Wilhelm II

This final volume of John C. G. Röhl's acclaimed ⸺ reveals the Kaiser's central role in the origins of t⸺ ⸺orld War. The book examines Wilhelm's part in the Boer War, the Russo-Japanese War, the naval arms race with Britain and Germany's rivalry with the United States, as well as in the crises over Morocco, Bosnia and Agadir. It also sheds new light on the public scandals which accompanied his reign, from the allegations of homosexuality made against his intimate friends to the *Daily Telegraph* affair. Above all, John Röhl scrutinises the mounting tension between Germany and Britain and the increasing pressure the Kaiser exerted on his Austro-Hungarian ally from 1912 onwards to resolve the Serbian problem. Following Germany's defeat and Wilhelm's enforced abdication, he charts the Kaiser's bitter experience of exile in Holland and his frustrated hopes that Hitler would restore him to the throne.

JOHN C. G. RÖHL is Emeritus Professor of History at the University of Sussex. His many previous publications include *The Kaiser and his Court* (1994), which was awarded the Wolfson History Prize, as well as the two previous volumes of his biography of Kaiser Wilhelm II — *Young Wilhelm: The Kaiser's Early Life, 1859–1888* (1998) and *Wilhelm II: The Kaiser's Personal Monarchy, 1888–1900* (2004) — which won the Einhard Prize for the biography of a major European figure in 2013.

WILHELM II

INTO THE ABYSS OF WAR AND EXILE 1900–1941

JOHN C. G. RÖHL

TRANSLATED BY

SHEILA DE BELLAIGUE AND ROY BRIDGE

CAMBRIDGE
UNIVERSITY PRESS

CAMBRIDGE
UNIVERSITY PRESS

University Printing House, Cambridge CB2 8BS, United Kingdom

Cambridge University Press is part of the University of Cambridge.

It furthers the University's mission by disseminating knowledge in the pursuit of
education, learning and research at the highest international levels of excellence.

www.cambridge.org
Information on this title: www.cambridge.org/9780521844314

Originally published in German as *Wilhelm II. Der Weg in den Abgrund 1900–1941*
by Verlag C. H. Beck München © John C. G. Röhl, 2008

First published in English by Cambridge University Press, 2014 as
Wilhelm II: Into the Abyss of War and Exile 1900–1941 © John C. G. Röhl 2014

English translation © John C. G. Röhl 2014
4th printing 2015

Printed in the United Kingdom by Berforts Information Press

A catalogue record for this publication is available from the British Library

Library of Congress Cataloguing in Publication data
Röhl, John C. G.
[Wilhelm II. English]
Wilhelm II : into the abyss of war and exile / John C. G. Röhl; translated by Sheila de Bellaigue and Roy Bridge.
pages   cm
ISBN 978-0-521-84431-4 (Hardback)
1. William II, German Emperor, 1859–1941.   2. Germany—Politics and government—1888–1918.
3. Germany—History—William I, 1871–1888.   I. De Bellaigue, Sheila, 1945–, translator.
II. Bridge, F. R., translator.   III. Title.
DD229.R641284 2014
943.08′4092—dc23   2013005149

ISBN 978-0-521-84431-4 Hardback
ISBN 978-1-107-54419-2 Paperback

For my grandchildren

BENJAMIN

SEBASTIAN

MAYA

LUKAS

JONATHAN

SOPHIA

EMILIANO

ANGELINA

Contents

Illustrations

ACKNOWLEDGEMENTS

Figure 1   Royal Collection Trust/© Her Majesty Queen
                    Elizabeth II 2012
Figure 3   Bildarchiv Preußischer Kulturbesitz/Staatsbibliothek
                    zu Berlin/Eugen Jacobi

Preface to the English edition

'He has been Emperor just over 30 years, he did great things for his country but his ambition was so great that he wished to dominate the world & created his military machine for that object . . . Now he has utterly ruined his country & himself & I look upon him as the greatest criminal known for having plunged the world into this ghastly war which has lasted over 4 years & 3 months with all its misery.'[1] These powerful words, written by King George V on 9 November 1918, the day his cousin Wilhelm II fled into exile, could well serve as an epigraph for this, the third volume of my biography of the last Geman Kaiser, covering the years from his breakthrough to undisputed power at the turn of the century to his death at the height of the Second World War in June 1941. True, the road from 1900 to the 'ghastly war' of 1914—18 was a long and winding one, with many diplomatic twists and turns on the way that might have led to a different outcome, and the Kaiser's decision for war, though considered frequently and with growing insistence as 1914 approached, was not finally reached until that summer. But the underlying conflict that eventually led to that fateful decision had been at the root of all the tectonic shifts that had transformed the international states system in the decade prior to war: the centuries-old irreconcilability between continental hegemony and the balance of power in Europe, in this case between Imperial Germany's ambition to 'dominate the world', as King George put it, and the determination of Great Britain, republican France and tsarist Russia to combine in an 'Entente' to avoid subjugation. Kaiser Wilhelm II and the twenty or so men who shaped Germany's policy under him in those pre-war years, building up the mightiest army and the second largest naval force on earth, had not by any means always had the intention to launch a war against her European neighbours. But they shared the conviction that their Empire's current constrained status was unjust and in the longer term wholly unacceptable, and in the last years of the armed peace their anger and frustration at being thwarted diplomatically reached boiling point.

The archival evidence for the mounting determination of Wilhelm II, the army and navy leaders and finally the civilian statesmen, too, to deploy military force to achieve their ambitious ends is quite overwhelming, and it is perhaps a measure of the profound and enduring consensus brought about in Germany by the 'Fischer controversy' of fifty years ago that these conclusions occasioned little comment there when the German edition of this volume was published in 2008. Instead, the book's lively reception was dominated by a subordinate question, that of the Kaiser's personal responsibility for the catastrophe. Had he, rather than 'the elites' in general, as structuralist historians had claimed, really wielded such decisive power, particularly after the twin domestic disasters of his reign, the disgrace of his favourite, Prince Philipp zu Eulenburg, in the homosexuality scandals of 1906—9 and the *Daily Telegraph* crisis of 1908?

Needless to say, this volume pays due attention to the 'elites' that governed the Prusso-German Kaiserreich. The testimony of the men in positions of power and of other insiders is liberally quoted and their responsibilities and shortcomings are analysed throughout. But what were the power relationships between them and the monarch? When there was dispute, as there always is in high politics, say between the army and the navy over resources, or between the navy and the Reich Chancellor and his advisers in the Wilhelmstrasse over negotiations with Britain, who had the final say? Who had appointed these army, navy and civilian leaders in the first place, and who had the right to dismiss them at will? The manner in which Wilhelm II operated the 'kingship mechanism' in order to dominate decision-making after Bismarck's dismissal in 1890 is the central issue addressed in the second volume of this biography,[2] but the distribution of power between the Kaiser and his predominantly military court on the one hand and the Chancellor, the state secretaries and the Prussian ministers on the other is also of fundamental importance in the years under the stewardship of Bernhard von Bülow (1900—9) and Theobald von Bethmann Hollweg (1909—17). So was Wilhelm II's will to power broken after the scandals surrounding his closest friends and the near-revolutionary public outrage over his 'interview' of 28 October 1908 in the *Daily Telegraph*? In August 1913, less than one year before the decision to launch a continental war in the guise of a defensive war against Russia, preferably sparked by a conflict between Austria-Hungary and Serbia in the Balkans, the veteran Austro-Hungarian ambassador Count Ladislaus von Szögyény-Marich confided to his Foreign Minister Count Berchtold in Vienna: 'If I ask myself the question who now really directs German foreign policy I can only come to one answer, and that is that neither Herr von Bethmann Hollweg nor [the Foreign Secretary] Herr von Jagow but Kaiser Wilhelm himself has his hands on the controls of foreign policy, and that in this regard the Reich Chancellor and the

Foreign Secretary are not in a position to exercise any significant influence on His Majesty.'[3] By this time, Szögyény had been in charge of the embassy in Berlin for more than two decades. Would he have been mistaken on a question of such existential importance to his disintegrating multinational Empire at such a critical time?

The issue of how much power and influence is to be attributed to the Kaiser in the system of Personal Monarchy bequeathed to the Hohenzollern dynasty by Bismarck — Wilhelm's closest associates referred to him proudly as 'the mightiest ruler on earth'[4] — has been the subject of numerous monographs and will no doubt go on being debated. One thing is not in dispute, however. As German Emperor, King of Prussia, Supreme War Lord and Supreme Bishop of the German Protestant Church, the hyperactive and hypersensitive monarch could not and would not be bypassed; he had the final say on all significant matters, most notably on all appointments to high office and in decisions affecting war and peace. Even if he was on occasions forced by circumstances to back down, as he was, and even if he sometimes found the task of choosing between contesting advisers irksome and even beyond his ability, as he did, it was nevertheless in his hands that all the threads — the military, naval, foreign and domestic policies being pressed on him for decision — came together. If we wish to see what those policies were, how they were arrived at and on what underlying assumptions they were based, we could hardly do better than to adopt as our vantage point the view from the 'mightiest throne on earth'. A biography of Kaiser Wilhelm II, based on thorough archival research, can hold the key to understanding how the world came to be plunged into the seminal catastrophe of the Great War one hundred years ago.

As German Kaiser and King of Prussia Wilhelm II held himself accountable only to his fearsome Lutheran–Calvinist God, duty-bound to follow in the footsteps of his illustrious Hohenzollern ancestors the Great Elector, Frederick the Great and his own revered grandfather 'Wilhelm the Great' to lead Prussia-Germany to domination in Europe so as to inherit Great Britain's position as Europe's global superpower. As the new century dawned and Germany powered ahead to become the most dynamic and successful Great Power on the old continent, he could confidently expect the lesser states to gravitate ever more closely to the imperial sun in Berlin and at the same time to 'unhinge' the existing international system — the concert of Europe — by exploiting the supposedly irreconcilable differences between Russia, the great land empire in the east, and Britain, the great oceanic empire in the west — the bear and the whale, as they were thought of. Within just a few years, those 'irreconcilable' differences were overcome, first by the Entente Cordiale between Britain and France (which had itself been allied to Russia since 1894) and then directly between Britain and Russia, too, in the Triple Entente of 1907. The Kaiser's Germany was now 'encircled', Bismarck's 'nightmare of coalitions' had become reality. With only the ramshackle Austro-Hungarian

Empire and volatile Italy as allies, Wilhelm's grand ambition of establishing 'Napoleonic supremacy' in Europe 'in the peaceful sense' had been frustrated.

Increasingly a siege mentality, paired with the determination to break out of the 'vice-like' grip of the Entente as soon as favourable circumstances presented themselves, predominated at the Kaiser's court, in military and naval circles and the Wilhelmstrasse. In the Bosnian annexation crisis of 1908–9, the Agadir crisis of 1911 and during the Balkan wars of 1912–13, Europe came within inches of war. In none of these three crises did Kaiser Wilhelm take the initiative, however. His endorsement, the *sine qua non* of their high-risk strategy, had to be 'extracted' by his advisers, who, in spite of the Supreme War Lord's characteristic bellicosity, could never be quite sure that his support would hold at the critical moment. Notably, in November 1912, the monarch agreed to the policy being urged on him by the General Staff, Reich Chancellor von Bethmann Hollweg and the Foreign Secretary, von Kiderlen-Wächter, to stand fully behind Austria-Hungary's plan to attack Serbia even if that conflict were to result in war with Russia and France. But then, in the notorious 'war council' of 8 December 1912, on learning of Britain's determination to prevent France from being 'crushed' by the German army, the Kaiser panicked and ordered a 'postponement of the great fight' until further preparations — among them a huge increase in the army and the completion of work on the Kiel Canal, scheduled for summer 1914 — had been made.

As that time approached, Wilhelm II repeatedly urged his Austrian ally to take the plunge by attacking Serbia. 'Now or never!', and 'I am with you!' he assured Vienna as early as October 1913. If the Russians backed down, as they had in the Bosnian crisis in 1909, the Central Powers would at least have gained predominance over the Balkan peninsula and the eastern Mediterranean; but if the Tsar took up the gauntlet, so much the better, as the time for war on the continent, the General Staff assured him, was now propitious. 'With head held high and hand on sword-hilt', Wilhelm was determined to 'settle accounts' with France and Russia 'once and for all' — albeit again on the assumption that Britain would stay out of the conflict, if only out of respect for 'his' battlefleet. With this hopeful scenario in mind, the generals, admirals and statesmen had little difficulty, when news of the assassination of his friend Archduke Franz Ferdinand reached him on 28 June 1914, in 'extracting' from their Supreme War Lord his 'blank cheque' in support of Austria's planned invasion of Serbia. He agreed to set off on his annual cruise along the coast of Norway to mask the plot that was afoot, but in Balholm, where the imperial yacht lay at anchor, ready at a moment's notice to sail home, Wilhelm was not only kept fully informed of the unfolding crisis, but engaged actively in the diplomatic and military preparations for war, prematurely ordering the bombardment of Russia's naval bases, the return of the fleet to base and the establishment of an exclusion zone in the western Baltic Sea. Not until he learnt, back at Potsdam, of Britain's threat to enter the war to maintain the European balance of power did the Kaiser's nerve fail — as it had in December 1912. His desperate last-minute efforts, along with his brother Prince Heinrich, to avert the calamity of an all-out global war, have perhaps not been accorded the recognition they deserve, but they, too, were inspired solely by fear of British intervention, as was shown by his triumphant call for champagne when, for a fleeting moment, it seemed as if Britain would stay neutral after all.

In view of such vacillation, and more especially in the light of the far greater horrors still to come, no one would now describe Kaiser Wilhelm II as 'the greatest criminal ever known'. But in many respects his authoritarian, militaristic, nationalistic and racist mindset, as well as his ambitions to dominate the continent, clearly presaged the calamities of a generation later. His plan to reward his victorious troops by settling them on 'ethnically cleansed' land in Flanders, his demand for almost limitless annexations in eastern Europe, the madcap conspiracy theories he evolved in exile to explain the enormity of the ruin he had brought upon himself, his house and his people — all this, and most particularly his genocidal diatribes against the Jews, is so redolent of Hitlerism that one rubs one's eyes when seeing them written down in the Kaiser's own hand. Those who encountered him even before his abdication in November 1918 — the party leaders in the Reichstag, for example, or Eugenio Pacelli (the future Pope Pius XII) — thought him distinctly unbalanced and wondered whether this condition had come on under the strain of war or whether he had always been this way. It almost goes without saying that Wilhelm hoped to be restored to the throne on the back of Hitler's seizure of power and that he exulted at the *Führer*'s diplomatic and military successes. The Second World War was, he wrote in English to an American friend in September 1940, revealing the trajectory of his own life's work, 'a succession of miracles! The old Prussian spirit of Frd. Rex ... has again manifested itself, as in 1870–71 ... The brilliant leading Generals in this war came from *My* school, they fought under my command in the [First] Worlds War as lieutenants, captains or young majors. Educated by Schlieffen they put the plans he had worked out under me into practice along the same lines as we did in 1914.'[5]

This book is not an exact translation of the volume that was published in Germany in the autumn of 2008. I have restructured the section on the First World War, turning two chapters into three by devoting one to the Kaiser's war aims. Much new material has appeared which I have tried to take into account without altering the essential character of the text. The Kaiser's political speeches have been published in a critical edition, as has his obscurantist correspondence in exile with the anthropologist Leo Frobenius. I am indebted to Dr Peter Winzen for his revealing research on the many homosexual men — Eulenburg, Bülow, Friedrich Alfred Krupp and others — whom Wilhelm II counted among his closest friends. Dr Annika Mombauer has kindly made her invaluable edition of the diplomatic and military documents on the origins of the First World War available to me for cross-referencing. Not everything has been a gain: the diary of Dr Alfred Haehner, the Kaiser's physician, which proved to be such a rich source for the first five years of his exile in Holland, was lost when the entire Historical Archive of the City of Cologne was swallowed up by the earth in a rainstorm in April 2009, but copies are preserved for inspection in my private collection.

Translating this large book has necessarily been a joint enterprise and I have been more than fortunate in being able to work alongside two brilliant wordsmiths who brought so much more to the task than linguistic skill, impeccable though that was. Lady de Bellaigue had already translated the entire second volume of this biography and was therefore thoroughly at home in the arcane world of the Hohenzollern court and Wilhelmine high politics. As a former Registrar of the Royal Archives at Windsor Castle she was able to ensure that everything in that marvellous treasure-house pertinent to this biography, most especially the then still unsorted papers of Lord Knollys, King Edward VII's Private Secretary, was made available to me. Our close collaboration has been a very long one, and I am overwhelmed by her devotion to this project and proud to think of her and her late husband Sir Geoffrey de Bellaigue as my friends. Once again I am deeply grateful to Her Majesty the Queen and the staff at the Royal Archives for the unrestricted access I have enjoyed over so many years. In Professor F. R. Bridge, Professor Emeritus of International History at Leeds University, I found a distinguished colleague with whom it was a delight not only to spar over the appropriate rendering of many an obscure German phrase but also someone able to put me right on the more esoteric aspects of Habsburg diplomacy and Balkan railway networks. Professor Matthew S. Seligmann piloted us safely through the treacherous reefs of German naval terminology. The translation was made possible by a grant from the City firm of Gissings, and I thank Mr Sean Breslin and his board once again for their most generous support. Sarah Turner has copy-edited the finished manuscript with meticulous accuracy while taking care to preserve the Kaiser's own idiosyncratic English style, and that master indexer Douglas Matthews has rendered my dense text more accessible not only by providing the reader with a myriad of individual threads to follow but also by cutting great swathes through the forest with general entries such as 'Wilhelm II', 'Germany' and 'Great Britain' to let in the light.

There have been times over the past four years when serious illness made the completion of this translation seem an unattainable goal. For their unfailing support in those troubled times I thank my friends Professor Holger Afflerbach, Dr Ragnhild Fiebig-von Hase, Manfred Graf von Roon, Prince

Rainer von Hessen, Professor Isabel V. Hull, Dr Annika Mombauer, Professor Hartmut Pogge von Strandmann, and not least, Mr Alec Nesbitt of Larkspur, Colorado, for riding shotgun on the gallop through death valley. It is impossible to find words to express my gratitude to our three children and their families. My most heartful thanks are once again due to my wife Rosemarie for the patience with which she has endured four further years of my dark obsession with the Kaiser when we could have been out on the Downs together in the sunshine.

John Röhl
Sussex, July 2012

Preface to the German edition

'How small a thought it takes to fill a whole life!' Wittgenstein remarked.[1] The small thought that has filled my professional life came to me half a century ago when it dawned on me, in the course of my archival research for my first book, that Kaiser Wilhelm was *the* central political figure of the Wilhelmine epoch. At the height of his powers he controlled every fundamental decision on matters of personnel, foreign and armaments policy, and in the first half of his reign the same was true also of domestic policy; it followed that his conception of his role as sovereign and the manner in which he exercised his power were immensely significant, far more so than had been acknowledged by historians of his era. The implications of this simple thought were momentous. All at once I recognised the historical significance of this powerful and controversial monarch's childhood and youth, on which very little research had ever been done. The difficult birth and its unfortunate medical consequences, the failure of the educational experiment attempted by his liberal-minded parents and the reactionary and militaristic spirit which began to develop in the young Prince Wilhelm of Prussia from an early age became the central theme of the first volume of my biography. My next task was to investigate and describe how Wilhelm II built up the position he inherited at the age of 29 as Kaiser and King, Supreme War Lord and Summus Episcopus of the Evangelical Church, to the point where he became the decisive factor in the increasingly strong German Reich which Bismarck had established by force of arms in the heart of Europe. His bitter battles for power — first with Bismarck, then with the latter's successors, Caprivi and Hohenlohe, and with the Prussian ministers of state — in which he was ably assisted by his favourite, the fawning Count (later Prince) Philipp zu Eulenburg, formed the principal subject of the second volume.

The present volume continues this investigation of the distribution of power. For which decisions taken under the Reich chancellors Bernhard von

Bülow (1900—9) and Theobald von Bethmann Hollweg (1909—17) was Wilhelm II personally responsible? In which areas of public life could the monarch successfully assert his authority, and in which did conflicts arise — with whom, and with what results? These are the questions that will be asked; and the sources, of which thanks to the admirable letter-writing and diary-keeping culture of Wilhelm's times there is an abundance, provide clear answers. They show that although Wilhelm's opportunities to control domestic policy diminished after the turn of the century and even more so after the major scandals and crises of 1906 to 1909, there is absolutely no doubt that despite the deeply dysfunctional state of the late Wilhelmine system of government, in the sphere of foreign and military policy he remained the decisive power until the outbreak of war in 1914.

This discovery leads compellingly to the perception that has shaped this third volume: if we are to understand the motives of German foreign policy and the accompanying military and naval preparations in the critical years which preceded the First World War and which were to lead to catastrophe in the summer of 1914, it is not enough to study the plans and strategies of the Reich chancellors, secretaries of state and diplomats of the Wilhelmstrasse (not to mention the Prussian ministers of state). Rather, we must direct our gaze above all at the mentality, motives and machinations of Kaiser Wilhelm II, his court clique and his paladins in the army and the navy, who chose the fatal course they steered through the rapids of the numerous pre-war crises into the vortex of the world war.

The biography of such a powerful, hyperactive ruler, who imagined himself entrusted by his fearsome Germanic God with a mission to perform great deeds for the land of his illustrious forefathers, who believed he knew better on every subject than civilian statesmen and diplomats, who insisted on making all important decisions himself — the biography of such a man rapidly becomes a kind of world history. The biographer is confronted with the — albeit attractive — challenge of describing the major events taking place in the world and setting them in their international context while at the same time not losing sight of the link with his subject. In this third volume, as in the others, I have tried to solve this problem by allowing Wilhelm II, his friends and his closest collaborators, as well as opponents bound up in the machinery of politics, to speak for themselves as often as possible. The reader will find scarcely a sentence in this volume that neither contains nor is based upon a written or spoken quotation from the time. Thus we see historical developments through the eyes of contemporaries and learn about their world from their words. This has meant that the concluding volume of the biography has had to be even longer than its two predecessors. But it has gained enormously in immediacy from the richly faceted and vivid nature of the documentation, and this sharpens our picture of Wilhelm's contemporaries and of their perception of the dramatic happenings of the Wilhelmine epoch, which is surely of inestimable value.

If we briefly survey the terrain that is to be examined in this third volume, the path leading into the abyss of war and exile can already be easily detected. As the second volume was able to show, even before the turn of the century the Kaiserreich, under its youthful, militaristic monarch, was preparing to make a breathtaking attempt to overturn the existing international balance of power in order to raise itself to a position of supremacy on the continent of Europe, thereby acquiring the status of a global superpower — becoming a *Weltmacht*, a World Power, in the parlance of the day. Grand Admiral Alfred von Tirpitz's accelerated fleet-building programme was to be the means by which Great Britain would be neutralised as guarantor of the European balance. The present volume begins with an examination of the ambivalent state of Anglo-German relations at the turn of the century, when Wilhelm II tried to make the most of his close connections with the British royal family in order to compensate for the hardening of public opinion on both sides of the North Sea during the Boer War. The assurances of friendship expressed by Queen Victoria's grandson were not taken at face value in London, however, and this was due partly to the expansionist ambitions in the Orient that Wilhelm manifested during the Boxer Rebellion in China and through the Baghdad railway project (Chapter 4), but also, and much more importantly, to the far from misplaced suspicion that the Kaiser's only reason for seeking better relations with Britain was to gain time to build his battlefleet and unite the continent under German domination (chapters 1–3). This suspicious interpretation of his intentions was confirmed by the deceitful policy that Wilhelm simultaneously pursued towards Russia: he tried to induce Tsar Nicholas II to break off Russia's alliance with France, turn his back on Europe and find his historic mission in becoming the defender of Christendom and the 'white race' against the heathen 'yellow peril' in the Far East (Chapter 7). With the outbreak of the Russo-Japanese War in February 1904, Wilhelm II's great goal seemed to be within reach. Plans for the occupation of Denmark were prepared, the Netherlands and Belgium each received an extraordinary ultimatum from the Kaiser — everything was ready for a military defeat of France (Chapter 12). Then for the first time the mobilisation of Britain's superior naval power acted as a deterrent. And in the end the trustful Tsar, enlightened by his ministers about the disastrous consequences of giving in to the Kaiser's blandishments, refused to exchange his alliance with France for a new *Dreikaiserbund* with the Central European Powers, Germany and Austria-Hungary (Chapter 11 and Chapter 14 on the Treaty of Björkö).

The German challenge soon led to a diplomatic revolution (Chapter 10), which Bismarck had always feared as the *cauchemar des coalitions* — the nightmare of encirclement of the German Reich by the outer ring of

European Powers. During the first Moroccan crisis (Chapter 13) and at the subsequent Algeciras conference (Chapter 16) Germany's isolation became clear for all the world to see: not only Great Britain, Russia, Italy, Spain and the smaller European states, but also the United States of America — which had long since grown suspicious of German intentions in the Caribbean and Latin America and not least of the Kaiser's bombastic utterances (Chapter 9) — made it plain that they would not accept the humiliation of France.

Inevitably, the setback at Algeciras had serious consequences for the prestige of the Crown in the Reich itself (chapters 20–5). The painful loss of face drew the attention of critics on both the Right and the Left to the dilettantish and peace-endangering way in which the Kaiser and his courtiers were gambling away Bismarck's heritage. This middle section of the book shows how, from then onwards, Wilhelm II's 'Personal Rule' was criticised quite openly and with a ferocity that had previously been heard only among the tiny handful of those in the know. This hostile atmosphere formed the background to the embarrassing sex scandals that shook the Hohenzollern court around 1906, as also to the *Daily Telegraph* crisis of November 1908, which provoked a real nervous breakdown in Wilhelm: he was haunted by paranoid delusions and began to believe that 'the Jews' were taking control of his country.

In the November storm of 1908 the Kaiser had found himself compelled to give a solemn assurance that he would in future conduct himself in accordance with the constitution. Where foreign and military policy were concerned, however, his decision-making power was in no way reduced; quite the contrary. Under the 'civilian Chancellor' Bethmann Hollweg, Wilhelm II's personal control of the course pursued by the Reich in foreign and armaments policy continued undiminished (Chapter 28). With an alarming lack of reflection, a reckless desire for prestige, a militaristic aggressiveness, a temperamental instability and emotionalism that bordered on the pathological, he talked in these years of the necessity of a great war in order to break out of the irksome ring of encirclement and bring about Prussia-Germany's rise to World Power status. As early as in August 1908, during negotiations at Kronberg, he openly threatened the British with war. In the Bosnian annexation crisis of 1908–9 (Chapter 26) he assured his intimate friend Archduke Franz Ferdinand that he would stand by Austria-Hungary 'through thick and thin' if the Habsburgs were to invade Serbia, in spite of the danger of a general European war. Meanwhile, in the spring of 1909, he gave orders for an extremely stern ultimatum to France to be drawn up. Only the fact that Russia backed down, still weakened by war and revolution as she was, prevented the outbreak of the great war in 1909 (Chapter 26).

Two years later, war in the west came within a hair's breadth when Britain again undertook to defend France with her still superior navy during the Agadir crisis (Chapter 30). As in the first Moroccan crisis, Britain's readiness to go to war proved a deterrent in the short term — Germany was again forced to give way humiliatingly — but with the Navy Bill ordered by Wilhelm II in the heat of the moment in the autumn of 1911, the Anglo-German antagonism became so intense that it seemed to many people to be only a matter of time before the conflict would have to be settled by force of arms. Where the Kaiser's interests in this conflict lay becomes clear in the negotiations conducted by the British Minister of War, Lord Haldane, in Berlin in February 1912. His goal was not the 'fantasy' of a colonial empire overseas, he declared, but a fundamental diplomatic revolution through which he would become 'leader of the United States of Europe' (Chapter 32). Great Britain was to be compelled by the murderous arms race to give up her ententes with France and Russia and to undertake to remain neutral in any war on the continent — even in the eventuality of a German attack on France. Wilhelm's expectations suffered a severe setback when it became apparent that Britain would not under any circumstances be prepared to expose her allies to attack by entering into an unconditional neutrality pact with the Kaiserreich.

Following the failure of the negotiations with Haldane, Wilhelm's attention was again drawn towards the east, where in late 1912 the war between the Christian Balkan states of Bulgaria, Serbia, Montenegro and Greece and the decaying Ottoman Empire promised to open the door to far-reaching expansion for Germany and Austria-Hungary. As if intoxicated, Wilhelm II dreamed of the Central European Powers enjoying 'preponderance' over the eastern Mediterranean and 'the whole Mohammedan world! (India)'. For obvious reasons, in this volume particular attention is paid to German policy in the eighteen months between the beginning of the Balkan wars in October 1912 and the outbreak of the First World War in the summer of 1914. The extent to which the Kaiser and his generals (in close cooperation with their allies, the statesmen and generals of the moribund Austro-Hungarian monarchy) were ready — indeed increasingly determined — to go to war is documented in detail (chapters 33–7). Several times during these months, as will become clear in these pages, a Balkan war was in imminent danger of breaking out. Such a war, it had to be assumed, would develop via the mechanism of the European network of alliances into a continental war, and in the event of Great Britain intervening, a world war. In December 1912, uncertainty over the still unsettled question of British neutrality had its deterrent effect for the last time (Chapter 34). In the summer of 1914, on the other hand, Wilhelm and his brother Prince Heinrich of Prussia kept their eyes firmly shut and pinned their hopes on a few casual remarks which Heinrich had elicited from King George V during a brief visit to Buckingham Palace. 'I have the word of a King, and that is enough for me!' Wilhelm exclaimed on 29 July 1914. Naturally, this volume also examines in detail the controversial role played by Wilhelm in the crisis of July 1914, which is the subject of no less than four chapters (38–41). Thanks to the unusually full source material, his conduct and the decisions he took during these weeks can be reconstructed from day to day, often from hour to hour, and his mood swings between determination to go to war and panicky readiness to negotiate can be shown in the context of the rapidly escalating crisis.

With the outbreak of the world war, power passed from the Kaiser to the generals with astounding speed. During the war Wilhelm II, as Supreme War Lord, was still institutionally the highest authority and could not be bypassed. As before, in accordance with the principles of the kingship mechanism, the Reich Chancellor and the leaders of the army and the navy still had to seek his approval if they wanted to carry through their chosen course of action. In sharp contrast to his almost manic activity in the pre-war period, however, Wilhelm now took a far more passive attitude to his role. The pitiful part he played in political and military affairs in the world war foreshadowed the complete collapse of the monarchy in November 1918 and the ex-Kaiser's years of embittered exile in Holland, which are the subject of the last three chapters of the book.

Just as for Wilhelm II's long reign, I have been able to draw on revealing new sources for his years of exile which throw a sharp light on his life and his psychological state in Amerongen and Doorn. The diary kept by his personal physician Dr Alfred Haehner, the records of conversations with him made by numerous visitors from Germany, his own letters to relations and well-wishers, together with the well-known diary of his adjutant, Sigurd von Ilsemann, bear witness to an appalling refusal to face up to reality. In Holland, Wilhelm denied any responsibility for the disaster of his thirty-year rule and built up a fantasy that the world war and the downfall of the Hohenzollern Monarchy were the result of an international conspiracy hatched by the Jews, the Freemasons and the Jesuits. His offensive hatred for the Jews — and for the modern democratic world in general — took on such a psychopathic nature from 1917 onwards, as will become clear in these last chapters, that visitors wondered in alarm, and not without justification, whether the Kaiser had been quite in his right mind when he still held the reins of power. It would not surprise me if readers of this book, on studying some of the outbursts of the last German Kaiser quoted in it, found themselves asking similar questions.

As in the preceding two volumes, I have wherever possible checked the quotations from the printed primary sources with the archival manuscript originals for their authenticity. Details of their provenance and of any discrepancies in the records are to be found in the notes section. The reader should regard these quotations as the forensic evidence that they actually are: in the same way as fingerprints or DNA evidence in a criminal case, correctly interpreted and seen in their context they testify to the actual motives and actions of Kaiser Wilhelm II, members of his family, his circle of friends, the generals and officials of the court, the statesmen and diplomats, as well as of the observers and critics inside Germany and abroad from the turn of the century to the First World War and beyond. The incontrovertible value of contemporary sources as evidence needs to be pointed out here in order to prevent the impression arising that the observations made in this book, some of which will undoubtedly be regarded as very controversial, are merely the subjective opinions, or even the prejudices, of the author. I am concerned only with finding out the truth; should I have overlooked relevant documents giving a different picture, or placed a wrong interpretation on the sources I have quoted, I would be glad of any correction.

Through my own archival research, which has now extended over more than half a century, I have in many instances been able to add considerably to the printed sources which have since become available in great quantity. As ever, the holdings of the Royal Archives in Windsor Castle proved a real treasure trove, and I again thank Her Majesty Queen Elizabeth II for allowing me the freedom to carry out research in this superb archive. My gratitude is due to the archivists, above all Lady de Bellaigue and Pamela Clark, for their friendly assistance over more than twenty years. An indispensable source for the life of Wilhelm II from his birth in January 1859 until his death in June 1941 is provided by the papers of his parents and of his youngest sister Margarethe, Landgravine of Hesse, preserved in the Hessisches Hausarchiv at Schloss Fasanerie near Fulda. I thank the archivist, Dr Christine Klössel, who has been constantly helpful; and above all I thank Prince Rainer von Hessen, who opened the doors of his family's archives to me many years ago and who has always supported my work in a spirit of friendship and trust. Special mention must also be made of the astonishingly frank letters which Wilhelm II wrote to his friends Max Egon II, Fürst zu Fürstenberg, and Archduke Franz Ferdinand of Austria-Hungary, which I was able to consult in Donaueschingen and in the Magyar Orszagos Levéltar Budapest respectively, and from which I have quoted extensively. The papers kept in the Military Archives in Freiburg, the Bundesarchiv in Koblenz and Berlin, the Geheimes Staatsarchiv at Berlin-Dahlem and the Haus-, Hof- und Staatsarchiv and the Kriegsarchiv in Vienna are almost inexhaustible sources for the biographer of Wilhelm II, and I thank the staff of these archives too for their help. The political archives of the German Foreign Office, the Auswärtiges Amt, formerly in Bonn and now in Berlin, contain countless autograph documents and marginal notes by the Kaiser, some of which I have been able to quote to complete and correct the officially published documents; I owe thanks above all to Dr Gerhard Keiper for his patience in answering my questions.

Many of the sources cited in this volume I did not find myself; they were sent to me by friends and colleagues from all over the world. I have acknowledged their help in the corresponding reference notes. In addition, however, I wish to express here the deep gratitude I feel towards a number of friends and colleagues for the selfless support that they have given me, often over decades, through word and deed. They are, above all, Professor Holger Afflerbach, Professor Dr Wilhelm Deist†, Dr Michael Epkenhans, Dr Ragnhild Fiebig-von Hase, Professor Dr Stig Förster, Dr Christoph Johannes Franzen, Manfred Graf von Roon, Professor Dr Lothar Machtan, Dr Annika Mombauer, Dr Stephen Nicholls, Professor Hartmut Pogge von Strandmann, Professor Dr Wolfram Pyta, Professor Matthew Seligmann and Dr Karina Urbach.

During my work on the text over the years help was always available to me thanks to the generosity of the British Arts and Humanities Research Council, the endowment fund of Deutsche Bank and Mr Sean Breslin of Gissings in London, so that this book could almost be regarded as a kind of communal enterprise, although the responsibility for the end product and any mistakes in it naturally remains entirely mine. When I set out upon the third volume Markus Bussmann, Dr Robert Gerwarth, Dr Anna von der Goltz and Björn Hofmeister assisted me in its formulation. In writing the chapters on Bülow's Chancellorship I was able to rely on the expert support of Dr Gerd Fesser with his specialist knowledge of Bülow. In the final stages I was helped by Bernhard Dietz and Dr Michael Obst to shape the over-long manuscript into its present form. Dr Obst, himself an authority on Kaiser Wilhelm II, deserves my very particular thanks; without him this book could not have appeared for a long time yet. Last but not least I thank Dr Stefan von der Lahr at C. H. Beck, who has now been editing my volumes on the Kaiser for fifteen years, giving my German the final polish and saving me from many mistakes.

I have now worked on this three-volume biography for exactly as long as Kaiser Wilhelm sat on the throne of his forefathers. Throughout all these years my wife has borne with good cheer and stoical calm the sacrifices that are the other side of the coin to my imperial preoccupation. She more than anyone else will be relieved that the biography is at last complete. I thank her and our children for their understanding. During my work on this volume, eight grandchildren have come into the world. They have often kept me from working but they have filled my whole life with light and happiness. To them — the future — this last volume is dedicated.

John Röhl
Sussex, April 2008

CHAPTER ONE

Death and transfiguration

Early in the evening of 22 January 1901 Queen Victoria died at Osborne House on the Isle of Wight, surrounded by more than twenty members of her close family. They included her eldest son Albert Edward the Prince of Wales, now to succeed her as King Edward VII, and her eldest grandson, Kaiser Wilhelm II, who knelt beside the dying Queen, supporting her with his arm until her last breath. Missing from those present was the Queen's eldest daughter Victoria, the widowed Empress Frederick, sister of Edward VII and mother of the Kaiser. She was gravely ill and unable to leave her home, Schloss Friedrichshof, among the wooded hills of the Taunus in Germany. Hopes for better relations between Britain and Germany ran high at this moment – only to revert all too soon to bitter recriminations on both sides. 'You have no idea, my dear William, how all of us in England appreciate the loyal friendship which you manifest towards us on every possible occasion. We hope always to look upon Germany as our best friend as long as you are at the helm', Edward wrote to his imperial nephew in the spring of 1900.[1] Yet only a few years after his accession the new King was venting his feelings about the Kaiser in terms which, as the Foreign Secretary Lord Lansdowne commented, 'make one's flesh creep'.[2] He would continue to be as courteous as possible to Wilhelm, the King declared, but he would *never* trust him. He was England's 'bitterest foe'.[3] Wilhelm was scarcely less harsh in his criticism of Edward, who he said was plotting against him everywhere; it was well-nigh incredible 'how much personal hatred this behaviour by his uncle revealed', indeed it was beyond belief 'what a Satan' the King was.[4] The Kaiser constantly repeated his deep-rooted conviction that Edward VII was the real instigator of the anti-German conspiracy of encirclement directed by the other World Powers against the German Reich. Even in late July 1914, with world war only hours away,

Wilhelm II and his closest advisers at the imperial court regarded the coming struggle against a hostile world as the very personal work of the King himself. Confused and fearful, the Kaiser exclaimed at this historic moment, 'Edward VII is stronger after his death than I, who am still alive!'[5] How did this fatal rift between the two closely related dynasties and peoples come about in so short a time? How justified was the King in concluding that his nephew's conspicuous friendliness at Queen Victoria's funeral, during his sister Vicky's long illness and on countless other occasions, was nothing but hypocrisy, designed to hide his real aims, which were so fraught with danger for Britain and the rest of Europe? In order to appreciate more fully the ambiguity of Kaiser Wilhelm's policy towards England at the turn of the century, it is worth taking a closer look at his behaviour within the close family circle, before investigating the political aims which he was in fact pursuing behind the smiling mask.

THE DEATH OF QUEEN VICTORIA

On the afternoon of 18 January 1901 Queen Victoria's physician, Sir James Reid, without the knowledge of the royal family, sent a secret telegram to the Kaiser saying 'Disquieting symptoms have developed which cause considerable anxiety.'[6] Wilhelm decided there and then to travel to England. Some time before he had confided to his closest friend, Prince Philipp zu Eulenburg, 'Of course the people have no inkling how much I love the Queen ... how intimately she is linked with all my memories of childhood and youth! That is why nobody understands my constant fear of suddenly hearing that she is hopelessly ill or has died, without my being able to see her again.'[7] The numerous guests invited to Berlin for Wilhelm's forty-second birthday on 27 January were told not to come.

At Osborne House the assembled members of the English royal family were far from pleased to hear that Wilhelm intended to join them. Like James Reid, they were afraid that the news of the Kaiser's arrival might precipitate the Queen's death.[8] The Prince of Wales decided to intercept the unwelcome guest in London and 'keep him at Buckingham Palace'.[9] He met his imperial nephew on the evening of 20 January at Charing Cross station. On his arrival Wilhelm, suspecting nothing, telegraphed to the Reich Chancellor Count Bernhard von Bülow: 'Very kindly received here by the Prince. Prince of Wales very warm, touched and full of gratitude that I have come. Freiherr von Eckardstein told me that when news reached London last night that I was coming, there was general pleasure and gratitude and, if I may say so, enthusiasm. Prince of Wales informed me Her Majesty's condition "unchanged, still serious", it is a "degeneration of the brain" and the nervous system is affected, with great weakness; he had not been able to see his own mother yet, as immediate death feared if any agitation!!'[10]

That same evening the Queen's condition was so alarming that Reid telegraphed to the Prince telling him that he should after all return to the Isle of Wight next morning, and bring the Kaiser with him.[11] So both uncle and nephew, together with Arthur Duke of Connaught and the Duke of York, the future King George V, travelled from Buckingham Palace down to Osborne on 21 January 1901. The Kaiser was so 'charmed by the Prince of Wales and his relations here' that Count Paul von Wolff-Metternich, the diplomat accompanying him, feared he might indulge in anti-Russian indiscretions, which would certainly be reported to St Petersburg. It was a fear shared by Bülow. 'At the first opportunity, when I am alone with H.M., I shall draw the All-Highest's attention to the danger of indiscretions', Metternich assured the Reich Chancellor.[12]

On the morning of 22 January Reid summoned all the members of the family to the Queen's room. She was by now blind, and her daughters, Princesses Helena, Louise and Beatrice, gave her the names of all those present, but hid from her the fact that Wilhelm II was also at her bedside. Hurt, the Kaiser asked the royal physician: 'Did you notice this morning that everyone's name in the room was mentioned to her except mine?', to which Reid replied: '*Yes*, and that is one reason why *I* specially wish to take you there.' Reid recorded in his diary: 'I took the Kaiser to see her, and sent all the maids out and took him up to the bedside, and said, "Your Majesty, your grandson the Emperor is here; he has come to see you as you are so ill", and she smiled and understood. I went out and left him with her five minutes alone.' Although the Queen was scarcely in a position to hold a meaningful conversation, she said to Reid afterwards 'The Emperor is very kind.'[13] At 4 p.m. the family gathered around the dying Queen once more. Most of them came and went at intervals; only the Kaiser and Alexandra, Princess of Wales, stayed in the room with Reid throughout. Sir Thomas Barlow, another of the Queen's physicians, wrote admiringly: 'The Emperor was the figure that to us was the most striking personality in the room next to the Queen. There he stood with his eyes immovably fixed on his grandmother, apparently with no thought but of her. When asked to speak he said he had come to tell her about the Empress Frederick, that she was a little better, she was taking drives again, that she sent her love and then quietly, he took his place of watching again — no self-consciousness or posing there but simple dignity and intense devotion. But in the earlier part of the day, when the family had been summoned he had showed himself so ready and deft in putting in a pillow here and there and when some of the others said "more air" he was away to the window to lift it himself if I had not forestalled him.'[14]

'There was much weeping as the end drew near, the German Emperor crying like the others', wrote another witness, who found Wilhelm's devotion 'beautiful & touching'. For the last hour Sir James Reid and a nurse, at the Queen's right, held her up in a half-sitting position, while Wilhelm knelt at the left side of the bed, supporting her with his right arm.[15] She died at half past six in the evening. Behind the doctor sat the Prince of Wales, who at that moment became King of Great Britain and Ireland and Emperor of India.

On the whole, his English relatives were favourably impressed by Wilhelm II's uncharacteristic restraint at Osborne. The Duchess of York, the future Queen Mary, commented that in the end the royal family was pleased that Wilhelm had come, and that 'dear Gdmama knew him & spoke to him'.[16] 'Nothing can be kinder & more thoughtful than the G. Emperor is', Edward reported a few hours before the Queen's death. 'He is only the grandson here & not the powerful Sovereign he is at home.'[17] Writing to his seriously ill sister Vicky, the new King again praised the unaccustomed modesty of her son's attitude during his stay in England. 'William's touching & simple demeanour up to the last will never be forgotten by me or anyone.'[18]

In the midst of the preparations for Queen Victoria's funeral Kaiser Wilhelm II celebrated his birthday at Osborne. His aunt, Grand Duchess Luise of Baden, sent him her good wishes in a letter which evidently came from the heart. He had, she said, 'played your part so wonderfully as grandson and son, accompanying that great life, whose passing we all mourn, to its end. I feel deeply affected; for me it brings to a close a wealth of precious memories of childhood and youth, beginning 50 years ago in 1851. What an uplifting time this must be for you, no doubt reminiscent of 1888. God bless you in all that you are living through over there, for it is of such great significance both now and for the future.'[19]

Sending his own good wishes, the Kaiser's former tutor Dr Hinzpeter also recognised the emotional complexity of these sad hours for Wilhelm. 'Not only the pain of losing so highly venerated a Grandmother, but also the heartening sense of bringing comfort and support to the grieving family; not only the pride with which, in your incomparable position at the head of the German ruling princes, you represented Germany as the most advanced of all monarchies, in the specifically monarchical homage which the European Sovereigns paid to their doyenne, the most admirable of monarchs, but also the uplifting knowledge that you were personally creating a firm bond between two great peoples which certain interests and passions seek to drive apart. The human soul that could feel all that at once must indeed have been elevated far above ordinary emotions.'[20]

To mark his birthday Wilhelm conferred the High Order of the Black Eagle on the Commander in Chief of the British army, Field Marshal Lord Roberts, and appointed the Duke of York, now the heir to the throne, à la suite of the German navy.[21] In return, King Edward appointed his German nephew Field Marshal in the British army and gave him the Star of the Order of the Garter in brilliants (see Figure 1). The young Prusso-German Crown Prince was made a knight of the Order.[22]

Wilhelm II was deeply moved, commenting to the Reich Chancellor that this was 'the work of the Lord!' 'I was completely stunned! But he [the King] had tears in his eyes and he has never been warmer or more affectionate!'[23] Later he wrote to his uncle Arthur of Connaught of his deep emotion at being promoted to Field Marshal: 'I shall allways [sic] be proud of this distinction to my dying days ... The moment is & allways will be engraved in my memory & the spot – the fire place in the dear Osborne drawing room – will never be forgotten as well as that memorable morning.'[24] Wilhelm's brother Prince Heinrich, whom Edward had appointed Vice Admiral in the Royal Navy, wrote mockingly: 'This is the first alms that our A[ll] H[ighest] Lord and Master has received from the hands of the English King for all his efforts the other side of the Channel!'[25]

As the Royal Navy's cannon salutes rang out, the Queen's coffin was conveyed by the royal yacht over to Portsmouth, and then taken to London by special train. From Victoria station the cortège processed on horseback and on foot to Paddington, and from there the journey to Windsor was completed by train. Solemn and stony-faced, the Kaiser, already wearing the uniform of a British Field Marshal, rode beside his two uncles, Edward VII and Arthur of Con-naught, directly behind the gun-carriage carrying the coffin. On 4 February the Queen was finally laid to rest in the mausoleum at Frogmore, beside her husband, Prince Albert, the grandfather who had died when Wilhelm was only two years old.[26]

The following day the King gave a magnificent banquet in Wilhelm's honour at Marlborough House. As well as the German guests, it was attended by the Foreign Secretary, Lord Lansdowne, Lord Roberts and the British ambassador at Berlin, Sir Frank Lascelles. After Edward VII had expressed his thanks to the Kaiser for coming so swiftly and staying so long 'at much personal inconvenience', Wilhelm rose to speak. As the English press reported, he said that nothing had given him more pleasure 'than to be present with his Uncles and Aunts during the last moments of the great and noble life of his beloved Grandmother, for whom from his earliest boyhood he had attended

Figure 1 Kaiser Wilhelm II in England after the funeral of his grandmother
Queen Victoria, resplendent in his new uniform as a Field Marshal
of the British army

the strongest feelings of love and veneration'. He thanked the King for
conferring on him the rank of a Field Marshal in the British army and drew
attention to the fact that 'this honour enabled him to wear a uniform similar to
that worn by the Duke of Wellington and Lord Roberts, and this compliment

would be highly appreciated by his Army. He heartily reciprocated His Majesty's feelings with regard to relations between the two Empires.'[27]

After the banquet the Kaiser and his suite left for home. As he boarded his ship he sent a telegram *en clair* to Eulenburg. 'I set out from here feeling deeply distressed', he declared, 'but grateful for all the wonderful and uplifting impressions I have received, and for all the proofs of affection and friendship shown me by both King and people. You are right: no one suspected how deeply devoted I was to this glorious grandmother, and only now have I learnt how much she loved me and how highly she thought of me. But at any rate an unshakeable foundation has now been laid, on which, with mutual understanding and regard, good and friendly relations between our peoples will be built, for the benefit of the world' — just as he had always hoped.[28] Eulenburg immediately forwarded the Kaiser's 'moving' telegram to Bülow and commented: 'His whole English nature, which was so rarely able to come into play precisely because of this beloved grandmother, gives vent to itself in these enthusiastic words — and gave vent to itself during the fortnight in England *because* the beloved grandmother lay in her coffin and could no longer say: "Dear Willy — it's time for you to leave now!" What a curious, childish, touching naivety there is in [these] words . . . Nonetheless, our beloved master's personal success has been so great that it has become a trump card in the political hand that you hold. The other great powers see it that way too.'[29]

The gratitude felt towards the Kaiser in Britain, both at court and among the population, was indeed extraordinary, even if, as was soon to become only too evident, it did not bear the hoped-for political fruit. Hundreds of drawings and photographs in the illustrated papers — for instance showing the Kaiser alone in the chapel at Osborne, praying and kissing his grandmother's coffin[30] — had acknowledged Wilhelm's grief. The length of his stay was all the more keenly appreciated in Britain because it was known that a storm of indignation was brewing in Berlin, not least because he had conferred an order on Lord Roberts, the conqueror of the Boers. The King wrote affectionately to Wilhelm: 'Your recent visit here will never be forgotten by the Nation & I shall always remember with the deepest gratitude your having come over here at such an intensely sorrowful & important an occasion.'[31]

One would certainly not wish to question the sincerity and depth of Kaiser Wilhelm II's grief at the death of his grandmother during the two weeks which he spent in England in January and February 1901. Throughout this time he showed not only impressive imperial dignity but also a very human distress that gives the lie to any suspicion that he was merely play-acting. And yet it is plain that there was an element of political reckoning in his demonstrative participation in the funeral ceremonies. The Kaiser's brother-in-law, the

Hereditary Prince Bernhard of Saxe-Meiningen, summed up the dual purpose of the hasty journey to London thus: 'The Kaiser's departure for England in order to hurry to his grandmother's bedside has not failed to make a good impression. In this decision human feeling and political calculation certainly played their part in equal measure. It was intended to work upon the public mood, and it has had the desired effect.' But with his spectacular dash to England Wilhelm was seeking to influence not only public feeling but also high politics in Britain, according to the cynical Prince Bernhard, who rated Wilhelm's chances of success in the latter arena much lower. 'The death of the old Queen begins a new phase in history, for in spite of everything she was still our best friend on that side of the Channel, and would never have allowed matters to come to open conflict.' He feared that under Edward VII British foreign policy would be given an anti-German slant. 'The former Prince of Wales is after all generally considered to belong to the "Prussian-hating" sect in Europe', the Hereditary Prince observed, 'and to that can be added a certain antipathy towards the German Emperor, which of course he will not show openly just now. On the contrary, he will drip with fine words and overflow with friendship. But I do not trust this peace and I am curious to know how things will work out in the future.'[32] Prince Bernhard's words were to prove prophetic.

ILLNESS AND DEATH OF THE EMPRESS FREDERICK

Queen Victoria's death was followed seven months later by that of her eldest daughter, Wilhelm's mother Victoria, the Empress Frederick. It had been apparent for some years that she was suffering from cancer, but it was only in May 1899 that the world-famous specialist, Professor Rudolf Renvers, told her that her illness was incurable. The Kaiser was deeply shocked when Renvers gave him the tragic diagnosis on 21 May. To his sister Victoria (Moretta), living at Palais Schaumburg in Bonn, he wrote an impassioned letter in the English in which the family conversed, exclaiming bitterly at 'this too terrible state of things ... That old rhinoceros of Wegner who has been observing this affair since *then never* recognised its seriousness & allways [sic] said it was *nothing*! Even in England the same doctor – Dr. Williams – said within 7 months, first that it was *nothing*, & then that it was very *serious* & ought to be *operated at once*! I am simply furious about this! They all for years and years have lulled poor mother into a false quiet till the evil itself shows her by pain etc. what it really is! Now my dear Vicky the situation is very serious! ... For the reason that the tumours on poor mothers side are so developed that there is danger of their breaking through her skin during the next months. That would mean a terrible mess, a fearful smell & stench, bandages all over, no gowns, use of narcotics morphia etc. & a life of awful pain and so on. If she were operated these things would all be removed & a state of more or less rest would be restored. Two men are within your reach who are first rate operators & very nice men, who could be invited — en passant — for lunch or tea to see mother. The one is Doctor [Max] Schede (Bonn) whom you must know, & the other Prof. [Vinzenz von] Czerny Heidelberg. Which you choose is the same to me, but one *must* see her, for Renvers — as I told you before — *not* being a *surgeon* can not be saddled with the *whole* responsibility for mothers life! It is for her own self & for her own rest & quiet that I implore you to do all [that] is possible in bringing one of these men to mother, for what is awaiting her, if she does not see him is too fearful to say! And Renvers is quite powerless to avert it without an operation! — It is too terrible I am quite ill about all this! And to have to keep all this terrible business to oneself, not to be able to help! O these confounded beasts of English Doctors! Why must our family be chosen to suffer from their idiotic stupidity or nastiness!'[33]

This letter full of horror and anger is the only surviving source bearing witness to the Kaiser's emotions on receiving the news of the inevitable, painful death his mother was facing. Did he, at that moment, feel any remorse for the appallingly bad relationship which they had had since his youth? Was he conscious of all she had suffered in the 1880s when he turned against his parents, personally and politically, and allowed himself to be used as a tool against them by Bismarck and Waldersee? One may have one's doubts. The furious outburst against the English medical profession at the end of the letter harks back both to the injury he himself suffered at birth (for which no British doctor was to blame) and to the mishandling of his father's cancer of the throat by Morell Mackenzie. But it gives little indication of any regret for his own behaviour at that difficult time. By pursuing an anti-British policy abroad while building up his Personal Monarchy at home, Wilhelm had sabotaged his parents' liberal, anglophile life's work, and in so doing he had perhaps even hastened the onset of illness in both. It was a reproach which his mother at any rate did not spare him when she wrote to him that 'the sorrows & grief, the anxieties & trials I have had to endure are the cause of what has now come'.[34]

Wilhelm proved only too right in fearing that the widowed Empress would resist any attempt to intervene. Her reply to her son's anxious plea to allow herself to be examined by a German surgeon was tantamount to a refusal. 'Pray do not worry on my account; or I shall regret so much having let you into my sad secret!', she warned him, and added, with the same mixture of medical

naivety and tactical optimism that had characterised her attitude in 1887 and
1888, 'I have full confidence in the persons I have consulted, & have my eyes
quite open as to the course I am pursuing. My case is not a desperate nor a
rapid one, & though I have a good deal of pain at times, at other times I am
quite comfortable! ... Though I cannot have *better surgical* advice & opinion
than I have had, and mean to continue with, yet if it is in the slightest degree a
satisfaction to you, I am quite ready to see the one at Bonn.' She admitted that
cancer was a serious illness, but 'a heart disease, or spinal complaint or
paralytic attacks, affected eyes or brain would be *far far worse*, & I am also
very thankful it is my *left* & not my right side as I can write & paint without
trouble. Please set your mind to rest on my account! I have plenty of courage
left − & intend to do all I can to live on & get well if I can ... Death has no
fears for me, − & I am quite ready when the time comes to lie down by the
side of dear Papa, Sigie & Waldie in my place in the mausoleum of the
Friedenskirche. Goodbye dearest Child. Pray burn this Letter *at once*.'[35]

Despite her suffering, in October 1899 the Empress travelled to Sarzana on
the Gulf of La Spezia to spend several months at the Villa Marigola, which her
marshal of the court, Hugo Freiherr von Reischach, had rented for her.[36]
Wilhelm put his yacht *Loreley* at her disposal during her stay on the Italian
Riviera.[37] He suggested considerately that she should not hasten her return to
Germany, as the weather in the north was 'beyond all description nasty &
horrible'.[38] In these letters it is apparent that relations between mother and
son were improving, which is further borne out by a lively correspondence on
the internal layout of the Berlin palaces, and of the new buildings and gardens
on the Museum Island and in the Academic quarter.[39]

The Empress's condition grew visibly worse, although she did not quite give
up hope of recovering.[40] 'The pain in my back makes my Life a misery', she
admitted in a letter to Wilhelm of November 1899. 'My nights are such a
torment as I cannot turn right or left!'[41] 'Sometimes I have to *call out*, *so* great is
the pain ... and [I] am *so* ashamed to be seen in this half crippled state ...
Morphia I have been offered very often but I *will not* take it, it *upsets* one so
much.'[42] The extent to which her own suffering was overshadowed by her
dreadful experience during her husband's illness was evident in particular from
her efforts to keep the cause of her illness secret. She wrote to her daughter
Sophie, the Greek Crown Princess: 'You know how indiscreet people at Berlin
are. I am not much loved, so I should not like to have people most likely
rejoicing over my misfortune and speculating on my coming decease before it is
necessary ... Did we not see enough of that in 1888! *No*, I want to remain
mistress of my actions and have no one interfere about my health or my private
affairs.'[43] She emphatically rejected Sophie's protests against this attitude.

'I bear no malice, but I also have no illusions, my experience of 42 years has taught me that. The ill-will so many bear my country is also extended to me, and at Berlin most people totally misunderstand me, and I am not to their taste. I have met with ingratitude and unkindness and disloyalty *untold* but I am not unforgiving … I should *not* like people at Berlin to know I am ill. My own friends would be sad and sorry, and also many a one among the townspeople, but the rest would be only too pleased to get rid of me! That was shown, written and said too plainly in 1888 for me to forget or misunderstand it … It is not my fault, but the fault of circumstances, which I had against me ever since I set my foot there in 1858, as a young girl only anxious to please … Had dear Papa been spared to reign for 10 or 20 years, things would have changed very much in that respect, as I would have had the *possibility* of rendering many a service which has been denied me.'[44] From the beginning Victoria made it clear to the Kaiser, too, that she wanted to keep her illness secret for as long as possible. 'As long as I am not the subject of conversation, gossip & discussion, & can continue to lead an active & useful Life, all is right, therefore I am so anxious nothing should leak out!', she told him in May 1899.[45] In the letters they exchanged Wilhelm and his mother camouflaged the subject as a precaution, speaking only of 'lumbago' or 'nerve pains'.[46]

In the course of 1900 quite a few relations and friends came to say goodbye to the gravely ill 59-year-old Empress.[47] In September 1900 her brother, still Prince of Wales, came to visit her and expressed a strong wish, on Queen Victoria's behalf as well as his own, that she make one last journey to England.[48] Renvers tried to forbid the journey, but she was unwilling to listen to him.[49] Had she gone, she might well have been present at Queen Victoria's death. Presumably she would then have died in England rather than at Friedrichshof. But there was no longer any question of such a journey. She was 'devoured with pain … with rarely an hour's respite', she admitted to her mother. 'I feel my patience & endurance well nigh worn out.'[50] In the following weeks her condition improved temporarily, and Wilhelm was able to tell his uncle Edward that his mother was able to leave her bed for the first time for a long time. 'We have spent most anxious days … & feel relieved to see her out of the immediate danger. She is slowly gathering strength, & of course still weak; but if she continues as she has done for the last 4 or 5 days, then we are in hopes that in a month or more, she will have recovered so far as to allow her beeing [sic] brought down & weather permitting into the open … Under the prevailing circumstances it is naturally impossible for her to go to England.'[51] (See Figure 2.)

But the improvement in his mother's state of health for which Wilhelm had hoped did not come.[52] In November 1900, one of her last letters to Queen

Figure 2 A last portrait of the Empress Frederick, Wilhelm's mother

Victoria reads: 'I am just as I was, the pain is fearful when it comes on, and the night sleepless. Tomorrow I shall have been 7 weeks in bed – & in pain, – not counting all the pain before – which I struggled with when I was still about! It is *hard*.'[53] When all her children (except Sophie) gathered at Friedrichshof two weeks later for her sixtieth birthday she expressed the fear that she would be able to see very little of them.[54] The Kaiser told Bülow, whom he had just appointed Reich Chancellor, that his 'poor' mother had to endure 'endless torment'.[55]

The attempts of her English relations to have the Empress treated again by Sir Francis Laking, who had visited her secretly in Italy, were blocked by the Kaiser's emphatic refusal to allow it. On 12 October 1900 Wilhelm telegraphed to Queen Victoria: 'Mama most thankful for the care of her doctors. Praised them to me today. She does not want anybody else. I can only repeat that any other doctors here would excite her and make her suspicious which must not be. Laking can see or hear nothing which could not be written to you and I would not allow him to see Mama. Besides it would create a most deplorable feeling here which must on no account be roused on account of Mama.'[56] The elderly Queen, consumed with worry though she was, had to give up her plan. 'I never doubted for a moment that Mama was in excellent medical hands and receives every possible care', she wired back. 'I merely wanted to have a verbal report. I shall certainly not send Laking as I do not want to cause disagreements, though it naturally increases my anxiety.'[57] Queen Victoria complained helplessly that she felt 'most cruelly cut off being unable to travel at this season so far else I would have gone to Darmstadt to be within reach when she was a little stronger to get a glimpse of her.'[58]

The sudden death of the Queen on 22 January 1901 was naturally a heavy blow for the ailing Empress in Kronberg. She bitterly lamented that she had not been able to see her mother one last time. When the distressing news reached Friedrichshof she was grief-stricken, writing: 'Words cannot describe my agony of mind at this overwhelming sorrow. Oh, my beloved Mama! Is she *really* gone? . . . To have lost her seems *so* impossible – and I far away could not see her dear face or kiss her dear hand once more. It *breaks* my heart . . . What a Queen she was, and what a woman! What will life be to me without her, the wretched bit of life left to me, struggling with a cruel disease?'[59]

The Kaiser was shocked when he saw his mother again after the funeral ceremonies in England. He wrote to his uncle Edward on 9 February 1901 from Kronberg: 'Mama has visibly changed since I last saw her in November. Her face is swollen a little, so that through its roundness & fullness the likeness to dear Grandmama has become very marked. The progress of the malady on her left side is great . . . Consequently she is weak & feels absolutely miserable. Her idea of going to England is a fantasy, which the doctor says is quite out of the question, she is totally intransportable. We are all fearfully pained by what we see & hear, & it is frightful to fancy what complications might arise besides. Poor mother is simply in a horrible state of suffering & discomfort;

so that one really sometimes is at loss to think wether [sic] she could not be spared the worst!'[60] The King was all the more astonished to receive a letter from his sister a few days later, expressing her 'ardent wish' to come to England at the end of February or the beginning of March, and saying that she was thinking of renting a house in Bournemouth for several months.[61] The desire to die in her beloved homeland was undoubtedly behind this plan. It also seems possible that the Empress had thoughts of smuggling her correspondence with her mother into England in this way.

But the doctors again forbade the journey as too risky,[62] and so the Empress saw her brother Edward for the last time at the end of February 1901 at Schloss Friedrichshof. The King arrived at Kronberg with one of his private secretaries, Sir Frederick Ponsonby, and Sir Francis Laking, whom he had appointed his personal physician. Although Edward had urged his nephew to treat his visit as purely private, when the three Englishmen in civilian dress stepped out of the train at Frankfurt they were met by Kaiser Wilhelm, surrounded by the military officers of the court, Adjutant-General Gustav von Kessel, Adjutant-General Friedrich von Scholl and Vice Admiral George Alexander von Müller, all resplendent in full uniform, together with Count August zu Eulenburg. In the following days, too, the Kaiser insisted on being present at every possible opportunity.[63] The King, however, succeeded in turning down his nephew's invitation to stay with him at the Schloss in Bad Homburg.[64]

On 15 June 1901, the anniversary of his father's death, Wilhelm II paid what was to be his penultimate visit to his mother at Friedrichshof.[65] In reply to a letter from Edward VII asking for news about his sister's condition,[66] the Kaiser wrote in deep dismay: 'When I saw her last on the 15th she suffered much pain & was very low in spirits & downcast. She often grew quite despondent & sometimes gave way to despair. This however not so much from the pain she is suffering — so the doctor says — but on account of the utter helplessness in which she is placed by this horrid illness ... The sight is most pitiful to one considering that one is utterly unable to give the slightest help. Morphia is used in long intervals & larger doses & does her much good giving her rest for several hours. The vital organs up to this date are quite free & in no way attacked, so that there is nothing to inspire any momentary anxiety; if things go on like at present the doctors think that it may go on for months even into the winter possibly. It is fearfully distressing!'[67]

Her torment came to an end in early August 1901. Her children and grandchildren, as well as some of her nieces and nephews, hastened to the dying Empress's bedside. Wilhelm broke off his northern cruise and arrived at Schloss Friedrichshof with Kaiserin Auguste Viktoria (Dona) on 3 August, two days before his mother's death. He sat by her bed throughout the last hours, and was there when her struggle finally ended. Edward VII, who had been preparing to leave for Germany in the hope of seeing his sister still alive, wrote to Wilhelm expressing his sympathy 'at the loss of your beloved Mama – & I know how you will miss her. She & I were devoted to one another – & my greatest pleasure was our weekly correspondence – now alas! a thing of the past. But one could not wish her life prolonged owing to her intense suffering.'[68] The King and his suite joined Wilhelm and his brother and sisters as they accompanied the coffin on the train journey from Kronberg to Potsdam. There the Empress was laid to rest in the Friedenskirche beside her husband and their two sons who had died young, Sigismund and Waldemar.

During her brother's last visit to her in February 1901 the widowed Empress had entrusted her letters to Queen Victoria to Fritz Ponsonby (who was a godson of her husband Friedrich III). She had hidden them, together with her other papers, in a secret room specially built on a mezzanine floor at Schloss Friedrichshof, to keep them out of her son's grasp. Not without reason she feared that the horrific events of the summer of 1888 might repeat themselves. 'I will send them to you at one o'clock to-night and I know I can rely on your discretion', Ponsonby claimed she told him in a private interview. 'I don't want a soul to know that they have been taken away and certainly Willie must not have them, nor must he ever know you have got them.'[69] According to his own later account, in circumstances reminiscent of a gothic mystery story, Ponsonby managed to smuggle the two trunk-sized boxes containing the correspondence out of the heavily guarded castle, under the very eyes of the Kaiser, who stood talking and gesticulating animatedly as they passed, and thence eventually to his own home near Windsor. After the Empress's death, he claimed, the grounds of Friedrichshof were completely encircled by mounted troops, with policemen posted all around the castle itself, 'while experienced secret police officers searched every corner of every room'.[70]

It is now clear that Ponsonby's dramatic account of how the correspondence came to be spirited away to England is untrue in several important respects.[71] For one thing, as Prince Wolfgang of Hesse was able to establish, the diary of his grandmother the Empress shows unequivocally that the Kaiser departed for Berlin on 26 February,[72] that is to say, four days before Ponsonby and the King left Friedrichshof for England on 2 March. There was thus no need for the trunks to be smuggled out of the Schloss under the Kaiser's nose. For another, no troops surrounded the Schloss and no secret policemen searched the rooms, if only because 'neither the Kaiser nor anyone else in his entourage could have realised that the letters the Empress had written to Queen Victoria had found their way back to Friedrichshof' – presumably to serve as the basis for an autobiographical account of her life as Crown Princess and Empress in Germany.[73] It was therefore only natural, as Prince Wolfgang observed, that his dying grandmother should have wished to see her letters to the Queen returned to the Royal Archives at Windsor where they properly belonged, and to have entrusted their transport to Sir Frederick ('Fritz') Ponsonby as the King's Private Secretary.[74] As there were no witnesses present at his meeting with the Empress it is impossible to say with any certainty whether she indicated her wish that her letters should not only be kept out of the Kaiser's hands but also one day be published by Ponsonby.[75] Their sensational publication in 1928–9 was to provoke a bitter row within the royal family on both sides of the North Sea, revealing the conflicting opinions in which the exiled Kaiser was held. As we shall see, Wilhelm tried in vain to prevent the publication of the letters with their painful details of his often shameful behaviour towards his parents in the 1880s.[76] But Ponsonby's controversial decision to publish did at least have the positive effect of giving voice at last to an astonishingly progressive English Princess and Empress who had long been silenced and maligned in Prussia-Germany.[77]

The Empress Frederick's death gave fresh impetus to the rumours which had been circulating for some years of a secret marriage to her Oberhofmeister Götz Graf von Seckendorff.[78] In 1897 Lord Esher, a close friend of Edward VII, was asked by a representative of the *Westminster Gazette* whether he had heard of any such marriage. Esher answered 'that although women were capable of any folly, this particular woman was too clever to sacrifice her position in Germany, which was just re-established, her relationship with the Emperor and with the Queen, for the sake of a man who had lived in her house twenty years! For a young Apollo, conceivably. But not for Polonius.' In his diary Esher added the cynical comment: 'This reply suffices whatever the truth may be.'[79] In the years that followed, it became generally accepted in diplomatic and journalistic circles worldwide that Seckendorff was not only the dowager Empress's confidante but 'peut être même l'epoux morganatique' – perhaps even her morganatic husband.[80] How forcibly Kaiser Wilhelm was prepared to defend his late mother's honour was apparent soon after her death. In response to these revived rumours he sent an open telegram to the Reich Chancellor on 28 August 1901: 'The Berliner Tageblatt has had the insolence and filth to say the vilest things about my mother. I have sent Plessen and von Löwenfeldt to their offices with sword and revolver and forced the editor to retract. I leave it to Your Excellency to publicly brand this swinish horde of newspaper pirates as they deserve, in whatever way is appropriate, through the Press.'[81] This was Wilhelm II's authentic voice.

The deaths of the old Queen and of the Kaiser's mother in 1901 severed a bond between Germany and Britain at a moment when it badly needed to be maintained. For the poisonous brew of jingoistic passions which was now boiling up in the press and on the streets of both countries – prompted above all by naval rivalry and by the outbreak of the Boer War in the autumn of 1899 – could scarcely be held in check any longer by either government. Kaiser Wilhelm II did indeed see himself as a bulwark against the hatred which threatened to drive the German and British peoples into a terrible fratricidal war. Yet at the same time, together with Bülow and the generals at court, aided by Tirpitz's massive battleship-building programme and all too often in collaboration with the chauvinistic forces within Germany, he was pursuing an ambitious strategy to gain supremacy. Its goal was to establish the German Reich, instead of Britain, as the foremost European Power. The ambiguity of the imperial strategy and the menace that it represented for Britain will become clearer if we disentangle the threads of Wilhelm's controversial role during the Boer War.

CHAPTER TWO

The Kaiser and England during the Boer War

In later years, and particularly in his notorious 'interview' in the *Daily Telegraph* in the autumn of 1908, Kaiser Wilhelm II constantly harked back to the stand he had taken during the Boer War as proof of his friendship for England. 'German opinion undoubtedly was hostile — bitterly hostile', he declared to the London newspaper, looking back on the South African War. But *official* Germany had not only taken no part in the anti-British press campaign, but had consciously held back, and he himself had even refused point-blank to receive the Boer delegates who were trying to bring about European intervention in the war, although the German people would certainly have garlanded them with flowers. And when Russia and France had approached him with a suggestion that in concert with Germany they should 'humiliate England to the dust', he, Wilhelm, had answered that Germany had to avoid any policy that risked bringing her into conflict with British naval power. But even that was not all, the Kaiser went on to assert in the 1908 *Telegraph* article. After the British defeats during 'Black Week' in December 1899 he had worked out a military plan of campaign, shown it to his General Staff for their comments, and placed it at the disposal of the British government. Almost as if claiming the British victory over the Boers for himself, the Kaiser added that 'the plan which I formulated ran very much on the same lines as that which was actually adopted by Lord Roberts, and carried by him into successful operation', and then asked, perplexed, 'Was that ... an act of one who wished England ill?'[1]

The major political crisis caused by this imperial 'interview' will be examined in detail in Chapter 25. Here we shall simply investigate the claims Wilhelm II made in this newspaper article and on countless other occasions as evidence of his pro-British attitude at the turn of the century, in the light of the available sources in the Royal Archives at Windsor Castle and elsewhere. What were the German Emperor's real intentions in this cruel war of conquest conducted by the British in South Africa, which caused such anger and horror throughout Europe? Why did he suddenly turn against precisely those nationalistic forces which he had stirred up against England with his 1896 telegram to Paul Krüger, and whose Anglophobia he continued to exploit for the benefit of his battleship-building progamme? Did he really send campaign plans which had been checked by the German General Staff to London, with a view to ensuring a British victory over the Boers? What was the truth of the matter with regard to the alleged proposal by Russia and France to form a continental league with Germany and bring England 'to her knees'? And why, if such an offer was made, did Wilhelm not accept it?

SECRET FANTASIES OF WORLD POWER AND THE FEAR OF A PREMATURE WAR

The war which broke out in October 1899 after years of tension between Great Britain and the two Boer republics, Transvaal and the Orange Free State, seemed to offer Germany great opportunities, but equally great dangers. On the one hand, there was a belief in Berlin that with the British Empire plunged into war in South Africa, the moment had come for a worldwide redistribution of power, from which the young and economically successful German Reich ought certainly to reap the first benefits. On the other hand, Tirpitz's battleship-building programme, through which it was hoped to bring Britain's naval supremacy to an end, was still only in its infancy. At this 'time of our weakness', as Wilhelm II called it,[2] a war with England would have disastrous consequences. Should Germany's longer-term goals become known during the 'danger zone', which would last until the fleet was ready, London might well be provoked into making political alliances or even undertaking a preventive strike against Germany. Even the popular enthusiasm which was needed for the fleet programme, and which was therefore assiduously fanned at the highest level, threatened to bring about an adverse reaction from Britain. More dangerous still were the vociferous tirades of hatred heard among many sections of the German population when imperialistic, plutocratic Britain took brutal measures against the small, Germanic, Protestant farming community in the Transvaal. The chances of a corresponding Germanophobia arising in England, and bringing a premature Anglo-German conflict nearer, were all too great. It was therefore necessary to camouflage real intentions and convey the impression that Russian and French money was at work subverting the public mood and influencing it against the Kaiser and official German policy. In addition, Wilhelm needed to show as amiable a face as possible to his English relations and to English public opinion, so as to keep them in the dark as long as possible. 'I am the only one who is still holding the English back, otherwise they will break out too soon and my fleet is not ready', he declared in a marginal note on a report from London, completely betraying his plan.[3] As he explained in March 1900 to Queen Wilhelmina of the Netherlands, who had proposed a joint German, Dutch, Russian and French peace initiative in support of the defeated Boers, the moment of reckoning for the British Empire had not yet come. It was true that 'the map of the world' was 'in the process of undergoing great changes', the Kaiser conceded, but in view of the increasingly passionate feelings of their peoples, statesmen needed to weigh up their policies with the greatest caution if they were to prevent a war breaking out unexpectedly and at the wrong time. For war must not come until 'the price paid by a people in misery and blood is worthwhile. It is true that such "Realpolitik" is often very harmful to Christian morality ... But whoever believes in the Lord God as Supreme Judge of the world order also knows that nothing in the life of nations escapes Him, and that He punishes wrongdoing with unsparing severity, when? And how? That is for Him to decide! So one must allow matters to take their course, in silence although in deep sorrow ... Yet one must look into the future and strive to make one's country strong and able to defend itself, so that at least one is prepared, should the Lord choose one to be his instrument some day!? Thus it is in the interest of world peace, as well as that of the Netherlandish-Friesian race on the continent, that there should be a powerful fleet on the sea! When it is afloat, then at last the banners of Orange and Brandenburg will fly side by side on every sea, as in days gone by ... Until then let us be silent and work.'[4] Similarly, the Kaiser told the French ambassador, the Marquis de Noailles, in October 1899 that for the moment 'England's fleet was equal to any coalition, while Germany had as good as no fleet. I was therefore not in a position to abandon the strictest neutrality, and had to acquire a fleet first. After twenty years, when it is ready, I shall change my tune.'[5]

Nowhere do Wilhelm II's secret aims at the turn of the century manifest themselves more clearly than in the pompously subservient letters which the then Foreign Secretary and future Reich Chancellor Bernhard von Bülow addressed to the Kaiser. Deliberately playing on his vanity and his cult of his Hohenzollern ancestors, Bülow wrote to Wilhelm in 1900: 'How true it is that in Your Majesty's reign the British are playing the same role as the French under the Great Elector and the Austrians under Frederick the Great. Dealing with the English is infinitely laborious, infinitely difficult, requires infinite patience and skill. But just as the Hohenzollern eagle drove the double-headed Austrian eagle from the battlefield and clipped the wings of the Gallic cock, so, with God's help and Your Majesty's strength and wisdom it will get the best of the English leopard too. Its wings are growing.'[6] As head of the Foreign Office, Bülow was well aware of Wilhelm II's antipathy towards the British Prime Minister, Lord Salisbury, and fostered it energetically. At the same time, however, he emphasised the need always to act 'cautiously, coolly, playing the waiting game' in regard to England until the battlefleet was ready.[7] 'There is probably no man in Europe with whom I am inwardly as angry as with the fat English Prime Minister' he wrote to the Kaiser in a key letter of August 1899. 'But I think like Odysseus, when he was provoked by the suitors before he had all his arrows in his quiver . . . Only when Odysseus had gathered his arrows and his bow together did he strike all the shameless suitors down onto the sand. After that he ruled in Ithaca, content, happy and undisturbed. He gave his enemies no hint of his intentions in advance. If Your Majesty, with Your uncommon skill in dealing with the English, succeeds in winning over Salisbury and in maintaining reasonably good political relations with him, until our fleet (to use Scharnhorst's words) is over the worst, it would be a political master-stroke.' Referring to the looming conflict with the Boers, Bülow added, with cynical calculation: 'If war were really to break out in South Africa, England would be far less able to take action in Asia and Polynesia, at least for a certain time, and would thus be more dependent on us. On the other hand we have no interest in the complete defeat of the Boers and Afrikaaners, which would be the most likely outcome of the contest. As far as I can judge, I think it would be best for us to remain completely neutral and to say nothing, for the time being, with regard to the dispute between England and the Transvaal.'[8]

A letter from Bülow of 8 November 1899 informing the Kaiser of the successful conclusion of the negotiations between Germany, Britain and the USA over the partition of the Samoan Islands gives an insight into the long-term aims, as well as the domestic motives, of German policy. 'Of course we did not give the English the smallest undertaking as to our future attitude, in particular with regard to the South African war, and we made sure our overall policy remained completely unfettered. Your Majesty has a free hand everywhere, just as before . . . So, with God's help and thanks to Your Majesty's energy, tenacity and wisdom, Upolu and Sawaii have been won for Germany, and Your Majesty's glorious banner will fly over both! These islands, where Germans have worked so long and so diligently, and which serve as a base for our trade in the Pacific Ocean with Polynesia, Australia and Western America, have great commercial value. Greater still is their maritime significance for our inter-oceanic shipping, in view of the future Panama Canal and the projected German world cable link. But the place which the islands occupy in the nation's heart is of even higher value ... Ineradicable memories and the blood of dear ones have long since formed a bond between these islands, which Your Majesty has now won, and Germany. Neither the Navy nor the people would ever have recovered from their loss; their gain will inspire both to follow Your Majesty further on the path towards world power, greatness and everlasting glory.'[9] Given Germany's far-reaching aims, and especially the hostility shown towards him personally, it is hardly surprising that Lord Salisbury saw no political advantage in an audience with Wilhelm during the Kaiser's visit to England in November 1899, as 'the real difficulties between the two countries depended on the fact that they were rival colonial Powers'.[10] The Prime Minister had long since suspected that Wilhelm's accusations against him were nothing but the expression of his malign intentions towards Britain.[11]

Although the great geopolitical confrontation they sought had to be delayed until the battlefleet was ready, Wilhelm II and Bülow nevertheless cherished breathtaking ambitions for a possible 'reordering of the map of the world' as a result of British entanglement in the Boer War. In the spring and summer of 1899 Wilhelm had again complained bitterly of 'the old, unscrupulous, self-interested, loutish English policy',[12] uttered warnings about the true nature of 'John Bull'[13] and expressed contempt for the English habit of accepting the friendly offices of other Powers without being prepared to return them. One was constantly reminded, he wrote sarcastically, 'how far one gets when one does England a good turn without previous clear and binding agreements, purely from the goodness of one's heart!'[14] In September 1899, when it was reported that Lord Salisbury was growing increasingly alarmed at the deteriorating situation in the Transvaal, Wilhelm wrote in triumph: 'Now we can name an even higher price if the English want something from us.'[15] Making no attempt to hide his satisfaction over Britain's difficulties, the Kaiser wrote, at the outbreak of war in October 1899: 'Now the disadvantages of "Glorious Isolation" are coming out. What is more, a feeling has arisen that all the other powers have been thoroughly antagonised by constant loutish, pushing behaviour, and that they are all glad that the lout has got his come-uppance now. He [the Englishman] senses that although we have constantly been badly treated, we have not let ourselves be swept away, and are therefore a constant reproach to him in our silent endurance. At any rate it is now apparent that "we've got the ships, we've got the men, we've got the money too", from the 1897 Jubilee days, certainly sounds very splendid, especially from *the very stage* — displaying the Union Jack — from which a short while ago in the winter the German Emperor was mocked in songs greeted by storms of wild applause, but when put into practice it has its problems after all, and will in any case cost a great deal of the last item! There's the rub! The game is getting too costly! John Bull isn't used to that! The risk has suddenly grown much greater!'[16] To Waldersee's suggestion that there would be political and material advantages to be gained from the situation if he gave the English the impression that the Germans were 'well-wishing friends in times of need', Wilhelm nodded in agreement and replied: 'I think that can be managed.'[17] The Kaiser cherished hopes of a Russian attack on Persia, Afghanistan or India. With Britain's involvement in South Africa the Russians would 'surely make their presence felt' in Central Asia, he commented, 'and then our gestures of friendship will begin to acquire a high value in the market! Especially in London.'[18] His jubilation at this initial stage of the South African war was irrepressible. 'May they [the English] get into a real pickle, and may India, Asia and Abyssinia join the dance!'[19]

Foreign Secretary Bernhard von Bülow, who had recently been raised to the rank of Count, beguiled his All-Highest sovereign with the ultimate prospect of the Reich becoming the foremost Power in the world. Not only South and East Africa, and the South Pacific with its connections to Australia, North and South America and the new Panama Canal, but also the entire Asiatic land bridge would come under German influence. As 'the great aims' of German world policy he listed no less than 'the Mediterranean, Byzantium, Persia [and] East Asia'.[20] The Reich must take full advantage of the 'momentarily so favourable situation' which had arisen from British difficulties in South Africa 'for the Baghdad railway, coaling station on the Red Sea, and other things'.[21] If only the fleet were ready! When Bülow again stressed that 'overseas policy' could be conducted only 'with adequate naval power' at one's disposal, the monarch wrote impatiently in the margin of Bülow's report that this was exactly 'what I have been preaching to those donkeys of Reichstag deputies every day for 10 years'.[22] At the beginning of the Boer War he exclaimed in frustration: 'What can we do? The English are so far beyond us that it is no use our grumbling.'[23]

The statesmen and generals around Wilhelm II, as their diaries and letters show, were similarly convinced that as long as German naval power remained inferior, England must not be unnecessarily provoked; only after the completion of the battlefleet in about a decade and a half would it be possible to take a strong stance against England. Alfred von Tirpitz himself explained at the beginning of 1900 to Eugen von Jagemann, Baden's envoy in Berlin, that the 'determined advocates of a peaceful policy' had 'altogether the upper hand' in the government, because it was recognised that 'a war at sea, unless perhaps France or Russia began the offensive', would 'destroy our navy in its infancy'.

If, however, war with England were to break out, according to Tirpitz it would certainly be 'in the interests of self-preservation to give France the alternatives of cooperating at sea or being attacked by us on land'.[24] Even the ever-militant Hereditary Prince Bernhard of Saxe-Meiningen, Commanding General in Breslau, recognised the enforced ambiguity in his imperial brother-in-law's attitude. After the first British setbacks in the Boer War he commented: 'There is surely no one happier in his heart than the Kaiser over the defeat of the English, who are for once getting a proper clout in their insolent faces. But in the true interest of the state he has to keep his thoughts secret . . . and must be silent, in order not to rouse English anger against us in our impotence. The stupidity and baseness of our beloved people's representatives have put him in this position' by constantly rejecting the Kaiser's demands for the navy.[25] The Prince complained bitterly to General Colmar von der Goltz of the powerless condition to which the Reich was, for the time being, condemned. 'We are thus forced to watch, while a small, courageous people is swallowed by the English, those hypocrites. I hope their stomachs will be upset for a good long time, for these Dutch folk are not an easily digested snack.'[26] A few weeks later Prince Bernhard wrote: 'The typically English, brutal behaviour towards the Transvaal, the war which the dear humane English are about to begin under the flimsiest of pretexts, this is what naturally interests me at present most of all.' Goltz had complained 'that Germany, which after all had an interest in not allowing the Boers to be annihilated, did not leap to their aid. But how are we to do that? Thanks to the obtuseness of our dear Reichstag we still have no fleet worthy of the name, for the few ships we have are not worth a powder shot against a naval power! How can we help the Boers? Words alone cannot do it! It has long since been clear to me that England is only lying in wait for a conflict so as to leave us with a choice between humiliation and the destruction of our trade. I expect events to build up to that in a few years, and in fact I am fairly sure of the timing: it will happen as soon as the Queen closes her eyes.'[27] At the height of the South African war the Prince comforted himself with a glance into the future. Without a strong battlefleet Germany had to 'hang around ignominiously in the corner of world affairs'; only when the fleet was ready around 1917 would one be able to hope for the rise of a generation which was not 'born with donkey's ears and blinkers', he commented.[28] With similar impatience Colonel Bruno von Mudra bemoaned German impotence at the outbreak of the Boer War: 'If only we were now in a position – which we are not, with our fleet – to take advantage of the war in South Africa, as soon as it is really alight, to attack [England].' Only 'in 14 years' time' would it be possible for 'combinations to arise in the relationship between the great powers in question' which would 'make the idea of a simultaneous landing on Britain's south and east coasts seem no longer in the least Utopian'.[29]

In view of British supremacy even Waldersee was forced to admit the necessity of letting slip the opportunities which the outbreak of the Boer War seemed to offer to the Reich, at least for the time being. To be sure, he welcomed the British defeats at the Cape in December 1899 and commented that as a result of these failures, the German Empire's position 'on the world stage' had 'unquestionably improved'; it was now important to take advantage of that fact.[30] He also took malicious pleasure in observing the growing dissatisfaction with British rule among native troops in Egypt and hoped for unrest in Britain itself and in Ireland. England could scarcely afford a further defeat 'without falling victim to general contempt', he commented in February 1900. 'What a chance France would have now if she had an energetic man at the helm!'[31] But Waldersee fully appreciated the bitter reality that British supremacy at sea placed severe limits on the Reich's scope for action. And more clearly than Wilhelm, Bülow, Tirpitz, Prince Bernhard and Colonel Mudra, the old Field Marshal foresaw that Britain would not simply accept the construction of the German fleet without responding. 'We are constantly dependant on England's good will and benevolence', he noted shortly before the beginning of the war in the Transvaal. 'Whenever we order a new ship, England immediately places an order for 2 or 3, so she always remains far superior to us. No intelligent person would ever believe that we can build a fleet equal to that of the English. Our only chance of countering them is through alliances, and we no longer have any.'[32] Waldersee foresaw very clearly the consequences of the German challenge when he wrote in February 1900: 'If England wins the war in South Africa, and if serious problems do not arise for her in Egypt or India in the meantime, it will not be long before conflict breaks out between us . . . God grant that we be spared such a calamity — for that is what war with England would be for us. The good Lord will certainly have to intervene in events to help us; our diplomacy cannot do it.'[33] It was just such a calamity that the Kaiser wanted to prevent by his personal charm offensive.

GERMAN ANGLOPHOBIA AND THE KAISER'S VISIT TO WINDSOR AND SANDRINGHAM

The temporising, outwardly strictly neutral and peaceable policy maintained by Wilhelm II and the Wilhelmstrasse was thwarted by the critical, increasingly anglophobic reaction of German public opinion to the war in South Africa.[34] The Krüger telegram and the government-led propaganda campaign in favour of the expansion of the fleet had already created the impression in

Britain that Germany was the country's most dangerous enemy. After the first Navy Law was passed in the spring of 1898 the Kaiser's mother complained that 'the *abuse* poured on England by the German Press day by day about everything and on every occasion is quite extraordinary. I fear it leads to a distressing conclusion in England, which is that she has no greater enemy than Germany and no more bitter foe than William.' She drew urgent attention to the danger that as a result of this hostility England might ally herself with Russia and France against Germany.[35] Eighteen months later, when the storm clouds of war were gathering over South Africa, she wrote – still the proud 'Engländerin' to the last – to her eldest son: 'Germany is in a state of Anglophobia which is no better than Russia or France. I am heart & soul with my country in this and admire what our troops have done till now.'[36] Again she warned Wilhelm of the consequences of the hate-filled anti-British tirades in the German press. 'It is *so* easy to excite blind unreasoning hatred! But it is *very* difficult to cure it & to calm it, & it breeds *mischief* & *only* mischief.'[37] Seriously ill as she was, she saw clearly that German anglophobia had become a two-edged sword for Wilhelm and the statesmen of the Reich. 'This wicked rubbish [anti-British feeling] is not convenient for the German Government, which wants now to be on the best terms with England on account of its colonial plans, etc. Yet on the other hand it finds that this Anglophobia is one of the chief impulses for moving people to vote money for the extension of the fleet.'[38] She complained bitterly at the German, French and Russian *Schadenfreude* over the defeats suffered by the British troops in December 1899. 'Oh, if I were a man, how I should like to knock a few people down!'[39] In a letter to her son in March 1900 she pointed out that the German agitation was far more wounding for Queen Victoria than the anti-British campaigns in France or Russia. 'Her Mother was German, her Husband was German, her sons in Law & daughters in Law (nearly all), her sympathies always *were* German, and her kindness & generosity have been constantly shown in 60 years in countless different ways! ... You can imagine *my* feelings when I see *her* made the subject of gross and insulting carricatures [sic] sent on Post cards through the Imperial Post at Berlin!!'[40]

It was not only Wilhelm's anglophile mother, however, but also the otherwise so anglophobic Waldersee, who immediately recognised the danger which lay in the mounting popular hatred for Britain. At the beginning of the war he had certainly shared the general indignation, heartily wished failure upon the British, and criticised what he saw as the 'ambiguous' attitude of the Kaiser and the Wilhelmstrasse.[41] But not long afterwards, when the second German Navy Bill was under public discussion, the General feared that it was being 'all too openly' stressed in parliament and in the press 'that we need a large fleet because of English superiority'.[42] He had similar reservations about the rebuke which Bülow thought fit to administer to Britain in a speech on this occasion in the Reichstag. 'There is no question that it caused great anger in England', he recorded nervously. 'Perhaps they have swallowed it down because of the defeats in Natal, but certainly very unwillingly.'[43] Only a few weeks later he observed with growing concern that the British newspapers were 'beginning to lose all shame in attacking us; it gives me the impression of a deliberate hate campaign'.[44]

In this risky situation, in order to avert dangerous countermeasures on Britain's part, Wilhelm and Bülow had to make strenuous efforts to separate official German policy from overwrought public opinion and to create the impression in London that the latter was directed against the Kaiser, or was even a Franco-Russian intrigue. As Bülow pointed out to the Grand Duke of Baden at the end of 1899, where foreign policy was concerned 'the sky is anything but cloudless. We must operate with great care. We must prevent the passionate excitement of German public opinion against England and the very bitter anti-English language of the German press from disturbing our relationship to this power (which despite its defeats in South Africa is still our superior at sea); but we must not allow this to endanger the independence of our existing policy in any way, nor put our good relations with Russia at risk.'[45] After some initial hesitation Kaiser Wilhelm fell in with this line. Reports reached Waldersee from court circles that the Kaiser had passionately attacked the German press, and 'complained that its anti-English stance was making matters very difficult for him politically'.[46] His words were followed by deeds.

In spite of the outbreak of war in South Africa the Kaiser stuck to his plans to visit Windsor and Sandringham in November 1899. This decision, highly controversial in Germany, served both to allay British mistrust of the German Reich and to show publicly that anti-British agitation among the German population had nothing in common with Wilhelm's personal intentions, nor with official German policy.[47] He instructed his friend Philipp Eulenburg to tell the British ambassador in Vienna, Sir Horace Rumbold, how much he yearned to be reunited with his grandmother, 'who had always been so good to him and was bound up with his earliest recollections'. The Kaiser, Eulenburg insisted, was 'absolutely furious' about the storm in the German press against his forthcoming visit to England, to which he had been looking forward for months. He took a passionate interest in the war in South Africa and indeed occasionally expressed reservations about British strategy there, but generally he spoke 'in terms of unstinted admiration' of the 'quality and demeanour of our troops', who — in Wilhelm's own words — fought like heroes, 'as indeed

British soldiers always did'. The Kaiser was absolutely convinced that 'the right policy for Germany was to keep on very cordial terms with Great Britain'.[48] When the Bismarckian press maintained that Bismarck, the 'Grand Master of all diplomatic statecraft', would have viewed the visit to England with profound misgiving, the Kaiser dismissed such criticism with the remark: 'Quite so! Because the Great Man was not in a position to take new circumstances into account, and could not get out of the attitude of small-minded mistrust and carping left over from Crimean War days.'[49] Now, apparently, it was time to aim for greater goals – those of world politics.

The assurances of friendship dispensed by the Kaiser and Bülow in Windsor and Sandringham acquired all the more urgency when the influential British Colonial Secretary, Joseph Chamberlain, who had done more than anyone else to promote an Anglo-German alliance, made it plain to both men that if the German press attacks on Britain continued, 'the Englishman' would come to the conclusion that 'the German' was his worst enemy.[50] In his audience with Queen Victoria on 23 November 1899 Bülow emphasised, as the Queen noted in her journal, that he was 'much distressed at the bad feeling in Germany against us ... He was in despair about the Press, which he said was most difficult to control, and spoke, just as William did, of the immense harm Bismarck had done by using all his influence to promote a bad feeling towards England and seek a close alliance with Russia, when it ought to be just the reverse. He spoke with great attachment of Vicky, and how much she wished for a good understanding between Germany and England.'[51] Similarly, in the conversations which he held at Sandringham, at the Kaiser's request, with Francis Bertie, Deputy Under Secretary of State at the Foreign Office, Bülow tried hard to play down the damaging impression which the German press attacks had created. He distanced himself from Bismarckian methods and reiterated that he was 'most anxious to cultivate good relations with England. He knew that alliances were not in vogue here but he hoped to be able to get over difficulties, as they arose, by friendly discussion, and goodwill would not be wanting on his part.'[52]

The Kaiser too, in his own animated manner, told the royal family and leading statesmen how much he deplored the German press denigration of Britain. He assured the Queen's Private Secretary, Sir Arthur Bigge, that the criticism did not at all coincide with his government's attitude; on the contrary, he said, he even believed 'that Russian money was being spent in Germany to influence the Press unfavourably towards England! He had tried to get at the few respectable Press authorities to stop this Anglophobe campaign.'[53] In a letter to his uncle Edward, the Kaiser depicted the anti-British press campaign in Germany as a fiendish intrigue by Russia and

France. 'With superhuman efforts Bülow & I we slowly got the better of the German Press, swamped as it was with articles, news, canards & last not least roubles & francs from both sides, with a view of creating a socalled anti English feeling, which was to be denounced by my kind neighbours to England.'[54] However obvious the Machiavellian calculation behind such assurances, it would be a mistake to see them purely as a tactical move. Waldersee could not believe his ears when he heard from an authoritative source that the Kaiser had complained not only to his English relations and British statesmen but also to Count Schlieffen, 'that it was only the *Press* which had whipped up the otherwise very sensible German people against the English − our natural allies − and that this had been brought about solely by Russian roubles!'[55] This idea of Wilhelm's was 'really incredible', Waldersee fulminated; he wondered who could possibly have suggested such a thing to the Kaiser.[56] Such accesses of anglophilia, however, always swung quickly back into hatred and envy of his 'motherland'.

After his return to Germany Wilhelm expressed the hope, in an affectionately worded letter of thanks to his uncle, that his visit to Windsor and Sandringham would usher in a new era in Anglo-German relations. 'Am quite convinced that my stay will benefit both countries & that intercourse with your leading men also with Bülow will bear good fruit in time for both of us & for the world at large. Bismarck's old saying still remains true when he told Grandpapa that he wished him to meet his colleagues once a year if possible. "It is always a good thing for the great lords to meet once a year, for one conversation is worth ten times more than ten written dispatches".'[57]

The temporising calculation that lay behind the visit and the Kaiser's other friendly gestures towards Britain was not lost on those in the know. Wilhelm's former tutor Hinzpeter wrote to his imperial pupil after the visit: 'It must be exceedingly difficult to steer the poorly-armed German ship of state out there on the ocean, far from our protecting coasts and their batteries, where any collision could prove disastrous and must therefore be carefully avoided. This journey by the Kaiser has been discussed more than any other before it; and the German populace has displayed only too clearly both its lack of political sense and its instinctive dislike for England. The latter is easy to explain psychologically. As long as the Germans were preoccupied only with literary or political or religious interests, they could be full of admiration for England, which possessed much that they themselves sought after. But since economic interests have come to the fore, they cannot but be full of enmity and jealousy towards the rivals who were once overwhelmingly superior and are still dangerous. Nor will matters improve until Germany has become so strong that she loses the vexing and embittering fear of competition, i.e. until the difference in economic power and also in naval power has become more tolerable. Furthermore, the German public is unfortunately not yet able to understand that the more fiercely the competitive battle rages between peoples and individuals, the more necessary it is for states to be peaceful and friendly towards each other. It is fortunate, and it bodes well, that the German Emperor thinks and cares for his people in this respect too.' Wilhelm accepted this interpretation of his aims with approval.[58]

The Kaiser's visit to Windsor did not dispel the danger which he attributed to the 'agitation by certain German papers for war against England, although our weakness at sea is obvious', and he was obliged to maintain a very cautious policy towards Britain.[59] With the British military successes in South Africa in the spring of 1900 public fury in Germany, Russia and France reached new heights, and made it even more difficult for their governments to steer a moderate course.[60] Wilhelm, however, defied this storm of protest and stood by his policy of non-intervention at all costs.[61] After the New Year reception at the Berlin Schloss the British military attaché, Colonel Sir James Grierson, commented that the monarch, who had spoken to him like a 'brother officer', was probably 'the only man in this nation who wishes us this success from his heart'.[62]

Wilhelm took particular trouble to nurture his relationship with the royal family, so as to dispel British mistrust. On 19 April 1900, when the Prince of Wales arrived at Altona on his way back to London from Copenhagen, he was surprised and touched to be greeted with full military honours by the Kaiser, who had hurried there from Berlin, in full dress uniform and accompanied by an enormous suite, with his brother Heinrich and the British ambassador, Sir Frank Lascelles.[63] And it was only gratitude for Wilhelm's personal resistance to the hostility of German public opinion and the anglophobia of those around him that persuaded the Duke of York (the future King George V) to accept the Kaiser's invitation, looked on with favour by Queen Victoria, Lord Salisbury and Lascelles, to go to Berlin for the celebration of the coming-of-age of the German Crown Prince on 6 May 1900.[64] On the other hand the Duke's mother, Alexandra, the Princess of Wales, believed that she had seen through Wilhelm's intrigues, writing scornfully to her son: 'Anyhow W. wishes at this moment to be extra civil but without offence I fear it is only to suit his own purpose & throw dust in our eyes – *his country* cannot disguise its *true* feelings against us – and all *his future* will show it with a vengeance.'[65]

The strange dispatch which Wilhelm sent to Reich Chancellor Prince Hohenlohe on 10 January 1900 demonstrates not only how much his attitude was determined by fear of war with Britain induced by the popular anglophobic frenzy, but also how useful this proved for his plans for the navy.

In it the Kaiser demanded the immediate introduction of the Navy Bill, as a kind of internal lightning-conductor. 'The mood throughout the population [against Britain] has become ... so angry, and disgust at the insult it has received is mounting so fast that sooner or later it will try to force its way through with elemental violence. The next thing will be public meetings, protest meetings and even more impudent attacks against England and the Queen herself than have already taken place. That would probably ... in the case of further setbacks, provoke the English to the utmost against us. So the fast expanding head of steam among our people must be diverted internally, into the path on which patriotism can most usefully serve our country.' And this path, he said, was the new Navy Bill.[66] In his excitement Wilhelm seems to have been unaware that his ambiguous attitude could be counterproductive. The British military attaché, however, realised at once that the Kaiser wished to take full advantage of the public unrest 'to get his naval bill passed'.[67]

In view of British sensitivities Wilhelm firmly refused to grant an audience to the deputation of Boers led by Dr Leyds, although they were received by Tsar Nicholas II.[68] In October 1900 the Kaiser rejected the demand of the Transvaal delegates that he should participate in the protests against Britain's 'more and more brutalising and inhuman' conduct of the war in South Africa, with the note 'non possum' – 'I cannot'.[69] Then Paul Krüger himself landed in Marseilles in November and was enthusiastically acclaimed in Paris, after which he announced his intention of coming to Berlin next. Wilhelm was faced with the acute dilemma of whether or not to accede to the demands of German public opinion and receive the South African politician, who was after all travelling through Europe as 'head of state'. If Krüger came to Berlin, the Kaiser foresaw that the mob would break the windows of the British Embassy, and that he would be forced to order troops to intervene to protect the building.[70] Replying by telegraph to his Foreign Office's report on the proposed visit, he pointed out that it was unprecedented for a head of state to come to Berlin without previously enquiring whether his visit would be welcome. This was 'an attempt at political rape' and that was reason enough to reject it. It was true, as Privy Councillor Friedrich von Holstein recorded, that in the past the Kaiser had 'sent the Krüger Telegram on his own initiative', but one should not forget that 'between the Krüger Telegram and today [December 1900] the Kaiser's relations with President Krüger have cooled as a result of various experiences, firstly the President's great reserve in responding to questions raised with him regarding German interests, and secondly his total disregard of the personal advice which we ... repeatedly offered him, while it was still possible to avoid conflict with England'. Consequently the Kaiser was 'freed from all moral responsibility towards

Krüger and the Transvaal, for they have always gone their own way and have regularly done the opposite of what we advised. I am not worried about the effect of the refusal', Holstein declared. 'The German Emperor, and even more so the King of Prussia, together and in complete agreement with his government, represents a power compared to which the pinpricks of franc-tireurs, court preachers etc from the rest of Germany and elsewhere count for nothing at all.'[71] Inwardly the Kaiser sympathised with the anti-British criticisms of the nationalist agitators.[72] But he saw clearly the threat to his grand designs for world politics represented by the excited state of German public opinion and 'our idiotic Press', as he frequently called it.[73] Moreover, the Kaiser was not slow to see how he could make diplomatic capital from his resistance to the chauvinists in his own country. He hoped, he told Bülow on 14 February 1901, 'that the English understood and appreciated what he was doing for them, against strong opposition from German public opinion'.[74]

THE KAISER AND THE WAR IN SOUTH AFRICA

Kaiser Wilhelm's outwardly pro-British stance during the Boer War was all the more striking because long after sending the Krüger Telegram in January 1896 he had continued to support the efforts of the two Boer republics, the Transvaal and Orange Free State, to gain their independence. When reports from London in the spring of 1897 indicated that war might soon break out in South Africa, Wilhelm at once ordered these rumours to be spread in the German press. The news was 'very serious' and would have 'unforeseeable consequences', he commented, expressing his suspicion that 'England has surely been pushed into acting more quickly by the Reichstag's vote on naval affairs, so as to exploit the time while we are weak.' He hoped that if there were war, the British would 'get the same thrashing as 15 years ago' – a reference to the defeat they had suffered in the first Transvaal war in 1881.[75] In 1897 Wilhelm still had every intention, as in January 1896, of ordering a direct military intervention on land in support of the Boers. In view of the imminent war he emphatically rejected the Reich Chancellor's proposal to reduce the strength of the army in the neighbouring German colony of South-West Africa (now Namibia). 'We must have enough troops at our disposal in South West Africa, firstly to put down immediately any revolts stirred up by England, but then so as to have a strong column available to come to the aid of the Afrikaaners and Boers, in alliance with Hottentots etc. For it is in our interest that they are preserved. Our strength at sea in comparison with England = 0, but on land it is rather different, especially with the support of the brave Boers. Therefore we must not only not reduce the army, but quietly and gradually strengthen it. 20–30 men must be sent out with every ship, and they could then be kept ready there, partly in the army, partly as settlers.'[76] In the spring of 1898 Wilhelm received the German Consul General in Capetown, Bruno von Schuckmann, who suggested a large-scale German settlement programme in South-West Africa to counteract the growing British influence in the southern half of the continent. The Kaiser commissioned him to write a report on 'the German presence in Cape Colony'.[77] Waldersee therefore had some grounds for suspecting, at the outbreak of the South African war in 1899, that the Boers had been 'really very much encouraged by Germany, or to be more precise, by the Kaiser' in their refractory attitude towards Britain.[78] Wilhelm's hostility towards Britain lasted until the eve of the Boer War. But as both the Kaiser and Bülow remembered the disastrous results of Bismarck's attempts at mediation at the Congress of Berlin of 1878, they realised from the start that it was essential to keep well clear of the South African conflict.[79] In August 1899 Wilhelm decreed: 'No! Not our business. *We* are keeping out of that!' He added sarcastically: 'The Hague Peace Conference can easily step in.'[80]

In the first disquieting weeks of the war Wilhelm's attitude swung bizarrely back and forth. In September 1899 Waldersee recorded that the Kaiser was apparently bent on sending German officers to the British army, and wrote in alarm: 'I hope it is not too late to dissuade him.'[81] At the beginning of the war Wilhelm spoke 'with great satisfaction of the success of the English and great hostility towards the Boers'.[82] At the end of October 1899, when news of British setbacks arrived, his attitude veered round to the opposite direction. While hunting in Blankenburg, Waldersee heard, the Kaiser had declared himself convinced that the cause of the Boer War had been 'the dirtiest money-grubbing and greed for gold'. It was news to Waldersee that, as Wilhelm stated, 'so many highly-placed people [in England] had got mixed up in nasty transactions that war had been chosen as the only way to get out of them'.[83] Shortly afterwards the Kaiser expressed the opinion that the British army was considerably worse than had been supposed in Germany. In mid December 1899, when news of the heavy British defeat at the Tugela River broke, Waldersee thought he could detect from the Kaiser's ambiguous reaction 'that although he had delighted in the humiliation of the English, he was beginning to feel sorry for them after such serious defeats, and especially that he felt very much for his grandmother'. Waldersee, on the other hand, considered it 'very good luck that this has happened'.[84]

The Kaiser's sympathy for the British royal family and his regret at the heavy losses suffered by British regiments in South Africa, some of whose officers he knew personally, is strikingly confirmed by sources in the Royal

Archives at Windsor – as he was to claim in the *Daily Telegraph* interview of 1908.[85] In reply to Queen Victoria's telegram informing him personally of the catastrophic defeat of the British army under General Sir Redvers Buller at the Tugela River, Wilhelm sent a message full of sympathy: 'Most grateful to have thought of me, had just read copy of Sir Redvers despatch. Am sincerely sorry for the terrible loss of life, which has occurred in the last fortnight, a proof of the dauntless courage of officers and men.'[86] That day he wrote to his mother: 'I know how deeply you must be concerned in the terrible desasters [sic] which overtook the British Army in Afrika [sic] in the last fortnight. How many friends, & friends sons are out there dead or wounded! The situation is most serious & gives me much anxiety too. But in all this misery at all events the pluck & dauntless courage of the officers & men stand out in a clear relief, & this will help to bear the heavy burden of sorrow which Providence has suddenly laid on Britains shoulders.'[87] His Christmas letters to his British relations likewise left them in no doubt about his sympathy over the heavy losses in South Africa.[88] 'Many brave officers & men have fallen or are disabled after showing pluck, courage & determined bravery! How many homes will be sad this year & how many sufferers will feel agonizing pain morally & physically in this day of holy pleasure & *peace*! What an amount of bloodshed has been going on, & is to be expected for the next months to come! Instead of the angels song "Peace on Earth & goodwill amongst men" the new century will be greeted by the shrieks of dying men killed & maimed by Lyddite shells & balls from Quickfirers! Truly "fin de siècle"! . . . May we soon hear of a good end & Peace in that part of the Globe, so that everyone can again breathe more freely! For the sight of White man killing white is not good for the Blacks to look on for too long; & the simple suspicion that they might find it practical for their prosperity to fall on the whites in general is enough to make ones blood run cold.'[89]

Such expressions of sympathy did not of course exclude the Kaiser's habitual aggression. On the very same day as Wilhelm wrote compassionate letters to his English grandmother and his Uncle Bertie, he reviled the Colonial Secretary, Joseph Chamberlain, who had protested at the participation of German officers on the side of the Boers, as 'cheeky Joe', and repeated his usual complaint: 'If we had had a fleet, Chamberlain would not have been so bold.'[90] The seizure of three German steamers by the Royal Navy, for suspected smuggling on behalf of the Boers – Dutch, Swedish, American and French ships were also searched, without this giving rise to international incidents – likewise aroused the fury of the Kaiser. On 2 January 1900 he ordered stronger action against Britain. 'In view of the marked unfriendliness, indeed hostility, of England towards us, which has shown itself in the seizure of German ships, among other things, I consider it right to emphasise our *neutrality* even *more intensively*. It would therefore be advisable, in the first instance, to place an absolute ban on the *export* of any and all war materiel ordered from us by England, shells, artillery from Krupp etc. . . . Then Italy should be reminded that as a member of the Triple Alliance she is in no way authorised to help England further, by supplying mules or by occupying Egypt so as to free the English garrison there which is to go to the Cape.'[91] In direct accord with the imperial command, the Reich government adopted an unusually harsh tone, culminating in Bülow's threat that if Britain insisted on maintaining her ruthless policy, Germany would be obliged to 'look for another combination'.[92] The robust condemnation in the Reichstag of the British anti-smuggling measures again met with the approval of Hinzpeter, who congratulated the Kaiser on 'such a decisive and dignified response'. It had been greeted with 'great and general satisfaction. With their strong antipathy for the English, the people took it for granted that the latter acted with malicious intent to cause offence and humiliation, and they feared that they would have to accept this treatment. So they feel all the more relieved and grateful for the strength and shrewdness with which the matter has been handled.'[93]

THE KAISER'S BATTLE PLANS FOR A BRITISH VICTORY OVER THE BOERS

Animated by these ambiguous motives towards Britain, but with the unambiguous intention of building up his battlefleet, in the winter of 1899–1900 Kaiser Wilhelm occupied himself with forging the battle plans for the British army which he was to quote as proof of his constant goodwill towards Britain eight years later in the *Daily Telegraph* interview. He followed the progress of the war with close attention, drew up detailed calculations of British losses from the beginning, and even in the early stages developed strategic plans which he showed to the British military attaché, Grierson.[94] The heavy defeats inflicted on the British in the catastrophic 'Black Week' in December 1899 strengthened his conviction that a great victory for the Boers was imminent.[95] In this spirit he set out a pessimistic forecast in the first of two memoranda, written in his own hand at the Neues Palais on 21 December 1899, under the heading 'Gedankensplitter über den Krieg in Transvaal' ('Notes on the War in the Transvaal'). The size of the British force fighting in South Africa, which was calculated in Berlin to be about 65,000 strong, was evidently insufficient, 'notwithstanding heroic bravery and efforts', to achieve the operational goals set for it. In order to overcome the resistance 'much larger numbers' − some

60,000 more soldiers with 550 to 600 extra officers − would be needed. This number, however, could now be made up only with volunteers, militia and yeomanry. 'It is doubtful and remains to be seen', the memorandum concluded, 'whether this material of men which is totally unaccustomed to tropical warfare and untrained in shooting, led by inexperienced officers, will succeed where "seasoned" and trained active troops, accustomed to warfare, have been unable to succeed?!'[96]

Contrary to this gloomy prognosis, the British army nevertheless achieved victories in the last days of 1899 which the Kaiser fully acknowledged in his correspondence with his English relations.[97] A few weeks later, at the beginning of February 1900, Wilhelm sent his uncle a second, longer memorandum entitled 'Further thoughts on the Transvaal War'. In it he offered the heir to the British throne concrete suggestions on the conduct of the war. Although written in Wilhelm's own hand, it was in German, from which it can be assumed that it was drafted by one of his aides-de-camp, perhaps by Helmuth von Moltke, the future Chief of the General Staff. Nonetheless, the Kaiser proudly declared that he had drawn it up as someone 'who has seen active military life since now 23 years & who commands & directs the training of the German Army since 88 i.e. 12 years... Pray make any use you like of my Memorandum according to your pleasure, perhaps it would interest Grand-mama.'[98] The memorandum summarised the course of the war since mid December 1899. Once again the Kaiser recommended increasing the number of combatants. After several months of preparation, perhaps lasting until the autumn, the British forces could then be concentrated 'at any point of the theatre of war' and 'attempt under one command' to defeat the Boers. 'Unity in the command and in the direction of the different Columns towards one fixed point of the extensive field of operations are however the indispensable preliminary conditions of success. To keep in view the main object with the neglect of all secondary considerations, however important these may appear, must be the aim of the Commander', Wilhelm pontificated. It was also imperative to ensure that foreign Powers would not intervene, at least until the autumn, which 'in the present situation of the world appears somewhat doubtful ... If therefore diplomacy *cannot guarantee* absolutely to secure the respite just referred to, it would certainly be better to bring matters to a settlement. Even the best football Club, if it is beaten, notwithstanding the most gallant defence, accepts its defeat with equanimity. Last year in the great Cricket match of England v. Australia, the former took the victory of the latter quietly with chivalrous acknowledgement of her opponent.'[99]

The Prince of Wales thanked the Kaiser and promised to forward the document, which he said he had read with great interest, to his mother.

But he showed his displeasure at the comparison at the end of the memorandum – which was undoubtedly Wilhelm's own work – between the life-and-
death struggle in Africa and a harmless sporting engagement. 'I am afraid I am
unable to share your opinions expressed in the last Paragraph of your Memo, in
which you liken our conflict with the Boers to our Cricket Matches with the
Australians in which the latter were victorious and we accepted our defeat', he
wrote. 'The British Empire is now fighting for its very existence as you know
full well, and for our superiority in S. Africa. We must therefore use every
effort in our power to prove victorious in the end!' He went on to express his
concern at the widespread anti-British attitude on the continent, and deplored
the enthusiastic reception given to the Boer leader Dr Leyds 'by all classes of
Society in Berlin'.[100] Edward did not hide his annoyance at Wilhelm's remarks
when he sent the memorandum on to Queen Victoria. 'I would call your
attention to the last two paragraphs in which he hints broadly that Foreign
Powers might intervene!', he commented indignantly.[101] The acting German
ambassador Count Metternich, with whom he discussed the Kaiser's paper,
openly expressed regret that this passage had ever been written.[102]

What justification did the Kaiser have for claiming to have been the spiritual
father of the British victories over the Boers, with his two 'Gedankensplitter'
memoranda? The first, of 21 December 1899, contained no practical advice,
but only the fatalistic prediction that even with double the number, the
quality of the British troops was insufficient to guarantee a victory over the
Boers. It is true that the Kaiser added to the memorandum a diagram in his
own hand showing the disposition of troops in Natal and in the western part
of the battle area. But this was limited to the British army and contained no
indications of the strength or disposition of the enemy's troops, which could
have been useful for the British conduct of the war.[103] So the British learnt
nothing that they did not themselves know – and far better – about their own
army. The longer memorandum of 4 February 1900 contained advice to
concentrate troops with a view to a decisive strike after a period of preparation
lasting several months. It is true that the document caused astonishment
among British generals at the knowledge and military competence of the
Kaiser,[104] but it arrived too late to influence the progress of the war in South
Africa. The news of the relief of Kimberley by Roberts and Kitchener arrived
in mid February 1900 – only a matter of days after the Prince of Wales
received the memorandum. This was followed on 21 February by the raising
of the siege of Ladysmith.[105] Even if Roberts had received the 'Further
thoughts' of the German Emperor in time – which was impossible with
the long sea routes – the memorandum would only have confirmed the
correctness of a strategy which the General had long since decided to adopt

anyway. That did not of course prevent Wilhelm from wanting at least to share the glory of victory with Roberts. In a telegram to his grandmother he greeted the news of the capitulation of the Boer army as proof that the concentration of the troops which he had recommended 'has immediately borne its fruit'.[106]

THE THREAT OF A CONTINENTAL LEAGUE

How did matters actually stand with what was perhaps the most explosive claim made by Wilhelm II in his 1908 'interview' with the *Daily Telegraph*, namely that he had not only repudiated the blandishments of France and Russia to take advantage of the Boer War to 'thoroughly humiliate' Britain, but had loyally informed the British government, via a telegram to his grandmother, of this perfidious proposal by the Dual Alliance?[107]

The idea of a continental league against Britain was already in the air when the war broke out in South Africa — also for reasons of German domestic politics, for the government was under considerable pressure from the conservative-agrarian press, which demanded a closer association with Russia.[108] The Kaiser at first rejected it with great passion, pointing to the superiority of the British navy and to the unreliability which both France and Russia had demonstrated when he himself had proposed a united front by the continental Powers against Britain three years earlier, after his Krüger telegram. A few weeks before the outbreak of war in South Africa Wilhelm, standing in Bülow's study, explained to the Foreign Secretary and the elderly Reich Chancellor, Prince Hohenlohe, why it was now necessary for him to hold back completely where the continental Powers were concerned. 'If the English did not reach their objective in South Africa and had to give in, they would look for another opponent to attack. That could only be the French, whom Russia would leave in the lurch. We would carefully hold back. If we had already possessed a decent fleet, we could join with France; but that is not possible now.'[109] On the eve of the Boer War he was convinced, as he commented angrily, that Paris would 'immediately join England against us again! As with the Transvaal 1896–97'.[110] At the opera on 28 October 1899 he spoke to the French ambassador, the Marquis de Noailles, about the situation which had arisen from the South African war. He repeated his complaint about the missed opportunity of forming a continental league against Britain in 1896. But he went on to say that it would be too dangerous for all the Powers to attempt such a thing at the present moment, given British superiority at sea. He rejected the ambassador's suggestion of joint Franco-German action against British expansion in Africa on grounds which he explained in a telegram to Bülow. 'We were witnessing the establishment of a second great colonial empire, probably in place of India. That could *now* no longer be *prevented*. If the English were disturbed in their business in any way now, with a mere nudge of the elbow they would throw the rest of us who sit on the periphery of Africa straight into the sea, and we would not be able to do the slightest thing about it. In 1896 the English fleet was unprepared and a third weaker, and my telegram [to Krüger] took the country completely by surprise. If all the states had associated themselves with us at that time, something could have been done.' But the French ambassador's predecessor, Herbette, like the then French and Russian foreign ministers, Hanotaux and Lobanov, 'had turned their backs on us with scornful laughter and pinned all their hopes on a clash between England and us'. Only in twenty years' time, when the battlefleet would be 'ready', would he be able to speak another language. As Wilhelm reported to Bülow, however, the French ambassador's comments revealed that 'Fashoda still rankles and the Russians still tweak the Gauls' hair at this tender spot, and so both want to harness us to their carriages.'[111]

After the relief of Kimberley and Ladysmith and the capitulation of the Boer army in Paardeberg in February 1900, the end of the Boer Republic was in sight and the international situation had fundamentally changed. Wilhelm II's reaction was to intensify his attempts at a rapprochement with Britain. By warning the British of the supposed intentions of Russia and France to create a continental league against Britain or to intrigue against Britain elsewhere in the world, he aimed to demonstrate to the government in London the value of German friendship – and the danger of having Germany as an enemy in league with the Franco-Russian Dual Alliance. From February onwards the Kaiser tried, in a series of remarkable letters and conversations, to convince the British royal family and government of the necessity of a rapid end to the war in South Africa, on the grounds that far greater dangers threatened Britain in Europe and Asia. He uttered dark warnings that Britain's real enemy was to be found not in South Africa but directly across the Channel in France. He knew for a fact 'that "sundry Peoples" are quietly preparing to take liberties & foster intrigues & surprises in other parts of the world. This is begining [sic] to be instinctively felt in Europe & is consequently causing much uneasiness in the Political World. I want a strong, unhampered England, it is eminently necessary for the Peace of Europe! Be on the look out! – The concentration of the Reserve Squadron at Portland is most wise, & will I hope create a quieting impression in "certain neighbouring quarters". To my opinion this measure ought allways [sic] to be taken as soon as the Channel Fleet leaves for its ordinary trip to Gib[raltar] etc.' The Prince of Wales should pay no attention to the 'Pharisaical protestations of good faith &

friendship' of the French and Russians. These Powers were 'Humbugs! Ware wolf! [sic] We must both keep our weather eye open.'[112]

On 8 February 1900 the Kaiser called on Sir Frank Lascelles. He read out the 'Further thoughts' to the astonished ambassador and sharply criticised the British conduct of the war. Wilhelm warned Lascelles too of the danger of 'foreign complications', should the war continue for much longer. The British had strayed into this extremely difficult war, he commented mockingly, 'as if it had been no more serious a matter than an expedition to dethrone King Thebaw or to knock the King of Coomassee off his stool'. Now they had seen their mistake and realised that they must work out a war plan which would require a considerable period of preparation. 'The question therefore arose whether Her Majesty's Government could avoid the complications which might arise in the meantime.' Rebellions might break out in the Sudan, in Egypt and also in Abyssinia, fanned by French and Russian money. The situation in the Far East was also dangerous: Russian influence in China was growing steadily, and according to reliable information Japan had mobilised her troops for an attack on Russia. The Russians had also increased their hold over Persia through a loan; one day, following the example of the British acquisition of the Suez Canal, they would suddenly take over. In his conversation with the ambassador, Wilhelm expanded further on the possibility that Britain would move her troops in Egypt to South Africa and have them replaced by an Italian garrison. Three weeks ago he had informed the King of Italy that he would not raise any objections to such a step. As a member of the Triple Alliance, Wilhelm explained, the King was obliged to discuss military undertakings with his allies. He, the Kaiser, knew very well how unpopular his consent to the exchange of troops would be in Germany, but he also knew that Italy depended on the British navy for protection against France, and if only for that reason she would be prepared to accede to British demands. When Lascelles said he was confident that Salisbury would regard this action by the Kaiser as a friendly gesture not only towards Italy but also towards Britain, the Kaiser replied: 'Yes, . . . it was intended as such, and I wished to tell you of it at the time, but then you were still being naughty about my ships, and I could not come to see you.' When the ambassador pointed out that the Germans had reacted much more angrily to the searching of their ships than the other nations affected, Wilhelm tried to dismiss the affair as merely a trivial family matter. What was much more serious, he said, was Britain's general attitude to German sensibilities. When the discussion turned to British plans to tax beet sugar, which was imported principally from Germany, the Kaiser commented jokingly: 'If you tax German sugar, I will send a Prussian army corps to Herat.'[113] Bülow was horrified when he heard of

Wilhelm's conversation with Lascelles. He felt compelled to withdraw the Kaiser's remarks point by point. There were no rebellions stirred up by Russia or France in the Sudan or Abyssinia; the news of the mobilisation of the Japanese army had not been confirmed; and he thought it unlikely that the British garrison in Egypt would be sent to South Africa and replaced by Italian troops. The only correct statement was that the Kaiser's agreement to such a step had been intended as a gesture of friendship.[114] In London such dizzying speculations did not inspire confidence, as can easily be imagined.

On 1 March 1900 the Kaiser had another very frank conversation with Lascelles in which he claimed to have fought throughout the winter against anti-British feeling in the German population and even in his closest entourage. He had roundly rejected the demands of the Russian and French press that he should seize the initiative to put a stop to the Boer War. He told Lascelles that 'he made politics with his head and not with his heart and although he had had much to suffer from the attacks of the English press both on himself and on Germany in general, he would certainly take no action which would embarrass Her Majesty's Government, and he took great credit to himself for having prevented any hostile action on the part of France or Russia which any encouragement on his part would easily have produced. He thought it was only fair that it should be known and recognised in England that his action had influenced the conduct of France and Russia, or, as His Majesty expressed it, "that he had kept these two tigers quiet".'[115]

Wilhelm's dark hints about the mischief which Russia and France were plotting against the British Empire took concrete form when a letter from him arrived in Windsor at the beginning of March 1900, with the news that the Russian Foreign Minister, Count Muraviev, had made a formal proposal to him of joint action with Russia and France against Britain.[116] The three continental Powers would take part in a 'collective action ... against England for the enforcing of Peace & the help of the Boers!!' 'I have declined', the Kaiser declared. 'I have answered that I thought it best that the organiser of the European Peace Conference at the Hague – H. I. M. the Tsar – were to inform himself directly in London, wether [sic] the British Government & People were in a mood to listen to such proposals as His I. M. Government was thinking of making. I had my doubts about it & personally thought I knew pretty sure what the answer would be from London! After enquiring what Russia would do in case of a "refus" from England the very reassuring answer was given "Nothing!" Sir Frank [Lascelles] has been informed by me of this preposterous step in a *very confidential* manner.'[117] When told of a comment by the Tsar that the courageous Boers would inevitably be lost unless a Great Power intervened in their favour, and that it fell primarily to the German

Kaiser to undertake this step, Wilhelm was equally firm in rejecting this, particularly because he knew that Britain was determined to pursue the war until the complete subjection and assimilation of the Boer Republic into the Empire had been achieved, and would therefore react very badly to any mediation proposal. This information from St Petersburg showed once again, Wilhelm wrote on the report, 'how false, lying and disloyal that scoundrel Muraviev's behaviour is, and how right I was to send him packing at once! If the Russian is itching to intervene, let him do so himself! Or with France!'[118] Muraviev was 'an insolent lying scoundrel without parallel!' the Kaiser railed.[119] He would not let himself be used by Russia as a front man against England and 'thereby fall right into it', he vowed.[120]

Both Queen Victoria and the Prince of Wales thanked Wilhelm warmly for his loyalty and expressed the hope that the other continental Powers would follow his example.[121] As Metternich, whom the Kaiser had sent to London as his special representative, was able to report, the Prince had described Wilhelm to some prominent members of Parliament as a true and trustworthy friend of Britain. The German Emperor, he said, thoroughly understood the South African question and had prevented an intervention by Britain's enemies. 'Bravo! Very good and quite right', Wilhelm wrote in surprise and delight on Metternich's dispatch. 'I'll be damned! That is extraordinary coming from the Prince of Wales, he has never taken our side so much before!'[122] Soon afterwards a letter arrived from the Prince, confirming Metternich's report to a remarkable degree. 'What you tell me about Mouraview's conduct does not surprise me as I believe there is nothing he would not do in conjunction with France to annoy us in every possible way . . . What your answer was I had little doubt of − you have no idea, my dear William, how all of us in England appreciate the loyal friendship which you manifest towards us on every possible occasion. We hope always to look upon Germany as our best friend as long as you are at the helm. It is of course deeply to be regretted that the feeling throughout Germany is not alas! very friendly towards us. One can only hope that it may improve in time, and when both countries become thoroughly satisfied, that to go hand in hand together in friendly rivalry is the mutual benefit of us both!'[123]

On 9 March 1900 Lascelles was asked to come at once to the Berlin Schloss, where the Kaiser had an important message for Salisbury to give him. In the course of an hour's conversation Wilhelm stated that he had done his best to discover the motives behind the Russian government's proposal of an intervention by the continental Powers to bring the war in South Africa to an end. 'With this view He had sent a copy of the Russian Note to all His Representatives abroad, with instructions to report what they could ascertain on the subject', Lascelles reported. 'The most interesting reply He had received was from Vienna where it appeared that the French Ambassador had recently shown a great deal of restless activity, and had pointed out that if England were allowed to achieve a complete success, her Power would be increased, and her arrogance would render her insupportable. The Russian Ambassador had been calmer in his language but had insisted that it was advisable to take advantage of opportunities which might not recur, and both were strongly of opinion that the German Emperor was the proper person to take the initiative. This was very kind of them [Wilhelm commented] but the German Emperor had no intention of doing anything of the sort, and He believed that the Russian Government had now realized that fact, as Osten-Sacken [the Russian ambassador in Berlin] had again spoken to Bülow on the subject and had received a very categorical reply in the negative. His Majesty did not think it likely that France and Russia would take any further steps in the matter, but He thought it right to tell me that the Emperor of Russia had now become pro-Boer ... and His Majesty [Wilhelm II] had ascertained that the Empress Mother had lamented her loss of influence over her son, and the sad fact that he had become anti-English ... A weak Emperor of Russia with a perfectly unscrupulous Minister like Mouravieff whose only idea was to maintain himself in Power, was a serious danger to the Peace of Europe ... He regretted that England had apparently lost the influence which she formerly possessed in Persia, and alluded to the recent Persian loan as a triumph of Russian over English Diplomacy.' Lascelles concluded: 'I need not repeat what I have reported in my private telegram of today as to The Emperor's belief in the possibility of a War between England and France, in which he believed that we should be entirely successful, whilst he would keep his bayonets fixed on the land side, nor as to the suggestions he would make if he were asked his opinion as to the terms of Peace to be made in South Africa, but he observed that the present War had set many stones rolling, and no one could say where they would stop, and had raised many questions which had much better have remained latent, and He asked what the position of Germany would be if she found herself confronted by a coalition of France, England and Russia when she would have to fight for her very existence. He was aware that he had adopted an unusual method in communicating his secret information personally to me. Had it been merely a question of maintaining good relations between the two Governments, He would not have departed from the usual Diplomatic course, but that He could not forget that He was the Grandson of The Queen for whom he had always entertained the deepest devotion, which had if possible been increased by Her noble attitude in these trying times.'[124]

THE KAISER AND THE BOER PEACE INITIATIVE

Wilhelm and Bülow were only too conscious of how sensitive the British were on the question of possible peace negotiations, and of how carefully they needed to operate. When the two Boer republics asked for the good offices of the German government in March 1900[125] the Kaiser and his Foreign Secretary rapidly came to an agreement that German mediation between London and the South African governments could be considered only if *both* sides wished for such assistance, and even then it would be best if it came from a third government which − unlike Germany − did not have any interests of its own in South Africa to look after. Bülow showed a draft telegram on these lines to the Kaiser on 10 March 1900 for his approval. Wilhelm accepted it but gave orders that the dispatch was 'to be communicated immediately, together with the request from Pretoria, to Lascelles and to our Embassy in London for His Royal Highness [the Prince of Wales], for as telegrams *went en clair* via *the English cable*, London knows about it and must hear of our answer at once, otherwise too much mistrust. Only absolute and complete openness will prevent misconception in this instance. Shall tell Her Majesty myself of the facts and our answer.'[126]

On Sunday 11 March 1900, from Heligoland, the Kaiser sent Queen Victoria and the Prince of Wales identical telegrams. He had repeatedly changed its English wording so as to achieve the right nuance.[127] He informed them that the government of the Transvaal, in the name of both South African republics, had asked the German government for 'friendly intervention' to restore peace. He had instructed his Foreign Office to respond to the request of the Boers as follows: 'The first and paramount question to be settled before steps for "Friendly Mediation" could be taken was whether *both* antagonists were ready to accept it, i.e. whether England was also ready to do so. Only in case this question should have been answered in the affirmative my Government would of course be happy to lend a hand to bring about a peaceful issue. My Government further suggests that the Republics would do well in order to find out whether Her Majesty's Government just now would be in a mood to accept mediation at all, to directly inquire in London and if this did not suit them, to refer to any third Power not vitally interested in South Africa, Germany being materially interested. It was the duty of my Government to refrain from taking any steps in this matter which would be liable to be misunderstood in England, and which could give rise to the suspicion that we were prompted by other than purely humanitarian motives. This would only jeopardise the cause of Peace instead of serving it.'[128] Salisbury expressed to Count Metternich his 'hearty and respectful thanks to the Emperor for the goodwill displayed in his communication to the Transvaal', but stated very firmly that Britain did not wish for any mediation.[129]

The short telegrams of thanks that the Queen and the Prince of Wales sent the Kaiser after consultation with the Prime Minister[130] gave no hint of the annoyance which Wilhelm's communication had caused in London, in spite of its friendly tone. The true feelings of both the royal family and the government found expression in the 'strong language' which the Queen used in a cipher telegram to Lascelles. Sir Frank should make it clear to the Kaiser 'that my whole nation is with me in a fixed determination to see this war through without intervention. The time for, and the terms of, peace must be left to our decision, and my country, which is suffering from so heavy a sacrifice of precious lives, will resist all interference. The Emperor has proved himself such a kind friend to England and so affectionate to me that I wish him to know the true position of things.'[131] Wilhelm had to put a brave face on it and replied to his grandmother that her view was 'exactly what I answered to Count Morawieff [sic] and in perfect harmony with the views I take of the actual situation and which I have always advocated. After nearly 14,000 officers and men have shed their blood for Queen and Country there can be only this issue.'[132]

THE GROWING MISTRUST TOWARDS WILHELM II

The Queen's rebuke was all the more hurtful to the Kaiser because he was convinced that he could expect her nation's gratitude. He was irritated that there were otherwise well-informed Englishmen who evidently had 'no inkling of the services which I have secretly rendered to Her Majesty, the government and the whole country!'[133] At the end of March 1900 he again reminded his grandmother of his loyal reaction to the alleged Russian and French proposal of a joint démarche against England. 'By my telegrams you are informed of the sudden surprises in the political phases of the war & I am most thankful to Providence that I was granted such an opportunity of saving your country from a most dangerous situation in warding off a combination aiming a blow at England in a moment which was vital to her. May your Government see in my action a renewed proof of my firm friendship & a sign of my determination that you shall have fair play.'[134] Salisbury, to whom the Queen showed this letter, expressed satisfaction at these 'earnest expressions of his goodwill'. But he could not suppress his doubts as to 'whether a proposal for a combination against England was ever really made by France & Russia to Germany'.[135]

The Prime Minister's distrust speaks volumes about his assessment of the Kaiser's intentions. Others went much further and suspected that Wilhelm II himself was the real instigator of the plan for a concerted intervention by the continental Powers against Britain. When his claims about a Russian plot which he had foiled out of loyalty to Britain appeared in the *Daily Telegraph* in 1908, the British diplomat Sir Cecil Spring Rice reported that he had heard from a reliable source how the Russian note had come to be sent. In Persia, Spring Rice's Russian colleague, Hartwig, had told him 'that the Kaiser had talked at a Court function to Osten Sacken about the necessity of intervening in the Boer War. Osten Sacken reported the conversation in a dispatch but the Foreign Office did not answer it. The Kaiser then sent to him to ask if he had an answer. Osten Sacken telegraphed to say the Kaiser was pressing for a reply. The Tsar gave orders to the Foreign Office that a "courteous communication" should be made. Hartwig said he drafted the answer: it was to the effect that Russia, as the initiator of the Hague Conference, was anxious to prevent this effusion of blood: and that the Russian Govt. would give the most favourable consideration to any proposal to that effect which the German Govt. would put forward. Hartwig said that Osten Sacken foolishly put down a paraphrase of the telegram in writing and communicated it to the German Foreign Office who at once refused to entertain the idea of intervention – but *kept the document.*'[136] If this version of events is true, it looks almost as though the Kaiser laid a trap into which Russian diplomacy innocently walked.

There were similar suspicions about Germany's relations with France during the Boer War. On 20 March 1900 Metternich reported from London that the Rothschilds in the city had received a telegram from their Paris cousins telling them that Germany had recently attempted to persuade the French government to intervene in the war; Germany, however, had made such exorbitant demands as the price of her own cooperation that Paris had roundly rejected the German proposal.[137] The Kaiser described these claims as 'a shameless lie', but the suspicions were not entirely unfounded. As Bülow stated on 3 March, Germany had to be especially careful to avoid complications 'with other Great Powers and particularly with other Naval Powers ... as long as we are uncertain of the attitude of our neighbour France. We could be certain only if there were an agreement under which the contracting Powers guaranteed each other's European borders for a considerable number of years. Such an agreement is therefore the essential prerequisite for us to consider whether we can enter into any new, broad combinations.'[138] In plain language that meant that Germany might after all be prepared to take part in a continental coalition against England, on condition that France formally recognised the rightful claim of the German Reich to Alsace and Lorraine.[139] A conditional acceptance on these lines was far removed from the indignant refusal of the alleged Russian proposal for a continental league which

Wilhelm II conjured up for the benefit of Queen Victoria, the Prince of Wales and the British government. Nor can it be claimed that the Kaiser knew nothing of the condition which his government had attached to participation in the continental coalition against Britain. Far from it: he expressly stated that a telegram from the French Foreign Minister Delcassé to the French ambassador in Berlin confirming that his government, without ulterior motives, recognised Germany's borders as laid down in the Frankfurt Peace Treaty, would be enough to satisfy this condition.[140] Lord Salisbury's scepticism about the German Emperor's repeated assurances of loyalty and friendship was thus by no means unfounded.

To Wilhelm's consternation it became evident a year later that Metternich had been justified in warning of systematic attempts on the part of both France and Russia to sow discord between Germany and Britain; furthermore, it appeared that these intrigues, which had been going on for some time, had succeeded to a certain extent in Britain.[141] On 6 April 1901 a secret telegram arrived from London with the news that Arthur Balfour, Lord Salisbury's nephew and soon to be his successor as Prime Minister, had asked one of the leading finance houses — presumably the Rothschilds — whether it was conceivable that 'His Majesty the Kaiser had quite suddenly put himself completely on Russia's side and against England'. Wilhelm wrote angrily on the telegram: 'Naturally old Salisbury believed that! Hell and damnation! To think me capable of such a thing! ... I don't understand the British! Such a lack of principle is downright outrageous. These people are incorrigible!'[142] In a letter to King Edward VII he complained bitterly that he was 'very grieved to hear from friends & private sources that the French & Russians are playing a violent game of intrigues at London, which has so far proved successful, that actually some members of the Government have given vent to the apprehension, that I was siding with the Russians against England! A most unworthy & ridiculous imputation.'[143] He was no less free with his 'severe criticism' of the British government in conversation with Lascelles.[144] It was only with difficulty that the ambassador succeeded in making clear to Wilhelm that Balfour's remarks had been inaccurately reported to him. Lascelles, like King Edward VII and the Foreign Secretary, Lord Lansdowne, deplored the Kaiser's propensity to listen to 'gossip'.[145]

CHAPTER THREE

'I am the balance of power in Europe.' Wilhelm between Britain, Russia and France

As a result of the South African war and other upheavals around the turn of the century – the Spanish–American war, the Anglo-French clash at Fashoda and the dramatic developments in China – the international order had begun to shift. The traditional diplomatic groupings in Europe – the Triple Alliance between Germany, the Austro-Hungarian Empire and Italy, the Franco-Russian alliance, Britain's Splendid Isolation – seemed to have lost their permanence. Furthermore, the old European Great Powers were confronted with the question of how the new World Powers, America and Japan, would position themselves in relation to Europe and to each other. In North and East Africa, the eastern Mediterranean, Central Asia, China, Korea and Manchuria, the South Pacific, the Caribbean, Central and South America, new conflicts loomed which seemed likely to lead, if not necessarily to war, then at least to new and unexpected factions between the Powers. A process of radical change in the international political landscape had begun, at the end of which, within only a few years, Germany was to find herself in isolation. Why? And what specific role did Kaiser Wilhelm II play in this fateful development?

It is astonishing to realise how clearly his contemporaries foresaw this development, catastrophic as it was for the Kaiserreich. In April 1900 Waldersee recorded that both Britain and Russia were treating Germany with increasing coolness and mistrust. 'I am more and more convinced that I was absolutely right when I stated many years ago that we had no friends. If I am indeed right, this would certainly be a damning verdict on our policy.'[1] Only two years later the Field Marshal saw his fears confirmed. He looked back over international affairs since the turn of the century and concluded that the situation had radically changed for two reasons, 'first because of the growing strength of the United States and its consequent tendency to intervene in all

international quarrels; and secondly because of the complete change in the
importance of Eastern Asia'. As a result of Germany's 'very muddled colonial
policy' and her unnecessary 'proclamation of a *Weltpolitik*', the Reich was
'more involved in the new groupings than is perhaps wise. Greater reserve
would certainly have done no harm and would probably have helped.'[2] Deeply
concerned, he asked if under the Kaiser's direction the Reich would continue
to prosper 'or will he lead it to destruction?'[3] And Waldersee was by no means
alone in his criticism. In the spring of 1900 – just at the time when the Paris
Rothschilds were circulating rumours of a German plan to set up a continental
league against Britain[4] – Waldersee heard that the influential Prussian
Finance Minister, Johannes Miquel, had said that 'an Anglo-French agreement
against us' would shortly come into effect. He immediately realised the danger
of such an alliance for Germany. 'As Russia must be regarded as allied to
France, this would mean a coalition of England, Russia and France against us,
in which case I have no doubt that Austria would also join it.' Again he
bemoaned the fact that such a prognosis amounted to 'a damning verdict on
our policy and our diplomacy'. Although he was not convinced that matters had
already gone as far as Miquel feared, Waldersee nevertheless worried about the
extent to which the Reich was equipped for a major European war. He
commented that Germany was 'financially unprepared for a war', for, as he
recorded with alarm: 'The Juliusthurm [the war chest] holds 120 million, a tiny
sum for today's needs; in the Reichsbank there is some 100 million, but that is
also far too little to maintain our credit ... I only wonder why nothing is done
to prepare us financially for a war, if it is thought that war is in prospect?'[5]

Kaiser Wilhelm and Bülow were at first far less apprehensive about the
situation. Misjudging the dangers, they took it for granted that an economically successful Germany, with an increasingly strong arms policy, could allow
herself a 'free hand' between Britain and Russia and play off these two
flanking Powers – and likewise Russia's ally France – against each other to
her own advantage. 'Today we no longer have to expect, as in the first decades
after the recovery of Strassburg and Metz, to find ourselves the object of a
concerted attack', Bülow asserted. 'The great goals over which international
interests are in conflict today – the Mediterranean, Byzantium, Persia, Eastern
Asia – are questions on which we have the freedom to decide for ourselves.'[6]
As if such a combination of excessive self-confidence and guile were not risky
enough in Europe, the Kaiser tried to turn Britain against America, America
against Britain and Japan, and Russia against Japan. With frenetic energy he
plied Britain, Russia, France and America with offers of one new treaty after
another. These might at first sight seem confusing and inconsistent, but all
had the same goal: to break out of the confines of the existing balance of

power in Europe in order to cement German supremacy on the continent and pave the way for *Weltmacht*, global superpower status. Since the true purpose behind these offers, which were of course immediately passed on to the other governments concerned, was crystal clear, this policy might in itself have caused the Powers under threat to close ranks. But on top of this, ambitious German plans for expansion in the Middle East, in China, Central and South America and North-West Africa deepened still further the mistrust felt by the other Powers towards Germany.

PRESSURE FOR AN ALLIANCE WITH BRITAIN

Even before the outbreak of the Boer War in the autumn of 1899 one of the foremost aims of the Kaiser's foreign policy had been to establish a binding alliance between Germany and the two Atlantic Powers, Great Britain and the United States. In January of that year Wilhelm II told the British ambassador, Lascelles, 'that the two great English-speaking nations and Germany should come to a good understanding and should act together but if these three horses are to be driven abreast, it was necessary that Germany should be protected from the kicks of the American horse'.[7] In the spring he went further, seeking an alliance between Germany, Britain, America and Japan.[8] Subsequently, the Boer War convinced him that in her hour of need Britain would ally herself to the German Reich, or even to the Triple Alliance — whether out of fear of international isolation, or (as we have seen) out of gratitude for the Kaiser's support in the face of hostile German public opinion and the alleged Russian and French intrigues. During his visit to Windsor in November 1899, on the advice of Bülow and Holstein, Wilhelm maintained a 'sphinx-like' reserve, in the hope that later on, after the German battlefleet had been built up, still greater concessions could be demanded in return for German friendship.[9] In a conversation with Sir Arthur Bigge, Queen Victoria's Private Secretary, on 20 November, he remarked that there was probably no question of a formal Anglo-German alliance, but a looser understanding might perhaps be possible. According to Bigge, the Kaiser said 'Lord Salisbury was afraid that Germany wanted to make an alliance: Nothing of the sort, for we know that is impossible; but an *understanding yes*. Then when a question arises which only interests England, Germany would not interfere, and vice versa. But as soon as the question involved common interests we would stand and act together.'[10] Wilhelm expressed himself even more clearly three days later in his interview with the Colonial Secretary, Joseph Chamberlain. When Chamberlain said that he wished for 'a general understanding between Germany, England and America', the Kaiser responded, in line with Bülow's advice: 'Such a general

understanding would have its drawbacks for both sides. While it did not accord
with English traditions to enter into formal alliances, Germany's excellent
relations with Russia would impose definite political limitations on her, at
least for the time being.'[11]

Bülow, on the other hand, struck a different note in his meeting with
Chamberlain. He urged the influential Colonial Secretary to make a public
speech expressly promoting an Anglo-German accord with American participation. Chamberlain obliged, in a celebrated speech in Leicester a week later.
In it he spoke of a 'natural alliance between ourselves and the great German
Empire' and of a triple alliance 'between the Teutonic Race and the two great
branches of the Anglo-Saxon race'. He stated with emphasis: 'It is not with
German newspapers that we desire to have an understanding or alliance; it is
with the German people.'[12] Bülow promised to do his part by speaking out
publicly in favour of an Anglo-German–American understanding.[13]

Chamberlain's dismay was thus all the greater when the German Foreign
Secretary made his notorious 'hammer-or-anvil speech' in the Reichstag on
10 December 1899. With one eye on the excited anti-British mood in Germany
and the other on the new Navy Bill, not only did Bülow ignore the idea of an
understanding between Germany, Britain and the USA, but while conceding,
with marked coldness, German willingness to live in peace and harmony
with Britain, he stated as a condition that this must be on the basis of 'full
reciprocity' and 'parity', also in naval and colonial matters. He added threateningly: 'We do not wish to tread too close to any foreign power, but we will not
allow any foreign power to tread on our feet, nor will we allow any foreign
power to push us aside.' Germany's security rested upon 'the unwavering Triple
Alliance, and our good relations with Russia'.[14] Holstein, Hatzfeldt, Eckardstein
and the other German diplomats who had seen a hopeful new development in
Chamberlain's offer of friendship, were horrified.[15]

Although Wilhelm II did not criticise Bülow's speech – the temptation to
exploit the 'furious' wave of anti-British emotion to get the second Navy Bill
passed was evidently too great[16] – in his impetuous way he nevertheless
persisted with his efforts to bring about an understanding with Britain. He
pinned his hopes on a complete revolution in the world order, which would be
brought about by Britain's difficulties in South Africa. As we have seen, the
serious illness of his mother and the death of Queen Victoria gave him plenty
of opportunities to present his British relations, senior military officers and
leading statesmen with lengthy and often astonishing suggestions for an
accord between Germany and Britain. But he became increasingly frustrated
and annoyed when his royal relations and the British statesmen – primarily
Salisbury – rejected his various offers. Thus in February 1900, in a

conversation with Lascelles, he berated the British, who 'seemed to forget that the German Empire was a young State which could not stand being kicked ... He had constantly striven to promote the most cordial relations between our two countries, and just when his endeavours seemed to be crowned with success, he had received a kick on the shins which had upset all his endeavours. In the spring of last year [1899] matters had appeared to have been placed on a satisfactory footing, but then came the miserable Samoan business, which undid all the good which had been done. Then again in the autumn he had paid his visit to the Queen in spite of the opposition which had been raised. He had, however, "faced the music", and his reception in England had caused an excellent impression in Germany, but then came the seizure of the German ships, which had irritated German public opinion to the utmost ... He was not, however, discouraged, and he would still continue to endeavour to bring about a good understanding between the two countries.'[17]

Salisbury's cool reception of these repeated attempts to curry favour were a hard test of the Kaiser's patience. On 31 July 1900 Wilhelm complained in a letter to the Prince of Wales about the Prime Minister's refusal to accept his offers. 'I have remarked with some astonishment', he wrote sarcastically, 'that whenever my Government has suggested a proposal or some idea in general latterly they have been received with no great "empressement" just in Downing Street. I think however that it might be useful in the future for an eventual understanding, if I were enabled to see my way more clearly as to the motives & aims which actuate the ... souls of the great men dwelling there, for up to now we have to put up with answers, that often are most enigmatic & leave one under the impression that their origin is not far from the tripod of Pythia; in the long run this wont do in Politics. Though animated by the best intentions I cannot of course be expected to play the game of "follow my leader" blindfolded where the interests of my country are at stake.'[18]

At the end of 1900 the Kaiser explained to his old friend Leopold Swaine, the former British military attaché, how he saw the future development of the world. Seizing on one of his favourite themes, namely that the 'Latin nations' (he expressly named Spain, Portugal, France and Italy) were all 'doomed' and 'in a state of decay',[19] he once again pressed for cooperation between Germany and England. But, he warned, 'I must feel and be made to feel that there is reciprocity. I think your people are gradually beginning to realize that I wish to live on good terms with them. Commercial rivalry is good for both of us and if we both spend our money on the same objects we shall soon put an end to our political rivalry. But we must stick together. There are only two Races in the World: The Teutonic & the Slave [sic]. The Latin Race is dropping down the Ladder and we need take no account of it. But the Teutonic People must stand shoulder to shoulder or the Slaves will destroy us. I suppose as long as Lord Salisbury influences your foreign policy so long I expect he will favour France at our expense. But believe me he is wrong. France will never forgive Fashoda and it cares little for your soft words. Beware also of America. America cares no more for what you did for her in her war with Spain. Such gratitude in an American is short lived ... America is now trying to mix herself in European Questions, and you will see that before long she will have a fleet in the Mediterranean.'[20]

Shortly after this memorable conversation with Swaine, when Wilhelm rushed to England to see his dying grandmother and was received by the Prince of Wales in London, he telegraphed triumphantly to Bülow saying that he seemed at last to be making headway with the British. 'So it appears that "they are coming", which is what we have been waiting for.' He wrote optimistically to the Reich Chancellor of his forthcoming conversations with Salisbury and the new Foreign Secretary, Lord Lansdowne. 'God grant me the right thoughts and words so that I may express them in the right way, and so that what we discussed may come to pass for the good of both countries. I shall let you know at once. Freiherr von Eckardstein tells me that Chamberlain has confidentially indicated that "splendid isolation" is over, England must choose between the Triple Alliance and Russia-France.' The Colonial Secretary himself and the British Foreign Office, Wilhelm reported, were convinced supporters of an alliance with Germany and were only waiting for Salisbury's departure for Cannes to begin negotiations with Germany.[21]

On 25 January 1901, a few days after the death of Queen Victoria, Wilhelm had a long conversation with Lansdowne at Osborne. To the latter's amazement, the Kaiser urged on him the need for Britain to join the Triple Alliance, as a European bulwark against Russian and American world domination. And that was not all: having only recently tried to goad Britain into war with France,[22] he now proposed that France, too, should become a member of the new coalition. Wilhelm later sent Bülow a lengthy account of what he said. He told Lansdowne that he knew for a fact that certain influential members of the British Cabinet were seeking a permanent understanding with Russia and France. 'I had no wish to stir up England against Russia, nor to cause trouble between England and France or France and Russia, as had perhaps been said of me previously. On the other hand I considered it my duty to portray the world situation to the English Foreign Secretary as I saw it. Thus, Russia would no doubt accept English concessions with pleasure and the friendliest assurances ... But would Russia be satisfied with that? Russia was curling herself round the Indian border like a snake and would use any concessions she received to throttle India.' Continental European diplomacy was more

systematic than its English counterpart, the Kaiser maintained, treating
Lansdowne to a lecture on the subject. 'While English diplomacy only ever
concerned itself with *one* object ... and in the process forgot everything else,
like an English Lord with a salmon on the line, the continental powers tried to
keep the whole picture in mind as well as the interests of the day, to draw
conclusions from small signs ... and set up alliances. Hence European
diplomacy was taken by surprise far less often than the English. This was
also because, in his indifference, the Englishman had hitherto cared very little
about the European continent, and had indeed considered himself as
something special, standing apart from Europe, as the expression "England
and the Continent" demonstrated. Herein lay the root of the evil and also the
possible remedy. The milestone in world history was coming ever closer, when
England must freely and unreservedly take her stand on Europe's side, and
both declare and feel her solidarity with Europe, or choose America. England,
America and Russia would undoubtedly form a powerful group, but it was
equally certain that England would be crushed between these two and swept
out of the way, if she allied herself with them. The United States were
determined, full of youthful vigour and arrogance, without scruples or any
sense of solidarity with others. They were sufficient unto themselves with
their vast and still partly undeveloped continent. At the same time they
applied the Monroe Doctrine only insofar as they wanted to keep all others
at bay; but they were themselves spreading out wherever they wanted. They
stood with one foot in Honolulu and the other in Cuba! It seemed to me
England's friendship in the war with Spain had been ill repaid. American
sympathies lay with the Boers, and they tore up a treaty with England with
unscrupulous egoism ... I put it to the Minister openly, whether people here
really still lived under the illusion of American friendship ... I asked him to
hear also what I had to say about how America and Russia were gradually
drawing together, which in itself seemed improbable. America had been
supporting Russian policy in China for years. She had on various occasions
tried to destroy the European concert, thereby fulfilling a Russian wish ... On
the other hand Russia treated American interests with the greatest consideration ... The rapprochement between Russia and America had thus been in
preparation for a long time. It rested on the fact that both were not European
Powers and thus took a hostile attitude towards Europe on many matters. Both
wanted to keep the Europeans, plus the English, well away from China. They
wanted to share China between them: one aimed to seize political, the other
commercial, control.' Once again parading his racist view of world order, the
Kaiser predicted that 'the Slav, with his numerical superiority, his passive, half
slumbering instincts which are nevertheless directed towards distinct aims,

emerging with elemental power, slowly and threateningly, into world history, and the American, with his toughness, his spirit of invention, his determination and the inexhaustible resources of his new land – these two would, if left to their own devices, absorb everything in the end.'

According to Wilhelm there was 'only *one* means of salvation, and that was to bring Europe together *with* England and France'. The alliance between France and Russia was invalid, the Kaiser insisted, as it had depended on two conditions which were no longer effective. 'The French wanted Alsace-Lorraine to be won back by the Russians, and the Russians wanted money from the French.' Since then, however, many Frenchmen had realised that the recovery of Alsace-Lorraine had been 'only a beautiful dream', and that Russia would never support a French war of revenge. The second condition of the Franco-Russian Entente, on the other hand, had been fulfilled, the Kaiser argued, since the Russians had received their money and the French no longer had it. But the Russian Finance Minister, Sergei Witte, needed more money 'to stave off state bankruptcy. He was therefore already looking around for a new creditor. This could well be Uncle Sam, who was rapidly developing from a debtor into a creditor of Europe. This was driving a wedge into the Franco-Russian friendship which, with the right encouragement, would eventually break it up.' A third development had led to a loosening of Franco-Russian relations, Wilhelm asserted – disappointment with the 'small, slight, timid' person of Tsar Nicholas. France at the moment was like 'a coquette . . . who, neglected by her lover, looks around for another', in Wilhelm's words. 'So it was a question of winning the French back for Europe. Here there was an important task for England. His Majesty the King of England, with his tact and his knowledge of the French character, could achieve a great deal in this peaceful work of unification.'

From all these circumstances it was evident, the Kaiser concluded, in this astonishing interview with the British Foreign Secretary, that 'on the one side stood Russia and America, as states with non-European interests; on the other stood Europe, which must be united again in order to provide a counterweight . . . The signs of the times indicated that the future would belong to either the Slavic or the Germanic race. The Latin peoples no longer led the way and could no longer play a decisive role in Europe and the world. It was therefore my opinion that the Germanic race had to stand all the more firmly together to face the problems which the future held . . . What mattered to me was to keep the peace, so that the German Reich had time to compress its mosaic elements into a solid mass, and thus allow German trade to pursue its peaceful course. I wished the same for England . . . The old English policy of so-called maintenance of the European balance of power, by which one was played off against the others, so that they held each other in check for the

Figure 3 'I am the balance of power in Europe!' Wilhelm II at the turn of the century

benefit of England, was [however] exploded. No one on the continent would fall into that trap again. I was the balance of power in Europe, whose duty it was, in accordance with the constitution of the Reich, to determine foreign policy. For that reason, incidentally, it did not really matter very much whether excessive sympathy was shown towards the Boers here and there in the German Reich. It was I who was responsible for policy.' The Kaiser finished his account with the self-satisfied but far from surprising observation that his remarks had clearly made a deep impression on Lord Lansdowne.[23] (See Figure 3.) On his return to Berlin, Kaiser Wilhelm had similar conversations with Lascelles. He repeated his wish 'to maintain the most friendly relations with England', but added: 'You must understand that all you have to do is to keep me in good humour, the rest does not signify.'[24]

The variety of alliances Wilhelm offered to Britain is bewildering. In the short period between 1899 and 1901 he urged the British government to agree to a combination of Germany and Britain *with* the United States (and Japan) *against* France and Russia (1899), an Anglo-German alliance *against* America (1900), a coalition between Germany, Britain and France against the USA and Russia (1901), and finally British entry into the Triple Alliance of Germany, Austria and Italy, once again with France joining as well (1901). Why did Britain accept none of these proposals, but choose instead, in the next few years, to form an alliance with Japan, safeguard friendly relations with the United States and establish an Entente with France and finally with Russia too? The answer is to be found as much in a deep mistrust of German aims as in cool calculation of national interests.

In the autumn of 1901 the prominent diplomat Sir Francis Bertie, in a secret memorandum showing significant foresight, analysed the offers of alliance which the Kaiser and his government had 'constantly and for some years past' made, always accompanied with a barrage of 'threats and blandishments'. He reached the unambiguous conclusion that Britain must avoid binding herself to Germany through a defensive alliance. 'Germany is in a dangerous situation in Europe', Bertie pointed out. 'She is surrounded by Governments who distrust her and peoples who dislike ... her. She is constantly in a state of Tariff war with Russia. She has beaten and robbed Denmark, and for that purpose she took as partner Austria and then turned round on her confederate and drove her out of Germany, eventually making her a rather humble ally. She has beaten and taken money and territory from France. She covets the seaboard and colonies of Holland and the Dutch know it, and, as the Belgians are well aware, she has designs on the Belgian Congo ... The internal troubles of the Austro-Hungarian Empire detract from its value to Germany as an ally, while the state of Italy politically, militarily, and financially, is not such as to inspire the German Government with much trust in effective Italian support.' In view of her endangered position in Europe it was necessary for Germany 'to endeavour to obtain the certainty of armed support from England for the contingency of an attack on Germany by France and Russia combined; for if England be not bound to Germany, and His Majesty's Government come to a general understanding with France and Russia, or either of them, the position of Germany in Europe will become critical'. For these reasons Germany was doing her utmost to create mistrust between Britain and Russia and between Britain and France.

'She is always ready with information for our consumption of Russian and French intrigues, and probably supplies the Russian and French Governments with particulars of our sinister designs.'

Outside Europe the interests of Britain and Germany were anything but identical, the diplomat asserted. The aim of the German Reich to become a great sea power compelled her to acquire coaling stations and naval bases along the shipping routes of the world. These, however, could only be bought from Spain, taken by force from Holland, stolen from Portugal and Siam, or won from France in war, and such a development would be detrimental to the position of the British navy everywhere, but above all in the Mediterranean. In American waters Britain could safely leave it to the United States to thwart German ambitions, Bertie argued. But following the participation of Australian and New Zealand troops in the Boer War, Britain had the moral duty to protect not only her own, but also these countries' interests in the Indian Ocean and the Pacific, against foreign attacks. Thus, in the diplomat's view, the disadvantages of an alliance with Germany far outweighed any advantages. 'If we had a formal alliance with Germany we should either have to shape our conduct over a large extent of the globe in accordance with her views and subordinate our policy to hers, as is the case with Austria and Italy; or, if we acted independently, whenever we took measures necessary for the protection of our interests in some distant part of the world, we might be told by Germany that we were bringing about a situation which might lead to an attack on us by France and Russia, obliging Germany without sufficient cause to take up arms in our defence; or Germany might find some moment opportune for herself, but inconvenient for us, for bringing on a war on a question in which we might not have a great interest ... If we had an alliance making it incumbent on each ally to come to the aid of his partner when attacked by two Powers, it might be difficult to decide whether, in some particular case, the *casus foederis* has arisen, for the attacking parties are not necessarily the real aggressors ... If once we bind ourselves by a formal defensive alliance, and practically join the Triplice, we shall never be on decent terms with France, our neighbour in Europe and in many parts of the world, or with Russia, whose frontiers and ours are conterminous, or nearly so, over a large portion of Asia. In our present position we hold the balance of power between the Triple and Dual Alliances. There is but little chance of a combination between them against us. Our existence as a great and strong State is necessary to all to preserve the balance of power, and most of all to Germany, whose representations as to the disasters which await the British Empire if His Majesty's Government do not make an alliance with her have little or no real foundation. Treaty or no Treaty, if ever there were danger of our destruction, or even defeat, by Russia and France, Germany would be bound, in order to avoid a like fate for herself, to come to our assistance. She might ask a high price for such aid, but could it be higher than what we would lose by the sacrifice of our liberty to pursue a British world policy, which would be the result of a formal defensive alliance with the German Empire?'[25]

THE KAISER AND RUSSIA AT THE TURN OF THE CENTURY

The Kaiser's restless pursuit of an alliance with Britain in the years 1899 to 1901 coincided with the failure of his repeated attempts to achieve a closer relationship with Russia. In the spring of 1899, commenting on a suggestion by the Russian Finance Minister, Sergei Witte, that an alliance between Germany, Russia and France would carry along all the other continental Powers with it, thus enabling them to act in concert against Britain and America, the Kaiser reacted bitterly: 'Quite so, but nothing new! That was discussed 4 years ago with the present Tsar [Nicholas II] and 2 years ago at Peterhof with Witte too, but both times without any success. I have so often been ready for it, but in Russia strength of will and determined action was always lacking at the last moment!'[26] Quite apart from political and economic conflicts of interest, the difficult personal relationship between Wilhelm II and Nicholas II was undoubtedly an obstacle to any alliance between the two neighbouring empires. Although the Kaiser had hoped for much from the young Russian ruler after he became engaged to Wilhelm's cousin and sister-in-law Alix of Hesse, Nicholas had for some time been given to expressing 'unfriendly sentiments about our Emperor's pestering ways, while the latter is full of mockery for the Emperor Nicholas's feebleness', as Waldersee observed.[27]

The conflicting personalities and political attitudes of the two emperors came into unusually sharp focus over the international disarmament conference which was held in The Hague, at the Tsar's suggestion, from 18 May (his birthday) to 29 June 1899. Publicly Wilhelm wished this peace initiative success.[28] In fact, however, he saw the Russian proposals, which he repeatedly vilified as 'hypocrisy, rubbish and lies',[29] as nothing but an attempt to prevent Germany from counter-arming, in order to safeguard the supposed lead which her financially weak eastern neighbour had over her. The 'whole swindle', the Kaiser suspected, was 'more or less directed against *our military* development ... which Russia would like to bring to a halt, so as to keep us in the subordinate, inferior position vis-à-vis herself! They are short of money! And we are in the process of arming to make up for 15 missed years in comparison with Russia! The East Prussian border will be sealed off [by Germany] with a chain of forts and rapid-fire cannon, and beyond that with infantry armed with repeating rifles, and that does not suit the programme of *the* great "raids" for which the [Russian] cavalry is massed on our border! Hinc illae lacrymae! But I shall not let that deter me in the least. I shall play my part in the Conference comedy, but I shall keep my sword by my side for the waltz.'[30] Wilhelm scornfully rejected the proposal that international disputes should in future be resolved through a permanent court of arbitration, commenting that other countries 'can none of them mobilise as quickly as us! The whole Conference is tailored to that, too.'[31] In a letter to Queen Victoria he complained that the Russian army had been kept at wartime strength for years, the Russian battlefleet had been built up at enormous speed, the construction of the Trans-Siberian railway had been pushed ahead, and now the Tsar was trying to ward off the economic effects of the Russian over-arming by convening an international peace conference.[32] The Kaiser ridiculed the Russian initiative in other ways too, and with it the peace movement in all countries. The announcement that there would be prayers every Sunday in American churches for the success of the Hague Peace Conference was repudiated by Germany's Summus Episcopus – Wilhelm was the supreme bishop of its Protestant churches – with the remark: 'May Heaven forgive these hypocritical Pharisees!'[33] He continued to mock the suggestion that a permanent peace bureau should be set up to settle disputes, and observed, referring to Europe's foremost pacifist, the Austrian Bertha von Suttner: 'O Lord! Chairman Frau von Suttner?!'[34] His greatest contempt, however, was reserved for the initiator of the peace conference, the young Tsar, whom he derided as a 'day-dreaming boy' or a 'boyish day-dreamer!'[35] As the Kaiser made no attempt to conceal his views, it is not surprising that they soon became known in St Petersburg.[36]

In the words of the editor of the collection of official documents published in the 1920s as *Die Große Politik der europäischen Kabinette 1871–1914*, Kaiser Wilhelm's comments on the results of the Peace Conference showed 'unparalleled malice'. He wrote, on 23 June 1899: 'In Wiesbaden I promised to grant the Tsar my help to find a satisfactory solution! So that *he* does not make a fool of himself before Europe, *I* agree to this nonsense! But in practice and in future I shall look to none but God and my sharp sword! And shit on all the resolutions! Wilhelm I.R.'[37] Bülow, who described the negotiations in The Hague as 'a detestable monument to human short-sightedness and stupidity', responded in honey-toned admiration of Wilhelm's attitude. The delegates at the Peace Conference were nothing but 'muddle-headed diplomats, newspaper scribblers, stockjobbers and old women, who imagined that merely by making speeches and resolutions they could change the divine order of the world which has prevailed since the Fall of Man and through the Fall of Man', he wrote to the Kaiser. 'But Your Majesty's wisdom, self-control and far-sightedness have succeeded in getting over this episode without giving the Russians and Tsar Nicholas any reason for justified complaints. I admire Your Majesty's self-control all the more sincerely because I know how much it goes against Your Majesty's manly and upright feelings to take part in such half foolish, half perfidious trivialities.'[38] Instead of parroting his master's words, the Kaiser's principal foreign policy adviser would have done better to consider the likely effect on foreign countries, and above all on Russian policy, of the monarch's blinkered, belligerent attitude.

With the end of the Hague Peace Conference in June 1899 German relations with Russia had reached a low point. Prince Cantacuzene, the Russian envoy in Stuttgart, who had recently spent several weeks at court in St Petersburg, warned of German 'greed' in the Near East, and of the likely annexation of the German-speaking Crown lands by Germany in the event of the disintegration of the multinational Habsburg Empire.[39] As 'particularly black marks' in Russo-German relations, Cantacuzene named the Kaiser's journey to Palestine and the German plans to build a railway through Anatolia, which implied 'if not plans for conquest, then certainly a wish to gain political influence in the country or to colonise'. As far as the possible annexation of the Austrian Crown lands by the German Reich was concerned, Cantacuzene stressed that Russia could not accept 'a transfer of power of such magnitude', especially since the population of the lands was not exclusively German, but partly Slav. Russia regarded the survival of Austria-Hungary as a necessity, but if it should nevertheless break up, it was difficult to see how a settlement could be found between Germany and Russia.

Kaiser Wilhelm, as usual, covered the report he received of the Russian diplomat's observations with endless marginalia, which only confirmed that Russia's fears were justified. Cantacuzene's warnings, he wrote, sounded as if Russia wanted to declare war on Germany in the event of the disintegration of the Habsburg Empire. 'These are the sort of expressions one finds in memoirs from the period around 66–70, often used about us, above all by France. God preserve Austria from collapsing, and us from inheriting the crown lands there. But if something like that should arise in the course of the century, and Russia wanted to prevent it for the reasons mentioned above, then she would quite rightly deserve, and receive, a powerful dose of hard German thrashing. If you want to swallow all China, Persia and India [sic!] and then refuse to allow your neighbour a route into Asia Minor, you deserve a hiding and the loss of everything [sic!] you already have. Furthermore it is not at all clear who will break down first, the Habsburgs or the Romanovs.'[40] When the Russian Foreign Minister, Count Muraviev, added his voice to Cantacuzene's admonitions, particularly with regard to German penetration of Asia Minor, and referred pointedly to the option of an agreement between Russia and Britain, Wilhelm repeated his conviction that Russia might soon collapse, and indeed earlier than the Turkish Empire.[41]

In September 1899 the Tsar's habit of visiting his wife's relations in Darmstadt without paying a courtesy call on the Kaiser in Berlin or Potsdam led to another outbreak of rage from Wilhelm. Nicholas had asked whether he could perhaps meet the Kaiser in Wiesbaden during his forthcoming visit to Hesse, whereupon Wilhelm invited him to Potsdam and Hubertusstock to shoot. The Tsar declined this invitation on the flimsy grounds of a family bereavement. The Kaiser sent an aggrieved telegram to Bülow: 'Considering all the due consideration I have shown to his – the Tsar's – exalted position, the standing of the Crown of Prussia and the Imperial German Crown demands that the Tsar should not disregard the proper observation of the international courtesies that are after all prescribed for ruling princes. He has already done this to me several times. (I refer to the instances in Wiesbaden and Darmstadt.) He takes it for granted that he can travel around unhindered in the German Empire, carefully avoiding the capital and its surroundings ... If Freiherr von Richthofen [the deputy Foreign Secretary] wishes for good relations with Russia, he is saying just what I think. But like marriage, that takes two. And if one is not willing (as in this case, out of passivity and laziness), there is nothing to be done, however hard the other tries. What is more, instead of earning thanks he will come under the suspicion, which is very easily aroused in the Russians, that he is running after them.'[42] Wilhelm's insistence that the Tsar and his wife visit Potsdam did little to improve relations with Russia. Weeks went by without Nicholas giving the slightest indication of when he would come. 'This kind of visit really shows how cold the relationship is, and it is also interesting to see that the Kaiser is fully prepared for a discourtesy', Waldersee observed.[43] In the end the meeting was arranged for 8 November 1899, but it was kept 'as short as it could possibly be. The Kaiser told us of it and was visibly in a bitter mood.' It was clear that the meeting was nothing but an act of cold-blooded duty, the General commented.[44]

Disappointed by the spectacular failure of his attempts at rapprochement, Wilhelm resorted to complaining of the personal weakness and political indecision of the young Tsar.[45] In March 1900 he told the British ambassador, Lascelles, that Nicholas had 'a decidedly peaceful disposition, but he lacked the strength of character necessary to rule a country like Russia'.[46] The Kaiser's disgust with the 'indecision of the Tsar and the traditional selfishness of Russian policy' was stoked by Bülow, who spoke contemptuously, in his fawning submissions to the Kaiser, of the 'indolent nature of His Imperial

Majesty' and joked about the Tsar's wish to be seen throughout the world as an 'angel of peace'.[47] Insiders spoke of 'an estrangement between the two Majesties' or at least of 'ill-humour on the part of the Russian Emperor'.[48] Given the frosty state of German–Russian relations, Wilhelm and Bülow agreed in September 1900 that a further meeting between the two emperors would be 'pointless' for the time being. The Foreign Secretary advised his master to maintain 'a (friendly) reserve', in the hope that this would make the Russians feel the need 'to draw nearer to Your Majesty again'.[49] Instead, relations between the Kaiser and the Tsar soon reached a new low point.

At the end of January 1901 Bülow, who had by now been promoted to Reich Chancellor, sent the Kaiser a draft telegram congratulating the Tsar on the bicentenary of the foundation of the Russian navy. Wilhelm, who was then in England for his grandmother's funeral, rejected the warm words suggested by his principal adviser in favour of a deliberately unfriendly message. 'I have put the telegram into curt and cool language', he explained, with evident anger and hurt pride, 'as H.M. [Tsar Nicholas] no longer feels inclined to observe the dictates of friendship and courtesy towards me which I, after all my attentions, was justified in expecting from him. The following will show you what I mean: Yr Excellency will remember the conversation with Grand Duke Vladimir which I related to you, in which he told me that traditions were finished with, they were a nonsense and not understood by young people etc. etc. and therefore that the Prussian paintings ought to go back to Berlin as they no longer had any value for them there etc. I did not tell Yr Excellency how the conversation ended, however, as the servant arrived with the sad telegram about Grandmama and I had to leave. Yr Excellency will remember that on 3 or 4 November I had informed Osten-Sacken, through Knorring, that I had been created Field Marshal by the Emperor of Austria and was also one at home. Now I knew that according to long-standing convention one is generally promoted in neighbouring armies in line with promotion in one's own army. Nevertheless Kaiser Franz Josef [sic] had been gracious. Six months had now passed, and the Tsar had taken no notice. As this rank was something exceptional, I asked whether H.M. might not, through a little note or a telegram, graciously express the intention and gratification of conferring this rank upon me in his army too. For if one were to become a colleague of Suvorov, Wittgenstein etc., for me that was such an honour that I would be glad to receive a little word of encouragement from the Sovereign ... Osten-Sacken reported accordingly. From 4 November to 18 January I had no news. When Vladimir mentioned this affair more or less in passing at the end of our conversation, and said with a laugh that it was nonsense, the Emperor [Nicholas] would not do it because it was not necessary!!! Of course we were promoted together and so it was quite superfluous and out of the question for the Emperor to show interest and take notice of it, and he *would do nothing of the kind!* So why didn't I just stick the damn twigs on my epaulettes myself! It was all I could do not to shove my baton into his mouth! I have been snubbed like a junior officer by the Russians!'[50] It is an alarming thought that the German Emperor and Supreme War Lord should allow himself to be guided by such childish concerns in deciding on the alignment of his powerful empire in the world political order! Not for the first time the newly appointed Reich Chancellor will have thrown up his hands in despair and asked himself what he had let himself in for.

A FRANCO-GERMAN ALLIANCE?

In his annoyance at the Russian rejection Wilhelm defiantly turned his thoughts to the idea of a separate alliance between Germany and Russia's ally, France.[51] The Franco-Russian Dual Alliance had its origins purely in French admiration for Tsar Alexander III, whose aura had only been 'enhanced by distance and unapproachability', he claimed. 'Tsar Alexander III, in spite of the pleas and urging of the French, had never been to Paris. Eventually Tsar Nicholas II had agreed to go, and when he, small, weakly, timid and with hardly a word to say to the French dignitaries, had appeared in Paris [in October 1896], the aura had vanished. Since then the French had gained nothing from the alliance, except for a quantity of Grand Dukes amusing themselves in Paris.'[52] From mid 1899 onwards Wilhelm did his best to drive a wedge between France and Russia with the aim of bringing about a German–French rapprochement.

During his North Sea cruise of July 1899 the Kaiser paid a visit to the French training ship *Iphigénie*, when for the first time since the foundation of the German Reich the German Emperor's standard flew from the mainmast of a French warship.[53] This gesture of friendship was all the more remarkable because since the Anglo-French clash at Fashoda, Wilhelm had made no secret of his hope for a war between Britain and France, and had even pressed for it in both St Petersburg and in London.[54] The first reaction in Paris, where feelings were running high over the Dreyfus case, was sceptical. The Kaiser dismissed this with the over-optimistic remark: 'No harm done! It will certainly have an effect, it takes time to do a thing well. Especially in Gaul.'[55]

It became even more evident that the visit to the *Iphigénie* was conceived as a diplomatic attempt at rapprochement with France when Wilhelm, soon afterwards, declared that at the forthcoming unveiling of a memorial to the fallen of the First Guards Regiment on the battlefield at St Privat, he intended also to honour the French fallen. He sent a wire to the German ambassador in Paris, Count Münster, saying: 'The memorial is in the form of a figure of an Archangel. It should be seen as representing the guardian of the graves of the fallen, both of the German and of the French armies. I intend, after the ceremony, to have a laurel wreath laid officially, in the name of the regiment and of my entire army, by my Adjutant-General, who will be accompanied by the gentlemen of my headquarters, on the most important French memorial in the area, of whatever regiment, as homage to the bravery of the French army.' The Kaiser went on to say that he would pass on to Münster the text of the speech he intended to make at St Privat, so that it could be given to General Gallifet, the French Minister of War.[56] In his address, on 18 August 1899, Wilhelm emphasised the unusual choice of a war memorial in the form of an archangel in armour resting peacefully on his sword. The figure, he said, was standing 'in this blood-soaked field, as the guardian, so to speak, of all the brave soldiers of both armies, both ours and the French, who fell here. For the French soldiers too went to their glorious graves fighting courageously and heroically for their Emperor and their fatherland; and when our flags bow before the bronze statue, greeting each other, and flutter sorrowfully over the graves of our dear comrades, may they also blow over the graves of our opponents, and whisper to them that we remember the brave dead with sorrowful respect.'[57]

There were constraints upon Franco-German détente, however, especially as any compromise on Wilhelm's part over the contentious question of Alsace-Lorraine was out of the question. When he received a report, in August 1899, that the Queen Regent of Spain had advocated greater independence for Alsace-Lorraine within the German Reich, so as to make allowance for French self-esteem, Wilhelm wrote contemptuously on the report: 'Stupid nonsense! Vanity is the chief devil of the Gauls and they must conquer it themselves. The territory is German and we shall do in *our* home whatever *pleases* us and France has nothing to do with it any more.'[58]

In these circumstances disappointment was inevitable, and the Kaiser, as so often, reacted with defiant aggressivity. As we have seen, he promised the British ambassador Frank Lascelles in March 1900 not only to remain neutral in what he believed was the forthcoming war between France and Britain, but also to ensure, through the protective power of the German 'bayonet', that Russia kept out of the conflict.[59] Nevertheless a Franco-German reconciliation remained a goal which Kaiser Wilhelm pursued during these years, and in a variety of ways. In his conversation with Lord Lansdowne at Osborne House on 25 January 1901 he pressed the British Foreign Secretary to mend fences with France, which, together with Britain, should then join the Triple

Alliance against Russia and America. 'The old French culture was useful and necessary for Europe', the Kaiser had asserted on this occasion, although only recently he had numbered the French among the 'doomed' Latin peoples. 'The lively, receptive, artistic spirit of the French acted for Europe like the pepper on the beefsteak', he now declared. It would thus be 'a mistake to leave France out of the reckoning'. The French were beginning to realise that a war of revenge to win back Alsace-Lorraine was impracticable, and that the Tsar would never offer his help; if they dared to go to war nevertheless, 'the most humiliating thrashing' would be the result. 'More than thirty years had already flowed over the war, and the French had long since begun to think more calmly about these things. Nor did I think that it had been in vain that I had taken every opportunity to show courtesy to the French', the Kaiser added. It was the joint historic task of Britain and Germany to separate France from Russia and win her over to join 'Europe'.[60] To Lascelles he declared that as a war between the Germanic and the Slav peoples was more than likely, he was anxious 'to induce France to withdraw from the Russian Alliance. This would take time, but it was not impossible.' The French were increasingly disappointed with the Russian alliance, which brought them no gain, but only obligations. 'No doubt, the memory of Alsace-Lorraine was still alive, but that was now a page of ancient history.' So he was hopeful 'that, when the conflict between the Teutons and Slavs broke out, France would not be found on the side of the latter'.[61]

In the months and years to follow Wilhelm continued sporadically to pursue his policy of rapprochement with France. In May 1901 the French General Bonnal took part in the exercises of the 2nd Guards Infantry Brigade at the invitation of the Kaiser. On this occasion Wilhelm proposed a toast to the French army and spoke of the comradeship in arms of the German and French troops in the China campaign.[62] During his Scandinavian cruise in 1901 Wilhelm received the former Prime Minister Pierre Waldeck-Rousseau, together with other influential men from the upper echelons of French society, as his guests on board the *Hohenzollern*.[63] That summer Bülow was able to heap flattery on the Kaiser with the observation that 'the process by which French social, artistic, scientific and military circles are being drawn closer to Germany – or more correctly, to the person of Your Majesty', had now become plain for all to see.[64]

Waldersee's diary also bears witness to the fact that 'reconciliation with France' was among the Kaiser's 'many plans for the future'. It was true, the General recalled, that even in Bismarck's time there had been no lack of attempts to reach an understanding with France, but 'the present Kaiser is more active, and certainly too active. The French, of course, see quite clearly what he is after; they accept all courtesies without allowing themselves to be blinded by them.' In spite of these reservations Waldersee was not against Wilhelm's policy towards France on principle. It was undoubtedly correct, in his view, that the great majority of Frenchmen no longer supported the revanchist aim of recovering Alsace-Lorraine, but only wanted to earn money. 'Nor is the French army at all anxious for war', he wrote, and 'to the great mass a war with England would be much more welcome' than a conflict with Germany. Serious politicians in France had been considering the question of reconciliation for some time, and no longer demanded the return of Alsace, but only of Lorraine. They were prepared 'to make some sacrifice for it, e.g. to give us Madagascar'. Waldersee was convinced, however, that Germany must keep Lorraine too. 'Gaining time is also very important in this matter, and time will gradually help the French get over Lorraine.' One should never forget, all the same, that 'given the character of the French' the revanchist spirit could be reactivated at any time. This would be sure to happen 'if we have a difference of opinion with England, which can very easily arise'.[65]

THE KAISER MEETS THE TSAR IN DANZIG IN SEPTEMBER 1901

Despite all his attempts to win favour in London and Paris, and despite his denigration of the Russians, Kaiser Wilhelm still cherished hopes of cooperation between the two neighbouring empires of Germany and Russia. One event − the visit of Tsar Nicholas to the German manoeuvres near Danzig from 11 to 13 September 1901 − is clear evidence of this. It was a telling episode, pulling together all the threads running towards France, Russia and Britain.

In April 1901 the Kaiser had sent the Tsar a brief telegraphic invitation to the combined naval and military manoeuvres planned for mid September near Danzig, and he had been gratified to receive an acceptance, albeit rather vaguely expressed.[66] His initial enthusiasm evaporated when the Russians made it clear that out of consideration for France they wished to keep the possible attendance of their monarch at the German manoeuvres secret for the time being. In mid May Wilhelm's uncle, Grand Duke Friedrich I of Baden, observed anxiously that the Kaiser was very prone to 'harsh criticism of Russia'. He had begged his nephew 'to differentiate between friendship and good relations for political expediency, all the more so because there is a strong inclination in St Petersburg to seek agreement with England on certain major questions, and English policy is concerned only with English interests'.[67] At Wilhelmshöhe on 20 August 1901 the Kaiser was surprised to receive the news that following his forthcoming meeting with Wilhelm at Danzig, Nicholas II intended to visit the French army at Compiègne and the French northern fleet at Dunkirk. He sent an angry telegram to Bülow saying that it was surely remarkable that neither the Russian ambassador in Berlin nor any source in St Petersburg had given the slightest hint of the Tsar's plans. 'This is how matters now stand, in my view', he wired. '1) Either all the Russians without exception have been leading us on and have kept this long-planned French visit a secret from us; and so as to throw us off the scent they have tossed us the news of the visit to me to console us and keep us busy. That would be possible except for the Tsar himself, who I cannot yet persuade myself to believe is such an arch swindler. Or 2) the state of affairs in Russia has become so bad that Mr Witte with his financial absolutism cannot cope any more. He needs a large loan, which can only be obtained in return for His Majesty in person, ergo the latter must be sent. Or 3) as a result of the Chinese affair relations between Germany and France, particularly between the two armies, and goodwill in France towards myself in person, have been so much strengthened and fortified that the Russians have been seized with blind panic and they think it necessary to try to dazzle the Gauls again with the brilliance of the white Tsar, which seems to have faded somewhat, and to bring back some of the Republic's pleasure in her amie and alliée.' In a characteristically defiant reaction to disappointing news the Kaiser briefly abandoned his plans for uniting Europe (including France) under his own leadership and withdrew into a vision of a militarily unassailable fortress Germany. 'This affair need be of no interest or concern to us', he wrote. 'We must continue to build our armoured forts on the Rhine and set up a series of new garrisons in Posen and West Prussia as agreed, for which incidentally I have already given orders to the Minister of War. Furthermore we must press ahead as fast as possible with the construction of our fleet. The ones who are going to get a nice fright are the English, and perhaps it is aimed at them too.'[68]

At the end of his dispatch to Bülow Wilhelm reverted to what really hurt him in the Tsar's behaviour – the secretiveness, as if the visit to Danzig needed to be kept out of the limelight, while the journey to France had been officially negotiated between governments and portrayed to all the world as an act of high politics.[69]

Shortly afterwards a personal letter from the Tsar, in belated response to a letter from Wilhelm of 13 June, went a long way to explain the mystery.[70] Not without *Schadenfreude* the Kaiser scribbled on reports of the Tsar's forthcoming French trip: 'So he had to go! he had no choice! Otherwise Witte got no money.' The visit evidently gave 'neither Gaul nor Russia . . . much joy! If not a kind of Canossa.'[71] Bülow was in no doubt that 'the pilgrimage of the Tsar to Gaul' was intended as a 'chess move against England'. The Tsar's surprising request that Wilhelm bring the Reich Chancellor with him to Danzig meant that this meeting too had become a matter of high politics, and it encouraged both the Kaiser and Bülow to hope for a diplomatic breakthrough. Bülow's initial reaction was to calculate that it would be very much in the German interest if the Tsar's visit to Compiègne and Dunkirk helped strengthen the republican government, for the present regime in Paris was 'far more comfortable for Your Majesty than an Orléans, a Bonaparte or a military dictatorship'. The French, for their part, would be 'all the more peaceable, the bigger their account with the Russians grows, and with it the material risk they run in the event of a continental war'. Bülow suggested that the Kaiser show great indifference towards King Edward VII and Sir Frank Lascelles, who were coming to Wilhelmshöhe after the funeral of the Empress Frederick on 23 August, and act as if he knew far more about the purposes behind the Tsar's visit to France than he was able to say.[72]

Without waiting for this advice from his Chancellor, the Kaiser wrote to tell the Tsar how overjoyed he was that he, Nicholas, who was Honorary Admiral of the German fleet, would be attending the naval manoeuvres off Danzig. Reckoning that he could manipulate Nicholas better without his advisers, Wilhelm urged him to leave behind his newly appointed Foreign Minister, Count Vladimir Nicolaevitch Lamsdorff, in St Petersburg. 'Regarding Count Lamsdorf [sic] I shall of course receive him should he be on board your yacht; should that not be the case, and as we are not on shore at all, please do not trouble the poor Minister to make the long voyage to Danzig.'[73] The Reich Chancellor's belated attempt to influence Wilhelm's answer, or at least to see it before it was sent, received short shrift. The Kaiser telegraphed to him on 25 August saying 'The wording of my reply to the Tsar's letter cannot be altered now because it is already in the Emperor's hands. In any case I do not think that my words differ materially from your suggestions. From the Tsar's letter it was clear that he does not want Lamsdorff with him in Danzig, otherwise he could simply have said that he was bringing him in case Count von Bülow would be there ... I believe I interpreted the Tsar's intentions correctly by allowing him to keep Lamsdorff away in a courteous manner. The main thing, in my view, is that we make sure of the *Emperor*.' Wilhelm added a handwritten comment: 'If you work on him [the Tsar] thoroughly, that is enough; and better for the after-effect if Count Lamsdorff is not there to water everything down again later or to betray it all to Witte, whose creature he is.'[74] The occasion for this correspondence may seem trivial, but the incident shows the dangers which were inherent in Wilhelm II's personal diplomacy, and which in the not too distant future — one need look no further than the fiasco of the Treaty of Björkö[75] — were to shake the relationship of trust between Kaiser and Chancellor.

Although the Tsar did in fact bring Count Lamsdorff, the meeting of the two monarchs in Danzig proved a great success. Bülow lost no time in making use of its propaganda value through the press bureau of the Foreign Office.[76] In Russia, too, statesmen, military authorities and newspapers, hitherto so suspicious of German intentions in Turkey and China, welcomed the improved relations with Germany. Suddenly concord between the neighbouring empires seemed to have come within reach. From St Petersburg Wilhelm received reports that the Danzig meeting had found favour there, unlike the Tsar's visit to France, which was regarded with 'unmistakable, if cautious, disapproval among all Russians of a monarchist disposition'. His reaction was to assert that this realignment was exactly what he was aiming at in the long run. Russian monarchists, it seemed, were convinced 'that the German and Russian Emperors, but not the latter and the President of the French Republic, can dictate peace to the world, if they act together'. Wilhelm wrote approvingly in the margin of this report: 'Indeed, and it shall be so, God willing.'[77]

Even now Wilhelm could not resist the temptation to play the card of the apparent rapprochement between Germany, Russia and France against Britain, in the hope that it might yet be possible to induce the latter to join the Triple Alliance.[78] On 23 August 1901 King Edward VII arrived at Wilhelmshöhe with Lascelles.[79] Both the British Foreign Office and the German Auswärtiges Amt had made precise preparations for the discussions between the two monarchs, but the surprising news of the Tsar's forthcoming visit to the French military and naval manoeuvres had such an impact that both Kaiser and King ignored the official agenda. By his own account Kaiser Wilhelm returned to his underlying idea of a union of the European Powers, including Britain, under German leadership. It was true, he declared confidently to his British guests, that there was 'an old school of politicians ... to whom Prince Bismarck once belonged, and even today e.g. Lord Salisbury and a few old-fashioned gentlemen in Paris, St Petersburg and Vienna, who saw it as the task of politics to move the individual states of the continent back and forth into different groups, play them off and incite them against each other. But this recipe did not work any more. Politics now pursued their course out in the world, and differences in Europe were fading. In recent times and especially since the Chinese expedition the continental states had been more closely united. For instance who would have thought it possible ten years ago that French and German troops would fight together under a Prussian General against a third party? The blood they spilt together had worked a miracle, and we now got on very well with our neighbours the other side of the Vosges. — Here I stand in the middle of Europe, with my strong army, and together with my allies, of whom I am sure, I shall see to it that all remains calm.'

England, the Kaiser continued, must therefore adapt her policy accordingly. She would not fail to have noticed 'that a strong current was flowing on the Continent in favour of a continental economic union against those who cause economic annoyance to the Continent. England will do well to bear this in mind. I cannot judge whether it is possible and useful for England to maintain her splendid isolation, or whether it is in her interest to take the side of the Continent or of America. I would only put forward for consideration that America and Russia are perhaps on a closer footing with each other than is dreamt of in London.' The Kaiser referred to Britain's exposed position, above all in East Asia, where without Japan's support she would not be able to defend her interests against the joint advances of Russia and America. Then he again insisted that 'England must decide on which side she wishes to stand; she will have to show her hand in the end. If she believes that her interests point towards the European Central Powers I shall be delighted; that would mean joining the Triple Alliance. After all that has happened recently and in the course of history, however – the experiences that Frederick the Great had with English politics are but one example – England cannot be surprised that we no longer react to generalised phrases about friendship and cooperation. We can only do business on the basis of firm agreements. Unless the English government lays a properly initialled, very clearly worded treaty before Parliament and gets it ratified there, so that all the world can see, there is nothing more to be achieved with us, that is, with the Triple Alliance, for I will agree to nothing without my allies.' At the end of his account the Kaiser recorded, in an access of arrogance, that he thought King Edward and Lascelles had been noticeably uneasy about the forthcoming meeting between him, Nicholas II and Bülow in Danzig, or about the Tsar's visit to France. 'Whether this will be enough to make the English and particularly Lord Salisbury give up their passive policy and open their eyes to the slow but inexorable decline of their prestige and of England's position in the world, remains to be seen.'[80]

The ultimate aim of Kaiser Wilhelm II's policy was not to conclude a treaty of alliance with Britain, France or Russia, but to play the three World Powers off against each other in order to attain German supremacy over Europe. What he really had in mind was clearly expressed in one of his marginalia in the spring of 1900. He wrote: 'Just wait! As soon as I have sorted things out with John Bull, Johnny Crapaud will be in for a thrashing.'[81] In other words: as soon as I have got the English bulldog on a lead I shall trample on the ugly French toad. And in January 1901, while in the Isle of Wight at the time of his grandmother's death, when Wilhelm affirmed his love of England and renewed his attempt to bring about an Anglo-German alliance, he was at

the same time living in hope of a collision of Russian and British forces in the
Persian Gulf. He annotated a report: 'That may turn out very nicely'; but it
was important that 'our stupid press' should be 'reasonably sensible and keep
its trap shut'.[82] In fact he himself constantly trumpeted his intentions and
intrigues to all the world. Needless to say, statesmen in London, St Petersburg
and Paris saw through this game and consequently reached agreements with
each other. Shortly before her death Queen Victoria told Nicholas II, who was
married to her favourite granddaughter, that Wilhelm always described
Russian policy as directed against Britain, which neither she nor Lord
Salisbury believed. She was worried, however, that 'William may go and tell
you things about us, just as he does about you to us. If so, pray tell me openly
and confidentially. It is so important that we should understand each other,
and that such mischievous and unstraightforward proceedings should be put a
stop [to]. You are so true yourself that I am sure you will be shocked.'[83] Slowly
but surely, as Bülow warned the Kaiser, the two great flanking Powers of
Europe, and France too, drew closer together.[84]

CHAPTER FOUR

The Boxer Rebellion and the Baghdad railway

It was not only in Europe that Germany's ambitious goal of becoming a World Power represented a threat for the established Great Powers, Britain, Russia and France. Overseas, too, these Powers saw the claims of the Kaiserreich colliding increasingly with their own interests, and this tended to drive them, despite their mutual rivalry, to make common cause against the uncomfortable intruder in their midst. Around the turn of the century this was the case above all in China and the Near East, apart from the bitter Anglo-German conflict over southern Africa. Both Germany's leading role in the suppression of the Boxer Rebellion in China in the summer of 1900 and her far-reaching plans to build a railway through Anatolia to the Persian Gulf via Baghdad aroused deep mistrust in the governments in London, St Petersburg and Paris. The sources show not only the global dimensions of German aims but also, once again, the almost overwhelming personal power of Kaiser Wilhelm, who was able to determine the Reich's policy down to the smallest detail. With some justification he claimed the punitive expedition to China as 'My Far-Eastern action' and the Baghdad railway project as 'My railway!'

`MY FAR EASTERN ACTION´: THE PUNITIVE EXPEDITION TO CHINA

From the spring of 1900 onwards frightening reports had been arriving in Berlin and the other European capitals from China. The Yihetuan rebels were marching on Peking, killing numerous Europeans and Chinese Christians, destroying churches and railway installations. From 20 June 1900 the foreign legations in the Chinese capital came under attack by the 'Boxers' while four hundred European, American and Japanese marines tried to defend them.

As telegraph communications with Peking were cut, for weeks there was uncertainty in Europe about what was happening in the Far East.

The 'Yellow Peril' had long been a cause of anxiety to the Kaiser and was the inspiration for his notorious sketch of 1895, 'Nations of Europe, protect your holiest possessions!'[1] As a result of the annexation of Kiaochow in November 1897 Germany had entered into competition with Russia and Britain, Japan and America over the future of the vast, dilapidated Chinese Empire, a matter in which Wilhelm II naturally took a serious interest.[2] But the Boxer Rebellion brought out in the Kaiser a bloodthirsty aggressiveness so extreme that it gave many observers the impression of a pathological state.[3] As early as 5 June 1900, when alarming calls for help arrived from the German envoy in Peking, Clemens Freiherr von Ketteler, he threatened: 'Agreed! Squadron commander must be given necessary instructions. If necessary, should anything happen to any German the city of Weih-Huan − an old den of pirates − not far from Kiaochow, is to be bombarded and occupied at once. The plan has already been prepared by HRH Prince Heinrich and the Chief of the Admiralty Staff is very much in favour of it.'[4] On the advice of the generals in his suite and of the Commander in Chief of the East Asia Squadron, Vice Admiral Felix Bendemann, Wilhelm decided at first to send an entire army corps to China, but allowed Bülow to dissuade him from this idea.[5] His agitation exploded into rage when news was received in Berlin that Ketteler had been murdered in Peking. The killer was a uniformed soldier of the regular Chinese army, not a 'Boxer'. In a dispatch to Bülow of 19 June 1900, which was a foretaste of his 'Hun speech' of 27 July, the Kaiser furiously demanded the complete destruction of the Chinese capital in retribution. 'After latest reports from China severity of catastrophe no longer in doubt ... In addition reports of riots in Yangtse-Kiang valley and on West River show that China as a whole is determined to throw out Europeans. Therefore preparations must be made immediately for *major military action of a concerted nature.* Summon [the foreign] Ambassadors at once who should seek instructions from their governments with a view to launching the action. Strong contingents must go out to the joint army. Peking must be thoroughly attacked and levelled to the ground ... I will gladly provide the Supreme Commander if necessary. For the whole action must be put into safe hands, and this means *European.* We must never risk allowing Russia and Japan to do it alone and cut out Europe. The German envoy will be avenged by my troops. Peking must be razed. England can take over command of action at sea. Marine infantry must also be sent out. It is the battle of Asia against all Europe!'[6]

Although the period from spring 1900 until spring 1901 was overshadowed by dramatic private, political and international developments − to cite but the illness of Wilhelm's mother, the death of Queen Victoria, the second Navy Bill, the change of Chancellor from Hohenlohe to Bülow, the Boer War and the ceaseless search, as described above, for a conclusive diplomatic coup in Europe – the events in China preoccupied the Kaiser to a most unusual degree. In taking such a strong stand he was undoubtedly driven by the wish to take revenge for the death of his envoy. Did he have any further objectives in mind? Initially Waldersee thought that 'apart from punishing the Chinese, he was not pursuing any definite aims. The Kaiser may well have had vague ideas about "dividing up China". The main thing, though, was probably the need to play a role in "Weltpolitik", without a clear idea of the consequences of this attitude.'[7] After a meeting with the monarch, however, the General reached a more soundly based conclusion. 'The Kaiser expressed great hopes of the expedition for the development of our trade in East Asia, he also confided to me that he hoped to obtain the highest possible war reparations from the Chinese, which he needed urgently for the Navy. So I realised that the monarch was intent on expanding our possession in Shantung, and that he would gladly have got his hands on Zhifu for this purpose.'[8] Indeed on 2 July 1900 Wilhelm ordered the occupation of the important international merchant city of Zhifu (Chefoo, now Yantai), with its ice-free port; the Chinese ships there were to be sunk and the Yangtse-Kiang region was to be claimed as belonging to the German sphere of interest. Although Zhifu lay on the north coast of the Shantung peninsula, not far from the British base at Wei-hai-wei and the Russian naval base at Port Arthur, Bülow gave his support to the Kaiser's orders in a circular telegram. Only when Vice Admiral Bendemann drew attention to the very dangerous general situation in China and to the inadequate resources of all the Powers engaged there, was the idea of occupation abandoned for the time being.[9]

The Director General of the Hamburg-America-Packet (Hapag), Albert Ballin, also advised expressly against annexations in China. Germany, he said, should aim only for 'concessions and no land'.[10] Accordingly the Kaiser assured the Prince of Wales on 31 July 1900 that the Tsar and he were pursuing the same policy in China. 'We both want China to remain whole & undivided, not split up in spheres of interest; & open door!'[11] For Wilhelm and Bülow the first consideration was to prevent Germany being forced out of trade in the Yangtse-Kiang region, the richest in China, which the British regarded as their zone of influence.[12] Helmuth von Moltke, the Kaiser's aide-de-camp and later Chief of the General Staff, who must have known Wilhelm's views well, showed how he saw the situation in a letter to his wife. 'Of course one must not go into the real motive behind the whole expedition, for if we are to be absolutely honest, it is financial greed that has persuaded us to cut into the great Chinese cake. We wanted to make money, build railways, start up mines, bring in European culture, that is, in a word, to make money. In that we are not one whit better than the English in Transvaal.'[13]

Once again Bülow felt compelled to draw the Kaiser's attention to the danger of the other World Powers drawing together against the German Reich. 'If Germany steps into the foreground in East Asia too soon and too much', he warned, 'it is possible, considering the Russians' jealousy, the latent hostility of the French and the unreliability of English policy, that the other powers might close ranks against us. We thought it wiser to hold ourselves ready for all eventualities, but not to show our hand prematurely ... In my respectful opinion, the greater the mistrust with which the other powers watch each other, the better the prospects for German interests. On the other hand it is likely that if Germany stepped forward as the principal interested party in Chinese affairs, one or other of the powers would use that as an opportunity to channel the mistrust of all towards Germany and to preserve their unity at the expense of Germany.'[14] Wilhelm, however, responded with a characteristically naive and impulsive reprimand. 'There is only one interest, and that is exemplary punishment of the people of Peking and the Boxers for the attack on our envoy. Everything else will follow! Blood has already been spilt in common, and that is the best basis!'[15] Given the general indignation at the excesses of the 'Boxers', Wilhelm at first expected that the European Great Powers would put aside their rivalries and act in unison to 'punish' the Chinese. But when he heard of differences that had arisen within the international force in the Tientsin district he reacted angrily, writing on 8 July 1900: 'The report from Tientsin of the quarrel between the English and Japanese and the Russians, which prevented a necessary attack on an enemy battery, is probably the most abysmal instance of political self-interest that has ever arisen in military history.'[16]

WILHELM'S 'HUN SPEECH' OF 27 JULY 1900

In a series of sensational martial speeches the Kaiser called upon the troops leaving for China to gird themselves for a merciless campaign of revenge. In his address to the expeditionary force, which seems to anticipate eerily his famous speech on the outbreak of war in 1914, he declared in Wilhemshaven on 2 July: 'The fiery torch of war has been hurled into the very depths of peace ... A crime of outrageous insolence and horrifying cruelty has been committed against my trusted representative and has swept him away. The envoys of other countries are in mortal danger, and with them the comrades who were sent to protect them. Even today, perhaps, they have fought their last fight. The German flag has been insulted and scorn has been poured upon the German Reich. That demands exemplary punishment and revenge ... So I send you out now to avenge the wrong, and I shall not rest until the German flags, together with those of the other Powers, fly victoriously over those of China and, planted on the walls of Peking, dictate peace to the Chinese.'[17] In a similar spirit, at the departure of a division of ships of the line from Kiel, the Kaiser proclaimed: 'I shall not rest until China is overthrown, and all bloody deeds have been avenged.'[18]

Afterwards Wilhelm left for his annual Scandinavian cruise, but the sea air did nothing to calm his excitable state of mind. From the *Hohenzollern* Eulenburg wrote to Bülow: 'I have the feeling that I am sitting on a powder keg and am *extremely* careful. Please keep political communications *as brief as possible* and ask for decisions only where they are unavoidable.'[19] A few days later, the Kaiser's friend added: 'I am sometimes really frightened, and I am seriously worried.'[20] It was in this over-excited condition, on his return from the cruise, that Kaiser Wilhelm II made the bloodthirsty 'Hun speech' at Bremerhaven which was to have a disastrous effect not only on public opinion in Germany and abroad, but also on the behaviour of the German soldiers in China. In the Middle Kingdom the German soldiers were to conduct themselves 'like the Huns under their King Attila a thousand years ago', evoking 'traditional German excellence', the Supreme War Lord commanded. 'The name of Germany' must become known in China to such effect 'that no Chinaman will ever again dare so much as to look askance at a German ... Pardon will not be given, prisoners will not be taken. Whoever falls into your hands will fall to your sword.'[21]

The Kaiser's call to arms, reinforced by the distribution of copies of his picture, 'Nations of Europe, defend your holiest possessions', inscribed with 'No pardon' and 'No pardon will be given', was received with enthusiasm by the departing troops, according to eye-witness accounts.[22] Not only did it represent an offence against the Hague Land Warfare Convention of 1899, as has recently been emphasised by several historians, but it can also be seen as 'the beginning of a German strategy of extermination which was continued in the colonial wars in Africa as well as in the First and Second World Wars'.[23] In his memoirs Bülow described the Hun speech as 'perhaps the most harmful speech that Wilhelm II ever made'.[24] He made half-hearted attempts to keep the worst passages of the speech out of the newspapers but soon saw that his efforts were pointless after the authentic text, taken down in shorthand by journalists present, appeared in the *Weserzeitung*, the *Bremerhavener Zeitung* and the *Hamburger Zeitung*. Discouraged, he instructed the Foreign Office that 'no attempt should be made to cast doubt on the complete text published by the aforementioned newspapers'.[25]

Although the devastating comments of German and foreign newspapers were shown to the Kaiser on Bülow's orders,[26] his behaviour at his public appearances in the following weeks showed little sign of change. At Bremer-haven he told the officers on the transport steamers *Adria* and *Rhein* that in China they would be dealing with a crafty enemy, who was 'cowardly as a dog by nature, but treacherous. Take special pride in strong discipline, spare the enemy population but be ruthless towards those who approach you weapon in hand! . . . And now go with God, gentlemen; show the world what Prussian discipline can do . . . Show the Chinese too that there is a Power that intends to castigate them for their lawless deeds, without regard to more distant practical goals. Wage the war until the goal that I have set you is achieved, and atonement is complete!'[27] On another occasion, bidding farewell to other troop transports setting out for China, the Kaiser declaimed 'very firmly and with strong emphasis': 'Do not rest until the enemy is thrown to the ground and begs on his knees for mercy.'[28]

WALDERSEE'S APPOINTMENT AS 'WELTMARSCHALL'

Immediately after receiving news of Ketteler's death the Kaiser had appointed Field Marshal Count Alfred von Waldersee, who happened to be with him on board the *Hohenzollern*, Commander in Chief of the German expeditionary force in China. He did so without consulting either the Reich Chancellor Prince Hohenlohe or Foreign Secretary Count von Bülow and against the wishes of Tirpitz.[29] As we have seen, in his telegram to Bülow of 19 June 1900 he had already intimated that if there were to be an international intervention force, he would want to provide the Commanding General.[30] Bülow shared the not entirely groundless hope that the Powers would agree to give overall command to a German general, who would be in a relatively 'neutral' position between the Anglo-Japanese and the Franco-Russian groupings. He warned strongly, however, against Germany taking the first step in this extremely sensitive matter.[31] But the Kaiser would not let it rest, and under pressure from his impatient demands German diplomats took soundings in the capitals of the Great Powers as to whether a German supreme command would be acceptable, and whether the other Powers might even be prepared to suggest it themselves.[32] The German approach was received with reserve on all sides. Count Hatzfeldt, ambassador in London, reported that the Prime Minister, Lord Salisbury, wanted to act in concert with Japan, but otherwise independ-ently, and had remarked meaningfully that neither in 1815 nor in the Crimean War had there been a Supreme Commander of the allied forces.[33] Meanwhile the German ambassador in St Petersburg, Prince Radolin, sent word that the Russian War Minister, General Kuropatkin, was clearly aiming for the supreme command himself.[34] Nevertheless, on Bülow's advice the Kaiser sent a telegram to Nicholas II on 5 August. In it he asked the Tsar whether he wanted a Russian general to be in supreme command; if not, Wilhelm suggested Waldersee for the post. Nicholas answered that he agreed with the Kaiser's suggestion.[35] Thereupon Wilhelm II immediately and mendaciously informed the Austrian Emperor, the King of Italy, the Emperor of Japan, the Prince of Wales and the French President, Émile Loubet, that the Tsar had not only placed his troops under Waldersee's command but had suggested the latter as Supreme Commander of the international intervention force in China.[36] The Grand Duke of Baden, who considered the East Asian expedition 'a very ill-starred enterprise', was strongly opposed to a German general taking on the supreme command, which would mean an additional burden for the country.[37] Wilhelm's sister Charlotte, too, was anything but enthusiastic. 'I do not like Waldersee's appointment! Not at all! That trickster, with his dishonesty, can run us straight into trouble.'[38] And his usually bellicose brother-in-law, Hereditary Prince Bernhard of Saxe-Meiningen, warned that it was 'a dangerous business into which we have somewhat recklessly jumped, but which we now have to carry on until success is at least half-way achievable'.[39]

Waldersee, mockingly described as 'Weltmarschall' (World Marshal), was in no hurry to go to China. By his own account he had himself briefed 'as thoroughly as possible' at the Foreign Office, and then defined the aim of his mission as 'after appropriate punishment of the Chinese, to help the country return to ordered circumstances, to encourage it to expand its trade relations with Europe and to make it solvent'.[40] When he left Hanover, travelling via Kassel, where the Kaiser bade him farewell as 'Leader of the united troops of the civilised world',[41] to Naples, and embarking there in the steamship *Sachsen-Coburg* on 22 August 1900, Waldersee and his enormous staff enjoyed what amounted to a triumphal progress through Germany, Austria and Italy. The crowds surging around his hotel and at the stations were greater than on any of the Kaiser's journeys, he wrote proudly to his friend General Verdy du Vernois. He commented with satisfaction 'that great crowds are still capable of national feeling'.[42]

In the Wilhelmstrasse it was feared that the Kaiser and Waldersee would pursue an independent policy over which the diplomats would have no control, fears which proved entirely justified. After his arrival in China the Field Marshal reported exclusively to the Kaiser, as Supreme War Lord, on his supposedly 'purely military' activity, so that the Foreign Office was obliged to seek the help of Philipp Eulenburg. On 27 September the Under Secretary of

State, Oswald Freiherr von Richthofen, wrote to Eulenburg: 'It would be of great importance to us always to be kept informed, as far as is possible, of Count Waldersee's messages. Count Schlieffen tells me that the Count only sends wires direct to His Majesty, so that it will not always be very easy to find out the content of his telegrams. But I would like to ask you, while you are with His Majesty, to do your utmost to help fulfil our wish.'[43] Three days later, for the first time, Eulenburg passed on a telegram from the Field Marshal to the Foreign Office.[44] He himself was deeply disturbed by the connivance of the two 'soldiers', bypassing the responsible statesmen and diplomats, and expressed his disapproval in a letter to Bülow saying that the Kaiser considered 'that the whole business of sending Waldersee was *entirely military*, it is nothing to do with the Foreign Office and moreover it is to be directed *by the Kaiser alone*, who is in charge. This attitude is neither *politically* nor *militarily* acceptable and can only lead to a catastrophe.'[45]

GERMANY BETWEEN ENGLAND AND RUSSIA

Bülow and his closest adviser, Friedrich von Holstein, were anxious to pursue their usual 'free hand policy' in the Chinese campaign, and hence to maintain the same degree of detachment from both Russia and Britain. Wilhelm's pro-British leanings were a serious obstacle from the beginning. Bülow therefore attempted to persuade the Kaiser to change his attitude, in the process playing a dangerous game with the vision of a future victorious war against Britain. 'The English are showing the cloven hoof of their ruthless selfishness more and more clearly', he wrote to the Kaiser on 6 August 1900. 'I have told the Russians, the French, the Americans and the Japanese that we would join in all international steps to preserve the international character of the Yangtse, without giving the Dual Alliance the impression that we would pull its chestnuts out of the fire if there's trouble with John Bull. The more we keep in line with the other interested parties in the Yangtse question, the sooner their relations with England may turn sour, and we need shed no tears over that.'[46] The hoped-for effect, however, was long in coming.

As Waldersee constantly emphasised in his reports to the Kaiser, the railway line between Shanhaiguan and Peking, which was built with British capital, was the principal cause of contention between the British and the Russians in China. But instead of keeping out of the quarrel, as recommended by the 'unbelievably weak' — Waldersee's description[47] — Wilhelmstrasse, the Kaiser inclined towards a pro-British position in his instructions to the 'World Marshal'. Eulenburg was horrified, writing to Bülow on 3 October 1900: 'That the Kaiser should direct Waldersee to take sides with the English over this railway, instead of standing aside when Russia and England are at logger-heads, is unbelievable!'[48] In the following weeks Wilhelm continued to interfere in the Anglo-Russian railway dispute through his direct orders to Waldersee, regardless of the fact that the Field Marshal's written reports took several weeks to arrive and might therefore have lost something of their relevance to the actual situation.[49]

The clash over the railway line in north China led the British to enter into the Yangtse Treaty with Germany on 16 October 1900. Both partners committed themselves – in full accord with Wilhelm II's views[50] – to the open-door principle, not for the Yangtse region alone, but for all Chinese river and sea ports. That both contracting countries declared themselves in favour of preserving China's territorial integrity gave the treaty an anti-Russian complexion, in view of the Russian seizure of Manchuria. Radolin, the German ambassador in St Petersburg, who knew nothing of the Anglo-German treaty until he read about it in the newspapers, complained irritably that his government was suddenly applying 'English policy' and as a result its 'differences with Russia were constantly increasing, in spite of our continuous assurances of collaboration'.[51] In the following months, too, German policy in China to a great extent took Britain's side against Russia, and the predicted consequences soon followed.[52] When it became apparent in the spring of 1901 that the Russians, as the Kaiser put it, would 'simply hold on to Manchuria without a treaty and not give it back', his fury knew no bounds. The Chinese had simply refused the Russian demands and 'betrayed the treaty conditions to the other Europeans, and now the ursus asiaticus [Russia] cannot get hold of the honey-pot by amicable agreement! He is angry that his neatly-woven little plan has come into the open, and so of course we are to blame! For now he will just "*steal*" the honey, when he would rather have avoided appearing to do so! Moreover it all costs money.'[53]

Meanwhile Wilhelm had been obliged to abandon his own plans to annex the port of Zhifu on the Shantung peninsula.[54] In spite of the danger of international complications Waldersee had at first had no reservations about fulfilling the Kaiser's original wish. On 24 November 1900 he had affirmed in a report to Wilhelm that since taking over command he had always had his eye on the occupation of Zhifu. He considered this action 'not difficult, and easy with the help of the armoured squadron'. Waldersee announced that 'when shipping recommences, that is at the latest on 1 March 1901', he would 'proceed to the capture of Zhifu'.[55] Wilhelm forwarded the report to his brother Prince Heinrich and to Bülow, both of whom spoke out against an attack on Zhifu. In a memorandum of 14 January 1901 Heinrich argued passionately that the seizure of Zhifu would be not only economically and politically unwise, but 'unworthy – and worthless'. Germany had repeatedly and solemnly declared that she 'was *not on any account* thinking of territorial expansion. The proposed action would give the lie to German policy and destroy the Anglo-German agreement. An inevitable consequence of this measure would be the *division* of China and the seizure of the *Yangtse Valley* by the English, if not the *setting alight of the firebrand* of a general war.' Furthermore the Prince advocated a conciliatory attitude towards China, in order to restore trust between the two sides. In his judgement, China had been sufficiently punished, 'not least through the sometimes outrageous behaviour of various Europeans'.[56] This time the Kaiser gave way, and in early February he called off the proposed occupation of Zhifu.[57]

In fact since Waldersee's appointment as Supreme Commander, the situation in China had changed very much to Germany's disadvantage. On 15 August 1900, four days before the Field Marshal left Berlin, British and Japanese troops had stormed Peking and freed the besieged embassies. Although this effectively rendered his mission redundant, Waldersee tried to salvage something positive from it, writing to Bülow: 'I consider the capture of Peking and the flight of the Chinese government into the interior – although it may have been a disappointment to our All-Gracious Lord – not at all unfavourable for our immediate interests. It prevents any single one, or – God forbid – all of our allies coming to separate agreements.'[58] This was precisely the danger. A separate peace treaty concluded before Waldersee arrived in Peking would wreck the Kaiser's and Bülow's plans. Their disappointment knew no bounds. Wilhelm telegraphed to his Foreign Office on 21 August: 'The report just received from St Petersburg that the [Russian] Emperor considers the war at an end following the capture of Peking . . . is extremely regrettable and surprising . . . The Russian news sounds disturbingly as if they are prepared to parley and it shows great dishonesty and unscrupulousness towards us. In short, this means: with your help we have Manchuria, to which we are not entitled, in our pocket; thank you very much. You have served your purpose, so off you go! As the French say, they mean to "débarquer" us. This outrageous affront must be repudiated as bluntly as it deserves.'[59] When the American government also signalled that it regarded the military action in China as completed and proposed an international conference to clarify the complicated situation, Wilhelm raged: 'Just wait until Waldersee is there, then it will soon be clarified! . . . The conference is nonsense! The circumstances are perfectly clear and it can only confuse them! We are staying in Peking and the Chinese are going to learn a lesson! The Generals are still in command!'[60] His own General's comment on this development, however, was pessimistic. 'I am truly sorry for the Kaiser, for Germany will not even come near achieving what she demands, and is being shamefully let down by most of her allies, above all by Russia, which has caused us problems from the very beginning.'[61]

Bülow agreed with the Kaiser that Germany must 'do everything to delay the start of peace negotiations until the arrival of Waldersee and the expeditionary force. We can also point out that there is no one there yet with whom proper negotiations can be undertaken; that the Boxer movement must be thoroughly rooted out if it is not to flare up again immediately; that it is in the interests of all the Powers to establish serious and comprehensive guarantees against the recurrence of such dangerous revolutionary movements in China; that adequate atonement must be made for the crimes which have been committed, to prevent the danger of similar excesses occurring again at the next opportunity; that pacification must make greater progress throughout China etc etc.' At the same time, however, Bülow again warned the Kaiser of the looming danger of Germany's self-isolation. As ever, the Kaiserreich must 'keep in contact as much as possible with all the Powers, in spite of the perfidious intentions which some of them of course secretly harbour', he stressed. 'If we offend the Russians we run the risk that they go straight to Salisbury and agree on a quick peace settlement with China. We must remain in harmony with Russia as long as possible, in token of monarchical solidarity and of our friendly attitude towards Russia in all north Chinese questions. If we turned away from England completely, on the other hand, that would not improve our situation either. We must act together with England, America, Japan and (as far as possible) also with France on the basis of the restoration of permanent facilities for trade and communication in China.'[62] But caution and discretion, the qualities which this extremely difficult situation demanded, were not exactly Wilhelm II's strong points.

On 21 September 1900 Radolin reported in great anxiety from St Petersburg about the increasingly hostile attitude of the Russians. 'It is becoming ever clearer here that they will not follow us on *our* military path in China. They would not be sorry to see us get *bogged down* on our own and perhaps bleed to death ... They do not trust us and the "Supreme Command" an inch in spite of all assurances of friendship that we are given.'[63] Six days later Waldersee at last took on the overall command of the intervention forces in the Peking area, which had meanwhile grown to 87,000 men. Since the Boxers and the Chinese regular army had already been defeated and peace negotiations had begun, the victories in battle of which Kaiser Wilhelm had dreamt were no more to be won. Those who, like Prince Heinrich, were well acquainted with circumstances in the Far East, were already pressing in October 1900 for the withdrawal of the warships which had been sent there, in view of the 'lack of action in China'.[64]

THE EFFECT OF THE KAISER'S SPEECHES

Waldersee proved himself active by ordering numerous punitive expeditions 'to cure the Chinese of their taste for war'.[65] Many of these military operations were linked with fearful massacres among the Chinese civilian population.[66] After his return from China Waldersee admitted the murderous conduct of war by the German soldiers. But he sought to relativise it by pointing to the 'cruelties and atrocities' that the British had committed in their 'war of extermination' against the Boers; moreover, he commented, it was 'a fortunate circumstance that human life is worth little in China, and it was not held very much against us that many people who had in fact done nothing bad were killed'.[67] Some German soldiers justified their murder and pillage to a British officer by saying that the Kaiser had declared in his speech at Bremerhaven that they should behave in exactly that way, and they were only following his orders.[68]

In Germany too, Wilhelm II's rabble-rousing speeches were becoming central to the growing protests against the luckless Chinese adventure. Since the summer of 1900 the Social Democratic and Progressive newspapers had been criticising the German intervention. The leaders of the SPD and the Progressive Party, August Bebel and Eugen Richter, demanded that the Reichstag be summoned to discuss the situation. The 'ill will' of these 'miserable wretches', as Waldersee contemptuously called them, was directed principally against the Kaiser.[69] 'All the parties . . . are hostile and suspicious towards H.M.', the Reich Chancellor Prince Hohenlohe wrote to his son just before he retired. 'They all want to give vent to their feelings, and as they cannot attack the Kaiser, they will fall upon me instead. But since I am not privy to the Kaiser's Chinese policy, nor can I make H.M. any different from what he is, I shall cut a very sad figure.'[70] Bülow, who with the Kaiser was chiefly responsible for the expedition, told Wilhelm that in his opinion a premature summoning of the Reichstag would be seen 'only as weakness on the part of the Crown'; on no account should parliament be summoned before Waldersee and the expeditionary force had arrived in China.[71] Not until mid November 1900, when the government was obliged to put forward a supplementary budget to pay for the intervention in China, was the Reichstag able to debate the expedition.[72] In the sittings of 19 and 23 November Bebel and Richter fiercely denounced the Kaiser's 'Hun speech'. Bebel read out extracts from the 'Hun letters'– written by German soldiers in China to their families at home – in which they described the atrocities which occurred on the German 'punitive' expeditions. 'Everything that fell into our hands butchered, neither women nor children were spared', a typical letter read. 'Towards the evening we burned down the whole town. September 11th was the bloodiest day that I have yet been through in China. That day I looked more like a butcher than a German soldier.'[73] Another soldier, as Bebel pointed out, referred directly to the Kaiser's 'Hun speech' in writing home from Taku: 'When we had won the first battle, you should have seen how we marched into the town. Everything in our way, whether man, woman or child, all were slaughtered. How the women screamed! But the Kaiser's order says: Give no quarter! — and we have given our oath to be loyal and obedient and we shall keep it too.' The leader of the Social Democrats added: 'I acknowledge that the Kaiser did not order that women and children should be murdered; on the contrary, he said: spare them! But, gentlemen, you can see how this order is interpreted in the minds of the soldiers, fanaticised and roused to the utmost.'[74] Waldersee may have been the 'General executioner', Bebel commented with withering ambiguity, but the 'moral responsibility' for the Chinese campaign lay with the Kaiser alone.[75]

In view of the criticism coming from all sides in the Reichstag — the National Liberal Ernst Bassermann and the Conservative Albert Freiherr von Levetzow also condemned the Kaiser's speeches — Philipp Eulenburg implored Wilhelm 'to desist *for the time being* from any *public* announcement, whether *civilian* or military, even if there were *only the very remotest chance* of it provoking or exciting feelings in some way. Especially *in regard to China*.'[76] Wilhelm answered his friend's telegram calmly: 'Am very grateful for your hints, which correspond fully to the course I have decided upon. It is also the course I have been following strictly hitherto.'[77] Yet that same day the Kaiser reminded young naval recruits at their swearing-in ceremony at Kiel of the bravery of the German troops in China, who had succeeded in 'cutting their comrades free from the enemy's clutches', and spoke melodramatically of those who 'sank to their rest, some carried off by deadly canon-fire, others by deadly bullets or fatal illness'.[78]

The Kaiser congratulated Bülow on his 'masterly shooting down' of the Left Liberal Eugen Richter in the Reichstag and told him he 'deserved the shooting medal for it'.[79] In his attempts to defend the monarch on that occasion, Bülow had been compelled to resort to the most threadbare of excuses. The Kaiser had received the news of the murder of Ketteler just before his speech in Wilhelmshaven on 2 July, Bülow stated, and this had 'made the blood course more swiftly through the German Emperor's veins'. In his 'Hun speech' in Bremerhaven Wilhelm had been mindful that in the meantime other European envoys had also been killed; accordingly he had 'spoken as a soldier at that moment'.[80] In fact, the new Reich Chancellor's support amounted to an exposure of the Kaiser.

THE OVERHASTY WITHDRAWAL

Only a few weeks later a different wind was blowing at the Kaiser's court. The 'struggle of Asia against the whole of Europe' was to be broken off, the four ships of the line that had steamed away to China for the punitive campaign in July 1900 were to be brought home with all speed, for more important tasks awaited them in the Baltic. On 9 May 1901 Under Secretary of State Richthofen informed the German envoy in Peking, Mumm von Schwarzenstein, that the Kaiser was very insistent on summoning the battleships back to Germany.[81] Bülow, who had hitherto restrained Wilhelm from excessively militant action, suddenly had to try to stop him ordering a premature withdrawal. Writing to the Kaiser on 10 May, he reported that the Chief of the General Staff, Count Schlieffen, had 'stated that the removal of the armoured squadron while the greater part of Your Majesty's expeditionary force is still on Chinese soil seemed to him to be highly questionable militarily'. The Reich Chancellor added: 'From my political standpoint I cannot ignore similar concerns. In particular the danger unfortunately exists that as soon as Your Majesty's expeditionary troops lose the armoured battleships which are their strongest support, the Russians could cause them difficulties ... Given such serious military and political reservations about the separation of expeditionary force and armoured fleet, I venture to ask Your Majesty, with the deepest respect, to agree to postpone the withdrawal of the fleet at the present moment.'[82]

The Kaiser listened to the advice of neither his Reich Chancellor nor his Chief of General Staff, and swept aside the objections of the Secretary of State at the Reich Navy Office, Admiral von Tirpitz, as beyond his competence. His telegram to Waldersee on 11 May 1901 betrayed what was really on his mind. 'Imperial manoeuvres near Danzig envisaged. Participation of fleet in grand style: landing manoeuvres, evolutions etc. Need armoured division for them. Tsar has already held out prospect of appearance for fleet manoeuvres.'[83] We have already seen how the Kaiser's expectations were roused by the Tsar's agreement to attend the Danzig manoeuvres, planned for September 1901.[84] In response to Bülow's submission of 10 May, Wilhelm appended a detailed explanation of why it was imperative for the ships of the line to sail home from China at once, and not to wait until June or July, when severe storms could be expected in the Indian Ocean. 'I cannot say I quite agree with the above remarks on all points. As to the armoured division being needed for the troops, it has no connection with them at all. The ships are scattered in distant harbours, have absolutely nothing to do, and that is not good for their crews. If the Reich Navy Office considers that the division can arrive in time for the manoeuvres if it leaves China in July, then it is quite wrong. The Reich Navy

Office is not in a position to pronounce on the tactical military use of the ships in squadron formation, nor is that its task, which is limited to matters of maintenance, construction and administration. On the basis of information I have gathered, 2 months must be allowed for the return voyage – as it will be in the bad season – and then at least 14 days to 3 weeks in the home harbour for repairs. After that HRH Prince Heinrich needs the division in the squadron for at least 4 weeks, to coordinate them with the others and to perform evolutions. For a naval *manoeuvre* in squadron formation in my presence will be out of the question if one division has trained in the Gulf of Petschili and the other at Kiel, as Adm[iral] von Tirpitz could have told Yr Excellency. Neither the ships nor HRH must be exposed to the danger of collisions, and that can only be achieved by exercising in *squadron* formation, which cannot be practised in China, and so it must be done at home. The above calculation works out at not quite 3 months, if all goes smoothly; the division *must* come back in *May*, that is my carefully considered decision based on military grounds! If Yr Excellency, after these observations, still declares yourself absolutely against this decision for political reasons, then I must call off the imperial manoeuvres and cancel my invitation to the Tsar; for nothing decent can be done with the miserable remnant at home! Whether this action will improve the mood in Russia, where . . . it is particularly unfriendly to us, I leave you to judge . . . But from all I know, their [the Russians'] mood will be considerably improved if they see that we too are making preparations to withdraw and begin our withdrawal by calling our ships home. The ships made neither England nor Japan nor America nor Russia more docile or obliging towards us, in spite of their presence for 6 months. They will certainly not make any more difference to the situation by *staying*. That Russia is ill-disposed towards us is of course nothing new, unfortunately, for the past 1½ years or so . . . In these circumstances we should make a start with our withdrawal, and our ships are needed at home.'[85] The Reich Chancellor hastened to assure the Kaiser that he would do 'everything in my power to enable Yr Majesty to recall the armoured squadron and the major part of the expeditionary force in the course of this month'.[86] In early June 1901 the Kaiser ordered his 'World Marshal' Waldersee to give up his supreme command and return to Germany.[87] Eulenburg commented indignantly on this decision: 'The carelessness and impatient haste with which China is to be stopped (simply to have a few armoured battleships in Danzig for a certain visit!) has something really frightening about it, when one thinks of the past summer.'[88]

The intervention in China had brought neither the military triumphs nor the political advantages hoped for; instead, as Bülow had warned from the beginning, it had led to endless squabbles with the Russians and the British.

During the campaign the Kaiser's main cause of complaint had been the Russians; now, as a result of Britain's rejection of his repeated attempts at rapprochement, and the renewed prospect that he might pull off a great coup with the Tsar's visit to Danzig in September 1901, he turned his ire on the British. Thus on 14 May 1901, temporarily reverting to Bülow's 'free hand policy' between Russia and Britain and contradicting his original attitude, he noted: 'Once again it is the infamous false British who want to push us into the middle so as to avoid a clash with Russia. That is why we must get out [of China] as soon as possible and leave the two of them alone.'[89]

'MY RAILWAY!' WILHELM II AND THE BERLIN TO BAGHDAD RAILWAY PROJECT

Even more than in China, the German plan to build a railway from South Anatolia to Baghdad and thence to Basra or Kuwait on the Persian Gulf brought the Kaiserreich into dangerous rivalry, at the turn of the century, with Britain, Russia and France in the Middle East, a region even then prone to crises of international significance. All these Powers had vital interests to protect in the enfeebled Ottoman Empire. For Britain the Near East was the line of communication with India, the 'great artery of the Empire'.[90] In British eyes it was unacceptable that a railway running from the Mediterranean to the Persian Gulf should be entirely in the hands of a foreign Power.[91] In Russia, Asia Minor and North Persia had for centuries been regarded as part of the Russian sphere of influence, and Russia aspired to gain control over the straits of the Bosphorus.[92] France, too, had significant historical, religious and above all financial interests in Constantinople to defend. Thus, with the Baghdad railway project, Imperial Germany was pushing its way into a region of which Bismarck had once declared that it was not worth the bones of a single Pomeranian Grenadier.[93] With the lively support of Wilhelm II, who had identified himself personally with the project since 1899 − the Baghdad railway 'is my railway!' he declared roundly in the summer of 1907[94] − the plan, together with the battlefleet, became the quintessential expression of Wilhelmine aspirations for world power.[95] As Gregor Schöllgen has written, one is presented here with 'the spectacle of an equal mixture of inexperience and ignorance composing German foreign policy in general and German Eastern policy in particular'.[96]

Since 1889, the year of Wilhelm's first journey to the Orient,[97] the Anatolian Railway Company, a German financial group controlled by the Deutsche Bank, had been building a railway line from Haidar Pasha, near Constantinople, to Ankara and Konya.[98] In the autumn of 1890 Sultan Abdul

Hamid II instructed his ambassador in Berlin, Tewfik Pasha, to seek support from Kaiser Wilhelm for the continuation of the railway line to Baghdad.[99] The Sultan wanted the project to be carried out by a German financial group led by Alfred Kaulla.[100] Wilhelm sent a telegram to the Sultan agreeing to give his support.[101] It had not escaped the wily despot Abdul Hamid that the building of the railway was of great military and economic significance to his empire. He saw the sovereignty and territorial integrity of Turkey as under threat primarily from Russia and Britain, and was therefore determined to place the much sought-after construction contracts with German banks and companies.[102]

The first protests from France and Britain against the railway project made themselves felt as early as in 1892.[103] As the Foreign Secretary Adolf Freiherr Marschall von Bieberstein pointed out: 'The affair has acquired more importance for us because His Majesty the Kaiser and King, at the Sultan's special request, conveyed to our All-Gracious Lord by the Turkish Ambassador here, has declared his interest in German firms taking on the construction of the railway in question. It would therefore compromise the person of His Majesty if the concession were not now awarded to the German applicants.'[104] With Marschall's appointment as ambassador in Constantinople in the summer of 1897, Germany's Turkish policy entered a new and active phase.[105] Marschall threw himself enthusiastically into his task at the Golden Horn and advocated an energetic expansion of German business in the Near East. A man of literary talent, he sent back to Berlin an enormous number of detailed, well-informed and vividly expressed reports which fascinated Wilhelm. Many of the submissions made by this 'fellow from Baden', on whom the Kaiser had previously poured so much scorn, now earned genuine praise from him. When Marschall referred to a Turkish proverb which, he said, meant 'Haste comes from the devil, but patient waiting comes from God', Wilhelm added an amused comment: 'I laughed so much reading this alone in my room that the windows rattled!' At the end of the report he wrote: 'Quite outstandingly well written. A model report. Thank and congratulate Marschall from me on his success and his skilful conduct.'[106] In early 1899 the ambassador drew up his 'Guide to German policy on the Baghdad Railway' – a 46-page report to Reich Chancellor Prince Hohenlohe.[107] The vision he evoked at the end of his analysis was revealing. 'If I picture the future, showing how matters will stand one day if Germany continues to expand economically in the Orient – the port of Haidar-Pasha, to which, by and large, German products will be brought in German ships, the railway line from there to Baghdad, a German enterprise which uses only German materials and at the same time provides the shortest link for goods and people between the heart of Germany and her

East Asian possessions – I can see the moment approaching when the famous remark [by Bismarck] that the whole of the Orient is not worth the bones of a Pomeranian Grenadier becomes an interesting historical reminiscence but is no longer an actual reality.'[108]

Wilhelm's second journey to the Orient in the autumn of 1898 attracted enormous international interest.[109] At that time the Turkish government was considering applications from both France and Britain for concessions to build railway lines to Baghdad.[110] For months the Kaiser had been preparing to make a decisive intervention with the Sultan on the railway question, and he did not fail.[111] Only a few weeks after the end of his tour the Anatolian Railway Company was given the concession to build a large commercial port at Haidar Pasha, and soon afterwards a preliminary concession for the construction of the Baghdad railway as well. From London Count Hatzfeldt reported that in the view of 'the leading papers' the award of the preliminary concession was 'a success which is in no small measure attributable to the personal influence of His Majesty the Emperor'.[112] In March 1899 Bülow, 'with most humble duty', informed the Kaiser that 'since Your Majesty's return from the Holy Land this plan has been the constant object of discussions and negotiations between the Foreign Office and Herr Siemens. It was vouchsafed to the latter not only that there were no objections from our side to the expansion of the Anatolian railway network, but that we were perfectly prepared to promote the railway plan wherever it went and to emphasise our support for it to the Porte.'[113] According to the well-informed diplomat Friedrich Rosen, Siemens, the Director of the Deutsche Bank, on being told of the imminent award of the concession, was 'beside himself at the burden which the Deutsche Bank would now have to bear, and exclaimed: "I do not give a damn for this concession and the whole Baghdad railway!"'[114] In this case, at least, the driving force behind the German Reich's imperialistic urge for expansion was not the financiers, as is often claimed, but the dreams of world power cherished by the monarch and his diplomats. The commitment of the Kaiser, Marschall and Bülow put the recalcitrant banker under ever greater pressure.

Bülow had announced to the Reichstag on 12 December 1898 that Germany had 'no direct political interests in the Orient' and was not seeking to exercise 'any particular influence in Constantinople'.[115] Until the outbreak of war in 1914 the Reich government constantly repeated the mantra that it was pursuing exclusively economic goals in Turkey. The Austro-Hungarian ambassador in Berlin, Count Szögyény, knew better, however. 'The significance of this latest German enterprise, according to the unanimous view of the papers here, and to similar pronouncements on the part of the government, lies exclusively in the sphere of commerce, and not at all in that of politics. — This interpretation may well be correct in the first instance', he commented. 'One can foresee, however, that numerous businesses here will progressively establish themselves along the new railway line, which in turn might well lead to a gradual settlement by subjects of the German Reich. That this process, a kind of commercial colonisation, will go hand in hand with the growth of Germany's political influence in Asia Minor, and thus also at the Golden Horn, seems to me more than likely.'[116] Privately, at any rate, Bülow made no secret of the fact that he was also interested in political influence in the Ottoman Empire. Thus in his submission to the Kaiser of 30 September 1898 he emphasised that it was necessary 'in the interest of Germany's political position in Turkey and especially of German influence in Asia Minor' that the Baghdad railway 'should come under German influence'.[117] Six months later the Foreign Secretary described the construction of the Baghdad railway as a precondition for the 'opening up of the country for German interests as a whole'. This too Wilhelm II annotated 'Agreed'.[118]

From early 1899 the Kaiser had been intervening more forcibly in the Baghdad railway project. In this regard his memorable meeting on 11 March 1899 with Cecil Rhodes proved highly significant. Rhodes asked the Kaiser bluntly 'why he did not go for Mesopotamia [Iraq] as a colonising ground', to which Wilhelm answered that 'this was a project he had had for years'.[119] Not long afterwards, when Hatzfeldt sent in a newspaper article according to which the Persian Empire would soon be divided up into spheres of influence of the European Powers, William commented: 'But then we must secure Mesopotamia for ourselves!'[120] In November 1907, during a discussion with the British Foreign Secretary about the Baghdad railway, the Kaiser described his conversation with Rhodes as the actual moment of decision. In a secret note to the King, Sir Edward Grey said that Wilhelm had told him of an occurrence which had deeply impressed him during a meeting with Rhodes. 'Mr. Rhodes had told him that he took a map to bed with him every night, and studied what parts of the world there were waiting for European development. He had perceived Mesopotamia to be one of these; and that was the place Germany ought to take in hand. Mr. Rhodes had said this spontaneously to the Emperor at the very moment that the latter had conceived the idea of the Bagdad Railway, and when there were only four persons, himself, the Sultan, the German Chancellor [meaning Bülow], and the German Ambassador at Constantinople, who knew of the project. The Emperor had said to Mr. Rhodes: "You are perfectly right, and that is what we intend to do."'[121] During his Scandinavian cruise a few months after the meeting with Rhodes, the Kaiser, in his characteristic 'energetic mood', as Eulenburg reported to Bülow, expanded on 'the thoughts

you know of about a "German" Asia Minor'.[122] When Marschall urged in April
1900 that negotiations with the Turkish side over the definitive contract should
be started without delay, Bülow agreed, observing: 'We must conclude the
business quickly now, not least because His Majesty is pressing for it.'[123]
An imperial command put an end to the resistance of the Prussian Minister
of Finance, Johannes von Miquel, who feared the financial risk of state
participation: 'To the Minister of Finance for information and *to be carried
out immediately*. Wilhelm I.R.' Miquel promptly backed down.[124]

Failing to recognise the danger of isolating the Reich, Wilhelm, Marschall
and Bülow tried to play off the World Powers which had been established in
the Near East for over a hundred years against each other. They grossly
overestimated Imperial Germany's room for manoeuvre in the region. Thus,
when a British protectorate over the sultanate of Muscat on the Gulf of Oman
was in the offing in February 1899, Wilhelm commented: 'One could of course
give the British a fright from time to time with the vision of a Franco-Russian
Entente in the Red Sea and indicate to them that if, for instance, they wanted
to seize Muscat, they would need our good will to do so. In return, compensation in the form of a coaling station on the coast of Arabia, and friendly
support for the Euphrates railway which would be useful *to them* against the
aforementioned entente![125] Hatzfeldt cautiously suggested that the hopes
apparent in Wilhelm's comment were illusory. It seemed doubtful, he wrote,
that 'drawing attention to the frightening vision of a Franco-Russian entente
cordiale in the Red Sea would prove particularly effective here [in London] or
would induce the English to agree to any concession to us in Muscat that they
would not otherwise have wished for'.[126]

On similar lines Otto von Mühlberg sent instructions from the Auswärtiges
Amt to Hermann Freiherr von Eckardstein, the First Secretary at the German
embassy in London, in a 'very secret' letter at the beginning of 1900. 'It is
essential, therefore', he wrote, 'to exploit the rivalry between England and
Russia in Asia for our own benefit, so that, with a bow to the British lion here
and a curtsey to the Russian bear there, we can push our railway through to
Kuwait on the Persian Gulf'.[127] With no apparent misgivings Marschall had
already declared in June 1899 that Germany need show no consideration
towards Russia in expanding in the east – an idea that Wilhelm considered
'excellent'.[128] Marschall saw Kuwait as the most appropriate point of contention between Russia and Britain, where 'the Russian would be forced to
declare himself with regard to the Persian Gulf and thus to choose between
England and (indirectly) ourselves'.[129]

Russia's protests against the German plans for the Baghdad railway soon
took on a menacing form. After a conversation with the Russian ambassador in

Berlin, Count Nikolai von der Osten-Sacken, on 15 April 1899 Bülow recorded: 'The Russian ambassador emphasised with some vigour that in view of the age-old memories, feelings and hopes of the Russian people, the Russian government and the Tsar regarded with concern any competition for Constantinople and everything connected with Constantinople. It was feared in St Petersburg that our economic foothold in Turkey would develop into German political supremacy, which in time would inevitably lead to a conflict that would not otherwise exist between German and Russian aspirations.'[130] Six weeks later the Russian Foreign Minister, Count Muraviev, declared himself ready to approve Germany's activities in Asia Minor 'provided, of course, that Germany, for her part, unambiguously recognised the traditional exclusive claims of Russia to the Bosphorus and used her influence on the other powers accordingly, should the need arise'.[131] Wilhelm II was infuriated by this remark and strongly objected to the Russian Foreign Minister's tone. 'That is no doubt the kind of language Nicholas I used to Friedrich Wilhelm IV! But it is damned different under me! I ask you!! Heels together and stand to attention, Herr Muraviev, when he speaks to the German Emperor.'[132] As for the minister's warning that if Russia could not agree with Germany she might come to an understanding with Britain, Wilhelm simply swept it aside.[133] When the Russian government complained about a visit by Major Curt von Morgen, the German military attaché in Constantinople and an imperial Flügeladjutant, to the Turkish-Russian border, the Kaiser was again enraged. 'The Russians have no business saying anything in Turkey, and my aides-de-camp will go wherever it pleases me. Whether or not it makes Muraviev happy . . . The Russians have run out of money, they feel that we are gradually catching up on Alex[ander] III's 10-year lead in armaments, and are closing and fortifying our borders and winning allies or friends, and that does not suit them, as it puts them too much on an equal footing with us and they are afraid of getting a good thrashing!'[134] And in response to an observation by Heinrich von Tschirschky und Bögendorff, the First Secretary at the German embassy in St Petersburg, on 27 February 1900, that 'our railway project in Asia Minor affects Russian self-esteem', Wilhelm commented: 'Incredible! What has Asia Minor got to do with Russia!'[135] A year later, a Russian prince declared 'before witnesses', as the Kaiser angrily remarked, that if Germany did not 'clear out of *Asia Minor* soon and take her hands off the *Baghdad railway*, we shall declare war on her in 2 years'. The Kaiser thought it entirely possible that Russia would use the 400 million that she had recently received from France 'to put a stop to our Baghdad railway and our influence in Turkey'.[136]

There was little indication at first that the British government was also uneasy about the German railway project. The huge importance of the railway in terms of military strategy naturally did not escape the British, especially as the German press made no secret of it. In his book *Die Bagdadbahn*, first published in 1901, the German 'liberal imperialist' Paul Rohrbach frankly discussed ideas which could not have been more threatening for the British Empire. 'From Europe, England can be attacked and seriously wounded in one place only: Egypt. With Egypt, England would lose not only control over the Suez Canal and communications with India and East Asia, but probably also her possessions in Central and East Africa. The conquest of Egypt by a Mohammedan power like Turkey could also have dangerous after-effects on the 60 million Mohammedan subjects of England in India, as well as in Afghanistan and Persia. But Turkey can think of Egypt only on condition that she has an extended railway system in Asia Minor and Syria at her disposal, that the continuation of the Anatolian railway to Baghdad enables her to fend off an attack on Mesopotamia by England, that she enlarges and improves her army and that her general economic situation and her finances make progress'.[137] London had already entered into secret treaties with the Sheikh of Kuwait in 1898 by which the projected terminus of the Baghdad railway – in effect the gateway to further expansion – came under British control.[138]

At the end of 1902 the Kaiser still found it incomprehensible, in view of the growing influence of the Russians on Persia, that 'there are still people' in Britain 'who talk of a rapprochement with Russia!'[139] Slowly but surely, however, Britain, Russia and France, which as World Powers had previously been at odds with each other, drew closer together in the Near East.[140] In January 1902 the Anatolian Railway Company received the definitive concession to build the Baghdad railway and in March 1903 the Baghdad Railway Company was set up. As the cost of the project was high, the company's President, Arthur von Gwinner, Siemens's successor as Director of the Deutsche Bank, clung to the hope that British capital could be attracted to help finance it. But in January 1903 his illusions were shattered. The Foreign Secretary, Lord Lansdowne, told him bluntly that 'until now, England had sole control of the shortest route to India. With the construction of the Baghdad railway this would no longer be the case. He believed, however, that the combined influence of England and Russia might perhaps suffice to prevent the building of the Baghdad railway.'[141] On 25 April 1903 the German chargé d'affaires in London, Johann Count Bernstorff, reported that Britain and Russia were negotiating the demarcation of their spheres of influence in Asia. The northern area was to go to Russia, the southern to Britain. Wilhelm II commented bitterly: 'Aha! to take away the Baghdad railway from us and keep the Yang-Tse.'[142] The next day Bülow had to tell the Kaiser that the attempt to involve British capital in the financing of the Baghdad railway had failed. 'English participation has fallen victim purely to the anti-German agitation in the English press and to the pressure of public opinion that has arisen in consequence of it.'[143] By the word 'press' Wilhelm wrote 'Russian-inspired'; by 'public opinion' he added 'influenced by Russia'. He commented angrily at the end of Bülow's report: 'Above all, however, Alvensleben [German ambassador in St Petersburg from 1901] must not mince his words but tell Lamsdorff immediately and plainly from me, that if he does not wish to see me in the Balkans anywhere but at his side, he must order his agents to halt their activities in London at once! Otherwise he has lost his chance with me.'[144] French investment in the building of the railway could not be attracted except on a small scale because the French capital market was not opened for the Baghdad Railway Company's bonds. Nevertheless in July 1903 construction began on the railway, and in October 1904 the 200-kilometre line from Konya to Bulgurlu was brought into operation. So the railway project retained its explosive potential in the coming years, as we shall see.

CHAPTER FIVE

The shabby compromise: Wilhelm II and Bülow's Chancellorship

How significant was the Chancellorship of Count (later Prince) Bernhard von Bülow, which lasted from 1900 to 1909, for the decision-making process of the Kaiserreich? Recent historiography continues to debate the point. Did Bülow – as is so often claimed – really attempt to push back the power of the Kaiser, which had (as the second volume of this biography has shown) increased so enormously since the fall of Bismarck, and to win back for himself and his ministerial colleagues the authority of the Chancellor and the 'responsible government', lost under Caprivi and Hohenlohe? And if so, with what success? Or did he tacitly accept what seemed to him to be an irreversible shift of political power in the 1890s and merely do his best to neutralise the worst excesses of Wilhelm's Personal Rule, as each case arose? These questions are of fundamental importance to the biography of Kaiser Wilhelm II. For upon the answers will depend the degree of responsibility for the catastrophic development of the Reich during Bülow's Chancellorship – from the international 'encirclement' of Germany to the debacle of the *Daily Telegraph* crisis of 1908 – that can be ascribed to the monarch himself.

KAISER OR CHANCELLOR? THE BÜLOW CONTROVERSY

The relationship between the Kaiser and the Chancellor during the Bülow years has remained the subject of controversy until the present day. Wolfgang J. Mommsen, in summing up the conclusions of his last book, *War der Kaiser an allem schuld?* [*Was it all the Kaiser's fault?*], published in 2002, claims: 'On closer examination it is evident ... that the Kaiser influenced central foreign policy decisions to a far lesser extent than his contemporaries believed and than is commonly accepted in research on the subject. In particular, Reich

Chancellor Bülow manipulated the monarch, using him on the public stage as the spearhead, in effect, of the Weltmachtpolitik he was conducting, although the Kaiser by no means always approved his strategy without reservation.' In the field of domestic politics too, according to Mommsen, the Kaiser's regime served as 'a bulwark for senior civil servants ... enabling them to maintain their own sphere in which to exercise largely uncontrolled power ... The governing classes in Germany exploited the Kaiser's rule in order to take preventive measures against the dreaded transition to a parliamentary system.'[1] (See Figure 4.)

It is seldom wise for a historian to disregard the perceptions of contemporary observers in forming his judgement. Nevertheless, Mommsen's assertions on this point represent something of a consensus among German historians today. Bülow's biographer Gerd Fesser takes a slightly more cautious but broadly similar line, stating that in the early days of his term as Chancellor, and above all in relation to domestic questions, Bülow was able to 'raise the authority of the Reich Chancellorship ... decisively'. Fesser qualifies this, however, by emphasising that in foreign policy Bülow's room for manoeuvre was 'strictly limited', since 'Wilhelm II was not prepared to make any cuts in naval armaments'. All in all, however, German policy in the years from 1900 to 1909, according to Fesser, was decided principally by Bülow and not by the Kaiser. 'Like no Reich Chancellor before or after him, Bülow succeeded almost throughout his period of office in controlling Wilhelm II to a great extent, through a combination of flattery and careful persistence', Fesser also maintains.[2]

Such views are current not only among German historians. In his biography of Wilhelm II, Christopher Clark writes of the crucial relationship between Kaiser and Chancellor: 'Once in power, the 51-year-old Bülow largely succeeded in setting his own agenda ... It was clear that Bülow's and Wilhelm's views diverged on many key issues and that it was Bülow who generally succeeded in imposing his own preferences ... Bülow took great care to conceal from Wilhelm the shift in the balance of power between chancellor and emperor that had taken place since the resignation of Hohenlohe. At every possible opportunity, he sought to persuade the emperor that it was he, Wilhelm, who deserved the credit for the government's successes in parliament and abroad, and that Bülow's schemes were all an attempt to realise the Kaiser's worthy vision of a national policy.' Unlike Mommsen and Fesser, however, Clark concedes that it was not long before Bülow's tactics of deception broke down. 'By 1902 there were signs that Wilhelm was becoming increasingly perturbed at his own exclusion from the political process, more critical of the direction of policy and more determined to challenge the

Bülow: Glauben Sie mir, meine Herren, es gibt in Deutschland kein persönliches Regiment!

Figure 4 'Bülow will be my Bismarck!' In the tongue-in-cheek caption Bülow averrs:
   'Believe me, gentlemen, there is no such thing as personal rule in Germany!'

chancellor on key symbolic issues ... Autumn 1902 marked the end of the
honeymoon with Bülow.'[5] By that reckoning, then, the Chancellor's subtle
domination of the Kaiser lasted for scarcely two years.
   Konrad Canis, a distinguished authority on the foreign affairs of Imperial
Germany, addresses the problem even more cautiously. It is true that he starts

from the premise that on his appointment as Reich Chancellor, Bülow, taking Bismarck as his model, set himself the goal of reviving the power of the Chancellor and Prussian Minister-President which had declined under Caprivi and Hohenlohe. At the same time, however, Canis concedes that such a goal could not be achieved under Wilhelm and the prevailing power structures of the Kaiserreich, for it was 'as much at odds with the constitutional and political circumstances as with the erratic character of the Kaiser'.[4] In his recently published third volume, covering the years 1902 to 1914, Canis again features Bülow as the chief architect of German foreign policy, but is then forced to show how over and over again the Kaiser thwarted the Chancellor's best-laid plans, finally ruining everything with his maritime obsession and his antagonism towards England. Clearly this otherwise magisterial diplomatic history would have been more persuasive still had Canis given due consideration to the monarch and his entourage at court.[5] Even the late Marxist historian Willibald Gutsche admitted that Wilhelm's contribution to the course that eventually led to the catastrophe of the First World War was considerable. 'To an increasing degree', he writes, 'Wilhelm II behaved not only as a figurehead but as an active trailblazer for the policy of German Junker-bourgeois imperialism'.[6]

There is no doubt that Bülow at first enjoyed a high level of 'All-Highest confidence' and was consequently in a position to restore something of the authority of the Reich Chancellor over the machinery of state in the Reich and in Prussia. The crucial question, however, is this: did Bülow really exercise this newly acquired power to get his own ideas accepted by the Kaiser? Did he succeed, as most historians believe, in persuading the monarch, through 'calculating subservience', that he was carrying out his will when in reality he was doing the opposite? Given the Kaiser's well-known narcissistic hypersensitivity and his enormous sense of power this assertion seems implausible. Were there any occasions, before the crises of 1905, when Bülow gambled with his extraordinary relationship of trust with Wilhelm, which was after all the essential basis of his position, by setting himself against the Kaiser? Such conflicts must have left their mark in the documentary record. Yet one searches in vain for them in these early years. Bülow's whole personality and career throw doubt on the supposition that he would have risked the highest office in the Reich for the sake of a political decision that he considered to be right.

Peter Winzen, the foremost authority on Bülow, has recently revealed in several brilliantly researched volumes both the extent of the cunning the fourth Chancellor of the Reich used to worm his way into power and the abject sycophancy vis-à-vis the Kaiser he deployed to become the latter's 'darling' and to stay in the monarch's good books.[7] From his *faisandé* marriage to the Italian-born Countess Marie Dönhoff (a *protégée* of the future Empress Victoria) in the 1880s[8] and his overtly homosexual courting of the Kaiser's favourite 'Phili' Eulenburg in the 1890s[9] to the ruthless destruction of his rivals such as Waldersee and — last but not least — Eulenburg himself in the 1900s,[10] no stratagem seems to have been too merciless, no flattery too fawning for this latter-day Machiavelli. Obviously, on taking office Bülow expected to be able to use his special relationship with the Kaiser to prevent further gaffes or at least to mitigate their effects. Perhaps he intended to play some of his cards close to his chest in the hope of avoiding the monarch's direct interference. But would such a man have risked his own hard-won position as Chancellor, dependent as it was on Wilhelm's day-to-day blind faith in him, to claw back the powers his predecessors in that office had forfeited?

The British historian Katharine Anne Lerman, who has examined the 'decisive relationship' between the Kaiser and his fourth Chancellor in detail, denies that Bülow had any intention of seeking the kind of power Bismarck had wielded. On the contrary, the new Chancellor accepted the system of 'personal rule in the good sense' on principle, if also on the assumption that his unprecedented relationship with Wilhelm would enable him to call a halt to the monarch's worst escapades. 'After the power struggles of the 1890s Bülow made no attempt to redress the balance which had swung in the monarch's favour', Lerman states convincingly in her aptly titled study *The Chancellor as Courtier.* 'Indeed rather than claw back some of the power the Chancellor had lost, Bülow chose to base his personal position on the Kaiser's authority and confidence, and he constructed his system on an identity of interest between Kaiser and Chancellor.' 'Bülow intentionally based his entire system of government on harmonious relations between Kaiser and Chancellor', she writes. 'Wilhelm's confidence was the source of the Chancellor's strength, authority and security within the executive … Wilhelm II displayed a remarkable trust in Bülow's judgement and repeatedly left to him the conduct of affairs … Nevertheless, his success in restraining the Kaiser, his relative freedom of manoeuvre and the new confidence which their harmonious relationship engendered in the system in the early years were only achieved at a terrible cost … Bülow was acutely sensitive to the fact that Wilhelm II alone had the power to dismiss him — hence his determination to sustain their friendship, his obsequious and ingratiating approach and predisposition to submit to the monarch in direct confrontation. All Bülow's energies were harnessed to the overriding need to avoid a conflict with the Kaiser.'[11]

The leading American expert on the Wilhelmine era, Isabel V. Hull, also recognises Kaiser Wilhelm II as the chief supporter and guarantor of Bülow's position, first as Foreign Secretary and then from October 1900 as Reich Chancellor. 'Bülow never doubted that Wilhelm's personal goodwill was the indispensable prerequisite to the discharge of his office . . . as Chancellor', she writes. He accepted this relationship between monarch and servant as 'fundamental to the "personal monarchy"' and as the quintessence of the principle of monarchical rule upheld by the Bismarckian constitution. The close relationship to Wilhelm, however, was also 'Bülow's heaviest burden', for 'to remain in favour with Wilhelm while at the same time restraining his usually disastrous personal interventions was a task worthy of a Sisyphus or a magician'. Moreover, according to Hull, Bülow's central strategy of allowing the Kaiser to believe that he was the actual creator of German domestic and foreign policy had two serious drawbacks. Firstly, the Chancellor could never oppose the Kaiser directly without running the risk of putting his relationship of trust with Wilhelm at stake. Secondly, Bülow's vigilance would inevitably decrease with time, so that a catastrophe in domestic or foreign policy was virtually a foregone conclusion.[12]

WILHELM II'S PERSONAL MONARCHY ON THE EVE OF BÜLOW'S CHANCELLORSHIP

A glance back at Wilhelm II's rule in the last years of Hohenlohe's Chancellorship very soon reveals how hopeless any attempt to reassert the constitutional rights of the office of Reich Chancellor would have been, even if this had been Bülow's aim. It is clear that in the period before Bülow's appointment to the Chancellorship the monarch had become increasingly highhanded and the power of the three Secret Cabinets and of the Kaiser's military entourage had grown. At the same time the cohesion and influence of the 'responsible' machinery of the state had declined. As the envoy from Baden, Eugen von Jagemann, reported at the end of 1899, the Reich Chancellor, the Prussian ministers of state and the secretaries of state of the Reich offices had long since ceased to be 'influential responsible advisers with their own ideas'. They had descended to the level of mere 'executive organs of a higher will' and could at any time be taken by surprise 'by unexpected orders from the Civil Cabinet'.[13] The ministers and secretaries of state did no more than accept 'the decisions of H.M., which were usually already fixed beforehand', Jagemann stated. No longer did anyone dare raise objections 'which did not meet the Kaiser's wishes'. Not only had collective steps by the ministry against the Kaiser and King (as in the Köller crisis) become unthinkable, but individual ministers and secretaries of state kept their heads down and no longer took responsibility for collective development. 'The two armed service ministers [the Minister for War, von Gossler, and the Secretary of State of the Reich Navy Office, Tirpitz] are in fact inclined to withdraw into their own departmental responsibilities and the Minister of Justice [Schönstedt] also considers himself more as a technical assistant, rather than having the ambition to enter into political matters. Even at the regular meetings of the ministers of state Count Bülow takes part only when his own department is concerned.'[14] There was widespread criticism that 'not only the parliamentary bodies but also the Chancellor and the Ministers ... are caught unawares by enunciations from the Kaiser'.[15] Everywhere people complained of the 'powerful presence of the imperial personality' and of the dominance of 'the Kaiser's personal policy' over 'purely business and objective matters', Jagemann reported to Karlsruhe, full of foreboding at this state of affairs.[16]

The liberal South German envoy was by no means the only one who was strongly critical of Wilhelm II's Personal Rule and its consequences in the years immediately before the turn of the century. The staunchly Prussian, reactionary militarist Count Waldersee recorded in 1899 that on all sides there were complaints 'about the increasingly autocratic inclinations of the Kaiser' — he 'interferes ruthlessly in all matters that happen to interest him at the time' without taking the slightest notice of the views of the ministers.[17] After a meeting with the German ambassador in Paris, Count Münster, Waldersee noted pensively: 'Münster very much deplored the fact that the Kaiser wants to make all policy himself whenever he can, and likes to deal with the ambassadors himself. In fact quite a lot of damage has already been done as a result.'[18] It was very unfortunate 'that the Kaiser always addresses himself personally to the important questions instead of letting his ministers act', Waldersee commented in the autumn of 1899. 'His inclinations are ... very autocratic ... and the ministers are so tame and weak-willed that they never stand up to him with determination.' Since Bismarck's departure there had been only two ministers, Waldersee thought, who had maintained their position with dignity, namely the Prussian Minister of Ecclesiastical Affairs, Robert Graf von Zedlitz-Trützschler, and the Prussian Minister of War, General Walter Bronsart von Schellendorf.[19]

In early 1900 Waldersee commented with dismay: 'I find my view confirmed increasingly, that the Kaiser not only wishes to rule autocratically, but in fact does rule autocratically. He no longer needs the advice of anyone, has a very definite opinion on everything in which he wishes to intervene, and demands unquestioning execution ... If Ministers summon up the courage to mention difficulties in the country or the Reichstag, he always thinks they are spineless. There is no such thing as opposition . . . No one has his own opinion any more, or at least no one dares to assert it, each of them silently submits, knowing that if he raised difficulties he would be removed. Where are the men of character to be found! Flatterers and cowards are being reared . . . How long it can go on like that it is impossible to say . . . But we can be sure of one thing: that if serious times should come, there will not be enough men around. The Kaiser ruins everyone he deals with.'[20] That such a system must 'lead to a bad end' was 'absolutely clear and indeed very many people feel it now'.[21] If setbacks or mishaps arose, which would be particularly dangerous in matters of foreign affairs, the survival of the monarchy itself would be threatened. For then people would say 'the Kaiser did everything himself and he is to blame', the General prophesied.[22]

That Wilhelm II maintained virtually no contact with his 'responsible' advisers — apart from the Minister of War and the Foreign Secretary — as Waldersee had discovered, was deplored by the ministers themselves. But this led to no concrete results. After a meeting with the Vice President of the Prussian Ministry of State, Finance Minister Johannes von Miquel, in January 1900, Waldersee wrote: 'The Kaiser takes not the slightest notice of the opinion of a minister . . ., nor of that of the government, if it does not suit him. These gentlemen, however, let everything wash over them, accept the inevitable and do exactly as they are bid.'[23] A few days later the General received further confirmation of his observations. 'The Kaiser rules autocratically and takes no account at all of the fact that there is a government . . . All the ministers — and it could not be otherwise — are discontented and feel quite rightly that they are in fact in a very degrading position. Of course those who come off best are the ones whose province interests the Kaiser little or not at all, for the time being; the most severely tested are the Minister of War — although he goes along with everything — and the Foreign Secretary, that is to say Bülow, as Hohenlohe is no longer taken seriously.'[24] The inevitable result of this mode of ruling, Waldersee felt, was a disastrous confusion and lack of responsibility among the highest authorities of the state. 'We have no Ministry presenting a united front, but only departmental ministers who are not governing ministers', he complained.[25] The spirit of resignation that this induced among the statesmen is evinced by General von Gossler's warning words in February 1900 about the new law placing restrictions on pimping. It was essential, he said, 'whatever happens . . . to be sure of His Majesty's views, in order to avoid a complete repudiation. I do not believe that His Majesty will resist the [puritanical] influences which are working on him now.'[26]

It was neither the recognition that such a system of government held great dangers for both the monarchy and the security of the Reich, nor the feeling that to continue in public office under such circumstances would be degrading for the ministers, which led the Kaiser to replace Hohenlohe with the considerably younger 'splendid fellow', Bülow, in mid October 1900. On the contrary, Wilhelm's decision to appoint a new Chancellor was prompted purely and simply by the fact that Hohenlohe, who was now 81, found himself in an untenable position with regard to domestic policy. A change in the relative power of Kaiser and Chancellor as a result of Bülow's promotion to the highest political office in the Reich was hardly to be expected.

BÜLOW AS FOREIGN SECRETARY

The story of Bernhard von Bülow's rise, first to Secretary of State for Foreign Affairs and then to Reich Chancellor and Prussian Minister-President, raises the question of whether this was a man with the capability and will to win back for the Reich Chancellor the enormous personal power which the Kaiser had built up for himself since Bismarck's dismissal.[27] Bülow's conduct from the time of his arrival in the Wilhelmstrasse in the autumn of 1897 certainly gave no hint of any such intention. During this transitional period he attempted to secure the Chancellorship for himself by means of three strategies. Firstly, the elderly Prince Hohenlohe was to be kept in office for as long as possible so as to give Bülow time to prepare the terrain for his own promotion.[28] Secondly, in order to avoid compromising or wearing himself out unnecessarily, he took care to keep out of disputes over domestic policy as much as possible and to make his name in the sphere of foreign affairs.[29] Finally, he sought above all to secure and retain for himself, using what amounted to brazen flattery, the All-Highest confidence that was now the indispensable basis of every career in the upper reaches of political life under Kaiser Wilhelm II.[30]

Soon after taking over the Foreign Office Bülow declared that the nurture of his personal relationship to Wilhelm II would be the focus of his entire political activity, for 'unless I maintain constant (verbal and written) contact with H.M., the status quo which was so painstakingly glued together will fall apart'.[31] It was precisely this realisation which compelled him to avoid all possible conflict with the Kaiser. As he himself put it in November 1899, in words which quite openly show the extent of his calculation: 'I cannot see any purpose in making suggestions to His Majesty that would have no prospect of practical success but only make the All-Highest lose faith in me.'[32] Bülow justified his attitude with the argument that he 'did not want to annoy the

Kaiser from the outset by opposing him' but that he had sought 'to establish my place first'. Waldersee's comment on this approach was scathing. 'The poor man evidently doesn't realise that he has lost the whole thing as a result. He should have established his place in the first 8 days and then let a serious clash arise; then the Kaiser would have given in. Now he knows that Bülow is weak and will never hesitate to treat him ruthlessly.'[33]

In the last years of Hohenlohe's Chancellorship Waldersee recorded with disgust that Bülow was prepared to make 'quite incredible' use of flattery.[34] Previously he had often criticised the Chief of the Military Cabinet, von Hahnke, and the Chief of General Staff, Count Schlieffen, to the Kaiser, describing them as spineless, but even they were men 'of a different calibre' from Bülow; they were not 'shallow flatterers' like him.[35] At first Bülow's calculation seemed to succeed to a certain extent. In March 1899 Waldersee recorded: 'All is still well between Bülow and the Kaiser, although perceptive observers claim that the former's nerves are severely tested.'[36] A few months later the Field Marshal again accorded a certain recognition to the Foreign Secretary's tactics, noting that Bülow's behaviour was 'unquestionably very skilful' and one could tell that the Kaiser was very satisfied with the man. 'Bülow says many flattering things to the Kaiser and never says no, but he has often acted differently afterwards, for he knows that the Kaiser is very quick to give his opinion and often forgets what he said in haste.'[37] It remains unclear, however, which specific measures Bülow managed to carry through against the Kaiser's wishes by such methods.

A relationship of trust built on such insincerity was bound to collapse sooner or later, as must have been evident to those close to Wilhelm and Bülow, especially as the Foreign Secretary found it increasingly difficult to distance himself from domestic squabbles.[38] In October 1899 Waldersee recorded: 'Bülow is apparently beginning to notice that it is not easy to do business with the Kaiser after all; it seems he sometimes finds it quite hard to show the same friendly face all the time, nor can it be to the Kaiser's taste in the long run to be constantly heaped with praise in the way Bülow does it. The Kaiser cannot think much of it, even if he puts up with a sizeable dose of it.'[39] At the beginning of 1900, nine months before Bülow's promotion to Reich Chancellor, the General believed that 'the first passionate love' between Bülow and the monarch was 'over'. Decisions on diplomatic appointments which Bülow would not have accepted had been taken by the Kaiser over his head: Wilhelm nominated Freiherr von Eckardstein, who lived in England, as First Secretary at the London embassy and promoted the former Hofmarschall (Marshal of the Court) in Coburg, Wilhelm von Schoen, to the post of envoy in Copenhagen.[40] Very few people knew what trouble Bülow had with the Kaiser, Waldersee

remarked a few weeks later. 'It is said he often longs to go back to the Palazzo
Caffarelli [the German ambassador's palace in Rome]'.[41] The Centre party
member of the Reichstag, Prince Arenberg, and the Bavarian envoy Count
Lerchenfeld likewise observed at this time that 'Bülow has a terrible time
simply preventing the very worst imprudences [of the Kaiser]'.[42]

As Wilhelm's behaviour became more and more autocratic, while the
internal state of the country worsened and the dangers of Germany's growing
isolation among the Great Powers loomed ever larger, Bülow felt an increasing
urge to throw in the towel and abandon all ideas of taking on the Chancellorship. In April 1900 Waldersee wrote in his diary: 'Secretary of State Bülow
finds himself in an extremely unpleasant situation; he is clever enough to see
the whole sad state of affairs and would rather get out today than tomorrow.'[43]
At the very latest after the Kaiser's intervention in China and his catastrophic
'Hun speech' in the summer of 1900, Bülow must have realised what he had
let himself in for. Yet even now he kept his opinion to himself. On his
appointment to the supreme command of the international China expedition
Waldersee was astonished to see how calmly and unprotestingly Bülow
accepted the Kaiser's high-handed rule. Above all, the fact that the monarch
had ordered the armoured squadron to China without consulting Bülow had
caused despondency and anxiety in the Foreign Office. Yet both the Foreign
Secretary and the Reich Chancellor had apparently resigned themselves to
their fate 'without resistance'.[44] Following a meeting with Bülow a few days
after the 'Hun speech', Arthur von Brauer sent a revealing report to the Grand
Duke of Baden. The Foreign Secretary had 'merely cast his eyes up to heaven
and sighed, but it spoke volumes'.[45] Nevertheless it was precisely this 'quality',
the ability to endure the autocratic conduct of the Kaiser to the point of
self-abnegation, that was to smooth the path to Bülow's appointment as Reich
Chancellor.

BÜLOW'S PROMOTION TO THE REICH CHANCELLORSHIP

On his dismissal in October 1900 Prince Hohenlohe reflected bitterly on the
unusual single-mindedness with which Bülow had directed his efforts towards
the Chancellorship. 'When Bülow took Marschall's place [in the autumn of
1897] I had a rival beside me ... Bülow worked slowly, carefully but unceas-
ingly towards the goal of replacing me at the Kaiser's side. There was nothing
I could do to prevent it. I could not unseat him from his position with the
Kaiser, who preferred him. So fate had to take its course until catastrophe
struck.'[46] In fact Bülow's appointment as Reich Chancellor on 17 October 1900
stands out in the history of the thirty-year reign of Kaiser Wilhelm II as the

only planned and smoothly executed change of Chancellor – all the others, the transition from Bismarck to Caprivi, from Caprivi to Hohenlohe, from Bülow to Bethmann Hollweg, not to mention the makeshift arrangements towards the end of the world war, were characterised by confusion and panicky indecision.

In Berlin, ever a hotbed of rumour, there was speculation until the last moment about other candidates for the Chancellorship. Although none of them had any real chance, that they should even be considered is indicative of Wilhelm's unpredictability, his autocratic behaviour and his dynastic attitude towards the highest offices in the land. 'There was much anxiety that the Kaiser might have appointed another straw man', Baroness Spitzemberg noted with relief in her diary.[47] This comment referred principally to the rumour that had been circulating for years that the Kaiser might replace Chlodwig Hohenlohe, the Kaiserin's uncle, either with her brother Ernst Günther, Duke of Schleswig-Holstein,[48] or with Prince Hermann zu Hohenlohe-Langenburg, another of the Kaiserin's uncles and Statthalter (viceroy) of Alsace-Lorraine at the time. The latter's appointment as Reich Chancellor, it was said even in serious-minded circles, would have two advantages for the monarch: firstly, he would gain another 'pitiful' Reich Chancellor who would 'never oppose the Kaiser ... and would thus be thoroughly agreeable to him'; and secondly Wilhelm would be able to make his sister Viktoria ('Moretta') financially secure by promoting his brother-in-law Prince Adolf zu Schaumburg-Lippe, who had come out of the dispute over the Lippe succession empty-handed, to the glamorous and highly paid post of Statthalter in Strassburg.[49] As late as in April 1900 Waldersee wrote angrily in his diary: 'If the Kaiser should in fact carry out this plan, it would certainly provoke a storm of indignation. I think the German Princes would be bound to revolt against such a totally incompetent man as Prince Adolf of Schaumburg being given one of the most important posts in the Reich.'[50] Similarly, when the former Oberhofmarschall (Senior Marshal of the Court) and ambassador in St Petersburg, Prince Hugo von Radolin, was spoken of as the probable successor to Chlodwig Hohenlohe, this choice was seen as nothing but a means of fulfilling the Kaiser's wish to continue and extend his autocratic rule. 'Well, why not?' Waldersee commented resignedly when he heard the rumour of Radolin's supposedly imminent appointment. 'He has one quality to recommend him very strongly, being so insignificant and contemptible; the Kaiser could scarcely find a more compliant Chancellor.' Radolin, the General feared, would certainly 'adapt himself to the Kaiser's every wish and whim'.[51] In fact, immediately after Bülow's appointment as Reich Chancellor Radolin was sent to Paris to take Münster's place as ambassador.[52]

At the beginning of October 1900, just before Chlodwig Hohenlohe's resignation, statesmen other than Bülow were still being discussed as candidates for his post. Some thought that 'for the sake of the Eulenburgs' the Kaiser would choose Count Botho zu Eulenburg, who had been the Prussian Minister-President and Minister of the Interior until his dismissal in 1894.[53] The Finance Minister, Johannes von Miquel, who had 'the ear of the Kaiser' and kept in close touch with the head of the Kaiser's Civil Cabinet, Hermann von Lucanus, was considered another likely candidate until the last moment.[54] The German ambassador in London, Count Paul von Hatzfeldt, also had high hopes of being appointed Reich Chancellor, it was said.[55] Wilhelm, however, was not to be deflected from his 'Bülowchen'.[56]

Once the long-planned transition from Hohenlohe to Bülow was accomplished, Philipp Eulenburg, who had done more than anyone else to ensure that this change took place without causing a crisis, congratulated the Kaiser on his success. 'When I recall the *frightful* convulsions at the birth of the last two Chancellors, I could not be happier thinking of my beloved imperial Master, for this third birth was such a pleasing, gentle glide from one to the other.' Bülow, he said, would be a 'steadfast servant, loyal to his Sovereign', who 'with true, deep personal love for Yr Majesty', would 'never desert the post which he thought it right, in all modesty, to accept'. Inevitably, with Bülow taking on the Chancellorship and the responsibility involved, which extended also to questions of domestic politics, there would be more 'room for friction between master and servant' than before, Eulenburg warned. 'But Bernhard will always consider Yr Majesty's commands and wishes sacred ... If he should ever oppose Yr Majesty's views on this or that, however, Yr Majesty will remember how differently that is to be understood when it comes from a Bernhard than, for instance, from a Bismarck. Yr Majesty said to me: "Bernhard shall become my Bismarck one day." Yes indeed, he will be that, but − *Gedanken und Erinnerungen* will not be written and the beacons on the German mountains will be lit for Wilhelm II.'[57]

The iron law of Personal Monarchy, under which the fourth Chancellor assumed the highest office in the Reich, had been irrevocably established for years. 'Bülow is not a man of iron', Hildegard von Spitzemberg commented, adding pertinently: 'But such a man would not remain Chancellor for long, and would soon be "shattered". Bülow will bend his back, as a clever man, but not an insignificant or incompetent one.'[58] Only a few years later the Baroness was shocked to hear from her brother-in-law, the Conservative member of the Reichstag Nikolai von Below-Saleske, that 'Bülow had told the Kaiser from the beginning that he considered himself as the executor of his master's thoughts and commands; he would naturally oppose and argue as far as this seemed feasible, but he would renounce the idea of having a policy of his own from the outset.' As Spitzemberg remarked in 1903, 'In fact that is what is happening, more or less, and hence the zigzag policy, the zigzag action and the increasingly tyrannical despotism.' She added somewhat sceptically: 'Nevertheless it seems to me unlikely that this was a *parti pris*, so fully "agreed" from the beginning; it has merely turned out thus, thanks to the pliant back of the servant and the violence of the master.'[59] Yet there is plenty of evidence that Below's report was correct almost to the letter.[60] The evidence shows that Bernhard Bülow's inner dependence on the so-called 'All-Highest confidence' was even greater than that of Caprivi and Hohenlohe. Skilled as he was with both the spoken and the written word, Bülow had to try, with all the unctuousness of a courtier, to preserve the friendly feelings that Wilhelm II undoubtedly entertained towards him, and to avoid any argument that could cast a shadow on their relationship. With characteristic cynicism Prince Herbert von Bismarck commented, when Bülow paid a visit to Friedrichsruh immediately after taking office: 'He sees the mistakes but has to go along with them so as to preserve himself, for that is all he cares about.'[61] Everyone wondered how long the Chancellor would be able to avoid coming into conflict with the unpredictable, autocratic, hyperactive and vainglorious Kaiser, whether over another provocative speech, a foreign policy démarche, a public appointment, a court scandal or a challenge in the Reichstag. Given the chronic excitability of the Kaiser and the risky state of affairs both within Germany and abroad, the next disaster would certainly not be long delayed.

THE KAISER AND HIS 'BÜLOWCHEN'

Before Count and Countess von Bülow moved in October 1900 into the Reich Chancellor's residence at Wilhelmstrasse 77, which had resembled a 'first class waiting room' under Bismarck and had deteriorated even further under Caprivi and Hohenlohe, they had it tastefully renovated for a quarter of a million marks.[62] Bülow made no attempt, however, to restore the political position of the Reich Chancellor which had been lost under Caprivi and Hohenlohe. Instead, he accepted the overwhelming dominance and autocratic conduct of the Kaiser as an unalterable fact, and as Chancellor he pursued the same tactics of 'calculating' flattery that he had demonstrated in his transitional period as Foreign Secretary. He recognised that the monarch's favour was indispensable to his position, and that it was only by remaining on friendly terms with the Kaiser that he could exercise any influence at all. He remarked that a Reich Chancellor who 'did not possess H.M.'s confidence in such high measure [as himself]' would have far less 'opportunity to conduct German policy independently'.[63] When Friedrich von Holstein warned him in 1902 of Wilhelm's increasing high-handedness, Bülow replied: 'The tendency you emphasise is in fact undoubtedly to be found in H.M. But towards me it is modified – or it might be better to say not applied – because of H.M.'s great personal generosity and friendship. H.M. does not want to lessen my personal standing, far from it. On the contrary he wants to help, support and back me ... But it is certainly true that as soon as a Chancellor in regard to whom no personal feelings [of the Kaiser] were involved came into office, the above-mentioned tendency would once more become as strongly apparent as it was before my nomination.'[64]

So as to retain, and cultivate, the Kaiser's confidence in him, the Reich Chancellor took sycophancy to the level of the black arts. Wholly in accordance with the monarch's sense of his position, he spoke of the 'gracious commands' which he expected to receive from the All-Highest authority.[65] He was 'enraptured' by Wilhelm's foreign policy initiatives, acclaiming them as 'so astoundingly simple that one wonders why no one else has yet hit upon them. But not everyone is a Columbus.'[66] Against his better judgement he praised Wilhelm II's Russian policy, to which alone (apart from divine Providence) peace in Europe could be attributed.[67] Nor did Bülow shrink from expressing his 'admiration' for the Kaiser's speeches. 'Your Majesty has a rare gift for saying the right thing to each person ... I often tell myself how far my ability falls short of my wish to serve Your Majesty. But such thoughts always spur me on afresh.'[68] Towards the end of the Kaiser's Scandinavian cruise in the summer of 1904 Bülow wrote to him: 'Above all I wish to express my heartfelt thanks for Your Majesty's gracious recognition on the occasion of the conclusion of the German-Russian trade treaty. Tschirschky has informed me by telegraph that Your Majesty did me the great honour of mentioning me to the commanders of Your Majesty's ships during dinner. I was deeply moved and it would have made me proud, were I not always mindful and fully aware how much my efforts fall short of what it is my wish and my endeavour to be able to do for Your Majesty.'[69]

This submissive and undignified conduct towards the Kaiser made a disagreeable impression on Bülow's contemporaries. His conception of his role as Reich Chancellor, his insincere 'bowing and scraping', was universally condemned as a betrayal of the constitution and the nation.[70] After Waldersee returned from China in the summer of 1901 he took careful stock of the Berlin scene and concluded that although Bülow's standing with the Kaiser remained firm, it was only at the cost of all responsibility and dignity. 'He suits the Kaiser because he flatters him a great deal and never openly opposes him. It is said to be positively repulsive to listen to him heaping the most insipid flattery on the high Lord, which inevitably gives the latter an inflated sense of his own capabilities. He is bringing a heavy responsibility on himself.'[71] For Waldersee it was beyond doubt that Bülow was completely under the Kaiser's control. The Chancellor, he recorded, had several times 'quite innocently' declared, 'I can do nothing about it, that was entirely the Kaiser's decision.' Bülow was thereby 'calmly' admitting 'that he is in fact not Chancellor at all, but it is the Kaiser who is running affairs'.[72]

The perspicacious Hamburg shipping Director Albert Ballin, who met Wilhelm II and Bülow on various occasions after the turn of the century, was horrified by the one-sided relationship, based entirely on flattery and deception, that existed between Kaiser and Chancellor. After a two-hour walk with the Kaiser in the summer of 1901 Ballin was 'quite crushed', as Holstein recorded. 'Ballin had gained the conviction that the Chancellor's position with the Kaiser was no longer what it was. The Kaiser was much too intelligent not to have noticed gradually that the Chancellor always agreed with him to his face, but then managed behind his back to get *his* way.' He predicted the imminent fall of the Chancellor.[73] Following another meeting with the Kaiser Ballin repeated his conviction, this time to Waldersee. With his many years of experience, the General knew better. The flattery had 'not yet become too much for the Kaiser'.[74] Two years later he recorded that Ballin had admitted that he had 'deceived himself when he had said the previous [sic] year that the Kaiser could not possibly put up with Bülow's flattery in the long run. Now he says: "Bülow is a misfortune for us, he is completely ruining the Kaiser by continually saying the most grossly flattering things to him and gradually leading him to a hugely exaggerated opinion of himself.'[75] Even Bülow's close colleague in the Wilhelmstrasse, Holstein, in a subtle appraisal of the situation, wrote in January 1902: 'In some ways I feel sorry for Bülow. He is not a strong character, and up till now has achieved everything by amiability and his cleverness in taking people. But this by itself is not enough in the face of H.M.'s constantly growing awareness of his position as ruler. From time to time H.M. disregards the Chancellor, perhaps *in order* to demonstrate who is master ... I do believe that he [Bülow] has on occasion dissuaded the Kaiser from doing something, but has never directly opposed H.M. Firmness is not one of B.'s distinguishing characteristics, nor is his persistence very great.'[76] As the historian Ragnhild Fiebig-von Hase aptly observes: 'In fact the Chancellor, who after all was formally responsible for the policy of the imperial government, was reduced by the Kaiser in a most degrading manner to the level of one of the rival parties competing for the monarch's ear. It would have caused any statesman of character to hand in his resignation.'[77]

Waldersee kept a keen eye on the further development of relations between Kaiser and Reich Chancellor. After accompanying Wilhelm and Bülow to Italy in the spring of 1903 he wrote: 'I like the Reich Chancellor less and less, having been able to observe him again on the Roman journey and also recently in Berlin. I had never seen such a thoroughly false person before and it is quite extraordinary that the Kaiser, who is so clever, does not recognise this hypocrite.'[78] Waldersee was only very occasionally prepared to concede that Bülow had 'a certain influence on the Kaiser after all'. He noted in the spring of 1903, for instance, that Bülow had brought the Kaiser round to a less hostile attitude towards the Centre party. One therefore had to recognise, he wrote, that the Chancellor exercised 'at least an indirect influence in some questions' on the Kaiser, and dealt 'at any rate skilfully' with him, without letting him feel that he was influencing him. 'On the other hand the Kaiser often carries on ruthlessly over his head and Bülow has to go along with everything. Under no circumstances will he stand up to the Kaiser firmly. What still amazes me is that the latter does not see through his Chancellor's complete lack of character.'[79] Again in 1904, shortly before his death, the Field Marshal complained that Bülow was 'absolutely unprincipled' and went along with 'every initiative that the Kaiser undertakes'.[80]

The eggshell brittleness of the relationship between Kaiser and Chancellor was obvious to all those around them, who waited with baited breath for the first sign of an estrangement. Already in the summer of 1901 there was talk in Berlin of 'serious differences between His Majesty and the Chancellor'.[81] When the Kaiser announced a few weeks later that he was coming to shoot at Liebenberg, Eulenburg's Schloss, the rumour at once went round that Bülow – like Caprivi and Botho Eulenburg in the autumn of 1894 – would be 'brought to the kill' there.[82] Although these early fears were unfounded, there was nevertheless a Chancellor crisis in October 1902 which revealed how totally dependent Bülow was on the Kaiser's whims, and compelled the Chancellor to make still greater efforts to keep Wilhelm's favour. As Holstein confided to his diary, the Kaiser had come to Potsdam and Berlin feeling disgruntled about Bülow's policy towards Britain, and had stayed there for a week without seeing the Chancellor. Bülow became uneasy and asked for an audience, which proved 'very lively'. The Kaiser had complained, Holstein noted after the meeting, that he was 'misunderstood by the German people as well as by the English, and that nothing was being done in the German Press to enlighten the two nations. In short, he was dissatisfied with the guidance of the semi-official Press and with the conduct of affairs in general.' After this very 'unpleasant' audience, during which Wilhelm 'got furious', calm was restored. Now they would have to wait and see how the relationship would develop, Holstein opined. 'Bülow boasted mightily of H.M.'s affection for him, but is nervous ... I do not believe ... that the Kaiser will dismiss Bülow; the Kaiser finds him convenient because of his tractability. But Bülow's influence in foreign affairs will be still further circumscribed.'[83] 'Bülow has lost his nerve', Holstein noted a few days later. 'For the first time he seems to fear that he is becoming estranged from the Kaiser. That is why he is keeping absolutely still. He allows the Press to say whatever it pleases, and is only concerned with what might annoy the Kaiser.'[84]

After this temporary upset the Chancellor managed to shore up his position of trust by clinging even more closely to the Kaiser and scarcely allowing him out of sight.[85] Indeed, after the Reichstag accepted the Customs Tariff Bill in December 1902 the Kaiser's proofs of favour went so far as to overshoot their target. Bülow's elevation to princely rank, which had already been approved, was torn up at his own urgent plea. As Baroness Spitzemberg sarcastically remarked, 'H.M. emptied the cornucopia of his grace again in so gross a fashion that those favoured do not know whether they should rejoice or turn red in the face.'[86] The future Chief of the Civil Cabinet, Rudolf von Valentini, accompanying the Kaiser and Bülow to Rome in place of Lucanus, who was ill, noted in his diary that the 'relationship of trust' between the monarch and the Chancellor was again 'in full bloom'; he fully understood how it was that 'this extraordinary man' exercised 'great influence on the Kaiser'.[87] The Württemberg envoy, Axel Freiherr von Varnbüler, made a similar comment in the summer of 1903: he thought that the Chancellor had 'an increasing influence on the Kaiser, whom he now wisely seldom allows out of his sight ... in particular because he has more or less skilfully rescued him from his dilemmas'.[88] The mere fact that Bülow was able to indicate in February 1903 in the Reichstag that he would gladly approve the members' allowances and was only prevented from doing so by the Kaiser's refusal, was generally interpreted as proof that he must be in an 'extraordinarily strong' position with the All-Highest authority.[89] The justification Bülow gave for his obsequious attitude to the Kaiser was, in effect, that it enabled him to prevent worse things happening. That there was a certain legitimacy in this argument is undeniable. The consequences of such a regime, however, were disastrous.

ADMINISTRATIVE ANARCHY IN THE EARLY BÜLOW YEARS

However submissively the new Chancellor behaved towards the Kaiser, it seemed legitimate to expect that Bülow, precisely because he enjoyed the monarch's trust, would be able to control the machinery of government in the Reich and in Prussia with a degree of authority that had eluded his two predecessors. At his first session as Reich Chancellor and Minister-President on 23 October 1900, in the Prussian Ministry of State, Bülow emphasised that he would be governing with the backing of the Kaiser. The 'Prussian Monarchy' must henceforward form the 'basis' for the position of the Kaiser in the Reich and in the world, he said. As a prerequisite for the steady and purposeful government expected of it, the Ministry must always present a united front, and there must likewise be no inconsistency between Prussian and Reich policy.[90] Naturally, the new Chancellor did not omit to send Wilhelm II the relevant extract from the minutes of the meeting, which the Kaiser returned to him through Lucanus, with approving annotations. What was taking concrete form here was the very power structure towards which Wilhelm, Eulenburg and Bülow had been steering since 1895–6, namely that of the monarch *with* the Reich Chancellor *against* the ministers of state. This was how the system of Personal Monarchy 'in the good sense' was to function.[91]

Such a system of government was already an anachronism at the turn of the century, however, and it would inevitably bring the Crown more and more into conflict with a German society which was modernising itself with breathtaking speed. In the new pluralistic world of the twentieth century with its numerous and increasingly influential parliaments, parties, interest groups and organs of the press, difficult internal issues could hardly be satisfactorily resolved by commands from the monarch — even after prior consultation with the Chancellor. Nor could this system guarantee harmony within the heterogeneous administration, both Prussian and German. But if strong disagreements within the government and between the government and the Reichstag or the Prussian Landtag were inevitable, so too were conflicts between the ministers and the Kaiser. And however hard he tried, as Reich Chancellor and Prussian Minister-President, Bülow would not always be able to keep out of them.

On the day of Bülow's appointment Jagemann, the Baden envoy, sceptically wondered whether the former Foreign Secretary, who had 'taken no interest in domestic politics' in the past three years, would now 'emancipate himself enough' from Foreign Office business 'so that he truly grows into a Chancellor and Minister-President, i.e. that he really directs domestic policy in the Reich and the state, or whether in this regard the undisciplined disintegration of the departments will continue'.[92] Almost as if answering Jagemann's question, Waldersee recorded in his diary in the autumn of 1902 that Bülow was occupying himself 'almost exclusively with foreign policy' and did not even take the trouble 'to acquaint himself with our internal affairs about which he knows so little. The Ministry is in chaos and there is no question of united action.' Even in the very important question of the customs tariff treaties Bülow 'scarcely makes his presence felt at all'; the Secretary of State for the Interior, Count Arthur von Posadowsky, had to bear the whole burden. 'Every serious and reasonably well-informed person to whom I have spoken is deeply unhappy and worried and no one knows what it will all come to', Waldersee recorded.[93] 'It is more and more evident that Bülow is not competent to deal with our domestic issues', he commented acidly in October 1902, exactly two years after the Chancellor took office.[94] In May 1903 he again criticised Bülow's weak control of the country's internal affairs. 'His ministerial colleagues know him, of course, and have not a jot of respect for him. I hear that his chairmanship of ministerial meetings is usually feeble and as a rule ends in compromises whenever there are differences of opinion.'[95]

The growing conflict of interests on the one hand, and the structural absence of a coordinating, supreme decision-making body in the Reich on the other, was in itself a recipe for 'polycratic chaos'. But this was aggravated many times over by Wilhelm II's autocratic rule. The diaries and letters of well-informed contemporaries seethe with complaints about the state of affairs behind the shining façade that Bülow succeeded in presenting to the outside world through his numerous press contacts. All the pernicious features of the Personal Monarchy which had caused so much concern and criticism in the last years of Hohenlohe's Chancellorship lived on under Bülow: Wilhelm II's autocratic claim to power, expressed in his letters, speeches and marginalia; the unsupervised influence of unofficial advisers who had the monarch's ear; the 'court travel mania' which made it difficult to find a suitable moment to bring important matters before the Kaiser for his decision;[96] the lack of any coordination and unity between the various government departments both in Prussia and the Reich; and not least, the criticism, now growing to a dangerous level for the Crown and expressed both in parliament and among the population, against such an anachronistic and irresponsible system of rule. At the end of April 1901, after a conversation with Miquel, Prince Hohenlohe recorded that the Finance Minister and Vice President of the Ministry of State told him that 'dissatisfaction was growing among the people. They do not want absolute monarchy. He is pessimistic about the future. The Kaiser no longer listens to the ministers, especially the whole Ministry of State.'[97] Less than five months after moving into the Reich Chancellor's residence Bülow found himself compelled to threaten resignation because of disputes between the departmental ministers.[98]

The major ministerial crisis which broke out at the beginning of May 1901 because of the Conservatives' rejection of the Mittellandkanal and the closure of the Prussian Landtag — dissolution of the House of Representatives was avoided because new elections could easily have degenerated into a plebiscite against the Kaiser – led to the dismissal of three of the most important Prussian ministers, and at the same time to a thorough reorganisation of the Ministry of State. Miquel, Hammerstein-Loxten and Brefeld all retired and were replaced by new men. The former Minister of the Interior, Georg Freiherr von Rheinbaben, succeeded Miquel as Prussian Minister of Finance; the former Secretary of State of the Reich Post Office, General Viktor von Podbielski, was appointed Prussian Minister of Agriculture; and the Ministry of Trade went to the industrialist and National Liberal member of parliament Theodor von Möller. Rheinbaben's place as Minister of the Interior was taken by Hans Freiherr von Hammerstein, and Reinhold Kraetke, a competent but politically unambitious official, was given the Reich Post Office in succession to Podbielski.[99]

The handling of the ministerial crisis of May 1901 can in several respects be considered as characteristic of the relationship both between Wilhelm and Bülow and between them and the other Prussian ministers. The Kaiser returned on 30 April from a shoot at Schlitz, in the Vogelsberg, the property of his boyhood friend 'Em' Görtz; only three days later he left to visit his new friend Max Egon II Prince zu Fürstenberg at Donaueschingen in the Black Forest. This 'sudden appearance and disappearance by the Kaiser, in order to slaughter three ministers in between two bouts of chasing mating capercaillie' struck Philipp Eulenburg as 'somewhat turbulent' behaviour. He hoped, he wrote caustically to Bülow, 'that not too many others have made the same observation'.[100] Baden's representative in the Bundesrat also drew attention to the prominent role that the Kaiser, in conjunction with the Chancellor and Lucanus, had played in overcoming the crisis. 'These things do not seem to be dealt with between colleagues in the Ministry of State', Jagemann was surprised to find, as he reported to Karlsruhe. 'Instead H.M., with the President of the Ministry of State and the Chief of the Civil Cabinet, was allowed to bring about the settlement himself.' Jagemann heard through a counsellor in the Foreign Office of the strange way in which the Kaiser and his 'Bülowchen' interviewed the various candidates for office. After a dinner for his birthday Bülow had 'gone into various rooms in which ministerial candidates, who were to be received separately, waited *en cachette* for discussions, and finally H.M. himself appeared, before his departure [for Donaueschingen]'.[101]

Although Bülow was anxious to present the reorganisation of the Ministry of State as a reshuffle he had been planning for a long time,[102] he and the Kaiser wrestled over the distribution of ministerial posts until the last moment. The choice of both Podbielski and Hammerstein can be unambiguously attributed to Wilhelm.[103] As the Austro-Hungarian ambassador Szögyény reported to

Vienna, General von Podbielski was 'one of the Kaiser's decided favourites and is a habitual guest at His Majesty's beer evenings and skat parties. Count Bülow, who claims the Kaiser's favour entirely for himself and does not like sharing it with others, was for this reason not particularly inclined to welcome the appointment of Herr von Podbielski ... nor that of Freiherr von Hammerstein.'[104] The Kaiser nearly succeeded in appointing still more of his favourites to the Ministry of State. He offered the Prussian Finance Ministry first to the Director of the Deutsche Bank, Georg von Siemens and then, when Siemens resisted, to the Silesian magnate Guido Count Henckel Prince von Donnersmarck; only after the latter had also refused to take on this thankless task did Wilhelm compel Rheinbaben to switch from the Ministry of the Interior to that of Finance.[105] Until 5 May, when he was already shooting in Donaueschingen, he cherished hopes of being able to give the Ministry of the Interior to Theobald von Bethmann Hollweg.[106] Like Wilhelm, Bethmann was an alumnus of the Borussia student fraternity of Bonn University, and he had been governor of the province of Potsdam. Bülow, however, succeeded in temporarily keeping out this rival, who was to take over the Ministry of the Interior in 1905 and in fact to become Bülow's successor as Reich Chancellor in 1909. But it was at the cost of agreeing to the appointment of Hammerstein, who had attracted the Kaiser's attention through his archaeological reports while he was District President in Metz.[107] Even in the choice of Möller as Minister of Trade, Wilhelm II's antipathy to social reform was decisive. When Hinzpeter ventured to remark in a letter to the Kaiser that as an advocate of social reform, the thought of 'the transition from Berlepsch via Brefeld to Möller' gave him 'a slightly chilly feeling', the All-Highest countered with a disparaging marginal note: 'We have reformed "socially" enough for the time being.'[108] To the very last Bülow had every reason to fear that the Kaiser could revert to his earlier idea of offering this post to the Saxon industrialist Jencke.[109]

Bülow's own position was never in danger during the reshuffle – 'You stand too far above such things as guardian of the state – the Ministers must pay the price when things do not go as they should', Eulenburg assured him.[110] But the episode cannot be seen as the creation of a 'real Bülow Ministry', still less as a victory of the Reich Chancellor over the Kaiser. On the contrary, one cannot but endorse Katharine Lerman's conclusion that the events of May 1901 showed that Bülow was always prepared to submit to the Kaiser's wishes if necessary.[111] Admittedly he had been able to get rid of his chief rival, Miquel, but that had in no way improved his position in the Ministry of State, especially as neither General von Podbielski nor 'the *new* Hammerstein', who in the eyes of both Philipp and August Eulenburg was 'obstinate', 'far too western' and 'completely unfamiliar with the whole of eastern Prussia', would support him against the Kaiser.[112] Even the decision to leave vacant the post of Vice President of the Ministry of State, held by Miquel since 1897, which Bülow represented as reinforcing his own authority, can definitely be seen as a further step in the breakdown of governmental harmony vis-à-vis the Crown, an inexorable process which had begun with Bismarck's departure.[113]

It is also clear that even after the ministerial changes of May 1901 the Kaiser maintained direct contact with only a few ministers; most of them he practically never received. This had the effect of fatally undermining the unity of the administration. Waldersee recorded at the end of 1901 that he had heard from a most reliable source 'that since the spring, apart from Bülow, Gossler and Podbielski the Kaiser had not seen any of the ministers again'. Viktor von Podbielski was 'apparently in very good odour with the Kaiser at the moment'.[114] Soon, thanks to this preferential treatment, Podbielski was even being talked of as a possible successor to Bülow.[115] In October 1902 Waldersee noted that there were rumours that Bülow was intriguing against Podbielski because the Kaiser received the new Minister of Agriculture too often.[116] When Karl von Thielen was dismissed in June 1902 from his post as Minister of Public Works, Hermann Budde became the third General (with Gossler and Podbielski) in the Ministry of State, and initially the Kaiser established good relations with him, too.[117] Not only in ministerial circles but also in the press fears were expressed that in order to remain in the Kaiser's good books, Budde would seek to please him by pushing ahead with projects that the country could not afford.[118]

Although the Minister of War, Heinrich von Gossler, was regularly received in audience by the Kaiser, his fellow generals continued to regard him as a mere puppet of the monarch, with whom he behaved like a 'court Jew-boy'.[119] Just as in Hohenlohe's day, the 'utterly spineless' minister was criticised for 'a total lack of willpower with the Kaiser', as Waldersee censoriously observed in December 1901.[120] When Gossler was replaced by General Karl von Einem in May 1903 there was relief in the army, but it was assumed that there would be no fundamental change in Wilhelm II's relationship with the Minister of War. Jagemann reported that it was said of the departing minister 'that it was he who had suggested to H.M. the Kaiser the many new regulations on uniform specific to the regiments. Also that he had been too lax in representing military interests to the Reichstag, and had sometimes resorted to untruths.' The real reason for his dismissal, however, was that like his predecessor Bronsart von Schellendorf he had forfeited the Kaiser's confidence. 'But what seems to me decisive', Jagemann wrote, 'is that H.M.'s relationship with Herr von Gossler, who by the way is the longest-serving military departmental head since Roon, had gone sour, and it reminds me of the real reason for his predecessor's dismissal. In conversation with H.M., Herr von Bronsart had said in response to some unreasonable demand that he could not answer to the Reichstag for it. He received the retort that the Minister of War did not have to answer to the Reichstag for anything at all and could simply declare that the Kaiser had commanded it.'[121]

While Wilhelm II openly favoured a few ministers, he took no interest at all in the others. He did not like either the Secretary of State for the Interior, Posadowsky, or his colleague at the Reich Treasury, Maximilian Freiherr von Thielmann, while Arnold Nieberding, the Secretary of State for Justice, was even considered *persona non grata* by him.[122] Admiral von Tirpitz, as Secretary of State at the Reich Navy Office, had regular audiences with the Kaiser but as we shall see, Wilhelm's relations with him, too, became increasingly tense. The inevitable consequences of this form of rule were confusion and servility at the highest level of government, the domination of the 'responsible' authorities by the three Secret Cabinets and other officials and soldiers of the court, and the growth of the influence of unofficial advisers on the Kaiser's decisions. In May 1903 Waldersee expressed his dismay at Wilhelm's attitude to Bülow and the Prussian ministers and Reich secretaries. 'The present people suit him very well; he can do what he likes with each of them; there is in fact no collective Ministry and one can hardly consider Bülow as Minister President.'[123] In 1904 the Field Marshal was damning in his verdict on the way the government was being run. 'The fact is that we have government by [Secret] Cabinet with the Kaiser's autocratic will, which he generally conveys to the ministers through Lucanus', he wrote. 'Bülow's position is an exception, as the Kaiser sees him often – in Berlin every day, and likewise the Minister of War and Tirpitz, who have an audience at least once a week; but here too, as the Kaiser is away so much, the Chief of the [respective] Cabinet often plays a more prominent role. Of the other Ministers, Podbielski used to have the most audiences, for which shooting expeditions usually provided the opportunity, but that happens far less often. Budde has the occasional audience now, but then he is still new. Schönstedt, Studt, Rheinbaben, Möller actually never have audiences.' On the other hand there were plenty of unofficial advisers, Waldersee observed.[124]

THE PERSONAL MONARCHY UNDER BÜLOW

There is no indication in the sources that Reich Chancellor von Bülow, the Prussian ministers or the Reich secretaries of state 'manipulated' and 'instrumentalised' the Kaiser without his knowledge, as numerous historians believe. It is of course correct that increasingly critical public opinion and both parliaments in Berlin imposed limits on the power of the monarch at home. It is also correct that Bülow and his colleagues sometimes could not avoid making this clear to him. In May 1904 Hofmarschall Robert Count von Zedlitz und Trützschler observed quite rightly that modern parliamentary and democratic trends were having an increasingly restrictive effect on the Kaiser's scope for decision-making. 'These safety valves', he wrote in his diary, 'hold in check much that could otherwise become excessive and bring about certain disaster: although autocratic behaviour, arbitrariness and caprice can make themselves felt, in general they cannot be conclusive in the most fundamental and important decisions'.[125]

From time to time the Chancellor even found himself compelled to sort out embarrassing blunders by Wilhelm which had become public knowledge. When Oberhofmarschall August Eulenburg jokingly reproached him in 1904 for being rather too ready to give in to the Kaiser, Bülow responded seriously: 'You have no idea how much I have prevented and how much of my time I have to spend setting to rights what our All-Highest Lord has upset.'[126] Jagemann spoke with a certain admiration of the parliamentary skills demonstrated by Bülow, who evidently considered himself as the 'intermediary between Crown and parliamentary majority'. The Reich Chancellor was 'undoubtedly ... a more parliamentary minister' than his two predecessors, Caprivi and Hohenlohe. Jagemann speculated that this could probably be attributed to his many years of experience in Italy.[127]

It would be wrong, however, to underestimate the influence of the Kaiser on Bülow's political decisions. In the highly contentious customs tariff question, for example, Bülow's tactical room for manoeuvre was severely restricted by Wilhelm II's strongly anti-agrarian attitude. In the spring of 1902, reporting on this from Berlin, Jagemann wrote: 'In connection with the tariff question all kinds of rumours are buzzing around about the personal attitude of H.M. the Kaiser. I think it foolish to try to interpret these as some kind of opposition to the Reich Chancellor, because Count Bülow's position on these questions was the same a year ago as it is now ... The attitude of the high Lord [i.e. Wilhelm II] in this question has also been quite consistent from the beginning, and even agrarian ladies can often be heard saying that because of H.M.'s declared will, nothing more can be done for agriculture.'[128] If Kaiser and Chancellor were of one accord on customs tariff policy, when it came to parliamentary allowances for the members of the Reichstag, which both Bülow and Posadowsky wanted to introduce as a concession to the democratic parties, the Kaiser's objections remained an insurmountable obstacle for months on end.[129] When the Reich Chancellor announced the so-called 'Klosettgesetz', an act providing for the introduction of envelopes for ballot papers and for the erection of polling booths, it was seen as showing 'that the Chancellor had wanted to make some concession relating to the constitution of the Reichstag. But the fact that this was only the Klosettgesetz was proof that in his attempt to grant the parliamentary allowances he had failed to win over H.M. the Kaiser.'[130] This supposition was confirmed by Bülow's speech in the Reichstag on 3 February 1903, in which he indicated that there was 'a difference of opinion between him and H.M. the Kaiser' over the allowances. 'In other words he was saying that he wanted to grant the allowances', but could not, 'because H.M. the Kaiser had not authorised the Chancellor to make a concession'. Jagemann rightly pointed out that this admission broke with 'the principle that the government is under an obligation to give its sincere support to the decisions of the Crown'.[131]

The Reichstag played no such part in foreign, military or personnel policy, and it was here that the predominance of the imperial will over the responsible authorities was most in evidence. Wilhelm watched the activities of his diplomats like a hawk, and upbraided the Foreign Office for its occasional attempts to circumvent the policy he advocated.[132] Not infrequently his tone towards the officials of the Wilhelmstrasse was shockingly rude. Just before leaving for his Mediterranean journey in the spring of 1904 he wrote 'a terribly rude marginal note' and said within earshot of three Foreign Office officials and numerous others: 'Those swine in the Ausw[ärtiges] Amt gave me a few hours work on the very day of departure.'[133] Only a few weeks later he wrote at the top of a letter: 'The Wilhelmstrasse has shitted itself in front of the foreign press yet again, and the offices there stink accordingly!'[134] Draft telegrams from the Foreign Office had to be shown to him for his approval; conversely, Bülow's attempts, in view of the tense international situation, to submit drafts carefully formulated in the Wilhelmstrasse for the Kaiser's correspondence with the Tsar were rejected as churlishly as were the Chancellor's requests to see Wilhelm's letters to the Russian monarch before they were dispatched.[135]

Far from being manipulated by the Reich Chancellor and the other senior civil servants, Kaiser Wilhelm enjoyed his power to the full in the first years of Bülow's term of office. Despite the black thunderclouds gathering on the horizon, for him this was the high summer of his Personal Rule. His 'extraordinary over-estimation of his political accomplishments' spoke out of his every word, as the wife of a German diplomat commented after an encounter with the 'loutish' Kaiser in May 1904.[136] Count Zedlitz reflected apprehensively on the 'forceful personality of the Kaiser', which was 'accumulating an enormous amount of power for the Crown'. This, he thought, would 'almost inevitably be disastrous for his successors'.[137] Basically the Kaiser wanted 'only to be admired, praised and confirmed in his own decisions', the Hofmarschall noted in August 1904, after 'the closest observation'. It was true that one could occasionally tell him unpleasant truths, but he usually took this 'as amusing small talk and a diversion', Zedlitz concluded. 'All in all he is so imbued with his own intellectual superiority that he sees such efforts as nothing but tiresome presumptuousness. The exceptions are usually only apparent exceptions, and even those are possible only in his rare favourable moods.'[138] Zedlitz was far from denying that the Kaiser had talent and elements of a modern outlook, but he feared that the autocratic, reactionary aspects of his personality would always have the upper hand. Whatever progressive insights Wilhelm might have, he unfortunately also possessed 'the tendency to keep everything in his own hands and rule in a completely autocratic way'.[139]

The Silesian Hofmarschall was by no means alone in his critical opinion. Rudolf von Valentini, Councillor in the Secret Civil Cabinet, who was increasingly obliged to stand in for the ailing Lucanus in his work, and above all on the Kaiser's numerous journeys, was struck by the bizarre traits which he observed in Wilhelm II, and which he described in a passage which was mostly omitted from his memoirs, published in 1931. 'During these journeys, when we were in close contact every day, the whole problematic nature of the strange man whom providence has placed at the head of the German people became more apparent to me than ever before. As a human being he shows unusually charming characteristics. When he greets his travelling companions cheerfully in the morning and pinches his favourites in the leg, when he does Dresky's exercises in the middle of the crowd, gives the order for a terrific round-dance at the end and is the wildest in the forward charge, when he laughs so heartily at the old sea-dog Mensing's funny stories and Count Hülsen's vulgar Berliner slang that the whole ship echoes with it, one cannot but enjoy this cheerful innocence and unaffected freshness. And he wants everyone to share his pleasure when he sees something beautiful or interesting, a cape sparkling with lights, a leaping dolphin or a whale spouting a jet of water into the air. But it is precisely his human kindnesses and failings that stand in the way of his being a great ruler. He is too impulsive, too much a man of feelings and instant judgement, to be able to master and assess great issues. His long political disquisitions are written from the point of view of a youngish Guards officer, who approaches the great world of politics with the naivety of the officers' mess. He lacks not only seriousness but, in particular, depth of judgement. Colossal self-confidence and much "Renomaya" [swagger], but little "courage". It is not too far off the mark to attribute the way he consistently emphasises and demonstrates his peaceful intentions in large part to the subconscious sense that the bravura he otherwise likes to display would not be equal to the serious test of a war. Thus he always gives way willingly to the strong, be it Russia, England or the Pope, while he has little regard for, or interest in, weaker countries. It is only in his own country that he cannot bear the strong and the self-confident. For him, the Agrarian, like the Social Democrat, is the naughty boy who refuses to accept the benevolent guidance of the master – the great merchant who pours worthless praise on him to curry favour, the industrial magnate who subsidises his favourite pastimes with meagre scrapings from his huge profits, are worth more to him than the silent peasant on whom the strength of his state ultimately depends. Since the state of affairs within the Reich is in many ways so unsatisfactory he is not particularly interested in it and prefers to busy himself with foreign policy, which still lives off the old glory of the great past, at least outwardly. And here the impulsive, emotional side of his nature manifests itself most dangerously, for cool calculation and consistency of action, which alone can ensure success, are switched off. Action is taken under the influence of momentary moods, and then it takes years of hard work to obliterate and set to rights the impression made by that ill-considered action.'[140]

The court and government officials who were able to observe the prevailing relationship between the Kaiser and the statesmen of the Reich day after day did not doubt for a moment who gave the orders under Bülow's Chancellorship. Zedlitz was deeply shocked by the 'undoubtedly absolutist inclinations' of Wilhelm II.[141] The German system of government had 'in fact become the Cabinet politics of the 18th century' and was therefore dangerous 'both externally and internally', he warned.[142] The 'absolute rule' of Wilhelm II – the Kaiser's habit of leaping into the breach at every opportunity – constituted 'a direct danger'.[143] The Hofmarschall pilloried the obsequiousness and dishonesty of the Chancellor, the ministers and secretaries of state and the senior military establishment. None of them had the courage, he wrote in November 1903, to resign when treated badly by the Kaiser. 'In days gone by there might have been such Ministers', Zedlitz observed; his father had been Minister of Ecclesiastical Affairs and had resigned in 1892. 'Today they probably scarcely think of such possibilities; they sway timidly from one side to the other and leave the rest to kind fate.'[144] After Wilhelm's New Year meeting with his commanding generals in January 1904 Zedlitz wrote anxiously: 'Here . . . the inadequacy of our system was shown up particularly harshly. What a lot of mischief it can cause! What inferior people the monarch has to advise him! Many of them doubtless think much more deeply in their own minds, but what use is that if in the end they do not dare to say a single word freely. That is the fundamental evil to which one constantly has to come back, and the fault that threatens our future.'[145]

The consequences of the Kaiser's Personal Rule were evident to anyone who could look behind the scene. Varnbüler commented quite rightly in 1903 that under Wilhelm II and Bülow Imperial Germany had a 'completely aimless government that acted only on a case-to-case basis'; moreover, it had to 'talk out of the way any serious concern'. Anyone who advised active measures was silenced. 'Not only H.M. but also the whole of the Wilhelmstrasse was separated by a Chinese wall from the country, of whose real state these gentlemen knew nothing at all.' In both foreign and domestic affairs Varnbüler was 'very pessimistic about the future', his sister Hildegard von Spitzemberg recorded.[146] She noted in her diary in April 1904 that all German diplomats were complaining about 'the initiatives and arbitrary action taken by H.M., who is not open to any advice, conducts only his own very personal policy and is leading glorious Germany into disaster unless God helps us!'[147] The 'forceful personality' of the Kaiser and his autocratic style were having a corrupting effect on the diplomatic service, the provincial administration, the officer corps, the upper echelons of society in general, and even on some academics. Diplomats complained of the Kaiser's habit of praising reports which recounted 'any comic or racy tale, a piece of bravado, a student prank', whereas he was bored by serious analyses and found fault with them.[148] Friedrich von Holstein, the head of the political division of the Foreign Office, taught the German ambassadors with whom he was friendly how to frame their reports if they wished to preserve their good name with the Kaiser. Writing to Radolin in Paris in late 1901, he commented: 'Your latest reports came closer to that lively style which H.M. likes. After all, he is very "personal" and likes the personal element in reports. Wangenheim's report on the marriage of Sultan Murad's daughters was praised by the Kaiser as no report had been praised for a long time. It reported what the Princesses *are supposed* to look like, what the bridegrooms look like ... etc. Your report about the King and the royalties at the Ritz Hotel was too involved and too cautious. The Kaiser ... reads too quickly to stop and ask himself: who is this, who is that? ... My advice therefore is to carry on along these lines, but in particular not to bury the spicy anecdotes in private letters, where they do you no good, *but to include them in the official reports*, like raisins in a cake. Believe me, this admixture is the secret of success.'[149]

If an ambassador or envoy did not report vividly or amusingly enough, he was in danger of dismissal. Prince Philipp zu Eulenburg retired from his post as ambassador in Vienna (among other reasons) for failing to express himself forcefully enough for Wilhelm II's liking on the anti-Prussian riot in Lemberg (Lviv).[150] Theodor von Holleben's days as ambassador in Washington were likewise numbered 'because he had not given a definite enough answer to a

query from H.M.' in January 1902. 'That's not the way to reply to me!' the
Kaiser angrily exclaimed.[151] 'Is it not unspeakable?' Baroness Spitzemberg
protested. 'It makes one sick to the stomach that distinguished officials in the
highest posts should be treated with such outrageous high-handedness and
barbaric cruelty and thrown out like lackeys! . . . It made my blood boil with
anger!'[152] A similar fate befell the President of the provincial government of
Hanover, Hans von Brandenstein, who had rendered valuable service to the
Kaiser before his accession as his mentor in affairs of state, but 'after severe
strife' with Wilhelm in 1903 was forced into 'an embittered departure . . .
from government service'.[153] Spitzemberg was indignant at the 'tyrannical'
behaviour of the Kaiser and wrote: 'What I find so distressing is the Kaiser's
mentality, which lies behind all these actions: he refuses to take advice
from his legal, responsible servants; instead, being a "Pfiffikus Schmärrle"
[a "slyboots"] and a tyrant, he hopes he will be better served by creatures who
owe him their unearned position, and sows envy, hatred, mistrust and servility
among his most senior officials, thus opening the door to every kind of
baseness.'[154] A few months later, when another reshuffle of diplomatic posts
was in the offing, she commented despondently: 'If H.M. again interferes
arbitrarily from on high, even Bülow's influence will be useless.'[155] The
Baroness bitterly condemned the Chancellor's 'absolute inability to stand by
his subordinates, as soon as the Kaiser goes so far as to frown'.[156]

The sycophantic spinelessness which spread in the upper reaches of
German society in these first years of Bülow's Chancellorship had a depressing effect on Zedlitz. In the autumn of 1904 he commented in his diary that
although life at court in Berlin was already demoralising enough, 'the servility
and flattery coming from people farther away . . . is so monstrous that a person
living constantly at court could not possibly manage, with all his physical
strength, to debase himself so much day after day'. Zedlitz listed a whole series
of episodes which he considered symptomatic of the pernicious influence
generated by Wilhelm II's style of rule. 'When Prince Dohna reports a good
stag at Rominten, he puts on an expression suggesting that it is so important
that he has come rushing up, and is quite out of breath with excitement
and haste. When we arrived at Danzig on the way back from Rominten
via Königsberg and the Marienburg, His Majesty was received at the station
by Lieutenant General v. Mackensen, who kissed him on his gloved right
hand . . . On our departure from the station General v. Mackensen even
went so far as to allow a few tears to appear in his eyes. On the journey from
Danzig to Hubertusstock Professor Slaby of the Technical High School in
Charlottenburg was on the train . . . After he had pointed out to the Kaiser
several times how much opposition his All-Highest self had encountered in a

variety of matters, and how his opponents would certainly be obliged to see their mistake in the end, it was only natural that the Kaiser eventually said: "Yes, that is quite right, my subjects ought simply to do what I tell them, but my subjects always want to think for themselves, which gives rise to all the difficulties".' The list of such episodes could be 'multiplied innumerable times', Zedlitz noted with dismay.[157]

Although the Hofmarschall had often expressed admiration for the openness with which Wilhelm II was prepared, 'in a truly modern way', regardless of birth or outward rank, to receive distinguished men of science or business for lively conversations, he foresaw all too clearly the deleterious effect of the Personal Monarchy even in these 'independent' circles. 'The position of absolute ruler that the Kaiser has created for himself there too may well be, one day, the most significant point for the future and for history. By the force of his personality, combined with the power of his position, he soon overwhelms even these people, who are not so close to him. However independent they are, in his presence they become courtiers, and within a short time they are often worse courtiers than those permanently appointed to that role ... For the Kaiser himself it is most deeply regrettable that even now, in peaceful times, he cannot find people who speak out frankly for their convictions. How much harder it will be for him in moments of danger and distress! Herein lies the explanation for much that may seem quite incomprehensible in times to come.'[158]

CHAPTER SIX

Wilhelm II and the Germans, 1900 to 1904

That Kaiser Wilhelm II enjoyed great popularity among the German people, despite his autocratic behaviour, his personal interference in every controversial aspect of public life and his insulting speeches and dispatches, is one of the most persistent legends of recent German history. That a monarchist and admirer of Wilhelm like Nicolaus Sombart should spread such myths in the context of his scapegoat theory is perhaps understandable; but for a leading academic historian like Wolfgang J. Mommsen to make the claim in his biography of Wilhelm II, published in 2002, that 'the Germans had the Kaiser they wanted – regardless of all problems', and to add that Wilhelm was 'popular among the people in spite of his extravagant conduct and offensive speeches',[1] is at variance with the evidence of the contemporary sources, and moreover imputes to the German people a degree of political naivety that they did not possess. On the contrary, it is probable that had the German public discovered even a fraction of what was going on day after day at the imperial court, Wilhelm II's irrational and completely anachronistic form of rule would have been rejected as intolerable by the overwhelming majority.

There is no doubt that the Kaiser, resplendent in one of his many colourful uniforms and mounted on his charger, cut an imposing, youthful and glamorous figure and could captivate the 'cheering masses' – including many women and schoolchildren who were regularly brought out to wave flags at parades and manoeuvres. Even as harsh a critic as Waldersee conceded in early 1900 that Wilhelm II was on the whole a popular figure. 'Leaving aside his political leaps and bounds and his speeches, which are not necessarily taken seriously because his lively temperament is well known, the masses are impressed by his whole manner, his energy and his restless activity, and indeed many a piece of ruthlessness, when crowned with success, has not failed to make a certain

impact on them. The fact that he is a good husband and the father of 7
children is enough to have put him in the good books of the entire female half
of the nation anyway.'[2] Such superficial and short-lived popular enthusiasm,
however, could not be considered genuine popularity, and not long afterwards
the Field Marshal was painting the future of the Hohenzollern Monarchy in
the darkest of colours. In February 1903 his diary reads: 'It is really distressing
to see how the high Lord is busily preparing the ground for revolution . . . The
powers of subversion are working more and more openly, the lower classes are
increasingly falling prey to them, and he hurts and embitters the great
majority of those in whose interest it is to uphold the state, and who are,
thank heavens, still supporters of the monarchy in our country nonetheless . . .
In spite of his 44 years the Kaiser still has not learnt that the cheering of the
masses is of little value. On the contrary, it pleases and impresses him very
much, even though for years the schoolchildren have always been brought
out for it.'[3]

    In October 1902 the former Foreign Secretary, Adolf Freiherr Marschall von
Bieberstein, now ambassador in Constantinople, commented that the Kaiser's
popularity was 'unfortunately in steady decline'. He took the view that
Wilhelm was 'too little King of Prussia and too much German Kaiser, an
office of which he has forged a completely wrong notion, wrong by law, and
wrong because it does not correspond to the feelings of his Germans. As a
result he is constantly offending his [German] royal colleagues and the other
German [non-Prussian] tribes, but also, and not least, offending the particular
sensibilities of his Prussians themselves, especially among the classes who are
his strongest supporters, the landed aristocracy and the conservative officials.
His play-acting with mystical, mediaeval concepts that are dead or dying out
makes him ridiculous.'[4]

    The second volume of this biography gave a full account of the alarm with
which the governing elite, the officer corps, diplomats posted in Berlin,
parliamentarians, journalists and political parties of all shades of opinion were
already reacting in the first years of Wilhelm II's reign, when confronted with
the absolutist arrogance of the young ruler. We saw how concerned they were
at the decline of respect for the monarchy evident at all levels of society, and
how from year to year indignation and displeasure at the Kaiser's domineering
and insulting demeanour grew.[5] The constant abuse of the Reichstag and the
Prussian Landtag, the bloodthirsty speeches about the intervention in China,
Wilhelm's journey to England at the high point of the Boer War and many
another provocation created turmoil on every side among the German people
at the turn of the century. When Bülow was appointed Reich Chancellor and
Prussian Minister-President on 17 October 1900 he found himself confronted

with the acute danger of a joint action by the federal princes and the Reichstag against the Kaiser which would threaten the very existence of the Hohenzollern Monarchy. As never before, the Crown was openly and directly criticised in parliament. Against this background assassination attempts were made on Wilhelm in Breslau and Bremen. Although they proved harmless, they were an unmistakable warning.

THE ATTACKS ON THE KAISER IN THE REICHSTAG

That relations between Wilhelm and a large number of members of parliament were deteriorating rapidly had been an open secret since the Left Liberal Democrat Eugen Richter's speech in the Reichstag in May 1897.[6] Richter's oratorical assaults on the Kaiser's Personal Monarchy, which were received with cheers of applause, were in fact only the signal for a whole series of increasingly critical attacks on Wilhelm II and his autocratic rule, which in many ways anticipated the debacle of the *Daily Telegraph* crisis of November 1908. In December 1899 both Richter and the Centre party leader Dr Ernst Lieber took advantage of the classic parliamentary vehicle, the budget debates, to denounce the insults that the Kaiser had directed at the Reichstag and the German people in his speech of 18 October 1899 in the city hall at Hamburg.[7] Wilhelm had complained bitterly of the Germans' lack of unity and of their unwillingness to make sacrifices in the cause of *Weltpolitik* and the construction of the battlefleet. 'I have observed with deep concern the very slow progress that Germans have made in developing their interest and political understanding of great, world-shaking questions.' Because of the rapid changes 'in the field of the national economic life of the nations ... the tasks before our German Reich and people have grown to a massive extent and require from Me and My government unusual and demanding efforts, which can only succeed if Germans stand behind us, unified and firm, renouncing factions. For this, however, our people must be resolved to make sacrifices. Above all they must lay aside their craving to seek the highest goal in ever more sharply defined party lines. They must cease putting the party above the welfare of the whole. They must contain their old, hereditary failing, that of making everything an object of unrestrained criticism, and they must stop at the limits set them by their own most vital interests. For it is precisely these old political sins which are now taking a heavy revenge on our naval interests and our fleet. If I had not been persistently prevented from strengthening them in the first eight years of my reign, in spite of urgent pleas and warnings, for which I was not even spared scorn and derision, how differently would we have been able to promote our flourishing trade and our overseas interests!'[8]

The Hamburg speech was seen as an outrageous provocation for the Reichstag, which only that spring had agreed to the Navy Bill and had thereby made 408 million marks available to build up the fleet. On 12 December 1899 the Centre party leader Lieber accused the Kaiser in strong terms of having implied that the German people lacked patriotism and did not understand the major aims of German policy. 'Indeed, I can say that the German people have never been more sharply rebuked, and not just at home, but openly, before all the world, than at that Hamburg celebration', he declaimed. 'I can only think ... that it was irresponsible advisers of His Majesty who have cast suspicion on the German people in this way.'[9]

The timid reaction of the government front bench to Lieber's criticism reflected the not unjustified anxiety of the ministers that the debate might broaden out into a general attack on the monarchy. Reich Chancellor Prince Hohenlohe answered immediately: 'I must express my lively regret that a speech of His Majesty the Kaiser should be subjected to such criticism.' The speech had sprung solely from 'the concern of the monarch for the power and the good name of the fatherland', Hohenlohe declared. 'In the great position which the German Emperor, who is at the same time King of Prussia, occupies, he cannot be debarred from admonishing the German people to unity in the pursuit of great goals, nor from giving strong, direct expression to his wishes.'[10] Lieber, however, was undeterred and retorted amid the applause of the house that he would never allow anyone to take away his right 'as a representative of the German people, to say, even in the presence of His Majesty the Kaiser, with all due respect but quite resolutely and frankly, what I consider it necessary to say'.[11] The Secretary of State for the Interior, Count Posadowsky, also spoke out against the Centre party leader's criticism, by order of the Kaiser − but in vain.[12] Shocked by this clash, Hereditary Prince Ernst zu Hohenlohe-Langenburg wrote to his father saying that the government was taking 'one beating after another, and Herr Lieber is, as usual, master of the situation'.[13]

Although Lieber's speech gave great cause for concern, fear of even stronger attacks by the Progressive party or the Social Democrats compelled ministers and courtiers to show great restraint. How careful they had to be is demonstrated by the secret memorandum written by the Chief of the Civil Cabinet to the Kaiser on 14 December 1899. 'In accordance with the All-Highest command' Posadowsky had made a statement that morning 'with reference to bringing Your Majesty's speeches into the debate of the Reichstag', Lucanus informed the Kaiser. With the courtier's skilful turn of phrase he continued: 'Your Majesty may perhaps find it somewhat tame, but care was required, because in the end it is not a question of an infringement of a written law, but only of a tradition, although a very important one. It is perhaps also best at the moment to avoid entering into conflict with the Reichstag. In my respectful opinion this cannot happen until the position of the Reichstag with regard to the Navy Bill can be clearly assessed. Otherwise it will harm the success of the Bill from the outset. What is certain is that the attitude of the federal governments to the affair was clearly expressed by the Secretary of State, that his statement, as the report of the session shows − Bravo! on the right, movement on the left − made a deep impression on the house and that, at least at first, no one said a word against it. In the event, which is not impossible, that the matter should again be mentioned in the Reichstag in an inappropriate manner, then it will be time to resort to heavier guns.' Not least in order to avoid endangering his fleet plans Wilhelm pronounced himself content with the 'perhaps somewhat tame' statement by Posadowsky.[14]

As the imperial advisers had feared, Lieber's speech marked the beginning, but neither the end nor even the climax of the storm of indignation let loose by the Kaiser's offensive remarks at Hamburg. On 14 December 1899 Eugen Richter made a speech aimed directly at Wilhelm, setting out his view of the principles involved. 'If the monarch makes use of his privileged freedom of speech to speak publicly to the people in that fashion, it is our duty to make use of our own freedom of speech to reply', the veteran parliamentarian declared. 'Unjustified charges were made against the Reichstag in that speech; it was accused of having persistently rejected reinforcements of the fleet during the first eight years of the present Kaiser's reign, and of having subordinated the good of the whole to party interests. To defend oneself against such accusations is not a question of showing manly pride before a royal throne; it is simply the duty imposed by self-respect. If a mere private person makes such charges against the Reichstag, it is beneath the dignity of the Reichstag to authorise a prosecution; but if these accusations emanate from such a high and privileged position it is the duty of the Reichstag to speak out against them.' The Left-Liberal leader asserted that the Kaiser misunderstood the function of parliament: it was 'the duty of the representatives of the people to criticise, and the more dangers there appear to be on the paths to be trodden, the sharper must be the criticism − which also applies to the Hamburg speech ... And since the people's representatives have not only the right but the duty to criticise, it is wrong to give the impression that their only calling is to stand united and with closed ranks behind governments and princes. No, gentlemen, that is to confuse the duties of the representatives of the people with the functions of a regiment of bodyguards. Princes too are fallible beings, and they are all the more prone to fallibility because of their secluded upbringing and the biased circles in which they move. Even a sense of responsibility before God, however strongly it manifests itself, cannot protect against these lapses.' Richter's speech, in which he repeatedly referred to Bismarck's recently published *Gedanken und Erinnerungen*,[15] culminated in an assessment of Wilhelm II's personal foreign policy. He commented perspicaciously that 'government policy at present is too impulsive, too erratic, too dominated by sudden inspirations and too little controlled by independent ministers for us to regard it with anything other than positive mistrust. We had little or no cause to oppose Prince Bismarck on foreign policy, although we opposed him strongly on domestic policy; but the foreign policy of the newest course, which is being developed under the watchword of *Weltreich* and *Weltpolitik* ... is, I will not say too fantastic, but too full of fantasy, to inspire any kind of confidence.'[16]

The hard-hitting attacks made by Lieber and Richter on Wilhelm II in December 1899 set a precedent. Only three months later the Social Democrat Paul Singer seized the opportunity offered by the review of the previous budget year's government expenditure to launch another bout of fierce criticism of the Kaiser in the Reichstag. The pretext for his speech was that the Foreign Office had exceeded its budget by 40,064.50 marks as a result of the travel expenses of the Kaiser's retinue for his Middle Eastern trip in the autumn of 1898. But the real target of Singer's stinging attack was never in doubt. 'I may therefore, without fear of contradiction, assert that the Kaiser's journey to Jerusalem was universally regarded as having arisen from the Kaiser's private initiative; and I believe people will be very surprised to see from the records of government over-spending in the year 1898 that Reich funds were used for this journey.' Amid the applause of the Social Democratic Party, Singer described this as an unprecedented case affecting matters of principle. In a dangerous development for the monarchy, a clear majority of the Reichstag was ready to support Singer's proposal that the entire survey of Reich expenditure and income for the 1898 budget year should be sent back to the parliamentary audit commission.[17]

When Bülow took over the Reich Chancellorship in October 1900 Wilhelm II's alarming unpopularity was among the most pressing problems with which he was confronted. On 22 November 1900 he warned Philipp Eulenburg in a secret telegram of the 'almost desperate' situation that had arisen because of the threat of joint action by the German federal princes and the Reichstag against the Kaiser. He implored Wilhelm's best friend to prevent the monarch from making any further public utterances.[18] That morning Eulenburg himself had been feeling anxious about the '*increasingly strong* shift of opinion against H.M.', exclaiming in a telegram to Bülow: 'How happy this whole Reichstag gang would be to go against [H.M.] with you!!'[19]

After receiving the Chancellor's dispatch he sent a 'very, very urgent' request to Wilhelm 'to refrain from any *public* pronouncement − whether civil or military' in the immediate future, in view of the dangerous mood in the Reichstag.[20] The events of the war in South Africa and Wilhelm's hurried journey to England to his dying grandmother's side further aggravated the crisis facing the monarchy in the following weeks. During a visit to Bavaria in February 1901 Eulenburg observed: 'The feeling against our dear master in Germany is really frightening!' Opinions at the Bavarian court and in influential circles in Munich were positively bursting with lèse-majesté, he told Bülow.[21] Wilhelm, however, took his friend's warnings lightly. He did indeed promise to hold himself back in future, but then added, in martial tones: 'My duty and my right to speak to my soldiers is naturally excluded, and I shall never allow it to be interfered with or restricted.'[22] It would soon be apparent that this very reservation held the seed of the next rebellion against him.

THE BREMEN ASSASSINATION ATTEMPT AND THE KAISER'S SPEECH TO THE ALEXANDER REGIMENT

The turn of the century brought a wave of assassination attempts on crowned heads which were bound to have a particularly unsettling effect on Wilhelm II, as the most prominent representative of the monarchical principle. In September 1898 Empress Elisabeth of Austria was stabbed to death by an anarchist at Lake Geneva;[23] in the spring of 1900 a young Belgian tried to kill the Prince of Wales;[24] on 29 July 1900 King Umberto of Italy fell victim to an attack in Monza.[25] But in Germany, too, attacks occurred which brought the fragility of the European monarchies into the limelight and led to renewed appeals to Wilhelm to retreat more into the background.

Only a few days after Bülow's appointment as Reich Chancellor a 'mentally deranged' woman threw an axe at the carriage in which the Kaiser was out driving in Breslau with his brother-in-law Hereditary Prince Bernhard of Saxe-Meiningen, but neither of them was hit.[26] Nonetheless 'It *might* have been horrid', the Empress Frederick quite rightly commented.[27] A mere four months later, in Bremen on the evening of 6 March 1901, a young workman 'of unsound mind' named Weiland threw an iron buckle at the Kaiser which cut open his cheek beneath the right eye, leaving a wound four centimetres long. A letter from the Chief of the Naval Cabinet affords us a precise insight into the physical and psychological effects of this act of violence (see Figure 5). 'On the temple or in the eye the blow could have been devastating. The wonder of it is that our All-Gracious Lord felt neither the object flying at him nor, in the rain, the copiously flowing blood; it was those around him who

Figure 5 The scar beneath the Kaiser's right eye, caused by the attempt
on his life in Bremen on 6 March 1901

drew his attention to it first. Last night was good, there is no fever and so the
result of the shameful deed will soon be obliterated. But the deed itself
indicates what grave times we live in and that even troops lining a route
provide inadequate security.'[28]

After the assassination attempts in Breslau and Bremen the court was more
cautious in announcing details of the Kaiser's travel plans. 'From a completely
reliable source' the Austrian chargé d'affaires, Count Thurn, learned that
henceforward 'the most comprehensive security measures, going far beyond
what was previously the custom', had been ordered.[29] The Kaiser's eldest sister
Charlotte, Hereditary Princess of Saxe-Meiningen, was convinced that the
Breslau and Bremen episodes had no political significance at all;[30] more
thoughtful observers, however, disagreed. Hinzpeter spoke for many when
he blamed the increasing criticism of the Kaiser in all parties and especially
among the Conservatives and in the officer corps, for the mood that had led to
the Bremen attack.[31] Writing to express his sympathy to his former pupil on
15 March 1901, he went so far as to say that 'the whole population' shared the
guilt for the 'abominable' assassination attempt. 'The irresponsible vilification
coming from all parties has succeeded in making the atmosphere in Germany
so electric that for minds of a particularly weak disposition it becomes quite

natural for insulting phrases to turn into abusive deeds ... Unfortunately a variety of factors encourages the incidence of outrageous insults like that in Bremen. In particular, the parties in general use immoderate language. Some declare: The peasant must now consider his King as his enemy! Others say: It is a disgrace that the Kaiser did not receive President Krüger! Again, others say: It is a sin and a shame that our Jesuits still have not been given back to us! Still others even preach that a King is a monster and no longer has any place in the civilised world of today. And all this is proclaimed in Germany with a pathos which is all the more vivid because the widespread democratic tendency inwardly resists the vigorous assertion of the rights of the monarch which is characteristic of the conduct of the Kaiser. A weak brain cannot withstand such a flood of vituperation and is led astray.'[32]

Hinzpeter's views found an echo in the defiant speeches that the Kaiser made on 22 March 1901 to the leaders of the Reichstag and the Prussian House of Representatives. He complained of the decline of support for the monarchy and pointed to the attack in Bremen as proof of the confusion prevailing in immature young heads. For decades, esteem for the Crown and the government had been dying out more and more. There was not enough respect for authority, and the blame for that lay with all classes of the population, who instead of serving the general interests of the people, pursued their special interests. The government and the Crown were being criticised 'in the most harsh and hurtful manner'.[33]

These remarks confirmed the fears of many observers that the assassination attempts might after all have had 'certain repercussions on Kaiser Wilhelm's nerves'.[34] In his letter to Wilhelm of 15 March 1901 Hinzpeter had cautiously expressed the wish that 'along with the external injury the painful wound of the soul will heal, and that Your Majesty will not let the misdeed of a person of unsound mind deter You in Your proud, fine, magnanimous attitude to the German people. Your Majesty must not allow Your life and Your happiness to be spoiled and embittered!'[35] After the Kaiser's speeches of 22 March the royal tutor felt compelled to repeat his words of warning. Although the physical injury had healed easily, Hinzpeter wrote, 'Your Majesty's reply to the parliamentary committee gives us cause to fear that the inward outrage will not disappear so quickly. With Your Majesty's permission, I wish to draw attention to the consideration that at the moment the monarchy naturally finds itself in a painful state of transition in relation to the mood among the population. The traditional, direct, so to speak innate liking and respect for the dynasty and the person of the monarch has inevitably suffered from the political, religious, social and economic struggles among the people, while the recognition that a strong monarchy is essential for a Germany threatened from outside, and also of vital importance for a thriving inner development, is dawning very slowly indeed. The extraordinarily great lack of political education in Germany prevents this recognition from spreading quickly. Similarly the consciousness that the honour of the monarch, as the personification of the nation, is also the honour of every individual citizen, that the good of one is also the good of the other, has not yet developed clearly enough. And therefore the feeling of responsibility for the safety of the Kaiser and for his dignity is not yet strong enough; but it must and will become strong enough at least to protect the monarch from insults by word or deed.' The Kaiser put a large black question mark in the margin beside this confident prediction.[36]

In the 'period of exacerbation' (as Jagemann sarcastically called it)[37] provoked by the Bremen attack, however, the former tutor's wise warnings fell on deaf ears. This was already evident on 28 March 1901, when Wilhelm II made speeches to the Alexander Regiment in Berlin in which he called upon the soldiers to sacrifice their lives for the King and his family if need be. He addressed the troops from horseback, speaking with 'extraordinary energy' and 'unusual gravity', accompanying his words 'with rapid, emphatic gestures with his Field Marshal's baton'.[38] In its new barracks on the Kupfergraben near the royal palace the regiment was called upon, the War Lord insisted, 'to be prepared, as it were like a bodyguard day and night, to risk life and limb for the King and his house if necessary. And if a time should ever come again in this city as it did before [this was a reference to 1848], a time of rebellion against the King, then, I am convinced, the Alexander Regiment would put all insubordination and impropriety against its royal Master firmly back in its place.'[39] Wilhelm's rage against his own people was slow to abate. On his Scandinavian cruise in 1903 the monarch ranted that in the forthcoming revolution he would mow down the Social Democrats, 'but only after they had first plundered the Jews and the rich'. He intended to 'take revenge for [18]48 – *revenge*!!!'[40] Soon after his appointment as Commanding General of Berlin, Gustav von Kessel complained: 'H.M. has already ordered me *twice*, on the most flimsy of pretexts and in open telegrams, to fire on the people.'[41]

Under the 'painful impression of recent events', no less a person than Grand Duke Friedrich I of Baden was moved to speak out. 'I must confess to you', the Kaiser's uncle wrote anxiously to Reich Chancellor von Bülow in March 1901, 'that the state of public affairs here in Germany seems to me to have reached a high point of inherent danger that compels us to take precautions for the future. The speeches of H.M. the Kaiser when the Kaiser Alexander Grenadier Guards Regiment moved into its barracks are the danger which I have just described as threatening ... One of the worst effects is the lowering of the authority of the Kaiser through thoughtless discussion of the remarks attributed to him. – This damage to his reputation also has the effect of gradually undermining public order throughout the Reich and brings in its wake an unfavourable assessment of the German Reich abroad, and with that a weakening of confidence in Germany's power and strength. I mention all this only to let you know the observations I have been able to make since the two speeches and how pervasive the dissatisfaction has become in many circles, not excluding those of the higher, experienced levels of the army. Such circles are particularly dismayed that a circumstance has been specified which would necessitate armed intervention, whereas all military discipline must be based on unconditional obedience, and one has hitherto always avoided emphasising such issues of potential conflict. This provokes thought, causes debate and thus gets openly discussed at the beer table, where the mischief-makers can play their game. In view of this state of affairs I see only one possibility for a lasting remedy, and that is to permit the publication of imperial speeches in the future only if their wording is officially confirmed. In future these speeches would have to be shown to the Civil Cabinet, which must show them to the Reich Chancellor, so that they could be modified as necessary. With the Kaiser's approval, however, it would be necessary to ensure that imperial speeches to closed troop units and toasts in officers' messes are not published at all ... Now I know very well that these suggestions of mine can only be put into practice with the approval of the Kaiser', the Grand Duke admitted, thereby touching on the sore point which had caused the failure of all previous damage-limiting exercises. His offer to Bülow to take the intiative himself this time does credit to the Grand Duke. 'I scarcely need to assure you of the convictions which guide me, for you know my admiration for the Kaiser and the high esteem in which I hold his outstanding abilities and excellent characteristics. That is exactly why I wish him to remain beyond any critical discussion, and his strength to be reserved for any expansion of power.'[42]

If Bülow, on taking office as Reich Chancellor, had expected that his special relationship of confidence with the Kaiser would enable him at least to stop the latter making controversial public appearances, now at the latest he saw his hopes disappointed. Directly after the Kaiser's speech to the Alexander Regiment rumours circulated in Berlin that the Chancellor had handed in his resignation,[43] and although the rumours were immediately denied, Bülow's consternation is beyond doubt. He admitted to the Grand Duke of Baden that the fierce criticism of the Kaiser both at home and abroad had caused him 'many a difficult hour'. It had long been his 'earnest and urgent endeavour to find some appropriate means by which such journalistic commentary on the Kaiser's speeches as lately and so regrettably appeared could be, if not completely obviated, then at least diminished to a degree that would from the outset prevent even more far-reaching and dangerous damage to the Crown.'[44]

The uproar over the speech and the speculation to which it gave rise in many newspapers about the Kaiser's mental state had not yet died down when Wilhelm made another speech on 31 March 1901, this time to the committee of the Prussian upper house, which caused downright despondency. With the iron buckle that Weiland had thrown at him in Bremen on the table before him, the Kaiser declared that 'all the theories that are being aired in the press about My frame of mind are based on complete ignorance and have no foundation at all. I have read everything which the newspapers have written about My alleged psychological state on the occasion of the incident at Bremen, but nothing is more mistaken than to assume that I suffered from it mentally in any way. I am the same as I was before; I have become neither elegiac nor melancholic . . . I stand in God's hand and I shall personally never allow myself to be deterred by such incidents from following the path which I have recognised it as my duty to follow. On My journeys I come into contact with all circles of the population and therefore I know very well what is said and thought about Me among the people. But anyone who thinks that I shall allow myself to be intimidated by such incidents in my other measures will be very much mistaken. Everything remains as it was before.'[45]

Although Bülow made an outward show of indifference and declared with a shrug that 'one simply has to accustom oneself to not taking the consequences of these remarks [by the Kaiser] too seriously', he admitted to the Prussian envoy in Munich, Count Anton Monts, that he was 'unhappy about the Kaiser's latest speeches and had made serious representations to H.M.'[46] In fact the 'representations' that he made were very limited. As he told the Grand Duke of Baden on 17 April 1901, 'the journalistic exploitation of the All-Highest's latest speeches' had not escaped the Kaiser's notice. 'As a result H.M. was gracious enough to show me the draft of a speech which the All-Highest intends to make on His forthcoming visit to Bonn. At my request H.M. consented to change a few passages in this draft.'[47] In addition Bülow persuaded the monarch to issue an internal order, as suggested by the Grand Duke, under which 'Speeches which the All-Highest makes on parade grounds, in barracks or in officers' messes to troops, institutes and the officer corps, are not to be published without the consent of the All-Highest.'[48] The Reich Chancellor had his doubts, however, as to whether the Kaiser would observe these regulations himself. As he wryly observed to the Grand Duke, it would be 'very pleasing . . . if H.M. were inclined to adhere to the principles of this All-Highest order', for, like the Grand Duke, he was convinced 'that it would be of crucial importance for the common good if the speeches of

H.M. were no longer made the object of criticism, as has happened only too often, when H.M. has spoken without previous consultation with his appointed advisers'. 'It seems to me that the most useful thing', Bülow continued, 'would be if the speeches which H.M. makes to gatherings of military men were no longer made public at all, because H.M., as is his right, starts from the premise that as Supreme War Lord He is entitled to speak without reserve to His soldiers, and also because the military tone is not always suitable for public use'. As the Kaiser was to travel to Karlsruhe shortly, the Reich Chancellor asked the Grand Duke, 'relying on your complete discretion', to use his influence with Wilhelm II with a view to achieving 'a gradual calming down of public opinion, which has been excited by all kinds of events in recent days'. He emphasised that it would be necessary to work 'very quietly and carefully now' within the country, and 'especially to avoid unhelpful provocations of the Reichstag'. Moreover it was 'absolutely necessary that H.M. the Kaiser and King should attend the forthcoming unveiling of the National Memorial to Prince Bismarck in Berlin [on 16 June 1901] in person, as the absence of the All-Highest Person would add grist to the mill of Bismarckian agitation and of the faction'.[49] That Wilhelm attended the unveiling ceremony 'only through gritted teeth' was, however, all too common knowledge.[50]

THE SOCIAL DEMOCRATS' 'HATRED FOR THE KAISER'

Although the Kaiser held back somewhat in his public utterances over the next few months, the risk of an angry outburst against the workers or the Social Democrats was never far away. In 1900, during a strike by the staff of the Berlin trams, he had telegraphed the Commanding General of the Guards Corps saying: 'I expect at least five hundred people to be shot when the troops intervene.'[51] When Hinzpeter drew his attention in December 1901 to the fact that for Berlin alone the number of unemployed was estimated at between 25,000 and 85,000, Wilhelm II commented brazenly that these people were at least 'good material for the cavalry!'[52] And in fact the next scandal was not long in coming. On 26 November 1902 Wilhelm II made a speech in Essen in honour of the industrial magnate Friedrich Alfred Krupp, who had committed suicide after accusations of homosexuality against him in the SPD newspaper *Vorwärts*.[53] (See Figure 6.) The speech contained extraordinarily strong criticism of the German Social Democrats. 'The particular circumstances accompanying this sad event have induced me, as Supreme Head of the German Reich, to come here in order to hold the shield of the German Kaiser over the family and the memory of the deceased', Wilhelm declared after the funeral. 'A deed has been done on German soil, so despicable and base that it

Figure 6 In Essen for the funeral of the homosexual industrialist
Friedrich Alfred Krupp in November 1902

has made all hearts tremble, and every German patriot should blush with
shame at the disgrace brought upon our entire people. The honour of a true
German, who only ever lived for others, whose only thought was always the
good of the fatherland, but above all that of his workers, has been impugned.
This deed, with its consequences, is nothing less than murder; for there is no
difference between the man who mixes and serves a poisoned drink to another
and the man who, from the safe hiding-place of his editorial office, destroys
the honourable name of a fellow being with the poisoned arrows of his
calumnies and kills him through the mental torments he has thus caused.
Who was it who did this abominable deed to our friend? – Men who previously
passed for Germans but who are now unworthy of this name, who have come
from the classes of the German working population, the very people who have
endless reasons to thank Krupp, and thousands of whom in the streets of
Essen, with tears in their eyes, are waving a last farewell to their benefactor's
coffin.' Addressing himself to the workers present, Wilhelm declared: 'You
Krupps workers have always remained loyal to your employer and stood by
him; gratitude has not been extinguished in your hearts; with pride I have

seen the name of our German fatherland glorified everywhere abroad through the work of your hands. Men who want to be leaders of the German workers have robbed you of your loyal master. It is for you to shield and defend the honour of your master and to protect his memory from opprobrium. I am confident that you will find the right ways to make the German working people feel and see clearly that for good and honourable workers, whose shield of honour has been besmirched, any further association or relationship with the originators of this shameful deed is out of the question. Whoever does not sever all ties with these people implicates himself morally in their guilt.'[54]

A few days later Wilhelm repeated his attacks on the Social Democrats. In an address to workers in Breslau on 5 December 1902 he renewed his call for German workers, not least because of what they owed to the Hohenzollerns, to break with the anti-Kaiser SPD. He declared: 'The social legislation introduced by the great Kaiser Wilhelm I's glorious message was continued by Me, and through it good, secure living conditions were created for the workers into their old age, by the imposition of often considerable sacrifices on the part of the employers; and our Germany is the only country in which legislation has continued to be developed to a high degree for the welfare of the working classes. On the grounds of all this care devoted to you by your Kings I am justified also in addressing a word of warning to you. For years you and your brothers have allowed agitators of the Socialist party to delude you into believing that if you did not belong to this party and declare your faith in it, you would be ignored and would not be in a position to make your justified interests heard so as to improve your situation. That is a gross lie and a serious error. Instead of representing you objectively, the agitators tried to stir you up against your employers, against other classes, against the Throne and the Church, and at the same time they have exploited, terrorised and enslaved you in the most ruthless manner, in order to increase their power. And for what did they use this power? Not to further your welfare, but to sow hatred between the classes and to scatter cowardly libels, to which nothing was sacred, and which in the end were aimed even at what is most noble. As honourable men you cannot and should not have anything more to do with such people, nor allow yourselves to be led by them any longer.'[55] In some factories the employers hung the text of the Kaiser's speech on the wall. In the Reichstag the leader of the SPD, August Bebel, bitterly castigated the 'impudence' with which the Kaiser's speeches were exploited against employees. 'They are fobbed off with starvation wages of the most wretched sort, and now they are expected to sign an address in which it is stated that good living standards are ensured for the worker in the Reich. Could there be a bloodier mockery?'[56]

It was not only with speeches, however, that Wilhelm II sought to separate
the 'simple, straightforward' German workers from the SPD and win them
back for the monarchy. In late 1902 the Kaiser summoned all provincial
governors to a meeting at which he 'instructed' them to take appropriate
measures in their respective provinces.[57] In the Ruhr, in Essen, Magdeburg
and Breslau, at the Vulkan shipyard in Stettin and in many other places
employees were compelled, on pain of dismissal, to produce so-called 'Loyal
Addresses', in which, as Bebel put it, they were expected, 'in the most
demeaning terms, to express their loyalty to the Kaiser's person and declare
their support for his attacks on the Social Democrats'. In the Ruhr region the
employers — Bebel continued — had 'even taken shamelessness as far as to
present the workers with an address to sign, containing a sentence like this:
"At the same time we most humbly beg Your Majesty to consent to take the
initiative for an amendment of the legislation in order to prevent further
poisoning of the life of our people through a reprehensible form of attack."' In
Bochum, Bebel reported, the employers had forced their workers to sign an
address 'in which the Kaiser was asked to have the existing legislation
tightened up so that freedom of opinion and perhaps also the freedom and
the right to vote in Germany will be restricted'.[58]

The Kaiser's drive against the Social Democratic movement was firmly
repudiated, and not only by the movement itself. Conservatives like Waldersee
dismissed Wilhelm's attempt to turn workers against the party, which they
attributed to the influence of Hinzpeter and Adolf von Harnack, as a hopeless
cause. In his diary for 11 January 1903 the Field Marshal commented: 'So the
Kaiser too is now under the illusion that it is quite easy to detach the workers
from the socialist leaders, if one simply takes an interest in them in a
benevolent fashion ... The disappointments seem to come all too soon this
time. Only a very short time ago he was very pleased and touched by an
address from the Vulkan workers, expressing their devotion to him. Now,
however, 1,600 workmen from the same factory have apparently declared that
this address was composed under all kinds of pressure (from foremen, bosses
etc). I have no doubt that the same kind of thing will happen again soon,
because the Social Democratic leaders are in a state of fury about the Kaiser's
conduct in the unfortunate Krupp affair ... They are plotting their revenge.'[59]

In January 1903 the SPD succeeded in raising the 'unfortunate Krupp
affair' in the Reichstag. It had become particularly embarrassing for the Kaiser
after his speech at the grave in Essen, as the criminal proceedings for libel
had had to be stopped: the 'accusation' of homosexuality against the 'true
German' industrialist had turned out to be correct. 'What makes the matter
difficult', Jagemann reported, 'is the circumstances in which the case was closed.

Frau Krupp, as I now know for sure, did not withdraw the action on her own initiative. The Saxon envoy told me today that he recently heard from the Minister of Justice himself that he had persuaded the widow to take this step, and that he had been obliged to do so simply in order to protect H.M. from a public defeat.'[60]

On 22 January 1903, in the Reichstag, August Bebel spoke out with unprecedented ferocity against the Kaiser's criticisms of his party, and was loudly applauded, not only by the Social Democrats. 'Only recently [we have] once again had occasion to observe that the present German Kaiser talks about the Social Democrats at every opportunity and that he expresses his antipathy towards us in the harshest and most cutting terms', he declared. 'We are attacked, violently attacked ... and cannot reply. Now if this relationship engenders a particular degree of resentment − indeed, gentlemen, to speak frankly − of *hatred* towards the person of the Kaiser among those who are attacked ... − are you surprised? Is it not natural? I ask the gentlemen on the extreme Right, the loyalest of the loyal: if you were continually kicked as much as we have been kicked for 13 years, would you still have the same feelings of loyalty ... that you have today? There was once a time when you gentlemen over there were in a very embittered mood, and I heard then from a very reliable source that there was more lèse-majesté uttered at that time in conservative circles in Prussia and Germany than anywhere in the German Reich.'

Aptly, Bebel drew attention to the difference between Wilhelm II and the other federal princes. 'Gentlemen, other German princes do not do what the Kaiser does. For instance, I cannot recall a Social Democrat newspaper or a Social Democrat speaker ever having been punished for insulting the Prince Regent of Bavaria or the King of Württemberg or the Grand Duke of Hesse or another of Germany's princes. Why not? − Yes, those gentlemen maintain the reserve that their position as constitutional rulers requires of them ... I must be frank: they do not behave in that aggressive fashion, they do not pursue, if I may express it thus, any personal or any party political aims ... With the German Emperor it is different. Yesterday the Reich Chancellor made a very fine attempt to justify this from his point of view; he says it is in fact a very good thing that the Kaiser is not like other people, that he is of an energetic nature and speaks his mind, that he is no Philistine. This word pleased me especially ... No indeed, that he is not! That is the good thing that I too can see in him ... He does not need to be a Philistine, nor should he be one, in my opinion; but the way he is, and the way he is towards us, pleases us extraordinarily little; *it displeases us to the highest degree* ... I should like to see the Speaker ... if I used a similar tone in speaking about the Kaiser as he does about the Social Democrats ... I should be in hot water then! ... For 13 years we have heard him speak over and over again, in a whole series of variations, of the "inner enemy" which is Social Democracy ... In the speech to the miners' deputation in 1889 it was: "For me every Social Democrat is the equivalent of an enemy of the Reich and the fatherland!" ... On 2 September 1895 we were called "a mob of people not worthy to bear the name of 'Germans'" ... On 13 October 1895, in connection with the assassination of the industrialist Schwarze in Mühlhausen, a murder for which we were as little responsible as the German Emperor, his telegram to his family says: "yet another sacrifice to the revolutionary movement fanned by the Socialists" ... At the swearing-in of recruits in 1891 they are told how they owe unconditional obedience to him – the Kaiser – even if he ordered them to shoot their father and mother ... And so it has continued, this charming and incessant refrain. Not only has our party been condemned wholesale in the harshest and most insulting fashion, but the attacks on *us*, the *representatives* of the party, have found their harshest expression in the Kaiser's recent speeches ... These contain a direct challenge to the workers to break with us because we are highly dangerous people ... Gentlemen, these are no less than attacks on the strongest party in Germany, which plays a very decisive role in the policy of the German Reich ... attacks that cannot be tolerated for any length of time ... Not only are we Germany's strongest party by far, after the next elections we shall be so to an even *greater* degree ... and we shall gradually have the majority of German voters on our side and perhaps one day the majority of members of parliament too ... But if the German Emperor attacks Social Democracy as a whole and us as the representatives of the party in particular in such a violent way, in the strongest words known to the German language, then *it is absolutely natural* that we *should protest in the strongest possible way against it ... and reject such an attack and such a manner of speaking in the strongest possible way as improper, inadmissible and insulting.* (Storms of applause from the Social Democrats. Shout: Damned disgrace! from the extreme left – Speaker's bell rung.)'

Not without *Schadenfreude*, Bebel pointed out the counterproductive effect of the Kaiser's attacks on his party. 'If a person attacks us in this way, it must be for some reason; he must surely believe that it will help his own position, that it will further the political aims he is pursuing. Do you believe that, gentlemen? Does a single one of you believe that? Do you believe that the German Emperor has created more monarchists in this way? Or do you believe that the German Emperor has reduced the number of Social Democrats by his speeches? *As far as one can judge, the opposite is the case* ... Yes, gentlemen, who knows whether we would have grown so much if it had not been for the Kaiser's speeches. (Much laughter.) I rate every speech by the Kaiser against us at about 100,000 votes gained. (Gales of laughter.) So if he wants to continue with this kind of agitation against us, we really have no objections.'

Bebel concluded by denouncing, in tones that echo those of the private diary entries of Waldersee, Zedlitz-Trützschler and Baroness Spitzemberg, the corrosive effect of Wilhelm II's Personal Monarchy on the entire life of court and state in Germany. 'The Reich Chancellor has declared that there is no Bonapartism and Caesarism in Germany ... those are foreign words,' he says. Yes indeed, they are foreign words, but unfortunately they have become very successfully naturalised in Germany ... And why? Because, as in the countries where these words originated, in Germany too a state of affairs has come about which corresponds only too well to these descriptions ... Gentlemen, we have Caesarism and Byzantinism in abundance here', the Social Democrat leader proclaimed, to widespread applause. 'For certain aspects and phenomena of the German Reich the only comparison that can be found is with the Rome of the Caesars or Byzantium in decline ... Byzantinism is rife because Caesarism prevails. Overweening social ambition and toadyism are rife in our country, to a worse degree than has ever existed among any people ... and especially among the upper classes in Germany ... One needs only to mix a little with these classes, to be only a little in the know, to realise how much cowardice, spinelessness, ambition and toadyism there is among them. (Lively shouts from the left: "Quite true! Quite right!") None of them has the courage any more to express an opinion that might cause offence in high places; they all bow down and grovel, they all try to grab money, positions and advantages for themselves ... They clench their fists in their pockets when the advantage they seek eludes them, but they are too cowardly to speak openly ... It seems to me, gentlemen, that all of you also have reason to stand up to this terrible cancer which is notoriously and indisputably gnawing at our national character, and to lead by your good example, that is, to prove your manly courage even before the thrones of Kings.'[61]

Bebel's angry attack on the Kaiser and his style of rule hit home like a thunderbolt. Jagemann rightly observed in his report of 23 January 1903 that 'the entire three-day budget debate now became principally a discussion about H.M. the Kaiser'.[62] Waldersee's verdict on the dramatic events in the Reichstag was sombre. Bebel, he said, had 'attacked and criticised the Kaiser and also the Crown Prince in an unprecedented way, without being either stopped or strongly opposed'. Apart from the shouts of bravo from the Social Democrats the house 'listened in silence', noted the General. Only the Reich Chancellor had roused himself to respond, with a 'very feeble-sounding speech defending, or to be more precise, excusing' the Kaiser, 'from which he quickly switched to foreign policy matters'. Waldersee's fury 'that we have come to this' knew no bounds. 'The leader of the Social Democrats attacks the Kaiser in the most violent way, and mocks the Crown Prince too, accuses him of governing by [Secret] Cabinet, nurturing flatterers etc., and he is heard out so calmly that it almost sounds like agreement! A scoundrel shouts out "Damned disgrace", referring to the Kaiser's speeches. Would one not expect that the entire house would jump up and demand that the man who shouted be thrown out, that the Speaker would intervene most indignantly, that the ministers would walk out and the public gallery be enraged? Nothing happened. The Speaker called for order without even trying to establish who the speaker was, and the Reich Chancellor merely said that the speaker was no doubt ashamed of himself. That is all. It cannot go on like this, but I am afraid that it will go on, and ever more clearly in a downward direction. Does it not look as if the Reichstag actually agreed with Bebel's remarks?' Waldersee wondered, with horror.[63]

A few days after the stormy debates in the Reichstag, when Waldersee went to Berlin for the Kaiser's forty-fourth birthday, he thought he could detect clear signs that Wilhelm had been affected by the criticism of him. 'The Reichstag session with Bebel's attacks has made a considerable impression on the Kaiser, thank God; whether it will be a lasting one is another question and will depend on whether he is attacked again.' Waldersee added: 'I have heard many opinions expressed in the last 2 days and I have been pleased to see that my view of the seriousness of the situation is in fact shared by very many people, even in very liberal circles. The monarchy has suffered a heavy blow from Bebel's speech and the fact that it remained as good as unanswered.'[64]

THE KAISER'S VACILLATION BETWEEN THE CONSERVATIVES AND THE LIBERALS

As we have observed, the physical attacks on the Kaiser in Breslau and Bremen had considerable symbolic significance, while the speeches full of democratic spirit made by Richter, Lieber, Singer and Bebel in the Reichstag were perceived as a real threat to the future of the Hohenzollern Monarchy. To judge the full extent of the crisis of confidence around Wilhelm II in the early years of Bülow's Chancellorship, however, it is necessary to take a close look at the sense of disorientation that prevailed within the so-called 'bourgeois' camp, a state of affairs that was attributable not least to the Kaiser's indecisive manoeuvring between the Conservative and Liberal parties.

As the long-standing representative of Bavaria in the Bundesrat, Count Lerchenfeld, commented in the spring of 1903, it was difficult to pin down the

Kaiser's attitude in domestic politics. The only certain thing was that in this sphere too, just as in foreign policy, he wanted 'to intervene in everything, to bear the responsibility for everything' and that he considered the ministers 'at least in theory purely as his executive organs'. It was true that he could not always follow the workings of the machinery of state in every detail, so it was mostly in 'favourite projects' that his intervention was noticeable. But there were some projects – Lerchenfeld named specifically the Mittelland canal, strongly opposed by the Conservative party – to which he was tenaciously attached. 'He is keener on the development of German world trade than on agrarian interests, and so although it is against his inclination he is now quite far away from Conservative circles.'[65]

Occasionally Wilhelm II professed, as he had done in the early 1890s, that his real aim was to create a great Conservative–Liberal block, excluding the Catholic Centre party and the Social Democrats. Thus in the autumn of 1904 he expressed the wish to bring about a 'union of all non-social democratic elements', in order to be freed from dependence on the Centre party in the Reichstag.[66] Speaking to his former classmate Siegfried Sommer in December 1903, he emphasised the need to bring together the upper levels of society, which were in competition with each other economically, in view of the threat from below. It was his aim, he said, to create 'real relationships' between the representatives of industry and 'his' aristocracy. 'I have organised the Kiel Week so as to mix them up thoroughly. Once they have spent a few days there together, it will be as if they had spent a whole year in each other's company. I am throwing them together like pellets in a drum and they are bound to rub each other smooth.' Above all with an eye to the increasing competition from America he, the Kaiser, had 'brought into his circle' personalities from industry like Albert Ballin, Heinrich Wiegand and Walther Rathenau.[67] But Wilhelm had failed to appreciate the unbridgeable conflict of interests between agriculture and industry. He may well also have underestimated the profound antipathy which the aristocracy east of the Elbe felt towards him and which was entirely mutual.

Wilhelm II's hostile attitude towards the Prussian landed aristocracy represented by the German-Conservative party, as exemplified by his conduct in the crisis over the Canal Bill in 1899,[68] continued to make itself felt in the new century. In the spring of 1901 the newspapers quoted highly critical comments by the Kaiser on the landowners. 'Until they swallow the [Mittelland] Canal', he was reported as saying, 'I shall not approve the customs tariffs, and I shall approve only those I wish to approve'.[69] The confusion caused by such aggression towards the governing elite of the Prusso-German Reich was immense. Writing to her doctor, Professor Schweninger, after her brother's strong words had appeared in both the *Börsen-Courier* and the *Tägliche Rundschau*, Hereditary Princess Charlotte commented in dismay: 'Après nous le deluge, God knows! One cannot but be deeply sad and serious, facing the future with *open* eyes! A state of affairs similar to that in your hospital!'[70]

As ever, the arch-conservative Waldersee bewailed the abysmally bad relationship between the Crown and its natural supporters, the peasant population. On 19 March 1902 he wrote in his diary: 'Unfortunately the Kaiser is still in a furious mood with the landowners and has also allowed himself to be persuaded that these are the East Elbian Conservatives, whereas at the moment the entire Centre party and a considerable number of National Liberals are of a decidedly agrarian turn of mind ... It is extremely regrettable that so many conservative elements are so embittered; it would be a great misfortune if a wide gulf opened up between them and the Crown.'[71] After a visit to Berlin Waldersee recorded in May 1902 that not only had he been confirmed in his impression that the Kaiser wanted to break with the Conservatives, but the Reich Chancellor, 'although he had previously sworn solemnly never to do such a thing, would join in with this move ... Several remarks by the Kaiser that I heard myself showed how roused his feelings are against the Conservatives.'[72] When at last an agreement was in sight between the Conservatives and the Centre party in the vexed question of customs tariffs, Waldersee found it incomprehensible that the Kaiser did not want to grasp this opportunity with both hands. 'I know from a completely reliable source that it is the Kaiser *alone* who refuses to concede to wishes of the majority in the Reichstag over the customs question', he exclaimed.[73] Again in September and October 1902 he expressed his bewilderment at Wilhelm's apparent intention to break with the Conservatives, although they were the only ones who would not 'rebel against his autocratic inclinations'. If the Kaiser went ahead with the break, the Conservative party leaders would lose their influence to a radical agrarian movement, Waldersee predicted. The Social Democrats would stand by, sure of victory, watching the state-supporting parties tearing each other apart.[74]

Wilhelm II's failure to appreciate the plight of agriculture was attributed by many of his critics at least partly to his personal experience as an – apparently – successful farmer on the west Prussian estate of Cadinen which he had acquired. The Kaiser had no idea, it was said, 'how much he was being swindled in Cadinen'.[75] His Hofmarschall, Zedlitz-Trützschler, commented bitterly in 1904 on the fantasies conjured up there to deceive the Kaiser.[76] And Rudolf von Valentini, who as Secretary of the Civil Cabinet had access to all the financial details of the estate, remarked angrily that 'to restore a decayed property with unlimited resources at his disposal' was no great feat for the

Kaiser; but it was quite wrong to draw conclusions about agriculture throughout East Elbia on the basis of the exceptionally privileged position of the monarch.[77] As in the Caprivi years, however, Waldersee also detected the liberal-bourgeois influence of Wilhelm's former tutor, Hinzpeter, and of the Chief of the Civil Cabinet, Hermann von Lucanus, in the Kaiser's unsympathetic attitude to East Elbian agriculture.[78]

Did Hinzpeter and Lucanus really exercise an anti-Conservative influence on the Kaiser? As far as Lucanus (the son of an apothecary) is concerned, it is impossible to judge, since his exchanges with the Kaiser were primarily *viva voce*, but the correspondence between Wilhelm and Hinzpeter has survived almost in its entirety. A few of the letters which reached Wilhelm from his old tutor in Bielefeld did ineed contain the advice, tailored to his autocratic tendencies, that he should turn away from the Conservatives and make himself 'completely free' to manage the parties at will. In a letter of 6 May 1901 Hinzpeter enthusiastically welcomed the recent ministerial reshuffle in Prussia, which he saw as an assertion of the Crown's independence of all special interests, and especially of all ties to the East Elbian landowning aristocracy. 'This crisis could bear particularly valuable fruit for all time ... if the monarchy, detached as it now is from the traditional close bond with the agrarian-conservative party and standing truly above all parties, thereby became completely free in all its decisions and movements. As the conservative-agrarian party has likewise become nothing more than a special interest group, this development would be both natural and favourable.' The 'good Doctor', as Wilhelm called him, spoke of the 'remarkable circumstance that all the parties are more confused than edified by the government's actions, they feel hindered rather than helped in their plans and are therefore very reticent and mistrustful in their reactions. The government is not winning applause from any party and has shown itself as truly non-partisan. Consequently, if one still believes that there is political wisdom in the much misused dictum about the government standing above the parties, it is tempting to regard the expression attributed to the Kaiser: I do not rule with parties! as literally true.'[79]

The Kaiser's latent wish to free himself from the Conservatives caused confusion not only among the parties but also within the government. The East Elbian aristocracy, after all, provided the foundation on which the Prussian state, and above all its provincial administration, was built. A Reich Chancellor who wished to govern liberally, and to assemble a majority in the Reichstag or in the Prussian parliament in favour of liberal measures, would have to 'begin by changing the whole body of officialdom from top to bottom', for the 'machinery of government' in Prussia was 'a strictly Conservative organisation', the Bavarian Lerchenfeld observed in March 1903.[80] And so it remained: in 1910 a senior government official remarked sceptically, in a conversation with the Democratic parliamentarian Georg Gothein, 'How is it possible for us to pursue liberal policies? For twenty-five years no Landrat, no Regierungsrat nor Regierungspräsident, hardly any Oberpräsident, no head of department, hardly the head of a single local council in East Elbia, has been appointed to office who was not conservative to the marrow. We find ourselves in an iron net of conservative administrators.'[81]

From time to time the Kaiser seemed to realise how impracticable it was to break with the East Elbian aristocracy. In the autumn of 1902 Bülow recalled a remark the Kaiser had made the previous winter at Hubertusstock, to the effect that in economic questions he did not always think like the Conservatives, 'but they are after all the only ones with whom one can govern. The Liberals just aren't gentlemen.' Now, in October 1902, 'the feeling is much the same, perhaps even more intense', the Chancellor thought. The Kaiser was 'understandably very bitter' about the 'incredibly stupid attitude of the Liberal Press', and if a crisis arose, 'a shift to the Right' could be expected.[82] Such moments of insight never lasted, however, and Wilhelm's aversion to the old aristocratic families of Prussia found frequent expression. In February 1903 Waldersee observed that 'the Kaiser's antipathy towards the Agrarian League' was becoming ever stronger 'thanks to deliberate attempts to whip up his feelings'. It would be no surprise, the Field Marshal commented, 'if His Majesty were not content with mere speeches and rebukes, but tried to vent his anger on individuals as well'. In Waldersee's eyes it would be a disastrous mistake if the government broke with the organisation which 'in fact includes the most conservative and monarchist elements that we still have in the country'. The Kaiser should be working for a reconciliation with the agrarian movement, not a break.[83] Even after the Reichstag elections of June 1903, in which the Social Democrats made dramatic gains in numbers of votes and seats, the Kaiser was still flirting with the idea of a break with the Conservatives. At a New Year reception in January 1904 he declared that he expected his ministers to 'push through the Canal Bill ... and threatened to appoint Liberal ministers'.[84]

The illogicality of the Kaiser's obsession with the idea of joining forces with the liberal parties constantly worried Waldersee. In April 1902 he commented that Wilhelm 'does not acknowledge that he wants to rule autocratically and that he does in fact do so, as far as the ministers are concerned. But how can this be combined with liberal ideas, which demand a proper constitutional King!'[85] Six months later the General reflected: 'In order to justify their existence, Left Liberals and Progressives or whatever these people may call themselves, seek first of all to establish constitutional conditions, thus making it impossible for the Kaiser to take autocratic measures.'[86] Waldersee noted with dismay in February 1903 that it was becoming increasingly clear that the Kaiser was moving in a liberal direction. As people were beginning to scent these liberal tendencies in the monarch, they were now making increasingly liberal demands, such as a fairer division of constituencies, which would give the Social Democrats and also the Progressives more seats in the cities. It would be logical, the General commented bitterly, for the Kaiser to appoint genuine liberals as ministers. 'But of course he does not think of that; he only has time for people who do his bidding unconditionally.'[87]

Wilhelm II's autocratic behaviour and the Liberals' growing criticism of his 'personal rule' did in fact hinder a shift towards liberalism, as Waldersee had recognised. The public outcry over the Kaiser's Swinemünde telegram to the Prince Regent of Bavaria[88] and the sharp criticism of his rejection of a fountain celebrating German fairytales planned by the city of Berlin in September of the same year provoked a defiant reaction from Wilhelm against the Liberals. In October 1902, as we have seen, this made a swing to the Right seem possible.[89] Then again in mid December 1902, when the Customs Bill was approved by the Reichstag, Waldersee saw reason to hope for an improvement in the relations between the Kaiser and the Conservative party, especially as 'the conduct of the pigheaded Progressives, who are threatening revolution, must surely open his eyes'.[90] If Kaiser Wilhelm II's unpredictable shifts between the Conservative and Liberal parties already created confusion enough, his anti-Catholic attitude, in view of the necessity of winning the support of the Catholic Centre party for any Bill that was to succeed in the Reichstag, had a positively paralysing effect on the government.

CATHOLIC GERMANY AND THE MYSTERY OF THE KAISER'S LETTER OF 7 AUGUST 1901

As German Emperor it should have been one of Wilhelm II's foremost duties to represent the German people with the greatest possible dignity and balance, thus acting as a symbol for the integration of the entire heterogeneous nation. Instead he often behaved like a Protestant zealot and made no secret of his deep abhorrence for the Catholic Church. In 1914, only a few months before the outbreak of the world war, all the German newspapers were preoccupied for weeks on end with a telegram and a letter of several pages which the Kaiser was said to have addressed to his widowed aunt, Landgravine Anna of Hesse, daughter of Prince Karl of Prussia, in the summer of 1901 when she informed him of her decision to convert to Rome. According to the press reports, which were based on the assertions of a number of Centre party members of parliament, in his letter to the Landgravine the Kaiser had not only expressed himself strongly about the Pope, the bishops and the Catholic clergy, but had challenged his aunt with the words: 'You are joining a superstition that I have made it my life's work to root out.' According to another version this sentence read: 'The religion to which you have converted is one that I hate.' If the Landgravine stood by her decision, he would give orders for her to be excluded from the Hohenzollern circle and denied all contact with his entire family.[91] These alleged remarks by the Kaiser understandably gave rise to bitter criticism, directed at the monarch in person. Not until 4 April 1914 did a statement appear in the official organ, the *Norddeutsche Allgemeine Zeitung*, to the effect that the Kaiser's letter to the Landgravine Anna in 1901 was 'purely a family matter' and contained 'no comment of any kind about the Catholic faith, the Catholic Church or the Catholics and the Kaiser's views on them'.[92] Shortly afterwards loyal newspaper articles appeared with headlines such as 'The forged imperial letter', dismissing the whole story as pure fiction.[93] But what had really happened in the summer of 1901, and what light does Wilhelm's quarrel with his aunt Anna of Hesse at that time throw on his attitude to the Catholic third of the German nation?

The sources are far from complete in this case, but what is certain is that on 24 July 1901 Wilhelm II sent the 65-year-old widow a telegram from Molde, in Norway, which read: 'If you persist in your intention to change your religion, I must tell you, as Head of the House of Hohenzollern of which you still have the honour to be a member, that you will no longer belong to it and all members of the Family will be obliged to break off contact with you at once and for ever. Wilhelm I.R.'[94] As the Landgravine was not prepared to give up her conversion to the Catholic Church, the Kaiser sent a written order to the Minister of the Royal Household, Wilhelm von Wedell-Piesdorf, that henceforth 'no one in my House is to have any further contact with the renegade'.[95] On 12 May 1902 he decreed, in a Cabinet order addressed to the House Minister: 'Since Her Royal Highness the Dowager Landgravine Anna of Hesse, Princess of Prussia, has converted to the Roman Catholic Church, it is My will that the members of My Royal House should henceforth refrain from all contact with Her Royal Highness. You are to convey My decision to the members of My Royal House.'[96] According to a report that was reprinted by the *Süddeutsche Zeitungsdienst* in 1925, Wilhelm II coldly informed his aunt Anna of her exclusion from the House of Hohenzollern with the words: 'I hereby no longer consider Your

Royal Highness as a member of our House, with whose sacred traditions you ... have broken. What I told you by telegraph therefore stands: in consequence of Your Royal Highness persisting in your intention, all contact with all members of My House is completely severed, and this has been notified to the Head of Your Royal Highness's Hessian line for further action. The House of Hohenzollern expels you and has forgotten your existence. Wilhelm I.R.'[97] Thus the expulsion of the Landgravine from the family, with which the Kaiser had threatened her ten months earlier during his Scandinavian cruise, is substantiated beyond doubt. But what of the letter of several pages in which, according to a member of the Reichstag, Dr Jäger, he is said to have declared that he had made it his life's task to 'root out' the Catholic 'superstition'?

The efforts of historians to find this letter, about which there was so much speculation in 1914, have so far proved fruitless. Wilhelm wrote it on 7 August 1901 in answer to the Landgravine's protest at her threatened exclusion from the House of Hohenzollern. In his *Denkwürdigkeiten* Bülow claims to have seen the draft, which was 'spitting with rage', and to have 'culled' the 'worst passages' in it; if that were true the draft would have been far worse than the finished version that was sent to the Landgravine, but it is doubtful that Bülow's account is correct in this case.[98] At any rate he was deeply shocked at the wording of the Kaiser's letter when he heard of it from Cardinal Georg Kopp, to whom on 12 August 1901 the Landgravine had sent copies of the telegrams and letters exchanged with Wilhelm. Both the Reich Chancellor and the Cardinal Prince-Bishop were firmly convinced of the need to keep the disastrous document secret. From Norderney Bülow wrote to Kopp on 7 September 1901 saying: 'In the delicate Hessian affair everything possible has been done to restore calm, and indeed I hope I can say it has succeeded. I can only be truly grateful to Your Eminence for the steps taken to achieve the same effect on the other side.'[99] Bülow saw to it that the Kaiser's letter was kept neither in the Reich Chancellor's safe nor among the Foreign Office records. As a result his successor Bethmann Hollweg was initially at a loss when in March 1914, a few days after Cardinal Kopp's death, rumours of the tirades of hate against the Catholic Church which Wilhelm II's letter of 7 August 1901 was alleged to contain appeared in all the newspapers.[100] Not until he was sent a certified copy of the Kaiser's letter by Prince Friedrich Karl of Hesse, Wilhelm's brother-in-law, was the Reich Chancellor in a position to issue a denial of the most serious allegations circulating in the press. The Kaiser's letter to his aunt the Landgravine, it was stated, had been limited to family matters and contained no comments of any kind about the Catholic Church or the Kaiser's Catholic subjects.[101]

The authentic text of the notorious letter of 7 August 1901, which as we have seen was copied several times and sent to various recipients, remains unknown. The fact that it was kept strictly secret indicates that it did indeed contain remarks by Wilhelm II which were 'spitting with rage' and which both sides felt compelled to suppress in the interest of religious peace. It is clear, however, that the version that made the headlines in spring 1914 was in fact a forgery. Arnold Wahnschaffe, Under Secretary of State in the Reich Chancellery, informed the Chief of the Civil Cabinet, Rudolf von Valentini, in April 1914 that 'We are now trying everything we can to find out who circulated the malicious forgery. Following a newspaper report I have tackled two Centre party members of parliament in writing, on the Chancellor's instructions, and hope that they will talk.'[102] It is not clear how far Wahnschaffe succeeded in his detective work before the outbreak of the world war compelled him to turn his attention to very different tasks. But a letter of May 1915 from the Landgravine Anna, which the archivist Christine Klössel found in her research in the Diocesan Archives at Fulda, throws an interesting light on the 'so-called "case of the Kaiser's letter"', which the elderly Princess bitterly denounced as 'a despicable business'. In it the Landgravine explained how Father Cyprian of the Capucine order, from Altötting, came to Rome to see her in the spring of 1902. 'F. Cyprian spoke to me with such sympathy that I, quite innocently and unsuspectingly, told him about those very upsetting events preceding my conversion. A priori, in my unreserved veneration for the sacred role of the priesthood – trusting in unconditional discretion as a matter of course. Unfortunately I was shamefully deceived. The Father irresponsibly misused his position, and moreover immediately afterwards took inaccurate notes which did not correspond to the facts, and distributed this account widely, with the undoubted intention of exploiting the conversation in his own interest. That the Catholic Church could not be well served by this, that simply by breaching the Kaiser's confidence the mistrust of his Catholic subjects had been aroused – that it was impossible to see the full extent of the harmful consequences – none of this dawned on F.C. in his short-sightedness. There are even grounds for suspecting that dishonest motives, hatred of Prussia and the desire to deal a blow to the King of Prussia, led him to publicise the matter.'[103]

Whatever dark designs might have been behind the affair of the Kaiser's letter, the religious division between Protestant Prussia-Germany headed by Wilhelm II as Summus episcopus[104] and the Catholic section of the population represented politically by the Centre party had now become a deep rift which Bülow had great difficulty in overcoming.[105] Like many in the Kaiser's more immediate circle[106] Waldersee, who was still haunted by the paranoid illusion that the German Reich was facing 'a grand conspiracy led by the Jesuits' whose object was 'to topple the Protestant Empire and make Germany the laughing stock of the world again', was passionately opposed to any kind of rapprochement with the Centre party.[107] In October 1902 he went so far as to malign Bülow's Italian wife Marie and her mother Laura Minghetti as secret agents of the Vatican. Bülow, he suspected, was 'already far too surrounded by Catholics'.[108] Although Waldersee's allegations were unfounded, it is incontestable that in the first years of his Chancellorship Bülow succeeded in wresting concessions to the Catholic Church and the Centre party from the Kaiser, despite the latter's resistance. Waldersee repeatedly noted that Bülow had maintained 'that he had no objection to the repeal of the Jesuit Law; only the Kaiser was against it'.[109] In January 1903 the Reich Chancellor stated quite openly that he aimed to bring about the readmission of the Jesuits and that he saw many advantages in this. He was not having an easy time with the Kaiser, he said, 'but I believe I can persuade him to agree'.[110] When the Chancellor announced the repeal of the Jesuit Law on 3 February 1903 Waldersee commented indignantly: 'So we go merrily on downhill! And the Kaiser approves it all! How often in the past has he sworn never to let the Jesuits in! We have sad times to come.'[111] Only the policy of suppression pursued against the Polish minority in Prussia by both Wilhelm and Bülow seemed to Waldersee to provide some kind of guarantee that no further overtures to the Centre were likely. 'If the Kaiser does not decide to give up the latest Polish policy again – six months is rather short; but I did not expect more than 2 years of consistency – he will again fall out with the Catholics, which would please me very much.'[112]

A direct result of the rapprochement between the Reich government and the Centre party, as Philipp Eulenburg had always foreseen, was the fall of the anti-clerical government of Count Christoph von Crailsheim in Munich. 'There is rejoicing in the ultramontane camp', Waldersee recorded on 21 February 1903. Crailsheim's resignation was 'regarded really by all sides as a victory for the ultramontane Catholics and for particularism. So that would be yet another step on the downward path. Surely the Reich Chancellor should be starting to feel somewhat uneasy about all this? His Catholic-friendly conduct is being repaid in a strange way. Nor can he say this time that he is giving in to pressure from the Kaiser, for it is the other way round: it is he who has persuaded the Kaiser, with great difficulty, to change direction. The Kaiser has always had the right sense that the ultramontane Catholics are our worst enemies, but he has constantly made the mistake of thinking himself cleverer than the Catholic priests, and even today he still thinks he will be able to manage them. He has some very sad discoveries to make.'[113]

VISIONS OF DOOM AND THOUGHTS OF *COUP D'ÉTAT*: THE REICHSTAG ELECTIONS OF JUNE 1903

The clumsy manoeuvring by the state authorities between Conservatives and Liberals, between Catholics and anti-clericals, between suppression of the workers' movement and social reform led, as could only be expected, to growing confusion among the parties and, not least, to an alarming inability to act on the part of the government itself.[114] The statesmen of the Reich contemplated the Reichstag election, due in June 1903, in a condition of helpless paralysis. Two weeks before the election Hinzpeter, writing from Bielefeld, sent the Kaiser a gloomy assessment of the increasingly democratic, socialist and pluralistic mood developing among the German people. Wilhelm covered the letter with underlinings and exclamation marks and forwarded it to Bülow. 'The electoral situation in our constituency is typical of the Reich in general', the royal tutor opined, 'in that the pro-Reich national parties, thanks to their disagreements and lack of political sense, make it easy for the anti-Reich international parties to win the mandate, so that, to be precise, the Catholic third defeats the Protestant two thirds. The battle here is in actual fact between the Centre and the Social Democrats alone, as the only united, firmly organised parties. It would not have been difficult for the National Liberals and Conservatives to win the mandate if they had been able to agree on one candidate. But in spite of all efforts this was not possible, because both put so much emphasis on their economic interests – industrial or agricultural – that there was no room left for general political calculations and considerations.' Hinzpeter's scepticism about the electoral prospects of the Conservatives and National Liberals was mingled with disquiet about 'how much the air is filled with socialist ideas today. Even among our slow-moving rural population there is an awakening of the class-consciousness that creates such a gulf between employers and workers in industry. The cottagers, hired hands and agricultural workers come to believe that their interests are different from those of the landowners – in this case not the aristocracy but large-scale farmers – and that to defend their interests they must bestir themselves and work together ... That they will gradually be drawn into the Social Democrat camp seems to me beyond all doubt ... For the moment they add to the confusion here and contribute to the chances of the Centre getting the mandate again, as before.'[115]

The results of the election of 16 June 1903 overshot the most pessimistic expectations of the court and produced a massive growth in the Social Democratic vote, to over three million (almost a third of all votes cast). This led, after the second ballot on 25 June, to an increase in the number of SPD seats in the Reichstag from 56 to 81. With 100 seats (19.7 per cent of the vote) the Centre remained the strongest party, with the deciding voice in the Reichstag. Particularly dangerous for the monarchy was the socialist movement's penetration of the rural population, 'to a considerable extent in some places', as Waldersee noted with concern.[116] The German-Conservative party won a mere 10 per cent of the vote and found itself with only 54 seats in the Reichstag.[117]

Devastating as the election results were for the government, Bülow at first reacted with ostentatious calm. After the first round of voting he congratulated the Kaiser unctuously on his speech in Hamburg, which he said had been 'so powerful that even the newspapers supporting the opposition most strongly could not escape its effect'.[118] In another letter, of 19 June 1903, he tried to justify the government's very noticeable reserve during the election campaign. 'Nothing annoyed the parties more', he maintained, 'than the fact that the government did not do them the favour of perching like an owl on the crows' hut, so that the party ravens could sh... on its head. The same people who raised a hue and cry when Your Majesty set up a beacon for public opinion in matters of really vital national importance were now wailing that a word "from above" was needed. One knows from long experience that people who are inclined to overestimate themselves are never so discouraged as when one takes no notice of them. If the final ballot turns out as the provincial governors expect, the new Reichstag will not be fundamentally different from the old one. There will be not quite so many Agrarians and a few more Socialists. If the latter behave like louts it can only contribute to the general disillusionment.'[119]

Waldersee was shocked by the apparent lack of concern of the Kaiser and the Chancellor, in view of the huge success of the Social Democrats. 'The Kaiser is far too easily misled by Bülow about the situation and he still sets the greatest store by the cheers of the masses', he commented on 21 June 1903.[120] When he tried to convince Wilhelm on 18 June – that is to say between the two rounds of voting – that the moment had come for him, as Kaiser, to 'take action', the General was sorely disappointed. 'I had expected to find him in a serious mood, and to some extent able to see the significance of the elections, but I was entirely mistaken. He repeatedly spoke of the Reichstag with the greatest disdain! Lucanus sees the situation in exactly the same way as he does, and doubtless it is the same with Bülow, whom the Kaiser spoke to in Berlin on the 17th.' That Bülow 'sat back and did absolutely nothing in the elections' was 'an unbelievable misjudgement and lack of knowledge of mankind and the world', in Waldersee's view.[121]

When the full significance of the SPD's election victory became clear after the final ballot, numerous highly placed people demanded the dismissal of

Bülow and the appointment of a strong man to carry out a policy of 'forceful reaction'.[122] Wilhelm II accused his government of 'slackness' and railed that 'the Social Democrat gang should be exterminated by fire and sword'.[123] Immediately after the ballot more and more voices were heard 'clearly expressing what I have felt for a long time', Waldersee wrote, namely 'that it cannot go on like this in our country and that Bülow must go . . . I would go so far as to say that we can only gain by a change of Chancellor; we could not have a worse one than him. Through his spinelessness and complete loss of nerve he is leading us straight into disaster. In foreign policy it has got so bad that we have *not a single* friend on whom we can count. Everyone distrusts us, and everyone heartily wishes us to come to grief. The whole world knows how dishonest he is. And on top of that the utterly mismanaged situation at home, the helplessness and the lack of courage — it really is not a pretty picture.'[124] A little later he noted: 'I am finding my view more and more confirmed, both orally and in writing, that it is Bülow who is causing our misfortune and that he will make complete fools of the Kaiser and all of us.'[125]

The feeling rapidly spread among the highest levels of society that great revolutionary upheavals lay ahead. 'The elections are just wonderful!! They suit our decadence, more and more covered up with speeches and festivities!' Wilhelm's eldest sister wrote scornfully to Schweninger.[126] Zedlitz, too, conceded that 'much in our present circumstances, both in high places and below' recalled 'times of the most serious political upheavals'. The sagacious Hofmarschall went on to say, however, that he did not count himself among the pessimists, 'unless we ourselves, the upper classes, by our alienation from and lack of understanding of the life of the people and of modern developments, allow ourselves to be pushed into a reactionary current, which could certainly lead to catastrophe'.[127]

Yet reactionary preventive measures were precisely what the military element and other influential voices at court and in the government were demanding. The former Minister of War, General Julius von Verdy du Vernois, painted fatalistic pictures of the bloody destruction to come. Those in power in Berlin were 'as good as blind' and deceived themselves with optimistic ideas, 'partly, no doubt, because they feel too weak to set about taking extraordinary measures', he complained in a letter to Waldersee. 'But what do constitution and parliament matter when it is a question of saving population and fatherland from the guillotine!' he exclaimed. 'The people can see that we are in fact already standing with both feet on revolutionary ground, which has been fertilised with the sewage of universal suffrage and coalition rights so as to rear poisonous plants! I often find myself engrossed in reading about the great French Revolution at the end of the 18th century. We have already climbed the first rungs of their ladder, exactly as in those days. What could still be curbed by suppressing a few uprisings now, which could easily be done, will cost much blood in a few years and soon after that will no longer be possible to overcome at all ... I am trying to find out more about how matters stand among the classes concerned. At any rate it is already *much* worse than most people believe.'[128]

Not surprisingly, the Field Marshal fully shared his friend Verdy's convictions. Even before the Reichstag elections he had compared the situation in Germany with that in France on the eve of the revolution of 1789 and demanded drastic measures against the Social Democrats and the Reichstag. When the debates on the tariff question led to riotous scenes in the Reichstag on 27 November and 1 December 1902, and the Kaiser declared that 'he would be quite happy for the riots to get far worse', the General had commented sceptically: 'I would be happy too, if I could be convinced that serious measures have been planned and if [there were] a firm determination to carry them out. But I do not believe it in the least. Nor does it seem likely that Bülow would advise any such thing. Unfortunately neither he nor the Kaiser realises how confidence in the Reich government is declining. The Social Democrats are playing an increasingly important role and as a result their reputation is growing in broad sections of the population.'[129] Bismarck, according to the man who was once his bitterest adversary, would have used the present conduct of the Social Democrats in the Reichstag as an opportunity to carry out an 'energetic coup' against them, as long as the army could still be counted upon. He himself had warned the Kaiser of the danger in 1894, Waldersee wrote. 'He did not take it amiss at all and even seemed to agree with me, but he did nothing.'[130] Before the Reichstag elections Waldersee repeatedly argued for the removal of universal suffrage by an 'act of brute force' before it was too late.[131] After the Social Democrats' election success in June 1903 he wrote in alarm: 'Comparisons are often made with the development of the French Revolution, and there are undoubtedly dreadful similarities.'[132] The Prussian Minister of Agriculture, General Viktor von Podbielski, and the Prussian Minister of War, General von Einem, also spoke out 'again and again for the amendment of the electoral law' as 'a most essential government measure' and as 'the remedy for everything', in the presence of the Kaiser and the commanding generals.[133] Even Count August zu Eulenburg was entirely in agreement with him, Waldersee said, although the Oberhofmarschall was 'too cautious to come out with an opinion in the Kaiser's presence'.[134]

The Kaiser, however, not only held on to Bülow; he continued to reject any idea of a *coup d'état* and cherished hopes of solving the social question in a monarchical way. Directly after the Reichstag elections of 1903 Waldersee

commented, bitterly disappointed, 'that the Kaiser has absolutely no intention
of taking any action against the Social Democrats. . . . But it is not a question
of superior intelligence — it is helplessness. What has happened to the energetic Kaiser who wanted to smash everything! Who volunteered to deal with
the Social Democrats on his own!'[135] A few months earlier the Field Marshal
had observed with concern that the Kaiser was 'very busy with the social
question'. Wilhelm 'liked to think that only a monarchy, that is to say the
Hohenzollern monarchy' was in a position to solve this question. 'I have been
unable to ascertain who in particular has influenced him in this.'[136] Waldersee
had the impression that it was the Secretary of State for the Interior, Graf
Arthur von Posadowsky, of all people, who had given the Kaiser this idea.
After a visit to Berlin he noted in the spring of 1903: 'To my regret I heard
very disparaging opinions — also from ministers — about Posadowski. He is
accused of slackness towards the Social Democrats. It seems to me that it is he
who is chiefly responsible for persuading the Kaiser that the Hohenzollerns
have a mission to solve the social question.'[137]

Demonstrably, as well as Posadowsky and Lucanus, Dr Hinzpeter played a
not inconsiderable role in advising Wilhelm II on the 'social question'. In his
letters to his former pupil he laid emphasis on social policy as 'the most
reliable measure of the cultural level of a people'. Social reform, he said, had
an 'incomparable' effect in elevating 'the entire nation . . . because it brings
material and moral help to the lower classes, an idealistic frame of mind and
moral aspirations to the upper classes, and thus strength and health to the
whole organism of the people'. The workers' protection measures of November
1881 and February 1890 were 'epoch-making in German development',
Hinzpeter maintained, 'because the movement that began with them gave
the German people cultural superiority over Europe and America'. If this
course of reform were energetically pursued it would also create 'the indispensable foundation of future *Weltpolitik*'.[138]

In November 1903 Hinzpeter took it upon himself to provide the Kaiser
with a detailed analysis of the factional struggles within the SPD, thereby
encouraging him to hope for a gradual rapprochement between the movement
and the existing order. 'The orthodox, i.e. revolutionary, section of the Social
Democrat party is trying to exploit the embarrassing fact that in spite of its
great exertions the party cannot get into the Prussian Landtag [because of the
three-class franchise] . . . as fresh proof that the workers can expect nothing
from efforts to achieve reform within the existing capitalist society, and that
they must therefore work for the violent overthrow of that society. But this
attempt by the orthodox group to hold on to the old revolutionary mood will
also prove fruitless. The orthodox doctrine of the Social Democrats with its

fantastic dogma and mysteries did not originate from the feelings of the workers, but was foisted on them as a creed by bourgeois radicals [here Wilhelm II wrote 'Richter and the Left Liberals' in the margin]. But for increasing numbers of workers, as they grow more intelligent and their situation improves, utopian visions of the future are losing their fascination; they demand practical efforts to raise their station even more, and join rapidly growing professional associations – social democratic, non-social democratic or anti-social democratic works associations – in order to achieve this. Just as the old political parties have put aside their political ideals – feudalism for the Conservatives, parliamentarism for the Liberals – and replaced them with agrarian or industrial-commercial ideals, so the Social Democrat party is replacing its politically revolutionary radicalism with socio-economic aspirations and is becoming really representative of the workers. Thus nothing remains of the gleaming organisation of political parties which the constitution of Prussia and the Reich created except a number of social groups which, as the French crudely express it, quarrel over the assiette au beurre, alike in their aims, more and more alike in their mannerisms.'[139]

Hinzpeter's observations did not fail to make an impression on Wilhelm, for in spite of occasional outbursts against the Socialists, the Left Liberals or the Centre party he had no intention at this time of adopting the *coup d'état* policy advocated by Waldersee, Verdy or von Einem. Although in his conversation with Siegfried Sommer on 23 December 1903 he made derogatory remarks about the right to vote in elections to the Reichstag – he himself would not have conceded it, he said, for it was absurd that 'people who had lived for years on alms ... should now suddenly have the same right as the highest in the land' – he did not demand its abolition. The Kaiser even expressed 'his indignation at the members of the Reichstag who were absent from sittings. In the previous winter', he told his former classmate, 'an occasion had arisen when there were 50 representatives of the government and 40 members of the Reichstag present. All in all the level of the Reichstag had fallen extraordinarily low. When one thought of the old days, there had never been imperative mandates. Each was expected to represent the general interest; now one person would be elected *for* the Canal – another *against* the Canal, one for this, another for that.' At any rate it was the Kaiser's view, according to Sommer's account of the conversation, 'that the right to vote must go hand in hand with the duty to vote'.[140] Again, in late 1904 Admiral von Müller expressed astonishment 'at the Kaiser's calm attitude' towards the Social Democrats.[141] Wilhelm II's relatively optimistic approach to the party at this time is all the more remarkable because a particularly brutal royal murder took place almost at the same time as the Reichstag elections of June 1903.

On the night of 10–11 June 1903 in Belgrade the Obrenovic dynasty was extinguished by a deed of a bloodthirstiness unprecedented even in Serbia. The enthusiasm among the Serbian people, even among the well-educated, knew no bounds.[142]

It is true, however, that by the end of 1903 the Kaiser was showing unmistakable signs of impatience with Bülow's policy towards 'anarchists and nihilists'. With almost insulting curtness Wilhelm rejected a draft letter in which the Reich Chancellor addressed the Tsar on the subject of a common stance 'in the great struggle against the enemies of monarchy and peace'. He wrote a furious note on the draft: 'This phrase has already been over-used to the point of nausea and has lost all its value, as it is nothing but an empty phrase as it always was.' The formulation that Bülow had used, he said, was 'so dreadfully hackneyed through permanent use in letters, notes, and your speeches that it has no resonance any more. All the more so as in your energetic attempt to get the governments to take an energetic position on this question – with regard to the murder of King Umberto – you have seen year after year pass without the least thing happening . . . Not until you submit an order to me for the collective execution of these villains shall I consider the above phrase to be true!'[143] It was by no means the last time that Kaiser Wilhelm would demand the execution of socialists and anarchists.

CHAPTER SEVEN

'We two make history and destiny is in our hands!' Kaiser and Tsar on the eve of the Russo-Japanese War

After the First World War former Russian, French and British diplomats who had been directly involved in the dramatic events leading up to the catastrophe made a grave accusation against Kaiser Wilhelm II: it was he who had been chiefly responsible for pushing the weak Tsar Nicholas II into war with Japan. In the three years before the outbreak of the Russo-Japanese War on 8–9 February 1904, it was alleged, Wilhelm had persistently sought to persuade Nicholas that it was his sacred duty before God to take up the struggle of the 'white race' and Christendom against the 'yellow peril' of the heathen peoples of the Far East and to conquer Korea and Manchuria for Russia. According to Alexander Savinsky, the closest colleague of the Russian Foreign Minister Count Lamsdorff, the Kaiser's aim had been not only to embroil Russia with Japan and the British Empire in the Far East. In addition he had tried to bring eastern central Europe, the Balkans and the whole of the Near East as far as the Persian Gulf under German control and to overturn the Franco-Russian alliance, or, alternatively, to form a continental league linking both France and Russia to the Triple Alliance. The former Russian official was by no means alone in taking this view. With regard to Wilhelm's war-mongering role in the Russo-Japanese conflict, at any rate, Savinsky saw eye-to-eye with leading French and British diplomats.[1]

The editors of the official German documents published in *Die Große Politik der europäischen Kabinette* in the 1920s disputed these assertions with unusual ferocity. Such allegations were 'completely false' and could not be proved 'by a single word'; the Kaiser's letters and telegrams from the time of the Russo-Japanese conflict contained 'not one word that could be interpreted as war-mongering; on the contrary, the German ruler's visible efforts to tell the Tsar the plain truth about Japan's determination to go to war, England's equivocacy and the unreliability of the French ally could only have had the effect of restraining the Tsar from ill-considered warlike decisions'. Far from pushing Russia into the ruinous war with Japan, Wilhelm II and Bülow had been 'anxiously intent on avoiding even the appearance of war-mongering'.[2]

The denials by the editors of *Die Große Politik* are unconvincing if only because the documents they themselves edited for publication include numerous sources which provide ample evidence for the accusations against Wilhelm. To cite but one example: in December 1903, just before the outbreak of war in the Far East, the Kaiser stated in a marginal note, published in *Die Große Politik*, 'Since 97 – Kiaochow – we have never left Russia in any doubt that we would cover her back in Europe, in case she intended to pursue a bigger policy in the Far East which could lead to military complications; (with the aim of relieving our eastern border from the fearful pressure and threat of the massive Russian army)! Whereupon Russia took Port Arthur and *trusting us*, she took her fleet *out of the Baltic*, thereby making herself *vulnerable to us by sea*. In Danzig in 01 and Reval in 02 the same assurance was given again, with the result that entire Russian divisions from Russian Poland and from European Russia were and are being packed off to the Far East. That would not happen if the governments had not come to an agreement!!'[3]

In the meantime international historiography has shown convincingly that German policy since the turn of the century was in fact aimed at fanning the flames of Russo-Japanese antagonism to the point of open war, albeit avoiding the '*appearance* of war-mongering'. Bülow, the Foreign Office, German diplomats and the military saw in the approaching war in the Far East a great opportunity to free themselves from the pressure of the Franco-Russian Dual Alliance and the danger of a war on two fronts. Furthermore, as the German ambassador and Foreign Secretary Wilhelm Freiherr von Schoen admitted in his memoirs, it was an opportunity to 'unhinge' the balance of power in Europe.[4] The goal of Germany's Russian policy in these years had been nothing less than the destruction of the Franco-Russian Dual Alliance and the union of the giant Russian Empire, now diverted towards the Far East, with Germany, which would thereby have achieved supremacy on the continent.[5] The outbreak of war between Russia and Japan, which was allied with Britain, was greeted with delight in the German Reich, for it hoped, having 'tipped the global scales' as Holstein put it, to reap great benefits from the conflict.[6]

Although impressive work has been done on this period, not enough light has been shed on the role that Wilhelm II played in the conception and execution of this extraordinary policy. In her seminal study of German–Russian relations during these years Barbara Vogel repeatedly stresses that it was not the Kaiser but Bülow and the Foreign Office who laid down German policy towards Russia. The Chancellor and Privy Counsellor Friedrich von Holstein, she says, had 'developed an unsurpassed mastery in politically programming their own sovereign' so that the latter, even if he occasionally missed the target, nevertheless moved 'within the framework of his government's political calculations'.[7] The American expert Jonathan Steinberg, in his otherwise brilliant essay on Germany's policy in the Russo-Japanese War, reaches a similar conclusion: 'The Kaiser's ... flamboyance, his interventions, his mercurial disposition and his lack of restraint certainly made a bad situation worse, but during the Russo-Japanese War ... the Kaiser played a peripheral part in affairs.'[8]

Wilhelm II's attitude to the Tsar, and especially his part in the growing tensions between Russia and Japan from 1902 to 1904, deserves a closer examination against this background. Is it true that he was largely a bystander in the dramatic international events of these years? Did the responsible statesmen in the Wilhelmstrasse succeed in using him as an instrument in their calculations? Did he disturb the otherwise cautious and considered policy of his Reich Chancellor from time to time by his flamboyant behaviour? Or should he be considered as the actual instigator of the German policy of driving Russia into war? He himself, at any rate, had no doubt about the decisive role which he personally had played in bringing about the conflict. At the beginning of the war in the Far East he explained proudly to his suite that it had been 'his intention from the beginning to drive Russia into this situation. This had been absolutely necessary to relieve the pressure on our eastern border, and when we captured Kiaochow he had foreseen everything for Russia exactly as it had now turned out.'[9]

IN EXPECTATION OF A JAPANESE ATTACK ON RUSSIA

The Kaiser's repeated assertion that since 1897 he had consistently pursued the aim of persuading Russia to go to war against Japan does not quite tally with the fact that after the occupation of Manchuria by Russia following the suppression of the Boxer rebellion, he at first took Japan's side and for a long time expected a Japanese attack on Russia. For a while he even entertained hopes that he would be able to draw Japan on to Germany's side against Russia. Thus in February 1901 he commented: 'Japan is so strong at sea and has such excellent equipment that her intervention on one or the other side in the Gulf of Petschili will be the deciding factor. It is therefore absolutely essential that Japan is brought over onto our side if possible. And not tempted by Russia, with declarations of l'Asie pour les Asiates!'[10] A few days later news reached him that the Chinese government had appealed to London and Berlin for help in its conflict with Russia over Manchuria. Speculating wildly, he played with various combinations, including, for the first time, the possibility of cooperation between Britain and Japan against Russia in the Far East, which seemed highly desirable to him. 'What an interesting situation!' he exclaimed. But he wondered what the real reason behind the Chinese call for help from Germany and Britain might be. 'I don't trust these scoundrels. A cry of distress from these rogues asking for help from "the red-haired barbarians", their worst enemies into the bargain, is extremely unnatural, and moreover for help against Russia, which is highly suspicious. Might not the Chinese have pulled this off to create a bone of contention between Powers who are at odds with each other? Or might not the Russians have put the Chinese up to this so as to see how far they can go with the English without coming to blows with them, and also to find out how far the casus foederis goes for us in the alliance I am supposed to have concluded recently in London?' Suddenly there rose before Wilhelm's eyes the possibility of a war with England and Japan on one side and Russia and France on the other, from which Germany could reap the benefit. 'If Japan and England took joint action', he calculated happily, 'together they could smash Russia completely in Petschili and the surrounding area, but they would have to do it soon, before the Russians get too strong. There would be no need for us to be actively involved at all and as soon as the English had committed themselves we could keep the French off their backs through extremely benevolent neutrality. That would be quite enough in the first instance and it would relieve the English and spur them on, if they had this support from us. We shall very soon arrive at the situation that I had always foreseen for the French, when they have to decide whether they want to take Europe's side in China, or take Russia's side against Europe. If they do the latter they will be hopelessly beaten by England and Japan, and will lose Annam and Tonking and all their colonies for ever.' He added wistfully: 'And how wonderful it would be if we had a few squadrons of battleships ready now.'[11]

At this stage the Wilhelmstrasse already felt compelled to preach restraint where German rapprochement with Japan was concerned. In an adroit memorandum of 27 March 1901 Holstein pointed out that an approach by Germany to Japan, a country that was obviously pursuing annexationist aims, would be seen as a change from the purely defensive stance hitherto maintained by the Reich to a policy of aggression, above all towards Russia. 'The task of inducing Japan to adopt an energetic policy ... is [therefore] best left to England', Holstein wrote. Germany had made a binding declaration in Tokyo that in the event of a Russo-Japanese conflict she would remain neutral and would 'by remaining neutral, also procure French neutrality'. He added: 'We cannot justifiably go beyond this declaration.'[12]

In view of the growing tension between China and Russia over Manchuria on the one hand, and on the other the resignation of the Ito Cabinet in Tokyo, which had been ready to come to an agreement, Wilhelm II spent the spring of 1901 believing that a war in the Far East was imminent. He sent a dispatch to the German envoy in Tokyo, Count Emmerich von und zu Arco-Valley, saying that Russia had already ordered preparations for mobilisation and instructing the Commander of the German squadron in the Far East, Bendemann, to withdraw his cruisers to Tsingtao in the event of war breaking out.[13] In a conversation with the Reich Chancellor on 26 June 1901 about the relative power of Japan and Russia in the Far East, Prince Heinrich, who since Kiaochow was regarded as a Far Eastern expert, expressed the view that although Japan had the 'guts' to attack, in the long term Russia would be victorious.[14] In July the Wilhelmstrasse instructed the sceptical German envoy to offer the Japanese government discreet encouragement to go to war by promising 'benevolent neutrality'.[15]

The 'great disappointment felt by the Kaiser at the passing of the clouds of war' was, as Barbara Vogel rightly points out, unmistakable.[16] In April 1901 he castigated the British government as 'unmitigated noodles' because they had missed the chance to use the Manchurian question to assert Britain's position in the Far East. The true motive behind the Kaiser's suggestion did not of course escape the British: they were supposed to fall into the trap prepared by Wilhelm, the purpose of which was to boost Germany's position in Europe through a war in the Far East.[17] His anger over the postponed Far Eastern war showed itself in a particularly crass manner on 23 August 1901 at his meeting, already mentioned, with King Edward VII and the British ambassador, Sir Frank Lascelles, at Wilhelmshöhe. Wilhelm told his astonished guests that the Russians were using French money to transfer troops from west to east, 'whether to Manchuria, to Korea or against Japan remains to be seen'. 'A propos Japan!' the Kaiser continued, according to his own record of the conversation. 'If I remembered rightly, in the winter of this year the Japanese envoy had enquired of my government what England's probable attitude to a Japanese conflict with Russia would be. At that time we told the Japanese that in our view England would surely maintain a very benevolent neutrality. After this I see Lord Lansdowne [in January 1901], mention this question to him, and this Minister says to me personally: "What do you mean, neutrality! No, British warships will fight alongside Japan, and we certainly must take their side." Summer comes and goes, the Japanese zest for war disappears and nothing happens. The answer to this puzzle came to me later from — the

Russian side! The Russians told us Japan wanted to start a war, asked England
for money and this money was *refused* them. At this point King Edward made
a remark expressing strong disapproval of this policy on the part of the English
Cabinet and affirmed that he had known absolutely nothing about it. Sir
Frank also protested vehemently and said that although he was being very
indiscreet he must state that on the contrary, the Japanese had refused to
accept English money. When I expressed doubt the ambassador came out with
it and said that England had indeed offered money, but she had made
conditions which Japan would have had difficulty in accepting. I responded
that it came to the same thing whether one simply refused something or
whether one made such conditions that the other person could not accept it. If
it behaved that way the English government could not be surprised if the
phrase "perfidious Albion" was still considered valid. I could only describe
such a policy as "betrayal". At this, lively protests from the King and Sir
Frank.' As the conversation continued, Kaiser Wilhelm warned his British
guests of the secret cooperation between Russia and America in the Pacific
Ocean. The American capture of the Philippines signified 'a step against the
Yangtse. Does England really believe she can stand up to Russia and America
in the Far East alone, without Japan?' In answer to this question the ambassador conceded 'that in the long run England cannot hold out in East Asia
without Japan at her side', whereupon the Kaiser declared that in that case
England's policy towards Japan was all the more incomprehensible. The
Japanese were an 'easily excitable, ambitious people who would not easily
forget an affront to their honour – of the kind that English policy had
undoubtedly caused'.[18]

THE ANGLO-JAPANESE ALLIANCE OF JANUARY 1902

Neither the Kaiser nor his advisers guessed that at this time the British
government had already embarked on negotiations with the Japanese
ambassador in London, Tadasu Hayashi, which would lead to a formal
Anglo-Japanese alliance in January 1902.[19] The British agreement with Japan
was partly motivated by fear of a growing international isolation, as had
occurred during the Boer War. In addition, both the enormous economic
potential of the United States and the expansion of the Russian and French
fleets – not to mention that of Germany – were putting increasing pressure on
the British fleet. In a secret memorandum of 4 September 1901 the First Lord
of the Admiralty, Lord Selborne, took the view that in the event of war
between Britain on the one hand and Russia and France on the other, the
decisive battles would take place in the Mediterranean and in the English

Channel. In order to be sure of victory Britain must therefore concentrate her fleet in European waters. On the other hand, the complete elimination of British naval power in the east could not be accepted, as this would mean the loss of the bases in Hong Kong and Singapore, just when a battle with Russia for India was to be expected. In the northern Pacific, however, the balance of power was shifting to Britain's disadvantage, principally because the Russian Baltic fleet was gradually being transferred from Kronstadt to Vladivostok and Port Arthur ... But any British attempt to redress the balance of power in the Far East would in turn mean a dangerous reduction of the presence of the Royal Navy in home waters. The dilemma would be solved overnight, Selborne argued, if Britain could come to an agreement with Japan. The alliance could take the form of a British pledge to come to Japan's aid if she were *simultaneously* attacked by Russia and France; in return Japan would have to promise to take part in a war if Britain should come into conflict with Russia and France at the same time. 'Such an agreement would ... add materially to the naval strength of this country all over the world, and effectively diminish the probability of a naval war with France or Russia, singly or in combination.'[20]

On the basis of views such as this, Salisbury's Cabinet gave almost unanimous approval to the agreement on 5 November 1901.[21] Silence was to be maintained towards the Germans in the first instance,[22] for in Downing Street it was feared that Germany might hear of the Anglo-Japanese understanding through Hayashi or Eckardstein, and would try to undermine it. Full of mistrust of German intentions, Sir Francis Bertie wrote to Knollys, the King's Private Secretary, on 23 November 1901: 'I suspect that the German Government have knowledge ... of the desire of H.M. Govt to extend the Agreement being negotiated with Japan to cover not only a case of an attack by any two Powers on Japan or England in the Far East, but to any double attack anywhere. This would not at all suit Germany for pleased as she might be to feel that her interests in the Far East would be safeguarded by an understanding between England and Japan limited to the Far East and that such an understanding when communicated to Russia – as it would be by Germany – would be a bar to an Anglo-Russian Agreement, she would feel that with a general alliance with Japan we could more easily than now dispense with German offers of alliance. Therefore the German Government have probably advised Japan to defer *any* Agreement with us till it is seen how we come out of the South African business, and meanwhile she will as the honest broker see what can be done at Petersburg.'[23]

Was Francis Bertie's suspicion justified? In fact Berlin had not got wind of the secret negotiations either via Tokyo or through Eckardstein. Nevertheless

the object of German policy remained, unquestionably, to bring about a war
between Japan and England on the one hand and Russia on the other, and to
prevent any understanding between Japan and Russia (or between England
and Russia).[24] In the course of their meeting at Danzig Nicholas II indicated
to the Kaiser that although he did not envisage an immediate war with Japan,
he expected it in two years' time. When he received a report from St Petersburg to the effect that Russia was trying 'to avoid serious complications in the
Far East for the time being and to prevent a premature aggravation of the
conflict of interests between Russia and Japan', Kaiser Wilhelm wrote on it
'Correct! Until 1904!'[25]

In the meantime Wilhelm continued his attempts to encourage Nicholas II
to confront Britain in the Persian Gulf. On 7 September 1901 he had already
made up his mind that Kuwait should become the point at issue between
Britain and Russia, 'for then the Russians will have to declare their intentions
in the Persian Gulf and choose between England and us (indirectly)'.[26] At the
beginning of 1902 reports reached Berlin that both Russia and Britain were
anxious to take Kuwait. In January a British warship landed cannon there,
allegedly as a deterrent to Russian intrigues.[27] Once more the Kaiser saw this
as an opportunity to stir up Anglo-Russian conflict. In a letter to the Tsar of
3 January 1902 he enthusiastically greeted the arrival of the Russian warship
Variag in the Gulf. 'It was a very wise thing', he wrote, 'to show your flag
there. As it seems not impossible that another Power [meaning Britain] was
intending to repeat the very successful experiment she carried out on the Nile
when she hauled down the Sultan's flag, landed men and guns, hoisted a flag
of some kind on some pretext or other and then said "J'y suis, j'y reste!" In this
case it would have meant unlimited control over all Persia's trade routes to the
Gulf, and thus over Persia itself, and with that "Ta-ta" to your intended
development of Russian trade, which you started so efficiently by bringing
Persia into the customs union.' Changing the subject to the importance of the
Baghdad railway, Wilhelm II went on to point out that the British action in
Kuwait showed 'once again the great need for the Baghdad railway, which
I intend to build with German capital. If the great Sultan had not dithered
over this question for so long the line would have been begun years ago and
would have given you the advantage now of being able to send a few
regiments from Odessa straight to Kuwait, and that would have upset the
calculations of the other Power, because the Russian troops would have
controlled the land routes to the interior, against which even the biggest fleet
is powerless for many reasons.'[28] In March 1902, when Metternich sent a
warning from London that there was a growing inclination in Britain to seek
an Anglo-Russian rapprochement and to accept the idea of allowing Russia

into the Persian Gulf, the Kaiser wrote scornfully in the margin of the report: 'England cutting off its nose to spite its neighbour! The Russian will laugh loudest over this nonsense, for they will be the ones to reap the benefits.'[29]

In his letter of 3 January 1902 Kaiser Wilhelm did not only encourage the Tsar to expand Russian interests in the critical Gulf region. He urged Nicholas to build up the Russian fleet more quickly and offered him the protection of the German battlefleet, itself growing at tremendous speed. Britain's action in the Persian Gulf, he argued, revealed 'the enormous advantages of a superior fleet ... which controls access from the sea to places which have no overland communications, and which the rest of us cannot reach because our fleets are too weak and without them our shipping is at the mercy of the enemy'. He drew the Tsar's attention to the latest addition to the strength of the German navy, several battleships which were about to be put into service, and assured Nicholas that they would 'undoubtedly make their presence very agreeably felt and prove useful, as long as they help you keep the world at peace'.[30]

On 3 February 1902 Lord Lansdowne revealed to the astonished German ambassador Count Metternich that England and Japan had concluded a treaty by which each of the two Powers undertook to stand by the other militarily until a mutual peace accord had been achieved, in the event that, while 'protecting their special interests' in China and Korea, one of them should find itself at war with two foreign Powers.[31] Wilhelm's reaction to the news was outwardly positive. Writing to his uncle Edward VII on 26 February 1902, he welcomed the Anglo-Japanese agreement as promoting peace. 'I congratulate you on the conclusion of the new Alliance, which we all here look upon as a guarantee of peace in the East', adding that he nevertheless continued to cherish hopes of 'the union among the Teutonic Races'.[32] In reality the Kaiser considered the treaty extremely damaging for Britain. For, as he saw it, the new alliance was 'aimed at Russia', and by blocking Russian expansion in the Far East it would transfer the full weight of the Russian Colossus on to Afghanistan and India. The result, inevitably, would be heavy dependence by Russia on German support.[33]

The Reich Chancellor and the Foreign Office were no less delighted and relieved than the Kaiser.[34] Their long-standing fear that Britain and Russia might join hands over Germany's head now seemed to have vanished.[35] A Russo-Japanese war, into which France and Britain could be drawn as allies of Russia and Japan respectively, had come within reach. Germany's position, as the real winner in the game between the two power blocks, seemed to have been enormously strengthened overnight.[36] In the Wilhelmstrasse, too, it was thought that Russia would now feel compelled to seek close cooperation in Europe with Germany, with her superior army and her rapidly growing battlefleet. His hopes riding high, the Kaiser intensified his efforts, through his special relationship with Tsar Nicholas, to draw the giant Russian Empire on to Germany's side and to play it off against the British Empire and its new ally, Japan. But in February and March 1902 his most senior advisers intervened in an ill-advised attempt to restrain him which, as we shall see, was to cause confusion all round.

THE REJECTION OF COUNT LAMSDORFF'S OUTSTRETCHED HAND

Within a few days of the Anglo-Japanese treaty becoming public knowledge the Russian Foreign Minister, Count Vladimir Lamsdorff, showed signs of anxiety at the incipient isolation of his country, just as the German leadership had anticipated. On 14 February 1902 Bülow noted that Wilhelm II took a certain amount of pleasure in this development. 'H.M. is delighted that Count Lamsdorff is taking a "very grave" view of this agreement. He is even more delighted that it has elicited from the Russian Minister the wish for "union between other powers". His Majesty remarked in passing that the agreement was a severe but not entirely undeserved punishment for the Russians' flirtation with England, their passivity during the South African war, their aloofness towards us, their failure to respond to His Majesty's well-meaning hints. It was becoming clear that Russia too had many an Achilles' heel, especially in the Far East.'[37]

When shortly afterwards the German ambassador in St Petersburg, Count von Alvensleben, reported that he had learned in a conversation with his Austrian colleague Baron Aehrenthal that Russia wished to turn her back on republican France and align herself with her monarchical neighbours, Germany and Austria-Hungary, Wilhelm II gleefully welcomed this development as the fulfilment of his boldest hopes. It would be 'a blessing! And the result of the impression left by Danzig and then Compiègne', if Russia resumed her traditional relationship with the two empires. Such a change of direction, he thought, would be not only 'very sensible!' but, in view of the Anglo-Japanese agreement, indispensable. The Tsar 'must do it, because of Japan and England! If he has to transfer troops to the East he will want to be sure of his neighbours.' The Kaiser rejected out of hand Aehrenthal's advice that Germany and Austria should react 'as indifferently as possible' towards any such change in Russian policy. Tsar Nicholas II, he wrote, 'is probably favourably inclined towards *us*, and that doesn't suit Aehrenthal, and so *we* are supposed to be *indifferent*!!' That was all 'humbug! Whether Austria behaves with indifference or not is quite irrelevant to the course of world history! She is our ally and will join in with whatever I agree with the Tsar!! We two make history and destiny is in our hands!'[38] The next day, in a conversation with Alvensleben, Lamsdorff raised the question of 'whether it might not be advisable, in view of the new treaty, if Germany and Russia were to renew the expression of their common policy in the Far East'. Through a joint 'declaration' Lamsdorff hoped to achieve 'unity between all the continental powers', for − as Alvensleben reported the conversation − 'Austria and Italy would presumably follow us [Germany], and he thought he could count on France joining in.'[39]

Although Bülow also aspired to an alliance with Russia as his ultimate aim, Lamsdorff's offer seemed to him to have come at an inopportune moment. Partly out of fear of Britain − the German battlefleet was by no means out of the 'danger zone' yet − and partly because he expected to obtain far better conditions from Russia once she was embroiled in military conflict in the Far East, the Chancellor not only rejected Lamsdorff's proposal but did so in unnecessarily harsh and wounding terms. In an arcane instruction of 22 February 1902, which Alvensleben was ordered to read out to the Russian Foreign Minister, Bülow began by giving flimsy economic reasons for turning down the Russian overtures. In a second, more hard-hitting passage he set out the 'political' considerations that supposedly weighed against an alliance between Germany, Russia and France. 'Count Lamsdorff will be well aware that the Triple Alliance is not likely to promote anti-Russian tendencies but, ultimately, rather the opposite. Equally, I assume that the Dual Alliance is likely to restrain possible tendencies on the part of France. One cannot fail to recognise, however, that in one particular the Triple Alliance and the Dual Alliance are fundamentally different, and that is, that aggressive action against Russia by a member of the Triple Alliance is highly unlikely, indeed one may say absolutely out of the question, if Germany disapproves of this action. On the other hand the case might well arise in which some political adventurer in France − dictator or monarch − seizes power for himself and then, because he cannot survive otherwise, hits out at once in the expectation that the Russian government, as in the last Turkish war, will be swept into the fight by a tidal wave of chauvinist and revolutionary elements. This French hope is nourished by the fact that the Russian government, in order to distract the Russian press from other questions, allows it to depict the German Empire as Russia's real enemy, day after day and year after year. For the Russian press the German is now what the Turk was before 1877. There is an apparent contradiction between this perception and the conviction that Germany nevertheless has nothing to fear from Russia. But the contradiction disappears as soon as one realises that France allies herself to Russia purely out of hatred and fear of Germany and has abandoned her 900-year-old Oriental policy.

In the unlikely event that Germany came out of the war diminished and France strengthened, the latter would at once revert to her traditional Mediterranean and Oriental ambitions.' In an allusion to the Crimean War coalition between Britain, France and Piedmont-Sardinia against Russia in the 1850s, Bülow added a warning that he was expressing 'more than mere supposition' when he said that France would be able to count on 'strong support' from Britain and Italy in adopting such a policy.[40]

On 25 February Bülow also read out his instruction to the Russian ambassador in Berlin, Count Osten-Sacken, who had called on him in order to discuss Lamsdorff's offer. In response to Bülow's arguments the ambassador pointed out that the revanchist tendency in France was dying out and that no Frenchman still thought seriously of attacking Germany. Nor did Russia have the slightest interest in a Franco-German war; her influence in Paris had become all-powerful in the meantime, and she would never allow a French attack.[41] But neither Osten-Sacken's objections nor a warning from the German ambassador in St Petersburg that the Chancellor's dispatch could do lasting damage to relations between Germany and Russia made any impression on Bülow.[42]

By overestimating the German Reich's room for manoeuvre in the new global situation, Bülow and Holstein convinced themselves they could detach Russia from France and persuade the former to join the Triple Alliance. They proceeded on the assumption that Russia would before long come into conflict with Japan, backed by Britain, and might also be badly affected by revolutionary unrest. As a result she would need to be able to rely on benevolent neutrality, if not active support, from Germany.[43] Konrad Canis rightly points out that this attitude on Germany's part was almost bound to increase Russia's growing mistrust of 'the real purpose of German foreign policy ... Blinded by its "free-hand" policy, German diplomacy allowed this opportunity to slip, and furthermore, by turning it down point-blank, gave rise to new and deep reservations in Russia', which in turn encouraged a rapprochement between Russia and Britain with the aim of circumscribing Germany's position of power.[44] Lamsdorff's anger at the brusque response accorded by Berlin to his cautious treaty proposal was to have important consequences for the future development of international relations, as will be seen.[45]

In her study of German policy towards Russia Barbara Vogel describes how Bülow, out of fear that the Kaiser, in his 'euphoric mood', might agree 'at once and with enthusiasm' to Lamsdorff's proposal, at first kept the monarch in ignorance of it. She states that it was not until 16 March, the day on which a joint declaration was issued by Russia and France against the Anglo-Japanese alliance, that the Reich Chancellor informed Wilhelm II of the Russian offer of friendship and showed him press reports depicting Germany as the real winner in the Far Eastern crisis.[46] If Vogel's account of this episode is correct, it would indeed be a striking example of Bülow's 'masterly' skill in 'politically programming [his] own sovereign'.[47] But is it really a fact that the Kaiser allowed his Chancellor to pull the wool over his eyes and manipulate him into taking an opposite view, over such a vital question as German–Russian relations, in which he took so close an interest? It is safe to assume that Wilhelm – just like Bülow and Holstein – recognised the obvious advantages of a cautious attitude. He also shared the belief of his most senior advisers that following the Anglo-Japanese accord Germany would be able to break up the Dual Alliance between Russia and France.[48] In mid March, after the publication of the Franco-Russian declaration against the Anglo-Japanese alliance, in which Germany had taken no part, criticism began to be voiced in Paris to the effect that this extension of the Franco-Russian Dual Alliance, which had hitherto been concerned only with Europe, could drag France into a war over Far Eastern issues and that Germany, by cleverly going her own way, would reap the greatest reward from the new situation in the Far East. At this Wilhelm II was jubilant, exclaiming: 'I hope so. Yes indeed! "La toute petite declaration" was made *without* our participation! It is better so.' Commenting on a reported French remark that following the Anglo-Japanese Alliance the Reich was in a position 'to play the arbiter between the two allied groups in any disputes', the Kaiser wrote smugly 'Oui Madame!' It was already evident, he said, that his help was being sought on all sides.[49]

Nevertheless it remains almost inexplicable that the Chancellor kept the Kaiser in the dark about the full significance of Lamsdorff's proposal as a possible starting point for a German–Russian alliance. If this was an example of Bülow's attempted manipulation of the monarch, no one, least of all Bülow himself, can have regarded it as a successful one. Not only did his cynical deception of the Kaiser have serious consequences which culminated in Wilhelm II furiously calling the Russian Foreign Minister a liar when the latter spoke to the Tsar of a proposed alliance which Germany had rejected.[50] In addition Bülow's high-handed response to Lamsdorff's overture threw away a real chance at reaching that closer agreement with Tsarist Russia for which the Kaiser and his Chancellor had been striving and would continue to strive for several years to come. What is certain is that Wilhelm, irrespective of how much he knew of Lamsdorff's proposal, continued his eager courtship of the Russian autocrat even after the agreement between Britain and Japan became public knowledge. As Bülow commented after his conversation with the monarch on 14 February 1902, 'His Majesty wishes that no doubts should be entertained in St Petersburg regarding the loyalty of our position. This is

especially important because our relations with Russia depend fundamentally
on the confidence that the Emperor Nicholas places in our All-Gracious
Lord.'[51] In his personal Russian policy, indeed, the Kaiser was to go considerably further than his advisers considered justifiable.

REVAL, AUGUST 1902: THE 'ADMIRAL OF THE ATLANTIC' MEETS THE 'ADMIRAL OF THE PACIFIC' IN THE BALTIC

In early January 1902 Wilhelm wrote to Nicholas II, thanking him for coming
to Danzig and asked when he could return the visit.[52] The Tsar responded by
sending his 'favourite adjutant' Obolensky to Berlin with birthday presents for
the Kaiser and suggesting a meeting at the Estonian naval port of Reval, now
Tallinn, in August.[53] The fact that the preparations for the Reval meeting
were made by the Russian naval attaché in Berlin, Captain Paulis, was
symptomatic of the power struggle that was raging in the Russian leadership.
Lamsdorff and the influential Minister of Finance, Sergei Witte, were seeking
to reach an agreement with Japan and hoped to find support for this in Tokyo
from the party around former Japanese Prime Minister Ito. Meanwhile,
however, a group of Russian grand dukes led by Alexander Bezobrazov and
Admiral Alexeiev, anxious – not least for their personal enrichment – to gain a
foothold in Korea and Manchuria, had found a ready listener in the Tsar.
Paulis saw himself as the representative in Berlin of the Russian pro-war party
and intrigued with Wilhelm II and the Chief of the Naval Cabinet, Admiral
Gustav von Senden-Bibran, against his own Foreign Minister, whose distrust
of Germany's intentions only increased as a result.[54]

In view of this Russian internal conflict the discovery that Lamsdorff would
not be coming to Reval became a matter of major political significance. The
German ambassador in St Petersburg saw it as indicating a Russian wish
'as far as possible to deprive the forthcoming meeting between the Emperors
of any political importance'. Alvensleben, pointing out that Lamsdorff had not
yet got over his annoyance with Germany for rejecting his offers of friendship,
warned strongly that the absence of the Russian Foreign Minister from the
Reval meeting would give 'a very regrettable impression of present relations
between Germany and Russia'.[55]

Like the ambassador, the statesmen in the Wilhelmstrasse constitutionally
responsible for the foreign policy of the Reich were convinced that
the presence of the Russian Foreign Minister at the forthcoming imperial
rendezvous was indispensable. The Reich Chancellor sent an urgent plea to the
Kaiser, who was on his annual Scandinavian cruise, to smooth Lamsdorff's path
to Reval. 'If Lamsdorff really did not come to Reval, in the present state of

our relations and in view of the general world situation it would be a political failure of the highest order for us', he argued on 11 July 1902. 'The absence of the Russian Minister for Foreign Affairs at the meeting between Your Majesty and His Majesty the Emperor Nicholas would be seen everywhere as a proof that the political significance of the interview at Reval was to be played down by the Russian side from the very outset . . . Lamsdorff will not be able to stay away from the interview if Your Majesty expresses the wish to His Majesty the Emperor Nicholas to see him there. In my most humble opinion the best manner of doing this would be for Your Majesty, in writing to His Majesty the Emperor Nicholas, to treat it as a matter of course that Lamsdorff will come, but at the same time to let it be understood how much it is Your Majesty's personal wish to see Lamsdorff on this occasion. If Your Majesty wished to add that Your Majesty would be glad to see Lamsdorff in Reval also because it was Your All-Highest intention to confer an honour on him there, the defeat of those who envy and oppose us would be plain for all to see. This honour could only be the Order of the Black Eagle, which until now every Russian Minister for Foreign Affairs has received, and moreover always soon after he took up office . . . If the high Order of the Black Eagle were not conferred at the second meeting between Your Majesty and His Majesty the Emperor Nicholas, it would be attributed not to the personality of Count Lamsdorff but to a worsening of relations between Germany and Russia.'[56]

The diplomat Heinrich von Tschirschky, who was accompanying the Kaiser on his Scandinavian cruise as representative of the Foreign Office, reinforced the Reich Chancellor's entreaty, but neither his nor Bülow's words made much impression on Wilhelm.[57] Not only was the Kaiser under the influence of the Chief of his Naval Cabinet, Senden-Bibran, who was hand in glove with the Russian naval attaché Paulis, but he was full of hatred for Lamsdorff, presumably, as Barbara Vogel assumes, because he suspected that the Foreign Minister might have seen through the deceitful German game.[58] Before Bülow's letter arrived on board the *Hohenzollern* Tschirschky had held an hour-long discussion with the Kaiser about Germany's Russian policy in the course of which he discovered that Senden had reported to Wilhelm on a long conversation with Paulis, and that this had 'considerably sharpened' his antagonism towards Lamsdorff. The core of the naval attaché's intrigue against the Foreign Minister, Tschirschky told the Reich Chancellor, had been 'the Russian offer to us to join the Franco-Russian Entente, and our "refusal".' 'His Majesty told me', Tschirschky wrote, 'that Paulis had said he would not rest until Count Lamsdorff had been overthrown, for as long as he was Minister good relations would never be established between Russia and

Germany'. The diplomat's warning that the German Reich should avoid giving any impression that it had a hand in the Russian intrigue against Lamsdorff fell upon deaf ears.[59]

Over the next few days there were increasing signs of the deep grudge which the Kaiser bore towards the Russian Foreign Minister. On 15 July 1902, when Tschirschky showed him Alvensleben's report on his conversation with Lamsdorff, Wilhelm wrote in the margin of the document: 'There you are, that is what the fellow is like.' When the diplomat tried to point out that 'important *German* interests would be at stake . . . if the Minister did not come to Reval', the Kaiser retorted that 'he could not dictate to the Emperor Nicholas who he should bring with him'.[60] On the same day Wilhelm II annotated both Alvensleben's private letter to Bülow of 5 July and the Reich Chancellor's submission of 11 July with hostile remarks of a coarseness that surpassed his worst outbursts. The news sent by the ambassador that it looked very much as if the Russian Foreign Minister would not attend the imperial meeting in Reval received the comment: 'Very satisfactory. We don't need the fellow.'[61] Bülow's suggestion that he might confer the Order of the Black Eagle on Lamsdorff was rejected out of hand. 'No!' he exclaimed. 'I have personally expressly agreed with H.M. [Nicholas II] that no one, whoever he is, shall get an order this year if he was decorated last year. Lambsdorff [sic] has constantly intrigued to turn the Tsar against me personally and against the Reval meeting, I know that through Paulis, and he certainly doesn't deserve an order from me for that! Lambsdorff is furious because you refused to join in the so-called "petite déclaration" in the spring against England-Japan. He has given the Tsar the notion that he has offered you an *alliance*, and that you had advised me to reject the *alliance*. On ne peut pas se fier à l'Empereur, are the authentic words spoken by him, which were *repeated* by *Loubet* [the President of France] to the Tsar and repeated by Grand Duke Alexander, the Tsar's brother-in-law, to Paulis. I personally do not care in the least whether that beast Lambsdorff comes or not. I did not discuss anything with him last year and when I decorated him he became very impudent! I shall agree *everything* with the Tsar *direct*. Moreover, for all we know the Tsar is already dropping Lambsdorff and finds him repugnant and so does not *want* to bring him. In that case surely I cannot force the Tsar to bring along a fellow who disgusts him and who is on his way out?!' In his letter Bülow had warned the Kaiser of the anti-German attitude of Admiral Alexeiev, whom Paulis wanted to succeed Lamsdorff as Foreign Minister, but even this argument made little impression on Wilhelm. He continued his tirade with the comment: 'I think something is certainly afoot with Alexeiev. Old Admiral Krämer was to have been in attendance on me [in Reval], because he speaks German.

This arrangement was suddenly overturned and the Tsar ordered Alexeiev to take his place. That could possibly mean that the Tsar wishes to bring Alexeiev into my presence so as to facilitate an exchange of views before he appoints him Foreign Minister. I think it possible that Lambsdorff will fall sooner or later as Niki does not like him. I cannot believe that his departure would be regrettable for us. He lies in wait, intrigues, ducks and weaves when he can and hates us. An Admiral who knows our fleet, its strength and its efficiency, who lived with it in China and even fought a common enemy with it, is in a much better position to form an opinion of us and of our value as friends and our dangerousness as enemies than that insipid tshinovnik [pen-pusher] who has not yet deigned even to look at me or the Reich Chancellor or to visit Berlin. Adm. Alexeiev may or may not be anti-German, but all the same − if he is a good soldier − he will calculate accurately − and much more accurately than a stinking bureau chief and pen-pusher in an office − how far it is *militarily* useful or necessary to get on bad terms with us. He can do so all the more effectively because he has also seen his friends from the nation amie et allié [i.e. France] fighting alongside our Grenadiers and sailors in China, and his verdict on the latter was in their favour, while the Gauls came out very badly. I would be glad if Alexeiev came. I shall do nothing for Lambsdorff and certainly not give him the Black Eagle Order. Wilhelm I.R.'[62]

What the Reich Chancellor, who was on holiday on the island of Norderney, privately thought of his sovereign's intemperate comments is not recorded. In his written response of 22 July 1902 he assured his All-Highest Lord that he had received his 'gracious marginal notes . . . with the most respectful thanks'. He continued in sycophantic vein: 'Everything Your Majesty says would be right if the Emperor Nicholas were a monarch like Your Majesty. But that is not the case. For that reason I am afraid that the Emperor Nicholas will not shake off Lamsdorff so soon, and in particular I am afraid that as long as Lamsdorff remains Minister he will maintain his influence on the Emperor Nicholas . . . The Tsar receives the Foreign Minister every week, far more often than all the others. If Lamsdorff, whom I personally find just as repugnant as Your Majesty does, becomes more and more of an enemy, he will make increasing use of the influence which the Tsar's character and his office gives him in order to frustrate Your Majesty's plans.' Once again the Chancellor set out the reasons why it was necessary for the Foreign Minister to be present at least briefly at the meeting of the emperors at Reval. 'Even if Lamsdorff is in Your Majesty's presence for a mere five minutes everything that could be said to diminish the importance of the meeting falls flat on the ground.' All that he was seeking to do, Bülow affirmed, was to make sure that 'Your Majesty's great thoughts and the effect of Your Majesty's powerful

personality are not hampered by petty tricks of servile vanity ... As on all
other occasions, nothing will happen in this case without Your Majesty's
knowledge and All-Highest approval. But I believe that unless arrangements
are made soon for Lamsdorff to come, he will take a holiday and thus get out
of going to Reval once and for all.' Again Bülow asked the Kaiser either to
write to the Tsar himself, or to leave it to him and Alvensleben to see that
Lamsdorff was invited.[63]

On returning from his cruise the Kaiser did in fact give Bülow permission
to invite Lamsdorff to Reval. His hostility towards the Russian Foreign
Minister, however, had in no way diminished. In a telegram of 28 July 1902
from Sassnitz he wrote to the Chancellor: 'Have received your two letters.
Lambsdorff [sic!] has lied in the most shameless way to Alvensleben. You are
quite right, firstly the Emperor [Nicholas] invited you in Reval [a mistake for
Danzig] in my presence. Secondly he sent me a message through Paulis saying
expressly that it should be *exactly* as in Danzig, the same people should
accompany us, and as the Ministers would be there the ambassadors did not
need to come. The scoundrel is trying the same manoeuvre for the second
time. He did not want to come to Danzig either, first I had to let him know
that I wanted to see him. It was all right there because I was the sovereign
who was receiving a visit. Now I am the guest who is paying a visit. Therefore,
however much I might like to do so I cannot personally take any step. I would
also lay myself open to the suspicion that I was *asking* the fellow and he
graciously accepted or refused. That cannot be. I must leave it to you to take
whatever steps seem appropriate to you, through Alvensleben or by other
means, to get Mosjö [Monsieur] to Reval. I might add that I do not share your
opinion that his appearance will make any impression whatever in the world.
He has already taken care that all the papers you cite keep quiet about the
meeting or deny that it has any significance, and that will be believed. If he
really comes he will simply put it about that he could not avoid coming, but
naturally did not discuss politics with me or anyone else. He has in any case
made sure the press said nothing about Reval up to now. Loubet's visit or the
Bulgarian's were talked about for weeks in advance. His conversation with
Alvensleben is a magnificent specimen of Slav mendacity and shamelessness
and a proof of how much he hates us.'[64]

In his *Denkwürdigkeiten* Bülow prided himself on having 'brought the
Kaiser into line' by 'mental massage', without making the slightest allusion
to this correspondence, so demeaning to him as Chancellor of the Reich. It is
true that in the end he succeeded in inviting Count Lamsdorff to Reval and in
persuading Wilhelm II that he must not only shake the Foreign Minister
by the hand but also, personally, confer the Order of the Black Eagle on him.

But the Chancellor could not prevent the Chief of the Naval Cabinet, Senden-Bibran, and the Russian naval attaché Paulis from continuing to intrigue both against Lamsdorff and against Britain.[65] He was even less successful in preventing one of the most embarrassing episodes of the reign of the last German Kaiser, in Reval. According to Bülow's account Wilhelm walked towards him, arm in arm with the Tsar, calling out loudly from some distance away: 'Do you know what we have decided to call ourselves in future? From now on the Emperor Nicholas is called the Admiral of the Pacific, and I shall call myself the Admiral of the Atlantic in future.' The Tsar was visibly embarrassed, Bülow recalled, but Wilhelm ignored the pleas of his most senior adviser, when they were alone again, to 'have done with this dreadful play on words'. Instead, 'with the wilfulness of an Enfant terrible ... to the evident discomfort of the Tsar', the Kaiser carried on with the 'joke' at the farewell dinner. When the Russian imperial yacht, *Standart*, weighed anchor and set off on the homeward journey to Kronstadt Wilhelm II's farewell message, sent to the Tsar by semaphore, was: 'The Admiral of the Atlantic bids farewell to the Admiral of the Pacific.' Nicholas sent only a brief 'Good-bye!' in response. When the whole story appeared in the international press a few weeks later it contributed in no small measure to the mistrust of the Kaiser's motives felt by the Atlantic Powers, Great Britain, France and America.[66] The Russian General Mossolov wrote a similar description of the episode, adding that when Admiral Nilov brought the Kaiser's signal to him, Nicholas whispered to the Admiral: 'He's raving mad!'[67]

Against these retrospective accounts by Bülow and Mossolov it must be said that, at least outwardly, there was no sign that the Tsar was put out by the incident. His supposedly embarrassed 'Good-bye' signal (according to Mossolov it was 'Pleasant voyage!') was no doubt an allusion to the childish English expression 'Ta-ta' that the two emperors had adopted in their communications with each other. Directly after his return from Reval Nicholas II sent Wilhelm an exuberant telegram expressing his satisfaction with their meeting. 'I cannot tell you how happy I am about your visit and that you were pleased with my gunnery school. Your signal was reported to me.'[68] When he received the German ambassador in audience four days later he spoke of the 'charming' days in Reval and, as Alvensleben reported, commented on 'our All-Gracious Lord's cheerful mood', which had proved to him 'that His Majesty the Kaiser and King had also been agreeably impressed. Altogether the Tsar spoke in the warmest terms of his pleasure at the present understanding with our All-Gracious Lord'. In particular, while discussing the newly introduced measures against the anarchists the Tsar had expressed 'his very great satisfaction at the firm agreement between Russia and Germany on this question', Alvensleben noted.[69] In a further report of 16 August 1902, which the Kaiser proudly ordered to be sent to every German embassy and legation in Europe – and there were twenty-three of them – Alvensleben wrote effusively of the dazzling impression that the meeting in Reval had made throughout the higher circles of Russian society. 'There is the greatest satisfaction on all sides at the Emperors' meeting in Reval … I had the opportunity of observing this at the audience granted to me by His Majesty the Emperor Nicholas, as also in my conversations with Count Lamsdorff and several others who participated in the meeting, and elsewhere too I hear nothing but favourable and pleasant comments. The warmth of the relations between the two sovereigns and the cordiality and kindness of our All-Gracious Lord cannot be praised highly enough.' It was recognised, the ambassador continued, 'that the meeting of the two powerful neighbours can only serve peaceful ends, and at the same time there was pride in the knowledge that what was demonstrated in Reval before the very experienced eyes of our All-Gracious Lord passed off so well. For the Russian Navy, the very marked manner in which their prowess in gunnery was honoured when the Tsar appointed the Commander of the Squadron as Admiral à la suite and later, after the warmest expressions of praise, embraced and kissed him in front of the assembled officer corps before the departure from Reval, was proof that they had also won the approval of the exalted guest.'[70]

Finally, the very serious intent, in terms of *Weltpolitik*, which lay behind the 'joking' allocation of the Pacific and Atlantic oceans to Russia and Germany respectively should not be overlooked. Since Nicholas II succeeded to the throne in November 1894 the Kaiser had constantly urged the young Tsar to regard himself as the defender of Christian Europe against the heathen 'yellow peril' in East Asia and to rely on the backing of the German Reich in Europe.[71] It was precisely this aim that Wilhelm was again pursuing in Reval, as the letter which he wrote on 2 September 1902 to the Tsar clearly shows. 'The whole visit was a particular delight for me, but it was more than that. The Naval Artillery School which was shown to me on your orders is the most vital part of the development of the fleet and of its preparation for its "business". By allowing this demonstration you have given me a special sign of your trust – albeit in response to what I showed you in Danzig – and it implies complete trust in the visitor, as is only possible between men of the same ideas and principles, and between monarchs it means united work towards a common goal, to preserve the peace of their countries. This confidence and this belief that you have shown me is not misplaced, I assure you, for it is entirely based on reciprocity. The proof of it is that the secret plans of my newest ships – not accessible to any foreigner – were confided to you and to the discretion of your naval authorities. Add to these facts that we both have the same interest in the development of our fleets, so that we have an innate passion for the sea; this is evidence enough that we need to regard our two fleets as *one* great organisation, which belongs to *one* great continent whose interests it has to protect along its coasts and in the open sea. This means in effect the peace of the world. For as rulers of the two leading Powers of the two great continental groups of nations, we can exchange views on any general question concerning their interests, and as soon as we have settled how it is to be approached, we can persuade our Allies to adopt the same point of view. But if both Alliances – that is five Great Powers – have decided that peace must be preserved, the whole world must keep the peace and will be able to enjoy its blessings. That is a convincing illustration of the fact that the two Alliances maintain the balance of Europe and the world if they remain in close agreement through annual meetings between their two leaders for the purpose of exchanging ideas. This is all the more necessary because certain circumstances in the East show that Japan is becoming a somewhat restless customer, and that the situation demands level-headedness and determination on the part of the peaceful Powers ... Twenty to thirty million trained Chinese, supported by half a dozen Japanese divisions, led by competent, intrepid Japanese officers, full of hatred for Christianity – that is a vision of the future that cannot be contemplated without concern, and it is not impossible. On the contrary, it is the realisation of the yellow peril which I described a few years ago, and I was ridiculed by the majority of the people for my graphic depiction of it ... Your devoted friend and cousin Willy, Admiral of the Atlantic.'[72]

Although in this letter the Kaiser professed to bring all five continental Great Powers together under Russian and German leadership, his policy was directed as much against France as against Japan and England.[73] This is already clear from the gloating comment that Wilhelm wrote on Radolin's dispatch of 6 September 1902 reporting on the feelings of astonishment and helplessness that the imperial meeting in Reval had aroused in Paris. 'Most satisfactory! It is a very good thing that the infamous Gauls should feel thoroughly put out!'[74] With or without France, the possibility that had always existed that England might ally herself with one or another Power or group on the continent had now, after Reval, disappeared, the Kaiser claimed triumphantly. In mid September he commented that the British Colonial Secretary, Chamberlain, who in a conversation with Eckardstein had let slip that he intended to go on exploiting the jealous rivalry between the continental Powers, was very much mistaken. 'We are no longer jealous[,] the two great continental coalitions have just come to an agreement.'[75] Shortly before his visit to England from 8 to 20 November 1902 Wilhelm told the Tsar what he proposed to say to British ministers if the subject of Reval came up in conversation. His chosen form of words, of which Nicholas expressed his approval, ran: 'His Majesty the Emperor of Russia as the head of the dual Alliance, I of the triple Alliance, we have both the one great object in view to secure Peace for our nations and our friends. We therefore work at the maintenance of Peace, and by this for interests common to the continental nations, who wish to strengthen and develop their commerce and their economical positions.'[76]

Nicholas thanked Wilhelm for his letter in a reply dated 8 September 1902, and seemed willing to accept his allotted mission to defend Europe's 'holiest possessions' against the Asiatic threat. He wrote with great warmth: 'The way in which you speak about your recollections of your stay at Reval touches me deeply. Above all I am happy you have felt, as I did at Danzig, the real sentiment of confidence by witnessing the methods of gunnery practice worked out for my navy, when we showed you and your officers every thin[g] we think useful in naval warfare . . . I beg you to believe me in what I say, that I was *not* among those who laughed at your picture of the "yellow Peril"; only it did not seem to me to be so near at hand. We are preparing ourselves for such a disagreeable eventuality. It won't be the first time that Russia will have to serve as a rampart to Europe, when the East poured the overflow of its inhabitants into our country. But God grant that may not happen so soon!'[77]

At Reval the two emperors had discussed not only the general aim of joint control of the Eurasian continent but also the timing of the Russian attack on Japan that was to usher in this German–Russian domination. In January 1904, immediately before the outbreak of war in the Far East, Wilhelm recalled that at their meeting the Tsar had declared bluntly to him: 'In 1904 I shall declare war on Japan.'[78] From numerous remarks by the participants it also emerges that the German attitude towards the Russo-Japanese War expected in 1904 was a central theme of the discussions at Reval. Kaiser Wilhelm himself, as already mentioned, stated unequivocally in December 1903 that both at Danzig in 1901 and at Reval in 1902 he had assured the Tsar of Germany's benevolent neutrality, 'with the result that entire Russian divisions from Russian Poland and from European Russia were and are being packed off to the Far East. That would not happen if the governments had not come to an agreement!!'[79] It is clear also from a record made by Holstein and a retrospective marginal note by Bülow that the Kaiser promised the Tsar his support in the event of a Japanese attack in East Asia. In a memorandum of 24 March 1902 Holstein stated that the assurances of neutrality which Germany had given Japan in June 1901 'would not prevent us declaring to the Russians, in accordance with the undertaking given by His Majesty in Danzig, that in a Russo-Japanese war Russia need not be concerned that Germany would cause any inconvenience'.[80] And in December 1902 the Reich Chancellor noted that 'the greatest caution and skill' were required, for 'His Majesty indicated to the Emperor Nicholas at Danzig and Reval that in the event of an attack on Russia in the East he would protect his back.'[81]

THE MEETING OF THE EMPERORS IN WIESBADEN AND WOLFSGARTEN, NOVEMBER 1903

After the Reval meeting Wilhelm continued his efforts to persuade Russia to strengthen her fleet in the Far East by withdrawing ships from the Baltic and the Black Sea.[82] The table of shipping drawn up in his own hand which the Kaiser sent to the Tsar on 2 September 1902 showed a clear preponderance of allied British and Japanese naval units in East Asian waters.[83] A month later he rejected as nonsensical the view put forward by some Russian statesmen that a war with Japan would chiefly entail action on the mainland rather than at sea. The sea was 'unavoidable!' in a war with Japan, he insisted; thus, he argued, the recent Japanese fleet expansion plans mattered to Russia because 'everything depends on whether the Jap[anese] fleet can defeat the Russian fleet so as to enable the transport fleet to throw the Jap[anese] army over to the mainland! Therefore *action at sea* is the first and most important thing.'[84] It was also with the aim of spurring Nicholas on to a faster ship-building programme that Wilhelm sent his eldest son to St Petersburg in January 1903 with a model of the latest German battleship.[85]

Despite Wilhelm's tireless efforts, in the months following Reval it looked for a time as if the appeasement politicians in St Petersburg and Tokyo would gain the upper hand. Bülow was disappointed to report to the Kaiser on 1 August 1903 that 'in East Asia the Russians and the Japanese are trying to outdo each other in backing out'.[86] Wilhelm remained convinced that 'there will be war! In good German, voilà tout!!', but he did not hide his fury at the Russian attempts to preserve peace and more especially at Lamsdorff's skilful diplomacy. In a 'wild outburst of hatred' (Vogel), which reveals both his fear of Russian power and his contempt for the Tsar whom he had so assiduously courted, the Kaiser wrote on 20 August 1903 on a report from St Petersburg: 'That Lamsdorff fellow is very good at handing out guaranteed "reassuring declarations" in empty phrases like this, and all the ambassadors and cabinets in Europe, shedding tears of emotion over this "honest, good, trustworthy man", fall straight into the trap! He "reassures" them all, while they see with their own eyes how Russia annexes whole continents, builds ships, forms squadrons, assembles armies, makes war preparations in the grandest style! They are "reassured" – because they want to be, in accordance with the principle "Mundus vult decipi, ergo decipiatur"! That is a very great talent and the Tsar should keep a servant like him nice and warm; he is invaluable. For he "reassures" the whole world until "the little Father" is ready to strike and laugh very heartily at us all, which he will have every right to do! I have never trusted Lamsdorff farther than I could see him, because I saw through this play-acting, in spite of his greasy mask of "bonhomie", and because I do not trust his *master*! The Russian has become a complete *Asiatic* and is justified in making a fool of stupid Europe; and one can only congratulate him that the diplomatic corps and cabinets of Europe contain so many simple-minded coffee-drinking old women and fall for this monstrous, indecent, insolent, shameless tripe, quite seriously and trustingly! It is a real humiliation for us "civilised states" to allow ourselves to be treated like this by the "Cossacks". That is my "Resumé"! W.' The report, with its marginal notes, had to be sealed before the Reich Chancellor handed it over to be filed.[87]

Bülow expressed doubts as to whether the Tsar would ever decide to go to war and advised caution. With an eye more to another Turkish war than to war against Japan, he warned that Germany must 'keep to the directive which Your Majesty previously laid down for this eventuality, that we do not tie ourselves down either for or against Russia without first obtaining serious Russian guarantees for our wishes. Our position will be all the stronger once the Russians are committed.'[88] In the meantime, however, the influence of the pro-war party at the Russian court was growing, while Lamsdorff and the other advocates of conciliation were effectively shut out of the decision-making process. In May 1903 the Tsar appointed Bezobrazov as secretary of state; in August he proclaimed the establishment of a governorship in East Asia and appointed the bellicose Admiral Alexeiev as Viceroy and Supreme Commander in the Far East. A group of grand dukes, who wished (as did Nicholas II himself) to exploit the forests and mineral deposits of Korea and Manchuria for their personal gain, formed a Far East committee and found a ready listener in the Tsar. The ministers who pressed for an understanding with Japan were left out in the cold.[89]

In mid October 1903 Wilhelm II's hopes were revived when Nicholas II, who was staying at Wolfsgarten, near Darmstadt, with Grand Duke Ernst Ludwig of Hesse (brother of Tsarina Alexandra and of Princess Irène of Prussia), sent word to the Kaiser that he would be glad to speak to him again before returning to Russia. Wilhelm immediately suggested a meeting on 4 November at Wiesbaden.[90] On 25 October Prince Heinrich, who was at the family gathering at Wolfsgarten with his wife Irène, telegraphed saying that

Nicholas wished to see Bülow as well, and would bring Lamsdorff with him to Wiesbaden.[91] The Tsar was accompanied by several court officials and adjutants-general as well as by Shebeko, the Russian military attaché in Berlin, so that the Wiesbaden meeting acquired a highly political significance.[92] It was to be held in an atmosphere dominated by the approach of war in East Asia and a looming crisis in the Balkans.[93]

As soon as the Reich Chancellor heard that the two emperors were to meet, he again felt obliged to warn Wilhelm to be reticent, in order not to unnerve the Russians. On 19 October 1903 he wrote to the Kaiser: 'With regard to the Far East, even the slightest suspicion that Germany was taking Russia's side would paralyse any opposition from Japan and England and would certainly make the Dual Alliance Powers [Russia and France] the masters in Asia. Already in the past week several English newspapers have published claims, perhaps Russian-inspired, that there is a secret East Asian agreement between Russia and Germany and that this makes any resistance by Japan impossible. In the event that Tsar Nicholas should raise this question, may I most humbly recommend to Your Majesty to maintain Your All-Highest present position, namely that Germany would be a neutral observer of a Russian–Japanese duel, and would remain so until the end, but that the intervention of other Powers could create situations whose consequences would be unforeseeable, and that in such an eventuality it would be impossible to commit oneself in advance. This general hint will probably suffice, and Your Majesty will be spared the necessity of referring to the difficult point of mutual territorial guarantees [by which Bülow meant, principally, Alsace-Lorraine] as a condition of any agreement. It would of course be best, as Your Majesty would be unable to comply fully with Russian wishes with regard either to the Far or the Near East, if Your Majesty were in a position to forestall any expression of such wishes.'[94]

The fears of the Chancellor and the Foreign Office seemed to be confirmed when the German chargé d'affaires in St Petersburg reported that the Russian papers were now also emphasising 'the natural relationship between Russia and Germany' and celebrating 'the traditional Russo-German community of interests'.[95] The danger that lay in these assurances of friendship seemed at first to escape the Kaiser. In the margin of the report he commented that if Russia's relationship with Germany was 'natural', then 'the Alliance with Gaul is *unnatural!* And that is right.' As for the community of interests between Russia and Germany, 'the Russ[ian] Press should accept it once and for all and act accordingly', he demanded.[96] He repudiated French attempts to prevent the impending Russo-Japanese War with characteristic bellicosity. 'The Gauls are afraid of losing money in the East Asian rumpus, and want us to stop the Russians for that reason! I have no intention of doing so', he wrote at the end of October 1903 on a report from Paris.[97] Even he was alarmed, however, when shortly before the Wiesbaden meeting the Havas news agency reported that the Tsar had expressed his satisfaction at the Franco-British understanding and at the recent rapprochement between France and Italy in a letter to President Loubet of France. As Bülow stated in a secret telegram to Holstein, the Kaiser considered that 'a general coalition against us was not impossible' and that he thought 'the Tsar's remarks at any rate proved that the assumption that a Crimean War group would form against Russia had become a phantasm'. As far as the meeting at Wiesbaden was concerned, Bülow continued, the Kaiser had promised him 'that he would give the Tsar no promises of any kind except on the basis of full reciprocity and reciprocal guarantees'.[98]

The two emperors met at Wiesbaden on 4 November 1903 and continued their discussions the next day at Wolfsgarten.[99] General Mossolov recalled that the Tsar had looked exhausted after his conversations with Wilhelm, but 'every interview that he had with the German Emperor unmistakably got on his nerves'.[100] Wilhelm took little notice of Bülow's plea for discretion and caution. With his characteristic exuberance he denounced the French and the Italians for their godlessness and unreliability and the English for their deceitfulness. These three western Powers, who were aiming at a 'Crimean War combination' against Russia, were also 'bound to each other by shared liberal ideas, by similar democratic institutions and by various common interests in the Orient', he reminded the absolute ruler of all the Russias. France, Russia's ally, was 'a declining nation with a clear downward tendency; the blood of the murdered King and the aristocracy stains this nation that is being destroyed by atheism'. Germany no longer had anything to fear from France in military terms; 'she had 38 million inhabitants, we have 56 million, that is almost 20 million more, which meant three million more men able to take up arms than France'. Wilhelm surprised the Tsar with the news that France would remain neutral in a war between Russia and Japan and that he, Nicholas, therefore need not fear that a Russo-Japanese War would broaden into a conflict with England. For according to the Anglo-Japanese alliance England was obliged to come to the help of Japan only if she were attacked by *two* Powers. The purpose of Edward VII's visit to Paris in May, Wilhelm asserted, had been to advise France to adopt a neutral stance in East Asia, so that England too could remain neutral.

The Kaiser gained the impression that even if the Tsar were not directly seeking war with Japan, he was nevertheless preparing for it. It may be, as Bülow recorded in his account of the discussions between the two monarchs at

Wolfsgarten, that Wilhelm did not expressly give the Tsar 'a promise ... of backing in East Asia', but the general aim of the conversation was, unmistakably, to allay the Tsar's fears about a war with Japan. According to the Kaiser's handwritten addition to the Chancellor's account, Nicholas II had emphatically stated, at the close of the talks, 'that in all great questions of Foreign Policy as well as home affairs, we entirely agree, as I have exactly the same opinion as You'.[101] Following the meeting it became apparent that Nicholas had put his trust unreservedly in Wilhelm. In Russian court circles it was said that 'for the Tsar there is only one authority at present: Kaiser Wilhelm. If the Tsar is showing a certain confidence at this difficult time it is thanks to Kaiser Wilhelm. The Tsar is firmly convinced that he can rely on the Kaiser, and therefore also on Germany, whatever the circumstances.'[102] What Wilhelm II hoped to gain from the fraternisation between Germany and Russia is indicated by the marginal remarks that he wrote on the French and Russian press reports of the meeting of the two emperors. Next to a comment that the rapprochement of Italy and Britain with France should be seen as a triumph of democracy he noted: 'Quite so.' An observation that the meeting of the two emperors seriously threatened to become the start of a Holy Alliance between Germany, Russia and Austria which could endanger the progress of democracy earned the remark: 'And so it should!'[103] Wilhelm took a particular interest in the press reports from Russia, which showed that the newspapers there, evidently with the blessing of the government, had treated the meeting of the two monarchs, with their ministers in attendance, as a matter of special consequence. Concern at the daily deployment of troops to the Far East, the insecure situation in the Balkans, the dependence of Russia's current ally, France, on the western Powers and not least the increasingly ominous internal situation in their own country, had, it seemed, given way to a sense of relief at all levels of Russian society as a result of the Wiesbaden meeting.[104] When Lamsdorff, on his return from Darmstadt, reverted 'again and again to the importance of unity between the three Imperial Powers', Wilhelm agreed, only commenting impatiently that the Russian Foreign Minister should 'just get his filthy press to support this better'.[105] Confident that he had restored the Three Emperors' League as a reactionary bulwark against the western Powers with their increasingly democratic tendencies, at the end of 1903 Wilhelm II looked forward expectantly to the coming conflict between the Russian Empire and Japan, Britain's ally.

CHAPTER EIGHT

The Anglo-German antagonism: the Kaiser, the King and public opinion

For a long time the Boer War cast a dark shadow over relations between Germany and Britain. The cruelty with which the British had often behaved in combating the guerrilla war waged by the Boers, above all the creation of concentration camps for over a hundred thousand women and children, aroused anger in other countries beside Germany, but German agitation was particularly resented in Britain, perhaps because the British were most keenly aware of their own vulnerability in relation to the 'German threat'. A recent study of British views of the Kaiser rightly sees the end of 1901 and the beginning of 1902 as the decisive 'turning-point in British public opinion about Germany ... Before the Boer War there was as yet no natural and fundamental hostility towards the Germans.'[1] Within a very short time Anglophobia in Germany and Germanophobia in Britain assumed horrifying dimensions which could scarcely be kept in check by the leading statesmen. Indeed even the latter – and, increasingly, the monarchs of both countries – were caught up in the tide of passionate accusations. Although both Edward VII and Kaiser Wilhelm consciously tried to bring their close dynastic relationship to bear against the tirades of public hatred, they had no lasting success. Even before the full extent of German hegemonial aspirations became apparent through the battlefleet-building programme, the relations between the two empires were acutely strained. What had seemed unthinkable only a few years earlier was now common talk: war. In the autumn of 1902 a German general wrote to his colleague, Freiherr Colmar von der Goltz: 'God grant that the land manoeuvres inaugurated by Your Excellency will signal the start of the revenge that history must and will take against the English for their infamous behaviour towards the Boers. For that, of course, we need a Chief of the General Staff who can make history.'[2]

THE STATE AND THE PEOPLE

In October 1901 an incautious speech in Edinburgh by the influential Colonial Secretary, Joseph Chamberlain, gave rise to an outburst of indignation in German public opinion.[3] In it he asserted that the nations which were accusing Britain of barbarity and cruelty in South Africa had themselves committed far worse offences before, and named the Russians in Poland and the Caucasus, the Austrians in Bosnia, the French in Tonkin and the Germans in the Franco-Prussian war of 1870–1. This, above all, was seen as a slanderous attack on the German army. The new German ambassador in London, Paul Count von Wolff-Metternich zur Gracht, was instructed to protest strongly against the 'extremely tactless and clumsy' speech.[4] In Germany there were mass rallies with 'immoderate accusations of every kind' against the British conduct of the war, which in turn provoked 'great bitterness' throughout Britain, as Metternich reported. The British saw the 'storm of indignation' as further evidence that 'hostility to England is more deeply rooted in the German people than among other nations'. The Prince of Wales (the future King George V), 'visibly upset', had shown Metternich a newspaper report about a resolution by the evangelical clergy of the Rhine province and had asked him why the Reich government did nothing to stop such infamies.[5] Attempts by Holstein, the Foreign Secretary, von Richthofen, the press officer Otto Hammann and others to persuade Bülow to condemn the German protest meetings in the interest of Anglo-German relations fell on deaf ears. Nothing could be more foolish, the Chancellor argued, than 'the English request for repression of the anti-English trend from above', for if he made a statement in the Reichstag which did not satisfy 'national sentiment', the anti-English mood in Germany would only be intensified.[6]

In this highly charged situation Kaiser Wilhelm at first maintained his composure. 'The Emperor has been calm and self-possessed all through', Holstein assured the anxious correspondent of *The Times*, Valentine Chirol.[7] The Counsellor emphatically denied rumours that Wilhelm was supporting the Anglophobic agitation; on the contrary, he claimed, the Kaiser was full of praise for Edward VII, which in the past had by no means always been the case.[8] In fact, Wilhelm saw an enviable patriotism in the united stand of the entire British people behind the army and against foreign criticism. 'Right or wrong, my country!' he exclaimed admiringly. 'When shall we in Germany reach that point?'[9] His attitude was a curious mixture of contempt for the civil government and solidarity with the British army. During a banquet in the Neues Palais in honour of King Edward's birthday on 9 November 1901 the Kaiser spoke to the British ambassador in such critical terms that even

Lascelles, who had a certain experience of such things, was shocked. 'His Majesty's language was marked ... by the severe criticisms of the action of His Majesty's Government to which he has accustomed me for the last two years', the diplomat wrote. The British government had missed several opportunities to put an end to the war in South Africa, with the result that the army, 'in which he took so great an interest, was being sacrificed to the interest of politicians'. Wilhelm turned down the ambassador's offer to transmit the Kaiser's advice to London as pointless. 'It was useless for him to make suggestions which were disregarded, and he was not going to "stick to us" any longer.' When Lascelles pointedly asked him to whom he wanted to stick, if not to England, the Kaiser at once replied 'To myself.' What England needed now, he said, was a strong man like Disraeli or Pitt. During the journey back to Berlin Bülow had tried to play down the Kaiser's remarks, the ambassador reported. 'His Majesty was a soldier and had little liking for parliamentary institutions and civilian Ministers, and he was especially irritated by the idea that the army was being sacrificed to the politicians, whom he held in little esteem. There could, however, be no doubt that His Majesty sincerely desired that England should be in no way weakened and that he regretted that the continuance of the war in South Africa hampered her freedom of action in other parts of the world.' The Chancellor then spoke of the anti-British feeling in Germany. 'There was no doubt that German public opinion was strongly in favour of the Boers to the extent, he should say, of 99 per cent of the population. This, however, was purely sentimental and did not imply hostility to England, and although public opinion in Germany did not influence the action of the Government as in England, he was convinced that, if a poll were taken, to decide whether measures should be taken which might lead to an estrangement with England, 99 per cent of the population would answer in the negative.'[10]

THE PRINCE OF WALES'S CONTROVERSIAL VISIT TO BERLIN

While the two nations on opposite sides of the North Sea continued to denigrate each other with increasing vehemence, Edward VII made an attempt to restore relations through his close ties with the Prusso-German royal family. He instructed Lascelles to impress upon Wilhelm II how much he hoped for a friendly Anglo-German 'entente cordiale' on all matters. The ambassador should also find out whether a visit by the young Prince of Wales on the occasion of the Kaiser's forthcoming birthday would be welcome.[11] During a reception at the Neues Palais on 28 December 1901 Wilhelm gave the impression of warmly accepting the hand of friendship proffered by his uncle. He echoed the King's wish for an 'entente cordiale' and seemed genuinely pleased at the prospective visit by the Prince of Wales, inviting him to come on 25 January, instead of arriving with the other princes on the following day, so that he could be received in a fitting manner.[12]

Two days later the Kaiser wrote a letter to his uncle which demonstrates better than any other document his conflicted attitude to his mother's homeland. In a strange mixture of sentimental memories of youth, grief for his deceased grandmother and mother, flattering admiration for the powerful British Empire, emphasis on the purportedly shared racial and religious heritage of the two 'Germanic' peoples, defiant autocracy and dark threats, it reads: 'The last time I wore highland dress at Balmoral was in 1878 in September when I visited dear Grandmama, & was able to go deerstalking on Lochnagar. Dear Grandpapa's gigantic old "Jäger" was still in waiting on Grandmama & looked after my rifles; whilst a very nice old but fine headkeeper with a good highland name & a splendid face stalked with me. All these memories came back to me . . . & made me think how the time flies past! . . . The vanishing year has been one of care & deep sorrow to us all, & the loss of two such eminent women, mothers & Queens as dear Grandmama & poor Mother is a great blow leaving for a long time a void, which closes up very slowly! Thank God that I could be in time to see dear Grandmama once more, & to be near You & Aunts to help you in bearing the first effects of the awful blow! What a magnificent realm, she has left you, & what a fine position in the world! In fact the first "world empire" since the Roman Empire! May it allways [sic] throw in its weight on the side of peace & justice! I gladly reciprocate all you say about the relations of our two Countries & our personal ones; they are of the same blood, & they have the same creed, & they belong to the great Tutonic [sic] Race, which Heaven has intrusted [sic] with the Culture of the World; for – apart from the Eastern Races – their [sic] is no other Race left for God to work His will in & upon the world except ours; that is I think grounds enough, to keep Peace & to foster *mutual* recognition & *reciprocity* in all what draws us together & to sink everything, which could part us! The Press is awful on both sides, but here it has nothing to say, for I am the sole arbiter & master of German Foreign Policy & the Government & Country *must* follow me, even if I have to face the musik! [sic] May Your Government never forget this & never place me in the jeopardy to have to choose a course which could be a misfortune to both them & us!'[13] The King sent extracts from this 'remarkable' letter to the Foreign Secretary, Lord Lansdowne, who at once forwarded them to the Prime Minister, Lord Salisbury, commenting to the King: 'The friendliness of His Imperial Majesty's tone is satisfactory, but the last sentence is certainly significant.'[14]

Shortly afterwards the King received a second letter from the Kaiser which was scarcely calculated to dispel the growing mistrust of the London government. Like the letter of 30 December, it contained an unmistakable threat that seems to foreshadow Bülow's unfortunate speech attacking Joseph Chamberlain a few days later, with its reference to biting on granite. 'Hoping that by dint of soothing and calming the more turbulent sons of my Fatherland & their Press, I had at last with great efforts managed to get the Papers quiet here. You may well imagine with what dismay & very deep regret I read the last speech of the most illadvised Colonial Secretary. It is a conglomeration of bluff, overbearing and secret insult to the other nations at large, which will do a great deal of harm, provoking sharp repartees & creating unnecessary uneasiness all over the world. It was a most unlucky thing to do, & if he does not stop these elucubrations, which he suddenly likes to spring on mankind in general, one fine day he will wake up to see his country in the greatest of muddles ever yet seen.'[15]

Bülow chose exactly this delicate moment to pour more fuel on the flames. Although ten weeks had passed since Chamberlain's Edinburgh speech, on 8 January 1902 the Reich Chancellor made a speech in the Reichstag recommending the German public, in connection with the British minister's critical remarks, to heed the words of Frederick the Great: 'Let the man be and don't get excited, he's biting on granite.'[16] Encouraged by this, the anti-Semitic deputy Liebermann von Sonnenberg castigated the British army in South Africa as 'a mob of thieves and robbers' and declared Chamberlain, who until lately had counted among the most high-profile advocates of an Anglo-German alliance, to be the 'most villainous knave on God's earth'.[17] Holstein thought the 'granite-biting speech' was the 'first major mistake' that Bülow had made. At first he expressed suspicion that the Chancellor might have made his speech in order that 'a rapprochement with England would be rendered impossible for the time being'.[18] Later he took the view that internal political reasons had prompted Bülow's action, which Holstein described as 'the Krüger Telegram on a small scale'. In any case the speech had had a damaging effect abroad, he concluded, and this in turn might put a strain on Bülow's relations with the Kaiser, above all 'once H.M. is affected by these repercussions, for example if the English visits cease'.[19]

In London Bülow's speech caused consternation. At court and in Downing Street it was assumed that Wilhelm II had seen the text in advance and must therefore have approved it.[20] The question was raised as to whether in the circumstances it was at all possible for the Prince of Wales to go to Berlin for the Kaiser's birthday.[21] Asked by the King what the Reich Chancellor's remarks meant, Lansdowne replied that he had read the speech 'with concern and surprise, for I had certainly supposed that, if there had ever been occasion for taking notice of Mr. Chamberlain's speech in the Reichstag, that occasion had passed by. This gratuitous resuscitation of the question has been most unfortunate. I regret the whole tone of the speech, and the ambiguous reference to assurances received from the other side is most mischievous.' He promised to convey the King's enquiry to the Prime Minister and discuss with him what should be done.[22] A diplomat spoke for many in Downing Street when he remarked sarcastically that he expected Metternich to put in an appearance soon with assurances of Bülow's unalterable devotion to Great Britain. 'The persistent way in which the Germans kick us in the street and kiss us in the cupboard is becoming tedious.'[23]

Lascelles did his best to smooth matters over. He cast doubts on the supposition that Wilhelm had known of Bülow's speech. 'I am convinced that the Emperor wishes to be on good terms with us, but he has not much confidence in the Govt. Public opinion is still very much against us, and I am afraid there is little hope of its changing until the war is over. Bülow's speech was not over friendly and will no doubt be resented in England but his position vis a vis of the Reichstag was not an easy one, and he no doubt thought it necessary to pose as the champion of the German army.' The ambassador urged strongly that the Prince of Wales's visit should go ahead. The Chancellor had meanwhile repudiated Liebermann's attacks on Chamberlain and the British army, and in a second speech he had publicly reaffirmed the wish for a good understanding with Great Britain, a country that had never waged war against Germany. 'I should be sorry if anything should be done at which the Emperor could take offence. It is true that he has more than once expressed his disapproval of the actions of the government, but he has never faltered in his expressions of friendship for the King and the Royal Family.'[24]

Although personally hurt by the British press attacks, for his part Wilhelm took steps to bring about reconciliation. He declared his intention of conferring the honorary command of a Prussian regiment on the Prince of Wales when he came to Berlin. He invited Lascelles and his sister and daughter to the Neues Palais again and impressed upon him that 'although he is hurt at the outburst of indignation in the English press which he regarded as directed against himself', he set great store by good relations between the two countries. Lascelles replied 'that although he was not surprised at the outburst which Count Bülow's first speech had occasioned in England, he had been disappointed that His Excellency's second speech, which he was convinced was intended to be friendly, should have been so unfavourably received.' The ambassador repeated his request that the Prince's visit be allowed to take place as planned. 'Sir Frank has no doubt that The Emperor will speak to the Prince of Wales with the frankness and openness which are habitual to him, and he hopes and believes that His Royal Highness will receive the impression that His Majesty, in spite of the criticisms in which he will probably indulge with regard to the action of some of Your Majesty's Ministers, and the conduct of the war in South Africa, is not only in favour of a good understanding with us, but is also convinced that this happy result will one day be attained.'[25]

King Edward did not at all agree with the conciliatory attitude of his ambassador.[26] He decided to write to the Kaiser himself expressing his opinion bluntly and threatening to cancel his son's visit unless Wilhelm apologised. He told his nephew 'that since reading the violent speeches which have been made quite recently in the Reichstag against England, and especially against my Colonial Minister and my army, which shows such a strong feeling of animosity against my Country, I think that under the circumstances it would be better for him not to go where he is liable to be insulted or be treated by the Public in a manner which I feel sure no one would regret more than yourself. It is very painful to me to have to write this, but I feel I have no other alternative. I regret also to read in the last paragraph of your letter of the 6th Instant, a very strong remark you make concerning Mr. Chamberlain, and, the speech to which you allude is I presume the one made on October 25th last year at Edinburgh. You are I am sure far too sensible, and know England too well, not to feel certain that he had not the slightest intention of saying anything disparaging to your fine and brave army. However the German Press took it up violently, and distorted to a great extent what he said. I had hoped that your Chancellor Count von Bülow would have explained to the Reichstag that, as Lord Lansdowne repeatedly told Count Metternich, Mr Chamberlain's words were not only not intended to reflect upon the armies of Germany, but that they appeared to my Government quite incapable of the interpretation which had been placed upon them. Unfortunately, however, he acted otherwise. Ever since my accession, now nearly a year ago, I have had but one desire, my dear William, and that is that our two Countries should "pull well" together in spite of the strong Boer feeling in yours, which, however, they have a perfect right to express without heaping insults on my brave army, of which you are a Field Marshal, and accusing them of having committed the horrors in South Africa with which they have been so unjustly charged. I must express my deep regret that these gross libels on my army should, as far as I am aware, have received no check or discouragement from your Government.' The King followed these hard words by expressing his pleasure at Wilhelm's proposal to make him an Admiral in the Germany navy; and as a birthday present, he said, he was sending a copy of the portrait of Frederick the Great which hung at Windsor.[27]

As soon as the King's letter arrived in Berlin on 16 January 1902, Lascelles forwarded it to the Neues Palais,[28] but told the King's Private Secretary frankly that he was sure the King's decision to forbid his son's visit to Berlin would bitterly disappoint the Kaiser. He could not but fear, he said, that the Kaiser would take offence at the King's assertion that the Prince of Wales might be insulted by the massed Berlin rabble. Furthermore, in his letter Wilhelm had not protested against Chamberlain's speech of the previous October, but against the most recent speech by the minister in Birmingham, in which Chamberlain had not thought fit to mention foreign Powers at all. 'I have frequently noticed in my conversations with the Emperor that he especially resents being treated, as he is in the habit of expressing it, as a "quantité négligeable", and the idea ... that he has been so treated, may perhaps explain the intemperate language in which he indulged in his letter to the King.' He, Lascelles, had argued from the beginning that the Prince of Wales's visit could do much good. 'I fear that its postponement will deeply wound the Emperor and will be commented on in the Press in a manner which will make the re-establishment of really friendly relations between our two Countries more difficult.' Although it was not impossible that the cancellation of the visit might give the German government a salutary shock, he feared that it might lead, if not to an outright break, then at least to a period of tension which would be in the interest neither of Germany nor of Britain.[29]

Just as he had done twelve years earlier, after the Vienna incident,[30] Lord Salisbury felt compelled to draw attention to the dangers of a quarrel between uncle and nephew. He wrote to the King on 22 January 1902 saying that much would depend on how Wilhelm II reacted to his letter. 'Of course he may reply to Your Majesty's letter by some kind of overture, which You can accept. If he does it will be the most satisfactory outcome.' Salisbury was afraid, however, that the Kaiser would not reply to his uncle's warning at all. If Prince George then went to Berlin after all, the German press would interpret this as a climb-down by the British, and British public opinion would respond accordingly. But if the visit was cancelled it would mean an open breach. The Prime Minister judiciously advised that if Wilhelm did not react appropriately to the King's letter, the Prince of Wales should resort to a 'diplomatic illness': a telegram could be sent on the Friday saying 'that H.R.H. has a bad cold, and fears that he will be unable to accept the Emperor's hospitality on Tuesday. Your Majesty does not need to be told that this is an ordinary diplomatic device — when it is desired to be absent from any ceremony for any public reason, without openly giving offence. Lord Salisbury does not suggest this course as wholly satisfactory: but it is preferable to any other that can be pursued. It avoids an open breach on the one side: on the other it evades any appearance of submissiveness to an insult.'[31]

Events seemed to confirm Salisbury's supposition that the Kaiser might simply ignore his uncle's letter and continue ostentatiously with preparations for the Prince of Wales's visit. During the memorial service in the English church at Potsdam on 22 January, the anniversary of Queen Victoria's death, a remarkable altercation took place between Wilhelm II and Lascelles. The ambassador had been surprised to see that preparations for the Prince of Wales's visit were going ahead, and asked the Kaiser whether he had not received the King's letter. The Kaiser claimed not to have seen any such letter and said it must have got lost on the way from Berlin to Potsdam. After the service Lascelles told the Kaiser what the letter had said and gave him the copy which had been sent for his own information. After reading it the Kaiser declared, with some agitation, that 'it was really a fatality which had caused that particular letter to go astray. He betrayed considerable irritation, and talked about another Fashoda and the possibility of having to recall Count Metternich.' Lascelles intervened to point out that 'if His Majesty recalled his Ambassador in England, my Mission would at once come to an end ... I reminded His Majesty that on my arrival at Berlin, I had warned both Count Buelow and Baron von Richthofen that the irritation in England in consequence of the violent abuse which had been lavished upon us for the last three years, had become very acute, and might become dangerous, and that I had repeated this to His Majesty himself at the first interview which I had with him at Potsdam. His Majesty nodded assent. I then said that Count Buelow's first speech had appeared to me to be distinctly unfriendly, and that I had told Herr von Mühlberg that he must be prepared for a sharp retort from England.' The indignation at this first speech had been so great that his second intervention in the Reichstag had been seen there as inadequate, indeed even as an aggravation of the first. 'The Emperor protested loudly against this interpretation of Count Buelow's language and said that the German phrase "Sie wissen zu sterben" conveys to a German mind the very highest compliment to soldiers.'[32] Later in the conversation, however, Wilhelm signalled that he was ready to make some concession in order to enable the Prince's visit to go ahead after all. For the Prince of Wales not to appear, now that all the German princes had been invited to Berlin and all the preparations had been made, would be 'a most serious matter'. The Kaiser promised to take every possible step to trace the King's letter and answer it.[33]

Lansdowne was relieved to be able to forward the ambassador's telegram to the King with the comment that the Kaiser was evidently prepared for some kind of 'overture'. Edward insisted, however, that he could do nothing further

until the Kaiser had acknowledged receipt of his letter and apologised.[34] In his
opinion the story that the letter had got lost could not be given the slightest
credence, particularly as Lascelles had been sent a receipt for it. The ambassador was instructed, through Lansdowne, to make clear to the Kaiser that the
King would give permission for his son's journey only if Wilhelm wrote or
telegraphed to him asking for it; furthermore he must guarantee that the
Prince would not be subjected to any unpleasantness in Berlin. 'Of course the
Emperor's letter must not be in any way aggressive or offensive in its tone.'[35]

Before these instructions arrived in Berlin Lascelles received a visit from
Wilhelm II, who read out to him a letter to the King which he wished to send
to London that evening by special courier. According to the ambassador's
report of the fast-moving events of the afternoon of 22 January 1902,
'At about two o'clock the Emperor sent me a message through the telephone
that the missing letter had been found. At half past three he sent me a further
message that he had not yet seen Count Buelow, who was engaged at the
Reichstag, and must therefore postpone his visit, which he would make
without fail in the course of the afternoon. He arrived at the Embassy at a
quarter before seven, and read me the letter which, after consultation with
Count Buelow, he had addressed to the King.' Wilhelm let it be known that it
had not been easy for him to win over the Reich Chancellor to his conciliatory
course of action. 'Count Buelow had at first expressed considerable indignation
at the construction which had been put upon his speeches, and at the slight to
the Emperor which the abandonment of the Prince of Wales' visit would
imply, but His Majesty had persuaded him that a further attempt should be
made to prevent a rupture between our two countries. He asked me whether
I thought the letter would have the desired effect, and I replied that I believed
it would.'[36]

Although the original of Wilhelm's letter cannot be traced in the Royal
Archives in Windsor, we know through both Lascelles and Metternich what it
said. The Kaiser dismissed as unfounded his uncle's fears about hostility
towards Britain in Germany, defended both speeches by Bülow and emphasised his own pro-British policy. In particular, his two visits to England, his
refusal to receive ex-President Krüger and the fact that he had conferred the
Order of the Black Eagle on Lord Roberts, 'all of which had caused dissatisfaction and considerable criticism in Germany', were proofs of his goodwill.
There was no danger of any unpleasantness towards the Prince of Wales from
the crowd in Berlin, the Kaiser continued, for 'No German would think of
insulting one of His Majesty's guests and the son of a great and powerful King.
He hopes that the King will not be influenced by the German press which is
constantly attacking the Government but which has no real significance as he

himself is the master in Germany (and) directs the foreign policy of the country. He concludes', according to Lascelles's résumé of the letter, 'by saying that the abandonment now of the Prince of Wales' visit would not only cause him great pain but would be considered by the public as a personal offence to him for which it would be difficult to find an explanation'.[37] The relief in London at this outcome was palpable.[38] The Prince of Wales arrived in Berlin, as planned, on the evening of 25 January. In a conversation with Bülow about the anger that his Reichstag speech had caused in Britain he did not mince his words.[39] An acute crisis in Anglo-German relations had been averted through the Kaiser's concession on the question of the visit, yet the mutual distrust was by now so deep-rooted that a rupture seemed possible at any time.

EDWARD VII′S POSTPONED CORONATION AND THE CRISIS IN ANGLO-GERMAN RELATIONS

At the end of February 1902 Metternich sent the Reich Chancellor an urgent warning of the rapidly growing distrust towards Germany that was apparent at all levels of British society. 'Mr Chamberlain's power has increased enormously, and there are people who see in him the next Prime Minister. Right now he is supposed to be very angry with us ... When talking over the development of German-English relations with politician friends, I find nearly everywhere the opinion that while *a good deal of irritation* [in English in the original] with Germany was the predominant feeling at present, this was only *skin-deep* [in English in the original] and would disappear again. Amongst the English people there was no real hostility towards us. On the other hand I do find a strongly-marked anti-German trend in all political publications, newspapers and reviews. Wherever something can be found which can be interpreted to the disadvantage of Germany or as a weakening of her alliance system, it is being joyfully exploited, as if there could be no greater political boon for England than a weakening of Germany. And these attacks in the Press are particularly directed against your person ... The only thing which to some extent still preserves the much loosened bond between Germany and England is the person of H.M. the Kaiser. If the force of circumstances should ever make H.M. oppose England publicly on some issue at dispute, I am firmly convinced that the last bond would be broken. We would have to reckon with England's declared enmity for a generation. England for her part would not consider at all the question whether we could inflict more damage on England than she could on us. For the moment I would summarise the general situation by the saying: "I wouldn't give twopence for Anglo-German relations" [in English in the original].'[40]

Metternich repeatedly drew attention to the possibility that Britain might come to an accommodation with Russia, France and Italy.[41]

In this tense state of affairs Wilhelm once again tried to bring his close relationship with the British royal family into play. He congratulated the King on the Anglo-Japanese alliance and asserted hypocritically that in Germany everyone regarded it as 'a guarantee of peace in the East'. He described the warm reception given to his brother Prince Heinrich in the United States as proof that Lord Salisbury's prediction of a 'union among the Teutonic Races' was at last beginning to come true.[42] But even in the closest family circle there seemed to be no end to the succession of squabbles.[43] The Kaiser was particularly enraged by Edward VII's decision to hand over Osborne House on the Isle of Wight, which cost millions to maintain, to the nation.[44] The place where Wilhelm had spent so many happy childhood days in the heart of the British royal family, and where his grandmother had died only a year ago, was to be turned into a college for naval cadets and a convalescent home for military and naval officers, while the reception rooms and terrace were to be opened to the public. He thought his uncle's plan 'downright shameless and outrageous'.[45] Princess Louise, Duchess of Argyll, Wilhelm's aunt, suggested to her brother the King that he give Osborne House to the Kaiser as a summer residence, but Edward VII turned down the idea as impracticable.[46] One cannot help wondering what would have happened if the King had agreed to his sister's suggestion. Would relations between the two royal families have become warmer as a result, or would the greater proximity merely have brought greater friction? How would statesmen, newspapers and peoples on either side of the North Sea have reacted to the Kaiser's ostentatious 'Anglomania'? Merely to ask such questions leads one into the realms of fantasy.

In May 1902 the Boer War showed signs of coming to an end. Wilhelm II heard through private contacts in South Africa that the Boers were ready to accept the British peace conditions, and telegraphed to the King sending him this news.[47] Edward thanked him for his 'most important Telegram', of which he immediately informed his government.[48] Four weeks later the Kaiser was able to send the King his congratulations on the peace treaty, adding that his uncle would know, from the way Wilhelm had followed all phases of the war with 'anxiety and sympathetic interest', how genuine a pleasure he took in its conclusion.[49] He wrote to Lascelles later the same night: 'Your letter just received in going to bed. Heaven be praised for these glad tidings! After all you see I was quite well informed when a month ago I told you about proposals for peace and their probable acceptance.'[50]

Edward VII's coronation, which had been due to take place on 26 June 1902 in Westminster Abbey, had to be postponed when the King suffered an attack of acute appendicitis and had an emergency operation. The German deputation which had already arrived in London for the ceremony included two men to whom the Kaiser had entrusted the task of putting Anglo-German relations on a better footing: Field Marshal Count Alfred von Waldersee and Count Götz von Seckendorff, the confidant of the late Empress Frederick. Both regarded the ailing King as comparatively pro-German, reason enough for them to wish him a speedy recovery.[51] It was all the more imperative to build up a good relationship with Britain, as Waldersee now put it, because Germany had 'gradually managed to reach the point of having not a single reliable friend'.[52]

The decision to send the anglophobic Field Marshal, of all people, to London, arose from an urgent plea from Metternich, the German ambassador. He recommended that in order to take the sting out of the anti-German feeling that was provoked, above all, by the violent attacks in the German press on British behaviour in the war in South Africa, Waldersee should make some favourable comment in public on this sensitive theme.[53] The Kaiser took up this suggestion and on 22 June 1902, at a dinner given by the British Commander in Chief, Lord Roberts, Waldersee read out a speech drafted by the German embassy in which the 'humanity' of the British conduct towards the Boers was acknowledged. 'It was a strange feeling for me to be expected to say such things', Waldersee recalled, 'as I am quite convinced that acts of cruelty and callousness have indeed been committed by the English army. But when the Kaiser bids me do so in the national interest, I cannot well do otherwise, and I must simply put up with the hostile attacks to which I shall be subjected at home because of it.'[54] Nevertheless Waldersee showed more understanding for the British conduct of the war than most of its critics. Shortly after his return from East Asia he expressed the opinion that the British were undoubtedly waging 'a deliberate war of extermination' in South Africa, and that the full extent of their 'cruelties and atrocities' would probably not come to light until later; on the other hand, however, it should not be forgotten 'that in 1870, starting with Sedan, we shot many franctireurs, and particularly in the Loire campaign and the operation at Le Mans we burned down numerous farms and also whole villages as punitive measures'. In China too, German military operations could be held responsible for the deaths of many innocent people.[55]

Thanks to his special connection with the British royal family Seckendorff was in a position to offer the Kaiser, in a 'strictly confidential' letter, unusual insights into the prevailing mood in London and into the concerns of the court at Windsor. The relationship of Great Britain to the German Reich, he said, was that of 'an old, civilising Great Power that is on the way down, to a young, strong and powerful nation which intrudes and competes everywhere where England formerly commanded and ruled alone and without competition, especially in the sphere of commercial policy. In addition, when one compares the two, the Germans undoubtedly show greater efficiency, sobriety and skill in adapting to the new circumstances. The comfortable life enjoyed by too many people has made the English soft. Jealousy on the one hand, on the other a sense of being insufficiently respected and recognised, and yet feeling superior. At the same time the press on both sides consciously and unconsciously stirs up hatred, as is happening here at the moment through a correspondent of the Times [Saunders] ... who openly preaches war against both Panslavism and Pan-Germany. – In these circumstances it is difficult to make use of the good relations between the two Royal Families. Yr Majesty knows how favourably inclined King Edward has become towards Yr Majesty. We must all hope that God grants him a long life. I have no justification for claiming that the heir to the throne cherishes anti-German sentiments – but so it is said ... Yr Majesty's name is revered by all, both high and low, but also feared, and as everything that Germany does or does not do is watched, Yr Majesty cannot but be aware that even the most trivial news travels from London via Copenhagen, Petersburg, Greece, Coburg etc. The whole population remembers with gratitude that Yr Majesty paid the last honours to Queen Victoria.' Seckendorff concluded by suggesting that portraits of Kaiser Friedrich III and his wife should be hung in the German embassy in Carlton House Terrace.[56]

The hopes of the Kaiser and the Chancellor for better relations with Britain received a fillip when the elderly Lord Salisbury retired on 12 July 1902 and his nephew, Arthur James Balfour, took over as Prime Minister. In a letter to Wilhelm II on 22 July Bülow expressed confidence 'that we shall get along better with Balfour than with his fat uncle, whose arrogance and Gallomania made it so difficult to establish a good relationship between us and England'.[57] The Reich Chancellor had no inkling, even two weeks later, that his master was planning to make an ostentatious gesture to improve Anglo-German relations.[58]

Wilhelm sent his brother Heinrich to represent him at the coronation, which finally took place on 9 August 1902, after Edward VII's recovery, and entrusted him with a very affectionate letter to the King. In it he expressed the wish to visit the King and Queen at Sandringham in the autumn. Edward willingly agreed and suggested 8–15 November, the King's birthday being on 9 November.[59] Wilhelm's dignified appearance at the unveiling of a statue of his mother in Bad Homburg also helped improve relations between the two monarchs.[60]

   The necessity, but perhaps also the futility, of such efforts by the monarchs
to achieve better relations is demonstrated by the reports of the German
chargé d'affaires in London, Freiherr von Eckardstein, at this time. On
14 September 1902 he described a recent meeting with Joseph Chamberlain,
who as a result of his great popularity had acquired an 'almost impregnably
dominant' position and was exercising an even stronger influence on British
policy in the new Cabinet than in Salisbury's government. Moreover he
controlled a major part of the London press, which inevitably followed his
lead. In the course of their conversation, Eckardstein reported, the Colonial
Secretary, who in the past had been emphatically pro-German, 'gave vent to
his rancour against Germany'. The 'vehemence' with which Chamberlain
spoke revealed that 'his ill-humour towards Germany was much more deep-
rooted and dangerous' than Eckardstein had assumed. The 'uncontrolled
outbursts of hatred against England' during the Boer War, Chamberlain said,
had shown him and his Cabinet colleagues the mortal danger threatening
their country from Germany. 'Apparently the idea had taken hold among the
German people that in the course of time Germany would have no difficulty
in bringing about the fall of England and her colonial Empire and in taking
over England's entire heritage herself.' British policy must henceforth take
account of 'the reality of an apparently unconquerable hatred towards England
on the part of the German nation', and the British people too, 'at all levels of
society, both in the mother country and in the colonies' were 'filled with such
hatred towards Germany that every Ministry ... for a long time to come'
would have to reckon with this factor. 'Of course no English statesman in his
right mind would think of suddenly starting a war with Germany. Any
provocation on the part of Germany ... would, however, put John Bull in
such a "temper" that no English cabinet would be able to resist it.' In 1896, at
the time of the Krüger telegram, war had been close, but in those days it had
been no more than 'a hysterical flare-up' of public opinion. Now, on the other
hand, distrust of Germany was so widespread and profound that even a minor
provocation would suffice 'to set everything on fire'. Chamberlain himself
hoped that it would never come to war between Germany and England, for a
conflict would be extremely harmful to both countries in the long run. But if
war should nevertheless come, England would be able to find at least one, if
not several, allies on the continent, even at the last moment. Chamberlain
went on to warn Eckardstein that the Kaiser's forthcoming visit to England
would not bring about any change in British public opinion, for 'antipathy
towards the German nation had already become too deep-rooted in all sections
of the population'. Kaiser Wilhelm, by now convinced that he had achieved
an understanding between the 'two great continental coalitions', the Triple

Alliance and the Dual Alliance, was unperturbed, annotating Eckardstein's report with optimistic remarks and concluding calmly, 'however furiously the grape-juice seethes, it will still only become wine'. Nonetheless he ordered this worrying information to be forwarded to the Chief of the General Staff, Count Schlieffen.[61]

THE QUARREL OVER THE RECEPTION OF THE BOER GENERALS

The 'provocation' which Chamberlain had predicted was not long in coming, and it brought Germany and Britain to the brink of serious conflict. In spite of warnings from Holstein, who considered it 'folly', Bülow suggested to the Kaiser on 17 September 1902 that he should grant an audience to the three Boer generals, De Wet, Botha and De la Rey, who had been received by Edward VII in August and were now planning a tour on the continent.[62] Wilhelm agreed on condition that the audience was arranged through the British ambassador, as the Boers were now British subjects.[63] What was already an explosive situation became even more dangerous when on 24 September the three generals issued a proclamation on behalf of the impoverished Boers containing bitter attacks on Britain.[64] When Lascelles informed London of Wilhelm II's intention to receive the Boer leaders, Edward VII instructed him to tell the Kaiser that this step, shortly before his visit to England, would be 'very unpopular'.[65] The British government – in contrast to the King – went so far as to reject the compromise suggested by Wilhelm that the audience should be sought through the British ambassador. The Kaiser's wish to receive the Boer deputation, they argued, was chiefly for internal political reasons, and was not at all in Britain's interest; nor, therefore, should the country's diplomatic representative be involved in arranging the audience.[66]

When the news of the planned audience for the generals in Berlin became public knowledge the British press 'went wild', as Holstein observed.[67] Eckardstein, who was running the London embassy in Metternich's absence, reported on 4 October 1902 on the 'widespread agitation' of public opinion there. 'The news that signatories of the manifesto are shortly to be received by His Majesty the Kaiser has . . . caused a fresh outbreak of the ill-humour and antipathy against Germany which were provoked by the events of the war and had hardly begun to calm down.'[68] Eckardstein thought it questionable that the Kaiser's journey to Sandringham could go ahead if the audience took place. His reports even mentioned the possibility of war with England, Holstein recorded.[69]

This time Edward VII proved more conciliatory than his ministers. He rejected a draft telegram to Lascelles, saying that he should not under any circumstances seek an audience for the Boer generals. Instead the King insisted on his earlier proposal that Lascelles should personally introduce the generals to the Kaiser and attend the audience himself. This would underline the status of the Boers as British subjects and avert an Anglo-German crisis. For the generals to be received without the ambassador being present would certainly, on the other hand, have a 'deplorable' effect in England.[70]

In Germany, too, strenuous efforts were made to find a diplomatic way out of the dilemma. Metternich, who was in Berlin at the time, put it to Lascelles on behalf of the Wilhelmstrasse that the best solution would be for the generals not to come to Germany at all; the ambassador should find some way of persuading them to cancel their visit. If they nevertheless came to Berlin, it would in fact be advantageous if Lascelles presented them to the Kaiser and remained with them during the audience. 'This would prevent their German friends from making capital in an anti-English sense . . . and disarm people in England who object to their reception by the Emperor.' If the ambassador should refuse to introduce the generals to the Kaiser, however, Wilhelm II would be faced with the dilemma of whether to receive them or not. An audience in these circumstances would be well perceived in Germany but very unpopular in England. If the Kaiser did not receive them, many people in Germany would accuse him of giving in to pressure from England because he did not want to risk the cancellation of his forthcoming visit. After all, the Kaiser was the best friend England had in Germany, and the English must think carefully about whether they wanted to confront him with such a difficult choice.[71] To everyone's relief the Boer generals, now in Holland, put themselves in the wrong with a declaration on 7 October 1902 that they could not themselves propose an audience with the Kaiser, but must be invited by the Kaiser himself.[72] With great presence of mind Holstein telegraphed to The Hague saying that this proclamation put an end to the question of an audience. A similar statement appeared the same day in the *Norddeutsche Allgemeine Zeitung*. Bülow thanked the Councillor sincerely for having sprung the trap for him.[73]

In fact the Kaiser, who was staying at Rominten in East Prussia, had already decided a few days earlier not to allow the audience to take place. Far from stubbornly insisting for a long time that he would receive the Boer generals, as Eckardstein later claimed,[74] Wilhelm II had accepted Bülow's proposal on the matter 'without any enthusiasm'.[75] On 3 October Bülow learned of the serious reservations which the Kaiser had about the audience. They arose principally from 'the concerns of Admiral Tirpitz, who had just left Rominten, about the threat to our overseas interests and in particular to the continuation of our fleet-building programme in the event of disputes with England', but the

Kaiser's planned visit to England had also influenced his attitude.[76] Two days later Wilhelm sent a frank telegram to Edward VII from Rominten putting the decision on whether to receive the generals entirely into the King's hands. 'As the three Farmer Boer Generals want to tour in Germany and may not improbably ask for audience I have ordered Government to privately enquire in London whether you countenance this idea, or are adverse [sic] to it. As they are your subjects they must apply through Sir Frank for reception: should he decline by your orders, there is an end of the matter. Should he accede I would see them informally and leave them in no doubt that they have to keep quiet in my country as I shall not stand any anti-British nonsense for a minute.'[77] Eckardstein's report on the agitated mood in England reached him while he was still in East Prussia, whereupon he took the decision on his own initiative not to receive the generals. Revealingly, he wrote at the top of the document: 'Under these circumstances the audience will not take place for I am the only one who is still holding the English back; otherwise they will break out too soon and my fleet is not ready. It is much better if the Engl[ish] government refuses, and we act accordingly!'[78] When the Boer generals were received a few days later in Paris by President Émile Loubet, the Prime Minister, Émile Combes and the Foreign Minister, Théophile Delcassé, the Kaiser showed that he fully understood the indignation in England and gave orders in a marginal comment that 'No member of my Government or civil service official is to get involved with the Boers, see them or take part in events arranged for them. The same applies to military officers, who are to be informed of this through the Military Cabinet. It would be better if they could be advised not to come to Berlin.'[79]

With the decision of both the Kaiser and the Wilhelmstrasse against an audience for the Boer leaders the worst of the crisis was over, but the anger of public opinion in both countries was to continue to reverberate for a long time to come. 'For as long as I have known England', Count Metternich reported from London, 'I have never experienced such bitterness against another nation as that directed against us today'.[80] As predicted, Wilhelm's decision not to receive the generals was sharply criticised by the German press, which in turn was commented upon in England 'in the most shameless way'. Naturally, as Waldersee noted on 12 October 1902, the English hate campaign would then give rise to 'still more resentment here at home'.[81] Eckardstein came to Berlin and was said to have told the Kaiser that 'the English would attack us some time within the next five years'.[82] Wilhelm complained peevishly to Bülow 'that he was misunderstood by the German people as well as by the English, and that nothing was being done in the German Press to enlighten the two nations'.[83] Since this incident the relationship of trust between Wilhelm II and Bülow had deteriorated. Holstein again described the Reich Chancellor as 'very nervous', because he was aware that in England he was considered 'the main obstacle to a German–English rapprochement'.[84] 'Bülow has lost his nerve', the Councillor wrote on 11 November 1902, while the Kaiser was staying with his uncle at Sandringham. 'He has only now realised how completely he has failed to persuade the Kaiser to take an anti-English line, and he has finally seen what he has done with his Chamberlain speech. For the first time he seems to fear that he is becoming estranged from the Kaiser. That is why he is keeping absolutely still . . . and is only concerned with what might annoy the Kaiser.'[85]

THE KAISER'S VISIT TO SANDRINGHAM IN NOVEMBER 1902

Against the background of popular agitation Kaiser Wilhelm and King Edward did their best to pour oil on troubled waters by demonstrating as much harmony as possible during their time together at Sandringham. As Wilhelm's visit from 8 to 15 November 1902 was classed as 'private', he was accompanied by neither the Reich Chancellor nor a representative of the Auswärtiges Amt. Nevertheless the political significance of the meeting of the two monarchs was unmistakable, and Edward had seen to it that the Kaiser would meet the most influential British statesmen at his home in Norfolk. The Prime Minister, Arthur Balfour, Joseph Chamberlain, Field Marshal Lord Roberts, the Secretary of State for War St John Brodrick and other leading personalities were invited as guests.[86]

On the first full day of his stay, the King's birthday, Kaiser Wilhelm seized the opportunity to convey to Balfour the necessity of a strong German navy and try to influence him towards Anglo-German cooperation in *Weltpolitik*. As Metternich reported in a telegram to Bülow from Sandringham on 9 November, the Kaiser explained the German fleet-building programme to the Prime Minister 'from a new viewpoint'. He maintained that 'while England constituted a complete national entity within its own confines, Germany resembled a mosaic picture in which the separate elements were still plainly visible and not yet fused together. This was also evident in the army, which was certainly imbued with the same patriotic spirit, but which was formed of contingents from the different states. The young German Empire, however, needed institutions in which it could see the unified idea of Empire clearly embodied. One such institution was the Navy. The Kaiser had command over it, Germans from all regions flocked to it, and it was a constant, living example of the unity of the Empire. For this reason alone it was necessary and it therefore had a warm advocate in His Majesty. In the course of the conversation, His Majesty went on to repudiate the foolish notion that we were building a fleet in order to attack others. He had no interest at all in gaining or losing a few palm trees in the tropics. Such questions of colonial borders could always be settled easily, with a little goodwill. We had enough distant territorial possessions to exercise and perfect our colonising capacities for a long time to come. The English were two hundred years ahead of us in their skill at colonisation. We still had to learn and we still had plenty to do in order to make good use of our colonies.'[87] Whether Balfour gave credence to the 'philosophical' exposition of the Kaiser's beliefs is open to doubt.

Three days later, after conversations with Lansdowne,[88] Chamberlain and other guests of the King at Sandringham, Kaiser Wilhelm sent Bülow a long telegram that was hardly calculated to dispel the anxieties of his increasingly 'nervous' Reich Chancellor. He had tried to make it clear to Chamberlain, the Kaiser wrote, that Bülow was regarded in Germany as pro-English and was even mocked as 'Lord Bülow ... But it did not have the desired effect. He is very angry with Your Excellency and the "Ministers" in general; he seems to be personally under the impression that he has been outrageously duped, and therefore feels injured, and this is the mood in which he judges our entire policy and our actions. This anger is reflected in the newspaper articles which he influences directly or indirectly, and it has transferred itself to a stubborn section of the population. That is a great pity, but nothing can be done about it at the moment. His authority is absolute, he is all-powerful in England and *all* classes of the people are absolutely behind him. The Ministry dances to his tune, does nothing important without him, and *never* does anything against him. In these circumstances it is vitally important, firstly to keep our press under strict control – for people here will not tolerate much more – and secondly, in foreign policy, to do nothing else that could cause unnecessary friction and disputes between us and England ... My reception here cordial and kind as always. Population likewise warm and obliging and very polite, so that I personally am very satisfied. But I believe that people here distinguish between "the Kaiser" and "the German Government", and wish the latter would go to the devil; just as in Germany they distinguish between the King and Chamberlain, of whom the latter can likewise go to hell ... This is a true reflection of the impressions I have received here. They are disagreeable politically, and must be overcome with much patience, tact – including in the Auswärtiges Amt – and "holding the tongue" by our press. If that does not happen, there is a danger of very serious consequences suddenly arising. So we must be careful! Here they have thirty-five battleships in service, and we have eight!!, and by about 1905 there will be 196 battleships, cruisers and protected cruisers ready for service in England against our 46!'[89]

After Wilhelm's departure on 15 November 1902 the two monarchs exchanged warm letters of thanks as evidence of their new relationship.[90] The Kaiser was particularly struck by his uncle's suggestion that they should deal directly with each other in future, without the diplomats intervening. He underlined Edward's words: 'I trust that too long a time may not elapse ere we meet again as we can personally discuss so many matters together without the necessity of diplomatic notes!' In truth the King was relieved to be rid of his uncomfortable guest. 'Thank God he has gone', he is said to have exclaimed, according to Eckardstein.[91] He turned down a suggestion that he should visit Berlin the following year, commenting that this was 'unnecessary and much too soon, apart from the fact that it would entail another return visit from the Emperor!'[92]

Great Britain and her King had also, on several occasions in 1902, let the German Reich feel their power and put the proud and ambitious young Kaiser, who understood the importance of British supremacy at sea better than most of his ministers and better than the excitable German public, in his place. Suppressing his fury at patronising British attitudes, Wilhelm II uttered the professions of friendship which he considered necessary to gain time for the construction of the German battlefleet. He had no intention of tolerating British supremacy and the international order in Europe and the world which British naval power guaranteed, on a long-term basis. In court and political circles in Berlin Wilhelm's audacious objective was no secret. 'Yes, the fleet which we lack and which we need in order to confront England's arrogance "with an armed fist" – that is the bitter thought that constantly recurs whenever the Kaiser expresses his views', the Württemberg envoy, Axel Freiherr von Varnbüler, reported to Stuttgart in December 1901.[93] A little over a year later Varnbüler's sister, Hildegard Freifrau von Spitzemberg, heard through Bethmann Hollweg's son-in-law that the Kaiser's 'fundamental aim' was 'to break England's position in the world and give Germany the advantage', for which he needed to build a strong fleet.[94] In December 1903 Waldersee noted in his diary that Reich Chancellor von Bülow had casually told a close friend that 'in foreign policy what mattered was to avoid complications until the fleet had reached the strength the Kaiser was seeking to give it'.[95]

With hindsight the idea that a war fleet of sixty ships of the line could be built in the North Sea by 1920 without the British, Americans or French getting wind of it seems completely insane. And indeed we shall see how soon statesmen, diplomats and journalists of the Atlantic Powers recognised the political and military threat to their countries inherent in the Tirpitz Plan and how they reacted to it. The repercussions of the naval arms race which began around 1902 on international relations were all the more acute because for a considerable time other rivalries had led to growing suspicion of Germany in British and American public opinion: in particular, beside commercial competition and scarcely concealed aspirations towards hegemony on the continent, Germany's colonial ambitions in Africa and China, in the Near and Middle East, in Samoa, the Philippines, the Caribbean and South America. It was not long before Edward VII considered his unruly nephew, in spite of all his assurances of affection and familial feeling, as 'the bitterest foe' Britain had in the world.[96] The King successfully used his enormous prestige to help bring about a diplomatic revolution in Europe with the aim of halting the dangerous increase in the power of the Kaiserreich. The fact that in this endeavour Edward VII was able to rely on the support of the United States of America, whose statesmen, business and industrial leaders and journalists felt no less threatened by the 'German menace', proved to be of great international political significance.[97] The following chapter will be devoted to the engrossing theme of German–American relations under Wilhelm II.

CHAPTER NINE

The Kaiser and America

In early 1903, a year before his death, Field Marshal Count Alfred von Waldersee expressed consternation at the deep gulf which had opened up between the German Reich and the United States of America. 'That Germany should give America cause for concern is sheer nonsense, but unfortunately it is true; they see all kinds of ghosts and they are arming themselves for war at sea.'[1] Why this should have surprised him is hard to explain, since for years he had been keeping a detailed record in his diary of the deteriorating relations between Germany and the USA.[2] In his view, the responsibility for this development lay in no small measure with the Kaiser, who had given offence by trying to acquire one of the Philippine Islands during the Spanish–American war.[3] Waldersee knew that in the event of war the Reich would not be able to do much damage to such a distant opponent, and would in any case have nothing to gain. 'Even if we were victorious in a naval battle and could then perhaps pay New York a visit, what would we achieve in the long run?'[4] Nevertheless he did not rule out the possibility of a German–American war. In view of the increasingly hostile mood in the United States 'we must keep watch on all sides and be careful, but also have the energy to take the initiative at the right moment', he commented in 1899.[5]

The belief that the growing antagonism between the two countries could result in military conflict was entirely shared on the other side of the Atlantic. Leading American statesmen were not slow to recognise the danger to their interests represented by the German Reich's ambitions in Central and South America. As early as in 1897 the future President Theodore Roosevelt had resolutely declared, in line with the Monroe Doctrine, 'that we did not intend to have the Germans on this continent'. 'If Germany intended to extend her empire here, she would simply have to whip us first.'[6] Shortly after the turn of the century he expressed his suspicion that the German armed forces intended 'to take some steps in the West Indies or South America, which will make us either put up or shut up on the Monroe Doctrine'.[7] In spring 1901 Roosevelt wrote to the US ambassador in Rome, Georg von Lengerke-Meyer, of the 'extreme desirability of keeping Germany out of this hemisphere'. He was coming to the view, the President said, that 'Germany's attitude towards us makes her the only power with which there is any likelihood or possibility of our clashing within the future.' While American relations with Britain had fundamentally improved in the last four years, the German Reich had risen to be a 'great growing power', whose 'ambitions in extra-European matters' were now so far-reaching 'that she may clash with us'.[8] Given Wilhelm II's unpredictability, the influential Senator Henry Cabot Lodge also considered such assessments of German intentions 'well within the range of possibilities' and predicted in 1901 that if there were to be war between Germany and the United States, it would be sparked off by German attempts to annex territory in Brazil.[9] The American ambassador in Berlin, Andrew Dickson White, warned in June 1901 that 'in view of the spirit now evidently dormant in the mind of the Emperor and among many who stand very near him', German annexation attempts in Latin America were to be expected as soon as 'Germany shall have developed a fleet larger than that of the United States'.[10] At around this time the *Washington Post* expressed the opinion that the Kaiser's plans embraced not only South Brazil but the whole world. 'There is nothing too fantastic or too ambitious for his scheme of imperial expansion'; it was only that he did not yet have the power to accomplish his aims.[11]

Recent historical research has established beyond doubt that the Americans' 'concern' at German intentions were by no means a figment of their imagination. The leading authority on German–American relations in the Wilhelmine era, Ragnhild Fiebig-von Hase, after decades of work on the sources, has reached the conclusion that 'the Kaiser, Bülow, the Foreign Office, the accredited diplomats in the USA and Latin America and the naval authorities [were] convinced that if German expansionist aims in Latin America were to be achieved, confrontation with the USA was inevitable'.[12] If the German naval attaché in Washington, Herbert von Rebeur-Paschwitz, repeatedly drew attention to the march of American influence in the West Indies, Central and South America and argued that the Reich must make military preparations for potentially serious conflict with the USA, such sentiments were far from being his 'personal fantasies'; they were views that were wholeheartedly approved and shared in Berlin, above all by Kaiser Wilhelm II.[13] Fiebig-von Hase points out that in addition to the unification of Europe under German leadership, the penetration of the South American continent had been a constant aim of the Kaiser. She adds: 'It was here that the ultimate goals of the Kaiser's ambitions, reaching far beyond European hegemony, became clear.'[14]

For the biographer of the last German Kaiser the importance of this research can scarcely be overstated. One is astonished to discover here a hitherto virtually unsuspected 'new world' that reveals more than anything else the extent of Wilhelmine Germany's global ambitions. Not only did the Kaiser and the powerful elite which he had assembled around him aspire to unite the continent of Europe under German domination, not only did they seek to acquire colonies, bases and spheres of influence in Africa, the Middle East, China and the Pacific, but a German Empire was to be established even in Central and South America, if necessary at the cost of military conflict with the United States. Around the turn of the century the Kaiserreich was engaged, as we shall see, in a feverish search for naval bases in the Caribbean, to protect German commerce in the western hemisphere against American competition and to encourage more German emigration to Latin America. In the Admiralty Staff lunatic plans were concocted for war with the USA, culminating in a land attack on New York. The conflict of interests between Germany and the USA reached such a pitch that in December 1902 and again in January 1903 the German battlefleet and the US navy came close to attacking each other off Venezuela. As a result Imperial Germany came to be seen by American public opinion as the USA's most dangerous enemy. In an astonishing overestimation of his own powers, and completely failing to recognise the dangers involved, Kaiser Wilhelm II declared at the end of 1903: 'South America is our goal.'[15] Just how did the monarch and his advisers think they could achieve this objective, so distant in every way?

GEOPOLITICAL RIVALRY: 'SOUTH AMERICA IS OUR GOAL, OLD BOY!'

Given the strong emphasis he placed on the monarchical principle at home one is not surprised to discover that abroad, too, Wilhelm II saw himself as the champion of the old European monarchies against the republican upstart in North America. In the autumn of 1897, when war was about to break out between the United States and Spain, the Kaiser demanded intervention by all the European monarchies except the British against the rising 'young' republic. He wrote to the then newly appointed Foreign Secretary, Bernhard von Bülow, telling him that 'a note from all of us Continentals to Uncle Sam and John Bull' must be sent, stating that 'we stand by each other and would not tolerate Cuba being stolen from H.M. [Queen Maria of Spain]'. Such a step, Wilhelm said, 'would fulfil a double purpose. Firstly the villains will see from it that Europe's Kings really stand by each other and share sorrow and joy together, and have no intention of giving way to republican moneybags; secondly it would be a much more effective lever to promote and consolidate the continental union against America which the Tsar and I have planned.'[16]

The creation of a 'continental union against America' mentioned here by the Kaiser had been a recurring theme of his ambitions since he came to the throne. The second volume of this biography showed this central idea taking various forms: in 1892 Wilhelm II declared that the 'underlying thought' behind his policy was to establish a kind of 'Napoleonic supremacy' in Europe; a year later he told the heir to the Russian throne, Tsarevich Nicholas, that he wanted to bring the European monarchies together, above all because 'the Republic of North America was showing ever more inclination to seize all trade, including that of South America, for itself'; in 1894 he announced in the Prussian Ministry of State that the 'supremacy' of the German Reich must be brought to bear not only militarily but also in commercial policy. In other words, old Europe must close ranks against the USA to stop the latter cutting off Germany from her principal market, South America.[17] In September 1896 he openly courted the young Tsar's support for 'a customs union against the United States' and pressed him to promote this idea in Paris too. After his meeting with Nicholas II the Kaiser told his friend Philipp Eulenburg that 'Our programme is: . . . to bring Europe together in the struggle against . . . America in a common defensive customs union, with or without England.' As we were able to demonstrate, Wilhelm and Eulenburg saw the Tsar's apparent acquiescence as providing 'the point of departure [for] the unification of Europe' and 'the programme, as it were, for the immediate future of the European world'. Kaiser Wilhelm's favourite foreign policy objective, the 'continental union against America, possibly also against England', seemed to them to be within their grasp in 1896. Their disappointment was all the greater when the Tsar failed to respond to the memorandum Wilhelm had personally drawn up and handed to him in Wiesbaden, entitled 'On the need to form a politico-mercantile coalition of the European states against the USA'.[18] Nevertheless the basic idea of a European continental league continued to be a leitmotiv for Kaiser Wilhelm in the Bülow era.

In the summer of 1900, during his Scandinavian cruise, he received the journalist Pierre de Ségur and other French tourists and 'unbosomed himself with extraordinary frankness in regard to the United States . . . toward which he evinced only very faint sympathy', as the American press later reported on the basis of an article in the *Revue de Paris*. 'To him there is a menace for the future in the colossal trusts so dear to the Yankee millionaire.' In order to protect itself against the American threat Europe must form a customs union, as in the days of Napoleon, the monarch declared to his French guests.[19] The Kaiser's remarks caused uproar in the USA and deep embarrassment in the Wilhelmstrasse when they appeared in numerous press reports in November 1901. And when the German ambassador in Washington, Theodor von Holleben, complained of the apparent Germanophobia of the American press, the *New York Herald* retaliated by asking 'whether the German press would not have been worked up into a fury had it been informed, correctly, or perhaps incorrectly, that Mr Roosevelt had expressed himself to a party of French tourists as in favour of a universal boycotting of German products because he did not approve of certain German business systems'.[20] Even several years later, in September 1905, Eulenburg was able to record that 'the idea of a *European coalition* against the yellow race (even more than against America) continues to dominate *the Kaiser's* thinking. Bülow is pursuing the same thought as regards the coalition − which I, like him, have cherished for years, although *only against America*.'[21]

As these remarks demonstrate, the Kaiser was in this case fully aware of the important role played by economics in the political rivalry between the two dynamic nations. In the summer of 1897, when he appointed Bülow Foreign Secretary and put Tirpitz in charge of the Reich Navy Office, he described German−American competition for the Latin American market as 'the beginning of a war to the death'.[22] At the same time he deliberately chose Holleben as ambassador in Washington because he needed 'a bold man there . . . who can wage the tariff war against America if necessary'.[23] Since 1899 he had seen 'great danger' for Germany in the efforts of American business to set up trusts, as they could be used 'to attack our industry and trade . . . Capitalist wars have much more fearsome effects than powder and shot.'[24] The takeover of three British shipping lines by a trust headed by the American railway magnate J. P. Morgan in the spring of 1901 aroused the fear that the USA would soon seize control of all passenger and goods traffic in the North Atlantic at the expense of the Europeans. 'That can only be prevented by all Continental lines including England joining together', the Kaiser commented on 30 April.[25] He dismissed Morgan's offers of cooperation with the characteristic remark: 'That, if I may say so, is tripe. Who the hell would believe him?'[26] In September 1901, on Wilhelm's orders, Bülow asked Albert Ballin, the Director General of the Hapag Line, to send him suggestions for the protection of German shipping which he would submit to the Kaiser.[27] Wilhelm then invited Ballin to his hunting lodge at Hubertusstock and together they devised the strategy intended to put a stop to any attempt by Morgan to acquire Hapag or the North German Lloyd Line. When news of American designs on more British shipping lines came in, Wilhelm was relieved to be able to shrug it off.

'That can't happen to us, thank God!'[28] And when Ballin succeeded in making a deal favourable to Germany with Morgan in February 1902, on the eve of a visit to New York by Prince Heinrich, the Kaiser sent him enthusiastic congratulations from Hubertusstock.[29]

The aims of the Kaiser's policy of *Weltmacht* included, as we have seen, not only the unification of the European continent under German leadership but also the economic and political penetration of Latin America, which brought Germany into direct conflict with the United States. When President Theodore Roosevelt suggested to him in December 1903 that he should give priority to expansion in the east, Wilhelm wrote cockily on the dispatch: 'Here's to you! The Russians are sitting tight there. No, South America is our goal, old boy!'[30] He followed the exploratory voyages of the American gunboat *Wilmington* on the Orinoco and the Amazon with intense interest, and declared 'We must do that too!'[31] Since the 1890s he had ardently supported a project to establish a 'New Germany' in southern Brazil, and he demanded impatiently that German emigration thither should be 'got under way as soon as possible'.[32] When his trusted friend Karl Georg von Treutler was appointed German envoy in Brazil in 1901 Wilhelm II gave him personal instructions to treat his role less as diplomatic than as economic, and above all to look after the German settlers in southern Brazil. He also arranged for the new envoy to be put in touch with the Hamburg business circles that had a particular interest in Brazil.[33] The German settlements were 'intended as the basis on which the systematic colonisation of southern Brazil with a German population could be achieved'.[34] On several occasions the Foreign Office pointed out to the Kaiser the important role that the building of railways could play in preventing 'North American influence and North American capital from taking hold in those lands brought under cultivation by Germans, and thus damaging German trade and German industry in territory where there is still great scope for German energy and initiative in the future'.[35] In November 1903 Wilhelm agreed to send a permanent diplomatic representative to La Paz, which Bülow had told him was essential because of the 'forthcoming struggle against North American competition'.[36]

The Kaiser's overarching aim, as he repeatedly made clear, was to overtake the USA in terms of political power by building up his naval strength.[37] It is true that the battlefleet-building programme introduced by Tirpitz in 1897 was directed principally against Britain, but from the beginning the Kaiser also had the United States in his sights as a potential opponent. In December 1897 he noted on a letter from the American ambassador Andrew Dickson White: 'We shall win the favour of America and England in proportion to how much we strengthen our fleet and thus make it inadvisable for either of them to molest or offend us at the risk of suffering damage as a result.'[38] According to a record made by Bülow in the summer of 1898, as a guideline for German foreign and armaments policy the Kaiser decided that 'problems and conflicts with the [North American] Union were to be avoided as long as this was compatible with the dignity of the Reich. Once our Navy had passed the transitional phase the moment might come to call the United States to account.'[39] Again and again, in connection with the growth of American power, the Kaiser urged the need for 'a strong fleet very soon', for 'then the rest will sort itself out'.[40] As Fiebig-von Hase has shown, for Wilhelm the building up of the fleet represented 'the only panacea' which could change the power relationship between the Reich and both the USA and Great Britain. When Holleben warned of the growing anti-German mood in America in the summer of 1898, the Kaiser responded that the battlefleet was the instrument through which England and America could be forced to show respect, and which could prevent an Anglo-American alliance. At this time he assumed that by 1901 Germany would already be in a position to 'go out and take action' at sea.[41] When the Navy Bill of 1900 was introduced he expressly named 'England and America' as the enemies at whom the measure was aimed.[42] In June 1900 he tossed aside admonitions that Germany should proceed more cautiously in Latin America with the remark: 'Once we have a decent fleet we can do as we like, to a certain extent, for South America will be none of the Yankees' business any more.'[43] A year later he was bemoaning the long years of neglect of fleet construction and his inability to send a cruiser squadron to the Caribbean to back up his policy in Central and South America.[44] And as late as December 1904, contemplating the progressive expansion of US influence in Latin America, he lamented: 'Oh you pig-headed German Reichstag! Why have you refused me the fleet for 10 years? If we were strong enough at sea by now, such a thing would be impossible.'[45]

GERMANY AS *TERTIUS GAUDENS* BETWEEN BRITAIN AND AMERICA

In every dispute with the United States the Kaiserreich needed to ensure the benevolent neutrality of Great Britain, for to fight both Atlantic Powers simultaneously seemed madness even to the hotheads in the Admiralty Staff. It was clear, however, that the two Anglo-Saxon nations were drawing ever closer together. Britain's exposure during the Boer War and the victory of the USA over Spain led to a tacit understanding, amounting to an admission that the British Empire had passed its apogee and would never again contest the claim of the United States to leadership either in the Americas or in the Pacific. Added to this were deeply rooted historical, linguistic, cultural,

economic and familial ties which underpinned this quiet diplomatic revolution. It was of course the beginning of a development that was to determine
the course of history up to the present day.[46]

At the Hohenzollern court the growing rapport between the two Anglo-
Saxon World Powers was regarded with anxiety, but the significance of the
tectonic shift which underlay it was not at first fully recognised. Kaiser
Wilhelm tried, through would-be cunning personal diplomacy, to set the
British against the Americans and vice versa. Not surprisingly, given the close
links between the leadership of the two countries, each side immediately
reported such attempts to the other, thus only deepening the distrust of both
towards Wilhelm. The memorable conversation that the Kaiser conducted in
1901 with the British Foreign Secretary, Lord Lansdowne, about the evil
intentions of the United States throughout the world has already been quoted
at length.[47] In the course of it he attempted to entice Britain to abandon her
bond with the USA in favour of alliance with Europe. According to his own
account he warned that 'the United States were determined, full of youthful
strength and high spirits, lacking scruples or feelings of solidarity with others'.
'They were sufficient unto themselves on their vast, still partly unexplored
continent. They applied the Monroe Doctrine only in order to keep all others
away; on the other hand they themselves spread out wherever they wanted.
They stood with one foot in Honolulu and the other in Cuba! It seemed to me
that England's friendship in the war with Spain had been ill repaid. American
sympathies were on the Boers' side ... I then asked him – the Minister –
frankly whether people here really still lived under the illusion of American
friendship.' After all, the Americans were trying, together with Russia, 'to
keep the Europeans, including the English, out of China. They wanted to
share China between them: one would take over political, the other commercial, power ... The Slav with his overwhelming numbers, his passive, half
slumbering instincts which were nevertheless directed towards specific objectives, who slowly and menacingly, with elemental power, came to the fore in
world history, the American with his toughness, his inventiveness, his determination and the inexhaustible resources of his new land – these two, if they
were allowed, would in time absorb everything.'[48] In August of that year,
when Edward VII and Lascelles arrived at Wilhelmshöhe for discussions with
the Kaiser, Wilhelm repeated his warning against American intentions. Their
capture of the Philippines signified 'a step towards the Yangtse', he claimed.
'Does England believe she can stand up to Russia and America in the Far East
alone, without Japan?'[49]

The Kaiser took malicious pleasure at every sign of an Anglo-American
conflict, from which he hoped to derive some advantage. Thus in 1901 he

commented on a report that London had given in over the Panama question: 'John Bull has to make concessions to Jonathan.'[50] When Roosevelt announced in February 1902 that he would send troops to Alaska if the negotiations with Britain over the position of the Canadian frontier did not yield the desired result, Wilhelm wrote: 'Here's to the President! John Bull will certainly put up with that too.'[51] Wilhelm's hopes were seconded by Bülow, who in 1899 expressed his delight to the Kaiser at the prospect of an imminent war between the USA and Britain, in which the issue would be American acquisition of Canada. 'I can see it coming', the future Chancellor rejoiced. 'So long as we don't allow ourselves to get entangled with America, John Bull will eventually have to face the alternative of letting Canada go or risking a disastrous clash with Uncle Sam.'[52] Again in the spring of 1903 Bülow played down the danger of an Anglo-American agreement against Germany when he assured the Kaiser that 'the British Empire has grown so big that it can no longer survive by its own strength alone. It must have an ally and would give a great deal to win over the Americans to such an alliance ... But America will think very hard before she joins forces with England. Such a commitment would contradict American traditions and inclinations. America is too egoistic not to say to herself that Uncle Sam can do better business with a free hand than in a joint enterprise with that fat and equally selfish John Bull.' The main conflict of interests between Britain and the USA was in China, in Bülow's opinion. 'In the Yangtse valley the English are using all possible means to gain supremacy. Thanks to the resistance they are meeting, particularly from America, they have not yet achieved it there ... America has the same interest as us in the "open door" on the Yangtse and will not give it up unless she believes she is under threat from a coalition brought together by us.'[53]

Animated by the belief that British and American interests were irreconcilable, at this time the Kaiser was already pursuing the hazardous aim of persuading the United States to join with Germany in taking action that would cause lasting damage to the British Empire. In October 1901, when London newspapers demanded a rapprochement between Britain and Russia, his reaction was to make it his 'duty' to 'come to an economic agreement with America'. The goal of this German–American cooperation would be 'the destruction of English world trade, their shipping etc', as he bluntly declared. Together with America the German Reich would inflict 'such heavy losses' on the English 'that for good or ill they will be forced to try to get on better terms with us politically. If these measures succeed', he predicted, 'all the other nations will want to join us'.[54] As this marginal comment makes clear, the Kaiser's motivation for these offers to America was, as always, his overriding aim of German supremacy in Europe. The collaboration with the USA was intended to force Britain to her knees and thus make her submit to German hegemonial plans.[55] In fact these approaches to the USA had the opposite effect, for naturally the Americans detected their manipulative purpose at once. The Kaiser's cunning proposals were immediately passed on to the British government, with the result that distrust of German policy, and particularly of Wilhelm's intentions, increased dramatically in both Washington and London.

After his successful collaboration with Albert Ballin over the negotiations with J. P. Morgan, Wilhelm considered himself a better connoisseur of the American industrial elite than the official representatives of the Reich in the USA.[56] Firmly convinced that his personal influence on the Americans would be far more effective than that of his diplomats, Wilhelm invited Morgan and his family to Germany in the summer of 1902. On 1 July the *Corsair*, the magnate's luxury yacht, arrived in Kiel, where the Kaiser was waiting for his guests on board the *Hohenzollern*. The monarch evidently felt in his element in this plutocratic atmosphere. Morgan's daughter Anne described the meeting of the two men in a letter to her mother. 'At three o'clock the Kaiser, Bülow, his aide de camp and an admiral all came on board the Corsair and stayed an hour and a half, and no words can say how perfectly delightful he made himself. Of course we were all scared to death and didn't know what to do, but he hates ceremony of any kind when he is off that way and insisted on doing everything as if he was one of us. As to his looks, he isn't a bit like his photographs or portraits there isn't one of them that begins to be strong enough. His eyes are perfectly marvellous very blue they look you through and through. Well I tell you it was the shortest hour and a half I ever spent.'[57]

Enthusiasm over the Kiel meeting was short-lived. Eckardstein was horrified to learn in London soon afterwards that the Kaiser, in the belief that he was addressing a purely American audience on board the yacht, had declared at the top of his voice that 'England was the common enemy, against which America and Germany had to stand together. But there had also been an Englishman aboard who had sat down and reported the Kaiser's speech by letter to the Foreign Office [in London]. There the letter was kept.' Eckardstein therefore concluded 'that it was useless to go on struggling against the flood of English bitterness', and asked to be released from the diplomatic service. As Holstein recorded in November 1902, Bülow confronted the Kaiser with this incident to bring him to his senses. 'The Kaiser got furious when he heard this story, denied everything, but was much quieter and less assertive afterwards.'[58]

British and American sources not only confirm the accuracy of Eckardstein's information; they show that the Kaiser's outbursts were in fact far worse and that they reached the political elite in London and Washington by other routes, causing enormous damage. On board the American yacht was the young and decidedly pretty fiancée of an American diplomat at the Berlin embassy named Hitt, with whom the Kaiser had a long and candid conversation. Hitt's father was not only a member of the House of Representatives but chairman of the Foreign Relations Committee. On the basis of what his future daughter-in-law told him, this influential US politician became convinced that Kaiser Wilhelm was 'the most reckless man in Europe'. The monarch had spoken to this young woman, a perfect stranger, 'with such brutal frankness that the girl was amazed'. He had abused his fellow sovereigns, 'especially his Uncle Edward'. The Washington correspondent of the *National Review*, A. Maurice Low, whose report reached the ears of the British government, summed up Hitt's description thus: 'The Emperor's characterisation of the King and the British people was evidently malevolently brutal, and his manner no less than his words showed how he hated all things English.'[59]

Morgan himself gave his London business partner Clinton Dawkins more details of his discussion with the Kaiser at Kiel, which Dawkins immediately passed on to influential British contacts. He told the Governor-General of South Africa, Lord Milner, in November 1902 that Wilhelm had 'admitted to Morgan when the "combiner" was at Kiel, that he had not thought it unfair to make a little trouble between us & the U.S. over ships. We must all woo your great Republic, he said, and the English thought they had advanced so far in your regard over the Spanish war that it was fair to disturb an attachment that was going so far.' In addition, 'before miscellaneous company at Kiel', the Kaiser had 'openly' used 'the most violent language' against the Colonial Secretary, Joseph Chamberlain, Dawkins reported. Not only was Chamberlain no gentleman; he was 'also corrupt & influenced all through the war [in South Africa] by corrupt motives which would sooner or later see the light!' In Dawkins's opinion Prime Minister Balfour and Joseph Chamberlain were the only members of the government who had understood the 'German menace'. But the Americans, too, had seen the danger. 'I think that they understand these things in America. They keep a very close watch on Germany in Washington where they seem to be well posted in foreign affairs in spite of (or because of) having no regular diplomatic service.'[60]

After the Kaiser's embarrassing indiscretions at Kiel had become known Metternich felt obliged to point out to Bülow the disastrous consequences of the incident for Germany's relations with Britain and the United States. On 4 February 1903, in a private letter to the Chancellor, he wrote: 'The story that His Majesty the Kaiser expressed himself unkindly about England and King Edward on an American yacht is apparently . . . being used to influence King Edward . . . His Majesty is said to have described England as "a rotten country" and made America shine by contrast. Of King Edward His Majesty is said to have remarked "that if he (the Emperor) had done what King Edward has done, he would have been turned out of his country."' Metternich went on to warn that King Edward was 'very pro-American at the moment', and that he could not help fearing that 'we have not reached the end of the yacht story yet and that "some mischief makers" will try to work on King Edward and create discord between him and our All-Gracious Lord'. The ambassador's fears were to prove justified.[61]

It was not long before the King's Private Secretary asked the British ambassador in Berlin how much of the 'yacht story' was true. Lascelles replied on 20 March 1903: 'It is evident that the Emperor did go on board an American Yacht last year, and used language which, to say the least, was indiscreet, more especially as there was an Englishman on board, whose name I forget, but who had been an honorary attaché somewhere, and wrote a report to Lord Lansdowne, which I saw at the F.O. This report said that His Majesty indulged in abuse of the English Government, but I do not remember that it contained any direct denunciation of The King. I remember that it struck me at the time that the Emperor had used equally strong language to me about the Government, but it is one thing for him to talk tête à tête with an Ambassador, who will of course report the conversation, and quite another to speak to a lot of people, whom he did not know, in a manner which must lead them to believe that he hated England and all things English. This I certainly do not believe, and although there can be no doubt that, on board the American Yacht, he used language which was quite inexcusable in the Company in which he found himself, we should remember that he always exaggerates and that people who do not know him well are apt to misunderstand him. The whole incident regrettable as it was is now ancient history, and might I think be allowed to drop altogether.'[62] But Lascelles's wise appeal to common sense fell on deaf ears at the court in Windsor.

PRINCE HEINRICH'S 'MISSION' TO AMERICA

The most flagrant of Kaiser Wilhelm's attempts to use personal diplomacy to launch a German–American coalition against the British Empire, or at least to undermine the growing fraternisation of Britain and America, was Prince Heinrich's 'political propaganda tour' of the USA in February and March 1902.[63] As Ragnhild Fiebig-von Hase has shown, Heinrich's visit to America was due 'exclusively to the Kaiser's initiative'. The idea of sending the Prince arose from 'the naïve expectation of the Kaiser that he could influence American policy by means of personal contacts and marks of favour, in the form of visits by imperial relations, awards of medals and gifts of statues', and thereby block out the real conflicts of *Weltpolitik* which existed between the two countries.[64] Wilhelm provided his brother with wide-ranging instructions aimed at achieving a German–American accord against Britain. Above all Heinrich was to use his influence to make sure that the agreement between Albert Ballin and J. P. Morgan for the regulation of North Atlantic steamer traffic was signed and sealed. The Prince was even to negotiate with the US government on the thorny question of Venezuela.[65] The officials of the Wilhelmstrasse were beside themselves with horror at the mission of the Prince, who was not exactly well-versed in diplomacy, especially since Heinrich, as a member of the royal family and 'as a sailor', claimed that he took his orders from the Kaiser and at first refused to accept the Reich Chancellor's instructions.[66] Particularly alarming was the news brought by the Prince's Hofmarschall, Albert von Seckendorff, that Heinrich thought it his duty to bring home 'some kind of political success' from his journey. But what caused the diplomats the most anxiety was the Prince's intention of making enquiries in Washington as to 'whether and to what extent it would be possible to create a German sphere of influence in South America'. The mere mention of this thought would be quite enough, Holstein was sure, 'to bring the President's mood down to freezing point'. Moreover the Prince wished to discuss the Philippine question with Roosevelt. The Chancellor and the Foreign Office were seriously afraid that Heinrich's mission to America would do more to serve 'the wishes and interests of our enemies and those who bear us a grudge than the interests of Germany'.[67] Eventually Bülow succeeded in convincing the Kaiser of the necessity of limiting the trip to a pure courtesy visit. On the Kaiser's authority the Reich Chancellor was able to brief the Prince on the guidelines of government policy on numerous contentious issues – Venezuela, the Danish Caribbean island of St Thomas, the press, commercial policy, shipping, emigration, cables and post. In a letter to Prince Heinrich of 30 January 1902 he made it clear that it would be a mistake 'to believe that any political initiatives were expected of Your Royal Highness in America'. The purpose of the journey was purely to win over the Americans by showing them courtesy and convincing them of the usefulness of good relations and of the Kaiser's goodwill towards the American people. On no account should Prince Heinrich mention the German attitude during the Boer War as this could be shown to contradict Wilhelm II's neutral stance on the war. In addition he was advised not to raise 'on his own initiative' any matters concerning South and Central America, and 'of course not to admit to any kind of intentions on the part of Germany in those areas'. He should dismiss as 'absurd fantasies' American fears about 'German ideas of acquiring land or influence as far as Central and South America were concerned', although he should of course avoid giving the impression of any binding commitment on the subject. The Reich Chancellor nevertheless emphasised to the Kaiser's brother that this was the most important journey for many years undertaken by a prince on behalf of the fatherland.[68] For his part Wilhelm too had high expectations of the trip, despite the strict constraints placed on his brother.[69] He turned down Waldersee's wish to go to the USA at the same time with his American wife, fearing that this might detract from the effect of the Prince's visit.[70]

The pretext for Prince Heinrich's American tour was the launch of the Kaiser's new racing yacht, *Meteor III*, which had been built on Shooter's Island, near New York, as a 'gesture of reconciliation' towards the United States.[71] The occasion was planned for 25 February 1902 and attracted great attention among the American public because Alice Roosevelt, the 16-year-old daughter of the President, was to launch the yacht. The news that the Kaiser's brother, accompanied by a high-ranking delegation, would attend the ceremony and then carry out a tour to Washington, Annapolis, St Louis, Chicago, Milwaukee, Philadelphia and Boston conferred an aura of high politics on the Prince's 'mission' to the United States.[72] Captain Georg Alexander von Müller, whom the Kaiser appointed as his Flügeladjutant on 27 January 1902, was made responsible for handling relations with the American press.[73] To lay the ground for the trip Prince Heinrich instructed Müller to put out appropriate information on his career. 'Please dress up my services rather more than you and I would consider decent and handle the whole affair with the kind of catch-phrases that would impress a Yankee reader. – This time, Georgie, we *must* hit the jackpot, much as I hate that kind of thing! The end must justify these distasteful means!'[74]

On 15 February 1902 Prince Heinrich, accompanied by no fewer than nine officers including Tirpitz and Müller, sailed for New York in the luxury steamship of the Hapag line, *Kronprinz Wilhelm*. He arrived on 23 February, after a stormy crossing.[75] All the participants in the eighteen-day tour of the United States found it impressive, but hectic and exhausting. Tirpitz commented afterwards that less would have been more, and that he had 'only put on a show of lasting it out'.[76] Apart from innumerable receptions in New York – of which the banquet given by J. P. Morgan for the thousand leading 'Captains of Industry' was the high point – Roosevelt invited the delegation to dinner at the White House in Washington and a meeting with members of Congress was arranged for them (see Figure 7). During a visit to Harvard Prince Heinrich was given an honorary doctorate.[77] Meanwhile, as we have seen, the cooperative agreement between Ballin and Morgan on which the

Figure 7 The Kaiser's brother Prince Heinrich of Prussia on his way to dinner
with President Theodore Roosevelt in the White House, February 1902

Kaiser congratulated the shipping magnate and his brother so enthusiastically,
had already been signed behind closed doors on 21 February 1902.[78]

The Americans saw at once that the Prussian Prince's 'mission' was conceived as a move against Britain.[79] It was no accident that the Wilhelmstrasse
chose precisely this moment to publish official documents which drew attention to Britain's allegedly dubious role in the Spanish–American war and
showed British statesmen in a bad light.[80] 'In England people are furious and
feel very downhearted' wrote Waldersee jubilantly. 'There could hardly be a
better way of creating public enthusiasm for the Prince's tour, and it is really a
stroke of luck that the mask has at last been stripped off the English and the
world sees what miserable hypocrites they are.'[81] Heinrich's visit would show
the Americans 'how systematically they [the English] have stirred up feelings
against us'.[82] When the tour was over Waldersee warned that strenuous
attempts would be made 'abroad, and especially in England' to 'destroy the
beneficial effects of the journey'.[83]

The Venezuelan crisis, which suddenly became acute at the beginning of
1902 and seemed likely to call for joint action by Germany and Britain,
threatened to overshadow the anti-British agenda of Prince Heinrich's
journey. When the British government signalled that it would be willing to

participate in an Anglo-German blockade of Venezuelan ports, Wilhelm II found himself faced with a dilemma. On 20 January 1902 Reich Chancellor von Bülow asked him 'most humbly' for his 'gracious permission to enter into contact with the British Government with a view to a possible joint measure against Venezuela'. Wilhelm rejected the request. No approach from London could be entertained in any way, he stipulated, 'unless we can be sure that the British will not see it as an opportunity to arouse American suspicions of us, and thus weaken the effect of my brother's visit. In any case no such steps must be taken until after the Prince's mission has been completed; and he can still be given instructions − in writing if necessary − about this proposed action, for Roosevelt.' Whether 'collecting the cash' in Caracas took place 'a few weeks sooner or later' was 'neither here nor there!'[84] Nevertheless the Kaiser did recognise that cooperative action by Germany and Britain in the Caribbean, together with his brother's simultaneous 'mission' in the USA, might be seen as the countries of the 'Germanic race' presenting a united front. In a letter to Edward VII on 26 February 1902 he wrote: 'Henry had an awful passage, which he is rapidly forgetting under the warmth of his reception, veryfying [sic] Lord Salisbury's prophecy some years ago of the union among the Teutonic Races, which he hoped would once take place. This is at least a beginning!'[85] After his return from the USA Heinrich took up the same notion of the importance of race. In April 1902 he wrote to the American journalist Poultney Bigelow, a friend of both Heinrich and Wilhelm since their youth: 'I believe that we are drifting towards a crisis in which the question of *race*, rather than that of *nations* will play a decisive part & I shall leave it to Your imagination & judgement to decide which *race* has a calling for the future, or at least should have. I consider the German & Anglo-Saxon race as one & the same.'[86]

Although Waldersee had enthusiastically approved of the Prince's journey, he was disgusted by the adulation with which it was treated in the German press.[87] Many newspapers reverted to 'their former tone of praising the Kaiser extravagantly as the originator of the trip, the man of clear vision and grand ideas. His Majesty must not grow vain and believe that he is really much cleverer than everyone else.' It would be better to wait and see the results of Prince Heinrich's visit, the General warned.[88] At the end of 1902 the Kaiser was still praising his brother's success, writing on a report from Washington: 'Heinrich's journey is the capital we are living on!'[89] On the occasion of his birthday in January 1903 he promoted the Prince to the command of the naval base at Kiel.[90] In reality the Prince's 'propaganda tour' had not achieved any lasting improvement in German–American relations. 'There was no question of the Reich becoming the real winner in the game of Anglo-American relations', Fiebig-von Hase concludes. 'As far as German–American relations and Germany's international position were concerned, the Prince's visit was no more than a temporary diplomatic success that had no profound influence.'[91] An influential German–American observer commented in early 1903 that the constant German attempts 'to sow discord between us and England' had had precisely the opposite effect. 'Over the last year Germany has pursued an altogether very unfortunate policy here in America and in spite of Prince Heinrich's visit, in spite of all the attempts to woo us and all the exaggerated professions of friendship, the dominant feeling here is distrust of the aggressive German *Weltpolitik*, which may have serious consequences in the future. We have no liking at all for a brutal, materialist, bragging Germany, unsettling the whole world.'[92] A few weeks after the American visit Kaiser Wilhelm commented bitterly that Gordon Bennett, the proprietor of the *New York Herald*, had declared that 'he would not rest until he had brought about war between Germany and America within the next 3 years'.[93] Even Poultney Bigelow publicly criticised Germany's aims.[94] By the end of 1902 Waldersee had to admit that Germany was far from winning the contest with Britain to court public opinion in the United States. 'We are competing with England in grovelling for American friendship', he commented. 'For the time being England still has a decided advantage, as there are strong links. But I believe that the Americans are clever enough not to be beguiled into bestowing their favour on either suitor.'[95]

THE SEARCH FOR NAVAL BASES IN THE CARIBBEAN

The Kaiser's attempts to bring about a rapprochement with the United States through personal diplomacy were doomed to failure not least because at the same time he had set himself the goal, with the backing of his Naval Cabinet and the Admiralty Staff, of acquiring naval bases in Central and South America, thus infringing the USA's Monroe Doctrine. The Chief of the Naval Cabinet, Admiral Gustav Freiherr von Senden-Bibran, did his best to stoke up Wilhelm's enthusiasm for this project. As Holstein complained, 'despite his notoriously mediocre intelligence', Senden-Bibran 'always had the Kaiser's ear' and had demanded that an island in the Gulf of Mexico be procured 'without straining our relations with America', which in Holstein's opinion was an impossible task.[96] Wilhelm pinned his hopes on the Danish West Indian islands of St Thomas and St John. In fact, he had himself missed an opportunity to obtain the Danish Virgin Islands in exchange for part of North Schleswig in 1896, when he had rejected Copenhagen's proposal with the comment: 'My subjects are not to be sold for a few islands! What [Kaiser] Wilhelm

I acquired, I intend to keep.'[97] With the outbreak of the Spanish–American war, however, it looked as if there might be another chance to establish a naval base in the Caribbean without any serious opposition from the United States. In April 1898 the Kaiser gave orders for the Foreign Office to consult with Tirpitz and come up with suggestions 'on the St Thomas question' to submit to him.[98] It was not long before the central dilemma of German policy, which had arisen from the simultaneous pursuit of *Weltpolitik* and of a bigger battlefleet, again became apparent. To Tirpitz, above all, the acquisition of overseas bases, with which the Kaiser, the Navy High Command and sections of the public were keen to push ahead, seemed too risky as long as his great ship-building programme was still in the danger zone.[99] The rapid victory of the USA over Spain, however, put an end to German hopes of fishing in troubled waters in the Caribbean. For fear of antagonising American public opinion, the Kaiser turned down an offer from the President of the Dominican Republic to take a lease on a port in Haiti, commenting: 'Oh what sweet innocence. I am not going to fall for a trick like that.'[100]

Wilhelm's enthusiasm for acquiring the Danish Antilles was rekindled when a speculator approached the Auswärtiges Amt in early summer 1899 with a project for the purchase of the island of St John.[101] Unlike the previous year, this time Tirpitz supported the idea and advocated it to the Kaiser and in the press. In May 1899 the Admiral hinted at the ambitious goals he had in mind with the acquisition of St John. 'It would depend on whether the Foreign Office, with an eye to the future, as soon as we had the strength at sea, were inclined to aim at, or to keep open as an option, a more active policy in America (e.g. planned promotion of German emigration to South America). In that case St John would be necessary, because with this island in our possession we need not be afraid of a conflict with America.'[102] Bülow and Holstein had to use their best efforts to persuade the Kaiser to reprimand Tirpitz for his all too open press campaign for the purchase.[103]

In the next few years the Kaiser, Senden, Tirpitz and the Admiralty Staff kept up the search for a naval base or at least a coaling station in the western hemisphere.[104] In their view there was an urgent need to acquire an operational base for the war with the United States which they increasingly saw as inevitable. In this regard, too, the Danish Antilles, together with the Dutch island of Curaçao, were considered to be the most suitable islands.[105] When Holleben advised that German territorial ambitions in the Caribbean should be roundly denied in view of the growing unrest on the subject in the USA, Wilhelm commented: 'Now now, Mr Ambassador! Tell them to control themselves; whatever is necessary for the Navy will be done, even if it displeases the Yankees.' Holleben must stop being so nervous, he added.[106] (See Figure 8.)

Figure 8 An American response to German ambitions in the Caribbean, 1902

When the Americans tried to acquire the Danish Virgin Islands for themselves Wilhelm saw this as a serious threat to German aspirations in Latin
America. He complained in December 1901 that 'Europe looks on silently and
has to let its interests go by the board because England is too slack, while we,
because of 10 years of the Reichstag's stupidity, lack the Navy which could
have been useful on this occasion.'[107] When Wilhelm von Schoen was
appointed German envoy in Copenhagen in January 1900 the Kaiser gave
him the task of reopening the very negotiations which he himself had blocked
in 1896: the exchange of the Danish Virgin Islands for part of north Schleswig.
Since the turn of the century the Kaiser had been cultivating his connections
with the Danish royal family with particular zeal, not least because they were
among the bitterest opponents of the sale of the islands to the USA.[108]

In a memorandum drawn up in April 1903 by the Admiralty Staff on the
need for naval bases, the Danish and Dutch islands in the West Indies were
once again identified as the most important objectives. The acquisition of
these bases was 'a matter of life or death' for Germany and it would be
achieved in due course, that is to say after the completion of the battlefleet,

through the union of Holland and Denmark with the Reich. Sooner or later, according to the memorandum, 'a bloody conflict between America and Europe' was inevitable and this war would certainly take place 'in the Caribbean Sea and off New York'.[109] That these breathtaking visions of world power were shared by Kaiser Wilhelm and his immediate circle is clear from the 'very secret' talks which the monarch and his confidant, Adjutant-General Hans von Plessen, held with Schoen in December 1904. They talked openly of bringing the smaller neighbouring countries of Belgium, the Netherlands and Denmark under German control. Plessen averred that 'it was highly desirable for us to get our hands not only on Denmark but also on Holland with her colonies, if only to establish the coaling stations that were so urgently needed'. When the diplomat remarked 'that such plans could not be accomplished without bloody conflicts with nearly all the Great Powers including America, the General conceded that their realisation was perhaps still a long way off'.[110] Until the great fleet programme was completed one would have to be satisfied with establishing an informal German influence in the Caribbean. In spring 1905 Ballin, acting for the Hapag line, succeeded in obtaining important concessions on St Thomas from Denmark. This 'brilliant' success was greeted with enthusiasm by the Kaiser, as he saw it as a preliminary move towards the eventual acquisition of the island as a naval base. In his eyes Denmark, with her colonies, was slowly drifting into 'dependence' on the German Reich.[111]

OPERATIONAL PLANS FOR A WAR AGAINST NORTH AMERICA

Since the American victory in the war with Spain, talk of a war between Germany and the USA had been constantly in the air. In spring 1899, in a memorandum for Prince Heinrich, Bülow drew attention to the danger inherent in the 'violent agitation against the Reich' taking place in the United States. The Foreign Secretary emphasised particularly that 'an armed conflict with the great North American Republic' was 'undesirable for us', because this would drive the USA into the arms of Great Britain.[112] At about the same time the German ambassador in Washington, Theodor von Holleben, warned that the USA might 'one day offend us so much that we would have no alternative but to draw our swords'.[113] But there were also Americans, such as Admiral George Dewey, the celebrated hero of the Spanish–American war, who declared openly in 1899 that the next war which the USA would have to wage would be against Germany.[114] Of course neither government deliberately sought war, but their conflicting interests, above all in Central and South America, made a military clash in the Caribbean seem increasingly likely.[115]

Of all people, the Kaiser, the Naval Cabinet and the Admiralty Staff failed to practise the reserve urged on them by the Wilhelmstrasse. When the Haitian warship *Crête-à-Pierrot* was hijacked by rebels in 1902 and challenged a steamer of the Hapag line on the high seas, the Kaiser ordered the gunboat *Panther* to be sent to Haiti, without consulting the Reich Chancellor or the Foreign Office. The rebel ship was bombarded and sunk, an action jubilantly commended by Kaiser Wilhelm with the words 'Bravo Panther!'[116]

Operational plans of a breathtaking audacity for war with the United States had been in preparation by the Admiralty Staff since 1898, and the Kaiser had been actively involved in them from the start. On 24 January 1900 the Chief of the Admiralty Staff, Vice Admiral Otto von Diederichs, submitted a 'Memorandum on a plan of operations for war between Germany and the United States of North America' to Wilhelm II.[117] A few days later the Kaiser expressly reserved for himself, as Supreme War Lord, the right to decide on the planning and preparation of such a war by ordering that 'the conclusions with regard to war operations arising from the Admiralty Staff's work, journeys, war games and manoeuvres' should 'in every single instance be submitted to him in audience, and his decision should be sought on how far the material should be made available to the officer corps in general'. The monarch himself would decide 'for which instance of war a particular plan should be submitted to him'. This plan should then be worked out by the Chief of the Admiralty Staff in person and should be kept 'strictly confidential' until mobilisation.[118] Wilhelm II repeatedly ordered the Admiralty Staff to consult with the Great General Staff on an operational plan for war with the USA.[119] The result was the 'Operational Plan III', of which the first draft was submitted to the Kaiser on 21 March 1903. In the following months and years the plan was revised several times until in May 1906 Vice Admiral Büchsel, Diederich's successor, pronounced it 'out of date' and it was shelved. The Entente Cordiale between Britain and France and the increase of British and American naval strength had rendered what were in any case harebrained operational plans for a war in the western hemisphere utterly illusory.[120]

What goals were to be achieved by a war with the USA, and how did the Kaiser and the Admiralty Staff imagine such a war could be conducted on the other side of the Atlantic Ocean anyway? In all the memoranda submitted to the Supreme War Lord the stated war aim is to establish German power in the Caribbean and in Central and South America on a firm political and economic footing. In his memorandum of January 1900 Diederichs had already suggested that Cuba and Puerto Rico, which the Americans had conquered in the war with Spain, might be 'desirable targets for us in the right circumstances'. Two years later the Chief of the Admiralty Staff pointed out in a submission to the Kaiser that Puerto Rico would make 'an extremely important and valuable base' for Germany. Furthermore this would achieve a 'breach in the principle of the Monroe Doctrine' that would be 'extremely valuable in the future'. In the Operational Plan III which the Kaiser approved in March 1903 it is stated that after a successful outcome in the war against the USA the German Reich would be in a position 'to put our trade with the West Indies, Central and South America onto a sound footing . . . The most important military imperative' was to acquire 'a secure position in the West Indies and a free hand in South America', a concession that would represent 'a break with the Monroe Doctrine'. Again in autumn 1903 the Admiralty Staff demanded the occupation of Puerto Rico as a 'bastion against the presumptions of the Monroe Doctrine'. This island, as well as providing 'a valuable guarantee for the peace negotiations', would give the German Reich 'the sought-after strategic base, and secure it for the future'.[121]

The lunacy of the German war plans becomes fully apparent when one considers the strategic dilemma that had to be solved. By what means could a democratic superpower like the USA be compelled, at such a distance, to give up its possessions and its claims? All the plans worked out by the Admiralty Staff took as their starting point the destruction of the US Navy, the essential prerequisite of military action on the American mainland, as a result of which Washington would be forced to seek peace. The German occupation of Puerto Rico would draw the American fleet out into a decisive battle in the Caribbean, it was thought. Only after the destruction of the US Navy would the second phase begin, when German troops would be landed on the northeast coast of the USA. Then, after the conquest of, say, Boston, New York, Philadelphia, Washington and Baltimore, the American government would be compelled to make peace![122]

In January 1900 a report by the German naval attaché in Washington, Herbert von Rebeur-Paschwitz, drew the Kaiser's attention to the necessity of land operations in the event of war with the USA. Wilhelm ordered the Admiralty Staff and the General Staff to make a joint submission to him. Schlieffen, however, considered the Admiralty Staff's plans so hazardous that when Diederichs sought his views on the suitability of Cape Cod as an operational base for an attack on Boston and New York he did not reply for several months, and then only after a further reminder. On 10 December 1900 the joint audience ordered by the Kaiser eleven months earlier took place at long last, and in the course of it Schlieffen succeeded in persuading the monarch to give up the idea of military operations on the American mainland. Wilhelm II gave orders that for the time being plans should be limited to the conquest of Cuba.[123]

Although the Chief of the General Staff calculated that at least 100,000 soldiers would be needed for operations against Boston and that many more would be required to attack New York, while even the capture of Cuba would take 50,000 men, the Chief of the Admiralty Staff spoke contemptuously of a military declaration of bankruptcy, and carried on with his plans without further cooperation with the General Staff. After lengthy preliminary studies, of which the Kaiser was kept informed in detail and to which he gave his blessing, on 21 March 1903 he finally approved the 'Operational Plan III' which, as we have seen, involved the capture of the American Caribbean islands. Both for reasons of prestige and to protect the Panama Canal which was then under construction the US Navy would be compelled to engage in a decisive battle. This plan also provided for an attack on New York from Long Island, for only thus could the USA be coerced into seeking peace. No discussions were held with the General Staff on the participation of the army in this second phase of the plan. The historian Fiebig-von Hase comments: 'The Navy now felt responsible only for the first stage, which was to be conducted exclusively as a war at sea, and left it to the Kaiser to work out what further steps would be necessary. This did not happen.'[124]

The strategic folly of these war plans becomes even clearer when one considers the position of the German Reich in the heart of Europe. How would Russia, France and Great Britain react if twenty-two German battle-ships and over 100,000 German soldiers became involved in a war with the USA thousands of kilometres away on the other side of the Atlantic Ocean? It would take all of forty days merely to transport the troops via the Azores to Puerto Rico. For the General Staff it would have been unthinkable to weaken the home front to that extent. Nor would Tirpitz ever have approved of putting his precious battlefleet at risk in an overseas escapade of this kind. The Chief of the Admiralty Staff himself recognised the Achilles' heel in his war fantasies in his introductory remarks to the Operational Plan III. 'The essential precondition for a war between Germany and the United States is *a political situation in Europe* which leaves the German Reich with a completely free hand in foreign affairs. Any insecurity in Europe would prevent the successful completion of a war against the United States.'[125]

Virtually alone among German historians at the time, Dr Fiebig-von Hase recognised the intimate link between the Kaiser's insistence on exercising direct military command and the damaging 'polycratic chaos' that was affecting decision-making at the highest level. 'He had personally reserved the right to decide on all questions relating to the war plans. Ultimately this meant that only the Kaiser and his military advisers were qualified to take decisions on what were often politically explosive questions concerning the deployment of the fleet in peacetime and in war.' The Reich Chancellor and the Foreign Office received only belated, incomplete and often indirect information about the bizarre plans hatched by the navy. The result, in Fiebig-von Hase's damning words, was 'a serious institutional weakness of the German system, because the Kaiser showed himself completely incapable of the task which fell to him of coordinating policy on security and foreign affairs.'[126]

THE VENEZUELAN CRISIS OF 1902–1903

The Kaiser and his advisers had been aware from the start that Germany's far-reaching ambitions in Latin America and the Caribbean were incompatible with the USA's claims, asserted under the Monroe Doctrine, to a monopoly of influence in the western hemisphere. When an American fleet gathered off Venezuela in 1895 Wilhelm thundered, in a marginal note: 'So Venezuela is in the process of going under because of the Monroe Doctrine! This is very serious! And we must soon decide, knowing how valuable South America is, whether we want to take precautions there or not.'[127] In a conversation with the Hanseatic envoy, Karl Peter Klügmann, in November 1897 the Kaiser launched into 'endless political tirades' against the North American republic. He regretted that Europe had not supported the southern states in the Civil War, he expressed the hope that the conflict of interests between the western and the eastern states would weaken the USA and complained: 'Nobody does us any favours. Everything in the world is governed by the question of power. Anyone who cannot kick the others in the shins goes under. We can do that in Europe, of course, but in the wider world we are at a disadvantage.'[128] A few days later the *New York Times* reported that Kaiser Wilhelm had threatened that unless the American policy of interference in the Caribbean stopped the German Reich would be compelled to teach the United States some manners.[129] It was at this time that Wilhelm II uttered his celebrated pronouncement that 'the trident must be held in our fist', and his promise to retaliate 'with a mailed fist' if anyone should ever encroach on Germany's rights.[130] On 6 December 1897 in the Reichstag Bülow expressed the Reich's new claim for world power in the words: 'We do not seek to put anyone in the shade, but we demand our place in the sun. In East Asia as in the West Indies we shall endeavour ... to protect our rights and our interests.'[131]

For the time being Germany simply lacked the ships needed for a major engagement on the other side of the Atlantic. When revolution broke out in Venezuela in summer 1899 the Reich still had no alternative but to call on the help of the Americans, of all people, to protect German interests.[132] Not until the cruiser *Vineta* was commissioned in the spring of 1900 was it possible for

Berlin to contemplate active intervention in Venezuela.[133] And indeed in
August 1901 the Commandant of the *Vineta* was instructed to investigate
the Orinoco and the approaches to Caracas with a view to troop landings, and
to prepare maps of these regions.[134] With the rapid development of the
German fleet the possibility of a conflict with the US navy in the Caribbean
or off Venezuela became ever more realistic. The Chief of the Admiralty Staff,
Diederichs, proved to be a determined champion of German expansion in
Latin America supported by military action, even at the risk of a clash with the
United States.[135] In an audience on 10 October 1901 he put forward the case
for sending two of the new twin-screw torpedo boats to Venezuela. This action
would have the added advantage, he argued, that it 'constitutes a welcome
preliminary trial for a possible military deployment there on a grand scale'.
Probably under the influence of Tirpitz the Kaiser initially turned down
Diederichs's suggestion.[136] Despite this setback, however, the Chief of the
Admiralty Staff continued to promote the idea of a major show of force against
American hegemonial claims, 'as proof of our firm determination'.[137]

Only two days after his audience Diederichs nearly achieved his wish.
Following a brawl between two officers from the *Vineta* and Venezuelan police
in Puerto Cabello, Wilhelm II reacted with fury: he wanted a specific apology
from the Venezuelan President, Cipriano Castro, as well as a twenty-one-gun
salute to the German flag, 'or else I shall order a bombardment'.[138] As Fiebig-
von Hase remarks, 'If all the considerations put forward by Diederichs and the
Foreign Office had failed to persuade the Kaiser to agree to a show of force
in Venezuela, this was now all but accomplished by his own unbridled temperament, his immense vanity and his over-sensitivity.'[139] It was only with
difficulty that Bülow and Tirpitz succeeded in dissuading Wilhelm from
issuing his demand to Venezuela.[140] Tirpitz's argument that the dispatch of
torpedo boats to the Caribbean would only lead to re-arming by the US navy
had the desired effect on the Kaiser. Once again Wilhelm complained bitterly
of 'the sins of the last 20 years of neglect' by the Reichstag of the fleet-building
programme. If the parliament had only listened to him, the cruiser squadron
which was now tied down in China would have been free to be deployed
'wherever it was needed and where there was trouble. How much more support
my wishes and my policy in Central and South America would have if . . . the
cruiser squadron . . . could suddenly appear off Venezuela!' he exclaimed.[141]

Although the Chancellor was able to prevent the Kaiser's unthinking rush
into action in October 1901, it was not long afterwards that he himself
suggested a measure against Venezuela which was no less likely to provoke
serious conflict with the USA. His aim was to achieve informal German
control over the crisis-riven country and thereby to strengthen German

influence throughout Latin America.[142] Bülow's proposal was an unmistakable challenge to the Monroe Doctrine and thus to the United States, but he deliberately concealed from the Kaiser the military implications of the blockade he advocated, which did not exclude at least a temporary occupation of the Venezuelan coast. Indeed he went so far as to claim, falsely, that the US government had 'no objection to our action'.[143] The Chancellor's reckless initiative is all the more inexplicable because Theodore Roosevelt's appointment as President had brought into power in Washington a man who had never made any secret of his deep mistrust of German intentions in Latin America.[144]

To the astonishment of the Reich Chancellor the Kaiser refused his consent to the risky project elaborated in the Wilhelmstrasse and took over the management of the Venezuelan crisis himself. It was for the Supreme War Lord and the naval authorities, not the civilians in the Wilhelmstrasse, to pronounce on this matter of military policy. Wilhelm's behaviour in this instance was all the more serious because Diederichs had proposed in a submission of 23 December 1901 that six cruisers should be sent to Venezuela.[145] Without giving the Reich Chancellor the opportunity of explaining his intentions again, the Kaiser received the Chief of the Admiralty Staff on 7 January 1902 in the presence of Senden and Plessen. After Diederichs had repeated his reservations about the so-called peace blockade recommended by the Chancellor, the Kaiser decided against it, 'because a successful outcome seemed uncertain'. On his own initiative Diederichs did not take the opportunity of putting forward 'suggestions for the military measures to be undertaken', but gained the impression that the Kaiser had already made up his mind before the audience.[146] Probably correctly, Holstein attributed this to the influence of Tirpitz, who had thus succeeded once again in dissuading the Kaiser from premature adventures overseas in the interest of the great battlefleet-building programme.[147] What was more, however, the visit to America by the Kaiser's brother and the agreement between Ballin and Morgan were in the offing and it was important that neither be put at risk by a military action in Venezuela. Even after the Foreign Office and the Admiralty Staff had agreed on a common line the Chancellor was unable to get his way with the Kaiser.[148]

Ragnhild Fiebig-von Hase accurately summarises the decision-making process at work here under the Personal Monarchy of Wilhelm II. Although the 'ill-defined structure of the governing hierarchy ... gave the Reich Chancellor the responsibility for policy, at the same time this all too often became a farce in view of the freedom of manoeuvre which the constitution accorded to the Kaiser through his prerogative in the sphere of foreign and security policy, and it was the Kaiser and his military advisers who determined the course of foreign policy'.[149] Fiebig-von Hase points to the disastrous results of this system. 'A policy which swung back and forth, with the Foreign Office and the Chancellor pressing for a major punitive action against Venezuela, the Admiralty Staff wanting to extend this to a show of force vis-à-vis the United States, the Reich Navy Office rejecting the whole action on grounds of cost and for fear of a clash with the USA during the dangerous stage of the fleet building programme, and the Kaiser, irritated over a minor incident on the Venezuelan coast, wanting to start a bombardment but then ... dropping the whole business – such a state of affairs could only create confusion and mistrust within the Kaiserreich and abroad.'[150] As the Venezuelan crisis pursued its course, the decision-making process in the Kaiserreich continued to be dogged by serious conflicts between the civilian leadership, the Admiralty Staff, the Reich Navy Office and the Crown.

After Prince Heinrich's return from the USA the season for major action in the Caribbean was over and further initiatives had to be postponed until the autumn of 1902.[151] In early September Wilhelm II gave Bülow permission to enter into negotiations with London on a joint peace blockade of Venezuela and to prepare the cruisers *Vineta*, *Falke* and *Gazelle*, the gunboat *Panther* and the training ship *Stosch*, all of which were stationed in the eastern Caribbean, for the action, only turning down the Chancellor's suggestion that the gunboat *Habicht* be sent over from Cameroon as well.[152] Whereas the British government had favoured a joint British–German blockade as the best policy in the event of a failure by Venezuela to meet the demands made on her, it now described the confiscation of the Venezuelan warships as the most appropriate response. The Kaiser agreed with Bülow that the government in London must make a binding declaration of what further measures it intended to take if the capture of the warships failed to have the desired effect.[153] The Reich Chancellor also warned his sovereign 'with the greatest respect' of the possibility that although the two European Powers were acting jointly, the government in Caracas might fulfil the British demands but refuse those of Germany. Since in such an eventuality Germany would no longer be able to count on British cooperation, she would be obliged, if only for the sake of maintaining German prestige in Central and South America, to enforce her demands alone. As well as the capture of warships, therefore, a German blockade of the most important Venezuelan ports would also be necessary to bring pressure to bear, with the landing of troops as a last resort. 'Accordingly, for reasons of both domestic and foreign policy, I venture most humbly to beg Your Majesty to give your gracious permission for this matter to be handled as proposed', the Chancellor requested.[154]

In his response the Kaiser continued to take a considerably more reserved line than the Reich government and the senior naval authorities.[155]

He maintained that the Reich still lacked the means for a major military action in South America and demanded improvised measures to increase the strength of the naval force. 'I must point out', he wrote, 'that in the event of further measures – that is to say a serious blockade, and if that fails, possible military landings etc – we do not have sufficient *matériel* and personnel. In my opinion, (in order to avoid detaching cruisers from the active squadron for as long as possible – because as is well known they are not intended for overseas but belong in the Ordre de bataille at home) other cruisers should be mobilised ad hoc and reserves called up to man them. Then these ships could go on trial voyages and prepare to go out if necessary. For this an additional budget must be announced; I cannot tell how much would be needed but it could well reach 10–20 million. If the action has to be carried out, the bill will soon amount to 50–60 millions. I cannot judge whether the objective justifies this expenditure. It will have a very disruptive effect on the unfavourable financial position of the Reich.'[156] In consequence of the Kaiser's comment Bülow called a meeting to discuss military policy which was attended by the three admirals, Tirpitz, Senden-Bibran and Büchsel, as well as the Foreign Secretary, Oswald Freiherr von Richthofen.[157]

Like the Kaiser, the Chancellor and the admirals recognised the advantages of taking joint action with Great Britain in Venezuela and were anxious that this cooperation should not be endangered by 'legal red herrings'.[158] After difficult negotiations an Anglo-German agreement was reached in early December 1902. Waldersee's diary expressed his surprise at this development. 'Now we are allied with England! Of course it is only a matter of an action against Venezuela to which America has given its blessing – that it had to be sought is a sign of the new times – but nevertheless it is still joint action. Will it help create better relations? I do not think so.'[159] Italy's decision to participate in the blockade with two cruisers was regarded by both Kaiser and Chancellor as a positive development. After several German warships and a British cruiser had sunk three Venezuelan gunboats on 8 December 1902 Wilhelm II wrote: 'Italy is welcome to join in, and the more ships the English send, the better. Our action will fade all the more into the background while theirs comes into the foreground. We are naturally joining in the English programme. I am also against sending out more ships from home! Our flag is represented[,] let us leave the *British* to take the *lead*.'[160]

Despite every precaution, in December 1902 Germany came within a hair's breadth of war with the United States. The increase of the European naval presence in the Caribbean, the sinking of the Venezuelan gunboats and the bombardment of forts on the coast caused great agitation in American public opinion.[161] On 10 December 1902 the new Chief of the Admiralty Staff,

Wilhelm Büchsel, had to break the news to the Kaiser that an American fleet had gathered off Puerto Rico and was simulating a battle with a European fleet that was attempting to capture Culebra and Puerto Rico – in other words, exactly the situation envisaged in the secret German operational plans.[162] The greatest possible restraint was vital if Berlin wished to avoid a clash with the United States. After detailed consultations between the Wilhelmstrasse and the Naval High Command Büchsel told the Kaiser on 17 December that 'following a requisition from the Reich Chancellor', he had 'given orders to the Commander of the Cruiser Division on the East American station', Scheder, that when the blockade was enforced, which was due to happen shortly, 'the German contingent should not be the first to turn away or arrest ships of the United States of America'. The German fleet should not stop American ships 'until further notice', but 'this should be as little obvious as possible to third parties'.[163] The Kaiser gave his consent to this procedure but pointed out that it made the blockade practically illusory. Furthermore, these measures could not remain secret in the long run. Indeed they would 'positively encourage the Americans to indulge in smuggling and blockade-running'. And quite rightly, he added, the other nations would 'take this special treatment amiss'.[164]

Although he declared himself content in principle with the measures taken, the way in which the Reich Chancellor, the Foreign Office and the Admiralty Staff had acted aroused the Kaiser's fury. He saw such cooperation between officials subordinate to him as an infringement of his prerogative as Supreme War Lord. On 17 December 1902 he angrily ordered the Chief of the Naval Cabinet to make it clear to the Chancellor and the Chief of the Admiralty Staff that it was inadmissible for decisions to be reached in this manner. 'Although I do not wish to withdraw my consent to the telegram at this late stage, I must protest very strongly against the impropriety of this procedure, which I resent', he raged. 'We are so to speak at war with Venezuela. I have supreme command and sole leadership as War Lord. My agency, the Admiralty Staff, can only pass on *My* orders, after they have been drafted. But the Admiralty Staff is never permitted to draft orders without *previous submission* to me, let alone to send them out! It may not arrange with *anyone* military measures which affect the control of operations, let alone – as here – accept "requisitions" from civilian authorities. The Reich Chancellor ought to ask *me* to have an instruction issued with the above contents. But he should never *approach the Admiralty Staff* with a direct *demand*. That is an infringement of my personal right to direct war operations. It was wrong and it should first have been checked and then immediately rejected by the Admiralty Staff! – If urgent orders are necessary, the Reich Chancellor must telegraph to *Me* and I will then have the rest done by telegraph or telephone through the Naval Cabinet. You are to explain the above to the Reich Chancellor and the Chief of the Admiralty Staff. Wilhelm I.R.'[165] When Senden confronted the Chancellor with the Kaiser's objections, Bülow asserted that the greatest possible speed had indeed been essential, as an American steamer was already on the way to Venezuela. The order sent to Scheder, he said, had been intended only as a temporary measure, for 'as soon the English had seized *one* North American ship' the German Commander could 'seize as many such ships . . . as he wanted'. As for the Chief of the Admiralty Staff, Senden reported, the Kaiser's orders had been sent to him in writing, 'so that from now on matters will be handled as Your Majesty wishes'.[166]

Only days later another serious incident occurred, again almost causing a German–American war. When the *Panther* came under fire from Fort San Carlos on 17 January 1903 Scheder, in accordance with the Kaiser's orders, decided to take punitive action. *Panther* and *Vineta* together pounded the fort to pieces. Hostility towards the Reich in America reached a high point. 'At no time since the beginning of the Venezuelan problems has feeling against us been as strong as now', Albert Count von Quadt, secretary at the Washington embassy, warned.[167] 'Are people in Berlin crazy?' exclaimed President Roosevelt, who like other statesmen in Washington was beginning to think seriously about preparations for a war with Germany. On 19 January 1903 Büchsel had to report to the Kaiser that the Americans had assembled their entire naval force under the flag, 'a state of affairs that otherwise only occurs in the event of mobilisation'.[168] Not least because of the events in Venezuela, the USA now decided to adopt a fleet-building programme involving the construction of forty-eight large ships of the line.[169] But instead of being induced to draw in its horns by this warning signal, the Admiralty Staff, with the consent of the Kaiser as we have seen, chose precisely this moment to work up operational plans for a war against the United States.[170]

All too soon the Venezuelan adventure proved itself to be an expensive failure in both military and political terms. As a result of the sinking of the Venezuelan gunboats and the bombardment of the coastal fort by German cruisers, public opinion not only in the United States, but also in England, France and other countries, turned against the Kaiserreich, which was seen as the principal instigator of these harsh sanctions.[171] Under public pressure Edward VII and the British royal family also turned against the Anglo-German action in Venezuela. On 28 January 1903 the King told Metternich that he wished to bring the affair to an end as soon as possible. It was much more important, he thought, to get the whole business 'out of the way with all speed, than to obtain agreement to our mutual financial demands'. Wilhelm

was indignant at his uncle's inclination to give way and commented mockingly: 'That really is too much to ask ... Serenissimus has lost his nerve!
Grandmama would never have said that!'[172] But in the end the Kaiser, too,
recognised the danger that lay in continued intransigence on the Venezuelan
question. On 15 February 1903 he gave in to the Reich Chancellor's 'most
humble' request to lift the blockade and return her captured ships to
Venezuela.[173]

A CHANGE OF AMBASSADORS IN WASHINGTON

In this critical situation the Kaiser did not alter his American policy but
instead pinned his hopes on a change of ambassador. The dramatic and
much criticised decision to replace Theodor von Holleben with Hermann
Freiherr Speck von Sternburg was 'taken by the Kaiser alone' and as Fiebig-
von Hase emphasises, only served to increase 'the general doubt about the
soundness of imperial policy'.[174] But Sternburg, who had an English mother
and an American wife, was regarded as a personal friend of Roosevelt and
Wilhelm II was convinced that he would restore the relationship of confidence
between the Reich and the USA.[175]

'Specky' Sternburg had recommended himself to the Kaiser as Holleben's
successor. In a report of 26 November 1902, carefully tailored to the monarch's
character, he praised the statesmanlike qualities of the departing French
ambassador in Washington, Jules Cambon. In masterly fashion, Cambon had
succeeded in gaining the most respected and influential status in the US
capital for France and had brought the two nations closer together. Sure
enough, this provoked the comment from Wilhelm II that 'The same really
should be the case, and with even more reason, with My Ambassador!!'
Sternburg had more to add: the new British ambassador, Sir Michael Herbert,
a personal friend of the President, was also working skilfully and successfully
to create more intimate relations between London and the White House.
Germany's position in Washington, on the other hand, could 'hardly be
described as advantageous at the moment. From remarks President Roosevelt
has made direct to me ... it is plainly and unequivocally the case that the
German diplomatic representatives in Washington are far from enjoying his
unreserved confidence to the full.' Roosevelt had complained that there was no
one in the German embassy with whom he could discuss important questions
freely and in complete confidence. Sternburg had also established in conversation with the Russian ambassador, Cassini, that Germany had the least
influence of all the Powers in Washington. Predictably, Wilhelm II was
appalled. 'In other words our ambassador won't do!' he commented on the

report.[176] Sternburg's wiles had succeeded. At the height of the Venezuelan crisis, in spite of loud protests in court society as well as in the Reichstag, Holleben was fired and replaced by Speck von Sternburg. This was the way to advance one's career under the system of Personal Monarchy. Holleben could scarcely object: after all, he had wormed his way into his predecessor's post by much the same method six years earlier.[177]

When the new ambassador reported shortly after taking office that he had been for a long ride with Roosevelt, the Kaiser felt justified in his choice. 'What a good thing it is for H[is] M[ajesty]'s German representative to be able to go out riding with the President!' he commented jubilantly in a marginal note in February 1903.[178] Bülow agreed that Sternburg, as Roosevelt's friend, was 'absolutely the right man' for the post.[179] All too soon the hopes which Wilhelm II and the Chancellor had of Sternburg proved to be an illusion, however, for Roosevelt made fun of the Kaiser's naivety and had not the remotest intention of making concessions to Germany out of friendship for Sternburg.[180] After only a few weeks rumours were circulating that Roosevelt did not take his friend 'Specky' seriously. The influential Polish grandseigneur Count Bogdan von Hutten-Czapski attended a dinner at which Albert Ballin 'could not have been more damning in criticising Speck's conduct since he arrived in America as harmful for German–American relations'. As Holstein was able to report to the Reich Chancellor, the other Hanseatic notabilities present had emphatically agreed with Ballin's verdict. In April officials at the Foreign Office were already wondering whether 'in view of the complexity and importance of the existing and forthcoming issues between us and America' a change of ambassador might be advisable, but Holstein advised them 'to try a thorough dressing-down first . . . to rid him [Sternburg] of his delusions of grandeur'.[181]

THE FIASCO OF WILHELMINE GERMANY'S AMERICAN POLICY

German naval activity in the Caribbean, the Reich's scarcely concealed ambitions in Latin America and its use of force against Venezuela had led to an international debacle. The attempt by Wilhelm and Bülow to manoeuvre the two Anglo-Saxon naval Powers into opposition with each other, and then to draw first the USA and then Britain on to Germany's side, had had exactly the opposite effect.[182] Waldersee recognised the historical significance of the diplomatic revolution that had taken place in Anglo-American relations, commenting in his diary at the end of 1902: 'Basically this is . . . proof of how strongly the position of the United States has improved in the course of a few years . . . The best thing now would be for us to stick firmly to England *against* America; then the worthy Yankees would be less cocksure. But that is out of the question with the mood in England. Over there we have been quite outdone in grovelling for America's favour, particularly as the entire nation does it, while here it is chiefly the concern of the government, which unfortunately no one in the outside world really trusts. German policy really has a very poor reputation.'[183] 'What has the Kaiser got out of all his civilities and friendly gestures etc to the Americans!' Waldersee asked.[184] A particularly serious development was the decision of the USA to build a large battlefleet, especially as the Americans left no room for doubt that they would use the navy against the German fleet too, if necessary. Roosevelt bluntly told Speck von Sternburg in February 1903 that during the Venezuelan blockade the German ships had 'seen their future opponent in Admiral Dewey's fleet, while Dewey's people had regarded Germany's ships as their next target', a remark to which Wilhelm reacted with irritation.[185] His fears were apparent at a dinner in honour of the Chief of the General Staff, Count Schlieffen, on 3 April 1903. Waldersee recorded afterwards that 'when the conversation came round to the growth of the American Navy he spoke very bitterly about England and especially about her feeble conduct in the Panama Canal question'. Wilhelm was also 'very annoyed about his failed attempts to win America's friendship'.[186] After a further meeting with Wilhelm in January 1904 Waldersee commented that the Kaiser took a very calm view of the situation. 'But he is angry about the bad feeling in England and America and said he was determined to demand a further increase of the fleet in 1904 . . . I gained the impression that he was thinking of a very large figure.'[187] At the end of his life Waldersee looked back with deep concern over the years of Wilhelm II's reign, which seemed to confirm his worst fears. The general situation was beginning to take on 'a very serious character', he concluded. 'If only the Kaiser would realise that he will get nowhere by polite gestures. We have already lost face far too much that way, in my opinion, and have reached the point where no one trusts either him or our policy; nor is anyone afraid of us any more. It seems to me that we are now beginning to reap the harvest of the policies we have pursued for the last 13 years, most of which I have found incomprehensible.'[188] The feared 'encirclement' of the mighty German Kaiserreich in the heart of Europe had come close to realisation.

CHAPTER TEN

Uncle and nephew: Edward VII and the 'encirclement' of Germany

From early in 1903 there were increasing signs of a revolutionary shift in the international states system which was to lead within a few months to the diplomatic isolation of Germany. Not least out of concern at the growing economic and military power of the Kaiserreich, with its ambitious, unpredictable ruler, the British, who had already formed an alliance with Japan and were on excellent terms with the United States, now turned their attention to St Petersburg, Paris, Madrid and Rome. The conviction that the 'splendid isolation' of the Victorian era could no longer be maintained and that Britain needed new allies was gaining strength. Neither in the government nor in public opinion, however, was there now any enthusiasm for an alliance with Germany. Above all, Germany's plans for her battlefleet, whose 'fundamental aim' was 'to break England's world domination to Germany's advantage',[1] were being 'kept under close scrutiny from England', as Prince Heinrich warned Admiral Tirpitz in October 1903. On the other side of the North Sea people were 'remarkably well informed' about German intentions, the Prince reported.[2]

KING EDWARD AND THE 'ENCIRCLEMENT' OF GERMANY

In February 1903 news reached Berlin that the French Foreign Minister, Théophile Delcassé, intended to enter into negotiations with Lord Lansdowne on the cession of Morocco to France.[3] Subsequently, when Edward VII embarked on a tour to Lisbon, Rome and Paris in the spring, the Kaiser was convinced that machinations by his uncle against him and his Reich lay behind the Anglo-French rapprochement.[4] From then on, in the eyes of the Kaiser and numerous other German decision-makers, the King was perceived as the authentic architect of the dastardly 'encirclement' by which all their fine dreams of world power were thwarted.[5] Soon after the King's return from Paris, Eckardstein, then First Secretary at the German embassy in London, learned that a Triple Entente between Britain, France and Russia might be in the offing.[6] Commenting on this later, he wrote: 'I have not the slightest doubt that during that spring [1903] . . . there was, to some extent, a "plot" to isolate Germany completely. At the time of King Edward's visit to Paris, and likewise during President Loubet's return visit to London, Monsieur Delcassé not only accepted English overtures to bring about an Entente with France, but also tried his best to engineer an Anglo-Russian rapprochement. If only out of pure hatred for Germany, the English side was ready to fall in with M. Delcassé's suggestion. In Russia too there was no lack of support for reconciliation with England.'[7] Soon, indications of a closing of ranks between the three great colonial Powers, Great Britain, France and Russia, began to multiply. Count Bernstorff, the German chargé d'affaires in London, reported on 25 April 1903 that negotiations with the Russian Empire were under way, with the aim of drawing a demarcation line between British and Russian spheres of interest throughout Asia. The Prime Minister, A. J. Balfour – 'a naïve young man' in Wilhelm II's eyes – envisaged, it was believed, a line from west to east stretching from Alexandretta in the eastern Mediterranean via the Hindu Kush to the mouth of the Yangtse.[8]

The Kaiser later boasted of having been practically alone in recognising this dangerous development from the beginning. Commenting in 1904 on Eckardstein's warning of an imminent Anglo-Franco-Russian Entente against Germany, he wrote that this was 'what I always said would happen but no one would believe me'.[9] In fact, Wilhelm at first made light of the possibility that Britain and Russia might settle their differences throughout Asia.[10] Bülow shared his master's optimism and assured him that the diametric opposition between the Russian 'bear' and the English 'whale' – the prerequisite for Germany's 'free hand' policy – was as entrenched as ever. The exploratory talks between the Russians and the British were nothing but the traditional means by which Russia's 'invariably very cunning and Machiavellian diplomacy' played off Britain against the German Reich in order to distract attention from her own expansionist cravings in the Near and Far East. 'In this situation we must constantly strive, in the manner adhered to by Your Majesty with distinction and success hitherto, to arouse neither English nor Russian nor American mistrust. We must neither give the English the opportunity to make the Russians suspicious of us, nor furnish the Russians with any reason to make the English suspect us', the Chancellor exhorted.[11]

Gradually, however, unmistakable signs were emerging that a \
Entente between the three great rivals, Britain, France and Russia,
established. In May 1903 Count Götz von Seckendorff was told
Blennerhassett, sister of the German diplomat Casimir Leyden, tha
VII had gone to Paris with the specific goal of 'creating an Anglo-Franco-
Russian coterie'.[12] After a stay at the British court, where he was a welcome
guest because of his close relationship with the Empress Frederick in the last
years of her life, Seckendorff sent a detailed report on the atmosphere there,
which had a far from reassuring effect on the Kaiser. 'England was now in a
generous mood where Russia was concerned', Seckendorff warned Bülow. If
the Russians had any anxieties about Germany, they could 'à tout prix come
to an agreement with Japan (= England)'.[13] He went on to explain that
'1. Dislike of us in England was very great, but this was due more to
commercial envy than to bitterness at the attitude of our public opinion
during the Boer War; 2. No one in England thinks of attacking us; 3. but
there is a strong tendency in England to reach an understanding with France
and in particular with Russia − partly due to fear, especially of the latter
Power, partly also because England feels the need of an ally but does not want
us as an ally at this stage, being cross with us.' Seckendorff had gained the
impression in London 'that in the Anglo-Russian flirtation, it is England who
is doing the courting while Russia is reserved'.[14]

In a wide-ranging report of 2 June 1903 Count Metternich attempted to set
out the deeper reasons for the dramatic change of direction of British foreign
policy in favour of France, but at the same time to avoid causing any panic in
Berlin. 'The history of recent decades has shown that England is not inclined to
form alliances on the European continent', he began. Although in the 1890s
Britain's isolation and the many interests she had in common with Germany
had led her to reflect on whether an alliance with Germany might not after all
be in her interest, 'her dislike of becoming involved in continental business
overcame all other considerations, and the manifold attempts at Anglo-German
rapprochement never went beyond the initial stages. Those attempts were
based, on the English side, partly on fear, partly on friendship. The fear that
German power might also turn against England has . . . subsided, as far as the
present time is concerned . . . The friendship disappeared with the Boer War . . .
The Anglo-French rapprochement is a product of a shared aversion towards
Germany . . . Without the estrangement between Germany and England the
anglophile mood in France would not have been possible, and Monsieur
Delcassé would still have a long time to wait for his wishes to be fulfilled.
Without the aversion towards Germany the English press would not have been
able to work for months on reconciliation with France, nor could Monsieur

Cambon have made conciliatory speeches. King Edward's visit to Paris is all his own work and, as I know for certain, it was arranged on his own initiative. Far be it from me to assume that King Edward intended to strike a blow against Germany. But as the mood on both sides of the Channel was so favourable, it was perfectly sensible from his own and from his government's point of view to play their part and to dispel the earlier tension . . . I am convinced, however, that the English government does not wish the current reconciliation with France, which has fallen so conveniently into its lap, to create any conflict with Germany. It has the satisfying feeling of having rid itself of one opponent without having to make any sacrifice . . . Reconciliation with one opponent . . . does not necessarily mean making an enemy of a third party. On the contrary, I know that the English government does not wish to break the link with Berlin, but to maintain it.' No political agreements with France had been made, Metternich affirmed, and attempts to come to an understanding with Russia had always been rejected by St Petersburg. The ambassador therefore felt sure at this time that Delcassé's efforts to create a new Triple Alliance between Russia, France and Britain were doomed to failure. 'The Russians and the English have no desire for a punitive expedition against Germany. To form an alliance one must after all have a purpose and an opponent. But where is either to be found for the future Triple Alliance? . . . It seems to me that the prophecy of a future Triple Alliance owes more to impressionism than to the visionary powers of the prophets, and that it is not yet necessary to summon Cincinnatus from his plough. But I would go so far as to assume that even in the event that England and Russia arrived at a modus vivendi . . . the English government, whether Conservative or Liberal, would not make use of this temporarily calm situation to pursue an anti-German policy. Why, in order to rid itself provisionally of one enemy, should it make a new enemy without any provocation? . . . Nevertheless we must not underestimate the anti-German current in England and, I may say, throughout the world. It was especially conspicuous during the Venezuela affair, when the whole world took sides against us, although we were fighting for a totally just cause, whereas England, which is not very popular otherwise, was only a secondary target for criticism. For the moment, calm and patience remain the best policy where the embittered and prejudiced mood in England is concerned.'

The Kaiser praised this report from Metternich as 'excellent' and 'accurate'.[15] Yet the government had every reason to fear his outbursts of frustrated rage, which could put further pressure on relations with Britain. The Chancellor continually reminded him not to allow himself to be distracted from 'our calm, patient attitude', for one could give the English 'no greater pleasure than by losing one's temper now'.[16]

IMPERIAL FRUSTRATION

It would have been obvious to anyone who knew the circumstances of Kaiser Wilhelm's youth and was familiar with his personality – the speed with which he took offence and the ambitious fantasies of world power which he had pursued since the mid 1890s – that he would react with frustration and rage to Britain's rapprochement with France, Russia and Italy. The fact that it was his mother's brother, of all people, who in his opinion had engineered the 'encirclement' of the Reich, must have awakened bad memories of his childhood; perhaps, too, it aroused his guilty conscience over his behaviour towards his parents. More strongly than ever before, Wilhelm was now developing an impatient sense of expectation, intensified by wounded pride and a desire for revenge.

It showed itself at first in the growing resentment he felt when his uncle, after his tour to Lisbon, Rome and Paris, refused to visit the German capital. He was 'hurt and disappointed' that the King had not been in Berlin since his accession, as he complained several times in the course of 1903.[17] How deeply offended he was is particularly evident from the comments he scrawled on a report in the *Daily Chronicle* on the State Visit by King Edward VII which was eventually scheduled for the summer of 1904. He complained that the article was 'positively insulting' and had presumably been written 'by one of the Jewish friends' of the King. 'It shows how the gesture of courtesy towards me and therefore towards the German Reich is regarded in England. It is likened to a business deal – almost like a meat market! If one compares it to the dithyrambs of enthusiasm the newspapers indulge in over the possibility of the Emperor Franz Josef [sic] appearing in England, one can see how far the temperature of feelings towards us in England has fallen.'[18]

Even the choice of Colonel Lord Edward Gleichen as British military attaché in Berlin failed to improve relations between the two royal families. Grandson of Queen Victoria's half-sister, Gleichen was related both to Kaiserin Auguste Viktoria and to Edward VII, and the latter had personally intervened to have him appointed.[19] Although Wilhelm showed his pleasure at this, in his letter of thanks to his uncle he could not resist criticising the circumstances of the appointment. 'I may venture to suggest that the next time the War Office intends to change the Milit. Attaché here, they would be more sensible if they recalled the old one *after* the new one had been presented to me & to the authorities, with whom he is to treat & correspond. But not as was the case this time, recall the acting one, *before* they knew who was to replace him, & leave the post vacant for many months!'[20]

The Kaiser's sense of grievance eventually expressed itself, as feared, in a speech which caused indignation in Britain and seriously worsened relations between the two royal families and the two nations. On 19 December 1903, in Hanover, Wilhelm II asserted that the British would have lost the Battle of Waterloo if Blücher, with his Prussian and Hanoverian troops, had not come to their aid in time. Once again the British press attacked the Kaiser, and Edward VII fulminated against his nephew's remarks, which he considered 'foolish, injudicious & historically untrue'.[21] The King's advisers had difficulty in persuading him not to send a letter of protest. It was hoped that Edward's projected visit to Kiel at the end of June 1904 would provide the occasion for a reconciliation. But before that much more was to happen in the world to excite the Kaiser's fury.

'CRIMEAN COMBINATION' OF THE WESTERN POWERS AGAINST RUSSIA, OR 'A GENERAL COALITION AGAINST US'?

Long before the signature of the Entente Cordiale between Great Britain and France on 8 April 1904 the fact that a new combination of the Great Powers was emerging had been recognised both in the Berlin Schloss and in the government offices of the Wilhelmstrasse. When a report arrived in September 1903 of close cooperation between Britain and France in the Middle East, the Kaiser was dismayed, writing in the margin of the report: 'So these two greyhounds are already hunting the Turkish hare à deux!'[22] It was becoming ever clearer to him that 'Gaul is sticking it out with England after all'; in every aspect of policy, feeling in England was directed against Germany.[23] In October 1903 he commented ruefully in the margin of a report on the growing understanding between Great Britain, France, Italy, the United States and Japan that 'the Crimean War combination with Japan as an ally and America in the background is not bad!'[24] Wilhelm saw the rapprochement of Britain with these Powers as a triumph of democracy, against which the three imperial Powers in eastern Europe must unite.[25] The new British ambassador in Washington, Sir Michael Durand, it seemed, had instructions to draw the United States into the Anglo-French Entente and undermine German influence in America. 'I expected that', the Kaiser wrote on a report from Sternburg.[26] When in December 1903 another joint move by England, France and Italy in the Middle East was in the offing, he remarked that it would soon be apparent 'what sort of plan of action against the imperial powers has been concocted in Paris and London by the "Crimean Combination". England cannot in any circumstances take part in it, and to give Italy the leadership would be tantamount to giving it to England.'[27]

The rapprochement of the two leading maritime Powers, Britain and France, had an almost irresistible magnetic effect on Germany's partner in the Triple Alliance, Italy, whose change of course into the Anglo-French camp could no longer be overlooked.[28] Like the German ambassador in Rome, Count Anton Monts, Kaiser Wilhelm considered that from now on an 'active military intervention [by Italy] on behalf of Germany' was 'out of the question'. Italy's 'neutrality in a potential military conflict on a larger scale', on the other hand, they considered to be a certainty; the German army was also 'quite clear' in this regard. Both the Kaiser and the ambassador attributed this development in part also to the hostile attitude of the young King Victor Emmanuel III towards Austria, and hence towards the Triple Alliance. The views of this ruler, who was 'certainly not without talent', were 'compromised by what amounts to blind hatred, as far as Austria is concerned', the two men agreed.[29] Time and again Wilhelm II deplored the unavoidable fact that Austria-Hungary 'is in conflict with Italy, and the Triple Alliance is coming apart as a result'. 'Does everything have to go wrong for us these days!?' he exclaimed in April 1904.[30]

At this time Kaiser Wilhelm was still describing the ever more apparent cooperation between Italy, France and Britain as the 'Crimean Combination'.[31] He was of course alluding to the coalition between Britain, France, Turkey and the northern Italian kingdom of Sardinia-Piedmont which had been formed to fight Russia in the Crimean War from 1853 to 1856. In 1903 such a coalition would at least have offered Germany a chance that the Franco-Russian Dual Alliance might break up and Russia ally herself with the German Reich and the Danube Monarchy. Gradually, however, Wilhelm was forced to confront the bitter possibility that the reorientation of British foreign policy which was under way was not aimed at creating a Crimean War coalition of the western Powers *against* Russia, as he had originally believed, but rather at bringing together these Powers *with* Russia, thus achieving the international isolation of Germany − a nightmare that would become a reality only a few years later. If things went on like this, he commented in October 1903, sooner or later Germany would be taken by surprise by 'a "global coalition" directed against us'.[32] As the Reich Chancellor telegraphed to Holstein, 'His Majesty ... was very much struck by the report ... received this morning ... that the Tsar, in his letter to President Loubet, expressed his particular satisfaction at the Anglo-French agreement and the Franco-Italian rapprochement. His Majesty considers a general coalition against us not unlikely, and thinks the Tsar's remark shows that in any case it was a fantasy to assume that a Crimean War group would come together against Russia.'[33] By the end of 1903 Wilhelm was no longer in any doubt that 'England is − privately − working flat out to isolate us.'[34]

At first the closer cooperation between Britain, France and Italy, with Russian support, was most in evidence in the Balkans, where even the Habsburg Dual Monarchy began to follow in the wake of the new constellation. In September 1903 Kaiser Wilhelm expressed himself strongly against Germany's ally Austria-Hungary, which suddenly joined forces with Russia in the contentious Macedonian question. 'That really is outrageous!' and 'an inglorious end to Austrian stupidity in the Balkans', he commented angrily. His reaction was defiant. 'We shall stick to my policy towards the Turks! I do not care a jot whether I am isolated or not! I am not joining in this highway robbery! My policy is not going to be dictated by Herr Bachmetieff [the Russian ambassador in Constantinople]!'[35] The other Powers, however, continued to deal with the crisis on the Balkan peninsula without involving Germany. Wilhelm was dismayed. 'England, Russia, Austria arrange matters in the Balkans, with Italy and France in the background, and we are left out! It will end up with Russia being offered Stamboul!'[36]

The pain of Germany's growing isolation was felt all the more acutely because the only dependable ally remaining to the Reich, multinational Austria-Hungary, seemed to be moving inexorably towards disintegration. The Reich Chancellor wrote to the Kaiser from Norderney in September 1903: 'Is the ancient Habsburg Monarchy already falling apart? I do not believe so for the time being, although I admit that it is showing Hippocratic symptoms ... This much seems certain: that Austria-Hungary would no longer have the strength and courage to do anything but ally herself to Russia in order to defend herself from a direct Russian attack.'[37] Bülow was concerned that in military, aristocratic, Slavophile and ultramontane circles in Cisleithania there was talk of seeking a rapprochement with Russia and France in place of the alliance with the German Reich; only the Magyars across the Leitha River could prevent such a diplomatic volte-face. Wilhelm II shared Bülow's concern, and treated his visit to Kaiser Franz Joseph in September 1903 as a public demonstration that 'Germany continued to see the Danube Monarchy as her faithful and fully equal ally'.[38] Nonetheless this crisis-ridden partner continued to be a source of great anxiety. When, following Wilhelm's visit to Vienna, Polish newspapers in Galicia deplored Austria-Hungary's close link with Germany, his reaction was to describe the Slav peoples of the Danube Monarchy as 'Bastards!'[39]

As war between Russia and Japan drew nearer in the winter of 1903–4, London and Paris intensified their efforts to come to an understanding, both governments being anxious to avoid being dragged into the coming conflict between their respective allies.[40] Despite his fears of international isolation for the German Reich, the Kaiser still saw the Anglo-French rapprochement above all as an opportunity to prise apart the Dual Alliance between Russia and France and conjure up a new Dreikaiserbund bringing together the German, Russian and Austrian empires. When the French premier, Maurice Rouvier, declared that his country's alliance with Russia did not extend to East Asia but only to Europe, Wilhelm greeted this announcement jubilantly with the remark: 'If that is the case, and Rado and Alvo [the ambassadors Prince Radolin and Count Alvensleben] must confirm it first, one can well imagine how furious the Russians must be about the "Crimean Combination"; and of course we shall have a much better hold over them!'[41]

The Kaiser was by no means alone in making this optimistic assessment, for the diplomats in the Wilhelmstrasse were also wedded to the 'free hand policy' between east and west. During a visit to St Petersburg the diplomat Wilhelm von Stumm discovered that the Russian government had virtually given up any expectation of help from France in a war with Japan.[42] In a memorandum of 16 January 1904 Holstein spoke of a complete 'about-face' of French diplomacy. The imminent end of the Franco-Russian alliance and the rapprochement of France with Britain and Italy had been 'patiently prepared and . . . unremittingly pursued' by Paris for years, he asserted. Holstein still relied on the assumption that the conflicts between Russia and Britain on the one hand and between Russia and America on the other were still insuperable and would remain so in the future. Both in East Asia and in the Middle East Russia thus faced diplomatic isolation. 'Germany is therefore the only Power to which Russia can turn for help.'[43]

There was, however, no lack of voices warning of the danger of the complete isolation of the German Reich. Eckardstein again cautioned that an American–British–French–Italian–Japanese combination might try to encircle Germany by drawing Russia into its ranks. But he saw a Russo-Japanese war as a chance to take the sting out of this threat. The explosive situation in the Far East had 'at least postponed into the distant future the danger that . . . an Anglo-Russian settlement could ever be reached'. No matter whether Russia or Japan won the war, the conflict in East Asia would strengthen Germany's position not only for the moment but for the future too, provided 'that we sit absolutely still', the diplomat stressed. 'I do not believe in "the yellow peril" for the time being, even if Japan won. If Russia won, she would cherish an unconquerable hatred not only for England but also for America, for many years to come.' It was true, however, that as far as the British were concerned, a Russo-Japanese war would 'reawaken the thought that . . . Germany, which is standing by at the ready, would be the deciding factor'.[44]

Eckardstein's observations found a ready ear in the Kaiser, who indicated on 24 January 1904 that he completely agreed with the memorandum.[45] He too was plagued by anxiety that French diplomacy might yet succeed in bringing Russia, France's ally of old, into the Entente Cordiale with Britain. 'Delcassé and Cambon have it all under control', he remarked bitterly in January 1904.[46] Like Eckardstein, Wilhelm saw a Russo-Japanese war as the best chance of separating Russia from Britain and France. He repeatedly deplored the Tsar's 'feeble' attitude to Japan and described him as an 'innocent angel'.[47] He greeted any sign of Anglo-Russian or Franco-Russian tension as 'music to my ears'. When he heard that the Tsar had said Britain was now behaving in exactly the same 'perfidious' way towards his country as she had towards Germany, he commented 'Oui madame'.[48]

With the conclusion of the Anglo-French Entente Cordiale on 8 April 1904 the coalition of west European Powers which Wilhelm II had been predicting for a year became a reality. Bülow tried to play down the significance of this development, at least outwardly. He issued statements to the press and in the Reichstag that the Entente was no more than a 'colonial agreement' which must be regarded as 'a new symptom of the peaceful state of world affairs'.[49] But the Kaiser realised what a profound change had occurred in international relations. On 19 April 1904 he telegraphed to the Reich Chancellor: 'The recent Anglo-French agreement still gives me food for thought on various fronts. In my opinion the French have shown remarkable skill in taking advantage of their present political situation. Without loosening their ties with Russia they have succeeded in extracting a high price from England for their friendship. The dominant position that they have now achieved in Morocco is undoubtedly a great prize for them, and they were able to pocket it cheaply by giving up their rights in Egypt, which were more theoretical than practical. As our commercial interests in Morocco are considerable I hope we have secured the necessary guarantees that our trade there will not suffer. England, for her part, has acquired a completely free hand in Egypt. The possible sources of friction between France and England have been substantially reduced by the agreement, and the latter has gained a great deal of freedom of manoeuvre elsewhere in the world as well. It is only to be expected that England's growing friendship with France, and the security it gives her *that she need fear nothing from that quarter, will make the English less and less likely to show us any consideration.* The language used by the English press also proves, at any rate, that people there are as ill-tempered towards us as ever.'[50] Bülow could not but agree with the Kaiser's conclusions and indeed took them further, pointing out that the Anglo-French combination would have an even more magnetic effect on Italy than before.[51] Wilhelm was not convinced by assurances from his diplomats that the Entente could be complemented by an Anglo-German rapprochement, commenting meaningfully:

'No, because we are too alike, and we shall be stronger than the French.'[52] Although he did not think war with Britain was inevitable, he kept it in mind for the future and agreed with the sentiments expressed by Bernstorff in a report from London of 16 April 1904: 'If, for the sake of German power and German expansion, it really becomes necessary to wage war with England some day, then every hour that this battle can be delayed is a bonus for us.'[53]

At the very latest with the signing of the Anglo-French Entente in April 1904, the policy of Weltmacht introduced by Kaiser Wilhelm II, Bülow and Tirpitz eight years earlier had failed. Not least in order to hold back the supremacist ambitions of the Kaiserreich a ring had formed, encircling the globe, against which Germany could not prevail. The World Powers of Great Britain, France, the United States, Japan and, latently, Russia too, joined forces and blocked the way to hegemony; Italy withdrew de facto from the Triple Alliance, leaving Germany alone with the disintegrating Danube Monarchy. But instead of altering course from their thwarted expansionist drive and seeking new allies, the Kaiser and the Reich government chose to continue with the naval and world-power policies that represented such a threat to the other Powers. Talk of a great and unavoidable war could now be heard on all sides.

THE MEDITERRANEAN CRUISE OF 1904

When Wilhelm II heard of the conclusion of the Entente Cordiale he had not been in Germany for several weeks, but had been cruising in the Mediterranean. He had left Bremerhaven on 11 March 1904 and only returned to Berlin, via Genoa, at the end of April. The North German Lloyd line had put the large, luxuriously appointed steamer *König Albert*, equipped to carry thousands of passengers, at the Kaiser's disposal, and he had settled in with a suite of twenty-five gentlemen and fifty servants. It was only two days before his departure and almost by chance that the Chief of the Admiralty Staff, Büchsel, and the Foreign Office heard of the Kaiser's intention of taking the most modern cruiser of the German battlefleet, *Friedrich Karl*, as a protective escort for his voyage.[54]

On 16 March 1904 the *König Albert* dropped anchor in the northern Spanish port of Vigo. There Kaiser Wilhelm, 'in the very best of moods', met the young King Alfonso XIII, whom he found 'simply enchanting'.[55] The two monarchs discussed the explosive question of the future of Morocco, in connection with which, as Metternich had reported from London, an Anglo-French agreement in France's favour was emerging at this precise moment.[56] Wilhelm calmly advised the young King to maintain the best possible relations with France and

Britain, but to beware of Portugal, as 'the Portuguese, above all the Court, . . . were no longer anything but vassals of the English'.[57] He expressly welcomed the 'arrangement' which Spain had just made with France over Morocco.[58] On the question of compensation for Germany the Kaiser expressed himself with uncharacteristic restraint, to the astonishment of his diplomats, who remembered his earlier greed for Moroccan acquisitions – whether a complete colony or limited coastal strips with ports for coaling stations.[59] From Vigo Wilhelm telegraphed to Bülow saying that he had congratulated Alfonso on the agreement with France over Morocco, which he 'approved and considered sensible', and that he had emphasised that Germany was seeking '*no territorial acquisition*' there, but only 'open ports, railway concessions and the import of her goods'. He even considered the idea put forward by the Wilhelmstrasse of acquiring the Sous estuary and the port of Agadir as 'impractical'.[60] Before the Kaiser's meeting with Alfonso XIII, Joseph Maria von Radowitz, the German ambassador in Madrid, had reminded him that German diplomats, in view of the imminent agreements between France and Britain, already envisaged the possibility of compensation in the Moroccan dispute and that this had been confidentially discussed with the Spaniards. Wilhelm II, however, had responded by saying that 'there was no reason now to go back to that; he was not seeking for anything in Morocco except advantages for our trade and for the spread of civilisation'. Radowitz was surprised to see how forcefully the Kaiser advocated this point of view in Vigo. 'Regarding Morocco, His Majesty said that *we* were not pursuing our own interest in any way, nor, in particular, any territorial wishes at all, and that we would limit ourselves exclusively to the preservation of commercial freedom and the furtherance of cultural activity. In that, Spain would always find us on her side.'[61] Wilhelm's emphatic denial on the question of territorial acquisitions in Morocco thus ran counter to the policy advocated by the Chancellor and the Foreign Office and sowed the seeds of future conflicts.

At the end of March 1904 Holstein was still under the impression that the Kaiser was seeking to acquire a port on the west coast of Morocco.[62] In fact Wilhelm's territorial ambitions lay elsewhere at this point. It was not the Sous estuary that he coveted, but the island of Fernando Po, off Cameroon, the present-day Macias Nguema, which he wished to acquire by 'payment'.[63] This island, a Portuguese colony, had great strategic significance for two reasons: as protection for the German colony on the mainland facing it, and – more importantly – as a naval base halfway between Gibraltar and the Cape of Good Hope. But the Kaiser deliberately left the young Spanish King in the dark about this. When he arrived in Minorca, on the other hand, he surprisingly expressed the wish to lease Port Mahon on the east coast of the island as a German coaling station. The Foreign Office quietly dropped this imperial suggestion as something completely unattainable.[64]

During his three-day stay at the British naval base of Gibraltar Wilhelm II's hyperactivity and his notoriously know-all attitude once again caused discomfort in London. The fortress made a powerful impression on him.[65] The Kaiser and his suite were surprised by the openness with which their British hosts escorted them through the casemates to the signalling station and showed them some of the defensive installations. When the *König Albert* left Gibraltar on 20 March to a thunderous salute from the Royal Navy, Wilhelm stayed on deck for a long time in a state of 'happy excitement. The Kaiser was very impressed by the reception he was accorded', noted Rudolf von Valentini, who was in the party as the representative of the Civil Cabinet. 'He almost felt like an Englishman and yet he does not realise that they must be suspicious of his naval policy. A fantastic idea of his importance as "Admiral of the Fleet" and the unfortunate saying "Blood is thicker than water" govern his ideas of his relationship with England.'[66] In reality the government in London had, with the King's agreement, taken precautions to keep the Kaiser away from the most sensitive areas of the defences at Gibraltar.[67] Naturally the restrictions imposed on him did not prevent the 'Admiral of the Fleet' from offering uninvited criticism of the installations and thereby offending the 'representatives of England's proud power'. After the visit to Gibraltar Wilhelm sent a 'remarkable' letter to Edward VII, which the latter forwarded to Admiral Prince Louis of Battenberg. Both he and the King reacted with astonishment and scorn. Battenberg rejected the Kaiser's criticism, commenting, 'Gibraltar, like all our naval bases, is defended to resist any *probable* attack, − not every *possible* attack. We cannot admit for a moment that during War a large fleet of hostile battleships would be at liberty to sit down in front of Gibraltar and pound it to pieces ... What "William II" [sic] has apparently not grasped is that the Naval Bases of the *inferior* side must necessarily be more strongly defended than those of the *superior* side.' The detailed criticisms the Kaiser had made, which were based on false assumptions, only proved 'how superficial his naval knowledge is'.[68] Whatever the Kaiser hoped to achieve by his remarks, they did nothing to improve the atmosphere between him and the King on the eve of the meeting they were to have in June.

A curious situation arose when it transpired that the French President, Émile Loubet, would be on a state visit to Italy from 24 to 28 April, at just the time when Kaiser Wilhelm was due to begin his homeward journey via Genoa. The idea of a meeting with Loubet and Victor Emmanuel III in Italy appealed to Wilhelm. In view of the Anglo-French rapprochement, however, Bülow and the Foreign Office regarded a meeting with the French head of state as most inopportune.[69] The responsible statesmen in the Wilhelmstrasse lived in fear of an act of imperial defiance for several anxious days.[70] On 28 April the news that the Kaiser had arrived in Karlsruhe without incident was therefore received in Berlin with relief.

KING EDWARD VII'S VISIT TO KIEL

On both the German and the British sides there were renewed efforts to play down the significance of the Entente Cordiale for Anglo-German relations by emphasising the close family relationship between the two ruling houses.[71] In political circles high hopes were placed in a visit by King Edward to Germany, although both sides recognised the danger of anti-British demonstrations. The Kaiser was also afraid that the Pan-German League, who had 'no sense!', would undermine the purpose of the visit.[72]

On 12 May 1904 Edward VII sent a very friendly letter to his nephew thanking him for his comments on the fortifications at Gibraltar and announcing that he would be coming for 'Kiel Week' in June.[73] But the King's visit was ill-starred. At the beginning of June the Kaiser exchanged extraordinarily strong words with the British ambassador about the repercussions on German rights in Egypt of the Anglo-French accord. In a conversation with Lascelles on 6 June Wilhelm, for the first time, threatened war in response to what seemed to him to be the outrageous attitude of the British government. He telegraphed to the Reich Chancellor: 'I have had a very serious discussion with the English Ambassador. He himself brought up the subject of the incomprehensible behaviour of the government in London regarding our negotiations. He said he had no explanation for it. He did not understand his own government any more. He had already sent as rude a telegram as possible, in very strong terms, to London and was going there himself tomorrow to clarify the situation. I gave him to understand that this behaviour was unacceptable, just at the moment when we are preparing a ceremonial reception for the King. It reinforced the pessimists in their assumption that England and France were plotting to do serious harm to Germany, which I had not wanted to believe before now. I would of course know how to defend myself against that, but I said that I must state that Germany had not given even the slightest reason for such a coalition to be formed against her, and therefore looked to the future with complete trust in God and with a good conscience. If England really intended to play off France against us, like Japan against Russia, we would show ourselves equal to this task; but I hoped that these assumptions, which were beginning to gain ground in Germany, were wholly unfounded, and that His Excellency would succeed in persuading people in London to see reason and learn good manners. This affair had to be settled before the King's visit; in any case I intended to keep a very close eye on British diplomacy in St Petersburg and to take very severe action against any intrigue.'[74] The dispute was in fact resolved after a Cabinet decision in London, but any thought of a more wide-ranging agreement with Germany 'has now dropped entirely into the background', as the Foreign Secretary, Lord Lansdowne, told the King.[75]

Although Edward VII had himself suggested attending Kiel Week, he was anxious for his visit to be treated as informally as possible. He asked Metternich to arrange for the honorary suite to be attached to him in Germany to wait until the Royal Yacht *Victoria & Albert* reached harbour at Kiel before coming on board, rather than boarding at Brunsbüttel. He also expressed the wish – promptly disregarded by Wilhelm II – 'that the visit of His Majesty the Kaiser ... should likewise take place only when the Yacht is anchored in the harbour at Kiel, that is to say, not as soon as she sails out of the Kaiser Wilhelm Canal'. In addition, the King asked for the text of the speech which the Kaiser intended to make during the welcoming ceremony on board the *Hohenzollern*. Metternich passed on this request, explaining that 'as the guest of His Majesty the Kaiser on a German ship, King Edward would also speak German in replying. In spite of his knowledge of German, however, he would like to have time to consider his answer in advance, as it is, after all, harder for him to make a speech in German than in English. He would therefore very much like to exchange toasts beforehand. King Edward also believes that it would be in the general interest if no political reference of any kind were made in the toasts to be given. I have the impression', Metternich added, 'that King Edward does not yet consider his Englishmen ready to listen to talk of ancestral ties or community of interests with the Germans without feeling inwardly uncomfortable, and I am afraid he is right'.[76]

On 20 June the Reich Chancellor received the draft of the toast which the Kaiser intended to give at the welcoming ceremony for the King in Kiel, with a request for his comments. It read: 'It gives me great satisfaction to bid Your Royal and Imperial Majesty welcome for the first time on board a German warship. Choosing the sea route, Your Majesty has reached the shores of Germany as the ruler of a great Empire that encompasses the globe by sea, and you also most kindly wish to participate in our German sailing events. Your Majesty was greeted by the thunderous salutes of the German Fleet, which is delighted to see its Honorary Admiral. It is the newest creation among the fleets of the world and an expression of the revived growth of the naval prestige of the German Reich which the Late Great Kaiser created anew. Destined to protect the Reich's trade and its colonies, the Fleet, like the

German Army, serves to maintain the peace that the German Reich has kept
for over 30 years and that Europe has shared in keeping. Everyone knows from
Your Majesty's words and deeds that all Your Majesty's efforts are directed
towards this same goal, the preservation of peace. Since I have done everything within my power to reach this goal too, may God grant success to our
endeavours. In grateful remembrance of the unforgettable hours we shared by
the death-bed of the great Creator of the Empire over which Your Majesty
now reigns, I raise my glass to Your Majesty's health. I drink to the health of
His Majesty the King of Great Britain and Ireland, Emperor of India.' Bülow
had not been able to assist in drafting the toast; it was only later that he
managed to change the word 'colonies' into 'territory' and to have the late
Queen described as 'great ruler' instead of 'great creator' of the British
Empire.[77] Apart from this, he was forced to accept the text, which was
regarded abroad as bombastic and threatening.[78]

   Although Edward VII was anxious to stress the sporting and family nature
of his visit as much as possible, the international political dimension of the Kiel
meeting at this particular moment could not be overlooked. Wilhelm, above
all, had very high expectations of his uncle's visit. Characteristically he insisted
on personally deciding every last detail of the meeting of the two monarchs.
Hofmarschall Robert Count von Zedlitz-Trützschler thought it positively
'strange ... how much importance the Kaiser attributed to this meeting.
He involved himself in everything, down to the trivia of the decoration of
the "Hohenzollern". A large tent roof was stretched over the promenade deck,
wonderful floral decorations were arranged, with little fountains and waterfalls
splashing among them to delight the eye. A dinner for 108 people and a tea
party for 220 were given in honour of the King. The Kaiser regarded these
things as so important that three quarters of an hour before the festivities
began he was already completely ready (in full dress), walking restlessly
around the deck, and could scarcely bear to wait for the time to go by.'[79]
Rudolf von Valentini was equally critical of Wilhelm's role in the arrangements for the 'memorable' visit by the King. 'The Kaiser had called up all
possible resources to prepare an impressive reception for his guest. The harbour
was full of warships of all sizes and vintages, even the oldest tubs were brought
out and fixed up so as to give the English as overwhelming as possible an idea
of our naval power. Whether this was wise seemed highly doubtful to us
outsiders even then ... And in the midst of this contingent of flag-bedecked
ships lay the black yacht "Victoria and Albert", with the threatening presence
on board of a man who was less likely to be taken in than anyone else, and who
in his heart was already determined to send all this to kingdom come ...
Everywhere we were struck by the cool, reserved manner of the guests, which

Figure 9 Uncle and nephew: Edward VII and Wilhelm II in Kiel, June 1904

even the urbane, jovial demeanour of the corpulent King himself could not disguise. This array of power and splendour only too clearly carried the message: "Friend, feel my strength and defend yourself." And this friend did not fail to draw the obvious conclusions from this gesture.'[80] (See Figure 9.)

Zedlitz was also struck by the contrast between the two rulers when he saw them together at Kiel. He was impressed by the King, who had become 'thinner' and 'more agile' and looked 'splendid', and admired the Parliamentary Monarchy, which Edward embodied, rather than the Personal Monarchy that Wilhelm II had established. 'What a difference between the two rulers! There may well have been much to reproach the King with in his private life. But now he has become a personage who is highly esteemed in his country. – I believe that in his lifetime he has managed to acquire a degree of experience of the world that is rarely accorded to a ruling prince; out of that grows a knowledge of human nature that is of inestimable value to a ruler. Furthermore there is the peculiarly English constitution by which he cannot be made responsible for failures, and yet has enough room for manoeuvre to maintain his position as a skilful and significant force for the good of his country . . . The reign of Queen Victoria will probably stand as historical proof of how extraordinarily favourable this form of government has turned out to be not only for the people but also for the strengthening of the throne in England. If one compares it with our system and the personality of our ruler, one cannot but concede that this "throwing-oneself-into-the-breach-at-every-opportunity" is one of the most dangerous forms of government. However great our Kaiser's gifts might be, they could only help him acquire real knowledge of human nature and of the world if he had truly lived in the world and among people.'[81]

The visit ended with the usual exchange of telegrams containing extravagant expressions of thanks and assurances of friendly relations between the two nations.[82] The Reich Chancellor reported to Holstein with obvious relief: 'The English visit passed off well. King Edward gave me the honour of repeated and lengthy conversations and met me with kindness and confidence. My general impression is that relations with England could improve in time, but that this cannot be achieved overnight, but only by patience and great tact.'[83] In fact the hopes which the Kaiser had pinned on his uncle's visit had not been fulfilled at all. Zedlitz rightly feared that the benefits of the Kiel meeting would be outweighed by its ill effects. 'Everyone will certainly pretend', he wrote, 'that we are on the best possible footing with England, and that through the two monarchs in particular all the problems have been more or less eliminated for a time; but in fact all the problems between the German and the English peoples still exist, and the people who work hard to stir up these conflicts will only be encouraged to do so with even more enthusiasm.'[84]

CHAPTER ELEVEN

East Asia in flames: the Russo-Japanese War and its consequences

In view of the historical significance of the constellation of Powers which formed in 1903–4, linking Britain, France, Italy, the United States and Japan, and considering the bitterness with which the Kaiser reproached his uncle Edward for instigating the 'encirclement' of Germany, the lack of concern with which Wilhelm II initially regarded the emergence of the 'Crimean Combination', as he repeatedly called it, is very striking. One explanation can be found in his expectation that he would be able to exploit this 'democratic' Crimean coalition to further his own grand designs. As we saw in the previous chapter, Tsarist Russia was to be persuaded to disengage from its republican ally, France, and to join forces with the imperial monarchies of Germany and Austria-Hungary instead. While London and Paris were engaged in negotiations over their differences in Egypt, Morocco and Canada, which were finally resolved with the Entente Cordiale in April 1904, Kaiser Wilhelm persistently incited the Tsar to attack Japan.[1] He tried to persuade Nicholas that world history had predestined holy Russia to be the defending champion of the 'white race' and of Christendom against the 'yellow peril'. He held out the prospect of the whole of Korea and even Peking belonging to the Russian Empire after the victory over the Japanese which Russia would undoubtedly achieve. The 'Admiral of the Pacific' and the 'Admiral of the Atlantic' would thereafter rule Eurasia between them. Together Germany and Russia would then be able to put an end to British supremacy at sea and divide the 'best' of the British colonies between them. France and the other 'democratic' Powers which had come together in the Crimean coalition would, in one way or another, decline into insignificance. The continent of Europe − naturally including Russia, which would in the end be entirely dependent on Germany − would then be safely in German hands.[2]

WILHELM THE WAR-MONGER

The inner world of Kaiser Wilhelm II is documented in more detail in the
weeks leading up to the outbreak of the Russo-Japanese War than at almost
any other time. Practically every day, as if intoxicated, he expounded his hopes
of world domination in personal letters and telegrams to the Tsar or in long,
excited annotations on diplomatic reports. Ever since the meeting of the two
emperors in Reval in 1902, when Nicholas II had declared his intention of
going to war against Japan in 1904,[3] Wilhelm had been confidently expecting
military action by the Russians in East Asia as soon as their fighting forces
on land and at sea were ready.[4] The closer the East Asian war came, the more
Wilhelm intensified his efforts to propel the Tsar into war with Japan.
In the three months between their meeting at Wiesbaden and Wolfsgarten
at the beginning of November 1903 and the Japanese attack on Port Arthur on
8–9 February 1904 the Kaiser wrote to the Tsar no fewer than nine times –
more than in the years from 1899 to 1903 together.

In a letter of 19 November 1903 Wilhelm, writing as always in his
idiosyncratic English, stressed not only their close family relationship but also
the strong community of interest between the three eastern European imperial Powers vis-à-vis the western Powers under parliamentary rule. He urged
the Tsar to beware of the growing influence of the Anglo-Franco-Italian
'Crimean coalition' in the Balkans, above all in Bulgaria. This development
proved once again, Wilhelm suggested to the Tsar, 'what I hinted at in our
conversation, that the "Crimean Combination" is forming and working
against Russian interests in the East. "The democratic countries governed by
parliamentary majorities, against the Imperial Monarchies." History always
will repeat itself.'[5]

During their meeting in Hesse Wilhelm had asked the Tsar for permission
to send him news of military matters from time to time and with this in mind
he had given Nicholas a 'private' cipher which would allow the two monarchs
to correspond without the mediation of their ministers. The 'autocrat'
Nicholas immediately passed the telegraph cipher to his Foreign Minister
and had all Wilhelm's secret telegrams decoded in the Foreign Ministry.[6] The
Reich Chancellor and the German Foreign Office, on the other hand, knew
nothing of the exchange of dispatches between the two sovereigns. On
3 December 1903 the Chief of the Admiralty Staff, Büchsel, had an audience
with the Kaiser at which he submitted a memorandum headed 'Are there
advantages for Japan in beginning a war with Russia during the winter'.[7] The
very next day Wilhelm telegraphed to Nicholas saying: 'The Officers in
Command of my troops in China have been for a long time already ordered

closely to survey the intercourse between Japs and Chinese Military and the growing influence of Japan with the Chinese Army, 2 days ago I got a report that the Japs are clandestinely arming the Chinese behind your and my backs against us ... The Chinese troops are drilling day and night and ... remarkably well! Commanded by Jap instruction officers, whose numbers are steadily increasing! Nice business! I believe the Chinese [ought] not to be allowed to have Japs in their Army! They are sure to rouse Chinese hopes and inflame their hatred against the White Race in general and constitute a grave danger to your rear in case you would have to face a Jap[anese] adventure on the Seashore. Begging your pardon for my liberty I have taken, I hope the Admiral of the Pacific will not be angry with the Admiral of the Atlantic's signals, who is always on the look out! Ta, ta.'[8]

Even without seeing Wilhelm's private telegrams to the Tsar the Reich Chancellor was concerned about the Kaiser's war-mongering and about the effect that this might have above all in Britain, Japan's ally. At the end of December 1903 Bülow, the man officially responsible for German foreign policy, found himself pleading desperately for German support for Russia's East Asia policy to be kept secret. He quite rightly feared that the covert goals of German policy would be exposed by Wilhelm II's excessive enthusiasm and would filter out of St Petersburg to Paris, London and Washington.[9] But the Kaiser would not allow himself to be tied down. In his marginal note on Bülow's letter the Supreme War Lord expressed his views on the coming Russo-Japanese conflict in terms that were nothing if not clear. '*What our relations with the Russians are*, any half-way intelligent politician in the world could have worked out perfectly easily, especially since Wiesbaden. Anyone who has read our press and the Russian press with attention – and can read between the lines – will not doubt for a moment that we will *not* take a hostile line towards the Russians in their East Asian conflicts.' Wilhelm reminded the Reich Chancellor that since the occupation of Kiaochow in 1897 he had never left the Russians in any doubt that he would protect them from the rear in a war with Japan, as a result of which large contingents of Russian troops had been moved from the western to the eastern border of the Russian Empire. 'That would not have happened if the governments had not been in agreement!! Even the stupidest Japanese or British "capman" [sic!] can understand that!'[10]

In his Christmas letter of 3 January 1904 Wilhelm assured the Tsar that he would be absolutely entitled to an ice-free port on the Pacific, as well as to Manchuria and the entire Korean peninsula. 'Everybody here understands perfectly that Russia following the laws of expansion must try to get at the Sea for an iceless outlet for its commerce. By this law it is entitled to a Strip of coast where such harbours are situated (Wladiw[ostock], Port Arthur) their

"Hinterland" must be in your Power so as to allow your building the Railways which are to carry the goods to the ports (Mandschuria). Between the two ports is a tongue of land which may – in one adversary's hand – become a new sort of Dardanelles. That is impossible for you to allow. These "Dardanelles" (Korea) must not threaten your communications, thereby hampering your commerce. That is already on the "Black Sea" and that is not what you [went] to the Far East for! Therefore it is evident to every unbiassed [sic] mind that Korea must and will be Russian. When and how that is nobody's affair and concerns only you and your country. That is the opinion of our People here at home and therefore there is no excitement or "emballement" or war rumors or anything of that sort *here*. They are sure and that Korea will once be yours is a foregone conclusion here like the occupation of Mandschuria, hence nobody trouble [sic] themselves about it here!'[11] Wilhelm angrily refused the Reich Chancellor's request to see in advance, and perhaps help to draft, this highly political letter to the autocrat of all the Russias. In the first place, he retorted, the letter had already been sent and could not be stopped. And secondly he wished to remark 'that some limit must be placed on the constant editing of my private correspondence with the Tsar. My letters are being made to seem more and more like notes or memoranda, which is not at all what they are otherwise. And it could make the Tsar much more suspicious if he ever had reason to believe that my "*private* letters" were drafted in the Reich Chancellery! I might also come to think it unnecessary ever to show you "private letters" in advance any more!'[12] Heedless of the Chancellor's concerns, Kaiser Wilhelm continued his breathtaking war-mongering correspondence with the Tsar.

As both sides prepared for war he followed their moves with feverish interest. In his view, time was on the side of Russia and against Japan. When, therefore, the Russians showed themselves temporarily willing to come to a compromise, he saw this at first as a brilliant chess move which would enable them to undermine both the Japanese claim to supremacy in East Asia and Britain's strong position in the Middle East. In a long and confused comment appended to a submission by the Chancellor of 8 January 1904, in which the latter discussed the Russians' willingness to make peace on the one hand and Japan's increasing determination to go to war on the other, Wilhelm expressed the opinion that if there were no war, '*Then Japan has de facto lost Korea*, for she has missed her "*last good opportunity*". Then Russia will certainly *seem* to be the one who "gives way" or "calls a halt"; but by waiting longer she will grow stronger and stronger, her superiority will no longer be in any doubt and Japan's prospects will be less and less favourable. If the Japanese, after all their threats and fuss and arming, abandon the idea of an expedition to Korea and demobilise without a battle, at the moment when Russia *is apparently backing*

away, I would consider it a heavy defeat for Japan and a great moral victory for
the Russians. For everyone will say: if the Japs do nothing to the Russians at
the *present opportune* moment, since it is clear that Russia is not yet ready,
they certainly will not dare to do so months or years later, when Russia has
been able to establish superior strength. i.e. *the Japanese*, more than all
"Asiatics" – more than all the yellow race, which they aspire to lead against
the Whites – are *morally dead*! So – provided the Japs keep quiet and disarm –
the present "backing out" by the Russians is perhaps a *great moral victory*!
Especially in the eyes of the *Asiatics*, who matter a great deal to Russia! The
consequence will be that wherever Russia's attention may be directed –
Afghanistan, Persia, Tibet – when she makes her wishes clear, the rulers of
those countries will be influenced by the thought: "Japan, *supported by
England*, did not dare rebel against the Muscovites, so England won't do so
alone either!"' The Kaiser's instruction caused consternation in the Wilhelmstrasse, especially as he had added that the Russian proposals for compromise
were particularly suitable for the arbitration tribunal at The Hague. This, in
the view of the experienced officials of the Foreign Office, sounded in the
present circumstances 'like some kind of mockery' and certainly could not be
passed on to the Russian government, as the Kaiser had demanded.[13]

Still more secret telegrams, again without any input from his official
advisers, were dispatched by the 'Admiral of the Atlantic' to the 'Admiral of
the Pacific', spurring him on to take action against Japan and reporting on
Anglo-Japanese intrigues against the Russian Empire, including allegations
that Britain was secretly giving assistance to the Japanese navy.[14] Huge
quantities of tinned food from the USA were being supplied for the Japanese
army and navy. The funds for these massive purchases had unquestionably
been placed at Japan's disposal by a 'very friendly' donor – meaning Britain,
the 'Admiral of the Atlantic' declared.[15] On the same day he wrote to his
'dearest Nicky': 'May God grant that everything will come off smoothly and
that the Japs may listen to reason; notwithstanding the frantic efforts of the
vile press of a certain country [England]. That also seems to have money left to
sink it into the Japanese mobilization abyss.'[16]

While Wilhelm could scarcely control his frustration at the peaceable
attitude of the 'soft', 'unmilitary' Tsar, he welcomed news of Japanese belligerence. From the Japanese point of view the decision to attack soon was 'quite
right', he declared, as Japan would otherwise miss her last chance of a
victory.[17] When a telegram arrived from Count Arco in Tokyo on 13 January
1904, announcing that all Japanese statesmen were now in favour of war,
Wilhelm reacted with enthusiastic approval. This decision was 'understandable!' he commented, for the longer the Japanese 'allow Russia to hold them

off with negotiations ... the heavier the expense will be, and the greater the
eagerness of the whole nation for the fray. If they do not achieve a spectacular
success by peaceful means, which can be presented to the people as a signal
humiliation for Russia, and thus give them complete satisfaction, the Ministers run the risk of having to face an immediate and violent revolution, which
would break out because of the useless waste of money and the battle they had
avoided! Demobilisation without a war becomes more expensive and more
difficult, as their state of mobilisation has already lasted too long and gone too
far ... So it is probable that without a spectacular moral victory of that kind –
which would satisfy the army and the people – demobilisation can scarcely be
declared, they have been playing with fire for too long and it has ignited the
people's passion. In this situation the Russ[ian] suggestion of further *negotiations* is of course the worst and most unpleasant of all things, as they can last
for an unforeseeable length of time, and to continue to keep the Jap[anese]
army and navy mobilised – even drawing heavily on London's purse – for such
a long time would probably be out of the question. So there is *no longer any
guarantee of peace* even in a conciliatory answer from Russia offering negotiations. *But only in her acceptance, unconditionally and without further ado, of
the Jap[anese] demands!* And even something as incredible and seemingly
impossible as this could not be entirely dismissed, given the soft, idealistic,
excessively peace-loving, unmilitary nature of Emperor Nicholas II, if his
counsellors could find the right sugar coating for the bitter pill. And such a
man will perhaps be found! ... Of course the effect on the Russ[ian] Army
would be devastating, and could possibly – considering the Emperor's lack
of popularity in the Army – have unexpected consequences to the detriment
of the "little Father" in the event of serious events *within the country.* Thus
here too there is a "wall" which is the limit to which the Russ[ian] Emperor
can withdraw! We are watching the spectacle of 2 of the most militaristic and
best organised martial nations on earth becoming embroiled in military
complications – almost helplessly, one might say – because they are governed
by 2 rulers who are completely incompetent in military matters, who do not
know what they want, who do not dare to do what they would like, and take
refuge in eternal war councils and state councils out of fear of the responsibility
with which they would gladly saddle their Ministers and Generals; who will
not be happy until their people have forced them to do what they really wanted
to avoid, namely to take up the sword which they fear! However this situation
resolves itself, it must lead to disaster in the end; above all, if there is now no
war, the fuel of unsatisfied passions will accumulate until one day it causes a
world-shattering explosion. The conduct of the Mikado and the Emperor
[Nicholas] deserves the title of "Drifting". Seldom has a great historical

moment found 2 such small minds at the head of two such nations! . . . It seems to me that neither of the governments has yet understood the full scale of the situation. It is not a question of the "open door" in Manchuria, through a Masampho or a condominium in Korea, but of whether Russia is equal to her task of undertaking the protection and defence of the White Race, and with it Christian civilisation, against the yellow race. And whether the Japs are determined to ensure the domination of the Yellow Race in East Asia, to put themselves at its head and to organise and lead it into battle with the White Race. That is the kernel of the situation; and therefore there can be very little doubt about where the sympathies of all half-way intelligent Europeans should lie. England betrayed Europe's interests to America in a cowardly and shameful way over the Panama Canal question, so as to be left in "peace" by the Yankees. Will the "Tsar" likewise betray the interests of the White Race to the Yellow, so as to be "left in peace" and not to embarrass the Hague tribunal too much? Wilhelm I.R.'[18]

The Supreme War Lord of Prussia-Germany was completely baffled by the Tsar's readiness to compromise. 'That is the language of an innocent angel! But not of the White Tsar!' he remarked contemptuously on 15 January 1904. Nicholas's idea that Russia and Japan could co-exist in peace was 'absolutely out of the question, considering Russia's long-terms aims, of which the Japs are aware!' In a 'Signal from A[dmiral] of A[tlantic] to A[dmiral] of P[acific]' of 19 January 1904 Wilhelm told the Tsar that the Japanese community in Chile had heard from Tokyo that the war would begin at the end of the month.[19] Nicholas's reply, indicating that he still hoped for a peaceful settlement with Japan and thought all the reports of war preparations originated from Britain, was treated to a scornful annotation by the Kaiser: 'You innocent angel!'[20] The Tsar simply did not understand, he wrote on a report from London, 'where Japan finds the nerve' to confront a great Power like Russia; in fact it came from 'the Tsar's own attitude!' Wilhelm condemned the Russian request to Britain to mediate in the East Asian conflict as an appalling 'humiliation' of Russia by the country 'which gives Japan ships manned with its own crews and pays for Japanese mobilisation!' Mediation to preserve peace must be 'prevented', the Kaiser commanded.[21] When London rejected a second Russian request for mediation as 'too late' on 8 February 1904, he saw this as 'slap in the face No. 2 from John Bull'. The forthcoming war with Japan, according to his highly critical view of Russian policy, was the result of 'their own shirking and cowardice as well as stupidity'.[22] He was incredulous at the Tsar's birthday letter to him of 24 January 1904 — signed 'Nicky Adm. of Pacific' — which spoke of his continuing hopes for a calm and peaceful agreement with Japan.[23] 'But for heaven's sake, how can he hope for a calm & peaceful solution!?' The

Tsar's belief that Japan wished to avoid war was positively crazy, Wilhelm commented. Nicholas was making 'a gross, incomprehensible mistake!! To continue to believe such a thing after all the information he has received is really inexplicable!'[24] Wilhelm II admitted to Bülow that he had hoped the warmth of his letter of 3 January 'would encourage the Tsar to use all his power against Japan. Instead Nicholas's attitude had remained as timid as ever, he seemed not to want to fight and it was not impossible that he would leave Manchuria to the Japanese in the end without a fight or after feeble resistance. Such a turn of events should at all costs be prevented.'[25]

WILHELM AS THE 'CHAMPION OF THE WHITE RACE' AGAINST THE 'YELLOW PERIL'

The Chancellor's constant attempts to persuade the Kaiser to be more reserved in his communications with the Tsar did not mean that he disagreed with the strategic aims of Wilhelm's policy. On the contrary, Bülow enthusiastically congratulated Wilhelm on his success in manoeuvring apart the Franco-Russian Dual Alliance which had been a threat to the German Reich for so many years. 'The fact that as far as anyone can judge, the danger of a Franco-Russian attack on us, which dominated European and especially German policy for decades, has now receded into the far distance, we owe, next to Divine Providence, to Your Majesty's consistently loyal, friendly and appropriate attitude to the Tsar and Russia', he wrote in the summer of 1904.[26] What concerned the Reich Chancellor was the tactical calculation that the Tsar must not notice that Germany was aiming to lure him into war with Japan. On 16 January 1904 Bülow recorded in a secret note that 'His Majesty quite agrees with me that we must keep quiet with regard to the Russo-Japanese conflict at present, and above all avoid anything which could give rise to the thought, especially in Russia, that we want to stir up a war.' On the other hand the Tsar and his people must 'be convinced that they have a loyal and trustworthy neighbour in the German Kaiser and the German government ... His Majesty told me today he thought it not impossible that if the situation became more acute Russia would request our support in some form. As one ought to prepare for all eventualities in matters of policy, he asked me to set down my thoughts straight away about what counter-demands we could make in such a case.' The Chancellor thereupon asked his advisers in the Foreign Office to draft a *pro memoria* for the Kaiser explaining in plain language the dilemma in which the Far East crisis placed Germany, in view of the increasingly clear evidence that a power bloc consisting of Japan, Britain, France and America was emerging.[27] Privy Councillor Holstein's response was deeply sobering. 'Germany has to . . . weigh the question of whether and under what conditions she wants to stand at Russia's side against Russia's enemies. What would be gained from it and what would be the risks? The issue of military power on land and at sea is of decisive importance for this calculation. If Germany takes sides with Russia she places herself not beside, but in front of Russia, for Germany is the more easily attacked of the two allies, not only through her maritime and colonial interests but also on the continent. Therefore a clear political overview is only possible on the basis of military and in particular – because this is where the greater danger lies – naval judgements.'[28]

It was true, however, that Wilhelm II 'as Sovereign' was also pursuing completely irrational, ideologically oriented aims which made no sense at all to his Chancellor, his diplomats and even his close entourage.[29] In a note recording a conversation with Wilhelm in February 1904 the Reich Chancellor commented on the monarch's extraordinary sense of mission, which in Bülow's eyes conflicted dangerously with the national interests of the German Reich. He warned the Kaiser that 'incautious German words of encouragement addressed to the Tsar' were the surest way of bringing about a premature and bad peace agreement between Russia and Japan. 'If the Tsar noticed that His Majesty wished him to sink his teeth firmly into Japan, it would make him let go at once.' To which Wilhelm replied, according to Bülow, 'that from the point of view of the statesman I might well be right. But he reacted as Sovereign, and as such he was hurt by the way the Emperor Nicholas laid himself open to attack through his feeble conduct. In so doing the Tsar was compromising all great sovereigns. For the sake of the reputation of monarchies something must be done to make the Emperor Nicholas act more forcefully. I responded', Bülow wrote, 'that His Majesty's duty was only to defend his own honour and the interests of the Prussian and German people. The German Kaiser was not responsible for other rulers and peoples. Kaiser Wilhelm I and Frederick the Great would not have fretted about the concerns of others . . . His Majesty answered that times had changed. In those days there had been no Socialists and Nihilists who benefited from the humiliation of monarchs. By his apathetic behaviour the Tsar was damaging the monarchical principle. He ought to go to Moscow and summon holy Russia to battle, mobilise the whole army etc.' Bülow repeated his warning that 'too much lecturing' would only annoy the Tsar and make him suspicious. The Kaiser again conceded, Bülow recorded, 'that my arguments were no doubt correct from the political standpoint', but as sovereign he, the Kaiser, took a broader view and could judge the situation better than statesmen and diplomats, who were concerned only with the present. As a mere politician he, Bülow, failed to see 'a terrible danger', namely the 'yellow peril. It was the greatest danger threatening the white race, Christendom and Europe as a whole. If the Russians gave way even more to the Japanese, the yellow race would be in Moscow and Posen in 20 years.' When Bülow interjected that he 'did not believe in this danger, and that in any case it affected other World Powers, Russia and England, America and France, more directly than us, His Majesty persisted in his view, which he wished me to put down on paper and place in the archives ... We had to draw the Tsar's attention to the gravity of the yellow peril, which he did not yet grasp. I argued that the only result of this would be that the Tsar would call on us to give him armed assistance against a danger that seemed to us to be so great. That would mean war with England.'[30]

When the Japanese declaration of war was announced, Wilhelm was ecstatic. 'Now we must use all means to grab the whole of East Asia, particularly on the Yangste', he exulted.[31] More than that: the staggering geopolitical objective which Kaiser Wilhelm hoped to achieve with his policy in the Russo-Japanese conflict, namely to unite the peoples of Europe under German leadership against the 'yellow peril', again found expression in a note he wrote on 9 September 1904, intended 'to be acted upon by my diplomats!' Japanese distrust of Europe would 'never diminish but only increase!' he commented on a report from Tokyo by Count Arco. As the rising power destined for predominance over the yellow race, Japan had every right to be suspicious of the 'wall' which was in the process of encompassing the white race, enhancing its strength for when the great final showdown between the yellow and white races broke out, in which Japan would lead the Chinese onslaught against Europe. 'At the same time it will be the final battle between the two religions, Christianity and Buddhism; Western culture and Oriental half-culture. It will be the battle which I predicted and drew in the picture, *the one* in which the whole of Europe, as "Etats Unis de l'Europe", should and must come together under German leadership to defend our holiest possessions! Thus there will *always* be bad feelings towards *us* in Japan, because we are beginning to be strong and dangerous *at sea*, and therefore in a position − if they *attack* Europe − to take the war to the shores of Japan, if necessary. Our Navy will represent another enemy for them! We must be prepared to see Japan[ese] squadrons off Heligoland, Kiel and Kronstadt soon! It is instinct which alerts *the same* feeling towards us in the minds of the Japanese, as Caesar felt towards Casca, and Wallenstein towards Butler! Hence the "bad feelings" which make Arco so very nervous! He should not worry a jot about them, for they are good signs that Japan is afraid of us! One should not forget that in the present war Japan is not fighting the Russians *qua* Russians, but because they belong to the white race! We all belong to it too, therefore we other Whites in Europe must always remind ourselves that in this battle "Tua res agitur"! The Russians are defending the interests and also the preponderance of the White race against the growing presumption of the Yellows. Whether the situation for *Europe* is favourable or unfavourable in relation to *Asia* will depend on how the war turns out. Therefore our sympathies must be with *Russia*! And therefore it is of the greatest possible importance that the Baltic Fleet – when ready and trained – should be sent out to win back supremacy at sea and snatch it from Japan. In the Gulf of Petchili the fate of the war will be decided by who ultimately wins maritime supremacy – and if it goes badly for Russia – even the fate of Siberia, which would then be lost; with that, the Asiatic would reach the Urals. It is a question of Russia's future, and indirectly that of the whole of Europe too! That being the case, I can understand Ito's frown or the Mikado's "ill humour", but I do not care in the least about them! Quite simply, I already expect their hostility, which is no longer an unknown quantity in the equation for me, as it is for so many of my compatriots and some of my diplomats too! I *know very well* that one day *we shall have to have a life-and-death struggle* with Japan, and therefore I assume that the Japanese think the same about us. So the situation is clear and I am preparing for it! At any rate the most unstinting benevolent neutrality towards Russia! They shall help us beat off the Japanese later; but it would be better still if they gave them a thorough drubbing now!'[32]

Again at Christmas in 1904, when the Russian Empire was plagued by revolutionary unrest and the Japanese were about to capture Port Arthur, Wilhelm II gave vent to his madcap racist ideology. The conflict in East Asia was 'above all a *purely racial question*! The Japs hate *all Whites*! They will play off one White nation against another and instead of the "open door" they will conjure up "Japano-Chinese Labours" and Produces [English in the original] of unimaginable abundance and cheapness, so that in spite of the "open door" the other products of Europe and America will simply be kept out, as they will be unable to compete. Once they have got hold of Europe with the help of England and America, then it will be the turn of those two, the countries whose production is the most expensive and which pay the highest wages to workforces that have the most expensive "standard of life" [sic]. Then the clash will come in the form of a massive "Labour Question" [English in the original] throughout the white cultural world, when the White Race will unite in arms against the Yellow Race to defend its own existence and to fend off the "Yellow (workers) Peril"!'[33]

THE KAISER AND THE RUSSO-JAPANESE WAR

In February 1904 the war between Russia and Japan which Kaiser Wilhelm II had worked to bring about for two years in his secret correspondence with the Tsar finally broke out. In the night of 8–9 February Japan carried out a surprise attack on the Russian naval base of Port Arthur. Two Russian battleships and a heavy cruiser were torpedoed and the Pacific Fleet was trapped in its harbour. This meant that Japanese troops could be landed in Korea without hindrance. In short order the troops pushed forward over the Yalu river, the frontier between Korea and Manchuria, and advanced towards Port Arthur, which they now besieged by both land and sea.

Two days after the attack on Port Arthur Kaiser Wilhelm took up his pen to console his "dearest Nicky" and stiffen his resolve. 'The outbreak of hostilities has had sad consequences for your brave Navy, which have deeply moved me!' he wrote on 11 February. 'How could it be otherwise seeing that I am Russian Admiral and proud of this rank too! Evidently the serious events show that the warning news I could send you through my ciphers were absolutely correct, and that since long the Japanese Government were in bitter earnest and decided to have war ... I can well imagine how sore at heart you must feel that all your pains to secure peace were of no avail. But on the other hand this gives you a good conscience and a clear one too, which allows a man – as I often say – to march to the fray without knapsack or impediments. It seems that Heaven – on whose help and will we both rely – has willed that it should be so! Then you must look upon the events in the light of a Trial for yourself and your country, which is to enable you and them to show and develop all the great qualities which are dormant in the Russians, which they already once proved in the great times of the first years of the 19th century! ... You may rest assured that day and night my thoughts are occupied with you all!' Once again Wilhelm enclosed with his letter precise details of Japanese arms supplies to China and made a point of condemning France's disloyal behaviour in this connection. 'The [raw] steel material is boxing produced in France (Creuzot) – your Ally! – and to be finished in Japan', he informed the Tsar.[34]

The Kaiser followed the course of the war in the Far East with the help of a map spread out on a billiard table, using it to discuss the situation with his Flügeladjutanten almost every evening.[35] He insisted on working out a precise war plan for the Russians at the very start of the war, although he kept it to himself initially. Not until August 1904, after both the Russian army and the Russian Pacific fleet had suffered crushing defeats, did he impart to the Tsar the different plan of action *he* would have followed, and tell him how the war could still be won. His mobilisation plan, he said, had been based on the number of Japanese divisions, and since these were estimated at 10 to 12, it would be necessary to send 20 Russian divisions, that is to say 10 army corps, to counter them, in order to achieve absolute superiority. Nicholas ought to have sent, in addition to the four Siberian army corps that were already

in Manchuria, six more corps from Russia. 'They would be formed in *2* armies
of *3* corps each served by a cavalry corps of *8* brigades with *4* mounted batteries
per *army*.' He had not ventured to pass these ideas on to the Tsar before, the
Kaiser asserted, 'as it is not my business to meddle with your affairs and I was
afraid of your telling me to mind my own business, as you know better what
Russia requires'.[36]

The fact that the Kaiser was in a position to send the Tsar detailed war
plans and military secrets from East Asia was to a considerable extent
thanks to a personal information network that he had built up shortly
before the war began, in addition to the official reports he received.[37] On
9 January 1904 the Chief of the Kaiser's Naval Cabinet suggested in a letter
to the Reich Chancellor that it would be very instructive for the country's
own navy if German naval officers could be admitted as observers to the
headquarters of the warring parties.[38] Immediately after the outbreak of
war a sharp-eyed corvette Captain, Albert Hopman, was sent to Port Arthur
via Peking. He sent highly informative reports direct to the Kaiser from the
beleaguered Russian naval base, until he was forced to leave the city
in August 1904 in dramatic circumstances.[39] In addition, Wilhelm had
been receiving excellent information about the state of affairs in Russia
from Paul von Hintze, who since July 1903 had been German 'Naval
Attaché for the Northern Empires residing in St Petersburg'. Although
Hintze, unlike Hopman, addressed his reports to Tirpitz, the latter forwarded them immediately to the Supreme War Lord, who covered them
with enthusiastic marginalia and had them sent on to the General Staff and
the Admiralty Staff – but not to the Reich Chancellor or the Foreign
Office.[40] Hintze's appointment as Flügeladjutant early in 1906 only confirmed what had long been obvious: the naval attaché enjoyed a particularly
high level of imperial favour.[41] At the Russian court too, Hintze's position
was unusual. At the end of 1904 he was even asked to write memoranda for
Nicholas II from time to time. The Tsar 'would like to be as well informed
as the Kaiser', he was told at Peterhof.[42]

The information which Hopman, Hintze and others sent to Berlin from the
East Asian theatre of war was to be of great significance for the development
of ship building and tactics in the German navy, but its effect on policy in
the Wilhelmstrasse remained minimal. With his blinkered military vision
Wilhelm II again gave orders that naval attachés and war observers should
behave like the commanders of his ships abroad; their reports were not to be
made available to the civilian authorities, but only to him and the military
and naval high command.[43] As Jonathan Steinberg has rightly observed, the
Chancellor and the Foreign Office would probably have been more reserved

in their dealings with Russia if they had received better and earlier information about the state of the Russian armed forces.[44]

As if that were not enough, in the summer of 1904 Kaiser Wilhelm reverted
to his favoured system of sending the Tsar one of his Flügeladjutanten as
his strictly personal military representative. Without the knowledge of the
Reich Chancellor or the Foreign Office, he wrote to Nicholas II on 6 June
1904 saying that he would send Major Count Gustav von Lambsdorff to
St Petersburg as military attaché, but in the special capacity of an authorised
military representative. 'He is instructed by me to consider himself as attached
to *your person solely*, as it was in the days of Nicolai I and Alexander II. He is
only responsible in his reports to me personally, and is forbidden once and for
all to communicate with anybody else either Gen. Staff, or Foreign Office, or
Chancellor. So you may entrust him with any message, enquiry, letter etc. for
me and make use of him in every respect as a direct link between us two.
Should you like to send me one of your suite who enjoys your full confidence,
I will receive him with pleasure, for I think it highly necessary during these
grave events, that you should be able to quickly communicate with me "le cas
échéant", without the lumbering and indiscrete apparatus of Chancelleries,
Embassies etc.'[45] In return, the Tsar sent his aide de camp Colonel Shebeko to
Berlin. But Shebeko rarely appeared at court and usually spoke only of the
weather to the Kaiser, as the latter complained.[46]

Needless to say, Wilhelm also continued to write to the Tsar encouraging
him in his battle with the 'yellow peril' and giving him military advice. He was
proud, he wrote in June 1904, 'in these days which are of course trying to you,
your army and the country', to be looked on as Nicholas's *real friend* . . . So it
is! And I can assure you that nobody follows all the phases of the war with
greater interest and assiduity than I do.' With clear manipulative intent,
Wilhelm congratulated the Tsar 'on the bravery and gallantry of your soldiers
and sailors who deserve all praise and who have fought very well!' He was
surprised, however, at the 'shortsightedness' of the Commander in Chief of the
Russian troops in Manchuria, Kuropatkin, who was inclined to go on the attack,
instead of remaining on the defensive as the Tsar had wanted. Kuropatkin
ought 'all the more to have followed your councels [sic], as you had been to
Japan yourself, and therefore were a much more competent judge of the Japs
than him. Your warnings were quite right and have been fully borne out by the
facts. I only hope to goodness the General won't jeopardise the final success of
your Forces by rashly exposing them to an "échec" before the whole of his
reserves have joined him, which are as I believe still partly on the way . . . one
can never be too strong for the battle; especially respecting the artillery: an
absolute superiority must undoubtedly be established to ensure victory.'[47]

At the same time Wilhelm pursued his efforts to separate the Tsar from his ally, France, and to nurture his hatred for Britain. Only lately, he wrote, he had expressed his surprise to the French military attaché in Berlin that the French had not sent their fleet out to hold Port Arthur open until the Russian Baltic Fleet had arrived. 'After many hints and allusions' he had found out 'what I always feared – that the Anglo-French agreement had the one main effect, viz. to stop the French from helping you! Il va sans dire, that if France had been under the obligation of helping you with her Fleet or Army I would of course not have budged a finger to harm her; for that would have been most illogical on the part of the Author of the Picture "Yellow Peril"!'[48]

Just a few days later Wilhelm reinforced his letter with a telegram to Nicholas which he again did not show to the Reich Chancellor. In it he told the Tsar that one of his Flügeladjutanten had by chance talked to a British diplomat who was passing through Berlin about the war in East Asia, and had asked him why the French had not come to Russia's aid. The Englishman had replied: 'Oh, no we could not allow that; we have stopped them from doing so; for that would have made us help the Japs, which we don't want to do.' The Kaiser went on to inform the Tsar that the Royal Navy intended in the near future to put in at both French and Italian ports in the Mediterranean.[49]

When Wilhelm II told members of his entourage in May 1904 that it had been 'his intention from the beginning to drive Russia into this situation', Hofmarschall Count von Zedlitz-Trützschler expressed the hope that the Russians would never learn of the Kaiser's remarks. But he feared the worst, for the Kaiser's temperament repeatedly led him into dangerous discussions, even with foreigners. In his diary Zedlitz recorded that Wilhelm's opinion on the outcome of the war had been 'as pessimistic as possible for Russia, both at home and abroad'.[50] Gradually Kaiser Wilhelm had to come to terms with the possibility of a Japanese victory. Already in early May 1904 he realised that the loss of Port Arthur as a stronghold would mean the end of Russian rule in Manchuria. It was quite conceivable that 'Japan will throw the Russians out [of Manchuria] and give it back to China', he remarked.[51] Shortly afterwards he declared that 'for months' he had 'always maintained' that the Japanese did not want to conquer anything for themselves, but would content themselves with giving Manchuria back to China and maintaining their privileged position in Korea.[52]

In spite of his pessimistic assessment of Russia's position, which was confirmed by the reports sent by Hopman from Port Arthur and Hintze from St Petersburg, Kaiser Wilhelm cynically persisted in pretending to the Tsar that his ultimate victory was certain. Even after the Russian fleet's attempt to break out of Port Arthur had failed he urged Nicholas on to further efforts.

He had no doubt, he wrote to the Tsar on 19 August 1904, that 'you will and must win in the long run, but it will cost both money and many men; as the enemy is brave and well led and can only be beaten by overwhelming numbers and time and patience. Of course the operations of the field army will be easier and will give better results, as soon as the Baltic Fleet will have arrived on the scene, and forced the Jap[anese] Fleet back into their ports, thus restituting the *command of the sea* [to] you, now lost by the inefficiency of the Admirals in command of the Naval Forces at Port Arthur. The *command of the sea* is an absolutely necessary equivalent to the final success of the land campaign of the army. As it deprives the enemy of his vast supports, reinforcements, &c. which he can now use freely for the pouring in of reserves, ammunitions, commissariat, evacuation of wounded, &c.'[53] Wilhelm gave this letter to his brother Heinrich, who travelled to St Petersburg on 24 August 1904 for the christening of the little Tsarevich Alexei. During those festivities the Russian army suffered a heavy defeat near Liau-jang.

As Bülow had warned from the outset, the Kaiser's open partisanship for Russia inevitably had serious repercussions for Germany both internationally and domestically. In July 1904 Wilhelm sent 'his' Russian regiment, the 85th Wiborg Infantry, which had been ordered to Manchuria, a goodwill telegram in such effusive terms that it was interpreted everywhere as an indication that Germany would very soon join in the war against Japan. King Edward VII, astonished, asked Sir Frank Lascelles what Wilhelm could have meant by the telegram. The ambassador replied: 'I do not know how far it is usual for Sovereigns who are the honorary chiefs of foreign Regiments to telegraph their feelings when such regiments are ordered to the front when war is going on, and I see in this morning's Times that a German newspaper points out that the Emperor sent a similar telegram to his English regiment when it was ordered to South Africa. It is certainly unfortunate that the Emperor should have used language which made some people think that he was preparing to take part in the war, but I do not believe that this was his intention and I look upon the Telegram as another example of His Majesty's exaggeration of expression. It is somewhat amusing to see how the German Press is attempting to minimize the importance of the Emperor's Telegram and point out that Germany will certainly not abandon her neutral attitude. This I firmly believe to be the case, and although it would have been better if the Emperor had used more moderate language or indeed had not thought it necessary to telegraph at all, I do not think that the Telegram will have any important result, as it is inconceivable to my mind that the Emperor should wish to join in the war when his doing so must inevitably bring about a general European war which it cannot be to Germany's interest to provoke.

But even if the Emperor were personally disposed to help Russia out of her difficulties, I don't believe that even he with all his authority would succeed in inducing the Reichstag to embark on a war in the Far East where German interests are of such relatively small importance.'[54] Kaiser Wilhelm himself, as monarch and soldier, saw it all with different eyes. Later, in October 1904, he thanked the Tsar for conferring countless orders on 'his' brave regiment.[55]

The Kaiser's telegrams to the Tsar could, however, adopt quite a different tone. When the Russian cruiser *Smolensk* seized the Lloyd steamer *Prinz Heinrich* and confiscated the post destined for Japan, the Kaiser, who was then on his annual Scandinavian cruise, telegraphed threateningly that this was 'a violation of international law [and] will create great surprise and disgust in Germany, considering the friendly feeling shown to Russia by our country, and if repeated, will, I fear, contribute to considerably reduce the sympathy still cherished for your country by Germany'.[56] The Tsar was forced to apologise for the excessive zeal shown by the *Smolensk*. Measures had been taken, he assured Wilhelm, to prevent this happening again. It would be 'too sad, if one episode were to spoil the excellent relations existing between our countries'.[57] But only a few days later the Russian Emperor received a second angry telegram from Norwegian waters. A Russian cruiser had captured the Hapag steamer *Scandia* with her officers and crew, Wilhelm complained. 'This act is an open violation of international Sea law and is nearly adequate to piracy. I think it is high time that the captains of the so-called cruisers should receive instructions warning them to refrain from committing such acts ... as they are able to bring about international complications.'[58] For the second time Tsar Nicholas was compelled to apologise.[59] In Britain, which had had a similar experience with Russian warships, the German dispute with Russia was greeted with a certain *Schadenfreude* over the fact that the German government, despite openly favouring Russia, had fared no better than the British.[60] This was exactly the effect that Tschirschky, who was accompanying the Kaiser as Foreign Office representative, had predicted. He sent a woebegone dispatch to the Wilhelmstrasse on 24 July 1904 reporting that he had done his utmost to dissuade the Kaiser from sending the telegram to the Tsar, but in vain. 'I represented to His Majesty the unpleasant impression that such critical language must make on the Tsar, and pointed out that in view of the similar incident pending between England and Russia, it would be politically wiser not to allow an intervention on our part to interrupt the disputes between those two nations. I also opposed His Majesty's view that the Russians were guilty of an "act of insolence towards Germany", as in my opinion the Russian captains had not set out to capture *German* ships, but merely to seize any ships in order to earn the high prize money. His Majesty, however, would not give up his intention; he had to teach the Tsar a lesson personally.'[61] The harsh telegrams were perhaps also a sign of the Kaiser's growing disillusion with the state of affairs in Russia.

The impressions gained by Prince Heinrich during his stay in Russia were not exactly calculated to enhance hopes of a Russian victory. True, Nicholas was full of 'inexplicable optimism' and had sent a message to Wilhelm saying: 'Willy need not be anxious at all, he may go fast asleep at night, for I vouch for it, that everything will come perfectly right'! But the Tsar had described the increasing activity of the Chinese as so dangerous that he was thinking of '*declaring war on China* (!!!)'. On the other hand, there was a general mood of dejection. The Russian grand dukes were 'as always . . . utterly apathetic and unenthusiastic'; they did not 'go out to the battlefield and do nothing but enjoy themselves'. The only good news Heinrich brought back from St Petersburg concerned Kaiser Wilhelm's apparent popularity in Russia. 'My person in great favour *for now* in every respect', he telegraphed to Bülow in high delight. 'Population in the country so devoted to me personally that in Moscow at the announcement of the birth of the heir to the throne, they immediately called for the German Kaiser to be invited to be godfather; this feeling is apparently also widespread around the country!'[62]

Slowly the storm clouds of revolution gathered over the Russian Empire. After a meeting with Sergei Witte, with whom he was negotiating – very much to Germany's advantage – the Russo-German Trade Treaty, Bülow wrote to the Kaiser: 'What I hear from Russia and also privately from Russians indicates that discontent with the reactionary system there has gradually become very great. It was already so under Alexander III, but his heavy, calm and steady hand kept the discontent from making itself felt so much, and he did not start any unfortunate and unpopular wars. Under his weaker, less consistent successor, who is too dependent on his close entourage, the revolutionary flames flicker more boldly, and bad mistakes in the government and in military preparations give them even more nourishment than they already draw from the traditional Russian system of administration. Witte does not believe in a revolution . . . but in the possibility of further assassination attempts, from which may God protect the Tsar. If the Tsar keeps his nerve and does not make peace prematurely and on weak terms without achieving military successes first, in my opinion the probability is still that the great Russian Empire and the House of Romanov, which is after all quite firmly anchored in the emotions of 100 million muzhiks, will survive the present trial, although it is certainly very serious.'[63]

At the beginning of the war Kaiser Wilhelm had taken for granted that in due time he would play a decisive mediating role in the peace negotiations.

It would be for him, and not the Reichstag, to decide on this; 'it is no business of that band of apes!'[64] In June 1904 he put it to the Tsar that if, in the course of events – naturally not at once, 'seeing that the war has only just begun' – he wished for mediation, he should turn to Wilhelm and not to Britain.[65] In view of the Russian defeats, however, even this prospect disappeared. In September 1904 Wilhelm was angered by indications that the role of peacemaker might fall to President Roosevelt. 'It seems the distinguished gentleman means to have his say in the world without standing on ceremony', he commented with disgust.[66] The Kaiser had very definite – typically monarchical – ideas of what form the peace treaty should take. Should the Russians lose the war, which in fact he now expected, in his view Korea would undoubtedly be 'quite simply annexed by Japan! Which they have richly deserved.' Manchuria 'will go back to the Chinese, to whom it belongs, and because it is the ancestral homeland of the ruling dynasty! *assuming that the Russians lose!* Roosevelt's idea of giving Manchuria neutral status under the control of a Chinese viceroy nominated by Germany was 'quite impossible' and 'pure nonsense, won't work at all!!', in Wilhelm's opinion.[67] 'I would not dream of it! . . . I refuse to agree to that!', he wrote. 'If Russia cannot hold it, it belongs to China, to whom it should be handed back as agreed by treaty!'[68] In his view, though, 'one should not divide up the bear's pelt until one has shot him! . . . My attitude remains the same as before, that Manchuria – if Russia were compelled to give it up altogether in consequence of her defeats, and was not able to re-conquer it in the 2nd campaign – definitely must be given back to China, which the Tsar had already pledged himself to do by treaty in 1901. The ruling dynasty must recover its ancestral burial places, the Bogdychan and the Dowager Empress must be able to pray at the tombs of their ancestors, and one day to be laid to rest at their side in free Chinese ground in Mukden! It is just as clear that Korea must go to Japan – in some form or other. Russia and Japan will be able to put forward their proposals as to that. It is essential that we have the "open door" everywhere attested in writing. The right to occupy Port Arthur will certainly be asserted by Japan, if she succeeds in taking the place and holding it permanently. If she is unsuccessful, the question will settle itself. I am quite happy to work together with Roosevelt but only for the "open door", which he must fully support and fight for, while we stay in the background. In addition the victors must be allowed – depending on the outcome of the war – to take, or keep, whatever they sought by way of pledges with as little interference as possible, if they give us significant trading advantages in return.'[69]

In October 1904 Kaiser Wilhelm advised the Tsar to carry on with the war for one to two years and not to seek peace until after major victories.[70] A Japanese negotiator had appeared in Paris and seemed to be authorised 'to try to get

France and England − l'entente cordiale! − to mediate in favour of Japan for peace ... This shows that Japan is nearing the limits of its strength in men and money and now that they have gained advantages over the Mandchurian army, they fancy that they can stop now and try to reap the fruit of their efforts by enticing other Powers to mix themselves in the matter and to get at Manchuria, by a Peace Conference. As I know your ideas on the further development of the war, and that after a severe reverse you will of course never lend a hand to such proceeding, I thought it my duty to inform you of what seems to be going on behind the scenes. I think the strings of all these doings lead across the Channel. Willy.'[71] The Tsar, who suspected that the Americans, rather than the British, were behind the peace feelers, replied confidently: 'You may be sure, that Russia shall fight this war to the end, until the last Jap is driven out of Mandchuria, only then can come the talk about peace negotiations and solely between the two belligerents. May God help us. Hearty thanks for your loyal friendship which I trust beyond anything. Nicky.'[72]

Even now, when the danger for Germany as well as for Russia was at its greatest, the Kaiser did not shrink from sending telegrams to the Tsar, without informing the Wilhelmstrasse, urging him to continue the war against Japan until victory was certain.[73] In a dispatch on 19 November 1904, which did not come to the knowledge of the Foreign Office until 1917, Wilhelm assured Nicholas that Japan had reached the limits of her strength and was putting out peace feelers, admittedly on conditions that were completely unacceptable to Russia. 'My suspicions accordingly, that the Japs are trying secretly to get other powers to mediate, because they are now at the height of their successes, have proved correct. Lansdowne has asked Hayashi to intimate to England the conditions, upon which Japan would conclude peace. They were telegraphed from Tokio, but were so preposterous, that even blustering Lansdowne thought them too strong and urged Hayashi to tone them down. When the Japs made a wry face and difficulties, Lansdowne added: "Of course England will take good care, that in the mediation Russia will be kept well out of Mandchuria, Korea, etc., so that de facto Japan will get all she wants"!! That is the point the British have in their eye, when they speak of friendship and friendly mediation. France, as I hear from Japan, is already informed of these plans and of course a party to this arrangement, taking − as usual in the new "entente cordiale" − the side of England. They are going to offer you a bit of Persia as compensation, of course far from the shore of the Gulf − ça va sans dire −, which England means to annex herself, fearing you might gain access to the warm sea, which you must by right, as Persia is bound to fall under Russian control and government. This would give you a splendid commercial opening, which England wants to debar you from. Probably your diplomatists will have reported all this to you before, but I thought nevertheless it my duty to inform you of all I hear, all of which is authentic serious news from absolutely trustworthy sources; Lansdowne's words are authentic too. So you see the future for your army is brightening up, and soon you will be able to turn tables upon the enemy. May God grant you full success, while I continue to watch everywhere for you. Best love to Alix. Willy.'[74]

During a visit to Silesia to hunt in November 1904 the Kaiser received news of Russian affairs which obsessed and enraged him. For days, Zedlitz observed, he talked 'almost constantly about the Russo-Japanese war'. The Cossacks were completely useless as a fighting force, he said; they had merely plundered and must be sent back home. He expressed indignation at the corruption in Russia and exclaimed: 'What else can one expect in that country, where not a single ship can be bought without the head of the Navy, Grand Duke Alexis, earning a quarter of a million roubles by it!' The Hofmarschall was surprised at how much 'fantasy' the Kaiser wove into what he said. 'In certain moods and with certain people he can be remarkably gullible, and his lively imagination and impulsive temperament incline him to embellish strange things and make them even stranger.' Although Wilhelm was very glad that thanks to the Russo-Japanese War 'the threat to us of a Franco-Russian alliance has been banished for the time being', on the other hand he was 'nevertheless very well-disposed towards Russia', Zedlitz noted. And yet Wilhelm became so pessimistic about the state of affairs in Russia that at the beginning of December 1904 he ordered the sale of all the Russian securities in his private possession.[75]

THE KAISER AND 'THE FLEET THAT HAD TO DIE'

Kaiser Wilhelm had great hopes of Russia's Baltic squadron, which was to sail halfway round the world in order to relieve Port Arthur. He considered 'very seriously', as he told his entourage, putting one of his most capable senior officers at the disposal of the Russians. The man could leave the German navy and reappear unobtrusively in the Russian fleet. 'In the end, however, the Kaiser decided to give up the idea for reasons of neutrality and because of the possible consequences with Japan', one of those present recorded.[76]

On 14 September 1904 an anonymous article, evidently inspired by the British Foreign Office, appeared in the London *Times*, warning of secret agreements between Germany and Russia.[77] The article caused disquiet in the German press and above all in the Wilhelmstrasse. Alarmed by the rapidly increasing distrust abroad, and above all in Britain, over Germany's open partisanship for Russia, Chancellor Bülow asked Albert Ballin in late September 1904 to cancel Hapag's contract to supply coal to the Russian Baltic

Fleet on its way out to the East Asian theatre of war.[78] In a letter to the former
Flügeladjutant Ferdinand von Grumme-Douglas, which the latter immediately sent on to the Kaiser, the Director of the Hamburg shipping line
described his dispute with the Chancellor. He had made it clear to Bülow
that only a direct order from the government would give him the right to
withdraw unilaterally from the coaling contract with Russia. The Reich
government must understand, however, that it would thereby deal Russia an
irreparable blow, 'for if I withdraw from the contract . . . the plan to send out
the Baltic squadron will fail. That would provide Russia with a perhaps not
entirely unwelcome opportunity to put all the blame for an unsuccessful
outcome to the war on to the fact that it was impossible to send the Baltic
squadron out because of Germany's interference.'[79] When the Kaiser read
Ballin's letter on 26 September 1904, he scrawled a furious note on it. 'The
Wilhelmstrasse has shitted itself again in front of the foreign press, and its
offices stink correspondingly!' He 'fully agreed!' with Ballin's remarks. 'The
argument he used with the Chancellor echoes my views completely, and is
almost in the same words as my answer to his questions!'[80] He told the Tsar, in
another telegram that was not seen in the Foreign Office until 1917, that he
had given orders 'that Hamburg-America Line is in no way to be hampered'.[81]
Only later did the Kaiser realise that by taking this attitude he was risking war
with the 'Anglo-Japanese group'.[82]

Wilhelm did not hold back with advice on the preparation and dispatch to
East Asia of the Russian Baltic Fleet. In a telegram to Nicholas II of 8 October
1904 he offered his views on the best way of training and deploying the
squadron and even on technical details. Thus prepared, the Russian Baltic
Fleet would achieve the decisive victory when it arrived in East Asia in spring
1905, he prophesied. 'Then the seapower is back in your hands and the Japs:
Land forces are at your mercy; then you may sound the "General advance" for
your army to crush the enemy! Hallali! . . . There is no doubt that the
appearance of a strong, fresh fleet with *many numbers* – though some may
be older ships – will do well and decide the day in your favour.'[83]

Two days later Kaiser Wilhelm followed this advice with a strong recommendation to Nicholas to add the Black Sea Fleet to the Baltic squadron,
although it would be a breach of the Paris Treaty of 1856 for the fleet to pass
through the Dardanelles, which would anger Britain above all. The combination of the Black Sea Fleet and the Baltic Fleet would 'ensure victory', he
wrote. 'As to the best manner of proceeding, I have, after ripely maturing the
question and after having taken information, come to the following conclusion. The best plan would be to silently and quietly prepare the [Black Sea]
Fleet for its destination, not to breathe a word about your intention to anybody

and any other Power. Then at the moment you think right, calmly and proudly steam through the Dardanells [sic]. The Sultan – as we both know for certain – will not offer the shadow of resistance and once you are out, we all shall be vis à vis of a "fait accompli", which we all shall quietly accept. I have not the slightest doubt that England will accept it too though the Press may fume and rage and their Squadrons steam about a little as they often do in the Mediterranean. But they won't stir in earnest when they see that the rest of the Powers remain quiet. The main point is, that it must happen quite suddenly and unawares and take the whole world by surprise, without letting the secret out beforehand ... Ever yours aff^ate Willy.'[84]

The unsought advice of the German Kaiser was not followed, and his expectations of a glorious Russian victory, as is well known, were fulfilled neither at sea nor on land. Instead of carrying out tactical exercises in the Baltic until spring 1905, as Wilhelm had suggested, the Baltic squadron set sail as early as 15 October 1904 on the long voyage to Port Arthur. It had only reached the North Sea when it became involved in a calamitous incident that almost caused a world war. On the night of 21–2 October the Russian fleet, apparently assuming it was under attack by Japanese torpedo boats, fired on some defenceless English fishing boats on the Dogger Bank off Hull. While both the British and the Russian governments did everything in their power to resolve this inexplicable affair peacefully, the London press erupted in a storm of abuse – not against Russia but against Germany.[85] Some newspapers, particularly the *Times*, went so far as to claim that the Reich had warned the Russian admiralty of a forthcoming Japanese attack in the North Sea with the definite intention of provoking a conflict between Russia and Britain.[86] This view was even shared by the First Sea Lord, Sir John Fisher, who wrote to his wife on 28 October: 'Things look very serious. It's really the Germans behind it all ... That German Emperor is scheming all he knows to produce a war between us and Russia.'[87]

Although the Reich government and the German press behaved with great restraint, Kaiser Wilhelm was infuriated beyond measure by the Dogger Bank episode. He had no scruples in discussing the most far-fetched theories with his entourage, even in the presence of the servants, as Zedlitz-Trützschler disapprovingly recorded.[88] He dismissed outright the suggestion that the Russian Admiral Rozhestvensky had suffered from hallucinations or had acted in a moment of sudden panic. 'That is out of the question with this calm Admiral! I know him!', he wrote. 'I am sure he saw torpedo boats under a foreign flag. Probably redundant English ones sold to Japanese.' The British press campaign, he was convinced, was aimed at forcing the recall of the Russian battlefleet. It was not the fleet that was a danger to the public, as the

English were claiming, but 'England is a danger to the public with its constant intrigues and attempts to stir up hatred'.[89] He considered the British government's proposal to set up a tribunal to investigate the incident as 'an outrage'. Such a thing 'has never happened before!' One could not 'allow *foreigners* to judge the conduct of one's *own* serving officers!' To settle the crisis in this way 'would be scandalous!' 'Naturally' Japan was also trying to pour fuel on to the flames, so that England would keep 'the Russ[ian] fleet away from them' by preventing it from continuing its journey.[90] When the German military attaché in London, Count von der Schulenburg, reported that the Foreign Secretary Lord Lansdowne had threatened to halt the Russian Baltic Fleet unless all demands were fulfilled within twenty-four hours, the Kaiser again reacted with fury, maintaining that this was 'a clear indication that the Japanese have told the English that they hold them responsible for stopping the Russ[ian] fleet from coming to East Asia. So they are using the Hull fishing fleet as a pretext and have set up the demands − as unfulfillable as possible − to give them a reason to detain the Russians for as long as possible.'[91]

At the height of the crisis between Russia and Britain, Wilhelm II finally realised what dangers he had brought about with his constant assurances of friendship to Nicholas II. On 30 October 1904 the Tsar told the Kaiser's military representative, Gustav Count Lambsdorff, that he was going to have a 'very serious' talk with the British ambassador, Sir Charles Hardinge, along the lines of the Kaiser's latest telegram. It was time 'to show, following Germany's example, that not all English demands need to be fulfilled', although he still expected the incident to be settled by arbitration. Lambsdorff emphasised that this significant remark by the Tsar 'need not necessarily be understood to mean that His Majesty [Nicholas II] was hoping for immediate *active* intervention by Germany' in order to reject exaggerated British demands. Nevertheless, from the Tsar's 'energetic language' and his 'elevated tone', Lambsdorff had gained the impression that he 'pins great hopes on Your Majesty's friendly attitude'.[92] The Reich Chancellor recognised the danger and sounded the alarm. It was clear from Lambsdorff's report, he warned, that in order to settle the Hull incident the Tsar 'would like to play us off against England. On no account must that happen, for as regards this incident . . . the French will not in any circumstances take action against England . . . Therefore the objective Your Majesty has in mind, namely to detach France from England and push her towards us and Russia, would not only not be achieved, but probably the opposite would happen.' It was therefore essential, Bülow insisted, that the Hull episode be settled before Germany and Russia formed an alliance and approached France.[93]

'THE FIRST FAILURE THAT I HAVE PERSONALLY EXPERIENCED'

Despite this setback, Wilhelm II, Bülow and Holstein continued to pursue their cherished idea of forming a continental league aimed against Britain. In a telegram to the Tsar of 27 October 1904 the Kaiser referred to the British hostility which Germany had incurred by supplying coal to the Russian fleet; in return for this he demanded a closer link between the German Reich and both Russia and France. The demand made by Britain and Japan that Germany cease her coal supplies to the Baltic squadron was tantamount to a threat of war against both Germany and Russia, and the two countries must stand shoulder to shoulder to confront it, he wrote. Together, Germany and Russia must also remind France of her contractual duty to support Russia. Wilhelm's language was unmistakably threatening. 'Though Delcassé is an Anglophile "enragé", he will be wise enough to understand, that the British fleet is utterly unable to save Paris!' he told Nicholas. 'In this way a powerful combination of 3 of the strongest continental Powers would be formed to attack, whom the Anglo-Japanese group would think twice before acting [sic].'[94] That the Kaiser and Bülow intended from the outset to use threats of force if necessary to 'detach France from England and push her towards us and Russia', as the Chancellor described it,[95] is clear from the aggressive anti-French comment that Wilhelm wrote on a dispatch from London on the same day. It was very significant, he remarked, 'that far from springing to the aid of the *Russians* as allies and escorting them with their fleet, the villain Cambon has persuaded the villain Delcassé – both England's friends – to offer his good offices to *England*. It is doubly necessary that the Gauls should be reminded, by Russia, whose allies they actually are; in other words they must put their cards on the table, pro or contra England. Wilhelm I.R.'[96]

The risks attached to their approach to Russia were brought home to Bülow and Holstein in an extraordinary crisis meeting the Chancellor summoned on 31 October 1904 with the Chief of General Staff Count Schlieffen, the State Secretary of the Reich Navy Office Admiral Tirpitz and Foreign Secretary Baron von Richthofen to consider Germany's propects should an alliance with Russia lead to a war with the two western Powers. Their expectation that if France could be brought into alignment with the continental bloc, war with England could be avoided, was not shared by the military men nor by Richthofen, however desirable an alliance between Germany, Austria-Hungary, Russia and France seemed to them too. Tirpitz declared that his fleet was still far from being able to take on the Royal Navy and pleaded for more time.[97] And Schlieffen was certain that, since England and France were bound to stand together, Germany could at best achieve only half a victory: the

invincible Royal Navy would destroy Germany's overseas trade, leaving
Germany no option but to conquer France with a lightning attack through
Belgium. A British declaration of war, he stated, 'must therefore be the signal
for Germany to mobilise her entire army and fleet and attack France if
necessary by a preventive strike'.[98]

Despite these warnings, the high-risk initiative Kaiser Wilhelm had set in
motion suddenly took an unexpectedly hopeful turn. Against the advice of the
Russian Foreign Minister, Count Vladimir Lamsdorff, who could see nothing
in Wilhelm II's suggestions but 'constant attempts to upset our friendly
relations with France', Tsar Nicholas took up the idea of a continental league
aimed against Britain and asked the Kaiser, in a telegram of 29 October 1904,
to draw up the outlines of a Russo-German agreement to which France would
have to accede.[99] Although Wilhelm had long dreamt of a German Europe
and in September 1904 had again described the unification of 'the whole of
Europe ... under German leadership' as his goal,[100] this time the decision to
offer the Tsar an alliance did not arise solely from his own initiative, but
rather from consultations with the Reich Chancellor, who in turn had
discussed it with Holstein.[101] The latter had until recently rejected the idea
of a Russo-German alliance as offering nothing but disadvantages and dangers
for Germany. Since the establishment of the Entente Cordiale, however, and in
view of the growing ill-humour towards Germany in Britain, he had come to
the conclusion that the Reich's international position was no longer 'intact'
and that it must be safeguarded by a pact with Russia.[102] The decisive step in
this 'question of world-historical importance', as Bülow called it, had therefore
been taken in conditions of the greatest secrecy, by all three men. Kaiser,
Chancellor and Privy Councillor were convinced of the need 'to guard the
secret from the Anglo-French party at the Russian court for the time being'. As
a telegram could easily fall into the wrong hands, while sending a Flügeladjutant would draw attention prematurely to the negotiations, Bülow advised
the Kaiser to write a letter to Nicholas and to have it delivered to St Petersburg
by courier.[103]

Promptly on 30 October 1904 — the day before the crisis meeting at the
Reich Chancellor's palace — Bülow submitted a draft reply to the Tsar's
telegram to the Kaiser, which Wilhelm copied out almost unchanged. With
his letter he enclosed the text of a treaty of alliance which, he said, he had
drawn up 'secretly' with the Chancellor. 'Nobody knows anything about it, not
even my foreign office; the work was done by Bülow and me personally.' 'Be it
as you say', the Kaiser wrote. 'Let us stand together.' 'If you and I stand
shoulder to shoulder the main result will be that *France must openly and
formally join us both* thereby at last fulfilling her treaty obligations towards

THE RUSSO-JAPANESE WAR AND ITS CONSEQUENCES

Russia which are of highest value to us, especially with respect to her fine harbours and good fleet, which would thereby be at our disposal too . . . This consummation once reached I expect to be able to maintain Peace and you will be left [a] free and undisturbed hand to deal with Japan.'[104] In spite of the secretive approach adopted in Berlin the Tsar showed the draft treaty to his Foreign Minister, Lamsdorff, who insisted that before it could be signed the accord must be submitted to France, as Russia's ally.[105] With that, the Kaiser's grand scheme was doomed to failure at least for the time being, for France would never willingly submit to German hegemonial plans. Boutiron, a French diplomat *en poste* at St Petersburg, detected at once that behind the Kaiser's courtship of the Tsar lay the desire to destroy the Franco-Russian Dual Alliance and the Anglo-French Entente.[106] Yet Wilhelm, Bülow and Holstein at first continued to spin their web. They still hoped that Russia could be 'turned round'.[107]

On 16 November 1904 Bülow sent Wilhelm the draft of another letter to the Tsar, which he and Holstein had drawn up for the Kaiser to translate into English and copy out. 'My justification for this presumption', the Chancellor explained, 'is that this is a question of a truly great and, for the watching world, utterly unexpected development.'[108] The letter reveals the anti-British tendency of Germany's Russian policy with unusual clarity, for in it the Kaiser encouraged the Tsar to attack Persia and India. 'Last not least an excellent expedient to cool British insolence and overbearing would be to make some military demonstrations on the Persic-Afghan frontier, where the British [think] you powerless to appear with troops during this war [against Japan]; even should the forces at your disposal not suffice for a real attack [on] India itself they would do for Persia – which has no army – and a pressure on the Indian frontier from Persia will do wonders in England and have [a] remarkably quieting influence on the hot headed Jingoes in London . . . The Indian frontier and Afghanistan are the only part of the Globe where the whole of her Battle-fleets are of no avail to England and where their guns are powerless to meet the invader. India's loss is the death stroke to Great Britain!'[109] The Kaiser carried out the task set him by Bülow, but not without complaining. He returned the completed letter, which was to be delivered to the Tsar this time by the military attaché Gustav Lambsdorff, to Bülow with the remark: 'No more changes are to be made. I have worked for 7 hours until a quarter past one last night, when I was more dead than alive . . . Please come for breakfast at 1 o'clock. W.'[110]

Yet this second approach was also frustrated by Nicholas's insistence that the text of the treaty be shown to the French before signature, as otherwise it would seem to them 'as if we tried to enforce the treaty on France'.[111] The Kaiser's

disappointment was 'boundless'.[112] After he had decoded the Tsar's telegram
with the help of two generals, Kuno Count von Moltke and Wilhelm Count
von Hohenau, he wrote bitterly to the Reich Chancellor: 'The great Lord
begins to get "cold feet" with regard to the Gauls, and is so feeble that he
will not even enter into this treaty with us without their permission — i.e. not
against them either. In my opinion it is impossible to let Paris hear anything
about it until we have the "little father's" signature. For a communication to
Delcassé before the signature means a telegram to [Paul] Cambon and the
same evening it will be printed in the Times and in the Figaro, after which
the whole thing will be over; for the row that would then break out in
London would perhaps persuade the "little father" to modify the treaty in
such a way as to make it worthless, or frighten him off completely from
concluding it. I am very discouraged, but not surprised, by this turn of events.
He has no backbone where the Gauls are concerned, because of the loans.'[113]
The Chancellor, recognising the danger that the Tsar might be driven 'into
the arms of England' if the wrong tone were adopted towards him now, was
careful to formulate the response to Nicholas, which the Kaiser again translated, so as to 'leave open for the Tsar the possibility of a Russo-German
understanding in the future, even if he shies away from it now'.[114]

There followed a tense wait in Berlin for Tsar Nicholas's answer[115] — 'he is
taking 2 months as usual', the Kaiser complained impatiently — during which
the highly dangerous drawbacks of Germany's Russian policy became all too
clear. The French government stressed 'with conspicuous eagerness', as Bülow
told the Kaiser on 6 December 1904, 'that the Dual Alliance remains
unchanged and Germany's efforts to win over Russia would fail'. Wilhelm
had no doubt that Bülow was right in suspecting that some of the secret
Russo-German negotiations must have 'filtered through from the Neva to the
Seine ... I think the news was simply passed on', he commented bitterly
in the margin. Far from showing its appreciation of the coal supplies and
other services rendered, the Russian government was distinctly cool in its
behaviour. At the same time the signs that the German Reich was facing
'an Anglo-Japanese action' — Wilhelm feared a strike 'against Kiaochow' —
were increasing alarmingly. It was high time, both the Chancellor and the
Kaiser thought, to force Russia to 'lay her cards on the table, so as to establish
how far we can depend on Russian help if, owing to the coal supplies, we come
into conflict [with Britain and Japan]'. Once again Bülow drew up the text of a
letter to the Tsar for Wilhelm to translate. In it he asked for 'absolutely
positive guarantees' of Russia's military support in the event that 'England
and Japan should declare war against me, on account of the Coaling of the
Russian Fleet by Germany'. If Berlin received no satisfactory answer, the

Chancellor would 'request Herr Ballin in Your Majesty's name ... not to supply any more coal to the Russians'.[116] The negotiations between Lamsdorff and Alvensleben on this thorny question proved extremely difficult.[117] Wilhelm adorned his ambassador's reports with intemperate marginal comments,[118] but in the end he was forced to accept that for the time being, the secret treaty negotiations with Russia had fallen through owing to the problem of French participation. On 21 December 1904 he sent the Russian military attaché Shebeko to the Tsar with a letter, most of which he had drafted himself. 'We shall under all circumstances remain true and loyal friends', he assured Nicholas. 'My opinion about the agreement is still the same; it is impossible to take France into our confidence *before* we two have come to a definite arrangement. Loubet and Delcassé are no doubt experienced statesmen. But they not being Princes or Emperors I am unable to place them ... on the same footing as you my equal, my cousin and friend. Should you therefore think it imperative to acquaint the French Government with our negotiations *before* we have arrived at definite settlement, I consider it better for all parties concerned to continue in our present condition of mutual independence, and of the spontaneous promotion of each others ends.'[119]

The year 1904 ended with great disillusionment in Berlin. The Kaiser was reminded of Prussia's desperate plight on the eve of the Seven Years' War; others spoke of her impending defeat by Napoleon in 1807.[120] Wilhelm II described the Tsar's answer to his letter as 'a clear rejection of any idea of an agreement without Gaul's prior knowledge'. This was 'a totally negative result after two months of honest work and negotiations', he complained – 'the first failure that I have personally experienced. I hope it will not herald a series of similar events ... Paris must get one in the eye from us one day! They certainly got wind of our negotiations and wrecked them.'[121] Bülow expressed similar disappointment at the way in which the Tsar had simply ignored the Kaiser's last letter; this confirmed the suspicion 'that the Russians attach no value to an alliance with us, or not as great a value as they should if they had a proper appreciation of the world situation and the balance of power on either side', he wrote to Wilhelm.[122]

The Kaiser was further enraged by the 'immoderately harsh language' of the Russian Foreign Minister, Count Lamsdorff.[123] Whoever believed the Russian minister's declarations of friendship should pay a thaler as forfeit; they were nothing but 'pretentious rubbish'. France intended to wage war against Germany, perhaps not at once, but 'some other time at a favourable opportunity!' and would rather die 'on the spot' than come on to Germany's side. In any case, 'as a civilian!' Count Lamsdorff was not capable of judging whether there was danger of war or not. His remarks to Alvensleben were 'a hidden but decided threat' that France would wage war against Germany 'if we are not as good as gold!'[124] Fuming with anger at alleged intrigues by the Russians against him in London, Kaiser Wilhelm turned abruptly away from Russia and towards Japan and America, as we shall see in a moment. The 'monstrous lies' of the Russians were 'utterly vile filth from St Petersburg via Paris', he raged. 'Lamsdorff wants to stir up trouble between us and England and has deliberately lied in the most shameless way at my expense – whether with or without his master's knowledge I will leave aside – in Paris and in London! . . . We must treat the Russians with the most complete and absolute coldness and mistrust, and keep on the right side of America and Japan!'[125]

VOLTE-FACE: THE DEMAND FOR A 'JAPANESE–GERMAN ALLIANCE WITH SUPPORT FROM AMERICA'

Filled with forebodings that the Anglo-French Entente might consolidate itself into a Triple Entente with Russia, the Kaiser suddenly demanded that the German Reich ally itself with Japan and the United States of America. On 26 December 1904 and again two days later he gave instructions to Bülow that 'America and Japan must now be cultivated all the more. The latter are no doubt very piqued with England and in a despondent mood, as not everything is going as they hoped.'[126] In February 1905 he again directed Bülow, not without an undertone of resignation, to pursue this course. 'We must respond to the [Anglo-Franco-Russian] grouping with a Japanese–German alliance supported by America!'[127] Again in March 1905, just before he set off on his Mediterranean trip, he demanded that Japan and the USA be brought on to Germany's side so that together they could make a stand against France, Britain and Russia.[128] The Reich Chancellor had to explain to the Kaiser that his demands could not be so easily fulfilled. In the first place an agreement with Japan was quite out of the question for the moment. 'The Japanese have an underhand policy and might well be capable of exploiting a further German approach in such a way as to try to push us into conflict not only with France – which would be less damaging – but also with Russia', he warned. In the end Bülow succeeded in winning Wilhelm round to his point of view.[129]

Not only was a rapprochement with Britain's ally Japan ruled out, but American support was also to prove as difficult to achieve as ever. On the occasion of the inauguration of the Berlin cathedral on 27 February 1905 Wilhelm II spoke to both the American ambassador in Berlin, Charlemagne Tower, and his colleague George Meyer, who was on his way to take up his appointment as ambassador in St Petersburg, of his admiration for President Theodore Roosevelt. His words were intended as an approach to the USA; but they also found their way to London via the British diplomat Cecil Spring Rice, to whom both American ambassadors recounted their conversations with the Kaiser, and who passed on the news to Edward VII's Private Secretary.[130] Very probably as a result of Wilhelm's advances, Roosevelt shortly afterwards wrote to King Edward assuring him of America's friendship for Britain and emphasising the common interests of the two countries.[131] Sir Frank Lascelles was able to report with satisfaction from Berlin that Wilhelm's 'attempts to sow distrust of us in other nations and more especially in America ... have signally failed, and I do not think are more likely to be successful in the future'.[132] The bizarre expedient of forming a diplomatic union between the German Reich, the victorious Japan and the republican United States had proved to be a fantasy. Scarcely less illusory, however, were the military solutions which now came under discussion in Berlin.

CHAPTER TWELVE

Operational plans for a war in western Europe

What a change had come about in the international situation of the German Reich in the course of 1904! At the beginning of the year Kaiser Wilhelm was still under the spell of an intoxicating dream of European domination – of a unified Europe under German leadership as a result of the Russo-Japanese War and an alliance with the Russian Empire. Instead of the hoped-for continental league aimed against Britain, however, the Anglo-French Entente Cordiale had come into being with Italy's tacit adherence and had found support not only from Japan but increasingly from the United States of America too. And now, at the end of the year, it became painfully clear to the Kaiser that Russia too, far from accepting Germany's secret offer of an alliance, would stick to her ally France and thus to the world constellation led by Britain. The 'encirclement' of Germany which Waldersee had always feared had become almost complete.

In this crisis a mood of defiant determination began to take hold in the Kaiserreich. The French diplomat Maurice Paléologue recorded with concern in 1904 that he had recently observed in Germany 'a kind of national mysticism that ascribes an exceptional and unexpected vocation to the Germanic race in the future government of humanity. The practical consequence of that is as follows: the leaders of Germany must develop the expansionist strength of Germanism to the maximum and must not hesitate to speak out in affirmation of its justified claim to hegemony over the world, to the *Welt-kaiserthum*.' When Paléologue expressed his fears to Delcassé, the French Foreign Minister, the latter exclaimed: 'That is absurd! That is megalomania! ... It will lead Germany straight into war. ... Wilhelm's policy of pretentious bragging can only end in war.'[1]

Instead of learning lessons from the diplomatic debacle and fitting peacefully into the world order now dominated by Great Britain (and, in the background, increasingly by the USA), the Supreme War Lord and his 'faithful paladins in the army and navy', as Bethmann Hollweg was to call the military entourage, decided to revive the operational plans for war against Britain, with or without French participation. With no threat from the east to their rear, in 1905 the Kaiser, the General Staff, the Minister of War and leading figures in the Imperial Navy were on the point of deciding to take a sword to the Gordian knot of encirclement to the west. The highly secret debates between the Kaiser, the army, the navy, the Chancellor and the Wilhelmstrasse in these critical months again throw significant light on the process by which decisions on military policy were taken in the Prusso-German Kaiserreich. Although ultimately it did not lead to catastrophe this time, it did not bode well for the future.

THE SUPREME WAR LORD AND HIS 'FAITHFUL PALADINS IN THE ARMY AND NAVY'

In early November 1904 Hofmarschall Count Zedlitz noted in his diary that the difficulties that had arisen between Britain and Russia as a result of the war in East Asia were 'preoccupying the Kaiser a great deal. – His imagination is so hard at work that for several days he has been discussing the various implications of it all, even when servants are present, and with almost everyone in his close entourage.'[2] On the one hand Wilhelm II was oppressed by the thought that France intended 'at some favourable opportunity' to unleash a war against Germany.[3] On the other, however, he feared a British attack on the still incomplete German fleet.[4] He took such a serious view of reports from the German naval attaché in London, Captain Coerper, 'of increasing bad feeling, articles openly inciting attacks, and conversations on the same lines with ladies from naval circles' that he defined 'the withdrawal of the [English] Mediterranean Fleet from the Mediterranean . . . into English waters' as a 'casus belli for us in this situation'. 'It would have to be seen as a direct threat of war with us . . . The situation begins to look more and more like the prelude to the 7 Years' War.'[5] Zedlitz recorded with concern on 21 November 1904: 'For a considerable time the Kaiser has regarded relations with England as very tense, and he constantly reverts to the opinion that the possibility of a war between us and England can scarcely be avoided, and thinks that for their part the English want to bring about this serious conflict.'[6] The most ominous possibility, however, was that both scenarios – war with France *and* Britain – could coincide.[7] Bülow's assessment of the situation, at Christmas 1904, was that 'England has paid for her entente cordiale with France with a heavy sacrifice. Her renunciation of Morocco in particular is surprising and suspicious. It makes one wonder whether England perhaps

wished to secure France's support against Germany or for an English policy of
acquisition in China or for the purposes of an Anglo-Russo-Franco-Japanese
grouping to be achieved through French mediation.' 'Both!' the Kaiser
commented laconically in the margin.[8]

In these days of crisis the Kaiser constantly questioned the highest authorities
of the Reich, the army and the navy as to how Germany should proceed in a
war with Britain. 'He gave the Chief of General Staff, the Minister of War, the
Secretary of State of the Reich Navy Office etc the task of answering this
question: "The English, who are now showing that they have sole power at sea,
are also interfering in German affairs and although they themselves frequently
supply coal to the Russians for the Baltic Fleet's outward journey, they demand
categorically that Germany should not do so and threaten to blockade her. What
should Germany do?" After a dinner at the Neues Palais the solution of this
question was discussed by His Majesty, over cigars in the billiard room, with
Lieutenant General v. Moltke . . . in the presence of the Crown Prince, Prince
Eitel Friedrich, a few invited guests, the Flügeladjutanten, the princely adjutants etc. He began by saying that all the solutions were wrong and that even
the Chief of the General Staff [Schlieffen] and General v. Moltke himself had
not given the right answer. The correct solution, however, was the following:
"Any action by the German fleet against the English is completely out of the
question, for the English fleet is so superior to the German in numbers that
even with the best leadership and great bravery, and even if it sacrificed
itself entirely, the German fleet could destroy only about half England's naval
power, and with such superiority our coast would therefore be completely
blockaded. − The German fleet should certainly not be sacrificed. On the other
hand, since the French are now so closely linked to the English that one can
treat them as their allies, in this difficult situation one should stick to them and
attack them."' In the view of Hofmarschall Zedlitz the 'solution' put forward by
the Kaiser was 'fantastic and utopian', for nothing would be more detrimental
for Germany and advantageous for England than a Franco-German war. Zedlitz
was astonished by Moltke, who meekly accepted the fact that the Kaiser
criticised his solution in the presence of ten officers of whom several were his
juniors, and presented his own solution as the only right one. 'As the Kaiser has
been praising this solution to the skies for several days', Zedlitz could only
assume 'that the other exalted personages in question maintained an eloquent
silence.' But there was 'great danger' in this.[9] Again in mid-December 1904
Zedlitz noted with alarm: 'It is remarkable how worried the Kaiser has been
lately about relations with England . . . I particularly dislike the idea of taking
advantage of France if we come into conflict with England. − I think this idea,
as so often, has not been thought through to the end.'[10]

As 1904 drew to a close, with Russia out of the count as a player, while Germany's conflict with the two western Powers grew immeasurably more intense, the scenario envisaged by the Kaiser and his highest-ranking generals becomes alarmingly clear from the conversations which the diplomat Wilhelm von Schoen had with the monarch and his Adjutant-General, Hans von Plessen, in Silesia in early December. The Kaiser declared that he was no longer willing to tolerate Britain's attempts to limit the building of the German battlefleet. 'His Majesty would regard it as essential, in any such event', Schoen reported to the Reich Chancellor, 'to call a halt by force of arms to Britain's outrageous presumptuousness and to prevent hostile actions against our North Sea and Baltic coasts by taking swift and extensive measures. In so doing His Majesty would have no choice but to set aside the consideration he has hitherto shown, and which has not everywhere been appreciated as it deserved, towards great and small neighbours and to confront them with the question, which must be decided within the shortest possible time, of whether they wish to be our friends and allies in the conflict, or to count themselves among our enemies. Ultimata on these lines would be delivered to Paris, Brussels, The Hague and Copenhagen, to the latter simultaneously with the occupation of a few strategically important points in and adjoining Danish waters. *Denmark* would of course point to her neutrality. As she possessed only pitifully inadequate means to maintain and defend it effectively, however, such an assurance was worthless.' In such cases one had to 'simply ignore' international treaties. 'Immediate action with military force would be taken against any of the aforementioned neighbouring countries . . . that did not at once and unambiguously decide for us. The point in time when a hostile act by England was to be expected would be regarded as having begun the moment that she brought her fleet out of the Mediterranean into home waters.' There was no danger that the German occupation of Denmark could drive Russia into the arms of England, as it could be anticipated that Russia would have to wage war in East Asia 'for several more years'. These All-Highest views were warmly seconded by Plessen, who added that in such a case Germany would certainly also acquire Denmark and Holland with their colonies. When Schoen warned that such plans would inevitably lead to 'bloody conflicts with practically all the Great Powers including America', Plessen replied that their realisation might 'perhaps have to be postponed to the distant future'.[11]

It seems curious, given his martial bombast, that the Kaiser initially took a back seat in the ruthless colonial war that broke out in 1904 against the Herero and Nama peoples in the colony of German South-West Africa, present-day Namibia. True, his first reaction had been to send the notorious

General Lothar von Trotha, who had distinguished himself by his brutality against the 'Boxers' in China, to suppress the uprising, but then he had been persuaded to change his mind. Holstein was more dismayed than anyone at the monarch's lack of involvement and in April 1904 regretted that the rumours that the Kaiser was directing the campaign personally from on board the *Hohenzollern* were unfounded.[12] Baroness Spitzemberg learned in August 1904 that Wilhelm was even refusing to allow discussion of the conflict in his presence, presumably, as she mockingly surmised, because there was 'no glory or fame to be had from it'.[13] All too soon, however, the Supreme War Lord's ruthless 'military culture' resurfaced to provide the underlying legitimation of one of the very worst atrocities of his reign: the near-annihilation of the Herero people. Overruling civilian objections, the Kaiser sent Trotha out to South-West Africa in June 1904, assuring him that he would have dictatorial command and have 'nothing to do with the Chancellor'.[14] It was as 'the Great General of the Mighty Kaiser' that Trotha promulgated his genocidal 'extermination order' of 2 October 1904 before driving the entire Herero people, men, women and children, into the Omaheke desert to their deaths.[15] No direct command from Wilhelm authorising this *Vernichtungspolitik* has ever been found, but historians are agreed that Trotha had every reason to believe that his policy of extermination had the Kaiser's full approval in the same way as his brutal behaviour in China had had.[16] Trotha's deliberate campaign of annihilation caused such revulsion in Germany that Bülow and the colonial officials in the Auswärtiges Amt begged Wilhelm II to rescind Trotha's 'extermination order', insisting, among other things, that it would 'demolish Germany's reputation among the civilised nations and feed foreign agitation against us'.[17] Only after protracted negotiations with Schlieffen and Hülsen-Haeseler did the Chancellor manage to persuade the Kaiser to retract the order on 8 December.[18] A livid Trotha threatened to resign but was mollified by Schlieffen's assurance that 'continuing the offensive against the mass of Herero is not supposed to be hindered by the All-Highest order ... but voluntarily surrendering Herero are not to be shot down but accepted'.[19] Trotha continued his war against the Herero and the Nama people further south, but instead of extermination through thirst and starvation, they were now to be rounded up in concentration camps (so-called *geschlossene Niederlassungen*) and worked to death.[20]

Whatever his involvement in colonial wars might have been, as German Kaiser, King of Prussia, Supreme War Lord and Commander in Chief of the Navy, Wilhelm II inevitably played a central part in the difficult strategic decisions which had to be taken in view of the fundamental change since 1904 in the Reich's international position. In both military and foreign policy matters he insisted on his prerogative as final arbiter. He made ceaseless attempts, often without consulting his principal advisers, to solve the nation's strategic problems through personal contacts and correspondence with his fellow monarchs, without stopping to think that he might thereby be betraying his country's most vital military secrets to potential enemies. Among the statesmen of the Wilhelmstrasse, the military authorities in the General Staff and the Ministry of War, not to mention the leading lights in the Admiralty Staff and the Reich Navy Office, opinions differed widely and often clashed over the strategic response to the challenge posed by the changed situation. Under the system of Personal Monarchy only the Kaiser had the right and the power to reconcile these rival views. He possessed neither the intellectual capabilities nor the equable character required for this superhuman task; moreover, in itself the autocratic command structure inherited from Frederick the Great worked against any rational assessment of the situation and prevented the coordination of the various options available. Nowhere is the lethal effect of the kingship mechanism more apparent than in the interplay between Crown and state, army and navy during the titanic disputes in which the course was set for the crisis-ridden development of the ensuing years.

In describing the relationship between Kaiser Wilhelm and his 'faithful paladins in the army and navy' it is difficult, as Zedlitz remarked in May 1904, to avoid writing satire. In the saloon car of his special train the monarch greeted the Prussian Minister of War, General Karl von Einem, and the Chief of the Military Cabinet, Count Dietrich von Hülsen-Haeseler, with the words: 'You old donkeys believe you know everything better because you are older than I am; but that is absolutely not the case.'[21] Every year Wilhelm personally led the army's manoeuvres with a retinue the size of a cavalry regiment[22] and, in the unanimous opinion of all the generals, with disastrous results for the efficiency of the army. Field Marshal Waldersee, now at the end of his life, had always deplored the practice by which the imperial manoeuvres 'were designed purely to help the Kaiser succeed, however great the mistakes he made'. In early 1904 he threw up his hands in horror at the war games 'which Schlieffen has to conduct in such a way that the Kaiser is always the victor. They have gradually been reduced to real childishness; when one hears that [Adjutant-General] Plessen writes Army Orders and [Adjutant-General] Scholl leads Cavalry Corps — and always with great success — that already gives one some idea of what is going on ... I have completely given up hope of the Kaiser changing his ways.'[23] Zedlitz complained after the autumn manoeuvres in 1904 that the Kaiser himself had 'stirred everything up so much' that 'the inevitable result was too much hurry and haste ... His

Majesty frequently rode into the firing line himself to drive the action forward even more strongly.' Everyone knew 'where the wind was blowing from' and acted in accordance with the Kaiser's wishes; neither for the troops nor for the General Staff were such manoeuvres of the slightest use.[24] The British military attaché Lord Edward Gleichen, who took part in the 1904 imperial manoeuvres as an observer, could not conceal his astonishment at Wilhelm's behaviour. The Supreme War Lord had commanded the blue side on the first day and by means of an impossible frontal attack (in closed formation) against a strongly defended position, combined with a late turning manoeuvre, had driven the red side back to the north-west, while the red cavalry successfully attacked the blue army. On the following day he took over command of the red side and this time led them to victory. The combined operations between land and sea forces, which the Kaiser had ordered simply to impress the public, were considered a farce by all the generals, according to Gleichen. They showed unmistakable signs of discouragement, he reported to London, not least because of the Kaiser's 'sudden impulses to change the order of things'.[25]

On the occasion of a controversial appointment in the army, one of the Flügeladjutanten commented that it was clear 'that in such appointments the Kaiser's wishes are absolutely decisive'.[26] This was soon to be confirmed at a very high level when Wilhelm, instead of appointing the experienced General Staff officer Hans von Beseler to succeed Count Schlieffen as Chief of the Great General Staff, as had been agreed with the Chief of the Military Cabinet after long consultations, surprisingly chose his Flügeladjutant and close friend Helmuth ('Julius') von Moltke for this vital post. Waldersee was horrified, commenting in his diary on 5 January 1904: 'The impression that this must have made on everyone in the army who has at least some judgement, is one of astonishment followed by profound sorrow. Moltke himself is intelligent enough to regret the Kaiser's decision . . . It is typical of the situation we are in that General Plessen has had a say in this highly important matter of filling the most crucial post in the army. Even people of the quality of General Scholl and the Flügeladjutanten occasionally have their say, and especially in this question. I do not believe there could be a greater humiliation for the General Staff . . . During the last imperial manoeuvres the Kaiser frequently expressed himself in the most derogatory fashion about the General Staff and this time . . . he went so far as to say that he did not need a General Staff, he will do everything alone with his Flügeladjutanten. It is no wonder that a mood of deep dissatisfaction has taken hold in the General Staff.'[27] As the details of Moltke's nomination as Schlieffen's successor were 'better not written down', the old Field Marshal, who felt 'completely defeated', made coded notes that speak volumes. The path followed by the Kaiser 'makes me more and more anxious', he noted. In him 'the sense of greatness is growing in a way that is becoming positively frightening'.[28]

Waldersee's damning verdict on Moltke's suitability for the post was echoed by other officers. The Chief of the Military Cabinet regarded Moltke as a spiritualistic visionary and threatened to resign over his promotion.[29] The 70-year-old General Wagner, who had taught Moltke in the War Academy, wrote apprehensively: 'This gentleman might prove disastrous.'[30] General Bruno von Mudra, who had expected General Freiherr Colmar von der Goltz to be appointed Chief of General Staff, was not yet ready to give up all hope, but he drew an alarming picture of Wilhelm II's autocratic conduct in the military sphere. Mudra learned from Brigade Commander Count Kanitz, who was in close contact with the imperial court, 'that the Moltke business . . . is apparently not at all settled yet'. It seemed that Moltke was 'a victim of the most direct case of sic volo, sic jubeo in this incomprehensible decision on his future. Moltke wrote at once to His Majesty — which at any rate does credit to his character — asking for his appointment as Chief of General Staff to be set aside as he did not feel at all equal to the demands of the post. Count Kanitz claimed to have heard this from a very direct source when he was in Berlin recently. H.M.'s answer — the appointment stands, for a Prussian officer must believe himself equal to anything and must also be able to do anything. Schlieffen is said to be furious at the choice of Count [sic] Moltke and cuts him dead completely . . . Be that as it may — in finally enforcing his wishes in this matter H.M. will have difficulties with his close entourage, and I expect the first of these will be Count Schlieffen's long face; and then it is quite possible, to judge by experience, that H.M. will hit out in the other direction and actually make the right man Chief of General Staff.' Apart from 'a few bigwigs', according to Mudra, the whole army wanted to see Colmar von der Goltz taking over from Schlieffen. Admittedly, Schlieffen himself preferred Beseler, but as Mudra pointed out: 'That the Kaiser, if he cannot get M[oltke] appointed — should give Schlieffen the satisfaction of choosing his candidate, would be a serious affront to the All-Highest infallibility — and therefore I do not believe in Beseler . . . Furthermore, as Count Kanitz also said, the Kaiser does not like him. — At any rate the crisis is not yet resolved — and therefore I am not yet giving up my best hope.'[31] As is well known, Wilhelm II stuck to his decision and appointed 'Julius' Moltke, who retained his status as the Kaiser's Adjutant-General, to be Schlieffen's successor as Chief of General Staff on 1 January 1906, remarking that Moltke could take care of what little peace-time work there was; in wartime he would be his own Chief of General Staff.[32] The only concession to which the monarch agreed was to promise to take a less active part in conducting manoeuvres in future. But he was not to keep even that promise.

However disastrous the Frederician decision-making system was to prove under Wilhelm II, and however inclined one is to believe that regular collective consultations between the responsible authorities – the Reich Chancellor, the Foreign Office, the General Staff, the War Ministry, the Admiralty Staff and the Reich Navy Office – would have led to a more realistic assessment of the situation, it is impossible to overlook the alarming degree of megalomaniac self-delusion to which even these highly placed advisers to the Crown were subject. In the light of modern research it can scarcely be disputed that the notorious Schlieffen Plan, which was formulated at this time and envisaged a lightning attack on France via Holland, Belgium and Luxembourg, could never have achieved its aims. The same is true of the Tirpitz Plan, which had already – at the latest with the signature of the Entente Cordiale and the fears of an Anglo-German war in November to December 1904 – proved itself to be a highly dangerous mistake. But the grandiose dreams of power of the leaders of the army and navy went much further. What is one to make of the attitude of the Kaiser's Flügeladjutant, Georg Alexander von Müller, the future Chief of the Naval Cabinet, when he demanded in February 1905 that the building of battleships should be speeded up, declaring portentously that if this should lead to war with Britain, 'Our answer must be: In that case, let it be world war, which will take our armies to India and Egypt'?[33] Or of the memorandum written by the future Chief of the Admiralty Staff, August von Heeringen, in April 1902 for Prince Heinrich of Prussia, in which he stated firmly that the only way in which Germany could achieve ultimate victory over the British Empire was by invading England, for which, however, it would be essential to gain control of the North Sea, and therefore first of all to occupy Holland and Belgium?[34] Or – to cite one last example, which has already been mentioned – the 'top secret' submission to the Kaiser made by the Chief of the Admiralty Staff, Vice Admiral Wilhelm Büchsel, on 21 March 1903, recommending an attack on New York in the event of war with the United States, so as to 'force' the American navy to fight, and to 'destroy' it?[35] In the face of such extreme intoxication with world power and such autistic over-estimation of Germany's capacities it seems questionable, after all, that further consultations between the departmental authorities would have helped materially to restore a sense of reality.

THE OCCUPATION OF DENMARK IN THE EVENT
OF 'WAR AGAINST ENGLAND ALONE'

This, at any rate, is the depressing conclusion to which one is led by a study of the operational plans for war with Britain that the Admiralty Staff prepared over many years on the orders of Kaiser Wilhelm and in close cooperation with the General Staff. The files of the Admiralty Staff, the Reich Navy Office and the Naval Cabinet preserved in the Military Archives at Freiburg provide a truly remarkable insight into the military decision-making process and the mentality of the leadership in Berlin during these years of radical change, when Great Britain ceased to be a potential ally of the German Reich and instead entered into the Entente Cordiale with France.

When the Kaiser was in Berlin or Potsdam the Chief of the Admiralty Staff was received in audience by the Supreme War Lord every Tuesday, and in addition to this official appointment Büchsel frequently found other opportunities to speak to the Kaiser of his concerns. He loyally assisted the monarch with long memoranda on the world situation, the state of preparation for war and the operational plans of the navy for every conceivable eventuality. It is above all in the reports submitted to the Kaiser by the Chief of the Admiralty Staff that the development of German plans for war with Britain can be traced.

Since the beginning of the battlefleet-building programme in 1897–8 the German naval authorities had been compelled to take account of the danger that as soon as the actual purpose of the Tirpitz Plan became apparent, the Royal Navy would aim a destructive blow at the nascent German fleet before it could become a deadly threat to Britain. From the outset the Admiralty Staff had a secret remedy in case war broke out with Britain during this 'danger zone': they planned a rapid attack on Denmark, with the help of the army, in the first days of the war. Not only Jutland and Funen but also the main island of Zealand, together with the Little Belt, the Great Belt and the Sund were to be brought under German control. As early as on the morning of the third day of mobilisation, according to the plan, German troops were to reach Copenhagen.[36] It was a plan with multiple aims: it would seriously disrupt Danish mobilisation, the Danish fleet would be destroyed or captured, and an initial success with powerful effects on the national morale would be achieved. The fundamental purpose of the assault on Denmark and the approaches to the Baltic Sea, however, was to give the German fleet, greatly inferior as it was, a better chance of success against Britain. With the dramatic attack on Denmark the Royal Navy was to be compelled to divide its forces and expose itself to the danger of a battle with the German war fleet in the Belts and the western Baltic. In an Admiralty Staff paper of early 1903 setting out the basis for war plans this key principle is enunciated with great clarity. 'In the first place the purpose of our strategic measures ... must be: to bring about the division of the English fleet. The separation of the two parts so far from one another that our line of communication through the [Kaiser Wilhelm] Canal ... is considerably shorter than that between the two English groups. In this way we intend to make it

possible to defeat one part of the English fleet with our concentrated forces
before the other part can come to its aid. Strong pressure on England will be
necessary to bring about this division because it is strategically wrong with
the numbers in question. How can this pressure be brought to bear? ... By
our forcing Denmark to ally herself with us or by taking hostile action
against Denmark, which will make the English government send a fleet to
support a friendly country calling for aid ... This pressure can be applied if
we declare war on Denmark or bring about a state of war by military action
without a declaration of war.'[37]

It goes without saying that Kaiser Wilhelm was kept fully informed of these
breathtaking operational plans from the beginning, and he had expressly
approved them in a 'declaration of the All-Highest will' of 12 December
1899.[38] Wilhelm gave orders to the Admiralty Staff to agree the details of
the operational plan with the General Staff – but not with the War Ministry
or the Reich Navy Office and certainly not with the Reich Chancellor or the
Foreign Office – and then to submit it to him in a joint audience. What
sounded like a simple order from the monarch, that the Admiralty Staff
should make 'certain firm arrangements with the Gen. Staff' and then 'report
direct' to him, proved difficult in practice, however.[39] Schlieffen at once
expressed reservations, as he feared that the German occupying forces could
be cut off on Zealand if the British fleet forced a passage through the Great
Belt.[40] The Admiralty Staff had to point out repeatedly that the military
occupation of Zealand was imperative if the purpose of the enterprise – the
blocking of access to the Baltic, the capture of Copenhagen and the splitting up
of the British fleet – was to be achieved. The devolved consultations between
representatives of the Admiralty Staff and the General Staff which began in
March 1900 ground to a halt in wearisome negotiations of details. A discussion
on 22 December 1902 seemed at first to lead to clarification of the disputed
points still outstanding. The Chief of the Admiralty Staff again explained to
the two army representatives 'the principal points of view of the operational
plan for the Fleet in the event of Germany making war against England alone:
the superiority of the English Fleet forces the German Fleet onto the defensive. Such defensive action has little prospect of succeeding in the North Sea; it
will be productive only if the English Fleet is induced to divide and move the
principal theatre of war to the straits leading into the Baltic Sea. In order to
achieve this it is essential that the German fleet controls the supply routes to
the Baltic Sea', and that in turn necessitated the seizure of the adjoining
Danish territories.[41] On 14 April 1903 the Kaiser approved the detailed plans
worked out for the proposed occupation of Denmark. Soon afterwards, however, Schlieffen gave clear expression to the doubts he had held from the

outset about the Admiralty Staff's operational plans: what guarantee had Germany that once war had broken out Britain would in fact remain the *only* opponent?

The *conditio sine qua non* of the Navy's plan of operations against Denmark had always been that Britain should have 'no ally on the Continent against us'. This was exactly the point stressed by Schlieffen in a letter to Büchsel of 6 August 1903, which came to the Admiralty Staff as a bombshell. 'In order to fulfil Your Excellency's intention of occupying Danish territory in the event of a war against England *alone*, about 2 army corps will be needed. These will certainly be available as long as England is Germany's sole opponent. But this situation is hardly likely to last long. It can safely be assumed that the unfavourable position into which we have been brought by a war against England, and into which we have put ourselves by making war against Denmark, will be exploited by other powers against us. We will then be faced with a war for which we will need every last man and in which we definitely cannot spare those 2 army corps occupying the Danish islands. The absence of both army corps from the theatre of war in which we must summon all our strength to gain victory will be all the more painful because they can contribute nothing to the outcome or to the settlement either of the general war or of the war against England alone. They will be waging war against Denmark which had no hostile intentions of any kind towards us, and only against England in the event that the latter really wishes it and does not restrict herself to the simplest and most natural means of destroying our trade. In these circumstances I most humbly beg Your Excellency to consider again whether the plan to occupy Danish territory cannot be abandoned.'[42]

In spite of this clear rebuff Büchsel managed, by referring expressly to the Kaiser's formal approval of the plans, to persuade Schlieffen to continue with the preparatory work and interdepartmental negotiations.[43] That the question of a possible occupation of Denmark remained unresolved until the summer of 1904, more than four years after the Kaiser's agreement in principle to the Admiralty Staff's proposals, suggests that war with Britain was not thought to be imminent.[44] But this was to change in the coming months and above all after the Dogger Bank incident in October 1904.[45] For the time being, however, Kaiser Wilhelm II and his military and naval paladins cherished hopes that the departure of the Russian armed forces to East Asia would give them an undreamt-of freedom of manoeuvre in western Europe. With gusto the ruler of Germany set to work, using his personal relationships with neighbouring monarchs to overcome the strategic dilemma of his central European empire, a dilemma that neither the army nor the navy had been able to resolve.

THE KAISER'S PLAN FOR A 'NORTHERN ALLIANCE
TO PROTECT THE BALTIC SEA'

Since March 1903 Wilhelm II had eagerly pursued the idea of a 'northern alliance to protect the Baltic Sea', which would include a 'rapprochement ... between Denmark and Germany' as well as other measures. To the utter amazement of the Russian ambassador, Count Osten-Sacken, the Kaiser told him that he aimed to form a 'union of the northern monarchies – Denmark, Sweden, Norway, Russia and Germany, to protect the Baltic Sea'.[46] Before his visit to Copenhagen in April for an early celebration of the eighty-fifth birthday of King Christian IX[47] the Reich Chancellor had had to warn him to be cautious and reserved in what he said, in view of British, Russian and American suspicions about Germany's motives. 'Although it was in fact Your Majesty who originally thought of a northern alliance to protect the Baltic, outwardly we must maintain the idea, and create the impression, that the initiative came from Russia, because otherwise we would draw down on ourselves both the English resentment that such a project can be expected to arouse and the English counter-attack to which it would lead.'[48]

The theme of Danish neutrality also became the subject of earnest discussion between Wilhelm and the Tsar at their meetings in Wiesbaden and Wolfsgarten in November 1903, in fact at the very moment when the General Staff was raising objections to the navy's operational plans in the north.[49] According to the notes that Wilhelm made for himself on his conversations with Nicholas II, he told the Tsar that Prince Johann of Schleswig-Holstein-Sonderburg-Glücksburg, the Danish King's brother, was constantly pressing for neutral status for Denmark and Danish waters; he, the Kaiser, had however made it clear to the Prince that 'that would be possible only if Denmark also had the military capacity to enforce respect for her neutrality from all Great Powers, including England, and the question was whether that was possible. The Prince had given His Majesty no answer to this. Therefore it was clear – as Tsar Nicholas himself would also have concluded in Denmark – that there was no such guarantee. So if a Great Power which had a quarrel with Russia abroad wanted to get into the Baltic, little Denmark would not be able to block access to it, and by ignoring her neutrality the Sund and the Belts could be forced and Kronstadt, Libau etc threatened. The Russian Emperor said: "Nelson did that 100 years ago, and the British or the Americans will certainly do it again. If the Danes – as is actually the case – are not in a position to guarantee the integrity of their waters they must authorise the two of us, who are threatened by this situation, to do it for them, so that we can prevent any enemy from coming into the Belts or the Sund, relying on the Danish forts and Copenhagen as our operational bases, instead of having to wait until the intruder reaches open sea in the Baltic and has seized Copenhagen and the exit routes.'" The two emperors agreed to discuss this idea 'with the King of Denmark himself at the next opportunity, and without any Ministers being invited'.[50] During King Christian IX's visit to Potsdam on 17 December 1903 Kaiser Wilhelm discussed the neutrality question privately with him.[51] Afterwards the Kaiser reported to St Petersburg that Christian had recognised how vitally important Danish neutrality was for Russia. He had frankly admitted that he could not guarantee the neutrality of his country, nor could he close the entrances to the Baltic against a superior fleet. He therefore greeted with relief the proposal that Russia and Germany should guarantee Danish neutrality. 'He has promised to say nothing about the matter to his minister — a radical parliamentary man — till you have decided how the affair is to be treated. H[err] v[on] Bülow to whom I referred the matter, is most pleased with the proposal, is also of opinion that, Danish Prime Minister, and before all their Parliament must be kept out of it. That it was to be an agreement secretly made between the 3 Sovereigns, through any instrument they like to draw up by their representatives; that in *case of war* Denmark was to immediately declare its neutrality, and that we two declare our firm intention to guarantee it, and if necessary to help to defend it by force.' Wilhelm assured the Tsar again that the King was '*obviously relieved*' at the thought that his two great neighbours were of the same opinion and in an emergency would hasten to his aid.[52] In actual fact, as Wilhelm had predicted, the elderly King of Denmark was 'crushed' by these menacing developments.[53]

On the basis of the 'detailed information' which the Kaiser gave him, shortly after Christmas 1903 Bülow directed his attention to the difficult tactical handling of the question. He came to the conclusion that 'the surest way to avoid either allowing ourselves to be pushed unnecessarily into the line of fire of the English navy for the sake of the Russians, or giving the Tsar a justifiable reason to be angry or suspicious of us, is for us to off-load the "project" we have been demanding ... onto the worthy King of Denmark'.[54] The draft for an appropriate letter to the Tsar which Bülow submitted to the Kaiser was, however, rejected by the latter in terms which were unusually curt, even for him.[55] He flatly refused to accept the Chancellor's suggestion that he should enclose a few Danish newspaper articles on the neutrality question with the letter. 'The Tsar writes asking whether Your Excellency could draw up something; your draft simply ignores this! That will not do, and would go down badly with him and make him suspicious. An answer must therefore be devised so that I can submit to him quotations from proposals made in "*Danish*" *newspapers* which he can use as the basis of a letter to the King, which the *King* is *expecting* from him. I would write to the latter saying that the Tsar will get in touch with him himself and write to him about this matter! This Danish neutrality question must be pursued vigorously as if it were *principally in Russia's interest*, with us helping out of kindness, as "honest broker". In reality, however, it is *vitally important* from the military point of view for *us*! It would mean doubling our strength in case of war, if we could rely on Danish support!' If Denmark did not take Germany's side it would be a simple matter for the British to destroy Germany with 'a couple of hammer blows ... Since His Majesty *the Emperor [Nicholas] himself* sets great store by keeping the possible agreements to guarantee Danish neutrality strictly secret, there is no reason to think that *he* will want to infringe them or allow them to be announced by his government. As far as England is concerned there is therefore no need for anxiety, as she will not hear about it. But even if she did find out it would not be a serious matter, for she herself has often stood up for the same thing in the past, and moreover His Majesty [Edward VII] would even be grateful to us if we have arranged for his dear old papa-in-law to be protected from any injustice.'[56]

The Danes did not go along with the Kaiser's 'plan'. Instead they strengthened Copenhagen's sea defences and assured Berlin that these and other measures would secure the country against a surprise attack; they had thus 'taken the first step towards safeguarding neutrality'.[57] Wilhelm took this news calmly, for in the meantime the Russo-Japanese War had broken out and Britain had declared that she would not intervene. It was understandable, he replied to King Christian on 26 February 1904, 'if you take appropriate military precautions in any case, in order to safeguard your country's neutrality'.[58] Yet the Kaiser's intention of seizing Denmark was not abandoned, but only postponed. As will be seen, his plans continued to arouse suspicion in Scandinavia, Britain, France, Russia and America for years to come. In the Wilhelmstrasse, too, they caused grave misgivings.[59]

'WINNING OVER BELGIUM' AND THE NETHERLANDS

At the beginning of 1904, just before the outbreak of the Russo-Japanese War, Wilhelm II also attempted, by means of his personal contacts with the Belgian and Dutch royal houses, to 'win over' Germany's neighbours to the west. He did this in the belief that the war in the Far East might give the Kaiserreich an opportunity of striking a blow against France. In the winter of 1903–4 the German General Staff, in making its plans for operations against France, had for the first time started from the assumption that any such action might be used by Britain as an opportunity to side with the enemy and send troops to

Holland or Belgium. The Admiralty Staff had to concede, in a submission to the Kaiser on 19 January 1904, that the German navy was utterly incapable of preventing any such troop landings – for instance in the Scheldt.[60] Given this scenario, the attitude of Belgium and the Netherlands naturally acquired even more significance.

From 26 to 28 January 1904, and thus only a few days after the Admiralty Staff's pessimistic assessment of the situation had been relayed to the Kaiser by Büchsel, King Leopold II of the Belgians visited Berlin for the Kaiser's birthday. Wilhelm was determined to seize the opportunity to bind Belgium more closely to Germany. As he told the Reich Chancellor: 'We must remind King Leopold of the splendour and magnificence of Burgundy in the old days ... If we give him the prospect of rising to similar heights through an alliance with us, Leopold will be ready for anything.' In his *Denkwürdigkeiten* Bülow described the painful scene that took place after the discussion between the Kaiser and the King on the evening of 28 January 1904. Leopold had looked 'extremely upset' on his departure; an adjutant noticed that in his agitation the King had put on his helmet the wrong way round, with the eagle at the back. Afterwards Wilhelm had complained to the Chancellor of the 'contemptibility' of his fellow monarch. He had spoken to the Belgian King of the old Burgundian Empire and told him that he could, if he wanted, 'stretch out his sceptre over French Flanders, Artois and the Ardennes'. When Leopold replied 'with a smirk' that neither his ministers nor the Belgian parliament would have anything to do with such ambitious plans, Wilhelm had lost all patience. 'I told the King that I could not respect a monarch who felt answerable to deputies and ministers instead of to our Lord God in Heaven alone. I also told him that I was not to be trifled with. Whoever was not for me, in the event of a European war, was against me. As a soldier I belonged to the school of Frederick the Great, the school of Napoleon I. Just as the former had begun the Seven Years' War with the invasion of Saxony and the latter had always forestalled his enemies at lightning speed, so I would allow myself, if Belgium were not with me, to be guided only by strategic considerations.' After Bülow had expressed his misgivings about this, the Kaiser had become 'more nervous and vehement than was usually his wont with me', and had finally declared: 'If that is what you think, I shall have to look around for another Reich Chancellor in the event of a war.'[61]

In view of the politically explosive nature of this episode, historians have often questioned whether Wilhelm could really have so crassly betrayed his General Staff's plans to violate Belgian neutrality in a war against France, at his meeting with Leopold II in January 1904.[62] Yet there can be no doubt of the authenticity of his ultimatum. Numerous contemporary sources confirm the incident. Thus, for instance, a German diplomat stationed in Brussels recorded after a conversation with Wilhelm II in December 1904 that by his own account the Kaiser had quite bluntly asked King Leopold II, during his visit to Berlin the previous January, 'what attitude he, the King, intended to adopt in case an armed conflict should break out between Germany and France or Germany and England'. He had 'categorically demanded of the King during a lengthy conversation in January of this year, that he, the King, should give him a written declaration now in time of peace to the effect that in case of conflict Belgium would take her stand on our side, and that to this end the King should amongst other things guarantee to us the use of Belgian railways and fortified places. If the King of the Belgians did not do so, he – His Majesty the Kaiser – would not be able to give a guarantee for either his territory or the dynasty. We would then, if the case arose, immediately invade Belgium and the King would have to suffer all the – to him – harmful consequences. If on the other hand the King were to make the desired declaration at this stage, he – His Majesty the Kaiser – felt inclined, though he did not like doing so, to give him not only a guarantee regarding the continued existence of the Kingdom of Belgium in its present form, but also to enlarge Belgium by granting it territory in Northern France – His Majesty at this point also used the term "Old Burgundy". King Leopold presumably realized clearly what he and the Belgian dynasty could expect from a victori-ous republican France.'[63]

King Leopold's reaction to his powerful neighbour's naked threats of war and occupation was of course also recorded in several Belgian documents. On his return to Brussels he immediately told the Foreign Minister, Baron de Favereau, and his Chief of Cabinet, Count Smet de Nayer, of Kaiser Wilhelm's extraordinary ultimatum. The Kaiser had criticised France, which had rejected his repeated efforts to create a continental bloc against Britain, and he had declared that he would not be so stupid as to wait until the French had finished making their preparations against him. 'The French want war. Good, they shall have it.' He had called on the King to ally himself with him. 'In the gigantic struggle that is to come Germany is sure of victory, but this time you must decide. You must be with us or against us . . . If you are with us, I will give you back the Flemish provinces that France wrongly took away from you. I will restore the Duchy of Burgundy for you. Think about my offer and about what awaits you.'[64] The Kaiser's remarks and the horror of the Belgians at the unmistakable threats issued by the Supreme War Lord quickly found their way to London and Paris. They also contributed, later, to the widespread conviction that Wilhelm was by then already intent on a great war.[65] In his biography of Leopold II, published after the First World War, Count Louis de

Lichtervelde commented: 'The King grasped what was being said and informed his ministers of it. He saw it as another reason to take action against the anti-militarist tendencies in his country and ... to strengthen ties of friendship with Great Britain, whose importance in the next war, in view of her undisputed supremacy at sea, he foresaw.'[66] Too late, the Reich Chancellor drew his sovereign's attention to the risks he had run in taking the line of an ultimatum to Belgium. Everything depended, he warned Wilhelm in July 1905, 'on the Belgians not suspecting in advance that if it comes to it we intend to confront them with such an either-or choice. Otherwise they would use their wealth to build fortifications against us, and tip off the French so that they too can adapt their plans accordingly.'[67]

The threats directed by Kaiser Wilhelm at the young Queen Wilhelmina of the Netherlands at exactly the same time were, if anything, even more shocking. Although no trace has been found of a purported letter from the Kaiser to the Queen about which rumours circulated later, there can be little doubt that Wilhelmina was alarmed by a secret communication from Wilhelm II in early 1904, in spite of several denials – it has been attested by too many sources. The earliest surviving reference to this episode dates from 16 February 1904, only a few weeks after Wilhelm's discussion with King Christian IX at Potsdam on 17 December 1903 and only a few days after the ultimatum to the King of the Belgians in Berlin on 28 January 1904. Just at this time Kaiser Wilhelm received Prince Heinrich of Mecklenburg-Schwerin, the Prince Consort of the Netherlands, whom Wilhelmina had married in 1901, for a private dinner. At their meeting the Kaiser expressed his concern about the Dutch coastal defences in the event of a war between Germany and Britain in such a way as to make a frightening impression on the Prince Consort, and through him on the Dutch Queen.[68] In a confidential private letter of 16 February 1904 the Colonial Minister, A. W. F. Idenburg, wrote to the Governor-General of the Dutch East Indies saying that the Queen had told him and his ministerial colleagues in confidence, a few days before the recent outbreak of the Russo-Japanese War, that if Britain sided with Japan, Germany and France would join Russia and wage war against Britain and Japan. Queen Wilhelmina had then added, according to Idenburg, that 'the Netherlands and Denmark, which were not in a position to safeguard their neutrality adequately, would then be given 24 hours' to decide whether they were for or against Germany; Belgium had already given a corresponding assurance to Germany. This announcement had seemed so 'fantastic' that the Dutch ministers were astonished and asked the Queen for the source of this ominous news. Wilhelmina had refused to name anyone, but from the indications she gave no one could have doubted that the German Emperor was the person in question, Idenburg wrote.[69]

In the years to come the secret of Kaiser Wilhelm's outrageous threat was constantly on the verge of being revealed. On 11 March 1905 a discussion took place between Queen Wilhelmina, Prince Consort Heinrich and General J. C. C. den Beer Poortugael, a member of the Council of State, on the situation of the Netherlands in the event of a European war. The Queen commented that the country would be 'the buffer ... if there were war between England and Germany' and expressed anxiety about Wilhelm II's impulsiveness. Prince Heinrich then said 'that the German Emperor had told him personally that in such an eventuality he would be in our country with an army, whether or not we were neutral'.[70] In November 1908, after the embarrassing episode of the Kaiser's 'interview' in the London *Daily Telegraph*, the Dutch newspaper *Het Vaderland* published a sensational leading article entitled 'Kaiser and Queen', based on confidential information from the diplomat and Member of Parliament Baron Jacob Derk Carel Van Heeckeren van Kell. In the article it was claimed that Wilhelm II had already decided during the Boer War, when he anticipated the outbreak of a European war, that it was imperative to occupy the Dutch seaports. 'So when the Japanese war broke out the Kaiser wrote a letter to the Queen in which he announced that to his most profound regret he would be obliged to carry out his intention, if the Netherlands found themselves unable to take up a defensive position against England immediately. The Queen, in a state of the greatest distress, communicated the threatening letter to the Minister, Dr Kuyper, whereupon Kuyper decided that it would be desirable to have a few fortifications put into working order ... Fortunately matters took a different turn. Nevertheless, the incident had left relations between Kaiser and Queen on a more or less unfriendly footing.' The German diplomat Richard von Kühlmann, chargé d'affaires at The Hague at this time, requested urgently that a denial be issued in response to the article, which touched on 'the most ultrasensitive aspect of German–Dutch relations' and was likely to cause 'serious damage to the relationship between the two countries, especially at the present moment'.[71] He lost no time in contacting Kuyper, who received the Queen's permission for a *démenti*, although its wording was not altogether convincing. Far from denying the Kaiser's threat of war, Kuyper merely declared 'that the Queen had never said a word to him about a letter received from the German Emperor in 1904, still less shown him such a letter'.[72] Wilhelm's conversation with the Prince Consort was not mentioned.

In spite of the denial the rumours of a sinister letter from the Kaiser to Wilhelmina would not go away.[73] On 9 February 1910 Baron Van Heeckeren again spoke out, this time not in secret through an anonymous newspaper article but openly during the budget debate in the First Chamber of the

States-General.[74] Heeckeren repeated the claim that in 1904 the German Emperor had threatened, in a letter to Queen Wilhelmina, to occupy the Dutch coast if the Netherlands did not strengthen their coastal defences.[75] The Foreign Minister, De Marees van Swinderen, firmly contradicted this version of events in the First Chamber on 18 February 1910. 'H.M. the Queen has never received a letter, a telegram, a note or any kind of written message from the German Emperor regarding the military defence of our fatherland. Furthermore the Queen has never discussed this subject in conversation with the Emperor', he declared solemnly.[76] Once again the Kaiser's threatening words to Prince Heinrich were passed over.

In consequence of this parliamentary episode, on 13 March 1910 Dr Kuyper recorded his memories of the events of January to February 1904 in a sealed note which was not to be opened until after his death. In it he made it clear that, as Idenburg had already indicated, it was not a *letter* that the Queen had received from Kaiser Wilhelm, but a message conveyed to her (probably verbally) through a relation, which she was obliged to take just as seriously. Kuyper wrote: 'During the international tension in 1904–5 H.M. the Queen informed me in an audience that she had received a report according to which it was very likely that the current tension could lead to a sudden war between Germany and France. If this war should actually break out, we could suddenly be faced with an ultimatum giving us 12 to 14 hours to decide what our stance towards Germany would be. When I asked . . . from whom H.M. had received this report or this warning, H.M. replied that she was not at liberty to tell me.' In the subsequent discussion by the ministers of this information it had become clear that it could only have come from German government circles. 'We therefore considered two possibilities: 1) that it came from the German Government itself, or 2) that a member of the German ruling family had conveyed it to H.M. after he had learned of the German Government's plans. In dealing publicly with this question, as a former Minister I could not of course reveal what H.M. had told me in audience. . . . I now record what happened, so that if necessary it can be made public after my death.'[77]

THE REVIVAL OF PLANS TO SEIZE DENMARK

The German navy's operational plans against Denmark, as we have seen, presupposed a war 'against England alone'. In issuing his threats to Belgium and Holland in January 1904, however, Kaiser Wilhelm was proceeding on the assumption that Germany would attack France in the near future, and that this would entail the risk of British intervention. The sense of his own military strength, which had underpinned both his conversation with Leopold II and

Figure 10 Admiral Wilhelm Büchsel, architect of the plan to seize Denmark
in the hope of luring the Royal Navy into the Baltic Sea

the ultimatum conveyed to Queen Wilhelmina, arose from the calculation that
with the departure of the Russian army for the east, the German Reich, freed
from any threat from the rear, could now achieve its aim of bringing all its
power to bear on the west, against both Britain and France. The shift in the
international political constellation which had come about with the outbreak
of war in East Asia meant that the Admiralty Staff, too, had new tasks to fulfil.
Its Chief, Büchsel, hoped that the plans he had harboured since 1899 for a
major action against Denmark would nevertheless still meet with All-Highest
approval (see Figure 10). In a letter of 2 November 1904 to Schlieffen, he
asserted that a war against France *and* Russia could be virtually ruled out for
the foreseeable future, whereas the likelihood that France would be drawn
into a conflict between the German Reich and Britain had increased. This
would relieve the pressure on the army but increase it on the navy. Büchsel
argued that it was therefore all the more important to shut off the Belts, and
in order to do so a significant participation by land forces would be essential.[78]
Although the General Staff continued to have reservations about diverting
troops to occupy Denmark, resistance to the plans of the Admiralty Staff came
from the Prussian War Ministry rather than from the General Staff.
Schlieffen, who became a legend after the world war, was considered by many

of his contemporaries as dull and markedly reluctant to speak out in the Kaiser's presence. The War Minister, General Karl von Einem, on the other hand, raised both formal and material objections to Büchsel's efforts to push through his plans with the backing of the Kaiser. He cited procedural rules previously approved by the Kaiser according to which only the War Ministry was authorised to make the army's preparations for war with Britain. Moreover Wilhelm II had stipulated that the Admiralty Staff should not transmit its wishes to the army via the Chief of General Staff but should convey them through the Secretary of State at the Reich Navy Office to the Prussian War Ministry. Von Einem therefore demanded that representatives of his ministry and of the Reich Navy Office should attend the interdepartmental discussions.[79] Kaiser Wilhelm, however, continued to support the Admiralty Staff's operational plans and ordered the consultations to proceed between the Admiralty Staff and the General Staff alone.[80]

The war panic that broke out in October and November 1904 after the Dogger Bank incident intensified the debates between the diplomats, the generals and the naval authorities to a considerable degree. Under the impact of the threatening British press campaign several informal crisis talks took place in Berlin between various combinations of civilian statesmen and military authorities.[81] On the evening of 18 November 1904 the Kaiser summoned the Reich Chancellor, the Chief of General Staff and the Secretary of State of the Reich Navy Office – Büchsel was away at Kiel for the launch of the imperial flagship *Deutschland* – to a crisis meeting. At this meeting, during which Schlieffen did not say a word, Wilhelm II took the line of the absent Chief of Admiralty Staff and ordered plans to be prepared for the occupation of Denmark with the support of the army. 'So the decision has gone the way we wished and now it is a question of striking while the iron is hot', Büchsel commented jubilantly.[82] Shortly afterwards the Kaiser approved a Cabinet order to the same effect.[83] During the subsequent consultations the Chief of Admiralty Staff, sure of Wilhelm's support, cheerfully ignored the continuing objections of the army to the idea of tying down a large contingent of troops in a secondary action against Denmark. It was the last straw for the War Minister. Writing to Tirpitz, he protested that when he had heard for the first time in February 1904 that the navy intended, in the event of war against England, to shut off the Great Belt, 'and that His Majesty had approved of this plan', he had assumed 'that it was a question affecting purely naval interests, in which the army's part would be merely to place military units at the navy's disposal'. But now he had been informed 'that the planned measures to close off the Great Belt were in the general interest of the country and the securing of the blockades would fall to the army alone, which would also have to bear the costs'. In these circumstances he was entitled, 'as the sole responsible representative of the interests of the army, to claim that presentations to His Majesty the Kaiser about such questions should not be made only [by] a representative of the navy'.[84]

Nevertheless the Admiralty Staff's risky operational plans continued to have the unconditional support of the Kaiser and his military retinue. As we saw earlier, in early December 1904 the monarch and his Adjutant-General, Hans von Plessen, were talking openly of their intention of delivering 'ultimata . . . to Paris, Brussels, The Hague and Copenhagen', in the latter case 'simultaneously with the occupation of a few strategically important points in and adjoining Danish waters'. In so doing, they would have to 'simply disregard' international treaties.[85] Büchsel, confident that he possessed the Kaiser's complete trust and that he had acted strictly in accordance with All-Highest orders, rejected the War Minister's protest and worked personally on the memorandum that he intended to present to the Kaiser at his audience on 3 December 1904. The 'very secret' document leaves no room for doubt that it was the intention of the navy, even in the event of war against Britain *and* France, to lure part of the British fleet into the Baltic in order to engage it in battle there. The Chief of Admiralty Staff wrote:

> With my most humble duty I have to report to Your Majesty that the negotiations with the General Staff concerning the occupation of Danish territory in the event of an attack by England came to the following conclusions:
>
> 1. To carry out the occupation of Denmark as necessary only for the direct defence of the blockades in the Great and Little Belts, one active Division will suffice, reinforced by heavy artillery supplied by the army in the field (guns etc. which do not belong to the Division).
> 2. This number of troops will not suffice if Denmark responds to the occupation of her territory by declaring war. In this case a further contingent must be sent in from the homeland, which will amount to about two army corps.
> 3. Therefore if Danish territory is occupied by troops, two army corps will be tied down on the coast whatever happens, unless Denmark allies herself with us.
> 4. These two corps can be made available without further ado if the army is not engaged elsewhere at the same time. It is conceivable, however, that even if the war begins by a surprise attack by England alone, France will be drawn in as a result. In this case the two army corps would be unavailable for operations against France.
> 5. Judging from the observations made by the Chief of General Staff, I am convinced that he does not think it right to hold back two active army corps on the coast in a war against England with the prospect of French participation, and that he can therefore only advise against adopting measures or ordering

operations which would result in holding back troops in this way. This therefore calls into question the possibility of bringing in troops to defend the blockade, and with it the possibility of closing off the Little Belt at the northern end and of defending the blockade in the Great Belt from the land. A decision on this matter is necessary for the mobilisation preparations of the navy, and I can only ask Your Majesty most humbly to come to this decision through a joint audience of the authorities concerned.

6. My position is as follows: it is not for me to judge whether the two corps are available, or whether the benefit that will arise for the conduct of the war in general if the blockades are defended from the land and if the war — possibly brought into the Baltic — takes place on Danish territory, is greater or smaller than the disadvantage entailed by the absence of the two army corps on the French border. One thing is certain, however. Germany cannot neglect to defend herself against the enemy coming through the Belts. Consequently she will have to make war preparations in the Belts, that is to say on Danish sovereign territory, thereby infringing Denmark's neutrality. That is unavoidable! If Denmark is inclined to be unfriendly to us, she will be able to use this as an excuse to declare war on us, in spite of the fact that England will likewise disregard Danish neutrality, because these infringements of her neutrality begin with us. Whether or not we occupy Danish territory, we must in any case take steps to defend our northern border and the Kaiser Wilhelm Canal against the Danish army, possibly joined later by an English army that could be landed there. Whether the territorial and auxiliary troops remaining in the country would be sufficient for this purpose it is, again, not for me to judge.

7. The consequences for the conduct of the war by Your Majesty's navy, if the troops cannot be provided to defend the blockades, would be as follows: The Little Belt cannot be blockaded at the northern end, but only at the southern end; as a result it will be 1) considerably more difficult to effect the blockade, 2) easier for the blockade to be removed by the enemy, 3) consequently our position in the Great Belt will be threatened from the rear and may therefore have to be abandoned prematurely. Furthermore the opportunity will be lost to launch an assault from the Little Belt on the rear of the enemy attacking the blockade in the Great Belt. The blockade in the Great Belt cannot be defended *from the land*; this has to be done by *ships*. During the night, when clearing work is done on the blockade, the ships are constantly exposed to gunfire and torpedo boat attacks (they have to keep their searchlights constantly on the blockade). The defence of the blockade will therefore be considerably weakened and, because of the high consumption of naval resources, it will only be possible to maintain it for a much shorter time than if the blockade is defended from the land, where the guns and searchlights need only be protected from attempted landings.

As a result of this weakening of the blockade positions, the purpose which Your Majesty expects them to fulfil, of inflicting on the enemy such heavy losses of ships that the battlefleet waiting behind the blockades has the prospect of completely annihilating the attacking fleet, will be achieved to a considerably lesser degree, indeed the losses on our own side would be considerably greater than on the enemy's side, since the defence of the blockade must be left to older ships, and it would be impossible to prevent the blockade being cleared away. So this blockade would achieve only a dearly bought delay of the attack by the enemy fleet on Kiel, or on its narrow blockade, but would not provide the opportunity for a battle with good prospects of success.[86]

Admiral Büchsel put these weighty considerations to the Kaiser on 3 December 1904, during a walk in the Thiergarten.[87] He noted on the memorandum that because his audience had been ordered to take place during the Kaiser's walk, 'the Chief of the Headquarters [Plessen] and the Cabinet Chief [Senden-Bibran] were not present'. Once again, Wilhelm accepted the arguments of the Chief of Admiralty Staff in full. Büchsel commented afterwards: 'H.M. expressed the view that the two Corps (IX and X) would have to stay in the North until the situation there was clarified. The occupation of Danish territory must take place in any case because of Esbjerg, quite apart from the defence of the blockades. He was of the opinion that the army could and must spare these troops. H.M. spoke of his intention of issuing a Cabinet Order which would provide a clear basis for the preparatory work ... We are therefore continuing to work in the first instance on the assumption that the troops will be provided, but we must now arrange for a stronger occupation of Zealand and Funen to come later as a second thrust – by sea.'[88]

On 9 December 1904 the Kaiser's Flügeladjutant Georg Alexander von Müller noted in his diary that the Kaiser was 'very busy because of the tension with England' and had spent the afternoon working on this question alone. Wilhelm had invited Count Schlieffen, the Chief of General Staff, Admiral Büchsel, the Chief of Admiralty Staff, and Lieutenant-General Helmuth von Moltke to dinner. 'At the end the Kaiser took the Chiefs of the General Staff and Admiralty Staff with him for a discussion.'[89] In order that the backing he had received from the Kaiser during these consultations should also be a matter of written record, Büchsel wrote to Schlieffen asking for a resumption of the interdepartmental discussions so that the matter could be resolved quickly. On the evening of 9 December, he said, the Kaiser had again ordered him verbally to establish once and for all, with the Chief of General Staff, 'what troops will be required by the army in connection with the planned deployment on non-German territory at the beginning of a war forced on Germany by England, and will therefore not be available for other purposes at first. As soon as the number and type of troops are settled, I most respectfully suggest that we report to H. Majesty in a joint submission, and by explaining at the same time the reasons for and against this deployment, give H. Majesty the basis on which to make a decision as to what measures are to be taken in the circumstances described, and how far the planned preparations for such measures should go. It will also be necessary to point out that the War Ministry has not been involved so far. – I should like to emphasise again that a rapid decision on this question is imperative for the Admiralty Staff, and if this suggested method of achieving a decision cannot be accepted, I would ask Yr Excellency to indicate some other method.'[90]

In accordance with All-Highest orders, Schlieffen agreed to do as the Admiralty Staff wished and told Büchsel on 20 December 1904 that he had begun a detailed examination of troop requirements for the operations in Denmark. 'I intend to make a submission to His Majesty giving the information necessary for a decision and most respectfully leave it to you to do the same.'[91] Despite this assurance several weeks passed without any sign of the Chief of General Staff's report to the Kaiser. On 23 January 1905 an irritated Büchsel informed Schlieffen that his own submission was ready to be sent to the Supreme War Lord, and demanded that Schlieffen tell him on which day he intended to hand in his report, for it was important that both reports should reach the Kaiser at the same time. Büchsel added a warning 'that I must obtain H.M. the Kaiser's decision punctually in mid-February on the deployment of H.M.'s Fleet'. It would be embarrassing for him, Büchsel concluded, if he were obliged on that occasion to point out the major gaps in the preparatory work on the operations 'which are there because the Kaiser has been unable to make a decision on what is after all the most likely scenario for war'.[92]

It was characteristic of the way in which such momentous planning was carried out in Wilhelmine Germany that it did not occur to the Chief of Admiralty Staff and the Kaiser until January 1905, while they discussed bringing the operational plans against Denmark into force, that it was essential for the Reich Chancellor, the Foreign Office, the War Ministry and the Naval Cabinet, all of whom had been ignored hitherto, to be involved. Büchsel's submission, which Wilhelm approved on 31 January 1905, included the statement: 'In order to prevent any serious delays occurring in the event of war, the participating or relevant authorities must be informed as far as is necessary, before war breaks out, of what we want in the war. In particular the Reich Chancellor must be aware of the general outlines of the o[perational] plan, as well as of the stance our military leaders in war propose to adopt with regard to questions of international law, in order to take account of our intentions, if necessary, in directing the policy of the Reich.' The monarch had signified 'His All-Highest intention', Büchsel noted on his submission, that his commands should be sought 'at a joint audience of all the authorities involved and of the Reich Chancellor'.[93]

The Kaiser's ruling for or against the navy's grand operational plan in the event of war between Germany and England alone, or England and France together, was now imminent. For five years Büchsel and the Admiralty Staff had worked towards this moment of decision. In a memorandum for the Kaiser the Admiral made one last attempt to emphasise the world-historical significance of the struggle against Britain and the primary role which would thus fall to the German fleet. 'Our national existence is at stake in the war against England!' he asserted. 'We must wager everything if we are to achieve our goal; if we lose, England will force us to submit unconditionally to her will; if so Germany can expect to be excluded for all time from the ranks of the world powers and will sink down to the status of a continental power.' It was true that the Reich might be able, 'by conquering a continental ally of England . . . to draw nourishment for a time from the enemy country' and thus to delay 'the moment when we must do England's bidding', but this could last only for a short time and it would not prevent England's final victory. That could be achieved only 'if we succeed in inflicting such damage on England's powers at sea that she sees the wisdom of breaking off this war and recognising Germany as a power factor with rights equal to hers, in order to maintain her own position as a world power'.

'In the war with England the final outcome rests solely with the fleet', Büchsel continued. 'Therefore Germany must use all her resources — including those of the army — to support the war conducted by the fleet.' He concluded: 'If therefore one course of action offers the prospect — even if it is not very great — of achieving the goal of our warfare at sea, this course must be adopted with the greatest possible effort and the greatest possible energy. The situations that we need must be created regardless of our neighbours and using the broadest possible interpretation of the rights of belligerent parties. All measures must be directed towards the one aim of supporting the war conducted by the fleet.' Given the superior power of the British navy and its permanent state of readiness for war, a battle right at the beginning of the war would be as hopeless for Germany as a strategic defensive in the German Bight. Purely defensive action was in any case 'incompatible with the aim of our warfare and incompatible with the spirit of those who have grown up in YM Fleet, incompatible with what the nation expects from the Fleet for which great sacrifices have been made, incompatible with the hope of receiving the means to continue building up our Fleet after the war until it is a decisive power factor in Yr Majesty's hands'. Büchsel brushed aside the objection that the British would keep their resources together in the North Sea and not fall into the trap of the heavily mined entrances to the Baltic, arguing that the Royal Navy's offensive spirit and the calls for help which could be expected from Denmark would win the day. He had to concede somewhat awkwardly that if the enemy did not after all behave as expected, 'if he remains in the North Sea, if he keeps the exits from the Baltic under surveillance only between Scotland and Norway, then of course our further measures in the Belt are in vain and Denmark has been driven into the enemy's arms for nothing. But nothing else has changed in our war situation vis-à-vis England. We are in no less favourable a position than before in relation to our principal enemy.' The fleet could console itself with the 'great moral advantage' that it had seized the offensive, even if on a limited scale, at the very beginning of the war and had 'done everything in its power'. Büchsel pleaded for a rapid decision by the Kaiser. 'The need to complete the war preparations against England, which have been going on for years, is extremely urgent in the present state of affairs. This requires a final decision now on the issue of whether and which Danish territory is to be occupied, regardless of whether France will be drawn into the war or not ... Without a final decision ... without careful pre-war preparations on the basis of this decision, it will be impossible to carry out this plan in the war. But these preparations need time, they require extensive collaboration with the War Ministry and the Reich Navy Office, neither of which has yet been heard, and therefore I venture most humbly to request that after Your Majesty has taken cognisance of the opinion of the Chief of General Staff and has heard the views of the War Minister and the Secretary of State of the Reich Navy Office ... Your Majesty will graciously consent to come to a decision ... For the operations of the Fleet in the war against England or England and France, are we to reckon with the occupation of part of Zealand with Korsør, Sprogø, Funen and part of Jutland with Esbjerg and Fredericia, as planned, and should all the preparations to mobilise for this be undertaken?'[94]

While Büchsel waited tensely for the Kaiser's decision, the General Staff's statement of opinion on the operational plan reached him at long last. Although it pointed out various logistical difficulties that would have to be overcome, it calculated that the navy's plan would be practicable. Schlieffen's memorandum of early February 1905 contained no objections in principle to the war in the north. On the contrary, it confirmed that the blockade of the Belts, with the troops and artillery necessary to defend it, just as desired by the navy, could be put in place by the fourth day of mobilisation.[95]

This statement by the General Staff was concluded on 4 February 1905, dispatched on 6 February and received by the Admiralty Staff on 8 February.[96] The Kaiser had therefore not yet seen it when he took his momentous decision on 7 February *against* the occupation of the main island of Zealand. One can well imagine the frustration and confusion in the Admiralty Staff on 8 February, when the letter from the Chief of the Naval Cabinet, Admiral von Senden-Bibran, with the Supreme War Lord's negative decision, arrived – at the same time as Schlieffen's positive statement of opinion. Senden wrote: 'His Majesty the Kaiser and King has today been pleased to decide, following Your Excellency's report of the 3rd, that ... for the operations of the fleet in the war against England or England and France the planned occupation of part of Zealand with Korsør is to be ruled out, because, on the one hand, the Reich Chancellor has expressed considerable reservations about it from the political point of view, and on the other, in a war against England and France the army cannot provide troops to the strength required for the occupation of Zealand without endangering its chances of success against France.'[97] The disappointed officers of the Admiralty Staff made a note on Schlieffen's statement that the matter was now 'settled by All-Highest decision'.[98]

The objections of the Reich Chancellor and the diplomats on the one hand[99] and those of the War Ministry on the other had in effect persuaded the Kaiser to turn on his heel. Although Wilhelm's negative decision of 7 February 1905 referred only to Zealand and Korsør and thus seemed to leave the occupation of Funen and Jutland open, Büchsel could not avoid the conclusion that as a result of the imperial decision the whole plan to split the British fleet by attacking Denmark was doomed to failure. A blockade of the Great Belt could not be maintained without occupying Korsør, and the political and military objections which the Reich Chancellor and the War Minister had raised to the invasion of Zealand were equally valid for the occupation of Funen and Jutland. In these circumstances Büchsel asked the Kaiser on 13 February 1905, 'since it is absolutely imperative to establish a firm basis for the deployment of Your Majesty's Fleet in the war against France and England ... to be pleased to command that the navy is *no longer in any way* to expect participation by the army in its conduct of the war in the Belt'. The Kaiser accepted this recommendation from the Chief of Admiralty Staff in audience on 16 February 1905.[100]

The imperial decision of 7 February 1905 against the occupation of Denmark in the event of war with England alone or with England and France together turned the operational plans of the Admiralty Staff, on which five years of intensive work had been expended, into so much waste paper. The basic idea behind the plans now had to be abandoned and a completely different strategy pursued. As Büchsel explained to the Kaiser at his audience on 21 March 1905, 'in the present circumstances' the only right course he could see was 'to assemble the entire active battlefleet in the Elbe, where it is held together in its Chief's control, ready for any action that the war situation may require'. Of course such actions would be limited, in view of the superior power of the British fleet for the foreseeable future. 'A strategic offensive on the English coast, as matters stand – at least for the time being – is out of the question. There remains only strategic defensive action, or to express it better, offensive warfare with support from our coast.' Kaiser Wilhelm approved these basic principles for the assembling and deployment of the fleet in a war against England on 21 March 1905.[101] Two days later he left Cuxhaven in the mail steamer *Hamburg* and set sail for the Mediterranean, where by landing at Tangier he was to provoke the first of the great pre-war crises.

DID WILHELM II WANT WAR IN 1904–1905?

Scarcely any other theme of pre-First World War history has aroused as much controversy as the question of whether the political and military leadership of the Kaiserreich in 1904–5 deliberately set out to use the opportunity offered by Russia's defeats and revolutionary unrest to bring about a so-called 'preventive war' against France. Despite intensive research of the sources opinion is still divided, but it is an incontrovertible fact that from the outbreak of the Russo-Japanese War in February 1904 the preventive war question was constantly discussed, and at the highest levels, in Berlin. On 19 April 1904 Prince Lichnowsky, Bülow's right-hand man, called on Schlieffen on the Chancellor's behalf and received from the Chief of General Staff, in response to an enquiry, the significant statement: 'If it should prove necessary for us to have a war with France, the present moment would undoubtedly be favourable for it.'[102] It was no coincidence that at just this time – to be precise, after the General Staff's journey of June 1904 – the first draft of the notorious Schlieffen Plan was produced. It bore the title 'War of aggression against France' and entailed the violation of Belgian and Dutch neutrality. Not until December 1905 – just before his departure – did Schlieffen re-name his war plan 'War against France allied with England', which reflected the stark reality. Significantly, there is no reference in it to a subsequent campaign against Russia.[103]

In spite of his almost uncontrollable belligerence towards Britain and France, Wilhelm II was held back from launching an attack in the west by the realisation that his army and especially his navy were not ready for war, and that the German population, too, would oppose a war of aggression. On 4 February 1905 Admiral von Müller recorded that the Kaiser was 'infuriated' by a speech by Arthur Lee, Civil Lord of the British Admiralty, in which Lee, alluding to the building of the German battlefleet, had emphasised the readiness for war of the Royal Navy and threatened a preventive strike like the sinking of the Danish fleet at Copenhagen in 1807. Wilhelm immediately summoned the British ambassador, Sir Frank Lascelles, and subsequently told Müller that he regarded 'this new English threat ... as an instigation to France ... whom it would suit very nicely if I lashed out. Naturally I have no intention of doing so, but I demand a categorical denial from Mr Lee.' The next day Wilhelm again talked excitedly about 'English threats and enlargement of the Fleet to be carried out nevertheless'.[104] On 15 February 1905, walking in the Thiergarten with Müller, he was 'very overwrought' and spoke again of the Kaiserreich's extremely tense relations with England and France. Referring to the rabid war-mongering of the Pan-German League, he complained of the 'inability of the Germans to understand [the] broad political situation' and explained: 'France as instigator of England against Germany and as the object of attack'.[105] The Kaiser's decision on 7 February 1905 to abandon the planned occupation of the main Danish island of Zealand in the event of war must be seen against this background. It points to the realisation that a war against Britain *alone* had become highly unlikely, if only because Germany, unable to defeat Britain, intended to conquer France by way of compensation for the loss of her fleet, her colonies and her overseas trade.[106] In a war against Britain *and* France, however, all available army corps would be needed for the offensive in the west.[107] Should one take on such a dangerous risk?

At the end of July 1905 Wilhelm II took the decision he had already announced eighteen months earlier of appointing Helmuth von Moltke as Chief of General Staff at the end of the year in place of the elderly Schlieffen. Schlieffen's son-in-law Wilhelm von Hahnke, the son of the former Chief of the Military Cabinet, told General Groener in 1926 how this decision finally came about. Hahnke recalled that several generals, including Plessen, Hülsen-Haeseler and Moltke, had been trying to get rid of Schlieffen as Chief of General Staff for some time. 'They came up against the Kaiser's resistance and needed heavy artillery. There was a meeting of the Council of State [sic] in 1905 during the Morocco crisis, presided over by Bülow; Tirpitz and Schlieffen were there, among others. There was a lot of blather back and forth. Finally Bülow asked Schlieffen for his opinion. Schlieffen said: "Russia is tied down in the East, England is still weak after the Boer War, France has fallen behind in her arms programme. The German Reich must prove its ability through a war sooner or later. Now is the most favourable time. Therefore my solution is: war with France." Tirpitz lost his temper, saying his fleet was not ready yet, and Bülow's heart sank into his boots, saying war is impossible with *this* Kaiser. He ran to the Kaiser and said, these are risky times, the Chief of General Staff is a frail old man, it is high time the Kaiser looked around for another Chief.'[108] By this account, therefore, only Tirpitz was opposed to bringing about a war in western Europe, because the battlefleet was 'not yet ready'. Bülow, on the other hand, completely accepted Schlieffen's view that under the prevailing circumstances the war against France which had to be waged 'sooner or later' had better be launched in the near future. According to Hahnke's evidence he had made only two conditions: the replacement of Schlieffen by a younger Chief of General Staff, and the Kaiser's assurance that he would not personally interfere in the conduct of the war. Moltke, for his part, took on the General Staff on condition that Wilhelm gave up directing manoeuvres himself.[109] This had been 'bitterly hard' for the War Lord, Moltke wrote to his wife, but it was at least a beginning.[110]

In an astonishing letter of 30 July 1905 Wilhelm informed the Reich Chancellor of his decision to dismiss Schlieffen and went on to say, evidently in the assumption that war might break out at any moment with Britain and France, without Russian involvement: 'I have ... talked over all the eventualities with Julius von Moltke ... The result is as follows: ... If England starts a war with us in some way or other, two dispatches must immediately be sent by Your Excellency to Brussels and Paris demanding that they declare within six hours whether they are for or against us. We must march into Belgium at once, however she declares herself. In the case of France it depends whether she remains neutral − which I should like to think is not entirely out of the question, even if the probability is slight −; then the Russian casus foederis [her commitment to stand by France] can be discounted. If she [i.e. France] mobilises, then that is a threat of war against us in favour of England, and in that case Russian regiments must march with us. I believe that to rape and pillage in beautiful Gaul would be a pleasant enough prospect to lure the Russians. It might be worth considering whether France could be offered a rounding-off at Belgium's expense as bait for good behaviour towards us, as a substitute for the lost Reich lands [of Alsace and Lorraine] ... We cannot count on *active* Russian help in the near future, as war and revolution is keeping the army busy and the fleet is no longer in existence. But it leaves us free to the rear! Very good *passive* help!'[111] So in July 1905 the Kaiser and Moltke had already reached this stage in their thinking and planning for a large-scale European war.

But were Wilhelm II and his most senior military advisers actively seeking war in the west at this supposedly favourable moment, or did they merely want to be strategically well prepared in case Britain and France instigated such a war themselves? Certainly Tirpitz's battlefleet was still some years away from being 'ready' for the decisive battle with Britain, while in the Prussian War Ministry too it was argued that the great military confrontation with France should be delayed for technical reasons connected with armaments.[112]

A few telling sources suggest that in December 1905 lively discussions took place which finally led to the decision that the war in the west should after all be postponed for a few months or even years. In 1936 a former General Staff officer, Riemann, wrote to the historian Rudolf Schwertfeger telling him that he had been assigned to the artillery division of the Great General Staff as First Lieutenant from March 1905. Riemann recalled: 'One day Count Hermann Sch[lieffen], a close friend of mine and nephew of the Chief of the Gen[eral] Staff, Count v. Schlieffen ... came to our room at about 10 a.m. looking very agitated ... Count Hermann Schlieffen said: "I have just come from Uncle Alfred [Schlieffen]. Do you know what happened? Last night at 1 o'clock the Kaiser summoned Bülow and Uncle Alfred to see him. This morning at 6 the War Minister too. Question of war with France." "And do you know", said Hermann Schlieffen, thumping the table, "whose fault it is that this unique opportunity has to be missed? It is your fault! (I am in the field artillery.) The War Minister declared that our artillery is altogether inferior to the French." ... Count Hermann Schlieffen was a great favourite with his uncle, who came to greet him almost every morning when he came on duty ... I have no doubt', Riemann asserted, 'that he was telling us his uncle's words that morning, and his embittered resignation'.[113]

That this dramatic nocturnal decision to delay the war in the west happened at the end of 1905 is clear both from Müller's diary and from the Kaiser's notorious New Year's Eve letter to Bülow. The Admiral's diary for December lists a whole series of audiences, which taken together bear witness to a lively conflict at the highest level.[114] The crucial discussion described by Riemann between the Kaiser, Bülow, Schlieffen and the War Minister, von Einem, seems to have taken place on the night of 20 to 21 December 1905, for Bülow and Schlieffen can be shown to have been together at the Schloss at that time. On 23 December 1905 there were several further 'military audiences and reports' at the Neues Palais, according to Müller.[115]

The staggering letter which Kaiser Wilhelm II wrote to Reich Chancellor von Bülow on New Year's Eve 1905 bears eloquent testimony to the content of these military–political consultations. In it the Kaiser expressly demanded the postponement of a 'world war' – his very words – until all Germany's armaments, especially her field artillery, had been brought up to date (just as Riemann reported) and her battlefleet completed, and until the support of Germany's allies was assured, the entire Islamic or Arabic world had been won round to the German cause, the German people roused to enthusiasm for war and Social Democracy within the country eliminated! The Supreme War Lord wrote: 'The news that in France 150 million has already been spent for war preparations without anyone noticing is extremely serious and disturbing ...

It has given the French a very considerable lead over us . . . To do England the favour of taking on the odium of attacking France on account of Morocco, so that the English at last have the desired opportunity to set upon us in the fine guise of "protecting the weak against aggression" is not in our interest, nor is it a programme likely to inspire the enthusiasm of our people . . . If you, my dear Bülow, are reckoning on the prospect of a possible war . . . you ought to be very active in seeking out our allies. It would be absolutely essential to call upon them for help, for their existence would then also be at stake, as it would be a world war. But above all an alliance ought to be concluded with the Sultan at once, coute qui coute [sic], which would place the Mohammedan forces to the furthest possible extent − under Prussian leadership − at my disposal, and likewise with all Arab rulers. *For on our own we are not in a position to wage war against an alliance of Gaul and England.* Next year is particularly unpropitious, as we are in the process of re-arming our artillery with a new (recoil) gun, which will take a year to complete. The infantry is also in the process of being re-equipped and is receiving new rifles and new ammunition. Around Metz there are still unfinished forts and batteries every-where, which are the first to be attacked. Thus in technical military terms we are not at a stage at which I as Supreme War Lord would happily agree to send our army into action without further ado.' At sea Germany was 'well-nigh powerless' because for years the Reichstag had refused to strengthen the fleet, the Kaiser complained. '*We are absolutely defenceless against a comb[ination] of France and England's navy.*' Therefore, Wilhelm continued, 'I would very strongly advise that matters should be arranged so that *as far as is at all possible, we are spared the necessity of deciding to go to war for the time being.* Furthermore, at a moment like this when the Socialists are preaching and preparing open rebellion, I cannot take a single man out of the country without the greatest danger to the life and property of its citizens. First [we must] shoot down the Socialists, behead them and render them harmless − if necessary by a bloodbath − and then [fight a] war against the foreign foe! But not beforehand and not a tempo.'[116] On the following day the Supreme War Lord announced to the commanding generals, assembled for their annual New Year's meeting in Berlin, that he would never fight a war over Morocco. They left the Schloss, the War Minister recalled, 'in silence and depressed'.[117]

With its passionate enumeration of all the reasons against an immediate war, the Supreme War Lord's notorious letter of 31 December 1905 in fact only goes to show that up to this point Wilhelm II had proceeded on the assumption that German policy, if not exactly aimed at bringing about such a war, had at least calculated on it as a strong possibility. As the Austrian military attaché reported on 12 December 1905, both the Kaiser and War

Minister Karl von Einem, while not pressing for a war, were doubtful whether peace could be maintained for long and determined to bring about a war 'at a point in time favourable to us'.[118] This conclusion throws significant light on the conduct of the monarch in the two major foreign policy moves of 1905 which will be examined in detail in the following chapters – the Kaiser's sensational landing in Tangier on 31 March 1905, and the signature of the secret treaty of alliance with the Tsar on the island of Björkö on 24 July 1905.

CHAPTER THIRTEEN

'Paris must get one in the eye from us one day!' The Kaiser and the first Morocco crisis

O n 31 March 1905, during his voyage to the Mediterranean, Wilhelm II paid a brief visit to the ancient port of Tangier on the Moroccan side of the Straits of Gibraltar, and in so doing caused a serious political crisis that brought Europe to the edge of a major war.[1] What was this provocative act designed to achieve, and whose idea was it? For a long time Edward VII was convinced that the Kaiser himself was behind it, and that his intention was to start a war.[2] From this point onwards he considered his nephew as Britain's most dangerous enemy.[3] The Kaiser, however, insisted (not when the Morocco crisis had developed into a fiasco for Germany, but well before that in the summer of 1905) that it was only for Bülow's sake that he had landed in Tangier. In his famous 'suicide telegram' to the Reich Chancellor of 11 August 1905 he protested: 'Do not forget that you made use of me *personally against my will* in Tangier so as to score a success in your Moroccan policy ... I landed for your sake, because the Fatherland demanded it, and mounted a strange horse in spite of being handicapped by my crippled left arm, and the horse came within a hair's breadth of *killing* me, which was *the risk you took*! I rode right through the Spanish anarchists because *you wanted it* and *your policy* was supposed to profit from it!'[4] In his memoirs the Kaiser put less emphasis on his fear of anarchists and strange horses than on the political reservations which he had supposedly expressed about the landing. 'I was afraid that this visit could be seen as a provocation, given the state of affairs in Paris, and that in London it would bring about an inclination to support France in the event of war.'[5] The diplomat Wilhelm von Schoen, who was in attendance on the Mediterranean voyage, recorded that the Kaiser justified himself by claiming that 'it had not been his intention to allow the journey to become a highly political and in some respects somewhat objectionable demonstration ... The Chancellor, however, presumably under the influence of Herr von Holstein, had insisted so strongly on a political emphasis that in the end, in accordance with constitutional principles, he had gone along with it.'[6] Schoen confirmed this account and commented: 'Not until several days later, in Naples, when the Kaiser received the first news of the powerful effect that the Tangier visit had created in the world, did he seem to realise fully the immense political significance of his action. Although the Kaiser did not say as much, I had the impression that he felt, on looking back at what had happened, that it would have been better to have stood by his original refusal.'[7]

Historical research has not reached a consensus, even after a hundred years, on the roles or motives of the three people chiefly responsible for Germany's Moroccan policy – Wilhelm II, Bülow and Holstein. But it is generally agreed that the Kaiser's visit to Tangier exacerbated international tensions and considerably increased the risks of a world war thereafter. Holstein's American biographer, Norman Rich, commented that the Kaiser's landing in Tangier 'set off what was probably the most serious international crisis in Europe in the era before the First World War'. The first Morocco crisis 'was to result in a crystallisation of diplomatic alignments that set the stage for the events of 1914'.[8] But historians are not alone in recognising the miscalculation behind the theatrical provocation; a number of contemporaries also saw it. Only a week after the Tangier landing the wise Count Zedlitz wrote: 'All that the visit has actually achieved is that the French have become extremely excited and we have well-nigh driven them into the arms of the English, which in the present situation is the worst possible outcome for us ... If the two powers take serious action in this matter we shall have to give way.' The incident, he thought, could have lasting repercussions in the same way as the 'very suddenly and hastily dispatched Krüger Telegram. At any rate the whole manner in which this affair has developed makes it one of the moments that may one day prove really dangerous for the country.'[9] Richard von Kühlmann, who was to be directly involved in the adventure, later blamed Holstein for the debacle, whose aim it had been to 'force France to her knees' in order to establish Germany's hegemony and preponderance in Europe.[10]

How did this blunder come about? What were the aims of the Reich Chancellor and Privy Councillor von Holstein in the Morocco crisis, and what attitude did the Kaiser adopt towards them? When, if at all, did he express misgivings about the Wilhelmstrasse's risky show of strength and attempt to take a different, more conciliatory line? Wilhelm was after all at the height of his personal power in 1905, and this was particularly true in the sphere of foreign and military policy. As we shall see, he initially repeatedly and proudly claimed credit for the landing as an essential prerequisite of the goal he kept constantly in his sights, a continental league against Britain.[11] In April 1905, shortly after his ride through Tangier, he wrote to Countess Annina Morosini: 'You will have noticed that all Europe now does my will – in fear of me.'[12] When Count Götz von Seckendorff, who was with the Kaiser on the cruise to Lisbon, Tangier, Gibraltar and Naples, asserted that the Moroccan adventure had not been the Kaiser's idea but that of the German Foreign Office and that Wilhelm had until the last moment expressed his reluctance to land in Tangier, the British Foreign Secretary, Lord Lansdowne, was not convinced. 'To the best of my belief the originator of the idea was Tattenbach, who succeeded in impregnating the Emperor's mind with it. The Emperor then took it up enthusiastically and made it his own. – But the truth may be somewhere between the two.'[13] The German ambassador in Paris, Prince Hugo Radolin, a close friend of Holstein, blamed the military at court for the fiasco: in his view the Kaiser was 'surrounded by bad advisors, viz. military men anxious to earn crosses and . . . he allowed himself to be pushed to a point which was near to war'.[14] Whatever the truth, Wilhelm's conduct during the first Morocco crisis throws much light on the acute tension between his personal diplomacy and the Reich government's foreign policy and thus merits close examination.

SPRING 1904: THE PRELUDE

That the Kaiser could have behaved in a very different way is demonstrated by his decisive attitude a year before the fateful landing in Tangier, during his Mediterranean cruise in spring 1904. At that time Bülow and the Wilhelmstrasse made plans for a show of strength in Morocco which the monarch repeatedly refused to accept. When the Pasha of Fez had the Moroccan agent of a German firm imprisoned, Bülow wanted to use the incident as a pretext to bring about 'a settlement, at last, of our . . . claims against Morocco, some of which have been outstanding for a considerable time'. 'Because of our political and economic position in Morocco, especially in relation to the other powers engaged there, it is . . . essential that we break this resistance and insist that we be given complete satisfaction for behaviour which is in breach of contract and is degenerating into open mockery of our rights.' The Chancellor suggested to the Kaiser in March 1904 that he should demand 'rapid and adequate atonement for the flagrant breach of contract in Fez', that is to say the immediate release and compensation of the German agent as well as 'severe punishment for the sherifian officials involved in the affair'. But Wilhelm II reacted negatively to these strong words, dismissing them with the resigned comment that as the

Moroccan authorities had the backing 'of Gaul and Britain together', they would not be punished anyway.[15] He therefore rejected his Chancellor's proposal 'to give emphasis to the subsequent negotiations by an increase of military strength' in the shape of German warships which would be sent to Tangier 'to back up our claims and complaints'.[16] In view of the 'very advanced stage' of the negotiations over the Anglo-French Entente, concluded shortly afterwards on 8 April 1904, the monarch argued, 'a unilateral warlike action by Germany at this moment' would 'undoubtedly arouse the suspicion of these powers, it would shake their belief in our repeated ... assurances that we claim no exclusive rights in Morocco and put the stamp of ambiguity on our policy'.[17]

So for once the Kaiser took a much more cautious view than his Chancellor and poured cold water on the latter's aggressive plans. Instead of unilateral action by the Kaiserreich he proposed a European and international resolution of the problem. Bülow saw what was actually a minor incident as a long-awaited opportunity and 'sufficient grounds for military action'; his sovereign, on the other hand, was worried about the threat of Germany's isolation, in view of the imminent conclusion of the Entente Cordiale, and expressed disapproval of precisely the policy of seesawing between the other great Powers that he himself so often pursued. The Chancellor, however, was reluctant to abandon his gunboat diplomacy. He drafted a reply to the Kaiser saying he considered it his duty to point out that the concessions which would have to be made to Paris, London and Madrid in order to achieve a joint action in Morocco 'could potentially have undesirable repercussions on the fate of the imminent new Navy Bill. The Opposition, which will turn anything it can find into ammunition, will have no difficulty in using our recourse to foreign help against Morocco as grounds for arguments against the fleet.'[18] This transparent attempt by Bülow to capitalise both on Wilhelm's fondness for 'his' fleet and on his aversion to the Reichstag came too late and was never sent – whether because the Entente Cordiale was already as good as signed,[19] or whether because in the end Bülow (as usual) lacked the courage to defy his monarch's explicit rebuff, must remain an open question.

At any rate the conclusion of the Entente on 8 April 1904 confirmed the Kaiser in his rejection of the show of strength in Morocco proposed by Bülow. Since England's 'possible points of friction with France' had now been 'considerably reduced', he commented on 19 April, *'any consideration for us will fade more and more into the background where England is concerned* ... In these circumstances it might well be seen as a blessing that no demonstration of our naval strength took place in Morocco.'[20] In the summer of 1904 the Kaiser again rejected a request from the Wilhelmstrasse for an ultimatum to be issued to the Sultan of Morocco and a warship to be sent to North Africa to back up Germany's demands.[21]

THE TUG-OF-WAR OVER THE TANGIER LANDING

In the following months Germany's international position had deteriorated considerably, principally because of the growing tension with Britain during the Russo-Japanese War. It was a situation that demanded the greatest possible caution and restraint, as Bülow and Holstein also recognised. Just before the Kaiser's Mediterranean voyage in March 1905 Bülow advised him to make himself agreeable to the Italian royal family, in order 'not to drive [Italy] completely into the French camp'. The 'general world situation', the Reich Chancellor opined, was 'so tense that we must try to lose as few tricks as possible'. This warning provoked an embittered retort from Wilhelm. 'If that has not already happened, in days gone by when the seeds for the present constellation were sown. The Triple Alliance loosened by Austria falling out with Italy, Russia unchanged or Indifferent [sic] towards us, England hostile, Gaul bent on revenge.'[22] On Bülow's prompting the Kaiser took forceful steps to bind Italy to the Triple Alliance by reproaching the Italian ambassador Count Lanza over rumours of a Franco-Italian treaty of neutrality. The purpose of this, as Bülow explained to the German ambassador in Rome, Count Monts, was 'to bring home to the Italian Government that it must keep its predilection for France under control, at least outwardly, and take more care to look after German–Italian relations than hitherto, since the accession [of Victor Emmanuel III]'.[23] Whether such steps did anything to achieve the aim of keeping Italy loyal to the Triple Alliance is doubtful, in spite of Bülow's assertion that 'the fact that we intimidated Italy was useful, if only to sound out the mood there, and also as a warning'.[24] What was more evident from these initiatives was the impotence of German policy in countering the growing isolation of the Reich.

In this situation it was France which was to give the Wilhelmstrasse the pretext for a daring attempt to break the chains of the Entente. For it transpired that the French government had omitted to inform Germany officially of the conclusion of its colonial agreement with Britain and to secure Berlin's recognition of the advantages France had thereby acquired in Morocco. Britain, by contrast, had come to an understanding with the Reich on the protection of German interests in Egypt and had in turn received Germany's formal agreement to British rule on the Nile. This had happened just before King Edward VII's visit to Kaiser Wilhelm for Kiel Week at the end of June 1904.[25] Through her omission France had unwittingly given an impetus to Germany's moves to prevent the practical application in Morocco of the agreements made with Britain. The aim was to demonstrate to the French policy-makers and in particular the Foreign Minister Théophile Delcassé, the architect of the Entente Cordiale, the worthlessness of their link to Britain and thus to destroy this important element of the encirclement threatening Germany. The Kaiserreich took the line of insisting on the independence – nominally still valid – of the Moroccan Sultanate so as to keep Morocco out of the French grasp and show up the Entente Cordiale as a mere scrap of paper of no real value to Paris. What more sensational way could there be of demonstrating this than an official visit to Moroccan territory by the German Emperor, bringing greetings to the Sultan – from sovereign to sovereign, thus acting as standard-bearer of the monarchical principle even in the Maghreb? With Russia's hands temporarily tied, it was strategically the ideal moment for such an action.

At the same time France was trying to cement her influence in Morocco. In the second half of January 1905 the French envoy Georges St-René-Taillandier travelled inland from Tangier, the diplomatic city on the Atlantic, to the court of the Sultan of Morocco, Mulay Abdul Aziz, at Fez. His mission was to secure French supremacy in Morocco, as accorded under the Entente settlement. Taillandier presented the Sultan with what amounted to a demand to turn his country into a French protectorate: France wanted to exercise financial control, keep out political influence from other countries and control the Moroccan army through French instructors.[26]

In their approach to the issue Holstein and Bülow were only too conscious that the Kaiser was still opposed to ostentatious action in Morocco. Wilhelm's refusal to send warships to North Africa in the spring and summer of 1904 and his renunciation of territorial ambitions in Morocco continued to have an effect.[27] The Kaiser persisted in his view 'that the Reich's policy is burdened with too many external and internal issues to get involved in an enterprise in Morocco'.[28] He also entertained the bizarre hope, as we have seen, that in the event of war the entire Mohammedan world would agree to be commanded by a Prussian general, and was consequently anxious not to jeopardise this dream by offending Islamic sensibilities in Morocco.[29] In view of the Kaiser's attitude the Auswärtiges Amt twice refused, in October 1904 and January 1905, the requests of their envoy and the German colony in Morocco to increase the German naval presence off the Moroccan coast.[30] Nevertheless there are interesting indications that the idea of a landing in Tangier may have originated with Wilhelm himself.[31] The American government was astonished to receive a request on behalf of the Kaiser at the beginning of 1905 for American cooperation with the planned action in Morocco, for he had thereby put himself into their hands. John Hay, the US Secretary of State, commented on 7 March 1905 that by informing Britain and France 'of what he has said to us in the last few weeks we could make very serious trouble'.[32]

During a consultation on the programme for the 1905 Mediterranean voyage the Kaiser told Oberhofmarschall Count August zu Eulenburg that he wished to cruise along the North African coast so as to see something of Morocco, and that he did not want to stop at Gibraltar for too long. Eulenburg took the precaution of asking the Chancellor whether he had any objection on political grounds, to which Bülow sent a written reply to the effect that 'in his view there could scarcely be any objection to merely sailing past close to Tangier'. Zedlitz, who as Hofmarschall worked closely with Eulenburg, his superior, reported that from Bülow's reaction 'it appeared that this plan did not entirely please him, and that he meant to advise gently against it. – But after a few days His Majesty spoke quite calmly of a possible short "landing" in Tangier, and Count Bülow no longer had the nerve to explain that this could in fact cause difficulties with the political state of affairs. It appeared from the whole situation that the Reich Chancellor thought the visit to Tangier very undesirable, but that he did not state this with sufficient firmness.'[33] The itinerary which Eulenburg sent to Bülow on 13 March 1905 already included a four-hour stop by the monarch in the Moroccan port. Under the influence of Holstein, however, Bülow now realised that the Kaiser's landing could be turned into a world political coup. On 19 March the semi-official *Kölnische Zeitung* reported a 'very definitely emerging rumour' that 'His Majesty Kaiser Wilhelm will put in at Tangier on the morning of the 31st of the month and will be received by a Moroccan dignitary on behalf of the Sultan [of Morocco]'. This news also attracted international attention. The London *Times* reminded its readers of Wilhelm's words of the previous year, that Germany sought no territorial advantages in Morocco, but only the maintenance of equal economic rights. Bülow had this and other articles reproduced without comment in the *Norddeutsche Allgemeine Zeitung* and sent them to the Kaiser with the remark: 'Your Majesty's visit to Tangier will embarrass Herr Delcassé, frustrate his plans and promote our economic interests in Morocco.' 'Tant mieux', the Kaiser noted with satisfaction on the margin of the Chancellor's letter. So there was as yet no sign of political reservations about the adventure, either at court or in the Wilhelmstrasse.[34]

At first Wilhelm seemed delighted that the planned visit to Tangier would give him the opportunity he had explicitly demanded 'to give Paris one in the eye'. But only a few hours later he was hesitant about exploiting this 'chance' after all. When he heard on 20 March from news agency reports 'that [the] German colony and Moroccans are preparing to take advantage of my visit and the British are using it against the Gauls', the Kaiser sent new orders to Bülow. 'A telegraph message must be sent to Tangier at once saying that it is *highly* doubtful that I shall land, and that I am travelling only incog[nito] as a tourist; therefore no audiences, no receptions.'[35] In the following days a very reluctant Wilhelm had to be virtually nursed along by Bülow and Holstein. The Chancellor reassured and flattered him. He assured him that the statement 'based on the declaration made by Your Majesty last year' and published in the *Norddeutsche Allgemeine Zeitung*, 'that Your Majesty does not aspire to any territorial advantages in Morocco, but only claims the same economic rights as other nations for Germany there, has put paid to all the sensational inventions by the press. In these circumstances I wish to recommend most humbly that nothing be changed in Your Majesty's existing travel plans as far as Tangier is concerned.' Bülow tried to make it a point of honour for Wilhelm: if it now became known that the Kaiser would only land at Tangier – if at all – incognito, the French Foreign Minister would publicly claim this 'restriction of the imperial itinerary' as a 'victory' for himself. 'I venture to believe that I am at one with Your Majesty in thinking that we have no grounds for allowing Herr Delcassé this triumph, which he would exploit with his usual virtuosity.' Wilhelm accepted this argument, two days before his departure.[36] Nevertheless he let it be known that when he stopped at Lisbon on his way southwards, he expected 'proposals' to be telegraphed to him as to whether he could 'disembark without risk to his safety. If so, His Majesty wishes to visit the sights and beauty spots of Tangier with Kühlmann [the German chargé d'affaires] as guide and then to take breakfast at Kühlmann's house. It must also be decided whom His Majesty is to receive on board as representative of the Sultan of Morocco.' So the Chancellor could by no means be sure of his wavering monarch. He made a note, in effect an instruction to himself and Holstein: 'All this must be carefully considered and settled, so that a detailed programme for Tangier is ready for His Majesty when he arrives in Lisbon, setting out what is to happen there, the situation there, what he is to say etc etc.'[37]

On 22 March 1905, at the unveiling of the monument to his father in Bremen, Wilhelm II made a remarkable speech in which, while presenting himself as a man of peace, he placed unmistakable emphasis on the growing power of the German Reich on land and at sea and revealed his ambitious goals for the future, even referring to world domination by the Hohenzollern dynasty. 'I swore a solemn oath when I came to the throne, after my Grandfather's powerful reign, that for my part bayonets and cannon should lie still, but that bayonets and cannon must be kept sharp and efficient so that envy and jealousy from abroad should not disturb us at home as we build our garden and our beautiful house. I vowed, because of what I had learnt from history, never to aspire to a fruitless domination of the world. For what has become of the great so-called world empires? Alexander the Great, Napoleon the First, all the great warrior heroes – they swam in seas of blood and left behind subjugated peoples who rose up at the first opportunity and caused the empires to fall into decay. The *Weltreich* [world empire] that I have founded for Myself [sic!] shall consist in the fact that, above all, the newly created German Reich shall enjoy the complete trust of all parties, as a quiet, honest, peaceful neighbour, and that if history should perhaps one day speak of a German *Weltreich* or of a *Hohenzollernweltherrschaft* [a Hohenzollern world supremacy], it shall not have been founded on conquests by the sword, but through mutual trust between nations aspiring to the same goals . . . I thank God that in this City Hall I do not have to sound the alarm, as I did once in Hamburg. The fleet is afloat and it is being built, the human resources are available. Their zeal and spirit is the same as that which inspired the officers of the Prussian Army at Hohenfriedberg and Königgrätz and Sedan, and with every German warship that is launched, one more guarantee of world peace is created, and our enemies will be the less likely to pick a quarrel with us and we shall be the more valuable as allies.' The task of German youth, Kaiser Wilhelm II declared, would be 'to avoid conflict, hatred, discord and envy, to rejoice in the German fatherland as it is, and not to strive for the impossible; to yield to the firm conviction that our Lord God would never have taken so much trouble with our German fatherland and its people if He did not have great things in store for us. We are the salt of the earth, but must also be worthy of it. Therefore our youth must learn self-denial, renouncing what is not good for them, eschewing what has been brought in from foreign countries and upholding morality, discipline, order, reverence and religious feeling . . . Then we shall be regarded from all sides with respect, sometimes also with love, as steady and reliable people; we shall be able to stand with our hand on our sword-hilt and our shield upright before us, and say: Tamen, let what will come, come.'[38] The next morning Wilhelm, in the best of moods, set sail from Cuxhaven on board the Hapag steamer *Hamburg* for his Mediterranean voyage.[39]

In Paris the news of the planned visit to Tangier created 'a strong impression', as the German chargé d'affaires reported. 'In the press, and even more in salons and clubs, the prevailing tone is one of disquiet and fear of complications.'[40] Bülow did his best to intensify this mood, instructing the Foreign Office 'to say nothing at all if diplomats ask about Tangier and Morocco . . . and to maintain a serious and impassive expression. For the time being our attitude in this connection should be like that of the sphinx, surrounded by curious tourists but betraying nothing.'[41] This opacity recommended itself not only for

its primary purpose of making France feel insecure, but also because the
German government itself could not be entirely sure of its monarch and his
ultimate intentions. Sending off a barrage of telegrams to Lisbon, Bülow tried
to convince the Kaiser that he should land at Tangier as proposed. 'Everyone is
watching, at home and abroad . . . This visit has put Delcassé in an embarrassing situation for the first time in a long time. If the visit to Tangier goes
according to plan, Delcassé with his anti-German policy will be seen as a
disgraced European.'[42] The Sultan of Morocco was 'highly delighted about
Your Majesty's visit to Tangier' and had already sent his great-uncle there with
three other important dignitaries as well as a handwritten letter.[43] In a further
telegram containing detailed stage directions on what the Kaiser should do and
say in Tangier, Bülow emphasised 'the safety of the stance we have adopted. By
standing up for equal economic rights for all nations, we also become, ipso
facto, protectors of the British commercial community in Morocco, whose
interests the English government has betrayed by the agreement with France.
The English merchant is too sharp not to know what it would mean for him, as
for all non-French colleagues, if Morocco were to be gradually forced into the
same form of protectorate as Tunis.' The French press had 'grown more
insolent again', among other things demanding 'e.g. the return of Metz', with
the aim of persuading the Sultan of Morocco 'that France was the stronger of
the two Powers [France and Germany] and was able to define the conditions
governing relations between the two Powers . . . To counteract this it would be
advisable, in my most humble opinion, for Your Majesty to receive the Sultan's
envoys with particular favour and expressly as the envoys of a Sovereign . . .
It is not in the German interest to promote the gradual assimilation of Morocco
by France by discouraging the Sultan. Apart from the fact that the systematic exclusion of non-French merchants and industrialists from Morocco,
after what happened in Tunis, would mean a considerable economic loss for
Germany, it also constitutes a failure to recognise our position of power if Herr
Delcassé has not thought it worth the trouble of entering into negotiations
with Germany concerning his Moroccan plans. Herr Delcassé has completely
ignored us with regard to this. It therefore seems advisable that Yr Majesty,
without saying a single unkind word about France, should not make any
reference at all to France in Morocco, and should also avoid doing the French
chargé d'affaires the honour of speaking to him but only give him a silent
greeting . . . Yr Majesty's visit to Tangier is the focus of world interest at this
moment. In Lisbon attempts will be made to draw Yr Majesty out on the
subject of our aims in Morocco. The more Yr Majesty acts the sphinx until
arriving in Tangier, and the less our attitude is discernible until then, the more
powerful the effect of the visit to Tangier will be.'[44]

The Reich Chancellor's constant flattery and blandishments failed to achieve any effect at first, especially as the news from Tangier sounded anything but encouraging. From Lisbon the Kaiser sent an anxious telegraph message to Bülow on 28 March 1905: 'All hell is already let loose in Tangier, yesterday an Englishman was almost murdered, I think the plan there is really very doubtful and as Tattenbach [the German envoy in Lisbon] who is an old hand also has doubts, I have ordered him to come with me and take a look at things first, before I go ashore.'[45] At this Bülow immediately set to work on Tattenbach, sending him no fewer than four telegrams on 29 March to persuade him to advocate a landing. 'If the Sultan stands firm and rejects the French demands in the main, so that France is confronted with the alternatives of a diplomatic defeat or a Moroccan war, Herr Delcassé's diplomatic prestige [will be] torn to shreds by his compatriots ... Delcassé's numerous enemies would like to take advantage of this embarrassment to bring him down ... It would therefore be no wonder if the Minister and his cronies were now doing their best to prevent His Majesty visiting Tangier by attempting to intimidate him.'[46] The implicit message was: whoever argues against a landing plays indirectly into France's hands. In addition, the Chancellor tried to allay fears about the Kaiser's personal safety. That Tattenbach should accompany the Kaiser to Tangier was 'particularly reassuring' for him, Bülow asserted. But the aforementioned Englishman, according to information from the German chargé d'affaires, had received 'only a very light scratch' and public opinion in Tangier was 'inclined to see the attack as a French machination to try to prevent His Majesty's visit to Tangier'. The Chancellor boldly claimed 'that since all the required measures have been taken, by the German and Spanish police as well, our All-Gracious Lord is facing hardly more of a risk in landing in Tangier than in going for his daily walk in the Tiergarten'.[47] It was true that 'the safety of the All-Highest Person' took precedence 'over everything else'; the Chancellor must, however, 'regard it as a misfortune for His Majesty and for the German Reich if the situation in Tangier was really such that the landing could not take place. The enemy press would of course spread reports that His Majesty had wished to avoid a supposed danger, which would afterwards be described as imaginary. You will agree with me that this opinion, if it gained ground, would inevitably dispel the awe which His Majesty's fearless vigour inspires in the world today. This awe has until now been one of the chief factors in the peaceful maintenance of Germany's position of power. If the prestige of the All-Highest Person were compromised, the conduct of foreign countries towards us would change and before long, as soon as an opportunity presented itself, we would find ourselves confronted with a choice between attacking and retreating.'[48]

Tattenbach replied that in the Kaiser's entourage there was certainly 'a strong feeling against His Majesty landing in Tangier', but he himself considered such fears misplaced and took the view, as did Oberhofmarschall Eulenburg, that 'whatever happens . . . the proposed visit ought not to be abandoned, after so much has been said and written about it'.[49] Once again Bülow put direct pressure on the Kaiser from afar, in a telegram which he deliberately kept 'very calm'.[50] 'Delcassé is sweating blood because Your Majesty's visit to Tangier will upset his finely-spun plans. He had let it be stated in Fez that France was acting on behalf of all the European Powers, who all agreed to and wished for Morocco's subjection to France. If Your Majesty now appears in Tangier, received with jubilation by all the Mohammedans, fêted by all the non-French Europeans, and without taking any notice of the French, Delcassé will be in the soup.'[51] Nonetheless the Chancellor himself still thought it possible that his efforts might not succeed, for he wrote to Holstein: '*Pejus eventum* we must think up a telegram in the event that H.M. should stay on board.'[52]

THE KAISER'S RIDE THROUGH TANGIER

Even after the three-day visit to Lisbon, where the uninterrupted festivities did nothing to calm nerves, it was evident to Schoen, who was travelling with the imperial party as the representative of the Auswärtiges Amt (and whom the Kaiser was to appoint Foreign Secretary two years later) that 'the Kaiser viewed the prospect of the Tangier adventure with some anxiety'.[53] Schoen, as Valentini observed, was 'in a state of great agitation from the very beginning. After all, Chancellor Bülow and the Foreign Office (Holstein!) had given him the carefully calculated task of *getting the reluctant Kaiser to Tangier, without fail.*'[54] The diplomat reported apprehensively to Berlin that the monarch had been 'wavering up to the last minute' as they approached Tangier, and inclined to avoid the visit 'on the pretext of landing difficulties'.[55] The 'All-H[ighest] mood' matched the weather off Tangier, Admiral von Müller recorded: a stiff wind was blowing from the east.[56] As there was no harbour wall and a heavy sea was running, the *Hamburg* could not simply sail into Tangier but had to anchor off the city (see Figure 11).[57] That was not all: the Kaiser was particularly nervous because he would be expected to ride through the narrow streets of the city on a strange horse.[58] 'The final struggle for the Kaiser's soul began in sombre weather and rough seas in the Tangier approaches', Valentini wrote to his family.[59]

The ultimate decision was brought about by the action of the German chargé d'affaires in Tangier, Richard von Kühlmann. He had been informed by Bülow of Wilhelm's doubts and had therefore come out to meet the

Figure 11 The Kaiser's provocative landing at Tangier on 31 March 1905

Hamburg. 'With remarkable elegance',[60] as Valentini testified, the diplomat climbed a pilot's ladder up the side of the great steamer, a feat not without danger. Completely drenched by the huge waves, Kühlmann presented himself to the Kaiser, 'still dripping', but in the full dress uniform of the Bamberg Uhlans, the regiment in which he had served. Wilhelm was 'visibly amused' by this spirited exploit. He praised Kühlmann 'for the initiative he had shown' and jokingly promised him 'a permanent position at the military school of gymnastics, in case things went wrong in the diplomatic service'. But he persisted in refusing to land because of the heavy swell and tried to sweeten this decision for Kühlmann by immediately conferring the Order of the Red Eagle on him. The young chargé d'affaires, however, was not deterred by this 'psychologically ... very interesting move' and read out to the Kaiser telegrams from Bülow which made it clear that the Chancellor would not hear of cancellation. Still wavering, Wilhelm ordered that an advance party consisting of Kühlmann, Tattenbach and Adjutant-General von Scholl should go ashore first to check on the situation and above all on the 'horse question'. Back on board, they reported positively on the preparations which had been made. Kühlmann again tried to apply 'rather strong pressure', exhorting Wilhelm not to forget that 'all Africa is watching Your Majesty'. Whereupon the Kaiser 'suddenly made up his mind, ordered battledress, buckled on his revolver and merely said curtly: "We shall land."'[61]

Kühlmann had prepared the Kaiser's ride through the narrow streets to the legation building with great care. Since no specially broken-in horse had been brought on this voyage for the Kaiser, as was the usual practice, before the *Hamburg* arrived the chargé d'affaires had 'spent many hours trying out horses brought in from all around to choose from, looking for complete calmness and imperviousness to gunfire . . . After much effort a reasonably suitable horse was eventually found, and it was prepared for its difficult task as well as possible in the short time available.'[62] Furthermore Kühlmann had established contact, through an informant, with the numerous Spanish anarchists living in Tangier and had contrived to portray the Kaiser to them as a potential saviour from the threat of French supremacy in Morocco. 'There was such hatred of the French appropriation of Morocco and such delight at a demonstration of opposition by Germany that I could even have employed the Spanish anarchists to protect the monarch without spending the considerable sum of money I had thought necessary. They went so far as to erect a special stand to watch the Kaiser's entry and they attracted his attention by their especially loud and demonstrative cheering during our ride through the city. When I told the Kaiser who was cheering so enthusiastically he was amused by the idea of this tribute from hard-bitten anarchists.'[63] (See Figure 12.)

Although the ride through the city went off without the slightest hitch, an incident occurred during the reception at the German legation which was to have repercussions on Franco-German relations in particular. When the Third Secretary at the French legation, Count Chérisey, 'conveyed Delcassé's respects and greetings and in effect welcomed His Majesty to Morocco in Delcassé's name', Wilhelm could not contain himself. He ignored Bülow's recommendation of sphinx-like reserve and – in distinct contrast to his other conversations at the reception, which were all 'bland' in tone – replied that his visit to Tangier signified that he 'demanded free trade for Germany and full equality with other nations; when Count Chérisey tried to assent magnanimously to this, His Majesty remarked that he intended to come to a direct agreement with [the] Sultan as the equal, free ruler of an independent country, that he would make sure that his All-Highest, fully justified claims were recognised and that he expected these claims to be properly respected by France too. Count Chérisey turned pale, tried to answer but was cut off by a brief dismissal and withdrew with bowed head.'[64] Not content with that, deliberately sidestepping Kühlmann's advice to take the sting out of the political clash by showing courtesy, Wilhelm conferred an order on the English officer commanding the Moroccan ceremonial guard, but not on his French colleague.[65]

Figure 12 The fraught ride through the streets of Tangier

Although Wilhelm's uncompromising outburst against Chérisey ran counter to the careful calculations made by Holstein and Bülow, they were not
displeased by it. In a letter to his sovereign the Chancellor spoke approvingly
of 'highly significant speeches, especially those to the French chargé d'affaires
and the German colony', which he said had 'made a lasting impression on the
mood both inside and outside Europe'.[66] It was a not unwelcome *fait accompli*
which Holstein too accepted calmly. With evident satisfaction he looked upon
the monarch's robust language in Tangier as proof 'that we want to pursue a
firm policy. Nothing else would be possible anyway after what the Kaiser said
to Chérisey. To retreat once one has taken up a position would have the same
consequences as shirking a duel. One exposes oneself to further and greater
humiliations.'[67]

THE EPILOGUE: THE MEDITERRANEAN CRUISE OF SPRING 1905

From the documentary evidence it is clear that Wilhelm, having resisted
landing in Tangier until the last moment, was after all extremely satisfied
with his visit and at first had no idea of what a furore his ride through the port

and his speeches would create. He was, as Kühlmann observed, 'visibly pleasantly surprised, given his great predilection for the Mohammedan Orient ... by the warmth of the reception accorded him [in Tangier]'.[68] Schoen reported to Berlin that the Kaiser appeared 'highly gratified by the visit, particularly also by the ... confidential message from the Sultan that he would not carry out any reforms without previous agreement with the Imperial Government'.[69] Similarly, when everyone was safely back on board the *Hamburg*, Müller recorded that the Kaiser was 'very satisfied with the political success' of his visit.[70] That the monarch had come 'within a hair's breadth' of being killed in Tangier, as he claimed in the 'suicide telegram' to Bülow already quoted,[71] that as Bülow wrote in his *Denkwürdigkeiten*, he 'had to be prepared to be bucked off his nag before the eyes of the astonished and gaping Moors and Arabs',[72] is a myth. All the eye-witness accounts confirm that the visit had 'passed off without incident'.[73]

The Kaiser's excellent mood held out for days. Even in Gibraltar, his next stopping point, in spite of his cool reception his manner was studiedly mild and complacent, evidently — as Valentini surmised — to 'obliterate the impression of this Moroccan special tour, to which he had reluctantly agreed, in the eyes of the English'.[74] On his arrival at Naples on 5 April Wilhelm received a reassuring letter from the Reich Chancellor, confidently predicting American support for the German demand for a conference to be convened by the Sultan on the future of Morocco. 'If a conference takes place we can already be sure of America's diplomatic support for the open door policy. England will shrink from taking a strong stand against America there, as everywhere else. Austria will not want to quarrel with us about Morocco, and I believe the same is true of Italy ... I therefore think it out of the question that a conference could result in pushing Morocco into France's exclusive sphere of influence and power ... France ... will probably remain isolated if she pursues her plans any further. Russia is preoccupied with herself, and for England it is very difficult, in view of the support of President Roosevelt and also of a considerable proportion of English public opinion for the open door policy, to show greater favour to France. In these circumstances Your Majesty, in Your powerful and legally unassailable position, can calmly await the settlement of the Moroccan question.'[75]

Thus, confident that the ball he had set rolling with his hazardous ride through Tangier would continue to roll in the direction planned by him and his Chancellor, Wilhelm was safe to enjoy the rest of his cruise. For four weeks he and his entourage toured Sicily, southern Italy, Corfu[76] and Venice, where he delighted in the company of the beautiful Countess Morosini. (See Figure 13.) In Sicily he talked endlessly and enthusiastically of Frederick II of Hohenstaufen, exclaiming when they visited Castel del Monte: 'Yes, when one

Figure 13 Contessina Annina Morosini in Venice

thinks of everything that great Kaiser accomplished! But if I could have you whipped and beheaded as he could, I too would be able to achieve more.'[77] Not infrequently his entourage bemoaned his imperious behaviour. When one of them asked the date, Schoen said with a sigh that it was 9 April, 'unless it is ordered otherwise'. Everyone on board had to do daily exercises under the personal command of Kaiser Wilhelm; on Sundays he himself read out long sermons which came across as 'dreadful hair-splitting stuff'. Expeditions ashore without the monarch were relished by the members of his entourage as 'golden freedom'.[78] Only very rarely were politics discussed during these weeks following the Tangier landing. According to Müller's detailed diary, throughout the entire time the Moroccan crisis was mentioned only once, and that with proud reference to 'the great day at Tangier'.[79]

THE AIMS OF GERMANY'S MOROCCAN POLICY

There is no doubt that the international tension which gripped European cabinets, stock exchanges and public opinion after the Kaiser's landing in North Africa was brought about intentionally. Friedrich von Holstein, the real architect of the Moroccan policy, was not necessarily aiming at a war in western Europe, as is sometimes maintained; nevertheless he pursued an intransigent course which deliberately took into account the possibility, if not the probability, of a war with France (and Britain). The French Republic was to be confronted with the choice of humiliating itself vis-à-vis Germany or of inviting invasion by the Prusso-German army, which was well acquainted with 'the road to Paris'.[80] Since the beginning of the Russo-Japanese War in February 1904 and the outbreak of revolution in Russia in January 1905, as a result of which the Germans could put aside any fear of war on two fronts for years to come, Germany had found herself in a uniquely favourable strategic position. The backing which France had secured from Britain through the Entente Cordiale was considered to be largely ineffective because British ships, as the Kaiser constantly pointed out, had 'no wheels' and could not protect Paris. Holstein, covered by Bülow, therefore insisted on an international conference to settle all questions relating to Morocco, which should be attended by the nations which had been signatories to the Madrid Convention of 1880 (Germany, Austria-Hungary, France, Great Britain, Spain, Italy, Portugal, the Netherlands, Belgium, Sweden, Norway and the USA). 'Contractual collectivity is a principle on which we can take a firm stand without ourselves appearing to harbour aggressive intentions', the Privy Councillor explained to the Chancellor on 5 April 1905.[81] In this way not only would France's 'Tunisification' of Morocco be thwarted, but Germany's neighbour and 'hereditary enemy' would also be publicly humiliated because her independent right to conclude international treaties with other Great Powers would be denied before all the world. German policy in the first Morocco crisis was not aimed at territorial or commercial gain – the confidential offers which the French made to Germany in the weeks and months following the Tangier landing were all rejected by Holstein. Nor was the downfall of the hated French Foreign Minister Delcassé on 6 June

1905, however welcome, enough to satisfy Berlin. Rather, the ultimate aim of
German intransigence was to separate France from her new Entente partner
Great Britain, whether indirectly, through French recognition that Britain
could not provide any protection against German military supremacy on land,
or directly, through war. Holstein kept in close touch with the Chief of the
Great General Staff and it was certainly no coincidence, as Chapter 12 has
shown, that the Schlieffen Plan for a lightning attack on France through
Belgium, Luxembourg and southern Holland was developed at precisely this
time and in this particular political and strategic context.[82]

However secretly Holstein operated – he concealed his real aims not only
from the French but also from most of the German ambassadors – there can be
no doubt that the Kaiser knew of and agreed with the calculations of the
Wilhelmstrasse. His reluctance to land in Tangier arose not from political
reservations but from sheer fear of the physical risk to himself. The documentary sources show that Wilhelm fully endorsed the aim of splitting up the
Entente and also, to this end, uttered threats of war when the occasion arose –
as for instance he did to Prince Louis of Battenberg at Gibraltar, as we shall
shortly see. In marginal notes on diplomatic reports from London and Paris he
repeatedly expressed his conviction that Great Britain would be powerless in a
Franco-German war. 'The English navy will not protect Paris from conquest by
us!'[83] The French statesmen were 'afraid' of Germany, he commented in early
May 1905, 'but that does not alter the facts of the matter'.[84] On 8 May Bülow
reported with satisfaction in a telegram to Holstein that 'H. Majesty completely
agrees with us on the Moroccan question.'[85] And on 22 May Holstein warned
that if the French reckoned 'that when the psychological moment came the
powers that be in Germany would not have the necessary guts' for war, they
would 'come a bad cropper'. He made himself clear: 'The Chancellor and, so I am
told, the Kaiser see quite clearly that it would be more dangerous, particularly
for Germany, to retreat than to stand firm. The war which would be avoided by
giving in now would certainly be forced upon us after a short interval under
some pretext and worse conditions.'[86] By her international humiliation France
was to be compelled, as Wilhelm II understood very well, either to wage war
against the Reich at an extremely favourable moment for Germany, or else to
join the continental league to which Germany aspired.[87]

THE DEBACLE

From the landing at Tangier on 31 March until 6 June 1905, the day of the
Crown Prince's wedding and of Delcassé's fall from power, which the Kaiser
celebrated by raising Bülow to princely status, nothing indicated that

Wilhelm's attitude during the Moroccan crisis was any less aggressive than that of Bülow and Holstein. But from the beginning their impulsive sovereign constituted yet another unpredictable factor – since it was he who had the last word – in what was in any case an extremely risky policy of threats.

In June 1905 Holstein once again came close to resigning, precisely because of the Kaiser's constant aggressiveness. As he wrote to Bülow: 'The Kaiser has always tended to be critical, but recently the occasions on which his complaints have been of an insulting nature, apparently on purpose, have grown more frequent . . . It can definitely be said that over the last hundred years no King of Prussia has treated a department of the central government with such marked contempt for such unimportant reasons.' As Bülow had talked him out of handing in his resignation in protest against the offence he had been caused, Holstein saw 'only one remedy, and that is that the attention of His Majesty should be drawn to the bad effects resulting from the violent tone of his reprimands'. He was ready, he said, to make a complaint to the Kaiser so as to 'bring to an end a situation which I regard as undignified', and if it led to his dismissal, this would be preferable to allowing 'the continuation of the present state of affairs with the repeated expressions of the Kaiser's contempt at shorter or longer intervals'.[88]

It was not only the Kaiser's barbed marginal comments, however, which caused Holstein's mood of discouragement. He was also convinced that Wilhelm had effectively stabbed him in the back by making conciliatory remarks aimed at the French government, thereby undermining all the calculations behind Germany's official Moroccan policy. As a result Delcassé's downfall had not led to a Franco-German understanding, as expected, but rather to a hardening of the French stance, even after Maurice Rouvier, the Prime Minister, took over the Foreign Ministry. Holstein found himself in the embarrassing position of having to write privately to Radolin, the ambassador in Paris, to find out what the Kaiser had actually told the French officers who had been invited to the Crown Prince's wedding, or who had taken part in the manoeuvres at Döberitz, about Germany's intentions. 'We, the Chancellor and I, know nothing . . . It seems to me that H.M. has a bad conscience, as he hasn't said anything to the Chancellor. Judging by the phlegmatic attitude which Rouvier adopted . . . I would assume that H.M. reassured the French regarding the danger of war.' Holstein went on to express the fear that at the Crown Prince's wedding the Kaiser had assured General Henri de Lacroix that German policy was 'all bluff'.[89] For months the Chancellor and the Foreign Office were left groping in the dark as to what the Kaiser had said to the French.[90]

In fact, convinced that he had almost reached the goal of his continental league policy, Wilhelm II did hold out a conciliatory hand to France at this time. Commenting on an article in an English journal which discussed the possibility of a German attack on France, he wrote: 'No! I will never be capable of such an action!'[91] During the wedding festivities on 6 June 1905 he reportedly told General de Lacroix that a war between Germany and France would be 'like a war between brothers'; he expressed pleasure at Rouvier taking over the Foreign Ministry, which he was sure would contribute towards reconciliation between the two countries; he had never set great store by Morocco and France was welcome to it.[92] When the ambassador Marschall von Bieberstein called on Holstein in the Wilhelmstrasse a year later, in the summer of 1906, the Privy Councillor told him 'about Morocco and how the defeat came about. When H.M. heard the news of Delcassé's fall he said to the French General, de la Croix, who was there for the Crown Prince's wedding, "maintenant je ne vous ferai plus de difficultés au Maroc". This was kept secret from the Foreign Office, but nevertheless the situation could still have been saved if H.M. had not given orders at the last moment that we should take a soft line.'[93] On a report from Radolin of 11 June 1905 with the news that Rouvier was willing to negotiate, the Kaiser wrote: 'Good, just what we want.'[94] He conferred a high-ranking order on the French financier Bezold, who had been involved in confidential negotiations between Paris and Berlin, on the grounds that 'He has saved us from a war.'[95] After the Döberitz manoeuvres he 'warmly' proposed a toast to the health of the French army[96] and said to the French military attaché, the Marquis de Laguiche, 'I am very glad that Monsieur Delcassé has gone. The dreadful policy he pursued in France frightened me and would have led you into a catastrophe, of that you may be sure.'[97] He had no intention of 'waging a war on account of this Morocco business'. Recognising the far-reaching significance of this remark, Laguiche expressly asked the Kaiser whether in that case he might be permitted to make use of it, and received the prompt answer: 'You may make use of it.'[98]

Now Bülow, too, considered resignation.[99] As Holstein later bitterly complained: 'it is something quite new in the history of diplomacy for a constitutional sovereign to keep secret from his own Government the concessions which he had made to a foreign Government, thus placing it in a situation where for a period of months it has to defend a position which the monarch surrendered long previously'.[100] In retrospect Bülow blamed the complete failure of the German policy on Morocco on Wilhelm's willingness to give way. 'After Delcassé's resignation (1905)', he wrote, 'I urged H.M. not to speak too kindly to the French (and especially General Lacroix) at once, as otherwise we would not obtain the necessary guarantees for Morocco from them; but H.M. could not be held back from doing so.'[101]

This conciliatory phase, however, lasted for only a few days. At the end of June 1905 Wilhelm himself realised with alarm that Rouvier, who had initially signalled his readiness to compromise, had reverted to the tough line taken by Delcassé. That his own utterances might have contributed to this sudden volte face did not of course occur to the Kaiser.[102] On 23 June 1905 he telegraphed to Bülow from Kiel, where he had a meeting with Prince Albert of Monaco, who was trying to bring his influence to bear in favour of a peaceful resolution of the conflict: 'Rouvier's present behaviour completely incomprehensible and in blatant contradiction of everything he told the Prince before. London possibly involved. Prince intends to write to Rouvier in this sense at once.'[103] On the basis of this telegram it was perfectly plain to Bülow that Germany was once again on the brink of a major war. For if Rouvier was indeed about to go ahead with Delcassé's programme and if he persisted in rejecting the international conference demanded by Germany, it would be incumbent on Germany to issue an ultimatum saying that the Reich considered itself under an obligation to intervene 'on behalf of the Sultan and the status quo . . . We are now at the turning point of the Moroccan question', Bülow wrote to Radolin. 'It therefore seems imperative to lose no time in putting Herr Rouvier right. Any further delay could strengthen his position in following the current Delcassé line and encourage him to go still further, which would not help the cause of peace.'[104]

Kaiser, Chancellor and Privy Councillor were thus of one mind again, for Wilhelm was equally determined to insist on the proposed conference.[105] Before Kiel Week was over, and again during a visit to the General Staff headquarters later, he made it clear, according to the French Consul General in Hamburg, 'that he did not want war, but that if he were forced into it by a policy of pin-pricks, he would go into battle convinced of the superiority of the German army'.[106] As Holstein was able to report to Radolin on 23 June 1905, on the previous day the monarch had been 'informed of the unfavourable situation of the Moroccan question, and right now . . . the Chancellor has received a long reply by telegram. The Kaiser entirely shares the Chancellor's point of view and finds it inconceivable that Rouvier should have set himself the task of realising Delcassé's programme, thus enhancing the latter's prestige. He told the Prince of Monaco what he thought of this in no uncertain terms. The Kaiser says that the Prince was completely overcome and intended to write at once to Rouvier. So this letter . . . will have been necessary if the theory of the two trends [of German policy on Morocco] is still current in Paris. The letter will kill it.'[107] On 1 July Holstein summed up the political line which he, the Kaiser and Bülow were pursuing as follows: 'the main aim of the Moroccan action [is] that we should demonstrate to the French *ad oculos* that it is better to treat us well rather than badly'.[108] A week later, on 8 July 1905, the French government gave in and agreed to the conference demanded by Germany. The next day, when the Reich Chancellor arrived on board the *Hohenzollern* at Swinemünde, the Kaiser ordered him to be 'greeted with 3 cheers', as 'a special honour in recognition of the agreement to the Morocco conference obtained from France'.[109]

All too soon, of course, it would emerge that Germany, rather than France, was isolated internationally. By pursuing a policy of threats in the Moroccan crisis Germany had succeeded in uniting all the Powers, including America, Italy and Russia, against her. In the end the only support Germany received at the conference in Algeciras came from her ally Austria-Hungary, herself threatened with decline. The decision-makers in Berlin therefore continued to be preoccupied over the following months by the question of whether the Reich's response to this encirclement should be war, while Russia was still unable to take action. The answer came only on New Year's Eve 1905, as we saw at the end of the previous chapter, with a decided 'No, not yet' from Kaiser Wilhelm II.[110] But in the three months between the Tangier landing on 31 March and France's acceptance on 8 July 1905 of the German demand for a conference the consensus between Wilhelm, Bülow and Holstein had held good for all but sixteen days in June. Their aim remained the same throughout: to separate France from Britain by threatening war and to compel her to join a continental league led by Germany. In June 1905 the Kaiser adopted a conciliatory tone towards France because he thought he had achieved this aim. As soon as he realised that he had acted prematurely he reverted to the line taken by Bülow and Holstein until France actually gave way.

That Wilhelm II had doubts about embarking on the Tangier adventure which Bülow and Holstein so strongly urged on him can be proved beyond question. But his reluctance did not stem from love of peace or from political foresight, as his loyalist defenders, after Germany's defeat in the world war, constantly asserted, but rather — to emphasise the point again — from fear for his personal safety in a foreign city. He fully endorsed the political goals of the Wilhelmstrasse. During his Mediterranean cruise and also after his return to Germany Kaiser Wilhelm II was animated by belligerence towards France and irritation with Britain for standing guard over France with her navy. On 1 April 1905, on board the British flagship *Drake* in the harbour at Gibraltar, he had a memorable conversation with Admiral Prince Louis of Battenberg, which the latter immediately reported to Edward VII. According to Battenberg the Kaiser not only justified his landing in Tangier with reference to the principle of the 'open door', but also declared himself convinced that the world would one day be divided between the Germanic and the Slavic races. 'As for

France', the Kaiser added brashly, 'we know the road to Paris, and we will get there again if needs be. They should remember that no fleet can defend Paris.'[111] Not least because of reports such as this, Edward VII became convinced 'that Germany's Moroccan policy is secretly aimed at bringing about war with France and England'.[112] Even with the Americans, whose support for the German demand for a conference was seen as indispensable, Wilhelm II spoke of his real aims with a clarity that left nothing to be desired.[113] President Theodore Roosevelt expressed his surprise at this in a letter to the British diplomat Cecil Spring Rice on 26 May 1905. 'The Kaiser . . . has shown an astonishing willingness to put down in black and white what his feelings are. Evidently he regards me as a gentleman and feels confident that the letters would never be published against him.'[114]

Several months after the landing in Morocco Wilhelm II was still claiming the credit for the apparently successful coup at Tangier. To both his circle of friends and to foreign diplomats he portrayed his dramatic appearance in Morocco as a brilliant chess move: through it he had both frustrated his uncle Edward's encirclement plans and forced France to give up her claims on Alsace-Lorraine and thus to recognise German supremacy. In endless conversations with his friend Prince Philipp zu Eulenburg in September 1905 the Kaiser expounded the thinking behind his Moroccan policy. 'The idea of a *European coalition*' was 'as dominant as ever *in the Kaiser's mind*', Eulenburg recorded. Wilhelm had told him that in order to 'prevent the imminent isolation of England' the 'very skilful and devious King Edward' had brought about an understanding with France through which France had been given a free hand in Morocco. 'But the agreement also contains a clause by which France and England would attack Germany together, should the need arise', the Kaiser had claimed, from which he had drawn the conclusion that 'we had to play gros jeu [for high stakes] and I allowed Bülow to use me as a *puppet* for the coup de théâtre at Tangier. *If* the French wanted to fight at all, they would have to do it now – if they did not want to fight, the Morocco crisis which we set in motion would have the effect of a cleansing storm and clear the way for an Entente between us and France.' The French government had heard through Prince Guido Henckel von Donnersmarck, who was a friend of Rouvier's son-in-law, 'that if England attacked Germany, Germany would immediately march into France and exact compensation from France for the damage England could not be stopped from inflicting on the coasts of Germany'. It had soon become clear that neither President Loubet nor the other ministers 'had any inkling of the danger to which Delcassé's policy and King Edward's friendship had exposed them'. The French statesmen voted unanimously against war, and Delcassé, who – as the Kaiser claimed – had already written out the order for armoured ships to be sent to Tangier, was brought down. This put an end to Edward VII's intrigues and cleared the way for the formation of 'a peaceful continental coalition'.[115] As we shall soon see, the Russian diplomat and later Foreign Minister, Alexander Isvolsky, was thunderstruck when Wilhelm II served up this abstruse interpretation of the first Moroccan crisis to him during a nocturnal conversation at Copenhagen.[116] The annoyance with which Bülow and Holstein regarded Wilhelm II's personal diplomacy during the Moroccan crisis, and their determination to put a stop to it, were to emerge in a curious fashion shortly afterwards, when the Kaiser was convinced that with the Treaty of Björkö he had at last achieved his dream of a continental league.

CHAPTER FOURTEEN

'A turning-point in the history of Europe' or the fiasco of Björkö

Kaiser Wilhelm II's personal diplomacy reached its inglorious climax when on 24 July 1905, on the imperial Russian yacht *Polarstern* off Björkö in the Gulf of Finland, he pulled the text of a German–Russian treaty of alliance out of his pocket and persuaded Tsar Nicholas II to sign it, without the countersignature of any responsible minister. True, the treaty had been drawn up in the Auswärtiges Amt and sent to the Kaiser by the Reich Chancellor. Wilhelm, however, had not only copied out the French text in his own hand but at the last moment, to overcome the Tsar's doubts, had added a rider under which the mutual defence pact was to be valid only within Europe, which in the eyes of Bülow and the Wilhelmstrasse deprived the treaty of much of its value for Germany. The only way in which Russia could be of assistance against Britain, they argued, was by attacking India; in Europe Russia was powerless, for she no longer possessed a fleet, and the Russian army could no more attack the British Isles than could the German army. The Russian ministers objected even more strongly when they learned of the Björkö treaty – although this did not happen until many weeks later – for the German–Russian alliance was aimed not only against Britain but at least as much against Russia's ally France, whose investments the crisis-ridden Russian Empire needed more than ever following the defeat by Japan.

Thus the Kaiser's spectacular initiative at Björkö, through which it seemed that his long-standing hope for a continental league under German leadership was at last to be fulfilled, ran miserably into the sand. The relationship of trust between Wilhelm II and his Chancellor, who handed in his resignation because of the arbitrary amendment of the text of the treaty, suffered a setback from which it never recovered. Not only that, but relations between Wilhelm and Nicholas II, which for a good ten years and despite numerous disappointments the Kaiser had constantly sought to rebuild and put to use, were never the same again after the fiasco of Björkö. All too soon Tsarist Russia was to turn away from Germany and seek protection with the Anglo-French Entente against the threat of German supremacy in Europe.[1]

WILHELM AND RUSSIA'S DEFEAT IN THE EAST

The road that was to lead the Kaiser and the Tsar to Björkö in the summer of 1905 was far from straight. At the end of December 1904 Wilhelm, as we have seen, had suffered 'the first great disappointment' of his foreign policy when Russia rejected an offer of alliance with Germany.[2] But only a few days later, on 2 January 1905, Port Arthur fell to the Japanese army. As soon as the news of the capitulation reached Berlin Kaiser Wilhelm took up his pen and wrote – once again without consulting the Chancellor or his Foreign Office – a letter of condolence to the Tsar, offering him his services with the peace negotiations. 'I hope you wont fancy that I intrude upon your privacy, when I address myself to you to beg you to tell me what your plans for the future are, so that, if possible I may make myself useful to you, and be enabled to shape my course of my policy . . . Now, I prefer being informed by yourself directly, instead in a round about way through other agencies, as I have firmly stood to you and your country from the first as your faithful friend!'[3]

The Kaiser then aroused vehement criticism both at home and abroad by conferring the order 'Pour le mérite' on both the Russian General Stoessel, who had capitulated at Port Arthur, and the Japanese General Nogi.[4] Count Zedlitz quite rightly deplored these awards to foreign military commanders as 'not without risk', for such things were 'for their own war leaders to decide', and moreover it was not at all certain yet 'how far their services [were] in fact recognised in their own armies'.[5] The award of the highest Prussian order to Stoessel 'for exemplary defence of the fortress' later proved particularly embarrassing, as he was condemned by a Russian military tribunal to a lengthy prison sentence when it transpired that the fortifications were unfit for defence at the time of the capitulation.[6]

Although the Kaiser's unpredictable initiatives did not make the conduct of diplomatic relations any easier, the Wilhelmstrasse nonetheless made frequent use of his personal correspondence with the Tsar. Over the thorny question of coal supplies for the Baltic squadron, for instance, in mid February 1905 Bülow submitted to the Kaiser telegrams drafted by Holstein which the latter then sent to the Tsar in Wilhelm's name.[7] Similarly when the question arose of whether Germany should offer to mediate for the Russians in the war against Japan, Bülow and Holstein took advantage of the Willy–Nicky correspondence. 'It would be a great boon for our position in the world and a great insult for England and France' if Germany, together with the USA, could bring about peace, Holstein commented on 20 February 1905; but first it was important to wait for the Tsar's reply to Wilhelm's latest letter.[8] This suggests that Bülow and Holstein might not only have known of the 'strange' 'historic' letter which the Kaiser sent to the Tsar on 21 February 1905, but also approved and perhaps even helped to draft it, as incredible as this may seem. Writing in his idiosyncratic English, in it Wilhelm adopted an astonishingly critical tone on the Russian conduct of war in Manchuria and on the Tsar's response to the revolutionary events within Russia. He tried to soften the wounding effect of his remarks by presenting them as a 'sketch which I have drawn of the European Public opinion with respect to the events in Russia', which he felt compelled, as an honest friend, to convey to the Tsar in his isolation at Tsarskoe Selo.

As far as the war against Japan was concerned, the Kaiser wrote bluntly: 'On one point all seem to agree in Europe as by common "consensus" that the Zar personally is solely responsible for the War. Its outbreak, the surprise caused by the sudden attack, the evidence of want of preparation is said to be his fault. They say that the thousands of families who have lossed [sic] their male relatives by the war or must miss them for long months lay the blood & their complaints at the steps of the Zar's throne. It is maintained that the Reservists called out to leave their homes, do it reluctantly detesting to fight in a country whose existence they do not know of, and for a cause which is unpopular to them. They are careworn when they think of their wife and children they leave behind, slowly sinking into poverty and helpless misery, they lay their anguish and their cares at the door of the Zar's Palace wishing he had left them at home. The reports from the Foreign and Russian correspondents with the army show it fighting an uphill fight against a most redoubtable foe. It had to begin war under very difficult circumstances, not having had time to properly prepare for the task, under the disadvantage of inferior numbers with which it was unable to stem the inrushing tide of mishaps and to meet the terrible onslaught of a foe known to have been preparing for this action during the last five years. For all this the Zar is thought to be responsible. Also the fearful losses of the Navy are shouldered upon him.' After commenting that 'the responsibility for a war is a very serious thing for a Ruler', Wilhelm went on to say that in the three wars his own grandfather had had to wage, the German people had supported him enthusiastically, 'the whole nation rising like a man and resolved to win or die, victory or destruction'. Such wars, Wilhelm asserted, 'are easy to be borne for the Ruler because his whole people share the burden with him. But the responsibility for an unpopular war is quite a different matter; when the glow of flaming patriotism is unkindled and when the nation as a whole takes no willing part in it, and suddenly sends its sons to the front because the Zar so wills it, but without making his cause their own that is a fearful and heavy load to bear; whose weight can only be lightened by the pureness of motives which give the Ruler the clearness of conscience necessary to enable him to expect his subjects to fight for him even if they are unable to discern the motives themselves.' The Tsar should ask himself whether Kuropatkin was the right man to command the army, though undoubtedly he was knowledgeable about the enemy and their manner of fighting. The solution of the dilemma, according to Wilhelm, could be that 'the Zar himself might perhaps personally take over the Command in Chief, & joining his brave troops, restore their confidence, cheer them by taking his share of hardships, electrify them by his presence & preserve the services of Kouropatkine for his troops, as he would act as chief of the Staff to his "War Lord" . . . The European Public as well as the Russian Nation is instinctively looking toward the Zar, & expecting that he will come forth & do something grandly, a great personal act; meant to show all that he is the Autocratic Ruler of his People & willing to allay their anxieties & pains as far as is in his power.' Wilhelm went on to urge the Tsar to show himself in the sacred, ancient capital city of Moscow. 'In former times your forefathers before they went to war used to repair to Moscow, pray in the old Churches & then assemble the Notables in the Kremlin inside, & the People outside in the courtyard & announce to them with great ceremony the necessity for the war & called upon their loyal subjects to follow them to the field of battle. Such a call from the Kremlin in Moscow — which is still the real Capital of Russia — never failed to find a response from the Russian Nation! Such an act, such a call to arms was expected by Moscow & Russia from you since the days following the 8th of February of last year, & they then were ready to answer with enthusiasm smarting under the fell blow, which had fallen on them unawares, & the Citizens of the great Capital looked eagerly forward to your coming: it is even hinted that the officials had your train got ready for starting. But the Zar came not.'[9]

Needless to say the Tsar took no notice of the Kaiser's advice. Only a few days after the letter arrived in Tsarskoe Selo the decisive Battle of Mukden began, culminating on 10 March 1905 with complete victory for the Japanese army. The news from Manchuria left Wilhelm II disappointed and perplexed. At a naval swearing-in ceremony at Wilhelmshaven on 9 March 1905 he made a speech which left an embarrassing impression on all those present. He was as convinced as he had always been, he declared, that 'only a good Christian . . . can be a good soldier'. So one should not conclude from the victories of the heathen Japanese over the Christian Russians 'that Buddha is above Christ Our

Lord'. No, not at all; 'if Russia was beaten, the reason was largely ... because Russian Christianity must be in a very sad state, while the Japanese were able to exhibit many Christian virtues. A good Christian, a good soldier!'[10] Zedlitz could only shake his head and comment that there was no denying the fact 'that in East Asia the Christians are constantly beaten by the non-Christians'. Wilhelm's remarks were 'impolitic' and the Russians above all would be 'displeased that their misfortunes are made the subject of the effusions of official speeches'.[11]

Two days later the Kaiser sent Bülow an angry telegram from Bremerhaven. 'News just received from "Wolff" concerning the peace negotiations by Gallo-English group on behalf of the Tsar shows that Rotschild is not prepared to pay for a lengthy war. These negotiations are probably the chief reason for sudden cancellation of King Edward's journey! He now wants to form a Gallo-British-Russ[ian] alliance, having got Tibet and Afghanistan in his pocket ... With all this going on it is outrageous that we, who loyally stood by the Tsar, with *advice* too, are left completely out in the cold again. The defeat at Mukden seems to have come very close to destroying the Russ[ian] army.'[12] The sudden swing of Wilhelm's inclinations towards Japan caused widespread irritation in diplomatic circles across the world.[13]

REVOLUTION IN RUSSIA

Not only did the disastrous defeats suffered by the Russian army radically alter the Kaiser's perception of the situation in terms of military strategy, but the revolutionary turmoil within the Russian Empire which followed the catastrophe in the east represented a fundamental challenge to the monarchical principle which he embodied and held sacred. The Social Democratic press derided Nicholas II and observed mockingly that even the conservative newspapers in Germany were treating 'the Little Father like an idiot'. 'Yesterday still the Lord of the world, today a miserable imbecile', *Vorwärts* commented on 17 March 1905.[14] When he heard the news of the catastrophe at Mukden, Philipp Eulenburg sounded the alarm to the Kaiser. 'And Russia?? Monarchical prestige in Europe will suffer a *considerable* setback if they do not make peace soon and restore order within the country ... A *Dreikaiserbündnis* [three-Emperors' alliance] is more necessary than ever − but take care. It is extremely unpopular in Germany now. We need reforms in Russia, not fusillades, to get an alliance accepted.'[15]

Kaiser Wilhelm II, however, proved to be an opponent of constitutional reform which would have reduced the personal power of the autocratic Tsar. He blamed the collapse of Russia principally on corruption, and prided himself on having preserved Prussia-Germany from a similar fate through his campaign against the Union Club and gambling in the 1880s.[16] In January 1905 he described constitutional reforms in Russia as 'suicide — hara-kiri by the government'. Zedlitz criticised this blinkered attitude and commented that the Kaiser believed 'rather too much in the necessity of ruling by force in Russia'.[17] When tens of thousands of workers, led by the priest Father Gapon, tried to gain access to the Tsar in St Petersburg on 22 January 1905 and several hundred of them were killed in front of the Winter Palace, Wilhelm sent a congratulatory letter to Nicholas. He urged him to take measures which would increase the popularity of the Tsar without infringing his absolute power. 'Many and most vague are the plans for reform in your country ... but the most sensible and best adapted to its people and their customs, seems to my humble notion, the formation of a body of men chosen from the best and ablest heads in the different "Zemstvos". This body would be attached to the "Imperial Council" and it could be given any question of importance having a vital Interest for the whole of Russia to be worked out and prepared for in the "Imperial Council"; also men well versed with the special theme under discussion, could be called upon to give their advice, being chosen from every part of the people ad hoc. And the comble [summit] would be if you from time to time presided yourself so as to be able to hear as many different men as possible, in order to be able to form a correct judgement on the question before them. Just like I did in 1890, when I called on the great Comittes [sic] for the elaboration of the "Social Laws" for the working classes, after the great Strike — and which I presided for weeks. In this manner the body would be able to provide the "Imperial Council" with every information it wants, enabling you in the same time to remain in touch with the great bulk of the lower classes; thereby ensuring to the latter every means to make themselves heard in matters appertaining to their welfare and thus forming a direct canal of communication between the simple folk and their "Emperor and Father". Besides you would be able — on account of your own information — to keep good watch and control on your "Imperial Council" and the "Comittes of Ministers" to see the work by them is done as *you* wish and your *People* want; this way ensures *the executive* once for all to the "*autocratic Czar*" and not to a leading *Minister* with a board of helpless Colleagues blindly following his lead.'[18] Unmistakably, these suggestions reflected Wilhelm II's own autocratic predilections and his conflict with Bismarck and his successors.

On 17 February 1905 Grand Duke Sergei of Russia, the Governor-General of Moscow, who was married to the love of Wilhelm's youth, Princess Ella of Hesse (sister of the Tsarina and of Princess Irène of Prussia), was killed in a bomb attack.[19] The murder of his hated rival prompted the Kaiser to write the 'historic' letter quoted above, of which its German editor Walter Goetz wrote that it must certainly be seen as 'extremely patronising' towards the Tsar.[20] 'What terrible tidings have come from Moscow!', he wrote in his inimitable English. 'These beasts of anarchists have perpetrated a dark & dastardly deed ... It is very hard for the fine old capital of Russia, that her walls should have been soiled by so foul a crime but surely she harbours no true citizen drawing a breath who can approve of it! I cannot believe that these demons have risen from the ranks of your Moskovite subjects, they were probably foreigners from Geneva. For the great bulk of your people still place their faith in their "Väterchen" the Czar & worship his hallowed person.' Throughout Europe, the Kaiser claimed, people held the view that the new Minister of the Interior, Svjatopolk-Mirski, 'too suddenly allowed the Press a greater liberty than before & dropped the reins – so tightly held by [his predecessor] Plehwe – too soon. Hence a sudden flood of unheard of articles & open letters addressed to the Ruler, a thing up to then thought impossible in Russia; some of them most insolent calculated to diminish the respect for the Autocratic Rule. This opportunity was seized by the Revolutionary party to get hold of the unsuspecting workpeople, to work them up into a state of ferment & to make them demand things – they were incapable of understanding – in a peremptory, disrespectful manner accompanied by language & acts which came very near to looking like revolution. This brought the working class – I am sure against their will – into direct opposition to the Government & into conflict with the Authorities, who had to maintain law & order. As these misguided & illinformed bands, mostly composed of men taught to look at the Zar as their "Father" & to "tutoyer" him as such, were under the impression that they would be able to place their wishes before him by coming before his Palace, it is suggested that it might have been more practical if the Zar had received a certain number of them – drawn up in the square amid a cordon of troops – & had addressed them from the Balcony of the Winter Palace, where he would have been accompanied by the highest Clergy & the Cross & his Suite as a "Father" speaks to his children, before the Military had to act; it was perhaps not impossible that in this manner bloodshed might have quite been avoided or at least dimished. The example of Nicolai I has often been quoted, [Wilhelm continued] who quelled a very serious rebellion by personally riding into their midst his child in his arms, & brought the rebels to their knees in short time. It is thought that now, as then, the person of the Zar has still an enormous hold on the simple people, & that they still bow down to his hallowed appearance. A word from such a position & in such an "entourage" would have awed & calmed the masses & sounded far away over their heads into the farthest corner of the Realm ... In an Autocratic Regime, it is argued, it must be the *Ruler himself* who gives out the password & the programme of action in an unmistakable official way. It seems that every body is expecting something of this sort by way of an act of will by the Zar personally. As long as this does not happen the impression at large will continue, that the announced reforms & law paragraphs are only ministerial work meant for show & to throw sand into the peoples eyes; & men will continue to anxiously miss the firm hand on the country's helm, guided by a master mind with a clear purpose, steering for a clearly defined goal. This state of things creates a feeling of uneasiness which in its turn evolves dissatisfaction generating "fault finding à tort et à travers" on a grand scale even with the mildest man of the very best intentions & actuated by the sincerest & purest of motives. In consequence the disappointed spectator – perhaps also the subjects – is more & more prepared to throw on the Zar's shoulders the responsibility for everything with which they are dissatisfied. In ordinary times this matters very little, & in constitutional Nations it is not so dangerous, as the Kings Ministers have to mount the breach & to defend his person. But in Russia, where the Ministers are unable to shield the sacred person of the Ruler, as they are known to be his tools simply, such troubles which fill the Russian minds with unrest & uneasiness, & which lead to the saddling of the Ruler with the odium for everything disagreeable that happens, are a very serious danger for the Ruler & his dynasty, because they tend to make him *unpopular*. Now, it is argued, that the "intelligentsia" & the Society in parts are allready [sic] dissatisfied, should the Zar also become *"unpopular"* with the masses the agitators might easily raise such a storm that it would be very uncertain, wether [sic] the Dynasty would be able to weather it.'[21]

In his letter Wilhelm II listed precisely which concessions the Tsar should make to the people and which reforms must be avoided. 'Not the promise of a general legislative assembly, no Constituante or Convention Nationale, but a Habeas Corpus Act & wider extension of the Conseil de l'Empire. No liberty of assembly or of the Press, but strict orders to all censors to abstain from any chicanes henceforth.' He even went so far as to suggest to the beleaguered Tsar where and how these measures should be announced. 'European observers think that it could be managed, that the Zar could make the expected "Grand acte" by going to Moscow & assembling the nobility & notables in his magnificent Palace speak to them.' Then the Tsar, '"entouré" by the Clergy with banners & cross & incense & holy Icons would go out on the balcony & read out the same speech he held before, as a Manifestoe to his assembled loyal subjects in the Court Yard below, encircled by the serried ranks of the troops ... When you tell them that you – in case you thought it necessary – would go to share the hardships of their brothers & relatives in the field, who had to go out by your command, & to cheer them & try to lead them to victory, it is argued that the People will be deeply touched & cheer you & fall to their knees & pray for you. The Zar's popularity would be recovered.'[22]

Whatever the Kaiser hoped to achieve by this highly undiplomatic letter, its effect was virtually nil. The Tsar answered on 25 February 1905 with a short, anodyne telegram of thanks,[23] but he went neither to Moscow nor to the front, and the situation inside Russia deteriorated alarmingly. Berlin society was outraged to hear from Prince Fritz Leopold of Prussia, recently returned from St Petersburg, that Nicholas II had taken hardly any notice of the brutal murder of his uncle and brother-in-law Sergei and had spent the evening in childish foolery on the sofa.[24] British diplomats reported that the attitude of civil servants and officers in Berlin to the state of affairs in Russia had completely changed. They were all appalled at the seriousness of the situation and the widespread corruption in the highest circles in Russia. Bülow feared the worst, 'not a revolution but a sort of jacquerie', and Wilhelm II was so obsessed by developments in Russia that he considered taking the Russian expert Professor Theodor Schiemann with him on his Mediterranean cruise.[25] When the German ambassador, Count Alvensleben, reported from St Petersburg on 17 March that the Tsar no longer listened to anyone but his mother and his wife, Wilhelm commented in horror: 'He is in great danger if that does not stop soon! The little Hessian Princess, who never heard anything about politics in Darmstadt, is handing out political advice?! . . . Fools rush in where Angels fear to tread!'[26]

PRINCE HEINRICH'S MISSION TO TSARSKOE SELO

Immediately after the bomb attack on his brother-in-law Sergei, Prince Heinrich had travelled to Berlin to obtain Wilhelm's consent for his wife to go to Russia for the funeral.[27] It seemed a good opportunity to send Heinrich himself on a mission to St Petersburg.[28] The letters that the Kaiser had sent Nicholas II had remained practically unanswered, and Wilhelm's hope that he could influence the Tsar by appointing his Flügeladjutant, Gustav Count von Lambsdorff, as his military representative in St Petersburg, had come to nothing. But brother-in-law Heinrich could not be given the cold shoulder at the Tsar's court; he was in a position, as Bülow put it, to say 'more or less anything' to the Tsar 'that even the closest relative can say to an Emperor'.[29]

On 2 April 1905, two days after the Kaiser's landing in Tangier, his brother Heinrich travelled to Tsarskoe Selo. Before leaving he called on the Reich Chancellor, who asked him, as the Prince recorded, 'to influence Nicky to persist with the war'.[30] Unusually for him, Heinrich kept a detailed diary

about the situation at the imperial court in revolutionary Russia. The entry for
4 April reads: 'Nicky rather depressed at first. Talks calmly about the war. Pins
his hopes on Rosestwenski [sic]. Wants to send 180000 more reservists to
theatre of war. Tells me there is a strong peace party. Admires the energy of
the Japanese.' On the afternoon of 8 April 1905 Heinrich went for a walk with
Nicholas II. He drew the Tsar's attention 'to all the dangers' and advised him
to visit Moscow at Easter. 'In response to his question "Why?" I answer
because religious and historic centre there. – He admitted arguments were
right. Wilhelm had already written to him on similar lines. I draw his
attention to danger of revolution. As to present position of the army Nicky
says it was not making a stand . . . near Charbin in order not put the railway at
risk (!). He said he did not give orders, only suggestions . . . Nicky drives me in
the sledge to the train, thanks me for my frank words.'[31] Bülow forwarded the
'very secret' telegrams which Prince Heinrich sent him from St Petersburg to
the Kaiser in the Mediterranean, so that Wilhelm heard at once of his
brother's consternation at what he found. 'My overall impression', Heinrich
reported from Tsarskoe Selo, 'is that situation at home and abroad utterly
hopeless. Russia is moving towards her inevitable fate. Reasons: complete
failure of personality on the part of the Sovereign, who is in no way equal
to the circumstances; moreover similar failure on the part of the Ministers,
who shun any responsibility. Even closest relations see no hope and are
in despair.'[32]

On his return to Kiel Heinrich wrote a letter to his brother summing up his
observations. In it he repeated his conviction 'that the present state of affairs
in the Russian Empire is utterly hopeless'. Only two things could put a stop to
the incipient anarchy and revolution, namely the victory of the Russian Baltic
squadron over the Japanese fleet, and the Tsar's appeal to his people at Easter
from Moscow. This was precisely the suggestion that he had been 'preaching
for months', Wilhelm noted in the margin of the letter on 15 April. Heinrich
had to admit, however, that he still doubted 'whether Nicky [would] make up
his mind to go to Moscow, and also to take the energetic measures to suppress
the anarchists which I was able to recommend to him'. Moreover, the letter
continued, the Tsar 'had considered the idea of visiting the army, he told me,
but had given it up because of the unrest in his own country'. It was altogether
uncertain that if the Tsar decided to go to see his troops he 'would ever reach
the army alive', in Heinrich's view. He had tried everything 'to shake Nicky
out of his incomprehensible and highly dangerous state of apathy – of inability
to summon up any will-power. I said things to him which ought to have made
him dispatch me over the border at once under armed guard, instead of
thanking me, as he actually did, almost weeping with emotion, for my

"frankness".' Nicholas was determined to go on with the war, Heinrich reported. 'He is convinced that "time" is on his side, provided that the necessary funds can be kept flowing, even though a strong current in favour of peace is constantly making itself felt, also in army circles within the country, and trying to influence Nicky.' The Tsar lived under the 'almost childishly naive' illusion that he could achieve peace without ceding any territory and without war reparations, and moreover demanded the right to keep a fleet of any size he liked at Vladivostok, which Wilhelm agreed was 'completely crazy!!!' When Heinrich demurred, saying 'I am afraid the Japanese will ask you more for their trouble', Nicholas had simply answered: 'Then they must wait.' 'Nicky is a psychological puzzle to me!' the Prussian Prince sighed. 'Physically well developed, intellectually gifted, a heart of gold, and no will-power, possessed by an unusual degree of fatalism that is in danger of becoming a disaster! To make matters worse, he has not a single man in his entourage or among his ministers who would be prepared to risk his neck or to take on responsibility.'[33]

Immediately after his conversation with Prince Heinrich in Berlin Bülow wrote to the Kaiser to pass on what the Prince had told him. He concluded that 'the future of Russia is thus more than ever a big question mark, but it is too massive and compact a block not to continue to play a certain part in the international state system. Therefore Your Majesty is quite right to remain a benevolent friend and neighbour to Russia, while at the same time cultivating our relations with all other nations, both great and small, which can be of use to us. And if Your Majesty continues to keep our sword sharp we can calmly wait and see what the Russian Vesuvius eventually disgorges. Old empires die hard, and Russia is so ill-suited to constitutional and liberal experiments such as France went through 115 years ago, that in the end it would not surprise me if what seems today to be the most improbable thing should happen and the Russian state structure outlasted the present feverish mood among the population and survived into the future, even if very much weakened by a severe blood-letting.'[34]

Kaiser Wilhelm's bitter disappointment at the catastrophic defeats of the Russian army and at the revolutionary unrest in the Russian Empire found expression in the speech which he made in Strasbourg in May 1905 on his return from his cruise.[35] Addressing the officers of the XV Army Corps and numerous foreign observers, he openly criticised the Russian army for drunken and dissolute conduct. 'The Japanese officer corps is extremely efficient and has fully proved its worth, and likewise the Japanese soldier.' The Russian army, by contrast, had been 'demoralised' at the Battle of Mukden 'through immorality and consumption of alcohol'. According to press

reports his expressions had been rather more crude. He went on to claim that
the Russian Commander in Chief, Kuropatkin, had made the mistake of going
to the front at Mukden, while his Japanese opposite number, Oyama, had
stayed behind in a place from which he could survey the entire battle and
calmly direct it, like a chess player, move by move. 'Germany may have the
task, since Russia has shown her weakness towards the yellow peril, of
preventing the spread of this peril', Wilhelm warned. The war in East Asia
had once more proved the value of traditional methods of defence — fox-holes,
hand-grenades, barbed wire — he pontificated.[36] As the British military
attaché, who was among the audience, reported, the speech led to widespread
comment as to whether it had been tactful of His Majesty to denigrate the
officers of the Russian army quite so publicly.[37] The Reich Chancellor and
Holstein were horrified, as was the Grand Duke of Baden, and they did their
utmost to prevent the Supreme War Lord from making any more belligerent
speeches against Russia.[38] In vain, through the *Norddeutsche Allgemeine
Zeitung*, the government repudiated the published version of the Kaiser's
speech, but without issuing a correction.[39] Everyone knew perfectly well that
the Kaiser's wounding remarks had been correctly reported. A year later, when
the by then dismissed Privy Councillor von Holstein initiated a campaign
against Wilhelm II's dangerous 'autocratic ways', it was precisely the Strasbourg speech which he recommended a publicist to take as his cue: in it the
Kaiser 'read a lecture to both the Russians and the Japanese as though he were
a global schoolmaster. With that speech he caused us untold harm, not only in
Japan. H.M. demonstratively displayed his displeasure against a man in high
position (not Bülow) who risked making a vigorous criticism.'[40]

THE GERMAN—RUSSIAN RAPPROCHEMENT AFTER THE
BATTLE OF TSUSHIMA

On 27–8 May 1905 the Russian Baltic squadron, which had sailed half round
the world under the command of Rozhestvensky, was destroyed by the
Japanese fleet off Tsushima in the Bay of Korea. With it the last hope of the
Russians for a happy outcome to the war was also destroyed. The Tsar was
forced to arrange peace negotiations and to reconsider the relations between
his country, devastated by military defeat and internal unrest, and the other
Great Powers. After Tsushima, Wilhelm II found fresh hope that his dream of
a continental league under his leadership might still be realised. In a very
affectionate letter of 3 June 1905[41] he strongly advised Nicholas to seek peace
and offered himself as an intermediary with President Roosevelt. 'From the
purely *military strategical* point of view the defeat in the straits of Corea ends

the chances for a decided turn of the scales in your favour; the Japanese are now free to pour any amount of reserves, recruits, ammunition etc. into Mandschuria for the siege of Wladiwostok, which will hardly be able to resist very long without a fleet to support it ... Formally it is of course possible, even under these adverse circumstances to continue the war for any amount of time. But then on the other hand the *human* part must not be overlooked. Your country has sent thousands of its sons to the fronte, where they died, or were taken ill and were left cripples for the rest of their lives. Now as I wrote to you in my last letter − Febr. 6th − the war is very unpopular and the people see their sons and fathers reluctantly, even unwilling leave their homes to fight for a cause they not only not espouse but abhor! Is it compatible with the responsibility of a Ruler to continue to force a whole nation against its declared will to send its sons to be killed by hecatombs only for his sake? Only for his way of conception of National honour? After the people by their behaviour have clearly shown their disapproval of a continuance of the war? Will not in time to come the life and blood of all uselessly sacrificed thousands be laid at the Rulers door, and will he not once be called upon by Him, the Ruler and Master of all Kings and men, to answer for those, who were placed under his control by the Creator, who entrusted their welfare to him? ... When a nations ways show that it has had enough ... is it not reasonable that also its Ruler should then ... draw the consequences and conclude peace? Even though it be a bitter one? Rather than risking through the prolongation of an unpopular war to create such a bitter feeling in his country that it would not even refrain from taking serious steps to eventually force the Ruler to comply to their wish and adopt their views? Of course there is the Army to be considered. It has fought and bravely fought − through heat and cold for 1½ years trying to win victoria for you and your country, but up to now Providence has withheld success from it. Defeat, fearful loss of life, and sufferings unspeakable have instead been sent to the poor Army and have been willingly borne by these capital, brave, quiet, selfsacrificing fellows your soldiers. That they should burn for revenge and be ready to do battle at every possible moment is quite natural. But is there any new leader or General among the Captains who is able to *guarantee* success, so that it would justify a new tremendous effort at the expense of thousands of the soldiers lives? Is the Army really absolutely convinced that it will yet be able to turn the scales? To this question you of course alone are able to know the answer. Should the answer however be given in the negative by your Generals in your Soldiers name, declaring on their honour that they could only die for their Emperor but hardly win any *decisive* victories for him, then I think your conscience may be at rest as to wether you ought to go on fighting or not, and you could

THE FIASCO OF BJÖRKÖ

open the Peace negociations which would be hailed with joy by all your loyal subjects throughout Russia after the tribute of blood they readily gave their Emperor ... Napoleon I and Fredrick the Great also suffered defeat! It must be looked upon as Gods will that things have taken this course! God has imposed this burthen on you, and it must be borne, but perhaps by His intentions and with His help, lasting good may come out of all this in the end; a new life and a new order of things for the development of Russia may spring from this time of trial, which would be a recompense your subjects richly deserved. Forgive the length of this letter, but I feel bound as your friend and colleague to tell you what I think is true and right! You know the motives that prompt me, and you are free to do with these lines what you think fit. Should however the ideas propounded in this letter coincide with yours and you think that I could be of any even smallest use to you for the preparatory steps to bring about peace, pray dispose of me at your leisure. I may perhaps turn your attention to the fact that no doubt the Japanese have the highest regard for America before all other nations. Because this mighty rising Power with its tremendous fleet is next to them. If anybody in the world is able to influence the Japanese and to induce them to be reasonable in their proposals, it is President Roosevelt. Should it meet with your approval I could easily place myself – *privately* – in rapport with him, as we are very intimate; also my ambassador there [Speck von Sternburg] is a friend of him.'[42] Shortly after this letter was sent Wilhelm II decided against sailing along the coast of Norway and to go instead on a cruise in the Baltic in the hope of a meeting with the Tsar. His aim was none other than to bring about personally, from monarch to monarch, a 'turning-point in the history of Europe'.

THE TREATY OF BJÖRKÖ

'This time we are not seeking the tranquil world of glaciers and white nights. We are sailing round and round and twisting the rope of policy', General Helmuth von Moltke wrote from the *Hohenzollern* in July 1905.[43] When he had taken leave of the Kaiser at Sassnitz Bülow had told Wilhelm that he would be 'delighted' if the Baltic cruise led to a meeting with the Tsar. 'It would be the greatest blessing for both nations and for the world; but we cannot suggest it from Berlin; if he suggests it or asks for it, then go, and God go with you!'[44] He suggested to the Kaiser that when he met the Tsar he should propose a German–Russian defensive agreement, but that he should leave the negotiations to the Russian Foreign Minister, Vladimir Lamsdorff, and himself, the Reich Chancellor.[45] Wilhelm, however, was obsessed with the idea of achieving an alliance with Russia without the responsible statesmen.

Figure 14 The Admiral of the Atlantic meets the Admiral of the Pacific in the Baltic

On 18 July 1905 he telegraphed to Nicholas II: 'I shall soon be on my way home, and cannot pass the entrance to the Sea of Finland without sending You warm greetings and good wishes. If it would please You to see me – either on shore or on Your yacht – I am of course at Your disposal. I shall come as a simple tourist without ceremony.'[46] Whereupon Nicholas suggested that they meet off the little island of Björkö, near the town of Wyborg. It was 'a pleasant, quiet place', and at such a serious time as this he could not go too far away from the capital.[47] Wilhelm now asked Bülow to send him the text of the German–Russian treaty of alliance which had been 'transmogrified by Count Lamsdorff' the previous year and had therefore been a failure.[48] The next day Holstein sent the text by telegraph to Bülow on the island of Norderney, from where Bülow forwarded it to the Kaiser.[49]

On 23 July 1905 Wilhelm II met the Tsar off Björkö (see Figure 14). With the exception of the diplomat Tschirschky, not even the Kaiser's entourage on board the *Hohenzollern* knew what was about to happen. Moltke recorded with emotion how the Kaiser had come to join them and said: 'Now, boys, get your full-dress uniform ready. In two hours you will be standing in front of the Emperor of Russia.' None of his travelling companions had guessed 'the reason for this sudden, secretly arranged visit', the future Chief of General Staff commented; 'but we were all conscious of the enormous political importance of the next few hours, whose consequences no one could predict'.[50]

Wilhelm himself was almost overcome by the significance of his meeting with the Tsar. On the following day his relief was evident from his letter to Bülow. 'These last days I have been thinking so hard that my head was buzzing, so as to be sure that I would do it right, keeping the interests of my country always in mind, but just as much those of the monarchical principle in general. In the end I lifted up my hands to the Lord who is above us all, and entrusted everything to Him, and asked Him to guide me according to His will, I was only a simple tool in His hands and would do what He told me, however hard the task might be ... Now I felt wonderfully strengthened and my will and my purpose grew ever firmer and more definite ... And what did I find? A warm, affectionate, enthusiastic reception such as could only be given to a sincerely beloved friend. The Tsar embraced me and pressed me to him as if I were his own brother, and looked at me constantly with eyes beaming with gratitude and joy ... Soon the Tsar took me on one side and said he was longing to have a proper conversation. We lit cigarettes and were soon in Medias Res. He was uncommonly pleased about our Morocco agreement, which would open the way to good and lasting relations with France, and he warmly applauded my hope that a permanent understanding, perhaps even an "agreement" with Gaul might blossom from it ... Then the conversation turned to England and it very soon became apparent that the Tsar bears a serious personal grudge against England and the King. He described Edw [ard] VII as the greatest "mischief maker" and most dishonest and dangerous intriguer in the world. I could only agree with him by remarking that I had particularly suffered from his intrigues in the past few years.' During dinner that evening on board the *Hohenzollern* the Tsar had been in a cheerful mood, Wilhelm's account continued, and Nicholas's entourage had also been in favour of a German–Russian–French alliance, in which even Japan might be able to participate later on, as 'the best solution of the situation'. The next morning Wilhelm had visited the Tsar's yacht, 'in happy anticipation'. Again the Tsar received him on the gangway with an affectionate embrace, and again, during breakfast, he criticised England and her perfidious influence on Russia's ally, France. 'Now I felt the moment had come', the Kaiser reported to Bülow, describing this world-historical episode. Edward VII of course had a weakness for little 'agreements', Wilhelm had said. 'How would it be if we also came to a "little agreement"? We had of course already discussed one in the winter, but it had not worked because of Delcassé and tension with France. All that was over now and we would become good friends of the Gauls, so there were no more obstacles?!' When the Tsar expressed his regret that he did not have the text of the treaty of December 1904 with him, Wilhelm exclaimed: 'I possess a copy which quite by chance I happen to have with me in my pocket.' The Tsar had taken him into his father's cabin and closed all the doors. 'His dreaming eyes sparkled with light as he did so', the Kaiser recorded. 'I pulled the envelope out of my pocket, unfolded the paper on Alexander III's writing table in front of the Dowager Empress's portrait ... and showed it to the Tsar. Once, twice, three times he read the text that has already been communicated to you. I sent up a fervent prayer that the good Lord should be with us now and guide the young ruler. There was a deathly silence ... Then I heard the Tsar's voice beside me saying "that is quite excellent. I quite agree!" My heart beat so loudly that I could hear it; I pulled myself together and said quite casually: "Should You like to sign it? It would be a very nice souvenir of our entrevue." He glanced over the paper once more, and then said: "Yes I will." I opened the inkwell, handed him the pen and he wrote in a firm hand "Nicolas"; then he handed me the pen and I signed, and when I stood up he embraced me emotionally ... My eyes were brimming with tears of happiness, – my forehead and my back were running with moisture too – and I thought, Fried[rich] W[ilhelm] III, Queen Louise, Grandfather and Nicholas I, they were perhaps nearby at that moment? At any rate they were looking down on us, and they will all have rejoiced! ... So the morning of 24 July 1905 at Björkö has become a turning-point in the history of Europe, thanks to the grace of God; and a great relief for my dear fatherland, which will at last be freed from the dreadful clutch of the Gallo-Russian pincers.' The 'work of rapprochement' had been 'crowned with success and the gamble has paid off', Wilhelm jubilantly declared after the signature. 'And now that it has happened, one is amazed and asks how such a thing is possible? The answer is very clear to me! God has ordained and willed it thus. In defiance of all the wit of man, making a mockery of all human efforts, He has brought together what belonged together! His ways are different from our ways and His thoughts are higher than ours! What Russia arrogantly repudiated last winter and, in her obsession with intrigue, tried to turn to our disadvantage, she has now accepted with gratitude and delight as a wonderful gift, because she has been brought down by the terrible, harsh, humiliating hand of the Lord.'[51] Euphoria at his successful coup, pride in his personal achievement, astonishment at his own daring, relief that nothing had gone wrong – scarcely any other of the fifteen thousand diplomatic documents printed in the collection of source materials assembled in *Die Große Politik der Europäischen Kabinette* displays as much emotion as this letter from Wilhelm II to the Reich Chancellor.

The Kaiser's elation lasted for several more days. On his return to Germany on 27 July he wrote the Tsar an effusive letter of thanks which betrayed the breathtaking extent of the hegemonial expectations he attached to the treaty.

'The 24th of July 1905 is a cornerstone in European Politics and turns over a
new leaf in the history of the world; which will be a chapter of peace and
goodwill among the great Powers of the European Continent, respecting each
other in friendship, confidence and in pursuing the general Policy on the lines
of a community of interest. The moment the news of the new "groupement"
will have become known in the world, the smaller nations, Holland, Belgium,
Danmark, Sweden, Norway will all be attracted to this new great centre of
gravity, by quite natural laws of the attraction of smaller bodies by the larger
and compacter ones. They will revolve in the orbit of the great block of powers
(Russia, Germany, France, Austria, Italy) and feel confidence in leaning on
and revolving around this mass. The dual Alliance combining with the Triple
Alliance gives a Quintupel Alliance, well able to hold all unruly neighbours in
order, and to impose peace even by force, if there should be a power hair-
brained enough to wish to disturb it.'[52] Imagining himself so close to his goal
at long last, the Kaiser was ill-prepared for the crushing disappointment he
was to face when Bülow handed in his resignation over the treaty he had just
signed at Björkö.

BÜLOW'S LETTER OF RESIGNATION

Neither the Kaiser nor the Tsar had a responsible minister with him in Björkö.
Wilhelm, however, was accompanied by a representative of the Auswärtiges
Amt in the person of the diplomat Heinrich von Tschirschky, with whom he
had discussed his secret intentions in detail. It was therefore Tschirschky who
was ordered to go over to the Russian imperial yacht after the two monarchs
had signed the treaty. Together with the Russian Minister of the Navy,
Admiral Birilew, he was to countersign the treaty as a witness.[53] His first
telegrams about the Björkö episode fully confirmed and supplemented the
Kaiser's bombastic description. At the first meeting of the monarchs on the
evening of 23 July the Kaiser had found the Tsar 'very angry with England
and especially King Edward'. Nicholas had spoken 'with indignation about the
policy of intrigue pursued by the King' and had assured the Kaiser, 'banging
the table with his fist', that he would never 'allow himself to get involved in
making pacts with England and least of all against the German Emperor'.
Wilhelm, Tschirschky continued, had taken advantage of the Tsar's bitterness
towards England to speak again of the danger of all the entrances to the Baltic
Sea being controlled by little Denmark: Russia and Germany, after all, had a
common interest in keeping the British navy out of the Baltic. Then the Kaiser
added the question of the Norwegian succession to his argument and obtained
the Tsar's agreement to join him in opposing Edward VII's intention of

putting his daughter Maud, who was married to Prince Charles of Denmark, on the throne of Norway.[54] He had also warned Nicholas of the possibility that England (as in 1807) might occupy Kristiansand, on the Skagerrak, in which case Germany would probably take Bergen in retaliation. 'The Emperor Nicholas was visibly alarmed at the idea of Norway being divided up and England possibly obtaining a firm footing there', Tschirschky reported. He sent the Reich Chancellor the text of the treaty which he had countersigned, without mentioning any reservations he might have had about it. On the contrary, he commented jubilantly that the Kaiser had found the Tsar in a mood 'in which he would have been prepared to sign quite different things as well, if the Kaiser had put them before him'.[55] In Norderney Bülow received the news from the Kaiser and Tschirschky of the signing of the treaty 'with deep emotion and sincere gratitude'. He wrote congratulating the monarch on his success, 'for it was Your Majesty alone who made this turn of events possible and brought it about'.[56]

When the Chancellor read through the Treaty of Björkö which Tschirschky had telegraphed to him, however, he discovered that the previous year's text had been modified in one important particular. By the insertion of the phrase 'en Europe' the mutual assistance clause had been limited to Europe. That signified, in particular, that in the event of a common war against Great Britain, Russia was not under any obligation to attack British India. Bülow anxiously enquired of Holstein: 'Are you of the opinion that the addition "en Europe" makes the treaty worthless for us, because in Europe Russia cannot help us at all with her worn-out fleet, nor is her army of any use to us against England? Under the circumstances should I invalidate the treaty by refusing to countersign it? Or do you think that even in this form the treaty has some value for us as a way of undermining the Dual Alliance?'[57] The *éminence grise* of the Wilhelmstrasse replied: 'The treaty in its present version is still decidedly advantageous for us.'[58] The next day Bülow heard that Wilhelm himself had added the words "en Europe" to the text of the treaty.[59] He telegraphed to the Kaiser on 28 July 1905: 'In the treaty I have reservations about the addition of "en Europe" to the first article. The only thing that the English really fear is a Russian attack on India. In Europe the Russians can do little to help us with their worn-out fleet, nor can they be of much use against England with their army. If the English know that if they attack Germany the Russians need only support us in Europe, and Russia is not under any obligation to attack India, they will be more prepared to come to blows with us than if India were in danger.'[60]

Wilhelm II was determined to justify himself. 'The passage "en Europe" was inserted by me after mature deliberation and I was fully aware of what

I was doing. Without it we would have been absolutely obliged to give our assistance in Asia. For in the event of a clash, e.g. in Afghanistan, if England harassed Russia there, Russia would rightly claim our military assistance in the form of troops.'[61] In response to Bülow's reference to England's fear of a Russian attack on India the monarch maintained that 'As far as the "pressure on India" is concerned, it is a popular slogan in diplomatic language and an item kept in the diplomatic dispensary for the defeat of England, but it is completely illusory. I had this question thoroughly studied again last year and examined from all sides by the General Staff. It is as good as impossible for a large army to set out on the march to India without years of really enormous preparations and expense. It would take so much time that England would have all the time she needed to make her preparations and countermeasures. And then it is questionable whether the attacking army would ever reach the Indian border still in a condition to fight, so that this idea really cannot be entertained in the world of sober "Realpolitik", all the more so because Russia is now in a very weakened state as far as troops and resources are concerned and will remain so for a long time; in addition she will lose billions in war costs and will need just as much again for reorganisation and reconstruction after peace has been concluded, so that she will be completely incapable of a military task such as the above for a generation ... If it should come to war with England, Russian help for us will *not* lie in *Asia* and the chimera of "pressure on India", but in the fact that Russia will guarantee us *absolute freedom from threat from the rear in Europe*, so that the "war on two fronts" on which we have worked for the last twenty years will turn into a war on *one* front, id est as in [eighteen-] seventy with the *entire* unified German army against *France alone*. Provided of course that France, in order to help England, mobilises against us, which is not ruled out ... No *active* help can be expected from Russia in the near future, as war and revolution are keeping the army busy and the navy no longer exists. But it leaves us free to the rear! Very good *passive* help!'[62]

At this point Bülow had no intention of handing in his resignation because of the Kaiser's interference with the text of the treaty. True, he deplored the insertion of the phrase 'en Europe' and wondered how the Tsar could be persuaded to sign the original version, but he too, like Holstein and Tschirschky, considered the agreement a great prize for Germany because it broke up the Franco-Russian Dual Alliance and gave the Reich a free hand in the west.[63] In his reply to Wilhelm II's bellicose telegram he emphasised that what the Kaiser had said 'about the value to us of freedom to the rear' was in his opinion absolutely correct. 'To have achieved this for us does Your Majesty the greatest possible credit.'[64]

It was not until 2 August 1905 that Prince Bülow took the decision to hand in his resignation on the grounds that he considered the addition 'en Europe' to be 'pernicious' and could not accept responsibility for it.[65] The assumption is that this decision was inspired by the influence of the Foreign Secretary Freiherr von Richthofen, who paid a visit to the Reich Chancellor in Norderney on 1 August.[66] The 'ungracious marginal comments' which the Kaiser scrawled on his most recent telegrams will likewise have contributed to Bülow's decision.[67] More generally, irritation and anxiety over Wilhelm II's personal style of ruling undoubtedly played a part too: it was after all only a matter of weeks since the Chancellor had considered resigning in protest at the monarch's independent policy towards France.[68] In August 1905, after the fall of Delcassé and his own elevation to princely status, Bülow found himself in a strong position with Wilhelm II. He knew that the monarch could hardly let him go. Evidently he saw the Kaiser's interference with the Treaty of Björkö as an opportunity to teach him an effective and lasting lesson for his high-handed behaviour, which as Reich Chancellor Bülow had accepted without protest for years.[69] He was nevertheless taking a risk. It was not so much his post in itself as the intimate relationship of trust which had formed the basis of the collaboration between Kaiser and Chancellor for ten years which was now at stake.

In his resignation letter of 3 August 1905 the Reich Chancellor wrote bluntly: 'I owe it to my Imperial Master to state openly that after calm and purely objective examination before God and my conscience I cannot but consider the addition of "en Europe" harmful and dangerous.' As a result of this insertion the agreement had become much more advantageous for the Russian Empire than for Germany. 'What does Germany set at risk?' he asked, in reference to potential conflict with England. The answer was 'A fine fleet, flourishing trade, rich coastal cities, our colonies. What does Russia risk, if Asia is excluded? A navy which scarcely exists any more, very little trade, insignificant coastal towns, no colonial possessions. The risks are quite disproportionate with the limitation of "en Europe".' Parity could have been ensured only if the British had had to fear a Russian attack on India. The Tsar and his Foreign Minister Lamsdorff would never give their consent to an alteration of this treaty which was so advantageous for Russia; even to suggest an alteration would be 'highly dangerous' because it might give the Russians the opportunity to 'back out' of the whole treaty. 'Therefore with the deepest respect I ask Your Majesty to be pleased to entrust the direction of foreign policy to *other* hands ... I do not need to say that I would of course explain my resignation on grounds of my health. Even less need I say that my most loyal, grateful and sincere good wishes would always remain with my

Imperial Master and that until my last breath my whole heart will beat for the happiness and glory of Yr Majesty.'[70]

Bülow's letter arrived at the Foreign Office on 4 August and was forwarded to the Kaiser, who arrived at Swinemünde the next day. Once again Wilhelm tried to convince Bülow that the inclusion of 'en Europe' in the treaty was sensible and necessary. 'We cannot *force* the Russians to plan operations against India if they are *unwilling* or claim to be unable, even without *"en Europe"'*, he pointed out. 'But they will be easier to persuade to do it when they have come to an agreement with Japan. The English *"strategists"* and Anglo-Indian politicians use the *"pressure on India"*, i.e. possibility of Russian attack, purely as a bugbear for home consumption — in London — so that they are given *sufficient* power and resources to use against their *enemies within India*, who since Japan's victories over the "white race" no longer believe in the latter's invincibility and have begun to be restless. I have been told by high-ranking English officers who formerly served in India that they do not fear any danger at all from Russia, for an attack with any relatively strong unit "of the army type" is impracticable. Your Excellency is quite right to say that the border is well fortified and prepared, yet another reason why it has become unassailable. It probably goes without saying that without *"en Europe"* the entire German navy would be obliged — at the request of the Russians — to put to sea and stop English troop transports everywhere from getting to India, and in the process, far from any home port as an operational base, they would be destroyed by the superior English navy.'[71]

Once again the Chancellor paused to consider whether Tsar Nicholas could be persuaded to accept the original version of the treaty. Wilhelm could perhaps explain in a letter to Nicholas that according to the German constitution the agreement was valid only if the Reich Chancellor countersigned it, and the latter objected to the words 'en Europe'. Or Germany could retain the agreed text of the treaty if the Tsar would make an express declaration 'that in the event of a war Russia would have to take action all along the line'.[72] Holstein, however, strengthened the Chancellor's resolve to oppose the agreement. He maintained that '1. 'En Europe' is damaging, for to have Russia as a "bogeyman" threatening India would have been very desirable for us, in order to keep the English Philistine at bay. 2. "En Europe" is unnecessary, for where our ships are concerned, war with England will be fought out in the North Sea and the Baltic. There is absolutely no question of using our fleet in distant seas.'[73] At the same time Holstein considered the Björkö treaty 'even in its present deformed version . . . too valuable' to wager on a 'wild card' like a letter from Wilhelm II to the Tsar, the result of which would be unpredictable. The treaty's value, he argued, lay 'in the devastating effect it will have on France, and the indirect repercussions this will bring about on England'.[74] In spite of this rather ambiguous advice Bülow became increasingly convinced that the Treaty of Björkö would be acceptable only if it could be ensured that in the event of war with England 'Russia were of course also obliged to take action in Asia'.[75]

On 9 August 1905 Adjutant-General Helmuth von Moltke arrived in Norderney as the Kaiser's emissary. Afterwards Bülow reported to the Foreign Office: 'General von Moltke told me . . . in the name of His Majesty the Kaiser that the All-Highest was deeply distressed by my request to resign. His Majesty did not understand how I could wish to leave him when he had full confidence in me. His Majesty the Kaiser could not believe that I would desert him in his present difficult position. I replied that I had not offered His Majesty my resignation in a state of temporary emotion, or out of self-opinionated stubbornness or even wounded pride, but because I was responsible to the German people for the course of our foreign policy. I could not carry this responsibility if changes of such consequence as the addition of "en Europe" were made by His Majesty, without seeking my advice, in such a decisive document as this draft treaty. I would remain in office only as long as I could serve the country. If this were made impossible for me, I would leave. I must reserve my final decision as to my resignation until after an interview with His Majesty, which I would now request in writing from the All-Highest himself.'[76]

That the Kaiser was deeply affected, indeed devastated, by Bülow's request to resign is apparent from his letter to the Chancellor of 11 August 1905. It is quoted here at length, for it is one of the most remarkable documents of the Kaiser's entire life. He wrote: 'On mature reflection, I am completely unable to see how "en Europe" could have made the situation so much more serious or dangerous for us than hitherto, that it has caused you to offer me your resignation. I have informed you of two facts which alone signify such enormous progress compared to the previous state of affairs that they must be regarded as of great value for us: 1) that His Majesty the Emperor [Nicholas] solemnly declared to me that for Russia the Alsace-Lorraine question was *un incident clos*. 2.) that he promised me faithfully never to enter into an agreement or alliance with England against us. If Bismarck had succeeded in obtaining even one of these two declarations from Alexander II or III he would have been beside himself with joy and would have been feted by the entire nation as if he had won a great victory. These are two such momentous facts that I believe that they alone mean greater security for our fatherland than all treaties and other safeguards . . . I thought I had worked for you and that I had achieved something special. Whereupon you send me a few cold lines and your resignation!!! You will perhaps excuse me, my dear Bülow, from describing my state of mind to you. To be treated in such a way by the best, closest friend I have ... without being given any valid reason, was such a fearful blow to me that I broke down completely and cannot help fearing I may fall victim to a severe nervous disorder! You say the situation has become so serious because of the treaty with "en Europe" that you cannot take any responsibility; towards whom? And in the same breath you believe you can answer before God, in the situation you regard as particularly acute and serious, for finding it in yourself to desert your Kaiser and Lord, to whom you have sworn loyalty, who has heaped affection and distinctions upon you, your fatherland and − or so I thought − your most loyal friend!? No, dear Bülow, you cannot do that to us both! We have both been called by God, and created for each other, to work and use our influence for our dear German fatherland ... Your person is 100,000 times more valuable to me and our fatherland than all the treaties in the world ... Do not forget that you *put me personally at risk* in Tangier in order to make a success of your Moroccan policy ... And now, after I have done all that − and, as I confidently believe, a great deal more besides − for you, you simply want to cast me adrift because my situation seems to you to be too serious!! But I do not deserve this from you, Bülow! No, my friend, you will remain in office and *at my side*, and you will continue to work together with me ad majorem Germaniae gloriam, indeed you are as good as under an obligation to me after putting me to use this year, you cannot and must not refuse me, you would be disavowing your own entire policy this year and I should be disgraced for ever! *Which will destroy me.* Allow me a few days to rest and collect myself before you come, for your letters have brought me into too great a state of nervous agitation and I am incapable of calm debate now. Your true friend Wilhelm I. R. PS I appeal to your friendship for me, say no more about intending to resign. Telegraph to me "all right" after reading this letter and then I shall know that you are staying! For if a letter of resignation arrived from you, the next morning *would find the Kaiser no longer alive!* Think of my poor wife and children!'[77]

Bülow had not expected Wilhelm II to react so melodramatically to his request to resign. The following day he wrote him a letter beginning with expressions of remorse and deep sympathy. 'The letter which I have just received from Your Imperial and Royal Majesty has grieved me deeply. To have caused Your Majesty disquiet and anxiety causes me bitter pain. I would give my life to spare Your Majesty distress, to clear away rocks from Your Majesty's path, to arrange everything for Your Majesty's benefit!' Then Bülow declared the Kaiser to be a 'highly gifted and chivalrous being, towering over all others in talents and intellect, nature and character'. Of his objections to the formula 'en Europe' he wrote: 'Before God, to whom I pray daily to increase Your Majesty's happiness and renown, I swear to Your Majesty that it was not out of arrogance or foolish sensitivity that I drew attention to the disadvantages and dangers of that addition, but because my conscience drove me to it.' 'Of course' he was ready to remain in office. 'As long as Your Majesty is able and willing to make use of me I shall follow Your Majesty with the sole wish and thought that God may give me the strength to serve Your Majesty in a manner fitting my duty and my love for Your Majesty.'[78]

Shaken by Bülow's threat to resign, Wilhelm II was now prepared to abandon the phrase 'en Europe' and wanted to put the appropriate amendment to the Tsar.[79] Holstein, however, continued to urge Bülow not to touch the treaty. His argument ran: 'Lamsdorff, who bears a grudge against our Kaiser for his previous contemptuous treatment, and of course most of all for being "taken by surprise" by Björkö, will use the request for an amendment to wreck not only the request but the whole treaty as well. Nothing could be easier. For if *we* want to make an alteration we cannot refuse the Russians an addition or a deletion.' Even with the insertion of 'en Europe', Holstein again maintained, the treaty was still valuable for the German side.[80] When Kaiser and Chancellor met again on 18 August 1905 at Wilhelmshöhe, Wilhelm assured Bülow that he had neither written nor telegraphed to the Tsar about the affair. He was perfectly willing to agree that nothing should be done to revise the treaty until further notice. He also fully recognised the need for 'absolute secrecy' about the treaty until it had been accepted by both sides and published.[81]

THE GERMAN—RUSSIAN RAPPROCHEMENT RUNS INTO THE SAND

If the German statesmen had had problems with the treaty agreed between the two emperors at Björkö, their objections – in any case ambivalent – paled into insignificance beside the resistance put up by the Russian ministers to it. The Tsar did not tell his Foreign Minister, Lamsdorff, of the treaty until 30 August 1905.[82] Far from laughing up his sleeve at the addition of 'en Europe', as Holstein at first suspected he would, Lamsdorff categorically rejected the entire treaty, which he rightly saw as a betrayal of Russia's ally, France, and an acceptance of German hegemony in Europe. The influential Russian statesman Sergei Witte had spent the summer of 1905 in the USA while negotiating the peace treaty with Japan. On his way back to St Petersburg he visited Paris, then Berlin and finally Rominten in East Prussia, where he met the Kaiser on 27 September 1905. Wilhelm was anxious not to be denied the pleasure of personally letting Witte into the secret of Björkö. 'Tsar tells me', he telegraphed to Bülow from Rominten, 'he has nothing against my letting Witte in on treaty; knows nothing about it ... *I* will therefore *personally* inform Witte about it; neither you nor Foreign Office must give him any hint of it.'[83] But Witte, who was appointed Prime Minister shortly afterwards, had no alternative but to reject the Treaty of Björkö too. It was of vital importance to the Russian state to take up a huge loan of 2¼ billion francs from France. But France would not have given a single franc of credit to a Russia which had concluded a treaty of mutual military assistance with the German Reich. Both Witte and Lamsdorff therefore made it clear to Nicholas II that he had been extremely foolish and that the treaty must not on any account be allowed to come into force.[84]

It would have been impossible, however, for the Tsar to go back on the treaty which he had solemnly signed. So he tried to worm his way out of it. In a letter to Wilhelm on 7 October 1905 he described the treaty as 'a document of immeasurable value'. But he went on to say that, unfortunately, he had not had the text of the 1894 Franco-Russian treaty of alliance with him in Björkö. He now considered that the Björkö treaty should not come into force until France's attitude towards it was clear. If France refused to accept the Björkö agreement, it would have to be altered in such a way as to render it compatible with the Franco-Russian treaty.[85]

Wilhelm implored the Tsar to stand by their agreement. 'The wording of the Treaty does not – as we agreed at Björkö – collide with the Franco-Russian Alliance, – provided of course the latter is not aimed directly at my country. – On the other hand the obligations of Russia towards France can only go so far as France merits them through her behaviour. Your Ally has notoriously left you in the lurch during the whole war [against Japan], whereas Germany helped you in every way as far as it could, without infringing the laws of neutrality. This puts Russia morally also under obligations to us; do ut des [I give so that you give].' The Kaiser concluded by once again appealing to the religious feelings of the 'Ruler of all the Russias': 'We joined hands and signed before God who heard our vows! I therefore think that the treaty can well come into existence ... What is signed, is signed! And God is our Testator!'[86]

Nicholas let five weeks pass and then wrote to Wilhelm: 'As You rightly said, what is signed – is signed. The same loyalty imposes upon me to fulfil what was signed by my Father & cannot be struck off by a stroke of the pen. Therefore in order to be able to fulfil just as loyally the clauses of the new treaty with Germany, Russia finds it necessary to complete the Bjorkoe [sic] understanding by the Declaration annexed.'[87] This declaration read: 'In view of the difficulties which stand in the way of the immediate adhesion of the French Government to the defensive treaty of alliance signed at Bjorke [sic] on the 11/24 July 1905 ... it is agreed that Article I of this act will not be applicable in the event of a war with France and that the mutual engagements which unite the latter with Russia will be upheld in their entirety until an accord between all three nations is established.'[88] As Wilhelm rightly pointed out in a letter to Bülow on 26 November 1905: 'The enclosed "declaration" is a direct annulment of the treaty in the event of war with France. And therefore a restoration of the status quo.'[89] The Kaiser also already foresaw what Bülow did not want to see – the formation of a Triple Entente between Britain, France and Russia. 'Since France will never attack us alone but only together with England, spurred on by the latter, even in the event of war between us and England, in which we would have to attack Gaul, the Tsar would immediately hide behind the declaration and go to the aid of the Two Powers, because he must remain loyal to his ally. The coalition is there de facto! King E[dward] VII has fiddled that nicely. Now the Gauls have land forces at their disposal ad libitum.'[90]

On 28 November 1905 Wilhelm tried once more to persuade the Tsar that there was no need to add a declaration to the Björkö treaty. 'If the French agreement is like ours, purely defensive, then there is no incompatibility between the two, and one does not exclude the other, so that no further declaration is required.'[91] The Tsar, however, responded: 'Our alliance with France is a defensive one. I think the declaration I sent you could remain in force until France accept [sic] our new agreement.'[92] Wilhelm now realised that the Russian side had written off the Björkö treaty. Commenting on a letter from the Tsar of 23 January 1906, he telegraphed angrily to Bülow: 'Enclosed I send you another delightful piece of work cobbled together by the ideological youth on the throne of Russia! The latest phase of the Russo-Gallic alliance "frise le ridicule", but shows how in Paris – at London's instigation? – a contrecoup is immediately launched against every rapprochement between the two Emperors, which the little Tsar falls for every time, or is dropped into by Lamsdorff, on the grounds of the "historic alliance" ... And it is all presented to one behind a tearful mask of undying intimate friendship! ... His Almighty Majesty ought to be too ashamed to do such things in front of his ancestors and mine, and of me; to write such letters to me, dictated to him by Lamsdorff!'[93] With that, the bold dream of a 'peaceful continental coalition'[94] under Germany's leadership was over, at least for the present.

CHAPTER FIFTEEN

Balance of power or hegemony? The Anglo-German conflict and the quarrel with King Edward

Unlike the Kaiser's landing in Tangier, which was conceived as a deliberate show of strength, the agreement which Wilhelm II and Nicholas II signed on 24 July 1905 on board the *Polarstern* was kept secret from the world for many years. Only with the abdication of the Tsar in February 1917 did any mention of the Björkö accord reach the press — it was at once assumed that Nicholas must have been drunk to have agreed to such a treaty with the German Kaiser. When the semi-official *Norddeutsche Allgemeine Zeitung* thereupon saw fit to confirm the existence of the Björkö treaty, the journalist Theodor Wolff asked the former Reich Chancellor Prince von Bülow for an explanation. Bülow commented mockingly on the dilettantism of the Kaiser, who had never mastered the art of diplomacy. He himself, before the Kaiser set off, had urged extreme restraint upon him, in view of the fact that his every word would be relayed to Paris and London. In spite of this the Kaiser had discussed a treaty of alliance with the Tsar at Björkö, 'and indeed he drew up a treaty there and then ... But it was done as a dilettante would do it. ... The Kaiser was of course delighted, he thought he was bringing home an enormous success', Bülow recalled, and continued patronisingly: 'As soon as I heard what had happened I submitted my resignation. The Kaiser, who is sometimes very touching, was very abashed and wrote to me at once begging me not to leave him in the lurch. I remained in office and tried to play for time over the matter, and at least to take care that it caused no ill-feeling between us and Russia.'[1]

However much Bülow tried to distance himself from Wilhelm II's actions and intentions by making them appear unrealistic and ridiculous in this interview and on other occasions, it is indisputable that he had had a hand in forming his sovereign's foreign policy not only over the Tangier landing but also at Björkö, and therefore shared the responsibility for it. As we have observed, the treaty with Russia was drafted in the Auswärtiges Amt – first in December 1904 and then again in July 1905 – and sent to the Kaiser by Bülow himself. Tschirschky, who was to be promoted to Foreign Secretary soon afterwards, was aware of Wilhelm's intention from the outset, and did not demur when the Kaiser put a limit on the application of the Russo-German agreement by adding 'en Europe'. Nor did Bülow hand in his resignation at once, but only after lengthy reflection, and even then his motive was more to deliver a rebuke to the Kaiser for taking diplomacy into his own hands. It is true that both he and Holstein regretted the restrictive insertion made by the Kaiser, but both were enthusiastic about the conclusion of the treaty in itself and warned strongly against trying to remove the insertion, thereby risking the loss of the signed treaty, which seemed to put German hegemony in Europe within reach.

BALANCE OF POWER OR HEGEMONY?

The 'Napoleonic supremacy' which the Kaiser, the Chancellor, the Foreign Office, the naval authorities and the army had striven to establish since 1897 at the latest, was unmistakably aimed against the existing European balance of power which in the end was upheld by Great Britain. Germany's world policy therefore clearly carried the risk of a world war from the very outset. Through his threats of war against France, Belgium, Holland and Denmark, and not least through the conclusion of the treaty of alliance with the Tsar at Björkö, for several weeks in the autumn of 1905 Wilhelm II imagined that he had come close to realising his grand plan of uniting Europe under German supremacy. Count Zedlitz-Trützschler recorded in his diary: 'The Kaiser's political hopes at the moment are in fact directed towards achieving such a feeling of closeness with Russia and France that, if possible, a kind of alliance comes about which will provide a counterbalance to the Anglo-Japanese alliance.'[2] The Kaiser explained the aims of his anti-British continental policy to Philipp Eulenburg in the course of endless conversations in autumn 1905. 'The thought of a *European coalition*' was 'as dominant as ever *in the Kaiser*', Wilhelm's closest friend recorded approvingly.[3]

Both sides, German and British, were already only too aware that the Kaiserreich's hegemonial policy could easily lead to military conflict. Metternich, the German ambassador in London, gave an unequivocal warning in a private letter to Bülow on 2 October 1905 of the great dangers that would arise from an anti-British alliance between Germany and Russia. 'A German-Russian rapprochement aimed against England will bring us no benefit but only harm and danger, for the simple reason that ... Russian help against England is about as valuable to us as the man in the moon. Russia has no fleet, she cannot protect our ports and our trade, and her army is of no use to us against England.' 'In war between England and Russia in which we became entangled' Germany would play the same role as France in a war between Germany and Britain, 'that is, we would have to pay for the pots cassés'.[4] The German policy of creating a continental league also carried the risk that France 'goes over to the English completely'. Kaiser Wilhelm, however, roundly rebuffed Metternich's warnings. If only 'because of her 10 billions of savings ... which are in Russ[ian] hands', France could not go over to the English, he maintained. 'The Ambassador is a civilian and does not understand what it means for us military men to have our back and arms free, instead of having to defend 2 fronts!' he wrote. 'As soon as Gaul realises that Russ[ian] bayonets are no longer pointing towards us, so that we have a completely free hand, she will take good care not to go over to England, whose fleet has "no wheels" and would be of no use at all to France! to protect her from us.'[5] Unlike Metternich, the influential First Secretary at the London embassy, Johannes Count Bernstorff, sided with the Kaiser and supported the conflict with Britain in principle, although in his view it should be postponed for as long as possible. For the time being war between Germany and Britain must be avoided, he argued in April 1905. 'If war really must be waged with England at some point, for the sake of German power and expansion, every hour that this battle can be postponed is a gain for us. The power of the German people is growing steadily, whereas no one, if he has eyes to see, can live among the island people of England without becoming aware that they have at least already reached their peak.'[6] A further 'excellently written' report from Bernstorff in the spring of 1905 won Wilhelm's warm approval; in it Bernstorff expressed the opinion that the British government and public opinion, 'instead of recognising the living forces in history and getting on good terms with us', wanted to make 'the attempt that throughout the entire course of world history has always failed', to stand in the way of a rising nation.[7] Tirpitz and numerous other leading figures in Berlin were similarly convinced that it lay in Germany's interest to postpone the decisive struggle with Britain for a long time to come.

On the British side 'the German menace' had long since been recognised and appropriate diplomatic and strategic countermeasures taken, which in turn provoked bitter complaints from the Kaiser and his military entourage, as if the British Empire ought to give up its worldwide position of supremacy to the Kaiserreich without a struggle. On 16 January 1905 the former Flügeladjutant Ferdinand von Grumme wrote a report on the mood in England for the Kaiser:

'People in England did not understand the agitation in Germany, or the feeling that England did not want to give us a chance. England would have to reckon with the fact that we were there and they could not use force against us without making fools of themselves in the world. The only explanation they could find was that the Government, and above all His Majesty, needed this mood in Germany in order to increase the speed of fleet building.'[8] In August 1905, a few days after the meeting of the two emperors in Björkö, the Chief of General Staff designate, Helmuth von Moltke, wrote to his wife: 'The worst thing for us is England's jealousy of our growing trade and our industrial development. When one looks at the English newspapers one is shocked by the systematic and spiteful anti-German hate campaign pursued by the papers of all parties. The press is positively bloodthirsty and would gladly eradicate us root and branch, so as to be absolutely free to rule and exploit the world. These press writers and bawlers make a lot of mischief and play with fire unscrupulously. If it comes to blows they of course don't need to risk their skin, they stay cosily at home, dip their pens in poison and gall and let the others kill each other.' It must be Germany's task 'to prepare seriously and with bitter energy for war'.[9]

Apart from the battlefleet-building programme, ever more dangerous for the British Empire, the Kaiser's threats against France, Belgium, Holland and Denmark and his mysterious meeting with the Tsar at Björkö gave the British leadership cause for alarm. As we have seen, on 1 April 1905, immediately after his sensational landing in Tangier, Wilhelm II had a conversation with Prince Louis of Battenberg in which he expressed his conviction that the world would one day be divided between the Germanic and the Slav races. As far as France was concerned, he added, the German army knew the road to Paris, which no fleet would be able to defend.[10] King Edward VII was almost speechless with anger when told by Battenberg of this barefaced threat of war by Wilhelm. 'I consider that the Tangiers incident was one of the most mischievous & uncalled for events which H.M. G[erman] E[mperor] has ever undertaken', he wrote to Prince Louis. 'It was a gratuitous insult to 2 Countries − & the clumsy theatrical part of it − would make me laugh were the matter not a serious one. It was a regular *case* of "Bombastes Furioso"! I suppose G[erman] E[mperor] will never find out as he will never be told how ridiculous he makes himself. − In all he said to you there is throughout a want of sincerity . . . I have tried to get on with him & shall nominally do my best till the end − but trust him − *never*. He is utterly false & the bitterest foe that E[ngland] possesses!'[11] It was only with great difficulty that the King could be persuaded that his nephew's Moroccan policy 'was not secretly working towards a war against France and England'.[12]

After the calamitous defeats of the Russian army and navy in the war against Japan and the revolutionary turbulence within the Russian Empire, British statesmen recognised that the balance of power in Europe had shifted massively in Germany's favour, at least for a few years to come. The diplomat Cecil Spring Rice, arriving in St Petersburg in the spring of 1905, commented almost resignedly that German hegemony over Europe could scarcely be prevented by peaceful means any longer. He set out his views in a perceptive analysis written for the King on 2 May. Since Russia could not contemplate war with Germany under present circumstances, there was no threat to Germany from the rear. Internally, too, the situation had changed radically. In the days of the old Kaiser, Wilhelm I, Germany had decided against war with France in 1875 and again in 1887, under pressure from Russia. But now the old Kaiser had 'given place to the new Kaiser, and the growth of the Socialistic party threatens the dynasty unless some great and striking achievement restore the prestige of the Hohenzollerns (so Prince Henry is reported to have said when he was in the East) . . . The sympathies of Russia (that is of the Government) are with the two Empires [Germany and Austria-Hungary]: England, France, and Italy are naturally antipathetic to her . . . It is quite evident that both monarchies [Germany and Russia] have the same enemy − the internal one, which is more to be feared than any other; and that their common action in support of one another is quite essential at the present moment. This is especially true of Poland. If they quarrel the internal enemy will profit, he can only be suppressed by joint action. This is the superlative danger and all other questions are subordinate to this. Germany can offer to the Czar security on the Western frontier, supplies for the war, money, and so on, and security against Revolution. In return all she asks is to be allowed a free hand in Western Europe, where after all Russia has no interests − and against that nation which is the source and origin of all Revolutions. It would be impossible to deny the force of this argument. This explains the fear of the French. A new "alerte" under much more dangerous circumstances to France may break out at any moment, and who is to save? . . . The French here are very grateful to us, but at the same time it is hard to answer the question − what can England do to save France from invasion if Russia guarantees Germany complete immunity on the Eastern frontier? (Please don't answer).'[13]

News of the meeting between Wilhelm II and Nicholas II at Björkö was thus greeted with deep suspicion in leading circles in Britain. Only a few weeks after the meeting a first eye-witness account of Wilhelm's Baltic cruise and his rendezvous with the Tsar arrived at the Foreign Office in Downing Street. Prince Otto zu Sayn-Wittgenstein had been travelling with the Kaiser and was asked to accompany him, together with Tschirschky, on board the *Polarstern*.

His confidential description of Wilhelm II's state of mind and of his breathtaking ambitions provoked a horrified reaction in London. While the Tsar had looked well and laughed happily at lunch, Wilhelm had left a very different impression on Wittgenstein. He had been 'restlessly talkative and silent in turn and seemed exceptionally preoccupied throughout the whole cruise'. According to the Prince, 'His Majesty talks vehemently on subject after subject, and suddenly relapses into complete silence, staring intently into space for several minutes together ... To his guests the demeanour and general appearance of the Kaiser has much changed for the worse during the last twelve months. The Emperor William's talk is ever of alliances and political combinations, and he gave utterance on the cruise to his cherished idea of now being able to effect a coalition between Germany, France and Russia, to the exclusion of Great Britain.' Wilhelm was very much afraid of the growing power of Japan and was anxious to conclude an alliance with the United States in order to pre-empt the threat of a pact between Great Britain, Japan and America.[14] The British Foreign Secretary immediately forwarded the secret report containing Wittgenstein's comments to the King and the Prime Minister, A. J. Balfour, who both saw in it the confirmation of their worst fears. 'Am more convinced than ever of G[erman] E[mperor]'s animosity towards England', noted Edward VII.[15] Lord Lansdowne commented: 'I must say that Prince Wittgenstein's description of the German Emperor's language and demeanour fills me with disquiet. What may not a man in such a frame of mind not do next?'[16] From St Petersburg the influential British ambassador Sir Charles Hardinge reported in September 1905: 'There is no doubt that the Kaiser is conducting a very active campaign of which the objects are to weaken the Franco-Russian alliance and to prevent any sort of friendly "rapprochement" [by Russia] with England ... No stone is being left unturned to excite distrust. Such manoeuvres have not so far affected the Govt. who realise the proper value to be attached to the Emperor's friendship which is dictated purely by self-interest and fear of isolation. There is no doubt however that the Emperor Nicholas has been greatly impressed by the recent interview at Biorki and is for the first time convinced of the sincerity of the Kaiser's professions of friendship.'[17] It was now clear to the British that an almost inevitable, relentless conflict had begun between their vast, worldwide empire, now gradually tiring, and the young, vigorous Prussian–German military monarchy on the continent. The Anglo-German antagonism was to cast a shadow over Europe for half a century.

THE KAISER'S DESIGNS ON DENMARK

For Great Britain as a maritime power, the practical significance of the Russo-German alliance concluded by Wilhelm and Nicholas in Björkö is evident not least from their plans to occupy Denmark on the outbreak of a war, and to remain in occupation afterwards as well. As has already been described, a few months before his Baltic tour of summer 1905 Wilhelm had reverted to his explosive idea of a 'Union of the Northern Kingdoms – Denmark, Sweden, Norway, Russia and Germany – for the defence of the Baltic Sea', and with this in mind he was hoping to bind Denmark, which held the key to the Baltic, more closely to Germany.[18] As we have seen, he and his Adjutant-General, von Plessen, told the German envoy in Copenhagen, Wilhelm von Schoen, in December 1904 that it was 'highly desirable' for Germany to 'get our hands on' Denmark. The Kaiser declared that Denmark would have to 'decide to put herself under the protection of the German Reich in some way or other, initially in the form of a customs union, and then through military concessions as well', adding that international treaties would have to be 'ignored' in the process. In the lifetime of the old King Christian IX he would 'show as much consideration as possible, but later this would be dropped'.[19] Wilhelm turned a deaf ear to warnings from Bülow and Schoen that any alliance between little Denmark and the powerful German Reich would look to the eyes of the world like an annexation of Denmark by Germany and would certainly turn Britain, France, Russia and America against the Reich. He declared bluntly that because of the war in the Far East, which would probably drag on for years, the danger of Russia and Britain joining forces on the grounds of the 'seizure of Danish territory and waters' by Germany was very slight indeed.[20]

In February 1905, when growing tension with France and Britain compelled him to abandon the Admiralty Staff's plan for the military occupation of Denmark, the Kaiser telegraphed twice in quick succession to Bülow, saying 'We must bring about a closer link with Denmark.'[21] After a conversation with Wilhelm the Reich Chancellor recorded on 6 February 1905: 'In connection with the English threats, H.M. again spoke of Denmark. He admitted that any threat against Denmark could have dangerous consequences, but did express his urgent desire for an alliance with Denmark in order to prevent thereby an English surprise attack on Kiel and the Baltic ports.'[22] At first Bülow agreed to 'academic' soundings in Copenhagen about a German–Danish alliance on these lines, but a memorandum from Friedrich von Holstein again alerted him to the dangers which Germany would bring upon herself. It was true, Holstein conceded, that the elderly King Christian might privately retain a certain affection for the Kaiser, but Denmark was a constitutional country and any alliance depended ultimately on popular feeling – which was fundamentally anti-German. Any rapprochement with the mighty Reich would immediately arouse the suspicion of the Danish people that Denmark was about to be made dependent on Germany. Any government which ignored these popular instincts would be swept away in no time, and even the Danish monarchy would be under threat. The court and the government in Copenhagen would therefore turn to Britain and Russia for help. Britain would happily seize the opportunity of setting herself up as the defender of a small country against a 'forced' German alliance, and France would call for joint British–French–Russian action to protect Danish independence and maintain the status quo in the Baltic. 'The plan of drawing Denmark within the outer ambit of the German Empire is a great idea for the future', the Geheimrat argued, but for the time being it was a dream fraught with danger, which could be realised only on one of two conditions: either the British navy must be tied down in some other way or the German navy, whether alone or in combination with an ally, must be of equal strength to the British. At the moment, Holstein warned urgently in February 1905, any step in the direction of a link between Denmark and Germany would play into the hands of the promoters of a Franco-Russian–British triple alliance against Germany.[23] Schoen, who had already drawn attention to the danger of a world war in December 1904, was equally blunt in opposing the Kaiser's wishes. He wrote to Holstein that raising this 'delicate question' at the present time would have dire consequences. 'For one thing the Danes themselves aren't ripe for it yet ... Russia probably would never forgive us if we used its present difficulties to seize the key of the Baltic, and as regards the British, they would in their present mood hardly hesitate to accuse us of an unfriendly act and in this they would probably be supported by France. In short, it seems to me ... that the present moment is as unfavourable as could be in order to work for a goal which as such is certainly desirable and will be achieved in time, but very gradually.'[24] The arguments put forward by the Wilhelmstrasse left the Kaiser unmoved, however, and for the time being he pressed on with his plans to annex Denmark in some way to Germany.[25] At his meeting with Nicholas II at Björkö there was 'also much discussion of Denmark', as he reported jubilantly to Bülow. The Tsar expressed the wish (according to Wilhelm) 'that we should consider whether some form could not be found by which we two could guarantee King Christian his territory in such a way that we could be sure of being able to conduct the defence of the Baltic from *north of the Belts* in the event of war'.[26]

These missives from the Kaiser set alarm bells ringing in Berlin, particularly since Wilhelm's next destination on his Baltic cruise was Copenhagen. Just before he arrived in the Danish capital on 31 July 1905 the Chancellor and the Foreign Office advised him strongly not to discuss Danish neutrality, so as not to 'rekindle England's constantly alert, pathological mistrust'.[27] Not least because of King Christian's refusal to broach any political questions at all with him, Wilhelm II abandoned his resolve and sent a message telling Schoen, to the latter's relief, that as far as the neutrality question was concerned 'an initiative on our part is impracticable at the moment and would be useless, and that there was reason to believe that Denmark herself would, in time, come to the conclusion that it would be in her own interest to ally herself with us and possibly with Russia if war really broke out'.[28] Nonetheless, until 1914 the British Foreign Office proceeded on the assumption that on the outbreak of war Germany would immediately occupy her small northern neighbour in order to block off access to the Baltic. In a letter to King Edward VII in the spring of 1907 Sir Charles Hardinge, who by this time had been appointed Permanent Under Secretary of State at the Foreign Office, wrote: 'We fear that at the outbreak of war German troops would overrun Denmark & Jutland, while German ships would mine the Belts & Sound, and thus practically endeavour to close the Straits. It is only by rapid naval action that this could be prevented, but Germany has a better geographical position than we have, and has probably everything ready for immediate action.'[29]

Astonishingly, in Copenhagen Kaiser Wilhelm chose to discuss his European policy objectives, as pretentious as they were risky, with none other than the Russian envoy there, Alexander Isvolsky, who was soon to be appointed Foreign Minister (1906–10) and thereafter ambassador in Paris (1910–17), and who was to prove, as we shall see, the bitterest opponent of the Kaiser's expansionist plans. Through his colleague Schoen, Isvolsky received an invitation to come to the German legation at night for a secret meeting with Wilhelm. Evidently in the belief that he was speaking to the representative of a Great Power which was now allied to Germany, the Kaiser revealed the covert aims of his foreign policy to Isvolsky. Years later this nocturnal conversation remained an indelible memory for the Russian diplomat. Wilhelm II argued eloquently that peace in Europe could be secured only by completely new methods, namely through an alliance of the three continental Great Powers, Russia, Germany and France, directed against Britain. Isvolsky, completely taken aback, drew attention to the unbridgeable gulf which had opened up between France and Germany since the annexation of Alsace-Lorraine, whereupon the Kaiser lost his temper. His 'displeasure developed into unmistakable anger, and it was in a voice almost beyond his control that he made this most astonishing declaration: "The question of Alsace-Lorraine", he cried, "I consider to be not only non-existent at the present hour, but as having been cut out for all time by the French people themselves. I threw down the glove to France, à propos of the Moroccan affair, and she dared not pick it up; having then declined to fight Germany, France has renounced for good and all any claims she may have had in respect of her lost provinces."' Isvolsky's account continued: 'I thought at first that this outburst was merely one of the *boutades* for which the Kaiser was famous, but I soon perceived that it was a deep-seated conviction of his, for he reverted several times in the course of our conversation to the strange idea that, from the moment that France had bowed to the German threat, at the time of the Moroccan dispute, she no longer had any right to invoke her long-standing grievances as a ground for refusing friendship with Germany . . . The Emperor surprised me still more by declaring that, if, after all, France persisted in her refusal to join the proposed alliance, there were ways to bring her into it *by force.*'[30]

After his return from the Baltic cruise Wilhelm II telegraphed to the Tsar saying that because of the mistrust planted by Britain in the mind of the Danish King and because of public opinion in Copenhagen, he had not after all broached the question of Danish neutrality, as agreed at Björkö. In any case it had been quite unnecessary, the Kaiser asserted, for 'I was able to gather that the actual Minister of Foreign Affairs, Count Raben, and a number of persons of influence, have already come to the conviction that, in case of war and impending attack on the Baltic from a foreign Power [Britain], the Danes expect, their inability and helplessness to uphold even the shadow of neutrality against invasion being evident, that Russia and Germany will immediately take steps to safeguard their interests by laying hands on Denmark and occupying it during the war, as this would at the same time guarantee the territory and the future existence of the dynasty and country.'[31]

This telegram caused consternation throughout Scandinavia when it was published in 1917 after the Russian Revolution.[32] Its authenticity cannot be doubted, however, for in a letter of 9 August 1905 – which has survived, even though on the advice of the Chancellor it was never sent – Wilhelm II repeated almost word for word his assessment of the situation in Copenhagen and confirmed his intention of establishing joint German–Russian military occupation of Denmark in the event of war with Britain – and of maintaining the occupation subsequently. He wrote, 'through Iswolsky and also Schoen I had heard that the sensible men in society as well as in Governmental circles – among others Count Raben, the foreign Minister – are on their own account, little by little, coming to the conclusion, that in case of war between us both and a foreign Power, the latter attacking our Baltic shores, Denmark would be unable to uphold her neutrality, falling an easy prey to the foreigner. He would create Denmark his base of operations, and thereby draw her on his side as his unwilling ally. This she would have to pay for – eventl. by loss of independence – after the war, as we would never allow her to suffer such a fate again. As we would not countenance such a development of things, and never allow the door of the Baltic to fall into the enemy's hands, in case of an outbreak of war, these men are resigned to expect a joint occupation from us, which however would guarantee their territory to remain undiminished, and their independence to remain untouched. As this is precisely what we want the Danes to think, and as they are already on the road to it, I thought "let well [al]one" and said nothing; they are slowly ripening to the fruit we wish and in time to come it will fall into our laps.'[33]

At the time of the Kaiser's visit to Copenhagen rumours were circulating throughout Europe that Wilhelm intended to declare the Baltic *mare clausum* and to put it out of bounds to all fleets except for those of the countries bordering on it, for the purposes of manoeuvres.[34] In London both the Russian ambassador, Count Benckendorff, and Germany's envoy, Metternich, assumed that Scandinavia, and in particular 'the question of shutting off the Baltic Sea', had been one of the main themes discussed by the Kaiser and the Tsar at Björkö and they agreed that a 'new German–Russian Baltic policy' with the object of closing the Baltic 'would be regarded here [in London] as *casus belli*'.[35] Wilhelm II denied ever having had any such intention: the claim that at Björkö he and the Tsar had discussed the question of blockading the Baltic was 'nonsense'; 'no one would dream of doing any such thing'.[36] Yet the rumours were not far off the truth, as we have seen. And Great Britain was ready with her response, as Benckendorff and Metternich foresaw.

On 15 August 1905 the Royal Navy's Channel Fleet left Spithead and a few days later sailed through the Belts into the Baltic. From 27 to 31 August the warships lay at anchor off Swinemünde and on 1 September off Danzig. London gave official assurances that this was simply a run-of-the-mill naval exercise,[37] but it was clear to everyone that the British fleet's visit to the Baltic could not be regarded as anything but a deliberate show of strength.[38] In his memoirs Isvolsky expressed the opinion that the dispatch of the fleet was a direct response to the rumours then in circulation that Germany and Russia intended to blockade the Baltic.[39] On the Kaiser's orders the German man-oeuvre squadron broke off its own exercises and set sail at once for Danzig to 'welcome' its sister fleet, but Wilhelm's dismay was evident. He telegraphed indignantly to the Auswärtiges Amt to ask whether London had given formal notice of its intention to send a battlefleet to visit two German ports, to which Mühlberg had to reply in the negative.[40] Wilhelm responded furiously to suggestions in the press that he might pay a visit to the British flagship, then at anchor off Danzig, as a gesture of friendship. 'I visited – unsuccessfully – 2 English flagships [in Gibraltar] in the spring this year! I would not dream of it! Kiss the cudgel that John Bull threatens me with!!!'[41]

Whatever the immediate motive for the show of strength may have been, it is clear that the danger of war between Germany and Great Britain had come much closer and was suddenly being talked about by everyone. Helmuth von

Moltke already visualised a great European war. 'The English are stirring up hatred in the most incredible way, the most disgraceful lies are being spread and Germany is represented throughout the world as the evil spirit. The first shot exchanged between England and Germany will certainly be the signal for a general European massacre and one shudders to think of the horror of it.'[42]

DISCORD OVER THE THRONE OF NORWAY

As if his plans to draw Denmark gradually closer to the German Reich were not grounds enough for disquiet, in the summer of 1905 the Kaiser aroused further mistrust in both Copenhagen and London through his behaviour over the succession to the Norwegian throne, and particularly through his intrigues against the candidature of Prince Charles of Denmark. For the Prince's wife Maud was the youngest daughter of King Edward VII and Queen Alexandra, herself a Danish Princess by birth.

The dissolution of the union of Sweden and Norway was proclaimed in the Storting, the Norwegian parliament, on 6 June 1905. In the course of the prolonged crisis which had preceded this dramatic step the elderly King Oscar II had several times sought the advice of the Kaiser. As Count Szögyény discovered, Wilhelm had at first regarded 'armed intervention as the only remedy' against the movement for independence in Norway, but eventually he had been obliged to acknowledge that in view of the ailing King's passive attitude and of the 'deplorable indifference' manifested by public opinion in Sweden towards events in Norway, the Swedish government was unlikely to take a firm stance.[43] In spite of the attitude of 'great restraint' which the Kaiser adopted thereafter, rumours persisted that he had ordered military action in Norway. When Crown Prince Gustaf of Sweden–Norway came to Berlin at the beginning of June 1905 for the wedding of the German Crown Prince he asked Bülow bluntly whether, if Russia intervened in Norway, the Kaiser would also take military measures, whereupon the Reich Chancellor gave him the ambivalent answer that he thought it hardly likely that Germany would follow the wishes of the Kaiser in this question.[44]

Although the proclamation in the Storting on 6 June 1905 effectively deposed King Oscar II as King of Norway, the Norwegian Prime Minister, Christian Michelsen, invited the Swedish royal family to choose a younger Prince from the House of Bernadotte to be King of the newly independent Norwegian state. Oscar rejected this request as an insult. A significant part in this crisis was played by the Norwegian diplomat accredited to Madrid, Baron Fredrik Wedel Jarlsberg, who had already had consultations with Kaiser Wilhelm during the latter's visit to Lisbon in March 1905. This first meeting had done little to allay the diplomat's suspicions about Wilhelm II's intentions. In his conversations with his British counterpart in Madrid, Fairfax Cartwright, Baron Wedel depicted Germany and Russia as 'thieves' out to secure naval bases and trading advantages for themselves in Norway at the first possible opportunity. Wedel considered Wilhelm II particularly dangerous. He told Cartwright that the pleasure given by Wilhelm's annual visits to the Norwegian coast was marred by a feeling among the population that the Kaiser's attention was focused not so much on the beauties of nature as on the search for a naval base. Unlike Germany and Russia, he pointed out, both Britain and France had a strong interest in Norway's territorial integrity. In his opinion there was only one effective guarantee of Norway's independence, and that was the rule of a sovereign related by blood to the British royal family.[45]

Wedel had already telegraphed a suggestion on these lines to Michelsen on 5 June 1905, the day before the latter's proclamation in the Storting. In his dispatch he not only emphasised the importance of maintaining the monarchical system and winning Britain's support for the new state, but referred specifically to Prince Charles of Denmark as by far the most suitable future King of Norway. The Prince was not only a blood relation of Queen Alexandra but also the husband of Alexandra and Edward VII's daughter Princess Maud, whom he had married in 1896. Directly after the dissolution of the union with Sweden Wedel travelled to Stockholm, where the embittered King Oscar made it plain to him that no member of his house would ever accept the Norwegian throne. Thus the way was cleared for negotiations with Prince Charles of Denmark. On 17 June the Norwegian national hero Fridtjof Nansen was sent to Copenhagen as a mediator and a referendum was arranged for 13 August 1905.[46]

In this extremely delicate situation the Kaiser felt compelled to maintain 'great restraint for the time being'. As a direct result of the crisis Wilhelm decided 'for reasons of courtesy and dynastic solidarity' to abandon his habitual voyage to the Norwegian fjords that summer.[47] During his Baltic cruise he continued to behave with the requisite discretion. At his request his meeting with the Swedish King and Crown Prince Gustaf on 13 July 1905 took place not in Stockholm, but as inconspicuously as possible in the small port of Gefle in the Gulf of Finland.[48] Nevertheless fears were voiced about the powerful neighbour with his imposing naval presence.[49] Rumours circulated that Wilhelm II wanted to have his second son, Prince Eitel Friedrich, elected as King of Norway. Other German princes were also canvassed as, supposedly, the Kaiser's preferred candidates.[50]

The Norwegian succession was indeed the main topic of conversation in Gefle, but the Kaiser expressed his support for the nomination of a prince from the Swedish House of Bernadotte, not a German prince.[51] It was only with difficulty that Crown Prince Gustaf succeeded in convincing him that this was now 'practically impossible'. In Gefle, Wilhelm openly deplored the candidature of Prince Charles of Denmark and his wife, as 'the presence of an English Princess on the Norwegian throne' would signify the 'vassalage of Norway to England'. He also expressed the fear that Britain would benefit from 'commercial preponderance' in Norway from now on.[52] Wilhelm II's disappointment was evident from his dispatch of 14 July 1905 to Bülow, in which he complained that the Swedish court showed 'complete indifference to the fate of Norway and the Danish candidature seems already to be taken for granted. With the English son-in-law on the Norwegian throne the likelihood of England getting her hands on the country has greatly increased.' It was therefore all the more desirable for Germany 'to achieve a closer relationship with Denmark'.[53]

At his meeting with Nicholas II at Björkö on 23 July Wilhelm lost no opportunity to exploit the tense negotiations with Oscar and Gustaf for his own ends. On the very first evening, finding the Tsar full of indignation at Edward VII's intrigues, above all over the Norwegian question, Wilhelm told him of the state of affairs 'as it appeared from the impressions received at Gefle. The reference he made in passing, to the influence likely to be exerted as a result of English domination if the Danish Prince were chosen or a republic were established, was by no means lost on the Tsar.' Confirming the fears of Wedel Jarlsberg and Crown Prince Gustaf, Tschirschky's report of the imperial conversations continued: 'In speaking to the Tsar of this, His Majesty was able to make use of something said very confidentially at Gefle by King Oscar, who in the course of a conversation let slip the remark that of course there was nothing to prevent Germany occupying Bergen, and in response to the objection that England might have something to say about that, went on to say yes, then they would probably seize Christiansand! The Emperor Nicholas was visibly worried by the idea of Norway being divided up and of England possibly establishing a firm foothold there, and commented that ... the dangers for Russia of a blockade of the Kattegat were of course obvious.'[54]

Wilhelm II told the Reich Chancellor that when he informed Tsar Nicholas that 'King Oscar did not care who his neighbour turned out to be, and indeed had nothing against a republic', Nicholas had clapped his hands together over his head and exclaimed: 'That too – that is all we need, as if we did not already have enough republics and monarchies like that in the world, what is to become of the monarchical principle!?' On the question of the Norwegian succession the Tsar had said that 'if no Swedish Prince went and Copenhagen were interested, Prince Waldemar [the youngest brother of the widowed

Tsaritsa Maria Feodorovna and of Queen Alexandra] could go. He had a certain amount of experience, an elegant and agreeable wife [born a Princess of Orléans], and fine sturdy children.' 'I agreed with him', Wilhelm's letter to Bülow continued, 'but pointed out that according to private reports from Copenhagen the King of England had already given his consent if his son-in-law were chosen. This came as a very unwelcome surprise to the Tsar, who seemed to know nothing about it, and commented that his cousin Charles was completely unsuitable for this post, as he had never been anywhere, had no experience, and was insignificant and lazy; Waldemar would be much better. With Charles, England would stick her fingers into Norway "by fair means or foul" and increase her influence, start intrigues and eventually close off the Skagerrak by occupying Christiansand and so shut us all into the Baltic; it would also put paid to his ports on the Murman coast in the North.'[55]

When Fridtjof Nansen arrived in Copenhagen on 17 July 1905 he declared that Prince Charles of Denmark was the most popular and most suitable candidate to be king of his country. He assured the British minister, Sir Alan Johnstone, that 'no other candidate need be feared although a ridiculous rumour reached M. Michelsen that the German Emperor preferred Prince Waldemar. Raben; Wedel; Nansen; all agree that this candidature is entirely out of the question.'[56] The rumours of the Kaiser's support for Prince Waldemar infuriated King Edward VII, who instructed his Private Secretary, Francis Knollys, to leave Johnstone in no doubt that he was backing his son-in-law's candidacy. 'The King is much surprised at your thinking German Emperor is promoting Prince Waldemar's nomination to Throne of Norway instead of Prince Charles of Denmark. Matters have now gone too far, & King would consider it most unfriendly towards him personally if German Emperor's wish is carried out.'[57] Just before Kaiser Wilhelm's arrival in Copenhagen Edward VII sensed a new threat to his plans to put his son-in-law on the throne of Norway. In a cipher telegram addressed to Prince Charles he implored the entire Danish royal family to stand firm against the Kaiser's machinations.[58] When the Kaiser reached Copenhagen on 31 July 1905 he was informed in unequivocal terms through the British minister that the government in London fully supported Prince Charles's candidature for the Norwegian throne 'and that the King would be glad to know that the Emperor shared his views'. In a conversation with Prince Albert of Schleswig-Holstein, who had come with the Kaiser, Johnstone added a warning 'that any opposition would be very deeply felt by His Majesty [Edward VII]'.[59] The minister was relieved to be able to report to the King that the Kaiser had assured Prince Charles of his support.[60] In a telegram which he sent to the Tsar on his return to Rügen on 2 August the Kaiser explained why he had been unable to do anything in Copenhagen to prevent Edward VII's son-in-law from succeeding to the throne of Norway. 'The question about Charles going to Norway has been arranged up to the smallest detail, England having consented to everything, and there is nothing to be done any more. I talked with Charles about his prospects, and found him very sober, and without any illusions about his task.'[61]

As the Danish government hesitated to allow Prince Charles to be sent to Norway until Sweden had finally renounced the candidature of a prince of the House of Bernadotte,[62] the question of the succession remained in the balance for weeks. Irritated at the delay and fearful that Wilhelm II might after all try to put one of his sons on the Norwegian throne, Edward VII, who was on a visit to Marienbad, decided to take a hand in the negotiations. He ordered the British ambassador in Vienna, Sir Edward Goschen, who was also in Marienbad at the time, to send a blunt message by cipher telegram to Johnstone in Copenhagen. 'If Prince Charles were not to accept Norwegian Crown now King Edward fears that he and his family will be covered with ridicule. It is generally expected that Prince Charles will go to Norway; should he not King Edward is convinced that German Emperor will send one of his sons and much fears intrigues from that quarter are already going on.'[63] On 18 November 1905 Prince Charles of Denmark, as King Haakon VII, acceded to the throne of Norway with his British wife, but the feud with the Kaiser had contributed to Edward VII's ill-feeling towards his nephew, with lasting effect.

THE RIFT BETWEEN UNCLE AND NEPHEW

Although the Anglo-German antagonism of these years before the First World War was undoubtedly deeply rooted, it is striking how often the two monarchs were held personally responsible, both in the highest circles and in the press, for the deterioration of relations between their countries. Thus, for instance, the British Prime Minister Balfour blamed the Kaiser for the tension and following a Cabinet meeting on 28 June 1905 begged King Edward VII to do everything in his power to avoid helping 'to increase the state of European "tension" which the Emperor of Germany has so laboriously striven to create'.[64] Conversely the *Magdeburgische Zeitung* earned warm applause from the Kaiser with an article of 1 August 1905 asserting that 'some of the spiteful remarks [in the British press] have their origin in a growing recognition of the intellectual significance of Kaiser Wilhelm. They have given up their earlier attempts to dismiss him as not worth taking seriously. For a time they tried to accuse him of unbridled bellicosity. Since the visit to Tangier . . . he has been seen as the foremost wire-puller in Europe . . . As soon as there is the merest presumption of German influence in some affair or other, the cry goes up that the bogy man is at work ... Kaiser Wilhelm has no such supremacist ambitions. That is not only evident from the way he has ruled Germany up to now and from his latest speech in the venerable City Hall of Bremen but, above all, it lies in the nature of things and in the character of the nation at whose head the Kaiser stands. Germany wants nothing more for her own development than the same peace and the same elbow-room that the other nations enjoy.'[65]

On 1 August 1905 Sir Frank Lascelles confided to his Austro-Hungarian colleague Count Szögyény that 'King Edward has taken against Kaiser Wilhelm to a quite exceptional degree. His Majesty claims that his imperial nephew's behaviour towards him cannot be described otherwise than by the English word "unfair". In matters both great and small he is met with the most hostile and spiteful antagonism from Kaiser Wilhelm.' Lascelles expressly mentioned the dispute over the Norwegian succession as an example.[66] For his part Wilhelm II regarded his uncle as his bitterest adversary and spoke of him not only to his closest confidants but also to foreign ambassadors 'in very unfriendly, indeed sometimes very violent terms'.[67] In this overwrought atmosphere it was enough for news to reach London of a book critical of Britain, or for the British military attaché to appear at the German court in the wrong uniform, for a diplomatic incident to break out, keeping embassies, governments and not least the crowned heads themselves busy for weeks on end.[68]

The Kaiser's continued efforts to spread suspicion of British policy throughout the world and particularly in America by no means escaped King Edward's notice. In March 1905, while Wilhelm was on his journey to Lisbon, Tangier and Gibraltar, Knollys told Lascelles 'that the King is full of distrust of the Emperor'. While sympathising with Edward VII's attitude 'after what we know of his [Wilhelm's] attempts to sow distrust of us in other countries and more especially in America', Lascelles considered that 'these attempts have signally failed and I do not think are more likely to be successful in the future, and however much he might like to set other Nations against us, I am convinced that he does not wish to quarrel with us himself'. He urged caution: 'I presume we do not wish to quarrel with him, and therefore I think that, whilst we are quite right to be on our guard, with respect to his intrigues with Foreign Countries, we should do our best, in the real interests of the two Countries to remain on good terms with him.' This remark related particularly to King Edward's decision that he would not after all allow his son George, the Prince of Wales, to go to Berlin for the Crown Prince's wedding on 6 June 1905, as originally announced, on the grounds that the King of Spain would be visiting London at that time. In view of the tension between the two countries Lascelles considered this decision as 'most unfortunate' and 'almost a calamity'.[69]

Not without reason, the Kaiser took his uncle's decision as a conscious slight, the painful effect of which was only increased when the King paid the French Foreign Minister, Delcassé, a 'private' visit in Paris at the end of April.[70] Wilhelm's pent-up irritation with Britain suddenly erupted at the beginning of June as he waited at the station to meet Prince Arthur of Connaught, who was to represent King Edward at the wedding celebrations in place of the Prince of Wales. Lascelles was also at the station, but although the Kaiser greeted him, he avoided all political topics 'in a conspicuously deliberate way'. When the ambassador, who was about to leave for England for a few days, asked the Kaiser whether he had any message for King Edward, Wilhelm replied 'in a brusque . . . extraordinarily unfriendly tone of voice': 'I have nothing to say either to your King or to your Minister or to anyone at all in England. I want nothing to do with any of those gentlemen until they behave better towards me.' Lascelles immediately went to see the Reich Chancellor and told him he could not accept such treatment, which he found incomprehensible, and he must draw the consequences and ask his government to recall him from Berlin. Bülow too was 'greatly dismayed' by the incident and urged Lascelles 'to calm down and not to forget that with Kaiser Wilhelm's impetuous temperament His Majesty's words cannot always be taken at face value'. A few hours later the Chancellor came in person to tell the ambassador in the name of the Kaiser that Wilhelm had not had the least intention of offending Sir Frank. 'Kaiser Wilhelm', Bülow continued, 'was extremely angry about the persistently hostile attitude of the English press and in this connection accused the English government of a serious sin of omission, for he felt certain that with a little goodwill it would have been possible to put a stop to the ceaseless campaign to stir up hatred towards Germany and himself personally'. The Kaiser had been further irritated by the information recently received in Berlin, Bülow explained, that the English government had offered to conclude an offensive and defensive treaty with the French that was aimed directly against Germany, but that had been rejected by France. These and similar reports had been the reason for the Kaiser's 'harsh words', but 'no further significance' should be ascribed to them. The Reich Chancellor repeated his plea to Lascelles to disregard the whole incident. For the sake of peace Lascelles declared himself ready to let the matter drop at least for the moment, but he confessed to the Chancellor that he could not help wondering whether it would not be better to get himself recalled from Berlin, for in his ten years en poste he had not succeeded, 'despite the most assiduous efforts . . . in establishing and maintaining friendly relations between England and Germany'.[71]

When Lascelles called at the Auswärtiges Amt on 1 August 1905 on his return from leave, the Under Secretary of State, Otto von Mühlberg, at once expressed his regret at the critical state of Anglo-German relations, which had led both countries to the brink of war. In Mühlberg's opinion relations had deteriorated without any real reason. 'There was no question pending between the two countries which could cause a serious quarrel, and yet there was a general impression that a war between Germany and England – which only a few years ago would have been considered beyond the range of possibility – had become a positive contingency.' Although Lascelles countered that he did not believe in a war which England certainly did not wish and which, he hoped, no one in the German government was seeking to bring about either, he admitted that the distrust on both sides, above all at a monarchical level, had grown to a dangerous degree.[72] The ambassador entirely agreed with Mühlberg's observation that 'relations between King Edward and the Kaiser were tense at present. King Edward believed that Kaiser Wilhelm was trying to frustrate English plans wherever he possibly could.' According to Mühlberg, Lascelles complained that 'this ill-feeling was probably much increased by unsubstantiated tale-bearing and distortions of comments by our All-Gracious Lord'.[73] When the ambassador brought up the subject of the visit by the British Channel Fleet and the supposed German plan to declare the Baltic *mare clausum*, Mühlberg passionately denied 'that the German Government had ever entertained so preposterous an idea'. The thought had merely been aired in a few unimportant newspapers and had been rejected by the government on 30 July 1905 in the semi-official *Kölnische Zeitung*, the Under Secretary insisted – and said not a word about his sovereign's active canvassing of this subject. Lascelles drew attention to another reason for the distrust between the two countries: the Kaiser's machinations over the Norwegian succession, which were obviously aimed at preventing the candidature of Edward VII's son-in-law, in which the King took a great personal interest. He concluded the discussion by expressing the hope that 'means would be found, if not of coming to a friendly understanding, at all events of averting the dire calamity of war, which could not bring advantage to either country and would entail enormous loss upon both'. After reading Lascelles's report, the King praised the ambassador's 'excellent' handling of his conversation with Mühlberg.[74]

A HOT SUMMER IN MARIENBAD

It is not without irony that Kaiser Wilhelm II, whose policies for world power and naval development were so clearly directed against Great Britain and the British-guaranteed balance of power in Europe, longed to be invited to England and was increasingly irritated that his uncle Edward avoided him on his visits to the continent. When it was reported in the press in the summer of 1905 that the King might possibly pay a visit to the Kaiser on his way to Marienbad, Edward VII had these reports denied by Knollys. For Wilhelm there was not the slightest doubt that the whole business was an English intrigue intended to humiliate him and his country. The news of the imminent meeting between the two monarchs was a canard that had been deliberately spread 'to enable the démenti to be published ... The plan is quite clear!' he wrote. 'England is giving us a box on the ears by saying No.'[75]

The situation was so serious, however, that feelers were put out from the German side as to whether, in the interest of German–British relations, a meeting might be arranged between Wilhelm and his uncle, now staying at Marienbad. Count Götz von Seckendorff, the former Court Marshal and confidant of the late Empress Frederick, was among those who deeply deplored the 'the unsatisfactory state of the relations between the two countries' and blamed the imperial entourage, 'who seldom lost the opportunity of stirring up His Majesty's animosity against England'.[76] In a personal appeal of 15 August 1905 Seckendorff begged the King to visit the Kaiser at Bad Homburg on his way home from Marienbad, in order to put an end to the prevailing 'most unpleasant and untenable situation between England and Germany' in the interests of the whole world. 'I think Your Majesty would easily find means of restoring peace to the whole of Europe, the world at large ... with the happy hand, which Your Majesty has proved to do so often ... I beg to suggest that a meeting [with] the Kaiser and talking to the Emperor might create wonders.' As it happened, the Kaiser would be staying at Bad Homburg from 7 to 10 September. The King could therefore attend the drumhead service in front of the memorial to the Empress Frederick on Sunday 10 September, lunch with the Kaiser in the Castle at Homburg, then drive with him to the Saalburg and spend the night at Schloss Friedrichshof near Kronberg.[77]

King Edward regarded this well-meaning suggestion as an impertinence and instructed his Private Secretary to make quite clear to Seckendorff that for various reasons he was not prepared to meet the Kaiser in Bad Homburg. Knollys was to explain in the King's name that as far as the German Emperor was concerned, 'I have no quarrel with him of any kind. I am on the same terms that I have always been since my *accession*. Friendly letters & telegrams have been exchanged in the course of the year. I sent my nephew [Prince Arthur of Connaught] to Berlin for 2 important functions this year wh. seemed to please the E., & instantly accepted the E.'s invitation for my nephew to attend the manoeuvres next month ... That the Press of England & Germany abuse one another I can neither help or remedy. I am certainly not going to run after the E. & propose a visit even if it were possible wh. it is not. I cannot tell if the E. has any personal affection for me or not — though fr. things I have heard I think not — so that paying him visits 3 times a year would not alter matters.' As proof of the King's goodwill Knollys might also mention in his letter 'that we are inviting the Crown Prince & Pss. of Germany to pay us a visit to Windsor in Nov: & that after the departure of the French Fleet from Cowes we invited Metternich, Eisendecher, Eckhardstein & Coerper to dine with us on our Yacht!'[78] Knollys wrote as instructed, adding on his own account that a meeting between the King and the Kaiser just now, while Franco-German relations were so tense because of Morocco, would certainly be regarded with suspicion in France, 'but there is no reason why one should not take place later on when Germany & France have come to an agreement respecting Morocco & are generally on better terms. A meeting might then be for the benefit of both England & Germany & might tend to remove the feeling of mistrust with which we unfortunately regard each other at present.'[79]

Lascelles was so astonished by Seckendorff's initiative that he more than once expressed the suspicion that the Count might have acted on a hint 'from a higher quarter'. He shared the view held by the King, Lord Knollys and the British government that a meeting between the two monarchs at the present moment would be politically undesirable, but he welcomed the news that Edward VII might be willing to meet the Kaiser once the Franco-German dispute over Morocco had been settled. 'Such a meeting at the proper time would not fail to be productive of much good', he assured the King. The invitation to the Crown Prince and Princess to Windsor would undoubtedly also make 'an excellent impression in Germany'.[80]

The next time that Lascelles met Wilhelm II after the outburst at the station in early June, he reported that the Kaiser was pointedly friendly towards him. On the other hand Wilhelm had mentioned neither Anglo-German relations nor the visit of the Royal Navy to the Baltic, 'and the general impression which Sir Frank received from the whole conversation was that His Majesty, whilst almost going out of his way to show him personal civility, or indeed friendship, avoided the more important questions which affected the relations between our two Countries'. Even more disappointing than his refusal to touch on political matters, however, was the Kaiser's announcement 'that the Crown Prince would not be able to accept Your Majesty's invitation, as the date which Your Majesty had fixed coincided with the time when the King of Spain would visit Berlin, and moreover about that time an important function would take place at which the presence of His Imperial Highness would be required'.[81] Lascelles later reported to the King that he had heard from Wilhelm's sister, the Crown Princess of Greece, that 'the real reason for the Emperor's refusal to allow the Crown Prince to accept Your Majesty's invitation' was jealousy. Wilhelm 'wished so strongly to pay a visit to England himself that he would not let the Crown Prince go there until he could go himself. "The fact is" said Her Royal Highness "that we all love England, and he as much as any of us."'[82]

This rebuff, understandably, aroused King Edward's anger. When the Crown Prince wrote to decline his invitation, Edward VII responded in a letter heavy with irony, on 5 September 1905: 'My dear Willy, I was indeed sorry & at the same time, I must say surprised to learn from your letter that you & Cecile are unable to pay us a visit at Windsor which we had also so looked for[ward] to. As you write that "unhappily your Papa objects to your going away to England this year" there is nothing more to be said on the subject. – Another year it will probably be the same story as I have reason to believe that your Father does not *like* your coming to England!'[83] On his journey home from Marienbad the King deliberately bypassed Bad Homburg without calling on the Kaiser.

The quarrel between the two monarchs now escalated to an alarming degree. As Lascelles confided to his Austrian colleague, Count Szögyény, it was now 'Kaiser Wilhelm's turn to feel injured and to remonstrate against the tone of the letter [to the Crown Prince]. In his impulsive way His Majesty did not seem to be satisfied to tackle this family matter merely by a direct exchange of letters; he also asked the English Ambassador to make representations in his name. Sir Frank told me he had at first wanted to protest against having this not very pleasant task imposed on him, and had again told His Majesty of his intention, which he had already declared once before, of leaving his post here.' Wilhelm, however, had refused to accept Lascelles's proffered resignation, commenting jokingly that it was for just such tasks that ambassadors existed. Lascelles asked the Kaiser 'at least to permit him to say in his report that Kaiser Wilhelm regretted the deterioration of his relations with King Edward. "Yes", was His Majesty's response after a moment's reflection, "you may say so, but you must also say that it is not my fault that it has gone so far." "In spite of the sad fact of the matter", Sir Frank commented, "I could not help laughing inwardly, for King Edward had used almost exactly the same words to me not long before."'[84]

Lascelles sent an anxious telegram to Lord Knollys reporting that Kaiser Wilhelm 'did not conceal his annoyance & irritation at the letter which the King had written to the Crown Prince, & about which he intended to write to H.M. himself, as the remarks about himself amounted almost to a personal insult. It seemed as if the King was seeking a quarrel with him, & he cited other instances which he considered gave him grounds for complaint. I will report fully by next Bag, but I think it right to ask you to tell the King that the Emperor intends to write to him & it will no doubt be a strong (?) letter.'[85] Lascelles dispatched his full report on the affair direct to the King on 13 September 1905. In it he repeated the Kaiser's complaint that the letter to the Crown Prince had contained remarks that amounted almost to a personal insult. The King had taken it amiss that the Crown Prince was declining an invitation to England for the second time, Wilhelm said, but in both cases there had been important reasons for refusing. The first invitation had arrived shortly after his son's engagement and it would have been 'scarcely decent' for him to have abandoned his fiancée. And now the Crown Prince had to attend an important reception in southern Germany immediately after the visit of the King of Spain. 'There was moreover a Rule of the House of Hohenzollern that the Princes of the House must obtain the consent of the Sovereign to their leaving the Country, and it was usual for any Foreign Sovereign who wished to invite them to ascertain beforehand whether this consent would be forthcoming. This course had always been pursued by Queen Victoria who used to obtain the consent of the Emperor William I before addressing an invitation to her Grandson. The King had not thought it necessary to follow this course and the Emperor considered that he had a right to feel aggrieved as it looked as if His Majesty was seeking to "get hold" of the Crown Prince without his father's consent . . . The Emperor said that he intended to write himself to the King on this point. It was entirely wrong to think that he had any objection to the Prince's going to England, and he thought that his acts had proved the contrary. Even before the Crown Prince had finished his University education, he had encouraged him to go to England in the hope that he might learn something of the People . . . It was true that there were certain incidents connected with His Imperial Highness's visit which might have made him hesitate about allowing him to return for some time. There had been unseemly romping in unlighted corridors. One lady had absolutely gone to the length of taking off her slipper, and another had appeared in a kilt without any stockings. It was only some time after the Crown Prince's return and by slow degrees that these incidents became known to the Empress who was naturally very much shocked. He himself most highly disapproved of what had taken place, more especially on account of the Crown Prince's youthful age at the time.'

After this the Kaiser brought out a whole catalogue of further complaints against his uncle which had built up over the course of time. Wilhelm had given the astonished ambassador to understand, the latter reported, 'that this was not the only matter on which he considered he had a right to feel aggrieved. The King on his return from Marienbad had passed in the near neighbourhood, and it would have been easy to arrange a meeting, which would have given him great pleasure, if His Majesty had asked it. He knew that the idea had been entertained. It was no good my shaking my head for he knew what had taken place. The Press had spoken of it approvingly and suddenly Lord Knollys caused a statement to be published to the effect that the idea had never been entertained. There did not seem to be any necessity for such a statement the curtness of which was generally taken in Germany as an insult to him. This was the second time in the course of the conversation that the Emperor used the word "insult". Then again the King had taken no notice of the reception given to His Majesty's Fleet in German Ports. The reception had been a good one and he had sent his Fleet to greet their English comrades. He thought he was not unreasonable in expecting that the King would have sent him some acknowledgement of what he had certainly intended as a civility. Barely a year had passed since the King's visit to Kiel at which His Majesty had expressed his satisfaction, and more especially at his reception in Hamburg, the cordiality of which His Majesty himself had said could not have been exceeded even at Liverpool. His Majesty had then had a political conversation with Bülow with which he had been perfectly satisfied. Now every thing was deranged, and the Emperor really did not know why unless indeed the King wished to quarrel with him. He would himself write to His Majesty about the invitation to the Crown Prince, and it would be for me to bring the other points to His Majesty's notice and to place his views before him.' Lascelles had protested that the Kaiser was putting him in a 'very difficult and delicate' position, but Wilhelm, 'in the most friendly manner', had replied 'Why that is what you are here for.'[86]

King Edward could not believe his eyes when he received Lascelles's report. He wrote indignantly to Knollys: 'Of course I know that the young man [the Crown Prince] could not come over here without his Father's permission, so the G. E.'s most silly remarks on that point are beside the question. The real truth is that he was jealous of my asking his son at all. ... The whole tone of G. E.'s language to Lascelles is one of peevish complaint against me. I consider it totally uncalled for. But he wisely does not touch on politics as that is the subject which might lead forcibly to a serious quarrel & is therefore best avoided ... The social matters alluded to by the G. E. are almost too trivial to be taken notice of.' He hoped that in time a meeting with the Kaiser could be arranged, 'but during the remainder of this year I do not think it will be possible'.[87]

Knollys did not mince his words in the reply sent to Lascelles on the King's instructions. 'The Emperor must really be anxious for a quarrel when he complains of the denial which appeared in the English newspapers as to a meeting between the King & him, & says that it was looked upon as an "insult to him". The absurdity of this statement & his ridiculous touchiness, make it unnecessary for me to enter into this complaint of his — one among many others equally trivial. I will only remark that the King (& I think he was perfectly right) considered that in the interests of the two Countries it was desirable to put an end to the reports, that were prevalent, that he intended to meet the Emperor on going to or coming from Marienbad, & that notwith-standing what the Emperor, with his superior knowledge on everything, said to you, both Balfour & Lansdowne thought that it would be very unpopular in this Country. I mean of course at that particular time. Have you any idea why, if the Emperor wants the King to pay him a visit, he uses the language he does about him ... & why [he] also constantly intrigues against England? If he ceased doing these two things, I have no doubt the King would be glad to meet him when a good opportunity presented itself. But you must remember that the King proposed to go to Berlin a year & a half ago, but was then told that the Emperor, who appears to suppose that nobody has any engage-ments but himself, was recovering from an illness & had to go to the Mediterranean, though it would only have been a question of a short post-ponement of his journey ... I fear the Emperor is rather a Bully. I am very glad he was so amiable to you the other day, especially when you alluded to your resignation ... but what an impossible man he must be to deal with.' There was no question of a meeting between Wilhelm and the King for the time being, Knollys declared. 'Perhaps *next year*, unless the Emperor continues to trump up imaginary grievances against the King & to intrigue, whenever he has an opportunity against this Country.'[88]

Finally the two ambassadors, Lascelles and Metternich, met to discuss the unfortunate state of affairs but came to the conclusion, considering the reciprocal accusations of the two monarchs and the animosity displayed by public opinion in each country towards the other, that an improvement in Anglo-German relations was unattainable at present. Even the possibility of a meeting between the two monarchs should not be discussed 'until the mutual suspicion which unfortunately existed in both Countries should have become somewhat allayed'.[89] In a private letter of 2 October 1905 Metternich told the Chancellor that it had transpired from his conversation with Lascelles that Edward VII claimed to have no quarrel with the Kaiser but was convinced that the Kaiser 'was trying to exert his influence everywhere against him, the King'. Metternich went on to say that it was apparent 'that the time was not yet ripe for a discussion or a reconciliation between Their Majesties. The more calmly His Majesty the Kaiser behaves in response to his royal Uncle's displeasure, the more the latter is put in the wrong, and the sooner a proper

relationship between the two rulers will be established. I know for certain that
the personal quarrel between Kaiser and King is already regarded by the
leading English statesmen as highly undesirable on political grounds. As soon
as it becomes clearer to them that the fault lies with the King, and that the
personal relationship between the two rulers threatens to give rise to political
disturbances, they will themselves try to act as mediators with the King, for
his subjects do not have the slightest desire to risk their lives fighting the
Germans just because the uncle doesn't like his nephew. His Majesty King
Edward is clever enough to give way himself as soon as he feels that he has
gone too far. Only one must leave this process of recognition to the English
themselves', Metternich warned. 'If we did anything that could be interpreted
as an attempt by us to turn the English against their own King, they would be
unanimous in supporting him and making a stand against us.'[90]

The chances that the Kaiser would behave calmly in order to put his uncle
in the wrong were not rated highly either by the two ambassadors or by
Bülow. With his sovereign's impulsive nature in mind the Chancellor sent a
warning to Wilhelm's friend Prince Philipp zu Eulenburg, who went to
Rominten at the end of September 1905 to join the Kaiser. 'The world
situation is very uncertain and tense at the moment. Our enemies are on the
lookout for us to show weakness. If we do, with the hostile mood in England,
the distrust of the Japanese, the unpredictability of the French and the
uncertainty in Russia, the consequences could be alarming for Austria-
Hungary and Italy. We must not show any nervousness outwardly, but behave
more than ever with firmness, calm and courage. Nor must we allow ourselves
any incautious or impulsive behaviour: it would be inappropriate to the
situation.' In the discussions he was about to have at Rominten with the
Russian minister, Sergei Witte, the Kaiser must at all costs avoid 'outraged
recriminations against England', nor must he 'show any nervousness'
regarding Japan.[91] The descriptions of the imperial mood which Eulenburg
sent him from Rominten certainly did little to reassure the Reich Chancellor.
With his old familiarity Wilhelm 'explained the *whole* course of the policy'
and decked it out 'with 100 details', so that Eulenburg often had difficulty in
distinguishing 'the line between reality and fantasy . . . At times he wants to
impress, at others to amuse – sometimes there is no purpose at all behind it –
just one of his habits . . . From all this the picture that seems to me to stand out
most truthfully is that of the antagonism between Uncle Berty and Nephew
Willy, and it seems very worthy of note because the *strongest* impulse driving
all actions – and so also in politics – will always be personal passion. In some
natures envy has the strongest influence, in others it is revenge. In Uncle Berty
both are perhaps combined, for the "moral indignation" of the nephew over

the playboy uncle has probably never been forgotten by the latter. Also as the leader of mighty England he now wants to make himself heard more than his nephew.'[92]

Until well into the winter Wilhelm II fumed with anger against his uncle and against Britain in general. Lascelles admitted to Count August Eulenburg, who had expressed concern about the ill-feeling between Germany and Britain, that 'if I had reported to London everything that your All-Gracious Lord has said to me, we would already have had war between England and Germany twenty times over'.[93] In October 1905 the Hofmarschall Count Zedlitz recorded: 'The Kaiser's ill-humour with the King of England is even more deep-rooted than I thought . . . I am afraid this mood finds its expression every now and then and of course it will not remain a secret but will increase the tension even more.'[94] The Kaiser told his entourage that he had asked the King, through Lascelles, whether he was trying to pick a quarrel with him by travelling through his country as he had, without taking any notice of the Kaiser. Lascelles had answered, on behalf of the King, that 'the King was put out that the Kaiser was spreading malicious gossip about him throughout Europe, and therefore he had not been able to pay him a visit'.[95]

THE POSTPONED WAR 'AGAINST ENGLAND AND GAUL'

Wilhelm II's conviction that King Edward, together with the French Foreign Minister, Théophile Delcassé, had been planning an attack on Germany and that this had been prevented only by his landing in Tangier and the related threat of a German invasion of France, was given a new lease of life when on 6 October 1905 the Paris *Matin* published what purported to be revelations about the fall of Delcassé. The newspaper reported that Britain had given the French government a verbal promise, in the event of a German attack on France, to mobilise her fleet, seize the Kaiser Wilhelm Canal and land a hundred thousand men in Schleswig-Holstein.[96] Downing Street's assurances that the British government had never made any such promise were scorned by the Kaiser as 'empty excuses!' 'The *King* promised [it] personally to Delcassé himself! Not the government.'[97]

Delcassé's 'revelations' put Wilhelm into a state of high excitement once again. On 11 October he wrote to the King's brother-in-law, Prince Christian of Schleswig-Holstein, who lived in England, a melodramatic letter about the rift between Germany and Britain. Enclosing a German press report on the Delcassé revelations, he fulminated: 'That is the *real reason* for the "Entente Cordiale", from Brest and Cowes! They quietly come to an agreement to attack a neighbouring country and even divide it up straight away!

Naturally your poor homeland [Schleswig-Holstein] has to be the one to suffer, as the operational target of a British invasion force to be landed at *Esbjerg* in *Jutland*. The British fleet carried out the necessary reconnaissance precisely there in the autumn, as the Danes told us. Now you can just imagine the mood here after this revelation from the Minister's own mouth! It is deeply felt; and our people, especially your compatriots here, are profoundly hurt! But the general view here is that the tried and tested Schleswig-Holstein territorial army will be enough to give uninvited visitors of that sort such a reception that they could neither go home nor come back again. Delcassé's indiscretions have revealed the real background behind the speeches of Mr Lee, Admiral Fitzgerald etc, and the suspicion that the English, in alliance with France, were planning an attack on German coasts is completely confirmed! We have been warned! And will not let ourselves be taken by surprise!'[98]

In an important dispatch of 18 October 1905 Metternich explored the question of what circumstances would have caused Great Britain to intervene in a war between France and Germany, and emphasised that the British government '[could] always interpret the grounds and the reason for the war in such a way as to put us in the wrong in English eyes'.[99] In marginal comments on this telegram Kaiser Wilhelm repeated his conviction that 'at any moment' a German attack on France could be 'provoked' through 'politically outrageous behaviour' on the part of the French. In a Franco-German war England would 'certainly' take the view that Germany was in the wrong and she would therefore give military support to the French. 'That was the most important thing, the explanation our Philistines needed!' he commented. The contrary view taken by the Liberal opposition in England would be of 'no significance', for 'the public [was] on the other side'.[100]

At the beginning of December 1905 the Conservative government in London resigned, as had long been expected. In the new Liberal Cabinet led by Henry Campbell-Bannerman, Sir Edward Grey took over the Foreign Office and Lord Haldane, who was known to be particularly pro-German, became Secretary of State for War. At the same time meetings were held both in London and in towns in the Midlands and the north of England at which strong support was shown for reconciliation between Britain and Germany. The impetus for these came from the Kaiser's friend Lord Lonsdale who, however, remained in the background, as he knew that King Edward was prejudiced against him.[101] At this point Metternich made what he thought might be the last possible attempt to improve German–British relations. He reported several signs that the British people were beginning 'to come to their senses and see reason' and warned strongly against rejecting their proffered hand of friendship. 'We are at the turning point in our relations with England', he telegraphed on 3 December 1905 following rallies at the Junior United Services Club and the Lyceum Club in London at which numerous prominent Britons, including Lord Avebury and Lady Aberdeen, had testified to their friendship for Germany. 'If we . . . now coldly reject significant and spontaneous demonstrations of conciliatory attitudes, we must give up for ever any hope of improving our relationship with England', for 'whether we shall ever have another opportunity of winning back public opinion in England, even if it is only very slowly, nobody knows'.[102] The next day Metternich appealed directly to the Reich Chancellor to make clear to the Kaiser that 'the psychological moment for a rapprochement between the two nations, at least as far as England is concerned, has come; that there is an unmistakable wish here for a reconciliation and that it has been expressed publicly . . . Why should we not grasp the proffered hand with caution and without exaggerated expressions of friendship? . . . It can only be beneficial to the German fatherland if the dangerous tension between the two nations is eased.' The ambassador added that he knew from a reliable source 'that His Majesty King Edward also wishes for a settlement of personal and political differences, no doubt from a feeling that he went too far in the opposite direction last summer'. The Kaiser should give a friendly reply to the conciliatory telegram from Avebury which had been sent to him, Metternich urged, and he should declare that he fully supported the efforts being made to bring about a rapprochement.[103]

Kaiser Wilhelm, burning with resentment, rejected Metternich's warnings and advice out of hand. 'It is too early for that – we have been too deeply hurt!' he wrote on his ambassador's dispatch. 'Unless H.M. [the King] takes part indirectly' in the demonstrations 'or expresses his interest in them! they are of little use!' He would not send a friendly answer to Avebury's telegram unless 'H.M. E[dward] VII does it too and takes official notice of the Meeting!' 'Metternich is somewhat optimistic', the Kaiser commented. 'It is certainly gratifying that after 10 years of continuous vituperation and intrigue a few ladies and gentlemen and a few – not the most important – representatives of the Press come together to express their sympathy with Germany. I am happy to welcome these events as the first signs and symptoms of the development of a better relationship. But this must first be put to the test in the actions of the government, in its *policy*. When it stops surrounding England and filling the North Sea with squadrons against us, when it stops stirring up trouble for us in Paris and offers to help bring the French into an Entente Cordiale with us, when it stops setting the Russians against us and inciting the Poles, when it stops intriguing against us in America and instead holds out its hand to us in all honesty, saying *pater peccavi* with the comment: *Soyons Amis Cinna!*; when the King publicly changes his attitude to me and my country, only then will I believe that England wants to keep on friendly terms with us. Until then I most certainly will *not*. A few dinners with a few well-meaning words are no longer enough to satisfy me, after what I have experienced! I cannot be bought so cheaply any more. Above all, H.M. E[dward] VII will have to approach me himself!'[104] 'The *King* and his Government and his Parliament must offer me *England's hand!* Not Lady Aberdeen!!!' The movement for reconciliation in England was 'no more than the result of the Delcassé revelations, which have made the British feel shamefully exposed and taken in, and now, since the attack on us failed, we are expected to forget it all immediately!!'[105] The Reich Chancellor could answer Avebury's telegram on his behalf, the Kaiser ordered. '*I* shall most *certainly not* do so! It is not impossible that the whole affair is no more than a cunning *coup* devised by the King to soften our anger and its military consequences! while he calmly goes on with his intrigues and hopes to catch us out like stupid fools! I do not share Metternich's optimistic views! The speeches of a few insignificant gentlemen and ladies at a meeting and in a ladies' club mean absolutely nothing with regard to the way the English *behave* and *act* towards us. Not until H.M. changes *his policy* towards me, not until his representative at the *Moroccan Conference* works hand in hand with mine, calms the French down and tries to reconcile them with us; not until the statesmen *emphasise* officially and publicly in parliament that it is necessary that peace with us *must* be maintained, *not until then* will I believe it and change my attitude and conduct! What is more, *at this moment* a new fleet of six ships aimed directly against Germany is being formed in the North Sea! That means more than all the speeches and dinners.'[106] If Britain wanted better relations with Germany, he wrote on 20 December 1905, 'the government must at long last put a complete stop to the secret English Press campaign against us in Gaul, Belgium, Russia and America'.[107]

DISILLUSIONMENT: WILHELM'S INTERVIEW WITH SIR ALFRED BEIT

It was only at the very end of the year that the Kaiser became aware, as a result of new information from Britain and France, of the enormous danger represented by a war with these countries. On 28 December 1905 he received Sir Alfred Beit at the Neues Palais in Potsdam. Beit, a British–South African diamond millionaire born in Hamburg, was a friend of Cecil Rhodes and also had contacts with Edward VII, though these were not as close as the Kaiser believed. Their conversation made a deep impression on Wilhelm, who described it in a long, excited letter to Bülow. 'When I remarked that it was very gratifying that on all sides in meetings etc people were bestirring themselves and trying to reduce the friction, he [Beit] interrupted in his rapid, animated manner, saying that he fully agreed, and all the more so because England certainly wanted nothing at all from us except to be on a good footing with us. Morocco was the only difficult point. When I asked why, he answered: because in England it was generally thought that we wanted to make war on the French *because* they had come to an agreement with England and had concluded the "Entente Cordiale". I told him that "it was utter nonsense"! The English could make as many "ententes cordiales" with France as they wanted, it made no more difference to us than the Gallo-Russian Alliance, which had not worried us either.' England, however, had not had any right to allow preferential rights in Morocco to France at the expense of the other countries. 'Moreover it was very improper that no one had seen fit to give us the slightest morsel of information about an agreement in which our rights were ignored. In addition the English intrigues in Paris, which had come out through the Delcassé revelations, were grounds enough for us not to be in the rosiest of moods, but rather to have the impression that we were dealing with two highwaymen who by prior arrangement were getting ready to attack a man out for a walk; one would naturally grab a revolver in those circumstances! Mr Beit interrupted me animatedly and declared that as far as the *offer* of armed help mentioned in the Delcassé revelations was concerned, "*that had been intended only in the event that Germany attacked France unlawfully!*" England felt bound to France in the Moroccan question as a result of the "Entente Cordiale" and would support the French claims because that had been stipulated in the agreement and they wanted above all to retain the friendship of France. Therefore, in the event of a war between Germany and France, England considered herself absolutely committed to come immediately to the aid of the latter, *and she would certainly do so.* But no one in England had any intention of starting a war with Germany or even attacking us alone on their own initiative; public opinion as a whole would be absolutely opposed to that, for the people wanted at all costs to be on good terms with us. The government, whose members he knew, also wished for this and would do everything to promote friendly feelings. But that was why it was enormously important that the wretched Moroccan question should disappear from the agenda, for it weighed very heavily on the English, precisely because of the prospect of war between Germany and France. When I again declared that there was no question of that, we would be able to cope with the French so long as London left them in peace, Beit said that in France people believed as much as in London in an *imminent outbreak* of war! Rouvier, whom he had been to see a few days earlier, had also told him this when they had discussed the [Algeciras] Conference, which he thought would probably work itself out gradually, but he was very worried about surprises, "car il est incontestable qu'il y a quelque chose dans l'air" [for it is undeniable that there is something in the air]. As if that were not enough, Beit had discovered in Paris that preparations for a war were being made in secret! The reserve officers had received their call-up orders for the end of February, the presumed date of the outbreak of war, and everywhere measures had been taken to prepare for it as far as possible short of direct mobilisation. The mood in Paris had been serious, worried but firm and determined. The fright they had felt in the spring was over and, knowing that English help was assured, people were in good spirits. I replied that since the revelations we had never doubted that England would stand by France – and in general would always be on the side of our enemies. All this fear of war among the French was ridiculous, bordering on madness; if they decided to behave in a *loyal* and *gentlemanlike* way at the Conference they would find the same attitude on our part, and I hoped that in the course of it a *good understanding* would develop. So there was no reason at all for any war or for any concern about an attack by us. But the cause of this whole disagreeable business was to be found not in France but in *London*! It was the cursed campaign of hatred against us organised by the English, working systematically and secretly in the Press of all countries, planting unscrupulous slander, lies and suspicion to prejudice and incite everyone against us! "Do you believe that the English government is doing this?" Beit asked. I answered "No! But English capital from rich men of private means who thereby render *indirect* service to the government! I have been informed by Frenchmen that England has put 300,000 francs into the Press in Paris for anti-German inflammatory articles! Beit *confirmed* this; he had not known the sum, but the *fact* was absolutely *correct*! The Russians likewise had sums of money that they set to work in Paris, also against us; there again I knew the sum, 360 000 frcs.! Beit added "monthly"! Likewise I knew from Belgium, where the Liberal party leaders, who were keen to be on friendly neighbourly terms with us, complained that they could not influence their Press because it was quite simply *bribed by England* and under anti-German editorial control! Just as in Russia, where influential papers have been bought and provided with poison against us! These operations abroad are complemented by the systematic calumny which has gone on for years in countless English periodicals in which the people who sign themselves Calchas, Diplomaticus, one who knows, Vales etc. have served up to the English public the most outrageous, shameless slanders and lies about Germany and myself, which are never contradicted and are therefore believed ... Then Beit went on to say that what I complained about was right, the Press had behaved quite indescribably and was chiefly to blame for the situation today ... It was also unfortunately true that much English money had been fed to the Press for corrupt and evil purposes. But the first step had now been taken towards an honest rapprochement, and he promised me to use all his influence to have the Press campaign of hatred stopped. He would do so all the more gladly because he was convinced by what I had said that I honestly wished for peace and did not intend to attack the French, as *he had been led to believe in London* and Paris. He was sure that His Majesty K[ing] E[dward] VII also only wanted peace; only recently an officer had said to him, speaking of the Boer War, that the *next* war would go better, they had prepared themselves better for it, whereupon H.M. exclaimed "there shan't be any more war. I [won't] have any more war, Peace, Peace, Peace!" That feeling was shared by all the members of the government and by both City and commercial circles throughout England. *None of them* wanted *war*; they were only worried because of Morocco and the possibility that they might have to come to the aid of the French if they were attacked. He would however allay this fear in London. I added that he would do well to take steps at once to get the Press campaign in Paris stopped, for although we had the best intentions and wanted to be loyal and remain peaceful, the danger could not be ruled out that if London continued to whip up the French, they might eventually — trusting to the English help of which they could be sure — be so rude, intractable and provocative in their behaviour towards us that our national honour would come into play and we would have to resort to arms for its sake; then we would have to strike out, which would provide grounds for England's assistance, i.e. the "unlawful attack" by us on France. And it was a monstrous act of perfidy to seek to bring about such a thing. Mr Beit said at once: that should and must on no account be allowed to happen; I shall say in London that in Berlin there is only one wish, that London should leave Paris in peace once and for all, so that Paris can get along with Berlin and find its *modus vivendi*. England made her Entente Cordiale with France without interference from Berlin; out of politeness she should now refrain from putting any difficulties in Germany's way, even if the latter wants to come to a similar Entente with France; on the contrary, London should support Berlin and encourage Paris to agree. As regards his earlier remarks about the government's love of peace, he had one more comment to add. For there was one person who wanted war, had made detailed preparations for it and was stirring up support for it, and that was Sir John Fisher. He had recently said: "We are now quite ready and as powerful as possible, the Germans are not yet ready and are weak, now is the time for us let us hit them on the head." I replied

that I had taken this for granted from Sir John Fisher and I had instituted
precautionary measures accordingly; as far as I was concerned all arrangements in the British Navy since November 1904 had been preparations for
mobilisation and war and had been taken into account as such. "Now",
Mr Beit responded, "do not take that to heart any further, Fisher is a hothead
but has no say on policy and *has to* fall in line with the government. Similarly
when Admirals make speeches after dinner you must not take that too
seriously, as for example the ridiculous threat to land 100,000 men on you,
that is of course nonsense and too stupid!" I then explained that it was not
nonsense at all but quite easy to accomplish, given the colossal numerical
superiority of the English navy, and in particular in Denmark, where the
British fleet had carried out reconnaissance this last summer. "Indeed?" said
Mr Beit, "that is possible?! Yes, but once they have landed you kill them all?!"
To that I replied: "That is quite another matter and it is purely our affair!"
He nearly burst with laughter.' Finally, when Beit told the Kaiser that the
Berlin correspondent of the *Times*, George Saunders, had 'only recently
telegraphed to London that he knew from an irreproachable source that *within
two months* – in other words by the end of February – *war was to be declared
from here*!!!', Wilhelm dismissed this as an outright lie.[108]

This lively discussion and the information given him by Beit gave the
Kaiser much food for thought. The next day, 29 December 1905, he drew up
a list for the Reich Chancellor of the "very important" insights he had gained.
'Firstly, that in the Moroccan affair England and France will act like two
allies. That Fisher is passionately keen to use the opportunity to destroy our
Navy and our Merchant Navy . . . That for this purpose the foreign – Parisian
Press – is being very strongly worked on, with English private capital, to
embolden the Gauls as much as possible and persuade them to provoke us, in
order to have the *casus foederis*. That our Chief of the Admiralty Staff saw and
judged the situation quite rightly in regarding the naval changes begun in
November 04 as preparations for war and not merely as ordinary rearrange-
ments. That the reports from Flotow [the ambassador] and Mutius [the German
military attaché in Paris] on the mood in Paris are perfectly correct; the Gauls,
determined to fight although with heavy hearts, stand solidly and firmly
united behind their government; they have in fact made and are still making
numerous preparations for war which will *prevent them being taken by surprise*
and make invasion considerably more difficult. That the deadline telegraphed
to London by Saunderson [sic] – although fictitious – is accepted as genuine in
London and Paris, which is clear from the fact that England has sent a cruiser
to Kiel to observe us and see whether we are already at the stage of secretly
preparing for mobilisation, and that the Gauls are *now* sending yet another

cruiser to Copenhagen to see whether defensive measures are being prepared in Denmark by the Danes or by us. It also tallies with the *new formation* – just completed – of the English North Sea (Eastern Squadron) squadron – 6 ships of the line, 5 cruisers – and the concentration of all English naval fighting forces – 33 ships of the line, 25 armoured cruisers – ordered for the beginning of *February*, off the coast of Portugal ... This deadline (February) has been confirmed to me from another quarter as well, by Mirbach [the Kaiserin's Senior Court Chamberlain], who has just spent a month in Belgium. More than a dozen mothers-in-law of French reserve officers from his [Belgian] wife's circle of family and friends came to see him in floods of tears, asking whether he knew if it was true that war would break out in two months. When he roared with laughter at this the ladies got very angry and told him they had heard from their sons-in-law that they had all been instructed to be ready to report for duty in February, as Germany was going to declare war then. And they had all written their wills! Mirbach earnestly admonished the ladies not to believe such rubbish and authorised them to write to Paris saying it was all nonsense and lies. The dragons did so at once, breathing sighs of relief. – That, moreover, in London only the cooperation with France over the Moroccan question leads to war; but otherwise – because then France would not be directly involved – England does not want war with us, it does not appeal to large sections of the population. That H.M. E[dward] VII has also become more peaceable and no longer wants war as such ... That – and this is the most important thing of all – *England really did make an offer of military support to France* – Mr Beit admitted it straight out, except for some qualifi- cations – and still maintains her support! So Lansdowne lied to Metternich, which of course we at once took for granted, and that is why he could not issue a démenti. – That the reports from our gentlemen in Paris are right and their observations are exact and correct, i.e. that the Gauls are no longer frightened of us as they were in the spring, which is also demonstrated by all their military literature.'[109]

The combined impact of the information given him by Alfred Beit on 28 December 1905, his consultations with his most senior military officers and the news of France's preparations for war at last compelled Wilhelm II to recognise that his great plan to unite Europe under his own leadership by forming an alliance with Tsarist Russia and threatening war against France had failed for the time being because of Britain's determined resistance, and not least also because of the growing opposition in Germany. In his infamous New Year's Eve letter of 31 December 1905, quoted earlier, the Kaiser ordered his Chancellor to change course from the foreign policy pursued hitherto, which carried a high risk of war, and to do everything possible to avoid a

European war until further notice. Germany must 'not do England the favour of taking on the odium of attacking France on account of Morocco, so that the English at last have the desired opportunity to set upon us in the fine guise of "protecting the weak against aggression",' the Kaiser ordered. 'If you, my dear Bülow, are reckoning on the prospect of a possible war which might arise from France's behaviour at the Conference, you ought to be very active in seeking out our allies.' Most important of all, since war against Britain and France would turn into a 'world war', Germany must seek to conclude an alliance with the Ottoman Empire 'which would place the Mohammedan forces to the furthest possible extent − under Prussian leadership − at my disposal, and likewise with all Arab rulers. *For on our own we are not in a position to wage war against an alliance of Gaul and England.*' War in the coming year would be 'particularly unpropitious', the Supreme War Lord warned, as the artillery was being rearmed with a new recoil gun; and the infantry, too, was being re-equipped with new rifles. 'Thus in technical military terms we are not at a stage at which I as Supreme War Lord would happily agree to send our Army into action without further ado, especially on account of Morocco.' The Kaiser went on to identify three further reasons for the weak position in which Germany found herself. 'The flaws in the situation arise from the fact that 1) our diplomats in England have completely failed to get on good terms with Edward VII and win him over; 2) our Press has mercilessly provoked and angered the English in the most shameless way − consciously and unconsciously; 3) the Reichstag, by refusing to expand and increase the fleet for the first ten years of our reign, has set us back in such a way in relation to the other naval powers that we are well-nigh powerless. *We are absolutely defenceless against a comb[ination] of France and England's navy.* We would also have done better in the past years to try out the system of balances and agreements which Edward VII follows in such a masterly way, rather than always putting ourselves in the position of the piqued injured party insisting on his rights. There again our scoundrel Press committed terrible sins! ... So I would very strongly advise that matters should be arranged so that as far as is at all possible, we are spared the necessity of deciding to go to war for the time being.' Finally, Wilhelm pointed out, the mood in Germany itself would make a foreign war a most hazardous undertaking at the present time. In a bloodthirsty postscript to his letter the Kaiser added: 'At a moment like this when the Socialists are preaching and preparing open rebellion, I cannot take a single man out of the country without the greatest danger to the life and property of its citizens. First [we must] shoot down the Socialists, behead them and render them harmless − if necessary by a bloodbath − and then [fight a] war against the foreign foe!

But not beforehand and not *a tempo*. With kind regards and good wishes for the New Year, and may it bring us blessings on our work, Your true friend Wilhelm.'[110] Two weeks before the beginning of the international conference on Morocco in Algeciras, which had been convened only under pressure from the Reich's threats of war against France, Kaiser Wilhelm gave an unmistakable signal that he was not after all prepared to go to war against Britain and France over Morocco.

CHAPTER SIXTEEN

Humiliation in Algeciras

On 16 January 1906 the international conference to settle the Moroccan question was convened in Algeciras, not far from Gibraltar. Apart from the German Reich and the other European Great Powers, Russia, Austria-Hungary, France and Great Britain, it was attended by the United States, Italy, Spain, Portugal, Belgium, the Netherlands, Sweden, Norway and Morocco. As there were only forty-six decent rooms available in the small southern Spanish port, most of the delegates found themselves living together for several months in the hotel *Reina Cristina*. Each diplomat's facial expressions were closely observed, every word was minutely analysed, discussed in whispers and reported back to the respective capitals.

While the French and German delegates in Algeciras spent weeks wrangling over the smallest questions of detail – the most contentious issue, together with that of international control of the port police, proved to be the supervision of the Moroccan Central Bank – in the sphere of Great Power politics a seismic shift of global significance was becoming apparent. It was only the German threat of war that had induced France, militarily unprepared at the time and lacking the support of her ally Russia, to agree in the summer of 1905 to submit her claims in Morocco to negotiation at an international conference. At that time, with the fall of Delcassé and the acceptance by his successor Rouvier of the German demand for a conference, Kaiser Wilhelm II believed he was close to his goal of a European continental league under German domination, aimed against Britain, America and Japan. Since then, however, the balance of power and with it the prospect of a German triumph at Algeciras had changed once more. Russia had not accepted the alliance with Germany offered at Björkö, and France had expended a great deal of effort in improving the defensive installations on her eastern border. Rouvier had proved no more tractable than his predecessor Delcassé. His decision to accept Germany's demand for a conference was attributable not least to the American President Theodore Roosevelt's assurance that the United States would not allow France to be humiliated. Furthermore, France had come to secret agreements with both Spain and Italy as a result of which she could expect support for her Moroccan policy from these countries too. The economic straits in which Russia found herself after her defeat in the war against Japan and the revolutionary upheavals at home were so acute that France could be certain that the Russians would be dependent on French financial aid. What was to prove the crucial factor was the support of the supreme naval Power, Great Britain, whose determination to stand by France to the last, as Sir Alfred Beit had again made clear to the Kaiser on 28 December 1905, was beyond dispute. Thus even before the opening of the conference, contrary to what had originally been expected, a humiliating defeat for Germany and the Kaiser at Algeciras was already looming. With the exception of Germany's ally Austria-Hungary every single Power, both great and small, was ranged behind France. It was not Great Britain but Germany which was diplomatically isolated.[1] Not without reason the Kaiser feared that at Algerciras the proud Kaiserreich was about to suffer a humiliation on the scale of the French climbdown at Fashoda in 1898.[2]

GERMANY'S OBJECTIVES IN ALGECIRAS

Of the grandiose German aims which had come to the fore in the spring of 1905 when Germany demanded a conference on Morocco – to break up the Entente Cordiale and force France into a continental alliance with Germany and Russia – there was now little evidence. For Privy Councillor Friedrich von Holstein, the guiding spirit of Germany's Moroccan policy, the maintenance of the dignity of Kaiser Wilhelm II had become a high priority. As he wrote to his friend Radolin in August 1905, 'safeguarding the prestige of our Kaiser by not trying to force him to hand over the Sultan [of Morocco] to the French for better or for worse six months after his speech at Tangier' was, along with the achievement of equal trading rights in Morocco for all nations, Germany's most important requirement from the conference. Already at this juncture, however, he expressed the fear that the British would seek to have the Sultan subjected to French rule, precisely 'in order to humiliate the Kaiser'.[3] But even this modest face-saving aim was hindered by the indifference demonstrated by Wilhelm himself, who loudly announced everywhere that 'a German war on account of Morocco' would be 'preposterous'. When the ambassador in Rome, Count Anton Monts, expressed the view in a report in January 1906 that

Delcassé would probably have been prepared to cede Germany 'a large part of Morocco' in April 1905, the Kaiser wrote dismissively on the report: 'What for? We don't need it.' In response to the repeated attempts by the ambassador to discuss what was to be done if the conference came to nothing the Kaiser, as Holstein noted with dismay, answered coolly: 'Not a disaster. Then we remain on the basis of the Madrid Conference' of 1880, and 'That will mean the Madrid status quo, which France would have to break up.' The confusion caused in the Reich leadership and among the German delegates in Algeciras by Wilhelm's lack of interest in the Moroccan question was perceptible everywhere. Holstein, at a loss, forwarded the Kaiser's comments to Joseph Maria von Radowitz, the German First Delegate at the Algeciras conference, adding: 'The Chancellor too wants to avoid war insofar as this can be done with honour, but he is clear about the fact that in case of a diplomatic defeat, the blame would be placed not only on the delegates but also on himself.'[4]

When Sir Donald Mackenzie Wallace, a friend of King Edward who was to attend the consultations at the conference in an unofficial capacity, called on the German ambassador in Paris on his way to Algeciras, the latter revealed almost shamefacedly that the need to keep the Kaiser's promise to the Sultan of 31 March 1905 would be one of Germany's principal concerns. As Radolin explained to his British visitor, when Delcassé was ousted, Germany had expected France to adopt a conciliatory attitude on Morocco, but Rouvier had proved just as inflexible as his predecessor. In view of France's obstinacy it had become very unlikely that a final solution of the Moroccan question would be achieved at the conference. As a war was out of the question – 'I can assure you . . . that war is the last thing the Emperor wants!' – Germany would have to be satisfied with a solution in Algeciras 'which will enable both parties to retreat from their advanced positions without too great a loss of dignity'. This modest aim was perhaps all that the Kaiserreich ultimately hoped to achieve at the conference, Wallace concluded. Radolin had made a frank admission to him: 'The Emperor promised the Sultan to support him and he cannot, within a few months, seek to elude that promise. In the future we shall see what can be done. We may some day allow France to have what she desires, *if she gives us compensation elsewhere.*' This had been said 'in a half-apologetic tone', Wallace wrote, 'and I felt inclined to ask him why the Emperor had placed himself in that position, but from obvious reasons I refrained from putting such an indiscreet question'.[5]

In view of the confusion in Berlin it was no wonder that the German negotiators in Algeciras behaved as enigmatically as sphinxes. From Washington the German ambassador Speck von Sternburg sent a warning that their secretive silence was being interpreted in America as a sign 'that we are looking for a quarrel with France'.[6] When Wallace arrived in Algeciras he observed that neither the French nor the representatives of the neutral countries could make out what Germany actually wanted to achieve. All were still 'completely in the dark regarding the views and intentions of Germany in the Moroccan Question', he reported on the twelfth day of the negotiations. The chief French negotiator, Paul Révoil, had 'a strong suspicion that the Berlin Foreign Office has not yet made up its mind what course it will take'. Wallace himself could only speculate on what Radowitz, who was 'as slippery as an eel' and his deputy Count Tattenbach, who behaved like a bulldog, hoped to gain by their inept tactics. 'The important question for the moment is why Germany is taking all this trouble instead of stating plainly what she wants and what she will *not* accept. Some suppose that she is really hesitating and seeking enlightenment, whilst others suspect that she is simply raising a cloud of diplomatic dust in order to conceal her present activity and plans for the future. Perhaps both theories have some foundation.'[7] Even Rouvier was bewildered by the inscrutability of German policy. As the British ambassador reported from Paris on 31 January 1906: 'Rouvier cannot make out what the Germans want in regard to Morocco ... He says that to him the powers of imagination of the Emperor, Bülow, Holstein etc. and their self denials are quite incomprehensible.'[8]

WAR IN SIGHT?

Even if the German government were not steering a deliberate course towards war, the danger of war if the Morocco conference failed was on everyone's mind. On 28 January 1906 Wallace warned of just such an eventuality and stressed the need for Britain to consider seriously how she would react if war broke out between Germany and France. In his judgement 'a rupture, though unlikely, is by no means impossible', especially since the French were not nearly as acquiescent as they had been only a few months before. 'The thinly veiled threat of war last summer produced among them alarm almost amounting to panic; and not without reason, because they were not prepared at that time to resist an attack on their Eastern frontier. Since that time they have made great military preparations, and they now believe, rightly or wrongly, that they have nothing to fear ... Military specialists say that there is no danger of war this year, because the reorganisation of the German artillery is not yet complete, but that next year the military situation will be greatly changed.'[9] In London, too, the Foreign Office considered that the danger of a German attack on France was slight for the moment, and that it was more probable that France might strike the first blow.[10]

These assessments accord with the views of Kaiser Wilhelm, the Reich Chancellor and senior German military officers, all of whom, as we have seen, had been anxious at least since December 1905 to avoid a war.[11] As Bülow commented in February 1906, not even the army would hear of a war over Morocco.[12] As General Freiherr Colmar von der Goltz quite rightly asserted, writing to a worried friend: 'The only basis for all the war rumours is that people think *we* have belligerent intentions. This view is particularly widespread in France. There is certainly some logic in the fact that people cannot see any other reason why we started up the wretched Moroccan question and made such a noise about it, although basically it was nothing to do with us. But the fact is that we have *neither* belligerent intentions nor belligerent feelings of any kind. Exactly the opposite is the case – I think it is truer to say that those in authority are afraid of any war.'[13]

Wilhelm II continued to make it quite clear that he was not prepared to wage war over Morocco.[14] He assured all and sundry of the peaceable nature of German policy.[15] In a private letter to Edward VII of 1 February 1906 – for which he rewrote most of the draft submitted to him by the Reich Chancellor – he affirmed his wish to live in peace with all his neighbours, including France. 'My policy with regard to Peace is as clear as crystal! & to mistake it ought to be impossible! Yet it is with pleasure that I seize this opportunity, once more to solemnly repeat, & I hope you will believe me, that it is my most earnest endeavour & wish to remain in Peace with *all Countries*, especially my neighbours. The German Programme adopted for the Moroccan policy & communicated to the conference at Algeciras is: Maintenance of the open door, – i. e. equal rights for the trade of all Powers concerned – & recognition of the exceptional position & rights of France all along the whole of her border with Morocco. This programme is eminently peaceful, practical & international & seems to have been recieved [sic] with allmost [sic] universal approval. It represents the base of our pourparlers with France upon which we both agreed to go to the Conference. The reports that I get from our representatives at Algeciras are favourable, the same I hear is the case in Paris, Petersburg & London. So that a satisfactory settlement may be hoped for.'[16]

Tsar Nicholas likewise received assurances of the Kaiser's peaceful intentions. At the end of January 1906 Cecil Spring Rice reported from St Petersburg that Kaiser Wilhelm's influence was virtually the deciding factor as far as Russia's attitude in Algeciras was concerned. If the French ambassador Bompard enquired about prospects in Algeciras, he always received the same reassuring response from the Foreign Minister, Lamsdorff: 'Tout va bien; il n'y aura pas de guerre.' If he asked how the Foreign Minister could be so sure, he was told 'that the Kaiser has told the Emperor what his intentions are and that the Emperor is perfectly convinced that there will not be war. When he asks what the Kaiser has told the Emperor the answer is that the personal relations between the sovereigns are not the concern of diplomatists.' Spring Rice added that the Russian Prime Minster, Witte, was equally convinced that a war was out of the question after the assurances that Kaiser Wilhelm had given. If only for fear of the Social Democrats, Witte said, the German ruler wanted to avoid a war. He knew for certain 'that if war breaks out, whether or not Germany is victorious, the Socialists will have a large accession of force and will be a very formidable element. In view of this danger the German Emperor, he thinks, will not dare to fight unless France by her precipitate action puts herself hopelessly in the wrong.'[17]

Wilhelm's protestations, however, ignored the fact that the French were not prepared to accept Germany's conditions. Dominance in the zone bordering on Algeria, as offered by Germany, was not enough to satisfy them: they insisted on exclusive control over the whole of Morocco, which after Tangier would have been tantamount to a slap in the face for the Kaiser and the German Reich. Holstein drew attention to this dilemma when he wrote on 7 February 1906: 'Whether the Conference has any result or whether we keep the status quo, we will still keep the peace. His Majesty is telling everyone that he wants peace, and France will certainly not provoke a war. It is difficult for us to negotiate *for this reason*: because H.M., with all his desire for peace, is holding fast to his well-known position of 31 March. He would take it very much amiss if we "sold out the Sultan to France". Under these circumstances, *if* Révoil holds to his old programme of French domination, it is hardly to be expected that the Conference will have any result.'[18]

If there was no desire for war in London, it was recognised that if need be, even this eventuality must be contemplated without flinching. To counter the Reich leadership's illusory hopes of a breakdown of the Entente Cordiale, British diplomats declared unambiguously that Great Britain would stand by France to the last. In early February 1906 Prince Heinrich, while visiting the British embassy in Berlin, spoke of his brother's great joy at the improvement of German–British relations, and especially of his relationship with his uncle Edward. It had been 'a great shock' for him, Heinrich, 'to realise that if a war had broken out between Germany and France, England would have been on the side of the latter'. Sir Frank Lascelles, with unaccustomed candour, told the Prince that he had never seriously believed in the danger of a war as he was firmly convinced that neither Germany nor France wanted to fight; but 'it was certainly the case that if such a calamity had occurred, England would certainly have been on the side of France. It was generally if not universally understood in England that German action in Morocco was directed against the Anglo-French agreement, and it would have been impossible for England to have abandoned France if she had been compelled to go to war in consequence of having entered into that agreement.'[19] The views expressed by the new British Minister of War, Lord Haldane, and the First Lord of the Admiralty Lord Tweedmouth, as reported by Metternich on 20 February 1906 from London, were equally unequivocal. Haldane had declared bluntly 'that the English government unconditionally supported the French position and considered France's claims moderate'. Tweedmouth had said there were grounds for supposing that Germany was aiming to acquire a port on the Atlantic coast of Morocco. He had recently discussed this suspicion with Sir John Fisher, who had replied with his customary belligerence: 'If we really ever had a war with Germany, we would have something to bombard.' Such reports did not fail to have an effect on the Kaiser.[20]

BETRAYAL BY THE `LATIN RACE´

On 20 February 1906 Kaiser Wilhelm showed that he was still unwilling to give ground on the contentious issue of international control of the Moroccan police. On being told that Rouvier could fall within forty-eight hours if he agreed to this German demand and that Delcassé might then return, Wilhelm commented defiantly: 'No harm done! The situation will become all the clearer. It is better for Delcassé to make his own policy than for it to be made by Rouvier! I shall stick to my point of view!'[21] But only a few days later his mood became one of bitterness and resignation in the face of French obduracy. On 21 February he and the Chancellor discussed the situation in Algeciras at length and came to the conclusion that Germany must set her sights on bringing the conference to a close as far as possible without losing face. The Kaiser was certainly 'firm', Bülow told Holstein, but everything now depended on 'our seizing the right moment for an acceptable compromise. We cannot tolerate a humiliation. The failure of the Conference would be, no matter how one looked at it, a diplomatic setback for us. Neither public opinion, Parliament, Princes, or even the army will have anything to do with a war over Morocco. The test of the correctness of the position we have taken will be whether we will be able to find an acceptable way out of this impasse.'[22]

The search for a reasonably dignified compromise was not helped by Wilhelm's increasingly neurotic behaviour. 'The longer the Algeciras conference lasted, the more agitated His Majesty became', Bülow wrote in his memoirs.[23] He reacted almost with panic to what were now unmistakable signs of German isolation. His cherished hopes for a Europe united under his leadership collapsed like a house of cards as one country after another indicated that it would take the Anglo-French side. The key to his great plan — the separation of France from Great Britain, leaving the latter isolated within Europe — had to be abandoned as a failure, to Wilhelm's bitter regret. His deep disappointment found expression in his reaction to a letter of 20 February 1906 in which, ironically, his uncle the Grand Duke of Baden spoke out passionately in favour of reconciliation with France and the unification of the continent against Great Britain. In order to avoid a war between Germany and France, the Grand Duke wrote, it was urgently necessary 'to detach France from England and bring her back to a continental policy . . . If this continental connection can be achieved, thereby uniting the European empires and states more and more closely, the community of interests will also emerge more clearly, and the points of conflicts will be reduced. English policy would be substantially modified as a result and England would have to try to get on a friendly footing with the other Powers.'[24] Although this was the fundamental idea that Wilhelm himself had advocated for many years, he rejected it now as illusory, 'naïve childishness!' As Britain had 'the strongest Navy in the world' she 'didn't give a damn for the other Powers', he exclaimed. The union with France which the Grand Duke 'so warmly recommended and desired' and treated 'as if it were an innovation', he, Wilhelm, had 'tried in vain to bring about for 18 years. It takes two, like marriage! If one partner is absolutely set against it, it does not work! The Gauls are more fearful and respectful of England's navy than of our army for the moment, therefore they listen to London, and London does not want a union of Germany and France! So it just does not work!'[25]

Coinciding with these expressions of the Kaiser's frustration, on 24 February 1906 Schoen, who had been appointed ambassador in St Petersburg in succession to Alvensleben, reported that the Russian Prime Minister was calling for greater solidarity between the continental Powers against America, which was 'using powerful means to pursue its aims with unscrupulous brutality', and against 'England, sneering at continental Europe'. Aggrieved, the Kaiser commented 'I have tried to put this idea into practice . . . in Europe, I have been snubbed by every country, especially Gaul and Russia, and they have all fought me together with America!' Russia's advice to France to treat Germany with as much good will as possible in Algeciras was 'simply ignored, as Russia carries no weight! England has drawn the better cards and advises exactly the opposite!'[26]

In the second half of February 1906 Kaiser Wilhelm could only watch helplessly as even Spain and Italy, the Mediterranean states of whose support he had felt certain, were persuaded to go over to the Entente camp by France's determined stand and Britain's naval might which underpinned it. Only a few

months earlier, when the young King Alfonso XIII of Spain visited Berlin in
September 1905, Wilhelm had gone so far as to propose 'an arrangement with
a view to common action by our armies!' Now, in February 1906, he wrote to
Bülow expressing the suspicion that Spain had made a secret pact with France
over Morocco involving 'some dirty items at our expense'. His suspicion was
increased by the fact that King Alfonso had been so 'impolite' as to refuse to
give him any information about the agreement with France.[27] Not long
afterwards, Wilhelm's worst fears were confirmed. News arrived from Madrid
that Spain would not accept the German demand for an international police
force in Morocco. Wilhelm realised with alarm that Spain had long since
gone over to the Franco-British side. 'Aha! so the truth is out!' he wrote on
the report. 'The [Spaniards] have already shared out Morocco with Gaul.' The
prospect held out by Spain of a future alliance with Germany as soon as the
German navy was strong enough 'to confront the English navy with some
likelihood of success' now seemed almost ironic and the Kaiser rejected it,
remarking bitterly, 'in that case we shall have to give that up! for it will never
happen'. 'So we are supposed to defend Spain against the Engl[ish] navy and
France as soon as we are strong enough, but the Spaniards won't do anything
about it themselves! and have committed themselves to [support] both of
them! A fine state of affairs! And on top of that the wretches won't even
admit what sort of a pact with the "devil" they have made!'[28]

Even more alarming than Spain's siding with the Anglo-French faction was
the desertion of Germany by her Triple Alliance partner Italy.[29] As early as on
11 February 1906 the Kaiser complained that Italy 'was being two-faced as
usual' and was conceding 'more and more French demands'.[30] The longer the
conference went on, the more convinced Wilhelm became that in spite of all
assurances to the contrary, Italy too had come to a secret agreement with
France and was consequently of no further military strategic value for the
Triple Alliance. 'The Bible says "No man can serve two masters", and so
certainly not 3 masters! France, England and the Triple Alliance, that is quite
out of the question! The result will be that Italy clings to the British-Gallic
group! We would be well advised to reckon on that, and to write off this
"ally"!'[31] As he put it a month later, 'we are played out in Italy for the
moment'.[32]

That Italy had in effect switched sides from the Triple Alliance to the
Anglo-French Entente, which Wilhelm had long since predicted with his
'Crimean Coalition' slogan, was confirmed by the reports arriving from
Count Monts in Rome. On 3 March 1906 he submitted a perceptive analysis
of the world situation as the Italian government saw it. Inevitably, its effect on
the Kaiser and the Wilhelmstrasse was deeply sobering. 'In England people are

well aware of the strengths and weaknesses of the [British] Empire. This has given rise to the system of friendships and alliances which present-day England has built up for herself, contrary to her earlier political principles: with Japan for the East; with the United States for the Atlantic region and for the free supply of foodstuffs; with France for the Continent. The Anglo-French Entente must not be regarded as something temporary. The English, at least, entered into it with the intention that its effect would last for at least a generation ... Since England means to stand by her agreements with France, she will also defend France's Moroccan policy through thick and thin.' If only for the vulnerability of her long coastline, Italy was therefore compelled to take account of the greatest naval Power in the world and her Entente with France.[33] The Kaiser acknowledged the accuracy of this depressing assessment. He wrote 'very good! and absolutely right!' on the report. It was clear that the rapprochement between Germany and France which he sought would be out of reach for decades. 'So for my generation there is no further hope of a link with Gaul', he commented. But he maintained that neither he nor official German policy was responsible for this; the blame lay with the agitation in the German press against Germany's western neighbours. 'The German press has coupled England and France in criticising them both, and now they are together and Gaul is under Engl[ish] influence; we have lost her for the time being. Italy has joined them − Crimean Coalition − and we have lost out.'[34] Wilhelm was well aware that the constellation of Powers in the Mediterranean would change fundamentally again if only Germany could find her way back to a better relationship with Britain. 'Italy will stay with us only so long as we are friends with England', he commented. 'If that is not put right again she will leave the Triple Alliance!'[35] Even now, however, the Kaiser entertained no thoughts of changing the course of the naval policy which was so threatening to Britain. Commenting on a report from Monts that in the opinion of the Italian government no one in Britain had aggressive intentions towards Germany, 'but many politicians feel compelled to conclude from a variety of speeches and newspaper articles that Germany wants to seize the trident', Wilhelm wrote confidently, 'It's already happening.'[36]

The Kaiser was not unjustified, as we now know, in believing that he had discovered the content of the Franco-Italian exchange of notes in the summer of 1902, by which each Power had committed itself to strict neutrality in the event of an attack on the other.[37] In spite of the secretiveness of the Italians he knew for a fact, Wilhelm wrote on 15 April 1906, 'that Italy has promised France never to supply a single soldier to help us against her!' In the agreements between them 'there are bad things ... against allies too!' Italian policy, he maintained, was aimed 'against everything *Germanic*!' and now Gaul was even demanding 'to be greeted as a *girl friend* on Unter den Linden, which is of course "compromising" when one is out for a walk with one's lawful wife'.[38]

After the conclusion of the conference the Kaiser's fury with Italy grew to the point of threatening war. The day after the signature of the Algeciras Act he told the Austro-Hungarian ambassador, as the latter reported, that 'he did not want to waste his breath talking about Italy, except to assure us that it would give him great satisfaction, if the occasion arose — which was by no means out of the question, given the unreliable policy of that kingdom — to combine with us, possibly with weapons in our hands, to teach the latter a salutary lesson'.[39] Two days later Szögyény quoted the Kaiser as saying that 'it was certainly quite unheard-of to envisage a possible war against an ally; nevertheless he must assure me that if Italy should take up a hostile attitude towards Austria-Hungary, he would seize the opportunity with real enthusiasm to join us and strike at Italy with all the military power at his disposal'.[40]

The Kaiser reacted to the 'betrayal' by Spain and Italy with an alarming retreat into racist irrationality. 'One might call it a "Latin Union" against the Teutons in Germany — supported by the Teutons in London', he raged in a letter to Bülow on 11 February 1906. 'This "Union" has probably already long ago divided up the entire Mediterranean littoral of Africa by mutual concessions and agreements — without us — and with the sanction of England, which could then drastically reduce its fleet at Malta, for a "Mediterranean Question" in the old Nelsonian sense would then no longer exist. Entente Cordiale between Paris and London — thereby releasing ships for the new *North Sea* fleet.'[41] Inflamed with fury against the 'Latin race', he wrote in March 1906: 'All the miserable, degenerate Latin nations are simply becoming instruments in England's hands with which to combat German commerce in the Mediterranean. Not only do we have no friends any more, but this generation of eunuchs from the ancient Rom[an] chaos of nations hates us with all its heart! It is like the days of the Hohenstaufen and the Anjous! All the scum of the Romance race betrays us right, left and centre and jumps into the open arms of England, which will use it against us! A battle between Germanic and Latin peoples all along the line! and unfortunately the former are divided!'[42] 'From time immemorial' the Italians had 'left the German Kaiser in the lurch and betrayed him', he complained to his entourage.[43]

RUSSIA BACKS AWAY

Bitterly disappointed as Wilhelm was over the conduct of Italy and Spain, Russia's decision to throw her weight behind France was of course far more serious. This decision, clearly, was heavily influenced by the financial dependence of the Tsarist Empire, in the grip of revolutionary turmoil, on France.[44] True, the Tsar and the Kaiser continued their friendly correspondence, in the spirit of Björkö, over the heads of their ministers and ambassadors, but harsh reality intruded with growing insistence on the daydreams of the two sovereigns. Cecil Spring Rice reported from St Petersburg on 16 February 1906: 'There is a general impression that the Emperor [Nicholas II] seems to feel himself bound to the Kaiser by special ties of gratitude. This is by no means the case with Witte who after his short lived German enthusiasm has rebounded strongly in the other direction ... The main question now is finance. This depends to a great deal on the general situation. If this remains strained then Russia cannot borrow the ninety millions that she requires before the beginning of next year. But this again depends on the settlement of the question between France and Germany. Witte is loud in his abuse of the Germans who he says have duped him ... It is probable that the settlement was to have been part of the scheme which he brought back with him from Germany, namely a combination against the Anglo-Japanese alliance. This the French refused to enter into and as that part of the scheme broke down the rest fell with it. Perhaps this is the reason for the reluctance of the Emperor to address a personal appeal to the Kaiser. In the latter's hands rests the situation. It is felt here that the Morocco question is an Imperial question in which the Kaiser's personality is deeply engaged.'[45]

For years Wilhelm II had bargained on Russia's friendship, but by the beginning of March 1906 at the latest he was forced to acknowledge that it had sunk to 'practically zero!' Russian friendship 'does not exist for us!' he remarked bitterly. Schoen reported that Russia had 'moved openly and decisively onto the French side'. The Kaiser recognised that Russia's desperate situation, which had compelled her to 'put herself meekly into the hands of her French friend and helper', was the chief reason for her present attitude. 'According to Russian logic, therefore, we must beat the retreat on the Moroccan question so that Russia's plight is not worsened', Schoen observed. Wilhelm agreed completely, writing 'Bravo!' and 'Well said' by the ambassador's racist comments on the so-called national character of 'the Russian', typified by 'a low cultural level' and lacking the remotest sense of moral responsibility towards a neighbouring state which had adopted a loyal and noble stance. 'Ingratitude and arrogance ... are, as always, the chief characteristics of the Russian', the diplomat and future Foreign Secretary declared. He went on: 'Added to that is the sense of national identity, strengthened by the constitutional movement, the racial antipathy of the Slavs towards the Germanic race, the hatred of the champions of freedom for Germany, which is seen as the bulwark of reaction; then there is general suspicion of Germany's

ever-increasing power and jealousy of her triumphant progress in the broad
sphere of trade and culture ... The Russian, whether of high or low station,
seems not to appreciate good treatment: the chinovnik and the mujik respond
only to dictatorial manners and rudeness.' Wilhelm II instantly took up these
prejudices, expressing the opinion that Germany would 'have to use' the tactic
of rudeness towards Russia again. It was 'most certainly high time for it!!', the
monarch wrote – high time for Germany to take every suitable opportunity to
bring home to her Russian neighbour, in the only way it would be clearly
understood, the value of German friendship. The Russians were 'plain insolent!' and had been 'getting fat at our expense for long enough'. If Schoen's
racist remarks were aimed at the Kaiser's own convictions, they certainly
reached their target. The ambassador's report, Wilhelm commented, was
'Outstandingly well written! and tells the truth at last! without whitewash
or whining about past times!'[46]

When the Paris newspapers published a statement by Russia that whatever
happened she would vote with the French in Algeciras, Kaiser Wilhelm could
no longer contain his anger. On 21 March 1906, at a court concert for an
audience of seven hundred, he railed against the Russian ambassador, who
had stayed away, declaring 'What a pity Osten-Sacken didn't come. I would
have given him a good dressing-down today. And if it had ended with him
going straight back home I should not have cared in the least.' The Reich
Chancellor, who heard this remark, said as he left: 'It was just as well that
Osten-Sacken didn't come to the concert.'[47]

Wilhelm's fury with Russia did not subside for some time. At the end of
March 1906 another report arrived from Schoen, which the Kaiser again
covered with spiteful abuse of Russia's statesmen. 'Schoen has done well; send
him a telegram saying so! firm and clear, also rude when necessary, that is what
is needed with the Slavs', he ordered. Lamsdorff's 'web of lies' was 'too crass' and
'shameless beyond belief!' 'These lazy, lying Russians put on a bold impertinent
manner, perjure themselves, then add a few more lies, to save their faces! They
no longer take any notice of us at all! This kind of treatment is really outrageous! *Adding insult to injury*' [English in the original].[48] When Bülow reported
that Russia's financial difficulties and borrowing requirements had increased
enormously Kaiser Wilhelm greeted this news with *Schadenfreude*. 'Very gratifying!' he wrote at the end of March 1906. 'They won't get a penny from us.'[49]

ABOUT-TURN: THE KAISER DRAWS BACK FROM THE BRINK

In the face of France's unflinching insistence on her claim to 'peaceful
penetration' of Morocco and Germany's diplomatic isolation it soon became

clear that the German government would not be able to achieve even the modest aim of saving its face in Algeciras. Nevertheless the ignominious and baffling end came as a surprise for all the participants. When and why did Wilhelm give the order to yield?[50] It is clear that right up to March 1906 both he and Bülow, in accord with the Auswärtiges Amt, steered an uncompromising course which could have led, if not necessarily to war, then certainly to the break-up of the conference and hence to a serious international crisis. At the end of February the Kaiser reacted with defiant bravado to the assertion of the chief German negotiator in Algeciras that 'isolation is still out of the question for us now'. 'Is that so?' he scrawled in the margin. 'Nous verrons but it wouldn't matter!' He then rejected yet another proposed compromise on the contentious police question with a sharp 'no'.[51] On Bülow's instructions these marginal comments by the Kaiser were forwarded to Radowitz on 7 March 1906, in order to boost the latter's courage 'now before the decisive sessions of the conference'.[52] On the very same day, astonishingly, in Algeciras Radowitz signalled German willingness to compromise on the police issue and thus opened the way to a peaceful agreement. How is this about-face to be explained?

On 5 March 1906 King Edward VII, who was in Paris on his way to Biarritz, invited the French President Émile Loubet and – even more significantly – the dismissed Foreign Minister Théophile Delcassé to lunch. The news of this conspicuous gesture of solidarity between the two west European Great Powers came as a bombshell to Berlin. Among Holstein's papers is an undated note which records the effect of the Paris lunch on the Kaiser and Bülow. 'The next day the Chancellor asked me to see him and informed me in strict confidence that the Kaiser had ordered a letter to be written to him that we must give in because our artillery and our navy were not in any condition to fight a war. This letter was written under the impression created by the news that King Edward had invited Delcassé to lunch.'[53] It is not clear whether the letter from the Kaiser to Bülow to which Holstein refers was in fact his notorious New Year's Eve letter, which the Reich Chancellor had received nine weeks before, or whether it was a new letter in which Wilhelm repeated his reasons for opposing a war in the near future. What is clear is the shock that the Privy Councillor received that day, 6 March 1906, when the Kaiser gave orders to sound the retreat.

In connection with the German decision of the beginning of March 1906 to give way in Algeciras, Ragnhild Fiebig-von Hase has drawn attention to the significance of the exchange of letters between the Kaiser and President Roosevelt. She shows that as early as in the summer of 1905, while agreeing to the international conference, Roosevelt had enjoined the Kaiser to remain moderate and had warned him that the United States would not be willing to countenance unjustified attacks on French interests. If the Kaiser refused to compromise on small questions of detail at the conference, 'he would necessarily cause a war of which the whole world would disapprove'.[54] Through his ambassador, Speck von Sternburg, Wilhelm II had promised for his part to follow Roosevelt's advice if a crisis arose during the forthcoming conference. In March 1906 the President made use of this correspondence to persuade Germany to give way. When Roosevelt also threatened to publish the whole disastrous 'Willy–Teddy' correspondence on the Moroccan question the Kaiser saw no alternative but to abandon the struggle in Algeciras.[55]

This curious sequence of events was soon no secret at the British court and in Downing Street. The Under Secretary at the Foreign Office, Sir Charles Hardinge, was able to report to the King as early as on 9 March 1906 how the 'volte-face on the part of Germany' had come about. 'The President of the United States has been pressing the German Emperor and finally reminded His Majesty that he promised last summer that he would accept any solution of the Moroccan question which he (Mr Roosevelt) might consider just and reasonable. The President stated that in his opinion the French proposals ... were both just and reasonable and he held the German Emperor to his promise to accept a solution in this sense. This happened only two days ago and the result was almost instantaneous.' 'The concessions granted by Germany are really very considerable', Hardinge commented, and Sir Edward Grey would press France to accept the proposed compromise.[56] A few days later Grey, the Foreign Secretary, received cheering news from Algeciras: 'Communications are now passing between German Emperor and President of the United States in regard to the police question', and Germany was expected to give way.[57]

The statesmen in the Wilhelmstrasse received only incomplete information about these proceedings at the highest level, and often not until after the event. None was more confused over the timing and the cause of the Kaiser's retreat than Privy Councillor von Holstein, who had the task of finessing the whole delicate manoeuvre. As we have just seen, Bülow surprised him on 6 March 1906 with a letter from the Kaiser in which he had decreed that 'we must give in because our artillery and our navy were not in any condition to fight a war'.[58] In a further note dated 29 March Holstein looks back over the past five weeks and wrongly gives Sunday 11 March 1906 – five days *after* the Kaiser's order to concede on 6 March – as the date when the decision was made. In this note Holstein cites a series of remarks by the Kaiser and the Chancellor as evidence that until that date both were determined to hold out. He goes on: 'On Monday, 12 March, the Chancellor in a conference informed the State Secretary, Under State Secretary, *Geheimrat* Hammann, and me that it was necessary to give in. With the exception of Hammann, we all opposed giving in and pointed out that if we stood firm we could be certain of mediation by the neutrals because they – Russia, Italy, and even Liberal England, – badly needed not only peace but complete calm ... The Chancellor, however, ordered that we should give in, and dictated the main points to Under State Secretary Mühlberg.'[59] But by the time this meeting took place in the Wilhelmstrasse, in Algeciras Radowitz had long since indicated that he was ready to give way. In another document, a letter to Maximilian von Brandt of 10 April 1906, Holstein recorded: 'In the Morocco question, the Chancellor, the State Secretary, the Under State Secretary, and I all took the point of view that we should wait calmly until the neutrals in need of money and peace – Russia, Italy, etc. – came up with mediation proposals. It would not have taken much longer. However, His Majesty ordered the retreat, and thereby justified the prediction of King Edward ... that Germany would lose her nerve. Out of this retreat there arises an indefinite danger of war, because the pressure method, which succeeded in Morocco, may be applied against us at the next opportunity.'[60] As is well known, Holstein handed in his resignation on 31 March 1906; on 5 April Bülow suffered a fainting fit during a debate on the Moroccan question in the Reichstag. Two days later the Algeciras Act was signed.

KAISER WILHELM'S PERSONAL HUMILIATION

Outwardly Wilhelm II put a brave face on it. He read out to his entourage an article from the newspaper *Der Deutsche*, which was supportive of the Reich Chancellor. It maintained that Germany had in fact won a great diplomatic victory in Algeciras. The Kaiser seemed 'very satisfied with it', as Zedlitz recorded.[61] In conversations with American diplomats he said he was 'particularly well pleased with the outcome ... He pointed out that the interests of the United States were identical with those of Germany and that the value of the conference would be appreciated more and more by these two nations.'[62] He told the elderly Emperor Franz Joseph of Austria that he was delighted with the 'universally satisfactory conclusion' that had been achieved in Algeciras.[63] In a telegram of 13 April 1906 that was to cause a furore he thanked the Austro-Hungarian Foreign Minister Count Goluchowski 'for your unflinching support for my representatives' at the conference. 'A fine action by a loyal ally. – You proved yourself a brilliant second in the duel and you can be sure of the same service from me in the same circumstances.'[64] The announcement of a visit by Kaiser Wilhelm to Vienna was widely seen as 'a demonstration against England and Italy'.[65] In fact Wilhelm was striking out alone with these gestures of bravado. Not a single member of the imperial entourage except the Flügeladjutant Gustav von Neumann-Cosel would have advised the Kaiser to send the telegram to Goluchowski, if he had been asked, Zedlitz noted despondently. It could only be explained by the monarch's habit of cocooning himself 'in certain one-sided trains of thought . . . At such times the Kaiser's temperament gets the better of him.'[66] The Wilhelmstrasse was aghast, and yet the 'responsible advisers of the Crown' felt obliged to take the blame. When the telegram was fiercely criticised in the Reichstag the newly appointed Foreign Secretary, Heinrich von Tschirschky, defended the Kaiser with the statement: 'If His Majesty chose to send such a dispatch through a personal telegram, it is undoubtedly His Majesty's right to do so, and he is also absolutely free to choose his words, like any private individual. Naturally the Reich Chancellor takes responsibility for the contents of the telegram.'[67]

Those close to Wilhelm II thought that he had 'comparatively few illusions' about the failure in Algeciras and that he even realised that the unanimous conduct of the Powers in taking sides against Germany had also been tantamount to a personal humiliation deliberately inflicted on him.[68] It was not long, however, before the Kaiser (and Bülow) had found in Holstein the scapegoat on to whom they could heap the blame for the Algeciras debacle. A year after the resignation of the elderly Privy Councillor, Wilhelm commented that his own Moroccan policy had often been implemented 'by Holstein in a completely wrong and unnecessarily anti-French way, against my will! . . . In his skilful way Herr von Holstein twisted my very precise orders and arrangements with the Chancellor so much that in the end the opposite happened. He constantly stirred up and injected poison against France and put such pressure on the Chancellor that the latter repeatedly asked me in his garden, to my utter astonishment, the same question – whether I wanted or wished for war with France! Whereas my instructions to Madrid and Richthofen stated expressly: "Algeciras-Conference is to be the stepping stone of the beginning of the agreement between France and Germany!" W.'[69]

In the capital cities of the Powers no one doubted that Kaiser Wilhelm II was the driving force behind the foreign policy of the Reich. As they saw it, he had provoked the Moroccan crisis by his visit to Tangier, forced the summoning of the conference by threats of war and impeded attempts to find a satisfactory solution for months.[70] Not without mockery and *Schadenfreude*, Donald Mackenzie Wallace reported from Algeciras on 25 February 1906 to Edward VII's Private Secretary that Wilhelm II 'must have a parental feeling of tenderness for the Conference as his own pet child, and that is probably why the rupture, which he is rendering inevitable, is postponed so long'.[71]

Similarly the French ambassador in London, Paul Cambon, commented in March 1906 that 'unless the German Emperor, whom he [Cambon] regards as the prime mover in this question, yields at the last moment, a rupture of the negotiations is inevitable'.[72] From St Petersburg Cecil Spring Rice reported that Tsar Nicholas had at last realised that the key to the settlement of the crisis lay with the Kaiser alone. He had now signalled his willingness, 'as a last resort, if all other means fail, to appeal to the Kaiser, in concert, if possible, with the King', but 'the Russians seem to take the view that the Kaiser is a bad horse to go up to in the stable and that they would rather not adventure their Emperor near his heels'.[73] In France, too, the Kaiser was seen as bearing the overriding responsibility for German policy: the luckless French ambassador, Baron de Courcel, who travelled from Berlin to Paris with mediation proposals, was not even given a hearing because his government assumed 'that he has been hypnotised by the Emperor'.[74]

Not only the political course which Wilhelm II had steered but also the disastrous decision-making system which his style of government had brought about over the years, together with his personality itself, became the focus of criticism. On 16 March 1906 the Hofmarschall Zedlitz had a wide-ranging conversation with Tschirschky on board the warship *Kaiser Wilhelm II*. The newly appointed Foreign Secretary spoke despondently of the Moroccan conference and of German foreign policy as a whole. In his view the Kaiser's 'daredevil policy' bore a large part of the blame for the unfavourable situation which the Reich now faced. In Algeciras, he said, Germany found herself 'in a hostile confrontation not only with the whole of Europe (except Austria) but with the whole world; we had constantly drawn back, step by step, and would quite naturally have to give way even more'. Tschirschky had no hesitation in comparing Germany's situation in Algeciras with Prussia's humiliation at Olmütz in November 1850. He went on: 'We cannot allow it to reach the point of war, nor will it do so. But with this daredevil policy, whether the moment will come sooner or later when we no longer have any choice in the matter only time will tell. Although in his heart the Kaiser does not want war because he knows very well how high the stakes would be, he always wants to achieve great things with little effort and to win laurels without endangering himself.'[75] Zedlitz thought the widespread negative attitude towards the German sovereign was partly due to his 'brilliant, exceptional personality' which in itself was enough to antagonise other monarchs and statesmen. But he also criticised Wilhelm's way of 'putting himself to the fore, interfering in everything including foreign affairs, and . . . the demanding and often ruthless manner in personal relations' which had earned him 'not only enmity but hatred . . . The King of England, the Emperor of Russia and also the King of Italy, in spite of his periodic attempts to court their favour and even running after them, are not only not friendly towards him but positively hostile. These personal animosities have been greatly intensified by the fact that the Kaiser has often, all too trustingly, expressed himself very frankly and freely about these gentlemen both in writing and speaking, which has of course come to their ears ... Thus it was apparent in Algeciras that the Kaiser's frosty personal relations with the monarchs of other states had a harmful effect on the progress of the negotiations, and the Kaiser feels this himself and it increases his personal antagonism towards these sovereigns still more.'[76] For Holstein, now retired, the central problem of German policy was equally clear. 'All provocations are either conceived by the Kaiser or are conceived to please him', he complained after the ostracism of Algeciras.[77]

Sir Donald Mackenzie Wallace summed up the deeper significance of the conference in a final report to King Edward from Algeciras. Germany, by staking so much on the conference, had demonstrated 'that in all international combinations, even when her interests do not seem to be directly concerned, she must not be treated as a *quantité négligeable*', he wrote on 19 April 1906. On the other hand the conference had completely failed to serve the purpose of undermining the Anglo-French Entente, 'and it accentuated, instead of diminishing, the semi-isolation of Germany in Europe ... To all the world it is evident that Germany has only one friend in Europe, and that one friend (Austria) has so many internal troubles of her own that she cannot be regarded as a very efficient ally in international complications. What then will Germany now do? Will she be content to improve her relations gradually with the Powers and thereby forward the interests of peace which she professes to have so much at heart, or will she endeavour to make in Europe some new "constellation" of the Powers so as to enable her to play a predominant part?' Wallace did consider that there was much likelihood of the Reich choosing the more peaceful path. Instead, he saw danger in the clear indications that the Kaiserreich would withdraw from the international system and rely on its own strength. 'Trust to ourselves alone, that must be our watchword', Tattenbach had said to him on leaving Algeciras, adding: 'What we chiefly suffer from is that we produce yearly a million human beings and we must find an outlet for them! Can you wonder that we sometimes make ourselves disagreeable to other Nations? ... The great mistake we make is that we throw ourselves about in all directions and meddle in all parts of the world. What we ought to do is to make ourselves irresistibly strong, and then strike hard!'[78]

CHAPTER SEVENTEEN

'Encirclement': caught in the web of the Entente

For the Kaiserreich and its Kaiser a whole world had collapsed at Algeciras in the spring of 1906. Not only had Germany's grandiose expectations of uniting the European continent under her domination proved unattainable; her Triple Alliance partner Italy and her prospective ally Russia, together with Spain and the smaller countries, had gone over on to the side of the Anglo-French Entente, which was also supported by America (and Japan in the background). Only the crisis-ridden Danube Monarchy had remained loyal. The crucial question which Sir Donald Mackenzie Wallace had posed regarding Germany's 'semi-isolation' in Algeciras now had to be answered: would the Kaiserreich content itself with the status quo in the world and try by peaceful means to regain the lost confidence of the international states system, or would it continue by means of a cold war *avant la lettre*, so to speak, to try to tear apart the net of the Entente in order to make the breakthrough to World Power status after all?

WILHELM II AND THE CONDUCT OF FOREIGN POLICY

The decision as to which direction foreign policy should now take still lay principally in the hands of Kaiser Wilhelm II. In all sections of the German population and not least as a result of his failed and dangerous *Weltpolitik*, criticism of the 'Personal Rule' of the monarch grew to a disquieting extent, as we shall see.[1] Yet for the time being it did not affect Wilhelm's decision-making power and 'the autocratic element in the personality of the Kaiser' continued to grow alarmingly.[2] After eighteen years on the throne the monarch exercised an almost unimaginable influence in precisely the sphere of military and foreign policy. 'The Kaiser has gradually become accustomed to Sultanesque methods of rulership', Friedrich von Holstein commented in September 1907.[3]

In addition to Holstein's resignation, the Moroccan crisis had claimed a few other victims in the Wilhelmstrasse, which further weakened the role of the Foreign Office as an occasional counterbalance or obstacle to the All-Highest will. The Foreign Secretary Oswald Freiherr von Richthofen, overworked beyond endurance, had died of a stroke at the beginning of January 1906. Very much against the will of the Reich Chancellor, who was reported to have handed in his resignation in protest,[4] Richthofen was succeeded by Heinrich von Tschirschky und Bögendorff, of whom it was said that he regarded it as his task as head of the Auswärtiges Amt to carry out the Kaiser's will.[5] To satisfy Wilhelm II, Tschirschky had made Holstein's departure more or less a condition of his acceptance of office,[6] and so the powerful Privy Councillor, the only man of sufficient talent and experience to be able to develop the outlines of an alternative foreign policy, left office full of bitterness in April 1906 'because of my incredible treatment by Tschirschky'. As Holstein quite rightly surmised, 'Tschirschky would not dare to do all that if he didn't have the Kaiser behind him ... H.M. finds me inconvenient and now wants to make foreign policy himself, without contradiction from the professional bureaucracy.' The Reich Chancellor would be equally unable to stand up to Tschirschky, Holstein predicted, 'because he [Tschirschky] has the Kaiser behind him'.[7] In August 1906 he quoted approvingly a comment by 'a very acute observer' who found Bülow diminished; there was 'no longer anything Olympian about him. Tschirschky is handling foreign policy and especially personnel questions directly with the Kaiser.'[8] Indeed, there was room for serious doubt as to whether Bülow 'is still allowed to do anything at all about foreign policy'.[9] In order to preserve at least the appearance of a share in decision-making the Reich Chancellor wondered whether he should summon the French ambassador to Norderney to see him, 'as it would do no harm from the point of view of domestic politics if I were to demonstrate a lively interest in foreign policy'.[10] The favoured new Foreign Secretary, however, was also fully conscious of his dependence on the 'All-Highest grace' and it was not long before he began complaining of the monarch's unpredictable interference. 'Fickle are the favours of the great', he wrote in May 1906 to Karl von Eisendecher. 'You can imagine that I am prepared daily for a turnabout in the imperial feelings towards myself. The foreign relations of Germany are at the moment very complicated, and the prime requisite in such a situation – the ability to await developments with calm nerves – is not exactly to the taste of H.M.'[11] What course, therefore, did Wilhelm steer after the debacle of Algeciras? What aims did he still hope to achieve, and what means did he propose to use?

THE TRIPLE ALLIANCE IN CRISIS

Almost as if they were whistling in the dark to give themselves courage, Wilhelm and Bülow played down the dangers for the Reich that lay in the increasingly tightly woven net of ententes and agreements between the other Great Powers. As Tattenbach had predicted on leaving Algeciras, the German Reich retreated with its only ally, Austria-Hungary, into the fortress of Middle Europe and relied on its 'invincible' military strength in the knowledge that at the appropriate moment it could 'strike hard'.[12] Germany was strong enough, the Kaiser declared in June 1907, to look at the ententes – which he described contemptuously as 'political antics' – 'with cool amusement'.[13] The agreements between the other Powers would be torn apart 'like spiders' webs' by a single event, he believed.[14] Such paper pacts had no value in the real world, the Kaiser and his principal advisers declared. In July 1907 the acting Foreign Secretary, Otto von Mühlberg, was exultant at the rivalries cropping up everywhere between Russia and France, France and Britain, the United States and Japan. As he saw it, 'we can play the spectator watching all these spasms, and learn a lesson from them about the dubious value of the epidemic of loudly trumpeted guarantee treaties and declarations that has broken out. As Your Excellency [Bülow] said, time is on our side, and nations unfriendly to us will find their paper missiles powerless against the solid block which we form together with Austria in Central Europe.'[15]

After the 'betrayal' by the 'miserable, degenerate Latin nations' in Algeciras Kaiser Wilhelm decided to abandon the extended Mediterranean cruise he had planned for the spring of 1906.[16] Instead, he seized upon the idea of paying a visit to the Emperor Franz Joseph in June, as an expression of gratitude for his loyal support at the conference – and as a reprimand to Italy for her desertion. The visit was intended as a demonstration of the strength of the monarchical principle and of the dual alliance between Germany and Austria; yet as the date drew near for the journey to Vienna the political situation in the Dual Monarchy became more and more opaque and problematic, with the result that the Kaiser's resolve began to falter. As the German ambassador in Vienna, Count Carl von Wedel, reported just before Wilhelm's arrival, the crisis in the multinational Habsburg Empire deepened immeasurably when Franz Joseph, without the agreement of the Austrian government and the Austrian parliament, gave the Hungarians authority to raise customs tariffs independently. Indignant speeches in the Vienna parliament showed 'how seriously this has shaken the old Emperor's popularity, which used to be so great and universal'.[17] Rumours abounded of forthcoming mass demonstrations. Abdication by Franz Joseph could not be entirely ruled out, Wedel warned. He had heard the view expressed on all sides that a solution to the crisis could be found only in completely reordering the constitutional structure of Austria-Hungary towards a federal system. An internal structural transformation of this order, however, would inevitably bring about 'a radical change in the relations between the Austro-Hungarian Monarchy and the outside world' and by bringing anti-German elements to the front line it would be detrimental to Germany's power and influence in particular.[18] After this report it is no wonder that Kaiser Wilhelm had doubts about the expediency of his journey to Vienna. He gave orders for a telegram to be sent to the Reich Chancellor in Norderney to ask 'whether my visit is still appropriate under the circumstances? Or had it better be abandoned.'[19]

This nervous enquiry from Kaiser Wilhelm crossed with a letter from Bülow in which the Chancellor stressed the great importance of the visit to Vienna in view of Germany's international isolation. He stated that he had discussed the situation with Tschirschky before leaving Berlin and agreed with the latter '1) that our relations with Austria have now become more important than ever, as the Empire is our only really reliable ally, 2) that we must make our relative political isolation as little apparent to the Austrians as possible.' In order not to be fleeced by the ally, 'in Vienna we must neither show too strong a need for support from Austria nor behave as if we felt at all isolated. The Austrians must be given the impression that whatever arises we have complete confidence in ourselves. We must therefore also depict our relations with Russia, Italy and England as better than they perhaps are in reality.'[20]

During his visit to Vienna Wilhelm struck up a friendly relationship with the heir to the Austrian throne, Archduke Franz Ferdinand, and agreed with him on a secret visit to Berlin in the spring of 1907. Through the Archduke's ineptitude, however, this became public knowledge and the press indulged in wild speculation: it was claimed that they had even discussed the Emperor Franz Joseph's possible abdication. Zedlitz conjectured that the background to the discussion had been the question of rank, with regard to Franz Ferdinand's morganatic wife in the event of his accession to the throne.[21] However that may be, the secret negotiations between Wilhelm II and the heir to the Austro-Hungarian throne were yet again symptomatic of the commanding position which the Kaiser occupied in the formulation of foreign policy. As Holstein warned the Reich Chancellor on 3 May 1907, after a meeting in Berlin between Bülow and the new Austrian Foreign Minister, Alois Freiherr Lexa von Aehrenthal, 'If Aehrenthal leaves here with the belief that ... Austria can rely more on H.M. than on yourself ... then the direct exchange of ideas between rulers, to the exclusion of the Chancellor, will become a regular custom. (H.M. will certainly do nothing to discourage it.) That Archduke Franz

Ferdinand has already acted in this manner is a fact whose significance must be considered if one intends to estimate the situation correctly ... The Archduke and the Minister will now compare notes about with whom it is easier to negotiate and who takes the firmer line, H.M. or yourself.'[22]

After the Italian 'betrayal' in Algeciras Wilhelm's relations with Italy, officially Germany's Triple Alliance partner, were at their lowest ebb. In September 1906 he spoke 'very harshly' about Victor Emmanuel III to the British ambassador, describing him 'as a complete Socialist'. He maintained that the King was 'particularly proud of his Socialist views. He also flirted constantly with [Italia] Irredenta and with the idea of seizing Albania.'[23] Military help from Italy in a war against the western Powers was now out of the question. Wedel expressed the opinion that 'in the event of a war between us and Austria-Hungary on the one hand and France and England on the other, Italy would not mobilise a single man to help us ... I do not think one can rule out the possibility that she would break the treaty and join our enemies.'[24] The long-serving German ambassador in Rome, Count Anton Monts, came to a similar conclusion. On 5 February 1907 he reported fatalistically that 'even without any written pact' Italy would be 'no less likely to be found at England's side ... at decisive and important moments than the Gaul who is fettered to the island kingdom by the entente cordiale, apparently for a long time to come'. Kaiser Wilhelm praised this dispatch as 'brilliant', 'quite right' and 'excellently written ... Italy has given us the slip, as I have maintained since 1904!' he wrote. Paris and Rome would come to an agreement 'via London', so that in a war the Italians would be 'at the Gauls' side too'.[25] In his view Italy would certainly call into question the continued existence of the Triple Alliance Treaty 'as soon as England really puts pressure on her!' England could make herself 'as unpleasant as possible towards Italy and join up with Gaul to make Italy do anything they like'. But if Italy pulled out of the Triple Alliance a war between Austro-Hungary and Italy, which would quickly spread into a European war, would be as good as certain. So once again 'everything depends on England!' the Kaiser concluded. 'If England succeeds in removing Italy from the Triple Alliance, Italy will be gone and a general convulsion will be inevitable. As England and Gaul have been allowed to get together it has become even more probable that a war will be triggered by threats or some other way.'[26]

GERMANY BETWEEN BRITAIN AND FRANCE

What routes were there out of the impasse into which the Kaiserreich had strayed? To Holstein it was clear that by the time of the Algeciras conference at the latest, the plan for a 'continental alliance directed against England' had failed. He was convinced that 'we must get closer to England, even though the personal jealousies of the two monarchs will make that rather more difficult'.[27] As he shrewdly observed, however, the Kaiser would have to give up the arms race at sea as a prerequisite for an understanding with Britain. 'He [Kaiser Wilhelm II] will probably not want to go to war against England and France. To give in before a clenched fist would have very serious consequences. Therefore the place at which to give in must be carefully prepared well in advance, with these two formulae in mind: 1. Can we ever, no matter how great our efforts, achieve naval parity with the combined fleets of England and France? In our own right? By alliance? 2. Will the sum total of German military strength be augmented or relatively diminished by an extreme programme of fleet building? A restriction of our land forces, a cause for war. Land forces essential for defence, but not the fleet. We cannot conduct a war against England without allies. No allies in sight. Against Japan we might perhaps proceed with America. Our conflicts with all other Great Powers will be decided on land.'[28]

Holstein reproached the Kaiser and Bülow with clinging to their continental league policy and continuing to seek rapprochement with France; they failed to see that this could not be achieved, because of British mistrust of Germany's hegemonial ambitions. 'It is indubitable', he wrote at the end of August 1906, 'that Bülow does *not* want an improvement in our relations with England ... Bülow has the burning desire to establish closer relations with France. I have the same desire, but do not think it can be achieved at this time. England does not want this rapprochement, and England, which safeguards France's East Asian possessions against Japan, is now more important to France than ever. Furthermore France has far more reason to hope for a "frontier rectification" or a "revision of the Peace of Frankfurt" from an isolated, intimidated German Kaiser than from an ally of France that feels confident of French friendship ... I fear that the Kaiser, in order to get to Paris, and Bülow, in order to get compensation for the alienation of England for which he is partially to blame, will evince a willingness to make concessions that, instead of hastening a rapprochement, will make it more difficult.'[29]

Although Holstein was no longer in office when he wrote these wide-ranging thoughts, he continued to keep in close touch with Bernhard von Bülow, who was now also beginning to see the need for a radical change of foreign policy. In a letter of July 1906 to his brother Alfred, himself a diplomat, the Reich Chancellor castigated the '*stupid*' tirades of hatred uttered by the Pan-German League against Britain, which invited 'the *danger of a world war*', he affirmed. 'I want to maintain good relations with England, on equal terms and on the basis of full German independence ... Our relationship with a great empire like England must be handled with confidence in ourselves as a nation, but also with calm intelligence, without irrational passions ... We have no reason at all to make a permanent enemy of England and to find ourselves on such bad terms with her that we can be sure from the outset that in any political constellation, she will be among our opponents.' In his opinion there was no issue over which, given reciprocal good-will, German and British interests could not be peacefully and fairly reconciled. If Germany were ever attacked, whoever the attacker was, she would fight to the bitter end. 'But in the absence of compelling reasons, to provoke a war which would plunge civilised nations ... into a fearful struggle whose consequences ... for the well-being of the whole world and for the cultural progress of mankind I need not begin to describe to you, is a responsibility which could not be incurred by anyone who is really seriously concerned for the country's welfare and whose love for the fatherland does not consist merely of resounding words.'[30]

It is significant that even in this protracted lecture to his brother the Reich Chancellor said not a word about the chief obstacle to the improvement of German–British relations: the Kaiser's determined support for Tirpitz's battlefleet-building programme. Far from drawing the monarch's attention to the harmful effect of the relentless naval arms race on relations with Great Britain, Bülow outdid himself in praising the accelerated building programme as the Kaiser's 'very own work' after the naval manoeuvres in the autumn of 1907.[31] Not until the months immediately before his dismissal, when it was practically too late, did Bülow dare to suggest to the monarch that both Germany's commitment to *Weltpolitik* and her fleet-building programme should be cut down in the interests of a rapprochement with Britain. Needless to say the suggestion fell on deaf ears.

Of course Kaiser Wilhelm was also well aware of the key role that Britain played in Franco-German relations. In his view the fact that the French generals had been so sure of victory in the Morocco crisis and that there had been such a marked revival in the self-confidence of the French in general was 'chiefly' attributable to their confidence in British help, as he commented in the autumn of 1906.[32] On 19 September he surprised the British ambassador by remarking that England could contribute greatly to improving relations between Berlin and Paris, if only she were willing; England could make sure that the French 'behave decently with me'.[33] Often he raged against the efforts of the British government, and above all of his uncle, Edward VII, to strengthen the ties of the Anglo-French Entente in order to frustrate German plans for a continental league. A plan for an Anglo-French military pact was 'already as good as complete', he commented bitterly in November 1906.[34]

The King's aim was obviously to build up the Entente Cordiale 'into an alliance!' he exclaimed in response to a report from London of 17 October 1906, 'thus putting the French army and navy at England's disposal in order to prevent *us* from getting onto good terms with France'. His concluding remarks on the report revealed the secret formula by which he hoped to force Britain to abandon her policy of maintaining the balance of power on the continent: 'England's attitude will remain unchanged until we are so strong at sea that we become desirable allies.'[35]

It often seemed as if only the fear that Britain might intervene — by dispatching 100,000 men to Schleswig or the Maas and asserting her supremacy at sea — prevented a German attack on France. At the beginning of July 1906 Bülow urged the Minister of War and the Chief of General Staff, in view of the fact that there was 'much jealousy, hatred and enmity towards us in the world' and that Germany was as good as isolated, to investigate whether the army was truly in a fit state of preparation for 'the real thing'. Although Bülow emphasised 'that His Majesty the Kaiser knows nothing of this letter',[36] there is no doubt that Wilhelm II was fully convinced of the battle readiness and superiority of his army. When the British Secretary of State for War, Lord Haldane, came to the imperial manoeuvres in September 1906 the Kaiser, full of good cheer, galloped up to him and said: 'A splendid machine I have in this Army, Ld. Haldane; now isn't it so! And what could I do without it situated as I am between the Russians and the French. But the French are your Allies, so I beg pardon.' Haldane replied that 'were I in His Majesty's place I should feel very comfortable with this machine, & that for my own part I enjoyed much more being behind it than I should had I to be in front of it.'[37] He saw quite clearly that the German army, which was geared solely towards a war with France and Russia, had now reached the peak of its development. 'The organisation of the whole German Army is now perfectly worked out, and probably nothing more in the way of organisation remains to be done. One must remember that the process has been going on for half a century, & that it is directed to a single purpose — war with France & Russia. They would have to do the whole thing over again if they had to face the problem of distant overseas expeditions. For this they have but little provision.'[38] In a conversation with Sir Charles Hardinge, the Under Secretary of State at the British Foreign Office, at Kronberg in August 1906, Kaiser Wilhelm spoke of the 'overwhelming army' which Germany now possessed, and asserted frankly that 'in any war with France, Germany would be able to place in the field three million more men than France and would crush France by sheer weight of numbers. As for Russia it would be a long time before the Russian army could be reorganised ... His Majesty then dwelt upon the attitude of the

French, remarking that the French nation is a bundle of nerves, and a female race not a male race like the Anglo-Saxons and Teutons.'[39]

After Algeciras Wilhelm continued to pursue the policy of rapprochement with France, although at the same time he was not averse to revealing, even when talking to strangers, how he envisaged a future 'friendship' between Germany and France. Thus on 4 April 1906, during a dinner at the American embassy, he spoke of the need to obtain more space for the rapidly growing German population at the expense of France. At his accession the population had numbered forty million; now it stood at sixty million. A growth rate of more than a million young people a year was certainly welcome in itself, but in the course of the next twenty years the question of feeding the population would become acute. Then he remarked 'in a half pleasant way that the time might be ripe to say to France that Germany was over-crowded, that France had a considerable domain not being properly developed or utilized, and would it specially discommode them to move inward a reasonable distance.'[40]

Wilhelm II took malicious pleasure in noting every sign of a weakening of France's world standing. 'The Gauls are very annoyed! That pleases me' became his motto.[41] In December 1906 he was exultant when France and Spain sent a force of three thousand men to Morocco, ostensibly to protect foreigners under threat in Tangier, but in reality with the 'secret intention', as he believed, of 'then being in a position to disembark and annex'. When the German envoy in Tangier suggested that German warships be sent to a port in southern Spain so that they could get to Tangier quickly if the situation became acute, the Kaiser turned down this idea out of hand, on the grounds that the fury of Islam should be directed against France and Spain but not against the German Reich. 'The French poodle and the Spanish mastiff are hunting the Mohammedan bone, Morocco! They will earn themselves a tremendous beating! Because nothing can be done with 3000 men! If they land and the Moroccans gather round the Green Banner to go to war against the Christians, not even 30,000 men will be enough! Let the two of them do as they like! Let the Gauls provoke the Moroccans with their show of strength; then advise the Sultan to let fly and throw the Gauls into the sea, if it is in Morocco's interest! Once the fisticuffs have begun and Gaul is well and truly caught up in a campaign – à la Mexico – then we shall still have time to send ships! But first the whole business must really get going! Then we shall be in a good position, considering our relationship with the Mohammedan world, to act as intermediary! On no account is a ship to go out there, as long as England does not send any from home ... This is a heaven-sent opportunity for the Gauls to be plunged into a second Mexico, and it must not be spoilt! Let them land and send troops and ships until they have sunk their teeth into the

Moroccan lion and he has them by the throat! That will cost a lot of money and many soldiers! God grant it! At the right moment the whole of Morocco, cleverly incited, must be set loose on the Gauls! The latter must fall into the trap without our lifting a finger militarily!'[42] A year earlier Wilhelm had already declared that 'in the present very tense circumstances, when we stand almost *alone* in the face of great coalitions which are being formed against us, our *last trump card* is *Islam* and the *Mohammedan world*'.[43] But the idea that Germany, as 'a Power on such friendly terms with the Mohammedans', would be able to play off Islam against the Entente, also proved illusory. At the very moment when Wilhelm was wishing 'a second Mexico' on the French in Morocco, the British and French governments were secretly buying up shares in a company which owned the rights of access to all the quays in the port of Constantinople. 'We realised at once that if the Germans got hold of them they would gain an enormous advantage at Const[antino]ple & that this would form an important link in their Bagdad Railway scheme', Hardinge told the King's Private Secretary.[44]

Both governments were also doing their best to prevent the Kaiserreich from exerting any influence in Spain, for as Sir Edward Grey put it in December 1906, 'a good deal turns upon Spain just now; it would be very awkward if she turned to Germany away from France & ourselves. The Morocco question would then become more embroiled than ever.'[45] Edward VII's meeting with the King of Spain and afterwards with the King of Italy in April 1907 led to 'grotesque' and 'absurd' attacks on the British King in the German press.[46] Comparisons were made between Edward's successful diplomatic journeys and the failed initiatives of his German nephew. Wilhelm's eldest sister spoke with admiration and envy of 'what my uncle has achieved in terms of standing and reputation in the world through *deeds* (not *hollow* words!!)'.[47] A German general commented despairingly: 'Have we no devil who is German and who would be ready to do deals on our behalf as unscrupulously as fat Edward does for England!? . . . If the situation continues to go downhill, one day we shall find ourselves having to play *va banque*.'[48]

THE KAISER INSISTS ON THE 'ALLIANCE OF FRANCE AND GERMANY'

In spite of all these setbacks Wilhelm did not give up hope of a Franco-German alliance.[49] The chances of such a revolutionary change in the European states system seemed suddenly to improve when he received a letter from Prince Albert of Monaco on 31 May 1907.[50] In the letter the Prince proposed to bring with him to Kiel Week the former French Minister of the Interior and of War, Eugène Étienne, as well as Léopold Mabilleau, the

Figure 15 The Kaiser with Prince Albert of Monaco in Kiel, 1907

President of the Fédération nationale de la Mutualité Française, which had more than five million members; both Frenchmen, 'and likewise the Prince himself', were trying to bring about 'a German-French rapprochement', the Kaiser assumed.[51] In a perfect example of personal diplomacy, Kaiser Wilhelm received the Prince of Monaco and the French ex-Minister at Kiel on the evening of 25 June 1907 (see Figure 15) and afterwards, from the *Hohenzollern*, dictated a telegraphic dispatch to the Reich Chancellor reporting at length on this remarkable meeting. Étienne had immediately brought up the subject of Morocco. 'He explained the French point of view with typical French animation and eloquence. The long and the short of it was as follows: Germany should acknowledge France's supremacy in Morocco. France's only wish was to establish peace and order there. An unsettled Morocco as neighbour to Algiers was impossible and intolerable in the long run . . . France went to Algeciras at Germany's request and in the belief that Germany would stand by her, to enable French preponderance to be recognised. That had not happened, hence the irritation with us. I had been expected to make une déclaration, un mot pour la France in Tangier. That had not happened, hence the bad feeling. There was nothing he longed for more than good relations between Germany and France. It lay in my hands to bring this about: un mot, un beau geste de l'Empereur, and all would be well. Then a bon accord between the two countries could be established and, more or less by way of compensation, border adjustments or corrections would be conceded to us in the colonies, e.g. in Africa. I answered as follows: France had concluded the Morocco agreement with England in the spring of 1904 behind our backs, without informing us, and therefore against us. Our interests had been considerably endangered as a result, and likewise those of all other European colonies in Morocco. I knew that personally from the leaders of the latter. I had given France a year to inform me of what had been agreed but this had not been done. That was why the Algeciras conference had been called into being, so that the regulation of Moroccan affairs could be settled by the Great Powers together. Morocco was a free country under an independent hereditary dynasty, over which no single Great Power could claim preponderance unless it was established by conquest or through a protectorate. The Algeciras Act, which is the basis on which we stand, prevented that. In the spring we had given definite proof of our goodwill towards France when she overstepped the border and occupied Oudjda ... On my advice the Sultan had shown himself willing to grant France's multifarious requests ... These were direct services I had rendered to France without having been compelled in any way to do so. But all these services received little thanks from France, and things remained as they had been. As far as the beau geste was concerned, I had made plenty of them in the course of my 19-year reign! ... Vous n'en avez pas tiré les conséquences. [You did not give them the credit they deserved.] I was very glad that he was in favour of an accord between our two countries, that was absolutely in France's interest and it was the only right thing to do. But an accord offering small favours in the colonies would no longer suffice. The great questions about the future which were arising in the world demanded a united Europe, and that required Germany and France to go hand in hand ... Germany was strong enough to regard such political antics [i.e. the ententes] with cool amusement. We could not be left out after all, in spite of all Ententes. The great nations of the future, Japan and America, were already taking us into account and positioning themselves with us. France, on the other hand, had forfeited her freedom of action and was being dragged along in England's wake; England dictated what she pleased to Paris, and France had become England's helpless slave ... The time for the beau geste was now over, it was France's turn to give us solid proof of her goodwill. I would take France's wish for prépondérance morale [supremacy] in Morocco into favourable consideration only après que la France aura conclu une alliance fixe avec l'Allemagne [after France had concluded a firm alliance with Germany]. If the French were my allies their wishes would receive a sympathetic hearing from me and things would go as well for them, and their existence would be as assured as that of Austria and Italy. I could no longer accept the principle France has followed hitherto: to offer an arm to the Russian, a hand to the Briton, but a mere greeting to the German. I now demanded the hand too, at the very least; better still would be the arm. My hand had been loyally held out to them for 19 years; France had offered her hand to everyone else but had turned her back on me. I still held it out, in spite of all that. I advised them to accept it before it was too late ... So first of all an alliance, regardless of her alliance with Russia, then prépondérance morale in Morocco.' At this Étienne had made 'a gesture of despair' while the Prince of Monaco, who was sitting next to the Kaiser, had agreed with the latter on every point. 'With that the drama came to to end.'[52]

The next morning Étienne repeated the whole conversation in the presence of Prince Albert and Mabilleau and, according to the Kaiser, exclaimed that the 'alliance of France and Germany' was 'the best thing' after all. After lunch Mabilleau came up to the Kaiser and confirmed that the former minister had been completely won over to the idea of an alliance; the Kaiser had been quite right to explain the situation to him so clearly. Mabilleau himself would at once go to see Léon Bourgeois, whom he described as the 'coming man', and 'would tell him everything and work on him to that end. He would also inspire his 5 million Mutuels with the same spirit, and that was a good weapon for Bourgeois to use to put pressure on those in high places.' By their attitude Étienne and Mabilleau showed, the Kaiser wrote to his 'Dear Bernhard', 'how much Morocco matters to them, so that they are even ready to go ahead with an alliance with us for its sake! Well, plenty of water will flow down the Seine and the Spree before that happens. But I believe that I have sown seeds that will one day grow into fine plants, God willing.'[53] When the Kaiser met the Prince of Monaco again at Tromsø during his Scandinavian voyage, the Prince was able to report to him on the very favourable effect of his conversations with Étienne and Mabilleau at Kiel. 'The question of a rapprochement with Germany was being eagerly discussed ... everywhere [in France], something that would have been quite impossible a year ago.'[54]

As so often, the Kaiser had been dealing with outsiders and had greatly overestimated their influence on the decisions of those actually in power. He was all the more annoyed to find that the new French ambassador in Berlin, Jules Cambon, had taken the meeting with Étienne amiss and had not been among the ambassadors who came to Kiel Week. He interpreted Cambon's absence as a deliberate snub by the French government.[55] France's decision not to send any warships to Kiel seemed to him to show equally malicious intent. When Cambon tried to explain that he had not come to Kiel because he had not received even an indirect hint that his presence was expected, and moreover that no other European Power had sent any warships to Kiel Week, the Kaiser was enraged. 'Nor did Inouye and Tower [the Japanese and American ambassadors] receive one; both simply informed me they would be there', he wrote angrily on Radolin's report from Paris. 'Monsieur Cambon is perfectly well aware that he showed colossal stupidity and tactlessness in not coming to Kiel. If he was unsure whether he should come or not – considering how many distinguished and important Frenchmen were there – he could have *asked*. All his excuses are just childish! – He, the man who said himself je vais à Berlin pour causer, misses the best opportunity to do so, Kiel Week, to which a great many people came pour causer: as if he had never heard of Kiel Week! . . . No! There are other reasons behind it! That he is lying is evident from his ridiculous remark about sending ships, as if other Europ[ean] states had to be there in order for Gaul to send us a ship! The man is an ass! What better opportunity to send a ship than the regattas for the Coupe de France, a wholly official affair! – No! Monsieur Cambon must spare me such lame excuses; I know too much about it!'[56]

In mid July 1907 Otto von Mühlberg took advantage of a diplomatic reception at the Auswärtiges Amt to read out to Cambon extracts from the Kaiser's telegram about his conversation with Étienne. The purpose of this, as the Under Secretary explained to Bülow, was to demonstrate to Cambon that the rumours constantly repeated by the French press of a conflict between the Kaiser's policy and that of the German government were completely untrue. 'And secondly he was to be made to understand that his offers of small agreements and arrangements would not suffice.' Cambon, however, would not give up his 'pet idea of smaller agreements' and expressed the hope 'that given the suspicious, nervous mood that prevails between our two countries . . . these delicate little palliative measures' might bring about 'a certain reassur-ance, an awakening of mutual trust'. Moreover, the ambassador had launched boldly into the crucial question of Alsace-Lorraine, and had stated point-blank that the annexation had been a mistake by Bismarck. If he had left the French-speaking districts to France and turned Alsace into an autonomous region, France could have lived in perfect peace with Germany.[57]

THE CONFRONTATION WITH EDWARD VII AT SCHLOSS FRIEDRICHSHOF

For the Kaiser there was no doubt who was responsible for the indestructible web of ententes and agreements that had spun itself around Germany since 1904. It was not for the first time on the outbreak of war in the summer of

1914 but ten years earlier that he accused Britain, and his uncle above all, of having plotted to prejudice the governments and newspapers of almost every other country against him.[58] In February 1907 Wilhelm raged against Edward VII, who he believed had travelled to Paris once again in order to frustrate 'Gaul's wish for an understanding with us'.[59] He complained bitterly to his entourage of how his uncle was 'intriguing against him. He said he knew it for a fact from private letters from France. But the King of England was working equally hard against him in other countries too. In fact the entire press, including the American, had already been turned against him by English money; it was incredible how much personal hatred was demonstrated in this behaviour by his uncle. He concluded these remarks by saying: "He is a Satan; it is quite unbelievable what a Satan he is."'[60] He saw the exchange of notes on 16 May 1907 between Britain, France, Spain and Italy, which preserved the status quo in the Mediterranean, as a coup by his uncle directed 'more or less against Germany, by freeing the English Mediterranean fleet'.[61] There was most certainly a danger, Wilhelm believed, of France being 'harried by England into a war with Germany', but 'we shall not do them this favour!'[62] In response to the assurances of the French ambassador in London that Edward VII was a 'playboy' who would find it too much trouble to wage a war Wilhelm observed bitterly: 'But he can let "others" wage it.' When Paul Cambon remarked that there were indeed certain dangers in the King's inclination to pursue policies 'very pointedly aimed against his imperial nephew', Wilhelm reacted scornfully with the words: 'I am not perturbed! and look down from my trusty beast upon the riff-raff far beneath.'[63] Edward and his island kingdom were trying to curry favour with everyone except Germany, 'the better to be able to attack us with the help of everyone!', he suspected.[64]

In this mood, convinced that 'time . . . is certainly on our side', Wilhelm was not at all inclined to take the first step towards reconciliation. Rather, after the humiliation of Algeciras, he chose to play a waiting game with Britain, 'until the time is ripe'.[65] He insisted that the first steps towards a rapprochement should come from Britain herself, and reacted impatiently to the London government's assertions that it was eager to establish better relations. 'In that case the gentlemen will have to make up their minds to get on with it at long last', he wrote in the margin of a report from London of 19 May 1906. 'Why should we always have to make the first move!'[66]

The most influential advocate of Anglo-German rapprochement in the British Cabinet – the Kaiser called him 'a white raven! [i.e. a very rare bird!]'[67] – was the Secretary of State for War, Lord Haldane.[68] In May 1906 Haldane, in conversation with Metternich, conceded that 'Germany would have to be given territories into which she could channel her energy and vigour.

We [the Germans] had arrived a hundred years too late with our colonial policy, when almost everything had already been spoken for. He thought it all the more necessary that England should not oppose any remaining possibility of extending German influence.' In the interests of reconciliation between Germany and Britain Haldane thought it 'of the greatest importance', Metternich reported, 'that His Majesty the Kaiser should resume personal contact with King Edward, and he hopes that a meeting between the two monarchs will take place in the not too distant future'.[69] 'I have no objection!' the Kaiser asserted. 'H[is] M[ajesty] is welcome to visit me.'[70] On both sides, however, the question of a meeting was treated with the utmost caution. In London there was concern that a reunion between the King and the Kaiser might be misinterpreted in France and have an unsettling effect on relations between the two countries.[71] For Wilhelm II, after the affront of September 1905[72] the question of meeting his uncle became an emotionally charged matter of prestige. When it was suggested that a rendezvous with Edward in the Mediterranean might be arranged, Wilhelm, clearly hurt, annotated Metternich's telegram with the remark that the King had 'shot down that kind of thing twice in the past year! Let him come and call on *me* if he wants to see me! A meeting in the Mediterranean *is not good enough for me* after the insults on his part last year.'[73] He doubted that even a 'friendly meeting ... between the two related Sovereigns' would be able to change German–British relations for the better, commenting: 'I don't think so! Barely two years have gone by since Kiel! Meetings with E[dward] VII have no lasting value because he is envious. Propter invidiam.'[74]

In July 1906 Wilhelm finally accepted the King's suggestion that they should meet at Schloss Friedrichshof outside Kronberg while he was on his way to Marienbad. But neither the Kaiser nor the Chancellor pinned any political hopes on the visit. Wilhelm telegraphed to Bülow: 'Friedrichshof will suit very well for the meeting with Edward VII. In point of fact nothing will change at all, as he will remain as jealous as ever and continue to intrigue against us; but outwardly it will contribute to calm in the world.'[75] Nevertheless until the last moment a matter of form threatened to wreck the meeting. From the very beginning the British had made it a condition that the German newspapers should not depict the meeting of the two monarchs as if it were a demonstration of the King eating humble pie.[76] Yet the Kaiser insisted that the initiative for the meeting must come from the King.[77] The Reich Chancellor considered that the Kaiser was 'quite right' to take this stand and instructed Metternich to act accordingly in London.[78] In the end the troublesome question of an invitation was settled through family channels: the King mentioned his wish for a meeting with the Kaiser to the Crown Princess of

Greece, Wilhelm's sister Sophie, who was on a visit to London and who passed on the message to her sister Princess Margarethe of Hesse. The interview between the two monarchs did, however, acquire a political dimension by virtue of Edward's wish to bring Sir Charles Hardinge, the Under Secretary of State at the Foreign Office, discreetly with him to Kronberg.[79] Lascelles, the British ambassador in Berlin, was also summoned.[80] This decision was made easier for the British by the news from Berlin that the Kaiser had invited Foreign Secretary Heinrich von Tschirschky to take part in the meeting.[81] Wilhelm went so far as to condemn an announcement in the *Daily Telegraph* that the forthcoming visit by the King was of a strictly non-political character as 'disgraceful' and confirmed his decision to take Tschirschky with him to Kronberg, now most particularly in order to underline 'the political significance of the visit'.[82]

The conversation between the two monarchs passed off, as Wilhelm reported to the Reich Chancellor on 16 August 1906, 'to my complete satisfaction'. They discussed the worrying developments in Russia and Austria-Hungary and agreed that on Franz Ferdinand's accession his morganatic wife should be recognised as Empress.[83] To Kaiser Wilhelm's 'great astonishment' the King expressed himself 'extremely critically' on the subject of the forthcoming second Peace Conference at The Hague, which Edward described as positively dangerous. In a record of his discussion with the King written partly in his own hand, Wilhelm stated that it was also his own 'strong belief that it would be better if the [Hague] Conference did not take place at all. But if it were too late to prevent the conference in The Hague from assembling, it seemed sensible to me ... for Germany and England to come to an understanding on a few major issues beforehand, if possible. These, in my opinion, included the maritime questions above all. If England and Germany came forward at the conference with a definitely agreed programme on precisely these questions, these would be as good as accepted in advance.'[84] The King, Hardinge and Lascelles promised to pass on the Kaiser's suggestion to the British government, and did so.[85] In his record Wilhelm expressly emphasised that in proposing to cooperate with London in this way his aim had been above all 'to achieve a basis for a direct agreement on some subject or other with England, as a result of which closer relations could develop gradually between us. Whether in concreto it will be possible to achieve a practical result is a secondary consideration.' He was therefore deeply disappointed when the London Cabinet completely failed to react to his suggestion.[86]

Of course Wilhelm was not motivated by purely altruistic wishes for a rapprochement, and the British government's refusal to respond was understandable. The Kaiser's attitude, in fact, was driven by his suspicion that discussions on disarmament at the Peace Conference would enable the British to discover the extent of Germany's naval plans. 'We have known that for a long time', he commented on a report that at The Hague Britain intended to demand explanations from Germany on the increase of her fleet. 'That is why it is essential that our old programme from the last Hague Conference is maintained. Only if the "disarmament question" is *completely excluded* shall I send representatives to the Conference, otherwise *not*.'[87] Even at Kronberg the Kaiser 'repeatedly and emphatically' told the King and Hardinge 'that Germany had to stand by the Navy Law which was laid down and published six years ago. But Germany was not building up her fleet with aggressive intentions towards one state or another, and would organise her naval power only in accordance with what was needed in her own interest to protect her trade.' With respect to the conference at The Hague, Wilhelm recorded, he had explained very clearly to Lascelles at Kronberg 'that my instructions to my Ministers had remained the same as for the first Conference: in the event that the disarmament question came up in any form whatever, Germany would refuse to participate. As neither I nor my people would ever tolerate foreigners giving us any kind of orders regarding our military and naval affairs.'[88]

In his lengthy negotiations with Hardinge the Kaiser sang the praises of militarism, surprising the British diplomat by remarking that 'when people talk of the reduction of military forces Germans only smile. The German nation has not forgotten the peace of Tilsit, and ever since they had been firmly resolved to exist by the strength of their own right arm, and for this they had built up their overwhelming army of the present day.' Hardinge raised the natural objection that the reason for the Franco-Russian alliance and the Anglo-French Entente lay precisely in Germany's military superiority. 'The Emperor replied by assuring me of his most peaceful intentions, and that the question of war with France during last winter had never been seriously contemplated although he was well aware of the fears entertained in France as to his alleged intentions, which were absolutely without foundation. His sole aim and policy were to find commercial outlets for the ever-increasing and superabundant population of Germany.' Summing up his conversations with the Kaiser and Tschirschky, Hardinge wrote: 'I was struck by their evident desire to be on friendly terms with us, and by the fact that they now seem at last to realise that friendly relations with us cannot be at the expense of our "entente" with France, but that if they are to exist at all they must be co-existent with our "entente". I took every opportunity of rubbing this in.'[89]

British policy towards Germany remained unchanged if only for the reason that the King and the government in London unanimously supported the Entente with France and the rapprochement with Russia as the only effective means of preserving the balance of power in Europe. The British diplomat Louis Mallet correctly analysed the hidden agenda behind Berlin's ostentatious friendliness when on 6 June 1906 he commented, in connection with the forthcoming meeting of the two monarchs at Kronberg, that the Germans had 'made a great failure of the brutal method of destroying the Entente and now they mean to try what can be done by means of Municipal visits, Press visits, artists exhibitions Ministers visits to Berlin. Above & beyond all they hope to achieve their end by a meeting of the King with the Emperor.' Such a meeting would be regarded with deep suspicion in France and would certainly be exploited by the Germans in Russia too, Mallet warned. At any rate Britain must not put the enormous gains of the last few years at stake, he urged. 'The position to which we have attained in Europe during the last 3 years is entirely due to the Anglo-French entente & it has made us stronger than we have ever been since Palmerston's day. For the first time for many years we are able to deal with Germany on a footing of equality & our relations are now quite normal with that country. It has also brought an entente with Russia almost in sight. These are great results & it seems to me essential that we should continue on the same course, treating France *as if* she were an ally. I am convinced that in this way we shall maintain normal relations with Germany who will accept the situation & be prepared to live on friendly terms with us, once she recognizes that our close friendship with France is indissoluble. I consider that the insidious method of smashing up the entente which will now be tried both in London & Paris more dangerous than the drastic measures wh. have failed.' King Edward had read Mallet's warning letter shortly before his departure for Kronberg.[90]

RUSSIA BETWEEN A THREE EMPERORS' LEAGUE AND THE TRIPLE ENTENTE

At the time of their meeting at Friedrichshof in August 1906 both Kaiser Wilhelm and his uncle Edward could entertain hopes of an agreement with Russia that would be crucial for the future of the European states system. A Three Emperors' Alliance between Germany, Russia and Austria-Hungary would not only have fortified the conservative, monarchical-militaristic states in central and eastern Europe against the onslaught of liberal and democratic forces but would also have given a considerable boost to German hegemonial ambitions on the continent. On the other hand the expansion of the Anglo-French Entente to bring in Tsarist Russia — which had already been firmly allied to France for ten years — through a direct agreement with Great Britain would have completed the containment, or the 'encirclement' as it was seen in

Germany, of the Kaiser's supremacist policy. Despite the fact that the Triple Entente came into being in August 1907 on the signature of an Anglo-Russian agreement, it should not be forgotten that this was by no means a foregone conclusion and that despite countless setbacks, Wilhelm II continued to hope for an alliance with the Tsar until the very last moment.

True, even he could not fail to realise that the cooperation between Europe's two flanking Powers at the Algeciras conference had brought an Anglo-Russian rapprochement closer. Negotiations between London and St Petersburg received further powerful impetus from the appointment of the influential Sir Charles Hardinge as Permanent Under Secretary of State at the Foreign Office and that of Alexander Isvolsky as Russian Foreign Minister in the spring of 1906. Wilhelm II reacted bitterly to the increasing signs that a Triple Entente between Britain, France and Russia was in the offing. When he was informed in April 1906 that the Austrian ambassador in St Petersburg had voiced the fear that the cooling of German–Russian relations 'would give King Edward a welcome opportunity to approach Russia and seek an understanding with her', the Kaiser stormed: 'It doesn't matter! and cannot be prevented!' Fear of a rapprochement between Britain and Russia would not persuade him to cultivate the old friendly relations with Russia. 'We have done our *cultivating*! to no effect! Now let the Russians *cultivate* for once!' The thought that as part of an agreement Britain would be ready to relinquish Constantinople and the Straits to the Russians aroused his fury. 'Aha! Another international accord to break without asking the other countries!' he wrote. On the other hand he refused to intervene actively to prevent the Russian–British Entente which was now on the horizon. 'No!' he wrote in the margin of a report from Wedel, for that would make sure that 'the two really do get together!!'[91]

Under Isvolsky the Russian Foreign Ministry also followed 'more and more in England's wake', which prompted the Kaiser to remark bitterly in September 1906: 'A nice prospect! So in future we can reckon on the Franco-Russian Alliance, the Franco-English Entente cordiale and the Anglo-Russian Entente, with Spain, Italy and Portugal as second-rank appendages!'[92] Immediately after his appointment as Foreign Minister Isvolsky received from the German ambassador in St Petersburg a warning that although the German Reich welcomed a peaceful agreement between Russia and Great Britain over their respective interests in the Middle East, it most certainly expected to be consulted on everything affecting German interests.[93] The impression this warning made on Isvolsky was all the greater because memories of Delcassé's fate after the Morocco agreement with London were still fresh. And during his visit to Berlin in October 1906, when he was received by both the Kaiser and Bülow, Isvolsky observed that the Germans were 'extraordinarily sensitive . . .

with regard to any arrangement which might be come to between any two countries without their having been consulted'.[94]

For a short while the possibility of an understanding between Germany and Russia flickered into life when, in May 1906, Tsar Nicholas reverted to a suggestion made by the Kaiser the previous year that they should meet after the naval manoeuvres in the autumn.[95] Wilhelm II responded willingly and proposed that the Tsar should come to Swinemünde at the beginning of August to meet him on his return from his Scandinavian voyage.[96] Even before his departure for Norway, however, the Kaiser began to doubt whether the Tsar would be able to travel abroad in view of the continuing revolutionary unrest in Russia. He telegraphed to the Reich Chancellor in early July: 'Since the "emeute" of the I. Bat. Preobrajensk I consider ... the situation very serious and extremely dangerous; therefore very doubtful whether Tsar can leave country. He might run the risk of receiving a request to stay out of the country permanently; with a ban on returning. I do not think a catastrophe can be ruled out.'[97] Bülow replied: 'The situation in Russia is undoubtedly very grave ... Your Majesty is therefore certainly right to leave it to His Majesty the Emperor of Russia to decide whether His Majesty believes he can leave his country now and under these circumstances. It is of course all the more important that nothing definite about the plan for a meeting leaks out, for otherwise it would be said later that the cancellation of the meeting was a sign of the cooling of our relations with Russia.'[98]

In fact the naval attaché, Paul von Hintze, reported from St Petersburg on 18 July 1906 that the Tsar would not be able to come to meet the Kaiser on 1 August as arranged, because of the internal situation in Russia; but Nicholas hoped that in six to eight weeks calm would have been restored.[99] The postponement of the emperors' meeting was greeted with relief both in Germany and in Russia, where it 'could have given rise to very unpleasant comments in the Press and other undesirable and dangerous manifest-ations'.[100] Bülow stated expressly that it was 'no misfortune if the meeting between His Majesty and the Tsar does not take place'. At any rate it was better that the Russians had given up the plan 'than if we had cried off'. As a result there was no reason 'to link comments on Russian–German relations with the cancellation of the meeting. All in all our attitude towards events in Russia can never be calm and cautious enough.'[101] It was a view which Kaiser Wilhelm fully shared.[102]

After his return from Norway the Kaiser was infuriated by rumours that he had sent a telegram to the Tsar proposing to intervene to suppress the revolution in Russia; the story was 'sheer lies'. When the Wilhelmstrasse suggested to him that in view of the difficult situation in Russia and its effect on German–Russian relations he should abstain from direct correspondence with the Tsar, particularly as Nicholas was known to have a habit of reading out the telegrams to his Foreign Minister, with the result that they then landed on the desks of the cabinets in Paris and London, the Kaiser exploded with anger. 'The blessed Pythia at Delphi herself' would have been given 'a fearful headache' by the convoluted train of thoughts of the Auswärtiges Amt, he mocked. 'I hope the instructions given to my diplomats are less baffling!' He rejected the Foreign Office's advice to have a secret message sent to Isvolsky, instead of telegraphing to the Tsar, with incredulity. 'So that is supposed to be a better way!! ... If Isvolsky wants to tell lies, then he will immediately lie to his master too, as well as to London and Paris.' The spurious rumour of the telegram 'about our alleged intention to intervene' in Russia was the proof 'that whether I telegraph or not such telegrams will be invented. So it is better and more loyal *towards the Tsar* to telegraph, for he is the *only* person who matters to me! As for his ministers or his entourage, they don't change, those swine.'[103] Assurances that even if Russia were to enter the ranks of the constitutional states she would always give pride of place to the monarchical principle, like Germany and Austria, fell on deaf ears with Wilhelm, who regarded them with as much suspicion as the alleged Russian desire for a 'strengthening of relations between the Dreikaiser Powers' – all this was mere 'fantasy', he claimed. The mission to uphold imperial power 'requires a different Emperor' from Nicholas II.[104] Nicholas was not false, but he was weak, and the end result was the same.[105] Nevertheless Wilhelm still thought of a Dreikaiserbund to defend the monarchical, conservative system as the ideal solution. He commented approvingly on 18 November 1906 on the 'very gratifying' and 'right' programme put forward by the new Foreign Minister in Vienna, Aehrenthal, who promised to uphold the Triple Alliance 'with special attention to German and Austrian relations with Russia', particularly because 'given the present world situation and the progress made by democratic attitudes and institutions in almost all countries, the survival of monarchy could be guaranteed only if the three imperial Powers kept together'.[106]

Isvolsky also reaffirmed his wish for unity between the three eastern empires, but Kaiser Wilhelm interpreted such statements as self-serving lies. 'Why did he not honestly and openly come over to *us* and join forces with *us!?*' he asked in March 1907. The Russian Foreign Minister constantly invoked 'the shared interests of the dynasties', but 'in practice he never makes use of them!' The recent agreement between France and Japan, which Isvolsky had promoted and welcomed, would soon cause him 'bitter regret!', in Wilhelm's opinion, especially as he had also induced the 'Gauls' to advance money to the Japanese for armaments. Obsessed as he was with the 'Yellow Peril', the Kaiser found the Russian attitude towards Japan completely incomprehensible. Why, if Isvolsky did not wish the Japanese to become too powerful, did Gaul 'lend them several billions with the consent of the Russians!' he asked. He poured scorn on the Russian minister's assertions that Russia had to show herself to be accommodating for fear of another threat of war from Japan. 'Oh for heaven's sake!' he wrote in the margin of the report from St Petersburg. 'He thinks he has already sunk so low.' The Kaiser rejected Isvolsky's claim that the rumours of an Entente à quatre between Russia, France, Britain and Japan were completely unfounded. 'I believe them and so do *all* my compatriots!' Russian policy, 'as the devil knows', was bizarre and mean-minded; 'as usual' Germany was 'not taken into consideration at all ... as if we did not exist!' Isvolsky's assurances of the warmth of his personal feelings towards Germany were 'Rubbish! Far from it!' the Kaiser thundered. On the contrary, he was aiming at a 'Triple Alliance!' with Britain and France. From now on Germany must be 'as cold as an icicle' towards the Tsarist Empire.[107]

Suddenly the tide turned again when Tsar Nicholas held out the prospect of coming to Swinemünde for three days at the beginning of August 1907 – a year later than originally planned. From his Scandinavian cruise Wilhelm set hectic preparations in motion which show what high expectations he had of this meeting of the two monarchs. He asked Bülow to come and stay on board the *Hohenzollern* from 1 August so that they would have sufficient time to get ready for the negotiations.[108] Under the seal of secrecy he ordered the Prussian envoy in Karlsruhe 'to convey *verbally* to Admiral von Tirpitz, who is at present in St Blasien, the All-Highest command to come on board the Hohenzollern at Swinemünde in the afternoon of 1st August, in order to attend the reception of the Emperor of Russia which will take place on 3rd August. His Majesty the Kaiser asks Your Excellency to say *nothing* to the Grand Duke and Duchess of Baden until further notice and also to enjoin the strictest secrecy upon the Secretary of State of the Reich Navy Office.'[109]

The principal item on the agenda for the Swinemünde meeting was the treaty of alliance signed by both sovereigns exactly two years earlier in Björkö, followed by the attitude to be adopted by the two countries at the Peace Conference at The Hague and the contentious question of the Baghdad railway.[110] With regard to the current position of the Björkö treaty, Tschirschky sent the Chancellor a note stating, curiously: 'We consider the defensive treaty of alliance between Germany and Russia signed by both Sovereigns at Björkö on 24 July 1905 as still legitimate. His Majesty the Kaiser did not agree to the additional declaration concerning France which His Majesty the Emperor of Russia requested later, since according to the

Tsar the Franco-Russian alliance is of a purely defensive nature, and therefore does not conflict with the German–Russian *defensive* treaty. Russia was reassured by this.'[111]

Whatever the Kaiser was expecting from the Tsar's visit to Swinemünde, politically he achieved nothing at all except a vague declaration from Nicholas II that he wished to remain on a good footing with Germany for reasons of monarchical solidarity.[112] The three days were filled with naval reviews, battle manoeuvres and banquets attended by both emperors, Prince Heinrich, Bülow, Tirpitz, Isvolsky, Plessen, Büchsel, Holtzendorff, Hintze and numerous other German and Russian naval officers and aides de camp. Tsar Nicholas made a surprisingly favourable impression on Lieutenant-Commander Albert Hopman. 'I liked him very much for his youthful bearing. One's first impression is of shyness, but behind it there is much gravity, thought and tact. His expression is very well-meaning and rather soft, for a man. But inwardly he is . . . much stronger and steadier than the world believes.' His own monarch's demeanour, on the other hand, dismayed this perceptive naval officer. Wilhelm had shown 'a very crass lack of judgement' by repeating to the Tsar, during the battle exercise, a remark made by Tirpitz: 'The "Dreadnought" ought to be out there now, with Fisher in the middle of her' [English in the original]. Hopman recorded that the Tsar 'gave a forced smile. Edward will probably hear of it soon.' And then in his farewell speech on board the *Standart* Kaiser Wilhelm, full of pride in the navy that Germany had achieved through serious hard work and devotion to duty, had expressed the hope that the Tsar would succeed in building up a similar navy in the same way. 'He might as well have given him [the Tsar] a box on the ears', one German naval officer commented.[113]

After the Tsar's departure Bülow and Isvolsky had statements issued to the press emphasising the peaceful, family nature of the meeting between the two emperors.[114] For his part, Hardinge was able to report with satisfaction that the encounter at Swinemünde had done nothing to disturb negotiations between Great Britain and Russia, now in an advanced state. 'To judge from the official communiqué the meeting of the two Emperors was all that it should be, and we should have no reason to regret it . . . I do not think he [Wilhelm] will have been able to do anything to upset our proposed agreement with Russia however tempted he may have been to do so.'[115]

At first, his meeting with Nicholas II filled Wilhelm with renewed hope of a united front of the three empires, each of which possessed a strong government and a powerful army, against the liberal tendencies promoted by the western Powers. 'Rubbish!' he wrote angrily on an English press report remarking on Edward VII's popularity in Germany. 'We are still on closer terms with the Tsar!'[116] 'Quite right' and 'very good' was his verdict on a report of 9 August 1907 on the mood in Moscow, in which attention was drawn to the alleged link between British and French foreign policy and the democratic movement in Russia. This was exactly what Germany and Russia must give each other strong moral support to combat, he commented.[117]

Three weeks after the Tsar left Swinemünde shattering news reached Berlin. A wide-ranging agreement had been signed between Russia and Great Britain.[118] According to the reports, it was to be ratified by the signatures of Tsar Nicholas II and King Edward VII and would not be published until after that. In a move heavy with symbolic significance, the King invited the French statesman Georges Clemenceau and the Russian Foreign Minister Alexander Isvolsky to Marienbad.[119] As ever, Reich Chancellor Prince Bülow gave orders for 'calm and objective' treatment of the Anglo-Russian agreement in the press. On no account was it to be 'blown up into an English-Russian alliance or needlessly depicted as injuring German interests'.[120] In reality, however, there could scarcely have been a greater setback for his, or rather the Kaiser's, ambitions for world power than the union of Europe's two flanking Powers, both of which were also allied to France. As Bülow's biographer Gerd Fesser puts it: 'Bülow's foreign policy plan of playing off the Kaiserreich's rivals against each other had ended in an unparalleled fiasco.'[121]

THE RESPONSIBILITY OF KAISER WILHELM II

After the conclusion of the Anglo-Russian agreement, which put the seal on the Triple Entente, Sir Charles Hardinge congratulated his King effusively on the great success of British policy, which had at last succeeded in building a barrier against the danger flowing from the Kaiserreich. 'I venture to express the opinion that no Sovereign has ever, by peaceful methods, contributed more than Your Majesty to the pursuit of a successful foreign policy and to the predominance of his country in the Councils of Europe. When a comparison is made of the position of England abroad in 1900 and what this country now occupies Your Majesty has every reason for a feeling of profound satisfaction.'[122] The verdicts of Germans on their own sovereign, who had led the proud Reich created by Bismarck into the cul-de-sac of isolation, sounded very different. The fiery patriot Maximilian Harden had nothing but scorn for the failure of German diplomacy all along the line. 'On rira', he wrote to Walther Rathenau. 'Russia–Japan, Russia–England, Italy–Austria, France–Spain–England (Italy as sleeping partner) have alliances. We rejoice. For "world peace" is ensured.'[123] Above all he castigated the 'disgraceful' policy of 'Wilhelm the Peaceful', which in his opinion had led to disaster.[124] 'Ceterum censeo', he wrote to Friedrich von Holstein in the winter of 1906. 'It is my sincere conviction, after considering the matter again and again: the personal policy of the Kaiser is at the root of all evil ... Not enough of a Coburger to drive a hard bargain, not enough of a Hohenzollern to maintain a dignified reserve, and, whenever necessary, to show himself brave and fearless. If this manner of conducting policy by impromptu inspirations, whose consequences are never thought through to their conclusion, does not cease, I can see no hope.'[125]

No one recognised as clearly as the elderly, dismissed Privy Councillor Fritz von Holstein the fatal combination represented by Kaiser Wilhelm's personal diplomacy on the one hand and the ambitious battlefleet-building policy aimed at superpower status and challenging the other European Great Powers, on the other. On the eve of the signature of the agreement between Russia and Britain Holstein provided the Reich Chancellor with an analysis of the shortcomings of the Kaiser's policy which was of a quality unequalled either at court or in any government office and which, if those in authority had only taken notice of it, could have led to prudent reconsideration and a change of direction even at this late stage. Alluding both to the manner in which Wilhelm II suddenly gave way at the height of the Morocco crisis in June 1905 and to his attitude during his recent meeting with the former French Minister of War, Étienne, at Kiel, Holstein was highly critical of the combination of threats of war and premature withdrawal which characterised the Kaiser's foreign policy. 'That is his speciality. He will, even if he reigns for another twenty-five years, always let *la proie* [the prey] get away and chase after *l'ombre* [the shadow]. His foreign policy is sterile, his naval policy is sterile, and neither one nor the other will have any practical result for both are built up on false principles. He likes to begin his foreign policy with an attempt at intimidation, but retreats if the opposition does not at once give in. (Krüger Telegram, speech at Tangier.) This characteristic, which at first was recognised only by Uncle Edward, is now common knowledge. For that reason it will be difficult to find anyone stupid enough to give in to us before H.M. has time to do so himself.' Holstein's criticism of the battlefleet programme was even more fundamental. 'The naval policy is of benefit to the naval trust (armour-plating, etc.) and the promotion of naval officers. For the rest of Germany it is detrimental and an indubitable danger both in foreign and domestic affairs', he warned. 'The Kaiser's speeches about the fleet, the Navy League, and the convulsive naval armaments – these are the things that have consolidated an overwhelming naval superiority against us. At no time and under no circumstances can our navy hope to hold its own against this superiority. For that reason this naval policy is sterile. If it is nevertheless continued ... – then this would fall into the category of dangerous playthings ... It is childish to state that our navy will be able to face the combined forces of England and France. It is also childish diplomacy when Étienne or Radolin dangle before us the possibility of drawing France away from England over to our side. What can England offer the French, and what have we to offer? Overseas? And a [German] attack along the Vosges no longer has to be considered [by the French]. Any worries that may have remained about *that* after Algeciras have been swept away by H.M.' Holstein saw as particularly dangerous 'the repercussion the Kaiser's sterile policy will inevitably have at home. This danger is a great one. When people once begin to see that the sacrifices that are being demanded *crescendo* for the navy are purposeless tomfoolery, then Hervéism [Holstein is referring to conscientious objection and calls for the class struggle] will develop to such an extent that a nervous character like H.M. will feel obliged to reckon with it. Then we will have reason to fear a *domestic* Algeciras, and that means – into the frying pan . . . I cannot get rid of the feeling that the way H.M. is conducting affairs – always arming and always ignominiously backing down or running after somebody – that this cannot go on much longer.'[126]

Reich Chancellor Prince von Bülow fully recognised the accuracy of Holstein's analysis, but had neither the courage nor the opportunity to act upon it against the Kaiser. On 31 August 1907, the day of the signature of the Anglo-Russian agreement, Holstein wrote to his cousin Ida von Stülpnagel: 'Bülow is perfectly capable of seeing what is right, but the Kaiser says and does what he wants, and Bülow is dragged along behind him.' The retired Privy Councillor was forced to acknowledge, fatalistically, that his once considerable influence had vanished. 'If the Kaiser has misguided ideas on foreign or naval policy I am powerless to prevent it.'[127]

Like Holstein and many others, Hofmarschall Count Robert von Zedlitz-Trützschler realised that the 'forced and unnatural' and 'by no means harmless' construction of the German battlefleet against Britain was the crux of Wilhelm II's policy which had led the other Great Powers to unite against the Reich. 'Why is it actually necessary to enlarge our navy so much?' he asked in 1907. 'The present result of our naval re-armament is that we have attracted the attention, mistrust and jealousy of the whole world towards us. England in particular feels threatened, and not without reason, for we are arming in such a way as to make ourselves more or less a match for England. The result of this is that England simply arms herself even more, and as England has more power at her disposal, we can in fact also assume that England will always remain superior to us. So why spend so much, why bring this disquiet and mistrust and jealousy into our foreign policy?'[128]

CHAPTER EIGHTEEN

Germany's 'Dreadnought Leap'. The Kaiser and 'his' navy

At precisely the time when watchful contemporaries like Holstein, Zedlitz and eventually even Bülow were urgently calling for a halt to the Tirpitz battlefleet plan,[1] Kaiser Wilhelm and his Secretary of State at the Reich Navy Office gave a further twist to the spiral of a murderous naval arms race. Already in March 1906 the decision had been taken through a *Novelle* (amendment) to the Navy Law to lay down six additional large cruisers; now, in September 1907, Tirpitz received the Kaiser's enthusiastic consent to a *Novelle* specifying that four ships of the line of the gigantic new Dreadnought class (instead of three, as hitherto) were to be built every year. Since at the same time the life-span of the older ships of the line was to be reduced by five years to twenty years, so that the battlefleet would virtually renew itself automatically, this decision signified a massive qualitative intensification of the arms race, to which Great Britain would have to respond accordingly.[2] In fact the decision in September 1907 to increase the rate to four ships a year (the *Vierertempo*) was, as we shall see, influenced less by the carefully calculated principles of the Tirpitz Plan than by the more far-reaching ideas entertained by an impatient Supreme War Lord, the naval officers in his entourage and their colleagues in active service, as well as by the hotheads of the German Navy League. It was with some bitterness that the Secretary of State noted on his return from Rominten that autumn that the Kaiser did not seem to understand or care about the fundamental idea behind 'the *Äternat* [permanent authorisation] of the three-ship building rate [*Dreiertempo*], . . . the one goal I have pursued incessantly for 10 years'.[3]

It is not without irony that the naval enthusiast Wilhelm II accorded so little recognition to the 'master builder' Tirpitz – who for a decade had worked tirelessly and single-mindedly to build up this battlefleet, often against apparently invincible opposition in the government, in parliament and not least within the navy itself – that Tirpitz thought the Supreme War Lord might have failed to grasp vital elements of his great plan. The best authority on the Tirpitz Plan, Volker Berghahn, even raises the question of 'whether the Kaiser realised the full extent of the danger involved in this policy of forcing the pace of arming at all costs', and answers that this was probably 'only partly the case', 'for it seems as if some strange psychological mechanism limited his insight'.[4]

In this chapter the focus will be on the crisis-ridden relationship between Kaiser Wilhelm II and Admiral Alfred von Tirpitz in the years from 1903 to 1907, when the Kaiserreich, by stepping up the construction of its own battlefleet, threw down the gauntlet to Great Britain both as leading maritime Power in the world and as guarantor of the European balance of power, and forced her to take diplomatic and strategic countermeasures. The long-term plans of the secretary of state were of course by no means uncontested in Germany itself, even among leading figures in the navy; they were opposed as too one-sided by the Naval Cabinet, the Flügeladjutanten in the Kaiser's entourage, the Admiralty Staff and the Commander of the High Seas Fleet. As All-Highest War Lord Kaiser Wilhelm II thus found himself in the not always enviable position of having the last word in these conflicts, too. Not without reason the navy was seen as his 'favourite child', which he had personally brought up and which he could contemplate with justifiable pride, especially after he had appointed his own brother to the command of the High Seas Fleet.[5] It should therefore be no surprise that the Kaiser developed definite ideas of his own and that although he appeared to agree with the grandiose 'ultimate goals' of the Tirpitz Plan, he was by no means always happy with the controversial methods employed by the Grand Admiral.

Conversely, Tirpitz was entirely dependent on the Kaiser's support in carrying out his plans and had to 'gear his arguments to the monarch's psychology', as Berghahn has commented.[6] 'Wilhelm II was the focal point of the Prusso-German constitutional system as it had gradually evolved up to the turn of the century', he rightly points out. Much as it went against his 'Bismarckian nature', the Secretary of State at the Reich Navy Office was fully aware that his audacious battlefleet-building plan was not based on popular support but depended ultimately on a strong authoritarian monarchy, and indeed that even after the death of Wilhelm II it would need the powerful personal support of his successor. Thus in 1909 he wrote to the young Crown Prince: 'The question of whether Germany will rise up among the great nations or sink down among the small ones will inevitably be resolved in this century. But if one believes in Germany's future it is essential to have a degree of naval power sufficient to obtain "fair play" from England for us. This idea goes against the traditions of our state and our people so much that ... it cannot be translated into reality unless the Majesty of the German Kaiser of the day personally takes charge of protecting and promoting naval interests ... Or in other words: if His Present Majesty the Kaiser should depart this life one day, Germany's naval interests will collapse without the strong personal intervention of His Majesty's successor. The roots of the tree have not yet penetrated deep enough into our nation for it to be able to stand and to flourish without "gardeners".[7]

THE KAISER AND THE TIRPITZ PLAN

Nowadays, following the seminal research of Volker R. Berghahn, Wilhelm Deist, Paul M. Kennedy, Michael Epkenhans and Patrick J. Kelly, the Tirpitz Plan is widely regarded among historians as an unmitigated disaster that caused untold damage to Germany from the perspective of both home and foreign affairs.[8] With enormous tenacity Tirpitz pursued a fleet-building policy that was precisely worked out from a technical point of view but nevertheless exhibited so many elementary weaknesses that its calculations were hopelessly askew and the breathtaking 'ultimate goals' of the plan could never have been achieved. By 1920 a battlefleet of some sixty ships of the line and large cruisers was to be built at the steady rate of three a year; they were to be stationed in either the North Sea or the Baltic, without the British noticing or minding, still less launching a surprise attack (such as in 1807 when the Royal Navy destroyed the Danish fleet at Copenhagen before Napoleon could seize it) to sink the German miracle weapon before it could become a threat to their country. In fact the government in London and the British public were very quickly alerted to the looming danger, not least thanks to the extensive official campaign of naval propaganda in Germany and the hot-headed agitation of the German Navy League. Both were aimed at persuading the Reichstag by stages to agree to the astronomical sums needed for the naval arms race, regardless of the fact that it was precisely the increasing tax burden that would plunge the Hohenzollern Monarchy into crisis at home, and that these funds could have been better spent for other purposes – even if only to increase the strength of the army. As for the hope cherished by Tirpitz that throughout the lengthy period when the Reich would be in the 'danger zone', extreme restraint would be the keynote of official German foreign policy so as not to alert other countries to the real aims of the fleet-building programme – this expectation proved, if for no other reason than the Kaiser's innate thirst for recognition, to be unrealistic.

Thus after only a few years unmistakable signs of failure were already appearing in the battlefleet plan initiated by Tirpitz in 1897. The British government rapidly grasped the dangers for Britain and the European balance of power represented by the Kaiserreich's ambitions for superpower status and her naval policy, and took both diplomatic and strategic countermeasures.[9] As we have seen, concerns about the maintenance of British supremacy at sea already played a significant role during the negotiations which led to the alliance with Japan in January 1902. The opportunity which this treaty of alliance gave the Royal Navy of bringing warships back into home waters was echoed in 1904 with the conclusion of the Entente Cordiale with France, for now the Mediterranean Fleet could likewise be moved back to Portsmouth, Dover and Scotland in order to increase the British naval presence in the English Channel and the North Sea, or to Gibraltar, from whence it could head north or east as necessary. Not only in the British press but also in the Admiralty influential voices advocated sinking the German Imperial Navy, Copenhagen-style, before it became too powerful. The panic about a possible war after the Dogger Bank episode in the autumn of 1904 and the open discussion in 1905 as to whether Britain should defend France not only at sea but also on land by sending an expeditionary force of a hundred thousand men, were clear evidence of how desperately close the danger of war between Germany and Britain had already become. Since 1904, under the determined leadership of Sir John Fisher, the First Sea Lord, the British had been modernising and enlarging their Home Fleet, which was increasingly geared towards use against the Imperial Navy in the North Sea. Meanwhile, technical advances were making it possible to build bigger and bigger warships, leading to endlessly spiralling costs which made nonsense of the supposedly 'rational' calculations of the Reich Navy Office. What was more, the changeover to the construction of large battleships of the Dreadnought class necessitated widening and deepening the Kaiser Wilhelm Canal connecting the North Sea to the Baltic – work which would not be completed until July 1914.

If we look back to the years from 1903 to 1907, when the systematically calculated but nevertheless grotesquely delusional Tirpitz Plan entered the notorious 'danger zone', it is plain that relations between Kaiser Wilhelm II and Tirpitz were anything but smooth. Like Tirpitz, the Kaiser wanted to build a huge battlefleet to defy Britain, and in principle he was therefore willing, although not always happy, to keep the secretary of state in office. But constantly spurred on as he was by the 'extreme views' of the Chief of the Naval Cabinet, Freiherr von Senden-Bibran,[10] and of the admirals of the 'Front', Wilhelm's sympathies were in fact much more with the 'unlimited' demands of the fanatics of the Navy League, who denounced Tirpitz's systematic procedure as far too slow and far too cautious.

THE KINGSHIP MECHANISM AND THE NAVAL LEADERSHIP

Tirpitz had not been in office long before he found himself facing strong criticism, above all from within the navy itself: a considerable number of officers believed that war with Britain was imminent and therefore demanded instant action to raise the navy to a higher level of war-readiness. The conflicts between Tirpitz and the Admiralty Staff under Büchsel, who was working out wide-ranging plans for the acquisition of naval bases in the Caribbean, the bombardment of New York and the occupation of Denmark, Holland and Belgium, have been described in Chapter 12 above.[11] At the same time Tirpitz became the target of harsh censure from the 'Front' in the person of the Commander of the High Seas Fleet, Admiral Hans von Koester, who was as unconvinced as Büchsel that war could be avoided until the battlefleet was ready in 1920 or thereabouts. Koester's demands for a boost to the war-readiness of what was still a young navy were all the more dangerous for Tirpitz because his views were fully shared by Senden-Bibran. Both admirals, of course, had unrestricted access to the Supreme War Lord, who persistently interfered in the quarrel. 'Wilhelm II's technical naval advice got out of hand in the years from 1902 to 1906', the author of a recent study on the development of German ships of the line has commented.[12] In mid 1903 Wilhelm aligned himself so passionately with the 'Front' against the secretary of state that Tirpitz, as Berghahn writes, 'was utterly amazed by the Kaiser's state of excitement' during one audience.[13] The 'fury' and 'ill-humour' with which the Kaiser reacted to the arguments that Tirpitz produced against Koester's and Senden's ideas caused the secretary of state to contemplate resignation as early as in the spring of 1903.[14] One cannot help wondering how the naval arms race and German–British relations in general would have developed had the monarch dismissed Tirpitz at this juncture.

Such an outcome remained a possibility for some time to come, for the conflict between Tirpitz on the one hand and Koester and Senden on the other reached an early climax in the next few months. In September 1903 Wilhelm II gave orders for the active fleet to be developed at the expense of the reserve fleet, thereby fundamentally undermining Tirpitz's careful calculations. In his preparatory notes for his audience with the Kaiser on the subject, Tirpitz cited the reasons why the measure ordered by the monarch would endanger 'our great chances in a world war, particularly against England and America [sic!]'. In the end the secretary of state was forced to realise that he would get nowhere with his plea for a slow, systematic development of the battlefleet, given the monarch's impulsive temperament and his craving for prestige. So he abandoned the attempt to use his audience 'to make H.M. understand that questions regarding the organisation [of the fleet] cannot be resolved by his getting on his high horse and issuing orders' and should only be tackled 'in connection with the possible or desirable further development of the fleet', and that this further development could be 'assessed only in the R[eich] N[avy] O [ffice], not at the Front and not in the Cabinet'.[15]

The differences of opinion between Tirpitz, Senden and Koester erupted in a violent quarrel at Rominten at the end of September 1903. When Admiral von Hollmann, who was also present, attempted to mediate he was silenced by Wilhelm II. Tirpitz, the Kaiser complained, 'always wants to take the credit'; Koester must at all costs be kept on as Commander of the Fleet; Senden was 'a very honest fellow who only wants the best for me'. At lunch next day Senden regaled the Kaiser with a long list of alleged defects of the navy, but then Tirpitz managed to turn the tables and win Wilhelm round to his point of view. On 28 September, when the Chief of the Naval Cabinet again attacked the command structure proposed by Tirpitz and tried 'to use Prince Heinrich's tactical work as a battering-ram', Senden was 'given a fearful rebuff' and 'told to pipe down' by the Kaiser. 'And for the last 3 years Koester has been committing us to some dogma of his', Wilhelm suddenly complained. For two stormy hours Tirpitz and Senden threw accusations at each other in front of the Kaiser. Afterwards, when the two admirals were alone, the secretary of state gave the Chief of the Naval Cabinet 'a few home truths', by his own account. He, Tirpitz, had been compelled to 'save the Kaiser from a disastrous error of judgement and slanderous accusations had been made'. Senden then put on 'a show of conciliation' which Tirpitz refused to accept, openly threatening to resign instead. Senden asserted that Koester was the only Commander of the High Seas Fleet available and tried to persuade Tirpitz to agree that Koester 'should seek orders only from H.M. and [could] report [direct] to H.M.' To this the secretary of state retorted angrily: 'So that you are the only one to have audience of H.M. even on matters for which I alone would be responsible. And so the Secretary of State is supposed to kneel before him merely to have the honour of being the whipping-boy.' 'I thanked him for that', Tirpitz recorded, 'and told him he would have to look for a different sort of man. But whether such a person would also be fit to fight others for the navy's sake certainly did not seem to matter to him. Organisational development [is] my affair and not the [Naval] Cabinet's.' In the end the conflict was resolved when Senden promised to hand over his influential post to the Kaiser's Flügeladjutant Georg Alexander von Müller the following autumn.[16]

After his adversary had left Rominten Tirpitz was told by another Flügel-adjutant, Ferdinand von Grumme, of the suspicions spread by Senden, Koester and others in the Kaiser's entourage in order to undermine him. He had been accused of being in the pay of Krupp and of having 'probably rather social-democratic views'. 'Just because I am not among the highest-born in the land', Tirpitz commented bitterly. Objectively, however, he could be satisfied with the result of the set-to at Rominten, having managed to dispel the Kaiser's ill-humour towards him and fend off the attacks of Senden and Koester for the time being. He was relieved to be able to tell the Reich Chancellor that 'the acute tension with H.M.' was over.[17] Neither Tirpitz nor Bülow, of course, was prepared to believe Senden would actually resign until they had seen it with their own eyes. The Chief of the Naval Cabinet was certainly a 'clown' but the Kaiser would find it difficult to do without him.[18] In addition, Tirpitz voiced doubts as to whether the Kaiser had really 'understood' that the counter-proposals put forward by Koester and Senden concerned 'more than tactical questions'. Their organisational ideas, Tirpitz argued, would in fact have represented 'a disastrously mistaken method of developing our battlefleet' and moreover would have led to the Kaiser losing his position as 'Commander-in-Chief on land'.[19] Grumme and Hollmann also gained a distressing impression of the superficiality of the Kaiser's judgement when they spoke to him shortly after the quarrel at Rominten. They reported that he was 'quite simply tired of the subject' and had said that 'Tirpitz ought to be satisfied now, because he had got everything he wanted and H.M. had done all he could'.[20]

Nonetheless the secretary of state's argument that the proposals put forward by Koester and Senden could have endangered the position of the Supreme War Lord as the actual Commander in Chief of the navy did not fail to have an effect on Wilhelm, as Tirpitz knew it would. As Tirpitz noted, the Kaiser seemed to realise that the two admirals were seeking to reintroduce a kind of structural Supreme Command, even though at present the monarch himself was Supreme Commander. Wilhelm had recognised, Tirpitz recorded, 'that I had been right and had the right course of development in mind'.[21] Indeed, after an audience at Hubertus-stock on 12 October 1903 the Kaiser decided that Koester should give up the role he had exercised hitherto as Inspector General of the Navy and moreover that he should no longer be in charge of the autumn manoeuvres. With the agreement of Tirpitz and against the will of the Chief of the Naval Cabinet, Wilhelm declared his intention of allowing the post of Inspector General to lapse. As for the autumn manoeuvres, since he personally held the Supreme Command he would direct them himself, he said, together with the Chief of the Admiralty Staff. Koester should content himself henceforth with the active fleet; he was only one party to the manoeuvres and would have to be 'fitted in'.[22]

Another question on which Tirpitz managed for the time being to assert himself against the views of Senden and Koester was that of the types of ship to be built. On 10 October 1903 the Kaiser sent an enquiry to the Reich Navy Office: 'On which type will the *Novelle* be based? Armoured cruisers or ships of the line?'[23] At an audience on 14 November 1903 Tirpitz obtained the Kaiser's agreement to his plans for the systematic enlargement of the home battlefleet, which ran directly counter to the demands of the Commander of the High Seas Fleet for an immediate increase in war preparations and for the creation of an overseas fleet.[24]

In a letter he wrote directly after this audience, and in which he told Tirpitz that he was appointing him a full Admiral, Kaiser Wilhelm showed that in one respect at least he understood the principles of the Tirpitz Plan very well. He was 'very glad', he declared, 'to see from your preparatory submissions on the principal matters affecting the development of our *home battlefleet* that we are of exactly the same opinion. If it is skilfully arranged and an announcement is made at the right time, with a certain brio and panache, to the astonished grumble-guts of the Reich and the water-hating members of parliament, that in order to spare the country's financial resources — and hence to comply with the wishes of the people's representatives — H.M. has, with a heavy heart, *renounced his undoubted right to demand an overseas fleet* in favour of concentrating all means and resources on building up the *forces at home*, this cannot fail to have the desired effect; not only will it strike dead the "unlimited navy rumours" for ever, but it will stop the British being able to stir up other people's fears about our presence abroad, when we have no presence abroad.'[25] Wilhelm also assured his brother Prince Heinrich that he was in full agreement with Tirpitz, a state of affairs which Heinrich '[could] not welcome warmly enough'.[26] So in this case the Kaiser had, as Berghahn comments, 'thoroughly grasped the principle at stake'.[27]

In spite of the victory he had thus achieved, Tirpitz could never be quite sure of the Kaiser's support for his long-term plan and had to face the constant fear that Wilhelm would rush ahead 'sooner than is right', as he had so often done before.[28] The secretary of state sensed that the monarch was 'not exactly grateful' to him; rather, he was annoyed that Tirpitz had been proved right. 'It displeases him that he is not yet in sole charge, and above all that he is not yet seen in well-informed circles in the navy as the only one in charge. The sad and distressing thing about such a talented monarch is that he values the appearance more than the essence. What is crucial for him is not the actual matter in hand but the question of whether he is at once seen as the only figure of authority. He completely overlooks the fact that only the essence, the thing itself, is lasting and that what lasts is credited to him alone, while the henchmen are soon forgotten [and] in the Prussian way they are also quite content when the thing is done.'[29]

Exactly a year after the furious dispute in September 1903 the same farce was played out again at Rominten between Wilhelm II, Senden and Tirpitz. Zedlitz commented on the conflict-ridden relationship between the three men in his diary entry for 1 October 1904. 'Since the naval manoeuvres [at the beginning of September] a sort of crisis has been in the air, because the Chief of the [Naval] Cabinet v[on] Senden and the Reich Secretary of State v[on] Tirpitz had a number of disagreements', he wrote, adding that it was even feared that Tirpitz might resign, which would have meant a serious loss for the navy. Zedlitz also noted the characteristic detail that on the day they arrived there was no time for Tirpitz and Senden to be received in audience 'for hunting reasons' and that their meeting with the Kaiser the following morning was broken off because a 'royal' stag had been sighted. In order to indulge his passion for the hunt the Kaiser compelled the two admirals to spend an extra day in the wilds of East Prussia. 'On the other hand, the audience in the afternoon of the 29th turned out satisfactorily', Zedlitz remarked. 'The conflicts have been put aside for the moment, and a mood of relief was perceptible in all those involved.'[30]

As in the previous year the quarrels in the autumn of 1904 centred around the fact that the Kaiser, spurred on by Koester and Senden, demanded faster expansion of the navy, while Tirpitz, as before, upheld the advantages of his phased plan as laid down under the original Navy Law. Reverting to his favourite metaphor, he warned that constantly putting forward 'minor extra demands' would be selling one's birthright for a mess of pottage. All 'side-shows which in fact disturb rapid development' must be avoided. It was intolerable for the Chief of the [Naval] Cabinet to 'constantly stab [him] in the back and upset careful plans'. The Kaiser, however, firmly rejected these complaints against Senden. Tirpitz was utterly mistaken if he regarded Senden as an intriguer, he declared. No, the Cabinet Chief was in fact 'an Old Prussian seigneur for whom such a thing' would be 'quite impossible'. When Tirpitz responded that he did not wish to attack Senden's character in any way, 'but he had no grasp of the situation and our plans', Wilhelm tried to console the secretary of state by assuring him that he protected him and so 'no one could get at him'. Therefore, he said, Tirpitz had 'the most independent position that existed' anywhere in the government. And after all he, the Kaiser, did 'everything that I [Tirpitz] suggested'.[31] Berghahn rightly points out how inadequately the Supreme War Lord exercised the decision-making power which he alone possessed in these conflicts within the naval administration. Faced with a difficult decision to make both with regard to personnel and to the type of ships to be built, the Kaiser could not make up his mind.[32] As a result the conflicts remained unresolved through the next, critical years.

THE CONFLICT WITH TIRPITZ OVER THE 'FAST SHIP OF THE LINE'

The stormy arguments between Wilhelm II and Tirpitz were not solely about personnel policy, the command structure of the naval authorities or the speed with which the battlefleet was built, however fundamental these questions were. The Kaiser also considered it entirely consistent with his role — the navy being his own personal creation — to give the orders, down to the smallest detail, on the technical aspects of the ships to be commissioned and of their armouring, thereby endangering the best-laid plans of the Reich Navy Office. Thus in December 1903 he gave the Office a 'commission to construct' a battleship displacing 13,300 tons, with four 28 cm and eight 21 cm guns, storage for 2,000 tons of coal and a top speed of 18 knots.[33] In February 1904 in another of his construction commissions he gave orders not only to the Reich Navy Office but also to the Imperial Shipyard at Kiel to develop a project with eight 24 cm rapid-fire cannon.[34] Zedlitz very aptly remarked that 'the navy gains great advantages from the lively interest taken in it at the All-Highest level, indeed without this it would hardly make any progress at all, so the Kaiser really is the creator of our fleet. But on questions of detail the Kaiser's interventions cause the senior naval officers difficulties and great concern.'[35]

Under the influence of Koester and Senden and out of anxiety that the home fleet was far from ready for war, Wilhelm II had been pressing for the construction of cruisers since 1902, thus calling into question the Tirpitz Plan, which provided for the phased construction of a battlefleet of forty ships of the line and twenty large cruisers.[36] As we have seen, in the autumn of 1903 the secretary of state appeared to have succeeded in winning the Kaiser's support for his grand plan. Since then, however, the Supreme War Lord had been preoccupied to an almost manic extent with the details of a new type of ship combining the speed of a cruiser with the fighting power of a battleship, which he termed a *Schnelles Linienschiff* — a 'fast ship of the line'. The 'Front' was also in favour of this initiative but the Reich Navy Office 'absolutely' refused to consider it.[37] Wilhelm feverishly prepared sketch models of the new ships — they were heavily armoured cruisers with powerful engines and large-calibre guns — and demanded that Tirpitz include ships of this kind in his fleet-building plan. On 21 November 1903 he surprised the secretary of state by showing him an article on these cruisers which he had written with Senden's help. Despite Tirpitz's reservations he insisted on publishing the piece in the January 1904 edition of the *Marine Rundschau* under the pseudonym 'L'. In it he wrote enthusiastically about the armoured cruisers *Rivardaria* and *Moreno*, built by the Genoese engineering company Ansaldo for Argentina and then bought by Britain and passed on to Japan. Thanks to its low tonnage, he argued, this new type of ship could travel faster than ships of the line by three to four knots, and yet it carried bigger guns and was therefore effective; moreover it was comparatively cheap.[38] 'From now on the monarch's professional naval output continued unbroken for some considerable time', Berghahn comments ironically. 'He seemed to want to put the concept of "Personal Rule" into practice even in the complex sphere of battleship construction.'[39]

Temporarily unable to speak after an operation in November 1903 to remove a polyp in his throat, the Kaiser gave vent to his fury with Tirpitz, who refused to agree with him, in a barrage of pencil notes giving instructions to his suite. When the secretary of state had the temerity to question the technical information which he had used in his article, Wilhelm gave orders for 'the Consul General in Genoa to request the material immediately from Ansaldo [the shipbuilders]'. As he jubilantly informed his entourage, he 'was able to show it to him [Tirpitz] yesterday! Tableau! He is furious with his gentlemen who missed the facts.'[40] Another of his notes reads: 'Yesterday I gave Tirpitz another treat. I proved to him, using comparisons and drawings, that "Constitucion" and "Libertad" which Chile has just bought from England and which, at 11,800 tons, are the same size as Wittelsbach', even though they were equipped with bigger guns and armour-plating, could take on more coal and move faster than the German ships of this class.[41] An exchange of letters with the Spanish Ministry of Marine further confirmed his belief in the advantages of the new type of ship. Supremely confident of the rightness of his own opinion, he wrote to the Chief of the Naval Cabinet towards the end of 1903: 'After the photos arrived from Ansaldo yesterday evening I spent the whole evening and the whole morning today in such delight at the prospect of Tirpitz's face that my wife simply couldn't understand what was the matter with me! It will just show Tirpitz that I am serious about this question, and will not be put off by a few empty generalisations casting doubt on it. The letter from the Spanish Ministry of Marine is of course exactly what I needed and at just the right time, as it says almost literally what I said in my article on the Moreno. One could not wish for better proof. Our shipbuilding companies do not have the slightest doubt that Ansaldo is efficient, reliable and competent. It is just arrogance on the part of our officials, who want to be seen as having thought up everything themselves and are extremely annoyed when I come along and show them that there are other people who are also clever and think things out.'[42] Tirpitz was feeling 'rather caught out, in a sense, just as if he had let down his own brother', the Kaiser commented mockingly in December 1903. 'That is of course exactly what has happened. For despite all the masses of comparative tables ... he has never shown me one like the enclosed although his officials, who provide him with the material for the other tables, could have drawn up this one as well. But it's that arrogance again! ... And now, as the table is very surprising and tells a convincing story, he suddenly says that Ansaldo's information is not reliable and that its ships cannot maintain that speed! Rubbish.'[43]

With his demands for faster and bigger armoured cruisers the Kaiser may have been in line with the international trend, but it evidently did not occur to him that it was not his place, as sovereign, to interfere in the technical details of battleship construction, nor that by doing so he was putting his relationship with Tirpitz and the Reich Navy Office under great strain and also creating chaos from a budgetary point of view. He clearly considered himself a great expert in shipbuilding affairs and thought he knew better than the drawing office. Thus in his pencil notes to the Chief of the Naval Cabinet he laid down the law, among other things, on details of warship armour-plating, on the inadequate penetrating power of middle-calibre naval artillery and on the tactical implications of this in naval warfare.[44]

The Kaiser's fixation with the new cruisers had a wider impact and soon took on global dimensions. Having acquired, through the Consul General in Genoa, the blueprints for the Argentinian armoured cruisers *Rivardaria* and *Moreno*, which were now in service in the Japanese navy, and having corresponded with officials of the Spanish Ministry of Marine on the merits of the new type of ship, on 9 January 1904 – just before the outbreak of the Russo-Japanese War – he sent his article in the *Marine Rundschau* to the Tsar and told him that he had received the secret plans for the armoured cruisers from the Italian arms engineers Ansaldo 'by express permission of the President of the Argentine Republic'. He tried to persuade the Tsar to have similar cruisers built for the Russian fleet too.[45]

As Secretary of State at the Reich Navy Office Tirpitz now felt compelled to restate his opinion, in a fourteen-page memorandum of 29 January 1904, on 'the development of our Large Cruiser', that 'as far as Germany is concerned the English navy represents the only great maritime danger for the next decade' and that in battle with the Royal Navy the outcome would be 'decided by the ships of the line' alone.[46] The Kaiser's fury at this riposte knew no bounds. After a walk with his brother on 31 January 1904 Prince Heinrich recorded that Wilhelm had 'complained about Tirpitz in the most abusive terms (liar, intriguer etc) because of the armoured cruiser business!'[47]

The Kaiser curtly dismissed the secretary of state's propositions as 'Nonsense!' and 'Absolutely wrong!'[48] In his comments at the end of the memorandum he argued that since the enemy already possessed a large number of Large Cruisers, Germany should also develop a type of ship that could fulfil a dual task. The Imperial Navy therefore needed a cruiser that was not only suited to traditional service overseas but was 'also "fit for the line"'. 'Our Large Cruisers must be able to be fitted into the "line" at home [and] must therefore also have the requisite qualities.' There would be no objection to such ships continuing to be officially called Large Cruisers, he said; but in reality they would be fast ships of the line.[49] But to merge the cruiser type with the capital ship and create a single large battleship in this way threatened to undermine the Navy Act through which Tirpitz had committed the Reichstag to his grandiose fleet-building programme.[50]

The crisis of confidence between the two deepened when the Kaiser sent the secretary of state a telegram on 23 February 1904 informing him that he had written a second article about the armoured cruisers which he intended to publish, like the first, in the *Marine Rundschau* under the same "L" pseudonym.[51] At the time of the first article Tirpitz had pointed out the drawbacks of a public discussion of types of ship but his advice had been ignored. This time he instructed Albert Hopman to write an article for the *Marine Rundschau* countering the Kaiser's arguments.[52] Meanwhile, in his response to Wilhelm's telegram and then in an audience on 27 February 1904, Tirpitz warned the Kaiser that his 'reputation would be damaged' if he continued to intervene in technical discussions. Since the first 'L' article it had become common knowledge that the Kaiser was the author, Tirpitz pointed out. The appearance of a second article would 'give the opportunity to individuals who had neither the authority nor the standing to do so, to make critical comparisons between their own opinions and those of our All-Highest War Lord'. Kaiser Wilhelm refused to concede 'how much his reputation could be damaged by publication' and stubbornly insisted on carrying out his intention, declaring that 'the subject really needed to be clarified, and that was what he had done'. The secretary of state could do no more than reply that the Kaiser could 'still think it over'. The next issue of the *Marine Rundschau* was in any case already with the printers, so there was no hurry. In the end he had only done his duty and 'warned Y[our] M[ajesty] against publication', Tirpitz asserted, whereupon the Kaiser replied irritably: 'Yes, you certainly have.' Tirpitz now had to make himself clearer. He explained to the Kaiser that since 1900 he had deliberately used tactics of concealment with the Reichstag, which had enabled him to keep the deputies in the dark as to the significance of the battleships to which they agreed; a second article by the Kaiser about armoured cruisers would draw their attention 'to this very thing'.[53]

In fact the second article was never published, but the Kaiser continued to be obsessed by the question of the fast ship of the line. On 17 March 1904, during his voyage in the Lloyd steamer *König Albert*, he wrote a 'Response' to Tirpitz's memorandum of 29 January.[54] As he cruised in the Mediterranean he commissioned the Director General of the Imperial Shipyard at Kiel, Max Fischel, to construct a fast ship of the line.[55] At the beginning of April 1904, against the advice of the Reich Navy Office, he gave orders for the German armoured cruisers which had just been completed to be equipped with 24cm, rather than 21cm, guns.[56] Once again Tirpitz was compelled to use all the power at his disposal to frustrate the Supreme War Lord's initiative, which threatened the legally sanctioned programme for the construction of the battlefleet. On 6 May 1904 he made a desperate appeal for Prince Heinrich's support. If the Kaiser's wishes were carried out, the result would be 'the collapse of our Navy Law', he warned. 'If His Majesty demands cruiser ships of the line on a larger scale', the only recourse under the law would be for these ships to be called ships of the line, and the Reichstag would have to be asked to provide for them as such. It would not be permissible to ask for a large cruiser and secretly turn it into a capital ship. Such a procedure could not remain hidden in the long run, especially as 'the large cruisers planned by His Majesty cost 6 million [marks] more than the recently approved large cruiser C.' Under the current Navy Law, which was 'most particularly' intended for the construction of ships of the line – there were two large cruisers to ten ships of the line – until 1910 there was provision for the construction of only one more cruiser. 'It really would be selling one's birthright for a mess of pottage to want to modify the basic principles of the Navy Law for the one remaining cruiser. A Cabinet Chief might perhaps envisage that, but not a Secretary of State, who watches over His Majesty's real interests and considers himself responsible for them. In the past, when we put our budgetary demands to the Reichstag nothing did us more harm than a certain restlessness and constant changes to projects and ideas; but now we have built up a certain capital of trust in precisely this area, which stands our demands in very good stead. We shall be handing the opposition powerful ammunition if we give them the opportunity to talk about erratic principles of warfare, zigzag courses etc again.'[57] After a lengthy discussion Heinrich succeeded in talking his brother out of demanding fast ships of the line for the time being.[58] But only a few months later the arguments broke out again.

On 28 April 1905 the Kaiser wrote Tirpitz a letter from the Adriatic which raised the conflict between them to an acute level. In it Wilhelm demanded nothing less than the introduction of the new type of ship instead of the planned ships of the line and large cruisers. What was more, this was to be put into the *Flottennovelle* projected for 1906. In Messina, he wrote, the Commander of the *Sardegna*, Admiral Bettolo, had shown him the plans for new Italian ships of the line which were equipped with eight 30.5 cm guns in four double turrets and twenty smaller guns; medium-calibre guns were to be dispensed with entirely. Bettolo was also in favour of 'high speed in the capital ship, so that the Admiral was always able to maintain the appropriate distance for his artillery, either by approaching or by steaming away', the Kaiser explained. 'When I asked him why great speed was considered so important for ships of the line in Italy, as armoured cruisers were better fitted for this task, he answered that the Italians took the view that their country could not afford both ships of the line and armoured cruisers. Therefore it had been decided not to build any armoured cruisers, but to design ships of the line with such good water-lines that they could comfortably maintain high speeds and carry out armoured cruiser duties if the need arose ... I was all the more struck by what the commander of the Sardegna said because he almost literally repeated the ideas which I have been developing for years about the advantages of the faster capital ship over the armoured cruisers ... The above particulars confirm me even more in the view I have often put forward, that the development of the capital ship into the "fast ship of the line" is the right way to provide powerful large cruisers for countries which, unlike England, are not able to call on unlimited sums of money for large squadrons of armoured cruisers as well as capital ships. The comparative figures can be found in the table I sent to Your Excellency ... The Regina Elena class is de facto the "fast ship of the line" which I wish to see developed – instead of the Roon and the C class – and which I was told was unattainable. The idea I suggested, of Wittelsbach's armour plating on a ship of about the tonnage of Braunschweig but of greater length, was not so fundamentally wrong after all! The fact is that the new Italian ships of the line displace only 12,600 tons and are more heavily armoured than Wittelsbach. For the new navy bill it would be very gratifying – in my opinion – if we could say: we have enough armoured cruisers and our main strength is still the capital ship. We shall develop it into a single, fast type and put these together in light divisions which will be given cruiser duties to carry out as far as possible ... A ship of a maximum of about 13,200 tons should be chosen ... No armoured battery casemates. If the artillery is set up in turrets rather than batteries the large loopholes and the long armour-plating are no longer needed, the ship can also be lower, which means that its weight is reduced and this benefits other elements, above all coal, for which sufficient provision is never made in our ships. These figures are to be regarded as general points of reference that are put forward purely from the point of view that the "fast capital ship", which can if necessary be used as an armoured cruiser, is indeed also "fit for the line", which cannot be said of either the Friedrich Karl class or the C [class]. For in comparison with all our *present* armoured cruisers the "Regina Elena" is superior, *despite* the fact that she is a capital ship, and our armoured cruisers could not contemplate engaging with her. She is far superior in artillery and coal and they are no more than equal in speed. Wilhelm I.R.'[59] Over the next few days Wilhelm busied himself feverishly with the new type of ship, fortified by reports from his naval attaché in Rome.[60] He drew up page after page of comparative tables and sketches which Admiral von Senden sent to Tirpitz on 4 May 1905.[61] Once again Senden proved himself to be 'anti-Tirpitz' on this question, Admiral von Müller observed.[62]

Understandably, Tirpitz was infuriated by this interference in the battlefleet-building plans which he had succeeded in anchoring firmly in the Navy Law. Responding to the Kaiser's proposals in a dispatch of 6 May 1905, he expressed his objections principally on technical military grounds. He pointed out that the new class of ship planned by Italy and demanded by the Kaiser for the Imperial Navy might well be suitable for the Mediterranean Sea, 'but could scarcely be of use to a nation which can only afford to build ships which are also capable of fighting in difficult conditions in ocean waters'. For numerous technical reasons, he declared, the Italian model was 'unacceptable for our nautical conditions'.[63]

The Kaiser was not prepared to have his cherished ideas rejected in this way, and he telegraphed angrily to Tirpitz: 'Great speed is still the chief weapon for future ships of the line; they must be capable of at least 22 knots. That is my − unalterable − opinion, and construction must proceed accordingly! . . . Be it ever so well armoured, a fleet that is too slow and cannot catch up with its enemy will always be a defenceless target, which when engaged by a faster opponent will be helplessly shot to pieces by him from whatever distance suits *him*, and such a fleet would be better left unbuilt. That is the opinion of all the foreign naval officers to whom I spoke in the Mediterranean, and also of those who were with me, as well as my own. We of all people need speed.'[64]

Wilhelm was not content with declaring his 'unalterable' wish. Anticipating resistance from the secretary of state, on 4 May 1905 during his return journey to Germany he gave Müller the 'thorny' task of writing to Tirpitz 'about the new fast capital ship'.[65] Müller asked Tirpitz for a meeting in Berlin, in order to 'explain the considerations which have led His Majesty to wish for an increase in the speed of our future ships of the line'.[66] In the course of two discussions, which took place on 9 and 10 May 1905, Tirpitz declared bluntly that quite apart from the military and technical objections he had already expressed, he could not 'give his support to the desired change in our ship-building policy in the *Novelle* for parliamentary and financial reasons'. He repeated that it was 'impossible to bring about what is wished now'. As Müller reported to the Kaiser, Tirpitz made it clear, above all, that 'the difficulty of the parliamentary situation lies in the fact that to proceed by leaps and bounds undermines confidence in the consistency of our naval development hitherto, and in Admiral v. Tirpitz's view this confidence is extraordinarily important, and is indeed virtually a condition for the passage of the next *Flottennovelle*, which Your Majesty has approved, with its simultaneous increase in the number of units and very considerable rise in the cost of each ship'.[67] Müller's report was returned with the Kaiser's annotation: 'Parliament has too little technical knowledge to judge what is a "leap" and what is not, in the type of ship. Consideration for Parliament must never induce us to give up making the desired progress, even if it requires extensive changes, or to allow other nations to overtake us.'[68] On 11 May Wilhelm II repeated his order for one type of ship to be built according to his sketches so as to be able to establish in good time before the parliamentary debates 'at what cost a further increase in the speed of ships of the line can be achieved'.[69] Tirpitz's imminent resignation was prevented only by a compromise allowing one ship to be completed in accordance with the Kaiser's wishes while work on the *Novelle* continued as before.[70]

Investigations in the drawing office of the Reich Navy Office showed that unless it had a greater draught the fast ship of the line ordered by the Kaiser would be likely to capsize, and that extensive model experiments would be necessary before construction could begin.[71] Tirpitz evidently hoped to be able to work on the project in as leisurely a fashion as possible, but he reckoned without the Kaiser's obduracy. During the Baltic cruise in July 1905 Müller suggested that Tirpitz should send the monarch an assessment of the latest state of the construction work.[72] Tirpitz condescendingly ordered his colleague Adolf von Trotha to cook up 'something or other of interest in the shipbuilding line' for the Kaiser; what he had in mind, he said, was to give the monarch 'a tub to play with'.[73] But this attempt to distract the Kaiser was a complete failure. Trotha commented resignedly in August 1905: 'H.M. has of course never followed the factual explanations in this question, for one thing because this is quite alien to the way he works, and probably also because he wants to be proved right whatever happens.'[74] The Kaiser's pet project became a frequent topic of conversation at court and on board the *Hohenzollern* over the next few years.[75] On 26 November 1906 Wilhelm summoned the admirals of the High Seas Fleet to the *Deutschland* and gave them a lecture, as Hopman recorded, 'on the project he has given the shipyards for a fast ship of the line, aiming a few little digs at the Reich Navy Office in the process'.[76] In March 1907 the Kaiser interrupted the 'extraordinarily tedious' speech of the Chief of the Admiralty Staff in order to make his own speech on the advantages of the fast ship of the line.[77] In the summer of 1906 he had also tried to drum up public support for his project by announcing a prize for the best design for such a ship, again making no secret of his displeasure with the 'blind' naval architects of the Reich Navy Office.[78] In the end the Kaiser's pet project came to nothing only because after the developmental leap forward represented by the British Dreadnought class the German navy, including the Reich Navy Office, was itself forced to make a fundamental reassessment of its shipbuilding policy.

THE DREADNOUGHT AND THE WIDENING OF THE KAISER WILHELM CANAL

As our investigation of the prolonged conflict over the fast ship of the line has shown, Kaiser Wilhelm followed the shipbuilding plans of other navies, and naturally of the British navy above all, with intense interest. He had been fascinated by the article entitled 'An Ideal Warship for the British Navy' published in 1903 by the Italian engineering designer Vittorio Cuniberti in the annual *All the World's Fighting Ships*.[79] When the German naval attaché in London, Carl Coerper, reported on 5 January 1905 that the Royal Navy intended to build a large battleship of the Dreadnought type with a displacement of 18,000 tons and four 30.5 cm guns as well as ten 25.4 cm guns, the Kaiser gave orders for the head of the drawing office to come 'for an immediate audience' and to show him 'our latest plans for comparison'. When Coerper wrote again confirming his initial report, the Kaiser exclaimed excitedly: 'So there it is after all! That is the project put forward 2 years ago by Cuniberti in "All The World's Fighting Ships".'[80]

In view of the news from London Tirpitz had no alternative but to consider increasing both the size of the ships planned for the Imperial Navy and the related expenditure. After hectic consultations in the Reich Navy Office he submitted four projects to the Kaiser at an audience on 18 March 1905. All, however, were below Dreadnought size. Although the Kaiser approved the model which Tirpitz preferred, which with a displacement of 15,700 tons and 28 cm guns would have a top speed of 18.33 knots and cost about 33 million marks, he continued to press for bigger and faster ships of the line.[81] 'We must match that!' he ordered, when Coerper sent further details of the new British ship: 18,000 tons displacement, a main battery of ten 12-inch guns and a speed of 21 knots.[82] On 4 June 1905, a Sunday, he summoned Müller before breakfast and had a long conversation with him in the garden 'about the need to increase the speed of our warships'. Once again 'much ill-feeling towards Tirpitz' was in evidence, Müller noted, adding that the Kaiserin and the princes had been obliged to wait for their breakfast until the end of the conversation. The Kaiser's displeasure with Tirpitz and his comparatively cautious construction plans was intensified when Paul von Hintze reported from St Petersburg that Russia was planning to build ships of the line with a displacement of 19,800 tons. He demanded that the drawing office show him drawings of the Russian ships immediately.[83] During a 'difficult' morning walk with Müller at Kiel the Kaiser complained about 'Tirpitz's character, in contrast to Senden and Hollmann and very much like Bismarck'.[84]

On 20 July 1905 Wilhelm sent an eleven-page autograph letter to Tirpitz, followed four days later by another letter. Both missives urged Tirpitz to speed up work on torpedo weaponry and to build bigger and faster ships of the line.[85] The secretary of state promised to fulfil the Kaiser's demand to reinforce the torpedo boats; as far as bigger and faster ships of the line were concerned, Tirpitz declared that he agreed in principle with the Kaiser's wish, but he must remind him that 'the outside limit for the Kaiser Wilhelm Canal' had already been reached. If even bigger ships were now called for, 'we should be compelled to state officially that these ships can no longer go through the Canal. But that reopens the whole Canal question. Considering the great difficulty which the Tax Bill and the *Flottennovelle* will cause next winter, I would strongly urge Your Majesty to postpone the Canal question.'[86]

It was inevitable that at the audience arranged for the beginning of October 1905 at Rominten there would be a fierce dispute over the Dreadnought type and the 'odious' related question of the widening of the Kaiser Wilhelm Canal, which would cost untold sums, take years to complete and arouse suspicion both at home and abroad. On 3 September Tirpitz asked his colleagues in the Reich Navy Office to provide him with memoranda on the 'consequences' of increasing the size of the current *Braunschweig*-Class (13,000 tons) to 17,000 or even 18,000 tons, 'before I leave for Rominten'.[87] On the same day he received a message from the Chief of the Naval Cabinet saying that the Kaiser had declared that the Kaiser Wilhelm Canal needed to be made wider and deeper and had already discussed this with the Reich Chancellor. They had agreed that the increase in commercial shipping should be cited as the motive for the expensive work involved. In the belief that with this decision he had also solved the problem of the type of ship that could be built, Wilhelm expressed the hope that when designing the new warships it would no longer be necessary to take into account the dimensions of the locks.[88] Tirpitz suspected that the Kaiser's aim in widening the Canal was to achieve his cherished idea of the fast ship of the line, which was 'highly uncongenial' to Tirpitz himself, 'as I would prefer to spend money and effort on fighting strength [than on speed]'.[89]

The secretary of state pointed out that the Canal question could not be solved 'quite as easily as H.M. seems to think'. 'Nobody' would believe the claim that the almost prohibitively expensive work to widen the Canal had become necessary because of the increased volume of merchant shipping.[90] He realised, however, that following the Kaiser's decision he would not be able to conceal from the Reichstag the need for the Canal to be widened, and that this would also lead to public discussion of the need for larger ships.[91] Before his audience he travelled to Baden-Baden to obtain Bülow's 'general' agreement – in the Reich Navy Office the presumption was that the Reich Chancellor was 'not informed in detail' – to an increase in the naval estimates.[92] In Rominten on 4 October 1905 Tirpitz submitted to the Kaiser a draft for supplementary naval estimates (*Flottennovelle*) which, as Berghahn puts it, 'had a momentous influence on the fate of the entire Tirpitz Plan and on the course of German policy up to 1914'. The new German capital ship, with a displacement of over 18,000 tons, was to be 135 metres long and 26 metres wide; armed with twelve 28 cm guns, it would cost 36.5 million marks. In all, the ships of the line and large cruisers which the Reichstag would be asked to approve in 1906 would cost 940 million marks and the work to widen the Kaiser Wilhelm Canal would require a further 60 million. Kaiser Wilhelm welcomed these proposals and in so doing initiated an open arms race with Great Britain, for the foremost naval Power in the world had no alternative but to take up the German provocation, which was tantamount to a challenge to her maritime supremacy and her position as a World Power.[93]

THE TIRPITZ CRISIS OF 1905–1906

However irksome he found the monarch's constant interference in his domain, Tirpitz occasionally resorted to the well-tried tactic of stirring up Wilhelm's autocratic instincts in order to get the better of his own enemies, by using the Kaiser's position as Supreme War Lord against them. Thus in the spring of 1905 he had succeeded in convincing the monarch that the inordinate demands of the German Navy League for the formation of a third double squadron of ships of the line were an infringement of his rights.[94] As so often happened, however, the Kaiser's reaction overshot the mark by a long way. He sent an aggrieved telegram to the acting chairman of the Navy League, Major General Wilhelm Menges, on 6 May 1905, provoking his resignation and that of the League's propaganda chief, Major General August Keim.

He had proof, the monarch wired, that the Navy League was following an inadmissible path by arrogating to itself the right to determine the type of ships in the Imperial Navy. That was 'a direct infringement of the All-Highest War Lord's sphere of command', he wrote, which he must 'most definitely reject as entirely improper'. Although it was the task of the Navy League to promote understanding of the navy, 'interference in things of a purely military, technical nature' could not 'be tolerated now or ever by the naval authorities'.[95] When, after the resignation of Menges and Keim, the respected Otto Prince zu Salm-Horstmar also threatened to step down as President of the Navy League Tirpitz, Bülow, Senden and Müller took action to prevent a general crisis.[96] Tirpitz expressed his regret to Baden's envoy in Berlin that Menges and Keim had been induced to resign 'by an ungracious telegram directed to both Generals from the All-Highest, reprimanding them'.[97] On 24 May 1905 Bülow and Tirpitz managed to persuade the Kaiser to set aside his concerns about his rights and clear the way for a compromise by sending another telegram.[98] Menges and Keim were re-elected to the committee and at the general assembly of the League in Stuttgart, in the presence of the King of Württemberg and of Prince Heinrich, who had taken on the patronage of the League at his brother's request, the compromise proposals were accepted. On 15 June 1905 Kaiser Wilhelm wrote expressing his satisfaction to the King of Württemberg: 'If the Navy League keeps to the path it has now rediscovered, as is to be hoped, it will be able to do real good and I shall welcome its work.'[99]

In fact Wilhelm II's plans for increasing the navy coincided far more closely with the reckless demands of the Navy League than with Tirpitz's carefully calculated building programme. While the latter was seeking the Kaiser's approval for his Dreadnought *Novelle* costing billions, Salm-Horstmar, Keim and Admiral Thomsen were advocating even greater naval expansion. The secretary of state feared that the promptings of the Navy League might persuade the Kaiser to step up the Bill he had only just approved, especially as the leaders of the League were arguing that 'the people expect a much more ambitious bill from His Majesty, the absence of which will signify a direct threat to the stability of the monarchy'.[100] Tirpitz complained bitterly that this 'extremely vigorous agitation' was aimed at 'inducing the Kaiser to set his sights on a much greater enlargement of the Navy'.[101] Berghahn rightly points out how characteristic of 'the internal mechanics of the Wilhelmine regime' the secretary of state's fears of the monarch's erratic behaviour were.[102]

The pressure from the Navy League began to look particularly threatening when Salm, Thomsen and Keim asked for an audience with the Kaiser in November 1905 and tried to win over his Flügeladjutant Admiral von Müller to 'a more substantial enlargement of the navy, using public opinion as their argument'. Tirpitz succeeded in persuading Müller how dangerous it would be for the German Reich 'to attempt to push on faster than the official speed'.[103] But Bülow, who had assured Tirpitz of his support in September, now seemed inclined to turn the *Flottennovelle* into 'a question of major national importance'.[104] On 8 November 1905 the secretary of state sent the Reich Chancellor a memorandum in which he again set out in the clearest possible terms his conviction that a 'steady and systematic development of the navy' was essential. Even the regular enlargement of the German battlefleet which he had carried out in accordance with the Navy Law, he argued, entailed an almost unacceptable challenge to Great Britain which would intensify the danger of a war. 'The fact that Germany intends to lay down 16 ships of the line of 18,000 tons in the next *4* years, together with the realisation that England will have to reckon with a future quota of 50 to 60 first class German ships of the line, will cause such a shift of *real power factors* that even with a peaceful and sensible policy England will be *forced* to conclude that she must strike down such an opponent before he has reached a level of military strength so dangerous for her position as a World Power. This will very greatly increase the possibility of military clashes in the next 4 years, even before a single one of the new ships of the line is ready.' A steady and systematic process was also indispensable from the point of view of domestic policy, Tirpitz warned. For if the Reichstag should notice that the government was constructing a fleet of which it could be assumed, 'not entirely without reason', that it would one day be 'equal to the English', it would be impossible to obtain a parliamentary majority for it. As it was, the 'enormous costs' of the Bill already agreed upon would undoubtedly entail 'great political risks'. If even more were asked for, failure and a consequent 'great loss of prestige both at home and abroad' were to be feared. The renewed unrest in Russia and Austria would undoubtedly have repercussions on the German Social Democrats, Tirpitz warned. 'Whether the German Reich today possesses the inner strength to overcome a "period of conflict" seems ... questionable'.[105] In an accompanying note Tirpitz admitted that his memorandum contained thoughts 'which one probably can or must think but which, actually, ought not to be written down'. It was the secretary of state's express aim to win back the Reich Chancellor's support against 'the incessant subversion from another source, whose impatience is constantly spurred on by fantasists and ill-wishers'. By which he meant, of course, the Kaiser.[106]

There is no doubt that Wilhelm, encouraged by Senden, was receptive to the 'extreme' agitation of the Navy League and continually pressed for a faster rate of construction.[107] In his marginal notes he criticised the secretary of state for not having begun building four large ships a year from an earlier date.[108]

He repeatedly demanded that the older battleships be replaced faster and the new ones built sooner.[109] At Tirpitz's audience on 3 February 1906 Wilhelm accused him of having 'made insufficient use of *public opinion* for the benefit of the navy'. He laid down an ultimatum, as Tirpitz recorded: 'Bring forward. Shorten life to 18 years. Higher demands. (There seems to be a wish to dissolve the Reichstag under the pretext of the navy bill.)'[110] Undeterred by the warnings of Tirpitz and Holstein, Bülow took the same line. In a discussion with the Kaiser on 5 February 1906 the subject of 'the imbalance between our navy and the powerful force now mobilised by England' came up, as Senden, the Chief of the Naval Cabinet, recorded in a memorandum. 'When the Reich Chancellor asked whether anything could be done to speed up the construction of our navy, His Majesty replied that it was probably feasible . . . to shorten the life of the ships of the line by six or seven years. It would be best . . . if this initiative came as a motion [from the Reichstag]. Then the Brandenburg Class – first keels laid down in 1889 – or the Siegfried Class – first laid down in 1887 and 1889 – would already be due to be replaced and a request for new keels to be laid down could be made. These new ships could be launched in about 1907and probably go on trial voyages at the beginning of 1909. The Reich Chancellor agreed with His Majesty's opinion, he also considered the shortening of the life of the ships of the line to be a very good idea . . . and it would not interfere with the Navy Law at all.'[111] On 8 February 1906 Tirpitz confronted the Chancellor, who denied having told the Kaiser that a Reichstag resolution in favour of faster enlargement of the navy was attainable and declared that there must be a misunderstanding. Yet when Tirpitz told the Kaiser at an audience at the Stadtschloss in Potsdam two days later that neither he nor Bülow saw any prospect of getting a resolution through the Reichstag, 'His Majesty answered very curtly that the Reich Chancellor had said the opposite yesterday (Friday)'. Once again Bülow had to admit that it would be impossible to persuade the parties in the Reichstag to adopt the resolution for which the Kaiser wished. Together he and Tirpitz drew up a written statement which Bülow read out to the Kaiser on 13 February 1906 in the presence of Tirpitz, who later described Wilhelm's reaction as follows: 'Afterwards His Majesty took the statement, read it through again and then exclaimed heatedly: "So I shall not get the ships. We shall see what happens next!" After that he made a remark I did not quite understand and which was directed more towards me: "If we then have no ships . . .?" . . . When I asked the Reich Chancellor afterwards what the Kaiser could have meant by that, he merely said "I cannot do any more for you".'[112]

After this episode Tirpitz again seriously considered handing in his resignation. Only after a 'hard struggle between wounded personal dignity and the sense of a great obligation towards the state' did he decide, as Müller attested, to stay in office at least until the *Flottennovelle* had been passed.[113] Relations between him and the Kaiser remained extremely tense.[114] After the *Novelle* was adopted in the Reichstag on 28 March 1906 Tirpitz felt that he had earned the Kaiser's gratitude for this success, which the latter of course claimed as his own. Instead of praise the Admiral received a newspaper cutting on which Wilhelm II had written in the margin: 'Tomfoolery! The demands put in were too low and one can see now that the people who say so are right!'[115] Tirpitz handed in his resignation on 4 April 1906. Not only the repudiation inherent in the Kaiser's note but the entire treatment to which he had been subjected recently by the Kaiser seemed to him to indicate that he no longer possessed the 'All-Highest approval' indispensable to the discharge of his office. 'His Majesty's deliberate remark more or less puts the whole situation in this light.'[116] At the same time he hoped that by resigning he would 'have some influence on the Kaiser by encouraging him to fight his own inclination to toss this kind of not quite fully developed idea at government departments'. In framing his resignation letter, however, Tirpitz rejected a first draft complaining about the Kaiser's marginal note and instead gave his ostensibly poor health as his sole reason for wishing to leave office, in order 'not to excite the Kaiser's feelings more than necessary'.[117] It is therefore no surprise that the secretary of state was satisfied with the 'gracious' letter in which the Kaiser conveyed his refusal to let him go.[118] Tirpitz later discovered that Wilhelm had at first forwarded his letter of resignation to the Naval Cabinet without comment and that it was Senden who had drawn up the 'gracious' letter of 5 April. The Kaiser told Senden that 'he could not understand the Secretary of State; he knew that various differences and difficulties had arisen between him and the Secretary of State, but subsequently, at the last court party, he had seated Frau von Tirpitz next to him and thus given her precedence over all the Princes; he found it incomprehensible that the Secretary of State had seen fit to send in his resignation after that. He had thought the Secretary of State would perhaps write to him saying that he knew that there had been various instances lately when His Majesty had been dissatisfied with him and had disagreed with him, but since the Kaiser had singled out his wife in such an unusual way recently, he would have given up the idea of submitting his resignation.' The Kaiser had added, according to Senden, that 'other ministers have far worse things thrown at them by him, and what would happen if everyone wanted to resign as a result'.[119] The Kaiser also complained to Müller about Tirpitz's refractory behaviour and remarked that 'the *Minister of War*, von Einem, always did whatever the Kaiser ordered, while the Secretary of State of the Navy constantly made difficulties for him'.[120]

Although Tirpitz took up his post again after a period of leave, he declared in a very frank conversation on 3 May 1906 with Müller, who had meanwhile been promoted to acting Chief of the Naval Cabinet, that he would remain in office only on condition that the monarch's constant interference ceased. He stated bluntly that he could not endure 'the Kaiser's behaviour. The constant doubt as to whether His Majesty would stay the course on the various questions paralysed his initiative. In shipbuilding and similar matters the Secretary of State was kept so busy by His Majesty that his attention was directed more towards prevention and putting on the brakes than towards production.' He therefore had serious doubts about whether he could remain in office. Müller was not without sympathy for the secretary of state's attitude. His resignation had been 'really very necessary to clear the air', he commented. The Kaiser had now realised that Tirpitz was not one to cling to office, but that on the other hand he could not do without him in the Reichstag.[121]

Nonetheless both the secretary of state and Müller had good reason to doubt that Wilhelm had really taken the lesson of the resignation to heart. Wilhelm was still 'in very close contact' with Prince Salm-Horstmar, Müller warned. Only recently the Kaiser had wanted to agree to the Navy League's programme, until Müller drew his attention to the situation that would arise if this should become public knowledge. Müller also confirmed Tirpitz's fear that the Kaiser continued to believe the secretary of state had missed the opportunity for an even greater expansion of the navy. Even now Wilhelm was still counting on the idea 'that within the year a major new *Novelle* would be forthcoming, which would bring about faster replacement of the old ships and reduction of their life-span, as a result of which we would achieve the *four-ship building rate* within the year'.[122]

As before, Tirpitz found in Prince Heinrich, whom the Kaiser appointed to succeed Koester as Commander of the Fleet in May 1906,[123] a counterweight both against the hotheads in the Navy League and against the Kaiser with his constant demands for faster expansion. At the end of 1905 Tirpitz had underlined to the Prince his basic conviction that from the financial, staffing and technical point of view a systematic development of the navy was the only right way to go. 'One can perhaps conjure up armies out of thin air, as Scharnhorst and Gambetta did; but to build up a navy with the requisite bases and reserves needs the lifetime of a generation. But the building of our fleet can only be set in train by the Navy Laws', which might now be called into question because of the impatience of the Navy League and the Kaiser.[124] In a speech at the general assembly of the Navy League in Hamburg on 20 May 1906 Prince Heinrich praised Tirpitz's achievements, while at Kiel he told his brother firmly that 'if he could not get on with the Secretary of State he should let him go'. The Kaiser responded that 'that was out of the question; he still needed him and his organisational talent'. It did not pass unnoticed, however, that when the *Flottennovelle* was finally adopted on 19 May 1906 Wilhelm failed to confer the Order of the Black Eagle on Tirpitz in recognition of this achievement. When the secretary of state informed him that the *Novelle* had been passed he responded with conspicuous coldness, saying merely 'Many thanks for the good news.'[125] Then in July 1906 a colleague confirmed to him that the Kaiser had been annoyed 'that he was not getting his ships' and was indeed still annoyed 'that you do not agree with him about his ... fast ship of the line'.[126]

With the long-awaited appointment of Georg Alexander von Müller as Chief of the Naval Cabinet on 9 July 1906 Tirpitz believed he had acquired a like-minded ally at court, something he had lacked during the tenure of Senden with his 'extreme views'.[127] Müller promised to shield the secretary of state from the monarch's impulsive interventions. It was his 'fervent wish', he declared, 'that I shall manage to keep unnecessary friction away from you and make sure that you receive a sympathetic hearing from the All-Highest Lord'. Tirpitz could rest assured that whatever happened, both the Kaiser and the Chancellor wanted to keep him as secretary of state. Müller was firmly convinced 'that in the autumn Your Excellency will find a completely tractable ... Kaiser, who will be entirely open to sensible ideas about the way forward, even if as a result of these ideas the building rate has to remain as it is for the time being. Nor will there be any battle over types of ship, which in my opinion is an advantage of the "fast ship of the line" which should not be underestimated. For until the projects for the prize competition are submitted the question of types is dead, and once the projects are submitted, even if they are totally impracticable for technical or tactical reasons, they will still, in their extreme form, bring a completely new clarity to the question, unlike the mongrel creations so casually dashed off [by the Kaiser] in pencil on a telegraph form and not based on any figures.'[128] (See Figure 16.)

THE NAVAL ARMS RACE WITH GREAT BRITAIN

The strained relationship between Kaiser Wilhelm II and the Secretary of State of the Reich Navy Office should not obscure our recognition that both were pursuing the same revolutionary goal, namely to build up, by 1918, a home fleet of sixty large battleships. Both wanted, as Volker Berghahn has shown in his seminal study of the Tirpitz Plan, 'to build a fleet which regularly renewed itself, which was independent of the Reichstag's budgetary

Figure 16 Kaiser Wilhelm's designs for new warships

control and which would serve as a power-political lever directed against England'. Tirpitz, however, saw more clearly than Wilhelm II and the naval agitators the limits 'which constrained the Imperial Navy in the effort to create a naval instrument of power for Germany's future breakthrough to the status of a World Power'.[129]

Of course the Kaiser knew very well what domestic and foreign policy goals Tirpitz was pursuing in building up the battlefleet. He was filled with glee at the game of hide-and-seek which the secretary of state had played to deceive the members of the Reichstag about the true aims of his plan. With the Navy Law he had 'taken in Parliament completely', Wilhelm boasted in April 1907. In passing the law the members of the Reichstag had 'not understood at all how elastic the consequences were; for the Navy Law lays down that whatever he demands must be granted . . . In fact with this Navy Law I can have any division of ships of the line that I want. It is a corkscrew with which I can open the bottle whatever happens. And I hope the spray will reach the ceiling. Those dogs shall pay up until they are blue in the face. They are completely in my hands now, and no power in the world shall prevent me from extracting as much as possible.'[130] In his jubilation Wilhelm even went so far as to welcome

the travelling diplomacy practised by Edward VII, which usually aroused his
ire. Edward's meetings with the kings of Spain and Italy had unleashed a wave
of anti-English feeling in Germany which the Kaiser intended to exploit to
obtain a further enlargement of the navy. 'It has had the happy result that the
Reichstag grasps the situation and at last takes a patriotic line on questions of
military credits.'[131]

Unlike the Reichstag, Britain was not taken in by the deceptions of
Wilhelm II and Tirpitz. Charles Hardinge, the Permanent Under Secretary
of State for Foreign Affairs, resisted every attempt to reduce the British naval
presence in the North Sea and the English Channel. Writing to the King he
asserted 'that if Germany ever attacks us it will be by "coup de main"'. The
Royal Navy must always be ready, he said, 'to repel a surprise attack' from
the Imperial Navy.[132] In June 1907 he commented: 'We really are, vis-à-vis of
Germany, in a situation of serious danger which, with our resources & naval
expenditure, I feel sure the country would not tolerate for an instant if they
knew all.'[133] In early 1907 he wrote to Lascelles in Berlin: 'Our programme of
new construction will depend greatly upon Germany and it rests with her to
force or slacken the pace as far as we are concerned (and indeed as far as
France is concerned too).'[134] Likewise the Foreign Secretary, Sir Edward Grey,
insisted that the responsibility for the arms race lay with the Kaiser and that
this must be clearly and openly stated. 'He can, if the Reichstag votes the
money, oblige us to add another ten or twenty millions a year to the Navy
Estimates in the next few years, but if this is done I want people here and in
Germany, who will have to vote the money, to realize that it is he, who has
forced our hand in spite of our wish to limit expenditure', Grey wrote to Lord
Knollys in November 1906.[135]

Hypocritically, the Kaiser poured scorn on the growing conviction of the
British that the German fleet was intended 'to seize control of the seas from
England', calling such ideas 'sheer nonsense!' and 'such balderdash!'[136] When
reports came from London that fears were spreading about 'Germany's
increasing armaments at sea and on land' Wilhelm repudiated them as
ridiculous. 'The army has been on the same footing for years! And the Navy
Law dates from 97–99!!!' he declared in January 1907.[137] Grey's assertion that
Britain must maintain her supremacy at sea vis-à-vis Germany because
Germany possessed an overwhelmingly strong army which would invade
the country if the Royal Navy were destroyed was treated with mockery
by the Kaiser. 'Such outrageous balderdash!!' he wrote in 1907; 'what sort of
a picture of the world has this man got in his head?'[138]

Every initiative to halt the trend towards bigger and more expensive
warships through international or bilateral agreement was rejected with fury

by Wilhelm II as an unacceptable infringement of his rights as Supreme War Lord and of the sovereignty of the Reich. When in May 1906, in view of the forthcoming second Peace Conference at The Hague, Grey expressed his government's wish for limits to be set to arms expenditure, the Kaiser saw this as nothing but a trap 'to prevent *us* building a big fleet!' He would 'certainly not' fall in with Grey's suggestion. 'If anyone can limit his armaments, it is England alone! Since it has such a colossal superiority! But because it has this superiority it wants to keep it for all time, and therefore the *others* are not allowed to develop their armaments i.e. naval construction. Especially not us!'[139] He rejected Grey's proposal that the Powers should inform each other of their naval plans at the Peace Conference with the ironic comment: 'Oh how sweet!' 'So that England has due warning and can remain the strongest naval power!'[140] In England naval plans were kept secret until the last moment; 'but not here! For we have laid down our limits on ourselves in the Navy Law.'[141] He described as 'nonsense', 'rubbish' and 'Jesuitism' Grey's further suggestion that the size of the two battlefleets should be fixed arithmetically in a proportion of 2:1 or 3:1. Again and again he disingenuously cited the Navy Law as justification for his refusal to cooperate. 'Thanks to our Navy Law, which was published 10 years ago, England has been in a position to know as long as 10 years in advance what we shall have in 1907–10!! And thus to prepare for it! We are the only country in the world that has had the courage up to now to commit ourselves so far in advance by law and to be open about it! The mystery-mongering about the "Dreadnought" and the completely secret construction of the "Invincible" Class, which is the same size, flies in the face of Grey's wishes, while we fulfilled them long ago through our Navy Law!'[142] Clearly the English were aiming to surprise the other countries with the question of international control of arms limitations, Wilhelm commented, in the hope of 'a fight with us arising out of the discussion!' There would be 'no harm done!' if the disarmament question remained unresolved and this led to an intensification of the British government's naval programme: 'let them get on with it as long as they are willing to pay for it!' Grey's warning that the Liberal government, like its Conservative predecessor, 'in its feverish concern to maintain the lead which its naval instruments of power had over those of Germany', would 'continue the work of perfecting and strengthening them' left the Kaiser unperturbed. 'None of us will stand in its way[,] we are making ourselves only as strong as our interests require, and so as to prevent England, conscious of its great superiority, being able to attack us suddenly in order to destroy our navy with "mathematical" certainty!'[143] He complained bitterly of the British attitude to disarmament. 'So France and America, Japan and Italy may build as many ships as they want! Only we may not! The rest will come out of the Hague Conference.'[144] In the spring of 1907 he commented that 'H[is] M[ajesty] [King Edward] is not as harmless as he is made out to be, and the Engl[ish] Government is not as angelically pure as it would like to appear.' 'Furthermore, apart from the one "Dreadnought", 7–8 are under construction or on order, and that is now known, so with the best will in the world the disarmament theory cannot be upheld.'[145] The Kaiser found himself in a dilemma, however, when President Roosevelt also put forward the proposal that at the Hague Conference Germany should join the United States, France and Italy in calling for the displacement of all battleships to be limited to 15,000 tons; this was the only practicable means of cutting down the enormous expenditure for purposes of war.[146] But the Supreme War Lord's instructions were perfectly clear. 'Refuse!' he ordered. 'Every state builds what suits it! No business of anyone else! 15/X 1906 W.'[147]

THE KAISER AND THE MOVE TO THE FOUR-SHIP-BUILDING RATE

Soon after the passage of the *Flottennovelle* in the Reichstag in May 1906, a worrying report had arrived from London that the British had commissioned the construction of a 34.3 cm gun for the ships of the line of the new Dreadnought series and were even planning a further increase of calibre to over 40 cm; the new ships would probably have a displacement of over 20,000 tons.[148] For Tirpitz, the news from England meant the alarming admission that he had probably asked for too little in the *Flottennovelle* of 1906 after all, just as the Kaiser had complained. Worse still, the growing size of ships marked the beginning of the end of his bold plan.

The constant increase in the displacement of battleships was, as Berghahn remarks, grist to the Kaiser's mill, for in his eyes it confirmed that he was right in demanding fast ships of the line. 'Ships of the line, then … exactly my principle', he wrote triumphantly on the report on the new British construction plans.[149] Since the funds approved by the Reichstag in the spring of 1906 were insufficient to increase the displacement of the large cruisers *and* of the ships of the line, Tirpitz found himself compelled in September 1906 to recommend an increase only of the large cruisers for the time being, with the result that this type of ship actually came to resemble more closely the fast ship of the line which the Kaiser wished for. Not least for this reason, at his annual audience at Rominten on 28 September the secretary of state found the Kaiser more than willing to approve the enormous extra expense. Tirpitz explained to the monarch that the English had gone further than could have been anticipated in 1905 in the development of their large cruisers of the *Invincible* class.

Germany would have to respond by immediately enlarging the cruisers she had planned to build. The new type of cruiser would cost at least 10 million marks more than had been calculated hitherto, he warned. Wilhelm enthusiastically approved the Admiral's suggestion that this extra cost should be concealed from the Reichstag for the time being, and that a further *Flottennovelle* should be laid before the Reichstag, but only after new elections, which would be brought forward.[150] At long last, on the occasion of his birthday on 27 January 1907, he conferred the Order of the Black Eagle on Tirpitz, which was greeted with 'universal pleasure, especially in the navy'.[151] On 15 June 1907 the Kaiser sent Tirpitz a bouquet to congratulate him on his tenth anniversary as Secretary of State of the Reich Navy Office and thanked him warmly for all he had achieved.[152] Gone was the constant friction between the monarch and the secretary of state with the 'character of a Bismarck' which had so often come close to causing the latter's dismissal.

The idea of dissolving the Reichstag and conducting an election campaign with nationalistic slogans gained even more appeal the more apparent it became that London intended to take up the gauntlet. If the goal of a battlefleet that would be the equal of the Royal Navy in fighting capability were not to be abandoned, a gigantic new Navy Bill would be indispensable.[153] The so-called Hottentot Election of January 1907 did indeed bring losses for the Social Democrats and a pro-navy majority in the Reichstag with which Tirpitz was able to implement the next stage of his grand plan. In a letter to his patron Prince Heinrich of Prussia the secretary of state was exultant at the 'amazing defeat of the Social Democrats', whose 'lack of patriotism' had weighed 'so heavily . . . on our nation'. Once again he stressed the advantages of his gradual, long-term strategy which had brought the great goal within sight. 'As a result of the moderation we have exercised in the past year we are now in a position that is as favourable as could possibly be achieved. It can be seen in the current "even" speed of construction. Where the Reichstag is concerned it is . . . particularly important to hold on to the present Navy Law as our basis and to graft onto it only as much as can be "legally" carried through for the time being. Our object is to keep the same kind of safeguard against Reichstag majorities as the army in fact enjoys through the constitution and the defence laws. I am absolutely delighted that His Majesty seems to have accepted these ideas, for what is at stake is, after all, the greatest glory of His Majesty's reign until now: to have created a navy that is "permanent", thus also for His successors.'[154] On 3 February 1907 Tirpitz was already telling his colleague Adolf von Trotha that he intended to 'take advantage' of the new Reichstag, 'perhaps quite soon', to push through another Navy Bill. 'May heaven favour our cause. For me everything depends on the crucial question of the three-ship building rate.'[155]

On 9 March 1907 Tirpitz explained to the Kaiser that in view of the increase in the fighting strength of the British navy, the German navy would soon have to follow suit. He proposed a fourth *Flottennovelle* which would not only provide for the construction of considerably bigger capital ships and large cruisers but also prescribe the reduction of the lifetime of ships of the line by five years. Furthermore, it would at long last bring about the *'Äternisierung'* (permanent parliamentary authorisation) of the three-ship rate of construction which had been planned from the outset and by which the fleet would renew itself almost automatically every twenty years, without any further intervention from the Reichstag. Kaiser Wilhelm welcomed this solution with delight, and a relieved Tirpitz was able to comment in his notes on the audience that 'H.M. the K. approved of this proposal, and in particular that I can if necessary make a statement to the effect that we do not intend to give up the 3-ship rate.'[156]

A new capital ship, according to the calculations of the Reich Navy Office, would cost 47 million marks and a new large cruiser 44 million.[157] Bülow's objections to this enormously expensive and highly dangerous arms escalation failed to make any impact on the Kaiser's unthinking support for Tirpitz's plans. As Berghahn comments, the Reich Chancellor had 'scarcely any alternative but to agree, once Wilhelm II had given his consent'.[158] On 27 May 1907 Tirpitz used his audience with the Kaiser to make doubly sure of the monarch's commitment to his plan of action and to brush aside the objections expressed by Bülow. If necessary the Kaiser must 'take a hard line' in the interests of the *Flottennovelle*, he warned. Wilhelm II again assured Tirpitz of his support.[159]

The secretary of state seemed to have every reason to believe that the strategy of providing for a regular increase of the navy at the three-ship rate of construction, which he had pursued doggedly since 1897 and had carried through against the clamour of the naval fanatics and often against the impatient demands of Kaiser Wilhelm, had been a success. In August 1907 he promised Bülow to portray the forthcoming *Novelle* 'as something entirely natural and merely a consequence of our naval plan, which remained unaltered and limited'. He would once again draft the Bill in such a way that it seemed 'as small and harmless as possible both abroad and at home'.[160] Tirpitz even told the Kaiser on 7 September 1907 that the political aim of his Navy Law, envisaged from the outset, would be achieved through the new Bill, namely the *Äternat*. The goal of the Bill, he said, was 'to create, in the course of the next winter, such a stable and inviolable structure for the navy that no partisan agitation can disturb it in the future, which will also ensure that any increase in the fighting strength of individual ships which Your Majesty might consider necessary and which cannot yet be foreseen at all, can be easily effected in future'.[161] It was all the more surprising, therefore, that the draft which Tirpitz decided to submit to the Kaiser at Rominten overturned the basic principles of his own naval construction plan and, by changing over to a four-ship-building rate for the years from 1908 to 1911, broke through the last barriers of financial and diplomatic 'common sense'.[162]

There were technical and parliamentary reasons for this astonishing decision, but the 'greatest threat' to the *Novelle* which he had originally planned came from the Kaiser. Tirpitz was quite rightly afraid that Wilhelm, spurred on by the Navy League and ignoring the consequences, might decide to change immediately to a four-ship-building rate. The monarch's enthusiasm for the navy had by no means diminished since the winter of 1905–6. On the contrary, in April 1907 he had written on a newspaper article about British naval construction: 'Speed up the building, then! And bring down the age of our ships of the line so that more replacements can be made sooner.'[163] So as not to get into the same unpleasant situation as in November 1905 Tirpitz took the bull by the horns and went to see Bülow in Norderney immediately before his audience at Rominten on 21 September 1907. There he told the Chancellor that on the one hand the mood in the country in favour of a large increase in the navy had 'swollen' unexpectedly so that it was no longer possible to 'stand by the 3-ship rate'; on the other hand it was now 'not dangerous' from a diplomatic point of view to speed up the building of the battlefleet. Surprisingly, the Reich Chancellor accepted these explanations and in so doing took responsibility for the secretary of state's highly dangerous naval construction plans.[164]

Shortly afterwards Tirpitz set off for his annual trip to East Prussia, where his audience with the Kaiser took place at the imperial hunting lodge at Rominten. Wilhelm's reaction to the proposal that the pace of naval armament should be stepped up by going over to the four-ship-building rate was described in striking terms by Tirpitz. 'H.M. accepted the bill as something to be taken for granted, a mere bagatelle. The Reich Chancellor had already written to him, he said, to say that he had discussed everything with the members of parliament and even the rabid [Liberal] peoples' party members were willing to agree to it. When I pointed out that the previous negotiations with the members of parliament had extended only to the bill planned in the spring and not to the present one, H.M. said that did not matter at all! H.M. does not consider the financial difficulties of any importance. England could say nothing, as quantities of Dreadnoughts were suddenly being built everywhere. H.M. remarked that it was a good thing that I had now also come round to the view that the life-span of the ships of the line must be shortened.

He seemed not to realise, or to disregard, the importance of the *Äternat* of the three-ship building rate achieved thereby. All in all this audience was depressing for me, seeing that this is the one goal I have pursued incessantly for 10 years.'[165] Under pressure from his impatient sovereign, who shared the unbounded ideas of the Navy League, Tirpitz had thrown 'all the dictates of common sense overboard', as Berghahn puts it, and transformed the carefully calculated Navy Bill into a provocative four-ship-building rate *Novelle*. At the end of March 1908 a broad majority in the Reichstag voted to raise the existing three-ship rate to four large ships a year until 1911.[166]

CHAPTER NINETEEN

The zenith of Personal Monarchy. The Kaiser and the government on the eve of the great crisis

WILHELM II AT THE HEIGHT OF HIS POWER

After eighteen years on the throne the Kaiser exerted such an extraordinary influence, especially over military and foreign policy and over public appointments, that precisely those contemporaries who knew most about the decision-making process drew attention to the dangers of this development. In May 1906 – immediately after his dismissal – Friedrich von Holstein warned: 'Not only abroad but in Germany the fear of personal rule is increasing. And rightly so.'[1] In the opinion of Count Zedlitz, who as Hofmarschall had daily opportunities to observe the monarch's conduct, 'the autocratic streak in the Kaiser's personality is growing and we are running into difficulties both at home and abroad with this system'. Wilhelm 'almost deliberately' trained people 'to tell him only what pleases him and what he wants', Zedlitz lamented in March 1906.[2] Eighteen months later he commented on the Kaiser's tendency to ignore facts and opinions which displeased him. 'One needs to have observed this talent for refusing to hear an adverse opinion in order to understand how situations so often arise in which one has the impression that scarcely anyone speaks a word of truth any more . . . The ability always to choose the subject of conversation, to change its course or to break it off, the Kaiser's compelling, idiosyncratic personality, his refusal to hear certain points of view and also the dependence [on him] of the majority of leading people, create this situation, which one has to reckon with since for the time being it is impossible to see how it can change.'[3] The Kaiser could not tolerate independent-minded men around him, the Hofmarschall wrote. He had a sixth sense for this kind of person. 'He does not grapple with them for long, and then he casts them aside. There is no question of their influencing him . . . None of them has ever succeeded in asserting his view against the Kaiser, and none has ever had a lasting, reliable, strong influence on him. Neither Prince Bülow nor Prince Eulenburg nor even Oberhofmarschall Count August Eulenburg is any exception. They are, in the true sense of the word, only henchmen, for in the end it is the Kaiser who commands, and they carry out his orders without a word. At the same time I do not deny that they use their skill to prevent many things from happening and to put many things right, but at the decisive moment, when matters are serious, not one of them will speak his own mind.'[4] Like Waldersee fifteen years earlier, Zedlitz observed in December 1907 that the Kaiser would have to be confronted with truly difficult times before he too realised 'that the idea of flirting with absolutism today does the greatest damage not only to him, but also to the development of the nation'.[5]

The excesses of autocratic behaviour which Wilhelm II permitted himself in his dealings with the most senior of government officials are breathtaking. In the summer of 1906 he ordered the Prussian Minister of Culture, Education and Church Affairs to commission a bust of his tutor Hinzpeter for the National Gallery.[6] He sent an 'interminably long' telegram en clair to the ambassador in Constantinople, in which he described highly placed Turkish officials as scoundrels and rogues and demanded their dismissal – 'a blindness to the most basic rights of the Sultan which borders on madness', as Baroness Hildegard von Spitzemberg observed.[7] In September 1906 the diplomat Hans von Wangenheim discovered that the Kaiser had sent a letter to President Roosevelt 'written in the tone of an infatuated third-year schoolboy writing to a seamstress'. The ambassador, Hermann Speck von Sternburg, had refused to pass the letter on to the President, but Wilhelm II ordered him to deliver it nevertheless. Only when Sternburg threatened to resign did the Kaiser give way, but the ambassador was treated with conspicuous unfriendliness when next he appeared at court.[8] When the former Foreign Secretary and long-serving ambassador in Constantinople, Adolf Freiherr Marschall von Bieberstein, asked for a fortnight's extra leave, Wilhelm annotated the request with 'Ten days are enough.' 'This to an ambassador, out of sheer childish mischief!' Spitzemberg commented indignantly.[9] In October 1906, when the story of the fraudulent 'Captain' of Köpenick was doing the rounds, the general opinion in political circles was that 'such an incident could only occur under a regime like the Kaiser's, when people think the most outrageous instances of arbitrariness and sycophancy are permissible'.[10] At court experienced officials were deeply concerned about 'the change in the Kaiser's character . . . or rather the lack of change from the young, impulsive ruler to the mature, serious, purposeful one'. The 'brutality is increasing, the impossibility of saying anything displeasing, the delusion about the real state of affairs'.[11]

Neither the Reich Chancellor, still less the ministers and secretaries of state, could summon up the courage or find an opportunity to challenge this sort of treatment. Zedlitz, as ever critical, recorded the obsequious behaviour of the statesmen at a dinner at court in February 1906: 'Such a gathering of ministers around their King is surely a very peculiar phenomenon in present times. When the Kaiser came into the Pfeilersaal ... the Ministers stood in a semi-circle in front of him. They all adopted a more or less military posture ... The comparisons which this gathering evokes are unavoidable: one is reminded of the Colonel of a regiment with his captains. After dinner, when Podbielski entertained the company with rather coarse and suggestive stories, one could not help thinking of the smoking clubs' at the court of Prussian kings in the early eighteenth century.[12] Scenes such as this are symptomatic both of the subordinate position in which the Reich Chancellor and the ministers found themselves from the 1890s onwards, and of the high-handedness of a sovereign who expected such obsequiousness from the most senior figures in government. In such a one-sided relationship it was impossible for either the Chancellor or the ministers to protect the monarch from the increasingly strident criticism coming from the public.

The grovelling behaviour of Prince Bülow towards the Kaiser now sank to new depths. After he had fainted in the Reichstag on 5 April 1906 the Chancellor seemed to many observers to be physically and mentally weakened, and it was rumoured that he had had a stroke.[13] The society doctor Rudolf von Renvers ordered strict bed-rest and sent Bülow to Norderney to convalesce.[14] He was not to resume his official duties fully until October 1906. Now more than ever he fell into a sycophantic dependence on the Kaiser which disgusted his contemporaries. 'It gives me the greatest happiness to be able to carry out Your Majesty's intentions and smooth the way for Your Majesty's important aims', the Kaiser's 'most humble servant' telegraphed to his sovereign 'with my most loyal devotion' on 20 May 1906.[15] This was followed a few days later by a further effusion. 'To increase Your Majesty's fame, happiness and well-being to the best of my ability will be the focus of all my thoughts, all my cares and all my efforts until I draw my last breath.'[16]

Although he had become a millionaire thanks to a legacy and although the Kaiser had raised him to princely status, Bülow clung to office and did not dare put up any serious opposition to the monarch.[17] Zedlitz deplored such submissiveness on the part of the most highly placed statesman in Prussia and the Reich. 'If only he showed the slightest reservation, or even gave some indication that he was not in fact dependent on his post, he could achieve great things, for as a public figure he is absolutely indispensable to the Kaiser. But unfortunately this is not in his nature.'[18] In the following months and years the Hofmarschall watched with abhorrence the servile and ingratiating attitude which the Reich Chancellor displayed towards the Kaiser. Domestic politics were 'in as great a shambles as possible', Zedlitz commented, 'and as far as foreign affairs are concerned we have a kind of Olmütz in Morocco, although by comparison we have never had such a strong army and navy and thus such relatively weak opponents. But a Reich Chancellor who, when on board the "Hohenzollern", the minute he is told "You are ruining the excellent weather prospects with your light-coloured trousers" immediately goes to his cabin and puts on dark trousers, a Reich Chancellor who makes notes on his cuff at every opportunity so as to be quite sure not to forget any of the wishes casually mentioned in conversation, a Chancellor who is incautious enough on one occasion to express a diametrically opposed opinion and, noticing this, is silent only for a short moment before immediately introducing the exact opposite of his earlier view with the words: "As Your Majesty so rightly observed, the matter stands thus . . .", such a Chancellor, for all his very great gifts, for all the very great instruments of power available, makes the worst imaginable policy. I am afraid history will not judge him kindly.'[19] And Zedlitz was by no means alone in his critical verdict.

After a break of several years, on his retirement in April 1906 Holstein resumed his attacks on Wilhelm II's 'Personal Rule'. Like Zedlitz, he warned against the enormous risks represented by the Kaiser's autocratic character and the Chancellor's spinelessness. The monarch would not tolerate any independent expression of opinion and systematically weaned all those around him away from any tendency to contradict. 'The Kaiser has a dramatic but not a political instinct, he considers the momentary effect but not the consequences, and is actually for the most part unpleasantly surprised by them', Holstein wrote to the journalist Pascal David in May 1906: 'The German Reich is on the brink of a period of danger and degradation and is perilously close to it . . . All provocations are either conceived by the Kaiser or are conceived to please him . . . Criticism, in order to be effective, must be outspokenly directed against the Kaiser . . . The Kaiser must be made to realise that his prestige will suffer if he follows every impulse. This applies above all to the personal remarks of His Majesty.'[20] Soon Holstein found in the influential journalist Maximilian Harden a potentially very dangerous ally in the struggle against the Kaiser and his entourage.

THE PODBIELSKI CRISIS

However hard Bülow tried to retain the Kaiser's confidence in him by unscrupulous flattery, it was only a question of time until a situation arose in which he would have no alternative but to take a stand against the monarch. It happened in the summer of 1906. In the Reichstag the Centre party leader, Matthias Erzberger, made serious allegations of corruption against officers and civil servants in the colonial department of the Foreign Office. A Major Fischer, head of the army clothing supply office, was arrested and accused of accepting bribes from the firm of Tippelskirch, suppliers to the colonial troops in German South-West Africa. The crisis broadened into an affair of state when it transpired that the Prussian Minister of Agriculture, General Viktor von Podbielski, a protégé of Wilhelm II, had close business links with the firm. Erzberger, Left Liberal members of parliament and the Social Democrats demanded his resignation. On 18 August the Kaiser and Bülow discussed this 'tiresome affair' at Wilhelmshöhe, but they were unable to reach any agreement. Wilhelm gave the Chancellor an 'unfriendly' reception and refused to drop Podbielski. Bülow, who 'feared ... for his position', felt compelled to climb down for the time being.[21]

The clash over Podbielski was generally considered to be a signal that Bülow's days as Chancellor were numbered. On 11 September 1906 Anton Monts wrote to Holstein: 'I hardly think that B. B[ülow] will be able to stay in office much longer. The Pod[bielski] affair, in which he came out second-best, was really a serious defeat for him; that is, it would have been a fine opportunity for him to resign with honour ... The Chancellor certainly is not lacking in intelligence, only in character and willingness to face a fight. Therefore, despite his great talents, he will in the end have to leave the stage without honour. It seems to me that he is still full of illusions, especially about H.M., and believes that the old relationship still exists.'[22] In fact Wilhelm II, as we shall see, had already begun looking for a successor to Bülow.[23] On 8 October 1906 Hildegard von Spitzemberg noted: 'What I wrote here just after the catastrophe has happened exactly as I said it would: Bülow has been put out of action; he is kept on and highly praised to the outside world as an orator, which Tschirschky is not; meanwhile H.M. makes the important policy decisions with Tschirschky as his tool and commits one act of gross tactlessness after another, alas!'[24]

The Podbielski crisis had not been resolved by Bülow's acceptance of defeat at Wilhelmshöhe, but merely postponed. In November 1906 the Prussian Ministry of State unanimously demanded the dismissal of the Minister of Agriculture, whose position had become untenable, before the Reichstag met. The Bavarian envoy Count Lerchenfeld, who was always well informed, was able to report that twice recently the Kaiser had given Podbielski direct orders to stay in his post, saying 'he would cover him'. In so doing the monarch had 'put himself into deliberate conflict with the Chancellor and the entire remaining Prussian Ministry of State', Lerchenfeld warned. He forecast that although Bülow would force Podbielski out of office, this would be 'a Pyrrhic victory which he would not be able to enjoy for long, for the relationship between the Kaiser and the Chancellor was very strained at the moment'.[25] On 11 November Wilhelm found himself compelled to agree to Podbielski's dismissal. The conduct of the Chancellor and the ministers in presenting him with an ultimatum must have awakened in him memories of the crisis of November 1895 when Prince Chlodwig zu Hohenlohe-Schillingsfürst and the entire Prussian Ministry had threatened to resign in order to force the dismissal of Ernst Matthias von Köller, the Minister of the Interior, against Wilhelm's express wishes.[26] Holstein, who had played a decisive role in the Köller crisis, could not but 'doubt that Bülow would stay for much longer. The Kaiser will not forgive him for getting rid of Pod.'[27]

THE PUBLICATION OF THE HOHENLOHE MEMOIRS

As if the Podbielski crisis had not already shown the public enough of what went on behind the scenes of Wilhelm II's Personal Monarchy, the astonishing publication of the memoirs of Prince Chlodwig zu Hohenlohe-Schillingsfürst in October 1906 laid bare authentic source material about the events, hitherto kept secret, leading up to Bismarck's dismissal and during Caprivi's Chancellorship. The two-volume exposé rapidly became a sensational best-seller. Not only the Kaiser but the whole political world was aghast at the breach of confidence which Prince Alexander Hohenlohe had committed by publishing his father's papers.[28] Kaiser Wilhelm sent Philipp-Ernst zu Hohenlohe-Schillingsfürst, Alexander's eldest brother, an angry telegram testifying to his 'indignation' at the publication. 'How could it happen that such material could be made public without My permission being sought beforehand? I cannot but regard this action as the height of tactlessness, indiscretion and impropriety.'[29] Baden's envoy in Berlin, Baron Berckheim, reported: 'H.M. is furious, not only with Prince Alexander but also with Prince Philipp-Ernst, of whom he says that he can no longer regard him as the head of his family, as he cannot keep his agnates in order.'[30] Of the elderly Statthalter of Alsace-Lorraine, Prince Hermann zu Hohenlohe-Langenburg, the Kaiser remarked that one could surely have expected him to have more authority over his cousins and subordinates – Alexander Hohenlohe was District President in Colmar in Alsace.[31] Commenting on the Kaiser's mood the Chief of the Military Cabinet, General von Hülsen-Haeseler, told a member of the family: 'Believe me, the whole Hohenlohe family might as well bury itself.'[32] Bülow later recalled: 'The Kaiser was hard to pacify. There were few things he hated more than publications about sovereigns, and particularly about himself, that were not expressed in a very obsequious, if not sycophantic and glorifying tone ... In this respect Wilhelm II was very like Louis XIV.'[33]

It was only with difficulty that the Reich Chancellor succeeded in persuading the Kaiser to drop his demand for disciplinary proceedings against Prince Alexander, who had come to Bad Homburg to beg for Bülow's help.[34] The Prince was forced to relinquish his post as District President, however, which merely gave the scandal further prominence. He telegraphed to his uncle Hermann, the Statthalter, on 16 October: 'As I no longer have any doubt about the forthcoming All-Highest decision, after what the Reich Chancellor has told me, I have every right to make public the facts about my departure from office, in order to counter all the discreditable rumours spread about me in the Press, and I cannot allow myself to be deprived of this right.' He refused to be dissuaded from giving an interview to the editor-in-chief of the French newspaper *Le Temps*, a friend of his, in which he justified the publication of his father's memoirs.[35]

In order to save his own position as Statthalter, Prince Hermann wrote to the Kaiser expressing his 'deepest regret' and his 'indignation at the behaviour of Prince Alexander'. 'As soon as I heard of the just rebuke which it pleased Your Majesty to utter, I sent for Prince Alexander and drew his attention to the indiscretion of his conduct, making it clear to him at the same time that it would be impossible for him to remain any longer in his official position and that he must submit his resignation to Your Majesty. Your Majesty will All-Graciously understand how deeply painful it is for me, both as Head of the House of Hohenlohe and as Prince Alexander's immediate superior, that he has been guilty of such an offence against Your Majesty. Should Your Majesty see in this occurrence a degree of failure on my part to carry out my duty, and should it reduce the confidence which Your Majesty has All-Graciously bestowed so richly upon me in the 12 years of my administration of the province, I most humbly ask Your Majesty to permit me to lay down the post of Your Majesty's Statthalter in Alsace-Lorraine while at the same time requesting, with the greatest respect, to be allowed to continue my administration long enough to arrange for the disbandment of my household.'[36] On 20 October 1906 the Kaiser assured Hermann Hohenlohe of his continuing confidence in him. But Hohenlohe's days as Statthalter were henceforth numbered, and a year later he received his marching orders from the Kaiser.[37]

THE DISSOLUTION OF THE REICHSTAG AND THE 'HOTTENTOT ELECTION' OF JANUARY 1907

To the numerous causes of conflict which threatened to impair Bülow's relationship with the Kaiser another was added in 1906: they disagreed over the Centre party, whose democratic wing, led by Matthias Erzberger, was taking an increasingly confrontational course.[38] Since the adoption of the Customs Tariff Bill of 1902 Bülow had enjoyed a largely undisturbed period of cooperation with the Centre, and this predominantly Catholic party had played de facto the role of a government party. In return for its pro-government stance it obtained, among other things, the introduction of expense allowances for members of the Reichstag and concessions for Catholic private schools, which constantly gave rise to the Kaiser's aversion for 'Ultra-montanism'.[39] When in May 1906, at Erzberger's instigation, the party fiercely criticised the brutal war being conducted against the Herero and Nama peoples in German South-West Africa and denounced the corruption of the officials, Wilhelm II was incensed by this 'shameful' behaviour: the Centre party, he raged, was acting hand-in-hand with the Social Democrats.[40] He telegraphed angrily to the Reich Chancellor on 2 July 1906: 'Is there really no available means of protecting the world of our officials and officers from that professional backstairs creeper, vilifier and slanderer Erzberger? There is great indignation in these circles and it is growing; it would be a good thing if the Government showed him and the Centre its teeth.'[41] In response, Bülow assured the Kaiser that he fully shared 'Your Majesty's indignation at the incredible calumnies and accusations of the anti-colonialists'; he had given 'strict instructions that legal proceedings will be instituted against all ground-less accusations and exemplary penalties will be sought. Erzberger's conduct is outrageous and will be condemned by his political friends too ... The present case does not as yet justify tackling the Centre party itself. For Erzberger is on closer terms with a few Liberals than with the leaders of the Centre, who have been jealous of him for a long time and to whom he is a great nuisance. Unfortunately the parliamentary kitchen is no cleaner and probably even more complicated than the diplomatic one. In my most humble opinion, in the first place legal proceedings must immediately be instituted against every case of groundless accusations, then the examination of guilty officials must be carried out with the utmost severity and ruthlessness, and the guilty must be dealt with unsparingly.'[42] Significantly, Bülow tried to use the Kaiser's favourite, Tschirschky, as a front man, writing to him: 'I would be very grateful to you, and I believe you would be doing a service to the Fatherland, if you would on your own account, without reference to me, draw H.M.'s attention to the fact that constantly complaining and getting angry about the Centre leads nowhere.'[43] Whether Tschirschky, who according to Bülow 'was only too inclined to join in with every change of His Majesty's mood and to be no more than His Majesty's echo', carried out this commission is more than doubtful.[44] At any rate there was no change in the Kaiser's attitude towards the Centre party.

In December 1906 the Chancellor decided at short notice to break with the Centre party and in future to seek the support of the Left Liberals, who had been in opposition to the Reich government since the foundation of the Reich in 1871. The decisive factor was not some sort of internal political change of attitude but rather, as Wilfried Loth has emphasised, Bülow's 'concern for his personal position as Reich Chancellor'.[45] The dissolution of the Reichstag which he now brought about was recognised also by many a contemporary as 'a desperate measure to hold on to his position'.[46] Political developments, however, played into the Chancellor's hands to the extent that on the one hand, the Left Liberals voted for the first time in favour of a Navy Bill, and on the other, the Centre voted against the establishment of a Reich Colonial Office, not least because the man expected to be put in charge of it was the head of the Colonial Department of the Foreign Office, Ernst Prince zu Hohenlohe-Langenburg, who was regarded as a Protestant zealot.[47]

Bülow saw which way the wind was blowing and told the Kaiser at the beginning of December 1906 that he might ask for permission to dissolve the Reichstag, but that this plan must be kept strictly secret.[48] Wilhelm replied: 'Agreed. You have My full consent and My authorisation even for the most serious measure.'[49] Bülow confided his intention to a select few only, namely the Chief of the Reich Chancellery, Friedrich Wilhelm von Loebell, the secretary of state designate of the Reich Colonial Office, Bernhard Dernburg, and his press officer Otto Hammann. Loebell and Dernburg advised him, in dissolving parliament and holding new elections, to beat the patriotic drum.[50] It was only on 11 December that Bülow told his colleagues in the Ministry of State what he was planning.[51]

On 13 December 1906 the Centre, the Social Democrats, the Poles and the Guelphs, who together made up a majority, rejected on its second reading the Reich government's supplementary budget for the colonial war in German South-West Africa.[52] Erzberger had committed his faction to a counter-motion to reduce the German forces in South-West Africa from 8,000 to 2,500. Such interference in the imperial power of command was bound to fill Wilhelm II with rage. After the vote Bülow read out the Kaiser's order dissolving the Reichstag. He had made no attempt beforehand to come to an agreement with the Centre over a third reading of the Bill. The future party-political constellation had already become apparent during the vote: the Left Liberals joined the National Liberals and Conservatives in voting for the government's Bill.

The Kaiser was in high delight. On 12 December 1906 he crowed in a telegram to Prince Max Egon zu Fürstenberg: 'Here the Centre has at last shown itself up in all its disgraceful malice and unscrupulousness and has brought down a terrific storm on its own head.'[53] He sent a wireless message on 13 December to the Commander of the Fleet telling him that the Reichstag had been dissolved, 'because it has turned down all the credits and troops for South-West Africa'. There was 'great rejoicing' among naval officers that there had been 'more action at long last, and a powerful blow aimed at the Centre by the Government'.[54] After the dissolution Berckheim reported to Karlsruhe: 'H.M. the Kaiser is said ... to have expressed himself very satisfied with the turn of events; people are also pointing out that it has made the Chancellor's position secure again at the All-Highest level.'[55] Princess Marie Radziwill recorded on 15–16 December that Wilhelm had dined with the Italian ambassador Carlo Conte Lanza and had said – 'loudly enough for everyone to hear': 'It was high time that the gentlemen of the Centre had a good thrashing. They were getting more and more insolent, indeed they were so presumptuous they wanted to rule me.'[56] Baroness Spitzemberg noted that the Kaiser was 'in the sunniest of moods, elated by the deed which has brought him a great deal of approval, but of which he barely understands the consequences'.[57]

At the Reichstag elections of 1903 the Reich government had held back. Now it intervened vigorously in the campaign. It stirred up nationalist and imperialist feelings and directed them against the Social Democrats and the Catholic Centre as well as against the Poles and Guelphs. It deliberately excluded economic and social problems and concentrated on colonial and military policy.[58] Bülow's speech in the Reichstag on 13 December 1906 already hinted at the direction this campaign was to take: 'The Government cannot give way to the wishes and interests of individual parties when its highest responsibility, that of the nation, is in question ... We shall do our duty – trusting in the German people.'[59] In his New Year letter, published on 3 January 1907, addressed to Lieutenant-General Eduard von Liebert, the chairman of the Reich Association against Social Democracy, Bülow accused the Centre of having put pressure on the government 'in a matter which affected German military honour and our standing in the world'. The Centre's vote on 13 December had been 'an attack on the Federal Governments and our national dignity'. Bülow set out as his election slogan: 'The fight for the honour and the good of the nation against Social Democrats, Poles, Guelphs and Centre.'[60] The Pan-German League and the Navy League distributed huge quantities of pamphlets and brochures calling for support for the Conservative and Liberal parties which were 'loyal to the Reich'.[61]

This 'national' agitation against the Centre and the Social Democrats aroused an astonishing degree of enthusiasm in anti-clerical circles among the aristocracy and bourgeoisie, and there were those at the imperial court in whom it produced a state of near ecstasy.[62] The Flügeladjutant Max Freiherr von Holzing-Berstett, who was from Baden, wept 'with emotion and enthusiasm' when he read about the decisive Reichstag session in the newspaper.[63] He wrote to his mother in a frenzy of anti-Catholicism: 'How can one complain at a time when the battle against Rome is under way! Isn't it glorious! At last, at last one can see a possible end to this cursed, guilt- and blood-ridden church. Onward and upward! ... There is a Germany without Rome, without any of this black, un-Germanic pestilence.'[64] Even in the 'national' camp, however, there was considerable scepticism as to whether Wilhelm II and Bülow were really determined to see the battle against the Catholic and socialist 'enemies of the Reich' through to the end. The war-mongering General Friedrich von Bernhardi, while all in favour of stirring up a *coup d'état*, attempted to bring his friend Holzing-Berstett back down to earth, writing to him: 'With all my heart I share your sincere hatred for the priests and Ultramontanes. But I am too old to have such an enthusiastic vision of the future. The whole movement has been unplanned. It is true that there has long been a desire to throw off the oppressive influence of the Centre. But no one had the courage to do so. At least the present action has come from H.M. Dernburg set the ball rolling. But our Government is very far from undertaking a battle against Rome.'[65] Wilhelm II's eldest sister Charlotte, Hereditary Princess of Saxe-Meiningen, also took a pessimistic view of the situation and doubted that new elections would bring any lasting improvement. 'The dissolution of the Reichstag was necessary', she wrote to her doctor, 'but the next one could be *worse still*!! What then! We are *not* prepared for the onslaught, and Bülow least of all!! The future looks very *very* dark to me.'[66] Too late, Bülow realised the danger that he had incurred with his electoral campaign against the Centre. When the subject of a possible pact between the Centre and the Social Democrats came up at a dinner he was attending on 27 January 1907, the Kaiser's birthday, he exclaimed that such an eventuality would be 'the greatest conceivable disgrace, bordering on a national disaster'.[67]

The general election took place on 25 January 1907, followed on 5 February by the run-off ballot. As a result of the propaganda campaigns of the Reich government and the 'national' associations, the turnout rose from 75.8% in the 1903 elections to a massive 84.3%. The increase benefited the bourgeois parties almost exclusively. The Social Democrats lost half of their seats, while the Centre party was able to maintain its position.[68] Thanks to the support of two splinter groups, the German Reform party and the Wirtschaftliche Vereinigung (Business party), the Conservative–Liberal 'Bülow bloc' now had an absolute majority in the Reichstag. On the night of 25–6 January and again after the final ballot a few thousand citizens who supported the 'national' cause gathered at the Reich Chancellor's palace and at the Schloss to celebrate the election victory. Even the usually critical Baroness Spitzemberg was surprised by the outcome and thought the 'ovations in the middle of the night outside the Crown Prince's and Bülow's palaces' were 'very strange symptoms'.[69] The Chancellor addressed the excited crowd with the words: 'My great predecessor [Bismarck], whom we all revere, said almost 40 years ago: "Let us put the German people in the saddle; they will know how to ride." I hope and believe that the German people have shown today that they can still ride. And if everyone does his duty at the final ballot the whole world will recognise that the German people are firmly in the saddle and will ride down everything that stands in the way of their welfare and of their greatness.'[70] The Kaiser was no less jubilant at the election results. 'It is clear that God has spoken to the hearts and consciences of our people, and happy has been the result; may He continue to be gracious to them and to all of us and lead us according to His holy will', he wrote to his Uncle Friedrich of Baden on 30 January 1907.[71] After the final ballot Wilhelm – to the dismay of his sister[72] – made an impassioned speech to the masses from the balcony of the Schloss, proclaiming that the German people could defeat all the Powers ranged against them 'if all classes and confessions stood firmly and solidly together'.[73] From the imperial headquarters came unanimous reports of Wilhelm's state of high delight after the Reichstag elections.[74] Although the rumours of a change of Chancellor did not die down entirely, Bülow's position was certainly considered to be safe, at least for the time being.[75] 'Bülow is triumphant now and we are holding on to him, *more firmly* than ever', Wilhelm's sister Charlotte wrote in February 1907.[76]

KAISER AND CHANCELLOR AFTER THE 'NATIONAL' ELECTION VICTORY

After the dissolution of the Reichstag and the open breach with the Centre party Bülow's political fate was indissolubly linked to the 'Bülow bloc', but for the time being he could rely on the support of the Kaiser, who made no secret of his satisfaction with the results of the bloc policy.[77] In a telegram to Bülow on 11 May 1907 he praised the Reichstag in terms never before heard from him. 'I have learned with great satisfaction from Your Excellency's report of the 7th how assiduously the Reichstag has worked in the session which has just closed and what a significant number of important bills and contracts it has dealt with. For this very pleasing result, the credit for which is due first of all to the skilful and tireless efforts of yourself and your colleagues, as well as to the patriotic attitude of the Reichstag, I wish to express once more to Your

Excellency, from my heart, My Imperial appreciation and My sincere gratitude.'[78] On 26 June 1907 Berckheim reported to Karlsruhe 'that the Reich Chancellor Prince Bülow, who is more certain of H.M. the Kaiser's confidence than he has been for a long time, is resolved to stand or fall with the newly inaugurated bloc policy; for him the bridges to the Centre have been conclusively destroyed'.[79]

The Reich Chancellor was able to use this propitious moment to persuade the Kaiser to make some of the ministerial changes he wished for. At the end of June 1907, at Bülow's suggestion, Wilhelm dismissed both the Secretary of State at the Reich Office of the Interior, Count Arthur von Posadowsky-Wehner, who was close to the Centre party and who had warned against the dissolution of the Reichstag, and also the decidedly conservative Prussian Minister of Ecclesiastical Affairs, Konrad von Studt. Bülow justified Studt's dismissal to the Ministry of State on the grounds that this minister no longer fitted in with the bloc policy.[80] An embittered Posadowsky left the office he had led for ten years. His dismissal was totally unexpected. The Minister of War, General Karl von Einem, confided to Berckheim that Bülow had probably seen Posadowsky as a rival. The secretary of state, a man of great merit, had been sent on his way 'in a shockingly inconsiderate manner', Einem said. 'He had not had the slightest idea until Herr von Lucanus called on him, and he was given no longer than an hour to compose his letter of resignation, which was published no more than four hours later; quite justifiably he was deeply, severely hurt on leaving office.' Nor had Studt gone willingly; he had asked to be allowed to stay in office for at least a few more months, but in vain. Posadowky's successor as Secretary of State at the Reich Office of the Interior was the former Prussian Minister of the Interior, Theobald von Bethmann Hollweg, who was simultaneously appointed Vice President of the Prussian Ministry of State. As is well known, two years later Bethmann rose − in circumstances which will be examined in Chapter 27 − to become Reich Chancellor and Prussian Minister-President.

Although Bülow had seized the initiative in the reshuffle of the Reich leadership and the Prussian government, it was obvious that the Kaiser was wholly in favour of the changes and that his personal feelings were also involved. The Minister of War confirmed Berckheim's impression that the ministerial reorganisation had been influenced by the fact that 'as is well known, the Kaiser has never really liked Count Posadowsky'. Berckheim rightly saw the changes as a sign that Bülow had regained the Kaiser's confidence. The Chancellor had used this opportunity 'extremely skilfully' to remove a possibly dangerous rival to himself, in portraying Count Posa-dowsky to the Kaiser as 'unreliable and pro-Centre'.[81]

During this harmonious phase Bülow even succeeded in exerting a moderating influence on Wilhelm II's public appearances. On 8 August 1907 he sent Rudolf von Valentini a 'very confidential' letter beseeching him to make sure that 'the speeches which His Majesty makes at the manoeuvres in Münster, particularly this year in view of the new Reichstag and the demands of the national bloc policy, are of an especially carefully considered, statesmanlike and calm nature, so that they do not in any way, either through unnecessary harshness or through possible distortion of their meaning, give the opposition any cause for disgraceful criticism'.[82] This was exactly the tenor of the speech which the Kaiser made on 31 August at a banquet for the province of Westphalia. He addressed himself to the people of both town and country as well as industrial labourers, calling on them to work together 'united by the same loyalty and love for the Fatherland'. He had expressly included the labourers, saying: 'I am thinking also of the workers whose strong hands perform their tasks in the mighty industrial enterprises, at the blast furnaces and underground in the tunnels. Care for them, for their well-being, has been My precious inheritance from My Grandfather who rests in God, and it is My wish and My will that in the sphere of social welfare we hold fast to the principles that are laid down in the unforgettable message of Kaiser Wilhelm The Great.'[83]

At the end of September 1907 Bülow was able to paint the successes of his bloc policy in glowing colours for the Kaiser. 'The bloc has already had the good effect of making the Centre more modest and reminding it of its national duties. This was evident not only in Spahn's speech on the navy but also in the peaceful outcome of the Catholic congress at Würzburg. With the Left Liberals I have been particularly concerned to insist that they must support the naval and military budgets, which Payer has promised me they will. He is a Swabian, the leader of the South German People's party. Anyone who prophesied 40, 20 or even 10 years ago that a Württemberg people's party man would vote for army and navy budgets would have risked being confined in a Maison de santé as insane.'[84]

Needless to say, as soon as enthusiasm among the Conservatives and Liberals over the election victory had died down, it became more and more obvious that carrying out government policy under the conditions of the 'Bülow bloc' would become difficult.[85] True, both Conservatives and Liberals supported *Weltpolitik* and the military policy of the Reich government. They were also united by their opposition to the Centre (although the Conservatives' hostility towards the Centre was not as fundamental as that of the anti-clerical Liberals towards 'Ultramontanism'). But where decisive issues of economic and domestic policy were concerned there were major differences between the

Conservatives and the Liberals, especially the Left Liberals. Bülow could not
risk seriously annoying the Conservatives because they could at any time
revert to their alliance with the Centre and thus deprive him of his majority
in the Reichstag. And the leaders of the Centre party, who had not forgotten
their anger over Bülow's attitude during the election campaign, were ready
with daggers drawn. As early as in November 1907 the Austrian embassy
reported to Vienna that as difficulties were beginning to emerge over financial
policy, Bülow might forestall a split in his 'bloc' by resigning.[86] On 22 January
1908 Szögyény referred with some surprise to Bülow's declaration that he
would remain in office only if he could be quite sure of his majority in the
Reichstag. That was a 'concession to parliamentary practices' and Wilhelm II
had repeatedly expressed himself 'very forcefully' against such a development.[87] The long-serving ambassador of the allied Danube Monarchy knew
very well that it was not parliament but 'the uninterrupted confidence of his
imperial Master' which was 'the Reich Chancellor's mainstay, as always'.[88]

AT THE ZENITH OF PERSONAL MONARCHY

Meanwhile little had changed in the crucial relationship between Wilhelm
and Bülow. Even after the formation of the Bülow bloc it was the Kaiser, not
the Chancellor, who determined the guidelines of German policy. Bülow
limited himself to using the methods of the courtier to prevent the worst
excesses of the monarch and to keep up appearances as well as possible. Sir
Frank Lascelles, the British ambassador, expressed his astonishment in the
spring of 1907 that Bülow 'no longer does anything but prepare his speeches;
he has long since ceased to guide and influence policy'.[89] Marschall von
Bieberstein commented, during a visit to Berlin, that 'Bülow was not following
any definite course ... People could say what they liked against him, but to
get through ten years with H.M. was an achievement of which he himself
would never have thought himself capable; people did not see the mistakes he
had been able to prevent in his position, but only the kind of things that had
been permitted and got away with.'[90] Maximilian Harden continued to fume
with anger and accused Bülow of merely covering up the dark side of Personal
Rule by being so malleable. 'It is impossible to conduct a serious and effective
policy with this Kaiser', he complained in September 1907. 'The Chancellor
sees to it that this does not penetrate to the general consciousness, and that
each morning everything is freshly varnished.'[91]

Holstein was more concerned than ever at the effect of this system, above all
on Germany's international position. 'The Kaiser says and does what He
wants, and Bülow is dragged along behind', he lamented.[92] The Chancellor

had been well and truly 'pushed out' even from what was really his own domain, foreign policy. 'That is now decided by the Kaiser alone.'[93] 'The way in which we are governed makes me shudder: Bülow, who after all still takes the most personal responsibility, is in fact completely excluded from foreign affairs, although as Chancellor he alone is accountable for it. Tschirschky is quite incompetent; he has no opinions of his own but merely looks to the Kaiser and follows every signal.'[94] Baroness Spitzemberg made almost the same observation on 21 April 1907. 'Bülow is just pushed aside completely, seemingly by Tschirschky but in reality by H.M., who finds the latter highly congenial for exactly this reason.'[95]

While he thus governed in person, the Kaiser continued to receive strong support in both domestic and foreign policy matters from his court officials, the three Cabinet chiefs and the military officers in his household, as well as from a clutch of favourites. Even as an old and sick man Hermann von Lucanus, the Chief of the Civil Cabinet, played a prominent political role. Thus as Zedlitz told his father, the former Minister for Ecclesiastical Affairs, in the autumn of 1907, 'As regards ... "age" and "combining many tasks", Lucanus is certainly a living example of how much one can do in that respect. Since last spring he has really grown so old that one worries even when he walks from one room to the next, and mentally it is also very noticeable, unfortunately. In spite of this he actually directs a large – and not the most unimportant – part of the work of all the Ministers. I know that his power is also subject to the limits which naturally apply with a [Secret] Cabinet government, but in a trial of strength between him and a Minister or an Oberpräsident, even today I would advise anyone to have no qualms about backing the insignificant-looking old gentleman.'[96] Nor should one underestimate the influence of the Oberhofmarschall and Senior Master of Ceremonies, Count August zu Eulenburg, who in addition took over the office of Minister of the Royal Household in October 1907. The amalgamation of these different functions at court was, as August Eulenburg himself confessed, 'rather a lot for an ordinary mortal! ... But the Kaiser hopes this accumulation of offices will simplify and ease the burden of the work, which indeed can be achieved through regular, and if possible daily, contact with the All-Highest Lord ... But it depends on the likes of us keeping our health and strength so as to cope with the great mass of work.'[97] It also depended above all, as Zedlitz rightly observed, on being 'persona grata' with the Kaiser, which is precisely what many of the most senior statesmen of the Reich and Prussia were not.[98]

The dominant power of the monarch over the Reich government was exemplified in the great reshuffle which Bülow was compelled to make in the autumn of 1907 on the orders of Wilhelm II. The Kaiser's aim was to engineer the resignation of Prince Hermann zu Hohenlohe-Langenburg as Statthalter of Alsace-Lorraine and to appoint the Hanoverian Carl Count von Wedel, the ambassador in Vienna, in his place, contrary to the wishes of the Chancellor. The new ambassador in Vienna was to be the incumbent Secretary of State at the Foreign Office, Heinrich von Tschirschky. The Chancellor had no alternative but to put a brave face on it. In a letter to the Kaiser he dwelt hypocritically on the advantages which made Tschirschky particularly suitable for Vienna – he knew 'Cisleithania and Transleithania, both the capital and the provinces, and he is also an expert on business and trade affairs. His wife, half Viennese and half Hungarian, will be useful to him there.'[99] Bülow was not even able to make his own choice of Foreign Secretary, the man who would be at his right hand in the conduct of foreign policy. He wanted to appoint either the Under Secretary of State, Otto von Mühlberg, or (as his second choice) Alfred von Kiderlen-Wächter, the envoy in Bucharest, to succeed Tschirschky, yet he did not dare propose his two candidates to the Kaiser, who had made clear his preference for the ambassador at St Petersburg, Wilhelm von Schoen. Instead Wilhelm asked the Chancellor to bring him a list of the diplomats who could be considered for the important post of Foreign Secretary – and chose Schoen.[100]

Then, promptly on 1 October 1907, Prince Hermann zu Hohenlohe-Langenburg received the letter of farewell drafted by Lucanus and copied out in his own hand by the Kaiser at Rominten.[101] In very warm but firm words, the Kaiser put it to his uncle that he should resign. Since the publication of his cousin Chlodwig's memoirs the previous year Hermann Hohenlohe had been in almost daily expectation of his dismissal; nevertheless he reacted bitterly to the 'All-Highest autograph letter'.[102] He confided to his son Ernst that 'the great Lord has given me a very heavily sugared pill to tell me that I may take myself off. Concern for my health is hardly likely to have played a part in it . . . Although I feel that I am no longer equal to my task in the long run, it still pains me to leave a post which was so interesting . . . I only hope that the Kaiser will allow me to stay on for the autumn and will not have my retirement announced at once.'[103]

On 3 October 1907 the Statthalter sent the Kaiser a reply in which he handed in his resignation on grounds of health as demanded. He had in any case had the 'definite intention' of asking to be allowed to retire in the near future. To avoid the impression that he had been 'dismissed by Your Majesty in disgrace', however, which 'would of course affect me most painfully after many years of service', the old Prince asked to be allowed to stay in office at least until Christmas.[104] His son commented gullibly that 'if H.M. has a trace of the affection that he shows in his letter, he cannot refuse to fulfil your

request'.[105] Neither father nor son reckoned with the poisonous scheming
which had characterised the high politics of the Kaiserreich for decades.

Even before his letter reached the Kaiser Hohenlohe received a telegram
from the Reich Chancellor which was to make the Statthalter's resignation a
fait accompli. In it Bülow warned against 'indiscretions and distortions in the
Press over the matter which has given rise to the correspondence between
Your Excellency and His Majesty' and asked Hohenlohe's permission to
publish the correspondence at once.[106] Prince Hohenlohe replied immediately that he could not allow the publication, 'if only in His Majesty's
interest'.[107] In a state of agitation, he telegraphed to the Kaiser too. 'As no
All-Highest decision has yet reached me on the letter which I wrote with my
most humble duty, nor do I know what it is proposed to publish, and as the
Press cannot possibly have gained knowledge of Your Majesty's All-Highest
autograph letter to me nor of my reply ... I was unable to give my
permission.'[108] In a draft letter to Bülow that was never sent, Hohenlohe
stressed that 'such an unexpectedly rapid publication, the contents of which
I do not even know, naturally distressed me deeply and caused me to express
my objections to Your Excellency. I could not suppose that H.M. had agreed to
an action so hurtful to me.'[109]

An imperial telegram the next day put him right. 'It is in the interests of all
sides and above all corresponds to my fundamental view of such matters, that
the changes of personnel which are decided by me do not reach the Press
through indiscretions but are made public through an official announcement.
I have therefore ordered that the fact of the forthcoming change shall be
officially announced tomorrow Monday evening in Berlin. Until this has
happened I demand and expect absolute secrecy from all sides. My letter to
you and your reply will of course not be published, but only the fact of the
change. Also it is of course not necessary for you to leave Strasbourg immediately; you may arrange your departure at your leisure. Wilhelm I.R.'[110] Prince
Hohenlohe was recalled from his post as Statthalter in the Reichsland of
Alsace-Lorraine on 1 November 1907 and replaced, as Wilhelm had planned,
by General Count Carl von Wedel.[111]

These events caused astonishment in all circles.[112] To Holstein, Bülow
claimed that he had himself brought about Wedel's appointment to Strasbourg
and Tschirschky's to Vienna, for in both cases the Kaiser had been 'rather
indifferent'. It had been 'really painful' for him, however, not to be able to
appoint either Mühlberg or Kiderlen as Foreign Secretary. 'You know how
much I value Mühlberg. And Kiderlen is indisputably the best political head
in our diplomatic service.' But in this case the monarch had insisted on having
an active ambassador as Foreign Secretary. The Reich Chancellor admitted

sheepishly that he did not know Schoen at all well; but he hoped to be able to manage with him.[113] Holstein recognised Bülow's assurances as expedient lies and berated him. 'Once again you have subordinated your sound common sense to the decisions – or let us say the whims – of the Kaiser.' After all, Tschirschky was nothing but a 'schemer from Saxony' who, with his Austrian wife 'out of the third or fourth drawer', was completely unsuitable for Vienna and would certainly be socially snubbed there. The Catholic Hanoverian Wedel, who had fought against Prussia in 1866, was equally unsuitable for the Strasbourg post. 'The trouble is, to be sure, that these matters are not decided according to your ideas, but according to the by no means infallible political instinct of the Kaiser. In this basic pattern of our national life nowadays, which is becoming more and more evident, there is a national danger, not only from abroad but perhaps even more *at home*, because slowly but surely people will lose confidence in this manner of ruling. What that means in dealing with the destructive forces that are at work, no one needs to tell you.' Echoing Harden's accusation, Holstein warned the Chancellor that with his system of 'simply letting things take their course' he was becoming the 'cover' for 'things for which you can hardly answer, or for which you should not answer'. The Kaiser had 'gradually become accustomed to Sultanesque methods of rulership', and these cases were 'after all only two isolated needles in a large coral reef'.[114]

The abject role which Wilhelm II expected his Reich Chancellor to accept was widely regarded as degrading. In November 1907 Zedlitz recorded in his diary an incident which gave 'well-informed courtiers' cause to fear 'a Chancellor crisis'. The Kaiser had been so infuriated by an article in the *Kölnische Volkszeitung* that he demanded that the Chancellor initiate proceedings for lèse-majesté against the pro-Centre party paper. 'It was extremely awkward for Bülow – he tried to get out of it – but for all his great skill he did not succeed.' He gave in and began proceedings. On 22 November, however, the *Volkszeitung* published a telegram from the public prosecutor announcing that the proceedings for lèse-majesté had after all been suspended. For Zedlitz this vacillation was symptomatic of the way in which the country was being governed under Bülow's Chancellorship. 'There is such a torrent of sudden impulses and ideas [from the Kaiser], to which the Chancellor is unable to put up any resistance, and then after formally obeying orders he tries to get out of it in some way or other. But even his skill is not always sufficient to prevent damage arising out of it.'[115] Baroness Spitzemberg felt 'faint' at the idea that in the event of war the Kaiser, 'whether at military headquarters or here [in Berlin], could interfere in everything, muddle everything, paralyse everything', and what she heard about 'the most incredible errors of leadership' made by Wilhelm at the manoeuvres, and about the marginal notes he scribbled on diplomatic documents, did nothing to calm her fears.[116]

A few months after the 'national' election victory of the Bülow bloc in January–February 1907 Bülow's position seemed in danger again. The monarch frequently reproached the Reich Chancellor for his lack of energy and skill, which Zedlitz interpreted as a sign that 'the chances of Prince Bülow remaining in office for much longer do not look good'.[117] The always well-informed Count Szögyény was able to report in January 1908 that 'in parliamentary circles the rumours of Prince Bülow's imminent fall have not died down, and there are very persistent reports in circulation that Kaiser Wilhelm is already preoccupied, albeit unwillingly, with the idea of finding a successor for him'.[118] Holstein was convinced that the Kaiser would appoint Marschall von Bieberstein as Chancellor. On 21 January 1908 he wrote to his cousin, Ida von Stülpnagel: 'Marschall's candidature for the Chancellorship has many supporters, except among the Conservatives. Marschall would be at least as docile towards the Kaiser as Bülow and less skilful in deflecting him.'[119]

Bülow may have planned, as he claimed in his *Denkwürdigkeiten*, 'to take the next available opportunity, in the interest of the country, to take energetic corrective steps against the imperial infringements which were endangering and damaging the well-being of the Reich, as was my duty',[120] but he only rarely succeeded in deterring Wilhelm from his autocratic interventions. Even in the explosive field of international policy the Kaiser continued to make mischief without hindrance. In March 1908, in a letter to the American President he refused to accept the appointment of the career diplomat David J. Hill as ambassador in Berlin, apparently because he did not consider him sufficiently wealthy. The news that the Kaiser had written 'yet another of his ill-omened private letters, this time to Roosevelt', provoked a fresh storm of indignation in the German press.[121] Spitzemberg regarded this new affair as 'the worst and most embarrassing example of tactlessness' committed by Wilhelm II and bewailed the fact that 'no bad experiences are of the least help with the Kaiser, and Bülow simply accepts all infringements and interferences'.[122] It was only with difficulty that the officials of the Wilhelmstrasse succeeded in averting a trial of strength with the United States. Hill's appointment was eventually approved and he represented his powerful country in Berlin until 1911.

For the dismissed Privy Councillor von Holstein it was the last straw. Writing to Bülow in May 1908, on the eve of the greatest constitutional crisis of the Kaiserreich, he discussed for the first time the possibility of Wilhelm II's abdication. 'As long as His Majesty intends to remain Kaiser, he must subordinate any personal impulses to national necessity', he insisted.

'H.M. simply behaves incautiously ... In his – that is, in the monarchical – interest, as well as in your own, for your position in history, you must compel him to stick more closely than he has done heretofore to the paths which we regard as normal and sensible.' The Reich Chancellor should not allow himself to be intimidated by Wilhelm's 'hysterical threats' to abdicate, for even if he carried them out, 'that would not be the worst thing that could happen. Under the *given* circumstances, your *first* duty is to *lead* the Kaiser, and it is only your secondary task to protect him *if* he allows himself to be led.'[123]

IRRESPONSIBLE ADVISERS: ADOLF VON HARNACK AND HOUSTON STEWART CHAMBERLAIN

In the fertile soil of Wilhelm II's autocratic rule the poisonous plant of favouritism, as Bülow was to describe it in the Reichstag, was able to continue to flourish under his Chancellorship. Not only the notorious 'camarilla' around Philipp Eulenburg, whose activities will be investigated in Chapter 21, but also respected men from the industrial or academic worlds, by virtue of their close contact with the monarch, acquired an influence which Bülow could not control. In the early Bülow years the Silesian magnate Prince Guido Henckel von Donnersmarck and the Kaiser's former tutor Hinzpeter exerted just such an influence, above all on domestic and personnel policy.[124] In the formulation of German policy in the western hemisphere, in the Russo-Japanese War and then in the critical pre-war negotiations with Britain the Hamburg shipping Director Albert Ballin played an immensely important role.[125] The anti-Russian influence on the Kaiser of the Baltic journalist and professor of East European history, Theodor Schiemann, had made itself felt since the spring of 1905, when he had travelled with the Kaiser on his Mediterranean voyage. During the Scandinavian cruise of 1906 the Reich Chancellor felt compelled to remind Schiemann of his duty to 'weigh his words carefully', for he bore 'a heavy responsibility'.[126]

In October 1901, at Eulenburg's Schloss Liebenberg north of Berlin, the Kaiser met two men who, although very different from each other, were to have a lasting influence on his ideas and thus also on German policy: Adolf von Harnack[127] and Houston Stewart Chamberlain.[128] Harnack, Bülow commented mockingly years later, had surpassed even Schiemann in the art of flattering the monarch.[129] This 'court theologian' had belonged to the numerous 'lickspittles, sycophants and grovellers' around Wilhelm II, who had been 'constantly ready' to 'change their shirts and even their skin, if necessary'.[130] Harnack had been the 'darling and the adoring admirer of His Majesty'.[131] In his *Denkwürdigkeiten* Bülow condemned Harnack's addresses on ceremonial occasions as 'outdoing in their obsequiousness anything civil servants or officers have ever achieved in our country'.[132] Many contemporaries like Waldersee assumed, however, that Bülow fostered Wilhelm II's relationship with Harnack with the aim of 'occupying the Kaiser with questions that captivate him and distract him from others'; Harnack was also 'exactly the kind of person to make an impression on the Kaiser'.[133]

In 1903 Wilhelm's friendship with Harnack was put to the test by a theological conflict. A year earlier the Assyriologist Friedrich Delitzsch had given a lecture in the Berlin Schloss entitled 'Babel and Bible', in which he postulated the superiority of the Babylonian religion over the 'Israelite' religion and thereby sparked a heated debate on the importance of the Old Testament in Christian belief. In a second lecture, given − likewise in the presence of the Kaiser − on 12 January 1903 Delitzsch went further, claiming that the Hebrew Bible was so infected with Babylonian culture that it had lost its validity as a basis for Christian belief; most of the text of the Old Testament should be removed from the Bible.[134] In the Babel–Bible dispute, which had serious consequences, not least for relations between Christians and Jews,[135] Wilhelm II felt compelled to intervene in a highly personal way, writing in his own hand on 15 February 1903 a letter which caused a sensation, although he had given it to the Chancellor to edit before it was published. He reproached Delitzsch with having deserted 'the viewpoint of the rigorous historian and Assyriologist' and strayed into 'theological-religious conclusions and hypotheses which were very nebulous or risky. But when he incautiously came to the New Testament it soon became clear that he was developing such extremely aberrant views regarding the person of our Saviour that not only could I not follow him in them, but I was confronted by a point of view diametrically opposed to My own. He does not recognise the divinity of Christ, and therefore concludes with regard to the Old Testament that it does not contain any revelation about Him as the Messiah ... He has approached the question of revelation in a very polemical way and has more or less rejected it ... That was a serious mistake.' Wilhelm's own opposing belief found characteristic expression: 'It is beyond even the slightest doubt that God constantly and for evermore reveals himself in His human race which He has created. He "breathed his breath" into man, i.e. gave him a piece of himself, a soul. With fatherly love and interest he follows the development of the human race; to lead it onwards and to further it he "reveals" himself in one or another great wise man, or priest or king, whether among heathens, Jews or Christians. Hammurabi was one, Moses, Abraham, Homer, Charlemagne, Luther, Shakespear [sic], Göthe [sic], Kaiser Wilhelm the Great. He chose them and deemed them worthy of His grace, to do glorious, immortal deeds for their peoples both in the intellectual and in the physical sphere, according to his will. How often did not my Grandfather expressly emphasise this, that he was only an instrument in the hands of the Lord. The works of the Great Spirits are the gift of God to the nations, so that they can continue to learn from them and feel their way onwards through the confusion of what is still unfathomable here below.'[136] This expression of Wilhelm's beliefs threw light not only on his staggering conception of his own historical mission, but also on the conviction widely held in Protestant circles that divine revelation was manifesting itself in the gradual ascent of Prussia-Germany to greatness.[137]

The strictly Protestant Waldersee greeted the Kaiser's profession of faith as a 'most welcome event'. The Kaiser's letter would be 'a great relief to many devout Christians who had begun to be seriously concerned about his association with Harnack', Waldersee predicted. 'It will of course give little pleasure to Messrs Harnack, Delitzsch and Co. I wish that it had not mentioned the names of the great wise men, priests or kings to whom God has revealed himself, for this is too provocative and there will be resistance. The Catholics will certainly feel offended.'[138] Harnack did indeed respond, expressing his more liberal opinion in an article in the *Preussische Jahrbücher*, which he sent to the Kaiser.[139] Wilhelm answered at once: 'What you sent me interested me very much ... The aberrant views which you mention in it have also been on my mind ... As regards the person of our Saviour, my point of view is the same, even after reading your remarks. Christ is the Son of God − God in human form − the Saviour of the world. Christmas tells us how he came into the world ... With the divinity of Christ the Scriptures as a whole stand or fall ... in short our entire religion. For these Scriptures, this world of the Bible is a collection of documents about God's work of revelation. Written by human hands, they are naturally subject to mistakes. But that does not change the revelations they contain.'[140] Harnack replied the same day. 'Most high, most mighty Kaiser and King! All-Gracious Kaiser, King and Lord! Yr Imperial and Royal Majesty's All-Gracious and benevolent letter has moved me to the depths of my soul and earned my everlasting gratitude. Yr Majesty's belief in our Lord and Saviour Jesus Christ is also my belief, and I would not remain a theologian any longer if I lost this belief. But theology, as an academic discipline, can reach at best only the boundaries of the most profound and most sacred ... This is the sense in which I understand Yr Majesty's warm and lucid explanation and I accept it joyfully.'[141]

Precisely because he had the wit to leave aside most questions of religious study from then onwards, Harnack rose to become the monarch's most important adviser on matters of educational policy. Together they discussed and came to decisions in the next few years on the Academy of Sciences, the expansion of the University of Berlin, the Prussian Historical Institute in Rome, the rebuilding of the Royal Library, reform of the library system, German–American professorial exchanges, the admission of women to university education, reform of the girls' school system and the foundation of the Kaiser Wilhelm Society, the forerunner of today's Max Planck Gesellschaft.[142] Harnack's appointment as President of the Kaiser Wilhelm Society, whose creation Wilhelm had announced in a speech at the centenary celebrations of the University of Berlin on 11 October 1910, surprised no one. The pre-eminent position he held in academic organisation thanks to Wilhelm II's support was exemplified on 22 March 1914, the birthday of Wilhelm's revered grandfather, Wilhelm I, at the grandiose inauguration of the Royal Library, of which Harnack was also Director General.[143]

In complete contrast to Harnack's desire to keep close to the source of power, Houston Stewart Chamberlain lived a secluded life, at first in Vienna and then, after his marriage to Wagner's daughter Eva, at Haus Wahnfried in Bayreuth. His quiet influence did not make itself felt in ceremonies or new academic institutions but in a growing racist anti-Semitism in the Kaiser. English by birth, German by adoption, he wrote to the monarch at the end of 1909: 'Living close to my brother-in-law Siegfried gives an insight into the quietly industrious, cheerful work of a true German artist'; this was 'a moving experience in the midst of our utterly Jew-ridden artistic life'.[144] A few years earlier Chamberlain's notorious book, *The Foundations of the 19th Century*, which became an early standard work of racist anti-Semitism, had made a deep impression on Wilhelm.[145] He read both this book and Chamberlain's subsequent writings on Kant, Wagner and Goethe aloud to his entourage 'with breathless excitement and enthusiastic agreement'.[146] As early as in 1902 Chamberlain urged the Kaiser in his letters to take drastic measures to deal with the 'race issue'. What was certain, he said, was that either Germany would lead the world, 'or we dissolve altogether in a heartless chaos ... of characterless racelessness'. He demanded a statistical survey of the Jews as one of the 'un-Germanic races of Europe'. Above all racial selection was necessary, for 'If we do not decide ... to think resolutely about this problem and to cultivate race as a matter of principle', he warned the Kaiser, 'it will soon be too late, and our Germanic species will be lost for ever'.[147] Under the influence of Chamberlain, and with the scandals and crises which rocked the Hohenzollern Monarchy in the latter years of Bülow's Chancellorship, the Kaiser's racist and anti-Semitic views took on an increasingly disturbing form.[148]

CHAPTER TWENTY

'Kings are only human, after all.' Scandals at the Hohenzollern court

In May 1907 the Flügeladjutant Max Freiherr von Holzing-Berstett painted a vivid picture of the enthusiasm aroused by Kaiser Wilhelm II when he was staying at Wiesbaden. 'It really is a sight worth seeing when the Kaiser goes out for a ride here. The whole way home from the woods down into the castle is thronged with women and girls of every age who give the Kaiser flowers, stand in front of his horse at the gallop, scarcely letting him through, cheering him frenetically. 4 grooms, the saddle master and each of us with our arms full of flowers, forming a merry cavalcade down the road in lovely sunshine. It brings everything together. The many unemployed people, the glorious spring, the great fascination of the Kaiser for women. There is something extraordinarily sunny, joyful and light-hearted about him.'[1] (See Figure 17.) Not long afterwards Holzing reported happily from Wilhelmshöhe that the Kaiser 'rode at the gallop as never before. At the charge too. Was blissfully happy and youthful.'[2]

Six months later the monarch's good mood still seemed untroubled. On 20 January 1908 his third son, Prince Adalbert of Prussia, a serving naval officer, held a fancy dress party in the Imperial Yacht Club at Kiel. A hundred guests were invited, including many pretty young women, and arrived in an array of ingenious disguises. Albert Hopman, one of the naval officers present, recorded in his diary: 'At 8 o'clock the Kaiser appeared, completely by surprise and quite unrecognised, in a black domino with a mask and surrounded by a few other dominoes. Very amusing scene when Prince Adalbert recognised him. He moved among the guests, unrecognised, for a few more minutes and then after removing his mask appeared in the costume of the Great Elector, which suited him superbly.'[3]

Figure 17 The Golden Age: the Kaiser rides out among his people

Wiesbaden in May 1907, Kiel in January 1908: two scenes from the life of a kaiser and king, but no outsider observing this cheerful activity at the Hohenzollern court could have guessed what scandals these months would see in the imperial family, in Wilhelm II's closest entourage and in the elite Prussian officer corps – scandals that shook the monarchy to the core. It is only against the background of the deep shame engendered by these court scandals that we can understand the universal outrage against Wilhelm which erupted in November 1908 after his 'interview' in the *Daily Telegraph*.

KAISER WILHELM AND SEXUAL MORALITY

On the occasion of his silver wedding on 25 February 1906 the Kaiser confessed to his uncle the Grand Duke of Baden that it seemed to him 'like a dream that 25 years should already have gone by! And I cannot kneel and thank God enough for allowing them to pass so well and so fruitfully, through His wholly undeserved grace, while protecting and preserving the beloved lives of all my dear ones, and above all for safeguarding my wonderful wife, my loyal helper, until now. The best part of the celebrations has been to see how rightly the people have judged the worth and the work of their Kaiserin, in full appreciation of what the Lord has also bestowed on them in her.'[4] Where religion and morality were concerned the Kaiser, and still more the Kaiserin, surrounded by her three bigoted 'Hallelujah Aunts', demanded the highest standards and generated a misplaced and puritanical moral fanaticism at the Hohenzollern court which was often bewailed by more enlightened observers. As Count Zedlitz remarked in 1906, Wilhelm II's letters and speeches showed a particularly penetrating 'religious–mystical' streak; on another occasion the Hofmarschall recorded with concern that the Kaiser was threatening to turn into 'a real fanatic'.[5] He made a habit of preaching from the pulpit.[6] In March 1905 Wilhelm alarmed the world with a speech in Bremen in which he called on the German people to remember that 'the workings of divine Providence' were to be seen in their great historical achievements, and 'if our Lord God were not still planning great things for us in the world, he would not have bestowed such glorious qualities and powers upon our people'.[7] He made a peculiar impression on the naval officers when he personally conducted a service on board the flagship *Deutschland* in November 1906. It seemed to Hopman that the sermon he read out contained 'many of his own ideas', but it was 'full of mysticism and the crassest orthodoxy'. The Kaiser was 'really a very strange person'.[8] In the autumn of 1910, on his donation of a cross to the Benedictine monastery of Beuron, he declaimed to the monks: 'What I expect from you is that you . . . support Me in My efforts to preserve religion in the nation. This is all the more important because the twentieth century has unleashed ideas which can be successfully fought only with the help of religion and with divine support. That is my firm conviction! The Crown which I wear can vouch for victory here only if it is grounded in the Word and the Person of the Lord. As a symbol of this I have donated the cross in this church, so as to demonstrate . . . that the reigns of

Christian Princes can only be conducted in accordance with the will of our Lord and that they should help strengthen the religious sense that is innate in the Teutonic peoples, and increase reverence for altar and throne. Both belong together and must not be separated.'[9]

In a world that was rapidly modernising itself Wilhelm II clung stubbornly to the outdated dynastic principles of his forefathers. Not only he himself but his entire court felt obliged to change their clothes as appropriate several times a day, which was a considerable burden, particularly for the Kaiserin, the princesses and the court ladies, with their elegant toilettes and elaborate hairstyles.[10] As head of the family he often caused pain by intervening with his strict monarchical and Protestant views in the private life of members of the extensive branches of the Hohenzollern family. As we have already seen, he banished his widowed aunt, Anna Landgravine of Hesse, from the family and from court in 1902 when she converted to Catholicism at the age of 65. 'No one from My House' was to have any further contact with the 'renegade', he ordered.[11] In December 1907 Prince Friedrich Wilhelm of Prussia, son of Albrecht, the Prince Regent of Brunswick who had died the previous year, asked the Kaiser's permission to seek the hand of Countess Paula von Lehndorff in marriage. Again, Wilhelm was implacable. 'He can marry her, but as I do not countenance morganatic marriages he must renounce title and property.'[12] The Prince renounced the Countess instead and in 1910 married 'standesgemäß' – in keeping with his social standing – Princess Agathe von Ratibor und Corvey, from the house of Hohenlohe-Schillingsfürst, although not before her father had promised the Kaiser that 'the wedding will be conducted in a wholly Protestant manner and the future descendants will be baptised as Protestants and brought up in Our religion'.[13] Prince Friedrich Wilhelm's brothers were not to be so easily subjugated by the head of the family, as we are about to see.

The antediluvian attitude maintained by Wilhelm and Auguste Viktoria came into its own where the sexual conduct of men and women in court society was concerned and even led them to ban the tango, the fashionable erotic dance from Argentina, at court and regimental balls. Especially after Bülow's 'treason against the Crown' in the *Daily Telegraph* affair of November 1908, opponents at court had no difficulty in exploiting gossip to prejudice the Kaiser against the Chancellor and the Wilhelmstrasse. At Christmas 1908 the monarch told his closest friend Max Fürstenberg indignantly that the head of the press bureau at the Foreign Office, Otto Hammann, was involved in a 'divorce scandal' which should have led to his immediate dismissal, but Bülow had been unwilling or unable to let him go 'under any circumstances'. Hammann had 'seduced the wife of an architect, Bruno Schmitz – an ultra-modern fellow – and then took her away, and now he is going to marry her! Anonymous letter and leaflet campaign about it against Schmitz, proceedings for perjury etc! Holstein, who hates Ham[m]ann like the plague, has also intervened in this feud, Hammann hits him back just as hard via the newspapers, as he detests Holstein as much as other people. In the middle sits Bülow in despair because he *needs them both*, and tries vainly to reconcile them, as he cannot let them go, or they him! A smear campaign by the B[erliner] Z[eitung] a[m] M[ittag] against Kiederlen [sic] about a so-called "housekeeper" adds the finishing touch to this fragrant bouquet, out of which all kinds of unpleasant stuff will come! Doux pays! That is how things look here! That is the disciplined, well-behaved, reliable German officialdom! In whose hands and under whose leadership the German Philistine at last feels safe ... In fact the description would fit Paris or St Petersburg, or Florence in the time of the Medici, better than modern, sober Berlin! *That is why* I do not want to live there, so as to keep away from this unspeakable, unscrupulous camarilla filth, that is what I need; the future is uncertain and demands calm, clarity, determination and real men, not intriguing women and the same in men's clothing!'[14]

Not without reason, if one thinks of the lifestyle of the Crown Prince or Prince August Wilhelm, for instance, the Kaiser justified this moralising severity on the grounds that he needed to protect his six growing sons from temptation.[15] Wilhelm himself, however, was from time to time a victim of the irresistible attraction of the opposite sex. While Ella Sommssich, Anna Homolatsch and eventually — albeit after lengthy and embarrassing negotiations — Emilie Klopp (Miss Love) could be silenced by generous pay-offs, as we saw in the first two volumes of this biography,[16] at the turn of the century Wilhelm was plagued by an old affair which until 1905 threatened to turn into an international scandal. In 1886 Elisabeth Bérard, the divorced Countess von Wedel, had hidden in the Persian legation in Berlin five love letters to her in Prince Wilhelm's own hand, which were rediscovered only in the 1950s in Tehran. Feeling persecuted by court officials, not least because of these missing letters, after her divorce from her second husband, Schlarbaum, she resumed her maiden name and emigrated to Switzerland. In July 1900 she had her sensational memoirs published by the firm of Caesar Schmidt in Zürich under the title, *My Relationship with H.M. Kaiser Wilhelm II*. The book was banned in the German Reich but could be obtained by post in a false wrapper.[17] In June 1901 she moved with her two children to Paris, from where, evidently not in her right mind, she sent a constant stream of letters to the German ambassador Prince Radolin, King Edward VII, the Grand Duke of Baden and numerous other prominent people, some of which were signed with the mysterious initials 'W.W.W.', which were intended to signify her intimate relationship with Wilhelm and Field Marshal Count Waldersee in the late 1880s.[18] In the letters she claimed to possess secrets that would preserve Europe from war, but which she would be prepared to betray to the press if the Kaiser did not receive her. In compensation for the wretched fate which she had supposedly suffered in consequence of her intimacy with Wilhelm II she demanded that her daughter be given a house.[19] On 10 February 1903 she wrote to the commandant of the city of Berlin demanding a meeting with the Kaiser and the Reich Chancellor at a Bonn hotel within forty-eight hours; otherwise a world war and a terrible bloodbath would follow.[20] She repeatedly threatened to publish the Kaiser's letters in facsimile.[21] When in April 1903 a retired Captain named Emil von Hartmann offered to act as intermediary, Waldersee and the imperial Private Secretary, Miessner, had a meeting and decided to put the whole increasingly disturbing affair in the hands of the Reich Chancellor and the Foreign Office. As Wilhelm's 1880s love letters had not yet been secured, in August 1903 Bülow and the Under Secretary of the Auswärtiges Amt, Otto von Mühlberg, could see no alternative but to enter into negotiations with Elisabeth Wedel-Bérard if a scandal was to be avoided.[22] But then the melodrama took an unexpected turn.

In November 1903 the Countess appeared in Basel, presented herself to the German consul Arthur Marschall von Bieberstein and threatened to bring about the downfall of Prussia with a new book unless the Kaiser came to Basel to fetch her. The consul stated expressly in his report that the now no longer very youthful 'beauté' did not give the impression of being mentally ill.[23] A few weeks later he reported that on 28 January 1904 the cantonal police had had to take 'the divorced Countess Wedel-Bérard' to the Friedmatt psychiatric institute. She had been running through the streets shouting that the German Kaiser was being held prisoner in Basel and was in danger of his life. She was examined, and it was concluded that she was suffering from a dangerous degree of paranoia. She was convinced that the Kaiser had married her and that she, not Auguste Viktoria, was the legitimate Kaiserin. As she was penniless, the Director of the institute intended to appeal to the authorities in Oppeln in Silesia, where she was registered under the name of Schlarbaum, with a view to having her taken back to Germany.[24]

Significantly, when they heard that the Countess had been admitted to the psychiatric institute in Basel, the Reich Chancellor and the Foreign Office suggested to the Chief of the Civil Cabinet, Hermann von Lucanus, that her treatment could perhaps be paid for, not from government funds but from the All-Highest Privy Purse, which Lucanus, after some initial hesitation, authorised in June 1904.[25] The normal charge for foreigners staying in Friedmatt was five francs a day, ten if (as was to be feared in this case) a padded cell were necessary. As the patient, imagining herself to be the Kaiserin, insisted on a single room and also demanded first-class care, Bülow advised on 31 July 1904 that the daily allowance paid by His Majesty's Privy Purse to the Basel clinic should be raised to seven francs.[26] But the situation was gradually becoming untenable. At the end of 1904 and again in June 1905 the new Director of the clinic requested the removal of his incurable patient, who was becoming more and more difficult, to a German institution.[27] In the summer of 1905 Under Secretary von Mühlberg and Rudolf von Valentini, representing the Civil Cabinet, agreed that this was indeed the only conceivable solution.[28] On 18 September 1905 Elisabeth Schlarbaum, 'the former Countess Wedel-Bérard', accompanied by two female guards, was brought in a closed railway compartment across the border to Lörrach and handed over to the poorhouse authorities there. The German consul Marschall von Bieberstein, who had dealt with this delicate affair, was unable to discover where the patient had been taken from there. The total costs of the treatment in Friedmatt and the transfer of the Countess to Germany amounted to 789 Swiss francs.[29]

While this sad and ignominious episode was playing itself out in Basel, Kaiser Wilhelm, elated by his sense of power, continued to prove susceptible to the fair sex, especially as the Kaiserin, who suffered from a heart complaint, now seemed far older than her years. Visitors to the Hohenzollern court often expressed their shock at how suddenly the Kaiserin had aged — she had become 'old & white'.[30] During his Mediterranean voyages of 1904, 1905 and 1909 Wilhelm visited the Venetian Countess Annina Morosini. The exact nature of their relationship, however, is unclear from the surviving sources. What is certain is that in the summer of 1905 there were dramatic scenes of jealousy over the ravishingly beautiful Contessa among members of the Kaiser's close entourage.[31] Around this time Wilhelm began an intimate correspondence with Mary Montagu, a young unmarried Englishwoman, daughter of Rear-Admiral the Hon. Victor Montagu, a man of pro-German views.[32] In October 1905 the Kaiser asked Admiral Montagu whether his daughter, whom he had met during his last visit to Cowes, was as beautiful as ever. 'I thought her the handsomest & nicest I ever met!', he wrote effusively.[33] Replying to a letter he subsequently received from Miss Montagu, he wrote on 17 October 1905: 'I well remember the conversation we had, while sitting on deck about death duties . . . The peach you prepared for me was excellent & I ever seem to taste it even now! You complain of my not coming to England & thus losing the opportunity of seeing me? Well my dear Miss Montagu, if you have had time or leisure to follow only a part of the publications in Reviews & Press of the United Kingdom for the last 3–4 years down to the last, you will understand the reasons prohibiting me. Your people must first learn manners again vis à vis to me & my country of which they seem to be sadly in want! It is incomprehensible to me how they can behave in such a manner to the eldest grandson of their Queen who was the last of her relatives she recognised & smiled upon before she died & in whose loving arms she drew her last breath!'[34] The correspondence continued in this vein for many years, until the outbreak of war in 1914, and we shall frequently have occasion to quote from it. Whether the relationship between the German Kaiser and the English admiral's daughter ever became closer, however, we do not know. It is conceivable, nevertheless, that the Kaiser's decision to take a three-week holiday on the south coast of England in the winter of 1907 was influenced by the hope of seeing Mary again, since her family home was close by.[35] All that is certain is that as late as in 1912 the Kaiser's 'dalliance' with this young Englishwoman led to outbursts of jealousy from Auguste Viktoria.[36] (See Figure 18.)

In the summer of 1906 observers were struck by the fact that the Kaiser insisted on setting off punctually for his annual Scandinavian cruise, despite the fact that Crown Princess Cecilie was due to give birth at any moment to his first grandchild and the possible future successor to the throne. This hasty departure even roused the suspicions of the elderly King Oscar II of Sweden that Wilhelm might somehow be intending to lay hands on Norway. King Oscar's relief was therefore all the greater when he found there was reason to believe the German sovereign's anxiety to depart for Norway on schedule was not out of territorial ambition but merely because of an affair of the heart. The King told the British envoy in Stockholm, Sir Rennell Rodd, that 'he thought he had discovered the real motive and it might be of interest to us to know what he believed it to be, as many people insisted on believing that the Emperor wished to establish a counterpoise to British influence there. He said he was practically sure that that attraction to Norway, and in fact to Bergen, was a very usual one and at the same time the most potent in the lives of men, namely a lady.'[37] The name of the lady concerned in the secret tryst at Bergen remains a mystery.

Harmless as such minor infidelities of the Kaiser may have been, historically they are worth mentioning because they seem to be evidence of his heterosexual orientation, which has been repeatedly called into question in view of the terrible scandals that destroyed several men in his closest entourage. Nevertheless Wilhelm's manner with some officers in his suite, on which contemporaries commented repeatedly and not without disgust, leaves a strange impression. Even after the scandalous affairs involving Willi Hohenau, Kuno Moltke and Philipp Eulenburg, which we shall discuss shortly,

Figure 18 Miss Mary Montagu, 'the most charming woman I have ever met'

at every encounter with certain members of his suite the Kaiser continued to pinch and tickle them until they made 'the most extraordinary noises'. His household lived in a state of constant terror that this 'childish' habit might become public knowledge. In December 1908 Zedlitz expressed his consternation at these antics, which were naturally seen and heard by the domestic staff. 'Just imagine what would happen if a spiteful and malicious article appeared about such a thing.'[38]

THE KRUPP SCANDAL OF 1902

Kaiser Wilhelm's sexual ambivalence, long the subject of speculation especially in the wake of the Eulenburg trials,[39] has recently come to the forefront of debate again through the meticulously researched work of Peter Winzen on the many homosexual men to be found among the Kaiser's closest friends, including (alongside the Liebenberg circle) the Reich Chancellor Bernhard von Bülow himself and Wilhelm's favourite Max Egon II Fürst zu Fürstenberg, as well as several of the officials at his court.[40] Of particular interest in this regard is the very active part Wilhelm II played in the first major homosexuality scandal to hit Germany during his reign, that surrounding the risky behaviour and sudden death − almost certainly by suicide − of his friend the eminent industrialist Friedrich Alfred Krupp on 22 November 1902.

For several weeks before that tragedy the arms manufacturer, whose steelworks at Essen employed some 50,000 workers, had been the subject of lurid articles about his lifestyle on the Isle of Capri which had appeared first in the Italian press and then in *Vorwärts*, the organ of the Social Democratic party of Germany (SPD). The SPD's attack on their capitalist *bête noire* 'the richest man in Germany' had culminated in a piece entitled 'Krupp on Capri' penned by Kurt Eisner which had been published in *Vorwärts* on 15 November 1902. Krupp was with the Kaiser at Kiel when the article appeared. He returned immediately to Essen and initiated libel proceedings against the newspaper, whose offices were ransacked by the police. One week later Krupp was dead. Magnus Hirschfeld, the unusually well-informed campaigner for gay rights, had no hesitation in accusing the reactionary penal code, in particular the notorious paragraph 175 which criminalised sexual acts between men, of responsibility for the tragedy. Not the newspaper articles of *Vorwärts* but '§ 175' had hounded the industrialist to his premature death. Almost one third of all suicides were brought about by the dreadful dilemma resulting from this inhumane law, he believed, which condemned homosexuals to a life overshadowed by the twin threats of blackmail and imprisonment.

The Kaiser, having just returned from visiting his uncle Edward VII at Sandringham, was at the shoot in Bückeburg when he was told the news of Krupp's death. Given that the embarrassing accusations against the steel magnate had not been disproved and that the libel charge against the editors of *Vorwärts* was still pending, his entourage was vocal in urging him not to attend Krupp's funeral, but Wilhelm, to his credit, insisted on travelling to Essen. At a shoot in Silesia hosted by Prince Guido Henckel von Donnersmarck Wilhelm told his (and Eulenburg's) close friend Axel Freiherr von Varnbüler, Württemberg's envoy to Berlin, that he had been 'stormed from all sides' to reverse his spontaneous decision to attend the funeral. 'When this proved unsuccessful one had even tried to hide behind the Kaiserin. But that proved a complete failure, Her Majesty had not wavered for one minute to see him pay his respects to the deceased as a self-evident Christian duty. One of the few whose heart had been in the right place had been the Reich Chancellor, who had immediately telegraphed his approval with the comment that he had been about to advise His Majesty to do just that.'[41]

When he arrived at Essen for the funeral the Kaiser sought assurances that Krupp had not been a practising homosexual and was informed by several people, as Hirschfeld later heard on the gay grapevine, that though the deceased had had 'an exceptionally soft, gentle, sensitive nature', he had been 'asexual' and had in fact abhorred all sexual activity. It was on the strength of these assurances that Wilhelm, now convinced more than ever that the *Vorwärts* had hounded his blameless friend to an early grave, gave his notorious speech in his capacity as 'Sovereign of the German Reich' condemning the Socialists as 'men unworthy of the name of German' for what amounted to the 'murder' of this 'truly German man'.[42] Bülow, while pleased that the monarch had attended the funeral, spoke of his alarm that Wilhelm in his passionate outburst had once again overstepped the mark, provoking the SPD into proving the veracity of their assertions in court.[43] The Social Democrats for their part warned of the dangerous precedent that the monarch, who was himself protected from criticism by the law of lèse-majesté, had set by involving himself in an ongoing court case. *Vorwärts* asked: 'Is it permissible for the wearer of the Crown to pass his sentence before a pending trial has even commenced, thus placing the court in the invidious position either of contradicting the Kaiser's word, or else creating the dreadful impression that the Kaiser's opinion had influenced its judgement?'[44] The embarrassment for the wearer of the Crown was all the greater when on 15 December the chief prosecutor Hugo Isenbiel, no doubt bowing to pressure from on high, announced that the case against the editors of *Vorwärts* was being dropped.[45]

Did Wilhelm II really think Friedrich Alfred Krupp was innocent of the accusations the newspaper had levelled against him? The industrialist's extremely incautious homoerotic lifestyle on Capri and in Berlin had long been the focus of attention, as had the irreparable breakdown of his marriage — both Friedrich Alfred and Margarethe Krupp were being treated for marital problems by Ernst Schweninger, physician also to the Kaiser's sister Charlotte[46] — and the Kaiser had involved himself actively in their troubles, taking Krupp's side on a number of key occasions.

Krupp made so little effort to hide his predilections for young men that he was well known to the Berlin police by the time Hans von Tresckow took over the surveillance of the homosexual scene in the city in 1900. To Tresckow's astonishment the multi-millionaire industrialist would spend night after night watching the wrestling in a downtown theatre. In the Hotel Bristol, where he stayed when in Berlin, Krupp displayed an intense interest in the young waiters, several of whom he had himself sent from Italy to work in the hotel, ensuring that they were properly fed, took regular baths and so on.[47] From 1898 onwards he spent several months at a time in Capri, living in the Hotel Quisisana and spending so lavishly on his favourites as to arouse the envy of the less fortunate, who took their revenge by spreading rumours about his true purpose on the island.[48] When these reports reached Germany in May 1902, it was Kaiser Wilhelm who warned his friend of the danger and ordered him to return home, urging him never to return to Capri.[49] As he told Admiral Friedrich von Hollmann, Tirpitz's predecessor at the Reich Navy Office and a close friend of Krupp, the Kaiser held detailed discussions with the industrialist on his return from Capri while staying at the Villa Hügel in Essen in June and expressed his satisfaction at Krupp's decision not to return to the island.[50]

The part Wilhelm II played in the final act in the breakdown of the Krupps' marriage was less admirable. As the tsunami wave of scandal reached Germany in early October 1902, Margarethe Krupp, with the support of the firm's board of directors, took the decision to declare her husband's incapacitation and to entrust the huge company to a management committee. With the intention of winning the Kaiser's approval for her takeover she set off for Cadinen, Wilhelm's estate in the north-eastern province of West Prussia, and on 10 October 1902 convinced him that Krupp's disempowerment was the only way to save the company and the family's honour. It was Admiral von Hollmann, who happened to be present at Cadinen, who alerted Krupp to the threatening palace revolution. As Krupp rushed back from London, where he was buying a yacht, Hollmann succeeded in persuading the Kaiser that it was not Friedrich Alfred but Margarethe Krupp who was of dangerously unsound mind and needed to be locked away in a lunatic asylum – a fate that threatened many women attempting to escape from marriage to a homosexual husband at this time.[51] On reaching Baden-Baden on 13 October, Krupp arranged for his wife to be admitted to the well-known psychiatric clinic in Jena run by Professor Otto Binswanger, cynically informing the Kaiser that his wife had 'today agreed to submit herself willingly to a thorough treatment' of unknown duration. He had felt obliged to insist on this step 'as the symptoms of illness in my wife were on the increase and the rumours she had set in motion were spreading to ever wider circles'. Krupp thanked the monarch profusely 'for the kind and gentle way in which Y. M. has intervened on behalf of my person and my interests'.[52] It speaks volumes for the shameful way she had been treated by Krupp, with the Kaiser's evident support, that Margarethe Krupp was declared fit and well the moment her husband died. She was immediately allowed to leave the clinic in Jena and was back in the Villa Hügel on 23 November 1902, but unlike the Kaiser she did not attend the funeral three days later.[53]

DIVORCE IN THE HOUSE OF HESSE

The painful dilemma into which Wilhelm's strict views on morality led him, as monarch and head of his family, became evident in November 1901 when he was informed that his cousin, Grand Duke Ernst Ludwig of Hesse-Darmstadt, intended to divorce his young wife 'Duckie', Princess Viktoria Melita of Saxe-Coburg-Gotha.[54] The reason for their separation was not in doubt: because of the Grand Duke's homosexual tendencies 'this marriage', as Prince Heinrich, Ernst Ludwig's brother-in-law, wrote to Wilhelm on 8 November 1901 from Darmstadt, had been 'a failure from the beginning', as there was 'a certain inability on the masculine side to satisfy a passionate woman like Duckie for long'. This state of affairs and the resultant friction 'turned both of their lives into a harrowing experience'. Heinrich suspected that this news might 'perhaps arouse your displeasure, certainly your astonishment and also, I hope, your sympathy'. The divorce, Heinrich added, would probably be formalised on 25 November 1901, the birthday of both husband and wife.[55]

Kaiser Wilhelm was very closely related to both Ernst Ludwig and Viktoria Melita, for all three were grandchildren of Queen Victoria. He had spent happy days in Darmstadt as a child and a student with Ernst Ludwig and his four older sisters Viktoria, Ella, Irène and Alix, the children of his mother's sister. He had wanted to marry Ella, Irène was married to his brother Heinrich and he had himself set in train the marriage of the young Alix with Tsarevich Nicholas of Russia when he was in Coburg for the wedding of Ernst Ludwig and Viktoria Melita. Wilhelm wrote his cousin Ernst Ludwig a letter of ten emotionally charged pages which sheds more light than any other document on his conception of the significance of royal marriage as the model for the general population. In it he does not reproach the Grand Duke for his homosexual inclinations but for the fact that, with these tendencies, he married at all and that now, instead of coming to an accommodation, he will bring the institution of marriage into discredit through his divorce. The step that Ernst Ludwig was about to take was 'sad' and 'deeply regrettable', Wilhelm wrote to him on 11 November 1901. 'Painful for your heart, which could not have reached such a decision except after exceptional struggles. Deeply distressing for your family and country [of Hesse], for whom the model of family life will be so abruptly removed and destroyed, and who will find themselves robbed all at once of their sovereign lady and of the prospect of an eventual successor for you. The caring hands of the noble lady who was called by God to create a home for you and to bring relief from need among the people, who was to be the guardian of family feeling and to set an example to women among the people, will all at once be taken away from the Hessians and replaced by barren emptiness. It is a step that is also deeply to be regretted in the monarchical sense in general. The mere fact of it will constitute a sad novelty in German history hitherto. A ruling German Prince divorces his wife, and that without a particular blame attaching to her, without a grave offence on her part which would have compelled him to take this step. Simply because the two cannot come to an understanding, or do not earnestly try, or are unwilling to do so. That would no doubt have meant sacrifices, perhaps very difficult ones; yet had they been tried earlier and made in good time they could have averted this terrible disaster. For it is a disaster. A bad example in this frivolous time, when divorce has almost come to belong to the ingredients of modern marriages in the middle and better classes. A blow to the esteem and standing of our German princely houses which will be bitterly felt by all of us, your colleagues, and which will come home to you; for we all consider ourselves one family! — After Ernie's [Hereditary Prince Ernst of Hohenlohe-Langenburg's] detailed report I could only conclude that the chief reason why the relationship between you two was disturbed from the beginning lies in physical factors in you which must already have been familiar and clear to you when, or before, you proposed marriage. Your courtship was received coldly at first and even rejected. That must have made you reflect that you did not arouse the full impression of a mature man in the young girl. You should have examined yourself all the more keenly and considered whether, if your renewed proposal should receive a favourable hearing, you were in fact in a position to fulfil the expectations of your future wife! and above all once married to make doubly and trebly sure that you took care of her if she now — perhaps with resistance and after persuasion by relations at the highest level — gave you her hand after all! It would have been no misfortune if you had waited a year or two more before you married, for after all she was only 17!! And now her hopes have not been fulfilled, and she has felt frustrated and neglected, and played the role of a clothes horse on which you could hang your toilettes and rivieres of diamonds and gemstone necklaces so as to show yourself off to the world with your beautiful wife! It has wounded her deeply! For she is fiery by nature, but with depth and greatness, and she needed a lord and master and husband whom she has not found in you. And who you are not, according to what Ernie [Hohenlohe] told me, even in your own words when you answered him: "A woman or a girl or a man does not awaken the slightest feeling or interest in me, I consider them only from the point of view of a statue." Unhappy creature! If that were so, how could you have the heart to woo this wonderful maiden and chain her to you, especially as she did not come to you with any enthusiasm?! What you did was a grave wrong towards her; and no wonder if in spite of outward appearances you were bound to make her life a burden to her. But even if that were all so, once entrusted to you before God you took on the responsibility before Him for her weal and woe, "for better for worse", through good and evil days; and that you still have, and it might well have been settled with more understanding between each other. From Ernie [Hohenlohe] I know that the discord arose between you almost from the beginning for the above reasons, so from the beginning the consequences of your over-hasty action in marrying too early made themselves felt. Therefore it should have been your first concern to think about how an acceptable state of affairs could have been brought about and the worst thing, which is now happening, avoided. You refer in your letter to the fact that I am a good friend to you, which I am, you are quite right, and with all my heart . . . If you regarded me as your friend, why did you not come to me and tell me your woes? As an older married man I would gladly have stood by you in word and deed and would have spared no effort to keep you together, even if only outwardly in the eyes of the world! But an arrangement would have been found and God would have helped us. I know many a marriage in which things are just the same as with you, but which have not ended in divorce. Once again my dear Ernie, I am very sorry for you but I am just as sorry that you let it go so far without calling for my help! Instead even Heinrich, who was with me, very wrongly concealed the matter from me, his brother and head of the family; and I only learned of the approaching catastrophe through a telegram from my diplomatic representative! I do not call that friendship! – Now nothing can be changed! You must bear what you have brought upon yourself. Marriage is much too highly regarded by the people of Germany for this event not to cause a fearful sensation, and you will hear many unpleasant things said. At any rate the divorce must be conducted in such a way that your poor, lovely young wife can remain absolutely untainted and blameless in the eyes of the world, and you take the wrong upon yourself; God help her, the sweet, fatherless child, and you; that is the wish of your friend and cousin Wilhelm.'[56]

The Kaiser's plaintive offers of friendship and marriage counselling proved short-lived. When Ernst Ludwig expressed the wish to come to Potsdam as soon as possible to talk things over with Wilhelm, the latter made no attempt to conceal his displeasure. The Grand Duke should not come until his affairs were in order, he decreed. '*He* wanted to come *at once*, and I refused', he wrote on 21 November 1901 on the telegram from the envoy in Darmstadt. In answer to the Grand Duke's request he had said that 'a journey to see me *now* would be like the humiliation [of King Heinrich IV by the Pope] at Canossa [in 1077], and would look as if I had only summoned him to give a report and to answer to me for the stupid things going on in his household. Remarks would be made again about "vassalhood" etc, and his people would hold that against him very much! He must take consequences of this himself, as he stirred it up himself; and he was master in his own house; his private affairs did not concern me as long as they were not directly harmful to or for the Reich; he would have to settle them on his own. If he wanted advice this was my opinion and that was that.'[57]

THE GALLANT PHILANDERER PRINCE JOACHIM
ALBRECHT OF PRUSSIA

Wilhelm's uncle Prince Albrecht of Prussia, Regent of the Duchy of Brunswick since 1885, had died on 13 September 1906 at Schloss Kamenz in Silesia. The 'rather unworldly' and 'very strictly religious' Prince Regent[58] was survived by three sons, Prince Friedrich Heinrich (1874–1940), Prince Joachim Albrecht (1876–1939) and Prince Friedrich Wilhelm (1880–1925), whose projected marriage to Countess Lehndorff, as we have already seen, fell foul of the Kaiser's objections.[59] Since 1906 the two eldest Prussian princes had been kept in the limelight by the gutter press.

Friedrich Heinrich and Joachim Albrecht had grown up in luxurious conditions in Berlin, where they lived at the Palais Prinz Albrecht in the Wilhelmstrasse. Each received an allowance of 30,000 marks per annum from the Privy Purse and an additional 30,000 from their father. This was augmented by considerable sums in interest from inherited capital funds.[60] It is not surprising that already in their early years both showed an ominously devil-may-care attitude to life. Robert Count von Zedlitz-Trützschler, who was later to become Hofmarschall, served as Joachim Albrecht's personal adjutant during his military service with the Dragoon Guards and was strongly critical of the life led by the officers of this glamorous regiment commanded by the future Minister of War, Erich von Falkenhayn, which was characterised by luxury and 'a great deal of alcohol, a great deal of noise, dancing ... or card games'. He goes on to comment in his memoirs: 'This officer corps was not the right one for the two Princes ... Prince Joachim Albrecht was rather easy-going by nature, he frequently got into very bad company and as a result often found himself in trouble ... There did not seem to be any possibility of keeping him on more or less the right track.' Among the chief problems Zedlitz had to deal with were Joachim Albrecht's endless love affairs.

He struggled in vain to protect the Prince from the disaster threatened by the 'wiles and trickery of Eve's daughters'. Even among ladies of the highest standing the good looks and musical talent of his protégé had given him the aura of a Prince Charming.[61]

In September 1906 rumours reached the German embassy in London that Prince Joachim Albrecht was about to marry a Viennese woman, Marie Blich-Sulzer, who following a sham marriage was now called — of all things! — Baroness Liebenberg. Although the Prince denied any intention of marrying, Wilhelm II sent the lovesick young man to German South-West Africa to join the colonial troops there. Separated by thousands of kilometres from his beloved Baroness Liebenberg, the Prince took a dramatic turn for the worse. 'From my own observation, since His Royal Highness left Berlin a change has undoubtedly taken place in his mental functions', reported Captain von Brandenstein, the Prince's adjutant. 'This shows itself in the fact that His Royal Highness not infrequently loses the measure of what he ought to say and do as a Prussian Prince. In particular as a result of the long separation his unfortunate passion for Baroness Liebenberg has increased to a degree which I find unnatural. His Royal Highness continues to feel a martyr, a victim of malicious people's vulgar minds and love of gossip. The Prince regards it — in his own words — as his highest and finest duty to carry out that for which he means to answer to God as the right thing, namely to hold fast to the "noble" woman, in defiance of all the world! He tells people who are not at all close to him that his friendship for the "good woman" is purely spiritual. Only vulgar people could think anything else. Even with his doctor and me he tries to deny the sexual relationship. Everything in the way of good qualities, love and willingness to make sacrifices which the Prince can command he devotes to this — in his words — "most distinguished of all women". The numerous attempts in every conceivable way to convince him of the necessity of breaking off this disastrous relationship have unfortunately failed. The last conversation on this subject with His Royal Highness ended with the Prince declaring curtly that no one could forbid two people to love each other and that he would sooner shoot himself than commit the iniquity of being unfaithful to this woman. An insight into the thoughts and feelings of His Royal Highness cannot but evoke sincere commiseration and the most intense sympathy. In the opinion of the . . . doctors the Prince's attitude in the Liebenberg affair also has a pathological basis.' The illness manifested itself 'in unbridled criticism of people in their absence, which he accompanies with highly excited gestures without regard for strangers around him', Brandenstein lamented. 'Improvement . . . of any kind' the adjutant considered to be 'quite out of the question'.[62]

A crisis loomed when Joachim Albrecht let slip in South-West Africa that he intended to travel incognito to Switzerland to meet the Baroness. As the Prussian Prince was unlikely to remain unrecognised, there was 'a danger that the purpose of the transfer to South-West [Africa] previously ordered at the All-Highest level' might be 'represented by the Press as having failed'. In order to prevent another scandal in the press Brandenstein expressed the opinion in April 1907 that it was 'imperative that His Royal Highness should find orders awaiting him at Naples to report to His Majesty at once, or alternatively, which is perhaps an even better idea, that a senior officer, e.g. General von Schenck, should be given the task of meeting His Royal Highness at Naples on 26 May and accompanying him to Berlin'.[63] General Count Dietrich von Hülsen-Haeseler, the Chief of the Military Cabinet, took the line that it should be left to the Prince, as an adult, to decide how he should behave towards Baroness Liebenberg, as long as he did not publicly compromise himself with her and also declared that he did not intend to marry her. After his audience with the Kaiser the Cabinet Chief, 'looking crestfallen', told Hofmarschall Zedlitz that the Kaiser 'would not hear of anything of the kind'. 'It is quite impossible to talk to him. He banged the table with his fist and shouted at me very angrily: "My sons don't have women. Why should others have them?"'[64] Finally Wilhelm approved an order which Hülsen-Haeseler submitted to him instructing Major General von Schenck, Joachim Albrecht's brigade Commander, to meet the Prince in Naples. It ran: 'His Majesty is confident that in future there will be no question of any relations *with* or connection of the Prince *to* Baroness Liebenberg. His Majesty as Head of the Royal House cannot in any circumstances tolerate that the Prince should give the public the slightest cause for remarks about his moral way of life, let alone that he should entertain any thoughts of matrimony with regard to the lady. His Majesty must assign to His Royal Highness as Prince, man of honour and officer, full and complete responsibility for all he does or does not do, and should the Prince not meet the expectations placed upon him and prove deaf to the strong warnings addressed to him, His Majesty will find himself compelled to take the most severe measures against him. His Majesty demands that the Prince keep in mind what he, as a Prussian Prince, owes to the honour and esteem of his House and expects that he will arrange and conduct his future life accordingly, and keep his escutcheon unsullied and pure. Only if the Prince leads an exemplary life before all the world will His Majesty take into consideration the reinstatement of the Prince in the Army. His Majesty expects to be given notice of every change of place of residence during the period of leave.'[65] When Hülsen showed the instructions to Zedlitz, the latter expressed surprise that it was formulated 'in very general terms'; one could just as well take it to mean that 'the Prince could now no longer live with his woman at all' as that 'he could live with her discreetly'. The Chief of the Military Cabinet agreed with this objection and merely responded: 'It was not possible otherwise, and the Kaiser would never approve other instructions.' He would, however, send written instructions to Schenck to read out the Kaiser's orders to the Prince, but then tell him that he 'could see his woman if he did not publicly compromise himself and if he did not intend to marry her'. Schenck later confirmed that everything had gone off as planned in Naples and that the Prince had given him a written promise to abide by both conditions. 'The Kaiser knows nothing of this verbal order. That is what happens when one tries to rule and reform the world on excessively virtuous principles.'[66]

The humane compromise which Hülsen, Zedlitz and Schenck were able to bring about more or less behind the Kaiser's back fell through, however, because of the unstable emotional state of the Prince. He was living with Baroness Liebenberg, who was not yet divorced, and continuing to run up large debts. In October 1907 a certain Professor Ziehen, on the basis of a military medical report which had been sent to him and without ever having examined the Prince himself, diagnosed a psychotic defect – the Prince, he claimed, was obviously suffering from either *dementia praecox* or *dementia paralytica*. The prognosis was unfavourable, Ziehen wrote, inasmuch as a complete cure was as good as impossible. Incapacitation proceedings on grounds of mental deficiency (not mental illness) would have every chance of success. Instead of incapacitation, which would have repercussions on the Prince's state of mind, however, one could consider the appointment of guardians, although the Prince would have to give his consent for this. Surveillance of the patient wherever he went would be essential in any event, as he was not in a position to look after his own affairs.[67]

On 25 February 1908 Kaiser Wilhelm II sent his cousin Prince Joachim Albrecht two All-Highest Cabinet orders. In the first, which the Prince 'gratefully' accepted, the monarch demanded that he hand in his resignation from the army. The second order asked the Prince to agree to the appointment of guardians, and at the same time offered him financial help to settle his debts. In his reply of 28 February 1908 the Prince rejected this imposition. 'I believe I can comply with all Your Majesty's justifiable wishes without submitting to a condition so humiliating and so cruelly damaging to my life. I may perhaps be allowed to point out that I would have to declare myself mentally ill and not responsible for my actions if I agreed to a guardianship. What value could my gratitude and any proof of my devotion to Your Majesty have if I declared myself in need of guardianship?'[68] A few days later Prince Joachim Albrecht of Prussia, Knight of the Order of the Black Eagle, was retired from the royal Prussian army, with the specific and degrading condition that he was henceforth forbidden to wear any military uniform.[69]

Zedlitz, and with him 'the majority of level-headed people', condemned this extreme action by Wilhelm II as 'incredible'. The Prince was accused of adultery 'because he is still living with a person who married a down-at-heel Baron Liebenberg in a sham marriage so that she could take his name. As she has never lived with this man and he is causing nothing but problems over the divorce so as to extract money, the accusation of "adultery" is in fact incomprehensible. – On the other hand an attempt has been made to persuade the Prince to place himself officially under a kind of "guardianship". On the recommendation of his legal adviser . . . the Prince refused to do this, whereupon he was retired without the right to wear uniform. – Not without reason the Prince asked: "What have I actually done that I should have to declare myself insane?" – The result of this retirement will be that the Prince will be kept out of "blameless" and decent society even more than before, that he will be driven even more into the arms of his woman, and that dubious elements of all kinds will impose themselves on him and only drag him further down morally, and exploit and deceive him. I deeply deplore this solution.' Just as strongly, Zedlitz condemned what seemed to him an incomprehensible willingness on Kaiser Wilhelm's part 'to destroy other existences in order to preserve his own sons' morals'.[70] Only after the collapse of the monarchy was Joachim Albrecht able to marry the woman with whom he had lived for thirteen years. And then, only a few weeks after the wedding Marie, Princess of Prussia, née Blich-Sulzer, died.

THE ROYAL GROOM: PRINCE FRIEDRICH HEINRICH OF PRUSSIA

At the very moment when the Kaiser dispatched Prince Joachim Albrecht to the war in Africa because of his relationship with a commoner, the Prince's older brother Prince Friedrich Heinrich of Prussia became embroiled in a homosexual scandal which was likewise to end in banishment. As we shall see, the affair triggered a whole avalanche of accusations against members of Wilhelm II's closest entourage, from which the Hohenzollern monarchy was never to recover.

Rumours about Prince Friedrich Heinrich's homosexual escapades had been circulating for years. He is said to have liked dressing up as a groom and to have demanded payment for his services. He was repeatedly followed by police officers and even received a warning from the President of the Berlin police force, Georg von Borries.[71] The rumours threatened to become dangerous when the Prince was elected Grand Master of the Order of St John of

Jerusalem at the beginning of 1907. Count Wilhelm von Wedel-Sandfort, Commander of the Order in the province of Westphalia, strongly advised the Prince not to accept the post in view of the stories going around, but Friedrich Heinrich ignored his warning. Eventually the Minister of the Household, Wilhelm von Wedell-Piesdorff, took it upon himself to write to the Prince 'in very precise terms'. In despair Friedrich Heinrich appealed to the Master of Ceremonies, Count Edgard von Wedel – himself a homosexual – in a letter asking him to bring the matter before the Kaiser in a manner that would steer him out of trouble. 'Incredibly', however, Edgard Wedel showed the letter to the Kaiser, as a result of which the Prince, as Zedlitz remarked, was 'done for, of course'. For Wilhelm immediately decided to appoint his own son Eitel Friedrich as Grand Master, thus in effect publicly confirming the rumours about Friedrich Heinrich. Wilhelm's over-hasty decision, which recalls his impulsive behaviour over the Kotze affair in 1894, was also to have dire consequences in other respects in the coming months. The Hofmarschall rightly condemned what had happened, which in his opinion had 'something horrible' about it. 'People with their delusions of virtue, their Pharisaism and their terrible severity and cruelty' seemed 'quite mediaeval' to him. As there were no proofs against the Prince, which even Borries had conceded, it would have been wiser to keep one's nerve, face it out and and deny the rumours if necessary, Zedlitz thought.[72]

The Kaiser's decision in March 1907 to appoint Friedrich Heinrich à la suite of the 2nd Dragoon regiment caused astonishment and disapproval. 'If one is prepared to accept in the first place that he cannot become Grand Master of the Order of St John of Jerusalem because of § 175, logically he cannot be appointed an officer à la suite of a regiment either', Zedlitz commented, for of course this offence meant immediate dismissal for any officer.[73] If this appointment had been intended as a mark of confidence in the afflicted Prince, its effect lasted for no more than a few days. In the weekly review *Die Zukunft* of 27 April 1907 Maximilian Harden openly accused Prince Friedrich Heinrich of Prussia of suffering from 'hereditary perversion of the sexual drive' and stated that he had been obliged to renounce the Grand Mastership of the Order of St John of Jerusalem for this very reason.[74] The result of this public exposure was devastating: in the eyes of court society the Hohenzollern Prince was utterly damned. Zedlitz recorded indignantly on 7 June 1907 that no one in Berlin would receive Prince Friedrich Heinrich any more; they thought 'he should live abroad and only, perhaps, be able to stay quietly at Kamenz from time to time. They want to take away his military aides de camp, as no officer could possibly be expected to be aide de camp to such a Prince ... The whole affair is terribly tragic, because the Prince is fundamentally a good, dutiful person.' For the critical Hofmarschall the Kaiser's decision to banish this cousin as well from the court was yet another glaring example of the ill-considered manner in which the monarch exercised his powers. 'How much we are ruled by chance events, and what sudden decisions they give rise to! To think of the kind of people whose advice is sometimes decisive! How little effort is made to talk something over calmly and objectively with the responsible authorities before rash decisions are made.'[75]

'LIKE HEATHEN ROME': COUNT HOHENAU AND THE POTSDAM GUARDS REGIMENTS

Because the Hohenzollern monarchy saw itself as primarily a military monarchy, it was acutely affected by the scandalous events in the Potsdam Guards regiments which came to light in 1907, especially as relations of the Kaiser were again among the chief culprits. Count Wilhelm von Hohenau (1854–1930), the eldest son of the second marriage of the elderly Prince Albrecht, youngest brother of Kaiser Wilhelm I, rose to be an imperial Flügeladjutant, a Lieutenant-General, Commanding Officer of the elite regiment of Gardes du Corps and finally of the 1st Guards Cavalry Brigade. He was married to Margarete, Princess zu Hohenlohe-Oehringen, and had three daughters. In May 1907 Hohenau was banned from court for homosexual offences and six months later dismissed from the army and forced to flee abroad. The reputation of his younger brother, Count Friedrich von Hohenau – whose wife had been the target of most of the spiteful anonymous letters during the Kotze scandal[76] – was likewise put at risk by allegations of homosexuality.

Also embroiled in the Potsdam scandal was Count Johannes von Lynar, who was married to the sister of Grand Duchess Eleonore of Hesse-Darmstadt. Lynar was considered one of the most elegant Guards officers and commanded the Bodyguard Squadron of the Gardes du Corps regiment. When the Crown Prince took over this command, Lynar acted as his right-hand man.[77] The illustrious status enjoyed by Lynar, Hohenau and others at the Hohenzollern court and in the Prussian officer corps was abruptly destroyed when on 23 October 1907, in the first court case of *Kuno Count von Moltke* v. *Harden*, Private Bollhardt affirmed under oath that he had for years taken part in homosexual orgies at Count Lynar's Villa Adler on the Heiligensee in Potsdam, and that he was certain that he had also recognised Count Wilhelm Hohenau there. Bollhardt's declaration naturally spread throughout the international press, as did Harden's claim that he had only called the soldier in his defence because he assumed that the accusations which had been made against Hohenau for many years were generally known. 'It is common knowledge, after all. If you pushed me further, I would bring you members of ruling houses who say: is it possible that anyone still disputes it!'[78] He was alluding to none other than the Kaiser's eldest sister Charlotte.[79]

The events in the Adler Villa on the Heiligensee even came under discussion in the Reichstag, in a heated debate at the end of November 1907. The Reich Chancellor Prince Bülow affirmed, in reference to the Hohenau and Lynar affair, 'that everything will be done by our military authorities to eradicate such abominations ferro et igni [with fire and sword]'. The Prussian Minister of War, Lieutenant-General Karl von Einem, conceded that there had been certain misdemeanours in the Gardes du Corps regiment but maintained that an order which he had recently published forbidding members of the regiment from going out in white breeches and black jackboots would help get rid of such evils in the future, for it would prevent 'assaults by the perversely inclined sectors of the civilian population' on the soldiers. Einem contested the idea that the Villa Adler had served more or less as a brothel. The goings-on there which had become known in the Moltke–Harden case had nevertheless provided a reason 'to institute immediate court martial proceedings against Count Hohenau and Count Lynar'. In response to the reproach that as Minister of War he, together with the Commandant of the Imperial Headquarters, Adjutant-General Hans von Plessen, and the Chief of the Military Cabinet, Count Dietrich von Hülsen-Haeseler, should have protected the Kaiser from contact with such men, Einem retorted that he had known nothing about the officers' inclinations and he must 'decline to collect his information from Berlin drinking-holes; I must decline to set any store by rumours, tittle-tattle, whispers or tale-telling'. It would be 'absolutely idiotic' for the Chief of the Military Cabinet 'to bring into proximity with His Majesty a man of whom he knew that he had such inclinations and indulged in activities following these inclinations'. Such a man would after all have been 'a sick man, a madman', and even leading medical experts would not have expected to find such men in the Kaiser's entourage. In conclusion the Prussian Minister of War concentrated on damage limitation. 'It has been said that His Majesty's entourage consists of nothing but such people. If there is one man who is guilty, gentlemen, it is Count Hohenau. So what does that leave of this entourage? I would not advise anyone to tell His Majesty's entourage, as it now is, to their faces that they indulge such inclinations.'[80] Only days before this Kaiser Wilhelm II, faced with the shattering revelations about the sexual behaviour of his most intimate friends, had broken down with the cry: 'Kings are only human, after all, and can sometimes be ill too!'[81]

CHAPTER TWENTY-ONE

Prince Eulenburg's downfall. The campaign against the Liebenberg 'Camarilla'

Embarrassing as the scandals in the collateral branches of the Hohenzollern family and in the Potsdam elite regiments were, they would not in themselves have shaken the monarchy to its foundations. This was to happen only when the sensational scandals of 1906–8 spread into the realm of high politics with the increasingly pointed attacks on the Kaiser's friend Philipp Prince zu Eulenburg-Hertefeld (see Figure 19) and the so-called 'Liebenberg Round Table', which was accused of forming a homoerotic, effete, fawning, spiritualistic, faith-healing and even – oh horror! – pacifist ring around the Kaiser in order to shield him from his people and the harsh realities of *Weltpolitik*.[1] The devastating weapon of public accusations of homosexuality in the campaign against this group of men was brought into action relatively late, in November 1906, and even then not primarily by the journalist Maximilian Harden but by the Reich Chancellor and his colleagues and advisers in the Wilhelmstrasse. The manner in which Bülow behaved in the Eulenburg affair, as he gambled with the future of the Prussian–German Crown in order to cling to what had long since ceased to be a position of any dignity, is positively breathtaking.[2]

THE MACHINATIONS OF THE 'LIEBENBERG ROUND TABLE'

As we have seen, the relationship of trust between Kaiser and Chancellor had been irreparably damaged by Bülow's threat to resign over the Treaty of Björkö and by the Algeciras debacle.[3] The Chancellor's fainting fit in the Reichstag on 5 April 1906 and his seven-month convalescence on Norderney could only strengthen the impression that he was worn out, and the resignation of the Prussian Minister of Agriculture, Viktor von Podbielski, which had

Figure 19 Prince Philipp zu Eulenburg-Hertefeld, the Kaiser's best friend

been forced on the Kaiser, had then fanned the smouldering fire of the crisis.[4]
Even the dissolution of the Reichstag in December 1906 and the election
victory of the nationalistic bloc parties could provide only a temporary
reinforcement of Bülow's position, for the Bülow bloc proved less than solid.
On both counts, therefore – with the monarch and with parliament – the
Chancellor seemed doomed to failure. It was certainly no coincidence, but
rather an absolutely classic manifestation of the system of Personal Monarchy,
that grotesque rumours now began to spread everywhere about sinister
machinations going on in the Kaiser's entourage.

Since the spring of 1906 there had been a widespread belief that Philipp
Eulenburg and his friends were intent on exploiting Bülow's weakness in
order to take over the highest offices of the state for themselves and their
associates. Observers noted with alarm that immediately after Bülow's fainting

fit and the dismissal of Holstein the Kaiser conferred the Order of the Black Eagle on his former favourite 'Phili', who had deliberately remained in the background for the past few years. The historian Professor Theodor Schiemann, who witnessed the manner in which the Kaiser informed Eulenburg of the high honour he was to receive, instantly suspected that the award would 'inevitably be linked with the Reich Chancellor's illness' and thought it imperative that the official announcement be delayed.[5]

The unexpected decoration of the Kaiser's favourite aroused deep mistrust and indignation. It was linked not only with Bülow's attack of weakness and Holstein's dismissal but also with the publication of the sumptuous volume entitled *Deutsche Gedenkhalle: Bilder aus der vaterländischen Geschichte* [A German Pantheon: Patriotic Pictures from History], which had been produced under the aegis of Eulenburg and presented to the Kaiser in April 1906.[6] In the *Zukunft* of 28 April 1906 Harden scoffed at the award of the highest Prussian order to Eulenburg. This new 'Knight of the Eagle' was, he wrote, 'a poet, a composer, a spiritualist (like the new Chief of the Great General Staff); and not, it seems, to be kept out of favour for very long. "He loves the Kaiser so deeply, lives only for a glance from him; and how good it feels to have this enraptured eye constantly fixed upon oneself." Whenever Phili's name crops up again, a shiver runs through the ranks. And now the Black Eagle; what for? . . . Phili has been "busy" again. This time . . . it is . . . a luxury volume that glorifies Wilhelm the Second and other men who seem great to the enraptured eye.'[7]

For Friedrich von Holstein, who held Eulenburg responsible for his downfall, it was now clear that his great adversary in the battle against the Personal Monarchy in the 1890s had resumed his role of 'chief adviser of the Kaiser'.[8] Even before the award of the Black Eagle the Privy Councillor had suspected that 'Phili' was aiming to get himself appointed ambassador in Paris, with the help of his intimate friend Raymond Lecomte, secretary at the French embassy.[9] After the Kaiser conferred the order on Eulenburg Holstein wrote bitterly to Schiemann: 'The ostentatious decoration of Phili at this precise moment clears the horizon. A few weeks ago someone who is now ill (i.e. Bülow) told me that Phili had said to him "But Holstein is driving us to war". So Phili has at any rate advised the Kaiser to be accommodating, and he has been rewarded for it . . . The battle against Phili's romantic politics was one of my principal tasks in the last 10–12 years. Now Phili has won.'[10] Unbelievably, a fatal duel with pistols between the 70-year-old retired Privy Councillor and the recently dubbed knight of the Order of the Black Eagle was only narrowly avoided!

When Schiemann wrote to Holstein telling him that Eulenburg had preserved 'every scrap of paper' in his archives at Liebenberg, Holstein took this as an attempt at intimidation. On 28 April 1906 he replied saying that he was 'unutterably astonished that somebody who had as much dirt sticking to him as Philipp Eulenburg, who is open to attack from any side you care to choose, should turn to threats. But such characters occasionally have moments of hysterical over-excitement.'[11] Three days later Holstein sent Eulenburg a letter which could hardly have been more insulting. It ran simply: 'My Phili! This greeting is not a mark of esteem, for "Phili" to-day among contemporaries signifies – nothing good . . . I am now free, I need exercise no restraint and can treat you as one treats any contemptible person with your characteristics.'[12] After receiving this note Eulenburg called on his old friend the Württemberg envoy Axel Freiherr von Varnbüler, and asked him to be his second in a duel with Holstein under the harshest conditions – with drawn pistols at five paces until one of the combatants was unable to continue the fight. Varnbüler agreed to deliver the challenge to Holstein, but pointed out that in view of the enormous scandal that a duel between two such prominent people would inevitably cause, it would probably be necessary to give notice of it to the Auswärtiges Amt, as the department concerned. Foreign Secretary Tschirschky heard Eulenburg out in the presence of Varnbüler and then, after discussing the matter with Under Secretary von Mühlberg, declared that he must try, 'in the interests of the State', to prevent the duel by persuading Holstein to withdraw his letter. After all, he suggested, Eulenburg's assurance that he had not been involved in any way in Holstein's dismissal provided him with a fair basis on which to do so. In the end Holstein agreed to withdraw the letter on condition that Eulenburg repeat, on his word of honour and in writing, his verbal assurance that he had had nothing to do either with Holstein's discharge or with the attacks against him. Although Varnbüler persisted in his view that 'only by a duel to the death can this *personal* insult be put aside', Eulenburg declared himself willing 'for *political* reasons' to agree to the settlement of this affair of honour.[13]

   Although the barely credible drama of the duel fizzled out into nothing, it was the prelude to the series of sensational trials which were to take their fatal course shortly afterwards. As a result of the involvement of the Foreign Office and Schiemann in the quarrel, now at the very latest there were many people who were able to testify to the accusation of pederasty which Holstein had made against Eulenburg.[14] But the Kaiser remained in the dark, and neither Bülow nor Eulenburg himself enlightened him. 'I had a long, very heated discussion with H.M. about Hol[stein], and very disagreeable it was for me', Eulenburg confessed in a letter to Varnbüler on 13 May 1906. 'If he should come to hear about my affair later he will not be able to forgive me for saying nothing to him on this occasion about what happened!'[15]

The fears preoccupying Bülow, Holstein and numerous others that Eulenburg and his Liebenberg coterie were about to make a political comeback were soon reinforced by further signs of imperial favour.[16] Immediately after the settlement of the duel affair, Eulenburg accompanied the Kaiser to Alsace to see the restored castle of Hohkönigsburg in the Vosges, and stayed at the imperial Schloss at Strasbourg with Wilhelm for three days. Not surprisingly, this revived the rumours of his aspirations to the illustrious and highly paid post of Statthalter of Alsace-Lorraine. In his memoirs Bülow claimed that the ambassador in Vienna, Carl Count von Wedel, sent him a message in late summer 1906 via his brother Karl Ulrich, who was the military attaché in Vienna, saying that 'there were people working hard against me, including and especially Philipp Eulenburg, who wanted the Chief of the General Staff, Hellmuth [sic] Moltke, to be Reich Chancellor. Eulenburg was leading the Kaiser to believe that I was much more ill than H.M. thought. "Bernhard's life is in danger." And by the by, one could get along even without "dear" Bernhard, in fact quite well. The Kaiser would have to manage foreign policy alone, supported by him, Eulenburg, and the loyal Tschirschky, but as far as domestic policy was concerned a strong man, that is to say a General, would be needed as the new iron broom to sweep everything clean.'[17] Such rumours seemed to be confirmed when Eulenburg travelled to Rominten with the Kaiser in October 1906 and reported to the Chancellor from there that Wilhelm was complaining of 'a certain lack of energy' in Bülow which stemmed from his illness. 'What is certain', Eulenburg went on, 'is that he knows of absolutely no one whom he could put in your place'.[18] On 10 October 1906 Holstein wrote to his cousin Ida von Stülpnagel: 'Bülow's Chancellorship is said to be coming to an end. The Kaiser is said to be completely finished with him ... It is Phili Eulenburg who is the gravedigger. He does not want to be Chancellor but wants to put forward someone close to him.'[19]

Thus there was a widespread suspicion in 1906 that Eulenburg, thanks to his proximity to the monarch, was on the point of engineering a virtual alternative government in the shadow of the throne. But how credible was such speculation? Holstein, Bülow and also journalists like Harden knew only too well what an immense and harmful influence Eulenburg had exercised in the 1890s with the establishment of Wilhelm II's Personal Monarchy. Yet since then he had been compelled to give up his ambassadorial post and retreat into the background politically, and his relationship with the Kaiser had from time to time been characterised by bitterness and deep concern about the latter's mental health.[20] At the age of 60 had he still the strength, the ambition and indeed the opportunity to move into action again as the man really in control of the Reich's destiny, as his numerous enemies claimed? Not entirely without reason, Zedlitz cast doubt on such fears among his contemporaries. 'Latterly everything that has happened in politics here has been attributed to the Eulenburg Round Table. This is a mistake. The Kaiser did not take either Prince Eulenburg or Count [Kuno] Moltke entirely au sérieux in political matters. Moreover Prince Eulenburg no longer had any political ambition at all. In particular, however, it is a long time since he has been in constant contact with the Kaiser. He was seen only once a year at Rominten, and the Kaiser would go to Liebenberg once in the autumn for a day or two. Apart from that, Eulenburg was invited to luncheon perhaps once or twice in the entire year and otherwise there was in fact no contact for any length of time.'[21] Again at the end of 1907 the Hofmarschall commented: 'If Prince Philipp Eulenburg had really had even a quarter of the influence ascribed to him, we should long since have found ourselves embroiled in difficulties and catastrophes such as scarcely anyone dares imagine. He is certainly a charming "grand seigneur" with very sophisticated, agreeable manners, but at the same time so full of fantasy and mysticism that I cannot understand at all how anyone can take him quite seriously. In fact he was neither ambitious nor hard-working ... All his endeavours were aimed at being the Kaiser's friend. That he certainly was to a very high degree. For with his agreeable manners and his very funny and witty stories he has won himself a firm place in the Kaiser's affections as a quite outstanding causeur. − As such a friend he has doubtless also had extraordinary influence on the Kaiser on many an occasion, and many a hasty, fantastical and mystical idea and decision may well be attributable to him. But he has never used this influence in a well calculated and well thought-out way.'[22]

However refreshing this appeal to common sense as a corrective to the exaggerated, almost paranoid suspicions of Holstein, Harden and Bülow appears to be, the fact is that the rumours of an imminent secret seizure of power by the Liebenberg clique gained an astonishingly pervasive hold over the leading political elite and, as Peter Winzen has shown in his most recent studies of the scandals, they were not unfounded.[23] The Prussian Minister of War, the Bavarian Prime Minister, the Badenese envoys in Berlin and Munich were all, as we shall see shortly, convinced of the accuracy of these rumours. What is more, we also have *direct* evidence bearing eloquent witness to the hubris prevailing within the inner circle around Eulenburg in the spring of 1906. On 6 April 1906, the day after Bülow's fainting fit and only a few hours after the Order of the Black Eagle had been conferred on Eulenburg, Theodor Schiemann and Kuno Moltke were invited to Varnbüler's house. At this meeting Count Anton Monts, the ambassador in Rome, was openly mentioned 'as the possible future Reich Chancellor'. Varnbüler himself was named both as Tschirschky's successor at the Foreign Office and as future Prime Minister in Stuttgart. Three days later Schiemann attended a breakfast meeting at Moltke's house at which Eulenburg and Varnbüler were also present. Once again the conversation was dominated by wide-ranging speculation about appointments. Schiemann noted in his diary: 'It seems that Tschirschky is unlikely to last long in his post; [Kuno] Moltke seems to want Monts to succeed him, and Varnbüler to succeed Schön [as ambassador in St Petersburg].'[24] If one considers that only a few days later Holstein was abruptly dismissed from office, it is hardly surprising that the fears of a takeover of the most important posts by the Liebenberg Round Table gained general currency. Indeed, Varnbüler admitted to his sister Hildegard von Spitzemberg that he considered the new Chief of General Staff, Helmuth von Moltke, as extremely well-suited to the post of Reich Chancellor. He was a 'magnificent' speaker, and 'if it ever comes to it, character is surely the most important thing in dealing with universal suffrage'. Varnbüler even revealed that the hoped-for appointment of the Chief of General Staff as Chancellor would entail some kind of *coup d'état* to change the electoral law.[25]

As always, everything depended on the decision of Wilhelm II, the 'man of unlimited possibilities', and the political world kept a tense watch on his behaviour towards the Chancellor on the one hand and the group around Eulenburg on the other.[26] After his visit to Alsace with the Kaiser, which provoked hostile comments in the press, Eulenburg at first retreated from the limelight, ostensibly because of a serious illness. He refused Wilhelm's invitation to join the Scandinavian cruise for the same reason, thereby putting his newly revived friendship with the monarch at risk.[27] Eulenburg's presence during the annual imperial shooting holiday at Rominten in October 1906 was regarded with suspicion; this, and the fact that he spent the night of 22–3 October at the Neues Palais in Potsdam, threatened to unleash a storm of protest.[28] In the end it was Wilhelm's visit to Liebenberg (see Figure 20) in November 1906 which provoked the scandal which was to plunge the Kaiser's best friends into the abyss and deal a blow to the Hohenzollern throne from which it never recovered.

THE KAISER'S VISIT TO LIEBENBERG IN NOVEMBER 1906

As Wilhelm had at first cried off because of a cold and then announced himself available again for a brief visit to Liebenberg on 7 November, Eulenburg had to improvise the guest list at very short notice. It was too late to reach Emil Count Görtz and Georg von Hülsen; but General Paul von

Figure 20 Schloss Liebenberg, Prince Eulenburg's castle in the
Mark Brandenburg, north of Berlin

Leszczynski, Jan Freiherr von Wendelstadt, Axel Varnbüler and a few neighbouring landowners were able to come. Kuno Moltke was also there, in the
Kaiser's suite. The presence of Raymond Lecomte, a secretary at the French
embassy and notorious as a homosexual, proved fateful; he was apparently
invited 'by imperial command'.[29] As Holstein reported to his cousin, 'the idea
that the Frenchman was with the Kaiser in a very small group of friends drove
little Harden ... into a veritable frenzy of rage'.[30] For his part Harden
recorded that Holstein turned quite pale when he heard of Lecomte's presence
at Liebenberg.[31] Even Princess Marie Radziwill, who was on close terms with
the French embassy and a friend of Lecomte considered that to have invited
him at the same time as the German sovereign showed 'dangerous imprudence'. The Kaiser seems not to have betrayed any state secrets at Liebenberg.
'But he talked' − according to Lecomte − 'without pausing even for a minute,
from morning till night. He spoke about art, roared with laughter at endless
old anecdotes which were basically completely uninteresting, recounted his
voyages, his musical impressions, his experiences at sea etc., and did not even
leave himself time to eat ... The Kaiser was like a schoolboy on holiday who
has not yet learned how to behave in society.'[32] The sheer superficiality of
his exalted guest even got on the nerves of his host. During the three days of
the Kaiser's visit, Eulenburg complained, there had been 'nothing but chatter'.
'It is *incomprehensible* how the Kaiser can bear it all! He talks incessantly with
the *greatest liveliness!*'[33]

However that may be, Wilhelm II's presence at the heart of the 'Liebenberg Round Table' caused uproar throughout the establishment. The Deputy Senior Master of Ceremonies, Bodo von dem Knesebeck, made 'very heated' comments about the three days spent by the Kaiser in the company of Eulenburg, who was a 'very dangerous friend for the Sovereign', for he was 'false, ambitious and incapable of grasping the broad principles of policy'.[34] On 7 November 1906 of all days, the day on which Wilhelm arrived in Liebenberg, the *Neue Gesellschaftliche Correspondenz*, which was close to the Chancellor, reported that a 'high-born bard' wanted to bring Bülow down and make the Chief of General Staff, Helmuth von Moltke, 'Reich Chancellor of the Interior'.[35] The Badenese envoy in Berlin, Sigismund Freiherr von Berckheim, sent the article, which was reprinted by several newspapers, to Karlsruhe with the comment that War Minister, General von Einem, had personally assured him that the information in it was 'unfortunately correct on all points'. Eulenburg had already brought Caprivi down and now wanted to get rid of Bülow too, because owing to financial difficulties he wished to obtain the highly paid position of Statthalter of Alsace-Lorraine. Berckheim continued scathingly: 'Prince Bülow now rightly considers the reappointment of Prince Eulenburg to high public office impossible, and that is for a reason which is in effect known to all the world here but which no one dares tell the Kaiser about, or even give him a hint of it; namely that the Prince is said to harbour passions which are allowed in the Orient and tolerated in Russia but punished as a criminal offence in this country ... There is said to be very incriminating evidence against him in the form of letters which in the event of publication would cause a huge scandal – and this the Chancellor wishes to avoid at all costs. But Prince Eulenburg himself obviously sees things differently and therefore he wants to push the Chancellor slowly but surely out of the way, by adding on a Vice Chancellor.' Eulenburg thought he had found 'a willing tool' in the new Chief of General Staff, von Moltke, whom he intended to direct through his confidant, Lieutenant-General Count Kuno von Moltke, the Commandant of the City of Berlin. Berckheim named his colleague from Württemberg, Axel Varnbüler, as 'the third member of the trio': he too was with the Kaiser at Liebenberg and likewise aspired to an ambassadorial post for reasons of financial need. Although the 'cunningly thought-out plan' had failed for the time being because the Kaiser had personally convinced himself that Bülow had regained his health, 'it still strikes one as strange that instead of going to Letzlingen he has now gone to Liebenberg for a few days'.[36]

The natural suspicion that Bülow and his press officer Otto Hammann were behind these newspaper attacks on the Liebenberg 'Camarilla' is strengthened by the Reichstag speech in which the Reich Chancellor effectively went public on 14 November 1906, in response to a critical interpellation by the leader of the National Liberal party, Ernst Bassermann, accusing the Kaiser of arbitrary use of power and of encouraging spiritualism and sycophancy.[37] In a clear allusion to Eulenburg and his circle Bülow declared that 'Camarilla' was not a German word; 'Camarilla is the word for a horrible foreign poisonous plant, and no one has ever tried ... to plant this horrible poisonous plant in our country without causing great harm to Princes and great harm to the nation.'[38] The speech was all the more significant because Bülow unequivocally criticised the Kaiser too − he deplored the 'excessive personal intervention' of the monarch 'without ministerial cover'.[39] In a letter to Wilhelm the Chancellor excused himself to some extent for his criticism by explaining that the German people were very sensitive to absolutist tendencies; the Kaiser had certainly never violated the constitution, but many of his speeches and telegrams had been used against him. Quite unperturbed, Wilhelm II wrote in the margin of Bülow's letter: 'Agreed! Many thanks! *I shall not change!* And the grumbling will continue.'[40]

HARDEN'S CAMPAIGN AGAINST THE 'LIEBENBERG ROUND TABLE'

As the reaction to the article in the *Neue Gesellschaftliche Correspondenz* showed, the homosexual nature of the Liebenberg Round Table was widely known even before Maximilian Harden launched his campaign against Eulenburg and Kuno Moltke. Holstein was already noting in his diary on 11 November 1906 that the two men were in the habit of describing the Kaiser in their letters as '*das Liebchen*' − 'the Sweetheart'.[41] And on 15 November the Bavarian Prime Minister, Freiherr von Podewils, disclosed to the Baden envoy in Munich that Eulenburg's 'moral defects' had already been a matter of speculation ten years before.[42]

On 17 November 1906, three days after the Reich Chancellor's speech in the Reichstag, Harden's first major attack on 'Phili' Eulenburg and his 'Round Table' appeared in the *Zukunft*, under the ominous title 'Prelude'. In it Harden recorded that in the 1890s no important post had been allocated without Eulenburg's involvement; but then 'his star seemed to wane. His protégé Bülow sat firmly in his place in the sun; he had become Count, Chancellor, Prince and incidentally the heir to millions as well ... Yet the Romantic came back from exile, was invited [by the Kaiser] again, was taken to the North Cape with him, received visits.' So it was no wonder if the Chancellor felt threatened. After all, Eulenburg had 'taken care of all his friends. A Moltke is Chief of General Staff, another [Moltke] who is even closer to him is Commandant of Berlin, Herr von Tschirschky is Secretary of State at the Foreign

Office; and it is hoped that another warm little corner will still be found for Herr von Varnbüler. All good people. Musical, poetic, spiritualist; so pious that they expect more healing from prayer than from the wisest doctor, and in their communications, both spoken and written, they show a touching friendliness. All that would be their private affair if they did not belong to the Kaiser's closest Round Table (I have by no means listed all the affiliates) and were not, visibly or invisibly, spinning fine webs which are beginning to stifle the German Reich.' At the centre of Harden's criticism was the accusation that Eulenburg had been responsible for encouraging the Kaiser's absolutist tendencies. 'That a German Emperor should wish to regulate everything himself may already be cause for concern; if he, with a temperament inclined towards dramatic eruptions, is advised by an unhealthy late Romantic and spiritualist, then even if he were supremely gifted, a policy à la Victor Hugo would be the only conceivable outcome ... Such a development would be an incalculable disaster for the Reich and for the monarchy and must therefore be prevented by all available means. Today I openly name Philipp Friedrich Karl Alexander Botho Fürst zu Eulenburg und Hertefeld, Count von Sandels, as the man who with unremitting zeal has whispered into the ear of Wilhelm the Second, and continues to do so to this day, that he is called to rule alone and that, as an incomparably blessed being, he may expect and beseech light and support only from the seat among the clouds, from the heights of which the Crown was bestowed on him; and to feel responsible only to that place. The calamitous influence of this man should at least not be allowed to continue in the dark.'[43]

A week later Harden published another attack in the *Zukunft* under the title of 'Dies irae', directed against Eulenburg ('the Harper') and Kuno ('Tütü') Moltke ('the Sweetie'), as a result of which the Kaiser's closest friend eventually fled abroad. In an allusion to a scene from Goethe's *Faust*, Harden wrote mockingly: 'November 1906. Night. Open field in the Uker region. The Harper: "Have you read it?" The Sweetie: "Yes, on Friday." The Harper: "Do you think there will be more?" The Sweetie: "We must consider it a possibility; he seems well informed, and if he knows the letters which mention the *Liebchen* ..." The Harper: "Unthinkable! But they are having it reprinted everywhere. They are desperate to get us." The Sweetie: "A coven of witches. It's all over! All over!" The Harper: "If only He [the Kaiser] does not find out about it!"'[44]

Through a mediator Harden, Eulenburg and Moltke secretly arranged a 'cease-fire' under which the journalist agreed to stop his attacks if and as long as Eulenburg left Germany. Although he was well aware that his flight would only confirm Harden's accusations, Eulenburg left on 10 December 1906 with his family for Territet on Lake Geneva. Kuno Moltke, who in Harden's eyes had acted only as a harmless intermediary between Eulenburg and Wilhelm, was able to stay on undisturbed at his post as City Commandant of Berlin after Eulenburg's retreat.[45]

For a long time Kaiser Wilhelm knew nothing of these dramatic events, played out in part quite publicly and in part among his closest friends. Eulenburg explained his abrupt departure for Switzerland to the Kaiser on the grounds of influenza and the sudden illness of his daughter Augusta ('Lycki'), who in truth was expecting a child by the family tutor, Edmund Jaroljmek, whom she then married much against her father's will.[46] Although Harden's poisoned arrows were aimed at the heart of Wilhelm's Personal Rule, neither the Reich Chancellor nor any courtier or military officer in his suite had the courage to inform him of the terrible accusations which had led his favourite to flee abroad. While her brother was kept in ignorance, Hereditary Princess Charlotte of Saxe-Meiningen followed Harden's campaign with fascination and enthusiastic approval. Its revelations were 'frighteningly wonderful', Wilhelm's sister wrote to her doctor Schweninger; she had positively 'devoured' the article in the *Zukunft*. She must not say more, however, nor should one draw comparisons, but 'the present state of affairs is *too* sad!'[47] After the two articles of 17 and 24 November attacking the Liebenberg clique she exulted: 'Harden's revelations were masterly but he *must* produce more, although what he discloses can only be distressing: our misery is . . . *frightening*.'[48] But she was quite alone in the family in holding such views, she wrote. They all condemned Harden as a 'vile scoundrel, insolent Jew, brute etc.'; at court 'blindness, mawkish sentiment, apathy, stupidity, false sympathy with H.M.' prevailed.[49]

Wilhelm was thus quite unaware of the danger when he stated that he fully expected Eulenburg to come to the Berlin Schloss on 18 January 1907 to be ceremonially received into the chapter of the Order of the Black Eagle. Eulenburg's decision to accept the invitation remains incomprehensible, since his reappearance at court would inevitably provoke Harden into renewing his attacks. And promptly on 2 February 1907 an accusation appeared in the *Zukunft* that Eulenburg, together with the French diplomat Lecomte – 'who as we know does not have to rely on the front entrance' – had put pressure on the Kaiser to give way in the Moroccan crisis.[50] The Prince hurried back to Lake Geneva, but only for a few weeks. His return from Switzerland in April 1907 proved disastrous for him, his family, his friends and not least the Hohenzollern monarchy, for it triggered Harden's decision to deal the death-blow to the alleged 'vermin' surrounding the Kaiser.[51] 'Look at this Round Table', he exclaimed in the *Zukunft* of 13 April 1907. 'Philipp

Eulenburg, Lecomte (whom *le tout-Paris* has known since before yesterday), Kuno Moltke, Hohenau, the Chancellor's Civil Adjutant Below. They do not dream of setting the world on fire; they are quite warm enough already.'[52] Two weeks later Harden's campaign reached its climax with the clearest allusion yet to Eulenburg's homosexuality. In an article of 27 April entitled 'Roulette' he denounced Wilhelm II's recent decision to confer the highest Prussian order of the Black Eagle on Prince Albert of Monaco. It was incredible, he wrote, that this 'prince of gambling-dens' and owner of the 'casino also world-famous as a female flesh market' should have spent ten days as the guest of the Kaiser and had now also received the Order of the Black Eagle. 'But this is a damned serious matter, is it not?' he stormed. 'Prince Friedrich Heinrich of Prussia had to renounce the Grand Mastership of the Order of St John of Jerusalem because he suffers from a hereditary perversion of the sexual drive. Are the statutes of the chapter of the Black Eagle more lenient? Among its members is at least One whose *vita sexualis* is no more wholesome than that of the banned Prince. And now there is to be One among them who tolerates the largest gaming room and the biggest whore-market in Europe and earns a rich return on both.'[53]

THE BANISHMENT OF KUNO MOLTKE AND PHILIPP EULENBURG FROM COURT

Although the danger that these accusations represented for the Kaiser and the monarchy was obvious, even now Bülow still refused to inform Wilhelm II of the article.[54] Questioned later in the Reichstag about this omission, the Reich Chancellor explained that he had taken no action because 'it was not until the spring of this year that any real or even plausible evidence' had been brought to his knowledge. Besides, it had not been the Reich Chancellor's duty but that of senior courtiers to warn the monarch of such attacks.[55] More flagrant testimony to the irresponsible attitude of the 'principal adviser to the Crown' can scarcely be imagined. It is true, however, that the Chancellor now instituted enquiries about Eulenburg through Count Bogdan von Hutten-Czapski of the Berlin police, from which it emerged that only recently Prince Eulenburg had 'slept with a rent boy in a hotel in Berlin'. After that he realised, he claimed, that Eulenburg was 'beyond saving'.[56]

Harden, as always alarmingly well-informed about events in the Kaiser's entourage, gloated over the 'laughable' news that the court had 'talked of nothing but "Roulette" for three days'.[57] There as in the Wilhelmstrasse helpless indecision, cowardice and neglect of duty prevailed. Even the elderly and infirm Chief of the Civil Cabinet, Hermann von Lucanus, who had little to lose, said not a word to the Kaiser.[58] Adjutant-General von Plessen, the Chief of the Military Cabinet, General von Hülsen-Haeseler, and the Minister of War, General von Einem, agreed that they should first speak to the two army officers, Wilhelm Hohenau and Kuno Moltke, and then report to the Kaiser. With regard to Eulenburg, who was still officially listed as a diplomat, the three generals enquired of the 'competent authority' whether 'anything' was known against the Prince. And since the response was negative they too, as the Kaiser's most senior military advisers, left their Supreme War Lord in the dark about the accusations raised against his best friend.[59]

Plessen, as Commandant of the imperial headquarters, interviewed Hohenau and Moltke on 1 May 1907. The following day, on the advice of Hülsen, the young Crown Prince showed his father the articles in Harden's *Zukunft* of 13 and 27 April.[60] The Kaiser, who supposedly knew nothing of such things and treated them as 'a crime',[61] was thunderstruck. 'Never in my life shall I forget my father's distraught, horrified face, staring at me in bewilderment as I talked to him in the garden of the Marmorpalais about the misdemeanours of his close friends', the Crown Prince recalled years later.[62] After his son had broken the news to him, it seems, 'H.M. did not want to believe it at first but in the end could not close his mind to the evidence.'[63] On 4 May 1907 Admiral von Müller had 'a long conversation about the consequences of the revelations in the Zukunft (Hohenau, Moltke, Prince Eulenburg)' with the Kaiser and recorded afterwards that the monarch had been 'very agitated'.[64] Harden was able to inform Holstein that 'H.M. is said to be angry with Ph. and to have demanded that he and Kuno clear themselves without delay.'[65] The Kaiser, it was said, was 'not exactly delighted' at the public commendation of the Crown Prince for having brought the attacks on the Liebenberg Circle to his attention.[66]

While Hohenau fled abroad Kuno Moltke, after sounding out Harden to no avail, felt compelled to ask the Kaiser to release him from his post as City Commandant.[67] Although he had assured Plessen that he had never had sexual dealings with men, he took the view 'that a person who had to suffer under such grave suspicions' could not remain 'in the Kaiser's immediate entourage'. 'Without a farewell audience, without a handshake' the General à la suite and Flügeladjutant who had belonged to Wilhelm II's most intimate circle of friends for fourteen years was suspended by Cabinet order on 24 May 1907.[68] His resignation was of course seen everywhere as an admission of guilt. Müller, to whom Moltke had often turned in his distress, was dumbfounded at this decision by the Kaiser, which he described as 'incomprehensible', for as a result Harden had come out of the affair 'as the victor'.[69] Hereditary Prince Bernhard of Saxe-Meiningen, Wilhelm's brother-in-law, wrote to his father after a visit to Berlin: 'The things that are happening here in the Kaiser's entourage are really alarming. His friend Count Kuno Moltke suddenly dismissed, likewise his Adjutant-General of many years, Willy Hohenau, his other friend Count [sic] Eulenburg fallen from grace, and in fact no one really knows why. The truth of what is rumoured cannot be checked: that the insinuations in an article in the Zukunft should in fact be the reason sounds so bizarre that it is difficult to believe. After all, one cannot base a charge on a malicious remark in a sensational article in the Zukunft, at any rate one cannot pass sentence, even if only a moral one, without having investigated the matter thoroughly. But nobody knows whether such an investigation has been thoroughly and objectively carried out. At the moment it all looks like heartlessly arbitrary behaviour.'[70]

The fall of Philipp Eulenburg, who as the leading figure in the Liebenberg Round Table was regarded as 'the most compromised',[71] now followed inexorably. On 4 May 1907 Wilhelm instructed his Adjutant-General, Gustav von Kessel, Eulenburg's cousin, to give the Prince an ultimatum. 'His Majesty the Kaiser and King has commanded me to write to you to say that the All-Highest Person expects to hear whether you have taken steps, and if so what steps, to start a legal action against certain suspicions expressed in one of the recent articles in the "Zukunft". It is said to contain, among other things, insinuations against a Knight of the High Order of the Black Eagle. His Majesty drew most particular attention to this and awaits an explanation as to whether you consider yourself beyond reproach with regard to these allusions. I am not familiar with the articles themselves. Your report is to be sent direct to His Majesty.'[72] To this harsh 'command' from the Kaiser Eulenburg replied: 'I declare to Yr. Majesty *that I consider myself beyond reproach*. I believe I may also assume that more than 20 years of life together and the extremely thorough knowledge of my nature and character which Your Majesty's perspicacious mind possesses *cannot* ever have allowed any doubt to arise on this score. Among the first steps which I have had to take in this wretched business was the challenge I issued to the man who in my opinion was the *real* instigator of those malicious attacks, Herr von Holstein. This very strong challenge was withdrawn after the insult received from Herr von Holstein had been atoned for in an agreed manner. That I have hitherto hesitated to react to the gibes of the Zukunft – which are *calculated* to provoke a politically scandalous lawsuit – was due *purely* to political considerations. I was described as the person who nourished Yr. Majesty's "autocratic cravings" (!), and I was linked with so many questions of a *delicate* political kind that I saw it as my *duty* towards Yr. Majesty and Yr. Majesty's Government to overlook many a personal attack in order to avoid *such* a lawsuit. Now it seems that recently, in issues of the *Zukunft* that I have not read – for I am lying in bed completely paralysed by neuritis (*inflammation* of the nerves) in both feet and knees – the personal attacks on me have taken on a malicious character. Under these circumstances I am indeed no longer in a position to maintain my silence. This is made easier for me since Yr. Majesty is willing to disregard the political consequences of a possible lawsuit. Nevertheless it appears appropriate, since I am still in Your Majesty's active service, for me to ask for disciplinary proceedings against myself. These are to take place in the next few days.'[73]

The Kaiser received this letter while he was attending the funeral of his uncle Grand Duke Friedrich I of Baden in Karlsruhe.[74] As reported to Eulenburg by his cousin August, Wilhelm spoke to him 'very kindly about the sad situation in which you find yourself, and also seemed to be in favour of the disciplinary investigation, for he completely accepted the information you gave in the report requested through Kessel'.[75] Only a few days later, however, Kaiser Wilhelm's attitude towards Eulenburg and Moltke had already changed again. On 23 May 1907 Harden heard from Emil Rathenau that 'H.M. says he doesn't want to see Phili any more and intends to find new people with whom to associate.'[76] A week later the Chief of the Naval Cabinet noted with dismay the 'terribly harsh' manner in which the Kaiser had spoken 'about the Moltke–Eulenburg case'.[77] Although at first he had been willing to content himself with barring Eulenburg from court and refused to demand the return of the Order of the Black Eagle, Wilhelm now decided to take this more rigorous step.[78] Bülow attributed the hardening of the Kaiser's attitude to the two Cabinet chiefs, Hülsen and Lucanus, and to the military retinue under Plessen.[79] On 1 June Harden discovered that the '*maison militaire* etc. is raving, wants to take away Kuno's uniform and Phili's Black Eagle'.[80] The former Chief of the Military Cabinet, Field Marshal von Hahnke, now Chancellor of the High Order of the Black Eagle, is said to have remarked that it was to Harden's credit that he had opened 'this abscess', and Hülsen even considered quitting the court so as to be free to tell the truth about Eulenburg.[81]

Possibly Wilhelm's decision to drop his intimate friends in such a 'heartlessly arbitrary' way was influenced by the fear that he might himself be suspected of having homosexual tendencies.[82] On the other hand we should not lose sight of the proven fact that Eulenburg, Moltke and other members of the Round Table did indeed harbour such tendencies and many – Eulenburg and Hohenau certainly – had actively indulged them. Of this the members of the Kaiser's military entourage were now quite convinced, and the court generals whom the Eulenburg camp criticised as 'wretched ... traitors',

Kessel, Hülsen-Haeseler, Plessen, Hahnke and Einem, were right to see the Liebenbergers' protestations of innocence as mere bluff. They advised the Kaiser to sever his ties with the accused men as quickly as possible in the interests of the monarchy.[83]

The loss of his two friends, Eulenburg and Moltke, hit the Kaiser particularly hard because other members of the so-called Round Table, as for instance Emil Count Görtz, felt compelled to take cover too.[84] In their place Wilhelm resolved to look for 'new people with whom to associate',[85] and his choice fell in the first instance upon the Badenese–Austrian grand seigneur Max Egon II Prince zu Fürstenberg, who was as keen as the military entourage to turn the monarch against those who had enjoyed the imperial favour before him.[86]

'AN ABOMINABLY CALLOUS ACT': THE KAISER'S ULTIMATUM

Whoever it was who influenced the Kaiser in this direction, the effect was lethal. Wilhelm sent word to the Reich Chancellor that he thought him 'too good-natured towards Eulenburg, not firm enough' and it was high time to 'pull himself together'.[87] On 12 May 1907 Eulenburg had written to Bülow reminding him of their long-standing friendship and begging him for his help. 'A press trial will bear evil fruit and it is what our enemies want. His Majesty is no doubt scarcely aware of the consequences. I feel myself to be untouched by the filth into which they want to drag me and with which they want to besmirch His Majesty . . . I am counting on your support insofar as your position allows you to give it. . . . If I claim anything for myself before God, it is my loyalty to you – and my belief in your loyalty, of which no one has been able to rob me. How much you have done for me – how much I have done for you! And how could I commit treachery towards the man I consider as the only possible Reich Chancellor – towards my friend?'[88]

Although the Chancellor assured Eulenburg of his sympathy,[89] he knew only too well that unless he 'cleared off' abroad, Eulenburg was irretrievably lost. Neither on political nor on personal grounds did Bülow have any intention of protecting his former friend and patron. Following the Kaiser's order to him to 'pull himself together' Bülow sent Eulenburg an imperial ultimatum which could hardly have been more heartless and which struck Eulenburg as 'an abominably callous act'.[90] On 31 May 1907 the Reich Chancellor wrote to him: 'I am commanded by His Majesty the Kaiser and King to make the following communication to Your Excellency: 1. His Majesty has learnt that Your Excellency was the subject of an attack in the "Zukunft" as early as in November last year and took no action against it, but contacted Herr Harden privately with the request that he abstain from further attacks.

In contradiction of this Your Excellency assured His Majesty in two letters at the beginning and at the end of May that you had no knowledge of the "Zukunft", did not read it and therefore did not know what was in it. 2. This, together with the circumstance that so far nothing has happened in response to the attack in the "Zukunft" of 27 April, leads His Majesty the Kaiser to suppose that Herr Harden is in possession of letters from you which make it impossible for you to take proceedings against him; these letters, in His Majesty's opinion, may perhaps have come from your correspondence with Count Moltke which has been purloined from him and put into Herr Harden's hands. His Majesty has recently become aware of part of the contents of the correspondence and the All-Highest considers it so compromising that He is forced to draw His own conclusions. 3. It has *now* come to His Majesty's knowledge that among the guests invited to Liebenberg by Your Excellency there were gentlemen of dishonourable reputation, one of whom [Wendelstadt] could not be invited to dinner by the [Prussian] Royal Envoy in Munich for that reason. His Majesty is outraged that Your Excellency took so little care in the selection of your guests and thereby put the All-Highest himself in a shameful situation for a monarch. 4. His Majesty accordingly expects Your Excellency to request permission to retire forthwith. Furthermore His Majesty wishes, insofar as the accusations of perverse tendencies made against Your Excellency are untrue and your conscience with regard to His Majesty is completely free and clear, to be able to look forward to an unambiguous declaration to this effect from you, on the basis of which proceedings would be taken against Herr Harden. Otherwise His Majesty expects Your Excellency to return the Black Eagle Order without causing a stir and to go abroad. Bülow.'[91]

Harsh as this letter was, privately the Chancellor tried to persuade Harden to make concessions and to smooth Eulenburg's path towards a lengthy stay abroad. His primary concern, he asserted, was to protect the Crown from further damage.[92] He summoned Varnbüler to see him and 'passed on' to him, as Varnbüler recalled in his memoirs, 'with a painfully distressed expression [and] the usual assurances of friendship for Phili ... the incriminating evidence that was being reported to him from all sides, especially by General von Kessel who as a close relation was after all above suspicion, but which was also stored in the safes of the Auswärtiges Amt in secret reports from the political and vice police of Vienna, Munich and Berlin. – Supposedly so overwhelming that it would be virtually hopeless for Phili to contest it in open court, and that at the very least it would mean a disastrous scandal for the Kaiser, as his friend, and for the reputation of the state. He implored me to back up his advice to Phili, as a friend: to go to the South at once, on sick leave, and to stay there until the storm had calmed down and grass had grown over it all. It was immediately clear to me that such "grass" would never grow even over Phili's grave, that he would be admitting his guilt *urbi et orbi* by fleeing abroad, and in this way would really compromise his friend the Kaiser, and I told B[ülow] so.'[93]

Varnbüler's objection was indeed justified, but the friendly advice Bülow gave Eulenburg undoubtedly represented the only remaining possibility of escaping the far worse disaster of a scandalous trial. The compromise solution proposed by the Chancellor would have had every prospect of success, for with the removal of the Liebenberg clique from the Kaiser's entourage Harden had already achieved his actual goal. Politically he had 'undoubtedly won' the battle, the latter commented on 3 June 1907. It was now considered impossible 'that the group should ever regain influence'.[94] The 'bag' had been quite respectable, he wrote triumphantly in a letter to Holstein. 'Willi [Hohenau] und Tütü [Moltke] are out, Phili's resignation . . . will be accepted. Lecomte gone and discredited, everything savouring of Camarilla at least made much more difficult.' Bitterly Harden bewailed the fact that no one told the Kaiser of his willingness to keep quiet from now on.[95] After all, he had 'frightful material' in his possession and could 'make a scandal that would rock the world', he warned. 'The man closest to the throne besmirched for ever. I wanted to avoid it and have gone to the limits of self-renunciation.' That it had to come to this was Bülow's fault.[96]

Harden's letter to the public prosecutor's office in July 1908, when the scandal reached its climax with the arrest of Eulenburg, gives a shocking impression of the 'crushing' evidence that he believed he had uncovered in the course of his campaign. The Kaiser's best friend had 'associated with nothing but pederasts all his life', including Fritz von Farenheid, Lecomte, Johann Lónyay, Jan von Wendelstadt, Edgard von Wedel and the two counts Hohenau. In addition to this were: 'Bismarck's evidence. Hundreds of police records . . . [Eulenburg's] conduct from the Prenzlau report up to today. 2 oaths. Danby, Trost, Riedel. Are they all lying? Although it would have been in their interest to say the opposite? Hasn't E. served up dozens of lies to the court? . . . With this criminal every step is calculated; likewise with Herr Tütü.'[97] It may well be that Harden, with the self-righteousness of the zealot, tended to exaggerate. It is also true that many of the names and crimes he mentioned here were investigated only in the course of the next twelve months. But Eulenburg himself certainly knew what kind of a life he had led, what was at stake for him, his family, his friends and not least for the monarchy, if he denied everything and faced down the truth! In view of the socially destructive potential of an accusation of homosexuality – which could still have regrettable repercussions in Germany until only a few years ago – in Wilhelmine society, the fact that this romantic poet–prince still indignantly rejected the only way he could have saved himself, by going abroad as inconspicuously as possible, seems to indicate a dangerous refusal to confront reality.

When Varnbüler delivered the imperial ultimatum, signed by Bülow, to Eulenburg at Liebenberg at the beginning of June 1907, in the presence of his legal adviser Karl Laemmel, and confronted him with the incriminating evidence produced by the Chancellor, Eulenburg 'categorically refused Bülow's demand that he "clear off" abroad'. He denied the accusations against him so resolutely, 'without hesitation or reflection', that Varnbüler, as he later maintained in his memoirs, was 'convinced of his innocence'.[98] Varnbüler's retrospective description cannot be taken quite literally, for he had been an intimate friend of Eulenburg and Moltke since their student days together in Leipzig and Strasbourg, and he of course knew as much as anyone about their sexual orientation. He had received letters from 'Tütü' Moltke, his 'Dachs', discussing 'old Philine', and like his two friends he, too, had called the Kaiser 'das Liebchen' in his letters.[99] But neither in June 1907 nor a year later, when his friend's castles in the air had long since vanished, was Varnbüler able to counteract Eulenburg's 'poetic fantasies'. In June 1908 he confided to his sister, Baroness von Spitzemberg, 'such strange things about Eulenburg' that she no longer had any doubt about his 'guilt', although she thought it possible that he 'truly and honestly' considered himself innocent.[100] Even after the catastrophe of his arrest in May 1908 Eulenburg clung to the 'fiction', as Varnbüler wrote to Moltke, 'that he is innocent and that I believe this – and I accept the fiction even though I do not believe it'.[101]

In his reply to Bülow of 4 June 1907, which he asked to be submitted to the Kaiser 'in full', Eulenburg made a series of excuses and then dealt with the central question of his homosexual inclinations. He was willing to answer this question only on the assumption, he wrote, 'that it has come direct from His Majesty, and that Your Excellency has merely conveyed it to me. For I should be compelled to reject such a question from anyone other than His Majesty as a most serious insult. On the above-mentioned assumption, however, although I have already given a direct answer to what was in effect the same question in my letter of 5 May, I wish to declare again here, in order to remove any further doubt, that my conscience with regard to perverse inclinations is completely free and clear.' Although he believed that he had thus refuted the reasons put forward by the Kaiser for his resignation, he had to recognise that he 'no longer possessed His Majesty's confidence' and therefore asked to be allowed to go into retirement.[102]

In a final letter to Bülow Eulenburg claimed that Wilhelm's 'withdrawal of his friendship' had not really surprised him. 'To lose my friend of many years

... was not the cruel disappointment which you perhaps assumed it would be for me, for I was only too familiar with the sailor who goes on putting on "oilskins" long after it is necessary. The disappointment lay only in the odious manner of killing me off. And yet I am objective enough to understand that a monarch would wish to get rid of an uncomfortable friend as soon as possible, given the distasteful turn my affairs ... took. For me the danger lies in the fact that I must now be as guilty and as worthless as possible for him so that he can publicly account for the way he has acted.' In spite of the Kaiser's 'abominable' ultimatum of 31 May which the Chancellor had signed, Eulenburg again begged Bülow to give him 'the protection of a friend' and praised his efforts to limit the scandal. He asserted that it was 'absolutely right', in his view, 'that you allowed these fantastic mistakes to be made without causing a crisis. You would only have immeasurably enhanced the position of the Generals, and as their influence has grown so great ... we could easily have had a Reich Chancellor Hülsen. You are leading us through the rapids in the only possible way and if you accomplish it, it will be a patriotic deed. From this you can see, beloved Bernhard, *how* I see the situation and how far I am from having taken offence at your participation in my final act.'[103] Whether this appeal for the Reich Chancellor's protection had any effect at all has been called into question, with good reason in view of Bülow's ambiguous attitude.[104]

THE FIRST MOLTKE–HARDEN TRIAL

Despite his constant protestations of innocence Eulenburg knew very well that he must at all costs avoid a trial in which he would have to make a declaration under oath regarding his sexual orientation. Instead of suing Harden, therefore, he instituted proceedings against himself on 1 June 1907 at the public prosecutor's office in neighbouring Prenzlau, for an infringement of § 175 of the criminal law.[105] This case, which was tried on 15 June 1907, was universally recognised as mere 'hocuspocus' and did nothing to bring about the desired 'purification', particularly as Harden was able to declare that he had never accused Eulenburg of any offence which would have been punishable under § 175.[106]

The efforts of Eulenburg, Bülow and others to avoid a disastrous series of scandalous trials failed because of Kuno Moltke. The General had been driven into a corner by Wilhelm II's over-hasty and ill-considered demand that he be 'either cleansed or stoned',[107] by the narrow-mindedness of his military superiors, who turned down an investigation by disciplinary tribunal and court martial, and finally by Harden's refusal to accept his challenge to a duel. Instead, he sued the journalist for libel.[108] In spite of Moltke's position as City

Commandant of Berlin, the public prosecutor's office, apparently with the approval of both the Kaiser and the Chancellor, denied that the prosecution of Harden was in the public interest so that in the end Moltke was forced to take the highly risky course of a private prosecution.[109] The Kaiser's sister Charlotte exclaimed in horror when she heard of the General's intention: 'Have these people gone mad? Do they really want to dispute this? The whole world knows about it.'[110] Harden quickly got to hear of this remark by the Hereditary Princess and, as we have seen, threatened to bring before the court those 'who say: Is it possible that anyone still disputes it at all!'[111]

The hearing began on 23 October 1907 before lay assessors in Moabit, presided over by a young district court judge and including a butcher and a dairyman. Although the admission tickets had run out days before, journalists were able to report in detail on the sensational revelations, with the result that the building was soon besieged by hundreds of curious spectators. The trial thus gave Harden, who was now bent on ruthless self-justification, the opportunity to raise publicly the 'very serious, important question for the whole of Germany', of 'whether the friends and advisers of the German Kaiser are worthy of their position'.[112] Both for Moltke and for Eulenburg the evidence of the witness Lilly von Elbe, Moltke's divorced wife, whom Harden had met in 1902 through Schweninger, proved absolutely catastrophic. She stated under oath that Moltke had described the institution of marriage as a 'filthy business' and the marital bedchamber as 'nothing but an institution for rape'; a woman was 'no more than a lavatory'. On the other hand her former husband, she said, had loved his male friends passionately, and above all Eulenburg, who had been his superior as ambassador in Vienna from 1897 until 1899. He had used pet names for Eulenburg such as 'my soul', 'my dear old boy', 'my only Dachs'. 'One day', as she recalled, 'Count Philipp Eulenburg had left his handkerchief behind in Count Moltke's room after a visit. When Count Moltke found the handkerchief he pressed it ardently to his lips and said "My soul! My love!"' (See Figure 21.) After his separation from her in November 1898 Moltke had said he wanted to go back to court as a Flügeladjutant, for 'Phili' needed someone close to the Kaiser in order to be kept well informed. Eulenburg and he had formed a ring around the Kaiser into which no one else could enter.[113]

It was this political aspect in particular that Harden made the core of his defence. His lawyer, Max Bernstein, declared to the court that his client had written his articles to fight 'against a state of affairs that was worth fighting against, and that it is to his credit if these men no longer have any political influence, if this state of affairs no longer exists. It was a feature of this state of affairs ... that the gentlemen who surrounded the All-Highest person were

Neues preußisches Wappen
(Liebenberger Entwurf)

A. Weisgerber (München)

Figure 21 'Prussia's new coat-of-arms.' An embarrassed response to the Moltke–
Harden trials. Philipp Eulenburg is depicted as the harpist, with Kuno
Moltke holding Eulenburg's monogrammed handkerchief to his lips

pederasts. Herr Harden did not say that in his articles, for at that time it was
not necessary to say that. I say it now ... I do not claim that the plaintiff
[Kuno Moltke] participated actively in these pursuits, but the plaintiff is the
only one in this group of whom I do not claim it. I do claim of the plaintiff,
however, that the nature of the other gentlemen can scarcely have escaped his
notice.' Bernstein left open the question of whether or not he numbered
Eulenburg among the active homosexuals; but he asserted 'that already at
the time when Prince Eulenburg was in Vienna, general rumours about his
homosexual disposition were in circulation' and that Moltke knew of them too.
He announced his intention of summoning as witnesses not only the sexologist
Magnus Hirschfeld but also the Kaiser's Adjutant-General von Kessel, the
Chief of the Military Cabinet Count von Hülsen-Haeseler and the Reich
Chancellor. He also wished to question Eulenburg under oath.[114]

The court decided to proceed to hearing the evidence concerning 'whether pederasty was practised in the circle of friends to which Prince Eulenburg, Count Wilhelm Hohenau and the plaintiff belonged'![115] The former Guards cuirassier Bollhardt testified that he believed he had recognised not only Hohenau but also Kuno Moltke and Eulenburg among the participants in the homosexual orgies in Count Lynar's Villa Adler, but that he could not be quite sure.[116] Eulenburg was summoned but did not appear, although he was staying – supposedly seriously ill – at his Berlin residence not far from the courtroom. Bernstein drew the obvious conclusion that Eulenburg wanted at all costs to avoid giving evidence under oath, in spite of the fact that he could have testified in defence of his friend Moltke. When the court decided to question the Prince on his sickbed and to confront him with Bollhardt there, Harden's lawyer declared bluntly: 'Prince Philipp Eulenburg is not giving evidence because he is afraid of the law that decrees imprisonment for perjury! That is why he has not appeared here and also why he does not want to see the witness Bollhardt. Everything else is pretence, show, play-acting!'[117] Bernstein had tracked down possible witnesses in the Munich area and now, menacingly, he issued a stern warning to Eulenburg: 'If Prince Philipp zu Eulenburg denies under oath that he has homosexual tendencies and that he has actively indulged these tendencies, I shall attempt to prove, by means of witnesses, that this assertion is untrue.' Furthermore he would be able to cite numerous comments known to have been made by Bismarck, who had 'described Prince Eulenburg in the most unmistakable way as a pederast'.[118]

Predictably, in his summing-up Bernstein interpreted the fact that Kaiser Wilhelm had dropped his two friends without listening to their side of the story as proof that he was convinced of their 'guilt'.[119] Harden, the lawyer made clear, had evidence that they had called the Kaiser 'das Liebchen' in their letters. 'I believe I can almost state it as a fact that Prince Eulenburg is a pederast', he exclaimed, 'and Herr Harden is right to wish to liberate the Kaiser from such an entourage'. Alluding to a line by Schiller, he continued: 'The singer should go with the King but the pederast should not go with the King! ... Anyone of such a disposition must be removed from His Majesty's entourage! ... The Kaiser should and must have full-blooded men around him, for otherwise we shall find ourselves with the most reprehensible body of courtiers in the German Reich, and may heaven preserve us all from that ... Make a sharp distinction between men like Eulenburg, Hohenau, Moltke and the men of Germany. Then you will be in tune with the general feeling!'[120] On 29 October 1907 the court delivered its crushing verdict: Harden had produced proof of the truth, he was not guilty of repeated libel of Moltke and was acquitted; costs were awarded against Moltke.[121] A cheering crowd carried Harden shoulder-high out of the courthouse.

'DREADFUL BOUTS OF MENTAL DEPRESSION': THE KAISER'S REACTION TO THE TRIAL

The monarchy was shaken to its very foundations not only by the verdict against the Kaiser's friend and Flügeladjutant but also, and above all, by the details which had emerged in the course of the trial about practices among Wilhelm II's closest entourage.[122] Lieutenant-Commander Albert Hopman expressed the hope that the trial, which had created such a sensation throughout the world, would have a 'thoroughly cleansing' effect and would ultimately bring about 'a gradual change in our constitution towards a purely parliamentary system', for which he considered the German people were gradually becoming ready.[123] Zedlitz looked back with horror on the luckless handling of the scandal, which he regarded as characteristic of the dysfunctionality of the Reich government in general. In his view 'we could not have settled the whole affair in a more foolish and compromising manner. I have no hesitation in saying that if someone had offered a prize for dealing with this scandalous business in the least skilful and most compromising way for the ruling house, the court and also the army, the prize would have to go to whoever gave the orders for what we actually did.' The handling of the scandals had shown clearly 'that we have already gone so far along the road to catastrophe that our state organism, although actually well developed, could not prevent such a moral collapse . . . Lack of a sense of responsibility and nervous toadyism have also produced a state of affairs in which the full extent of the helplessness and incompetence at work here has not been recognised.'[124]

As early as on the first day of the trial the head of the Reich Chancellery, Friedrich Wilhelm von Loebell, reported to the Chancellor that 'the Harden case is taking a highly unfavourable course for Count Moltke. The descriptions of scenes from the Count's married life given in completely open hearing make his abnormality look proven and are destroying him personally. Very strong evidence is also being produced of the political influence of the Round Table. Among other things constant reports from Moltke to Eulenburg about everything happening at court in both the political and the personal sphere. Remarks in letters: "We are forming a tight circle around the Kaiser; no one can get to him without us" etc. have been read out.'[125] Bülow sought an audience of the Kaiser and expressed his deep disapproval of the course the trial was taking. 'The scandalous revelations that are now occupying the thoughts of the sensation-hungry public can best be overcome', he declared, 'by our pursuing a firm and dignified policy that will lift the nation out of this morass and guide it to great ends'.[126]

Wilhelm II, too, had followed the trial day in and day out. The Reichstag stenographer, Neufort, had kept a shorthand record of the proceedings which formed the basis of daily reports to the Kaiser.[127] Extracts from the press at home and abroad were provided for him. At the very outset he had exclaimed despairingly: 'Why didn't that feeble Kuno behave like a brave officer and defend his honour at once? Then we should not have had this horrible mess.'[128] When the trial came to an end Zedlitz commented: 'The Kaiser has been more deeply affected by the affair ... than anyone expected. He has followed the court hearings and in the process has heard things that were completely withheld from him before. While he usually assiduously avoids the truth when it might sound unpleasant to him, this time for once he was interested to hear everything. The effect on him has been quite profound, for the time being ... In general his mood, in accordance with his nature, expresses itself in extremes. He has moments when he is profoundly despondent and senses that the whole affair is a deep disgrace. Then when Prince Eulenburg and Count Moltke are momentarily in favour he has the fantastic idea that he must accord them a rehabilitation of a quite unprecedented kind. Then again, when he is very angry about a newspaper article that has been passed to him he thinks quite seriously of demanding a direct explanation and says with complete conviction: "If the newspapers don't stop it now I shall send a Flügeladjutant over and have an editor shot dead." In short he has, so to speak, lost control of himself.'[129] After the verdict was declared against Moltke, Kaiser Wilhelm suffered a nervous breakdown accompanied by 'dreadful bouts of mental depression' which even led to a temporary cancellation of the state visit to Britain that he had been planning to make for months.[130]

At the end of November 1907, while the Kaiser was recuperating on holiday at Highcliffe in the south of England, the court scandals of the past year came under discussion in the Reichstag. In contrast to the remarks he had made in the spring about a 'Camarilla' in the Kaiser's entourage, Bülow now declared: 'In order to flourish, the first prerequisite for this poisonous plant is surely the isolation and lack of independence of the monarch. Our Kaiser has certainly been criticised sometimes, just as everyone is criticised for one thing or another; but that he isolates himself from contact with others and has no will of his own is something of which, to the best of my knowledge, he has never been accused. I think, therefore, that it is high time to put an end to the gossip and murmurs and whispers about camarillas.'[131] Bülow's assertions were regarded by many deputies as mere 'playing with words'. The south German democrat Friedrich Payer declared that nothing could hide the fact 'that for years the Kaiser's entourage has included influential persons whom we consider second-rate because of their personality or the company they keep'. For the SPD August Bebel drew attention to the views held by Bismarck on Eulenburg and his circle of friends, as revealed at the trial. 'The men behind in both senses, including physically, sit at Liebenberg. These people surround the Kaiser and isolate him. The Kaiser believes that no one influences him . . . That is true for his official advisers; but these people . . . these male weaklings keep everything away from him as they see fit. The worst thing is that such people always share their ruling Master's opinion . . . When the Kaiser says something and looks around him he sees nothing but worshipping faces gazing at him. They always tell him that he is right and thus they create a counterweight to the advisers whose duty it is to oppose him.' Bebel recalled the Liebenbergers' intrigues against Bülow in the autumn of 1906. In his eyes 'such a state of affairs' was 'shaming for Germany'; in a country with parliamentary government such 'backstairs business' would be unthinkable. While the Social Democrat pointed out that § 175 was untenable and demanded its abolition, the leader of the largely Catholic Centre party, Martin Spahn, expressed indignation at the facts which had come to light during the Moltke–Harden trial, 'of which one can only say that they correspond to the moral scenery of heathen Rome'. The anti-Semite Liebermann von Sonnenberg thought fit to demand that all homosexuals be dispatched to a 'South Sea colony supervised by well-paid, strong-armed washerwomen'. Representatives of the parties of the Right protested against the impression which the trial had created, above all abroad, of a general moral decline. There could certainly be no question, Bassermann declared for the National Liberals, 'that our German people, our German officer corps, our German aristocracy are morally corrupt and degenerate'. Bülow and the War Minister, General von Einem, also strongly repudiated this implication, 'as if the German people and the German army were not entirely healthy at their innermost core'. It would be unjust and foolish to infer 'corruption of the aristocracy and contamination of the army' from the misdemeanours of individual members of the higher social classes, the Chancellor asserted.[132]

On his return from England the Kaiser showed himself anything but appreciative of the difficulty the Reich government had faced in dealing with the universal indignation in the Reichstag. He was, as Zedlitz recorded on 18 December 1907, 'still very aroused about the Harden trial'. He took offence at the openness with which the revelations had been discussed in parliament and again reproached Bülow, who in his opinion should have prevented the debate altogether, with 'lack of energy and skill'. 'All the Kaiser's resentment over the behaviour of the people's representatives in this case burst out', the

Hofmarschall recorded, 'when he broke off the conversation . . . and said as he left . . . "And one is expected to govern such a rabble. They are absolutely not ready for a constitution."'[133] But the storm that had already caused such enormous damage was very far from over.

BÜLOW AND THE ADOLF BRAND TRIAL

After the catastrophic outcome of the Moltke trial influential people again tried to bring about a settlement. 'In the interests of the Kaiser and of the Fatherland we must prevent a repetition of this trial', urged the former Minister of Agriculture, General Viktor von Podbielski. 'Who will stem the flood once passions are unleashed?'[134] But the lesson provided by the trial — that the revelations about conditions at the Hohenzollern court had had a far worse effect than the unfavourable outcome for the plaintiff — was not learnt; instead, the steamroller of litigation rolled inexorably onwards, and this time with strong support from the state, which adopted for itself the slogan attributed to the Kaiser: 'No turning back until the fellow [Harden] is in jail.'[135] When Kuno Moltke lodged an appeal against the verdict on 31 October 1907 the public prosecutor's office suddenly accepted the public interest argument it had previously rejected and took over the prosecution against Harden. Three weeks later Eulenburg gave notice of legal proceedings against Harden and Bernstein on the grounds of the 'most gravely slanderous remarks and insults' that they had uttered in the first Moltke trial.[136]

As if all this were not more than enough, on 6 November 1907 another sensational trial began in Berlin, and once again the question of homosexuality in the highest circles was the central issue. The writer Adolf Brand, an ardent pioneering champion of gay rights, had asserted in a pamphlet that the Reich Chancellor Prince von Bülow was 'in exactly the same situation as Prince Eulenburg' and had himself been saddled with a blackmail episode years ago. Several of Bülow's closest colleagues in the Reich Chancellery and in Norderney — Brand named the officials Max Scheefer, Paul von Below-Schlatau and William Seeband — were homosexual and in particular Scheefer was the Chancellor's 'better half' and 'inseparable companion'.[137] Brand's accusations began to look ominous for Bülow when Below-Schlatau was forced to flee abroad because of Harden's attacks.[138]

Bülow reacted to Brand's 'shameless' claims with a vehemence which in the opinion of one of his biographers sounded like 'a declaration of war on his alter ego'.[139] The Chancellor assured his close friend Friedrich Wilhelm von Loebell, the Chief of the Reich Chancellery, on 27 September 1907 that to him 'every homosexual inclination has been not only disgusting but simply incomprehensible all my life. I have never, even only in my thoughts, felt that kind of repugnant impulse in any form or to any degree whatever.'[140] On the other hand Brand, as it turned out, was in possession of highly explosive information about Bülow's double life while he was ambassador in Rome. He referred to witnesses from the Roman gay community who would testify that Bülow moved in their circles in the 1890s and had been known among them by the nickname Concettina. Max Scheefer, now a Privy Councillor, had already been his constant companion at that time, and had exchanged 'rapturous words, tender embraces, pressing hands, looks' with him. Brand went on to affirm that the Roman police knew of Bülow's intimate relations with Scheefer and therefore had him listed as a homosexual. In Rome Bülow seems, as Peter Winzen was able to establish on the basis of the personnel records of the Auswärtiges Amt, 'to have lived out his homosexual tendencies with a maximum degree of anonymity. Since mid-1895 he was always accompanied in this by Max Scheefer, who as a 30-year-old secretary in a railway company had joined the staff of the Auswärtiges Amt in May of that year and had worked at the German embassy in Rome since 1 August ... Scheefer was to follow his master to Berlin two years later and to have a brilliant career as Private Secretary to the Reich Chancellor.'[141]

With the full force of state power behind him the Reich Chancellor succeeded, in a case before the second criminal division of the Berlin district court on 6 November 1907, in producing proof that 'all and every homosexual inclination, disposition and feeling in every form and every degree' was foreign to his nature.[142] Scheefer also denied under oath that he had had intimate relations with Bülow. Brand was given the maximum penalty of eighteen months' imprisonment, but he had to be released early because of illness, emigrating to Switzerland. Scheefer contemplated suicide and was eventually compensated by Bülow with the post of Vice-Consul in Trieste.[143] Such a solution had already suggested itself because Scheefer was making ominous claims that William Seeband was an intimate friend of Eulenburg's Private Secretary Karl Kistler, and that they called each 'Du' and exchanged kisses; just as he had brought Kuno Moltke to the Kaiser's court as an informant, so Eulenburg had infiltrated Seeband into the closest circle around the Chancellor.[144]

As the second volume of this biography and the more recent studies by Peter Winzen have shown, Bülow's relations with Eulenburg and his circle of friends reached far back into the past and were a great deal more intimate and intertwined than he was now willing to admit. Bülow's younger brother Alfred had been a very close friend of Eulenburg and Varnbüler since their student days in Strasbourg;[145] another brother, the military attaché

Karl Ulrich, was generally known to be a homosexual,[146] and a nephew of the Chancellor with the same name had shared an apartment in Berlin with Edmund Jaroljmek, the 'former darling and private secretary of Prince Eulenburg', who had run away with Eulenburg's daughter Augusta ('Lycki') and had supplied Harden with letters stolen from his father-in-law.[147] With the same deliberation which Bülow had shown in 1886, in marrying the divorced Countess 'Contessina' Dönhoff, a good friend of Crown Princess Victoria, (see Figure 22) he revealed himself to Eulenburg as a 'sisterly' kindred spirit from 1892 at the latest, and proffered himself as the man who would know how to put Eulenburg's ideals into practice. When Eulenburg suggested to his 'old Bernhard', whom he loved 'with all his heart' in 1893 that they call each other 'Du', the future secretary of state and Reich Chancellor wrote to his 'dearest Philipp' that they shared 'a true inward affinity' because 'we think and feel the same in the depths of our being ... As sisters our souls once rose from the mysterious fount of all being; only we were given different sheaths and different coloured wings.' He too, Bülow, loved Eulenburg 'with his whole soul'. Together they would be able to guide Kaiser and Reich on to the right path.[148]

Bülow owed his meteoric political ascent entirely to the backing which Eulenburg had given him with the Kaiser, but in order to survive as Reich Chancellor he allowed his patron to be brought down by the Brand trial and on 6 November 1907 portrayed him publicly as a homosexual. Under oath Bülow stated that he had certainly known Eulenburg 'for a very long time and ... very well', but 'unfavourable rumours' had not reached his ears 'until the last few years'.[149] Eulenburg, summoned as a witness, now could not avoid taking an oath, which he had previously done everything in his power to avoid. He declared 'quite categorically' that he had never in his life been 'guilty of criminal acts in relation to § 175'.[150] In saying this he had not really committed perjury, for not all homosexual acts were punishable offences, but as events would prove, he had walked into a fatal trap.

'HE'S GONE!' THE KAISER AND EULENBURG'S END

In the presence of numerous journalists, both German and foreign, the second *Moltke* v. *Harden* trial began on 19 December 1907 at Moabit.[151] To Wilhelm II's horror it even looked for a time as if his eldest sister Charlotte and her husband Bernhard, Hereditary Prince of Saxe-Meiningen, might be summoned.[152] The Kaiser complained furiously in a letter to Houston Stewart Chamberlain soon after the case began: 'A close circle of friends that is suddenly broken up through Jewish impudence, slander and lies. To have to

Figure 22 Prince and Princess von Bülow

see one's friends' names dragged through the dirt of all the gutters of Europe for months on end and not to be able or allowed to help them is frightful!' The 'mud' was being flung 'as high as the rooftops', he raged, and even the Reichstag had 'wallowed in it with relish like swine in the muck!'[153]

Under oath the apparently seriously ill Eulenburg, called as a witness, repeated his assertion that he had never offended against § 175 of the criminal law. This statement was just what Bernstein had been waiting for. The lawyer insistently asked the Prince whether this declaration under oath 'also meant that he had never committed homosexual acts at all, even unpunishable ones'. Bernstein specifically named Georg Riedel and Jakob Ernst, who would testify that they and Eulenburg had masturbated together. Eulenburg, still under oath, nevertheless continued to deny ever having indulged in such 'filthy acts'.[154] Not least as a result of this statement, on 3 January 1908 Moltke was declared 'morally pure' and 'untainted' and Harden crushingly condemned to four months' imprisonment and the reimbursement of the costs of the trial.[155] Suddenly Eulenburg had become the innocent victim. Baroness Spitzemberg noted on 5 January 1908: 'One has to believe in Eulenburg's innocence from the sexual point of view not only because he has sworn it but because he has challenged the whole world to indict him of such a crime.'[156] Kaiser Wilhelm was 'very pleased' with the outcome of the second trial and thought of bringing about Eulenburg's and Kuno Moltke's immediate and demonstrative rehabilitation.[157] After the trial, in which Eulenburg had 'again sworn himself clean', Holstein believed, Bülow was unlikely to remain in office long, because the Liebenbergers would now be 'in the ascendant again'.[158] Bülow's successor would be 'a partisan of Eulenburg, presumably Marschall, who ... would do the Kaiser's bidding and protect Eulenburg as much as possible'.[159]

In the end the voices at court warning against an ostentatious rehabilitation of the two accused men prevailed. They managed to restrain Wilhelm from such an 'exposure [to attack] of the All-Highest Person'.[160] Three weeks after his condemnation Harden lodged an appeal at the Reich court in Leipzig. He was out for revenge and actually had 'devastating' evidence to hand.[161] For about six years he had known about Eulenburg's sexual relations with young fishermen on Lake Starnberg at the time when he was working as Prussian Secretary of Legation in Munich. He also received anonymous tips from the local population. Out of sympathy for Adolf Brand, the Munich dairyman Riedel called on Bernstein and declared himself ready to testify against Eulenburg. In addition, Harden engaged a detective who collected further incriminating evidence in Munich, Berlin, Vienna, Hamburg and other cities.[162] As early as on 19 January 1908 Harden and Bernstein hit upon the tortuous idea of having themselves libelled in a newspaper so that Riedel and other witnesses could be questioned under oath in a fake trial, this time before a Bavarian court.[163] They persuaded the Munich editor Anton Städele to publish an assertion in his *Neue Freie Volkszeitung* that Harden had received a million in hush money from Eulenburg so as to stop him uncovering further evidence.[164] The case of *Harden* v. *Städele* was fixed for 21 April 1908 at the Munich district court.

The statements made under oath by Riedel and the Starnberg fisherman Jakob Ernst, which could not have been more painfully clear,[165] destroyed Eulenburg's reputation for ever. Hildegard von Spitzemberg wrote with horror in her diary: 'All conversation is polluted and poisoned by the Eulenburg affair, and every day new, even more dreadful and upsetting details and symptoms emerge, which are already dragging the Kaiser himself into the foul atmosphere!!'[166] In consternation the Baroness's brother Axel Varnbüler wrote to Justizrat Karl Laemmel saying that only by committing suicide could their mutual friend save his family's honour. After the witnesses' statements in Munich he saw 'nothing but the inexorable, irrevocable fact: he is irretrievably lost.' Prosecution for perjury and the reopening of the Moltke–Harden case were inevitable. 'But still more dreadful than this outward catastrophe is the inward collapse of belief in one's friend. That he lied to us, swore to us falsely — that could be *forgiven* as an act of desperation by a man hounded almost to death, if he did it not just on his own behalf but also to save the honour of his family, of his name. But then he would be compelled to pass sentence on himself before being judged by others — inconspicuously departing this life, as his illness would make possible ... The bullet [is] even now the most merciful solution — even if it can no longer save him and his family from disgrace ... And at least it would be a tragic end — an end at last to all this nauseating filth.' Varnbüler urged the lawyer to advise Eulenburg to commit suicide. 'However hard and cruel it may seem — it would still be the greatest act of compassion. Will he not himself come to see this as the only solution? I feel as if the news must arrive at any moment from L[iebenberg]. Or does he lack the moral courage?'[167]

On 30 April 1908 and in the following days Eulenburg was questioned before a judicial commission.[168] The Prussian Minister of Justice, Maximilian von Beseler, kept the Kaiser up to date with the inexorable fall of his best friend of so many years.[169] On 1 May he told him that at the hearing the Prince had 'categorically denied all guilt', but that the commission was still considering whether to issue an arrest warrant.[170] On 9 May the minister reported: 'Prince Eulenburg was questioned at Schloss Liebenberg on the afternoon of the 7th of the month ... The two Munich witnesses, Ernst and Riedel, were brought face to face with the Prince and in spite of insistent rebuttals on the part of the Prince they stood by their incriminating statements and also swore them on oath. The Prince denied all guilt equally firmly and declared that he was baffled. After the examination was over the investigating judge ... issued an arrest warrant against the Prince on strong suspicion of perjury and, after hearing evidence from the court doctor ... and the Prince's family doctor, gave orders for him to be transferred to the Charité.

The transfer took place yesterday afternoon ... by automobile. The Prince's application to be released from arrest on bail was refused by the investigating judge ... on the grounds ... that there were circumstances which gave reason to believe that the accused would induce witnesses to make false statements.'[171] At the same time the Prussian Ministry of State, under Bülow's chairmanship, ordered the confiscation of all Eulenburg's personal papers.[172] Kaiser Wilhelm, meanwhile, was staying at Donaueschingen with his new friend Max Egon zu Fürstenberg. On his departure he wrote to thank Fürstenberg for the 'charming days' he had spent with him, adding the words 'He's gone!'[173] Nevertheless he repeatedly showed signs of sadness and remorse over his lost friend. Thus Varnbüler told his sister at the end of June 1908 that instead of his earlier outbursts of rage Wilhelm now thought of Eulenburg 'with great sorrow'. He had exclaimed: 'Why did he do that to us, why did he not confide in anyone?' The Kaiser was 'deeply shamed at being thus let down by his friend'.[174]

The judicial investigation brought more and more incriminating evidence to light and dragged other members of the Kaiser's entourage into the abyss. In the library at Liebenberg 'indescribable' homosexual publications were found, in which the name of the Kammerherr [Gentleman of the Bedchamber] Edgard von Wedel-Gerzlow had been written in Eulenburg's hand. On 2 June 1908 the Minister of Justice was compelled to tell the Kaiser that Wedel had admitted having committed 'a similar moral misdemeanour to those with which Prince Eulenburg is charged at present'. In the end Eulenburg confessed that the books belonged to him; he had written Wedel's name on them because he was a bachelor and their discovery would thus have been less damaging for him. Wedel lost his post as Kammerherr and the official apartment which went with it.[175] Most damning for Eulenburg was the discovery of a letter which he had written on 22 December 1907 – thus immediately after he had testified under oath at the second Moltke–Harden trial that he had never engaged in 'filthy acts' – to Jakob Ernst, imploring him to deny everything that had happened between them if he were summoned as a witness, especially as it had all been 'far too long ago'. The public prosecutor rightly pointed out that this letter amounted to an admission 'that filthy acts between the accused and Ernst did take place'.[176]

These extremely unpleasant developments and the ensuing charge against Eulenburg for double perjury and inducement to commit perjury were reported to the Kaiser by Justice Minister von Beseler on 5 June 1908.[177] The effect on Wilhelm II was shattering. Those who saw him at the time were 'horrified at the Kaiser's nerviness, the tension in his face, his restless expression and his manners'.[178] Three weeks later the case against Eulenburg began

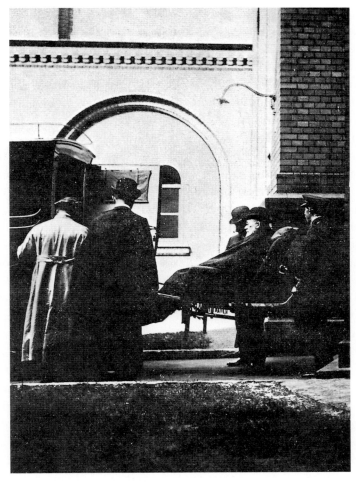

Figure 23 Eulenburg being carried on a stretcher from his hospital
bed to the courtroom

at the district court in Moabit. Reporting on the course of the proceedings,
Beseler told the Kaiser that the chief witnesses, Ernst and Riedel, had stood
by their statements and had again sworn them. Ernst's statement, above all,
had given the impression of complete credibility.[179] On 17 July, by which
time the Kaiser was on his Scandinavian cruise, Beseler reported that the
proceedings had been broken off because in the opinion of the court doctors
the accused's life was in danger as a result of hardening of the arteries,
swelling of the knee joints and blockage of the veins; even an attempt to
continue the proceedings by the Prince's sickbed in the Charité had had to be
abandoned (see Figure 23).[180] No date was set for the resumption of the trial,

at which time all the evidence would have to be presented again. Eulenburg, who remained under arrest for the time being, made an 'impressive' speech protesting against the suspension of the proceedings.[181] When this news reached him on board the *Hohenzollern* the Kaiser was confused and angry. He telegraphed to Bülow on 18 July 1908: 'I am very disagreeably surprised by the sudden unfortunate decision of the court in rebus Eulenburg! That whole shambles was for nothing, and the wretched business is going to start again from the beginning! Don't these people realise what immense damage it does to our reputation abroad!? On the one hand the doctors declare him not in a condition to be questioned, and on the other he makes a long speech in his defence! How does that fit together? The trial ought to have continued, even if E[ulenburg] were doomed! That would still be better for him than to vegetate under arrest for months on end, with the trial threatening in the background, and then for it to begin again right from the beginning! In this affair I find the judicial authorities harder to understand than ever!'[182]

At the end of September 1908 Eulenburg was released on bail for 100,000 marks and was able to go home to Liebenberg. The court was nevertheless concerned that in spite of his illness the Prince might soon travel abroad and especially that he might go to one of the countries that 'do not extradite for perjury'.[183] In May 1909 there was general astonishment at the news that Eulenburg, who was supposedly unfit to stand trial, was planning to travel to Bad Gastein in Austria. At the request of the public prosecutor's office bail was raised to 500,000 marks. A medical deputation that arrived unannounced at Liebenberg now declared 'that the Prince's illness in the Charité and the court room − was entirely simulated!!' The Under Secretary at the Foreign Office, Wilhelm Stemrich, ordered the re-arrest of 'the demonic person' who had 'shamefully duped all the doctors at the Charité'.[184] Even now, thoughtful observers wished that Eulenburg would simply flee abroad. But Baroness Spitzemberg put her finger on a sore point when she commented in her diary on 9 June 1909: 'It is of course the worry that he could publish dubious letters from H.M. if he were attacked too strongly that is tying people's hands in this case.'[185] Eulenburg was compelled to stay at his Berlin residence under medical supervision. An attempt to resume the main hearing against him had to be suspended, for after only a short time on 5 July 1909 he collapsed unconscious. He was taken back to Liebenberg, which he was never to leave again until his death in September 1921.[186] It was not until the 1980s that his 'dubious' correspondence with the Kaiser was made available to historians.

CHAPTER TWENTY-TWO

The Kaiser's visit to Windsor and Highcliffe, November to December 1907

The sexual scandals at the Hohenzollern court, which seriously damaged the reputation of the Crown, prepared the ground for the greatest internal political crisis of Wilhelm II's reign in November 1908. They also led to a considerable loss of prestige abroad – and this at a time which, with the expansion of the Entente Cordiale into the Anglo-Franco-Russian Triple Entente, could hardly have been more critical. While many Germans turned their backs on the monarchy after the painful revelations, others responded to profound feelings of shame and disgrace by taking refuge in the unreal world of the Pan-Germans and the naval fanatics, with their megalomaniacal ideas of the Reich's historic mission to rise to *Weltmacht* in defiance of all deterrent warnings from the international states system. It was certainly no coincidence that at the precise moment when the threat of a great European war drew dangerously closer with the publication of the new German Navy Bill in November 1907, a glittering visit by the German Emperor and Empress to the British capital was planned, with a view to soothing tense Anglo-German relations. Yet even this state visit, intended as a gesture of friendship and so very controversial on both sides of the North Sea, hung in the balance for a time because of the scandalous revelations about life at court in Berlin.

FRIENDLY OVERTURES

The Kaiser's visit of November 1907 was ill-starred from the outset. In the twelve preceding months Wilhelm II had showered his British relations with such assurances of his attachment and goodwill that the Liberal Prime Minister, Sir Henry Campbell-Bannerman, was reminded of the 'ugly' Italian proverb: he who is kinder to you than is his wont has either injured you or wishes to do so.[1] A plaintive letter to his aunt Louise, Duchess of Argyll, in December 1906 reveals how unjustly the Kaiser considered himself treated by English public opinion. 'And to think that I, who have looked upon my task to draw the two nations closer together, to teach them to know eachother better, & to slowly learn to honour & cherish eachothers traditions, I the grandson of Britains greatest Queen, should year by year be hooted, jeered at, cavilled & slandered, & held up to ridicule by the British Press & literature mercilessly & endlessly. To have every event which does not turn out according [to] British expectations in any corner of the globe invariably saddled on me quite as a matter of course as one of my usual intrigues! That is very hard! For it hinders me from coming over as often as I wished to visit my friends & the places where I once was a happy child! May Providence grant that 1907 may show us the beginning of better feeling among nations who are threatened by a common danger!'[2] The British royal family was well aware of Wilhelm's ambiguous feelings for England, the 'curious mixture' of his 'two natures, the German and the English'.[3]

Not least thanks to friendly overtures by the Kaiser – gifts, appointments and a particularly welcoming attitude towards British diplomats – and in spite of many a setback, Anglo-German relations improved noticeably in the course of 1907,[4] as even the ever-suspicious Under Secretary of State Sir Charles Hardinge observed. 'Without being unduly optimistic I really think that the German Emperor, with the visit to Windsor in view, is trying to behave in a sensible manner and not to spring any surprises on us.'[5] Beneath the surface, however, Wilhelm II's feelings for his mother's homeland were characterised as before by a high degree of irritability and aggression. His peculiar mixture of affection and bitterness towards his English relations showed itself in a typical fashion in August 1907 when Bülow passed on warnings about the dangerous gossip put about by Prince Albert of Schleswig-Holstein. Albert, a cousin of Wilhelm II and ten years younger than him, was a Major in the Prussian army and since 1899 had regularly accompanied the Kaiser on his summer cruises along the Norwegian coast. A few weeks before Wilhelm's state visit to Windsor Prince Arthur, Duke of Connaught, accused this young Prince of having contributed greatly to the worsening of relations between the two courts by his 'gossiping'. Wilhelm repudiated this criticism. 'He has *never* gossiped to *me* about King Edward; whether he has done so to him about me I do not know!' he declared. 'Prince Albert even behaved very well at the worst time in '04–'06, when war with England seemed to be threatening. When his passionately anti-German mother expressed herself in the most unbelievable way about me and Germany in the presence of family and friends and stirred up feeling against us, as she has unfortunately made a habit of doing for a long time, he said quite bluntly that in the circumstances he would ask my permission to resign so that he could go into battle even against his own family in the forthcoming war; but if people wanted peace, then they should not talk like that in his presence about his War Lord and the Prussian Army.'[6] As Wilhelm can only have heard of this clash between mother and son through Prince Albert himself, the Kaiser's marginal comments in fact merely confirmed the fears of his uncle Arthur.

A DIFFICULT INVITATION

While feelings on both sides were so laden with potential conflict it is not surprising that even the invitation to pay a state visit to Windsor proved extremely complicated. In the summer of 1906 a visit by the German Emperor still looked anything but desirable in view of the tense relations between France and Germany over Morocco, the negotiations pending between Britain and Russia and, not least, the inflamed state of public opinion in Germany and Britain. It was not until April 1907 that Edward VII took up the question again. The King reminded Hardinge and Grey that since Queen Victoria's death Wilhelm II had come to Britain only once, and that had been for a private visit to Sandringham in November 1902. The Kaiser had not yet returned the King's official visit to Kiel and Hamburg in the summer of 1904. He was therefore of the opinion 'that it would be neither polite nor politic to delay the return visit'.[7] Edward VII's meetings with the kings of Spain and Italy, however, which in April 1907 led to 'grotesque' and 'mad' attacks against the British monarch in the German press, cast renewed doubt on the Kaiser's state visit. On 30 April Hardinge wrote to the King saying: 'I have discussed with Sir E. Grey the question whether it would not be possible to say something to the German Ambassador to the effect that Your Majesty is very anxious to be able to invite the German Emperor to a state visit to Windsor in November, but that you feel that it will be very difficult to carry out your wishes and to insure the success of the visit, if the German press continues its present attitude and if the antagonism to France in Morocco is maintained.'[8] In the end it was not until June that the formal invitation could be sent to the Kaiser and once again it was the King who pressed the hesitant Foreign Office to agree to it. When Hardinge consulted Grey the latter commented, not exactly with enthusiasm, 'that as it has to take place it would be better that it should take place soon, & as November is the month when the visit would be most convenient to the King he agreed that if the Lord Mayor's visit to Germany … passes off without any contretemps the moment would seem to have arrived when the invitation should be given'.[9]

While the former Hofmarschall to the Empress Frederick, Hugo Freiherr von Reischach, who had been visiting England to buy horses, hurried to Hamburg with the King's letter of invitation, the ambassador in London, Count Metternich, sent a series of dispatches to the Auswärtiges Amt in Berlin about the apparent origin of the invitation, which again cast serious doubt on the hoped-for effect of the visit. Metternich reported that the distinctly anti-German First Sea Lord, Admiral Sir John Fisher, of all people, was claiming credit for having persuaded the King to send the invitation. Fisher had 'asked his Sovereign whether the right moment had not now come to issue an invitation to His Majesty the Kaiser, and when King Edward warmly agreed, Sir John Fisher expressed, and was granted, his wish to be seconded to the personal service of His Majesty the Kaiser if the invitation were accepted. The Admiral is apparently trying to clear himself of suspicion of anti-German policy', Metternich telegraphed. 'His wish to get to know His Majesty the Kaiser better is an old one; his endeavours to show himself as pro-German are new.'[10] When Metternich's dispatches were submitted to the Kaiser they provoked a roar of outrage. Freiherr von Rücker-Jenisch, the diplomat in the Kaiser's suite, reported to the Auswärtiges Amt that 'the All-Highest was extraordinarily angry about the content of Count Metternich's reports because it was clear from them that Admiral Sir John Fisher was behind the intrigues against Germany and that he was chiefly to blame if relations between Germany and England had not improved hitherto despite many attempts. Now, because it suited Sir John Fisher, He *was allowed* to come to England again; His Majesty was practically a plaything in the hands of the English Admiral, who was pushing himself forward in an outrageous way. His Majesty the Kaiser shares Your Excellency's opinion that *before* a visit by His Majesty to England King Edward must pay an official visit to the All-Highest, whether on his way to or from Marienbad.'[11]

In a further telegram Metternich expressed the opinion that there must be a publicly recognisable Anglo-German rapprochement before the Kaiser could accept the invitation to Windsor. It was 'not to our advantage', he warned, 'for the English court and the English government to get hold of the idea that the German Emperor will rush over to England at the first summons, as soon as it fits in with the political scheming here. There is a general suspicion in Germany that England is working busily to isolate us, and this suspicion will be strengthened by the new Mediterranean agreement ... so that an All-Highest visit to England will neither be understood nor have a calming effect in Germany unless there were a moment of calm in the meantime.'[12] The Kaiser shared the Reich Chancellor's opinion that there could be 'no question' of refusing the invitation. Nevertheless, like Metternich, he expected a public signal of rapprochement between Britain and Germany. He said it was 'absolutely essential that an official visit by King Edward to Berlin should precede his visit to Windsor. For King Edward had never been to Berlin officially.' As Jenisch reported to the Wilhelmstrasse, he had to point out to the Kaiser repeatedly 'that King Edward had wanted to pay an official visit to Berlin in 1904, but this did not suit His Majesty at that time and King Edward had been asked to come to Kiel instead. His Majesty disputed this, until I told Him that it was recorded in the files. My aim was to try to prevent His Majesty already becoming all too set on demanding an English visit to *Berlin* now, as it would probably be very difficult to get this accepted.'[13]

As Edward – albeit unwillingly – agreed to the suggestion of a meeting at Wilhelmshöhe,[14] Wilhelm's annoyance over Fisher's role and his thwarted desire to make his uncle visit Berlin soon evaporated. During his Norwegian cruise he spoke in tones of triumph to senior naval officers 'for almost half an hour about the English navy and English affairs. The invitation for the visit planned in November came from the King, who is said to have been put up to it by Fisher, and was a great surprise to H.M. He thought the explanation for it was that in England the [King's] journeys to Spain etc. did not go down well because they were aimed too much against Germany and that they now want to cry off. The Kaiser made a characteristic remark that one had to be blunt and rude to the English; that was the way to get the most out of them.'[15]

Events both abroad and at home continued to cast a shadow over the forthcoming state visit until the last moment. The news that Sir John French, the Commander in Chief of the British army, was to go to St Petersburg with the French General de Lannes to visit the Chief of the Russian General Staff, Palytzin, alarmed and angered Kaiser Wilhelm. The '*present* meeting of the Generalissimo of the British Army Sir J. French with Gen[eral] de Lannes (France) at Palytzin's headquarters' was a sure sign that England was continuing to pursue her anti-German policy, he wrote furiously in October 1907. 'The policy of encirclement goes on in its calm unchanging way in spite of the invitation to Windsor, which is only a trick and intended to pull the wool over the eyes of the fools in both nations. To send French to St Petersburg 3 weeks before I come to London is *outrageous*; all the more so when one knows that for 40–50 years *no German* army commander has ever been officially allowed into Russia!'[16]

THE MYSTERIOUS CANCELLATION

The Kaiser, like the entire court, was deeply shaken by his close friend Kuno Moltke's sensational libel suit against Harden, which was heard before the court at Moabit in the last week of October and which, as we have seen, ended with Harden's acquittal on 29 October 1907.[17] Haunted by the scandal, Wilhelm suddenly decided to cancel his visit to Windsor, pleading influenza. In the evening of 31 October, without even informing the Reich Chancellor, he telegraphed from the Berlin Schloss telling his uncle that he could not come and asking whether the Crown Prince, together with the Kaiserin, would be welcome in his place.[18] Incredulous, the King wired back: 'Your telegram has greatly upset me – as your not coming to England would be a terrible disappointment to us all, the family and the British nation. Beg of you to reconsider your decision and trust you may be much better next week. We will lessen the programme as much as you like.'[19] He sent the Kaiser's telegram and his reply to Knollys with the request that he consult the Prime Minister, Grey, Hardinge and Metternich that same night as to what to do. 'The G[erman] E[mperor] has placed me in a most difficult & unfair position', he complained. 'The fact is after all these dreadful revelations during the recent lawsuit at Berlin – he dare not "face the music" & has probably been told that he will get a bad reception in England. I do not see how his son could well take his place with the Empress. It would be too evident that he is afraid of coming over just now. Of course he is (unberufen) as well as I am. It is a regular "impasse". His Telegram to me is very unfair – but he will not know how to answer my reply to his Telegram ... I cannot describe how upset I am by all this & its consequences. Nobody beyond Grey & Hardinge should see this letter.'[20]

Knollys, Grey and Hardinge all hoped that the Kaiser could still be persuaded to stick to the original programme for the visit. In a telegram to ambassador Lascelles and in a conversation with Metternich the Foreign Secretary stressed 'that a favourable reception for the Emperor is now assured here, now more than ever, for sympathy is felt for him at the pain, which recent revelations must have given him and some admiration at the courage with which he has had them exposed.' If a postponement of the state visit were unavoidable, however, then it should be for no more than a few weeks and the new date should be announced at once. But if it proved impossible to rearrange the Kaiser's visit because of the King's other engagements, in the opinion of the Foreign Office the best solution from the political point of view would be for the Crown Prince to come instead of his father.[21] Hardinge even considered that a visit to Britain by the German Crown Prince might have more lasting advantages. 'The Crown Prince would receive a tremendous ovation, and although he is said to be already very friendly to this country his visit would no doubt confirm him in this attitude, which would be an asset to us in the future. It would however be infinitely better if the Emperor came himself.'[22]

The Reich Chancellor knew nothing of his sovereign's momentous decision to cancel the state visit which had been planned for many months and with great difficulty. It was only in the afternoon of 1 November 1907 that he received a long, agitated telegram from the ambassador in London. Metternich reported that the King's Private Secretary Lord Knollys had told him that the King was 'very angry' and was convinced 'that His Majesty did not *want* to come . . . The King is afraid . . . that the scandalous trial has made such a depressing impression on the Kaiser that the All-Highest does not want to go on a journey abroad at this time . . . The King and Lord Knollys are of the opinion that the English people would not understand the cancellation and would suspect that reasons arising from a less friendly disposition of His Majesty the Kaiser towards England lay behind it. Lord Knollys, who . . . has been working hard for a year and a half to bring about the visit, is afraid that if the visit is definitely cancelled the improvement in relations between the two countries which is well under way will be undone.' The ambassador added: 'With Lord Knollys I maintained the formal line that illness could be the reason for the cancellation. I share the view held by the King and Lord Knollys, however, if there were indeed other reasons involved. In view of this serious situation may I ask Your Excellency for information, whether for myself personally or for discussion with His Majesty the King.'[23] Two hours later another telegram arrived from Metternich telling Bülow that Grey fully shared the views of the King and Knollys and regretted the cancellation.[24]

Astonished, Bülow submitted the two telegrams to his sovereign, who covered them with the most extraordinary comments. Wilhelm confirmed Metternich's report that he had cancelled the state visit to England in a telegram to the King. 'I was so unwell yesterday', he declared; 'I had a *sudden fainting fit* and would have fallen to the ground had I not grasped the back of a chair as I fell, which threw me onto the sofa; I was brought round with champagne by the Kaiserin who rushed in by chance. As I felt very unwell and weak, I telegraphed to H[is] M[ajesty] asking whether my son could represent me and accompany H[er] M[ajesty], or whether the visit could be postponed until next spring. He answered that he hoped that in 8 days I would have recovered enough to come after all. Consequently from today I have begun to ride and to go out, and will try to go to the theatre and to mix with people in order to prepare and strengthen myself at least a little, and to get used to people, as I have not even eaten with my household up to now. I have had a complete collapse! Also partly caused by dreadful bouts of mental depression; as well as by a complete lack of sunshine on my body in this terrible year of rain, I who need the sun so much, so that I may have to spend the winter in the South. I therefore considered it my duty to notify H.M. at once. I shall do my utmost to get myself going to some extent, but cannot yet definitely accept ... I shall do everything I can to regain my strength through exercise in the fresh air, riding etc. and hope for the best; but I have had a hard knock and influenza is probably partly to blame. Mucus secretion is still severe!' Wilhelm rejected the assertion that he did not *want* to go to England because of the Harden–Moltke trial as 'an outrageous insinuation'. 'That has nothing to do with it. I happen to be suffering from severe bronchial catarrh, with a cough and a cold, and that weakened me and led to the fainting fit, which has *never* happened to me before! Kings are only human, after all, and can sometimes be ill too!'[25] Not until 4 November 1907 did Kaiser Wilhelm finally decide to go ahead with the planned visit to England, and then to spend three weeks on the south coast to cure his catarrh.[26]

THE STATE VISIT TO WINDSOR

After all the difficulties which had preceded it, outwardly at least the Kaiser's visit was a resounding success. Foreign Secretary Wilhelm von Schoen later recalled the decidedly favourable impression made by the Kaiser's speech at the banquet at Windsor Castle, when he spoke with great warmth of his youthful memories and of his veneration for the 'great Queen'.[27] The high point of the visit was the imperial couple's drive through London from Paddington station to the Guildhall on 13 November, which proved to be the occasion of a hearty mass demonstration of Anglo-German friendship.[28] On his return to Windsor that evening Wilhelm telegraphed jubilantly to the Reich Chancellor: 'Our visit to the City favoured by splendid weather went off highly satisfactorily. Tremendous crowds kept in exemplary order in the streets greeting us enthusiastically throughout drive. Reception at Mansion House solemn and magnificent. Very costly present offered to us, Lord Mayor's speech and mine received with loud cheering.'[29] Bülow immediately sent his congratulations and assured Wilhelm that 'the news of the fine reception given to our Kaiser and Kaiserin in England' had produced 'universal gratification here at home'.[30] The next day Kaiser Wilhelm reported to his Chancellor on the measures which the London police had taken to prevent outbreaks of violence during his drive through the city. 'English Socialists held a meeting at Townhill [sic], from where they intended to move out into the streets with a view to demonstrating. Police Chief let them do as they pleased at the meeting, but when they wanted to move out, had all exits blocked. Thus they could only rage uselessly. German and other foreign Socialists had also come over aiming to hold disruptive demonstrations and had taken up a position on a street corner. The English police sent detectives to mingle with them, who would have drawn their truncheons at the slightest attempt at a disturbance. The Socialists wisely kept as quiet as mice, so that there was not the slightest note of discord.' Not least as a result of these measures his drive through the streets of London had been a remarkable success. The London police chief had told the King 'that to his knowledge no foreign Sovereign had ever been given such a warm reception as I had yesterday', Wilhelm telegraphed. At Windsor Castle too, 'everyone is highly delighted at how well yesterday went and at the speeches, which have produced a very friendly response in the press today'. The previous evening a Welsh choir had sung 'Deutschland über Alles', the Kaiser added jubilantly, 'in *German*, for the first time in Windsor Castle'.[31] Indeed, as the Princess of Wales reported to her aunt in Germany: 'Here so far everything goes smoothly, both German Majesties couleur de rose, making themselves charming & agreeable to everyone, in fact nothing could be better. The London reception was excellent, a glorious day & thousands of people all the way from Paddington to Guildhall. William's speech at the lunch was charming.'[32]

Charles Hardinge's opinion was considerably more muted. After the Kaiser's departure for Highcliffe Castle he wrote a thoughtful assessment of the events of the past few days. 'The German Emperor's visit passed off most successfully. I should describe his reception by the crowds in the streets as good but not enthusiastic but in the Guildhall he had a very good warm reception. Unfortunately the value of the Emperor's peaceful assurances has been somewhat discounted in the eyes of the public by the almost simultaneous publication of the German naval estimates which give food for thought. I saw a great change in the Emperor from what he was when the King went to Wilhelmshöhe – he has evidently suffered from the anxiety of recent incidents in Berlin. He has been in a curious frame of mind. It will interest you to know that ten days before he started he chucked his engagement and telegraphed that he would send the Crown Prince in his place. He was evidently afraid to face the music – Metternich & Bülow were both told that the refusal at the 11th hour would make a very bad impression and that whatever we might say or do the public would say that he had not come because he was mixed up in the scandals & was afraid ... When at Windsor they both [Wilhelm and the Kaiserin] expressed themselves enchanted with their visit & the cordiality of their reception and as far as I know the visit passed without a single hitch.'[33]

THE KAISER'S INITIATIVE ON THE BAGHDAD RAILWAY QUESTION

Even in the political sphere agreement was achieved. The German and British foreign offices had each drawn up lists of the points upon which negotiation might be possible during the state visit. The British had identified the

Baghdad railway, the Anglo-Russian agreement on Persia and the Moroccan question as possible themes, while the Germans put forward reflections on the Hague Disarmament Conference, the Macedonian situation, Britain's Mediterranean agreement with Spain and Italy and the Herero rebellion in German South-West Africa.[34] Already on the first full day of the visit the Kaiser had a wide-ranging conversation about some of these questions with Sir Edward Grey, in the course of which he expressed views which were not at all in line with the briefing notes prepared for him by the Wilhelmstrasse. He launched straight into the question of the dangerous state of affairs in the Balkans, the Foreign Secretary recorded. 'The Emperor spoke with emphasis of the way in which the different nationalities treated each other. He said that Italy always had her eye on Albania, which was her "vis-à-vis", and that he was quite sure Austria would never tolerate any attempts by Italy to get a footing across the water. He ... said it was the ambition of Prince Ferdinand [of Bulgaria] to make himself King of the Balkans, with Constantinople as his capital. The Emperor said that the Turkish Government was more fit to rule than any of these other nationalities. It was tolerant as between different religions to an extent which they were not. I told him that I feared the Turkish Government made it impossible for the country to develop. It did not pay its officials or soldiers, and the Palace clique at Constantinople made it impossible to secure good Governors.' Whereupon the Kaiser brought up the subject of the Baghdad railway, Grey reported. 'The Emperor spoke with great appreciation of the qualities of the Turkish population. He said the development of the country in which the Anatolian Railways were had been extraordinary ... When the last extension of the railway southwards was made the people had travelled hundreds of miles to see it, and had expressed their thanks most enthusiastically for the building of the railway. Germany desired to go on with this work of development, and to continue the railways ... It would be necessary for Irrigation to go hand in hand with the progress of the railways. Germany had engineers who were specially suited for this work, and the Emperor's view was that Germany should do in Mesopotamia what we had done in Egypt, and when his opinion had been asked on this point he had always said it was quite right that German capital should go there.[35] ... Germany's view with regard to the Bagdad Railway was entirely commercial. Germany desired no further territory. Her own Colonies were ample for her needs. And besides there were large German places of business flourishing in British Colonies ... I observed that, with regard to the Bagdad Railway, there must necessarily be a strategical as well as a commercial side. The Emperor said that this was no doubt the case, and the Railway would shorten the way for us to India. I said that, as the Railway had a strategical value, public opinion here would be very suspicious if the undertaking was entirely under the control of a foreign Power. – The Emperor said there would be no ground for any suspicion. Germany was not going to acquire any territory in Mesopotamia, and the Turks would not be able to use the Railway against us. I told him that, when the Bagdad Railway was last discussed in this country, it was the political rather than the commercial side which had been emphasised, and it might be so again. The Emperor said he knew that France and Russia had put a political construction upon the project, and Germany had offered some time ago that there should be English and French co-operation. This offer had been refused, and now, though the Germans would be quite willing to have English and French capital, they felt that they must certainly carry through the undertaking themselves.'[36]

Not until two days later did the Kaiser inform the Reich Chancellor of the initiative he had taken in this matter of serious international concern. He telegraphed in high delight to Berlin on 14 November 1907 saying that Grey had been 'completely changed' by his visit and his speeches. 'I had a discussion with him and Mr Haldane about the Baghdad railway in which I successfully refuted all the prejudices prevailing here. I believe the English will give up all opposition if we leave the end of the railway on the Persian Gulf to them as a gate making it a condition that it must always be left open. Probably more on this tomorrow.'[37]

After he had also discussed the Baghdad railway with the King while they were out shooting together, the Kaiser decided on a dramatic move. In a note which he handed to the Minister of War, Haldane, he suggested that Germany and Britain should cooperate in building the last stretch of the railway; the terminus on the Persian Gulf could be in British hands, on condition that 'the gate should always remain open for peaceful purposes'.[38] With the agreement of Edward VII intensive consultations took place, first between Grey, Hardinge and Haldane[39] and then between Wilhelm II, Haldane, Schoen and Metternich, but in the end they came to nothing. The following day Haldane dictated a note on his negotiations with the Kaiser and the German diplomats, which had begun in the evening of 14 November 1907 and were continued in the early hours of the next morning. 'At 7 [in the evening] I saw the Emperor. I found him very enthusiastic about the possibility of an agreement, and eager to say that about the strategic question of the gate Germany would make no difficulty of any sort.' To this Haldane replied 'that there was another part that would require attention. The footing on which we stood with Russia and France was now so friendly that it was impossible that we should discuss matters without keeping them informed, and that it was really essential that the discussion should go on "à quatre" instead of "à deux". The Emperor expressed himself in a quite friendly spirit on this, but with considerable vehemence. He said he knew that Russia was opposed to the whole project, and would at once make difficulties. Also, he felt confident that France would at once proceed to make claims for further recognition about Morocco, in exchange for what she was asked to do about the Railway. He said, further, that the concession was really a German affair, and that it was all very well for Germany to discuss the matter freely with a Power with which she was on as good terms as she was with England, but that her people would certainly object to her having "pourparlers" with France and Russia.' Nevertheless the Kaiser promised to think about the suggestion. Just before dinner Schoen came up to Haldane and told him that there had been a misunderstanding. The Kaiser had been unaware, he said, that Schoen, while still ambassador in St Petersburg, had discussed the whole question of the Baghdad railway with the Foreign Minister, Isvolsky, 'and that they were entirely at one and would have negotiated and signed an agreement had M. Isvolsky not been taken ill. He added that the Emperor considered that this altered the whole features of the difficulty, and made matters much more easy, and that after the theatrical performance which was to follow the dinner party that night the Emperor wished to see me in his private room. I went to the Emperor's private room at 1 o'clock in the morning, and the conversation lasted till 2. Herr von Schön and Count Metternich were present. The Emperor said that he had not known of M. Isvolsky's conversations with Herr von Schön, and that he was now of opinion that there would not be the smallest difficulty. As regards France, he said there would be no difficulty either, because he had gathered from the French that they would have liked to have come into the business, but would not do so unless we were ready to come in also. Now that matters were upon such a friendly footing, he did not anticipate any difficulty.' The four men then went through the document drawn up in the British Foreign Office which Haldane had given to the Kaiser before dinner. 'The Emperor said that he completely understood the necessity on our part of proceeding at every step with the full knowledge and concurrence of the French and Russian Governments; that in our position this was quite legitimate; and that it was further in accordance with his own wishes. Count Metternich, at an earlier stage in this second interview, had said that he did not think a Conference of the four Powers was desirable. The project belonged to Germany, and ought not to be thrown open in such a fashion. But I had explained that I did not think Sir Edward Grey meant any thing more than this: that the business men should meet in Berlin, and should define what each of them wanted. They might not get what they wanted. The Emperor might not be willing to concede things out of his commercial rights. But, on the other hand, the difficulties might be diminished, and even might all disappear. As a result, after a long discussion which lasted till 2 in the morning, the Emperor said that he cordially concurred in the note as the basis on which to proceed; that we were "ganz einverstanden"; and that what he would like would be to get on as quickly as possible. He was very hopeful, now, that good business would come to all the four Powers concerned, and he would ask Herr von Schön to proceed to London that day (the 15th), to take the initiative by making a proposal from Germany, which he understood Sir Edward Grey desired to have as a first step. By the end of this interview, Count Metternich's critical attitude had become so greatly modified that he observed that there should be no difficulty about a discussion in Berlin "à quatre" in the sense now made plain, and that it was not only legitimate but quite natural that we should wish to proceed in full consultation with France and Russia.'[40]

Following these nocturnal negotiations Haldane confidently asserted to King Edward that the Kaiser's visit would prove to be 'of far reaching importance'. 'Mr Haldane may mention that he had the honour of an audience from the German Emperor which lasted till 2 this morning, & that all points arising in the discussion appeared to have been satisfactorily met. Mr Haldane informed the Emperor of Your Majesty's views & the Emperor expressed his belief that he could give effect to these views on all points.' Hardinge showed equal satisfaction when he wrote to Knollys on 15 November: 'During the last two days we have given the Bagdad Railway a good shove forward. Whether an agreement will be arrived at, it is as yet premature to say, but the Emperor & Schön have both admitted our right to have a gate of which we are to hold the key, i. e. a section of the Railway. This is a great step forward. When discussions begin, & the initiative for them has been thrown upon Germany & accepted by the Emperor, they will have to be conducted on business principles. The Germans can now no longer say that we are blocking the railway. We are very pleased at the turn which this affair has taken.'[41] Grey likewise had the impression that 'the whole visit of the Emperor' had been 'a great success, and beneficial from every point of view'. Above all, the Baghdad railway question had taken an extremely favourable turn as a result of Haldane's conversation with the Kaiser.[42] The Foreign Secretary suspected, however, that the Kaiser had acted on his own initiative without prior consultation with the Reich Chancellor.[43]

The fact that this imperial initiative came to nothing was due partly to Russia's continuing opposition to the Baghdad railway as a whole[44] and partly as Grey had feared to the objections raised by Bülow. Schoen, who had supported Wilhelm's action at Windsor even against the advice of Metternich, with hindsight drew attention in his memoirs to the important reasons why negotiations with Russia and France would not have been desirable. 'At the negotiating table we would have found ourselves alone, confronted with three other players who were not well-disposed towards us and were in alliance with each other. Nor did it seem advisable to give Russia and France reason to believe from the outset that we were inclined to accord the same weight to their not at all well-founded interest in the matter as to that of England, which was far more closely involved. It must also have appeared doubtful whether Sir Edward Grey's wish for those two Powers to be involved was prompted purely by the idea of a general equilibrium, or whether it was not also determined by an inclination to allow a new power grouping, of which only the vague outlines could be made out at that time . . . to emerge into the light of a certain recognition. The matter therefore went no further and gradually petered out.'[45]

THE KAISER AT HIGHCLIFFE

While the Kaiserin and her retinue returned to Germany, on 18 November 1907 Kaiser Wilhelm II began a three-week convalescent holiday at Highcliffe Castle, Colonel Edward James Stuart Wortley's home on the south coast of England, opposite the Isle of Wight. As is well known, it was there that the conversations took place which, when they were published a year later in the *Daily Telegraph*, caused an international sensation and nearly cost the Kaiser his throne.[46] (See Figure 24.)

Before the Kaiser's arrival in England both Count Metternich and his First Secretary, Wilhelm von Stumm, thought it their duty to warn against exaggerated expectations. In a letter to the Chancellor of 7 November 1907 explaining his views, Metternich defended the deliberately reserved line he had taken in drafting the Kaiser's speeches, and at the same time gave a prophetic warning of the consequences which could arise from an exaggerated emphasis on the blood relationship between the royal families and the two nations. He was sure the German sovereign would receive a hearty welcome in England, but a political rapprochement between Germany and Britain would not be feasible. 'People here do not want any friction or tension. They want to live in peace with Germany. But they do not want any warmer political rapprochement. This is reserved for France, and perhaps also for others if they are to be had, but not for us. For they are afraid of us and of our intentions and we are seen as the possible future enemy, for reasons not of commercial but of naval rivalry. Therefore they do not want to run the risk, by too pronounced a rapprochement with Germany, of arousing the suspicion of the French and thus putting their friendship at stake.' For this reason it was important to avoid 'stressing the blood and dynastic relations' in the Kaiser's speeches and addresses, the

Figure 24 The Kaiser and his entourage at Highcliffe, November 1907. Front row
from left to right: Adjutant-General Hans von Plessen, Prince Max Egon zu
Fürstenberg, Edward Stuart Wortley, the Kaiser, Colonel Legge, Count Dietrich von
Hülsen-Haeseler. Admiral von Müller is standing top left and Count August zu
Eulenburg is behind Hülsen-Haeseler on the right of the photograph

ambassador advised. Expressions of that kind would be 'passed over in embarrassed silence by officialdom in England, but many other elements would
seize the opportunity ... to respond with malicious criticism. Whether the
mood in our own country is ripe for His Majesty the Kaiser to emphasise the
dynastic relationship with England can best be judged by those who live there.
I doubt it.' This would be the tenor of his advice to the Kaiser when he arrived
in England, the ambassador added apprehensively.[47]

Stumm took a similar view, commenting after the Kaiser's departure for
Highcliffe that the enthusiasm of the crowds in the streets of London should
not be seen as a symptom of political rapprochement, for the two Powers
disagreed too profoundly on foreign and arms policy. Although the visit of the
imperial couple could justifiably be called a success in every respect, it would
be a mistake to indulge in illusions about the removal of the tensions existing
between Germany and Britain in the past few years. 'For the time being two
factors will always stand in the way of a greater degree of warmth in Anglo-
German relations: consideration for France and the expansion of the German

navy.' The recently announced German naval programme had 'once again caused great unease' in London. Even the most convinced advocates of a pro-German policy maintained the view that for every new German ship the British must build two. Stumm expressed the hope, however, that with time the British would become accustomed to the idea 'that Germany possesses a strong navy', and that in Germany too it would gradually be recognised 'that the English navy will always be superior to the German'. Then, he predicted, 'the value of French friendship would also decline in the eyes of English statesmen', which would render it possible 'to raise Anglo-German relations above the level of correct politeness which characterises it at present'.[48]

Although Kaiser Wilhelm's marginal comments on Stumm's report advising restraint signified his agreement — it was all 'quite right', and 'we have known that for a long time' — he persisted in his attempts to convince the British of his honourable intentions and the necessity of an Anglo-German alliance. On 1 December 1907, at Highcliffe, he took his British host Colonel Stuart Wortley aside in the library and confided to him: 'When history is written, it will be shown how the British public has misjudged me. At the commence-ment of the Boer war, when everything was going wrong for you, the Queen wrote me a letter saying how anxious she was about the state of affairs. Although nearly all my people were in favour of the Boers, from a purely sentimental point of view (a bible reading, protestant people being oppressed by a great nation of a like religion), personally I knew that the majority of the Boers were not bible reading and I realised, with a view to the future of my own colonies, the extreme importance of the ultimate victory of the mother country. I immediately set to work with my general staff and having considered the situation as it was, I recommended a certain line of military action. Queen Victoria thanked me most deeply. I do not wish to say it was owing to my advice, but the strategy followed by Lord Roberts on arrival in South Africa was exactly that which I had recommended. When two German ships were stopped near Delagoa Bay for carrying contraband of war, that is rifles, guns and ammunition, I telegraphed to Hamburg at once to say I must have absolutely definite information as to whether any German ships had left the port thus laden, and that I would permit no such smuggling. I received a reply that it was absolutely untrue. These ships on being examined were found to contain nothing ... Early in 1900 the French and Russian governments approached my government, asking for my support if they intervened against you on behalf of the Boers. My government was sorely tempted; but I absolutely declined to do so, and thus saved England from a most dangerous position ... And on the top of all this, you flash the "entente cordiale" in my face ... The French nation will kiss you today but tomorrow they may be all against you: they are not to be trusted. I have colonies which will take years to develop and to pay their cost: but they will eventually pay. So with you, the world is big enough for us both. We ought to work together. Do not trust in France: a rotten reed.' Wilhelm II went on to remind Stuart Wortley that he had refused to receive the South African agitator Willem Leyds in Berlin 'and was much abused accordingly in the German Press'. He also claimed always to have instructed his agents in Egypt to support British interests there and to resist the numerous French intrigues.[49]

The next day the Kaiser explained to the British Colonel why he had been obliged to dismiss Bismarck: the Chancellor had wanted to have the socialists shot down by troops, whereas he had maintained that 'as the ruler of a great nation' he was responsible only to the Almighty, and 'that I would never incur before the Almighty the responsibility of shooting down my people'. Stuart Wortley then asked him whether he had had any presentiment in 1904 that the Russian army would be defeated by the Japanese. 'No, none whatever', the Kaiser responded. 'In fact, my agents reported to me that the Russian army was in an excellent condition in every way. Only one man, an English Professor in a Japanese college at Tokio, came to me in Berlin and told me that the Russians would not win a single battle. I laughed him almost to scorn. Shortly after the war began, I was at the opera in Berlin with several members of my Head Quarter Staff. After the first act a telegram arrived from my military agents in Corea stating that the Japanese had forced the passage of the Yalu. I handed the telegram to my Chief of the Staff who said it must be false, as it was impossible: the flower of the Russian army being on the Yalu. After the second act of the opera a second telegram was handed to me, giving me exact details of the battle – the number of killed and guns taken – and stating that the Japanese success was due to the murderous fire of their recently purchased Krupp field gun. Then I had no more surprises, for my agents reported to me the deplorable condition of the Russian army. The General in command of communications imported a large number of cocottes for the various dépôts on the line and took 60 p.c. of their "earnings" for his own pocket.' The Kaiser regarded it as a 'disgrace' that the Russian grand dukes had not gone to the front in the war against Japan.[50]

In a further conversation with Stuart Wortley Kaiser Wilhelm made the absurd claim that he had built up the German battlefleet not against Britain but against the Japanese, to protect the white race. With reference to the growing tensions between the United States and Japan, he declared: 'I foresaw the danger of the Yellow Peril 20 years ago, and that is why I built my fleet – just to be ready to lend a helping hand ... If there was a war between the United States of America and Japan, you [Great Britain] would be placed in a very awkward position. You could never take part with Japan against the United States, people of your own flesh and blood. Your position would be a very difficult one, for throughout the whole of the west coast of America – even from Vancouver which is Canadian – there is a feeling against yellow labour competition against white labour. You would be obliged to support your Canadian subjects and yet you have an alliance with Japan.' The alliance with Japan was, for Britain, 'a very dangerous policy which you will regret. But, much as I may be misunderstood, I have built my fleet to support you.' He concluded this twaddle with the claim that the British army was completely corrupt and that Admiral Sir John Fisher was 'a most dangerous and overrated man' who controlled the Royal Navy through venal subordinates.[51] Stuart Wortley immediately related these sensational comments by his exalted guest in letters to his wife, whose brother was the influential diplomat Sir Rennell Rodd.[52] The Colonel's record of the Kaiser's remarks at Highcliffe and of further utterances vouchsafed to him by the monarch in September 1908 formed the basis of the notorious 'interview' in the *Daily Telegraph* that led to a storm of indignation in November 1908. Yet already a year before that well-known national crisis a 'newspaper interview' of Kaiser Wilhelm II gave cause for alarm.

AN EARLY EMBARRASSING INTERVIEW WITH THE KAISER

While Wilhelm II was trying to persuade Colonel Stuart Wortley at Highcliffe that he was the actual initiator of the British victory in the Boer War and that he was building up his battlefleet purely in order to support the British Empire and protect it from the yellow peril, the *Daily Dispatch*, a regional newspaper based in Manchester, published an alleged interview given by the German sovereign to a 'senior diplomat' which caused surprise and dismay in London and Windsor.[53] According to a report of the interview which appeared on 4 December 1907 in the London *Times*, the Kaiser had described the strong German fleet as essential to the future development of his country. 'We are obliged to secure new markets for the export of our own industries. As these countries are inhabited in most cases by half-civilized nations, we are bound to show them our power. Some more men-of-war would bring in millions of money to our commerce, as we would get much better conditions in our commercial treaties than we get now ... After all, we must have our colonies for our ever-increasing population if we are not to lose millions of our own people. There are no countries in Europe we could conquer without damaging ourselves. Let us begin with the north. The Scandinavian countries are very beautiful indeed, but they are very poor; in consequence they are not at all desirable for us. Of course there is much of the old Germanic strength and tenacity in their populace; but this would only make more difficult their political and national assimilation. Holland's populace shows very much the same tenacity of national character. Even more would this be the case with Belgium. Switzerland? It serves as the very best Buffer state we could wish. One may say about Switzerland, if it did not exist, it would have to be invented. Russia? It is quite true the Baltic provinces have been German once; but they are not German any longer! The Russification of these provinces makes progress daily, and we would be very much mistaken if we believed that we should be received there with open arms. Besides, even if we could conquer the Baltic provinces it would become for us nothing more than a matter of permanent difficulty. The extension of our East frontiers would put us in a worse strategical position than now. Our position as regards Russia itself would become untenable. And this would not be the worst. We would make Russia our permanent and irreconcilable enemy. We should have to fight Russia, which would observe very likely the same military tactics against us which the Russians practised against Napoleon during the war of 1812. No! We should never think of such a conquest! We need Russia, and Russia needs us.' When the subject of Anglo-German relations came up, the Kaiser grew 'very animated', the newspaper report stated. 'I am glad to see the quarrels in the Press of these two countries ended', he exclaimed. 'We do not want to take anything from England; and England cannot take or even wish to take anything from us. England and Germany have therefore every reason[54] to hold together and to help each other as long as the vital interests of the nations do not force the Governments into controversy. What difficulty could possibly arise between England and Germany which would be incapable of a friendly and amicable settlement? Besides our blood relation to England we have every interest to see England strong and powerful. We would feel ourselves very soon any weakening of England. A German statesman who would go to war with England for the sake of getting perhaps a little colony from Great Britain – and that would be all we would expect even after a victorious war – would not deserve his place at the helm of the Empire. No, no', the Kaiser declared, 'we want nothing of this sort; all we want is peace and again peace to develop our commerce, our industry, and our national culture.'[55]

The German embassy immediately issued a *démenti* of this press report, but the editor of the *Daily Dispatch* resolutely insisted on the authenticity of the Kaiser's remarks, of which he said he could produce documentary proof. The record of the conversation, he declared, had originally come into his hands about two weeks earlier. Realising the importance of the document he had sent the text to Count Metternich at Highcliffe Castle asking him to submit it to the Kaiser for verification. A few days later the London correspondent of his paper had received a telegram summoning him to the German embassy, where he was informed that the text contained some imaginative passages, for instance one concerning the interference of the Pope in European politics and another about German interests in South America, and therefore it would probably be better for these statements to be left unpublished. A revised version omitting these passages was agreed, however, and this the correspondent took back to the embassy for authorisation. He was summoned to the embassy a second time by telegram, where Stumm read out a letter from the ambassador, written from Highcliffe, confirming that although the Kaiser had no direct recollection of the conversation, 'the views reported were certainly shared by the Kaiser'. The text was returned to the correspondent with a few handwritten corrections by Metternich, and he was given express permission to publish the text as in accordance with Kaiser Wilhelm II's opinions. As proof of the accuracy of this account the editor quoted, word for word, the handwritten corrections which Metternich had made. Adroitly, he asked why the ambassador would have taken such pains to edit the text he had been sent if, as the embassy now claimed, it was a 'pure invention'. In a second *démenti* Stumm was forced to concede in *The Times* of 6 December 1907 that the published text, if not verbatim, had conveyed the general sense of Kaiser Wilhelm's views.[56]

These embarrassing events, which were reported by *The Times* and by the international agency Reuters, were of course closely followed at the highest level in London. When the first article appeared in *The Times* on 4 December Sir Charles Hardinge, anticipating the horrified reaction of German nationalist circles to such interviews with the Kaiser, wrote to Lord Knollys: 'Have you seen the Emperor's extraordinary statement to a reporter of a Birmingham [sic] newspaper? It really is too extraordinary. I do not know what his own Pan-Germans would say to it.'[57] At first Hardinge and Grey believed Metternich's protestations that the whole so-called interview had been apocryphal,[58] but then found the editor's riposte wholly convincing. Hardinge wrote to Knollys on 6 December: 'There is absolutely no doubt as to the truth of the statement of the Manchester Despatch, and the German Embassy made a great mistake in publishing such a "démenti". Stumm, the 1st Secretary, who is a very honest straightforward fellow, evidently spoke the truth when he said the article represented the views of the Emperor. The corrections made are quite conclusive. I hear privately that the Diplomatist with whom the conversation is supposed to have taken place was, not an Englishman, but a German, and the points made by the Emperor were the arguments which H.M. was to use in discussing Anglo-German relations with English people! I also hear that the Editor of the Despatch wrote a very strong letter last night to Metternich warning him that he would not take yesterday's démenti, which was a barefaced lie, lying down etc . . . It is thought that this letter wrung from the German Embassy the modified démenti of today with which the Editor is said to be not at all inclined to be satisfied. It is rather amusing as showing what bunglers the Germans are.'[59]

So the 'interview' given by Wilhelm II to a 'diplomat of European rank' published on 4 December 1907 was not a matter of 'gaffes' by a monarch supposedly given to impulsive utterances, but of a deliberate action in which the Wilhelmstrasse and the German embassy in London were deeply involved, in order to pull the wool over the eyes of the British public about Germany's true intentions and above all to gain time for the expansion of the battlefleet. That these protestations failed to achieve their goal in Britain, France, the Netherlands and Scandinavia and gave rise in these countries to renewed fears of invasion plans did not prevent Wilhelm and Bülow, as is well known, from repeating the attempt a few months later in grander style, through an 'interview' between the Kaiser and Stuart Wortley in the *Daily Telegraph*.[60] They were encouraged in their belief in the effectiveness of bogus interviews with the Kaiser by the positive response in the American press to the interview published in the *Daily Dispatch*. At the end of December 1907 Speck von Sternburg reported from Washington on a very gratifying leading article in the *New York Tribune* entitled 'Peace, Peace and Peace again'. According to the ambassador, the paper had commented that 'in spite of the fact that His Majesty stood out among all the world's leaders in being known as "War Lord", and that originally it was widely believed that under his All-Highest rule Germany and Europe would soon be embroiled in war, in the last 19½ years exactly the opposite had happened. Germany could be regarded as the most peace-loving of all the European Great Powers. Almost all the other countries had fought wars during that period or had contemplated them more than Germany. Therefore the Kaiser's remarks coincided with the facts and should be taken as sincerely meant. The reasons given by His Majesty for this policy were equally true; there was no land in Europe that Germany could conquer without endangering herself. It was in Germany's interest to maintain Russia's integrity and friendship, as well as England's welfare and power. France was not mentioned because it would have been impossible to say anything about her without running the risk of being misunderstood. But it was clear that Germany's own interest indicated peace with France just as strongly as with any other Power. The Kaiser's reasons for peace were applicable to all countries. The conquest of even the smallest of countries would affect others and would almost inevitably lead to dangerous complications for the conqueror.' These comments by the *New York Tribune* were 'particularly welcome', Sternburg observed, 'because they counteract the repeated attacks, stemming from English and French sources, made by various newspapers on Germany's alleged policy of conquest towards Holland.' Kaiser Wilhelm was pleased with Sternburg's report and gave orders for copies to be sent at once to the embassies in London, Paris, St Petersburg and The Hague. In an excess of zeal the Wilhelmstrasse forwarded the gratifying report to all the remaining thirty-three legations as well.[61]

BRITISH ASSESSMENTS OF THE 'GERMAN DANGER'

Far from taking Kaiser Wilhelm's protestations of peace and friendship at face value, both the court at Windsor and the statesmen in Downing Street credited the German Reich with breathtaking ambitions. Almost as if in preparation for the Kaiser's visit, in September 1907 King Edward VII gave his friend the journalist Donald Mackenzie Wallace a copy of the book *Germany's Swelled Head* by the Hungarian scholar Emil Reich,[62] which he had just read, and asked Wallace to give him his opinion on the author's alarming assertions. In an initial assessment Wallace had no hesitation in commending the book: it contained facts that often escaped the English and which could bring about 'disastrous consequences for the British Empire'. The author had probably somewhat exaggerated the danger represented by the Pan-Germans, Wallace commented, for the great majority of the German population was sensible and peaceable. Hence the danger came less from the people than from above, and principally from Wilhelm II. 'The danger of the wild Pan-Germanic ideas', in Wallace's view, lay 'in the possibility of their being taken up seriously by the Emperor. That he has a certain sympathy with them is unquestionable ... But it must be remembered that he is much more imprudent in words than in acts ... There is no doubt that His Majesty, while occasionally displaying Pan-Germanic Spread Eaglism [sic] in his speeches, has not allowed it to permeate into his policy, and it has certainly never led him into war. What we have, as a nation, to fear is, I submit, not megalomania of the vulgar type called "swelled head", but the quiet persistent carrying out of a well considered policy which aims at destroying our naval supremacy, with a view to appropriating a large portion of our Colonial Empire.' Wallace summed up Emil Reich's conclusions thus: 'The Emperor ... pursues a well founded, well organised policy. His subjects, being a prolific race, feel the need of expansion, but they find that expansion in Europe is impossible, *firstly*, because they are surrounded by countries already densely populated, and *secondly* because any attempt to make large European conquests would produce a hostile coalition of Powers, such as checked the aggressive schemes of Louis XIV and Napoleon. They have to look, therefore, for possibilities of expansion in distant, thinly populated regions, and they are consequently forced into worldwide imperialism. In this field of national activity they meet with three formidable rivals, England, the United States, and Japan. Of the three opponents England stands in the first rank, and her naval supremacy must be broken before Germany can realise her Colonial ambitions. Humanly speaking, therefore, a life-and-death struggle between England and Germany is inevitable, but as it will not begin until the German plan of attack has been carefully and completely prepared, both in the diplomatic and the military sense, we have a certain breathing time, and we ought to utilize it for making counter-preparations of a defensive kind. Unfortunately the great majority of Englishmen have not yet come to understand the real aims and methods of German policy, and those who perceive the danger are unwilling or unable to take the measures for averting it. Too much confidence is placed in the invincibility and ubiquity of the British fleet, and consequently no adequate land force is created. No doubt the British Navy is at present greatly superior in strength to the German, but the Germans are rapidly overtaking us in naval armaments, and it is quite possible that in a few years they may try conclusions with us. If a great naval battle takes place, the stakes will be very unequal, because Germany will risk merely her fleet, her Colonies and a portion of her maritime trade, whereas England will risk her position as a Great Power.'[63]

Not without reason, Edward VII and his Private Secretary Lord Knollys were dissatisfied with the experienced journalist's rather circumlocutory comments on a matter of such vital importance, particularly since Wallace's own views on the Kaiser had disappeared beneath those of the Hungarian professor. In response to their request for clarification Wallace therefore made a more precise statement of 'my own conception (subject to future correction) of a very complicated and enigmatical character'. On 11 October 1907, that is only four weeks before the arrival of the Kaiser at Windsor, he drew a fascinating character sketch of the German sovereign. 'Certainly the Emperor William is by nature impulsive and flighty, and these natural characteristics of his often find expression both in words and in acts; for, so far from attempting to conceal them, he loves to startle the world from time to time by a theatrical display of his personality ... But behind his impulsiveness and flightiness he has a certain amount of latent prudence which generally awakens at critical moments and prevents him from making the fatal plunge into war. At once vain and ambitious, he is anxious and impatient to extend his influence and his dominions both in Europe and in other parts of the world, but he is intelligent enough to perceive, in his calmer moments, the obstacles and dangers with which he is surrounded. As to Europe, though he sometimes coquettes with Pan-Germanism, he knows very well that any attempt to imitate Louis XIV or Napoleon in their wild schemes of territorial aggrandisement would soon produce a great European Coalition which would finally crush him. Already he is regarded everywhere with suspicion, and the Powers most exposed to his aggressive tendencies are now drawing together, so that he must already have at least a presentiment of future isolation. In this respect the Algeciras conference was a premonitory warning to him, and he felt it so keenly that he foolishly showed his irritation in the famous communication to Count Goluchowski ... As to Colonial expansion the position is very similar. Here the extreme wing of the Colonial party corresponds to the Pan-Germanists, and His Majesty often coquettes with them, but he never entirely loses sight of the fact that the Power which has command of the Sea has to be taken into consideration. Though he may send off a telegram full of sympathy and encouragement to an enemy of England, he carefully refrains from supporting his message by the dispatch of a fleet! Fortunately for himself and his country the diplomatic campaigns which his restless ambition induces him to undertake are like military manoeuvres in which the troops engaged use merely blank-cartridges. This ought not, however, to put us off our guard or make us relax our watchfulness, because it is pretty certain that if we had the misfortune to find ourselves seriously hampered by international or internal complications, he would take advantage of the opportunity and order ball-cartridge to be served out. For a good many years he has been waiting and watching and hesitating between two opinions. As German colonial expansion can be effected only in one of two ways, either by means of friendship and cooperation with England or by hostility and defiance of her, he has oscillated between the two policies, trying now to cajole and now to frighten us into accordance with his wishes. Any competent person with the secret archives of our Foreign Office at his disposal could write a most interesting and instructive sketch of these oscillations ... When we next meet', Wallace wrote to Knollys, 'I shall be curious to know whether you agree, to any extent, in my conception of the Kaiser's character and aims.'[64] Wilhelm II's activities in the coming months were to confirm the gravest forebodings of the British government.

CHAPTER TWENTY-THREE

The hot summer of 1908. On the verge war with Britain

BRITISH FOREBODINGS OF WAR WITH GERMANY

How sincere were Wilhelm II's solemn affirmations of friendship at Windsor, at the Guildhall in London and at Highcliffe Castle? How well grounded – to put the question the other way round – were Sir Donald Mackenzie Wallace's fears in October 1907 that in the long term the Kaiser harboured far-reaching plans for conquests in Europe and overseas which would rock the British Empire and disrupt the international states system around the globe? On 18 November 1907, the day of the German sovereign's arrival at Highcliffe, the new German Navy Bill was published in Berlin. Since Tirpitz had formulated the Bill in deliberately obscure terms, it took the British naval attaché, Captain Philip Dumas, two weeks to work out and report to London the gigantic extent of the naval building programme, adding the new ships authorised by the Bill to those already provided for under the Navy Bill of 1900 and the replacement ships which would be built as a result of shortening the period of service of older ships. According to his calculations, by 1914 the Imperial Navy would possess thirty-six battleships (of which sixteen would be of the Dreadnought type) and nineteen large cruisers (including five of the Invincible class). And since under the new programme there would be a break in shipbuilding in 1911, in his view a further Bill would inevitably be demanded then to fill the gap.[1]

As if this development were not worrying enough, in December 1907, while Wilhelm was fervently asserting his friendly intentions towards Britain at Highcliffe, the 'still very secret' news reached London that Germany and Russia, had, as the Kaiser had striven for years to arrange, come to an accord over the maintenance of the status quo in the Baltic and that they intended to bring Sweden into the accord too. In Hardinge's judgement, this agreement was aimed against France and Britain, and he commented to Edward VII that it was significant that Denmark was not included, for 'If Germany was at war with us her first step would be to occupy part of Denmark, & if Denmark were included in the agreement both Russia & Sweden would be bound to prevent Germany from doing so.'[2] At the same time as this initiative with regard to the Baltic, Count Metternich put forward another proposal in the name of the Kaiser which Hardinge considered no less 'insidious'. Ostensibly in order to dispel the rumours circulating that the Kaiser had designs on Holland, an agreement should be reached between Britain, Germany, Denmark and Holland – but not France – over the maintenance of the status quo in the North Sea. This suggestion, in Hardinge's view, was an attempt to drive a wedge between Britain and France.[3]

As was only to be expected, the announcement of a massive expansion of the navy and the rumours of German intentions with regard to Denmark and the Netherlands aroused fears of a war and even of an invasion not only among the British public but also at the highest government levels in London.[4] But they also hardened British resolve to take the necessary counter-measures by land and by sea and to seek even closer diplomatic ties above all with France and Russia. Already in September 1907 the Foreign Office had drawn the King's attention to an article in *The Times* in which the military correspondent Charles à Court Repington had called for the greatest possible vigilance with regard to German naval policy. 'The German navy is not only powerful, but it is always concentrated, and obeys a single impulse. It is not permissible to neglect a single precaution by sea or land when we are considering the chance of the hostility of this Power.'[5] Sir Charles Hardinge, Admiral Sir John Fisher and Viscount Esher, all close friends of the King, played a key role in the coordination of foreign and naval policy against the German threat, and Esher had gone public with a letter which was published in *The Times* on 6 February 1908.[6] Fisher wrote bluntly to the King on 14 March 1908: 'Russia & Turkey are the two Powers and the *only two* that matter to us as against Germany and that we have eventually to fight Germany is as sure as anything human can be.'[7]

The danger that Kaiser Wilhelm could order an invasion of the British Isles was taken quite seriously in the Foreign Office. Although Tirpitz, in a conversation with the British naval attaché Dumas in February 1908, tried to play down such ideas as absurd and completely impracticable, Hardinge and the Foreign Secretary Edward Grey were decidedly of a different opinion. The former wrote: 'There are many indications that the future invasion of England is being carefully prepared in Germany and, if ever the moment should arise, it will almost certainly be found that no precaution has been neglected to ensure its success.' And Grey commented: 'There is no doubt whatever that the Germans have studied and are studying the question [of an invasion], German officers on leave come here and explore our coast and no doubt send in reports which are interesting and welcome to their own authorities. No doubt also the German Staffs work out possible plans. We too continue to work out the best methods of making any such plans miscarry. As long as we have sufficient superiority of Navy the risk will be too great for the Germans to run it in cold blood, but it is a danger to us to be borne in mind in all contingencies.' The leading expert on Germany at the Foreign Office, Eyre Crowe, commenting on the naval attaché's report on his conversation with Tirpitz, wrote: 'We may have our own idea whether an invasion can be prevented or repelled, but it is too well known that the German military authorities not only regard it as feasible in certain circum- stances, but have studied the ways and means and made plans. I believe it is on record that so great an authority as Moltke regarded the invasion of England as practicable. It is certain that the Great General Staff at Berlin is of the same opinion. It is only 2 or 3 years ago that Baron von Edelsheim, then a captain on that Staff published, with the authorization of his chief, a pamphlet dealing in detail with the measures to be taken for the purpose; that the pamphlet was immediately afterwards suppressed; and that Baron von Edelsheim was sent back in disgrace to his regiment, because the Emperor was very angry that the pamphlet having been noticed in the English press, threatened to cause bad feeling and impair the political relations. It is also a fact which I myself got to know through the indiscretion of one of the officials of the Hamburg-America Line, and which I brought to Lord Lansdowne's notice at the time (some 2 or 3 years ago, I think) that the Emperor with his own hand made a number of blue pencil corrections and alterations in the designs of 2 new liners, then about to be built, because H[is] M[ajesty] maintained that the designs as submitted to him would not permit of these ships taking their allotted part in the transport of 2 divisions to England. In view of these facts and other considerations of a more general character which need not here be set out, Admiral Tirpitz's bland remarks to Captain Dumas do not, I think, deserve to be taken very seriously. It is of course his business to prevent if possible any suspicions from arising as to possible German plans.'[8] Against this background the Foreign Office now decided to send the King the memoran- dum on the global historical significance of the German challenge written by Crowe a year earlier, which later became so famous. In his accompanying letter Hardinge emphasised the special qualifications possessed by Crowe, who was a 'very able young fellow'. 'He has exceptional opportunities for knowing what Germans think, as his mother was German, his wife is German and his sisters have married Germans. Consequently all his relations are Germans! I think there is a good deal in what he has written.' Edward VII received the memorandum with great interest.[9]

WILHELM'S LONGED-FOR ALLIANCE WITH THE UNITED STATES AND CHINA

While Wilhelm II presented himself outwardly as a friend of England before, during and after his visit to Windsor, London and Highcliffe, he considered the British Empire, with its Entente policy, as Germany's worst enemy. Immediately after his return from England he wrote to the Reich Chancellor expressing his views. 'England's whole policy in the last few years is clear! To make her position in Europe unassailable for us, in order to keep us in Europe and tie us down by naval means while they seize the Yang-tze region, so that we are kept cowering and don't disturb their robbery. Hence all those Ententes with the Mediterranean powers, so as to have bases everywhere, and on top of that launching France into the Morocco affair. This was supposed to lead to a clash between us, so that the British could get rid of the pair of us and have the tasty morsels all to themselves! That was also the reason for the Entente with Russia over Persia, so that Russia is pacified and quiet and does not interfere. And hence also the colossal fury of the British now over the American navy's move [into the Pacific], of which they made no secret to me; the balance of power at sea is hopelessly upset and is changing to their disadvantage in the East. Therefore we must see to it that the [American] navy remains in the Pacific and if possible also goes to the Philippines and China! It will provide cover for the Yangtze until we are ready with our navy! *England will never dare do anything against America*; if she sees that we two are acting resolutely together to preserve China, she will perhaps even co-operate with us, like a true Pharisee! And in that way Japan is made harmless. So there is a great work to be done here; onwards, we have thought about it long enough! Enough words have been exchanged; now let us see deeds! Wilhelm I. R. Give this to Schön to read.'[10]

The 'great work' which the Kaiser had been striving towards for years was nothing less than bringing about an 'Entente' between the German Reich, the USA and China, thus creating a global counterweight to the Anglo-Franco-Russo-Japanese combination. Already in June 1907, when he heard of Roosevelt's intention to send the American Atlantic fleet into the Pacific, Wilhelm had written to the President offering to send the entire German navy to protect the American Atlantic coast.[11] A few months later, when speculation arose about an imminent war between the United States and Japan, the Kaiser sent Roosevelt another letter, this time offering to send a Prussian army corps over to protect the Californian coast.[12] On the eve of his visit to Windsor the Kaiser received the welcome news that China was at last showing interest in an alliance with Germany and America. 'That's the result of the constant "Entente" business by the British, who treat other countries like a herd of cattle for the sake of their own interests', he exulted.[13]

On his return from Windsor and Highcliffe in December 1907 the Kaiser received a report from the German envoy in Peking, Count Arthur von Rex, which gave the impression that an alliance between Germany, America and China was now within reach. He had 'worked for years!' for this moment, Wilhelm rejoiced.[14] In a series of excited marginal comments on this 'excellent' report, he recorded happily that such an alliance with the United States and China against the Anglo-Franco-Russian Entente was something that he had 'already suggested *a year ago!*' The report contained 'exactly my sentiments, which I also expressed to [the former Chinese envoy] Yin-cheng! Not only [the Chinese statesman] Juan-shi-kai but also Yin-cheng has brought about this enquiry to us, as a result of the suggestion for an Entente with us which I made direct to H[er] M[ajesty] [the Empress-Regent Tsu-Hsi]! That was *a year ago*, and up to now we have done *nothing* about it! But now we shall get to work! *At once*, subito!'[15] Confident of success, he wrote to the Chancellor on 30 December 1907: 'My dear Bülow, Today I have read Rex's secret report, which I had been expecting for a long time, with interest and pleasure. It is a frank, clear opinion and a clearly defined goal. I completely agree with his views. They are in part only reiterations of what I have long been preaching to the Ausw[ärtiges] Amt. But unfortunately I have never been able to spur the latter into action, since among us Germans the "pale cast of thought" constantly paralyses "enterprises of great pitch and moment". In the autumn of last year, as arranged with you, I had a conversation about China's future with Yin-tschang, who was about to leave. I told him how much we had China's interests at heart and how anxious I was to smooth the Empress's path for her, which was demonstrated by the fact that I had given orders for my troops to be withdrawn. I asked him to tell H[er] M[ajesty] this from me. You will remember, or find in your records, how successful this step was. It was decisive, and China began to trust us again. At that time, with your agreement, I asked Ying-tschang to convey to H[er] M[ajesty] the Empress a proposal for an *Entente Cordiale* which *guaranteed* the most important parts of China (not the extensive outer provinces) and Kiautschou for us together with support in the event of attack. He promised me to do that. As he has only *now* achieved respect and influence, he has only just set the affair in motion, and that at a very appropriate moment.

Rex's suggestion coincides completely with mine and must be made the basis for *immediate* negotiations. An Entente Cordiale with China for the *preservation of the status quo* is absolutely necessary for us! Otherwise our entire Weltpolitik will be ruined. That is why I was glad to see that the Americ [an] fleet had set sail [for East Asia]. The fact that they are coming round into the Pacific of course makes a mess of all the British and Japanese calculations. Whether they like it or not the British will have to send a strong squadron back to the East, which they imagined was safe under Jap[anese] protection; that will inevitably reduce their strength against us in Europe. The Japanese of course want China for themselves, but also want all whites out of Asia. But they have not yet got their navy ready, and so are not inclined to fight America *now*. Therefore for them and us the situation is *favourable*, as the pressure of 19 ships of the line, 15 armoured cruisers and the biggest Navy in the world under *a single command* will do a fine job in keeping the others from attempts to divide up China and to put us and America at a disadvantage there. So it is *also* in the American interest to conclude a similar Entente Cordiale with China for the preservation of the *status quo* so that their trade does not suffer. In the long run Russia too – when these people have properly grasped the situation – will be inclined to come to a similar agreement because she does after all have a great interest in preserving China and not acquiring other unwanted Europeans as her Eastern neighbours as well as Japan. The Emperor [Nicholas II] has already hinted as much to me and I have commended to him particularly warmly a good relationship with China. All the Europ[ean] nations have concluded their ententes here for particular purposes, to protect themselves and to safeguard their interests. It is absolutely essential for us to do the same now, as our most important future export interests are at stake; these require China's continued existence *in her entirety*! With the predatory carve-up that those 3 beggars have in mind we shall be lost and done for! The modus operandi can only be chosen in such a way that China comes to an entente with each of us separately. We can of course put heavy pressure on Rooseveldt [sic] through Sternburg, so that when he gets the request he will accept it with goodwill. We absolutely must conclude the entente as soon as possible! I have striven and worked for this moment for years! It was not easy! Whenever I raised the question with Tschirschky he simply wrung his hands and said "China, oh yes, China!" That was all! The fact that we would incidentally also get the Russians – apparently – into something of a headlock, which hypocrites like Lamsdorff and Isvolsky thoroughly deserve, did not have the desired effect either! But now it is high time to *seize* a favourable opportunity *boldly*, not to look around constantly to see what other people say! The others have never bothered about us, so tit for tat! — The article from the *Finanzchronik* which I sent you yesterday shows how viable China is. Chinese self-esteem is not to be underestimated either, and if we could do something to support and influence the reorganisation of their army that would be a good thing!'[16]

THE KAISER'S LETTER TO LORD TWEEDMOUTH

Spurred on by hopes of joining forces with China and the USA, Wilhelm felt able to adopt quite a different tone towards Britain from that of his Guildhall speech. The Reich Chancellor urged moderation upon him, above all on naval policy, but succeeded only in arousing the Supreme War Lord's displeasure. In his memoirs Bülow recalled that Wilhelm had asserted that with the British, 'ruthless, even brutal frankness is the only way'; Germany had 'no cause to tread softly, and more especially, no reason at all to slow down the pace of naval construction or to come to any kind of arrangement with Albion on naval matters'. It was this mentality that gave rise to the 'regrettable' letter which the Kaiser wrote to Lord Tweedmouth behind his back, Bülow complained.[17]

On the evening of 16 February 1908 Admiral von Müller, now head of the Naval Cabinet, was attending a theatrical performance at the Crown Prince's Palace in Berlin when he was summoned to the Schloss. In his study the Kaiser showed Müller two letters which he had written to Lord Tweedmouth, the British First Lord of the Admiralty, and to King Edward VII, without the prior knowledge of the Reich Chancellor, the Foreign Secretary von Schoen, or Admiral Tirpitz.[18] The letter to Tweedmouth amounted to one of the worst independent initiatives ever taken by the Kaiser, and one which caused serious damage internationally to his own reputation and that of the German Reich. It ran: 'During my last pleasant visit to your hospitable shores I tried to make your authorities understand what the drift of German naval policy is, but I am afraid that my explanations have been either misunderstood or not believed, because I see "German danger" and "German challenge to British naval supremacy" constantly quoted in different articles. This phrase, if not repudiated or corrected, sown broadcast over the country and daily dinned into British ears, might in the end create the most deplorable results. I therefore deem it advisable, as Admiral of the Fleet, to lay some facts before you to enable you to see clearly that it is absolutely nonsensical and untrue that the German naval bill is to provide a navy meant as a challenge to British naval supremacy. The German fleet is built against nobody at all; it is solely built for Germany's needs in relation with that country's rapidly growing trade. The German naval bill was sanctioned by the Imperial Parliament and

published ten years ago, and may be had at any large bookseller's. There is
nothing surprising, secret, or underhand in it, and every reader may study the
whole course mapped out for the development of the German Navy with
the greatest ease. The law is being adhered to, and provides for about thirty to
forty ships of the line in 1920. The number of ships fixed by the bill included
the fleet then actually in commission, notwithstanding its material being
already old and far surpassed by contemporary types. In other foreign navies
the extraordinary rapidity with which improvements were introduced in types
of battleships, armaments, and armor made the fleet in commission obsolete
before the building programme providing additions to it was half finished.
The obsolete fleet had to be struck off the list, thus leaving a gap, lowering the
number of ships below the standard prescribed by the bill. This gap was
stopped by using the finished ships to replace the obsolete ones instead of
being added to them as originally intended. Therefore, instead of steadily
increasing the standing fleet by regular additions it came to a wholesale
rebuilding of the entire German Navy. Our actual programme in course of
execution is practically only the exchange of old material for new, but not an
addition to the number of units originally laid down by the bill of ten years
ago, which is being adhered to. – It seems to me that the main fault in the
discussions going on in the papers is the permanent ventilating of so-called
two to three or more power standard and then only exemplifying on one
power, which is invariably Germany. It is fair to suppose that each nation
builds and commissions its navy according to its needs and not only with
regard to the programme of other countries. Therefore, it would be the
simplest thing for England to say: "I have a world-wide empire and the
greatest trade of the world, and to protect them I must have so and so many
battleships, cruisers, &c., as are necessary to guarantee the supremacy of the
sea to me, and they shall, accordingly, be built and manned." That is
the absolute right of your country, and nobody anywhere would lose a word
about it, and whether it be 60 or 90 or 100 battleships, that would make no
difference and certainly no change in the German naval bill. May the
numbers be as you think fit, everybody here would understand it, but
the people would be very thankful over here if at last Germany was left out
of the discussion, for it is very galling to the Germans to see their country
continually held up as the sole danger and menace to Great Britain by
the whole press of the different contending parties, considering that other
countries are building, too, and there are even larger fleets than the German. –
Doubtless, when party faction runs high there is often a lamentable lack of
discrimination in the choice of weapons, but I really must protest that the
German naval programme should be only one for her exclusive use, or that

such a poisoned view should be forged as a German challenge to British supremacy of the sea. If permanently used mischief may be created at home, and the injured feeling engendering the wish for retaliation in the circle of the German Naval League as a representative of the nation which would influence public opinion and place the Government in a very disagreeable position by trying to force it to change its programme through undue pressure, difficult to ignore. – In a letter which Lord Esher caused to be published a short time ago he wrote that every German, from the Emperor down to the last man, wished for the downfall of Sir John Fisher. Now I am at a loss to tell whether the supervision of the foundations and drains of royal palaces [an allusion to Lord Esher's former employment in the Office of Works] is apt to qualify somebody for the judgement of naval affairs in general. As far as regards German affairs, the phrase is a piece of unmitigated balderdash, and has created immense merriment in the circles of those here who know. But I venture to think that such things ought not to be written by people who are high placed, as they are liable to hurt public feelings over here. Of course I need not assure you that nobody here dreams of wishing to influence Great Britain in the choice of those to whom she means to give the direction of her navy or to disturb them in the fulfillment of their noble task. It is expected that the choice will always fall on the best and ablest, and their deeds will be followed with interest and admiration by their brother officers in the German Navy. It is, therefore, preposterous to infer that the German authorities work for or against persons in official positions in foreign countries. It is as ridiculous as it is untrue, and I hereby repudiate such calumny. Besides, to my humble notion, this perpetual quoting of the German danger is utterly unworthy of the great British Nation, with its world-wide empire and mighty navy. There is something nearly ludicrous about it. The foreigners in other countries might easily conclude that Germans must be an exceptionally strong lot, as they seem to be able to strike terror into the hearts of the British, who are five times their superiors. – I hope your Lordship will read these lines with kind consideration. They are written by one who is an ardent admirer of your splendid navy, who wishes it all success, and who hopes that its ensign may ever wave on the same side as the German Navy's, and by one who is proud to wear a British naval uniform of Admiral of the Fleet, which was conferred on him by the late great Queen of blessed memory. – Once more the German naval bill is not aimed at England and is not a challenge to British supremacy of the sea, which will remain unchallenged for generations to come. Let us all remember the warning Admiral Sir John Fisher gave to his hearers in November, when so cleverly he cautioned them not to get scared by using the admirable phrase "if Eve had not always kept her eye on the apple she would not have eaten it, and we should not now be bothered with clothes." ... Wilhelm I.R. Admiral of the Fleet.'[19]

The Kaiser's letter provoked horrified reactions in both Britain and Germany, as its contents gradually became known. Since Wilhelm had written to his uncle alerting him to his letter to Tweedmouth, King Edward invited the First Lord to dinner at Buckingham Palace on 19 February, together with Fisher.[20] It is not difficult to imagine the King's anger at the insulting attacks on his friends, the manifest lies about the building of the German battlefleet and the very fact that the German monarch had written a political letter to the First Lord of the Admiralty, the ministerial head of the British Navy. On 22 February 1908 he sent his nephew an indignant – and now celebrated – reprimand: 'Your writing to my First Lord of the Admiralty is a "new departure", and I do not see how he can prevent our press from calling attention to the great increase in the building of German ships of war, which necessitates our increasing our navy also.'[21]

Although this letter from the King had arrived in Berlin by 24 February,[22] eleven days were to elapse before the Reich Chancellor, the Foreign Secretary and Admiral von Tirpitz got wind of their sovereign's incredible behaviour, via the press and reports from London.[23] Tirpitz, who felt particularly betrayed because the Kaiser had 'almost childishly made a whole series of false statements which the English had of course recognised as such straight away',[24] threatened to resign and had to be pacified with a seat in the Prussian House of Lords.[25] Princess Marie Radziwill describes how the Chancellor and the Foreign Secretary, both beside themselves with anger, hurried to the British embassy to ask whether the story they had read in *The Times* of 6 March was true. 'When Lascelles said it was in fact true Bülow fell back into his armchair with his head thrown back and his face so red Lascelles thought the Chancellor was going to have a fit on the spot.'[26] Stunned, Prince Bülow sent a telegram to the Kaiser, who was visiting Wilhelmshaven: 'May I respectfully ask Your Majesty for a copy of the letter to Lord Tweedmouth so that we are prepared for all eventualities and I can report to Your Majesty on further developments after Your Majesty's return.'[27]

As Wilhelm had not kept a copy, Bülow was eventually forced to send a trusted emissary secretly to London to obtain the text of the Kaiser's deplorable letter.[28] Before knowing how it was worded, he asked the Kaiser for his consent in principle for the publication of the letter, 'if necessary omitting personal passages, for instance that concerning Lord Esher'.[29] Quite unperturbed, Kaiser Wilhelm wired back saying that he 'agreed to publication'.[30] Not surprisingly when the complete text of the letter with all its odd and extremely insulting expressions reached the Wilhelmstrasse, Bülow and Schoen abandoned the idea of publishing it.[31]

The Tweedmouth letter was not published in full until after the outbreak of the world war. But more than enough of its contents leaked out to cause a serious crisis both in London and in Germany. Metternich risked his ambassadorial post by reporting on 6 March 1908 from the British capital on the disastrous effect of the Kaiser's letter and warning that 'all those elements friendly towards us will be weakened and the Jingoists strengthened. His Majesty the Kaiser's popularity in England will also suffer and suspicions about our policy will increase again.'[32] In London the affair of the letter was discussed in both houses of Parliament. For the first time, the German imperial navy was explicitly named as a probable opponent when the British naval estimates were set.[33]

In Berlin Maximilian Harden described the letter to Tweedmouth as 'the great crisis. Much much worse than the Krüger Telegram.'[34] Marie Radziwill expressed doubts about the mental health of a monarch who had acted so autocratically and irresponsibly on such a dangerous question. 'Never has such unparalleled imprudence, lack of tact, and abysmal forgetfulness of the position of the Head of State been seen before', she sighed. 'I am beginning to be absolutely convinced our Sovereign isn't well and that his brain is no longer quite normal. If it had been clear, he would never have committed such an appalling blunder as this last. This time it's really worse than a bloomer ... It is certain that the Emperor, as we know him, only wrote it because he hoped to influence British naval construction in such a way as to give himself more time for the German programme ... There are undoubtedly treacherous depths on both sides, as well as the peculiar desire of the Emperor's to direct everything in this world. For a long time now his character has been becoming more and more autocratic, liking to give advice when it is not wanted and wishing to dominate everything.'[35]

In his memoirs Bülow scoffed at the explanation with which the Kaiser sought to excuse himself for his irresponsible initiative. At the time 'when he was working away on his letter' the Reich Chancellor had had a cold, and the monarch 'could not expose himself to catarrh because of his old ear complaint'.[36] He, Bülow, had however come to the decision, in view of the Tweedmouth letter, that in the national interest he would no longer tolerate independent initiatives by Kaiser Wilhelm. 'It is understandable', he wrote, 'that an unauthorised action of that kind, overstepping to an alarming extent the boundaries of what is permissible, could not fail not only to annoy me but to cause me deep anxiety and to strengthen me in my resolve to take advantage of the next available opportunity, in the interests of the country, for a vigorous condemnation of the imperial infringements which were so dangerous and harmful to the well-being of the Reich, in accordance with my duty'.[37]

For a long time, however, Wilhelm II persisted in maintaining that he had acted rightly, and he pursued his totally uncompromising policy on the naval question to the very brink of war with Britain. During the annual ambassadors' dinner at the Schloss on 11 March 1908 the French ambassador recorded with astonishment that the unfortunate affair of the letter had caused the Kaiser more satisfaction than annoyance, 'and that it was not causing him the smallest embarrassment'; indeed he saw no problems at all in the incident and would happily do exactly the same again.[38] Metternich's dispatch recounting the harmful effect of the letter on the British government's naval policy did not cause the Kaiser any concern; he merely commented: 'I do not share Metternich's fears. The English have not yet gone so completely mad. The attack in the Times comes from the King who is worried that the letter [to Tweedmouth] might make too reassuring an impression.'[39] The ambassador attempted to make it clear, in simple and unsparing language, why the English thought that Germany's battlefleet construction threatened their most vital interests and thus felt compelled to pursue their Entente policy. But this was spurned by Wilhelm in a torrent of uncomprehending denials. Metternich's assertions were 'all English mistakes!' and nothing but 'Rubbish!' The ambassador's statement that 'a battle lost in the North Sea means the end of the British Empire' was countered with the remark, 'far from it! no reason at all for that!' Similarly, Wilhelm dismissed the observation that Britain feared that alliance with a strong Germany would 'lead to political dependence on us and she therefore prefers to seek support from others', commenting significantly, 'they have always done that and it is simply wrong! and a bad mistake, as in the long run it is bound to make our people suspicious and angry!' Finally, justifying the letter to Tweedmouth once again, he thundered: 'This reasoning by the English and also by the Ambassador is not new and it must and can only be constantly put to rights by corrections and explanations. That was what the letter was for. Besides, according to the above exposition the English are doing absolutely the wrong thing and making a political mistake, if they "prefer to seek the support of others" rather than to have friendly relations with us! That is a mistake ex fundamentis which will reveal itself through its consequences in all kinds of impossible situations with which England itself will be burdened. In these circumstances one cannot simply calm down; one must provide "relief". All this is *not our Navy's* fault, but that of the whole *insane "Dreadnought" policy* of Sir J. Fisher and His Majesty, who thought they were putting us "en demeure" with it. And now they and the hoodwinked British realise that they have made a complete mistake and that they have thereby destroyed their old, great, former superiority, since *all states* are now copying them. That has made the British nervous, as they have only just found it out. They will just have to get used to our Navy. And from time to time we must assure them that it is not against them.'[40]

ON THE THRESHOLD OF WAR WITH BRITAIN

Wilhelm II's aggressive sentiments towards Britain and her King reached a positively alarming degree when he learned that in June 1908 Edward VII was planning to travel with Hardinge, Sir John Fisher and the Commander in Chief of the army, General Sir John French, to meet Tsar Nicholas II at the Russian naval base of Reval. The Anglo-Franco-Russian Entente, he declared, was 'only a mask for an anti-German grouping like before the 7 Year War! . . . So reform the Reich's finances! Many *indirect* taxes; strong Navy, strong Army! Powder dry!'[41] In 'the most violent language' he criticised his uncle and the British politicians to the Russian ambassador – abuse which was of course not only reported to St Petersburg but also reached London at lightning speed.[42] Very soon a whole series of belligerent remarks found their way via Russia into the German press too.[43]

On 29 May 1908, during brigade exercises at Döberitz, the Kaiser gave a talk to the officer corps which caused an international furore as news of its wording gradually leaked out. In mid-June the *Dortmunder Zeitung* reported that at Döberitz the Kaiser had spoken for the first time of the 'encirclement' of Germany. He was alleged to have said: 'Now, it looks very much as if an attempt is being made to encircle us and face us down. We shall be quite capable of dealing with that. The German has never fought better than when he has had to defend himself on all sides. Let them come and get us. We are ready.'[44] At first the Kaiser emphatically refuted alarmed enquiries as to whether he had in fact struck such a belligerent note. 'The lies at my expense have taken on such horrendous dimensions that I am losing my patience. There is *nothing* true in anything that has been said! It is all invention and must be strongly denied. I declare categorically once again that in Döberitz I held purely official, military consultations *without a trace of politics*; I made no speeches, especially none like the one reported in the newspapers.'[45] Several weeks later he described the journalist who had reported on his speech at Döberitz in the *Dortmunder Zeitung* as a 'swine'.[46]

Bülow's resolve 'to take advantage of the next available opportunity, in the interests of the country, for a vigorous condemnation of the imperial infringements which were so dangerous and harmful to the well-being of the Reich, in accordance with my duty'[47] was now put to the test. The Chancellor finally felt obliged to bring home to the monarch the terrible damage he had done with his brash remarks. 'I continue to believe that for economic and financial reasons England would only very reluctantly take the decision to go to war. I believe that Russia needs and wants peace. And finally I believe that even France, although she has not yet got over Alsace-Lorraine and the loss of her 250-year-old prépondérance légitime on the continent and has not given up the idea of revenge, has doubts about running the unpredictable risks of a war. But at the same time I believe that it is in the interest of these Powers to make us appear on edge and restless. That is our enemies' tactic if only because every real or apparent threat from our side induces the French to fortify their Eastern border even more, the English to build even more Dreadnoughts, the Russians to move even more troops to their Western border. It is therefore regrettable that Y.M.'s address, intended only for the officers at Döberitz, has become more widely known through indiscretion. We must work as quietly as possible to make our Army swift to strike and ready for war, but outwardly we must avoid anything that draws attention unnecessarily to our work and to us and exposes us to fresh suspicions and intrigues.'[48] Again Wilhelm refused to accept any responsibility. 'Your letter is based on a mistake', he replied to the Chancellor's admonition. 'I did not make any such address to the assembled officers in Döberitz.'[49] The whole rumpus was a product of the guilty conscience of the Entente politicians. Edward VII, above all, was working to bring about war and trying to put the blame on him, Wilhelm. 'He wants war!' Wilhelm exclaimed at the end of June 1908. 'Only somebody else is to wage it; and I am to start it, so that he escapes the odium!'[50] This is an early hint that the idea was dawning on Wilhelm II that in unleashing a European war one must shift the blame on to the enemy. In the summer of 1908 this realisation led him, as we shall soon see, to the alarming conclusion that Britain must be provoked into attacking Germany in order for Germany to be seen by the world and her own people as the victim.[51]

Kaiser Wilhelm's characteristic denial that he had ever uttered the words ascribed to him at Döberitz lost any remaining credibility when on 20 June 1908 he was given a tumultuous welcome by massed crowds of cheering, singing people in Hamburg, and Albert Ballin persuaded him that this patriotic tribute was the result of his speech at Döberitz. People were 'delighted that a strong, unmistakable message had been proclaimed to other countries, because they expected the warning contained therein to have the best possible effect in the interests of peace', Ballin assured him. As reported by the envoy Georg von Treutler, who was present as representative of the Wilhelmstrasse, 'Herr Ballin added that the person guilty of leaking the speech deserved the "Order of the Black Eagle"'. Suddenly Wilhelm II felt reinforced in his bellicose views. He noted excitedly that this was the first time for ten to fifteen years that he had heard 'Die Wacht am Rhein', the patriotic song which the assembled crowd had spontaneously started to sing. He gave orders that the 'extraordinary warmth of his reception and the large numbers participating in it' should be officially recorded.[52] A few days later, in a speech at Brunsbüttel, referring to his lively reception by the people of Hamburg he declared: 'As I wondered what had caused this outbreak of enthusiasm, there rang out spontaneously, at first gradually and then growing louder and louder, our old German storm song. Then I knew. Gentlemen, I thank you for it; I understood you. It was the pressure of a friendly hand held out to a man who follows his path with determination and who knows that he has behind him someone who understands and wants to help him.'[53]

THOUGHTS OF WAR ON THE NORTH SEA VOYAGE

When the *Hohenzollern* put to sea with the Kaiser and his retinue on 6 July 1908 – this time the company included the Chief of General Staff, Helmuth von Moltke, the Chief of the Military Cabinet, General Count Dietrich von Hülsen-Haeseler, and the Chief of the Naval Cabinet, Admiral Georg von Müller[54] – the danger of war was on everyone's lips. Hereditary Prince Ernst zu Hohenlohe-Langenburg wrote to his father about a conversation he had had with the elderly Prince Guido von Henckel-Donnersmarck. Henckel did not believe there would be war in the near future, he reported, 'as the French are afraid of having to pull England's chestnuts out of the fire for her and the Russians are still suffering too much from the wounds inflicted by the last war. But the situation remains rather disturbing all the same'.[55] As the Royal Navy was holding its summer exercises in the Skagerrak while the Imperial Navy, for once, was leaving its home port to sail out to the Azores, Anglo-German relations were particularly tense at this time.[56] The Commander of the High Seas Fleet, Admiral Count Baudissin, considered the deployment of the British navy in the Skagerrak to be a kind of mobilisation and anxiously stressed the necessity of staying in daily contact with the Supreme War Lord to keep him informed of developments. The Foreign Secretary, however, affirmed that the political situation gave no cause for concern. Captain Hopman agreed. 'The English have no intention of hitting out', he commented on 30 June 1908. 'They are only distrustful and want to intimidate us a little. If they attack us there will be a huge European war and they cannot tolerate that.'[57] Prince Heinrich also considered war with Britain 'most unlikely' and 'effectively out of the question'. Nevertheless he gave orders that if war broke out the German navy should return to the North Sea via the northern route round Scotland.[58]

Wilhelm II did not believe any more than his brother did that the British had any immediate intention of going to war.[59] But his conviction that Edward VII himself was the driving force behind the anti-German 'encirclement policy'[60] was reinforced by a piece of information given him by Albert Ballin. He telegraphed angrily to Bülow after his conversation with the Director General of the Hapag company, saying that the latter had been told by the influential Anglo-German financier Sir Ernest Cassel 'that he had heard from the King that His Majesty [Edward VII], in order to have a "springboard" with the Tsar so as to detach him from me, had made out [at Reval] that the Sanjak railway project had been hatched by me personally, and that I then put the Austrians up to it, to annoy the Tsar, inflict a political defeat on him and make him the laughing-stock of Europe. As a result the Tsar had suffered a defeat at my hands just as he had at the hands of the Japanese. The Tsar ought not to take such a thing lying down or tolerate it from me. Sir Ernest added that it seemed the Tsar had believed this. I have no words for the perfidy of such a pack of lies. Cassel [was] utterly horrified when Ballin told him this was a despicable lie, as King Edward firmly believed it. When Ballin declared on his honour (which I can confirm) that I knew nothing of the whole story and first heard of it through the newspapers like everyone else, Cassel declared that he must tell the King of this at once, to dissuade him from believing such rubbish.'[61]

The Kaiser's extreme irritation with Britain and with his uncle in particular persisted throughout the Norwegian voyage and created – no doubt also under the influence of Moltke – a dangerously belligerent mood. British statesmen's fears, relayed to the Kaiser through Metternich's reports, of an attack on England by the German navy, merely provoked his scorn. Those 'fellows' in London who were so afraid of an invasion ought to be 'sent for a cold bath cure!' he thundered. 'We shall never be so stupid! That would be Hara-Kiri ... It is crazy nonsense to imagine we would want to attack, ambush or indeed "sweep away" the English purely out of jealous rivalry! The only thing we want is to be left in peace by them so as to be able to expand our trade undisturbed.'[62] But only a few days later Wilhelm adopted a different tone. Suddenly he was determined to press ahead with his fleet plans regardless of the British reaction, calling out in defiance: 'If they want war, let *them start* it, we are not afraid of it!'[63] What had happened to increase the Kaiser's belligerence?

In mid July at Odde, in Norway, he received direct reports from his old friend Albano von Jacobi, his military plenipotentiary at the Russian court, of conversations Jacobi had recently had with the Russian Minister of War, Rediger, and the Foreign Minister, Isvolsky. These reports encouraged the Kaiser and the Chief of General Staff to hope for Russian neutrality in the event of a war between Germany and the two Great Powers in the west.[64] It transpired from Rediger's remarks to Jacobi, as Wilhelm telegraphed excitedly to the Reich Chancellor on 15 July, 'that Russia has no intention of going to war against us at the moment, nor is she ready to do so ... On the other hand he hinted that it was not out of the question that in the event of a complication between England and us, Russia would perhaps remain neutral and confidential talks with us would not be rejected out of hand ... Isvolsky declared that he had subjected the completely "impossible" English proposals regarding Macedonia to careful revision and toning down. It was now entirely up to us to put our relations with Russia onto a permanently favourable footing in the future; for everything would depend on our reaction to the Russ[ian] proposals and how we treated them. If we accepted them Russia would no longer follow the pro-English course which he had been *forced* to take by Austria's and our conduct in the Sanjak railway affair. If we rejected them Russia would continue resolutely on that course, and would attach herself ever more closely and firmly to England and abandon us. Gen. v. Jacobi is of the opinion that Rediger and Isvolsky spoke to him in accordance with a mutually agreed plan; he thinks Isvolsky's last remark was "bluff". Moltke has seen both reports. He declared that it is *absolutely essential* that Rediger's "invite" [sic] is accepted. In the event of war with England it would be of the most vital significance for the Army Command to know that Russia was neutral and to keep her so; our entire deployment would depend upon it. Our diplomats must therefore try by every means to secure the declaration of neutrality. In addition to that, the outbreak must then be contrived in the right way, which is that England must attack us and if she gets France to join in, France must also declare war on us. Thus we are *the ones being attacked* and with that, the casus foederis for Russia is invalid where France is concerned, as it comes into play only in the event of an *attack by us* ... I do not think Isvolsky's words are just an empty bluff, for after all we know what devilish methods England employed at Reval. I entirely share Moltke's point of view. See to it that we come to an agreement of a *military* nature with Russia as soon as possible, under which she promises us her neutrality, so long as the casus foederis is not brought about by some ineptitude on our part. In the event of serious complications, organise our tactics in such a way that England and France attack us, so that we are the victims and Russia, free of the casus foederis, can declare her neutrality. In that situation Moltke and I can cheerfully face even the heaviest trials with complete calm and confidence, trusting in God. But Russia must be made fast now.'[65] Similarly, when Pourtalès, the ambassador in St Petersburg, wrote to the Auswärtiges Amt on the possibility of Russian neutrality in the event of war between Britain and Germany, the Kaiser noted on his report: 'That must be absolutely clearly and *incontestably settled* by negotiation with Russia. Our Army Command must demand it whatever happens.'[66]

THE INCREDIBLE HALE INTERVIEW OF 19 JULY 1908

At the same time as the reports from London and St Petersburg, news reached the *Hohenzollern* in mid July 1908 from Peking which revived the Kaiser's long-cherished hopes for an agreement between Germany, the United States and China to counterbalance the grouping of Britain, France, Russia and Japan.[67] Wilhelm described the hesitant Chinese negotiator Yuan-Schi-Kai impatiently as a 'fusspot!' The principal points of the agreement had been explained to the Chinese as long as a year ago, he protested. Everything had been 'agreed with Roseveldt [sic] already! and the Sons of Heaven have been informed!' 'It has been agreed with America that we make a statement of policy! Nothing in writing and no alliance', he commented on the report from Peking.[68]

In the expectation of an agreement with the USA and China, the Kaiser received the American clergyman and journalist Dr William Bayard Hale for an interview on board the *Hohenzollern* off Bergen on 19 July 1908. It was an interview which the US President and the leading statesmen in London concurred in thinking might have unleashed a world war had its content – as the Kaiser had intended – become public knowledge. In the interests of peace Roosevelt, King Edward VII and the British Foreign Office advised strongly against publication, and even the text censored by the German Foreign Office and released for printing was bought up and pulped at the last minute when, in November, it became obvious that after the catastrophe of the *Daily Telegraph* crisis the publication of a second interview would almost inevitably have led to Wilhelm II's abdication. Nevertheless, by August 1908 the governments of every foreign Great Power including Japan were in possession of the complete, undoubtedly authentic text of the Hale interview; only the German Reich Chancellor, kept in the dark by his sovereign and the Wilhelmstrasse, knew virtually nothing of the true content of the hair-raising conversation of 19 July 1908 until the very end of the year.

Hale had been recommended to the Kaiser by the ambassador Johann Count von Bernstorff and the Auswärtiges Amt after the journalist had published a laudatory article on Roosevelt.[69] Immediately after his memorable two-hour conversation with Wilhelm II the American wrote detailed notes for himself on everything that the monarch had 'eagerly and impulsively' told him.[70] The same evening he sent a résumé to the owner of the *New York Times*, adding a warning. 'Germany is expecting to fight England, and, in my judgment, the Emperor does not care how quickly. He poured a steady stream of insults upon the English for two hours.'[71] On his return to New York Hale described to the astounded editors of the newspaper the key points of what the Kaiser had said. He repeated 'that the Emperor was most bitter against England during the whole interview and that Germany was ready for war at any moment with her and the sooner it came the better. He claimed that Great Britain looked upon Germany as her enemy because it was the most dominant force on the continent of Europe and it had always been England's way to attack the strongest Power. France and Russia were now out of the running, he said, and she was friendly with them, so everything was directed against Germany. The Emperor said that Great Britain had been degenerating ever since the Boer war which was a war against God and for that she would be punished as all nations have been who have done wrong to a weaker Power that was in the right. He believed that a war would come, and he was aching for the fight, not for the sake of war, but as something that was unpleasant and inevitable, and the sooner the better. With regard to India the Emperor appeared to be thoroughly posted and said that within nine months that country would be overrun by one of the bloodiest rebellions ever known in history. He blamed this upon the Japanese who, he said, had their goods in every bazaar and their agents sowing sedition and treachery in every quarter. Dr Hale said that he gathered from the Emperor that his ambition was to take Egypt from the British and later the Holyland from Turkey thereby emulating the deeds of the Crusaders in taking the land of Christ from the Infidels. He appeared to be very bitter against his Uncle King Edward and accused him of trying to set the other Powers against Germany. As to France and Russia he said they were not worth talking about from a military or naval point of view ... During the whole interview the Emperor walked the floor and spoke forcefully and earnestly delivering each word so that Dr Hale could understand him thoroughly. He seemed to be full of electricity, and his eyes snapped when he spoke of England, his bitterness was so intent.' An editor of the *New York Times* passed on this highly explosive information confidentially to the British press magnate Lord Northcliffe, assuring him that not a line of it would appear in the American paper, 'but you can rely safely that every word I have written to you was actually spoken by Wilhelm, and if he is in such a frame of mind that he opens out to an American clergyman at the first time of meeting him, there is a danger of something happening before long'.[72]

According to Hale, the Kaiser's confidence in victory was based on his conviction that the British Empire was in the process of breaking up, and that the imminent world war would represent a final battle between the 'yellow' and the 'white' races, in which the German Reich would fight shoulder to shoulder with the United States of America and China; it evidently did not bother him in the least that according to his world view the British, the French and the Russians would be on the 'yellow' side and the Chinese on the 'white' side. He declared proudly to the American journalist, in a reference to 'Nations of Europe, protect your holiest possessions!', the picture warning against the 'yellow peril' which he had sketched fifteen years earlier: 'So I painted the yellow peril. I dare say the world smiled. The world does not smile now. The time for smiling is passed. Everybody understands what must come to pass between the East and the West, the yellow race and the white. It is imbecile folly for us to close our eyes to the inevitable, for us to neglect to prepare to meet the inevitable. We are unworthy of our fathers if we are negligent of the sacred duty of preserving the civilization which they have achieved for us and the religion which God has given us. All the world understands that the greatest contest in the destiny of the earth's population is at hand.' In this battle for the future of mankind the Germans and the Americans were natural allies, Kaiser Wilhelm II affirmed. 'Vast number of Germans and men and women of German descent ... of your big country constitute already a necessary bond between us. Our religion [is] the same. Our race [is] the same. Nowhere, no longer now, even in the nightmares of agitators, is there imagined to be a shadow or possibility of an issue between us.' President Roosevelt, who had reviewed all these questions with him, shared this conviction. 'Oh! This has gone much further than anybody dreams. It has been on my mind for four or five years in this form and it is working out. [The] main trouble is [that] China is so slow.' Yet 'one of these days, very soon now, I hope very soon, an emissary of the highest rank [from China] will visit [the] United States and will revisit us and let us know what China's conditions are, and then we can go ahead. Germany and [the] United States [of] America, declaring that we guarantee Chinese territory and the open door in all part[s] of [the] Chinese Empire. Oh ... Ho! ho! I wonder what they will say to that.' 'Here His Majesty laughed loudly and capered about on deck', Hale recalled, going on to quote the Kaiser further: 'Oh! It will come out all right ... The future belongs to [the] white race; it does not belong to the yellow nor the black nor the olive-colored. It belongs to [the] blonde man, and it belongs to Christianity and Protestantism. We are the only people who can save it. There is no Power in any other civilization or any other religion that can save humanity, and the future belongs to us, the Anglo-Teutons, the man who comes from northern Europe.'[73]

The deadly enemy of the white northern race was the Japanese, Wilhelm announced. 'We know this much about him', he explained to the perplexed Hale, 'he hates the white man, worse than the white man hates the devil. He hates every thing belonging to the white man. He is a miracle at imitation but at heart he despises all that he parodies for the moment.' 'The Japanese are devils', the Kaiser exclaimed; 'that is the simple fact. They are devils.' The first battle between them and the white race had been fought in 1904–5, he stated. 'Russia was fighting the white man's battle. Many did not see it then. All do now. What a pity it was not fought better! What a misfortune! Those Russians were not fit to fight this fight. What a pity it should have [fallen to] them to do it.' The Kaiser's face reddened and he raised his fist, Hale noted. Then he exclaimed: 'My God! I wish my battalions could have had a chance at them; we should have made short work of it.'

The great danger did not lie in the Japanese alone, but in 'Japan at the head of a consolidated Asia, the control of China by Japan which is sharply and bitterly antagonistic to the white man's civilization. That would be [the] worst calamity. That could threaten the world.' He, the Kaiser, had recognised this danger many years ago and demanded that the east be divided up. It was the historic duty of the white man 'to prevent Japan's swallowing China'. Germany and the USA must together guarantee China's integrity; this was the only possible salvation, for the other white nations were useless. 'It is no good talking about Great Britain, a traitor to the white man's cause', Wilhelm railed. 'The ninnies there have got that government in an absolutely impossible position. I tell you that Empire is going to pieces on this rock if that alliance of theirs with Japan is persisted in. I do not see how the British Empire can be saved from dismemberment.' Australia and New Zealand were already seeking the protection of the American navy against the yellow peril. Canada was threatening to leave the Empire because of immigration from Asia, and in South Africa the race question had reached a critical point. The British people were not in favour of the alliance with Japan, 'but the ninnies who run the Government are determined to stick to it. England is in the position of a traitor to this white man's cause, and England is outside any programme which other western countries devise to meet the conditions which the awakening of the East has produced. Then if you go on to consider what other Powers are bound to England by treaty of alliance or diplomatic understanding, what other Powers must be considered as excluded from any programme against England's Eastern ally. This counts out France and Russia ... What Power remains then interested and unfettered? [The] United States.'[74]

On the return journey from Bergen to Berlin Hale wrote an article about his interview with the Kaiser. Although he omitted or toned down Wilhelm's most offensive remarks in it, the newly appointed American ambassador, David J. Hill, advised strongly against its publication, even in this watered-down form.[75] The editorial staff of the *New York Times* decided unanimously not to print a single line of it. They sent their political correspondent in Washington to President Roosevelt with the letters in which Hale had recorded the Kaiser's most pointed remarks. Roosevelt also expressed strong opposition to their publication, as they would cause 'a great deal of harm'. Scarcely able to believe what he had learned, the President told the former US Secretary of State, Elihu Root, that the Kaiser 'had spent two hours talking to this unknown newspaperman in language which would invite an international explosion if made public'.[76] 'The publication of the interview would really jeopardize the peace of the world', he warned in alarm.[77] Although they remained unknown to the wider public, however, Wilhelm II's words did not fail to have an effect on the foreign policy of the United States. Roosevelt admitted to the British Admiral Arthur Lee that he had been compelled to revise his assessment of the danger to world peace represented by the German Reich in the light of Wilhelm's utterances. Hitherto he had considered British fears about the German danger as 'slightly absurd' and had not believed 'that there was a need of arming against Germany'; after the Kaiser's remarks to Hale, however, which had shown that the monarch 'regarded war between England and Germany as inevitable and as likely to take place soon', he had changed his mind. Roosevelt now recognised the unpredictability of the 'jumpy' Kaiser as a danger to world peace. 'If he is indiscreet enough to talk to a strange newspaperman in such a fashion it would be barely possible that sometime he would be indiscreet enough to act on impulse in a way that would jeopardize the peace', he commented anxiously.[78] From this time Elihu Root also regarded Wilhelm II and his Reich as 'the great disturber of the world'.[79]

Wilhelm II's remarks spread like wildfire from government to government. As has already been mentioned, the editor of the *New York Times* passed on the gist of the interview to the British newspaper baron Lord Northcliffe.[80] Northcliffe too decided against publication but sent the synopsis that he had received from New York to Sir Edward Grey.[81] Soon the truth of the reports about the Kaiser's remarks was no longer in doubt, especially when the complete, uncensored text of the interview with the Kaiser, as written down by Hale on the return from Bergen to Berlin, found its way into the hands of the British government in November, via none other than Britain's ally Japan. As early as at the end of August the Japanese embassy in Washington had obtained Hale's article — by what means it is not clear — and sent it to Tokyo where it made the worst possible impression, as one can well imagine.[82]

The French ambassador in Washington also succeeded in getting sight of the text of the interview, and this version was also passed on to the Foreign Office in London.[83]

Grey and Hardinge sent a copy of the synopsis to the King, who was incredulous. 'This account is a very strange one! Can it be considered authentic?'[84] When he was shown the complete text of the interview, however, Edward VII had no further doubts as to its authenticity. 'I am convinced in my mind that the words attributed to the German Emperor by Mr. Hale are perfectly correct. I know the German Emperor hates me and never loses an opportunity of saying so (behind my back), whilst I have always been kind and nice to him.'[85] Like the statesmen in Downing Street the King recognised the enormous danger of allowing the Kaiser's remarks to become public knowledge. On 17 November he urged Hardinge to do everything to prevent publication in the *Morning Post*. 'We sent for the Editor this morning and he says that he is in possession of the account of the interview but he has faithfully promised not to publish it', the Under Secretary of State reassured the King's Private Secretary next day. He added that the notorious Germanophobe, Leopold Maxse, was planning to force the Kaiser to abdicate by publishing the interview in the *National Review*, but that the Foreign Office would prevent this publication too. King Edward was relieved at this intervention. 'All's well that ends well!' he replied to Hardinge. 'Maxse must really be spoken to seriously.'[86]

When a few of the Kaiser's worst comments nevertheless leaked out to the press, the French Prime Minister, Georges Clemenceau, demanded that the full text of the interview be published, with a view to laying bare the true goals of German policy and thus showing the world 'what a danger to peace is its Emperor'.[87] Only with difficulty did Grey and Hardinge succeed in preventing publication. They did this not least in the belief that the appearance of the Kaiser's interview in a foreign newspaper would give rise to a wave of patriotic indignation in Germany, which could do much to restore Wilhelm II's damaged reputation after the *Daily Telegraph* crisis. The best chance of achieving a normal relationship with Germany, in Grey's opinion, lay in the Kaiser's current weakness, 'with his megalomania'. 'Never has the Emperor's position been so low in the world', Grey observed with satisfaction. 'Why then not let well alone!'[88] Hardinge, for his part, commented that Wilhelm II was obviously 'in a very excitable & ill-balanced frame of mind which with provocation might become dangerous'; he ought not to be driven further into a corner, for then he would truly become 'a danger to Europe'.[89]

Nevertheless, in Britain, too, the Hale interview caused a major shift in the government's attitude towards Germany. In November 1908 Grey told the French ambassador that as a result of the Kaiser's remarks there had been a change of heart in favour of France among some of his Cabinet colleagues, and notably 'chez Mr. Winston Churchill', and Hardinge confirmed that there was now even a majority in the Cabinet 'if necessary prepared to support a policy of intervention in favour of France'.[90] The disastrous effect of the interview on the attitude of leading circles in Britain alarmed the King of Sweden during his visit to Windsor in November 1908. While staying with his brother-in-law Grand Duke Friedrich II of Baden afterwards, Gustaf V described to the Prussian envoy at Karlsruhe, Karl von Eisendecher, the impressions he had gained in London. Eisendecher passed on this information in a private letter to Bülow, reporting that King Gustaf had told him 'that the mistrust of Germany prevailing on the other side of the Channel must unfortunately be blamed for the most part on His Majesty ... Over there it is believed that our All-Gracious Lord controls German policy almost exclusively and that in spite of all his well-publicised pro-England talk, at heart he is an enemy of the British Empire. The majority of the people and the press, and perhaps to a greater or lesser extent King Edward too, share this feeling. They cannot be persuaded that the German navy is not to be used for aggressive purposes against England and the nightmare of invasion is constantly present in their minds.' Evidently Edward VII had given the Swedish King very precise details of the content of the Hale interview, for Gustaf spoke of his concern that the Kaiser's terrible outburst might still be published. The wording of the conversation was known 'both to the Foreign Office in London and to the King', he warned. 'The comments attributed to the Kaiser therein would have to be taken very seriously in England, if they were true, as they show unmistakable hostility.' The King of Sweden was absolutely convinced, Eisendecher wrote, that the 'true content of Hale's report ... should not come to light under any circumstances', for it would 'arouse a storm of indignation among the British against our All-Gracious Lord and Germany's supposedly two-faced and aggressive policy ... King Gustaf talked on this subject with evident anxiety about further evils that could possibly arise from it, and at the same time made it quite plain that in his view a war between the two great civilised nations would not only be the greatest possible disaster for the participants but would have an absolutely devastating effect on the position of power and the progress of the whole of Europe.'[91]

ANGER AT EDWARD VII'S FAILURE TO VISIT BERLIN

In view of the extremely militant attitude towards Britain adopted by Wilhelm II in the summer of 1908 it is no surprise that his meeting with his uncle Edward, which after a long tug-of-war finally took place on

11 August 1908 at Schloss Friedrichshof in the Taunus, was ill-starred from the outset. Wilhelm was particularly enraged that the King had evaded the invitation he had issued at Windsor for a return visit to him and the Kaiserin in Berlin and instead decided to visit the Russian imperial family at Reval. It was outrageous, the Kaiser felt, that King Edward 'after *accepting* my invitation [to Berlin] later turned it down in order to visit someone else instead of me! Which is considered an insult among Sovereigns, and one which no one has ever dared to offer me before.'[92] When he heard that the King would be accompanied on his journey by Queen Alexandra, Wilhelm's anger boiled over. 'That would make my wife the only one who has never received a visit from the Queen!' he exclaimed furiously.[93] Metternich was instructed to discuss the question of the return visit by the British royal couple with Lord Knollys. In a private letter to Bülow, Metternich advised strongly against forcing the issue, and pointed out that although the Danish-born Queen harboured 'no personal animosity towards our All-Gracious Lord, her dislike of Berlin and Prussia will probably never disappear, and whether raison d'état will ever overcome it I cannot say, given the Royal Lady's obstinate character'. Wilhelm annotated this observation with 'Raison d'état *must* prevail, otherwise it is an affront to my wife!'[94] Bülow and Schoen only narrowly succeeded in cancelling an order which the Kaiser had already issued, by way of revenge for the 'unfriendliness' apparent from Edward VII's behaviour, under which British officers would not be allowed to attend the imperial manoeuvres except at the express invitation of the Kaiser himself.[95]

On 5 July Metternich wired to say that he had heard through Sir Ernest Cassel that King Edward wanted to visit the Kaiser at Kronberg on his way to Marienbad, as he had done two years before. He also wished to use this opportunity to discuss in more detail his and the Queen's state visit to Berlin.[96] In the mistaken assumption that he would be in Stockholm at the time of his uncle's journey to Marienbad, Wilhelm suggested to the Reich Chancellor in all seriousness that the meeting with the British King should take place during the latter's return journey instead, and in Alsace or Lorraine, of all places![97] Horrified, Bülow had to spell out to his sovereign that he would only be playing into the hands of the King and the French by proposing such a thing. From a recent conversation with Ballin in Norderney, Bülow wrote, he had 'discovered a great deal about the relationship between Your Majesty and His Majesty King Edward'. 'Evidently the King sets out to provoke you with all kinds of pinpricks. Nothing amuses the King more, Ballin said, than to see signs of a bad mood here. The King regards that as evidence that he has achieved his goal. But at the same time the King would like to make it appear to the world that he has been slighted by Your Majesty. This is a tactic which the royal gentleman practises with forethought and skill. Our tactics must therefore be to avoid showing any weakness and to make it impossible for the King to find reasons to complain about us with regard to either practical or formal matters. That is precisely what is needed in the case of the visit. The King would be pleased if we appeared to be disgruntled because Your Majesty's visit to England last year has not yet been returned. He would be gratified to conclude that he had succeeded in angering us. For serious political reasons, however, we must hope that the English visit to Berlin will take place.' A meeting with Edward, for instance at Homburg, Kronberg or Baden-Baden, would be a good start, as it would give them an opportunity to discuss a later visit to Berlin, but, 'the King will not come to Strassburg or Metz. It would be wrong to suggest a meeting with him there, for His Majesty would undoubtedly refuse, which would only make him even more popular than before in France.'[98] Finally, on 20 July, a letter arrived on board the *Hohenzollern* from King Edward, proposing that he and the Kaiser meet at Schloss Friedrichshof in Kronberg on 11 August – after Wilhelm's return from Sweden. 'I could arrive in the morning and stay till after dinner', he wrote.[99] To the Chancellor's relief the Kaiser accepted this suggestion.[100]

`IF ENGLAND WANTS WAR, LET HER START IT´

As yet, Bülow had no inkling of the disastrous interview that Wilhelm had just given the American journalist William Hale at Bergen. But the Kaiser's telegram of 15 July, ordering him to secure Russian neutrality in an Anglo-German war and to make sure that Britain would be branded as the aggressor, was in itself enough to make the Chancellor fear that when the two monarchs met at Kronberg the Kaiser might go too far on the naval question, in order to provoke Britain. In his memoirs Bülow even compared Wilhelm II's tactics at Kronberg with the confrontation between Wilhelm I and the French ambassador Benedetti in Bad Ems in July 1870, which had led to the Franco-Prussian war.[101]

The dangerous attitude to the naval question which Wilhelm II adopted in the run-up to the Kronberg meeting was also evident to the Chancellor from the violent remarks which the Kaiser scribbled on reports from London. Wilhelm's fury over the British demand for a deceleration of the naval arms race had grown uncontrollably during the Scandinavian cruise. Such demands were nothing but 'the result of English lust for excessive power and their habit of seeing ghosts everywhere', he ranted. They only dared make them 'because they think my diplomats are shitting themselves and can be intimidated by war cries'. He, the Kaiser, would regard any attempt to limit German naval construction as a declaration of war and 'respond with grenades'. 'If England intends to do nothing more than hold out her hand graciously to us and tell us we must limit our navy, that is an incredible piece of impertinence which carries with it a serious insult to the German nation and its Kaiser . . . France and Russia have as much right to demand that we limit the arming of our land forces. As soon as one allows a foreign state to meddle with one's own arms programme, under whatever pretext, one abdicates responsibility, like Portugal and Spain! The German navy has not been built *against* anyone, and not *against* England either! But according to *our* needs! That is quite clearly stated in the Navy Law and has gone unchallenged for 11 years! This law will be fulfilled down to the last iota; whether it suits the British or not is of no consequence! If they want war, let *them start* it; we are not afraid of it!'[102]

A further report on the attitude of leading British statesmen to German naval construction inspired the Kaiser's rudest marginal comments. He furiously repudiated Grey's observation that the Germans were the only nation in Europe that was building a large, strong, unified modern navy with Dreadnoughts, and moreover that they were doing so not far from the British coast. The German navy, Wilhelm claimed, would 'never' become a threat to Britain. The 'Gauls' were also building a large navy and were 'even closer' to the British coast than Germany. Grey was an 'ass!' if he believed no other Powers had Dreadnoughts. 'They are all building them!' He was also 'quite wrong!' not to take America into account and to believe that a conflict between Britain and the United States had become unthinkable. Mockingly, the Kaiser asked whether war between Britain and America would be 'as unthinkable as the loss of India thanks to Japan!?' In response to Metternich's report that the influential Chancellor of the Exchequer, David Lloyd George, saw the spectre of war looming on the horizon despite the desire of both governments and both peoples to avert it, Kaiser Wilhelm scrawled angrily in the margin 'nothing could be further from my mind! If England wants war let her start it [,] we will give her what she wants!' He rejected out of hand Lloyd George's urgent warnings that both sides must cut back on the naval arms race, which he described as '*outrageous*!' Such ideas were 'Rubbish!', 'humbug' and 'nonsense!' The Chancellor of the Exchequer's assertion that the British navy must always be a good bit stronger than the German navy in order to guarantee the British nation a sense of security and to 'prevent any wilful aggressiveness . . . from arising' in Germany, provoked another savage outburst. 'That is the kind of language that has only been used for China or Italy or other such types before! Disgraceful!!' he wrote. After such expressions he would '*never*!' agree to slow down the pace of naval construction. 'No! No, no and no again!' 'The kind of conversation that has gone on between L. George and Metternich is really degrading and provocative for Germany! I must insist that in future he should strongly repudiate such expectations. In this case he has simply listened, patiently accepted the opinions and orders of English statesmen and merely limited himself to protests that had no effect. He must give the gentlemen who are so anxious to *"prevent our wilful aggressiveness" from arising* a straight answer like "Piss off etc." So that these fellows see sense for once! That L. George should even dare to come out with a diktat *to determine our* rate of naval construction is incredible, but the result of it is that in his first conversations Metternich has got onto the slippery slope of *"possibility not absolutely ruled out"*. The clever British will fasten onto that, and sooner or later they will use it against him and catch him out, regardless of "private conversation", "expression of opinion without prejudice" etc! He ought to have rejected it *ab ovo* with the remark: "No state allows another to prescribe or meddle with the extent and nature of its arms preparations; I refuse to hold such a conversation"! And furthermore tell them to read the Navy Law – public knowledge for 11 years – and Nauticus! Metternich should get a thorough kick in the behind; he is too soft!' By His Majesty's command copies of Metternich's report were made for the Chief of General Staff and admirals Tirpitz, Müller and Baudissin.[103] Bülow only just succeeded in ensuring that the insulting marginal comments by the All-Highest were omitted from the copies. Nevertheless it was not long before they became known further afield.[104]

THE CONFRONTATION AT KRONBERG ON 11 AUGUST 1908

The Chancellor must have guessed what direction the talks on the naval question which were now in store at Kronberg would take. On the morning of 11 August 1908 Edward VII arrived at Friedrichshof. The two monarchs quickly agreed that the retiring British ambassador in Berlin, Sir Frank Lascelles, should be succeeded by the ambassador in Vienna, Sir Edward Goschen, and harmony prevailed on various other matters[105] – but only because the King hesitated to bring up the troublesome naval issue.[106] He left this task to his Under Secretary of State, Sir Charles Hardinge, who did not mince his words.

Kaiser Wilhelm recorded his own version of the conversation with Hardinge in a long, dramatic telegram in three parts to Bülow, which was quite rightly regarded as a key historical document when it became known after the war.[107] The Kaiser proudly reported to his Chancellor that after they had left the table the British Under Secretary very soon brought the conversation round to the naval question. 'He spoke of the *grave apprehension*

[English in the original] which was felt in every circle in England about our naval construction. When I expressed surprise and asked why this was so, since it was limited by law and the law had been public knowledge for 11 years, he responded that it was because it was always concentrated at home. I replied that we needed our navy to protect the rapid growth of our trade. He said: "But it always stays at Kiel or Wilhelmshaven and in the North Sea." I said: "As we have no colonies and no coaling stations, that is our base; we have no Gibraltar or Malta." He replied: "Your trade cannot be protected from your base. Why do you not sail around more?" I said: "Because our London embassy and officials abroad were of the opinion that the less the British see our navy, the better; if it appeared in the Channel it would cause displeasure." He asked: "No doubt you are joking?" I replied: "I am deadly serious, my crews have found it hard enough to bear having to serve their time entirely in northern waters." He said: "That is quite incredible. In England it was interpreted quite differently." I said: "This summer I sent my fleet overseas during your great manoeuvre in the North Sea, an unmistakable sign of my peaceful intentions and my trust in England." He said: "That was excellent, it had a very good effect; just send your ships away often, then our people will be very much calmer. Nonetheless it would be more desirable to allay our anxiety about naval construction, as you will have reached our strength in a few years." (!) ... "You are making such rapid progress in building Dreadnoughts that in a few years, let us say in 1912, you will match and even overtake us in strength. The English people are very agitated and deeply concerned about that." I replied: "That is absolute rubbish. Who has spun you such a nonsensical yarn?" To which he said: "It is not nonsense at all, it is authentic information from the English Admiralty." I replied: "It is still nonsense, even if your Admiralty told it to you, and at the same time proof of how little English statesmen and the English people know about maritime matters and how ill-informed they are about their own strength, if they can imagine such a thing. After all, you have long since overtaken the Two Power Standard, without realising it, and you have already reached the Three Power Standard." He said: "That is quite impossible. Our Admiralty says it can scarcely maintain the Two Power Standard, precisely because of German naval construction, which is of a threatening nature." I responded: "Your Admiralty must know better and it is amusing itself bluffing you and your compatriots with scare stories. I can prove to you that I am right, from the Nauticus." He said: "You cannot have any more authentic information than what the Admiralty has given me." I replied: "Your information is wrong, I am an Admiral in the English Navy, which I know very well, and I understand it better than you who are a civilian and know nothing about it." I had the Nauticus brought down and showed

Sir Charles the tables of which Your Excellency knows, with the naval construction graphs. His face showed speechless astonishment . . . After a long silence Sir Charles asked: "Who is this Nauticus? I have never heard of him before." I replied: "He is a series of gentlemen, leading experts from all professions and classes, who have access to authentic information." He said: "Those gentlemen cannot claim to be better informed than the Admiralty. This table is quite arbitrary and I do not attach the slightest value to it . . . We must put a stop to this competitive ship-building and come to an arrangement to slow down the rate of construction. For otherwise our Government will have to bring in a major programme next year to build new ships, and as it lacks the means to do so, new taxes will have to be imposed. That will be very unpopular, the people will grumble and it might bring the Government down." I said: "If instead of regarding the Nauticus tables as fictitious you accepted them as correct, you would see that a supplementary building programme of that sort to maintain your superiority is completely superfluous. We are not engaged in *competitive ship-building*; our rate of building is laid down by law, the number of ships likewise, and you know it. *You* are the ones engaged in competitive building, and it is a competition that exists only on the English side and was invented by your Admiralty.' He then said: *"Can't you put a stop to your building? Or build less ships?"* [English in the original.] I replied: "The strength of Germany's navy is governed by German interests and alliances, it is defensive and certainly not directed against another nation, least of all England. It is no threat to you; you are all frightening yourselves imagining things at the moment." He responded: 'But nevertheless an arrangement ought to be reached to limit building. *You must stop or build slower.*" [English in the original.] To which I said: *"Then we shall fight for it is a question of national honour and dignity."* [English in the original.] And as I spoke I looked him firmly and intently in the eye. Sir Charles turned bright red, bowed to me, asked my pardon for his words and expressly begged me to consider them as inadvertent remarks in a private conversation, which he hoped I would forgive and forget. He had conducted the conversation in a rather irate and almost dictatorial tone. I do not doubt for a moment that he had received his instructions and marching orders from Fisher. In the evening I talked to him again and he was quite a different man, charming, jovial, seasoning his conversation with anecdotes . . . The frank discussion with me, when I showed my teeth in no uncertain terms, had its effect. That is how one always has to behave with the English.'[108]

Clearly the Kaiser believed that thanks to his special skill in dealing with the English as 'half an Englishman' himself, and to his expert knowledge as 'Admiral of the English Navy', he had achieved a momentous victory over the

British civilian. In his memoirs Bülow wrote scornfully of Wilhelm II's 'telegraphic effusion', which had appalled him. It had been immediately evident to him from the 'fantastically exaggerated' telegram that for his own greater glory the monarch 'wanted to turn this into an event something like the historic scene that had been played out between Wilhelm I and Benedetti at Ems in July 1870'. The Kaiser had greeted an official from the Auswärtiges Amt with the words: 'I really gave Sir Charles a piece of my mind, don't you think?' The Reich Chancellor, who had at last recognised the enormous danger that lay in Anglo-German naval rivalry and asked the Kaiser to be more careful, soon noticed that Wilhelm was 'in a very bad mood' with him. Bülow's 'cool demeanour' after receiving the description of his great victory at Kronberg had 'bitterly disappointed' the monarch. Wilhelm had expected 'thanks and praise' for having 'in a trice, won round not only Hardinge but also his uncle the King to himself and his point of view'. From then onwards the Kaiser had become 'even more stubborn' on the naval question than he had been before, Bülow recalled. Altogether, the Kronberg conversations had again brought out strongly His Majesty's tendency 'to conduct foreign affairs as much as possible on his own', which was particularly dangerous with regard to Britain.[109] Over the following months the Kaiser 'frequently' boasted to his courtiers that at Friedrichshof he had openly threatened the English with war if they continued to demand a limitation on German naval armament; and England could 'have [this war] at once, if she really wants it'.[110]

Immediately after his conversation with the Kaiser, Hardinge repeated all the arguments he had used with Wilhelm to Freiherr von Jenisch, the diplomat in attendance on the Kaiser, and indicated that even 'the smallest sign' of a slowing down of the expansion of the German navy would be enough for the British government to desist from increasing its own naval strength. Jenisch was forced to admit that in view of Wilhelm II's attitude any concession was as good as ruled out. 'I did not myself believe that His Majesty the Kaiser would allow himself to be influenced with regard to the execution of our naval programme', he reported lamely to his superiors in the Wilhelmstrasse.[111]

Inevitably, Kaiser Wilhelm's explanation of why the German fleet always remained concentrated in home waters seemed absolutely ridiculous to Hardinge. Nor did he give any credence to the naval construction graphs from *Nauticus* which the monarch showed him. The King's Private Secretary, Sir Frederick Ponsonby, immediately wrote to the young Prince of Wales summarising the principal points of the argument between the British states-man and the Kaiser. 'After luncheon Charlie Hardinge had an innings and appears to have put things very straight to the Emperor. He pointed out that as long as they continued to build ships we should be forced to do likewise. He asked for what purpose the Germans were building such a large fleet. Obviously it was not necessary for fighting France, Austria or Russia and therefore we were forced to the conclusion that it was directed against us. The Emperor replied that it was to protect their commerce! Hardinge thereupon asked why it was kept at Kiel instead of being allowed to go & protect commerce in China etc. The Emperor replied that he understood our feelings would be hurt if he allowed the Fleet to go cruising about (this was weak). Hardinge pointed out that if a large increase of expenditure on the Navy was made next year the people of England would realize that it was entirely owing to Germany and the feeling between the two countries would become yet more acute ... The Emperor said that the shipbuilding programme of Germany had been promulgated in 1900 and noone had said a word. Yet when they carried it gradually out, all England cried out. He said that Fisher hoodwinked everybody. The Press were made to believe that we were below the two power standard but he could prove that 2 years ago we had reached a 3 power standard and that in 2 years time we should be very nearly up to the three power standard again. Did we expect Germany not to protect itself but to remain in a weak state to be mopped up whenever it suited us. He gave Hardinge a book showing how we stood and giving chapter & verse about every ship. He ended up by saying that not only would he not diminish the shipbuilding but he refused to enter into any discussion on the subject. There was a good deal of plain speaking and Lascelles was afraid the Emperor was annoyed at being tackled like this. However I don't think he was ... The feeling in Germany seems to be very antagonistic to us and now all sorts of stories are started about the King. Trench [the military attaché] told me that the hatred of the King was intense. They all accused him of trying to humiliate their country. My own feeling after hearing so much is that nothing is further from the thoughts of the Emperor and his advisers than to go to war with us but that they may be carried away by the bad feeling against us which they have fostered and eventually they may be unable to stifle the popular wish for war.'[112]

After his return to England Hardinge also wrote to the Prince of Wales reporting on his dispute with Wilhelm II at Kronberg. 'At the very first opening I raised the whole question of German naval armaments, their motives & intentions. I persisted in thrashing out the whole question with the Emperor who evidently did not much like it, but, to sum up, the result arrived at was a categorical statement by His Majesty that the naval programme, which had been sanctioned by law, would and must be completed by the dates fixed, and that no discussion or slackening of the rate of construction would be tolerated. He was full of friendly protestations that there was no underlying intention of attacking England, but he failed to give any satisfactory reason for the necessity of so large a fleet ... I cannot see that our relations with Germany can ever be really good until there has been some modification of the building programme.'[113]

In the days following the Kronberg conversation Hardinge set down his impressions of it in a long memorandum. 'While smoking his cigar after luncheon', he recorded, 'the Emperor did me the honour of calling me up to speak to him. In the course of a conversation on the popularity of military service in Germany, which had become an ingrained principle in the education and development of the national character of the German people owing to the devastation and misery from which the Germans had suffered during the Thirty Years War, the Seven Years War, and the Napoleonic campaigns, but from which the British isles had been happily spared, allusion was made to the relations existing between England and Germany, which the Emperor declared to be quite satisfactory except for the evil results of the campaign of the yellow press in both countries. I replied that I was sorry to be unable to share the Emperor's opinion, since there could be no concealment of the fact that a genuine apprehension was felt in England as to the reasons and intention underlying the construction of a large German fleet. This apprehension was felt, not in England alone, but also in Europe, where happily it remained as the only element of unrest in the international situation. No cause for disagreement existed between England and Germany, and the diplomatic relations between the two countries were perfectly friendly and natural, without the smallest cloud on the political horizon likely to cause anxiety in the future. The knowledge of these facts made it difficult for thoughtful people to reconcile the friendly assurances of the Emperor and German Government with the acceptance by the German Parliament of the extensive naval programme, which could only be realized at considerable sacrifice on the part of the German people. The execution of the German programme would necessarily entail a corresponding increase in our expenditure on naval armaments, since the naval supremacy of Great Britain had now become a cardinal principle of British policy, which no Government of whatever party could afford to ignore. Although nobody could have the right to dictate to any Power a programme of naval construction, it had been fully realized in England that, if the present German programme is completed, the German navy will, in a few years' time, be in superior position to the British navy as regards the largest type of battle-ship, and British supremacy at sea would thus be endangered. Unless it were possible for some sort of friendly discussion to take place between the two Governments resulting in a modification or slackening of the present rate of shipbuilding, it would be necessary for the Government next year to submit to Parliament an extensive shipbuilding programme and to explain how the necessity for it had arisen. There could be no doubt that Parliament would accept whatever burdens the Government might propose, but there could be no doubt that this naval rivalry between the two countries would embitter their relations to each other, and might in a few years' time lead to a very critical situation in the event of a serious, or even a trivial dispute arising between the two countries. The Emperor maintained that there was absolutely no cause for apprehension in England as to the German naval programme, and that no sensible person in Germany had ever thought for a moment that the German fleet was intended for an attack upon England . . . He therefore failed to see any reason for nervousness in England, or for any increase in the British fleet on account of the German naval programme. This programme was not a new one; it had been passed by law; and it had become a point of national honour that it should be completed. No discussion with a foreign Government could be tolerated; such a proposal would give rise to internal troubles if the Government were to accept it. He would rather go to war than submit to such dictation. I at once pointed out to the Emperor that, in suggesting a possible friendly discussion between the two Governments, there had been no question of dictation and that my words could hardly bear that interpretation, to which His Majesty assented. I said that I was at a loss to understand how His Majesty arrived at the figures of relative strength of the two navies in battle-ships in 1909, and could only assume that the sixty-two first-class battle-ships of the British fleet comprised every obsolete vessel that could be found floating in British harbours and that had not been sold as scrap iron. The Emperor at once sent an Aide-de-camp for a publication of this year by "Nauticus" giving the above figures and presented me with a copy for my own edification and conviction.' Hardinge explained to the Kaiser why supremacy at sea was an existential question for Britain: she had no standing army, and her coasts were open to attack at any time. The strength of the German battlefleet, on the other hand, was justified neither by the Royal Navy nor by the French or Russian fleets; moreover it was not suitable for the protection of German trade abroad. To this the Kaiser retorted 'with some warmth that the talk of invasion was sheer nonsense, and that such an idea had never been contemplated by any serious person in Germany. Moreover, it was he that directed the foreign policy of Germany, and was it likely that he would ever tolerate such an idea for an instant? He maintained that the figures given by "Nauticus" were correct, and that those given by the Admiralty were intended to deceive public opinion in

England. It was in England that the first "Dreadnought" had been built in the greatest secrecy, and on its completion Admiral Fisher and the press had at once announced that she was capable of sinking the whole German navy. These statements had forced the German Government to begin building ships of a similar type to satisfy public opinion in Germany. Although England had previously increased the size of her battle-ships Germany had kept to the smaller size of heretofore, until provoked by the action of the British Admiralty to build ships of the largest size. As for the German fleet to be kept at Kiel, he kept it there because Count Metternich had reported to him that the Foreign Office and public opinion in England were sensitive, and did not like the German fleet passing up and down the Channel. Moreover, Germany had not the numerous bases which England possessed in distant seas, and German ships had in consequence to be kept at home. He had, however, now sent his ships to the Canaries, and, to show his confidence in British policy, he had done so at a moment when the North Sea was full of British war-ships engaged in naval manoeuvres. The Emperor repeated that the German naval programme of thirty-eight battle-ships and twenty cruisers must be completed by 1918 at the various stages prescribed by law, and that no further increase would then be made, but that the navy would be maintained at that strength. As for His Majesty's Government they were of course free to build as they pleased.' Hardinge pointed out that in that case, if no countermeasures were taken the danger of an invasion of the British Isles would always remain. He expressed regret at the Kaiser's determination to stick to the ship-building programme without any cuts, and dismissed the idea that the English would be made nervous by the German navy passing through the English Channel. His memorandum continued: 'Reverting to the general question of naval expenditure, I expressed the hope that the moderate counsels would still prevail, and that although friendly discussion between the two Governments might, as the Emperor insisted, be barred, still I was convinced that His Majesty's Government would require no written formula nor verbal statement from the German Government, but only a visible proof that the programme of naval construction had been modified or slackened, in order to make similar modification or slackening in their own. Without some such proof it would be quite impossible for His Majesty's Government to resist the pressure of public opinion, and a large counter-programme of naval construction would be inevitable. The conversation here ceased, but two hours later I had an interview with Herr von Jenisch, who had been out on a motor drive, and had had no means of communicating with the Emperor in the meantime ... Herr von Jenisch gave me precisely the same replies as the Emperor had already given ... It is to be regretted that the German

Government have assumed such an uncompromising attitude towards any discussion or modification of their actual programme of naval construction.' Still, Sir Charles reflected, it was just as well to know the worst and make one's preparations accordingly.

After dinner the Kaiser, who was in an excellent mood, had summoned him again and discussed a series of other matters with him, Hardinge recorded. The Young Turks' *coup d'état* in Constantinople, the 'Yellow Peril' and the Sanjak railway were among the subjects that came up, and here Wilhelm emphasised that Germany would never accept the domination of a European Power in the Balkan peninsula. 'During the course of this conversation the Emperor made several satirical allusions to England's policy and her "new friends", and endeavoured to show what a good friend he had been to England in the past.' The Kaiser claimed that during the Boer War Russia and France had wanted to form a coalition with Germany against Britain – a demand that he personally, against the advice of his government, had decisively rejected. Furthermore, at that time he had ordered a plan of campaign for the war in South Africa to be worked out by his General Staff and had sent it to his grandmother, after which Lord Roberts had implemented it to the letter against the Boers – claims which were to create a universal furore when they were published just a few weeks later in the notorious 'interview' with Wilhelm in the *Daily Telegraph*.[114] Hardinge's memorandum continued: 'The Emperor complained that no British statesmen ever visited Berlin, and that consequently it was impossible for them to understand German sentiment and the German people. He constantly sent his statesmen to England to study various questions, but he could only remember two instances of English statesmen doing the same. The two instanced were those of Lord Rosebery many years ago and Mr. Haldane quite recently . . . Towards the close of the interview an Aide-de-camp came to the Emperor and announced that the King was ready to leave for the railway station. As I somewhat hurriedly rose and asked permission to fetch my coat and hat, the Emperor stopped me and said in a very emphatic manner: "Remember that I fully adhere to and mean every word that I uttered at the Guildhall last year. The future of the world is in the hands of the Anglo-Teuton race. England, without a powerful army, cannot stand alone in Europe, but must lean on a Continental Power, and that Power should be Germany." There was no time or opportunity to continue what might have been an interesting discussion of a somewhat ambitious policy. On thinking over the Emperor's words and the general trend of the conversation, I cannot resist the conclusion that his last sentences were the climax to which he had been gradually leading, and that he wished to urge once more the great advantage to England of friendship with Germany over the understandings with France and Russia which have already shown such beneficent and practical results during the past few years.'[115]

Hardinge's impression that Kaiser Wilhelm's obviously carefully prepared fighting talk at Kronberg was in fact aimed at achieving an Anglo-German agreement is astonishing, when one thinks of the open threats of war with which the monarch repeatedly reacted to English demands for the pace of German naval construction to be slowed down. And yet the Under Secretary's conclusion was not so very wide of the mark. Even at the peak of his rage over Edward VII's meeting with the Tsar at Reval, when at Moltke's instigation he urged Bülow, if war threatened, to provoke Britain into an attack on Germany,[116] the Kaiser had visions of an 'entente' between Britain and Germany which would supersede that between Britain, France and Russia.[117] Wilhelm heartily endorsed the former Prime Minister Lord Rosebery's criticism of the Entente Cordiale with France. The British government's policy, Rosebery mockingly observed, amounted to 'protecting oneself against a country with 60 million inhabitants and the strongest army by making friends with other countries, instead of making friends with the strong country itself.' 'Exactly what I always say!' Wilhelm commented; if British statesmen had sought a rapprochement with Germany instead of France and Russia, no one would be worrying about either the German danger or the German navy in London now.[118]

Wilhelm's wishful thinking about an Anglo-German understanding was completely illusory at this juncture, not least because he — unlike Bülow, who was now in favour of a concession — still stubbornly refused to modify the battlefleet-building programme even by 'an iota'. The marginal comments which he wrote, even after the confrontation at Kronberg, on the reports from London warning of the feeling there reveal how recklessly he continued to toy with thoughts of war with Britain. A reduction in his building programme was absolutely out of the question, he declared, even at the risk of war with England. After all, Germany would have 'a good chance' in such a war. English assurances of friendship were 'all completely meaningless, as they all see a reduction of our navy as a prerequisite of their friendship; and that is just what we would not do! The British should just wake up to the fact that war with Germany means the loss of India! and of their position in the world as a result.'[119] When news arrived from Vienna that Emperor Franz Joseph had expressed displeasure to Edward VII over the Anglo-Russian meeting in Reval, Wilhelm commented approvingly: 'Bravo! The more the British are punished for their impertinence, the better.' He was particularly delighted to hear that the Austrian Foreign Minister, Aehrenthal, had become 'almost

abusive', telling Sir Charles Hardinge that 'in view of the Entente policy
which King Edward has seen fit to inaugurate, no one could really blame
Germany for persistently continuing to expand her fleet'. It was a good thing,
the Kaiser observed, 'that that insolent fellow' should have been 'taken to task',
and 'very good! that he should occasionally hear it from a third party too'.
Hardinge would 'go back to England *a sadder but a wiser man*!' [English in the
original.] This news was all 'very gratifying!' Wilhelm exulted; 'it does me
good to hear it!'[120] A few weeks later the Kaiser repaid Aehrenthal's loyalty to
Germany, as we shall see, by his ill-considered backing of the reckless
annexation of Bosnia and Herzegovina.

It was precisely Wilhelm's readiness to provoke war with Britain and
France, provided that Russia could be persuaded to remain neutral, that had
confirmed the effectiveness of the Anglo-Franco-Russian Entente in maintaining peace. Had Britain broken off her ententes with France and Russia in
order to enter into an alliance with Germany, as Wilhelm II periodically
envisaged, this would have meant conceding domination of the whole of
Europe to the Kaiserreich. Not only would France and Russia have been at
the mercy of the Prusso-German army, but Great Britain herself would have
been confronted with a united continent and would have been defencelessly
exposed to German military power on land and at sea. It is therefore hardly
surprising that Hardinge did not for an instant consider accepting Kaiser
Wilhelm II's suggestion that Britain give up the ententes with France and
Russia in favour of uniting the 'Anglo-Teuton' race under German leadership.

Hardinge's stance was confirmed by the disastrous Hale interview, news of
which landed on his desk only a few days after his return from Kronberg.[121]
Looking back at the numerous conflicting statements Wilhelm II had made
over the past year, in December 1908 following the *Daily Telegraph* affair
the Under Secretary of State set down his impressions. The interview with the
Kaiser in the *Daily Telegraph*, he wrote, 'corresponds almost exactly with
what the Emperor said to me at Cronberg last August, and, although it may
appear very contradictory to you, I believe that it really represents his feelings.
At the same time there is no doubt that, at the beginning of the month of
July, he gave expressions to entirely opposite views in his interview with
Mr. Hale ... The explanation of this extraordinary *volte face* is, I believe,
the following: After the interview between The King and the Emperor of
Russia at Reval in June, the Kaiser was quite mad, and raved to everybody
against England. This I know for certain, because he had the imprudence to
use the most violent language about England at the beginning of July to the
Russian Ambassador in Berlin, who reported it to his Government. In abusing
England, he abused also The King. Nevertheless, when he had got over his

rage at the Reval interview, he still expressed friendly fee
England, and nothing could have been more friendly than l
with The King at Cronberg. He is either, therefore, a friend of
greatest knave that exists and a very good actor. It is very unfc
impulsive nature carries him away in such a manner, and man.
foolish things. He has had his wings clipped for the time being; but at the ι_b
of fifty it will not be easy to change the man.'[122]

CHAPTER TWENTY-FOUR

'Our Kaiser and his People!' The crisis of Wilhelm's Personal Monarchy

THE KAISERREICH AND THE DEMOCRATIC TREND OF THE TIMES

The diplomatic isolation of the Kaiserreich that had become increasingly evident since 1904 also had a domestic political dimension: Wilhelm II's Personal Monarchy, by international standards, looked more and more like the last remaining stronghold of a long since outmoded autocratic form of government. Particularly after the Russian Revolution of 1905 and Nicholas II's promulgation of a parliamentary constitution, Bülow feared that the forces of progress would no longer see the Russian Empire but 'the German Kaiserreich and the Prussian monarchy . . . as a bulwark of . . . monarchical-conservative order' and therefore as their principal opponent.[1] With the collapse of the strongest bastion of reaction in eastern Europe Kaiser Wilhelm and his advisers could not but fear that this democratic development would also have serious consequences for the two Central European empires, as well as for the Turkish Empire. Wilhelm II was perturbed by a report from Count Metternich in July 1906 that London newspapers were maliciously suggesting that a collapse of autocracy in Russia would also undermine the monarchy in the German Reich, 'which on its own can no longer remain the last refuge of the autocratic principle in Europe'.[2]

Bülow had no illusions about the danger that the downfall of the absolutist Tsarist Empire would represent for Germany. Writing to the Kaiser on 17 July 1906, he stressed the point. 'What we are now seeing is, as far as can humanly be judged, the collapse of the Russian autocratic system that for a hundred years was the bane and often the terror of democratic Europe, but also the hope and sometimes the prop of monarchical and conservative Europe.' Although it made Germany's position easier in foreign policy terms, the

Russian changeover to parliamentary government was to be regretted 'because the difference in the development of the eastern monarchies from that of the western states is now too clearly visible. Constitutional and liberal England, which openly sympathises with the Russian revolutionaries, is doing splendidly; powerful opportunities in the future are opening up for the American republic; the French republic, which Socialists either secretly or openly share in governing, enjoys universal approval and its capital is the favourite rendezvous of all Kings. Even in Italy prospects are not as bad as is sometimes thought; small democratic countries like Denmark, Belgium, Holland and Norway are enjoying great domestic prosperity, while in that centuries-old stronghold of monarchical and conservative principles, the venerable Habsburg monarchy, everything is falling apart, and as for Russia, which seemed to be the indestructible citadel of autocratic, militaristic and orthodox principles, its very foundations, framework and roof-beams are shaking. Even for as strong a monarch as Your Majesty this makes the situation more difficult, although I am not at all pessimistic about it provided that we combine firmness with prudence and caution in our domestic policy, and do not confuse the trivial with the important, in a word continue to operate fearlessly, calmly and sensibly ... The dear old gentleman on the Danube and the charming young gentleman on the Neva have succeeded, through a series of mistakes, omissions and over-hasty actions, in achieving the result that there is once again a widespread belief that salvation lies more with the Left than with the Right. In consequence, much of what Your Majesty's powerful personality and noble aspirations would have accomplished for the monarchical principle has been ruined. We must take this as a warning to act with firmness and wisdom both abroad and at home, but also as a challenge to go bravely onward, trusting in the old God of Prussia.'[3]

The Chancellor could not predict what would happen in Russia, but he did not believe that the Russian people, who 'at their innermost core ... are not Germanic but Slavonic-Tartar, not European but Asian', would be able to 'tolerate free institutions of the English or American type'. Expert opinion differed widely about the future development of Russia, he commented. 'Some people foresee a general revolt of the peasantry with all the horrors of an agricultural revolution or scenes of murder like three years ago in Belgrade; others believe that as in Central Europe after 1848 things will sort themselves out in one way or another.' The disaster was entirely due to the fact that Tsarist Russia had set its face against a long-overdue modernisation, Bülow observed. Nicholas II, like his father before him, had misjudged the times. 'They thought that a great movement which, basically and despite all its excesses, the freedom movement in Russia is, could only be suppressed by

Cossacks wielding their whips, Uhlans their lances and Grenadiers their guns, and not by allowing any reforms or timely concessions. That was a fatal mistake ... As soon as an unlucky war – which a personal and absolutist regime is particularly ill-equipped to endure – came along, the debacle followed, and even Alexander III's heavy handed severity might have been able to hold it up but could scarcely have prevented it.'[4]

Wilhelm II of course also recognised the inner link between this alarming development abroad and the exposed position of the monarchy at home. In a letter of 1 February 1906 to thank his uncle, the Grand Duke of Baden, for his birthday congratulations, Wilhelm looked back over the past year which had brought the Russian Revolution and the Moroccan crisis and clearly sensed that these events would not be without repercussions on the principle of Personal Monarchy that he embodied. 'It was certainly a difficult year! And an eventful one too!' Worries within the family 'were soon joined by political worries; sometimes in the West, in our diplomatic relations, at other times in the East, where anxiety about war and its conclusion alternated with concern about the outcome of the struggle for the throne and the survival of the dynasty as the country reorganised itself! One was besieged by a mass of problems and it was not easy always to find the right, practicable and honourable path to follow. But with God's manifest help all went well, and He will continue to help us.'[5] A year later he admitted to his now 80-year-old uncle how laborious ruling the country had sometimes seemed to him. 'It has been an immensely difficult and thorny task to mould the demands of modern times in such a way that the transition from the great era to the present one was accomplished without rifts, shocks and drawbacks for our people and our fatherland. Anyone who had tried to tackle this without the conviction that God had set the task and He would also help solve it, would soon have lost heart and given up. It was only with God's wonderful help and His blessing that we were able to get as far as we have!'[6]

The realisation that where foreign policy was concerned Germany was now largely dependent on her alliance with Austria-Hungary did little to reassure the German leadership, in view of the chaotic state of affairs in the multi-national Danube Monarchy. Wilhelm followed the signs of disintegration, which in May 1906 were compounded by tumultuous demands for universal suffrage in the Viennese parliament, with consternation. He told his close friend Max Egon Prince zu Fürstenberg (see Figure 25), that he was 'quite horrified' at the 'so-called programmatic speech' which the Austrian Prime Minister, Konrad Prince zu Hohenlohe, had just made in parliament. 'It is not a programme at all, but a speech to be made over a beer or a meal at the students' union or at an election dinner. It is a toast to Universal

Figure 25 The Kaiser out walking on the south coast of England in November 1907 with his new friend Prince Max Egon zu Fürstenberg

Suffrage! ... It ought properly to have finished with three cheers for the right to vote! It does not look like the work of a statesman; especially as he refrains from making any concrete suggestion and is only too grateful to accept any such suggestion from the members of parliament. So he does not seem to be quite clear what he wants or should do. It does not promise much for the future.'[7] The crisis in the Habsburg Dual Monarchy deepened a few days later when Kaiser Franz Joseph, without the agreement of the Austrian government and the Austrian parliament, granted Hungary the authority to raise its own customs tariffs. As the German ambassador Count Carl von Wedel reported on 30 May 1906, the fiery speeches made in the Austrian parliament showed 'how seriously the once great general popularity of the old monarch has been shaken'. It was not the uncouth remarks of individual desperadoes against the occupant of the throne which had forced this depressing realisation upon him, Wedel asserted, but the fact that such attacks had been listened to without protest and frequently with secret agreement. 'What left the deepest and most disturbing impression was the speech of the leader of the Christian Socialists, the Mayor of Vienna Dr Lueger', which had been received with stormy applause and ended with a challenge to the Emperor Franz Joseph: 'Kaiser, do you want to take the responsibility in the eyes of history for bringing the ancient Habsburg Empire, rich in honours and triumphs, to such a wretched end?' The Pan-German Karl Hermann Wolf also attacked the Emperor fiercely. The man who had gone furthest, however, was the notorious Czech party leader Count Sternberg, when he said that he had refrained from putting forward a particular motion only because it would not have been admissible under the constitution. The motion would have been 'To request His Majesty to transfer the business of government into younger hands'. Wedel emphasised that the bitterness and despondency prevailing in Vienna had never before found such clear expression. The phrases used by Lueger, who was supported by the broad mass of the people, particularly by the petty bourgeoisie of the capital, were 'hammer blows at the dynasty, not only at the ruling Kaiser'. Rumours were rife in Vienna of mass demonstrations in the offing. On all sides Wedel was hearing the opinion expressed that only by completely changing the constitutional structure of Austria and moving towards federalism could a solution be found to the Empire's crisis. Such a change of internal structure, however, would inevitably entail 'a radical alteration in the relations of the Austro-Hungarian Monarchy with the outside world' and it would be detrimental primarily to Germany's position because anti-German elements would come to the fore.[8] As we have already seen, the decision to go ahead with Wilhelm II's planned state visit to Vienna in spite of this delicate situation was heavily influenced by the desire to strengthen the monarchical principle on the Danube.[9] As is well known, the visit failed to have the intended effect. The internal disintegration of the allied Dual Monarchy advanced at headlong speed and continued to horrify Wilhelm II over the following months. On 12 December 1906 he wrote to Fürstenberg: 'The description of what is going on in Hungary is incredible; the behaviour of these people is tantamount to madness, and almost borders on treason! And concessions are still being made to them! ... Meanwhile in Austria parliament *falls into universal suffrage*, which was originally meant only to threaten the rebellious Magyar Excellencies and nobility, and which the Hungarians will never bring in *like that*! It drives one to despair!'[10]

SAFEGUARDING THE MONARCHY AGAINST THE MENACE OF REVOLUTION

The bomb attack on the newly wed King of Spain and his bride in the summer of 1906[11] gave rise to reflection in Germany as to how such dangers could be effectively prevented. In his fury at the incident Wilhelm II initially suggested a simple remedy to the Reich Chancellor: 'Best way to prevent assassination attempts is simply to seize the known anarchists and lock them up, likewise all suspicious persons. That is what the Sultan did for our visit and it proved to be a success. Recommend passing this on to Vienna. I must add that I find it absolutely astounding that no one has put forward any suggestion, no government has shown the slightest indication of taking action against those bastards of anarchists. If after every assassination attempt in every country the known anarchists were arrested and beheaded there and then, that would soon put a stop to the whole business. But no government has the guts to do it, not even ours. So we can no doubt expect more trouble. The blood of Kings is on the head of the ministers of their governments.'[12] He called on the Chancellor to try out 'appropriate measures' to prevent 'such outbreaks of political fanaticism'. As Bülow informed the Prussian Ministry of State on 31 August 1906, the Kaiser had expressed 'the wish for the closest possible surveillance of the terrorist movement' and had 'particularly emphasised the need to keep a close watch on, and if necessary expel, the Russian students who are at present in this country'. He had replied to the Kaiser that the Prussian Interior Ministry and the Berlin police headquarters were already carrying out this surveillance 'with the utmost vigour'. Internationally too, action against anarchism was making progress. Switzerland and the USA had recently shown more resolve and energy in taking preventive measures, and an international conference in Rome had agreed on inter-governmental cooperation in the surveillance of 'dangerous socialist and anarchist elements'. A general agreement on the extradition of known anarchists to their home countries, however, had fallen through because of opposition from Britain, which insisted on maintaining its traditional right to grant asylum. Bülow had also drawn the Kaiser's attention to the fact that the Ministry of State had already been working for months on 'the question of combating social democratic and revolutionary activity and particularly on preventing such influences from penetrating the Army'. In the end, however, he had been obliged to tell the Kaiser the truth and had said to him 'that His life was in God's hands', for 'no police precautions can be wholly successful . . . against bomb attacks'.[13]

The ensuing discussions in the Ministry of State as to whether it was 'necessary and practicable' to 'strengthen existing legal powers to combat anarchism' merely revealed the helplessness of the authorities. The Prussian Minister of the Interior, Theobald von Bethmann Hollweg, did not think that a strengthening of the penal code would stand a chance in the Reichstag and also doubted the effectiveness of keeping Russian emigrants under surveillance and expelling them if necessary, as it was always possible 'that there are other fanatical and dangerous elements of this kind in the country'. Nevertheless, particularly extensive police precautions had been put in place for the Kaiser's journey to Silesia for the manoeuvres, because the socialist stronghold of Breslau provided 'fertile ground' for trouble. The ministers pointed out that Wilhelm II offered favourable opportunities for assassination attempts, especially when out walking and on his return from parades, when he customarily rode at the head of the escort to the colour. The Reich Chancellor and the Minister of War, however, refused to draw the Kaiser's attention to these dangers: the monarch, said Bülow, 'was imbued, where His personal safety was concerned, with a high degree of trust in God and a certain fatalism, and it would be difficult to persuade him to accept restrictions on his freedom of movement'. 'The state of affairs in Germany', Bülow added, 'was fortunately not to be compared with Russian conditions, and preventive measures such as have been adopted there . . . would hardly be understood by our people. There was in any case no sure defence against bomb attacks, as the sad incident in Madrid had once again demonstrated.'[14]

THE GROWING DISCONTENT WITH KAISER WILHELM II

Unlike in Russia, Austria-Hungary, Spain and Portugal, Italy and Serbia, the danger to the Hohenzollern Monarchy stemmed less from revolutionary mass rebellions or anarchist attacks than from the rapidly spreading feeling at every level of society that the 'Sultanesque methods of rulership' practised by Wilhelm II were completely anachronistic and put the German nation to shame.[15] On 9 November 1906 Baroness Spitzemberg noted in her diary: 'The tone which newspapers of all shades of opinion are adopting against the Kaiser's autocratic and retrograde rule is really alarming – they are positively threatening.'[16] She drew a sad comparison between Germany's political development and that of Britain and lamented the fact that 'at a time when our nation has become richer and politically more powerful than ever, we have a sovereign who wants to keep the patriarchal, autocratic principle alive artificially, or even to bring it back to life, although it has long been dead in the hearts of his people, and in so doing he is nurturing only sycophancy and servility on the one hand and on the other, discontent and passive – for the time being – resistance.'[17] The departing British ambassador Sir Frank Lascelles, in a conversation with her, 'shook his head gravely over the new, critical, rebellious spirit among our people'.[18] In 1908 the Baroness found it 'positively shocking how bluntly the ... Generals ... speak about the Kaiser's interference in personnel questions and about his policy'.[19]

The increasing ill-feeling towards Wilhelm and his 'Personal Rule' was by no means limited to the ruling elite; it was common to all classes of society and all religious denominations. The mood throughout Germany was 'wretched', observed the ambassador Count Anton Monts, who was widely tipped as the next Reich Chancellor, in September 1906. He added far-sightedly: 'Our working men, who were driven into Social Democratic courses by the manifold mistakes of Bismarck and are being driven further along this course principally by H.M., must be steered into other channels. In the long run a country cannot be ruled without the working men, or against them, for, whether we like it or not, Germany has already become an industrial state. The principles of the old Prussian class state are no longer applicable, particularly when the ruling classes show so little political judgement. By a timely recognition of the signs of the times, much could have been saved that was good and vital. But why should a proletarian feel any sympathy for Crown or Altar when he sees daily that under these banners the most despicable egoism is simply seizing special advantages for itself? ... The class state and rule by the Grace of God are no longer tenable in the light of modern times.'[20]

In Berlin and other cities thousands took to the streets to demonstrate in favour of the abolition of the three-class franchise in Prussia; the excessive security around the Berlin Schloss was generally interpreted as evidence of weakness and fear.[21] In the Catholic Centre party, on whose support in the Reichstag the government had depended until the end of 1906, an increasingly critical mood took hold under the leadership of Matthias Erzberger and Hermann Roeren. Hinzpeter drew his erstwhile pupil's attention to the fact that both the Social Democratic workers' movement and the Catholic Centre party had a very strong popular base. In a letter to the Kaiser of 31 March 1907 he pointed out that the Social Democrats and the Centre were 'in essence very closely related, in that they both have a uniformly demagogic organisation and demagogic tendencies. And so it has been from the very beginning with the Social Democratic party, as a horizontal section of the population, because it embraces the lowest social class, while the Centre comprises a vertical section. Thus initially the Centre was controlled by the upper class, the worldly and spiritual aristocracy. But in accordance with the democratising trends of the time, here too power has passed to the lowest class, groups of which are in the hands of the lower levels of the clergy. The latter are also of a very demagogic turn of mind.'[22] 'With the growth of industry' the Social Democratic party would also 'grow inexorably', he warned. 'The power of the Centre' had become 'too great and well-grounded' to be 'substantially weakened in a single onslaught'; that would require 'the work of generations'. At best one could hope for a split in both these popular movements.[23]

Hinzpeter counselled moderation and patience — above all where the question of the workers was concerned. On 1 September 1906 he wrote to Wilhelm drawing attention urgently to the growing gulf between the trade unions, whose first concern was to demand better working conditions from employers, and the idealists of the Social Democratic party, who wanted the mass strike to be 'incorporated into the doctrine and tactics of the party as an important new weapon of the proletariat for the overthrow of Capitalist society'. These ideas of the 'empty-headed windbags' in the party, however, were increasingly regarded by the trade union leaders as 'impractical non-sense' for which they were not willing to risk their organisation and their very considerable means. The Kaiser received this letter on 3 September 1906, just before the imperial manoeuvres in Silesia which had given rise to the discussions in the Ministry of State about the security of the monarch.[24] Only a few days later Wilhelm made a speech in Breslau in which he described God as Prussia's old ally and called on his audience to join the battle against all 'prophets of doom'.[25]

HALF-HEARTED ATTEMPTS TO INCREASE THE POPULARITY OF THE MONARCHY

Of course the Kaiser was not universally disliked, and he continued to be decidedly popular in some sections of the population. Bülow pressed him to make use of this personal popularity and the traditional splendour of the Crown to stabilise the monarchy. He advised Wilhelm to exploit to the full the susceptibility of the masses to the magic of imperial family celebrations. When

Crown Princess Cecilie gave birth to her first son in July 1906 the Reich Chancellor saw this as an opportunity to embed the popularity of the dynasty more deeply in the nation. He wrote to the Kaiser that this happy occasion reminded him of the birth of the present Crown Prince Wilhelm in 1882, when he, then a young secretary at the embassy in Paris, had declared: 'Today the glorious Hohenzollern dynasty, to which the German people are bound by a thousand bonds, stands before them in four generations.' On the occasion of the baptism of the new Prince, Bülow suggested that the gratitude of the Kaiser and Kaiserin to their 'loyal people' should be expressed through a 'graceful Cabinet Order', and that at the same time a large donation should be made towards the foundation of an infant hospital for the benefit of all families.[26] Very much against the will of the Crown Prince and Princess (see Figure 26), who had been 'most anxious to celebrate the christening of their son very simply and if possible en famille', the Kaiser insisted that his grandson be christened 'with full ceremony' and that as in 1882, friendly monarchs should be asked to be godparents to the child.[27] Bülow particularly welcomed the fact that Wilhelm II chose his uncle Edward to be a godfather, and suggested that he ask the President of the United States if he too would take on this role.[28]

To mark the birth of the Kaiser's first grandchild the majority of the Prussian ministers of state declared themselves in favour of an amnesty, even in cases of lèse-majesté, as an act of grace of this kind would be 'of the greatest significance politically'. But an additional proposal by Bülow to reduce heavier sentences slightly was rejected, for the ministers feared that this might also include criminal offences 'on account of which action is constantly having to be taken against the Social Democratic press'.[29] The consultations resulted in the All-Highest decree of 27 January 1907, the Kaiser's birthday, and an order by the Justice Minister the following day which held out the prospect of a significant legal limitation on the penalty for offences of lèse-majesté.[30] When the Ministry of State discussed the draft of a new law on lèse-majesté on 23 March 1907, Bülow was able to state 'that His Majesty the Kaiser and King will certainly consent to everything that seems appropriate to limit the penalty for lèse-majesté'. The Ministry of State agreed on a law that exempted from punishment all cases in which the act had been committed 'out of ignorance, thoughtlessness or hastiness or otherwise without malicious intent'. The Secretary of State of the Reich Justice Office, Arnold Nieberding, drew attention to the fact that in South Germany it was 'already very rare for convictions to be obtained for insulting the Kaiser'; in future such insults would probably 'go completely unpunished, to all intents and purposes'.[31] The relaxation of the law was welcomed as a long-overdue modernisation — likewise the simultaneous decision of the Ministry of State to confer more honours in future.[32]

Figure 26 The Crown Prince with his bride, Cecilie Duchess of Mecklenburg

Surprise and delight were caused by yet another decision, that the German translation of the book *Lui devant l'objectif caricaturel* by the Frenchman John Grand-Carteret, which contained some 300 international caricatures of the Kaiser, would not be banned. In a decree of February 1906 the state authorities were instructed on 'All-Highest orders' 'to refrain from any prosecution or confiscation on account of the contents of this work'. Following this, a caricature of Wilhelm II appeared in Germany for the very first time with Olaf Gulbransson's drawing 'H.M.' on the title page of *Simplicissimus.*[33]

There were of course limits to the success of such attempts to help the imperial monarchy increase its popularity. The magnificent court functions which Kaiser Wilhelm often took the leading role in planning and preparing always had 'something of the masquerade' about them, as Zedlitz observed after the ceremonial investiture of Prince Eitel Friedrich as Grand Master of the Order of St John of Jerusalem on 18 March 1907. The ceremony had been rehearsed in the presence of the Kaiser four times, each time for an hour and a half.[34] Shortly before his appointment as Chief of General Staff, Helmuth von Moltke complained after a court ball: 'It always makes a very strange impression on me when I see the procession of the court into the White Hall; the Kaiser always brings such a breath of the Middle Ages in with him . . . It is as if the dead were resurrected, with pigtails and powder.'[35]

The luxurious life at court and in the exclusive Potsdam Guards regiments aroused increasingly strong criticism. A son of the Kaiser's, Prince Adalbert of Prussia, had become a naval officer but refused, contrary to orders, to live on his warship. Instead he took up residence in a 'fantastically furnished' villa in Kiel and behaved, as Zedlitz complained, more like a Russian Grand Duke than as if he embodied 'the traditional, quite unpretentious and dutiful model of a Prussian Prince'.[36] The Kaiser himself had been negotiating with Emperor Franz Joseph and his daughter Princess Gisela of Bavaria since 1905 to buy the 'Achilleion', the beautiful little palace on Corfu which had belonged to the Empress Elisabeth. In April 1907 he instructed the ambassador in Vienna, Carl Wedel, to purchase the house and surrounding grounds for 1 million francs.[37]

Above all, Wilhelm's hostility towards parliament, the political parties, the press and broad sections of the population repeatedly made itself felt so blatantly that it hindered the efforts of his advisers to anchor the monarchy more firmly in the nation's affections. In August 1906 both Bülow and Tschirschky urged the Kaiser to make at least a symbolic gesture by authorising a few concessions to the parliamentary and democratic tendencies of the day; this would even be advantageous to the Kaiserreich's foreign policy, they argued. In a submission to the Kaiser the Foreign Secretary commented that 'at the moment our international situation is unfortunately such that public opinion almost everywhere in the world, in ignorance of the real state of affairs, regards us, or at least pretends to do so, as reactionary, quarrelsome and out to conquer others, whereas in reality our policies are peaceful, not aggressive. Other powers which are less peaceful and moderate than we are have succeeded in clothing themselves in the mantle of modern, humane and liberal attitudes.' For this reason Bülow and Tschirschky favoured the suggestion made by Metternich from the London embassy that Berlin should for once be put forward as the venue for the Interparliamentary Conference. Wilhelm II, however, at first refused point-blank to listen to the advice of his principal advisers.[38] Only four months later, when Bülow and Tschirschky again approached him, did the Kaiser agree to the Conference being held in Berlin in September 1908, but only with the proviso that no attacks 'against the Prussian Army or the German Navy' were made at the congress.[39]

The world of court and military ceremonial in which Wilhelm II moved made an anachronistic impression in a highly industrialised country which, with a Reichstag elected by universal adult male suffrage and a modern mass-circulation press, was wholly familiar with vital elements of democracy. In 1906 the Kaiser described criticism of his long-standing Chief of the Civil Cabinet, Hermann von Lucanus, by the leader of the German Conservatives, Ernst von Heydebrand und der Lasa, as 'extremely rude'. He wrote to Bülow: 'Such an honourable, diligent old official deserved better treatment from the Conservatives; especially as he is my official.' When the Left Liberal *Vossische Zeitung* complained that the imperial court had taken no notice of the death of the great parliamentarian Eugen Richter, Wilhelm reacted with 'great hilarity'.[40] Zedlitz was a lone voice at court with the view that it would have been tactically wiser to have taken notice of Richter's funeral in some appropriate way, as he had undoubtedly been a man of great significance.[41]

Wilhelm's attitude to the press fluctuated between contempt and aggression. He was convinced that most foreign newspapers were bribed by foreign Powers to denounce him and his Reich. The press was of course completely in the hands of 'European pan-Judaism', he declared in 1908. More than once, when he was particularly angered by an article, he threatened to send one of his Flügeladjutanten to the newspaper's offices to shoot the editor. The remarkable order he addressed to the Civil Cabinet on 30 August 1908 shows what he thought of the growing criticism of his 'Personal Rule'. 'The inventions about the person of His Majesty the Kaiser and King and about his intentions and plans are increasing to such an extent that it seems scarcely possible or desirable to continue denying them one by one. His Majesty wishes, however, that a list of all these false reports should be drawn up in the course of the year and published at the end of the year in the hope that the Press will draw a salutary lesson from it.'[42]

On 8 September 1906 the Kaiser's nervous irritation found an outlet in his notorious 'prophets of doom speech' at Breslau. 'Just as the great King [Frederick the Great] was never let down by his old Ally [i.e. God],' he proclaimed, 'our Fatherland and this beautiful province will always be close to his heart. And so let us forge a new vow from the wonderful treasure of memories and from the golden loyalty that has greeted Me here: to dedicate ourselves from now on to one single task, for which we must summon up all our mental and physical strength, and that is to take our country forwards, to work for our people, every man in his estate, no matter whether high or low, with confessions joining together to combat unbelief, and above all to keep our vision untrammelled for the future and never to lose faith in ourselves and our people.' This call to arms was followed by a threat: 'I will not tolerate prophets of doom, and anyone who finds the work uncongenial should go away and find himself a better country if he wants.'[43] The speech worsened the mood throughout the country and was harshly criticised even in Conservative circles.[44]

'GERMAN ANXIETIES' OF A 'PROPHET OF DOOM'

If one wished to name a moment when the impressive structure of Wilhelm II's Personal Monarchy began to sway noticeably, one would not be far wrong in pointing to the autumn of 1906. In October 1906 Maximilian Harden bore witness to it. 'The personal policy of the Kaiser is at the root of all evil ... If this manner of conducting policy by impromptu inspirations, whose consequences are never thought through to their conclusion, does not cease, I can see no hope. And with all due consideration for the monarchy, I do not know whether a great, hard working people can today still be circumscribed by such characteristics of a single person.'[45] In November 1906, when the entire German press was full of rumours about the alleged intrigues of Philipp Eulenburg and the Liebenberg Round Table,[46] Hildegard von Spitzemberg was horrified by the tone of an interpellation in the Reichstag by the National Liberal member Ernst Bassermann, which was 'clearly aimed at H.M. in an astonishing and shocking way' and in which 'arbitrariness, spiritist influences [and] sycophancy' were evoked; 'everything only too true but never before so openly expressed!'[47] And a few weeks later Max Weber wrote to the prominent liberal Friedrich Naumann: 'The amount of contempt which we as a nation receive abroad (Italy, America, everywhere!) – and *rightly*, that is the crucial thing – *because* we "put up with" *this* rule by *this* man, really has now become a factor of first-rate "world political" importance for us ... We are becoming "isolated" because this man rules us in this way and we tolerate and find excuses for it.'[48]

In the autumn of 1906, shortly after Kaiser Wilhelm had used his Breslau speech to order all 'prophets of doom' out of his Reich,[49] an obscure publishing house in Freiburg brought out a brilliantly written anonymous work entitled *Unser Kaiser und sein Volk! Deutsche Sorgen. Von einem Schwarzseher* [*Our Kaiser and his People! German Anxieties. By a Prophet of Doom*], to which

court society and political circles reacted with a mixture of shocked appreciation and profound alarm.[50] The identity of the author is still unclear today,
but at the time insiders were quite certain that it must have been someone at
the highest level, with personal experience of the Kaiser, so accurate were his
observations on every subject. Baroness Spitzemberg noted in her diary on
26 November 1906: 'Lately I have been reading, with burning interest, an
anonymously published brochure, "Our Kaiser and His People!" ... The
author must be well versed in everything and at the forefront everywhere,
for he knows a great deal about military matters, politics, the Reichstag, the
court and details about individuals, and he must also have been in personal
contact with the Kaiser. He takes a very grave view of our situation at home
and abroad.' Her son Lothar von Spitzemberg, who was a gentleman in
waiting to the Kaiserin, was also 'very shocked' by the brochure.[51] Holstein
admired the 'elegant, very modern style' in which the 'sensational brochure'
was written and had 'very little doubt' that the author was 'a senior officer', for
there was 'more than one among them who knows how to write'.[52]

The anonymous author exposed the conduct of government under Wilhelm
II unsparingly and with astounding insider knowledge. He asserted that the
fundamental cause of the growing concern throughout Germany, not only
among the perpetually carping 'horde' of Socialists and Democrats but also
among the 'hundreds of thousands of warm-hearted, unreservedly pro-
monarchical compatriots', lay in the autocratic personality of the Kaiser, which
was absolutely incomprehensible 'except in terms of his firm belief in the
divine right of Kings'. There was 'simply no field left in which he did not
demand recognition as an expert'.[53] Wilhelm II insisted on keeping all the
reins in his hands and on making all decisions, even on minor matters, 'so as to
leave no room for doubt that he really is his own Chancellor'.[54] 'And so he goes
on treading a perilous path beside the precipice of a dilettantism that destroys
his prestige; he makes his own life and that of others inordinately difficult;
and above all he impedes the machinery of government by seeking to be its
driving force, whereas even the most competent man, in his place, is only
entitled to be its chief supervisor.'[55] 'The penchant for over-hasty judgements,
Wilhelm II's impulsivity, the naïve subjectivism ... and finally the urge to
assert supreme command everywhere, an urge which refuses to tolerate
anything but yes-men and keeps all strong characters at bay, for its suspicion
never sleeps; inevitably, all this imposed a very distinct framework on the way
in which a man like Bernhard Bülow could function as Chancellor from the
outset ... He found the Chancellor's position so restricted already that the
limits of his own capabilities almost exactly matched the framework which
Wilhelm II had designed for the activity of his principal servant and adviser.'[56]

It had gradually become impossible to give the Kaiser a complete, realistic picture of the true state of affairs in the Reich. Undeniably, since Bismarck's departure, subsequent chancellors had no longer adopted the position of leading statesmen but rather that of subordinate officials. Equally, none of his responsible advisers had shown sufficient strength or spirit of self-sacrifice to tell the Kaiser unpleasant truths. Nonetheless the blame for the growing estrangement between monarch and people lay above all with the Kaiser, for Wilhelm was animated by the urge to shine and to dominate. 'At an audience, the adviser has often not yet reached his third sentence when the Kaiser starts speaking himself, expounds his own views on the subject, which he always believes he has fully mastered, and asks questions only to answer them himself at the same time; he easily ... gets carried away from one subject onto another and at the end of the prescribed time he has usually given the adviser an extremely lively hour but at the same time has made it impossible for him to fulfil his duty to provide information and put forward his own opinion.' Anyone who failed to follow the Kaiser's entertaining flights of intellect – as for instance Posadowsky – but stuck doggedly to his duty and tried to return to his theme, quickly gained the reputation with Wilhelm of being a 'tedious fellow' or a 'wooden bureaucrat'. If on the other hand a minister knew how to make the Kaiser laugh heartily with a crude joke – an obvious reference to Podbielski – he could defy even the strongest attacks of public opinion.

Bülow had 'flattered his way into his imperial Master's heart as an amusing conversationalist', the anonymous author commented. The Reich Chancellor could, however, 'rightly claim for himself that he has, even if it was often by very roundabout and devious means, at least told the Kaiser what was absolutely essential and, by a constant intellectual sacrifice in minor matters, has after all enabled Wilhelm II to see more clearly as far as some of the more important questions were concerned. As long as our Kaiser lives among an entourage trapped in attitudes originating from centuries ago, as long as this entourage manages to keep the Kaiser firmly inside the circle of those who share these ideas and to give him information from within it, and thus from a completely one-sided point of view, that is no small achievement.'[57] Bülow had been a career diplomat and knew 'how to get along with Wilhelm II. He has prevented much; he has been obliged to let much happen; he has done nothing of his own ... In many instances he has heard for the first time from the Press about something for which he had to take responsibility. It's just as if the Kaiser derived satisfaction from the fact that his principal adviser is seen by the whole world as a mere accessory. Don't even mention Caprivi and Hohenlohe in this respect. But Bernhard Bülow has admittedly been more than a mere tool of the Kaiser's initiatives. But even so, foreign countries were to be given the impression that only the Kaiser himself could take responsibility for the entire policy of the German Reich.'[58]

Ever since 'the centre of gravity of government was shifted into the [secret] Cabinet' under Wilhelm II, Bülow had been obliged, in his attempts to prevent the Kaiser's 'all too questionable deviations', or at least to cover up for them after the event, to 'mix with the competition' and use the methods of a courtier himself. 'It can be regarded as a national disaster that the Chancellor of the German Reich, although he is not himself a product of the camarilla, nevertheless not only provides cover for a kind of Cabinet government, but is also constantly obliged to compete with the courtiers on their ground, instead of being the independent and determined initiator of a strong policy for which he can put the case to his imperial master with his head held high. It will be deeply deplored if the Reich Chancellor can be continually surprised by political actions on the part of his Sovereign because he, like any other courtier, does not have eyes and ears everywhere, so that he must always be prepared to have obstacles put in his way. A catastrophic turn of events can be predicted if German policy continually fails to follow any straight line because the Chancellor can at best achieve only compromises, is far from being able to prevent all deviations and often cannot himself give sufficient reasons for actions whose consequences are unforeseeable.'[59]

Convinced that he was 'really the most talented and efficient strategist in his army', Wilhelm II had 'taken it upon himself to be his own Chief of General Staff even more cheerfully than to be his own Chancellor'. The role the Kaiser had assigned to the actual Chief of General Staff had therefore been even humbler than that of the Chancellor in this system, the 'prophet of doom' pointed out with dismay. 'It is characteristic of the alarming degree of importance which our Kaiser accords to purely outward factors that a Moltke was appointed to this post as soon as one was available. In the long run Wilhelm II would no more have tolerated a man like the "great silent one" [i.e. the old Field Marshal Count Moltke] as his principal military adviser than he could put up with a Bismarck as Chancellor. But "his Moltke" he did want. It looked so decorative.' The younger Moltke could not stand comparison with a von der Goltz or a Beseler, in the writer's opinion. 'But he was a Moltke. And when old Schlieffen had to be sacked, title and task passed to the man long since designated for it. Schlieffen had advised against it. Audible grumbling from the Commanding Generals, at any rate strong enough to warn the favourite. At the eleventh hour he himself asked not to be appointed. But then he was appointed anyway!'[60] No wonder that Holstein, who had such an intimate knowledge of events behind the scenes, thought the author was a senior army officer. One cannot help thinking of General Bruno von Mudra who, as we have seen, had expressed very similar views about Moltke's appointment as Chief of General Staff in his letters to Colmar von der Goltz.[61]

The conclusion that the 'prophet of doom' drew from Kaiser Wilhelm II's eighteen-year reign was damning. 'The young ruling Prince who wanted to be Chancellor and Chief of General Staff of his country, senior Bishop of the united Evangelical Church, ultimate authority on all questions of art and science, who wanted to direct the foreign policy of the Reich, to point out new paths for industry, trade, agriculture, education and sport, to be the stimulus for every social, economic and technical achievement, also had to be personally present wherever a foundation stone or a keystone was put in place, wherever a ship was named, a church or a barracks dedicated, a new gun tested, a memorial unveiled, an exhibition opened, a music festival celebrated, a horse or automobile race held, a regatta arranged. Through his presence he wanted to stamp even trivial occasions with his personality.'[62] Like Holstein, the author compared Wilhelm's autocratic government with the 'Sultanesque methods of rulership' which prevailed in the declining Ottoman Empire of Abdul Hamid II. 'In our country today the situation is in fact not very different from that of Turkey, where the Porte ekes out a shadowy existence, the seraglio pulls all the strings, changes of mood in the Yildiz dictate both domestic and foreign policy, the camarilla triumphs and the ministers no longer work towards a fixed programme of government under a unified leadership but merely try to read the wishes of their ruler from the expressions of his face, and fear nothing *more* than to go against *his* intentions. Restricting the authority of the Grand Vizier was also one of the first acts of Abdul Hamid's reign; Abdul Hamid too wanted to be his own Chancellor, his own Chief of General Staff. He too wants obedient servants above all, puts an excessive value on good manners and conversation to chase away the doldrums, listens to sycophantic toadies singing his praises without reflecting that the airs which sound so sweetly flattering to him get on the nerves of the great mass of the people and stir up stronger and stronger opposition.'[63] 'The personal will of the ruler first and last!' the anonymous author exclaimed bitterly. 'The Chancellor as rival to the court camarilla, simply to prevent the most dangerous extravagances! – The civil service constantly keeping an eye on the court authorities over its head! – The bureaucracy corrupted and partly ruined! – Parliament spineless to the point of self-destruction! – No counterweight to camarilla and cabinet rule anywhere to be seen! – And that is how Germany is governed in the first flush of the twentieth century.'[64] The catastrophe that the 'prophet of doom' and countless others foresaw in the autumn of 1906 was not long in coming.

CHAPTER TWENTY-FIVE

Nemesis. Wilhelm II and the *Daily Telegraph* affair

In the late summer of 1908 Kaiser Wilhelm II took a keen interest in the rehearsals of the ballet *Sardanapalus, the Last Days of Niniveh,* which received its first performance on 1 September 1908 in the Royal Opera House in Berlin. In preparation for it he had brought in the leading German and foreign Assyriologists and had had historically accurate scenery constructed. As well as his didactic and archaeological aim, the 'popularisation of scholarly research in the Mesopotamian ruins',[1] he had a topical and highly political purpose: he announced to the prominent international guests invited to the dress rehearsal that the point of the production was 'to strengthen monarchical feeling among the people by showing them how truly Personal Rule leads a state to glory and greatness'.[2]

Only a few weeks later the system of Personal Monarchy collapsed. The discontent over Wilhelm's anachronistic high-handedness, which had already made itself felt soon after his accession and had recently increased to an alarming degree − not least as a result of the dangerous international isolation of the Kaiserreich and of the embarrassing sexual scandals at court − erupted in a wave of indignation against the Kaiser's 'Personal Rule'. His abdication was openly discussed and at times the future of the Hohenzollern Monarchy itself seemed to be in doubt. What triggered the 'November storm' that swept through all parties and social classes and also had damaging repercussions abroad was, famously, an 'interview' given by Wilhelm to a then unnamed Englishman, which appeared with the Kaiser's express permission in the London *Daily Telegraph* on 28 October 1908. The very idea that the monarch had held a 'private conversation' with a foreigner in which he had spoken about the aims of German policy aroused fury enough; but apart from this, the interview contained three '*horrenda*', as Bülow called them, which caused particular offence to German public opinion:

1. Evidently in an attempt to dispel British suspicions about German naval construction, the Kaiser had claimed that the battlefleet was not aimed against Great Britain but was intended for the struggle against the 'Yellow Peril' – Japan and China – in the Pacific.

2. The German people, above all the lower and middle classes, certainly had hostile feelings towards England, but he himself had always done everything in his power to defend England's interests. Thus for instance he had worked out a plan of campaign against the Boers with his General Staff and sent it to his grandmother Queen Victoria.

3. At the same time he had not only rejected an initiative by Russia and France, who wanted to form a Continental League during the Boer War in order to 'humiliate England to the dust', but he had immediately reported this perfidious plan to London. The English were 'mad as March hares' if they thought they could see him, the German Emperor, as anything but a friend.

How this fatal 'interview' came about and what Kaiser Wilhelm intended to achieve by it will be explained shortly, on the basis of the documentary evidence. No less revealing, however, is the question which has been debated for decades, of what role the Reich Chancellor and the German Foreign Office played in the publication of the article. Until recently international scholarship, with very few exceptions, has taken at its face value Bülow's claim that he never read the draft of the interview, which was written on thin paper in a scarcely legible English hand, either when he received it at the beginning of October 1908 or after it had been checked by the Auswärtiges Amt, but that he had allowed the manuscript to be returned to the Kaiser on the assumption that the Wilhelmstrasse, which had suggested only a few corrections, had released the interview as safe for publication. Those to blame for the catastrophe, therefore, were the worthy official, Reinhold Klehmet, who had not recognised the explosive nature of the article, and the Under Secretary, Wilhelm Stemrich, whose job it was to deputise for the Foreign Secretary, Freiherr von Schoen, during the latter's absence; Stemrich, however, was too new to his post to realise what repercussions the publication of the Kaiser's remarks would have. Finally, a considerable proportion of the blame rested also on the envoy Felix von Müller, who was acting as assistant to the Chancellor during his stay on Norderney, for he had failed to draw Bülow's attention to the dangers of publication.[3]

This more or less 'official' version of events relating to the genesis of the Kaiser's 'interview' in itself throws a harsh light on the state of affairs that had been allowed to develop behind the glittering façade of the Personal Monarchy. But since the publication of Peter Winzen's comprehensive documentation of the *Daily Telegraph* affair at the latest it has been exposed incontrovertibly as a cynical cover-up by Bülow.[4] The mere fact that the text of the interview had not been written by hand on inferior paper but typed in double spacing on the particularly heavy paper used by the London newspaper,[5] and that on Bülow's orders three more typed copies were made at the Foreign Office, proves that we are dealing with a cunning manipulation of the facts in which not only the Reich Chancellor but very probably also the Foreign Secretary, Wilhelm von Schoen, who did not go on leave until after the decisive consultations, took part.

But if Bülow did in fact read the embarrassing text of the interview and send it back to the Kaiser for publication, what are the conclusions to be drawn from this astonishing discovery? Contemporaries suspected that Bülow had consciously exposed the Kaiser in the pursuit of an ambitious plan to convert the Kaiserreich to parliamentary government in three stages: through the dissolution of the Reichstag and the elections of January–February 1907 he had created parliamentary backing for himself in the 'Bülow bloc'; by supporting the attacks on Eulenburg and the 'Liebenberg Round Table' he had got rid of the secret camarilla around Wilhelm II; and now by deliberately humiliating the Kaiser he aimed to break his powerful will in order to bring him finally under the control of the responsible Reich and Prussian state authorities. This bold interpretation of the events of November demands examination, but it must be said at the outset that even if it is not without elements of truth, it seems unconvincing as it stands, if only because of Bülow's personality and his style of government. When French newspapers indulged in speculation along similar lines in mid November 1908, the Württemberg envoy Axel Varnbüler expressed doubts that Bülow had either the bad or the good qualities required to devise such long-range, single-minded plans. 'I do not credit him either with such unscrupulousness in the choice of his methods or with the determination and persistence to carry out such broad and ambitious aims, but consider him more as an opportunist, a step-by-step improviser good at exploiting given situations. But in so doing he certainly shows very imaginative talent, very acute calculation and – what is by no means to be despised – he is unusually lucky.' At the same time, however, Varnbüler concluded that Bülow had at least temporarily 'emerged from this last crisis in a stronger and more secure position in relation to the Kaiser and the nation than any Reich Chancellor before him had ever enjoyed since Bismarck's time – and even than the latter under the "new Master".'[6]

As a monarchist, Bülow certainly did not want to set in train the parliamentarisation of Germany. But did he really think he would be able to teach the Kaiser a 'pedagogic' lesson in order to break his will to power and thus make his own position as Chancellor unassailable? In the end, given his long experience, Bülow must have known, as his contemporaries also realised soon after the November crisis, that his days as Reich Chancellor were numbered from the moment when he had forfeited the Kaiser's confidence in him by his 'betrayal'. We shall see whether Bülow's conduct in the weeks before the appearance of the Kaiser's interview in the *Daily Telegraph* is not rather to be explained by his notorious submissiveness towards Wilhelm, than by a conscious intention to wrench the tiller from his grasp and transfer the focus of power from the court back to himself and his colleagues in the Wilhelmstrasse, specifically with a view, as Canis suggests, to slowing down the naval arms race and improving relations with Great Britain.[7]

Whether or not he read the manuscript of the interview beforehand, it is clear that Bülow was completely taken aback by the storm of indignation it aroused, as Winzen has proved beyond doubt. This fact too speaks against a carefully considered and resolute plan on the part of the Chancellor to humiliate the Kaiser. Neither the monarch nor the Reich Chancellor nor the Foreign Office foresaw the effect which the Kaiser's assertions, which were aimed purely and solely at British policy, would have on German public opinion. Wilhelm II was convinced not only that he had acted constitutionally in this case, because he had personally sent the English text to the Chancellor for his appraisal, but also that in his interview he was following a political line agreed with Bülow.

THE PRELUDE TO THE INTERVIEW

In order to understand the Kaiser's remarks which appeared in the *Daily Telegraph* at the end of October 1908 it is essential to bear in mind that we are not dealing with convictions honestly expressed by Wilhelm II but with a half-naive, half-dishonest attempt to fool the British about the true goals of German policy and to foment suspicion against their Entente partners, France and Russia, as well as against their ally Japan. For years Wilhelm had stressed his close family relationship to the British ruling house – for example by recalling the genuinely reverent role he had played at his dying grandmother's bedside – in order to dispel the growing mistrust in London of Germany's foreign and naval policy.[8] He brusquely rejected the somewhat reserved speeches drafted in the London embassy for his visit to Windsor in 1907, calling them 'wretched', 'scandalous' and 'abominable', and demanded emotionally charged language emphasising his family ties to the royal family, despite warnings that this would be counterproductive in England. In his own hand he added the following sentences to the draft speech: 'Ties of close relationship & many dear memories of bygone days link me to Y. M. family. Among these memories stands foremost the figure of my revered Grandmother the great Queen Victoria whose image is imperishably engraved in my heart. While the remembrance of my beloved mother carries me back to the earliest days of a happy childhood spent under the roof & within the walls of this fine old Windsor Castle.'[9] This was how he wanted the British to see him.

Wilhelm's assurances of friendship for Britain were, however, increasingly characterised by frustration and bitterness over the fact that his uncle the King showed him so little warmth, British statesmen practically never came to Berlin and the London press continued to be animated by profound suspicion of the 'German danger'. As early as in October 1905 he had declared in a letter to Mary Montagu, already quoted in Chapter 20, that he could not come to England again for the time being because the newspapers there had been full of hatred for him and Germany in the last three to four years.[10]

As well as evoking the memory of the late Queen and of his idyllic childhood experiences at Osborne, Wilhelm constantly reminded English interlocutors that during the Boer War he had worked out a plan of campaign for the British army and sent it to his grandmother. As we have already seen, the Kaiser brought out this story for the benefit of his English host at Highcliffe, Colonel Stuart Wortley, alongside the third '*horrendum*' of the *Daily Telegraph* interview: the claim that he had turned down the Franco-Russian proposal of a Continental League and loyally reported it to London.[11]

After his return from England in December 1907 Kaiser Wilhelm repeated these *idées fixes* in numerous further conversations with British statesmen and diplomats, including Lascelles. In January 1908 the *Strand Magazine*, apparently with Wilhelm's express consent, published a biographical article by the British journalist J. L. Bashford, in which the Kaiser was quoted as saying: 'I cannot comprehend the ill-feeling against me in England. I have acted loyally to England. An offer was made to Germany simultaneously from two powerful sides to take advantage of the situation and to interfere in British policy, and I refused point-blank. I instantly telegraphed the nature of the offer to my uncle.'[12]

Again on 11 August 1908, in his set-to with Sir Charles Hardinge at Schloss Friedrichshof, Wilhelm II had made the same claims, word for word, as appeared ten weeks later in the *Daily Telegraph*. In his record of the Kronberg conversation Hardinge had noted how the Kaiser, after their sharp disagreement over the German battlefleet-building programme, had adopted a different tone in the evening and had stressed 'what a good friend he had been to England in the past. Thus he repeated the statement previously made (I think) to His Majesty's Ambassador at Berlin that, during the Boer War, he had been approached by the French and Russian Governments to make a coalition against England, but that he had absolutely declined to do so, and had threatened to make war on any Power that dared to make an unprovoked attack on England at that time. I did not think it is worth while to mention that this account does not tally at all with that given by M. Delcassé and the Russian Government of this transaction. So also His Majesty told me that, after our early reverses in the Boer War, he had received a letter from the late Queen Victoria, full of grief at the losses suffered by the British troops, which had touched him deeply. He had at once instructed his General Staff to draw up a plan of campaign, which he had sent to the Queen, and that this plan had been followed by Lord Roberts in all its details. "And yet," His Majesty added, "I am said to be the enemy of England!"[13]

There can be scarcely any doubt that these efforts at the All-Highest level to soothe British fears came to the ears of the Reich Chancellor, especially as Bülow's cousin Martin Freiherr von Rücker-Jenisch was a permanent member of the Kaiser's suite as representative of the Wilhelmstrasse. Rather, everything indicates that Bülow welcomed the Kaiser's anglophile assurances, for it was during that summer that the Chancellor had at last become convinced that an Anglo-German rapprochement was urgently needed.[14] Bülow's fundamental agreement with the Kaiser's attempts to dispel British concerns, coupled with his subjection to the sovereign, which had become his habit over many years, and no doubt also with a degree of demoralisation in view of the role allotted to him as Reich Chancellor – these factors, rather than a Machiavellian attempt to show up the monarch before all the world so as to break his personal power will have been behind Bülow's behaviour when the draft of the Kaiser's interview arrived in Norderney on 1 October 1908.

THE GENESIS OF THE *DAILY TELEGRAPH* INTERVIEW

As soon as the 'interview' was published in the *Daily Telegraph* the guessing-game began over the identity of the 'former diplomat' who had apparently written this explosive account of it. Many thought the recently retired British ambassador in Berlin, Sir Frank Lascelles, was the author; others named the journalists J. L. Bashford, Lucien Wolff and John Alfred Spender as possible candidates.[15] Not until 1930 did it become known that Edward Stuart Wortley was responsible for the article.[16] Following the research by Peter Winzen and others the genesis of the interview is now to a large extent clear.[17] As a thank you for his hospitality at Highcliffe Castle, Kaiser Wilhelm had invited 'Eddy' Stuart Wortley, who had meanwhile been promoted to Brigadier General, to take part in the autumn manoeuvres in Lorraine.[18] On 10 September 1908 a conversation took place on the manoeuvre ground between Wilhelm and the British General, which was to lead directly to the publication in the *Daily Telegraph*. Stuart Wortley later recalled: 'On the concluding day of the manoeuvres the Emperor sent for me. He was on his horse in the middle of a ploughed field. He told his staff to clear away for some distance, and proceeded to recount to me all that eventually appeared in the interview which was published. He concluded by saying he wished me to use my discretion and to have the gist of the interview published in a leading English newspaper ... The Kaiser did not mention any particular paper in which he wished this interview to be published, but left the matter entirely in my hands.'[19] The monarch promptly informed his Reich Chancellor, in a written comment on a report from London, that Stuart Wortley had just declared to him: 'My countrymen are as mad as marchhares [sic], even in September. Even General Sir John French believes firmly in a forthcoming german attack!' The Kaiser had authorised Stuart Wortley 'to take home the message from me that the British gave the impression of a set of raving lunatics'.[20] Six weeks later these remarks were to appear, word for word, in the *Daily Telegraph.*

With the help of the respected editor of the *Daily Telegraph*, John Benjamin Firth, Stuart Wortley put together an article in the form of an interview and sent the text — the original manuscript, which is preserved among the General's papers, consists of ten typed pages with a broad margin for corrections — to the Kaiser on 23 September 1908 requesting his permission to have it published. His covering letter leaves no doubt that his intentions were honourable. 'The great honour which Your Majesty did to me at the recent manoeuvres and on previous occasions, during Your Majesty's stay at Highcliffe, in talking so openly concerning the most regrettable tone of a portion of the Press of this country regarding your actions and intentions towards this country, have so deeply impressed me that, in my humble opinion, it is high time that the sincerity of Your Majesty's good feelings and intentions, as publicly expressed on more than one occasion, should through the medium of a leading newspaper be placed prominently and strongly before the British public. If this is done, and done well, I have no doubt whatever that a great change will come over the most ungracious and improper tone of certain organs of the Press — and be productive of much good. On my return from the manoeuvres I communicated most confidentially with a friend of mine [Harry Lawson] whose father is the proprietor of the Daily Telegraph, a paper which has never adopted the tone concerning Your Majesty which is so much to be regretted. As a result of my interview, the enclosed draft of a supposed communiqué has been made at my instigation, veiled as from a retired diplomat. I think that it embodies all that Your Majesty expressed to me. Before, however, taking any further steps in the matter, or allowing any use to be made of it, I submit it for Your Majesty's perusal – and in the hope that if Your Majesty disapproves of it in any way, you will be gracious enough to tell me. I am only one of Your Majesty's great admirers in this country, whose great wish is to prove to the people of England Your Majesty's firm desire to be on the best terms with them.'[21] On 30 September Kaiser Wilhelm sent a telegram from his East Prussian hunting lodge at Rominten expressing his thanks for the draft and saying that he would have it examined.[22]

THE TEXT OF THE INTERVIEW AND THE SO-CALLED 'RESPONSIBLE GOVERNMENT'

The Kaiser received Stuart Wortley's draft at a moment when European peace seemed threatened by crises both to the west and to the east, and when he was becoming acutely aware of Germany's isolation. On the one hand his fury against his uncle Edward, whose Entente policy he blamed for the international isolation in which the Kaiserreich found itself, reached new heights at this time.[23] On the other hand, however, in view of the uncertain situation arising from the Young Turks' takeover of power in the Ottoman Empire, he felt that an Anglo-German rapprochement was urgently needed. On 12 October 1908 he defined the line he wished German policy to follow: 'We must try, amidst this terrible chaos, to get back onto a better footing with England ... England and Germany are the two Great Powers who it seems were not informed in advance throughout the whole business, and therefore have a more or less free hand and ought to come to an agreement.'[24] It was precisely this goal that the forthcoming 'interview' in the *Daily Telegraph*, the draft of which the Kaiser had forwarded to the Reich Chancellor in Norderney for his inspection, was supposed to achieve.

In addition to the tensions caused by the Young Turks' revolution, Bulgarian attempts to gain independence and the annexation of Bosnia and Herzegovina by the Habsburg Empire – crises to which we shall return in the next chapter – serious trouble had also arisen in Morocco.[25] In this connection Wilhelm II had violently reprimanded his Foreign Office for not keeping him up to date with important business.[26] The Kaiser's fury with the Wilhelmstrasse partly explains his express orders to Bülow to examine the manuscript of the interview for the *Daily Telegraph* himself and *not* forward it to the Auswärtiges Amt.[27] Wilhelm's autocratic attitude perhaps also explains why the leading officials in the Wilhelmstrasse were apparently somewhat intimidated when, despite the Kaiser's orders, they received the text of the interview from the Chancellor with instructions to check it. At any rate the poor communication between the court camp at Rominten, the Reich Chancellor in Norderney and the Foreign Office in Berlin is evidence of dangerous strains on the conduct of government which were to lead to catastrophe over the handling of the text of the interview.

Stuart Wortley's draft and his covering letter to Wilhelm II reached Bülow in Norderney on the evening of 1 October 1908. In forwarding the two documents to the Chancellor, Rücker-Jenisch had emphasised several times, on the Kaiser's behalf, the explosive nature of what it was planned to publish, and requested Bülow to review it with the utmost discretion and without involving the Foreign Office. 'His Majesty is glad of Stuart Wortley's offer and of the fact that a distinguished Englishman is also offering his services to help bring about good relations between Germany and England. He thinks that the article is well written and that it gives a truthful account of his own words . . . His Majesty has instructed me to send you the letter and its enclosure for your attention, with the request to return them, and asks you to make whatever changes you think fit to the article and to write these next to the present English text. For this purpose the article ought perhaps first to be copied onto one side of a divided sheet of paper. His Majesty also wishes a copy with the amended text to be kept for us . . . I have already drawn His Majesty's attention to the fact that in several places the words put into His All-Highest mouth needed correction because they did not accord with the facts, for instance . . . with regard to the negotiations during the Boer War etc. His Majesty seems very keen to receive an answer from you soon.'[28]

Thereafter the progress of the manuscript through the various offices can now be clearly established. It was not until the beginning of November, when the well-intentioned publication had proved to be a disastrous mistake, that Bülow hit upon his cover story that the text of the interview had been written on thin paper in a very indistinct English hand and that he had therefore sent it on, unread, to be checked in the Foreign Office.[29] As Winzen has been able to show on the basis of the sources, the Chancellor worked on the missive received from Rominten and forwarded it to the Wilhelmstrasse on 2 October with 'very secret' instructions to check the article over carefully and write in any corrections, additions or omissions that seemed desirable in the margin of a typed copy of it.[30] In the Foreign Office the Under Secretary, Stemrich, who held this post for only eleven months, and the more experienced but subordinate Councillor, Reinhold Klehmet, scrutinised the English text closely. Both recognised its dubious nature but assumed, especially as the Chancellor had not raised the question of how opportune publication would be, that Bülow would take the final decision on this highly political matter.[31] Klehmet therefore corrected three factual mistakes in the article, which Stemrich sent back to the Chancellor in Norderney on 5 October, together with a typed copy of the article, the original manuscript, Stuart Wortley's covering letter and Jenisch's letter to the Chancellor. On 7 October Stemrich sent the additional typed copy for the Kaiser which Bülow had requested.[32] Thus the Reich Chancellor now had *three* typed copies of the article in his possession, while a fourth copy was retained in the Foreign Office. On 10 October Bülow asked the envoy Felix von Müller, who was with him as the representative of the Foreign Office, to send all the documents collected in Norderney back to the Wilhelmstrasse, and returned there himself on the night of 11–12 October.[33]

On 12 October 1908 Bülow lunched with the Kaiser at the Reich Chancellor's palace.[34] As Foreign Secretary von Schoen recalled in his memoirs: 'After luncheon the Kaiser had a long conversation with the Chancellor in the garden, at which I was not present. As I gathered later from a remark by the Kaiser, they talked about the publication in question. The Kaiser asked for the matter to be finally settled, and the Chancellor agreed to this.'[35] While Wilhelm left for Döberitz next day to go hunting, Bülow discussed the article and the amendments suggested by Klehmet and Stemrich with Schoen, before sending off the document to Jenisch, who had meanwhile gone to Klein-Flottbeck, on the afternoon of 13 October.[36]

Jenisch sent the draft article with the three marginal corrections by Klehmet, together with Stuart Wortley's letter, back to the Kaiser. His accompanying letter declared, untruthfully: 'The article, as Your Majesty was pleased to command, has been thoroughly examined by the Reich Chancellor, bypassing the Foreign Office as far as possible, and there are only three passages in which exception can be taken to the wording. I have inserted the changes suggested by His Excellency in the margin of Stuart Wortley's draft; a copy of the draft has been retained for the record. With regard to each of the changes Prince Bülow has made the following comments: 1) It might be better to tone down somewhat, for an English newspaper, the acknowledgement that the majority of the German people have unfriendly feelings towards England. 2) The statement about Consul Vassel's journey to Fez had to be amended in accordance with the actual circumstances, 3) likewise that relating to our reply to the Franco-Russian proposal for an intervention in the Boer War. This, as is well known, was on these lines: we had to be particularly careful to avoid complications with other Great Powers, especially Sea Powers, as long as we were not sure how we stood with France, and the only way we could be sure was through mutual territorial guarantees for a period of many years. The remarks ascribed to Your Majesty should perhaps not deviate too far from this motivation, in which there is no trace of the threat of armed intervention by Germany in favour of England ... Providing that the few changes proposed meet with Your Majesty's approval, I most humbly enclose a draft reply to Colonel Stuart Wortley which, once Your Majesty has perused it, could be encoded again by the cypher-clerk, All-Graciously authorised by Your Majesty and then dispatched with Colonel Stuart Wortley's article as a registered letter.'[37]

The Kaiser signed the covering letter and sent the draft article, with the handwritten corrections which Jenisch, on Bülow's instructions, had inserted in the margin, back to Stuart Wortley on 16 October. On both sides of the North Sea the few who knew about it were confident that the article would lead to a distinct improvement in Anglo-German relations. 'I firmly hope that it may have the effect of bringing about a change in the tone of some of the English newspapers', the Kaiser told the British General, who replied on 22 October: 'I have taken steps which I hope and believe will tend to correct the stupid impressions concerning Your Majesty's feelings towards this country, which certain organs of the press have created. The profound admiration and regard which I have for Your Majesty dictates to me a duty ... to put before the British public the true feelings that You have towards us. I shall be overjoyed if good comes out of it.'[38] Wilhelm II sent Stuart Wortley's letter to the Foreign Office, where Bülow and Schoen can be proved to have taken note of it on 26 October.[39] None of those involved in the formulation of the article seems to have foreseen the impression the Kaiser's interview would make on public opinion in Germany.[40]

'SHAME ON THE GERMAN REICH!' THE REACTION TO THE INTERVIEW

On 28 October the article which was to send shock-waves around the world was published on page 11 of the *Daily Telegraph* in London. Under the headline 'The German Emperor and England. Personal Interview. Frank Statement of World Policy. Proofs of Friendship' the reader learned that Kaiser Wilhelm II did not share the anti-English feelings which prevailed in broad sections of the middle and lower classes of his people, and that he was, so to speak, in a minority in his own land. As proof of this he quoted his refusal to receive the Boer generals, who would have been cheered by the German people, in Berlin in the summer of 1900. Furthermore, at the height of the Boer War he had rejected a proposal by France and Russia to make use of the British involvement in South Africa to 'humiliate England to the dust'. He had replied to both Powers, which were now England's friends, that 'so far from Germany joining in any concerted European action to put pressure upon

England and bring about her downfall, Germany would always keep aloof from politics that could bring her into complications with a sea power like England.' He had informed England's sovereign of this reply; it was still in the archives of Windsor Castle and was proof of how he had acted in the days of English adversity. As further evidence of his pro-English stance Wilhelm II spoke of the fact that after the heavy defeats suffered by the British army in December 1899 he had personally worked out a plan of campaign which he asked his General Staff to check and then sent to England, where it was to be found among the state papers at Windsor, awaiting the verdict of history. His plan had been largely identical to that followed by Lord Roberts in leading the British troops to victory. 'Was that . . . an act of one who wished England ill?' he asked. Wilhelm's assurances culminated in the claim that the German battlefleet was not being built against England, but on the contrary, was intended for the joint struggle, with the Royal Navy, against the Yellow Peril in the Far East. 'Look at the accomplished rise of Japan; think of the possible national awakening of China, and then judge of the vast problems of the Pacific. Only those Powers which have great navies will be listened to with respect, when the future of the Pacific comes to be solved; and, if for that reason only, Germany must have a powerful fleet. It may even be that England herself will be glad that Germany has a fleet when they speak together on the same side in the great debates of the future.'[41]

The effect of these remarks by the Kaiser on public opinion in Britain was anything but what was intended. In the German embassy in London there was utter despair. Count Metternich sighed that one might as well shut up shop completely, and the First Secretary, Wilhelm von Stumm, described his sovereign as the 'greatest gaffeur' in Europe.[42] King Edward had intensive enquiries made into the identity of the 'English diplomat' who had passed on the Kaiser's comments to the newspaper. He angrily rejected any attempt to play them down as 'well-intentioned' and dismissed the plea of the former ambassador in Berlin, Sir Frank Lascelles, that allowances should be made for the Kaiser's well-known tendency to exaggerate.[43] The London press interpreted the German monarch's expressions of friendship as an attempt to dispel suspicion about German naval construction and to sow discord between Great Britain and her allies, Japan, Russia and France. Almost as if in response to the Kaiser's assurances, in the House of Commons on 14 November 1908 Herbert Henry Asquith, the Prime Minister, confirmed the British government's determination to maintain the country's superiority at sea whatever happened.[44] In America President Roosevelt wrote to the publisher of the *New York Tribune*, Whitelaw C. Reid, saying he literally did not dare tell the paper what he knew and thought about the Kaiser's latest interview.[45]

The negative reaction abroad, however, was far exceeded by the disastrous effect of the interview on German public opinion.[46] Schoen took the view on the spur of the moment that the Kaiser's opinions as published in the London newspaper ought best to be withheld from the German public, but it was already too late.[47] The 'interview' was published in full in the evening editions of the German newspapers, provoking a storm of horrified indignation in all political parties and social classes. Baroness Spitzemberg spoke for the overwhelming majority of her countrymen when she wrote in her diary on 30 October 1908 that Wilhelm's remarks were 'the most shaming, despicable, indiscreet and questionable thing that the Kaiser has ever done! . . . The Kaiser is ruining our political position and making us the laughing-stock of the world, while his son applies for a patent for a new kind of cuff-links!! It makes one despair and wonder if one is in a madhouse!'[48] In passages which reflect the discontent of the entire nation with two decades of anachronistic and incompetent rule by Wilhelm II, she gave vent to her indignation at the interview. 'That was a fearful day, for one really felt like beseeching all the saints in heaven to help, just as if one had lost a battle, as misery gave way to anger, anger to misery!' Her friends and acquaintances all reported on 'the devastating impression . . . that this dreadful affair had created everywhere, amongst the most diverse sorts of people. The Kaiser — I might almost say unfortunately — cannot be reproached with organising the publication without consulting his ministers this time; I say unfortunately because he will therefore not feel at all guilty, whereas what is certainly much worse than yet another piece of high-handedness is the fact that he could make such unstatesmanlike, tactless, baseless, rash statements and that he privately blurted out state secrets and political agreements in such a criminal way. There is something so unmanly and childish in this talkativeness itself, which seems positively contemptible in ordinary mortals. Quite natural that the press, this time in complete accord with the entire population of all parties, calls for a remedy for a state of affairs on which practical limits must be imposed, since the sovereign's nature and behaviour will stay the same, alas.'[49]

Maximilian Harden saw his very worst fears confirmed by the interview. In his *Zukunft* he published three irate articles entitled 'Against the Kaiser'.[50] Not without reason he interpreted the fiasco as a typical consequence of Wilhelm's Personal Rule, and especially of the Eulenburg scandal, which seemed to him to be 'the fundamental cause of the present crisis'. 'Since then, complete loss of balance at the top. One thing after another.' He wrote to the retired Friedrich von Holstein on 15 November 1908 expressing the opinion that stern measures must be taken to compel Wilhelm to abdicate, for otherwise the only way out of the crisis was to start a war. 'I no longer have any confidence in promises and reservations; this monarch will *never* change, and is simply in the hands of [English] blackmailers ... In England there are still a vast number of letters. In Highcliffe *everything* was discussed, before journalists, and *everything* has been written down ... To clear ourselves of shame and ridicule, we will *have* to go to war, soon, or face the sad necessity of making a change of imperial personnel on our own account, even if the strongest personal pressure had to be brought to bear.' The Kaiser could be forced to abdicate, Harden thought, if he were threatened with public disclosure of his excursions on Lake Starnberg in the 1880s with Eulenburg and the chief witness for the prosecution, Jakob Ernst. If Wilhelm stayed on the throne, Germany would 'slip into the abyss'. Any of the other federal princes, even King Friedrich August of Saxony or 'even a child', would make a better Kaiser than Wilhelm. 'He wasn't cut out for it', Bismarck had always said. 'And can he, after everything that has now been said abroad and at home, think – seriously think – that he can again play the Kaiser and the highest authority? This is the end; and the only question is whether we will have the courage to perform the operation, or whether we prefer the slow decomposition of the body of the Reich.'[51]

These were certainly drastic suggestions, and yet they cannot be dismissed as the embittered over-reaction of a lone fanatic, for no less a person than Charlotte, Hereditary Princess of Saxe-Meiningen, the Kaiser's own sister, saw the situation very similarly to Harden. 'Poor Reich!!' she wrote on 18 November 1908. She was filled 'to the depths of my being' with shame for Germany. She had suggested that the ruling princes should make a joint approach to the Kaiser, under the aegis of Prince Ludwig of Bavaria, with the aim of introducing a kind of collective regency.[52] 'Now that my brother has got himself into an impossible situation *no one* helps him; only I try to do so! (*Please keep this secret!*) I want to persuade the German Princes to go to the Kaiser *unanimously* (if possible), putting their silly individual rights aside *for once*, and offer him their help in the interest of the *Reich* and in the name of *their* peoples, under clearly-stated conditions. To act together and keep together is in my view absolutely essential! and the only thing that could still make an impression on him. Ludwig would have to be the spokesman, in the name of his father [Prince Regent Luitpold of Bavaria] and of the Grand Dukes, Saxony and Württemberg ... My husband laughs and says I won't be able to get the gentlemen to do it. Shame on the German Reich! Then they are not worthy to remain ruling princes. *I* would like to help my poor brother (one *has* to take him as he is). Bülow and his cronies are his undoing!!! ... I can see through *everything* now!! The Bundesrat is a comedy, the Ministers likewise, we are left standing alone, sunk in the deepest mire, and as a loyal Prussian I am *ashamed*.'[53]

A sense of shame, a hysterical feeling of impending doom gripped the entire nation and even the officer corps was not immune. People were ashamed of the sovereign who had made his people the laughing-stock of the whole world. Many were reminded of Friedrich Wilhelm IV, who had died insane.[54] In the officers' messes Prussian staff officers on active service were reported to be declaring out loud that 'the Kaiser is positively pathological', that he 'ought to be locked up at Babelsberg for three months opposite portraits of Bismarck and the old Kaiser', 'we shall lose the next war because the Kaiser will lose his nerve', and 'the Kaiser ought to be placed under a regency'.[55]

BÜLOW'S 'TREACHERY TOWARDS THE KAISER'

When his 'interview' with Stuart Wortley appeared in the German press Wilhelm II was still at Wernigerode as the guest of Prince Stolberg. It was only on their return journey on 29 October 1908 that the monarch and his suite read the newspaper reports in the dining car of their train. The Chief of the Civil Cabinet, Rudolf von Valentini, at once realised how much resentment the Kaiser's remarks 'were bound to arouse in a whole series of foreign states, but not least in his own people', for the interview had exposed to the public gaze 'highly questionable revelations about the most delicate issues of foreign policy and our relationship with England, Russia and France'. As he later recalled: 'We were all horrified, but the Kaiser, who was sitting with us and read the article too, remained completely silent.'[56] When they arrived at Potsdam Wilhelm certainly seemed very agitated and made a speech to some recruits in which he emphasised Germany's readiness to defend herself, if need be, against all those who bore her a grudge for her success.[57] Yet it was not until many days later that Wilhelm was to realise the full extent of the catastrophe brought about by his remarks in the *Daily Telegraph*.[58]

His loyal 'Bülowchen', of all people, dealt him an early blow. In a breathtaking, almost farcical about-face the Reich Chancellor suddenly claimed not to have had any prior knowledge of the fatal interview and tendered his resignation on 30 October 1908. In his submission to the Kaiser of that day he regretted that he had not read 'Colonel Wortley's long composition, which was very illegibly written on bad paper', but had sent the manuscript – against the express orders of the Kaiser – to the Foreign Office to be checked. Had he read the article he would have advised strongly against publication. The responsibility for the lamentable mishap therefore lay not with him but with the bureaucrats in the Foreign Office, who had not followed his instructions to examine the document carefully. Should his conduct nevertheless meet with the Kaiser's disapproval, Bülow offered to resign. At the same time, however, he stressed the advantages for the Kaiser of leaving him in office as Reich Chancellor, for only then would he be in a position to 'respond openly and emphatically to the unjustified attacks on my imperial Master'. As a first step in Wilhelm's defence Bülow promised to declare officially that the Kaiser had acted completely in accordance with the constitution by sending him the manuscript to be checked.[59]

The Kaiser flatly refused to accept Bülow's resignation.[60] In two hours of conversation at the Reich Chancellor's palace on the evening of 31 October 1908, both men managed largely to avoid the thorny subject of the interview, so that for days on end the Kaiser remained firmly convinced that Bülow was in general agreement with his remarks to his English interlocutor and that his only reservations were about the timing of the publication.[61] At the Chancellor's suggestion and to Wilhelm's visible satisfaction the Foreign Office press bureau issued a statement to the *Norddeutsche Allgemeine Zeitung* and launched a full-scale campaign to exonerate the Kaiser, the Chancellor and the Foreign Secretary and pass the buck to the subordinate advisers of the Wilhelmstrasse.[62] On 31 October Admiral von Müller recorded in his diary that Schoen had been summoned to see the Kaiser 'because of the blunder in the Foreign Office regarding the publication in the Daily Telegraph'; he had come away 'quite happy again, after all'.[63] The Kaiser had told him 'he was only glad that he would no longer be the focus of the usual criticism from all sides and that it would be aimed at the Foreign Office; it was up to those gentlemen to work out how to cope with it!'[64] As the Bavarian envoy, Count Lerchenfeld, recalled: 'At first, when the row about the interview broke out in the Press, the Kaiser was amused and told his entourage with a kind of malicious pleasure that a scandal was brewing, but it was nothing to do with him; the Foreign Office was responsible and had got itself into trouble.'[65] Completely failing to recognise the 'deep seriousness of the situation', Kaiser Wilhelm left the capital on the evening of 3 November, 'without a care in the world', as the Baden envoy reported, to go 'back to Austria and Donaueschingen to hunt for the next 10 days!'[66]

Wilhelm put his trust in his Chancellor's parliamentary skills and loyalty and did not suspect that Bülow, in view of the storm of indignation that continued to rage undiminished, would decide not to protect his imperial master any longer. In order to stay in power Bülow committed 'treachery towards the Kaiser', as Winzen has described it.[67] He instructed Jenisch, who was accompanying the monarch on his ten-day visit to Austria and Baden as the representative of the Foreign Office, to prepare Wilhelm for the changed situation. Jenisch therefore told the Kaiser frankly on 4 November that his talkativeness with foreigners was 'painful' to the German people, 'that such remarks coming from him could cause serious damage to our policy; that in general H.M. was all too often excessively trustful and had political discussions which would be better left to his responsible advisers'. After this conversation, in which the Chief of the Military Cabinet, Hülsen-Haeseler, also took part, Jenisch had the feeling that he had made a lasting impression. As he reported to the Chancellor, 'Hülsen backed me up very intelligently, and we both had the impression that H.M. accepted this, as he did not respond. At luncheon H.M. was visibly quiet and preoccupied, but perfectly friendly.'[68]

Wilhelm's prolonged stay with Archduke Franz Ferdinand at Eckartsau, after which he paid a brief visit to Franz Joseph in Vienna and then went to stay with his friend Max Egon Prince zu Fürstenberg in the Black Forest, proved to be a serious mistake. Inevitably, it only deepened the gulf between the seemingly carefree monarch, away on a shooting spree, and his angry people. Yet instead of advising the Kaiser to return to Berlin, as the Kaiserin, Adjutant-General von Plessen and others at court advocated, Bülow took care to keep him away, on the pretext that a sudden interruption of the imperial itinerary could have an 'alarmist' effect abroad.[69]

In the Kaiser's entourage it was Hülsen-Haeseler who took the lead in speaking out 'very bluntly' to him about the gravity of the situation and urging him to return to Berlin. Shortly after they arrived at Eckartsau on 4 November he confronted Wilhelm with the truth about what was happening. The Kaiser was astonished, saying afterwards to Jenisch: 'Hülsen has just put matters in a different light. Until now I believed that in general Bülow agreed with my remarks to the Englishman and considered only the timing of the publication inopportune. Now Hülsen tells me that the reason for the uproar among the German people and in the Press is that they see from the statement in the N[orddeutsche] A[llgemeine] Z[eitung] that I had a political discussion of that kind with a foreigner without the agreement of the Reich Chancellor.'[70] When Müller reported to Hülsen that Albert Ballin had asked him 'to persuade H.M. to return to Berlin instead of shooting foxes at Donaueschingen as if the huge uproar over the Steward-Wortley [sic] interview was nothing to do with him', Hülsen replied: 'It has been my opinion from the outset that H.M. must cancel his stay here but if the Reich Chancellor does not feel that and say so, there is probably no hope of H.M. returning sooner now. And the Chancellor certainly never told H.M. that he wanted to resign because H.M. had made statements to foreigners which were not in accord with Reich policy and which he was not in a position to approve or countersign. H.M. believed that Bülow had covered for him completely in the declaration in the *Norddeutsche* and disagreed *only* with the timing of the publication. I told H.M. on the journey here how things stood and that the entire nation, including myself, was deeply upset and extremely angry, rather like in 1870, that H.M. should have spoken to foreigners openly criticising the policy of the Reich, and I told H.M. the plain truth as far as I was able. You can be sure that I too would do all in my power to urge the Kaiser to return soon, if the Chancellor suggested it.'[71]

THE 'NOVEMBER STORM' IN THE REICHSTAG AGAINST THE KAISER'S 'PERSONAL RULE'

The two-day debate on the Kaiser's interview in the *Daily Telegraph* that took place in the Reichstag on 10 and 11 November 1908 constituted 'a milestone in Germany's parliamentary history', as the future Prime Minister of Bavaria and Reich Chancellor, Georg von Hertling, testified.[72] Never before in the history of the Kaiserreich had there been such scenes. With rare accord speaker after speaker denounced the autocratic rule which Wilhelm II had exercised for two decades. The leader of the National Liberals, Ernst Basser-mann, spoke of an almost 'unanimous protest . . . against what in this country is called Personal Rule'. In the name of his party he demanded 'secure guarantees against the interference' of the Kaiser in politics. 'No personal moods and impulses, no fervent proclamations, no policy of excessive friendliness alternating with a box on the ears.'[73] For the Progressive People's party Otto Wiemer described 'the constant intervention of Personal Rule' as the 'greatest evil' of constitutional reality in Germany. 'What moves the German people today, what rouses it to anger from the depth of its soul, is the clear recognition that this Personal Rule is so far-reaching and is exercised in such a way that it is not in accord with the interests of either the monarchy or the state. Impetuous expressions of monarchical subjectivism, emotional outpourings and sudden impulses are at their least appropriate . . . in the sphere of foreign policy.' With Bülow and the ministers and secretaries of state in his sights he demanded that the advisers to the Crown 'should not be malleable courtiers who assume responsibility after the event even if they have not been consulted beforehand, not bureaucrats or civilian adjutants who fit themselves as well as they can into whatever office is entrusted to them, but they should be real statesmen who are fully conscious of their responsibility to the country as well.'[74]

Hertling, who was then spokesman for the opposition Centre party but also a convinced monarchist, found himself in a painful predicament, as he admitted. 'Where the All-Highest Person is concerned, criticism should fall silent. But, gentlemen, the days of the French Sun King and the days of the English Stuarts lie far behind us, and today in the modern world even the holder of supreme power must be willing to submit to the criticism of the representatives of the people if he has given rise to it through his actions.' He gave a statesmanlike warning of the diplomatic consequences of Wilhelm II's remarks. In the past the Reichstag had often spoken of 'the King of England's policy of encirclement'. But now, after the publication in the *Daily Telegraph*, he had the impression 'that on the German side a policy of repulsion is being pursued that will inevitably bring us into conflict with all other Powers'. The 'isolated position' in which Germany now found herself was 'only safe if it was carried off with calm dignity, with a sense of our own strength and with the restraint that such a position renders absolutely essential, and if any impulsive remark that can awaken the suspicion of other Powers is avoided'.[75] Hertling concluded by reading out a declaration by the Centre party repudiating the Kaiser's remarks in detail and demanding responsible government through the Reich Chancellor in future. The declaration stated that the Kaiser's claim that anti-English feeling prevailed among the German people was not borne out by the facts. Furthermore, Wilhelm's actions during the Boer War showed him going against the feeling of the German people and were very regrettable. Finally, the Kaiser had 'described intervention by the German Reich in the Pacific region as the goal of our naval expansion. This remark contradicts all official statements, which were decisive for the Reichstag in passing the Navy Bill. Moreover it entails a grave threat to the preservation of peace.' In future the Reich Chancellor must exert strong influence to prevent declarations of such political consequence by the monarch, which were liable 'to put the reputation of the German Reich in very serious danger and to shake confidence in its leaders'. In order to safeguard peace and dispel mistrust, everything 'that is likely to give rise to doubts either at home or abroad about the federal and constitutional principles of the Reich' must be prevented. 'According to the constitution the Reich Chancellor alone is responsible to the Reichstag for Reich policy. The German people must demand that the Reich Chancellor possess the will and the strength to bring the kind of influence to bear on the Kaiser without which his constitutional responsibility loses all meaning.'[76]

For the Social Democrats Paul Singer quite rightly castigated the official version of the events leading up to the publication as 'so grotesque and at the same time so absurd that this campaign by the Wilhelmstrasse really cannot be taken seriously'. With Bülow's statement in the *Norddeutsche Allgemeine Zeitung* that he had not read the manuscript 'the Kaiser tragedy gave way to a Reich Chancellor farce'. Like the other speakers, however, Singer pointed out that the most important aspect of the crisis was not the question of how the Kaiser's remarks came to be published but the fact 'that these remarks could be made at all'. The Reich Chancellor himself had acknowledged how harmful the Kaiser's assertions had been when he declared that he would have advised against their publication if he had only known of them in advance. Clearsightedly, Singer demanded that in the interests of the German people and of world peace the Personal Monarchy should be transformed into a parliamentary form of government. He called for 'a constitutional change that would put decisions on war and peace into the hands of the people's representatives. For in the last analysis it is surely war that hovers like a ghost on the horizon, war that becomes possible and is an increasing danger if irresponsible policy, this Personal Rule, continues to prevail in Germany. In the end, after all, it is the German people who have to put their lives, their health, their property and their blood in the balance if, as a result of such irresponsible policy, as a result of this kind of event, the situation becomes as acute as has unfortunately happened in the past few weeks.' The Reichstag must be given the right to participate in the appointment of the Reich Chancellor, for 'the Kaiser's right to appoint' offered 'no adequate guarantee for the safety and welfare of the people . . . The unilateral confidence of the Kaiser, which . . . suddenly changes from one day to the next, the Kaiser of whom we have no idea what he expects from ministers, of his minimum requirements in terms of the knowledge and competence that a minister must possess . . . the unilateral confidence of the Kaiser is not sufficient . . . to reassure the German people about their future and to safeguard them from ministerial posts being occupied by unsuitable and incompetent people . . . In England and France it is unknown for ministers not to have the confidence of the majority in Parliament. In England and France the ministers are taken from the ranks of the majority in Parliament; and to bring about this state of affairs in some form will be the task of the Reichstag if it seriously wants to prevent such events recurring.'[77]

The deputies, like the spectators in the crowded galleries, waited eagerly to see how the Reich Chancellor would respond to these attacks on the monarch. Bülow had had his speech drafted by Otto Hammann and (as always) he had learned it by heart. It was — in the words of the Social Democrat Wolfgang Heine — an 'extremely skilful dance on eggshells'.[78] It contained a series of half-truths and deliberate lies, aimed above all at extricating the Chancellor himself from an embarrassing episode. The subordinate officials of the Foreign Office were again made scapegoats. He himself had at once realised the 'disastrous effect' of the Kaiser's utterances when he saw them for the first time on 28 October in the *Daily Telegraph*, the Reich Chancellor brazenly declared. The 'most serious and difficult decision' that he had ever made in his political life had been 'to stay in office, in accordance with the Kaiser's wishes'.

As Reich Chancellor he intended to see to it that in future the Kaiser would observe, 'even in private conversations, that restraint which is equally essential in the interests of a consistent policy and for the authority of the Crown. Without this, neither I nor a successor of mine could bear the responsibility.' Winzen rightly characterises Bülow's defence of himself to the Reichstag as 'shameless play-acting'.[79] Although he knew better, the Chancellor asserted that 'His Majesty the Kaiser has at various times made private remarks to private English personalities which were put together and published in the "Daily Telegraph". I must assume that not all the details of the conversations have been accurately reproduced.' As an example he cited the 'story of the plan of campaign'. The Kaiser's comments, which he had expressly described as 'aphorisms', were purely theoretical observations without practical significance for the British conduct of the war. 'The Chief of General Staff, General von Moltke, and his predecessor, General Count Schlieffen, have declared that the General Staff ... has never examined or forwarded to England a plan of campaign or a similar piece of work relating to the Boer War by the Kaiser.' Bülow then criticised the fact that 'several excessively strong expressions' had been used in the *Daily Telegraph* article; for instance the Kaiser was reported to have said the majority of the German people were anti-English. On the contrary, 'on the basis of mutual respect' all parties in Germany wanted peaceful and friendly relations with England. 'The passage relating to our interests in the Pacific Ocean is also too highly-coloured', Bülow went on. 'German naval construction is as free of aggressive tendencies in the Pacific as in Europe.' He made only a feeble attempt to protect the Kaiser, by drawing attention to 'psychological' factors. 'For two decades our Kaiser has worked, often in difficult circumstances, to bring about friendly relations between Germany and England. These honest efforts have met with obstacles which would have discouraged many others ... Our intentions were misjudged, we were accused of hostile plans against England which had never been in our minds. The Kaiser, rightly convinced that this state of affairs was a misfortune for both countries and a danger for the civilised world, never gave up the goal he had set himself ... I can understand that the Kaiser ... felt hurt when he was repeatedly made the object of attacks which treated his best intentions with suspicion. Indeed, people went as far as to attribute his interest in the German Navy to secret plans to attack vital English interests, plans of which he would never dream.'[80]

Such assurances of Wilhelm II's good faith did little to calm feelings. On the second day of the parliamentary debate the speakers' attacks on Wilhelm's 'Personal Rule' intensified. Amid applause, the Württemberg Democrat, Conrad Haussmann, called out to the Reichstag: 'Remember this: neither yesterday nor today has anyone come forward in this German Reichstag to defend the actions of the German Kaiser, not even a Conservative ... In Germany all sections of the population agree in their judgement of the situation; they are annoyed and their tempers are aroused. ... In Germany someone uttered the phrase: "I will not tolerate prophets of doom", – and the mouth that uttered this phrase has created prophets of doom in their millions! ... At present the German fatherland finds itself ... in danger into which it has been led by its well-meaning Kaiser.' The Reich Chancellor had expressed doubts as to whether all the details of the interview had been accurately reproduced. The Reichstag, however, wanted to know about this for certain, and would be only too glad if it were so. 'That is something the German Kaiser must know, and the German Kaiser surely had to be asked whether these details were correct! The German Kaiser, to whom his own interview was sent, must surely have read his interview – or did the German Kaiser not read his interview either, which his friend sent to him?' The Kaiser's good intentions, as Bülow had affirmed, were indeed beyond doubt, yet 'all those arguments the German Kaiser used in his discussions with Englishmen were attempts to achieve his ends by completely inappropriate means ... It is also a fact, which all yesterday's speakers made clear, that the German Kaiser has not exactly increased Germany's popularity abroad.' The Reich Chancellor had spoken of difficult days. But, Haussmann asked, 'were they difficult days for the Kaiser too?' Would it not have been right for him, as the person principally involved, 'to be at the centre of government business during those days, and to enable our leading statesman to explain matters in a way that would have reassured the German nation?' Like other speakers before him, Haussmann deplored the fact that under the existing power structure the responsibility ascribed to the Reich Chancellor under the constitution was 'merely a fiction, a matter of form, an outward cover and an inward sham'. In future the Reich Chancellor must genuinely direct affairs himself, and only if he had a parliamentary majority behind him would he be able to carry this through against the Crown. In view of the unanimous opinion of the entire Reichstag that 'something must be done', Haussmann proposed that an address should be sent to the Kaiser in which the concerns of the people were clearly expressed. 'It would be an honest attempt to bring about the change with the Kaiser's cooperation; and that would surely be the happiest of all solutions. After all, we do not have the right to believe that our Kaiser would be the only one not to realise what the whole of the German people wishes and realises.'[81]

An even harder line was taken by the Social Democrat Wolfgang Heine, who reeled off a 'colossal list of accusations against "Personal Rule" and its practitioner' and called on the Reichstag to overthrow Bülow so as to make it plain to the Kaiser 'that no Chancellor can survive if he does not take vigorous action against his [the Kaiser's] tendency to interfere in policy'.[82] But the Reich Chancellor said nothing. He did not listen to his advisers, Loebell and Hammann, who exhorted him to protect the Kaiser against these 'wild and unjust' attacks. Instead he listened to Bethmann Hollweg, who advised strongly against any further intervention by the Chancellor, in view of the 'disorderly mood' in the chamber.[83] In vain a few Conservatives pleaded for the Chancellor to say at least one more word in the Kaiser's defence. One really could not just 'leave [the Kaiser] to stew'; indeed, Bülow's silence would mean 'total abandonment of the monarch by his most senior official and that will not do, if we want to uphold the monarchical principle'.[84] While the Chancellor continued to remain silent, the Conservative Elard von Oldenburg-Januschau seized the opportunity to make an impassioned declaration of loyalty. The Reichstag, he said, had no right to criticise the actions of His Majesty the Kaiser and King. For Haussmann and his party friends the Kaiser might be merely 'a fixture'; 'for us [Conservatives] he is a person ... and we shall serve His Majesty the Kaiser and King personally for as long as we live, without fear but with the old loyalty which we have never denied him, until our dying breath'. During this speech, which was greeted by a storm of cheers to the right of the house and mocking laughter to the left, the Reich Chancellor and the ministers of state looked on, without a word.[85]

As soon as the Reichstag session ended Bülow summoned the Prussian Ministry of State for a special session. The ministers were all reeling under the shock of the debate, for as one of them commented, never had 'a German Kaiser or a Prussian King been exposed so defencelessly to the attacks of Parliament' as in the past two days.[86] Bethmann Hollweg, who according to the memoirs of the Minister of War was 'in a state of collapse', was apparently only able to stammer: 'One more day like that and we shall have a republic.'[87] As Bülow also assured his ministerial colleagues that he had not read the fatal interview and would naturally have advised against its publication if the Kaiser had only consulted him, they too were full of indignation at the irresponsible remarks that the monarch had made in private conversations, especially with a foreigner. Among the sternest critics were General von Einem and Admiral von Tirpitz, who openly expressed their 'horror'.[88] The former declared that 'dissatisfaction with the Kaiser's conduct and demeanour, the excessive growth of Personal Rule, the Kaiser's temperamental outbursts and his moods, was becoming more and more widespread, even in the officer corps'.[89] Yet even now, typically, the ministers gave vent to their criticism only on condition that they would not be named in the minutes, for they all knew only too well the effect their words would have on the Kaiser's confidence in them – which was still essential to their remaining in office. They expressed unanimous regret at the enormous loss of prestige that 'the monarchy and the person of His Majesty the Kaiser' had suffered as a result of this affair and voiced the fear that if such a thing happened again it might be 'disastrous for Kaiser and Reich, for King and Prussia'. 'The Ministry of State therefore asks the Reich Chancellor and Minister President, acting also on behalf of the Ministry of State, to seek audience of His Majesty in order to acquaint Him with the gravity of the situation and impress upon Him the necessity of avoiding anything which could give rise to similar criticism.'[90] That same evening Bülow sent a telegram to the Kaiser at Donaueschingen requesting an audience.[91]

THE HOUR OF TRUTH AT DONAUESCHINGEN

While the floodtide of criticism rose higher and higher in the press, the Reichstag, the government, the officer corps and the general population, Kaiser Wilhelm was enjoying himself fox-hunting at Donaueschingen as the guest of Max Fürstenberg. Harden, well-informed as always, reported to Walther Rathenau: 'H.M. in high spirits; at least *for show*.'[92] The Auswärtiges Amt and even the young Prince Friedrich Wilhelm of Prussia sent him critical press cuttings, but the Kaiser was unmoved. 'I never read newspapers', he declared defiantly.[93] At first his suite did what they could to protect Wilhelm from the agitation against him. The future Austrian Foreign Minister, Count Ottokar Czernin, invited to Donaueschingen to hunt, arrived with a tale of an 'almost revolutionary' incident that had occurred during his journey. In an overcrowded station restaurant all the travellers had criticised the Kaiser violently and one of them had even made an inflammatory speech against the monarch. The Kaiser's suite implored Czernin to say nothing to Wilhelm about this disturbing experience, but one of the gentlemen – it might well have been Hülsen – 'strongly objected and declared that on the contrary, the Kaiser must be given the full details of the story and ... even undertook ... to carry out this probably not very pleasant task himself'.[94] In spite of such attempts to enlighten him the Kaiser was largely unprepared for the furious debate in the Reichstag.[95]

On 10 November, the first day of the debate, Wilhelm went on an excursion to Lake Constance with his suite for the test flight of a Zeppelin (see Figure 27). As Admiral von Müller noted, the Kaiser would have liked to go up in the airship himself, 'but the Kaiserin had made him promise not to do so'.[96] Afterwards, at the investiture of Count Ferdinand von Zeppelin with the Order of the Black Eagle, Wilhelm gave an address which was a perfect example of the 'emotional

Figure 27 The Kaiser and Fürstenberg (on the left in uniform) watch the maiden flight of Zeppelin Z1, with the Crown Prince on board, at Donaueschingen in November 1908

outpourings' that were attracting fierce criticism in parliament that very day. 'Our fatherland can be proud to possess such a son, the greatest German of the twentieth century, who through his invention has led us to a new phase in the development of the human race. It would not be too much to say that today we have experienced one of the greatest moments in the development of human civilisation.'[97] Those in the Kaiser's entourage who had only recently heard him castigating Count Zeppelin 'almost daily' as 'the stupidest' of all South Germans, were certainly not the only ones to shake their heads in disbelief at this exotic praise.[98]

Not until 11 November did Wilhelm begin to sense the extent of the political crisis which almost swept him from the throne. In the morning he appeared, as Müller recorded, 'almost an hour later' than planned for the shoot. But he 'apologised, for once. Had been reading Reichstag proceedings, was very worried. Nevertheless in a very cheerful mood at the hunt luncheon in the tent.'[99] In the evening Fürstenberg and Hülsen-Haeseler explained to him 'the reasons for, and the extent of, the ill-feeling among the people'. This revelation had a dramatic effect. As Rudolf von Valentini heard on his arrival at Donaueschingen, the Kaiser had been 'completely floored' by it. He could not understand 'how his good intentions had been so misunderstood, and how his political activity could be judged so harshly and disparagingly. Tears of anger and disappointment rose to his eyes.'[100] The Chief of the Civil Cabinet was surprised at the 'severity' of the Military Cabinet Chief's judgement of the Kaiser 'and at the serious concern for the future expressed by a General who is as close as he is to the monarch'.[101] Hildegard von Spitzemberg heard later that the Kaiser had been 'in a furious temper at Donaueschingen'; in spite of that, however, 'Hülsen spared him nothing'.[102] Zedlitz, who was also at Donaueschingen throughout the visit, reported to his father afterwards that the Kaiser became 'deeply depressed' on 11 November, although this very soon manifested itself in his refusing to read anything more about what had happened and trying to 'take his mind off his gloomy thoughts . . . In spite of a variety of diversions, however, a certain depression remained until our return.'[103]

When Valentini arrived at Donaueschingen on 13 November 1908 he found the Kaiser 'looking pale and strained'. He had succumbed to a mood of 'uncomprehending disappointment' and was 'very downhearted and worried about what would happen next'. As they drove to the hunting ground Wilhelm asked the Chief of the Civil Cabinet in consternation: 'Tell me, what is really happening? What does all this mean?'[104] When the Kaiser and his Cabinet Chief took up the conversation again in the evening of 13 November Wilhelm protested that he had never 'decided on policy without the Chancellor or

against him'. 'Everything I have done or said has either been discussed with
him beforehand or fully approved by him afterwards. Especially the conversation with [Stuart Wortley] at Highcliff[e] Castle in the autumn of 1907, which
is causing such an immense uproar now after its publication in the Daily
Telegr., for I reported it verbatim to Prince Bülow when I next saw him in
Berlin, and the Prince was touched and thanked me for supporting his policy
so effectively. When I received the transcript of the conversation at Rominten
several things in it seemed wrong and not clearly expressed, and I therefore
told Herr v. Jenisch to send the manuscript to the Chancellor with the request
that he should *himself personally* check it to see whether there would be any
objection to its publication. I considered the matter so important that I did not
want to rely on the judgement of anyone of a subordinate rank in the Foreign
Office. After my return from Rominten I asked the Chancellor what had
happened to the manuscript; he gave an evasive answer, saying it was still
being checked with regard to form etc. A few more weeks went by and then
I received the manuscript with a few corrections and the Chancellor's covering
letter saying that in his view there was no objection to publication! . . . Thus in
this case too, he – H.M. – had done everything possible to cover himself
constitutionally. He certainly could not have assumed that the Chancellor
would not even read a document sent to him in circumstances of such gravity!
At any rate he could not be reproached for anything. But he was willing to
accept responsibility for this too, just as he had accepted the abuse about the
visit to Tangier . . . He had said nothing in response to it all and he would
continue to say nothing. But in the proceedings of the Reichstag on 10 and
11 November he had been subjected to a "judicial murder" and the Chancellor, who no doubt knew it would happen, had used "a fencing foil instead of a
battleaxe" to defend him.'[105] Although Valentini had expected him to demand
Bülow's dismissal, to his relief Wilhelm did not do so but accepted 'with
admirable calmness' the need to keep the Chancellor in office for the time
being, in the national interest. Finally the Kaiser decided to return early to
Berlin. He was ready 'to receive the Chancellor and give him the assurances
which he demands in the interests of the future, and which will mean the
renunciation of personal intervention by the ruler in the machinery of
government. Having taken this decision, he feels relieved.'[106] The
Fürstenbergs gave a festive dinner party to say farewell to their guests. But
even that was to be interrupted by a truly bizarre tragedy.

Valentini wrote a vivid eye-witness description of the strange death of
General Count Dietrich von Hülsen-Haeseler, the sternest critic in the imperial entourage, on the final evening of the Kaiser's stay at Donaueschingen
(see Figure 28). The regimental band was playing a waltz while the monarch

Figure 28 General Dietrich Count von Hülsen-Haeseler, head of the Military Cabinet
until his untimely death while dancing for the Kaiser at Donaueschingen in
November 1908

and all the guests stood talking in the hall, when suddenly there appeared
'a grotesque figure: Count Hülsen-Häseler, who had been in a particularly good
mood all day, had put on a brightly-coloured balldress belonging to our hostess
and a large hat decked with ostrich feathers, and was dancing gracefully to the
music, holding a fan coquettishly in his hand. He was rewarded with resounding applause as he left the hall, stepping backwards and throwing kisses to the
ladies, and went out through a glass door. – Then all of a sudden there were
hurried footsteps, murmurs and whispers. Everyone rushed towards the door
and behind it lay stretched out on the floor the man who had only just been so
full of the joys of life – dead! His outer clothing was removed, the doctor
prostrate over him trying everything medical science prescribes to restore
life – in vain – he fell down *because* he was dead! And by his head stood
the Kaiser, by the body of the man who had been closer to him than any other
in recent years, and who had only very lately rendered him the service of a
friend by frankly and honestly telling him the truth. Truly a drama!'[107]

Hülsen's death, just as the Kaiser was facing the most serious crisis of his
reign, signified a bitter, almost unbearable loss for Wilhelm. In his telegram to
the Kaiserin announcing the death of the Chief of the Military Cabinet he

called Hülsen his truest friend.[108] During prayers by the coffin next morning
the Kaiser, Valentini recorded, was 'quite beside himself'. The funeral took
place on the morning of 15 November 1908. The Kaiser knelt 'by the coffin
next to the widow, in a rather theatrical way', before he and his suite left to
take the train to Potsdam.[109]

THE CONFRONTATION WITH BÜLOW ON 17 NOVEMBER 1908

Soon after Wilhelm's arrival on the morning of 17 November the Reich
Chancellor came to the Neues Palais for a private audience with the Kaiser
which lasted two hours. Holstein had urged Bülow to stand firm and had
expressed the fear 'that for the sake of the Kaiser you want to make a false
peace between the Kaiser and the people, nay, between the Kaiser and the
Reich'. But if he did so, 'within a few months you will be miserably ruined.
For who will there then be to defend you?' 'Be firm, Bülow, do not let them
pull the wool over your eyes. The Kaiser will think twice before he lets you go,
at this time. But if the worst should happen, if he will not listen to reason, it
would be better for you to go now, as a great man, than in a few months as a
despised one.'[110]

Commenting on Wilhelm's 'irritable' and 'forbidding' attitude during the
audience, the press officer Otto Hammann recorded that the monarch had
'maintained a forced calm. The Chancellor tried in vain to present a convincing case to the Kaiser, by referring to diverse occasions on which sudden
decisions, autocratic interference in every possible sphere and ill-considered or
wounding speeches had repeatedly provoked criticism. He answered only in
monosyllables and gave little indication that it was beginning to dawn on him
that he had deceived himself for twenty years about his personal role.'[111]
Wilhelm had responded to Bülow's reproaches 'with obvious distaste' or
exaggerated expressions of compliance such as 'of course there is no need for
me to write any more letters at all'.[112] He nevertheless approved, if only
'silently', the Chancellor's request for the publication in the *Reichsanzeiger* of
a declaration in which the monarch promised in future to guarantee 'the
stability of Reich policy while observing constitutional responsibilities'.[113]
Immediately after the audience Bülow gave Holstein an account of how it
had gone. 'Mood more irritated, opposition more stubborn, conversation more
difficult than I had assumed . . . I held firmly to all the demands listed in my
notebook, without toning anything down. I left no doubt that I would otherwise resign at once. The communiqué for the *Reichsanzeiger* (drafted by me)
I forced through in opposition to the idea of a manifesto or a Cabinet Order
(which was again proposed!).' If his action won the support of the Reichstag

and the Prussian parliament, 'there is the possibility that from now on there will be a different kind of rule, and a good many things can get better.' If, however, everything remained as it was, he would resign.[114] The Reich Chancellor told the Centre party leader, Hertling, that the audience had been 'extremely difficult'. 'He had had to inform the Kaiser of the ill-feeling which had arisen before, and not only on account of the publication in the Daily Telegraph. He had drawn his attention to all the earlier incidents, speeches, telegrams &c, but although, on the one hand, he had been obliged to make the Kaiser realise that he must change his attitude, on the other hand he had to avoid publicly humiliating the Crown ... The Kaiser had been very shaken, his eyes had constantly filled with tears and in his "god-fearing frame of mind" he took it all as an "affliction visited upon him". He had promised not to send any more telegrams or make any more speeches without first obtaining the Chancellor's agreement.'[115] Of course, for Wilhelm's sister Charlotte 'the resolution at Potsdam' provided no guarantee of fundamental change. 'H.M. thinks himself infallible, Bül. carries on juggling and I ... cannot stop being deeply pessimistic about the future of our German political, dynastic and governmental affairs', she commented fatalistically.[116]

The Chief of the Civil Cabinet, whom the Kaiser sent for after Bülow's audience, found Wilhelm 'pale and agitated' and had the impression 'that he had only temporarily given way under heavy mental pressure, but would never forgive the Chancellor for this hour.' From this moment onwards, according to Valentini, the Kaiser had spoken to him of Bülow 'only in the bitterest terms'. Wilhelm again affirmed that he had reported every detail of his conversations at Highcliffe to the Chancellor, who had expressed his warm approval of them. Wilhelm had sent him the interview and it had been returned to him 'without a single word of warning', but now the Chancellor was accusing him of acting on his own authority and had branded him at home and abroad as a trouble-maker. 'His confidence in him [Bülow] had been completely destroyed and could never be revived.'[117] When the War Minister, General von Einem, arrived later for an audience the Kaiser shouted at him: 'You Ministers are all swine.' To him too Wilhelm insisted that he had 'written or telegraphed to Bülow every day from England giving him the content of all his conversations with English friends' and that he had 'always received the Chancellor's full approval'. 'He had asked for the papers, but they had not been found at the Foreign Office. Bülow must have destroyed them, he said.'[118] Soon afterwards Bülow discovered to his irritation that the Kaiser was spreading the story that a year earlier he had been asked by the Chancellor to speak on the lines of the *Daily Telegraph* interview when he went to England; he had sent the Chancellor a 24-page letter informing him that he had done so and had received the latter's warmest thanks. Subsequently, however, Bülow had himself leaked the matter to the press 'in the most perfidious way'.[119] Months later Wilhelm was still trying to clarify the behaviour of the Chancellor over the origin of the interview by writing privately to those involved.[120] He always maintained that before his departure for England in November 1907 he had spent hours in the garden of the Reich Chancellor's palace walking up and down with Bülow discussing the line he should take in London, that he had regularly reported to Bülow from Highcliffe on his conversations with Stuart Wortley and that he had also related them to him in detail after his return, whereupon the Chancellor had thanked him 'with tears in his eyes' for supporting his policy towards England.[121]

However much truth there may have been in these claims – and no letters from Wilhelm to the Chancellor from Highcliffe have ever been found – the Kaiser seemed incapable of understanding that the storm of indignation was not just directed against such details, but was rather the expression of a deeply felt disquiet about his disastrous style of rule as a whole. Bülow tried in vain to explain to him not only that his claims about the genesis of the interview were 'untenable' but also that ill-feeling against him had been widespread long before the publication in the *Daily Telegraph*. 'I never advised His Majesty to speak to anyone, least of all to private individuals in England, about what H.M. had written to Queen Victoria as "military aphorisms" and about the Franco-Russian mediation proposals. Nor is the version given by H.M. of both episodes consistent with the facts, because it is very exaggerated. For 11 years I have always protected H.M. and always put myself in the line of fire, even when H.M. did not ask me first (the Swinemünde telegram, the telegram to Prince Lippe, the "Hun speech", the Krupp speeches etc. etc.). The present unrest comes from the fact that there have been too many, too often repeated instances of rash acts being committed (the seconds telegram [of 1906 to Austria-Hungary], the prophets of doom speech, the letter to Tweedmouth, the case of [US ambassador] Hill etc.).'[122] In truth the Reich Chancellor would have had a far longer list to cite had he wanted to do justice not only to the well-known 'rash acts' but also to the overwhelming dominance of the Kaiser in the formulation of German domestic and foreign policy since 1897.

A 'SEVERE SHOCK TO HIS NERVES'

In the days following his confrontation with Bülow Wilhelm's state of health declined markedly. Indeed, on the very next day – 18 November – Prince Heinrich received news that his brother would not be coming to Kiel for the swearing-in ceremony of recruits, as had been planned.[123] By 20 November

Harden heard that the Kaiser was in bed, suffering from 'some cerebral irritation'.[124] On 22 November Wilhelm wrote to his friend Max Fürstenberg: 'After all that trouble, now I feel as tired, drained and worn out as if I had been on an exhausting walking tour ... It is a fearful trial for me to see or meet other people; I can't yet get used to the sight of them.'[125] Soon afterwards his condition deteriorated to such an extent that it would not be going too far to call it a genuine nervous breakdown. What had happened?

At Bülow's audience on 17 November 1908 he and Wilhelm had also discussed the possibility that the Kaiser's interview with the American, William Bayard Hale, on board the *Hohenzollern* the previous August, reports of which were circulating in the newspapers, might be published. At such a critical moment this would certainly have brought about Wilhelm's abdication, and perhaps even the collapse of the Hohenzollern monarchy itself. The Kaiser, however, assured the Chancellor 'that He had not said a word to Mr. Hale about politics and especially not about our English policy and our relations with England'. Nevertheless Bülow had thought it advisable to prevent publication and order all copies of the interview text to be bought up.[126] On 21 November he sent the Kaiser a transcript of the passages in the Hale interview of which the publication would be 'particularly undesirable', asking Wilhelm 'not to show this extract to anyone in the world' but to return it to him at once to be destroyed. The Kaiser still appeared to be quite unconcerned, describing the article as 'highly exaggerated and partly invented'. He wrote at the top of the document: 'Many thanks! A great deal of fantasising and gross exaggeration.'[127] But on the morning of 23 November, when he read a summary of the Hale interview in the *Berliner Tageblatt*, he realised that even in this watered-down form it contained enough explosive material for a political catastrophe of unimagined dimensions. For the newspaper article reported the Kaiser's horrendous remarks to Hale, of which we have already heard,[128] by and large correctly.[129] Suspecting the kind of impression this article would make worldwide, after the storm over the *Daily Telegraph*, Wilhelm sent a telegram to Bülow at 10.34 a.m. saying 'Have read unbelievable stuff in the *Tageblatt* purporting to be Hale interview. I authorise you to deny it at once. If some word of explanation needs to be sent to England for H.M. [the King], please let me have a draft.'[130] In the next few hours Wilhelm II collapsed under the strain of this latest disaster. A telegram in which Bülow asked permission to deny the *Tageblatt*'s report as a 'flagrant hoax' was returned to him from the Neues Palais with a note that 'His Majesty had been taken ill and his doctor was not allowing His Majesty to see any documents for the time being.'[131]

Hofmarschall Zedlitz recorded this dramatic episode in his diary. 'Two days ago Schulz, the valet, came to the room of the Flügeladjutanten at the Neues

gitated state and said he had been ordered by His Majesty to call
ancellor on the telephone at once and say that His Majesty
o be told that he had received such a severe shock to his nerves
ts of recent days that he was compelled to withdraw from all
and over his duties as ruler to the Crown Prince. Schulz was told
         down and it was made clear to him that he could not possibly carry out
this order, to which in the end he agreed. Then Count [August] Eulenburg was
contacted by telephone, and after he had been informed of the facts he
conferred with the Kaiser, the Reich Chancellor and the Cabinets and restored
calm to the situation.'[132] The Oberhofmarschall and the Chancellor agreed on
a statement to be issued to the press explaining that Wilhelm had contracted
influenza and required a few days' rest.[133] Baroness Spitzemberg, however,
heard the truth from one of the Kaiserin's chamberlains: the Kaiser was
suffering from 'serious depression', he had 'taken to his bed, was seeing no
one, holding no audiences, having his meals alone without his suite, in short,
he was still very confused'.[134] Some years later the Crown Prince recalled how
on that day he was 'summoned urgently to the Neues Palais' and carefully
prepared by his mother before going to talk to the distraught Kaiser. 'Minutes
later I was with my father, who was in bed. I was deeply shocked by his
appearance ... He told me to sit down and talked very fast, insistently and
accusingly about these events. He was consumed with disappointment, despondency and resignation; at the same time his bitterness constantly broke
through at the injustice he saw in what had happened ... In the end we
agreed that for a short time and until he had completely recovered from his
illness I would act as a kind of deputy to the Kaiser.'[135] The monarch was
persuaded to give up the idea of abdication.

Writing to Max Fürstenberg on 25 November 1908 the Kaiser told him self-
pityingly that: 'What I suspected and predicted to you has indeed happened to
me! 3 days ago I suffered a proper collapse and have been in bed for 3 days,
asleep or half asleep, after a violent fit of weeping woke me up from a dead
faint. Sleep, invalid food, complete prohibition of all work etc. are the consequences. [His personal physician Dr] Ilberg is treating me with fir-needle
baths, carbonic acid baths, massages, valerian drops etc! Poor fellow! He says it
was caused by too much motoring and by overwork!! As if 4 weeks of such
hellish *mental* torment could be banished by *such* cures!! What is doing me a
great deal of good is the complete release from all work! I needed to have a
break! But see how the politicians and scribblers have brought me down!!'[136]

Instead of recognising his mistakes and drawing lessons for the future from
the disaster caused by his quasi-absolutist manner of ruling, Wilhelm II still
refused to accept any blame. Although he had no alternative but to restrain

himself in his speeches for the time being, in his letters and conversations —
above all with foreign sympathisers — he gave vent to extravagant tirades of
hatred for those who he considered had 'betrayed' him. It was not long before
he saw himself as 'the greatest martyr of his time'.[137] As far as his conduct and
the much criticised system of Personal Monarchy were concerned, the *Daily
Telegraph* affair made little difference, as we shall see. Among his entourage
the feeling of sitting on a powder-keg did not diminish, but increased markedly. 'Fundamentally the Kaiser is in fact still the same as before', Zedlitz
observed. Although Wilhelm was 'still deeply depressed', the Hofmarschall
commented on 22 December 1908, physically he was 'quite well' again. There
was even a certain danger that he had 'something violent' in mind. 'Whether
failure has made him more inclined to violent action than before is difficult to
judge. On the whole that is probably not the case, as after the last collapse of
his system he seemed to have become rather soft and weak. Nevertheless there
are so many different sides to him that the tendency towards forceful words
and actions may come back again.'[138] Those familiar with life at the heart of
the court continued to deplore the Kaiser's habit of 'always being the only one
to speak and . . . conducting the conversation almost exclusively alone, in front
of everyone, both at table and afterwards, throughout evening after evening'.
But it was no use hoping for any improvement.[139] Wilhelm repeatedly and
loudly proclaimed his fury at the Reichstag, which he accused of throwing
mud at him and persecuting him with envy and hatred, and at the newspapers, which he would never read.[140] The court lived in a state of constant
fear of further revelations.

CHAPTER TWENTY-SIX

Upheaval in the Balkans. Kaiser Wilhelm and the Bosnian annexation crisis of 1908 to 1909

I t did nothing to calm the situation that the *Daily Telegraph* affair, the most serious constitutional crisis since the foundation of the Reich, coincided with the appearance of a threat of war over the Near East. The overthrow of the tyrannical despotism of Abdul Hamid II by the Young Turk movement in July 1908, and the announcement of western-style parliamentary elections throughout the Ottoman Empire were certainly welcomed by most of the Sultan's subjects, Christian and Moslem alike; but whether the concomitant displays of fraternisation really portended a permanent solution to the Empire's internal problems was less than certain. Externally, the revolution at Constantinople and its repercussions in the Balkans had serious consequences for the relations of the Great Powers with each other, startling Europe, according to Bülow's memoirs, like a thunderclap: the continent had 'not been so agitated for many years'.[1] For which group of Powers – the Triple Entente or the Triple Alliance – would the new rulers in Constantinople decide? What would be the consequences of the revolution for the delicate question of the Straits, and for Russia's relations with Britain and France? Whose influence – Russia's, Britain's, Austria-Hungary's or Germany's – would prevail in Bulgaria, which was on the brink of declaring its independence of Turkey? How would Russia on the one hand and Austria-Hungary on the other react to Pan-Serbian aspirations emanating from Belgrade? And how would the world empires, British, French and Russian, cope with their millions of Moslem subjects, in the likely event of an awakening of Islam from Calcutta through the Caucasus to Casablanca?

These world-shaking questions have been thoroughly examined by historians since the First World War. Here, we are concerned specifically with the attitude of Wilhelm II towards the disturbances in the disintegrating Ottoman

Empire. What hopes did he have of Islam, and what did he think of the seizure of power by Young Turkish officers who had mostly been educated in Germany? What was his attitude towards the gambler's throw of his only remaining reliable ally, Austria-Hungary, when Vienna not only encouraged Bulgaria to declare its independence of Turkey, but caused a serious international crisis by annexing Bosnia and the Herzegovina – to Wilhelm's utter surprise. How long, if at all, would the Kaiser stand by the promise wrung from him in the *Daily Telegraph* affair to keep out of politics in future? And how far would this be affected by, on the one hand, his very difficult relations with Bülow after their confrontation of 17 November 1908, and on the other his seemingly blind trust in his two Austrian friends, Max Egon Prince zu Fürstenberg and Archduke Franz Ferdinand? As we shall see, Wilhelm's emotional, racist and militarist behaviour in the Near Eastern crisis of 1908–9 points uncannily towards his policy in July 1914, when the constellation of the Powers was in a number of respects the same.

'OUR *LAST TRUMP* CARD: *ISLAM* AND THE *MOHAMMEDAN WORLD*'

Ever since his spectacular trip in the autumn of 1898 to Constantinople, Jerusalem and Damascus, where he proclaimed himself the protector of the world's 300 million Moslems,[2] it had been a favourite idea of Wilhelm II's that he would one day be able to ally himself with the world of Islam against the great imperial Powers Britain, France and Russia. In 1901 the Kaiser had declared the penetration of the Ottoman Empire to be a central aim of German policy.[3] For years, he held firm to his pet scheme of a German–Austrian–Turkish axis stretching from Berlin to the Persian Gulf. The Baghdad railway project was a part of this scheme, and was linked to the notion of some day being master of Mesopotamia (Iraq), and possibly Egypt and the Holy Land as well.[4] On the eve of the Algeciras conference of 1906, Holstein had lauded the fact that by his 'persistent efforts over the years' the Kaiser had gained the sympathies of 'the peoples of Islam';[5] and it was this very idea that the Kaiser had seized on as his hopes of a strategic breakthrough in the Moroccan crisis began to fail. In November 1905 the Chancellor asked the Kaiser for his 'gracious permission' to send a ship, the *Loreley*, to join the naval demonstration that Britain, France, Italy, Russia and Austria-Hungary were organising to force the Sultan to accept a more rigorous international control of the finances of Macedonia. The Kaiser refused, not least because he feared the negative repercussions in the Moslem world: 'Given the present strained relations, when we are confronted, almost alone, by great coalitions forming against us, our *last trump* card is *Islam* and the *Mohammedan world*.

I absolutely refuse to stir that up against us as well, and alienate it by participating in this really pathetic, ridiculous comedy.' German participation in the planned demonstration would 'be particularly hurtful to the Islamic world, if we joined in with its mortal foes'.[6] When, in October 1908 the visit of the Russian Foreign Minister, Isvolsky, to Paris and London signalled a reinforcement of the Triple Entente, Kaiser Wilhelm thought of replying by bringing Turkey into the Triple Alliance.[7] As we shall see, Turkey and the whole Islamic world played a central role in the Kaiser's dizzying world-political schemes in the Near Eastern crisis of 1908–9 (and again in the Balkan wars of 1912–13).

The Kaiser was by no means alone in his desire to play off the Ottoman Empire and the world of Islam against the Triple Entente. A group of generals round Field Marshal Baron Colmar von der Goltz, on whom the Kaiser bestowed the Order of the Black Eagle on 27 January 1907, regarded this very strategy as a promising path to World Power status. They demanded of German diplomats, 'and not least those in Constantinople . . . a certain diabolical ruthlessness . . . that will only make use of the fig leaf of bourgeois honour until they have clearly gained the advantage over their opponents. It is all a question of using all the tricks of heaven and hell to retain the friendship of the Turks and to make them the enemies of England and France.'[8]

THE YOUNG TURK REVOLUTION

In July 1908, with Sultan Abdul Hamid II's restoration of the Turkish constitution of 1876 and the seizure of power by the Young Turks, the Kaiser's plan for a German–Austrian–Turkish axis to oppose the Anglo-French–Russian bloc seemed to come unstuck. On 25 July the Chancellor telegraphed to the Wilhelmstrasse: 'H.M. the Kaiser and King regards the Sultan's action in restoring the constitution as evidence of weakness, which could possibly be very damagingly exploited by England.'[9] Nor did English and Russian newspaper reports representing the Young Turk movement as anti-German fail to make an impression.[10] Yet a few days later, Wilhelm welcomed the success of the Turkish national movement, which he hoped would put an end, not only to the abysmal conditions and corruption within the Ottoman Empire, but also to the 'machinations of the English and the Russians' at Constantinople and in the Balkans. He told himself that the Young Turks' objectives had 'always been the fundamental idea' of his own policy. 'And this is now at last being fulfilled, with the summoning of a Turkish parliament whose members will, it is to be hoped, themselves take over the "reforms" and check once and for all the interventionist aspirations of meddlesome Europ[ean] Great Powers.

That will be good for the Christians as well as for the Moslems in Turkey, and is therefore exactly what I have always been striving for. I am very satisfied with this solution.'[11] Warnings from his diplomats that with the establishment of an English- or French-style constitution the Ottoman Empire would turn away from Germany and towards the Entente were firmly brushed aside. By late August 1908 he was fully confident that he could count on the Turkish army: 'The revolution is not the work of "Young Turks" from Paris or London, but of the army alone, and indeed, exclusively of the "so-called German officers" educated in Berlin. A purely military revolution. These officers are in control and they are entirely German in feeling.' The change of regime in Constantinople would even lead to the dissolution of the Anglo-Russian Entente', the Kaiser prophesied, because 'Russia will not in the long run tolerate the strengthening of Turkey with English assistance. And this will cause serious disagreements in the future.'[12]

Indeed, Wilhelm even envisaged the possibility of an Islamic uprising stretching from India to Morocco that would signal the end of British, Russian and French rule in these regions. He lauded as 'excellent!', and 'a truly classic piece of work!', a dispatch of 3 September 1908 from his ambassador at Constantinople, Baron Adolf Marschall von Bieberstein, on the upheavals that had occurred in the Ottoman Empire. He was delighted to see that Marschall's analysis confirmed his own conviction − partly the product of wishful thinking − that the Young Turk movement was a 'national-turkish *islamic* movement', and not a movement embracing all Ottoman subjects whatever their race and creed. 'Quite right!', Wilhelm noted in the margin of the report, 'I have for years been warning against trampling on Islam and provoking it, and the whole of Europe laughed at me and called me a Turkish stooge.' The Kaiser also welcomed Marschall's prediction that the Moslem Turks would now become the masters in their country: 'at last! and they must be too'. Intervention in favour of the Christians by Vienna, London or St Petersburg would call forth a 'furor islamiticus' from India to Morocco. Marschall's report was 'a complete confirm-ation of everything I have so often discussed with Marschall, Goltz, and Tewfik since my last visit to Stamboul. It has now come to pass, although neither Salisbury, nor Lobanov, nor Muraviev, nor Balfour would believe me; they all of them, in their crazy stupidity, pigheadedness and incredible arrogance, and despite my warnings, mistreated, insulted and trampled on Islam for years until it could stand it no more and has risen up united. It only needs one more intervention from outside with "reform proposals" etc., which Aehrenthal is "not yet" prepared to drop, and the Sultan, whether he likes it or not, will have to unfurl the green flag of the Prophet, the name of "Allah" will resound in all corners of Asia and Africa, and that will be the end for the Christians.'[13] In the

event the Young Turkish movement, which won the parliamentary elections
hands down, turned out to be radically secularist and demonstratively pro-
British.[14] In October 1908 the Kaiser railed against his uncle Edward, who
had succeeded in replacing German influence in the Balkans and Constantinople by the hegemony of England, France and Russia. Thus, Wilhelm's long-
term Turkish policy had, as he himself said, 'gone up in smoke'. It amounted to
'a great triumph for E[dward] VII over us'.[15] He was soon cursing the Young
Turks as 'lackeys of England', and raged: 'That is a grandiose coup! We are now
finally thrown out of the Near East and can pack up. Now London alone lays
down the law there! Very hard!'[16] His misjudgement of the new power relationships in Constantinople was by no means the only unpleasant surprise the Kaiser
had to face in the Near Eastern crisis of 1908.

The revolution in Constantinople had serious repercussions throughout the
Balkans, which Wilhelm regarded with dismay as a further success for Edward
VII. Bulgaria was still formally a vassal state of the Ottoman Empire and its
ruler, Ferdinand of Saxe-Coburg-Koháry merely had the title of Prince. Now
Ferdinand — whom the Kaiser had detested for years[17] — saw in the upheavals
in Constantinople an opportunity to proclaim the full independence of his
country and assume the title of Tsar. Already in September there had been
signs that the Bulgarians were becoming restless, when they nationalised the
branch of the Orient railway line that ran through the principality; and when
Franz Joseph further nourished Bulgarian aspirations by receiving the visiting
Ferdinand with full royal honours in Budapest on the 23rd, Wilhelm had no
doubt that his uncle was again involved: 'I hold this whole Bulgarian action to
be a coup engineered by King Edward in Marienbad. The prince is entirely in
his hands and is collaborating with him. The King is trying wherever he can —
according to my informants in the City — to damage German capital; and as
this is heavily involved in the Orient Railway, the coup is explicable.' Wilhelm
considered Franz Joseph's ceremonious reception of Ferdinand 'an unheard-of
stupidity'.[18] A rift had opened up between his own Near Eastern policy and
that of his ally on the Danube. When on 6 October 1908 the Austrians went on
to proclaim the annexation of Bosnia and the Herzegovina, which conjured up
a possible danger of war, without first taking the Kaiser into their confidence,
the Alliance was threatened with dissolution.

THE BOSNIAN ANNEXATION CRISIS

The Austro-Hungarian Foreign Minister, Alois Lexa Count von Aehrenthal,
had been thinking for some time about the possibility of establishing the Dual
Monarchy's supremacy in the Balkans with the help of Bulgaria. The two

provinces of Bosnia and the Herzegovina had been subjected to Austro-Hungarian administrative and military authority in 1878; but in legal terms they remained a part of the Ottoman Empire. The Vienna government's decision of 19 August 1908 to respond to the Young Turks' announcement of parliamentary elections throughout the Empire by annexing Bosnia and the Herzegovina in full sovereignty was a clear breach of the Treaty of Berlin. At the same time, however, Aehrenthal's plans also owed something to the drastic deterioration of Austro-Serbian relations since the bestial murder by Serbian officers of the King Alexander Obrenovic and his wife Draga in 1903. As the new king, Petar Karageorgevic, was determined to avoid the fate of his predecessors, and allowed the officers who had carried out the coup – nationalists to a man – to run the country, the tendency of Obrenovic policy to waver between Vienna and St Petersburg gave way to a decidedly pro-Russian and anti-Austrian stance. From Belgrade, propaganda for a Pan-Serbian state (including Bosnia and the Herzegovina) went out to the Serbian inhabitants of Austria-Hungary.[19]

Aehrenthal was attempting by means of the annexation to demonstrate the futility of Pan-Serbian propaganda and to reinforce the Dual Monarchy's Balkan position for the future. In preparing his bold action, he took the German Chancellor and the Foreign Secretary von Schoen into his confidence to a degree, but not Kaiser Wilhelm. Already on 21 July 1908 – weeks before any decision had been taken – Bülow had assured Aehrenthal of his full and unreserved support for his Balkan policy.[20] On 5 September Aehrenthal visited Schoen, on holiday in Berchtesgaden, and told him that he was looking, beyond the annexation, to 'the complete destruction of the Serbian revolutionary nest'. Serbia was to be partitioned between Austria-Hungary and Bulgaria.[21] When he then met the Russian Foreign Minister Isvolsky at Buchlau in Moravia on 16 September, he obtained his consent to the planned annexation. In return, Aehrenthal promised his support for the opening of the Straits to Russian warships. That done, he thought he had got everything ready for his coup. In a letter of 26 September to the German Chancellor he announced the annexation as imminent; and he was 'entirely confident of Germany's support'.[22]

This support, Germany's 'Nibelung loyalty' to the Dual Monarchy as Bülow was to call it,[23] was never in doubt. At the end of October 1908 the Chancellor again assured Aehrenthal that he would regard 'the decision that you finally come to as the one that the circumstances demand'.[24] He was assuming that the risk that the crisis might escalate into a general war was slight. Russia, he believed, would not dare to intervene in an Austro-Serbian war, for fear of Germany's military superiority; and the information he was receiving from

Russia confirmed this.[25] Thus, the ambassador in St Petersburg reported on 13 November 1908: people were 'quite clear that a war could mean financial ruin for Russia and the rekindling of the flames of revolution with unforeseeable consequences'.[26] Together with Russia's military weakness, it was the very noticeable reserve of Russia's alliance partner, France, that encouraged Bülow in his optimistic assessment.[27] Holstein, now in retirement, confirmed Bülow further in his attitude; and on 7 November the Chancellor brought an energetic and forceful assistant into the Auswärtiges Amt: Alfred von Kiderlen-Wächter, who ten years before had fallen into disgrace with Wilhelm and had been sent by way of punishment to Bucharest.[28] The course of German policy in the Bosnian crisis was determined, on the whole, by Bülow, Holstein, and after November, Kiderlen. But what role did Wilhelm II play in this, the 'most serious and momentous of all Balkan crises'?[29]

Aehrenthal's explosive letter of 26 September 1908, announcing the imminent annexation of the two provinces and relying on Germany's unconditional support, only reached the Kaiser in Rominten on 6 October, together with Franz Joseph's personal letter of 29 September and supporting comments from Bülow and Heinrich von Tschirschky, now Germany's ambassador at Vienna.[30] By that time Franz Joseph had already proclaimed the annexation of Bosnia and the Herzegovina and Prince Ferdinand had announced Bulgaria's independence as a kingdom. Wilhelm was enraged, not just because he was informed so late, but above all because the annexation confronted him with a direct conflict of loyalties between Austria-Hungary and the Ottoman Empire.[31] 'That we cannot do anything to oppose the annexation is obvious! But I am personally most deeply hurt in my sentiments as an ally that H.M. [Emperor Franz Joseph] did not in the slightest take me into his confidence beforehand! The first news of the impending annexation reached me yesterday (5th) evening from a Turkish source in Stamboul. The polit[ical] changes in Stamboul, which H.M.'s letter puts forward as the reasons for the annexation, took place in July. It would surely have been feasible for the ambassador to have informed me − personally − on 18 August, in the strictest confidence, that something of the kind was in train. Thus I am the last person in Europe to find out anything at all! . . . I deeply regret the way in which the affair has got off the ground. The lying hypocrite Ferdinand and the venerable old Emperor appearing together on the luridly illuminated stage as plunderers of Turkey!! The English will now indeed claim that everything was arranged in advance by Austria and us with Bulgaria − that is to say *against Turkey* − and that our stance on the Orient Railway question was a dirty comedy act. From the Turkish point of view the position now arises that, after 20 years of political friendship on my part, my best ally is the first to give the signal for the partition of Europ[ean] Turkey! A nice situation for us in Stamboul ... If the Sultan in his desperation should declare war and unfurl the Green Flag of Holy War, I should not particularly blame him, and as for the Christians – false gallows-birds – in the Balkans it would serve them right!'[32] On 7 October the Kaiser noted bitterly: 'I regret that ... Aehrenthal's frightful stupidity has put me in the dilemma of not being able to protect our friends the Turks and stand by them, because my *Ally* has wronged them. Instead of which I have to watch England advising and protecting the Turks in my place, and to make matters worse, with arguments from international law that are formally incontestable and after my own heart. Thus my Turkish policy, laboriously built up over 20 years, goes up in smoke.'[33]

Wilhelm followed events as they now developed with passionate interest. Though he might be boiling with rage, outwardly he had to put a good face on things. In a personal letter to Franz Joseph he assured him that he was 'very well able to appreciate' the reasons for annexing Bosnia and the Herzegovina: 'In this question too you can count on my unchanging personal friendship and veneration and on the close friendship that binds our two empires together as allies.'[34] In his marginal comments, however, his resentment against the Austrian ally continued to find expression all too clearly. On a report of 9 October from Marschall about Austria's proceedings Wilhelm noted bitterly: 'It is simply a felony! the "thanks of the House of Habsburg"!'[35] Three days later he declared angrily: 'Aehrenthal's action is coming to look increasingly like a trooper's prank. He told us nothing; gave Tittoni and Izvolski such veiled hints that they both feel totally deceived; left the Sultan – who is after all more involved than anybody – totally out of consideration; has burdened his master with the appearance of complicity with the treaty- and peace-breaking Ferdinand; brought the Serbs to boiling point; irritated Montenegro beyond measure; enraged the Cretans; thrown overboard our Turkish policy, laboriously built up over twenty years; angered the English and helped them to replace us in Stamboul; seriously annoyed the Greeks through his friendship for Bulgaria; smashed the Treaty of Berlin to pieces and caused irreparable confusion in the Concert; enraged the Hungarians because Bosnia should have been annexed by them, and infuriated the Croats because they were intending to annex it! As an overall achievement that is a European record that no diplomat has yet managed to bring off. But a far-sighted statesman he certainly is *not*!'[36]

Holstein, still aggrieved at what he felt to be the Kaiser's stab-in-the-back in the Morocco crisis, complained to Bülow in a letter of 8 October 1908: 'H.M. has as usual made a false start. He is against Austria and for the Turks, that is, he is working for Uncle Edward. H.M. has just no sense for the political, nothing can be done about that.'[37] But the fears of the overanxious old diplomat proved unfounded: on 12 October, after the Kaiser's return from Rominten the Chancellor managed in a lengthy conversation in the Chancellor's palace garden to 'turn him round completely'. The Kaiser, Bülow later recalled, had been 'extremely agitated' about events in the Balkans. Even after the fall of his 'special friend' Abdul Hamid, the Turks were still 'his darlings' and he was furious at the humiliation inflicted on them by the annexation. He was hardly less angry about the fact that Ferdinand had made so bold as to assume the royal title of Majesty without asking his permission. 'In a stormy rush of words the Kaiser . . . told me that we should change course completely. In Vienna we must demand the immediate withdrawal of the Emperor Franz Joseph's annexation proclamation and the simultaneous resignation of the Minister Aehrenthal. The style of "Majesty" usurped by the brazen Bulgarian must never be recognised, now or ever.' Gradually, so Bülow boasted, he had managed to make the Kaiser see that it would not do to drive either Austria-Hungary or Bulgaria 'into the camp of our enemies by kicking them'. From this day on, he and the Kaiser were again in agreement about Balkan policy.[38]

Indeed, after his meeting with Bülow on 12 October the focus of Wilhelm II's anger shifted from Austria-Hungary to the Triple Entente Powers. Isvolsky, who, with his eyes on the Straits, had agreed to the planned annexation, now declared himself duped and demanded the summoning of a conference of the signatories of the 1878 Treaty of Berlin to discuss Serbia's demands and the question of the Straits.[39] The governments and the press in Great Britain and France also called for a conference to resolve the dangerous situation in the Balkans. People in London and Paris sympathised with the Young Turks and emphatically condemned Aehrenthal's action. Germany's Triple Alliance partner Italy also condemned the annexation. Neither in London nor in Paris, however, were ruling circles prepared to support the Russian demand for the opening of the Turkish Straits to Russian warships.

To these developments Kaiser Wilhelm reacted with the fiery impulsiveness so typical of him. After his experiences at Algeciras the idea of an international conference was quite abhorrent to him. On a report from St Petersburg he noted: 'Isvolsky has been thoroughly fooled by Aehrenthal a number of times, over the Sanjak Railway, the annexation, and the deal with Bulgaria, and feels totally ridiculous. For months he has been going round Europe – apart from Germany – in an attempt to save his face in Russia and to come home with some success or other. This is now to be the conference. And we as usual are supposed simply to agree good-naturedly to the far-reaching agreements he has made with London and Paris without asking us. That I shall certainly not do. For the last 1½ years Isvolsky has behaved so badly towards me and my country – personally, in his policy, and in his press – that he must be taken down a peg and given a box around the ears. I am against the conference because, as H[is] H[ighness] the Reich Chancellor rightly remarked, it would after all end with the other Powers coming together against us. For Austria too, it is best not to attend, in order to avoid giving the impression of appearing before a tribunal. If the Russians want compensation, they should copy Aehrenthal's modus procedendi and simply sail though the Dardanelles, and that would settle the question without a conference!'[40] The conference demanded by Isvolsky 'will not be', he declared, 'and we shall not attend it, Austria does not want to have Bosnia at the conference, and Russia not the Straits, so what is the point of a conference!?'[41]

'IF ONLY IT WOULD START!' WILHELM AND THE PROSPECT OF WAR

In mid October 1908 Wilhelm became convinced that the Balkan crisis was rapidly moving towards a war between Bulgaria and Turkey. At the same time the Serbian government called up 110,000 reserves and prepared for war with Austria-Hungary. The Bulgarian government had made Ferdinand 'Tsar, and wishes to give him Stamboul as his capital, and for that the present moment is the best', Wilhelm thought, because Russia was 'disorganised and Turkey unprepared and undisciplined! With Austria as a co-conspirator!'[42] He soon hit on the idea, that he would long hold fast to, that the Russians were behind Bulgaria's desire for Constantinople. 'The Russians want to see the Bulgarians in Stamboul, so that they can get the Straits *from them* for *themselves alone*. The fait accompli, which is now in fashion for tearing up treaties, will be played out here too.'[43] But he was not worried about a war in the Near East, coolly explaining that 'whatever happens, it will be to the good! A solution resulting from a discharge [of Turkish rage] against Bulgaria is more logical, as it is merited, than a general massacre of Christians! Enraged Islam and the threat to the constitution will be the two effective driving forces.'[44] When Radolin, the ambassador in Paris, reported on 17 October that Isvolsky had just told him that 'his information from Bulgaria was very serious and he fears the outbreak of hostilities',[45] Wilhelm remarked: 'if only it would start! Then we should not get this damned conference! That can only be troublesome and damaging for us! Isvolsky has made himself totally ridiculous and wants both to save face and to break up our alliance. I shan't support him in either quest.'[46] When he met the Austro-Hungarian ambassador Count Szögyény on 21 October the Kaiser reminded him 'very forcefully' that already thirteen years before he had not 'conceived of alliance loyalty only in terms of the letter of our treaty of alliance, but would stand loyally by our [Austria-Hungary's] side in all questions great and small'. The Emperor Franz Joseph was indeed 'a Prussian Field Marshal, and so only has to give the order and the whole Prussian army will obey his command'.[47] At the end of October 1908 Wilhelm reacted to the prospect of war between Serbia and Austria with the impatient exclamation: 'Get on with it! Then there will be a relaxation of tension.'[48]

The international conference proposed by Great Britain, France and Russia to deal with the new situation in the Near East was unanimously rejected by Wilhelm, Bülow and the Wilhelmstrasse.[49] No doubt whatever could be allowed to arise regarding the German Reich's loyalty as an ally of Austria-Hungary. He would not be 'the bailiff who implements the Anglo-Gallo-Russian judgement against Austria-Hungary!' Wilhelm II declared, and went on: 'Count Hoyos, whom I met today at the shoot, told me that Austria wants no conference and will certainly never attend if Bosnia is on the agenda. I encouraged him and said I had no expectations of a conference, which after all only wanted to sit in judgement over the Emperor [Franz Joseph]. I would not go to it if Vienna does not.'[50] The proposal of the French Foreign Minister, Stephen Pichon, that 'France and Germany should co-operate over important questions', Wilhelm countered with the comment: 'not *without* Austria, and certainly not *against* her.'[51] Fearful of arousing the distrust of his last reliable alliance partner, Wilhelm refused altogether to assume the role of mediator in the Balkan crisis. 'Thank you very much! So that we should be blamed if Austria is unwilling, or should take the Straits from Turkey for Russia!'[52]

As Isvolsky wanted to visit Berlin too, after London and Paris, and as Wilhelm II had never concealed his contempt for the Russian minister,[53] Bülow was obliged to advise the Kaiser to be extremely careful. 'Herr Isvolsky naturally hopes to hear from Your Majesty as much sensational information as possible about the situation in the Near East and our relations with the other Powers, in order to twist and exploit it as he thinks fit ... So I make so bold as to suggest for Your Majesty's gracious consideration, whether it might not be appropriate if Your Majesty yourself should not tell him anything of political significance, but simply refer him to the Secretary of State and me, with the observation that Your Majesty is not particularly interested in the specialised matters in question.' Wilhelm not only readily accepted this advice – 'that was my intention', he replied, 'I wanted to let him talk and not commit myself to anything whatever' – but also Bülow's suggestion that he hint at the possibility of his some day being appointed ambassador at Berlin. It was important to be kind to him personally, so that he could not play the martyr.[54] On 25 October 1908 Bülow gave a big dinner party for Isvolsky in Berlin (see Figure 29).[55] Three days later, with the publication of the *Daily Telegraph* interview the Personal Monarchy's house of cards collapsed. What was the impact

Figure 29 Reich Chancellor Prince von Bülow with the Russian Foreign Minister
Alexander Isvolsky in Berlin in October 1908

of this most serious internal crisis on Wilhelm's attitude towards the smouldering conflict in the Balkans?

`I STAND BY YOU THROUGH THICK AND THIN.' WILHELM AND ARCHDUKE FRANZ FERDINAND

After his exceedingly frosty confrontation of 17 November 1908 with Bülow
and his ensuing nervous breakdown the Kaiser withdrew 'sulking' from
politics for weeks.[56] While he concealed his intentions from his 'responsible'
advisers, he put himself trustingly in the hands of his Austrian friends. These
included not just Max Egon II Prince zu Fürstenberg, who held an influential
position among the Austrian high aristocracy,[57] but also the imperial and royal
heir apparent, Archduke Franz Ferdinand, who was thought to be the real
driving force behind the Bosnian annexation and boasted of having made
Aehrenthal Foreign Minister.[58]

From 4 to 6 November 1908, as we have seen, Wilhelm stayed with Franz
Ferdinand for a shoot in Eckartsau, before travelling via Schönbrunn to
Donaueschingen. His visit to Franz Ferdinand caused a good deal of unease,
not only because of the crisis in Germany, but also in view of the turmoil in
the Balkans. Almost in a panic, Isvolsky expressed the fear that Wilhelm
would support the military party in Vienna, led by Franz Ferdinand, which
was 'very warlike', and pushing for war with Serbia;[59] but the Kaiser
restrained himself. Bülow had asked him not to touch on the Dardanelles
question in talking to the Austrians.[60] On 5 November Wilhelm telegraphed to
the Chancellor from Eckartsau: 'In our talks so far, in which I was merely in
the role of listener, Franz Ferdinand dealt with the annexation question very
vigorously. He was involved in it everywhere, and, in fact, as a driving force.
Spoke very well of Aehrenthal, whom he had sought out himself. Extraordinarily warm about our attitude as allies, almost enthusiastic, very sharp about
King Edward VII and England ... spoke of Isvolsky with hatred and scorn.
The Emperor Nicholas II had *recently* sent him a *secret* message promising
always to maintain his friendship for Austria, and in the event of possible
warlike complications (with Serbia) Russia will not mobilise one single man
against Austria ... Good hunting! Straits question not touched upon.'[61] Next
day, the Kaiser reported further about Franz Ferdinand's intentions. 'Bosnia
and the Herzegovina are to be incorporated as an imperial province, and
administered like our Reichsland [Alsace-Lorraine]. He is glad that everything
went off so well, thanks to our loyal support, which he cannot emphasise too
much. Only one thing annoys him: that the Bulgarian carried out his coup at
the same time, and that he is now always spoken of and cited together with
His Majesty the Emperor; that should have been avoided ... Do not have the
impression that any warlike complications are envisaged for the moment,
unless Serbia and Montenegro are totally mad.'[62]

In the course of November, as we have seen, Wilhelm's idyllic world
collapsed.[63] Convinced, in his paranoia, that his own Empire was now being
ruled by Harden and Holstein, who had Bülow completely in their hands,
after the *Daily Telegraph* crisis Wilhelm turned trustingly to Prince Max and
Princess Irma zu Fürstenberg, to the long-serving Austro-Hungarian
ambassador Count Szögyény, and to Archduke Franz Ferdinand direct, promising them Germany's support. To his friend Max Fürstenberg he wrote on
1 December 1908: 'What you write about the Austrian view of me and my
policy gives me great satisfaction. Yes, Austria can count on me, and I stand by
you through thick and thin! According to today's news, there seems to be
complete anarchy in Prague; now that Czech mob will have to be fired on ...
You may by all means tell Franzi of the condition I am in.'[64]

A week later Wilhelm received the Austro-Hungarian ambassador for a heart-to-heart audience in the Neues Palais. Szögyény reported on 9 December 1908 that he had found the monarch 'quite extraordinarily depressed'. 'This may be partly the result of His physical discomfort, but chiefly it is still the after-effects of the depressing impact of recent events on His Majesty. His Majesty assured me that he needed to talk to me quite openly and – as He put it – "to pour out His heart". But He must ask me to regard what He said as strictly confidential and only to report it to His I[mperial] and R[oyal] Apostolic Majesty. Until now only the Kaiserin and His children were fully aware of His anxieties about the situation that has arisen and how hurt he has been. Otherwise, only Archduke Franz Ferdinand knows about His innermost feelings, from their long conversations in Eckartsau.'[65] A few days after this repudiation of his Chancellor vis-à-vis the representative of a foreign Power, Wilhelm took up his pen to pour out his grief to the Archduke in person (see p. 735 below).[66] The developing intimacy between the German Kaiser and the Austro-Hungarian heir, apparent at the height of the Bosnian Crisis, was to have far-reaching consequences.

WAR AGAINST RUSSIA OR A CONTINENTAL LEAGUE AGAINST ENGLAND?

The renunciation of political activity that Wilhelm had imposed on himself after his 'nervous breakdown' of 23 November did not last long. Just three weeks later he was back on duty with his usual passion. When it was reported from St Petersburg that Isvolsky was again talking of a possible formal alliance between Russia, France and England, the Kaiser raged that the Russian Foreign Minister must have 'a damned bad conscience! He was flirting with England when he was threatening us in the spring over the Sanjak Railway affair. But the flirtation doesn't seem to have brought him the Straits, only the settlement that England wanted in Asia. Now Isvolsky is constantly bluffing us with the Engl[ish] alliance, in order to draw us away from Austria. Russia must get the Straits from Austria *and* from us, but not from London, and certainly not from London alone. I am *quite certain* that it was *Isvolsky* who *used* the term Engl[ish] Alliance and *publicised it himself.* He did just the same thing with the text of the conference programme in the autumn, leaking it in London, only to issue a dementi from Paris the next day, when it didn't have the effect he expected!'[67]

Wilhelm's position in the Near Eastern crisis now swung erratically between readiness for the great war against Russia – up to this point in time he had only envisaged war against the western Powers, not against Russia – and his old desire for a restoration of the Three Emperors' Alliance between

Germany, Austria-Hungary and Russia (with or without France) against
Britain. Some months earlier, in the summer of 1908, he had asserted that a
'preventive' war against Russia 'would be the only right thing to do militarily.
Frederick the Great would have done it, and he would have been correct.'[68]
This analogy came to dominate his thinking in the Bosnia crisis. On 10
December the military attaché in St Petersburg reported that the Russian
War Minister had stated 'in drastic terms' that there was 'no question' of
Russia's going to war for Serbia.[69] The attaché also gave a detailed account of
the Russian army's shortcomings in terms of armaments and organisation.
This moved Wilhelm to declare: 'Then from a military point of view the
present would be the best moment to settle accounts with the Russians.'[70] The
following day the ambassador Count Pourtalès reported a dramatic conversation with Isvolsky. Referring to newspaper reports that there already existed a
firm alliance, beyond the terms of the Triple Entente, between Russia,
England and France, Pourtalès had declared to the Russian Foreign Minister
that 'such an alliance would mean the closing of the ring which would make
Germany's position in Europe intolerable. At the very first sign that such an
alliance was impending I am sure that a considerable part of German public
opinion, peaceable as it otherwise might certainly be, would press for an
aggressive policy to break up the ring if possible, before it was completed.'[71]
This too was greeted with delight by Wilhelm: 'definitely yes, take preventive
action, as Fred[erick] the Great did in his day'. Enraptured, he remarked on
the dispatch, à propos the ambassador's forceful words: 'Excellent! I endorse
every word! Pourtalès's language was well considered, truthful and spirited. It
is good that Isvolsky got to hear it. The fellow has manoeuvred himself into
such a corner with his perpetual bluffing, intrigues, lying and finessing that he
is caught in his own net and cannot free himself again!'[72]

On 13 December 1908 Wilhelm received confirmation from his military
plenipotentiary in St Petersburg, Captain Paul Hintze, that Russia was not at
present prepared to go to war for Serbia, and that her real aim was only to
secure free passage through the Dardanelles for her warships.[73] Suddenly, the
Kaiser's hopes for a combination of the three eastern empires against England
revived. The Tsar, he demanded, must be 'drawn over to' Germany and
Austria-Hungary. With the disagreement between Russia and England over
the Straits question the chance of a diplomatic revolution had appeared which
Germany must seize with both hands. 'That could perhaps bring about a very
different Power constellation', he wrote to Bülow. 'In any case it should not be
impossible, with a little skill, to draw the 3 empires closer together and to
strengthen the monarchical idea. If Austria and Germany ... accommodate
the Tsar in the Straits question and strive to remove difficulties, as we now

know he attaches such importance to this point that he would not shrink from going to war about it, then that would help him to achieve a new success – bringing him in opposition to London – satisfy Russ[ian] public opinion, and do Isvolsky a great service. France will have to choose between going along with her Russian ally – that is, with the empires – and standing by England. She will no doubt choose the first, on account of the 12 billions. England will be faced with the choice of either supporting Turkey, as hitherto, and *opposing* the opening of the Straits, or demanding their opening to *all*, that is for *herself* too, which Russia does *not* want. She will have to take upon herself the hatred of the Russians or the Turks, i.e. come into conflict either with the Slav or the Mohammedan world. In the latter case the deleterious consequences should be felt very soon in Egypt and in India. For it is this very unrest in these countries that is at the root of England's present Turcophilia. The Russians are counting on this already and are arming for a war, in which we too would be involved; we are not afraid; but I think it could perhaps still be avoided by the opening of the Straits, which, if offered by 2 emperors to the third could lead to a harmonious relationship between the 3 empires which France would have to join, like it or not, and Italy too; and England would at the very least become very polite. At any rate, the situation is very serious. And in this state of affairs it is indeed a delightful irony that at this very moment the cuts-demon is leaping around in the Reichstag and celebrating real orgies, which, at this of all times, is preventing the army and navy from *discreetly* preparing for coming events as they would otherwise do ... Now the task is to be armed and get ready to fight! On top of that, the reduction of the Navy budget by 50 mill[ions] makes it impossible to get the mines, of which we are hundreds short, to defend our harbours and estuaries, a bad start, almost treasonable given the present situation! How many billions could that cost us in ruined trade! Even to attempt to make great savings at the expense of the armed forces in such disturbed times looks like weakness and encourages the enemy to attack. The last sentence in yesterday's St Petersburg telegram, "that the Tsar is my friend as before and I can rely on him" – following on the brusque declaration "he wants the Straits" – shows how his friendship can be gained, strengthened and made use of. Berlin must therefore get to work soon, together with Vienna, to handle the Straits question with St Petersburg. In this way the Tsar can be drawn towards the imperial Powers, and Isvolsky's vanity be satisfied at the same time.'[74]

Bülow's reply to these 'All-Highest directives' was drafted by Kiderlen-Wächter. In principle, he explained, a return to the Three Emperors' Alliance between Germany, Austria and Russia would be welcome. And accommodating the Russians over the Turkish Straits could indeed be the starting point for an improvement of relations with Russia. This could best be arranged along the lines of the secret Russo-German Reinsurance Treaty of 1887, because even after that treaty had expired in 1890 Germany's benevolent attitude in the Straits question had not changed. But Bülow and Kiderlen warned urgently against taking the initiative in this question. 'The most regrettable hostility towards us that prevails in England, and to some degree in France, is so great that our coming forward would imperil Russia's objectives rather than further them.' Therefore, it would be more in Russia's interests to ask France to mediate with England. Such negotiations would soon show that England, given the prevailing 'enthusiasm of the English for the liberal-revolutionary element in Turkey' and the need to 'consider its own Mohammedan subjects in India and Egypt' was not prepared to take account of Russia's wishes in the Straits question.[75]

As in the old days, Wilhelm II covered his Reich Chancellor's submission with endless imperious minutes and marginal comments. Bülow's proposal was 'the exact opposite of what I want', he scribbled. 'It would be almost as if designed to drive the Tsar into the arms of the English.' He, Wilhelm, on the other hand, wanted to split off Russia (and France) from England and draw it towards Germany and Austria. 'If England says No, then the friendship between it and Russia is finished, and the offended Tsar will then come to Austria and to us, and France with him, and then he will get permission and consent from the rest of us and it will be up to England, whether to stand *alone* in the way of the Russians who have all Europe behind them. That is the way to finesse it . . . The chief thing here is to drive a wedge between London and Isvolsky. That will be done if we and Austria give Russia our consent and together warmly support the Russ[ian] demarches and the Tsar's wishes in Paris and London . . . Hence, I do not agree with the proposal; and the instruction [to the ambassador in St Petersburg] must be modified accordingly. It is less a question of successful demarches than of confronting England with the dilemma I outlined yesterday, of giving the Tsar a spectacular demonstration of our and Austria's assistance, and of bringing about a rift between London and St Petersburg.' Hintze's telegram was indeed, 'especially with its personal conclusion – . . . an *appeal to me . . . for help*', Wilhelm declared. 'The Tsar . . . wants the Straits; une question d'amour-propre. He has already been rebuffed with his proposal in London in the autumn . . . and he has now turned to me. I cannot now advise him to try again with the help of Paris! There they certainly helped him as much as they could the first time. Besides, that would amount to deliberately pushing the Tsar directly into the arms of England, and bringing about that very Anglo-Franco-Russian grouping. He has shown his trust in me in asking me to help him succeed. We must make use of that, by ensuring that the empires now interest themselves in his plan and support it, together with Paris, in London, because Paris in this case can do nothing else. If London again says No, then the rift with St Petersburg will be wide open, we have diligentiam prestiret and shown the Russians that we mean them well; and they can now choose their path, with or without England: take it or leave it. If London says Yes, then Vienna and Berlin — together with Paris — have helped Russia to fulfil her wishes and Russia is content and will draw closer to us, Paris too indirectly, because it always joins in whatever St Petersburg does, and Isvolsky's vanity is satisfied, which is very important. Russia must get *the Straits* from *Vienna* and *Berlin*; those were Bismarck's and Schweinitz's words to me!'[76] In the end, Bülow, Schoen and Kiderlen-Wächter managed to convince the Kaiser that to support Russia's wishes at the present moment, when the annexation crisis had not yet been settled, would be interpreted as weakness: Isvolsky would be able to tell the Tsar 'that we were intervening not from love but from fear'. But even so, the idea of a restoration of the Three Emperors' Alliance remained a longer-term aim of the civilian statesmen in Berlin, too.[77]

The desire for a renewal of the continental alliance of Germany, Austria and Russia, chiefly directed against Britain, cropped up again in the letter of 31 December 1908 that Wilhelm II sent, without informing the Reich Chancellor, to Franz Ferdinand. 'My dear Franzi', he wrote to the Archduke, 'We are taking serious questions with us into the New Year that have still to be resolved . . . The key to the situation lies with that certain maritime Power we have often talked about and about whose behaviour we are both in complete agreement. It is pursuing an unprincipled, savage campaign against our two countries in all corners of the world. In Paris, Madrid, Rome, above all in St Petersburg and Stamboul. Its aim is a great *continental* war of all against all, so as to fish in troubled waters and weaken us *all*. Russia, however, does *not want* a war — because it *cannot fight at the moment*. Even so, the intention is recognisable in *Isvolsky's* speech to construct a Balkan league of the *Slav brother races* against you, which would suit the other Power's plans quite well. This league can best be countered, it seems to me, if you bind Bulgaria closely to you and make it go along with you. In so far as it shows itself openly at your side it demonstrates that its interests are being safeguarded by you, *even though* it is *Slavic*. That *fact* will cut the ground from under those who talk of a threatened Slavdom, and Isvolsky will have one weapon fewer for trouble-making. Romania will also be on your side. So you have the two best Balkan states and armies on your side, which must be a factor in making calculations if things should get serious. The Turks are I think also to be had. They "urgently need a lot of money". It would be a pity if they got it *all* from beyond the seas and became even more dependent on those people's wishes. The Oriental is very susceptible to gifts, and so long as the Baksheesh is not too small, it should not be without effect ... It would surely be nice if the negotiations brought the 3 empires back together again as a "community of interests". At any rate I have let people know in Sofia that my vote for recognition and my goodwill in future will depend solely on whether Fernando Naso [Ferdinand of Bulgaria] stands resolutely by your side, which I can only advise him to do. For the rest, I keep myself prepared for everything that God may wish to send and keep my powder dry and am on guard. That you can count on us, you know, and whether our army is worth anything you are best able to judge.'[78]

GERMANY AND THE DANGER OF WAR BETWEEN AUSTRIA AND SERBIA

While Wilhelm would have preferred a restoration of the Three Emperors' Alliance, the closing sentences of his New Year's letter to Franz Ferdinand show that he by no means ruled out a general war, which could easily have arisen out of Austro-Russian differences over the Balkans. At his New Year's reception for the commanding generals on 2 January 1909 the Supreme War Lord identified himself with an article of Schlieffen's, which painted a fatalistic picture of the international scene and took the 'encirclement' of Germany and Austria-Hungary for an accomplished fact.[79] Bülow felt obliged to bring his sovereign back to earth with a letter criticising the pessimistic standpoint of Schlieffen's article (and thereby, indirectly, of Wilhelm II) and setting out the guidelines of his own policy, which was aiming at a huge forward thrust in the Near Eastern crisis: 'While the military points of the *Deutsche Revue* article were certainly excellent, its political arguments are unfortunate. What is now important is to stiffen the Austrians, who have taken a stand, not just for themselves, but ultimately for us too against the Entente Powers. It is a matter of convincing the Austrians that the Russians will not be fully capable of action for years yet; the Italians are not strong or spirited enough to attack Austria; England cannot do much against the Austrians and also has reason, on commercial as well as political grounds, not to start a war with us; France is still in awe of our superiority. It is, moreover, not true that Austria would not be in a position to lend us support. Austria can indeed very well support us against Russia, and it is plain to see that the latest turn of Austrian policy has made Austrian co-operation against Russia more certain than it was before the annexation of Bosnia and the Herzegovina. Finally, it is untrue that in the event of a European conflagration Austria must concentrate on the southern front. On the contrary, Austria would do well in its own interests as well as ours, to throw all its forces against Russia and to stand on the defensive against Italy and the Serbian and Montenegrin robber-states.'[80]

From the fact that his speech to the commanding generals was already known in the Russian embassy by the next day and was apparently passed on from there to the progressive *Berliner Tageblatt*, Kaiser Wilhelm concluded, encouraged in this belief by the Chief of General Staff Helmuth von Moltke, that the 'indiscretion' was the work of the Russian military plenipotentiary, Tatishchev; and he suspected that its purpose must be to sabotage the impending visit of the British royal couple to Berlin.[81] While Wilhelm was thus turning against Russia again, he was impressed by Britain's enhanced standing at Constantinople (and hoping, no doubt, for English neutrality in a war against Russia). On 14 January 1909 (when the Turks accepted an Austrian offer of monetary compensation for the annexed provinces) he congratulated Franz Ferdinand on the 'gratifying' resolution of the conflict — an outcome he attributed partly to British influence. 'The offer was efficacious and seems to have been welcomed by the Turks . . . It was very amusing that people in London should tell us quite unashamedly that they had given the Turks clearly to understand that they should accept the offer. So Albion gives the orders there, stirring up and pacifying quite as it wishes and as suits it. Our standing together impressed London, and so they gave way.' Evidently England was seeking a rapprochement with Germany and Austria and turning away from Russia.[82]

Once Austria-Hungary had settled with the Young Turks, the danger of European war now threatened to come not from Constantinople but from a conflict between the Dual Monarchy and the 'robber-states' Serbia and Montenegro, whose demands for compensation for the annexation of Bosnia and the Herzegovina had been supported by Russia and rejected by Austria-Hungary. At the turn of the year 1908–9 the critical question was posed in acute form: how would Russia and Germany react to a war between Austria-Hungary and Serbia? In a letter to Wilhelm of 25 December 1908, Tsar Nicholas expressed the fear that Austria would attack Serbia, and asked that Germany should give Vienna to understand that an Austro-Serbian war would endanger the peace of Europe.[83]

Wilhelm's reply of 8 January was drafted in the Auswärtiges Amt in English, and Bülow expressly asked the Kaiser to copy out the letter unchanged, since every word in it had been carefully considered. Exceptionally, apart from a few very minor deviations, Wilhelm followed the Chancellor's advice,[84] telling the Tsar that he wished 'that Germany and Russia should be as closely united as possible' as 'their union would form a powerful stronghold for the maintenance of Peace and monarchical institutions'. But the letter also contained many complaints about Russian policy, which clearly in the previous two years had been 'gradually drawing away from us more and more, evolving always closer towards a combination of Powers unfriendly to us'. Russia's mistrust of German policy was however unfounded. Berlin had had no advance knowledge of the annexation of Bosnia and the Herzegovina, for which Germany was held to blame. There was no reason to expect an Austrian attack on Serbia such as the Tsar feared. 'I also feel it is my duty to tell you quite frankly that I am under the impression that your views about Austria's intentions are too pessimistic, and that you are overanxious, more than is necessary. We here at any rate have not the slightest doubt that Austria is not going to attack Serbia. That would not at all be like the Emperor Francis Joseph, who is wise and judicious and such a venerable Gentleman. Nor do we believe that Aehrenthal harbours any such plans. Of course the small Balkan states must necessarily be prudent and loyal and avoid all provocations and put a stop to warlike preparations. These small states are an awful nuisance! Quantités négligeables!? The slightest encouragement from any quarter makes them frantic . . . Six years ago these very small people were looked upon with disgust and horror by the whole world as the murderers of their King!'[85]

Despite these assurances, a danger of war did indeed exist. The Austrian Chief of General Staff, Franz Freiherr Conrad von Hötzendorf, was pressing doggedly for an offensive war against Serbia.[86] True, at the beginning of January 1909 his German counterpart Moltke had maintained that it would be advisable not to provoke a war with Serbia, because so long as Austria 'confines herself to standing on the defensive against Serbia, Russia will have no reason to take action'.[87] However, on 21 January 1909 Moltke, with Bülow's agreement, assured his Austro-Hungarian colleague of Germany's full support in a war against Russia. 'I believe', he wrote to Conrad, 'that only an Austrian invasion of Serbia might lead Russia to intervene actively. With this, the casus foederis would arise for Germany.' Moltke even took into account the possibility that the French would then lend their Russian ally military support. But even then, he declared, 'the position of the allied empires [Germany and Austria] would have to be regarded as serious, but not threatening'.[88]

What was Kaiser Wilhelm's attitude towards this crucial question? At the end of January he expressed his conviction that the annexation crisis was solely the result of the irresponsible personal rivalry of Aehrenthal and Isvolsky and should certainly not drive the world to war. 'One has to look at Russ[ia]'s whole Balkan policy in the light of the deeply slighted, boundless vanity of Isvolsky', he declared. 'He has made himself ridiculous coram publico, and now wants to get his revenge partout on Aehrenthal. The desire for vengeance that arises from injured vanity is the most dangerous of all; especially when, as in this case, political naiveté, frivolity and limitless mendacity are involved; it would not bother their consciences to start a world war to satisfy their desire for revenge. I should not actually take the matter itself too tragically, were it not for the poor, weak, Tsar, completely made a fool of by Isvolsky. He has once already been driven − completely unsuspectingly, and despite all pleas and warnings − into war with Japan, and here I see the seeds of a similar idiocy in the Balkans. A conflict arising from the envy and jealousy of two statesmen has once before put two countries in great danger: Bismarck versus Gortschakoff! The result of that: the Russo-Gallic alliance!'[89] With satisfaction he noted the increasing indications that France would hold Russia back from war. Over a conflict in the Near East 'la belle France will not go into the fire', he mocked; there was no enthusiasm for that in France, if only 'for fear of losing 5 billions of investments through a war in Turkey'. Germany must under no circumstances participate in any mediation; 'the Gauls must do that *alone* on their own account, it will not bring them much joy in Petersburg'.[90]

In February 1909 Wilhelm received from Franz Ferdinand a furious tirade against the Hungarians, whom the Archduke denounced as 'the most infamous anti-dynastic, mendacious and unreliable characters' in his multinational Empire. The Magyars were in fact 'the root of the evil' in the Dual Monarchy's problems, 'the instructors for all those elements' who wanted to dissolve the Habsburg Empire 'by revolutionary pressure and excesses'. The 'shameless' advance of the Slavs in all parts of the monarchy was nothing more than an imitation of Magyar behaviour. The Archduke explained to the Kaiser: 'I am completely convinced ... that the moment the dreadful activity of the Magyars is checked (which can be done *quite* easily, as the Magyar, being a real Hun and Asiatic, always only blusters, but immediately bows to force), the Slavs will also stop their violent behaviour and once more submit calmly and quietly to the culturally far more advanced Germans. If the Austrian Monarchy is to have peace and order, and the chance of pursuing, together with its allies, a forceful foreign policy for the benefit of all its peoples, then there is only one remedy, and one necessity, and that is to break this *preponderance of the Hungarians*! Otherwise we shall with absolute certainty become a Slavic empire and Trial-ism, which would be a disaster, would be established!'[91]

In his truly dizzying answer of 12 February 1909 to this philippic, the German Kaiser sprang to the defence of the Hungarians as important allies of the 'Teutons', the English and the Turks in their inevitable common struggle against 'the united power of Slavdom' and the 'Romance (Latin) nations'. 'My dear Franzi', he wrote, 'the dangers which you apprehend regarding the future internal development of the Monarchy in relation to Hungary I found very interesting. Certainly, the Hungarian, with his chauvinism and vanity is not easy to handle: and as you say, these tendencies have been strengthened even more by too much giving way, so that it is difficult to draw a clear line marking the end of concessions. That they should not be made at the expense of the army, which would thereby lose homogeneity and strength, is obvious. On the other hand, recent months have exposed the Slav danger, in its delusions and its ferocity in a surprising way. According to your own account, Belgrade and Prague are operating with a common programme, which is quite clear from the funds being spent. Moscow is behind both of them, and how far Cracow and Lemberg [i.e. Lvov or Lviv] are involved I cannot judge. Now for Austria this *Pan*-Slav danger is the greater of the two, because it is beginning to work against Austria and its Imperial House inside the country itself, through the Czechs, and to threaten the existence of the Monarchy *because it has recently incorporated Slav provinces*, and is thereby in process of evolving into a *second Slav Great Power* (alongside holy Slav Russia). We shall have to reckon increasingly in future with this *Pan*-Slav hostility – fostered by other Great Powers – and resulting from a fear of competition, and of a *division* of Slav power *between* you and Russia, which will always make Russia mistrustful. The best defence against the Pan-Slav danger and its machinations is a) a good, firm relationship with Romania b) the same with Bulgaria and c) with Turkey. In addition, the hatred of the Hungarians for everything Pan-Slav would make them a good support against all Slav tendencies, particularly in the south. For the chauvinism of the Hungarians arises from a fiery patriotism, even if it is of a particularist hue; and if properly managed it could certainly be put to good use for the benefit of the fatherland as a whole.'

Wilhelm continued: He had recently spoken to the new Turkish ambassador in Berlin 'about the future political plans of the Young Turks'. 'He explained that their main programme included firm friendship with Austria, Romania, possibly Bulgaria, Germany, and, he hoped, England, so as to dig a deep ditch across Europe between the Romance (Latin nations) and the Slavs dependent on Russia. The Latins and the Slavs are both too similar in their characteristics and racial peculiarities, and are therefore always drawn towards each other. Turkey had always had bad experiences with both races, and could also only expect the same; each one on its own was a danger for Turkey; together they represented a dangerous threat that Turkey could only counter through a close connection with the other Great Powers, Austria, Germany and England. I naturally urged him seriously to establish good relations with you, and told him that all such stupidities as the boycott should be ended as soon as possible.' The annexation of Bosnia and the Herzegovina had been mentioned during

King Edward's recent 'very successful' visit to Berlin, 'but without recriminations, and where differences of opinion cropped up it was easy for me to exert
a clarifying and calming influence'. Even the 'thorny issue' of naval construction had now been 'cleared up', the Kaiser asserted. Confident of a diplomatic
rapprochement between the Triple Alliance and Great Britain, as well as
Turkey, Romania and Bulgaria, Wilhelm ended this highly political letter,
which, naturally, he did not show to Bülow — just as if there had never been a
Daily Telegraph affair.[92]

In this phase of the Balkan crisis Kaiser Wilhelm lived in constant hope of a
realignment of the Great Powers of Europe against the Slav danger. At the
beginning of March 1909 he still believed that Russia's advance into the Near
East would 'some day' lead to a 'clash with the European cultural and Teutonic
world'. 'Therefore [there must be] a coming together of Teutons and Anglo-
Saxons, possibly with the Gauls!'[93] But this optimistic assessment of the
situation that prevailed in the wake of Edward VII's visit to Berlin, was put
in question again by reports that Russia's Balkan policy would meet with
sympathy in London and Paris. On 20 February Wilhelm II peremptorily
declared himself 'in agreement' with Bülow and Kiderlen that Germany
should refuse an Anglo-French proposal for a common démarche in Vienna
to resolve the Austro-Serbian conflict: 'No! I shall not join in.'[94] He agreed
with the Chancellor that it was not Vienna but Belgrade that was the right
place to exert pressure. When Aehrenthal rejected Anglo-French soundings,
Wilhelm gloated: 'Good! Rebuffed! that'll teach the Gauls a lesson.' 'I stand by
my refusal! I shall certainly *not* join in such steps against Austria!'[95] A British
suggestion that Austria might compensate Serbia for the annexation by a small
cession of territory drew Wilhelm's sarcastic comment: 'England can cede
Walfisch Bay or Jersey and Guernsey!'[96]

THE PLANNED ULTIMATUM TO FRANCE

The moment of decision over war and peace was now approaching fast. On
20 February 1909 the Kaiser welcomed Aehrenthal's unconcealed intention
'to clear up the situation with Serbia' in the coming month.[97] On 23 February
he was shown a letter from Aehrenthal to Bülow talking of 'a chastisement of
Serbia by Austria' and the possibility of proceeding against Serbia 'by force of
arms'. Bülow thought 'Russian intervention hardly probable, however much
the Slavs might rage', because the army was unprepared, Russia's finances
would not stand a war, and above all the dynasty would be endangered.
Besides, France, which certainly wanted to avoid a war, would put pressure
on its ally to prevent Russian intervention in an Austro-Serbian war.[98]

Wilhelm agreed with this comforting analysis and added: 'We can see how clever it was of us to agree with the Gauls about Morocco. Because they now have their hands free and can more easily press the Russian Allié energetically to keep calm. This will annoy Isvolsky immensely and not strengthen the friendship.'[99] St Petersburg's warnings that in the event of an Austrian attack on Serbia the Russian government would not be able to withstand the pressure of public opinion, the Kaiser dismissed as 'a bluff'.[100]

For Wilhelm the assumed unwillingness of the French to be drawn into war over a Balkan questions was the cornerstone of Germany's Balkan policy.[101] To compel France to restrain Russia he gave orders (with Moltke's agreement) on 24 February 1909 for a breathtaking intervention in Paris, in the form of an ultimatum. 'In view of the serious situation, we must *immediately* get in touch with *Paris* and demand that France join with us in putting pressure on Russia to force her to adopt a clear position with regard to Serbia (joining in pressure on Belgrade). It must be made clear to France that in the event of Russia's intervening against Austria, the *casus foederis* arises for us immediately, i.e. mobilisation. France must be forced to make a binding and clear declaration that it will in this case *not go to war with us at all*. Not at the start of the war, nor later. A declaration of neutrality is not sufficient. If France refuses to make this declaration, that is to be taken by us as a casus belli, and the Reichstag and the world informed, that France, despite our invitation to tread together with us the only possible path to maintain the peace of Europe, has refused and has therefore *willed the war*. This clarification, in this form, is necessary so that we can start our mobilisation in the first instance against France and finish her off. In no case can the army get into the position where one half is engaged against Russia and the other half standing guard against an unreliable France. We must throw everything against the West or everything against the East. In the former case, if France refuses to declare that she will in no event intervene in a Russo-Austro-German war. In the latter case if France declares that she will join us in pressing Russia to keep the peace, and, should Russia refuse to back down, will refrain from attacking us if we support Austria against Russia. To be dealt with immediately in Paris. Wilhelm I.R. Chief of General Staff is in agreement.'[102]

Never before had the fatal mechanism that was to lead five years later to the catastrophe of the First World War been so clearly delineated as in these remarks of Wilhelm II's in February 1909. It is not surprising, therefore, that after that catastrophe the editors of the official German documents on the origins of the war, *Die Große Politik der europäischen Kabinette*, should have striven to make light of these imperial utterances. They mocked the Kaiser's 'extraordinarily characteristic' marginalia and pointed out that Wilhelm was only 'seeking to counter Isvolsky's bluffing with a similar policy of bluff, but that he was by no means thinking of adopting a policy that could cause a war'. Bülow, they claimed, had also not taken the minute seriously and had 'simply ignored' it. And Wilhelm had been 'quite content when the Auswärtiges Amt refrained from demanding that Paris declare itself as the monarch was demanding: a certain proof that in this as in so many other cases he regarded his marginalia, formulated as categorical commands, as mere expressions of opinion, the consideration of which he left to the Auswärtiges Amt as the proper authority'.[103] What is true is that at the end of February there were increasing signs that even without German pressure France was advising restraint in St Petersburg, which for the moment robbed the ultimatum to Paris demanded by the Kaiser of its relevance. That it continued to be central to his military calculations, however – and to those of the General Staff – was demonstrated, not merely by his behaviour in the July crisis of 1914, when Bülow and Schoen were no longer in the Wilhelmstrasse, but by many other statements of Wilhelm's from the pre-war years which were not accessible to the editors of the *Große Politik*.

On 1 March 1909 Wilhelm received the Saxon War Minister Baron Max von Hausen for a confidential talk about 'high political questions, present and future'. According to Hausen's secret memorandum, written two days later, Wilhelm II expressed the following sweeping ideas: 'The French people at the moment hold Russian bonds to the value of about 25 billion francs. Hence the duty of the French government to keep Russia from going bankrupt. If it came to a war now, that would be at a time when Russia has not yet re-established her army and has no navy, so Russia would certainly be completely destroyed. But this would not be without repercussions on the French, who if Russia collapsed would lose a great part of their national wealth. This consideration obliges France to hold Russia back from war for the next few years, and to influence her policy accordingly. Russia, who would like to recover her old prestige in international politics soon, finds her impotence very painful, and does not find either her dependence on French capital or the French government's influence particularly edifying. Hence, the Franco-Russian Entente, from the Russian point of view, is not completely trouble-free. For us it is no longer appropriate to seek Russia's friendship as we used to. Instead of that, it is desirable to keep on a good footing with Turkey and to develop and strengthen such an entente. Without any doubt, with the cultural development of Japan, and the upturn that China is now experiencing, the *Yellow Peril* will be a problem for Europe before long. If *Russia* can fend off this threat and protect Europe from it, as is her duty thanks to her geographical position vis-à-vis China, then Tsarist Russia would recover its old position in world politics at a stroke. In order to give Russia the time and the opportunity to develop her armed forces to implement such a policy, it will be necessary to keep Russia's hereditary foes — the Mohammedans — from disturbing her recovery. Such a policy, led by Germany and taking account of Russia's interests, directs us towards maintaining *the friendship of Turkey*. But we also have need of this friendship if Russia should fail to ward off the Yellow Peril, and if the task then falls to us of warding it off ourselves. For if in such a contest we had the Turks as our enemies, on the side of the yellow races, the struggle would be immeasurably more difficult for us than if we were on a good footing with the Mohammedans, if possible in alliance with them. Finally, one must bear in mind that present developments in the Balkans might, if Russia recovers her powerful position, [drive] *Panslavism* to turn against an Austria that is steadily advancing in the Balkan peninsula. — Also the Czechs in Bohemia are promoting Panslav ideas. In such an event, i.e. if Russia turns against the Austrian Empire, we are obliged to intervene to help Austria. Then it would be desirable to have Turkey too among Russia's opponents, and for this reason too, we must retain her friendship. I think that within 5 years there will be a conflict between Russia, and either Austria, or the Balkan states (the latter if the centre of gravity of Slavdom should shift to the Balkans, to Russia's disadvantage). If the conflict remains confined to Russia and the Balkan states, then we have no reason to interfere. But the moment France threatens to help Russia to Austria's disadvantage, and does not immediately stop if I give my word of honour as Emperor to refrain from all military action in return for French neutrality — I will send a 24-hour ultimatum to France (secret) — and order the mobilisation of the whole German army against France. In this case, too, *friendship with Turkey* would be useful. It would bring our allies — the Austrians — an immediate addition of strength, and would be advantageous to us too in so far as we could move against Russia with fewer forces and should be able to put up a bigger force against France.'[104] In the Balkan wars of 1912–13 and again in June and July 1914, such breathtaking trains of thought played a not inconsiderable role.

'WELL THEN, LET HIM GET IN THERE!' A BLANK CHEQUE FOR WAR AGAINST SERBIA

In Wilhelm's case, this alarming vision of the future was combined, since the murder of King Alexander and Queen Draga in 1903, with a deep, indiscriminate hatred of the Serbs. At the height of the annexation crisis, Holstein, now gravely ill, pointed to the disturbing fact 'that the Kaiser, with whom the personal aspect always predominates, is violently prejudiced against the Serbs as regicides'.[105] The stubborn refusal of the Serbs to recognise the annexation of Bosnia and the

Herzegovina further deepened Wilhelm's aversion towards them. When in March 1909 the Serbian Prime Minister asked for consideration for Serbia's dignity and national feeling, Wilhelm minuted: 'there's no such thing!'[106] This execrative national arrogance, too, was to play a fatal role in July 1914.

In mid March 1909 Aehrenthal brought matters to a head by threatening to publish documents to prove that at Buchlau Isvolsky had indeed consented to Austria's annexation plans. Wilhelm welcomed Aehrenthal's humiliation of Russia, which had become necessary 'because for 6 months Austria has had troops mobilised on the frontier because the Serbs absolutely refused to show their colours. That has cost 200 mill[ions] so far and just cannot go on! It must come to a conclusion, which Isvolsky is dragging out!'[107] Two days after Aehrenthal's move Germany's military plenipotentiary in Russia, Paul von Hintze, reported on a secret meeting of the Duma in which Guchkov, the leader of the nationalist Octobrist party, had stated without contradiction that the Russian army was 'not ready for war'.[108] The previous day Isvolsky had described the foreign situation to the party leaders in similar terms and had demanded an enormous increase in military expenditure. Wilhelm noted: 'in 3 or 5 years the Dardanelles will be taken by arms'.[109]

Hintze's report led the Kaiser to encourage the Austrians to attack Serbia. With the words 'I shall stick to it!', he again promised the Dual Monarchy his military support.[110] Szögyény reported that the Kaiser had, with Bülow's consent, emphasised 'that Germany, just as she has so far fully supported our efforts to keep the peace, will also stand wholeheartedly at our side in the event of war'.[111] Diplomatic reports from Belgrade or St Petersburg that talked of a readiness to seek agreement were spattered with Wilhelm's aggressive marginalia: 'Disarmament etc, no question of it! Absolute rubbish! Isvolsky's diktat' or 'Dreadfully lame excuse! like Butler with Piccolomini! You have sharpened the arrow etc!'[112] Isvolsky had 'driven the Serbs into this' and obviously wanted to 'put a brake' on Austria!'[113] Despite clear signs of a Russian retreat – on 17 March Pourtalès telegraphed that Isvolsky had assured the Austrian ambassador that 'if it comes to an Austro-Serbian war, Russia will in no event depart from her neutrality'[114] – Wilhelm continued to urge an Austrian attack on Serbia. 'Now that at last is a clear statement!' he crowed. 'So forward and invade!'[115] A few days later came the Berlin government's quasi-ultimative demands that forced Russia to give way.

On 21 March 1909 Bülow instructed Pourtalès to inform Isvolsky that the German government was prepared to propose to Austria that she ask the signatories of the Treaty of Berlin to agree to the nullification of Article 25 of the treaty regarding Bosnia and the Herzegovina. At the same time the Wilhelmstrasse gave the Russian government clearly to understand that if Russia did not agree to the annexation of Bosnia and the Herzegovina, the German government would give Austria a green light to attack Serbia. The Russians knew all too well that if they then came to the assistance of Serbia and the German army intervened, Russia would be no match for them.[116]

This 'ultimatum' Pourtalès delivered on 22 March. On his telegraphic report that Isvolsky had said that before giving a definitive answer he would have to consult the Tsar and the council of ministers,[117] the Kaiser scornfully minuted 'Coward!'[118] On the same day Nicholas II appealed to Wilhelm to prevent the impending Austrian invasion of Serbia, warning that in view of the anger prevailing in Russia, it would hardly be possible to localise an Austro-Serbian war; but even if that were possible, a war in the Balkans would inaugurate an era of great alarm and nervousness in Europe. It would 'put an end to every possibility of a good understanding in the future between Austria and Russia', while 'any final estrangement between Russia and Austria is sure to affect also our relations with Germany'.[119] Two days later Isvolsky gave way and announced that Russia would recognise the annexation if Austria and the other signatories of the Treaty of Berlin should ask for it.[120]

To the astonishment of Wilhelm and the German diplomats the British and French governments, angered by what they considered to be Isvolsky's abject surrender to German pressure, did not associate themselves with Russia's action but demanded guarantees of a peaceful settlement of the new order in the Balkans.[121] As ever, the Kaiser rejected any idea of a conference with acerbity: 'Heavens!!! The British want to smuggle a whole lot of other questions into the conference, to make it a sort of Algeciras II. Possibly thereby also to burden the continental Powers with the task of defending the Dardanelles and denying them to Russia.'[122] 'Here London has for the first time got into direct opposition to Petersburg, unless the coup has been secretly agreed with Isvolsky, to make it easier (apparently) for him to agree.'[123] When Count Metternich reported from London that the British, French and Italian governments would continue to refuse to recognise the annexation, Wilhelm minuted bitterly: 'Well, that is what all our courtesy towards Paris has brought us! An unreliable pack, totally under *London's* influence!'[124] 'The two hounds [Great Britain and France] are hunting the hare à deux!'[125] '!! Lying seems to have been elevated into a principle in London', he complained, adding: 'Italy is leaving us in the lurch after all.'[126] When Aehrenthal hinted that, despite all mediation efforts of the western Powers, a war with Serbia would still suit him, Wilhelm minuted impatiently, 'Well then, let him get in there!'[127]

`A WONDERFUL TRIAL-RUN FOR THE SHOWDOWN'

With the retreat of Russia and Serbia the Austro-German bloc had won a prestige victory with which the Kaiser could now be well content.[128] On 9 April 1909 he boasted in a letter to Archduke Franz Ferdinand: 'Those were very interesting months that we now have behind us, and their result, even it didn't bring a solution by the bayonet, is to be highly valued all the same. It was a real pleasure to me to be a good second to you for once, and by holding unflinchingly to our alliance, to demonstrate to the world that if the two empires stand together Europe simply has to listen to them. And the secret of this bloc is the granite foundation of the two allied armies! The two best armies in the world arm in arm and determined not to stand any nonsense, and to get obedience and respect for their countries, that is a fact which all other diplomats and states *must* come to terms with, whether they like it or not. As Pappenheim's cuirassier says in Wallensteins Lager: "Why can we laugh at them? Because there are so many of us." And may things stay that way! Then Europe will also hold its peace! In these weeks the advantages of the alliance have also been demonstrated to its two peoples, and I have been as gratified by the approval shown for our attitude by all races of your fatherland, just as much as I have, especially, been deeply moved by your unreserved emphasis on it. Certainly I can imagine that, from a purely military, technical point of view, *Conrad*, you yourself, and the whole army, must have hoped to go to war, and that for the ordinary lieutenant the outcome should have been different. On the other hand, however, you have been able to have a wonderful trial-run for the event of a showdown, and to test whether everything would work. And it succeeded brilliantly! Everybody – of whatever race – streamed to the colours, and the prompt and exact operation of the whole military mechanism was a great success for your General Staff, War Ministry, and the whole army. You have shown what you can do as allies and you are highly esteemed. So highly that the presumed foes didn't even attempt any counter-measures! Bravo: I congratulate you on it most warmly. It confirms what I once said to my officers: "If the Emperor of Austria mounts his horse, then all his peoples will follow him!" The [Young Czech] deputy Kramarz, who would like to see us Germans driven from the face of the earth, once said "The Austro-German alliance is a played-out old piano that has no more melodies in it." Excuse me, the gentleman was mistaken! Events have given the lie to him; the piano is still in good order and has 2 wonderful marches in reserve which never fail in their effect: the Radetzky and the Yorck Advance! Aehrenthal has done his job superbly and has displayed above all a fabulous patience, which has been highly appreciated everywhere; he has always kept us informed about everything in the most gracious and open way, so that it was a real pleasure to work with him, a great, true statesman, who has steered his country away from petty internal trivialities towards broader international points of view, an invaluable skill. May God keep him for you!'[129]

The Kaiser's militaristic Nibelung loyalty to the declining Habsburg Empire, which he displayed from the start of the annexation crisis in October 1908, did not bode well for the future. True, Germany's 'unflinching' loyalty to her ally had compelled Russia, still militarily weak after the war with Japan, to retreat, but the readiness of Wilhelm and his generals in March 1909 to go to war at Austria's side against Russia and if necessary France, cannot be doubted. The idea that Russia would have rearmed 'in 3 or 5 years' lodged itself in their minds and led Wilhelm too to consider whether Germany should not seize the initiative with a preventive strike to break up the ring that was growing ever tighter around the Reich. In top military circles, as with Wilhelm himself, there was unconcealed disappointment that the allegedly inevitable conflict had not already broken out.[130] The Chief of General Staff, von Moltke, made no secret of his conviction that he would have preferred it if Austria-Hungary had launched its well-prepared war against Serbia and Montenegro. He assured his Austrian counterpart Conrad von Hötzendorf that he too profoundly regretted 'that the opportunity has been allowed to pass unused, and will probably not come back so soon under such favourable circumstances. I am convinced that it would have proved possible to localise the war between Austria-Hungary and Serbia, and the Monarchy would have been so strengthened internally and externally by its victory as to gain a preponderance in the Balkans that would not be that easily shaken. Even if Russia had moved and a European war had resulted, the chances for Austria and Germany would have been better now than they would probably be in a few years. Still, Your Excellency, let us look confidently to the future. So long as Austria and Germany stand shoulder to shoulder, each ready to acknowledge the "tua res agitur" in the fate of the other, we shall be strong enough to break up any ring. On this central European bloc, a great many can break their teeth.'[131] To his niece Maria, Moltke admitted on 11 April 1909, 'it would not have taken much this spring for me to have been subjected to the test of fire, of whether I was fit for my post or not. For we were really close to it, everything was prepared and we were ready to strike . . . Now everything is calm again and if the cousins across the Channel don't go quite mad, which they seem to be on the way to doing, we shall probably have 3–4 years of quiet. The conflict between Germandom and Slavdom — because that is fundamentally what Austria's Balkan action is about — will come nevertheless, it is only postponed because the biting [dogs] that bark all around us are afraid of the German whip.' No doubt with the Kaiser's 'bad nerves' in mind, Moltke added: 'the calm steadiness of our foreign policy during the whole period of tension was a joy to my heart. May we remain so, calm and collected, with hand on sword, not provoking, not boasting, ready for action but sparing with words, looking the future firmly in the eye, true to our pledged word, relying on God, and trusting in ourselves.'[132] The new head of the Military Cabinet, General Moriz Freiherr von Lyncker, had also reckoned Germany's chances as 'favourable, both against France and against Russia' if it had come to war, and had indeed thought it 'desirable to bring about a war at the present moment, in order to get out of our internal and external difficulties'. But when Count Zedlitz remarked 'that the Kaiser's nerves were bad and we had very much to take account of his difficult personality', Lyncker conceded: 'I agree with you, Moltke is not afraid of the French or the Russians, but he is very afraid of the Kaiser.'[133]

The German prestige success in the Bosnian annexation crisis proved very soon to have been a Pyrrhic victory, however. 'We succeeded all along the line', Zedlitz wrote on 9 April 1909, 'of course with the heaviest artillery, as we were in fact prepared to strike. How we shall fend off the hatred that this diplomatic success has earned for us, is a cura posterior. But it all amounts to this: "How badly our policy turned out in the past 20 years whenever His Majesty intervened, and how rapidly we were able to gain a diplomatic success when these interventions did not occur".'[134] The disadvantageous consequences of the 'success' were not long in coming. The Triple Entente, a rather loose arrangement hitherto, became firmer. On the other hand Italy, who received no compensation for Austria-Hungary's territorial gain, drew further away from her partners in the Triple Alliance.[135] The enmity between Germany and Russia and Austria-Hungary and Serbia, was exacerbated. Russia's ruling circles saw her retreat as deeply humiliating.[136]

With flattering private letters to the Tsar Wilhelm II did what he could to make good the damage caused by Germany's 'ultimatum' in St Petersburg. On 3 April he praised Nicholas II for his retreat of 22 March: 'It is thanks to your high-minded and unselfish initiative that Europe has been spared the horrors of a universal war, and that the Holy Week will remain unsullied by human blood, which would have been spilt.'[137] He developed this theme in a letter which Hintze took to the Tsar in person: 'A few weeks ago when affairs threatened to become dangerous, your wise and courageous decision secured peace for all the nations. I was most gratified that through my helping co-operation you were able to fulfil your task ... If you and I join in loyal co-operation for the maintenance of Peace – which is my most fervent wish – I am thoroughly convinced that Peace will not only be maintained but will not even be troubled. There is not a shadow of doubt, that peace guarantees the vital interests, the security of our peoples, as well as of our dynasties.'[138] But these threadbare efforts did no good. On 29 May 1909 Hintze reported: 'As is well known, Your Majesty's mediation proposal of March was initially interpreted at court here as meaning that Austria had decided to invade Serbia and that Germany was prepared to take all the consequences upon herself, including the possibility of war with Russia. The wording of the mediation offer reawakened terrible memories of the last communications of the Japanese minister in 1904. Russian public opinion [here Wilhelm minuted; 'the Gallo-English press'] then turned it into a German ultimatum.'[139]

Although Bülow was to claim after the world war in a letter to Tirpitz that the Bosnian crisis had by no means led to a deterioration of Russo-German relations,[140] in reality those relations were seriously and lastingly damaged. For ruling circles in Russia the Bosnian crisis and above all the German démarche of 21 March that was perceived as an ultimatum was a traumatic experience.[141] The British ambassador in St Petersburg reported at the end of March that Russia had never before undergone such humiliation and been forced to submit to the dictation of a foreign Power.[142] Nicholas II wrote to his mother, the sister of Queen Alexandra in London: 'Germany's behaviour towards us has been brutal, and we shall not forget it.'[143] Fearful of not being able to cope in future confrontations with the Austro-German bloc, Russia now made extraordinary efforts in the field of armaments.[144] When in July 1914 a crisis arose similar to that of 1908–9, Russia was militarily stronger and did not retreat, and the confrontation ended in catastrophe.

CHAPTER TWENTY-SEVEN

The 'pantomime': from Bülow to Bethmann Hollweg

Bülow's relationship with Kaiser Wilhelm in the last months of his Chancellorship was harmonious enough outwardly, and his eventual departure on 24 July 1909 seemed to take place in an atmosphere of mutual agreement. Immediately after his resignation Bülow tried to counter rumours emanating from pro-Kaiser loyalist circles, the so-called *Kaisertreuen*, that since the *Daily Telegraph* crisis he had 'no longer enjoyed H.M.'s confidence, except "officially"', and had been unable to win it back again'. In reality, he insisted in a long letter of self-justification to his successor Theobald von Bethmann Hollweg on 28 September 1909, the relationship of trust between the Kaiser and himself had been completely restored by the spring of 1909 at the latest. 'H.M. twice refused to accept my resignation and each time he emphasised his confidence in me. After the detailed discussion I had with Him *in March* [1909] He assured me most graciously and warmly that I had His full and unshakeable confidence. He frequently invited himself to meals with me, visited me, invited me to Potsdam and treated me in the most gracious and friendly manner whenever we met in Berlin, Potsdam, Wiesbaden etc. When he said goodbye to my wife and me he invited us to come to Potsdam for H.M. the Kaiserin's birthday. On many occasions (on my birthday, on 3 May, before His visit to the Tsar and again after the rejection of the inheritance tax) he telegraphed to me warmly and in a way which left me in no doubt that he wished me to remain in office. In Kiel, when I tendered my resignation, he talked over the whole situation at home and abroad, as well as the choice of my successor, in a friendly and trusting manner. It was only after a long discussion at Kiel that I managed to convince H.M. that after the rejection of the inheritance tax I could not remain Reich Chancellor, in view of the course I had adopted in domestic policy since the last elections. How does it make

H.M. look, if that was *all a pantomime*! But I am convinced that it was not a pantomime and that H.M. did not want to part with me. Just as I for my part would not have resigned if the outcome of the Reich financial reform had not compelled me to do so.' But Bülow's 'pro-Kaiser' opponents were claiming that the opposite was true, and in order to defend his honour against this 'despicable slander' he threatened to take legal action, a plan which could not have been more damaging to the monarchy. He had after all been 'a Minister for 12 years and Reich Chancellor for 9, in difficult circumstances and not without success'. Where would it lead, he asked, 'if this campaign of slander continues and it comes to legal proceedings, and if alleged remarks by His Majesty are set against statements made by me under oath? It would be one of the sorriest episodes in German history, and one which I would wish to spare the country.'[1] No such suicidal court case ensued, of course; had it done so, as Bülow made clear, not only the *Daily Telegraph* interview and the Bosnian crisis would have come under scrutiny, but also the Kaiser's letter to Lord Tweedmouth, his protest against the appointment of the American ambassador David J. Hill, the Swinemünde telegram to the Prince Regent of Bavaria, the telegram to the Prince of Lippe, the 'Hun' speech in the summer of 1900 and the 'prophets of doom' speech of September 1906. The outcome of such a trial, however, would by no means have been to Bülow's advantage, for Wilhelm's own letters and his remarks to trusted members of his entourage prove beyond doubt how deeply rooted his hatred of Bülow was, indeed how obsessed he was with the delusion that under Bülow Germany had been manipulated by a Europe-wide Jewish conspiracy. It was not the defeat of the inheritance tax Bill in the Reichstag that brought the Chancellor down – that merely gave the Kaiser a pretext to rid himself of the 'traitor to the Crown'. Since November 1908 his relationship with Bülow had indeed been *'nothing but a pantomime'*.

THE KAISER AND THE `KAISERTREUEN' AFTER BÜLOW'S `TREACHERY TO THE CROWN'

Only a few days after the Kaiser's nervous breakdown in November 1908 the always well-informed Zedlitz reported to his father that in his own mind the monarch had 'worked out an account of events according to which he can be seen as the greatest martyr of his time. Although he is keeping Bülow on for the time being, he still bears him a strong grudge.'[2] Shortly afterwards the Austrian ambassador, Szögyény, reported that Wilhelm had complained bitterly 'that Prince Bülow had tried to excuse his own misdemeanours at the expense of his imperial master – and had not even attempted to defend him – Kaiser Wilhelm – against brutal and completely unjustified attacks. It was purely as a result of this that it had become possible for public opinion to put the blame for all the major and minor mistakes that had actually been made in Germany's domestic and foreign policy onto His, Kaiser Wilhelm's, personal rule.'[3]

After the *Daily Telegraph* affair a faction of loyalists — the Kaisertreuen — formed around Wilhelm and actively encouraged his hostility towards Bülow.[4] As early as on 6 December 1908 the journalist Eugen Zimmermann reported to the Chancellor that 'certain circles' (he did not yet name names) were working against him. Also involved were 'inactive ministers with far-reaching connections, magnates etc.' This group, to which Prince Fürstenberg, the historian Theodor Schiemann and the journalist Adolf Stein belonged, claimed that during the *Daily Telegraph* crisis Bülow had 'systematically hoodwinked' the Kaiser. It was *he* who had had the interview published because he 'wanted to gain a hold' over the Kaiser; there was open talk of Bülow's 'taking over the reins'.[5] Under the demagogic influence of the loyalists a curious 'reinterpretation' took place, as Huber has commented: 'The pro-Kaiser campaign transformed the "smooth courtier" Bülow into an unscrupulous intriguer who, in order to safeguard his own position of power, had put the reputation of the Kaiser, the prestige of the monarchy and the safety of the Reich at stake.'[6]

Wilhelm, spurred on by the loyalists and by a disturbing sense of deep injury, developed pathological conspiracy theories and plotted revenge on his own 'incredibly cowardly' government, the 'disgraceful and monstrously vile' Reichstag, the 'lying' press and 'Europ: Pan-Jewry', which had 'completely pulled the wool over the eyes of the poor, utterly deceived German people'.[7] He wrote to Mary Montagu, who had expressed her sympathy with him, on 21 November 1908 saying: 'It is true that heavy trials are the best means of showing where ones friends are & what & how they feel for you: that is most comforting & reassuring. From all parts & classes in England letters like yours have poured in upon me full of sympathy & kindness during the time at home I was for weeks assailed by a thoughtless rabble calling itself a parliament & following a base & ruthless press in the last stage of hysterics. I shall not speak a word of defence & quietly bear up with all this; I look upon this as sent by Providence as a trial, which must be borne with a bowed head & lips closed. But shall never forget, how my People treated me after 20 years hard work for them which raised them to the position they now hold! And all that without giving so much as a hearing.'[8]

To his entourage Wilhelm gave the impression of a trapped, wounded animal which might resort to an act of extreme violence.[9] As his correspondence shows, at this time he drew particularly close to Max Egon II, Prince zu Fürstenberg, and his wife Irma, born Countess Schönborn-Buchheim.[10] The Kaiser's letters to these 'semi-foreigners' reveal better than any other source how he really felt after Bülow's 'treachery'. The tone of the replies from the Prince and Princess surpassed even the gushing extravagance of those which Wilhelm had once received from Philipp Eulenburg, and had a visibly heartening effect on him.[11] So it was his intimate friend Max who was 'the first and only one' whom Kaiser Wilhelm let into 'the secret of that terrible hour' after his confrontation with the Reich Chancellor on 17 November 1908.[12]

After Wilhelm II's nervous breakdown on 23 November 1908 Fürstenberg beseeched the monarch not to lose heart completely: 'My heart aches to see that my dear Imperial Master feels unwell and *still*, and *again and again*, suffers from the consequences of this wretched business! I confess that I have always been terribly afraid that something of the kind would happen – but I beseech Your Majesty on my knees to fight against this dreadful state of depression with all the great, admirable strength of will which is certainly in Your Majesty's nature! In spite of everything that has, alas, happened, Your Majesty *must* and *need not* be too pessimistic about the future! Your Majesty's heroic decision to listen *calmly* to what the Chancellor had to say and to accept his proposals *calmly* – has opened the eyes of thousand upon thousand of Your Majesty's loyal subjects who had been *misled*, and awakened admiration within our German Fatherland and beyond!'[13]

While his Austrian friends heaped sympathy upon him, the Kaiser continued to cold-shoulder his Reich Chancellor.[14] Apart from attending the centenary celebrations of the municipal reforms introduced by Freiherr vom Stein in 1808 with Bülow on 21 November, when he ostentatiously read out his prepared speech, Wilhelm stayed in the Neues Palais at Potsdam, avoided all contact with the Chancellor and kept out of affairs of state as much as possible. Outwardly, he was at pains not to allow his feelings to become apparent. According to Bülow he had 'even become more considerate in many respects, rarely and reluctantly contradicted me and only got annoyed over the navy question, and even then only when I brought up this topic'.[15] In fact, however, Wilhelm's fury remained undiminished. His Christmas letter to Fürstenberg expressed contempt for the Chancellor. 'Here matters are much the same as always; but the situation is not without interest. As a result of my burying myself in the Neues Palais, Renvers [Bülow's doctor] recently sent Ilberg [the Kaiser's personal physician] to me. The latter explained, on the former's instructions, that the "*poor*" Chancellor was so dejected and miserable that he was worried about him. The reason, he said, was that he "*felt*" the fact that he could no longer see me and discuss matters with us. I retorted that the Chancellor needed only to request an audience and he would be sent for. What was more, it was in fact his own doing, for he had of course *recommended* that I keep aloof; if *he* was suffering from it, then that was his affair and not mine, for it suited me very well.'[16]

In his self-imposed isolation Wilhelm deluded himself that he had been the innocent victim of a treacherous conspiracy in which Bülow, Holstein and Harden had pulled the strings. The German people had been 'misled' and in fact still supported him, their Kaiser. On 1 December 1908 he thanked Fürstenberg for his 'kind, loyal letter'. 'My wife is looking after me in the most touching and self-sacrificing way', he reported. 'We are doing a lot of reading together, for she reads to me while I sketch, or study battle plans and correct the manoeuvres. I am not yet allowed to attend to business and cannot yet hold audiences; nor do I read newspapers, so that I know nothing about anything. Except that yesterday I read in Sunday's "Graphic" from *London* that now, as the Kaiser is keeping his distance, the Chancellor has become All-powerful. But that, they say, is the worst of all worlds! They prefer an indiscreet absolutist Kaiser to a Chancellor who governs the Reich with the help of his two *"thugs"*, *Holstein* and *Harden*! So foreigners have picked up the same trail that in this country was only suspected by insiders! . . . I am firmly convinced that God will help me through this and that the *people* will come to their senses, but will the politicians and the Press?? Dear old [August] Eulenburg, in his fury, has lambasted the Conservatives and run them down so much that they are ashamed and creep around like curs after a whipping! . . . I hope Germany will not be dragged down into the dirt too much by Holstein and Harden. That the latter is still alive after what he has done to me is strange! What a shame not a single sub-lieutenant, not a single court lackey has had the nerve to rid us of this pestilence!'[17]

In the following days and weeks Wilhelm's interpretation of the events of November as a malicious conspiracy directed against him by Bülow, Holstein and Harden became even more firmly fixed in his mind, not least as a result of irresponsible gossip conveyed by Schiemann. At Christmas 1908 he wrote a long letter to Fürstenberg which bears eloquent witness to this dubious idea. Full of self-pity, he complained: 'I have really been under a great deal of strain! In 1907 Kuno Moltke and Hohenau, and throughout the year the Eulenburg affair which went on into the spring of 1908. Then in 1908 the events we know well! It really has been a bit too much for a sensitive disposition! This new campaign against me has made me prick up my ears, however, and other men who are loyal to me likewise. Enquiries and investigations have now been made by the latter. So far the results have been as follows. Holstein has a firm agreement with Harden; they hunt as a pair. Holstein has fully recovered his old influence over Bülow and is the irresponsible controller of our policy, as he was over the Moroccan question. To show how far it goes, recently, after one of Bülow's latest Reichstag speeches, for which he was praised in the European press, Holstein sent the Chancellor [a copy of it] with annotations and also wrote him a critical letter in which he pointed out all the mistakes in the speech and then gave him a strong dressing-down for it.[18] A charming state of affairs! ... This Holstein has a lady friend, Frau v. Lebbin. Her salon is the mustering-place for the Press scoundrels or their instigators, who gather there to receive their instructions for the campaigns that are to be conducted. The Vice President of the Reichstag, the *National*!!! Liberal [Hermann] Paasche, is also in touch with Harden. His son married Harden's daughter not long ago. Paasche supplies the Nat. Lib. Press with poison, above all the Hanover newspapers, hence the angry outbursts from there, which I could not understand. Herr Witting − Harden's brother, whom I personally honoured and decorated as Mayor of Posen − also works with Paasche ... It is this choice circle which − the impulsive unconstitutional Kaiser having been excluded − runs the German Reich indirectly through Bülow, under Holstein's direction. Where that will lead the devil only knows; I do not care, nothing can be done about it. Of course neither the Chancellor nor his gang suspects that I know about it, so do not give it away. My supporters want to get hold of incontrovertible *documentary* evidence first. Only then can we discuss striking a blow ... The future is uncertain and requires calm, clarity, determination and real men, not scheming womenfolk or the same in men's clothes! My time will come, and then they will have to come running to me again, when trouble and danger threaten!'[19]

As ever, Fürstenberg backed up his imperial friend in his deluded belief that he was the victim of a diabolical plot. He gave him hope that he would recover his self-confidence and all his former power. 'It would be *a triumph* precisely for these opponents if they managed to rob Your Majesty of all confidence in your subjects and thus of all pleasure in your work! That is of course the whole point of unleashing the press hounds! They want to sound the death halloo over Your Majesty, so that Your Majesty "gives up the ghost", and *then* the field would be open for the others − no, no, a thousand times no! That must not and *shall* not happen! There will be, there *must* be, a great national awakening; the countless right-thinking people who for a thousand reasons ... have been unable to resist the pressure of the clamouring critics and agitators − they will all suddenly see the abyss towards which they are being steered, and the scales will fall from their eyes! As we have so often seen in history, they will recognise the so-called benefactors of the people for what they are, turn their backs on them and return penitently to their Kaiser and King! They will sense how much pain they have caused their Sovereign in their blindness and then Your Majesty's time will come again! ... I hold firmly to the belief that the people *are* good − those who incite and provoke them are the only bad ones!' With a childish naivety that bordered on irresponsibility Fürstenberg added: 'I have just been at the distribution of Christmas presents, where we said a heartfelt and loyal prayer to the Christ child ... asking Him to bless our most beloved, dear Kaiser with the most beautiful and glorious gifts that our dear Lord can bestow: peace in His heart and renewed trust in and love for His people! – The Christ child will hear our prayer! I am convinced of it!'[20]

Another consequence of Wilhelm's conviction that his intentions had been particularly well understood by the Austrians (and the English) while his own statesmen, parliamentarians and journalists had betrayed him shamefully, was that he sought solace in his friendship with the heir to the Austro-Hungarian throne, Franz Ferdinand. He poured out his heart – and this at the height of the Bosnian annexation crisis – to his 'dear Franzi' in a woebegone letter of 16 December 1908: 'You are mostly *au courant* with what has happened and can therefore judge what an effort it has been for me to behave as if everything were in order and to continue working with the people whose neglect of their duty and moral cowardice deprived me of the protection which in any other country would be afforded to its head of state as a matter of course. It is particularly comforting for me to have received so many proofs of sympathy from Austria; strangely, the same is true of the countless letters which I am receiving, mostly from people I do not know, from all levels and classes of the people and society in England. They unanimously and very strongly condemn the loutishness of the German Press, the disgraceful and monstrously vile conduct of the German Reichstag and likewise the incredible cowardice of the government officials who shamefully *failed to stand up for* their Sovereign. This last is the feeling of which the poor German people are only beginning to be aware, for they have had the wool pulled over their eyes completely and have been utterly deceived by the lying press of Europ[ean] Pan-Jewry, but are now gradually emerging from under the spell of the Jewish Press charade. They are taking stock and beginning to notice what has been done to them and how they have been misled. There are more and more signs of a growing realisation that I have been outrageously and shamefully wronged. Meanwhile I have put some clever bloodhounds on the trail of the Press "swine" and have already achieved quite nice results. As I expected, a whole consortium of first-rate scoundrels from all classes and professions has been revealed. They don't yet suspect anything, these fellows!'[21]

It is plain that this highly contrived interpretation of the *Daily Telegraph* affair blocked any insight the Kaiser might have had into his own responsibility and thus made any amendment of his own behaviour seem superfluous. Of course there were wiser heads at the imperial court who saw clearly that the disaster of November 1908 was the almost inevitable result of the system of Personal Monarchy exercised under Bülow for over ten years. Zedlitz rightly took the view that in the crisis 'a lengthy process of fermentation led to a serious eruption, and that where the people were concerned, the fear of being plunged into an adventure with unforeseeable consequences also played a part'.[22] In December 1908 the veteran Oberstallmeister (Senior Master of the Horse), Hugo Freiherr von Reischach, a Württemberger, wrote to his Badenese colleague Freiherr von Holzing-Berstett, whom the Kaiser had just appointed as his Flügeladjutant, that it was his belief 'that the Chancellor should stand in front of the Kaiser and not behind him. I would have covered for him and then resigned because this mistake took place within my area of responsibility.' Reischach also saw clearly that the *Daily Telegraph* affair was a systemic crisis arising from the style of government practised by Wilhelm II and Bülow. He hit the nail on the head in asserting that Bülow ought to have resigned also because as 'the leading statesman [he] has never in the last 10 years had the manly courage to tell His Majesty seriously and categorically that he must restrain himself more. When one speaks to His Majesty alone one can, with all the deference due to the monarch, say everything to him that concerns one's area of responsibility, and the Chancellor has seen him alone God knows often enough in ten years. But if one never says anything oneself, if one does everything to surround the monarch with soft, weak and insignificant men like Jenisch, Schoen etc., one should not be surprised if everything falls apart. But then one certainly does not also have the right to use a case of this kind to strengthen one's own position. Bülow is a diligent, immensely cultivated, very clever, very well-read human being, I would say the most highly civilised human being of the current century, but he is not a statesman, nor a productive person, nor a man, and it is men who make history, not people who merely manoeuvre.'[23] By assigning the principal responsibility for the catastrophe to Bülow and not to the monarch, however, Reischach underestimated the Kaiser's 'will to power' which underlay the system of Personal Monarchy. Nor was it long before the Kaiser unleashed a new storm of indignation and with it a new crisis of confidence between him and the Chancellor.

'ONE IS GRADUALLY TURNING INTO A CONVINCED ANTI-SEMITE'

At the reception for the commanding generals at the Berlin Schloss on 2 January 1909 Wilhelm II read out the article by the former Chief of General Staff, Count Alfred von Schlieffen, which has already been mentioned.[24] It had just been published anonymously in the *Deutsche Revue* under the title

'Der Krieg in der Gegenwart' ('War in the Present Day') and it drew an extremely pessimistic picture of the military position of the German Reich and of Austria-Hungary. These two Powers, according to Schlieffen, stood 'unprotected in the middle . . . surrounded on all sides by the other Powers behind ramparts and trenches . . . At the given moment the gates will be opened, the drawbridges lowered and armies of millions will pour over the Vosges, the Maas, the Königsau, the Niemen, the Bug and even the Isonzo and the Tyrolese Alps in a devastating and destructive torrent. The danger is enormous.'[25] As he read out the essay to his audience of forty generals the Kaiser made it quite plain that the views expressed in it matched his own. Holstein was stunned by this fresh indiscretion and advised Bülow to hand in his resignation immediately. 'The Schlieffen article and its adoption by the Kaiser is a very pointed reversion to the practices of the past', he wrote; 'one could even call it a mockery of constitutional forces. In its way clever. The Kaiser can always appeal to the "indiscretion" (which was of course part of the plan). In fact, it could not be more harmful. Fearful, as at the time of Algeciras, discouraging for Austria (that is the worst of it), and encouraging for the encirclement Powers. We again have two types of foreign policy: the policy of the bureaux that is for firmness, and the Kaiser's policy that considers firmness to be dangerous.' Holstein added: 'If I were Chancellor, I would tomorrow calmly hand in my resignation and say to myself: "Either it is accepted, and then I go out in triumph; or − 5 to 1 − it is not accepted, and then the Kaiser will have to behave and I will with one stroke have achieved the authoritative position in history that a Chancellor must possess in the interests of the Reich, *especially now*".'[26]

Although Bülow, too, considered the Schlieffen article harmful − he heard from his brother in Vienna that there was much head-shaking over it there; 'our friends are precisely the ones who least understand such a lukewarm attitude'[27] − he did not hand in his resignation. To Holstein he replied: 'I must prevent that unbelievably foolish (or perfidious) article from having too discouraging an effect on Austria; but I must also avoid offending the feelings of the army and the acute military sensibilities of the majority of the nation.'[28] As for the Kaiser, the Reich Chancellor contented himself with a mild reprimand.[29] In fact, the 'traitor' Bülow's words of warning made very little impression on Wilhelm compared with the letter he received from his friend in Donaueschingen, which brimmed over with sympathy and righteous indignation, stoking the Kaiser's anger. 'It is outrageous the way the Press is behaving yet again!' Fürstenberg wrote on 9 January 1909. 'One positively fumes with rage that this gang dares to stir up public opinion again when it had only just calmed down a little, and to launch yet another dishonourable, infamous Press campaign! How dare these people turn a perfectly unexceptionable event, which the consultation and Your Majesty's reception on 2 January certainly were, into a subject for their impertinent comments!? It is nothing but a continuation of the events of December or November! There is *something fishy going on* – even a blind man could see it and would think that it was done to order, or at least *tolerated*! These senseless fools are attacking the most sacred thing they have, they are undermining the authority, the position and the inviolable right of their Kaiser to speak to the army exactly as the All-Highest War Lord thinks fit! ... It cannot, it must not go on! That these infamous newspaper writers have the audacity to attack our dearly beloved Kaiser again and again, and that this is tolerated, must be condemned in the strongest possible language by every loyal subject of Your Majesty! It is astounding that there is no power in the state that will stop these goings-on and call a halt to this traitorous, perfidious, terrible campaign! One cannot but think that there is a system behind it, a carefully considered and devilishly executed plan which will inevitably have unforeseeable, dreadful consequences for our fatherland, for the Kaiser and for the Reich! I do not know whether I am right to say all this, but I cannot do otherwise! When one's heart is full the words overflow! I had to write like this because I know how much Your Majesty, my revered Lord, must be suffering again because of this unspeakable affair! ... But we are *unshakeably* convinced that hundreds of thousands of people think and feel this way and ardently yearn for Your Majesty to receive relief and reassurance!'[30] This tirade matched the Kaiser's thinking exactly. 'Quite agree with your views!' he telegraphed on 11 January. 'The Golden International has our Fatherland in its grip and plays ball with our holiest possessions through the press which it controls! One is gradually turning into a convinced anti-Semite. If the German *Volk* ever wakes from the torpor of the hypnosis induced by the Jewish press and becomes seeing, we could be in for a nice surprise!'[31]

This incident only strengthened Wilhelm's paranoid feeling that he was being spied on everywhere. He told his aides de camp and court officials that foreign journalists had repeatedly disguised themselves as footmen and photographers so as to listen to what he said at meals.[32] His bizarre conviction that his Reich was being secretly ruled by Harden, Holstein and the Jewish 'Golden International' persisted for several more months. When Sir Charles Hardinge accompanied King Edward VII and Queen Alexandra on their visit to Berlin in February 1909, he gained the impression at the imperial court that Bülow's position was in danger. The Kaiser and the entire imperial family deeply distrusted the Chancellor, not only because of his behaviour over the *Daily Telegraph* affair but also because of his close association with Holstein.[33]

After the Chancellor's audience on 2 February 1909 Admiral von Müller noted in his diary: 'H.M. and Reich Chancellor both in a very good mood.'[34] But the Kaiser frequently abandoned the pretence and reviled the Chancellor who, he contended, was operated by remote control by Holstein and Harden.[35] After a conversation with the Kaiser on 13 January 1909 Zedlitz noted that Wilhelm was 'in fact very angry' with Bülow and accused him, among other things, of having 'no idea ... how to pick the right people'; 'that is why we have so many failures' in foreign policy.[36] The Kaiser also spoke 'very disapprovingly' about a speech that Bülow made in the Prussian Chamber of Deputies on 19 January 1909.[37] On 13 February 1909 he rejected as 'incredible blindness!' an assertion by the Chancellor that during the *Daily Telegraph* crisis he had been unable, 'in the interests of Your Majesty, the Crown and the country, to act in any other way', given the prevailing situation and mood in Germany. Bülow's obsequious claim 'that in this case too, my conduct was determined purely and exclusively by loyalty to Your Majesty's House and sincere love for Your Majesty's All-Highest Person' earned a contemptuous comment from the Kaiser. 'Damned little of that was in evidence! Impertinence.'[38] He described Bülow to the War Minister, Karl von Einem, as a 'traitor to the Crown' and threatened him with a 'dishonourable discharge'.[39]

In February 1909 Wilhelm complained to his aunt Luise, Grand Duchess of Baden: 'One moves about in an atmosphere of dishonesty, mistrust, watchfulness and insincerity. One hides one's anxious thoughts and feelings for fear that they could be misinterpreted by people of ill will. Questioning, doubting faces everywhere, and sullen people performing their tasks half-heartedly. A very perceptible reaction against the events of last November has begun among the people and in public opinion. One feels duped into believing one has committed an act of enormous folly or blatant injustice.'[40] Soon after this he bewailed his situation in comments recorded by the Chief of the Civil Cabinet, Rudolf von Valentini. 'Unhappy man that I am, what sin have I committed that God should punish Me by making Me ruler of this nation! ... The Ministers make the most flagrant mistakes and then when things go wrong they creep behind the King! And that is called "constitutional rule"!' Alluding to Maximilian Harden, Wilhelm exclaimed: 'I am treated as an outlaw! I refuse to accept any longer that a Jew (Harden) should go around in my own country making money out of insulting me. He gets 2000 M[arks] from his impresario every evening that he gives his lecture "Against the Kaiser"! If there are no laws against such misconduct I shall take matters into my own hands.'[41]

At the heart of the Kaiser's conspiracy theory was his belief that Bülow had deliberately set him a trap with the *Daily Telegraph* interview so as to compromise him before all the world and thus seize power for himself. This interpretation of events is clearly expressed in a letter of 22 February 1909 written by Wilhelm to the diplomat Felix von Müller, who had been seconded to assist Bülow with day-to-day business in September to October 1908 during his stay in Norderney. In the letter the Kaiser complained bitterly: 'When I sent the manuscript of the so-called Daily Telegraph Interview to the Reich Chancellor last October, there was a covering letter with it from Freiherr von Jenisch, which contained among other things a deliberate order to the Chancellor not to let the document out of his sight, and above all not to allow it to go to the Foreign Office or to get into the hands of Foreign Office officials. In a later conversation in October H.S.H. [Bülow] told me of his own accord that he had read it and would read it through again once it had come back from the Foreign Office, and then send it to me. To my considerable astonishment, after the publication I was informed by him, and it was stated in all the newspapers, that he had not read the document at all and had not known its contents. The subsequent handling of the affair brought months of attacks of the vilest and rudest kind upon me, buried the Crown in a deep layer of filth, greatly harmed the Old Prussian Kingdom and the prestige of the German Imperial Crown, undermined our reputation abroad, brought boundless shame and disgrace on the House of Hohenzollern and unspeakable suffering and sorrow on myself and the Kaiserin. I said nothing. But now it is being increasingly recognised that a terrible wrong has been done to me; and as a result the feeling among the people and in society has begun to swing round powerfully in my favour. Above all, one encounters the view on all sides that the Chancellor lied to the entire German people, Parliament and Ministry when he claimed that he had not read the contents of the interview.' Wilhelm appealed to Müller's 'sense of honour as a cavalier and a gentleman, and to the fealty that you swore to me as a civil servant and that you owe me' to send him a 'detailed and truthful account of everything that happened in Norderney regarding this manuscript'.[42]

THE 'RECONCILIATION' OF 11 MARCH 1909

In the spring of 1909, as Bülow asserted in the self-serving letter to Bethmann Hollweg quoted above, some sort of reconciliation was nevertheless achieved between Kaiser and Chancellor. This was undoubtedly partly due to Bülow's uncompromising policy in the Bosnian crisis and his willingness to face a major war over it, which Wilhelm acclaimed as a resounding success.[43] When the two men met at the Berlin Schloss on 11 March 1909 the Chancellor announced that he felt he no longer enjoyed the Kaiser's confidence and therefore wished to resign. Wilhelm refused to accept his resignation: in the national interest, he declared, Bülow must first complete the reform of the Reich's finances. It is not clear from the sources what Wilhelm's real intentions were at this moment. Even members of his closest entourage were uncertain whether there had been a genuine reconciliation or whether their sovereign was still putting on an act.[44] Immediately following the two-and-a-half hour audience Wilhelm said to the Flügeladjutant in waiting, Hans von Gontard: 'I have finished with Bülow', and a little later he remarked to August Eulenburg: 'After the finance reform I shall appoint a new Chancellor.' Zedlitz, on the other hand, gained the impression that 'this time Bülow has won all along the line'.[45] This interpretation is supported by a note of 4 April 1909 written − with evident satisfaction − by Wilhelm to Irma Fürstenberg: 'Max will already have told you of the Chancellor's about-turn and peccavi, and his support for Aehrenthal has of course been very successful. He is taking a breather in Venice.'[46] This would indicate that the Kaiser believed his Chancellor had apologised for his conduct and promised to submit to the Kaiser's will in future. As we shall see, the monarch's restored self-confidence manifested itself particularly clearly wherever his prerogative as Supreme War Lord was involved.

On 13 April 1909 Wilhelm set off for Corfu and did not return to Berlin until 23 May.[47] As Fürstenberg also went on this journey there are no letters to him from the Kaiser at this crucial time, so that we are deprived of the intimate insights we might otherwise have had into Wilhelm's attitude towards Bülow. Nor do the surviving sources make the picture any clearer. The day after the Kaiser's departure Szögyény reported to Vienna that 'now that the reconciliation between him and his imperial master has been fully and finally achieved and the threatening storm clouds over the Balkans have taken on a more favourable outlook, [Bülow] has taken himself off to Venice in a cheerful holiday mood'.[48] There the Chancellor had another meeting with the Kaiser, but those who observed it came away with an ambiguous impression, especially as the Kaiser had also invited the German ambassador in Rome, Bülow's enemy Count Anton Monts, to meet him. On board the *Hohenzollern* Monts − whom Valentini described as 'a dubious character, but certainly very clever' − had 'very confidential conversations, also after Bülow had left', with the Kaiser.[49] In his *Denkwürdigkeiten* Bülow recounts that while in Venice he was told by 'a completely trustworthy gentleman in the All-Highest entourage' that the Kaiser had 'loudly and audibly' greeted Monts with the words 'Bülow has betrayed me! You must take his place.'[50] Whatever his intentions were, on 3 May the Kaiser, pointedly and in the friendliest of tones, congratulated Bülow on his birthday and declared emphatically that 'the present difficult state of internal political affairs will be overcome. At any rate I do not intend to allow parliamentary pressure to shake My confidence in you or to influence My decisions.'[51] But no sooner had Wilhelm arrived at the little palace of Achilleion on Corfu than the relationship between Kaiser and Chancellor suffered another setback.

THE SUPREME WAR LORD AND THE DETHRONEMENT
OF THE SULTAN

After the dreadful experiences of the previous winter the idyllic holiday of several weeks on Corfu, when the Kaiser busied himself enthusiastically with archaeological excavations, provided badly needed rest and recuperation.[52] The idyll was suddenly interrupted by the news that on 27 April 1909 Sultan Abdul Hamid II, who had already been declared incapacitated, had been deposed by a military revolt.[53] The Sultan's dethronement hit Wilhelm II hard, especially since it was so incomprehensible 'for us soldiers', as the Kaiser's Adjutant-General, Gustav von Kessel, put it, 'that the army had put itself at the disposal of the revolution under parliament, against its ruler'.[54] 'One could see why the Kaiser reacted to this event almost as if it had been a blow against himself', Valentini commented.[55] Through the Chief of the Military Cabinet, Moriz von Lyncker, Wilhelm ordered General Colmar von der Goltz, who was acting as military adviser in Constantinople, to send him a report on the upheavals in Turkey.[56] Within days this new Oriental crisis led to serious differences of opinion between Wilhelm and the Reich Chancellor, the Foreign Office, the Admiralty Staff and the Reich Navy Office.

Already on 17 April 1909 the Kaiser had refused to approve the dispatch of more warships to the eastern Mediterranean to protect German citizens, which the Wilhelmstrasse advocated. 'Not even another pinnace at this moment!' he wrote. 'There will be so many ships of the Mediterranean Powers there that calm will be maintained in the ports. I shall not send a single ship unless and until England *deploys ships* from her *home fleet!*'[57] When he was informed that not only Britain but also France, Austria and Russia would be sending ships and that two German cruisers were to be got ready and ordered to Piraeus for the time being, the Kaiser astounded Bülow by ordering him to demand money from the Reichstag to replace the two ships.[58] When Bülow attempted to dissuade him from this idea by pointing out the uproar that such a measure would cause, especially abroad, Wilhelm flew into a rage. 'My God, as soon as any simple routine measure is needed here at home, *abroad* always has to be brought up!' he scrawled on the Chancellor's telegram. 'It really is quite appalling.'[59] In the long telegram he sent in response, the Kaiser rejected

Bülow's proposals in an arrogant, know-all tone and behaved just as if he were the Supreme War Lord who need only say the word wherever naval matters were concerned.[60] It did not trouble him that such decisions were bound to have an effect on the German Reich's foreign policy. That Prince Bülow gradually lost the desire to serve as Reich Chancellor under such circumstances is not surprising.

THE REICH FINANCIAL REFORM AND THE FALL OF BÜLOW

During the 'reconciliation' audience on 11 March 1909 Wilhelm II had evoked the subject which would in the end prove Bülow's undoing: the Reich financial reform. On this issue there were no material differences between the Kaiser and the Chancellor. The growing expenses of the Reich, and not least the naval construction which was so close to the Kaiser's heart, meant that additional revenues of 500 million marks were needed for the 1909–10 annual budget. On 3 November 1908 the Reich government had therefore tabled draft bills for new taxes in the Reichstag. Four-fifths of the projected extra revenues were to be raised through indirect taxes (on beer, brandy, wine, tobacco, gas and electricity). The remaining fifth was to be obtained by raising the inheritance tax as a Reich tax and extending it to spouses and descendants.[61] The leading politicians of the German-Conservative party and the Agrarian League were determined to block the inheritance tax, which would have affected the big landowners most of all.[62] Torpedoing the financial reform, they thought, would also give them an opportunity to break up the 'bloc' with the Left Liberals established in 1907, and to bring down the 'traitor' Bülow himself. Another factor which caused the Conservatives to turn away from Bülow was his vague announcement that he intended to reform the reactionary Prussian three-class suffrage.[63] Wilhelm's hostility towards Bülow, of course, was no secret among the Conservatives. But in order to avoid any misunderstanding after the Kaiser's gestures of 'reconciliation' on 11 March 1909, the Crown Prince informed the Conservative member of parliament Elard von Oldenburg-Januschau that his father would in any case dismiss the Chancellor in the foreseeable future, whatever transpired with the Reich financial reform.[64]

The decision of the Conservative faction in the Reichstag to vote against the inheritance tax seemed incomprehensible to the Kaiser. As the Chief of the Civil Cabinet reported on 6 May 1909 from Corfu, Wilhelm was inclined 'to see the solution of the puzzle in the "defiance of the Junker"' against the Crown, a view which Valentini shared. 'There is a certain brutal dogmatism in the party's attitude which might easily ... lead them into a serious catastrophe. And it seems quite possible to me that *that* could put an end to their days of glory and power for ever, given the way in which the general mood of the people has developed. So they are playing for high stakes – perhaps without quite realising it.' At all events Wilhelm firmly envisaged the dissolution of the Reichstag as a last resort. 'There are clear signs that this thought holds no terrors for the All-Highest – quite the contrary', Valentini wrote to the head of the Reich Chancellery, Friedrich Wilhelm von Loebell. 'What the Kaiser absolutely and categorically rejects is the other eventuality – to part with the Chancellor as a result of parliamentary combinations of whatever kind. He will *never* accept the latter's resignation if offered in consequence of these problems. This thought was of course also fully expressed – by way of a preventive measure – in the congratulatory telegram of the 3rd of the month and Prince Bülow definitely must and can depend on it. Of the two so to speak constitutional courses – dissolution or change of Ministers – the Kaiser will agree to the former without hesitation if it is recommended to him; to the latter he will never agree.' When Valentini asked what would happen if the Reich financial reform came to nothing, the Kaiser had replied: 'Things will simply remain as they were before for another year. We shall add to our debts of however many billions by another half and carry on negotiating the financial reform on the basis which has been accepted as correct, or begin again from the beginning, until the Reichstag is worn down or only too ready to give in. All that is necessary is for us to *keep our nerve* and not to think that the world or at least the Reich will collapse if "not every blossom-laden dream bore fruit" ["nicht alle Blüthenträume reiften", a quotation from Goethe's *Prometheus*]. The Turks say "this too will pass" and we too must make this our watchword in our struggle which, in the broad context of things, is not so very surprising!'[65]

After his return from the Mediterranean the Kaiser received the Chancellor in audience at Wiesbaden on 18 May 1909. Bülow later summed up the impression he gained from this interview. 'He wished me to resign; he wanted to get rid of me. But he wanted to decide for himself when and under what circumstances I should go and what form my departure should take.'[66] Evidently Wilhelm was not contemplating a crisis in the near future, for on 30 May he invited Bülow to accompany him on his journey to meet Nicholas II and the whole imperial family in the Finnish archipelago, which had been arranged for 17–18 June 1909.[67] He was also proceeding on the assumption that the controversial Reich financial reform would eventually be accepted by the Reichstag.[68] Wilhelm took a personal interest in the formulation of the reform and, for instance, refused 'categorically to agree to an increase in the tax on coffee' on the grounds that 'he had no desire to risk losing the friendly relationship only recently established with Brazil for the sake of the Reichstag's squabbles over taxation!' As Valentini told Loebell, during the audience the Kaiser had also expressed the opinion that 'matches could carry a much higher tax, and for the rest some other solution must be found. He constantly comes back to the bachelor tax.'[69] Clearly the Kaiser was once again participating in the formulation of domestic policy, as in days of old.

On 24 June 1909 the inheritance tax was rejected by a narrow majority in the Reichstag consisting of members of the German-Conservative party, the Free Conservative Reich party, the Centre and the Polish party. Wilhelm initially stood by the solemn assurance he had given Valentini in Corfu that he was absolutely determined 'never' to part company with the Chancellor as a result of pressure from parliamentary combinations.[70] The day after the defeat he urged Bülow to fight the Reichstag, telegraphing to him: 'Vote was a farce! Four votes not a majority. Use the Press to get the country really going against the Reichstag, which is working against its interests, so that wavering members of parliament are persuaded to change their minds. Am ready if necessary, if the majority against the bill at third reading is again so small or even smaller, to impose the tax law outright. The country is on our side and ultimately only force is any use.'[71]

In response to a telegraphic request from Bülow the Kaiser summoned him to Kiel on 26 June 1909. The international Kiel Week was in full swing and the Supreme War Lord's delight at being in the midst of 'his' navy had once again induced a kind of intoxication. 'Faced with this overwhelming preoccupation with naval matters the Kaiser's interest in what was happening disappeared almost completely', Valentini commented bitingly.[72] The audience on board the *Hohenzollern*, at which Valentini was present as Chief of the Civil Cabinet, lasted from 9.30 a.m. until midday. Bülow tendered his resignation. The Kaiser accepted it but demanded that before he left office Bülow should get the Reich financial reform passed without the inheritance tax. The Chancellor made it clear that he considered the dissolution of the Reichstag to be an 'impossibility', for new elections would 'bring in 40 more Social Democrats'. He hoped 'nevertheless to bring about an acceptable financial reform without inheritance tax by mid-July'.[73] During this crucial meeting with the Reich Chancellor who had conducted the affairs of the Reich in accordance with his wishes for twelve years to the day, the Kaiser scarcely listened, but repeatedly looked at his watch, as he had been invited to lunch on board a French chocolate manufacturer's yacht.[74]

THE CHANCELLORSHIP MERRY-GO-ROUND IN KIEL

Scarcely any episode in the later stages of the Wilhelmine Reich shows as clearly how much power the Kaiser could still exercise, even after the *Daily Telegraph* crisis, and how much influence the 'irresponsible' men in his immediate entourage had retained, as the appointment of the fifth Reich Chancellor. At the same time the scandalously superficial manner in which this decision was taken provides a perfect illustration of the anachronistic farce of the 'Personal Rule' which had been at the centre of public criticism for years. Since 17 November 1908 Bülow's departure had in fact been a foregone conclusion, and yet until the last moment Wilhelm did not know whom he should appoint to the highest post in the Reich and in Prussia! While he waited impatiently for the settlement of the Chancellor crisis, which threatened to interfere with his Scandinavian cruise, the Kaiser sailed around in the Baltic for hours on end. On 9 July 1909 he complained in a telegram to Franz Ferdinand: 'I am lying around here waiting to see what happens as far as that damned Parliament is concerned, now that the Centre, the Poles and the Conservatives have given themselves the pleasure of suddenly bringing down Bülow! What a fine pack of scoundrels! I am afraid that my holidays will be sadly shortened by this dirty trick and that the search for a replacement is very difficult.'[75]

The Kaiserin, who had involved herself more in politics since the *Daily Telegraph* crisis, argued in favour of keeping Bülow. 'She gave too little weight to the strong desire for revenge that had taken hold of the Kaiser since the November affair', Valentini rightly recalled.[76] This vengeful feeling was increased by Schoen, the Foreign Secretary, and Theodor Schiemann, who made 'disparaging remarks' about Bülow. Schoen informed the Kaiser that the departing Chancellor had described the *Daily Telegraph* crisis to him as 'very useful, in fact', while Schiemann told the monarch that he 'could not stand the whole journalistic kettle of fish under Bülow any longer'. The Chief of the Naval Cabinet deplored the fact that 'everyone, including those who were probably brought to the fore by B[ülow], is now attacking him'; it was 'a sad spectacle'. Meanwhile on 6 July the Kaiser made bad-tempered comments to Müller about the 'difficulty of finding a new Reich Chancellor'.[77]

Since the crisis of November 1908 the names of several generals, ambassadors, courtiers and government officials had been traded as possible successors to Bülow. At first General Alfred von Loewenfeld, Wilhelm's Flügeladjutant, whom he had recently promoted to Adjutant-General, Commander of the Palace Guard and Commander of the Xth Army Corps, was spoken of as a candidate for the Chancellorship.[78] Shortly before Christmas Adjutant-General Hans von Plessen, while out hunting, discussed the succession question with the Bavarian envoy Count Lerchenfeld who, as Wilhelm told his friend Fürstenberg, expressed the very decided opinion that 'H.M. must choose a Prussian, above all *not* a South German or a Bavarian; that *never* works; Hohenlohe showed us that.'[79] At the end of February the German ambassador in Paris, Prince Hugo Radolin, was spoken of at court and in industrialist circles as the future Reich Chancellor.[80] In April on the journey to Corfu Wilhelm 'promised'– as we have seen – Count Anton Monts that he would be Bülow's successor.[81] The retiring Chancellor succeeded in enlisting the help of the Chief of the Civil Cabinet to prevent Monts's nomination.[82] Using the curious argument that in the coming years 'the most difficult problems' would be in the sphere of domestic politics, not foreign affairs, Bülow advised the Kaiser to appoint Bethmann Hollweg as his successor. (See Figure 30.) But when Valentini suggested his name on 3 July, Wilhelm rejected it, remarking: 'I know exactly what he is like. He is an arrogant, pig-headed schoolmaster; I can't work with him.'[83] Wilhelm's antipathy towards Bethmann was endorsed by the Kaiserin, who thought him 'too philosophical, unworldly and ponderous'; moreover he had an uncongenial personality and (metaphorically) 'a rather too crooked back'.[84] Three further candidates for the highest office in the Reich, the brothers August and Botho zu Eulenburg and the Statthalter of Alsace-Lorraine, General Count Carl von Wedel, turned down the Chancellorship when it was offered to them. On 6 July the well-informed Austrian ambassador, Count Szögyény, reported to Vienna that apart from Carl Wedel and Bethmann Hollweg, the Prussian Minister of Finance, Georg Freiherr von Rheinbaben, had the best chance of becoming Chancellor.[85] When Valentini reported for duty on board the *Hohenzollern* in the afternoon of 7 July he found the Kaiser 'very bad-tempered about the delay'. Suddenly Wilhelm reverted to 'the idea he had already touched upon earlier, of nominating General Colmar Frhr. v. der Goltz as Chancellor'. He ordered the Chief of the Civil Cabinet 'to take the Orient Express to Constantinople at once!' While Valentini was studying the train time-table, however, he was summoned by the valet to see the Kaiser in his cabin again. 'In the meantime His Majesty had changed into tennis clothes and he received me on his way out of the door. He had thought the matter over again, he said; it would be unfair to the Turks to take away the General now, when he had an important mission to fulfil there; he was willing to have Bethmann, and I should now make all the necessary arrangements quickly!' The Kaiser could finally leave for his Scandinavian cruise. When one considers that appointing the Reich Chancellor and Minister-President of Prussia constituted the foremost responsibility of the monarch, it is difficult to imagine a more damning example of a dereliction of duty than this flippant shilly-shallying between two such contrasting candidates. If Wilhelm had stuck by his preferred choice of Field Marshall von der Goltz instead of dashing off to play tennis, war or a *coup d'état* (or both)

Figure 30 Bülow with his replacement, Theobald von Bethmann
Hollweg, in July 1909

would almost certainly have followed swiftly.[86] In the event, it was Theobald von Bethmann Hollweg who, on 14 July 1909, 'with a melancholy
expression, yet not unwillingly', took on the highest and thorniest office in
the land.[87] It was to be his lot as the fifth Chancellor of the German Reich,
a man utterly inexperienced in foreign affairs, to plunge the world into the
catastrophe of the Great War in the summer of 1914.

CHAPTER TWENTY-EIGHT

Wilhelm and the direction of foreign policy under Bethmann Hollweg

At the end of August 1909, only six weeks after Bülow's replacement by Bethmann Hollweg, *Simplicissimus* carried a caricature by Th. Th. Heine entitled 'A Chancellor's Education' which depicted in four stages the rapidly changing relationship between Bethmann and the monarch (see Figure 31). In the first picture, Wilhelm is looking up respectfully at the tall figure of the new Chancellor; in the second the two men eye each other on an equal level; in the third the Chancellor has become very small in comparison; in the last, the Chancellor has to resort to a telescope, so enormous has the military monarch, booted and spurred, become in the plenitude of his power and self-aggrandisement.[1] If the caricature rather exaggerated the dominance of the Kaiser, it is nevertheless astonishing how swiftly and completely Wilhelm II recovered from the setbacks of the previous two years – the horrific scandals at court and the *Daily Telegraph* affair – and with what self-confidence he resumed control of German policy. In the field of foreign and military policy particularly (on the domestic front, not much could be done anyway, given the predominance of the Conservatives and the Centre party in the Reichstag) the new Reich Chancellor soon got used to his role as the executive organ of the imperial will, even if he found himself obliged from time to time to urge moderation on his impetuous sovereign. Wilhelm, for his part, who had only agreed to Bethmann's appointment with reluctance, could soon congratulate himself on his choice. By December, he was pleased to report to Archduke Franz Ferdinand that 'our Chancellor has got off to a good start and done a lot to calm things down at home and abroad'.[2] How did Wilhelm see the world in the first years of Bethmann's Chancellorship, and what influence was he able to exert on the formation of foreign policy under Bethmann? Is it even true, as Bülow later insinuated, that the Kaiser had chosen this lacklustre bureaucrat

Figure 31 'A Chancellor's Education', 1909. Bethmann Hollweg is
quick to learn the ropes

bereft of international experience precisely with the intention of directing
foreign policy himself?[3] If so, he must have been delighted by the success of
his stratagem. In August 1913, after twenty years in the capital of the
Habsburg Empire's only ally, its ambassador Count Szögyény could assure
his superiors in Vienna: 'If I ask myself the question who now really directs
German foreign policy I can only come to one answer, and that is that neither
Herr von Bethmann Hollweg nor Herr von Jagow but Kaiser Wilhelm himself
has his hands on the controls of foreign policy, and that in this regard the
Reich Chancellor and the Foreign Secretary are in no position to exercise any
significant influence on His Majesty.'[4]

THE AFTER-EFFECTS OF THE BOSNIAN `HAMMER BLOW´

Fundamental to Wilhelm II's stance in the years from 1909 to 1911 was his conviction that with the 'hammer blow' against Russia in the Bosnian annexation crisis he had discovered a recipe for victory against the intrigues of the Entente. Thus, he wrote in triumph to Franz Ferdinand on 13 August 1909 that 'the cooking up of ententes across the water has led to nothing. For it only needed Austria and us to come together to put a stop to the whole business; and the dear friends who, intoxicated by their ententes, were acting as the masters of Europe, sobered up and preferred not to pursue matters to extremes as one of them [i.e. England] had so heartily wished, as it would have come out of the conflict as the sole gainer! Result: rather a hangover and Austria is *also* building "Dreadnoughts"! Apparently a quite unexpected and very disturbing result for people "over there"!'[5] In a further letter to Franz Ferdinand in January 1910 he reaffirmed that Austria's and Germany's 'standing firm together' in the Bosnian crisis had 'saved Europe from a catastrophe ... preserved the peace of the world, and shown the futility of the intrigues and ententes set in train against our alliance'.[6] As late as the summer of 1911 Wilhelm threatened a British admiral with a repetition, if necessary, of the Bosnian show of force: 'This Herzegovina affair has shown how powerless England really is on the continent. *It was I* who settled it, after my own fashion, for my friend Austria, and you had nothing to say in the matter. And I shall do the same again if the occasion arises.'[7]

Germany's alliance with Austria-Hungary was to be turned into a sort of Central European fortress,[8] and extended towards the south and east by a military agreement with a Turkey whose strength, in turn, was to be revived with German help. Although Kaiser Wilhelm assumed that the Tsarist Empire would be 'incapable of action' for 'about five years',[9] from the autumn of 1909 he advocated a secret military convention between Austria-Hungary, Turkey and Romania against Russia. Here, he was taking up the suggestion of the Turkish ambassador to Berlin, Osman Nizami Pasha, but he insisted, characteristically, that discussions of the *casus belli* between Vienna and Constantinople should take place not at a diplomatic, but at a purely military level.[10]

Wilhelm and Bethmann Hollweg discussed this plan at length with Franz Ferdinand during his visit to Potsdam and Letzlingen in late 1909. As the Chancellor was able to inform Aehrenthal on 15 November, the talks revealed 'complete mutual agreement ... in all questions of foreign policy'. 'Just before we left Letzlingen', Bethmann continued, 'His Majesty my Most Gracious Master showed the Archduke a highly confidential report that had just arrived from our military attaché in Constantinople, according to which the Turkish ambassador here, Osman Nizami Pasha, who is at present on leave in Constantinople, had spoken to your plenipotentiary Baron Giesl von Gieslingen about the idea of a military convention between Turkey and Austria-Hungary. My Most Gracious Master had, I might tell you in strict confidence, prima vista taken up this idea with enthusiasm. I myself should not like to comment on it before I know your views. The question of the consolidation of the new regime in Turkey seems to me to be a crucial one in this connection.'[11]

A few days later Kaiser Wilhelm pressed the Archduke directly to support the conclusion of a secret military convention with Turkey. 'It was very valuable for me to learn from what Aehrenthal told us that my ideas about your relations with Turkey had received such speedy confirmation. The approach of the Turkish ambassador in Berlin, Osman Nizami, to Aehrenthal is very welcome and deserves to be met with trust and sincere goodwill. The Turks are looking to the future, are fearful for their possessions and their security, and — naturally and reasonably — are seeking a connection with the Central Powers. Purely technical, secret military agreements between general staffs would seem best to meet the situation. The diplomats do not need to be involved — they are always indiscreet — and the minister can always pretend to know nothing. The presence of Gen. v.d. Goltz [in Constantinople] guarantees security and makes the situation easier.'[12]

The Austrians' reluctance to fulfil the German Emperor's wish arose partly from a not unfounded fear that their powerful neighbour might take them in tow and push them forward against Russia. In September 1910 Bethmann Hollweg set out for the Kaiser with perfect clarity the calculation that, four years later, he was to make the guiding idea of his policy in the July crisis: 'We must of course wish that, if it comes to war, the first [Russian] attack is launched against Austria, who will then need *our* help, and not against us, which would leave it up to Austria to decide whether to fulfil her alliance obligations.'[13] This was exactly the idea that Wilhelm was pursuing in 1909 when he pressed for a secret military convention between Vienna and Constantinople. The Austrians and Turks 'must be *brought together militarily*; then the Austrians will be nailed down vis-à-vis the Russians and out of favour in St Petersburg. That is why Aehrenthal wants to have nothing to do with the military convention with Turkey. Once that is signed and sealed, the Russians will never forgive the Austrians! and it will be an apple of discord between them.'[14] When it was falsely reported in the Vienna press in 1910 that a military convention had already been concluded, on the Kaiser's initiative, between Germany, Austria-Hungary and Turkey, Wilhelm observed that that was, alas, too good to be true: 'would that we had got that far!' However, 'just don't issue a *démenti*' of the false report, and 'let the canard fly on unharmed'.

He was quite unimpressed by Bethmann's warning that such rumours had already caused concern in Paris, London and St Petersburg. The 'three scoundrels are heartily welcome to their nervousness', 'just let them get worked up!' He was equally sharply opposed to the Chancellor's view that before going any further towards a military convention with Turkey the Allies should take their Triple Alliance partner, Italy, into their confidence. To inform Italy of their secret plans would be 'very undesirable! What three know, the world knows!!' 'Under no circumstances' should Bethmann put out feelers to Rome. 'We were never asked by Rome, either, when they made agreements with Paris without us! Or by other states! when they made agreements with each other!'[15]

THE ENTENTE'S ADVANCES IN THE NEAR EAST

The hopes that the Kaiser had had of an Austro-German–Turkish axis in the aftermath of the Bosnian crisis were frustrated by the steadily increasing influence of Britain, France and Russia in the Balkan peninsula and the Near East.[16] On 17 August 1909, only a few days after he had boasted to Franz Ferdinand about the effectiveness of Austro-German solidarity in frustrating the 'cooking up of ententes', Wilhelm was raging against the interference of the Entente Powers in the internal affairs of Turkey. An Anglo-French suggestion that the two Central Powers should participate in an international action to pacify Macedonia reawakened Wilhelm's feelings of hatred for England, and for King Edward in particular, to whom he ascribed this 'unheard of' proposal and obvious 'trap!!!' 'Last year's revolution in Turkey was brought about precisely with the very clear objective of putting an end once and for all to the meddling of any Power other than Turkey in Macedonia, and we all recognised this at the time, and Germany welcomed it as a blessed relief! We could at last see an end of the dreadful sea-serpent! To seek to re-open the Macedonian question now, given the highly unstable conditions prevailing in Turkey, is pure madness, and is bound to damage Turkey's self-esteem to a provocative degree. Edward VII has suggested this to Gaul, in order to set us completely at odds with Turkey! I refuse to have anything at all to do with such stuff! ... All such proposals, veiled or open, indirect or direct, are to be *rejected* jointly with Vienna!'[17]

In November, Wilhelm was very much put out by a report that the British, patently with Russia's approval, were seeking a monopoly of navigation on the Tigris and Euphrates – an 'unheard of piece of insolence'. 'The cloven hoof is plain to see!' 'The Turks must be stiffened to resist!' he ordered: 'It is a move against the Baghdad Railway.'[18] The Kaiser entirely shared ambassador

Marschall von Bieberstein's suspicion that 'the early stages of a world-historical catastrophe could lie in these English manoeuvres', which 'amounted to a blow at the heart of the Ottoman Empire'.[19] When he learned from the newspapers that England would only consent to a raising of Ottoman import duties if the Turks dropped their guarantee for the Baghdad railway, Wilhelm regarded this as 'such a direct attack by England on us, and on the great cultural mission that Germany has set herself', that he instructed the Chancellor to make it clear to London that in such circumstances it would 'hardly be possible to go on talking about a general understanding with England'. London's move at Constantinople constituted 'interference by a foreign Power in the right of self-determination of a second Power, to the direct disadvantage of a third'. In the end, Bethmann managed to calm the monarch down somewhat by pointing to the dissolution of the British parliament and the uncertain outcome of the impending elections.[20]

The possibility of war between Greece and Turkey over Crete, leading to European intervention in support of Greece, with Serbia and Bulgaria also joining in, was one of Wilhelm II's constant anxieties. This would end, he feared, with the seizure of Mesopotamia and Crete by the British, and the annexation of Constantinople and the Dardanelles by Russia.[21] In the summer of 1910 he was worried that London was 'working to "liquidate" Turkey, the Baghdad Railway, Crete, Egypt, Dardanelles etc!'[22] The position in the eastern Mediterranean was a 'wonderful mess! But that is just what England wants in order to swallow up Egypt, Suda Bay, Baghdad Railway etc! when the fighting starts!'[23] His hopes of delaying the British takeover of the Middle East were placed, remarkably enough, in Russia, who he reckoned was still too weak herself to participate in the partition of Turkey. He wrote on a report from St Petersburg in June 1910: 'Isvolsky *is afraid* of the *unholy mess* in the Near East that England so longs for. That would enable England to grab Suda Bay, Egypt, Arabia and Mesopotamia, and she would allow Russia to take the Dardanelles. As Isvolsky knows, however, that Russia is *at present* quite incapable of fighting the Turks, who are occupying Stamboul, with any hope of success, he wants to *postpone* the partition, and to this end wants to retain Russian troops in Crete to prevent a *premature* seizure of Suda Bay by England.'[24]

It was not only the overwhelming influence of the British navy in the eastern Mediterranean that the Kaiser felt to be an almost insuperable obstacle in the way of his own Near Eastern ambitions, but also the enormous financial power of the French in Constantinople. Bitterly, he denounced the activities of French financiers in the Turkish capital as 'unheard of insolence' and sheer extortion. 'That is pure blackmail!' he exclaimed, 'The Gauls treat the Turks like a 5th-rate negro state! An attitude that is simply insulting.' The Turks would have to 'stand firm. We must stiffen them. We too can supply them with money.'[25] Under no circumstances must they submit to the Caudine yoke of French demands. 'The Turks must be informed of the fact that money is readily available in Germany', he ordered on 22 October 1910. 'They must never fall in with this French insolence.'[26]

WILHELM AND THE BALKAN STATES

Of the smaller Balkan states, only Romania was regarded by Wilhelm as a friend at this time. The Hohenzollern King Carol was 'a noble, upright character and has done a lot to raise the level of his people and stabilise conditions in the country', he assured Franz Ferdinand. 'He is a valuable ally in the eternally restless Balkans, as he is well informed about conditions there and manages them with a cool, clear head and a judgement fortified by experience.'[27] Wilhelm had only contempt for George I, the 'flabby' King of the Hellenes, notable only for his 'irresponsible lack of willpower'. Writing to his aunt, Grand Duchess Luise of Baden, the Kaiser poked fun at the King's respect for the constitution, which might lead him to start a war with Turkey 'just for the sake of the constitutional principle that the King must in absolutely every case do what the chamber and the people demand!'[28] 'There is no king in Athens any more', he wrote to Franz Ferdinand, 'only a helpless, cowardly milksop who has betrayed his dynasty!' For his part, he 'gave up the dynasty for lost'.[29]

In Greece and in Serbia too, Wilhelm felt that British influence was inexorably increasing. The Greek Prime Minister Venizelos, Wilhelm wrote bitterly to Max Fürstenberg in March 1910, had recently declared in Crete that 'the King will be thrown out, but it is not certain who should replace him, as Prince George (grandson), whom he wants, is *not* wanted by *England*, because he is too closely related to the German Emperor!! And what England does not want just does not happen in this world.'[30] Referring to England's overweening influence in Athens the Kaiser rejected Marschall von Bieber-stein's proposal to strengthen Germany's position in the eastern Mediterranean by selling the warship *Blücher* to Turkey. This, Wilhelm decided, would 'not be to our advantage! and risky as Greece is supported by England, who has turned against Turkey and towards Greece. It would also go against my family loyalty to strengthen the enemies of the Greek dynasty, related to mine by blood and at present facing such threatening dangers. For it stands and falls with the hope of the union of Crete with Greece! Now Greece is *arming*! Perhaps with English money, of course. If I were *now* so ostentatiously to supply ships to Turkey with the result that in the event of war with Greece she defeats the latter with the help of a German battleship supplied for the occasion; then we should be in trouble not just with Greece but with England, who would intervene with the Mediterranean fleet. We have so far refused in principle to allow ourselves to be dragged into the Cretan question. The sale of the "Blücher" to Turkey *now* would be seen as our taking sides directly *in this quarrel* in favour of Turkey; and would turn the whole Greek world, which still counts for a lot in the East, against us, just as England too would resent it. I am against the sale, therefore.'[31] Serbia, he complained in September 1909, was no less than Greece 'under the sceptre of England'. 'Quite a charming gentleman, Uncle E[dward] VII!'[32]

The hatred the Kaiser developed for Ferdinand of Bulgaria ('Fernando Naso' as he mockingly called his long-nosed Coburg cousin) was of a veritably pathological intensity – especially after Ferdinand assumed the title of Tsar in October 1908. He noted with glee in 1910 that Ferdinand had been accorded a cool reception when he visited St Petersburg; indeed, that, contrary to the normal rules of courtesy between sovereigns, Nicholas II had refused to make him Colonel-in-Chief of a regiment.[33] In fact, Wilhelm's behaviour towards his Bulgarian cousin was soon raising eyebrows in society worldwide. In January 1910, for example, Baroness Spitzemberg learned from the banker Paul Schwabach of an astonishing scene at a wedding in Brunswick: 'The Kaiser and the Tsar of Bulgaria were standing back-to-back talking to other people. Suddenly [Ferdinand] received a mighty blow on his behind, and turned round in fury to see the Kaiser roaring with laughter.' A few days later the Baroness encountered a court official who confirmed 'with concern the story about long-nosed Ferdinand, whom H.M., even before the notorious blow on the backside, treated so appallingly, just because he can't stand him, that he left for home, incandescent with rage ... I am just surprised, the Baroness added, that not one of the princes who are so furious gives the Kaiser such a dig or blow back!'[34] Another version of the tale reached the British Foreign Office from the legation in Sofia some months later: 'It appears that King Ferdinand was leaning out of the window looking at something in the street, when the Emperor, whose fondness for horseplay is notorious, came up behind His Majesty, and could not resist the temptation of applying a hearty spank to the Royal Posterior. The King's breeches were tight and the spank stung, possibly more than was intended. King Ferdinand, pale with rage, told the Emperor he had taken an unpardonable liberty. The Emperor replied to the effect that it was a cousinly joke, and advised Ferdinand not to make an ass of himself. King Ferdinand replied, haughtily, that he did not admit of such jokes being played upon him. The Emperor turned his back and went off in a rage, leaving King Ferdinand fuming, and probably longing to rub the place that hurt the most.' The mutual hostility between the two monarchs surfaced again when they met at the funeral of Edward VII in May 1910. On this occasion, too, Kaiser Wilhelm treated Ferdinand 'most rudely', leading an astonished Theodore Roosevelt to remark that 'he had never seen anything like the Emperor's rudeness to his Bulgarian relative'.[35]

THE CONTEST WITH RUSSIA FOR PREDOMINANCE IN THE BALKANS

The Anglo-German rivalry in the Near East was accompanied by a sharp conflict with Russia over predominance in the Balkans that threatened to drive the Powers ever closer to the brink of war. Even after the Tsarist Empire's retreat in the Bosnian crisis Wilhelm II nourished an unbridled hatred of the Russian Foreign Minister Isvolsky.[36] Austria and Germany, he warned, must continue to 'keep a close eye on him', for he was, 'as before, Aehrenthal's most rabid enemy, and detests us likewise'.[37] Besides, the 'Jesuit' Isvolsky acted according to the principle that 'the purpose of words is to conceal our thoughts!'[38] If he had initially been inclined to attribute Russian foreign policy to Isvolsky's injured vanity, Wilhelm had to admit in due course that Russian Balkan policy was determined by state interests. Therefore, as he acknowledged in September 1909, a change of personalities on the Neva would not make any appreciable difference. The Russians were intoxicated with pan-Slav predelictions for 'Russia's historic mission in the Balkans', and would continue 'to entertain themselves with these visionary images until one day the Mongols are in the Urals! Then they will recognise too late where Russia's "historic mission" really lay! namely, the protection of Europe from the Yellow Peril!'[39]

Wilhelm regarded Isvolsky's engineering of a visit by the Tsar to the King of Italy at Racconigi on 25 October as a slap in the face. That the Tsar, in travelling from Darmstadt to Italy, should have made a long detour to avoid Austro-Hungarian territory, he saw as a calculated affront to the venerable old Emperor Franz Joseph.[40] The secret talks between Isvolsky and the Italian Foreign Minister, Tittoni, led to an exchange of notes which indeed spoke of the maintenance of the status quo in the Balkans but envisaged a reordering of the peninsula in line with the national principle if Ottoman rule in Europe should collapse; and while Tittoni recognised Russia's interests in the Straits, the Russians recognised Italy's interests in Tripoli and Cyrenaica.[41] Kaiser Wilhelm immediately suspected that Isvolsky had 'done some dirty work with Tittoni behind our backs',[42] and condemned the double-dealing of his Triple Alliance partners as 'truly jesuitical and absolutely truly Italian'.[43] The public obligation of the two Powers to maintain the status quo in the Balkans he dismissed as 'Rubbish pour la Gallerie! The poor status quo — what it has already had to put up with! The meaning of the agreement is far more: "sounding the death halloo over Turkey!"'[44] Talk of preserving the status quo in the Balkans was, he remarked in a typical marginal note, 'just a cover for the Balkan League cigar' that 'would be made from Turkish tobacco'. For Vienna, however, a strong Turkey was a vital interest! And it could only be maintained if there was no 'upgrading' of the Balkan states — such as could only come about with Russian help and at Turkey's expense.[45] The claim by the Russians 'that the intrusion of the Islamic Ottoman Empire into Christian Europe was an insufferable anomaly' was, Wilhelm declared, 'as clear as we could wish' and proved that they were striving for 'a Balkan League! against Austria'. 'Russia is engaged in forming a Balkan League for the *Liquidation* of Turkey — Dardanelles etc. — and the hemming in of Austria, against whom the "Slav brothers" are to be united.' Again he demanded that 'Austria must make sure of Romania and Turkey, if necessary by alliances or military agreements.'[46] Thus, it was clear to the Kaiser that, should Russia intervene in the Balkans, 'for us the *casus foederis*', leading to military action, would arise.[47] As usual, he suspected that British influence lay behind Russia's forward policy, and asked how France, 'with her 5 billions invested in Turkey' would react.[48]

THE KAISER AND FRANZ FERDINAND

Faced with Germany's growing isolation Kaiser Wilhelm redoubled his efforts to cultivate the friendship of Archduke Franz Ferdinand and the aristocratic clique that had formed round the heir apparent. Already in September 1909 Wilhelm's participation in the Austrian army manoeuvres at Groß-Meseritsch in Moravia, in the presence of not only the Archduke but the revered Emperor Franz Joseph, had demonstrated the unity of the two empires.[49] The visit of the Archduke and his wife Sophie to Potsdam and Letzlingen in the following November set the seal on the friendship. As Wilhelm's letters show, he lost no opportunity to express an exaggerated respect for the Archduke's morganatic wife who was ostracised at the court in Vienna.

The brilliance and charm of the aristocratic clique round Franz Ferdinand greatly impressed the Kaiser's Prusso-German entourage, not a few of whom were worried that Wilhelm might be more enchanted by them than was good for Germany. As one of the Flügeladjutanten who accompanied the Kaiser to Max Fürstenberg's estate at Donaueschingen in November 1909 reported to his wife: 'The "party" is perhaps the finest and most noble to be found anywhere in the world ... Despite all the fun, shouting and drôlerie,

Fürstenberg himself and a Count Nostitz are to be taken seriously. Both politically active in Austria, and not without an agenda and purpose in their conversations with the Kaiser, who in his glorious openness and inexhaustible loquaciousness always has plenty to say. As both gentlemen are closely related to all the influential people in Austria, I think this harmless shooting party is not without political importance – as the Kaiser is aware. Especially as it is clear that these days Austro-German solidarity is the whole world's sheet anchor.'[50]

As has already been seen, Wilhelm II had for some time been carrying on a lively correspondence with Franz Ferdinand about racial questions in the Dual Monarchy and in the Balkans that was to have serious geopolitical implications.[51] In December Kaiser Wilhelm continued this disturbing exchange of views with reference to the latest international developments. In congratulating him on his birthday, he explained to the Archduke that: '*Racconigi* was for *Isvolsky* simply a personal act of revenge against Aehrenthal in which the Tsar was at first strongly opposed to joining him. The *Balkan league* seems to have been discussed, or at least support for the Balkan *slavs* at the expense of the other races (Germans, Magyars, and Turks) with the warm, benevolent and advisory participation of England, who is working especially hard in Belgrade and Sofia. The latest speeches of the Czechs leave no doubt about the aims of the "Slavic Union" which, through Kramarc, is commanded and directed from St Petersburg, where at the moment Sir A Nicholson [sic! British ambassador] is an absolute autocrat and has Isvolsky completely in his pocket. Kokovtsov's journey to Harbin was aiming for an entente with Ito and Japan in order "to have some peace" in the East! Thanks to Ito's death, that has not succeeded for the moment, but the Russians say quite openly "We are not strong enough for 2 sides, therefore we want to *wind things up in the East*, so as to deal more effectively with the Balkans and the rotten *West*. They are giving up their great historic mission in Asia in order to act against Europe!" This completely confirms what I told you and what you at first did not want to believe: "If the Yellow peril or Wave rolls up, the Slavs will *not* – as their duty and geographical situation demand – defend Europ[ean] culture against the East but will, alleging the pretext of the struggle against Pangermanism, unite with the Yellows against us, and they have in addition managed to get the help of the Latin-Romance race in this![''] That is the naked truth, facta loquuntur! So you must now make sure of the Moslems and get them on your side! At last England – who is involved in all these things – has her hands full at home. There things are looking jolly. Lansdowne's ill-considered move is said to have been inspired by E[dward] VII himself, and so everybody is annoyed with him. How it will end, nobody knows. Probably small majorities, frequent parliamentary and ministerial changes, and the Irish and the Labour party holding the balance.'[52]

While Wilhelm drafted this extremely controversial letter behind the backs of his 'responsible' advisers, the Archduke engaged his Chamberlain, Karl Baron von Rumerskirch, to draft his congratulatory letter on the Kaiser's birthday.[53] If its somewhat formal tone led the German monarch to suspect that the Archduke was seeking to distance himself from him, his fears were confirmed by signs of an Austro-Russian rapprochement which Wilhelm saw as designed to drive the Dual Monarchy and Germany apart. According to the Paris press, it was only the 'brutal hammer blow' that Germany had delivered to Russia in the Bosnian crisis that was responsible for the regrettable tension between Austria and Russia; so these two Powers would do well to join together against the troublemaker in Berlin. The Kaiser was in no doubt as to who was behind these 'damned clever' intrigues: the British ambassador to Russia, Sir Arthur Nicolson, was 'the organising spirit behind the campaigns originating in St Petersburg' in collaboration with the British and French ambassadors in Vienna, Cartwright and Crozier, and the anti-German journalist Gabriel de Wesselitzky.[54] The 'Supreme Commander' of these attempts to lure away even Germany's last ally, however, was Edward VII himself.[55]

Almost in a state of panic, Wilhelm wrote the Archduke an effusive letter to dispel his mistrust and to explain the 'true' background to the perfidious plot. Only Austro-German solidarity in the crisis of the previous year had, he repeated yet again, 'saved Europe from a catastrophe and preserved world peace, by exposing the futility of the intrigues and ententes directed against our alliance. Herr Wesselitski's visit to Aehrenthal was, in my view, yet another attempt in that direction – and not the last ... Wesselitzki is the most fanatical Germanophobe and most rabid agitator against both me personally and my country, and lives in London. For over a dozen years he has been launching the most monstrous and slanderous attacks on us that you can imagine, in *English*, and under a pseudonym, in all the English reviews and journals, and it will be no thanks to him if it doesn't come to war with England. In St Petersburg too, he makes use of "Novoye Vremya" reinforcing there in Russian what he writes against us in English in London. I personally have suffered a great deal from him. This creature, Aehrenthal has received in audience, without suspecting that he had been sent to him by [the British ambassador] Cartwright and [the French ambassador] Crozier; but the actual instigator of the intrigue is Sir Arthur Nicholson [sic] in St Petersburg. I spotted it at once and was amused that such a clever man as Aehrenthal should fall for such a clumsy manoeuvre. The funniest thing about the story was that while Aehrenthal told us that the attempt at a rapprochement came from St Petersburg, Isvolsky told me that Aehrenthal had begun to approach him. You can imagine that I must have smiled to myself at this. Consu de fil blanc! not worth the ink and paper it was written on.'[56] Meanwhile, Wilhelm's efforts to ingratiate himself with the Archduke were reinforced by displays of laudatory flattery for his friend's military capacities and of gushing cordiality towards his wife.[57]

A few days later Wilhelm wrote the Archduke a further letter, warning him again of attempts to separate the Dual Monarchy from Germany. 'All Austria-Hungary, Croatia and Bohemia is enmeshed in a network of Anglo-French correspondents (4 have been spotted in Agram alone) designed to agitate and cause unrest in those provinces, with a view to undermining the Dual Alliance and arousing suspicion of me and my country amongst you. Wesselitzki has just delivered a big public lecture in St Petersburg at which diplomats – especially from the Slav states – and the high society of St Petersburg were strongly represented. Full voice was given to the most evil suspicions against us, and the need for everybody – above all Russia and England – to co-operate closely, against whom is not difficult to guess! So watch out, something is brewing!'[58]

To back up his theory of an Anglo-Franco-Russian plot to undermine his friendship with Franz Ferdinand Wilhelm turned to their common friend, Prince Max Egon zu Fürstenberg, writing to him on 18 February 1910 in high indignation: 'According to a report of Tschirschky's, who has just lunched with Franzi, my letter has had a good effect, as the Archduke was very satisfied. It came at the right time, for to judge from private information from Vienna, Russia's rapprochement game – i.e. to break up the Austro-German bloc using Anglo-Franco-Russian press and other agents goes merrily on. Herr Wesse-litzki is the leading actor and manipulator. He has recently, in St Petersburg, proclaimed to the whole world that he knows the Archduke thinks nothing of me, receives no real information from here either, and is a far too independent character to be taken in. He must be brought to St Petersburg very soon. To prepare an agreeable reception for him there he will now get the "Vremya" to publish some favourable articles about Franzi based on material he got in Vienna. A Viennese gentleman – a friend of Wesselitzki's – will feed these articles to the Archduke to encourage him to come to St Petersburg one day instead of going to Berlin all the time. The idea is devilishly cunning! ... As last year the two of us together paralysed England, we must at all costs be driven apart. The old Emperor said recently in Vienna that "the Russians had literally *forced themselves* on him, and he just simply had to listen to them."! Meanwhile in St Petersburg Isvolsky declares that he is unable to fend off the Austrian advances!!! That the two countries are having talks and are winding up the ministerial quarrel is certainly desirable, but the choice of persons and methods for achieving this are very singular ... Franzi must be warned!'[59] Fürstenberg took it upon himself, with the Kaiser's express approval, to warn the Archduke 'in the sense of Your Majesty's gracious letter against the monstrous intrigues and machinations of the Russians and their crew'. He felt it *essential* to work on the Archduke like this *all the time*, in order to [head off] all foreign influence in advance'.[60]

WAR WITH RUSSIA?

Wilhelm's fear, expressed to the Archduke in December 1909, that Russia might 'in alliance with the Latin-Romance race ... and using the pretext of the struggle against Pangermanism unite with the Yellows against us'[61] was temporarily allayed in January 1910 when his brother Prince Heinrich returned from the funeral of Grand Duke Michael in St Petersburg with friendly assurances from his brother-in-law the Tsar. Delighted, Wilhelm informed the Chief of General Staff von Moltke that the Tsar had said 'that he would withdraw 4 army corps from our frontier. These would be used, in the first place, for garrison-towns in the interior and further into central and eastern Russia ... so as to be available in the event of revolts, and for the economic advantage of the garrisons; then, because H.M. described the position in the East as insecure, and above all did not trust the Japanese, who were apparently arming, planning to annex Korea, and seemed to be developing more far-reaching plans against Russia's East Asian possessions. In view of this, the army massed in Poland was unfavourably positioned, and should be deployed more towards the centre and the eastern frontier to facilitate its faster transportation to the points under threat.'[62] On the very next day, Wilhelm wrote in obvious relief to the Tsar: 'Henry faithfully repeated all the messages you entrusted him with for me. I entirely share your views. I can perfectly well understand that developments in the Far East are absorbing your attention. The communication made to him about your decision to withdraw 4 Army Corps from our frontier has given me great satisfaction. The more so as Henry told me, that ... you referred in the heartiest terms to the traditional friendship of our 2 countries and to their brotherhood in arms established a century ago. You well know how I always had and will have these sacred relations at heart, and I need not tell you how deeply gratified I am at your kind and touching words.' He proposed a meeting with his 'dearest Nicky' in August after his annual northern cruise.[63]

Wilhelm's reawakened confidence in Russia's intentions was short-lived, resting as it did on his over-estimation of the Tsar's power and determination.

His nervousness regarding his eastern neighbour reached a new intensity at the end of August, when his military plenipotentiary in St Petersburg, Paul von Hintze, reported to him that the dispositions adopted in the Russian army manoeuvres had been quite openly based on the assumption of a war against Germany or Germany and Sweden.[64] In Wilhelm II's view, Hintze's alarmist report was 'the most serious and truthful that we have so far received from there'. 'He has no doubts about the purposeful, energetic military preparations against Germany, with whom war is to be waged in the near future. He describes the theme of the manoeuvres as a public endorsement of the long-prepared and generally *popular* plan for an early war against us to compensate for the war with Japan.'[65] The news from St Petersburg confirmed Wilhelm in his view that he, as a military man, had always assessed the situation more correctly than his civilian advisers. 'Whether my ministers will now at last believe me, that Russia is up to something and we must build up our armaments!!?' he exclaimed; and diplomatic protests against the explicit naming of Germany as the presumed opponent were, he felt, 'too mild. Against such Russian insolence a different tone is called for.'[66] It was, after all, a matter of 'systematic agitation and the blackening of Germany among all classes in Russia, which we shall now have to take into account. Hintze's report hits the nail on the head. The fellows want to calm us down, because they are not yet ready, that's all!'[67] The incident was only irksome to the Russians because it gave Germany 'advance warning of what is threatening us'.[68] Their intention was obviously 'to so provoke Austria in the Balkans that it comes to a war, and we are dragged in by the casus foederis', he wrote in August 1910 – in an eerie presentiment of the events of August 1914. 'The Russians are arming for a possible war against Austria and us!'[69]

The effect on Wilhem II of Hintze's reporting alarmed not only the Chancellor and the diplomats, but the generals at the Kaiser's court. Even Adjutant-General von Plessen sharply opposed Hintze's view 'that Russia is arming against us ... and that the Balkans would provide the sought-for opportunity'.[70] But for the time being the Kaiser held firm to his military plenipotentiary – not least because his chances of securing a 'new military budget' might be increased by Hintze's report, on which he minuted: 'I think this material should certainly be enough for the Chancellor and the War Minister.'[71]

At the same time, however, he recognised that the possibility of a Russo-German war brought with it the danger that Austria-Hungary might seek to keep clear of the threatening conflict by reaching an agreement with Russia behind Germany's back. Such a scenario seemed nearer realisation in September 1910 with the transfer of Isvolsky from the Foreign Ministry in

St Petersburg to the Russian embassy in Paris; and with the consequent diminution of the personal animosity between the foreign ministries in Vienna and St Petersburg. Bethmann had some reason to be nervous about any Austro-Russian rapprochement between Germany's imperial neighbours. He made a great effort to convince Wilhelm of the need, during his forthcoming visit to Austria-Hungary (16–20 September) to let nothing transpire about the crisis in Russo-German relations. If a war broke out with Russia it would be desirable for Germany, the Chancellor declared, that Russia should first strike against Austria, who would then have to appeal to Germany for help, 'and not against us, which would leave it up to Austria to decide whether to fulfil her alliance obligations'.[72] On the eve of his departure for Vienna Wilhelm declared himself in agreement with this idea, although he recognised how difficult it would be to carry out: 'Yes, but whether it *turns out* like that depends on very clever policy in Berlin!' An Austro-Russian understanding at Germany's expense was by no means out of the question, for 'if the two of them seriously want to, they can and will get on without us!' 'The only obstacle is the Hungarians! who will not tolerate such a policy!' Wilhelm promised the Chancellor that he would 'not talk about the Russians . . . at all' in Vienna – 'except perhaps insofar as they are stirring up trouble in the Balkans and being disagreeable to the Austrians and Turks'.[73]

THE TSAR'S VISIT TO POTSDAM IN NOVEMBER 1910

The replacement of Isvolsky on 10 September 1910 by Sergei Dmitrievich Sazonov (a German-speaker) was in fact the prelude to an – albeit brief – Russo-German rapprochement such as the Kaiser had been hoping for in January.[74] Wilhelm continued to regard an improvement in Russo-German relations as 'very desirable', but he doubted the Tsar's readiness to respond. Since the end of August Nicholas II had been staying with his family in the Wetterau in Hesse, where the ailing Tsarina was taking the cure, and then with his brother-in-law Grand Duke Ernst Ludwig in Wolfsgarten near Darmstadt, but for weeks he had been evading Wilhelm's invitations to visit him in Potsdam.[75] 'He has been humming and hawing for weeks!?', Wilhelm complained in October 1910, 'As always! in politics too!'[76] In his increasing frustration he accused the Tsar of having at least tolerated Isvolsky's anti-German policy. 'Why did he allow it then? If he was aware of it, why did he not change it!? . . . Soft words and feelings are no use any more, with the Triple Entente and the 6 new Russian army corps in formation! Now only deeds count, and facts!'[77]

Only Sazonov's visit to Berlin on 1 November 1910 and the following two-day visit of the Tsar to Potsdam brought new hopes of an understanding based, as Bethmann put it, on 'the strong, effective monarchies intrinsic to both countries'. The Tsar's wish 'to speak freely and openly with Your Majesty about political affairs' received an enthusiastic welcome from the Kaiser: He had 'been hoping for this for years, but it had never happened!' He was, of course, sceptical about the new Foreign Minister's claim that the days of Russia's expansionist policy were over, and that that had enabled Russia to reach an agreement with England. 'The force of events will certainly not permit that! If the two of them agree on a partition of Persia, then they will become territorial neighbours in Asia, and Russia will be drawn willy nilly into the Indian sphere!!' The prospect of a new Anglo-Russian clash in Persia reawakened Wilhelm's hopes of winning Moslem sympathies: 'If the Emperor [Nicholas] is determined to partition Persia, naturally we cannot prevent it. We *must* secure guarantees of commercial equality, freedom and the open door for ourselves. We *can* point to the dangers of a partition. We can lead the awakening *self-consciousness* of the Mohammedan peoples, which would probably greatly resent the annexation of Moslem territory. The *feeling of solidarity* among the Moslems shown by the collections for the Turkish fleet in India; the repercussions of Mohammedan agitation on the Moslem subjects of the other Great Powers. These are aspects that we could warn about in a friendly fashion. That enables us in the event of an annexation of territory to assure the Mohammedan world that we tried as best we could to safeguard and speak up for their interests.'[78]

After an open exchange of views with the Tsar in the Neues Palais on 4–5 November[79] Wilhelm was hopeful 'that Russo-German relations have now taken a favourable turn, and that in future the governments too will speak openly to each other'.[80] Seizing the opportunity, Wilhelm announced that he would call on the Tsar in Wolfsgarten on 11 November, where he was able, according to the representative of the Wilhelmstrasse Freiherr von Jenisch, 'to confirm . . . the good impression of the Tsar's friendly disposition that he had gained in Potsdam'. 'In long talks with the Tsar, at which the Grand Duke [Ernst Ludwig] and Prince Heinrich were also present, His Majesty gave a detailed acccount of our naval policy and our relations with England. The Japanese too were discussed, in similar terms as at Potsdam.'[81]

To seal the new relationship the troublemaker in St Petersburg, Paul von Hintze, had to be sacrificed. During Wilhelm's visit to Wolfsgarten on 11 November his host, Grand Duke Ernst Ludwig told Jenisch that his brother-in-law the Tsar had 'completely . . . lost confidence' in Hintze. 'The Tsar knew very well that H.M. the Kaiser attaches the greatest weight to every word that Herr von Hintze reported or related', and that the ambassador's influence was 'nil' in comparison.[82] Initially, Wilhelm dismissed the attack on Hintze as 'a vile intrigue of jealous people around him'.[83] Bethmann Hollweg, however, insisted on the recall of the bothersome military plenipotentiary in the interests of the 'marked change in Russian policy in the wake of Potsdam';[84] and as a result, at the end of November Wilhelm asked Nicholas confidentially whether he wished Hintze to be withdrawn.[85] The Tsar replied immediately that he had indeed lost confidence in Hintze. 'In the last eighteeen months I saw, or rather felt, that the man had changed. He avoids me, never looks me in the eye, and if I manage to get to talk to him — he gives answers of one syllable — in short, he is not the Hintze I knew before . . . What the reasons are for this change, I don't know, but I am bound to admit that in the circumstances it would be better if he were replaced by another of your aides-de-camp.'[86] Against the Kaiser's wish to give Hintze an ambassadorial post, Bethmann managed to have the ambitious naval officer appointed minister to Mexico.[87] He was destined to become Germany's Foreign Secretary in 1918.

Immediately after the Potsdam meeting the Kaiser ordered the Chancellor to draft a telegram to the Emperor Franz Joseph reporting on its encouraging outcome.[88] Archduke Franz Ferdinand was gratified by the resultant improvement in Germany's relations with her eastern neighbour, which he expected would have a positive effect on Austria-Hungary's relations with Russia.[89] On 14 November Bethmann sent Aehrenthal a detailed account of the Tsar's visit: 'The personal relationship between the two emperors was friendly and relaxed. I have the distinct impression — and this was confirmed by both sides — that both sovereigns were absolutely satisfied with their meetings and conversations, both here and in Wolfsgarten.' The Chancellor described at length his discussions with Sazonov, who had 'made a very good impression . . . as a calm, serious, and sensible politician, with whom it will always be possible to speak openly'. True, the Russian Foreign Minister had voiced two fears in Berlin: 'In the first place, he is very much afraid of an expansionist policy on Austria-Hungary's part in the Balkans, and of our supporting it, then he believed that we are inciting Turkey to an aggressive policy both in the Balkans and particularly towards Persia, and that we are striving to supply her with the necessary means.' He had managed to put both fears to rest, Bethmann assured Aehrenthal. Germany was firmly convinced 'that Austria-Hungary was not considering any kind of expansionist policy in the Balkans. Similarly, we had never pledged ourselves to support expansionist plans of Austria-Hungary in the Balkans, and she had never approached us with a request to do so. M. Sazonov was so relieved to hear these assurances that he spontaneously promised me that Russia, much as she was striving to come to terms with England, would never join with her in a hostile combination directed against Germany. I must ask Your Excellency to treat this last with the strictest secrecy.' He had further agreed with Sazonov that Russia and the Triple Alliance must work to maintain the status quo in the Near East, and that that required a peaceful internal development of the Balkan states and the maintenance of a strong regime in Turkey. 'Should it prove impossible, contrary to expectation, to maintain the status quo, then it would be the task of the Powers to localise the resultant conflict and to agree as to further measures.' Altogether, in his letter to Aehrenthal, Bethmann emphasised with relief the fact that 'a start has again been made towards a confidential discussion with Russia that will also have its effect on Austria-Hungary's relations with Russia ... I think I may expect this meeting to lead to a real alleviation for the policies of both our Empires.'[90] 'Our alliance relationship', so he told Aehrenthal at the end of 1910, 'is coming ever more clearly to the fore as the political fulcrum of the whole of Europe'.[91]

The reciprocal pledges given during the Potsdam meeting, that neither the German nor the Russian government had joined or would join any combination which could be aggressively directed against the other, were made public in the Chancellor's speech to the Reichstag on 10 December — which incurred the Kaiser's displeasure. After reading a newspaper report of it he thundered: 'I know nothing of this! No such promise was tendered to me, nor have I given one! I only know that Russia will not help England against us if England starts a war!' He was afraid that such a declaration might make the Triple Alliance useless, as 'it would formally cancel the *casus foederis* vis-à-vis Austria in the event of a Russian war, and endanger the main supporting pillar of the Triple Alliance'.[92] True, the Chancellor was able to calm the Kaiser down by pointing out that the language he had used in the Reichstag was quite compatible with Germany's obligations to Austria and Italy, especially as Vienna had repeatedly made binding declarations that it was not pursuing any aggressive designs in the Near East,[93] but the incident revealed a difference between Kaiser and Chancellor that was to prove by no means a trifling one, as events developed in the next four years. For Wilhelm II, Germany's absolute loyalty to the 'old emperor' in Vienna had long been a sacrosanct principle that was not to be questioned.

Quite apart from this, Wilhelm saw in Bethmann's declaration in the Reichstag an infringement of his role as the real director of German foreign policy. Thus he complained, in commenting on the Chancellor's letter of 11 December defending his speech: 'I should have been informed of it in good time. For I knew nothing of it! and it was a step of some importance, after all ... It is a factor of great political significance, about which the *director* of foreign policy, the *sovereign*, must not be left in the dark. In future, the content of any forthcoming political declaration and steps taken vis-à-vis foreign governments are to be reported to me in advance.'[94] After the war, the editors of the *Große Politik* condescendingly made light of these marginal comments of the Kaiser's, as arising 'obviously ... from a welling up of his hypersensitivity about sovereignty', but after years of experience the officials of the Wilhelmstrasse would certainly not have been so dismissive of the power of the monarch.[95]

It may well be, as foreign observers maintained, that after the Eulenburg affair and the *Daily Telegraph* crisis Wilhelm II no longer followed any fixed course in foreign policy, that he reacted to developments rather than determining their course. Certainly, at home, he found himself subjected to sharper criticism than ever before, and largely left the routine matters of government to his statesmen and diplomats. Even so, it would be wrong to underestimate his influence on world events. On the one hand, his powers of decision remained undiminished and almost absolute in matters of political appointments and in the field of military command. On the other, all decisions, especially those about foreign policy, had to have the monarch's approval, which meant that certain solutions were tacitly given preference, while others were rejected in advance as being certainly unacceptable to the Kaiser. The 'kingship mechanism' that allowed Wilhelm to have the last word whenever two opposing lines of conduct were recommended to him, proved especially effective in what was perhaps the most important foreign policy question of these years – negotiations with England over naval construction – which will be dealt with in the chapters that follow.

Apart from this, in the course of conversations and correspondence that were beyond his advisers' control with high-ranking representatives of other World Powers, Wilhelm II indulged in dizzying, extravagantly phrased tirades about the future that aroused deep mistrust about the ultimate objectives of German policy, and in many cases awakened suspicions that the powerful monarch was not quite sane. Wilhelm's correspondence with the Tsar on the eve of the Russo-Japanese War, his meeting with him in Björkö, the fatal interview he gave to the American journalist William Hale in 1908, his bellicose threats to Sir Charles Hardinge at Kronberg, his remarks to Colonel Stuart Wortley that shocked the German public when they appeared in the *Daily Telegraph* in October 1908 – the Kaiser continued in this embarrassing vein even after the November crisis of 1908 and the departure of Bülow in 1909.

CHAPTER TWENTY-NINE

The King is dead, or new hopes of an agreement with England

Wilhelm II's continental policy was primarily directed against Britain and the international system she presided over, the *pax britannica* with its concomitant, the European balance of power. This did not mean that the German Empire would not have welcomed an alliance with the leading seapower. In the view of the Kaiser and his advisers, however, such an alliance would have had to recognise Germany's 'equality of status' with the British Empire not just in Europe, but in the world, a condition which the British rejected out of hand, as they recognised that it would open the door to a German domination of Europe that was bound in the end to lead to their own downfall. By dint of an extraordinary admixture of dynastic ingratiation and unrelenting competition in the field of naval armaments Wilhelm hoped to bring the British to abandon their ententes with France and Russia in favour of a 'political agreement' with Germany. The ever-sharpening Anglo-German antagonism of the pre-war years thus developed into a life and death struggle between the principle of the balance of power represented by Great Britain, and the domination of Europe that Germany was striving for. British foreign policy, with its guiding principle, as Metternich defined it in 1909, that the maintenance of the balance of power in Europe required a counterweight to the Central Powers, was therefore for Wilhelm II the greatest obstacle to the realisation of his own hegemonial plans. To his mind the British principle of the balance of power was nothing more than an attempt 'to prevent Europe from uniting and to keep us in a permanent state of impotence'.[1]

THE NAVAL ARMS RACE AND CONTINENTAL HEGEMONY

Despite the agitation of the Navy League and the Pan-German League Germany's policy towards England was not predetermined or laid down in advance. If the Chancellor and the diplomats rather than the Kaiser and Tirpitz had been in control, tolerable relations with London would have been perfectly attainable. Even Bülow had recognised, towards the end of his Chancellorship, the immense damage that naval rivalry had done to Anglo-Geman relations.[2] His efforts at slowing down naval construction in return for more amicable relations with Great Britain were taken up by his successor, who assured the Austrian Foreign Minister Aehrenthal in November 1909 that he considered a lessening of tension between public opinion in England and the German Empire to be 'a most desirable ... objective ... not only in terms of my own country's specific interests, but also because I cannot imagine an Anglo-German conflict that would not drag in the whole continent'.[3] However, Bethmann's attempts to slow down naval construction came up against fierce opposition from Tirpitz, who could rely on the Kaiser to back him up.

In August 1909, only a few weeks after his appointment, Bethmann, with the Kaiser's consent, proposed to the British ambassador, Sir Edward Goschen, a limitation of battleship building linked to a 'general' political agreement.[4] But before the negotiations could really get going Wilhelm urged the need for restraint in view of the political crisis in England. On 30 September, after Tirpitz had visited him in Rominten, he telegraphed to the Chancellor that the English 'must be left to approach us, as we have been the first to show our hand', and hence 'a dilatory procedure would seem to be entirely appropriate'. The present moment was in any case the worst possible time to negotiate a naval agreement since the British government would be less willing to compromise during the impending election campaign. Moreover, he must absolutely reject the reductions in the naval budget being demanded by Adolf Wermuth, the Secretary of State at the Treasury, because 'as Supreme War Lord, I can never allow the naval power of the Reich to be put in question like that'.[5]

Bethmann's proposal met with distrust and rejection, not only in the Reich Navy Office, but in the Foreign Office in London and at the court in Windsor. 'The German proposal is startling in its suddenness', Sir William Tyrrell told the King's Private Secretary on 1 September, 'considering that a year ago at Cronberg the Emperor refused even to discuss the question of naval expenditure. From all accounts Bethman-Hollweg [sic] is a sincere & honest man, but Goschen is perturbed by those above and around the new Chancellor whose motives may not be quite above suspicion.'[6] The Permanent Under Secretary,

Sir Charles Hardinge, thought he could see through the German proposal: 'I feel that it is an insidious attempt to sow distrust between us & France & Russia & the greatest caution is necessary ... What they really want is to secure from us a promise of neutrality in certain eventualities and we should be juggins' to give this.'[7] Indeed, Hardinge hoped that the German proposals would prove 'quite unacceptable', and he was 'not at all sure that it would not be best for our country that they should be so. Germany is already feeling the pinch of taxation and it becomes each year more evident that she will have the greatest difficulty in finding money for her navy. Some people may draw the conclusion that this might precipitate a conflict but our supremacy at present is so considerable that the Germans would not be such fools as to provoke it, and if we are such fools as to ever allow that supremacy to be endangered we shall richly deserve anything we may get.'[8] He was, of course, afraid that some Cabinet ministers such as David Lloyd George or Winston Churchill might be inclined to fall for the German bait. 'The invitation of the German Emperor to Winston to attend the manoeuvres is I am sure part of this policy, and his aim is to secure a reduction next year of our naval expenditure.'[9] (See Figure 32.)

The German initiative in the naval question was indeed directed towards drawing the British over to the side of the Triple Alliance and getting them to turn their backs on their Entente partners, France and Russia. When, in a further meeting with Goschen in November, Bethmann elaborated on his concept of an Anglo-German agreement Hardinge saw his fears confirmed: 'The Chancellor's proposals are most insidious and dangerous, and I think it is high time now to drop them. I shudder however at the thought of what the fate of such proposals might be with a Cabinet in which L[loyd] George & Winston Churchill had the controlling influence.'[10] Sir Edward Grey spoke openly of his readiness to resign as Foreign Secretary should the Prime Minister side with Lloyd George and reject the construction of the six further Dreadnoughts that the Foreign Office deemed necessary.[11] Edward VII agreed entirely with Grey and Hardinge. As the King's Private Secretary, Knollys, told Hardinge on 13 November, Edward was convinced that a naval agreement with Germany purchased by a promise of British neutrality in the event of a continental war would be a fateful error, as 'Germany would have the power of demolishing her enemies, one by one, with us sitting by with folded arms, & she would then probably proceed to attack us.'[12] After the King's death, Knollys confirmed that along with 99.9 per cent of people in England Edward VII had regarded Germany with 'considerable distrust' all his life.[13]

To British apprehensions the Kaiser simply refused to listen. When the Germanophile War Minister Lord Haldane said that if England were to join

Figure 32 The gathering storm: Winston Churchill with Wilhelm II at the 'Kaiser manoeuvres' of the German army in 1909

together with the Triple Alliance the other continental Powers would be 'so disturbed that the peace would be perpetually imperilled', the Kaiser dismissed this argument as 'rubbish!' and claimed that the other European Powers — primarily France and Russia — 'would join in too', and so the whole continent would be united.[14] His reaction was much the same when in February 1910 Metternich reported a four-hour-long private conversation with the former Prime Minister A. J. Balfour, who explained that Great Britain's policy towards Germany was fundamentally due to 'fear of Germany's growing sea-power', and concern lest it could ultimately 'destroy England's position' and render her 'dependent on Germany'. Again Wilhelm II roundly dismissed these anxieties as 'Rubbish!', 'Nonsense!' and 'Hallucinations'. Balfour's arguments were 'perfectly lamentable and childish excuses' that did not deserve to be taken seriously. 'He should be ashamed of such silly talk.'[15]

The negative attitude of the British govenment and public constantly drove the Kaiser into a rage. To his young friend Mary Montagu he described the excitement in the United Kingdom as simply mass hysteria. 'The poor German Nation is being painted in all possible colours to suit the end of the scaremongers! It is quite distressing to see the wholesale lying & slandering going on in the mouth of Englishmen at the expense of me & my country & its Services. Such ways are totally undignified of a large world-governing country as England with a Fleet 3 times stronger than any other on the waters. Your countrymen seem to have lost their senses completely! Providence grant that they may soon find them again! It is hightime!'[16] The admiral's daughter's attempts to get the Kaiser to understand British anxieties only aroused his indignation: 'With regard to your political celebrities & so called great statesmen, their behaviour towards me & my country, seen from here, can only awaken pity & mirth, for they really make the impression of people all let loose together from Bedlam! In order to "rouse" your people they go & invent, & tell the most unheard of nonsense, fables, & even brazenfaced lies about the intentions, or supposed intentions, of my country they mostly never have seen, certainly not studied & of its ruler whom they dont know & who has never honoured them with any of his views!! Well if children do such things they get an olivedraught & are sent to bed, & when serious grown up peoples, go in for such bad jokes, they ought to be sent to Bedlam! Your politicians seem like actors in a pantomime, they are a set of screaming clowns or hysterical old women! as far as their utterances about Germany & its plans are concerned! ... You also say that it would be well that our two countries should stand together. That is my ideal I am working for since 20 years of my reign. But the violent press & the violent & senseless speeches in England make the task next to impossible. As for having to sink my ideas & feelings at the bidding of the people, that is a thing unheard of in Prussian history or traditions of my house! What the German Emperor, King of Prussia thinks right & best for his People he does; if he thinks Peace is necessary – as I am convinced – he will maintain Peace, notwithstanding all the bellowing of your People to the contrary, & in this he fullfills the wishes of his own subjects, who only desire to be on good terms with England. Scream & shout as much as you like to rouse the "slumbering Britons", but leave me & Germany out of the mess! There is America, Japan, Russia etc. all growing & developing even more rapidly than we are! Why are they not also referred to??!'[17]

THE COMBINATION OF `THE ANGLO-SAXON & THE TEUTONIC RACES´

Hardly anything demonstrates the ambivalence of Wilhelm's attitude to the United Kingdom so clearly as the hopes he cherished, at the end of 1909 and early in 1910, of a revival of the conflict between Russia and Japan, both of whom had links with England. His lively imagination seized on the possibility that the dispute over railways in Manchuria might result in a new Russo-Japanese war, into which the USA might be drawn – thereby becoming dependent on German support, possibly against the UK. Cheerfully, he minuted on the Chancellor's report at Christmas 1909, 'at last a great International point of view with broad perspectives. That is refreshing and gratifying. The Teutonic races co-operating in the East! The Mongols and Tartars will look sour . . . This will demonstrate to the world for the first time the coming together – even if only abroad – of the Teutonic-Anglo-Saxon countries! A great gain!'[18] Over the next weeks, Wilhelm's hopes of a global realignment of Powers along racial lines increased, and he rubbed his hands over the growing tension in the Far East. 'Then the quarrel will start between America and England. And also the dilemma for England, between the *yellow* ally and the *white* brother.'[19] Friction was also increasing, he gloated, 'between Japs and Yankees . . . and that is good'.[20]

Almost feverishly, he expatiated in his correspondence with Franz Ferdinand on the possibilities that these events seemed to offer. 'Developments in the Far East are following exactly the course I described to you', he wrote to the Archduke on 30 January 1910. 'Russia is retreating before Japan, and wishes to "liquidate" as they put it, in order to make trouble in the Balkans. Japan is arming further in order to gobble up the former Amur provinces and Vladivostok. America has taken up the cause of the poor Chinese and is starting to promote the interests of the White Race in the opening up of China by a policy of building railways, which I support. The repercussions that this has had in London, Tokyo and St Petersburg and the (sometimes very sharp) recriminations, offer material for a comedy! All to the good that America has seized the lead energetically! The other Whites will eventually join in. England seems to me to have enough on her plate with her own affairs for the time being.'[21]

A week later the Kaiser again gave his fantasy free rein, constructing a bizarre scenario of a second Russo-Japanese war and a combination of Germany and America against Japan and possibly against England as well. 'Things in the Far East look amusing', he wrote to Franz Ferdinand. 'After reconnaissance work near the Manchurian Railway and in Korea Japan is building field hospitals and munitions depots everywhere. The siege guns for Vladivostok are . . . already in position on the continent in North Korea . . . The Japanese will naturally . . . push Russia out in the long run and also swallow up North Manchuria in the end. Then it will be Vladivostok's turn. If it falls, that will be the first rap of the Asian peoples on the European door, and then the "Yellow Peril" will really be on the move. People here generally assume that the position will be definitively clarified by 1915. The Panama Canal is supposed to be completed in that year, which will allow the United States to concentrate its whole fleet in the Pacific. *Before that* the Japanese – if they still have designs as hitherto on *that* ocean – will have to contend with America for possession of it – so people think in America; if it comes to that, the Americans will need the German fleet to cover them in Europe – together with America's warships in the Atlantic – in case England should act as Japan's ally – though this is not likely. Hence the rejection a limine by the Americans of the English offer of last autumn . . . to make common cause with them against us. The combination (America-Germany) that may possibly emerge from this is gradually beginning to dawn on John Bull, hence in part his anxiety and nervousness about us!'[22]

When reports reached him in the summer of 1910 of the conclusion of a Russo-Japanese agreement over the Manchurian railway, Wilhelm saw here too the harbinger of a global conflict, this time between the 'Teutonic-Anglo-Saxon' peoples and the 'Yellow Peril' backed by the 'Slavs'.[23] It was in the first instance, he believed, a question of the 'partition of China!', from whom 'Japan is to take Manchuria and Russia, Mongolia, and this at a moment when England – because the alliance was and is an act of folly – is drawing away from Japan. If it were to come to a clash between America and Japan in which England found herself having to support America, then Russia would be *forced* to stand by Japan in Asia (India), otherwise she will lose Vladivostok, and Mongolia and Eastern Siberia too. If we helped America and England, which would be natural, then we should (theoretically) have the Russians against us.

That proves what I said in 1908, that in the event of an assault on Europe by the "Yellow Peril", the Slavs would not only not resist it, they would support it against Europe.'[24]

Not only events of worldwide significance in the Far East, but internal conditions in Great Britain strengthened Wilhelm's conviction that the maritime world Empire was on the brink of collapse. In February 1910 he declared, according to Zedlitz, that 'England was totally decadent, the upper classes were demoralised, and in the army and navy this showed itself in corruption and incompetence. Above all, commercial life was stagnating and this showed that the development of the English people had reached a stage of hypertrophy that made it unable to keep up in the competition between the peoples. The mediocrity of its achievement was evident everywhere, and the world would experience the decline and fall of the English world Empire with frightening speed.'[25]

Fully confident that Germany, thanks to its commercial, scientific and military development, had now gained the upper hand, Wilhelm replied on 30 January 1910 to his uncle Edward's letter congratulating him on his birthday. 'Your remark: "that it is essential for the Peace of the world that we should walk shoulder to shoulder for the good of civilisation & the prosperity of the world" strikes a familiar note in my heart. This wish has allways been the leading maxim of my policy & the goal which I have ardently striven to reach. It is a firm part of my political creed that the future of the world would be assured & safeguarded if the Anglo-Saxon & the Teutonic Races worked together. They are the powerful guardians of the Ideals of Christian Faith & Christian civilisation & it is their common duty to proclaim & disseminate them over the world. This task is imposed on them by Providence! It ought by its scope & greatness alone suffice to put a stop to all heckling & squabbling between them. It must remind them, that Providence is waiting for them to return to their work, which they are in danger of neglecting. This once brought home to the People & fully realized & understood by them, they will soon I trust sink their differences & agree to join hands in the common cause.'[26]

What Wilhem was aiming for with this letter to the King he described a few days later in a remarkable conversation with the United States ambassador David Jayne Hill, which the latter set down in writing the same evening. 'He said that a curious thing had just occurred on his birthday, it was a letter from his Uncle Edward, who for the first time in his life had discussed politics. "He has never thought it worth while before", he said. "He has always regarded himself as my superior and has felt a good deal nettled that I am an older sovereign than he while only his nephew. Now that he sees that we are strong and that the political situation in E[ngland] is bad he wants to have a better understanding and begins to think his poor nephew may be of some account ... I have never understood why the English should be so suspicious of us, even both parties. Part of it is due to the Daily Mail. It is dreadful the way the newspapers misrepresent us in England and Northcliffe is the most to blame for this. It was his Daily Mail that started the fiction of the toast by our naval officers "Zu Dem Tag", ("The Day when they would fight England"). My brother Henry speaking as the head of the navy has denied it absolutely, but they will not believe him, and they do not believe me. It was different in Grandmama's time. She would have put a stop to this long ago as she did when it began about Kruger. (This is what he told me last summer on the Meteor as he stood before Queen Victoria's picture and uttered his splendid eulogy of her.) What do they think in England? If they do not trust my word of honor, why do they not reason? What would I have to gain by invading the island? What could I do with it if it were mine? Do they think I want to run off with the Wallace Collection! It is a scandal the way they talk about Germany, and the King has not seemed to care. But he is beginning to care now. He begins to see that we have some ships. We do not want as many as they have. We do not want their colonies nor the dominion of the sea, we only want to have our rights respected. Germany is now almost as rich as England. We are competing with them successfully everywhere and all we want is an equal chance. They have tried to hold us up as a menace to Europe, but we have menaced no one. They have tried to array Europe against us, but their entente is weakening. As for the Latins, they have had their day. I do not believe the Slavs are to be the leaders of the future. Providence has designs, and it would not be a compliment to Providence to believe that it is to the Slavs and not to the Germanic race that Providence looks for the civilization of the future. No, it is the Germanic race, – we here in Germany, the English and the Americans, – who are to lead the civilization of the world. What a pity to be divided! It is all wrong to distrust one another. I am hoping for better things. I have replied to my Uncle's birthday letter in this sense. I have told him that it is his fault if we have not had a better understanding and an earlier one, for until now I have never felt free to discuss politics with him. I have tried to be understood but I could not open this subject with him until he did with me. As for what has been said of me personally, I never care about that; but I do care for my mission as German Emperor, and I do not intend to let the dignity of that office sink in my hands or to forget its responsibility. Germany has kept the peace of Europe ever since my Grandfather was chosen Emperor. I have had many occasions when I might have broken it, many other occasions when others would have broken it – for me, but in these twenty-two years we

Figure 33 Kaiser Wilhelm II with President Theodore Roosevelt in 1910

have had peace. In what forty years of European history has Europe had unbroken peace, which it has enjoyed since the founding of the Empire, and yet they say Germany is a menace to Europe!'[27]

On 10 May 1910 the former American President Theodore Roosevelt came to Berlin for five days (see Figure 33). He was generously entertained by the Kaiser and had long conversations with Bethmann Hollweg, Tirpitz, and the Foreign Secretary, Wilhelm von Schoen.[28] 'The Emperor, as everyone knows, talks with the utmost freedom with almost anyone', Roosevelt noted. Wilhelm declared his love for England, emphasising that 'I was brought up in England, very largely; I feel myself partly an Englishman. Next to Germany I care more for England than for any other country.' True, the Kaiser had abjured all thought of a war against England, but even so, the perceptive American observed, 'this does not mean that I regard his attitude toward England as free from menace. I do not believe that Germany consciously and of set purpose proposes to herself the idea of a conquest of England, but Germany has the arrogance of a very strong power ... Germany would like to have a navy [so] strong that whenever England does something she does not like she could at once assume towards England the tone she has assumed toward France ... If she had a Navy as strong as that of England, I do not believe that she would *intend* to use it for the destruction of England; but I do believe that incidents would be very likely to occur which might make her so use it.' Wilhelm had spoken equally openly about the threat posed, in his view, by Japan, which Roosevelt welcomed, as he had always recognised that 'it would be a serious situation if Germany, which ... is the only white power as organized as Japan, should strike hands with Japan. The thing that prevents it is Germany's desire to stand well with Russia. The Emperor was sure that Japan intended to organize China, and then, at the head of the Mongolian race, threaten the white dominance of the world ... I could not forbear asking him why, as he felt so keenly that the Christian powers should stand as one against the Yellow Peril, he did not feel the same way about Turkey.' Roosevelt summed up his overall impression with the words: 'In international affairs, he at times acts as a bully, and moreover a bully who bluffs and then backs down.' Certainly neither the Kaiser nor his country was an easy neighbour. 'Yet again and again, and I think sincerely for the moment at least, he dwelt to me on his desire to see England, Germany and the United States act together in all matters of world policy.'[29] After the former President's departure Wilhelm sent him photographs of them together at the manoeuvres in Döberitz, with the ringing inscription: 'Total agreement about the general maxims of life + policy between Amerika + Germany ... The Germanic + Anglo Saxon Races combined will keep the world in order!'[30] A few days later Wilhelm was to meet Roosevelt again in London, at the funeral of Edward VII, who had died on 6 May.

THE FUNERAL OF KING EDWARD VII

With the death of his uncle Edward, Wilhelm's hopes revived of an understanding with Great Britain that would recognise Germany's 'equality of status' in the world. Alongside Roosevelt, who was, however, no longer in office, the Kaiser now seemed to many to be the most important personality on the whole planet. As one of the Flügeladjutanten who accompanied the Kaiser to the funeral remarked, Wilhelm II was, 'now that the royal uncle is dead, more than ever the decisive factor in the world. He and Roosevelt will in the immediate future be the masters of history. The young King ... will be in a quite different relationship to him from the dominant King Edward.'[31] Here, the aide-de-camp was echoing a theme of the British newspapers that declared that 'since the death of King Edward, Kaiser Wilhelm was indisputably the leading political personality among the monarchs and the only one who thanks to the power of his personality and influence was in a position to carry on the life's work of the late King, namely, maintaining and safeguarding the peace of Europe'.[32]

Wilhelm himself immediately recognised the opportunities opened up by the change and strove assiduously to cultivate his relations with his cousin George V.[33] His reply to the Chancellor's telegram of condolence announcing the death of his uncle was pensive: 'An outstanding Polit[ical] personality has suddenly disappeared from the European stage, leaving a perceptible gap. At such a moment one forgets a lot of things. Engl[ish] policy as a whole will ex off[icio] not change very much. But there will be some remission in the active organisation of intrigues that always had Europe holding its breath and would not allow it to settle down and enjoy some peace and quiet. The personally constructed combinations will, now the head is missing, disintegrate: For they were held together by the magic effect of Person[al] influence and persuasive eloquence on the leaders of the various states. It is a serious blow for France. And many a *right thinking* and *rational* Gaul may well quietly scratch his head and ask whether France ought after all to have had better relations with her neighbour, rather than having to try to improve them now. Isvolsky too will feel really lonely now that his guiding star is extinguished! I think on the whole that there will be more calm in Europ[ean] politics; and even if that were all, it would still be a gain. If nobody is stoking up the various fires, they will burn less fiercely. Apart from his own people, E[dward] VII will be mourned chiefly by the Gauls and the Jews.'[34]

Although the Chancellor approved of Wilhelm's going to the funeral, he was worried about the political damage that the Kaiser might do by careless talk. His anxiety increased when Wilhelm remarked the present moment was a good one for 'putting down a marker' in London, and he appealed to Metternich to prevent the monarch from engaging in political discussions wherever possible. 'I need not say, dear Count, that I doubt whether political discussions are opportune at the moment. Apart from the reserve prescribed by political tact in view of the national mourning, any attempt by His Majesty to initiate political discussions would be especially undesirable because influential people in England might discern in it a personal desire on the part of our most gracious Master to win the King over to Germany's side and away from the close friendship with Russia and France.' He had tried to make it clear to the Kaiser that it would be better if he did not even touch on political questions when in London, but he was 'not sure whether any impression I made will be a lasting one ... I ask you, therefore, to ... act in the same sense, which, given your expert knowledge of His Majesty's disposition and your proven tact, should not be difficult.'[35]

Bethmann's apprehensions seemed to be confirmed by Wilhelm's first telegram, describing the warm reception he had received from George V, and touchingly describing how the King had accompanied him to the catafalque in Westminster Hall. 'After we had both knelt in silent thought, we went up to each other and joined hands, deeply moved. A moment of historic importance when, amidst his grieving subjects who bore witness to the occasion, standing by King Edward's coffin, England's King held the German Emperor's hand in a firm grip.'[36]

Early next morning the second dispatch arrived, with Wilhelm's reports on his conversations wth George V, Roosevelt, the French Foreign Minister Stephen Pichon, and other personages assembled in London. Although most of the British statesmen had little sympathy for the idea of cooperation between the Germans and the Anglo-Saxons, and a few of them were even 'quite hopeless' in matters of 'general politics, such as the East Asian question, co-operation between the white races etc.,' Wilhelm remained confident that the magic of his personality could bring about a change; and he was quite enchanted with the brilliant reception he had received.[37] He was equally proud to describe to the Chancellor the role of honour that George V had assigned to him in the magnificent and 'deeply moving' funeral ceremony. (See Figure 34.) Early in the morning, the King had ridden, 'with all his royal guests through streets lined with troops and the silent multitude to Westminster Hall'. 'There, the King ordered that apart from the Duke of Connaught, the Queen Mother, and [her sister] the Dowager Empress of Russia, I alone of all the foreign princes was to dismount and go with him into Westminster Hall . . . After the coffin had been mounted on the gun carriage the mighty funeral procession, several kilometers long, began to move. The Duke of Connaught and I both rode, as Field Marshals, on either side of the King, who wore a general's uniform. It was the most imposing demonstration of mourning by a whole people for its beloved sovereign that I have ever witnessed . . . Here too I could often hear whispers from the crowd of "the King and the German Emperor" . . . The ceremony ended with a luncheon for everybody at Windsor Castle. When I got there I had been assigned the rooms of my parents, where I had often played as a little boy, and which were famous for their magnificent view over the whole of Windsor Park. There were so many memories filling my heart as I moved through the rooms where I had played as a child, stayed as a youth, and enjoyed as a man, and later as ruler, the gracious hospitality of the great Queen and of His late Majesty. They reawakened in me my old feelings which bind me so fast to this place, and which for me personally have made the last few years, in political respects, particularly hard to bear. I am proud to call this place my second home country, and to be a member of this royal house, as which I am always treated most warmly by everybody. It was very remarkable how when I left Windsor Castle in an open carriage, and passed through the same crowd that had latterly been standing there in silent

Figure 34 Wilhelm II and his cousin George V at the funeral of King Edward VII

mourning, it was suddenly as if an electric shock went through the crowd as they recognised me. At this moment the cry arose, ever more insistently, "the German Emperor", until suddenly a loud voice shouted: "Three cheers for the German Emperor", which was taken up by the massed crowds and resounded through all the streets as a thunderous triple "Hurrah" from the massed crowds. I had tears in my eyes and my neighbour, the King of Denmark, said to me: "How the people here like you! That is marvellous, that the people give you such an enthusiastic reception despite their deep sorrow for dear Bertie." I think this entirely spontaneous welcome can be regarded as a good omen . . . I feel very well here and am living in Buckingham Palace in the beautiful ground-floor Belgian rooms with a view of the lovely garden that is so big that one doesn't notice the noise of the city of millions . . . Here too, I played a lot as a child, and still have a memory of the spot where I was colossally sick after eating too much pudding.'[38] The touching trustfulness with which the sovereign here recounted his childhood memories testifies to the familiar relations that he had established with the Chancellor over the past year. At the same time, however, the accompanying conviction that his personal magnetism had gained him the hearts of the English people included the dangerous illusion that the maritime Empire would remain aloof from conflicts on the continent – an illusion that was strengthened by the impact of the internal political crisis that he was witnessing in London. It was in vain that Metternich tried to make it clear to him that the sympathies he met with on all sides in London 'should certainly not be underestimated' and might indeed 'in due course produce tangible results'; but that they were 'for the moment . . . only a mood', which could easily be dissipated if real differences arose.[39]

Metternich's warnings were timely, as despite Bethmann's attempts to restrain him, the Kaiser, as was his nature, involved himself in busy political activity in London. On 23 May he telegraphed to the Chancellor: 'I have in the course of my stay had a number of conversations with my relatives, with courtiers and a few old acquaintances, and have in particular been witness to many conversations between many people. In short, the position is this: People are completely preoccupied with the internal situation and their uncertain future. In general the picture is really black. The government is veritably detested. The language used to describe the Cabinet cannot be sharp enough. Nobody sees any solution for the moment. People note with satisfaction that in the days after the King's death and at the time of the funeral the prime minister and other colleagues of his were hissed in the streets, and expressions such as "you have killed the King" were heard. People regard the tremendous demonstration of grief on the day of the funeral as a demonstration against the government and think a swing to the Conservatives not impossible. The growth of the Socialists is also causing concern, even if they behave more reasonably and have less far-reaching plans than ours do.' In discussing the world situation in detail, including the position of the British in Egypt, with Sir Ernest Cassel, Wilhelm had spoken up 'strictly as a private individual' for the annexation by Britain of Egypt, and cited Roosevelt's similar opinion: he had always been surprised 'that after the enormous sacrifices of blood, gold and manpower England had not annexed Egypt in some form or other long ago'. When the financier objected that England did not know 'what Europe would say about that, and was especially worried about Germany's attitude on the question, as we were very distrusted', he replied that the British colonial administration was excellent, German trade was flourishing in all the British colonies, and would certainly be in agreement with a British annexation of Egypt. 'Politically, of course, there were a lot of difficulties to resolve, especially given our friendly relations with Turkey, and a fair amount of water would have to flow down the Nile before a solution was found. However, if in the event of general unrest which might spread to India, England found herself forced for strategic (Suez Canal) or other reasons to consolidate the position in Egypt in that way, I personally should fully understand, and we could talk about it. I did not think that in such an event Germany would come forward to oppose England. However, I had never handled the question from that point of view and did not know what the government thought about it. Sir Ernest replied that if that was my view, and if it ever became known in England, the distrust against us would be banished at a stroke, and, above all, Anglo-German friendship on a political level would take an enormous step forwards, and a great part of the mistrust against us would disappear. Could he tell Sir E. Grey anything of this? I replied that that would not be appropriate, as it was only a private conversation and I should first have to discuss it with Your Excellency. He said: "I have had the honour to earn the confidence of my late master over the years, and I should like to do the same for Your Majesty. I shall remain silent until Your Majesty sends me further commands."'[40]

Although King George was 'very preoccupied with the internal situation' and had not talked to him about foreign policy, Wilhelm had great hopes of his influence over his cousin.[41] When the Chancellor congratulated him on his success in England and remarked that in the negotiations with London and St Petersburg over Persia 'a more moderate view, less plagued by fears of a trouble-making Germany' was already beginning to prevail, the Kaiser strongly urged him to hold back, as the King had first to get used to his job. 'Getting his bearings and working his way into all these foreign matters will take time. He will have to construct a new framework for handling Political questions. Either as in the past or differently. But at this time of deep sorrow for him and the entire nation, it would be considered in very bad taste and lacking in tact for pressure to be applied from outside to settle these questions now. I very much wish that extreme caution and quiescence should prevail in our relations with London at the moment ... Wait and see! Any bustling or premature schemes in the field of foreign policy – on the part of our newspapers too – could do us a lot of damage here! Because they are very sensitive here at the moment. It needs a lot of tact, and it would be best to remain respectfully silent; until H[is] M[ajesty] speaks. In any case, for us now to propose a discussion of what is actually a purely theoretical Persian question, which is in terms of the position here of no importance whatever, would really be a faux pas and would have the most unpleasant consequences. Which would totally destroy all I have achieved here. Let us be satisfied with the good effect of my presence here; and wait and see what comes.'[42] The Kaiser's exaggeration of the role that George V could play within the British parliamentary system was to have fatal consequences in the July crisis of 1914, as we shall see.

At least outwardly, Wilhelm's five-day stay in London must be counted a success. Count Metternich was full of praise when the Kaiser left for home: the feelings of 'warmth and enthusiasm' expressed in the London newspapers as soon as his visit was announced had lasted for the whole of his stay. 'They wrote at length about His Majesty's personal qualities. The imposing dignity of his appearance, his almost unlimited, always surprising virtuosity, his pious religious faith, his invincible vitality, his persistence in pursuing hs political objectives, his honesty of purpose and conviction, the modern progressive spirit that he embodied, were eloquently described. There was special praise for the piety and familial loyalty with which the Kaiser, as formerly at the death of Queen Victoria, so now on this tragic occasion, had hastened to come and express his sympathy ... The general tone that rang though the whole press, including those papers otherwise noted for their Germanophobia, was the desire and expectation that His Majesty the Kaiser's visit would serve to maintain world peace and lead to a sincere rapprochement between Germany and England.'[43]

During his annual northern cruise Wilhelm tried to develop his friendship with the new King. 'My dear Georgy', he wrote to him from Norway on 8 July 1910, 'Let me thank you for the kind thought of sending me the photo of the 9 Sovereigns at Windsor. A souvenir of a sad but ever to be remembered day of mourning, which never can be effaced from my memory. That I was permitted to come over to stay with you through all those hours has created a link between us which I allways shall cherish.'[44] The King thanked the Kaiser for his letter in very friendly terms. 'The many kind words you use with regard to your last sad visit to this Country have touched me deeply; the heartfelt sympathy which you showed on that occasion was greatly appreciated not only by my family but by my people at large.'[45] For a short time it seemed that thanks to the Kaiser's charm offensive a new era was dawning in Anglo-German relations. But Wilhelm's hopes were soon to be badly disappointed again, because, as before, behind the fine speeches and gestures of friendship on stage, the underlying Anglo-German contest between hegemony and the European balance of power continued unabated.

THE RESUMPTION OF NEGOTIATIONS FOR AN ANGLO-GERMAN ENTENTE

Following his promising visit to London and the alarming Russian army manoeuvres of August 1910 in which Germany was directly named as the enemy, Wilhelm again took up the demand for a 'political entente with England', without, however, being prepared to make concessions in the matter of naval construction.[46] But this was the very question that continued to divide the two countries by a wide gulf. On 14 August in Wilhelmshöhe the British ambassador, Sir Edward Goschen, presented the Reich Chancellor with a memorandum that was hardly more than a proposal for occasional exchanges of views. To this, the Kaiser replied with an eleven-point programme setting out his ideas for a 'general political understanding' with England that could hardly have been more far-reaching. From what he evidently thought was a position of superiority, he made demands of the British that they could not possibly accept. Before anything else, he insisted, a 'political agreement' must be reached in which Great Britain must give up the Entente she had concluded with France and Russia and conclude instead an Entente with Germany. 'England wishes the political agreement [with Germany] to be one that can include the Powers with whom she stands in an entente relationship, i.e. England (to reassure them!) should immediately inform them of it. Here we demand reciprocity, i.e.: The Franco-Russian alliance is a military alliance with detailed engagements directed against us. (Pretext alleged threats of attack from Germany). In 1904–05 England joined a directly anti-German coalition, one recognised as such, and offered France military assistance on the continent. England declares nevertheless that she has not agreed to anything against us in her Ententes with Germany's enemies, and that she bears us no ill will. That is a self-deception. The very fact of England's joining the Franco-Russian alliance amounts in principle, from the German point of view, to an unfriendly act. Agreements in this or that direction have nothing to do with the case. If England therefore wishes to communicate the entente we have in prospect to other Powers, then we demand first of all admission to her Ententes with Russia and France, the content of which was not communicated to us beforehand. The basis for the entente with us, policy on parallel lines in the world. Above all, common defence of the open door. That is attractive to commercial circles of every kind in England and in the City above all, and is also popular in Germany. It is possible that there might be talk later of a guarantee of India, as there is great anxiety in England about India. Envisage in exchange a guarantee of Alsace-Lorraine and a promise of rear cover and possibly maritime assistance.' Only after England had accepted these conditions would it be possible to discuss with her the relationship between the two battlefleets. And on this point too the Kaiser's demands were completely unrealistic. England, so he explained in his eleven-point pro-gramme, was demanding 'a standstill in German naval construction . . . while offering English reciprocity. This, as Germany is more or less bound by a detailed law is apparently an attempt to head off any German *Novelle*. England has no fixed law, and can lay down any number of ships as she likes and according to need. How can this be construed as reciprocity? England must first present us with a construction programme that she is obliged to stick to, and which clearly indicates the future development of the English navy.'[47]

Predictably enough, within weeks Wilhelm's hopes of a large-scale under-standing with England had been dashed. In a dispatch from Rominten to the Reich Chancellor on 30 September 1910 he raged against the British-led Triple Entente's plans, now becoming obvious to all the world, 'to encircle Germany financially and strangle her'. 'Everywhere, British bankers and industrialists are . . . fighting to the death against every opportunity for orders for German industry or its commercial advancement, and even against Gernan capital investment abroad. The Entente Powers are using financial harrass-ment against the countries which are allied to us or on friendly terms with us, to try to ruin them, and by worsening their financial plight – so long as they are allied to us – to drive them to break with us. In *commercial* terms, therefore, *war* with England and the Entente is in fact *fully under way*, without its being noticed in Germany apart from in the world of high finance, where the situation is regarded as very serious. In these circumstances the English memorandum that was presented at Wilhelmshöhe is worth even less than it was at the time. It completely pushes aside our demand for a 'political' entente as the basis for a *maritime* one and says no more about it, which makes the whole sorry effort look like just an embarrassed manoeuvre ut aliquid facere, so as to be able to blame us again afterwards for failing to agree to it. So long as England is striving so openly, and using all means including her alliances to damage us in our justified commercial enterprises, there can be no question of an entente.' He ordered the Chancellor to 'discuss the position with the big banks in Berlin, so that we can defend ourselves in good time'.[48] When Bethmann assured him that the German reply to the British memorandum had 'again, and entirely in line with Your Majesty's command, sharply emphasised the need for a political agreement in connection with a naval agreement' the Kaiser crossly replied: 'that can come later, as given France and Russia's enthusiasm for [naval] construction we cannot bind ourselves by an agreement with one side alone when we have to build against a coalition of several states'.[49]

Wilhelm was pained by Germany's isolation, which continued to grow even after the death of Edward VII, and his reaction was one of sulky defiance. When in September 1910 his diplomats warned that any strengthening of China by Germany would be unwelcome to Tokyo, and would automatically bring the German Reich into opposition to Japan, the Kaiser declared: 'that is now here to stay! ... I am fully in agreement with the idea of supporting China ... Whether the Japanese or anyone else pulls a long face about it doesn't matter in the least. [The Brazilian President] Fonseca has asked me for German officers and France has made a fuss about it. The Turks have bought ships from us, France-England-Russia threw a fit! England has divided up Persia with Russia *without us*, Russia has divided up China with Japan without bothering about us, and we have neither done nor said anything against it. Therefore, it must be all right the other way round! China and Turkey are the only two countries that trust us and where we can still accomplish anything. If we lose these two out of pusillanimity, neglect, laziness, or connivance with perceived opponents who might take offence, we shall disappear from the scene, and deservedly so. Both must be supported by all − including financial − means against England's policy of financially encircling Germany!'[50]

KAISER WILHELM'S LAST VISIT TO LONDON

The Kaiser's hopes of an understanding with Great Britain rallied again when in February 1911 he received an invitation from his cousin George V to attend the unveiling of the memorial to Queen Victoria in London, planned for 16 May. Wilhelm and the Kaiserin could spend a few days in Buckingham Palace and were to bring their daughter Victoria Luise with them too, on what would be a private visit.[51] He at once spotted an opportunity to make political capital out of his close relationship with the British royal family and his personal popularity in England, as he had done at his uncle's funeral. Enthusiastically, he replied to the King's invitation: 'You cannot imagine how overjoyed I am at the prospect of seeing you again so soon & making a nice stay with you. You are perfectly right in alluding to my devotion & reverence for my beloved Grandmother, with whom I was on such excellent terms. I shall never forget how kindly this great lady allways was to me & the relations she kept up with me though I was so far her junior, she having carried me about in her arms. Never in my life shall I forget the solemn hours in Osborne near her deathbed, when she breathed her last in my arms! Those sacred hours have riveted my heart firmly to your house & family, of which I am proud to feel myself a member. And the fact that for the last hours I held the sacred burden of her – the Creator of the Greatness of modern Britain – in my arms, in my mind created an invisible, special link between her country & its People & me, which I fondly nurse in my heart.'[52]

Yet whereas on a dynastic level cordial family feelings held sway, in official relations between the two countries distrust and frustration continued to prevail. The German demand for a 'general political' understanding as a precondition of a naval agreement confronted the British Cabinet with a dilemma. In a memorandum of March 1911 the government pointed out that neither the Entente with France nor that with Russia, which had both settled existing material differences, had embodied such a general political formula; the agreement proposed by Germany might therefore 'be considered as something more comprehensive, far-reaching, and intimate' than the agreements that had been concluded with Paris and St Petersburg and would be likely to give rise to distrust there. As a compromise, the British proposed negotiations about the Baghdad Raiway and railways in Persia, that could be carried on at the same time as talks about a reduction of naval armaments.[53]

These tentative negotiations were overtaken by an apparent British 'capitulation' when the First Lord of the Admiralty Reginald McKenna and the Foreign Secretary Sir Edward Grey announced in the Commons on 13 March that as the expenditure on armaments had become unsustainable, Britain would be satisfied with a naval ratio of 3:2 with Germany. Tirpitz observed retrospectively: 'With this "Capitulation" to the formula of 2:3, while we maintained the Navy Law, everything was achieved that we had ever sought ... *The German Chancellor only needed to seize the opportunity* ... Yet instead of seizing it with both hands, the Kaiser hesitated. What he was thinking of, I don't know.'[54] In fact, there was nothing mysterious about the attitude of the Kaiser, who wanted to turn the screw ever tighter and demanded that the competition in armaments continue unrestrained, in order to force the British to abandon their ententes with France and Russia. The British 'capitulation', he rejoiced, was 'a great success for our perseverance!' 'Had we stopped building 4 or 5 years ago as Metternich and Bülow wanted, we should now be at war "Copenhagen". Thus, they [the British] respect our firmness of will and have to yield to facts. So, just carry on building. And when the higher tempo ceases, perhaps instead of 2 battleships and 1 heavy cruiser, 1 battleship and 2 heavy cruisers. So that we can make up the deficiency.'[55]

At this time, the German naval attaché in London, Captain Wilhelm Widenmann, believed that the British had still not grasped the full implications of the German Navy Law that would become automatically self-renewing after 1917.[56] However, when he met the Kaiser on board the *Hohenzollern* on 14 May, he told him he suspected that the British government had now become aware of the trap after all, and that it was only for this reason that they had proposed a fixed ratio of 3:2. Excitedly, Wilhelm telegraphed to Tirpitz: Widenmann had discovered 'that the English government, after studying the Navy Law, had at last come to recognise that, according to the Law, after 1917 replacements would automatically transform the 2-er tempo into a 3-er tempo. England is seeking, by its *apparent* concession, to tie us down to making the 2-er tempo permanent, thereby taking the Law out of our hands. He [Widenmann] urgently warns us not to accept this in any circumstances. The contingent offer of a ratio of 2:3, which we should have been prepared to accept in [19]08 and [19]09, is now in [19]11 worthless, as in the meantime the figures have been altered by an enormous number of new Engl[ish] ships. Hence, the purpose of the Engl[ish] agreement about naval construction is to tie the Germans to a 2-er tempo and pulverise the Navy Law. The fact that an agreement has been offered is proof of the effectiveness of the Navy Law and of our fleet. The latter has had a direct impact then, as a spur to make an agreement with us; its unimpeded development and expansion according to the Navy Law – while also keeping open the possibility of an earlier move to a 3-er tempo if unexpected progress by our neighbours should make it necessary – absolutely essential.'[57]

In his reply to this 'command' Bethmann did what he could to calm the Kaiser down. 'Whether England is ready to jump this ditch will only become clearer when we know if she wishes to make any proposals at all, and what these are.' 'It would be in our best interests, therefore, to carry on talking calmly and soberly, without being too pressing and at the same time (as we have always done in carrying out Your Majesty's gracious commands hitherto) keeping the political agreement to the fore. In our last memorandum we made it clear that the implementation of the Navy Law is a sine qua non for us. The consequences of this in terms of our 2er- and 3er-tempo . . . will only have to be spelt out to the English if it becomes clear from the nature of any proposals which they should make to us, that they are now ready for a political agreement. Otherwise they would, I fear, again become suspicious.

While I fully share Your Majesty's position, that only the actual building up of our navy will bring the English to reason, at the same time the growing confidence in the constancy of Your Majesty's policy has also contributed to improving relations, and, given the political character of the English, without such confidence we shall not be able to achieve our aim. Besides, Your Majesty's personal relationship with King George, as demonstrated by the present invitation, happily guarantees that our relations with England will continue to develop favourably.'[58]

On his visit to England in May 1911 the Kaiser, as in 1907 and 1910, placed his reliance on the brilliant effect of his personality on the Londoners. Delighted with his reception, he telegraphed to the Reich Chancellor that the unveiling of the memorial to his grandmother Queen Victoria in front of Buckingham Palace was 'simple but very grand and enthralling'. The 'King mentioned my visit in very gracious, cordial terms which – I later discovered – met with universal approval ... I spoke to Asquith, Sir E. Grey, Haldane. Nothing special concerning us. With the usual English tact, no political questions touched on ... In all my meetings I was struck by a refreshing openness and relaxed (in a good sense) attitude on everybody's part compared to earlier. Whenever we drove out there were crowds of people greeting us with cheers ... down to the simplest labourers. Usually, therefore, I drove through London bareheaded, hat in hand ... The wish to stand well with us really very clear.'[59] The Kaiser went on to sum up his impressions for Bethmann of the general mood in England: 'The "people" had shown by their attitude and the spontaneous warmth of their demonstrations that they not only admired him, the Kaiser, but also wanted an understanding with us. How far this feeling had penetrated into the upper ten thousands [sic] who had been worked on by King Edward in the opposite sense, remained doubtful. Within the royal family the tone had never been so free, open and cordial as this time.'[60] Wilhelm rated the favourable effect of his visit to England very highly; and covered with furious marginalia such as 'Rubbish' and 'Nonsense' an article in the *Wiener Zeitung* that claimed that the private and family nature of his visit to London had deprived it of any political effect. 'This ass does not know London, London life, and life at court at all! Otherwise he would not write such drivel.'[61]

Before the Kaiser left for London, fears had been expressed in the Wilhelmstrasse that he might be 'very susceptible to English influences' and commit himself to a dangerous degree on the question of an agreement.[62] In fact, on his return to Berlin Wilhelm assured the Chancellor that during his stay in England, he had not engaged in political dicussions, apart from touching on the Moroccan question with the King. He conceded that he had talked 'at length about our relations with England' to Sir Ernest Cassel and Prince Louis of Battenberg, but he could count on their discretion. According to a memorandum of Bethmann's, the Kaiser had told Cassel that 'we could not allow ourselves to be "differentially treated" by England . . . England had reached agreement with France in 1904 over Morocco, and then with Russia in Reval, without asking us. Now she makes the consent of Russia and France a precondition of a political understanding with us. That was discriminatory treatment which we could not put up with and which would not get us any further. His Majesty did not say', the Reich Chancellor noted lamely, 'whether he had discussed the naval question with these two gentlemen'.[63]

In actual fact, when he was leaving London, Wilhelm had given vent to one of his most horrendous tirades in a reign studded with indiscretions and *faux pas*, and one which was to have a fateful effect on British policy. On 20 May 1911, speaking on board the *Hohenzollern* to Prince Louis of Battenberg, who was soon to have supreme command of the Royal Navy, Wilhelm said that he sincerely desired the most cordial political relations with England, 'but you must not *differentiate* in the way you have been doing of late. You must not preface every conversation with the condition that you cannot come to an agreement with us on this or that subject if it were to affect the interests of France or Russia', and he vehemently rejected Battenberg's argument that the good relationship between Great Britain and those two countries was 'the natural & necessary counterpoise to the Triple Alliance'. 'The Emperor fired up & proceeded with more & more warmth, not to say heat, to ridicule this conception of the balance of power in Europe', Prince Louis recorded. 'You must be brought to understand in England that Germany is the sole arbiter of peace or war on the Continent', Wilhelm had exclaimed. 'If we wish to fight, we will do so with or without your leave. And why? Because we Continental powers dispose of armies counting millions. Of what possible use would it be for you to land your 50,000 men anywhere? I am convinced you would never attempt anything so foolish, as those beautiful lifeguards & grenadier guards would be blown sky high by my submarines before they could set foot on shore. − As to those French, we have beaten them once & we will beat them again. We know the road from Berlin to Paris. You know you can't mount your Dreadnoughts on wheels & come to your dear friends' assistance. In the meantime I wish them joy in their Morocco business. The more millions & the more soldiers it will cost them, the better. − That [Bosnia-]Herzegowina business showed how powerless England really is on the Continent. *I* settled it my way, for my friend Austria and you had not a word to say in it. And I will do so again if the occasion arises. Let me impress upon you one thing. Any attempt on your part to come between me & Russia I will look upon as the most *unfriendly* of all actions. There are ties between Germany & Russia which no one must touch. For one thing we went through the great wars of liberation from Napoleon's yoke together (sic!), for another the two dynasties are closely related & devotedly attached to one another. Then there is another consideration, which you in your democratic country do not appreciate or understand. To us the monarchical principle is a sacred thing. If a revolution were to endanger the throne in Russia, the Emperor of Austria & I would instantly march in shoulder to shoulder, and re-instate the Emperor Nicolas.' Sardonically, Battenberg recalled the cynicism with which Wilhelm had pushed the Tsar into the war with Japan, and the *Schadenfreude* with which he had greeted Russia's subsequent catastrophic defeats. Altogether, he gained the impression that the Kaiser wished his views to be passed on to the decision-makers in London, presumably 'as a piece of bluff, to frighten them into a more cautious attitude as regards friendly relations with France, but especially with Russia'.[64]

Battenberg sent his memorandum on this conversation to the King who immediately sent it on to Asquith, who in turn showed it to the Foreign Secretary. All were shocked, and asked themselves if the German monarch was quite sane. Asquith wrote: 'The Emperor has long since ceased to have any settled policy, and is (I believe) every year taken less & less seriously by his own subjects. One is almost tempted to discern in some of the things he said to Prince Louis the workings of a disordered brain; but (even if that is so) they are none the less dangerous.'[65] In the Foreign Office, the conviction became increasingly deep-rooted that Germany was striving for 'hegemony in Europe'.[66] As Battenberg's wife, Princess Victoria of Hesse-Darmstadt, was the sister of the Tsarina Alexandra, one can assume that Wilhelm's boasting also became known in St Petersburg. At any rate, the Kaiser's threatening expostulations contributed to the London government's decision to stand by France to the end when the second Moroccan crisis inaugurated the next great trial of strength over predominance on the continent.

CHAPTER THIRTY

Agadir: the leap of the *Panther*

Of all the European Great Powers Germany's republican neighbour to the west was the one with whom Wilhelm II had least contact. While the British and Russian monarchs were welcome in Paris and Wilhelm was received with enthusiasm in Vienna and London, a visit by a German emperor to Paris had been simply unthinkable since 1871. Of course, there could be no question in the French case of any personal correspondence between monarchs, such as Wilhelm engaged in with the Tsar and Archduke Franz Ferdinand, and, with an appropriate degree of reserve, with his British relatives. Hence, Kaiser Wilhelm's contacts with the French state were confined to occasional telegrams of congratulation or condolence to this or that French statesman, general, or artist or their widows. True, he did not shrink in some of his speeches – in Strasbourg in September 1908, for example, from threatening France with war – just as he brashly informed Prince Louis of Battenberg in May 1905 and again in May 1911 that the German army knew the way from Berlin to Paris and would not if the case arose be deterred from attacking France by British Dreadnoughts, which after all could not run on wheels. He even told an American diplomat that in view of the steady growth of Germany's population he might one day have to ask France to evacuate broad stretches of territory in the north and east so that Germans could settle there.[1] On the other hand, at least for the time being, Wilhelm II was also concerned to maintain tolerable relations with his western neighbour, an attitude which quite often exposed him to ridicule and charges of cowardice and pacifism from nationalists at home.[2] On several occasions, in fact, the Kaiser adopted a more conciliatory line towards France than his diplomats in the Wilhelmstrasse, especially over the Moroccan question, politically so explosive ever since 1904.

'MY VERY OWN PERSONAL ACHIEVEMENT.' THE BACKGROUND TO THE MOROCCAN QUESTION

Already in the autumn of 1908, even before the *Daily Telegraph* crisis, Wilhelm II had made known his strong personal interest in the Moroccan question, expressing his displeasure at the slow pace of the Franco-German negotiations and the 'pettifogging' attitude of his officials. That September blows had actually been exchanged in Casablanca when German consular officials had tried to prevent the arrest by French marines of three German deserters from the French foreign legion. The Kaiser had taken up a decidedly conciliatory position, ordering the dismissal of the German officials who he said had only been acting 'out of francophobia'.[3] Instead of issuing a strong protest, let alone sending warships to Casablanca, as the Wilhelmstrasse and the young Crown Prince were contemplating, Wilhelm pressed for a resolution of the conflict from the start, and telegraphed, as the crisis deepened, that such an incident was what he had 'always feared'. 'I am confirmed in my worst fears, which I have long held. Recommend a formula be found as soon as possible, as otherwise there will be indiscretions and publications by the Gauls, and then the apology from us will be a *unilateral* one, which will be a great humiliation! If one is in the wrong one should honestly admit it.'[4] Indeed, Wilhelm seemed so set on conciliation that Bülow expressed the fear that, as in 1905 at the height of the first Morocco crisis, his sovereign's pusillanimity could make the French less inclined to compromise.[5]

In 1908 the Kaiser was striving impetuously for an agreement with France and Britain about the future of Morocco over the heads of the Chancellor and the Foreign Office. True, he had originally welcomed Bülow's decision to recognise the pretender Muley Hafid as Sultan – 'Yes! The sooner the better!'[6] – but when the German move met with protests from England, France and the United States, he urged a swift conclusion to the conflict with the western Powers.[7] He expressed his displeasure that the diplomatic correspondence over negotiations with London and Paris had been withheld from him by the Wilhelmstrasse: 'How is it', he enquired in a telegram of 24 September 1908 from Rominten, 'that I did not receive notice of either the communication of the French note on Morocco or its content, nor of the reply to us?'[8] When the documents finally arrived at the imperial hunting lodge in East Prussia on 26 September Wilhelm was furious that the negotiations had been completed without his prior knowledge or approval. 'On 22 IX the Ausw[ärtiges] Amt submitted, in the name of my government, i.e. in my name, a reply of which I was completely ignorant, to my note which I had not been able to see!!! That is indeed something quite unprecedented in Pruss[ian] history!; *which I hope will never be repeated!* If the note causes a Europ[ean] crisis, then I shall deny responsibility for it!' The note from Paris should first have been presented to him 'to obtain my views and consent in respect of a reply'; and 'the draft reply – as always but especially in such an important matter affecting the whole of Europe – should have been put to me *first* for examination and approval before it was finalised or sent off!'[9]

In Bethmann Hollweg's Chancellorship too, Wilhelm insisted on publicising the decisive role he personally had played in resolving Franco-German differences over Morocco. That was strikingly demonstrated in November 1909, when he sent the Chancellor a telegram from Silesia, asking him to include an expression of his satisfaction at the Franco-German Moroccan agreement in the forthcoming speech from the throne.[10] After much thought Bethmann advised against such a demonstration of gratitude towards France, arguing that 'such a compliment from Your Majesty in a ceremonious speech from the throne' would be 'unusual in itself' and also problematical 'in terms of consideration for other states'. A friendly reference to France would point up the failure to refer to England, and perhaps also Russia, all the more sharply and give rise to unwelcome comments.[11] Wilhelm, however, had no time for such gestures of consideration for other countries. 'The Ausw[ärtiges] Amt and numerous chancellors have been preaching this to me for 20 years and we have ended up totally isolated in the world! Only Austria still wants anything to do with us! We must defend our interests regardless of other people's moods!' As for unfriendly comments in the British or Russian press, he 'couldn't care less'. 'They have been going on the whole year. My government ought actually to be getting used to them.' He insisted on including an expression of thanks to France in the speech from the throne. 'If we have any intention at all of reaching agreement with France, we have to take their vanity into account! There can be no question here of consideration for other countries. They have never shown any consideration for us in their relations with each other. In any case, the Moroccan question is one between us and France alone! How we stand with regard to France and how we treat her is our business alone and nobody else's! If we go on like this, being mindful of everybody, showing endless consideration, weighing things up and enquiring, then we shall be throwing away our position. France has been polite to us, and we have replied in kind, as befits polite people. What other people think or don't think about it is quite immaterial! That is how England, Russia etc behave at every opportunity. If we do the same it will have a good effect! And the objective, to flatter the Gauls and please them is a good one! The Moroccan agreement is my very own personal achievement, brought about by me despite the procrastination and faintheartedness of my officials, and it has proved beneficial to both countries! ... I neither consulted any other countries, nor bothered about them! The interests of my country were at stake and it just had to be done! England showed no consideration for us in the 1904 treaty with France over Morocco! Russia showed no consideration when she made the Racconigi agreement with our ally [Italy], behind our very backs! So, if I wish to greet the Gauls, I don't need to ask permission from anybody! A reference from Y[our] Exc[ellency] in the Reichstag would certainly be gratefully received, but a mention by me would carry a lot more weight; and the agreement was made by me before you became Chancellor. Hence my desire for a brief reference in the speech from the throne.' The Reich Chancellor had to give way and insert a corresponding passage in the speech with which the Kaiser opened the Reichstag on 30 November 1909.[12]

But the hopes of fruitful cooperation with the French that Wilhelm had placed in the agreement were not fulfilled. The transformation of Morocco into a French colony went ahead. In March 1911 an uprising broke out against the Sultan Abd al-Hafiz, who was regarded as a French puppet. France used it as a pretext to send troops to the Moroccan capital, Fez, in contravention of the Act of Algeciras. Kaiser Wilhelm, however, persisted in his conciliatory attitude. On 30 April, from distant Corfu, he telegraphed to Bethmann Hollweg: 'Have just received the Wolff telegram, which you no doubt know about, regarding the slaughter of the Moroccan garrison in Fez and the Sultan's flight to the French consulate. If the news is confirmed, the French will probably ... have to send a large military expedition to Fez. It can only suit us if French troops and money are heavily engaged in Morocco, and in my opinion it is not in our interests to prevent this. If the French thereby contravene the provisions of the Act of Algeciras we can initially leave it to the other Powers, above all Spain, to protest. Presumably, the demand to send warships will again make itself heard in Germany. But we cannot do anything with warships, as Tangier is not threatened and the field of action lies inland. I ask you therefore to stand up to any cry for warships in advance.'[13] A week later Jenisch, who had accompanied the Kaiser to Corfu, wrote to the acting Foreign Secretary, Alfred von Kiderlen-Wächter: 'Your Excellency is sufficiently well informed of His Majesty's view of the Moroccan question. The Kaiser wishes us to do absolutely nothing to discourage the French from involving themselves heavily there. When I pointed out to him that we had after all signed the Act of Algeciras and had made other agreements too, which could not be disregarded altogether, His Majesty said: if it suited their policy the French would simply ignore such agreements, even if other Powers protested, and then we should be left with nothing, as, after all, we did not want a war over Morocco. Naturally, the French would have to guarantee the open door for our trade.'[14] However, under the influence of Bethmann Hollweg and Kiderlen-Wächter, Wilhelm's attitude was to change soon after his return to Berlin.

GUNBOAT DIPLOMACY: KIDERLEN-WÄCHTER AND THE LEAP OF THE *PANTHER* TO AGADIR

The brash, self-assured, heavy-drinking Swabian Kiderlen-Wächter (whom Harden, in an allusion to his predecessor in office Count Herbert Bismarck, characterised as 'a super-Herbert')[15] – was as Secretary of State at the Auswärtiges Amt subject to the Chancellor's orders, but de facto he soon established himself as being in charge of foreign policy: while Bethmann's dispatches to the Kaiser kept up the appearance that the Chancellor was in control, they were in fact written at Kiderlen's dictation.[16] Unlike Wilhelm II Kiderlen was determined to exploit the impending French occupation of Fez (which finally occurred on 21 May 1911) for a spectacular forward move.[17] As he said to the Prime Minister of Württemberg, Karl von Weizsäcker, on 23 April, he was 'thinking in terms of sending a German warship to the coast of Morocco ... The French had to be reminded that Germany still existed. They would indeed soon become aware of this if only Germany would show herself undaunted.'[18] At the beginning of May he had the office draw up a memorandum on policy in Morocco which contained the decisive passage: 'The occupation of Fez would be the start of the absorption of Morocco by France. To protest would bring us nothing, and we should then be facing an almost intolerable moral defeat. We must therefore secure some object that would make the French disposed to offer compensations in the ensuing negotiations.'[19]

To back up the forceful action he was planning in Morocco, Kiderlen had established contact with nationalist circles and the world of heavy industry, thereby playing with fire, as the hopes he conjured up for a German south Morocco were never to be banished. On 19 April he met the President of the Pan-German League, Heinrich Class, to gain his support for a press campaign in the 'national' spirit.[20] Like the Pan-Germans, industrial circles were demanding that the Reich should not stand idly by 'while the French "Tunisified" Morocco' but should annex the southern part of the country (the Sus region) which was rich in raw materials.[21]

On 1 July 1911 the German gunboat *Panther*, flying the battle flag of the imperial German navy, suddenly appeared off the small south Moroccan port of Agadir, (followed a few days later by the small cruiser *Berlin*) and provoked the second Morocco crisis (see Figure 35).[22] Officially Kiderlen justified this bold action by referring to German commercial interests in southern Morocco,

Figure 35 The gunship *Panther* off Agadir, 1911

allegedly threatened by native unrest.[23] From the beginning, however, his real aim was to secure 'compensations' in other parts of Africa. He reckoned that the days of the Belgian and Portuguese colonial empires in Africa were numbered, and he hoped to succeed to their inheritance. In this way a German 'Mittelafrika' would be created — a huge colonial empire that would include German South-West Africa, German East Africa, the Belgian Congo, the French Congo, the Cameroons and Togo, Angola and Mozambique.[24]

The 'national' German papers greeted the 'leap of the *Panther*' enthusiastically as a deliverance, the reawakening of the post-Bismarckian 'Sleeping Beauty'. They made demands on France and even in some cases sounded a clarion call for war. On 2 July 1911 the *Rheinisch-Westfälische Zeitung*, the mouthpiece of the Rhineland and Ruhr heavy industrialists, published an article that caused a sensation: 'At last a deed, a liberating deed, to dispel the fog of bitter discontent in Germany. For two decades after the departure of the great Chancellor [Bismarck], his incompetent successors have piled failure upon failure. In cowardly fear the unworthy successors of the heroes of 1870 have given way step by step to the provocations of foreigners. The Caprivis and Hohenlohes and Bülows have heaped a multitude of humiliations on our people, as if we were not the most populous nation in Europe, as if we could not back up our rightful claims to power with an army of 5 million bayonets and a fleet that can no longer be discounted, as if we were not a people whose enormous proficiency and high endeavours have to an increasing degree enabled it to surpass centuries-old nations in markets all over the globe. Our people have begged, warned and complained, deepest discontent and

nationalistic despair have driven millions to vote for the illusions of Social
Democracy: this did not bother those called upon to fulfil the people's will,
who continued to misgovern Germany all the more. Now at last a deed, a
liberating deed! It was urgently needed. The honour of our people is at stake,
which the Kaiser pledged at Tangier, which Bülow committed at Algeciras,
and which Kiderlen-Wächter brought into play yet again in the Franco-
German agreement of 1909. The French have paid no heed to the Kaiser's
word or to treaties, they have perpetrated one provocation after another, they
have insolently torn up the treaties, they are proceeding to annex the rich
north-west African territory completely: regardless of our justified claims and
our rightful interests. Very well! The path they have chosen, we can tread too.
If they take it upon themselves "to restore order" in Morocco, we can do the
same. They have given us a free hand, we shall make use of our freedom of
action. There is now a German warship at Agadir. It still remains open to
them to agree with us about a partition. If they do not wish to, then may the
Panther have the effect of the Ems telegram.'[25] In Paris and London the
suspicion arose that the Germans were seeking by threatening war to acquire
part of Morocco with Agadir as a naval base.

THE KAISER AND THE SECOND MOROCCO CRISIS

It is not unthinkable that by stirring up the 'national' campaign Kiderlen was
also trying to put pressure on the wavering Kaiser. It is clear that both among
the incensed right-wing public and in the offices of the Wilhelmstrasse – and
there, not least, on account of his dispatches from Corfu – the fear prevailed that
the monarch, who had the final word, might at the last moment 'back down'
(*umfallen*). Bethmann's assistant, Kurt Riezler, noted on 29 May 1911: 'In the
A.A. they rightly think that we shall only get anything worthwhile from the
French, despite their willingness to pay compensation, if we have seized a
bargaining counter. The Chancellor is to put this to the Kaiser on the basis of
an office memorandum drafted by the A.A. – but he has actually got doubts
himself. Meanwhile, His Majesty can interfere and spoil everything. [The
Kaiser's banker] Leo [Ludwig] Delbrück, who was shooting with him in
Madlitz, told him that people in Paris had told him that we could have all the
colonial compensation we wanted, and a billion (!!) as well, if only we did not
disturb them in Morocco. The Kaiser said we ought to make an offer. He wants
nothing to do with sending a little ship. But it won't work without it. If we make
an offer we shall get nothing but commotion in the press and cries for war.'[26]

Yet how well-founded were these fears that at the decisive moment Wilhelm
might back down (as he had allegedly done in the first Morocco crisis) rather

than hold firm to the end? Already on 5 May 1911 Bethmann Hollweg read to the Kaiser in Karlsruhe a memorandum of Kiderlen's in which the aim of the planned action – to secure a pledge 'that would incline the French to pay compensation' – was clearly set out, and Wilhelm gave the memorandum his full approval.[27] Kiderlen noted with satisfaction: 'The Kaiser has approved my Morocco programme (including ships to Agadir).'[28] And in the following days and weeks up to the decisive moment Wilhelm repeated his unconditional support for sending warships to Agadir and demanding the French Congo. Significantly, reckoning that annexations in Morocco might rouse the world of Islam against Germany, the Kaiser's aim was to acquire colonial territory, not in southern Morocco, but in Central Africa.[29] On his return from London at the end of May he told the Chancellor that he had discussed the Moroccan question with George V at King Edward's funeral and had emphasised that although Germany would 'never' go to war over Morocco, she had to secure for herself the principle of the 'open door' and might also possibly demand compensation from France from her colonial territories in Africa.[30] Later, when Great Britain came forward to protect France, the Kaiser expressed to the British Chief of General Staff, Sir John French, his amazement at London's 'provocative' and 'dangerous' attitude, which surprised him all the more as he had himself during his visit to England in May informed the King of the action he was planning. He even implied that he had informed the British government in advance of his intention to send a warship to Agadir.[31] Likewise, he told his friend Lord Lonsdale after the event that he had in May 'had a long conversation with the King of England in the garden of Buckingham Palace about Germany's intentions in Morocco, that territorial acquisitions in Morocco were not on our programme at all, whereas compensation elsewhere certainly was. That the King had been quite in agreement, but that he had then clearly not (as his constitutional duty would have dictated) said a word to his ministers about his conversation with the Kaiser – hence, in large part, the surprise.'[32] It is therefore clear beyond any doubt that from the beginning of May 1911 Wilhelm II was fully aware of his government's intention to press for compensation in Central Africa by means of a dramatic protest against the French advance in Morocco, and that he had given the démarche his formal approval.

In the following weeks Bethmann and Kiderlen – almost as if they did not really trust their sovereign to hold firm – continued to seek assurances from him that he was in agreement with their high-risk plan, and would stick with it to the end. They received express confirmation of this at the beginning of June, when Wilhelm came away from the Döberitz manoeuvres to discuss the latest state of affairs with Bethmann in Berlin.[33] The final decision to send the *Panther* was taken during the Kiel regatta week, when the Kaiser received the Chancellor and Kiderlen in audience on 26 June 1911 and gave them the green light.[34] Kiderlen's mistress Hedwig Kypke commented disapprovingly on the Kaiser's behaviour: 'When Kiderlen asked permission to report to him about Morocco the Kaiser allowed him just about ½ an hour. And H.M. complained later that K. had taken up his valuable time! And yet the question then was one of war and peace!'[35] Wilhelm, however, explained his impatience in Kiel by claiming that Kiderlen's audience was in fact superfluous, as he had already given his consent to the sending out of the *Panther* at the beginning of May and again at the beginning of June.[36] After the event – on 4 September – he claimed 'to have disliked the action very much. But, as a constitutional monarch, he had allowed the Reich Chancellor and Kiderlen to have their way, while leaving the responsibility (but also any glory that might result from it) to them. He had, however, specifically pointed out that the German cruiser in Morocco would give offence in England and would render illusory all that had been achieved by the imperial visit to London.' At this, Kiderlen had declared: 'England would complain but not do anything.'[37] Be that as it may, immediately after reporting to the Kaiser at Kiel on 26 June, Kiderlen telegraphed to the Under Secretary of State at the Auswärtiges Amt: 'Ships approved.'[38] The naval authorities carried out the orders of the Supreme War Lord without being initiated into the intentions of the Wilhelmstrasse. Admiral von Müller, the head of the Naval Cabinet, recalled with some irritation how 'suddenly during the Kiel Week ... the decision of the A.A. and the Chancellor' was taken to send 'a gunboat and later a cruiser (*Berlin*) to Agadir "in order to protect endangered Germans there"', whereby 'neither the Secretary of State at the R[eich] N[avy] O[ffice] nor the Chief of the Adm [iralty] St[aff] nor I ... was informed of the political purpose of the action'. 'We are defending your cruiser on our western frontier' was all that Kiderlen said to them. If the navy had been asked for its opinion on the Agadir action beforehand 'it would have advised against it', especially as it is 'at the moment in a particularly unfavourable stage of development (Canal, Heligoland, submarines, mines, torpedoes)'.[39]

On 5 July 1911, accompanied as usual by his 'Nordic cruise companions', including, yet again, the Chief of General Staff von Moltke, Wilhelm embarked on his voyage along the Norwegian coast. The first press comments on the 'leap of the *Panther*' came in even before he left, and Müller found them 'quite alarming' – he later remarked that the pleasure trip had been 'altogether a mistake' in the circumstances.[40] But the cruise took its usual carefree course. On 6 July Müller noted in his diary: 'A lot of tomfoolery at gymnastics this morning. His Majesty cut through [Adjutant-General] von Scholl's braces with a penknife.'[41] Far from having misgivings about

Kiderlen's action, Wilhelm showed impatience and irritation at the slow pace of the negotiations that were supposed to compel France to cede the entire French Congo to Germany. Kiderlen, in speaking to the French ambassador, Jules Cambon, on 20, 21 and 22 June had merely hinted vaguely at Germany's demands.[42] Not until 9 July did he give Cambon to understand that Berlin was ready to leave Morocco to the French if she received compensation from France in return. The 'Congo' was mentioned, and also 'Togo', but Kiderlen was not more explicit on this occasion either.[43] The Chancellor's report on these negotiations (almost certainly written at Kiderlen's dictation) displeased Wilhelm immensely, and he vented his ire on the Foreign Secretary: 'This is a damned farce!', he minuted. 'If they want to cede the Congo, what can be clearer than that! . . . Well then, nothing achieved at all! I cannot conceal my amazement at this report. *At the beginning of June*, during the inspection of the cavalry at Döberitz, I came to Berlin to see the Chancellor. He told me of Cambon's conversation with him and Kiderlen in which Cambon first made mention of *compensations* in the col[onial] field. The Chancellor then asked for my *authorisation* to specify something like the *Congo*, as we could not take possession of Mohammedan territory. I gave my *consent* to this and the Ausw[ärtiges] Amt was informed. The Chancellor went on to mention that in talking to Cambon, Kiderlen had said, in response to his offer: "But it will have to be a big chunk", to which the ambassador responded with a nod of approval. Now I should like to know what authorisations are still required? *Mine* was asked for *4 weeks ago* and *granted*. For a second time, and unnecessarily, Kiderlen served up all the material to me in Kiel, in the presence of H[is] E[xcellency] yet again, and again sought *my authorisation*, which I immediately *granted*. What the devil then still remains to be done? This is just pure farce! They negotiate and negotiate and no one shows his hand! If we waste our precious time like this, the British and Russians will stiffen the backs of the terrified French and dictate to them what they should, at the most, graciously concede to us!! — At the beginning of May in *Carlsruhe* the Chancellor set out for me the whole programme for our negotiations over Morocco, I declared myself *in agreement*, and now at the beginning of *July* we are exactly where we were! This kind of diplomacy is too rarefied and too elevated for my brain.'[44] It may be, as the editors of the *Große Politik* complain, that the Kaiser was in error about the detailed chronology of the decision-making process; but there can be no doubt about his determined support for Kiderlen's policy of compensations. By the following day, Wilhelm had calmed down somewhat, but he still held firm to his desire to gain the entire French Congo. As Georg von Treutler, the diplomat attached to the imperial suite, reported to Kiderlen on 11 July, the Kaiser had made 'very strong marginal comments' on the Chancellor's telegram, but had meanwhile settled for the following 'watered down' reply: 'His Majesty is of the opinion that the tempo of the negotiations ought not to be unduly slowed down at the moment, because otherwise He fears an undesirable intervention by other Powers. The agreement of 1909 must form the basis of our deal with France, which must be similarly bilateral . . . As the Secretary of State and M. Cambon have now made mention of the words "compensation" [and] "Congo, Togo", the French must be compelled by gentle pressure to come forward with their offer . . . I ought to add that His Majesty attaches especial importance to the Congo.'[45]

At long last, in a further conversation with Cambon on 15 July, Kiderlen revealed that it was for him not a matter of Morocco, but of the French Congo – 'in fact, the whole of it'. 'The ambassador almost fainted', and declared, as Bethmann reported to the Kaiser, that no French government could consent to that. It had become clear to Kiderlen, the Chancellor warned, 'that to secure a favourable outcome we should at any rate still have to act very forcefully'.[46] This statement, which conjured up the danger of a major war, threw the Kaiser into a panic: 'Then I must return home at once. For I cannot allow my government to take such a line without being on the spot to supervise the consequences carefully and keep control of them! That would be inexcusable and too much like a parliamentary monarch. Le roi s'amuse! And meanwhile we are heading for mobilisation! *with me away* that cannot be allowed to happen! But then our allies must first be informed! For it affects them!'[47] Angrily, the Kaiser repeated his accusation that Kiderlen with his dilatory negotiations had thrown away the favourable opportunities that had existed earlier on. 'The Gauls have recovered from the first shock; found time to get advice from Petersburg and London – which I was always afraid of with the incredible delays – and on London's advice are cutting back . . . The offer is ludicrous and minimal in comparison with what they were indicating to us *2 months* ago, when they were still *isolated* and therefore afraid of us. I remember what Delbrück told us when he came back from Paris *at the end of May*. Months were allowed to elapse without taking up the thread and managing the affair *à deux*, on the basis of: "Cambon must be the first to utter the word 'compensations', in the name of Gaul." At last he did so, and then we went to Agadir. That immediately aroused alarm and distrust in London, which sprang to the aid of its ally to stiffen them up, and now we are in fact negotiating indirectly with London via Paris. Then, St Petersburg interferes as well, so that again we have half a conference working against us. In the Balkans, the Austrians are being played off against Turkey to divide them from us and prevent their support-ing us in the event of *serious* complications with France, which is supposed to go along with Russia!'[48]

In a telegram of 17 July 1911 Treutler emphasised that Kiderlen's remark
that Germany would have to 'act very forcefully' against the French had
'obviously greatly irritated' the Kaiser. He warned Kiderlen to bear in mind
that it 'will be very difficult to gain His Majesty's consent to steps that he fears
will lead to war'.[49] Immediately Kiderlen wrote to the Chancellor requesting
permission to resign, and a second request followed on the 19th.[50] In the first
letter Kiderlen formulated in all clarity the far-reaching aims that he was
pursuing in his Moroccan policy: 'We must have the whole of the French
Congo — it is the last opportunity, without fighting for it — to get anything
useful in Africa. Bits of the Congo with rubber and ivory, fine as they may be,
are no use to us; we must get to the Belgian Congo, so that we can participate
if it should some day be partitioned, and so that we, so long as it continues to
exist, can maintain across that territory a connection to our [colony] East
Africa. Any other solution represents a defeat for us, which we can only avoid
by standing absolutely firm ... I do not believe that the French will take up
the gauntlet, but they must be made to feel that we are prepared to go to the
utmost extreme ... We shall only get a satisfactory solution ... if we are
prepared to go all the way, i.e. if the others feel and know that we are.
Whoever declares in advance that he will not fight can not achieve anything
in politics.'[51] Kiderlen justified his second letter of resignation in terms of his
clearly having lost 'the All-Highest confidence': 'His Majesty has ... deigned
to state expressly I have "wasted precious time", and that this policy was "too
subtle and too elevated" for His Majesty. Moreover, His Majesty has deigned
to interpret the language I used to Your Excellency, that we should still have to
act very forcefully, as uttering threats against France. As is clear from the
context, I only wished, and was indeed obliged, to point out that the fulfilment
of our demands on France would meet with a more stubborn resistance than
His Majesty seemed to have expected, and that we should therefore have to
speak very sternly to the French. It is still a long way from that to direct
threats. Even so, such a degree of tension might arise in the course of
negotiations, if we were to take them seriously, that we might have to tell
the French straight out that we were prepared to go to the utmost extreme.
And if this were to be effective we must ourselves be inwardly determined to go
that far. Obviously, for such a serious step the All-Highest authorisation would
have to be obtained in advance. I am obliged to recognise, therefore, to my
great regret, that His Majesty takes me for either so inexperienced or lacking in
conscience, as to threaten a foreign state without a special authorisation from
His Majesty.'[52] Bethmann presented neither of Kiderlen's requests to the
Kaiser. He managed to calm the monarch down. Wilhelm accepted the Reich
Chancellor's explanations and telegraphed on 21 July 1911: 'Your Excellency is

authorised to continue the negotiations in accordance with your instructions so far.'[53] Thus Kiderlen had, as his biographer Ralf Forsbach remarks, regained 'his old freedom of action' as far as the Wilhelmstrasse was concerned.[54] On the very same day, however, his reckless plans suffered a tremendous blow from quite a different quarter.

LLOYD GEORGE'S MANSION HOUSE SPEECH

On 21 July 1911 the British Chancellor of the Exchequer, David Lloyd George, delivered a speech at the Mansion House in London, the text of which he had drawn up together with H. H. Asquith, the Prime Minister, and Sir Edward Grey, the Foreign Secretary.[55] 'I would make great sacrifices to preserve peace. I conceive that nothing would justify a disturbance of international goodwill except questions of the greatest national moment. But if a situation were to be forced upon us in which peace could only be preserved by the surrender of the great and beneficent position Britain has won by centuries of heroism and achievement, by allowing Britain to be treated where her interests were vitally affected as if she were of no account in the Cabinet of nations, then I say emphatically that peace at that price would be a humiliation intolerable for a great country like ours to endure.'[56] If the declaration was couched in general terms, its practical significance was nevertheless clear: should it come to a war between Germany and France, then Great Britain would intervene on the side of her Entente partner.[57] Lloyd George's speech was expressly endorsed by King George V.[58]

Yet again Europe stood on the brink of a major war. Müller recorded the atmosphere on board as 'rumours of war' reached the *Hohenzollern*. Treutler was 'very agitated', he noted, especially when a Wolff Agency telegram reported that the British fleet had called off its voyage to Sweden and Norway and was being concentrated in home waters. The Kaiser, however, took the rumours of war calmly. He personally brought the Wolff telegram with him into the mess and said, 'the English are concentrating their fleet'; but he then sat down along with the Moselle club and joked with them until midnight. Many others on board, however, 'were horrified, and saw war as already having broken out, and themselves as captured by English warships as they sailed for home'.[59]

On the evening of 28 July the *Hohenzollern* reached Swinemünde and next day Bethmann and Kiderlen came on board.[60] The tension had risen dramatically in the wake of Lloyd George's speech. After Cambon had rejected Kiderlen's demand for the whole of the French Congo, the Foreign Secretary said to Bethmann straight out: 'Our reputation abroad is in ruins, we must fight.'[61]

The Chancellor was deeply concerned and feared that Kiderlen was out for war. In a truly grotesque entry of 30 July 1911 Kurt Riezler recorded in his diary how German policy was being conducted in this crisis: 'Yesterday Bethmann and Kiderlen alone together in the evening. Bethmann wanted them both to drink a lot in order to get Kiderlen to talk. But what he said was very serious, with the result that the Chancellor believes that K[iderlen] is not merely considering the possibility of a war, but is actually out for one ... Bethmann's information is not complete. Kiderlen will not let anyone see his cards, says that the Chancellor should find someone else if he does not trust him.'[62]

Müller made a note of the confused discussion that took place in Swinemünde on the evening of 29 July 'before the widest forum' and in the presence of the Kaiser and the Chancellor. 'Kiderlen made a brash speech (with side-swipes at the stupid public and the Pan-Germans) about the pointlessness of trying to preserve an independent Morocco. Territorial gains in Morocco were pointless for us, because it is not a territory for settlement and we had in any case no surplus of agricultural labour. Therefore better to round off the Cameroons in the direction of the Congo while sacrificing a strip on Lake Tchad which is only swamp anyway. Later perhaps to exchange Togo for more territory towards the south. War with France very inopportune at the moment, as England certainly on the side of France and then our allies more or less worthless. H.M. very quiet. In agreement, however. Altogether a sorry picture.' On the following day Kiderlen declared that he knew perfectly well what a 'terrific howl' there would be if he contented himself with 'compensations' in Central Africa instead of a piece of Morocco. But he was not bothered about that. In politics one must set oneself grand objectives. 'The additional gains we may make in Central Africa are part of a plan across Africa as a counter-project to an English Africa from the Nile to the Cape.'[63] Kiderlen succeeded yet again in enlisting the Kaiser's support for his adventurous course. Riezler noted on 1 August: 'The Kaiser was very subdued in Swinemünde. Kiderlen came back very cheerful.'[64] The journalist Paul Weitz found the Foreign Secretary 'highly satisfied' after his audience with the Kaiser: 'H.M. absolutely firm and supportive of the Bethmann-Kiderlen policy ... H.M. gave Bethmann and Kiderlen *complete* freedom of action.'[65] Even so, doubts as to Wilhelm's ability to hold firm continued to be raised.

INDIGNATION IN GERMANY AGAINST 'WILHELM THE PEACEFUL'

At the height of crisis, the Württemberg envoy in Berlin, Baron Axel von Varnbüler, fearful lest the Kaiser lose his nerve and order a humiliating retreat, wrote to his sister, Hildegard von Spitzemberg: 'Morocco! Things have

looked really touch and go there in the last few days . . . Let's hope we hold on;
Kiderlen, I can trust to do so, he has nerves of steel. But the other one, who
writes this slogan all too often on photographs and in golden books . . . That is
the question!'[66] It was widely asserted that the Kaiser's support for Kiderlen's
extremely risky policy did not necessarily stem from conviction, but partly
from a feeling that he had to demonstrate his strength in order to avoid a
second *Daily Telegraph* crisis. Prior to the audience with Bethmann and
Kiderlen in Swinemünde on 29 July Riezler had thought: 'This time H.M.
will have to say yes and amen to everything. Those two will surely stand firm,
and if they quit and the policy is put into reverse, then there will be another
November storm but stronger, and the disappointment among the people will
be fearsome. This time we must go through with it.'[67] Riezler's prognosis
seemed all too soon to become a threatening reality. During the Kaiser's
absence in Norway there had been open speculation in Paris and London as
to whether he would on his return disavow his government and back down to
preserve peace.[68] In British newspapers Wilhelm was called 'the Peacemaker',
in French ones 'Guillaume le Timide'.[69] In Germany, however, such hopes
expressed abroad only aroused the ire of 'national' circles, which talked of an
impending 'Olmütz' or 'Bad Ems'. On 4 August 1911 the *Post*, the organ of the
Free Conservatives, attacked the Kaiser with hitherto unparalleled asperity.
'Has Prussia changed, has the old Prussia perished, have we become a race of
women . . . have all feelings of national honour, all great political responsibility, all vision, perished in Germany, are we no more than a laughing-stock
for foreigners? What has happened to the Hohenzollerns, from whom sprang a
Great Elector, a Frederick Wilhelm I, a Frederick the Great and a Kaiser
Wilhelm I? Is the Kaiser going to be the strongest support of English and
French policy, a support far stronger than fifty French divisions? Is he to
become the hope of France? We cannot yet believe this, we do not wish to
believe it. Nor do we wish to believe what the English and French newspapers
have been saying for weeks: just wait until your Kaiser returns, then the
retreat will be sounded, then Germany will give way.'[70] Next day, Maximilian
Harden published the derisive article 'Wilhelm the Peaceful' in the *Zukunft*.[71]
Even if the Supreme War Lord had been inclined to back down, the anger
prevailing in the country would have made this practically impossible.

   Wounded by the invective from the Right, Wilhelm II demonstrated his
'determination'. In a 'strictly secret' telegram of 9 August 1911 Jenisch
informed Kiderlen that the monarch was 'greatly upset' by the newspaper
articles. 'His Majesty told me that the current that had set in since Swinemünde was very alarming and must be checked. It must be made clear to
public opinion that the Kaiser is ready at any moment to act with all vigour.'[72]

Kaiserin Auguste Viktoria urged her husband to take an unbending militaristic line with the French and British 'lest afterwards the accusation be heard that a Hohenzollern had bowed to these opponents and backed down'.[73] With astonishment, Baroness Spitzemberg noted in her diary on 8 September that Kiderlen had said that 'H.M. had been by no means flabby, but even more aggressive than his ministers!'[74]

This aggression was demonstrated in exemplary fashion when Kiderlen began to turn away from his collision course and steer towards a compromise with France: he renounced his claim to the whole of French Congo and the French, for their part, declared themselves ready to cede a portion of that colony. In what was clearly a misunderstanding the French premier Joseph Caillaux (who was only imperfectly informed of Kiderlen's retreat) chose this moment to announce that he wanted to send a warship to Agadir and that a British ship would go there too.[75] Kiderlen thereupon telegraphed to Jenisch: 'Please report to His Majesty the Kaiser that mediator ... has not yet been able to speak to the minister, who is away from Paris for a few days, but was convinced for his part that M. Caillaux will provide a perfectly satisfactory explanation.'[76] This report drew from Wilhelm a reaction that Erich Eyck has characterised as a 'childish tantrum'.[77] The Kaiser scribbled on it: 'That is a new piece of insolence! if, in the middle of such serious negotiations, they utter such threats, then we shouldn't wander off to have a picnic but demand an answer. As things stand we are faced with his impudence, and he then lets us await his pleasure! Such a thing after making us wait for 3 days! Unheard of!' As for Kiderlen's assertion that Caillaux would provide a satisfactory explanation in the end, Wilhelm wrote: 'That is no longer enough, they must include a clear dementi, and that *immediately*! The mediator must see Caillaux at once and make it clear to him that he has to apologise *within 24 hours* for treating me with such insolence, or *I* shall break off the negotiations.'[78] Next day the Kaiser sent Kiderlen a telegram in the form of an ultimatum threatening to break off the negotiations and resort to 'other measures' if the French did not '*immediately* make the Reparation d'honneur due to us' within twenty-four hours. 'Nobody has ever threatened me directly until now! ... This is a colossal piece of impudence on the part of the French, and after all our forbearance and patience, I take it as a box over the ears!' The tone that the French were adopting in the negotiations was out of keeping with 'the dignity of the German Reich and Nation'.[79] In much the same way, Jenisch reported on 9 August that Wilhelm II had the impression 'that the French were trying to drag out the negotiations until we discharged our reserves in the autumn. He will not do them that favour.'[80] In the end Kiderlen managed in an audience with the Kaiser alone to bring him back on course, noting with self-satisfaction after the meeting: 'It was easy to calm His Majesty down ... When I have to deal with His Majesty, I am forced to recognise time and again, even when he is of a different opinion, that he is fundamentally intelligent. He can also put up with contradiction, only it has to be substantiated and presented in a form that spares his feelings.'[81] Kiderlen then went on holiday to Chamonix, where he met the Russian-born Baroness de Jonina, a known French agent; and in the room they shared he deliberately left secret documents lying about, the content of which he evidently intended the spy to report to Paris.[82]

READINESS FOR WAR

While Kiderlen, with Bethmann's support, was engaged in negotiations, frustration prevailed among the army leadership. Moltke's *cri de coeur* in a letter of 19 August 1911 to his wife is notorious: 'If we once again emerge from this affair with our tail between our legs, if we cannot bring ourselves to make energetic demands which we would be ready to force through with the sword, then I despair of the future of the German Reich. In that case I will leave.'[83] Looking back in October 1911, the Prussian War Minister, Josias von Heeringen, judged that the army had been 'absolutely prepared for the event of war with France, without, however, desiring it, as had the younger officers and the Pan-German party'.[84]

There are many statements from the crisis months that show that Wilhelm II too, while not looking for a war, went on reckoning with war against both western Powers if the negotiations with France should fail. True, in talking to Müller on 1 August 1911 about a possibly imminent war, he said, 'one doesn't like to think of it, when all one's sons are at the front';[85] but he soon spoke in far more militant tones.[86] When Count Metternich reported that England would support France not merely with words, but if necessary with deeds and was in a position to land '90,000 men on the French or Belgian coasts within a fortnight', Wilhelm countered with, 'and we have got submarines'.[87] As we have just seen, on 9 August he threatened to break off the negotiations and resort to 'other measures'.[88] Eight days later he wrote: 'The French must clear the ditch somehow or other, or feel our spurs.'[89] Far from shrinking from the thought of war, Wilhelm discussed with the Chief of General Staff and the Prussian War Minister what measures ought to be taken to put Germany in a position to mobilise as soon as possible. Thus, he saw to it that the negotiations with France were so managed that they would not be broken off before his troops were back from manoeuvres. In a telegram of 28 August 1911 to the Reich Chancellor he pointed out that the French troops were stationed in their garrisons and would therefore 'in the event of mobilisation ... have the advantage over us, as we are still engaged in our great manoeuvres and far away from our garrisons ... Hence, the negotiations must be so managed that any failure does not occur while the manoeuvres are going on.'[90] Shortly afterwards the Austrian military attaché reported to Vienna that talks had taken place between the General Staff and the Auswärtiges Amt, after which measures necessary for mobilisation and concentration had been put in place. 'Otherwise, however, they think — almost with regret — that the Moroccan question is almost certain to be resolved peacefully.'[91]

When on 27 September 1911 the French inhabitants of Agadir raised the Tricolor on the fortress there Kiderlen threatened military action if it should turn out that 'the hoisting of the flag ... had been ordered by the French consul in Mogador',[92] but Wilhelm now utterly rejected the idea of a war, for technical military reasons — the time for a war in his view had passed. He termed the incident over the flag 'a silly schoolboy prank', and Kiderlen's sharp reaction to it 'Nonsense! ... Consuls are occasionally seized from time to time with the furor Consularis, and act without instructions. Once the government disavows, perhaps dismisses, him, the matter is over! To rattle the sword just now on account of such an idiocy is quite outrageous! That would be, in the first place, doing exactly what England has been waiting for for months in order to have a casus foederis et belli, and in the second place my reserves have been sent home, the fleet is disbanded and dispersed in various harbours for repairs, and the torp[edo]-boat flotillas are out of service. All this with the consent of the Reich Chancellor, who was consulted beforehand! Moltke is on holiday in Italy or hunting in Hungary! So the choice of this moment to engineer a provocation is the most foolish one possible.'[93]

Soundings of the Allies, Austria-Hungary and Italy, indicated little willingness to participate in a war between France and Germany. The Austrian Chief of General Staff Franz Conrad von Hötzendorf told the German military attaché Count Kageneck on 9 September 1911 that he had asked the Emperor Franz Joseph for permission to embark on 'pourparlers' with Berlin over 'how Austria-Hungary stood, if it came to a war between Germany and France, what preparations our army was to make (concentration, deployment etc.)'. The old monarch did not think 'that the time had yet come for this', 'as he did not believe that it would come to a war'.[94] More surprising, by contrast, was the assurance given by the King of Italy to Crown Prince Wilhelm during an ibex-shooting expedition in the Alps and which an almost incredulous Kaiser passed on to Archduke Franz Ferdinand in Kiel on 5 September 1911: Italy would have fulfilled her Triple Alliance obligations 'to the last man' if the Moroccan question had resulted in a Franco-German war. 'This was the first time since the death of His Majesty King Humbert I', Wilhelm told the Archduke, 'that he knew of any pronouncement on Italy's attitude and loyalty to the alliance in so definite a form'. It had been 'worth a great deal to him to know that in the event of war Italian troops . . . would be fighting alongside'.[95]

In the end, Bethmann Hollweg was able to inform the Kaiser on 2 November 1911 that the Franco-German negotiations over the Congo had been successfully concluded. Visibly relieved, Wilhelm replied: 'Best congratulations on ending this delicate affair.'[96] By the agreement, France ceded 275,000 square kilometres of the French Congo to Germany.[97] True, this territory was mostly swamp land infected with sleeping-sickness; but as part of the plan to create a great German colonial empire in Central Africa it was not entirely worthless. Even so, it was clear that the high-risk game that had led to the Mansion House speech of 21 July stood in no relation to the 'Sleeping-sickness Congo' that had been acquired. Nationalist circles in Germany were particularly furious. As Kiderlen had concealed his real objectives for so long, while at the same time encouraging the Colonial Society and the Pan-German League in their agitation, he had aroused hopes that he was neither able nor willing to fulfil. As an embittered Ernst Bassermann, leader of the National Liberal party, declared in the Reichstag: 'When the news arrived that we were not seeking territorial acquisitions in Morocco, there was great disappointment in Germany. National feelings had been mightily inflamed, and people were reckoning with the possibility of war. One can well say: Hardly ever had there been such a resolute determination to fight, among all classes of our population, as at that time. Then the news suddenly arrived: we are only seeking compensation, and that not in Morocco but in the Congo.'[98] As will be seen, the outcome of the second Morocco crisis, so widely regarded as a humiliation in Germany, gave rise to a conviction that a war against Britain would soon be inevitable.

Wilhelm II was not the initiator or the driving force behind the disastrous 'leap of the *Panther*': that was Kiderlen-Wächter. True, the Kaiser had approved of Kiderlen's action from the beginning, had personally signalled it during his visit to London in May 1911, and repeatedly spurred the Wilhelmstrasse on to a more energetic stance against France. If he occasionally had doubts about the wisdom of Kiderlen's policy, he time and again allowed himself to be brought round to Kiderlen's way of thinking in personal interviews with the strong-willed Foreign Secretary, who was fully backed by Bethmann. In his heart, however, Wilhelm was always sceptical about the enterprise. His objective was not *Mittelafrika* but primacy in Europe and − beyond this − territorial acquisitions and spheres of influence in the Near and Far East. On 11 January 1912 he drew up a telling memorandum looking back on the Agadir crisis and describing colonial acquisitions in Africa as a diversion from the real aims of his *Weltmachtpolitik*. 'In the Moroccan affair, England has gravely insulted the German people in word and deed, and they have been deeply stirred. This will be translated into an Army and Navy budget. England knows this; and the people of England have taken fright at it, and at the storm of discontent that they have unleashed in Germany. England does not want a war ... Hence the hints given to us in all quarters about a *colonial* empire to be built in *Africa* ... England's game is clear', Wilhelm declared, 'but my officials cannot see through it. By the delusion of a '*colonial* empire' in Africa, with acquisitions at the expense of *others* we are to be drawn into conflicts and drawn *away* from *Welt*politik, i.e., they want to settle the great Asiatic question *without us* ... The settlement of the Asiatic question *with us* is the basis of my whole policy, of the development of the Navy too, and of my milit [ary] concentration in Europe. That is why it is such a bugbear, and why it is to be dissipated in *Colonial* acquisitions and fragmented.'[99] It might have been possible to make colonial gains in agreement with Great Britain, but not the shift in global power that the Kaiser was striving for with his military concentration in Europe and Asia. So, after the confrontation with Russia over Bosnia and the rash threat to France over Morocco in 1911, the island kingdom that had proved itself yet again, in the Agadir crisis, to be the guarantor of the existing European states system moved unmistakably into the foreground as the chief opponent of the Kaiser's *Weltmachtpolitik*.

CHAPTER THIRTY-ONE

'The enemy identified.' The acceleration of the naval race and the growing menace of war

ooking back over the Agadir crisis at the beginning of 1912, Helmuth von
Moltke observed to the Austrian military attaché that 'the past year had
shown that it was England who was Germany's enemy. It was remarkable how
England was almost hypnotised by Germany and was doing all she could to
injure her, while being quite remarkably conciliatory towards other Powers.'[1]
Like the Chief of General Staff, the Kaiser too believed after the second
Morocco crisis that he had identified England as Germany's chief enemy. In
September 1911 he wrote to the Chancellor: 'We have identified our opponents, experienced their veritably humiliating activity, and had to bear it with
gritted teeth. They seem to have no interest in our friendship for the present.
So we are not yet strong enough. They are only impressed by force and
power.'[2]

Wilhelm II's irritation with England came out in all his political statements
and actions.[3] He was convinced that the hidden hand of 'perfidious Albion'
was at work in everything that happened in the world, however far away. He
was enraged by Italy's totally unexpected 'felonious attack' on the Ottoman
Empire in Libya in September 1911, not only because he felt his own ally had
deceived him, but also and above all because he saw in it a cunning English
plot to destroy the cordial relations between Turkey and the Triple Alliance
and stir up the entire world of Islam against Germany. Hence, on Kiderlen's
report announcing the Italian attack on Tripoli, he scribbled furiously:
'England wants to use Italy in Tripoli to get the *Mohammed[an]* world to
suspect the rest of us of portraying the *Turkish* (Stamboul) *Caliphate* to the
Moslems as impotent, as it has been unable to prevent the loss of the ancient
Mohammedan lands of Tripoli, Tunis and Morocco. Thus, the *Arabian*
Caliphate cloaked in an *Anglo-Egyptian* protectorate, is to be sold to the

Mohammedans ... Once Stamboul has been driven back, then England comes forward as guarantor and protector of the new Caliphate and the rest of us can all stand by and watch.'[4]

THROWING DOWN THE GAUNTLET: THE NEW NAVAL *NOVELLE*

Lloyd George's Mansion House Speech of 21 July 1911 had given rise to two currents of opinion, both among the German public and within the ruling elite.[5] While the Reich Chancellor, the Auswärtiges Amt and the diplomats sought a rapprochement with Britain, the Navy League, the Pan-German League, and a number of other 'bourgeois' circles demanded an increase in naval armaments – even at the risk of war – in reply to the humiliation that England had inflicted on the German Reich. In this national fervour, Wilhelm II and Tirpitz saw a welcome opportunity to move to an even faster tempo for the construction of large battleships, beyond the terms of the Navy Law. By 3 August, Tirpitz was already recommending exploiting the 'Morocco spirit' among the German public to bring in a 'strong' supplementary budget, or *Novelle*, for the Navy as early as the coming winter. 'The English have already got wind of the new *Novelle* ... and are shouting about it', he noted, 'but that cannot hold us back. If the English try to veto the *Novelle*, then we have the grounds for war that everybody in Germany will understand, and then we must let fate take its course.' The Grand Admiral adopted this irrational position even though he clearly recognised that 'as regards a naval war the moment was as unfavourable as possible. Every year gained puts us in a better position.' He listed the measures that would actually have to be completed before the German Reich could have any chance whatever of victory in a war against the superior power of Great Britain: 'Heligoland, [Kiel] Canal, Dreadnoughts, U-Boats etc.'[6]

The Kaiser, too, demanded the immediate introduction of a supplement to the Navy Bill. That was 'the only thing that will put us on equal terms with them [the British]!', he declared at the height of the Agadir crisis.[7] 'Only by means of an even stronger fleet' could 'the British be brought to reason'.[8] In an after-dinner speech to the Senate of Hamburg on 27 August 1911, he praised the progress that the Hanseatic city had made in the 23 years of his reign and continued: 'The safeguarding of trade and seafaring is the achievement of the German people in recent decades, through the development of the powerful German battlefleet, universally noted for its manly spirit and discipline. It is this fleet that embodies the determination of the German people to play a role at sea. This young fleet, just coming into bloom, is of quite special interest to the people of Hamburg. If I have correctly understood their expressions of enthusiasm, I think I am right in assuming that they intend to go on strengthening our Navy in the future too, so that we can be sure that no one will be able to contest our rightful claim to our place in the sun.'[9] On the Prussian envoy's report of the enthusiastic reception of his speech by the people of Hamburg the Kaiser minuted, significantly: 'The people sang "Die Wacht am Rhein" for the first time in 40 years! avis au lecteur!'[10] (He had clearly forgotten for the moment that the same song had been sung in Hamburg after his militaristic speech in Döberitz three years before.)[11]

The Kaiser had delivered his speech without informing Tirpitz before-hand.[12] The Reich Navy Secretary was eager to use the occasion, however, to take up the question of the *Novelle*, though at first he had no clear idea of what he should ask for. As will be seen, his ideas went far beyond the mark, not only in the view of the Reich Chancellor, the diplomats and the Reich Treasury, but also in the opinion of a considerable number of naval authorities. The head of the Kaiser's Naval Cabinet, the Commander of the High Seas Fleet, the Chief of the Admiralty Staff, and even a few of Tirpitz's colleagues in the Reich Navy Office, urged internal improvements to the fleet rather than yet another *Novelle*. Albert Hopman remarked perceptively in November 1911 that Tirpitz's demand for more big battleships meant 'an over stretching of our financial and military capabilities, creating new, incalculable difficulties for our policy without presenting a clear objective that the world can understand. In the clear light of day it appears to be a fancy of the Kaiser's, whose mechanical toy destroys his clear political and military vision. I think Tirpitz would be glad to have been more reserved in presenting his demands . . . They bring us a fleet that will be a hothouse plant . . . Where shall we go in the end with 60 capital ships? England cannot be blamed if she sees this figure as a constant threat. The England–Germany ratio will always be the same, about 2:1, and, in my view, England cannot even consider agreeing to 3:2. Her fleet has duties all over the world, ours only in the North Sea.'[13]

It was exactly considerations such as these that made Bethmann Hollweg, Kiderlen-Wächter and Adolf Wermuth, the State Secretary at the Reich Treasury, take a determined stand against the plans of Wilhelm II and Tirpitz. Four days after the Kaiser's speech Tirpitz told the Chancellor that a 'stronger fleet was absolutely necessary so as to be able to pursue *Weltpolitik*'. He claimed that war 'had been decided upon' anyway in England, and 'could not be avoided'. When the Chancellor anxiously enquired whether he could undertake to guarantee a victorious outcome, Tirpitz replied, according to his own evidence, 'No one can do that, but we must run the risk or abdicate politically.'[14] On the following day Bethmann, who had in the meantime consulted Kiderlen and Wermuth, was 'much more negative', specifically on account of the 'danger of war with England' and Germany's financial constraints.[15] In view of growing criticism at home – five months later four and a half million electors were to vote for the (at least nominally) Marxist and republican Social Democrats – the Chancellor also had reason to doubt whether the people had been as 'passionately' in favour of the new demands for naval expenditure as the Kaiser and Tirpitz repeatedly claimed.[16]

In the event, Wilhelm's Hamburg speech of 27 August 1911 gave rise to one of the most serious crises in domestic and foreign policy of the pre-war years. In accordance with the dictates of the 'kingship mechanism' the monarch was allowed – indeed obliged – to decide between Tirpitz and Bethmann, between challenging England and her Entente partners or seeking agreement with them – in the final analysis, therefore, between war and peace. As will be seen, he made no secret of his feelings. Even if circumstances in the end obliged him to reduce his original demands, Wilhelm II sided with Tirpitz, and often in the crassest manner that displayed his contempt for the 'civilians' in the Wilhelmstrasse.

Early September 1911 saw a big naval review at Kiel in the presence of Archduke Franz Ferdinand. On 4 September, Wilhelm declared to Georg von Müller, head of the Naval Cabinet, in a mood of 'exaltation': 'The German nation was livid with England, in the best mood for a naval *Novelle*, and was, indeed, definitely expecting one.' The admiral replied that to move up to a *Dreiertempo* (that is, laying down three capital ships a year) immediately after the Moroccan crisis could give rise to a 'danger of war with England' and that the navy 'was at the moment in a particularly unfavourable state (Kiel Canal, Heligoland, U-Boats, Mines, Torpedoes)'. These objections Wilhelm brushed aside regardless: 'I have always been confronted with this lack of readiness whenever things got critical. But now is the time to go ahead in any case. The people demand it. If the Reich Chancellor, and Kiderlen and Wermuth don't want to co-operate, then they are out on their necks. The Reich Chancellor should find out more about the feelings of the people. Why did he not accept the invitation to the reviews in Altona and Stettin, where he could have seen for himself what the people are thinking? . . . The Secretary of State [Tirpitz] is quite prepared for a new Navy Bill, and is just looking for the proper form. There is enough money available, the Reich Treasury does not know what to do with all the money, and the Conservatives would be glad to make good their gross error in refusing to agree to the inheritance tax by responding to a national appeal.' At the same time, Wilhelm also rejected Müller's advice to talk to Admiral Henning von Holtzendorff 'about the Navy's readiness for war'. The Commander of the High Seas Fleet 'could not tell him anything new at all', the Kaiser replied; so it was 'quite superfluous for me to ask him yet again'. To prevent any misunderstandings, Müller defined his own position in this debate: 'I am myself entirely of the view that a war with England cannot be avoided in the long run. But I am also of the view that the present is the most unfavourable time conceivable for the Navy. The ill-feeling against England will still be available to be used later as an effective means for getting a Navy Bill through.'[17] From this point on, the question of the most suitable moment to risk, or even to bring about, a war against England was never off the agenda.[18]

The next day nevertheless witnessed a clash between the Supreme War Lord and the Commander of the High Seas Fleet, von Holtzendorff, when the admiral emphasised to the Kaiser that 'H.M. would jeopardise his most personal achievement (the existence of the Navy) if war were to break out now.'[19] Bethmann Hollweg too, on Müller's advice, asked Holtzendorff for 'his views about the possibility of war',[20] after which the Chancellor could report to Müller that both Holtzendorff and the Chief of the Admiralty Staff August von Heeringen were 'quite of the same mind' as he.[21] Bethmann's confidence proved ill-founded, as Müller, as we have seen, unlike Holtzendorff, thoroughly approved of 'the need to move up to a *Dreiertempo*', and was merely pleading for a postponement of 'inevitable' war with England. Heeringen, too, although he doubted the readiness of the Imperial Navy, was to reveal himself to be a supporter of the *Novelle*.[22] All the same, in Holtzendorff the Chancellor had gained a powerful ally in his struggle against the naval plans of the Kaiser and Tirpitz, and for a short time, he succeeded in persuading Wilhelm to postpone the supplementary estimates.

On 6 September 1911 the Kaiser had a long talk with Bethmann. 'I told the Reich Ch[ancellor]', he later reported, 'that he was far too noble-minded to understand the English. Metternich too failed to understand the English, and that is why he must leave his post ... I then agreed with the R[eich] Ch[ancellor] that the outcome of the Moroccan affair must first be awaited, and only then, according to the public reaction, should the fleet *Novelle* be taken up. Perhaps it would be necessary to postpone the fleet *Novelle* for a year, perhaps until [19]13 (completion of the Canal).' Müller expressed his satisfaction over this postponement and said that in his view 'nobody could take the responsibility for a war with England at the present moment'. Above all, the completion of work on the Kaiser Wilhelm Canal between the Baltic and the North Sea – the task of widening it would be completed, not in 1913, but only at the end of June 1914 – seemed to him, as for Holtzendorff, an essential precondition for risking a conflict with the vastly superior naval Power.[23]

The decision to postpone the *Novelle* until 1913 or 1914 only lasted a few days. In mid September, during the army manoeuvres at Boitzenburg, the

Kaiser hit on the idea of concealing his much desired naval expansion by a subterfuge: instead of the training vessels envisaged by the Navy Law, Germany would build armed cruisers, justifying this development in terms of increases in the French and Japanese navies.[24] An agitated Chancellor summoned the head of the Naval Cabinet, showed him the 'pressing letter' that he had just received from Wilhelm, and pointed out that it was 'simply childish to try to conceal the anti-English implications in this way. Nobody would fall for that. We then spoke', Müller reported, 'of how mistaken H.M. was about the feelings of the public. He ought to consider what the rush on the savings banks and the fall on the stock-exchange can tell him about this.' Müller's diary continues: 'I again defined my position. We cannot limit ourselves to a *2er tempo* [laying down two capital ships per year] until 1917 because we need to accelerate the construction of new types.' True, he 'could not judge whether bringing in a naval *Novelle* for the fleet now or next year would mean war with England'. But should this danger exist, then in his opinion it would certainly be 'in the interests of the Navy ... to postpone this war, which is indeed inevitable in the long run, until the Canal has been completed'.[25]

ROMINTEN SEPTEMBER 1911: THE 'DECISIVE TURNING-POINT IN THE HISTORY OF OUR FATHERLAND'

Meanwhile Tirpitz was preparing for his annual audience in East Prussia, at which Wilhelm II would have to define the German Reich's policy on armaments and foreign affairs. On the one hand the Reich Chancellor, the Auswärtiges Amt, the diplomatic corps, the Reich Treasury, the Commander of the High Seas Fleet and (with reservations) the head of his Naval Cabinet were all urging him strongly to avoid any provocation of Great Britain; on the other stood the powerful Grand Admiral Alfred von Tirpitz with his Reich Navy Office, no longer demanding a *Novelle* for cruisers, such as the Kaiser had been thinking of up to now, but a dramatic strengthening of the battle-fleet by building Dreadnought-class ships-of-the-line.[26] On 26 September 1911 in the hunting lodge at Rominten, Wilhelm made his decision in favour of the Grand Admiral's breathtaking plan to bring the strength of the German fleet up to a permanent ratio of 2:3 in relation to the Royal Navy by building three instead of two capital ships per year. The Reichstag was to be asked to supplement the Navy Law by funding a third active squadron of battleships and two squadrons of heavy cruisers. Tirpitz's ultimate aim was still the '*Äternat*' – a guaranteed, self-perpetuating figure – of sixty Dreadnought-class battleships in the North Sea, which would, he calculated, give the High

Seas Fleet 'a militarily realistic chance against England' – unless the English found themselves compelled by their shortage of manpower and money to back down beforehand and recognise Germany's pre-eminence, both in Europe and overseas. That kind of *'Alliance with England'* would, he declared, be *'the coping stone of our naval policy'*.[27] As a concession to the Chancellor, Tirpitz declared himself prepared to defer the *Novelle* until the autumn of 1912, and Müller, who was present at the audience, could record that 'H.M. was very much in agreement and seemed relieved that such an unaggressive approach had been found.'[28] The new objective of a permanent ratio of 2:3 in relation to the Royal Navy was to be announced simultaneously in the Reichstag and in a note to England. 'His Majesty is fully in agreement with the principle of the procedure, which His Majesty had already declared to be desirable and attainable, but thinks a communication to England *before* the introduction of the *Novelle* would be expedient, and is of the view that we are dealing here with an historic moment, which cannot be announced to the German people by the Secretary of State or the Reich Chancellor, but must be included in the speech from the throne.' When Tirpitz expressed his doubts as to whether the English would be at all prepared to accept a ratio of 2:3, the Kaiser confidently explained that 'the financial situation in England would force them to accommodate us, indeed, they would gladly seize the opportunity to ease the heavy burden of arms expenditure ... By fixing a ratio of 2:3 we have for the moment, in a way, secured some territory. The question of whether we now build on this territory immediately, or faster or more slowly according to economic circumstances, can remain open.'[29]

That same evening Müller drafted the letter in which the monarch informed the Reich Chancellor of the result of the discussions at Rominten. In view of Bethmann's objections to the *immediate* introduction of the *Novelle*, the monarch had declared himself content to defer it by a year; as to the matter itself, however, he must remain firm. He 'had to point out that this was not merely a matter of life and death for the future development of the *Navy*, but for the future foreign policy of *the Reich*'.[30] One of the weightiest of decisions, concerning – precisely – 'a matter of life and death for the future foreign policy of the Reich', had thus been taken yet again in the absence, and against the will, of the constitutionally responsible Reich Chancellor.

Not content with the letter drafted by the head of his Naval Cabinet, the Kaiser on 30 September, in a long letter redolent with euphoric wishful thinking, explained the motivation behind his decisions. 'My dear Bethmann', he wrote, 'The head of the Naval Cabinet will have handed to you [on 13 September] a letter about the "cruiser *Novelle*". I consented to this solution with a very heavy heart, and only did so in order to make the situation

easier for you at home. That, however, was before Italy's felonious attack
which launched the war against Turkey and which can have incalculable
consequences in the Near East. Now things are different. My sense of responsibility as Supreme War Lord compels me to take up again the question of our
maritime strength and to bring it urgently to your attention ... I wish,
therefore, in what follows, to give you a sketch of what I think my future
naval policy will be ... It is now no longer a question of a so-called "cruiser
Novelle", but of a clearly recognisable objective that is to be laid down for the
future of my Navy, and thereby also for the future of the Reich, in so far as it
affects our relations with England. Certainly, up to now the aim behind our
naval development has been the Risk Theory, as was also clearly explained in
the preamble to the Navy Law: our fleet must be so strong that even the
strongest naval Power could not attack it without suffering considerable
damage. In opposition to this Risk Theory (of which England has only very
recently become aware) England had its "no risk" theory, in the form of the
"two Power standard" or two keels to one (German) standard. The Risk
Theory has fulfilled its purpose and is finished. We now need another, firmer,
more easily recognisable objective in order to direct our people and accommodate their desire for a role at sea. This aim must be expressible in figures,
must at the same time be a source of effective propaganda that the people can
easily understand, and must make clear the limits to our intentions in both
financial and naval political terms. It must be expressible in a short slogan
which the common man can quickly grasp and use — as in England the
"two power standard" was used and understood by everybody, king or beggar.
It can be found in the term which Your Excellency has already agreed to (in
the conference with Tirpitz in Wilhelmshöhe in 1909): *a ratio of 2:3* for the
German and British fleets. It has the advantage of curtailing and deflecting all
criticisms from petty minds and scaremongers about "boundless naval plans"
etc. On the other hand, with regard to the English, it readily concedes to them
a considerable supremacy and removes in advance all grounds for talking
about "bidding for the sovereignty of the seas etc." At the same time, it
represents a certain commitment, *vis à vis* the British, that they have always
wanted; and guarantees there will be no surprises from our side, as it lays
down the ratio once and for all. As it is a question of the relative strengths of
the fleets as a whole, which are clear and fixed for all the world to see, the
tempo of the annual *construction* programmes, hitherto the cause of so much
excitement and misunderstanding in England, drops out of the argument. In
future it will not be important for England whether we reach our target by
building 2 or 3 or 4 ships a year, the aim we are striving for is well known, and
has been openly and frankly avowed, and German naval construction is

thereby no longer sinister and mysterious. England is now free to pursue whatever construction plans she wishes, fast or slow, many or few, that does not concern us, we shall always hold fast to the ratio. What vessels the ratio is to apply to must remain for the moment an open question. For the moment it seems to me expedient to base it on the number of battleships and armoured cruisers under 20-years old in operation in the front line. This question will still, of course — as regards bringing in the *Novelle* etc — need further discussion and consideration. For within this ratio of 2:3 (which we are still far from attaining) the annual increase in personnel and material must be fixed by a *Novelle*. — I should think it right and proper to announce our plans in a speech to the Reichstag (possibly in the speech from the throne, in which I tell my people what they are aiming for). Just as loyalty and the open management of the affair demand that a communication be made to England *in advance*. Whether she for her part accepts the ratio or not does not concern us. We have done what we can to show that we are not planning anything outrageous against England, or anything hostile, and the rest of the world will take an appreciative view of our wise self-restraint. If the British should nevertheless resort to an overwhelming building programme, they burden themselves in the eyes of the world with the *odium* of *provocation* and hostile *intentions* towards us, which in view of our proposals they would have difficulty denying, and that they would be extremely reluctant to take upon themselves, given their obsession with presenting themselves as innocent and spotless to the world. As moreover, according to all accounts, the state of their finances is by no means brilliant ... I think the commercial world and the stock exchange will be very pleased by our proposal, as the government can no longer claim that we are morally forcing it to undertake a massive building programme because they do not know our intentions. As for the date for bringing in this *Novelle*, that must be determined by the world situation, which has been suddenly and totally changed by the unexpected [Italo-Ottoman] war. We shall see when I next discuss these matters with Your Excellency, how far your objections to an early introduction of the *Novelle* have changed or not. The latest date — if it is not to be this autumn — for announcing the Navy's new objective — a 2:3 ratio — to the people would have to be about February of next year. That would be the *preliminary move* for the *Novelle*, which would then follow in the *autumn of 1912*. It is undeniable that we are at a decisive turning point in the history of our fatherland. We have identified our opponents, experienced their veritably humiliating activity, and had to bear it with gritted teeth. They seem to have no interest in our friendship for the present. So we are not yet strong enough. They are only impressed by force and power, when they appear in a form that cannot possibly be misunderstood. Our people expect the government that "is known for talking" to take some "action", as they say. It is time for a national deed that steers the enthusiasm of the Germans in the right direction without giving their opponents grounds for action. That is the direction I have sketched out, the announcement of the 2 to 3 ratio for the German [fleet] in relation to the British. As Y[our] Exc[ellency] will see from the above, the procedure I am proposing frees you from the necessity, when you put forward the *Novelle* in the Reichstag, of having to take a "high line" towards England, which you told me you were so afraid to do lest it appear dangerously provocative. In view of our publicly limiting the ratio to 2:3 that would be quite superfluous, as everybody knows that we are still only at 1:2, and in armoured cruisers 1:4; and that in itself means we still have to reach the limit in the first place. I have sent a rough sketch of these guidelines of Mine to Adm. v. Müller and von Tirpitz; both have declared themselves completely in agreement and they did not hesitate to find my solution a very good and felicitous one ... Wilhelm I.R.'[31]

HESITATION ON THE BRINK OF WAR

In emphasising his own role the Kaiser was not motivated solely by vanity (although this factor was clearly also involved) but much rather by the desire to increase the pressure on the Reich Chancellor to consent to the new navy policy. On 3 October 1911 Müller and Tirpitz met Bethmann to discuss the Kaiser's 'extremely rude letter' that had just arrived. Müller noted: 'Reich Chancellor remarkably patient, but nevertheless very much against any provocation of England by a *Novelle*.'[32] The Chancellor was staking everything on getting the Rominten decision reversed. He was supported, as before, by Kiderlen, Wermuth and the ambassador in London, Count Metternich, but he also found support among the leadership of the navy itself. Hopman, who was witness to the bitter debates in the Reich Navy Office, spoke in very sceptical terms about the *Novelle*'s chances of success and favoured an agreement with England, so as to secure at least Germany's leading position in the continent. As he noted on 2 October 1911: 'If England makes the *Novelle* a reason for war we shall come off badly, given the general political situation at the moment and the inadequate development and leadership of our Navy. It would be better to wait ... Go on building slowly and without a fuss, alliance with Russia or England, not against both. England's position as a World Power is too strong for us to overthrow at present. Better to co-operate with her and uphold predominance on the continent. Bismarckian policy. England is only frightened of us because we go on and on relentlessly with our naval armaments. Yet we cannot catch up with her. She would strike us dead before we did, and she could manage to do that now, I am firmly convinced ... We have wanted to soar too fast and too high in the world and, and as parvenus, have talked too big. The guilty one is Wilhelm II. The nation too is now going to find out where his zigzag policy has brought us in the end.'[33] Only a few days later Hopman feared that Tirpitz might have gone too far in his conflict with Bethmann. True, the secretary of state was 'a tremendous fellow', who 'if he gets his way this time [would] emerge victorious from the hardest fight he has ever fought. Then Wermuth, and perhaps Bethmann too, would indeed have to go. [But] perhaps Tirpitz has now strung the bow too tight. After all, if England shows her teeth, Wilhelm will only back off again. That is, in my view, the snag with the whole thing.'[34]

The Chancellor continued to receive valuable assistance in his battle with Tirpitz from Admiral von Holtzendorff, who argued for improving the preparedness of the existing fleet, and continued to oppose a *Novelle* as 'uncalled for'.[35] To counter the influence of this 'fantasist' Tirpitz felt obliged to put before the Kaiser a 'memorandum on the extreme resistance of the commander at the front in the matter of the future development of the Navy', insisting that the navy commanders should only be allowed to present any divergent views they might have on the development of the fleet 'to His Majesty alone, and not to the Reich Chancellor and the secretaries of state at the Auswärtiges Amt or the Reich Treasury'. According to Tirpitz's record of the audience, Wilhelm had been 'very indignant' to learn of Holtzendorff's meddling.[36] On the other hand, Müller pointed out to the Kaiser that Tirpitz was at odds with the commanders at the front and the Admiralty Staff over the inadequate internal condition of the Navy; and that he himself as head of the Naval Cabinet had no easy task in keeping the peace among the various naval leaders.[37]

Bethmann was actively seeking the support of the naval commanders when on 4 October 1911 he confronted them with the critical question: 'how far are our chances in a war with England dependent on the completion of the [Kiel] Canal and the facilities on Heligoland?'[38] Both Tirpitz and the Chief of the Admiralty Staff, August von Heeringen, replied that Germany's prospects in such a war were at the moment 'not good at all'. Completing the Canal and the defences on Heligoland would improve Germany's chances somewhat, they said, 'but not to any significant extent'. Both thought it unlikely, however, that England would declare war on account of the planned *Novelle*.[39] Tirpitz sent these assessments to the Kaiser, who was waiting impatiently, and despite acknowledging the risks involved in a war, pressed for an early introduction of the *Novelle*. 'I humbly present to Your Imperial and Royal Majesty, in compliance with the order just transmitted to me by the head of the Naval

Cabinet, two reports to the Reich Chancellor, which set down in writing the content of the discussions between the Reich Chancellor and me. As Your Majesty will graciously see, I made the point to the Reich Chancellor that it would be in our best interests to choose the earliest of the dates envisaged by Your Majesty: Announcement by the Reich Chancellor in the old Reichstag, i.e. before the elections [of January 1912]. Introduction of the *Novelle* in the budget for 1912, i.e. immediately after the elections. That would, of course, make Your Majesty's naval policy into a slogan for the election. I fully recognise that it is also, given its links to questions of taxation, a matter of the greatest importance for domestic policy.'[40]

Henning von Holtzendorff took a very different view (see Figure 36). While conceding that the announcement of the new programme would meet with widespread approval in Germany, he was emphatic that in England the *Novelle* would have a 'provocative' effect and 'probably' lead to war. He pleaded strongly for postponing all provocation of England, at least until the widening and deepening of the Kaiser Wilhelm Canal was completed in the late summer of 1914. 'Our fleet is at the moment in a particularly unfavourable condition for war against England. A considerable weakness on our side lies in the unfavourable ratio of big battleships, which is yet further accentuated by the unfinished state of the Canal ... We shall never be able to avoid a period of risk if we go on to develop the Navy as planned, but it will lie, to some extent, in our hands to determine the right moment to start ... In choosing this moment, considerations of internal and foreign policy must, in my view, take second place to purely military ones, i.e. we must not burden ourselves with the consequences of provocative behaviour unless our fleet, with its present complement in terms of manpower, is fully prepared for war and equal to the enemy in terms of quality ... As far as I know the naval authorities were until very recently united in the view that our Navy is not at the present moment in a condition to fight, and that such a moment will only occur a) when our High Seas battlefleet consists entirely of modern battleships and cruisers and b) the Canal is able to accommodate them ... That is, the autumn of 1914 would be the time to bear in mind after which we might look forward with confidence to the effect our intention to expand beyond the Navy Law might have on our opponent, secure in the knowledge that our Navy would be able to inflict such damage on him as to justify spending so much of our national resources on naval armaments ... Even if, in terms of domestic politics, the introduction of a *Novelle* just now would fall on fertile ground, the probability of war associated with it would nevertheless find the Navy inadequately prepared until 1914, and could lead to national catastrophe. Therefore, to await the moment, to make use of the time

Figure 36 The Kaiser with the Commander of the High Seas Fleet,
Admiral Henning von Holtzendorff

meanwhile, and then to go forward as planned on a firm military footing to
establish that position relative to the English Navy that Germany's vital
interests require, would seem logical to me.'[41] This memorandum by the
Commander of the High Seas Fleet, while indeed remarkable in historical
terms, did not play any part in the immediate conflicts between Tirpitz and
Bethmann, as the Chancellor did not receive it until the end of October, by
which time important decisions had already been taken.

DITHERING IN HUBERTUSSTOCK

There was every indication that on 14–15 October 1911 in the Hubertusstock hunting lodge Kaiser Wilhelm would decide in favour of Tirpitz and against Bethmann. Of course, he found it an extraordinarily difficult choice, as he could not afford, for reasons of domestic politics, to sacrifice either the Grand Admiral or the Reich Chancellor. Neither the parties concerned nor the members of his entourage could fail to note the signs of 'nervousness' and of shying away from responsibility. Wilhelm complained of being overburdened and short of information, saying that he had to do everything himself, and the Chancellor and the ministers no longer called on him. Increasingly, he relied on his three heads of Cabinet, whose influence now grew substantially, and the advice of his Flügel-adjutanten and various visitors to the court. The 'kingship mechanism' through which he had been wont to issue his imperious commands gradually became a burden for him. Outwardly, of course, he made a show of strength, often indulging, as will be seen, in coarse abuse of his civilian advisers.

Since the Rominten audience of 26 September 1911 Wilhelm had been 'firmly determined to bring the ratio of the German to the English fleet up to 2:3'. According to Baron von Jenisch all his marginal notes showed that 'His Majesty was very irritated with England.'[42] Indeed, his rage continued to blaze undiminished, and above all in his reaction to Metternich's reports warning incessantly against a war with England and France, Wilhelm showed himself absolutely unrelenting. 'The good Metternich [is] quite besotted and deeply affected by these dear Englishmen', he mocked; the reduction of naval expenditure on both sides that the ambassador was urging was 'rubbish!'; there could be no talk of an agreement with England before 'we have the right basis, with a ratio for 2:3 for the German and English fleets. Then, there can be negotiations over arms reductions, *not before!*'[43]

Bethmann asked the head of the Naval Cabinet to try to calm the Kaiser down. 'He could not now, in the autumn, make a statement' in support of a *Novelle* for the fleet, and he thought 'the Tirpitz plan with a ratio of 2:3 provocative'. The Chancellor spoke 'very bitterly' about the Kaiser's only summoning him to report to Hubertusstock on 15 October – a day after Tirpitz. Müller promised to 'try to calm him, but asked in return that in his speech the Chancellor should at least not rule out the presentation of the naval budget in the spring. This he somewhat reluctantly promised me.'[44] More and more, the head of the Naval Cabinet was taking on the role of honest broker between Tirpitz and Bethmann, which he felt all the more obliged to do as he was becoming increasingly anxious about 'the Kaiser's state of mind and the general confusion in our affairs'.[45]

When Tirpitz arrived at Hubertusstock on 14 October 1911 the Kaiser immediately complimented him 'on his truly statesmanlike reply to the Chancellor's written questions', and offered him a stag to shoot, 'which the vain gentleman accepted with obvious delight'. 'In view of Plessen's presence' during the audience, Tirpitz said he felt obliged to speak with 'great reserve': he understood the Chancellor's difficulties and did not wish to press for a statement in the Reichstag this autumn. The Kaiser was relieved to hear from Müller that the Chancellor had for his part agreed not to 'rule out' the naval estimates in the spring of 1912.[46]

During the audience, to the amazement of both admirals and the Adjutant-General, the Kaiser produced a letter to the King of England, drafted by himself, and informing his cousin 'Georgy' of his intention to introduce a *Novelle* for the fleet 'based on a ratio of 2:3'. Müller noted: 'A few neat turns of phrase in it, but of course, as a whole absolutely impossible. Tirpitz, asked for his opinion, was complimentary about the skilful wording, but added the caveat that such a letter was a political document, and he could not presume to express an opinion as to its expediency. When I was asked, I expressed very strong misgivings as to the impact of the letter in terms of the constitutional position of the King of England.' For this comment the head of the Kaiser's Naval Cabinet was rewarded with the 'ungracious' retort: 'But this letter will be written, you can say what you like.'[47] Even so, when the Kaiser came back to his idea next day, Müller again spoke out 'very decidedly' against the sending of the letter. He pointed out that 'the King would pass the letter on to Asquith, the Liberal Cabinet would rebel against this policy-making between monarchs, the letter would certainly become known in Germany and, given past experience, would be badly misinterpreted by the public. Furthermore, in constitutional terms the King has very little to say in England, nor can he, as a person ... be considered a deciding factor. His Majesty did not like to hear this.'[48]

In the evening of 14 October 1911 Müller spoke up for the Reich Chancellor and the Treasury Secretary Adolf von Wermuth: if the naval *Novelle* was to be implemented successfully both men would have to be brought round to support it. His Majesty did not like to hear that, either. 'Wermuth is not my minister at all, but a parliamentary minister', he complained. 'He does not bother about me, but does as he likes. Why doesn't he come and report to me like the other ministers? He has been to see me once, babbling about the Treasury's having no money.' When Müller pointed out that the Treasury Secretary was a subordinate of the Chancellor and could not simply apply for an audience, the Kaiser replied: 'No, he is my minister, he is paid by me.' The Admiral then pointed out that Bethmann had been 'very pained' not to have

seen the Kaiser 'for so long ... and particularly in such troubled times'.
Wilhelm ought to remember that the Chancellor's public standing would be
diminished if he did not receive him regularly. 'The newspapers keep an exact
record.' But the monarch was unmoved. 'That is his fault', he said. 'Why did
he not come to Rominten? I do not exist for him. I hear nothing about the
course of political negotiations.' Müller explained that Bethmann was simply
'too modest. He does not wish to inconvenience Y[our] M[ajesty] and waits to
be summoned when Y[our] M[ajesty] wishes to see him.' He suggested that
the Kaiser might like to invite Bethmann to spend a second day at Hubertusstock. 'The R[eich] C[hancellor] was very put out that he had only been
summoned for Sunday, when there were such urgent matters to discuss' – to
which the monarch replied: 'If the R[eich] C[hancellor] knew what my life is
like here, he would understand why I am inviting him for Sunday. I am not
asking him for a short report – he is supposed to come for walks and talk
politics with me. During the week I never get round to going for walks, as
I have to go stalking immediately after breakfast and immediately after
luncheon ... He is full of doubts and is completely dominated by fear of
England. But I shall not let England dictate to me what I should and should
not do. I have told the R[eich] C[hancellor] he should remember that I am
descended from the Gr[eat] Elector and Fred[erick] the Gr[eat], who did not
hesitate to act when they thought the time right. I also told the Reich
Chancellor that he must take Divine Providence into account, which will
certainly see to it that a people that has so much to answer for as the English
will also be brought low some day.' In the end Wilhelm agreed to invite
Bethmann Hollweg to spend the night at the imperial hunting lodge.[49]

Despite Müller's intercession, Bethmann's audience during the next morning's walk was anything but trouble-free, and he complained afterwards that
the Kaiser had been 'very fierce' with him. He had in the end managed get the
monarch to drop the idea of an immediate announcement in the Reichstag.
The *Novelle* was to be introduced in the spring of 1912, and even then only 'if
it was possible at that time'. Müller even managed, to the Chancellor's relief,
to talk the Kaiser out of sending his letter to the King of England. 'The
R[eich] C[hancellor] was touched and gave me his hand.' Wilhelm, too, was
satisfied with the outcome of the negotiations, praised Müller for his mediation, and declared himself 'quite in agreement again with the Chancellor'. He
instructed Müller to inform Tirpitz of the result to the audience.[50]

In the Reich Navy Office Hopman had already suspected that the Kaiser
would 'topple over' again, and noted: 'H.M. seems to want [the *Novelle*], but is
at the same time very undecided ... Tirpitz is fighting everybody. Reich
Chancellor, Wermuth, Kiderlen, Plessen, and Müller too is not keen either and

sticks up for Bethmann (kindred spirit).'[51] When Müller's letter arrived with
the news that there was not now to be an announcement in the Reichstag after
all and that even the introduction of a *Novelle* in the spring of 1912 was again
in doubt, although 'His Majesty ... personally was very much' counting on
it,[52] Tirpitz's position seemed to be 'shattered'. According to Hopman, the
Chancellor now had 'the upper hand'. Tirpitz was 'quite gloomy' and believed
'H.M., the Chancellor and their associates would not be brought to change
their minds again.' Tirpitz's cause was 'as good as lost. The key point is the
indecision of H.M., who is afraid of England and who wishes to avoid war at
all costs. He is, as Tirpitz himself says, very nervous yet again ... Tirpitz still
sets his hopes on directly influencing the Kaiser. I don't believe in this any
more', especially as Müller and Holtzendorff were engaged in 'a dubious
game'. Even so, Hopman conceded that the arguments Bethmann had used
to win the Kaiser over − 'danger of war against England, serious domestic
conflict, influence on the impending elections, large sums soon to be
demanded for the army' − were indeed very weighty ones.[53]

TIRPITZ OR BETHMANN? THE CHANCELLOR CRISIS OF THE WINTER OF 1911−1912

The success that Bethmann achieved in Hubertusstock − thanks to the influence of Müller, Holtzendorff and Plessen − on 15 October 1911, proved short-
lived. A fortnight later at an audience in the Neues Palais at Potsdam Tirpitz
won Wilhelm over to the idea of a *Novelle* yet again, by telling him that he
had to choose between 'two currents': the one, led by Holtzendorff, which
wished to avoid all provocation of England before the widening of the Kiel
Canal had been completed, and only 'make good the deficiencies' in the
meantime, and the other which would 'both make good the deficiencies and
pay due regard to the future development of the Navy'. 'Settled', Tirpitz noted
afterwards with satisfaction: 'H.M. was entirely of the opinion that the
right way to make good the deficiencies was also through the *Novelle*.' It
was decided all the same, should war break out suddenly, to transfer all
the Dreadnought-class battleships that could not pass through the Canal to
Wilhelmshaven on the North Sea. Moreover, fifteen more U-boats were to be
built by the summer of 1913, the U-boat base and the defensive installations
on Heligoland were to be completed (200 rounds of munitions were immediately dispatched to the island), the preparation of the torpedoes was to be
completed and mines purchased to the value of 1.6 million marks.[54]

On 3 November 1911 Tirpitz called on Müller with a draft of the *Novelle*,
and asked him to present it to the Kaiser, as a meeting of the Prussian

Ministry of State prevented him from doing so himself. Together the two admirals considered how they might inform the Reich Chancellor 'in a few words' that the draft had been sent direct to the Kaiser.[55] In discussing the draft the monarch, who was 'immensely' interested, promised 'not to talk to the Reich Chancellor about the *Novelle* before the Chancellor had himself received it'.[56] Hopman was afraid, quite rightly, that the Reich Chancellor would not accept such trespassing on his authority. Again he predicted that Bethmann and Kiderlen would gain the upper hand as they 'would use the spectre of war with England to win H.M. round all over again'.[57] The Chancellor was striving 'with all his might for a rapprochement with England' and wanted 'to avoid even the possibility of a war'. Behind Bethmann's efforts to maintain the peace 'there of course stood one higher personage whose hollowness', Hopman complained, 'becomes more apparent by the day'.[58]

On 11 November the Kaiser arrived in Kiel for the swearing-in of recruits and the launching of the battleship *Kaiserin*. In the previous two days the debate in the Reichstag over the Moroccan debacle had witnessed tumultuous scenes, for which the Crown Prince had made an appearance.[59] Tirpitz made use of the heated discussion in order to press ahead, insisting that a *Novelle* really must be brought in now, to restore Germany's reputation as a Great Power; if this was not done, 'Lloyd George's box over the ears' would be followed by a second blow.[60] True, Wilhelm II praised Bethmann's forceful defence of German policy in the Agadir crisis,[61] but he also saw in the 'national' fervour manifested in the Reichstag another chance to push through the naval increases he so much desired. 'The German people's hatred of England', he declared to the Württemberg envoy Varnbüler, 'their national enthusiasm and willingness to make sacrifices, must be put to practical use – with speed – while the iron is hot'.[62] Hence the Kaiser's telegram from Kiel to the Reich Chancellor: 'Heartfelt congratulations on yesterday's speech! It made an excellent impression here too, in all circles, military, naval, and civilian; just as I arrived to find Kiel in ecstasies after the first speech. A good write up in the foreign press too. Yesterday's speech really will make a good impression abroad! Just don't lose your sense of humour! I gather from private sources in [political] party circles that feeling is so favourable to a strengthening of the fleet – as the applause in the House at that point also shows – that it is a great pity that the *Novelle* is not being introduced this autumn. It would easily get through. The government would be in an excellent position, as it would be translating popular sentiment, and the deep-seated emotions that have been aroused, into a useful action. Perhaps Your Excellency will think this over again with Tirpitz. I shall see him today and could instruct him in this sense. The people are expecting something like this now and would celebrate it as a national deed. So let's get to work!'[63] The head of the Civil Cabinet Rudolf von Valentini tried to sweeten the bitter pill for the Chancellor by explaining that this dispatch arose from 'an off the cuff decision of the Kaiser',[64] but whether Bethmann's dismay was really diminished by this may well be doubted. Tirpitz was no less surprised when at the banquet after the swearing-in of recruits the Kaiser pushed over to him a menu card on which he had written: 'Have telegraphed to His Excellency the Reich Chancellor and after congratulating on speech, pointed to feeling in the Reichstag for increasing the battlefleet. I had been struck by this and I had private information from parliamentary circles that feeling favourable to *Novelle*. The people would celebrate new *Novelle* as national deed, and I was asking him, therefore, to think again about introducing it, *even this autumn*.'[65]

Fortified by the imperial menu card, Tirpitz again pressed for the immediate introduction of the *Novelle* and, in an attempt to strengthen his hand, threatened to resign. On 14 November 1911 he explained to Müller that to move from a construction tempo of four ships a year down to two would amount to a second retreat in the face of England. Müller made it clear to him 'that if I [Tirpitz] raised the question of my resignation the Kaiser would be very displeased and would not accept it'; to which he replied 'that the Kaiser could very well tell me that I should double the size of the *Novelle*, but the Kaiser could not ask me to defend a measure that in my view implied abdicating before England'.[66] In the end, Müller said he was prepared 'to put [Tirpitz's request] to His Majesty'; and in the audience that followed the Chief of the Naval Cabinet got the Kaiser to 'agree to work on the R[eich] Ch[ancellor] to have the *Novelle* introduced immediately into the discussions of the budget in the Bundesrat'.[67] That same evening Müller informed the Grand Admiral that the Kaiser had sent him to the Reich Chancellor with the command to introduce the *Novelle* into the Bundesrat, together with the budget for 1912, before the end of the year.[68]

Müller was fully aware of the gravity of the situation, for with this decision the crisis had come to focus on the issue of Bethmann or Tirpitz. In a letter to his colleague Valentini the head of the Naval Cabinet warned of the danger of a Chancellor crisis, as it could no longer be expected that the Kaiser would give way over the naval question again. Should Bethmann Hollweg refuse to carry out the Kaiser's command, Tirpitz would resign, which would amount to 'a very regrettable ... confirmation of a policy of abdication to England'. Valentini should try to influence Bethmann to put his financial and foreign policy objections in second place to 'the National aspect of the *Novelle*' and 'thereby also avoid disavowing His Majesty the Kaiser, who has committed himself so strongly to the *Novelle*.[69] After Müller's lengthy meeting with Bethmann, he could note with relief that the Chancellor had 'come to terms with the idea of the *Novelle*'.[70]

While Wilhelm, as Müller noted, held 'firm to the *Novelle*',[71] Bethmann continued to try to postpone any decision on the question. On 28 November he informed the Kaiser that he had not yet included the *Novelle* in the budget as commanded because he first had to agree with him the taxation measures that the supplementary naval estimates would entail.[72] At the same time, at Wermuth's suggestion, he enquired of the army leadership whether a new Army Bill ought not to be given priority over the naval *Novelle*.[73] After talking to Tirpitz and the Chancellor on 29 November Müller noted the latter's ambivalence: Bethmann 'very undecided. Extremely uncomfortable with *Novelle*. Saw great danger of war with England. Afraid lest, if the *Novelle* provokes another box over the ears from England, we should again just put up with it and not draw the sword ... He is plagued by his doubts. Poor man.'[74]

Stubbornly, the Chancellor refused to carry out the Kaiser's order to announce the *Novelle* when the budget was discussed in the Bundesrat. When the navy chiefs appeared together before the Kaiser in the Neues Palais on 9 December Tirpitz, Müller and Heeringen pointed out that this refusal was 'blocking' the *Novelle* and making it 'politically unfeasible'. Müller's diary describes the Kaiser's fury on that morning: 'H.M. very strong for the *Novelle*. If the R[eich] Ch[ancellor] does not want it he must go. Political isolation of Germany ... Need to cut the Gordian knot. I must be my own Bismarck. At any rate, the Secretary of State should rest assured, the Kaiser will push the *Novelle* through. Bitter criticism of the indecisiveness of the otherwise "tremendously decent" Chancellor and of our diplomacy.' Yet again Wilhelm II sent Müller to the Chancellor with the order, 'come what may', to announce the impending introduction of a *Novelle* for the navy during the forthcoming Bundesrat debate over the budget. The Admiral found the Chancellor depressed and 'completely pessimistic about everything'.[75]

The same day saw a violent showdown between Bethmann Hollweg and the Kaiser, which the latter described to Müller in a letter. 'Reich Chancellor was just here. He started straight away ... about the bills for the Army and Navy ... The budget is healthy and if published before the elections as it now stands would make a good impression. If the Army and Navy bills are to be added in, there would have to be a whole package of new taxes, and the inheritance tax would have to be included; and the entire body of Conservatives ... and the Liberals too, have already definitively pronounced against these. These taxes would be dangerous, furthermore, in that the parties plan to extend them to all the German royal houses, which would greatly exasperate the royals in

South Germany, and could not be refused by the Bundesrat. Without these taxes it would be very difficult – before the elections – to introduce the bills. He would like, therefore, to bring in a small supplementary budget (2 ships) and announce it before the elections, and the Army and Navy bills afterwards, in the winter, as a supplementary budget. I objected that that was a betrayal of his own people, who were fiercely demanding a *Novelle*, and that England, once reassured by the small budget, would, if a supplementary budget for 3 ships were suddenly introduced, get into precisely the mood he was seeking to avoid. At the moment, people over there are prepared for a *Novelle*, they have taken it into account so to speak, and would be just as astonished as our people if none appeared. The Chancellor said: such an Army and Navy *Novelle* has never been brought in as part of the budget before, but always as a special law, as a supplementary budget. That made matters so terribly difficult, as did the fact that Tirpitz had indicated to him that in the contrary case he would resign. That would never do at all, I declared I should not let him go under any circumstances. The Chancellor remarked that Heeringen (War Minister) had told him he could not finish the task before the 15th, and hence it would hardly be possible to incorporate the whole budgetary requirement in the budget [before] the debate in the Bundesrat, and a supplementary budget would be better. In the end, he said one should think about whether to do the thing by a loan rather than by taxes. Such a loan would however look very warlike. He was afraid that in response to the *Novelle* England, even if she does not go to war with us directly, will needle us and tread on our toes for so long that *we* shall be forced to resort to an Ems telegram and thereby to an *offensive* war. I said, they had been doing enough of this already without its having come to a war, and it was the task of our diplomacy to preserve us from such a result and to put England in the wrong. Finally, after a lot of to-ing and fro-ing I managed to get H[is] E[xcellency] to agree to discuss with Tirpitz and Heeringen yet again the procedures for bringing in the *Novelle* (either as part of the budget or as a supplement); in the *latter* case I *demanded*, when the so-called little budget was presented, a *public announcement* – for our people and for England – that a supplementary budget with proposals for increasing our readiness for war will be brought in as soon as the preparatory work is completed and the financial aspect settled. He is ready to do this and will ask the gentlemen to see him tomorrow ... He wondered however whether the III Squadron wasn't more important than the construction *Novelle*, he could include the personnel requirements for the former in the budget *immediately*, and that would be something tangible, actually existing, and ready for use at once, whereas the 1st ship of the *Novelle* will only be delivered in 3 years, and who knows if England will wait that long. I replied that the *Novelle* was of a piece and that we needed Dreadnoughts for the III Squadron too, above all, Dreadnought-class cruisers. Please inform Tirpitz – *strictly confidential, by word of mouth, immediately.* He should just negotiate and discuss tomorrow sine ira et studio. The Chancellor, by the way, is determined to present the combined bills in February–March. So, the discussions should not give rise to any conflicts.'[76] Müller welcomed 'the Kaiser's firm stance' and took the letter to Tirpitz.[77]

At the end of December 1911 Tirpitz declared himself prepared to reduce his original demands, in view of the Reich Chancellor's resistance, the impending elections, and, above all, soundings from England about a possible colonial agreement. He continued to demand the construction of three new ships of the line in addition to the ships envisaged by the Navy Law, but he was now prepared to reduce the number of replacement cruisers from three to one. Müller promised to put these 'offers' to the Kaiser during his audience of 23 December; and Wilhelm instructed him to see Valentini and the Chancellor, and to report back to him. Müller found the Chancellor, however, 'as always undecided'.[78] The bitter conflict between Bethmann Hollweg and Tirpitz was to cast a shadow over German policy for many months to come.

THE KAISER'S READINESS FOR WAR

In these weeks around the turn of the year 1911–12 Wilhelm's thoughts revolved continually round 'the Navy, England, the Reich Chancellor, the Conservatives, the financing of the *Novelle*, the inheritance tax, but also the latest literature about Fred[erick] the Gr[eat]'.[79] A report by August von Heeringen, the Chief of the Admiralty Staff, on the British preparations for war in the summer of 1911 and on 'the need to be prepared ourselves, especially by concentrating our ships in the North Sea' must have given him food for thought.[80] Still, he remained determined, come what may, to push through the *Novelle* for the fleet. On 9 January 1912 the Neues Palais was witness to an unusual assemblage – at the Kaiser's invitation – of military and naval leaders, statesmen, financiers and academics, at which plans for the military and naval budgets were discussed, with reference to England, and to Germany's own lack of preparedness. The participants included the Chief of General Staff, von Moltke; Admiral von Müller; the bankers Arthur von Gwinner and Ludwig Delbrück; the Secretary of State at the Reich Colonial Office Wilhelm Solf; the Under Secretary of State at the Auswärtiges Amt, Arthur Zimmermann; and Professor Theodor Schiemann. Müller summed up the 'drift' of the discussion in the words: 'Just no more building battleships now, when we have the best chance to get on good terms with England and make great colonial gains (Portuguese and Dutch colonies). The same old story. H[is] Maj[esty] remained harsh and unyielding.' Gwinner pointed to Germany's 'quite inadequate financial preparation for war', and this impressed Moltke in particular, but the Kaiser blurted out: 'That's all the same to me!'[81]

As to his willingness to risk a war with Britain and France on account of his *Novelle*, Wilhelm II left no one in any doubt. On 15 January 1912, in the presence of Müller and Valentini, he denounced the 'feebleness and timidity' of Bethmann Hollweg and the Wilhelmstrasse 'in the sharpest terms. He was getting no help at all from this Reich Chancellor and had to do his work with Heeringen, Tirpitz and Julius [i.e. Moltke] unaided.'[82] On the same day he discussed Anglo-German relations with the former ambassador in Madrid, Ferdinand Baron von Stumm. When the latter, too, gave him the advice: 'just don't build any Dreadnoughts', his sovereign replied, according to his own account: 'I will tell you something, you diplomats have filled your pants, the entire Wilhelmstrasse stinks of ***.'[83]

Not until 25 January 1912 could agreement be reached (partly as a result of the catastrophic results of the Reichstag elections) to reduce still further the *Novelle* the Kaiser had started on its way five months before in his Hamburg speech. Of the three ships of the line and three heavy cruisers originally demanded there now remained only the battleships (in addition to those prescribed by the Navy Law) which were to be laid down in 1912, 1914 and 1917 respectively. On 7 February 1912 the *Novelle* was announced, in the speech from the throne in the White Hall of the Schloss.[84] Even in this truncated form the *Novelle* represented a distinct sharpening of the threat to Great Britain, especially as, quite apart from the new ships, the *Novelle* envisaged an increase in the personnel of the High Seas Fleet from 67,000 to 101,500. As the newly appointed First Lord of the Admiralty, Winston Churchill, exclaimed, when he received an outline of the *Novelle* on 31 January: 'This is certainly not dropping the naval challenge.' In reply, London would have to double its expenditure on the Royal Navy and transfer its battleships stationed in the Mediterranean to the North Sea. Churchill asked himself how long such an armaments race could be sustained.[85] He was by no means alone with his fears. The Foreign Secretary, Sir Edward Grey, had recently had to reckon with the possibility that the Germans might suddenly attack the British fleet.[86] And Churchill's implacable predecessor Admiral Lord Fisher declared in December 1911 that the decisive contest would start 'in September 1914'. 'That date suits the Germans, if ever they are going to fight. Both their army and Fleet then mobilised and the Kiel Canal finished and their new (naval) building complete.'[87] The Agadir crisis and the German reaction to the 'humiliation' of Lloyd George's Mansion House Speech had nevertheless 'brought Europe a large step closer to war'. The feeling prevailed on both sides of the North Sea that 'the great contest had become inevitable sooner or later'.[88] Even the negotiations of 8–9 February 1912 in Berlin, between the British War Minister, Lord Haldane, and Bethmann Hollweg, Tirpitz and the Kaiser only served to point up the incompatibility between the vital interests of the two empires.

CHAPTER THIRTY-TWO

'Already leader of the United States of Europe?' Wilhelm and the debacle of the Haldane mission

The visit of the British War Minister Viscount Haldane to Berlin in February 1912 is rightly regarded as a decisive event in the years leading up to the First World War. Seldom was the incompatibility between Great Britain's balance-of-power policy of maintaining the status quo and the German Reich's claim to the leadership of continental Europe so strikingly displayed as in the negotiations that started on 8 February in the Chancellor's palace and continued in the Schloss on the following day. An examination of Wilhelm II's numerous, often very emotional utterances, before, during and after the Haldane mission shows what exaggerated expectations he had of it. It was not the proffered colonial empire from coast to coast across Africa, but the prising apart of the Anglo-French Entente Cordiale, leading to Germany's supremacy on the continent, that was the overriding objective that, for a brief moment, Wilhelm thought he had achieved. By remorselessly building up his fleet he had, he believed, forced Britain to yield. In February 1912, as this chapter will show, he acted on the assumption that the United Kingdom would give up its Entente with France and embark instead on one with Germany, involving a treaty obligation to observe unconditional neutrality in any Franco-German war, that is to say including one initiated by Germany. Only after the conclusion of such a treaty was Wilhelm prepared to consider slowing down the German naval programme as a quid pro quo.

Not surprisingly, Haldane, Sir Edward Grey, and the recently appointed First Lord of the Admiralty, Winston Churchill, saw in this proposal Wilhelm II's desire to destroy France's position as a Great Power, either by war or the threat of war. After the inevitable failure of the negotiations – at which the Kaiser was greatly exercised – the British strengthened their North Sea presence by pulling back the Mediterranean Fleet into home waters, and further undertook to come to the assistance of France if Germany attacked her.

In parallel with the tug-of-war between the two Great Powers, the momentous struggle within the ruling elite in Berlin over the direction of policy described in the last chapter continued unabated. Tirpitz regarded the British offer of negotiations as nothing more than a trap to kill the planned new supplementary Navy Bill, the *Novelle*, offering Germany worthless overseas colonies unaccompanied by any firm promise of neutrality, and fought tooth and nail against any concession in the naval field. He was opposed by the Reich Chancellor, the Foreign Secretary, Alfred von Kiderlen-Wächter, and the ambassador in London, Count Metternich, who were pressing desperately for concessions over naval armaments because they saw in an agreement with England the last chance to preserve world peace, whereas a failure of the negotiations would sooner or later end in world war.

As so often it fell to Kaiser Wilhelm to decide between these two camps. He made it perfectly clear that his heart was with Tirpitz and that he despised the pusillanimous 'civilians' in the Wilhelmstrasse and at the London embassy. True, in February 1912 he declared himself prepared to agree to a reduction in the naval programme, but only because Bethmann Hollweg persuaded him that the destruction of the Triple Entente and a united Europe under his leadership were now within his grasp. When it dawned on him a few weeks later that the English were determined to continue with their 400-year-old balance-of-power policy and maintain their lead at sea, he returned to his earlier militaristic position.[1]

WILHELM AND THE SEARCH FOR AN AGREEMENT WITH ENGLAND

With the despairing courage of a man who knew his position was hopeless, Metternich had been urging Berlin ever since the Agadir crisis not to string the bow too tight in the matter of armaments, but to seize instead the British government's proffered hand of friendship. The ambassador enjoyed the strong backing of his deputy at the embassy, Richard von Kühlmann, while their efforts were subverted by the naval attaché in London, Captain Wilhelm Widenmann, who reported in the most spiteful terms on the anti-German feeling in England and particularly on the alleged machinations of Winston Churchill at the Admiralty.[2] The Chancellor's attempts to hold the naval attaché's highly political reports back from the Kaiser until Metternich − Widenmann's superior − could put forward his dissenting opinion were taken very ill by Wilhelm II,[3] who made it perfectly clear that he fully shared the attaché's harsh judgements and despised the 'civilian' ambassador's conciliatory approach.[4]

Metternich warned urgently that although the *Novelle* would not necessarily cause Britain to declare war immediately, it would convince the whole country 'that a war with Germany was inevitable'. This being so, the British would not leave Germany the time to complete her battleship-building programme but 'would seek an occasion for a war ... before the build-up of our fleet has been fully completed'. In any case, England would be determined to maintain the existing advantageous ratio in relation to the German navy (of about 2:1), and that, too, could render social and economic pressures in England 'so intolerable' as to make war appear the lesser evil. These views earned the Kaiser's fierce condemnation: Metternich was acting like a 'scared rabbit' and talking 'nonsense', 'tripe' and 'incredible rubbish'. If the British government declared war, Wilhelm scoffed, that would not bother him: 'Just let them! ... Then they will get the odium that England always tries to avoid ... We have had our ears boxed [in the Agadir crisis]; and now we are supposed not to build any ships!' The ambassador's report was 'the usual Metternichian advice! Just don't build in Germany, then England will be in a good mood! I do not agree with the ambassador's view! The naval attaché is right!'[5] Brusquely, he telegraphed to the Chancellor from Silesia on 27 November: 'Metternich's position exactly the same as over the *Novellen* of 1904 and 1908. Had I listened to him then we should have *no fleet at all* today! *His argument subjects our naval policy to the influence of a foreign Power in a way that I, as Supreme War Lord and Kaiser, cannot and will not accept, now or ever*! And which amounts to a *humiliation* for our people. The *Novelle* stays!'[6]

Another dispatch from London arrived which Wilhelm covered with marginal comments that testify eloquently to his intentions. Metternich, alluding to Grey's keynote speech to the Commons of 27 November 1911, declared himself convinced that with the conclusion of the Moroccan crisis the peace of Europe must now be assured. 'As we do not wish to wage aggressive war in the East or in the West, and as no wars can be expected to arise in the foreseeable future that might tempt England to intervene, there is nothing for the moment that is likely to revive our differences with England.' This assessment Wilhelm dismissed with the exclamation: 'sancta simplicitas!' Vehemently he rejected Metternich's endorsement of Grey's proposal to work for an agreement over a German colonial empire in Central Africa. What the Kaiser demanded instead was 'the abandonment of England's ententes' with France and Russia, and as London was not prepared to agree to this, there was 'nothing to be done!' As one could never be absolutely certain that England would not intervene against Germany – 'that is the chief thing'– then one must go on arming, the Kaiser concluded. Metternich's warnings that the present favourable climate of opinion in England would change the moment naval construction was intensified, and that the Anglo-French Entente could then easily become a regular alliance, made little impression on Wilhelm. He was no longer reckoning on a reconciliation with England, he declared, and the transformation of the Entente into a formal alliance would happen 'anyway' and 'that would clarify the position'. 'There is no helping the poor man!' he jeered at the end of Metternich's dispatch. 'He still insists, just don't arm at home, then England will stay in a good mood! nothing more!'[7] All this indicates that Wilhelm would only have been ready to refrain from intensifying the naval arms race in exchange for a binding British promise to remain neutral in the event of a continental war. The impracticability of such a bid for hegemony was recognised by no less an authority than Tirpitz's colleague at the Reich Navy Office, Albert Hopman, who described Grey's speech to the Commons as an 'expression of England's clear and firm policy', and one 'against which Wilhelm II must always be doomed to fail if he wishes to challenge it. As for my own political convictions, I need say no more. They are with England, and not with Wilhem II, who has made a mess of everything and will go on doing so.'[8]

Meanwhile, Wilhelm's anti-English bellicosity was intensifying. On 6 December 1911 he wrote to his friend Franz Ferdinand: 'To judge by the behaviour of the English in the past year – and Grey's blathering makes no difference – we shall have to expect a few surprises from that quarter and take precautions by building more ships. Only strength and brutal power makes any impression across the Channel. Politeness is seen as weakness. We have the *manpower*, and they [the English] are not in a position to keep up.'[9] When on 12 December he was presented with a telegram from Baron Marschall von Bieberstein about the impact the Anglo-Franco-Russian Entente was having in Constantinople, he raged: 'Unheard of! We are again being cut out! ... If the exclusion of German industry goes on unchecked like this: then we shall have to take up arms and get our way sword in hand. So – armaments!'[10] It was no coincidence that a few weeks later Kaiser Wilhelm chose Marschall as Metternich's successor at the London embassy.

Wilhelm sharply rebuffed all Metternich's and Kühlmann's efforts to secure an agreement with England. Grey, he complained, would never make concessions that were any use. '*He just* will *not*! and would only be forced to do so by the weight of hard facts!' Furiously, he minuted on a report from Metternich: 'Pah! You are very humble and undemanding, Mr Ambassador. That is *not* enough for *me*! That amounts to *nothing*! ... That is not the manner in which the German Kaiser and his German people can and must expect England to approach them if they are to change their political attitudes and behaviour. They dictate and we are supposed to accept! There can be no question of that!

We must be approached & taken at *our own valuation*, or everything will stay as it was! At any rate, we must push ahead with our shipbuilding! London must sing a very different tune before I let myself in for anything. In sum, one can see that so long as Grey remains in office no real *political* agreement will be possible! So long as the English government does not feel morally compelled to agree with us, nothing can be done. Apart from arming!' By forcing the pace of naval armaments Great Britain was to be compelled to abandon the Entente policy she had been pursuing since 1904, in which 'the Waterloo ally [i.e. England] is *participating at the side of France* in the anti-German *military* offensive alliance against us!'[11]

THE KAISER AND THE 'MIRAGE' OF A COLONIAL EMPIRE IN AFRICA

Wilhelm II's primary aim, then, was not colonial acquisitions overseas but the breakthrough to supremacy in Europe. The inevitable consequence of this policy of continental hegemony was that the other European Powers − great and small − sought protection, under the aegis of Great Britain, from the threatening German predominance. Moreover, it was precisely on account of his preoccupation with supremacy in Europe that Wilhelm rejected as deceitful the British offers to help Germany to acquire a colonial empire stretching right across Africa. Evidently London's underlying motive was to divide the German battlefleet concentrated in the North Sea by luring its ships thousands of miles away! Only the Wilhelmstrasse and the diplomats of the London embassy, he declared, had 'swallowed the British bait!!' and failed to spot the perfidious intention behind it.[12] When Kühlmann reported on 8 January 1912 that Britain was prepared to help Germany to acquire a great colonial empire in Central Africa − i.e. precisely the aim of Kiderlen's adventurous *Panthersprung* of 1911 − the Kaiser was up in arms, disputing in countless minutes and memoranda Kühlmann's claim that German policy now faced a choice between two clear and sharply divergent courses of action − 'on the one hand, the chance of peace with honour, colonial expansion, successful cultural activity and growing prosperity, on the other the revival of the old feud, strengthening anti-German activity everywhere and conjuring up serious dangers.' 'No!', Wilhelm raged, 'We have enough colonies! If I want some I shall buy them or get them without England!' In any case neither the Portuguese colonies nor the Congo basin, the subjects of the preliminary talks in London, belonged to England. 'They want to offer us things that do not belong to them! Like Morocco!' Whatever African territory Germany might get was 'not that important! The chief thing is, first of all, a *political* rapprochement! Until that takes place I shall not make any colonial deals

with England. They will not change the cost of my military budget one iota.'
The British intention was clear: Germany was 'to have a scrap with France
over the Congo ... just as over Morocco!' He would 'not even think' of
accepting the English proposals, he declared. 'As the territory belongs to
neither England nor us, we should immediately be forced to proceed against
the owners with our army, and then England would certainly find an opportunity to stab us in the back ... England does not wish us to have colonies, but
colonial wars and *entanglements*.' Besides, she wants to weaken 'our concentration of power and strength' in the North Sea. Kühlmann was 'an eager pupil
of Metternich's and therefore reproduces all the rubbish that has been served
up to me ever since I have been building my fleet; only it has never impressed
me. I shall therefore refrain from contradicting this stuff. I do not want any
gifts of colonies from England, as these are always offered *at the expense of
others* and carry the seeds of conflicts, the end of which cannot be foreseen.
The strengthening of our armed forces that I hold to be necessary must and
will go on.'[13]

Although Wilhelm said he could not be bothered to refute Kühlmann's
arguments, he could not resist sending the London embassy a long memorandum expounding his views to the contrary. 'The report is based on false
premisses', he fulminated on 11 January 1912. England wanted to avoid a
war and wished, after insulting Germany in the Agadir crisis, 'to put us in a
"good mood" again like a whipped child, with the offer of a carrot after Lloyd
George's *stick*. Hence, the hints to us from all quarters about a *colonial* empire
to be built up in *Africa*. Naturally we are offered, in true British fashion, the
possessions of *others* over which England does *not* have the right of disposal.
Portugal has not so far indicated that she intends to get rid of her colonial
possessions; and she will probably demand quite a few millions which we shall
probably not have available. France has got a preemptive right over the Congo
Free State; and there is no chance that she would accommodate us in her
present frame of mind. On the contrary, the moment our intentions became
known she would be quite capable of offering the Belgians 1 billion – which
she always has ready – to snap it up from under our noses. So the British
"presents" turn out to be Greek gifts, which would bring us into the same
position vis-à-vis their owners as France is in Morocco vis-à-vis Spain; Italy in
Tripoli etc. These gifts would, as soon as we seriously attempted to grab them,
land us in the ugliest situations – thanks to agitation in the newspapers and
England's diplomatic lies – and sap our strength and concentration of power,
financial, military and naval, in Europe. England's game is obvious, but my
officials cannot see through it. Germany is to be drawn, by the delusion of a
"*colonial* empire" in Africa and acquisitions at the expense of *others*, into

entanglements, and distracted from *Welt*politik, i.e. they want the great Asian question to be resolved à trois *without us*, by the Triple Entente, Japan and America, and we are *not* to be involved. But if Asia is partitioned our exports – industrial production – will suffer permanent damage and we should have to secure the open door for them by warships and grenades. The solution of the Asian question *with us* is the basis of my whole policy, including the Navy and my military concentration in Europe. That is why it is regarded as a nuisance, to be dissipated in *colonial* expansion and fragmented. So that we have no voice in Asia – or anywhere else in the world! That is why I will not accept the English offers. Already in the autumn H[is] E[xcellency] the Reich Chancellor established the principle, with my express approval, that before any *detailed* agreement there must first be a Political Working agreement with England, i.e. recognition of our *Political* importance and *Political* equality, and the general bringing into line of our *policies* in the *world*. Apparently England does *not* want this, but wants to fob us off with *Colonial* crumbs, to clear us off the *world* stage, and possibly also go on manoeuvring *against* us! So the offer is a waste of time! When H[err] v[on] Kühlmann dreams of the great German colonial empire in Africa, he forgets the *method* of its creation, the *means* – our lack of funds – and the *personnel* – our lack of suitable trained officials. He would also do well to stick his nose into a work on naval history. Then he could learn that being a *Great Colonial Power* means *at the same time* being *a Great Naval Power*. Without the latter, the former is nonsense. The history of Spain shows that. She was a mighty *colonial* Great Power, but neglected her navy and lost her whole *colonial* empire. The last phase was St Jago de Cuba! A great colonial empire cannot be maintained without a *strong fleet*. For the great colonial empire mentioned above, therefore, I should have to demand *in the first instance*, a doubling of the naval budget and the building of great fortified harbours and naval stations! The military budget remains in force regardless of such dreams!'[14] Wilhelm's attitude remained unchanged until news from London led him to hope that Britain was indeed prepared to give up her ententes with France and Russia in favour of a comparable agreement with Germany.

IN EXPECTATION OF THE ʻENTENTEʼ WITH ENGLAND

On 10 January 1912 Bethmann Hollweg explained to the Kaiser, just as Metternich and Kühlmann were doing, that an understanding with England had become attainable. Germany would ʻbe able to build up a great colonial empire (Portuguese colonies, Belgian Congo, Dutch colonies)ʼ and – this was the decisive point – would ʻdrive a wedge into the Triple Ententeʼ. The navy could have money for personnel, U-boats, and other 'auxiliary weapons', the Chancellor assured him, 'only no more Dreadnoughts'.[15] Wilhelm was at first 'beside himself' at Bethmann's suggestion, but he soon became convinced that he could at last achieve his great aim, the break-up of the Entente and German supremacy in Europe. On 7 February, the day Haldane arrived in Berlin, Admiral von Müller, after talking for hours with the Kaiser and Tirpitz 'about English ententes and neutrality agreements with colonial prospects', noted: 'H. Maj. very enthusiastic. Saw himself already as leader of the United States of Europe, and a German colonial empire stretching right across Central Africa.'[16]

When exactly Kaiser Wilhelm first learned of the intention to send a prominent British statesman to take soundings in Berlin is not absolutely clear. It is only certain that the impetus came from Albert Ballin, who won over the influential British financier Sir Ernest Cassel for his plans (see Figure 37).[17] The governments in London and Berlin each assumed that Ballin and Cassel were acting on instructions from the other, which was to give rise to endless misunderstandings. Grey told Metternich that early in January Cassel had suggested, on instructions from Kaiser Wilhelm, that Churchill might visit Berlin, but the Kaiser firmly denied having taken the initiative. Grey's claim was 'Nonsense!', he wrote. 'I had nothing to do with Cassel until the end of January, when he thanked me for his decoration and came out with Grey's offer.'[18] But here the Kaiser was glossing over the mediatory role that Ballin had played. It seems almost unthinkable that the latter, who saw the Kaiser and Bethmann in the middle of December 1911,[19] would have dared to take the initiative in such a delicate question without first assuring himself that the Kaiser was in agreement. It is also true that at the end of 1911 Ballin sent the Kaiser an article from the *Westminster Gazette* headed 'Towards an Anglo-German Detente', on which Wilhelm wrote the remarkable comment: 'Quite good, apart from the ridiculous idea that we are striving for hegemony in Central Europe: *We are* in fact Central Europe. And that other smaller states lean on us or come within our orbit through the law of gravity, is quite natural. The English do not want that, because it absolutely shatters their theory of the "Balance of Power" − i.e. playing the European Great Powers off against each other ad libitum − and would create a united continent, which they will do anything to thwart, hence the lies about our craving for hegemony! Just as they claim and practise it in the world at large! We Hohenzollerns have never yet striven for such overweening and nebulous aims. And shall, God willing, never do so!'[20] Whether Ballin felt the distinction between 'hegemony' and a mighty German 'Central Europe' to be more than hair-splitting, we do not know. At any rate, he must have seen in the Kaiser's reaction an encouraging sign and embarked with Cassel's assistance on the attempt to bring a British negotiator to Berlin.

Figure 37 Wilhelm II with Albert Ballin, Managing Director of the
Hapag shipping line

Originally, Winston Churchill was to have gone to Berlin for talks, but
as newly appointed First Lord of the Admiralty, he did not feel in a position
to play the role of mediator.[21] He was, however, actively involved in the
discussions that resulted in the sending of the War Minister, Viscount
Haldane. On 27 January 1912 Grey, Lloyd George and Cassel met at
Churchill's house and drafted the short *note verbale* about possible negotiations with Germany which Cassel presented to Bethmann Hollweg in Berlin
two days later.[22]

The insuperable obstacles in the way of an Anglo-German understanding were already apparent at this early stage. Germany's hopes of what Müller termed 'England's attempt to draw close to us' were always set far too high: Müller spoke of England's 'offering ententes'.[23] On the other hand it was clear that the *Novelle*, agreed upon only a few days before, would constitute a major obstacle (albeit one less extreme than the original draft would have made it) to an agreement with England. True, the Kaiser felt obliged to inform the British of the *Novelle*, at least in outline, but it was significant that he sent Müller, as head of his Naval Cabinet, to Bethmann Hollweg to draft the communication to London, and not Tirpitz, who he feared 'would make trouble for the Chancellor'.[24] The Grand Admiral's obdurate resistance to any concessions whatever to the British was to make the negotiations very difficult indeed.

The outlines of a possible agreement emerged after a discussion lasting several hours between Ballin, the Kaiser and the Chancellor on 31 January 1912. Müller listed in his diary the three elements – a slowdown in the speed of naval increases, colonial expansion, and a promise of neutrality – that were to be weighed against each other: '1. Recognition of England's claim to a superior naval force in view of her geographical position, colonies etc., 2. support for German attempts to expand in so far as same are compatible with British interests, 3. support to be given immediately once Germany indicates where she wants to take action, 4. Mutual obligation not to join any coalition directed against the other party. Duration of the Entente, for the time being, 20 years.'[25]

On 3 February the Kaiser again discussed 'the Ballin-Cassel political disclosures' with the head of his Naval Cabinet 'under the seal of strictest secrecy', and instructed Müller to report, 'by 6 o'clock this evening, on the possibility of a further reduction of the *Novelle* with a view to reaching an understanding with England'.[26] On the following morning Wilhelm, Bethmann and Ballin drafted the reply to the British *note verbale;* neither Tirpitz nor Cassel was involved, and Kiderlen, too, felt bypassed.[27] In this reply – Wilhelm dictated the English text personally – the Kaiser demanded, as a quid pro quo for slowing down the tempo of German naval construction, a 'political' agreement in which 'both Powers agree not to take part in any plans, combinations or acts of war directed against either of the said parties'.[28] Wilhelm told Müller 'that he could not do other than enter into negotiations with England. A refusal means war in the spring – and war on 3 fronts at that.'[29]

Müller urgently advised including Tirpitz in the discussions, whereupon the Kaiser ordered him to bring the secretary of state to the Schloss that evening. The three of them walked up and down in the Star Chamber, 'T. as usual ungracious, not to say arrogant and difficult. But he had in the end to admit that negotiations could not be declined and that this morning's dispatch for Ballin, Cassel, and the Embassy in London had been skilfully drafted.'[30] But a grudge against the Kaiser, who had 'given way' again, was still in evidence, especially as Tirpitz felt he had been sidelined.[31]

Feverishly, Wilhelm prepared himself for the negotiations with Haldane that appeared so promising. In an 'All-Highest draft' of 5 February he defined the chief aim as reaching an 'Alliance- or neutrality-treaty, on the basis of which we could adopt a slower tempo for the *Novelle*'.[32] Next day, after further discussions with Bethmann, the Kaiser sent Tirpitz some handwritten notes, which read:

Re discussions with Haldane, the following agreed with the Chancellor:

General

1) Haldane is coming (*assumption*) in a *private* capacity to *take soundings* and *prepare* the terrain.
2) Clarification as to whether this is the case, or whether he declares himself to be (empowered by the Government as a whole) to start negotiating now.
3) In the *first* case, point out that he comes as the representative of a government *committee* which is nonbinding and has *so far* not committed itself. Whereas the government here, by contrast, is directed by *1 man*, the Kaiser, i.e. the Chancellor speaks in his name. Therefore, for the moment, in the *first* case, the Chancellor will only be expressing *his private* opinion, and not that of the Kaiser.
4) Exercise great care and reserve in the conversations, to allow Haldane to show his hand first.
5) Clearly expressed determination to maintain the [naval] budget. Influence of foreign state on it impermissible.
6) In discussing exchanges of information, construction plans, and any limitation of armaments, *incisive emphasis* on *reciprocity* – if something is done here, the same to be done in England.[33]

The 'political' question of British neutrality, which was the kernel of the negotiations, was not mentioned in these notes for Tirpitz, as it did not fall, as he complained, in his sphere of responsibility as Secretary of State of the Reich Navy Office. The Grand Admiral was firmly convinced that the English were far from inclined to give up their centuries-old balance-of-power policy – and specifically their ententes with France and Russia – in exchange for a relaxation of the naval armaments race. The 'equality of *political* status . . . in the *world*'[34] that the Kaiser was demanding could only be attained, Tirpitz argued, after an unrelenting competition in naval construction had practically forced the United Kingdom to capitulate. So the secretary of state poured 'a lot of water in the wine' of a 'quite ecstatic' Kaiser who on the eve of Haldane's visit saw himself 'already as leader of the United States of Europe'.[35] As he bluntly informed the monarch: 'I believe that there are no grounds whatever for assuming that the English really want to give up the policy they have been pursuing for years and embark on an entirely new course.'[36] Tirpitz was to be proved right, which made Wilhelm's fury at the outcome of the negotiations all the more bitter.

What the Kaiser was demanding as a quid pro quo for a slowing down of the rate of German naval construction amounted in British eyes to the abdication of the UK as a World Power, the abandonment of her ententes with France and Russia and the consequent acceptance of German supremacy on the European continent. As recently as September 1911, in a memorandum for George V, Sir Arthur Nicolson had set out the arguments against an Anglo-German alliance. Only the ententes with France and Russia had protected Britain against a German hegemony in Europe. 'The policy of England has always been to maintain a balance of power and to resist the predominance of any one Power. Had we not settled our outstanding questions with France and Russia we should have offered both these Powers opportunities of creating serious embarrassments and difficulties to us in Egypt, Newfoundland, New Hebrides and in the Middle and Far East.' An alliance with Germany would have given England no protection against such dangers. On the contrary, 'we should soon have found ourselves compelled to do the bidding of Germany, and we should have been drawn into any adventures to which her policy might lead us. Our alliance with Germany would have maintained a constant friction with France & Russia and might possibly have led to war ... Compare the situation before 1904 with the present – and there can hardly be a question that our own international position is far stronger and the security for peace far greater.'[37] On 8 February, the very day on which Haldane started his negotiations in Berlin, Nicolson expressed grave doubts about the course that was being adopted: 'I do not myself see why we should abandon the excellent position in which we have been placed, and step down to be involved in endeavours to entangle us in some so-called "understandings" which would undoubtedly, if not actually impair our relations with France and Russia, in any case render the latter countries somewhat suspicious of us. Moreover, is it likely that we shall be able to obtain from Germany an undertaking of a really formal and binding character that she will not increase her naval programme – and will always be content to leave us in undisputed and indisputable supremacy?'[38] Clearly, only huge concessions of world-historical importance by one side or the other could have led to an agreement, and they were not to be expected.

LORD HALDANE IN BERLIN

The choice of Viscount Haldane as negotiator was a natural one. The War Minister, whose predilection for German philosophy had earned him the sobriquet of 'Schopenhauer' from Asquith, spoke fluent German, had studied in Göttingen, translated German books into English, and often spent his holidays in Germany. He knew the Kaiser personally and had invited him to his house in Queen Anne's Gate the year before.[39] But Haldane's status as negotiator was unclear all the same. In his first conversation with the Chancellor on 8 February he explained 'that I had come here officially with the approval of the King and the Cabinet, but merely to talk over the ground, and not to commit either myself or my own Government to any propositions'.[40] Moreover, it was striking that the minister, who was accompanied only by his brother (the renowned scientist), stayed at the Hotel Bristol, not at the embassy. Officially, both Haldanes had come to Berlin on university business.[41] However, it was not questions of formal status, but very weighty differences of substance that caused the negotiations to fail.

The first round of soundings between Haldane and Bethmann Hollweg on 8 February went off satisfactorily, but also showed clearly the limited possibilities for agreement. The British minister pointed to the growing power of Germany as causing the other European Powers to draw together. 'Germany had built up, and was building up, magnificent armaments, and with the aid of the Triple Alliance she had become the centre of a tremendous group. The natural result was that other Powers had tended to approximate.' Haldane made it clear that Britain would not be able to accept the crushing of France by Germany. The Chancellor replied that he could see, even if he did not particularly like the term 'balance of power', that Great Britain would always lean towards the weaker grouping in Europe. He had, however, drawn up a neutrality formula which he hoped might bridge the differences between the two camps, Triple Alliance and Triple Entente,[42] and which ran: 'should one of the High Contracting Parties become involved in a war with one or more Powers, the other will observe towards it at least a benevolent neutrality, and work for the localisation of the conflict.'[43] Haldane pointed to the 'fatal' difficulty with this formula. What would happen, he asked the Chancellor, if 'for example' Germany should attack France? In such a case Great Britain could not sit back and watch with hands tied. Only if the neutrality formula were expressly confined to 'aggressive or unprovoked attacks' could this awkward consequence be avoided. The Chancellor pointed out how difficult it was to define the aggressor when war broke out, but he conceded that an 'unconditional' neutrality clause was problematical. He would think further

about the question; the chief thing was the goodwill between the two countries. 'For two and a half years he had been striving to bring about an
agreement between Germany and England. This had been the aim of his
policy ... He would take counsel over our talk and communicate with me
shortly again. I have reason to think that he went immediately to see the
Emperor', Haldane noted.[44]

His negotiations with Tirpitz, scheduled for the next day, promised from the
start to be a good deal more difficult. The incompatibility of the two points of
view was clear from the notes the Grand Admiral drew up on the eve of the
encounter: England was professing, he wrote, to offer Germany the same
relationship she had with France, 'but is not in fact doing so. Proof: E[ngland]
wants to stay neutral if F[rance] attacks G[ermany]. E[ngland] keeps a free
hand if G[ermany] attacks F[rance]. The principle does not apply in reverse,
for E[ngland] does *not* want to stay neutral if G[ermany] attacks F[rance].
France, therefore, has a different entente. Apart from this, who is the aggressor? F[rance] can so insult G[ermany] under this agreement that G[ermany] is
forced to go to war.' From Germany's point of view the whole point of the
negotiations with Haldane was that 'England should not participate in a war
between G[ermany] and F[rance], and that is just what England refuses to
agree to. If, however, England is to participate in such a war, then we need
to build up our armaments.' The British were obviously seeking, according to
Tirpitz, to get Germany to abandon the *Novelle* without tying their own
hands.[45] On the eve of the decisive meeting with the British negotiator Tirpitz
summed up his position incisively in a note for the Kaiser. The 'political
demand' that Germany would have to ask for as a quid pro quo for slowing
down her naval building programme was: 'England may not participate in any
war between Germany and France, regardless of who is the "aggressor". If we
cannot get this guarantee, then we must go on arming in order to be a match
for the Anglo-France entente, which is to all intents and purposes an offensive
alliance.'[46]

Tirpitz's note crossed with one from the Kaiser who continued to cherish
high hopes of the negotiations: there was 'such a great amount' at stake.[47] He
assumed that an Anglo-German Entente was there for the taking, and used all
his influence to bring Tirpitz into line. He sent Müller a letter to read to the
Grand Admiral before his meeting with Haldane, warning that 'the Chancellor ... has been made frightfully mistrustful of Tirpitz (by the Ausw. Amt)
and he is very worried that Tirpitz could make a mess of things by sticking too
rigidly to a departmental line with regard to the timing of the Bill and the
tempo [of shipbuilding] ... The Ausw. Amt – so I hear on the quiet – is
furious at not being officially involved, out of vanity and a desire to get all the

glory — which of course it doesn't want to see going to the Kaiser personally, let alone Tirpitz. So long as Tirpitz doesn't put a spoke in our wheel, we are in the clear in so far as the Entente can be concluded *politically*, but he mustn't upset things for us any more. At the same time the Chancellor urgently begs that nothing be said by Tirpitz *about the 2 power standard*, unless Haldane himself expressly raises the matter. There is no doubt the fate of the [Anglo-German] Entente very much depends on today's conversation between Tirpitz and Haldane, and with it the fate of Germany and the whole world — surely Tirpitz must see that. He must operate with bold, free, plain strokes, free from mistrust and ulterior motives! ... If Tirpitz can sufficiently accommodate Engl[and]'s wishes when she puts them to us, so that we get the Entente [with England] signed and sealed, then I shall see to it that the world hears that he was the man whom Germany and the world have to thank for peace, and for a pile of colonial territory too. Then he will have a position in the world that no German minister has had since Bismarck, and in the Reichstag too, which he will be able to twist round his little finger! The Chancellor showed us today on the map, just what England wants to help us to get. 1) The whole of Angola, which is bigger than the whole of S W Africa, 2) the part of Mozambique that is assigned to us, 3) Zanzibar and Pemba too if we want it, and 4) the southern half of the Congo State (later) if we want it. So that East Africa and S W Africa can be joined up. As payment for all this, the island of Timor.'[48]

Originally the Kaiser wanted, as Müller advised, only to participate in the conversations of 9 February until Tirpitz and Haldane had 'warmed to each other', but then 'as things ... really got going H.M. could not resist keeping his hand in the game'. He stayed in it to the end and boasted that he personally had brought about the agreement.[49] While strolling afterwards with Müller in Döberitz he took the opportunity to 'pour out his heart to him about the meeting'. 'Thank God that I was there!', he cried. 'Tirpitz's pigheadedness had brought the discussion to a complete dead stop. T. wanted to give up absolutely nothing from the *Novelle* and got on to the two power standard as well. Then I leapt in and said we ought to divide the purely political from the naval-political. The *Novelle* would have to be brought in in its present form, but once there was a political entente, then I as All-Highest War Lord can declare that the creation of the III Squadron is not now all that urgent, and that the ships we need will therefore be built at a slower rate, the first in 1913, the second in 1916 and the third in 1919. An attempt by Haldane to interfere with the Navy Law itself I ruled out immediately, saying that that is a Law and cannot be touched. I also reserved my right to build in a faster tempo if I saw that France and Russia were going ahead faster, whereupon Haldane immediately said that the British would naturally ask the French and

Russians to build in a moderate tempo. Haldane is very satisfied with the discussion and says that the result will be greeted with joy in England, especially by the King. He will now go straight back and arrange for Grey to come to Berlin at once with the text of the treaty for signing, and for the agreement then to be published immediately.'[50]

With high hopes Wilhelm wrote to the Reich Chancellor, who on his express orders had not participated in the negotiations on 9 February: 'The difficult session has ended – and ended *very well* in fact! Of course, despite all our care and good intentions, the two-power standard 2:3 and everything else one wanted to avoid came up for discussion. But in the end everyone's "steam was expended" and I permitted myself to propose the following basis, which was accepted all round. 1., the agreement – which is to be *purely political* – will contain *nothing at all* about naval strengths, standards, and construction. 2., as soon as the agreement – which is to be *purely political* – is published and as soon as the budget is brought in, I shall have Tirpitz explain, *à propos* the agreement, that although we are demanding a *Novelle* with a third squadron, in view of the agreement and to avoid prejudicing its beneficial effects, the first ship will not be asked for until 1913 and the other two at intervals of three years, in 1916 and 1919. Haldane was in agreement; Tirpitz too. English government will proceed in the same way and reduce its building programme accordingly. So my position on my *Novelle* and vis-à-vis my people has been preserved.'[51] Triumphantly, the Kaiser informed Ballin of the breakthrough that very evening. 'Agreement brought about by me', he wrote proudly, and after explaining the agreements, declared: 'I went *a long way* to come to an accommodation. But this is now *the end!* He [Haldane] was very nice and sensible and perfectly understood my position as Supreme War Lord and that of Tirpitz vis-à-vis the Reichstag over the *Novelle*. So I think I have done everything that it was in my power to do!!!'[52]

In the evening Haldane and Bethmann had another talk in the Wilhelm-strasse. Unlike the Kaiser both recognised how difficult it would be to come to an agreement, for if London could not accept the new *Novelle*, even in a yet more attenuated form, the agreement would fail 'and things would get even worse'. An agreement with England, the Chancellor again declared, was 'his life's dream', and yet it was nevertheless doomed to failure thanks to Tirpitz's naval policy. Bethmann promised to go on doing his best, 'but the forces he had to contend with were almost overwhelming'.[53] Next day, at the funeral of Field Marshal Wilhelm von Hahnke, the former head of the Military Cabinet, a gloomy Chancellor told Müller: 'Things are very much worse. Haldane has a very unfavourable impression of Tirpitz, I really don't know what it will all come to.'[54] Wilhelm II, however, cherished the illusion for days that he had convinced Haldane of the inevitability of Germany's supremacy. According to Walther Rathenau, an elated Kaiser had explained to him on 13 February: 'Haldane has learned the truth and was very depressed. England acknowledges that she has to reckon with our navy. They are seeking an agreement. Haldane was given the answer: The political questions must be cleared up first . . . The Kaiser just needs to be in Cowes again, then he will put everything in order. The King trusts him. His plan is: United States of Europe against America. This was not unappealing to the English. Then five states (including France) could get something done!'[55]

`MY PATIENCE AND THAT OF THE GERMAN PEOPLE IS AT AN END!'

Of course, in the Kaiser's view, the fundamental change he had so hoped for in British foreign policy had resulted, not from an agreement freely arrived at between the two Great Powers, but from a naval arms race that had forced the United Kingdom to give in. He therefore persisted with his *Novelle* unmodified and his aim of a ratio of 2:3 for the two battlefleets, and categorically rejected all appeals from the Chancellor and the Foreign Secretary to show some flexibility in furtherance of a naval agreement with England; and in the conflict between Tirpitz and Bethmann Hollweg, in the last analysis a conflict between war and peace, he continued to side with Tirpitz against the 'civilians' in the Wilhelmstrasse. On 24 February 1912 Tirpitz went so far as to inform the head of the Naval Cabinet and Wilhelm's Adjutant-General Hans von Plessen that he was convinced 'that the Kaiser would seriously jeopardise the most important, if not the only credit item on his government's balance sheet if he authorised a one-sided retreat, i.e. giving way to England'. Plessen promised to tell the Kaiser at the next opportunity that 'he must not back down!'[56] After his audience with Tirpitz, according to a note of Muller's, 'His Majesty the Kaiser expressly affirmed today that he was certainly not thinking of dropping the naval *Novelle*. Nor was there for him any question of bringing in the *Novelle* without additional warships.'[57]

Against the Supreme War Lord, the Reich Navy Office, the Naval Cabinet and the Adjutant-General, Bethmann and Kiderlen could not prevail.[58] A request from the Chancellor to call the naval attaché Widenmann to order, as his activity was threatening to sabotage relations with England, Wilhelm rejected in 'unnecessarily' sharp terms.[59] 'No!' he exclaimed; Widenmann was 'an officer and can only be disciplined by the Supreme War Lord, never by civilian superiors'.[60] On 24 February Wilhelm complained to Kiderlen that he had 'learned with regret from the Reich Navy Office that, unfortunately, the result of the discussion between you and the Secretary of State at the Navy

Office was negative. Your Excellency expressed the fear that the neutrality clause in the Anglo-German agreement would prove unobtainable if the three new battleships necessary for the completion of the third squadron remain in the *Novelle*. You further urged the Secretary of State to drop the ships until they can be ordered at a later date, and to bring the *Novelle* in without them, which the Secretary of State – quite rightly – refused to do. He cannot do that without my authorisation, which he will not get. I am amazed that Your Excellency should presume to reopen a question which has already been dealt with by me and Lord Haldane and settled in the presence of the Secretary of State. I have expressly agreed with Lord Haldane that the *Novelle cannot* and *must not* be touched, as a matter of principle. At the same time, however, that I was willing to accommodate the wishes of the English government that he represented, with regard to the *tempo* of naval building. The proposed reduction of the *Tempo* was accepted by Lord Haldane straight away and declared to be sufficient. I reported this outcome to the Chancellor who received it with grateful thanks … Since that day I have not had the slightest indication of any development that might change anything in my conversation with Lord Haldane. England is completely silent … How Your Excellency can conclude, therefore, that the neutrality clause could only *be obtained* with difficulty, or not at all, unless the three battleships are *dropped*, is inexplicable, as it was accepted by Lord Haldane *with the battleships*. You must have – perhaps from private sources – more recent news than I have received. I therefore call Your Excellency's attention to the fact that, at the Chancellor's express wish and in full agreement with him, I personally took charge of the naval-political part of the negotiations – not without success, apparently – and that I intend in future too, *personally* to take this matter *independently* in hand, as it can easily be compromised by too much diplomacy. I command Your Excellency, therefore, to send me all information – including private information – that may come to your knowledge officially or unofficially.'[61] Kiderlen asked for an audience and assured the Kaiser 'with deepest reverence' that he had 'only, within the parameters of activity prescribed for me by Your Majesty, dutifully and openly spoken my mind, as Your Majesty has the right to expect. That I did not wish, and shall never wish, to pre-judge any decision of Your Majesty's whatever, goes without saying; but I also know that Your Majesty always permits a loyal servant to express his opinion – even if it is wrong – openly and without reserve.'[62]

At last, on 25 February 1912, a report arrived from Metternich of a conversation he had had with Grey and Haldane three days before,[63] from which Tirpitz, Müller and Wilhelm II concluded that no agreement could be reached with England after all.[64] The head of the Naval Cabinet declared

himself 'shocked at England's effrontery' and advised strongly against any
further concessions in the naval question.[65] Tirpitz once again explained to the
Kaiser the incompatibility between the German and British standpoints: 'We
are demanding that England should reorientate her whole policy, abandoning
her existing ententes while we take the place of France. England is
demanding that we should reorientate our naval policy, so that our Navy can
no longer pose any kind of danger to England.' He no longer believed that
such a far-reaching agreement could be achieved and recommended sticking
to the building plan ostensibly agreed with Haldane, for three additional
battleships.[66]

Tirpitz's submission made no bones about Germany's heady ambitions, but
the Kaiser used it as a basis for a letter to the Chancellor, quoting Tirpitz
almost word for word.[67] 'My dear Bethmann! I have ... considered the
situation, at length and from all angles, and have come to the following
conclusions. I. General situation. 1. *We* are after all demanding that England
should reorientate her *whole policy* to the extent of abandoning her present
ententes, while we more or less take the place of France. 2. *England* is
demanding that we should reorientate our *naval policy* so that our fleet can
no longer pose any kind of danger to England. The difficulty for us is that it is
solely and alone our naval policy, drawn up and until now uncompromisingly
pursued by me, that has brought the English to consider whether it might be
desirable to turn towards us; and that, if they do so, alone guarantees that the
change will be sincere and lasting, and that we shall, moreover, if we pursue
the entente with England in future, be strong enough to ensure our equality of
status vis-à-vis even the strongest entente partners. 4. The difficulty *for
England*, on the other hand, lies in the fact that, now as always – let us not
deceive ourselves – she sees the *Entente with France* as the best security
against an over-powerful *Germany*. She will now only be further confirmed
in this by the tempting alliance offers from Paris that Cassel was talking
about. The result, 5. is a vicious circle, from which it will be difficult to find
a way out, and on which it will be even more difficult to base an agreement
that satisfies both parties. This seems to be acknowledged in England
already ... *Our* last word must remain the agreements made with Haldane ...
Wilhelm I.R.'[68]

Next day, when a second report from Metternich arrived confirming the
reluctant attitude of the British, the Kaiser flew into a rage and covered the
document from top to bottom with furious marginalia. 'If Metternich had
understood his job properly, he would have told Grey immediately, 8 days ago,
that his proposal represented a complete disavowal of Lord Haldane's negotiations with H[is] M[ajesty], and that he refused to forward such a proposal to

Berlin. His job was to negotiate a political agreement, not a unilateral one about our *Novelle*; for that would amount to an infringement of Germany's freedom of decision and an interference with the powers of the Supreme War Lord!' 'So, they are now going on about the *Novelle*! Just as I suspected from the start! It must be underlined yet again for our diplomats and their activity: it was the English who made the first move for an agreement. They made proposals through Haldane (reduction of building tempo) with the agreement of *the whole cabinet*, which we, with a heavy heart, *accepted*. We proposed a neutrality agreement. That has *not* so far been accepted by them. Now they are throwing over the Haldane basis that we had accepted, sans façon, and are demanding more or less the abandonment of the *Novelle*, *without* the *slightest offer* to us in terms of a *pledge of neutrality*! Such one-sided proceedings are absolutely unacceptable! They should *first* send *us* the draft of a *neutrality agreement*, and then we shall decide what we shall do! Grey openly admits – as my letter of 27th and 28th to the Chancellor suggests – that Haldane has been disavowed, and the points he agreed with me abandoned. Instead of negotiations for a political agreement (treaty) between two nations *of equal status*, there is to be an 'understanding' or 'consensus' regarding a law that one of the two contracting parties is to introduce, to the effect that its implementation will be prevented because it does not suit the other party: i.e. an insolent interference with the free power of decision of one great nation by another. That is no longer negotiating, but exerting pressure and calling to order! I shall not go along with that sort of thing! *My* basis for negotiations is the one agreed with Lord Haldane, whose proposals were – as he expressly emphasised himself – *endorsed* by the *whole* English *cabinet*. I shall *not* budge from that. Any discussion of the details of my *Novelle*, I rule out a limine. It has nothing to do with the agreement!'[69]

On 27 February Wilhelm bluntly informed the Reich Chancellor that Grey's attitude was 'an astonishing piece of British shamelessness' and totally 'unacceptable'. 'So it amounts to this: England wants to force us to *renounce* the *Novelle* and give up *the chance to defend ourselves* against England in order to *purchase* a very dubious declaration of neutrality of very questionable sincerity! I must, as Kaiser in the name of the German Reich, and as Supreme War Lord in the name of my armed forces, *reject* such a proposition once and for all as *incompatible with our honour.*' He went on to voice his 'most determined and urgent desire', which was felt 'in all circles – not merely military but even political and ministerial too – *that the whole defence budget (military and naval together) should at last be brought in as soon as possible*, as further delay would be irresponsible and could lead to serious difficulties. From a political point of view I cannot understand why, for example, the

Ausw. Amt in handling the negotiations with England, only has the English point of view in mind, i.e. the English promise of neutrality is treated as something of great importance, while ours is never similarly appraised in terms of its enormous value to England. That is more than modesty, it is almost pusillanimity; to know that the Kaiser with his redoubtable, respected, growing power is on their side rather than against them is just as important for the British as the other way round. So we want to stick firmly to our point of view, in full consciousness of *what we are worth*, and let them see our teeth for once. *England proposed* the agreement and *took the first steps*, we showed ourselves accommodating, and it is up to England to complete the business. But not at the *price* of a piece of our national security! I shall *never* go along with that. Wilhelm I.R.'[70] The head of the Kaiser's Civil Cabinet, Rudolf von Valentini, noted in his diary that the Kaiser was 'very upset about Bethm[ann]' and altogether 'a nervous wreck'.[71] In the evening the Kaiserin summoned the head of the Naval Cabinet and read him a letter that she had written to the Chancellor, urging him 'to take a firm stand and to spare the Kaiser', whose 'nerves were quite shattered by the eternal delays'.[72]

It was with incredulity that Tirpitz noted that the diplomats wanted to go on negotiating despite what he regarded as London's humiliating response, and were even prepared to consider dropping the three planned battleships. According to his information, the Under Secretary of State at the Auswärtiges Amt, Arthur Zimmermann, had declared: 'Either we make further concessions over the *Novelle* or there will be no political agreement. In the latter event, it will certainly come to a war with France, where a dangerous chauvinism is already widespread. France will not wait while we complete our arms pro- gramme; they think they have the advantage at the moment . . . The problem is that if the situation becomes critical His Majesty will not go through with it; so this element of uncertainty had to be taken into account . . . They [the Wilhelmstrasse] were now hoping to achieve political success without war, by means of a political agreement with England. If a political agreement can be concluded, this would have a beneficial effect on the mood in France and Russia.' The Grand Admiral was flabbergasted: 'So we have now come to this! They say the *Novelle* will lead to war. They approve of [Wilhelm II's going to] Corfu and [appearing at] Cowes. The plan which the Wilhelmstrasse e tutti quanti have been steadily pursuing since the autumn . . . The clever English really have pulled a fast one on us!'[73]

On the evening of 28 February 1912 the Chancellor 'at last' agreed, 'in accordance with Your Majesty's wish', to the official publication of 'the substantive content of the defence budget without going into the question of its financing'. He also promised to have an appropriate communication sent to the British in the form of a detailed memorandum 'drawing their attention to the clash with Haldane's statements'.[74] Bethmann was of course aware of 'the importance and indeed decisive significance' this memorandum would have for 'the development of our relations with England', and when Metternich notified him of an imminent new conversation with Haldane, decided to postpone its transmission to London.[75]

Believing that Bethmann's memorandum had already gone off, the Kaiser telegraphed Metternich on 3 March to ask how the British had received it. The ambassador had to reply that the document had not yet arrived in London. In some irritation, the Kaiser telegraphed to the Chancellor: 'Metternich replies in answer to my question, memorandum not yet arrived, I was promised it would go off on Friday evening.'[76] Bethmann's explanation for the delay did nothing to calm him down: 'I should have been informed immediately of Metternich's talk with Haldane, and my permission should have been sought to postpone the dispatch of the memorandum that I had ordered. I should all the more have been informed as I had told H[err] v[on] Kiderlen, expressly and in writing, that he had to keep me permanently informed, immediately, of every official and unofficial phase and disclosure relating to the English affair, as I have *personally* reserved to *myself* the command over the handling of the affair. I demand that in future this order be complied with absolutely, and no step taken without me! The memorandum for England is to be sent to me at once in writing, as I have not yet got to see it. Wilhelm I.R.'[77] Next day he telegraphed a further order to the Reich Chancellor: 'Memorandum must be presented tomorrow the 6th. The defence budget is therefore to be published on the evening of the 6th. If that is not done, I shall give the order to the War Minister and the Secretary of State at the R[eich] N[avy] O[ffice] to publish the budget themselves. My patience and that of the German people is at an end!'[78] To the ambassador in London the Kaiser telegraphed on the same day: 'Report immediately, as soon as you have presented the document.'[79]

The monarch's disturbing state of excitement reached new heights when he received Metternich's account of his conversation with Haldane. With derision he dismissed the ambassador's assurance that the War Minister had affirmed the British government's desire for an agreement with Germany, to which end it was offering its 'full support for her acquisition of a broad belt of territory across Africa from coast to coast'. Haldane's warning that it would not be in England's interest 'if we did eat up France' – Metternich quoted Haldane's words in English – threw Wilhelm into a rage. He was even more infuriated by the War Minister's declaration that England would reply to the *Novelle* by a new supplementary budget and 'an increased concentration of the Fleet by drawing on ships from the Mediterranean fleet'.[80] This warning Wilhelm interpreted as a 'mobilisation'. Incensed he wrote: 'The proposal is in fact a deviation from the basis of 9 February, which I am not prepared to see changed. All the less so as the Mediterranean fleet too is to come into the North Sea. That will be regarded here as such a threat that the agreement will be totally destroyed. This displacement must be abandoned. Please declare firmly to Metternich in London, and through him to Haldane, that moving the Mediterranean fleet into the North Sea will be regarded by us as a warlike act that will be answered by a *strengthened Novelle* in its old form and mobilisation.'[81] In the same sense, the Kaiser telegraphed to the Chancellor on 5 March: 'The summoning of the Mediterranean fleet into the North Sea would be answered by a strengthened *Novelle* in its old form and mobilisation.'[82] At the same time, he telegraphed to Metternich, 'should England withdraw her ships from the Mediterranean to England – North Sea – that will be regarded here as a threat of war and will be answered by a strengthened *Novelle* – 3er Tempo – and possibly mobilisation.'[83] Müller was horrified at the 'incredibly coarse language' of the dispatches to the Chancellor and Metternich. 'I assumed the Kaiser wished to provoke the Chancellor to resign. Of course he could have got that for less trouble.'[84]

BETHMANN HOLLWEG'S OFFER OF RESIGNATION

The Chancellor, Foreign Secretary von Kiderlen-Wächter and Count Metternich had been putting up with this disgraceful treatment for months without protest, in the cause of maintaining the peace – although all three suspected that the Kaiser intended to dismiss them 'once the English negotiations are over'. Baron Adolf Marschall von Bieberstein was already being spoken of as both a candidate for the Chancellorship and as Metternich's successor in London.[85] Now, however, Bethmann had had enough. On 6 March 1912 he made the Kaiser's bellicose dispatches the reason for handing in his resignation. The monarch's telegraphing Metternich directly, announcing a mobilisation behind the Chancellor's back and threatening to have the defence budgets published by the Secretary of State for the Navy and the Prussian War Minister in contravention of the constitution, showed clearly, Bethmann wrote, that the Kaiser 'had excluded the Reich Chancellor from the direction of foreign policy'. Yet if such behaviour alone had led him to consider resigning, it was the warlike policy itself that the Kaiser was pursuing and for which he, as Chancellor, could not take responsibility, that had made his resignation a 'pressing necessity'. He explained that the negotiations now starting with England must be managed in such a way that their eventual failure should not appear too blatantly. 'Above all we must push the blame for failure on to England. If we do not do that, not only will our relations with England be fatally damaged, but the chauvinism that is now being fanned into flame in France will be encouraged in the most foolhardy aspirations. France will become so provocative and presumptuous that we shall be forced to attack her. In such a war, France will automatically be assisted by Russia and doubtless by England, while for our allies the casus foederis does not arise – indeed, we should be obliged to beg for their assistance or neutrality. I cannot accept the responsibility of contributing, for our part, to such a situation. If war is forced upon us, then we shall fight and with God's help we shall not perish. But that we, for our part, should conjure up a war when our honour or vital interests are not involved, I should regard as a sin against Germany's destiny, even if according to all human calculation, we could hope for an outright victory. But even that is not the case, at least not at sea.'[86]

Bethmann's letter of resignation reached the Kaiser on 7 March, during the gunnery exercises of the fleet at Cuxhaven. Müller recorded: 'H.M. was still sulking. Valentini came to report at noon. Afternoon, long discussions, H.M. with Valentini and – Ballin. I was only brought in for the drafting of the pacificatory letter to the Chancellor.'[87] The Kaiser's mood was captured in his marginal comments on a report from London once again refusing to consider concessions beyond the offer to Haldane of 9 February. England, he raged, had wanted 'to prevent our building the 3 extra ships in order to establish a permanent 2-er Tempo and to reduce our future naval strength by ⅓. I am no more prepared to allow anyone to meddle with my naval personnel than France or Russia have ever allowed us to prescribe to them how many battalions, cavalry troops or batteries they might include in their military budgets ... This really is *after all* an attack on the *Navy Law* ... which our [civilian] government people were prepared to undermine. They were well on the way to doing England the favour!'[88] On returning to Berlin Wilhelm summoned Bethmann to the Charlottenburg Schloss where, according to Müller, 'H.M. and Reich Chancellor walked up and down in the vicinity of the Mausoleum and effected a reconciliation at this sacred spot. He told Valentini, Plessen and me about it, but at the same time came up with a new idea for possibly toning down the *Novelle*.' Müller was ordered 'to discuss the matter with the Chancellor and Tirpitz'. The 'eternal vacillation and hesitation' therefore continued.[89]

The Kaiser's new readiness to drop the three new battleships and pursue a political agreement with Britain provoked an immediate threat of resignation from Tirpitz, who loudly lamented the 'collapse' of Wilhelm's resolve. In his view, the abandonment of the new battleships meant 'that we are striking our colours before England and changing the direction of our naval policy'. Although the *political* decision as to whether this was necessary lay with the Chancellor and the Kaiser, he for his own part was so firmly convinced of the necessity of the present naval policy towards England, and had publicly committed himself to it to such a degree, 'that His Majesty himself would think it out of the question for me to go along with such a change and defend it'. Shortly afterwards Müller telephoned Tirpitz to say that the Kaiser was 'very angry' with him, but had now again decided to bring in the *Novelle* unchanged. Tirpitz was invited to luncheon at the Schloss, but was not to talk about the naval question, as the Kaiser was 'too upset'.[90]

On the evening of 11 March Tirpitz was again summoned by the monarch, who greeted him with the words: 'We have won.' Wilhelm explained that the Chancellor had promised him in writing 'that he would take on the *Novelle* in accordance with agreements with Haldane. Her Majesty the Kaiserin had been to see the Chancellor this morning and told him that though she did not meddle in politics, she could bear it no longer, the Chancellor must come to a decision and must not give way to England. Moreover, Sir Ernest Cassel had told Ballin that Churchill had only been furious because it was Haldane who had been sent to Berlin, but for the rest he was quite indifferent to the *Novelle*, even with the three ships, in fact they were not at all bothered about the ships ... So, just as we have always preached to the Reich Chancellor.' Bethmann's hesitancy was 'quite pathological', the Kaiser declared; on the other hand, he was 'universally trusted abroad, and therefore had to be kept on'.[91]

THE FAILURE OF THE NEGOTIATIONS

Bethmann's principled protest of 6 March against Wilhelm II's autocratic approach to government and the bellicose tendencies of his policy thus produced no lasting change. True, the Chancellor continued for a time to try to dilute or delay the *Novelle*, but the Kaiser reverted to the harsh militaristic tone of recent weeks, declaring that he 'would not even think!' of any change in his naval policy. The English only wanted to obstruct the transition to an automatic '3er-Tempo' planned for 1917 and to vitiate the Navy Law. England's threatened counter-armaments 'need not bother us at all!' '*Our* programme satisfies *our* needs, and what England does about it is immaterial!'[92]

For one moment Wilhelm II believed that thanks to his refusal to yield he had achieved his great aim, the disruption of the Anglo-French Entente, after all. On Sunday 17 March 1912 Albert Ballin, who had again been negotiating with Haldane and Churchill in London, and who now saw 'an offensive and defensive alliance in process of formation', entered the Schloss in Berlin and

announced to the Kaiser, in the presence of Valentini and Müller: 'Your
Majesty, I bring you the alliance with England.' The 'English cabinet's
decision on our neutrality proposal' was 'on its way' and would 'arrive this
very afternoon'.[93] All the greater the disappointment, therefore, when early
that evening the British government's final rejection arrived.

Metternich had pressed Haldane to get the Cabinet to offer some sort of
neutrality formula so as to enable the Chancellor to insist on modifications to
the *Novelle*, the publication of which was imminent; if the British government
was not satisfied with the modified Bill it could always take back its offer later.[94]
As Grey's Private Secretary William Tyrrell remarked when reporting this to
Lord Knollys, Metternich's proposal was breathtaking.[95] After a Cabinet meeting on 14 March Grey put to the German ambassador, in the presence of
Haldane, a formula that London would be prepared to accept, provided that
agreement could be reached over the *Novelle*. According to this: 'England will
make no unprovoked attack upon Germany and pursue no aggressive policy
towards her. Aggression upon Germany is not the subject and forms no part of
any treaty, understanding or combination to which England is now party, nor
will she become a party to anything that has such an object.'[96] Metternich saw
straight away that the formula would not satisfy Berlin, and next morning put
to Grey two alternative proposals expanding the neutrality formula in line with
German wishes. The first said: 'England will therefore observe at least a
benevolent neutrality should war be forced on Germany'; the second, slightly
weaker: 'England will therefore as a matter of course remain neutral if a war is
forced upon Germany.' The Foreign Secretary told Metternich straight out why
he objected to both, explaining 'quite frankly how the growing strength of
Germany had given rise to an anxiety in this country that a day might come
when a German Government might desire to crush France. If such a contingency arose, . . . we might not be able to sit still: for we should feel that, if we
did sit still, and allowed France to be crushed, we would have to fight alone
later on . . . On the other hand, I had given France clearly to understand that, if
France was aggressive towards Germany, no support would be forthcoming from
us, or would be approved by British public opinion. Our formula, as it stood,
expressed this situation. I was afraid that the words which he suggested would
give an impression going beyond the literal sense of the words, and might be
taken to mean that under no circumstances, if there was war on the Continent,
could any thing be expected from us. I told him frankly my difficulties, and I had
hoped that the formula which we had suggested would be sufficient.'[97] On 16
March the two met again and Grey once more explained that he wished to avoid
the word 'neutrality' altogether, as it could give the impression 'that more was
meant than was said'. At the same time, he warned the ambassador that the

negotiations over a formula would become quite pointless if Germany announced that she was expanding her battlefleet 'because the naval increase would destroy the good effect produced by the formula'. As Metternich had hinted that Bethmann Hollweg might fall over this question, he, Grey, felt it important to stress that both he and Haldane had confidence in the Chancellor. 'We believed genuinely that he wished to pursue a straightforward policy of peace: and, as long as he remained German Chancellor, he might rely upon our co-operating with him to preserve the peace of Europe, each of us not only abstaining from aggression upon the other, but each also using what influence we had with others to prevent war.' At the same time, Grey continued, he must point out 'that a formula could not be made a purely personal guarantee. For instance, if we were to exchange with Germany now a formula which made relations between us and any other country more distant, we could have no security that Herr von Bethmann-Hollweg might not be overthrown a month or two hence: when we should be in the position of having gained nothing as regards the policy of Germany, and we should have lost something elsewhere.'[98]

When in the early evening of 17 March 1912 Metternich's report of his discussion with Grey reached the Hohenzollern court, where only a matter of hours before Ballin had been forecasting an alliance with England, the reaction was one of profound indignation, but at the same time, of 'remarkable . . . relief all round'. 'H.M. was really cheerful. We now know where we are.'[99] The English proposal was, as Müller wrote, 'completely unacceptable. Qualified neutrality conditional on our dropping the *Novelle*. The object of the whole exercise − getting rid of the *Novelle* − is revealed in all its starkness. Naturally the English proposal will be rejected.'[100] Wilhelm II reacted in exactly the same way to Grey's formula, that only offered 'a very limited neutrality! not a general one'. The formula 'leaves it entirely to England to judge' whether an attack was 'unprovoked' or not. Grey's statement that he could not pursue the neutrality issue so far as to endanger the Entente with France enraged the Kaiser, who minuted, 'so we are only in the second rank! Outrageous!!' Above all, Wilhelm took offence at the British Foreign Secretary's expression of confidence in Bethmann Hollweg: the policy of the Reich did not depend on the Chancellor 'but on *me*!', he exclaimed; and Grey's remarks showed his 'distrust *of me*, therefore!' Like a sulky child, the Kaiser wrote on the dispatch from London that signalled the failure of the Anglo-German negotiations: 'Never in my life have I heard that one can make an agreement with only one statesman − and one particular one -- in mind, independently of the sovereign concerned. From the above it is clear that Grey has no idea who is actually master here and that *I* rule. He is now telling me who my minister should be if I am to make an agreement with England.'[101]

One last time the Chancellor took up the cause of an Entente with England, the cause, in the final analysis, of the maintenance of peace. He conceded that London had 'not yet put forward an adequate formula' but declared himself convinced that, with a little goodwill in the question of armaments 'a political agreement' must be possible after all; whereas a failure of the negotiations would, as Churchill had said to Ballin, force England to increase her armaments and 'necessarily lead to war within the next two years ... The question is therefore ... whether by publishing the *Novelle* we wish to give the signal for an arms race that will render an Anglo-German war (and the necessarily concomitant land wars) likely this year or next. I humbly await Your Majesty's orders.'[102]

How did Wilhelm II answer this fateful question? In response to the plea from his leading statesman he wrote on 18 March, the anniversary of Bismarck's dismissal: 'The English reply note absolves me from the task of replying to your letter. It makes a mockery of the negotiations so far, and is such a piece of cool insolence that there is nothing more to say. I reject *this agreement*. But I recommend pursuing the negotiations in such a way that *England is put in the wrong by refusing our proposal*. By dropping Haldane the English government has departed from and thrown over its own basis for negotiations and disavowed him. That puts an end to the agreement. Now *new* negotiations start on a different basis. I propose offering to England − as out of consideration for France she *won't* give us neutrality − instead of the neutrality clause, an offensive and defensive alliance that will include France. *If England rejects that, she has put herself flagrantly in the wrong before the whole world*, if she accepts, then our standing vis-à-vis the German nation is enhanced in respect to the *Novelle*. At the same time Paris is to be informed that, although French behaviour towards the German army and nation has been outrageous, the government here does not nourish any evil designs, and in negotiating with England has expressed its willingness to take France into the alliance too. If that is rejected, then the matter is clear, and we have done our duty. If it is accepted, the peace of Europe is assured. However, the *Agreement of the Haldane negotiations* is dead. I shall not discuss it any further!'[103]

THE INTERNAL REPERCUSSIONS OF THE FAILURE OF THE HALDANE MISSION

The failure of the Haldane mission was to have serious consequences abroad; but given the high hopes that Bethmann Hollweg, the Wilhelmstrasse, Metternich, Kühlmann, and, from time to time the Kaiser, had had of the negotiations with England, there were bound to be repercussions on power relationships in Berlin. Seldom did Wilhelm II behave more autocratically than after the failure of the Anglo-German negotiations in the spring of 1912. Above all the position of the Chancellor and the ambassador in London (Kiderlen's standing had already suffered a blow after the Agadir crisis) were henceforth regarded as badly shaken. When he received Tirpitz and Müller in audience on 18 March Wilhelm told them that he had found the Chancellor 'very crestfallen' that morning at the turn his policy had taken. Bethmann was 'very ashamed at the failure of the English negotiations'. He was indeed, the Kaiser said, 'a totally broken man and he felt really sorry for him'. The monarch, by contrast, was 'in very merry and, as he said, totally relaxed mood', urging Bethmann to drink a glass of port as a stiffener, and advising him not to break off the negotiations abruptly, but to push the odium for the failure on to England and France. This proposal the chastened Bethmann had accepted. 'These old gentlemen from Bismarck's time, like Bethmann and Kiderlen', the Kaiser mocked, 'simply cannot break free from their narrow continental-European existence'. He had ordered the Chancellor to inform the ambassador in London 'that he was absolutely astonished that Metternich could have even agreed to receive such proposals'. He insisted on Metternich's removal the moment things started to calm down.[104]

After the failure of the Haldane mission the Kaiser felt, according to Tirpitz, 'that he could no longer rely on Bethmann Hollweg'. Wilhelm's self-aggrandisement grew markedly as a result of the crisis, and along with it the influence of irresponsible advisers and of the three heads of Cabinet.[105] In a letter to George V which he drafted on 18 March but apparently never sent, Kaiser Wilhelm II set out to explain to the King the power-relationships within the German Reich. 'The Chancellor as well as the Foreign office are both purely officials of the Emperor. It is the Emperor, who gives them directions as to which policy is to be pursued and they have to obey and follow his will.'[106] For the Chancellor, the Auswärtiges Amt and the diplomatic corps, all of whom had allowed themselves to be duped by Haldane and the British government, Wilhelm felt nothing but contempt. He summoned Bethmann Hollweg to Corfu with the express intention, as he told his bosom pal the Austrian Prince Fürstenberg, of humiliating him; Bethmann, he said, 'must be made to feel *quite small*'.[107] Self-righteously, on 31 March 1912, he scribbled on a report from England: '*We* are jeered and laughed at for taking these proposals and speeches as *serious*, even *binding*. *I myself* suspected something like that, and therefore pressed for months for the publication of the defence budget *independently* of these proceedings. My diplomats took, contrary to me, a different view, accepted everything that came from London at face value, definitive, conclusive; continually put enormous obstacles in the way of my exercising my powers and duties as Kaiser and Supreme War Lord – responsible for the military capacity and defensibility of my people – in the illusory hope of concluding an agreement! The mirage of an African colonial empire dazzled them, while the component parts of it on offer belonged to others; with whom we might perhaps get involved in armed confrontations! Our people were left in the dark about the defence budget which was delayed for 6 weeks to no purpose, until the English minister Churchill revealed it in the English parliament. Much valuable time, effort, and labour and endless aggravation ensued. Result!= 0! ... I hope that my diplomats will draw the lesson from this, to pay more attention to their master and his commands and wishes in future than hitherto, especially when it is a matter of doing anything with England, whom they do not know how to handle; while I know England well! It was a *real English bluff* that my diplomats fell for. Thank God that nothing of the *Novelle* was sacrificed, that would have been impossible to justify to the German people.'[108]

Unlike the Chancellor and the Wilhelmstrasse – so the Kaiser claimed in a truly astonishing minute – he had seen through the dirty tricks of the English from the start. 'The English government's plan, on which their whole action was based, was ... broadly as follows: The discussions with Haldane and the British offer of a transcontinental colonial empire were to get the German government ... *to drop the Novelle*. At the same time, in the political clauses, the term *neutrality* was *rejected* as too difficult to define. Haldane was supposed to bring *home* this *success* ... That would have been a *colossal* success for the English people and parliament: the Germans had lost their *Novelle*, had received *no pledge of neutrality*, and the prospect of an *ephemeral colonial empire* in Africa, to be constructed out of the possessions of *other nations*, would have involved Germany in first-class conflicts with the nations that were *to be robbed*! That, in nuce, was Haldane's mission. I saw through him and his shady colleagues in time, and really spoiled their game. I have saved the German people's right to sea power, and their right of self-determination in matters of armaments; and shown the English that to interfere with our armaments is biting on granite – thereby perhaps reinforcing their hatred, but also earning their respect.'[109]

TWO AMBASSADORIAL CHANGES AND THE DEATH OF KIDERLEN-WÄCHTER

After the crisis over the Haldane mission the Kaiser, happy as a child going on holiday, had fled to Corfu, and did not return to Berlin for ten weeks.[110] In a melancholy letter of 7 May to Mary Montagu, he said how sad he was to be leaving Corfu 'where I have had a delightful holiday, surrounded by olives, roses, orange blossom, gloxinias, gladioli, laburnums etc etc, mountains and sea. Heavenly paradise and nobody to disturb my peace, not even political questions interest me! I have been busy instead with picnics and excavations, which were extremely interesting. Now I am leaving this earthly paradise to return to my duties, i.e. trouble and work, a sisyphean task for which nobody is grateful, and a lot of criticism from all quarters.'[111] The imperial suite would have been just as glad as the statesmen in Berlin if the Kaiser really had confined his activity to picnics and excavations and left the direction of policy to them. But that was not to be the case.

While en route to Corfu the Kaiser was considering the immediate dismissal of Kiderlen-Wächter, Bethmann's right-hand man in foreign policy affairs. The Chancellor felt obliged to appeal urgently to the head of the Kaiser's Civil Cabinet in Corfu to assuage the Kaiser's ill will against the Foreign Secretary. Kiderlen was irreplaceable, he insisted, and must be kept on, even if he had fallen into disfavour with the Kaiser. Valentini reassured him: he had managed to fend off the danger of Kiderlen's dismissal for the present. 'Y[our] Exc[ellency] is quite right, his departure now would be a heavy blow, not just for Y[our] Exc[ellency], but in terms of the whole business. *All* competent observers regard him as our most skilful diplomat today; his departure, and his replacement by some lesser light like Bernstorff would be incomprehensible, and would certainly turn out badly for the service, quite apart from the fact that people would give Y[our] Exc[ellency] the blame yet again for 'this grovelling to France'. It was with sincere conviction, therefore, that I worked to get H[is] Maj[esty] to change his mind about Kiderlen – I think not unsuccessfully ... The same advice has come at other times and from other quarters, and I think that it has had an effect. At any rate, there is no more talk of an immediate change as there was when we arrived here. The chief thing now seems to me to be that K[iderlen] himself should not throw in his hand out of pique. That must not happen: it would be too disgraceful if the bad boys in positions high and low should achieve their aim and get rid of perhaps the only man who can match up to the Cambons, Greys and Co.'[112] That Kiderlen could only be kept in office thanks to the ability of the head of the Civil Cabinet and other members of the Kaiser's entourage to exert influence on the monarch residing in Corfu, says enough about Wilhelm II's methods of governing, even at this late stage in his reign.

How touchy the monarch was about all – even imaginary – infringements of his prerogatives was shown by his furious reaction to the Wilhelmstrasse's handling of the *Titanic* disaster: not the officials but he alone as Kaiser had the right of decision over such matters. As Valentini reported from Corfu, the sinking of the *Titanic* on 14 April 1912 had made a 'quite incredible' impression on the Kaiser 'and now dominates the conversation almost completely. He wants to keep all steps and measures regarding it in his own hands.'[113] Wilhelm went so far as to make his participation in the launching of the *Imperator* on 24 May conditional on the equipping of the super-liner with 'the most advanced safety devices prescribed by His Majesty'. Behind this demand, Müller informed Tirpitz, lay the Kaiser's plan for 'international legislation on maritime safety under Germany's aegis'.[114] 'Very incensed', the Kaiser, in a telegram from Corfu, rebuked the Auswärtiges Amt for having, without seeking his permission, taken steps towards an international regulation of maritime traffic after the *Titanic* disaster. 'On the basis of what instruction or order was this done? I should have first been asked for my permission . . . A step of such great international importance can only be devised and ordered by a sovereign, not by one of his subordinate agents without his knowledge and authorisation. I regard this area as a special prerogative of the Crown and shall keep the whole matter in my hands. Hence, any necessary papers for approval or proposals are to be submitted to me and will then be dispatched in my name.'[115]

For Kiderlen, even more unbearable than the Kaiser's meddling in the everyday running of affairs was his insistence on his right to appoint ambassadors himself, over the heads of the Reich Chancellor and the Foreign Secretary. As has been seen, ever since the Agadir crisis the Kaiser had been demanding, very much against the wishes of Bethmann and Kiderlen, that Metternich be replaced in the supremely important London embassy by Baron Marschall von Bieberstein. The appointment of Marschall was not only a blow for those who were still working for an Anglo-German rapprochement, but also a personal affront to the Foreign Secretary. According to a report of the Austro-Hungarian military attaché in Constantinople of 4 May 1912, 'relations between Baron Marschall and the Secretary of State Herr von Kiderlen-Wächter have recently become quite impossible'. True, they had never been very good, but they had now, 'after Russia's latest moves in the Straits question, become terrible'.[116] Kaiser Wilhelm had no intention of supporting the policy of his minister, but sided emphatically with the ambassador: 'My Near Eastern policy, pursued for twenty years, and superbly represented by Marschall, remains absolutely the same.' This policy he often threatened 'to defend, sword in hand, together with the Turks'.[117] Even after the crisis passed, the relations between Marschall and Kiderlen 'were in such a state that co-operation between the two . . . hardly [seemed] possible'.[118] And now in May 1912 Wilhelm II was appointing Marschall, of all people, who had never even been to England and who even 'in his outward appearance had nothing about him to attract the English', to succeed Count Metternich as ambassador in London.[119]

As it happened, Marschall died in the London embassy on 24 September, only weeks after taking up his post. This news, Harden said on hearing it, was bound to make the bibulous Kiderlen 'drunk with joy'.[120] Almost timorously, the Chancellor wrote to the Kaiser proposing the septuagenarian Anglophile Prussian envoy in Karlsruhe, Karl von Eisendecher, as Marschall's successor. Eisendecher had in the past shown his ability as a diplomat in Tokyo and Washington, he wrote, 'and has always been a true and proven servant of Your Majesty. But above all, people in England know that as he has often accompanied Your Majesty on visits there, he enjoys Your Majesty's special confidence, and he will also meet with sympathy and trust on the other side of the Channel. He is persona grata at the royal British court and especially with His Majesty King George; and in the course of his annual visits to England has made a lot of friends among persons of influence. In my humble opinion it is now a matter of sending to London a representative whose personality proves in advance that Your Majesty wishes for closer and warmer relations with England. The envoy von Eisendecher should be in a position to prepare the ground for negotiations for a rapprochement, and also as an old naval officer to be fully alive to the futility of the concept of disarmament.'[121] In the same letter Bethmann tried to head off the appointment of Prince Karl Max von Lichnowsky, who had formerly been Bülow's right-hand man (and Marie von Bülow's cicisbeo),[122] but had now withdrawn to his estates in Silesia. He explained to the Kaiser that Lichnowsky was 'not himself unsuitable' for the post; but his eccentric wife Mechthild, who lived only for her artistic interests, would not be able to establish for herself the position in society necessary to support her husband.[123]

The Kaiser replied to his Chancellor in a highly agitated, angry letter of 30 September 1912: 'It is striking how the English press, in its articles on Marschall's arrival in London and in the obituaries, always talks of *his* services, labours and efforts in the cause of Anglo-German unity, and never of any English ones. One hears the same in private letters coming from England. That is, people in London have got used to the idea that it is up to *us* to devise the means of bringing about the work of union (that they too – apparently – desire) and then present it to them for their approval. People in London treat us as a kind of staff-hiring agency whose function is to supply the proud Englishman with suitable servants who know how to keep him happy and who, if they succeed will be treated with condescension and benevolence. The butler Metternich, for example, was very passable, and left with an excellent reference. The butler Marschall was welcome and they expected great things of him – in terms of sensitivity to English moods and desires – now he is dead, and they are waiting patiently to see if the agency can or will find another good butler. Of course, he will not have it easy. This quite perverse attitude of England's – humiliating for all of us – really must first be put right. Now is a good time for this. By sending Marschall *we* made it plain and clear from here what *we* wanted, and this was gratefully understood by London and the whole world. Now what has *England*, for her part, *done* towards the 'great work'? She coolly leaves us with Goschen – whom his own countrymen call a darned ass, as we are not worth anything better! So long as England does not *change* her ambassador in Berlin, even a Marschall can achieve nothing! It always takes 2 for a marriage! Now our man is dead. Now we are to send a replacement. But that can only happen when *England* for once shows some good will on her part, and sends us the *best* man she has got. That is the quid pro quo which we, after all the press lies and polemics, ententes and conventions, must absolutely *demand* if we are to maintain our dignity with the British. So, *no hurry about a replacement*. And a hint to London through diplomatic channels that as our 'great' man is dead, it is now up to them to send us a 'great' man from their side, as we do not keep them in stock by the dozen. When the frogs asked Zeus for a king, he sent them a log, on which they hopped and jumped about and had fun. That was Metternich. After this he sent them a snake, which bit them and drove them into a mousehole, that must be Metternich's successor! If London does not follow our suggestion and Goschen stays then we know what is what, and can calmly get our mobilisation plans out of the drawer, because everything will be clear.'[124] The Chancellor's proposal to send the diplomat Wilhelm von Stumm, who had a great fortune and knew England well, as ambassador to London, received a vehement rejection from the Kaiser: 'No! He is far too *afraid* of the English! And hates my Navy', he thundered. 'I shall only send to London an ambassador who enjoys *My* confidence, obeys *My* will and carries out *My* orders. With *one* instruction: If Grey asks him on his arrival in London, "What have you brought with you?" Answer: "Nothing. I am to hear what you have to offer." ... That is how to deal with the bigwigs in the Foreign Office!'[125] Without further contacting the Chancellor, Wilhelm II appointed Prince Lichnowsky to what was indeed the most important diplomatic post and ordered the new ambassador to report his experiences in London to him directly by means of private letters.[126]

So nothing had changed in the Kaiser's attitude to England. Newspaper reports that stated the obvious – that an Anglo-German rapprochement would only be possible if Germany abandoned her quest for maritime supremacy – were spattered with his characteristic marginalia: 'All British insolence and boundless effrontery! Because they are running out of money and breath, we should stop!!' The articles, he said, confirmed the reports of the naval attaché Widenmann, according to whom 'England's struggle against our Navy Law . . . will go on with undiminished force, including attacks on the person of the Secretary of State Tirpitz himself! Well then, Attention! Eyes wide open! I won't stand for it!' For the Kaiser, there could be no question of an agreement with England 'as *long as we have no agreement with France!*' Now too, he emphasised that for him it was not a question of colonies but of the reordering of Europe. Colonial acquisitions 'are not the issue at all! But Germany wants to get on with and agree with her neighbours *in Europe*, especially France, but 'England's interests' will not permit this, and she tries to prevent it. That is the main point! Not islands in the tropics.' It was clear to the Kaiser: the British balance-of-power policy, with its fear of German predominance, was hindering the uniting of the European continent against the growing power of the USA. 'England just does not want the continental Powers to get on, as they might then come under German direction, and that − i.e. the united continent of Europe − is against well-known British interests! Hence the continuing incitement − naturally against the potential predominant Power. Meanwhile America is growing ever stronger, ever more powerful, and will gradually absorb England's power and establish the English-speaking world empire, in which England will be reduced to an American outpost against the European continent.'[127]

The Kaiser's 'fixed aim' was, as Bethmann put it on 3 October 1912, 'a broadly-based, realistic agreement with England' that would take account of Germany's natural predominance on the continent. The Chancellor conceded that the British ambasasador in Berlin, Sir Edward Goschen, was 'certainly not the man' to set such an agreement in train, but he warned against letting it be known that Germany was seeking his replacement by an 'important personality', because 'the English gentlemen' would make it sound as if 'England's friendly countenance was of such overriding importance to us'. A second danger might be that 'the English, if they learn of our wishes, might indeed send us a "prominent" personality, but one who was not the right one for improving relations'. A brash imperial minute soon cast this warning aside: 'Well then, we should know where we are and see clearly! That might not be a bad thing either.'[128]

On the last day of 1912 Alfred von Kiderlen-Wächter died from a stroke in his office in the Wilhelmstrasse. His fellow Württemberger and friend, Hugo Baron von Reischach, praised Kiderlen's extraordinary achievements in a letter to Prince Fürstenberg, lamenting above all his long years of exile in Bucharest at the instigation of the slippery Bülow. Reischach thought

Kiderlen's death a national loss, 'especially at this moment. It is a veritable disaster how often death has robbed the Kaiser of his best men at a relatively young age. He was a good man, even if he inherited a strong streak of our Swabian national vice of fondness for a good joke at somebody else's expense and coming out with some malicious remark. But he was loyal, a good German and devoted to his Kaiser. Such men are better and more valuable than those who are always smiling and bowing. We do not produce the latter, of course, south of the Main. It was one of the dirtiest tricks — I think it was Bülow — to tell H.M. about the content of the letters which he [Kiderlen] wrote in his capacity as Jenisch-Treutler [i.e. the representatives of the Wilhelmstrasse in the Kaiser's suite] from his travels, which were of course full of jokes, including some about H.M. . . . Of course, the person concerned only showed these letters to His Majesty in order to ruin Kiderlen's career for ever. As the Bülow era people had no time for strong minds and characters, given their eternal and justified fear that they might expose their own hollowness and tightrope-walking and cause them to fall off, and being in power was so nice. Just think, how many things could have gone differently if Kiderlen had been in the foreign secretary's post instead of Richthofen, Tschirsky [sic] and Schön . . . But complaining and brooding is no good, let us hope that we get a good man as his successor.'[129] Wilhelm's choice, of course, fell on Gottlieb von Jagow, who in the summer of 1914 was to lead the Auswärtiges Amt into world war.

CHAPTER THIRTY-THREE

November 1912: the strategic switch from west to east

The British decision of July 1911 to protect France by threatening Germany with war and mobilising the Royal Navy had strengthened to an alarming degree the aversion felt in broad sections of the public in Germany and among the ruling elite towards Great Britain. The fatalistic belief gained ground that sooner or later war with the naval Power and its Entente partner France was inevitable.[1] A few hotheads even longed for a war as a 'liberation', as a release from the perceived impasse at home and abroad.[2] The hate-filled denunciations of England in nationalist circles and notably in the Flottenverein were particularly ominous. In his pamphlet *West-Marokko deutsch!* the leader of the Pan-German League, Heinrich Claß, openly called for war with France. Only at the last minute was the Auswärtiges Amt able to persuade him to delete a passage in his inflammatory pamphlet that demanded breathtaking annexations: France, according to the original text, must cede to Germany the whole territory from the Somme estuary on the Channel to Nancy in the East, and southwards from Nancy to Toulon on the Mediterranean – and all this 'free from inhabitants'.[3] In 1912, under the pseudonym Daniel Frymann, Claß published the defamatory, antiliberal and anti-Semitic *Wenn ich der Kaiser wär'* [*If I were the Emperor*], in which he called for a holy war to gain command of the world.[4] The same year saw the appearance of the retired General Friedrich von Bernhardi's notorious book *Germany and the Next War*, demanding a war against England, France and Russia 'at all costs'. Only by conquering France, creating a Central European league of states, and founding a great colonial empire could Germany rise to the ranks of a *Weltmacht* – a 'World Power'.[5]

This sort of talk was also to be heard at the imperial court, among army and navy officers, and in the Wilhelmstrasse, but in these circles, which bore the responsibility for the fate of Germany, opinions were rather more diverse. They covered a broad spectrum ranging from the desire for a war to cut through the entanglements of political realities to the wish for an agreement with Great Britain and France to forestall a threatening catastrophe. Behind the scenes a violent struggle had broken out over the future course of German policy, in which ultimately the issue was that of war and peace. For was not Germany's claim to World Power status foreordained by World History or Providence, and were not the attempts of Great Britain with its Entente to stand in the way of this justified expansion perfidious and unjust? Was the proud Prusso-German Reich to renounce the achievement of its aims simply for the sake of peace? And if the decision was for war, against whom should it be waged – England alone, England and France together, Russia alone or together with France, or perhaps indeed against the entire Triple Entente? And when? As the conflict was obviously inevitable in the long run, would it not be better to bring it about at a favourable moment, rather than to leave the initiative with the enemy? What military measures and what diplomatic steps ought still to be taken in order to be optimally prepared for the conflict? And how could the German people, who had voted in their millions for the peace-minded Social Democrats in the Reichstag elections of 1912, be brought round to support a bloody war against their European neighbours? Our main task here is to define, with the help of the sources, the position of Wilhelm II in particular in these many-faceted debates. It will become clear that in the course of 1912 an important change occurred in the strategic planning of the Kaiser and his generals: for them it was no longer primarily perfidious England, but the 'Slavic' Tsarist Empire that was the enemy to be defeated.

THE KAISER AND THE 'NEXT WAR'

As shown in Chapter 31, after the humiliating 'Olmütz' of the second Morocco crisis, war with Great Britain was regarded as inevitable, above all in military and naval circles and in the nationalist Conservative party.[6] At the same time, however, it was these very circles that doubted whether Kaiser Wilhelm would ever summon up the courage to launch a war against England. As the future War Minister, General Erich von Falkenhayn, observed a few weeks after Agadir, 'outwardly, our political situation has improved ... but internally nothing has changed, in so far as H.M. is as determined as before to avoid a war ... Whether the general dissatisfaction with this way of managing the Reich's affairs, which is growing daily and in increasingly influential circles, will in the end force the Kaiser to go to war is another question.'[7] In December 1911 the same General wrote: 'As far as one can judge a war between Germany and England has become inevitable. No more than the humiliations of St Germain, Tilsit, and Olmütz, will those which our dear blood-brothers have inflicted on us in this year of discontent ever be forgotten by the spirit of Prussia and Prussian pride. What [the Conservative party leader] Heydebrand said about it in the Reichstag is entirely in accord with the feelings of all good Prussians and of most Germans. Neither the "great" Emperor of Peace . . . nor Bertha's supporters [i.e. Bertha von Suttner and the Peace Movement] will be able to change this.'[8] Even Baroness Spitzemberg noted that 'everybody' thought the Kaiser 'basically a coward' and therefore lacking in 'the courage of the strong, who maintain the peace as long as possible, but not at any price. He is afraid of the responsibility, the disturbance to his life, the work, the sacrifices of all kinds.'[9] And the ever-critical naval officer Albert Hopman noted in his diary: Wilhelm II was 'not a Frederick the Great, so after the fanfare of Agadir we shall indeed sound a parley. It is all the bill for our utterly aimless policy towards England which has made the whole world our enemy, and it should be charged to W's most personal private account.'[10]

Within the imperial family the young Crown Prince made himself the spokesman for the Pan-Germans and the militarists. On 5 November 1911 he sent his father some scornful press articles about 'the heroic deeds of Bethmann Hollweg' to show him 'that there is no one in the whole fatherland so mocked and ridiculed as our Reich Chancellor . . . Bethmann is not a man, that is the nub of the matter'.[11] Together with his New Year's greetings for 1912 the younger Wilhelm sent the Kaiser a demand for a great and glorious war: 'I personally hope for a war, and not from any rash desire for a fight, but from calm and sober calculation. The German people have reached a turning point, and will go either up or down. As people begrudge us our place in the sun, we must take it by force. Besides, I am convinced that the political situation at home, so fragmented and muddled with its internal party interests, would improve at a stroke if all the country's sons had to take up arms for their land, and I am convinced that people abroad will stare in horror and amazement at a Germany awakened and set on fighting to the bitter end. I have just the one desire, to prove to you then at the head of my fine regiment, that we can still attack and die just as well as in the days of the Great King [Frederick II].'[12]

True, the Kaiser had prudently banished his eldest son to Danzig precisely because of his warlike attitude, but even there the Crown Prince represented a threat to the Chancellor and his policy of reconciliation. During the stormy parliamentary debate about Morocco from 9 to 11 November 1911, in which both Bethmann Hollweg and Kiderlen-Wächter defended their policy vigorously against the attacks of the Conservatives and Pan-German nationalists, the Crown Prince made a demonstrative appearance in the Reichstag. Not only did all the newspapers comment on his presence and behaviour there, but according to a report in the *Nationalzeitung*, which proved to be true, the Crown Prince had telegraphed to his brother Prince Eitel Friedrich and his mother the Kaiserin, asking them to join him in taking action against the Chancellor.[13]

But what was Wilhelm II's own attitude in the face of these expectations that a great war was in the offing? Did he deserve to be mentioned in the same breath as Bertha von Suttner, winner of the Nobel Peace Prize? At the end of 1912 none other than Emanuel Nobel himself wanted to put the German Emperor forward for the Peace Prize. Both the Chancellor and those around the Kaiser immediately said no, not only because the award would have exacerbated the differences between the Crown and the Nationalist Right beyond measure, but also, surely, because it would have been greeted with howls of laughter all over the world, and especially among the Social Democrats in his own country.[14] Certainly there cannot have been in modern European history a crowned monarch who felt himself to be so utterly a 'military man', looking down scornfully on 'civilians' and diplomats, constantly comparing himself to the Great Elector, The Sergeant King, Frederick the Great and his own 'always victorious' grandfather 'Wilhelm the Great', and continually − even in the presence of foreigners − talking in the most undiplomatic terms of the necessity for war.

In speaking to the British Chief of General Staff, Sir John French, at a troop inspection at Altengrabow on 2 and 3 August 1911, Wilhelm II criticised Lloyd George's Mansion House speech sharply, 'describing it as provocative, encouraging France to resist him, & dangerous to the peace of Europe'. Menacingly, according to French, the Kaiser added: 'If we [the British] interfered in the affairs of Germany, we must take the consequences.' Sir John quoted the Kaiser as saying, 'I don't mean to interfere with you nor do I mean you to interfere with me and if you do you will find how sharp the sword is.' French then went on: 'Speaking of France the Emperor said he had no fear but that he could over-run her whenever he liked. He did not think France would ever fight him unless egged on & supported by us & our press.'[15] In London, General French's report gave rise to a debate at the highest level about Wilhelm II's readiness to go to war. Lord Knollys took the view that French was 'mistaken in implying that the German Emperor would be not unwilling to go to war. I believe myself that he would do everything in his power to prevent a war for the reasons I have more than once mentioned to you, but of course if he finds himself in a "tight place" owing to the indiscretion of his Minister for Foreign Affairs, or if he is over-persuaded by his Generals, he may

of course find it difficult, if not practically impossible, to avoid declaring war.'
Knollys passed on French's report to King George V who found it 'very
interesting' and thought that 'the Emperor may be driven into war whether
he likes it or not'.[16]

In September 1911 Wilhelm pressed the Chancellor to take a firmer line
against England even if this meant risking war. He told the head of his Naval
Cabinet that he had 'had a walk with him in the garden of the Neues Palais
before I left for the manoeuvres. But I did not achieve anything. He is full of
doubts and paralysed by fear of England. But I shall not let England dictate to
me what I may and may not do. I told the R[eich] Ch[ancellor] that he should
remember that I am descended from the Gr[eat] Elector and Fred[erick] the
Gr[eat] who did not hesitate long to take action when it seemed to them the
right time. I also told the Reich Chancellor that he must, after all, take Divine
Providence into consideration too, which will see to it that a people that has so
much to answer for as the English will also some day be brought low.'[17] As so
often, dynastic-historical mythology had combined in the Kaiser's mind with
unrestrained militarism and a blind faith in God to invalidate the laws of
raison d'état.

It was with lively satisfaction that Kaiser Wilhelm read an article by the
Bonn Professor Philipp Zorn in the *Kölnische Zeitung* of 30 December 1911,
with its summons to 'struggle for our national existence ... with all vigour
and strength' if England did not fundamentally change its attitude towards
Germany. 'Good', 'Yes', and 'Right', he noted in the margin when the Professor
declared that 'things cannot stay as they are'. It was a question of 'victory or
perish', and the German people would 'if necessary not shrink from taking on
the whole world'. The world war that would then ensue would indeed be
frightful, but 'we have done what we could − indeed, perhaps even more − to
avoid it ... We now have nothing more to say. Enough words have been
exchanged. We are waiting for deeds to testify to England's love of peace, on
which "Peace on Earth" depends.' These sentences, too, the Kaiser found
'Excellent'.[18]

January 1912, the bicentenary of the birth of Frederick the Great, saw a
new edition of the four-volume biography of the Prussian King by Reinhold
Koser, whom the Kaiser received in audience several times.[19] On the occasion
of the anniversary Wilhelm made a speech in the officers' mess of the elite
First Regiment of Guards in Potsdam, in which he again compared himself to
the Great King, saying that, like the latter, he was an optimist. 'That is the
only possible way', he boasted, 'to master the huge task of ruling a German
Reich successfully. I too am an optimist today in regard to the future of my
fatherland, the status which is its due, and which it must have. People love to

draw comparisons and find parallels, and so they often compare the situation before the Seven Years' War with that of today. And they are not wrong. If I, in such a situation, can look towards the future without fear, indeed, even with a smile, I do so . . . because I hope that, just as I cherish my army and live and work for it, the army, from field marshal to lieutenant, has placed its unconditional trust in me. If that is so, then I too can readily adopt the stance of daring everything if the honour of Our People demands it. Just as in those days the King's command was decisive for civilians and the military, so it is today, and so I should not hesitate for a moment if it is necessary to draw the sword for the honour of my fatherland. Then I should let nothing hold me back. The existence of all of you may be at stake, Gentlemen, and of everything we have. But it can only be done if one command, one will is decisive for all, and if that command is obeyed without question . . . If it is, then I should not be afraid of confronting even a whole world in arms; for we Hohenzollerns are used to dealing with such situations; other people who are not brought up to it may take fright, we Hohenzollerns are used to looking such things coolly in the eye — just as He did while reckoning with the possibility of going down with glory; and I too wish to emulate my great ancestor. Only I must have you all solidly behind me; then I shall say, like the Great King, my best allies are my troops and my generals, and, thank God, I can also say my ships and my admirals.'[20] When three days later, on the occasion of the Kaiser's birthday, the *Leipziger Tageblatt* declared that Wilhelm II would not hesitate for a moment to draw his sharp sword if Germany should be seriously in danger, the Supreme War Lord's minute on this was 'correct!'[21] On holiday in Corfu in May 1912 Wilhelm told the King of Greece that he was 'really furious' with the British government and the way it had treated him. 'I do not want a war', he exclaimed, 'but England apparently wants one & if they want it we are quite ready'.[22] On his return from Corfu the Kaiser presented his Chief of General Staff 'Julius' von Moltke with an inkwell with an image of Mars, the god of war, writing to him: 'Regard this as a token of my unchanging confidence in your valuable contribution to the military training of the Army and to its readiness to strike. I am glad that the passage of the military budget has given you and the general staff much of what you want.'[23]

After the manoeuvres in September 1912 Wilhelm declared in his assessment: 'I was pleased with the infantry. I saw all the battalions with a few exceptions. I could see from looking at the men that they had been through a lot; but when they heard my car or saw me approaching, or when the battle order was given, they pulled themselves together, gritted their teeth, and came to attention . . . I am convinced that no army in the world can equal us in such manoeuvres. Others wouldn't dare to ask so much of their men. The main thing for all of us, however, is character. Character means the will to victory; to strike, and when the enemy is sighted, the first thought: he will be beaten. What happens after that depends on the enemy's fire and his formations. In war, only character is decisive. I point to Blücher and Constantin von Alvensleben at Vionville, who did not ask what formation to fight in, but simply attacked. Character counts for more than mediocre textbook correctness, from which may the Lord God preserve us for all time!'[24]

'NON-INTERVENTION AT ALL COSTS': WILHELM AND THE FIRST BALKAN WAR

After the failure of the Haldane mission the Kaiser turned his attention again towards the east, in the hope of luring the Tsar away from France and England. The King of Greece was convinced that the Kaiser was 'at the moment trying to bring about an alliance with Russia & to alienate her from France'.[25] But the auspices for the meeting with Nicholas II at Baltic Port (Paldiski in Estonia) on 4 July 1912, at which Bethmann Hollweg, the Russian Prime Minister, Count Vladimir Kokovtsov and Foreign Minister Sergei Sazonov were present, but not Kiderlen-Wächter, were from the very start unfavourable. Wilhelm was put out by the report that the Russians wanted to confine the visit to two days, and were asking him to avoid arriving too early out of consideration for the state of health of the Tsaritsa. Scornfully, he replied to the Reich Chancellor's report: 'Not true. I had the same conditions put to me in previous years when the Empress [Alexandra] was still in good health! The fellows just don't want to have to get up too early . . . I shall only agree to the programme if you have time in the 1/2 days for *detailed* talks with the ministers. Otherwise the rest of the hostile Europ[ean] press will say that we were there for such a short time that nothing serious can have been discussed!'[26] After a further report from St Petersburg that the Tsar, following the precedent of the Potsdam meeting in November 1910, would not propose a toast to the Kaiser, Wilhelm lost patience altogether, minuting on the ambassador's dispatch: 'The Tsar has never made a speech on such occasions. I intend, following the precedent of the Potsdam meeting, to wear underpants and, in case of rain, an oilskin coat! even if the foreign office or the embassy would prefer a cloth greatcoat. One ought also to find out whether galoshes may be worn . . . I assume that, as before at Björkö, and again in Swinemünde, we shall be eating with knives and forks! And the kvass will be drunk out of glasses and not from the bottle!'[27] The encounter with the German monarch at Baltic Port proved to be every bit as intimidating and irritating as the Russians had feared, with Wilhelm confessing to a startled Sazonov for over an hour that his parents had never loved him, and then haranguing both the Tsar and Kokovtsov endlessly on the need to establish a pan-European oil trust to counter competition from America. The meeting was nevertheless deemed a diplomatic success, and Wilhelm could send to the old Emperor Franz Joseph the 'gratifying' news from Baltic Port 'that Russia, whatever happens in the Italo-Turkish war, will not allow herself to be drawn into a policy of surprises and upheavals. Her readiness to put a brake on any warlike tendencies of the little Balkan states has been clearly stated once more. All in all an apparently sincerely felt need for peace, which can only be of benefit to the peaceful policy of our two empires, and that is the main thing.'[28]

In view of the many reported sayings of Kaiser Wilhelm in the wake of the Agadir crisis and the Haldane mission that testify to his increased willingness to contemplate a general war, his apparently pacific attitude when the Balkan wars broke out in the autumn of 1912 is at first sight puzzling[29] – all the more so as the Kaiser had been for many years, as we have seen, an energetic advocate of the stabilisation and strengthening of the Ottoman Empire. One motive for his indifference to the fate of Turkey was undoubtedly the deposition of Sultan Abdul Hamid II (27 April 1909). With his surprising stance towards the turmoil in the Balkans, sarcastically characterised by his suite as 'non-intervention at all costs', Wilhelm II was, however, also pursuing breathtaking political objectives. As will be seen, the upheavals in the Balkans awakened his expectations of an 'Imperium' that would establish the preponderance of Germany and the Triple Alliance in the Eastern Mediterranean and, overland, as far as Odessa and the frontiers of India and Egypt.

The widely expected offensive by the Balkan states against the Ottoman Empire – by now seriously embarrassed by the war with Italy, an Albanian revolt and a governmental crisis at Constantinople – drew nearer when the Montenegrins attacked Turkish frontier positions in August 1912. As the first reports reached Berlin the Under Secretary Arthur Zimmermann telegraphed to the Kaiser: 'As Your Majesty's gracious intention is to prevent a war in the Balkans, I humbly beg to consider myself authorised to work through Your Majesty's ambassador in Constantinople ... for a peaceful resolution of the conflict.' Surprisingly, the Kaiser demanded a different policy and replied to Zimmermann: 'No. Wait. I do not think that is necessary! I do not care what Montenegro does. Keeping her in order is Austria's and Italy's business! We do not want to involve ourselves prematurely in every little thing in the Balkans. Await developments calmly and do not rush to play the policeman.'[30] The very obsequiousness of Zimmermann's language testifies to the Wilhelmstrasse's subordination to the monarch, and sure enough, the Under Secretary hastened to alter his instructions to the ambassador at

Constantinople and to the minister in Montenegro in accordance with Wilhelm's marginal comments.[31]

Tension increased dramatically when news reached Rominten on 30 September 1912 of Bulgaria's and Serbia's mobilisation and of a trial mobilisation of a few Russian units. Baron Jenisch, the Wilhelmstrasse's representative at the imperial hunting lodge in East Prussia, telegraphed to the Reich Chancellor: 'As Your Excellency will imagine, His Majesty is quite excited at the news from the Balkans. His Majesty inclines to the view that it will come to war.'[32] Bethmann Hollweg's assurance 'that there is no reason for us to be worried even if war breaks out in the Balkans' drew from the Kaiser the brash comment 'a war never worries me'. He would stay confidently in Rominten, 'as I can order mobilisation from there just as easily'.[33]

In the Kaiser's entourage, however, fears were widespread that given the 'very exposed' position of Rominten close to the Russian border, the imperial party could be overrun by Cossacks and the Kaiser taken prisoner.[34] 'One wonders whether the person of His Majesty the Kaiser is not in danger here, a few kilometres from the frontier, which is bristling with Russian cavalry divisions', Jenisch informed the Chancellor, 'and asks whether His Majesty ought to be advised to move the imperial party to Cadinen or Hubertusstock'. 'The fact is that a Russian Cossack detachment could reach the imperial hunting lodge without resistance in a matter of hours.'[35] Bethmann made haste to restore calm, replying reassuringly on 1 October 1912 to the dispatches from Rominten: there was 'every indication' that if it came to war in the Balkans, the Great Powers would not be involved. 'Nor is there at the present moment the slightest reason to cut short the imperial sojourn in Rominten. Such a flagrant beach of the peace as a sudden attack on the Kaiser's place of residence would be so unprecedented as to be absolutely inconceivable. Please impress this on the military members of the suite and point out that it would be irresponsible to bother H.M. with such baseless speculations. The responsibility for safeguarding His Maj[esty] from attacks from abroad rests with the Reich Chancellor.'[36] This was, for Bethmann Hollweg, an unusual display of manly courage, but it did no good: the imperial party moved to Cadinen in West Prussia, where they could feel secure from a Cossack attack on the German Emperor.

The Kaiser's assessment of the situation was reported by Jenisch to Bethmann on 2 October 1912. 'His Majesty is naturally impressed by the warlike news from the Balkans, believes that hostilities will break out, is very suspicious of Russia and England (who have undoubtedly reached agreement at Balmoral on the fate of the Dardanelles) and doubts that the Great Powers are sincere about wanting to prevent a Balkan conflagration. His Majesty goes so far ... as to describe the outbreak of war in the Balkans, once relations have reached such a crisis point, as no great misfortune. Therefore His Majesty wants us to refrain from any attempt to influence the Balkan states and to allow events to take their course. I continue to try to make it clear to His Majesty that the maintenance and strengthening of Turkey-in-Europe is altogether in our interests. But of course His Majesty, as Your Excellency knows, has for some time wanted to have nothing more to do with Turkey.'[37]

The Kaiser followed the development of the crisis, first from Rominten, then from Cadinen, with intense interest. 'Are all my representatives asleep?!!' he wrote angrily on a dispatch from the Chancellor of 1 October 1912. 'The fellows should report at once! telegraph!'[38] When dispatches on the situation in the Balkans reached him at last, on 3 October, he made no secret of his displeasure. 'And the Ausw. Amt does not report that to me immediately!! The devil take the lot of them! This is unheard of!' he thundered. He should have 'received the dispatches immediately without fail!!! It is very wrong to leave me in the dark like this!' With great determination Wilhelm II seized personal control of Germany's Near Eastern policy. 'From now on *everything* from the Balkan states or from the Great Powers is to be forwarded to me immediately. I want to form *my own* judgement, and not to be kept in leading strings by the Aus[wärtigen] Amt that is not infallible.'[39]

Now too, on the very eve of the First Balkan War, in which Bulgaria, Serbia, Greece, and Montenegro joined to strike at Turkey, Wilhelm II demanded absolute restraint. The territorial expansion of the little states at Turkey's expense was only 'natural' and would do no harm. 'I am against interfering at the moment. Rather let them let off steam, and talk after the bloodletting, when everybody will be more ready to listen. Turkey must now show whether she is still the Great Power she claims to be or not!'[40] Again, he stressed 'what a delicate matter intervention could be'; the only right policy for the Great Powers was to localise the conflict.[41] There was at this moment, Wilhelm was convinced, 'no reason whatever' for an Austrian attack on Serbia that would probably lead Russia to intervene.[42] On the contrary, he welcomed the Serbo-Bulgarian agreement pledging Serbia to send her whole army into Bulgaria for the joint attack on Turkey.[43]

It was with his nerves seriously overwrought that on 4 October 1912 the Kaiser dismayed the Wilhelmstrasse with an 'agitated memorandum' peremptorily demanding that the four Christian Balkan states be allowed to proceed against Turkey unhindered. 'This eternal emphasis on peace on all occasions – appropriate and inappropriate – has in the past 43 years of peace produced a veritably eunuchoid mentality among the leading statesmen and diplomats of Europe. Today, for example, everybody says: "The Great Powers must intervene, they must keep, maintain and safeguard the peace, they must prevent the Balkan states from going to war, or — if that proves impossible — must prevent their making territorial gains and expanding after the war!" How do they think they can do this? 1) Mobilisation is a serious step, and more consequential than a mere threat. It has been — it is clear — forced upon the governments — which are shaky — by their populations. Now to try to use external pressure to force them to demobilise would, in the first place, burden them with the hatred of their subjects, and in the second, virtually deliver these rulers, forced by the people to go to war and then prevented by the Powers from doing so, to the Revolution. For it is likely that if they yield to the external pressure they will all be thrown out by their enraged subjects, and perhaps even murdered. That is, the Powers assume the responsibility for the possible overthrow of the Balkan dynasties. If it has been difficult enough to maintain order *with* them, how much less will it be possible with Slav republics dependent on Russia! And all for what? Just for the sake of safeguarding the rather problematical existence of Turkey?! 2) Things as they stand are simply bound to lead to a clash between the Balkan states and Turkey-in-Europe. It is better it should happen now — when it *does not suit* Russia & Gaul, — because *neither* is *ready* to take us on, than later, when they are prepared and ready. 3) People see in the behaviour of the Balkan states "an attempt to blackmail" Turkey!? Why? Was — from an Austrian point of view — the young Frederick's behaviour towards Maria Theresia before the First Silesian War any different!? The Balkan states believe they must expand, and feel driven to do so; and that can only be done at the expense of a — perhaps decadent — Turkey; and as it cannot be done peacefully, there will be a fight, and they have joined together ad hoc in pursuit of their development and expansion. And that the Great Powers simply wish to deny them point blank??! By what right? To whose advantage? I shall certainly not join in. Just as we did not allow anyone to meddle in our "rightful development" in '64, '66, and '70, so I cannot and will not obstruct and thwart others. 4) Just let it come to a war. Then the Balkan states will show at last what they are capable of, and whether they have the right to exist. If they defeat Turkey decisively then they have been right and they deserve some reward. If they are beaten, they will pipe down and there will be peace and quiet for a long time; and the territorial question will disappear. The Great Powers must hold the *Ring* where the conflict *takes place* and has to *remain*; we for our part must keep calm and do nothing over-hasty. That means above all, in my view, no overkeen interference now for the sake of the so-called "peace", which would be a bad one, full of evil consequences. Just let these people get on with it; either they will receive blows or deal them out, and there will always be time to talk afterwards. The Eastern Question must be resolved by blood and iron! But at a time that suits us! That is now. Wilhelm I.R.'[44]

Kaiser Wilhelm continued to pour scorn on the efforts of the Great Powers to resolve the eastern crisis peacefully. It was 'a quite hopeless story, a confession of Europe's bankruptcy'. The Great Powers had made fools of themselves 'brilliantly' and had yet again demonstrated 'their complete impotence as a European Concert – to the Asiatic peoples!'[45] At the end of October Wilhelm described the Russian Foreign Minister's attempts to maintain the Balkan status quo by summoning a 'businesslike conference' as 'Nonsense! ... M. Sazonov is a superficial, very shallow person, who quite fails to appreciate the successes others have achieved through material sacrifice, blood, courage and devotion! That will not get him very far with military-minded nations.'[46] 'The very cool negative position of England and Germany is the only correct one!'[47] While he denigrated the efforts of statesmen and diplomats to keep the peace, the Supreme War Lord left no one in any doubt as to his admiration for the fighting forces of the Balkan states.[48] 'Civilians', he blustered, could not judge the situation, 'that is a matter for the military'.[49] The course of arms alone should decide the future of the Near East. Only if Turkey was victorious could the Sultan's sovereignty and the integrity of the Ottoman Empire survive, 'otherwise, simply expulsion [from Europe] and partition!' If, on the other hand, 'the "little ones" win and occupy the territory, then they will want their voice to be heard, which they cannot fairly be denied, and which Russia will support.'[50]

Kaiser Wilhelm made no secret of his admiration for the rapid military successes of the Bulgarians, Serbs, Greeks and Montenegrins. On 25 October 1912 he wrote rapturously on a dispatch from his minister in Belgrade: 'Macedonia is lost, and the Sanjak too! L'Intégrité de l'Empire Ottoman – in Europe – finished! Stamboul is threatened. If the Turks can be pursued fast, the Bulgarians can be before, or in, Stamboul in 8–10 days. The Turks have not been able to win a single battle, nor to hold a single city – apart from Scutari – their rule in Europe is shattered. They have proved themselves absolutely incapable of holding the country; and they must go. Greeks, Serbs and Montenegrins have fought with unexampled courage. The Bulgarian leadership has been masterly and they have been brilliantly deployed, no conference of Powers will be able to deprive them of one village. I, at any rate, shall absolutely vote against it if I am asked. They have honourably taken by conquest what they wanted, and have drummed their way into the Concert of Europe – which needed some new blood and spirit. Perhaps we shall see Ferdinand I as Tsar of Byzantium? As leader of the Balkan league? The Balkan states have won their qualifying duel and no decision of any Europ[ean] synod of elders can reject them.'[51]

The victories of the Balkan armies against the Turks only strengthened Wilhelm's determination not to intervene in the conflict. In a postscript to his minute on the above-cited dispatch from Belgrade he wrote: 'Yesterday I asked H.M. the King of Saxony what he thought of the situation and the chances for the "Intégrité de L'Empire Ottoman" in the event of further reverses. H.M. replied in the presence – in the small room – of many ladies: "If those Turkish shitheads [Scheißkerls] are such pathetic pricks [Jammerpinsel] that they can't any longer defend their own country themselves, then the swine should clear out of Europe and the Balkan states should fight each other for the inheritance. That doesn't concern us. The bones of a Saxon or Pomeranian grenadier are too good to be deployed because of Serbs in Uesküb or Bulgarians in Stamboul. Anyway there can be no question at all, given their courage and military achievements, of taking what they have conquered away from them." These words, spoken in a loud voice, made a great impression on the company, which fell suddenly silent, while many embarrassed ladies looked at the floor! He was speaking after my own heart. Of course M. Poincaré and the dabbling diplomats will be shocked. But he is right!'[52] As late as the end of November 1912 the Austrian military attaché was amazed to discover, after talking to members of the Berlin General Staff, that 'His Majesty's sympathy lies entirely with the Balkan League' and 'especially with the Bulgarians'.[53] When the Greeks took Salonica, an enthusiastic telegram of congratulation that the Kaiser sent to his sister Queen Sophie on 21 November caused consternation in both Turkey and Germany.[54]

THE AIM: 'PREPONDERANCE IN THE MEDITERRANEAN' AND 'THE WHOLE MOHAMMEDAN WORLD! (INDIA)'

The Kaiser's remarkable enthusiasm for the cause of the smaller Balkan states was anything but altruistic; and even his proclaimed admiration for the heroic deeds of their armies only partly explains his attitude towards the forward push of Bulgaria, Serbia, Greece and Montenegro. The expectations he had of the advance of the Balkan League towards Constantinople were expressed in his marginal comments of 3 November 1912 in which he defined 'our own objectives' in breathtaking terms: the '4-Power League' of Balkan states must be taken into the Concert of Europe 'as a 7th Great Power', and, in fact, 'aligned with Austria and the Triple Alliance! Perhaps by actually joining it.' He warmly welcomed Austria-Hungary's readiness to come to terms with the new situation in the Balkans and said, with regard to the Russians' desire to return to the pre-war status quo, 'just let them try! Then the unity of the Slav brotherhood disappears for a start, and the league of 4 immediately gravitates towards Austria, together with Romania.' In his bedazzlement, Wilhelm already saw himself as the leader of a great Central European empire stretching to the Black Sea and deep into the Middle East. Austria must 'give the construction of a "United States of the Balkans" . . . her energetic support. For in such a formation the Balkan states will soon get themselves into opposition to Russia, and will then quite naturally have need of Austria and hence of the Triple Alliance, for which they will provide a very desirable reinforcement and an offensive flank against Russia. If they are clever, they will make an alliance with Turkey post pugnam. Our policy ought to operate as outlined above in conjunction with Austria! [Tsar] Ferdinand is welcome to go into Stamboul!'[55] With the victory of the Balkan League and Austria-Hungary's renunciation of territorial expansion Wilhelm thought that he had at last achieved the breakthrough to World Power status.[56]

He was appropriately brusque in resisting Turkish appeals for mediation. 'The victors dictate the terms', he declared on 4 November 1912. 'Turkey's request may be forwarded to the Balkan League. But *together with a statement of my position*, and H.M. [Tsar Ferdinand] refuses to allow pressure to be exercised. Procedure: let the other Powers come to us and inform us of their intentions. If one of them (France or Russia) wants to go ahead, let it do so *alone*. I *forbid* our participation in any action that might be interpreted by the League of 4 as intending to hold them back, even if this means risking offending several members of the Concert. Inform Rome and Vienna of my position, and the 4-power League too.'[57] 'I refuse *to participate at all in any action* to restrain the Bulgaro-Serbo-Greeks in their triumphal progress, or to propose or impose terms on them that do not suit them. I am now for fair play, free fight and no favour! And for the interests of those fighting! Let them and the Powers be so informed at once.'[58] 'I shall not lift a finger', Wilhelm was still declaring on 8 November. 'The Bulgarians will and must go in!'[59] This attitude seemed to the Kaiser all the more unexceptionable as his brother Heinrich had reported after meeting Tsar Nicholas that the latter had assured him 'emphatically' that he himself 'was not thinking' of occupying Constantinople; 'he would *not take Stamboul even if it was given to him* and he did not care if the Bulgarians went in. The cross would then be on the Hagia Sofia again, and that was the main thing.'[60] As late as 15 November Kaiser Wilhelm lived in joyous anticipation of Tsar Ferdinand's entry into Constantinople and ordered the ambassador Hans von Wangenheim 'to refrain from all military-political interference' that might strengthen Turkey against the victorious Balkan states. Wangenheim's attempt to raise the Turks' spirits was 'absolutely improper behaviour. He is stepping outside the strict neutrality I prescribed and is compromising me and my government vis-à-vis the Bulgarians. For if the latter lose a lot of men in the fighting . . . and my embassy's activity gets to be known, the Bulgarians will charge their losses to our account for giving the Turks moral support . . . Turkey-in-Europe is finished, she must get out, and the fewer difficulties she makes the better.'[61]

Naturally Wilhelm's great dream of a 'seventh European Great Power' proved totally illusory. The huge increase in the power of the Triple Alliance in the Balkans that he hoped for soon showed itself to be unacceptable to the 'Concert of Europe', and the much vaunted 'United States of the Balkans' were soon to be engaged in a brutal war among themselves. But the Kaiser continued to set great store by an expansion of Triple Alliance power towards the south-east, even if in a modified form: not the four Balkan states that had defeated Turkey, but an alliance between Bulgaria and Turkey was to produce his much desired breakthrough to world power and secure German influence as far as Odessa, Egypt and India. By December 1912 Wilhelm had to admit that the 'Quadruple Alliance' of the Balkans states would 'not last!' 'The Bulgarian will break away' and this would, he hoped, frustrate the machinations of the Entente in the Near East.[62] When on 1 December 1912, during a fox-hunt at Donaueschingen, he received news (which later turned out to be false) that Tsar Ferdinand had offered the Turks an alliance, Wilhelm II saw himself already as master of a great world empire; and he hastened to send a giddy telegram to the Auswärtiges Amt: 'The Turkish report of Ferdinand's alliance offer has not surprised me, any more than his betrayal of his allies. It is a brilliant, grandiose concept! The protector of broken-down Turkey and leader of regenerated Turkey coming together to fend off the Russians and hold the Serbs down. Austria must enter a military alliance with Turco-Bulgaria, and we must cooperate in strengthening and regenerating both states. Such a power combination will drive Greece and even Serbia helplessly towards Austria. Thus, Austria will become the predominant Power in the Balkans and the Eastern Mediterranean, and together with Italy and a regenerated or newly constructed Turco-Bulgarian fleet, will be a powerful counterweight to England, whose communications with Alexandria could be threatened. Russia will then be finished in the Balkans and Odessa threatened. Then the Triple Alliance Powers will be preponderant in the Mediterranean, and have control of the Caliph and thereby of the whole Mohammedan world! (India). Serbia will then get it in the neck! and we can take up our Turkish policy again.'[63] It is all too understandable that the editors of *Die Große Politik der europäischen Kabinette* should have tried to draw a line between these imperial 'fantasies' that seemed to anticipate the Mitteleuropa plans pursued during the First World War and official German foreign policy in the pre-war years. In his 'exceedingly characteristic' manner, they mocked, the

Kaiser had 'in a trice constructed veritable castles in the air' which did not, they insisted, 'have any further consequences'. But be that as it may, few documents reveal Wilhelm II's expectations and objectives in the Balkan crisis of 1912 more clearly than this dispatch of 1 December 1912 from Donaueschingen.[64]

THE THREAT OF WAR BETWEEN AUSTRIA AND SERBIA — AND RUSSIA

Together with the growing tension between the Balkan states, an insuperable obstacle to the realisation of the Kaiser's hopes for a Central European empire stretching from Hamburg to the Hindu Kush was Austria's refusal to allow the victorious kingdom of Serbia access to the Adriatic.[65] At first, Wilhelm was anything but sympathetic to Vienna's position, writing to Kiderlen-Wächter on 7 November: 'I see absolutely no threat to Austria's existence or even prestige in a Serbian port on the Adriatic. I think it is dangerous to oppose Serbia's desire unnecessarily. Russia would support Serbia immediately, and we should be back with the old pre-war Sanjak situation . . . These are . . . to some extent "conceits" that Vienna thinks necessary, but their realisation, *with all their possible consequences (war etc.)* only concerns *Austria* and *not her ally*. If I wanted to avoid the casus foederis, and indeed did avoid it, when the Serbs moved into the Sanjak and Uesküb at the outbreak of the war, I am even less inclined to recognise it because the Serbs are in Durazzo or Albania. Such a far-reaching obligation is not in accordance with the spirit of the Triple Alliance, which was from the start designed to guarantee *actual possessions*; nor do the Austr[ian] Monarchy's actual vital interests and conditions really require it. Certainly Vienna finds many of the changes in the Balkans resulting from the war really uncomfortable and also undesirable, but none of them is so crucial that we should on that account expose ourselves to the danger of war, for which I could not answer either to my people or my conscience. In 1908 things were quite different, as it was then a question of an *actual part* of Austria, that had belonged to her for a long time. That must be the guideline for our policy.'[66]

The Kaiser and his suite were only too well aware of the mechanism which could transform a local conflict between Austria and Serbia into a general war. As early as 1 October 1912 the Flügeladjutant at Rominten, Max Freiherr von Holzing-Berstett, had explained in a letter to his wife: 'Germany can get drawn into war even against its will, thanks to its alliance commitments to Austria. That the latter will have to fight is not improbable. That France will strike the moment we mobilise (even partially) in the East, seems certain. That England will seize the moment, equally certain. And Italy will attack

Austria.'[67] Alert to the incalculable risk of escalation, Wilhelm II told the Reich Chancellor during a shoot in Letzlingen (near Magdeburg) on 9 November 1912 that he refused to involve Germany in a conflict between Austria-Hungary and Serbia that might lead to war with Russia and France, insisting, as he telegraphed to Kiderlen afterwards, 'that *under no circumstances* will I *march against Paris and Moscow* on account of Albania and Durazzo'.[68] But then, later that very day, there was a dramatic shift in Wilhelm's attitude towards an Austro-Serbian conflict. The longer-term consequences of this change of heart were to prove momentous and deserve to be examined in detail.

'YOU CAN COUNT ON US.' THE KAISER'S DECISION FOR WAR

If Wilhelm was most definitely not working for a European war during the first phase of the Balkan wars, he nevertheless viewed Russian and French policy with deep suspicion, believing that these Powers might seize on the conflict to attack the Triple Alliance. He saw the presence in France of the Russian Grand Duke Nicholas Nikolaievitch and his Montenegrin wife, and their provocative visit to the fortifications on the German frontier, as propagandistic preliminaries for such an attack. He further suspected that the representatives of the Balkan states had agreed the plans for their attack on Turkey in Paris, under the Grand Duke's chairmanship. 'Then the visit to Nancy & Toul was a symptom', he wrote excitedly on 4 October 1912, 'of the fact that the Grand Duke, being privy to the Balkan states' intentions, hopes that Austria will strike at Serbia, who will bring Russia in, raising the casus foederis for us, in which case Gaul is immediately to attack us in the rear. The whole business on our frontier was arranged in order to give the Gauls courage and to stir up hatred. Then it was not a comedy at all, but preparation for bitter realities.'[69] Wilhelm ordered the ambassadors in Paris, Rome and Constantinople to report to him everything they had been able to discover about the secret conversations of the representatives of the Balkan states in Paris. At the same time, Count Pourtalès in St Petersburg was instructed to report to him whether tendencies were discernible among the Russian public and in the army to make common cause with their Orthodox co-religionaries in the Balkans.[70] Marginal notes of 11 October 1912 on a report from Kiderlen show that Wilhelm was convinced that only the premature outbreak of war against Turkey had frustrated Russia's machinations. According to the Russian plan, he believed, the attack 'should only take place when Russia was ready to take us on, and when she thought the right moment to strike had come'. But even now Wilhelm was still afraid the Balkan conflict might escalate into a general war if Austria should feel obliged to use force to expel the Serbs from the Sanjak of Novibazar. For 'the Panslavs in Russia would make such a commotion that Russia would have to go to war willy-nilly'.[71] 'Russia', he declared, 'simply wants a war, and wants to use Austria as a pretext! Because she wants to go to Stamboul!'[72] As a countermeasure to Russia's supposed machinations, on 11 October 1912 he ordered the Auswärtiges Amt to work for a rapprochement with England and a military agreement with Japan![73] The beginnings of a strategic reorientation from west to east were unmistakable. Two days later, on the Kaiser's initiative, the Hubertusstock hunting lodge was the setting for a crisis meeting with the Reich Chancellor, the Prussian War Minister, the Chief of General Staff, the head of the Military Cabinet and the Foreign Secretary, at which Wilhelm demanded a large increase in the military budget. True, the War Minister, Josias von Heeringen, managed initially to persuade him to drop this demand, but in the General Staff, now under the influence of the new Quartermaster-General Count Georg von Waldersee and of Erich Ludendorff, Chief of the 2nd Section since 1 October, 'the Kaiser's initiative' was taken up 'with fresh energy' and plans for the massive army budget increase were drawn up that, as will be seen, would be accepted by the Reichstag in the Spring of 1913.[74]

On 9 November 1912, during his stay at Letzlingen, Bethmann Hollweg gained the impression that despite the Kaiser's declaring that he would '*under no circumstances march against Paris and Moscow*' on account of a Serbian port on the Adriatic,[75] he had now come round to see that in certain circumstances it would be necessary to support Germany's Triple Alliance partner in a war against Serbia. 'Today, back on a sound basis', the Chancellor telegraphed to Kiderlen with obvious relief.[76] This 'sound basis' consisted, as will soon become clear, in Russia's putting herself in the wrong (or being put in the wrong) to provide the Geman people with an effective slogan for the 'war of annihilation' − as Wilhlem himself termed it.

Immediately on his return from Letzlingen on 9 November 1912 Wilhelm discussed the menacing situation in the Balkans with Kiderlen, after which he set down his views in another extraordinarily revealing memorandum. 'Serbia is demanding access to, and ports on, the Adriatic, Austria rejects this out of hand. Russia seems to want to support Serbia's aspirations, and she and Austria could get into such a clash that it comes to an armed conflict. Then the casus foederis arises for Germany, as Vienna is attacked by St Petersburg − according to the treaty. This commits Germany to mobilising and fighting on 2 fronts, i.e. in order to be able to march against Moscow, Paris must first be taken. Paris will undoubtedly be supported by London. Germany must, therefore, embark on a struggle for existence with 3 Great Powers in which *everything* will be at stake, and in which she might possibly perish. All this follows from Austria's unwillingness to have the Serbs in Albania or Durazzo. It is clear that this objective cannot serve Germany as a slogan for a war of annihilation [Vernichtungskrieg], let alone enable us to inspire the German nation to start a war for such a reason, and nobody can square it with his conscience and his responsibility to God and his people to gamble with Germany's existence for such a reason. That would be to go beyond the scope of a treaty, even beyond the scope of the casus foederis, which should never be open to the interpretation that the German Army and People should be placed directly in the service of the foreign political whims of another state, and held, so to speak, at their disposal! The Triple Alliance Treaty guarantees only the actual *possessions* of the 3 states, but does not commit them to unconditional support in disputes about the possessions of others! Of course the casus foederis arises if Austria is attacked by Russia. But only if Austria has *not provoked* Russia to attack. Now such a situation could arise here regarding Serbia. And that Vienna must avoid at all costs. Vienna should listen to, or make, mediation proposals about the Albanians and their future, and leave it to the *Russians* to quash them and incite the Serbs to go for broke. If the Russ[ians] should *reject* an acceptable Austr[ian] mediation proposal approved by the other Powers the *Russians* put themselves *in the wrong* vis-à-vis Vienna, burden themselves with the disapproval of the Powers, arouse the suspicion that they are actually pressing for war with Austria (with Albania a mere threadbare pretext), and would, as troublemakers, earn the ire of all reasonable people, and so if it comes to war, as the *provocative* party that will not leave Vienna in peace, they would provide our government with a good slogan for mobilisation!' After the Kaiser's meetings with Bethmann and Kiderlen on 9 November 1912, therefore, the focus was no longer on avoiding a great war, but on the idea of representing Russia as a troublemaker in the hope of finding an effective slogan to win over the German people and to isolate Russia diplomatically. The Kaiser's increased readiness for war was also expressed in the little verse that he appended to his memorandum:

> For years we have practised forgiveness
> As the Gods have always taught us
> But the weight of the yoke is rough
> It's time for us to shake it off.[77]

On 11 November 1912 Wilhelm ordered the Auswärtiges Amt, through the Minister of the Royal House, Count August zu Eulenburg, to prepare copies of 'all His All-Highest Majesty's handwritten memoranda, telegrams and marginal commands relating to the Balkan crisis since this September.

His Majesty intends to secrete this collection of documents in the archive of the Royal House.'[78] Was this intended, one wonders, to serve as proof of the Kaiser's peacefulness in the preceding weeks in the event of war?

The days that followed brought news of troop reinforcements in Russian Poland and Austrian countermeasures on the Galician frontier. Kiderlen informed Vienna in response to an anxious query from the Kaiser's close friend Prince Fürstenberg that 'in the event of further developments' Germany 'would not hesitate for a moment to fulfil our alliance obligations'; Austria-Hungary should, however, endeavour to put itself in the right 'and appear not as the provocative but as the provoked' party.[79] Wilhelm was convinced that a war between the two eastern empires into which Germany, France and Britain would be drawn, could now hardly be avoided. 'The question and answer game of diplomacy will now begin, countermeasures from the other side, resentful enquiries from this side and that, and then an incident on the Serbo-Bosnian frontier and the explosion is there, and with it the casus foederis! . . . Caveant Consules! We must put proposals to the Reichstag to improve the training of our 100,000-strong reserve. And high time too!'[80]

The Kaiser saw the approaching Great Power conflict as a racial struggle of Germans against Slavs. The question of whether Germany would be prepared to defend the vital interests of Austria-Hungary, and especially of 'Germandom', against the advance of 'Slavdom' he answered on 20 November 1912 with, 'absolutely'. The symptoms of decay in the multinational Danube Monarchy must give way to a policy of force, for 'only blood and iron can now cure those ruffians', the non-German peoples. Austria had forgotten, Kaiser Wilhelm declared, 'that it cannot be ruled in the Czech fashion, nor the Bohemian, nor the Polish, nor the Magyar, as has been tried, but *only in the German*! The *German* House of Habsburg has subjugated all these peoples with the help of the *German* Austrians. With the Slavs, divide et impera is the only feasible way.' Every parliamentarian who resisted this policy deserved to be hanged.[81] In very similar language the Austrian War Minister, Moritz Ritter von Auffenberg-Komarów, declared: 'We need at least half a century of peace in the Monarchy to get the South Slavs in order, and we can only achieve this if all South Slav hopes of Russian support have been finally destroyed. Otherwise, the Monarchy will go to pieces.' On 21 November the news reached Berlin that the Emperor Franz Joseph had ordered mobilisation in East Galicia. Auffenberg confirmed that the German General Staff was fully informed of all the measures taken by the allied army.[82]

Wilhelm was aware of the significance of the Austrian decision. On 21 November 1912 he spoke to the Austrian military attaché Freiherr von

Bienerth of 'his anger at the "insolence" of the Serbs ... and went on to say that Austria-Hungary could count unconditionally on the support of the German Reich. Regarding Bulgaria, His Majesty stated that he was certainly hoping to draw her into the Triple Alliance camp; Bulgaria was thoroughly tired of Russia's eternal chivvying. His Majesty concluded by declaring: "Germany's sword is already loose in its scabbard, you can count on us."'[83] On a report from ambassador Heinrich von Tschirschky in Vienna Wilhelm wrote that for Germany, too, this was 'a moment of profoundest seriousness'. 'It can turn into the Europ[ean] War and for us possibly a struggle for existence against 3 Great Powers. For us, it is a matter of getting a clear picture from London and Paris quickly.'[84] In a telegram of 21 November 1912 the Kaiser gave Kiderlen-Wächter to understand that he was now indeed ready for war, as Russia had put herself in the wrong and was seen as a Power pressing for war. 'From the whole Europ[ean] press – in particular the English – it appears that Austria is generally regarded as the provoked party, and with that the situation that I had hoped would emerge has been achieved. If Russia should resort to countermeasures or demands that compel Emperor Franz Josef [sic] to start the war, then he will have right on his side, and I am ready – as I told the Chancellor recently in Letzlingen – to apply the casus foederis in full, and with all the consequences. I think it essential, therefore, that the ambassadors in *Paris* and *London* must be ordered *at once* to ascertain *with absolute clarity* and to report to me, whether in such circumstances *Paris* would definitely go along with Russia immediately, and what side England will take. The ambassador in St Petersburg is to report as soon as possible how Russia reacts to the Austrian demarche – as soon as it takes place – and to inform me as soon as possible how he regards the present situation there. All the ambassadors must inform their military attachés and work together with them, and report personally to me at all times.' The Supreme War Lord continued: 'At the order of Emperor Franz Joseph', Field Marshal Blasius Schemua, Conrad von Hötzendorf's successor as Chief of the Austro-Hungarian General Staff, would be arriving in Berlin in the morning, 'to discuss possible military operations with Moltke. Afterwards, both gentlemen will come to see me.'[85]

THE KAISER'S AND MOLTKE'S SECRET MEETING WITH THE CHIEF OF THE AUSTRO-HUNGARIAN GENERAL STAFF, 22 NOVEMBER 1912

In this case too, the editors of the official *Die Große Politik der europäischen Kabinette* were concerned to play down the significance of the Kaiser's telegram for the history of the origins of the First World War. They stressed that the timing of Schemua's 'brief' visit to Berlin was uncertain; and the General was in any case back in Vienna on 23 November without having come into contact with 'those leaders responsible for making policy'. The directives 'dashed off' by the Kaiser had also been without practical consequences 'of any kind'. Both in talking to Schemua in Berlin and when he was with Archduke Franz Ferdinand in Springe over the next few days, Kaiser Wilhelm had restated 'yet again the standpoint that he had consistently held to, that he did not wish to be drawn into a war on account of a Serbian harbour. All reports agree that on the occasion of the visit of the Austrians Kaiser Wilhelm II and his advisers counselled moderation.'[86] Possibly the confusion is partly attributable to the necessity for the strictest secrecy − even Archduke Franz Ferdinand's Chamberlain was allowed to learn nothing of the real purpose of the meeting.[87] Thanks to sources which were not available to the editors of the *Große Politik*, however, it is now possible to reconstruct the actual course of the momentous Austro-German military conversations in Berlin and Springe.

General Schemua arrived at the Friedrichstrasse station in Berlin on Friday 22 November 1912 at 7.35 in the morning and at 9.00 o'clock went on foot and, to avoid recognition, in mufti, to the General Staff Headquarters.[88] He found his colleague Helmuth von Moltke confident in his assessment of the strategic situation.[89] Moltke confirmed what Bienerth had reported just before Schemua left Vienna for Berlin, namely that neither France nor England constituted a serious threat to the Triple Alliance. Several officers of the German General Staff had told him, Bienerth wrote, 'that there is at present hardly anything to fear from France. As regards England, I heard the view that she too, by sending such a strong naval force − 8 modern battleships − into the Mediterranean, had lost her former substantive superiority in the North Sea. If last year, despite having all her forces available in the North Sea, England hesitated to strike, then this is even more likely to be the case today.'[90] Schemua's talks with Moltke on 22 November, therefore, saw 'complete unanimity in assessing the overall situation'. Moltke, the Austrian Chief of General Staff later recorded, 'entirely understood our assessment of our situation vis-à-vis Russia and Serbia ... He also promised me not merely to stand guard, but to launch a forceful offensive action in parallel with ours. He repeatedly emphasised Germany's alliance loyalty, saying that we could count absolutely on Germany if Russia threatened us, and that it was also an eminent interest of Germany's too that we should not be weakened. The seriousness of the situation was clear to him. German mobilisation would automatically entail that of France, and to have two mobilised armies standing alongside each other was an untenable situation which was bound to lead to a clash. But then the first consideration, naturally, must be to crush the enemy in the West first — which he hoped to do in 4 to 5 weeks — and then to transfer the spare capacity in forces to the East.' Doubts expressed by the Austrian — who thought the short time allocated to the defeat of France 'very question-able' — Moltke sought to dispel by talking of possible replacement divisions. Schemua's memorandum continued: 'While we were engaged in our lively exchange of views it was reported that the Kaiser had just arrived, and a few moments later H. Majesty entered the room . . . H.M. started by discussing the latest reports that had come in, including one stating that an industrialist who was just back from a long motor-car tour all over France had not been struck by anything that pointed to preparations for war or a warlike mood; and he mentioned further a letter from a person of high standing in the Tsar's entourage to the effect that Russia was not yet adequately prepared for war; but that she would be in 2 years' time — so the match would then end in a draw. H.M. then deigned to hear what I had to say. When I remarked that I could not banish my anxieties regarding Italy's attitude, H.M. told me that these were groundless, and related the following episode: When his eldest son, Crown Prince Wilhelm (H.M. said 'my boy') was staying as a hunting guest of the King of Italy 2 years ago, the Crown Prince had said in his impulsive way (it was just at the time of the Franco-German tension after the Moroccan crisis) that in the event of war Italy would probably not go along with us, to which Victor Emmanuel replied in very decided terms that Italy would loyally fulfil the obligations she had undertaken. H.M. added that the King was a reserved, but a reliable man. When San Giuliano [the Italian Foreign Minister] was last in Berlin he had spoken in the most loyal terms of the Alliance . . . and declared himself ready to renew the treaty at once. Turning to Moltke, H.M. said that it might perhaps be advisable to appear to be in touch with the Chief of the Italian General Staff in order to demonstrate the military unity of the Triple Alliance to the public. H.M. then turned back to me and stressed emphatically that we can count fully on Germany's support under all circum-stances. Conditions in Russia with all the internal political disruptions are not clear; but Hartwig, the Russian minister in Belgrade, and Isvolsky the ambas-sador in Paris are doubtless the chief agitators. Besides, the fear of political and revolutionary unrest helps to determine military measures in Russia. After a few personal enquiries H.M. . . . took his leave, remarking that he had now to go to receive . . . Archduke Franz Ferdinand at the station. I talked for a while longer with . . . Moltke, who emphasised that he too was fully aware that impending events will be critical for the very existence of our states. He was counting on the continuance of our relations of trust and thanked us for our frequent support in matters of military intelligence.' Then, while Moltke left for the shoot with the Austrians at Springe, Schemua returned to Vienna.[91]

Figure 38 'I'll stand by you through thick and thin!' Wilhelm II and his friend
Archduke Franz Ferdinand at their crucial meeting at Springe in November 1912

At Springe (near Hanover) the Kaiser left Archduke Franz Ferdinand in no
more doubt than the allied Chief of General Staff that he was prepared to
support Austria-Hungary 'under all circumstances', even if this should lead to
a world war 'against the three Entente Powers'.[92] Given the tense situation,
the shooting party at Springe was highly political in character, including as it
did the Austrian Court Chamberlain Baron von Rumerskirch, the Austrian
military attaché Karl von Bienerth, Reich Chancellor von Bethmann Hollweg,
the Chief of General Staff, Grand Admiral von Tirpitz, the three Secret
Cabinet chiefs, the court officials Count August zu Eulenburg and Max von
Lyncker and Adjutant-General Gustav von Kessel (see Figure 38). Bienerth
was emphatic that at Springe Franz Ferdinand had had the opportunity for
thoroughgoing discussions with Bethmann, Moltke and Tirpitz.[93] On reports
that spoke of the readiness of the Tsar, under the influence of Rasputin, to risk
a 'great war' for Serbia's demands for access to the Adriatic, Kaiser Wilhelm
minuted: 'That is all we wanted to know' and 'now we have certainty'.

Wilhelm was reckoning on war, even if Tsar Nicholas were to attempt to avoid it. 'The situation is that of 1877–8 – exactly!' he declared. 'Alexander II insisted that he did not want a war, and so there would be no war! And at the railway station he encountered the volunteers from his regiments, in uniform, setting off for Serbia against his will! Within 4 weeks he had declared war! It will be the same again!'[94] Archduke Franz Ferdinand took with him from Springe 'the certainty of German assistance in the event of war'.[95]

On 25 November 1912 the German General Staff confirmed that no mobilisation measures were discernible either in Russia or in France. On the other hand, Austria was obviously 'on the threshold of decisive measures' against Serbia, and 'if Austria strikes that would probably draw Russia out of her waiting attitude. A German mobilisation against Russia would then perhaps be an unavoidable consequence.' As the Bavarian military plenipotentiary Wenninger reported to Munich, the Kaiser was 'in a very nervous state'. At any rate, the situation was 'extremely tense', and 'the acceleration of various military measures' had been ordered.[96] Older army officers, including the Kaiser's brother-in-law, Hereditary Prince Bernhard of Saxe-Meiningen, were pensioned off without notice. 'My husband has received his dismissal from the army, *coldly & curtly*', Wilhelm's sister Charlotte complained on 23 November. 'H.M. has no further use for him *whatever* . . . I shall try to keep my outrage to myself . . . But it's of a piece with everything else!'[97] After talking to Moltke on 27 November, the War Minister, Josias von Heeringen, could confirm that 'the German Army can look to the future with complete confidence',[98] and Moltke himself defined his position thus: Germany could 'at the moment contemplate a war quite calmly . . . because Russia is not ready, and France is on the one hand deeply engaged in Morocco and on the other facing a threat from Italy's co-operation with Austria and Germany. The military-political situation is, therefore, at present favourable to us. But it can change.' If it did not come to a war now, a big new Army Bill would have to be brought in, for Germany must then 'be strong enough to rely on her own strength, and the further enlargement of her armed forces would brook no delay'.[99] To his niece, Moltke said, 'if war is to come, I hope it comes soon, before I am too old to manage things properly'.[100]

CHAPTER THIRTY-FOUR

Deterrence: the unresolved problem of Britain's neutrality

At the end of November 1912 the German Reich was very close to committing itself – as the previous chapter has clearly shown – to supporting its ally Austria-Hungary in an offensive war against Serbia, even at the risk that such a forward move in the Balkans might lead to a European war between the Central Powers and the Franco-Russian alliance. Why did the closing months of 1912 not witness the frightful world war that was to be triggered by precisely this mechanism eighteen months later? As we shall now see, the answer to this controversial question lies in the revelation which – despite Lloyd George's Mansion House speech and the failure of the Haldane mission – took the Kaiser completely by surprise: Great Britain was determined to maintain the balance of power in Europe and made it clear that she would not allow her Entente partners to be 'crushed'. Deterrence, the *raison d'être* of the Triple Entente, thus functioned for what was to be almost the last time in the winter crisis of 1912–13. Why it failed to work a year and a half later, in the summer of 1914, is a question that will preoccupy us in this chapter as well as in those that follow.

PRINCE HEINRICH'S FIRST MISSION TO ENGLAND

Just as the danger of general war seemed to draw closer in November 1912, so the question of Britain's attitude in a Balkan conflict became increasingly urgent. As we have seen, Wilhelm II had on 21 November peremptorily ordered the ambassadors in Paris and London to tell him 'straight out' whether France would immediately join Russia, and what side England would take.[1] Moltke, in his discussions with his Austro-Hungarian counterpart, Blasius Schemua, had assumed that England would initially stay out, and this

was also the impression that Prince Lichnowsky had gained in the short time
he had been ambassador in London. As he informed the Kaiser in a private
letter of 23 November 1912, Sir Edward Grey was visibly striving to make
Anglo-German relations 'as close as possible ... Like the great majority of
politicians here', he desired 'to live in peace and friendship with us, without of
course sacrificing his relations with France and Russia on that account. To him
too, the thought that a general war might break out over Northern Albania
seems absurd.' As for the key question, what Great Britain would do should
such a war nevertheless break out, Lichnowsky could of course give no clear
answer: 'Whether in the event of a general war on account of Serbs and
Albanians — which we can hardly ask of the German people either — the
government here would intervene, is difficult to say, and surely depends in the
end on the secret agreements existing between the Entente Powers. But to go
by my impressions here, I do not believe that England would decide for active
intervention so long as somehow a possibility existed of keeping out of the
conflict.'[2]

The confidence in its ability to cope with all situations that characterised
the German army was lacking in the Imperial Navy, however. There the
prospect of war with England was viewed with as much nervous apprehension
as in the Wilhelmstrasse. The Admiralty Staff warned Kiderlen-Wächter that
the Royal Navy had been 'brought up to a state of extreme war-readiness',
whereupon the Auswärtiges Amt asked the navy to abstain 'for the present'
from measures 'that England could regard as directed against her'.[3] In an
audience on 3 December 1912 the Chief of the Admiralty Staff reported to the
Kaiser that the redeployment of the Royal Navy, while not of a decidedly
offensive character as in 1911, was not run-of-the-mill either, and would 'if the
case arose, permit the concentration of naval power *en masse* in the shortest
possible time'. Admiral von Heeringen confessed that Germany's military
position at sea in the face of Britain's overwhelming superiority was hopeless —
against sixteen English heavy cruisers ready for immediate action, Germany
could 'at the moment' muster only two (*Blücher* and *Moltke*) actually capable
of fighting.[4] Wilhelm agreed to the proposal to order the *Goeben* and *Breslau*
to return from the Mediterranean immediately, as they would not be able to
pass the Straits of Gibraltar if war broke out.[5] Tirpitz for his part took the
relaxed view 'that the political situation at the moment is not so threatening as
to justify orders that are of no lasting validity, do not fall within the guidelines
laid down for the next few years, and will cost more than we have means
available'. Even he, however, declared himself in agreement with moving the
U-boat flotilla to Heligoland and taking some precautionary measures to
enhance the readiness of the fleet for war.[6]

Not least on account of Lichnowsky's and Kühlmann's optimistic forecasts of the waiting attitude that London would probably adopt in a continental war, Kiderlen and Bethmann Hollweg took a sanguine view of Germany's situation in the Balkan crisis. They assured Admiral von Müller that the situation was 'decidedly more favourable to us than in 1909 with Austria's annexation of Bosnia', especially as 'today, we have both Italy and England on our side'.[7] Both statesmen therefore – Kiderlen in the Bundesrat on 26 November and Bethmann in the Reichstag on 2 December 1912 – formally declared Germany's readiness to stand 'firm and unflinching' by Austria if the Dual Monarchy had to 'fight to defend its Great Power status'; after all, in such a conflict it would not be only Austria's existence but 'the maintenance of our own position in Europe' and 'our own future and security' that would be at stake.[8] As the Austrian military attaché Baron von Bienerth discovered, it was Moltke who had 'pressed for' this militant wording in the Chancellor's speech.[9] But these declarations, while heartily welcome to Vienna, caused alarm in London.

Wilhelm II likewise proceeded on the assumption that England would stay neutral in the event of a war between the Triple Alliance and Russia and Serbia, while France's role (like that of England in the event of a Franco-German war) remained, as hitherto, altogether unclear. Quite unperturbed, he added in his own hand the words 'be it in peace or in war' to the birthday telegram he sent to the Chancellor from Donaueschingen on 29 November 1912.[10] As we have seen, in these 'very jolly' days in the Black Forest, he was living in the expectation of an alliance with Turkey and Bulgaria that would make the Central Powers predominant in the Balkans and the eastern Mediterranean and supreme in 'the whole Mohammedan world!' as far as India; Russia would then be 'finished, and threatened in Odessa'.[11] When on 3 December he received Lichnowsky's letter with its hopeful assessment of Grey's policy, the Kaiser was 'strongly impressed by England's rather surprising rapprochement with Germany'. All the same, he was determined not 'to fall for words any longer, but to wait for deeds'.[12]

In this uncertain situation Prince Heinrich's visit to his cousin King George V at Sandringham acquired a particular significance. While Wilhelm was slaughtering a hundred foxes at Donaueschingen[13] the Kaiser's brother left Kiel on 30 November, saw Lichnowsky (who continued to take an 'optimistic' view of the situation) on 2 December, and in the evening of 4 December called on his sister-in-law Princess Victoria of Battenberg and her husband Prince Louis, who had just been made First Sea Lord under Churchill at the Admiralty.[14] As a result, Battenberg felt obliged next day to warn his cousin the King that Heinrich and Wilhelm were obviously quite wrong in their estimation of Great Britain's attitude in a European war. 'Harry of Prussia', he wrote, '(who presumably reflects his brother's views) does not appear to realise that if War were to break out between Germany & Austria v[ersus] Russia & France, we here cannot permit either of the two latter countries, especially France, to be crippled – consequently we *cannot* stand out in certain circumstances'.[15] His warning did not fail to make an impression on George V.

On 6 December 1912 Prince Heinrich went to Sandringham to see the King, who said he was entirely satisfied with the relations existing between the two countries, but warned him, as Heinrich noted cryptically in his diary: 'If Europ[ean] war, then England, France and Russia against us and Triple Alliance! But otherwise never provoke a war. Our Fleet war.'[16] After Heinrich's departure the King felt obliged to report to Sir Edward Grey on the Prince's somewhat unsettling visit: 'In the course of a long conversation', Prince Heinrich had asked him 'point blank, whether, in the event of Germany and Austria going to war with Russia and France, England would come to the assistance of the two latter Powers. I answered "undoubtedly, Yes – under certain circumstances". He expressed surprise and regret, but did not ask what the certain circumstances were. He said he would tell the Emperor what I had told him. Of course Germany must know that we would not allow either of our friends to be crippled.'[17] The King had spoken without consulting his responsible ministers, but Grey approved his language retrospectively and in return told him how, by a 'remarkable coincidence', Lichnowsky had put the same question to Haldane at the same time and had received the same answer.[18]

Prince Heinrich's enquiry as to England's attitude towards a continental war made such an impression on the King that weeks later he reported on it at length to the Russian ambassador Count Benckendorff and his French colleague Paul Cambon in the presence of Churchill and Lloyd George.[19] After a visit to Windsor, Cambon reported to his superiors in Paris: 'The brother of the Emperor Wilhelm, envisaging the possibility of a conflict between Austria and Russia which would necessarily lead to the intervention of the army of Germany and France, asked King George whether England would take part. "Certainly yes, His Majesty responded, in certain circumstances." Prince Heinrich objected, saying that in Berlin one could not imagine the possibility of a war between Germany and England; that these two countries united by bonds of blood, by their interests and their traditions could not fight one another without denying their history; and that such a conflict would be all the more incomprehensible because British interests were not involved. "We both have our friends, the King replied, you call yours your allies, we do not have allies other than Japan; but our friends are no less entitled to count on us. You proclaim your loyalty to your allies, we are in honour bound to

remain loyal to our friends." Prince Heinrich then tried to indicate to the King
the disadvantages for England of her intimacy with France. "My father, the
King responded, was concerned throughout his reign which lasted nine years
to reach and develop our entente with France and Russia. He had his reasons.
How do you expect me, whose reign is not yet two years old, to change this
policy all of a sudden? That's impossible."' Cambon continued: 'The King
added that Prince Heinrich probably came to England to put this question to
him.' The ambassador admitted that he and his Russian colleague had been
unable to ask the King what he had meant by the expression 'in certain
circumstances', but they were both sure that he had had in mind 'an aggression by Austria in Serbia and some ultimative demands addressed by Germany
to France'.[20]

It can indeed be taken as certain that Heinrich went to Sandringham in
December 1912 on the instructions of his brother. His journey just at this
critical time seems of historical significance and all the more remarkable in
that, as will be seen, he was to go to England again, in the last week of July
1914, i.e. a few days before the outbreak of the world war, and in a private
conversation with the King in Buckingham Palace was to ask exactly the
same question about England's attitude in the event of a European war.[21] Both
in December 1912 and in July 1914 Prince Heinrich gave his brother –
presumably with the best intentions but all the same highly irresponsibly –
a rosy account of the King's reply that was far removed from the truth: he even
admitted to the King that in his report to Wilhelm he had left out 'the one
sore point' of their conversation in Sandringham, viz., England's determination not to let her two Entente partners be crippled.[22] The King had
instructed him, Heinrich reported to his brother on 11 December, to tell the
Kaiser that 'if you, Georgie and Nicky would strive to maintain the peace,
all serious danger would disappear. – England is not harbouring any thoughts
of war whatever, and wants to maintain the peace and avoid a European
conflict, just as Germany does.' George's answer to the critical question
about British neutrality was metamorphosed by the Prince from an expressed
royal opinion into a mere 'general impression' he had gained in London – and
even this was further toned down.[23] In his view, England was 'peace loving'
and wished 'to avoid any conflict with us ... Should a serious European
conflict break out which obliged Germany to stand by her treaty obligations
to Austria, then as things stand at present one could perhaps count on
neutrality, but not with England's joining in on Germany's [!] side, for
England will be concerned, as always, to regulate as far as she can the balance
of power on the continent, and presumably throw her weight on the side of
the loser, i.e. the weaker.' As for the King's and Battenberg's clear statements

that in a war Great Britain would stand by France and Russia, Prince Heinrich's letter did not mention them at all.[24]

THE 'ANGLO SAXONS' AND THE 'FINAL STRUGGLE BETWEEN SLAVS AND TEUTONS'

It may well be that Prince Heinrich's performance in London left not only the King and the Battenbergs, but Downing Street too with the impression that Kaiser Wilhelm and Germany's leaders were basking in the illusion that England would be neutral in the event of war on the continent. Certainly their anxieties about German errors of judgement increased with Bethmann's speech in the Reichstag on 2 December, in which the Chancellor, at Moltke's urging, formally assured the Austrians of Germany's support should they have to 'fight' Russia. The very next day Lord Haldane, in a conversation with Lichnowsky, spoke of British support for France in terms that could not be misunderstood: 'In a general European conflict that might arise from an Austrian invasion of Serbia' it was 'hardly likely that Great Britain would be able to remain a passive observer'. The principle of the balance of power was simply 'an axiom' of British foreign policy and had led the United Kingdom to align itself with France and Russia. In Great Britain 'the feeling was general that the balance of power ought to some degree to be upheld' and 'England could therefore under no circumstances tolerate the crushing of the French, which he, as a great admirer of our army and our military establishment, felt would be fairly certain. England cannot be, and is not willing, to be confronted afterwards by a united continent under the leadership of one Power.'[25]

Wilhelm II received Lichnowsky's report clarifying the British position on the morning of Sunday, 8 December 1912. In violent marginal comments and elsewhere he gave free rein to his rage at Britain's balance-of-power policy which was 'nonsense' and would 'make England our enemy for ever'. In the grip of a racialist frenzy, he predicted that in the impending 'final struggle between Slavs and Teutons ... the Anglo-Saxons' would find themselves 'on the side of the Slavs and Gauls' as 'loyal supporters of the Gallo-Slavs against the Teutons!' 'Because England is too cowardly openly to leave France and Russia in the lurch in this event, and is too envious of us and hates us, other nations are not supposed to draw the sword to defend their interests, as then England would go against us after all, despite all her assurances, despite Marschall and Lichnowsky. A real nation of shopkeepers! And they call that a policy of peace! Balance of Power!'[26] As he telegraphed excitedly to his Foreign Secretary, Haldane's declaration to Lichnowsky 'tears apart the veil of uncertainty. Out of envy and hatred of Germany, England will definitely support France and Russia against us. The struggle for existence that the Teutons in Europe (Austria, Germany) may have to wage against the Slavs (Russia) supported by the Romanics (Gauls) finds the Anglo-Saxons on the side of the Slavs. Reason: envy, fear of our becoming too great! A desirable clarification which must be the basis of our policy from now on. We must make military agreements with Bulgaria and Turkey, and with Romania too. We must also make such an agreement with Japan. Any Power we can get to help us will do. It is a question of to be or not to be for Germany.'[27]

Next day the Kaiser impressed on Archduke Franz Ferdinand the need to conclude at last the agreement with Turkey that he had been advocating for so long. The chances were good: 'we must strike while the iron is hot'. He also told him of Haldane's statement that 'if Germany by supporting Austria, became involved in war with France and Russia, England would without hesitation join France, as *she could not permit* our crushing France and *the Continent's becoming united* under German influence, that would be unacceptable to England! He [Haldane] was here in the winter as England's *dove of peace* offering the *neutrality clause* in the event of a European war! Now it sounds different, but really English! Full of venom and hatred and envy that our alliance and our two countries are doing so well! It did not surprise me and the necessary measures are in hand. It is a desirable clarification that reduces the maundering of the English press about peace and friendship to its proper proportions and really exposes its policy in Europe − balance of Power − playing off the Great Powers against each other to England's advantage, in all its shameless nakedness.'[28]

On 10 December 1912 Wilhelm, looking 'very grave and worn out', had a remarkable conversation with the Swiss minister, Alfred de Claparède. 'In agitation', the Kaiser explained to him that the war of the Balkan states against Turkey had been 'simply a racial war, a war of Slavdom against the Germandom', and that Russia had been behind it. 'Her whole idea was gradually to win over all the Slavs in other states, particularly Austria-Hungary, and to weaken Austria militarily by the loss of so many million Slavs . . . Austria had long since recognised this threat, as we had in Germany too, and we would not leave our ally in the lurch: if diplomacy fails, we shall have to fight this racial war.' Wilhelm had then gone on to talk about England, giving vent to his anger at Haldane's statement to Lichnowsky: this 'so-called friend of Germany' had declared 'that England would never tolerate Germany's assuming a predominant role in Central Europe *vis à vis* her neighbours. Is not this an impertinent statement that should really be met by breaking off diplomatic relations with England! Is it not unheard of . . . that these Anglo-Saxons, linked to us by a common origin, religion, and civilising mission should wish to make themselves the tools of the Slavs. It was rather easier to understand that the Romanics, although their civilisation is quite different from that over there in the East, should combine against us in this racial war!' Kaiser Wilhelm then proceeded to explain to the Swiss diplomat 'very forcefully' and 'agitatedly' that 'the creation of a strong Serbian empire directed against Austria and Germany must be prevented. It was a vital necessity for both countries not to let themselves be encircled by a Slav ring. We have renewed the Triple Alliance, and people in St Petersburg know how things stand. If this question – a vital one for us – cannot be settled by diplomacy, then the issue will be decided by force of arms. A solution can be deferred. But the question will come up again in 1 or 2 [years], and then Turkey will have to be reinvigorated: that was my initial policy: a state will have to be created in the Balkans that does not look to St Petersburg, but to Vienna; – on the other hand, Italy will hold the line against the West.' The 'racial struggle could not be avoided', the Kaiser repeated. 'It will take place, perhaps not now, but probably in one or two years' time.'[29]

When on 12 December 1912 Wilhelm received his brother Heinrich's letter misreporting what King George had said at Sandringham he minuted angrily: 'Grey seems to have stuffed the good King full of lies.' The question of England's neutrality was 'already settled! She will go with France!'[30] He informed his brother, to put him right, that Haldane had meanwhile told Lichnowsky 'that in the event of a European war in which Germany was fighting Russia and France, England would *not* remain *neutral* but would *help France against* us. In justification of this statement he explained that England could not tolerate our becoming the strongest Power on the continent and uniting it under our leadership!!! So, to put it bluntly, a *moral declaration of war* which amounts to an *alliance* relationship with France. My diplomats are very taken aback. Not us military men. We have always reckoned with the English as probable enemies, and now they have themselves – dispelling all doubt – declared themselves to be so. We have got a clarification in a *negative* sense, which makes it easier for us to take preparatory measures. By an irony of fate it is that same Haldane who came to Berlin in February with the proposal for a *neutrality clause* – which we accepted – who now, as a possible Europ[ean] war approaches, says the opposite. And now one is supposed to engage in politics with such fellows!' Heinrich's conversations with 'Georgy' showed, the Kaiser continued, 'that the good King hasn't got a clue about politics, and that he has no contact at all with his government, who apparently give him either no information at all – or false information. This is very regrettable, as the weal and woe of Europe depends on his and Nicky's decisions; both great empires are in the hands of very weak rulers with questionable, if not dishonest, advisers!

For us, this all means a need to strengthen our armaments on land and sea. It is only *our* armaments that are upholding the crumbling peace of Europe now.'[31] The thought that his brother might have deliberately misrepresented the King's vitally important statements (which were entirely in accordance with government policy) did not occur to Wilhelm – let alone the thought that he himself, with his injured vanity, his autocratic hyperactivity, his unrestrained militarism and his racialist drive for expansion, constituted a far greater danger to world peace than the 'weak' rulers of England and Russia.

On 13 December 1912 Wilhelm went on to inform the Bavarian envoy Count Lerchenfeld (on whom he had called to express his condolences on the death of the Prince Regent Luitpold) that Haldane had told Lichnowsky 'that if war should break out between the four Powers, regardless of whether Germany attacked or was attacked, England would declare war on Germany. Great Britain could not allow Germany to crush France, and there then to be only one Power on the continent, which would exercise an absolute hegemony.' According to Lerchenfeld's report to Munich, 'H.M. in his account of the affair could not conceal a certain *Schadenfreude* that Bethmann and Kiderlen had been wrong. He said that neither of them has ever had any idea of what people are thinking in England. "I know the English, they will never give up their traditional policy of playing the continental Powers off against each other".' True, Wilhelm conceded that Haldane's declaration did not indicate a desire to go to war, but much rather to move Germany to exert a pacifying influence on Austria. But he stuck to his view 'that if war comes, England will be on the side of our enemies'. The Kaiser had exclaimed: 'The Teutonic English will fight alongside Frenchmen and Russians for the Slavs and against their racial comrades.' For Lerchenfeld, however, the crux of the 'extremely agitated' utterances of the Supreme War Lord was the statement that it would be 'a case of all or nothing for Germany soon, perhaps very soon. Threatened on three sides, we must be prepared for everything and must leave nothing undone to strengthen the army and navy. The German people themselves feel this and are prepared for any sacrifice. People understand that a lost war is far more costly than any number of taxes.' If the Reich Chancellor made difficulties for him, Wilhelm added, he would have to go. In addition to spending on the army and navy Germany must 'look for alliances everywhere', he declared. 'The Romanians are already close to us. Now a treaty should be concluded with Bulgaria.' To Lerchenfeld, too, the Kaiser spoke disparagingly of the Tsar and the King of England. Not that all this made a very favourable impression on the long-serving representative of Bavaria, who confessed to his chief in Munich that 'I could have wished for more cool composure and and a less rhapsodic approach to affairs.'[32]

The Kaiser's agitation was still undiminished and he was still raging against what he alleged to be Great Britain's incomprehensible attitude when he insisted to Albert Ballin in a letter of 15 December that support for Austria-Hungary in her struggle against Serbia and her 'unruly' Slav subjects at home was a vital matter for Germany. 'Austria had reached a turning point and it was a question of *life and death* whether she remained *German* and was ruled in a *German* fashion – and hence remained viable *as an ally* – or whether she was overwhelmed by Slavdom and became *unviable as an ally*. If we are forced to go to war, we should be helping *Austria* not merely to fend off Russia, but to ward off the whole Slav threat and to remain *German*. Id est, a *racial struggle* was impending between the Germans and the overweening Slavs. A *racial struggle* that we shall just have to face, as it is a question of the future of the Habsburg Monarchy and the *existence* of our fatherland. (That was the real theme of Bethmann's forceful speech.) In short, a *question of life and death* for the *Teutons* on the continent. In this, it had been of value that until today England had supported the Austro-German point of view. As now, however, war with Russia means immediate war with *France*, it was of interest to know whether in this – purely *continental* case – England could not quite well declare the neutrality she had proposed to us in February. On 6 [sic!] December Haldane now came to Lichnowsky, apparently on Grey's instructions, and bluntly informed the astonished ambassador: If Germany were involved in a war with Russia and France, England will *not* stay *neutral*, but *immediately* fly to the assistance of France. The reason for this was: England cannot and will *not ever* allow us to establish a predominant position on the continent that would allow it to unite. Hence, England can in no circumstances allow us to crush France. What effect this news had on the whole Wilhelmstrasse you can well imagine! I myself was not surprised by it – as you know, *militarily*, I have always counted England as an enemy – but it amounts to a welcome *clarification*, even if in a *negative* sense.'[33]

WAR DEFERRED UNTIL 1914? THE 'WAR COUNCIL' OF 8 DECEMBER 1912

Anyone reading the above-cited statements of the Kaiser in their entirety will conclude that Europe was already in December 1912 on the brink of a catastrophe such as that which occurred in the summer of 1914. The decision to stand by Austria-Hungary in the '*racial struggle* ... of the Teutons against the overweening Slavs' was clearly a considered one and was even, under pressure from Moltke, announced by Bethmann Hollweg in the Reichstag on 2 December 1912. If Wilhelm had only had his brother's deliberately distorted reports of King George V's statements to go on, a world war might well have broken out at the end of 1912. Only Lichnowsky's report of Haldane's clarification of London's position, which Wilhelm received on the morning of 8 December, destroyed the illusions he had been cherishing about British neutrality. For days on end the Supreme War Lord was only too clearly in a state of racialist and militaristic intoxication. As a 'military man' he had always counted England as an enemy; now it was a question of taking preparatory measures against 'three sides' and of 'leaving nothing undone to strengthen the army and navy'.[34]

Given the extent of the powers he still exercised as Kaiser, King, and Supreme War Lord within the decision-making structure of the Prusso-German military monarchy, the extreme agitation that had seized Wilhelm II was bound to have serious consequences. Immediately on receiving Lichnowsky's report that Sunday morning he telegraphed his 'paladins from the army and navy' — but not the Reich Chancellor or the Foreign Secretary — summoning them to the Schloss to discuss the situation.[35] A whole series of accounts of this conference (which Bethmann angrily described as a 'war council') have survived which, if they do not agree on every point, nevertheless give a reliable picture of the general drift of the discussions. The head of the Naval Cabinet, Admiral Georg von Müller, was present at the meeting and wrote in his diary that same evening that the Kaiser, referring to Lichnowsky's report, had informed the assembled generals and admirals of Haldane's statement that 'England, if we attack France, would unconditionally spring to France's aid, for England could not allow the balance of power in Europe to be disturbed.' Wilhelm, according to Müller, had welcomed the information 'as a desirable clarification of the situation' for those who had felt sure of England. The Kaiser went on to say: 'Austria must deal energetically with the foreign Slavs (the Serbs), otherwise she will lose control of the Slavs in the Austro-Hungarian Monarchy. If Russia supports the Serbs, which she is evidently does (Sazonov's declaration that Russia would immediately move into Galicia if Austria moves into Serbia) then war would be unavoidable for us too. We could hope, however, to have Bulgaria and Romania and also Albania, and perhaps also Turkey on our side. An offer of alliance by Bulgaria has already been sent to Turkey. We have exerted great pressure on the Turks. H.M. has also pressed the Crown Prince of Romania, who was passing through on his way back from Brussels, to come to an understanding with Bulgaria. If these powers join Austria, then we shall be free to fight the war with full fury against France. The fleet must naturally prepare itself for war against England. The possibility mentioned by the Chief of the Admiralty Staff in his last audience of a war with Russia alone cannot now, after Haldane's statement, be taken into account. Therefore immediate submarine warfare against English troop transports in the Scheldt or by Dunkirk, mine warfare in the Thames.' Tirpitz was ordered by Wilhelm to build more U-boats as fast as possible. At this point the Chief of General Staff von Moltke intervened: 'I believe a war is unavoidable and the sooner the better. But we ought to do more through the press to prepare the popularity of a war against Russia, as suggested by the Kaiser's discussion.' The Kaiser welcomed this proposal and ordered Tirpitz to make use of his press contacts to this end. The Grand Admiral argued, however, for 'the postponement of the great fight for 1½ years'.[36] The Chief of the Admiralty Staff August von Heeringen, who was also present at the meeting, actually quoted Tirpitz as saying that 'our chances are at the moment very unfavourable. But in 1914 when the Canal and Heligoland are ready, things will be different'; and this assurance had 'visibly impressed' the Kaiser.[37] The following morning Tirpitz told his colleague Hopman that he had opposed Moltke's pressure for an early war in the meeting, arguing that 'it was in the interests of the navy to postpone the war for 1–2 years if possible. The army too could do a lot in that time to make better use of our surplus population.'[38]

   Although the so-called 'war council' only became known to historians in the 1960s, when it played a central role in the second phase of the Fischer controversy,[39] the military-political gathering of 8 December 1912 very quickly became a topic of conversation in well-informed circles at the time. The military plenipotentiaries of Saxony and Bavaria, in close touch with the General Staff and the Prussian War Ministry, soon discovered 'that the picture behind the scenes is very different from that presented on the official stage'. The Bavarian General von Wenninger reported on 15 December 1912 that the Kaiser was 'in an openly war-like mood': on the previous Sunday he had summoned Moltke, Tirpitz and Müller and informed them, 'in a most agitated state', that Haldane had told Lichnowsky that 'England would stand on the side of Germany's enemies, whether Germany attacked or was herself attacked (Echo of the Chancellor's speech!). England could not look on while France was thrown completely to the ground and a power arose on the continent which possessed absolute hegemony in Europe. Moltke wanted to launch an immediate attack; there had not been a more favourable opportunity since the formation of the Triple Alliance.' Tirpitz, Wenninger continued, demanded 'a postponement for one year, until the Canal and the U-Boat harbour on Heligoland were finished. The Kaiser agreed to a postponement only reluctantly. He told the War Minister the following day only that he should prepare a new large Army Bill immediately. Tirpitz received the same order for the Fleet ... The Kaiser instructed the General Staff and the Admiralty Staff to work out an invasion of England in grand style. Meanwhile his diplomats were to seek allies everywhere, Romania (already partly secured), Bulgaria, Turkey etc.'[40] It was clearly in consequence of this report that on 19 December the new Prince Regent (later King) Ludwig of Bavaria anxiously enquired of the Reich Chancellor as to the Kaiser's intentions. 'In recent weeks the idea has generally got about that His Majesty is pressing for war', he told Bethmann, who denied this just as categorically as he rejected Ludwig's claim that 'His Majesty was planning an invasion of England' and had had a military plan drawn up for it. Bethmann did what he could to convince the Prince Regent that neither he nor the Kaiser personally was harbouring any aggressive intentions whatever towards England.[41]

Was the World War really 'deferred' on the morning of Sunday 8 December 1912, as Fritz Fischer claimed in his controversial book *War of Illusions*, until the work on the Kiel Canal had been completed in the summer of 1914?[42] Did the Kaiser, as Wenninger reported, only consent 'reluctantly' to the 'postponement'? Did he continue to think in terms of a *racial struggle* between Germandom and Slavdom that was inevitable and would 'probably start in one or two years'? The violent criticism to which Fischer's 'deferred war' thesis gave rise in the 1960s is to some extent understandable if one recalls those years, in which professional historians in the Federal Republic still thought in terms of a general 'slithering over the brink' into a war that no Power wanted. But times change, and historians change with them. Today the prime responsibility of the German and Austro-Hungarian governments for precipitating the Great War in July 1914 is no longer seriously questioned; and the 'war council' of 8 December 1912 no longer appears as merely the inexplicable and inconsequential aberration of a politically insignificant and not quite rational monarch. As has been shown, the military-political discussions on that Sunday morning fit seamlessly into a decision-making process whose origins went far back, and which finally led to Armageddon in the summer of 1914. Fischer's opponents would have found it easier to refute his 'deferred war' thesis if the world war had not broken out at the very time that was singled out in December 1912 — immediately after the completion of the Kiel Canal — and on the pretext of a long-anticipated *racial war* between Austria and Serbia.

THE BATTLE WITH THE CHANCELLOR OVER THE ARMY AND NAVY BILLS

If the imminent danger of war had been dispelled for the moment, nothing much had changed as regards the tense political situation and the confrontational constellation of Powers in Europe that winter. On 5 December 1912 the

Triple Alliance between Germany, Austria-Hungary and Italy was renewed
ahead of schedule, but the encirclement of this Central European bloc by the
flanking Powers, France, Russia and Great Britain, was still considered an
unacceptable restriction on the legitimate development of the burgeoning
Wilhelmine Empire. When on 20 December Lichnowsky pointed out yet
again that England, in the interests of preserving the balance of power, would
'in all circumstances extend her protecting hand over France', Wilhelm
again made it abundantly clear that he would not let that deter him from
attacking in the west. Britain's balance-of-power policy, he reiterated, meant
nothing more than 'playing off the continental Powers against each other to
England's advantage!' He simply 'refused to put up with' the 'hemming in' of
Germany by Britain; and he was quite outspoken in his confidence that
France, even with 'British help', would not be in a position to fend off
Germany's superior might.[43]

To strengthen Germany's position vis-à-vis the Entente, the Kaiser had on
8 and 9 December ordered a new Navy Bill and a massive increase in the size
of the army. Both measures amounted to a challenge, not only to England,
but to the continental Powers France and Russia, and a major step in the
direction of war; 'the whole future policy' of the German Reich depended, as
Bethmann recognised, on these decisions.[44] One can well understand the
Chancellor's indignation that the Kaiser, without his participation, or even
knowledge, had summoned a military Areopagus which had taken decisions
about war and peace and made plans for military legislation that he was now
supposed to implement. He had been pained to discover that the Bavarian
Prince Regent had been better informed about the 'war council' of 8 December
than he, the 'responsible' director of German policy. As he complained bitterly
to Eisendecher a fortnight later, Haldane's statement to Lichnowsky had been
'in no way so serious' as the Kaiser had made out. 'It only repeated what we
have known for a long time, that England as ever supports the balance of
power and would therefore stand up for France if the latter is in danger of
being completely annihilated by us in a war. H.M., who despite his policy
demands that England fall all over us, got terribly agitated about it and
immediately – naturally behind my back and Kiderlen's – held a war council
with his paladins from the army and navy – ordered the drawing up of
Army *and Navy* Bills, and trumpeted Haldane's words – fantastically embroi-
dered – to God and the world ... If H.M. wishes, together with Tirpitz, to
make the links [between England and France] absolutely unbreakable, he
should manage this without difficulty with the aid of a new naval *Novelle* ...
England ... does not wish for a continental war, precisely because she would
become entangled in it, and she has herself no wish to fight ... But we, for our

part, ought not to pursue any nervous jumping-jack policies, otherwise the others will some day lose patience.'[45]

On receipt of this cry of alarm Eisendecher wrote a courageous letter to the Kaiser on 23 December, hoping to dissuade him from a new Navy Bill, at least. Haldane's statement, he explained, was obviously 'honest and well meant.' England had an urgent need of peace and did not want to be put in a position of having to fulfil her military obligations to the Entente. It was quite superfluous to embark on further armaments against England. On the contrary, 'sooner or later the two Great Germanic Nations of Europe will have to stand together on the world stage, if Slavdom, Yankees and in the end the yellow race, are not to prevail. Indeed, the time will surely come for the whole of western Europe to unite with Germany and England in the lead.' As the far-sighted old diplomat pointed out – not without a touch of sarcasm – to the navally besotted Kaiser: 'Of course if one thinks that the great conflagration and war with England are inevitable' and that 'the time is right', a new Navy Bill 'would probably be the best way to bring the conflict about'. Like Bethmann, Eisendecher argued for increasing the size of the army; but he regarded new demands for the navy as only justified 'if we want war'.[46]

Informed by Adjutant-General Hans von Plessen of the Kaiser's orders regarding armaments policy, the Reich Chancellor asked the War Minister and Tirpitz to explain what seemed to him to be 'totally impracticable projects'. Both men assured him that the initiative for the new bills had lain, not with them but with the Kaiser. Tirpitz even said that 'His Majesty had already been pressing him for a Navy Bill in the summer.' Very forcefully, Bethmann insisted that the two ministers must 'not commit themselves behind my back, even to His Majesty', and made it clear that he 'could not tolerate any kind of press campaign in favour of the projects'.[47] Aware that Germany's 'whole future policy depended' on these questions of armaments, Bethmann on 18 December 1912 launched a passionate appeal to the Kaiser to leave the military bills aside, at least for the moment, in order not to drive England irretrievably into the arms of France and Russia. As he explained: 'That for us a war with Russia also means a war with France is certain ... On the other hand, it is ... at least doubtful whether England will actively intervene if Russia and France appear plainly as *provoking* the war. Then the English government would have to reckon with public opinion at home. Statements such as Haldane's only show that England would intervene in favour of a defeated France after the event – and even then probably only diplomatically ... In these circumstances it is most desirable that while the present London negotiations [over the Balkans] are going on, the public should not get to know of any German plans for army and navy increases.

That could easily be used against us as a provocation, and would, if it came to a war, do nothing to strengthen us, while it would be likely to shake the confidence of wide circles in Germany in the strength of our existing armaments and give English chauvinists the opportunity they seek to intervene in the war against us immediately. I have the honour most humbly to beg Your Imperial and Royal Majesty, therefore, to instruct the military and naval authorities that any preparations for eventual legislation be kept absolutely secret, and also that the federal states be not informed of them before the Reich departments have come to a decision about them.' Bethmann went on to castigate as 'downright dangerous the agitation in favour of a bigger navy that has already started in the press' (which he rightly ascribed to Wilhelm's order of 8 December to Tirpitz) and asked the Kaiser to instruct the Grand Admiral to stop the press campaign at once.[48]

Bethmann's letter of 18 December 1912 was, let it be said, no plea for peace. On the contrary, the Reich Chancellor was actually assuming that war between Germany and Austria on the one hand and Russia and France on the other was virtually inevitable in the near future, and was only considering by what devices, when it came to contriving this war, England could be kept out of it. Here, he seized on the idea that had already been central to the discussions at the time of Haldane's mission to Berlin: if it could only be managed to represent Russia or France or both as the aggressors, England might possibly stay neutral and only intervene in favour of a moderate treatment of France later during the peace negotiations. This was also the argument employed by the head of the Naval Cabinet, Georg von Müller, when he regretted that it had not been decided on 8 December 'to present Russia or France or both with an ultimatum which would unleash the war with right on our side'.[49]

Kaiser Wilhelm, however, dismissed the Chancellor's optimism as dangerous wishful thinking. Once again, he knew best. He 'did not doubt for one moment' that in the event of a Franco-German war the English would go into action at once. 'Haldane has declared expressly that the possibility of [France's] being crushed cannot be tolerated, therefore England's *immediate* intervention is certain, and not *afterwards*!' The idea that Germany could count on England's neutrality provided she herself avoided all provocation Wilhelm held to be a 'grave fallacy! . . . We can have avoided all provocation as *we* see it, and will still be *represented* as the *provocative party*, as soon as it suits our opponents and the newspapers *in their pay*!' Of course, at the start of every war a provocation 'can *always be concocted* with the aid of some fairly skilful diplomacy and a cleverly managed press (e.g. Spanish Candidature 1870) and must *always be kept ready to hand*'. The Reich Chancellor's arguments against the introduction of new military bills were nothing more than 'the same old stuff that people here bring up against these bills every time! Exactly the same was said last winter against the *Novelle* and it didn't happen anyway!' Even Bethmann's request to restrain the propaganda of the national organisations and the Reich Navy Office met with a harsh rebuff from the Kaiser. The agitation in the press was, 'given the overall situation very understandable and good and worthy of acknowledgement! ... Our people are very disturbed about the situation and are giving expression to their feelings!' Tirpitz had 'nothing to do with it!' The Kaiser sent Bethmann's letter with his marginal comments to all three heads of Cabinet with the order to transmit their contents orally to Tirpitz, the War Minister, and the chiefs of the General and Admiralty Staffs at once. He promised not to say anything about his armament plans to the federal states for the time being, 'but that does not alter the fact about the demands which are to be made later and which I am determined to have'.[50]

Despite all the Reich Chancellor's objections, therefore, Kaiser Wilhelm II stood by his demand for a substantial strengthening of both the navy and the army. As early as 4 January 1913 he ordered Tirpitz at his next audience to present 'proposals for a faster building tempo for the big battleships'. The time had come, he said, to introduce the *dreier Tempo* – i.e. to build three Dreadnoughts per year; the Reichstag would, he was sure, make no difficulties.[51] On the Kaiser's instructions the head of the Naval Cabinet informed the Reich Chancellor 'that H.M. is expecting at long last to receive next Saturday proposals for a naval *Novelle* (stabilisation of the *3er Tempo*)'.[52]

Now, however, Bethmann Hollweg was determined to make a clear stand against a new Navy Bill. On 5 January 1913 he informed Müller that he was prepared to ask the Reichstag for an additional 3–400 million marks for the army, but a simultaneous naval *Novelle* he regarded as 'out of the question'.[53] On the same day he had an audience with the Kaiser which decided the matter. He informed the monarch, who was 'very pleasantly surprised', that he intended to bring in a huge Army Bill, but that 'in view of our relations with England which are becoming more friendly, there must be no naval *Novelle* at the moment. The stabilisation of the *3er Tempo*, while justified in itself, must be postponed for a year.'[54] With this compromise the Kaiser declared himself 'definitely in agreement'.[55] Next day, he sent for his three Cabinet chiefs and told them that he had made 'this concession' to the Reich Chancellor. Müller was given the task of informing Tirpitz of the imperial decision.[56] The Secretary of State at the Reich Navy Office raged 'in very grandiloquent and derogatory' terms about the Kaiser who had again 'toppled over'; but he had no choice but to come into line.[57]

The abandonment of the Navy Bill the Kaiser was demanding had averted for the time being that provocation of England that the Chancellor feared. The idea that England would remain neutral in a continental war, provided that the Dual Alliance, especially Russia, could be cast in the role of aggressor, was gaining ground. Bethmann's decision in favour of a massive army increase therefore implied a thrust towards the east, even though for obvious strategic reasons, to quote Bethmann, 'war with Russia means for us a war with France too'.[58] The Austro-Hungarian General Staff noted with satisfaction that the German Army Bill, which envisaged an increase of nearly four army corps, meant 'a quite extraordinary alleviation of the task of mobilisation and a substantial improvement in the army's readiness for war'.[59] To a certain extent, however, the decision in favour of the Army Bill had implications for future decision-making in respect of timing, too. For the Reich Chancellor was well aware that such a massive increase in the army strengthened the argument for an early strike. He had discussed this very question with Field Marshal Freiherr Colmar von der Goltz on 10 December 1912, explaining that the Reichstag would indeed approve any demands whatever for the army, but 'if we ask for so much now, then we should have to be definitely planning . . . to strike soon'. Goltz confirmed this assessment and reminded Bethmann that Bismarck too had fought three 'preventive wars' that had been 'a blessing for his country'.[60]

The deterrent effect of Lord Haldane's warning of December 1912, that England could not tolerate the crushing of France by the German army, therefore proved short-lived. Instead of bringing Germany to abandon a course that was leading to war, as Haldane had intended, the clarification he gave Lichnowsky had only led to a postponement of the great struggle for supremacy in Europe. Meanwhile — a timespan of one or two years was settled on — Germany's armaments were to be strengthened, the German people enlisted for a war against 'Slavdom', new alliance partners sought in the Balkans and the Near East, and finally, ingenious ways devised of bringing Great Britain, at the decisive moment, to abandon her Entente partners after all. In the first instance, however, it was a question of persuading Austria-Hungary, who had been given a formal and public promise of German support for an attack on Serbia, that the time for this had not yet arrived. The 'final struggle between Slavdom and Germandom' had been postponed but not abandoned.

CHAPTER THIRTY-FIVE

'Berlin has warned us off again.'
The 'postponed racial war against Slavdom'

The war between the four Christian Balkan states and Turkey had given way, on 3 December 1912, to a fragile ceasefire. While the Greeks had been able to take Salonica and the Serbs Üsküb (Skopje), Monastir, and Durazzo (Durrës) on the Albanian coast, the Bulgarian advance on the fortress of Adrianople (Edirne) had been checked. Attempts by the European Great Powers at the London conference of ambassadors to establish a lasting peace in the Balkans foundered on the refusal of the Turks under Enver Pasha to cede Adrianople, and the fighting resumed on 3 February 1913. The Balkan League continued its triumphal march, with the Greeks capturing Janina, the Bulgarians Adrianople, and the Montenegrins Scutari. Europe was several times on the verge of a great war as a result of the simmering conflict between Austria-Hungary on the one hand and, on the other, Serbia or Montenegro, both of whom were protected by Russia. As the British ambassador in St Petersburg wrote on 20 February: 'If we get over this crisis without a European war it will be a miracle.'[1] Only at the end of May did the the Great Powers manage to draw up a preliminary peace, creating an independent Albania that blocked off Serbian access to the Adriatic; but on 29 June, the even bloodier Second Balkan War broke out, when Bulgaria attacked her former allies and found herself at war with Turkey and Romania too. In the Treaty of Bucharest of 10 August 1913, concluded between the belligerents themselves without Great Power intervention, Bulgaria, who had been looking to Vienna for support, was deprived of the greater part of her gains from the First Balkan War, together with Silistria and the Southern Dobrudja, which were taken by Romania.

The upheavals in the Balkan peninsula amounted to a severe setback for the Dual Monarchy, and therefore for the Triple Alliance too. However, fear of a Russian attack and uncertainty as to whether Germany and Italy would then fulfil their alliance obligations held Vienna back from attacking Serbia, now a disquietingly strong neighbour. Kaiser Wilhelm II followed the twists and turns in the Balkans and the complicated negotiations in the 'Concert of Europe' assembled in London, with an intensity that was unusual even for him.[2] After bringing himself to the point, in mid November 1912, of being prepared to help Austria in a war against Russia (and France), on 8 December, as we have seen, after Haldane's warning that Great Britain could not allow France to be crushed, he had accepted Tirpitz's advice to avoid a European war if possible, at least until the completion of the widening of the Kiel Canal in the summer of 1914. The decision-makers in Vienna came to feel the effects of this reversal soon enough: Kaiser Wilhelm and his brother Heinrich, the Chief of General Staff von Moltke and Chancellor von Bethmann Hollweg gave their allies in Vienna to understand, in no uncertain and often wounding terms, that they could not for the present count on Germany's support in the event of war against Russia after all. But the Balkan situation remained critical, and more than once in the months after the 'war council' of 8 December the Kaiser, the generals and the governmnent in Berlin found themselves confronted with the question of whether they really could advocate a further postponement of the conflict which they regarded as 'inevitable'. Thus it might almost have come to a European war in May 1913 if the Montenegrin troops besieging the Albanian town of Scutari had not been withdrawn at the eleventh hour. But although relations between Vienna and Berlin continued to be strained, the moment of decision was nevertheless approaching inexorably. In October 1913 Wilhelm II told the Austrian military and political leaders straight out that he was now ready for the great struggle. It was then, already, that he issued the Austrians with a blank cheque for the war against 'Slavdom' that they were to present for payment in July 1914.

'BERLIN HAS WARNED US OFF AGAIN'

With the ceasefire of 3 December 1912 and the meeting of the London ambassadors' conference the tension in the Balkan situation relaxed at last, and the feverish bellicosity that Haldane's warning had stirred up in Wilhelm II also gradually faded away. On 17 December the Austrian ambassador in Berlin reported after a luncheon in the Schloss that Wilhelm was definitely hoping that peace would be preserved. There was no danger threatening from Russia for the present, as she needed peace more than any other state in Europe. 'In Germany no special measures have been taken for the event of war, but there was no need at all for them anyway, as the German army can be fully prepared for war within six days.' Kaiser Wilhelm had assessed

Austria-Hungary's position as 'quite good'. Bulgaria was 'veritably sucking up to' her, Greece and Montenegro were also looking towards Vienna, 'and he would have to be very mistaken if Serbia, despite her provocative attitude so far, did not give way at the decisive moment'.[3]

In mid December Baron Franz Conrad von Hötzendorf was recalled to the key position of Chief of the Austro-Hungarian General Staff in place of Blasius Schemua. Pleased though Wilhelm II might have been by Conrad's reappointment,[4] on the question of war and peace the views of the Kaiser and the General were at this moment diametrically opposed. Without the backing of the — in his view — 'unreliable' Kaiser the 'new' Chief of General Staff could not get his way in his demand for war against Serbia and/or Russia, especially as after mid December Archduke Franz Ferdinand too supported the concili-atory policy of Franz Joseph and his Foreign Minister Leopold Count Berchtold.[5]

Austrian fears that Germany could, in the event of a Russian '*attack* on Austria *alone* (in the South) sit and do nothing', as the Kaiser put it, were not groundless.[6] In January 1913 Berchtold sent Count Friedrich Szápary on a secret mission to Berlin to consult the Reich Chancellor, Under Secretary Zimmermann and possibly Moltke too, 'to ascertain 1) whether and how far our ally can be counted on in the various possible cases of a serious threat to our interests and 2) what assurances Germany has that Italy would intervene in the event of a general conflagration'.[7] Szápary's report that the German leaders were unwilling to go to war at the present time was received with consternation in Vienna. Conrad, in particular, pleaded now more than ever for war against Serbia into which, if Russia intervened, Germany would be 'dragged' willy-nilly.[8] On 27 January 1913 he unashamedly demanded an immediate war, for fear of Austria's being dragged into a war for German interests at some later moment.[9]

Vienna learned through various channels of the German decision of December 1912 not to risk a war, at least until the completion of the Kiel Canal in the summer of 1914. On 25 January 1913 the Austro-Hungarian naval attaché in Berlin, Captain Hieronymus Count Colloredo-Mannsfeld, had a long audience with Prince Heinrich, in the course of which the Kaiser's brother openly admitted 'that for Germany a war at the present moment would be extraordinarily undesirable'. In an obvious allusion to Lichnowsky's conversation with Haldane and the decisions of the 'war council' of 8 December, Prince Heinrich explained that 'although the same outright aversion to war prevails there, England would, in accordance with its declarations to the German government, certainly stand by Russia and France and intervene actively if the Triple Alliance as such should move towards war. The German

fleet was in a very difficult position vis à vis the English. The problem of
uniting the German Baltic and North Sea squadrons before the completion of
the Canal has been thoroughly explored both in theoretical studies and in
manoeuvres and one can say that the odds on success and failure are more or
less equal. The English naval forces are so superior that if they were all to be
sent against the German North Sea fleet, it would be really difficult to see
what the German fleet could do against them. These remarks of the Prince',
Colloredo noted, 'sounded very pessimistic in comparison to the views one
normally encountered in the German navy'.[10]

In other respects, too, a rift opened up between Vienna and Berlin in the
wake of the 'war council'. On 28 January 1913 the Bavarian military plenipotentiary in Berlin, Karl Ritter von Wenninger, reported that 'people in ruling
circles here are not satisfied with Austria's attitude in Balkan matters'. The
London ambassadors' conference had agreed to allow Montenegro to extend
her territory in the direction of the Adriatic while giving Scutari to Albania,
which was to form an autonomous principality ruled by a Turkish prince
under the control of the protecting Powers. Now, however, the Austrians had
raised objections to this solution. In their view, Montenegro should get
nothing and Albania should be controlled by Austria herself under a Roman
Catholic prince. The result of this mistaken policy, Berlin feared, would be a
revolution in Montenegro that would drive it into the arms of Serbia, who
would thereby gain access to the Adriatic.[11]

These unmistakable signals from Berlin were decisive, if not always welcome in Vienna, where the struggle between the Chief of Staff pressing for
war and the Foreign Minister inclining towards restraint was reaching a
critical point. On 8 February 1913 Berchtold decided that the Dual Monarchy
had absolutely no interest 'in letting things come to a war with Russia'; rather,
it should try 'to solve' the Serbian question 'at a more favourable time, when it
is not threatened with attack from Russia'.[12] Berchtold's doubts about Conrad's
war policy were strengthened immeasurably when a letter of 10 February
1913 from the German Chancellor made it certain that the Dual Monarchy
could not after all count on German support in a war against Serbia and
Russia. After talking to the Kaiser, the Chancellor explained to the allied
Foreign Minister with almost insulting clarity that Germany was not disposed
to fight a world war for the sake of Austria's concerns in the Balkans – all the
more as she hoped, given time, to move England to give up her ententes with
France and Russia. It was certain, the Chancellor argued, 'that the forces
behind the Panslav agitation [in Russia] would gain the upper hand if Austria-
Hungary should get herself into war with Serbia. In that event, whether there
was more sympathy or less for the motives of the I[mperial] and R[oyal]

government would be immaterial. Moreover, if one looks at the matter objectively one must admit that it is almost impossible for Russia, given her traditional relations with the Balkan states, to stand idly by while Austria attacks Serbia without suffering an enormous loss of prestige. The advocates of a peaceful policy, among whom we can certainly count Messrs. Kokovtsov and Sazonov, would simply be swept away by the tide of public opinion if they should attempt to resist it. But the results of a Russian attack are clear as day. They would amount to a war between the Triple Alliance — which Italy would probably *not* support with great enthusiasm — and the Triple Entente, in which Germany would have to bear the whole weight of the Anglo-French attack . . . I should not fail in this connection to point to something which in my view deserves the most serious attention: the changing political attitude of England in recent years. During the annexation crisis [1908–9] England was a driving force behind Russia and pursued a prestige-policy that made a peaceful compromise extremely difficult to achieve. Today, England constitutes a mediatory element, through whom we have time and again been able to exert a calming influence on Russia . . . England's attitude is one of a number of signs that indicate that the policy of ententes has passed its peak, and that we can look forward to a reorientation of English policy, if we succeed in getting out of the present crisis without a war. Of course, it is a question of developments that are in their early stages and which will need some time to mature. But I should deem it an error of immeasurable proportions to resort to a solution by force — even if a number of the Austro-Hungarian Monarchy's interests should call for it — at the present moment when there is even a remote chance of our being able to wage the war on substantially more favourable terms for us.'[13] Berchtold, clearly rattled, forwarded Bethmann's letter to Franz Ferdinand: it expressed 'the German position, that we should not move lest the tender little plant of Anglo-German reconciliation be crushed, with a frankness that one might term impertinent!'[14]

In parallel with Bethmann's warning to Berchtold, Moltke wrote to his opposite number Conrad on 10 February in language that could not have been clearer: the great war between Germans and Slavs would have to be fought 'sooner or later'; but the present moment would be premature. 'The management of a great war between the Triple Alliance and the Triple Entente, or even one against Russia and France alone', Moltke declared, 'will require, if we are to bring it to a successful conclusion, the engagement of all available forces and the exploitation of every chance. To divide our forces would then be more hazardous than ever. If Austria needs all her forces to fight Russia, the same applies to Germany in a war with France. I should recommend, therefore, that even the troops we have standing ready in the East should be

committed in the West, if the need to consider Austria did not prevent it. For
I believe the settling of scores between Germany and France to be central to
the whole European war, and even Austria's fate will in the end be determined
not on the Bug but on the Seine.' He went on to point to the importance of
popular enthusiasm in such a war, claiming (as the Kaiser had so often done)
that this could not be discerned in the present tension between Austria and
Serbia over access to the Adriatic; indeed, Russia must instead be made to
appear the aggressor if an effective slogan for the war was to be found. He
explained to Conrad: 'Your Excellency knows that a war in which the existence
of the state is the issue requires the consent, sacrifices and enthusiasm of the
people. The feeling of loyalty towards Austria as an ally is strong and vital in
Germany, and it would no doubt express itself with elemental force if Austria's
existence should be threatened by a Russian attack. But it would be difficult to
find an effective slogan if the Austrians were now to provoke a war for which
there was no sympathy among the German people.' Instead of starting a war
with Serbia now, Conrad should rather wait for the Balkan League to break
up. In the conflicts between Bulgaria and Serbia, which were sure to follow
once Turkey was defeated, Austria must join with Bulgaria, for then 'Austria
will have complete freedom of action against Russia.' The 'European war'
which 'must come sooner or later' would 'in the last analysis . . . be a struggle
between Germandom and Slavdom', he repeated, quite in the tone of
Wilhelm II. 'To prepare for this is the duty of all states which carry the
banner of Germanic culture. But the attack must come from the Slavs. Anyone
who sees this conflict approaching will realise that it will require: the rallying
of all our forces, the exploitation of every opportunity, but above all the full
sympathy of the people for a decision of world-historical significance.'[15]

In his reply Conrad made much of the pressure of time under which the
Triple Aliance, and particularly the multinational monarchy, was operating.
Against Moltke's view that a European war must come sooner or later, Conrad
pointed out 'that if we wait for the hostility to assume this form − a racial
conflict − we shall then hardly be able to count on the enthusiasm of our Slavs,
who amount to 47% of the population, for the fight against their racial
comrades. At present, the feeling of being bound together by historical ties,
and the cement of army discipline still count − whether they would still do so
in future in the case in point is questionable. The Monarchy, therefore, cannot
let these conflicts develop into a racial struggle; but must try to divide the
South and West Slavs culturally and politically from the East Slavs; to draw
them away from Russia's influence. One of the first preconditions for this is to
check the growth and sovereignty of an independent Great Serbia which
Russia could use as a tool to destroy the Monarchy.' Compared to this

primordial threat, the question of a Serbian port on the Adriatic was in fact a secondary affair for which the monarchy must certainly not go to war. 'But if we just watch while Serbia develops independently and becomes a powerful ally of Russia and a point of attraction for our Southern Slavs, then undoubtedly that Slav menace will grow that will in the end strike at the heart of Germany; and she too will then have to think about when it must counter this threat.'[16]

Conrad received further indications of the motives behind Germany's sudden retreat at the end of 1912 from the report of the military attaché Karl von Bienerth on his conversation with Moltke on 19 February. In response to Conrad's letter, Moltke declared straight out that Germany did not yet wish to take upon herself the risk of war against Russia, France *and* England. 'Starting a world war needs careful consideration. The immediate future is still completely uncertain. It was still an open question whether it will be possible to devise a definitive Balkan settlement without a European war. Here, one should note that despite various attempts to stir her up, France wished to avoid a war. He suspects it is the same with England, but he believes that England has promised France in a written treaty to co-operate in a war against Germany, and so her intervention would have to be reckoned with.'[17] In view of these statements, which sounded so different from the bellicose assurances of November and early December 1912, it is not surprising that the Chief of the Austrian General Staff complained to the German military attaché Count Kageneck at the end of Febraury 1913 that 'Berlin has warned us off again'.[18]

Without doubt, Wilhelm II agreed with his brother, the Chancellor and Moltke that a European war had to be avoided for the time being. On 30 January 1913 he told the Austrian ambassador: 'Whether a future settling of accounts with Russia can be avoided lies in God's hands; but the present moment would be an unfavourable one for either Austria-Hungary or Germany to expose themselves to a world war.'[19] In this conversation, the Kaiser also revealed to Szögyény that he was 'pursuing and striving for the maintenance of peace, but that in the event of the Monarchy's being involved in a war, he would certainly come in with the full force of the Reich. His Majesty said it would be difficult to convince the German people of the need to go to war, as they would not understand the "Durazzo" question. He thought that matters should not be pushed to breaking point on account of a few Albanian towns.'[20] That this was all a matter of a temporary tactical delay until a suitable patriotic slogan was found, the great army budget safely passed, and other preconditions fulfilled, is clear from, among other things, the Kaiser's announcement on the following day (quite in the style of Moltke) that the great showdown between Germans and Slavs was inevitable and now only a matter of time.[21]

At the end of February 1913 the Austrian military attaché listed what he thought were the reasons for the German desire to 'postpone the great decision'. 'I think that in His Majesty's case the idea of spending what is after all his silver jubilee year at peace may count for something, and then, in addition, the fear of England.' As regards the latter, Bienerth continued, his colleague the naval attaché had already reported on a conversation he had had with Prince Heinrich to the effect that 'the German navy would be at a disadvantage so long as the Kiel Canal was not open to heavy battleships of the line and the union of the Wilhelmshaven and Kiel squadrons was possible only by sailing round Denmark. And the fact that the fortification of Heligoland had not been completed also played a role.' On the other hand, Bienerth reported, 'the General Staff is once again emphasising that if the great decision is further postponed, both France and Russia will be able to make good their deficiencies in heavy field artillery and mortars.'[22]

On 24 February 1913 Wilhelm urged on Franz Ferdinand a reduction of the dangerous tension with Russia: 'For the great majority of people in Europe . . . the present state of affairs is a veritable calamity. Especially trade, exchange, communications, finance and credit, not only in your country and Russia, but in Germany and the whole world, are beginning to suffer quite severely from the intolerable tension that has weighed so heavily on Europe for six months now! To alleviate it would be a really epoch-making work of peace, worthy of a *man of energy*, who has the *Moral* courage to utter the *liberating* word, even if it is not always immediately understood, and might even make him moment-arily unpopular with certain groups. And then I often ask myself whether the matters at issue − for example: grazing lands for the goats of Scutari, and that sort of thing − are really so important that you and Russia should still be confronting each other half in arms? . . . ! For, to tell the truth, it is the military measures that Austria-Hungary and Russia have taken that are the chief reason why things cannot calm down. These measures, however, cost a fortune and oppress so many thousands of poor families in need. It is my humble opinion, which I here permit myself to put to you trustingly and in all openness as your loyal well-meaning friend, − that you could without any risk consider gradually reversing these measures, provided, naturally, that Russia does the same à tempo; and, according to my private information, Russia would undoubtedly cooperate . . . I should welcome this wholeheart-edly. Austria-Hungary would, on the one hand, prove to the whole world that she is not nervous, and on the other gain the sympathy of all those in the world who have been hit by the prolonged crisis and are starting to become alienated and look at you askance. A really appropriate time for starting the "disarmament" – and also for presenting it to the outside world to the best effect – would be the 300-year jubilee of the House of Romanov, which would certainly give the Emperor Nicholas sincere and heartfelt pleasure; and enable him to stage the celebrations against a peaceful instead of a warlike background! ... Now this would be a really excellent opportunity, would have a grandiose effect, and be welcomed with sheer joy all over the world.'[23]

When shortly afterwards Franz Ferdinand wrote to inform him of a letter, drafted by Berchtold, which he had written to the Tsar,[24] the Kaiser congratulated his 'dear Franzi' in enthusiastic terms: 'What great pleasure your dear letter gave us! In this case one can justly say "Les beaux esprits se rencontre!" Bravo my friend! You have handled it and carried it out brilliantly! It has certainly not been easy, and the task demanded effort, patience and staying power! But afterwards the success, which makes up for all the hardships involved. You have rendered an immortal service, for you have broken the spell that was crushing Europe. Millions of grateful hearts will remember you in their prayers. I think that the Emperor Nicholas will also be glad that he can send his reservists home! Everybody will breathe again when that happens.'[25]

'WITH WEAPON IN HAND': THE KAISER AND AUSTRIA IN THE SCUTARI CRISIS

Wilhelm II continued his policy of pushing Austria towards reconciliation with Russia in the spring too, when the Montenegrins and Serbs resumed their attack on the fortress of Scutari that had been assigned to Albania. Aware that Serbia's advance could soon lead to a world war, the Kaiser initially displayed an astonishing willingness to leave the whole of Albania and Montenegro to Serbia. Thus, he minuted on a report of the incursion of Serbian troops into Albania on 6 April 1913: 'Then they should in the devil's name stay in there and finish off Albania altogether! ... And the Serbian troops going in there are intended for the *occupation* of Montenegro. Then Serbia would stretch from the Austrian-Bosnian to the Greek frontier, and include Albania. A grand concept, for which the troops are well positioned and which cannot be prevented; except by putting the whole Austrian army in the field!' Wilhelm continued: 'I am of the view that in this most serious situation the Albania plan can no longer be maintained. It looks as though Serbia will not get out, and she has made herself at home there; just as she is going about assembling enough troops in Montenegro to render her totally dependent. If Serbia is firmly determined to hold these territories with the help of her whole army, then no diplomacy, no notes, no naval demonstrations will be of any use. To dislodge her would require a campaign of several months by the whole Austrian army, and that would constitute the casus belli for Russia and the world war would be here! Either the [London] conference immediately offers Nikita [King of Montenegro] an equivalent for Scutari, province and town – possibly at Albania's expense – or Serbia does so herself and shares Albania with him, if she doesn't swallow him up too! Anyhow, Serbia now becomes the chief actor and behind her *unofficial Russia*!'[26] In view of the danger of war, Wilhelm demanded that Austria should give up her demands for an autonomous Albania; independent action by Austria-Hungary against Serbia and Montenegro would mean 'withdrawing from the Europ[ean] conference' and would conjure up the danger of a war with Russia. 'In any case', he added, 'it must be pointed out to Vienna that the leadership rests with London, and that Vienna, like all of us, must calmly await what London does . . . The Europ[ean] conference has to decide. Not Vienna alone.'[27]

On this occasion, too, the lack of German backing proved decisive for the policy-makers in Vienna, where Conrad (as always) was pressing strongly for war, while Franz Joseph, Franz Ferdinand and Berchtold continued to strive to keep the peace. On 22 March 1913 Conrad begged Berchtold to send Serbia and Montenegro an ultimatum demanding the evacuation of Albania, and in the event of a refusal to mobilise against both states. 'I must stress the necessity for action in the grand manner as the only right one in military terms, and speak out against all half measures and footling enterprises . . . The danger arising from Russia's attitude must be taken on board, – but a firm attitude on Germany's part could perhaps avert a threat from this quarter.'[28] True, the uncertainty as to 'how far Germany and Italy would throw their loyalty as allies into the balance' made even Conrad hesitate.[29] On 15 April, however, he again explained to the aged Emperor 'that a satisfactory outcome of the Balkan crisis would only be possible for the Dual Monarchy if it decided to leave the Concert of the Powers and pursue its interests by force of arms'.[30]

Franz Joseph still refused to take this fateful step, but the pacific attitude that Wilhelm II had assumed since 8 December 1912 was to change in the course of spring 1913. The more acute the crisis on the Adriatic became, the more impatient he grew at the inability of the 'Concert of Europe' assembled in London to take action.[31] In the hesitation of the conference of ambassadors to decide on energetic measures to compel Montenegro and Serbia to withdraw from Northern Albania Wilhelm discerned a Russian conspiracy, in which Grey had evidently joined. Furious, he wrote on a telegram from Lichnowsky of 26 March 1913, 'so, the Russians don't want to! Then Grey doesn't want to either! Then the whole thing is dropped! That is, the Russians are in the commanding position in the conference of ambassadors and we have to come into line! Extraordinarily dignified for the rest of us Great Powers! . . . Then Panslavism (sub nomine Sazonov) is in the end the master of the ambassadors' conference, which only carries out his ideas. That, I am *not* inclined to put up with in the long term. Grey must show exactly the same consideration for the wishes of the public in Austria, Italy and Germany as for the public in Russia! Lichnowsky must tell Grey this in all friendliness but with all clarity!'[32] Elsewhere, he scolded: 'The Russians do not *want* to put pressure on Montenegro under any circumstances. They are playing a shameless double game with us, dragging things out to prevent our intervention and stiffening the resistance of the Balkan states! This is disgraceful behaviour!'[33] On 4 April the Kaiser expressly welcomed Tschirschky's report that he was reminding the decision-makers in Vienna of the necessity, if they resorted to force against Montenegro, of 'so arranging things that Russia is in the wrong and that she or her satellites appear as the aggressors'.[34]

Gradually the Kaiser began to fear that for Austria to abandon her demands for an autonomous Albania would amount to a severe loss of prestige for the Dual Monarchy. At the beginning of April 1913 he spoke of Austria's and Italy's 'absolute obligation' to stand united 'in defence of Albanian autonomy, if necessary by *military* force'. 'That is, a common Austro-Italian action against *Serbia* . . . It is to be hoped that Rome and Vienna reach agreement on this as rapidly as possible and let us know what they have decided to do. Obviously, I support their action. For it might serve to salvage Vienna's one political success in the total shambles of its failed Balkan policy, namely an autonomous Albania. And we must help Vienna to achieve such a success coute qui coute – even with weapon in hand! Moreover, this united action by Austria and Italy would strengthen and improve the relations between them and consolidate the 3 Alliance.'[35]

The Kaiser adopted this martial tone, significantly, on the assumption that Great Britain would join the Triple Alliance Powers for a naval demonstration against Montenegro, in which neither Russia nor France would participate. That would at last produce the power-constellation he had long striven for. As he wrote with glee: 'England at the side of the 3 Alliance in the Mediterranean demonstrating against Slavdom! Who would have thought such a thing possible a year ago! Almost too good to be true. One has to see it to believe it!!! oh Triple Entente!!!? . . . That is, the civilisation of Europe united against Asiatic Slavs and Tartars! . . . We are coming! . . . A ship must be sent there immediately. If there is a senior Engl[ish] or Austr[ian] admiral on the spot, the "Goeben", if not, then the "Breslau", as we don't need to take over the leadership of the demonstration.'[36] In the hope that as a result 'the 3ple

Entente could break up' the Kaiser crowed: 'It now shows how incredible, foolish, wrong-headed and contrary to England's interests English policy has been so far, of going with the 3ple Entente against us. Now England is faced with the choice between upholding her prestige and interests in association with the 3 Alliance while letting the 3ple Entente go; and working with the 3ple Entente against her own interests.'[37]

Of course, Great Britain did not join the Triple Alliance, nor did the Triple Entente break up; rather, Grey supported Russia and France, which sharpened the confrontation between the two blocs in the Balkans once again. As the Kaiser indignantly exclaimed on 6 April 1913: 'Then the 3ple Entente would stand against the 3 Alliance, the Conference would be derailed, and it would be Europ[ean] War!'[38] Perhaps it was the feeling of being on the brink of historic catastrophes that lay behind Wilhelm's repetition on 17 April of his order of November 1912 to the Auswärtiges Amt, to send him copies of 'all the All-Highest handwritten memoranda, telegrams and marginal commands relating to the current Balkan crisis in order to secrete them in the archive of the Royal House'.[39]

The crisis came to a head when news arrived that Montenegrin troops had taken Scutari on 23 April 1913. The bafflement of the ambassadors in London in the face of Nikita's stubborn refusal to evacuate the city only confirmed Wilhelm's disdain for the Concert of Europe and transformed his attitude towards a unilateral military action by Austria-Hungary. The 'pussyfooting!' London conference was engaged in an 'ostrich-policy', he thundered. 'Given such pathetic, lamentable behaviour, Nikita can do whatever he likes. For example, invite the whole corps diplomatique to the victory parade!' A proposal that officers from the international squadron assembled at Durazzo might be sent to Scutari, he rejected with scorn: 'For God's sake, the poor fellows! To play the roles of policemen and burgomaster in Scutari!! Far from their ships!!! ... Sweeping the streets! Brothels! ... That will be nice! Frightful nonsense!' If no better solution could be found, 'then Austria will take action!'[40] 'If S[ir] E. Grey doesn't *take action* swiftly, energetically and decisively, the unity of the Powers will come to an abrupt end! They cannot respond to the seizure of Scutari with mere resolutions.' An Austrian decision to proceed, either alone or with Italy, against Monetenegro was '*bound* to be taken, given that Grey and the ambassadors' conference do not respond with anything stronger than phrases to the capture of Scutari, which is a direct slap in the face for the Powers! Austria cannot put up with such insolence for ever, as it would mean the end of her sole political achievement (the creation of Albania).' Grey's desire to maintain the Concert of Europe to hold Austria back from unilateral action was '*impossible in the long run* and we cannot go

along with such lamentable feebleness in aeternum without seriously damaging our self-esteem ... In short, if Grey does not decide on milit[ary]
intervention very soon, the ambassadors' conference is over for me! For high
words do not do any good any more!'[41] Already on the next day the Kaiser had
to accept that Italy would not join in an Austrian military action. He now had
to fear that 'in that case ... the 3 Alliance is going to pieces!' while on the
other hand there were signs that 'the 3ple Entente is coming together again!'
He was affronted to see that 'the desire to hold the Triple Entente together is
still stronger than to knock Nikita down and make him obey!'[42] From Bad
Homburg Kaiser Wilhelm sent orders to propose to the London conference a
kind of military sanction against Montenegro, to be implemented by Austria
and Italy under British leadership. 'Should England unexpectedly let us down,
then Lichnowsky would have to propose that Austria *and* Italy, or, if that were
not attainable, Austria alone, should receive a mandate.' Failing such a
mandate, however, Austria would 'absolutely' have to be held back 'from
unilateral action at the moment'.[43]

As the Kaiser ordered, Lichnowsky was instructed to ask the ambassadors'
conference to give Austria and Italy a mandate for intervention, under British
leadership, against Montenegro. The ambassador recognised, however, that
both the British and Russian governments wanted to gain time, and were
asking whether cessions of territory elsewhere and financial inducements
might not yet bring Montenegro to evacuate Scutari. When France and Italy
endorsed this initiative, Lichnowsky refrained from making his proposal. On
27 April 1913 the Auswärtiges Amt instructed the ambassador to declare at the
conference that if the other Powers did not agree to entrust Austria and Italy
with a mandate, Germany alone would give Austria-Hungary her permission
to take military action. In Rome, too, the Germans took diplomatic steps to
induce Italy to support Austria, at least formally.[44]

This 'energetic and clear attitude [of Berlin] in favour of the Austrian
position', gratefully received in Vienna, was expressly endorsed by Kaiser
Wilhelm.[45] He poured scorn on the efforts of George V to calm the Austrians
down. The King's recommendations were 'Rubbish!' and 'Nonsense!' Neither
George nor anyone else could say what should be done if Nikita should
establish himself in Scutari, 'newly fortified, reprovisioned, and with fresh
supplies of money and ammunition'. Nobody had the courage 'to face up to
this possibility and to resort to shooting. To make great speeches – gladly; but
to defend one's honour and point of view by armed force, no! There could be a
firefight! The British want to watch that *from the outside*!' 'Incredible rubbish!', was the comment of the Supreme War Lord of the German Reich when
King George said that he did not wish to send troops to Scutari because he

could not risk English soldiers being fired on. 'Why not?' Wilhelm asked, 'are they only to be used against Germany now? Otherwise, they have already been fired on by the whole world.' The King had proved yet again that he was 'not a military man'. England was withdrawing from the game, 'and when it comes to an explosion *on the Continent*, will *at first* stick to the comfortable role of tertius gaudens and let her leadership of the Europ[ean] Conference fade away without so much as a whimper. Only later will the sacred soldiers be sent into action, *against us!*'[46]

In the event of an Austrian military action against Scutari the Kaiser and the Wilhelmstrasse were calculating, significantly enough, that if Serbia decided to intervene she would put herself in the wrong and that therefore England would initially stay neutral in any major war that might then arise. This thought was clearly expressed in a private letter that Gottlieb von Jagow sent to Tschirschky on 28 April 1913: 'We declare in St Petersburg that the Austro-Montenegrin and Austro-Serbian conflicts are local ones in which the other Great Powers have no grounds for intervention and must therefore keep quiet. We should also have to make the same declaration in Paris and London, alluding to the inevitable consequences that must follow if Russia attacks Austria. It is very important for us to have the role of provoked party as I think that England would then – and only then – be able to stay neutral.'[47] As we shall see, it was exactly this miscalculation that, fourteen months later, lay at the root of German policy in the July crisis.

Very much in the same vein, on 30 April Wilhelm II advised putting limits on any military action by Austria. 'If she goes in, she should confine herself to *Montenegro*, and possibly the Sanjak; but *leave it up to* Serbia, whether she wishes to take *action* against Austria. If she does, Serbia puts herself in the wrong and Russia is not necessarily compelled to attack Austria.'[48] On the other hand, the Kaiser pressed for immediate Austrian action against Montenegro, and was decidedly opposed to Grey's attempts to find a peaceful solution to the Scutari question through concessions to Montenegro. 'Here it is a question of enforcing the will of Europe on a defiant Nikita, not of concessions to him!' When Grey proposed that the impending chastisement of Montenegro by Austria-Hungary should be 'moderate', Wilhelm asked sarcastically 'What is a moderate war?!!!' In Grey's hesitation over approving unilateral action by Austria-Hungary Wilhelm discerned partisanship for Russia and France against the Triple Alliance, and he wrote in great excitement on Lichnowsky's telegram: 'Vive la triplice . . . France is victorious and the 3 Alliance falls for it! Exactly as I predicted! At the first whiff of gunpowder England runs for cover! . . . Grey has opted for France! and against us!'[49] When Italy, too, declared for Grey's compromise proposal, the Kaiser exclaimed '3 plice + Italy! This is getting nicer and nicer!'; and he also objected when the ambassadors' conference agreed to a brief delay in taking action against Monetenegro. 'What's this?' he asked. 'Can take months! It's all just to cheat Vienna out of taking action ... How long are the Austrians *to go on* waiting?' The suggestion that Grey might criticise Austria's attitude in the Commons drove him into a fury: 'If he is so incredibly insolent as to do this, the Conference is finished! It is not for him to tell H.M. the Emperor [Franz Joseph] what to do, nor has he either to approve or disapprove.' Austria's patience had already been tried to the limit. England's unconcealed dependence on France was, in the Kaiser's view, shameful: 'Poor England, to have fallen so low, what would Nelson have said!!' On the other hand, Germany evidently 'counted for nothing' with the British Foreign Secretary. All the efforts of the Powers were being directed towards 'making it impossible for Austria to intervene!' In a blazing rage, he scribbled on a telegram from Tschirschky on 1 May 1913: 'I think the limit has been reached for Austrian hesitation, and only a quick decisive blow can resolve this situation, which has got bogged down to the point of becoming ridiculous. The more Austria goes on temporising and giving way and putting things off, the more untenable her situation becomes, externally *and internally* too ... Grey has for long been of the Gallo-Russ[ian] opinion that Montenegro *can* stay in Scutari. And to cover up his total lack of character, cowardice and the abandonment of all his fine phrases and notes to Montenegro – in Chinese, to save his face – he assumes the role of "saviour" and "upholder" of a) the 3 plice and b) the *unity* of the Conference *at the expense of Austria and the 3 Alliance*! That is, he is *deliberately* pursuing an anti-Austrian policy, as he is perfectly well aware of Austria's situation *externally and internally* and it is clear, and he must tell himself this, that she *cannot* act otherwise! The suggestion that he might include a disparaging remark about Austria in his statement to Parliament is an act of disgraceful disloyalty. The result would be an instant explosion in Austria, and here too, and in Russia most of all: so the *leader* of the Europ[ean] conference, its so called *"upholder"*, *deliberately* gives the signal for the world conflagration! A truly British concept, but politically dishonourable and disloyal to the highest degree! One cannot remain on political terms with such a man.'[50]

If on this occasion the peace was saved at the last moment, this was not attributable to any lack of readiness on Germany's part to support the Dual Monarchy. On the contrary, Under Secretary Zimmermann informed the Bavarian military plenipotentiary Wenninger on 2 May 1913 that 'after Berlin had stiffened the backbone of the Austrian foreign policy leadership last Saturday, their energy soon began to flag; only Conrad von Hötzendorf was for decisive action as before, while Berchtold and even Archduke Franz Ferdinand again appeared to waver. It will need another push of support from Germany if Austria is to go through with it. In Rome, too, cross-currents are constantly surfacing that call in question the results of German advice – the agreed parallel action with Austria. "The best thing for us would be," Zimmermann said, "if Austria and Italy divided Albania between themselves, Austria taking the northern and Italy the southern half, that would be the simplest solution of the Albanian question".' When Wenninger questioned whether Russia and the Balkan states would tolerate this, 'Zimmerman replied that Russia had throughout the entire business demonstrated a remarkable love of peace in order, he suspected, to hide her fear of war and revolution. The Balkan states would not be asked.'[51]

A European war seemed imminent and Germany was ready to put the notorious Schlieffen Plan, as modified by Moltke, into operation. On 5 May 1913 the Quartermaster-General of the General Staff, Georg Count von Waldersee, told the Bavarian military plenipotentiary that the reports that Scutari had been evacuated were untrue and that 'the situation was more serious and more confused than ever'. He enquired as to the readiness of the two Bavarian army corps for war and told Wenninger that there was to be 'a conference between the General Staff and the Admiralty Staff' that very afternoon – 'what the subject would be, Count Waldersee was not allowed to say'.[52] The following day Waldersee let slip that those who had attended this new war council had been reckoning absolutely with the outbreak of a European war, and said to his Bavarian colleague straight out: 'Even if today – with the easing of the situation – we can no longer say that we are on the point of mobilising, I can tell you now that my enquiry yesterday about sending the Bavarian army corps into action was in fact a last check up.' With the announcement of Nikita's readiness to evacuate Scutari, the acute danger had passed for the moment, but 'so long as Scutari has not actually been evacuated and occupied, without a hitch, by the troops that have been landed ... and so long as it is not absolutely clear that Austria and Italy are finally renouncing any Albanian expedition, then, given the "uncertain" attitude of England and Russia and the apparent propensity of France for "Putsches" the danger of war is still imminent'.[53]

THE 'UNAVOIDABLE STRUGGLE BETWEEN SLAVS AND TEUTONS'

Even if the Germans had been prepared to face the risk of a European war over Scutari in May 1913, they still preferred a later date for the great settling of accounts. In Vienna Tschirschky stressed to Berchtold that 'all the last wars have been won by those who prepared for them for years ... We [Austrians] ought to prepare for a war that should bring us Serbia, Montenegro and North Albania, Italy Valona, and Germany the victory over Panslavism.'[54] Moltke, who had not been present at the critical meeting of 5 May — he had been taking the cure in Karlsbad — discussed the situation with the Austrian military attaché on his return to Berlin and emphasised that the 'purely diplomatic solution of the Scutari question' that had been achieved was 'only a postponement, not a solution. Hence the strengthening of the German army.' He now expressed the hope that Conrad von Hötzendorf too 'would strive to strengthen the I[mperial] and R[oyal] army as much as possible'.[55] In their next conversation on 18 June Moltke could tell the attaché of his pleasure at the increase in the Dual Monarchy's fighting forces that had since been decided on. 'As in his opinion the next war can only be a European one, involving all the continental states, so the aim must be to create the most favourable conditions possible for it, in order to act with maximum effectiveness. In earlier times Turkey had still counted as a power-factor on the continent. Now she has been eliminated, and instead we have to reckon with the Balkan states that are now stronger and will probably tie down a considerable part of the Monarchy's forces.' These considerations were 'one reason for the new increase in the German army'; and by strengthening its own army the Dual Monarchy was now for its part improving 'its position vis-à-vis the East'.[56]

Kaiser Wilhelm II was no less convinced than his Chief of General Staff that, even if it had been avoided for the moment, a great war would come in the foreseeable future. Brashly, he minuted on a report of 6 May 1913 from St Petersburg: 'The struggle betw[een] Slavs and Germans can no longer be avoided and will surely come. When? We shall see.'[57] As monarch and War Lord he dismissed with scorn the efforts of the diplomats to maintain the fragile peace. 'Thank God' it was not the diplomats but the crowned heads of Europe who were in charge; they took the decisions which 'the diplomatic gentlemen will have to obey', he noted at the end of May, after meeting Nicholas II and George V in Berlin on the occasion of his daughter's wedding (see Figure 39).[58]

During the wedding celebrations Kaiser Wilhelm had a long and far-ranging talk with King George's Private Secretary, which Lord Stamfordham (as Sir Arthur Bigge now was) thought so indicative of the mindset of the German monarch that he reported on it in no fewer than four memoranda, so as to miss none of its nuances. As regards the war in the Balkans, Wilhelm told the astonished Englishman: 'This war has upset the whole of the East & it will some day raise a question not British, or Russian but international, for it will

Figure 39 The cousins Wilhelm II and George V at Potsdam for the wedding of
Princess Viktoria Luise, the Kaiser's daughter, on 24 May 1913,
Queen Victoria's birthday

be racial. – The Slavs have now become unrestful & will want to attack
Austria. Germany is bound to stand by her ally. – Russia and France will join
in & then England – fighting against the Anglo-Saxons & the Culture of the
world. He cannot understand how we wish to join the Latin Races in
preference to the Teutons. "I know this, that you are engaged to help the
French."' When Stamfordham pointed out 'that only an unprovoked attack
would involve us', the Kaiser mockingly replied: 'And will you tell me what an
unprovoked attack is – Is it enough to knock your cap off or must I kick your
shins. Look at that Morocco business: I know that [Sir John] French was over
in France or your Staff Officers were & you promised to send 100,000 troops &
that's what made us so sore. I am a man of peace – but now I have to arm my
Country so that whoever falls on me I can crush – & crush them I will.'
Wilhelm went on: he had given the Tsar clearly to understand 'that if Austria
is attacked, he would be absolutely obliged to support her: he could not desert
the old Emperor Franz Joseph, with all his past defeats, his sorrows etc.' 'How
could I do anything other than stand by him?' he cried. The English, Wilhelm
said, 'talk a good deal about the balance of power & that to maintain it you
joined the *Entente*: but *Germany* holds the balance of power'. 'He must arm

every man available, especially considering the combination against him.' Over and above that, the course of events would be determined by Providence. 'I am always telling people that in their calculations they forget Providence but I do not.' Then the Kaiser went on to speak 'earnestly about the yellow peril & said Japan was working against us in India: he had seen a copy of an anti-British proclamation 600,000 of which had been distributed by Japan in India. We [the English] have withdrawn all our ships from the Pacific: as soon as the Panama Canal is open America & Japan will compete for supremacy in those waters – and we have assembled all our ships in the North Sea, & why? because we are idiotic enough to think that he wants to attack us – ! We don't prevent other countries from building ships & really must not think they are intended to use against us – we must not be like Nero who, when he saw people laughing in the streets, was sure they were laughing at him! There was room enough for us both in the world & he was a man of peace & wished above all to be at peace with England.'[59]

During the Scutari crisis of May 1913 when the General Staff and the Admiralty Staff assembled for the second time in six months for a sort of war council, the question of the still unfinished Kiel Canal became acute again. Shortly after the crisis meeting of 5 May the new head of the Admiralty Staff, Hugo von Pohl, declared that in view of the danger of war and Haldane's well-known declaration of December 1912, the big battleships that could not yet pass though the Kiel Canal would have to be based in the North Sea. Germany, he wrote to Tirpitz on 9 June 1913, must 'at all events remain prepared for a war with England. That seems to me all the more necessary as Lord Haldane, as Your Excellency knows, told our ambassador in London that in the event of a conflict between the Triple and Dual Alliances England will take the side of the Dual Alliance, if it cannot prevent the conflict.'[60] Like the Kaiser, the Wilhelmstrasse and the General Staff, the Imperial Navy clearly preferred to postpone the 'great struggle', at least until the widening of the Canal had been completed.

'WILL O' THE WISPS'. THE OBJECTIVES OF WILHELM II'S NEAR EASTERN POLICY

The efforts of Bethmann Hollweg, the Auswärtiges Amt, Lichnowsky and Kühlmann to bring about a rapprochement with Great Britain by working closely with Sir Edward Grey at the London ambassadors' conference were undermined by Wilhelm II's warlike impatience. Repeatedly he threatened to abandon the 'Concert of Europe'. 'I am not going along with these embarrass-ing farces of the Europ[ean] Concern – not Concert – any more, and shall from now on go my own way in dealing with the belligerents, as is best for us and without regard for others!' he exclaimed.[61] He accused the British Foreign Secretary of always giving way to Russian and French pressure, and so sacrificing 'all the interests of Austria and the 3 Alliance! ... I cannot go along for ever with such a Schweinerei without protesting! ... Nor can we expect our people to put up with them!'[62] 'For such home-baked feeble tosh we did not need either the Pacificator Mundi Grey or a months-long London Conference! He has made a brilliant fool of himself!' the Kaiser declared in June 1913, on the eve of the Second Balkan War.[63]

In contrast to Grey, striving to prevent further bloodshed by tireless manoeuvring between the six Great Powers of the ambassadors' conference and the representatives of the Balkan states and Turkey, who were engaged in parallel negotiations in London, the Kaiser, as a 'military man', continued to insist that only after a decisive result on the battlefield would a solution be attainable. 'I am for fighting first, then for working out clear preliminaries of peace on the battlefield, in which the Powers can intervene. But there can be no intervention so long as there is no concrete instrument of peace between the belligerents. The one party must first win a decisive victory and the other admit defeat.' Otherwise the result will only be 'nonsense and confusion'. 'Nothing is decided, no victor, no loser, nobody gives way, and the one demands to be treated just as well as the other. Anybody who now *prevents a conflict* will take upon himself all the odium of *both sides* over the peace terms. I shall have no part in it!'[64] The different solutions proposed by Grey for the tiresome question of Adrianople Wilhelm II dismissed as 'rubbish', declaring that 'I have had enough of this muck and shall not join in such nonsense any longer! Let the ruffians fight each other and bring the matter to a conclusion that clarifies the situation.'[65] The Turkish government's proposal to occupy Adrianople jointly with the Bulgarians Wilhelm rejected out of hand as 'absolute idiocy!' Instead of a compromise he again demanded a clear military decison on the battlefield. 'Such silly proposals will not be agreed to by any victorious opponent. Adrianople or War! That is the Bulgarian slogan. A joint occupation of the city is complete madness! The French and us in Metz!'[66]

With the recapture of Adrianople by the Turks in the summer Wilhelm II began to hope that if Russia intervened in favour of Bulgaria she would appear as the disturber of the peace of Europe.[67] Grey's suggestion that Germany might join with Russia in moving the Turks to evacuate Adrianople, precisely in order to prevent a unilateral action by Russia, met with an impassioned rejection from the Kaiser. 'If he is *afraid* of single-handed action by Russia – which I am not – then let *England* act together with Russia and try to bully the Turks out, and earn the odium of the Moslem world; why should we be so stupid as to do this for England?' To the Kaiser it was clear: 'What Herr Grey cannot do himself, as it is too prickly for him, the maid Germania is to do, as Britannia wants to go fishing and shooting grouse! – I am not worried that Russia might undertake anything *alone* against Turkey, for the simple reason that she is not in a position militarily to do so and is too weak. Should she do something nevertheless, well, so much the better, as she will split herself off from England and possibly France too, and the 3ple Entente will be in ruins. That can only suit us. For Russia and Germany to *"propose"* – as Grey suggests – that Turkey should evacuate Adrianople is really naïve! Because he is afraid of his Indian Mohammedans, we are supposed to do England's work and take the odium upon ourselves. We should not dream of doing so! It is up to Stamboul to consider carefully whether it wants to stay in Adrianople at all or not! And to take its decisions *free* from any pressure from us. If it should then reach the conclusion that it would be more practical to follow the earlier advice of the Powers and leave the city to the Bulgarians, then Stamboul will take that path and agree about it with Bulgaria *directly*. If, on the other hand, the pressure of the Mohammed[an] world is too strong, and if for reasons of prestige Stamboul has to stay there for the present, then it is not for Germany to offend Moslem feelings unnecessarily and turn them against herself by giving advice to the contrary. Hence, Grey's suggestion of a German-Russ[ian] action against Stamboul over Adrianople must be absolutely rejected! It is now a matter of the sensitivities of the government in Stamboul and of its relations with the Turkish Army! In other words: Grey is afraid that his ally Russia might withdraw from the Entente, and we are supposed to help him to hold onto Russia! I wouldn't dream of it!'[68]

Wilhelm's position in the Balkan crisis was still determined by far-reaching geopolitical expectations of a breakthrough to German supremacy in the Near and Middle East; but with the return to power of the Young Turks under Enver Pasha in Constantinople on 23 January 1913 and the advance of Bulgaria, where Russian and French influence prevailed, his original concept of a power constellation to achieve his long-term objective had changed. Instead of setting his hopes – as he had done at the start of the Balkan wars – on a combination of all the Balkan states as a seventh Great Power, and instead of dreaming of an alliance between Bulgaria and a regenerated Turkey to give Germany command of the Near and Middle East as far as Odessa, India and Egypt, he now demanded the construction of an 'iron ring' round Bulgaria and a combination of the Triple Alliance and the remaining Balkan states (including Serbia) and Turkey. Wilhelm II's anti-Bulgarian policy brought him increasingly into opposition to the government in Vienna, which was counting precisely on Bulgaria for support against the Pan-Serbian aspirations of Belgrade. At the same time, Wilhelm's support for Greek ambitions in the Adriatic offended not only Austria, but, as will be seen, Germany's other Triple Alliance partner, Italy.

As soon as Austro-Russian relations began to relax in February 1913 Wilhelm came forward with his new Balkan project. A rapprochement between the Habsburg Monarchy and Serbia, Greece, Romania and Turkey should establish 'a solid ring round Bulgaria' and further the extension of Triple Alliance influence in the Near East. After consulting his friend Max Egon Prince Fürstenberg, he suddenly pronounced on 5 March 1913: 'It is in Austria's interests to get on with Serbia, politically and commercially, and to further her development. If she does, there will no longer be any need for an Austr[ian] army on the Serb[ian] frontier. Moreover, the *announcement of the fact* that troops or reservists were being withdrawn from the Serbian frontier, and that Austria *wants* to live on good terms with Serbia, would give satisfaction to Russia without involving anything unpleasant for Austria. Vienna's policy towards Serbia was wrong! Let them recognise their error and put it right, and give Serbia the support against Bulgaria that she needs and wants. As Serbia has already allied with Greece to the same end, that state too would co-operate with Austria. Thus, Vienna could, by an exercise of flexibility and skill, construct a solid ring round Bulgaria, which Turkey could later join! Prince Fürstenberg has been informed and is fully in agreement.' The best way 'to get on to good terms with Belgrade' was, 'in Fürstenberg's opinion, the revision of the commercial treaty which Serbia has voluntarily offered'. Wilhelm's instructions were forwarded *in extenso* to the loyal Tschirschky in Vienna, who put them to an anything but enthusiastic Berchtold.[69]

Contrary to the new Balkan policy being urged by Berlin, Berchtold insisted that the Austro-Hungarian government's prime objective was 'to draw Bulgaria *and* Romania together towards the Triple Alliance'; but Kaiser Wilhelm knew better, countering with: '! – Serbia and Romania is much easier'. Austrian attempts to win over Bulgaria would 'not succeed!' in any case, as Bulgaria was 'firmly attached by "golden" bonds to Russia and France'. 'I am still of the view, as before', he wrote, 'that the combination Serbia, Romania, Greece under Austria's leadership is the more natural and better one; because Turkey too will attach herself to it rather than to a Bulgarian one. Then Austria would have a preponderant influence over at least 3 Slav Balkan states, which could be formed under her aegis into an iron ring round Bulgaria. In the long run Sofia would not be able to resist such pressure, and would herself gradually find her way towards them when the tutelage of her friend Russia becomes too much for her. At any rate,

with Austria, Serbia, Greece and Romania in alliance the much feared
Panslav surge will be utterly split up. Whereas by the methods Berchtold
intended to adopt, all the Slavs would be driven willy-nilly into Russia's
arms.' These imperial marginal notes, too, were forwarded by Jagow to the
Vienna embassy as a guideline.[70] For months Kaiser Wilhlem continued to
cling to the idea of encircling Bulgaria by an Austro-Serbian-Greco-Romanian
'iron ring' – which gave rise to a serious crisis of confidence between Berlin
and Vienna.[71]

Behind the Bulgarian advance on Constantinople Wilhelm discerned
Russia's intention of getting to the Dardanelles herself. It was to be feared
that Russia had 'reached a secret agreement with Bulgaria . . . that Bulgaria
could also take Stamboul too – for Russia'.[72] It was not Russia, however, but
the German Reich that should prevail in Asia Minor and Mesopotamia. The
view of the German ambassador at Constantinople, Hans von Wangenheim,
that the 'resurrection' of Turkey could only come about if she could rely on
both Germany *and* England, Wilhelm dismissed with the remark, 'can't be
done! either or!'[73] Over Palestine and Syria, so he believed, the English and
French were already engaged in a 'life and death' struggle. 'So watch out,
be careful that the partition isn't implemented without us. I shall take
Mesopotamia, Alexandretta [Iskanderun], Mersina! The perceptive Turks are
already patiently awaiting this "fate".'[74] At his daughter's wedding in May
1913 Wilhelm did not shrink from astonishing Lord Stamfordham with an
explanation of the aims he was pursuing in the Near East, speaking at length
about Mesopotamia and the development of Alexandretta into a 'great commercial port'. He seemed to know every detail about the Baghdad railway and
sketched out on a piece of paper the planned route that it would take through
the Taurus mountains. 'He was glad that the Koweit question had been settled.
He seemed to approve of the railway's not being extended beyond Basra, with
goods being transported to and from the coast via the Schatt-al-Arab' water-
way.[75] Jagow expressed himself in exactly the same sense in a dispatch to the
ambassador at Constantinople: Turkey was 'only of interest to us, in that she
should continue to exist in Asia until we have consolidated our position in our
zones of activity there and are ready to annex'.[76]

Wilhelm's support for Greece's desire to extend her Adriatic frontier as far
as the northernmost tip of Corfu was so flamboyant that it was generally
ascribed to his feelings for his brother-in-law Constantine who, after the
murder of his father, King George I, in Salonica on 18 March 1913, had
succeeded to the throne in Athens.[77] His own diplomats could only shake their
heads as his policy threatened to arouse mistrust, not only in France and
England, but above all in Italy and Austria. In contrast to Wilhelm, his two

alliance partners assumed that Greece, which was seeking to make the Straits between Corfu and the mainland into a naval base, would in the foreseeable future fall under the influence of the Triple Entente. As usual, the Kaiser dismissed such anxieties as 'Nonsense!', 'Rubbish!' and 'Idiotic!' Greece would in future belong not in the sphere of influence of the Triple Entente, but of the Triple Alliance. 'The territory that lies opposite Corfu must certainly go to Greece ... If Greece is to be so intolerably badly handled as [the Italian Foreign Minister Marquis di] S[an] Giuliano seems to intend, then of course it will certainly go over to the *Triple entente*! Which it has so far had no reason whatever to do! They — as far as Russia is concerned — are backing Greece's mortal enemies, the Bulgarians, as France is too! ... The [Italian] minister's view is nonsense, as he has no knowledge whatever of the terrain opposite Corfu. And as for the construction of a naval base there, naturally it cannot be sited *between* Corfu and the mainland — geographical nonsense — but in Corfu. If Hellas wants to build a fortified harbour there, that is no business of either the Italian General or Admiralty Staff! I at any rate shall take Greece's side in decidedly opposing this nonsense.'[78]

German diplomats reacted with genuine dismay to the pro-Greek shift in German Balkan policy, which they attributed to Wilhelm personally. On 18 April 1913 the naval attaché in Rome, Werner Freiherr von Rheinbaben, reported to the Reich Navy Office on a wide-ranging talk he had had with the First Secretary at the London embassy, Richard von Kühlmann. Kühlmann had been 'quite appalled' to learn from the ambassador at Rome, Hans von Flotow, 'that we have now quite suddenly, apparently on the basis of an All-Highest hint, made ourselves eager advocates of *Greek* wishes regarding the southern Albanian frontier. Instead of continuing to follow the simple and clear political line — *strengthening of the Triple Alliance with a commercially beneficial rapprochement with England, playing the Balkan states, including Greece, off against each other to prevent further building of blocs* — German policy was again getting mixed up with muddled ideas such as "support for Greekdom against the Slav onslaught", which again marks us out as unreliable characters. What business of ours is the northern frontier of *Greece*? We should now be standing up energetically for *Italy*! Italy was already seriously put out, describing this attitude of Germany's as a poor reward for the premature renewal of the Triple Alliance. Away with the will o'the wisps — that Germany had to *support itself* on Greece, Romania and Turkey in future. These were fragile reeds to lean on! Herr v. K[ühlmann] will do his best from London to work against such a mistaken German policy.'[79] Certainly the Kaiser's Greek policy not only put a strain on German–Italian relations but cast a cloud over relations between Berlin and Vienna as well.

THE CRISIS IN AUSTRO-GERMAN RELATIONS

At his daughter's wedding the Kaiser assumed for a moment the position that he had always regarded as his God-given right. For him, it was not the ambassadors' conference in London but the areopagus of three anointed European sovereigns under the aegis of the German Kaiser in the German capital that constituted the real 'Concert of Europe', governing the fate of smaller, weaker states, and, not least, even the internal affairs of the Dual Monarchy. In this state of elation, he informed the Austro-Hungarian heir apparent, in a 'secret!' letter of 27 May 1913, of all that he and his British and Russian crowned colleagues had agreed behind his back. 'Dear Franzi', he wrote, 'I take the opportunity of Max [Fürstenberg's] return to send you these lines about the course of our meeting. From a political point of view it was altogether gratifying and auspicious. There was absolute unanimity between King George V, the Emperor [Nicholas] and me about the affairs of the Balkan states. The following was agreed as a common line of policy. 1) The vengeful, restless and unreliable King of Bulgaria to be told once and for all to hold his peace and see reason. With the knowledge and approval of the King of England, the Emperor [Nicholas] and I have sent him two sharp telegrams that leave no room for misunderstanding. The Emperor holds Bulgaria responsible, if she continues the struggle against Greece, for all disasters that might follow in the Balkans. 2) Whatever happens, Turkey is to be reorganised and helped back on to her feet; she is to be preserved from collapse and partition. Reorganisation of the Army, the Navy, Gendarmerie etc. Refortification of the capital, in view of the threateningly close Bulgarian frontier. Stamboul to remain Turkish and the Sultan's residence without question. 3) The allied Balkan states should be prevented from quarrelling over the division of the spoils. The Emperor has therefore assumed the office of arbitrator between Serbia and Bulgaria at the request of both states. 4) Greece's wishes are to be supported, in order not to deprive the victorious commander of the fruits of his victory and to give the new ruler [King Constantine] a good start and a good position vis-à-vis his people ... In a private conversation with the Emperor a chance remark of his gave me the opportunity to describe to him in detail and at length Austria's internal political difficulties (Slav question) and to gain an insight into his attitude to the Balkan question. The Emperor showed his complete, deep understanding and – to my great delight – spoke highly of Kaiser Franz Josef's [sic!] attitude, fully appreciating the difficulties of his position. Both the King of England and the Emperor are in complete agreement with me and firmly determined to keep Bulgaria's unbridled hunger for expansion at Turkey's expense within strict limits, and to secure the best possible conditions for preserving and strengthening Turkey. At any rate, Stamboul must in no event fall into Bulgaria's hands. May you regard this communication as a new proof of my staunch confidence in you, dear Franzi, and see how important it is for me that you should be well informed about the objectives which should be pursued in the Near East in future.'[80] It is more than questionable whether Nicholas II or George V knew very much about the world-shaking decisions that Wilhelm put in their mouths in this letter. As the meeting had not been a political one but a purely private family celebration, the monarchs had come to Berlin without their ministers. True, the King later admitted that he had discussed the future of Turkey with the Kaiser and the Tsar in Berlin; and that all three had agreed that Turkey must be helped to hold on to her possessions in Asia. But these discussions had, George insisted, remained at a very general level.[81]

The ruthless arrogance with which Wilhelm in his letter to Franz Ferdinand ignored the interests and aims of the allied Dual Monarchy reflected the contempt and growing impatience which he, his generals, and the Wilhelmstrasse too, had meanwhile come to feel for the policy of Vienna. Berchtold, the Kaiser complained, was simply 'helpless, knows nothing, and deceives himself and others with phrasemaking'. His equivocal policy, his refusal to take up a clear position against Russia, was 'the root cause of the whole Balkan mess', Wilhelm declared. 'Austria has done everything she could to repudiate the commanding role she could have played. Now only one thing can save Vienna — to befriend the Balkan state against which the Tsar decides, and to bind it to her, in order to make a breach in the Panslav edifice.'[82] Berchtold's demand that in the end Austria-Hungary must give her consent to any definitive Balkan settlement was greeted by the Kaiser with scorn. Austria's consent would 'hardly be needed any more'; she would 'indeed, not be asked for it'. Franz Ferdinand was not wrong when he remarked in July 1913 that the Kaiser was 'mad with rage' [*fuchsteufelswild*] at Austria's Balkan policy.[83] Berchtold was obliged to beg the Archduke when he replied to Wilhelm — 'while objectively setting out our point of view with the necessary clarity' — to avoid a polemic 'as far as possible'.[84] Bitterly, he complained that 'Berlin ... leaves us completely in the lurch in this historic hour of destiny';[85] and the old Emperor Franz Joseph, too, had to admit that 'at a time of decision when our very existence is at stake, we are virtually isolated'.[86] It was patently obvious that Imperial Germany was taking over more and more the leading role in the Near East that had hitherto been exercised by the Dual Monarchy.[87]

Both Vienna and Berlin welcomed the outbreak of the Second Balkan War on 29 June 1913, in which the Balkan states fought over the division of the territories they had taken from Turkey. For a time the threat of a combination of Balkan states under Russian auspices had been banished. 'May this Slav monster perish', the Kaiser crowed, 'and may the war between the Balkan Slavs deal a heavy and long-lasting blow to Panslavism!'[88] In his efforts to keep the peace, Grey had 'quite failed to see what the fraternal conflict in the Balkans means in Continental terms! The collapse of Russia's policy and prestige in the Panslav world!'[89] But the Austrian government's plans continued to be diametrically opposed to the Balkan policy of Wilhelm II. While the Kaiser stood up for Greek interests as before, both Austria and Italy feared the creation of a new naval Power in the Adriatic; while Wilhelm was striving to draw Romania towards the Triple Alliance in order to isolate Bulgaria, it was precisely Bulgaria's military support against Serbia that Berchtold was pursuing; and while Wilhelm was working to associate Serbia closely with the Dual Monarchy so as to free the latter to face up to Russia, for the Austrians it was precisely the inordinately strengthened Serbia that was threatening their most vital interests.

In sharp terms, Wilhelm condemned the negative attitude of both of his Triple Alliance partners towards Greek demands in the Adriatic. 'If Austria and Italy are unreasonable towards Greece that is not our fault! We are not obliged to join in *every* idiocy these two are planning. We have already taken on quite enough in this respect for the sake of our allies. If they ... just go on making their position worse, we can warn them, but not stop them; but we don't need to join them.'[90] He did not mince his words in demanding a complete reversal of Vienna's Bulgarian policy. When on 29 June the Second Balkan War began, with a Bulgarian attack on Greek positions in Macedonia, he told the Austrian naval attaché straight out: 'He hoped so much that the Bulgarians would be soundly beaten and cut down to size as they deserve and that they would not find any support for their ambitious aspirations.' The Dual Monarchy, he went on, 'would commit a grave error if it wanted to support Bulgaria at Romania's and Serbia's expense'. For Austria had now 'probably the best opportunity to win Serbia's lasting gratitude and secure all the advantages she wishes, and the King of Romania too deserved every possible consideration for his loyal support for the Triple Alliance over the years, whereas one will never be able to count on Bulgaria, given her absolute unreliability'.[91] Conrad von Hötzendorf was not wrong in suspecting that the Kaiser's 'pronounced hostility' to Bulgaria was 'chiefly directed against the ruler of that country', Tsar Ferdinand.[92]

The subjection of the ancient Danubian Monarchy to the powerful northern Empire was painfully felt in Vienna.[93] In a lamentation to Archduke Franz Ferdinand at the end of July 1913, Berchtold listed the many differences between his Balkan policy and that of Berlin that was making his task so difficult: 'As for our relations with Germany, the long crisis has naturally given rise to a few "dissonances", which are attributable to the fact that Germany wishes to handle the Balkan questions which are primarily of interest to us solely to suit her own convenience, and has at various times been to blame for developments that are unfavourable to us ... If we have this alliance [with Germany] to thank for the unpleasant fact that the French and English money markets are closed to us and we are heading for a financial catastrophe, they should at least lend us political support in the one area of foreign policy where the Monarchy has vital interests at stake. Instead of which, the German diplomats put their heads together with the Italians ... and discuss in touching harmony how they can diplomatically cripple their ally in the Balkans! Having to swallow all this and a lot more belongs to the pleasant duties of my office! But I am well aware that we cannot offend Germany and have to bear in mind that we might possibly have to rely on German support at a conference or elsewhere. Besides, it would be impractical in the long run to pursue two kinds of Balkan policy and make things easier for our opponents. It is therefore absolutely necessary for us to engage in a discussion with Berlin about the new situation that the Balkan War has created on our south-eastern frontier.'[94]

At the same time, Berchtold had a meeting with Conrad, in the course of which the latter, too, made no bones about his dissatisfaction with Germany's selfish policy. He went so far as to wonder whether it might not be better for Austria to attempt her move against Serbia 'in agreement with Russia' rather than with Germany. At any rate, any 'further military measures' which might be impending should not be used for 'trivial' purposes, but 'for the great objective of restoring or extending our position in the Balkans; and this time Germany must not be consulted as in 1909, because she is working to sabotage our expansion in the Balkans and regards the independent states there as a fruitful terrain for her commercial ambitions'.[95]

That summer, relations between Wilhelm II and Berchtold reached their lowest point. In a retrospective telegram of 16 August 1913 the Kaiser emphasised that he had had grave doubts about Austria's policy from the start of the Balkan crisis. In the early stages, in order to avoid a clash between the two Great Power groups, he had felt it advisable to demonstrate 'the indivisible solidarity of the Triple Alliance'. To that end he had 'made the sacrifice' of 'endorsing certain Austrian wishes that he actually disapproved of, which went by the names Sanjak, Durazzo, Scutari and autonomous Albania'. In the meantime, however, both Austria-Hungary and Russia had made so many mistakes 'that their so-called influence in the Balkans' had suffered 'a perhaps irreparable blow'. With the outbreak of the Second Balkan War the pursuit of what had hitherto been the chief aim of German policy, namely preserving the peace of Europe, had moved into the background. Now, the Kaiser declared, it was no longer primarily a question of maintaining the peace, but of 'correctly assessing the new relationships that are forming in the Balkans and preparing the ground for possible future combinations. Hence, I could not go along with Austria's new and most serious error. Austria, who had hitherto served as a connecting link between the Triple Alliance and Romania, has failed in her important duty as an ally, allowing her stubborn pursuit of her erroneous Serbian policy to draw her into such close contact with Sofia that the traditional relations with Bucharest were bound to suffer at such a critical time. The timing of such an error was all the worse, in that at the same time Russia and France were obviously redoubling their efforts to win Romania for the Entente to the disadvantage of the Triple Alliance. I *was obliged*, therefore, in the name of the Triple Alliance, to try to correct this error, even at the risk of temporarily offending Austria. Similarly, I had to see to it that the new order of things in the Balkans was as favourable to us as possible. It must be our task — not for dynastic reasons, but by making use of existing dynastic links — to draw the obviously rising power of Greece over to our side. Here I deliberately put the emphasis on Greek expansion in and on the Aegean Sea, lest overambitious Greek aspirations in the Adriatic should make the inclusion of Greece in the sphere of influence of the Triple Alliance difficult and problematic for Italy. My policy towards Turkey in the Adrianople question followed very similar aims. I think the only right thing to do is to let conditions there ripen in their own time. In any case, I want to see no interference whatever from our side.' As soon as peace was concluded in the Balkans, it would be a question of 'convincing our own allies, and notably Austria, of the correctness of our policy and of dispelling the present irritation. A change in the personnel directing Austrian policy, which I have repeatedly been told is probable, will make our task (for which the press too must be given a directive) considerably easier, especially as I know that a great number of Austrian diplomats judge and condemn Berchtold's policy just as I do.'[96]

This expression of the imperial will of 16 August 1913 was immediately circulated to the relevant embassies and legations. Tschirschky, who was instructed to put its contents to the hapless allied Foreign Minister as gently as possible, reported on the 22nd: 'The minister was undoubtedly strongly impressed by His Majesty's declaration and will report on it to his imperial master without delay. Count Berchtold said he would be glad to see the position in the same light, but he was afraid that in future the new situation in the Balkans would hold many unpleasant surprises for Austria's (and hence Germany's) interests.'[97]

In this instance Wilhelm II's criticism carried all the more weight in so far as it was by no means just an eccentric solo effort on the part of the monarch. Complaints about Austria-Hungary's 'unfortunate Balkan policy' which had recently often deviated 'from the general interests of the Triple Alliance' were heard both in the Auswärtiges Amt and in military circles in Berlin, where Vienna was accused of 'anachronistic leanings towards Bulgaria' and 'turning away from Romania'. As the Bavarian military plenipotentiary reported on 12 August 1913, German diplomacy had been 'trying with success to banish Romanian resentment. Moreover, there is the heartening prospect ... of bringing the now stronger Greece to align herself with Germany politically, despite her French suitors. They are even hoping for a firm alliance-like combination, of Romania, Greece and Turkey, inclining towards the Triple Alliance, which would not only significantly relieve Austria's right flank in the event of a European war ... but would also (especially thanks to the rising Greek navy) represent a welcome addition to the naval forces of Austria and Italy in the Mediterranean.'[98]

'NOW OR NEVER!' 'I AM WITH YOU!' THE KAISER'S BLANK CHEQUE OF OCTOBER 1913

The pressure on Berchtold intensified steadily, especially as Kaiser Wilhelm and Moltke drew increasingly close to Conrad von Hötzendorf with his demands for war. Already at the end of June the Austrian military attaché in Berlin could inform Conrad that he had just learned from the Kaiser's Military Cabinet 'that His Majesty the Kaiser and King' would invite 'Your Excellency to this year's imperial manoeuvres', scheduled for Silesia in September. Presumably the idea came from Moltke, 'whose keenest desire is to bring Your Excellency into closer contact with the Italian General Staff'.[99] Moltke confirmed this, writing in person to his Austrian counterpart on 29 June: 'Let us look again with trust and confidence into the future. Whatever it brings, we shall face it hand in hand. The present oppressive atmosphere is building up for a storm ... I do not know what line your government takes towards Balkan affairs, I only know this, that if it comes to fighting, the Triple Alliance will do its duty.'[100] Conrad knew very well, therefore, that his views would meet with more sympathy from his German opposite number than from his own government.

On 7 September 1913, during the manoeuvres in Silesia, Wilhelm II received a letter from Franz Ferdinand that could not have been more cordial. The Archduke congratulated the Kaiser on 'the success of your policy, which I have again followed as always with the *greatest* admiration, and with which,

Figure 40 The Triple Alliance: the Supreme War Lord with the chiefs of the
Italian, Austrian and German General Staffs, Pollio, Conrad von
Hötzendorf and Moltke in 1913

if I may say so in all modesty and deepest devotion, I fully identify myself.
Allow me, Your Majesty, to tell you how much I long to discuss the latest
political events with you, for which there should be an opportunity either in
Leipzig, where I have the honour to see you again, or in Konopischt. I could
tell you much that, in my humble opinion, is of interest.'[101] Delighted,
Wilhelm said that he would come to Konopischt in the last week of October.[102]
The editors of the *Große Politik der europäischen Kabinette* take the Archduke's 'fully identifying' with the policy of Wilhelm II as proof that the latter,
too, was motivated by an 'absolute desire for peace', but this interpretation is
very much open to question.[103]

During the imperial manoeuvres in Silesia on 7 and 8 September 1913 (see
Figure 40) intensive discussions took place between Wilhelm II and Conrad, in
which Moltke and Waldersee also participated. Conrad claimed that the
position of the Triple Alliance had been gravely damaged by events in the
Balkans and insisted that if it came to war with Serbia, Austria must have
the right to choose her allies (naturally, he meant Bulgaria) herself. True,
Kaiser Wilhelm clung to the idea of Serbia's joining the Dual Monarchy,

because otherwise Austria would always have a South Slav state for a neighbour that in the event of a war with Russia could attack her in the rear. But he
stressed that neither in 1909 nor in the current Balkan crisis had he held
Conrad back from striking at Serbia. In the Bosnian crisis he had declared
'that Germany will be entirely on your side', and recently too, Austria could
have moved against Serbia at any time. 'Why did this not happen?' he asked.
'Nobody was stopping you!' Wilhelm readily accepted Conrad's suggestion for
a binding link between Romania and the Triple Alliance – mere promises
were not sufficient; and he agreed with him that Romania must 'join [the
Triple Alliance] on the same terms as the other allies. That is a good idea! We
must pursue it.' The Triple Alliance would have Greece, too, 'on our side'.
Greek public opinion was evidently pro-French and not pro-German, but 'now
after his victory the King can do in his country as he pleases. He will
implement the policy that *he* wants.'[104] On his return from the manoeuvres
the Kaiser ordered 'copies of all Balkan reports of military interest to be sent
immediately to the General Staff'.[105] In his negotiations with Moltke and
Waldersee Conrad urged that in view of the strengthening of Serbia, the
Germans should put up more troops against Russia. Moltke countered that
Germany 'if it came to a war would attack France with her main forces and
could only turn east after that'. True, he had 113 divisions at his disposal, but
'we have to think of the English, who will certainly be on France's side'.[106]

    With fresh energy Conrad now stepped up his demands for a war. In an
audience on 2 October 1913 he urged Franz Joseph to seize on the renewed
advance of Serbian troops into Albania, either to incorporate Serbia into the
structure of the monarchy by 'peaceful' means, or else to go to war to crush her
once and for all.[107] On the following day he made – according to the German
military attaché Count Kageneck – a 'brilliant' speech in the council of
ministers in which he referred to 'the inevitable and necessary conflict with
the embryonic Great Serbia'.[108] On 10 October, Conrad explained to Berchtold:
'Either we allow things to take their course, at the risk of perishing, or we
strike out, send an ultimatum, and go to war. To mobilise yet again without
acquiring any territory would be too much for the Army to bear.'[109] Berchtold
found himself obliged to address a sharp warning to Belgrade, telling the
German chargé d'affaires Prince Stolberg on 15 October that if the answer was
unsatisfactory he would present Serbia with an ultimatum. This time, the
Foreign Minister emphasised, Austria-Hungary was 'firmly determined . . .
not to give way'. A retreat would amount to the Dual Monarchy's 'total
abdication . . . which would be 'especially disastrous in respect of its own
South Slavs', whose 'centrifugal tendencies would be strengthened by a
weakening of the Monarchy. In the event of Serbia's continuing to resist,

therefore, he would have to go to war and for this he had got both the unanimous consent of the Austrian and Hungarian governments and the full support of His Majesty the Emperor Franz Joseph. He allowed himself to hope, therefore, that Germany, who indeed had a great interest herself in holding back the Slav flood, would morally stand firmly behind Austria-Hungary in this question; for it would probably only be a question of moral support, as neither Russia nor France wanted war.'[110]

Kaiser Wilhelm and the Wilhelmstrasse were entirely in agreement in giving their ally the 'moral support' it was asking for. Acting Foreign Secretary Zimmermann, when he sent Stolberg's dispatch to the Kaiser, who was staying with his sister Victoria in Bonn, declared: 'In accordance with the directives of His Majesty the Kaiser and King, we have during the crisis of last winter repeatedly and emphatically stated it to be our view that the solution of the Albanian question in acordance with Austria's wishes is a vital interest of the Dual Monarchy. If we were now to deny our ally our support, or even appear to be lukewarm, this would certainly be taken very badly in Vienna, where the advocates of an alignment with France and Russia are busily at work. A German refusal could also result in Austria's seeking salvation in a single-handed, perhaps over-hasty, action. I think we ought, therefore, to declare to Vienna that Austria can count on our moral support ... It would be advisable ... to raise the matter in London without delay, with a pressing invitation to the English government to participate in the demarche in Belgrade in order to stave off a single-handed action by Austria that might trigger off European complications. Paris and Petersburg only need to be informed of what has happened.' Zimmermann asked for the monarch's 'All-Highest decision' to be sent by telegraph, but he did not wait for it to arrive (clearly because he felt certain of the Kaiser's approval) and promised Berchtold on 16 October 1913 that the German Reich stood 'firmly behind Austria-Hungary'.[111] The Foreign Minister was 'highly pleased' at this communication and expressed his 'most sincere thanks for Germany's support'. On 17 October he repeated that 'while Austria-Hungary certainly does not wish to provoke conflicts, she would go through with this to the end, whatever happened. The Emperor [Franz Joseph] was despite his great age firmly determined to go to war if necessary, and had today given him permission to give Serbia an eight-day time limit for the complete evacuation of Albania'.[112] An ultimatum to this effect was presented in Belgrade at midday on 18 October 1913.

Kaiser Wilhelm's approval of Vienna's decision, which met with 'strong objections' not only in Paris and Petersburg but also in London and Rome,[113] was never in doubt. From Bonn, he instructed the diplomat in his suite, Count

Botho von Wedel, to telegraph to the Auswärtiges Amt: 'His Majesty the Kaiser and King has received the news with great satisfaction that Austria-Hungary is this time firmly determined not to give way to Serbia, and wishes the Austrian chargé d'affaires to be told that Austria-Hungary can be absolutely certain of our support. Your Excellency's proposals for dealing with the affair are also approved by His Majesty in every other respect.' Zimmermann immediately forwarded the telegram to Vienna 'for the information of Count Berchtold'.[114] The Foreign Minister 'received the All-Highest decision ... with great pleasure and asked me to transmit his deeply felt thanks', Stolberg telegraphed to Berlin. 'Germany's firm attitude, which he had never doubted, strengthened his confidence that Serbia will observe the eight-day time limit that starts today, and will not let it come to war.' In the event, the Serbs, who were isolated, found themselves forced to withdraw within the time limit. But a Serbian retreat was not at all what Wilhlem II was wishing for as the result of the Austrian ultimatum. 'That would be very regrettable!' he wrote on Stolberg's report – in eerie anticipation of the fatal marginal note that would initiate the July Crisis eight months later. 'Now or never! It is high time that peace and order were established down there!'[115]

On the day of the delivery of the Austrian ultimatum in Belgrade Wilhelm had a further conversation with Conrad von Hötzendorf, during the dedication of the massive monument to commemorate the Battle of Leipzig. After the ceremonial dinner in the Gewandhaus the Kaiser sent for Conrad, and told him, with regard to Serbia: 'The cup is full, [he] approved of the energetic action and confirmed that he stood wholly on the side of the Monarchy.' Verbatim, the Kaiser said: 'I go along with you. The other [Powers] are not ready, they will not do anything against it. In a few days you must be in Belgrade. I was always for peace; but that has its limits. I know a lot about war and know what it means, but in the end a situation arises in which a Great Power can no longer stand by and watch, but *is obliged* to take up the sword.'[116]

After the ceremony in Leipzig Wilhelm left for several days in Austria,[117] arriving on 23 October at Franz Ferdinand's castle of Konopischt in Bohemia, where he met a large contingent of the Bohemian and Hungarian high nobility. Three days later he called on Franz Joseph in Schönbrunn and had a long talk in the German embassy with Count Berchtold, who recorded the pronouncements of the German monarch in a veritably historic memorandum. According to this, the Kaiser had declared in no uncertain terms 'that nowadays we are not dealing with transient phenomena created and shaped by the activity of diplomats, but with a world-historical process comparable to the Völkerwanderungen, the Migration of Peoples, in this case, of a mighty advance of the power of the Slavs, even if not entirely in accordance with the wishes of the Panslavs. Panslavism and Russia with it, are of course a spent force in the Balkans; but at the same time the Slav states there have been so strengthened as to give Germany and Austria food for thought. War between East and West is in the long run unavoidable and if Austria-Hungary should then be exposed to invasion by a respectable military Power on her flank, that could be ominous for the outcome of the struggle of the peoples . . . The Slavs were not born to command but to obey, and this must be got into their heads. And if they believe that they can expect salvation from Belgrade, then they must be cured of this belief. With Serbia, there can only be one relationship for Austria-Hungary, that of the dependency of the smaller on the greater, as in the planetary system – in fact, the Kaiser simply cannot imagine any order in the Balkans other than the predominance of the Monarchy vis-à-vis all the states there. His Majesty imagines the solution of the problem thus: that we attract Serbia to us by dint of everything that they need, i.e. 1) Money (from the King downwards they are all to be had for money); 2) military training; 3) commercial concessions. On the other hand, Serbia must be made to obey the Monarchy, put her troops (who have shown in the war that they are quite capable) at the disposal of Austria-Hungary, and thereby guarantee that there will be no need to fear surprises on the Monarchy's southern frontier.' Berchtold's doubts as to the practicability of this programme the Kaiser countered 'by observing that the Central Powers' shortage of funds was of course a nuisance, but, on the other hand, France would not have all that much money to spare for the Balkan states either'. Berchtold's further objection that the 'implacable animosity of the Serbian race towards the Monarchy . . . stood in the way of the conclusion of a military convention', Wilhelm dismissed with the remark 'that in this respect one shouldn't beat about the bush'. He imagined 'that Serbia would be prepared, in return for the protection that our army would offer her against external attack, to put her army at our disposal, and subordinate it to ours, as it were. If they should refuse to do this, then force would have to be used, for "when His Majesty the Emperor Franz Joseph demands something, the Serbian government must submit, and if it does not, Belgrade will be bombarded and occupied until His Majesty's will has been fulfilled." And of this you can be sure, that I stand behind you and am ready to draw the sword whenever your actions make it necessary. (His Majesty accompanied these words by moving his hand to his sabre.)' The Kaiser also urged that Romania be drawn in 'to put pressure on Serbia to make her accept our demands. The German minister in Bucharest would receive instructions to keep in close touch with his Austro-Hungarian colleague to this end.' Wilhelm then went on to discuss the future of Turkey at length. 'His Majesty had used the meeting with the Russian and English monarchs at the Cumberland wedding [in May] to sound out their intentions regarding Turkey. Both sovereigns had spoken up for the preservation of Turkey and the Tsar, especially, had stressed that he did not want to occupy Armenian territory which, given its revolutionary population, would be of very questionable value to Russia. He too was absolutely in favour of Constantinople's remaining Turkish, "as the Porte is the best guardian of the Dardanelles". The King of England had mentioned that the Turkish government had approached England about the organisation of the Turkish gendarmerie. Kaiser Wilhelm had taken the opportunity to mention the further training of the Turkish army by Geman instructors, to which neither King George nor the Emperor Nicholas raised any objection . . . As regards our relationship with Bulgaria, His Majesty did not go into this; but he took the opportunity to accuse King Ferdinand of a thing or two *en passant*, viz. his coming forward to gain possession of Samothrace (he had assured Kaiser Wilhelm that he needed the island for the security of his coastline, he tried to tell the Tsar that he only intended to plant vineyards there, and King George had been led to believe that the island was the right place to accommodate Ferdinand's exotic birds), and further the fact that King Ferdinand had offered Constantinople to Russia. (He had asked the Emperor Nicholas for permission to take the city, declaring himself prepared to lay it at the feet of the Tsar.) As far as Russia was concerned, His Majesty regards a return to the traditions of the Holy Alliance and the Three Emperors' Alliance to be out of the question. He had been brought up in this tradition, but had to recognise that since Alexander III we have had to reckon with a different Russia, a Power that is hostile to us and working for our destruction, in which quite other elements are ruling than the Emperor. For the moment Kaiser Wilhelm is not worried about Russia; for the next six years we can be safe from that quarter. He had discovered this in March, when after a war council in Tsarskoe Selo, a Baltic German he knew personally had repeated to him a remark of the Emperor Nicholas: "Dieu soit loué, nous ne ferons pas de guerre, avant six ans c'est impossible!" Until then the army would not be ready to fight, and besides the ghost of revolution is going about.' When Berchtold remarked that the danger of revolution would probably be even greater in six years and represented a threat to the monarchical principle in general, Wilhelm II replied 'spiritedly that if it came to a war, he wouldn't give a damn for such considerations, for then it will be a life and death struggle for existence, where we two will stand together against a common foe, and then it would after all be immaterial in what way the opponent perished. Close sits my shirt, but closer my skin! Whenever during our talk, which lasted an hour and a quarter, the opportunity arose to touch on our alliance relationship,

His Majesty ostentatiously seized the opportunity to assure me that we could count on him fully and entirely. That was the red thread that ran through the Highest Lord's words, and when on departing I alluded to this and thanked him, His Majesty deigned to assure me that whatever came from the Vienna foreign office was for Him a command ...'[118] Tschirschky confirmed, in a report to Bethmann Hollweg, that the Kaiser had given Berchtold very clearly to understand that the Dual Monarchy must '*incorporate* Serbia somehow, *come what may*, especially in the military field, so as at least to have a guarantee that *in the event of war with Russia* it will have the Serbian army, not against it, but on its side'.[119]

CHAPTER THIRTY-SIX

Kaiser and Reich. Wilhelm's Personal Monarchy on the eve of war

The time has come to interrupt the narrative of events that preceded the fatal leap in the dark in the summer of 1914, and to cast an eye over the Personal Monarchy of Kaiser Wilhelm II in the twenty-fifth year of his reign. He had let it be known that he wanted to live out the year 1913, the year of his jubilee, in peace. He intended to celebrate it in glorious splendour, and to exploit it, together with the hundredth anniversary of the War of Liberation against Napoleon, to anchor the Hohenzollern Monarchy more firmly in the hearts and minds of the nation. Not least, the German people were to be pledged to future wars and sacrifices. As we shall see, this second objective was achieved, at least in part; but this was hardly the case with the first.[1] The gulf was too great between aspiration and reality, between the last Kaiser's anachronistic claims to autocratic power and the political maturity of the great majority of Germans.

In the twenty-five years of Wilhelm's reign the German Reich had made breathtaking progress: in terms of trade and industry, the natural and humane sciences, the arts and culture, it was incontestably among the leading nations of the world; but its political system was hopelessly outdated, backward-looking, and irremediably contaminated with the ideals of the Frederician military monarchy. Nevertheless, the democratic spirit of the times was noticeable everywhere. Universal male suffrage and the modern mass news-paper press had stimulated a vibrant political culture, and demands for the abolition of the three-class franchise in Prussia and for a central government responsible to the Reichstag became ever louder, especially from the growing numbers of Social Democrats. Alarmed by the rising democratic tide, reactionary voices at court, in the officer corps, in the German-Conservative party and the Pan-German League called vehemently for a reactionary *coup d'état* against parliament, universal suffrage, freedom of the press, Social Democrats and Jews – unless, that is, the problems at home could be solved by a swift successful war abroad. Towards the end of 1913 such ideas were gaining ground as the Crown Prince pushed himself forward as the spokesman of Pan-German hot-heads and as the Kaiser's blinkered attitude in the Zabern affair cast an alarming light on the domination of the military vis-à-vis the civilian authorities.

This chapter will also look again at the question of the distribution of power within the executive, a question inextricably bound up with the fierce controversy over the aims of German policy before and during the July crisis of 1914. Who had the decisive say in Berlin – the Kaiser with his entourage and the three secret cabinets? The Chief of General Staff, von Moltke, the War Minister von Falkenhayn and the other military leaders? Or the Reich Chancellor, the Wilhelmstrasse and the diplomatic corps? Were these three centres of power united in their aims, or were they at loggerheads, and if so with what result? The answers to these questions, key questions in a biography of Wilhelm II, have been obscured by the shadows cast by the bitter controversy of the years after 1918. In response to the so-called war guilt clauses of the Treaty of Versailles, crucial documents were suppressed, published in a tendentious form, or even destroyed. In particular, Wilhelm II's role before the world war was trivialised and played down as far as possible – not only because he was threatened with extradition as a 'war criminal', but also and above all because his were the words and deeds that seemed most likely to prove the allegation of the victorious Powers that the German Reich had brought about the war deliberately as part of a long-term plan. The innumerable aggressive comments that Wilhelm had scribbled on the diplomatic documents could not be erased. Between the wars patriotic German historians therefore strove assiduously to represent them as regrettable but in the end meaningless aberrations, which they alleged had had no influence on official policy-making.[2] It was not the 'impulsive' Kaiser but the 'responsible' Reich Chancellor, not the military but civilian statesmen and diplomats, who had determined German policy up to the outbreak of war. In 1932 the influential constitutional historian Fritz Hartung drew the declining curve that was claimed to show the political significance of the monarch's power after the fall of Bismarck: after high points in the early years of the reign, it had declined rapidly towards the end of the century, and after the *Daily Telegraph* affair of November 1908 Wilhelm II had completely lost the ability to translate his threatening words into policy.[3] This apologetic interpretation of the interwar years was extraordinarily long-lived after the Second World War, even though as early as the 1950s preliminary investigations of the evidence in the GDR archives in Potsdam and Merseburg had raised doubts as to whether Hartung's thesis held good for the years of Bethmann Hollweg's Chancellor-ship.[4] The present biography has been able to demonstrate, in the light of the rich archival sources available, the enormous power of decision that Kaiser Wilhelm II exercised to the very end of Bernhard von Bülow's Chancellorship — and that indeed in all spheres, not just foreign policy and military affairs. We were also able to show how under Bethmann Hollweg Wilhelm could exercise without restraint, if not indeed actually extend still further, his dominance in the determination of foreign policy. But what was the relationship between Kaiser and Chancellor in the field of domestic affairs in these last years before the outbreak of the war, years which were marked — admittedly by no means only in Germany — by serious constitutional crises? Was the deadlocked position abroad, into which the Reich had manoeuvred itself under Wilhelm, matched by such a feeling of hopelessness about the situation at home as to make a victorious war seem, if not unavoidable, then at least worth considering?

JUNE 1913: THE KAISER'S SILVER JUBILEE

According to the Austrian military attaché Baron Karl von Bienerth, one reason why Wilhelm II had so far been reluctant to let the Balkan crisis escalate into a general war was his desire to commemorate the year 1913, the twenty-fifth anniversary of his accession, in peace.[5] The pleasure with which the monarch was looking forward to these festivities was clear from the fact that two years before, at the height of the Agadir crisis, he was already starting to draw up instructions for how and where the great event was to be celebrated. The Chancellor could not believe his ears when in August 1911 Wilhelm formally expressed 'his will' that 'the celebrations for the twenty-fifth anniversary of his reign [should be] on the broadest possible basis and open to all classes of society' in the stadium that was as yet still under construction in the Grunewald — later the site of the 1936 Berlin Olympic Games. He had charged the former minister General Viktor von Podbielski with preparing the celebrations. Bethmann was speechless: 'I received this information in silence', he confessed, but since then he had become convinced that it was 'quite impossible' now 'to prepare festivities like this to take place in two years' time. We cannot know today whether we shall be holding celebrations in 2 years' time', he warned. 'Should anything leak out to the public that we are already busy with the celebrations for the 25th anniversary of His Majesty's reign the consequences, given the critical times we are living in, could be nothing less than fatal.'[6] Nevertheless, the construction of the

'German Stadium' went briskly ahead under Podbielski's supervision, and in fact it proved possible to open it punctually on 8 June 1913. Some 30,000 athletes and gymnasts paraded 'before their Kaiser'.[7]

For the jubilee itself the Hohenzollern family assembled in the capital (see Figure 41). The Schloss theatre gave productions of Joseph Lauff's *Der Große König*, with music composed by Frederick the Great, on 14 June, and on the following evening of *Lohengrin*. The actual jubilee started on 16 June, a beautiful sunny day, with a morning serenade by Berlin schoolchildren in the courtyard of the Schloss. Numerous deputations marched past the palace (see Figure 42), the Kaiser acknowledging their salutes from the balcony. At the banquet that night the Kaiserin, who had been suffering from a weak heart for years, collapsed and had to be taken to her rooms.[8]

In the university the rectors of all the universities of the Reich assembled for a festive ceremony. The German cities sent their burgomasters to celebrate in the imperial capital. Students organised a torch procession. Just as at the Kaiser's accession twenty-five years before, the federal princes too, now all of them sunk into political insignificance, gathered round Wilhelm II and bickered, just as then, over matters of precedence and decorations and other such frippery.[9] More important to many of his subjects than such childishness or the award of 'jubilee medals' to the First Regiment of Guards[10] was the Kaiser's decision to mark the occasion by granting an amnesty in all the German states: prison sentences of under three months were cancelled altogether, and in other cases the 'worthiness' of the prisoner was to be the deciding factor.[11]

Well-timed for the jubilee was the luxury publication *Our Kaiser. Twenty-five Years of the Reign of Kaiser Wilhelm II*, containing nine glossy colour portraits of Wilhelm and 449 black-and-white illustrations.[12] For more discriminating readers there was the three-volume *Deutschland unter Kaiser Wilhelm II.*, with contributions from eminent scholars and a number of former statesmen. Foremost among these was Bernhard Prince von Bülow, whose survey of German foreign policy since 1888 was even then contentious; the contribution about the army was written by no less a figure than General Friedrich von Bernhardi, and the conclusion by the former head of the Reich chancellery Friedrich Wilhelm von Loebell, soon to be appointed Prussian Minister of the Interior.[13] Although Loebell, together with the former minister, currently President of the Rhine province, Dr Dr Freiherr von Rheinbaben and the Speaker of the Prussian Landtag, Hans Count von Schwerin-Löwitz, were named as the 'editors', this lavish production was not organised by the state. The initiative came rather from the editor of the *Konservative Monatsschrift*, Herbert von Berger, who had recruited these and other state officials

Figure 41 Silver jubilee: the imperial family on the steps of the Neues Palais in Potsdam on 15 June 1913

Figure 42 The march past of the chimney sweeps in celebration of the Kaiser's
twenty-five years on the throne, 15 June 1913

by appealing to them – significantly – to raise the prestige of the monarchy;
and claiming that the three-volume luxury set would 'pay off a debt of
gratitude to His Majesty and counteract the irrational pessimism that is
becoming increasingly widespread ... The great danger for the German
nation is that with its eternal self-criticism and perpetual faultfinding it will
lose its old proud self-confidence ... It is a patriotic duty, therefore, to work
against the pessimistic mood that is continually gnawing away by pointing to
the positive achievements of recent times to show how we are making progress
after all, in all spheres of our national life, and how we have gathered and
moulded forces of which the past had no conception, and which have made us
stronger than at any previous time. The past quarter century embraces the
work of our Kaiser's prime years. Everything that was done then was done
under his gaze, and the twenty-five year labour of ruling has given him grey
hairs and furrowed his brow. He has indeed the right to expect that leading
Germans in all fields who have worked together with him and have received
honours and encouragement from him, should demonstrate to the nation, on
the occasion of his jubilee, the great, positive, and fruitful achievements of
these twenty-five years. The nation can be given nothing greater or more
essential than such a work, from which the German can learn to be proud and

confident again, and in recognising what has been achieved can feel assured that even greater things can be achieved in the future.'[14]

In their articles and in speeches, leading nationalist intellectuals such as Hans Delbrück and Hermann Oncken, while regretting the Kaiser's decision to sack Bismarck 23 years before, nevertheless praised him for uniting the German people around the throne and guiding the Reich to greatness.[15] The Kaiser 'has never been as popular as now', groaned Reich Chancellor von Bethmann Hollweg on 25 June 1913. 'It is almost frightening for anyone compelled to look behind the scenes. "Now the November Days [i.e. the *Daily Telegraph* crisis of 1908] have been ground to smithereens", he [the Kaiser] said to me.'[16]

'MIT GOTT FÜR KÖNIG UND VATERLAND' — A CALL TO ARMS

Although after his disastrous experiences in November 1908 Wilhelm II became somewhat more restrained in his public utterances, his own completely anachronistic views of his role as one who ruled by the grace of God still found expression from time to time and did not fail to give rise to acrimonious debates, not only in the Reichstag, about his Personal Rule. The whole country still smarted from the speech that he had made in Königsberg on 25 August 1910, in which he had emphasised the divinely ordained character of his position: 'Seeing myself as the instrument of the Lord, I go my way regardless of the views and opinions of the day.'[17] On 6 March 1913 Wilhelm used the occasion of the opening of the new city hall in Bremen to link his jubilee with the heroic deeds of Frederick the Great, the hundredth anniversary of the Battle of the Nations at Leipzig, and the victory over the French at Sedan in 1870. He was convinced, he proclaimed, that the victory over Napoleon a hundred years before had been the result of 'the intervention of Providence, the intervention of God, who casts peoples down, but also raises them up again'. The German people should remember 'divine Providence . . . that has in these hundred years brought us this change of fortune, and should remember with deep gratitude the great advances the nation has made . . . May the present generation show itself worthy of its forefathers, and emulate and strive to match them. May the youth of today take the youth of those days as models of devotion to the Fatherland . . . Just as in those days, our people are faced with the task of strengthening their fighting capacity, building up their armaments, and matching their forefathers of a hundred years ago in patriotic enthusiasm and readiness to make sacrifices.'[18]

Wilhelm was by no means alone in making such baleful appeals for self-sacrifice in the service of God, King and Fatherland. The Prusso-German

monarchical myth was invoked in countless speeches by the pillars of the old
order in an effort to attune the nation's youth to the idea of a possibly
imminent war. The Kaiser's most loyal paladin General August von Mackensen, for example, in his glowing address on Wilhelm's fifty-fourth birthday
(27 January 1913), similarly invoked the glorious past in order to draw 'lessons'
for the present. 'The year 1813 has been called the Prussians' greatest year.
A great past must not be forgotten. Especially now, where a new generation
believes it stands at the summit, we must remember how difficult it was to
climb to that summit. Godly enthusiasm and glowing love of the Fatherland,
readiness to make sacrifices and German idealism created the heroes of that
time. Who fought the most battles? Who fought the decisive battles? Prussia!
. . . It was Prussiandom that . . . finally put paid to the Emperor [Napoleon].
Not with force of numbers did they achieve this, nor with the superiority of
their arms, but with their moral strength. And we must bear this last consideration in mind, gentlemen, especially today. The new year in the life of our
Kaiser and King looks upon us with a grave countenance. We are certainly not
a warlike people; but we must remain a people ready to fight, and a fighting
people that can manfully stand up for itself . . . We do not want to extend our
frontiers. But just as Prussia was tough, and unloved, and even in 1813 and
1815 was only rewarded with ingratitude, so too "Prussianised" Germany
with its economic progress is surrounded by those who envy us. In a future war
our position in the world will be at stake. So it is a matter of not weakening
ourselves with internal quarrels, but of strengthening and consolidating our
moral forces. What led us to victory on the battlefields of 1870/71? . . . It was
the moral content of our army, of our people in arms! The moral strength
which − not least − is rooted in faith in our leaders and in our single-minded
devotion to the monarchy. Only the forces that created an Empire can also
sustain it . . . Who created Prussia, who, through Prussia, re-created Germany,
nationally and politically? The Hohenzollerns! The monarchical power they
exercised, the army they created, the nation-in-arms imbued by them with an
iron sense of duty, Hohenzollern rulers like the Great Elector, Frederick
Wilhelm I, Frederick the Great and Wilhelm the Ever-Victorious, set their
seal on Prussiandom, that Prussiandom that by way of Fehrbellin and Ross-
bach, Tauroggen and Möckern, Marslatour and Sedan − here at last united
with all the German tribes − achieved the crown imperial for its King. The
strong monarchical state power, which has welded into a unity within it the
trinity of nation, state and ruling house! Today this strong monarchical power
is personified in our King and Kaiser Wilhelm II.'[19] Again and again,
Mackensen appealed to the traditional inner bond between the Hohenzollern
Monarchy, the Prussian Army and the German nation. 'Life is nothing to us,

King and Fatherland everything. So thought our fathers a hundred years ago
when they went into battle under the sign of the iron cross and with the
battle-cry "With God for King and Fatherland" . . . We too, comrades, want to
go into battle with this watchword when the King summons us.'[20]

One year later, on the occasion of Wilhelm II's fifty-fifth birthday, Mackensen railed against the values of a modern democratic industrialised society
threatening to undermine Prussian militarism and once more invoked 'loyalty
to the Crown' and 'warlike manly virtues' as the only antidote to such poisons.
'The spirit of subversion, insubordination and sedition is infecting minds and
threatening the healthy spirit of our people – is threatening our youth', he
cried. No royal house, Mackensen averred, had bestowed on its subjects
four monarchs of the greatness of the Great Elector, Frederick Wilhelm I,
Frederick the Great and 'King Wilhelm the Victorious'. Now Prussia-Germany
was again blessed with a monarch of such a forceful character as the present
King and Kaiser. And he warned: 'States can only be preserved by the means
by which they were created. Good fortune abandons states that change their
character. That is a lesson of history.'[21] The Borussian military cult also found
succinct expression in the letter that Houston Stewart Chamberlain wrote to
Wilhelm II to congratulate him on his birthday in January 1914. After
thundering against Englishmen, Americans, Jews and journalists, Cosima
Wagner's English son-in-law, who now lived in Bayreuth, extolled Prussia-
Germany as the embodiment of the strong Christian–German military monarchy and a bulwark against the chaotic modern world. 'Thanks and praise be
to God', he exulted, 'that a Germany exists, and in Germany a Prussia, and in
Prussia a Prussian heart, with, as the heart of the army, the House of
Hohenzollern!'[22]

If such warlike, reactionary appeals met with little sympathy outside the old
Prussian provinces, among the Social Democrats and Left Liberals or in
Catholic Germany, they fell on more fertile ground in the capital itself.
A high point of the anti-parliamentary movement was the 'Christian-national
mass demonstration' – 'Christian-national' was code for anti-Semitic – staged
on 26 April 1914 in the Zirkus Busch in Berlin, again with the slogan 'With
God for King and Fatherland'. On this occasion Count Kuno von Westarp,
leader of the Conservatives in the Reichstag, made an impassioned speech
defending the Prusso-German system of government of personal military
monarchy against the ever-growing demands for a parliamentary system. Like
Mackensen, Westarp invoked the historical successes of the Hohenzollern
kings but also praised – in contrast to the General – the achievements of
Bismarck, while hardly mentioning Wilhelm II directly. He too pointed to
the organisational advantages of a strong monarchy, especially in waging war.

In view of her geographical position, Westarp argued, Germany was threatened from two sides: in the west by a France intent on revanche and in the east by the growing menace of Pan-Slavism. 'That is a situation in which we must always bear in mind the old motto of Frederick the Great "Toujours en vedette", and must always be ready if it should some day be necessary to draw the sword to defend our existence, our honour, and our way of life in the world. For that, we need a united leadership.' Whereas the French Republic had always to be afraid that after a victorious campaign a generalissimo like Napoleon could set up a dictatorship, this danger did not exist in the Prusso-German system. 'We here know who our generalissimo will be: our Kaiser, King and War Lord from the House of Hohenzollern, that has shown for generations what great warriors it can produce, and whose historical tradition is that all its members, including future rulers, pursue a soldier's career, not as a game but as a serious profession for life. And if our War Lord then returns victorious, with increased prestige and increased power at the head of a people's army that is intimately linked to him personally, we shall never need to see in that a danger, but, given all our historical experience, a valuable and splendid success in the life of our whole nation.'[23] It was not far from this to the idea of a quick victorious war to polish up the tarnished halo of the Wilhelmine Monarchy.

For in reality, the slogan of 'One Volk, One Kaiser, One Reich' so frequently invoked in patriotic speeches and rallies in these final years of peace had long had a hollow ring. The overwhelming victory of the Marxist–republican Social Democrats in the Reichstag elections of January 1912 – the SPD polled 4,250,000 (34.8 per cent) of the twelve million votes cast – together with the undiminished strength of the predominantly Catholic Centre party (1,997,000 or 22.8 per cent) and the democratic spirit of the times that was noticeable everywhere (and often scornfully dismissed as 'Jewish' in right-wing circles) had exposed the profound crisis in which the Hohenzollern military monarchy found itself after 25 years of Wilhelm II's reign. Conservative elites and the authorities on the one hand and the great majority of the population on the other were facing each other in a confrontation that seemed impossible to resolve. Even the arch-reactionary *Kreuz-Zeitung* had to admit on 15 June 1913, on the occasion of Wilhelm's jubilee, that the German people, normally the most convinced monarchists in the world, had never before in their history been so critical towards the monarchical idea as now.[24]

Kaiser Wilhelm himself was naturally deeply unsettled, as he admitted in a letter to his son the Crown Prince in November 1913, by the 'excesses of parliamentarism, the Jews and the press' in his country.[25] As the French ambassador Jules Cambon perceptively observed: 'The older Wilhelm becomes, the more his thoughts are influenced by dynastic traditions, the rigorism of the Kaiserin, reactionary tendencies at court and above all the impatience of the officers.'[26] The thought that it might be the duty of the Crown to smooth over political and cultural conflicts by political conciliation, and to integrate society not by bombastic historicising but by a dignified and modest demeanour, never occurred to Wilhelm II. The Hohenzollerns and the Reichstag dominated by Social Democrats and the Centre party were worlds apart. As he exclaimed in 1912: 'I am too good a Prussian to let myself be strangled by this democratic Reichstag!'[27] His comment on a report from the Reich Chancellor about the problems the government was facing in parliament in May 1913 was totally − and typically − uncomprehending: 'That is the thanks of the Reichstag to Me and the princes.'[28]

When in the spring of 1913 the maiden voyage of the enormous Hapag liner *Imperator* − Germany's answer to the *Titanic* − had to be delayed for three weeks, the Kaiser took this as a sabotage action of socialist shipyard workers − he derided them as 'Sozen' − directed against him personally. Furiously, he wrote on a report from Hamburg: 'Because the ruffians had organised a great strike so that the ship would not be ready for *my* voyage. Was arranged by the *Sozen* as a personal insult to me.' The delay in the launching was 'caused by the Socialists throwing a pickaxe in the turbine to ruin *my* ship, which bears my title . . . It was simply a long-prepared action by the *Sozen* who *did not want* me to launch the liner *Imperator*. They succeeded completely. They are *in fact ruling* this country, thanks to our flabby legislation and totally passive governments! That is the truth!'[29]

Even if the fear that was alleged to haunt the Kaiser of some day being executed on the Berlin Schlossplatz seems exaggerated − kings are not beheaded in Germany − there was always the possibility of an assassination attempt. In April 1913 the court decided, after rumours of a planned attack, that the monarch should travel to Karlsruhe by car rather than by train. As the Auswärtiges Amt was informed, Wilhelm had no idea of the real reason for the change of plan, and assumed 'that it was only on account of the fine weather'.[30]

THE KAISER AND THE GOVERNMENT ON THE EVE OF WAR

Many a loyal German burgher will have taken consolation − like Thomas Mann in his 1918 book *Betrachtungen eines Unpolitischen*[31] (Reflections of an Apolitical) − from the thought that not the Kaiser but the worthy Reich Chancellor Dr Theobald von Bethmann Hollweg and a dozen highly respected officials determined the course of German domestic policy. But what in reality was the relationship between the Sovereign and the higher state bureaucracy in this late phase of Wilhelm II's Personal Monarchy? The importance of this question and the historiographical problems it raises have been touched on in the introduction to this chapter. The answer that emerges from the sources is anything but reassuring.

The tone adopted by the monarch in his dealings with the Chancellor, the secretaries of state, the Prussian ministers and the diplomatic corps even in the later years of his reign defies the imagination. Wilhelm defined himself, as we have repeatedly seen, as a military man and spoke scornfully of civilians who lacked the energy to act decisively and spent their time searching for compromises. This view influenced above all his behaviour towards the Reich Chancellor, about whose ponderousness he often spoke mockingly or with frustration. 'The Chancellor', Wilhelm joked to Tirpitz, 'has to be seen as a pathological case, he sees a line across his path and cannot steel himself to cross it'.[32] In March 1913 Wilhelm sent Bethmann Hollweg an English newspaper cutting describing Germany as a country ruled by timid, inert bureaucrats. The Kaiser minuted 'Correct' in the margin and ordered the Chancellor to forward the cutting to the War Ministry and the General Staff. Bethmann took the Kaiser's marginal note as referring to him and replied that he could not accept such a verdict, especially not now when, with the Army Bill, he was engaged in one of the most critical political battles in German history. He did not wish to offer his resignation directly, but he must refuse to forward the article to the military authorities in question, as if the Kaiser's criticism became known it would make it impossible for him to work with the generals. Wilhelm reassured him that he had 'never yet regarded [Bethmann] as a bureaucrat, nor as the autocratic ruler of the German Reich – as that article described the bureaucracy'. As for newspaper articles, the Chancellor should not be so sensitive and 'get himself a thicker epidermis'. But this jovial tone was insincere: in fact, Wilhelm had been extremely angry over what he regarded as Bethmann's pusillanimous handling of the Army Bill; and he characterised the Chancellor as 'flabby and ponderous in action. Conceited and touchy.'[33]

What he actually felt about his Reich Chancellor Wilhelm revealed in November 1913 to his eldest son, who had again demanded Bethmann's replacement by a 'strong man' who would act by force against universal suffrage, 'the brutalisation of parliamentarism', the poisoning of the people by Social Democracy and not least the steady growth of 'Jewish influence in the press'. He was 'by no means blind to the fact', Kaiser Wilhelm confessed, 'that my government has often failed to display as much energy and spirit as might be desired in the struggle against these and other abuses. I am constantly struggling to drive them in this direction and spur them on. But we just do not have any strong men with the spirit for the fight, and if there are any, they have so many failings in other directions that one cannot employ them in positions of authority'. Bethmann Hollweg, Wilhelm hinted, he was keeping on despite his weaknesses, primarily for reasons of foreign policy. 'This is of such enormous importance for our Reich, surrounded by hostile neighbours, that one cannot entrust it to a firebrand. If I have a man whose honest policy inspires confidence abroad, and who follows my directions, then I have to put up with this and that weakness of his domestic policy.'[34] That was not exactly a vote of confidence.

Although Bethmann was a very different character from Bülow, he was just as disinclined as his predecessor to see it as his task to contradict the Kaiser, let alone to force him to make fundamental changes in his style of Personal Rule. Only when serious external dangers or a threatening parliamentary crisis made it inevitable was he prepared to step in to moderate a policy Wilhelm had embarked on. For the rest, Bethmann functioned as 'the executive tool of His Majesty'. Sometimes he delivered himself of professions of devotion that could well have come from the pen of his oleaginous predecessor. In January 1913, for example, he did not shrink from assuring his Sovereign that 'of all that has contributed in the past twenty five years to enhancing the greatness, honour and power of Prussia and Germany so marvellously, there is nothing that was not rooted in Your Majesty's foresight or drew invaluable succour from Your Majesty's energy'.[35] And the following year, his letter congratulating the Kaiser on his birthday predicted that although the Hohenzollern Monarchy might be faced with yet another 'assault from democracy', 'the spirit of the people will be healed again ... by their faith in Your Majesty's noble person'. The nation was 'thank God, not synonymous with the parties' and would continue to look in hope to the Kaiser.[36]

In fact, Bethmann suffered, ever since he had taken office as Reich Chancellor, from the feeling – that was not without foundation – that he did not possess the Kaiser's full confidence. It was characteristic of him that he should ask the head of the Naval Cabinet in the summer of 1911, after Wilhelm had been treating him badly for some time, to give him 'a tip if H.M. had decided to drop him'. Admiral von Müller lamented the Chancellor's submissiveness and advised him 'not to put up with so much from H.M.'[37] As Bethmann's courage repeatedly failed him he thought of giving up his thankless office, resignedly remarking in 1913 that things 'could certainly not go on like this for much longer'.[38] Even on the eve of the war, as his wife lay dying, he was toying with the idea of resignation, not for personal reasons but out of sheer vexation.[39] In the spring of 1914 the head of the Reich Chancellery Arnold von Wahnschaffe and the head of the Kaiser's Civil Cabinet, Rudolf von Valentini, were discussing between themselves, in almost condescending terms, the question of whether Bethmann had better stay or go. 'I don't in fact believe that the Chancellor has decided to go', Wahnschaffe remarked, 'But I always think of what you said to me in the winter: "He won't stay in office much longer." Not that I think that this is a response to the mood of His Majesty, which I believe to be very loyal. I am sure that if the Chancellor so wishes he can go on working with the Kaiser for a long time. But he has now been a minister for 9 years, and I often have the impression that these years have taken a great toll on him mentally and in terms of morale – physically he is in good shape. Now is the worst time of course, at the end of this endless winter; perhaps the summer will freshen him up. If he talks to Your Excellency about the question of "going or not" I should advise you to point the pistol at his chest and tell him that he must decide definitely to stay on. He must get out of this perpetual school-leaver's mood. Because it stops him making any plans at all.'[40]

From time to time, certainly, the stolid, melancholic and overly conscientious state official Bethmann Hollweg made known his doubts about his master's commands, but the course of German domestic and foreign policy was determined not by him, but by the Kaiser and the men who had his ear at court. The Secretary of State at the Reich Treasury, Adolf von Wermuth, one of the few higher officials who courageously stood up for their views, trenchantly described Bethmann's dependence on the 'All-Highest's confidence' in his memoirs: 'His primary concern was not what he should do, but what he was *not* allowed to do ... The moment he was afraid of giving offence somehow, all attempts to move him were in vain. His position with the Kaiser preoccupied him above all else. It was the bedrock of his own authority. Quietly he would first assure himself of the Kaiser's opinion. Then he would confidently declare that so long as he could rely on the All-Highest's confidence he did not intend to yield.'[41]

Examples abound of this system of decision-making, which may be termed 'negative personal rule'. In the spring of 1912 the head of the Civil Cabinet made it clear to the Chancellor through a private letter (to avoid official channels, as he openly admitted), that in view of the Kaiser's determined attitude, he was under no circumstances even to consider reforming the Prussian electoral system. As Valentini wrote to him from Corfu on 2 May, Wilhelm was 'more than ever convinced, in view of the intemperance of the *Sozen*, that the Prussian electoral system must remain, and he will never be persuaded to permit any reform. I warn you urgently not to attempt anything in this direction.'[42]

In dealing with the state secretaries of the Reich offices and the Prussian ministers the Kaiser was even more inclined to operate in accordance with military notions of command and obey. A phalanx of Reich Chancellor and ministers in solidarity against the Crown, such as had arisen in the Köller crisis of 1895 and the Bronsart affair of 1896 under Prince Hohenhohe, or over the dismissal of Podbielski under Bülow, would have been unimaginable under Bethmann Hollweg. In February 1914 Tirpitz's colleague Albert Hopman aptly described the Reich Chancellor as the Kaiser's 'rubber-neck' whom the monarch always used to force the few ministers who tried to stand up to him to lie down again.[43] When the Colonial Secretary Friedrich von Lindequist asked to be relieved of his office in 1911 the Kaiser commented uncomprehendingly: 'I think it quite unheard of that such a high state official should simply throw away his portfolio at such a serious time and for quite trivial reasons! It sets the bureaucracy a very bad example of disobedience ... It testifies on the one hand to an exorbitantly high estimate of his own personal worth (vanity) and on the other to a quite hair-raising lack of tact.'[44] The Kaiser's reaction was much the same when the Prussian Minister of Agriculture, Bernd von Arnim-Kriewen and the Minister of the Interior, Friedrich von Moltke, tendered their resignations.[45] On the other hand, Wilhelm never made any secret of his readiness to dismiss even the highest officials on the spot if they trespassed on anything he regarded as 'sacred' ground: the prerogatives of the Crown, the navy, his absolute power of command in the military field and the three-class franchise in Prussia.[46]

The insulting manner in which Wilhelm treated his advisers even at this late stage in his reign extended to his closest retainers and the very highest military circles. The Commanding General of the Guards, Karl Freiherr von Plettenberg, wrote to his wife on 6 March 1914: 'Today ... I reported to the Kaiser, who dragged me by the ear into his room, but then tried to be very gracious.'[47] None other than the long-serving head of the Naval Cabinet, Admiral Georg von Müller, complained bitterly in 1912 that he had 'when making his oral reports during the northern cruise, personally ... met with such rudeness that could not have been more sharply expressed even as marginal comments'.[48]

THE CROWN PRINCE AS FRONDEUR

If the Reich Chancellor often had misgivings about carrying on in his uncomfortable position, influential voices were loudly demanding that he should go. Crown Prince Wilhelm, by now in his thirties, was becoming more and more the spokesman of fanatics on the radical right who were urging the

Kaiser to dismiss Bethmann and the Foreign Secretary Gottlieb von Jagow, and who were working for a *coup d'état* at home and a war against France and Russia abroad. The telegram of support that the Crown Prince sent to the Pan-German League at its Breslau conference in September 1913 attracted widespread attention.[49] At this very moment the Bavarian General Konstantin von Gebsattel sent to the Crown Prince (who forwarded it to his father and to Bethmann Hollweg) a memorandum demanding war on 'Jewish intrigues and the incitements of Social Democrat leaders' that were 'corrupting the monarchical spirit of the German people'. As the Germans were in fact 'Christian, monarchical, constitutional, but not parliamentarian' and wanted 'a king who actually ruled, not a puppet in monarchical guise', universal suffrage for the Reichstag must be abolished and replaced by a plural voting system, either by means of a *coup d'état* or perhaps after a 'successful' war. The General went on to demand draconian measures to 'solve' the 'Jewish question': subjection of the Jews to the laws governing foreigners, double taxation compared to 'Germanic' taxpayers, their exclusion from the state administration and journalism, a ban on the acquisition of landed property, and measures to prevent the miscegenation of 'the Jewish and Germanic races'. Gebsattel urged the need to act with all haste, as discontent with the monarchy and the government had already reached a pitch at which 'French' conditions would soon prevail. In his view, even a war that went badly would be preferable to a 'long cowardly peace', as Germany was certainly strong enough to recover quickly from a defeat. If the German Reich showed its neighbours its 'iron fist' there was 'nobody on the continent (and not even England either) who would not give way ... We cannot be destroyed, and for the others there is too much at risk for them to dare to attack', the General continued; and he appealed to the Crown Prince to assert these principles when he came to the throne: 'There can be no greater and more beneficent crowning action than when the predestined leader of his people strides ahead along the necessary path.'[50]

Bethmann Hollweg lost no time in replying to the Crown Prince à propos this poisonous document, explaining that 'every unsuccessful coup d'état is either foolish or criminal ... The chances for a successful coup d'état are lower in Germany, a federal state, than in a unitary state. Although, so long as order prevails, the federal governments stand absolutely firm together, they would under no circumstances be united on a programme for a coup d'état. It is also extremely doubtful that they would stand so firm together and hold out in the revolution that would necessarily follow this coup d'état.' Like Friedrich von Holstein twenty years before, Bethmann pointed to the danger that in the event of such upheavals in Germany hostile states, above all France, might interfere. 'On top of the civil war at home we should then have war abroad,

that is, we should manoeuvre ourselves into the sort of position that Germany
was in during the Thirty Years' War or Russia at the end of the Russo-
Japanese War.' The idea of starting a war simply for prestige reasons he
rejected equally decisively, warning the Crown Prince that 'in any future
war, if it is undertaken without a pressing reason, not only the crown of the
Hohenzollerns but the future of Germany would be at stake. Of course our
policy must be a bold one. But to rattle the sabre in every diplomatic complication when the security and the future of Germany are not threatened, is not
only foolhardy but criminal.'[51]

The Kaiser asked the head of his Civil Cabinet to draft his reply to his son
with regard to Gebsattel's memorandum. His reactions to the firebrand's
demands come down to us, therefore, not in Wilhelm II's usual abrasive
language, but only indirectly, in the elegant text that Valentini put before
him for signature on 22 November 1913 (the content of which, of course,
nevertheless reflected the views of the monarch). The Kaiser warned the younger
Wilhelm against making himself the advocate of critics, who were running
rampant everywhere. 'These days any incident in our public life, however
insignificant, brings forth a flood of Cassandra-like cries ... So it is not
difficult to put together a whole collection of newspaper material every day
that could convince the innocent reader that conditions here at home are
rotten and heading inescapably for disaster. Well, I should like to see a state
that had such well-ordered conditions, such an industrious, healthy population, and such steady progress in prospect, as the German Reich. A glance at
internal conditions in England, France, Austria and Russia is enough to prove
this. We do not want to let our joy over our success in all fields of human
endeavour be spoiled by the caustic criticism and carping of such people who,
in the old German tradition, always know better ... Not that I wish to close
my eyes at all to certain serious faults in our political and social life today: the
electoral law for the Reichstag with its demeaning drift and the coarsening of
parliamentary life is most regrettable; Social Democracy is poisoning large
sections of the population and behaves insolently as everywhere; Jewish influence is steadily increasing in the press, in social life and throughout the arts;
the press is for the most part dreadful.' However, the 'weird dreamer'
Gebsattel was not offering any solution to these problems. 'For him, the only
remedy for the excesses of parliamentarism, the Jews and the press is a coup
d'état, or as he calls it − without having any idea as to the legal regulations − a
"state of siege". He wants to see this measure adopted in the midst of peace, as
it seems to him that after a "successful war" it would be "ungrateful" towards
the people (!). Coups d'état may in South and Central American republics
count as part of the art of government, in Germany they have, thank God, not

been the custom and must not become so, either from above or below. Those who advocate such things are dangerous people, more dangerous for the monarchy and its continuance than the wildest Social Democrat. For even the thought of such a measure would be bound to shatter the firm bond of trust which here still, thank God, binds together the ruler and the broad mass of his subjects. Changing the constitution by force is only conceivable after the crushing of a bloody revolution, from which God preserve us!' Gebsattel's recommendations for 'expelling the Jews from the Reich' were dismissed by Valentini as 'really childish'. It would set Germany's economic progress back by a hundred years while at the same time she 'would drop out of the ranks of civilised nations'. 'However, we must certainly direct our efforts towards excluding Jewish influence from the army and the bureaucracy with all rigour, and limiting it as far as possible in the fields of art and literature. As for Jewish influence in the press, I agree with you: here Jewry has found its most dangerous stamping ground. Reining it in and putting a stop to its dirty appetite for scandal and slander is a most important task. But it is a difficult one and can only be achieved if the freedom of the press is not otherwise restricted. For this is useful and essential in the modern state as a safety valve for all sorts of complaints and discomforts that might otherwise find expression in a dangerous way.' In conclusion, the Kaiser admonished his son to be more discriminating in future and 'always to remember that those who rule must look at things from a higher perspective than the celebrities of the day'.[52]

Not that the hot-headed Crown Prince (see Figure 43) followed his father's advice. Again he demanded Bethmann Hollweg's replacement by a 'real man who doesn't fear death or the devil; who takes decisive action both at home and abroad, even if it means treading on other people's toes. I believe that the confidence Bethmann enjoys abroad is worth less than the fear of a really strong man in his place.'[53] By the same token, the Crown Prince demanded the replacement of Jagow at the Auswärtiges Amt by the more forceful Under Secretary Arthur Zimmermann.[54]

One result of these conflicts and of the Crown Prince's agitation in the Zabern affair (see below) was the transfer of the heir to the throne from Danzig to service in the General Staff in Berlin.[55] In January 1914 he was allotted a Civil-Adjutant to have a moderating influence on him and prepare him for his future role in government.[56] Nevertheless, the nationalist-militarist clique who had gained his ear remained a thorn in the flesh for the Kaiser and the civilian statesmen right down to the outbreak of war. In May 1914 Dr Paul Liman published a 300-page work, *The Crown Prince. Thoughts on Germany's Future*[57] that caused something of a stir. It was written in the knowledge, as the author made clear, of 'how strong the impact

Figure 43 Father and son: Kaiser Wilhelm with the troublesome
Crown Prince at Königsberg, 1913

of the personality of the monarch made itself felt, even in the modern state,
and despite the restrictions of the constitutional system'. For this very reason,
therefore, it was necessary to know more about 'the Kaiser of the future, who
would be the leader in happy and in difficult times'. Although the book was
not intended to be 'a panegyric', its purpose was to 'awaken and enliven
confidence in the future and destroy that tedious pessimism that is being
busily disseminated with demagogic solicitude'.[58] The Kaiser, unsettled, gave
orders for a semi-official notice in the *Norddeutsche Allgemeine Zeitung* 'that
the book was not in any sense inspired by the Crown Prince, who, on the
contrary had nothing to do with it'. The Chancellor had to point out 'that such
a semi-official notice would only serve to publicise Liman's book'. It would be
wiser simply to pretend the book did not exist. Next day Valentini could report
to Bethmann that the Kaiser had accepted his arguments and would refrain
from any official comment.[59]

THE KAISER AND THE ZABERN AFFAIR

Frustrating as he found the internal situation, and impatient as he was in his
dealings with the gloomy, overly cautious Reich Chancellor, in the military
field Wilhelm II wanted to live life to the full and to his heart's content. Above
all, in personnel matters in the officer corps and the navy, the Supreme War
Lord had the last word, even if the two Cabinet chiefs Moriz Freiherr von

Lyncker and Georg von Müller occasionally felt obliged to present him with counterproposals. At the end of 1913 Müller wrote to his colleague Admiral Adolf von Trotha: 'You know how December always brings the Cabinet particular tasks of an unpleasant nature. This year, however, it seemed to me especially difficult to make the right decisions regarding personnel changes, all the more so as at the All-Highest level personal preferences (even if justified) clashed with service interests.'[60]

Like the civilian Reich and Prussian officials, those in charge of the army and navy were constantly afraid that the Supreme War Lord might seek advice from some unaccountable person or other, and make use of the kingship mechanism to frustrate their plans. Despite his earlier promise to Moltke Wilhelm continued to take an active part in army manoeuvres and at their conclusion to deliver detailed and sometimes impressive critical commentaries.[61] He personally determined the building of fortifications, the provision of aeroplanes and guns, the deployment of warships, and many other matters.[62] He informed the Austrian military attaché in June 1912 that on his orders a new fortress was being built near Metz that was primarily designed to protect the Moselle valley.[63]

Wilhelm II's personal identification with the military, coupled with his scorn for civilians, whether high officials, diplomats, politicians, journalists or even mere inhabitants of towns and villages, led in the closing weeks of 1913 – the jubilee year he had hoped would be one of peace and patriotic celebrations – to the most serious constitutional crisis in Germany since the November storm of 1908. Wilhelm had always been suspicious of the new constitution granted to the Reichsland of Alsace-Lorraine. In May 1912 he threatened openly to smash it to pieces unless conditions in the border territory improved;[64] and eighteen months later he proved himself an uncompromising defender of Prussian military power against the constitution and the law, against the Reich Chancellor and the Statthalter in Strasbourg, against the Reichstag and international public opinion.[65]

On 28 October 1913 in the small Alsatian garrison town of Zabern (Saverne) an incident occurred that was not in itself of much importance, but which in the weeks that followed – thanks partly to mishandling, partly to deliberate provocation by the military – was to escalate into a major crisis: a young lieutenant, Günter Baron von Forstner, had ordered his men, in the event of clashes with the town population (whom he insultingly referred to as 'Wackes') to make full use of their bayonets, 'and if you run such a Wackes through in the process, that won't do any harm'; he even offered a reward of ten gold marks for every 'Wackes' stabbed.[66] When the public learned of these insults and demonstrations occurred, Forstner ordered his troops to patrol the streets of Zabern with fixed bayonets. On 9 November 1913, on the orders of the local regimental Commander, Colonel Ernst von Reuter, and with the consent of the Commanding General in Strasbourg, General Berthold von Deimling, machine-guns were brought into the little town and the proclamation of a state of emergency was threatened.[67] The matter assumed international proportions when it was reported that Forstner had also shouted to his troops, 'You can shit on the French flag.'[68] Deimling had ten soldiers, who had allegedly denounced this vilification to the newspapers, arrested out of hand. On 28 November the affair reached its inglorious climax with the random arrest of twenty-seven persons by military patrols under Reuter's command.[69]

Fatally, Kaiser Wilhelm II identified himself wholeheartedly with the illegal proceedings of the military, whom he was determined to protect against all criticism from the civil authorities and the public. In late November 1913 he was, as always at this time of year, hunting in Donaueschingen in the Black Forest and had no civilian advisers with him apart from the diplomat Karl Georg von Treutler. Even the latter was ignored by Wilhelm, however, who regarded the affair as a 'purely military' matter. 'Unfortunately, I continue to be shut out', Treutler complained to the Chancellor on 4 December. 'His Majesty obviously doesn't wish to talk to me about Zabern.'[70] To Wilhelm's mind the excesses of the military in Alsace were the fully justified response to the agitation of the French government and press in Alsace-Lorraine. 'The whole Zabern story', he raged on reading a newspaper report on 2 December, 'provides stunning evidence of the terrific French agitation that has been at work burrowing away under the noses of our civilian authorities until it has achieved this result in what was once a German town ... The German press and the Reichstag have taken the matter up, as usual, and are making a mountain out of a molehill.'[71] 'For the last 2 years', Germany had been 'reviled and insulted, not just in the entire French press ... but even at home by "Wackes" stirred up with French money. It may well be *our* patience that runs out!' he warned.[72]

The Kaiser was stiffened in his 'purely military' approach by his eldest son, who wrote brashly to his father, as usual, that he very much hoped that 'in the Zabern affair they will make short work of the damned rabble and that recruits from Alsace will be stationed again in Prussia and elsewhere to make them lose all their appetite for such things'.[73] He pressed his father to stand firm: 'Jewish democracy wants nothing more than to undermine your power of command, and they will use any means to achieve this.'[74] To Deimling and Reuter the young 'Kaiser of the future' sent telegrams that caused horror when they were leaked to the public: 'Bravo!' 'Just hit them hard!' 'An example must be set to make the natives lose their appetite for such things.'[75]

It was clear to the Statthalter of Alsace-Lorraine, Count Carl von Wedel, from the start that in his bitter dispute with Deimling over the illegal excesses and provocations on the part of the military in Zabern, the monarch would side with the Commanding General. In a bitter letter to Bethmann Hollweg on 23 November Wedel had already predicted that Wilhelm would be prejudiced in favour of the military. 'After all, H.M. believes that commanding generals have a better understanding of state policy and the measures that should be adopted towards the population than the state government. Forcefulness is trumps these days, whether it is appropriate or not.'[76] Wedel, who had a military career behind him before becoming ambassador to Vienna and Statthalter in Strasbourg, was to be proved all too right.

When Wedel asked for an audience with the Kaiser in nearby Donaueschingen to inform him in person about the 'serious excesses and illegalities' of the military, Wilhelm refused: he would have the head of his Military Cabinet report to him on the basis of Deimling's report; Wedel should send him his interpretation of events in writing.[77] In a telegram of 29 November 1913 the Kaiser berated the Statthalter and his civilian officials as complete failures: it was not the Viceroy but the Commanding General who bore 'the responsibility for peace and order in the military district'. At the same time, he telegraphed to Deimling, giving him a free hand to 'maintain peace and order', and adding that he should 'not spare the necessary energy in doing so'.[78]

In his written submission of 1 December 1913 Wedel pointed out that the Kaiser's decision limited the Statthalter's authority 'in a manner incompatible with his position and dignity' and offered his resignation.[79] The Reich Chancellor, like Wedel, recognised that the military in Zabern had committed 'grave infringements of the law'; and like the Statthalter he demanded Reuter's transfer and the sending of a senior officer to the town to defuse the situation.[80] The Chancellor's request that the Kaiser should qualify his order to Deimling to maintain peace and order with the phrase 'within the limits of the law' Wilhelm at first rejected. Only when Bethmann made him realise, by himself threatening to resign, that in the event of further illegal actions by the military 'the most serious dangers would arise for the Army and the Crown, because the whole country would hold the imperial power of command responsible for the unconstitutional situation', did the Kaiser yield and promise 'again to instruct' General Deimling, during his forthcoming visit to Donaueschingen, 'to remain strictly within the limits of the law'. A declaration to this effect then appeared in the *Norddeutsche Allgemeine Zeitung*.[81]

As the crisis deepened alarmingly Treutler suggested that Valentini might ask the Kaiser whether he ought not after all to come to Donaueschingen to be

at the monarch's side. After consulting Bethmann, the head of the Civil
Cabinet telegraphed the Kaiser to this effect, but the latter refused the offer
point-blank: it was, after all 'purely a question of the power of military
command'.[82] Instead of Valentini the newly appointed Prussian War Minister,
Erich von Falkenhayn, went to Donaueschingen, where he managed to get
General Kühne sent to Alsace to investigate, but the Kaiser insisted that this be
given no publicity: a purely military matter must not be discussed in parliament. Kühne's first report from Zabern did little to enlighten the monarch,
who concluded from it that 'the swinish press must take ¾ of the blame!!';[83]
and the order went out from the Black Forest to the Reich Chancellor, due to
face the enraged Reichstag on 3 December, to 'stand firm'.[84] The profession of
loyalty that Bethmann made, against his better knowledge, about events in
Zabern, culminating in the declaration that 'the King's uniform must be
respected in all circumstances', was indeed far from sufficient to calm the
storm: on 4 December 1913 the Reichstag passed a vote of no confidence in the
Chancellor (by 293 votes to 54 with 4 abstentions).[85] Thus Bethmann had
managed to stay in office but only 'by submitting to the chauvinistic current in
military and court circles', as Fritz Fischer sarcastically observed.[86] However,
the mood of excitement in the Reichstag and among the population was
primarily directed against the Kaiser, not against the Chancellor, who was
regarded as merely his mouthpiece. The leaders of the Centre party and the
Left Liberals warned 'that the suspicion was widespread that the Kaiser
himself had prevented atonement being made for the wrongs that had been
committed. The bitterness over this went deeper than in the November days'
of 1908.[87] When he learned from Admiral von Müller that the 'harsh line in
the Zabern affair' was indeed 'attributable to H.M.', Albert Hopman clasped
his hands above his head. 'Yet another disaster by way of "sic volo sic jubeo".
He won't ever learn.'[88]

     After the catastrophic vote in the Reichstag Adjutant-General Hans von
Plessen tried to persuade the Kaiser to return to Berlin, but Wilhelm refused.[89]
So the Chancellor had to decide at short notice to go to Donaueschingen,
travelling overnight and arriving in the morning of 5 December at Fürstenberg's palace in the Black Forest, where he also encountered Deimling and
Wedel.[90] The crisis meeting lasted no more than three-quarters of an hour as
Wilhelm was leaving for a function in Stuttgart. According to an eye witness,
the Statthalter 'shouted at Deimling and Wilhelm II so loudly that his voice in
the Schloss could be heard in the park'.[91] (See Figure 44.) Wilhelm was shaken
when Wedel declared that he and the whole government of Alsace would
resign. He refused to accept the Statthalter's resignation and suggested instead
that, to calm the situation down – but also to teach the population a lesson,

Figure 44 The Zabern crisis: the Kaiser strides away in anger from Bethmann
Hollweg and Count Wedel, the Statthalter of Alsace-Lorraine, at Donaueschingen,
5 December 1913

as they were economically dependent on the troops – the battalions stationed
in Zabern be transferred to a military training ground far from Alsace. This
proposal, together with an assurance that Forstner and Reuter would be
punished, persuaded Wedel to stay on as Statthalter for the time being.[92]
Had he insisted on going, which would have been all too understandable in
view of the Sovereign's treatment of him, then (according to Wahnschaffe in
the Chancellery) 'the position of the Reich Chancellor' would have become
'untenable'. But with the fall of the Chancellor 'all the accusations of illegality'
would then be directed against 'the one who held the military power of
command'.[93] Thanks to Wedel's giving way, therefore, not only had Bethmann
been able to save his own skin (for the second time in 48 hours) but the
Hohenzollern Crown and the All-Highest power of command had been
protected from 'the most serious' danger of revolution.[94]

Of course, Wedel's days as Statthalter were now numbered. True, his
successor – the conservative Prussian Minister of the Interior Hans von
Dallwitz – was soon selected, but there ensued weeks of delay, it being
impossible to find someone suitable to replace him at the ministry. Crown
Prince Wilhelm was not the only one who made it clear to the Kaiser that he
must under no circumstances appoint someone 'who might favour a reform of
the Prussian voting system. What a disaster that would be for the state one

need hardly say.'[95] Naturally, Wilhelm II stood absolutely firm by his right to decide such personnel matters himself. In this particular shake-up, affecting as it did the composition of the Reich government and the Prussian Ministry of State, the wishes of the Reich Chancellor were hardly taken into account; indeed, all the talk was again about the possibility of Bethmann Hollweg's replacement. On 26 March 1914 Valentini informed Bethmann that 'in today's audience H.M. immediately raised the matter of the newspaper reports about the appointment of Dallwitz as St[atthal]ter. How was it possible that it has got into the press? He had mentioned it to no one, nor had he reached a final decision . . . I replied that Your Exc[ellency] had not been able to reach a final decision either, because the matter of a replacement for Dallwitz was causing problems, and there could be no question of sending Schorlemer [to Strasbourg] because he cannot be sent anywhere at the moment in view of a possible change of Reich Chancellor. To this, H.M. replied that He absolutely rejected a change of Chancellor, there was not the slightest reason for this. Those whom I suggested as possible candidates for the post of minister of the interior . . . He rejected decisively. Trott was in just the right place in ecclesiastical affairs; Eisenhart could neither read nor write and was not ready for a ministerial post anyway . . . Rebus sic stantibus D[allwitz] would simply have to stay; he had in fact already had doubts about making him Statthalter. [The Minister for Agriculture Clemens Baron von] Schorlemer was much more suitable and also much easier to replace. He wanted a decision in this sense to be taken soon, if only to put an end to newspaper talk. The Kaiser instructed me expressly to tell Your Exc[ellency] this at once . . . I should be happy', Valentini added, 'if Your Exc[ellency] would accept His Maj[esty]'s decided refusal to part from Your Exc[ellency] as a definitivum. In other respects too, I think the solution a thoroughly felicitous one. In Strasbourg Schorlemer will remain available for all eventualities too, and the question of a replacement for Dallwitz really hardly admits of a solution at the moment.'[96] The appointment of Dallwitz as Statthalter proved possible nevertheless, as Friedrich Wilhelm von Loebell, who had been head of the Reich chancellery under Bülow, declared himself prepared to take over the Prussian Ministry of the Interior; and he, as Wahnschaffe reported to the Kaiser, was certainly not one to be thinking of 'electoral-law surprises', but would 'above all re-establish a normal relationship with his old fellow conservatives and disappoint the Liberal friends of the Bloc'.[97]

The Zabern affair was an exemplary illustration of the overweening militarism that had seized the Prussian officer corps, the Pan-Germans, the national-conservative Right, and not least the Kaiser, the Crown Prince and their military entourage at court. Blinkered and obstinate when faced with the ever-rising democratic flood at home, these circles had taken refuge on that narrow strip – ever diminishing in terms of its acceptability to the people – that was the army, the heart of Prussia, 'with, as the heart of the army, the House of Hohenzollern!' True, Bethmann Hollweg had been able to fend off the worst consequences of this attitude for the moment, but for the course of German policy in 1914 – particularly, as shown by the Kaiser's hostile marginalia, against France – the excesses of military arrogance on the western frontier boded nothing good. The edge of the abyss was now perilously close.

CHAPTER THIRTY-SEVEN

'With head held high and hand on sword-hilt!' Preparations for war 1913 to 1914

By 1913 the tension, not only in the Balkans, but between the European Great Powers in general, had risen to such a high degree that to many observers a world war appeared almost inevitable. The French military attaché in Berlin expressed alarm that the mixture he detected there of wounded national pride, irritation with France, determination to break out of the constraints of encirclement, fear of being attacked at a later date, and not least unbounded confidence in Germany's own war machine might soon – not immediately, but in a year or so when everything was judged to be ready – lead to an outburst of national arrogance and anger that could 'force the Kaiser's hand' and start a war.[1] In the spring of 1913, the British ambassador in St Petersburg, Sir George Buchanan, mused: 'I trust that when we get over the Balkan Crisis, we shall not be confronted with a European one; but I confess that I feel very nervous about Franco-German relations. I do not believe that either France or Germany will be able to tolerate the strain of their increased armaments for long; and Delcassé is convinced that Germany intends to precipitate a war whenever she thinks that the chances are in her favour. I only hope that he is mistaken.'[2] More than a year later, at the beginning of June 1914, Buchanan's French counterpart, Maurice Paléologue, had the feeling 'that we are going into the storm. At what point on the horizon and just when it will break out, I could not say exactly. But from now on the war is both predetermined and not far off.'[3] Admittedly, the feeling of sitting on a powder keg arose primarily from the realisation that the build-up of armaments on land and sea could not go on for ever. But it is equally true that these misgivings were fed by certain statements and actions of Kaiser Wilhelm II and the German military.

Ever since the autumn of 1912 Wilhelm had been proclaiming *urbi et orbi* his conviction that the great racial war between Germans and Slavs was unavoidable and that its outbreak was only a matter of time. These ethnic terms were remarkably elastic, as he might include the Turks, and on occasion even the Chinese, along with the Germans, while sometimes counting the English among their enemies. What he understood as 'Germandom' and its tasks for the future came out on 31 July 1913 when, during his twenty-fifth northern cruise, he unveiled two gigantic statues of mythical heroes at Balestrand on the Norwegian coast.[4] In his speech, in the presence of King Haakon VII, he thanked the Norwegians for their hospitality over the years, and then announced: 'But this ferocious hero [Fridtjov] is not meant to be simply an expression of my gratitude to the Norwegians! No, he has a greater, more general significance. He should be a symbol for Scandinavians, Germans, Anglosaxons and all those races that are proud to count themselves part of the powerful group of Indo-Germanic peoples! How he stands there, at ease with his sword, used to his sword, and leaning on his good sword "Angurwadel", which "always smote the wicked and never suffered wrong", the favourite and the most noble weapon of the Teutons: in manly pride and fearless self-confidence, may he remind all Indo-Germans that they are one family, one blood; that thanks to God's grace it has been vouchsafed to them in the past to do great things for the development of the world and its culture; and that they must stand together, true and firm, so that in the future too they may solve in common the great tasks that God will put before them for the benefit of mankind.'[5]

As Wilhelm's silver jubilee year, 1913, drew to a close, the great Army Bill was safely passed, and the final stages of the work to widen the Kiel Canal and fortify the harbours on Heligoland were approaching, some of the conditions that the Kaiser had laid down in December 1912 and earlier for starting a great war had been fulfilled. But is there evidence to suggest that in 1914 he and his advisers had in mind the dramatic discussions of November and December 1912 and were – as presaged by the 'war council' – actually steering towards such a war? In line with Fritz Fischer, Adolf Gasser and a number of other historians, Willibald Gutsche affirmed in his short biography of Wilhelm II (1991) that 'from the turn of the year 1913–14 the Kaiser was only waiting for a favourable opportunity to start the war in the manner envisaged by the military and civilian leadership, namely, by disguising it as a defensive war, and avoiding British intervention as far as possible', but this interpretation remains the object of controversy to this day.[6] Let us try, on the basis of the evidence surviving from these last months of peace, to reconstruct the thoughts of the Kaiser and his closest advisers in the army and navy. Were they counting on an early war? Were they taking practical steps to prepare for one? These questions have been asked many times in the century that has come to separate us from the catastrophe of the First World War, and they have received a great variety of answers. Today, in contrast to the heated controversies of the interwar years, the points at issue are largely a matter of academic nuance.

`TO SETTLE ACCOUNTS WITH THEM ONCE AND FOR ALL!'
WILHELM AND THE FRENCH

Shortly after the decision of December 1912 to postpone 'the racial war against Slavdom' Wilhelm II began to display a sharpened hostility towards France. In April 1913, when German tourists in Nancy were subjected to verbal abuse from French students, he raged: 'It is absolutely loutish and uncivilised, like in a barbarian country! That comes from the anti-German rabblerousing!' 'The Nancy affair following directly on the indescribable behaviour of the inhabit- ants of Lunéville towards the crew of the Z4 [the Zeppelin that had crashed there in 1908] is really too much! It shows the French population on the frontier to be in a state of hostile excitement that borders on the behaviour of Red Indians or Hottentots. It is high time for My ambassador to speak sharply for once, and point out that the German population will regard such behaviour if it goes on as a provocation that can no longer be tolerated!'[7] In December 1913, at the height of the Zabern affair, the Kaiser gave vent to his wrath at the anti-German feeling in France with a warning that he could soon lose patience.[8] He would later blame the outbreak of war in 1914 on the revolu- tionary mood of the people of Alsace against the military that had been brought about by the events at Zabern.[9]

It was against the background of increasing Franco-German tension over events in Alsace that on 5 and 6 November 1913 the Neues Palais in Potsdam was the scene of some highly alarming conversations between Wilhelm II, Moltke and King Albert of the Belgians (see Figure 45), reports of which (like the Kaiser's interview with the American journalist Hale five years before)[10] spread like wildfire from government to government, and subsequently served to confirm the belief that the Kaiser and his generals had deliberately caused the war. Just as he had spoken threateningly to King Leopold II in January 1904,[11] so Wilhelm now declared to the new King that war against France was 'inévitable et prochaine'. France herself, he claimed, wanted war, she was arming for this purpose, and the language of the French press testified to a growing hostility towards Germany; the French people's desire for revanche was finding increasingly aggressive expression. Albert's objection, that the

Figure 45 Wilhelm II with King Albert of the Belgians in 1913

French were in fact on the whole peaceloving, the Kaiser rejected emphatically. He repeated his view that the conflict was inevitable and added, 'given the overwhelming superiority of her army, Germany is sure of victory'. He did not doubt that in these circumstances the Belgian King would remember his family connections with the House of Hohenzollern (King Albert's mother was a Princess of Hohenzollern-Sigmaringen).[12] In striking unanimity with his sovereign, Moltke confirmed to their royal guest that war with France was imminent and that this time they must finish the job. 'Cette fois, il faut en finir.' 'Your Majesty can surely imagine how the whole German people will be swept along in irresistible enthusiasm on that day ... There will be no resisting the *furor teutonicus* once it is unleashed.' And just as the Kaiser had threatened King Leopold in 1904, so now Moltke spoke of the dire consequences that would follow if Germany's little neighbour (and the other small states of Europe) should stand in the way of her advance. 'The small states would be very well advised to go along with us, as the consequences will be hard for those who are against us.'[13]

The impression that the King was bound to get, that Wilhelm and Moltke had agreed what to say, and that in both cases it amounted to a kind of ultimatum, was confirmed by remarks made by Moltke to the Belgian military attaché, Major de Melotte. When the latter argued that Europe could surely now look forward to a long period of peace, Moltke strongly dissented and told him that he should have no illusions. 'War with France is inevitable, and much nearer than you think. We do not want it. We have nothing to gain in that quarter. But we have had enough of these eternal alerts that retard our progress. It is absolutely necessary that France should stop cramping us and provoking us, otherwise we shall call her to order. The sooner the better ... I repeat, we do not want war. We shall only wage it to put an end to the matter. And we shall win. We are quite sure of victory.'[14] The Belgian historian Jean Stengers has rightly emphasised that the Kaiser's and Moltke's aggressive language was not the expression of a fleeting impulse that was not to be taken seriously. He cites, not only Wilhelm II's earlier threatening words to Leopold II, but also the fact that a few days after King Albert's visit the Supreme War Lord wrote in the margin of a report from Paris: 'Just let them come! Then we will *finally*, with God's help, *settle accounts* with them.'[15] Shortly afterwards another imperial minute declared: 'It is a question of our standing in the world, which is under attack from all sides! So head held high and hand on sword-hilt.'[16] As late as February 1914, when President Poincaré said that France 'had only one aim, the maintenance of the concert of Europe and of peace', Kaiser Wilhelm observed: 'We have heard this rubbish before and it does not impress us at all! As soon as they have the opportunity to attack us they will do so without further ado. Especially as it is becoming increasingly clear that with their lack of manpower they will not be able to keep the 3-year military service in the long run.'[17]

Wilhelm's and Moltke's warlike utterances understandably had a devastating effect on the Belgian King. Although he did not record them word for word, he told the Belgian envoy in Berlin, Baron Eugène de Beyens, about them and authorised him to pass them on to his French colleague, Jules Cambon.[18] Cambon initially promised to keep Beyens's information to himself, but in view of its explosive nature he felt unable to keep his word. On 22 November 1913 he sent a secret dispatch to the French Foreign Minister, Stephen Pichon, the contents of which were to go round the world with lightning speed. According to Cambon, until the Potsdam encounter of 5 and 6 November, King Albert had believed that as Wilhelm had so far exercised his influence in critical situations in favour of the maintenance of peace, he would be minded to do so in future. However, 'this time he was completely different: Wilhelm II is no longer the upholder of the peace against the bellicose tendencies of certain circles in Germany. The Kaiser has become convinced that war with France is inevitable and that it must come to that sooner or later. He thinks that French policy ... has been inclined for some time to take every opportunity to accuse Germany and to work against her and he is convinced that the idea of Revanche has not ceased to dominate French minds. The Kaiser, it goes without saying, is convinced of the crushing superiority of the German army and believes its success assured. General Moltke spoke exactly like his sovereign. He too declared *war to be necessary and unavoidable*, but he showed himelf even more confident of victory, "for, as he told the King, this time the job must be finished and Your Majesty will certainly be able to imagine the irresistible enthusiasm that will sweep the German people along on this day".'[19]

Pichon showed Cambon's dispatch to the President, Poincaré, and to the head of the political section in the Quai d'Orsay, Maurice Paléologue, who insisted that it be communicated to the Chief of General Staff, Joseph Joffre. Pichon himself regarded the Kaiser's statements to King Albert as extremely serious, and according to Paléologue, was unable to sleep because of them.[20] A few days after receiving the dispatch he discussed the Kaiser's and Moltke's remarks with the Russian ambassador, Alexander Isvolsky, who reported to St Petersburg on 4 December that Pichon had received 'very reliable information' from Cambon in Berlin, according to which Kaiser Wilhelm, 'who personally had hitherto been noted for his entirely pacific feelings towards France, and was even always dreaming of a rapprochement with France', was now beginning 'to draw ever closer to the view of those around him, particularly in military circles, who are convinced of the inevitability of a Franco-German war, and therefore believe that the sooner such a war breaks out, the better Germany's chances will be'.[21] As Jules Cambon had sent a copy of his dispatch to his brother Paul, the French ambassador in London, the utterances of Wilhelm and the Chief of the German General Staff were known there, too.[22]

After the outbreak of hostilities, the French *Livre Jaune* on the origins of the war included, as proof of Germany's premeditated policy in July 1914, an (admittedly somewhat distorted) version of Cambon's dispatch of 22 November 1913 on King Albert's conversations in Potsdam.[23] In the peace negotiations at Versailles, too, and in the bitter debate over 'war guilt' between the wars, the statements of the Kaiser and his Chief of General Staff to King Albert constituted the key point of the accusation of the victorious Powers that Germany's leaders had deliberately started the war. Thus, the Special Commission on the Causing of the War, sitting in Versailles, stated in its report, under the rubric 'premeditated war': 'Several months before the crisis of July 1914 the German Kaiser had ceased to behave as an exponent of peace. Convinced of the crushing superiority of his army, he gave free expression to his hostility towards France.'[24] Moltke's later claim that the document published in the *Livre Jaune* was 'an invention from beginning to end' did not, as the documents show, accord with the truth.[25]

`WE HAVE BECOME FOES!' KAISER WILHELM AND RUSSIA

Long gone were the days when Wilhelm II had dreamt of reviving the Three Emperors' League, or cherished the hope that he could inveigle Nicholas II into a crusade against the 'Yellow Peril' in the east. Early in 1913 he declared that he had been deeply suspicious of Russia's intentions 'for a long time!' 'But people never believe me!'[26] His repeated attempts by means of threats and promises to bring about the break-up of the Franco-Russian alliance had come to an end with the second Morocco crisis. Even the elation he had felt at his daughter's wedding in May 1913, when together with the Tsar of Russia and the King of England, he thought he could determine the fate of Europe, had turned out to be a short-lived illusion. His belief, on this occasion, that he had secured the consent of Nicholas II and George V to the appointment of a German general (Otto Liman von Sanders) as military adviser and Commander of a Turkish army corps at Constantinople had led to bitter disappointment. On 23 November 1913 Wilhelm noted on a report from Jagow: 'Russia fears our strengthening of Turkey and the enhancement of her milit[ary] powers of resistance and of her utility to us against Russia if she should some day attack us. She wants to preserve Turkey in a moribund state and to keep Stamboul as easy readily available prey! ... In her hunger for territory Russia *devours* Manchuria, Mongolia, North Persia without our batting an eyelid. When we, however, send officers to Turkey, then Russ[ian] "public opinion" gets excited!! If we were to submit to Russia's wishes, it would all be over with our prestige in the Mohammedan world!'[27] When France joined Russia in protesting against the Liman von Sanders mission Wilhelm complained angrily: 'The Russians and French are simply insolent and shameless. I informed H.M. the Tsar of Turkey's request for a German military mission when he was in Berlin in June [sic], in the presence of H.M. the King of England. The King said: "It is quite natural that they should turn to you for officers to reorganise their Army. We are asked to send people to reorganise their Police & Gendarmerie, which we shall do."'[28] The disclosure by the British ambassador at Constantinople that Britain understood Germany's attitude in the Liman affair and was only supporting the Russian position lest Russia be isolated, provoked the Kaiser to an angry outburst on

19 December: 'That seems to be becoming a habit these days! – At *our* expense!! For Grey we are always good enough for doing new little favours for Russia at our expense! – I'm blowed if I'm going to take such treatment. Grey's behaviour has been despicable! For how long will he wobble along between the two sides? If it is to be Russia, let him go openly with her; if us, then let him go openly with us!'[29]

In February 1914 Wilhelm II sent General Oskar von Chelius, 'one of my most intimate personal friends', to St Petersburg as military plenipotentiary 'attached to His Majesty the Tsar of All the Russias in person',[30] but just at this very moment relations between the German and Russian emperors received a blow from which they were never to recover. On 11 February the Russian Prime Minister and Finance Minister Kokovtsov resigned. Wilhelm wondered if the change of ministers in Russia was 'possibly the precursor of war in the Balkans?!' and minuted on a dispatch from Vienna 'So, Russia wants *another* Balkan war!'[31] The Tsar knew very well that the Kaiser was displeased with the new Russian ministers. In a private letter to Sir Arthur Nicolson in March 1914 the British ambassador at Berlin, Sir Edward Goschen, reported on an extraordinary conversation he had had with the journalist and son-in-law of Field Marshal Colmar von der Goltz, Paul Krause, according to whom the strained relations between Germany and Russia were the result of a bitter quarrel between the two monarchs. After Kokovtsov left office Wilhelm had given the Tsar advice as to whom he should appoint as his successor and whom he should not. Nicholas was furious at this interference and made it clear to Wilhelm that the choice of the Russian Prime Minister was none of his business. At this, Krause continued, Wilhelm had declared in a speech to some army officers 'that Russia was behaving in an intolerable fashion and that before 1914 was out He would put things in order!' The journalist had then asked the Foreign Secretary Jagow, who did not know of the speech, what was to be made of it, and had received the reply that His Majesty had at the time been 'exceedingly nervous and irritable and that when he was in that state he often said things which were better left unsaid, and to which much attention should not be paid.' Krause for his part alerted the minister to the enormous danger if a country was ruled by a sovereign 'who from sudden accesses of nervousness or irritation was capable of speaking as he had done before a lot of eager and probably hot-headed young officers'. To Goschen, Krause added that the danger that could arise from this was indeed great, but that he thought it 'extremely improbable' that Wilhelm would ever actually steel himself to declare war. However warlike his language might be, 'there was not much fear that he would ever take it upon himself to declare war . . . except under the very greatest pressure from his people'.[32] Be that as it may, it is well documented that after this incident Wilhelm lost hope of any improvement in relations between Germany and the Tsarist Empire. 'Russo-Prussian relations are dead forever. We have become foes!' he declared in February 1914.[33] He was confirmed in his hostility to Russia by the Crown Prince, who, now an active member of the General Staff, spurred his father on to warlike measures against Russia. 'Russia has been behaving very strangely of late', he wrote to the Kaiser on 21 February 1914, 'and needs to be brought down a peg or two. This could perhaps be done by drawing Sweden into the Triple Alliance. Sweden could tie down at least 3 Russian corps in the event of war, very important for us.' Wilhelm II did not reject his son's advice in principle, merely commenting on the proposal to add neutral Sweden to the Triple Alliance: 'for this 2 are needed, as for a marriage'.[34] As we shall see, he personally took up the idea in July 1914.[35]

Within weeks of the Kaiser's warlike address to the young officers, anti-Russian utterances in the semi-official press and newspapers close to the government increased perceptibly. The Austro-Hungarian General Staff noted with satisfaction that the press department of the Prussian War Ministry had been expanded.[36] At the beginning of March 1914 the *Kölnische Zeitung* carried an article under the headline 'Russia and Germany' that was interpreted as a bugle call for the impending continental war, and that attracted attention not least because it was generally regarded as having been inspired by the Wilhelmstrasse or the War Ministry.[37] The Bavarian military plenipotentiary reported to his superiors on 6 March that although the article was described by the Auswärtiges Amt as 'not semi-official', it was nevertheless based on a sound knowledge of the situation and deserved attention. Wenninger explained that 'French official circles are at the moment suffering from a terrible hangover: They feel that Russia has led them into a cul-de-sac – 3-year military service – from which there seems to be only one way out – shameful retreat. For a nation like the French that is doubly difficult. Feelings towards the Russian ally, who is generally blamed for this fatal situation, are very irritated … To regain France's trust and unreserved friendship, and thereby her financial support, Russia is displaying what can only be termed an ostentatious enthusiasm for war against Germany. It started with her grumbling about the German mission to Turkey and is now continuing in a more or less earnest pursuit of armaments increases. Russia hopes thereby, probably in vain, to persuade France to retain the 3-year military service. The French cabinet, however, has already taken the first steps towards abandoning this system, which the shortage of manpower makes it impossible to implement … So long as this reversal is not an historical fact, the French army will continue to suffer from a great weakness: for the present, 2 badly trained contingents of recruits constitute the foundation of the French army. Russia is up to her neck in reforms and reinforcements of her army and navy that have hardly got started. The wellspring that supplies her need for loans looks like drying up. To depict this whole situation as a rare opportunity for a far-sighted German policy is the hidden purpose of the *Kölnische Zeitung* article. If this favourable situation is not exploited, then Germany will have demonstrated yet again her unswerving love of peace in the most striking fashion, but the Reich may in return find its magnanimity ill rewarded by its opponents once they have recovered their strength. The suspicion that the publication was designed as a precursor of further increases in the German army and navy seems not to be well founded. On the other hand, it is an open secret that the Reich Chancellor is about to come forward with a demand for large sums for strategic railways. These are intended to recover the advantage that France has gained in terms of transporting troops to the western frontier . . . and to increase Germany's chances of defeating France quickly in a two-front war.'[38]

It is not surprising that the *Kölnische Zeitung* article caused a sensation in Russia. When newspapers in St Petersburg protested against the paper's suggestion that Russia was planning to wage war on Germany in three or four years' time, Wilhelm II was sure that he had correctly perceived this to be precisely her intention and, as 'a military man', he would take appropriate action. 'That is certainly the case! Absolutely!', he wrote in mid March on a report in which Pourtalès had taken a sceptical view of the alleged Russian war programme. Russia's arming to wage war on Germany was, the Kaiser claimed, 'a *racial question*! and a matter of feelings, in which so-called "ruling circles" are swept along and have no say'. The Tsar's love of peace counted for nothing, the Kaiser declared, as Nicholas was weak and had demonstrated 'his absolute unreliability and weakness in the face of all kinds of influence'. Pourtalès had questioned whether anybody could foresee what the situation would be in three or four years' time, but Wilhelm did not hesitate to claim the gift of clairvoyance for himself and his fellow monarchs: 'This gift does occur! Among sovereigns quite often, rarely among statesmen, among diplomats hardly ever.' In three or four years' time Russia would have 'half a dozen army corps more!' and would then, in contrast to the previous winter, be ready for war. Even if the Russian leadership was hesitant, '*racial* principles will enable the army and the people to impose their will and go to war as soon as it suits them'. For the ambassador's attempts to depict Russia's policy as unthreatening, Wilhelm had nothing but scorn: 'Our dear Pourzel would have done better to leave this dispatch unwritten! He will totally confuse people who are not Russia experts along with the weak, apprehensive characters among his readers! But he is not in the least convincing . . . Here, we are in the no-man's land between the military and the political, a tricky and unclear area, but one where the diplomat usually goes astray. I, as *a military man*, do not have the slightest doubt that Russia is systematically preparing for war against us; and I make my policy accordingly. Wilhelm.'[39] If, after 1918, the Kaiser had been brought before an international tribunal as the victors of Versailles were demanding, this effusive marginal comment, together with the threats of November 1913 to the Belgian King, would surely have been more than enough to convict Wilhelm of Hohenzollern of having deliberately sought war.

There is no doubt that the assessment of the European situation that is revealed in the inspired article in the *Kölnische Zeitung*, in General von Wenninger's résumé, and in the Kaiser's marginal notes reflects the convictions that prevailed in the General Staff and which were to be decisive for German policy in the summer of 1914. In these weeks before the outbreak of war, both the Chief of General Staff and the influential Quartermaster-General, Georg Count von Waldersee, drew up memoranda that matched Wilhelm II's utterances almost word for word.[40]

`ENGLAND IS *DRAWING TOWARDS US*, NOT DESPITE, BUT *BECAUSE OF MY IMPERIAL NAVY*!!'

Great Britain played only a subsidiary role in the calculations of the German army leadership. The General Staff assumed that the British would gain advantages overseas from the war, but would not intervene in military operations on the continent. They had simply no idea of the implications of British seapower — even if the Royal Navy adopted a waiting position — for the reinforcing of German troops advancing towards France through Belgium. But what of Kaiser Wilhelm, whose task it after all was to coordinate the demands of the army with harsh diplomatic realities and the limited capabilities of a fleet that was still under construction? How was it that the deterrent effect of the Anglo-Franco-Russian Triple Entente that had saved Europe from war — most recently in the winter of 1912–13 — suddenly failed to function in the summer of 1914? Why did Grand Admiral von Tirpitz declare himself for war even though he knew better than anybody that he still needed many years to complete his great naval plan? And how did the Kaiser and the Admiralty Staff envisage fighting a naval war at all under such circumstances? Or was Wilhelm even now, despite all the declarations to the contrary, still under the illusion that — provided Russia could be cast in the role of aggressor — the British would not react if the Prusso-German army marched with overwhelming force through small, neutral, Belgium in order to 'make an end' of their

Entente partner France? Was he even aware of the full extent of Moltke's plan to sweep through the whole of Belgium to the Flanders coast and to take Paris from behind? Was he, who claimed to understand the British better than all his diplomats, assuming that – whether from fear of the German navy, civil unrest in Ireland, crises in parliament and the suffragette movement; whether they had been promised that their overseas territories would not be touched; or whether simply because otherwise the Netherlands and Denmark too might be occupied – the British would simply abandon their centuries-old balance-of-power policy in Europe?[41]

Since the British position had been made clear by Lord Haldane, Prince Louis of Battenberg and King George V in December 1912 there had been attempts on both sides to achieve a better relationship, which revived the hopes of Berlin, and not least of the Kaiser, that Britain might stay neutral in a European war. In February 1914 Wilhelm took soundings as to whether he ought to come to London in the summer, but then gave up the idea on Lichnowsky's advice.[42] His expectations of English neutrality had been strengthened by his brother, who reported to him after a visit to London in April 1913: 'In contrast to the impressions I got in December, I found Georgie much calmer, very well informed about the whole position in Europe, and, which will hardly be news to you, in complete agreement with your government's expressed views in this field.'[43] In May 1914, too, when Prince Heinrich went to England again for the funeral of the Duke of Argyll, George V 'used the term Entente Cordiale' in talking to him – presumably with reference to the state of Anglo-German relations at the time.[44]

In March 1913 the British Prime Minister made a speech in the Commons that spread alarm in Paris and roused false hopes in Berlin: the claim was false, Asquith declared, that England was obliged in the event of a continental war to send a large body of troops across the Channel. Wilhelm noted with glee the consternation which this declaration aroused in France and questioned the claim of a few Parisian newspapers that England would indeed have to support France, if only to maintain the balance of power in Europe. 'That won't be the case', he gloated, adding that, 'according to my private information from financial circles in the City the English government has told the French government *in writing*, that it will under no circumstances support Paris in starting a revanchist war to recover Alsace-Lorraine, whether *provoked* or *unprovoked*. France must get such follies out of her head.'[45]

In contrast to Bethmann Hollweg, Lichnowsky, and the Secretary of State at the Reich Colonial Office, Wilhelm Solf, who were working for an Anglo-German rapprochement by way of a colonial agreement, the Kaiser attributed the recent positive signals emanating from London to his battleship-building programme, which he believed would in the end force the British into neutrality. He interpreted every sign of a more conciliatory attitude as proof of the deterrent effect of Tirpitz's risk theory and concluded that the naval construction screw must be wound ever tighter. He was overjoyed at Churchill's speech to his constituents in Dundee, attributing the improvement in Anglo-German relations to the feeling of security produced by the increase in British naval armaments: 'My risk theory! best thanks for the compliment Wi[nston] Churchill. This finally disavows and puts an end to the Fischer-M'kenna [sic] era of lies. Haldane too, and the Building holiday.' By adopting his own risk theory, Wilhelm continued, 'the British First Lord of the Admiralty implicitly accepts the German Navy Law in its entirety. Especially the *Risk paragraphs*! For me and all who together with me have created and expanded the Navy Law, defending it with our whole strength against all attempts from abroad, and especially at home, to weaken or break it, there could be no better justification imaginable or possible. A great triumph for Adm[iral] von Tirpitz before the whole world, which has been well earned and will give him an outstanding position in the world. A new proof of the old theory I have so often expounded, that only the *ruthless, manly, fearless pursuit* of one's own interests *makes an impression on an Englishman* and in the end *forces him* towards *a rapprochement*, whereas being what is termed accommodating never does, as he always regards it as giving up and cowardice. I shall *carry on*, therefore, mercilessly and ruthlessly, and regardless of all opposition at home, with *implementing* the Navy Law *fully* and to the last detail, and shall if necessary expand it! England is *drawing towards us* not despite, but *because of My Imperial Navy!!* Avis au lecteur!!'[46] Churchill's proposal that the two Powers should temporarily stop building and embark on a 'naval holiday' was 'self-evidently' unacceptable to the Kaiser.[47]

The disagreement between Wilhelm II and the Chancellor with regard to England was again apparent when on 9 December 1913 Bethmann made a speech reviewing foreign policy in the Reichstag, in which he welcomed the 'so satisfactory and continuing improvement of our relations with England' and the general rapprochement between the two related peoples. But when British newspaper commentaries on the speech pointed out that there could be no question of any such rapprochement so long as England felt her naval predominance to be threatened by the German naval programme, the Kaiser made it clear that he would never agree to an understanding with England on such terms. British maritime supremacy 'is on its way to the scrap-heap!' he exclaimed. Such a condition was incompatible with any *'lasting improvement'* in Anglo-German relations and 'simply a pipe dream!' 'Friendship that is conditional on one party's acknowledging the permanent *superiority* of the other is a nonsense; that is simply a protectorate! and amounts to Germany's capitulation as a maritime power, which I shall never sign up to, now or ever. Then we shall just have to manage without it.'[48]

Given his sovereign's absolutely rigid position on the naval question, the efforts of the Chancellor and the diplomats in the direction of an Anglo-German rapprochement were doomed to failure. In February 1914 London once more proposed a mutual reduction of expenditure on armaments. With characteristic obsequiousness Bethmann Hollweg asked the Kaiser to decide on this central issue of German foreign and defence policy. He 'made so bold', he wrote, 'as humbly to beg Your Majesty to deign to inform me through a marginal note of Your Majesty's All-Highest decision'.[49] Wilhelm's reply was appropriately definite: 'I have no desire to see the whole endless, dangerous, chapter concerning arms limitation ... opened up yet again. One way or another it amounts to England's objecting to my right to determine the sea power necessary for Germany, and in the end, to an attempt to undermine the Navy Law. If the English government is prepared to make proposals on the basis of the fixed figures for *both* nations, i.e. squadrons of eight ships of the line, and battle fleets (five squadrons to eight), we would consider them. These proposals must see to it that other Great Powers do not go on to increase their armaments disproportionately. As for the naval holiday, I share Your Excellency's opinion that it cannot be implemented in practice, and Your Excellency must appreciate that there is no possibility that I could ever agree to it. How exactly we formulate our rejection of it, I leave to Your Excellency.'[50]

TIRPITZ AND THE APPROACHING WAR

Despite the Kaiser's very determined adherence to his naval construction plan it was Tirpitz himself who at the end of 1913 was overcome with doubts that his final objective could ever be achieved. He was deeply mistrustful of Bethmann and accused him of working with Solf, Lichnowsky and Kühlmann, and behind the backs of the Kaiser, the Reich Navy Office and the Auswärtiges Amt, for a rapprochement with England at the navy's expense. As late as May 1914 he scented a danger that the Kaiser might appoint Lichnowsky Chancellor, make a tacit agreement on the home front with the Left Liberals, as in Caprivi's and Hohenlohe's day, and conclude an alliance with Great Britain. He was forced to recognise that with the huge expansion of the army in 1913 the funds would simply not be available for the navy to expand the battlefleet further as he had planned. Above all, within the naval leadership itself his long-standing critics were gaining more and more influence over the Kaiser with their argument that instead of building for years ahead, the navy should prepare itself for an early war. According to Hopman, Heeringen's successor as Chief of the Admiralty Staff Hugo von Pohl was claiming, much to the annoyance of Tirpitz, that thanks to his connections with the court and the Chancellor and his wife *he* was the one 'in control of Germany's destiny'.[51] Even in the matter of naval building the monarch tried to go behind the back of Tirpitz's Reich Navy Office.[52] In February 1914 Hopman reported to Trotha that Prince Heinrich and a few other naval officers had told the Kaiser that 'the Navy had too few cruisers, too little oil and coal, too few men etc. H.M. then deigned to express himself in strongly-worded marginalia to the effect that this was a scandal, 4 small cruisers should be put into service at once, an appropriate supplementary budget brought in, people conscripted, the Chancellor asked etc. As everyone knows, however, even at the imperial high table the soup is never eaten as hot as it is cooked, and after a long lecture (which was, of course, not very well received) from the Secretary of State, the demand was reduced to supplying one cruiser more for the Navy in the summer.'[53] As late as 26 May 1914 the Kaiser stressed in an audience with Pohl 'the need to replace the cruisers withdrawn from the Navy by this autumn'.[54] If Tirpitz generally managed to fend off such interventions of the Supreme War Lord, they continued to represent a latent threat and at the end of 1913 contributed to his throwing his enormous weight, too, on the side of those demanding war.

On 9 October 1913 Tirpitz made a speech to his staff in the Reich Navy Office in which he openly admitted that his grand plan was faltering and concluded that if Germany was not to content herself with the status of a second-rank continental European Power she must soon enter on the gamble of a world war (see Figure 46). The English, the Grand Admiral declared, were attempting by clever propaganda to represent the Navy Law as the sole cause of Germany's political isolation, her grave financial embarrassments and her social crisis, to estrange the Kaiser from him. His policy was also being obstructed by the great expansion of the army in recent years, as there was no longer an adequate supply of funds needed to build more and bigger ships. 'If there is no money, and if the Reichstag does not grant the means, the whole Law is simply a scrap of paper. But a demand for an extra 150 millions, to be covered by new taxes, will be needed as soon as we revert to the *Dreiertempo* [building three new ships each year]. That will be the critical moment for the Navy Law ... For Germany, however, the *Dreiertempo* is an absolute necessity, as only this tempo validates the Risk theory and makes it impossible for England to counter it by doubling her own tempo. If we do not hold to it, the whole navy policy will have been a mistake.' Faced with this startlingly realistic

Figure 46 Grand Admiral Alfred von Tirpitz

analysis, which should have led to an about-turn in German naval policy, Tirpitz took refuge in fantasy and demanded a war, even if it should lead to Germany's downfall. He ended his speech with the words: 'The question, generally speaking, of whether Germany should fight against England, if necessary, for her world position – with the enormous effort that such a struggle would involve – or confine herself in advance to the position of a European continental Power of the second rank, this question is in the last resort a matter of political conviction. In the end it would seem more worthy of a great nation to fight for the highest objective and perhaps to perish with honour, than ignobly to renounce the future.'[55] Given such an irrational stance, the deterrent effect of Britain's superior seapower was simply set aside.

The Grand Admiral's decision, so momentous in view of his political influence, in favour of an early war would have been made easier for him because the preconditions that he had laid down in December 1912 for

starting a war — the widening of the Kaiser Wilhelm Canal and the fortification of the U-boat base in Heligoland — would both be completed by the
summer of 1914. On 18 March 1914 the Reich Office of the Interior informed
Tirpitz that work on the Kiel Canal was so far advanced that a trial passage of
a Dreadnought would be possible by June.[56] (In the event, the trial run,
originally planned for 28 May, had to be postponed for about a month, as
the work on the embankment wall under the Grünenthaler bridge took longer
than planned.)[57] The fortifications on Heligoland were completed at about the
same time.[58]

These months also witnessed other preparations that pointed to the navy's
heightened readiness for war. In the spring of 1913 the General Staff began to
consider who should represent the navy at imperial headquarters in case of
war. A demand of 27 March from Admiral von Müller, head of the Kaiser's
Naval Cabinet, that both the Reich Navy Office and the Admiralty Staff
should 'renounce any representation at supreme headquarters in the event
of war' gave rise to a dispute between him and the two bodies concerned that
was a veritable textbook example of the functioning of the 'kingship mechanism'.[59] According to Pohl, Chief of the Admiralty Staff: 'The present system
is that the supreme command over the Navy rests with His All-Highest
Majesty the Kaiser himself. Therefore decisions ... can only be taken by
His Majesty. As these will, in wartime, generally be very urgent, His Majesty
must have the officials who deal with them directly to hand. If the Chief of
the Admiralty Staff stays in Berlin while His Majesty goes to the battlefields at
the front, the affairs of those directing the naval war would be dealt with by
handwritten or telegraphic reports.' This would take time, 'and the task
of reporting [to the Kaiser] at All-Highest headquarters ... would fall to
the Chief of the Naval Cabinet. This would burden the latter with a
great responsibility for matters which do not otherwise belong in his sphere
of activity.' The proposal from the Naval Cabinet, 'that the Chief of the
Admiralty Staff could on the basis of his general knowledge of the Kaiser's
intentions, himself issue urgent directives "on All-Highest command"', Pohl
rejected, arguing, significantly, 'that even directives issued in Berlin "on All-
Highest command" would not carry the same weight as if they came directly
from those around His Majesty'. Moreover, such an arrangement would be
damaging for the unity of direction of the war at sea and and would make for
uncertainty among the various commanders. 'I fully appreciate', Pohl stated,
'that the position of a Chief of Admiralty Staff at the Supreme Headquarters
of the Army will not be a comfortable one, but I think this must be accepted in
order to avert the very real dangers that the present system with the separation of the Chief of the Admiralty Staff from the decision-making centre

would entail in time of war'.[60] After both the Reich Navy Office and the Admiralty Staff eventually agreed to reduce their representation, the Military Cabinet could inform the Naval Cabinet on 24 May 1913 that the representatives of both naval bodies would belong to the first echelon of Supreme Headquarters and would therefore be members of the Kaiser's retinue in the event of war.[61]

THE LAST WAR GAMES OF THE IMPERIAL NAVY

How did Wilhelm II, the Supreme War Lord who prided himself on having chosen Nelson and Napoleon as his role models,[62] plan to wage a naval war against England with a battlefleet that was still under construction? Together with Pohl he presided over a series of war games in the winter of 1913–14 that were to illuminate with startling clarity the insoluble strategic dilemma of the Imperial Navy. In an audience of the Chief of Admiralty Staff on 20 October 1913, the Kaiser laid down for the High Seas Fleet the strategic assignment – assuming that when war broke out between Triple Alliance and Triple Entente it found itself on its spring cruise off northern Spain – of getting back home. In another assignment the North Sea Station was given the task of fighting France and Russia 'having secured England's neutrality, which can be assumed so long as she does not see her Great Power position as under threat, especially in the Mediterranean'. In this scenario the greater part of the German fleet was to wage 'a vigorous offensive war against Russia ... All the big new battleships and part of the lighter fighting forces are available for the western theatre. The task of the force in the North Sea is to protect our own commerce, destroy the enemy's commerce, and threaten the coasts of France.' In such a war, i.e. assuming England's neutrality, the Baltic Station should simulate the war against Russia and, should the opportunity arise, 'annihilate' the Russian fleet 'as speedily as possible ... by hit-and-run style surprise attacks on its bases'. Finally, as the war game for the cruiser squadron, the Kaiser prescribed a war against England, in the event that the latter, instead of a close blockade of the German coast, opted for a blockade of the approaches to the North Sea in the Channel and between Scotland and Norway in an attempt to lure the German High Seas fleet into attacking as far away as possible from home waters. In this – realistic – scenario, the naval command should wage an offensive war and 'bring the merchant cruisers into play' as soon as possible. These war games were supposed to clarify what the chances of success would be for such offensive operations and what would be their best targets.[63] The exercises devised by Pohl and the Kaiser did indeed show how the High Seas Fleet was to get home in the event of war; and they

showed how war was to be waged against France and Russia if England's
neutrality was guaranteed; but for the crucial question — what strategy the
battlefleet should adopt in the most probable case, with Britain coming to the
aid of her two Entente partners against a German attack — the last war games
of the Imperial Navy had no answer at all.

The plans that the Kaiser and his little 'Pöhlchen' worked out for waging a
naval war against Great Britain would look almost laughable if they were not
so serious and irresponsible. As usual the Chief of the Admiralty Staff pressed
hard for a strategy — at least for part of the navy — that Tirpitz had been
tenaciously resisting for two decades: cruiser warfare. A memorandum which
Pohl presented to the Kaiser on 29 April 1913 is eloquent testimony to
Wilhelm II's involvement in the detailed planning for a naval war against
England. 'Your Majesty has deigned to command that in the event of war our
ships stationed abroad are to engage in *cruiser warfare*. In a cruiser war *against
England most targets* will be found *in the Atlantic Ocean* across which almost
all of England's imports of *food* and *raw materials* are transported.' Pohl
conceded that '*for us*, waging *cruiser warfare in this area* ... entails particular
difficulties', as Germany had no bases in the Atlantic. He set his hopes on
the Norddeutsche Lloyd's fast steamers, *Kaiser Wilhelm der Große, Kaiser
Wilhelm II., Kronprinz Wilhelm* and *Kronprinzessin Cecilie*, which could
attain a speed of 23 nautical miles per hour, and in the steamers of the
Hamburg-Südamerikanische Dampfschiffahrtsgesellschaft. Those steamers
which found themselves in New York or the Atlantic when war broke out
would have to be 'transformed (in accordance with *an integrative plan that was
to be worked out in peacetime*)' into auxiliary cruisers, with the assistance of
the gunboats *Panther* and *Eber* or of training ships, before the training ships
'*themselves likewise* join the *cruiser war*'. 'Those *fast steamers of Norddeutscher
Lloyd which are in home waters on the outbreak of war* ... are to be armed in
Bremerhaven and then ... *escorted* through the English blockade. Once they
are through, they must try to make use of their speed to evade the enemy and
get into the Atlantic via the north of Scotland.' From the start, these fast
steamers were to be manned '*entirely with Navy personnel*'. If on the other
hand, their transformation into auxiliary cruisers takes place abroad, 'then the
core of the crew including the commander will be *supplied from* the crew of a
gunboat ... *or*, if they are armed *from a training ship*, from the first officer of
the latter and a few of the guncrew, together with their weapons, while in
both cases almost all of the *civilian crew remain on board*. This is assured in
that Lloyd has declared itself willing to appoint as deck crew or in the engine-
room ... only persons who are either reservists in Your Majesty's Navy or who
commit themselves in writing to stay on board in the event of war.'

The greatest difficulty in waging a cruiser war against England, Pohl explained, would be the securing of coal supplies. However, there were coaling stations in German hands in Madeira, Tenerife, Las Palmas, St Thomas, and in Buenos Aires, Montevideo and the Cameroons, 'with whose owners the necessary agreements have been concluded'. Provision had also been made for supplies of coal 'in the larger South American ports to be *bought up* as far as possible *before the outbreak of war* by reliable persons *and shipped* to certain places for the use of Your Majesty's ships. They will receive appropriate payment from the Reich Navy Office through our big banking houses. As all readily available supplies will only suffice for a start, we have established contact with the Hamburg-Amerika-Line to send, though its agency, a steady supply of North American coal in neutral steamers to the places in question. The Hamburg-Amerika Line is prepared to take on the task . . . Suitable bays with no traffic where coaling ships can wait for weeks without their presence being known, are . . . no longer to be found. We have therefore adopted the expedient that the coaling steamers should seek to rendezvous, moving up and down near strategically favourable points but as far removed as possible from other traffic, to await the warships. The latter should then go with the steamer to the nearest suitable bay and there, regardless of whether it is discovered, load the coal and disappear again before enemy vessels can reach the spot.' After his audience, Pohl noted with satisfaction at the end of April 1913 that the Supreme War Lord had 'approved the principles and directives laid down for the cruiser war in the Atlantic and given the order to continue with the necessary preparations for conduct of the cruiser war as planned'.[64]

In a further audience of 17 March 1914 the Kaiser authorised the Commander of the cruiser fleet, in the event of war with England 'under favourable circumstances' to consider 'an immediate attack on the enemy navy . . . in order to paralyse English commerce by gaining command of the sea'.[65] As will be seen, on 19 July 1914, i.e. several days before the Austrian ultimatum to Serbia, Wilhelm ordered that the Norddeutsche Lloyd and the Hamburg-Amerika-Line should be 'alerted in good time' by the Auswärtiges Amt 'so that they can take action in time and send instructions to steamers in foreign waters'.[66] The Admiralty Staff's plans for a cruiser war in the Atlantic with converted passenger steamers, which the Kaiser approved on 29 April 1913 and again on 17 March 1914, were a deadly threat to Britain's survival and were, as Matthew Seligmann has recently shown, taken extremely seriously by the Admiralty in London.[67] In the event, however, no fewer than fifteen German passenger steamers, including *Kaiser Wilhelm II., Kronprinz Wilhelm* and *Kronprinzessin Cecilie* – were detained in American ports when war broke out in 1914. The *Kaiser Wilhelm der Große*, which should likewise have been turned into an auxiliary cruiser, and the fast steamer *Cap Trafalgar*, on which Prince Heinrich and his wife had recently travelled to South America, were both sunk at the beginning of the war.[68] As we know it was not the cruiser war with converted fast steamers but the new U-boats that were almost to achieve the planned objective: to cut off the supplies of foodstuffs and raw materials to the British Isles.

The role of U-boats and torpedo boats in a war against England was discussed by Pohl and Wilhelm II on 26 May 1914. The admiral reported to the Kaiser at length on the lessons the navy had learned from the latest war games. After the audience Pohl noted on his report: 'His Majesty was in complete agreement with the execution of the game and with the conclusions that arose from it. "However important the defensive, don't drop the idea of the offensive!" His Majesty attaches great importance to close co-operation between the U-boats and the High Seas Fleet, and to sending the former into action before the battle.' As regards the role of torpedo boats, too, Wilhelm insisted on offensive warfare. 'His Majesty emphasised here again', Pohl noted, 'that it was absolutely necessary that the torpedo boats, even in battles in daylight, should close with the enemy.'[69]

In an audience on 9 June 1914 Pohl put before the Kaiser the orders that naval commanders would receive for handling encounters with enemy armed merchantmen in wartime. The Kaiser approved the Admiralty Staff's proposal to use 'every means to break' the resistance of such a merchantman. 'The responsibility for endangering passengers and the property of neutrals lies with the enemy government. The crew are to be treated as prisoners of war. The passengers are to be released, if they cannot be proved to have participated in resistance.'[70] In the same audience the war game was again discussed that had shown that if the High Seas Fleet found itself off northern Spain on the outbreak of war it would not be able to get home, either through the Channel or round Scotland. The Kaiser then made the astonishing proposal that the Admiralty Staff 'should look into and work on the question of sending the Fleet into the Mediterranean in a case like the one in the wargame'. 'The Mediterranean would offer in every respect a worthy target for the activity of the Fleet, whereas the war game indicates that returning home would lead to its annihilation.'[71]

When on 18 June the Kaiser proudly informed Tirpitz of his idea the Grand Admiral could hardly believe his ears. He took Pohl to task with a 'top secret' enquiry: 'His Majesty the Kaiser has told me that Your Excellency had spoken to him about possibly sending the whole High Seas Fleet into the Mediterranean in the event of war, and that it will therefore have to be permanently equipped with coaling-, oil-, repair- and other auxiliary ships. As such a demand would involve substantially altering the development plans for our whole naval forces, I have the honour to ask Your Excellency to be so kind as to give me an explanation.'[72] To this provocation, Pohl replied that there must be a misunderstanding. The question had only been touched on in his last audience while discussing the results of the war games of the past winter. The exercise that the Kaiser had fixed was how to bring the fleet home if it found itself off northern Spain when war broke out. The war games had shown that the fleet would have to do battle against a considerably superior English force. This being the case, the thought had arisen, of whether the threatened annihilation of the fleet could be countered by shifting its activity into the Mediterranean. 'I told His Majesty the Kaiser, in discussing this idea, that given the lack of bases, the inadequacy of the dockyards of our allies, the impossibility of getting sufficient supplies of coal and materials, munition replacements, and the lack of torpedo boats and auxiliary ships, I thought any long-term successful action in the Mediterranean by the Fleet cut off from its homeland to be out of the question ... His Majesty said, however, that in the Mediterranean the Fleet would be able to find a target worthy of its activity in every respect, and that the obstacles to this must therefore be overcome. Consequently His Majesty also regarded it as the duty of the Admiralty Staff to look further into this kind of warfare.'[73]

Naturally the Kaiser and the General and Admiralty Staffs continued to take precautions against a British attempt to land troops in Belgium, the Netherlands, Schleswig-Holstein or Denmark. As we have seen, in the crisis meeting of 8 December 1912 the Kaiser had urged the speedy construction of more U-boats and had ordered 'U-boat warfare against English troop transports in the Scheldt or by Dunkirk' immediately on the outbreak of war.[74] The Admiralty Staff had already been considering the wording of the ultimatum to be sent to the Belgian and Dutch governments in the event of war with England. According to a memorandum of 24 August 1912, 'If those responsible for the war on land are not in a position to refrain from occupying the territory of one or both of these states, the state concerned will have to give up its neutrality and declare either for or against us ... If, on the other hand, it is decided to respect the neutrality of one or both of those states, the state to be spared will on the outbreak of war be asked for a clear statement of its intentions. It will be expressly stated that we can only respect its neutrality so long as it tries to defend, and can actually defend, itself against a violation of its neutrality by our opponents, and *especially against enemy troop landings*. Should we have reason to doubt that it is willing or able to do this, we should for our part reserve the right to take action – including the use of its territorial waters – to prevent enemy troop landings.'[75] The government in Copenhagen was informed in the same peremptory language that in the event of war

Denmark would have to reckon with a German occupation unless that country could itself fend off any attempt whatever by the British to land troops. In June 1913 the Austro-Hungarian military attaché von Straub reported to Vienna that when the German minister in Copenhagen, Count Brockdorff-Rantzau, had taken up his post in August 1912, he had told the Danish Foreign Minister straight out: 'We are neighbours after all, and I hope you will support me in keeping our relations on a friendly, neighbourly basis. Our respective positions one to the other seem to me clear: should it come to a war between Germany and England ... there are two possibilities, either Germany will win or England will – which you would perhaps wish for, and I understand you. If Denmark has not in actual fact upheld her neutrality with all her strength in this struggle, then in the event of our victory you are finished, believe me. But if Germany is defeated – and that could only be at sea – then we shall compensate ourselves at your expense and France's.' This at least showed, the astonished attaché observed, 'that the minister's instructions must have been remarkably clear'.[76]

WILHELM II AND THE STRENGTHENING OF
THE TRIPLE ALLIANCE

In the expectation of an early war Kaiser Wilhelm committed himself personally to strengthening the ties that bound his partners in the Triple Alliance, Austria-Hungary and Italy, to each other and to Germany. King Victor Emmanuel III's visit to Kiel in July 1913 was followed in the autumn by that of the Duke of Abruzzi to the Kaiser in Potsdam. It was of more than symbolic importance that General Pollio, Chief of the Italian General Staff, stayed in Germany for more than two weeks, attending military parades in Potsdam, Posen, Breslau and Berlin, as well as the imperial manoeuvres. The appointment of the German military attaché in Rome, Major von Kleist, as an All-Highest Flügeladjutant was particularly appreciated, as hitherto only the German military attaché in Vienna had been so honoured.[77]

These declarations of friendship between Germany and Italy were set against a background of top-secret discussions between the Italian, Austrian and German naval authorities. On 11 June 1913 Pohl reported to the Kaiser on the conference then meeting in Vienna to facilitate joint operations between the navies of the Triple Alliance Powers in the Mediterranean. He pointed to the personal interest that the Emperor Franz Joseph and the King of Italy were taking in the discussions and stated: 'Your Majesty's ambassador in Vienna believes, just as I do, that the main value of the planned co-operation lies in the strengthening of the Triple Alliance idea, in the disappearance of the distrust between Italy and Austria, and in the spirit of the offensive embodied in the planned agreement.'[78] The Kaiser was fully aware of the explosive potential of the secret agreement if it should become known in London, Paris or St Petersburg. 'His Majesty pointed to the need to keep the agreement and these goings-on absolutely secret. Special precautions must be taken when informing the Auswärtiges Amt, the General Staff and the Secretary of State at the Reich Navy Office of the conclusion of the agreement as far as it concerns them. Likewise the Chief of the Mediterranean Division. And the Head of the Kaiser's Naval Cabinet, in so far as the commanding of officers is concerned.' The Reich Chancellor was not directly mentioned in Pohl's memorandum.[79]

The keystone of the naval agreement between Germany, Austria-Hungary and Italy was the adoption by all three navies of a secret code devised in Berlin, the Triplecodex. In his audience with Pohl on 26 May 1914 the Kaiser 'took full cognisance' of the Codex and expressed his great appreciation for the important and thorough work the Admiralty had put in. Pohl, for his part, stressed the overall significance of the Mediterranean Agreement: '15 years ago in the Schloss at Kiel, Your Majesty declared "Sea power is Reich power". The truth of that has since been proved. Nothing binds the German tribes together so much as the Navy Law and the success that the Navy has achieved abroad and in building up its power at sea. The same will be true for Austria, where already today the imperial idea is held high among the ships' officers and crews, and where the whole nation is proud of the emergent maritime Power. The Naval Agreement can surely be expected to have the most beneficial effects on the unity of the Triple Alliance.'[80]

In these circumstances, Kaiser Wilhelm's five-week holiday on Corfu in the spring of 1914 assumed a highly political significance, as his journey to the Ionian Sea via Vienna and Venice gave him an opportunity to meet the Emperor Franz Joseph, Archduke Franz Ferdinand, King Victor Emmanuel and his brother-in-law King Constantine of the Hellenes. While staying at Schönbrunn on 23–4 March Wilhelm also had talks with the Foreign Minister, Count Berchtold, and the Hungarian Prime Minister, Count Istvan Tisza, in which the latter statesmen emphasised the need to cooperate in a far-sighted Balkan policy designed to win Romania back to the Triple Alliance and to enlarge Bulgaria at Serbia's expense.[81]

With regard to Romania, the Kaiser was extremely dismissive of the disturbing rumour that the 20-year old Prince Carol (whose mother was a princess of Saxe-Coburg-Gotha and a granddaughter of both Queen Victoria and Tsar Alexander II) was about to marry one of Tsar Nicholas II's daughters. Wilhelm explained, according to Berchtold, that 'Prince Carol was still far too young, as he himself recognised, and it would be "utter madness" for him to marry now. King Carol had no wish to see a marriage that would make Russian influence predominant, the close family ties and the haemophilia in the family made the connection seem undesirable, and finally, neither of the two daughters of the Tsar who were of marriageable age could be seriously considered, as the elder was supposed to stay in Russia as a possible successor to the throne if the sickly Tsarevich should not live to reign, and the second one had a heart condition. – Whether despite all these arguments His Majesty is certain that the marriage in question can be ruled out, I cannot say', Berchtold concluded. 'But his explanations rather gave me the impression that in this case the wish was father to the thought.'[82]

From Venice, Wilhem sent a postcard to inform his friend Max Fürstenberg that 'in Vienna everything went off well, as here'.[83] Treutler and Valentini reported 'how the warmth and cordiality of the meeting with the King of Italy surpassed all expectations. Things went so far that H.M. praised him yesterday evening as one of the . . . cleverest of people!'[84] Fatefully the Kaiser interpreted Victor Emmanuel's cordiality as an 'express promise' that Italy would enter the war, if it came, on Germany's and Austria-Hungary's side.[85] On 27 March the *Hohenzollern* sailed into Miramar, where Archduke Franz Ferdinand came on board to exchange greetings. Together the Kaiser and the heir apparent reviewed the Austro-Hungarian fleet before they adjourned for luncheon in the beautiful castle.[86]

TURMOIL IN THE BALKANS AND THE CRISIS IN
THE TRIPLE ALLIANCE

The bloody strife in the Balkans cast its shadow over the sunny holiday in Corfu and continued to call into question the improvement in relations between the Triple Alliance Powers after the Kaiser and his court returned to Berlin. In April 1914 Admiral von Müller reflected that changes were occurring in the Balkans 'that carried within them the seeds of European conflict'.[87] Already before his journey south, Wilhelm had received news of the possible union of Serbia and Montenegro. However, whereas Conrad von Hötzendorf saw in an amalgamation of the two states – giving Serbia access to the Adriatic – grounds for military intervention, the Kaiser continued, as before, to regard Montenegro's joining Serbia as natural and inevitable. He warned the Austrians straight out that they would not be able to count on Germany's support in a war over this issue. 'It is absolutely impossible to prevent the union', he wrote in mid March 1914, 'and if Vienna should attempt to do so, it will be committing a great act of folly and conjuring up the danger of a war against the Slavs that would leave us completely cold'.[88]

In May, he still clung to his view that the union of the two Balkan states could not be prevented: 'one must recognise that *à la longue* Serbia and Montenegro will come together after all, as Tisza said'. It was high time for Austria and Italy to reach agreement about the matter.[89]

It was not Serbia, but Bulgaria, ruled by the Kaiser's *bête noir* Ferdinand of Saxe-Coburg-Koháry, that was still in his view the real enemy in the Balkan peninsula. Behind the bloody conflicts between Albanians and Greeks in Epirus Wilhelm discerned the influence of Bulgaria who, he telegraphed from Corfu on 4 April, had stirred up the disturbances 'in agreement with Russia-France, naturally ... so as to damage us'. 'A sharp word to Sofia would indeed be in order.' The Reich Chancellor was 'most grateful' for the monarch's 'most gracious telegram' and promised in reply that 'the Bulgarian intrigues will be the subject of a sharp complaint to Sofia'.[90]

In these last months before the outbreak of the Great War Wilhelm was much preoccupied with the rebellion that had broken out in January 1914 against Prince Wilhelm of Wied, whom the Great Powers had established as Prince of Albania. Angrily, he condemned what he regarded as the utterly mistaken policy of his two Triple Alliance partners.[91] 'Everything is coming to pass that I feared two years ago when Austria started with this Albanian nonsense. She is now reaping what she has sown!' he declared in May 1914. From the start, it would have been better to have appointed a well-disposed Moslem like Prince Fuad of Egypt as Prince of Albania instead of Wied.[92] When Wied asked for a 3,000-strong force of international troops the Kaiser was aghast: 'He must be mad! Then we might as well carve it up and keep it! ... Such horrendous nonsense. It is better if he clears off and Fuad Pasha or a Mohammedan prince replaces him! He can't cope on his own! And international troops in Albania is a nonsense that I shall have no part in under any circumstances.'[93] At the same time, however, he declared it 'essential to curtail' the influence in Albania of Italy and Austria 'who under the feeble Wied are becoming all powerful'.[94]

Most of all, it was Wilhelm II's relations with Italy that were plagued by the Albanian question in the last weeks of peace. A report from Rome at the end of May 1914 roused him to a fury: 'Unheard of feebleness, defeatism and falsehood, utterly Italian! A bit of lying, a bit of cowardice, a bit of Comorrha [sic]!'[95] As a 'military man' the Kaiser flamboyantly rejected Italy's pressure for international control of Albania with Italian, Austrian, German and British participation. 'Nonsense! How does the gentleman think that could work? Everybody occupies a strip and *keeps* it!! And can shoot it out with bandits!' If at all, then complete Italian regiments must be sent to Albania, and not small European units in any circumstances. 'I think sending *small* detachments would be *fatal*! These are military matters that civilians just don't understand, diplomats least of all! Down there one can only operate with Brigades and Divisions, as the Turks did before, and even they did not achieve anything. Send Prussian brigades to Albania – that I shall never agree to ... These fellows have given no peace for 1,000 years! they will laugh at the *small detachments* and attack them, forcing *large* ones to be sent after them. The country can only be pacified by an army of 40–50,000 quartered in strong garrisons in all the towns, and permanently engaged in expeditions into the mountains. *Who* should exercise a *unitary* command over the *international* force? If there is *no unitary* command and if the commanders of detachments are also in charge of *districts*, then the row will start up in no time between Austrians, Italians, Germans and Englishmen and the tribes will be played off against each other by the *governments* that control the detachments! The best thing would be to put a number of officers at the Prince's disposal to form a militia as soon as possible from *loyal* and *devoted troops* and equip them with mountain artillery from Rome and Vienna. For the Albanian will not take orders from any *foreign soldier* in the long run ... Besides which one must not forget that as soon as fighting starts in Albania, then all the Balkan comtadjis, Turks, Bulgarians, Serbs and Montenegrins will organise themselves as bands and join in!'[96] As always, Wilhelm was afraid that the intervention of foreign troops might estrange the Moslem world. 'It will be very easy afterwards', he warned on 30 May 1914, 'to depict Europ[ean] intervention as directed against the Mohammedans, and then we shall have alienated the whole Moslem world for ever! And at that price Albania is not enough for me!'[97] On 3 June 1914 the Kaiser welcomed London's decision not to send any troops to Albania and said that he was decidedly of the same opinion.[98] Two weeks later he was foaming with rage at the 'mean spirited' attitude of the Italians towards the Prince of Wied, treating him as an opponent while he was fighting for his life and had '*no one* to support him'. 'Italy has betrayed the Prince, and he has noticed that he is supposed to behave as if he had *not* noticed anything, and say nothing about it!' Italy's policy in Albania was 'quite unheard of!' he stormed. 'Italy is false, treacherous and mean in this business ... A jolly state of affairs! Nice ally! Deceitful Latins!'[99]

At the beginning of July 1914 Wilhelm was still refusing to have anything to do with the suggestion of international intervention in Albania. This would end up as 'a permanent European garrisoning of the whole country' which would be simply unaffordable. To conquer and pacify the country would require '6–8 infantry divisions and 300–400 million Marks'. The political consequences would be unforeseeable, for 'if, in the present state of excitement throughout the Balkans, such a mass of troops were sent into action, the war would start again. Who was to put up such numbers of troops, pay for them, feed them? Who would command them? Where should they be drawn from? What guarantees would be given to the states that supplied troops that their expenses would be refunded? and from where? I shall not contribute one company.'[100] When on 1 July 1914 the Kaiser penned this impassioned refusal to send German troops to the Balkans, the Sarajevo murders were already three days old. A few days later, in another marginal note, he gave the signal for the Austro-Hungarian army to march against Serbia, and, as things turned out, for the world war. How did it come to this?

CHAPTER THIRTY-EIGHT

Summer 1914: the decision for war

Kaiser Wilhelm's last stay in the Achilleion on Corfu (see Figure 47) had been nothing less than idyllic. Excavations on the island had revealed the remains of a pre-Christian temple which particularly interested him. 'The excitement is great', he telegraphed to the archaeologist, Professor Dörpfeld, on 11 April 1914;[1] and to his aunt the Grand Duchess of Baden he reported that 'the excavations have unearthed very important things that are of great interest to the archaeologists'.[2] On 15 April, when the Reich Chancellor too had arrived at the Achilleion with his adjutant Baron von Sell, the Kaiser reported with delight that 'everything here is still lovely. The Chancellor has recovered his health and had a good rest, and is very pleased with his talks with His Majesty [King Constantine of the Hellenes] and the statesmen here.'[3] A fortnight later, on the eve of his return to Berlin, he wrote melancholically to Mary Montagu: 'Our stay here is coming to a close. It was heavenly. 5 weeks of absolute splendid summer weather, with a burning hot sun. The vegetation especially in my garden beyond description lovely ... We made very interest-ing excavations, which will give the archaeologists many a nut to crack. Yesterday we had a great treat 180 young Greek ladies had come over in a special steamer, & in the afternoon danced old national dances in costumes, that came from all parts of Greece & were quite unique. The effect of all the different colours under the olive trees in the sunlight were simply magical ... It was all like a fairy tale or a dream. I am very sorry to leave this paradise of light, beauty, charm & light, but duty calls & I must return to the tread mill! We are pleased by the announced visit of a British Squadron under Admiral Warrender, which will come to Kiel for our "week" ... Ever Yours devotedly William I.R.'[4] At the beginning of May Wilhelm returned to Berlin. Just eight weeks later the German Reich and its Austro-Hungarian ally found

Figure 47 'This paradise of light, beauty, charm & light, but duty calls.' The
Kaiser on the balcony of the Achilleion at Corfu, 3 May 1914

themselves at war with a host of enemies. Could the Kaiser, when he left his
beloved Achilleion, have had any sense of the heavy responsibility that
awaited him in the Berlin 'treadmill'? It is not unthinkable.

WILHELM AND THE GENERALS BEFORE THE SARAJEVO ASSASSINATIONS

As Kaiser, King, and Supreme War Lord, Wilhelm II was simply bound to be
central to the decision-making process in July 1914, and a heavy responsibility
rests on his shoulders for the terrible catastrophe that befell the world that
summer. As Baron Beyens, the long-serving Belgian envoy in Berlin, observed
at the height of the crisis: 'MM. Jagow and Zimmermann would not use such
language without express instructions to do so from the Kaiser.'[5] The French
chargé d'affaires in London was convinced that 'the German ministers would
not dare to alter the guidelines laid down by the Kaiser without an express
command to do so'.[6] The Austrian diplomats, who were in an even better
position to judge this, for them existential, question, also had absolutely no
doubt that it was Wilhelm II rather than the Reich Chancellor or Foreign
Secretary who directed Germany's foreign policy.[7] And yet, in these crucial
five weeks that were to lead to war, the Kaiser played a less active role than
might be supposed. As we shall see, at the start of the July crisis the actual

wire-pullers behind Germany's fatal policy were indeed the Chancellor and the Foreign Secretary, together with the Under Secretary in the Auswärtiges Amt, Arthur Zimmermann, and the Director of its Political Department, Wilhelm von Stumm. At a somewhat lower level, the diplomats Alexander Count Hoyos of the Vienna Foreign Office and Dietrich von Bethmann Hollweg, the Chancellor's nephew at the German embassy in Vienna, played a very active role in promoting war.[8] In the last week before the outbreak of war the generals Erich von Falkenhayn and Helmuth von Moltke then took control. The Chancellor sent Wilhelm off on his annual cruise along the coast of Norway, partly in order to create the impression that Germany had no foreknowledge of the bomb about to explode in the Balkans, but partly also to prevent the unpredictable monarch from interfering with the *circulos* of the Wilhelmstrasse. There is evidence that the Kaiser was to some extent manipulated, and at times even misled, both by Bethmann and by the military leaders, particularly when, after his return to the capital at the end of July, he sought to prevent Britain's entry into the war. Despite his frequent and vehement affirmations, since November 1912, of his willingness to fight France and Russia, Wilhelm's unpredictability was seen both in Berlin and in Vienna as a problem that would need to be managed. The Austro-Hungarian General Staff and the German ambassador in Vienna were in March 1914 still considering how the Supreme War Lord could be brought to sanction a 'preventive war' they regarded as necessary or desirable. Both the Kaiser and Archduke Franz Ferdinand, it was agreed, would have to be 'forced' to do so, by being faced with a situation 'in which there was nothing for it but to strike out'.[9] When Moltke and Conrad met at Karlsbad at the end of May 1914, they were again in full agreement 'that at the moment things were still favourable for us, that one should therefore not hesitate on a suitable occasion to proceed with vigour and, if necessary, to begin the war'; though persuading the civilian statesmen to take 'energetic measures' would be a problem.[10] And when on 6 June 1914 the Chancellor, in talking to the Bavarian envoy, Count Lerchenfeld, about the 'preventive war that many of the military were demanding', pointed out that Conservative circles, too, were expecting 'that a war would clear up the internal situation in Germany', he added that 'the Kaiser has not waged a preventive war and will not wage one'.[11] Such doubts as to Wilhelm's readiness to fight are difficult to explain in the light of his identification with the militant attitude of the generals demonstrated repeatedly in earlier chapters of this book. Even in the weeks immediately preceding the murder of Franz Ferdinand and his wife in Sarajevo on 28 June there is plenty of evidence of his determination to fight Russia and France. Nevertheless, having decided that the time was as propitious as it would ever be to begin their war, the Reich's military and civilian leaders were not prepared to run the risk that the Supreme War Lord might after all panic and spoil their carefully laid plans.

The train of thought among the generals – often characterised by historians as 'absurd' – in that spring and summer, has now been well documented.[12] The Bavarian military plenipotentiary, Ritter von Wenninger, was able to report, à propos Moltke's calculations in the July crisis: 'The Chief of the General Staff . . . is doing all he can to exploit the unusually favourable situation for striking out; he points out that France is at the moment in difficulties militarily, that Russia does not feel at all sure of herself in military terms, that the time of year is favourable, with most of the harvest in, and the training of the new recruits has been completed.'[13] Just before the outbreak of war Lerchenfeld summed up the thinking of the generals as follows: 'Military circles here are in very good spirits. The Chief of General Staff von Moltke declared, some months ago now, that the present moment is militarily more favourable than it can ever be again in the foreseeable future.' In justification Moltke cited Germany's superiority in terms of artillery and infantry weaponry and shortcomings in the training of French recruits in recent years owing to the reintroduction of the three-year service.[14] Significantly, Lerchenfeld made no mention of the attitude of Great Britain in a European war; whereas in fact, the most serious miscalculation on the eve of the great catastrophe was the notion that Germany could launch an offensive war against France and Russia without having to fear the intervention of the British Empire.

Moltke's belief in the advisability of a continental war while Germany had the clear advantage, if only as a hedge against some indistinct future menace, was common currency among the German generals. On 18 May 1914 the Quartermaster-General, Georg Count von Waldersee, sent his superiors a memorandum setting out the arguments for an early 'preventive war' – i.e. for striking at France and Russia so long as a speedy German victory was certain (and pointing out, expressly and repeatedly, that an attack on Germany was not to be expected in the foreseeable future). 'For the moment we do not need to contemplate that Germany's opponents might begin a war; however, the signs are increasing that they are arming ceaselessly and are making preparations in the most manifold areas in order to attack the Triple Alliance . . . or preferably even Germany on her own when the time is right, albeit at a time a few years hence. It cannot be said that this year in particular is inviting Germany's opponents to attack the Triple Alliance. On the contrary, for the moment none of the main participants can really gain anything from bringing about the armed fight.' The French army was inadequately trained and had no serviceable heavy artillery; Russia's would still need 'several years' to organise the army and build strategic railways; England, thanks to the Irish question and other domestic difficulties, had 'no inclination at all' to participate in a war. On the other hand, the 'motley Monarchy' on the Danube was becoming ever more precarious as Germany's ally, and Italy too was threatening to defect from the Triple Alliance. 'From this contemplation it can be deduced that Germany will not have to endure an attack in the immediate future in a normal course of events, but that, on the other hand, she not only has *no* reason to avoid a conflict whatever the situation, *rather*, that the prospects for surviving a great European war quickly and victoriously are *today* still very favourable for Germany and also for the Triple Alliance. Soon this will no longer be the case.' The German Reich would do well to consider this position clearly and calmly, unless it wishes to seek peace at any price. True, Waldersee recommended a further increase in the army to prepare for the great struggle — further evidence that at this point (mid May 1914) he did not reckon that war was about to break out immediately — but his own logic led him perforce to the conclusion that the sooner the war on two fronts could be brought about, the better.[15]

On 19 May, Moltke, having received Waldersee's memorandum, asked Gottlieb von Jagow to meet him to discuss it. 'The prospects for the future he found very depressing', the Foreign Secretary later recalled. 'In two or three years Russia would have completed her armaments. The military superiority of our enemies would then be so great that he did not know how we could cope with it. At present we could match them to some degree. There was in his opinion nothing left for it but to wage a preventive war to defeat the enemy so long as we could to some extent survive the struggle. The Chief of General Staff accordingly left it to me to conduct our policy with a view to bringing about an early war.'[16]

At this very time — the end of May 1914 — Colonel Edward House, the closest adviser of the American President Woodrow Wilson, came to Germany on his peace mission. His ambitious objective was to save world peace by establishing a sort of 'Anglo-American–German world oligarchy'.[17] He had lengthy discussions with Tirpitz, Zimmermann, Falkenhayn and other leaders in Berlin, and on 1 June, on the occasion of the *Schrippenfest* festival in Potsdam, half an hour alone with the Kaiser.[18] The American's account of this memorable meeting gives us an arresting picture of the Kaiser's political views on the eve of the world war. 'I found him much less prejudiced and much less belligerent than von Tirpitz. He declared he wanted peace because it seemed to be in Germany's interest. Germany had been poor, she was now growing rich, and a few more years of peace would make her so. "She was menaced on every side. The bayonets of Europe were directed at her", and much more of this he gave me. Of England he spoke kindly and admiringly. England, America and Germany were kindred peoples and should draw closer together. Of other nations he had but little opinion . . . He spoke of the folly of England forming an alliance with the Latins and Slavs, who had no sympathy with our ideals and purposes and who were vacillating and unreliable as allies. He spoke of them as being semi-barbarous, and of England, Germany, and the United States as being the only hope of advancing Christian civilization . . . I told him that the English were very much concerned over his ever-growing navy, which, taken together with his enormous army, constituted a menace; and there might come a time when they would have to decide whether they ran more danger from him and his people making a successful invasion than they did from Russia, and the possibility of losing their Asiatic colonies. I thought that when this point was reached, the decision would be against Germany . . . In my opinion, there could be no understanding between England and Germany so long as he continued to increase his navy. He replied that he must have a large navy in order to protect Germany's commerce in an adequate way, and one commensurate with her growing power and import-ance. He also said it was necessary to have a navy large enough to be able to defend themselves against the combined efforts of Russia and France . . . I asked the Kaiser why Germany refused to sign the "Bryan treaty" providing for arbitration and a "cooling-off period" of a year before hostilities could be inaugurated. He replied: "Germany will never sign such a treaty. Our strength lies in being always prepared for war at a second's notice. We will not resign that advantage and give our enemies time to prepare . . . He said . . . that Great Britain had nothing to fear from Germany, and that he personally was a friend of England and was doing her incalculable service in holding the balance of power against Russia.'[19] Two weeks later, after taking soundings in Paris, too, Colonel House summed up the disturbing impressions he had gained in Berlin and Potsdam for Sir Edward Grey in London: 'I told of the militant war spirit in Germany and the high tension of the people, and I feared some spark might be fanned into a blaze. I thought Germany would strike quickly when she moved; that there would be no parley or discussion; that when she felt a difficulty could not be overcome by peaceful negotiation, she would take no chances but would strike. I thought the Kaiser himself and most of his immediate advisers did not want war, because they wished Germany to expand commercially and grow in wealth, but the army was militaristic and aggressive and ready for war at any time.'[20]

Clearly, the inhibition level against launching a war was particularly low amongst the military in the Prusso-German monarch's entourage, and given the symbiotic relationship between Wilhelm and his generals, there was always the danger that he, too, as 'a military man', might give his decisive vote to the war party. And indeed, within a few days of Colonel House's visit, the Kaiser was talking quite like Moltke, Waldersee and the generals at court. On 9 June he prophesied, à propos of a threatening Greco-Turkish conflict over the Aegean Islands, that there would soon be a 'bust up' over the partition of Turkey, and added what may seem to us an uncanny marginal comment: 'We shall soon be coming to the 3rd chapter of the Balkan Wars, in which we shall all be taking part, hence the strenuous and colossal war preparations of France and Russia!' In expectation of a great war between the Triple Alliance and the Franco-Russian alliance he ordered his policy-makers – just as in 1912 – to 'clarify the position in relation to England. W.'[21]

From 11 to 14 June Wilhelm stayed with Archduke Franz Ferdinand at his castle of Konopischt near Prague. According to the Chief of the Austro-Hungarian General Staff, Conrad von Hötzendorf, at this meeting the Kaiser was pressing the Archduke over the need for war: if the Austrians 'did not strike, the position would get worse; Russia was not ready for war at the moment'.[22] On his return, he was presented on 15 June – the twenty-sixth anniversary of his accession – with an article in the *Berliner Lokal-Anzeiger* reporting on the Russian War Minister's insistence on the retention of the three-year military service term in France. Wilhelm covered the article with marginal notes that showed him to be, if not exactly wishing for an immediate war, then at least strongly identifying himself with his General Staff and its militarist mindset. He dismissed the claim that Russia and France did not wish for war as 'rubbish': their armaments and the development of Russia's railway network were 'all directed against Germany'. As 'my General Staff has always claimed!' he wrote, Russia's rearmament had started two years before, in accordance with agreements with France. 'That calls for a clear decisive answer in the form of action!' he thundered. 'Well then! the Russians have shown their cards at last! Anybody in Germany who still does not believe that Russo-Gaul is working at high pressure for an early war against us, and that we must take appropriate countermeasures, deserves to be sent to the lunatic asylum in Dalldorf at once! Stiff new taxes and monopolies, and the 38,000 unconscripted into the army and navy at once!'[23] These demands were exactly in line with the thinking of Moltke, Waldersee and the War Minister Erich von Falkenhayn.

The Kaiser's bellicose marginalia carried the weight of instructions for the Reich leadership in the Wilhelmstrasse. On 16 June, twelve days *before* the Sarajevo assassinations, Bethmann Hollweg informed Prince Lichnowsky that the Kaiser and other top authorities in Berlin were inclining to the view that Russia was working according to plan for an early offensive war. Calls were being heard for a further immediate and comprehensive strengthening of the army, to be accompanied by an increase in the navy. The Kaiser, Bethmann emphasised, 'was now quite at home with this way of thinking'. To 'clarify' the British attitude in the event of a European war, as the Kaiser was demanding, Lichnowsky should point out in London that 'any sort of clash of interests, even quite a minor one, between Russia and Austria-Hungary could ignite the torch of war'. Whether a renewal of the Balkan crisis would lead to a European conflagration would depend, Bethmann warned, on the attitudes of Great Britain and Germany.[24] Not only Bethmann, but the highest-ranking military officers took Wilhelm's warlike attitude as a welcome signal for decisive action. On the very day that Bethmann informed Lichnowsky that the Kaiser and the generals were inclining towards a preventive war, Waldersee asked the military plenipotentiaries of the three non-Prussian kingdoms (Bavaria, Saxony and Württemberg) to cease sending written reports to their respective war ministries forthwith. Emissaries from the General Staff were already on their way to Munich, Dresden and Stuttgart to explain the situation to their war ministers in person.[25] What foreseeable developments in the next few days and weeks Waldersee had in mind, and whether he had even perhaps got wind of the impending outrage in Bosnia, must remain a matter for speculation.[26]

On 20 June, just eight days before the Sarajevo assassinations, the Kaiser, when speaking to the banker Max Warburg during his visit to Hamburg for the launching of the *Bismarck*, was again contemplating the possibility of a preventive war. According to Warburg, 'Russia's armaments and her extensive railway construction constituted in [the Kaiser's] opinion preparations for a war that could break out in 1916 . . . Oppressed by his anxieties the Kaiser was even considering whether it might not be better to strike out rather than to wait.' Warburg countered that 'Germany would become stronger with every year of peace. By waiting she could only gain.'[27] As we know, this wise advice was to be disregarded.

A few days later Wilhelm went to Kiel to welcome the British squadron that from 23 to 30 June was making a courtesy visit on the occasion of Kiel Week.[28] He had invited all the British Admiralty staff, and was disappointed that neither the First Lord, Winston Churchill, nor Prince Louis of Battenberg, the First Sea Lord, could be present.[29] Colonel House's desire to travel to Kiel together with Sir Edward Grey for secret discussions about détente with the Kaiser also went unfulfilled, not least because the British Foreign Secretary was afraid of offending French and Russian susceptibilities.[30] Despite the studied politeness, the atmosphere between the British and German naval officers was tense. 'There was a certain frostiness between us', the head of the Kaiser's Naval

Cabinet recalled after the war. 'Measures were taken against English espion-
age . . . and we were accordingly careful when we went on board English ships
not to seek to see more than the social character of the visit necessitated. The
Kaiser himself, for example, when he went aboard the English flagship,
declined the invitation to examine the interior of a gun turret.'[31] As the Kaiser
explained in a marginal comment: 'I was on an expressly "private visit" and
did not "inspect" anything, lest I might have to make concessions in return.'[32]

To the German naval authorities their British guests appeared to be more
than usually concerned to use the visit to find out about the Kiel Canal and the
number and capabilities of German U-boats.[33] They were embarrassed, therefore, when the squadron Commander, Admiral Warrender, approached Prince
Heinrich directly for permission for the cruisers *Southampton*, *Birmingham*
and *Nottingham* to make their return journey through the Kiel Canal. In the
end, however, no objections were raised to the three warships' sailing though
the newly widened Canal.[34] Five weeks later the British and German navies
were facing each other in a fight to the death.

REACTIONS TO THE ASSASSINATION OF FRANZ FERDINAND

In the afternoon of Sunday 28 June 1914 the Kaiser was aboard his yacht
Meteor, taking part in the regatta in the Kiel fjord. At 2.30 the head of the
Naval Cabinet received a telegram from Consul-General Eiswaldt in Sarajevo,
reporting that Archduke Franz Ferdinand and his wife had fallen victim to a
revolver attack. Müller immediately went by motor-launch to inform the
Kaiser, whose initial reaction he recorded in his diary: 'Do you think we had
better cancel the race?' The Kaiser decided to return to Potsdam next day, but
to allow the regatta to continue.[35] On 29 June the imperial couple were
greeted on their arrival at the small 'royal station', Wildpark, by Prince August
Wilhelm and his wife, the Reich Chancellor, Bethmann Hollweg, and the
head of the Civil Cabinet, Valentini. To all appearances, there was as yet no
sign of any intention to make the Sarajevo murders a motive for military
action in the Balkans.

Over the next few days the decisions were to be taken that four weeks later
led to the outbreak of the First World War. Historians have generally seen the
Kaiser's notorious marginal comment of 3 or 4 July – that 'now or never' the
Serbs must be 'sorted out' – as the decisive signal that after some initial
hesitation determined German official policy to take a hard line against
Serbia. But how did this imperial minute originate? After all, a full seven days
had elapsed since the regicidal murder in Sarajevo, which, given Wilhelm II's
notorious impulsiveness and his belligerent mood in the preceding weeks and

months, must give food for thought. There must have been some process of decision-making, albeit difficult to reconstruct for lack of evidence, in the first days of July. Whom did the Kaiser talk to in those days, what consultations and agreements ensued in the General Staff, the Prussian War Ministry, the Reich Navy Office, the Admiralty, the Wilhelmstrasse and in the Neues Palais?

To all appearances, life at court went on as normal in the days after the imperial couple returned from Kiel. There was as usual ample opportunity for serious discussions, though as to their content we have practically no information. On Tuesday 30 June Wilhelm received a joint oral report from the War Minister, Erich von Falkenhayn, and the head of the Military Cabinet, Moriz von Lyncker. On the same day, the Austro-Hungarian ambassador, Count Ladislaus von Szögyény-Marich, was invited to luncheon; and the Reich Chancellor came to dinner. The Wednesday morning saw an audience with the head of the Civil Cabinet, Valentini, followed by a session to discuss the furnishing of the new imperial yacht with his naval colleague, Müller, the Captain of the *Hohenzollern* and a naval construction engineer. On the next day, 2 July, the War Minister and the head of the Military Cabinet returned for another joint audience.[36] Just how little Wilhelm was thinking of a major war in these first days after the murders in Bosnia is clear from the fact that on the evening of 3 July he was still talking about the journey he was planning to make to Bucharest in the autumn.[37]

Originally the Kaiser intended to go to Vienna with his brother Heinrich for Franz Ferdinand's funeral on 3 July, returning to Potsdam on the 4th, but surprisingly this plan was abandoned 'on account of a slight indisposition' on the Kaiser's part, as the court circular put it.[38] In reality, the Consul-General in Sarajevo had learned that some dozen conspirators had been dispatched from Belgrade to carry out further assassinations, whereupon he had 'most urgently advised against' the Kaiser's going to Vienna.[39] The Austro-Hungarian Foreign Minister Count Berchtold, too, told Tschirschky on 2 July of a 'report, according to which 12 murderous thugs were on their way to assassinate Kaiser Wilhelm' – which might, he added, 'open people's eyes in Berlin to the danger that threatens from Belgrade'.[40] Wilhelm accepted the Chancellor's advice to abandon his journey to Vienna, but attached importance to the Emperor Franz Joseph's learning the real reason for his decision.[41] Both his fear of assassination and his rage at having been forced to give up his visit are bound to have affected his mood. On 3 July Admiral von Müller learned from his colleague Lyncker, who had been in the Neues Palais the day before, 'that the abandonment of the journey to Vienna is connected with uncertainty regarding assassinations, and that the uncertainty arising from the whole Austro-Serbian conflict is putting the northern cruise in doubt'.[42]

This was an early reference to a possible military action in the Balkans and the serious consequences that could ensue.

Crown Prince Wilhelm, in these early stages of the July crisis, was demanding not war, but the dismissal of the Chancellor Bethmann Hollweg and a *coup d'état* followed by a policy of repression that would very probably have led to civil war in Germany. On 4 July the heir presumptive, now 32 years old, wrote from Zoppot near Danzig rejecting his father's accusation that he had neglected to express his sympathy over the Sarajevo murders: his silence, he truculently contended, had been deliberate, 'as every word said or written about this shocking affair' seemed to him 'so banal and platitudinous'. He assumed, moreover, 'that you would know your eldest son well enough to know that it needed no words to show how deeply I understand your grief. – But deeds are more important than words. The opportunity must now be grasped to proceed energetically against the whole socialist rabble and the infamous guild of anarchists in this country at last. Reintroduction of the [Anti-]Socialist Law, revision of the wretched Reich association law, a new, stiff law to protect those willing to work. These things must be done while the spirit of the people is still at fever heat, i.e. fast. Of course, it can't be done with the present Reich Chancellor, so, along with millions of right-thinking Germans, I urgently beg you to let this hapless man go, and hand over the country to a man of iron, such as we need. Forgive this digression, but if the death of the poor heir to the throne has this result, we here in this country would bless him.'[43] As late as 9 July the hot-headed Hohenzollern Prince in Zoppot showed that he still had no idea of the policy that had been adopted in Berlin, telegraphing directly to the 'hapless' Reich Chancellor: 'I see from the newspaper that Serbs living in Berlin have been planning to assassinate His Majesty. If this should prove to be the case it would be desirable to expel at once all the filthy Serbs hanging around in Germany, especially the students. Expect energetic measures. Best regards. Wilhelm, Crown Prince.'[44]

At first there was uncertainty in official circles in Berlin and Vienna as to how to react to the Sarajevo murders. There were in both capitals advocates of a conciliatory line as well as those who thought the moment had come to 'settle accounts' with Serbia. In addition there were, as has been seen, numerous and powerful advocates of a 'preventive war' against Russia and her ally France. The Saxon envoy at Berlin, Ernst Freiherr von Salza und Lichtenau, reported on 2 July, after making enquiries in the Wilhelmstrasse, that plans were being made in Austria for energetic action against Serbia. The authorities in Berlin, he added, had advised Serbia to be as conciliatory as possible, and Russia had also been asked to exercise a moderating influence in Belgrade. According to this report, therefore, people in the Wilhelmstrasse believed that war between Austria-Hungary and Serbia could probably be avoided. 'If it nevertheless breaks out, then . . . Russia . . . would mobilise and the world war would no longer be preventable.' Yet this was the very situation, Salza went on to report, that the generals were seeking to bring about: 'Military circles are again urging that we should let it come to a war now, while Russia is not yet ready, but I do not believe that His Majesty Kaiser Wilhelm will let himself be inveigled into this.'[45]

Not merely German generals, but also some high-ranking civilians in the Wilhelmstrasse greeted the Sarajevo assassinations as a welcome opportunity to launch the so-called preventive war against Russia and France under what they thought would be favourable circumstances: neither Russia nor France was militarily 'ready', and England, faced with the Irish problem, the militant suffragette movement and other difficulties, could not go to war, and had moreover recently shown herself friendly towards Germany.[46] The German journalist Dr Victor Naumann had already called at the Foreign Ministry in Vienna on 1 July to explain (citing the Director of the political division of the Auswärtiges Amt, Wilhelm von Stumm) that 'people in Berlin were very worried . . . about Russia's armaments'. Naumann had seen for himself that in the German capital 'not only in military and naval circles, but in the Foreign Office too people were no longer quite so hostile towards the idea of a preventive war as a year ago. They have reached agreement with England about Africa and the Portuguese colonies, and the visit of the English fleet to Kiel had been arranged in order to document the improvement in relations. They therefore believed they could be certain that England would not intervene in a European war.' Stumm had told Naumann that the war 'which Germany could have whenever she liked' was now 'no longer impossible'. An annihilating Austrian strike against Serbia, Naumann went on to argue, was a matter of life and death for the Habsburg Monarchy. 'For Germany [it would be] the test . . . of whether Russia wanted war or not . . . France would probably be compelled for financial reasons to influence Russia in the direction of peace, but if it nevertheless came to a European war, then the Triple Alliance was at present still strong enough.'[47] As a matter of established fact the Wilhelmstrasse decided immediately after the Sarajevo assassinations and in agreement with the General Staff that the situation was unusually favourable, and pressed for strong action by Austria against Serbia even though this clearly involved the danger of war on a continental or even a worldwide scale.

In the mind of Prince Lichnowsky, the German ambassador in London, the instruction that Bethmann Hollweg had sent on the Kaiser's orders on 16 June had aroused the horrified suspicion that not only Wilhelm and the military, but also the civilians in the Wilhelmstrasse thought the moment had come to

settle accounts with the Franco-Russian Alliance; and he therefore decided to
go to Germany at the end of June for the celebrations connected with the visit
of the British squadron to Kiel. Lichnowsky's discussions in the Wilhelmstrasse on 29 June confirmed his fears that his own government wanted to use
the regicide in Sarajevo as a pretext for war against Russia; and he expressed
serious reservations about taking such a gamble. At the beginning of July,
therefore, the General Staff prepared, expressly for the doubting ambassador, a
secret memorandum about the armaments and strategic railways that Russia
was planning to undertake over the next few years; and it was on the basis of
this document that the Under Secretary, Zimmermann, explained the political
situation to Lichnowsky on 5 July.[48]

In the original version of a memorandum that was published in the spring
of 1918 under the sensational title *Die Schuld der deutschen Regierung am
Weltkrieg*, Lichnowsky describes his encounter with Zimmermann as follows:
'On my return from Silesia on 5 July I had a talk, shortly before my train left,
with the Under Secretary of State. He told me that a letter had just arrived
from the Emperor of Austria, saying that Vienna now wanted to take energetic
action to put an end to the intolerable situation on the Serbian frontier. The
Under Secretary seemed to think that if we could not now after all avoid a
war — thanks to Russia's unfriendly attitude — it would perhaps be better to
fight it now rather than later. I did not fail to express my serious objections to
this view, and pointed out that an Austrian war against Serbia would without
doubt lead to a world war.'[49] Later, Lichnowsky regretted his failure to stay in
Berlin on 5 July and to declare that he could not go along with a policy that
was aiming at war.[50] All this seems to show clearly that the General Staff, the
Foreign Office and the Reich Chancellor were already united on a course of
action involving war against Russia immediately after the Sarajevo assassinations, and before the Kaiser indicated his agreement to Austria's taking
military measures against Serbia in his marginal note of 3–4 July.

Naturally, the naval leadership was also involved in these decisions. As
early as 3 July Admiral Pohl asked the Reich Navy Office 'whether the work
on the Kaiser Wilhelm Canal had reached a stage where Dreadnought-class
ships could pass through, and when the still outstanding trial passage would
take place'.[51] A few days later the acting Secretary of State at the Reich
Navy Office, Eduard von Capelle, emphasised that both Pohl and the
Commander of the High Seas Fleet, Friedrich von Ingenohl, felt it to be
of 'the greatest importance, from a military point of view, that a Dreadnought should pass through the Kaiser Wilhelm Canal immediately'.[52] The
naval and civil authorities pressed on vigorously with reinforcing the weak
points in the banks of the canal, with the result that early in the morning

of 25 July 1914 the Dreadnought-class *Kaiserin* could undertake the trial run with the Kaiser's express authorisation.[53]

THE KAISER AND THE PROSPECT OF CONTINENTAL WAR

As German support for an Austrian action against Serbia could not be promised without the Kaiser's consent, the eyes of all those advocating war were turned, from the start of the crisis, on Wilhelm II. That he was personally deeply affected by the bloody murder of his friend 'Franzi' was shown by his sincere displeasure over his eldest son's failure to express his sympathy in writing.[54] The Kaiser's fear that a similar fate could befall him or another member of the imperial family was certainly genuine and by no means new.[55] As for Wilhelm's probable *political* reaction to the murder of Franz Ferdinand, there were of course, initially, wide differences of opinion. In the Wilhelmstrasse and the General Staff there were doubts as to whether he would particularly regret the death of the Archduke.[56] The Kaiser, however, agreed with the assessment of his ambassador in Vienna, Heinrich von Tschirschky, that the death of the heir apparent amounted to a great loss for 'the German element in the Austrian state'.[57] Wilhelm praised Franz Ferdinand's politics, even though he had been 'Russia's best friend', and had 'always' wished 'to restore the old Three Emperors' League'.[58] The Hungarian Prime Minister's suggestion that Franz Joseph might exploit the Kaiser's outrage at the regicide in Sarajevo 'to combat ... His Majesty's predilection for Serbia and to get his energetic support for our Balkan policy',[59] soon became a reality even without pressure from Vienna, when in a marginal note Wilhelm raged against the Serbian government for trying to implement its expansionist policy in the Balkans by means of 'murder and bombs'.[60]

Altogether, during these first critical days the Kaiser's mood swung back and forth between war and peace, with the result that the Wilhelmstrasse and the General Staff found themselves obliged to 'extract' from the monarch the decisions they desired. In the above-cited discussions of 1 July Victor Naumann told the highly influential Count Alexander Hoyos of the Vienna Foreign Office 'that Kaiser Wilhelm, if one talks to him properly at the present moment, when he is shocked by the murder in Sarajevo, will give us [Austrians] any assurance we want, and will this time [!] stand firm to the point of war, because he recognises the threat to the monarchical principle'. The Berlin Foreign Office, Naumann added, would 'not discourage this sentiment, because they regard the time as favourable for bringing about the great decision'.[61]

Vienna, too, was considering how the German Emperor could be brought to support military action against Serbia. At first, it was assumed that there would be negotiations with Wilhelm II on the occasion of Franz Ferdinand's funeral in St Stephen's cathedral.[62] Once Wilhelm cancelled his journey, policy-makers in Vienna decided – astutely capitalising on the Kaiser's psychological state – to send him a handwritten letter from the old Emperor Franz Joseph, whom he so deeply revered.[63] At the same time Waldersee saw to it, in agreement with Zimmermann, that the Kaiser should on 3 July receive none other than Major Günther Bronsart von Schellendorff, the German military attaché in Bucharest, who had been agitating against Russian policy as late as the middle of June.[64] The Kaiser had 'reviled everybody, and praised only the Greeks', Waldersee reported back to Zimmermann after Bronsart's audience.[65] What else the Kaiser and the attaché discussed we do not know; but it was perhaps hardly a coincidence that it was just at this moment that Wilhelm wrote the sharply anti-Serbian minute which both the generals and the civilian policy-makers could now interpret – with some relief – as a command.

A report of 30 June from Tschirschky had reached Berlin on the afternoon of 2 July, and the Kaiser sent it back to the Foreign Office on 4 July, castigating in angry marginalia the restraining line that the ambassador had adopted towards Vienna's planned action against Serbia. 'Who authorised him to do this?' Wilhelm thundered. 'That is very foolish! It does not concern him, as what Austria intends to do about it is her business alone. Then it will be said afterwards, if it fails, that Germany did not want it. Tschirschky should kindly drop such nonsense! The Serbs need sorting out – *and soon.*' It was 'now or never', he declared, for a thoroughgoing settling of accounts with the Serbs.[66]

News of the Supreme War Lord's bellicose mood spread rapidly from the military at court and Wilhelm II's civilian entourage to the army, the navy and the Wilhelmstrasse. Tschirschky altered the advice he was giving to the statesmen in Vienna at a stroke, even before the Emperor Franz Joseph's letter could be handed to the Kaiser.[67] On Saturday 4 July he received the influential *Frankfurter Zeitung* correspondent Hugo Ganz, and told him 'emphatically and repeatedly' (obviously intending that Ganz should pass the word on to the Austro-Hungarian Foreign Ministry) that 'Germany would support the Monarchy through thick and thin, whatever it might decide to do against Serbia ... The sooner Austria-Hungary strikes, the better. Yesterday would have been better than today, but today is better than tomorrow. The Kaiser and the Reich would stand by Austria-Hungary without fail.'[68]

Wilhelm's crucial minute of 3/4 July was not, therefore, an unconsidered impulsive reaction to the assassination of his friend six days previously, but a deliberate instruction, even if he had to a certain degree been manipulated into giving it. It was completely of a piece with his militaristic and bellicose cast of mind that had in the past few weeks and months coloured his conversations and marginalia on precisely this Balkan question. That the Kaiser was acting in full awareness of the gravity of the possible consequences of his decisions was shown by his negotiations on 5 and 6 July in the Neues Palais with the Austro-Hungarian ambassador and then with the leaders of the government, the army and the navy before he left in the early morning of 6 July for his annual cruise in northern waters.

On 5 July Kaiser Wilhelm invited Szögyény (who had been received by the Reich Chancellor on the previous day)[69] to the Neues Palais, to hand over the Emperor Franz Joseph's letter and a memorandum from the Vienna Foreign Office, which had been brought to Berlin by Count Hoyos. The 'frightful catastrophe' at Sarajevo, Franz Joseph wrote, was the result of agitation by Russian and Serbian Pan-Slavs set on the destruction of the Habsburg Monarchy and the weakening of the Triple Alliance. The threads of the 'well-organised conspiracy' led to Belgrade, where the government was striving for the union of all the South Slavs under the Serbian flag. As the continuation of this state of affairs was 'a threat to my dynasty and my lands', his own government must henceforth work for 'the isolation and diminution of Serbia', i.e. for the elimination of Serbia 'as a political power-factor in the Balkans. You too . . . will be convinced that there can no longer be any thought of reconciling the differences that divide us from Serbia, and that the conservative policy of peace of all European monarchs will be in danger so long as this focus of criminal agitation in Belgrade continues unchecked.'[70]

Kaiser Wilhelm's reaction to this letter is contained in the telegram — drafted by Hoyos — that Szögyény sent to Vienna that same evening. According to this famous document the Kaiser assured the ambassador that although 'he had expected some serious action against Serbia on our part, he had to admit that in view of His Majesty the Emperor's arguments, he had to keep serious European complications in view, and could not therefore give a definitive answer before he had spoken to the Reich Chancellor'. Szögyény continued: 'After luncheon, when I again strongly emphasised the seriousness of the situation, His Majesty authorised me to report to His Majesty the Emperor that in this case too we could count on Germany's full support. As I said, he must first hear the Reich Chancellor's opinion, but he has not the least doubt that Herr von Bethmann Hollweg will share his opinion entirely. This is especially true in regard to our taking action against Serbia. However, in his (Kaiser Wilhelm's) opinion we must not wait to take action. Russia's attitude will inevitably be hostile, but he had been prepared for this for years, and if it should come to war between Austria-Hungary and Russia, we could be confident that Germany will, as usual, stand by our side as a loyal ally. Russia was, moreover, as things stood today, by no means prepared for war, and will certainly think twice about resorting to arms. But the other members of the Triple Entente will agitate against us and fan the flames in the Balkans ... But if we really see military action against Serbia as necessary, then he (Kaiser Wilhelm) would regret it if we did not make use of the present moment, which is so favourable to us.'[71] With this, the Habsburg Monarchy's decision for war was as good as taken. As a staff officer inside the Austrian War Ministry told the German military attaché Count Kageneck 'with a triumphant smile' on 7 July, 'this time war is certain'.[72]

After offering this strong support to Austria, far beyond the oft-cited 'blank cheque' (as Imanuel Geiss points out), the Kaiser summoned such political and military advisers as he could get hold of to the Neues Palais that same afternoon.[73] He received Bethmann Hollweg together with Zimmermann in the park. 'No one else was present', the Chancellor stated in his memoirs — though as we shall see several generals were present for at least some of the time Bethmann and Zimmermann were with the Kaiser.[74]

Both civilians had seen copies of the Austrian documents and were in complete agreement with Wilhelm. As Bethmann later recalled in his memoirs, at this meeting the Kaiser declared that 'he could have no illusions about the seriousness of the situation that Pan-Serbian propaganda had created for the Dual Monarchy. But it was not for us to advise our ally as to what should be done about the bloody crime in Sarajevo. Austria-Hungary must decide that for herself. We should be all the more careful to refrain from giving direct advice, as we must strive by all means to prevent the Austro-Serbian dispute from escalating into an international conflict. However, the Emperor Franz Joseph must be told that in her hour of need we shall not abandon Austria-Hungary.'[75] After the catastrophic defeat in the world war it is all too understandable that Bethmann's retrospective account should be something in the nature of an apologia.

The Kaiser also saw his top military and naval advisers in the Neues Palais on that Sunday afternoon. At 5 o'clock he received the War Minister, von Falkenhayn, together with his Adjutant-General, Hans von Plessen and the head of his Military Cabinet, Moriz von Lyncker. The Kaiser read out to them parts of Franz Joseph's letter and the Vienna Foreign Office memorandum, and pointed out — as Falkenhayn testified to the parliamentary investigating commission in 1919 — 'that very serious consequences might follow from the obviously firm decision of Austria-Hungary now to put an end to Pan-Serbian propaganda, and asked me whether the Army was prepared for all eventualities. In accordance with my convictions, I affirmed this in a word and without any reservations, and only asked, for my part, whether there were any preparations to be made. H.M. denied this equally tersely and dismissed me.'[76]

There are further details of this important military–political discussion in Plessen's diary, written immediately after the meeting, in which he recorded: 'H.M. summons me to the Neues Palais for 5 o'clock. I find there the head of the Military Cabinet Lyncker and the War Minister Falkenhayn. H.M. reads us a letter from the Emperor of Austria and a memorandum from the Aus [trian] For[eign] Minister Count Berchtold, according to which the Austrians are preparing for war against Serbia and want to be sure of Germany in advance. The Reich Chancellor and the [Under]Secretary of State also appear. We are of the opinion that *the sooner* the Austrians strike at Serbia *the better* and that the Russians – although friends of Serbia – will not join in.'[77] This contemporary source is an unvarnished record of the unanimous stance taken by the Kaiser, the Reich Chancellor and the army leadership. There was no disagreement amongst them. One even has the impression that the path to be taken was agreed between the generals and the civilian leaders before they went to Potsdam. The talks and correspondence between Waldersee and Zimmermann referred to above also suggest collusion.[78]

Last but not least the Kaiser summoned Captain Hans Zenker, head of the tactical division of the Admiralty Staff, and standing in for Admiral von Pohl who was on leave, to Potsdam on that fateful Sunday. In November 1919, after the war had been lost, Zenker wrote, à propos of this audience: 'H.M. the Kaiser told me, for the information of my superiors, that at midday on 5 July the Austro-Hungarian chargé d'affaires [sic!] had asked him whether Germany would fulfil her alliance obligations in the event of an Austro-Hungarian war with Serbia that might give rise to tensions with Russia. H.M. had promised this, but did not believe that Russia would stand up for Serbia, who had soiled herself with the assassination. Nor would France let it come to a war either, as its field army was deficient in heavy artillery. But even if war against Russia and France was unlikely, it must nevertheless always be kept in mind as a military possibility. Even so, the fleet must muster for its visit to Norway, fixed for mid-July, just as he would also start his Norwegian cruise according to plan.'[79] Immediately after his audience on Sunday 5 July 1914, the Captain had stated rather more strongly that he had 'understood H.M. to be saying ... Austria wants to put unacceptable demands to Serbia in order to bring about war'.[80]

Before leaving for Kiel on the morning of 6 July Wilhelm spoke to Lieutenant-General Hermann von Bertrab, who was in charge of the General Staff while his chief, Helmuth von Moltke, was taking the cure at Karlsbad and Quartermaster-General Waldersee was on leave. According to Bertrab's post-war testimony, the Kaiser had put before him 'without witnesses' his view of the situation created by the measures Austria was intending to take against Serbia. There was no need for any special directives, Wilhelm emphasised, because 'he did not believe that serious complications would arise from the Sarajevo crime'.[81] On 8 July 1914, however, Bertrab informed Waldersee that during his audience the Kaiser had told him that he had promised the Emperor Franz Joseph Germany's armed support 'if complications arose from Austria-Hungary's planned action against Serbia'.[82]

GERMANY'S TWIN-TRACK POLICY IN THE JULY CRISIS

The minimum aim of German policy was the elimination of Serbia as a power-factor in the Balkans, thereby improving the starting position for the Triple Alliance in a war that might be brought about against Russia later; the maximum aim was the immediate unleashing of a continental war against 'Russo-Gaul' in what were thought to be favourable conditions. This two-track strategy, which came out in the Kaiser's apparently ambivalent stance, depended on preparing the army and navy for the second possibility without attracting attention. As a result of the Potsdam discussions of 5–6 July it was 'decided', as the Under Secretary in the Foreign Office Hilmar Baron von dem Bussche-Haddenhausen stated in 1917, 'at all events to initiate preparatory measures for war. Appropriate orders then went out.'[83] The generals did not need to do anything at first because, as both the War Minister and Waldersee averred, 'the army [was] ready for all eventualities'.[84] As regards the navy, the Kaiser expressly ordered Admiral Capelle on 6 July 'to prepare to mobilise the fleet. Care was to be taken in particular to ensure – without causing a political stir – that the new ships nearing completion, *Derfflinger*, *König*, *Großer Kurfürst* were ready for service and that as many torpedo-boats and U-boats as possible should be ready for war.'[85] With the Kaiser's consent the sailing of the gunboat *Panther* for the West Indies, fixed for 10 July, was postponed for two weeks;[86] and a number of other preparatory measures were discreetly taken on Capelle's orders to arm the fleet in case of war.[87]

Since 28 June Moltke had been taking his second cure within a short period at Karlsbad, and during these first weeks of the July crisis Tirpitz was in Switzerland. Of course, both were kept fully informed of developments in the capital.[88] On 8 July Falkenhayn too and – 'at the express wish of the Reich Chancellor'[89] – Waldersee as well, went on leave. Bethmann Hollweg himself was officially absent from Berlin until 25 July, although he travelled to the capital several times in secret.[90] Geiss is quite right to talk of the 'deceptive veil of holiday travels' designed to conceal the real intentions of both German

SUMMER 1914: THE DECISION FOR WAR

and Austrian policy.[91] However, the most striking proof to the world that the decision-makers in Germany did not have an international crisis on their minds was to be provided by the fact that the Kaiser departed, as he did every year, for his Norwegian cruise.[92] As he told Capelle early in the morning of 6 July, he was setting out on his northern voyage 'on the Reich Chancellor's advice ... to avoid causing disquiet'.[93] The Machiavellian intention behind this was clear to 'the few *cognoscenti*': As the Bavarian chargé d'affaires reported from Berlin on 18 July, the political leaders would claim, 'citing the fact that the Kaiser was on his northern cruise and both the Chief of General Staff and the Prussian War Minister on leave, that they had been just as much taken by surprise by the Austrian action as the other Powers'.[94] It can be assumed that Bethmann was also aiming by this manoeuvre to shut out the Kaiser as an 'element of uncertainty' from the decision-making process in the critical weeks to follow.[95]

Even as Wilhelm II left for Norway the statesmen in Berlin took care that Vienna should be in no doubt as to what Germany was expecting. In speaking on 5 July to Szögyény and to Count Alexander Hoyos, who had drafted the two Austrian documents and brought them to Berlin, Bethmann had reaffirmed that he had been 'authorised by his imperial master' to clarify the German government's view, that Austria-Hungary must decide for herself how she wished to proceed in regard to Serbia and Russia's plans for a Balkan League. The Austrians could, however, 'whatever our [i.e. Austria's] decision might be, count with certainty on Germany's backing as the ally and friend of the Monarchy'. Szögyény added that 'the Reich Chancellor too, like his imperial master, sees an immediate action by us against Serbia as the most radical and the best solution to our difficulties in the Balkans. From an international point of view he regards the present moment as more favourable than later.'[96] To Hoyos, Bethmann declared straight out that 'if war was inevitable the present moment was better than later'. On 8 July Tschirschky carried out Wilhelm's command to inform Berchtold '*as emphatically as possible* that Berlin is expecting the Monarchy to act against Serbia' and would not understand it if Austria 'allowed the present opportunity to pass without striking a blow'.[97] According to a long report of 12 July from Szögyény describing the situation in Berlin, 'not only His Majesty Kaiser Wilhelm but all other decisive factors here too are not merely [standing] firmly and loyally behind the Monarchy, but are encouraging us most strongly not to allow the present moment to pass, but to act against Serbia as energetically as possible ... That Kaiser Wilhelm and the whole German Reich would in all eventualities most loyally fulfil their alliance obligations towards us' − that was something Szögyény had never had any reason to doubt in all his years of service as ambassador in

Berlin. But the fact that just at this moment 'authoritative circles in Germany, not least His Majesty Kaiser Wilhelm Himself, are – one might almost say actually pressing us towards possibly taking military action against Serbia', Szögyény attributed to a number of 'general political considerations'. First and foremost was the conviction that although Russia was arming for a future war, she was 'not adequately prepared for one at the present moment'. Hence there was 'absolutely no certainty' that Russia would help Serbia militarily if she became involved in war with Austria-Hungary. 'And should the Tsarist Empire nevertheless decide to do so, it is at the moment far from militarily prepared and far less strong than it will be in a few years' time.' In the second place the German government believed there were clear signs that England, who is 'at the moment far from eager for war', would not 'get involved in a war that breaks out over a Balkan state, even if it led to war with Russia and possibly with France'. 'In general', Szögyény concluded, 'the political constellation is at present as favourable to us as it can possibly be'. Added to this was the outrage of the whole civilised world at the 'bloody deed at Sarajevo', and especially, in the case of Kaiser Wilhelm, 'as I gather from a reliable source that enjoys His Majesty's complete confidence, there is the purely personal factor of an unlimited enthusiasm for our Most Gracious Master, and for the admirable energy – exhibited in His letter – with which His I[mperial] and R[oyal] Apostolic Majesty is minded to defend the interests and prestige of the lands entrusted to Him'.[98]

There is no doubt that it was with the Kaiser's approval that the German government had included the 'great war' in its calculations. On 5 July Zimmermann gave Hoyos his own assessment of the situation: 'Yes, 90% likelihood of a European war if you undertake something like that against Serbia.'[99] The Under Secretary was equally frank in talking to the head of the foreign section of the Admiralty Staff, Captain Graßhof: if it came to an Austrian invasion of Serbia and it was not possible to hold Russia back, it would come to 'the great continental war', in which Germany must reckon on 'England's being on the opposite side from us'.[100]

CHAPTER THIRTY-NINE

The Kaiser's last Norwegian cruise

THE NORTHERN CRUISE CURTAILED

Shortly after 9 o'clock in the morning of Monday, 6 July, the Kaiser left Potsdam for Kiel. En route, the situation 'arising from the planned Austrian invasion of Serbia' was discussed 'incessantly' in the restaurant car of the imperial train. On arriving at Kiel the Kaiser immediately 'buttonholed' the Admiral Gustav Bachmann and the Commander of the High Seas Fleet, Friedrich von Ingenohl, 'and reviewed the situation with them' − which was in Müller's opinion 'quite superfluous', especially as the Kaiser had declared that 'the decision regarding Austria's measures would only be taken in about 9 days' time'.[1] This evidence alone gives the lie to the official claim made after the war that Germany had no inkling of Austria's intentions until the presentation of the ultimatum to Serbia on 23 July. That the Kaiser was fully aware of the enormous risks involved is shown by the assurance he gave to the industrialist Gustav Krupp von Bohlen und Halbach as many as three times that evening: 'This time I shall not topple over.' If Russia mobilised, he declared, he would answer with war. 'The Kaiser's repeated emphasis on how nobody will be able to accuse him this time of indecision was almost comic.'[2] That war was not a foregone conclusion is, however, indicated by his order to his brother Heinrich before leaving Kiel on 6 July to attend the autumn manoeuvres in the first week of September.[3]

On 7 July the *Hohenzollern* sailed out from Kiel through the Belt, past Skagen and along the coast of Norway as far as the Sogne fjord before anchoring on 11 July at Balholm, about eighty miles north of Bergen (see Figure 48). Although the northern cruise had been planned to last until the evening of 2 August,[4] the curtailment of the voyage (which on earlier

Figure 48 Waiting for the storm to break. The imperial yacht *Hohenzollern*
at anchor in the Sogne fjord, July 1914

occasions had extended several hundred miles further north) already
suggested that an international crisis was expected that could necessitate the
speedy return of the Supreme War Lord to Berlin.[5] Wilhelmshaven or
Cuxhaven could be reached from Balholm within 22 hours, and Kiel within
2 days.[6]

The cruise was supposed to give the impression that the Kaiser had no idea
of Austria's planned challenge to Belgrade and Russia, and of the international
crisis that would in all probability result from it. In reality, the summer
idyll in the Sogne fjord was constantly interrupted by news from home. The
Berlin Foreign Office sent dozens of telegrams and dispatches from Vienna,
St Petersburg, Paris, London, Rome, Belgrade, Athens, Constantinople and
Bucharest to the *Hohenzollern*, to keep the Kaiser and his tiny handful of
advisers up to date (apart from Wilhelm and Müller, only the representative of
the Auswärtiges Amt, Georg Count von Wedel, and Moriz Baron von Lyncker
were let in on Berlin's calculations).[7] Although the government later professed
to know nothing of Austria's intentions, it soon had precise information about
the planned ultimatum, formulated to be unacceptable, that Vienna intended

to present to Belgrade on 23 July with a deadline of a mere 48 hours. The Austro-Hungarian envoy in Belgrade, Wladimir Baron von Giesl, had already received instructions on 7 July to break off relations, whatever the Serbian reply to the ultimatum might be; 'it has to come to war'.[8] Like Bethmann Hollweg, the Auswärtiges Amt, the ambassador Tschirschky and the German military, Kaiser Wilhelm, too, was pressing for a speedy and irrevocable Austrian action against Serbia.[9] When he arrived in Balholm he covered Tschirschky's 'most secret' dispatch of 10 July about the slow development of the Dual Monarchy's plans with martial minutes, commenting on the report that the Emperor Franz Joseph now thought that a decision would have to be taken, with the words: 'That is taking a long time, as H.M.'s memorandum is 14 days old.' People in Vienna had 'had enough time' to formulate concrete and unambiguous demands to be put to Serbia. They should simply force Serbia to give up the Sanjak of Novibazar acquired in 1913, then war in the Balkans would be certain. 'Evacuate the Sanjak', Wilhelm demanded in a marginal note, 'then the rumpus will start at once! Austria must certainly get it back, to prevent the union of Serbia and Montenegro and the Serbs getting to the sea!' He condemned Count Tisza's more reserved policy as 'nonsense!' One could not behave like a gentleman 'towards murderers, after what has happened'. Austria was behaving 'rather as she did at the time of the Silesian Wars', he wrote angrily at the bottom of the document, and cited Frederick the Great: 'I am against war councils and discussions, since the more timid party always has the upper hand.'[10] Only when Tisza swung round towards war was Wilhelm content: the Prime Minister of Hungary was 'a proper man after all!'[11] In Balholm the Kaiser signed the draft of a letter to Franz Joseph that his Foreign Office had sent him on 9 July, in which he spoke of the 'serious danger' that 'threatens your lands and in consequence the Triple Alliance, from the agitation of Russian and Serbian Panslavs'. He recognised the need, Wilhelm assured the old Emperor, 'to free the southern frontiers of your states from this heavy pressure'.[12] 'May Heaven grant that!' he wrote on 22 July, on a report that spoke of Austria's giving Serbia a 'much needed lesson'.[13] Energetic and speedy action against Serbia was 'absolutely' necessary: 'what a pity!' was Wilhelm's reiterated comment on the Austrian decision, in an attempt to make coordinated Franco-Russian intervention more difficult, to delay the presentation of the ultimatum until the French President Poincaré had left St Petersburg;[14] and he described Vienna's sending the Austrian War Minister and the Chief of General Staff Conrad von Hötzendorf away for a time in order 'to forestall any alarm' as 'childish' – although he himself and several German officers and statesmen had gone on leave for this very same reason.[15]

MORE STRIFE WITH THE CROWN PRINCE

The success of the Wilhelmstrasse's scheme to simulate normality and to deny any foreknowledge of Austrian intentions until the unacceptable ultimatum had been presented to Belgrade, was jeopardised by the impetuous public gestures of the hot-headed Crown Prince in Zoppot. In mid July he seized on a pamphlet retailing a strongly nationalistic speech about Bismarck by Professor Gustav Buchholz to utter a strident demand for a forceful continuation of Bismarck's policy. If this were not enough, in a telegram thanking Lieutenant-Colonel Herman Frobenius for his book *Des deutschen Reiches Schicksalsstunde* (also published as *Germany's Hour of Destiny*, New York, 1914), the heir to the Prusso-German throne identified himself with the author's aggressive attacks on German policy of the day.[16] The Wilhelmstrasse had good reason to fear, as Jagow told Bethmann, that 'when the Austrian ultimatum becomes known – the telegram from Danzig [would give rise to] the most awful clamour'.[17]

At this critical moment the Reich Chancellor could not possibly accept such a disavowal. On 17 July he ordered the drafting of a formal rebuke to the Crown Prince, emphasising that, precisely in the present international crisis, the political consequences of such pronouncements were incalculable. 'The external situation, which is at the moment already tense owing to the Austro-Serbian conflict, demands that Germany react in a way that is both clear and considered. Even if we cannot today foresee further developments, it is nevertheless absolutely in our interests at the moment that if we give Austria our determined support we should not appear to others as the ones who are working for a European conflagration by stirring up national passions . . . It will only be possible to pursue a consistent and purposeful policy if there is no risk of cross-currents. Given the nature of the diplomatic game, it is not only possible but probable that such a counter-move, undertaken out of context, might not only help our opponent but also produce a result the opposite of that intended . . . May I therefore, with all respect, ask Your Imperial Highness to refrain from this kind of pronouncement in future.'[18]

Next day, to reinforce this reprimand the Chancellor telegraphed to Balholm asking the Kaiser to call his son to order himself, and to forbid any further disruptive interventions. The 'English, French and Russian press have interpreted his pronouncements as a sign that the Crown Prince is opposing Your Majesty's policy and working for war. But I also know from a reliable source that in government circles in the Triple Entente the emergence of the Crown Prince is taken seriously as a worrying sign.' He, the Chancellor, had sent the Crown Prince a long letter explaining how, in the present tense international situation, such demonstrations could 'compromise and cut across' the policy of the government, but he was by no means sure that the Crown Prince would comply with his request to refrain from such actions. Rather, he was 'seriously' afraid 'that His Highness, if the Austrian ultimatum now becomes known, will come out with things that, after all that has gone before, will be regarded by our opponents as deliberate warmongering, whereas it is our task, according to my instructions from Your Majesty, to localise the Austro-Serbian conflict. The accomplishment of this task is in itself so difficult that even small incidents can be decisive. I make so bold, therefore, as to humbly ask Your Majesty graciously to telegraph at once, prohibiting any kind of political intervention by His Imperial Highness.'[19] The Kaiser immediately complied with the Chancellor's wish, telegraphing to his son on 21 July: 'I appeal to your sense of duty and honour as a Prussian officer, who has to keep his promises without fail, and I am fully confident in my expectation that you will once and for all abstain, in the present tense situation and, indeed, altogether, from any political statement whatever to third parties that can only interfere with my policy and that of my responsible advisers.'[20] In his reply to Balholm the Crown Prince telegraphed simply: 'Orders will be carried out'; but in a telegram to the Reich Chancellor he let it be seen that he had understood the hint that Bethmann's dispatch conveyed between the lines: 'The content of the telegram which Your Excellency sent to H.M. on the said matter was of great interest to me.'[21] In a long letter to the Chancellor which does not seem to have survived, the Crown Prince demanded 'War and a Socialist Law, Struggle and Force.' 'Stupid phrases', sighed Kurt Riezler, Bethmann's closest adviser: 'Whatever has become of those educated officers who once made Prussia great?'[22]

WILHELM'S BID FOR NEW ALLIES

The Kaiser was not merely kept informed by the Wilhelmstrasse of top-secret developments in the Austro-Serbian crisis, he took a hand in shaping events himself. From Balholm he personally directed the efforts of German diplomats to get Turkey and Bulgaria, and as far as possible Romania and Greece, to commit themselves to the Triple Alliance and the impending general struggle against the 'Slavs'. On 20 July a telegram reached the *Hohenzollern* from Hans von Wangenheim, the ambassador at Constantinople, referring to the possibility of an agreement between Turkey and Greece over the thorny question of the Aegean Islands. An alliance between Turkey and a Greece that was linked by a defensive alliance to Serbia, however, might in the event of an Austro-Bulgarian attack on Serbia, drive not only Greece but Turkey too into the

Triple Entente camp. Wilhelm expressly approved the advice Wangenheim had given to the Grand Vizir, 'with a cautious allusion to the possibility of a serious turn in the Austro-Serbian relations' to conclude 'no alliances at all'; and he instructed his Foreign Office to see to it that there was 'no agreement' between Greece and Turkey, and to pass this instruction on to the minister in Athens, Albert Count Quadt-Wykradt-Isny.[23] On a further dispatch from Wangenheim, stating that Bulgaria, Romania and Turkey would stand 'wholeheartedly on the side of the Triple Alliance' in the event of Austria's taking action against Serbia, Wilhelm commented on 22 July, 'let us remind the gentlemen of this when the time comes'.[24] The time soon came. Three days later, as the *Hohenzollern* was sailing back to Kiel, Wilhelm wrote on a report from Sofia that Bulgaria wished to join the Triple Alliance, 'then get on with it!'[25]

The diplomatic scene in the Near East was becoming increasingly unclear as the Austro-Serbian conflict approached. On 23 July – i.e. before the presentation of the ultimatum at Belgrade – Wilhelm received from the Foreign Office a report from Constantinople saying that the head of the German military mission in Turkey, General Liman von Sanders, was convinced that Greece was on the verge of attacking the Dardanelles. Immediately, the Kaiser ordered the Wilhelmstrasse to tell his brother-in-law, King Constantine, that he was to refrain from the planned military action as Turkey's support would be needed in the coming struggle against the Slavs. Quadt was '*personally* . . . to give the King this message from *me* . . . Turkey wishes to join the Triple Alliance, i.e. to come to an understanding with Austria. This will make her valuable to us, and H.M. [King Constantine] must not for petty selfish reasons attack a friend of the Triple Alliance who is valuable to *me*, if it wants to support Austria *against the Slavs*. On the contrary, H.M. must side with Austria *himself*, otherwise my friendship is at an end.' On the very next day Wedel sent the Kaiser's marginalia to the Foreign Office, which forwarded the imperial order to Quadt in Athens.[26]

Already in the evening of 23 July a report reached Balholm from Wangenheim that the Turkish government was now convinced that it needed the support of one or other of the Great Power combinations. The Grand Vizir and other leading statesmen considered that 'the Triple Alliance was militarily stronger than the Entente and would be victorious in a world war [sic!].' Turkey and Bulgaria had already reached agreement about a treaty of alliance but Sofia had doubts about signing it without the 'patronage' of the Triple Alliance. The Turkish government was now pressing to join the Triple Alliance, but if it met with a rejection in Berlin it could also opt, if with a heavy heart, for the Triple Entente. The Kaiser immediately ordered the conclusion of alliances with Turkey and Bulgaria, and also, if possible, a stronger alliance with Romania, minuting on the report: 'It is now a matter of gaining every rifle in the Balkans that is ready to shoot *on Austria's side* against the Slavs, hence a Turco-Bulg[arian] alliance linked to Austria must indeed be accepted! That is an opportunistic policy, and it must be pursued here.' For want of better, the Bulgarians were to be 'included so long as they are ready to fight on Austria's side'. In a concluding comment that the Wilhelmstrasse telegraphed almost word for word as an instruction to Constantinople, the Kaiser declared: 'Agreed. If it can't be managed otherwise and Constantinople is absolutely set on an alliance "under the patronage of the *Triple Alliance* or of *one of its members*", then just let it try to get Romania and Bulgaria together and put itself at the disposal of Austria. I have nothing against it. It is after all better than raising theoretical objections and driving the Turks over to the Triple Entente.'[27] On that same evening he again forcefully expressed his expectation that Bulgaria, Turkey and, 'it is to be hoped', Romania, would join the Triple Alliance. Turkey, he wrote, 'is openly offering herself!!! A refusal or a snub would amount to her going over to Russo-Gaul, and our influence is gone once and for all! Wangenheim should certainly be accommodating to the Turks regarding their joining the Triple Alliance and take on board and report their wishes. In no circumstances whatever must we turn them down.'[28] Again, the imperial wishes were telegraphed from Balholm to Berlin and thence to Wangenheim in Constantinople.[29] Four days later Turkey made an official request for a secret alliance with Germany against Russia which, as will be seen, was concluded on 2 August 1914.[30]

IN EAGER ANTICIPATION OF THE AUSTRIAN ULTIMATUM

The famous 'Halt in Belgrade' proposal that Kaiser Wilhelm made on returning from his northern cruise on 28 July is often taken as evidence that he wished to prevent an Austro-Serbian war and avoid the threatening conflict with Russia and France. What the Kaiser really intended by his 'pledge' idea will be considered below. What is clear is that the apparently pacific attitude implied by his initiative of 28 July reflected a sudden later change of mood on the Kaiser's part that was in no way typical of his attitude during the three weeks of his northern cruise. In those weeks there was no question of the Kaiser's diverging from the line taken by the Wilhelmstrasse with regard to the Austrian note. Throughout his cruise he was thirsting for war with the 'Slavs', and the French too, and he held firmly, if with increasing trepidation, to the fateful course he had agreed with Bethmann, Zimmermann, the generals and the navy at Potsdam in the first week of July. Admittedly it was not true, as Sir Maurice de Bunsen, the British ambassador at Vienna, was informed, that Tschirschky telegraphed the text of the Austrian ultimatum to Kaiser Wilhelm before it was sent off.[31] But by 5 or 6 July at the latest he knew of Vienna's intention, 'in about 9 days' or 'in three weeks', to take some firm action against Serbia that might end in a major war – as we have seen, during the train journey from Potsdam to Kiel the head of his Naval Cabinet, Admiral von Müller, was already talking of 'Austria's intention to invade Serbia'.[32] In Balholm Müller noted in his diary on 19 July: 'His Majesty greatly excited about the consequences of the ultimatum that Austria is to present to Serbia on the 23rd.'[33] Wilhelm's correspondence of 20 and 21 July with Bethmann Hollweg about the Crown Prince's war-mongering – like his pressing for the speedy conclusion of alliances with Turkey, Bulgaria and Romania on 20 July – indicated that he was perfectly well-informed about the impending ultimatum and its possible consequences.[34] On 21 July he decided to postpone the sale of four torpedo boats to Greece.[35]

During the three weeks in which he was at anchor in Balholm Wilhelm spoke continually and in the fiercest terms about the 'Slavs' in the east and their ally, the 'absolutely socialist-sansculotte republic' of France in the west.[36] In determining his policy he had 'naturally' taken Russia's 'boundless scornfulness' and 'growing arrogance' towards the Habsburg Monarchy into account, he declared in a minute on a report from Count Pourtalès in St Petersburg that reached him shortly after his arrival in Balholm; and he added mockingly: 'Pride comes before a fall!'[37] On 23 July Wilhelm received a report of a heated discussion between Pourtalès and Sergei Sazonov, the Russian Foreign Minister, about the threatening conflict between Austria and Serbia. In numerous marginal comments on this document he made no secret of his conviction that the 'annihilation of Serbia' by Austria would 'be the best thing'. Sazonov's warning that if Austria attempted that she 'would have to reckon with Europe' the Kaiser rejected out of hand: 'No! Russia would! as the perpetrator and defender of regicide!!!' Even Sazonov's clear declaration that Russia would not be able to allow Austria to browbeat Serbia by threatening military measures, Wilhelm dismissed with a nonchalant 'qui vivra verra!'[38]

Within a matter of hours the Kaiser's expectation that 'Europe' would accept Austria's attack on Serbia and even turn against Russia if she endorsed the Sarajevo 'regicide' proved to be naive wishful thinking. A dispatch from Lichnowsky that reached the Kaiser on the evening of 23 July reported the British government's willingness to exercise its influence in favour of a peaceful settlement of the Austro-Serbian conflict, provided that Vienna's demands were compatible with Serbian sovereignty. This report Wilhelm covered in furious marginalia characteristic of his monarchical ideology. Whether the demands made on Serbia were moderate or not was not for

Grey to judge: 'that is a matter for H.M. the Emperor Franz Josef! [sic!]'.
Grey's remark that he could of course not make any representations in
Belgrade on the basis of frivolous accusations, enraged the Kaiser: 'what is
frivolous? How can Grey apply such a word to the venerable old gentleman!'
There was 'no such thing' as Serbian national honour. London's expectation
that Germany would not identify herself with 'unrealisable' demands of
Austria-Hungary's that 'are obviously designed to bring about a war' or merely
to serve as a pretext to fulfil Austria-Hungary's Balkan ambitions drove the
Kaiser into a rage. 'How could I do this? Not my business at all! What does
unrealisable mean? The ruffians have pursued their agitation to the point of
murder and must be sorted out. That is a monstrous piece of British shamelessness. It is not my business to give orders like Grey does to H.M. the Emperor
[Franz Joseph] about defending his honour!' The Kaiser heartily welcomed
Jagow's intention to tell Lichnowsky, as a guide for his language in London,
that Berlin had not been informed of the Austrian terms, regarded them as an
internal affair of Austria-Hungary's, and had therefore no right to interfere.
'Right!' the Kaiser commented: 'This must be seriously impressed on Grey
with all clarity! So that he can see that I shall not stand any nonsense. Grey is
making the mistake of putting Serbia on a level with Austria and other Great
Powers! That is unheard of! Serbia is a band of robbers that must be arrested
for their crimes. I shall not meddle at all in what is a matter for the Emperor
[Franz Joseph] alone to judge! I expected this dispatch and it does not surprise
me! Truly Brit[ish] way of thinking and condescending dictatorial manner
that I am determined shall be repulsed! Wilhelm I.R.'[39] On the same day
Count Wedel passed these imperial marginalia on to the Foreign Office, which
forwarded them to Lichnowsky.[40]

The day the Austrian ultimatum that was to start the war against Serbia
expired – 25 July 1914 – proved full of drama. First came the telegraphic
report that Count Berchtold had gone to Ischl, to await there, together with
Franz Joseph, the arrival of the Serbian reply.[41] Müller's diary describes these
fateful hours: 'In the morning when he went aboard – the text of the
ultimatum had meanwhile arrived from the Norddeich news agency – the
Kaiser read out a Wolf telegram, reporting consternation in Belgrade and
Russia's declaration that she could not stand aside. Great excitement.'[42] When
Müller spoke to Wedel about his misgivings regarding the 'unprecedentedly
sharp tone' of the ultimatum, he received the 'characteristic reply' of the
Wilhelmstrasse's representative: 'Our only worry is that the Serbs might
swallow the note.'[43] In a memorandum written after Germany's defeat in
1918 Müller recalled the eventful days before the war broke out: 'The Kaiser
came to me on deck, as usual, before breakfast, and said to me (as I had the

Norddeich telegram in my hand) "That is indeed a strong note for once, what?" I replied, "Yes, the note is strong, but it means war!" The Kaiser replied that the Serbs would not dream of risking a world war.'[44] However, the wild marginalia with which Wilhelm covered the newspaper reports that reached him that morning show no sign of any expectation of a peaceful outcome to the crisis. The articles from St Petersburg on the farewell speeches of the French President and the Tsar on 23 July he spattered with his favourite dismissive expressions: 'Quatsch!' 'Rubbish!' and 'Lies!' The Dual Alliance between France and Russia had been concluded, he was convinced, 'for a combined robber attack on us!'[45] While the newspapers speculated as to whether the war clouds blowing upon the horizon could be dispersed by a personal meeting between the French President and the German Emperor in the course of their return journeys, the Kaiser cursed Poincaré as a 'Gallic swine' and made arrangements with the Wilhelmstrasse and the Admiralty Staff to avoid a rendezvous with him in the Baltic at all costs.[46]

In the afternoon of 25 July a telegram reached Balholm with the news that Crown Prince Alexander of Serbia had appealed for help to Queen Elena of Italy, by birth a Montenegrin princess; that the military in Serbia, by contrast, were demanding the rejection of the Austrian note and war; and that Serbia's mobilisation was already in full swing.[47] In these critical hours Wilhelm II, while holding to a hard line, seems to have been reckoning on the Belgrade government's unconditional surrender, the occupation of Serbia by the Austro-Hungarian army, followed by its partition. He was expecting a Russian retreat, leading to a decisive shift of power in favour of the Triple Alliance, not merely in the Balkans but in Europe as a whole. On the dispatch from Belgrade, according to which the Serbian government had been utterly surprised by the ultimatum and was now discussing its reply under the presidency of Crown Prince Alexander Wilhelm noted with glee: 'Bravo! One wouldn't have thought the Viennese could do it! It seems that H.M. [King Petar of Serbia] has got cold feet! The proud Slavs! How hollow the whole so-called Great Serbian state now looks, and so it is with all Slav states! Just stamp firmly on the rabble's toes!'[48] Even so, that the Kaiser, for all his rejoicing over the expected diplomatic coup, was perfectly prepared for a war against Russia (and therefore against France too) was shown by the orders he gave when the flagship of his fleet, *Friedrich der Große*, with Admiral von Ingenohl on board, anchored off Balholm at 10.00 a.m. on 25 July. That morning, Müller's diary reveals, the Supreme War Lord gave the Commander of the High Seas Fleet 'what amounted to an order for operations against Russia, destruction of Reval [Tallinn] and Libau [Liepaja]. Ingenohl managed to remain quite calm.'[49] At midday, in view of the sharpening situation and the growing tension with Russia, the Kaiser gave orders to ask Denmark and Sweden what their position would be in the event of war.[50]

THE QUARREL WITH THE 'CIVILIAN CHANCELLOR' OVER RECALLING THE HIGH SEAS FLEET

The more the 'rumpus' on the continent loomed, the more critical became the position at sea. That the Kaiser was reckoning, even in the course of his Norwegian cruise, with the possibility of England's going to war could be seen as early as 19 July, a full four days before the presentation of the ultimatum in Belgrade. On that day he instructed Count Wedel to enquire of the Wilhelm-strasse whether the time had not come to let the directors of Hapag and the Norddeutsche Lloyd, Albert Ballin and Karl-Anton Freiherr von Plettenberg, know 'secretly and in strict confidence' that an 'Austrian ultimatum was to be expected on the 23rd'. Wedel telegraphed to Berlin: 'In view of the unforesee-able and possibly very swift consequences, it seems to H.M. desirable that the two great shipping lines be alerted in good time so that they can make timely arrangements and send instructions to their steamers in foreign waters.'[51] Already on the evening of 20 July Jagow could report to Balholm that he had with the Reich Chancellor's consent just spoken in confidence to Ballin and asked Plettenberg to come to see him next day 'about an important matter'.[52] What was expected of the Hapag and Lloyd fast steamers in terms of waging war on England has been described in Chapter 37.

In the North Sea a critical situation had arisen, the German High Seas Fleet having sailed on 15 July for exercises between Skagen and the southern coast of Norway, while at the same time the British Grand Fleet had been concentrated in the Channel for a grand review. The authorities in Berlin had to do all they could to give the impression of being set on peace, so that the British ships would disperse and return to their home bases on the 27th, as planned. If they did so, the German Admiralty Staff believed they would have at least six days in which to make a dash for safety.[53] If the German fleet were recalled ahead of time, however, the British might become suspicious and keep their warships together, with unforeseeable consequences.[54] The fact that Wilhelm II had power of command over the navy which, as Supreme War Lord, he could exercise from Balholm — after 23 July he was in direct telegraphic communication with the fleet[55] — thus constituted a serious threat to the calculations of the civilian authorities in Berlin, who attached the highest importance to ensuring British neutrality, at least in the first weeks of a continental war. There is no better illustration of the nervousness and perplexity of the Wilhelmstrasse about this than Jagow's hair-raising enquiry of the Admiralty Staff on 20 July whether 'we could not exert pressure on England by threatening in the event of her intervention [in the war] to grab Holland'. As the admirals put it, the Foreign Secretary could not have suggested 'anything more stupid'.[56]

Even at this stage a sharp conflict was developing between the Supreme War Lord and the government over the question of recalling the High Seas Fleet. Already on the evening of 19 July the Kaiser ordered its exercises to be 'so organised that the Fleet can immediately be concentrated for returning home'; it would only be allowed to call at Norwegian ports with special permission, which must be sought from him personally in Balholm.[57] The Chancellor and the Wilhelmstrasse expressed their displeasure at the incalculable Kaiser's interference with their carefully designed plans.[58] As Bethmann telegraphed to Jagow from his estate of Hohenfinow on the evening of 21 July: 'H.M.'s order for keeping the Fleet together until the 25th makes me fear that, if the ultimatum is then rejected, orders could come prematurely from Balholm for conspicuous naval movements. On the other hand, it could be fatal if the Fleet were in the wrong place in a crisis. As I cannot pronounce on the question from a military point of view, it would be well to talk to the Admiralty Staff, so that Count Wedel can then make a report to H.M. about the political factors that must be taken into account alongside the military ones.'[59]

That the Chancellor's fears were only too well-founded was shown by the telegram that Wilhelm fired off to the Admiralty Staff on 23 July: 'In my opinion the political tension forbids the dispersal of the Fleet to Norwegian harbours, and hence it would be better to give the order now to return home. I ask you to consult the Foreign Office and then telegraph your proposal to me.'[60] In the afternoon of 23 July Jagow telegraphed to Wedel in the Chancellor's name that the Austrian ultimatum, due to be presented in Belgrade on that day, would expire on the evening of the 25th. For the moment, Germany's official position would be that it was a matter of a local conflict between Austria and Serbia. 'Only the intervention of another Power would draw us into the conflict. That this would happen *at once*, that England in particular would *immediately* decide to intervene, is not likely ... Any recalling of our Fleet ahead of schedule could give rise to general concern and be regarded as suspicious, especially in England. After consulting Admiral von Müller please report in this sense to H.M.'[61]

The Reich Navy Office and the Admiralty Staff were no less alarmed than the Wilhelmstrasse by the Kaiser's interventions. Albert Hopman reported to Tirpitz, who was still in Switzerland, that the Chancellor had 'in a telegram from Hohenfinow expressed his fear that the Kaiser, by ordering the Fleet to stay away from the Norwegian ports and to return, could make the situation much worse and very seriously endanger the peaceful solution he was striving for. The immediate return of the Fleet must be prevented in all circumstances.' In fact, Hopman was convinced that the problem did not admit of any solution that would meet both the political and military requirements, as 'from a political point of view any change of plan that might attract attention must be avoided, while from a military viewpoint, i.e. reckoning with the possibility of war, the Fleet must return to Wilhelmshaven or Kiel at once.' Only if the statesmen could affirm that a British declaration of war need not be expected in the next six days might it not be necessary to recall the fleet immediately.[62] In the end, after consulting Zimmermann, Vice Admiral Paul Behnke telegraphed to the Kaiser that he did not regard the High Seas Fleet 'as threatened for the present, [but] recommended ... that it call in [at Norwegian ports] soon and break off its visit if the political tension between Germany and – [sic!] continues to increase'.[63] What the Kaiser would decide remained completely uncertain.[64]

On 24 July Wilhelm II did indeed give the fleet 'permission to enter Norwegian ports', as Bethmann and Jagow had demanded, adding the proviso that 'in granting leave, the possibility of a shortened stay was to be taken into account'.[65] At 9.30 next morning, however, 'during his walk' in Balholm the Kaiser issued a 'secret' order to 'speed up the coaling' of the battleships and to 'prepare them to leave port'. The two training ships in the vicinity received orders to return home immediately.[66] 'Meanwhile H.M. declared', Müller noted, 'that he was not relying on the Admiralty Staff's bringing the Fleet home on their own initiative'.[67] On the afternoon of 25 July the head of the Naval Cabinet was negotiating with Admiral von Ingenohl 'about the return of the Fleet. We reached agreement in the evening of the following day. At 6 o'clock Ingenohl got the Kaiser's consent and weighed anchor.'[68] The Kaiser's over-hasty action aroused the Reich Chancellor's ire. As Riezler later recalled, Bethmann spoke 'rather bleakly about the "dilettantism" with which the Kaiser and his friends were looking forward to a war – and a victorious one, for there could be no question of any other. "What does this puffed-up lieutenant (W.II) intend to do with the world?" Bethmann said to me.'[69]

Early on 26 July a telegram reached the *Hohenzollern* from the Reich Chancellor 'virtually accusing the Kaiser of having ordered the Fleet to prepare to return home simply on the strength of a Wolf telegram'.[70] Bethmann begged Wilhelm to hold back from ordering the fleet home as the Royal Navy, as had been hoped, had not resorted to any untoward measures, nor was Sir Edward Grey 'for the moment considering England's direct participation in a possible European war'.[71] Wilhelm covered this document in furious marginalia which testify to his state of extreme nervous excitement, but also to his readiness to go to war with Russia and France: Bethmann's telegram he found 'unheard of!' and 'incredibly impertinent!' He had 'never dreamt of' preparing the fleet to return home on the strength of a mere Wolf Agency report. He had given his orders 'on the basis of my minister's report of the mobilisation in Belgrade! This *can* lead to Russia's mobilisation and *will* lead to Austria's mobilisation! In that event I must have my fighting forces *together* on land and sea. There is not a single ship in the Baltic!! Nor, moreover, is it my habit to decide on military measures on the strength of *one* Wolf telegram, but in the light of the general situation, and this the *Civilian* Chancellor still fails to comprehend ... If Russia mobilises, my Fleet must already be in the Baltic, hence it is coming home!' The Royal Navy under Battenberg's command did not need to take any further measures. 'It is already prepared for war footing as the review has just demonstrated and has mobilised!'[72] Müller viewed the 'very angry' Kaiser's irritation with sympathy: his orders to the fleet had been 'perfectly justified in the light of the general situation, and that he had given them on the strength of a Wolf telegram – thanks to the complete lack of information from the A[uswärtiges] A[mt] – was a charge that reflected on Berlin'. Wilhelm instructed him together with Wedel to draft an appropriate reply to Bethmann.[73]

Even before the Kaiser's angry telegram reached Berlin the Chancellor took the opportunity of a report from the naval attaché in London[74] to appeal once more to the Supreme War Lord to leave the High Seas Fleet in Norway. The British were sending their crews on leave according to plan and wanted to embark on mediatory action in St Petersburg, where the mood was clearly vacillating. But Wilhelm II knew better than his '*Civilian* Chancellor'. There was also 'a Russ[ian] Fleet!' as well as an English one, he minuted in the margin of Bethmann's admonition. '5 Russ[ian] torpedo-boat flotillas are already engaged in exercises in the Baltic, and some or all of them can reach the Belts within 16 hours and close them. Port Arthur should be a lesson! My Fleet has been ordered to sail to Kiel, and that is where it will go! W.' Moreover, that Russia had started to waver, as the Reich Chancellor claimed, was *not* apparent from the material he (the Kaiser) had to hand.[75] This violent dispute between the War Lord and the Chancellor did not augur well for their cooperation once the Kaiser returned to the capital.

THE SUPREME WAR LORD'S 'PREMATURE' RETURN TO KIEL

The closer the presentation of the Austrian note to Belgrade loomed, the more problematical became the absence of the Supreme War Lord, who alone had the authority to issue mobilisation orders to the army and navy. Already in the early evening of 18 July Jagow was asking for information about the Kaiser's travel plans after the 23rd, as developments after that — i.e. the reaction to the Austrian ultimatum — would determine 'whether H.M.'s presence would be needed here ... As we wish to localise any Austro-Serbian conflict, we ought not to alarm the world by H.M.'s returning prematurely, on the other hand His All-Highest Majesty must always be contactable, lest we too should be compelled by unforeseeable events to take important decisions (mobilisation). Perhaps one might think in terms of a cruise in the Baltic for the last days of the voyage.'[76]

For the time being the *Hohenzollern* remained in the Sogne fjord. But as the moment of truth approached, the tension increased. On 21 July the head of the Military Cabinet Moriz von Lyncker reported to his wife: 'Since yesterday, it looks rather like war again; the situation is expected to get worse on the 25th in particular. We are ready to return at any moment. But that will hardly be necessary.'[77] A few hours later he wrote home again: 'The political situation certainly seems to be coming to a head, and I wish we were in Germany. If we have to, we can get to Cuxhaven in 22 hours; that is still some consolation. There is no fresh news today, by the way, and nothing decisive is expected until the 25/7. That is 4 days off ... Now what will you do if I suddenly return to Berlin? That is not impossible.'[78] At midday on 22 July Lyncker continued his running commentary: 'We — i.e. a small circle of initiates — are nevertheless rather in suspense as to how things will develop. What will Russia do if it now — as seems very likely — comes to a war between Austria and Serbia? Our own role is laid down. Things will be clearer in a few days.'[79] He wrote again a few hours later: 'The storm clouds on the political horizon are getting ever darker ... We can't tell how things will turn out. Otherwise don't worry before you have to; such crises have often passed, and one can hardly imagine that a great world war should break out over this band of robbers in Serbia.'[80]

On 23 July Lyncker's colleague Müller noted: 'Anxiety growing ... Ultimatum to be handed in today.'[81] In the evening, Lyncker reported to his wife: 'All of us, i.e. those in the know, are rather in suspense; the Austrian note has been presented in Belgrade today; it is supposed to be very harsh. What will the Serbs do? No doubt that will depend on whether they have Russia behind them or not? Austria has probably given them a deadline of only 48 hours, and so we shall perhaps be able to see more clearly within 2 or 3 days.'[82] On that same day the Kaiser reported optimistically to the Admiralty Staff that he 'intended, failing an incident, to arrive at Swinemünde on 1 August'.[83]

On 25 July, Müller, Lyncker and Wedel, although they had 'no official news from Berlin', unanimously agreed that the Supreme War Lord should return immediately to the capital, because 'a state of affairs in which the Kaiser was

engaged in a pleasure trip at such a critical time [was] really quite unacceptable'.[84] The head of the Naval Cabinet, who had for some time regarded the
whole northern cruise as a mistake, and one that had now become quite
'untenable',[85] described in his diary how in the course of 25 July the decision
was taken. 'At 3 o'clock I therefore ordered the commander [of the *Hohenzollern*, Captain von Karpf] to get steam up, I would answer for this, and prevail
on the Kaiser to return home. When the Kaiser had been wakened from his
afternoon sleep at half past 4 I went to him in his bedroom. I told him that
after consulting C[oun]t Wedel and Gen[eral] von Lyncker I considered the
situation in Balholm untenable and proposed that H.M should sail for home at
6 o'clock that evening. I had already ordered the captain to get steam up.
Meanwhile the minister in Belgrade had telegraphed that there was great
excitement there and no question of a reply to the ultimatum within the
specified time. The Kaiser, still in bed, thought for a moment and then said:
"Yes. Agreed. Can I still go on land for half an hour." I said he could. He went
on land to say his farewells.'[86] Those northern lands, where he had cruised
every year since 1889, Kaiser Wilhelm II was never to see again.

The aggressive marginal comments that the Kaiser penned on the numerous dispatches that arrived in the course of his stormy homeward voyage, do
not indicate any doubts about the course that had been adopted, let alone a
change of mind. Tschirschky's report that Count Berchtold had explained the
Austrian position to the Russian ambassador in sober and conciliatory terms,
emphasising that the Dual Monarchy was not claiming any Serbian territory
whatever, triggered the angry imperial comment that this was 'totally superfluous!' Berchtold would only thereby 'give an impression of weakness and of
apologising, which is quite wrong in dealing with Russia and must be avoided.
Austria has her good reasons and has made her demarche on that basis, and it
cannot now after the event be made a subject for discussion as it were!' The
Austro-Hungarian Foreign Minister was an 'ass' if he renounced Serbian
territory. Austria '*must* take back the Sandjak, otherwise the Serbs will get
to the Adriatic'. A shift in the existing power-relationships 'in the Balkans and
in Europe', which Berchtold had said was not an aim of his policy, would, the
Kaiser was convinced, 'come about of its own accord and must come. Austria
must become preponderant in the Balkans *vis à vis* the other smaller states, at
Russia's expense; otherwise we shall have no peace.'[87]

The Kaiser endorsed Sir Edward Grey's view that a state that accepted the
terms of the Austrian ultimatum would cease to be an independent state, but
he commented that 'that would be very desirable. [Serbia] is not a state in the
Europ[ean] sense, but a band of robbers!' The Balkan peoples, he said, were
'simply not' *Kulturvölker* and if Russia did not agree 'then the Russians are

simply no better either'. The Kaiser was counting on an Austrian invasion of Serbia as a certainty, even at the risk that it might trigger a war between Austria-Hungary, Germany and Italy on one side and Russia and France on the other. He rejected as 'useless' the British offer to join Germany in sounding out Vienna about an extension of the deadline in the hope of thereby finding a way out of the crisis. Equally, he brusquely rejected as 'superfluous' Grey's proposal that the four as yet uninvolved European Powers, Great Britain, Germany, France and Italy, should mediate: after all, 'Austria has already put Russia in the picture . . . and Grey has nothing else to propose. I shall not join in', Kaiser Wilhelm declared on 26 July, 'unless Austria expressly asks me to, which is unlikely. In questions of honour and of *vital* interests one does not consult others'; and he simply dismissed as 'nonsense' the danger foreseen by the British Foreign Secretary that even a localised war between Austria and Serbia could become a long-drawn-out bitter struggle in which the Dual Monarchy might 'bleed to death'.[88] Count Wedel telegraphed these imperial pronouncements to the Wilhelmstrasse that same evening.[89]

No less militant were the Kaiser's comments on a dispatch from the ambassador in Paris, Baron von Schoen. French protestations of wishing to work for the peace of Europe Wilhelm yet again dismissed as 'Rubbish' and 'sheer mumbo jumbo!' The Paris government's proposal that Austria-Hungary might negotiate with Belgrade about the points of the ultimatum that Serbia did not feel able to accept immediately provoked the angry observation: '*Ultimata* are complied with or not! But they are not *discussed* any more! Hence the name!'[90]

The mounting evidence that Russia would not accept the subjugation of Serbia by Austria-Hungary and the concomitant shift of power in the Balkans and in Europe made no impression on Kaiser Wilhelm, even during the voyage from Balholm back to Kiel. Just before leaving on 25 July he had instructed his ambassador in St Petersburg to speak to Sazonov 'clearly, seriously, and very firmly'.[91] Now, en route for home, he would have nothing to do with Sazonov's demand of 24 July that the Austrian charges against Serbia be 'put before a European areopagus'. That, he would 'quite certainly not!' permit, he wrote on a telegram from St Petersburg. 'For when its vital interests are at stake a Great Power cannot subject itself to a tribunal.' Russia, 'since her fraternisation with the French socialist republic is no longer aware of' her obligations to the monarchical principle, he declared on the evening of 26 July. The 'very excited' Russian Foreign Minister's warning that 'if Austria-Hungary swallows Serbia we shall go to war with her' made no impression on the Kaiser, who shrugged it off with the marginal comment: 'Well then, go ahead!'[92] But what, in such an event, would England's reaction be?

CHAPTER FORTY

Confusion in Potsdam: the fear of Britain's involvement

FROM KIEL TO POTSDAM

Despite the lively exchange of dispatches between the *Hohenzollern* and the capital, and despite his warlike language in Balholm and even on the homeward voyage, the Kaiser had not quite given up hope that Russia would back down at the last moment and the Austro-Serbian conflict would not give rise to a general war. As he made for Kiel on 25 and 26 July he repeatedly talked of continuing his holiday as planned with the Kaiserin in Wilhelms-höhe after just a short stay in Berlin. Thus, on 26 July, the head of the Military Cabinet wrote to his wife from the *Hohenzollern*: 'The Kaiser wishes to go directly from Kiel to the Neues Palais, where he will arrive with his suite tomorrow afternoon ... Now if we too should mobilise, the Kaiser will naturally stay on in the Neues Palais; but if − as is still very possible − Russia stands aside, then we too shall not move, and the Kaiser will perhaps (?) [sic] go to Wilhelmshöhe. That is all very uncertain.' After talking to the Court Chamberlain, Count Platen-Hallermund, at 6 o'clock, Lyncker added that the Kaiser had just telegraphed to the Kaiserin that 'he wishes, after putting himself in the picture in Berlin, to come to Wilhelmshöhe. That', Lyncker concluded, 'does not exactly suggest that we are on the brink of a war involving Germany'. Three hours later, after the arrival of the telegram reporting the sharp exchange between Sazonov and Pourtalès, Lyncker wrote that the Kaiser was 'for the time being' sticking with his plan 'of going to Wilhelmshöhe after a fairly short stay in the Neues Palais'. Even on the following morning, 27 July, the Monday, half an hour before they entered Kiel harbour, Count Platen told Lyncker that the Kaiser 'is going on to Wilhelmshöhe this very evening'. It would all depend, Lyncker added, 'on what the Chancellor says in Berlin'.[1] Of course, it became clear to the Kaiser soon after he arrived in Kiel early that morning that there could be no question of a summer holiday with the Empress in Kassel. In fact on that same day, in Schloss Wilhelmshöhe, Auguste Viktoria changed her last will and testament and returned to Potsdam.[2]

Reports reaching the *Hohenzollern* during the final hours of its homeward voyage left no doubt that the crisis was deepening. At midnight the Reich Chancellor telegraphed that King Petar and the Serbian government had left Belgrade for the south.[3] In the early hours Bethmann forwarded to the Kaiser by wireless a dispatch from St Petersburg reporting that Russian troop exercises had suddenly been broken off and the regiments ordered back to barracks. In Russian headquarters there was 'great excitement at the behaviour of Austria'; and Russia would probably mobilise against the latter.[4] On arriving in Kiel the Kaiser received a long report from his Flügeladjutant and boyhood friend Oskar von Chelius, now military plenipotentiary at St Petersburg, about the extremely angry mood at the Tsar's court: the sharp language of the Austrian note had aroused 'great indignation' in St Petersburg; Russia felt deeply hurt by the ultimatum; people were saying that never before had a state used such language against a weaker party. Russia could not permit Serbia to be 'crushed'. When Vienna refused Russia's request for an extension of the time-limit to allow negotiations to take place, the mood had swung round to one of 'extreme indignation against Austria'. The Tsar's entourage had given him, Chelius, clearly to understand that 'a war between Austria and Serbia . . . means war with Russia', and had asked him whether Berlin had had prior knowledge of the Austrian note and had approved it.[5]

The Chancellor's urgent advice to the Kaiser – to stay calm as the agreed 'localisation policy' demanded – only evoked a series of imperial exclamation marks and a scornful marginal note: 'Keep calm and carry on! Just keep calm! always keep calm!! But a calm mobilisation is indeed something new.' Bethmann should not come to meet him at Kiel, as he had offered, but 'he should wait for me in Berlin; I shall go there, or to Wildpark', the little railway station serving the Neues Palais in Potsdam.[6] The Chancellor, concerned to put Russia in the wrong, replied that the Kaiser should not go to Berlin, but to Potsdam, as in Berlin there might be anti-Serbian demonstrations that Russia could construe as meaning 'that we are seeking war with her', while it is Russia who, 'come what may, must at all costs be put in the wrong in the eyes of the world'.[7] This advisory directive also aroused the Kaiser's ire. As Admiral von Müller noted in his diary, Bethmann was 'treated ungraciously' by Wilhelm on his arrival at Wildpark 'because he had asked the Kaiser not to come to Berlin on account of the demonstrations that might be expected'.

'It gets crazier all the time', the monarch grumbled to the head of his Naval Cabinet, 'Now the man is telling me that I may not show myself to my people.'[8]

Far from allowing himself to be frightened out of his previous belligerent mood by reports from St Petersburg or warnings from the Reich Chancellor, when Kaiser Wilhelm landed at Kiel early in the morning of Monday 27 July he issued orders that both Bethmann and the naval authorities (Tirpitz had by this time returned from his holiday) regarded as bordering on the insane. The Kaiser put the Commander of the naval station, Admiral Bachmann, personally in charge of controlling the entrances to the Baltic.[9] Hopman's diary testifies to the horrified consternation of the naval authorities: 'At 2.30 a.m. something like the following cypher telegram arrives from the Baltic Station: "H.M. has ordered the station commander to look to the security of the western Baltic, and to this end has given him charge of SMS Kaiser, Rostock, and the V and VII Torpedoboat flotillas." I take this extraordinary thing to Tirpitz, who is with Capelle. His impression is the same as mine, and he puts it into words: Now he is playing at soldiers! I inform Behnke, who is also shocked and tells me that Pohl has been ordered to Potsdam for H.M.'s arrival. Hebbinghaus in Kiel tells me in reply to my telephonic enquiry, that H.M. had urgently and personally made Bachmann responsible for the task in question, which he too finds quite incredible. I tell him what I think too, and Tirpitz, who happened to be in my room while I was telephoning, only says that I ought to tell Hebbinghaus that he considered the matter militarily nonsensical and a political error. Capelle, to whom I then report, describes the order as "pathological" ... Tirpitz is not optimistic about the future and thinks that the affair will end in a humiliation for us.'[10] The hapless head of the Admiralty Staff, Hugo von Pohl, was only partially successful in getting the Kaiser's order revoked. As Hopman noted, almost in disbelief, after the Admiral's return from his audience in the Neues Palais on 27 July, 'Pohl has ... not found out very much from H.M., who only told him about the ... security order he issued in Kiel and Pohl did not oppose it unfortunately. Then this morning the Admiralty Staff proposed the withdrawal of H.M.'s order, and received the reply: "Alert can be dropped, but continue observation".'[11]

On the train journey from Kiel to Potsdam the Kaiser received a memorandum from the Reich Chancellor listing the matters that would be on the agenda when he arrived in Potsdam: Austria would in all probability not be able to undertake military operations before 12 August; Serbia, who had accepted almost every point in the ultimatum, would adopt a purely defensive posture if attacked; England, France and Italy desired peace; Russia, seemed according to latest reports to wish to start negotiations with Vienna. Germany's position was still that the Austro-Serbian conflict was an affair that concerned only those two states; Russia had been warned 'most emphatic-ally' by Bethmann 'about the consequences of any military measures that might in any sense be directed against us'.[12]

THE AUDIENCES OF 27 JULY 1914 IN THE NEUES PALAIS

When the Kaiser's special train pulled into Wildpark station at ten past three on 27 July he found the Chancellor and the Chief of General Staff (who had already been long in conference together)[13] and the head of the Admiralty Staff together with all the Generaladjutanten and Flügeladjutanten awaiting him.[14] Bethmann Hollweg, in what was his first audience since 5 July, gave the Kaiser his assessment of the situation on the basis of the latest reports. He explained that despite pressure from the Berlin government to display 'the greatest speed in its military operations and declare war as soon as possible . . . in order to forestall the danger of intervention by a third Power' the Chief of the Austro-Hungarian General Staff, Conrad von Hötzendorf, had declared that he could only 'start general operations [against Serbia] about 12 August'.[15] The government in Paris had begun to suspect 'that we are the driving force behind Austria-Hungary and are seeking war', but it was nevertheless anxious to calm St Petersburg down, provided Berlin would also advise moderation at Vienna.[16] Of the fourteen reports and dispatches on which Bethmann was basing his account, no fewer than seven had arrived from Russia in the last few hours. They contained the most contradictory information. On the one hand, the mobilisation of the Kiev and Odessa military districts was said to be as good as certain, while rumours of the mobilisation of several Russian army corps on the German frontier were pouring in by the hour. On the other hand, both Pourtalès and Chelius in St Petersburg had got the impression that people were 'very nervous and anxious'; the Foreign Minister Sazonov seemed 'to have rather lost his nerve', perhaps as a result of reports from Paris and London.[17] Despite the apparently wavering attitude of the Russian leaders, Wilhelm II rejected as premature the Reich Chancellor's suggestion that he might now send the Tsar a communication that the Auswärtiges Amt had already drafted for him.[18]

While he was still at Balholm the Kaiser had ordered the Wilhelmstrasse to put pressure on the Austrians to offer Rome generous compensation for their own impending expansion into the Balkans, in order to bring the wavering Italians into the war.[19] As he was sailing back to Kiel he had received 'worrying' news of a 'rather heated' meeting lasting several hours between Hans von Flotow, the German ambassador, Antonio Salandra, the Italian Prime Minister, and Marquis di San Giuliano, the Foreign Minister, about

the Austrian note to Serbia. The Italian statesmen were furious that the
ultimatum had been handed over without informing them in advance. Its
tone, moreover, was 'so aggressive and inept' that public opinion all over
Europe was outraged; and the Italian government was unable to fight against
that sort of mood at home. The Kaiser, however, interpreted this altercation as
merely an Italian attempt at blackmail to extort more compensation. Italy's
objections were 'rubbish!' he scribbled disdainfully in the margin of the report.
Italy had wanted 'to steal Albania on the sly and Austria has put paid to that.
The little thief always has to have something for himself too.' Just before he
landed in Kiel he had remarked, à propos Rome's objections: 'That is a lot of
nonsense and will sort itself out in the course of events.'[20] Now, during the
Chancellor's audience, he was extremely disconcerted to receive a dispatch
from Flotow reporting further 'sharp exchanges' with the Italian Foreign
Minister; and he now − rightly − saw a serious threat in San Giuliano's
repeated declarations that even if Russia and France intervened, Italy would
not be prepared to recognise the *casus foederis*, as Austria's action against
Serbia was not defensive but clearly offensive; indeed, that Italy might find
herself moved to intervene *against* Austria. Clearly recognising that a continental war might be imminent, Wilhelm again ordered the Chancellor to press
Vienna to offer Italy substantial compensations. After the audience Bethmann
noted: 'H.M. thinks it absolutely necessary that Austria should reach agreement with Italy about the question of compensations *in time*. Herr von
Tschirschky has to be told this for passing on to Count Berchtold on H.M.'s
express instructions.'[21] A telegram containing this imperial command went off
to Vienna that same evening.[22]

    After the audiences in the Neues Palais Müller thought he could discern a
certain easing of the international crisis. However, there had been no change
in the aims of German policy, which included a continental war in its
calculations; as Müller placidly summed it up, 'the tendency of our policy'
was: 'staying calm, letting Russia put herself in the wrong, but then not
shrinking from war'.[23] The head of the Naval Cabinet explained the momentous results of the Potsdam audiences of 27 July to his colleague Captain Ernst
Freiherr von Weizsäcker: according to Bethmann, 'England wishes to remain
neutral, on that we can count with fair certainty . . . France is not especially
keen to join in. Our policy is directed towards forcing Russia into the role of
provocateur. But we are not trying to hold Austria back from further action. At
the moment it is not, on the whole, likely that the conflict will spread. Austria
will not be ready militarily until 12. VIII. A lot can change before then. To the
outside world we must avoid giving the impression of being in a warlike
mood.'[24] The Prussian War Minister Erich von Falkenhayn was not involved

in the Potsdam discussions, but he too later learned 'on the quiet' and much to his satisfaction, that it had been decided to go through with the matter 'whatever it might cost'. Already on 27 July he commanded the troops who would otherwise have gone on exercises to return to barracks and gave orders for the safeguarding of the railways and the purchase of large quantities of grain.[25]

On this day, 27 July, there was no sign of any backing down or rethinking on Wilhelm's part. His marginal comments on the reports that reached him during or shortly after Bethmann Hollweg's audience indicated no change of attitude towards either the approaching conflict in the Balkans or its possible consequences. When Flotow telegraphed from Rome that an Austro-Serbian war might possibly be prevented as Serbia now seemed inclined to accept the Austrian demands if they were presented to her in the name of Europe, Wilhelm, true to form, dismissed this as 'Quatsch!'[26] He likewise rejected a British proposal for an ambassadorial conference between Germany, France, Italy and Russia, with the comment: 'I am not getting involved in anything.'[27] A French suggestion for German mediation in Vienna to save the peace he rejected equally sharply, declaring that the decision on war and peace rested not with Berlin but 'with St Petersburg alone!'[28] When on 27 July Tschirschky reported that Austria would declare war on Serbia next day or the day after at the latest, 'in order to pre-empt any attempt at mediation', Wilhelm accepted this without comment.[29] He declared himself in agreement when the Wilhelmstrasse put before him a secret instruction for the minister in Copenhagen, Count Brockdorff-Rantzau, to inform Denmark when the time came that 'in the event of a European war' Germany had 'no intention whatever of endangering the integrity of the Danish state. However, military events might, whatever we wish or intend, lead to operations that encroach on Danish waters. Denmark must take account of the seriousness of the situation and turn its mind to what position it will adopt in that event.'[30] As late as the evening of 27 July there were no more doubts about the agreed bellicose policy on the Kaiser's part than in the Wilhelmstrasse or among the generals. The latter were all the more staggered, therefore, when on the next morning, immediately before Austria's declaration of war on Serbia, Wilhelm indicated his readiness to relent. What had happened? Why did the Kaiser seem suddenly to have lost his nerve, when since the beginning of the month he had been backing the decision to risk a great war and had often been even more warlike than his advisers? Not surprisingly, this — albeit fleeting — change of mood was a direct response to the possibility that was beginning to loom on the horizon that England might not after all be prepared to stand aside.

'CONFUSED SPEECHES': THE KAISER'S HALT-IN-BELGRADE
PROPOSAL OF 28 JULY

Wilhelm's readiness for war both during the return voyage to Kiel and even
after his audiences with Bethmann, Moltke and Pohl in the afternoon of
27 July is attributable in part to reports from London that King George V had
personally assured Prince Heinrich of Prussia that England would stay neutral
in a war between the continental Powers.[31] On that day Bethmann confidently
declared that England's neutrality could be 'counted on with fair certainty'
and that it seemed 'that England's inclination towards neutrality is having a
very sobering effect on Russia and France'.[32] True, these reports were at odds
with warnings from the ambassador in London, Prince Lichnowsky, that an
Austrian invasion of Serbia must 'inevitably' lead to world war, but in Berlin
these warnings were brushed aside. In fact, the Reich Chancellor and the
Wilhelmstrasse well knew that nothing would be more likely to cool the
Kaiser's readiness for war with Russia and France than the fear of British
intervention. For this reason in handling the Kaiser they refrained – highly
irresponsibly – from putting all their cards on the table, tampering with
important passages in dispatches from London and simply withholding from
the Kaiser other reports from Lichnowsky that made it clear that, in the
approaching trial of strength between Triple Alliance and Triple Entente,
'England would certainly stand by France and Russia.'[33]

In his audience on the afternoon of 27 July Bethmann presented the Kaiser
with a copy of a dispatch from Lichnowsky that had been deliberately falsified –
by the elimination of the British Foreign Office's warning that the Russian
government could not possibly permit Austria to cross the Serbian frontier, but
would be obliged, 'if it did not wish to lose its standing in the Balkan states for
ever', to go to war with Austria. Before handing the telegram to the Kaiser, the
Chancellor also removed the concluding paragraph, with the ambassador's
urgent warning that Germany's policy of localisation was an illusion, and his
passionate appeal 'that our stance be determined solely by the necessity of
sparing the German people a struggle in which they have nothing to gain and
everything to lose'.[34] This manipulation of the text can only have been
intended to deceive his own sovereign as to the consequences of an Austrian
invasion of Serbia and the attitude of Great Britain. 'Presented to H.M.', the
Reich Chancellor smugly noted on the doctored copy of the telegram from
London. 'H.M. disapproved of Lichnowsky's point of view.'[35] From then on,
important information was withheld from the ambassador by his own government, on the grounds that he was too trusting and 'blunderingly tells
Sir Edward [Grey] everything'.[36]

While Bethmann was with the Kaiser in the afternoon of 27 July another dispatch from Lichnowsky reached the Wilhelmstrasse, reporting Grey's astonishment at Serbia's conciliatory reply to the Austrian ultimatum, which was obviously attributable to massive pressure from St Petersburg. If Austria now refused to negotiate about the few outstanding points of difference, let alone if she crossed the Serbian frontier and occupied a completely defenceless Belgrade, it would then be patently obvious that she had only been seeking a pretext to crush Serbia. The real objective of such an action would be, in Grey's view, to expel Russian influence from the Balkans, which would be unacceptable to Russia. 'That could cause the most frightful war that Europe had ever seen, and nobody could know what it could lead to.' The British Foreign Secretary was urgently asking the German government 'to use our influence in Vienna to bring the Austrians to accept Belgrade's reply as either adequate, or as the basis for further negotiations.' Lichnowsky went on to warn: 'For the first time I found the Minister annoyed . . . In any case I am convinced that if it were now to come to war, we should no longer be able to count on English sympathy and on support from Great Britain.'[37]

The men in the Wilhelmstrasse saw at once what the effect of London's attitude would be on the Kaiser's overwrought nerves, but they saw no possibility of keeping this explosive dispatch from him. In a note for the Reich Chancellor, Gottlieb von Jagow asked: 'Should the telegram be put before H.M.? Surely it can hardly be kept from H.M.?' On his return from Potsdam Bethmann Hollweg gave orders for Lichnowsky's dispatch to be taken 'by messenger to the Neues Palais early tomorrow'.[38] The report arrived there in the early hours of the morning of the 28th and did not fail to have the effect on the monarch that the Wilhelmstrasse had feared, especially as the day brought, as Müller noted, 'yet further alarming reports'.[39]

In forwarding Lichnowsky's telegram to Tschirschky in Vienna Bethmann Hollweg again made plain the calculation underlying his policy when he stressed that 'we must appear to be the ones who are forced to go to war'.[40] Even before the British mediation proposals arrived Jagow had summoned the Austro-Hungarian ambassador and assured him 'most definitely' that the German government was 'decidedly' opposed to taking London's proposals for mediation into account. It was only forwarding them to Vienna to prevent 'England's making common cause with France and Russia . . . just now . . . If Germany were to tell Sir E. Grey straight out that she did not wish . . . to forward his proposals to Vienna, that would create the very situation that, as mentioned above, must be avoided at all costs.'[41] When he sent Lichnowsky's telegram to the Kaiser the Reich Chancellor also explained to him in no uncertain terms why he had, 'in accordance with Your Majesty's wishes', forwarded the British mediation proposals to Vienna. 'If we were to reject every mediatory role out of hand, especially as London and Paris are continuing to put pressure on St Petersburg, then we should appear before England and the whole world as responsible for the conflagration, and as the real warmongers. That would, on the one hand, make it impossible for us to keep morale up at home, and on the other put an end to England's neutrality.'[42] Kaiser Wilhelm II's complicity in this Machiavellian duplicity is, therefore, undeniable.

At the same time − early in the morning of 28 July − that he was reading the telegram from London, the Kaiser received the full text of the Serbian reply to the Austro-Hungarian ultimatum, which was only now sent on to him from the Wilhelmstrasse.[43] On this document he wrote the famous words: 'A brilliant achievement for a mere 48-hour time limit. That is more than could have been expected! A great moral victory for Vienna; but with it disappears every reason for war, and Giesl [the Austro-Hungarian envoy] ought just to have stayed on in Belgrade. *I* should never have ordered mobilisation after that.'[44] At ten o'clock, after speaking to his Adjutant-General Hans von Plessen,[45] Wilhelm drafted in his own hand that remarkable letter to Jagow which, if it had only been implemented, might perhaps yet have prevented the world catastrophe that was about to occur. 'After reading the Serbian reply, which I received this morning, I am convinced that on the whole the wishes of the Danube Monarchy have been fulfilled. The few reservations that Serbia has made regarding individual points can in my opinion certainly be cleared up in negotiations. But the most humiliating capitulation is hereby proclaimed urbi et orbi, and as a result *every reason for war* disappears. However, neither the piece of paper nor its contents can have more than limited value so long as they have not been translated into *deeds*. The Serbs are orientals, and therefore liars, false, and masters of delay. To ensure that these fine promises become real facts there will be a need for a *douce violence*. That could be done in such a way: that Austria seizes a pledge (Belgrade) to enforce the implementation of the promises and holds it until her demands are actually fulfilled. That is also necessary in order to satisfy the honour of the army, mobilised *to no purpose* for the third time, to allow it a show of success in the eyes of the outside world, and the feeling that it has at least stood on foreign territory. Otherwise, if there is no campaign a strongly hostile feeling may develop against the dynasty, which would be very dangerous. If Y.E. agrees with me, I should propose saying to Austria: Austria has forced Serbia to make a very humiliating retreat, and is to be congratulated in this. Naturally, *there is no longer* any reason for *war*. However, there must certainly be a *guarantee*, that the promises will be *fulfilled*. That would be obtainable through a *temporary* military occupation of part of Serbia. Rather like our stationing troops in France in 1871 until the billions had been paid. On *this basis* I am prepared to mediate for *peace* in Austria. Counter-proposals or protests from other Powers I should reject out of hand, all the more so as more or less everybody is openly appealing to me to help to maintain the peace. I shall do that in my own fashion, and sparing Austria[n] *national sentiment* and the *military honour* of the *army* as much as possible. For the latter has already been appealed to by the Supreme War Lord, and it is in process of complying with his appeal. So it is essential that it gets a visible *satisfaction d'honneur*; that is a *precondition* for my mediation. So I wish Y.E. to draft me a proposal along these lines that can be sent to Vienna. I have already written to the Chief of the General Staff in the above sense through Plessen, who completely agrees with me. Wilhelm I.R.'[46] Momentarily, Wilhelm's hopes rose of soon being able to leave for Wilhelmshöhe: he informed Tirpitz that it was doubtful if he would still be in Potsdam for his audience on 1 August. In other words, he considered the situation to be, as Hopman noted, 'quite peaceful'.[47]

As late as midday on 29 July Wilhelm confirmed his conviction that there was no longer any reason for a major war. As he explained in a handwritten 'Assessment of the Situation': 'Serbia has actually already capitulated morally to Austria through her reply, and the justification for war has thereby disappeared. As, however, Serbia is a land of rabble and bandits, a paper promise is worthless. Austria must have cast-iron guarantees that the promise will *in fact* be carried out. That can be achieved by occupying part of Serbia until the conditions are fulfilled! As we in '70 remained in France until the billions had been paid. Hence, a punitive expedition and war [sic]. That would not give Russia or other Powers *any reason at all* to intervene in favour of the murderers of kings and princes. Whoever does that is an accomplice. Wilhelm I.R.'[48]

The Kaiser's promising initiative of 28 July remained without influence on the course of events. With studied cynicism, the Reich Chancellor and the leading officials of the Foreign Office saw to it that his suggestions were transmitted to Vienna in garbled form. True, the dispatch drafted by Stumm, the influential Director of the Political Department, that the Chancellor sent to Tschirschky in Vienna on the night of 28–9 July contained the proposal that Austria might declare for a second time that she was not seeking to acquire Serbian territory and would only occupy Belgrade temporarily as a guarantee that her demands would be met and out of consideration for the military honour of the army. But as for the Kaiser's main point, that with Serbia's submissive reply all grounds for war between Austria and Serbia had disappeared, there was not a single word. Moreover, the dispatch was sent off to Tschirschky so late that it only arrived in the early hours of 29 July, long after

Austria-Hungary's declaration of war on Serbia, and Berchtold, as hostilities had started, rejected the English mediation proposal as having reached him 'too late'.[49]

Bethmann's telegram to Tschirschky revealed that for the Wilhelmstrasse the issue was simply one of tactical advantages. The German government, the Chancellor explained to the ambassador, had been put in an extremely difficult position by Austria's delaying her invasion of Serbia until 12 August, as it was being pressed by all sides to mediate; and if it continued to reject all mediation proposals it would incur 'the odium of having brought about a world war [sic!], even in the eyes of the German people too. But that is no basis for starting and waging a successful war on three fronts. It is absolutely imperative that, whatever happens, the responsibility for any extension of the conflict to those not directly involved must lie with Russia.' Austria-Hungary must therefore again declare that she was not seeking territorial gains in Serbia and would only occupy Belgrade until her conditions had been met in full. 'If the Russian government does not admit the justice of this point of view, then it will have against it the public opinion of the whole of Europe, which is at the moment starting to turn against Austria. A further consequence will be that the general diplomatic, and probably also the military, situation will shift very substantially in favour of Austria-Hungary and her allies.' Tschirschky was to be careful to avoid giving the impression in Vienna 'that we wanted to hold Austria back'. It was simply a question, Bethmann explained, 'of finding a means of realising Austria-Hungary's aim of paralysing the vital nerve of pan-Serbian propaganda without at the same time unleashing a world war, and — if in the end the latter cannot be avoided — of improving as far as possible the terms on which we shall have to fight it'.[50] The motives and tactics of the German decision-makers in the July crisis could hardly have been more clearly formulated, but the Kaiser's initiative of that morning formed no recognisable part of them. It is not surprising, therefore, that the Chancellor did not show Wilhelm the dispatch to Tschirschky, as the monarch had expressly demanded. Even so, Bethmann allowed Wilhelm to believe that he had sent orders for 'the demarche as commanded' to Vienna — and had indeed, sent them by telegraph because, he claimed, there was 'no longer any regular railway communication with Vienna'.[51]

The confusion that arose from the Chancellor's misrepresentation of the Kaiser's orders is documented in the sources. As late as the evening of the following day (30 July) Wilhelm showed his bewilderment when he complained to Admirals Tirpitz, Müller and Pohl that 'he did not know what the Austrians wanted. He was being pressed from all sides and had therefore wanted to send someone from the Foreign Office to Vienna, but the railway lines were closed. So Tschirschky had been ordered by telegraph to demand of Berchtold a categorical statement of what they actually wanted. The Serbs had after all given way over everything except a few trivial points. He could understand that the Austrian army needed to satisfy its honour after mobilising three times against Serbia with no result, but a pledge would be adequate for that.' The Kaiser went on to explain, according to a memorandum by Tirpitz, that 'since the communiqué which he had received four weeks ago the Austrians had told him nothing of what they wanted. He had believed that appropriate steps would be taken immediately. Then they said that would take another 17 days, then there was a delay so as not to disturb the Poincaré visit, and after the ultimatum had been rejected they did not and could not take any action, but asked for a further 17 days before starting operations. He could not understand it.'[52] On the following day the Kaiser was still expressing his frustration that Austria seemed unwilling to fall in with his Halt-in-Belgrade proposal.[53] The illusion that his mediatory action was still under way partly explains his dismay when early on 30 July the news reached him of Russia's mobilisation against Austria-Hungary. The Kaiser had not seen through the double game his Chancellor was playing; but neither had he taken any action to make his pledge proposal effective.

While attaching all due weight to his initiative of 28 July – it was certainly a step in the right direction – one must question whether his proposal, even if it had not been thwarted by the Wilhelmstrasse, was at all likely to halt the course of events once they had got going. There had been no change in Wilhelm's attitude towards the conflict in the Balkans. He held as firmly as before to his demand for a massive shift of power in favour of Austria-Hungary at Serbia's and Russia's expense, even if he momentarily believed that this could now be achieved without an Austro-Serbian war. His idea that the Austro-Hungarian army could march into Serbia unopposed and occupy Belgrade and surrounding areas until the ultimatum was complied with seems an illusion: both Russia and Great Britain had made it clear that an invasion of Serbia by Austrian troops in any circumstances whatever would be an unacceptable provocation for Russia. The idea of handing over for a decision by the Hague Tribunal the points still in dispute between Vienna and Belgrade was still peremptorily dismissed by Wilhelm as 'Blödsinn!' [Nonsense] even now: a Great Power such as Austria could not go along with that, he insisted. The suggestion that he, as German Emperor, should give the allied Habsburg Empire some well-meaning advice against stringing the bow too tight he had dismissed already during the night of 28–9 July, remarking that 'those are phrases designed to push the responsibility on to me; and I will have nothing to do with it'.[54]

In any case, the mood in which Wilhelm II made his suggestion of 28 July did not last. When Falkenhayn came for his audience in the Neues Palais that evening he was initially shocked by the Supreme War Lord's frame of mind, that had 'changed completely'. 'He makes confused speeches, from which the only clear thing that emerges is that he does not want war any more and to this end is even determined to leave Austria in the lurch.' But the General, who was set on war, soon managed to convince the Kaiser of the correctness of the course pursued so far: 'I point out to him that he is no longer in control of the matter.'[55] By the following day the War Minister could note with satisfaction that the Kaiser was again convinced that 'the ball which has started to roll cannot be stopped'.[56]

THE FATAL EFFECT OF 'THE WORD OF A KING': PRINCE HEINRICH'S SECOND MISSION TO LONDON

The change in the Kaiser's mood in favour of a continental war was attributable at least in part to the arrival in the Neues Palais on 29 July of a letter from Prince Heinrich concerning a personal conversation with King George V that revived hopes of British neutrality. How did it come about that at the height of the July crisis the King was discussing England's attitude in an impending European war with his Prussian cousin – just as they had done eighteen months previously in December 1912?[57] The Prince's diaries only show that on 22 July he broke off his holiday with his family in St Moritz and returned to Kiel, from where he left for London on Friday the 24th, arriving the next morning.[58] He informed the King of his arrival and received that same evening a reply that described the international situation in gloomy terms.[59] 'I quite understand that you will be very busy until you go down to Cowes on Tuesday, where I hope to have the pleasure of seeing you next Saturday if the political situation enables me to leave London. I fear things look very black between Austria & Servia. The Austrian Minister & the Staff of his Legation left Belgrade this evening. I think Europe is nearer a general war at the moment than it has been for many years. Please God peace may be maintained.'[60] Early next morning (Sunday 26 July) the Prince replied using racialist and militaristic expressions that were not likely to assuage the King's fears: 'Dearest Georgie', he wrote, 'Thanks so much for Your dear letter! – Alas – I can not, but look upon the situation in the same light, as You do, & should I find the news confirmed that William has left for Germany, I shall return to Kiel, tomorrow morning! – As You say, please God, we may yet prevent a European war, & may our two countries stand together & avoid a general smash up, since it may end in the question of "race"! Au revoir dearest, we must each follow his call, happen what may. You will in future, as in the past find a true friend in Your always devoted cousin Harry PvP.'[61]

The Prince nevertheless called briefly at Buckingham Palace on that Sunday morning, at the King's request. The assurance that George V was supposed to have given him during this meeting – that England would stay neutral in the approaching continental war – became, as we shall see, both in the final stage of the July crisis and after the outbreak of war, an important element in the Kaiser's apologia to the effect that Grey had deliberately led him into a trap in order to destroy Germany.[62] Wilhelm claimed repeatedly to have been acting in the firm belief that the King had 'sent him officially . . . through Prince Heinrich a clear declaration of neutrality' that Grey then withdrew at the critical moment.[63] What actually transpired on that Sunday morning, and what did Heinrich tell his brother about what cousin Georgie had said?

The Prince's diary entry about his meeting with George V is extremely terse: 'Visit him at 9.45, Proposal Intervention, Germany, England, France, Italy to localise war between Austria and Serbia.' As a postscript Prince Heinrich added – whether days or even years later is not clear – in the bottom margin of the page the King's purported remark: 'We shall try & keep out of it, we shall probably remain neutral.'[64] Nor did the King, who was rushing off to church at 10 o'clock, make any notes on the conversation at the time. He only made a short entry in his diary – which was also added between the lines: 'Henry of Prussia came to see me early, he returns at once to Germany.'[65] Only afterwards – just when is not known – did the King write down (clearly with reference to the note he had received from Heinrich) – on a separate piece of paper an account of his conversation with the Kaiser's brother: 'Prince Henry of Prussia came to see me on Sunday July 26 at 9.30 AM. & asked me if there was any news, I said the news was very bad & it looked like a European war & that he had better go back to Germany at once. He said he would go down to Eastbourne to see his sister (Queen of Greece) & he would return to Germany this evening. He then asked what England would do if there was a European war. I said I don't know what we shall do, we have no quarrel with anyone & I hope we shall remain neutral. But if Germany declares war on Russia & France joins Russia, then I am afraid we shall be dragged into it. But you can be sure that I & my Government will do all we can to prevent a European war. He then said, well if our two Countries should be fighting on opposite sides I trust that it will not affect our own personal friendship. He shook hands & left the room having been with me about 8 minutes.'[66]

British court officials and statesmen soon learned of the King's conversation with the Prussian Prince; and although they had no inkling of any promise of neutrality, they immediately suspected that it had been Heinrich's intention to obtain something of the kind. As early as 26 July the King's Private Secretary, Lord Stamfordham, told the Permanent Under Secretary Sir Arthur Nicolson, who immediately informed Grey, that 'Prince Henry came over yesterday and breakfasted with the King this morning. Prince Henry said if Russia moved there would be internal revolution and the dynasty be upset. This is nonsense — but it shows how anxious they are to make out to us that Russia will remain quiet and to spread about that we will be equally quiescent — a foolish procedure — (Prince Henry has gone back to Germany).'[67]

After his brief visit to Buckingham Palace Heinrich hastened to the neighbouring German embassy, where he saw Prince Lichnowsky and the naval attaché Captain Erich von Müller. Shortly before noon the ambassador telegraphed to the Auswärtiges Amt: 'Prince Heinrich asks me to report to Y.E. that H.M. the King has expressed his keen desire that Great Britain and Germany acting as partners together with France and Italy may succeed in mastering this extremely grave situation in the interests of peace.' Lichnowsky did not mention any assurance given by the King as to the neutrality of Great Britain in a European war;[68] but that Heinrich believed he had received such an assurance is clear from the 'most secret' telegram that the naval attaché sent on the same day, 26 July, to his superiors in Berlin, who immediately passed the news on to the Reich Chancellor: 'King of Great Britain stated to Prince Heinrich of Prussia that England would be neutral if war should break out between continental Powers.'[69] From the embassy Prince Heinrich went down to Maresfield, the country house of Prince Alexander von Münster-Derneburg in Sussex, where he was visited by his two sisters, Queen Sophie of the Hellenes and Princess (later Landgravine) Margarethe of Hesse and their children, coming for the day from Eastbourne.[70] (See Figure 49.)

It is hardly imaginable that Heinrich would have come to London except 'on the Kaiser's orders' even if we cannot say exactly when he received such a command.[71] In any case, the impact of his conversation with the King on the Kaiser's decisions in this critical phase of the July crisis was catastrophic, as Wilhelm interpreted his brother's report of George V's hesitant off-the-cuff remark as amounting to 'a clear official declaration of neutrality'.[72] We have seen above how Captain von Müller's telegram of the 26th confirmed the Kaiser in his readiness for war after his return to Potsdam.[73] When Heinrich returned to Kiel on the 28th — just at the time when Lichnowsky's warnings were making Wilhelm start to waver and draft his Halt-in-Belgrade proposal — he informed the Kaiser by letter that 'before I left London, on the Sunday morning in fact, I had a brief talk at my request, with Georgie, who was fully aware of the seriousness of the present situation and assured me that he and

Figure 49 Prince Heinrich of Prussia (standing, second from the left) at
Maresfield in Sussex on Sunday 26 July 1914

his government would do all they could to localise the Austro-Serbian conflict,
and that was why his government had proposed, as you already know, that
Germany, England, France and Italy might intervene and try to hold Russia
back, and he hoped that Germany would be able, despite her alliance with
Austria, to endorse this proposal to prevent the European war to which, he
said, we were closer than ever before; and he added, word-for-word, "we shall
try all we can to keep out of this and shall remain neutral". That this
statement was sincerely meant, I am convinced, as I am that England will
also remain neutral at the start, but whether she will be able to do so in the
long run I cannot say, but I have my doubts, in view of her relationship with
France. − Georgie was very serious, but thinking logically and was most
earnestly and sincerely concerned to prevent a possible world war, whereby
he was counting very much on your co-operation ... For the rest, there was no
sign of any popular excitement in London, which was no doubt attributable to
the effect of the "weekend", which a country that is in such an advantageous
position geographically as England can afford. − Lichnowsky, whom I saw
again on Sunday, assured me once more of the integrity and sincerity of
Sir Edward Grey's attitude in the present crisis.'[74] After the war the Prince
conceded, both in a letter to the *Süddeutsche Zeitung* and in conversation with
the archivist Kurt Jagow, that the King's statement had in no way constituted a
promise of neutrality.[75]

ιe very next morning, 29 July, Heinrich received a telegram from the ιsking him to come down from Kiel to Potsdam immediately. He ιn the Neues Palais early in the evening,[76] and had to give Wilhelm -- ..... Bethmann an account of his impressions of England at once. As he recorded in his diary: 'Make myself available for mission to St Petersburg. W. thinks this pointless, but possibly London, which would be preferable.'[77] The Kaiser's brother, as we know, did not come to make a second journey to London. Instead, it was decided that the Kaiser should exchange messages with both the King and the Tsar, in the first case, to persuade the British to remain neutral, in the second to push on to Russia the blame for the outbreak of war.

THE SO-CALLED 'POTSDAM CROWN COUNCIL' OF 29 JULY 1914

Prince Heinrich arrived at the Neues Palais just when a series of discussions were taking place that have sometimes been called the 'Potsdam Crown council'. This term is misleading, not only because it was not a question of a Crown council in the constitutional sense of the King's presiding over a sitting of the Prussian Ministry of State, but because the monarch received the army and navy leaders in separate audiences.[78] Even at this moment of greatest danger the idea did not occur to the Kaiser to gather his highest military and civilian advisers (who were all in the Palace at the same time waiting for an audience) round one table together. At 4.20 p.m. the Reich Chancellor, the Prussian War Minister, von Falkenhayn, the Chief of General Staff, von Moltke, and the head of the Military Cabinet von Lyncker reported to him. When, shortly after 6 o'clock, they were dismissed, Prince Heinrich was allowed in for three quarters of an hour; and as an admiral, remained in the room when Tirpitz, Pohl and Müller came in for the naval audience at 7.15. Such a division of business made it easier for the Kaiser, as ever, to dominate most of the discussions.

Since the return of Bethmann Hollweg, Falkenhayn and Moltke to Berlin on 25 July the crisis had entered on its final phase. But they were in serious disagreement over tactics, although the final decision rested with the Kaiser alone. As early as the evening of the 28th the War Minister had managed, against the express will of the Reich Chancellor, to extract from the Kaiser the order to summon those troops who were away from barracks back to base.[79] Now, on 29 July, Falkenhayn described in his diary his altercations with Bethmann and Moltke and the Kaiser's decisions: 'Morning, reliable reports that France and England (the latter with the fleet) are mobilising and we are sitting still!! Session with Reich Chancellor about proclaiming state of

war in Berlin. Naturally he is refusing to budge. With Moltke to see the Reich
Chancellor, to win his support for military protection of important railway
tracks and buildings. This is Moltke's proposal, while I am more for proclaiming a "threatening danger of war". The Reich Chancellor naturally for
the former. With Moltke to H.M., who sided with the Reich Chancellor.
H.M.'s mood has changed again. Believes, as he says, that the ball that has
started to roll cannot be stopped any more. For that reason, agrees with me,
but topples over again when Reich Chancellor and, surprisingly, Moltke too,
push him in the opposite direction. So, the decision stands.' In practice, the
proclamation of a 'threatening danger of war' that Falkenhayn was
demanding would have meant mobilisation and the invasion of Belgium,
Luxembourg and France. For that reason the War Minister showed some
understanding for the Kaiser's decision when he remarked with a shrug:
'Naturally, whoever still believes in the maintenance of peace, or at least
desires it, cannot join us in proclaiming a threatening danger of war. Of
course, this decision puts us militarily at a disadvantage, but if Moltke can
bring himself to support it, I cannot oppose it.'[80]

For many years historians lamented that the only records of the important
debates in Potsdam on 29 July 1914 consisted of fragmentary memoranda
written after the event.[81] In the meantime, however, an authentic contemporary source has been found that throws new light on events and especially on
the effect of George V's supposed promise of neutrality on the Kaiser's frame
of mind. The diary of Admiral von Müller, the head of the Naval Cabinet,
describes these events as follows: 'Afternoon. Audience in the Neues Palais.
Before us (Tirpitz, Pohl and myself) Reich Chancellor, Chief of Gen[eral]
St[aff] and War Min[ister] had been received in audience. Talked to the latter
pair in the Adj[utants'] room, were in good spirits, being confident of
England's neutrality for the time being (the King had promised this to our
Prince Heinrich). Reich Chancellor was very red in the face. Our "audience"
was confined to a lengthy account of the situation from the Kaiser. The Reich
Chancellor had said that if the crisis could be got over, it would then be very
possible to reach an understanding with England over the naval question.
H.M. flatly rejected that. We all agreed. The Kaiser then told us of a statement
of the King of England to Prince Heinrich — who was present at the audience —
and about his exchange of telegrams with the Tsar about the war with
Serbia, which the White Tsar had called an ignoble war. Tirpitz then came
up with a few unimportant things. Kaiser was very exhausted. I therefore
proposed that Pohl's audience be postponed until tomorrow. That was indeed
done, but Pohl nevertheless spoke up and talked of the need to appoint a
supreme commander for the Baltic fleet, whereupon the Kaiser immediately

proposed Prince Heinrich, who heard this. I said I would make a proposal to H.M. after Pohl's audience about directing the war.'[82]

Müller's diary goes far to confirm the content of the memorandum that Tirpitz later penned about this naval audience in the Neues Palais. Writing in the third person he recorded: 'H.M. first explained that Prince Heinrich had returned today from England with the word of His Majesty the King of England that England would stay neutral in the war. Sir Edward Grey had of course declared that things would be different if we defeated France. His Majesty asked: "What does that mean?" To which Secretary of State Tirpitz replied that Grey's speech showed clearly that England was reserving her position and was not coming clean. Only if England declared her loyalty straight out would it not come to war. His Majesty replied: "I have the word of a king, and that is enough for me." His Majesty went on to say that a dispatch had been sent to London stating that we did not intend to take territory from France, that we were only defending ourselves from attack and would respect the neutrality of Belgium and Holland provided the other side did so too. After the war we should strive to reach a firm understanding with England. The Reich Chancellor had proposed that we should promise the same in regard to the Navy. That he had refused to do. There was no point in a naval agreement. He could not assume the responsibility for one in the eyes of his people, the Navy Law must be fully implemented. Secretary of State v. Tirpitz said he thanked His Majesty for this decision. To make such a promise at this moment would mean going on one's knees to England, and His Majesty could not answer for it before History and his own Person. He believed that Admiral v. Müller was of the same opinion, which Admiral v. Müller confirmed. Prince Heinrich agreed as well.'[83] The two Hohenzollern brothers and the three most senior admirals were therefore unanimously in favour of continuing the suicidal naval building programme against England, despite the protest of the Reich Chancellor, even if the Balkan crisis was peacefully resolved.

The military plenipotentiaries of Bavaria, Saxony and Württemberg noted that Falkenhayn, Moltke and the Kaiser himself were in a thoroughly warlike mood on 29 July 1914. Immediately prior to the Potsdam conferences the Bavarian General von Wenninger reported: 'The War Minister, supported by the Chief of General Staff, is urgently requesting military measures appropriate to the "tense political situation" and what is after all the "threatening danger of war". The Chief of General Staff wishes to go further; he is exerting all his influence in favour of seizing the unusually favourable moment for striking out.' On the other side, the Reich Chancellor was trying to avoid anything that could lead to similar measures in France or England and 'start the ball rolling'. It was for this reason that Bethmann had been opposed to the

Kaiser's coming home early and to recalling the fleet; and he had asked Tirpitz and Delbrück and other heads of government departments to stay on holiday.[84] On the next day Wenninger informed Munich that the Potsdam negotiations had led to no definitive result: 'The only concession obtained was that German military measures might gradually slide into the "threatening danger of war" stage.'[85] By the evening General Wild von Hohenborn was confidently declaring that 'we are sliding slowly but surely into mobilisation'.[86] Similarly, and at that same moment, the Württemberg envoy in Berlin, Axel Baron von Varnbüler, was reporting that the General Staff continued to regard 'the moment to be favourable to us from a military point of view', and that the Kaiser's mood was 'calm and resolute'.[87]

Even if Bethmann Hollweg was striving to hold the military back from over-hasty measures, his concern was, even now, not to prevent a major war, but to push the blame for the 'great bust-up' on to Russia, as he was convinced that only so would it be possible to get the German people to support the war, and to persuade England to remain neutral, at least initially. In the evening of 29 July he was still rejecting the War Minister's demand for mobilisation, on the grounds that Russia's mobilisation against Austria did not yet mean war, and that therefore 'the casus foederis had not yet arisen. However, we had to wait for that to happen, because otherwise we should not have public opinion on our side, either at home or in England. This last was desirable, for in the Reich Chancellor's view England would not be able to side with Russia if the latter, by attacking Austria and unleashing a general war, were thereby to take upon herself the blame for the great bust-up.'[88]

DISINGENUOUS DISPATCHES FOR THE TSAR

The Reich Chancellor and the Auswärtiges Amt had long been intending to bring the dynastic links between Wilhelm II and Nicholas II into play in the last phase of the crisis, both to delay Russia's mobilisation and to put her morally in the wrong. Bethmann had already sent Wilhelm the draft of a telegram to Nicholas, which reached Wilhelm on his way back from Balholm to Kiel but the Kaiser had dismissed it as premature.[89] On the evening of 28 July the Chancellor repeated his request that the Kaiser might 'now be so gracious ... as to send a telegram to His Majesty the Tsar. If it should then come to a war after all, such a telegram would expose Russia's guilt in the most glaring light.'[90] This time the Kaiser agreed to the idea, although he made several alterations to the English text that Stumm had drafted. The final text, sent off in the early hours of 29 July, read: 'It is with the gravest concern that I hear of the impression which the action of Austria against Serbia is creating in your country. The unscrupulous agitation that has been going on in Serbia for years has resulted in the outrageous crime to which Archduke Franz Ferdinand fell a victim. The spirit that led Serbians [in 1903] to murder their own king and his wife still dominates the country. You will doubtless agree with me that we both, you and me, have a common interest, as well as all Sovereigns, to insist that all the persons morally responsible for the dastardly murder should receive their deserved punishment. In this politics play no part at all. On the other hand, I fully understand how difficult it is for you and your Government to face the drift of your public opinion. Therefore, with regard to the hearty and tender friendship which binds us both from long ago with firm ties, I am exerting my utmost influence to induce the Austrians to deal straightly to arrive at a satisfactory understanding with you. I confidently hope that you will help me in my efforts to smooth over difficulties that may still arise. Your very sincere and devoted friend and cousin Willy.'[91]

This first telegram from the Kaiser crossed with one from the Tsar that Wilhelm received early in the morning of 29 July, when he was still in a state of shock after Lichnowsky's telegram of the previous day: at 7.30 in the morning he underscored the words and phrases that upset him (indicated below in italics) and covered the document with lengthy, angry marginal comments. 'Am glad you are back', Nicholas telegraphed. 'In this most serious matter I appeal to you to help me. An *ignoble* war has been declared on a *weak* country. The *indignation* in Russia, *shared fully by me*, is *enormous*. I foresee that very soon I shall be *overwhelmed* by the *pressure* brought upon me, and be *forced* to take extreme measures which will *lead to war*. To try and avoid such a calamity as a European war, I beg you in the name of our old friendship to do what you can to *stop* your *allies* from *going too far*.'[92] Suddenly, Kaiser Wilhelm beheld the full dimensions of the crisis that his policy had conjured up – war against the entire Triple Entente. The prisoner of his archaic monarchical ideology, he suddenly felt let down in his expectation that Nicholas would take his stand against the Belgrade 'regicides' and, as a ruler by the Grace of God, declare his solidarity with him, 'H.M.' the Emperor Franz Joseph and 'H.M.' King George V.

In reply to a submission from the Reich Chancellor he demanded 'solidarity of monarchs against band of regicidal brigands against which Austria is in the process of taking punitive action'. In his confusion he tried to clarify his thoughts. '1. Gist of the Tsar's telegram: An "*ignoble* war" had been unleashed against a poor little state, and this had given rise to immense indignation in Russia, which he – the Tsar – *fully shared*. He foresaw that he would be "*overwhelmed*" by public opinion and *forced* to take measures that were bound to lead to war. He was appealing therefore to my friendship, that I might "stop your allies from going too far". 2. *My telegram*, that crossed with the Tsar's said, more or less: the spirit that once drove the Serbs to regicide has continued to run amok among the population and has finally struck down the poor Archduke and his wife too. It was in the *common* interest *of all monarchs*, that those responsible should receive stern and exemplary punishment for the "dastardly murder". Politics had nothing to do with this case at all. I therefore appealed to H.M.'s friendship that has long bound us together, to help me to see to it that this punishment is carried out – to localise. I was fully aware of the difficult position that H.M. and the Russian Government found themselves in *vis à vis* public opinion. I had therefore urged Vienna to tell the Tsar quite openly and honestly what its motives were and what ultimate objectives it had in mind. (I too still do *not know* what these are to this day.)'[93] Again, on 30 July Wilhelm wrote bitterly on a Russian newspaper article: 'I could not assume that the Tsar would take the side of bandits and regicides, even to the extent of risking unleashing a European war. A Teuton is simply incapable of thinking like that, it is Slavic or Latin.'[94]

The Tsar's telegram, he grumbled in a marginal note for the Chancellor, was 'a confession of his own weakness and an attempt to push the responsibility on to me. The telegram contains a concealed threat! and something resembling a command to hold our ally back. If Y.E. sent my telegram off yesterday evening it must have crossed with this one. We shall now see what effect mine has. The term "ignoble" does not point to monarchical solidarity on the Tsar's part, but to a Panslav approach, i.e. a fear of a capitis diminutio [losing face] in the Balkans in the event of Austrian successes. But the overall effect of these is something that they could easily wait to find out. There will always be time later for negotiating and if need be for mobilising, for which Russia has no grounds whatever *at present*. Instead of summoning us to stop our allies, H.M. should turn to the Emperor Franz Josef [sic] and negotiate with him to discover H.M.'s intentions. Should we not send copies of both telegrams to London for the information of H.M. the King?'[95] Bethmann entirely shared Wilhelm's view that the Tsar's telegram was 'such a confession of his own weakness' that he thought 'it ought to be taken with a pinch of salt. At any rate it shows how necessary it was for Your Majesty to remind the Tsar of the real background to the Austro-Serbian conflict and its significance for the monarchies of Europe. I crave of Your Majesty, if I may, a short time to reflect on how Your Majesty might frame your reply. The form of the communication to London will also depend on that.'[96]

The reply to the Tsar's telegram was drafted by Gottlieb von Jagow in the Foreign Office and the English translation sent to the Neues Palais, from where, after the Kaiser had again amended the text in several places, it was sent off to St Petersburg at 18.35 on 29 July. That this dispatch too was not sent in cypher shows clearly that it was primarily intended as a propagandistic move to win over public opinion. The final version read: 'I received your telegram and share your wish that peace should be maintained. But as I told you in my first telegram, I cannot consider Austria's action against Serbia an "ignoble" war. Austria knows by experience that Serbian promises on paper are wholly unreliable. I understand its action must be judged as trending to get full guarantee that the Serbian promises shall become real facts. Thus my reasoning is borne out by the statement of the Austrian Cabinet that Austria does not want to make any territorial conquests at the expense of Serbia. I therefore suggest that it would be quite possible for Russia to remain a spectator of the Austro-Serbian conflict without involving Europe in the most horrible war she ever witnessed. I think a direct understanding between your Government and Vienna possible and desirable and as I already telegraphed to you, my Government is continuing its exertions to promote it. Of course military measures on the part of Russia which would be looked upon by Austria as threatening would precipitate a calamity we both wish to avoid and jeopardise my position as mediator which I readily accepted on your appeal to my friendship and my help.'[97]

Meanwhile, the Tsar telegraphed thanking Wilhelm for his 'conciliatory and friendly telegram' of the previous day, but adding that 'official message presented today by your Ambassador to my Minister was conveyed in a very different tone. Beg *you to explain this divergency.* It would be right to give over the Austro-Serbian problem to the *Hague conference.* Trust in your wisdom and friendship. Your loving Nicky.'[98] Later on during the night of 29–30 July (at 1.45 a.m.) a further telegram from the Tsar arrived in the Neues Palais which caused even more concern and confusion. Nicholas announced that he was 'sending [his military plenipotentiary General Ilya] Tatishchev this evening with instructions', adding, in an attempt at reassurance, that '*the military measures which have now come into force were decided five days ago* for reasons of *defence on account of Austria's preparations.* I hope from all my heart that these measures *won't in any way interfere* with your part as mediator which I greatly value. *We need your strong pressure on Austria* to come to an *understanding with us.*'[99] There could be 'no question', Wilhelm raged in a marginal note on this telegram, of strong German pressure on Austria. 'Austria has after all only carried out a *partial* mobilisation in the *south* against *Serbia.* At this the Tsar – as he here admits himself – has taken military measures, which have *now come into force* against Austria and us, and that 5 days ago. That is, therefore, almost *a week ahead of us.* Measures for *defence* against *Austria,* who is not attacking him *at all*!!! I can no longer involve myself in mediation, as the Tsar who was calling for it was at the same time secretly mobilising, behind my back. It is only a manoeuvre to hold us back and to increase the advantage they have already gained over us. My task is finished! W.'[100]

Historians have repeatedly pointed out that here was a case of a momentous misunderstanding, for by the term 'decided' the Tsar had only meant to say that measures which had been decided on as early as 24 July, had only been implemented now, on the 29th.[101] Imanuel Geiss remarks, à propos of this strange incident: 'Clearly, here Wilhelm II was either falling victim, in his excitement, to a verbal misunderstanding (which would be difficult to explain given his sure command of English) or he was reading into the English text, consciously or unconsciously, whatever suited him politically. Be that as it may, the political leaders of Germany interpreted the harmless word "decided" exactly as the Kaiser did.'[102]

Early in the morning of 30 July a telegram arrived from Pourtalès in St Petersburg confirming the news of Russia's mobilisation against Austria-Hungary. The Kaiser's fury knew no bounds. At 7 o'clock he wrote on the Chancellor's accompanying note: 'According to this the Tsar was merely fooling us with his appeal for my assistance and has really taken us for a ride! For one doesn't ask for help and mediation when one has already mobilised! W.' 'Then I too must mobilise!' he exclaimed, as Russia's mobilisation against Austria had already started 'on 24 VII'. 'According to the Tsar's telegram it was ordered 5 days ago, i.e. on the 24th, immediately after the presentation of the ultimatum to Serbia. That is, long before the Tsar asked me by telegraph for my mediation. In his first telegram he stated explicitly that he would probably be forced to take measures that would lead to a Europ[ean] war. That is he takes the blame upon himself. In reality, however, the measures were already fully under way and he simply lied to me. Tatishcheff's mission and the request that I should not let his mobilisation measures disturb me in my role as mediator are childish, and just designed to lead us up the garden path! I regard my mediatory action as having failed, as the Tsar, instead of loyally awaiting its outcome had already mobilised behind my back without any indication to me! W.'[103]

Although they were no longer counting on Russia's drawing back, Bethmann, Jagow, Zimmermann and Stumm continued their farcical charade with the Willy–Nicky exchanges. Towards midday on 30 July the Reich Chancellor sent over the draft for a further imperial telegram, which Jagow had drawn up in German, and which Wilhelm translated into English and sent back to the Chancellor. Bethmann ordered it to be sent immediately – *en clair* again – to the Peterhof palace: 'Best thanks for telegram. Its quite out of the question that my Ambassador's language could have been in contradiction with the tenor of my telegram. Count Pourtalès was instructed to draw the attention of your Government to the danger and grave consequences involved by a mobilisation. I said the same in my telegram to you. Austria has only mobilised against Serbia and only a part of her army. If, as it is now the case, according to the communication by you and your Government, Russia mobilises against Austria, my role as mediator you kindly intrusted me with, and which I accepted at your express prayer, will be endangered if not ruined. The whole weight of the decision rests solely on your shoulders now, who have to bear the responsibility for peace or war.'[104] What Bethmann Hollweg was now seeking was crystal clear from his appeal to the Kaiser – 'as this telegram will become an especially important document for History' – he begged the monarch 'to refrain from stating in it that Your Majesty's All-Highest mediatory role has already ceased'.[105] The aim of German tactics was, as Wilhelm II was fully aware, 'to increase Russia's guilt . . . and to document it before the whole world'.[106]

THE GAME OF POKER OVER BRITISH NEUTRALITY

The 30th of July was a black day for Wilhelm II – the day when his whole house of cards collapsed. The above-mentioned report that Russia had mobilised against Austria, allegedly some five days previously, was followed by telegrams from Prince Lichnowsky and the naval attaché in London, Erich von Müller, that shattered the illusion of British neutrality that had arisen, not least, from Prince Heinrich's optimistic account of his conversation with George V.

In the so-called 'Potsdam Crown council' on the evening of 29 July Wilhelm had informed Admirals Tirpitz, Müller and Pohl that a dispatch had been sent to London in which Germany offered to take no territory from France and to respect the neutrality of Belgium and Holland, provided Great Britain remained neutral.[107] That was something of a misunderstanding. In fact, the German offers were made, not in a dispatch, but by Bethmann Hollweg to the British ambassador Sir Edward Goschen, by word of mouth. These revealing negotiations took place on 29 July after the Chancellor's return from Potsdam – by which time it was 10.30 p.m. In the eyes of the ambassador and the Foreign Office in London this 'offer' demonstrated not only Germany's determination to go to war, but the full extent of the German Reich's expansionist ambitions in western Europe. In his meeting with Goschen, Bethmann explained that as Germany was not seeking 'to crush France', she was not seeking to upset the European balance of power either. 'We can assure the English Government – *provided* it stays *neutral* – that even in the event of victory, we are not seeking any territorial acquisitions at the expense of France in Europe. We can further promise to respect the neutrality and independence of Holland so long as our opponents do so. As regards Belgium, we do not know what counter-operations France's actions in an eventual war may compel us to take. But provided Belgium does not take sides against us, we should in this case too be prepared to give an assurance that the integrity of Belgium will not be infringed after the end of the war.'[108] From these proposals it was only too clear that Germany intended to infringe Belgian neutrality and occupy the country until the war was over. Even if Great Britain remained neutral the Reich Chancellor reserved the right to annex the French colonies and to impose severe terms on France. Moreover, if England entered the war, the implication was that Germany would feel entitled to annex French territory, too.[109]

In the Neues Palais on the morning of 30 July Kaiser Wilhelm and his brother were putting together a telegram from Prince Heinrich to George V that was supposed to secure British neutrality, at least for the first few weeks of the war, and at the same time – as Admiral von Müller put it revealingly – to 'push on to' the King the blame for the coming European war.[110] 'Am here since yesterday', Heinrich telegraphed, 'have informed William of what you kindly told me at Buckingham Palace last Sunday who gratefully received your message. William, much preoccupied, is trying his utmost to fulfill Nickys appeal to him to work for maintenance of peace and is in constant telegraphic communication with Nicky who to-day confirms news that military measures have been ordered by him equal to mobilisation, measures which have been taken already five days ago. We are furthermore informed that France is making military preparations, whereas we have taken no measures, but may be forced to do so any moment, should our neighbours continue which then would mean European war. If you really and earnestly wish to prevent this terrible disaster, may I suggest you use your influence on France and also on Russia to keep neutral, which seems to me would be most useful. This I consider a very good, perhaps the only chance to maintain the peace of Europe. I may add that now more than ever Germany and England should lend each other mutual help to prevent a terrible catastrophy [sic] which otherwise seems unavoidable. Believe me that William is most sincere in his endeavours to maintain peace, but that the military preparations of his two neighbours may at last force him to follow their example for the safety of his own country which otherwise would remain defenceless. I have informed William of my telegram to you and hope you will receive my informations in the same spirit of friendship which suggested them. Henry.' Prince Heinrich took the telegram personally to the Reich Chancellor, who arranged for its immediate dispatch – significantly again *en clair* – to London.[111]

When the two brothers were drafting their telegram they knew nothing of two dispatches that had meanwhile arrived from London, stating that the British Foreign Secretary had made it absolutely clear that if Germany attacked France it would be impossible for Britain to stay out of the war. One dispatch, from the naval attaché Müller, that had arrived just before midnight,[112] Admiral Pohl took with him when he presented himself in the Neues Palais at 11 o'clock on 30 July; and the head of the Naval Cabinet describes in his diary the impact of the news on the Kaiser: 'On the way to the Palace he [Pohl] showed me a dispatch … from the naval attaché in London, according to which Grey had told Lichnowski personally that England could not stay neutral in a Franco-German war, but would send her fleet into action immediately. That was the hardest blow in these days … The Kaiser, remarkably enough, did not yet know of this telegram, which had arrived during the night. He was greatly taken aback when he read it, but remained outwardly calm.'[113]

Although the Chief of the Admiralty Staff in his audience of 30 July started by presenting his operational plans on the assumption that England would be neutral, and the Kaiser approved them,[114] Wilhelm at the same time, in view of the new situation, issued an imperial order of command for the North Sea battle area. Acording to this 'the English fleet' was to be damaged 'by offensive operations against its surveillance- or blockade-ships in the German Bight and by a ruthless assault, right up to the British coast, with mines and if possible U-boats … Once these operations have achieved a balance of forces, we must try after preparing and gathering all our forces to send our fleet into battle on advantageous terms. If a favourable opportunity should arise beforehand, we must seize it.'[115] That morning the Kaiser, Pohl and Müller also laid down the principles that were to be applied against English troop transports. According to a 'top secret' memorandum approved by the Kaiser it was 'possible that circumstances will demand an *immediate* attack on the transports. In this case His Majesty will fix the time for operations against the transports … His Majesty wishes that the attacks shall then be carried out, if possible, primarily by U-boats and by saturating the deployment areas of the transports and the approaches to the embarkation and disembarkation ports with mines. But His Majesty does not wish the main body of the fleet to be employed for these operations without his express command.'[116] The Kaiser also went on to approve the orders put before him by the Admiralty Staff concerning the German fleet's treatment of the potentially neutral states such as Denmark, Sweden, Norway, Holland and Belgium.[117] The Secretary of State for the Interior was instructed 'from now on … to keep the water-level in the Kaiser Wilhelm Canal constantly high enough to enable big battleships to use the Canal at any time'.[118] At 1.15 p.m. the Kaiser gave the order to 'secure' the fleet. Despite all this, Prince Heinrich and his Adjutant, who drove directly from the Neues Palais to the Reich Navy Office, reported that 'H.M. is calm.'[119]

Immediately after the naval audience, the Kaiser minuted on a submission from the Reich Chancellor: 'Meanwhile a telegram arrived this morning from the naval attaché in London to say that Sir Edward Grey told Lichnowsky in a private conversation that if we got into war with France England would *forthwith, immediately* attack us at sea with her fleet. We are already taking appropriate countermeasures against such attacks etc. (à la Port Arthur) as far as it is possible to do so unobtrusively. I am surprised that Lichnowsky has not so far sent any report.'[120] In the margin of a cutting from the London *Morning Post* the Kaiser wrote a long comment in English that is eloquent of his confusion at this critical time: 'The *only possible way* to ensure or enforce peace is that England must tell Paris and Petersburg – its allies – to remain quiet i.e. neutral in the Austro-Servian conflict, then Germany can remain quiet too. But if England continues to remain silent or to give lukewarm assurances of neutrality; that would mean encouragement to its allies to attack Austro-Germany. Berlin has tried to mediate between Petersburg & Vienna on the appeal of the Zar. But H.M. silently has *mobilised before* the appeal; so that the mediator – Germany – is placed "en demeure" & his work becomes illusory. Now only England alone can stop the catastrophe by restraining its allies, by clearly intimating that – as Sir E. Grey declared – it had nothing to do with the Austro-Servian conflict, & that if one of its allies took an active part in the strife it could not reckon on the help of England. That would put a stop to all war. King George has communicated Englands intention to remain neutral to me by Prince Henry. On the other hand the Naval Staff have this morning – 30. VII. – received a telegram from the German Military [sic] attaché in London, that Sir E. Grey in a private conversation with Prince Lichnowsky, declared, that if Germany made war on France, England would immediately attack Germany with her fleet! Consequently Sir E. Grey says the direct contrary to what his Sovereign communicated to me through my brother & places his King in the position of a double tongues liar vis-à-vis to me. William I.R.' Towards one o'clock the Kaiser – presumably after receiving Lichnowsky's telegram – added a confused postscript (again in English) to this marginal note that testifies to his dismay: 'The whole war has plainly been arranged between England, France and Russia for the annihilation of Germany, lastly through the conversations with Poincaré in Paris and Petersburg, & the Austro-Servian strife is only an excuse to fall upon *us*! God help us in this fight for our existence, brought about by falseness, lies and poisonous envy!'[121]

Quite in the spirit of this postscript the Kaiser then covered Lichnowsky's telegram with marginal comments and a concluding minute in rabid language that pointed, as Admiral von Müller feared, to an incipient nervous breakdown – if it was not another cynical manoeuvre to shift the blame on to England and George V. Grey's 'very serious' warning that if his proposal for four-Power mediation by England, Germany, France and Italy was not taken up immediately Europe would be on the brink of a 'catastrophe' threw the Kaiser into a rage. Grey's statement was, he declared, 'the greatest and most unheard of piece of English hypocrisy that I have ever seen! I shall *never* make a naval agreement with such scoundrels!' Grey's 'vile, mephistophelian but typically English' mediation proposal amounted to 'our leaving Austria in the lurch', otherwise, England would 'attack us'. 'England shows her colours the moment she believes we are at bay and so to speak finished! This wretched shopkeeper rabble have tried to deceive us with dinners and speeches. The worst deception the King's message to me through Heinrich: "We shall remain neutral and try to keep out of this as long as possible." Grey makes the King a liar and his words to Lichnowsky are the outpourings of a bad conscience, as he now feels he has deceived us. Besides, it is actually a threat combined with a bluff, to draw us away from Austria and hinder our mobilisation, and to push the blame for the war on to us. He knows very well that if he were to utter one serious, sharp word of warning in Paris and St Petersburg and advise them to stay neutral, both would quieten down immediately. But he takes care not to say that word, and threatens us instead! Dirty bastard! [*Gemeiner Hundsfott*!] England *alone* bears the responsibility for war and peace, and not us any more! That must also be made clear to the public. W.'[122]

Early in the evening of 30 July the copy of a dispatch from St Petersburg arrived at the Neues Palais, which the Kaiser covered from top to bottom with accusations against Russia and England that testified not only to his bitter disappointment and alarm, but to a veritably delusional remoteness from reality, to which the mistaken belief that the Russians had mobilised against Austria as early as 24 July again made a fatal contribution. He took violent objection to Sazonov's claim that the partial mobilisation of the Russian army against Austria was in reply to Austria's mobilisation and could no longer be reversed: 'If mobilisation can no longer be reversed – *which is not true* – then why did the Tsar ever invoke my mediation 3 days later without mentioning the mobilisation order? That proves that the mobilisation seemed over-hasty even to him, and that he afterwards approached us *pro forma* and to calm his troubled conscience, although he knew that it was pointless, as he did not feel strong enough to *stop* the mobilisation. Rashness and weakness are driving the world into the most frightful war, the ultimate aim of which is the destruction of Germany. For of this there is in my mind no doubt: England, Russia and France have conspired – turning to good account the *casus foederis* that commits us to Austria – to use the Austro-Serbian conflict as the pretext for launching a *war of annihilation* against us. Hence Grey's cynical remark to Lichnowsky "so long as the war remains *confined* to Russia and Austria England would keep out, only if we and France *joined in* would he be compelled to take action against us." I.e. we either shabbily desert our ally and *sacrifice* it to Russia – thereby breaking up the 3 Alliance – or on account of our *loyalty to the alliance* we are attacked by the whole 3 Entente and *punished*, which will at last satisfy their envy by totally *destroying* us both. That is, in nuce, the naked truth of the situation, which was slowly but surely contrived by Edward VII, carried on and systematically built up in disavowed discussions with Paris and St Petersburg; finally concluded and set into operation by George V. At the same time, the stupidity and clumsiness of our ally has been made into a trap for us. Thus, the famous *"Encirclement"* of Germany has become a concrete fact, despite all the efforts of our politicians and diplomats to prevent it. The net has suddenly been closed above our heads and with a scornful smile England has achieved the most brilliant success for her tenaciously pursued, purely *anti-German Weltpolitik*, against which we have proved helpless, while, as we are struggling isolated in the net, she weaves from our alliance loyalty to Austria the noose for our political and economic annihilation. A terrific achievement that deserves admiration, even from one who is ruined by it. Edward VII is in death stronger than I am in life! And that there are people who believed England could be won over or pacified by this or that little thing !!! Tirelessly, relentlessly, she has pursued her aim, with notes, naval-holiday proposals, scares, Haldane etc, until she was ready. And we fell for it and even introduced a one-tempo in shipbuilding in the touching hope of pacifying England!!! All warnings, all appeals on my part, fell on deaf ears. And now we have England's so-called thanks for this! From the dilemma of our loyalty as allies of the honourable old Emperor a situation is constructed that gives England the pretext she was seeking to annihilate us, hypocritically disguised as the right to assist France in order to maintain the notorious balance of power in Europe, i.e. the manipulation of all the European states to England's advantage and against us! All these goings-on must now be mercilessly exposed, the mask of Christian kindness publicly and forcibly torn off, and this pharisaical cant about peace denounced for what it is!! And our consuls in Turkey and India, agents etc must incite the whole Mohammedan world into wild rebellion against this detested, lying, conscienceless nation of shopkeepers; for if we are to bleed to death, then England must at least lose India. W.'[123] As for General Liman von Sanders, who was seeking to return to Germany from Turkey, the Kaiser now gave the order: 'Must stay there, and also stir up the war and rebellion against England.'[124]

Naturally Grey's sharp statement of intent did not fail to have a deterrent effect on the Kaiser. As early as the evening of 30 July he ordered Foreign Secretary Jagow to send him a draft dispatch for Emperor Franz Joseph repeating his Halt-in-Belgrade proposal. The telegram, which he sent off to Vienna at 7.15 p.m. read: 'I did not think I could reject the Tsar's personal appeal for an attempt at mediation to prevent a world conflict and maintain world peace, and I had my ambassador present proposals to your Government yesterday and today. The sense of them is, among other things, that Austria after occupying Belgrade or some other places should state her requirements. I should be sincerely grateful if you would inform me of your decision as soon as possible.'[125] But this time, too, the Reich Chancellor saw to it that the Kaiser's move remained without any practical effect. In an urgent telegram to Tschirschky, Bethmann yet again laid bare the cynical calculation that lay at the root of his policy in the July crisis. 'If Vienna . . . rejects all concessions, it will then hardly be possible to push on to Russia the blame for the European conflagration that is breaking out. H.M. has at the Tsar's request undertaken to mediate in Vienna, because he could not refuse without arousing the irrefutable suspicion that we wanted war.' If Austria now rejected the mediation proposal from London 'then Vienna will be documenting that it is absolutely set on a war, into which we shall be drawn, while Russia will remain free from blame. That will put us in a quite impossible position *vis à vis* our own nation.' In his negotiations with the Austrian statesmen, therefore, Tschirschky was to interpret the Kaiser's telegram 'immediately and most emphatically in this sense' – i.e. as a mere tactical manoeuvre.[126]

Later in the evening the Kaiser recovered his nerve, no doubt influenced by the warlike enthusiasm of his brother and his sons, who had gathered round him.[127] As the head of the Civil Cabinet wrote to his wife the next morning: 'Yesterday evening the Crown Prince, Prince Heinrich, Adalbert, Eitel Friedrich, Joachim dined with the Kaiser, all frightfully warlike and sorry that we still hadn't mobilised! It is actually quite a good thing that the Kaiser has been confronted by these bold spirits, he is in a frightfully difficult position . . . All the same, the impression I got from a long and thorough discussion with H.M. after dinner in the Neues Palais (in the open air!) is that we shall not be able to avoid mobilising. Negotiations are still going on in all the capitals, and all ways and means are being tried, but given the attitude of England, who is certainly in a position to say the decisive word, but who seems apparently to have committed herself through an alliance with France, there is not much hope that war can be avoided. But the *timing* is still completely uncertain. Yesterday one thought the next 24 hours would be decisive, today there is a ray of hope again!'[128]

Wilhelm's mood brightened further when a conciliatory telegram from George V to Prince Heinrich arrived shortly before midnight on 30 July. The King was 'so pleased to hear of William's efforts to concert with Nicky to maintain peace', he wrote. 'Indeed I am earnestly desirous that such an irreparable disaster as a European war should be averted. My government is doing its utmost, suggesting to Russia and France to suspend further military preparations, if Austria will consent to be satisfied with occupation of Belgrade and the neighbouring Serbian territory as a hostage for satisfactory settlement of her demands other countries meanwhile suspending their war preparations. Trust William will use his great influence to induce Austria to accept his proposal thus proving that Germany and England are working together to prevent what would be an international catastrophe. Pray assure William I am doing and shall continue to do all that lies in my power to preserve peace in Europe.'[129] Between the lines of the telegram Wilhelm noted that Austria had 'this evening put forward the same proposals' – a mystifying statement that will be examined below.[130] Next morning at 6.45 Wilhelm asked the Reich Chancellor for a 'draft for a telegram to the King of England and for a possible communication to H.M. the Tsar, about England's and Vienna's proposals that are almost identical to mine'.[131]

On the other hand, the conciliatory tone of the King's telegram contributed perceptibly to a stiffening of Wilhelm's stance towards Russia. Early on 31 July he received a dispatch that had arrived during the night from General von Chelius, about Russia's partial mobilisation against Austria-Hungary. The Kaiser entirely agreed with the military plenipotentiary that Russia had mobilised as a result 'rather of fear of impending events' than of any aggressive intentions, and she 'had now taken fright at what she had done'. The Russians, he said, would now have to reckon with the mobilisation of the German army. Their aim was obviously 'at all events to gain time and to be ready before we are!' St Petersburg's argument that Austria's assurances that she wished to take no territory from Serbia could no longer be believed was dismissed by the Kaiser as 'Rubbish!' and 'Impudence'.[132]

By the morning of 31 July those close to Wilhelm II unanimously agreed that the outbreak of war was inevitable, 'but it might yet take some time all the same!' The head of the Civil Cabinet could report: 'If we mobilise, the Kaiser will initially move to Berlin and the headquarters will remain there for the first three weeks at least.'[133] On that morning, in a top-secret memorandum, the Kaiser described for the information of the Reich Navy Office, the Admiralty Staff, and later for the General Staff and the Prussian War

Ministry, the negotiations which had taken place with England over the last 24 hours. 'After the head of the Admiralty Staff informed me yesterday – 30 July – of the telegram from the naval attaché in London about Sir E. Grey's discussion with Prince Lichnowsky in which Germany was given to understand that only the betrayal of her ally by not participating in the war against Russia could save her from an immediate English attack, the ambassador's report confirming this conversation arrived soon afterwards, and was sent on here by the Foreign Office without comment. It was clear to me that here Sir E. Grey was telling me that his own King, who had just sent me a clear declaration of neutrality (transmitted verbally on 29 July) was a liar. As I am now convinced that the whole crisis was caused by *England alone*, and can only be resolved by *England alone* (by putting pressure on the allied Russians and Gauls) I decided to send a private telegram to tell the King, who is apparently still unclear as to his role and responsibility in the crisis, . . . that in my opinion the only chance now to prevent a world-wide conflagration, which England cannot desire either, lay in *London*, not in *Berlin*. I was asking H.M. the King, instead of making proposals for conferences etc, to tell the Russians and Gauls straight out – they are after all *his allies* – to *stop* mobilising immediately, to stay *neutral*, and to await Austria's proposals, which I shall send on as soon as I receive them. The full responsibility for the most frightful world-wide conflagration that has ever raged rested entirely on *his shoulders*, and he would some day stand condemned by the world and by History for this. There was nothing more I could do *directly;* it was up to him now to intervene and give proof of England's love of peace. He could rest assured of my loyal and most heartfelt support. Attached is the King's telegram in reply . . . In St Petersburg, according to the ambassador's report today, absolutely *no* enthusiasm *at all* for war, on the contrary a mood of depression, as yesterday evening again violent street fights between revolutionaries and troops and hangovers at court and in the military as sobriety dawns and they are horror-struck by what they have done, and may yet do, with their premature mobilisation. Wilhelm I.R.'[134]

This screed – dated by the Kaiser as '31/VII 14.12 h' – was apparently written somewhat earlier, and above all in ignorance of the news of Russia's general mobilisation, which reached the Wilhelmstrasse at 11.40 a.m. It is a remarkable document, not merely on account of the blatancy with which it pushes the blame for the impending catastrophe on to England. Wilhelm refers to reports from St Petersburg of a 'hangover feeling' that were four days old and therefore long out of date.[135] Nevertheless, together with the accompanying telegram from George V, it made a deep impression on the naval leadership (although not on Bethmann Hollweg and the generals). As Müller wrote in his diary: 'At noon, a guards officer came directly from the Kaiser with a very conciliatory telegram from the King of England in reply to Prince Heinrich. Very much for peace, hopes that if Austria contents herself with Belgrade and surrounding districts as a pledge for fulfilment of her demands other states will halt their war preparations etc. But how does that square with Grey's naked threat that if war breaks out between France and Germany the English fleet would immediately go into action against us. At the same time H.M. sent a memorandum about the situation as a whole. He still has some hopes of peace through his proposed pledge idea. He also writes that in St Petersburg, according to reports from the ambassador, enthusiasm for war has given way to a hangover feeling. An interesting document ... Later discussed both documents with Tirpitz. He asks, rightly, then what is the point of a war. He wants to put this point of view to the Reich Chancellor. I encourage him to do so.'[136] As Tirpitz was rushing off to see the Chancellor at 12.30, he learned of the Russian general mobilisation and the Kaiser's order meanwhile to proclaim a 'threatening danger of war'. Surprised, he referred to the Kaiser's memorandum he had just received, from which he read Bethmann excerpts that indicated a wide area of agreement between Vienna, London and Berlin. But the Reich Chancellor assured the Grand Admiral that 'in this memorandum the Kaiser was mixing up different things. The Kaiser was indeed heavily engaged in mediation, and then partial mobilisation – and today full mobilisation – was announced in Russia. That was such an unheard of proceeding against us that we could not put up with it.' In the course of the discussion Tirpitz repeated his pet idea that instead of going to war with Russia, Germany should ally with the Tsarist Empire and proceed jointly with it against England! As he explained to the Reich Chancellor, 'we should come to an arrangement with Russia. For it is clear that neither Russia nor Germany could have anything to gain from tearing each other to pieces – only the others.' Remarkably, Bethmann agreed with this, but observed with a shrug that Russia had responded to Germany's constant mediatory efforts by mobilising.[137]

THE KAISER'S LAST ATTEMPT AT MEDIATION

Immediately after the outbreak of war Wilhelm II claimed that he had at the last minute embarked on a promising attempt at mediation between Vienna, London and Berlin that only failed owing to the unexpected Russian mobilisation. Thus, in a telegram of 14 August 1914 to President Wilson of the United States, he stated that King George V had asked him to forward to Vienna a proposal by which 'Austria was to take Belgrade and a few other Servian towns and a strip of country as a "mainmise" to make sure that the Servian promises

on paper should be fulfilled in reality. This proposal was in the same moment
telegraphed to me from Vienna to London quite in conjunction with the
British proposal ... As both were of the same opinion I immediately transmitted the telegrams vice versa to Vienna and London. I felt that I was able to
tide the question over and was happy at the peaceful outcome. While I was
preparing a Note to H.M. the Czar the next morning to inform him that
Vienna, London, and Berlin were agreed about the treatment of affairs,
I received the telephones from H.E. the Chancellor that in the night before
the Czar had given the order to mobilise the whole Russian army, which
was of course also meant against Germany.'[138] As neither the King nor the
government in London received any such communication from Berlin this
claim of Wilhelm's has remained a mystery until now. When the Kaiser's
telegram to Woodrow Wilson was published in 1917 there was speculation in
London as to whether Wilhelm was lying for propaganda purposes or had
imagined the whole thing in order to justify himself. Another possibility was
that the Kaiser had in fact drafted a telegram to the King but that the central
offices in Berlin had not sent it on. A third, albeit very unlikely explanation
was that the telegram was sent off but suppressed by Lichnowsky in
London.[139] What had happened in reality?

A mediatory action was in fact started by Wilhelm II. One of the last things
he did before moving from Potsdam to the Schloss in Berlin on 31 July 1914
was to send a telegram in reply to the King of England from the Neues Palais
at 12.55 p.m. After affirming that the King's 'proposals coincide with my ideas
and with the statements I got this night from Vienna which I have forwarded
to London', he continued, dramatically: 'I just received news from Chancellor
that official notification has just reached Him that this night Nicky has
ordered the mobilization of His whole Army and Fleet. He has not even
awaited the results of the mediation I am working at and left me without any
news. I am off to Berlin to take measures for ensuring safety of my eastern
frontiers where strong Russian Troops are already posted.'[140]

Likewise, in the memorandum that he drew up on the morning of 31 July
for the naval chiefs, he was very explicit about his peace initiative: the
proposals put forward by George V in his last telegram 'fit in with mine that
I put to the Vienna Cabinet, who have left us without an answer for 6 days,
and which were likewise telegraphed to us yesterday evening from Vienna.
Diplomatic conversations have at last started between Vienna and Peterhof,
and Peterhof has also appealed to London to mediate.'[141]

The mediation proposal from Vienna that the Kaiser mentioned seems to be
a report from Tschirschky of 30 July, which, after the Kaiser had seen it and
covered it with marginal comments, was sent back to the Auswärtiges Amt on

31 July. Both Lichnowsky and Pourtalès were sent copies, but obviously without the Kaiser's marginalia, who therefore remained unaware of the significance Wilhelm attached to the dispatch. The report in question related to a forthcoming meeting between Berchtold and the Russian ambassador at Vienna, Shebeko, in which the Foreign Minister intended to declare (for purely tactical reasons, as Berlin had suggested) that the Vienna government had no desire for territorial acquisitions in Serbia and would only remain in occupation of Serbian territory as a pledge for the fulfilment of its demands. In this, Wilhelm recognised his own 'pledge-proposal' and minuted approvingly: 'So, more or less my proposal accepted and proceeding as I told the Tsar I was recommending.' At the same time, however, he expressed the fear that 'in view of the colossal military measures now announced by Russia all this is ... too late'. Nor is there any trace in the Kaiser's minutes of an instruction to telegraph Tschirschky's dispatch or its contents to the King or the government in London.[142]

The question of why Wilhelm was nevertheless convinced that he had forwarded an inportant mediation proposal from Vienna to London and a similar one from London to Vienna can now be resolved with the help of the diary of Prince Heinrich who noted, in an entry for 30 July 1914: '10 p.m. first news from Vienna for 6 days that territorial acquisitions not planned. 11 p.m. answer from Georgie very favourable, immediately inform Wilhelm who is on his way to bed. Receive order to go at once to Bethmann to tell him this. Vienna too to be informed of it, and furthermore London to receive Vienna communication. − 11.30 left by car, 1.15 arrive Berlin Chancellor's Palace, where Bethmann and Jagow present. − Carried out order. − 1.30 left, 2.20 arrived N[eues] P[alais] Potsdam.'[143] Despite the dramatic midnight mission of the Hohenzollern Prince, the Reich Chancellor and the Foreign Secretary, fully aware that Berchtold's intended declaration was only a tactical manoeuvre suggested by themselves, simply ignored the Kaiser's instructions, while leaving the monarch to believe that he had launched an important peace initiative.

The reckless policy the German decision-makers had been pursuing since the end of June 1914 was grounded in the assumption that if they could only manage, by using the Balkan conflict, to provoke Russia to declare war on the Triple Alliance, the nation would be ready to 'defend' Germany against the 'aggressor', England would stay neutral, at least at the start, and Italy would fulfil her alliance obligations. Four weeks later this whole house of cards had collapsed. True, Austria-Hungary, being in the vanguard in the Balkans, was bound to the German Reich with bonds of steel; and the German people were largely convinced of the justice of their cause − especially in a war of defence against 'barbaric' Russia. In this respect the machinations of the decision-makers were successful. But the assumption that the German army could now, without having to fear British intervention by land and sea, invade Belgium, Luxembourg and France and gain a quick victory in the west before joining with the Dual Monarchy, Italy, Bulgaria and Turkey, and possibly also Greece and Romania, to take on the ponderous Russian colossus, proved mistaken by 30 July at the latest. To back down in recognition of this fact would have required both moral courage and a formidable strength of character and would have involved a severe loss of face; but it could still have prevented the immeasurable catastrophe that was impending. However the decision-makers in Berlin lacked not only the necessary flexibility and courage, but even any real insight into the consequences once the most important premiss of their policy, British neutrality, had proved to be an illusion. The generals continued to believe in the invincibility of the troops and the Chancellor and the Wilhelmstrasse continued their duplicitous gamble, designed to land Russia with the blame, to the bitter end.[144]

The Kaiser, too, physically exhausted and with shattered nerves, was neither willing nor able at this late stage to insist on a radical change of course. True, he hesitated for three days, from 28 July to the late evening of the 30th; and his hesitation grew, above all, as he was confronted with the prospect of England's entry into the war, together with Italy's withdrawal from the Triple Alliance. In these three days he suggested – alone among the tiny group of decision-makers in Berlin – that Austria-Hungary and Serbia negotiate on the basis of his Halt-in-Belgrade proposal; but always hesitantly and fitfully, until the next gleam of hope from London seemed to banish the danger of British intervention and re-ignited his belligerence against Russia and France. Most importantly, he never realised that his own Reich Chancellor, with the connivance of the Auswärtiges Amt, was himself systematically undermining his half-hearted attempts at mediation. He spoke scornfully of the Tsar's weakness in handling his ministers and generals, and he was furious when Sir Edward Grey failed to stand by 'the word of a king' and honour the promise of neutrality that George V was supposed to have given to Prince Heinrich, but he quite failed to perceive that his own ministers were pulling the wool over his eyes to a quite criminal degree. Bethmann, Jagow, Zimmermann and Stumm falsified Lichnowsky's reports that warned against the illusion of British neutrality in order to mislead the Kaiser as to the consequences of German policy. They forwarded his Halt-in-Belgrade proposal to Vienna in a much attenuated form and far too late, while expressly emphasising that even this was only being done for appearances' sake – and that Vienna should not by any means take it up. In the end, Wilhelm II accepted the cunning deceptive manoeuvres of his own government as genuine, and still believed in the night of 30–1 July that he had set in motion a mediation plan that Vienna, Berlin, London and St Petersburg could all live with.

All the same, the differences of opinion between Wilhelm II and the Wilhelmstrasse in the three days prior to the outbreak of war should not be blown up into a conflict over matters of principle. There were a number of differences within the small group of decision-makers in Berlin in the last phase of the July crisis, but most of these were over matters of tactics and cannot in any sense be taken as evidence for the existence of a 'peace party' alongside the 'war party'. This applies to both Wilhelm's Halt-in-Belgrade proposal and to his frantic efforts at the eleventh hour to secure England's neutrality. He had been incessantly demanding a 'final struggle between the Germans and Slavdom' for a good eighteen months, and looking with scorn on the civilian Chancellor and the diplomats who did not understand the military profession. In October 1913 he had urged Count Berchtold to incorporate Serbia – peacefully if possible, otherwise by force – so that the Habsburg Monarchy would have its back free for the approaching struggle with Russia. That would have been the very situation that would have resulted from an occupation of Belgrade and surrounding districts by Austrian troops, and a sufficient explanation of why the Russian government could not agree to it. For almost two decades Wilhelm had been trying, partly by means of his family connections, partly by means of power-political levers such as an enhanced rate of naval construction, to persuade the British to leave Germany a free hand on the continent. The British had twice made it abundantly clear – in the two Moroccan crises of 1905 and 1911 – that they would not accept the crushing of France or a German hegemony in Europe. Twice – during the Haldane mission and in Haldane's statement to Lichnowsky in December 1912 – they had made it painfully clear to Berlin why they were determined to stand by the principle of the balance of power. That after all this, Kaiser Wilhelm should still see in a few off-the-cuff remarks made by King George to his brother Heinrich while hastily leaving for church one Sunday morning, 'a clear official declaration of neutrality'; and that in his childish belief in monarchical solidarity he should elevate these remarks into 'the word of a King' that could set at nought the solemn assurances of the responsible government of Great Britain was evidence, not of a love of peace, but of panic, confusion and a loss of touch with reality that bordered on the insane.

CHAPTER FORTY-ONE

Into the abyss: the outbreak of war

Whatever misgivings the Kaiser may occasionally have had after his return from his northern cruise disappeared in the last few days before the outbreak of war. Not only did he cease to raise objections to going to war, he acted with determination as head of the decision-making structure with the task of resolving any differences – even if only of a tactical nature – between the civilian leadership, the generals and the navy. And in this he was not acting merely as a constitutional rubber stamp, but in the glowing conviction that the war against France and Russia would shortly end with the heroic victory of his troops and secure Germany's predominance in Europe (and beyond) for all time. According to a report of Wenninger's of 30 July 1914 to his superiors in Munich, 'H.M. is decidedly on the side of Moltke and the War Ministry' who were both impatiently pressing for war;[1] and, as Wilhelm himself told the Austro-Hungarian ambassador on the evening of 1 August, he was 'determined to settle accounts with France' and was expecting to be 'completely successful'.[2] It was his declared aim, from the start of the July crisis until the outbreak of war, 'to free the Balkans from Russia for ever!'[3] True, until the end he was hoping that Great Britain would be neutral, and that Italy, Greece, Turkey and Bulgaria would actively support Germany, but he remained set on war even when British intervention loomed and when it was clear that Italy, Greece and Romania were turning away from the Central Powers. Even in the night of 1–2 August, i.e. after the unleashing of war on the continent, Wilhelm II expressly praised 'the manly bearing of the Reich Chancellor' who had correctly implemented his master's wishes.[4] In all this he was encouraged by his brother Heinrich and by his sons, and even the Empress Auguste Viktoria was pushing her husband towards war. As Adjutant-General Karl Freiherr von Plettenberg, Commander of the Corps of Guards, recorded in his memoirs: 'In the end it was Her Majesty the Empress who felt — certainly with a heavy heart — that she had to press her husband to come to a decision. When our ambassador Lichnowsky, ensnared by English diplomacy, sent yet another telegram that led His Majesty to believe there was still hope of peace, Her Majesty said, before witnesses, "Now war is the only thing left, and my husband and my 6 sons are going off to it." (The expression she used was an even stronger one)', the General recalled.[5]

'BEAMING FACES EVERYWHERE': THE OUTBREAK OF WAR ON THE EUROPEAN CONTINENT

Since Thursday 30 July the War Minister, Erich von Falkenhayn, and the Chief of General Staff, Helmuth von Moltke, had been pressing the Reich Chancellor to put an end to the 'intolerable' situation facing Germany by proclaiming a 'state of threatening danger of war' — the preliminary stage of inevitable general mobilisation.[6] Late in the evening, after 'endless negotiations' between Falkenhayn and Moltke on one side and Bethmann Hollweg, Jagow and Zimmermann on the other, there was a violent dispute — according to Falkenhayn's diary — between the Chancellor and the Chief of General Staff as to 'who had to bear the responsibility for any war' that might ensue. 'In the end, Moltke and I managed to insist that by noon tomorrow at the latest a decision must be taken about declaring a threatening danger of war.'[7]

The Chief of General Staff had already, early that morning, summoned his Adjutant Major Hans von Haeften by telegraph to return to Berlin, and when he arrived at midnight Moltke told him that 'war was as good as inevitable', and asked him 'immediately, this night, to draft an "Appeal to my people" and an "Appeal to the Army and Navy", so that he could present both to His Majesty at his audience in the morning'. The political situation was such, he explained to Haeften, that 'unless there was a miracle — i.e. the Russian mobilisation is cancelled — war looks inevitable. Germany can now only save the peace at the price of a great national humiliation, for any negotiation in the shadow of a Russian mobilisation will amount to a national humiliation. But if we mobilise, that means war. If Germany now hesitates to take this step, say, to gain time for negotiations, this means that if, predictably, the negotiations fail, Germany will go to war under the most unfavourable circumstances imaginable. We should thereby be allowing our opponents to bring the war on to German soil. If we delay with our mobilisation our military position will become worse by the day, and this, if our probable opponents steadily go on with their preparations, can have the most fatal consequences for us.' In deadly seriousness Moltke continued: 'This war will become a world war, with England joining in too. Few people can have any idea of the extent, duration and result of this war'; and he concluded by observing that 'at noon tomorrow ... the decision will be taken regarding war and peace. The Reich Chancellor, the War Minister and I together have an audience with His Majesty.'[8]

On Friday 31 July the War Minister and the Chief of General Staff, who was still 'unfortunately very nervous', were with the Reich Chancellor again when at 11.40 a.m. – i.e. twenty minutes before the deadline they had themselves decided on – a telegram arrived from Pourtalès in St Petersburg confirming Russian general mobilisation.[9] The military leaders, the Chancellor, the Foreign Office, and any other statesmen and officers who learned of it, reacted to the news with relief. They could now make use of the Russian mobilisation, as they had intended from the start, as a pretext for proclaiming a threatening danger of war and launching attacks on France and Russia. As for the mood in the War Ministry, the Bavarian military plenipotentiary noted in his diary: 'Beaming faces everywhere, handshaking in the corridors; they are congratulating each other on having cleared the ditch. Rumours of an ultimatum to France – somebody asks whether it is necessary to go after France as well who is running like a scared rabbit; General v. Wild says: "Well, we'd like those chaps to be in it too."'[10] A dispatch of 31 July from Lerchenfeld, the Bavarian envoy in Berlin, confirmed that 'in military circles here' people were 'in the best of spirits', as they had long thought 'that militarily the moment was more favourable than it will ever be in the foreseeable future'.[11] Even in the navy and the civilian administration people were relieved and gleeful. After a morning ride in the Tiergarten the head of the Naval Cabinet went into his office where 'very soon ... my gentlemen [came in] with a message from the Admiralty Staff that war had "at last" been decided on'.[12] The Secretary of State in the Reich Office of the Interior, Clemens von Delbrück, was also 'in the happiest of moods' after the threatening danger of war had been proclaimed.[13]

Kaiser Wilhelm was no exception. At 7.30 he went for his morning ride in Potsdam, and as Prince Henrich noted in his diary, 'everything seemed to be going well when suddenly at 12.30 the news arrrived of the mobilisation of the whole Russian army and navy. W. calm, composed, gives orders for move to Berlin by automobile.'[14] Lerchenfeld reported the same day that 'after some fluctuations in his mood at the start of the crisis' the monarch was 'now very serious and calm';[15] and he made a 'very determined calm impression' on the Austrian ambassador too.[16]

As the orders for declaring a threatening danger of war and for mobilisation itself could only be issued by the Kaiser it had long been agreed that Wilhelm should move from Potsdam to Berlin at short notice. Falkenhayn recorded that

Figure 50 From Potsdam to Berlin, 31 July 1914: on the road to the abyss of war

after the news of the Russian general mobilisation arrived at 11.40 'the Kaiser was immediately ... requested by telephone to order a state of "threatening danger of war" to be proclaimed throughout the Reich. It is also put to him that he should now move to the Schloss in Berlin. Russia is to be presented with a 12-hour ultimatum, either she undertakes to stop all preparations against us and Austria immediately or we would mobilise, which means war. France to be asked to state within 18 hours what her position would be in the event of war between Germany and Russia. In the event of an evasive or neutral reply, she is to be asked to hand over Toul and Verdun to us as pledges for the duration of the war.'[17] Kaiser Wilhelm immediately telephoned the order for the proclamation of a state of threatening danger of war, which was issued by Falkenhayn at one o'clock. A few minutes later the Reich Chancellor informed Tschirschky in Vienna that Berlin had replied to the Russian general mobilisation by proclaiming a threatening danger of war, to be followed within 48 hours by German mobilisation. 'This means war is inevitable.'[18]

Immediately before leaving the Neues Palais in the early afternoon of 31 July (see Figure 50) Georg Count von Wedel presented Wilhelm with another Foreign Office draft of a telegram to the Tsar. This document (to which Wilhelm as usual made numerous corrections and additions) must therefore have been drawn up before confirmation of the Russian general mobilisation had been received. The text of the telegram as it was sent (just after two o'clock) read: 'On your appeal to my friendship and your call for assistance I began to mediate between your and the Austro-Hungarian Governments. While this action was proceeding your troops were mobilised against Austria-Hungary my ally. Thereby, as I have already pointed out to you, my mediation has been made almost illusory. I have nevertheless continued my action. I now receive authentic news of serious preparations for war on my eastern frontier. Responsibility for the safety of my Empire forces preventive measures of defence upon me. In my endeavours to maintain the peace of the world I have gone to the utmost limit possible. The responsibility for the disaster which is now threatening the whole civilised world will not be laid at my door. In this moment it still lies within your power to avert it. Nobody is threatening the honour or power of Russia who can well afford to await the result of my mediation. My friendship for you and your Empire, transmitted to me by my grandfather on his deathbed, has always been sacred to me and I have honestly often backed up Russia when she was in serious trouble, especially in her last war. The peace of Europe may still be maintained by you, if Russia will agree to stop the military measures which must threaten Germany and Austria-Hungary. Willy.'[19]

In the afternoon the army leaders awaited the Kaiser in the Berlin Schloss. As Lyncker reports: 'In the Sternensaal stood the Kaiser with Generals von Moltke, von Plessen, von Falkenhayn and me, and again explained the position to us in the light of further telegrams ... During this review, which lasted about a quarter of an hour, the Chancellor – who had been sent for – arrived and the talk continued calmly along the same lines. The Chancellor requested and received permission to put two questions, by telephone, to St Petersburg and Paris, the wording of which ... was described as a sort of ultimatum, to be answered within 12 hours; it was probably about four o'clock in the afternoon when this took place, and when the Chancellor telephoned the pursuant instructions to Foreign Secretary von Jagow.'[20]

Lyncker's account of this historic scene can now be complemented in several important respects by the diary of the Prussian War Minister, Falkenhayn, who wrote: 'Between 2 and 3 to H.M. in the Sternensaal. He gives an exposé of the situation and pushes all the blame on to Russia. His bearing and language are worthy of a German Emperor! Worthy of a King of Prussia! The order regarding threatening danger of war which I am holding in my hand is signed as we stand. Then Moltke reads out Major von Haeften's draft of an Appeal to the People which made an excellent impression, as his voice if at times choking with tears was nonetheless full of energy. The same author's Appeal to the Army that Moltke gave me, will have to be very substantially amended. The Chancellor, who has meanwhile turned up, takes over the Appeal to the People, and clearly shows his displeasure that Moltke has been trespassing on his territory here, which leads to a clash between the Reich Chancellor and H.M. At Moltke's request H.M. designates the Crown Prince as leader of the 5th Army. I fetch him from the next room and the Kaiser and father adjures him, in language as beautiful as it is grave, to obey, and to avoid any Prince of Homburg-style escapades.'[21]

In the afternoon of 31 July both the Kaiser and the Reich Chancellor made public speeches from the balconies of the Schloss and the Chancellor's Palace respectively which were to leave a deep impression on the public mind. 'An hour of hardship has come for Germany', Wilhelm II declared. 'All those who wish us ill are driving us to defend our just right. The sword is being forced into our hand. I hope that if my efforts at the eleventh hour to bring our opponents to reason and to maintain the peace should fail, we shall with God's help so wield the sword that we can return it to the scabbard again with honour. We shall show our opponents, however, what it means to provoke Germany. And now I commend you to God. Now go to church, kneel before God, and seek his aid for our brave army!'[22] Although Falkenhayn thought the Kaiser's speech 'very feeble',[23] Admiral von Müller considered both speeches 'to the enthusiastic people' to be 'excellent' and most effective. 'Mood brilliant', he noted triumphantly in his diary. 'The government has succeeded very well in portraying us as the attacked.'[24] Thus, one of the most important aims of the leaders of Germany in the July crisis – putting Russia in the wrong in order to get the support of the German people for the war[25] – had been achieved. Now they had to ensure that while the German army was striking out at France, Austria-Hungary would take the field against Russia. It was precisely here that Kaiser Wilhelm II could bring his influence to bear.

SECURING AUSTRIAN COMRADESHIP IN ARMS

While the two Hohenzollern brothers, the Reich Chancellor and the four highest generals were gathered together in the Sternensaal in the afternoon of 31 July, a telegram arrrived from the Tsar, which had crossed with the one the Kaiser had sent from the Neues Palais. Nicholas II expressed his hope that Wilhelm's mediation might yet produce a peaceful solution to the crisis. 'It is *technically* impossible', he continued, 'to stop our military preparations which were obligatory owing to Austria's mobilisation. We are far from wishing war. So long as the negotiations with Austria on Serbia's account are taking place my troops shall not take any *provocative* action. I give you my solemn word for this. I put all my trust in God's mercy and hope in your successful mediation in Vienna for the welfare of our countries and for the peace of Europe.'[26]

The Tsar's words fell on deaf ears in Berlin. Moriz von Lyncker described the Kaiser's reaction on reading the telegram: Wilhelm had admitted that 'the Tsar of course still protested his love of peace, for which he pledges his "sacred word of honour" in his last telegram . . . but that on the other hand, Russian mobilisation is going ahead, because, as the Tsar pleads by way of excuse, it was "in actual fact not possible" to cancel the military measures and especially the mobilisation. This shows quite clearly', Lyncker concluded, 'that the Tsar has no will of his own and is being driven by the Russian war party'.[27] The Chancellor and the generals were no more prepared for serious negotiations than in preceding weeks, but they now exerted strong pressure on the Dual Monarchy to fulfil its treaty obligations. 'We expect Austria's immediate active participation in the war against Russia', Bethmann Hollweg declared in a sort of ultimatum to Vienna.[28] But the action to make sure of Austria's support was really initiated by Kaiser Wilhelm himself, when in the afternoon of 31 July at the request of the Wilhelmstrasse he drafted a telegram to the Emperor of Austria which reflected the power relationship between the two allies with brutal clarity. Austria-Hungary's request for German cover for a war against Serbia was now replaced by a German ultimatum demanding that Austria stop the war against Serbia — 'a mere side-issue' — and devote her entire armed forces to providing Gemany with cover against Russia. The telegram that the Kaiser sent to Franz Joseph at four o'clock read: 'The measures that I have today ordered prior to the mobilisation of my entire army and navy will be followed very soon by their actual mobilisation. I am reckoning on 2 August as the first day of mobilisation and am ready in fulfilment of my alliance obligations to start the war against Russia and France immediately. In this mighty struggle it is of the greatest importance that Austria should commit her main forces against Russia and not divide them by a simultaneous offensive against Serbia. This is all the more important as the greater part of my army will be tied down against France. Serbia's role in the gigantic contest that we are embarking on shoulder to shoulder is entirely subsidiary and calls for only the very minimum of defensive measures. We can only hope for a successful war and the continued existence of our Monarchies if we together confront our new and powerful opponent with our combined forces. I also beg you to do all you can, by being accommodating, to induce Italy to participate, everything else must yield to ensuring that the Triple Alliance enters the war united.'[29]

To the same end, namely 'to give the Austro-Hungarian Monarchy the greatest possible boost for striking at Russia', the Kaiser sent for the Austrian military attaché, Karl von Bienerth, towards five o'clock on that Friday afternoon and explained to him that 'Germany must first direct the main body of her forces against France and only after crushing her can she go on the offensive against Russia, so Austria-Hungary must bear up against the initial Russian onslaught, and must reckon on having to face at least fourteen corps, because according to our information only six Russian corps are to be employed against Germany for the moment.'[30] What would happen if Great Britain sided with France and Russia, the Supreme War Lord could not say; but he admitted to Bienerth that 'he was convinced that Germany would have to reckon with England's active intervention against the Triple Alliance; and how the German fleet was supposed to cope with the far superior Anglo-French fleet, God only knew'.[31]

A promise that the Austro-Hungarian army would be chiefly deployed against the Russians was not long in coming, Franz Joseph replying on 1 August that 'as soon as my General Staff learned that you are determined to start the war against Russia at once and to pursue it with all your power, the firm decision was taken here too to muster the greater part of our main army against Russia'.[32] In Berlin, early in the afternoon of that same day, the telegraph office in the Schloss received a final telegram from the Tsar to the Kaiser: 'Understand that you are obliged to mobilise but wish to have the same guaranty from you as I gave you, that these measures *do not* mean war and that we shall continue negotiating for the benefit of our countries and universal peace dear to all our hearts. Our long proved friendship *must* succeed, with God's help, in avoiding bloodshed. Anxiously, full of confidence await your answer.'[33] Of course, Kaiser Wilhelm was unable to give any such 'guaranty', for even Germany's initial deployment plans envisaged the invasion of Luxembourg and the seizure of Liège: in short, Germany's mobilisation, unlike those of France and Russia, meant war.

MOBILISATION

Once the Kaiser had signed the order proclaiming a state of 'threatening danger of war' on the afternoon of 31 July war against Russia was a foregone conclusion for both the German Reich and its Austro-Hungarian ally. And as Russia had been allied to France for twenty years, and Germany had only the one war plan, involving a lightning offensive in the west, a Franco-German conflict was equally certain. The attitude of Great Britain to such a war, by contrast, still seemed very much an open question. Would the British really calmly accept the 'crushing' of their French Entente partner by the German army and navy, as the decision-makers in Berlin were all hoping? Would they even tolerate the violation of Belgian neutrality if Germany promised to restore the territorial integrity of the little country after the war? As the safeguarding of the Channel coast and the maintenance of the European balance of power had been a prime aim of British foreign policy for centuries, such a degree of self-restraint would have seemed extremely unlikely to most objective observers – but was there not 'the word of a king', the promise of neutrality that King George V was supposed to have made to Prince Heinrich in Buckingham Palace on the morning of Sunday 26 July? Given the vast importance of British sea power, not only in terms of the military operations themselves, but of the influence it could exert over all states with vulnerable coastlines such as Italy and Greece, Kaiser Wilhelm and the whole political establishment in Berlin clung to the last to their hopes of British inaction.

It was precisely because of the calculation that London might stay out if Russia could be cast in the role of aggressor that Bethmann Hollweg and the Wilhelmstrasse tried to delay German mobilisation for as long as possible, but the War Minister and the Chief of General Staff were pressing for a speedy attack on Luxembourg, Belgium and France. As the conflict between civilian and military leaders grew sharper by the hour Falkenhayn called on the Chancellor in the evening of 31 July 'to make clear to him, yet again and with urgency, the military disadvantages of delaying mobilisation'.[34] When in the afternoon of 1 August Haeften learned of Bethmann's view that France might yet decide to stay neutral, he hastened to inform Moltke, who struck his fist on the table and cried out in agitation: 'Then I demand the whole country as far as the Meuse, including the whole fortified Meuse-line with the fortresses of Verdun, Toul, Épinal, and Belfort as guarantees of French neutrality. If France agrees to that, her power is broken and we can attack Russia with our main forces without worrying about the rear ... For the time being, naturally, we are sticking to our offensive in the West. Only when, if France declares her neutrality, we have the Meuse fortresses in our hands can we attack Russia.'[35]

In the late afternoon of 1 August Wilhelm II came out on the side of the military in this dispute, as Falkenhayn dramatically describes in his diary. 'Since, although the ultimatum expired at noon, there is no reply from Russia by four o'clock, I drive to the Reich Chancellor's to get him to go with me to the Kaiser to ask him to give the order for mobilisation. After a lot of demurring he agrees and we telephone Moltke and Tirpitz. Meanwhile, H.M. himself telephones and tells us to come to him with the order for mobilisation.'[36] Wilhelm himself felt, therefore, that general mobilisation should not be delayed any longer. As Falkenhayn noted: 'At five o'clock, H.M. signs the order on the table carved out of wood from Nelson's *Victory*.

I say: May God bless Y.M. and your arms, may God protect the dear Fatherland. The Kaiser then gave me a prolonged handshake, both of us had tears in
our eyes.'[37] At that same moment Count Pourtalès handed in the German
declaration of war in St Petersburg.

ANOTHER TRAGI-COMEDY ABOUT BRITISH NEUTRALITY

Once the mobilisation order was signed, Moltke and Falkenhayn hastened to
leave the Schloss to make a start on 'the bloodiest enterprise that the world has
ever witnessed'.[38] Hardly had Falkenhayn got to the war ministry when
Wahnschaffe of the Reich Chancellery appeared with the latest cypher
telegram from Lichnowsky: Sir Edward Grey wanted to see the ambassador
at once and was likely to propose that 'if we did not attack France, England
would stay neutral and guarantee that France would refrain from action'.[39]
Falkenhayn immediately gave the order, on his own authority, that no German
patrol was to cross the French frontier, and the 16th Division's invasion of
Luxembourg was also to be halted.[40] He rushed back to the Schloss, where
meanwhile Moltke, Bethmann, Jagow, Valentini, Plessen, Lyncker, Müller and
Tirpitz had reassembled. According to Lyncker, Lichnowsky's telegram had
the effect 'of a bomb', since 'it now suddenly appeared that instead of facing
3 opponents we might have to deal with only 1'. Everyone agreed that 'the
Kaiser would have to show the people and the world that he was magnanimously grasping the proffered hand'.[41] After reading out the telegram to the
Chief of General Staff the Kaiser declared: 'We must accept this, of course, and
hold back the advance in the west for the time being.'[42] 'Therefore', the
Supreme War Lord commanded, 'we simply march east with the whole army!'[43]

Apart from Moltke, all those present were completely in agreement with
the Kaiser's decision. One witness, the Flügeladjutant Max von Mutius, was
struck by Wilhelm's objective reaction to the British offer. The Kaiser, he said,
had asked Moltke whether it was still possible to prevent the army from
crossing the frontier. As the Chief of General Staff did not know the answer,
Colonel Gerhard Tappen was summoned from the Operations Department,
who said that it was. Only then were the appropriate orders issued to stop the
advance. The army was to complete its deployment in the west without
crossing the frontier, before being redirected in an orderly fashion to the
eastern front. In short, Mutius felt, as Holger Afflerbach observes, that 'to
this extent the Kaiser had reacted perfectly rationally and professionally and
had shown himself tactful in his handling of Moltke'.[44] There was thus no
question here of a single-handed action by the Kaiser, a sudden panic attack, or
even a heroic, but in the end illusory, attempt to save world peace — it was

simply a cool calculation that if Grey's offer held good, the war against Russia could be fought in well-nigh ideal circumstances. Moltke, however, was thunderstruck, remarking bitterly to Mutius: 'That is what I was always afraid of, we would have won the two-front war.'[45] He pointed out, in some agitation, according to his own account, that the deployment of an army of millions had entailed years of work and could not be simply improvised. 'If His Majesty insists on sending the whole army to the east, this would not be an army fit for fighting but a wild mob of disorganised armed men without provisions.' But 'the Kaiser insisted on his demand and was very angry, saying to me, among other things, "Your uncle would have given me a different answer!", which I found very hurtful.' Moltke's proposal to demand the fortresses of Toul and Verdun as guarantees for French neutrality during a Russo-German war was rejected, as was his insistence on occupying Luxembourg, which he insisted was essential to the German deployment. 'In my presence the Kaiser turned, without asking me, to the Flügeladjutant on duty, [in actual fact it was Adjutant-General Hans von Plessen] and ordered him to telegraph the order immediately to the 16th Division in Trier not to invade Luxemburg. – I felt my heart was about to break . . . I tried in vain to convince His Majesty that we needed the Luxemburg railways and had to secure them, but I was seen off with the remark that I should make use of other railways instead. He stood by the order.'[46]

According to Haeften's memorandum, Moltke felt especially bitter about Falkenhayn. 'Instead of supporting him against the Kaiser's nonsensical plan' the War Minister had 'held his tongue'.[47] Yet if we are to believe the memorandum, Falkenhayn had already, even before the meeting in the Schloss, issued the 'nonsensical' orders that the Kaiser was now also issuing. But the War Minister was acting in the knowledge that the bloody dice of war could no longer he stopped; and he himself recalled a conversation with Moltke in a corner of the Sternensaal: 'He claims to be a completely broken man, because this decision of the Kaiser's shows that he is still hoping for peace. I console Moltke. I share his view of H.M.'s ideas, but I cannot see anything for Moltke to take offence at in the fact that a few of his orders have been held back for a time, and the Kaiser's humanitarian spirit does him honour. Obviously I do not believe for one moment that the telegram will change anything in the huge drama that started at 5 o'clock.'[48] When the Crown Prince also came up and asked whether the negotiations with London would affect the mobilisation order, the War Minister replied that war was now inevitable.'[49]

While he still had all his civilian and military advisers around him Wilhelm instructed the Reich Chancellor, Jagow, Falkenhayn and Moltke to draft an open telegram 'from government to government' in response to Lichnowsky's telegram.[50] The War Minister claims in his diary that 'after violent scenes between the Chancellor and Moltke', he had himself 'at the Kaiser's command' dictated to Jagow the text of this reply,[51] in which Germany guaranteed that she would not cross the French frontier if by 7.00 p.m. on Monday 3 August England committed herself, with all her armed forces, to vouch for France's unconditional neutrality throughout the entire Russo-German war.[52] At the same time, at the other side of the Sternensaal, the Kaiser, Müller and Tirpitz 'hammered out' a telegram to King George V himself, accepting England's offer to guarantee French neutrality with her army and navy and promising – despite the German mobilisation which had already begun and which for technical reasons would have to continue – that 'I shall of course refrain from attacking France & employ my troops elsewhere. I hope that France will not become nervous. The troops on my frontiers are in process of being stopped by telegraph & telephone from crossing into France.'[53] After the Reich Chancellor had approved it, this telegram was sent off to the King at 7.05 p.m.

Moltke returned to the General Staff an utterly broken man. He was, his wife recalled, 'blue and red in the face and so agitated inside that he could not get a word out. In the end the tension gave way to a fit of weeping, in which he repeatedly blurted out: "I am happy to wage war against the French and the Russians, but not against such a Kaiser."'[54] As he himself later wrote about his physical and mental state: 'It is impossible to describe the mood in which I came home. I was as it were broken, and weeping tears of despair. When the telegram to the 16th Division was laid before me, repeating the order already given by telephone, I threw my pen down on the table and said "I shall not sign it."'[55]

While Moltke was weeping tears of despair in his office, the mood of triumph in the Schloss was further heightened by the arrival at 8.30 p.m. of a second telegram from Lichnowsky, this time with the news that in an hour's time Grey wished 'to present proposals to him for English neutrality, even in the event of our being at war with both Russia and France'.[56] The head of the Naval Cabinet made a euphoric entry in his diary: 'What a fabulous turn of events! Glasses of champagne in the adjutants' room. The Kaiser in very elated mood but very nice.'[57]

The Reich Chancellor, confident that England would now after all, as he had hoped all along, leave Germany a free hand on the continent, got Wedel to draft an ultimatum to the Tsar that he 'most humbly' put before the Kaiser for signature at 9.45 p.m. This time, too, the Kaiser altered the text in various places and returned it a few minutes later to the Chancellor, who ordered it to be sent *en clair* to St Petersburg immediately: 'I yesterday pointed out to your government the way by which, alone, war may be avoided. Although

I requested an answer for noon today, no telegram from my Ambassador conveying an answer from your Government has reached me as yet. I therefore have been obliged to mobilise my Army. Immediate, affirmative, clear and unmistakable answer from your Government is the only way to avoid endless misery. Until I have received this answer, alas, I am unable to discuss the subject of your telegram. As a matter of fact I must request you to immediately order your troops on no account to commit the slightest act of trespassing over our frontiers. Willy.'[58] To this telegram the Tsar was no longer able to reply, but could only minute on it, in dismay, 'Received after the declaration of war.'[59]

Late in the evening of this eventful 1 August the Kaiser sent for the Austro-Hungarian ambassador Count Szögyény,[60] who reported to Vienna on the Kaiser's confident mood, and his full support for war against both Russia and France. 'During our long conversation the Kaiser emphasised above all that he was continually exchanging telegrams with the Tsar but had to admit, to his deepest regret, that he could not understand Tsar Nicholas's present state of mind at all. Nor did he know whether the Russian Emperor had agreed the telegrams he sent him, Kaiser Wilhelm, with his advisers; the Tsar's chief adviser at the moment was probably the War Minister, but it seemed that the faith healer Rasputin was still exerting a decisive influence over him. The Tsar's telegrams were always full of contradictions, and unfortunately he could not find any other word to describe them than "lies". There had still been no reply to the enquiry Germany had made with a fixed time limit. A telegram had arrived – as usual in English – from the Emperor of Russia assuring him (Kaiser Wilhelm) that the mobilisation ordered in Russia was *not* directed at Germany. The reply from Paris had contained only empty "phrases"; on the other hand Sir E. Grey had telegraphed, with his royal master's consent, to offer to guarantee French neutrality in the event of war between Germany and Russia. Obviously he (Kaiser Wilhelm) would demand a "pledge" from France. He had the impression that France had been deeply shocked by Germany's mobilisation. In these circumstances it would be a question of holding, calmly, but with great determination, to the course we have followed so far.' Although he was at this moment convinced that England would both stay neutral and guarantee France's neutrality, Wilhelm made no secret of his intention to subjugate France. He was 'above all . . . determined', he told Szögyény, 'to settle the score with France and hoped to do so completely successfully'. At this moment Bethmann Hollweg's policy in the July crisis enjoyed the Kaiser's wholehearted approval: 'The Kaiser spoke in terms of high praise for the manly bearing of the Reich Chancellor and for the felicitous way in which he had implemented his plans.'[61]

Disillusionment came that same night. In London, George V summoned Sir Edward Grey to Buckingham Palace where the Foreign Secretary drafted the King's telegram in reply, explaining that Lichnowsky's dispatch was evidently based on a misunderstanding.[62] Consequently Moltke was again summoned to the Schloss, at 11.00 p.m. As he recalled: 'The Kaiser received me in his bedroom, he had already gone to bed, but got up again and threw on a dressing gown. He gave me a telegram from the King of England, in which he said he knew nothing of any guarantee that England would hold France back from war. Prince Lichnowsky's telegram must be a mistake or he must have misunderstood something. – The Kaiser was very agitated and said to me: "Now you can do what you like." I went straight home and telegraphed to the 16th Division that the invasion of Luxemburg should go ahead.'[63] Despite this decision, the basis of trust between Moltke and his Supreme War Lord had been destroyed for ever. As Moltke's adjutant noted, 'his whole nervous system . . . had been badly affected'. When headquarters moved to Koblenz the Chief of General Staff had to be accompanied by his wife, in the guise, on the Kaiser's orders, of a manageress of a Red Cross hospital.[64]

That same night a further telegram from Lichnowsky arrived in the Wilhelmstrasse, from where it was forwarded immediately to the General Staff, the war ministry, the Admiralty Staff and the Reich Navy Office, but was only put before the Kaiser on the afternoon of 2 August. The ambassador reported a conversation with Grey, who pointed out in the name of the whole Cabinet that the violation of Belgian neutrality would be of decisive import- ance for the attitude of the government in London and public opinion in the country towards a continental war. Apart from that, Grey had wondered whether in the event of a Russo-German war, Germany and France really could stand facing each other fully armed without coming to blows. When Lichnowsky asked whether France would accept such a pact, which Germany would indeed accept in order to secure Britain's neutrality, Grey promised to enquire, although he was only too conscious of the difficulties.[65] At 2.30 a.m. the leaders of the German government, the army and the navy – Bethmann, Jagow, Zimmermann, Hammann, Moltke, Falkenhayn and Tirpitz – assembled in the Chancellery for a review of the situation, which resulted in another 'furious' row between the civilians and the military over the declar- ation of war on France and the plans to invade Belgium.[66]

The generals had already criticised the declaration of war on Russia at 5.00 p.m. on 1 August as 'premature' and 'foolish', and had sought to prevent it.[67] They now had no time at all for the argument put forward by Bethmann and the Foreign Office, that war must now be declared on France in order to justify marching through Belgium. 'The invasion of Belgium could only be justified by the war on France, and that latter only by the war on Russia', Jagow later explained. 'It was now up to the political leadership to take the appropriate diplomatic steps to prepare the way for it.'[68] In this dispute, too, it was of course only a question of tactics, not of any difference of principle. Bethmann Hollweg expressly endorsed the Moltke–Schlieffen Plan, with its attack on France through Belgium and Luxembourg, with the telling argument that the alternative plan – for an offensive in the east while standing on the defensive in the west – would have amounted to confessing that Germany would be content with an indecisive 'draw', and 'such a watchword would never suffice to lead an army and a people into a struggle for existence'.[69] It was the Kaiser's task to mediate these differences between the statesmen and the soldiers the following day.

Early in the morning of 2 August the Reich Chancellor summed up for the monarch the dramatic events of the last few hours in terse style. 'According to report from General Staff (today at 4.00 a.m.) attempt to disrupt railways and advance of 2 squadrons of Cossacks towards Johannisburg [in East Prussia]. Thereby, in fact, state of war. Above reported immediately to Vienna and Rome, with request for statement about fulfilment of alliance obligations, and additional statement to Rome that we foresee a French attack. Russian ambassador has received passports. After agreement with War Ministry and General Staff, presentation of declaration of war on France not necessary today, for military reasons. Has not yet taken place, in the hope [sic!] that the French attack us.'[70]

Towards 10 o'clock the Kaiser presided over an agitated discussion in the Schloss between Bethmann, Moltke, Tirpitz and Plessen. While the Reich Chancellor insisted on a formal declaration of war on France, as without one he could not present the ultimatum to Belgium, neither the Chief of General Staff nor Admiral von Tirpitz could see the point of this. Against his better knowledge Moltke cited a whole list of hostile actions by the French that were supposed to prove that war had in fact already broken out: attempts to poison a well in Metz with cholera bacteria and to blow up a tunnel on the Moselle railway, the bombing of Nuremberg by French aircraft and other 'reports of barbarism'.[71] Numerous marginal comments by Wilhelm II show that he accepted these fabricated reports at face value. He instructed Bethmann 'to inform England that it is only circumstances and the actions of the French that force us to march through Belgium, and that we would in every other respect have regard for Belgian sovereignty and would pay for everything. Even after a victorious war we should remain most firmly determined not to infringe the integrity of Belgium in any way.'[72]

On the afternoon of 2 August the Kaiser covered Lichnowsky's telegram of the night before with furious marginalia that testify to his disappointment and anxiety: 'Grey's drivel shows that he has absolutely no idea what to do', he scrawled. 'Just heard that England has already cut the cable to Emden. I.e. an act of war! While she is still negotiating.' The British Foreign Secretary was 'a treacherous scoundrel'. His assurance that England had not the slightest intention of taking hostile action against Germany was 'a lie! He told Lichnowsky so himself 4 days ago!' As for Grey's speculation as to whether despite the war in the east the mobilised armies of Germany and France could remain facing each other without fighting: 'The fellow is mad or an idiot.' The Kaiser went on to state, contrary to the truth: 'Besides, with their aeroplanes dropping bombs it is the French who have started the war and the violation of international law.' Lichnowsky's assurance to Grey that Germany did not wish to destroy France or take territory from her was termed 'Drivel!' by Wilhelm II, who concluded: 'My impression is that Herr Grey is a false dog who has taken fright at his own infamy and treacherous policy, but doesn't want to come out openly against us, and rather wants us to force him to do so.'[73] As Jagow remarked to the British ambassador Sir Edward Goschen, the Kaiser was terribly depressed and thought that his reputation as 'the Kaiser of Peace' was now in tatters.[74]

WILHELM'S RENEWED SEARCH FOR ALLIES

The Kaiser's alarm about Great Britain's entering the war was all too understandable, for he was aware not only of the strategic threat from the Royal Navy to Germany's land and sea offensive in the west, but also of the implications that British hostility might have for Germany's actual or potential allies, especially in the Mediterranean and Scandinavia. On the eve of Britain's entry he described the constraints that even a waiting attitude on her part would impose on Germany's military operations against France: 'The English fleet is protecting the north coast of France by tying down our fleet. That is *assistance* to an *ally*. Instead of the attitude of a neutral. For England is *hindering* the *co-operation* of my fleet with my *army* against my *opponent*, who is already at war with me, and who started the war, without any declaration, and in breach of international law. Things cannot go on like this. England simply has to show her colours *immediately. One thing or the other.*'[75]

He had long been equally alive to the connection between England's attitude and the loyalty of Italy, with her endless, unprotected coastline, to the Triple Alliance.[76] When Lichnowsky's telegrams of 1 August seemed to point to British neutrality, Wilhelm ordered this hopeful news to be forwarded to Rome immediately, 'as Italy will never go along with us in the 3 Alliance so long as she is afraid that England might be hostile'.[77] Moreover, England's hostility and Italy's desertion threatened to have devastating effects on the hopes Wilhelm still cherished that Romania, Bulgaria, Turkey, Greece and even Sweden, too, might fight on the side of Germany and Austria-Hungary.

As we saw earlier, Wilhelm had already been negotiating while anchored at Balholm with Turkey, Bulgaria and Greece with a view to gaining their active support in the coming war with Russia.[78] Likewise, from the start of the July crisis he had been pressing the Austrians to offer Italy generous compensation – he was thinking of the whole of Albania[79] – for the expansion of their own influence in the Balkans, in order to secure her cooperation in the war against France.[80] Towards the end of the crisis, as the great war loomed, the Kaiser intensified his efforts, in close cooperation with the Wilhelmstrasse, to hold on to Italy, to persuade his relatives King Constantine in Greece and King Carol in Romania to join the Central Powers, and to bring the negotiations that had started between Turkey and Bulgaria to a speedy conclusion. In no other area, he believed, could he bring his personal influence so effectively to bear as in this field of dynastic diplomacy. Early in the evening of 31 July, after the proclamation of a state of 'threatening danger of war', a confident Wilhelm II explained to the Austrian military attaché that in the war against Russia and France that was now definitely impending, Germany and Austria-Hungary could count on the military support not only of Italy, but of Romania, Bulgaria, Turkey, Greece and Sweden as well. 'He had telegraphed to King Carol of Romania that as head of the House of Hohenzollern he was counting on his active support to implement the written treaty. Count Hutten-Czapski, who had just returned from Romania, told Kaiser Wilhelm he was absolutely convinced that Romania would intervene actively on the side of the Triple Alliance. Kaiser Wilhelm then remarked that Austria-Hungary ought to promise Romania Bessarabia ... Furthermore, he had sent the King of Bulgaria a very firm summons to side with Austria-Hungary in the general conflict.' With regard to 'Turkey's intentions, His Majesty said he could tell me, in strictest secrecy, that he was engaged in concluding a treaty with Turkey that committed her to send five army corps ... into action against Russia ... As regards Greece, he had sent a telegram to the King to say that he would sever all connections with him if Greece went along with Russia. He had further put it to the King of Greece that given the superiority of the fleets of Austria-Hungary and Italy his country was defenceless anyway, especially as the Greek army was still in process of reorganisation. If he, King Constantine, nevertheless wanted to intervene, he must do so against Russia. According to an exchange of views with the King of Sweden King Gustav wants to mobilise and, once war has broken out, to intervene. Kaiser Wilhelm's Flügeladjutant Colonel von Kleist, a former military attaché in Rome, was on his way to Italy with a letter urgently summoning King Victor Emmanuel to honour his treaty commitments by mobilising all his land and naval forces and sending an army group to the Alps as promised. Of course, what he was chiefly expecting from the appearance of Italian troops on German soil against the French was a strong effect on morale.'[81] Again, when Wilhelm received ambassador Szögyény in the night of 1–2 August, he was full of confidence in describing his 'continuing efforts to gain new and make sure of old allies'. He emphasised that 'he was continuing in every way possible to work on Italy, he had written very categorical letters to the kings of Romania, Bulgaria and Greece, and, as he could tell me in strict confidence, was in the process of signing a treaty with Turkey'.[82]

The Kaiser's expectations of Swedish support were based on nothing more substantial than the conversation King Gustaf V had had with the German envoy Franz von Reichenau on 26 July 1914. According to Reichenau's report, which was furnished with enthusiastic marginal comments by Wilhelm II on 31 July, the King had laid stress on his country's 'feeling of Germanic solidarity against Slavdom', praised Berchtold's note to Serbia, and spoken mockingly of President Poincaré.[83] Clearly these remarks fell far short of a promise to mobilise and fight once hostilities had broken out.

That same evening Kleist set off with the Kaiser's letter to King Victor Emmanuel[84] brusquely summoning him to order the immediate mobilisation of the Italian army and navy and to provide Gemany with the assistance promised by the treaty of alliance; any deviation from this would amount to a 'vile felony'. Some of the expressions in the Kaiser's letter were so insulting that the ambassador Hans von Flotow had to remove them before presenting it to the King.[85] Wilhelm's demand was obviously, given the anti-German mood of the country, completely unrealistic; the Italian government had long since made it clear that the country would be neutral;[86] and on 2 August the Auswärtiges Amt sent the Kaiser a telegram from Flotow which underlined this yet again.[87] The Italian Foreign Minister had told the ambassador once again that the *casus foederis* had not arisen for Italy, 'as this was a case of a war of aggression'; and he even claimed there was a risk of revolution if Italy entered the war. What really determined the Italian government's decision, however, was the fear of having England as an enemy.[88] Furiously, the Kaiser scribbled on the decyphered text: 'So, if we don't respect the neutrality of Belgium, England attacks us and Italy deserts us, that is the position in nuce! Betrayal by our allies – that's all we need!'[89] On 3 August a telegram arrived from King Victor Emmanuel, justifying Italy's neutrality with reference to the

defensive clauses of the Triple Alliance. Again, Wilhelm termed Italy's decision a 'betrayal' and cursed the King as a 'scoundrel!', whose assertions were
'lies' and 'sheer insolence'.[90] Then in the evening a telegram from Kleist
confirmed the King's negative attitude: although Victor Emmanuel had assured
him that 'personally' he was 'wholeheartedly on our side', he complained that
'Austria's incredibly maladroit handling of Italian national sensitivities in
the last few weeks had so stirred up public opinion against Austria that
co-operating with her now would unleash a storm ... As the people do not
understand the difference [between Germany and Austria] Austria's clumsiness means that Italy must also let Germany down, about which he, the King,
was deeply pained.'[91] Bitterly, the Kaiser added a sentence in his own hand to
the Foreign Office draft of a telegram to Emperor Franz Joseph: the King of
Italy had 'shamefully abused our trust and has not fulfilled his alliance
obligations'.[92] Even so, Wilhelm did not quite give up hope of a change of
heart, declaring on 4 August: 'come what may, Vienna must make binding
promises and offer large compensations which are attractive enough to be
effective, should have been done long ago'.[93]

Wilhelm II was expecting to the end that both Greece and Romania would
join Germany, Austria-Hungary, Bulgaria and Turkey in the fight against
Russia, but this hope soon evaporated as well. Early in the morning of 31
July he had approved with a few minor alterations the texts of the telegrams
drafted by his Foreign Office to the kings of Greece and Romania. Both were
clearly designed to draw these two states, like Bulgaria and Turkey hopefully,
towards the Triple Alliance side. 'I take it for granted', the Kaiser told his
brother-in-law King Constantine, 'that the memory of your murdered father
alone will hold you and your country back from supporting the Serbian
assassins against my person and the Triple Alliance. But purely from the point
of view of Greece's self-interest it seems to me that the place for your country
and your dynasty is on the side of the Triple Alliance ... Nobody has looked
more askance at Greece's marvellous ascent under your leadership than
Russia. There will never be a better moment than the present for Greece to
shake off, under the mighty shield of the Triple Alliance, the tutelage that
Russia is striving to establish over the Balkans ... Should you, against my
confident expectations, opt for the other side, Greece will be exposed to
immediate attack from Italy, Bulgaria and Turkey, and our personal relations
too would be damaged for ever.'[94] Constantine replied on 2 August that the
thought of helping Serbia had never even occurred to anyone in Athens; on
the other hand, it was quite impossible for his country 'to pounce on her'.
Instead, Greece must remain strictly neutral and support the maintenance of
the status quo in the Balkans. The Kaiser's marginal notes on Constantine's

telegram are clear evidence of the continuity of his anti-Russian policy in the July crisis. 'Inform Athens', he ordered, 'that I have concluded alliance with Bulgaria and Turkey for war against Russia and shall treat Greece as an enemy if she does not join us at once: have just said that to [the Greek envoy] Theotoki personally, while informing him that we are allied to Turkey and Bulgaria.' It was 'impossible' for the Greeks to stay neutral, 'you should march against Russia! . . . The Balkans are on the march . . . If Greece does not join in at once, she will lose her status as a Balkan power and we shall no longer support her ambitions but treat her as an enemy. It is not a question of the balance of power in the Balkans but of a common undertaking of the Balkan states to liberate the Balkans from Russia for ever! W.'[95]

Wilhelm dealt in much the same way with Romania. Jagow's draft telegram to King Carol, to which the Kaiser added a postscript in his own hand, was equally peremptory: 'After the wicked deed in Sarajevo the Emperor Franz Joseph, our honourable friend and ally, has demanded expiation from Serbia. Russia, who claims hegemony over the Balkans, is, by standing up for Serbia, making the latter's efforts to undermine the Austrian Monarchy her own. I too am forced to recognise that the Panslav movement is seeking, by destroying the Danube Monarchy, to disrupt the Triple Alliance, isolate and weaken Germany, and entrench Russia's control over the whole of south-east Europe. Alliance loyalty, honour, and self-preservation direct me to side with Austria. In this grave hour my thoughts turn to you, who have created a Kulturstaat [civilised state] in the eastern marches as a dam against the Slav flood. I trust that you as a Hohenzollern will stand loyally by your friends and fulfil your alliance obligations to the letter. Wilhelm.'[96] In the afternoon of 2 August the Kaiser peremptorily demanded that 'Romania must publish the treaty with Austria at once and immediately mobilise against Russia.'[97] When the Romanian Prime Minister Bratianu hinted that given the anti-Austrian feeling in the country, Romania might be neutral, Wilhelm, as usual, dismissed this as 'Nonsense' and again demanded that 'H.M. [King Carol] must mobilise! against Russia.'[98] He had himself pressed Austria-Hungary to offer Romania Bessarabia as a reward for entering the war. Now he seized on a suggestion from the ambassador at Constantinople that Romania might be persuaded to ally with the Central Powers by an offer of Turkish and Bulgarian assistance in conquering Bessarabia.[99] But in Bucharest, all these allurements failed, all the more so as Italy's declaration of neutrality made a deep impression there. On 4 August, after a Crown Council meeting with the King in the chair, the Romanian government informed the German and Austro-Hungarian envoys that it could not recognise the *casus foederis* as it had not been consulted in advance about the Austrian démarche in Belgrade.

Bitterly, Wilhelm had to recognise that his diplomatic efforts had failed, and pushed the blame for this on to his diplomats. 'Even before the war our allies are dropping off like rotten apples! A total débâcle of German and also Austrian diplomacy. That should and could have been avoided. W.'[100]

In the end, only Turkey and (over a year later) Bulgaria decided to fight on the side of Germany and Austria-Hungary.[101] Italy joined the war in 1915, Romania in 1916, and Greece in 1917 – but all on the side of the Entente. On 2 August 1914 Denmark, Sweden, Norway, the Netherlands, Switzerland and Belgium declared their neutrality. The situation that confronted the German Reich at the start of the war bore little relation to the fine hopes that had been celebrated with champagne in the adjutants' room of the Berlin Schloss just a few hours before.

THE VIOLATION OF BELGIAN NEUTRALITY AND BRITAIN'S ENTRY INTO THE WAR

It had been clear for years that in the event of war with France the German army would storm through neutral Belgium, come what may. As Lerchenfeld reported on 4 August, Moltke had said straight out that 'even English neutrality would be too dearly bought if the price was observing the neutrality of Belgium, since an offensive war [sic!] against France was only possible through Belgium'.[102] Although Wilhelm II, too, was fully aware that the violation of Belgian neutrality would almost certainly lead to 'England's intervention against us', he decided in the evening of 2 August that the German ultimatum should be presented in Brussels as planned. For a pretext, he fell back on the propaganda lies about French air raids on Germany. 'Our fear, which we have already referred to in the note to be presented to Belgium this evening, is confirmed by the fact that already today France has, in contravention of international law, embarked on warlike operations against us (aeroplanes dropping bombs on German territory, cavalry patrols crossing the frontier). Instruct the minister in Brussels to emphasise this when handing in the note.'[103] France's alleged activities also had to serve as a justification for the invasion of Luxembourg. 'Aeroplanes have flown to us over Luxemburg', the Kaiser declared on 3 August. 'Flying over a Neutral state for the purposes of war is a breach of neutrality.'[104]

On the same day the Wilhelmstrasse received a report from Claus von Below-Saleske, the minister in Brussels, that the Belgian government was rejecting the terms of the German ultimatum and would oppose any violation of Belgian neutrality with armed force.[105] At 5 o'clock a personal appeal from King Albert of the Belgians to the Kaiser arrived at the Schloss: 'Your Majesty and Your Government have repeatedly given us valuable proofs of your friendship and sympathy, and accredited persons have promised in the event of a new war to respect the neutrality of Belgium. We do not doubt that the feelings and intentions towards us of the mighty Empire whose destiny Your Majesty controls, remain unchanged. The ties of blood and friendship that bind our two families closely together move me to write to you today to ask you in this grave hour graciously to renew the expression of these feelings towards my country.'[106] The Kaiser sent Albert's letter to the Reich Chancellor and the Chief of General Staff and demanded an immediate telegraphic reply.[107] This telegram, drafted by Jagow, and insisting on Belgian compliance with the terms of surrender, was sent at 8.20 p.m. directly from the Schloss to Brussels on the Kaiser's orders.[108] In the evening of 4 August King Albert's bitter reply (*en clair*) arrived at the Schloss: he had not believed for one moment 'that Y[our] Maj[esty] would force us, before the eyes of the whole of Europe, to make the cruel choice beween war and dishonour, between respect for treaties and disregard of our international obligations'. Wilhelm sent the telegram on to his Foreign Office without comment.[109]

In the illusory hope of softening the impact of the German invasion of Belgium in London the Kaiser, Moltke and Bethmann had already agreed to promise the British the restoration of the territorial integrity (but not the sovereignty!) of Belgium *after* the war.[110] Indeed, as Wilhelm II wanted to ensure that this proposal — unlike his Halt-in-Belgrade proposal of 28 July — really was delivered, he wrote personally to the Reich Chancellor on 3 August: 'Further to our recent conversation, please let me know immediately by telephone whether, when London was informed of our ultimatum to Belgium, it was also made clear that Germany will give the Engl[ish] government a binding promise to guarantee the existence of the Belg[ian] state, even in the event of war with Belgium. If despite the written request of the Gen[eral] Staff, this was not done, then let it be done at once. Wilhelm I.R.' Jagow could assure the Kaiser that such a communication had in fact gone off to London.[111] But the German offer simply confirmed the British government's worst fears about Germany's intentions. At 7.45 p.m. Jagow received the ultimatum from the British ambassador demanding that Germany promise by midnight to respect Belgian neutrality, otherwise Great Britain would consider herself at war with Germany.[112]

On the morning of 4 August, while the German army was invading Belgium, the Kaiser returned to the charge that England could have prevented the war if she had only held her allies back and given his mediation efforts a chance. He wrote in English: 'If Grey wanted really to preserve peace he need only as Prince Henry suggested on 29th July intimate that the two allies

France & Russia — not to mobilize but to wait, till the pourparlers which I am directing had succeeded or otherwise, between Vienna and Russia. W.'[113]

At one o'clock on that day, in the White Hall of the Schloss, Kaiser Wilhelm II opened the Reichstag. This was where, almost exactly twenty-six years before, in the presence of Bismarck and the elder Moltke, he had confidently made his first speech from the throne. Now he said: 'In this hour of destiny I have gathered around Me the elected representatives of the German people. For almost half a century we have been able to stay on the path of peace. The patience of our people has often been severely tried by attempts to ascribe warlike intentions to Germany and to constrict her place in the world. Unswerving in its integrity, and in challenging circumstances too, My government has pursued the advancement of all moral, intellectual, and commercial energies as its highest aim. As the world can bear witness, in all the pressure and confusion of recent years, we have striven untiringly in the first rank to spare the peoples of Europe a war between the Great Powers. The most serious dangers arising from events in the Balkans seemed to have been overcome. Then, with the murder of My friend, Archduke Franz Ferdinand, an abyss was opened up. My noble ally, the Emperor and King Franz Joseph, was compelled to take up arms to defend the security of his empire against the dangerous machinations of a neighbouring state. In pursuing its just interests the allied Monarchy has been obstructed by the Russian Empire. It is not only our obligations as an ally that summon us to Austria-Hungary's side. It is also our gigantic task of protecting the ancient cultural community of the two empires against attack from foreign forces. It is with a heavy heart that I have had to mobilise My army against a neighbour at whose side it has fought on so many battlefields. It was with deep sorrow that I witnessed the shattering of a friendship that Germany had loyally cherished. The Imperial Russian government, yielding to pressure from an insatiable nationalism, has taken the part of a state that by its encouragement of criminal assaults caused the disaster of this war. That France too has sided with our opponents could not surprise us. All too often have our efforts to establish friendly relations with the French Republic come up against old yearnings and old grudges. Gentlemen! Whatever human foresight and energy can do to arm a people for this decisive struggle has with your patriotic co-operation been done. The hatred that has been building up in east and west for a long time has now burst into bright flames. The present situation is not the result of passing conflicts of interest or diplomatic combinations, it results from an ill-will that has been at work for years against the power and prosperity of the German Reich. We are not driven by any desire for conquest, but by the unflinching determination to preserve the place which God has granted us, for ourselves and all the future generations. You will see from the documents before you how My government and above all My Chancellor have striven to the last moment to prevent the worst. Now, being compelled to defend ourselves, and with a clear conscience and clean hands, we take up the sword. To the peoples and tribes of the German Reich My call goes out to defend, with all our power and in fraternal unity with our allies, that which we have created by peaceful labour. Following the example of our fathers, strong and loyal, grave and gallant, humble before God and fearless before the enemy, we put our trust in the eternal Almighty, that He may strengthen our arms and grant us success! It is to you, Gentlemen, that the whole German people, gathered around their princes and leaders, look today. Make your decisions with one accord and with speed — that is My profound desire.'[114]

Admiral von Müller found the speech 'very uplifting' and 'H.M. very disgnified'; but he well knew what a frightful catastrophe was about to unfold. As he reflected in his diary, hanging over the solemn ceremony in the White Hall was 'the oppressive atmosphere of the war with England that everybody regarded as inevitable. That evening, as he sat together with Tirpitz, came the news that the British ambassador had asked for his passports. 'So war with England has arrived. It has come because our politicians have no idea of the importance of superior naval power. A terrible test for Germany. How will this end?'[115]

Grey had presented the ultimatum to Germany with tears in his eyes. King George V, wringing his hands, had asked the American ambassador in London: 'My God, Mr Page, What else could we do?' For days the Austrian ambassador, Count Albert von Mensdorff-Pouilly, sat bewildered in the embassy and wept.[116] The grief-stricken Prince Lichnowsky was wandering like one demented through the rooms of No. 9 Carlton House Terrace when his American colleague called on him to take over the affairs of the embassy in the afternoon of 4 August 1914. 'He came down in his pajamas — a crazy man. I feared he might literally go mad', Page reported to President Wilson. 'He is of the anti-war party and he had done his best and utterly failed. This interview was one of the most pathetic experiences of my life. The poor man had not slept for nights.' Princess Mechthild Lichnowsky, Page added, had swept the portrait of Kaiser Wilhelm II from her writing table with the cry: 'That is the swine that did this.'[117]

CHAPTER FORTY-TWO

The Supreme War Lord in the First World War

When the Great War broke out in the summer of 1914, the Supreme War Lord cut a sorry figure. An embarrassing and painful ailment caused him increasingly to shun the public gaze (see p. 1130 below), his political influence, so decisive up to that point, declined rapidly, and he came nowhere near to attaining the aim to which he had previously laid claim of directing the conduct of the war in person. Power slipped almost overnight from his hands into those of the generals at Supreme Headquarters. The years 1914 to 1918 witnessed not only Wilhelm's own political and military decline, they also presaged the implosion of the Hohenzollern Monarchy along with that of all the lesser German monarchies in November 1918.[1] Even so, we must be careful not to overstate his powerlessness in these war years. The vital decisions that needed to be taken – the appointment and dismissal of military leaders and top statesmen, the conduct of the war at sea and the unleashing of unrestricted submarine warfare against neutral shipping, for example – still required the monarch's consent, and in this rather passive sense the kingship mechanism continued to operate throughout the war. By dismissing Moltke after the disaster on the Marne, by standing by Falkenhayn in the face of mounting criticism, by resisting the appointment of Hindenburg and Ludendorff until the summer of 1916, and by steadfastly backing Chancellor von Bethmann Hollweg until July 1917, Wilhelm II, closely chaperoned by his three Cabinet chiefs and his Adjutant-General Hans von Plessen, was in practice still determining German policy in a crucial way. To be sure, the role he now played was hesitant and reactive when compared with the hyperactive, often bullying manner in which he had ruled before the war, and for this reason his activities in the 1914–18 period receive less intensive scrutiny in this biography than I have devoted to his life heretofore. His lifestyle and his attitudes in these last four years of his reign are nevertheless of great interest, and readers seeking a fuller account could not do better than to consult Holger Afflerbach's edition of the wartime papers of two of the Supreme War Lord's closest associates, Hans von Plessen and the head of the Military Cabinet, Moriz Freiherr von Lyncker.[2] The following account draws heavily on this meticulous documentation.

JUBILATION IN AUGUST 1914: 'TODAY WE ARE ALL GERMAN BROTHERS'

Ever since the Austrian ultimatum to Serbia on 23 July 1914, large crowds collected daily outside the Kaiser's Schloss in Berlin. The citizens of the capital were traditionally inclined to regard the Brandenburg Gate, the Unter den Linden and the Lustgarten as places of historic significance and to gather around the monarch at such fateful times.[3] Hans von Schoen, Bavaria's deputy envoy in Berlin, observed in late July 1914: 'What distinguishes these demonstrations ... from previous such gatherings is the fact that the crowds are not made up of people from the lower orders but largely from the educated classes.'[4] It was they who cheered Wilhelm on 31 July as he drove from Potsdam to Berlin, and they who greeted his address from the balcony with cheers and patriotic songs.[5]

When mobilisation was announced on the afternoon of 1 August 1914, a large crowd once again gathered outside the Schloss. That evening Wilhelm addressed the masses with another speech: 'I thank you for all the love and loyalty which you have shown me in the past few days. They were grave as never before! If there is to be conflict, all parties will cease to exist! I too have been the object of attack by this party or that. But that was in peacetime. Today I forgive them with all my heart! Now I know no parties or confessions; today we are all German brothers. If our neighbour insists, if he will not allow us to live in peace, then I hope to God that our good German sword will emerge victorious from the fight.'[6] (See Figure 51.) This conciliatory tone had been urged on the Kaiser by Bethmann Hollweg in response to rumours that a number of Social Democratic members of the Reichstag were thinking of refusing to approve the war credits; they were still resentful at the Kaiser's earlier insults, when he had referred to them as 'unpatriotic scoundrels', 'a horde unworthy of calling themselves German' and a 'plague' that ought to be eradicated.[7] This second speech, too, was greeted with joy, as the Kaiserin's lady-in-waiting, Countess Mathilde von Keller, recorded in her diary: 'It was an indescribably moving, wonderful moment, the jubilation, the enthusiasm was overwhelming.'[8]

Figure 51 'Today we are all German brothers.' The Kaiser proclaims the outbreak of
war from the balcony of the Berlin Schloss on 1 August 1914

The unity of the nation was marked even more strikingly at the opening of the Reichstag on 4 August 1914. The Kaiser set the tone when, after reading the speech from the throne,[9] he added a spontaneous declaration of his own: 'You will have read, gentlemen, what I said to My People from the balcony of the Schloss. *I repeat, I no longer know any parties, I only know Germans.* (Wild applause!), and as witnesses to the fact that you are firmly resolved to stand with Me to the death come what may without regard for political, social or religious differences I call upon the party leaders to step forward and pledge this on oath with their hand in Mine.'[10] With these words the Kaiser had caught the national mood at the outbreak of war. The unanimous vote for the war credits by the Reichstag and in particular by the Social Democrats appeared to usher in a new era of national unity which stood in stark contrast to the conflicted pre-war years.[11] The expectation was widespread that the new *Burgfrieden* – the peace within the citadel – would continue for the duration of the war. The behaviour of the crowds in Berlin, their demand to see their Kaiser, was seen as proof of his ability to rally the nation around the throne. 'Suddenly the ideal of national Kaiserdom for which Wilhelm II had always striven appeared to have been realised.'[12] The Kaiser's speeches had enhanced his personal popularity enormously. Even his sternest critics were unstinting in their praise.[13]

It is not without irony that, with the outbreak of hostilities, the Kaiser was able to benefit from his reputation as a man of peace and even from the nationalist slur that he had been '*pacifiste*' and '*timide*'. He now personified the ideal of a monarch who had had war forced upon him. Even critics such as Albert Ballin and the former Chancellor Prince von Bülow, who had some inside knowledge of what had actually taken place behind the scenes in July 1914, were convinced that Wilhelm himself had played at best a marginal role in that crisis.[14] The belief in the Kaiser's desire for peace also helped to ensure the continuing support of the Social Democrats for the government's course when the war dragged on and the call for large-scale annexations grew louder. Thus Arnold Wahnschaffe, Bethmann's right-hand man in the Chancellery, could inform the Chief of the Kaiser's Civil Cabinet, Rudolf von Valentini, in June 1915: 'Several Social Democrats have told me that nothing counteracts the dangerous agitation of their own radicals so successfully as the belief, which is also widespread among Social Democratic workers, in the Kaiser's genuine desire for peace. The view could often be heard that "if the Kaiser had been *able* to avoid the war he would have done so, therefore this war could not be an unjust war of conquest."'[15]

Despite his renewed popularity and the initial support of the entire nation for the war, the Kaiser himself suffered under the burden of responsibility for having led the Reich to war. Outwardly he appeared resolute and confident of victory, as when, on 11 August 1914, for example, he sent the First Regiment of Guards to the front with the cry: 'The sword has been plucked from the scabbard and I shall not be able to sheath it again with honour unless we are victorious. And all of you must and will vouchsafe that I shall be able to dictate the peace to my enemies. Onwards into battle with the foe and down with the enemies of Brandenburg!'[16] Inwardly, however, the Supreme War Lord was racked by doubt. 'So many enemies', he was heard to sigh.[17] Bülow was shocked when he was received by Wilhelm for the first time since his dismissal in 1909. 'I was profoundly shaken when I saw his pale, frightened and I am tempted to say disturbed face. He looked agitated and at the same time exhausted. His eyes flickered restlessly ... He put a friendly arm around my shoulder as in old times and remarked that the "terrible" events of the past two weeks had taken their toll on him physically. On moving to Berlin he had had to spend forty-eight hours in bed. "A little nerves rest cure", he added [in English] with a sad smile.'[18] The monarch seemed 'as if transfixed' when the head of the army's railways department had his audience on 9 August.[19] As he left for the front three days later, the Kaiserin tried to reassure her husband with the words: 'But God will bring you back to me in good health, that is what you must always tell yourself whenever your poor nerves and your poor heart feel so depressed. Then you must always remember that I sense it from afar, [and] even though I cannot be with you, in my prayers I am always close to you and will try to calm you. – Don't take it all so much to heart, my darling, you can face the world with a clear conscience. Your country is fighting calmly for its holiest values and the Lord will show it the way forward ... May God protect you. – Take it easy whenever you can my darling.'[20] Protecting him and trying to prevent the ever-present danger of a total nervous breakdown became the foremost task facing the Kaiser's entourage.

DISASTER ON THE MARNE. THE FAILURE OF THE SCHLIEFFEN–MOLTKE PLAN

On 2 August 1914, the carefully laid plans of the General Staff were set in motion. While a single army took on the defence of the border with Russia, no fewer than seven armies were concentrated on the western frontier with the aim, in accordance with the Schlieffen Plan as modified by Moltke, of scoring a quick and decisive victory over France. The first vital step – the capture of the great fortress of Liège in order to allow the unhindered advance of the German right flank through Belgium – proved to be more difficult and more costly than Moltke had anticipated. Though unaware of the finer details of the situation,

Wilhelm II gave his Chief of General Staff a furious dressing-down on 6 August. Then, just a few hours later, on receiving more encouraging news, he praised him to the skies and elaborated plans for the territory he intended to annex from Belgium.[21] Alarmed by such lability, Plessen gave the order that 'the Kaiser's spirits must be kept up, whatever it takes'.[22]

For as long as the German army continued its seemingly unstoppable advance through Belgium, Luxembourg and northern France, optimism prevailed. On 16 August 1914 Wilhelm moved from Berlin to Supreme Headquarters at Koblenz in order to be closer to the action.[23] On 18 August the right flank of the army began its swing southward with the aim of encircling the entire French force. By early September, less than three weeks after the attack had begun, German troops were within fifty kilometres of Paris and the French government fled to Bordeaux. The mood was ecstatic. Lieutenant-Colonel Gerhard Tappen, Moltke's right-hand man, declared: 'In six weeks this whole thing will be over.'[24] Even the otherwise sceptical head of the Military Cabinet, Moriz von Lyncker, believed victory to be within grasp. 'Unless I'm very much mistaken the main campaign against France will be decided in a matter of days', he noted on 24 August.[25]

Meanwhile on the eastern front the German army was in serious trouble. The Commander of the 8th Army, General von Prittwitz, facing a superior Russian force, contemplated a withdrawal behind the Vistula and thus the abandonment of East Prussia. This news had a devastating effect back at headquarters and particularly on Wilhelm, as Admiral von Müller recorded. 'The Kaiser, who was in a very depressed mood, went for a walk with Lyncker and me in the garden for about 1½ hours. Finally he sat down on a bench and said: "Sit down too." The bench was very short. So we went to fetch another bench. Whereupon the Kaiser said: "So you already despise me so much that no-one wants to sit next to me." This was more than just a figure of speech', Müller noted. 'He really believed himself to be an outcast because his policies had resulted in large parts of his country being overrun by the enemy.'[26] The Austrian representative at German headquarters also had the impression that Wilhelm took the threat to East Prussia personally, feeling it to be 'very painful' and 'a severe insult to his self-esteem'.[27] After his audience with the monarch on 24 August Plessen noted: 'East Prussia, Gumbinnen and Allenstein occupied by the enemy. The Russians are burning and destroying everything! – We must see to it that we finish things off here in the west as quickly as possibly so as to come to the aid of the east.'[28] Moltke's fateful decision to divert two army corps from the west to the eastern front – the troops would be sorely missed in the imminent Battle of the Marne – was motivated at least in part by the mounting desperation at headquarters, however much this was later denied by all those involved, Wilhelm included.[29] In 1922 the ex-Kaiser was to declare that, although the fate of East Prussia had naturally been close to his heart, 'He would never have allowed Himself to be guided in His decisions by other than purely objective considerations. The withdrawal of 2 A[rmy] C[orps] from the French theatre of operations to the east had been recommended to him in an audience on the grounds that these Corps were no longer required in the west.'[30] As is well known, it was the newly appointed Commander of the 8th Army, Paul von Hindenburg, and his Chief of Staff Erich Ludendorff who succeeded at Tannenberg in late August 1914 in halting the Russian advance, thus laying the foundations for the legendary reputation of both.[31]

Just as relief came in the east, so the situation on the western front gave growing cause for concern. On 4 September Moltke was forced to admit that his grand plan to annihilate the French army had failed. 'Let us not delude ourselves. We have had a number of successes but we have not yet been victorious. Victory means destroying the resistance of the enemy. When armies numbering millions of men confront each other, the victor will have taken prisoners. Where are our prisoners? ... The relatively small number of captured enemy guns also shows me that the French have retreated according to plan and in good order. The heaviest task still lies ahead of us.'[32] Two days later the Battle of the Marne began with a counterattack by the French army on the exhausted German troops in their exposed positions. On 8 and 9 September the 1st and 2nd armies were forced to retreat; on 11 September Moltke gave the order for the retreat of the 3rd, 4th and 5th armies as well, with a view to re-establishing a unified front line. The Chief of General Staff feared an enemy breakthrough and took this decision during an inspection of the commanding officers – against the express will of the Kaiser and without his prior consent.[33] The Supreme War Lord responded with indignation. 'H.M. received the report quietly enough, but then thumped the table with his fist and forbad any further withdrawal. – This rather loudly expressed command was unfortunately not designed to make much impression on those present, since we are on the defensive and therefore unable to act without reference to the enemy', as Plessen commented on the Kaiser's outburst.[34]

Moltke, whose health had never been strong – he suffered from a swollen liver and kidney complications – and whose irritability had been causing concern ever since the outbreak of war, now had a nervous breakdown.[35] On 12 September Wilhelm observed to Plessen that the Chief of General Staff 'seemed rather nervous'.[36] Two days later, after the Chief of the Military Cabinet had also voiced his conviction that Moltke had become untenable, a dramatic change was made in Germany's High Command: 'In the evening a great crisis. The Chief of the Military Cabinet Lyncker together with his departmental head Marschall implore H.M. . . . to sack Moltke and to confer on War Minister Falkenhayn the responsibility for the duties of the Chief of the General Staff of the field army. And H.M. agrees without further ado. Moltke is called in together with Falkenhayn. H.M. breaks the news to M[oltke] that he is to go on sick leave due to exhaustion, and that the condition of his nerves will require a prolonged rest − 14 days! Moltke says: "That I will not do! I am not ill. If Y[our] M[ajesty] is dissatisfied with the way I am directing operations, then I shall go!" There ensues a discussion in which Lyncker takes a very aggressive stance. The outcome of the saga is: Moltke stays, [Quartermaster-General] Stein gets an Army corps, Falkenhayn takes on the duties of Quartermaster-General *alongside* those of the War Ministry.'[37] In actual fact, in an All-Highest Cabinet Order of 15 September 1914 Wilhelm II conferred all the responsibilities of the Chief of General Staff on Falkenhayn (see Figure 52), who was however not formally appointed to that office until November. In this way the change at the top of the army command was kept hidden from the public − and indeed from Germany's ally Austria-Hungary[38] − on the grounds that an announcement immediately after the Battle of the Marne would have amounted to an admission of defeat.[39] Naturally his sudden and astonishingly nonchalant dismissal by the monarch who had for decades assured him of his personal friendship came as a bitter blow to Moltke, who, faced with a humiliating situation at headquarters, found it impossible to resist participating in the intrigues that were now spun against Falkenhayn.[40]

Although the appointment had been urged on him by the Military Cabinet,[41] the choice of Falkenhayn as Chief of General Staff was very much the Kaiser's own: Wilhelm had considered him for this post ever since 1912, even before appointing him as Prussian War Minister in 1913.[42] But the new Chief of General Staff was no more successful than his predecessor in achieving a breakthrough on the western front. The short-war illusion was finally shattered in November 1914 with the heavy losses sustained in the attack on the British positions in Flanders. In the west, the advance ground to a halt at trenches stretching from the Channel coast all the way to the Vosges and the Swiss border; in the east, the Russian army proved unexpectedly resilient; and to make matters worse Germany's economy was largely cut off from global markets by the British naval blockade. The Central Powers found themselves facing a war of attrition against a superior coalition of World Powers. Their leaders struggled to find solutions to a situation for which they were quite unprepared. The vital task of coordinating the German war effort and in particular of mediating between the civilian and military leadership fell to Kaiser Wilhelm II as Supreme War Lord.

Figure 52 Erich von Falkenhayn, Moltke's successor as Chief
of the General Staff 1914–16

THE KAISER AND THE ARMY HIGH COMMAND UNDER FALKENHAYN

According to Article 63 of the Reich constitution, with the outbreak of war
Kaiser Wilhelm II had assumed supreme command over the armed forces of
the entire German Reich. In practice, this right had long since been transferred to the Chief of the Great General Staff acting in the monarch's name.[43]
Before the war Wilhelm had often boasted of his military prowess and had, as
we have seen, even 'reassured' those who were aghast at the younger Moltke's
appointment that in the event of war he would be his own Chief of General

Staff.[44] Now, in August 1914, after a fitful attempt to intervene,[45] he was forced to admit that he was not qualified to command an army of millions. As a rule he accepted the operative plans of the General Staff without demur while insisting that at least the appearance of his prerogative be upheld. In June 1915 he complained: 'I hear nothing of the detailed preparations, if I want to know what's going on I have to send my Flügeladjutant to find out … I try to intervene as little as possible, but outwardly Falkenhayn must be sure to preserve the fiction that I direct everything myself.'[46]

It was partly in order to maintain this 'fiction' that the Kaiser and his suite were based − with the exception of occasional state visits and a few sojourns in Berlin − for the duration of the war at Supreme Headquarters in its shifting locations: initially at Koblenz and Luxembourg, then in Charleville-Mézières in the French Ardennes or at Pless in Silesia, later in Bad Kreuznach on the Rhine and finally at Spa in south-eastern Belgium. As the generals remained wary of his interference, the Kaiser was systematically excluded from the decision-making process. The Chief of General Staff reported to him daily on the military situation but his accounts were deliberately manipulative. As Falkenhayn explained to the Bavarian military plenipotentiary in the early days of the war, Wilhelm 'is not given any more information than that provided to the diplomats and courtiers. Chiefly the number of prisoners, cannons etc. … Actually he is now no longer being told what is afoot, but only events that have already taken place and even then only the favourable ones.'[47] Two years later the Austro-Hungarian delegate at Supreme Headquarters, Alois Klepsch-Kloth von Roden, reported that Falkenhayn had 'very few scruples concerning the information that he passes on to H.M.' and was 'not at all choosy' in the methods he used to manipulate the Kaiser.[48] Vice-Admiral Albert Hopman of the Reich Navy Office noted as early as October 1914 that the army had totally sidelined Wilhelm − and recommended that the navy treat him in the same way, since in his view the Kaiser exercised too much influence in naval matters.[49]

Naturally, Wilhelm did not fail to notice his exclusion from decision-making. In November 1914 he complained to Prince Max of Baden: 'The General Staff tells me nothing and never asks for my opinion. If they imagine in Germany that I command the army then they are very much mistaken. I drink tea and saw wood and go for walks, and then from time to time I hear that this or that has been done, just as the gentlemen [the generals] think fit. The only one who is a bit nicer to me is the head of the army railway department who tells me everything he is doing and plans to do.' This comment may have been spoken in jest, but, as the head of the Naval Cabinet observed, it nevertheless reflected 'the tragic truth'.[50] In June 1916 Wilhelm complained to the War Minister General Wild von Hohenborn 'that Falkenhayn keeps the Supreme War Lord too much

in the dark'; he had not known even of the attack on Verdun until he had read of
it in the newspapers. 'If he was of such little use here he might as well go and
live in Germany.'[51] And Plessen noted after speaking to the Kaiser in November
1914: 'H.M. very mauvais humeur! He was being totally sidelined by the Chief
of General Staff, was being told nothing. All he could do was to say "Yes" to
everything, and that he could do just as well from Berlin!'[52] The Adjutant-
General cleverly reassured the monarch with the argument 'that He, the
Supreme War Lord, could not possibly be troubled with details considering
that such an army numbering millions of men was far larger than anything
ever commanded by Alexander the G[reat] or Napoleon I or Wilhelm I. That
was why he had a Chief of General Staff. He was the one who had to deal with
the details and submit only the essentials to him for his decision.'[53] But even
this reassurance, though well-meant, was a distortion of the truth. It would
have been quite unthinkable for the Kaiser, even if he had been kept more fully
informed, to have overridden the plans worked out by the General Staff with all
its expertise and its enormous technical apparatus. In the last analysis the
Supreme War Lord never even attempted to form an independent judgement
on the military situation. His entourage was astonished to observe that the
Kaiser's interest was confined to curious incidents and the odd anecdote.[54] Not
once throughout the entire course of the war did he ask how many of his own
people had been killed or wounded.[55]

   Even if we allow for the well-meant misinformation fed him by his
generals and his own inexcusable head-in-the-sand lifestyle, the superficiality
of the Supreme War Lord's understanding of the realities of the war was
shocking. The staff officer of the IX reserve corps noted after a visit from the
monarch: 'His Majesty looked well, he was gracious [but] spoke largely
in platitudes. What he said about the war is best passed over in silence.
Exc[ellency] v[on] Boehn [the Commanding General], who is otherwise so
very loyal to the monarch, turned as white as a sheet. Does His Majesty
realise, one wonders, what is at stake in this war − for him personally too, for
the sceptre and the crown, and for the Hohenzollerns as a whole?!'[56] To an
officer whose troops had just managed to repulse a fierce French attack with
severe losses the monarch gave the completely inappropriate advice: 'Issue the
order to fix bayonets and drive the bastards back again.'[57] Many gained the
impression that the Kaiser had only the vaguest notion of conditions at
the front, and his authority within the army declined dramatically.[58] The
fact that Prince Heinrich (as Commander of the naval forces in the Baltic
Sea) and Crown Prince Wilhelm (as Commander of the 5th Army) also held
important military positions even though their competence was very much in
question further contributed to the collapse of the Hohenzollern dynasty's

military reputation, as did the undeserved promotion of the Kaiser's other sons to high rank and in some cases to cosy sinecures.[59]

If the Kaiser was nevertheless able to exercise a certain, and by no means insignificant, influence on the strategic conduct of the war at least in the early years, this was because his right — in conjunction with his Military Cabinet — to appoint men of his choosing to the most important positions of command remained intact despite attempts by the statesmen, the military and even members of his own family to gain influence over him. From Falkenhayn's appointment as Moltke's successor in 1914 to his dismissal in August 1916, the Chief of General Staff remained a highly controversial figure. The army resented both his lack of seniority — at 53 Falkenhayn was younger than any of the commanding generals — and his lack of experience within the General Staff.[60] His arrogance had made him numerous enemies. 'Ninety-nine per cent of all the officers are against Falkenhayn', one observer commented in 1915.[61] Criticism of his leadership rose to fever pitch after the bloody failure of the campaigns in Flanders in 1914 and at Verdun in 1916, yet he was given little credit for the successes of 1915 — the occupation of Russian Poland after the breakthrough at Gorlice-Tárnow and the conquest of Serbia.[62] Bethmann Hollweg, too, was critical of the Chief of General Staff, in part because he shared the doubts over Falkenhayn's military capabilities, but in part also because he saw in him a rival with ambitions to become Chancellor himself.

On top of all this came Falkenhayn's never-ending conflict with the legendary heroes on the eastern front, Hindenburg and Ludendorff, who vehemently accused him of withholding reinforcements with which they believed a decisive victory over the Russian army could be achieved. In the face of their demands that priority be given to their front in order to knock Russia out of the war first, Falkenhayn persisted in concentrating on the western front in the not unreasonable belief that, given the endless expanse of Russia, a decisive blow against the Tsarist Empire was beyond reach. This rancorous dispute compelled Wilhelm II to play the thankless role of arbiter, which — thanks in large part to his entourage — he managed with considerable success.[63]

The high regard in which Falkenhayn was held by the Kaiser was based not least on a liking for him personally: his panache, his boundless energy and capacity for work, and the eloquence of his oral reports. 'The army hasn't yet got to know General v. Falkenhayn', the monarch responded to his critics. 'He is a wholly exceptional general. When the army commanders come to me to make their report, he shows that he is far better informed on the situation in the trenches of each individual Army than they are themselves.'[64] Moreover, Falkenhayn knew both how to play to Wilhelm's sense of self-importance and to preserve the trappings of the Supreme War Lord's overall power of command.[65]

Wilhelm and Falkenhayn also held basically the same view of the military situation Germany was facing: both of them (the Kaiser albeit not always consistently) regarded the long-term prospects of the Central Powers in a pessimistic light, saw little chance of a decisive breakthrough and hoped for a resolution of the conflict in particular through a separate peace with Russia.[66]

On the other hand, it is also evident that Wilhelm's determination to retain Falkenhayn was motivated by his wish to safeguard his own position as Supreme War Lord. The opponents of the Chief of General Staff were demanding that he be replaced by Hindenburg and Ludendorff, whose reputation for military genius had become boundless ever since the battles of Tannenberg and the Masurian Lakes in September 1914 and February 1915 respectively.[67] Not without reason, as events were to show, the Kaiser feared that an Army High Command under the immensely popular duo of Hindenburg and Ludendorff, whom, once appointed, he would be unable to dismiss, would overshadow him and deprive him of the last remnants of authority. 'The Kaiser is said to be furious at the suggestion that he should take the popular mood in Berlin into account. That would be tantamount to his abdication, and Hindenburg would thereby take his place as a tribune of the people', noted the Chief of the Naval Cabinet in July 1916.[68] Ludendorff was in any event detested by the monarch, who referred to him as 'an odious character devoured by personal ambition'.[69]

For the best part of two years Wilhelm remained steadfast in his support of Falkenhayn in the face of savage criticism, on the one hand from Hindenburg, Ludendorff and Moltke — who did not scruple to mobilise the Crown Prince and the Kaiserin against him — and on the other hand from a number of influential figures including Crown Prince Rupprecht of Bavaria, some of Germany's federal princes and Bethmann Hollweg. The Kaiser was encouraged in his stance by the Military Cabinet, whose Chief, Moriz Freiherr von Lyncker, and departmental head, Ulrich Freiherr von Marschall, shared the monarch's high regard for the embattled General. Lyncker exclaimed in admiration in December 1915: 'F[alkenhayn] is a damned energetic and clever chap. His nerves are made of steel, as perhaps too is his heart. At any rate he has an excellent and absolutely steady overview of the task facing him. When one recalls that our troops are on the North Sea and the Black Sea, at the gates of Saloniki, in the Tirol, at Riga and in Flanders, and our officers as far away as Mesopotamia and Persia!'[70] Furthermore, safeguarding the Kaiser's prerogative of appointing men of his own choice against outside interference continued to be one of the main responsibilities of all three of his secret Cabinets. Falkenhayn's ability 'to deal with' the Kaiser provided the Military Cabinet with one more argument for keeping him in charge. For this reason alone they held the Chief of General Staff to be irreplaceable.[71]

It was not until the crisis of 1916 that the Kaiser's support for Falkenhayn began to waver. The first blow was the unsuccessful attack on Verdun which had begun in late February of that year. Falkenhayn's bloodthirsty aim in attacking the symbolic and strategically vital fortress of Verdun was later described by Wilhelm in the following terms: 'We were trying to establish a position from which we could rain down death on Verdun, a position which would enable us to inflict maximum losses on the French when they counter-attacked, as they were bound to do.'[72] However, the German attack was halted before the heights on the eastern banks of the Meuse, essential to the bombardment of the city, were taken. Falkenhayn nevertheless continued the attack well into August 1916 in the forlorn hope that the losses inflicted on the French would prove unacceptable.[73] Instead, when the battle finally ended in November 1916 with the German troops being forced back into their original positions, the imperial army on the Meuse had itself suffered no fewer than 337,000 casualties.

To make matters worse, in June 1916 the Russian army achieved a surprising breakthrough in Galicia, inflicting huge losses on the Austro-Hungarian forces. For a time it seemed as if Germany's ally would be overrun. Falkenhayn's opponents – and in particular Bethmann Hollweg, who had lost all faith in the Chief of General Staff after the mass slaughter at Verdun – used the crisis to force upon the Kaiser the extension of Hindenburg's powers of command to include almost the entire eastern front.[74] Wilhelm only agreed to this highly contentious reorganisation of the command structure when the Austro-Hungarian situation became so desperate that his worst fears of a separate peace between the Danube Monarchy and Russia seemed imminent. His influence then proved decisive in breaking the resistance of Conrad von Hötzendorf, the Austrian Chief of General Staff, to such an extension of Hindenburg's powers.[75]

In the crisis into which the German war effort was thrown by the concerted attacks of the Triple Entente on all fronts in the summer of 1916 – in late June the massive Anglo-French assault began on the Somme – Wilhelm was implored on all sides to throw Falkenhayn to the wolves. With Hindenburg as Chief of General Staff, the argument ran, the Kaiser would if necessary be able to accept 'bad' peace terms; otherwise not only the monarch himself but also the entire dynasty would be blamed for the disastrous outcome of the war and be swept away.[76] In the course of July and August 1916 the signs increased that the Kaiser and the Military Cabinet were preparing to abandon Falkenhayn. Even so, as late as 24 August 1916 the monarch proclaimed his total trust in the General, assuring him: 'We will stay together to the end of the war.'[77]

Falkenhayn's fate was sealed when Romania declared war on Austria-Hungary on 27 August 1916. To the last the Kaiser had felt certain that his Hohenzollern cousin Ferdinand would preserve the neutrality of his Balkan kingdom.[78] News of Romania's entry into the war on the side of the Entente reached Wilhelm that evening as he was playing cards with his Cabinet chiefs and it devastated him: the collapse of Austria-Hungary and hence the defeat of Germany seemed to be at hand. Müller noted that the Kaiser appeared to lose all hope. 'Let there be peace – everything else was of no interest to him. By any reckoning a sad evening.'[79] Lyncker , the Chief of the Military Cabinet and Falkenhayn's last supporter in the Kaiser's entourage, now came under immense pressure, not least from Plessen and Valentini, and was forced to accept that the Chief of General Staff had become untenable.[80] On the following morning he advised a tearful Wilhelm to drop Falkenhayn and appoint Hindenburg in his place.[81] On 29 August 1916, the 'third Supreme Army Command" with Hindenburg as Chief of General Staff and Ludendorff as First Quartermaster-General took over responsibility for the conduct of the war (see Figure 53).

Falkenhayn's replacement by the Hindenburg–Ludendorff duo amounted, as Gerhard Ritter has observed, to a 'political turning point of the first order'.[82] With the appointment of the two legendary and practically unsackable generals, the Kaiser slipped even further into the background, not only in military matters but on the home front as well. It is true that Falkenhayn had also tried to exercise some political influence over Wilhelm, but by and large he had respected the formal separation between the military and the civilian spheres. In particular he had accepted as 'unassailable' the monarch's right to arbitrate in his conflicts with the statesmen, admitting that 'after all he could not tender his resignation' to get his way.[83] Hindenburg and Ludendorff had no compunction in intervening in politics. They were even prepared to invade the innermost sanctum of the Kaiser's prerogative – his right to appoint and dismiss men of his own choosing. Simply by threatening to resign the irreplaceable pair were able to exercise immense leverage both against the civilian statesmen and the monarch himself.

THE SUPREME WAR LORD AND DECISION-MAKING IN THE FIRST WORLD WAR

The constitutional right of military command enjoyed by the German Kaiser and King of Prussia – his *Kommandogewalt* – had a downside which revealed itself starkly during the First World War: the absence of any institutional link between the civilian and military spheres. The supposedly 'responsible'

Figure 53 The transfer of power to Supreme Army Command: the Kaiser with
Hindenburg, Bethmann Hollweg, King Ludwig III of Bavaria and Ludendorff

Reich Chancellor had no direct say in the military prosecution of the war.
Theoretically, the Herculean task of coordinating the entire war effort of the
German Reich therefore fell to the monarch. It was obvious to all that no one
person could possibly have shouldered such a burden. But Wilhelm II appears
not even to have understood the nature of the problem.[84]

Germany's strategy was decided by Supreme Headquarters – the *Grosses
Hauptquartier* – which encompassed, apart from the Kaiser and his immediate
suite, the General Staff, the head of the Admiralty Staff, parts of the Prussian
War Ministry and the three secret Cabinets, representatives of the Reich
Chancellor, the Foreign Office and the Reich Navy Office and also the military
plenipotentiaries of Germany's allies and of the three non-Prussian German
kingdoms Bavaria, Saxony and Württemberg.[85] Numbering some 5,000 men,

Supreme Headquarters thus had the potential to become the nucleus of coordinated decision-making in wartime. In reality, however, its functionality was impaired by several flaws. For one thing the Chancellor was based in Berlin and visited Headquarters only when his presence there was required. Most of the Reich offices and Prussian ministries likewise remained wholly or partly in the capital. Moreover, whenever Supreme Headquarters was transferred from one front to another, as was frequently the case, some of its departments were initially left behind. Such dislocation and the long distances between the various centres were hardly conducive to coherent policy formulation. A bad situation was made worse by the fact that the rivalries between the various departments and the mutual suspicion between the civilian and the military authorities that had bedevilled decision-making before 1914 continued unchecked throughout the war.[86] In the overwhelmingly martial atmosphere of Headquarters, representatives of the Reich government and other civilians were frequently treated with disdain and deliberately misinformed.[87] Wilhelm II, in his own estimation quite the front-line warrior, 'liked to take the soldier's part against that of the diplomat', as indeed he had done all his life.[88] Karl Georg von Treutler, the Foreign Office's representative, observed in the very first days of the war that the Supreme War Lord greeted the fact that 'the centre of gravity for everything was now shifting to the General Staff' with undisguised satisfaction.[89] Members of the government complained of 'the difficult mentality of the Kaiser', who saw threats everywhere to his jealously guarded prerogative of military command.[90] 'In wartime politics must keep its mouth shut until strategy permits it to speak again', was the Supreme War Lord's watchword.[91] Any objection raised by a civilian was prone to be condemned by him as a scandalous 'interference in the military conduct of the war'.[92] Matters were made worse by the fact that − especially after the dismissal of Treutler in the summer of 1916 − no diplomat of any standing was attached to Headquarters.

In these circumstances the three Cabinet chiefs who controlled access to the monarch were able to exercise an even greater influence than before the war. Right-wing agitators complained that Rudolf von Valentini, as head of the Civil Cabinet, and Georg von Müller, Chief of the Naval Cabinet, were shutting the Kaiser away behind a 'Great Wall of China'. Certainly − we shall come back to this point in a moment − efforts were made to keep bad news from the excitable monarch, but this was hardly the work of the two heavily criticised Cabinet chiefs. Quite the reverse: it was their loyal support for Bethmann Hollweg that alone ensured that the civilian statesmen continued to have access to, and thus a degree of influence upon, the Kaiser in a situation that structurally and psychologically favoured the military, and it was precisely this channel open to the 'responsible' statesmen to which the reactionary and nationalist critics so vehemently objected. The Cabinet chiefs were determined to uphold the monarch's right to have the final say precisely because they recognised that the conflicts between the political and military spheres were systemic rather than personal, and that the growing power of the generals, however justified by the war, also held grave dangers.[93]

If Wilhelm was effectively sidelined in military decisions, in domestic matters he was completely out of touch. As the war dragged on and complaints about his isolation grew louder, his Cabinet chiefs urged him to spend more time in Berlin. In September 1916 Müller proposed that the monarch and his entourage be moved permanently to the capital, arguing: 'The bad mood in the country is naturally directed in the first instance against the Chancellor as the personification of the government ... This makes it all the more important that the Chancellor is backed up by a well-informed, that is to say a not one-sidedly informed, Kaiser who shares the trials and tribulations of the people. But this can only be achieved if as a matter of course the Kaiser lives in Berlin.'[94] Such a view was, however, at odds with the traditional Hohenzollern notion of the Supreme War Lord as Commander of the armed forces tenaciously upheld by the Kaiser's military entourage and above all by his Adjutant-General, Hans von Plessen. The Kaiser himself, clearly more at home in the martial atmosphere at Headquarters than in Berlin, was in any case reluctant to travel to the capital, where he would have to confront the intractable problems on the home front. As the head of the Military Cabinet noted in June 1917: 'The idea of going to Berlin has come to nothing. Once again he [Wilhelm II] doesn't want to go; is afraid of unpleasant confrontations ... It would be such a good thing if the newspapers were once again able to report that he had conferred in Berlin with the Chancellor and spoken to this or that individual.'[95] Müller's diaries similarly record the evident distaste the Kaiser felt for the capital. 'During the evening promenade Valentini made an ill-starred attempt to get His Majesty to agree to a brief stopover in Berlin on the forthcoming trip to Vienna. The suggestion was rudely rejected and I was accused of having "forced" His Majesty to go to Berlin twice already. "And what good did it do me! He wouldn't dream of going to that ... again." When I replied that surely His Majesty's visit to Berlin had been received with much gratitude, all he said was: "Not a soul is grateful to me."'[96] Even in the severe crisis of July 1917 which was to lead to Bethmann Hollweg's dismissal the entourage had the greatest difficulty in getting Wilhelm to agree to spend some time in the capital.[97] He had his own way of demonstrating his displeasure over such 'forced' visits to Berlin. Müller recorded: '9 o'clock in the morning arrival in Berlin. That is to say one hour

later than originally planned. The Kaiser insisted on first taking breakfast and
a bath in Schloss Bellevue. The conferences with the Reich Chancellor,
Helfferich, Count Rödern and Batocki were therefore limited to a brief
three-quarters of an hour and consisted – as Valentini told me – of the Kaiser
chatting about the harvest in Pless, about the progeny of the zebu bull in
Cadinen and about the instructions he had given to Hindenburg. The gentlemen were quite appalled at such a complete lack of earnestness.'[98] As the
Kaiser also insisted on departing on schedule at 11 o'clock, this particular visit
to Berlin lasted no more than two hours.[99]

The monarch's almost total self-isolation led the administrative departments more and more to take decisions without his prior approval.[100] Though
Wilhelm had delegated some of the more routine matters to the Prussian
Ministry of State at the outbreak of hostilities,[101] he had nevertheless been
able to exercise a degree of influence, on the one hand through his control over
appointments and on the other through his right to arbitrate whenever there
was a dispute. Such differences were usually resolved in an improvised 'Crown
council' in which both sides were able to present their point of view. But
even this rather passive exercise of imperial authority often seemed to be
beyond Wilhelm. Müller complained that 'His Majesty is unable to keep such
discussions on an objective track.'[102] In March 1916 Lyncker wrote of the
crucially important conflict over unrestricted U-boat warfare: 'The matter
must be decided now and in fact by the parties involved in the dispute. The
Kaiser must not be burdened with this decision. It is too much for him.'[103]
Increasingly Wilhelm made clear his dislike of being confronted with difficult
decisions and complained of the strain involved in such meetings.[104] Wavering
uncertainly between one view and the other he tended to prevaricate. Sometimes the 'Crown council' meetings ended without any formal decision, more
often than not with a superficial patch-up of no lasting value. A typical
example of such irresolution is provided by the dispute over U-boat warfare
in March 1915 in which the Kaiser first adopted Bethmann's position, then on
the following day allowed himself to be persuaded of the opposite course by
Falkenhayn before finally deciding, after hearing both of them, to postpone a
decision altogether.[105] Such vacillation only served to poison the atmosphere
among the conflicting parties, since frequently the defeated side refused to
accept the Kaiser's decision as final and banked on his notorious mood swings
to attain a different outcome.[106] The confusion was made worse by the
existence of numerous rival authorities, in particular within the naval command, all with direct access to the Kaiser.

As Germany's lack of success on the battlefield came to be blamed by many
on Wilhelm's indecisiveness, plots were hatched to force him to abdicate in

favour of a regency, the accession of the Crown Prince or a military dictatorship. In April 1915 Admiral von Tirpitz approached the Kaiser's personal
physician to sound him out on whether he would be prepared to declare
Wilhelm II unfit to rule.[107] All such plans came to nothing, however, in part
because the monarchical principle was still inviolate, especially within
Wilhelm's immediate entourage, but in part also because with the Kaiser's
growing (self-)exclusion from power the problem solved itself. But the fact
that his abdication was being discussed at all was a worrying indication of
how far the esteem of both the monarch and the monarchy had sunk even
within the officer corps.[108]

`VERY BUSY DOING NOTHING': THE KAISER AT WAR

Though members of his entourage were at pains to stress how frustrating the
Kaiser 'with his lively temperament' found it to be kept in safety a hundred
or so kilometres from the front, the Supreme War Lord soon settled into a
daily routine seemingly untouched by the dramatic world-historical events
that were unfolding (see Figure 54).[109] On 19 August 1914 the head of the
Civil Cabinet wrote to his wife from Koblenz: 'We eat in the Garden Park,
the first breakfast at 8–9 without the Kaiser, who doesn't get up till later and
then breakfasts with his adjutants at 10. At lunch and in the evening he eats
with all of us, about 25 people altogether … At 12 o'clock midday H.M.
drives to the General Staff and then we hear this or that from him, but
usually only things which you too will later read in the newspapers … If
we have something to report to the Kaiser, as I did today, we go back to the
palace garden where one is sure to find him. There are always some people
with the Kaiser … Naturally the conversation is not an easy thing as
everything morose has to be avoided … Supper is at 7.30 and afterwards
there are cigars on the palace terrace … Everyone leaves at 9.30 and goes to
bed quite tired … There is no talk whatever of visits to the front, in the
afternoons the Kaiser usually goes for a drive in the Westerwald, yesterday
he was in Nassau and Ems. He then goes for a walk in the woods with the
adj[utants].'[110] This routine − the report of the General Staff at noon, all
other government matters dealt with at no fixed time, often during a
promenade in the park, the afternoons taken up with excursions, long
evenings dominated by imperial monologues or spent playing cards with
the entourage − changed little throughout the war.[111] As the Bavarian envoy
Count Lerchenfeld recorded: 'From all I hear the Kaiser continues to be very
busy doing nothing and has thereby in a sense excluded himself' from
playing any part in affairs.[112]

Figure 54 The unicorn in winter: 'Our Kaiser in the field'

Wilhelm's suite complained of his frequent mood swings. 'One moment despondent: The war would never be over. The next the loud-mouthed boast: He was as hard as steel, they [his enemies] would all have to kneel down before him.'[113] Whenever there was a crisis his closest advisers feared he would suffer a nervous breakdown, and not without reason: in December 1914 after the sinking of the German cruiser squadron in the Battle of the Falkland Islands, for example, and again in September 1918 he took to his bed for several days and was 'completely overcome by apathy, much as in November

1908 after the Bülow Affair'.[114] In the autumn of 1916 Lyncker noted with concern that Wilhelm had 'for some time now once again been terribly excited to the point of breaking down'; one had to ask oneself 'whether his nerves will stand the strain'.[115] When the newly appointed papal nuncio, Eugenio Pacelli, the later Pope Pius XII, visited the Kaiser in Bad Kreuznach in June 1917 he was alarmed to find him 'exalted' and seemingly 'unbalanced', and wondered whether this condition was the result of the strain of three years of war, or whether the monarch had always been like that by nature.[116]

In his more ecstatic moods the Kaiser would retell bloodcurdling martial anecdotes, ridicule his enemies or grossly exaggerate Germany's victories, crediting these to himself or to his son the Crown Prince. After a visit from King Ludwig III of Bavaria, Valentini recorded: 'We are relieved that the meeting is over. As ever it was a most unfortunate event on account of our "All-Highest's" unbelievable behaviour. But the old King is reported to have said: "Well, we know what he's like, don't we!" This is a bad business ... about which it's best to keep quiet. But it is hard to put up with this awful boasting and this overweening arrogance which is already implicit in the myth now being peddled that the real author of the victory is our Crown Prince. True, his Army fought bravely and twice repulsed the determined attack of the French. But to credit him alone with our success is to go much too far. I pray that God will not punish us for such arrogance.'[117] The Kaiser's entourage, and especially those of its members who had sons in the field or relatives who had fallen in battle, were deeply pained by such bombast.

Wilhelm was by no means alone in his vulgar racist contempt for Germany's enemies and on occasions for her allies. The letters of his entourage, too, are peppered with references to 'disgusting Japs', 'filthy Cossacks', 'ghastly Walloons', 'detestable Austrians' and 'dirty Americans'.[118] A General Staff officer who was later to serve as the Kaiser's Flügeladjutant wrote of the British army: 'On our operational maps we have marked the position of these animals in yellow, since that is the colour of the shit the vultures leave on the rocks in the zoo and therefore suits them best.'[119] But the All-Highest's railing against his enemies often took on a murderous tone.[120] He may have bewailed the destruction of churches and libraries by German troops on their advance through Belgium, but he had no compunction in justifying the atrocious reprisals on Belgian civilians as a deterrent to sniper fire.[121] Outraged that the people of Alsace were unafraid to show their sympathy for the French, Wilhelm directed that they be 'ruthlessly strung up and shot dead, with no exceptions made for priests or parliamentarians!'[122] After the Battle of Tannenberg in September 1914 he proposed that the 90,000 Russian prisoners of war should be left to perish on the Kurische Nehrung, a barren spit of sand in the Baltic Sea. It was left to Falkenhayn to protest 'in suitable form' against such barbarism.[123] The entourage realised that such bloodthirsty outbursts were not always meant literally, of course. Lyncker thought they were essentially 'panic attacks', but 'at the same time he secretly entertains hopes of peace which are then always dashed again. And this exhausts him, and his fear then surfaces in the form of monstrous bragging. It is often unbearable to hear him trying to delude himself.'[124]

    The Supreme War Lord's alarming mood swings also had another cause which remained hidden even from his immediate entourage. For some years before the outbreak of war Wilhelm had suffered from an ailment which inhibited his mobility, made riding increasingly difficult and gave reason for grave concern. During the last holiday in Corfu in spring 1914 Admiral von Müller complained of the monotony of life at the Achilleion; not even the walks which the Kaiser had previously enjoyed could now be taken by him. 'Apparently his knee, which has often given him trouble in the past, is playing up again. But one daren't discuss it. Emperors must not have any imperfections.'[125] The true cause of the Kaiser's disability was not clinically diagnosed until three years later. When Müller arrived at Schloss Bellevue on 16 February 1917 for his routine audience, he was informed that 'H.M. will not be receiving "any reports at all" this week. What was the trouble? H.M. is said to have had a furuncle removed from his leg and the Kaiserin is watching over him like a Cerberus to ensure that nobody comes near him.'[126] The Kaiser had in fact had an operation not on his leg but on his scrotum, which had in the course of the years swollen to an alarming size, measuring 32 centimetres in circumference and 19 centimetres in length. On that 15 February 1917 the monarch's personal physician, Dr Otto von Niedner, succeeded in removing three spermatoceles each the size of a hen's egg together with a hydrocele of similar dimension from the imperial testicles. The doctors concluded that these sacs full of semen or water had been caused not, as previously assumed, by a riding accident, but were − like his lame arm, the torticollis and the problem with his ears − the belated consequences of the trauma he had suffered at birth.[127]

    Altogether, there was little sign in Kaiser Wilhelm II in wartime of that freshness of youth that had been such a 'powerful talisman' at the beginning of his reign a quarter of a century earlier.[128] One of his generals was disturbed to note in November 1914 that the monarch's face had changed, had become longer and redder, and that his hair − now grey − was worn too long.[129] A visitor to Supreme Headquarters in the first months of the war reported: 'The Kaiser looked exhausted and not at all well . . . His hair is now quite grey and the oedema on his forehead has grown larger still.'[130] It is unclear why exactly the Kaiser should have been suffering, as was frequently the case, from 'oedema', 'furuncles' and 'swellings' on his forehead and neck. But it is not without interest that his sister Charlotte, who was tormented all her life by variegate porphyria, similarly suffered, among other painful symptoms of that dominant genetic disorder, from watery blisters on the skin. Evidently assuming that her brother had inherited the same disease, Charlotte wrote to her physician Professor Schweninger that Wilhelm was treating his oedema in 'a stupid and completely mistaken' fashion.[131]

LOSING TOUCH WITH THE NATION

When the Kaiser left Headquarters, it was usually to show himself to the troops on the front. These visits were always carefully staged – the Austro-Hungarian delegate was reminded of 'Potemkin villages'[132] – but they gave the Supreme War Lord little sense of the conditions in the trenches. Naturally he had to be kept out of harm's way and so his visits tended to be confined to the relatively safe area well behind the front line. The inspections and parades put on for his benefit had all the hallmarks of the carefree times before the war, 'with music etc. just as at Tempelhof'.[133] As someone who accompanied Wilhelm to the eastern front in February 1915 noted: 'I found the totally unwarlike character of the arrangements embarrassing, and I gained the impression more and more that these so-called front visits, which go nowhere near to the front, only serve to cause resentment among the troops, who have to endure long marches and parade drill when the Kaiser puts in an appearance.'[134] The entourage acknowledged that these visits were largely pointless, but they went along with Plessen's arrangements if only because they had a welcome effect on the War Lord's frayed nerves. As Lyncker told his family: 'This afternoon we are once again going to the front; though there is really no point. Rather it is for the Kaiser's benefit, as he finds it very hard to put up with this tense inactivity and uncertainty' back at Headquarters.[135]

Always concerned that Wilhelm's fragile nerves would not stand the strain, his suite did what they could to distract or entertain him, closing their eyes to his thoughtless disregard for the feelings of his hosts, as for example when he shot deer or felled trees on the Silesian estate of Prince Pless.[136] His retinue was relieved whenever a guest arrived who could shoulder the burden of conversation, urging the visitor to 'talk away as much as possible'.[137] As a rule the entourage, and Plessen in particular, sought to keep bad news from the psychologically unstable monarch or at least to break it to him gently and at a carefully chosen moment.[138] And Wilhelm himself encouraged the habit, skilfully avoiding unwelcome topics and at times punishing the bearer of bad news by turning his back.

The patience of the long-suffering men around the Kaiser had its limits. They drew the line when his own behaviour threatened to damage the carefully cultivated public image of the monarch as the heroic Supreme War Lord. In May 1917 the head of the Military Cabinet was outraged when Wilhelm, instead of returning to Headquarters, chose to visit an art exhibition in Frankfurt instead. 'I made it clear to him in no uncertain terms what his responsibilities were towards his starving and long-suffering people. There was a massive row between us which ended with his running out of the room, shouting in fury and violently slamming the door loudly behind him . . . But unfortunately that's the way it is: His own comfort and his own amusement always come first. I live in fear that one day we shall have to pay for this. Already there is widespread grumbling about the Kaiser; the way he leads his life at times like these is no secret. Surely one has to stop him from cutting himself off more and more and becoming an irrelevancy. He doesn't even sense this decline himself and that is quite dreadful.'[139] Shortly after this incident Admiral von Müller made it 'quite plain' to the Kaiser's brother Prince Heinrich 'how out of place all of us felt we were here in Homburg and that the Kaiser had no right to take off such "Weekends". In this terrible war which called for such heavy sacrifices from the people the Kaiser must live for his duty alone. Our stay in Kreuznach too was nothing but a leisurely pastime. No one should imagine that the people don't realise these things. The Kaiser should be far more active, e.g. visiting munitions factories etc. The future position of the Kaiser in peacetime will depend on the Kaiser's behaviour during the war. The Prince listened to me like a good boy. Then in the afternoon he went for the usual drive with the Kaiser along the Rhine valley.'[140] The head of the Civil Cabinet also bewailed the 'peacetime and holiday atmosphere' at court. 'The Kaiser discusses temple construction (at the fountain), designs officers' rest homes, goes for drives and excavates at the Saalburg as if we were perfectly at peace and the fighting out there had nothing whatever to do with him.'[141] The entourage was shocked by the ever more frequent visits paid by the Kaiserin to Headquarters. Though Wilhelm clearly welcomed her company, it was all too obvious that her visits gave the lie to the image of the Supreme War Lord as the soldier-king sharing the harsh conditions of his troops. 'The entire hero legend is fading fast!' Valentini noted with alarm.[142] Yet Wilhelm convinced himself that he was loyally fulfilling his duty. Congratulating his youngest son Prince Joachim on his marriage in March 1916 he justified his absence from the wedding with the boast: 'The entire nation has taken up arms and is fighting, dying and suffering in defence of its holy soil, its liberty and all it holds sacred against a world of vile enemy scoundrels. In this struggle I belong in their midst in order to share all the hardship with my brave comrades and also to experience all that is uplifting and joyful.'[143]

The Kaiser's closest advisers were dismayed at how little understanding of the desperate plight of the nation he showed, at how he continued to put his hobbies, his hunting trips and drives through the countryside first, even declaring at one point that deciphering the Hittite language would prove to be of greater historical significance than the entire war.[144] Lyncker's opinion of Wilhelm II could hardly have been more dismissive: 'Unhappily the truth is that he excludes himself from many things and puts his own comfort before everything else. He has always done so, even before the war. He is simply very weak, and strong only in standing up for his own personal interests, especially in pursuit of a comfortable lifestyle with as little interruption as possible. This is unfortunately all too apparent.'[145] The Kaiser's 'war experience' thus had no deep or lasting effect on his character. It is shocking to read of the Supreme War Lord's habit of cancelling important conferences with members of the government because they clashed with the walks he was due to take with his Flügeladjutanten.[146]

The decline in his own standing as well as in that of the monarchy as an institution was evident not just to his entourage and to monarchists in general but on rare occasions even to the Kaiser himself.[147] In July 1916 Wilhelm noted with alarm that 'there was nothing about him in the papers'.[148] In 1915 a Berlin publisher proposed that, since the Kaiser had faded so much from public view, the Civil Cabinet should commission a pamphlet on the 'daily life and thoughts' of the monarch in wartime.[149] Such a book did eventually see the light of day in 1916 under the title *Der Kaiser im Felde*, but all it did was to reveal the pointlessness of his life at Headquarters: its 450 pages listed his travels, inspections, the visits of royal dignitaries and his stereotyped addresses to the troops.[150] The volume was intended primarily as an inspiration to the soldiers fighting in the trenches, but it can hardly have made much of an impression. The sporadic efforts undertaken by the imperial retinue to remind the soldiers and the hard-pressed people at home of the Kaiser's existence were no more effective. After the German success in the Battle of the Dobrudja in September 1916, for example, the Flügeladjutant Friedrich Mewes suggested calling attention to the role played by Wilhelm II in securing the victory. 'Publishing the news in the form of a telegram from the Kaiser to the Kaiserin is something I arranged last night. This is the traditional form in which the people out there were told of our victories, as in 1870/71. In this personal way the Kaiser's person is given somewhat more prominence, and that is only to be desired in the interest of the monarchy. The Kaiser and Ludendorff readily accepted my suggestion.'[151] But instead of the hoped-for propaganda coup Wilhelm's 'Dobrudša-Telegram' proved to be a public relations disaster because it was interpreted as an attempt to divert attention from the bloodletting simultaneously taking place on the Somme.[152] Furthermore, his seclusion at Supreme Headquarters and the censorship of all information about him helped to feed the wild stories circulating about his mental state. In the summer of 1916 it was rumoured, for example, that Wilhelm II was about to abdicate in favour of the Crown Prince 'because his temperament was too soft for the war'.[153] According to another story doing the rounds, the Emperor was in the throes of a religious fervour, spending hours on his knees praying for victory.[154] From 1917 the army's 'patriotic education' programme attempted to raise the monarch's public profile, but with little success.[155] By this time demands for his abdication were being submitted to the Military Cabinet.[156] Just as Admiral von Müller, General von Lyncker and Rudolf von Valentini had predicted, Wilhelm II's shallow self-indulgent lifestyle in wartime had served to pave the way for the revolution of November 1918.

CHAPTER FORTY-THREE

The Kaiser's war aims

Nothing demonstrates Kaiser Wilhelm's failure to grasp the implications of the mass slaughter taking place all around him better than the fact that, despite his fury at the 'betrayal' of his crowned cousins Nicky and Georgie, he held fast to the belief that a settlement, when it came, must be reached through agreement from monarch to monarch. This anachronistic conviction came vividly to light in conversations he had with the American ambassador James Gerard in late 1915, after the war had been raging for eighteen months. As Colonel House noted, 'the Kaiser talked of peace and how it should be made and by whom, declaring that "I and my cousins, George and Nicholas, will make peace when the time comes." Gerard says to hear him talk one would think that the German, English, and Russian peoples were so many pawns on a chessboard. He made it clear that mere democracies like France and the United States could never take part in such a conference. His whole attitude was that war was a royal sport, to be indulged in by hereditary monarchs and concluded at their will.' House asked the ambassador whether the Kaiser 'was crazy or whether he was merely posing'.[1] Admiral von Müller also records the Kaiser's view that the peace negotiations must be conducted not by elected representatives of the people but by the crowned heads involved in the conflict. 'A clever middleman should propose a meeting of the three emperors of Germany, Austria and Russia and the Sultan on the basis that the monarchs are after all responsible to God for the terrible sacrifices that their peoples have had to make, and that the pointless bloodletting must surely now be brought to an end through an agreement between the monarchs. In the other countries a conscienceless lawyer class without any sense of responsibility to God is at the helm.'[2]

THE 'GENERAL AIM OF THE WAR'

What would Wilhelm's terms have been, had he been able to dictate them? Surprisingly little is known in detail of the aims he pursued in the first two years of the war; not until 1917, after the collapse of Tsarism, did he write down what he regarded as an appropriate settlement for Germany in the event of victory. He seems not to have had sight of Bethmann Hollweg's infamous 1914 'September Programme' with its breathtaking list of demands for the subjugation of Europe 'for all time'. While he had moments of despair, at one point shocking his entourage by saying that if Germany were to lose the war this would have to be accepted 'as the will of Providence',[3] the Supreme War Lord naturally thirsted for conquest over France and Russia and was determined to overcome Great Britain and her 'perfidious' balance-of-power policy. If his input into the detailed plans being worked out by the statesmen and the military for outright annexations and more informal control over the Reich's neighbours was sporadic, this should not lead us to conclude that he was anything but passionately interested in those deliberations. His steadfast support of his Chancellor against all his rivals to the Left and Right is evidence in itself that he fully shared Bethmann's war aims.

One reason for the Kaiser's apparent reluctance to involve himself in detailed war aims planning was Bethmann Hollweg's insistence that, both to allay suspicions of German intentions abroad and to preserve social cohesion at home, the monarch must keep a low profile on such a contentious issue.[4] Bethmann implored the Kaiser to distance himself from the annexationist hotheads who believed Germany could and should 'revise the map of Europe at will'.[5] The carefully judged statement issued in the Kaiser's name on 31 July 1915 on the first anniversary of the outbreak of war was therefore largely defensive in tone, and even though it hinted euphemistically that the eventual peace settlement would have to guarantee Germany 'the necessary military, political and economic security for the future and fulfil the conditions for the unrestricted development of our productive forces at home and on the open seas', it was welcomed by moderates as proof that Wilhelm was 'by no means wildly annexationistic'.[6] But as we shall see, Wilhelm's real views – and those of his family and entourage – differed markedly from the public declarations he made on the Chancellor's advice.

The fact is that no one at Headquarters, and least of all the Supreme War Lord, was prepared to return to the status quo *ante bellum*. In 1917, when his exhausted ally Austria-Hungary pressed for a peace without annexations, the Kaiser declared that that was 'quite impossible' and totally 'out of the question ... That is something I cannot ask my Army and People to accept.'[7]

When Prince Lichnowsky — who made no secret of his conviction that his own government had wanted the war and was vilified in turn for having failed to keep Britain out of the conflict[8] — urged Count August zu Eulenburg to eschew annexations in Europe and settle for the Congo and a financial indemnity instead, the veteran Minister of the Royal Household replied that it would be quite unacceptable to reach a settlement without 'an improvement of our strategic frontiers in the east and the west'. No party except possibly the Social Democrats would agree to a peace that did not include at least a part of Poland and a part of Belgium. Were the Kaiser to propose such terms, Eulenburg warned, his position would quickly become untenable.[9]

With such views, August Eulenburg was very much a moderate in the imperial entourage. His fiery colleague Baron Hugo von Reischach, who had attended the Kaiser's mother when she was Crown Princess and was now the reigning monarch's Oberhofmarschall, longed to be posted to the front. Along with most others at Wilhelm's court, Reischach castigated the 'stupid policies' of Prince von Bülow, who as Reich Chancellor had twice failed — first when Britain was preoccupied in South Africa and then again when Russia was fighting the Japanese — to 'fall upon France' and seize Belgium. Reischach did, however, caution against provoking America, adding ominously that it would be for the next generation of Germans to fight that particular struggle. In contrast to Bülow, Reischach wrote, his successor, Bethmann Hollweg, was a 'true Prussian' with a clear head, a steadfast character and a heart of gold.[10]

In spite of major differences over precisely how it might be achieved, the consensus at Headquarters, fully shared by Wilhelm II, was that the Reich must fight on until domination over the continent had been reached — the 'general aim', as Bethmann euphemistically put it in his 'September Programme', of ensuring 'security for the German Reich in west and east for all imaginable time'.[11] In March 1915 the Danish diplomat Hans Niels Andersen came first to Berlin and then, accompanied by Bethmann, to Supreme Headquarters at Charleville to speak to Kaiser Wilhelm on behalf of the King of Denmark in the hope of initiating a peace process. It quickly emerged that neither the Chancellor nor the Kaiser was remotely prepared to accept a return to the status quo before the war. The former insisted that Germany had not entered the war 'for the conquest of new land, nor for the extension of her frontiers, but for the attainment of a lasting peace for her development, and that a peace that did not secure her these factors would never be accepted by Germany'. But Bethmann went on to emphasise that, 'even if the war had been commenced solely for attainment of the big aims already mentioned, events had developed in such a way that the German nation would not be content with a peace that brought Germany no compensation, or an important economical position in Belgium'. Referring bitterly both to Edward VII's 'designs of isolating Germany' and to the failure of the Haldane negotiations in 1912, he argued that the root cause of the war had been Britain's refusal to accept Germany's rightful demand for a greater say in world affairs. London, he complained, had shown nothing but 'contempt for Germany and lack of understanding of the demands of 70 million people of a calibre like the Germans'. Britain had been unwilling 'to grant Germany the place in the world she was entitled to as a result of the ethical position of the German people and for their industry and progress'. When Andersen spoke to the Kaiser at Charleville on 19 March 1915, Wilhelm used extremely undiplomatic language when referring to the Tsar and King George. In line with Bethmann's advice he blamed Edward VII and Sir Edward Grey for trying to isolate Germany 'to keep her down, & in this way hamper her peaceful world development'. King Edward, he claimed, 'had treated Germany with great arrogance and contempt'. He, the Kaiser, had loved England so dearly that he had incurred the mockery of his own countrymen, but 'his feelings for England had been trampled upon'. Now Germany was militarily and financially strong, her army was deep into France and French soil was undergoing economic Germanisation 'to assist in the future supplies of the German people and the German armies'. It must be clearly understood, Wilhelm declared, that the peace to come would need to be a lasting peace, 'concluded on a dignified basis for the German people and in harmony with the sacrifices made by them. This comprised Great Britain admitting German equality and not to regard her as an inferior partner ... who had to enquire first in Great Britain if, and when, Germany might build ships.'[12]

Freed from the constraints imposed on him in his dealings with the neutral Danish mediator, on his visit to Vienna a few months later the Kaiser spoke 'like a firework' of his plans for Europe when victory was his. As the Austro-Hungarian Foreign Minister, Count Stephan Burián von Rajecz, recorded in his diary on 29 November 1915, Wilhelm said his goal was 'Germany's greatness'. 'After the war', the monarch told him, 'he was going to carry out all his plans for reform without any consideration for the will of the parties. A central European association [would be] invincible because of its economic cohesion ... He would never ally with England. He sees revolution coming in Russia, in France he predicts a terminal decline. He wants to put an end to the English "balance of power" and, on a smaller scale, to that in the Balkans, with Bulgaria becoming dominant ... He thinks Serbia must be destroyed, and Montenegro put under *our* [i.e. Austrian] dominion etc.'[13] When in January 1918 the Austro-Hungarian diplomat and future Foreign Minister Count Gyula Andrássy offered to arbitrate as an 'honest broker' between

Germany and Britain with a view to securing 'a new European balance of power', the Kaiser flared up angrily: 'Thanks very much! don't need one! We'll get there under our own steam! with the sword! Heaven save us from this!' He opined that Andrássy needed to spend some time in a sanatorium, adding in English: 'There is a tile off this man's roof!'[14] As these tirades demonstrate, the Kaiser's vision for peace not only presupposed a complete military victory over France and Russia and thus domination over the continent; it would have provided the German Reich with an unassailable launch-pad for further expansion over the oceans and would for this reason alone never have been acceptable to Britain and the wider international community. Wilhelm seems to have been unaware of the contradiction between his own grand hegemonial designs and his repeated assertions that it was the Entente Powers who had engineered the war.

BELGIUM AND FRANCE: GERMANY'S WAR AIMS IN THE WEST

The consensus on the 'general aim' of the war can thus readily be seen as a continuation of German pre-war policies by other means: either through outright victory on the battlefield or by the offer of tempting terms in order to achieve a (temporary!) separate peace, one or other of the links in the chain of encirclement that had formed around Germany to contain her burgeoning power had to be broken, so enabling her to defeat the others and take her rightful place as a global superpower. When it came to determining the Reich's war aims in detail, however, the Kaiser was presented with conflicting advice, much of which had a surreal quality so long as victory over at least one of the Reich's enemies remained elusive. The notorious 'September Programme' drafted by Bethmann Hollweg and his assistant Kurt Riezler in expectation of a lightning victory over France in 1914 contained detailed plans for the reorganisation of western Europe: the annexation from France of the iron-ore field of Longwy-Briey and the strategically vital western slopes of the Vosges with the fortress of Belfort; the imposition of a war indemnity on France so large that she would for all time cease to be a Great Power; and the exclusion of British goods from the French market. Belgium was to be reduced to a German vassal state, with Liège and Verviers annexed to Prussia, other parts of south-eastern Belgium attached to Luxembourg, which would then become a German federal state and a German corridor through to the port of Antwerp. French Flanders, with the Channel ports of Dunkirk, Calais and Boulogne, was to be added to the new German-controlled rump Belgium. After victory in the west, the whole of continental Europe was to be brought under German economic domination under a central European association, to be supplemented by a continuous central African empire stretching from coast to coast. Except for a hint that 'Russia must be thrust back as far as possible from Germany's eastern frontier and her domination over the non-Russian vassal peoples broken', together with a vague reference to 'Poland', the precise aims to be pursued in eastern Europe were left open in Bethmann's memorandum of 9 September 1914.[15]

At the same time, Bethmann Hollweg's predecessor and rival, Bülow, developed even more precise plans for the German domination of western Europe and proposed the annexation of Russia's Baltic provinces, but he warned against the establishment of a Polish state in any shape or form. Going well beyond Bethmann's September Programme Bülow suggested that at the conference table Germany should demand 'Antwerp (Dunkirk, Boulogne, Calais), Flanders (both Belgian & French), the old Belgian-Dutch fortification barrier: (Lunéville, Toul, Verdun), Montmédy, Charleville, Maubeuge, Lille – the line of the River Maas [Meuse], essential on military-strategic grounds, since we will not be able to break through at Liège-Namur a second time. The minette field of Briey. The Belgian-French coal fields. With that F[rance], which does not have any other ore or coal . . . would be finished economically.' In the east, Bülow urged, the Reich should annex Russia's 'Baltic provinces & their hinterland (Suwalki, Kowno, Wilna)' but avoid creating a Polish satellite state, since 'a resurrected Poland would become the natural ally of F[rance], England, Austria, Italy, of everyone except us'. An Austria freed from the Russian threat would gravitate towards the western Powers, Bülow warned, and the attachment of Poland to her, as some were proposing, would only increase this tendency as well as strengthening clericalism within the Danube Monarchy.[16] At the Kaiser's court there was nothing but contempt for Bülow and his proposals, which, as August Eulenburg made clear, would have entailed a separate peace with Russia à tout prix, that is to say the abandonment of all Germany's plans with regard to Poland. 'His Majesty is firmly opposed to all these machinations, thank God', the Minister of the Royal Household commented. Wilhelm would never agree to the reappointment of Bülow as Chancellor, not only because he could never forgive him for his betrayal in the Daily Telegraph crisis of 1908, but also because he fully shared Bethmann's aim of creating a Polish satellite state.[17]

Bülow's former right-hand man at the Chancellery, Friedrich Wilhelm von Loebell, now the Prussian Minister of the Interior, was even more cautious with regard to annexations in eastern Europe, recognising that the expansionist expectations being raised by nationalist agitators could become a grave danger to the monarchy if they proved to be unobtainable, which he feared they would be. Loebell pointed out that victory in war could not be the end of

Germany's struggle for greatness but only a halfway point towards that goal, and that serious consideration had to be given to international relations after the war. His preference was to continue Germany's pre-war expansionism overseas, both in Asia and in central Africa, where he demanded a German Empire stretching from the South Atlantic to the Indian Ocean. Such a policy would be directed primarily against the western Powers and in particular against Britain, which in his view would always remain the Reich's chief rival. For the continuing contest with Britain, Germany would need to strengthen her military and economic position in the west by acquiring better harbours and an extensive North Sea coastline with unhindered access to the world's oceans and to her own expanded colonial Empire. Belgium should therefore be partitioned, with parts going to France, Luxembourg and Holland, but the central segment, though notionally 'autonomous', must be militarily and economically under German control – Britain, Loebell warned, would never accept the *outright* annexation of Belgium by Germany. In Europe, he urged, the main thrust of the war effort should be aimed against France, the historical enemy, from whom the Reich also had the most to gain. Germany's western borders should be amended to give her 'the key to France'; the French coal and ore deposits should be annexed; and France forced to pay an indemnity large enough to prevent her from ever again playing any role to thwart German interests. In the east, however, the only annexations Germany should demand were those designed to strengthen the frontier of East Prussia. Like Bülow, Loebell warned passionately against the restitution of Poland in any form. Germany, he believed, had no basic quarrel with Russia and should at all cost avoid causing the Tsarist Empire lasting resentment, since Russia would be Germany's most useful ally in her future global contest with the British Empire. Rather than being given control over Poland, Austria-Hungary should seek expansion in the Balkans and the Mediterranean, just as Germany's other main ally Turkey should be rewarded with gains in the Caucasus and Persia.[18]

Whereas the Kaiser and Bethmann aimed at expansion in both western and eastern Europe, and Bülow and Loebell wanted to spare Russia, seeing in France and Belgium the main prize of a victorious war, Hindenburg and Ludendorff were at this early stage surprisingly restrained in their aims on both fronts. On 1 April 1915 Ludendorff complained to the disgraced Chief of General Staff Helmuth von Moltke of the 'grossly exaggerated demands' being considered in Berlin, listing his own war aims as 'Liège together with a border strip and the Congo state, financial indemnity, the ore field of Briey, here in the east only minor border corrections. Austria will have to forfeit Lemberg [Lvov/Lviv] ... receiving compensation in Poland.'[19] A few weeks later he repeated: 'It is probably too early to think of the prize [to be demanded] when peace comes. In my dreams I see Liège, the French coal field, Belfort and the polit[ical] dependency of Belgium. In the east we must acquire some farm-land, not too much, but the eastern army must be satisfied.'[20]

The incorporation of Belgium with the ports of Antwerp, Zeebrugge and Ostend along with the coast of French Flanders from Dunkirk and Calais down to Boulogne was thus the primary German war aim in the west, common to all the proposals being put forward. Even Albert Ballin, bitter critic though he was of Bethmann's reckless policy in July 1914, insisted that Belgium must be brought into economic dependency on Germany, since otherwise it would 'become a glacis for the English'.[21] Wilhelm II, who had demanded the annexation of Belgium from the very beginning,[22] had a direct, if bizarre, input into Bethmann's plans for Belgium and northern France. On sending his programme from Supreme Headquarters to Clemens von Delbrück, the Secretary of State for the Interior, on 9 September 1914, the Chancellor confided that he had been under pressure from the Kaiser for some time to pursue a policy of what would today be termed ethnic cleansing in Belgium and northern France. 'His Majesty the Kaiser keeps harping on the idea that those territories which might be annexed from Belgium and France should be evacuated and settled by military colonies in the form of land grants to deserving non-commissioned officers and men. I cannot deny', the Reich Chancellor went on, 'that this idea has much to commend it, even though in practice it will be very difficult to implement. All the same we should consider whether we cannot find a formula by means of which we could impose such an expropriation to a certain extent upon the defeated state in the preliminary peace treaty.'[23]

When Antwerp fell on 9 October 1914, the Kaiser made a speech in which he insisted that the city must remain German – his 'diplomats would be strung up if they failed to ensure this'.[24] Throughout the war, Wilhelm demanded that Belgium, if it could not be annexed outright, must in practice become a German satellite state. In February 1915, after Bethmann had played on his resentment against Catholics,[25] the Kaiser declared that he would not dream of retaining the entire country; he intended 'only' to demand the Belgian fortresses and the coast, along with Antwerp.[26] After a visit to Ostend, Zeebrugge and Bruges in October of that year he said: 'I shall never give this up again, that I promise you!'[27] Bethmann murmured that 'since his last visit to Flanders' the Kaiser had 'once again become greedy for Belgium'.[28] When his spurious peace offer of December 1916 met with rejection by the Entente powers, Wilhelm reacted with defiance, informing the Wilhelm-strasse 'that there could be no more talk now of a compromise with France and Belgium. After turning down our offer for the third time, King Albert would never be allowed to return to Belgium, the coast of Flanders must be ours.'[29] As late as March 1918 he scribbled: 'No more mercy, they [the Belgians] must be partitioned.'[30]

Wilhelm also gave his full support to the demands of the Imperial Navy to use Ostend, Zeebrugge and Antwerp as U-boat bases and urged his admirals to prepare these ports for an invasion of England in a future war.[31] In response to the Vatican's peace initiative of 1917, Wilhelm seemed briefly to be prepared to give up his claims to Belgium, the *conditio sine qua non* of any meaningful negotiations with Britain.[32] Believing a general settlement to be within reach, he told the newly appointed Foreign Secretary Richard von Kühlmann in triumph: 'Well, Kühlmann, now you have a free hand, now show us what you're made of and secure us peace by Christmas.'[33] Not least because the German reply to the papal note made no reference whatever to the future of Belgium, Kühlmann's feelers met with a frosty response from London and Paris, and the Holy See's initiative came to nothing. But the episode nevertheless sheds a stark light both on Wilhelm's ambitions and the pressure he was under from the annexationists and navalists at home.

As if to prove the truism that we often appreciate the value of something when we think we are about to lose it, the Kaiser, facing the possibility of having to abandon his cherished western war aim in order to reach a settlement with Britain, wrote to the new Reich Chancellor, Georg Michaelis, in September 1917: 'By giving up the coast of Flanders my Navy is losing the aim for which it is fighting and gaining *nothing* in return, thus returning to the *Status quo ante!* People will say "*Skagerrak* [i.e. the Battle of Jutland] *was fought for nothing!*" and a very angry mood will seize hold of the already somewhat disgruntled officers and men in the Fleet. Tirpitz, Reventlow etc. will seize the opportunity to attack us with all the means at their disposal, so creating a situation for Your Exc[ellency] at home which could prove very awkward for the negotiations . . . The matter is so *serious* for me *personally* in my relationship with my Navy that I shall not be able to face the officer corps of the Navy ever again *without an equivalent* compensation for the abandonment of Flanders; since I am too *committed* in this question in favour of *retention* . . . If I *give up all* these things in order not to jeopardise the peace which *may* be attainable, then I am doing so for my *people*; but in respect of my milit[ary] institutions and the probable Milit[ary] future of my country I will be in a painful position from which Your Exc[ellency] must help me to extricate myself . . . In the eyes of the *Navy* and the *Hanseatic towns* this abandonment [of the coast of Belgium] will mean – and rightly so – *defeat* at the hands of England, and that will be the theme which Tirpitz with all his skill and cunning will use in his new "movement" to set the people and the

Fleet against us. It will be extremely awkward and dangerous for Your Exc[ellency] and my government and must not be underestimated. *He* was supposed to be and wanted to be Chancellor, and everyone who has taken his place is his sworn enemy. Should he come to hear of the abandonment of the coast which *he* has armed and fortified for us in such a masterly fashion, he will raise such a storm in the German lands as to make the July Days and Bethmann's fall seem like child's play. All this can therefore only be prevented by Your Exc[ellency] if very weighty *equivalences* and *compensations* are proposed which everyone can readily appreciate. I beg you once again urgently not to underestimate the mood of the officer corps of My Navy – which still contains many closet Tirpitzians – and to take My very difficult position with respect to them into account.'[34]

THE EASTERN AIMS: POLAND AND THE BALTIC LANDS

If the Kaiser's pet plan of colonising Flanders with German veterans came to nothing, another initiative of his was to have momentous consequences for the future of Europe. On 31 July 1914, immediately after issuing the fateful order to mobilise, he summoned the German–Polish magnate Count Bogdan von Hutten-Czapski and proposed – as he had in the early 1890s[35] – that Russian Poland be revolutionised. 'It is My decision', he declared, 'if God grants us victory, to re-establish an independent Polish state'.[36] Within days Hutten-Czapski was able to report to the Kaiser that his initiative had been received with jubilation by the Polish clergy in Posen. 'Bishop Dr. Likowski is deeply grateful for Your Majesty's remarks which I have conveyed to him! He will immediately promulgate a pastoral letter pointing out that it is the duty of every Catholic to fight against Russia with all available means . . . This step is most significant for the mood in Russian Poland, where the pastoral letter could be distributed by our troops as they advance.'[37]

Implementing the Kaiser's idea proved more difficult than anticipated. Neither he nor his top advisers could decide on the form a future Polish state should take. In September 1915 the monarch accepted the plan put forward by the Wilhelmstrasse of annexing a Polish 'border strip' and the Russian Baltic provinces to Germany, but handing over control of the new Poland to Austria-Hungary on condition that the Dual Monarchy integrated itself more closely in economic, political and military terms with the Reich. But when these plans ran into difficulties and both the Chancellor and the generals reverted to the idea of attaching all of Poland to Germany, the Kaiser, in the course of a general discussion of 'the annexations and reorganisation in the East', agreed that 'the whole of Poland must stay with Germany'.[38]

After a visit to Warsaw in mid February 1916, the Kaiser again turned his mind to the Polish question, now venting his anger at Austria's demands for control over that country. In a meeting with Hutten-Czapski in Potsdam on 13 June 1916 he outlined his plans in detail: Poland would be a 'completely independent state with close links to Germany'; treaties would secure for Germany a controlling influence over Poland's foreign policy and the Kaiser would personally assume supreme military command over her army; the Polish railways would be integrated with those of Prussia and there would be trade agreements giving Poland access to the sea through Danzig and other German ports. The creation of a Polish state closely linked to Germany had been his unswerving aim since before the war, the Kaiser declared, and he was more determined than ever to put his plan into effect.[39] The imperial proclamation of a Polish kingdom on 5 November 1916 was therefore very much Kaiser Wilhelm's brainchild.[40]

In the early years, several attempts were made to inveigle the Tsar into abandoning his two western Entente partners, but when hopes of reaching a separate peace with Nicholas II were dashed in late 1915,[41] Kaiser Wilhelm reverted to the original annexationist ambitions in the east by declaring 'that the enemy which with God's help must be weakened most completely and most extensively is *Russia*'.[42] Referring to the Baltic provinces of the Tsarist Empire he demanded: 'The Russian must be thrown out of the ancient German lands. He must no longer be allowed to keep a fleet in the Baltic Sea!'[43] With victory over Romania in November 1916, Wilhelm believed his goal of domination over the European continent to be within grasp. In euphoric mood he predicted that revolution would now break out in Moscow and St Petersburg, that England was facing starvation and France was down to her last man. 'Whoever is now still a pessimist should have his ears boxed', he announced. 'You would have thought our enemies were lying prostrate on the ground and we could simply dictate our peace terms', the German ambassador in Vienna, Count Botho von Wedel, sighed.[44] After visiting Romania in September 1917 and marvelling at her fertile plains and rich oil deposits Wilhelm saw himself in control of this country too, with unhindered access to the Black Sea and beyond.[45]

THE 'WRONG WAR'? THE KAISER AND THE 'SECOND PUNIC WAR' AGAINST BRITAIN

The international order which Kaiser Wilhelm II and his Reich had sought to revolutionise since the turn of the century was underpinned by the sea power of Great Britain and her Empire and, increasingly as the twentieth century unfolded, that of the United States of America. Britain's own territory may not have been the object of German war aims, but it would be quite mistaken to see her decision to stand by her Entente partners France and Russia in 1914 as opting for 'the wrong war', as has been suggested.[46] On the contrary, the overthrow of the balance of power in Europe and the domination of the continent by Imperial Germany amounted to a direct threat to Britain's security and her position in the wider world. With the Channel ports from Antwerp to Boulogne in German hands, German veterans settled along the Flemish coast, France reduced to an economic and military satrapy of the Reich, the entire continent from the Atlantic to the Black Sea, from the Gulf of Bothnia to Malta, united economically in a German-dominated Mitteleuropa, with a belt of annexations and satellite states stretching from Finland, Estonia, Latvia and Lithuania in the north to the Ukraine and beyond in the south, with the Baghdad railway threatening Egypt and the Gulf, German warships based in Brest and Bordeaux, in Madeira, the Azores and the Cape Verde Islands, and the entire Congo along with Togo, the Cameroons, East and South-West Africa in German hands, Great Britain would have sunk to the status of a minor offshore island at the mercy of the Imperial High Seas Fleet and the U-boats, which would have enjoyed unhindered access to the world's oceans.

The ineluctable interconnection between the bloody struggle taking place on the continent and the Anglo-German conflict at sea was clear to all. It was because her entry into the war made Germany's victory over France and Russia so much more uncertain that England became Germany's 'most hated enemy' overnight.[47] Indeed, for many in powerful positions in the Reich – the Crown Prince, the Kaiser's brother Heinrich, Field Marshal Colmar Freiherr von der Goltz and Grand Admiral von Tirpitz, to name but a few – the First World War was first and foremost a war against Britain, the conflict on the continent no more than a prelude to that larger, more decisive struggle still to come. In Goltz's eyes the entire war would be lost if Germany were to be victorious on land but fail to destroy British power in the world. In his letters to his father the Crown Prince – 'Little Willy', as he was derisively nicknamed in England – continued his relentless attacks on Bethmann Hollweg and Jagow as the men who had failed to prevent the entry of Britain and her allies into the war and who were even now hesitating to drop bombs on London.[48] On 6 October 1914, the younger Wilhelm vented his fury against the British, writing to the Kaiser that it was perfidious Albion that had 'set the Japanese and half-wild Indian hordes at our throats . . . The ultimate aim of the current war', he thundered, 'is the crushing of England, victory over France and Russia is only a means to that end. Anyone who has scruples or resists pursuing this aim with *all* the methods at our disposal is sinning against the Monarchy and our people, who desire nothing more ardently than the attainment of this goal.'[49] In February 1915 the heir presumptive to the Hohenzollern throne urged Grand Duke Ernst Ludwig of Hesse-Darmstadt to persuade his brother-in-law Tsar Nicholas to sign a separate peace so that German troops could be brought back from the eastern front to defeat France in the west. 'This alliance between Russia and France is altogether too ridiculous' and merely served to promote England's interests, he opined.[50] Congratulating his father on his fifty-sixth birthday in January 1916, the Crown Prince, in line with the ideas of Tirpitz, urged on him the signing of a separate peace with Russia and Japan in order to pre-empt the domination of the world by the English-speaking peoples.[51] He warned his father against any peace feelers that might be put out by Britain and America, as these would merely be attempts by Jewish high finance to cheat Germany out of the just rewards of her imminent victory.[52] For Prince Heinrich, too, the main aim of the war was to break out of the constraints of the European balance-of-power system underpinned by Great Britain. 'England has become our hereditary enemy!' the Kaiser's brother cried shortly after the outbreak of war, echoing a sentiment that was widely held. 'May the outcome of this war bring England her just punishment!'[53]

Kaiser Wilhelm may have outraged Tirpitz when, on 6 August 1914, he refused to allow the High Seas Fleet to engage with the Royal Navy in the North Sea; for the first three years of the war he may have accepted Bethmann Hollweg's advice and constrained the U-boats in their attacks on neutral commercial shipping for fear of bringing the USA into the war, but there is no doubting his bitter fury at Britain's decision to stand by her Entente partners. As Lichnowsky and several others at Headquarters informed the journalist Theodor Wolff: 'The Kaiser's rage is directed entirely against England, he is quite set on attempting a landing over there ... even though most of the military are against it.'[54] The bombing of London, Liverpool, Cambridge and other cities by Zeppelin airships which began in February 1916 received his full approval,[55] as had the sinking of the *Lusitania* in May 1915.[56] 'Those English brutes must sue for peace!' he insisted in May 1917. 'Until they do so we must continue to thrash them and shoot them and fight them with our U-boats! They must be made to swallow our terms!'[57]

As we have seen on many occasions in this biography, one of Wilhelm's favourite ideas throughout his reign had been the revolutionisation of the entire Islamic world against the empires of Russia, France and particularly Britain. On hearing of the latter's declaration of war on 4 August 1914 the Kaiser railed against 'this hated, lying, conscienceless nation of shop-keepers' with its 'pharisaical hypocrisy' of maintaining the balance of power in Europe, which was nothing more than 'playing the card of all the European nations in England's favour against us!' And he demanded that, 'if we are to be bled to death, England shall at least lose India'.[58] Ten days later he ordered: 'H.M. the Sultan must call on the Mussulmen in Asia, India, Egypt, Africa to fight the holy war for the caliphate.'[59] Four days later again, when reports of Turkey's probable entry into the war on the side of the Central Powers reached Supreme Headquarters, the Kaiser greeted this news with jubilation 'because now perhaps the entire world of Islam could go against England'.[60]

Destroying Britain's global power was so central to the Kaiser's overall war aim that with time he came to accept that this goal might have to be achieved in a 'Second Punic War' to be fought at a later date, after victory over France and Russia had been secured. His reasoning, as he put it in a vehement letter to Bethmann Hollweg's successor, Georg Michaelis, in September 1917, went as follows: 'I know England and the English better than my countrymen do, certainly better than my officials and the For[eign] Office! If Y[ou]r Exc[ellency]'s predecessors in office had only listened to my suggestions and followed my advice instead of pursuing their continental political theories and ignoring what I told them, our treatment of these brutes would have been a different one and much would have turned out differently too! What Y[ou]r Exc[ellency] *needs to understand* is this: England is our bitter sworn *rival* full of hatred and envy and as such it speculated that it would surely win this contest; if it loses, its hatred will only grow deeper still; and the struggle will *continue mercilessly after the peace*, economically . . . England has *not won* the First Punic War and − God willing − has therefore *lost* it; but we have *not defeated* it either and don't seem to be able to do so for the moment. Therefore the Second Punic War − hopefully under better conditions as far as our allies and prospects are concerned − must now be absolutely and *immediately* prepared for. *Because it is definitely coming.* Until one of the two of us has come out on top *alone* there will be no peace in the world! *Great Britain* will never accept a *condominium*; therefore it must be thrown out. It's the same situation we faced in '66 with Austria; which was the precondition for '70! . . . That's the way it is with England in the world. In order to *crush it* properly it is imperative that the necessary milit[ary] and *naval* preconditions are put in place now in the peace settlement.'[61] And this was no isolated incident: Wilhelm was so obsessed with the idea that victory in Europe would merely be the prelude to a second war against Britain that he trumpeted such ravings to his ministers, diplomats and parliamentarians for months on end. It was not only the Social Democrat leaders Friedrich Ebert and Philipp Scheidemann who recoiled in horror when the monarch, in 'a hail of words', told members of the Reichstag in July 1917: 'When HE has defeated all the others, HE will start a second Punic War and finish off England.'[62]

To Kaiser Wilhelm II the Anglo-German conflict was not simply a power struggle between two empires, one in decline and the other on the threshold of world-historical grandeur, but also a profoundly religious fight between good and evil, monarchy and democracy. When Ludendorff's great offensive began in the spring of 1918, Wilhelm declared that when the English or French came to sue for peace, they would first have to go down on their knees before the imperial standard, 'for this will be a victory of monarchy over democracy'.[63] In January 1917 he proclaimed in a letter to Houston Stewart Chamberlain: 'The war is a struggle between 2 *Weltanschauungen*: the Teutonic-German for morality, right, loyalty and faith, genuine humanity, truth and real freedom, against the Anglo-Saxon [*Weltanschauung*], the worship of mammon, the power of money, pleasure, land-hunger, lies, betrayal, deceit and . . . treacherous assassination! These two *Weltanschauungen* cannot be "reconciled" or "tolerate" one another, one must be *victorious*, the other *go under*!' The war, he asserted, was a German 'crusade against *evil* − Satan − in the world, prosecuted by us as *tools* of the Lord . . . We, the *warriors of God* will fight until . . . the *foes of the Kingdom of God* lie in the dust!, whose coming into the world would be rendered completely impossible by the Anglo-Saxon Weltanschauung, but which will be assisted by our victory! God wants this struggle, we are his tools, He will direct it, we need not worry about the outcome, we will suffer, fight and be victorious under His Sign! Then we shall have . . . the *German* peace, God's peace, in which the entire liberated world will breathe a sigh of relief! Without congresses and lawyers' fine speeches, solely by virtue of the victory of the Germans! Therefore forwards with God!'[64] The German *Volk*, Wilhelm declared in June 1918 on the thirtieth anniversary of his accession to the throne, was now 'the chosen people'; 'the Jews, who used to be, are [the chosen people] no longer'.[65]

THE KAISER'S LAST CARD: THE U-BOAT CAMPAIGN AND AMERICA'S ENTRY INTO THE WAR

If the Supreme War Lord was forced to accept that he possessed neither the ability nor the authority to direct the operations of an army numbering millions, this was not the case with regard to the war at sea. He rejected outright the demand of Grand Admiral von Tirpitz that a 'Supreme Command' be set up for the fleet, declaring: 'I reserve the right of supreme command to myself and do not wish anyone to come between me and the Navy.'[66] In January 1915 he was again reported as saying that 'the direction of operations of the army was in good hands and was no burden to him (the Kaiser) in any way, commanding the little navy was therefore something that he could quite easily undertake himself.'[67] For once such boasting was not empty rhetoric. The Kaiser was indeed able to exercise a considerable, if not always consistent, influence on the deployment of his hobby horse the Imperial Navy.[68] That responsibility brought with it a number of agonising dilemmas, however.

Prior to the outbreak of hostilities, Wilhelm II had ordered that, if the circumstances seemed propitious, the entire battlefleet should sail out to engage the enemy in the North Sea. In August 1914, however, much to Tirpitz's chagrin, he held the fleet back until such time as the numerically superior Royal Navy had been sufficiently weakened through mine warfare and submarine raids to give Germany at least a chance of victory. In this the monarch was following the advice of Bethmann Hollweg, who at that stage still hoped to use the battlefleet as a bargaining counter at the peace conference. The loss of several ships in skirmishes near Heligoland in late August 1914 and on the Dogger Bank in January 1915 confirmed Wilhelm in his determination to hold the fleet back. Its Commander, Admiral von Ingenohl, was ordered to undertake no sorties without the Kaiser's express approval.[69] The proponents of offensive action may have scoffed that Wilhelm was simply afraid of losing his favourite 'toy',[70] but their efforts to restore some freedom of action to the Commander of the High Seas Fleet and to permit forays further into the North Sea were firmly resisted. As ever, Tirpitz's problem was that he was unable to say how he intended to force the enemy into making the error of abandoning its wide blockade and engaging in a pitched battle.[71] In March 1915 the Kaiser decreed 'he didn't wish to see any more memoranda. He had ordered the Fleet to stay at home and that was that.'[72] Hugo von Pohl, whom Wilhelm appointed Commander of the High Seas Fleet after the battle on the Dogger Bank, eventually got him to agree that engagements with the enemy might be risked so long as they took place in a zone from which the German ships could reach the safety of their port within one day.[73] Of course the stranglehold of the British blockade, which cut Germany off from overseas markets, could not be broken by such tactics.

The most effective answer to that blockade was to counter-blockade the British Isles with U-boats, a tactic which had proved remarkably successful in the early months of the war. Deploying submarines against merchant vessels was not without its grave dangers, however. Once they surfaced the U-boats were an easy prey to enemy warships. Submarine warfare was therefore almost suicidal without breaching international law which called for merchant vessels to be searched and for their passengers and crew to be disembarked before the ships were sunk. In February 1915 Pohl managed to persuade Wilhelm – even though the issue was still being hotly debated by the civilian statesmen, the General Staff and the naval authorities[74] – to declare the waters around the British Isles a war zone within which enemy merchant shipping would be sunk without warning. Initially the Kaiser had expressed moral reservations, announcing to a group of naval officers in November 1914: 'Gentlemen, always remember that our sword must remain pure. We are not fighting a war against women and children. We want to fight a decent war, whatever the others do.'[75] But now he justified the new tactics as having been forced on him by the equally unlawful British blockade.[76]

On 7 May 1915 the U 20 torpedoed the British liner *Lusitania* off the Irish coast with the loss of almost 1,200 lives, including many Americans. In response to massive protests from Washington, Wilhelm restricted the conduct of submarine warfare by forbidding the U-boats to attack passenger ships.[77] Bethmann Hollweg, Admiral von Müller and Falkenhayn all approved of this decision for fear of triggering the entry of the last non-belligerent Great Power (followed possibly by several other neutral states) into the war against Germany.[78] Tirpitz and the head of the Admiralty Staff, Gustav Bachmann, handed in their resignation in protest, thereby breaking with a Prussian military tradition forbidding resignations which were designed to blackmail the monarch into submission. 'No! At a time like this, that is a felony. He will stay and must obey. No! Stay and obey!' commanded the outraged War Lord.[79] The issue came to a head again when more American lives were lost with the sinking of the British steamer *Arabic* on 19 August 1915. The Chancellor insisted on a public declaration to the effect that henceforth no passenger liners would be attacked without prior warning. Once again Tirpitz threatened to resign and once again Wilhelm announced that no one was permitted 'in war-time to ask to be relieved from his post on account of differences of opinion concerning the deployment of warships over which I as Supreme War Lord and in full awareness of My responsibilities have the final say.'[80] He went on: 'I have created and built up the Fleet as my weapon, how, where and when I decide to deploy it is solely my concern as Supreme War Lord. Everyone else has to hold their tongue and obey. America had to be stopped from participating in the war as our active enemy. It could provide our enemies, who are now in serious financial trouble and unable to match our own financial strength, with unlimited amounts of money and thereby give them a massive advantage over us. As Supreme War Lord it was my duty to prevent this from happening at all costs. That was prudent politics. That is why with a heavy heart I *had to* order *restrictions* to arrive at the desired goal ... First the *war must be won*, and to that end it is absolutely essential to keep any new opponent out of the

war; how that is achieved — whether with more or less sacrifices — is immaterial and entirely *my business*. How I deploy my Navy to that end is also
solely my business. Wilhelm I.R.'[81] With his second threat to resign Tirpitz
had finally forfeited the monarch's confidence: an All-Highest Cabinet Order
of 30 August 1915 dismissed him from his functions as adviser in matters
relating to the conduct of the war at sea; Bachmann was replaced by Admiral
Holtzendorff, who on 18 September called a temporary halt to the U-boat
attacks on merchant shipping.[82]

The agitation for its resumption and indeed intensification continued
unabated, however. The navy promised that the U-boats would starve Britain
into submission within six months and the public, desperately anxious for
victory and unaware of the dangers, grew ever more vocal in its demands.[83]
The issue became acute in the winter of 1915–16, particularly as Falkenhayn,
believing that the threat of America's intervention had receded, now changed
sides.[84] The Kaiser was torn this way and that by the conflicting advice he was
given. He had to ask himself, he said: 'Could he, against the view of his
military advisers, accept the responsibility for prolonging the war on humanitarian grounds, thereby sacrificing the lives of so many more brave ordinary
soldiers? He was facing the most difficult decision of his life. It was all very
well for Falkenhayn to talk. He did not have an overview over the political
consequences and underestimated the participation of a hostile America.'[85] In
this instance Wilhelm II had a more realistic appreciation of the significance
of the USA and of what submarine warfare could and could not achieve than
his military advisers. As he assured the Chancellor in March 1916, Germany
had 'far too few U-boats to be able to crush England and he would never be so
"stupid" as to provoke a war with America'.[86] At the same time he took
seriously Falkenhayn's warning that time was not on Germany's side and that
her allies might well collapse before the year was out.[87] In the end he opted
for a compromise proposed by Bethmann under which U-boats were permitted
to sink only *armed* merchant vessels without warning.[88] The hope was that the
American government would accept this solution, especially as it had itself
objected to guns being mounted on Entente freighters.

With this solution Bethmann hoped not only to have averted the dangers
inherent in unrestricted submarine warfare but also to strike a blow against
Tirpitz as its most vocal advocate.[89] Wilhelm reacted in fury to the continuing
propaganda in favour of unrestricted attacks on merchant shipping emanating
from Tirpitz's Reich Navy Office, seeing therein yet again a challenge to his
authority. On 3 March 1916 his anger boiled over when a spokesman for
Tirpitz grossly exaggerated the number of U-boats available for a blockade of
the British Isles. Tirpitz was provoked into submitting his resignation by a

sharply worded All-Highest Cabinet Order instigated by the Chancellor, and this time the Kaiser agreed to the dismissal of the man with whom he had built up his battlefleet but with whom he had now lost all patience.[90] Though Falkenhayn continued to press for unrestricted U-boat attacks,[91] Tirpitz's successor at the Reich Navy Office, Eduard von Capelle, declared much to the Kaiser's relief that such a campaign would not be a realistic option before the autumn. 'What an abyss lies behind us!' sighed Karl Georg von Treutler, the representative of the Foreign Office at the imperial court, on hearing the news.[92] When Treutler told the Kaiser that the German people would one day be grateful to him for not giving in to the U-boat lobby, the monarch retorted: 'You must be very much under the influence of the Wilhelmstrasse if you believe me to be such an ass as to bow to such agitation!'[93]

The disastrous consequences of the resumption of the submarine attacks became evident almost immediately: On 24 March 1916 a U-boat torpedoed the unarmed French steamer *Sussex* which the Captain had mistaken for a warship. Once again American lives were lost.[94] The USA threatened to break off diplomatic relations if the Reich continued the U-boat campaign in defiance of international law.[95] The German naval leaders quickly gave way, with Admiral Scheer, the new Commander of the High Seas Fleet, declaring that U-boat attacks on merchant shipping must cease altogether.[96] However, Falkenhayn now claimed that he would have to halt the massive army offensive at Verdun unless it were backed up by a U-boat campaign.[97] And Wilhelm supported the Chief of General Staff, telling the astonished Chancellor: 'The operations at Verdun were now ready and could only be carried out under the express precondition that England be simultaneously weakened so much through U-boat warfare that France is forced to abandon all hope of being saved by England. If U-boat warfare is abandoned − and that would mean a return to cruiser warfare − continuing the operation at Verdun would be pointless, since then even the most massive loss of life would not bring about the collapse of France. In the war of attrition which would then follow we would not be able to withstand further losses on our side, would have to give up Verdun and confine ourselves to passive defence on all fronts. With that the war would be lost ... The maintenance of [friendly] relations with America holds no positive advantage for us but it deprives us of the only means open to us of winning the war.'[98] On this occasion it was the head of the Admiralty Staff who saved the day by pointing out that if the USA came into the war, not even an unrestricted U-boat campaign would persuade England to sue for peace, an argument which enabled Admiral von Müller to bring the Kaiser round once more.[99] Even so, the further the prospect of victory receded, the greater the temptation grew to go all-out for the 'miracle weapon' of unrestricted U-boat warfare.[100] As Moriz von Lyncker noted in January 1917: 'In the entire country the situation is getting ever more desperate, we are running out of everything everywhere. It is absolutely essential to bring the war to an end quickly. But how? The U-boat [campaign] will probably come; but will it bring a decisive success? Nobody knows. It is a leap into the dark. But we must take the risk, and we shall.'[101] The stakes could not have been higher. As Kurt Riezler put it in January 1917: 'the death sentence' or 'an inheritance of millions', 'Wilhelm the Truly Great' or 'Wilhelm the Last' — both outcomes were on the cards.[102]

On 31 May 1916 the Imperial Fleet and the Royal Navy engaged in the Battle of Jutland without significantly altering the balance of power at sea.[103] The Kaiser was initially exultant, crying: 'The first mighty hammer blow has been struck, the nimbus of English global domination has been ripped down, the tradition of Trafalgar torn to shreds.'[104] He was nevertheless forced to accept Scheer's judgement that the German battlefleet would never be able to damage the Royal Navy to the extent that Britain would be forced to sue for peace; only unrestricted U-boat warfare could persuade her to capitulate.[105]

On taking over the General Staff in August 1916, Hindenburg and Ludendorff, though in principle in favour of an unrestricted submarine campaign, did not press for it for the time being, less for fear of provoking America's entry into the war than because of the danger that the neutral states of Europe might side with the Entente. By the end of 1916, however, the two generals thought the time had come to take the risk. Wilhelm concurred and set early February 1917 as the date for the campaign to begin.[106] The peace initiative of the Central Powers of 12 December 1916 was launched not least with the intention of using its (expected) rejection as a justification for the resumption of unrestrained attacks on commercial shipping. Kaiser Wilhelm insisted on 'appearing personally as the initiator and embodiment of the peace action'.[107] In a letter to the Chancellor he trumpeted: 'The proposal to make peace is an ethical act which is necessary to free the world from the burden weighing upon everyone. Such an act must be undertaken by a sovereign who has a conscience and feels himself responsible to God and has a heart both for his own people and for the enemy ... I have the necessary courage and am willing by God take the risk.'[108] To his American dentist, 'laughing hilariously', he described his motives in rather different terms: 'We've got the English and the French Governments in a nice predicament, trying to explain to their people why they don't make peace. They're wild with rage at us for surprising them in this way.'[109] The sincerity of the Kaiser's peace initiative was called into question by another of his notorious gaffes. In a speech to his troops which found its way into the international press and was greeted with horror both at home and abroad, he was reported as saying: 'In the certain knowledge that we were the clear victors he had yesterday proposed to the enemy to begin talks on whether to continue the war or make peace. What would come of it he did not yet know. But it was now down to them if the struggle went on. But if they think that they have still not had enough, then I know for sure that you will ***' − 'with that the Kaiser concluded with a soldierly expression which brought a grim smile to the faces of all the soldiers.'[110]

With the failure of his peace initiative and that of President Wilson which followed it, Wilhelm II saw no alternative to a resumption of the U-boat campaign with no holds barred. The fateful decision fell on 8 January 1917 after Holtzendorff's audience. Müller records: 'At 7 o'clock in the evening report to the Kaiser, who had suddenly and rather unexpectedly convinced himself of the need for ruthless U-boat warfare and declared himself very strongly in its favour, even if the Chancellor were to oppose it. He took the most remarkable view that U-boat warfare was a purely military matter which was of no concern to the Chancellor. If there needed to be a change of personnel [at the top], that would be no great matter!'[111] Finding himself facing a determined phalanx of U-boat warriors − even Müller now sided with them[112] − Bethmann Hollweg, depressed and ill, finally gave way. The Kaiser 'then signed the pre-prepared order without delay ... As he did so he remarked that he reckoned almost certainly with America's declaration of war.'[113]

What followed is well known. In early February 1917 the USA broke off diplomatic relations with the German Reich, followed two months later by her declaration of war. Wilhelm II reacted to these world-historical developments with his usual militaristic bombast. 'That's an end once and for all now to negotiations with America! If Wilson wants war, then let him bring it about and have it!'[114] The assurances of the Admiralty Staff that unrestricted submarine warfare would without fail force England to sue for peace turned out to be a catastrophic miscalculation. True, the tonnage sunk in the early part of 1917 was far greater than in the entire previous year, but the introduction in May 1917 of convoys protected by warships proved to be an effective countermeasure to the U-boat menace. For a time Kaiser Wilhelm exulted at the 'rapid advance of starvation in England',[115] but soon even he had to recognise that the U-boat campaign was an expensive failure that might well cost Germany the war.

THE RUSSIAN REVOLUTIONS OF 1917

The revolutionary upheavals in Russia − the abdication of the Tsar in February/March 1917 followed by the Bolshevik seizure of power in October/November − naturally had a dramatic effect on Germany's strategic position. If Wilhelm was dismayed by the personal tragedy of his cousins Nicky and Alix and their children, he greeted the political opportunities offered by the collapse of the Romanov dynasty with delight.[116] Though he warned Bethmann Hollweg that England might try to exploit the events in Russia to undermine monarchist sentiment in the Reich,[117] on the whole he seemed unperturbed by the precedent set by the democratisation of the Tsarist Empire.[118] When the Provisional Government's efforts to continue the war against the Central Powers foundered with the failure of the Kerensky offensive, he rightly took this as a sign that Russia was close to collapse. With Lenin's translation in the famous sealed train from Zürich through Germany to the Finland station in St Petersburg, the way seemed clear for an armistice or even a peace treaty with the enemy in the east, enabling German troops to be moved to the western front for a final push against France and Britain before the American presence became too strong. Despite the failure of the U-boat campaign, a German victory and the great prize it would bring appeared to be close at last.

What the world map would have looked like had the Kaiser been able to dictate the peace terms became evident in a series of memoranda he himself penned in characteristic style after the February Revolution; perhaps more clearly than any other source these documents show us what the First World War was really about. On 19 April 1917, in preparation for the summit meeting convened to discuss Germany's war aims, and very much in line with proposals put forward by the General Staff and the Admiralty Staff, the Supreme War Lord demanded nothing less than the seizure of Malta, the Azores, Madeira and the Cape Verde Islands as naval bases for the Imperial Fleet, the acquisition of the Belgian Congo, the ore field of Longwy-Briey, and the direct or indirect annexation to the Reich of Poland, Lithuania and Courland (Kurzeme, i.e. southern Latvia) in the east. Anticipating the complete disintegration of the Tsarist Empire he listed as further aims the 'autonomy' of the Ukraine, Livonia (i.e. northern Latvia) and Estonia. In addition, he intended to demand an indemnity of 30 billion dollars each from Britain and the USA, 40 billion francs from France and 10 billion from Italy.[119] Almost all of these aims were officially adopted a few days later at the Bad Kreuznach war aims conference.[120]

On 13 May 1917, Wilhelm II again set down 'My wishes and those of My armed forces' for the forthcoming negotiations with Russia. Under the pretext that the longer-than-expected duration of the war now justified even greater compensation for Germany's sacrifices, he listed his 'minimal' aims in thirteen points which again included the annexation of Longwy-Briey, the cession of Malta, the Azores, Madeira and the Cape Verde Islands, the French and

Belgian Congo along with the return of all of Germany's former colonies in Africa, German suzerainty over Belgium (partitioned into Flanders and Wallonia), and in the east Poland, Courland and Lithuania and an 'autonomous' Ukraine. Cyprus, Egypt and Mesopotamia were to be handed to Turkey and Gibraltar restored to Spain. To the enormous British, American, French and Italian war indemnities he had envisaged on 19 April 1917 the Kaiser now added the further demand for twelve billion marks each from China, Japan, Brazil, Bolivia, Cuba and Portugal, to be paid not in cash but in grain, oil, cotton and wool, copper, nickel and other raw materials.[121]

The Kaiser may indeed, as is often said, have learnt of the plans to spirit Lenin and thirty other emigrés from their Swiss exile to Russia from the newspapers, but he gave them his full approval, joking that the Bolsheviks should be presented with a copy of his speeches to take to Russia with them.[122] As we have seen, he had expressed his intention of revolutionising the Tsarist Empire in the event of war as early as 1913.[123] There is no doubt that Wilhelm II fully shared the aim of his Foreign Office, which Count Ulrich von Brockdorff-Rantzau, the chief architect of the plan, summarised in the words: 'Victory and as its prize the first place in the world is ours if we can manage to revolutionise Russia in time and thus break up the coalition.'[124] The Kaiser discounted the danger that Bolshevism might pose to his own regime, responding to a warning of the menace of international revolution from the Austro-Hungarian Foreign Minister Count Czernin by insisting that in Germany the monarchical principle was more firmly anchored than in the Habsburg Empire and therefore revolution held no dangers for the Hohenzollerns.[125]

With the advance of the German armies deep into western Russia in 1917, tempting new opportunities for expansion presented themselves. 'With God's help Riga is ours!' the Kaiser exulted in September. 'A wonderful proof of the efficacy of the iron will to victory of our wonderful troops! Forwards with God!'[126] 'The Baltic lands are indivisible and *I* will be their ruler', he cried a few weeks later. 'I have *conquered* them and no jurist can take them away from me.'[127] After the Bolshevik seizure of power, Wilhelm hailed the peace negotiations with the Soviet delegation led by Trotsky at Brest-Litovsk in December 1917 (see Figure 55) as 'one of the greatest successes of world history, whose true significance only our grandchildren will be able to appreciate'.[128] In January 1918 he crowed: 'Germany's victory over Russia was the precondition for the [February] revolution, this in turn the precondition for Lenin, and that for Brest! The same must now be done in the west! First victory in the west with the collapse of the Entente, then we will impose our terms which they will simply have to accept! And they will be tailored purely

Figure 55 German generals greet the Bolshevik delegation at
Brest-Litovsk, December 1917

to our own interests.'[129] 'Europe must be saved by the German character,
through our sword', he proclaimed.[130] Humanitarian ideas such as the freedom and happiness of the individual or the self-determination of nations had
no place in the 'victor's peace' that would now be imposed on the vanquished;
'only one's *own* naked self-interest and the guarantee of one's *own security* and
greatness must count'.[131] 'All those nebulous notions of internationalism, of
the brotherhood of man, of world democracy etc. have been burnt off by the
sun of the German army. God has granted us this victory which we have
imposed by our shining sword! The German Kaiser has smashed the Bolshevik
plans to revolutionise Europe's royal thrones – including those of his enemies –
and has prevented a "democratic peace".'[132]

Wilhelm justified the eyewatering expansion of German power up to the
Gulf of Finland and south to the Black Sea, the Caucasus and beyond not only
to advance the cause of monarchism but also in racial terms, arguing that real
peace 'between the Slavs and the Teutons was a complete impossibility ...
Peace with Russia could only be upheld through fear of us. The Slavs will
always hate us and remain our enemies. They are afraid of and have respect
only for those who thrash them! See Japan! That's how it will be with us too!

The Entente – which brought it [Russia] into the war – will always be able to do whatever it wants in Russia, especially as my diplomacy is so stupid; but our preponderance in the Teutonic [i.e. Baltic] lands is essential to keep Russia far away from our eastern frontier for all time.' No negotiated agreement with Russia, however favourable, would ever be able to achieve as much as outright annexation.[133]

Given this attitude, Wilhelm II was naturally predisposed to side with the annexationist generals in their conflict with the chief official German negotiator at Brest-Litovsk, the Foreign Secretary Richard von Kühlmann, however much he might have yearned for a quick end to the war. Whereas Kühlmann was intent on prising the western provinces of the Tsarist Empire away from Russia under the cover of national self-determination so as to establish a German-dominated *Cordon sanitaire* between the Reich and the socialist Soviet Union, the generals were bent on annexing the Baltic lands and large areas of Poland to Germany even if this meant prolonging the conflict.[134] Wavering between the two camps and complaining that he was being kept out of the loop by both sides,[135] the Kaiser contributed to his own exclusion from the deliberations at Brest-Litovsk by shutting himself off for weeks on end at Bad Homburg, where his wife was ill with a weak heart. His frustration and impotence expressed itself in angry marginal comments, as when he threatened to send recalcitrant members of the Reichstag to the western front.[136] But his marginalia also leave no doubt of his confidence in a resounding military victory and his consequent rejection of a negotiated peace, an idea he described as 'utter rubbish'.[137] He saw himself marching in triumph into the newly occupied Russian territories and praised the uncompromising stand being taken by the annexationist military negotiator at Brest, General Max Hoffmann,[138] while growing increasingly impatient with the endless diplomatic word games being played by Kühlmann and Trotsky.[139] The monarch seems to have been oblivious to the catastrophic impression the exorbitant German demands at Brest were bound to make on his enemies and allies alike, not to mention the sorely tried and starving German people.

In January 1918, Wilhelm was faced with a bitter conflict over the so-called 'Polish border strip', that is to say that area of Poland which Germany intended to annex should the body of Poland be assigned to the Austrian sphere of influence. On this issue Hindenburg and Ludendorff demanded the inclusion of a substantial part of Polish territory into the German Reich, whereas both Kühlmann and Hoffmann argued for the annexation of a far narrower strip. The Supreme War Lord, still theoretically the fulcrum of the 'kingship mechanism', sided with Hoffmann's more moderate proposal, not least in the hope of appeasing his exhausted and war-weary Austro-Hungarian ally. He told Kühlmann: 'I shall this evening inform the gentlemen of Army High Command of this boundary line and at the same time make it clear that this is my decision as Supreme War Lord and that this boundary is the one to be adopted.'[140] Kühlmann warned the monarch that Hindenburg and Ludendorff would not take kindly to his siding with their subordinate General Hoffmann, but Wilhelm, ever the military man, thought he knew his soldiers better than the Foreign Secretary. 'Well, Kühlmann, this is yet another of your typically diplomatic ideas. All of you diplomats are naturally jealous of one another, none of you is willing to recognise another's success. You obviously don't know my army at all. We soldiers are not like that. The Field Marshal [von Hindenburg] has so far always given way when I have ordered something as Supreme War Lord, and I am therefore confident that in the Crown Council this evening I shall be able to push the thing through to your and everybody else's satisfaction.'[141] In fact it was the Kaiser, not the diplomat, who had misjudged his generals: the Crown Council of 2 January 1918 ended with Ludendorff making such a furious scene that Wilhelm was forced to reconsider his decision.[142] Afterwards he complained that 'Ludendorff had angrily declared that the Army High Command could not accept this [decision]. As if I myself were not the Army High Command! But I shall try to abolish this unfortunate term "Army High Command"!'[143] In the heated controversy that ensued, Reich Chancellor Michaelis conceded that the generals had the right to be heard in all political questions, while insisting that he alone carried responsibility for government policy as a whole. That might have been formally correct on paper, but the confrontation over the Polish border strip had revealed all too clearly where power now really lay.[144]

If the Kaiser grew ever more impatient with the slowness of the negotiations at Brest-Litovsk, he certainly understood Trotsky's purpose in spinning out the talks for as long as possible. On 11 January 1918 he remarked that the Soviet delegation would agree to the independence of Poland only on a 'revolutionary, socialist basis' and went on: 'The Bolsheviks are trying to ensure that *all countries* – including those with which they are negotiating – adopt this form. That's why they are jabbering on so endlessly in the hope of enflaming the socialists among their enemies to influence the existing governments in their direction or if they refuse to overthrow them. Trockij hopes and expects that revolution, which he thinks could break out here at any moment, will bring about the "self-determination" of the peoples of the Central Powers! *Then* he wants to make peace with the "people", not with the "governments". We must be sure quickly to deprive him of all hope that any such thing might occur.'[145] The notorious Treaty of Brest-Litovsk was finally signed on Lenin's instruction on 3 March 1918.

It goes without saying that Kaiser Wilhelm II abhorred the radical rulers in Russia and the de facto alliance his own government had formed with them. Naturally he accepted the argument of the Wilhelmstrasse that the Bolshevik regime had to be supported, since it alone could guarantee the implementation of the Brest-Litovsk agreement. But he made no secret of his distaste, saying 'the Bolsheviks want revolution, want to make a huge workers' porridge', and that they needed to be 'clubbed to death because they are revolutionary'.[146] The Russian leaders were nothing but 'robber chieftains in charge of a thieving cheeky *Proletenjanhagels*', he exclaimed in May 1918[147] and referred to the representative of the Soviet Union in Berlin, Adolf Abramovič Joffe, as a 'swine' and a 'Jew boy'.[148] Wilhelm's anti-Semitism, which had grown more intense since the *Daily Telegraph* affair and the Eulenburg trials, now plumbed new depths. In February 1918 he observed: 'Apart from Lenin all the Bolshevik leaders everywhere are *without exception Jews*! supported by *Entente-Jews*! ... This is the *Jewish International*, for the sake of which the *Christians* are expected to beat each other to death.'[149]

Although Wilhelm was in theory keen to maintain relations with the White counter-revolutionary forces in Russia, when they demanded the restoration of the pre-war frontiers of the Tsarist Empire, that is to say the reincorporation into Russia of the Ukraine and the Baltic provinces which Germany coveted, his fury knew no bounds. 'Nonsense!' he exclaimed, revealing the extent of his worldwide ambitions. 'They have been put up to this by the Entente! On no account! These are the English terms, on which they *might* come to an understanding with us *if* we accept them! Then our domination of the Baltic Sea and the threat we pose to India and our link to the Caucasus would be gone and our victory would have been for nothing!'[150] As late as summer 1918 Wilhelm dreamt of parcelling Russia up into four 'Tsardoms': the Ukraine, the eastern Caucasus, Siberia and Rump Russia.[151] Faced with the choice on the one hand of supporting the Reds they abominated and continuing their advance towards the Hindu Kush, and on the other hand of aiding the Whites with whom they sympathised, but who were intent on restoring the Russo-German frontier of 1914, the Kaiser and his advisers had no hesitation in opting for the former course.

One week after the signing of the Treaty of Brest-Litovsk, the Kaiser, believing that victory would now follow in the west, declared any discussion of a 'peaceful future for the world' to be 'beside the point!' and set out his own vision in these terms: 'God willing we shall be able to impose the coming peace upon our enemies, which we must do. They will only sue for peace when they have been beaten so badly that they have had enough. Once they admit to that they will have to accept a peace which takes into account the *new* and heavy loss of blood suffered by the German people *solely* as a result of their *pigheadedness*. The peace must – if needs be at *their expense* and *without regard* for their *feelings* in the future – contain such *real guarantees* for us that a world combination such as the present one can *never* again be successfully put together against us. That is to say a genuine, proper, common-or-garden peace of the kind that has so far always been signed after a victorious war. There is no place in such a peace for dreams of human happiness or humanitarian cosmopolitanism, only one's *own* naked self-interest and the guarantee of one's *own security* and greatness must count. The vanquished must submit to his fate!'[152] He rejected out of hand any suggestion of an international order not based upon the military and economic predominance of Germany and her allies. When the *Berliner Tageblatt* complained that there was no mention in the Treaty of Brest-Litovsk of multilateral disarmament or arbitration or any kind of League of Nations, the monarch commented: 'because that is all rubbish! for which serious people don't give a toss!'[153]

Naturally the new German imperium that was emerging from the terrible conflict of the past four years had to be a bastion of Personal Monarchy on the Lutheran–Calvinist Hohenzollern model. Not only would Lithuania and Courland be bound in personal union to the Prusso-German Crown, that is to say ruled by himself,[154] the other German satellite states that were being set up as the Russian Empire disintegrated were also to be monarchies ruled by German or Austrian princes. In the closing days of the war the husband of his youngest sister Margarethe, Prince Friedrich Karl of Hesse, was chosen to be King of Finland, a plan that was abandoned only when Britain and France made it clear that they would 'consider the choice of Kaiser Wilhelm's brother-in-law to be one of Germany's war aims'.[155] Austrian archdukes might be enthroned in the Ukraine and elsewhere well to the south and east, but certainly not in the German sphere of influence further north. In the summer of 1918 Wilhelm railed in alarm against an alleged conspiracy of the Vatican to place a Catholic prince of Habsburg-Parma on the throne of Lithuania. 'The ultra-bigotted House of Parma, hand-in-glove with its fanatical father-confessors and championing a pigheaded mediaevalism, hates the Protestant House of Hohenzollern. It is seeking the Catholic encirclement of Germany ruled by the hated House of Hohenzollern. Led by Vienna it is striving for an *alliance* uniting it with Italy – won over by the restoration to it of the Trentino and the Tirol – France, Poland and Lithuania all the way *to the sea*! Hence the demand for *Poland's independence* … Hence the calls for an *independent* Lithuania under a *Cathol[ic]* prince; hence the resistance against our attaching the *Baltic lands*, including Livonia and Estonia, to us, which they plan to attach to Lithuania and convert to Catholicism in order to cut us off from the sea.' To the Kaiser's mind the arch-villain in this paranoid melodrama was that 'rascally traitor' and 'poisoner of wells' Matthias Erzberger, the leader of the Catholic Centre party, who was an agent, so Wilhelm believed, of Rome, Parma and the Habsburgs against Germany and the Hohenzollerns and had to be stopped.[156] That such crazed conspiracy theories should take hold of the imperator's mind at the very highpoint of German expansion is perhaps symptomatic of a terrifying realisation on his part that the end was nigh.

CHAPTER FORTY-FOUR

Downfall. The collapse of the Hohenzollern Monarchy

THE SACKING OF REICH CHANCELLOR THEOBALD VON BETHMANN HOLLWEG

Years of total warfare had inevitably had a devastating effect on the political and social situation at home. The Left Liberals and Social Democrats in particular were insistent that the immense war effort put in − and the hardships suffered − by millions of ordinary Germans must be rewarded through a significant democratisation of the Reich and Prussian constitutions.[1] Chancellor von Bethmann Hollweg was also keen for reform, not only to secure the people's immediate support for the continuation of the war, but also to place the Hohenzollern Monarchy on a firmer footing in the long run.[2] The most pressing precondition for any constitutional reform was the abolition of the antiquated three-class franchise to the lower house of the Prussian legislature, the Landtag, through which conservative forces were able to dominate the hegemonial state of Prussia and from there Reich politics as a whole. In his speech from the throne at the opening of the Landtag in January 1916, Wilhelm II announced his intention to reform the Prussian electoral system when the war was over, but such vague promises satisfied no one, least of all the starving population driven to distraction by the agitation for boundless annexations and unrestricted U-boat warfare which was prolonging the war.[3]

In face of the hardship of the 'turnip winter' of 1916–17, and fearful that the Russian Revolution might prove contagious, Bethmann became convinced that meaningful constitutional reforms, most notably a cast-iron pledge that direct and equal suffrage for the Prussian parliament would be introduced as soon as the war was over, had become inescapable.[4] The Kaiser seemed impressed by the Chancellor's argument that it would be unthinkable to introduce a reform Bill granting 'a poor worker decorated with the Iron Cross First Class a vote that counted for less than that enjoyed by a wealthy shirker in the same constituency'.[5] Nevertheless, like the Conservative Prussian ministers and the generals at Supreme Headquarters, he refused to commit himself to the introduction of equal votes for all.[6] In his 'Easter Message' of 8 April 1917, all he announced was a reform of the Prussian House of Lords along with unspecified changes to the voting system for the lower house, the House of Representatives, once the war was over.[7] As ever when he felt his *Kommandogewalt* – his prerogative to command in military matters – to be under threat, Wilhelm reacted with fury when, despite these 'concessions', the Reichstag demanded that military appointments and dismissals should in future be countersigned by the Minister of War.[8] He demanded that any further moves towards parliamentarisation be vigorously resisted. In a letter to Bethmann Hollweg he set out at length the reasons why, in his view, the parliamentary system would be quite unsuitable for Germany. 'This system has suffered total shipwreck in England a[nd] France. In England in particular – the mother of parliaments – both the parliament and the people have been completely sidelined, are consulted and kept informed about nothing, and have had to give way without resistance to the *dictatorship of one* Prime Minister with unlimited powers at the head of a *committee* of a handful of men. That is to say the old '*Directoire*' in its purest form. This amounts to a backward revision from a pure parliamentary regime in England to an *absolute autocracy*! At a time like this I will not tolerate that experiments in *old* parliamentary traditions are conducted here which have already been shown *to be dead* in England. It is impossible for us to try out such things since we do *not* have 2 parties – as in the old England – but a whole heap of them. In Prussia the idea that ministers should be appointed merely *because* they belong to the *parliament* would be impossible. For one thing this would infringe the right of the king to appoint and dismiss his ministers as he chooses, and for another there is no prospect of any practical success. In his day Bülow, *against my advice*, tried this by appointing the leader of the Liberals Exc[ellency] v. Möeller [sic] as Minister of Trade. It was a failure because his party out of envy immediately went into opposition against Moeller and brought about his fall ... Moreover a ministry composed of party members would include a Socialist, which is unthinkable. Similarly a parliament[ary] regime is out of the question for the Reich, since there the *Centrum* has the deciding votes. It can therefore combine with the Left to bring about the fall of a Conservative minister or coalesce with the Right to throw out a Liberal! Thus within a short time the Reich government would be totally in the hands and at the mercy of the Centre. In Edenkoben H.M. the King [of Bavaria] and his advisers made it very clear that the [federal] Princes and governments, while wholly appreciating and approving the *Easter Message*, would be absolutely opposed to any plans *going beyond that*. The *Easter Message* will be *implemented – after the war*, beyond that *I will not go under any circumstances*.'[9]

With the appointment of Hindenburg and Ludendorff to Supreme Army Command in August 1916 Wilhelm II came increasingly under their sway and almost always sided with them against the civilian statesmen.[10] 'The Kaiser has withdrawn totally into the shadow cast by the two soldiers', one influential official complained, and was 'drifting in their wake without a will of his own'.[11] For his part Wilhelm seemed relieved to have offloaded some of the responsibility resting on his shoulders to the powerful duo, remarking to one of his Flügeladjutanten: 'You know, I'm in seventh heaven with these two men.'[12]

Their opposition to Bethmann's reform course reached a crescendo after the Kaiser's Easter Message, with Ludendorff angrily complaining that the imperial pronouncement amounted to 'kowtowing to the Russian revolution'.[13] He and Hindenburg vehemently opposed any further concession as a sign that Germany's commitment to the war was faltering.[14] They had long regarded the Chancellor as ponderous and weak, accusing him not only of opposing the far-reaching annexations they intended to make at Russia's expense but also of failing to stabilise the home front.[15] The two generals now determined to work for the dismissal of the man who had been their ally in their long-running conflict with Falkenhayn. The gulf between Bethmann and the military was shown to be unbridgeable at the Bad Kreuznach war aims conference of 23 April 1917, at which, as we have seen, Wilhelm sided with the generals and approved their breathtaking annexationism, so scuppering any chance of a negotiated separate peace with post-Tsarist Russia desired by the Chancellor and the diplomats.[16] Hardly a day passed without the supreme military commanders bad-mouthing Bethmann and stirring up the monarch against him.[17] They brought in the reactionary governor of East Prussia, Friedrich von Berg, who (true to form) promptly told the Kaiser that 'the Reich Chancellor had lost the confidence of the fatherland and the majority of the parties', urging that Bethmann be sacked and replaced with Ludendorff. The Adjutant-General Hans von Plessen was delighted: 'H.M. received this information graciously.'[18]

The crisis came to a head in July 1917 when the need for further war credits forced the Reichstag, prorogued since May, to be recalled. The country was facing the prospect of a fourth starvation winter and the mood was bleak. The half-hearted promise of electoral reform announced in the Easter Message had failed to stem the tide of discontent, and the Social Democrats now called for the immediate introduction of universal suffrage in Prussia and the open acceptance of the principle of peace without annexations.[19] In this febrile atmosphere the Centre party leader Matthias Erzberger declared in the Reichstag on 6 July 1917 that the military and economic position of the country was so grave as to necessitate an immediate initiative to secure peace without annexations. The substantial and stable support (212 votes against 126 with 17 abstentions) his celebrated 'peace resolution' received from the three parties of the centre and left – the Social Democrats, the (largely Catholic) Centre and the Progressives – proved to be a milestone on the road to peace and constitutional reform.[20]

On the day after Erzberger's peace initiative, Hindenburg and Ludendorff turned up in Berlin to take up the fight against the Reichstag's 'defeatism'. Plessen noted in his diary: 'Field Marshal Hindenburg and Ludendorff ... came in response to a telegram from the War Minister in which he had described their presence in Berlin as essential for internal reasons ... H.M. expressed his disapproval of the War Minister's action in no uncertain terms, since the latter should properly have summoned Hindenburg only with H.M.'s prior approval. The War Minister denies summoning Hindenburg, claiming that all he did was to inform him of the events in the Reichstag after telling the Reich Chancellor he was doing so. But the latter had the telegram in his hand which clearly showed that he [the War Minister] had indeed asked Hindenburg to come ... An embarrassing affair.'[21] The Kaiser listened to the objections raised against the forthcoming Reichstag resolution but brusquely told the generals that they had no right to interfere in domestic politics – 'the entire matter was still in flux and in any case none of their business, they should simply go away again'.[22] This did not stop Ludendorff from spreading the malicious rumour that Bethmann had prevented them from speaking in the Reichstag themselves.[23]

On the following day, 8 July 1917, the Chancellor again pleaded with the Kaiser to concede equal suffrage for elections to the Prussian lower house.[24] Wilhelm agreed to summon a Crown Council to consider the vexed question of electoral reform, yet that very evening he discussed with Rudolf von Valentini, the Chief of his Civil Cabinet, who might replace Bethmann should the decision go against the Chancellor. Since no acceptable candidate emerged – the Kaiser rejected Prince von Bülow, Prince Hermann von Hatzfeld-Trachenberg and Count Siegfried von Roedern (currently State Secretary of the Reich Treasury) out of hand – the monarch sent Valentini to talk to the veteran Bavarian envoy in Berlin, Count Hugo von Lerchenfeld-Koefering, who strongly urged that Bethmann be retained 'on the grounds that he enjoyed the greatest trust of the South German courts and the allies, especially Austria'.[25] The next morning Wilhelm again discussed the Chancellorship with Valentini and the Minister of the Royal Household, Count August zu Eulenburg, a staunch opponent of electoral reform, whose plea for the appointment of Bülow once more fell on deaf imperial ears.[26] However, this time Valentini got the Kaiser to agree to appoint Roedern if Bethmann fell, even though, as the monarch himself told Plessen and Lyncker after the meeting, Roedern 'too was in favour of universal, equal and secret suffrage in Prussia'.[27] Admiral von Müller rightly observed that Roedern's appointment to the Chancellorship would be pointless, 'since he is known to lean towards liberal concessions'.[28] The absurdity of the situation was highlighted when, in answer to the question of why in that case a change in the Chancellorship was being considered at all, the only response to be heard was the delphic: 'stormy seas demand a sacrifice'.[29] The Crown Council ended inconclusively: the Prussian ministers and the Reich secretaries attending the meeting were divided – the Chancellor was supported by Breitenbach, Beseler, Sydow, Helfferich, Roedern and Solf, while Loebell, Schorlemer, Trott zu Solz, Lentze, Kraetke and Stein spoke against reform. Wilhelm, who appeared remarkably unconcerned throughout the deliberations,[30] reserved his position and summoned his son the Crown Prince to Berlin.[31] On the morning of 10 July Valentini found the Kaiser in an agitated state: 'He had had a sleepless night; the Kaiserin had made a most terrible scene when he told her after returning from the Crown Council of what had transpired.'[32]

The head of the Civil Cabinet described the Chancellor's stand in the audience which ensued as 'a magnificent plea in favour of "The Kaiser in the People's State [*Volksstaat*]"', in the course of which Bethmann had spoken 'with idealistic enthusiasm of the overwhelming achievements of the people in this war, in the light of which the last hint of suspicion or the withholding of constitutional rights seemed unjustified. It was not the crisis of this moment, but his profound inner belief in the readiness of the Prussian people for equal universal suffrage that had informed his decision. This [reform], granted freely by the Crown, would bring not a diminution but rather an extraordinary strengthening and consolidation of the monarchical idea. The impression made by the words and by the entire personality of the Chancellor, so full of strength and the profoundest conviction, was so strong not least upon the Kaiser that he said to me when Bethmann had departed – at around 2 o'clock – "and *this* is the man I am supposed to sack, who stands head and shoulders above all the rest!"'[33] Valentini managed to bring even the Crown Prince round to accepting the need for equal suffrage in Prussia.[34] Once the Kaiser's approval had been secured the decision of the Prussian Ministry of State was a mere formality — on 11 July 1917 Wilhelm II officially requested Bethmann Hollweg in his capacity as Prussian Minister-President to draft a Bill introducing universal, secret and equal elections to the Prussian House of Representatives.[35] The Kaiser's relief at the thought that his concession had resolved the crisis was short-lived, however.[36] 'The Electoral Law Decree has had no effect', noted the influential journalist Theodor Wolff. 'The Right is livid, the Left is lukewarm. The Pan-Germans, the Voss[ische] Z[ei]t[un]g and the Lokalanzeiger are continuing their personal hate campaign against Bethmann.'[37] The Reich Chancellor was now in a 'desperate mood', particularly as the Reichstag debates on the Peace Resolution were making no real progress.

To make matters worse the Crown Prince, who had agreed to the electoral reform only reluctantly, now involved himself in an intrigue against Bethmann.[38] Under the influence of the reactionary Hans Jaspar Freiherr von Maltzahn and Colonel Max Bauer of Supreme Army Command, the heir presumptive summoned a number of party leaders to discuss the situation with him on the morning of 12 July 1917. Almost all of them spoke in favour of the Chancellor's dismissal; only the Progressive People's party leader Friedrich von Payer wanted unequivocally to keep Bethmann.[39] When the younger Wilhelm attacked Bethmann that afternoon, accusing him of undermining the rights of the Crown, Valentini told him to his face that the rights of the monarchy 'could hardly be more severely undermined than by the heir to the throne officially asking the representatives of the parties in the Reichstag whether they were calling on the Kaiser to dismiss his Prime Minister!'[40]

Already disappointed that his Electoral Decree had failed to calm the mood in the Reichstag and the country as a whole, the Kaiser was devastated by the news which reached him from Bad Kreuznach on the evening of 12 July that Hindenburg and Ludendorff were about to submit their resignations on the grounds that they could no longer work with Bethmann.[41] The monarch was incensed at this act of insubordination and ordered the generals to meet him in Berlin, where he intended to reject their letters of resignation in person. But Bethmann Hollweg, forced to admit both that dismissing the popular duo would be out of the question and that he could no longer collaborate with them, submitted his own resignation on the morning of 13 July 1917, which Wilhelm accepted even before Hindenburg and Ludendorff reached the capital.[42] It was nevertheless clear to all that the Crown had in fact been forced to capitulate to the joint pressure of the military, the Reichstag and public opinion. 'In that case I might as well abdicate straight away', the dejected monarch exclaimed.[43] The right of the German Kaiser to choose his own Reich Chancellor and Prussian Minister-President had in effect been taken from him.

'CLUELESS': THE FARCICAL SEARCH FOR A NEW
REICH CHANCELLOR

In his resignation letter Bethmann Hollweg had recommended the Bavarian
Prime Minister Count Georg von Hertling as his successor, but he turned the
post down on account of his age – he was approaching his seventy-fourth
birthday – and his differences with the Supreme Army Command on the
question of war aims.[44] The suggestion made by the Bavarian envoy
Lerchenfeld that Count Bernstorff, the former ambassador to Washington,
might make a suitable Chancellor met with Wilhelm's 'lively objection',
though tellingly he declared himself ready to appoint Bernstorff 'should
Hindenburg find him acceptable'.[45] When Valentini refused to secure the
Field Marshal's approval on the grounds that the generals had no right to be
consulted on the Kaiser's choice of his Reich Chancellor, Wilhelm sent him to
talk to the head of the Military Cabinet General Moriz von Lyncker.
Together the two Cabinet chiefs went through a list of possible candidates,
in their desperation even leafing through the *Almanac de Gotha* and the
Handbook of the Royal Prussian Court and State in the hope of finding
someone suitable.[46] Later the 75-year-old Adjutant-General Hans von
Plessen joined them, noting in his diary: 'I chanced upon Valentini in the
Military Cabinet. Clueless. Lyncker ditto. In my presence they went through
all the possible and impossible candidates a second time: Dallwitz, Bülow,
Tirpitz, Gallwitz, Bernstorff, Rantzau. All of them in Valentini's opinion
unsuitable for this reason or that. Silent pondering. Then I proposed
Dallwitz once again. Rejected, since he is supposed to have declared on an
earlier occasion that he would always refuse this post. Then I proposed
Hatzfeld. But H.M. didn't want him or Bülow or Tirpitz either. Then
I suddenly thought of Under Secretary of State Michaelis, whom someone
had described to me as clever, lively and reliable! Valentini delighted! That
would be a suitable fellow. Valentini, Lyncker and I go along with this
proposal first to Hindenburg. He and Ludendorff are in full agreement.
Thereupon all three of us to H.M. – The All-Highest declares himself in
agreement even though he had seen him only once, saying he was short, a
dwarf.'[47] This then was the farcical way in which, at the most critical
juncture of the world war, after the Supreme Army Command had given
its blessing, the highest office of state in Prussia and the Reich was filled by a
political nonentity with absolutely no experience of foreign affairs whom the
Kaiser barely knew – Valentini noted: '[H.M.] is surprised but gives his
consent.'[48] The monarch's role in the choice of Bethmann Hollweg's successor was limited to blocking the appointment of men such as Bülow or Tirpitz

against whom he held a personal or political grudge, even though they enjoyed strong support both from the military and the general public.[49]

The circumstances in which Georg Michaelis was appointed Chancellor in July 1917 have rightly been seen as symptomatic of the bankruptcy of the Kaiser's Personal Monarchy in its dying days.[50] In the triangle formed by the (in many ways mutually antagonistic) forces of the Crown, the Supreme Army Command and the Reichstag, there seemed to be no alternative to giving the post that the mighty Bismarck had once fashioned for himself to a colourless and completely unknown bureaucrat who would offend none of them. Taking the helm of an exhausted empire in the middle of a deadly global conflict, the new Chancellor of the Reich admitted that 'he had hitherto walked alongside the waggon of international politics as an ordinary citizen', doing his best 'to keep abreast of events by reading the newspapers'.[51]

FIRST STEPS TOWARDS PARLIAMENTARY MONARCHY

Caught as he was between the irreconcilable forces of the army on the one hand and the Reichstag on the other, Michaelis soon found himself in deep trouble, and the Kaiser's interventions did not help. Gratuitous comments by both men on the Peace Resolution — Wilhelm declared he would never sign a 'soft peace' — exacerbated tensions with the parliament.[52] An attempt by Karl Helfferich, State Secretary of the Interior, to broker an agreement between the monarch and the party leaders on 20 July 1917 turned out, as his closest advisers had feared, to be a public relations disaster.[53] Talking incessantly with characteristic swagger Wilhelm II expressed his delight that the Reichstag, too, now wanted a 'compromise peace' — that 'compromise', he announced, would consist of 'our taking from the pockets of our enemies their money, their raw materials, cotton, minettes [and] oil and putting them into our own pocket'.[54] He speculated wildly on the alliances he would form after the war, spoke with utter disdain of the weakness of the Tsar and ranted on about the Second Punic War which he planned to launch against Britain once he had reached an understanding with France to become the master of a united European continent. He made no secret of his contempt for the assembled members of parliament, addressing them like young recruits and telling them: 'Democracy ends there where my Guards are in command.'[55] For Matthias Erzberger this meeting with the monarch was 'the deepest cut signalling the beginning of the end of the old regime'.[56] The five Social Democrats invited came away from the audience with the conviction that they had been ruled for years by a madman.[57]

The brief episode of Michaelis's Chancellorship did little to bring the government and the Reichstag closer together. True, some individual members of parliament were appointed as Prussian ministers, Reich secretaries and undersecretaries of state, but these appointees generally had no links with the three parties of the centre and left now forming the majority in the House, and they had in any case, in accordance with the constitution, to give up their seats on assuming office. Michaelis soon revealed himself to be an opponent of both parliamentarisation and the Peace Resolution.[58] The crisis came to a head on 8 and 9 October 1917 when the SPD and the more radical USPD (the left wing of the Social Democrats, which had split off to form an independent party) accused the government of supporting the annexationist propaganda of the ultra-nationalistic Deutsche Vaterlandspartei.[59] The government's response – Michaelis accused members of the USPD of subversive activity in the navy, and the State Secretary of the Reich Navy Office, Capelle, went so far as to name three members of the Reichstag as co-conspirators in a naval mutiny that had recently been put down – only poured fuel on the flames. Furious, the deputies of the centre-left majority declared that they were no longer prepared to work with the Chancellor.[60] The Kaiser, about to embark on a state visit to Bulgaria and Turkey, initially failed to understand the gravity of the situation: 'It's all the same to me', he told the head of the Naval Cabinet, 'the Reichstag can do what it likes. I have the nation and the army behind me, and Michaelis has the revolver – in the shape of my prorogation order – in his pocket.'[61]

Though the situation had not improved by the time of his return to Berlin on 21 October, the Kaiser was determined to keep Michaelis in office.[62] The majority parties continued to demand his dismissal, and, while leaving the choice of his successor to the Crown, they insisted that the new man submit his programme to parliament for approval. Their key demands were that Germany should respond positively to the papal peace initiative and that equal suffrage be introduced in Prussia as speedily as possible.[63] On submitting their demands to the Chief of the Civil Cabinet on 23 October 1917, the majority parties added the carefully worded request that 'the Kaiser, *if* he should decide upon a change in the person of the Chancellor, should instruct the person chosen by him to consult with the representatives of the majority parties prior to his formal appointment with the aim of agreeing a common programme as far as possible'.[64] The monarch rightly saw in this polite request an attack upon his constitutional right 'to dismiss and appoint the Chancellor entirely in accordance with his judgement'.[65] Valentini also perceived the grave constitutional implications of the Reichstag's initiative but favoured a compromise, especially as Michaelis's 'proven incompetence' had in any case made his removal unavoidable.[66] Michaelis, realising that his position as Reich Chancellor had become untenable, proposed that the Kaiser should relieve him of the Chancellorship but keep him on as Prussian Minister-President charged with steering the electoral reform Bill through the House of Representatives. As his successor as Reich Chancellor he proposed Count Hertling, who this time — as opposed to three months earlier — agreed on 28 October 1917 to serve, albeit on the momentous condition that he first assured himself of the Reichstag's support.[67] As Valentini commented, 'the Kaiser — now! — finds all this quite natural and has declared himself in agreement'.[68] In the course of complicated negotiations with parliament,[69] the idea of separating the Chancellorship from the highest Prussian post was dropped, Michaelis was dismissed and — to the dismay of many a staunch Prussian Protestant conservative, not least the bigotted Kaiserin herself[70] — the Catholic Bavarian Count Hertling was appointed as both Reich Chancellor and Prime Minister of Prussia on 1 November 1917. The Kaiser, irritated that the crisis had dragged on for so long, refused to listen to Valentini's advice that he should seek the views of others before reaching such a momentous decision, saying (as Valentini recorded): 'The outcome would be the same anyway, and he didn't much care for long-drawn-out discussions.'[71]

The events surrounding Michaelis's dismissal and Hertling's appointment only deepened the fears of the parliamentarians that the monarch was no longer of sound mind. On 27 October 1917 Erzberger came bursting into the Reichstag with news he had heard in the Foreign Office that Wilhelm had had another of his preposterous rants, this time in front of ministers, state secretaries and other high-ranking officials. As the Social Democrat Philipp Scheidemann later recalled, in his speech 'the Kaiser pointed to splendid victories in Italy, and declared they had been won not according to Hindenburg's and Ludendorff's plans, but according to his very own. Brilliant victories were coming! Italy would be knocked out like Russia. They would get even with France, as she would come over to our side. When the war was over a military Bill would be laid before them that would make all the world wonder. Then would come the Second Punic War, which he would conduct, and destroy England. He formerly thought about expelling [King] Albert and incorporating Belgium with the Empire. He had given up that idea, for, in dealing with Belgium, we should get more chatterers, and we had enough of them in the gossip shop — the Reichstag.' Of the reaction in parliament to these ravings Scheidemann noted: 'We all thought that the word "insane" only inadequately expressed the Kaiser's condition. The best thing would have been to send him to an asylum.'[72]

Slowly but surely in the crucible of total warfare the Personal Monarchy that Bismarck had imposed on the German Reich half a century before was inching towards a parliamentary system. The majority parties of the Reichstag succeeded in securing the appointment of Friedrich Payer of the Progressive People's party as Vice Chancellor and of Robert Friedberg of the National Liberals as Vice President of the Prussian Ministry of State. Wilhelm at first approved this profound shift in constitutional reality without demur,[73] but then allowed himself to be stirred up against Valentini by the Kaiserin, the Crown Prince and Plessen. 'Step by step Valentini has pressed me to give up the rights of the Crown', the monarch grumbled, evidently needing a scapegoat to justify the concessions he had been forced to make.[74] Weeks later he was still accusing the parliament of having 'pursued a policy of blackmail against him. He would pay the brutes back one day . . . As soon as the soldiers with their Iron Crosses came back home the Reichstag would be in for it.'[75] As we shall see, Wilhelm would delude himself to the last into thinking that his troops would fight against their fellow countrymen to keep him on the throne.

If the parliament was pulling in one direction, Supreme Army Command was pulling in the other. Hindenburg and Ludendorff were determined to remove the Kaiser's 'most dangerous' advisers from court, and since they held Valentini responsible for the lurch to the Left that had set in with the Reichstag's Peace Revolution, it was he who had to be the first to go.[76] The two generals found willing allies in the Crown Prince and the Kaiserin, who accused the head of the Civil Cabinet of having sold out the rights of the Crown.[77] When Hindenburg and Ludendorff once again issued an ultimatum to the effect that they would resign if Wilhelm did not sack the man who had been one of his most loyal and wisest counsellors for well over a decade, Valentini volunteered to go, to release the Kaiser from his dilemma. To the heir presumptive to the Hohenzollern throne who had allowed himself to be used as the messenger boy of the generals, Valentini exclaimed: 'What an undermining of the authority of the monarch! This time it is the generals who are forcing the Kaiser to make a change in the counsellors who stand closest to him, the next time it will be parliament! And then the Kaiser will no longer be free in his choice of a successor but will have to take whoever the Reichstag wants!'[78] Wilhelm II was as ever outraged at such a drastic intrusion into the most sacred sphere of his royal prerogative, but knew he was powerless to prevent it. 'So now the era of such enforcements has begun,' he bitterly remarked to Admiral von Müller, 'and there is absolutely nothing I can do about it.'[79] Valentini was replaced, as already mentioned, by the arch-conservative Friedrich von Berg, an old friend of Wilhelm's but also a trusted ally and willing tool of Hindenburg and the Supreme Command. Caught in the dichotomy between the parliamentary majority and the generals, between peace and annexations, the Kaiser's – and Germany's – fate would be decided on the battlefields of the western front.

`OUR ARMY SIMPLY CANNOT GO ON`

'Operation Michael', the massive offensive through which Ludendorff hoped to achieve a decisive breakthrough against the British, French and American armies, began between Cambrai and St Quentin on 21 March 1918.[80] The stunning initial German advances convinced the Kaiser that 'the battle is won, the English are totally beaten'; when they sued for peace they would have to kneel before the imperial standard, as this was nothing less than 'a victory of monarchy over democracy'.[81] After the advance had ground to a halt at Amiens, Ludendorff still hoped to wear the Allies down with a series of 'hammer blows' – in Flanders in April, at Chemin des Dames in May and at Noyon in June. The Supreme War Lord, sure of imminent victory and taking a keen interest once again in the military operations, fully approved of Ludendorff's strategy.[82] His entourage expressed concern at his exuberance which was based, they felt, on an over-optimistic estimation of what such localised 'hammer blows' were capable of achieving.[83]

Still confident of victory, the generals of Supreme Army Command continued their campaign to rid themselves of political opponents whose penchant for diplomacy they feared could rob Germany of the great prize to be had at the conference table. Ever since their clash at Brest-Litovsk, Richard von Kühlmann was the object of their most passionate hatred. On 24 June 1918 the Foreign Secretary made a speech in the Reichstag intended both to prepare the people at home for the need to settle for a compromise peace and to signal Germany's readiness to negotiate to the government in London.[84] His speech included the observation, anathema to Supreme Headquarters, that 'in view of the enormous scope of this coalition war and the number of Powers, some of them from overseas, involved, we can hardly expect to be able to bring it to an absolute conclusion by military decisions alone, without diplomatic negotiations of any kind'.[85] Hindenburg and Ludendorff immediately accused Kühlmann of defeatism, bewailing the 'demoralising' effect his words were bound to have on the army, and insisted on his dismissal. Hertling urged Wilhelm to keep Kühlmann at least for the time being in the hope of initiating peace talks with Britain. But then Friedrich von Berg, in a confrontation with the monarch bordering on insubordination, forced the Kaiser to change his mind once more. As Berg himself reported the incident: 'I had not expected *such* weakness in the Kaiser. I had the feeling that the ground on which I was standing was beginning to shake and, highly excited as I was, told him exactly what I thought of him. I declared that it was impossible to govern in this manner, that I refused to go along with this weak-kneed policy, that the Kaiser himself would have to bear the

responsibility if he wanted to throw his crown into the dirt, and if he carried
on like this he was sure to lose it ... Several times the Kaiser asked me if
I were prepared to accept the responsibility [!], which I naturally affirmed as
I would not otherwise be advising His Majesty to take this step.'[86] Wilhelm
not only sacked Kühlmann but appointed his personal friend Admiral Paul
von Hintze to the Auswärtiges Amt in the face of opposition from both the
Reichstag and the Wilhelmstrasse itself. Even at this late stage, then, the
Kaiser showed himself to be powerful enough to appoint a candidate of his
choice to high office, at least so long as the Supreme Army Command did not
oppose him, but this was to be the last time.[87] A few days after Kühlmann's
dismissal Berg persuaded Wilhelm to sack Moriz von Lyncker, his Chief of
Military Cabinet for the past ten years, as well, on the grounds that Lyncker –
a broken man since the death of two of his sons on the front – had also
expressed doubts on whether the war could still be won.[88]

Ludendorff's next 'hammer blow', a major attack on Reims beginning on 15
July 1918, was a disaster. Thereafter the German army had virtually nothing
in reserve and morale among the troops – which had been kept high only by
the prospect of a speedy end to the war – now sank to new depths.[89] Three
days after the attack on Reims the French mounted a successful counter-
offensive, and on 8 August 1918, the 'black day of the German army' as
Ludendorff called it, the British broke through the German positions at
Amiens. The huge number of men surrendering to the British left no doubt
that the German army had suffered a serious blow to its morale.[90] Wilhelm's
response to the disaster, after the initial shock, was resigned: 'I see that we
must take stock', he announced. 'We are at the limit of our capabilities. The
war must be brought to an end.'[91] He did, however, send von Berg to Brussels
to ask the Governor-General Ludwig von Falkenhausen whether he was
prepared to take over as Reich Chancellor with a view to establishing a
military dictatorship.[92]

In a Crown Council held under the Kaiser's chairmanship at Spa in
southern Belgium on 14 August 1918 the political and military leaders of
the Reich assembled to consider the consequences of the military setbacks.[93]
For the first time Ludendorff admitted that victory in the west was now
beyond reach, though he did maintain that the enemy's will to continue
the fight could still be broken by a German withdrawal behind unassailable defences on occupied territory.[94] Wilhelm dreamt of being able to rouse
the nation to hold out until acceptable terms were on offer. 'To weaken the
enemy's confidence in victory, to raise the confidence of the German people it
would be necessary to form a propaganda committee', he announced. 'Blazing
speeches must be held by prominent private individuals ... but also by the

statesmen.'[95] Yet he himself spent the following weeks in isolation from his people at Schloss Wilhelmshöhe outside Kassel, where Auguste Viktoria was recovering from a heart attack. It was there that news reached him of the collapse of his army along the entire western front. On 2 September 1918, evidently close to a nervous breakdown,[96] he exclaimed: 'We have lost the campaign. Our troops have now been retreating ever since 18 July. The fact is that we are exhausted. I can't understand what the people in Avesnes [i.e. the operations department of Supreme Army Command] thought they were doing. When the offensive across the Marne was begun on 15 July, I was assured that the French had no more than eight divisions in reserve, the English perhaps 13. Instead of that the enemy ... has hit us in our right flank and forced us to retreat. Ever since then it's been one blow after another. Our army simply can't go on.'[97]

THE PARLIAMENTARISATION OF THE HOHENZOLLERN MONARCHY

As everyone in the imperial entourage was forced to admit, the military reverses of the late summer of 1918 had had an alarming effect 'on the mood of broad sections of the population against the government and the Kaiser'.[98] Prince Max of Baden was among the many who appealed to Wilhelm to give up his seclusion and seize the initiative. 'The people are looking for their Kaiser and must find him if serious damage is to be averted. Rightly or wrongly they fear a growing sense of estrangement from Him, whereas they are ready to follow His leadership provided they are secure in the knowledge that He understands them.'[99] Acting on his own idea of mounting a propaganda offensive, on 9 and 10 September 1918 the Kaiser visited the Krupp works at Essen (see Figure 56) with the intention of 'reaching out to the workforce and, by means of a personal appeal which would be most effective in Essen as the centre of the armament industry, to counter the threatening unrest within the working class of the nation'.[100] Ignoring the manuscript that had been prepared for him, Wilhelm II trotted out his Hohenzollern monarchist ideology replete with the tired old shibboleth of the irreconcilable struggle between the godly chivalric Germanic virtues and the devilish plutocratic Anglo-Saxon vices, warning the exhausted, hungry and dejected Krupp workers that the war might last for many years to come and threatening anyone spreading defeatist rumours with the gallows. The Emperor's pep talk went down like a lead balloon, with hecklers shouting 'hunger!' and demanding 'when will there be peace?'[101] As usual the speech was substantially redacted for publication[102] but was nevertheless heavily criticised in the socialist and democratic press, whereas Wilhelm took comfort

Figure 56 'Each of us has his duty to perform and his burden to carry, you at
your lathe and I on my throne!' Kaiser Wilhelm II with workers at the
Krupp factory in Essen, 10 September 1918

from the praise its pious tone was accorded in some conservative newspapers,
deluding himself into believing that with his speech in Essen he had secured
the loyalty of the German working class.[103] Just a few days later he addressed
some four hundred officers of the torpedo division in Kiel with the words: 'The
goal is in sight, our muskets at the ready, defeatists must be stood up against
the wall.'[104] And then the news reached him that Germany's allies were
collapsing like dominoes.

On 25 September 1918 Bulgaria asked for an armistice. That the Ottoman
Empire and the Danube Monarchy would not be able to continue the war
became clear when the Syrian front began to waver and the Austrians put out
peace feelers.[105] As the crisis mounted Foreign Secretary von Hintze put
forward his plan for a 'revolution from above' as the quickest and simplest
way out of the lost war.[106] He proposed that the Kaiser head off the looming
political and social upheaval by appointing party leaders, including some
Majority Socialists, to the government and conceding parliamentary responsibility in the German Reich. The new democratic government would also, it
was hoped, be more effective in appealing to President Woodrow Wilson for
fair terms than the Hertling regime, which ever since the Peace of Brest-Litovsk

and the sacking of Kühlmann was seen in Washington and elsewhere as the footstool of the Supreme Army Command.[107] Ludendorff was himself now forced to admit that the war was lost and that catastrophe threatened to engulf the army itself: overnight, fearing a complete rout on the western front and the disintegration of the units retreating homewards, he demanded an immediate ceasefire and the opening of peace talks. Not least in the cynical calculation of exculpating himself and his fellow generals from the stigma of defeat, he gave his support to Hintze's plan with the telling words that the time had come *'to bring those circles into the government whom we have in the main to thank for the mess we are in . . .* They should now make the peace that *must* now be accepted. They must lie in the bed they have made for themselves.'[108]

Kaiser Wilhelm II shared Ludendorff's stab-in-the-back interpretation of the catastrophe facing his country. 'Our politicians have failed miserably' was how he reacted to the news of Germany's military defeat.[109] Bewildered and crestfallen, he dismissed Hertling and agreed to concede parliamentary government.[110] A decree of 30 September 1918 promulgated the Kaiser's wish 'to see the German people more closely involved than hitherto in the running of the affairs of the fatherland. It is therefore my will that men who enjoy the confidence of the people should have a significant share in the rights and responsibilities of government.'[111] Having only recently demanded that a squadron of soldiers should be ordered to send the Reichstag packing,[112] Wilhelm now rejected the idea favoured by some in his entourage of appointing a general as Reich Chancellor and proroguing the Reichstag,[113] declaring the notion of a military dictatorship in such dire circumstances to be 'nonsense'.[114] He still hoped, however, to 'preserve for the Crown the fullest possible initiative in forming the government'.[115] Accordingly, he insisted even now on exercising his imperial prerogative of choosing Hertling's successor without reference to the Reichstag.[116] A further clash with the majority parties, which were bent on thoroughgoing constitutional reform and at long last apprised of the military catastrophe facing the country, appeared inevitable.[117]

In their discussions with Vice Chancellor Friedrich von Payer and state secretary Count Roedern, who were sent by the Kaiser to sound them out, the party leaders made clear that they would settle for nothing less than genuine parliamentary responsibility, including a say in the appointment of the Chancellor himself. It was only because of the relentless pressure of time – Ludendorff was insisting on an immediate formation of the new government which could then declare an armistice[118] – and the refusal of both Payer and Constantin Fehrenbach of the Centre party to take on the post that a member of parliament was not appointed to the Reich Chancellorship. The Reichstag was, however, able to secure almost all of its other demands, with several deputies from the Centre party, the Progressive People's party and the Majority Social Democrats joining the government as state secretaries (some without portfolio) or under secretaries of state. Payer stayed on as Vice Chancellor; reactionaries such as von Berg the Chief of the Civil Cabinet, Paul von Hintze the Foreign Secretary and Hermann von Stein the War Minister were forced to resign. The Kaiser had lost the ability both to keep men of his choosing in office against the will of the parliamentary majority and also to exclude members of the Reichstag of whom he disapproved – most notably the 'rascally traitor' Matthias Erzberger – from the government.[119] From this time on (in contrast to the appointment of Payer and Friedberg in autumn 1917) the new men in the government retained their status as members of the Reichstag, and with that the transformation of the Kaiserreich into a Parliamentary Monarchy had come another significant step closer. Even the appointment of Wilhelm's younger 'colleague'[120] Prince Max of Baden as Reich Chancellor could hardly disguise the fact that the Kaiser had finally lost control over the composition of the government. Constitutional reforms pushed through in October 1918 completed the parliamentarisation of the Hohenzollern Monarchy: the monarch's prerogative of untrammelled military command, his *Kommandogewalt*, was subjected to ministerial countersignature, as was his right to make pronouncements on political issues; his right to declare war and sign international treaties would in future require parliamentary approval; and the responsibility of the Reich Chancellor to the Reichstag was firmly anchored in law.[121]

With that most of the demands of the majority parties had been formally attained. The big question remained whether the concessions made by the Crown and the military were genuine or merely tactical moves designed to secure their position in face of the looming defeat.[122] Was it credible that Wilhelm II, who for thirty years had trumpeted his anti-parliamentary and anti-democratic ideology and championed his Frederician notions of Personal Monarchy by Divine Right, had undergone an eleventh-hour conversion and was now prepared to accept the new constitutional forms? Abdication, the symbolic act which would have signalled to the nation and the wider world that a new order had indeed begun, was a step Kaiser Wilhelm II refused to consider until it was too late.

'AS IF HE WERE A LITTLE CHILD': THE KAISER'S FLIGHT TO HOLLAND

In the small hours of 4 October 1918 the government of Prince Max of Baden, under constant pressure from Supreme Army Command, asked President Wilson to arrange an armistice and accepted his celebrated 'Fourteen Points' as the basis for the forthcoming peace negotiations.[123] The hapless Chancellor, unhappy that his first act in office was to sue for the de facto capitulation of his country, was told by Wilhelm II, mindless militarist to the last: 'The Supreme Command consider an armistice necessary and you have not been brought here to make difficulties for the Supreme Command.'[124]

When the USA had declared war on Imperial Germany in April 1917, Kurt Riezler had sensed that this might spell not just the defeat of the Reich but the end of the Hohenzollern Monarchy as well. 'What if the Entente should publicly declare its readiness to negotiate with the German people but not with the Hohenzollerns?' he had asked.[125] Such forebodings now proved to have been well-founded. Wilson's first reply of 8 October 1918 already contained a hint that regime change could be a precondition for negotiations, since it posed the telling question of who really ruled in Berlin. The President felt justified in asking, the American note said, 'whether the Imperial Chancellor is speaking merely for the constituted authorities of the Empire who have so far conducted the war'.[126] In the second Wilson note of a few days later the US government, in an unmistakable reference to the Hohenzollern military monarchy and its responsibility for the war, declared as its general war aim 'the destruction of every arbitrary power anywhere that can separately, secretly and of its single choice, disturb the peace of the world'.[127] Naturally Wilhelm was quick to see the implications. Describing Wilson's reply as 'a piece of unmitigated frivolous insolence' he ordered the Chancellor 'to call upon our entire nation to rise up as one man around its Kaiser in defence of its most sacred values, just as its government must stand before him! The insolence of this interference in our political affairs must be shown up for what it is.'[128] The military terms for an armistice laid down in the second Wilson note – including a peaceful withdrawal from all occupied territory and an immediate cessation of submarine warfare – brought about a change of heart at Supreme Army Command, too. Suddenly the generals, having pressed for an immediate armistice, called for the negotiations to be broken off and for the entire German nation to be mobilised for a final defiant showdown with the western Allies.[129] Only by threatening to resign was Prince Max able to persuade the Kaiser to override the demands of the generals and admirals and order an end to the U-boat campaign.[130]

With Wilson's third note of 23 October 1918, the issue of the Kaiser's abdication rose to the very forefront of the domestic agenda.[131] In it the President roundly declared: 'It is evident that the German people have no means of commanding the acquiescence of the military authorities of the Empire to the popular will; that the power of the King of Prussia to control the policy of the Empire is still unimpaired; that the determining initiative remains with those who have been masters of Germany ... The nations of the world do not and cannot trust the word of those who have hitherto been the masters of German policy ... If the Government of the United States must deal with the military masters and the monarchical autocrats of Germany now, or if it is likely to have to deal with them later ... it must demand not peace negotiations but surrender.'[132]

Without so much as a word to the monarch or the civilian statesmen, Ludendorff responded to Wilson's third note by issuing an order to the army which in effect broke off negotiations with the USA.[133] Prince Max and his Cabinet, humiliated in the eyes of the world, were now determined to secure the dismissal of this General who had first driven them into seeking a hasty armistice and then done everything in his power to avoid responsibility for this fateful step. The Chancellor demanded that Wilhelm II put an end to the 'dual government' by sacking Ludendorff, threatening otherwise to resign himself.[134] The Kaiser gave way, saying 'it really is intolerable that such promulgations are issued without my or the Reich Chancellor's approval. I see no alternative to agreeing to the Chancellor's demand. Any other decision would lead to insoluble political difficulties.'[135] Ludendorff was sacked on 26 October 1918 and replaced by the Württemberger Wilhelm Groener. Hindenburg was persuaded to stay at his post, destined (as we know) to play a key part in the events leading to Wilhelm's abdication two weeks later — not to mention his fateful role as President of the Weimar Republic.[136]

Meanwhile the situation of the starving and disillusioned population at home and within the army was rapidly becoming intolerable. Since the Kaiser was seen to be the most obvious obstacle to ending the war, and since more favourable peace terms could be hoped for if he were toppled, a revolutionary atmosphere gathered pace throughout the country. Within the government the view gained ground that the monarchy could and should be saved, at least as an institution, if Wilhelm II (and his equally unpopular and discredited son the Crown Prince) could be persuaded to give up the throne in a timely, voluntary and dignified manner, to be replaced in the first instance by a regency.[137] But they reckoned without the Kaiser, who fumed at the President of the United States: 'That brute is demanding my removal and that of all the other monarchs in Germany. He has now thrown aside the mask and will get what is coming to him. The chap simply has not the foggiest idea of the situation in Germany.'[138] Deluding himself into thinking that the German people were still staunchly monarchist, he developed a wholly unrealistic plan of resistance. 'With every new note they are asking for more, and each time we give way. Wilson wants to dictate to us which constitution Germany should have and demands our total surrender . . . I am not going anywhere; if I were to, the Reich would fall apart, therefore it is my duty to stay put and if necessary go down together with my people. This time we cannot give way; if the government nevertheless wants to do so it will have to be kicked out. Then either a new government with a different majority or a military dictatorship; at the same time a call to the people to rise, the strengthening of the army, and then we will fight. Recently the troops have fought brilliantly. The Chancellor is not on top of the job, the Foreign Office has completely filled its pants.'[139] In spite of such hot air the monarch was forced to accept the realities of the situation and agree to the American terms for an armistice. In late October he even declared his public support for the recent democratic reforms.[140] After thirty years of loudly proclaiming the very reverse his people refused to believe a word, judging his declaration to be nothing but a cowardly bid to save his own skin and keep his throne.[141]

On the evening of 29 October 1918, on the urging of his entourage and very much against the wishes of the Chancellor, Wilhelm II left Berlin, where he had been since the beginning of the month, to rejoin the generals at Supreme Headquarters in Spa; he would never again set foot on German soil.[142] His departure proved to be disastrous, not only because he was now once again out of touch with the rapidly changing developments in the capital, but even more so because it was widely interpreted as a 'flight' from the moderating influence of the civilian statesmen back to the detested policies of the military.[143] Prince Max had come to the conviction that Wilhelm's abdication was now unavoidable, but as the heir presumptive to the Grand Duchy of Baden he had misgivings about advising his older 'colleague' to relinquish his crown in person.[144] On 1 November he therefore dispatched the hapless Prussian Minister of the Interior, Bill Drews, to Belgium to urge the Kaiser in the name of the government to abdicate. Supported by his generals, the monarch refused point-blank. Giving poor Drews a regular dressing-down, he insisted in his own words: 'I wouldn't dream of abdicating. The King of Prussia must not leave Germany in the lurch, least of all at a time like this; I too have sworn my oath and will keep it. I won't dream of quitting my throne on account of a few hundred Jews or 1,000 workers – you go and tell that to your masters in Berlin.'[145] Still convinced that the army was solidly behind him, the Kaiser vowed to put down the insurrection at home by force. 'My duty as Supreme War Lord forbids me to abandon the army', he proclaimed. 'The army is engaged in a heroic struggle with the enemy. Its determined cohesion depends on the person of the Supreme War Lord. If the latter departs, the army will disintegrate and the enemy invade our homeland without let or hindrance.' If there were any more talk of abdication, he would answer 'with machine-guns in the streets, even if my Schloss is thereby shot to pieces, but order there must be'.[146]

On that very day revolution began to spread like wildfire throughout the whole of Germany from Kiel, where the sailors had disobeyed orders to engage in battle with the Royal Navy in what would have been a suicide mission to save the 'honour' of the Imperial Fleet – the fact that the uprising had begun in 'his' navy was an especially bitter pill for the Kaiser to swallow.[147] As the revolution spread, the German monarchies came crashing down one by one: on the night of 7–8 November the ancient House of Wittelsbach was dethroned in Bavaria, followed the next day by most of the others. With a general strike and mass demonstrations scheduled for Berlin, the Majority Social Democrats, fearing chaos if they lost control of the streets, demanded the immediate abdication of the Kaiser, otherwise they would leave the government.

But Wilhelm was still certain that he had the might of the army behind him.[148] To establish whether the troops really would be prepared to take up arms against the revolutionaries at home the Supreme Army Command summoned the commanders of the divisions in the vicinity to Headquarters at Spa. On the morning of 9 November 1918 they were confronted with two questions: first, 'What is the attitude of the troops to the Kaiser? Will it be possible for the Kaiser marching at the head of the troops to reconquer the homeland by force of arms?', and secondly: 'What is the attitude of the troops to Bolshevism? Will the troops engage in armed conflict against the Bolsheviks in their own homeland?'[149] The answers to both questions were sobering in the extreme: Only one of the commanders answered the first question with 'Yes', fifteen judged the attitude of their soldiers to be uncertain and twenty-three answered with a resounding 'No'. Similar doubts about the reliability of the troops were expressed when it came to the question of their willingness to put down the revolution. Colonel Wilhelm Heye who conducted the survey summed up the results in the words: 'In general what emerged was that the troops felt no particular dislike for the Kaiser, that they were in fact quite indifferent to him, that they only had the one wish to return home as soon as possible to peace and quiet ... The troops are completely exhausted and battle-weary, all they want is to go home and live in peace there; the soldier at the front will take up arms against his fellow countryman at home only if and when his own hearth and home, his wife and child are threatened by the Bolsheviks.'[150] With that the Kaiser's plans to re-take Germany at the head of his army fell to the ground.

The news now reaching Spa from Berlin could hardly have been more alarming. The Independent Socialists had called a general strike, crowds of

Figure 57 Revolution! The Kaiser's Schloss in Berlin in December 1918

workers were milling in the streets, blood had been shed, the supposedly loyal troops in the capital were going over to the revolutionaries (see Figure 57). In the hope of averting civil war and possibly of saving the monarchy, the government again demanded the Kaiser's immediate abdication. Prince Max informed Headquarters that it was now a matter not of hours but of minutes.[151] Adjutant-General von Plessen and General Count Friedrich von der Schulenburg came up with the idea that Wilhelm should abdicate as German Kaiser but stay on as King of Prussia — a suggestion that had been considered and rejected by the government as unworkable long ago, as the two crowns were constitutionally inseparable. Wilhelm nevertheless clutched at this straw. In the late morning of 9 November 1918, the confused message was relayed by telephone to Berlin: 'The matter had now been practically decided, they were now working on the wording — the Kaiser had agreed to the abdication. We will be getting the wording in half an hour.'[152]

On the basis of this telephone call Prince Max could hardly have guessed that Wilhelm II intended to remain on the throne of his Prussian ancestors, relinquishing only the imperial Crown. The dilemma in which the Chancellor found himself at midday on that fateful 9 November is graphically described in his memoirs: 'The half hour went by without any sign of the promised wording from Spa. At any moment the Kaiser's dethronement could be proclaimed on the street. We had no way of stopping that from happening. The dethronement could only be pre-empted by declaring the abdication. If we were to achieve even the slightest advantage for the Kaiser and his House, the abdication had to be made public immediately and could not be announced as an appendage to the dethronement. We tried over and over again to reach the Kaiser. One telephone . . . was off the hook, the other one engaged. I was faced with the dilemma of either waiting and doing nothing, or of acting on my own initiative. I knew that I was not formally entitled to publish [the abdication] without the Kaiser's express consent. But I held it to be my duty to proclaim the Kaiser's decision, which had been reported to me as firm, while there was still some point in doing so.'[153] Prince Max thereupon authorised the official government news agency to announce 'The Kaiser and King has decided to give up the throne.'[154] Even this panicky proclamation, made over the head of the monarch who was still dithering at Spa, came too late, however; a few hours later, again to pre-empt the revolutionaries in the streets, the Social Democrat Philipp Scheidemann proclaimed the German Republic from the balcony of the Reichstag.

At Headquarters the pressing issue was now the monarch's personal safety. Only too aware of the bloody fate suffered by the Tsar and his family, and unsure of the loyalty of the guards regiment stationed at Headquarters, the Kaiser's entourage heard with alarm that revolutionary troops were on their way to Spa.[155] To the last the generals hesitated to inform the Supreme War Lord that the army no longer stood behind him. When finally they advised him that the game was up and that he must flee secretly across the border to the Netherlands, General Groener had the impression that in that awful moment the Kaiser's life had come to an end. 'He said nothing, just looked – looked from one to the other, with an expression first of amazement, then piteous appeal, and then – just a curious wondering vagueness. He said nothing, and we took him – just as if he were a little child – and sent him to Holland.'[156]

CHAPTER FORTY-FIVE

The unicorn in winter. A new life in exile

Early on Sunday morning, 10 November 1918, a spectral little motorcade drew up at the Belgian–Dutch border in the town of Eijsden. Accompanied only by his Adjutant-General Hans von Plessen, the two Flügeladjutanten Georg von Hirschfeld and Sigurd von Ilsemann, his physician Dr Otto von Niedner, Freiherr Werner von Grünau as the representative of the Foreign Office and a couple of attendants, the German Kaiser and King of Prussia had left Supreme Headquarters at Spa in the small hours in the gleaming white-and-gold royal train, but after just a few kilometres, fearing an attack from their own soldiers, the Supreme War Lord and his suite had switched to two waiting automobiles in the hope of reaching the safety of the neutral Netherlands undetected. For several hours Kaiser Wilhelm II had to put up with the catcalls of the good people of Eijsden while he paced, smoking, up and down the platform (see Figure 58) waiting for the royal train containing the remainder of his entourage and more than seventy servants to catch up with the advance party.

Although her equerry General van Heutsz had been in attendance at Spa from 5 to 9 November 1918, both Queen Wilhelmina and her government at The Hague were taken by surprise by the German monarch's sudden appearance on Dutch soil.[1] The telegrams which Paul von Hintze had dispatched from Headquarters on the evening of 9 November reached Friedrich Rosen, the German envoy in the Dutch capital, only after Wilhelm II's arrival at Eijsden. The Dutch Prime Minister Charles Ruys de Beerenbrouck and Foreign Minister Herman van Karnebeek made frantic telephone calls in the search for a suitable place for the imperial refugee and his entourage to stay. As it was still unclear whether Wilhelm had indeed abdicated, as was being claimed in Berlin, or not, the Dutch Cabinet turned down an offer from

Figure 58 The flight to Holland. On the railway station at Eijsden,
10 November 1918

the Queen – prompted in part no doubt by the terrible fate which had befallen the Tsar and his family – to make one of her own castles available to her Hohenzollern relative. Eventually Count Godard van Aldenburg-Bentinck agreed to put up the Kaiser at Amerongen, his moated castle in the province of Utrecht, for a few days. It was almost midnight on 10 November before Wilhelm received the Queen's telegram granting him asylum in the Netherlands. While the armistice was being signed in a railway carriage at Compiègne north of Paris, the Kaiser's train, accompanied by hostile demonstrations, made its way via Maastricht, Nijmegen and Arnhem to Maarn, where Count Bentinck met his guest and took him to Amerongen. Bentinck could not know that his visitors would spend the next eighteen months in his castle, nor that it would be there that, on 28 November 1918, Wilhelm of Hohenzollern would formally and for all time renounce 'his rights to the Crown of Prussia and thereby to the rights of the German Imperial Crown bound to it'.[2]

A NEW LIFE IN AMERONGEN AND DOORN

To find room for the Kaiser, his suite and the servants, Bentinck had to lease both guest houses in Amerongen, find emergency accommodation all over the town and ask the Dutch government to send in supplies and fuel. Wilhelm

Figure 59 The moated castle of Amerongen in winter. Wilhelm's
bedroom is marked with an X

was assigned rooms commanding a view of the Rhine and containing a bed
reputedly once slept in by the Sun King Louis XIV of France (see Figure 59).
Though his quarters were comfortable enough – by contrast, the Crown
Prince, who had also been forced to flee to Holland, had to make do with
extremely straitened circumstances on the island of Wieringen – Wilhelm II
was in effect under house arrest at Amerongen. His mail and telephone calls
were censored, and he was not permitted to leave the castle grounds without a
Dutch escort. As he had crossed the border before the signing of the armistice,
in field uniform and in the company of serving officers, his status remained
unclear: Was he to be treated as a private individual or as the King-Emperor
and Supreme War Lord of a belligerent Power? No less problematical were his
material circumstances: For how long was the Dutch taxpayer expected to
defray the cost of the upkeep of this foreign sovereign, his retinue, his guests
and his staff? At the request of the Dutch government the imperial entourage
was soon reduced to just two gentlemen, a physician (from November 1919
onwards Dr Alfred Haehner) and a handful of manservants. The seriously ill
Kaiserin, who had followed him in November 1918 with a staff of eleven, was
forced to make do with one lady-in-waiting (Countess Mathilde von Keller),
one chamberlain and six lackeys. Even so, the imperial household at
Amerongen numbered no fewer than twenty-four persons.[3]

On 30 November 1918 the revolutionary government in Berlin decided to
freeze the assets of the House of Hohenzollern, but this draconian step was

followed shortly afterwards by the transfer to the Netherlands of many millions of marks to enable the Kaiser and Kaiserin to lead a life in accordance with their estate: 652,000 Reichsmarks were sent to Wilhelm's accounts at the Von der Heydt'schen Bank in Amsterdam and Zandvoort in November 1918, followed by eight million marks in January 1919, 1.2 million in August 1919, six million in September 1919 and a further ten million Reichsmarks in October 1919. Another 38 million marks were sent him on the sale of two of the royal palaces on the Wilhelmstrasse. In the first twelve months of exile no fewer than 66 million marks were transferred from Berlin to his Dutch accounts.[4] But even these huge sums were not enough to cover the expenses of the Kaiser and his rump court in Holland, estimated to run at around 450,000 guilders per annum. In May 1921 Wilhelm's veteran Minister of the Royal House, Count August zu Eulenburg, asked the Berlin government for a further 10 million marks from public funds, which were duly approved, if under protest.[5]

From the outset the ex-Kaiser had the contents of the royal train, including some 300 plates and the silverware to go with them, at his disposal. On 1 September 1919 the Social Democratic Prussian Minister of Finance Albert Südekum approved the release of 'the furniture and other objects designated for the living quarters of the former Kaiser and King',[6] including priceless treasures from the Berlin Schloss, the Schloss Bellevue, the Schloss at Charlottenburg and the Neues Palais in Potsdam. The list itemising these objects ran to seventy-one pages; no fewer than fifty-nine railway carriages were required to transport them all to Holland.[7] The Social Democrats Hermann Müller and Philipp Scheidemann warned the government in vain against showing such generosity towards this 'failed monarch' whom 'millions upon millions regard as one of the men most guilty for the war and all the suffering it has caused'.[8]

After a plebiscite held in June 1926 to determine whether all the German princes should be dispossessed without compensation − Wilhelm referred to the 14.4 million (37 per cent of the electorate) German men and women who voted in favour of the motion as 'Schweinehunde!'[9] − a final agreement was reached on what belonged to the state and what to the Hohenzollerns. A contract dated 29 October 1926 between 'the formerly ruling Prussian Royal House' and the Prussian government awarded one third of the sixty royal castles − among them Bellevue, Babelsberg, Monbijou, Königswusterhausen, Cecilienhof, Oels, the Palais Kaiser Wilhelm I, the Niederländisches Palais on the Unter den Linden and the Prinz-Albrecht-Palais in the Wilhelmstrasse, together with one half of the Burg Hohenzollern in Württemberg − to the Hohenzollerns, along with the hunting lodge at Rominten in East Prussia, the

Cadinen estate in West Prussia, the Achilleion on the Isle of Corfu and two farms in what had been the German colony of South-West Africa.[10] Wilhelm was now able to repay the loan of one million guilders he had received from his banker Eduard von der Heydt. When he died at Doorn in June 1941, his estate after taxes was valued at almost 13 million marks.[11] No other exiled monarch in modern history was treated as generously as was Wilhelm II in Holland. This did not stop him from complaining bitterly of the 'barefaced robbery at the hands of the damned republic'.[12]

With the funds flowing from Berlin, Wilhelm had little difficulty in finding the 1.35 million guilders needed to purchase Huis Doorn with its park of 59 hectares from Baroness van Heemstra on 16 August 1919.[13] He had the manor house renovated, central heating and a lift installed and a new gatehouse to the park erected. In Doorn, to where he and the Kaiserin moved at the beginning of May 1920, the Kaiser was able to surround himself with memorabilia from the palaces he had left behind: 'Busts, paintings and etchings of the Gr[eat] Elector, Frederick the Great, Grosspapa and Papa . . . along with pictures of the Prussian Army throughout its years of glory! Hochkirch and Leuthen, Hohenfriedberg and Königgrätz decorate the walls', he wrote happily on 4 May 1920.[14] Even the saddle on which he had sat while working at his desk in the Schloss in Berlin now found a new home in the tower room in Huis Doorn. He took personal charge of the park, helping to fell trees and chop wood.

In spite of his wealth, however, a small-minded miserliness pervaded life at Doorn. Visitors were often expected to walk or take the tram to and from the station to save petrol. They complained of the poor quality of the food they were served. Dr Haehner, the Kaiser's personal physician, was forced to supplement his salary from his savings, and the wages of the chauffeurs and the fifty servants – twenty of them Dutch female day labourers – were so low as to cause much disaffection and a rapid turnover.[15] The dissatisfaction was blamed on the Marshal of the House Lieutenant-General (retired) Hans von Gontard, formerly the governor of the Kaiser's younger sons.[16] He in turn suffered 'a complete nervous breakdown' in 1922 and was obliged to spend four months on holiday on doctor's orders. But he returned to his post and served as the Kaiser's House Marshal until 1930.[17]

The 'courtiers' at Doorn gossiped and intrigued, the neighbours proved mostly prudish and dull, the Kaiser's movements outside of his walled park were severely restricted and he felt spied upon by The Hague government. Soon it became difficult to persuade talented men to take on duties at the isolated court and resentment grew, too, among those who volunteered to administer his financial affairs in the Generalverwaltung in Berlin. Not a few loyal Prussian monarchists were appalled by the indignity of Wilhelm's new

existence and expressed the hope that the humiliation he was enduring in
exile would soon be curtailed by a timely death.

THE THREAT OF EXTRADITION AND TRIAL AS A WAR CRIMINAL

In Amerongen and in the early years at Doorn Kaiser Wilhelm lived in
constant fear of kidnap and assassination. On taking his afternoon nap he
never failed to place a loaded pistol on his bedside table. He let his beard grow,
not least, as he said, because he didn't trust anyone 'to come near his throat
with a razor'.[18] The greatest danger he faced came from the victorious Allies,
however, who meeting in London in early December 1918 demanded
his extradition to face an international tribunal as the 'criminal chiefly
responsible for the war'.[19] (See Figure 60.) They held back from issuing an
ultimatum to the government in The Hague at this stage only because
President Woodrow Wilson considered it more prudent to postpone the vexed
'Kaiser Question' until it could be discussed at the forthcoming peace conference in Versailles.[20] Nevertheless, the threat of a blockade or even an invasion,
of the confiscation of its colonies or the loss of Dutch territory to Belgium was
taken so seriously in The Hague that on 6 December 1918 the Cabinet
demanded that Wilhelm leave the Netherlands. After speaking to Herman
van Karnebeek, Friedrich Rosen summoned Gontard to the capital to inform
him of this demand, while at the same time Count Lijnden van Sandenburg,
the governor of the province of Utrecht, was instructed to convey to the Kaiser
at Amerongen the government's expectation that he leave the country within
days.[21] On 8 December 1918 the deposed monarch agreed to leave Holland.
But where could he go?

Defeat in war, revolution at home, the 'betrayal' of his generals at Spa, the
abject flight across the border and now the threatening expulsion from the
Netherlands – the Kaiser had a nervous breakdown and on 14 December took
to his bed, just as he had done on several occasions both before and during the
war. For six weeks he refused to leave his rooms even for meals; until the end
of March 1919 he went around the castle grounds with his head swathed in
bandages, claiming that his old earache had returned to trouble him. Rumours
were circulated that Wilhelm was mentally ill; a Swiss psychiatrist was
summoned from Antwerp and spent a week in Amerongen. Foreign Minister
van Karnebeek was said to have expected the Kaiser to take his own life.[22]

If the monarch's nervous breakdown was genuine and a matter of serious
concern not only to the Kaiserin but also to the doctors,[23] it is equally true that
the entourage was intent on using the illness, if the need arose, to spirit
Wilhelm away in an ambulance to a temporary safe haven somewhere in

PUNCH, OR THE LONDON CHARIVARI.—May 19, 1915.

WILFUL MURDER.

The Kaiser. "TO THE DAY——"   Death. "——OF RECKONING!"

Figure 60 'Hang the Kaiser!' Demands for Wilhelm to be tried as a war criminal
were to be heard from the outset, as this *Punch* cartoon of 1915 shows

Holland or Germany such as a sanatorium, a monastery, the estate of the
Hereditary Princess of Salm or even a pleasure steamer on the Rhine, in the
hope of finding a new refuge for him later, perhaps in Scandinavia.[24] Partly
with the idea of disguising his identity Wilhelm now grew the white beard he
was to keep for the remainder of his life, and dyed his hair and wore
spectacles. The embassy at The Hague provided him with a false passport

and suitable clothes and placed a car at his disposal.[25] As the agitation in the press abated and the Dutch government grew less insistent on his immediate departure, these bizarre escape plans were for the moment shelved, but the danger of a kidnap attempt or extradition to London or Paris remained acute.

At nightfall on 5 January 1919, a certain Mr Luke Lea, the Senator for Tennessee, turned up at Amerongen wearing the uniform of a colonel in the US army and brandishing a letter from his government. As he told journalists after the event, his intention had been to kidnap the ex-monarch and hand him over to the American army on the Rhine. The Senator and the five American soldiers accompanying him were led away by the police.[26] Several further threats to seize the Kaiser were taken seriously, as was the news that a Belgian pilot was planning to drop bombs on the Schloss. In winter the ice on the castle moat was broken up each night to keep intruders away from the Kaiser.[27] As late as autumn 1920 Gontard handed out live ammunition on the strength of rumours that a band of Englishmen was planning to abduct the monarch in an airship.[28]

In the spring of 1919 the victorious Allies returned to the 'Kaiser Question', revealing a wide range of opinion. As a place of banishment they rejected Switzerland as being too democratic and Corfu as too insecure and for that matter, too pleasant. Well aware of French sensibilities, the British refrained from proposing that Wilhelm be sent to St Helena; the French for their part wanted to dispatch all the Hohenzollerns to Algeria, but this idea found little favour. The Falkland Islands, the Dutch East Indies, Devil's Island and Curaçao were all seriously considered, whereas the humane request from the Netherlands for permission simply to deposit the unwanted guest by means of a Dutch-registered ship in Argentina, Chile or Peru was ignored.[29]

There was much disagreement, too, on what charges were to be laid against 'William of Hohenzollern'. In the 'Commission on the Responsibility of the Authors of the War and on Enforcement of Penalties' which had been meeting since January 1919 the British and the French delegates argued for harsh punishment, the Italians prevaricated, and the Americans and Japanese seemed anxious to avoid a trial altogether.[30] Such divisions became deeper still when the Big Four met in Paris in April 1919. Whereas Lloyd George and Clemenceau insisted on a public trial, or at least on Wilhelm's banishment to the Falklands or to Devil's Island, President Wilson proved unwilling to take any action against the exiled monarch. In the end they agreed on a high-minded but imprecise paragraph which was to find its way into the Treaty of Versailles as Article 227: 'William II of Hohenzollern, formerly German Emperor', was to be publicly tried by a special tribunal composed of five judges from the United States of America, Great Britain, France, Italy and Japan respectively 'for a supreme offence against international morality and the sanctity of treaties'. The tribunal would be 'guided by the highest motives of international policy, with a view to vindicating the solemn obligations of international undertakings and the validity of international morality. It will be its duty to fix the punishment which it considers should be imposed.' The question of where the special tribunal would sit was left undecided.[31]

As the terms of the peace settlement being reached at Versailles became known in early May 1919, the Dutch government assured the Kaiser that they would not extradite him to the Allies; should the latter threaten the Netherlands in an ultimatum, however, they would not put any obstacles in the way of his flight to Germany. Soon the monarch convinced himself that the extradition question had now been 'resolved'; he dreamt of his return to Germany in triumph.[32] Such illusions were shattered when the embassy in The Hague reported Karnebeek's comment that, if the Entente Powers really were to threaten to use force to secure the Kaiser's extradition, Wilhelm should either put a bullet through his brain or else one of his adjutants should take it upon himself to ensure that he was no longer around to suffer the indignity of arrest and arraignment. Once again plans were hatched in Amerongen, at the embassy in The Hague and among monarchist army officers in Germany to spirit the Kaiser to some secret location.[33]

The 'Kaiser Question' came to a head in the summer of 1919. On 28 June Clemenceau, speaking for the Allies, issued a demand to the Dutch government for the immediate extradition of Wilhelm II and the Crown Prince. Lloyd George formally proposed that the trial should take place either in Britain or the United States. Ignoring President Wilson's warning that it would be prudent to avoid holding such a tribunal in a major city, on 2 July the Allies agreed on London as the venue. The Prime Minister announced this decision in the House of Commons on the following day without first informing the King, a discourtesy which understandably upset him.[34] The Kaiser for his part was outraged by the suggestion made by both Hans von Plessen and Admiral von Müller that, for the sake of his own reputation and that of his House, the good of the fatherland and of the monarchical principle at large, he should give himself up to the Entente Powers of his own free will; he never forgave either man their impertinence.[35] Wilhelm similarly rejected the suggestion made by the Archbishop of Cologne that he should pre-empt his extradition to face trial in London by voluntarily submitting himself to the judgement of a tribunal consisting of Pope Benedict XV, Queen Wilhelmina and King Alfonso XIII of Spain.[36]

Protests flooded in not only against a tribunal in London but against any kind of trial of the deposed monarch. In a joint submission to George V the former kings of Saxony and Württemberg and the Grand Duke of Baden argued that any humiliation suffered by Wilhelm II would damage the monarchical principle as a whole and therefore pose a threat to the British Crown itself. Many feared that a public trial of Wilhelm II would prove incalculable in its scope and its consequences. Lord Esher thought the whole idea 'idiotic' and warned that embarrassing aspects of British pre-war policy such as the tacit promises of support given to France and Belgium could come to light; surely one should not repeat the mistake made in banishing Napoleon to St Helena, thus turning the German Kaiser into some kind of martyr.[37]

As matters dragged on – the Dutch government remained adamant in refusing to hand him over – and interest in the issue of his trial and punishment was beginning to wane, Wilhelm's fateful role in the events that had led to war were brought into sharp focus by the publication by Karl Kautsky of the monarch's militant marginal comments on the diplomatic exchanges of July 1914.[38] These revelations of what had really gone on behind the scenes in those crucial weeks caused 'general consternation' and did 'untold damage' to Wilhelm's standing, especially in Holland, leading to renewed demands for his extradition and trial.[39] Once more plans were made in Amerongen for the Kaiser's return to Germany, whatever the cost. The British minister in The Hague, Ronald Graham, reported that German monarchists had hidden weapons including some 2,000 machine-guns along the Dutch–German border.[40] In late November 1919 Gontard informed the monarch's physician Dr Haehner that the Allies were clearly determined on securing the Kaiser's extradition. 'But everything had now been prepared for such an eventuality, there will not be a repeat of the way things were handled on that unfortunate day in November 1918. Should the demands of the enemy be met [by the Dutch], then the Kaiser would simply have to take the necessary extreme action. I gathered from his words [wrote Haehner], that the Kaiser would then slip back in total secrecy across the border. That this would almost certainly lead to civil war was clear to all ... Whether or not this would spell the end of the Kaiser was of no consequence, in such circumstances one's honour mattered more than one's life ... We must never permit the ignominy to reach the point where the Kaiser falls into the hands of the enemy.'[41] Dr Johannes Kriege, the former legal expert in the Auswärtiges Amt who came to Amerongen at the end of 1919 to advise on the extradition question, was also convinced that Wilhelm's return would bring civil war and a further incursion of Entente troops into Germany in its train.[42] The prospect that her husband, the Crown Prince and her son Prince Eitel Friedrich might be handed over to the Allies also brought about a serious deterioration in the condition of the Kaiserin.[43] It was obvious that she would not survive the banishment of the Kaiser to some remote island on the other side of the globe.

When the foreign ministers of the victorious Powers met in Paris in January 1920, they agreed – but again without the express consent of the USA and Japan – on a formal demand to The Hague for the extradition of Wilhelm II in accordance with Article 227 of the Treaty of Versailles. The accusations levelled against him personally read like a propagandistic catalogue of all the atrocities committed by the German army and navy in the west[44] – events on the eastern and southern fronts received not a mention. The Kaiser was charged with the cynical violation of the neutrality of Belgium and Luxembourg, the shooting of hostages in Belgium, the mass deportation of entire populations, the kidnap and rape of the young women of Lille, the systematic laying to waste of great swathes of territory and unrestricted submarine warfare against passenger liners and merchant vessels. All these violations of the highest principles of humanity were laid at the door of the Supreme War Lord who, having ordered them or acquiesced in them, bore, it was claimed, at least the moral responsibility for them. To exert pressure on the government of the Netherlands, the note pointed out that, had Wilhelm still been in Germany, his name would have been included in the list of the many hundreds of suspected war criminals whose extradition was required by Article 228 of the Treaty. Signed by Clemenceau as chairman of the Peace Conference, the note was handed to the Dutch envoy in Paris on 6 January 1920.[45] Once again the whispered wish could be heard in the corridors of power at The Hague that the troublesome guest should disappear 'without a trace'.[46]

The Dutch government, under the not-unjustified impression that such a decision would not be entirely unwelcome to the Allies, unanimously refused to comply with the demand for the Kaiser's extradition. When His Excellency J. B. Kan turned up at Amerongen on his bicycle with this news, the relief was palpable: the Kaiserin burst into tears and Wilhelm was elated. 'That evening the Kaiser's mood was better than it has been for a long time', noted his doctor.[47] 'There is still a God in Heaven who ensures that justice is done!' Wilhelm wrote to his sister Margarethe.[48] In a trice he once again saw himself back on the throne, this time in fact at the bidding of the British, who would, he believed, first join with Germany to rid the world of Bolshevism and then proceed to subjugate Japan in the Pacific! Incredulous, his doctor commented: 'He was quite delirious with this totally utopian idea and even named his terms: complete restoration of the borders as before the war, restitution of all the confiscated materials, ships and so on, generally compensation for all the things the enemy had forced us to give up in the peace treaty. There is no way of dissuading the Kaiser from the idea that he would take up governing the country again.' The restoration of the monarchy and the rearmament of

Germany by the very Powers who had been her enemies and had deposed him would, so Wilhelm exulted, 'then be the greatest triumph of his life!'[49]

But how did London and Paris really react to the refusal of the Netherlands to hand the Kaiser over? Downing Street was adamant in regarding Wilhelm as an 'enemy of the human race' and insisted that he be interned 'in some spot or island where he will be rendered incapable of again molesting the peace of the world'.[50] In a second Note dated 14 February 1920 Lloyd George and the new French Premier Millerand threatened their defenceless Dutch neighbour with serious reprisals.[51] At the same time, though, the British hinted at their willingness to forego a public trial on condition that Wilhelm be interned — albeit to live in comfort and dignity with his family — on the Falklands or one of the Dutch islands such as Java or Batavia.[52] The Cabinet in London agreed to adopt this compromise course on 5 February 1920; to save face the government in The Hague was to be urged to take the initiative itself. The other Allies supported the British proposal.[53]

Karnebeek turned down even this solution, however, and offered only to meet the concerns of the Powers by briefly hardening the terms of the ex-monarch's internment in the Netherlands before allowing him to live out his life in some distant land such as Chile or Peru. As the indecision and disunity of the Allies became ever more apparent — talk of war or a blockade of Holland struck everyone as absurd — the situation was suddenly complicated by the pronouncement of Wilhelm's son and heir, the Crown Prince, on 9 February 1920 that he was prepared to submit himself to the Entente in his father's stead.[54] Ignoring the younger Wilhelm's offer, the Allies issued a new Note complaining of the refusal of the Dutch government to move 'the ex-Emperor far from the scenes of his crimes [and] make it impossible for him to exercise his evil influence in Germany in the future', but they remained frustrated.[55] They had to content themselves with the written assurance extracted from Wilhelm under protest on 10 March 1920 that he would not leave Huis Doorn (see Figure 61) and the surrounding area without prior notice, would desist from all political activity and agree to the censoring of his correspondence.[56] Four days later Queen Wilhelmina formally proclaimed the conditions under which the exiled German Sovereign could remain in the Netherlands.[57] The ex-Kaiser showed neither appreciation of the dilemma in which the Queen found herself nor gratitude for permission to stay in the country. He described the stand she had been obliged to take as 'absolutely scandalous', adding that he would 'never' forgive her. It was only thanks to him, he maintained, 'that her country had not also been involved in the war. Twice the Army High Command had had the intention of undertaking something against Holland, and on both occasions it was he who had prevented it.'[58]

Figure 61 Huis Doorn in the province of Utrecht

The Allies' fears that Wilhelm, if allowed to remain in Holland, could involve himself in German politics or even return to Germany acquired a new urgency with the Rightist Kapp Putsch of 12 March 1920.[59] In their final joint Note of 24 March 1920 they warned the Netherlands of this continuing danger and held its government responsible for any consequences that might ensue. With that, and Wilhelm's move from Amerongen to Doorn on 16 May 1920, the troublesome 'Kaiser Question' was for the moment shelved.

THE IMPERIAL FAMILY AFTER THE REVOLUTION

When Dr Alfred Haehner took up his post as physician to the Kaiser and Kaiserin at Amerongen in November 1919 – alongside the diary of the Kaiser's Flügeladjutant, Sigurd von Ilsemann, the doctor's diaries provide us with a remarkable insight into the monarch's life in the first years of exile[60] – he was briefed by Hans von Gontard, Friedrich von Berg and Countess von Keller on the physical and emotional state of the imperial couple. They agreed in describing the gravely ill Kaiserin as a woman who had unfailingly devoted herself to the task of protecting her husband from unpleasant truths; in the last months of the war in particular, her determination to shield Wilhelm from harsh realities had contributed not a little to the collapse of the monarchy.[61] The Kaiser, on the other hand, was in their view a cold, self-centred egotist with 'the soul of a child' and a tendency to hide behind grandiloquent bombast. They warned the physician that side by side with his violent outbursts of rage 'the Kaiser would from time to time suffer a complete nervous breakdown, when he would simply take to his bed and be dead to the world . . . The last such breakdown occurred when he had gone to Holland and received the news that the Dutch government intended to ask him to leave the country again. At such times the doctor had to make a determined effort to get the Kaiser to pull himself together and get out of bed.'[62]

Just weeks after his arrival, Haehner encountered precisely such a breakdown which he was, however, able to avert at the last minute. As we have seen, the publication in late 1919 of the Kautsky documents on the July Crisis of 1914 sharply increased the danger that the Kaiser would be extradited to face trial as a war-monger. On 4 December 1919 the Kaiserin summoned the doctor to tell him that her husband was 'very downcast' and in danger 'of abandoning himself to his depression which would take hold of him completely, he would then simply lie in his bed refusing to see anyone and become more and more obsessed with his dark musings'. Haehner did indeed find the Kaiser still in bed in the early evening. Wilhelm told him he had suffered 'a little collapse' on reading the Kautsky documents. But the doctor managed to talk the Kaiser round and persuaded him to get up.[63] Fortunately, Gontard had delayed giving Wilhelm news that would almost certainly have plunged him into even deeper despair: his sons August Wilhelm and Joachim were both suing for divorce.[64]

From time to time the Kaiser was visited in Amerongen and Doorn by some of his siblings and all of his children, but it cannot be said that any of these encounters brought the exiled monarch much joy. Wilhelm was never to see his eldest sister Charlotte again: she died in Baden-Baden on 1 October 1919 from the effects of the porphyria which she had inherited from her Hanoverian ancestors.[65] His second sister Victoria (Moretta) Princess of Schaumburg-Lippe visited Doorn only once, when Wilhelm got re-married in November 1922. As Haehner recorded in his diary, she made an 'appalling' impression on the assembled wedding guests. 'The life she has led was written clearly on her face for all to see', it was as if one had come 'face to face with the madame of a brothel'. The Kaiser, too, was horrified and thought her 'sharp face utterly covered in thick powder . . . quite dreadful'.[66] As mentioned in the second volume of this biography, Victoria Schaumburg was to die in penury in November 1929 as the abandoned wife of the Russian confidence trickster Alexander Zubkov; she was buried at Kronberg.[67] Wilhelm's sister Sophie, whose husband Constantine had been forced to relinquish the Greek throne in 1917 — he was restored to the throne in 1920 but deposed again two years later — was never able to visit him in the Netherlands. Of his four sisters it was therefore only the youngest, Margarethe (Mossy), later Landgravine of Hesse, who became a regular visitor, along with her husband Friedrich Karl (Fischy). As we shall see, the Kaiser's correspondence with his sister provides us with perhaps the best insight into his mindset in exile right up to his death in 1941.

The occasional visits of his tanned and sporty brother Prince Heinrich of Prussia — by contrast Wilhelm appeared 'really puffy' and 'spongey' [68] — were anything but stimulating for the Kaiser. Haehner noted that Heinrich regarded his elder sibling first and foremost as an emperor, then as the head of the House of Hohenzollern and only in third place as his brother. The Prince, he said, 'stood almost blindly in awe of his brother and most readily subordinated himself to him in all things'.[69] For his part the Kaiser found it difficult to take his brother at all seriously, seeing him 'rather as an absolute child in politics for whose opinions he couldn't give tuppence'.[70] Heinrich, a chain smoker, was to die of cancer in 1928.

Nor could Wilhelm take any pride and joy in the visits of his six sons Naturally there was the usual systemic rivalry between the exiled monarch and his ambitious and impatient heir to the throne the Crown Prince, a theme to which we shall return below. But the Kaiser's relationship with his other sons was no less frosty.[71] Since the Crown Prince had also been forced to seek asylum in Holland, the Kaiser had on 23 November 1918 appointed his second son Eitel Friedrich (Fritz) to represent him in his capacity as Head of the Royal House of Brandenburg-Prussia in respect of all family and financial matters.[72] Not known for his patience or tact, Eitel Fritz soon came into conflict with the elderly Minister of the Royal House Count August zu Eulenburg, referring to the man who had served his father loyally for thirty-two years as a 'totally senile ... old ass'.[73] On a visit to Doorn in July 1920 Eitel Fritz had 'a violent set-to with his father, so that it is even being said, and in fact by his siblings, that he will never come here again'.[74] The aversion was mutual, with Wilhelm complaining that his son's 'repulsively obese figure' was the result of alcoholism which had obviously 'softened his brain'.[75]

For his son August Wilhelm (Auwi), who turned up at Amerongen at the end of 1919 after the failure of his marriage — his wife had run off with one of the servants [76] — the Kaiser felt something approaching disgust. Dr Haehner also found it difficult to suppress his distaste at this imperial Prince's appearance. 'To me he looked very much like a foppish young hairdresser or shop assistant. Very little manliness in his entire manner, on the contrary quite womanly with jewellery everywhere. The lower part of the little finger on both hands is completely covered with rings, and there are rings on the other

fingers and fancy bracelets on each wrist.' It was little wonder, the physician
noted, that Auwi's marriage had failed. 'That his manner, his entire being is
incapable of satisfying a woman with a strong desire for masculinity is ... only
too clear ... The Kaiser it seems has very little liking for this particular son.'[77]
When Auwi came to Doorn in December 1920 to be with his mother on her
deathbed, his father refused to let him live in the house 'because he thought
him too much of a softy and could not bear to see him walking around the
house all day'.[78] Wilhelm von Dommes, the Kaiser's Chamberlain, described
the Prince as 'unbelievably boorish, dreadfully superficial and soft'.[79] We shall
come back to the troubled relationship between Kaiser Wilhelm and his son
Auwi in a later chapter.

As for his son Adalbert and his wife Adelheid, by birth a Princess of Saxony-
Meiningen, Wilhelm appeared 'totally indifferent' to both.[80] Adalbert really
was not 'a particular favourite of the Kaiser', Haehner observed, and his 'exalted
and highly-strung' wife only got on his nerves. He could hardly wait for them
to leave.[81] In fact Adalbert's 'cold' and 'arrogant' manner put off everyone at
Amerongen and Doorn, with Friedrich von Berg remarking that he was
probably 'the most stupid of all the sons'.[82] Wilhelm's relations with his fifth
son Prince Oskar were initially overshadowed by the latter's morganatic
marriage to Countess Ina von Bassewitz, and it was not until their visit to
Doorn in August 1921 that the Kaiser got to know his daughter-in-law somewhat better. But even then observers were struck by the absence of warmth
between father and son. 'There is something cold, something military in their
relationship to one another', noted Ilsemann.[83] And that relationship hardly
improved when Oskar objected to his father's re-marriage the following year.[84]

Most problematical was the Kaiser's youngest son Prince Joachim, a source
of great worry for both parents from birth. At the end of the second volume of
this biography I quoted from the disturbing report that the celebrated psychiatrist Professor Robert Gaupp had submitted to the imperial family in May
1918 on the incurable '*innate abnormal tendency*' of this Prussian Prince. The
report stressed Joachim's extraordinary psychological and sexual excitability
and spoke of the uncontrollable attacks of rage which periodically took hold of
him like an avalanche.[85] In 1916 Joachim had married the 18-year-old
Princess Marie Auguste of Anhalt, but the marriage was a disaster from the
beginning. As Gontard told Dr Haehner in December 1919, Joachim was
'quite out of control and had beaten his wife, herself just a slip of a girl'.[86]
The Prince accused his mother repeatedly of having ruined his life by
forbidding his marriage to Elisabeth Urach on the grounds that she was a
Catholic.[87] As Joachim's marriage fell apart in the summer of 1920, there were
'terrible scenes' with his father in Doorn, ending in a 'regular fit of raving

madness'.[88] Kaiser Wilhelm went so far as to accuse the Entente of bribing an opera singer to undermine his son's marriage with the intention of 'ruining the reputation of our House'![89] On 17 July 1920 Prince Joachim of Prussia shot himself.[90] The Kaiser reacted with fury to the news of his son's suicide, outraged 'that the oaf should have done this, too, to us and especially to his mother!' Joachim had brought nothing but worry and pain to the Kaiserin. Both Wilhelm and Haehner thought it better to let the Empress think the death of her youngest son had been an accident. 'The Kaiser broke the news to the Kaiserin in person. He said to me afterwards', the doctor continued, 'that as he entered the Kaiserin's room and told her that Joachim had had an accident, the Kaiserin had immediately interrupted him: "He has shot himself!"' She wanted desperately to believe that his death had been accidental – the thought that she would not now see him in the afterlife she found unbearable – but she knew better.[91]

Of all his children Wilhelm got on best with his mercurial daughter Viktoria Luise (Sissy), the Duchess of Brunswick, who was the one most similar to him in temperament. As the family gathered together in November 1920 in the belief that the Empress was dying, Haehner observed that the little Duchess was 'just like her father, impulsive, jumping from one extreme to the other, a stranger to the middle ground'. She 'has the same lively temperament as her father, with the result that she finds it irksome to sit still in the sickroom and just for once take proper care of her mother'.[92] The Kaiser always found her visits 'invigorating' and a great joy.[93] All the deeper was his disappointment when his darling Sissy vehemently opposed his re-marriage – to a woman only a few years older than herself.

Apart from the family several old friends and acquaintances also came to visit the exiled monarch in Doorn. Among the most welcome was the South German and Austrian Prince Max Egon zu Fürstenberg, whose familiar manner – he addressed the Kaiser as 'Du' – astonished Haehner. The two men, the doctor recorded, greeted one another with a 'kiss on both cheeks and on the mouth'.[94] In late 1920 the erstwhile Flügeladjutant Max von Mutius took up service as the Kaiser's 'Hofmarschall'. Like the others at Doorn – Gontard, Ilsemann and even the ancient Countess von Keller – this retired General had to suffer the indignity of (for example) having the monarch dip his spoon into his pea soup to fish out bits of sausage.[95]

In the late summer of 1921 the 82-year-old Hans von Plessen, who had served the Kaiser blindly for almost thirty years as his Adjutant-General, came to Doorn to pay his respects to his Sovereign for what would probably be the last time. He was to leave in tears on account of Wilhelm's abysmal treatment of him. 'Plessen has become a ruin', cried the Kaiser on seeing the old General again.[96] Only once did he go for a walk with Plessen. 'The old gentleman just sat like a schoolboy in the officers' quarters waiting to be called, in his desperation reading through one newspaper after another', Ilsemann told Haehner on 4 September 1921, adding: 'Plessen has been so to speak driven out of Doorn by [Wilhelm's] bad behaviour' and was obliged to spend the remainder of his stay at Amerongen.[97] The Crown Prince was disgusted by the way Plessen had been treated in Doorn. He told Haehner: 'The man might well have had a quite mistaken, harmful influence on the K[aiser], and always shut the K[aiser] off [from the outside world] as if by a wall. But in fact he lived only for the K[aiser]. And now, having wished to see the K[aiser] one last time before dying, he has been treated in such a rude manner.' On arriving on Wieringen and relating to the Crown Prince how he had been received by the monarch, the old man 'broke down in tears and declared: he was now completely finished with the K[aiser]'. In the Crown Prince's opinion this was just 'another example of the K[aiser]'s inexplicable heartlessness and tactlessness which had done him such immense harm thoughout his life'.[98]

THE DEATH OF THE KAISERIN AND WILHELM'S MARRIAGE TO 'HERMO'

Auguste Viktoria had been suffering for many years from heart disease. In the summer of 1918 she had had a stroke at Wilhelmshöhe which had paralysed the left side of her face and her left arm.[99] She died at Doorn on 11 April 1921. Alfred Haehner sought out the Kaiser 'in order to pre-empt if need be a nervous breakdown of the kind that had been described to me as a possibility on the basis of earlier difficult times'. But he found Wilhelm 'outwardly composed. In response to my questions about how he was feeling he gave me reassuring answers and firmly refused any medication: surely I could see he was not some old washer woman, he had already experienced so many deaths in his family!' Even so his children arriving at Doorn expressed concern at the Kaiser's condition.[100] For days he looked 'very pale and terribly grave, one could see that he was making a huge effort to pull himself together'.[101] He was particularly saddened not to be able to attend his wife's funeral in Potsdam, writing bitterly to Irma Fürstenberg: 'What every common worker can do, namely follow his wife's coffin to the grave, even *that* has been made impossible for me by my traitorous people ... Now comes the road to loneliness, the yawning emptiness at one's side! One feels so orphaned & abandoned!'[102] All the same, Haehner noted as early as 25 April that the Kaiser had resumed his regular activity in the garden. He was 'once again very lively, apparently in good spirits, teases us again and makes the occasional joke. But one cannot rid oneself of the feeling that he is trying quite hard to drown his sorrows.'[103]

It had always been the intention of Wilhelm and his advisers to turn the progress of the Kaiserin's coffin from Doorn to Potsdam and the funeral ceremony in the park of Sanssouci into a mass demonstration for the restoration of the monarchy.[104] Back in 1918 the Kaiser had commissioned the construction of a mausoleum in the grounds of the Neues Palais, but as the revolutionary upheavals of that winter had prevented its completion, the burial was now planned to take place in the Antikentempel where Joachim had been buried the previous year.[105] Thousands lined the railway tracks as the train with Auguste Viktoria's coffin made its way through the Netherlands and Germany to Potsdam; hundreds of thousands walked behind the catafalque as it processed from the little station at Wildpark to Sanssouci. Six thousand officers formed the guard of honour at the ceremony on 19 April 1921 attended by the imperial princes Eitel Friedrich, August Wilhelm, Adalbert and Oskar, Crown Princess Cecilie, the generals Hindenburg and Ludendorff, Grand Admiral von Tirpitz and numerous monarchist organisations, as the Kaiser noted with 'great pride'.[106] Years later he would still refer to the grave of his Empress as 'a permanent place of pilgrimage' for all those wanting to demonstrate their loyalty. In 1924 he noted that a steady stream of schoolchildren and monarchist associations had again been filing past the temple where she lay.[107]

After the death of the Kaiserin, Wilhelm's loneliness gave rise to serious concern, with Dr Haehner expressing alarm at the 'psychological condition' of his patient. He urged family members and the entourage to invite more varied and interesting guests for the Kaiser to talk to, for 'if he continues to isolate himself so completely and doesn't from time to time see people other than the faces he sees day in day out', there was a 'grave danger' that he would shut himself off and avoid human contact altogether. Wilhelm had earlier received scholars, engineers, captains of trade and industry, but nowadays he saw almost nobody other than the trio Gontard, Berg and Dommes. 'The danger of the Kaiser's becoming a recluse was great, especially now that, with the death of the Kaiserin and in the absence of the balance she had provided, there was a marked tendency in him towards bitterness', Haehner continued. The Crown Prince agreed with the physician and stressed the need for his father to have some female company, too.[108] Soon there was to be an embarrassment of riches in this regard.

Not long after Auguste Viktoria's death, a procession of ladies 'eager to wear the ermine' began to turn up at Doorn, barely hiding their hopes of ensnaring the 62-year-old ex-monarch. A 'fabulous' doctor from Finland who 'completely entranced' the Kaiser with her 'visions', a Countess – a 'marvellous character' – from South Germany, an 'old girl friend from Potsdam' plus two 'very lively' Hungarian women occasioned much head-shaking in the imperial household in the summer of 1921.[109] That August the suite noted that Wilhelm was spending far more time with Gabriele von Rochow than he had ever devoted to any of his daughters-in-law. On the afternoon of 27 August 'he even ordered tea for himself and his guest in his study – something that had apparently never happened before'.[110] On a stroll through the park on 1 September the Kaiser astonished Ilsemann by declaring: 'The times are over when the German royals could marry one another. The results of such inbreeding could be seen today in almost of all the royal houses. And what scandals there have been everywhere! Just to think of my own sons Auwi and Joachim! . . . Yes, for us Hohenzollerns – if one considers that cousins and Catholics are out of the question – there is hardly anyone left to marry. That's why we must break with the old tradition . . . The princes should simply take a healthy woman from the nobility or the people for a wife . . . Yes, and, my dear Ilsemann, spare a thought for me! The children keep writing that I should not remain so alone. But if I should decide to marry again, who on earth would be a suitable match for me? Why should I not take a woman from our nobility? . . . The best would be someone of about my own age with whom I can share memories of our youth together – and a woman who does something for me!' Not surprisingly Ilsemann saw in these quite uncharacteristic musings the influence of Frau von Rochow, who had often been Young Wilhelm's dancing partner back in the old days.[111]

From the late summer of 1921 the charming 25-year-old Lily van Heemstra – a distant relative of the later film star Audrey Hepburn – was an almost daily guest at Huis Doorn. Ilsemann wrote in his diary on 23 September: 'The Kaiser has recently had much pleasure from the visits of Baroness Lili van Heemstra; he often goes for walks with her in the park, converses with this little lively person about literature, politics and generally enjoys her sunny disposition. Indeed he refers to her as his "sunshine of Doorn" . . . One shouldn't begrudge the Kaiser such pleasures; but I'm afraid the little "sunshine" is hoping that the Kaiser will marry her, even though she is only 25 years old. But the Kaiser has made it quite clear to her that he is not considering any such step.'[112] During a film show in Amerongen on 30 September 1921, the audience remarked not only on the Kaiser's own loud interruptions throughout the performance but also on the Baroness, who spent the entire evening in animated conversation with the monarch, never leaving his side.[113] Several weeks later Ilsemann could still note: 'Baroness Sunshine has won a large place for herself in the Kaiser's heart, he is daily more enamoured of her because she is so warm and understanding. He discusses all things with her, more openly than with any other person since the death of the Kaiserin.'[114] Obviously in love, Wilhelm referred to his young friend in a letter to his sister Mossy as 'my dear little ray of sunshine Lily'. He praised her as 'a financial genius & an administrative talent of the first order!' She was 'the most expert head butler and a banker to boot! And at the same time such lovable golden warm little heart!' When Ilsemann read out an embarrassing account a female visitor had written about the Kaiser's life in Doorn, Lily had held Wilhelm's hand and kissed it. 'I was tempted to give the dear child a big kiss for that', wrote Wilhelm to his sister.[115]

The Hohenzollern family was divided in its response to this altogether rather fetching liaison between the 62-year-old monarch and the young Dutch girl. Whereas Prince Adalbert and his wife offended the Kaiser by raising objections, the Crown Prince, who knew the beautiful young lady very well himself – he admitted to Haehner that she had been his mistress – warmly encouraged the relationship, telling the good doctor: 'His father should indeed begin to flirt with her, he could understand that very well. The Cr[own] Pr[ince] interprets her almost daily visits to Huis Doorn in terms of her "eagerness to wear the ermine", but is otherwise not unduly concerned.'[116] Princess Margarethe, too, was genuinely delighted that her brother was enjoying 'so much sunshine in his lonely life' in exile. The story took an unusual twist when both she and her brother – and indeed Lily herself – hit on the idea that the young Baroness should marry one of Margarethe's four sons. As Ilsemann observed: 'The Kaiser has now advised his young girl friend to marry one of the four sons of his sister [Margarethe]. Lili has agreed' and was on her way to Kronberg to get to know the Hessian princes. To Ilsemann's wife, Count Bentinck's daughter, Lily confided: 'Best of all I'd like to marry the Kaiser, but that would have to be as soon as possible, since he probably won't live much longer. If such a marriage turns out not to be possible, then I'd be quite happy to take one of the Hessian princes!'[117] When the time came for her to leave for Kronberg, Wilhelm wrote to his sister: 'I commend my dear little ray of sunshine to you, who is unfortunately leaving me now for quite some time; be good to her; perhaps something will come of her & one of your boys; she would be an ideal daughter-in-law, and for me an ideal niece ... May she bring sunshine into your house as she did in ours, I shall miss her terribly.'[118] Just how hard that parting was for him became evident when, shortly after she had left for Kronberg, the Kaiser wrote her a letter full of the 'most shocking sexual propositions' and suggesting that, if she could not be his wife, then at least she should be his concubine. Little Miss Sunshine did not hesitate to hand the embarrassing missive to her former lover the Crown Prince, who in his turn discussed it with Haehner and other members of the entourage at Doorn.[119]

After Lily's departure Gabriele von Rochow returned to Doorn to work her magic on the monarch. On Wilhelm's sixty-third birthday Haehner recorded: 'Frau v. Rochow is already giving herself airs as if she were the mistress of the house. The manner in which she behaves towards the K[aiser] shows clearly that she now enjoys the K[aiser's] confidence to a high degree. Her demeanour is not attractive, she is really quite snooty, especially now that she is aware, which is undoubtedly the case, that she has a certain amount of power over the K[aiser].'[120] In February 1922, after Rochow's departure – some months later she shocked the Kaiser by giving an interview to a British newspaper about her life at Doorn – another woman came to visit whom the entourage, and Haehner in particular, thought very much more suited to be Wilhelm's companion: the 50-year-old widow Auguste von Tiele-Winckler was, in the doctor's view, 'a full-blooded aristocrat ... clearly at home in the big wide world'.[121] She was strongly of the opinion that the Kaiser should re-marry – 'but a suitable woman and not someone of the kind that had been to Doorn hitherto'.[122] The physician actually urged the Kaiser to marry Frau von Tiele-Winckler, pointing out that 'even her majestic outward appearance made her brilliantly suited' to be his consort. Wilhelm replied that he did indeed 'like her very much, but when he had once before posed the question she had replied that she had no wish to marry again and in any case she was – not of the blood!' Haehner recounted this conversation to Frau von Tiele, who was 'quite shocked' and declared she would never re-marry, her husband had been absolutely devoted to her and there was no place in her heart for anyone else.[123] It would in fact have been too late for such a match, for by this time the Kaiser had committed himself to someone else altogether.

Without the knowledge of his family or the entourage, since Easter 1922 Wilhelm II had been corresponding with the widowed Princess Hermine of Schönaich-Carolath, the daughter of Prince Heinrich XXII of Reuss elder line, a woman whom he had never met and who was barely older than his own daughter. 'Hermo' arrived in Doorn on 9 June 1922 and took up residence in two rooms which had been prepared for her. Within hours the Kaiser had proposed to her, and two days later they were secretly engaged.[124] Evidently much in love, Wilhelm wrote to his friend Max Fürstenberg: 'So I have found a woman's heart after all, a German princess, an adorable, clever young widow has decided to bring sunshine into my lonely house & to help share my solitude and make it beautiful with her warm, devoted love. Peace and happiness have taken possession of my torn, tormented heart now that she has given me her hand ... My happiness knows no bounds.'[125] Haehner

Figure 62 The ex-Kaiser with his second wife, Hermine

remarked with some concern on the elderly monarch's sexual Indian Summer, and Friedrich von Berg openly declared, not without distaste, that in his view the Kaiser was 'no longer normal'.[126] Nevertheless, despite the undoubted passion, an element of calculation was not wholly absent from Wilhelm's decision, and still less from Hermine's. He convinced himself that by choosing a blue-blooded royal he had taken the wind out of the sails of his monarchist critics at home. Had he married someone 'not of the blood', he maintained on the eve of his marriage to Hermine, he would have lost his chance of being restored to the throne; but 'by choosing a princess undeniably of the blood' his return to Germany was now assured. 'The Princess was entitled to be and would indeed *become* the Kaiserin.'[127] (See Figure 62.)

When the official engagement was announced on 18 September 1922, barely seventeen months after Auguste Viktoria's death, the reaction within the imperial family, the entourage and among conservative supporters of the monarchy in Germany was hostile in the extreme.[128] Wilhelm told his son Oskar, who had raised objections to the match, to mind his own business; after all Hermine was, in contradistinction to Oskar's own wife, 'of the blood'.[129]

To a 'shameless' letter of protest from his son Auwi the Kaiser determined not to reply at all, saying that 'silly oaf ... was so limp he had not even managed to keep his own wife!'[130] His beloved daughter Viktoria Luise eventually despaired of changing her father's mind, but she could barely wait to leave Doorn and was resolutely determined not to attend the wedding.[131]

That contentious event took place at Doorn on 5 November 1922. The Kaiser wore the field-grey uniform of a general in the First Regiment of Guards with the orange sash of the High Order of the Black Eagle; for his bride he had personally designed a pale mauve wedding gown which had been made for her in Breslau. Wilhelm's brother Prince Heinrich, his sisters Victoria Princess of Schaumburg-Lippe and Margarethe Princess of Hesse, his sons Crown Prince Wilhelm and Prince Eitel Friedrich (but not August Wilhelm, Adalbert or Oskar, nor his daughter Viktoria Luise) and his friend Max Fürstenberg attended the wedding.[132] In his speech at the banquet Heinrich referred to the bride as 'Her Majesty the Empress and Queen'.[133] In her new passport, however, she was named only as Princess Hermine Reuss, wife of Kaiser Wilhelm II. She had not been accorded the coveted title of 'Kaiserin'.

The canny physician Alfred Haehner was in no doubt that the Kaiser had made a grave mistake in his choice of consort. Hermine's 'sole motive' in marrying the 'elderly Kaiser' had in his opinion been her expectation that the monarchy would be restored. The marriage would fail the moment she saw that there was no chance of the Kaiser's returning to the throne. 'When she comes to the realisation that the game is absolutely up for her, and then considers all the things she has given up or put up with for the sake of her ambition, this will cause the marriage to fall apart', he predicted in October 1923 and went on: 'As these disappointments start to mount, her bitterness will grow, and when there is nothing left but disappointment, the bitterness will turn into hatred. This woman will never accept a life of uncomplaining resignation, she will blame the K[aiser] for the failure of her overweening ambitions ... She will not allow the rift to become public ... but she will increasingly leave the K[aiser] on his own, go on her travels for longer and more frequently and lead a life wholly in keeping with her own desires.'[134] Ominously, Hermine had already insisted as a precondition for their engagement that she would be allowed to spend a sojourn of two months in Germany twice a year.[135]

The honeymoon mood held for several weeks, with Wilhelm writing to his sister Mossy (in English) obviously still very much in love: 'For me Hermo is the embodiment of the spirit of love itself. I am wrapped up in the warmest love given me by a loveable, enchanting, sweet young woman

with a glorious & fiery temperament. She is absolutely my ideal of woman-
hood, made for me ... I am quite indescribably happy! I have found what
I have been longing for & have had to do without for so long!'[136] Such
delirium never lasts, of course, and soon there were mutterings in the imperial
entourage to the effect that Hermine was 'totally' dominant, imposing her will
on the elderly monarch, with him, often silent and depressed, obeying her
every whim.[137] With the arrival in Doorn of her five children from her first
marriage, for whom the Kaiser had very little liking – the gatehouse and the
orangerie had to be extended to house them – Wilhelm became 'even less
lively than usual'.[138] The newly married couple got on each other's nerves, and
there were 'all sorts of grounds for irritation between them'.[139] The Crown
Prince and Wilhelm's daughter, too, grew 'very concerned' at the situation
within the marriage. They thought their father 'rather down and not looking
well' and 'above all psychologically' in a poor state. On a visit in August 1923
Viktoria Luise was quite shocked at what she observed. Haehner recorded her
as saying: 'It was at times really sad to see and to hear how sharply critical they
both were of one another. From her father's letters she had expected to find
joyous happiness and total harmony ... She was ... painfully disappointed at
what she found here. Her father had gone ahead and taken the step she would
never be able to condone, but in spite of all that she had hoped that things
would turn out well. But that was not at all her impression and her heart was
very heavy indeed.' Haehner could only confirm Viktoria Luise's worst fears:
Wilhelm was looking unwell, he was 'in a very depressed frame of mind and
had visibly aged. It was evident that the marriage was indeed not agreeing
with him.'[140] For her part Hermine complained of her husband's lack of
consideration. She cherished her freedom and was too much of an individualist
always to subordinate herself to him. '*Perhaps it would have been better if she
had not re-married at all!!*', the doctor wrote that she confessed to him. He
commented: 'There was quite a strong undertone of bitterness in her words, it
appears that she has only now realised what a burden she has taken on when
she took this step. It may well be that her ambition to "play at being a
Majesty" presented itself to her in such a brilliant light that she completely
failed to see the dark shadows.' Now her ambition had been thwarted, 'for she
must surely realise that the K[aiser] will never again play any part in politics,
and being addressed and treated as "Her Majestät" by this little circle here has
lost the attraction of novelty. She now sees only the hard life ahead, the
isolation, the loss of personal freedom. Someone with her character will not
come to terms with that, but will on the contrary grow ever more bitter. How
will it all end –? Certainly not well.'[141] Shortly before her first wedding
anniversary Hermine complained 'how dreadful she found their joint

bedroom, how the K[aiser] was always disturbing her, how inconsiderately he behaved towards her'.[142] On Wilhelm's face was written 'a strong dislike' for his wife, he regarded her with a cold criticism such as he had 'never before seen in the K[aiser]', Haehner observed in August 1923.[143]

Thus the happiness, the sunshine, which the Kaiser had craved after the death of his first wife proved to be all too fleeting. In view of the gloomy conditions pertaining in Huis Doorn it was little wonder that even his closest advisers thought it would be a mercy if death were to release the exiled monarch from the indignity of such an existence. Friedrich von Berg, who was appointed as Count August Eulenburg's successor as Minister of the House in 1921, remarked after a visit to Doorn that the Kaiser was so strongly embittered, held 'such eccentric opinions and refused to listen to anyone else's views', that it 'truly would be ... for the best if he died soon. He respected the Kaiser very much and really felt personally quite close to him, having known him for such a long time. For that very reason he would be only too glad if the Kaiser did not have to put up with a life such as the present one, which was so very awful, for much longer.'[144] Kaiser Wilhelm, of course, lived for another twenty years in exile in Holland and continued to plot his return and his bloodcurdling revenge. His activities in this final phase of his life make for anything but a glorious chapter in the history of the House of Hohenzollern.[145]

CHAPTER FORTY-SIX

'Blood must flow, much blood!' The Kaiser and the 'swinish' Weimar Republic

With his flight to Holland Kaiser Wilhelm II appeared to lose touch with reality altogether. In Amerongen and Doorn he inhabited a nightmarish world of views so extreme that one hesitates even to report them. The historian stands bewildered and ashamed before the mountain of evidence documenting the crazed and racist opinions espoused by the exiled monarch in these final years of his life, though admittedly such views were all too prevalent in *völkisch* and right-wing circles at the time, and by no means only in Germany. Traumatised by the loss of his throne, Wilhelm fell victim to the most bizarre conspiracy theories. The world war had been started not by him, his generals or Germany's statesmen with their hegemonial ambitions, but rather by the Austro-Hungarian Foreign Minister Count Berchtold in league with the Vatican, the Wittelsbachs, the Jesuits, the Freemasons and World Jewry with the intention of destroying the Protestant Hohenzollern Reich. Then again, it had been the Anglo-Americans, secretly in the pockets of the Jews, who had been plotting the downfall of Germany and its Emperor for years. To the last Wilhelm held fast to the belief that his long-dead uncle Edward VII had conspired to bring the English, the French, the Russians, the Italians, the Americans and the Japanese together to overthrow the Hohenzollern Monarchy by means of war and revolution. The German politicians of the Weimar Republic trying their best to govern the country after the havoc wreaked by war, defeat and revolution were in his mind all Jews and Freemasons, or at any rate in the clutches of such 'dark forces', and were being bribed and manipulated by Rome, the Entente or for that matter the Bolsheviks in Moscow. On his return to the throne there would be a bloodbath, the Jews would be 'destroyed and exterminated from German soil'; indeed, he would take his revenge on *all* those who had betrayed him. 'Blood must flow, much blood, [the blood] of the officers and civil servants, above all of the nobility, of everyone who has deserted me', he was still threatening on Hindenburg's death in 1934.[1] Visitors in Holland were appalled by the abyss of ignorance and hatred that opened up before them, dismayed by the fantastic schemes they encountered on talking to the exiled monarch. Not without reason they asked themselves, like the papal nuncio Pacelli and the Reichstag deputies before them, whether such disconcerting characteristics had not been in evidence even before the war and the abdication, when Wilhelm had held the reins of power. 'Completely flabbergasted', one such visitor observed in 1919: 'All his life, evidently in keeping with his entire personality, he must have lived in a world of his own imagining which he then imposes upon reality and experience . . . The view of the world which he made for himself and outlined for us was wrongheaded to a grotesque, truly tragic degree.'[2]

THE UNSUCCESSFUL REHABILITATION

In his isolation at Doorn the Kaiser had only one thing in mind — his restoration to the throne of his forebears. To this purpose he worked — alongside his archaeological studies and felling the trees in his park — at a number of apologetic texts designed to justify his long reign. In the spring of 1921 there appeared — initially without his consent in a Dutch newspaper — his *Vergleichende Geschichtstabellen von 1878 bis zum Kriegsausbruch 1914*, comparative chronological tables intended to prove that the world war had been caused by the Entente and its policy of encirclement.[3] The aim of the book, as he told his doctor, was clear: 'The more evidence comes to light that Germany and therefore he himself had not been guilty of starting the war . . . the revolution which was based on such lies would collapse completely and the awakened nation would then have to draw the necessary conclusions.'[4] One year later Wilhelm published the first volume of his memoirs entitled *Ereignisse und Gestalten in den Jahren 1878–1918*, the manuscript of which had been heavily redacted by the Pan-German publicist Eugen Zimmermann.[5] Several hundred thousand copies were quickly sold and the book was translated into many languages — sale of the world rights brought in 70 million marks[6] — and yet the hoped-for political effect was not achieved, not least because both the authorities in Berlin and the patriotically minded German historical fraternity were united in the belief that the national interest would be better served by discounting the role that Wilhelm II had actually played. Rudolf von Valentini, who had personally witnessed many of the events described in the Kaiser's memoirs, commented that the most shocking aspect of the book was 'the untruthfulness . . . with which he stands things on their head in order to place himself in the best light'.[7] The former head of the Reich Chancellery Arnold Wahnschaffe sighed that it really was 'as if the unfortunate Hohenzollerns are driven by some demon to provide the world with the written evidence to support its otherwise wholly one-sided & in many respects unjust condemnation of them ... The many enemies of the Hohenzollern monarchy were sure to greet [the memoirs] with absolute glee.'[8] The consensus in government circles was that the book could hardly have been more superficial.[9] Dismayed, Admiral von Müller put the work down with the comment that the Kaiser and the Crown Prince 'had surely both now dug their own graves'.[10]

There was in fact little the Kaiser might have said in his defence to counter the damning evidence in Kautsky's edition of the diplomatic documents of July 1914, Wilhelm's correspondence with the Tsar which had been published by the Bolsheviks, or the revelations in the memoirs of German statesmen that were now hitting the headlines. On reading the notorious Willy–Nicky correspondence, one nationalistic history professor sighed that all one could now do was to cover one's head in shame and crawl off into some dark corner.[11] When Emil Ludwig came to write his critical biography of Wilhelm II in 1925, he was already able to draw on the memoirs of Tirpitz and Valentini, the diaries of Waldersee and Zedlitz-Trützschler, parts of the correspondence of Philipp Eulenburg and the early volumes of the official diplomatic records published under the title *Die Große Politik der europäischen Kabinette*. It was not without reason that General von Dommes expressed the fear that Ludwig's 'book of shame' would be 'widely read and do both His Majesty and the monarchical ideal immense harm'.[12] The ex-Kaiser never tired of claiming that Emil Ludwig, whose surname was Cohn, was a 'lying Jew-boy' and his book therefore proof that he, Wilhelm, was the victim of a Jewish world conspiracy.[13] The account of his childhood and youth, which the monarch dictated to his Flügeladjutant Fritz von Mewes and which appeared in 1927 under the title *Aus meinem Leben 1859–1888*,[14] failed in its aim of winning support for his restoration, as did the various publications on archaeological and cultural anthropological themes designed to strengthen the monarchical principle in its struggle against western notions of freedom which the Kaiser defined as the 'negative, *anti-national* spirit of Rome and Juda'.[15]

From 1925 Wilhelm II concentrated his publicity campaign on the United States of America, as well as Germany. Through his lively correspondence with the German–American anti-Semite George Sylvester Viereck, who liked to hint that he was an illegitimate son of Kaiser Wilhelm I, with his childhood friend Poultney Bigelow and with Professor Harry Elmer Barnes, as well as with two female historians from the USA, the imperial exile sought to gain converts to his campaign against the Versailles 'war guilt lie' and propagate his vile racist and theological notions.[16] He published several articles, some of them under a pseudonym, gave interviews and worked tirelessly to promote his memoirs on the other side of the Atlantic. Soon he was forced to admit that all his efforts there were falling on deaf ears, just as they were in Germany. And why? 'The slandering and lying on the part of my enemies – especially the *Jews* – against my person and house [are] worse than ever', he told Viereck in 1927. 'The German Press under *Stresemann's and Jewish* control have ignored *all* the articles ... the Germans know nothing whatever about them.'[17] He broke off relations with Viereck in November 1928 on suspecting that he too had 'unfortunately now fallen under Jewish influence'.[18] He informed his friend Bigelow that Viereck was not descended from Kaiser Wilhelm I at all, but was rather the grandson of a certain Baron von Prillwitz who had had an affair with a Jewish actress named Viereck at the court theatre in Berlin; George Sylvester, Viereck's father, had been a socialist who had been forced to flee to the USA when Bismarck brought in his Anti-Socialist Law.[19] Viereck's extensive apologia for Wilhelm, which appeared in late 1937 under the title *The Kaiser on Trial*, was therefore written without any direct input from the monarch himself.[20]

In the summer of 1927 the Kaiser decided to place his campaign for rehabilitation in the tried and tested hands of Karl Friedrich Nowak. As he wrote full of enthusiasm to Prince Max zu Fürstenberg after Nowak's first visit to Doorn: 'The Austrian historian Nowack has been charged by me with the task of collecting together all the material on my epoch and my policy ... He is totally loyal to *me* and fabulously well-informed. He has already gone through all my own documents. He is a fanatical seeker after the truth and determined to destroy all the infamies against me once and for all.'[21] Nowak began by ghostwriting the much admired foreword to the German edition of the Letters of the Empress Frederick, which Sir Frederick Ponsonby had published in London without the Kaiser's permission and which caused considerable controversy both within the Hohenzollern family and the royal family at Windsor.[22] The first volume of Nowak's defence of Wilhelm and his reign appeared in October 1929 bearing the not exactly auspicious title *Das dritte Deutsche Kaiserreich*.

Though he was anxious to base his account on an objective scrutiny of the evidence, Nowak soon found himself becoming dependent to an unhealthy extent on Wilhelm's subjective version of events. In the course of his numerous visits to Huis Doorn he sat for days at a time with the Kaiser in his study taking copious notes from which he would dictate a first draft to Princess Kropotkin in their hotel room in Utrecht in the evenings. The ex-monarch then corrected in his own hand the typescript Nowak gave him to read the next morning. The whole of the second volume was compiled in this collaborative manner in the spring of 1931. Nowak's request to be allowed to collate the Kaiser's idiosyncratic recollections with the written sources (such as the correspondence between the monarch and Bülow) was turned down by Wilhelm as 'undesirable'.[23] Shortly before the publication of the second volume in October 1931 the all-too-predictable clash between Wilhelm's apologetic intentions and the scholarly integrity of his biographer took the form of a 'most furious' row between them.[24] Nowak died in December 1932 at the age of 50, before he could begin work on the crucial third volume of his biography. When, just a few months later, the Nazis publicly burnt the books of all Jewish authors, it must finally have dawned on Kaiser Wilhelm that he had entrusted the campaign for his rehabilitation and restoration to a member of what he himself termed the 'hated tribe of Juda'. In the ghastly terminology of Hitler's racial state Karl Friedrich Nowak would have been classified as a 'Volljude'[25] and all his works − including his 'fabulously thrilling' biography of the Kaiser and his times − were banned.[26]

Meanwhile the torrent of revelations of what had really gone on at the very highest level behind the glittering façade of the Second Reich continued unabated. In 1929 the third volume of Bismarck's *Gedanken und Erinnerungen*, so damaging to Wilhelm's reputation in right-wing circles, made its long-awaited appearance,[27] to be followed a year later by the four volumes of ex-Chancellor Prince von Bülow's reminiscences and in 1931 the *Denkwürdigkeiten der Reichskanzlerzeit* of Bülow's predecessor, Prince Chlodwig zu Hohenlohe-Schillingsfürst, containing many hundreds of authentic papers from the years 1894 to 1900. With Hitler's seizure of power in January 1933, critical voices of the centre and left were silenced,[28] but the attacks on the Personal Rule of Wilhelm II emanating from militaristic and nationalist circles grew if anything shriller still.[29]

All the more ironic, then, that it should have been an 'Englishman' who provided the reading public of the Third Reich with its most influential glorification of the Kaiser in the form of Jacques Daniel Chamier's 'sporting' apologia of the monarch, entitled *Fabulous Monster*. The German translation, *Ein Fabeltier unserer Zeit. Glanz und Tragödie Wilhelms II.*, became a huge publishing success in Nazi Germany and was reprinted several times even after the war.[30] But in this instance too, not everything was as it seemed. The author was not an 'Englishman', but one Barbara Chamier, born in 1885 in India as a general's daughter who had not been able to study at any university and knew little or no German. It is unclear how she hit on the idea of writing a biography of Wilhelm II − whether of her own accord or with a little encouragement, as seems likely, from monarchist circles in Germany. What is beyond doubt is that the German translation that was undertaken by Dora von Beseler, the daughter of the Prussian Minister of Justice Max von Beseler and the niece of a Prussian general, was sent to the Kaiser and corrected by him in Doorn before publication.[31] It is a telling reflection on the poverty of the Kaiser's campaign to restore his standing in the eyes of his countrymen that, far from recruiting a respected German historian to his cause, he was reduced in pursuit of his return to the throne to relying on the manipulated translation of an English amateur biography.

RESTORATION AND RETRIBUTION

If they failed signally in their main aim of securing his restoration, Wilhelm II's apologetic literary efforts nevertheless played their part in undermining the Republic by bolstering nationalist and militarist mythmaking and obscuring the truth about the recent past. Even so, his public pronouncements, filtered as they were through a variety of ghostwriters and intermediaries, were anodyne when compared with the vengeful and bloodthirsty opinions he dished up in private. In his table talk and private correspondence the exiled monarch gave vent to such a terrifying, murderous hatred of Jews, Freemasons and Catholics as to suggest he was suffering from a paranoid delusional world conspiracy complex. More than a decade before Hitler's seizure of power Kaiser Wilhelm II was demanding the bloody execution of the 'November criminals' of 1918 and the dispossession and expulsion of all Jews from Germany, from time to time even, as I shall show in a moment, calling for their extermination.

Visitors making the pilgrimage to Amerongen and Doorn were as unsuccessful as his entourage in talking the Kaiser out of such madness. 'It is still as it always has been, the K[aiser] has learnt nothing whatever from all that has happened. He simply closes his ears to anything he doesn't like', his physician sighed in 1923.[32] Shortly after taking up his duties in November 1919 Alfred Haehner complained of the monarch's pigheadedness in refusing to listen to reason when ranting on about the supposed world conspiracy of the Jews, the Freemasons and the Catholic Church against the Protestant Hohenzollern Monarchy. 'Once he has got such stuff into his head there is hardly any way of changing his mind, especially as it seems up to a point to confirm the interpretation he has constructed for himself of the cause of and the responsibility for the revolution.'[33] After four years of being in daily contact with him the good doctor opined that though the Kaiser might have an impressive memory he certainly lacked wisdom. 'His own ideas are very often quite

absurd, always moving along the same tracks like fixed ideas. E.g. everything
that he considers has befallen him is solely the work of the Freemasons and
Jesuits ... Whatever happens in the world, he sees the hand of the "Grand
Orient" at work.' If the Kaiser read something in the newspapers that did not
fit in with his own preconceptions, then it was simply a lie. He showed no
understanding whatever of the problems facing Germany at home. 'Each and
every event is seen solely from the point of view that every government since
the revolution has been incompetent. The only one to have governed well was
"He" himself. But he had been chased away with black ingratitude. Now the
Germans were getting their just deserts and it was only right that they were
suffering. He goes in for a great deal of metaphorical sabre-rattling, everyone
in Germany is so pitifully soft ... All this from the man who through his lack
of energy, his hesitancy, his sabre-rattling at the wrong time and place has
done so much damage! But one can now see how everything came about as it
did. Especially if one adds the K[aiser's] great receptiveness to flattery and
adoration. The sins of his immediate entourage among others in this regard
are quite incalculable.'[34] Haehner was anything but alone in the severity of his
criticism. In June 1921 the former Prussian Minister of Education, Friedrich
Schmitt-Ott, whom the Kaiser had known at the Gymnasium in Kassel and
therefore addressed as 'Du', came to stay at Doorn.[35] Frustrated and dismayed,
Schmitt-Ott was anxious to leave after just a few days: Wilhelm's opinions and
conversations always moved along the same lines; all he did was complain
about the 'cowardly and rotten' German people.[36] Even the Crown Prince, on a
visit from Wieringen in August 1921, was 'utterly perplexed' by the 'totally
fixed ideas with which his father was obsessed'; his father had 'shut his eyes'
and was absolutely out of touch with reality.[37] And Ulrich Freiherr von Sell,
who was charged with looking after the Hohenzollerns' interests in Berlin,
asked himself in 1928 after a visit to Doorn: 'Is it really still worth working
oneself to the bone for this dynasty ... when one sees over and over again that
the Kaiser will never change ... when one realises that he does not understand the important things and does not even want to know.'[38]

Betrayal, restoration and revenge were the themes that ran through the
obsessive expectorations of the embittered exile. 'The punishment will be
terrible', he raged in 1919. 'Such a total betrayal of a ruler by all his people is
without precedent in world history.'[39] As one guest recorded after a visit to
Amerongen in October 1919: 'Most drastic and violent of all was [Wilhelm's]
description of the betrayal and the felony he had suffered at the hands of his
people.' He had been 'lied to, deceived and betrayed on all sides!', there had
been 'betrayal, downright felony, cowardice right up to the very top!' The
Kaiser had used the harshest words and threatened to exact the harshest

punishment.[40] In February 1920 Wilhelm told his brother-in-law Prince Friedrich Karl of Hesse that he would certainly return to Germany, 'but only if begged to do so on bended knee, and then heads would roll'.[41] To Field Marshal August von Mackensen he wrote in 1920 that the November revolution had been a 'betrayal of the ruling house & the army by the German people who had been deceived and lied to by the Jewish rabble!' and would be 'severely punished!'[42] When the Allies were reported to have threatened to starve the Germans into compliance, the Kaiser proclaimed: '*Those* people deserve everything they'll get, nothing is too bad for them. No nation is as beastly as the German people or has ever behaved as basely!'[43] Haehner also recorded him as saying: 'Altogether the German people were a totally miserable lot, a band of scoundrels. They had chased him, the K[aiser], away but were now chasing after the foreigners. It was quite right that the people were suffering so severely. After all the things they had done to their K[aiser] they deserved no better fate.'[44] Five times he had been betrayed, Wilhelm counted in 1920: '1) by the Tsar, 2) by the Italians 3) by the Romanians 4) by Kaiser Karl & 5) finally by his people.'[45]

Repeatedly and even in the presence of foreign guests the Kaiser threatened to exact brutal and bloody revenge on his return to Germany. On the first anniversary of his flight to Holland he proclaimed that the 'revolutionary heroes' would all have to be 'hanged ... as soon as the new times dawn'. The first time Dr Haehner heard such bloodcurdling talk he assumed that the words 'weren't really meant literally ... but what is certain is that he would deal extremely severely with these men' if the chance arose.[46] When in January 1920 the Kaiser repeated his intention of 'wreaking really draconian punishment ... upon the Socialists and the Republicans' on his restoration to the throne, the doctor again comforted himself with the thought that these were mostly just 'big words of the kind he loves, whether they would really be acted upon if things got serious is something I very much doubt'.[47] As time went on, however, Haehner came to the view that these were indeed fixed ideas that the Kaiser meant quite earnestly. Wilhelm was intent on following in the footsteps of Napoleon who had 'simply had the lot of them shot. We too would have to have a dictatorship, a civil war would probably be unavoidable. The cowardly bourgeoisie would then have to show which side they were really on. And after that there would need to follow a violent expulsion of the Jews. He had been told that all our Socialist leaders had been out at the revolution to enrich themselves, Ebert, Scheidemann, Erzberger were all now multimillionaires.' Erzberger was 'sitting on 32 millions and Scheidemann too had not gone to Switzerland for nothing'. 'But one would know how to recoup the money when the time comes, these louts will get their just deserts.'[48]

The execution of the revolutionary leaders who had forced him from the throne formed a persistent leitmotiv of Wilhelm's table talk. He intended to put 'all 6,000 of them' up against the wall and shoot them; and those aristocrats (such as that 'Schweinehund' Prince Pless) who had sided with the Republic would also 'pay with their lives' for deserting him.[49] Livid, he expressed astonishment that the 'arch traitor' Prince Max of Baden — Wilhelm considered him a Freemason — was still alive.[50] The President of the Republic Friedrich Ebert 'would one day be paraded in chains down the Unter den Linden!' he announced.[51] Even Gustav Noske, who was credited with putting down the Spartakist uprising in Berlin in January 1919, 'deserved to be hanged!'; one should 'never forget that this lout had totally destroyed his life's work, the Fleet'.[52] When news reached Doorn in late August 1921 of the murder of Matthias Erzberger, the Kaiser celebrated his death with champagne.[53] Ilsemann told Haehner afterwards 'that the Kaiser had virtually danced for joy on receiving the news, so delighted was he that this man, whom he had always regarded as his most bitter foe, had got his just deserts'. The physician reflected: 'Certainly no other event has occasioned such great jubilation since I have been with the Kaiser.'[54] Wilhelm fully subscribed to the absurd notion that Erzberger's 'elimination' had been ordered by his own party.[55] And when Walther Rathenau was assassinated by the nationalist Organisation Consul on 24 June 1922, he exulted: 'It really serves him right!'[56] In November 1928 he responded to an offer from the Rathenaubund to facilitate his return to Germany with the words: 'The Rathenaubund can lick my . . .!'[57]

The western statesmen responsible for his and the Kaiserin's banishment to Holland, 'those wretches Lloyd George, Poincaré, Millerand and their ilk', would also get what they deserved, Wilhelm promised. 'The righteous God will pay them back, they will have to suffer for the crime that they have perpetrated. As he spoke his eyes lit up, he clenched his fists, he was utterly seized with fury and indignation against these people', Haehner recorded after speaking to the Kaiser.[58] The explanations Wilhelm gave for his downfall became ever more abstruse. In 1920 he declared that he had discovered from a reliable source that Woodrow Wilson had only been elected President of the USA thanks to the financial help he had received from King Edward VII. 'Now we can understand what Wilson is up to', he wrote to the Dutch statesman J. B. Kan: 'Away with the Hohenzollerns, hence the 14 Points to turn the Germans *against* our dynasty. The revolutionisation of Germany from Moscow with Lenin and Trotsky. The minute the Hohenzollerns had fallen the 14 Points disappear again, they were just a stratagem to trick the Germans into betraying their Kaiser. Then the destruction of

Germany, since as a democracy it was helpless!'[59] In 1928 he went so far as to describe Wilson as a 'paralytic madman'.[60]

Wilhelm poured scorn on the generals, the nobility and the conservative Deutschnationale Volkspartei for their failure to work actively for his return to the throne. The Fascist March on Rome and Mussolini's seizure of power in October 1922 were for him models of how the right-wing forces in Germany should act. It was absolutely 'pitiful' how 'the German people were behaving compared with the weak Italians. What on earth are all those field marshals, generals, staff officers doing in Germany, what is keeping them? – They're simply biding their time. None of them can find the courage to rise up to send the government to the devil and install a dictatorship at last, they're all too cowardly for that!'[61]

If Wilhelm reacted with mixed feelings to the two early attempts to overthrow the Weimar Republic by force – the Kapp Putsch of March 1920 and the Hitler–Ludendorff coup fiasco of November 1923 – this was because in both cases he could not be sure of being restored to the throne. When news of the Kapp Putsch reached him in Amerongen on 13 March 1920, the Kaiser was at first hesitant; the initial reports seemed to him to be too good to be true, the attempted coup 'over-hasty and badly planned'.[62] 'But then he showed himself hugely delighted at this turn of events', noted Haehner.[63] Once the putsch had failed it was the old story again: 'The people at home are all too weak. All it really needs is a little shove and the government will go flying, making way for a return of the old regime.'[64] Just as double-edged was Wilhelm's response in November 1923 to news of the Munich putsch, which he received, as Haehner put it, with tears in one eye and a twinkle in the other. On the one hand he was overjoyed that the detested Republic was about to be overthrown, on the other concerned that the coup had been attempted in Bavaria. As news arrived of the putsch's failure, everything was suddenly clear to him: the Kaiser, his doctor recorded, jumped on his old hobby horse and pronounced: 'The Catholics hadn't wanted the Protestant Ludendorff at the helm. Then he ranted against the former. Jews and Jesuits, both were in cahoots, both were without a fatherland, both would have to be exterminated!'[65] The failure of the putsch clearly showed, he claimed, that only he was in a position to restore order in Germany.[66] To the ever-loyal Mackensen he wrote on 19 December 1923: 'The Munich events were most unfortunate, though hardly surprising. You can't set up a new Reich from a beer hall! Ludendorff is a magnificent soldier but when it comes to politics he is clueless. The restoration of the Reich will come through Prussia & its restoration must begin in Potsdam or Stettin, never in Munich, with or through Bavaria! The ultimate conclusion to be drawn from your letter & those of others is: there is no point in speaking *only of the monarchy*. The *people* long for the *Führer*; therefore one must speak to them of the *monarch*; & make it clear to them that they should plead with their betrayed lord to come back to them! He will come! But the people must call him, & preparing the people to act in this way is the task and duty of every man loyal to his king!'[67]

MILITARY DICTATORSHIP, *FÜHRERPRINZIP*, *GLEICHSCHALTUNG*: THE POLITICAL PROGRAMME OF THE KAISER IN EXILE

Even in these early years in Holland the Kaiser was foreshadowing many of the ideas which we now associate with the Third Reich. He and he alone had a rightful claim to be the *Führer*, or dictator, of the German *Volk*, he insisted. The Divine Right of Kings and the monarchical principle, notions which had served as the ideological underpinning of his Personal Monarchy for thirty years, now formed the basis of his own version of the *Führerprinzip*, the leadership principle. In 1921 he told his doctor: 'God must give the *Volk* a *Führer* who would then act as the mediator between "Our Lord" and the *Volk*. He would receive his instructions from heaven above which he must then, with divine guidance, put into practice. All this could of course not be revealed to an entire *Volk*, but only ever to one person, namely the King given to the *Volk* by God!'[68] In a sermon of 1925 Wilhelm defined his notion of the leadership principle in the following terms: Only 'the *Führer* idea revealed by God to mankind' had any legitimacy. The *Führer* must exercise his rule 'on behalf of God, always conscious of his *responsibility towards Him*, under *His control, limited and bound* by it'; being 'bound by God and exercising leadership on behalf of God' had been his unswerving guiding principle and indeed that of his forebears on the Hohenzollern throne for 500 years.[69] To Tirpitz, who had argued that Germany's recovery would have to be effected through the parliamentary system of the Weimar Republic, Wilhelm responded on 1 January 1925: 'No republic, no Weimar, no parliament will ever rebuild Germany, they have reduced the country and the people to the state they're *now in*, and have demonstrated their *total* incompetence. The people are fed up to the back teeth of Weimar and the parliament and want to have nothing more to do with them. *All* the so-called "Great Men" of Germany have failed totally, whether as party leaders or as individuals. Only a *single* personality can now still save things through a *dictatorship*. *Without* the *Army* all is lost! It *must* be resurrected. That it can do only through its Supreme War Lord, the Kaiser, & for that to happen Versailles *must* fall . . . Germany is free! It should call, he will come!'[70] In September 1928 he told the writer and pacifist Fritz von Unruh: 'The hereditary monarch simply is the natural *Führer*, this has surely been demonstrated beyond doubt by all we have gone through with leaders elected by the people.'[71] As late as August 1931 he was insisting: 'May the German *Volk* finally prove through its deeds that it sees in its Kaiser alone its saviour in these desperate times.'[72]

In the light of the frequent changes of government in Berlin the Kaiser said he was 'almost proud of himself for having been able to rule such a mob in reasonable order for 30 long years'.[73] In 1921 he also opined: 'Now the world can at last see what a bunch of scoundrels I had to govern with . . . what I had to put up with throughout my reign.'[74] On his return to the throne he would sweep away the federal structures of the Bismarckian constitution and centralise the country, for 'the entire foundation of the Reich in 1870 had been made rather on the hoof . . . The individual states, Prussia, Bavaria, Württemberg, think that because they are kingdoms they are nations. That is wrong, they are tribes and all belong to one nation: the German.'[75] He also intended to keep the Auswärtiges Amt, 'the worst and most incompetent of all the departments', as he called it, on a very short leash.[76] 'Our diplomacy is even worse today than it was in My day', he trumpeted in 1926. 'When I come back I'll organise a thorough clear-out.'[77] Indeed he would ensure that in future 'the Kaiser . . . will be his own chancellor!'[78] Only as Kaiser would he be able to 'restore order in place of all this chaos'.[79] He would certainly get things 'moving again as dictator!', he promised. 'Just wait and see!'[80]

THE KAISER AND THE NEXT WAR

It goes without saying that Wilhelm thought of his future reign primarily as a military regime which would take ruthless action against both the internal and the foreign foes of the Reich. The stab-in-the-back legend in its most brutal guise was a stock-in-trade of his crazed ideology in exile. 'Another two to three months and victory would certainly have been ours', he declared in October 1919; only through 'treason at home' had Germany lost the war.[81] Defeat had come 'from behind, from home, from Juda's money . . . While commanded by Me, My generals and officers the brave army was achieving victories at the front, the war was lost by the people *at home*, led by their incompetent statesmen, lied to by the Jews and the Entente, bribed and incited to rebellion.'[82] Within months of his flight to Holland Wilhelm was hatching plans to appoint Ludendorff as his Chief of General Staff.[83] He wrote to Ludendorff: 'God *was* with us! He will be with us again as soon as the German *Volk* turns to him again, begging for mercy and forgiveness and pleading for his help. He will pull it out of the Jewish-Bolshevik mire into which it has sunk under Jew[ish] leadership back to the old religion, to its old loyalty to the

King and to its old strength! I still hope one day to have you at my side as my
Chief of General Staff when together we shall rebuild our old glorious army!
May God grant it!'[84] Even so, the monarch's anger at Ludendorff's behaviour
in 1918 had by no means abated. Ludendorff seemed to have forgotten, he
complained, that 'it was *he* who *lost his nerve in Spa to such an extent* that in an
audience with me he urgently *demanded* that we offer an armistice as well as
introduce a changed form of government with a new chancellor! And that
immediately! With that *he* set the stone of revolution rolling and cost me
my throne.'[85]

   To Field Marshal von Mackensen, who had questioned the feasibility of
a return to the old regime, Wilhelm wrote in the summer of 1920: 'The
unprecedented victories that you were allowed to gain over an enemy that
outnumbered us many times over were *granted to you by God*! If He grants
you something, He must hold you in high regard and *expect* something *in
return*! Out of the great successes in the great war that God has given you, you
should forge the golden shield of unshakeable faith against which the arrows
of Satan such as doubts about the future, despair, hopelessness, disgust,
pusillanimity will simply bounce off! I am doing just the same, I am working,
arming myself, thirsting for revenge! Waiting for the moment when the
fatherland in its hour of greatest need will want us all, when we shall *have to
spring to its aid* whether we are called or not, *you too*! You are destined for
greatness still!'[86] Until his own return to Germany Mackensen should become
the dictator, with Ludendorff in charge of military matters and Karl Helfferich in charge of domestic affairs.[87] Wilhelm told visitors from home: 'There
must be a military dictatorship to create order. Ludendorff or von der Goltz
or . . . Lettow-Vorbeck. Nowadays a small number of reliable troops will
suffice. One can see that in the case of Fiume, where a minor Italian Jewish
poet [the reference is to Gabriele D'Annunzio] is cocking a snook at the entire
Entente.' In Germany one should force the Entente into compliance by taking
the international commissioners hostage. 'Then order will be restored to the
country and then I shall come back to sweep the country clean with an iron
broom. Starting at the top. I have noted down the names . . . and once we
have restored order at home . . . we shall gallop full tilt at the enemy!'[88] In
May 1921 Wilhelm again called for a dictatorship which would raise a
powerful army. 'There must be a levy en masse of volunteers even if they
are armed only with scythes and hunting rifles. Then we will first throw out
the Poles and then move against the Entente!' Parliamentary government
had let the people down. 'In the old days under a King it would have been a
different matter. He would simply have issued the mobilisation order, called
the army together and ordered it to attack.'[89] In July 1921 he wrote in

expectation of a war against Poland: 'Will one of the "old ones" emerge as *Führer* at last, to awaken & rally the *Volk?*'[90]

With the occupation of the Ruhr by French and Belgian troops in 1923 his fury knew no bounds. The Germans had lost all sense of honour, were allowing themselves to be kicked in the teeth by all and sundry, there were no 'real men' around any more to rise up against the invaders, it would not be long before the French were in Berlin and the Poles in Küstrin and General Foch set up his headquarters in the palace of the 'great' Kaiser Wilhelm I. 'The spirit of 1813 must be reawakened', Dr Haehner noted him as saying. 'Then the Prussians had risen armed only with scythes, flails and hunting rifles and they were victorious, but today no one had the pluck ... After all there were enough weapons around. He had recently been told that cannons had been hidden away, machine guns too, even the great "Wilhelm" cannons were still in existence ... But you just wait and wait, until in the end a Bavarian King will be sitting as German Kaiser on the throne (!!).'[91]

The madcap plans the exiled Emperor dreamt up for Germany to break out of the shackles of Versailles to become a World Power were every bit as dizzying as his grandiose schemes in the years before the war. In October 1919 he declared that, given the sorry state of the French and British economies, the Germans had 'in effect already won the war ... We must only take care to come to an alliance with Russia, under a sensible government, then we will have freed ourselves from the "dual alliance forceps" ... Then we shall first hit the Poles over the head so as to gain some room for manoeuvre in the east ... The Alsatians will get their autonomy ... That way we shall have room to move in the east and the west. In the south we are rid of the whole Austrian caboodle, and German-Austria will join us, the rest cast off out of harm's way to the Balkans. America is preoccupied with Japan and Japan I will attach to Russia in the east, and then we'll march together with Russia against England! France will probably join us too, in such circumstances ... We have won the war, we'll come out on top again. All we need is the courage to stand up to and beat the English.'[92]

After the abortive Hitler-Putsch in Munich Wilhelm again proclaimed his intention of returning to Germany in order to start a civil war as a prelude to launching an attack on France in the west. In a chilling echo of his notorious letter to Bülow of 31 December 1905 he exclaimed on 12 November 1923: 'First the sword against the Sozis, then against the French ... However, if war against France were to come first, no one would be able to keep him in Holland, in that case he would come back straightaway, and if they didn't want him as King he would simply take over a batallion, against the hereditary enemy he would join the fray whatever the circumstances.'[93] Without cease the ex-Kaiser dreamt of his restoration to the throne and the victory over Germany's foes which would then follow. 'If God should ordain that he should return, then the old army would have to be resurrected ... Then we would win the war after all.'[94] He greeted with glee the impending conflict between the Bolsheviks and the British in Asia. 'Those ruffians are no nationalists, they have no more than the vaguest notion of a fatherland. Now that Russia has been grazed bare they will simply move on to another place where they can realise their ideas. That is exactly the plan laid down by the Jewish-masonic wirepullers as revealed in "the Elders of Zion".'[95]

In exile Wilhelm lived in expectation of a new world order which would come into being the moment the other Powers in their fear of Bolshevik Russia realised the need for a reinvigorated, monarchical Germany. On the outbreak of the Russo-Polish War in 1920 he predicted that the Red Army would overrun Poland and then 'invade Germany to lay it waste together with the Spartakists in order to export Bolshevism across the Rhine & the Channel to western Europe & England! At that point the Entente will be forced to unite with Germany! Then our time will have come!'[96] When the Russian 'asiatic hordes fall upon Poland and defeat it, it will be for Germany to arise and hurry to the eastern frontier in the struggle for existence!' he cried.[97] Germany's task would be to 'beat back the *Yellow Peril*, to be joined by the whole of Europe, including the neutrals. Then the Peace of Versailles will be in tatters! God with us.'[98] The war of annihilation which Europe would then fight against Bolshevism would in the Kaiser's view bring about a total reversal of the 1919 peace settlement. If Germany were to stand firm against the communist hordes in the east to save the skin of the western Powers, it must be allowed to rearm. 'If it comes to a struggle against Bolshevism, that war would be an even bigger war than the last one, costing billions and billions and an untold number of deaths. For one thing was certain: prisoners would not be taken in such a war. If Bolshevism was to be smashed, every single proponent must be clubbed to death, that was the only way to exterminate it altogether. The coming year was bound to face us with events of the most significant and staggering kind', the Kaiser predicted.[99] Over and over again he warned: 'If Germany is not re-armed, Bolshevism will sweep right over her to reach the borders of France and Holland. If these countries want to avoid being overrun, they would have to strengthen Germany again and rearm her regardless of all the stipulations of the peace, and furthermore there would have to be a grand coalition of all the erstwhile enemy Powers against the Russian foe. In such an event however Germany must be led by only *one* man ... On this the Kaiser based the hope that he would be recalled by those responsible for his abdication. That would then be the greatest triumph of his life!'[100]

In October 1923 such hopes of a campaign against the Soviet Union fought by Germany under his leadership and in league with the democratic Powers of western Europe were abruptly turned upside down after a visit to Doorn by the cultural anthropologist Leo Frobenius. Germany, Kaiser Wilhelm now declared, belonged on the other side and must lead the east against the west! Alfred Haehner recorded the 'striking' effect Frobenius's lecture had upon the Kaiser. Wilhelm, who had initially heckled the speaker, 'soon became very still, one could see that Frob[enius]'s words were exciting him greatly. At the end he said only: "That was phenomenal. I have never heard anything like it in all my life!"' The following evening the Kaiser 'recapitulated' Frobenius's lecture 'with a twist of his own' to Dutch guests at Amerongen. 'He now pronounced all the French and English to be negroes and berbers, suddenly felt himself to be an oriental and even declared that after this lecture he would have to reverse his map of the "Peoples of Europe etc." to read: "Peoples of the East unite against the West". Frob[enius] was presented by him with a portrait with the inscription: "The West can go under but Germany never will. It is the face of the East." This morning [the] K[aiser] told me that Frobenius was the greatest German he had ever met!' Haehner noted and added sarcastically: 'As [the] K[aiser] met with so much enthusiasm and interest (??) for Frobenius among the Dutch (!) at Amerongen ... he has asked for the lecture to be repeated on Monday evening, to which he intends to invite many more Dutch people (!!) in order to demonstrate to them where their friendship with France and England has led them!' When Frobenius took his leave on 16 October 1923 Haehner minuted with astonishment: 'I have never seen any guest so honoured by the K[aiser] nor that [the] K[aiser] allowed himself to be spoken to by anyone as Frobenius did, as if he were a schoolboy asking his teacher questions.'[101] Ilsemann too remarked on the epiphanic effect Frobenius's lecture had had on the Kaiser. 'At last I know', Wilhelm had cried, 'what the future holds for the German people, what we shall still have to achieve! In all these years since the revolution it has been troubling me, now I finally know the answer: We shall be the leaders of the Orient against the Occident! I shall now have to alter my picture "Peoples of Europe". We belong on the other side! Once we have proved to the Germans that the French and English are not Whites at all but Blacks – the French e.g. Hamites – then they will set upon this rabble.'[102] To the archaeologist Professor Wilhelm Dörpfeld the ex-monarch enthused: 'Frobenius was here and I have enjoyed many a splendid hour with this clear-minded & quintessentially *German* man. What confidence in the future of our nation lives within him, from what great heights does he look down on what is happening in the world, what marvellous tasks await the Germans the moment they are united once more under the mailed fist of the clear-sighted Kaiser and have rid themselves of all things non-German and all those of alien origin!'[103]

From this first meeting in October 1923 to Frobenius's death in August 1938, a close relationship flourished between the exiled monarch and the controversial anthropologist, so much so that Frobenius could be ranked alongside Eulenburg, Waldersee, Bülow and Fürstenberg as one of Wilhelm's most intimate and influential friends. Their recently discovered and meticulously edited correspondence, comprising 121 letters from the Kaiser and 96 replies from Frobenius, throws a lurid light not only on their previously unsuspected mutual solicitude, with the 'scientist' encouraging the monarch in the belief that he was the Christ-like sacrificial victim of 'hateful' evil forces,[104] but also on both men's fascistoid mysticism and utter rejection of all western values.[105]

In 1925 Kaiser Wilhelm condemned the Locarno treaties and Stresemann's policy of reconciliation with France as 'a *crime* against the German *Volk*, against the White Race, against our proven German-Russian traditions. Turks, Russians, Bulgarians, Scandinavians, Germans and Hungarians all belong to the *same cultural circle*: it is now closing itself off, do the Germans want to remain outside? *Never!* So *Away* with *Locarno!* We must never give up so much as an inch of German soil! Least of all the truly ancient quintessentially German Reichsland [Alsace-Lorraine] reconquered by all the German tribes under the leadership of Kaiser Wilhelm the Great and Crown Prince Friedrich Wilhelm! The very thought makes one ashamed . . . in view of the fallen of both wars lying there and their great leaders such as Moltke and Bismarck! That must not be! The honour of the German Volk will not permit it!' Stresemann's Locarno policy would lead to the enslavement of the Germans at the hands of the French, the ancient imperial cities of Speyer, Worms, Koblenz and Cologne would become French cities, the German General Staff and the regiments of Frederick the Great come under French command.[106] Many years later Wilhelm was still proclaiming: 'Our European culture is divided into two halves which are *diametrically* opposed to one another: that of *Western* Europe (England, France and the Mediterranean lands) and that of Eastern Europe (Germany, Scandinavia, Holland, Austria-Hungary, Russia). The moment one intrudes into the other, catastrophe will ensue. East is east and West is west!'[107]

Wolfgang Krauel, the son of the Director of the Colonial Department under Bismarck, came away 'utterly thunderstruck' from a visit to Wilhelm II in Amerongen in October 1919. It took some time for the monstrousness of what he had experienced to sink in. 'The entire revolution has passed him by without trace. He behaved like a Prussian officer who has been cashiered as a result of intrigues but who hopes to get his regiment back and then to punish the guilty. Devoid of any sense of reality he is still completely steeped in the vanished values of yesteryear.' Most disturbing of all was Krauel's realisation that Wilhelm's alienation from the real world dated not from his abdication but from much earlier, from the long years when he had exercised so much power. Krauel listed the bewildering *idées fixes* obsessing the monarch in exile. Germany had only lost the war because the imperial house had been overthrown; the minute it was restored order would be re-established and victory over the enemy secured. Before that happened the domestic constraints in the shape of the Centre party and Social Democracy must be destroyed and Prussia's hegemony over the Reich reasserted. 'Then the Kaiser would resume his rightful place at the head of the Reich, which would first of all destroy the Poles in the east in order to form an alliance with Russia. In the west an autonomous Alsace would be created as a bulwark against France, just as German-Austria and Italy would form a close union with Germany, the former as protection against the Slavic Balkans. The German–Russian alliance would break the Russian-French ring, bring in Japan as a new Triple Alliance partner and turn once again and this time with victory assured on England, which would probably in this new struggle be abandoned by France. Therefore *at home* the struggle of Prussian Protestantism against international democracy and the Centre party, and *abroad* a continental Bloc against England as the centrepiece and foundation of the new world order: He, the Kaiser and his House! *It's as if we were all back in the time of the crusades and the peregrinations of the Hohenstaufen emperors through Italy*! . . . The impression it made was *dreadful*!'[108]

JEWS, FREEMASONS, JESUITS: WILHELM'S WORLD CONSPIRACY COMPLEX

The aggression with which Wilhelm anticipated his return to the throne, be it as military monarch, dictator or *Führer*, is indeed frightening, but it is as nothing when compared with the paranoid madness of the bizarre world-conspiracy theories haunting his mind in exile in Holland.[109] It was his unshakeable conviction that 'Jesuitism' had allied itself 'with the Jewish Freemasons in order to bring down the German monarchy as the predominant force of Protestantism'. Without cease Wilhelm regaled his Rhenish Catholic physician Alfred Haehner, his equerry Sigurd von Ilsemann and all the other staff and guests at Amerongen and Doorn with the assertion that these Jewish–Masonic–Catholic conspirators had been the real perpetrators of the world war and therefore of his abdication. Soon after Haehner's arrival at Amerongen the

Kaiser informed him in no uncertain terms that the Catholic Centre party 'along with the Pope and the Jesuits . . . and in league with the Masonic-Jewish grand lodges were responsible for bringing about the fall of the Protestant monarchy'.[110] 'It was now clear to him, the Kaiser said, that [the Austro-Hungarian Foreign Minister] Count Berchtold had unleashed this war in order to reduce Prussia-Germany to the role it had played prior to 1866, so re-establishing a South German Empire under Austrian hegemony. That is why the Count had left his German ally totally in the dark at the beginning of the war as to the steps he had taken against Serbia. Quite simply, Berchtold had had the aim of defeating Germany with the aid of the Entente, intending to sign a separate peace early enough to ensure that Austria could withdraw from the war on favourable terms.[111] 'The international Jewish rabble, the Centre party and the South German princes' had pursued the goal of eliminating Prussia and its Protestant Kaiserdom for all time, replacing it with a Confederation of Princes with an Austrian monarch at the helm.[112] 'The brains behind this Austrian anti-German policy' had been none other than Matthias Erzberger, the Kaiser asserted, 'whose intention it had been to unseat the Protestant House of Hohenzollern and replace it with a Catholic Kaiser-reich of the Habsburgs. Erzberger had pursued this goal with extraordinary single-mindedness from the beginning and was now intent on the final destruction of Prussian domination by dismembering Prussia itself'.[113] Seven years later Wilhelm II convinced himself − again quite absurdly − that Admiral Paul von Hintze, once his favourite Flügeladjutant and the man who had served as the representative of the Wilhelmstrasse at Imperial Headquarters in Spa, had in reality been a perfidious agent of the Catholic Church and the chief culprit behind his flight to Holland in November 1918. He had discovered from a reliable source, His Majesty wrote on 4 January 1927, that Hintze was a '*Roman Catholic* and a long-term close associate of the *Jesuit Order*. In Rom[an] circles he boasts that *he* had forced me at Spa to agree to the introduction of a parliam[entary] regime; *he* had deprived me of my powers of supreme command; *he* had packed me off to Holland in majorem Dei gloriam!!! So *Rome* a[nd] the *Jesuits* were behind the *betrayal of Spa*, using my Flügeladjutant in league with the *Soziis* and *Jews* at home!'[114] In August 1931 Kaiser Wilhelm II fumed against Reich Chancellor Heinrich Brüning as '*someone educated by the Jesuits* and therefore an enemy of all things Lutheran-Hohenzollern-Prussian . . . A Jesuit at the head of the Reich!! Unbelievable.'[115]

The appointment of Walther Rathenau as Minister for Reconstruction in the minority coalition government of Joseph Wirth in May 1921 only served to confirm the Emperor's paranoid notions of a world conspiracy of Catholics,

Freemasons and Jews against his Lutheran–Calvinist dynasty. As he remarked to his physician: 'It had taken a *Cath[olic]* Cabinet to appoint the first Jew as a government Minister ... This showed once again the connection between Ultramontanism and international Jewish Freemasonry bent solely on keeping down the Prot[estant] Kaiserdom. To this end Ultramontanism would stop at nothing. Behind it all were the Jesuits working at the behest of Rome and using Erzberger as their tool.' Haehner's counter-arguments fell on deaf ears. As the physician noted after the conversation: 'The Kaiser is simply obsessed by the fixed idea that the Catholics are virtually persecuting him in this way.'[116] In 1923 Wilhelm persuaded himself that Rome had abandoned the House of Habsburg and had now 'chosen the House of Wittelsbach as the instrument of its antigermanic policy' instead, promising 'to attach the Austrian crown lands to Bavaria!'[117] Rome and the Jesuits, he declared in 1924, were 'absolutely determined to erect a large Catholic Reich. The Jewish Freemasons were behind it all, they were using the unsuspecting Jesuits for their purposes. Their aim was to bring about even greater chaos on the Continent with a view to then establishing their world empire.'[118] In 1928 he assured an American friend, 'the Jews & the Jesuits were always hand in glove against Protestantism & the Aryan race all over the world'.[119]

THE KAISER AND THE JEWS

In exile in the Netherlands the Kaiser's anti-Semitism, which he had espoused with particular fervour ever since the entry of the United States into the war and the Bolshevik seizure of power in Russia in 1917, assumed a genocidal intensity. On 2 December 1919 he wrote in his own hand to the most loyal of his generals, August von Mackensen: 'The deepest, most disgusting shame ever perpetrated by a people in history, the Germans have done unto themselves. Egged on and misled by the tribe of Juda whom they hated, who were guests among them. That was their thanks! Let no German ever forget this, nor rest until these parasites have been destroyed and exterminated [*vertilgt und ausgerottet*] from German soil! This poisonous mushroom on the German oak-tree!'[120]

At Amerongen and Doorn Wilhelm devoured the most abysmal anti-Semitic literature such as the notorious forgery *The Protocols of the Elders of Zion*,[121] Artur Dinter's *Die Sünde wider das Blut*,[122] Friedrich Wichtl's *Weltfreimauerei, Weltrevolution, Weltrepublik*,[123] Friedrich Andersen's book *Der Deutsche Heiland*,[124] and Houston Stewart Chamberlain's late work *Mensch und Gott*[125] and propagated their message of hate to all and sundry. While sawing wood in November 1919 he praised Dinter's book − a vile diatribe in which a married German girl is punished for the 'sin' of an earlier relationship she had had with a Jew by giving birth to handicapped children — and declared that after reading this book no one would ever trust a Jew again.[126] Some days later he told his physician 'that after all that had happened he too had now become an embittered enemy of the Jews. As soon as we had another regime these people would have to be rendered harmless. Not a single Jew, not even one who had had himself baptised, must ever again be allowed to hold public office.' Haehner recorded in his journal: 'Especially through reading the Dinter book, for which he is making a great deal of propaganda, the Kaiser has become fiercely hostile to the Jews. It has turned him, as he says himself, into a convinced and determined anti-Semite.' Wilhelm responded with delight to Haehner's observation that the book was making quite a splash in Germany, remarking it could not be distributed widely enough.[127]

Unsuspecting visitors to Doorn were taken aback when the Kaiser launched into his anti-Semitic diatribes. Max von Mutius, once a Flügeladjutant at the imperial court, could hardly believe his ears when the exiled monarch told him in December 1920 that 'the world, and Germany in particular, would not rest in peace until all Jews had been clubbed to death [tot geschlagen] or at least been driven out of the country'. When the General remarked that 'unfortunately it would not be practicable to club all of them to death', His Imperial Majesty countered angrily: 'My dear child, I can do it and will do it. Just you wait and see.' The Jews would have to be banned from politics and the public service. 'They must be expelled from all positions, from the press, the state parliaments and the Reichstag. They must be forbidden from acting as leaders of the masses.' With his drawing 'Völker Europas' he had warned many years ago of the danger that was threatening from the east.[128]

In March 1921 Wilhelm informed his dinner guests how the Jews all over the world were ganging up to destroy Germany. Again it was Dr Haehner who put the Kaiser's words on record: 'The Engl[ish], French and German Jews were all in cahoots with one another. Their sole aim was to establish the Jewish domination of the world. Therefore they first had to enslave the German people completely. The Engl[ish] Prime Minister [David Lloyd George] was completely in the hands of the Jews . . . When a new era dawned once more in Germany the Jews would meet their fate in no uncertain terms. They had syphoned off some 80 billions out of the country. They would have to repay all of this, the government must start by demanding 15 billions immediately. They would have to forfeit everything, their art collections, their houses, all their property. They would have to be removed once and for all from all their public offices, they must be thrown completely to the ground.'[129] Year after year it was the same story, the All-Highest, full of venom, pronouncing that 'a Jew is the ... most obnoxious scoundrel on earth'.[130]

When Friedrich Schmitt-Ott, the one-time Prussian Minister for Education, visited the Kaiser in Doorn in July 1921, he too was shocked by the depth of Wilhelm's abhorrence for the Jewish people. He listened in disbelief as the monarch explained his theory of how the Jewish masonic lodges in France, Britain and Italy had conspired to bring about the Great War. On departing the Kaiser handed him a silver brooch in the shape of a swastika with the words: 'Now you have been admitted into the order of the decent people', adding that the late Kaiserin had also worn such a brooch.[131]

On reading the news of the death of Friedrich Wichtl, the author of the vicious pamphlet *Weltfreimauerei, Weltrevolution, Weltrepublik*, in Vienna in August 1921, the Kaiser was in no doubt that Wichtl had been 'killed by Jewish Freemasons' who were 'absolutely furious with him for having revealed their secrets'.[132] In March 1923 the Kaiser vented his anger on a distinguished guest who had dared to question his assertion that the occupation of the Ruhr was the work of the Freemasons. 'Well, haven't you read the book by Wichtl? Which proves everything with the relevant documents!' To the visitor's admission that he did not know the book the ex-monarch responded angrily: 'Then it really is high time that you read it. How can you be so foolish as to come here so ignorant! ... If even you and your circle of friends do not know this book, how can you expect the broad masses to be familiar with it!'[133] In a letter to Ludendorff written in 1927, Wilhelm II was still citing Wichtl as his authority for the conviction that 'international Jewish Freemasonry' was Germany's deadliest foe.[134]

In the course of 1921 the Kaiser's anti-Semitism received new impetus from two books, Friedrich Andersen's *Der Deutsche Heiland* – on the 'Aryan Jesus' – and Chamberlain's *Mensch und Gott*.[135] Both works confirmed his belief that 'the Christian religion needed to be purged of its Jewish adjuncts'.[136] After reading the first chapter of *Mensch und Gott* he ranted against the 'Jewish world press' as 'the work of Satan' and told his doctor: 'All the Jews needed to be expelled from the press, none of them could be allowed to work their poison in this way, one day I would see, on his restoration, what a pogrom there would then be, but of a different and more effective kind than all those in Galicia!' Wilhelm considered Houston Stewart Chamberlain to be a new prophet, a second Luther[137] and shared the renegade Englishman's belief that Germany 'could only return to good health by purging its religion, Christianity, of all the accessories rooted in the Jewish spirit'. As his tutor Hinzpeter had always taught him, the Old Testament was not the word of God but only a history of the Jewish people.[138] 'Therefore let us free ourselves from the *Judentum* with its Jawe!', the Kaiser cried.[139] He was firmly convinced that Jesus Christ was 'a *Galilean*, that is to say *not a Semitic Jew*', since the latter were 'not permitted to live in Galilee!'[140] On 3 June 1923, in his last letter to Chamberlain, Kaiser Wilhelm raved that Jesus was '*not a Jew!* but a Galilean, a man 'of exceptional beauty ... tall and slim, with a noble face inspiring respect and love; his hair blond shading into chestnut brown, his arms and hands noble and exquisitely formed'.[141] For years to come the monarch handed out copies of Chamberlain's *Mensch und Gott* to his visitors at Doorn.[142] In a letter to Chamberlain's widow, Richard Wagner's daughter Eva, he again averred: 'Our Christian God, the merciful, forgiving God, the personification of eternal love, our father, as Christ has taught us, has absolutely not the slightest thing in common with the vengeful bloodthirsty, angry old Jaweh of the Jews.' On the contrary, 'the old Jew-God Jaweh is ... identical with Satan!'[143] In a letter of August 1929 to Hans Blüher, himself the author of a book on the 'Aryan Jesus',[144] the Kaiser again proclaimed the Jewish God Jahwe to be identical with Satan, and went on: 'It was Jahwe, the prince of this world, of banishment, who allowed Jehuda to nail his foe the Son of God to the cross. Thenceforth Jehuda is cast out for all time & will always be the enemy of Christ and those who believe in him!!'[145] On another occasion Wilhelm demanded the formation of a 'Christian International' to fight the 'struggle first against the *Verjudung* of Germany' and 'then after the purification of Germany the struggle against *das Judentum* in the world'.[146]

In countless letters to his American admirer George Sylvester Viereck the Kaiser ranted that 'world Jewry' – 'Juda' – was striving for domination over all the nations on earth. '*This Juda* crucified the Lord and is the same who let loose the worlds Revolutions, the murders of Princes and Sovereigns and Statesmen, and finally plunged Europe into the Worlds War; it is personified in the "International Capital", the "Golden International" and in "Bolshevism".' In this letter the Kaiser called Maximilian Harden 'a loathsome, dirty, Jewish fiend, who prepared the anti-imperial atmosphere against me and thereby the Revolution'. He described Rathenau as a 'mean, decieving [sic], rascally traitor' who had belonged to the inner circle of the 200 'International World Rulers of Jewish descent in whose hands the modern statesmen are the puppets and their Nations, Entente, Russia, America the "catspaw" to be used for the destruction of Christian "Culture"; the backbone of which were the Teutonic Race, the German Empire, the Hohenzollerns and the German Kings and Princes'.[147] The Jewish question was, he insisted, not a religious but a racial question. The Jews had their origins in Africa, they still showed negroid traits, hence their hatred for all the Aryan white races and most especially for the Germans, their race, their monarchy, their princes and their spirit. 'They belong to the *Coloured* Races and not to the *European White Race* ... which they intend to enervate, subjugate and destroy!'[148] In an article entitled 'The Jew Today' intended for publication in the USA, the Kaiser expounded this drivel at greater length. It was evident, he claimed, that there existed a devilish Jewish conspiracy to take over the world. This plan, which had been revealed in *The Protocols of the Elders of Zion*, had made astonishing advances in the past ten or twenty years. 'Nobody nowadays doubts that there is a ring of "International Jews" who now wearing the mask of "High Finance" attempt to upset or make puppets of all governments, and camouflaged as Bolshevists try by the World Revolution to upset every existing system of Statepower in the World ... The Teutonic Race, the German Empire, the Hohenzollerns, the German Kings and German Princes were the backbone of Christian Culture. Hence the "Jewish Inner Ring" decreed their destruction.'[149]

To his boyhood American friend Poultney Bigelow the Kaiser exclaimed in English in 1927: 'The Hebrew race are my most inveterate enemies at home and abroad; they remain what they are and always were: the forgers of lies and the masterminds governing unrest, revolution, upheaval by spreading infamy with the help of their poisoned, caustic, satyrical [sic] spirit. If the world once wakes up it should mete out to them the punishment in store for them, which they deserve.'[150] In another of his letters to Bigelow the Emperor railed that the Jews were determined 'to ruin the world – as they are ruining my country – & to infect it with the poison of their base, sensual, lascive [sic], degrading spirit, so as to be able to become the masters of mankind! May Heaven help us all who are of Germanic extraction & staunch adherents of the Lord to defeat their Satanic plans! Amen!' Providence had chosen the German race and the Hohenzollern dynasty to fulfil its cultural mission, and he, the Kaiser, was predestined by instinct and by birth to lead it, Wilhelm bragged. 'History showed me that Luther, Wieland, Goethe, Fichte, Kant, Great Elector, Fr. the Great, all the greatest thinkers the world ever saw & never can emulate, were not given to us for *nothing*. Their gift to us was clear proof that Providence was following a line in which Prussia-Germany & my House were called to play a conspicious part ... For 500 years my House continued building the foundations for this work of Providence, the *"Kulturmission"* to the world ... till the German Empire was refounded by William the Great & I was put in the place to put it into practice ... Then the Jews fearing this spirit & its influence as dangerous to their *"World Rule"*, because money & mammon had no influence with me, poisoned the worlds spirit, incited the Anglo-Saxon envy at the growth of prosperity in Germany.'[151] He called for a 'regular international all-worlds pogrom à la Russe' as 'the best cure' against the rising Jewish menace.[152] 'Retribution' was sure to come, and then there would be a 'general cleansing ... the Jewdom included, which is at the bottom of all this dirt!'[153] On 15 August 1927 he wrote in his own hand to Bigelow that the 'Press, Jews & Mosquitoes ... are a nuisance that humanity must get rid of in some way or another. I believe the best would be gas?'[154]

In view of the admiration in which he always held his elder brother it will come as no surprise that Prince Heinrich fully shared the Kaiser's pathological hatred for the Jews. Like Kaiserin Auguste Viktoria, Heinrich's wife Irene, the Tsarina's sister, had worn the 'Aryan' swastika even before the First World War.[155] On 8 December 1920 Heinrich looked back on the two years since the overthrow of the monarchy and wrote to the right-wing propagandist Franz Sontag (Junius Alter), anticipating the Nazi Nuremberg Laws by some fifteen years: 'There is no longer any room for doubt that Juda is chiefly responsible for all our troubles and I want to draw your attention to the work "The Protocols of the Elders of Zion", edited by Gottfried zur Beek, which has recently been published by the publisher "Auf Vorposten". I have ordered several copies of the popular edition of this work in order to distribute it widely! Our *Volk* must be alerted to the political dangers of Semitism and taught to realise that the Jew is a foreigner, an alien individual. − I believe that the future development of this most significant question must involve legislative action, as in the past, against this foreign race, namely: deprivation of their German civil rights, ghettoisation in certain quarters and towns, abolition of their freedom of movement, prohibition of their holding any public office and of their studying at any university whatsoever. − Strict measures against marital relations with Jewesses; thorough purification of the Aryan race. These measures will take generations to take effect, and they will require an anti-Semitic majority in the government and in parliament, but a start must be made if we are not to perish.' Heinrich boasted that he had submitted for use in a patriotic calendar the slogan: 'The future of the German *Volk* − and therefore of Europe − is a *racial question*. If Siegfried is to flourish, Juda must vanish!' He and his imperial brother had been brought up, he said, 'to be as respectful and courteous to Semites as to our own countrymen, a rule we followed religiously − with the results we now see!'[156] Even the Crown Prince criticised the anti-Semitism of his father the Kaiser and his uncle Prince Heinrich as too undiscriminating. In the opinion of the younger Wilhelm it was wrong to fight the Jews in general, 'on the contrary one should instead win over the *nationally* inclined Jews and make use of them. Naturally one had to keep international Jewry at arm's length. In this respect a wholly mistaken selection had been made in the past, what one had allowed to attend court were the international grand Jewish capitalists. The national Jews were prepared to make considerable sacrifices for national purposes.'[157]

The recently discovered diary of his physician Dr Haehner, the table talk recorded by the numerous visitors to Amerongen and Doorn, his own letters to friends and acquaintances, his literary output and last but not least the identical views expressed by his brother Heinrich provide us with a glimpse into the soul of Wilhelm II in exile – and what we see there is shameful and terrifying. The ex-monarch's virulent tirades of hate against the Jews are virtually indistinguishable from the vile ravings of Hitler, Himmler, Göring, Goebbels and their ilk.[158] Wilhelm's brutal anti-Semitism was of course by no means unique – as we know, similar attitudes, perhaps always latent, gained widespread currency once they were sanctioned and propagated by the authority of the state after 1933, leading ultimately to the suffering and death of countless millions of innocent people from all over Europe. What makes the Kaiser's racial inhumanity particularly disgraceful is his claim to exalted status as a sovereign by Divine Right speaking on behalf of his Lutheran God and a supposedly Aryan Jesus. Certainly Kaiser Wilhelm II had no ideological compunction, no moral qualms against seeking his restoration to the Prusso-German throne with the help of the National Socialist movement.

CHAPTER FORTY-SEVEN

Monarch by the grace of Hitler? Wilhelm II and the Third Reich

What was Kaiser Wilhelm II's relationship to National Socialism? What hopes did he entertain of a return to the throne with the support of that demagogic mass movement, and how for that matter did Hitler, Göring and the other Nazi Party leaders feel about a restoration of the monarchy? When did Wilhelm recognise the criminal nature of the Third Reich? Did his Christian faith, his self-esteem as head of an ancient dynasty or his three decades at the helm of a great empire in the heart of Europe perhaps restrain him from getting too close to the violent rabble-rousers now in control of Germany? Even though we search the record in vain for anything amounting to public criticism of Hitler's dictatorship, did the exiled Kaiser, towards the end of his life and out of harm's way in the Netherlands, at least express dismay in private at the unspeakable horrors being perpetrated in his own country and beyond, in terms that his monarchist defenders – yearning for any such sign after 1945 – could have construed as a protest and thus have served as an alibi? These are painful questions to which the sources provide no comforting answers.

THE HOUSE OF HOHENZOLLERN AND THE STRUGGLE TO RESTORE THE MONARCHY

In his early years in exile, as we have seen, the Kaiser thought of his return to the throne primarily in terms of a violent overthrow of the Weimar Republic: the generals of the old regime were to fetch him back in a coup, to be followed by a bloody civil war and the exacting of revenge on all his enemies. Only slowly did it dawn on him that to effect his restoration he would need – or need to create – some popular support. 'I shall certainly not move a finger and will not place myself at their disposal again unless they beg me to', he said of the German people as late as 1922. 'They have chased me away and I shall not come back until they call me.'[1] No one felt this reactionary stance, this lack of a popular base, to be an insurmountable obstacle to a restoration more keenly than his own sons. The Crown Prince sighed that his father was 'terribly out of touch with the real world', he should have lived at the time of Louis XIV; his tragedy was to have been born too late, his notions of rule by Divine Right had no place in the modern world and had made him many enemies.[2]

In his final days on the throne the Kaiser had sensed the danger that his sons might outbid him in the public's esteem. On taking leave of his family in Potsdam on 29 October 1918 on his way to Spa he had required all six of his sons to swear in writing that they would never accept a regency or the succession in his place.[3] In the turmoil of defeat and collapse the Reich Chancellor Prince Max of Baden had indeed attempted to save the monarchy by placing one of the Crown Prince's young sons – the 12-year-old Prince Wilhelm or his brother Louis Ferdinand – on the throne with perhaps the Kaiser's fourth son Prince August Wilhelm, the least compromised of the Hohenzollerns, as regent. The project failed, not least because Prince 'Auwi' showed little inclination at this point to shoulder any such responsibility.[4]

In the Kaiser's eyes it was not the 'effeminate' Auwi but Crown Prince Wilhelm who presented the gravest threat.[5] In the revolutionary days of November 1918 the younger Wilhelm had indeed made a bid to take over the ancestral throne, if not as Emperor then at least as King of Prussia. His offer of February 1920 to stand trial before an international tribunal in his father's stead was also widely interpreted as a bid for the Crown.[6] 'Shocked and disgusted' by this 'most deplorable' act his father wrote to him: 'Keep your hands off politics, which you don't understand anyway! ... By this step you are vindicating the Entente's claim that Germany was guilty for the war and are thereby saddling your fatherland and me and our House for centuries to come with the guilt for the war.'[7] 'That green boy is committing one foolishness after another and is ruining so much that can never be put right again', Wilhelm II complained to his physician. 'He has caused us nothing but trouble.'[8] The ex-monarch was furious when in 1922 the Crown Prince published his memoirs at the same time as his own.[9] The greatest setback to the Kaiser's hopes of a restoration, however, was his eldest son's return to Germany in the autumn of 1923, even though it soon became apparent that the Crown Prince was 'almost as unpopular' there as his father.[10]

The Crown Prince's return to Germany took his father completely by surprise.[11] While his adjutant Louis Müldner von Mülnheim was busy negotiating the details of his homecoming with the authorities in Berlin, the

younger Wilhelm confided to the Kaiser's physician in Doorn that 'given his
father's character' he could not tell him of his intentions to his face but would
have to explain them to him in writing. His return to Germany was bound to
cause a 'huge sensation', the Crown Prince said, but he intended initially to
keep his head down; restoring the monarchy would not be practicable for a
very long time. 'He would do his utmost to prevent the question of monarchy
from coming to a head prematurely, the burden of the past weighed far too
heavily for a monarch to be able to survive at the present time ... and the
prospects for the future might then be ruined for ever.'[12] The Crown Prince's
letter arrived at Doorn on 10 November 1923, the day after the fiasco of the
Hitler-Putsch in Munich. Haehner observed how the Kaiser, 'in deadly earnest, with somewhat reddened eyes almost as if he had been crying', addressed
his entourage with the words: 'I have to inform you that the Crown Prince has
slunk back to Germany.' 'Then with a somewhat exaggerated gesture he
unfolded the Crown Prince's farewell letter and read it out to us. When he
had finished reading the letter the K[aiser] said to us: I give you my solemn
word of honour that I had no prior knowledge of this decision of the Cr[own]
Pr[in]ce's, it was all planned and carried out behind my back ... I fail to
understand how the Cr[own] Pr[in]ce could behave like this ... How is it
possible for him to ask permission from the government of the likes of
Stresemann, Hilferding, Braun & their comrades. From a government that
had thrown his father and him out. That is simply discreditable. And how does
he imagine his future?'[13] His son's return to Germany, the failure of the
Hitler–Ludendorff Putsch and reports warning of the unpopularity of the
monarchist cause at home were all too much for him. In late 1923 Wilhelm II
suffered another prolonged bout of depression.[14]

      In the course of time Kaiser Wilhelm came to realise the need to mount a
propaganda offensive if there was to be a return to the throne.[15] He drew
renewed hope from the loyal address he received on 9 February 1927, the
fiftieth anniversary of his commission in the First Regiment of Foot Guards,
from the officers of the old Army, and from a visit from his favourite General,
Field Marshal August von Mackensen.[16] The strategy he proposed to follow
was a curious mixture of the old and the new. In his 'Guidelines on the Way
Germans Should Think and Act' of 1927 the Kaiser declared that the
comrades who had sacrificed their lives in the war had done so for 'German
freedom ... German *space [Raum]*' and 'German *honour*'; the aim of the
monarchist movement must be the '*protection* and *preservation* of the
Germanic Race. Its base is the German *Fatherland*, its symbol the *German
Kaiser*.'[17] And in directives issued to Germany's many patriotic associations he
demanded 'the *unleashing of a great national movement* with utmost passion,

the sharpest logic and the clearest sense of purpose, with the aim of *restoring the monarchy* so as to conquer in this way a *new German Reich under me*. And this *far removed* from any party, party politics, party organisation ... That is to say *opposed to* any sort of *parliamentarism* in whatever form. The latter is totally western, therefore *un-Germanic, un-German* ... Till the day dawns when the *great, pure, holy German movement for Kaiser and Reich* smashes *to smithereens* the thoroughly deceitful *parliamentary edifice* along with all its parties!'[18] In 1928 Wilhelm charged the retired Admiral Magnus von Levetzow with the coordination of all monarchist elements.[19] On his seventieth birthday on 27 January 1929 the Hohenzollern family (including nineteen grandchildren) gathered in Doorn together with thirty 'generals and colonels of my old victorious army under the leadership of F[ield] M[arshal] Mackensen'.[20] Dressed in the 'field grey' uniform of the First Regiment of Guards and carrying his field marshal's baton, the Kaiser told them: 'The first place at home belongs to me and to no one else.'[21]

   That 'first place at home' was being challenged primarily by his eldest son and Crown Princess Cecilie but increasingly also by the Princes Eitel Friedrich, Oskar and August Wilhelm who all joined the anti-democratic, paramilitary Stahlhelm movement in 1927.[22] Such rivalry within the imperial family was anathema to the monarchist cause. Just a few years after their formal abdication, the Hohenzollerns had ceased to function as a coherent and effective political unit.[23] Beset by intrigue and denunciation, they jockeyed for individual advantage and descended into disarray, especially when faced with the rising Hitler movement.

THE IMPERIAL HOUSE AND NATIONAL SOCIALISM

Kaiser Wilhelm's attitude to the *völkisch* and radical–nationalist movements flourishing in the Weimar Republic wavered in line with his perception of their position on the key question of his restoration. In November 1920 Rudolf von Valentini told the former Reich Chancellor Theobald von Bethmann Hollweg that he had heard from a general who had just returned from Doorn 'that the Kaiser is leaning towards "National-Bolshevism" a[nd] is convinced that with their help he will be able to ascend the throne again'; but then the monarch's mind had always been 'a fertile ground for such mystical notions', Valentini added ruefully.[24] In 1924 both Wilhelm and Prince Heinrich were enthused by the prospect of a merger between the conservative DNVP (the Deutschnationale Volkspartei) and the radical Deutsch-Völkisch movement, but soon both brothers were forced to admit that there was little support within the latter for a monarchist restoration. Disappointed, Heinrich wrote to the Kaiser on 12 March

1924: 'The Deutsch-Völkisch movement is terribly similar to the National Socialist movement; the latter consists for the most part of riff-raff and uses the term "National" simply as a cover! — Just look at the utter failure of that demagogue Hitler! ... It will therefore be best to treat the Deutsch-Völkisch movement with distrust, in much the same way as the Hitler-Socialsocialists [sic], who failed so utterly, as did their Führer, especially when the shooting started.'[25]

It was not until Hitler's move to the Right in 1928 and the founding in the following summer of Alfred Hugenberg's 'Reichsausschuss für das deutsche Volksbegehren', demanding a plebiscite against the 'War Guilt Lie' of Versailles and an end to reparations that Wilhelm II thought he spied the chance of undermining the Weimar Republic and restoring the monarchy by rallying all the so-called 'national' forces including the Nazis. As Hjalmar Schacht was signing the Young Plan in Paris, the Kaiser wrote to his former Flügeladjutant Admiral von Grumme-Douglas: 'There's a big move to demand a plebiscite against Schacht's betrayal of the nation in Paris! That's excellent! But it must be directed *"against the War Guilt Lie"*, using that slogan will bring *all of them* together at home! ... *All of them must get involved*! Patr[iotic] Leagues, Farmers' leagues, Stahlhelm, veterans organisations, N.D.O. [National Association of German Officers], D o B [German Officers League] etc. in one great action! Once we have gathered the nation together under this slogan, then we will throw out the Dawes [Plan], Versailles & a*ll sorts of other things*! *America expects this action of us*! Full steam ahead!'[26]

With the staggering electoral successes of the NSDAP and the transition to a presidential regime in Berlin the question of how best to achieve a monarchist restoration presented itself in a new light. Several members of the various German royal houses now joined the Nazi Party, while others, such as Wilhelm's cousin Charles Edward of Saxe-Coburg and Gotha, had been prominent supporters of the movement for years.[27] Since the summer of 1929 the Kaiser's son August Wilhelm had enjoyed close contact with Hermann Göring and through him with Adolf Hitler, who exploited his support to the full by immediately inviting the Prussian Prince as his guest of honour to the Nuremberg rally.[28] In December 1929 August Wilhelm formally joined the NSDAP, not least in the hope of enhancing his chances of acceding to the throne.[29] (See Figure 63.) In a letter the Kaiser fell short of demanding that his son rescind his Nazi Party membership, but he did warn him that he risked expulsion from the royal family should his association with the movement bring discredit on the House of Hohenzollern.[30]

Alongside Prince Auwi, and in open competition with him, 'Kaiserin' Hermine showed herself to be a glowing admirer of Hitler. Since 1927, when she had furnished some rooms for herself in the Berlin palace of the old Kaiser Wilhelm I,

Figure 63 The Kaiser's son Prince August Wilhelm of Prussia in
the uniform of Hitler's brownshirts, the SA

Hermine had been active, together with Levetzow, in winning support for a
restoration in right-wing circles including the National Socialists. In August
1929 she took part – uninvited – in the Nuremberg party rally. She spoke at
length to Hitler, urging him to put her husband back on the throne and insisting
that the Kaiser, delighted as he was at the growth of the *völkisch* movement, set
greater store by the NSDAP than by the Stahlhelm and the other nationalist
leagues; and as for the conservative DNVP, he had abandoned all hope that they
would ever take decisive action to resurrect the monarchy.[31] Later, Prince Auwi
remarked to Ilsemann that Hermine 'had asked Hitler whether he couldn't bring
the Kaiser and her back to Germany, but he had said no'.[32]

Figure 64 Hermann Göring on one of his visits to the Kaiser at Doorn in 1932

After a personal meeting with Hitler in November 1930 Levetzow tried to persuade the Nazi leader to visit the Kaiser in Doorn.[33] As a first step he set up a two-day visit by Hermann Göring and his wife Karin, symbolically scheduled for 17 and 18 January 1931, the sixtieth anniversary of Bismarck's proclamation of the German Reich in Versailles. Hermine regarded Göring as the 'pace-maker on the road to the throne' and took it upon herself to 'court him mightily'. At Doorn Kaiser Wilhelm and Göring got on like a house on fire, talking endlessly of politics, archaeology and cultural morphology. As to the 'crucial' issue of monarchy, Göring opined that 'to be sure the Kaiser must return, but the other German sovereigns should not be allowed back on their thrones!' To the former Court Chamberlain Count Schwerin, Göring affirmed 'quite clearly' that 'he approved of a return of the Kaiser to the throne'.[34] (See Figure 64.)

In the following months the burgeoning relationship between the Hohenzollerns and the Nazi leadership was cultivated avidly. The Crown Prince, Hermine, the royal family's Commissioner-General, Leopold von Kleist, Admiral von Levetzow and the Court Chamberlain Alexander Grancy-Senarclens all met with Hitler and/or Göring. Kleist presented Göring with priceless pieces of furniture and works of art from the royal collection and invited him to the shoot on the Hohenzollern estates; the Crown Prince gave Ernst Röhm, the leader of the Brown Shirts, a horse.[35] If the Kaiser regarded the intimacy of his son August Wilhelm with Hitler and

Göring with suspicion, he recognised its propaganda value quickly enough. And when Auwi was hit by a policeman's truncheon during a Nazi rally in Königsberg, his imperial father saw this as a golden opportunity to get into Hitler's good books. 'Through this my son has become a martyr!' he rejoiced. 'Now people will go over to the Nazisozis in their thousands.'[36] He congratulated Auwi on having become a martyr to the great national movement and enclosed a letter to Hitler which Auwi presented to his *Führer* in person in early April 1931. As the Nazi Prince remarked to Putzi Hanfstaengl after the meeting: 'Hitler has every reason to be satisfied. My father has agreed in no uncertain terms to support him in every way possible.' Naturally, Auwi continued to consider himself, rather than his father, as 'the best horse in the Hohenzollern stable'.[37] One way or the other, the Hohenzollerns believed themselves to be within sight of their goal. 'For months now the only thing one hears in Doorn is that the National Socialists will put the Kaiser back on the throne', Ilsemann noted over Christmas 1931. 'All hopes, all thoughts, all conversations and all letters are based on this belief.'[38] A visit by Hitler to the Kaiser in Doorn seemed imminent.[39]

In February 1932 direct negotiations took place between Leopold von Kleist and Hitler but the outcome was disappointing. As the Hohenzollerns' Commissioner-General reported after the interview, Hitler was reluctant to commit himself. True, he had declared himself 'in favour of the monarchy', but at the same time he had expressed reservations against both the Kaiser and the Crown Prince 'on the grounds that they would be rejected by the masses'.[40] From another source we learn that at this point Hitler was thinking of installing Prince Alexander of Prussia, August Wilhelm's son, as Emperor.[41] Wilhelm II's own hopes were kept alive by Göring, who during a second sojourn in Doorn on 20 and 21 May 1932 repeated his earlier assurances. 'It was not exactly pleasant to observe the venerable old Kaiser sucking up to such an upstart', remarked Ilsemann. 'On Göring's first visit the Kaiser still kept his distance, but this time there was no sign of that at all.' Hopes were still high that Hitler himself would soon be coming to Doorn.[42]

The Crown Prince was also doing his best to stay in personal touch with Hitler,[43] but, influenced by his wife Cecilie and his friend General Kurt von Schleicher, he sided rather with the paramilitary Stahlhelm and the Reichswehr and in 1932 declared his willingness to stand for the Reich presidency as the candidate of the 'national front'. Once in office he planned, he said, 'to mount a coup d'état à la Napoleon Bonaparte for the restoration of the monarchy'.[44] The Kaiser, sensing the danger to his own ambitions, forbade his son to stand for the presidency. 'If you take on this office', he wrote, 'you will have to swear an oath to the Republic. If you do that and keep it, you are finished as far as I am concerned, I shall disinherit you and throw you out of my House. If you swear the oath only to break it at the first opportunity, you will be perjuring yourself, cease to be a gentleman and also be finished as far as I am concerned . . . It is an impossible thing for the Hohenzollerns to return to power via the red republican presidential seat of an Ebert.'[45] Faced with this threat, the younger Wilhelm withdrew his candidacy but caused a sensation by declaring his intention of voting for Hitler instead of Hindenburg.[46] 'I believe I have thereby won over some 2 million votes for Hitler from among my Stahlhelm comrades and the German nationalists in general', the Crown Prince is said to have boasted.[47] In the coming crucial months, always in expectation of a restoration, he praised the 'wonderful movement' of Adolf Hitler.[48]

Prince Auwi continued to be much closer to Hitler than his elder brother, whom he castigated on account of his 'senseless relations with the grand Jews' and his habit 'of bathing from the banks [of the Wannsee] at Cecilienhof with his Jewish girlfriends'. Auwi accompanied the *Führer* on his legendary flights across Germany and stood at his side at dozens of mass rallies.[49] In April 1932 Hitler placed this Prince of Prussia at the head of the NSDAP's list of candidates for the elections to the Prussian Landtag, and this with the public approval of the Kaiser who declared: 'In full appreciation of the great national popular movement to which you are committed I hereby give you my permission to heed the call that has gone out to you.'[50]

With the dramatic success of the NSDAP in the Reichstag elections of 31 July 1932 Hitler came within reach of the highest office. His decision to turn down Hindenburg's offer of the Vice Chancellorship together with the post of Prime Minister of Prussia and to hold out for the Reich Chancellorship[51] was condemned by Wilhelm II as a grave mistake. The letter which the Kaiser wrote to the Crown Prince on 17 September 1932 reflects his bitter disappointment. To Hindenburg's statement that he could not square it with his *conscience* to entrust the *entire* power of the Chancellorship to the Nazis, Hitler should, in the opinion of the abdicated monarch, have retorted: 'Your Exc[ellency]'s *conscience* freely permitted you for years on end to entrust the *entire* power to those enemies of the Reich a[nd] of the Hohenzollerns the *Centre Party* in league with Red Sozis, Radicals, Jews a[nd] Bolsheviks and to stand by while these criminals ruined the country to its very foundations and strangled and fought against each and every national impulse. Surely now your conscience can turn towards the National movement! Which has emerged victorious from the elections!' The ex-Kaiser was equally critical of Hitler's decision to reject Hindenburg's compromise offer, however, complaining: 'It fills me with deep sorrow and concern to observe the outrageous *unscrupulousness* with which the *demagogic* leaders of the Nazis are ready senselessly to squander the capital of national energy gathered together in their national movement. The strong *National forces* that are even today still present in the Nazi-Party must be rescued from the totally irresponsible demagogic hustle and bustle of some of the leaders and orators and brought behind the National government. H[itler's] refusal was a dreadful howler and a grave disappointment for all nationally-minded people.' Hitler was 'wholly devoid of any political *flaire* or knowledge of history', the ex-monarch claimed, 'otherwise he would realise "Whoever has Prussia has the *Reich*! First *Prussia* must be cleansed and restored to law and order, obedience a[nd] discipline a[nd] *re-armed*, then the Reich!" So the offer he was made would have enabled him within a few months, thanks to his position in Prussia, to be the decisive voice in the Reich! He is *no* statesman, that is why he gives in to the pressure from the *extremists* in his entourage and has missed the chance. Against this *demagoguery of the moment* our *House* must present a *firm, solid united front* which is clearly and unmistakably visible *to the outside world*; to it the National elements of all circles made insecure and confused would then be able to rally … Give my regards to my beloved Rominten a[nd] the foresters! Be careful, don't commit any gaffes that might spoil your future chances … Please show this letter to your brothers.'[52]

The Kaiser's letter, written in despair at the supposed missed opportunity of dismantling the last remnants of the Weimar Republic, fell into the hands of the Nazis and wiped out whatever chance there might have been of a restoration of the Hohenzollern Monarchy by the grace of Hitler. As Schwerin reported in a telephone call to Doorn on 1 October 1932, on reading the letter Göring announced that 'he had been on the very point of going to Hitler in order to discuss with him the question of the monarchy in the Kaiser's interests; that was now quite out of the question'.[53] Wilhelm suffered a further blow when the Crown Prince informed him that Hitler had rejected his, the Kaiser's, plea to reconsider his decision to refuse to serve as Vice Chancellor in Franz von Papen's Cabinet.[54] Hitler's response was 'incredible', the Kaiser cried. 'From it we see that Hitler thinks only of himself, that he is suffering from megalomania and, like Ludendorff, is mentally overexcited. He never even mentioned the word "monarchy".' Wilhelm had at last been forced to realise, Ilsemann noted after an hour-long discussion with him in his study, that 'in relying on the Nazis he had been backing the wrong horse'. He now intended to ask Hugenberg and his newspaper empire 'to raise the imperial standard, his hour had come now or it never would. He would now tell everyone who had so far cast their vote for Hitler that they must vote *deutschnational*', i.e. for the more conservative DNVP.[55]

Wilhelm continued to be furious with Hitler long after the Reichstag election of 6 November 1932 in which the NSDAP lost two million votes as compared with the elections in July. On 10 November 1932 he wrote to his sister Margarethe Landgravine of Hesse that Hitler was crazy 'to demand influence & power, having rejected it when it was offered to him!' He was driving towards National Bolshevism while the right-wing parties were fighting one another to the delight of the Socialists and Catholics. 'High time for the sensible people to recall me, or else the Fatherland goes to the devil!'[56] Evidently fearing a scandal that could damage the Hohenzollern cause, the Kaiser now forbade his homosexual son Auwi to engage in any further activity on behalf of the Nazi movement and sent him temporarily abroad.[57] More than ever after the collapse of the Schleicher Cabinet Wilhelm saw in the restoration of a strong monarchy the only hope for Germany. On 24 January 1933, one week before Hitler's 'seizure of power', he complained: 'The mess at home frightful! The behaviour of Hitler shows a lamentable lack of talent for statesmanship, no discipline, no knowledge of national economy! He is only possible under a firm, strong hand in a limited area.'[58] Just days before Hitler's appointment to the Chancellorship the Kaiser cried: 'Call me and I'll come! Amen!'[59] But when, on 30 January 1933, the 'government of national concentration' was formed with Hitler as Chancellor and Papen as Vice Chancellor, the ex-Kaiser was overjoyed. Ilsemann noted: 'With the formation of the new government in Germany ... the question of the Kaiser's return to the throne has once again moved into the foreground. From all sides Doorn is being asked whether and when the Kaiser is going back to Germany.'[60] The union of the right-wing forces under Adolf Hitler was 'the Kaiser's best birthday present', his wife Hermine exulted.[61]

NEGOTIATIONS WITH THE *FÜHRER* FOR A RETURN TO THE THRONE

The notorious 'Day of Potsdam' in the Garnisonskirche on 21 March 1933 with its emphasis on the Prussian military traditions appeared to presage the return of the Hohenzollerns (see Figure 65). President Paul von Hindenburg, attired in the uniform of a Prussian general, saluted the Crown Prince with his field marshal's baton.[62] Princes Eitel Friedrich, August Wilhelm and Oskar also played a prominent part. True, the seat reserved for the Kaiser remained empty, but his restoration seemed to be just a question of time. On this day he remarked at Doorn: 'I am the only one not bound by party, therefore my return must now be pursued with vigour. I do not want to attain this without the Nazis; the upturn in Nazi support must of course be made use of, but the main thrust must surely come from the Black-White-Reds, above all from the Stahlhelm.'[63] Even so, Wilhelm was acutely aware of the slight implied in the choice of venue for the revivalist pageant: Instead of gathering at the grave

Figure 65 Another kind of restoration: on 21 March 1933, the Day of Potsdam, Kaiser
Wilhelm II's portrait is re-hung in the town hall of Berlin

of Frederick the Great in Potsdam, the nationalists should in his view have
met at the tomb of his grandfather Wilhelm I at Schloss Charlottenburg 'in
order to lay the wreath at the grave of the Great Kaiser', in which case the
speeches would necessarily have focused on the last three German emperors,
'recalling that Wilhelm I had founded the Reich and that Friedrich III and he
himself had strengthened it'.[64] And then, not long after the 'Day of Potsdam',
Wilhelm's hopes of returning to the throne were dashed when Hitler declared
an imminent restoration of the monarchy to be 'out of the question'. This
news 'struck him like a blow to the heart', Ilsemann recorded. 'I observed the

noble Lord very carefully, his expression became tense, the eyes widened alarmingly, he was unable to utter more than the one word "So!". The manner in which he said this sounded like the acceptance of his sentence by a man condemned to death.'[65]

On three occasions in the early months of the 'Third Reich' negotiations took place between Hitler and representatives of the House of Hohenzollern. On 9 May 1933 Hitler, accompanied by the War Minister Werner von Blomberg, met in Königsberg with Friedrich von Berg, formerly the head of the Kaiser's Civil Cabinet. Hitler stipulated his standpoint on a restoration in the following terms: '1.) He regarded the monarchy as the culmination of his task. 2.) For him there was only one German monarchy; he rejected monarchies in the federal states (the Länder). 3.) For the monarchy only the House of Hohenzollern could be considered. 4.) The time had not yet come for the reinstitution of the monarchy: a.) putting the monarchical idea into practice at the present time would be doing it no favour at all; b.) reintroducing the monarchy at present would interfere with the National Socialist programme of reconstruction; c.) and would bring about great difficulties in foreign policy. 5.) Hitler was – so Blomberg said – first and foremost a soldier. As such he believed it possible for the monarchy to come back through a plebiscite or something of that kind. Only the army could return the Kaiser to the throne after a victorious war.'[66]

In spite of this obvious rebuff, Wilhelm did not abandon hope. Confident that the collapse of the Hitler Cabinet was imminent, he felt sure that when the crisis came Germany would call him and then his hour would come.[67] In October 1933 General von Cramon submitted a memorandum to President von Hindenburg entitled 'Arguments in Favour of a Return of His Majesty the Kaiser and King to his Rights on the Occasion of his 75th birthday'.[68] In December the Kaiser assured Mackensen, who had once again expressed forebodings with regard to the monarchist cause: 'For all of us waiting for a change at home there is the one prayer: May the Lord preserve you for us and the nation-in-arms and the Fatherland for when it once again has a Supreme War Lord and an army!'[69]

On 26 September 1933 General Wilhelm von Dommes, as the representative of the House of Hohenzollern, having first discussed the matter with Hindenburg,[70] met the head of Hitler's Reich chancellery, Dr Hans Heinrich Lammers, to negotiate the restoration of the monarchy. Lammers stressed that, though Hitler was a monarchist, he believed that 'many years of preparation' would be needed before the people were ready to accept a crowned head again.[71] On 24 October 1933 Dommes was granted a personal interview with Hitler. The General pointed to the enthusiasm with which the Kaiser and his sons had greeted the national awakening of the German people. He laid stress on the need for Hitler to restore the monarchy if his achievements were to outlast him personally. Once again Hitler ducked the crucial question. 'With regard to the form the state will take, he wanted for the time being to put everything on hold ... Naturally he was aware that a system could not rest upon one pair of eyes alone but needed to be founded on a House. He did not have a family, his name was engraved in Germany's history, in a few years it would be anchored there for all time. He had no ambition beyond solving the tasks he had set himself: above all saving Germany from Bolshevism a[nd] liberating it from the domination of the Jews [*Befreiung von der Judenherrschaft*].' He thought it doubtful, the *Führer* added, whether a monarchy could be tough enough to take upon itself the bloody conflicts which such a programme would entail. 'Very few people understood his position in the Jewish question ... And here Hitler became very passionate [Dommes continued]: he went into great detail on how and why the Jews had become Germany's misfortune, had made the revolution etc. etc. The Jews would therefore have to be eliminated [*ausgeschaltet*]. This had been his aim from the beginning. He would not be blown off course. As I gained the impression that H[itler] was indirectly criticising His Majesty for being friendly to the Jews I interrupted him a[nd] told him something His Maj. had said to me in 1911 after a lunch at Admiral Hollmann's: "The Sovereign has the duty to ensure that all the strengths present in a nation are put to good use. If one excluded the Jews from the army and a career in the civil service, then one had to provide them with a safety valve through which they could use their intelligence and their capital to the best advantage of the nation; that was scholarship, the arts a[nd] charitable activities."' Dommes's all-too-naive anecdote made little impression on Hitler, who simply reiterated that 'the casting down [*Niederwerfung*] of Communism a[nd] Jewry were the tasks he had set himself a[nd] had to solve. He did not know how much time he would have to achieve his aims.' Dommes, clearly out of his depth when faced with the enormity of Hitler's intentions, made one last bid to change the *Führer*'s mind. 'I rejected the notion that the monarchy would be unsuited to solving the problems he had outlined and then asked Hitler directly whether he agreed with my conviction that this was indeed the case. He did not answer my question but instead returned to the Jewish question. Then he brought the conversation to an abrupt end.'[72]

A speech in the Reichstag by Hitler on 30 January 1934, the anniversary of his 'seizure of power' and three days after Wilhelm's seventy-fifth birthday, together with an order issued simultaneously by Göring dissolving all mon-archist associations, finally put paid to all these illusions.[73] Bewildered, the Kaiser exclaimed: 'The enemy is on the Right! Declaration of war on the

House of Hohenzollern and the German Kaiserdom! The monarchists loyal to the Kaiser are placed on the same level as the Bolsheviks!'[74] In a letter of 2 April 1934 to his sister he moaned: 'Our poor country!!? – God help us!! – – – ! Chaos!'[75]

In this tense atmosphere Hitler and Dommes held a second meeting on 27 April 1934, this time on the former's initiative. Hitler had taken umbrage at a telegram the Kaiser had sent in November 1933 to the National League of German Officers asserting that only under 'its Kaiser and the German Federal Princes' would Germany be able 'to stand on a firm and lasting foundation and find its way back to its former power and glory'.[76] On this occasion Hitler made no secret of the deep grudge he bore the monarchist movement. 'Back in the old Germany he had held monarchy to be the best state form. He had nothing against the monarchy, especially not against the House of Hohenzollern. But it had been a bitter experience for him to realise that the middle classes, the intellectuals and the Princes had shown no appreciation of his struggle.' The Bavarian Crown Prince had even castigated his movement as 'guttersnipes wet behind the ears ... Since the Princes had failed him, he, a little man, had had to save Germany with little men. His aims were: to save Germany from Bolshevism, the extermination [*Ausrottung*] of the criminals of the November Revolution, the inner purification, [and] the rearmament of the Reichswehr so as to restore Germany's prestige abroad as well. For all this he needed time – something like 12 to 15 years. Throughout this time he must not be disturbed.' Dommes repeated his pathetic assertion that many of these aims were surely 'identical' with those striven for by the Kaiser, but his plea fell on deaf ears. Hitler had set his mind firmly against a restoration.[77]

THE KAISER AND THE HITLER REGIME

At first, like Dommes and so many other contemporaries, Kaiser Wilhelm failed utterly to comprehend the true nature of the Nazi regime (see Figure 66). He was overjoyed at what he called the 'self-liberation' of the German people from the 'rule of terror' exercised by the Bolsheviks, the Socialists, the Democrats and especially by the Jews over the past fourteen years.[78] On 20 March 1933 he greeted the violent attacks of the SA, the brownshirted *Sturmabteilung* of the Nazi Party 'against the political criminals' as 'heart-warming'.[79] 'The Kaiser absolutely appreciates the greatness and the earnestness of the movement and is most impressed by the recent speeches', the besotted Hermine assured Cramon on 19 May 1933.[80] But then doubts and disappointments set in. Finding his letters were being opened and his telephone calls monitored, Wilhelm wrote to his sister in July 1933: 'I must say

Figure 66 The German Crown Prince takes the salute at a march
past of the SA in Breslau, 1933

I am most seriously anxious at what is going on in my poor Fatherland now in
the hands of untried & inexperienced youths!'[81] 'What an ignominious situation to be deprived of all rights acquired by birth & tradition', he exclaimed
in October 1933. 'May Providence repay them the kicks they deal out to me
nearly weekly! It is horrible to have our feelings trampled on like that! No
tradition any more! Brutality!'[82]

The murderous character of the regime was revealed all too clearly to
Wilhelm, too, when on 30 June 1934, in the 'Night of the Long Knives', not

only the leadership of the SA under Röhm, but General von Schleicher and his wife, along with numerous other supporters of a restoration of the monarchy, were brutally killed or silenced politically.[83] Louis Müldner, the Crown Prince's adjutant, was arrested and incarcerated for weeks. The Kaiser's son Eitel Friedrich underwent a terrifying interrogation at the hands of the Gestapo. Göring took sadistic pleasure in informing his loyal comrade Prince August Wilhelm that his name had been on the proscription list and he had only been spared execution because of his (Göring's) protection.[84] The Kaiser could barely disguise his satisfaction that his son had fallen foul of the Nazis: 'Auwi is now finished with his National Socialism. I have forbidden him from taking any further part in the Party. His fanaticism was almost pathological. And what thanks did he get and what has he achieved? Absolutely nothing!'[85]

What with Dommes's confrontation with Hitler on 27 April 1934, the prohibition of the monarchist associations and the bloody murders in the night of 30 June 1934, the Kaiser was finally forced to recognise that a return to the throne was out of the question. On Hindenburg's death he warned that many people were still deluding themselves about Nazi rule: 'the awakening will be terrible!'[86] And yet, spurred on by his wife and overjoyed at Hitler's foreign policy triumphs, with which he identified completely, Wilhelm gradually regained his faith in the *Führer*. In May 1934 Hermine gushed in a letter to a friend: 'May Hitler succeed in all his great plans . . . It always touches me to the heart . . . that he wants and strives for the goals which the Kaiser instinctively and fervently pursued but was prevented from attaining by those working with Him and by His reactionaries who boycotted or watered them down. From the bottom of my soul I wish Hitler complete success in the great things he is planning!'[87] On the reintegration of the Saarland into the Reich on 1 March 1935 the Kaiser hoisted the national flag to mark 'a German political achievement' and spoke with admiration of 'the determination with which the Führer had stood up to England'.[88] 'One's heart leaps when one thinks of what the Fuehrer has again given Germany this past year – universal military service!' Hermine cried in December 1935 in a letter to Mackensen. 'God preserve this man whose aims are so very pure.'[89] 'We are all so proud of our new army – what an achievement by the Führer, what a leap over the ditch of the Treaty of Versailles!', she wrote to another officer.[90]

Wilhelm justified Hitler's reckless decision on 7 March 1936 to reoccupy the Rhineland and renege on the Locarno treaties on the spurious grounds that these were defensive measures to ward off an imminent Franco-Russian threat. As he informed his friend and admirer the British General Wallscourt Hely-Hutchinson Waters: 'This step had to be taken. France . . . continued to fortify her Eastern Frontier, & to rearm & increase her Armaments instead of disarming as she was bound to do & as Germany did. Germany remained in a state of Disarmament for 17 years during which all the Powers signatories of Versailles rearmed to the teeth. This situation ludicrous in itself became dangerous when France had managed to surround the Disarmed country by a ring of Nations by concluding antigerman Pacts with all of them. The last link in this antigerman Ring was forged by the Franco-Sovjet Military Convention aimed at Germany & published in a violent antigerman spirit excluding all doubts as to its meaning! How could England allow her Ally such an insult to European Civilisation & become the sleeping partner to a Pact concluded against the only bulwark able to bar the inrush of Bolshevism into Europe?!! The reoccupation of the Rhineland Garrisons was dira necessitas as an answer to the Franco-Russian menace of War in deepest Peace; an act of Political brigandage on the part of a supposed cultivated civilised Nation to ally herself to Red Bolshevism, which is ready to destroy every vestige of Civilisation in the World!'[91] Naturally Hermine was no less fervent in her admiration of her adored *Führer*. 'Deeply moved' she told the General: 'Of course I feel in my heart and for the Kaiser the great strain that another man – not he himself can rule Germany – but I am thankful to Hitler and glad for Germany that after all these disgraceful years since 1918 to 1933 a man stood up and saved Germany from shame, slavery, death. England may not repeat 1914 – may not treat Hitler as it treated my poor Kaiser.'[92] Her husband, she never tired of repeating, was 'enchanted by Hitler's policies'.[93]

The Spanish Civil War was greeted by Wilhelm as an opportunity for the whole of Europe to stem the tide of Bolshevism. To his American friend Poultney Bigelow he wrote in August 1936: 'The Bolshevist System in Spain will I hope soon be smashed & arson & wholesale murder punished by the army & loyal Spaniards! May this be an eyeopener to all socalled statesmen who up to now underrated the danger of Moscow inspired vandalism, & help to combine the Powers for a common action for the destruction of this World Pest!'[94] In November 1936 he blamed Paris and London as well as Moscow for the bloodbath in Spain.[95] He was enthusiastic in his approval of the military support Hitler was providing to Franco's fascists. As Hermine assured Mackensen in December 1936: 'The Kaiser is exceptionally pleased at our intervention against Spain, against the red tide and at our combination with Japan against Bolshevism. England's behaviour is incomprehensible; the awful thing is that it will not only be England but Europe which will suffer if the red flood is not stemmed in time. What madness and what blindness.'[96] Wilhelm was utterly perplexed by the growing British suspicion of Hitler's intentions, writing to his sister in January 1937: 'The State of Europe ghastly; the policy of England disgusting, led by lunatics, becoming the sleeping partner of Bolshevism! All German Proposals answered with kicks & snarls; exactly as in my time!'[97]

The Anschluss of Austria in March 1938 occasioned further rejoicing at
Huis Doorn. 'How swift at just the right moment and how terribly audaciously
the matter has been handled', crowed Hermine.[98] She reported happily that her
husband was 'well and alert, following world events with immense interest –
He's exceptionally interested in the build-up of the armed forces; He cannot
hear and see enough of it, is deeply involved.'[99] In Wilhelm's eyes the tense
stand-off between Hitler and Britain and France over the Sudentenland was
nothing but perfidious trickery on the part of London. Thus he told his sister
on 16 June 1938 in all seriousness: 'The last Prague War-hoax was engineered
in London, by the *British Intelligence Service* telephoning to Prague that the
Germans were marching for the frontier!!! That nearly started a World
War!!!'[100] He was relieved to learn of Neville Chamberlain's readiness to
negotiate with Hitler over the partition of Czechoslovakia. Two days after
the Munich Agreement of 29 September 1938 he wrote to the widowed Queen
Mary: 'May I with a grateful heart relieved from a sickening anxiety by the
intercession of Heaven write my warmest, sincerest thanks to the Lord with
yours & those of the German & British People that He saved us from a most
fearful catastrophe by helping the responsible statesmen to preserve Peace.
I have not the slightest doubt that Mr. N. Chamberlain was inspired by
Heaven & guided by God who took pity on His Children on Earth, by
crowning his mission with such relieving success. God bless him.'[101] In much
the same exalted tone he wrote to his sister Margarethe, once again seeing in
Hitler's success a continuation of his own struggle against their uncle Edward
VII: 'What an *awful week of suspense* is behind us! It was an inspiration of God
that influenced Chamberlain to save the Peace! A clear proof of the influence
of Heaven on Earthly affairs. The agreement of Munich which *enforced* Peace
on Warpromoters has shattered Uncle Berties Policy against us, & brought
about by common consent of the People the *European Conclave* I vainly
wished for for 30 Years! The experience of the Worlds-War still alive in the
Peoples minds frightened them into listening to the Commands from Heaven.
War would have been a *Crime & our Country would have perished for ever*!'[102]
His sister was right to draw a contrast between 1914 and 1938. 'If Grey in 1914
had behaved as Chamberlain did in 1938, there would have been no World
War. But 1914 the British People *wanted* War, 1938 they *feared* it! Thank God
Providence influenced Chamberlain to take the bull by the horns & smash the
Bluff!'[103] In a Christmas message to General Waters sent on 12 December
1938 the Kaiser praised Britain's appeasment policy but asked himself how
long the peace would endure.[104]

The hostile reaction of the Powers to the annexation of Bohemia and
Moravia (and of Memel) into the German Reich in March 1939 briefly filled

Wilhelm with foreboding. 'The world seems to be subjected to attacks of hysterics & political lunacy', he exclaimed. The speeches being made in London and Paris caused him 'concern for the future of our beloved country'.[105] Hermine, however, thought it 'most refreshing to see how Wilhelm waxed furious at this renewed encirclement by the old Entente and at the insults levelled at Germany under the address of the Fuehrer'.[106] The British declaration of 31 March 1939 guaranteeing the frontiers of Poland was in the Kaiser's opinion 'detestable'.[107] In a characteristic letter to Queen Mary written on 30 August 1939, on the eve of the German invasion of Poland, Kaiser Wilhelm opined: 'I suggest that as the worlds Nations Committee at Geneva is dissolved, their Palace may be turned into an Asylum for Political Lunacy, to recieve [sic] all the Europ: Statesmen for a cure till they recover their senses! May Heaven preserve us from the worst!'[108]

THE SECOND WORLD WAR AND THE PERSECUTION
OF THE JEWS OF EUROPE

At the outbreak of war on 3 September 1939, the little town of Doorn was garrisoned by 3,000 Dutch soldiers. Isolated in their mansion and its walled park the imperial couple followed the dramatic events, full of admiration for Hitler's strategy. 'The Kaiser and I are watching all these great events unfold from the bottom of our hearts and are proud of our troops', wrote Hermine on 5 October 1939. 'God bless Germany.' Repeatedly she likened this new war to the First World War, and Hitler to Wilhelm. 'How wisely has the Fuehrer and those who have not deserted him, those who kept faith with him, the civilians and the military, arranged and achieved everything – how great is the unity. If only all those involved in 1914–18 had done their duty in the same way, we would never have had a 1918. I believe I can say in all honesty that the Kaiser and I are delighted from the bottom of our hearts that the Fuehrer has not had to confront the difficulties which the Kaiser experienced both militarily and at home, and during the war as well, alongside all his great concerns for the war and the Fatherland.'[109] 'My husband is wonderful in His proud delight at the achievements of the troops and all the great things the Führer is doing for Germany', Hermine told the Kaiser's old friend Max Egon Prince zu Fürstenberg during the Polish campaign.[110] The policy of the British government, which he was convinced had brought about the Second World War, was declared by Wilhelm on 18 October 1939 to be 'simply disgraceful & criminal! They feed the British with lies continually to keep up their spirit, because the *People* dont want war; certainly not the French, they detest it. May Providence help our brave army & navy to defeat the Plans of our Enemies as Heaven has done till now! The Polish Campaign was marvellous. Old Prussian spirit, the Leaders "My school"!'[111] 'How fabulous are our achievements, especially at sea and in the air', Hermine cried in December 1939. 'Wilhelm is so proud of it all and is totally absorbed by these great events.'[112] To one of her husband's grandsons she wrote: 'Grandpapa is wonderfully alert, takes a tireless interest in everything that is happening, full of confidence in you, the armed forces, in the wise commands and plans of the Führer', and she added: 'How shamefully England is carrying on.'[113] And a few days later she wrote tellingly in another letter: 'We do not doubt that he [the *Führer*] will succeed in bringing perfidious England to its knees and to conquer for Germany the place in the sun which it needs and deserves. With all our thoughts and wishes we are back home and at the fronts where such great things are being achieved. The Kaiser is proud of the young Wehrmacht and delighted at all the blows raining down on England.'[114] The occupation of Denmark and Norway in April 1940 was celebrated at Doorn as nothing less than a 'heavenly miracle'.[115]

On 10 May 1940 the Wehrmacht invaded the Netherlands and Queen Wilhelmina and her government fled to London. Four days later, German troops appeared at Doorn bearing a letter from Hitler and orders to mount a guard at the park gates for the protection of the monarch. Hermine reported in delight: 'The first German soldier in front of the steps to the house was such an incredible relief that I cannot find words to describe it. I shall never forget the expression on the Kaiser's face as he stood on the steps together with the commanding officer of a regiment – suddenly he was 30 years younger.'[116] To the Kaiser's daughter Viktoria Luise she wrote: 'You won't believe how He has been rejuvenated by all these events and how delighted He is that the Dutch pressure has been lifted from Him. At times he has the bearing he had 18 years ago. Every soldier He sees brings Him the greatest joy, and the news is playing its part in making Him proud and happy.'[117] (See Figure 67.)

The invitation of the British government, issued with the express approval of King George VI, to take up residence in England was rejected by Wilhelm II with the disdainful comment 'that he would rather allow himself to be shot in Holland than flee to England. He had no wish to be photographed alongside Churchill.'[118] To his American friend Bigelow he justified his decision with the words: 'I considered the British offer as a temptation of Satan therefore I refused it placing my whole confidence & trust in *God alone*. His answer to this resolve was: the Germans in Doorn & our immediate deliverance next day! Direct act of Providence!'[119] 'It would have been quite grotesque for us to go over to the enemy and besides a satiric drama if we had then to meet with the Queen of this country who has always slighted us here', Hermine explained in a letter to her sister-in-law.[120] Hitler's 'beautiful and dignified'

Figure 67 The Kaiser greets soldiers of the Wehrmacht at Doorn, May 1940

offer to choose a residence in Germany was gratefully declined by Wilhelm. Hermine informed Margarethe: 'I must say that Wilhelm has not been treated by any important German authority since 1918 with anything even remotely like the respect now being shown him by our gracious Fuehrer.'[121]

The catastrophic rout of the British army at Dunkirk and the fall of France were greeted at Doorn with wild delight. On 30 May 1940 Wilhelm rejoiced: 'The British Army is smashed & running for their lives leaving all their arms, artillery, war material behind. Their transports are being sunk by dozens!'[122] The following day he triumphed: 'The ordeal of Juda-England has begun. Destruction in Flanders.'[123] Two weeks later, as German troops entered Paris, the Kaiser sent the *Führer* a glowing telegram setting this victory in the context of the Prusso-German conquests attained by his own forebears. 'Under the deeply moving impression of France's capitulation I congratulate you and all the German armed forces on the God-given prodigious victory with the words of Kaiser Wilhelm the Great of the year 1870: "What a turn of events through God's dispensation!" All German hearts are filled with the chorale of Leuthen, which the victors of [the Battle of] Leuthen, the soldiers of the Great King sang [in 1757]: Now thank we all our God!'[124] As with the Munich Agreement and the campaign against Poland, Wilhelm II saw in the fall of France the justification for and the completion of his own hegemonial policy. As he wrote to the archivist Kurt Jagow on 5 July 1940: 'I was deeply moved by the incomparable achievements of the German Wehrmacht, leading to such prodigious successes. I followed the development of operations in minute detail with the aid of maps. Under brilliant leadership all sections of the armed forces displayed the greatest courage to achieve deeds that were quite stunning. The ignominy of November 1918 in the forest of Compiègne has been wiped out and the Diktat of Versailles torn up!'[125] Hitler's war, the Kaiser exulted in September 1940, was 'a succession of miracles! The old Prussian spirit of Fr[e]d[ericus] Rex, of Clausewitz, Blücher, York, Gneisenau etc. has again manifested itself, as in 1870–71 ... The brilliant leading Generals in this war came from *My* school, they fought under my command in the [First] Worlds War as lieutenants, captains and young majors. Educated by Schlieffen they put the plans he had worked out under me into practice along the same lines as we did in 1914 ... 1914–1918 is in no manner placed in the shadow by this war!'[126] At long last the balance-of-power policy pursued against Germany by Britain since the reign of Edward VII had been smashed and the continent united under German domination, the Kaiser proclaimed. 'Over here the new U.S. of Europe are in formation, shaping the Continent into one block of Nations', he warned Bigelow in November 1940. 'So for the foreigner "Hands off from Europe"! European Monroe Doctrine!'[127] And to his sister he wrote: 'The hand of God is creating a new World & working miracles. To think that France has finally dropped the poisonous Entente Cordiale Uncle Bertie's with Britain & sided with Germany & Italy in cooperation, ignoring the Kings appeal, is a *miracle*! We are becoming the *U.S. of Europe* under German leadership, a united European Continent, nobody ever hoped to see!'[128] The Kaiser was overjoyed 'to be experiencing the atonement for Versailles and the reconstruction of Germany – how he has suffered under the years of ignominy since 18', Hermine sighed.[129]

Britain's determination to hold out against Germany's domination of the continent initially met with disbelief in Doorn. 'Yes, over there [in England] they are blind & mad, suffering from moral insanity! Buckingham Palace!!!' the Kaiser cried in November 1940.[130] The situation into which Churchill had manoeuvred his country instead of grasping the outstretched hand of Hitler was in Hermine's opinion a scandal.[131] But then the well-worn explanation for the stubbornness of the islanders across the Channel resurfaced: it was all the work of the Jews and the Freemasons!

Up to this point in time the sources suggest that Kaiser Wilhelm had paid scant regard to the fate of the Jews under the terror regime of the Nazis. There is evidence neither of the pathological anti-Semitic world conspiracy theories he had spouted throughout the 1920s[132] nor of serious criticism of the disgraceful and mounting persecution of the Jews back home. In the very early days of the Third Reich Wilhelm even claimed that newspaper reports of thuggish brutality against Jewish citizens at the hands of the SA were nothing but lies put about by the Jews themselves to gain sympathy and damage the reputation of the Fatherland.[133] He was, however, shocked by the violence of the 'Reichskristallnacht' of 9 November 1938, berating his son Auwi (who had declared himself in 'complete agreement' with the attacks on Jewish lives, synagogues and property) by insisting that 'every decent person' must surely condemn such behaviour as 'gangsterism'.[134] To Queen Mary he wrote, on 13 November 1938: 'I am absolutely horrified at the late events at home! Pure bolshevism!'[135] But he made no public criticism of the unprecedented violence. And then, in the summer of 1940, his madcap anti-Semitic hatred of the 1920s resurfaced with a vengeance. He raved of the need to *'liberate'* England − *'thoroughly contaminated [durchseucht]'* as he claimed it was by Jews and Freemasons and therefore the land of Satan − *'from the Antichrist Juda'*. 'We must drive [*vertreiben*] Juda out of England just as he has been chased [*verjagt*] out of the Continent. The *Antichrist Juda must be expelled* [*hinausgestoßen*] from England as well as from the Continent.' It was the Jews and the Freemasons who had twice − in 1914 and again in 1939 − 'on the *orders* of Satan' and with England's help unleashed a war of destruction against Germany with the aim of erecting the 'world empire [*Weltreich*] of Juda', but 'then God intervened and *smashed* their plan! ... Juda's plan has been smashed to pieces and they themselves swept out [*weggefegt*] of the European Continent!' Now the continent was 'consolidating and closing itself off from British influence after the elimination [*Entledigung*] of the British and the Jews'. The happy result would be the establishment of the 'United States of Europe!'[136] At Christmas 1940, the ex-Kaiser informed his erstwhile adjutant Alfred Niemann that Britain's global domination had been based on the Liberalism of 'international Freemason-Jewry'. By virtue of 'Jewish dodgery' these forces had 'unleashed' the First World War and 'won it thanks to Jewish-American money'. Now world Jewry had 'initiated another war of "extermination"', but the power of England and France had been 'defeated and exterminated on the Continent'.[137] In his last letters to his sister the Landgravine Margarethe of Hesse he wrote in jubilation: 'The Jews are beeing [sic] thrust out of their nefarious positions in all countries, whom they have driven to hostility for centuries.'[138] As late as 20 April 1941 Wilhelm was still proclaiming: 'The feats of our brave troops are wonderful, God gave them success. − May He continue to help them to peace with honour, & the victory over Juda & Antichrist in British garb.'[139] (See Figure 68.)

One would have to judge these utterances to be the delusions of an insane mind were it not for the disturbing fact that millions of others had evidently

Figure 68 Wilhelm as the 'gardener of Doorn'

also succumbed to the collective psychosis of phobic hypernationalism. Which-ever way one looks at it, however, one thing is clear: precisely because he pinned the blame for the disaster of his own reign on the imagined machin-ations of mysterious dark forces, Kaiser Wilhelm II was incapable even at the last of grasping the enormity of the world catastrophe unfolding before his very eyes. As Hitler and the Wehrmacht made their final preparations for the war of extermination – the *Vernichtungskrieg* – and the Holocaust in the east, Germany's last Emperor was dreaming happily of his country's ultimate victory, her '*Endsieg*'.[140]

DEATH AND TRANSFIGURATION

Wilhelm II died on 4 June 1941 at the age of eighty-two. For some years his doctors had expressed concern over an irregular heartbeat and an enlarged prostate. From time to time the strikingly red colour of his urine caused consternation since 'even when the urine was deeply discoloured there was only ever evidence of small droplets of blood' – possibly a further indication (along with the ominous 'accesses of anger' noted by Erichsen many decades earlier and the stubborn vesication of the forehead recorded in the spring and summer of 1914) of porphyria inherited from George III, from which Wilhelm's sister Charlotte is now known to have suffered.[141] But in Wilhelm such symptoms were intermittent. When Dr Sotier took up his duties as his personal physician at the beginning of 1937, he found the Kaiser in robust good health: the voice was strong, the eyes bright, the skin well nourished and the stance erect. The lively interest the Kaiser took in the dramatic events of those years, accompanying them as he did with 'healthy criticism' and vigorous gesticulation, further confirmed Sotier's positive assessment.[142] On 18 March 1938, however, Wilhelm suffered an attack of angina pectoris, complaining 'that he had never in his whole life felt such pain'.[143] An irregular pulse, dizziness and – for a time – difficulty in speaking gave rise to fears of a serious deterioration.[144] But the Kaiser recovered from this setback, too. Hermine and all the visitors to Doorn over the next few years remarked on how admirably fresh he seemed.[145] Then, on 1 March 1941, Wilhelm suffered a dizzy spell while hacking wood – his favourite pastime – in the park. He complained of goutish pain. On 24 May an acute intestinal complaint seemed to signal the end: the children were summoned, but apart from his daughter Viktoria Luise they all left again when the Kaiser appeared to recover. Suddenly in the early evening of 3 June 1941 an embolism in the lungs caused him immense pain in the chest and abdomen and a shortness of breath. He cried out: 'This is the end of me, I am sinking, I am sinking!' He thanked Hermine and said goodbye to her, his daughter and his grandson Louis Ferdinand. In the night he lost consciousness and died at 11.30 on 4 June 1941.[146] The loyal Adjutant-General Wilhelm von Dommes recorded his All-Highest master's end: 'The fervent love of His Majesty for Germany found moving expression again and again throughout his illness. One hour before the agony began His Majesty was still urging us all to fight to the last for the Fatherland ... His last prayer was for Germany.'[147] (See Figure 69.)

No fewer than fifty-five family members and other royal relations attended the funeral in Doorn on 9 June 1941, among them the Kaiser's sister the Landgravine Margarethe, Crown Prince Wilhelm with his wife Cecilie, the other four surviving sons, Eitel Friedrich, Adalbert, August Wilhelm and Oskar, his daughter Duchess Viktoria Luise with her husband Ernst August of Hanover and Princess Irene, the widow of Wilhelm's late brother Prince Heinrich. (See Figure 70.) The Wehrmacht sent a guard of honour and a military band played the chorales 'Wenn ich einmal soll scheiden' and 'Ein feste Burg ist unser Gott' which the Kaiser had himself chosen for the occasion.

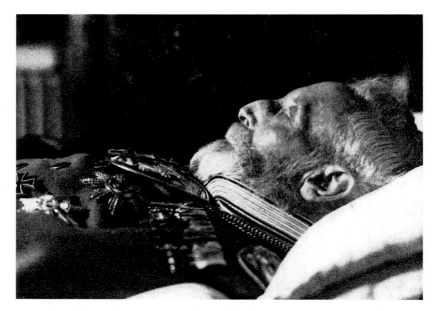

Figure 69 Death and transfiguration

Figure 70 The funeral at Doorn, 9 June 1941: the Crown Prince (now theoretically
Kaiser Wilhelm III) stands with Seyss-Inquart (Hitler's Reich Commissar for the
Netherlands) and the veteran Field Marshal August von Mackensen

Figure 71 The wreath sent by the *Führer* Adolf Hitler

Although preparations for the attack on the Soviet Union had reached a critical stage – 'Operation Barbarossa' was to be launched just thirteen days later – Berlin dispatched a high-ranking delegation to the funeral in Holland: the army, the navy and the Luftwaffe were represented by General Paul von Hase, Admiral Hermann Densch and Air Force General Friedrich Christian Christiansen respectively and the Supreme Command of the Wehrmacht by Admiral Wilhelm Canaris. A place of honour was reserved for the nonagenarian Field Marshal August von Mackensen. Hitler was represented by the Reich Commissar for the Netherlands, Dr Arthur Seyss-Inquart, who laid an enormous wreath from the *Führer* on the coffin of the last German Kaiser and King of Prussia (see Figure 71). Some of the guests at the funeral on that summer's day in Doorn would be executed a few years later as members of the Resistance, others would meet again as accused at the International War Crimes Tribunal at Nuremberg. Either way, the little ceremony in occupied Holland in the middle of the Second World War brought together representatives of the old and the new German governing elite, symbolising the numerous continuities between the Wilhelmine era and the Third Reich so palpably personified by the long life of Kaiser Wilhelm II.

Notes

PREFACE TO THE ENGLISH EDITION

1 King George V, diary for 9 November 1918, Royal Archives Windsor (RA), GVD.
2 John C. G. Röhl, *Wilhelm II. The Kaiser's Personal Monarchy 1888–1900*, Cambridge 2004.
3 Szögyény to Berchtold, 12 August 1913, *Österreich-Ungarns Außenpolitik, von der Bosnischen Krise 1908 bis zum Kriegsausbruch 1914. Diplomatische Aktenstücke des österreichisch-ungarischen Ministeriums des Äußeren*, 9 vols., Vienna and Leipzig 1930, VII, pp. 116–18.
4 Bülow to Eulenburg, 30 October 1895, John C. G. Röhl, ed., *Philipp Eulenburgs Politische Korrespondenz*, 3 vols., Boppard am Rhein 1976–83 (cited below as *Eulenburgs Korrespondenz*), III, No. 1581.
5 Kaiser Wilhelm II to Poultney Bigelow, 14 September 1940, quoted in John C. G. Röhl, *The Kaiser and his Court. Wilhelm II and the Government of Germany*, Cambridge 1994, p. 211.

PREFACE TO THE GERMAN EDITION

1 Ludwig Wittgenstein, *Vermischte Bemerkungen. Eine Auswahl aus dem Nachlass* (1895), Berlin 1946, p. 98.

1   DEATH AND TRANSFIGURATION

1 Albert Edward Prince of Wales to Kaiser Wilhelm II, 7 March 1900, J. Lepsius, A. Mendelssohn Bartholdy and F. Thimme, eds., *Die Große Politik der europäischen Kabinette, 1871–1914*, 40 vols., Berlin 1922–7, XV, No. 4480.
2 Lord Lansdowne to Sir Frank Lascelles, 25 September 1905, Roderick R. McLean, *Royalty and Diplomacy in Europe, 1890–1914*, Cambridge 2001, p. 123.
3 King Edward VII to Prince Louis of Battenberg, 1 April 1905, ibid., pp. 114f.
4 Robert Graf von Zedlitz-Trützschler, *Zwölf Jahre am deutschen Kaiserhof*, Stuttgart, Berlin and Leipzig 1925, p. 153.
5 Kaiser Wilhelm II, marginal note on Pourtalès to Jagow, 30 July 1914, Imanuel Geiss, ed., *Juli 1914. Die europäische Krise und der Ausbruch des Ersten Weltkrieges*, Munich 1965, No. 135.

6 Sir James Reid, diary for 18 January 1901, Michaela Reid, *Ask Sir James. Sir James Reid, Personal Physician to Queen Victoria and Physician-in-Ordinary to Three Monarchs*, London 1987, pp. 203f.

7 Eulenburg to Kaiser Wilhelm II, 26 January 1901, Röhl, *Eulenburgs Korrespondenz*, III, No. 1443.

8 Sir James Reid, diary for 19 January 1901, Reid, *Ask Sir James*, pp. 204–6.

9 Ibid.

10 Kaiser Wilhelm II to Bülow, 20 January 1901, *Große Politik*, XVII, No. 4982.

11 Sir James Reid, diary for 20 January 1901, Reid, *Ask Sir James*, p. 209.

12 Metternich to Bülow, 22 January 1901, printed in Norman Rich and M. H. Fisher, eds., *The Holstein Papers. The Memoirs, Diaries and Correspondence of Friedrich von Holstein 1837–1909*, 4 vols., Cambridge 1956–63 (cited below as *Holstein Papers*), IV, No. 765.

13 Sir James Reid, diary for 2 January 1901, Reid, *Ask Sir James*, pp. 210ff.

14 Sir Thomas Barlow to J. R. Barlow, 23 January 1901, RA VIC/Add U143a.

15 G. R. Theobalds, memorandum of 22 January 1901, RA VIC/Add U131.

16 Mary Duchess of York to Augusta Grand Duchess of Mecklenburg-Strelitz, 27 January 1901, RA GV/CC 22/55.

17 Albert Edward Prince of Wales to Princess Eduard of Saxe-Weimar, 22 January 1901, RA VIC/Add A7/345.

18 King Edward VII to Empress Frederick, 7 February 1901, RA VIC/Add A4/199. See Lamar Cecil, *Wilhelm II: Emperor and Exile, 1900–1941*, Chapel Hill, London 1996, p. 78.

19 Grand Duchess Luise of Baden to Kaiser Wilhelm II, 26 January 1901, GStA Berlin, BPHA Rep. 51 W Nr 2a. Cf. the birthday letter of Empress Frederick, AdHH Schloss Fasanerie. See also Kaiser Wilhelm II to Chlodwig Fürst zu Hohenlohe-Schillingsfürst, 26 January 1901, Karl Alexander von Müller, *Denkwürdigkeiten der Reichskanzlerzeit*, Stuttgart, Berlin 1931, p. 601 (cited below as Hohenlohe, *Denkwürdigkeiten der Reichskanzlerzeit*).

20 Hinzpeter to Kaiser Wilhelm II, 9 February 1901, GStA Berlin, BPHA Rep. 53J Lit. H Nr 1.

21 Kaiser Wilhelm II to King Edward VII, 27 January 1901, RA VIC/Add A7/298.

22 King Edward VII to Empress Frederick, 7 February 1901, RA VIC/Add A4/199.

23 Kaiser Wilhelm II to Bülow, 26 January 1901, PA AA Asservat No. 4.

24 Kaiser Wilhelm II to Arthur Duke of Connaught, 9 February 1901, RA VIC/Add A15/6434.

25 Prince Heinrich of Prussia to Senden-Bibran, 28 January 1901, BA-MA Freiburg-im-Breisgau, Senden Papers N160/4.

26 Reid to his wife, 1–5 February 1901, Reid, *Ask Sir James*, pp. 219–21.

27 RA Court Circular, 5–6 February 1901. On Wilhelm's speeches see the study by Michael A. Obst, *'Einer nur ist Herr im Reiche.' Kaiser Wilhelm II als politischer Redner*, Paderborn, Munich, Vienna and Zürich 2010. See also Michael A. Obst, ed., *Die politischen Reden Kaiser Wilhelms II. Eine Auswahl*, Paderborn, Munich, Vienna and Zürich 2011.

28 Kaiser Wilhelm II to Eulenburg, 5 February 1901, *Eulenburgs Korrespondenz*, III, No. 1444.

29 Eulenburg to Bülow, 6 February 1901, ibid., No. 1445.

30 See *The Graphic* of 9 February 1901.

31 King Edward VII to Kaiser Wilhelm II, 13 February 1901, GStA Berlin, BPHA Rep. 53 No. 19; Lady Emily Ampthill to Kaiser Wilhelm II, 29 January 1901, ibid., Rep. 53J Lit. A Nr 4; Princess Louise Duchess of Argyll to Kaiser Wilhelm II, 6 March 1901, ibid., Rep. 53J Lit. A Nr 8. On the Kaiser's reception by the British press see Lothar Reinermann, *Der Kaiser in England. Wilhelm II. und sein Bild in der britischen Öffentlichkeit*, Paderborn, Munich, Vienna and Zürich 2001, pp. 212–43.

32 Hereditary Prince Bernhard of Saxe-Meiningen to Colmar Freiherr von der Goltz, 24 January 1901, BA-MA Freiburg-im-Breisgau, von der Goltz Papers, N737 Zug. 228/95.

33 Kaiser Wilhelm II to his sister Victoria Princess zu Schaumburg-Lippe, 21 May 1899, AdHH Schloss Fasanerie.

34 Empress Frederick to Kaiser Wilhelm II, 23 May 1899, GStA Berlin, BPHA, Rep. 52T Nr 13.

35 Ibid. See also Empress Frederick to Kaiser Wilhelm II, 10 June 1899, ibid.

36 Empress Frederick to Kaiser Wilhelm II, 25 October and 7 November 1899, ibid.

37 Kaiser Wilhelm II to Empress Frederick, 4 November, 3 and 16 December 1899, AdHH Schloss Fasanerie. Also Kaiser Wilhelm II to Queen Victoria, 21 December 1899, RA VIC/I 62/76.

38 Kaiser Wilhelm II to Queen Victoria, 31 March 1900, RA VIC/I 62/90.

39 See, for example, Empress Frederick to Kaiser Wilhelm II, 25 October and 7 November 1899, GStA Berlin, BPHA, Rep. 52T Nr 13; Kaiser Wilhelm II to Empress Frederick, 4 and 18 November 1899, AdHH Schloss Fasanerie. See also Empress Frederick to Kaiser Wilhelm II, 7 and 19 March 1900, GStA BPHA Rep. 52T Nr 13; Röhl, *The Kaiser's Personal Monarchy*, pp. 894–5.

40 Empress Frederick to Kaiser Wilhelm II, 19 March 1900, ibid. See also Franz Herre, *Kaiserin Friedrich. Victoria, Eine Engländerin in Deutschland*, Stuttgart 2006, pp. 324–8.

41 Empress Frederick to Kaiser Wilhelm II, 7 and 10 November 1899, GStA Berlin, BPHA Rep. 52T Nr 13. See also Empress Frederick to Crown Princess Sophie of Greece, late September, 20 and 27 October 1900, A. G. Lee, ed., *The Empress Frederick Writes to Sophie*, London 1955, pp. 335ff. et passim.

42 Empress Friedrich to Kaiser Wilhelm II, 2, 9 and 21 December 1899, GStA Berlin, BPHA Rep. 52T Nr 13.

43 Empress Frederick to Crown Princess Sophie of Greece, early 1900, Lee, *The Empress Frederick Writes to Sophie*, pp. 322f.

44 Empress Frederick to Crown Princess Sophie of Greece, January 1900, ibid, pp. 324f.

45 Empress Frederick to Kaiser Wilhelm II, 23 May 1899, GStA Berlin, BPHA Rep. 52T Nr 13.

46 Empress Frederick to Kaiser Wilhelm II, 2, 9 and 21 December 1899, ibid.

47 Empress Frederick to Queen Victoria, 2, 6 and 18 August 1900, AdHH Schloss Fasanerie.

48 Empress Frederick to Crown Princess Sophie of Greece, September 1900, Lee, *The Empress Frederick Writes to Sophie*, p. 335.

49 Empress Frederick to Queen Victoria, 21 August 1900, AdHH Schloss Fasanerie.

50 Empress Frederick to Queen Victoria, 18 and 21 August 1900, ibid. See also Hereditary Prince Bernhard of Saxe-Meiningen to Georg II Duke of Saxe-Meiningen, 16 August 1900, ThStaMgn, HA 341.

51 Kaiser Wilhelm II to Albert Edward Prince of Wales, 21 October 1900, RA VIC/I 62/111c.

52 Empress Frederick to Kaiser Wilhelm II, 31 October 1900, GStA Berlin, BPHA Rep. 52T Nr 13 vol. III.

53 Empress Frederick to Queen Victoria, 1 November 1900, AdHH Schloss Fasanerie.

54 Empress Frederick to Queen Victoria, 18 November 1900, ibid. Also Empress Frederick to Queen Victoria, 1 and 25 December 1900, ibid.

55 Kaiser Wilhelm II to Bülow, 23 November 1900, PA AA R 3474.

56 Kaiser Wilhelm II to Queen Victoria, 12 October 1900, RA VIC/I 62/111b.

57 Queen Victoria to Kaiser Wilhelm II, 12 October 1900, RA VIC/I 62/111b.

58 Queen Victoria to Kaiser Wilhelm II, 14 October 1900, GStA Berlin, BPHA Rep. 52 W3 Nr 11.

59 Empress Frederick to Crown Princess Sophie of Greece, 23 January 1901, Lee, *The Empress Frederick Writes to Sophie*, p. 343; Empress Frederick to Kaiser Wilhelm II, 27 January 1901, GStA Berlin, BPHA Rep. 52T Nr 13 vol. III.

60 Kaiser Wilhelm II to King Edward VII, 9 February 1901, RA VIC/L 4/82.

61 King Edward VII to Kaiser Wilhelm II, 13 February 1901, GStA Berlin, BPHA Rep. 53 Nr 195.

62 Ibid.
63 Kaiser Wilhelm II to Arthur Duke of Connaught, 26 February 1901, RA VIC/Add A15/6434.
64 King Edward VII to Empress Frederick, 21 February 1901, cited in Hannah Pakula, *An Uncommon Woman. Empress Frederick, Daughter of Queen Victoria, Wife of the Crown Prince of Prussia, Mother of Kaiser Wilhelm*, New York 1995, p. 593.
65 Prince Heinrich of Prussia to Empress Frederick, 14 June 1901, AdHH Schloss Fasanerie.
66 King Edward VII to Kaiser Wilhelm II, 18 June 1901, GStA Berlin, BPHA Rep. 53 Nr 251.
67 Kaiser Wilhelm II to King Edward VII, 24 June 1901, RA VIC/X 37/44.
68 King Edward VII to Kaiser Wilhelm II, 7 August 1901, GStA Berlin, BPHA Rep. 53J Lit. F Nr 11.
69 Sir Frederick Ponsonby, ed., *The Letters of the Empress Frederick*, London 1928.
70 Sir Frederick Ponsonby, ed., *Briefe der Kaiserin Friedrich*, Berlin 1929.
71 Wolfgang Prinz von Hessen, 'Zum Geleit', in E. C. Conte Corti, *Wenn ... Sendung und Schicksal einer Kaiserin*, Graz, Vienna and Cologne 1954, p. viii.
72 Empress Frederick, diary for January–July 1901, AdHH Schloss Fasanerie.
73 Wolfgang Prinz von Hessen, 'Memorandum über die Briefe der Kaiserin Friedrich an die Königin Victoria', typescript, no date [1954], p. 6, AdHH Schloss Fasanerie.
74 Ibid., p. 2.
75 Cf. Ponsonby, *Letters of the Empress Frederick*, pp. xviff. (*Briefe der Kaiserin Friedrich*, pp. 14ff.); Sir Frederick Ponsonby, *Recollections of Three Reigns*, London 1951, p. 111.
76 See below, p. 1217.
77 Ponsonby, *Recollections of Three Reigns*, pp. 112ff.
78 See the memorandum of the Empress's librarian, Gustav Adolf Leinhaas, 'Die Beziehungen zwischen der Kaiserin Friedrich zu ihrem Oberhofmeister, dem Grafen Götz von Seckendorff', cited in John C. G. Röhl, *Young Wilhelm. The Kaiser's Early Life 1859–1888*, Cambridge 1998, p. 670.
79 Lord Esher, diary for 30 November 1897, Churchill Archives Centre, Cambridge. This passage has been omitted in Maurice V. Brett and O. Esher, eds., *The Journals and Letters of Reginald Viscount Esher*, 4 vols., London 1934–8.
80 P. de Margerie (Washington) to Delcassé, 19 November 1901, Archives du Ministère des Affaires Étrangères Paris, États-Unis 10, Politique Étrangère, Relations avec l'Allemagne. I thank Dr Ragnhild Fiebig-von Hase for drawing my attention to this report.
81 Kaiser Wilhelm II to Bülow, sent on by the latter to the Auswärtiges Amt on 28 August 1901, PA AA R 3488.

2   THE KAISER AND ENGLAND DURING THE BOER WAR

1 'The German Emperor and England. Personal Interview. Frank Statement of World Policy. Proofs of Friendship', *The Daily Telegraph*, 28 October 1908.
2 Kaiser Wilhelm II, marginal notes on a report from London of 18 March 1897, PA AA R 14631.
3 Kaiser Wilhelm II, marginal note on Eckardstein's report of 4 October 1902, *Große Politik*, XVII, No. 5101. See Lamar Cecil, *Wilhelm II: Prince and Emperor, 1859–1900*, Chapel Hill, London 1989, p. 327.
4 Kaiser Wilhelm II to Queen Wilhelmina, 27 March 1900, *Große Politik*, XV, No. 4494.
5 Kaiser Wilhelm II to Bülow, 29 October 1899, ibid., No. 4394.
6 Bülow to Kaiser Wilhelm II, 6 August 1900, GStA Berlin, BPHA Rep. 53J Lit. B Nr 16a vol. II.
7 Bülow to Grand Duke Friedrich I of Baden, 17 April 1899, Walther Peter Fuchs, ed., *Großherzog Friedrich I. von Baden und die Reichspolitik 1871–1907*, 4 vols., Stuttgart 1968–80, IV, No. 1975.

8 Bülow to Kaiser Wilhelm II, 6 August 1899, GStA Berlin, BPHA Rep. 53J Lit. B Nr 16a.

9 Bülow to Kaiser Wilhelm II, 8 November 1899, ibid. Cited in part in Gerd Fesser, *Der Traum vom Platz an der Sonne. Deutsche 'Weltpolitik' 1897–1914*, Bremen 1996, p. 75. On the projected railway from Delagoa to Tiger Bay in Angola see Harald Rosenbach, *Das Deutsche Reich, Großbritannien und der Transvaal (1896–1902)*, Göttingen 1993, pp. 169ff.

10 Lord Salisbury to Lord Gough, 15 November 1899, RA VIC/I 62/62a. Cf. Lord Salisbury to Kaiser Wilhelm II, 20 November 1899, GStA Berlin, BPHA Rep. 53J Lit. S Nr 15.

11 See Röhl, *The Kaiser's Personal Monarchy*, pp. 991–8; George P. Gooch and Harold Temperley, eds., *British Documents on the Origin of the War, 1898–1914*, 11 vols., London 1926–38, I, Nos. 319–20 et passim.

12 Kaiser Wilhelm II, marginal note on Hatzfeldt's report of 27 August 1899, *Große Politik*, XV, No. 4374.

13 Kaiser Wilhelm II, marginal note on Münster to Hohenlohe, 24 March 1899, ibid., XIV, No. 3944.

14 Kaiser Wilhelm II, marginal note on Hatzfeldt to Hohenlohe, 4 April 1899, ibid., No. 3950.

15 Kaiser Wilhelm II, marginal note on Bülow to Auswärtiges Amt, 25 September 1899, cited in Peter Winzen, *Bülows Weltmachtkonzept. Untersuchungen zur Frühphase seiner Außenpolitik 1897–1901*, Boppard am Rhein 1977, p. 213.

16 Kaiser Wilhelm II, marginal note on Tattenbach's report of 9 October 1899, *Große Politik*, XV, No. 4392.

17 Waldersee, diary for 17 December 1899, GStA Berlin, Waldersee Papers; cf. Heinrich Otto Meisner, ed., *Denkwürdigkeiten des General-Feldmarschalls Alfred Grafen von Waldersee*, 3 vols., Stuttgart and Berlin 1922–3, II, pp. 439f. (Cited below as Meisner, II or III).

18 Kaiser Wilhelm II, marginal note on Hatzfeldt's report of 27 August 1899, *Große Politik*, XV, No. 4374. See Rosenbach, *Transvaal*, p. 189.

19 Kaiser Wilhelm II, marginal note on Tattenbach's report of 9 October 1899, *Große Politik*, XV, No. 4392. Cf. his marginal note on Hatzfeldt's telegram of 11 October 1899, PA AA Asservat Nr 4.

20 Bülow to Wedel, 17 December 1901, *Große Politik*, XVIII/2, No. 5709.

21 Bülow's note on Eckardstein to Holstein, 21 December 1899, *Holstein Papers*, IV, No. 723. See Rosenbach, *Transvaal*, p. 199.

22 Kaiser Wilhelm II, marginal note on Bülow's report of 1 April 1899, *Große Politik*, XIV, No. 4053.

23 Waldersee, diary for 23 October 1899, GStA Berlin, Waldersee Papers; cf. Meisner, II, pp. 436f.

24 Jagemann to Brauer, 10 January 1900, Fuchs, *Großherzog von Baden*, IV, No. 2060. See Alfred von Tirpitz, *Erinnerungen*, Leipzig 1919, p. 141; Volker R. Berghahn, *Der Tirpitz-Plan. Genesis und Verfall einer innenpolitischen Krisenstrategie unter Wilhelm II.*, Düsseldorf 1971, pp. 380–4; Rosenbach, *Transvaal*, p. 199.

25 Hereditary Prince Bernhard of Saxe-Meiningen to Colmar Freiherr von der Goltz, 3 November 1899, BA-MA Freiburg-im-Breisgau, von der Goltz Papers, N737 Zug. 161/95. See also Carl Alexander Krethlow, *Generalfeldmarschall Colmar von der Goltz Pascha. Eine Biographie*, Paderborn, Munich, Vienna and Zürich 2012.

26 Hereditary Prince Bernhard of Saxe-Meiningen to Colmar Freiherr von der Goltz, 28 September 1899, ibid. See Feroz Yasamee, 'Colmar Freiherr von der Goltz and the Boer War', in Keith Wilson, ed., *The International Impact of the Boer War*, New York 2001, Chapter 12.

27 Hereditary Prince Bernhard of Saxe-Meiningen to Colmar Freiherr von der Goltz, 10 October 1899, BA-MA Freiburg-im-Breisgau, von der Goltz Papers, N737 Zug. 161/95.

28 Hereditary Prince Bernhard of Saxe-Meiningen to Colmar Freiherr von der Goltz, 23 December 1899, ibid.

29 Mudra to Colmar Freiherr von der Goltz, 2 and 9 October 1899, ibid. Zug. 228/95 and 161/95.

30 Waldersee, diary for 17 December 1899, GStA Berlin, Waldersee Papers; cf. Meisner, II, pp. 439f.

31 Waldersee, diary for 4 February 1900, ibid.; not in Meisner, II, p. 444.

32 Waldersee, diary for 23 October 1899, ibid.; cf. Meisner, II, pp. 436f.

33 Waldersee, diary for 7 February 1900, ibid.; omitted in Meisner, II, p. 444.

34 Hans Delbrück, 'Deutschland, Transvaal and der Besuch des Kaisers in England. Die neue Flottenforderung', *Preußische Jahrbücher* 98, 1899, 586–90; Pauline R. Anderson, *The Background of Anti-English Feeling in Germany 1890–1902*, Washington 1939, pp. 285ff.; Rosenbach, *Transvaal*, pp. 218ff.

35 Empress Frederick to Crown Princess Sophie of Greece, March 1898, Lee, *The Empress Frederick Writes to Sophie*, p. 277.

36 Empress Frederick to Kaiser Wilhelm II, 25 October 1899, GStA Berlin, BPHA Rep. 52T Nr 13. See Empress Frederick to Crown Princess Sophie of Greece, autumn 1899, Lee, *The Empress Frederick Writes to Sophie*, p. 312.

37 Empress Frederick to Kaiser Wilhelm II, 10 November 1899, GStA Berlin, BPHA Rep. 52T Nr 13.

38 Empress Frederick to Crown Princess Sophie of Greece, November 1899, Lee, *The Empress Frederick Writes to Sophie*, pp. 317f.

39 Empress Frederick to Crown Princess Sophie of Greece, December 1899, ibid., p. 320. See also Empress Frederick to Kaiser Wilhelm II, 21 December 1899, GStA Berlin, BPHA Rep. 52T Nr 13.

40 Empress Frederick to Kaiser Wilhelm II, 19 March 1900, ibid. See General Freiherr von Loë to Grand Duke Friedrich I of Baden, 20 March 1900, Fuchs, *Großherzog von Baden*, IV, No. 2074.

41 Waldersee, diary for 17 September, 12 and 23 October 1899, GStA Berlin, Waldersee Papers; omitted in Meisner, II, pp. 434ff.

42 Waldersee, diary for 5 February 1900, ibid.; not in Meisner, II, p. 444.

43 Waldersee, diary for 28 January 1900, ibid.; omitted in Meisner, II, p. 443.

44 Waldersee, diary for 1 April 1900, ibid.; omitted in Meisner, II, p. 444.

45 Bülow to Grand Duke Friedrich I of Baden, 31 December 1899, Fuchs, *Großherzog von Baden*, IV, No. 2054. On Bülow's policy during the Boer War see Winzen, *Bülows Weltmachtkonzept*, pp. 208–10.

46 Waldersee, diary for 23 October 1899, GStA Berlin, Waldersee Papers; cf. Meisner, II, pp. 436f.

47 Kaiser Wilhelm II, marginal note on Hatzfeldt to Hohenlohe, 16 August 1899, PA AA Preußen 1 Nr 4, Bd. 5; Bülow to Auswärtiges Amt, 11 September 1899, *Große Politik*, XV, No. 4083; Salisbury to Queen Victoria, 22 July 1899, RA VIC/I 62/28; Lascelles to Bigge, 26 August, 29 September, 14 and 15 November 1899, RA I62/37, I62/40, I62/60 and I62/62; Prince Heinrich of Prussia to Empress Frederick, 20 September 1899, AdHH Schloss Fasanerie; Queen Victoria to Kaiser Wilhelm II, 19 September 1899, GStA Berlin, BPHA Rep. 52 W3 Nr 11; Kaiser Wilhelm II to Queen Victoria, 25 September 1899, RA VIC/I 62/39; August Eulenburg to Bigge, 12 October and 5 November 1899, RA I62/42 and I62/46; Knollys to Bigge, 28 October, 8 and 10 November 1899, RA VIC/I 62/45, I62/50 and VIC/I 62/55; Prince Heinrich of Prussia to Empress Frederick, 30 October 1899, AdHH Schloss Fasanerie; Lascelles to Kaiser Wilhelm II, 14 November 1899, RA I62/59 (not sent).

48 Rumbold to Salisbury, 21 November 1899, RA VIC/I 62/66.

49 Kaiser Wilhelm II, marginal notes on an article in the *Hamburger Nachrichten*, 2 November 1899, PA AA R 3699.

50 *Große Politik*, XV, No. 4398; Winzen, *Bülows Weltmachtkonzept*, pp. 219f.

51 QVJ (Queen Victoria's journal), 23 November 1899, printed in George Earle Buckle, ed., *The Letters of Queen Victoria*, third series, 3 vols., London 1930, III, p. 423. Cf. Bülow's very different account of this conversation in *Große Politik*, XV, No. 4398.

52 Sir Francis Bertie, report of 26 November 1899, RA VIC/I 62/68. Cited in part in Winzen, *Bülows Weltmachtkonzept*, pp. 218f.

53 Bigge to Salisbury, 22 November 1899, quoted ibid., p. 217, note 128 and p. 219, note 138.

54 Kaiser Wilhelm II to Albert Edward Prince of Wales, 23 February 1900, RA VIC/W 60/89. Cf. the Kaiser's incomplete copy as printed in *Große Politik*, XV, No. 4509, and the Prince of Wales's reply of 28 February 1900, ibid., No. 4510. Further Lascelles to Salisbury, 9 February and 2 March 1900, Gooch and Temperley, *British Documents*, I, Nos. 311 and 313.

55 Major Johannes Scheibert to Waldersee, 10 February 1900, Meisner, II, p. 444.

56 Waldersee, diary for 15 March 1900, GStA Berlin, Waldersee Papers; cf. Meisner, II, p. 444, where this entry is mistakenly dated 10 February.

57 Kaiser Wilhelm II to Albert Edward Prince of Wales, 1 December 1899, RA VIC/L 4/81. On the Kaiser's visit see Reinermann, *Der Kaiser in England*, pp. 197–201.

58 Hinzpeter to Kaiser Wilhelm II, 3 December 1899, with the monarch's marginal notes, GStA Berlin, BPHA Rep. 53J Lit. H Nr 1.

59 Jagemann to Brauer, 10 January 1900, Fuchs, *Großherzog von Baden*, IV, No. 2060.

60 See Radolin to Hohenlohe, 11 March 1900, *Große Politik*, XV, No. 4486; Sir Condie Stephen, report from Dresden of 15 March 1900, RA I62/88; Metternich to Bülow, 19 March 1900, *Große Politik*, XV, No. 4456; Metternich to Hohenlohe, 24 March 1900, ibid., No. 4458.

61 See Sir Horace Rumbold, report from Vienna of 9 May 1900, RA VIC/I 62/103; see also the marginal comment on Dönhoff's report from Dresden of 4 March 1900, *Große Politik*, XV, p. 487.

62 Colonel Grierson to Bigge, 6 and 13 January 1900, RA VIC/I 62/76b and VIC/P 5/93.

63 Albert Edward Prince of Wales to Empress Frederick, 25 April 1900, RA VIC/Add A 4/158.

64 George Duke of York to Queen Victoria, 18 April 1900, RA GV/AA 12/83; Mary Duchess of York to Augusta Grand Duchess of Mecklenburg-Strelitz, 25 April 1900, RA GV/CC 22/34.

65 Alexandra Princess of Wales to George Duke of York, 28 April 1900, RA GV/AA 32/21.

66 Kaiser Wilhelm II to Hohenlohe, 10 January 1900, Hohenlohe, *Denkwürdigkeiten der Reichskanzlerzeit*, p. 547. See Röhl, *The Kaiser's Personal Monarchy*, pp. 1037f.

67 Colonel Grierson to Bigge, 13 January 1900, RA VIC/P 5/93.

68 See *Große Politik*, XV, Nos. 4500, 4501 and 4504.

69 Kaiser Wilhelm II, marginal note of 18 October 1900, ibid., p. 549.

70 Swaine to Bigge, 1 January 1901, RA VIC/I 62/114.

71 Holstein to Hohenlohe. 4 December 1900, Hohenlohe, *Denkwürdigkeiten der Reichskanzlerzeit*, pp. 598f. See Lee, *The Empress Frederick Writes to Sophie*, p. 340.

72 See, for example, the Kaiser's marginal comments on the report from Darmstadt of 3 January 1901, PA AA R 3062.

73 Kaiser Wilhelm II, marginal notes on Eckardstein to Bülow, 2 and 5 January 1901, *Große Politik*, XVII, Nos. 5339 and 5340; Kaiser Wilhelm II to Bülow, 5 March 1901, ibid., XVI, No. 4824; Bülow to Kaiser Wilhelm II, 6 March 1901, ibid., No. 4825.

74 Bülow, marginal note of 14 February 1901, ibid., No. 4814.

75 Kaiser Wilhelm II, marginal notes on a report from London of 18 March 1897, PA AA R 14631. On the war of 1880–1 in the Transvaal see Iain R. Smith, *The Origins of the South African War, 1899–1902*, London and New York 1996, pp. 28ff.

76 Kaiser Wilhelm II, marginal notes of 6 April 1897 on Hohenlohe's report of 6 March 1897, PA AA R 14631.

77 See Rosenbach, *Transvaal*, pp. 167f.

78 Waldersee, diary for 14 October 1899, GStA Berlin, Waldersee Papers; Meisner, II, p. 436. See J. A. S. Grenville, *Lord Salisbury and Foreign Policy. The Close of the Nineteenth Century*, London 1964, p. 182.

79 Bülow to Kaiser Wilhelm II, 27 December 1899, *Große Politik*, XV, No. 4459. See Rosenbach, *Transvaal*, pp. 184f.

80 Kaiser Wilhelm II, marginal note on Hatzfeldt's report of 9 August 1899, *Große Politik*, XV, No. 4370. See Rosenbach, *Transvaal*, pp. 184f.

81 Waldersee, diary for 17 September 1899, GStA Berlin, Waldersee Papers; omitted in Meisner, II, p. 434.

82 Waldersee, diary for 23 October 1899, ibid.; cf. Meisner, II, pp. 436f.

83 Waldersee, diary for 29 October 1899, ibid.; cf. Meisner, II, pp. 437f.

84 Waldersee, diary for 17 December 1899, ibid.; cf. Meisner, II, pp. 439f.

85 Kaiser Wilhelm II to Queen Victoria, 2 December 1899, RA VIC/I 62/75; Kaiser Wilhelm II to Albert Edward Prince of Wales, 1 December 1899, RA VIC/L 4/81.

86 Queen Victoria to Kaiser Wilhelm II, 16 December 1899, together with the Kaiser's reply to the Queen and the Prince of Wales, GStA Berlin, BPHA Rep. 53J Lit. G Nr 13.

87 Kaiser Wilhelm II to Empress Frederick, 16 December 1899, AdHH Schloss Fasanerie. Cf. the letter Prince Heinrich wrote to his mother on 13 December 1899, ibid.

88 Kaiser Wilhelm II to Queen Victoria, 21 December 1899, RA VIC/I 62/76. See also Kaiser Wilhelm II to Queen Victoria, 30 January 1900, RA VIC/I 62/80.

89 Kaiser Wilhelm II to Albert Edward Prince of Wales, 21 December 1899, RA VIC/W 60/26.

90 Kaiser Wilhelm II, marginal notes on Hatzfeldt to Auswärtiges Amt, 20 December 1899, *Große Politik*, XV, No. 4402.

91 Kaiser Wilhelm II, note of 2 January 1900, cited in Rosenbach, *Transvaal*, p. 232.

92 Bülow to Hatzfeldt, 6 January 1900, *Große Politik*, XV, No. 4425. See Rosenbach, *Transvaal*, p. 237.

93 Hinzpeter to Kaiser Wilhelm II, 22 January 1900, GStA Berlin, BPHA Rep. 53J, Lit. H Nr 1.

94 Rosenbach, *Transvaal*, p. 226.

95 Bülow to Eulenburg, 6 December 1899, *Eulenburgs Korrespondenz*, III, No. 1407.

96 Kaiser Wilhelm II, 'Gedankensplitter über den Krieg in Transvaal', 21 December 1899, RA VIC/W 60/28–29; the English translation is in RA VIC/W 60/27.

97 Kaiser Wilhelm II to Queen Victoria, 29 December 1899, RA I61/83. See Queen Victoria to Kaiser Wilhelm II, telegram, 8 January 1900, GStA Berlin, BPHA Rep. 53J, Lit. G Nr 13; Kaiser Wilhelm II to Albert Edward Prince of Wales, 13 January 1900, RA VIC/I 62/76c.

98 Kaiser Wilhelm II to Albert Edward Prince of Wales, 4 February 1900, RA VIC/W 60/66, printed in *Große Politik*, XV, No. 4507.

99 Kaiser Wilhelm II, 'Weitere Gedankensplitter über den Transvaalkrieg', 4 February 1900, RA VIC/W 60/67, printed in Sir Sidney Lee, *King Edward VII. A Biography*, 2 vols., London 1925, I, pp. 805–10. Cf. the version printed in *Große Politik*, XV, pp. 554–7. See Lascelles to Salisbury, 9 February 1900, Gooch and Temperley, *British Documents*, I, No. 311.

100 Albert Edward Prince of Wales to Kaiser Wilhelm II, 8 February 1900, RA VIC/W 60/73 and 74, printed in *Große Politik*, XV, No. 4508. See ibid., No. 4510.

101 Albert Edward Prince of Wales to Queen Victoria, 8 February 1900, RA VIC/P 6/46.

102 Albert Edward Prince of Wales to Empress Frederick, 11 and 26 February 1900, RA VIC/ Add A 4/146 and 148.

103 Kaiser Wilhelm II, graphic representation of British army units in South Africa, 21 December 1899, RA VIC/W 60/29.

104 General Wolseley to Bigge, 15 February 1900, RA VIC/W 15/159.

105 Kaiser Wilhelm II to Queen Victoria, telegram, 16 February 1900, RA I62/82; Kaiser Wilhelm II to Albert Edward Prince of Wales, 3 March 1900, RA VIC/W 60/105.

106 Kaiser Wilhelm II to Queen Victoria, telegram, 27 February 1900, RA P6/228a; Kaiser Wilhelm II to Albert Edward Prince of Wales, 23 February 1900, RA VIC/W 60/89. The version printed in *Große Politik*, XV, No. 4509 is incomplete. See the Prince of Wales's reply of 28 February 1900, ibid., No. 4510.

107 For the controversy over Kaiser Wilhelm's role in this murky issue see Fritz Heilbron, 'Deutsche Intriguen gegen England während des Burenkriegs', *Deutsche Revue*, September 1908, 266; Otto Hammann, *Zur Vorgeschichte des Weltkriegs. Erinnerungen aus den Jahren 1897–1906*, Berlin 1918, pp. 89ff.; Otto Hammann, *Um den Kaiser*, Berlin 1919, pp. 103ff; *Große Politik*, XV, p. 523.

108 Konrad Canis, *Von Bismarck zur Weltpolitik. Deutsche Außenpolitik 1890 bis 1902*, Berlin 1997, pp. 338–55.

109 Chlodwig Fürst zu Hohenlohe to his son Alexander, 6 December 1899, Hohenlohe, *Denkwürdigkeiten der Reichskanzlerzeit*, p. 548.

110 Kaiser Wilhelm II, marginal note on the report of 6 September 1899 from the military attaché Freiherr von Süßkind, *Große Politik*, XIV, No. 3635.

111 Kaiser Wilhelm II to Bülow, 29 October 1899, ibid., XV, No. 4394. In a letter of 27 March 1900 to the Queen of the Netherlands Wilhelm II complained of the refusal of Russia and France to join him in forming a continental league against England at the time of the Jameson Raid in January 1896. See ibid., No. 4494.

112 Kaiser Wilhelm II to Albert Edward Prince of Wales, 23 February 1900, RA VIC/W 60/89. The version printed in *Große Politik*, XV, No. 4509 is incomplete. See the reply of the Prince of Wales of 28 February 1900, ibid., No. 4510.

113 Lascelles to Salisbury, 9 February 1900, Gooch and Temperley, *British Documents*, I, No. 311.

114 Lascelles to Salisbury, 10 February 1900, ibid., No. 312.

115 Lascelles to Salisbury, 2 March 1900, ibid., No. 313.

116 On the Russian proposal and Germany's wary response, see Bülow to Radolin, 3 March 1900, *Große Politik*, XV, No. 4472.

117 Kaiser Wilhelm II to Albert Edward Prince of Wales, 3 March 1900, RA VIC/W 60/105.

118 Kaiser Wilhelm II, marginal notes on Pourtalès to Hohenlohe, 6 March 1900, *Große Politik*, XV, No. 4479.

119 Kaiser Wilhelm II, marginal notes on Radolin to Hohenlohe, 11 March 1900, ibid., No. 4486.

120 Kaiser Wilhelm II, marginal notes on Radolin to Auswärtiges Amt, 5 March 1900, ibid., No. 4476.

121 Queen Victoria to Kaiser Wilhelm II, 7 March 1900, RA VIC/P 7/69.

122 Kaiser Wilhelm II, marginal notes on Metternich to Hohenlohe, 5 March 1900, *Große Politik*, XV, No. 4475.

123 Albert Edward Prince of Wales to Kaiser Wilhelm II, 7 March 1900, ibid., No. 4480.

124 Lascelles to Salisbury, 9 March 1900, RA VIC/I 62/83.

125 See *Große Politik*, XV, Nos. 4481 and 4482.

126 Kaiser Wilhelm II to Bülow, 10 March 1900, ibid., No. 4483.

127 See the Kaiser's own heavily corrected drafts in PA AA R 14786.

128 Kaiser Wilhelm II to Queen Victoria and Albert Edward Prince of Wales, telegram, 11 March 1900, RA VIC/P 7/103 and VIC/W 60/114. See Buckle, *Letters of Queen*

Victoria, III, p. 508. Cf. the draft in *Große Politik*, XV, No. 4484. The Queen immediately sent Sir Arthur Bigge to Lord Salisbury to ask how she should respond to the Kaiser's telegram. RA/QVJ.

129 Salisbury to Queen Victoria, 11 March 1900, RA VIC/I 62/84.

130 Queen Victoria to Kaiser Wilhelm II, 11 March 1900, RA VIC/P 7/104; Albert Edward Prince of Wales to Kaiser Wilhelm II, 11 March 1900, PA AA R 14786.

131 Queen Victoria to Lascelles, 11 March 1900, Buckle, *Letters of Queen Victoria*, III, pp. 508f.; Lascelles to Kaiser Wilhelm II, 12 March 1900, RA VIC/I 62/85, printed in part in Buckle, *Letters of Queen Victoria*, II, p. 509; Salisbury to Bigge, 12 March 1900, Bigge to Queen Victoria, 13 March 1900, ibid.

132 Kaiser Wilhelm II to Queen Victoria, 14 March 1900, RA VIC/I 62/86; Kaiser Wilhelm II to Lascelles, 14 March 1900, RA VIC/I 62/87.

133 Kaiser Wilhelm II, marginal note on Metternich to Hohenlohe, 24 March 1900, *Große Politik*, XV, No. 4458.

134 Kaiser Wilhelm II to Queen Victoria, 31 March 1900, RA VIC/I 62/90, printed in Buckle, *Letters of Queen Victoria*, III, pp. 519f.

135 Salisbury to Queen Victoria, 10 April 1900, RA VIC/I 62/92.

136 Spring Rice to Knollys, 2 November 1908, RA King Edward VII's papers on Foreign Affairs, X series.

137 Metternich to Hohenlohe, 20 March 1900 with the Kaiser's marginal notes, *Große Politik*, XV, No. 4493.

138 Bülow to Radolin, 3 March 1900, ibid., No. 4472.

139 See Théophile Delcassé to the French ambassador in Berlin, Marquis de Noailles, 26 March 1900, ibid., p. 518.

140 Kaiser Wilhelm II, marginal note on Radolin's telegram of 5 March 1900, ibid., No. 4476.

141 Metternich to Hohenlohe, 20 March 1900 with the Kaiser's marginal notes, ibid., No. 4493.

142 Hatzfeldt, telegram of 6 April 1901 with the Kaiser's marginal notes, ibid., XVII, No. 4999.

143 Kaiser Wilhelm II to King Edward VII, 10 April 1901, RA VIC/X37/37.

144 Lascelles to King Edward VII, 13 April 1901, RA VIC/X37/40.

145 Lansdowne to King Edward VII, 13 April 1901, RA VIC/X37/38.

3 'I AM THE BALANCE OF POWER IN EUROPE.' WILHELM BETWEEN
BRITAIN, RUSSIA AND FRANCE

1 Waldersee, diary for 1 April 1900, GStA Berlin, Waldersee Papers, omitted in Meisner, II, p. 444.

2 Waldersee, diary for 25 December 1902, ibid.; Meisner, III, p. 198.

3 Waldersee to Engelbrecht, 31 December 1902, cited in Konrad Canis, *Der Weg in den Abgrund. Die deutsche Außenpolitik 1902–1914*, Paderborn, Munich, Vienna and Zürich 2011, pp. 17f.

4 See above, p. 46.

5 Waldersee, diary for 3 April 1900, GStA Berlin, Waldersee Papers; not in Meisner, II, p. 444.

6 Bülow to Wedel, 17 December 1901, *Große Politik*, XVIII/2, No. 5709. See Bülow to Kaiser Wilhelm II, 10 January 1901, ibid., XVII, No. 5341.

7 Lascelles to Salisbury, 20 January 1899, quoted in Rosenbach, *Transvaal*, p. 221. See Christopher M. Clark, *Kaiser Wilhelm II*, London 2000, p. 137; Gregor Schöllgen, *Imperialismus und Gleichgewicht. Deutschland, England und die orientalische Frage 1871–1914*, Munich 2000, pp. 86–106.

8 Kaiser Wilhelm II, marginal note on Radolin's report of 2 April 1899, *Große Politik*, XIII, No. 3537.

9 Bülow to Hatzfeldt, 28 May 1900, ibid., XVII, No. 5163; Bernhard Fürst von Bülow, *Denkwürdigkeiten*, 4 vols., Berlin 1930–1, I, p. 310; Holstein, memorandum of 17 November 1899, *Holstein Papers*, IV, No. 718; Holstein to Bülow, 10 and 22 November 1899, cited in Rosenbach, *Transvaal*, p. 220.

10 Bigge to Salisbury, 22 November 1899, cited in Winzen, *Bülows Weltmachtkonzept*, p. 217, note 128 and p. 219, note 138.

11 Bülow, memorandum of 24 November 1899, *Große Politik*, XV, No. 4398. See Winzen, *Bülows Weltmachtkonzept*, p. 217.

12 Quoted in James L. Garvin, *The Life of Joseph Chamberlain*, 3 vols., London 1934, III, pp. 507f.

13 Winzen, *Bülows Weltmachtkonzept*, pp. 220ff.

14 Johannes Penzler, ed., *Fürst Bülows Reden*, 3 vols., Berlin 1907–9, I, pp. 91ff. See Rosenbach, *Transvaal*, pp. 223f.

15 See Winzen, *Bülows Weltmachtkonzept*, pp. 225–30.

16 See Röhl, *The Kaiser's Personal Monarchy*, pp. 1034–9.

17 Lascelles to Salisbury, 9 February 1900, Gooch and Temperley, *British Documents*, I, No. 311.

18 Kaiser Wilhelm II to Albert Edward Prince of Wales, 31 July 1900, RA VIC/T 10/126.

19 Lascelles to Salisbury, 21 December 1898, Gooch and Temperley, *British Documents*, I, No. 124.

20 Swaine to Sir Arthur Bigge, 28 December 1900, RA VIC/I 62/113. See also Swaine's letter of 1 January 1901, RA VIC/I 62/114.

21 Kaiser Wilhelm II to Bülow, 20 January 1901, *Große Politik*, XVII, No. 4982.

22 See above, p. 43. See also Kaiser Wilhelm II, marginal note on Münster's report of 24 March 1899, *Große Politik*, XIV, No. 3944. Further, Holstein's correspondence with Eckardstein of March 1901, ibid., XVI, p. 335.

23 Kaiser Wilhelm II to Bülow, 29 January 1901, ibid., XVII, No. 4987.

24 Lascelles to Salisbury, 28 February 1901, Gooch and Temperley, *British Documents*, I, No. 322.

25 Francis Bertie, memorandum of 27 October 1901, RA VIC/W42/42.

26 Kaiser Wilhelm II, marginal notes on Radolin's report of 2 April 1899, *Große Politik*, XIII, No. 3537.

27 Waldersee, diary for 6 May 1899, GStA Berlin, Waldersee Papers; cf. Meisner, II, pp. 428f.

28 Kaiser Wilhelm II, speech of 18 May 1899 in Wiesbaden, Johannes Penzler, ed., *Reden Kaiser Wilhelms II. in den Jahren 1896–1900*, Leipzig 1904, p. 151. On the Hague peace conference see Wolfgang J. Mommsen, *Großmachtstellung und Weltpolitik. Die Außenpolitik des Deutschen Reiches 1870–1914*, Berlin 1993, pp. 158f.; Jost Dülffer, *Regeln gegen den Krieg? Die Haager Friedenskonferenzen 1899 und 1907 in der internationalen Politik*, Frankfurt a.M., Berlin 1981, pp. 103ff.

29 Kaiser Wilhelm II, marginal comment on Münster's report of 17 July 1899, *Große Politik*, XV, No. 4351.

30 Kaiser Wilhelm II, marginal comment on Bülow's report of 14 May 1899, ibid., No. 4257. On Wilhelm II's concerns about Russian rearmament see Hohenlohe's journal of 27 February 1899, Hohenlohe, *Denkwürdigkeiten der Reichskanzlerzeit*, p. 486.

31 Bülow to Kaiser Wilhelm II, 21 June 1899, with the Kaiser's marginal notes, *Große Politik*, XV, No. 4320. See also Wilhelm's comments on Münster's report of 28 May 1899, ibid., No. 4276.

32 Kaiser Wilhelm II to Queen Victoria, 29 December 1898, RA VIC/I 61/83.

33 Bülow to Kaiser Wilhelm II, 21 June 1899, with the Kaiser's marginal notes, *Große Politik*, XV, No. 4320.

34 Kaiser Wilhelm II, marginal note on Bülow's report 14 May 1899, ibid., No. 4257.

35 Bülow to Kaiser Wilhelm II, 21 June 1899, with the Kaiser's marginal notes, ibid., No. 4320.

36 See Derenthall's report of 21 June 1899, ibid., XIII, No. 3539.

37 Kaiser Wilhelm II, marginal comment of 23 June 1899 on Bülow's report of 21 June 1899, PA AA R 122. Cf. *Große Politik*, XV, No. 4320.

38 Bülow to Kaiser Wilhelm II, 6 August 1899, GStA Berlin, BPHA Rep. 53J Lit. B Nr 16a.

39 Grand Duke Friedrich I of Baden to Hohenlohe, 4 March 1899, Hohenlohe, *Denkwür-digkeiten der Reichskanzlerzeit*, pp. 487f.

40 Derenthall's report from Stuttgart of 21 June 1899 with the Kaiser's marginal notes, *Große Politik*, XIII, No. 3539.

41 Radolin's report of 29 June 1899 with the Kaiser's marginal notes, ibid., XIV/2, No. 4022. See also Wilhelm II's comments on Radowitz's report of 5 October 1899 from San Sebastian, ibid., XV, No. 4212.

42 Kaiser Wilhelm II to Bülow, 14 September 1899, ibid., XIII, No. 3540. See also the Kaiser's marginal note on the report from Darmstadt of 30 October 1899, PA AA Asservat Nr 4.

43 Waldersee, diary for 25 October 1899, GStA Berlin, Waldersee Papers; omitted in Meisner, II, p. 437.

44 Waldersee, diary for 29 October and 9 November 1899, GStA Berlin, Waldersee Papers; cf. Meisner, II, pp. 437f.

45 See Sir Francis Bertie's report on his talks with Bülow at Sandringham on 26 November 1899, RA VIC/I 62/68.

46 Lascelles to Salisbury, 9 March 1900, RA VIC/I 62/83.

47 Bülow to Kaiser Wilhelm II, 22 August 1900, GStA Berlin, BPHA Rep. 53J Lit. B Nr 16a.

48 Alexander Hohenlohe to Chlodwig Hohenlohe, 30 September 1900, Hohenlohe, *Denkwürdigkeiten der Reichskanzlerzeit*, p. 587.

49 Kaiser Wilhelm II to Bülow, 13 September 1900; Bülow to Kaiser Wilhelm II, 13 September 1900, PA AA R 3623.

50 Kaiser Wilhelm II to Bülow, 26 January 1901, PA AA Asservat Nr 4.

51 Alexander Hohenlohe to Chlodwig Hohenlohe, 18 September 1899; Chlodwig Hohenlohe to Alexander Hohenlohe, 24 September 1899, Hohenlohe, *Denkwürdigkeiten der Reichs-kanzlerzeit*, pp. 526f.

52 Kaiser Wilhelm II to Bülow, 29 January 1901, *Große Politik*, XVII, No. 4987.

53 Eulenburg to Auswärtiges Amt, 6 July 1899, ibid., XIII, No. 3569.

54 See Röhl, *The Kaiser's Personal Monarchy*, pp. 984—9.

55 Kaiser Wilhelm II, marginal comment on the report from Paris of 10 July 1899, *Große Politik*, XIII, No. 3570.

56 Kaiser Wilhelm II to Münster, 16 July and 4 August 1899, ibid., Nos. 3571 and 3574.

57 Kaiser Wilhelm II, speech of 18 August 1899 held on the battlefield of St Privat, Penzler, *Reden Kaiser Wilhelms II. in den Jahren 1896—1900*, pp. 163f.

58 Kaiser Wilhelm II, marginal note on the report of 12 August 1899 from San Sebastian, *Große Politik*, XV, No. 4211.

59 Lascelles to Salisbury, 9 March 1900, RA VIC/I 62/83, quoted above, pp. 42f.

60 Kaiser Wilhelm II to Bülow, 29 January 1901, *Große Politik*, XVII, No. 4987. See above, pp. 53ff.

61 Lascelles to Salisbury, 28 February 1901, Gooch and Temperley, *British Documents*, I, No. 322.

62 See *Große Politik*, XVII, No. 5020 and XXI/2, No. 7230 with marginal comments.

63 Tschirschky to Auswärtiges Amt, 11 July 1901, PA AA R 3747.

64 Bülow to Kaiser Wilhelm II, 21 August 1901, PA AA R 3624, printed in *Große Politik*, XVIII/1, No. 5390.

65 Waldersee, diary for 22 February 1902, GStA Berlin, Waldersee Papers; Meisner, III, pp. 179ff.

66 Kaiser Wilhelm II to Tsar Nicholas II, 20 and 21 April 1901, PA AA R 3623, *Große Politik*, XVIII/1, No. 5384; Tsar Nicholas II to Kaiser Wilhelm II, 21 April 1901, PA AA R 3623; *Große Politik*, XVIII/1, No. 5384; Bülow to Auswärtiges Amt, 21 April 1901, PA AA R 3623. On the emperors' meeting at Danzig see Mommsen, *Großmachtstellung und Weltpolitik*, p. 163; Barbara Vogel, *Deutsche Rußlandpolitik. Das Scheitern der deutschen Weltpolitik unter Bülow 1900–1906*, Düsseldorf 1973, p. 107.

67 Grand Duke Friedrich I of Baden to Bülow, 18 May 1901, Fuchs, *Großherzog von Baden*, IV, No. 2190.

68 Kaiser Wilhelm II to Bülow, 20 August 1901, PA AA R 3623, printed with minor changes in *Große Politik*, XVIII/1, No. 5388.

69 Bülow to Kaiser Wilhelm II, 21 August 1901, PA AA R 3624, printed ibid., No. 5390.

70 Kaiser Wilhelm II to Bülow, 22 August 1901 and Bülow to Auswärtiges Amt, 22 August 1901, PA AA R 3624, printed ibid., No. 5389; Kaiser Wilhelm II to Tsar Nicholas II, 13 June, 8 July and 22 August 1901, Walter Goetz, ed., *Briefe Wilhelms II. an den Zaren 1894–1914*, Berlin 1920, pp. 71–6 and 319ff.

71 Kaiser Wilhelm II, marginal notes on the report from St Petersburg of 23 August 1901, *Große Politik*, XVIII, No. 5895. The '*Gang nach Canossa*', a reference to the humiliating crossing of the Alps by King Henry IV to seek absolution from Pope Gregory VII in the winter of 1076–7, was a byword in German political parlance for abject surrender.

72 Bülow to Kaiser Wilhelm II, 23 August 1901, PA AA R 3624.

73 Kaiser Wilhelm II to Tsar Nicholas II, 22 August 1901, ibid., printed in Goetz, *Briefe Wilhelms II. an den Zaren*, pp. 74–6 and 320f. The Tsar's reply is in PA AA R 3624.

74 Kaiser Wilhelm II to Bülow, 25 August 1901, PA AA R 3624.

75 See Chapter 14 below.

76 Bülow to Auswärtiges Amt, 12 September 1901, PA AA R 3624. See Tsar Nicholas II to Kaiser Wilhelm II, 23 September 1901; Kaiser Wilhelm II to Tsar Nicholas II, 24 September 1901, *Große Politik*, XVIII/2, Nos. 5397 and 5398.

77 Pückler's reports from St Petersburg of 16 and 20 September and 7 October 1901 with Kaiser Wilhelm II's marginal notes, PA AA R 3624.

78 See Bülow to Holstein, 5 August 1901, *Holstein Papers*, IV, No. 784.

79 Cf. Lascelles to Salisbury, 25 August 1901, Gooch and Temperley, *British Documents*, I, No. 323.

80 Kaiser Wilhelm II to Bülow, 23 August 1901, *Große Politik*, XVII, No. 5023.

81 Kaiser Wilhelm II, marginal note on Radolin to Holstein, 11 March 1900, PA AA R 14786, cited in Norman Rich, *Friedrich von Holstein. Politics and Diplomacy in the Era of Bismarck and Wilhelm II*, 2 vols., Cambridge 1965, II, p. 618. Cf. *Große Politik*, XV, pp. 530f., where this note has been omitted.

82 Kaiser Wilhelm II, marginal notes on Eckardstein's report of 2 January 1901, *Große Politik*, XVII, No. 5339 and 5340.

83 Queen Victoria to Tsar Nicholas II, undated, probably March 1900, RA VIC/I 62/22.

84 Bülow to Kaiser Wilhelm II, 31 March 1903, cited in Canis, *Abgrund*, pp. 16f. See the warning signs of Germany's impending isolation recorded by Mensdorff, Metternich and Eckardstein, ibid., pp. 23f.

4 THE BOXER REBELLION AND THE BAGHDAD RAILWAY

1 See Gerd Fesser, 'Gelbe Gefahr', in Kurt Pätzold and Manfred Weißbecker, eds., *Schlagwörter und Schlachtrufe*, Leipzig 2002, I, pp. 150ff. On Wilhelm II's obsession with the Yellow Peril see Röhl, *The Kaiser's Personal Monarchy*, pp. 745ff. and 909f. On his language

in general see Volker Wittenauer, *Im Dienste der Macht. Kultur und Sprache am Hof der Hohenzollern. Vom Großen Kurfürst bis zu Wilhelm II.*, Paderborn 2007, pp. 219–92.

2 See Röhl, *The Kaiser's Personal Monarchy*, pp. 954ff.

3 Robert K. Massie, *Dreadnought. Britain, Germany and the Coming of the Great War*, New York 1991, pp 282f. See Bülow, *Denkwürdigkeiten*, I, p. 358.

4 Kaiser Wilhelm II, marginal comment on Bülow's telegram of 5 June 1900, PA AA R 18275. Cited in part in Bernd Martin, 'Die Ermordung des deutschen Gesandten Clemens von Ketteler am 20. Juni 1900 in Peking und die Eskalation des "Boxerkrieges"', in Susanne Kuß and Bernd Martin, eds., *Das Deutsche Reich und der Boxeraufstand*, Munich 2002, pp. 85f. On Germany's intervention in China see Wolfgang J. Mommsen, *War der Kaiser an allem schuld? Wilhelm II. und die preußisch-deutschen Machteliten*, Munich 2002, pp. 103–08; Canis, *Von Bismarck zur Weltpolitik*, pp. 338–55.

5 Hereditary Prince Bernhard of Saxe-Meiningen to his father Duke Georg II of Saxe-Meiningen, 16 August 1900, ThStaMgn HA 341; Kaiser Wilhelm II to Auswärtiges Amt, 2 July 1900, *Große Politik*, XVI, No. 4540.

6 Kaiser Wilhelm II to Bülow, 19 June 1900, ibid., No. 4527; Kaiser Wilhelm II to Albert Edward Prince of Wales, 18 July 1900, RA VIC/T 10/125.

7 Waldersee, memorandum, printed in Meisner, III, pp. 2f.

8 Ibid., p. 6.

9 Kaiser Wilhelm II, order of 2 July 1900; Bülow to Auswärtiges Amt, 3 July 1900; Admiralstab to Bülow, 8 July 1900, PA AA R 18438. See Martin, 'Ermordung des deutschen Gesandten', pp. 89f. Cf. Meisner, III, p. 6.

10 Peter Franz Stubmann, *Albert Ballin. Leben und Werk eines deutschen Reeders*, Berlin 1927, p. 215.

11 Kaiser Wilhelm II to Albert Edward Prince of Wales, 31 July 1900, RA VIC/T 10/126.

12 Bülow to Auswärtiges Amt, 29 July 1900, *Große Politik*, XVI, No. 4594.

13 Eliza von Moltke, ed., *Generaloberst Helmuth von Moltke, Erinnerungen, Briefe, Dokumente 1877–1916*, Stuttgart 1922, p. 324.

14 Bülow to Kaiser Wilhelm II, 19 June 1900, *Große Politik*, XVI, No. 4529.

15 Ibid., note 4.

16 Kaiser Wilhelm II to Bülow, 8 July 1900, ibid., No. 4558. See Canis, *Von Bismarck zur Weltpolitik*, p. 342.

17 Kaiser Wilhelm II, speech of 2 July 1900 in Wilhelmshaven, Penzler, *Reden Kaiser Wilhelms II. in den Jahren 1896–1900*, pp. 205ff.; Obst, *Die politischen Reden Kaiser Wilhelms II.*, pp. 197ff. See also Obst, *'Einer nur ist Herr im Reiche'*, pp. 223–54.

18 Kaiser Wilhelm II to Queen Victoria, 1 and 2 July 1900, RA VIC/I 62/107 and VIC/Q 16/268; Kaiser Wilhelm II, speech of 6 July 1900 in Kiel, Penzler, *Reden Kaiser Wilhelms II. in den Jahren 1896–1900*, p. 209.

19 Eulenburg to Bülow, 14 July 1900, *Eulenburgs Korrespondenz*, III, No. 1419.

20 Eulenburg to Bülow, 18 July 1900, ibid., No. 1420.

21 See the complete text in Bernd Sösemann, 'Die sog. Hunnenrede Wilhelms II. Textkritische und interpretatorische Bemerkungen zur Ansprache des Kaisers vom 27. Juli 1900 in Bremerhaven', *Historische Zeitschrift*, 222 (1976), 349f. See also Obst, *Die politischen Reden*, pp. 201–9; Röhl, *The Kaiser's Personal Monarchy*, pp. 1042ff.

22 Thoralf Klein, 'Der Boxeraufstand als interkultureller Konflikt: zur Relevanz eines Deutungsmusters', in Susanne Kuß and Martin Bernd, eds., *Das Deutsche Reich und der Boxeraufstand*, Munich 2002, p. 50. See also Ute Wielandt and Michael Kaschner, 'Die Reichstagsdebatten über den deutschen Kriegseinsatz in China: August Bebel und die "Hunnenbriefe"', ibid., p. 194.

23 Susanne Kuß, 'Deutsche Soldaten während des Boxeraufstandes in China: Elemente und Ursprünge des Vernichtungskrieges', in Susanne Kuß and Martin Berndt, eds., *Das*

Deutsche Reich und der Boxeraufstand, Munich 2002, pp. 165, 174. See also Sabine Dabringhaus, 'An Army on Vacation? The German War in China, 1900–1901', in Manfred F. Boemeke, Roger Chickering and Stig Förster, eds., *Anticipating Total War: The German and American Experiences, 1871–1914*, Cambridge 1999, pp. 459–76; Isabel V. Hull, *Absolute Destruction. Military Culture and the Practices of War in Imperial Germany*, Ithaca 2005.

24 Bülow, *Denkwürdigkeiten*, I, p. 359.

25 Bülow to Auswärtiges Amt, 27 and 29 July 1900, printed in facsimile in Martin, 'Die Ermordung des deutschen Gesandten', pp. 99–102. See Sösemann, 'Die sog. Hunnenrede Wilhelms II.', and also Jagemann to Brauer, 20 November 1900 and Bodman to Brauer, 23 November 1900, in Fuchs, *Großherzog von Baden*, IV, Nos. 2127 and 2129.

26 Bülow to Auswärtiges Amt, 27 and 29 July 1900, printed in facsimile in Martin, 'Die Ermordung des deutschen Gesandten', pp. 99–102.

27 Kaiser Wilhelm II, speech of 2 August 1900 in Bremerhaven, Penzler, *Reden Kaiser Wilhelms II. in den Jahren 1896–1900*, pp. 219ff.; Obst, *Die politischen Reden*, pp. 214f.

28 Kaiser Wilhelm II, speech to departing marines of August 1900, Penzler, *Reden Kaiser Wilhelms II. in den Jahren 1896–1900*, pp. 221ff.; Obst, *Die politischen Reden*, pp. 215ff.

29 Waldersee to Verdy, 28 January 1901, GStA Berlin, Waldersee Papers, Nr 53; Hohenlohe, *Denkwürdigkeiten der Reichskanzlerzeit*, pp. 578f.; *Holstein Papers*, IV, Nos. 194 and 201; Peter Winzen, *Die Englandpolitik Friedrich von Holsteins 1895–1901*, Cologne 1975, pp. 291f.; Hermann Freiherr von Eckardstein, *Lebenserinnerungen und Politische Denkwürdigkeiten*, 2 vols., Leipzig 1921, II, p. 187.

30 Kaiser Wilhelm II to Bülow, 19 June 1900, *Große Politik*, XVI, No. 4527. See above, p. 74.

31 Bülow to Kaiser Wilhelm II, 22 June 1900, *Große Politik*, XVI, No. 4529. See ibid., Nos. 4548 and 4561.

32 Hatzfeldt to Eckardstein, 18 and 20 July 1900; Eckardstein, *Lebenserinnerungen*, II, pp. 189–91; Annika Mombauer, 'Wilhelm, Waldersee, and the Boxer Rebellion', in Annika Mombauer and Wilhelm Deist, eds., *The Kaiser. New Research on Wilhelm II's Role in Imperial Germany*, Cambridge 2003, pp. 99ff.

33 Hatzfeldt to Auswärtiges Amt, 12 and 18 July 1900, *Große Politik*, XVI, Nos. 4568 and 4573; Derenthall to Hatzfeldt, 31 July 1900, ibid., No. 4595.

34 Bülow to Kaiser Wilhelm II, 5 August 1900, ibid., No. 4601, note.

35 Kaiser Wilhelm II to Bülow, 6 August 1900, ibid., No. 4602.

36 Waldersee to Verdy, 28 January 1901, GStA Berlin, Waldersee Papers, Nr 53. See Eckardstein, *Lebenserinnerungen*, II, p. 193. Also Walter Goetz, 'Kaiser Wilhelm II.' (unpublished manuscript), BA Koblenz, Goetz Papers, N/1215 Nr 350, p. 425.

37 Grand Duke Friedrich I of Baden to Bülow, 18 May 1901, Fuchs, *Großherzog von Baden*, IV, No. 2190.

38 Hereditary Princess Charlotte of Saxe-Meiningen to Ernst Schweninger, no date, BA Berlin, Schweninger Papers, Nr 132.

39 Hereditary Prince Bernhard of Saxe-Meiningen to Colmar Freiherr von der Goltz, 4 December 1900, BA-MA Freiburg-im-Breisgau, von der Goltz Papers, N 737 Zug. 228/95.

40 Waldersee to Bülow, 19 August 1900, GStA Berlin, BPHA Rep 53J Lit B, Nr 16a.

41 Kaiser Wilhelm II, farewell address to Waldersee in Kassel, 18 August 1900, Penzler, *Reden Kaiser Wilhelms II. in den Jahren 1896–1900*, pp. 228f.; Obst, *Die politischen Reden*, pp. 220f.

42 Waldersee to Verdy, 28 January 1901, GStA Berlin, Waldersee Papers, Nr 53; Kaiser Wilhelm II to Albert Edward Prince of Wales, 10 August 1900, RA VIC/W 16/47.

43 Richthofen to Eulenburg, 27 September 1900, *Eulenburgs Korrespondenz*, III, No. 1431.

44 Eulenburg to Richthofen, 30 September 1900, ibid., No. 1432.

45 Eulenburg to Bülow, 3 October 1900, ibid., No. 1435.

46 Bülow to Kaiser Wilhelm II, 6 August 1900, GStA Berlin, BPHA Rep 53 J Lit B Nr 16a, vol. II.

47 Waldersee to Verdy, 28 January 1901, GStA Berlin, Waldersee Papers, Nr 53.

48 Eulenburg to Bülow, 3 October 1900, *Eulenburgs Korrespondenz*, III, No. 1435.

49 Waldersee to Kaiser Wilhelm II, 25 September 1900, Meisner, III, pp. 15ff.; Kaiser Wilhelm II to Waldersee, 11 November 1900, ibid., p. 46; Kaiser Wilhelm II, marginal notes on Waldersee's report of 7 October 1900, *Große Politik*, XVI, No. 4735.

50 Kaiser Wilhelm II to Auswärtiges Amt, 22 August 1900, ibid., No. 4712.

51 Radolin to Holstein, 14 November 1900, *Holstein Papers*, IV, No. 758. See Canis, *Von Bismarck zur Weltpolitik*, pp. 344ff.

52 Bülow to Kaiser Wilhelm II, 6 January 1901, *Große Politik*, XVI, No. 4770, with marginal note; Kaiser Wilhelm II to Waldersee, 10 January 1901, Meisner, III, pp. 83f.

53 Kaiser Wilhelm II, marginal notes on Richthofen's report of 4 April 1901, *Große Politik*, XVI, No. 4838.

54 See above, p. 75.

55 Waldersee to Kaiser Wilhelm II, 24 November 1900, Meisner, III, pp. 54f.

56 Prince Heinrich of Prussia, memorandum for Kaiser Wilhelm II of 14 January 1901, GStA Berlin, BPHA Rep 52 V1 Nr 13a. See Bülow to Kaiser Wilhelm II, 17 January 1901, *Große Politik*, XVI, No. 4778.

57 Kaiser Wilhelm II to Waldersee, 2 February 1901, ibid., No. 4779.

58 Waldersee to Bülow, 19 August 1900, GStA Berlin, BPHA Rep 53J Lit B, Nr 16a.

59 Kaiser Wilhelm II to Auswärtiges Amt, 21 August 1900, *Große Politik*, XVI, No. 4615; Kaiser Wilhelm II, marginal note on Radolin's report of 30 August 1900, ibid., No. 4625. See Waldersee's memorandum in Meisner, III, pp. 5f.

60 Kaiser Wilhelm II, marginal notes on Richthofen to Metternich, 7 September 1900, *Große Politik*, XVI, No. 4633.

61 Waldersee to Verdy, 28 January 1901, GStA Berlin, Waldersee Papers, Nr 53.

62 Bülow to Kaiser Wilhelm II, 22 August 1900, GStA Berlin, BPHA Rep 53J Lit B Nr 16a.

63 Hohenlohe, *Denkwürdigkeiten der Reichskanzlerzeit*, p. 584.

64 Prince Heinrich of Prussia to Senden, 16 November 1900, BA-MA Freiburg-im-Breisgau, Senden-Bibran Papers, N 160/4.

65 Waldersee to Verdy, 28 January 1901, GStA Berlin, Waldersee Papers, Nr 53.

66 See Dabringhaus, 'An Army on Vacation?', pp. 459–76.

67 Waldersee, diary for January 1902, GStA Berlin, Waldersee Papers; omitted in Meisner, III, p. 177.

68 Richard O'Connor, *The Spirit Soldiers: A Historical Narrative of the Boxer Rebellion*, New York 1973, p. 298.

69 Waldersee to Verdy, 28 January 1901, GStA Berlin, Waldersee Papers, Nr 53.

70 Chlodwig Hohenlohe to Alexander Hohenlohe, 10 October 1900, Hohenlohe, *Denkwürdigkeiten der Reichskanzlerzeit*, p. 589.

71 Bülow to Kaiser Wilhelm II, 22 August 1900, GStA Berlin, BPHA Rep 53J Lit B Nr 16a.

72 See Kaiser Wilhelm II's speech from the throne on the opening of the Reichstag on 14 November 1900, Penzler, *Reden Kaiser Wilhelms II. in den Jahren 1896–1900*, pp. 241–4; Obst, *Die politischen Reden*, pp. 222–4.

73 Quoted in Fesser, *Der Traum vom Platz an der Sonne*, p. 61.

74 August Bebel, 'Chinapolitik und Sozialdemokratie vor dem Reichstag', in August Bebel, *Ausgewählte Reden und Schriften*, VII/1, Munich 1997, p. 85.

75 *Stenographische Berichte über die Verhandlungen des Reichstages*, Berlin, 1871–1918, 10. Legislaturperiode, 2. Session, Bd. 179, pp. 26ff. (19 November 1900) and pp. 113ff. (23 November 1900). See Clark, *Kaiser Wilhelm II*, p. 171; Mommsen, *War der Kaiser an allem schuld?*, pp. 106f.

76 Eulenburg to Kaiser Wilhelm II, 22 November 1900, *Eulenburgs Korrespondenz*, III, No. 1440.

77 Kaiser Wilhelm II to Eulenburg, 23 November 1900, ibid., No. 1441.

78 Kaiser Wilhelm II, speech of 23 November 1900 in Kiel, Penzler, *Reden Kaiser Wilhelms II. in den Jahren 1896–1900*, pp. 244f.; Obst, *Die politischen Reden*, pp. 224f.

79 Kaiser Wilhelm II to Bülow, 23 November 1900, PA AA R 3474.

80 Bülow, speech of 23 November 1900, *Stenographische Berichte über die Verhandlungen des Reichstages*, 10. Legislaturperiode, 2. Session, Bd. 179, p. 125. See Wielandt and Kaschner, *Die Reichstagsdebatten über den deutschen Kriegseinsatz in China*, pp. 192f.

81 Richthofen to Mumm, 9 May 1901, *Große Politik*, XVI, No. 4910.

82 Bülow to Kaiser Wilhelm II, 10 May 1901, ibid., No. 4911.

83 Kaiser Wilhelm II to Waldersee, 11 May 1901, Meisner, III, p. 138, footnote.

84 See above, p. 67ff.

85 Kaiser Wilhelm II, marginal comment on Bülow's report of 10 May 1901, *Große Politik*, XVI, No. 4911.

86 Bülow to Kaiser Wilhelm II, 11 May 1901, ibid., No. 4912.

87 On Waldersee's recall Wilhelm's sister Charlotte mocked: 'Wald[ersee's] return home is of no interest whatever to me, unless, that is, he is perhaps to be made Reich Chancellor as a reward for his heroic deeds!' Hereditary Princess Charlotte of Saxe-Meiningen to Schweninger, 10 June 1901, BA Berlin, Schweninger Papers, Nr 130.

88 Eulenburg to Bülow, 4 June 1901, *Eulenburgs Korrespondenz*, III, No. 1449.

89 Kaiser Wilhelm II to Bülow, 14 May 1901, *Große Politik*, XVI, No. 4917.

90 Ludwig Dehio, *Gleichgewicht oder Hegemonie. Betrachtungen über ein Grundproblem der neuen Staatengeschichte*, Darmstadt 1996, p. 325.

91 The British government's position with regard to the Baghdad railway project was defined on the occasion of Wilhelm II's visit to England in November 1907. See Gooch and Temperley, *British Documents*, VI, Nos. 62–6. See also below, pp. 589–94.

92 On Russia's attitude see Isvolsky to Benckendorff, 6/19 December 1907, printed ibid., p. 101.

93 Andreas Hillgruber, 'Zwischen Hegemonie und Weltpolitik. Das Problem der Kontinuität von Bismarck bis Bethmann Hollweg', in Michael Stürmer, ed., *Das kaiserliche Deutschland. Politik und Gesellschaft 1870–1918*, Kronberg 1977, p. 199.

94 Kaiser Wilhelm II, marginal note on Metternich to Bülow 17 June 1907, *Große Politik*; XXI/2, No. 7223.

95 On the romantic associations of the term 'Bagdadbahn' in Germany see Friedrich Rosen, *Aus einem diplomatischen Wanderleben*, Berlin 1931–59, I, p. 65; Fesser, *Der Traum vom Platz an der Sonne*, p. 49.

96 Schöllgen, *Imperialismus und Gleichgewicht*, p. 117. See Curd-Torsten Weick, *Die schwierige Balance: Kontinuitäten und Brüche deutscher Türkeipolitik*, Münster 2002, pp. 11ff.

97 See Röhl, *The Kaiser's Personal Monarchy*, pp. 125f.

98 See Karl Helfferich, *Georg von Siemens. Ein Lebensbild aus Deutschlands großer Zeit*, 3 vols., Berlin 1923, III, pp. 55ff.

99 Sultan Abdul Hamid II to Tewfik Pasha, 6 October 1891, *Große Politik*, XIV/2, No. 3961, annex.

100 On Kaulla see Helfferich, *Georg von Siemens*, III, pp. 31ff.

101 Marschall to Hatzfeldt, 6 January 1893, *Große Politik*, XIV/2, No. 3965, note.

102 On Abdul Hamid II see Joan Haslip, *Der Sultan. Das Leben Abd al-Hamids II.*, Munich 1968; Wolfgang Gust, *Das Imperium der Sultane. Eine Geschichte des Osmanischen Reiches*, Munich 1995, pp. 339ff.

103 Radolin to Caprivi, 23 December 1892, with the Kaiser's marginal comment, *Große Politik*, XIV/2, No. 3963.

104 Marschall to Hatzfeldt, 6 January 1893, ibid., No. 3965.

105 See Röhl, *The Kaiser's Personal Monarchy*, pp. 840f.; Bülow, *Denkwürdigkeiten*, I, pp. 15f.

106 Kaiser Wilhelm II, marginal notes on Marschall's report of 2 February 1902, *Große Politik*, XVII, No. 5247.

107 Johann Manzenreiter, *Die Bagdadbahn als Beispiel für die Entstehung des Finanzimperialismus in Europa (1872–1903)*, Bochum 1982, p. 193. The report was omitted from the official publication *Große Politik*. It is printed in its entirety in Schöllgen, *Imperialismus und Gleichgewicht*, pp. 444–52.

108 Ibid., pp. 451f.

109 On Wilhelm II's visit to Constantinople, Haifa, Jerusalem, Bethlehem, Beirut and Damascus in the autumn of 1898, see Röhl, *The Kaiser's Personal Monarchy*, pp. 944–54.

110 Helfferich, *Georg von Siemens*, III, p. 87.

111 Mumm to Marschall, 17 May 1898, Bülow to Kaiser Wilhelm II, 30 September 1898, *Große Politik*, XIV/2, Nos. 3976 and 3977; Schöllgen, *Imperialismus und Gleichgewicht*, p. 121.

112 Hatzfeldt to Hohenlohe, 30 November 1899, *Große Politik*, XIV/2, No. 3995.

113 Bülow to Kaiser Wilhelm II, 17 March 1899, ibid., No. 3980.

114 Rosen, *Aus einem diplomatischen Wanderleben*, I, p. 66.

115 Penzler, *Fürst Bülows Reden*, I, p. 32.

116 Ladislaus von Szögyény-Marich to Agenor Graf Goluchowski, 6 December 1899, HHStA Vienna, PA III Preußen, Karton 152, Bl. 358f.

117 Bülow to Kaiser Wilhelm II, 30 September 1898, *Große Politik*, XIV/2, No. 3977.

118 Bülow's submission to the Kaiser of 17 March 1899 with Wilhelm's marginal notes, ibid., No. 3980.

119 Grierson to Bigge, 18 March 1899, RA VIC/I 62/6, cited in Röhl, *The Kaiser's Personal Monarchy*, p. 988.

120 Kaiser Wilhelm II, marginal note on Hatzfeldt's report of 11 May 1899, *Große Politik*, XIV/2, No. 4004.

121 Grey to King Edward VII, 13 November 1907, RA VIC/W 52/58.

122 Eulenburg to Bülow, 10 July 1899, *Eulenburgs Korrespondenz*, III, No. 1396.

123 Bülow's marginal note on Marschall's report of 4 April 1900, *Große Politik*, XVII, No. 5220.

124 Kaiser Wilhelm II to Auswärtiges Amt, 19 August 1900, Miquel to Bülow, 29 August 1900, Kaiser Wilhelm II, marginal note on Marschall's report of 5 September 1900, *Große Politik*, XVII, Nos. 5223–5.

125 Kaiser Wilhelm II, marginal comment on Bülow's report of 2 February 1899, ibid., XIV/2, No. 3996.

126 Hatzfeldt to Hohenlohe, 17 March 1899, ibid., No. 3997, note.

127 Mühlberg to Eckardstein, 31 January 1900, ibid., XVII, No. 5213.

128 Kaiser Wilhelm II, marginal comment on Marschall's report of 6 June 1899, ibid., XIV/2, No. 3988.

129 Kaiser Wilhelm II, marginal note on Richthofen's report of 6 September 1901, ibid., XVII, No. 5298 See Chapter 7 below, p. 170.

130 Bülow's memorandum, 18 April 1899, *Große Politik*, XIV/2, No. 4017. See the comments of the Russian ambassador Count Osten-Sacken in A. S. Jerussalimski, *Die Außenpolitik*

und die Diplomatie des Deutschen Imperialismus Ende des 19. Jahrhunderts, Berlin 1954, p. 691, note 142.

131 Radolin to Hohenlohe, 29 June 1899, *Große Politik*, XIV/2, No. 4022.

132 Kaiser Wilhelm II, marginal note on Radolin's report of 29 June 1899, ibid.

133 Ibid. See above, p. 62.

134 Kaiser Wilhelm II, marginal note on Bülow's report of 4 July 1899, *Große Politik*, XIV/2, No. 4025.

135 Cited in Schöllgen, *Imperialismus und Gleichgewicht*, p. 117.

136 Kaiser Wilhelm II, marginal comments on Bülow's report of 10 May 1901, *Große Politik*, XVI, No. 4911.

137 Paul Rohrbach, *Die Bagdadbahn*, Berlin 1911, pp. 18f.

138 Helfferich, *Georg von Siemens*, III, pp. 109f.

139 Kaiser Wilhelm II, marginal note on a report from Tehran of 5 November 1902, *Große Politik*, XVII, No. 5356.

140 See Wilhelm II's sharply critical comments of 24 October 1901 on Russia's Foreign Minister Lamsdorff and the collaboration of Russia and France in Constantinople, ibid., XVIII/1, No. 5677.

141 Rosen, memorandum of 31 January 1903, ibid., XVII, No. 5252.

142 Kaiser Wilhelm II, marginal note on Bernstorff's report of 25 April 1903, ibid., No. 5361.

143 Bülow to Kaiser Wilhelm II, 26 April 1903, ibid., No. 5262.

144 Kaiser Wilhelm II, marginal comment on Bülow's submission of 26 April 1903, ibid.

5   THE SHABBY COMPROMISE: WILHELM II AND BÜLOW'S CHANCELLORSHIP

1 Mommsen, *War der Kaiser an allem schuld?*, pp. 7–12 and 92ff.

2 Gerd Fesser, *Reichskanzler Bernhard Fürst von Bülow*, Berlin 1991 (Leipzig 2003), pp. 63f., 78, 131 and 156.

3 Clark, *Kaiser Wilhelm II*, pp. 94–9.

4 Canis, *Von Bismarck zur Weltpolitik*, pp. 342 and 350f.

5 Konrad Canis, *Der Weg in den Abgrund. Deutsche Außenpolitik 1902–1914*, Paderborn 2011.

6 Willibald Gutsche, *Wilhelm II. Der letzte Kaiser des Deutschen Reiches. Eine Biographie*, Berlin 1991, p. 111.

7 See in particular Peter Winzen, *Im Schatten Wilhelms II. Bülows und Eulenburgs Poker um die Macht im Kaiserreich*, Cologne 2011, passim. See also Peter Winzen, *Bernhard Fürst von Bülow. Weltmachtstratege ohne Fortune – Wegbereiter der großen Katastrophe*, Göttingen and Zürich 2003; Peter Winzen, *Reichskanzler Bernhard von Bülow. Mit Weltmachtphantasien in den Ersten Weltkrieg*, Regensburg 2013.

8 See Röhl, *Young Wilhelm*, p. 549.

9 See especially Winzen, *Im Schatten Wilhelms II.*, passim. See also Peter Winzen, *Freundesliebe am Hof Kaiser Wilhelms II.*, Norderstedt 2010.

10 Peter Winzen, *Das Ende der Kaiserherrlichkeit. Die Skandalprozesse um die homosexuellen Berater Wilhelms II. 1907–1909*, Cologne and Weimar 2010.

11 Katharine Anne Lerman, *The Chancellor as Courtier. Bernhard von Bülow and the Governance of Germany, 1900–1909*, Cambridge 1990, pp. 248ff. See Katharine Anne Lerman, 'Bismarck's Heir: Chancellor Bernhard von Bülow and the National Idea 1890–1918', in John Breuilly, ed., *The State of Germany*, London 1992, pp. 103–27. See also Katharine Anne Lerman, 'The Kaiser's Elite? Wilhelm II and the Berlin Administration, 1890–1914', in Annika Mombauer and Wilhelm Deist, eds., *The Kaiser. New Research on Wilhelm II's Role in Imperial Germany*, Cambridge 2003, pp. 63–90.

12 Isabel V. Hull, 'Bernhard von Bülow (1849–1929)', in Wilhelm von Sternburg, ed., *Die deutschen Kanzler von Bismarck bis Schmidt*, Königstein/Ts. 1985, pp. 69f.

13 Jagemann to Brauer, 8 November 1899, Fuchs, *Großherzog von Baden*, IV, No. 2027. See Röhl, *The Kaiser's Personal Monarchy*, pp. 873ff.

14 Jagemann to Brauer, 1 December 1899, Fuchs, *Großherzog von Baden*, IV, No. 2042.

15 Jagemann to Brauer, 20 November 1899, ibid., No. 2036.

16 Jagemann to Brauer, 24 November 1899, ibid., No. 2040.

17 Waldersee, diary for 29 January 1899, GStA Berlin, Waldersee Papers; cf. Meisner, II, pp. 426f.

18 Waldersee, diary for 21 January 1899, ibid.; cf. Meisner, II, p. 425.

19 Waldersee, diary for 5 October 1899, ibid.; omitted in Meisner, II, pp. 434f.

20 Waldersee, diary for 12 February 1900, ibid.; omitted in Meisner, II, p. 444.

21 Waldersee, diary for 16 May 1900, ibid.; omitted in Meisner, II, p. 447.

22 Waldersee, diary for 5 October 1899, ibid.; omitted in Meisner, II, pp. 434f.

23 Waldersee, diary for 9 January 1900, ibid.; omitted in Meisner, II, p. 441.

24 Waldersee, diary for 20 January 1900, ibid.; cf. Meisner, II, pp. 442f.

25 Waldersee, diary for 22 August 1899, ibid.; Meisner, II, pp. 431f. See also Waldersee's diary for 20 January 1900, ibid.; partly in Meisner, II, pp. 442f.

26 Goßler to Hohenlohe, 18 February 1900, Hohenlohe, *Denkwürdigkeiten der Reichskanzlerzeit*, p. 562. The Chancellor feared the interference of the Kaiserin and of 'the entire pious clique of Berlin'. Chlodwig Hohenlohe to Elise Hohenlohe, 19 February 1900, ibid., pp. 562f.

27 The recent research of Peter Winzen has thrown astonishing new light on Bülow's character and his rise to power. See Winzen, *Bernhard Fürst von Bülow. Weltmachtstratege ohne Fortune*; and in particular Winzen, *Im Schatten Wilhelms II.*

28 Bülow to Grand Duke Friedrich I of Baden, 13 February and 31 December 1899, Fuchs, *Großherzog von Baden*, IV, Nos. 1941 and 2054; Hohenlohe's journal, 16 October 1900, Hohenlohe, *Denkwürdigkeiten der Reichskanzlerzeit*, pp. 591f.

29 Jagemann to Brauer, 28 June 1898 and 18 October 1900, Fuchs, *Großherzog von Baden*, IV, Nos. 1868 and 2114.

30 Bülow's strategy is searchingly analysed in Winzen's *Im Schatten Wilhelms II.*, pp. 312–25.

31 Bülow to Lindenau, 20 November 1897, cited in Katharine Anne Lerman, 'The Decisive Relationship. Kaiser Wilhelm II and Chancellor Bernhard von Bülow 1900–1905', in John C. G. Röhl and Nicolaus Sombart, eds., *Kaiser Wilhelm II. New Interpretations*, Cambridge 1982, p. 223. See Winzen, *Im Schatten Wilhelms II.*, p. 315. Also Szögyény's report of 2 February 1898, quoted ibid., p. 319.

32 Bülow to Holstein, 24 November 1899, Lerman, 'Decisive Relationship', p. 227.

33 Waldersee, diary for 29 January 1899, GStA Berlin, Waldersee Papers; cf. Meisner, II, pp. 426f.

34 Waldersee, diary for 16 May 1900, ibid.; omitted in Meisner, II, p. 447.

35 Waldersee, diary for 21 January and 29 October 1899, ibid.; cf. Meisner, II, pp. 425 and 437f.; also the diary for 16 May 1900, ibid.; not in Meisner, II, p. 445.

36 Waldersee, diary for 22 March 1899, ibid.; omitted in Meisner, II, p. 428.

37 Waldersee, diary for 14 September 1899, ibid.; cf. Meisner, II, pp. 432f.

38 See Wilmowski to Hohenlohe, 23 October 1899, Bülow to Hohenlohe, 15 March 1900, Hohenlohe, *Denkwürdigkeiten der Reichskanzlerzeit*, pp. 532f., 568.

39 Waldersee, diary for 29 October 1899, GStA Berlin, Waldersee Papers; cf. Meisner, II, pp. 437f.; also the diary for 16 May 1900, ibid.; not in Meisner, II, p. 445.

40 Waldersee, diary for 20 and 28 January and 10 February 1900, ibid.; cf. Meisner, II, pp. 442ff. Waldersee's suspicion that Schoen's appointment was the work of the Empress Frederick is not borne out by the available evidence.

41 Waldersee, diary for 29 March 1900, ibid.; omitted in Meisner, II, p. 444.

42 Rudolf Vierhaus, ed., *Das Tagebuch der Baronin Spitzemberg. Aufzeichnungen aus der Hofgesellschaft des Hohenzollernreiches*, Göttingen 1960, diary for 9 July 1900, pp. 398f. Cited below as Vierhaus, *Tagebuch*.

43 Waldersee, diary for 24 April and 16 May 1900, GStA Berlin, Waldersee Papers; cf. Meisner, II, pp. 445ff.

44 Waldersee, diary for November 1900, ibid., omitted in Meisner, III, p. 6.

45 Brauer to Grand Duke Friedrich I of Baden, 5 August 1900, Fuchs, *Großherzog von Baden*, IV, No. 2105.

46 Hohenlohe's journal, 17 October 1900, Hohenlohe, *Denkwürdigkeiten der Reichskanzlerzeit*, p. 592.

47 Spitzemberg, diary for 19 October 1900, Vierhaus, *Tagebuch*, p. 401.

48 Jagemann to Brauer, 1 March 1899, Fuchs, *Großherzog von Baden*, IV, No. 1951.

49 Waldersee, diary for 29 January 1899, GStA Berlin, Waldersee Papers; omitted in Meisner, II, p. 426. See Hohenlohe's journal, 15 and 16 October 1900, Hohenlohe, *Denkwürdigkeiten der Reichskanzlerzeit*, pp. 590ff.

50 Waldersee, diary for 24 April 1900, GStA Berlin, Waldersee Papers; omitted in Meisner, II, p. 445.

51 Waldersee, diary for 19 February 1899, ibid.; not in Meisner, II, p. 428.

52 See the bitter complaints of the dismissed ambassador in Münster to Hohenlohe, 2 December 1900, Hohenlohe, *Denkwürdigkeiten der Reichskanzlerzeit*, p. 598.

53 Hohenlohe's journal, 15 and 16 October 1900, ibid., pp. 590ff.

54 See Hohenlohe to Bülow, 27 October 1899, Hohenlohe to Posadowsky, 29 October 1899 and Chlodwig Hohenlohe to Alexander Hohenlohe, 17 December 1899, ibid., pp. 535f. and 551. See also Hohenlohe to Grand Duke Friedrich I of Baden, 20 November 1899, Fuchs, *Großherzog von Baden*, IV, No. 2037.

55 Spitzemberg, diary for 19 October 1900, Vierhaus, *Tagebuch*, p. 401.

56 Jagemann to Brauer, 4 and 5 May 1901, Fuchs, *Großherzog von Baden*, IV, Nos. 2180 and 2181.

57 Eulenburg to Kaiser Wilhelm II, 22 October 1900, *Eulenburgs Korrespondenz*, III, No. 1438.

58 Spitzemberg, diary for 19 October 1900, Vierhaus, *Tagebuch*, p. 401.

59 Spitzemberg, diary for 23 February 1903, ibid., p. 426.

60 See in particular Bülow to Eulenburg, 23 July 1896, quoted in Röhl, *The Kaiser's Personal Monarchy*, p. 826. Hildegard von Spitzemberg assumed, probably correctly, that Below had his information from her own brother, Axel Varnbüler, the Württemberg envoy in Berlin and Eulenburg's intimate friend.

61 Herbert Fürst von Bismarck to his brother-in-law Kuno Graf Rantzau, 4 November 1900, cited in Canis, *Von Bismarck zur Weltpolitik*, p. 351.

62 Spitzemberg, diary for 10 May 1901 and 1 February 1901, Vierhaus, *Tagebuch*, pp. 407 and 413.

63 Bülow to Holstein, 1 August 1902, *Holstein Papers*, IV, No. 804.

64 Bülow to Holstein, 4 October 1902, ibid., No. 808.

65 Bülow to Kaiser Wilhelm II, 31 August 1903, GStA Berlin, BPHA Rep. 53J Lit. B Nr 16a.

66 Bülow to Kaiser Wilhelm II, 2 April 1902, ibid.

67 Bülow to Kaiser Wilhelm II, 2 August 1904, ibid.

68 Bülow to Kaiser Wilhelm II, 31 August 1903, ibid.

69 Bülow to Kaiser Wilhelm II, 2 August 1904, ibid.

70 See Brauer to Grand Duke Friedrich I of Baden, 28 July 1904, Fuchs, *Großherzog von Baden*, IV, No. 2476.

71 Waldersee, diary for late December 1901, GStA Berlin, Waldersee Papers; cf. Meisner, III, p. 176.

72 Waldersee, diary for 19 October 1902, ibid.; cf. Meisner, III, pp. 191f.

73 Holstein to Bülow, 4 August 1901, *Holstein Papers*, IV, No. 783.

74 Waldersee, diary for late December 1901, GStA Berlin, Waldersee Papers; cf. Meisner, III, p. 176.

75 Waldersee, diary for 16 November 1903, ibid.; cf. Meisner, III, p. 220.

76 Holstein, diary for 11 January 1902, *Holstein Papers*, IV, No. 792.

77 Ragnhild Fiebig-von Hase, *Lateinamerika als Konfliktherd der deutsch-amerikanischen Beziehungen 1890–1903*, 2 vols., Göttingen 1986, II, p. 871.

78 Waldersee, diary for May 1903, GStA Berlin, Waldersee Papers; omitted in Meisner, III, pp. 214f.

79 Waldersee, diary for 28 May 1903, ibid.; omitted in Meisner, III, p. 215. A similar comment was made by Waldersee on 2 February 1903, ibid.

80 Waldersee, diary for 31 January 1904, ibid.; not in Meisner, III, pp. 228ff.

81 Bülow to Holstein, 3 August 1901, *Holstein Papers*, IV, p. 234.

82 Spitzemberg, diary for 31 October 1901, Vierhaus, *Tagebuch*, p. 411.

83 Holstein, diary for 7 November 1902, *Holstein Papers*, IV, No. 811.

84 Holstein, diary for 11 November 1902, ibid., No. 812.

85 Spitzemberg, diary for 26 July 1903, Vierhaus, *Tagebuch*, p. 432.

86 Spitzemberg, diary for 21 December 1902, ibid., p. 423. See also Bülow to Holstein, 4 October 1902, *Holstein Papers*, IV, No. 808.

87 Bernhard Schwertfeger, ed., *Kaiser und Kabinettschef. Nach eigenen Aufzeichnungen und dem Briefwechsel des Wirklichen Geheimen Rats Rudolf von Valentini*, Oldenburg 1931 (cited below as Valentini, *Kaiser und Kabinettschef*), p. 60.

88 Spitzemberg, diary for 26 July 1903, Vierhaus, *Tagebuch*, p. 432.

89 Jagemann to Brauer, 4 February and 5 March 1903, Fuchs, *Großherzog von Baden*, IV, Nos. 2370 and 2396. Cf. Jagemann to Reck, 21 March 1903, ibid., No. 2404. See below, pp. 119f. See also, for Bülow's behaviour in the succession crisis in Lippe in 1904, Spitzemberg, diary for 24 October 1904, Vierhaus, *Tagebuch*, p. 443; Brauer to Bodman, 2 December 1904; Fuchs, *Großherzog von Baden*, IV, No. 2490.

90 Minutes of the meeting of the Prussian Ministry of State on 23 October 1900, GStA Berlin. See *Die Protokolle des Preussischen Staatsministeriums 1817–1934/38, Acta Borussica, Neue Folge*, ed. Reinhold Zilch for the Berlin-Brandenburgische Akademie der Wissenschaften, 1. series, IX, Hildesheim, Zürich and New York 2001, IX, pp. 49f. See also Bülow, *Denkwürdigkeiten*, I, pp. 389f. Also Lerman, *Chancellor as Courtier*, pp. 49f.; Canis, *Von Bismarck zur Weltpolitik*, pp. 350f.

91 See Röhl, *The Kaiser's Personal Monarchy*, p. 826.

92 Jagemann to Brauer, 18 October 1900, Fuchs, *Großherzog von Baden*, IV, No. 2114.

93 Waldersee, diary for late September 1902, GStA Berlin, Waldersee Papers; this passage was omitted in Meisner, III, pp. 186ff.

94 Waldersee, diary for 25 October 1902, ibid.; not in Meisner, III, p. 192.

95 Waldersee, diary for May 1903, ibid.; not in Meisner, III, pp. 214f.

96 Mudra to Colmar Freiherr von der Goltz, 24 October 1900, BA-MA Freiburg-im-Breisgau, von der Goltz Papers, N 737/20.

97 Hohenlohe's journal, 28 April 1901, Hohenlohe, *Denkwürdigkeiten der Reichskanzlerzeit*, pp. 606f.

98 Jagemann to Brauer, 31 March 1901, Fuchs, *Großherzog von Baden*, IV, No. 2166.

99 The ministerial crisis of May 1901 is analysed at length in Lerman, *Chancellor as Courtier*, pp. 66ff.

100 Eulenburg to Bülow, 14 May 1901, *Eulenburgs Korrespondenz*, II, No. 1448. In a letter to Wilhelm II Hinzpeter had the temerity to refer to the 'frayed nerves of the Kaiser', but he went on to praise the decisive manner in which the monarchy had overcome the confusion and 'cleared the way for a renewed attempt to be made to reach its immovable goals'. Hinzpeter to Kaiser Wilhelm II., 6 May 1901, with the Kaiser's marginal comments, GStA Berlin, BPHA Rep. 53J Lit. H Nr 1.

101 Jagemann to Brauer, 4 and 5 May 1901, Fuchs, *Großherzog von Baden*, IV, Nos. 2180 and 2181.

102 Bülow to Eulenburg, telegram, mid May 1901, *Eulenburgs Korrespondenz*, III, p. 2018; Lerman, *Chancellor as Courtier*, pp. 71–3. See Spitzemberg, diary for 9 September 1901, Vierhaus, *Tagebuch*, pp. 409f.

103 On this see Lerman, *Chancellor as Courtier*, p. 70.

104 Szögyény to Goluchowski, 6 May 1901, quoted in *Eulenburgs Korrespondenz*, III, p. 2018.

105 Lerman, *Chancellor as Courtier*, p. 70.

106 Jagemann to Brauer, 5 May 1901, Fuchs, *Großherzog von Baden*, IV, No. 2181.

107 Lerman, *Chancellor as Courtier*, p. 71.

108 Hinzpeter to Kaiser Wilhelm II, 6 May 1901, with the Kaiser's marginal comments, GStA Berlin, BPHA Rep. 53J Lit. H Nr 1.

109 Jagemann to Brauer, 5 May 1901, Fuchs, *Großherzog von Baden*, IV, No. 2181.

110 Eulenburg to Bülow, 14 May 1901, *Eulenburgs Korrespondenz*, III, No. 1448.

111 Lerman, *Chancellor as Courtier*, p. 112.

112 Eulenburg to Bülow, 14 May 1901, *Eulenburgs Korrespondenz*, III, No. 1448; August Eulenburg to Philipp Eulenburg, 16 May 1901, ibid., p. 2019.

113 Cf. Jagemann to Brauer, 5 and 8 May 1901, Fuchs, *Großherzog von Baden*, IV, Nos. 2181 and 2182.

114 Waldersee, diary for late December 1901, GStA Berlin, Waldersee Papers; cf. Meisner, III, pp. 174f. On the state of Waldersee's health see Spitzemberg, diary for 12 December 1901, Vierhaus, *Tagebuch*, p. 412.

115 Waldersee, diary for 15 February 1902, GStA Berlin, Waldersee Papers; Meisner, III, pp. 178f.

116 Waldersee, diary for 12 October 1902, ibid.; omitted in Meisner, III, pp. 190f.

117 Waldersee, diary for 17 December 1902, ibid.; Meisner, III, p. 198. Cf. Wilhelm II, *Ereignisse und Gestalten aus den Jahren 1878–1918*, Berlin, Leipzig 1927, p. 149.

118 See Lerman, *Chancellor as Courtier*, p. 113; *Berliner Tageblatt*, 26 June 1902, Nr 319.

119 Mudra to Colmar Freiherr von der Goltz, 13 May 1903, BA-MA Freiburg-im-Breisgau, von der Goltz Papers, N 737, Mappe 23.

120 Waldersee, diary for late December 1901, GStA Berlin, Waldersee Papers; cf. Meisner, III, pp. 174f.

121 Jagemann to Brauer, 18 May 1903, Fuchs, *Großherzog von Baden*, IV, No. 2415.

122 Jagemann to Brauer, 20 October 1900, ibid., No. 2115.

123 Waldersee, diary for 28 May 1903, GStA Berlin, Waldersee Papers; not in Meisner, III, p. 215.

124 Waldersee, diary for 31 January 1904, ibid.; cf. Meisner, III, pp. 228ff.

125 Zedlitz-Trützschler, diary for 24 May 1904, *Zwölf Jahre*, pp. 66f.

126 Cited in Zedlitz-Trützschler, diary for 3 November 1904, ibid., p. 88.

127 Jagemann to Brauer, 4 February and 5 March 1903, Fuchs, *Großherzog von Baden*, IV, Nos. 2370 and 2396. Cf. Jagemann to Reck, 21 March 1903, ibid., No. 2404.

128 Jagemann to Brauer, 10 March 1902, ibid., No. 2270.

129 Jagemann to Brauer, 11 and 27 March 1902, Jagemann to Grand Duke Friedrich I of Baden, 6 April 1902, ibid., Nos. 2272, 2276 and 2279.

130 Jagemann to Brauer, 30 January 1903, ibid., No. 2369.

131 Jagemann to Brauer, 4 February 1903, ibid., No. 2370.

132 See e. g. Kaiser Wilhelm II's marginal notes on Eckardstein to Bülow, 6 April 1901, *Große Politik*, XVII, No. 4999; Rich, *Friedrich von Holstein*, II, pp. 631 and 645f.

133 Holstein to Marie Bülow, 5 July 1904, *Holstein Papers*, IV, No. 835. Cf. Holstein to Bülow, 25 June 1904, Holstein to Hammann, 6 July 1904, ibid., Nos. 828 and 836.

134 Kaiser Wilhelm II, marginal notes of 26 September 1904 on Ballin to Grumme, 24 September 1904, GStA Berlin, BPHA Rep. 53 Nr 361.

135 Kaiser Wilhelm II, marginal note on Bülow's report of 4 January 1904, *Große Politik*, XIX/1, No. 5972. See below, p. 266.

136 Spitzemberg, diary for 29 May 1904, Vierhaus, *Tagebuch*, pp. 440f.

137 Zedlitz-Trützschler, diary for 24 May 1904, *Zwölf Jahre*, pp. 66f.

138 Zedlitz-Trützschler, diary for 22 August 1904, ibid., p. 81.

139 Zedlitz-Trützschler, diary for 1 October 1904, ibid., pp. 81ff.

140 Rudolf von Valentini, manuscript, 'Aus meinem Leben', Teil II, Bundesarchiv Koblenz, Valentini Papers, Kl. Erw. Nr 341–1. Cf. Valentini, *Kaiser und Kabinettschef*, pp. 72f.

141 Zedlitz-Trützschler, diary for 24 December 1904, *Zwölf Jahre*, pp. 104f.

142 Zedlitz-Trützschler, diary for 29 November 1903, ibid., pp. 54f.

143 Zedlitz-Trützschler, diary for 27 February and 21 July 1904, ibid., pp. 65f. and 77ff.

144 Zedlitz-Trützschler, diary for 24 November 1903, ibid., p. 54.

145 Zedlitz-Trützschler, diary for 3 January 1904, ibid., pp. 59f.

146 Spitzemberg, diary for 26 July 1903, Vierhaus, *Tagebuch*, p. 432.

147 Spitzemberg, diary for 15 April 1904, ibid., p. 439.

148 Spitzemberg, diary for 24 October 1902, ibid., p. 421.

149 Holstein to Radolin, 12 December 1901, *Holstein Papers*, IV, No. 790. See also Holstein to Radolin, 6 November 1902 and 13 January 1905, ibid., Nos. 810 and 874.

150 Holstein to Radolin, 12 December 1901, ibid., No. 790.

151 Holstein to Radolin, 31 January 1902, ibid., No. 797.

152 Spitzemberg, diary for 7 January 1903, Vierhaus, *Tagebuch*, p. 424.

153 Valentini, *Kaiser und Kabinettschef*, p. 57. See Bülow, *Denkwürdigkeiten*, I, pp. 63ff.

154 Spitzemberg, diary for 18 January 1903, Vierhaus, *Tagebuch*, p. 425.

155 Spitzemberg, diary for 28 August 1903, ibid., p. 433.

156 Spitzemberg, diary for 14 March and 8 May 1903, ibid., pp. 427ff. and 430. In April 1904 Baroness Spitzemberg complained of the 'unbounded arbitrariness and frivolous superficiality' of the way the Kaiser appointed people to high office. Ibid., p. 440.

157 Zedlitz-Trützschler, diary for 1 October 1904, *Zwölf Jahre*, pp. 81ff.

158 Zedlitz-Trützschler, diary for 22 February 1904, ibid., pp. 61ff. See also the diary for 24 May 1904, ibid., pp. 66f.

6   WILHELM II AND THE GERMANS, 1900 TO 1904

1 Mommsen, *War der Kaiser an allem schuld?*, pp. 7–12, 92ff.

2 Waldersee, diary for 20 January 1900, GStA Berlin, Waldersee Papers; printed in part in Meisner, II, pp. 442f.

3 Waldersee, diary for 2 February 1903, ibid.; Meisner, III, p. 205.

4 Spitzemberg, diary for 24 October 1902, Vierhaus, *Tagebuch*, p. 421.

5 See Röhl, *The Kaiser's Personal Monarchy*, chapters 19 and 20.

6 See ibid., pp. 851f. Cf. Clark, *Kaiser Wilhelm II*, p. 171.

7 See Röhl, *The Kaiser's Personal Monarchy*, pp. 1033f.

8 Kaiser Wilhelm II, speech in Hamburg on 18 October 1899, Penzler, *Die Reden Kaiser Wilhelms II. in den Jahren 1896–1900*, pp. 176f.; Obst, *Die politischen Reden*, pp. 191–3.

9 *Stenographische Berichte über die Verhandlungen des Reichstages*, 12 December 1899.

10 Hohenlohe-Schillingsfürst, 12 December 1899, ibid.

11 *Stenographische Berichte über die Verhandlungen des Reichstages*, 13 December 1899.

12 Lucanus to Kaiser Wilhelm II., 14 December 1899, GStA Berlin, BPHA Rep. 53J Lit L Nr 12. See below, pp. 131ff.

13 Hereditary Prince Ernst zu Hohenlohe-Langenburg to his father Hermann Prince zu Hohenlohe-Langenburg, 15 December 1899, Hohenlohe-Zentralarchiv, Schloß Neuenstein, NL Hermann Hohenlohe-Langenburg, Bü 64.

14 Lucanus to Kaiser Wilhelm II, 14 December 1899, GStA Berlin, BPHA Rep. 53J Lit L Nr 12.

15 Otto von Bismarck, *Gedanken und Erinnerungen*, 2 vols., Berlin and Stuttgart 1898.

16 *Stenographische Berichte über die Verhandlungen des Reichstages*, 14 December 1899.

17 *Stenographische Berichte über die Verhandlungen des Reichstages*, 22 March 1900.

18 Bülow to Eulenburg, 22 November 1900, *Eulenburgs Korrespondenz*, III, No. 1439.

19 Eulenburg to Bülow, 21 November 1900, ibid., p. 2010.

20 Eulenburg to Kaiser Wilhelm II., 22 November 1900, ibid., No. 1440. See above, p. 85.

21 Eulenburg to Bülow, 16 February 1901, ibid., No. 1446.

22 Kaiser Wilhelm II to Eulenburg, 23 November 1900, ibid., No. 1441.

23 See Empress Frederick to Crown Princess Sophie of Greece, September 1898, Lee, *The Empress Frederick writes to Sophie*, pp. 282f.

24 See Empress Frederick to Kaiser Wilhelm II, 6 April 1900, GStA Berlin, BPHA Rep. 52T Nr 13; Empress Frederick to Crown Princess Sophie of Greece, September 1898, Lee, *The Empress Frederick Writes to Sophie*, pp. 282f.; Kaiser Wilhelm II to Albert Edward Prince of Wales, 31 July 1900, RA VIC/T 10/126. Also Queen Victoria to Kaiser Wilhelm II, 12 August 1900, GStA Berlin, BPHA Rep. 53 W3 Nr 11; Dowager Queen Margherita of Italy to Kaiser Wilhelm II, 17 August 1900, GStA Berlin, BPHA Rep. 53 Nr 225.

25 Empress Frederick to Crown Princess Sophie of Greece, July 1900, Lee, *The Empress Frederick Writes to Sophie*, p. 333.

26 Kaiser Wilhelm II to Queen Victoria, 17 November 1900, RA VIC/I 62/112. See Theodor Herzl to Grand Duke Friedrich I of Baden, 17 November 1900, Fuchs, *Großherzog von Baden*, IV, No. 2126.

27 Empress Frederick to Queen Victoria, 17 November 1900, AdHH Schloss Fasanerie.

28 Senden-Bibran to Paul Hoffmann, 8 March 1901, Hoffmann Papers, in the possession of Dr Margot Leo, Freiburg-im-Breisgau. See also Kaiser Wilhelm II to Hereditary Prince Ernst zu Hohenlohe-Langenburg, 8 March 1901, Hohenlohe-Zentralarchiv, Schloß Neuenstein, Ernst Hohenlohe-Langenburg Papers; Max Egon II Fürst zu Fürstenberg, 24 March 1901, FFA Donaueschingen; Spitzemberg, diary for 7 March 1901, Vierhaus, *Tagebuch*, p. 407; August Eulenburg to Lord Knollys, 27 March 1901, RA VIC/Add C 07/2/Q.

29 Thurn to Goluchowski, 23 October 1901, HHStA Vienna, Hofnachrichten: Preußen.

30 Hereditary Princess Charlotte of Saxe-Meiningen to Schweninger, 10 March 1901, BA Berlin, Schweninger Papers.

31 See e. g. Karl von Eisendecher to Bülow, 7 March 1901, Fuchs, *Großherzog von Baden*, IV, No. 2156.

32 Hinzpeter to Kaiser Wilhelm II, 15 March 1901, GStA Berlin, BPHA Rep. 53J Lit H Nr 1.

33 Kaiser Wilhelm II, speech to the speakers of the Prussian House of Deputies and the Reichstag, 22 March 1901, Johannes Penzler, ed., *Die Reden Kaiser Wilhelms II. in den Jahren 1901–Ende 1905*, Leipzig 1906, pp. 14f.; Obst, *Die politischen Reden*, p. 228. See Obst, '*Einer nur ist Herr im Reiche*', pp. 255ff.

34 Thurn to Goluchowski, 23 October 1901, HHStA Vienna, Hofnachrichten: Preußen.

35 Hinzpeter to Kaiser Wilhelm II, 15 March 1901, GStA Berlin, BPHA Rep. 53J Lit H Nr 1.

36 Hinzpeter to Kaiser Wilhelm II, 24 March 1901, ibid.

37 Jagemann to Brauer, 29 March 1901, Fuchs, *Großherzog von Baden*, IV, No. 2163.

38 Ibid. See Bülow, *Denkwürdigkeiten*, I, pp. 519f.

39 Kaiser Wilhelm II, speech to the Kaiser-Alexander-Regiment in their new barracks, 28 March 1901, Penzler, *Reden Kaiser Wilhelms II. in den Jahren 1901–Ende 1905*, pp. 16–19; Obst, *Die politichen Reden*, pp. 229f., '*Einer nur ist Herr im Reiche*', pp. 257ff.

40 Eulenburg to Bülow, 9 August 1903, *Eulenburgs Korrespondenz*, III, Nr 1499. Cited in John C. G. Röhl, 'The Emperor's New Clothes', in John C. G. Röhl and Nicolaus Sombart, eds., *Kaiser Wilhelm II. New Interpretations*, Cambridge 1982, p. 31.

41 Ibid.

42 Grand Duke Friedrich I of Baden to Bülow, 31 March 1901, Fuchs, *Großherzog von Baden*, IV, No. 2165.

43 Jagemann to Brauer, 30 and 31 March 1901, ibid., Nos. 2164 and 2166.

44 Bülow to Grand Duke Friedrich I of Baden, 5 and 17 April 1901, ibid., Nos. 2168 and 2171.

45 Kaiser Wilhelm II, speech of 31 March 1901 to the leaders of the Prussian House of Lords, Penzler, *Reden Kaiser Wilhelms II. in den Jahren 1901–Ende 1905*, pp. 15f.; Obst, *Die politischen Reden*, pp. 231f.

46 Bodman to Brauer, 11 April 1901, Fuchs, *Großherzog von Baden*, IV, No. 2169.

47 Bülow to Grand Duke Friedrich I of Baden, 17 April 1901, ibid., No. 2171.

48 Imperial order of 16 April 1901, quoted ibid., pp. 307f.

49 Bülow to Grand Duke Friedrich I of Baden, 26 April 1901, ibid., No. 2173.

50 Spitzemberg, diary for 16 June 1901, Vierhaus, *Tagebuch*, pp. 408f.

51 Quoted in Zedlitz-Trützschler, *Zwölf Jahre*, p. 75.

52 Hinzpeter to Kaiser Wilhelm II, 2 December 1901, PA AA R 3901.

53 For the most recent analysis of the circumstances leading to Krupp's death see Peter Winzen, 'Der erste politische Homosexualitätsskandal im Kaiserreich: Friedrich Alfred Krupp (1854–1902)', in *Archiv der Kulturgeschichte*, 93. Band, Heft 2 (2011), 415–50; cf. Dieter Richter, 'Friedrich Alfred Krupp auf Capri. Ein Skandal und seine Geschichte', in Michael Epkenhans and Ralf Stremmel, eds., *Friedrich Alfred Krupp. Ein Unternehmer im Kaiserreich*, Munich 2010, pp. 157–77.

54 Kaiser Wilhelm II, speech at the funeral of Friedrich Alfred Krupp in Essen, 26 November 1902, Penzler, *Reden Kaiser Wilhelms II. in den Jahren 1901–Ende 1905*, pp. 136–8; Obst, *Die politischen Reden*, pp. 250ff. See Obst, '*Einer nur ist Herr im Reiche*', pp. 264ff.

55 Kaiser Wilhelm II, address to a delegation of workers in Breslau on 5 December 1902, Penzler, *Reden Kaiser Wilhelms II. in den Jahren 1901–Ende 1905*, pp. 141f.; Obst, *Die politischen Reden*, pp. 254f. See Obst, '*Einer nur ist Herr im Reiche*', pp. 266f.

56 August Bebel, speech of 22 January 1903, *Stenographische Berichte über die Verhandlungen des Reichstages, 244. Sitzung*, p. 7488. For the background see Dieter Groh, *Negative Integration und revolutionärer Attentismus: die deutsche Sozialdemokratie am Vorabend des Ersten Weltkrieges*, Frankfurt a.M. 1973; Peter Domann, *Sozialdemokratie und Kaisertum unter Wilhelm II.*, Wiesbaden 1974; Dieter Groh and Peter Brandt, '*Vaterlandslose Gesellen*'. *Sozialdemokratie und Nation 1860–1990*, Munich 1992.

57 Waldersee, diary for 11 January 1903, GStA Berlin, Waldersee Papers; cf. Meisner, III, pp. 199ff.

58 August Bebel, speech of 22 January 1903, *Stenographische Berichte über die Verhandlungen des Reichstages, 244. Sitzung*, p. 7488.

59 Waldersee, diary for 11 January 1903, GStA Berlin, Waldersee Papers; cf. Meisner, III, pp. 199ff.

60 Jagemann to Brauer, 20 January 1903, Fuchs, *Großherzog von Baden*, IV, No. 2363.

61 August Bebel, speech of 22 January 1903, *Stenographische Berichte über die Verhandlungen des Reichstages*, 244, Sitzung, 7467ff.

62 Jagemann to the Baden Foreign Minister, 23 and 24 January 1903, Fuchs, *Großherzog von Baden*, IV, Nos. 2365 and 2366.

63 Waldersee, diary for 23 January 1903, GStA Berlin, Waldersee Papers; the second half of this important entry is omitted in Meisner, III, pp. 202f.

64 Waldersee, diary for 29 January 1903, ibid.; cf. Meisner, III, pp. 203ff.

65 Lerchenfeld to Podewils, 28 March 1903, printed in Peter Rassow and Karl Erich Born, eds., *Akten zur Staatlichen Sozialpolitik in Deutschland 1890–1914*, Wiesbaden 1959, pp. 138ff.

66 Zedlitz-Trützschler, diary for 14 November 1904, *Zwölf Jahre*, pp. 92f.

67 See Hartmut Pogge von Strandmann, 'Der Kaiser and die Industriellen. Vom Primat der Rüstung', in John C. G. Röhl, ed., *Der Ort Kaiser Wilhelms II. in der deutschen Geschichte*, Munich 1991, pp. 111–29; Hartmut Pogge von Strandmann, 'Rathenau, Wilhelm II and the Perception of *Wilhelminismus*', in Annika Mombauer and Wilhelm Deist, *The Kaiser. New Research on Wilhelm II's Role in Imperial Germany*, Cambridge, 2003, pp. 259–80.

68 See Röhl, *The Kaiser's Personal Monarchy*, pp. 882–7.

69 Newspaper article of 2 April 1901, Kaiser Wilhelm und der Getreidezoll, BA Berlin, Schweninger Papers, Nr 130, Bl. 188f.

70 Hereditary Princess Charlotte of Saxe-Meiningen to Schweninger, 4 April 1901, ibid.

71 Waldersee, diary for 19 March 1902, GStA Berlin, Waldersee Papers; cf. Meisner, III, pp. 181f. See Cecil, *Wilhelm II: Emperor and Exile*, p. 118. For the background see Hans-Jürgen Puhle, *Agrarische Interessenpolitik and preußischer Konservatismus im wilhelminischen Reich (1893–1914): Ein Beitrag zur Analyse des Nationalismus in Deutschland am Beispiel des Bundes der Landwirte und der Deutsch-Konservativen Partei*, Bad Godesberg, Bonn 1975.

72 Waldersee, diary for 4 May 1902, GStA Berlin, Waldersee Papers; cf. Meisner, III, p. 185. See also Waldersee's diary for late September 1902, ibid., but omitted in Meisner, III, pp. 186ff.

73 Waldersee, diary for 12 October 1902, ibid.; Meisner, III, pp. 190f.

74 Waldersee, diary for late September and 12 October 1902, ibid.; Meisner, III, pp. 188f. and 191.

75 Waldersee, diary for 5 December 1902, ibid.; cf. Meisner, III, pp. 194ff.

76 Zedlitz-Trützschler, diary for 18 June 1904, *Zwölf Jahre*, pp. 72–4.

77 Valentini, *Kaiser and Kabinettschef*, pp. 64–6.

78 Waldersee, diary for 4 February and 21 December 1903, 31 January and 19 February 1904, GStA Berlin, Waldersee Papers; cf. Meisner, III, pp. 206, 228ff., 223f. and 231f.

79 Hinzpeter to Kaiser Wilhelm II, 6 May 1901 with the Kaiser's marginal notes, GStA Berlin, BPHA Rep. 53J Lit H Nr 1.

80 Lerchenfeld to Podewils, 28 March 1903, in Rassow and Born, *Akten zur Staatlichen Sozialpolitik*, pp. 138ff.

81 Gustav Schmoller, Schmollers Jahrbuch 1910, pp. 1267ff. Cited in Röhl, *Kaiser and his Court*, p. 145.

82 Bülow to Holstein, 4 October 1902, *Holstein Papers*, IV, No. 808.

83 Waldersee, diary for 4 February 1903, GStA Berlin, Waldersee Papers; cf. Meisner, III, p. 206.

84 Waldersee, diary for 5 January 1904, ibid.; cf. Meisner, III, pp. 224ff. See also the entry for 31 January 1904, ibid.; cf. Meisner, III, pp. 228ff.

85 Waldersee, diary for 28 April 1902, ibid.; omitted in Meisner, III, p. 185.

86 Waldersee, diary for late September and 12 and 25 October 1902, ibid.; Meisner, III, pp. 188f. and 191f.

87   Waldersee, diary for 2 February 1903, ibid.; partly omitted in Meisner, III, p. 205.

88   See Canis, *Abgrund*, pp. 18f.

89   Bülow to Holstein, 4 October 1902, *Holstein Papers*, IV, No. 808. See above, p. 150.

90   Waldersee, diary for 14 December 1902, GStA Berlin, Waldersee Papers; Meisner, III, p. 197.

91   *Vossische Zeitung*, Nos. 159 and 160 of 28 March 1914.

92   *Norddeutsche Allgemeine Zeitung*, No. 81 of 4 April 1914.

93   Wirklicher Geheimer Kriegsrat Dr. jur. Romen, 'Der gefälschte Kaiserbrief', *Der Tag*, No. 82 of 7 April 1914; Romen to Kaiser Wilhelm II, 7 April 1914, GStA Berlin, 2.2.1 Nr 3087.

94   Kaiser Wilhelm II to Anna Landgravine of Hesse, 24 July 1901, quoted from the copy in the Hessen-Thüringisches Provinzialarchiv of the Franziscan Order. I thank Frau Christine Klössel, the archivist of the Hessische Hausstiftung, Schloss Fasanerie, most warmly for sharing this document with me.

95   Kaiser Wilhelm II to Wilhelm von Wedell-Piesdorf, May 1902, Hausarchiv Burg Hohenzollern.

96   Kaiser Wilhelm II to Wilhelm von Wedell-Piesdorf, 12 May 1902, AdHH Schloss Fasanerie.

97   Kaiser Wilhelm II to Anna Landgravine of Hesse, no date, cited from the *Süddeutsche Zeitungsdienst*, 17 March 1925, Nr 63, 5. Jahrgang.

98   Bülow, *Denkwürdigkeiten*, II, pp. 97f.

99   Bülow to Kopp, 7 September 1901, PA AA Hessen 56 Nr 1, Band 1. See ibid., R 2934.

100 Bethmann Hollweg, minute of 30 March 1914, PA AA AS 510.

101 Wahnschaffe to Valentini, 9 April 1914, GStA Berlin, Valentini Papers, Nr 21.

102 Ibid.

103 Landgravine Anna of Hesse to Professor Victor Thielemann, 29 May 1915. Again I thank Frau Christine Klössel for sharing this document with me.

104 For Wilhelm's role as Supreme Bishop of the Lutheran-Calvinist Church in Germany see the contributions in Stefan Samerski, ed., *Wilhelm II. und die Religion. Facetten einer Persönlichkeit und ihres Umfelds*, Berlin 2001. See also Thomas Hartmut Benner, *Die Strahlen der Krone. Die religiöse Dimension des Kaisertums unter Wilhelm II. vor dem Hintergrund der Orientreise 1898*, Marburg 2001.

105 Olaf Blaschke, *Katholizismus und Antisemitismus im Deutschen Kaiserreich*, Göttingen 1997; Norbert Schloßmacher, *Der Antiultramontanismus im Wilhelminischen Deutschland. Ein Versuch*, in Wilfried Loth, ed., *Deutscher Katholizismus im Umbruch zur Moderne*, Stuttgart 1991, pp. 164–98; Wilfried Loth, *Katholiken im Kaiserreich. Der politische Katholizismus in der Krise des wilhelminischen Deutschlands*, Düsseldorf 1984.

106 See below, p. 508.

107 Waldersee, diary for 4 May 1902, GStA Berlin, Waldersee Papers; Meisner, III, p. 185.

108 Waldersee, diary for 19 October 1902, ibid.; these passages have been mostly omitted in Meisner, III, pp. 191f. See also Waldersee's diary for 11 January 1903, ibid.; cf. Meisner, pp. 199ff.

109 Waldersee, diary for 19 October 1902, ibid.; cf. Meisner, III, pp. 191f.

110 Waldersee, diary for 19 January 1903, ibid.; Meisner, III, pp. 201f.

111 Waldersee, diary for 4 February 1903, ibid.; Meisner, III, p. 206.

112 Waldersee, diary for 4 May 1902, ibid.; cf. Meisner, III, p. 185.

113 Waldersee, diary for 21 February 1903, ibid.; cf. Meisner, III, pp. 207f.

114 Waldersee, diary for 16 February 1903, ibid.; not in Meisner, III, p. 207.

115 Hinzpeter to Kaiser Wilhelm II, 29 May 1903, GStA Berlin, BPHA Rep. 53J Lit H Nr 1.

116 Waldersee, diary for 21 June 1903, GStA Berlin, Waldersee Papers; cf. Meisner, III, pp. 217f.

117 See Ernst Rudolf Huber, ed., *Dokumente zur deutschen Verfassungsgeschichte*, 3 vols., Stuttgart 1963–78, pp. 538f.

118 Bülow to Kaiser Wilhelm II, 24 June 1903, GStA Berlin, BPHA Rep. 53J Lit B Nr 16a.

119 Bülow to Kaiser Wilhelm II, 19 June 1903, ibid. Cf. Spitzemberg, diary for 26 July 1903, Vierhaus, *Tagebuch*, pp. 432f.

120 Waldersee, diary for 21 June 1903, GStA Berlin, Waldersee Papers; cf. Meisner, III, pp. 217f.

121 Waldersee, diary for 20 June 1903, ibid.; cf. Meisner, III, pp. 216f.

122 Ibid.

123 Kaiser Wilhelm II, marginal note of 13 July 1903, quoted in Gutsche, *Wilhelm II.*, pp. 119f.

124 Waldersee, diary for 29 June 1903, GStA Berlin, Waldersee Papers; printed in part in Meisner, III, p. 218.

125 Waldersee, diary for 3 July 1903, ibid.; omitted in Meisner, III, p. 219. See also Waldersee's diary for 19 February 1904, not in Meisner, III, pp. 231f.

126 Hereditary Princess Charlotte of Saxe-Meiningen to Schweninger, 26 June 1903, BA Berlin, Schweninger Papers, Nr 130.

127 Zedlitz-Trützschler, diary for 30 November 1903, *Zwölf Jahre*, pp. 55f.

128 Verdy to Waldersee, 20 November 1903, GStA Berlin, Waldersee Papers Nr 53.

129 Waldersee, diary for 5 December 1902, GStA Berlin, Waldersee Papers; cf. Meisner, III, pp. 194ff.

130 Waldersee, diary for 5 December 1902, ibid.; cf. Meisner, III, pp. 194ff.

131 Waldersee, diary for 4 January 1903, ibid.; Meisner, III, pp. 198f.

132 Waldersee, diary for 8 December 1903, ibid.; printed in part in Meisner, III, pp. 221ff.

133 Ibid. Zedlitz-Trützschler, diary for 3 January 1904, *Zwölf Jahre*, pp. 58ff.

134 Waldersee, diary for 20 June 1903, GStA Berlin, Waldersee Papers; cf. Meisner, III, pp. 216f.

135 Waldersee, diary for 3 July 1903, ibid.; not in Meisner, III, p. 219.

136 Waldersee, diary for 4 March 1903, ibid.; not in Meisner, III, p. 208.

137 Waldersee, diary for 3 and 5 April 1903, ibid.; cf. Meisner, III, pp. 208f.

138 Hinzpeter to Kaiser Wilhelm II, 8 March 1902, GStA Berlin, BPHA Rep. 53J Lit H Nr 1.

139 Hinzpeter to Kaiser Wilhelm II, 28 November 1903, ibid. See Bülow to Kaiser Wilhelm II, 27 December 1903, *Große Politik*, XIX/1, No. 5970.

140 Siegfried Sommer, memoir of his audience with Kaiser Wilhelm II on 23 December 1903, Sommer Papers, Centre for German–Jewish Studies, University of Sussex.

141 Müller, diary for 4 December 1904, BA-MA Freiburg-im-Breisgau, Müller Papers.

142 Sir G. Bonham to Lord Lansdowne, 12 and 14 June 1903, RA VIC/W 43/93–4. For a graphic account of this outrage see Christopher Clark, *The Sleepwalkers. How Europe Went to War in 1914*, London 2012, pp. 3–13.

143 Kaiser Wilhelm II, marginal comments on Bülow's submission of 27 December 1903, *Große Politik*, XIX/1, Nos. 5970–1.

7 'WE TWO MAKE HISTORY AND DESTINY IS IN OUR HANDS!' KAISER AND TSAR ON THE EVE OF THE RUSSO-JAPANESE WAR

1 Alexander Savinsky, 'Guillaume II. et la Russie. Ses dépèches à Nicolas II. 1903–1905', *Revue des deux Mondes*, 1922, No. 12, 765–802, here in particular p. 771. See Maurice Paléologue, *Guillaume II et Nicolas II*, Paris 1935, pp. 95ff. See also Lascelles's report of 8 January 1904, in Gooch and Temperley, *British Documents*, II, No. 273, together with the observations of Erich Eyck in *Das Persönliche Regiment Wilhelms II. Politische Geschichte des Deutschen Kaiserreichs von 1890 bis 1914*, Zürich 1948, p. 360.

2 See the comments of the editors on Mühlberg to Arco, 27 October 1903, *Große Politik*, XIX/1, No. 5928 and on Holstein's memorandum of 24 March 1902, ibid., No. 5920.

3 Kaiser Wilhelm II, marginal comments on Bülow's submission of 27 December 1903, ibid., No. 5971.

4 Wilhelm Freiherr von Schoen, *Erlebtes. Beiträge zur politischen Geschichte der neuesten Zeit*, Stuttgart and Berlin 1921, p. 28.

5 See Vogel, *Rußlandpolitik*. See also Winzen, *Bülows Weltmachtkonzept*, pp. 408ff.; Cecil, *Wilhelm II: Emperor and Exile*, pp. 89ff.; Clark, *Kaiser Wilhelm II*, pp. 139f.

6 Holstein to Ida von Stülpnagel, 21 January 1904, in Helmuth Rogge, ed., *Friedrich von Holstein, Lebensbekenntnis in Briefen an eine Frau*, Berlin 1932, pp. 227f.

7 Vogel, *Rußlandpolitik*, especially pp. 45, 48 and 121.

8 Jonathan Steinberg, 'Germany and the Russo-Japanese War', *American Historical Review*, 75/2, 1970, 1986.

9 Zedlitz-Trützschler, diary for 1 June 1904, *Zwölf Jahre*, pp. 71f.

10 Kaiser Wilhelm II, marginal comment on Bülow's report of 20 February 1901, *Große Politik*, XVI, No. 4814, note.

11 Kaiser Wilhelm II to Bülow, 5 March 1901, ibid., No. 4824.

12 Holstein, memorandum of 27 March 1901, ibid., No. 4837.

13 Vogel, *Rußlandpolitik*, p. 106.

14 Ibid.

15 Bülow to Kaiser Wilhelm II, 4 February 1902, *Große Politik*, XVII, No. 5045.

16 Vogel, *Rußlandpolitik*, p. 106.

17 Francis Bertie, memorandum of 27 October 1901, RA VIC/W 42/42.

18 Kaiser Wilhelm II, memorandum of 23 August 1901. See above, pp. 70f. Cf. Lascelles's report of 25 August 1901 on the conversations in Wilhelmshöhe, Gooch and Temperley, *British Documents*, I, No. 323.

19 As a note of Lord Salisbury's Private Secretary makes clear, the King was let into the secret from the beginning but Lascelles was not. McDonnell to F. Ponsonby, 26 August 1901, RA VIC/W 42/29.

20 Selborne, memorandum entitled 'Balance of Naval Power in the Far East', 4 September 1901, RA VIC/W 42/40.

21 Francis Bertie, memorandum of 27 October 1901, RA VIC/W 42/42. See Winzen, *Bernhard Fürst von Bülow*, p. 99.

22 Lansdowne to Knollys, 7 November 1901, Knollys Papers, RA VIC/Add C 07/2/Q.

23 Bertie to Knollys, 23 November 1901, RA VIC/W42/43.

24 Bülow to Auswärtiges Amt, 13 September 1901, cited in Vogel, *Rußlandpolitik*, p. 107.

25 Kaiser Wilhelm II, marginal note on Alvensleben's report from St Petersburg of 4 December 1901, *Große Politik*, XVII, No. 5042.

26 Kaiser Wilhelm II, marginal note on Richthofen's report of 6 September 1901, ibid., No. 5298.

27 See Marschall's report of 28 January 1902 with the comments of Kaiser Wilhelm II, ibid., No. 5323.

28 Kaiser Wilhelm II to Tsar Nicholas II, 3 January 1902, printed in Goetz, *Briefe Wilhelms II. an den Zaren*, pp. 79–83, 322–5. See the Kaiser's rough draft and copy of this letter in PA AA R 3625. Further Kaiser Wilhelm II, marginal notes on Marschall's report of 2 February 1902, *Große Politik*, XVII, No. 5247.

29 Kaiser Wilhelm II, marginal notes on Metternich's report of 14 March 1902, ibid., No. 5351.

30 Kaiser Wilhelm II to Tsar Nicholas II, 3 January 1902, printed in Goetz, *Briefe Wilhelms II. an den Zaren*, pp. 79–83 and 322–5. Cf. the Kaiser's own rough draft and copy in PA AA R 3625.

31 The text of the Anglo-Japanese treaty is printed in Gooch and Temperley, *British Documents*, II, Nos. 124–5. See Metternich to Bülow, 21 February 1902, *Holstein Papers*, IV, No. 799.

32 Kaiser Wilhelm II to King Edward VII, 26 February 1902, RA X37/55. See McLean, *Royalty and Diplomacy*, pp. 47ff.; Volker Ullrich, *Die nervöse Großmacht. Aufstieg und Untergang des deutschen Kaiserreichs 1871–1918*, Frankfurt a.M. 1997, pp. 204f.; Cecil, *Wilhelm II: Emperor and Exile*, p. 87.

33 Metternich's reports of 3 February and 14 March 1902 with marginal notes by Kaiser Wilhelm II, *Große Politik*, XVII, Nos. 5043 and 5351. See Bülow's memorandum of 14 February 1902, ibid., No. 5048. See also Waldersee, diary for 15 February and 22 March 1902, GStA Berlin, Waldersee Papers; Meisner, III, pp. 178f. and 182f.

34 See Alvensleben's report from St Petersburg of 13 February 1902, *Große Politik*, XVII, No. 5047.

35 See Metternich to Bülow, 21 February 1902, *Holstein Papers*, IV, No. 799; Bülow to Metternich, 13 March 1902, *Große Politik*, XVII, No. 5046; Canis, *Von Bismarck zur Weltpolitik*, p. 393.

36 See Werner Stingl, *Der Ferne Osten in der deutschen Politik vor dem Ersten Weltkrieg (1902–1914)*, Frankfurt a.M. 1978, pp. 359ff.

37 Bülow, memorandum of 14 February 1902, *Große Politik*, XVII, No. 5048.

38 Kaiser Wilhelm II, marginal notes on Alvensleben's report from St Petersburg of 18 February 1902, ibid., XVIII/2, No. 5900.

39 Alvensleben's report of 19 February 1902, ibid., XVII, No. 5049. See Vogel, *Rußlandpolitik*, pp. 108ff.

40 Bülow, order of 22 February 1902, *Große Politik*, XVII, No. 5050. See Holstein's memorandum of 15 March 1902, ibid., No. 5062.

41 Bülow, memorandum of 25 February 1902, ibid., No. 5051.

42 Alvensleben to Bülow, 26 February 1902, ibid., No. 5052; Alvensleben to Bülow, 27 February 1902, ibid., XVIII/1, No. 5402; Alvensleben to Bülow, 2 March 1902, ibid., XVII, No. 5054.

43 Bülow to Alvensleben, 27 February 1902, ibid., No. 5053. See Holstein to Radolin, 24 March 1902, *Holstein Papers*, IV, No. 801.

44 Canis, *Von Bismarck zur Weltpolitik*, p. 394.

45 See Alvensleben to Bülow, 12 March 1902, *Große Politik*, XVII, No. 5060; Bülow to Alvensleben, 17 March 1902, ibid., No. 5063. Cf. Vogel, *Rußlandpolitik*, pp. 109f.

46 Vogel, *Rußlandpolitik*, pp. 109ff.

47 Ibid., p. 48. See above, p. 165.

48 Radolin to Bülow, 26 February 1902, with marginal notes by Kaiser Wilhelm II, cited in Vogel, *Rußlandpolitik*, p. 240.

49 Kaiser Wilhelm II, marginal notes on Radolin's report from Paris of 21 March 1902, *Große Politik*, XVII, No. 5901.

50 See below, pp. 176–9.

51 Bülow, memorandum of 14 February 1902, *Große Politik*, XVII, No. 5048.

52 Kaiser Wilhelm II to Tsar Nicholas II, 3 January 1902, printed in Goetz, *Briefe Wilhelms II. an den Zaren*, pp. 79–83 and 322–5.

53 Kaiser Wilhelm II to Tsar Nicholas II, 30 January 1902, printed ibid., pp. 84f. and 325f.

54 Vogel, *Rußlandpolitik*, pp. 112ff.; Eyck, *Das Persönliche Regiment Wilhelms II.*, p. 360.

55 Alvensleben, report of 5 July 1902 with the Kaiser's marginal note, PA AA R 3625; Alvensleben to Bülow, 5 July 1902, ibid., printed in *Große Politik*, XVIII/1, No. 5413 annex II. See also Alvensleben's report of 23 July 1902, ibid., XVIII, No. 5412.

56 Bülow to Kaiser Wilhelm II, 11 July 1902, PA AA R 3625, printed in *Große Politik*, XVIII/1, No. 5413 annex I.

57 Tschirschky to Bülow, 15 July 1902, PA AA R 3625, printed ibid., No. 5413 annex III.

58 Vogel, *Rußlandpolitik*, pp. 46 and 55.

59 Tschirschky to Bülow, 15 July 1902, PA AA R 3625, printed in *Große Politik*, XVIII/1, No. 5413 annex III.

60 Alvensleben, report of 5 July 1902 with marginal note by Kaiser Wilhelm II, PA AA R 3625; Tschirschky to Bülow, 15 July 1902, ibid., printed in *Große Politik*, XVIII/1, No. 5413 annex III.

61 Kaiser Wilhelm II, marginal notes on Alvensleben to Bülow, 5 July 1902, PA AA R 3625. Some of the Kaiser's more objectionable remarks have been omitted in *Große Politik*, XVIII/1, No. 5413 annex II.

62 Kaiser Wilhelm II, marginal notes on Bülow's report of 11 July 1902, PA AA R 3625; cf. the version printed in *Große Politik*, XVIII/1, No. 5413 annex I.

63 Bülow to Kaiser Wilhelm II, 22 July 1902, ibid., No. 5413 annex IV. See also Bülow to Kaiser Wilhelm II, 7 September 1903, GStA Berlin, BPHA Rep. 53J Lit. B Nr 16a.

64 Kaiser Wilhelm II to Bülow, telegram, 28 July 1902, PA AA R 3625.

65 Bülow, *Denkwürdigkeiten*, I, p. 580.

66 Ibid., p. 581.

67 Aleksandr A. Mossolov, *At the Court of the Last Tsar*, London 1935, pp. 202f.

68 Tsar Nicholas II to Kaiser Wilhelm II, telegram, 9 August 1902, PA AA R 3625.

69 Alvensleben, telegram of 13 August 1902, ibid.

70 Alvensleben, report of 16 August 1902, ibid.

71 See Röhl, *The Kaiser's Personal Monarchy*, pp. 749ff..

72 Kaiser Wilhelm II to Tsar Nicholas II, 2 September 1902, printed in Goetz, *Briefe Wilhelms II. an den Zaren*, pp. 86–90 and 326–8.

73 See Wilhelm's 'euphoric' comments to the Austrian ambassador Szögyény, cited in Canis, *Abgrund*, p. 36.

74 Kaiser Wilhelm II, marginal notes on Radolin's coded telegram of 6 September 1902, PA AA R 3625.

75 Kaiser Wilhelm II, marginal notes on Eckardstein's report of 14 September 1902, *Große Politik*, XVII, No. 5094. See Kaiser Wilhelm II, marginal notes on Bülow's report of 22 October 1902, ibid., XVIII/1, No. 5654. See also the Kaiser's remarks on the reports from Marschall of 24 November 1902 and from Metternich of 27 November 1902, ibid., Nos. 5662 and 5663.

76 Kaiser Wilhelm II to Tsar Nicholas II, 31 October 1902, ibid., Nos. 5417–19.

77 Tsar Nicholas II to Kaiser Wilhelm II, 8 September 1902, PA AA R 3625.

78 Kaiser Wilhelm II, marginal note on Alvensleben's telegram of 15 January 1904, *Große Politik*, XIX/1, No. 5940.

79 Kaiser Wilhelm II, marginal comments on Bülow's submission of 27 December 1903, ibid., No. 5971.

80 Holstein, memorandum of 24 March 1902, with Richthofen's note that the Kaiser was in complete agreement with its content, ibid., No. 5920. Cf. the apologetic interpretation offered by the editors, ibid., p. 4.

81 Bülow, marginal note on Richthofen's instruction to Arco, 6 December 1902, ibid., No. 5923. See Arco, report from Tokyo of 29 October 1902, ibid., No. 5922.

82 See the Kaiser's lengthy marginal note on Bülow's submission of 22 October 1902, ibid., XVIII/1, No. 5654.

83 Kaiser Wilhelm II, draft of his letter to the Tsar, dated Neues Palais 1 September 1902, with tables representing the strength of the fleets, PA AA R 3625. According to Wilhelm,

England and Japan together had twelve battleships of the line and fifty-seven cruisers in the North Pacific, as compared with the twelve ships of the line and twenty-four cruisers of the Franco-Russian alliance stationed there. The German East Asian squadron with one battleship and six cruisers was negligible in comparison.

84 Kaiser Wilhelm II, marginal notes on Arco's report of 29 October 1902, *Große Politik*, XIX, No. 5922.

85 Kaiser Wilhelm II to Tsar Nicholas II, 14 January 1903, Goetz, *Briefe Wilhelms II. an den Zaren*, pp. 91ff. and 329f.

86 Bülow to Kaiser Wilhelm II, 1 August 1903, cited in Vogel, *Rußlandpolitik*, p. 116.

87 Kaiser Wilhelm II, marginal notes on Alvensleben to Bülow, 20 August 1903, as cited in ibid., p. 273.

88 Bülow to Kaiser Wilhelm II, 7 September 1903, GStA Berlin, BPHA Rep. 53J Lit. B Nr 16a.

89 Savinsky, *Guillaume II*, pp. 765–70 and 779f.; Vogel, *Rußlandpolitik*, pp. 115ff.; Eyck, *Das Persönliche Regiment Wilhelms II.*, p. 360.

90 Kaiser Wilhelm II to Tsar Nicholas II, telegram, 17 October 1903; the Tsar's replies of 17 and 19 October 1903 are in PA AA R 3626.

91 Prince Heinrich of Prussia to Kaiser Wilhelm II, 25 October 1903, ibid.

92 Mühlberg to Lucanus, 27 October 1903, ibid.

93 Vogel, *Rußlandpolitik*, pp. 148f.

94 Bülow to Kaiser Wilhelm II, 19 October 1903, *Große Politik*, XVIII/1, p. 70.

95 Romberg, report from St Petersburg of 26 October 1903, PA AA R 3626. See Mühlberg to Arco, 27 October 1903, *Große Politik*, XIX/1, No. 5928.

96 Kaiser Wilhelm II, marginal note on Romberg's report of 26 October 1903, PA AA R 3626.

97 Kaiser Wilhelm II, marginal comment on Radolin's report of 29 October 1903, *Große Politik*, XVIII/2, No. 5917.

98 Bülow to Holstein, 31 October 1903, ibid., No. 5918.

99 'Programm für die Reise Seiner Majestät des Kaisers und Königs von Wiesbaden nach Wolfsgarten und Wildpark im November 1903', PA AA R 3626; Grand Duke of Hesse and the Rhine Ernst Ludwig to Kaiser Wilhelm II, 4 and 6 November 1903; Tsar Nicholas II to Kaiser Wilhelm II, 6 November 1903, ibid.

100 Mossolov, *At the Court of the Last Tsar*, pp. 202f.

101 Bülow, memorandum of 7 November 1903 with numerous additions by Kaiser Wilhelm II, *Große Politik*, XVIII/1, No. 5422. See Bülow, *Denkwürdigkeiten*, I, pp. 630–3; Bülow to Auswärtiges Amt, 5 November 1903, PA AA R 3626; Vogel, *Rußlandpolitik*, p. 156.

102 Radolin to Bülow, 28 February 1904, cited ibid., pp. 45f.

103 Kaiser Wilhelm II, marginal notes on Radolin's report from Paris of 6 November 1903, PA AA R 3626.

104 Romberg, report of 7 November 1903 with approving marginal notes by Kaiser Wilhelm II, ibid.

105 Romberg, report of 26 November 1903 with the Kaiser's marginal notes, *Große Politik*, XVIII/1, No. 5425. See Alvensleben to Bülow, 30 November 1903, ibid., No. 5426.

8 THE ANGLO-GERMAN ANTAGONISM: THE KAISER, THE KING AND PUBLIC OPINION

1 Paul Kennedy, *The Rise of the Anglo-German Antagonism, 1860–1914*, London and Boston 1980; Reinermann, *Der Kaiser in England*, pp. 244f.; Dominik Geppert, *Pressekriege. Öffentlichkeit und Diplomatie in den deutsch-britischen Beziehungen (1896–1912)*, Munich 2007. See also: Martin Schramm, *Das Deutschlandbild in der britischen Presse*

1912–1919, Berlin 2007; Peter Alter, 'Herausforderer der Weltmacht. Das Deutsche Reich im britischen Urteil', in Klaus Hildebrand, ed., *Das Deutsche Reich im Urteil der großen Mächte und europäischen Nachbarn (1871–1945)*, Munich 1995, pp. 159–77; Wolfgang J. Mommsen, 'Zur Entwicklung des Englandbildes der Deutschen seit dem Ende des 18. Jahrhunderts', in Lothar Kettenacker, Manfred Schlenke and Hellmut Seier, eds., *Studien zur Geschichte Englands und der deutsch-britischen Beziehungen. Festschrift für Paul Kluke*, Munich 1981, pp. 375–97; Willy Schenk, *Die deutsch-englische Rivalität vor dem ersten Weltkrieg in der Sicht deutscher Historiker*, Aarau 1967.

2 Mudra to von der Goltz, 29 October 1902, BA-MA Freiburg-im-Breisgau, von der Goltz Papers, N737, Mappe 22. See Waldersee, diary for 25 April 1903, GStA Berlin, Waldersee Papers; not in Meisner, III, p. 209.

3 See Valentine Chirol's letters to Holstein of 23 November and 18 December 1901, *Holstein Papers*, IV, Nos. 786 and 791.

4 Metternich to Bülow, 19 November 1901, *Große Politik*, XVII, No. 5073. See Lansdowne to Buchanan, 26 November 1901, Gooch and Temperley, *British Documents*, I, No. 326.

5 Metternich to Bülow, 19 November 1901, *Holstein Papers*, IV, No. 785.

6 Bülow to Holstein, 25 November 1901, ibid., No. 787.

7 Holstein to Chirol, 28 November 1901, ibid., No. 788.

8 Holstein to Chirol, 11 December 1901, ibid., No. 789.

9 Kaiser Wilhelm II, marginal notes on Metternich's report of 19 November 1901, *Große Politik*, XVII, No. 5073.

10 Lascelles to Lansdowne, 9 November 1901, Gooch and Temperley, *British Documents*, I, No. 324.

11 King Edward VII to Lascelles, 25 December 1901, RA VIC/X 37/49; Lascelles to King Edward VII, 27–8 December 1901, RA VIC/X 37/50.

12 Lascelles to King Edward VII, 27–8 December 1901, RA VIC/X 37/50.

13 Kaiser Wilhelm II to King Edward VII, 30 December 1901, RA VIC/X 37/51. The second part of this letter is printed in *Große Politik*, XVII, No. 5029.

14 Lansdowne to King Edward VII, 6 January 1902, RA VIC/W 42/45a. See Knollys to Lascelles, 7 January 1902, RA VIC/X 37/53.

15 Kaiser Wilhelm II to King Edward VII, 6 January 1902, RA VIC/X 37/52; Lansdowne to King Edward VII, 6 January 1902, RA VIC/W42/45a. Cf. Eckardstein to Knollys, 9 January 1902, Knollys Papers, RA VIC/Add C 07/2/Q.

16 Holstein, diary for 11 January 1902, *Holstein Papers*, IV, No. 792; Bülow, speech of 8 January 1902, as quoted in Penzler, *Fürst Bülows Reden*, I, pp. 241–5. See Fesser, *Reichskanzler Fürst von Bülow*, p. 99.

17 As quoted in *Holstein Papers*, IV, p. 244. Cf. Winzen, *Bülows Weltmachtkonzept*, p. 384.

18 Holstein, diary for 11 January 1902, *Holstein Papers*, IV, No. 792.

19 Holstein, diary for 14 January 1902, ibid., No. 794. See also Holstein's retrospective memorandum of 7 November 1902, ibid., No. 811.

20 Lascelles to Knollys, 17 January 1902, RA VIC/W 42/61. Cf. Christian Wipperfürth, *Von der Souveränität zur Angst. Britische Außenpolitik und Sozialökonomie im Zeitalter des Imperialismus*, Stuttgart 2004, pp. 154f.

21 See Lansdowne to Lascelles, 14 January 1902, Gooch and Temperley, *British Documents*, I, No. 330.

22 Lansdowne to Knollys, 10 January 1902, RA VIC/W 42/47.

23 Eric Barrington to Knollys, 11 January 1902, RA VIC/W 42/50.

24 Lascelles to Knollys, 11 and 17 January 1902, RA VIC/W 42/51 and 61; Lascelles to Lansdowne, telegram, 11 January 1902, RA VIC/W 42/52.

25 Lascelles to King Edward VII, 14 January 1902, RA VIC/W 42/54. See Lascelles to Lansdowne, 16 January 1902, Gooch and Temperley, *British Documents*, I, No. 331.

26 Lascelles to Knollys, telegram, 17 January 1902, RA VIC/W 42/59; Lascelles to Knollys, letter of 17 January 1902, RA VIC/W 42/61.

27 King Edward VII to Kaiser Wilhelm II, 15 January 1902, RA VIC/W 42/58. The final wording was moderated on the advice of the Foreign Secretary. Lansdowne to Knollys, 14 January 1902, RA VIC/W 42/48.

28 Lascelles to Knollys, telegram, 17 January 1902, RA VIC/W 42/59.

29 Lascelles to Knollys, letter of 17 January 1902, RA VIC/W 42/61.

30 See Röhl, *The Kaiser's Personal Monarchy*, pp. 77–101.

31 Salisbury to King Edward VII, 22 January 1902, RA VIC/R 22/65.

32 Lascelles to Lansdowne, 24 January 1902, Gooch and Temperley, *British Documents*, I, No. 336.

33 Lascelles to Lansdowne, telegram, 22 January 1902, RA VIC/W 42/64.

34 Schomberg McDonnell to 'Sidney', 22 January 1902, RA VIC/W 42/62.

35 Knollys to Lansdowne, 22 January 1902, RA VIC/W 42/65; Lansdowne to Lascelles, 22 January 1902, Gooch and Temperley, *British Documents*, I, No. 334.

36 Lascelles to Lansdowne, 24 January 1902, ibid., No. 336.

37 Lascelles to Lansdowne, 22 January 1902, ibid., No. 335. Knollys, memorandum of 23 January 1902, RA VIC/W 42/66.

38 Lansdowne to Knollys, 24 and 25 January 1902, RA VIC/W 42/67 and 68.

39 Lascelles to Lansdowne, 31 January 1902, Gooch and Temperley, *British Documents*, I, No. 337.

40 Metternich to Bülow, 21 February 1902, *Holstein Papers*, IV, No. 799.

41 Metternich, report of 14 March 1902, *Große Politik*, XVII, No. 5351.

42 Kaiser Wilhelm II to King Edward VII, 26 February 1902, RA VIC/X 37/55.

43 Knollys to Lascelles, 16 April 1902, RA VIC/W 42/76a.

44 Seckendorff to Kaiser Wilhelm II, 13 July 1902, GStA Berlin, BPHA Rep. 53J Lit. S, Nr 15–21.

45 Kaiser Wilhelm II, marginal note on Metternich's report of 11 August 1902, cited in Roderick R. McLean, 'Kaiser Wilhelm II and the British Royal Family: Anglo-German Dynastic Relations in Political Context, 1890–1914', *History*, 86/284, October 2001, 482.

46 Louise Duchess of Argyll to Kaiser Wilhelm II, 19 April and 12 June 1902, GStA Berlin, BPHA Rep. 53J Lit C–D.

47 Kaiser Wilhelm II to King Edward VII, 2 May 1902, RA VIC/W 60/161.

48 King Edward VII to Kaiser Wilhelm II, RA VIC/W 60/162.

49 Kaiser Wilhelm II to King Edward VII, 1 June 1902, RA VIC/X 15/21.

50 Lascelles to King Edward VII, telegram in code with the text of the Kaiser's telegram to him, 2 June 1902, RA VIC/W 42/81. See Metternich's reports of 2 and 3 June 1902, *Große Politik*, XVII, Nos. 5081 and 5082.

51 See ibid.

52 Waldersee to Verdy, 12 July 1902, GStA Berlin, Waldersee Papers, Nr 53.

53 Metternich, reports of 2, 3, 14 and 15 June 1902, *Große Politik*, XVII, Nos. 5081–4.

54 Waldersee, diary for late September 1902, GStA Berlin, Waldersee Papers; Meisner, III, pp. 186f.

55 Waldersee, diary for January 1902, ibid.; omitted in Meisner, III, p. 177. See above, p. 84.

56 Seckendorff to Kaiser Wilhelm II, 7 July 1902, GStA Berlin, BPHA Rep. 53J Lit. S, Nr 19.

57 Bülow to Kaiser Wilhelm II, 22 July 1902, *Große Politik*, XVIII/1, No. 5413 annex IV.

58 Bülow to Holstein, 1 August 1902, *Holstein Papers*, IV, No. 804.

59 King Edward VII to Kaiser Wilhelm II, 14 and 16 August 1902, PA AA R 3700; Metternich to Bülow, 19 August 1902, ibid. See King Edward VII to Lascelles, 28 August 1902, RA VIC/W 42/107c.

60 Lascelles to King Edward VII, 21 August 1902, RA VIC/W 42/97.

61 Eckardstein to Bülow, 14 September 1902, *Große Politik*, XVII, No. 5094. See Eckardstein, *Lebenserinnerungen*, II, pp. 397–404.

62 Bülow to Kaiser Wilhelm II, 17 September 1902, *Große Politik*, XVII, No. 5093.

63 Lascelles to Knollys, 3 October 1902, RA VIC/W 42/123. See Holstein, diary for 7 November 1902, *Holstein Papers*, IV, No. 811.

64 Eckardstein to Bülow, 4 October 1902, *Große Politik*, XVII, No. 5101.

65 Knollys to Lascelles, 2 October 1902, RA VIC/W 42/122.

66 Bertie to Lansdowne, memorandum of 1/2 October 1902, Lansdowne to Lascelles, 3 October 1902, RA VIC/W 42/137. Knollys to Lascelles, 4 October 1902, RA VIC/W 42/125. See Wipperfürth, *Von der Souveränität zur Angst*, p. 180; Kennedy, *Rise of the Anglo-German Antagonism*, pp. 265f.

67 Holstein, diary for 7 November 1902, *Holstein Papers*, IV, No. 811.

68 Eckardstein to Bülow, 4 October 1902, *Große Politik*, XVII, No. 5101.

69 Holstein, diary for 7 November 1902, *Holstein Papers*, IV, No. 811. See Eckardstein, *Lebenserinnerungen*, II, pp. 406ff.

70 King Edward VII to Lansdowne, 6 October 1902, RA VIC/W 42/128.

71 Lascelles to Lansdowne, 7 October 1902, RA VIC/W 42/135.

72 Bülow to Kaiser Wilhelm II, 8 October 1902, *Große Politik*, XVII, No. 5102.

73 Holstein, diary for 7 November 1902, *Holstein Papers*, IV, No. 811.

74 Eckardstein, *Lebenserinnerungen*, II, pp. 406f.

75 Holstein, diary for 7 November 1902, *Holstein Papers*, IV, No. 811.

76 Bülow to Auswärtiges Amt, 3 October 1902, *Große Politik*, XVII, No. 5099.

77 King Edward VII to Lansdowne, 8 October 1902, enclosing a copy of the Kaiser's telegram of 5 October 1902, RA VIC/W 42/130. See King Edward VII to Knollys, 8 October 1902, RA VIC/W 42/131.

78 Kaiser Wilhelm II, marginal note on Eckardstein's report of 4 October 1902, *Große Politik*, XVII, No. 5101.

79 Kaiser Wilhelm II, marginal note on Bülow's submission of 14 October 1902, quoted ibid., p. 233.

80 Metternich's report of 22 January 1903, cited in Canis, *Abgrund*, p. 30.

81 Waldersee, diary for 12 October 1902, GStA Berlin, Waldersee Papers; this passage is omitted in Meisner, III, pp. 190f.

82 Holstein, diary for 7 November 1902, *Holstein Papers*, IV, No. 811. See Eckardstein, *Lebenserinnerungen*, II, pp. 399f.

83 Holstein, diary for 7 November 1902, *Holstein Papers*, IV, No. 811.

84 Ibid.

85 Holstein, diary for 11 November 1902, ibid., No. 812. For the reaction in the British press to the Kaiser's visit see Reinermann, *Der Kaiser in England*, pp. 244–62.

86 Eckardstein to Bülow, 13 October 1902, with the Kaiser's marginalia, PA AA R 3700.

87 Metternich to Bülow, 9 November 1902, cited in *Große Politik*, XVII, pp. 115f.

88 The Kaiser discussed the question of the Straits with the Foreign Secretary and boasted later that he had given Lansdowne 'the brush-off'. See ibid., XVIII, Nos. 5659 and 5663.

89 Kaiser Wilhelm II to Bülow, 12 November 1902, ibid., XVII, No. 5031. Bülow's reply of 13 November 1902 is printed ibid., No. 5032. See Holstein, diary for 13 November 1902, *Holstein Papers*, IV, No. 813.

90 Kaiser Wilhelm II to King Edward VII, 19 November 1902, RA VIC/ADD A5/34; King Edward VII to Kaiser Wilhelm II, 25 November 1902, PA AA R 3701. See *Große Politik*, XVII, p. 116.

91 Eckardstein, *Lebenserinnerungen*, II, p. 415.

92 Hardinge to Knollys, 29 October 1902, RA VIC/Add C 07/2/Q.

93 Varnbüler, report of 14 December 1901, quoted in Winzen, *Bernhard Fürst von Bülow*, p. 67.

94 Spitzemberg, diary for 14 March 1903, Vierhaus, *Tagebuch*, pp. 427ff. See below, p. 245ff.

95 Waldersee, diary for 8 December 1903, GStA Berlin, Waldersee Papers; cf. Meisner, III, pp. 221ff.

96 King Edward VII to Battenberg, 15 April 1905, cited in McLean, *Royalty and Diplomacy*, pp. 114f. See below, p. 384.

97 See Magnus Brechtken, *Scharnierzeit 1895–1907. Persönlichkeitsnetze und internationale Politik in den deutsch-britisch-amerikanischen Beziehungen vor dem Ersten Weltkrieg*, Mainz 2006.

9   THE KAISER AND AMERICA

1 Waldersee, diary for 18 February and 4 March 1903, GStA Berlin, Waldersee Papers; not in Meisner, III, pp. 207f.

2 Waldersee, diary for 18 January 1899, ibid.; not in Meisner, II, pp. 423ff.

3 Waldersee, diary for 24 April 1900, ibid.; not in Meisner, II, p. 445.

4 Waldersee, diary for 6 May 1899, ibid.; omitted in Meisner, II, pp. 428f.

5 Waldersee, diary for 29 January 1899, ibid.; cf. Meisner, II, pp. 426f., where several key passages have been omitted.

6 Roosevelt to Spring Rice, 13 August 1897, quoted in Fiebig-von Hase, *Lateinamerika*, II, p. 746.

7 Roosevelt to Lodge, 27 March 1901, quoted ibid., p. 770.

8 Roosevelt to Lengerke-Meyer, 12 April 1901, quoted ibid. See also Roosevelt to Spring Rice, 3 July 1901, ibid., p. 780.

9 Roosevelt to Lodge, 27 March 1901; Lodge to Roosevelt, 27 March 1901, quoted ibid., p. 770.

10 White to Hay, 5 June 1901, quoted ibid., p. 774.

11 Fiebig-von Hase, ibid., II, p. 772. See *New York Herald*, 2 June 1901, quoted ibid., p. 780.

12 Ibid., I, p. 38. On German–American relations in the Wilhelmine era see also: Ute Mehnert, 'German Weltpolitik and the American Two-Front Dilemma: The "Japanese Peril" in German–American Relations, 1904–1917', *The Journal of American History*, 82, 1996,1452–77; Hans-Jürgen Schröder, *Deutschland und Amerika in der Epoche des Ersten Weltkrieges 1900–1924*, Stuttgart 1993; Manfred Jonas, *The United States and Germany, a Diplomatic History*, Ithaca 1984, pp. 65–94; Howard K. Beale, 'Theodore Roosevelt, Wilhelm II. und die deutsch-amerikanischen Beziehungen', *Die Welt als Geschichte* 15 (1955), 155–87.

13 Fiebig-von Hase, *Lateinamerika*, I, pp. 337f. and 340f.

14 Ragnhild Fiebig-von Hase, 'Die Rolle Kaiser Wilhelms II. in den deutsch-amerikanischen Beziehungen, 1890–1914', in John C. G. Röhl, ed., *Der Ort Kaiser Wilhelms II. in der deutschen Geschichte*, Munich 1991, p. 234.

15 Kaiser Wilhelm II, marginal note on Speck von Sternburg's telegram of 12 December 1903, as quoted in ibid., p. 244.

16 Kaiser Wilhelm II to Bülow, 28 September 1897, cited in Reiner Pommerin, *Der Kaiser und Amerika. Die USA in der Politik der Reichsleitung 1890–1917*, Cologne and Vienna 1986, pp. 73f.

17 See Röhl, *The Kaiser's Personal Monarchy*, pp. 366–70.

18 See ibid., pp. 929–32.

19 Quadt to Bülow, 8 November 1901, enclosing a newspaper clipping, PA AA R 17380.

20 The Kaiser and America, *New York Herald*, 9 November 1901, PA AA R 17380. For this incident see Fiebig-von Hase, *Lateinamerika*, I, p. 328; Fiebig-von Hase, 'Die Rolle Kaiser Wilhelms II. in den deutsch-amerikanischen Beziehungen', p. 233.

21 Eulenburg, memorandum of 25 September 1905, printed in *Eulenburgs Korrespondenz*, III, No. 1509.

22 Kaiser Wilhelm II to Hohenlohe, 1 August 1897, quoted in Fiebig-von Hase, 'Die Rolle Kaiser Wilhelms II. in den deutsch-amerikanischen Beziehungen', p. 239.

23 Holleben, memorandum of 22 August 1897, quoted ibid., p. 233.

24 Kaiser Wilhelm II, marginal notes on a consular report from Havana of 14 March 1899, printed in Jürgen Kuczynski, *Amerikanische Krisen und Monopolbildung in deutschen diplomatischen Berichten*, Berlin 1968, pp. 46f. See Ragnhild Fiebig-von Hase, *Lateinamerika*, I, p. 327.

25 Kaiser Wilhelm II, marginal note on Coerper to Tirpitz, 30 April 1901, PA AA Amerika Generalia 13. I thank Dr Ragnhild Fiebig-von Hase for drawing my attention to this document.

26 Kaiser Wilhelm II, marginal note on Bülow's telegram of 20 September 1901, cited in Fiebig-von Hase, *Lateinamerika*, I, p. 328.

27 Bülow to Kaiser Wilhelm II, 20 September 1901, PA AA Deutschland 138, Bd. 20.

28 Kaiser Wilhelm II, marginal notes on Coerper to Tirpitz, 11 November 1901, quoted in Fiebig-von Hase, *Lateinamerika*, I, p. 328.

29 Kaiser Wilhelm II to Ballin, 21 February 1902, GStA Berlin, BPHA Rep. 53 Nr 358. See Fiebig-von Hase, *Lateinamerika*, I, p. 328; Fiebig-von Hase, 'Die Rolle Kaiser Wilhelms II. in den deutsch-amerikanischen Beziehungen', p. 233. Vivian Vale, *The American Peril. Challenge to Britain on the North Atlantic 1901–1904*, Manchester 1984, pp. 81f. Also Sommer, memorandum on his audience with Kaiser Wilhelm II in the Neues Palais in Potsdam on 23 December 1903, Centre for German–Jewish Studies, University of Sussex, Siegfried Sommer Papers.

30 Kaiser Wilhelm II, marginal note on Sternburg's telegram of 12 December 1903, as quoted in Fiebig-von Hase, 'Die Rolle Kaiser Wilhelms II. in den deutsch-amerikanischen Beziehungen', p. 244.

31 Kaiser Wilhelm II, marginal note on Rebeur-Paschwitz to Tirpitz, 18 April 1899, cited in Fiebig-von Hase, *Lateinamerika*, I, pp. 335f.

32 Kaiser Wilhelm II, marginal note on Krauel to Hohenlohe, 6 October 1896, quoted in ibid., pp. 221f. See Jürgen Hell, *Der Griff nach Südbrasilien: Die Politik des Deutschen Reiches zur Verwandlung der drei brasilianischen Südstaaten in ein überseeisches Neudeutschland (1890–1914)*, D.Phil. thesis., Rostock 1966; Gerhard Brunn, *Deutschland und Brasilien (1889–1914)*, Cologne and Vienna 1971.

33 Fiebig-von Hase, *Lateinamerika*, I, pp. 226 and 234. Karl-Heinz Janßen, ed., *Die graue Exzellenz. Zwischen Staatsraison und Vasallentreue. Aus den Papieren des kaiserlichen Gesandten Karl Georg von Treutler*, Frankfurt a.M. 1971, pp. 78–85.

34 Mühlberg to Bülow, 18 February 1905, as quoted in Fiebig-von Hase, *Lateinamerika*, I, p. 238.

35 See Auswärtiges Amt to Kaiser Wilhelm II, 1907 and 1909, quoted ibid.

36 Bülow to Kaiser Wilhelm II, 23 November 1903, quoted in ibid., pp. 350f.

37 Kaiser Wilhelm II, marginal note 'I fervently hope so!' to a clipping from the *Scientific American* of 31 March 1900, quoted in ibid., p. 424.

38 Kaiser Wilhelm II, marginal note on White to Bülow, 8 December 1897, cited in ibid., p. 411.

39 Bülow to Kaiser Wilhelm II, 19. August 1898, as quoted ibid., p. 418. See Alfred Vagts, *Deutschland und die Vereinigten Staaten in der Weltpolitik*, 2 vols., New York 1935, p. 1374.

40 Kaiser Wilhelm II, marginal note on a report of 6 July 1898 from Dresden, quoted in Fiebig-von Hase, *Lateinamerika*, I, p. 418.

41 Kaiser Wilhelm II, marginal notes on Holleben's report of July 1898; Bülow, memorandum on Kaiser Wilhelm II's deliberations of 20 May 1898, ibid., pp. 417f.

42 Kaiser Wilhelm II to Bülow, 29 October 1899, *Große Politik*, XV, No. 4394.

43 Kaiser Wilhelm II, marginal note on Holleben's report of 18 June 1900, cited in Fiebig-von Hase, *Lateinamerika*, I, p. 410.

44 Kaiser Wilhelm II, marginal notes on a telegram from Pilgrim-Baltazzi of 11 October 1901 and on Bülow's submission of 15 October 1901, quoted in ibid., II, p. 865. See below, p. 236. Cf. Fiebig-von Hase, 'Die Rolle Kaiser Wilhelms II. in den deutsch-amerikanischen Beziehungen', p. 239.

45 Kaiser Wilhelm II, marginal note on Bussche to Bülow, 23 December 1904, cited in Fiebig-von Hase, *Lateinamerika*, II, p. 1088.

46 See Brechtken, *Scharnierzeit 1895–1907*, passim.

47 See above, pp. 53–6.

48 Kaiser Wilhelm II to Bülow, 29 January 1901, *Große Politik*, XVII, No. 4987. See above, Chapter 3.

49 Kaiser Wilhelm II, memorandum of 23 August 1901. See above, pp. 70f. Cf. Lascelles's report of 25 August 1901 on the conversations at Wilhelmshöhe, Gooch and Temperley, *British Documents*, I, No. 323.

50 Kaiser Wilhelm II, marginal note on Metternich's report of 1 October 1901, cited in Fiebig-von Hase, *Lateinamerika*, II, p. 948.

51 Kaiser Wilhelm II, marginal notes on Speck von Sternburg's report of 19 February 1903, *Große Politik*, XVII, No. 5151.

52 Bülow to Kaiser Wilhelm II, 11 August 1899, GStA Berlin, BPHA Rep. 53J Lit. B Nr 16a. Cf. Pommerin, *Kaiser und Amerika*, p. 100.

53 Bülow to Kaiser Wilhelm II, 31 March 1903, GStA Berlin, BPHA Rep 53J Lit. B Nr 16a.

54 Kaiser Wilhelm II, marginal notes on Metternich's telegram of 29 October 1901, quoted in Fiebig-von Hase, 'Die Rolle Kaiser Wilhelms II. in den deutsch-amerikanischen Beziehungen', p. 234. See her *Lateinamerika*, II, p. 947.

55 Fiebig-von Hase, 'Die Rolle Kaiser Wilhelms II. in den deutsch-amerikanischen Beziehungen', p. 234.

56 Kaiser Wilhelm II, marginal notes of 30 December 1901 on Holleben to Bülow, 29 December 1901, as quoted in Vagts, *Deutschland*, p. 475.

57 Anne Tracy Morgan to Frances Tracy Morgan, 7 July 1902, Pierpont Morgan Library New York. See Jean Strouse, *Morgan. American Financier*, New York 1999, pp. 470–3.

58 Holstein, diary for 7 November 1902, *Holstein Papers*, IV, No. 811.

59 Maurice Low to the editor of the *National Review*, 3 February 1903, RA VIC/W 43/63.

60 Dawkins to Milner, 6 November 1902, Bodleian Library, Oxford University, MS. Milner dep. 215.

61 Metternich to Bülow, 4 February 1903, PA AA, England 78 secr.

62 Lascelles to Knollys, 20 March 1903, RA VIC/W 43/63.

63 Georg Alexander von Müller, memorandum, in Walter Görlitz, ed., *Der Kaiser … Aufzeichnungen des Chefs des Marinekabinetts Admiral Georg Alexander von Müller über die Ära Wilhelms II.*, Göttingen 1965, pp. 23f.

64 Fiebig-von Hase, 'Die Rolle Kaiser Wilhelms II. in den deutsch-amerikanischen Beziehungen', pp. 246f.; Pommerin, *Kaiser und Amerika*, pp. 107f.

65 Fiebig-von Hase, *Lateinamerika*, II, p. 951.

66 Fiebig-von Hase, 'Die Rolle Kaiser Wilhelms II. in den deutsch-amerikanischen Beziehungen', pp. 234f.

67 Holstein, memorandum of 29 January 1902, cited in Fiebig-von Hase, *Lateinamerika*, II, pp. 952f.
68 Bülow to Prince Heinrich of Prussia, 30 January 1902, *Große Politik*, XVII, p. 243, note; Pommerin, *Kaiser und Amerika*, pp. 109f.
69 See the examples given in Fiebig-von Hase, *Lateinamerika*, II, pp. 959f.
70 Waldersee, diary for 1 February 1902, GStA Berlin, Waldersee Papers; Meisner, III, pp. 177f.
71 For the construction and launch ceremony of the *Meteor III* see Kristin Lammerting, *Meteor. Die kaiserlichen Segelyachten*, Cologne 1999, pp. 86–96. Cf. Fiebig-von Hase, *Lateinamerika*, II, p. 943; Pommerin, *Kaiser und Amerika*, p. 107.
72 Waldersee, diary for 1 February 1902, GStA Berlin, Waldersee Papers; Meisner, III, pp. 177f.; Pommerin, *Kaiser und Amerika*, pp. 107ff.
73 See the memorandum of Admiral von Müller in Görlitz, *Der Kaiser*, pp. 23f. and pp. 53–8.
74 Prince Heinrich of Prussia to Müller, 7 January 1902, printed ibid., pp. 57f.
75 See ibid., pp. 23f. and pp. 53–8. Prince Heinrich of Prussia to Tirpitz, 2 January 1902, BA-MA Freiburg-im-Breisgau, Tirpitz Papers, N253/183. On Heinrich's crossing see Kaiser Wilhelm II to Albert Ballin, 21 February 1902, GStA Berlin, BPHA Rep. 53 Nr 358.
76 Tirpitz to Prince Heinrich of Prussia, 7 May 1902, BA-MA Freiburg-im-Breisgau, Tirpitz Papers, N253/183.
77 See Görlitz, *Der Kaiser*, pp. 53–8; Lammerting, *Meteor*, pp. 91f.
78 See above, p. 217.
79 See Fiebig-von Hase, *Lateinamerika*, II, pp. 954ff.
80 Ibid., p. 950.
81 Waldersee, diary for 15 February 1902, GStA Berlin, Waldersee Papers; cf. Meisner, III, pp. 178f.
82 Waldersee, diary for 22 February 1902, ibid.; omitted in Meisner, III, p. 181.
83 Waldersee, diary for 19 March 1902, ibid.; cf. Meisner, III, pp. 181f.
84 Bülow to Kaiser Wilhelm II, 20 January 1902, with the Kaiser's marginal notes of 21 January 1902, *Große Politik*, XVII, No. 5106.
85 Kaiser Wilhelm II to King Edward VII, 26 February 1902, RA VIC/X 37/55.
86 Prince Heinrich of Prussia to Poultney Bigelow, 7 April 1902, Bigelow Papers, New York Public Library.
87 See Pommerin, *Kaiser und Amerika*, pp. 111ff.
88 Waldersee, diary for 19 March 1902, GStA Berlin, Waldersee Papers; cf. Meisner, III, pp. 181f.
89 Kaiser Wilhelm II, marginal comment of 13 December 1902 on Speck von Sternburg's report of 26 November 1902, PA AA R 17380.
90 Prince Heinrich of Prussia to Senden-Bibran, 25 January 1903, BA-MA Freiburg-im-Breisgau, Senden-Bibran Papers, N 160/4.
91 Fiebig-von Hase, *Lateinamerika*, II, p. 951.
92 Cited in ibid., p. 960.
93 Kaiser Wilhelm II, marginal comment on Metternich's telegram of 3 June 1902, *Große Politik*, XVII, No. 5082.
94 Prince Heinrich of Prussia to Poultney Bigelow, 7 April 1902, Bigelow Papers, New York Public Library.
95 Waldersee, diary for 7 December 1902, GStA Berlin, Waldersee Papers; cf. Meisner, III, p. 196.
96 *Holstein Papers*, I, p. 176.
97 Kaiser Wilhelm II, marginal note of 12 September 1896 on Kiderlen to Hohenlohe, 1 September 1896, cited in Fiebig-von Hase, *Lateinamerika*, I, p. 439.
98 Tirpitz to Kaiser Wilhelm II, 24 April 1898, cited in ibid., p. 436.

99 Ibid., pp. 440ff.; Tirpitz to Kaiser Wilhelm II, 24 April 1898, ibid., pp. 443f.
100 Kaiser Wilhelm II, marginal note, *Große Politik*, XV, No. 4203; Pommerin, *Kaiser und Amerika*, p. 114; Fiebig-von Hase, *Lateinamerika*, I, pp. 445f.
101 Ibid., pp. 450f.
102 Klehment, note on a conversation with Tirpitz on 27 May 1899, cited in ibid., p. 454.
103 Bülow to Tirpitz, 12 February 1899, cited in ibid., pp. 452f.; Tirpitz to Auswärtiges Amt, 24 January 1900, *Holstein Papers*, I, note 15.
104 See Fiebig-von Hase, *Lateinamerika*, I, pp. 458ff.
105 Ibid., pp. 462f.
106 Kaiser Wilhelm II, marginal notes on Holleben to Bülow, 9 February 1902, cited in ibid., p. 471.
107 Kaiser Wilhelm II, marginal note of 12 December 1901 on Holleben to Bülow, 25 November 1901, cited in ibid., p. 469.
108 See ibid., p. 465.
109 Schröder, memorandum of 15 April 1903, ibid., pp. 467f.
110 Schoen to Bülow, 2 December 1904, printed in Bülow, *Denkwürdigkeiten*, II, pp. 66–8. See below, p. 297.
111 Kaiser Wilhelm II, marginal notes on Schoen to Bülow, 23 March 1905, cited in Fiebig-von Hase, *Lateinamerika*, I, pp. 193 and 467.
112 Bülow, report on the general political situation for Prince Heinrich of Prussia, 3 March 1899, cited in ibid., pp. 418f.
113 Holleben, memorandum of June 1899, cited in ibid., p. 423.
114 Ibid., pp. 421; II, p. 753.
115 Ibid., I, p. 425.
116 Quoted in Vagts, *Deutschland*, pp. 1794ff.; Fiebig-von Hase, *Lateinamerika*, II, pp. 847, 990, 1059.
117 Diederichs, memorandum of January 1900, ibid., p. 475.
118 Diederichs, memorandum of 26 February 1900 for submission to the Kaiser, cited in ibid., pp. 476f.
119 Diederichs to Schlieffen, 1 May and 28 November 1900; Schlieffen to Diederichs, 1 December 1900, ibid., pp. 475 and 495. See below, p. 234.
120 Fiebig-von Hase, *Lateinamerika*, I, pp. 477f.
121 Memoranda of January 1900, 15 January 1902, 21 March and 3 October 1903, cited ibid., pp. 484f.
122 Ibid., pp. 491–4.
123 Memorandum for submission to the Kaiser on the reconnaisance of Cape Cod Bay of 9 December 1900 with marginal notes on Wilhelm's decision, ibid., pp. 495f.
124 Ibid., pp. 478, 496f. and 499.
125 Büchsel, 'Operationsplan III' of March 1903, cited ibid., p. 487.
126 Ibid., pp. 479f. See also ibid., p. 500.
127 Kaiser Wilhelm II, marginal note on Bodmann to Hohenlohe, 17 March 1895, cited ibid., p. 369. Cf. Kaiser Wilhelm II, dictation for the Reich Chancellor, 21 January 1895, cited ibid., p. 370.
128 Klügmann's report of 16 November 1897, cited ibid., pp. 403f.
129 *New York Times*, 12 December 1897, ibid., p. 403.
130 Kaiser Wilhelm II, speeches of 18 June and 15 December 1897, printed in Penzler, *Reden Kaiser Wilhelms II. in den Jahren 1896–1900*, pp. 52f. and 78ff; Obst, *Die politischen Reden*, pp. 159f., 167f.
131 Bülow, speech in the Reichstag on 6 December 1897, *Stenographische Berichte der 9. Legislaturperiode*, V. Session, 4. Sitzung, p. 60.

132 Richthofen, report to the Kaiser of 25 September 1899, Fiebig-von Hase, *Lateinamerika*, I, pp. 406f.

133 Ibid., pp. 410 and 440.

134 Ibid., II, p. 859.

135 Ibid., pp. 860f.

136 Diederichs, report for the Kaiser of 7 October 1901, ibid., II, pp. 861f.

137 Ibid., pp. 862f.

138 Kaiser Wilhelm II, marginal note on Pilgrim-Baltazzi's telegram of 10 October 1901, cited ibid., p. 864.

139 Fiebig-von Hase, *Lateinamerika*, II, p. 864.

140 Bülow to Kaiser Wilhelm II, 15 October 1901, quoted ibid., p. 864.

141 Kaiser Wilhelm II, marginal note of 16 October 1901 on Bülow's submission of 15 October 1901, cited ibid., p. 865.

142 Bülow to Kaiser Wilhelm II, 30 December 1901, cited ibid., p. 856.

143 Bülow to Kaiser Wilhelm II, 30 December 1901, cited ibid., p. 871.

144 Ibid., p. 867.

145 Ibid., p. 872.

146 Diederichs to Richthofen, 8 January 1902, cited in ibid., p. 873.

147 Holstein, diary for 11 January 1902, *Holstein Papers*, IV, No. 792.

148 Kaiser Wilhelm II, marginal notes on Bülow's report of 20 January 1902, *Große Politik*, XVII, p. 243, notes 1–2. See above, pp. 216f. and pp. 226f.

149 Fiebig-von Hase, *Lateinamerika*, II, p. 858.

150 Ibid., pp. 879f.

151 Bülow to Kaiser Wilhelm II, 1 September 1902, *Große Politik*, XVII, No. 5107.

152 Kaiser Wilhelm II, marginal notes of 4 September 1902 on Bülow's submission of 1 September 1902, ibid., No. 5107.

153 Kaiser Wilhelm II, marginal notes on Bülow's submission of 3 November 1902, ibid., No. 5108.

154 Bülow to Kaiser Wilhelm II, 3 November 1902, ibid., No. 5108.

155 Fiebig-von Hase, *Lateinamerika*, II, pp. 879f.

156 Kaiser Wilhelm II, marginal notes on Bülow's submission of 3 November 1902, *Große Politik*, XVII, No. 5108. See Fiebig-von Hase, *Lateinamerika*, II, p. 996.

157 Bülow to Kaiser Wilhelm II, 5 November 1902, *Große Politik*, XVII, No. 5109.

158 Bülow, marginal note on Metternich's report of 9 December 1902, ibid., No. 5119.

159 Waldersee, diary for 10 December 1902, GStA Berlin, Waldersee Papers; cf. Meisner, III, p. 197.

160 Kaiser Wilhelm II, marginal note on Bülow's submission of 12 December 1902, *Große Politik*, XVII, No. 5120. Cf. Fiebig-von Hase, *Lateinamerika*, II, p. 1040.

161 Bülow to Kaiser Wilhelm II, 12 December 1902, *Große Politik*, XVII, No. 5120.

162 Büchsel, report to the Kaiser of 10 December 1902, Fiebig-von Hase, *Lateinamerika*, II, pp. 1040f.

163 Büchsel to Kaiser Wilhelm II, 17 December 1902, BA-MA Freiburg-im-Breisgau, RM2/v.2008.

164 Kaiser Wilhelm II, marginal notes on Büchsel's submission of 17 December 1902, ibid.

165 Kaiser Wilhelm II to Senden-Bibran, 17 December 1902, ibid. Once again I thank Dr Ragnhild Fiebig-von Hase for kindly drawing my attention to this document.

166 Senden-Bibran to Kaiser Wilhelm II, 18 December 1902, ibid.

167 Quoted in Fiebig-von Hase, *Lateinamerika*, II, p. 1059.

168 Büchsel, memorandum of 19 January 1903, cited in ibid., p. 1068. For Roosevelt's critical judgement of the Kaiser and his role in foreign policy, see Cecil, *Wilhelm II: Emperor and Exile*, pp. 64, 95 and 105.

169 Fiebig-von Hase, *Lateinamerika*, II, p. 1060.

170 Ibid., p. 1068. See Peter Overlack, 'German War Plans in the Pacific, 1900-1914', *The Historian*, 69 (1998), 579-93; Nancy Mitchell, *The Danger of Dreams: German and American Imperialism in Latin America*, Chapel Hill 1997.

171 Metternich's report of 13 December 1902, *Große Politik*, XVII, No. 5122. See Speck von Sternburg to Auswärtiges Amt, 19 February 1903, ibid., No. 5151.

172 Metternich's report of 29 January 1903 with the Kaiser's marginal notes, ibid., No. 5140.

173 Kaiser Wilhelm II, comments of 15 February 1903 on Bülow to Kaiser Wilhelm II, 14 February 1903, *Große Politik*, XVII, No. 5150.

174 Fiebig-von Hase, 'Die Rolle Kaiser Wilhelms II. in den deutsch-amerikanischen Beziehungen', p. 247.

175 Fiebig-von Hase, *Lateinamerika*, II, p. 1052. For the dislike felt for Sternburg in court circles see Spitzemberg, diary for 7 and 18 January 1903, Vierhaus, *Tagebuch*, pp. 424f.

176 Speck von Sternburg to Bülow, 28 November 1902 with the Kaiser's marginal notes of 13 December 1902, PA AA R 17380.

177 Theodor von Holleben, memorandum of 22 August 1897, in private hands.

178 Kaiser Wilhelm II, marginal note on Speck von Sternburg's report of 19 February 1903, *Große Politik*, XVII, No. 5151.

179 Waldersee, diary for 20 January 1903, GStA Berlin, Waldersee Papers; Meisner, III, pp. 202f.

180 Fiebig-von Hase, *Lateinamerika*, II, p. 1052.

181 Bülow to Auswärtiges Amt, 12 April 1903; Holstein to Bülow, 12 April 1903, PA AA R 17380.

182 Fiebig-von Hase, 'Die Rolle Kaiser Wilhelms II. in den deutsch-amerikanischen Beziehungen', pp. 243f.; *Lateinamerika*, II, pp. 850-942 and 984-1083.

183 Waldersee, diary for 25 December 1902, GStA Berlin, Waldersee Papers; not in Meisner, III, p. 198. But see the entry for 4 January 1903, Meisner, III, pp. 198f.

184 Waldersee, diary for 12 February 1903, ibid.; not in Meisner, III, p. 207.

185 Kaiser Wilhelm II, marginal notes on Speck von Sternburg's report of 19 February 1903, *Große Politik*, XVII, No. 5151.

186 Waldersee, diary for 3 April 1903, GStA Berlin, Waldersee Papers; printed in a distorted manner in Meisner, III, p. 208; *Berliner Neueste Nachrichten*, 23 April 1903, as quoted in Fiebig-von Hase, *Lateinamerika*, II, p. 1082.

187 Waldersee, diary for 11 January 1903, GStA Berlin, Waldersee Papers; Meisner, III, pp. 199f.

188 Waldersee, diary for 16 February 1903, ibid.; omitted in Meisner, III, p. 207.

10   UNCLE AND NEPHEW: EDWARD VII AND THE 'ENCIRCLEMENT' OF GERMANY

1 Spitzemberg, diary for 14 March 1903, Vierhaus, *Tagebuch*, p. 428.

2 Prince Heinrich of Prussia to Tirpitz, 5 October 1903, BA-MA Freiburg-im-Breisgau, Tirpitz Papers, N 253/183.

3 See *Große Politik*, XVII, Nos. 5192-4.

4 Kaiser Wilhelm II, marginal notes on Tattenbach's report of 7 April 1904, cited in McLean, *Royalty and Diplomacy*, pp. 105f.

5 Kaiser Wilhelm II, marginal notes on Wedel's report from Vienna of 29 April 1903, *Große Politik*, XVIII/2, No. 5539; marginal notes on Alvensleben's report of 20 December 1903, ibid., XIX/1, No. 5929. Cf. Hermann Kantorowicz, *Der Geist der englischen Politik und das Gespenst der Einkreisung Deutschlands*, Berlin 1929, pp. 376 and 379.

6 Eckardstein to Bülow, 10 May 1903, *Große Politik*, XVII, No. 5369.

7 Eckardstein, memorandum of 17 January 1904, ibid., XIX/1, No. 5945.

8 Kaiser Wilhelm II, marginal notes on Bernstorff's report of 25 April 1903, ibid., XVII, No. 5361.

9 Kaiser Wilhelm II, marginal notes of 24 January 1904 on Eckardstein's memorandum of 17 January 1904, ibid., XIX/1, No. 5945.

10 Kaiser Wilhelm II, marginal notes on Bernstorff's report of 25 April 1903, ibid., XVII, No. 5361.

11 Bülow to Kaiser Wilhelm II, 31 March 1903, GStA Berlin, BPHA Rep. 53J Lit. B Nr 16a.

12 Bülow to Holstein, 15 May 1903, Holstein, *Geheime Papiere*, IV, No. 815, not in *Holstein Papers*. On the question of Germany's 'encirclement' see Klaus Hildebrand, *Das vergangene Reich. Deutsche Außenpolitik von Bismarck bis Hitler, 1871–1945*, Stuttgart 1995, p. 236; Canis, *Von Bismarck zur Weltpolitik*, p. 401; Thomas Nipperdey, *Deutsche Geschichte, 1866–1918, II, Machtstaat vor der Demokratie*, Munich 1990, p. 699.

13 Bülow, marginal note on Mühlberg's memorandum of 15 July 1903, *Große Politik*, XIX/1, No. 5924.

14 Bülow to Holstein, 16 May 1903, *Holstein Papers*, IV, No. 816.

15 Metternich, report of 2 June 1903 with the Kaiser's approving marginalia, *Große Politik*, XVII, No. 5376.

16 Bülow to Kaiser Wilhelm II, 19 June 1903, with the Kaiser's approving marginal notes, GStA Berlin, BPHA Rep. 53J, Lit. B Nr 16a.

17 McLean, *Royalty and Diplomacy*, p. 106.

18 Kaiser Wilhelm II, marginal notes of 29 December 1903 on an article in the *Daily Chronicle* of 24 December 1903, PA AA R 3701.

19 Kaiser Wilhelm II to Bülow, 1 August 1903, ibid.

20 Kaiser Wilhelm II to King Edward VII, 16 August 1903, RA VIC/X 37/57. Quoted in part in Matthew S. Seligmann, 'Military Diplomacy in a Military Monarchy? Wilhelm II's Relations with the British Service Attachés in Berlin, 1903–1914', in Annika Mombauer and Wilhelm Deist, eds., *The Kaiser. New Research on Wilhelm II's Role in Imperial Germany*, Cambridge 2003, p. 182.

21 Knollys to Lascelles, 23 December 1903, cited in McLean, *Royalty and Diplomacy*, p. 108.

22 Kaiser Wilhelm II, marginal notes on Bernstorff's report of 16 September 1903, *Große Politik*, XVIII/1, No. 5606.

23 Kaiser Wilhelm II, marginal notes on Metternich's report of 23 December 1903, ibid., XIX/1, No. 5968.

24 Kaiser Wilhelm II, marginal notes on Bernstorff's report of 12 October 1903, ibid., No. 5925.

25 Kaiser Wilhelm II, marginal notes on Radolin's report of 6 November 1903, PA AA R 3626.

26 Kaiser Wilhelm II, marginal notes on Speck von Sternburg's report of 26 December 1903, *Große Politik*, XIX/1, No. 5969.

27 Kaiser Wilhelm II, marginal notes on Marschall's report of 5 December 1903, ibid., XVIII/1, No. 5636.

28 Kaiser Wilhelm II, marginal notes on Wedel's report from Vienna of 29 April 1903, ibid., XVIII/2, No. 5559.

29 Monts to Bülow, 26 April 1904 with the Kaiser's approving marginalia, ibid., XX/1, No. 6404.

30 Kaiser Wilhelm II, marginal notes on Marschall's report of 20 April 1904, ibid., XXII, No. 7432.

31 Monts to Bülow, 26 April 1904 with the Kaiser's marginalia, ibid., XX/1, No. 6404.

32 Kaiser Wilhelm II, marginal note on Monts's report of 20 October 1903, cited in McLean, *Royalty and Diplomacy*, p. 107.

33 Bülow to Holstein, 31 October 1903, *Große Politik*, XVIII/2, No. 5918.

34 Kaiser Wilhelm II, marginal notes on Bülow's report of 27 December 1903, ibid., XIX/1, No. 5971.

35 Kaiser Wilhelm II, marginal notes on Richthofen's submission of 2 September 1903, ibid., XVIII/1, No. 5600.

36 Kaiser Wilhelm II, marginal notes on Romberg's report of 5 September 1903, ibid., No. 5602.

37 Bülow to Kaiser Wilhelm II, 7 September 1903, GStA Berlin, BPHA Rep. 53J, Lit. B Nr 16a.

38 Wedel, report from Vienna of 24 September 1903 with the Kaiser's approving marginalia, PA AA R 3647.

39 Kaiser Wilhelm II, marginal note on Wedel's report of 23 September 1903, ibid.

40 Metternich, report of 8 January 1904, *Große Politik*, XIX/1, No. 5931.

41 Kaiser Wilhelm II, marginal note on Bülow's telegram of 12 January 1904, ibid., No. 5936.

42 Lichnowsky, memorandum of 8 January 1904, ibid., No. 5930.

43 Holstein, memorandum of 16 January 1904, ibid., No. 5944. See Bülow to Holstein, 16 January 1904, *Holstein Papers*, IV, No. 818.

44 Eckardstein, memorandum of 17 January 1904 with the Kaiser's marginal notes of 24 January 1904, *Große Politik*, XIX/1, No. 5945.

45 Ibid.

46 Kaiser Wilhelm II, marginal note on Metternich's telegram of 20 January 1904, *Große Politik*, XIX/1, No. 5948.

47 Kaiser Wilhelm II, marginal note on the telegram from Tsar Nicholas II of 21 January 1904, ibid., No. 5947.

48 Alvensleben, telegram of 27 January 1904 with the Kaiser's marginalia, ibid., No. 5953.

49 Bülow, memorandum of 9 April 1904, ibid., XX/1, No. 6374. See Bülow's statement in the Reichstag of 12 April 1904, cited ibid., p. 12. See also Schöllgen, *Imperialismus und Gleichgewicht*, pp. 187ff.

50 Kaiser Wilhelm II to Bülow, telegram of 19 April 1904, *Große Politik*, XX/1, No. 6378.

51 Bülow to Kaiser Wilhelm II, 20 April 1904, ibid., No. 6379.

52 Kaiser Wilhelm II, marginal note on Metternich's report of 9 April 1904, ibid., No. 6375.

53 Bernstorff, report of 16 April 1904 with the Kaiser's marginal notes, ibid., No. 6376.

54 Büchsel to Senden, 9 March 1904, cited in Steinberg, 'Germany and the Russo-Japanese War', 1972.

55 Kaiser Wilhelm II to Bülow, 16 March 1904, *Große Politik*, XVII, No. 5208; Radowitz to Richthofen, 23 March 1904, ibid., No. 5209. See Valentini, *Kaiser und Kabinettschef*, p. 68.

56 See Metternich's report of 26 November 1903, *Große Politik*, XVII, No. 5207.

57 Radowitz to Richthofen, 23 March 1904, ibid., No. 5209.

58 Kaiser Wilhelm II to Bülow, 16 March 1904, ibid., No. 5208.

59 See Röhl, *The Kaiser's Personal Monarchy*, pp. 777f.

60 Kaiser Wilhelm II to Bülow, 16 March 1904, *Große Politik*, XVII, No. 5208; Radolin to Bülow, 30 March 1904 with the Kaiser's marginalia, ibid., No. 5210.

61 Radowitz to Richthofen, 23 March 1904, *Große Politik*, XVII, No. 5209.

62 See Holstein to Richthofen, 28 March 1904, *Holstein Papers*, IV, No. 826. For the reaction of Delcassé, see Maurice Paléologue, *Un Grand Tournant de la Politique Mondiale 1904–1906*, Paris 1934, pp. 97f.

63 Kaiser Wilhelm II to Bülow, 16 March 1904, *Große Politik*, XVII, No. 5208.

64 Holstein to Richthofen, 28 March 1904, *Holstein Papers*, IV, No. 826; also *Große Politik*, XX/1, Nos. 6481, 6512 and 6513.

65 Kaiser Wilhelm II to Tsar Nicholas II, 29 March 1904, Goetz, *Briefe Wilhelms II. an den Zaren*, No. XXXIII, pp. 113–16 and 338–40.

66 Valentini, *Kaiser und Kabinettschef*, p. 70.

67 Balfour to King Edward VII, no date, RA VIC/R 24/67.

68 Battenberg to King Edward VII, 13 May 1904, RA VIC/W 56/119.

69 Radolin to Bülow, 4 February 1904, *Große Politik*, XX/1, No. 6431. See Radolin to Holstein, 21 February 1904, *Holstein Papers*, IV, No. 822. See also Bülow to Monts, 6 March 1904, *Große Politik*, XX/1, No. 6389.

70 Monts, telegram of 17 March 1904, ibid., No. 6436; Monts to Holstein, 18 March 1904, *Holstein Papers*, IV, No. 825; Holstein, memorandum of 9 April 1904, ibid., No. 827.

71 Kaiser Wilhelm II to King Edward VII, 9, 11 and 12 April 1904. RA VIC/W 44/64a, 64b and 65a.

72 Kaiser Wilhelm II, marginal notes on Bernstorff's report of 16 April 1904, *Große Politik*, XX/1, No. 6376; marginal note on Bernstorff's report of 17 May 1904, PA AA R 3701.

73 King Edward VII to Kaiser Wilhelm II, 12 May 1904, PA AA Berlin R 3701.

74 Kaiser Wilhelm II to Bülow, telegram, 6 June 1904, *Große Politik*, XX/1, No. 6463.

75 Lansdowne to King Edward VII, 16 June 1904, RA VIC/W 44/110.

76 Metternich to Auswärtiges Amt, 17 June 1904, PA AA R 3701; Bülow to Kaiser Wilhelm II, 18 June 1904, ibid.

77 Bülow to Auswärtiges Amt, 20 and 21 June 1904, ibid.

78 Paléologue, diary for 25 June 1904, *Un Grand Tournant*, pp. 105f.

79 Zedlitz-Trützschler, memorandum of 21 July 1904, *Zwölf Jahre*, p. 78.

80 Valentini, *Kaiser und Kabinettschef*, pp. 74f.

81 Zedlitz-Trützschler, memorandum of 21 July 1904, *Zwölf Jahre*, pp. 78f.

82 King Edward VII to Kaiser Wilhelm II, 30 June and 1 July 1904; Kaiser Wilhelm II to King Edward VII, 1 July 1904, PA AA R 3702.

83 Bülow to Holstein, 29 June 1904, *Holstein Papers*, IV, No. 829. See Bülow's memorandum of 26 June 1904, *Große Politik*, XIX/1, No. 6038.

84 Zedlitz-Trützschler, memorandum of 21 July 1904, *Zwölf Jahre*, pp. 77f.

11   EAST ASIA IN FLAMES: THE RUSSO-JAPANESE WAR
AND ITS CONSEQUENCES

1 See Canis, *Abgrund*, pp. 79ff.

2 See Roderick R. McLean, 'Dreams of a German Europe: Kaiser Wilhelm II and the Treaty of Björkö of 1905', in Annika Mombauer and Wilhelm Deist, eds., *The Kaiser. New Research on Wilhelm II's Role in Imperial Germany*, Cambridge 2003, pp. 119–42.

3 See above, pp. 164 and 184.

4 Kaiser Wilhelm II, marginal notes on Romberg's report from St Petersburg of 7 November 1903, *Große Politik*, XVIII/2, No. 5919.

5 Kaiser Wilhelm II to Tsar Nicholas II, 19 November 1903, Goetz, *Briefe Wilhelms II. an den Zaren*, pp. 95ff. and 330f.

6 Savinsky, 'Guillaume II', 771f.

7 Steinberg, 'Germany and the Russo-Japanese War', p. 1969.

8 Kaiser Wilhelm II to Tsar Nicholas II, 4 December 1903, Goetz, *Briefe Wilhelms II. an den Zaren*, pp. 98ff. and 332f.

9 Bülow to Kaiser Wilhelm II, 27 December 1903, *Große Politik*, XIX/1, No. 5970. See also Eckardstein, memorandum of 17 January 1904, ibid., No. 5945; Speck von Sternburg, telegram of 21 March 1904, ibid., No. 5992; Metternich, memorandum of 25 December 1904, ibid., XIX/2, No. 6156; Boutiron to Delcassé, 24 and 26 October 1904, *Documents diplomatiques français 1871–1914*, ed. Ministère Étrangère, 41 vols., Paris 1929–36, 2nd series, V, Nos. 385 and 394.

10 Kaiser Wilhelm II, marginalia on Bülow's submission of 27 December 1903, *Große Politik*, XIX/1, No. 5971.

11 Kaiser Wilhelm II to Tsar Nicholas II, 3 January 1904, Goetz, *Briefe Wilhelms II. an den Zaren*, pp. 102ff. and 333ff.

12 Kaiser Wilhelm II, marginal note on Bülow's submission of 4 January 1904, *Große Politik*, XIX/1, No. 5972.

13 Kaiser Wilhelm II, marginal notes on Bülow's submission of 8 January 1904, ibid., No. 5933. See the memoranda of Richthofen and Bülow, ibid., Nos. 5934–5.

14 Kaiser Wilhelm II to Tsar Nicholas II, 7 January 1904, printed in a French translation in Savinsky, 'Guillaume II', 772f.

15 Kaiser Wilhelm II to Tsar Nicholas II, 9 January 1904, printed in a French translation ibid., 773.

16 Kaiser Wilhelm II to Tsar Nicholas II, 9 January 1904, Goetz, *Briefe Wilhelms II. an den Zaren*, pp. 106ff. and 333ff.

17 Kaiser Wilhelm II, marginal notes on Eckardstein's telegram of 8 January 1904 from London, *Große Politik*, XIX/1, No. 5931.

18 Kaiser Wilhelm II, marginal note on Arco's telegram of 13 January 1904 from Tokyo, ibid., No. 5937. See Kaiser Wilhelm II to Tsar Nicholas II, 14 January 1904, printed in a French translation in Savinsky, 'Guillaume II', 776.

19 Kaiser Wilhelm II to Tsar Nicholas II, telegram, 19 January 1904, *Große Politik*, XIX/1, No. 5946. See Savinsky, 'Guillaume II', 777.

20 Tsar Nicholas II to Kaiser Wilhelm II, telegram, 21 January 1904, *Große Politik*, XIX/1, No. 5947.

21 Kaiser Wilhelm II, marginal notes on Metternich's telegram from London, 20 January 1904, ibid., No. 5948. See also his marginal notes on Radolin's telegram from Paris, 30 January 1904, ibid., No. 5954.

22 Kaiser Wilhelm II, marginal notes on Metternich's report of 8 February 1904, ibid., No. 5957. See Zedlitz-Trützschler, diary for 7 December 1904, *Zwölf Jahre*, pp. 101–3.

23 Tsar Nicholas II to Kaiser Wilhelm II, 24 January 1904, *Große Politik*, XIX/1, No. 5952.

24 Kaiser Wilhelm II, marginal notes on Alvensleben's report of 27 January 1904, ibid., No. 5953.

25 Bülow, memorandum of 14 February 1904, ibid., No. 5961.

26 Bülow to Kaiser Wilhelm II, 2 August 1904, GStA Berlin, BPHA Rep 53J, Lit. B Nr 16a.

27 Bülow, memorandum of 16 January 1904, *Große Politik*, XIX/1, No. 5943.

28 Holstein, memorandum of 16 January 1904, ibid., No. 5944. See also No. 5951.

29 Bülow to Holstein, 15 January 1904, ibid., No. 5942; Bülow, memorandum of 16 January 1904, ibid., No. 5943. See also Kaiser Wilhelm II, marginal notes on Eckardstein's report of 17 January 1904, ibid., No. 5945; Zedlitz-Trützschler, diary for 1 June 1904, *Zwölf Jahre*, pp. 71f.

30 Bülow, memorandum of 14 February 1904, *Große Politik*, XIX/1, No. 5961.

31 Kaiser Wilhelm II, marginal note of 8 February 1904 on Alvensleben's report of 7 February 1904, cited in Canis, *Abgrund*, pp. 95f.

32 Kaiser Wilhelm II, marginal comment of 9 September 1904 on Arco's report of 11 August 1904, *Große Politik*, XIX/1, No. 6047.

33 Kaiser Wilhelm II, marginal comment of 25 December 1904 on Bülow's submission of 24 December 1904, ibid., XIX/2, No. 6274.

34 Kaiser Wilhelm II to Tsar Nicholas II, 11 February 1904, Goetz, *Briefe Wilhelms II. an den Zaren*, No. XXXII, pp. 109–12 and 337f. For the background see David Schimmelpenninck van der Oye, *Towards the Rising Sun. Russian Ideologies of Empire and the Path to War with Japan*, DeKalb, IL 2006; David Wolff, ed., *The Russo-Japanese War in Global*

Perspective: World War Zero, Leiden 2007; Josef Kreiner, ed., *Der Russisch-Japanische Krieg (1904/05)*, Göttingen 2005.

35 Zedlitz-Trützschler, diary for 19 November 1904, *Zwölf Jahre*, p. 94; Müller, diary for 22 November–1 December 1904, BA-MA Freiburg-im-Breisgau, Müller Papers.

36 Kaiser Wilhelm II to Tsar Nicholas II, 19 August 1904, Goetz, *Briefe Wilhelms II. an den Zaren*, No. XXXV, pp. 122–6 and 342–4.

37 See the comment of the editors of *Große Politik*, XIX/2, p. 390.

38 Senden to Bülow, 9 January 1904, cited in Steinberg, 'Germany and the Russo-Japanese War', 1969.

39 On Hopman's mission see Michael Epkenhans, ed., *Albert Hopman. Das ereignisreiche Leben eines 'Wilhelminers'. Tagebücher, Briefe, Aufzeichnungen 1901 bis 1920*, Munich 2004, pp. 101–19; Müller, diary for 21 November 1904, BA-MA Freiburg-im-Breisgau, Müller Papers.

40 See Johannes Hürter, ed., *Paul von Hintze. Marineoffizier, Diplomat, Staatssekretär. Dokumente einer Karriere zwischen Militär und Politik, 1903–1918*, Munich 1998, pp. 121ff.

41 Ibid., p. 33.

42 Hintze to Tirpitz, 21 December 1904, Steinberg, 'Germany and the Russo-Japanese War', 1969f.; Hürter, *Hintze*, p. 32.

43 Order of 10 February 1904, repeated on 5 February 1905, cited in Steinberg, 'Germany and the Russo-Japanese War', 1970.

44 Ibid.

45 Kaiser Wilhelm II to Tsar Nicholas II, 6 June 1904, Goetz, *Briefe Wilhelms II. an den Zaren*, No. XXXIV, pp. 118–21 and 340–2. The version printed in *Große Politik*, XIX/1, No. 6035 is probably based on an earlier draft.

46 McLean, 'Dreams of a German Europe', p. 125.

47 Kaiser Wilhelm II to Tsar Nicholas II, 6 June 1904, Goetz, *Briefe Wilhelms II. an den Zaren*, No. XXXIV, pp. 118–21 and 340–2. Cf. *Große Politik*, XIX/1, No. 6035.

48 Ibid.

49 Kaiser Wilhelm II to Tsar Nicholas II, 12 June 1904, *Große Politik*, XIX/1, No. 6037. For Lambsdorff's position in St Petersburg see Gustav Graf von Lambsdorff, *Die Militärbevollmächtigten Kaiser Wilhelms II. am Zarenhofe 1904–1914*, Berlin 1937. See McLean, *Royalty and Diplomacy*, p. 49.

50 Zedlitz-Trützschler, diary for 1 June 1904, *Zwölf Jahre*, pp. 71f.

51 Kaiser Wilhelm II, marginal notes on Speck von Sternburg's report of 9 May 1904, *Große Politik*, XIX/1, No. 5994.

52 Kaiser Wilhelm II, marginal notes on Romberg's report of 10 June 1904, ibid., No. 6036.

53 Kaiser Wilhelm II to Tsar Nicholas II, 19 August 1904, Goetz, *Briefe Wilhelms II. an den Zaren*, No. XXXV, pp. 122–6 and 342–4.

54 Lascelles to Knollys, 13 July 1904, with the King's approving comment, RA VIC/W 44/117.

55 Kaiser Wilhelm II to Tsar Nicholas II, 8 October 1904, *Große Politik*, XIX/1, No. 6057.

56 Kaiser Wilhelm to Tsar Nicholas II, 17 July 1904, ibid., No. 6062.

57 Tsar Nicholas II to Kaiser Wilhelm II, 20 July 1904, ibid., p. 231.

58 Kaiser Wilhelm to Tsar Nicholas II, 23 July 1904, ibid., No. 6064.

59 Tsar Nicholas II to Kaiser Wilhelm II, 31 July 1904, ibid., p. 232.

60 Metternich, telegram of 23 July 1904, ibid., No. 6065.

61 Tschirschky to Auswärtiges Amt, 24 July 1904, ibid., p. 232.

62 Kaiser Wilhelm II to Bülow, 28 August 1904, ibid., No. 6049. See also Bülow to Kaiser Wilhelm II, 15 July 1904, ibid., No. 6043; McLean, 'Dreams of a German Europe', pp. 123–5.

63 Bülow to Kaiser Wilhelm II, 2 August 1904, GStA Berlin, Rep. 53J Lit. B Nr 16a.

64 Kaiser Wilhelm II, marginal note of 2 September 1904 on Pourtalès's report of 24 August 1904, *Große Politik*, XIX/2, No. 6264 annex.

65 Kaiser Wilhelm II to Tsar Nicholas II, 6 June 1904, Goetz, *Briefe Wilhelms II. an den Zaren*, No. XXXIV, pp. 118–21 and 340–2. Cf. *Große Politik*, XIX/1, No. 6035.

66 Kaiser Wilhelm II, marginal note of 1 September 1904 on Bülow's submission of 31 August 1904, ibid., XIX/2, No. 6264.

67 Kaiser Wilhelm II, marginal notes of 2 September 1904 on Pourtalès's report of 24 August 1904, ibid., No. 6264 annex.

68 Kaiser Wilhelm II, marginal comments of 1 September 1904 on Bülow's submission of 31 August 1904, ibid., No. 6264.

69 Ibid.

70 Kaiser Wilhelm II to Tsar Nicholas II, 8 October 1904, ibid., XIX/1, No. 6057.

71 Kaiser Wilhelm II to Tsar Nicholas II, 19 October 1904, ibid., XIX/2, No. 6163.

72 Tsar Nicholas II to Kaiser Wilhelm II, 30 October 1904, ibid., No. 6064.

73 Kaiser Wilhelm II to Tsar Nicholas II, 15 November 1904, ibid., No. 6170.

74 Kaiser Wilhelm II to Tsar Nicholas II, 19 November 1904, ibid., No. 6174, printed in Charles Louis Seeger, ed., *The Memoirs of Alexander Iswolsky*, London 1920 (cited below as Isvolsky, *Memoirs*), pp. 47f. For the Japanese peace feelers in London, Paris and Washington see Holstein to Radolin, 25 November 1904, *Holstein Papers*, IV, No. 863.

75 Zedlitz-Trützschler, diary for 2 and 7 December 1904, *Zwölf Jahre*, pp. 101–3.

76 Zedlitz-Trützschler, diary for 7 December 1904, ibid., pp. 101f.

77 'Russia and Germany: A Far Eastern Understanding', *The Times*, 14 September 1904; Wallace to Knollys, 19 September 1904, RA VIC/W 45/1; Lascelles to Knollys, 19 September 1904, RA VIC/W 45/2; Lascelles to Lansdowne, 22 September 1904, cited in Steinberg, 'Germany and the Russo-Japanese War', p. 1976. Wallace believed Valentine Chirol to be the author of the article.

78 See Lamar Cecil, 'Coal for the Fleet That Had to Die', *American Historical Review*, 69/4, 1964, 990–1005.

79 Ballin to Grumme-Douglas, 24 September 1904, GStA Berlin, BPHA Rep. 53 Nr 361.

80 Kaiser Wilhelm II, marginal notes of 26 September 1904 on Ballin to Grumme-Douglas, 24 September 1904, ibid.

81 Kaiser Wilhelm II to Tsar Nicholas II, 8 October 1904, *Große Politik*, XIX/1, No. 6057.

82 Kaiser Wilhelm II to Tsar Nicholas II, 27 October 1904, ibid., No. 6118.

83 Kaiser Wilhelm II to Tsar Nicholas II, 8 October 1904, ibid., No. 6057.

84 Kaiser Wilhelm II to Tsar Nicholas II, 10 October 1904, Goetz, *Briefe Wilhelms II. an den Zaren*, No. XXXVI, pp. 128f. and 345f.

85 See J. A. White, *The Diplomacy of the Russo-Japanese War*, Princeton 1964, pp. 179–83.

86 Flotow, report from Paris of 26 October 1904 with the Kaiser's marginal notes, *Große Politik*, XIX/1, No. 6105; Metternich to Bülow, 1 November 1904, ibid., No. 6111. See also Lascelles to Prince Christian of Schleswig-Holstein, 1 November 1904, RA VIC/Add A18/Y10; Metternich to Knollys, 5 November 1904, RA VIC/W 45/72.

87 Fisher to his wife, 28 October 1904, cited in Arthur J. Marder, *From the Dreadnought to Scapa Flow*, 5 vols., London 1961–71, I, p. 111.

88 Zedlitz-Trützschler, diary for 3 November 1904, *Zwölf Jahre*, pp. 86f. See below, p. 295.

89 Kaiser Wilhelm II, marginal notes on Metternich's report of 24 October 1904, *Große Politik*, XIX/1, No. 6101.

90 Kaiser Wilhelm II, marginal notes on Metternich's report of 27 October 1904, ibid., No. 6104.

91 Kaiser Wilhelm II, marginal note on Schulenburg's telegram of 27 October 1904, ibid., No. 6106.

92 Lambsdorff to Kaiser Wilhelm II, telegram, 30 October 1904, ibid., No. 6122 with note.

93 Bülow to Kaiser Wilhelm II, 31 October 1904, ibid., No. 6123.

94 Kaiser Wilhelm II to Tsar Nicholas II, 27 October 1904, ibid., No. 6118.

95 Bülow to Kaiser Wilhelm II, 31 October 1904, ibid., No. 6123. See above, p. 286.

96 Kaiser Wilhelm II, marginal note on Schulenburg's telegram of 27 October 1904, *Große Politik*, XIX/1, No. 6106.

97 Adolf von Trotha, note of 31 October 1904; Tirpitz to Richthofen, 1 November 1904, Niedersächsisches Staatsarchiv Bückeburg, Trotha Papers, E Nr 1. See Steinberg, 'Germany and the Russo-Japanese War', p. 1977. Also Canis, *Abgrund*, p. 106.

98 Schlieffen to War Department, 7 October 1904; Einem to Bülow, 17 October 1904, cited in Canis, *Abgrund*, p. 110.

99 Tsar Nicholas II to Kaiser Wilhelm II, 29 October 1904, ibid., No. 6119. See ibid., p. 303, note.

100 Kaiser Wilhelm II, marginal comment of 9 September 1904 on Arco's report of 11 August 1904, ibid., No. 6047. See above, pp. 270ff.

101 See Rich, *Friedrich von Holstein*, II, pp. 688f.

102 Tirpitz to Richthofen, 1 November 1904, Niedersächsisches Staatsarchiv Bückeburg, Trotha Papers, E Nr 1.

103 Bülow to Kaiser Wilhelm II, 30 October 1904, *Große Politik*, XIX/1, No. 6120.

104 Kaiser Wilhelm II to Tsar Nicholas II, ibid., No. 6120 annex I with note. See Goetz, *Briefe Wilhelms II. an den Zaren*, No. XXXVII, pp. 130–4 and 346–8.

105 Tsar Nicholas II to Kaiser Wilhelm II, 7 and 23 November 1904, *Große Politik*, XIX/1, No. 6124 with annex and No. 6216, annex.

106 Boutiron to Delcassé, 26 October 1904, *Documents diplomatiques français*, 2nd series, V, No. 394; McLean, 'Dreams of a German Europe', p. 125.

107 Bülow to Kaiser Wilhelm II, 16 November 1904, *Große Politik*, XIX/1, No. 6125.

108 Bülow to Kaiser Wilhelm II, 16 November 1904, ibid., No. 6125 with annex.

109 Kaiser Wilhelm II to Tsar Nicholas II, 17 November 1904, Goetz, *Briefe Wilhelms II. an den Zaren*, No. XXXIX. See Canis, *Abgrund*, p. 107, note 85.

110 Kaiser Wilhelm II, marginal note of 17 November 1904 on Bülow's submission of 16 November 1904, *Große Politik*, XIX/1, No. 6125, note. The letter to the Tsar is printed in Goetz, *Briefe Wilhelms II. an den Zaren*, pp. 349ff.

111 Tsar Nicholas II to Kaiser Wilhelm II, 23 November 1904, *Große Politik*, XIX/1, No. 6216 annex.

112 Fesser, *Traum vom Platz an der Sonne*, p. 81.

113 Kaiser Wilhelm II to Bülow, 23 November 1904, *Große Politik*, XIX/1, No. 6126.

114 Bülow to Kaiser Wilhelm II, 24 November 1904, ibid., No. 6127 with annex.

115 See Tsar Nicholas II to Kaiser Wilhelm II, 7 December 1904, ibid., No. 6131; Zedlitz-Trützschler, diary for 10 December 1904, *Zwölf Jahre*, pp. 103f.

116 Bülow to Kaiser Wilhelm II, 6 December 1904, with the Kaiser's marginal notes, *Große Politik*, XIX/1, No. 6088; Kaiser Wilhelm II to Tsar Nicholas II, 7 December 1904, ibid., No. 6130; Goetz, *Briefe Wilhelms II. an den Zaren*, pp. 150 and 353. See also *Große Politik*, XIX/1, No. 6132.

117 Bülow to Alvensleben, 12 December 1904, ibid., No. 6135; Bülow to Holstein, 15 December 1904, Holstein to Bülow, 15 December 1904, Holstein to Metternich, 16 December 1904, *Holstein Papers*, IV, Nos 869–71.

118 Kaiser Wilhelm II, marginal notes on Alvensleben's report of 11 December 1904, *Große Politik*, XIX/1, No. 6134.

119 Kaiser Wilhelm II to Tsar Nicholas II, 21 December 1904, Goetz, *Briefe Wilhelms II. an den Zaren*, pp. 152f. and 354. Cf. the draft printed in *Große Politik*, XIX/1, No. 6141.

120 See Canis, *Abgrund*, pp. 107 and 113.

121 Kaiser Wilhelm II to Bülow, 28 December 1904, ibid., No. 6146. See Tsar Nicholas II to Kaiser Wilhelm II, 25 December 1904, ibid., No. 6145.

122 Bülow to Kaiser Wilhelm II, 26 December 1904, ibid., XIX/2, No. 6178.

123 Kaiser Wilhelm II, marginal note on Alvensleben's letter to Bülow of 26 December 1904, ibid., No. 6158.

124 Kaiser Wilhelm II, marginal notes on Alvensleben's report of 26 December 1904, ibid., XIX/1, No. 6144.

125 Kaiser Wilhelm II, marginal comment on Alvensleben to Bülow, 26 December 1904, ibid., XIX/2, No. 6158.

126 Kaiser Wilhelm II to Bülow, 28 December 1904, ibid., XIX/1, No. 6146. Bülow to Kaiser Wilhelm II, 26 December 1904, with the Kaiser's marginal notes, ibid., XIX/2, No. 6178. See the Kaiser's marginal notes on Erckert's memorandum of 18 November 1904, ibid., No. 6176. Also Kaiser Wilhelm II, comment of 16 January 1905 on Bülow's submission of 15 January 1905, ibid., No. 6280.

127 Kaiser Wilhelm II, marginal note on Bülow's submission of 14 February 1905, ibid., XIX/1, No. 6093.

128 Kaiser Wilhelm II, marginal note on the text drafted by the Auswärtiges Amt for a letter from him to the King of Italy, submitted by Bülow on 10 March 1905, ibid., XX/1, p. 98, note.

129 Bülow to Kaiser Wilhelm II with the Kaiser's marginal notes, 18 February 1905, ibid., No. 6186.

130 Spring Rice to Knollys, 2 March 1905, RA VIC/W 45/122.

131 President Roosevelt to King Edward VII, 9 March 1905, RA VIC/W 45/126a.

132 Lascelles to Knollys, 24 March 1905, RA VIC/W 45/146.

12   OPERATIONAL PLANS FOR A WAR IN WESTERN EUROPE

1 Paléologue, *Un Grand Tournant*, pp. 96ff.

2 Zedlitz-Trützschler, diary for 3 November 1904, *Zwölf Jahre*, pp. 86ff.

3 Kaiser Wilhelm II, marginal notes on Alvensleben's report of 26 December 1904, *Große Politik*, XIX/1, No. 6144. See his marginalia on Metternich's report of 12 January 1905, ibid., XX/1, No. 6425.

4 Cf. Bülow to Kaiser Wilhelm II together with the latter's numerous comments, 26 December 1904, ibid., XIX/2, No. 6157. This document is incomplete in *Große Politik*; the full version is in PA AA R 18858.

5 Kaiser Wilhelm II to Bülow, 23 November 1904, *Große Politik*, XIX/1, No. 6126.

6 Zedlitz-Trützschler, diary for 21 November 1904, *Zwölf Jahre*, p. 97.

7 Kaiser Wilhelm II, marginal note on Alvensleben to Bülow, 26 December 1904, *Große Politik*, XIX/1, No. 6144.

8 Bülow to Kaiser Wilhelm II with marginal note, 24 December 1904, ibid., XIX/2, No. 6274. These deliberations represented an early draft of a reply to President Roosevelt.

9 Zedlitz-Trützschler, diary for 3 November 1904, *Zwölf Jahre*, pp. 86ff.

10 Zedlitz-Trützschler, diary for 10 December 1904, ibid., p. 103.

11 Schoen to Bülow, 2 December 1904, as cited in Bülow, *Denkwürdigkeiten*, II, pp. 66–8.

12 Holstein to Ida von Stülpnagel, 23 April 1904, Holstein, *Lebensbekenntnis*, p. 232.

13 Spitzemberg, diary for 28 August 1904, Vierhaus, *Tagebuch*, p. 442.

14 Trotha to Hülsen-Haeseler, 7 December 1904, cited in Hull, *Absolute Destruction*, p. 63.

15 David Olusoga and Casper W. Erichsen, *The Kaiser's Holocaust. Germany's Forgotten Genocide*, London 2010, pp. 149f.

16 See the compelling evidence in Hull, *Absolute Destruction*, pp. 28ff. See also Jeremy Sarkin, *Germany's Genocide of the Herero: Kaiser Wilhelm II, his General, his Settlers, his Soldiers*, Cape Town 2011.

17 Bülow to Kaiser Wilhelm II, 24 November 1904, cited in Hull, *Absolute Destruction*, p. 64.

18 Ibid., pp. 64f.

19 Trotha to Schlieffen, 13 December 1904, cited ibid., p. 65.

20 Ibid., pp. 66–9; Olusoga and Erichsen, *Kaiser's Holocaust*, pp. 158–61.

21 Zedlitz-Trützschler, diary for 24 May 1904, *Zwölf Jahre*, p. 68.

22 Holzing-Berstett to his mother, no date [September 1904], GLA Karlsruhe, Holzing-Berstett Papers, 116/11.

23 Waldersee, diary for 5 January 1904, GStA Berlin, Waldersee Papers; cf. Meisner, III, p. 226. See Annika Mombauer, *Helmuth von Moltke and the Origins of the First World War*, Cambridge 2001, pp. 58ff.

24 Zedlitz-Trützschler, diary for 1 October 1904, *Zwölf Jahre*, pp. 83f. See also p. 42.

25 Gleichen, report on the imperial manoeuvres, 6 October 1904, RA VIC/W 45/3.

26 Holzing-Berstett to his father, 4 January 1904, GLA Karlsruhe, Holzing-Berstett Papers, 116/11.

27 Waldersee, diary for 5 January 1904, GStA Berlin, Waldersee Papers. Cf. Meisner, III, p. 225.

28 Waldersee, notes dated 5 January and 6 February 1904, ibid., VI.HA-B.I No. 7 (Engelbrecht).doc, Blatt 206. I thank Dr Annika Mombauer warmly for showing me this coded passage in Waldersee's Papers. For Moltke's appointment as Chief of General Staff see Mombauer, *Moltke*, pp. 42ff.

29 Bogdan Graf von Hutten-Czapski, *Sechzig Jahre Politik und Gesellschaft*, 2 vols., Berlin 1936, I, p. 410; Mombauer, *Moltke*, pp. 51ff.

30 Wagner to von der Goltz, 19 January 1904, BA-MA Freiburg-im-Breisgau, von der Goltz Papers, N737 Mappe 16.

31 Mudra to von der Goltz, 8 March 1904, ibid., Mappe 15.

32 Hermann von Stein, *Erlebnisse und Betrachtungen aus der Zeit des Weltkrieges*, Leipzig 1919, p. 36. See also Groener to Strube, 7 January 1931, cited in Mombauer, *Moltke*, p. 67.

33 Müller to Tirpitz, 8 February 1905, in Alfred von Tirpitz, *Der Aufbau der deutschen Weltmacht*, Stuttgart and Berlin 1924, p. 15.

34 Heeringen, memorandum of 12 April 1902 'betreffend den Krieg zwischen Deutschland und England', in Ivo Nikolai Lambi, *The Navy and German Power Politics 1862–1914*, Boston, London and Sydney 1984, pp. 215f.

35 Büchsel, notes for an audience with the Kaiser, 21 March 1903, BA-MA Freiburg-im-Breisgau, RM5/885.

36 Minutes of the discussions in the Admiralty Staff of 14 November 1902, ibid., RM5/1601.

37 Memorandum 'Grundlage für Erwägungen, betreffend den Krieg zwischen Grossbritannien und Deutschland', no date, [early 1903], ibid.

38 Memorandum of the Admiralty Staff of 17 May 1902, ibid.; Lambi, *Navy and German Power Politics*, pp. 210–13.

39 Memorandum 'Bemerkungen z. eventl. Berücksichtigung bei späterer Fortsetzung der Verhandlungen mit Gr. Gen. Stab betr. Mob.-Maßnahmen im Krieg gegen England', November 1901, BA-MA Freiburg-im-Breisgau, RM5/1601.

40 Lambi, *Navy and German Power Politics*, p. 214.

41 Schlieffen to Büchsel, 15 December 1902, BA-MA Freiburg-im-Breisgau, RM5/1601; minutes of the meeting of 22 December 1902 'über Operationsplan gegen England', ibid.

42 Schlieffen to Büchsel, 6 August 1903, ibid.

43 Büchsel to Schlieffen, 13 August 1903, note by Souchon of 15 October 1903, cited in Lambi, *Navy and German Power Politics*, p. 223.

44 Prussian Ministry of War to Admiralty Staff, 18 July 1904, BA-MA Freiburg-im-Breisgau, RM5/1601; also Admiralty Staff to Reich Navy Office, 6 January 1904, ibid..

45 See above, pp. 285f.

46 Kaiser Wilhelm II to Bülow, 29 March 1903, *Große Politik*, XIX/1, No. 5962, note.

47 See the speeches and telegrams of the King and the Kaiser in Copenhagen of 2 April 1903, in Penzler, *Reden Kaiser Wilhelms II. in den Jahren 1901–1905*, pp. 153–5.

48 Bülow to Kaiser Wilhelm II, 31 March 1903, GStA Berlin, BPHA Rep. 53J Lit. B Nr 16a. See Holstein to Ida von Stülpnagel, 20 April 1903, Rogge, *Friedrich von Holstein, Lebensbekenntnis*, pp. 220ff.

49 See above, p. 305.

50 Kaiser Wilhelm II, personal additions to Bülow's text of 7 November 1903, *Große Politik*, XVIII/1, No. 5422; Kaiser Wilhelm II to Tsar Nicholas II, 15 December 1903, ibid., XIX/1, No. 5963; Tsar Nicholas II to Kaiser Wilhelm II, 16 December 1903, ibid., No. 5964.

51 Kaiser Wilhelm II to Tsar Nicholas II, 3 January 1904, Goetz, *Briefe Wilhelms II. an den Zaren*, No. XXX, pp. 102–5 and 333–5.

52 Kaiser Wilhelm II to Tsar Nicholas II, 17 December 1903, *Große Politik*, XIX/1, No. 5965.

53 Tirpitz, memorandum of 14 November 1903, cited in Steinberg, 'Germany and the Russo-Japanese War', 1967.

54 Bülow to Kaiser Wilhelm II, 27 December 1903, *Große Politik*, XIX/1, No. 5970.

55 Kaiser Wilhelm II, marginal notes on Bülow's draft of 27 December 1903, ibid., No. 5970, annex; Kaiser Wilhelm II, marginalia on Bülow's submission of 27 December 1903, ibid., No. 5971. See also No. 5972 above; Vogel, *Rußlandpolitik*, pp. 163f.

56 Kaiser Wilhelm II, marginalia on Bülow's submission of 27 December 1903, *Große Politik*, XIX/1, No. 5971.

57 King Christian IX of Denmark to Kaiser Wilhelm II, 16 February 1904, ibid., No. 5974.

58 Kaiser Wilhelm II to King Christian IX of Denmark, 26 February 1904, ibid., No. 5975.

59 See below, pp. 386–92. Also Holstein, memorandum for Bülow, 31 July 1905, *Holstein Papers*, IV, No. 904.

60 Büchsel to Kaiser Wilhelm II, 19 January 1904, BA-MA Freiburg-im-Breisgau, RM5/886.

61 Bülow, *Denkwürdigkeiten*, II, pp. 72–6.

62 Gerhard Ritter, *Der Schlieffenplan. Kritik eines Mythos*, Munich 1956, p. 99; Gordon A. Craig, *Germany 1866–1945*, Oxford 1978, p. 317; Paul Kennedy, ed., *The War Plans of the Great Powers, 1880–1914*, Boston 1985, pp. 206f.; Arden Bucholz, *Moltke, Schlieffen and Prussian War Planning*, Providence and Oxford 1991, pp. 196f.

63 Hans Adolf von Bülow, memorandum of 30 December 1904, printed in *Holstein Papers*, IV, No. 904 annex. Cf. Bülow, *Denkwürdigkeiten*, II, pp. 72–6.

64 Robert Devleeshouwer, *Les Belges et le Danger de Guerre, 1910–1914*, Louvain and Paris 1958, pp. 53f.

65 See Baron Van der Elst, 'La Préméditation de l'Allemagne', *Revue de Paris*, 1 August 1923.

66 Comte Louis de Lichtervelde, *Léopold of the Belgians*, New York and London 1929, pp. 267f.

67 Bülow to Kaiser Wilhelm II, 30 July 1905, as quoted in Bülow to Auswärtiges Amt, 30 July 1905, *Große Politik*, XIX/2, No. 6229.

68 See Cees Fasseur, *Wilhelmina. De jonge Koningin*, Amsterdam 1998, p. 419.

69 Idenburg to Governor-General Rooseboom, 16 February 1904, printed in *Bescheiden betreffende de buitenlandse politiek van Nederland, 1848–1919*, third series, II (1903–7), The Hague 1958, No. 159, note 2. Cf. Fasseur, *Wilhelmina*, p. 419. I am grateful to Dr Ragnhild Fiebig-von Hase for drawing my attention to this and the following document.

70 As cited in Fasseur, *Wilhelmina*, p. 415.

71 Kühlmann to Bülow, 12 November 1908 enclosing a translation of the leading article 'Keizer en Koningin' in *Het Vaderland* of 11 November 1908, printed in *Bescheiden*

betreffende de buitenlandse politiek van Nederland, 1848–1919, third series, III (1899–1910), IV, The Hague 1958, No. 67.

72 Kühlmann to Bülow, 14 November 1908, printed ibid., IV, No. 68.

73 Kaiser Wilhelm II, marginal note on Müller's letter of 20 August 1909, cited in Marc Frey, *Der Erste Weltkrieg und die Niederlande. Ein neutrales Land im politischen und wirtschaftlichen Kalkül der Kriegsgegner*, Berlin 1998, pp. 32f.

74 Ibid., p. 32.

75 *Bescheiden betreffende de buitenlandse politiek von Nederland, 1848–1919*, third series (1899–1910), II (1903–7), No. 159, note 2.

76 Ibid.

77 Ibid. See Kuyper to De Marees van Swinderen, 18 May 1910, ibid.

78 Büchsel to Schlieffen, 2 November 1904, BA-MA Freiburg-im-Breisgau, RM5/1602.

79 Einem to Tirpitz, 18 July 1904, ibid., RM5/1601.

80 Büchsel to Tirpitz, 2 November 1904, ibid., RM5/1602.

81 For these deliberations of 31 October, 4 and 12 November 1902 see above, p. 302f.; and Müller, diary for 4 and 12 November 1904, BA-MA Freiburg-im-Breisgau, Müller Papers.

82 Büchsel, memorandum of 19 November 1904, BA-MA Freiburg-im-Breisgau, RM5/1602.

83 Memorandum on the discussions in the Admiralty Staff on 21 November 1904; draft of an instruction to Büchsel, 23 November 1904; memorandum 'Besondere Maßnahmen für O.P.II', 24 November 1904, ibid.

84 Einem to Tirpitz, 23 November 1904, ibid.

85 Schoen to Bülow, 2 December 1904, as quoted in Bülow, *Denkwürdigkeiten*, II, pp. 66–8. See below, p. 297.

86 Büchsel, memorandum of 2 December 1904 'Zum Immediatvortrag', BA-MA Freiburg-im-Breisgau, RM5/1602.

87 Müller, diary for 3 December 1904, BA-MA Freiburg-im-Breisgau, Müller Papers.

88 Büchsel, marginal notes of 3 December 1904 on draft memorandum of 2 December 1904, BA-MA Freiburg-im-Breisgau, RM5/887. A copy of Büchsel's marginalia is to be found ibid., RM5/1602. See Steinberg, 'Germany and the Russo-Japanese War', 1978.

89 Müller, diary for 9 December 1904, BA-MA Freiburg-im-Breisgau, Müller Papers.

90 Büchsel to Schlieffen, 10 December 1904, BA-MA Freiburg-im-Breisgau, RM5/1602.

91 Schlieffen to Büchsel, 20 December 1904, ibid.

92 Büchsel to Schlieffen, 28 January 1905, ibid. The last sentence quoted here was toned down in the final version.

93 Büchsel to Kaiser Wilhelm II, 31 January 1905 with the Kaiser's marginal notes of the same day, ibid., RM5/888.

94 Büchsel to Kaiser Wilhelm II, 3 February 1905, ibid., RM5/1602.

95 Schlieffen, memorandum of 4 February 1905, ibid.

96 Schlieffen to Büchsel, 6 February 1905, ibid.

97 Senden-Bibran to Büchsel, 7 February 1905, ibid. I am grateful to Oberstleutnant Gerhard P. Groß of the Militärgeschichtliches Forschungsamt in Potsdam for drawing my attention to this document.

98 File note of 16 February 1905 on Schlieffen's letter to Büchsel of 6 February 1905, ibid.

99 See Chapter 15, below.

100 Büchsel to Kaiser Wilhelm II, 13 February 1905 with the Kaiser's marginal notes of 16 February 1906, BA-MA Freiburg-im-Breisgau, RM5/1602. The draft of this submission to the Kaiser is to be found ibid., RM5/888. The Kaiser's momentous decision was passed on to the Commander of the High Seas Fleet, the head of the Baltic Station, the

Reich Navy Office, the head of the North Sea Station and the Chief of General Staff of the Army on 16 February 1905, ibid., RM5/1602.

101 Büchsel to Kaiser Wilhelm II, 20 March 1905, ibid., RM5/888. For the views of the Commander of the High Seas Fleet Admiral Felix Bendemann see his memorandum 'Gedanken über die augenblickliche kritische Lage' of 3 December 1904, in Steinberg, 'Germany and the Russo-Japanese War', 1978.

102 Lichnowsky, memorandum of his conversation with Schlieffen of 19 April 1904, with marginal comments by Holstein, *Große Politik*, XIX/1, No. 6031.

103 Ritter, *Schlieffenplan*, pp. 43ff.; Vogel, *Deutsche Rußlandpolitik*, pp. 167ff. See Hans Ehlert, Michael Epkenhans and Gerhard P. Groß, eds., *Der Schlieffenplan. Analysen und Dokumente*, Paderborn, Munich, Vienna and Zürich 2006.

104 Müller, diary for 4 and 5 February 1905, BA-MA Freiburg-im-Breisgau, Müller Papers. For the speech by Sir Arthur Lee see Oron James Hale, *Publicity and Diplomacy with Special Reference to England and Germany 1890–1914*, New York 1940, p. 271; Arthur J. Marder, *British Naval Policy 1880–1905. The Anatomy of British Sea Power*, London 1941, I, pp. 111f.

105 Müller, diary for 15 February 1905, BA-MA Freiburg-im-Breisgau, Müller Papers.

106 See Canis, *Abgrund*, pp. 135ff. and 173ff.

107 See above, p. 305.

108 Hahnke to Groener, 26 April 1926, BA-MA Freiburg-im-Breisgau, Groener Papers, N46/38.

109 See Mombauer, *Moltke*, p. 64.

110 Moltke to his wife, 16 September 1905, Moltke, *Erinnerungen, Briefe, Dokumente*, pp. 341ff.

111 Kaiser Wilhelm II to Bülow, 30 July 1905, as quoted in Bülow to Auswärtiges Amt, 30 July 1905, *Große Politik*, XIX/2, No. 6229.

112 Karl von Einem, *Erinnerungen eines Soldaten 1853–1933*, Leipzig 1933, pp. 110ff.

113 Riemann to Schwertfeger, 28 April 1936, cited in Heiner Raulff, *Zwischen Machtpolitik und Imperialismus. Die deutsche Frankreichpolitik 1904/06*. Düsseldorf 1976, pp. 131f.

114 Müller, diary for 5 December 1905, BA-MA Freiburg-im-Breisgau, Müller Papers.

115 Müller, diary for 21 and 23 December 1905, ibid.

116 Kaiser Wilhelm II to Bülow, 31 December 1905, originally published in *Berliner Tageblatt*, 14 October 1928; cited here as printed in Josef Reimann, *Fürst Bülows Denkwürdigkeiten und die deutsche Marokkopolitik (1897–1909)*, Würzburg 1935, pp. 110f.; cf. the distorted version in Bülow, *Denkwürdigkeiten*, II, pp. 197f. The Kaiser's infamous letter is cited more fully below, pp. 415–17.

117 Einem, *Erinnerungen*, p. 114.

118 Alois von Klepsch-Kloth, report of 12 December 1905, cited in Canis, *Abgrund*, p. 174.

13   'PARIS MUST GET ONE IN THE EYE FROM US ONE DAY!'
      THE KAISER AND THE FIRST MOROCCO CRISIS

1 For German intentions in the First Morocco crisis see Canis, *Abgrund*, pp. 117ff. See also Raulff, *Zwischen Machtpolitik und Imperialismus*; Albrecht Moritz, *Das Problem des Präventivkrieges in der deutschen Politik während der ersten Marokkokrise*, Bern and Frankfurt a.M. 1974; Martin Mayer, *Geheime Diplomatie und öffentliche Meinung. Die Parlamente in Frankreich, Deutschland und Großbritannien und die erste Marokkokrise 1904–1906*, Düsseldorf 2002.

2 Sir Francis Bertie to King Edward VII, 22 April 1905, RA VIC/W 46/1; Metternich, report of 27 June 1905, cited in Moritz, *Problem des Präventivkrieges*, p. 327. See below, p. 385.

3 King Edward VII to Battenberg, 15 April 1905, cited in McLean, *Royalty and Diplomacy*, pp. 114f. See below, p. 384.

4 Kaiser Wilhelm II to Bülow, 11 August 1905, *Große Politik*, XIX/2, No. 6237.

5 Kaiser Wilhelm II, *Ereignisse und Gestalten*, pp. 90f.

6 Schoen, *Erlebtes*, p. 19.

7 Ibid., p. 22. Cf. Mommsen, *War der Kaiser an allem schuld?*, p. 116.

8 Rich, *Friedrich von Holstein*, II, p. 695.

9 Zedlitz-Trützschler, diary for 7 April 1905, *Zwölf Jahre*, pp. 127f.

10 Richard von Kühlmann, *Erinnerungen*, Heidelberg 1948, p. 221.

11 See his remarks to Isvolsky in Copenhagen, quoted below, p. 389; also the information received from Prince Otto zu Sayn-Wittgenstein, quoted in Reginald Tower to Lansdowne, 13 August 1905, National Archives, Kew, Lansdowne Papers, F.O. 800/130, fols. 82–5.

12 As quoted in Tower to Lansdowne, 13 August 1905, ibid. On Wilhelm II's relationship with Countess Morosini see below, p. 528.

13 Lansdowne to Tower, 20 August 1905, National Archives, Kew, Lansdowne Papers, F.O. 800/130, fols. 86ff.

14 Sir Francis Bertie to Knollys, 17 October 1905, RA VIC/Add C 07/2/Q.

15 Bülow to Kaiser Wilhelm II with marginal notes, 30 March 1904, *Große Politik*, XVII, No. 6512.

16 Ibid.

17 Tschirschky to Bülow, signed by Kaiser Wilhelm II, 3 April 1904, ibid., No. 6513. See Canis, *Abgrund*, pp. 85f.

18 Bülow to Tschirschky (draft), 6 April 1904, *Große Politik*, No. 6514.

19 This was the assumption made by the editors of the *Große Politik*, XVII, p. 201.

20 Kaiser Wilhelm II to Bülow, 19 April 1904, *Große Politik*, XX/1, No. 6378.

21 See ibid., Nos. 6528ff. Cf. Raulff, *Zwischen Machtpolitik und Imperialismus*, pp. 68f.

22 Bülow to Kaiser Wilhelm II with marginal note, 10 March 1905, *Große Politik*, XX/1, No. 6429.

23 Bülow to Monts, 21 February 1905, ibid., No. 6426.

24 Bülow to Kaiser Wilhelm II, 5 March 1905, ibid., No. 6428.

25 Cf. *Große Politik*, XX/1, Chapter CXLIII; Lansdowne, 'Memorandum on questions pending with Germany', 16 June 1904, RA VIC/W 44/112.

26 Cf. Kühlmann to Bülow, 28 November 1904 and 7 January 1905, *Große Politik*, XX/1, Nos. 6538 and 6545.

27 See above, pp. 331f.

28 Report of the Bavarian envoy in Berlin, Count Lerchenfeld, 26 March 1905, Geheimes Staatsarchiv München, MA 76004, cited in Moritz, *Das Problem des Präventivkrieges*, p. 111.

29 See above, p. 327.

30 Richthofen, memorandum for Bülow, 7 October 1904, *Große Politik*, XX/1, No. 6534; Mühlberg to Bülow with the latter's marginal notes, 20 January 1905, PA AA R 15571; Canis, *Abgrund*, p. 90.

31 Cf. Raulff, *Zwischen Machtpolitik und Imperialismus*, p. 83.

32 Hay, diary for 7 March 1905, as cited in Ragnhild Fiebig-von Hase, 'The Uses of "Friendship". The "Personal Regime" of Wilhelm II and Theodore Roosevelt, 1901–1909', in Annika Mombauer and Wilhelm Deist, *The Kaiser. New Research on Wilhelm II's Role in Imperial Germany*, Cambridge 2003, p. 168.

33 Zedlitz-Trützschler, diary for 7 April 1905, *Zwölf Jahre*, pp. 126f. See the similar entry for 1 July 1905, ibid., pp. 128f.

34 Bülow to Kaiser Wilhelm II with marginal note, 20 March 1905, *Große Politik*, XX/1, No. 6563.

35 Kaiser Wilhelm II to Bülow, [20] March 1905, ibid., No. 6564, printed in facsimile in Bülow, *Denkwürdigkeiten*, II, p. 112. Emphasis in the original.

36 Bülow to Kaiser Wilhelm II, 20 March 1905 with the Kaiser's marginal notes of the following day, *Große Politik*, XX/1, No. 6565.

37 Bülow, memorandum of 21 March 1905, ibid., No. 6566.

38 Kaiser Wilhelm II, speech in Bremen of 22 March 1905, GStA Berlin, Rep. 89 Nr 671. Cf. Penzler, *Reden Kaiser Wilhelms II. in den Jahren 1901–Ende 1905*, pp. 240f. See also Obst, *Die politischen Reden*, pp. 263–6 and Obst, *'Einer nur ist Herr im Reiche'*, pp. 277ff.

39 Kaiser Wilhelm II to Tirpitz, 23 March 1905, BA-MA Freiburg-im-Breisgau, Tirpitz Papers, N 253/8; Valentini to his wife, 24 March 1905, BA Koblenz, Kl. Erwerbungen, Nr 341–3; Müller, diary for 23 March 1905, BA-MA Freiburg-im-Breisgau, Müller Papers.

40 Flotow to Auswärtiges Amt, 23 March 1905, *Große Politik*, XX/1, No. 6570.

41 Bülow, memorandum for Richthofen, Mühlberg and Holstein, 24 March 1905, ibid., No. 6573.

42 Bülow to Kaiser Wilhelm II, 27 March 1905, ibid., No. 6574.

43 Bülow to Kaiser Wilhelm II, 26 March 1905, ibid., No. 6575.

44 Bülow to Kaiser Wilhelm II, 26 March 1905, ibid., No. 6576.

45 Kaiser Wilhelm II to Bülow, 28 March 1905, ibid., No. 6580.

46 Bülow to Tattenbach, 29 March 1905, ibid., No. 6581. Cf. Bülow's instruction to Holstein on the evening of 28 March 1905, *Holstein Papers*, IV, No. 881: 'We must immediately telegraph Tattenbach setting out the political situation as a whole, over my signature.'

47 Bülow to Tattenbach, 29 March 1905, *Große Politik*, XX/1, No. 6582.

48 Bülow to Tattenbach, 29 March 1905, ibid., Nos. 6583 and 6586.

49 Tattenbach to Bülow, 29 March 1905, ibid., No. 6585.

50 Bülow's instruction to Holstein for the final draft; Bülow to Holstein, 28 March 1905, *Holstein Papers*, IV, No. 881.

51 Bülow to Kaiser Wilhelm II, 29 March 1905, ibid., p. 328.

52 Bülow to Holstein, 28 March 1905, ibid., No. 881.

53 Schoen, *Erlebtes*, p. 19.

54 Valentini, *Kaiser und Kabinettschef*, p. 76.

55 Schoen to Auswärtiges Amt, 31 March 1905, *Große Politik*, XX/1, No. 6588.

56 Müller, diary for 31 March 1905, BA-MA Freiburg-im-Breisgau, Müller Papers.

57 Valentini to his wife, 1 April 1905, BA Koblenz, Kl. Erwerbungen, Nr 341–3.

58 Schoen, *Erlebtes*, p. 19.

59 Valentini, *Kaiser und Kabinettschef*, p. 79.

60 Ibid.

61 Richard von Kühlmann, *Erinnerungen*, Heidelberg 1948, pp. 229f.; Müller, diary for 31 March 1905, BA-MA Freiburg-im-Breisgau, Müller Papers. Cf. Schoen, *Erlebtes*, p. 20.

62 Kühlmann, *Erinnerungen*, pp. 227f.

63 Ibid., pp. 226f.

64 Schoen to Auswärtiges Amt, 31 March 1905, *Große Politik*, XX/1, No. 6589. Cf. Kühlmann, *Erinnerungen*, p. 231.

65 Ibid., p. 232.

66 Bülow to Kaiser Wilhelm II, 4 April 1905, *Große Politik*, XX/2, No. 6599.

67 Holstein to Radolin, 11 April 1905, *Holstein Papers*, IV, No. 883.

68 Kühlmann, *Erinnerungen*, p. 231.

69 Schoen to Auswärtiges Amt, 31 March 1905, *Große Politik*, XX/1, No. 6589.

70 Müller, diary for 31 March 1905, BA-MA Freiburg-im-Breisgau, Müller Papers.

71 Above, p. 329.

72 Bülow, *Denkwürdigkeiten*, II, p. 111.

73 Schoen to Auswärtiges Amt, 31 March 1905, *Große Politik*, XX/1, No. 6589. But see the later account in his memoirs, Schoen, *Erlebtes*, pp. 21ff.; Kühlmann, *Erinnerungen*, p. 231.

74 Valentini, *Kaiser und Kabinettschef*, p. 81. Cf. Schoen, *Erlebtes*, p. 23.

75 Bülow to Kaiser Wilhelm II, 4 April 1905, *Große Politik*, XX/2, No. 6599.

76 On the Kaiser's somewhat chaotic visit to Corfu on 11 April 1905 see Ratibor's lengthy report of 22 April 1905, which Wilhelm covered in angry marginalia in Strasbourg on 10 May 1905, PA AA R 3739. Also Schoen to Bülow, 11 April 1905, ibid. On the purchase of the Achilleion see Wedel to Kaiser Wilhelm II, 2 April 1905, PA AA R 3476.

77 Zedlitz-Trützschler, diary for 31 July 1905, *Zwölf Jahre*, p. 130.

78 Müller, diary 5 April to 4 May 1905, BA-MA Freiburg-im-Breisgau, Müller Papers.

79 Ibid.

80 For this controversial question see Fritz Fischer, *Krieg der Illusionen. Die deutsche Politik von 1911 bis 1914*, Düsseldorf 1969, p. 100; Bernd F. Schulte, *Die deutsche Armee 1900–1918. Zwischen Beharren und Verändern*, Düsseldorf 1977, p. 387; Fritz Klein, *Deutschland von 1897/98 bis 1917*, Berlin 1986, p. 135; Fesser, *Der Traum vom Platz an der Sonne*, p. 105; Raulff, *Zwischen Machtpolitik und Imperialismus*, passim; Moritz, *Das Problem des Präventivkrieges*, passim; Rich, *Friedrich von Holstein*, II, pp. 696ff.

81 Holstein to Bülow, 5 April 1905, *Holstein Papers*, IV, No. 882.

82 See, above all, Raulff, *Zwischen Machtpolitik und Imperialismus.*

83 Kaiser Wilhelm II, marginal notes on Bernstorff's report from London of 22 April 1905, *Große Politik*, XX/2, No. 6846.

84 Kaiser Wilhelm II, marginal note on Radolin's report from Paris of 1 May 1905, ibid., No. 6848.

85 Bülow to Holstein, 8 May 1905, PA AA R 3476.

86 Holstein to Radolin, 22 May 1905, *Holstein Papers*, IV, No. 888.

87 See Eulenburg's memorandum of 25 September 1905, cited below, pp. 352f.

88 Holstein to Bülow, 17 June 1905, *Holstein Papers*, IV, No. 892.

89 Holstein to Radolin, 14 June 1905, ibid., IV, No. 891.

90 Raulff, *Zwischen Machtpolitik und Imperialismus*, pp. 26 and 124f.

91 As quoted in Wilhelm Groener, *Lebenserinnerungen. Jugend, Generalstab, Weltkrieg*, ed. Friedrich Freiherr von Gaertringen, Göttingen 1957, pp. 83f.; Ritter, *Schlieffenplan*, pp. 114f.

92 Radolin to Bülow, 24 June 1905, as cited in Raulff, *Zwischen Machtpolitik und Imperialismus*, p. 124. Cf. Moritz, *Problem des Präventivkrieges*, p. 115. See Canis, *Abgrund*, p. 140.

93 Marschall, diary for 18 July 1906 and 15 May 1907, cited in *Eulenburgs Korrespondenz*, III, pp. 2110f.

94 Kaiser Wilhelm II, marginal note on Radolin's report of 11 June 1905, *Große Politik*, XX/2, No. 6685.

95 Kaiser Wilhelm II, marginal note on Bülow's submission of 12 July 1905, ibid., p. 409. Canis, *Abgrund*, p. 132.

96 Lerchenfeld, report of 9 June 1905, cited in Moritz, *Problem des Präventivkriegs*, p. 115.

97 Laguiche to Berteaux, 14 June 1905, *Documents diplomatiques français*, 2nd series, VII, No. 59.

98 Zedlitz-Trützschler, diary for 26 November 1907, *Zwölf Jahre*, p. 174.

99 Holstein to Bülow, 23 June 1905, *Holstein Papers*, IV, No. 895.

100 Holstein to Bülow, 19 September 1905, ibid., No. 913.

101 Bülow's retrospective memorandum, cited in Raulff, *Zwischen Machtpolitik und Imperialismus*, p. 125.

102 See Holstein to Radolin, 15 September 1905; Radolin to Holstein, 18 September 1905, *Holstein Papers*, IV, Nos. 911–12.

103 Kaiser Wilhelm II to Bülow, 23 June 1905, quoted in Bülow to Radolin, 24 June 1905, *Große Politik*, XX/2, No. 6730.

104 Bülow to Radolin, 24 June 1905, ibid., No. 6730.

105 See Kaiser Wilhelm II's marginal comments on President Roosevelt's arbitration proposals of 24 and 25 June 1905, ibid., Nos. 6731 and 6738.

106 Lefaivre to Rouvier, 31 December 1905, *Documents diplomatiques français*, 2nd series, VIII, No. 302. Cf. Moritz, *Problem des Präventivkrieges*, pp. 122f.

107 Holstein to Radolin, 23 June 1905, *Holstein Papers*, IV, No. 896.

108 Holstein to Radolin, 1 July 1905, ibid., No. 898.

109 Müller, diary for 9 July 1905, BA-MA Freiburg-im-Breisgau, Müller Papers.

110 See above, pp. 326–8.

111 Battenberg, record of his conversation with Kaiser Wilhelm II on 1 April 1905, cited in McLean, *Royalty and Diplomacy in Europe*, p. 114. See below, p. 384.

112 Metternich, report of 27 June 1905, quoted in Moritz, *Problem des Präventivkrieges*, p. 327.

113 See in particular Bülow to Speck von Sternburg, 30 May 1905, *Große Politik*, XX/2, No. 6668; Speck von Sternburg to Roosevelt, 31 May and 9 June 1905, in Fiebig-von Hase, 'The Uses of "Friendship"', pp. 168f.

114 Roosevelt to Spring Rice, 26 May 1905, Theodore Roosevelt, *The Letters*, ed. Elting E. Morison, John M. Blum and John J. Buckley, 8 vols., Cambridge, MA 1951–4, IV, p. 1194.

115 Eulenburg, memorandum of 25 September 1905, *Eulenburgs Korrespondenz*, III, No. 1509.

116 See below, p. 389.

14 'A TURNING-POINT IN THE HISTORY OF EUROPE', OR THE FIASCO OF BJÖRKÖ

1 On the Kaiser and the Treaty of Björkö see Rich, *Friedrich von Holstein*, II, pp. 714ff.; Clark, *Kaiser Wilhelm II*, pp. 140ff.; Ullrich, *Die nervöse Großmacht*, pp. 207f.; Mommsen, *Großmachtstellung und Weltpolitik*, pp. 170f.; Cecil, *Wilhelm II: Emperor and Exile*, pp. 100f.; Canis, *Abgrund*, pp. 147ff.

2 See above, pp. 287–92.

3 Kaiser Wilhelm II to Tsar Nicholas II, 2 January 1905, Goetz, *Briefe Wilhelms II. an den Zaren*, No. XLIII, pp. 154–6 and 355f. Cf. the (somewhat inaccurate) copy of this letter, which was not deposited in the files of the Auswärtiges Amt until 1917, *Große Politik*, XIX/2, No. 6180.

4 After the Japanese victory at Mukden the Kaiser wanted to send a congratulatory telegram to the Emperor of Japan and to award the former Japanese Chief of Staff Oyama the order Pour le mérite. Kaiser Wilhelm II to Bülow, 11 March 1905, ibid., No. 6187.

5 Zedlitz-Trützschler, diary for 30 January 1905, *Zwölf Jahre*, p. 107.

6 Goetz, *Briefe Wilhelms II. an den Zaren*, p. 154.

7 Tsar Nicholas II to Kaiser Wilhelm II, 14 February 1905; Bülow to Kaiser Wilhelm II, 14 February 1905; Kaiser Wilhelm II to Tsar Nicholas II, 15 February 1905; Bülow to Kaiser Wilhelm II, 15 February 1905; Kaiser Wilhelm II to Tsar Nicholas II, 15 February 1905, *Große Politik*, XIX/2, Nos. 6092–6.

8 Holstein to Bülow, 20 February 1905, *Holstein Papers*, IV, No. 878.

9 Kaiser Wilhelm II to Tsar Nicholas II, 21 February 1905, printed in facsimile in Goetz, *Briefe Wilhelms II. an den Zaren*, pp. 425–32; see Goetz, ibid., p. xv.

10 Kaiser Wilhelm II, speech to recruits at Wilhelmshaven on 9 March 1905, Penzler, *Reden Kaiser Wilhelms II. in den Jahren 1901–Ende 1905*, pp. 239f.; Obst, *Die politischen Reden*, p. 262.

11　Zedlitz-Trützschler, diary for 9 March 1905, *Zwölf Jahre*, p. 121.

12　Kaiser Wilhelm II to Bülow, 11 March 1905, *Große Politik*, XIX/2, No. 6187.

13　Durand to Lansdowne, 30 March 1905, RA, Knollys Papers 1905.

14　'Der Zar hat Kopfschmerzen', *Vorwärts*, 17 March 1905.

15　Eulenburg to Kaiser Wilhelm II, 11 March 1905, *Eulenburgs Korrespondenz*, III, No. 1505.

16　Zedlitz-Trützschler, diary, late March 1905, *Zwölf Jahre*, pp. 123–6.

17　Zedlitz-Trützschler, diary, mid January 1905, ibid., p. 106.

18　Kaiser Wilhelm II to Tsar Nicholas II, 6 February 1905, Goetz, *Briefe Wilhelms II. an den Zaren*, No. XLV, pp. 161–5 and pp. 358–60.

19　Hardinge to Knollys, 1 March 1905, RA VIC/W45 120.

20　Kaiser Wilhelm II to Tsar Nicholas II, 21 February 1905, printed in facsimile in Goetz, *Briefe Wilhelms II. an den Zaren*, pp. 425–32; see ibid., p. xv.

21　Kaiser Wilhelm II to Tsar Nicholas II, 21 February 1905, cited according to the facsimile reproduced in Goetz, *Briefe Wilhelms II. an den Zaren*, pp. 425–32.

22　Ibid.

23　Tsar Nicholas II to Kaiser Wilhelm II, 25 February 1905, cited in *Holstein Papers*, IV, p. 326, note. The telegram began with the words: 'I thank you from the depth of my heart. Your long letter interested me greatly.'

24　Bülow, *Denkwürdigkeiten*, II, p. 161.

25　Spring Rice to Knollys, 2 March 1905, RA VIC/W 45/122.

26　Kaiser Wilhelm II, marginal note on Alvensleben's report of 17 March 1905, PA AA Rußland No. 82 Nr 1 Bd. 53, cited in Roderick R. McLean, 'Kaiser Wilhelm II and his Hessian Cousins: Intra-state Relations in the German Empire and International Dynastic Politics, 1890–1918', *German History*, 19/1, 2001, 44.

27　Prince Heinrich of Prussia, diary for 17 and 18 February 1905, MSM Hamburg.

28　Hardinge to Knollys, 29 March 1905, RA VIC/W 45/150.

29　Bülow to Kaiser Wilhelm II, 10 April 1905, GStA Berlin, BPHA Rep. 53J Lit B Nr 16a.

30　Prince Heinrich of Prussia, diary for 2 April 1905, MSM Hamburg.

31　Prince Heinrich of Prussia, diary for 2 to 10 April 1905, MSM Hamburg.

32　Prince Heinrich of Prussia to Bülow, 7 April 1905, GStA Berlin, BPHA Rep. 53J Lit. B Nr 16a.

33　Prince Heinrich of Prussia to Kaiser Wilhelm II, 11 April 1905, GStA Berlin, BPHA Rep. 52 V1 Nr 13.

34　Bülow to Kaiser Wilhelm II, 10 April 1905, ibid. Nr 16a.

35　See below, p. 597.

36　Kaiser Wilhelm II, speech in Strasbourg on 8 May 1905, Penzler, *Reden Kaiser Wilhelms II. in den Jahren 1901–Ende 1905*, pp. 252f.; Obst, *Die politischen Reden*, pp. 268f.

37　Gleichen, report of 17 May 1905, RA VIC/W46 25. See Müller, diary for 13 May 1905, BA-MA Freiburg-im-Breisgau, Müller Papers.

38　Gleichen, report of 17 May 1905, RA VIC/W46 25. Bülow to Holstein, 8 May 1905, Bülow to Mühlberg, 8 May 1905, PA AA R 3476. See Penzler, *Reden Kaiser Wilhelms II. in den Jahren 1901–Ende 1905*, pp. 254–6.

39　Kaiser Wilhelm II, speech in Strasbourg on 8 May 1905, ibid., pp. 252f.

40　Holstein to David, 13 May 1906, *Holstein Papers*, IV, No. 980.

41　On the genesis of the letter of 3 June 1905 see Kaiser Wilhelm II to Bülow, 25 July 1905, *Große Politik*, XIX/2, No. 6220, p. 461.

42　Kaiser Wilhelm II to Tsar Nicholas II, 3 June 1905, Goetz, *Briefe Wilhelms II. an den Zaren*, XLVII, pp. 370–3. The Kaiser drafted the letter personally and handed the text to the Auswärtiges Amt for transmission to St Petersburg. See *Große Politik*, XIX/2, No. 6193.

43 Moltke to his wife, 26 July 1905, Moltke, *Erinnerungen, Briefe, Dokumente*, p. 330.

44 As quoted in Kaiser Wilhelm II to Bülow, 11 August 1905, *Große Politik*, XIX/2, No. 6237.

45 Bülow, *Denkwürdigkeiten*, II, p. 137.

46 Kaiser Wilhelm II to Tsar Nicholas II, 18 July 1905, as quoted in *Große Politik*, XIX/2, No. 6202, annex.

47 Tsar Nicholas II to Kaiser Wilhelm II, as quoted in Bülow to Auswärtiges Amt, 20 July 1905, ibid., No. 6202, note and No. 6208.

48 Bülow to Auswärtiges Amt, 22 July 1905, ibid., No. 6208. See above, pp. 287–92.

49 Holstein to Bülow, 21 July 1905, *Große Politik*, XIX/2, No. 6203.

50 Moltke to his wife, 26 July 1905, Moltke, *Erinnerungen, Briefe, Dokumente*, p. 326. See Birgit Marschall, *Reisen und Regieren. Die Nordlandfahrten Kaiser Wilhelms II.*, Heidelberg 1991, p. 147.

51 Kaiser Wilhelm II to Bülow, 25 July 1905, *Große Politik*, XIX/2, No. 6220.

52 Kaiser Wilhelm II to Tsar Nicholas II, 27 July 1905, Goetz, *Briefe Wilhelms II. an den Zaren*, No. XLVIII, pp. 373–6.

53 Tschirschky to Bülow, 24 July 1905, XIX/2, No. 6218. A facsimile of the Treaty of Björkö is included in Bülow, *Denkwürdigkeiten*, II, pp. 140f.

54 Marschall, *Reisen und Regieren*, p. 149. See below, pp. 392–6.

55 Tschirschky to Bülow, 24 July 1905, *Große Politik*, XIX/2, No. 6218; Kaiser Wilhelm II to Bülow, 24 July 1905, quoted in Bülow to Auswärtiges Amt, 24 July 1905, ibid., No. 6215. See Marschall, *Reisen und Regieren*, pp. 148f.

56 Bülow to Kaiser Wilhelm II, 24 July 1905, *Große Politik*, XIX/2, No. 6216. Cf. Bülow to Holstein, 25 July 1905, ibid., No. 6217.

57 Bülow to Auswärtiges Amt, 26 July 1905, ibid., No. 6222.

58 Holstein to Bülow, 26 July 1905, ibid., No. 6223.

59 Bülow to Auswärtiges Amt, 27 July 1905, ibid., Nos. 6224 and 6225.

60 Bülow to Auswärtiges Amt, 28 July 1905, ibid., No. 6228.

61 Kaiser Wilhelm II to Bülow, 30 July 1905, as quoted in Bülow to Auswärtiges Amt, 30 July 1905, ibid., No. 6229.

62 Ibid.

63 Holstein, memorandum of 28 July 1905, *Große Politik*, XIX/2, No. 6227; Tschirschky to Bülow, 27 July 1905, ibid., No. 6225.

64 Bülow to Kaiser Wilhelm II, 30 July 1905, as quoted in Bülow to Auswärtiges Amt, 30 July 1905, ibid., No. 6229.

65 Bülow to Auswärtiges Amt, 2 August 1905, ibid., No. 6230.

66 Ibid., pp. 481f., note.

67 Bülow, *Denkwürdigkeiten*, II, p. 139.

68 See above, p. 349.

69 Fesser, *Reichskanzler Fürst von Bülow*, p. 112. Cf. Cecil, *Wilhelm II: Emperor and Exile*, pp. 100f; Clark, *Kaiser Wilhelm II*, pp. 140ff.; Winzen, *Bernhard Fürst von Bülow*, p. 107.

70 Bülow to Kaiser Wilhelm II, 3 August 1905, Bülow, *Denkwürdigkeiten*, II, pp. 139–44.

71 Kaiser Wilhelm II to Bülow, 5 August 1905, as quoted in Bülow to Auswärtiges Amt, 5 August 1905, *Große Politik*, XIX/2, No. 6233.

72 Bülow to Auswärtiges Amt, 5 August 1905, ibid., No. 6233. Cf. the Kaiser's draft of a letter to Tsar Nicholas II of 9 August 1905 and Bülow's suggested changes, ibid., annex A and B.

73 Mühlberg to Bülow, 10 August 1905, ibid., No. 6236.

74 Holstein to Bülow, 6 August 1905, ibid., No. 6234.

75 Bülow to Auswärtiges Amt, 9 August 1905, ibid., No. 6235.

76 Ibid.

77 Kaiser Wilhelm II to Bülow, 11 August 1905, *Große Politik*, XIX/2, No. 6237.

78 Bülow to Kaiser Wilhelm II, 12 August 1905, GStA Berlin, BPHA, Rep. 53 J, Lit. B Nr 16a, vol. III.

79 Kaiser Wilhelm II to Bülow, 12 August 1905, as cited in Bülow to Auswärtiges Amt, 12 August 1905, *Große Politik*, XIX/2, No. 6238.

80 Holstein to Bülow, 14 August 1905, ibid., No. 6239.

81 Bülow, memorandum of 18 August 1905, ibid., No. 6240.

82 See ibid., p. 505, note.

83 Kaiser Wilhelm II to Bülow, 27 September 1905, ibid., No. 6242.

84 Rosen, *Aus einem diplomatischen Wanderleben*, I, pp. 245f.; Vogel, *Deutsche Rußlandpolitik*, pp. 227ff.

85 Tsar Nicholas II to Kaiser Wilhelm II, 7 October 1905, *Große Politik*, XIX/2, No. 6247. Bernhard Schwertfeger, *Die Diplomatischen Akten des Auswärtigen Amtes 1871–1914. Ein Wegweiser durch das große Aktenwerk der Deutschen Regierung*, 8 vols., Berlin 1923–7, IV, 1, pp. 234f.

86 Kaiser Wilhelm II to Tsar Nicholas II, 12 October 1905, *Große Politik*, XIX/2, No. 6248; Schwertfeger, *Die Diplomatischen Akten*, IV, 1, p. 236.

87 Tsar Nicholas II to Kaiser Wilhelm II, 23 November 1905, *Große Politik*, XIX/2, No. 6254; Schwertfeger, *Die Diplomatischen Akten*, IV, 1, p. 238.

88 Ibid.

89 Kaiser Wilhelm II to Bülow, 26 November 1905, *Große Politik*, XIX/2, No. 6255.

90 Ibid.

91 Kaiser Wilhelm II to Tsar Nicholas II, 28 November 1905, *Große Politik*, XIX/2, No. 6257; Schwertfeger, *Die Diplomatischen Akten*, IV, 1, p. 240.

92 Tsar Nicholas II to Kaiser Wilhelm II, 2 December 1905, *Große Politik*, XIX/2, No. 6258; Schwertfeger, *Die Diplomatischen Akten*, IV, 1, p. 240.

93 Kaiser Wilhelm II to Bülow, 23 January 1906, as quoted in *Große Politik*, XIX/2, No. 6258, note.

94 Eulenburg, memorandum of 25 September 1905, *Eulenburgs Korrespondenz*, III, No. 1509.

15 BALANCE OF POWER OR HEGEMONY? THE ANGLO-GERMAN CONFLICT
AND THE QUARREL WITH KING EDWARD

1 *Norddeutsche Allgemeine Zeitung*, 13 September 1917; Theodor Wolff, diary for 18 September 1917, Bernd Sösemann, ed., *Theodor Wolff, Tagebücher 1914–1919. Der Erste Weltkrieg und die Entstehung der Weimarer Republik in Tagebüchern, Leitartikeln und Briefen des Chefredakteurs des 'Berliner Tageblatt' und Mitbegründers der 'Deutschen Demokratischen Partei'*, 2 vols., Boppard am Rhein 1984 (cited below as Wolff, *Tagebücher*), I, No. 608. See Hammann, *Die Vorgeschichte des Weltkrieges*, pp. 218ff.; Goetz, *Briefe Wilhelms II. an den Zaren*, pp. xxf.

2 Zedlitz-Trützschler, diary for 9 October 1905, *Zwölf Jahre*, p. 130.

3 Eulenburg, memorandum of 25 September 1905, *Eulenburgs Korrespondenz*, III, No. 1509. See above, pp. 352f.

4 Metternich to Bülow, 2 October 1905, *Große Politik*, XX/2, No. 6871.

5 Kaiser Wilhelm II, marginal notes on Metternich to Bülow, 2 October 1905, ibid., No. 6871.

6 Bernstorff, report of 16 April 1905, PA AA R 3703.

7 Bernstorff, report from London of 22 April 1905 with marginal notes by Kaiser Wilhelm II, *Große Politik*, XX/2, No. 6846.

8 Grumme to Müller, 16 January 1905, GStA Berlin, BPHA Rep. 53J Lit. G Nr 15.

9 Moltke to his wife, 3 and 25 August 1905, Moltke, *Erinnerungen, Briefe, Dokumente*, pp. 332 and 337f.

10 Battenberg, record of his conversation with Kaiser Wilhelm II on 1 April 1905, cited in McLean, *Royalty and Diplomacy*, p. 114.

11 King Edward VII to Battenberg, 15 April 1905, cited ibid., pp. 114f. The King sent Battenberg's account on to the Foreign Secretary with similar acerbic comments. See King Edward VII to Lansdowne, 15 April 1905, in Lee, *King Edward VII*, II, p. 340.

12 Metternich, report of 27 June 1905, cited in Moritz, *Problem des Präventivkrieges*, p. 327.

13 Spring Rice to Knollys, 2 May 1905, RA VIC/Add C 07/2/Q/2 May 1905, copy in RA VIC/W 46/3.

14 Reginald Tower to Lansdowne, 13 August 1905, National Archives, Kew, Lansdowne Papers, F.O. 800/130, fols. 82–5. I am grateful to Dr Ragnhild Fiebig-von Hase for drawing my attention to this important document.

15 King Edward VII, note on Tower's report of 13 August 1905, National Archives, Kew, Lansdowne Papers, F.O. 800/130.

16 Lansdowne to Tower, 20 August 1905, ibid., fols. 86ff.

17 Hardinge to Knollys, 27 September 1905, RA VIC/Add C 07/2/Q.

18 Kaiser Wilhelm II to Bülow, 29 March 1903, *Große Politik*, XIX/1, No. 5962 note. See above, pp. 306–8.

19 Schoen to Bülow, 2 December 1904, as quoted in Bülow, *Denkwürdigkeiten*, II, pp. 66–8.

20 Ibid. See also ibid., pp. 79f. and *Große Politik*, XIX/1, Nos. 5962 and 5966–9.

21 Kaiser Wilhelm II to Bülow, February 1905, as cited in Bülow, *Denkwürdigkeiten*, II, p. 79.

22 Bülow, memorandum of 6 February 1905, cited in *Holstein Papers*, IV, p. 324, note.

23 Holstein, memorandum of 6 February 1905, ibid., No. 876.

24 Schoen to Holstein, 11 February 1905, ibid., No. 877.

25 Kaiser Wilhelm II to Bülow, 14 July 1905, as cited in Marschall, *Reisen und Regieren*, p. 146.

26 Kaiser Wilhelm II to Bülow, 25 July 1905, *Große Politik*, XIX/2, No. 6220.

27 Bülow to Kaiser Wilhelm II, 30 July 1905, cited in Bülow to Auswärtiges Amt, 30 July 1905, ibid., No. 6229. Holstein, memorandum for Bülow, 31 July 1905, *Holstein Papers*, IV, No. 904.

28 As quoted in the footnote to Kaiser Wilhelm II to King Christian IX of Denmark, 6 January 1904, *Große Politik*, XIX/1, pp. 89f.

29 Hardinge to King Edward VII, 16 March 1907, RA VIC/W 51/46.

30 Isvolsky, *Memoirs*, pp. 77f.

31 Kaiser Wilhelm II to Tsar Nicholas II, 2 August 1905, as cited ibid., pp. 75f.

32 Ibid., p. 77.

33 Kaiser Wilhelm II to Tsar Nicholas II, 9 August 1905, draft of a letter not sent, printed in *Große Politik*, XIX/2, No. 6235, annex A.

34 Johnstone to Lansdowne, 31 July 1905, RA VIC/W 46/128.

35 Mühlberg to Kaiser Wilhelm II, 4 August 1905, with the text of Metternich's telegram, *Große Politik*, XX/2, No. 6869.

36 Kaiser Wilhelm II, marginal notes on on Metternich's telegram of 4 August 1905, ibid.

37 Cf. Lansdowne to Hardinge, 31 July 1905, RA VIC/W 46/130.

38 Moltke, *Erinnerungen, Briefe, Dokumente*, pp. 330f.

39 Isvolsky, *Memoirs*, pp. 73f.

40 Lascelles to Lansdowne, 2 August 1905, RA VIC/Add C 07/2/Q.

41 Kaiser Wilhelm II, marginal notes on Metternich's report of 9 August 1905, PA AA R 3703.

42 Moltke, *Erinnerungen, Briefe, Dokumente*, pp. 330f.

43 Szögyény, reports of 20 February and 14 June 1905, as quoted in Fritz Fellner, 'Die Verstimmung zwischen Wilhelm II. und Eduard VII. im Sommer 1905', *Mitteilungen des österreichischen Staatsarchivs*, XI, 1958, p. 508.

44 Memorandum by Trolle of 3 June 1905, as cited in Marschall, *Reisen und Regieren*, p. 140.

45 Cartwright to Lansdowne, 8 and 11 June 1905, RA VIC/Add C 07/2/R.

46 Fredrik Wedel Jarlsberg, *1905: Kongevalget*, Oslo 1946, p. 39. See Grand Duke Friedrich I of Baden to Crown Prince Gustaf of Sweden, 14 July 1905, Fuchs, *Großherzog von Baden*, IV, No. 2512.

47 Bülow to the Consul General in Christiania, 13 June 1905, PA AA R 3750.

48 Article 'Die Fürstenzusammenkunft in Gefle', *Dagbladet*, 17 July 1905, PA AA R 3674.

49 See the newspaper reports in Marschall, *Reisen und Regieren*, pp. 137ff.

50 Ibid., pp. 143ff.

51 The Grand Duke of Baden, whose daughter Viktoria was the Crown Princess of Sweden, also favoured this solution. Grand Duke Friedrich I of Baden to Crown Prince Gustaf of Sweden, 14 July 1905, Fuchs, *Großherzog von Baden*, IV, No. 2512. See Grand Duke Friedrich I of Baden to Bülow, 22 July 1905, ibid., p. 595, note.

52 Rodd to Knollys, 26 July 1905, RA VIC/Add C 07/2/R; Rodd to Knollys, 30 September 1905, RA VIC/W 47/321.

53 Kaiser Wilhelm II to Bülow, 14 July 1905, as quoted in Marschall, *Reisen und Regieren*, p. 146.

54 Tschirschky to Bülow, 24 July 1905, *Große Politik*, XIX/2, No. 6218.

55 Kaiser Wilhelm II to Bülow, 25 July 1905, ibid., No. 6220. See Marschall, *Reisen und Regieren*, p. 149.

56 Johnstone to Knollys, 20 July 1905, RA VIC/Add C 07/2/R.

57 Knollys to Johnstone, 30 July 1905, RA VIC/Add C 07/2/R.

58 King Edward VII to Prince Charles of Denmark, 30 July 1905, RA VIC/W 46/75.

59 Johnstone to Lansdowne, 31 July 1905, RA VIC/W 46/136.

60 Johnstone to Knollys, 1 August 1905, RA VIC/W 46/141.

61 Kaiser Wilhelm II to Tsar Nicholas II, 2 August 1905, as quoted in Isvolsky, *Memoirs*, pp. 75f.

62 Johnstone to Lansdowne, 18 August 1905, RA VIC/W 46/254.

63 Goschen to Johnstone, 18 August 1905, RA VIC/W 46/255.

64 Balfour to King Edward VII, 28 June 1905, RA VIC/R 26/46. On the attitude of the British press see Reinermann, *Der Kaiser in England*, pp. 277–81.

65 'Die Verdächtigungen Deutschlands', *Magdeburgische Zeitung*, 1 August 1905, with approving marginalia by Kaiser Wilhelm II, PA AA R 3627. For the Kaiser's speech in Bremen see above, pp. 336f.

66 Szögyény, report of 1 August 1905, as cited in Fellner, 'Die Verstimmung zwischen Wilhelm II. und Eduard VII', p. 509.

67 Szögyény, report of August 1905, as cited ibid., pp. 509f.

68 See e.g. Knollys to Lascelles, 27 July 1904, PRO FO 800/12; Lascelles to Knollys, 27 July 1904, RA VIC/W 44/183; Gleichen to Knollys, 27 July 1904, RA VIC/W 44/184; King Edward VII to Knollys, 29 July 1904 and Knollys, memorandum of 2 August 1904, RA VIC/W 44/185; Lascelles to Knollys, 5 August 1904, RA VIC/W 44/188; Gleichen to King Edward VII, 2 September 1904, RA VIC/W 44/199; Lascelles to Knollys, 2 March 1905, RA VIC/W 45/121; Spring Rice to Knollys, 2 March 1905, RA VIC/W 45/122; Gleichen to King Edward VII, 2 March 1905 and 10 March 1905, RA VIC/W 45/123 and 126; Lascelles to Knollys, 2 and 10 March 1905, RA VIC/W 45/121 and 127. Cf. Seligmann, 'Military Diplomacy', pp. 181–3.

69 Lascelles to Knollys, 24 March 1905, RA VIC/W 45/146; George Prince of Wales to Knollys, March 1905, RA VIC/W 45/147.

70 Szögyény, report of 11 April 1905, Fellner, 'Die Verstimmung zwischen Wilhelm II. und Eduard VII', pp. 503f.; Sir Francis Bertie to King Edward VII, 22 April 1905, RA VIC/W 46/1; *Große Politik*, XX/2, No. 6848.

71 Szögyény, report of 14 June 1905, as cited in Fellner, 'Die Verstimmung zwischen Wilhelm II. und Eduard VII', pp. 504–6.

72 Lascelles to Lansdowne, 2 August 1905, RA VIC/Add C 07/2/Q.

73 Mühlberg, memorandum of 1 August 1905, *Große Politik*, XX/2, No. 6868.

74 Lascelles to Lansdowne, 2 August 1905, RA VIC/Add C 07/2/Q, with a marginal comment by King Edward VII.

75 Kaiser Wilhelm II, marginal notes on Metternich's reports of 9 and 10 August 1905 and on an article in the *Magdeburgische Zeitung* of 15 August 1905, PA AA R 3703.

76 Lascelles to Knollys, August 1905, RA VIC/W 46/202.

77 Seckendorff to King Edward VII, 15 August 1905, RA VIC/W 46/231.

78 King Edward VII to Knollys, 18 August 1905, RA VIC/W 46/252.

79 Knollys to Seckendorff, 23 August 1905, RA VIC/W 46/285; King Edward VII to Lascelles, 20 August 1905, RA VIC/X 37/61.

80 Lascelles to King Edward VII, 18 and 21 August 1905, RA VIC/Add C 07/2/Q; Lascelles to Knollys, 22 August 1905, RA VIC/W 46/284.

81 Lascelles to King Edward VII, 26 August 1905, RA VIC/W 46/294; Lascelles to Knollys, 31 August 1905, RA VIC/Add C 07/2/Q.

82 Lascelles to King Edward VII, 13 September 1905, RA VIC/W 47/205.

83 King Edward VII to Crown Prince Wilhelm, 5 September 1905, GStA Berlin, BPHA Rep. 54 No. 33. copy in RA VIC/Add C 07/2/Q.

84 Széchényi, report of late summer 1905, as cited in Fellner, 'Die Verstimmung zwischen Wilhelm II. und Eduard VII', pp. 510f. Also Lee, *Edward VII*, pp. 348f.

85 Lascelles to Knollys, 10 September 1905, RA VIC/Add C 07/2/Q.

86 Lascelles, report of 13 September 1905, RA VIC/W 47/206.

87 King Edward VII to Knollys, 17 September 1905, RA VIC/W 47/253.

88 Knollys to Lascelles, 22 September 1905, RA VIC/W 47/315.

89 Lascelles to Knollys, 28 September 1905; Knollys to Lascelles, 2 October 1905, RA VIC/Add C 07/2/Q.

90 Metternich to Bülow, 2 October 1905, with marginal notes by Kaiser Wilhelm II, *Große Politik*, XX/2, No. 6871.

91 Bülow to Eulenburg, 22 September 1905, *Eulenburgs Korrespondenz*, III, No. 1507.

92 Eulenburg to Bülow, 23 September 1905, ibid., No. 1508. Cf. Bülow, *Denkwürdigkeiten*, II, pp. 171f.

93 Zedlitz-Trützschler, diary for 10 October 1905, *Zwölf Jahre*, pp. 132f.

94 Zedlitz-Trützschler, diary for 9 October 1905, ibid., p. 130.

95 Zedlitz-Trützschler, diary for 10 October 1905, ibid., pp. 132f.

96 Bülow to Auswärtiges Amt, 8, 10 and 12 October 1905, *Große Politik*, XX/2, No. 6872 with note, Nos. 6874 and 6875.

97 Kaiser Wilhelm II, marginal notes on Metternich's telegrams of 9 and 18 October 1905, ibid., Nos. 6873 and 6879.

98 Kaiser Wilhelm II to Prince Christian of Schleswig-Holstein, 11 October 1905, along with a copy of Prince Christian's reply of 19 October 1905, RA VIC/Add A 18/Y 10.

99 Metternich to Bülow, 18 October 1905, *Große Politik*, XX/2, No. 6879. See also Metternich to Bülow, 2 November 1905, ibid., No. 6881.

100 Kaiser Wilhelm II, marginal notes on Metternich to Bülow, 18 October 1905, ibid., No. 6879.

101 Lonsdale to Kaiser Wilhelm II, 24 December 1905, Lonsdale Papers, Cumbria Record Office, Carlisle. For Lonsdale and his relationship with the Kaiser see Röhl, *The Kaiser's Personal Monarchy*, p. 776.

102 Metternich to Bülow, 3 December 1905, *Große Politik*, XX/2, No. 6882.

103 Metternich to Bülow, 4 December 1905, ibid., No. 6883.

104 Kaiser Wilhelm II, marginal notes on Metternich's telegram of 3 December 1905, ibid., No. 6882.

105 Kaiser Wilhelm II, marginal notes on Metternich's telegram of 4 December 1905, ibid., No. 6883.

106 Kaiser Wilhelm II, marginal note on Bülow's submission of 4 December 1905, ibid., pp. 683f.

107 Kaiser Wilhelm II, marginal note on Metternich's report of 20 December 1905, ibid., No. 6886.

108 Kaiser Wilhelm II to Bülow, 29 December 1905, ibid., No. 6887

109 Ibid.

110 Kaiser Wilhelm II to Bülow, 31 December 1905, originally published in the *Berliner Tageblatt*, No. 487, 14 October 1928, quoted here from Reimann, *Bülows Denkwürdigkeiten*, pp. 110f.; cf. Bülow, *Denkwürdigkeiten*, II, pp. 197f. Cited in part above, pp. 326f.

16 HUMILIATION IN ALGECIRAS

1 On the conference of Algeciras see Rich, *Friedrich von Holstein*, II, pp. 696ff.; Lerman, *The Chancellor as Courtier*, pp. 141ff.; Mommsen, *Großmachtstellung und Weltpolitik*, pp. 173ff.; Cecil, *Wilhelm II: Emperor and Exile*, pp. 108f.; Canis, *Abgrund*, pp. 169ff.

2 Kaiser Wilhelm II to Bülow, 31 December 1905, originally published in the *Berliner Tageblatt*, No. 487, 14 October 1928; Reimann, *Bülows Denkwürdigkeiten*, pp. 110f.

3 Holstein to Radolin, 22 August 1905, *Holstein Papers*, IV, p. 364.

4 Holstein to Radowitz, 16 January 1906, ibid., No. 926.

5 Wallace to Knollys, 14 and 21 January 1906, RA VIC/W 48/9 and 48/12.

6 Sternburg to Holstein, 16 January 1906, *Holstein Papers*, IV, p. 387.

7 Wallace to Knollys, 28 January, 13 and 18 February 1906, RA VIC/W 48/17, 48/48 and 48/55.

8 Bertie to Knollys, 31 January 1906, RA VIC/W 48/27.

9 Wallace to Knollys, 28 January 1906, RA VIC/W 48/17.

10 Hardinge to Knollys, 6 February 1906, RA VIC/W 48/35.

11 See above, pp. 325f.

12 Bülow to Holstein, 22 February 1906, *Holstein Papers*, IV, No. 936. See below, pp. 410ff.

13 Goltz to Alexander, 27 February 1906, BA-MA Freiburg-im-Breisgau, von der Goltz Papers, N737 Zug. 228/95.

14 Holstein to Radowitz, 16 January 1906, *Holstein Papers*, IV, No. 926, see above, pp. 419f.

15 Kaiser Wilhelm II, marginal notes on Metternich to Bülow, 4 February 1906, *Große Politik*, XXI/1, No. 6945; Moltke to Bülow, 26 January 1906, ibid., No. 6944.

16 Kaiser Wilhelm II to King Edward VII, 1 February 1906, RA VIC/X 37/62, printed in *Große Politik*, XXI/1, No. 6962. The draft of the Auswärtiges Amt is in GStA Berlin, BPHA Rep. 53J Lit. G Nr 11.

17 Spring Rice to Knollys, 31 January 1906, RA VIC/W 48/26.

18 Holstein to Radolin, 7 February 1906, *Holstein Papers*, IV, No. 931.

19 Lascelles to Knollys, 8 February 1906, RA VIC/W 48/40.

20 Metternich, telegram of 20 February 1906 with marginal notes by Kaiser Wilhelm II, *Große Politik*, XXI/1, No. 7022.

21 Kaiser Wilhelm II, marginal notes on Metternich's telegram of 20 February 1906, ibid., No. 7023. See Wilhelm II's marginal notes on Radowitz's report of 26 February 1906, ibid., No. 7044; Bülow's memorandum of 7 March 1906, ibid., No. 7069. See also Holstein, memorandum of 29 March 1906, *Holstein Papers*, IV, No. 948.

22 Bülow to Holstein, 22 February 1906, ibid., No. 936.

23 Bülow, *Denkwürdigkeiten*, II, p. 209.

24 Grand Duke Friedrich I of Baden to Kaiser Wilhelm II, 20 February 1906, Fuchs, *Großherzog von Baden*, IV, No. 2547. Cf. Bülow, *Denkwürdigkeiten*, II, p. 209.

25 Kaiser Wilhelm II, marginal notes on Grand Duke Friedrich I of Baden to Kaiser Wilhelm II, 20 February 1906, GStA Berlin, BPHA Rep. 53J, Lit. B Nr 4. Cf. the official response of 1 March 1906, sent by Bülow to the Grand Duke in the Kaiser's name, Fuchs, *Großherzog von Baden*, IV, No. 2548.

26 Kaiser Wilhelm II, marginal notes on Schoen's report from St Petersburg of 24 February 1906, *Große Politik*, XXI/1, No. 7029.

27 Kaiser Wilhelm II to Bülow, 11 February 1906, *Holstein Papers*, IV, No. 933. The agreement of 3 October 1904 between France and Spain is printed in *Documents diplomatiques français*, 2nd series, V, No. 358.

28 Kaiser Wilhelm II, marginal notes on Stumm's report from Madrid of 20 February 1906, *Große Politik*, XXI/1, No. 7024.

29 See especially Holger Afflerbach, *Der Dreibund. Europäische Großmacht- und Allianzpolitik vor dem Ersten Weltkrieg*, Vienna, Cologne and Weimar 2002, pp. 533–91.

30 Kaiser Wilhelm II to Bülow, 11 February 1906, *Holstein Papers*, IV, No. 933.

31 Kaiser Wilhelm II, marginal comments on Monts's report from Rome of 8 March 1906, *Große Politik*, XXI/1, No. 7150.

32 Kaiser Wilhelm II, marginal notes on Monts's report of 6 April 1906, ibid., No. 7143.

33 Monts, report of 3 March 1906, ibid., No. 7064.

34 Kaiser Wilhelm II, marginal note on Monts's report of 3 March 1906, ibid.

35 Kaiser Wilhelm II, marginal comment on Monts's report of 11 March 1906, *Große Politik*, XXI/1, No. 7103.

36 Kaiser Wilhelm II, marginal note on Monts's report of 3 March 1906, ibid., No. 7064.

37 See Afflerbach, *Dreibund*, pp. 463ff.

38 Kaiser Wilhelm II, marginal notes on Monts's report of 8 April 1906 and Jagow's report of 15 April 1906, *Große Politik*, XXI/1, Nos. 7143 and 7151.

39 Szögyény, report of 8 April 1906, cited ibid., p. 333. See Afflerbach, *Dreibund*, pp. 547 and 566.

40 Szögyény to Goluchowski, 10 April 1906, cited in *Große Politik*, XXI/1, p. 333.

41 Kaiser Wilhelm II to Bülow, 11 February 1906, *Holstein Papers*, IV, No. 933.

42 Kaiser Wilhelm II, marginal comment on Stumm's report from Madrid of 9 March 1906, *Große Politik*, XXI/1, No. 7082.

43 Zedlitz-Trützschler, diary for 13 March 1906, *Zwölf Jahre*, p. 139.

44 Kaiser Wilhelm II, marginal notes on Schoen's report from St Petersburg of 24 February 1906, *Große Politik*, XXI/1, No. 7029. See the correspondence between Witte and Philipp Eulenburg, ibid., pp. 195ff.

45 Spring Rice to Knollys, 16 February 1906, RA VIC/W 48/54.

46 Schoen, report from St Petersburg of 4 March 1906 with marginal notes by Kaiser Wilhelm II, *Große Politik*, XXI/1, No. 7068. See also the Kaiser's marginalia on Schoen's report of 24 February 1906, ibid., No. 7029, together with the correspondence between Witte and Eulenburg, ibid., pp. 195ff.

47 Zedlitz-Trützschler, diary for 22 March 1906, *Zwölf Jahre*, pp. 147f.

48 Kaiser Wilhelm II, marginal notes on Schoen's telegram of 25 March 1906, *Große Politik*, XXI/1, No. 7125.

49 Kaiser Wilhelm II, marginal note on Bülow's submission of 31 March 1906, ibid., No. 8503.

50 Cf. the account in Bülow, *Denkwürdigkeiten*, II, pp. 209ff., according to which the Kaiser decided against war for technical military reasons in early April 1906 and ordered his diplomats to give way. In fact the decision was taken three weeks earlier for quite different reasons.

51 Kaiser Wilhelm II, marginal note on Radowitz's report from Algeciras of 26 February 1906, *Große Politik*, XXI/1, No. 7044.

52 Bülow, memorandum of 7 March 1906, ibid., No. 7069.

53 Holstein, undated memorandum, printed in *Holstein Papers*, IV, p. 405.

54 See Fiebig-von Hase, 'The Uses of "Friendship"', p. 172.

55 Ibid., p. 174.

56 Hardinge to King Edward VII, 9 March 1906, RA VIC/W 48/84.

57 Hardinge to King Edward VII, 16 and 23 March 1906, RA VIC/W 48/87 and 94. See Szögyény to Tschirschky, 23 March 1906, *Große Politik*, XXI/1, No. 7127.

58 Holstein, undated memorandum, printed in *Holstein Papers*, IV, p. 405.

59 Holstein, memorandum of 29 March 1906, ibid., No. 948.

60 Holstein to Brandt, 10 April 1906, ibid., No. 959.

61 Zedlitz-Trützschler, diary for 17 April 1906, *Zwölf Jahre*, pp. 148f.

62 O'Brien to Hay, 7 April 1906, National Archives Washington DC, Records of the Department of State, Dispatches from US Ministers to Denmark, 5 June 1905–6 August 1906 (Microfilm Series) M 41 Roll 28.

63 Kaiser Wilhelm II to Emperor Franz Joseph, 5 April 1906, *Große Politik*, XXI/1, No. 7139.

64 Kaiser Wilhelm II to Goluchowski, 13 April 1906, printed ibid., p. 332. See Afflerbach, *Dreibund*, p. 566.

65 Holstein to David, 13 May 1906, *Holstein Papers*, IV, No. 980.

66 Zedlitz-Trützschler, diary for 17 April 1906, *Zwölf Jahre*, pp. 148f.

67 Tschirschky, statement in the Reichstag of 24 May 1906, as cited in *Große Politik*, XXI/1, pp. 332f.

68 Zedlitz-Trützschler, diary for 17 April 1906, *Zwölf Jahre*, pp. 148f.; Canis, *Abgrund*, p. 187.

69 Kaiser Wilhelm II, marginal comments on Stumm's report of 17 April 1907, *Große Politik*, XXI/2, No. 7252.

70 On Washington see Fiebig-von Hase, 'The Uses of "Friendship"', pp. 151–4 et passim.

71 Wallace to Knollys, 25 February 1906, RA VIC/W 48/69.

72 Hardinge to King Edward VII, 16 March 1906, RA VIC/W 48/87.

73 Spring Rice to Knollys, 1 March 1906, with approving comments by King Edward VII, RA VIC/W 48/75.

74 Bertie to Knollys, 2 March 1906, RA VIC/Add C 07/2Q Knollys Papers.

75 Zedlitz-Trützschler, diary for 17 March 1906, *Zwölf Jahre*, pp. 146f.

76 Zedlitz-Trützschler, diary for 13 March 1906, ibid., pp. 139f.

77 Holstein to David, 13 May 1906, *Holstein Papers*, IV, No. 980.

78 Wallace to Knollys, 19 April 1906, RA VIC/W 49/3. Also Wallace to Knollys, 16 May 1906, RA VIC/W 49/19.

17 'ENCIRCLEMENT': CAUGHT IN THE WEB OF THE ENTENTE

1 See Chapter 21.

2 Zedlitz-Trützschler, diary for 13 March 1906, *Zwölf Jahre*, p. 145.

3 Holstein to Bülow, 26 September 1907, *Holstein Papers*, IV, No. 1051.

4 Berckheim to Marschall, 25 January 1906, Fuchs, *Großherzog von Baden*, IV, No. 2541.

5 See Brauer to Berckheim, 12 January 1906, ibid., No. 2538; Berckheim to Marschall, 25 January 1906, ibid., No. 2541. See also Tschirschky to Radolin, 26 January 1906, *Holstein Papers*, IV, No. 928 annex. For Tschirschky see Friedrich Graf von Hatzfeldt, *Heinrich von Tschirschky im Spiegel der Archive und der Geschichtsliteratur*, Cologne 1996.

6 Berckheim to Marschall, 9 April 1906, Fuchs, *Großherzog von Baden*, IV, No. 2551; Tschirschky to Eisendecher, 13 May 1906, *Holstein Papers*, IV, No. 981. See Otto

Hammann, *Bilder aus der letzten Kaiserzeit*, Berlin 1922, pp. 36–40; Hammann, *Zur Vorgeschichte des Weltkrieges*, pp. 233f.

7   Holstein to Bülow, 31 March 1906, *Holstein Papers*, IV, No. 950. See Holstein's diary for 17 April 1907, ibid., No. 1017.

8   Holstein to David, 29 August 1906, ibid., No. 990.

9   Holstein, diary for 5 March 1907, ibid., No. 1014.

10 Bülow to Mühlberg, 9 July 1907, *Große Politik*, XXI/2, No. 7268.

11 Tschirschky to Eisendecher, 13 May 1906, *Holstein Papers*, IV, No. 981.

12 See above, p. 436. On Austria-Hungary's policy at Algeciras see Fritz Fellner, *Vom Dreibund zum Völkerbund. Studien zur Geschichte der internationalen Beziehungen, 1882–1919*, Vienna and Munich 1994, pp. 92–106. On the crisis in the Triple Alliance after the conference see in particular Afflerbach, *Dreibund*, pp. 547–67.

13 Kaiser Wilhelm II to Bülow, 26 June 1907, *Große Politik*, XXI/2, No. 7257. See below, pp. 446ff.

14 Kaiser Wilhelm II, marginal note on Stumm's report of 22 August 1907, *Große Politik*, XXV/1, No. 8533.

15 Mühlberg to Bülow, 14 July 1907, *Große Politik*, XXI/2, No. 7270.

16 Szögyény, report of 27 March 1906, HHStA Vienna, Hofnachrichten: Preußen. Kaiser Wilhelm II, marginal note on Monts's report of 8 June 1906, ibid., No. 7157.

17 Wedel, report of 30 May 1906, PA AA R 3648.

18 Ibid.

19 Kaiser Wilhelm II, marginal note on Wedel's report of 30 May 1906, ibid.

20 Bülow to Kaiser Wilhelm II, 31 May 1906, GStA Berlin, BPHA Rep. 53J Lit. B Nr 16a; Tschirschky to Bülow, 3 June 1906, Wedel to Tschirschky, 3 June 1906, PA AA R 3648.

21 Zedlitz-Trützschler, diary for 19 March 1907, *Zwölf Jahre*, p. 156.

22 Holstein to Bülow, 3 May 1907, *Holstein Papers*, IV, No. 1025. The sentence in brackets was deleted again from the draft by Holstein.

23 Pourtalès to Bülow, 25 September 1906, PA AA R 5094.

24 Wedel, report of 2 November 1906, *Große Politik*, XXI/2, No. 7162.

25 Kaiser Wilhelm II, marginalia on Monts's report of 5 February 1907, ibid., No. 7167.

26 Kaiser Wilhelm II, marginal comments on Wedel's report of 2 November 1906, ibid., No. 7162.

27 Holstein to Radolin, 23 April 1906, *Holstein Papers*, IV, No. 966. Radolin gave this letter from Holstein to Sir Donald Mackenzie Wallace to read on his way through Paris; Wallace sent on certain passages to Windsor. Wallace to Knollys, 16 May 1906, RA VIC/W 49/19.

28 Holstein, memorandum of 17 May 1906, *Holstein Papers*, IV, No. 983.

29 Holstein to David, 29 August 1906, ibid., No. 990.

30 Bernhard Fürst von Bülow to Alfred Graf von Bülow, July 1906, as cited in Bülow, *Denkwürdigkeiten*, II, pp. 229–38.

31 Bülow to Kaiser Wilhelm II, 9 September 1907, GStA Berlin, BPHA Rep. 53J Lit. B Nr 16a. Cited in part in Fesser, *Traum vom Platz an der Sonne*, p. 117.

32 Kaiser Wilhelm II, marginal notes on Flotow's report of 18 October 1906, *Große Politik*, XXI/2, No. 7237.

33 Pourtalès to Bülow, 25 September 1906, PA AA R 5094. Partially printed in *Große Politik*, XXI/2, No. 7201.

34 Kaiser Wilhelm II, marginal notes on Radolin's report of 4 November 1906, ibid., No. 7231.

35 Kaiser Wilhelm II, marginal comments on Metternich's report of 17 October 1906, ibid., No. 7202.

36 Bülow to Einem, 1 July 1906, as quoted in Bülow, *Denkwürdigkeiten*, II, pp. 226ff.

37 Haldane to King Edward VII, 2 September 1906, RA VIC/W 49/100.

38 Haldane to Davidson, 19 September 1906, RA VIC/W 50/5.

39 Hardinge to Grey, 16 August 1906, RA VIC/W 49/95; Hardinge to King Edward VII, 19 August 1906, RA VIC/W 49/94. See below, pp. 454ff.

40 O'Brien to Root, 7 April 1906, National Archives Washington DC, Records of the Department of State, Dispatches from US Ministers to Denmark, 1811–1906, M 41 Roll 28. Cited in Vagts, *Deutschland*, p. 1878, note.

41 Kaiser Wilhelm II, marginal note on Flotow's report of 8 June 1906, PA AA R 3648.

42 Kaiser Wilhelm II, marginalia of 2 December 1906 on Bülow's submission of 1 December 1906, *Große Politik*, XXI/2, No. 7291.

43 Kaiser Wilhelm II, marginal comments on Bülow's submission of 13 November 1905, ibid., XXII, No. 7566. See Holstein to Bülow, January 1906, *Holstein Papers*, IV, No. 919.

44 Hardinge to Knollys, 28 December 1906, RA VIC/W 50/134.

45 Grey to Knollys, 30 December 1906, RA VIC/W 50/139.

46 Hardinge to King Edward VII, 30 April and 2 May 1907, RA VIC/W 51/74 and 75; Stumm, report from London of 27 April 1907 with marginal notes by Kaiser Wilhelm II, *Große Politik*, XXI/2, No. 7217.

47 Hereditary Princess Charlotte of Saxe-Meiningen to Schweninger, 25 April 1907, BA Berlin, Schweninger Papers, Nr 131.

48 Mudra to von der Goltz, 19 April 1907, BA-MA Freiburg-im-Breisgau, von der Goltz Papers, N 737/14.

49 Harden to Holstein, 3 May 1907, *Holstein Papers*, IV, No. 1024.

50 Prince Albert of Monaco to Kaiser Wilhelm II, 27 May 1907, GStA Berlin, BPHA Rep. 53J Lit. B Nr 16a.

51 Jenisch to Bülow, 15 June 1907, *Große Politik*, XXI/2, No. 7255; Canis, *Abgrund*, pp. 231f.

52 Kaiser Wilhelm II to Bülow, 26 June 1907, *Große Politik*, XXI/2, No. 7257.

53 Kaiser Wilhelm II to Bülow, 26 June 1907, ibid., No. 7258. See also the Kaiser's marginal notes on Radolin's report of 14 July 1907, ibid., No. 7271.

54 Jenisch to Bülow, 16 July 1907, ibid., No. 7272.

55 Kaiser Wilhelm II to Bülow, 26 June 1907, ibid., No. 7257.

56 Kaiser Wilhelm II, marginal notes on Radolin's report of 6 July 1907, ibid., No. 7267.

57 Mühlberg to Bülow, 17 July 1907, ibid., No. 7273.

58 Kaiser Wilhelm II, marginal notes on Schoen's report of 7 April 1906 and on Metternich's report of 26 April 1906, ibid., XXV/1, Nos. 8504 and 8505.

59 Kaiser Wilhelm II, marginal note on Metternich's telegram of 1 February 1907, ibid., XXI/2, No. 7207.

60 Zedlitz-Trützschler, diary for 19 March 1907, *Zwölf Jahre*, p. 153; Kaiser Wilhelm II to Bülow, 17 January 1907, *Große Politik*, XXI/2, No. 7203.

61 Jenisch to Bülow, 16 June 1907, cited ibid., p. 570, footnote.

62 Zedlitz-Trützschler, diary for 19 March 1907, *Zwölf Jahre*, p. 153; Kaiser Wilhelm II, marginal note on Monts's report of 18 April 1907, *Große Politik*, XXI/2, No. 7215.

63 Ibid.

64 Kaiser Wilhelm II, marginal note on Metternich's report of 8 May 1906, *Große Politik*, XXI/2, No. 7181.

65 Kaiser Wilhelm II, marginal note on Tschirschky's submission of 12 May 1906, ibid., No. 7184.

66 Kaiser Wilhelm II, marginal notes on Stumm's report of 19 May 1906, ibid., No. 7185.

67 Kaiser Wilhelm II, marginal note on Tschirschky's submission of 12 May 1906, ibid., No. 7184.

68 Kaiser Wilhelm II, marginal note on Metternich's report of 8 May 1906, ibid., No. 7181.

69 Metternich, report of 8 May 1906, PA AA R 3703, printed in *Große Politik*, XXI/2, No. 7181.

70 Kaiser Wilhelm II, marginal notes on Metternich's report of 8 May 1906, ibid., No. 7181.

71 Hardinge to Knollys, 7 April 1906, Knollys Papers, RA VIC/Add C 07/2/Q.

72 See above, pp. 399–407.

73 Kaiser Wilhelm II, marginal note on Metternich's telegram of 26 April 1906, PA AA R 3703.

74 Kaiser Wilhelm II, marginal notes on Metternich's report of 4 May 1906, *Große Politik*, XXI/2, No. 7180.

75 Kaiser Wilhelm II to Bülow, 2 July 1906, Bülow to Kaiser Wilhelm II, 30 June and 2 July 1906, PA AA R 3628, copies in R 3703.

76 Hardinge to Knollys, 9 June 1906, RA VIC/W 49/47.

77 Kaiser Wilhelm II to Bülow, 13 July 1906, PA AA R 3703.

78 Bülow to Kaiser Wilhelm II, 14 July 1906, PA AA R 3703.

79 Grey to Knollys, 30 July 1906, RA VIC/W 49/83.

80 Metternich to Auswärtiges Amt, 9 August 1906, PA AA R 3704.

81 Hardinge to Knollys, 31 July 1906, with marginal comment by King Edward VII, RA VIC/W 49/85.

82 Jenisch to Bülow, 13 August 1906, Bülow to Auswärtiges Amt, 13 August 1906, PA AA R 3704.

83 Kaiser Wilhelm II to Bülow, 16 August 1906, *Große Politik*, XXI/2, No. 7197.

84 Kaiser Wilhelm II, memorandum of 15 August 1906, ibid., XXIII/1, No. 7815.

85 Hardinge to Grey, 16 August 1906, RA VIC/W 49/95.

86 Kaiser Wilhelm II, memorandum of 15 August 1906, *Große Politik*, XXIII/1, No. 7815.

87 Kaiser Wilhelm II, marginal notes on the article 'Abrüstungskomödie' in the *Tägliche Rundschau* of 10 August 1906, cited ibid., p. 81.

88 Kaiser Wilhelm II, memorandum of 15 August 1906, ibid., No. 7815.

89 Hardinge to Grey, 16 August 1906, RA VIC/W 49/95; Hardinge to King Edward VII, 19 August 1906, RA VIC/W 49/94.

90 Mallet to Knollys, 9 June 1906, RA VIC/W 49/46.

91 Kaiser Wilhelm II, marginal notes on Wedel's report of 30 April 1906, *Große Politik*, XXV/1, No. 8506.

92 Kaiser Wilhelm II, marginal comment on Miquel's report from St Petersburg of 19 September 1906, ibid., No. 8518.

93 Lascelles to Grey, 29 October 1906, RA VIC/W 50/39.

94 Ibid.

95 Tsar Nicholas II to Kaiser Wilhelm II, 12 May 1906, PA AA R 3628.

96 Kaiser Wilhelm II to Tsar Nicholas II, 14 June 1906, ibid.

97 Kaiser Wilhelm II to Bülow, 2 July 1906, ibid., copied in Bülow to Tschirschky, 3 July 1906, ibid.

98 Bülow to Kaiser Wilhelm II, 2 July 1906, ibid., copied in Bülow to Tschirschky, 3 July 1906, ibid.

99 Hintze to Kaiser Wilhelm II, 18 July 1906, ibid.; Kaiser Wilhelm II to Hintze, 19 July 1906, ibid.

100 Schoen, report of 18 July 1906, passed on by Tschirschky to Jenisch, 18 July 1906, ibid.

101 Bülow to Tschirschky, 19 July 1906, ibid.

102 Jenisch to Tschirschky, 20 July 1906, ibid; Bülow to Kaiser Wilhelm II, 17 July 1906, GStA Berlin, BPHA Rep. 53J Lit B Nr 16a.

103 Kaiser Wilhelm II, marginal notes on Bülow to Jenisch, 14 August 1906, PA AA R 3704.

104 Kaiser Wilhelm II, marginal comments on Wedel's report of 2 November 1906, *Große Politik*, XXII, No. 7365.

105 Kaiser Wilhelm II, marginal comment on Schoen's report of 16 March 1907, ibid., XXIII, No. 7877.

106 Kaiser Wilhelm II, marginal notes of 18 November 1906 on Bülow's memorandum of 16 November 1906 on his conversations with Aehrenthal, ibid., XXI/2, No. 7164.

107 Kaiser Wilhelm II, marginal notes on Miquel's report from St Petersburg of 17 March 1907, ibid., XXV/1, No. 8541.

108 Kaiser Wilhelm II to Bülow, 13 July 1907, PA AA R 3628, printed in *Große Politik*, XXII, No. 7374.

109 Jenisch to Eisendecher, 13 July 1907, PA AA R 3628.

110 Mühlberg to Bülow, 22 July 1907, ibid., printed in *Große Politik*, XXII, No. 7375.

111 Tschirschky to Bülow, 25 July 1907, PA AA R 3628. Cf. Mühlberg to Bülow, 22 July 1907, *Große Politik*, XXII, No. 7375 annex I.

112 Holstein, diary for 13 August 1907, *Holstein Papers*, IV, No. 1046. Canis, *Abgrund*, pp. 233f.

113 Hopman, diary for 3–5 August 1907, Hopman Papers, BA-MA Freiburg-im-Breisgau, N 326/6.

114 Bülow to Auswärtiges Amt, 5 August 1907; Schoen to Auswärtiges Amt, 6 August 1907, PA AA R 3629; Kiderlen-Wächter to Auswärtiges Amt, 13 August 1907; Bülow to Auswärtiges Amt, 14 August 1907; Rantzau to Auswärtiges Amt, 14 August 1907, PA AA R 3630.

115 Hardinge to Knollys, 7 August 1907, RA Knollys Papers, VIC/Add C 07/2/O.

116 Kaiser Wilhelm II, marginal note on Metternich's report of 6 August 1907, PA AA R 3706.

117 Kaiser Wilhelm II, marginal notes on Kohlhaas's report of 9 August 1907, PA AA R 3630.

118 Miquel to Auswärtiges Amt, 31 August 1907, *Große Politik*, XXV/1, No. 8534.

119 Hardinge to King Edward VII, 26 August 1907, RA VIC/W 52/15; Goschen to Grey, 6 September 1907, RA VIC/W 52/21.

120 Bülow, marginal note on Miquel's telegram of 31 August 1907, *Große Politik*, XXV/1, No. 8534.

121 Fesser, *Traum vom Platz an der Sonne*, p. 119.

122 Hardinge to King Edward VII, 4 September 1907, RA VIC/W 52/20.

123 Harden to Rathenau, 23 August 1907, Hans Dieter Hellige and Ernst Schulin, eds., *Walther Rathenau* Gesamtausgabe, VI: *Briefwechsel Walther Rathenau – Maximilian Harden*, Munich and Heidelberg 1983, p. 536.

124 Ibid.

125 Harden to Holstein, 27 October 1906, *Holstein Papers*, IV, No. 1001.

126 Holstein to Bülow, 29 August 1907, ibid., No. 1047.

127 Holstein to Ida von Stülpnagel, 31 August 1907, Rogge, *Friedrich von Holstein, Lebensbekenntnis*, p. 287.

128 Zedlitz-Trützschler, diary for 19 April 1907, *Zwölf Jahre*, pp. 158f.

18　GERMANY'S 'DREADNOUGHT LEAP'. THE KAISER AND 'HIS' NAVY

1 See above, pp. 462f.

2 See Berghahn, *Tirpitz-Plan*, in particular pp. 565f.

3 Tirpitz, addendum to notes for his audience with the Kaiser on 29 September 1907, as cited ibid., p. 588. See below, pp. 496f.

4 Berghahn, *Tirpitz-Plan*, p. 445. See also Wolfgang König, *Wilhelm II. und die Moderne. Der Kaiser und die technisch-industrielle Welt*, Paderborn, Munich, Vienna and Zürich 2007, pp. 19–43.

5 See below, p. 465.

6 Berghahn, *Tirpitz-Plan*, p. 357.

7 Tirpitz to Crown Prince Wilhelm, 15 April 1909, as cited ibid., pp. 457f.

8 Volker R. Berghahn, 'Zu den Zielen des deutschen Flottenbaus unter Wilhelm II.', *Historische Zeitschrift*, 210/1 (1970), 34–100; Berghahn, *Tirpitz-Plan*; Herbert Schottelius and Wilhelm Deist, eds., *Marine und Marinepolitik im kaiserlichen Deutschland 1871–1914*, Düsseldorf 1972; Wilhelm Deist, *Flottenpolitik und Flottenpropaganda. Das Nachrichtenbureau des Reichsmarineamtes 1897–1914*, Stuttgart 1976; Michael Epkenhans, *Die wilhelminische Flottenrüstung 1908–1914. Weltmachtstreben, industrieller Fortschritt, soziale Integration*, Munich 1991; Rolf Hobson, *Maritimer Imperialismus. Seemachtideologie, seestrategisches Denken und der Tirpitzplan 1875 bis 1914*, Munich 2004; Jan Rüger, *The Great Naval Game. Britain and Germany in the Age of Empire*, Cambridge 2007; Patrick J. Kelly, *Tirpitz and the Imperial German Navy*, Bloomington 2011; Matthew S. Seligmann, *The Royal Navy and the German Threat 1901–1914. Admiralty Plans to Protect British Trade in a War against Germany*, Oxford 2012.

9 See Berghahn, *Tirpitz-Plan*, pp. 429ff.

10 Müller, diary for 10 February 1906, BA-MA Freiburg-im-Breisgau, Müller Papers.

11 See above, pp. 228–31 and 315–23.

12 Axel Grießmer, *Linienschiffe der Kaiserlichen Marine 1906–1918. Konstruktionen zwischen Rüstungskonkurrenz und Flottengesetz*, Bonn 1999, p. 18.

13 Berghahn, *Tirpitz-Plan*, p. 346.

14 Ibid., pp. 346f.

15 Tirpitz, notes for his audience with the Kaiser, 16 September 1903, as cited ibid., pp. 344–6.

16 Tirpitz, memorandum of 25–9 September 1903, cited ibid., pp. 347–9.

17 Tirpitz, notes on the events and negotiations of October 1903 to January 1904, as quoted ibid., p. 350.

18 Ibid., pp. 350f.

19 Tirpitz to Hollmann, 30 September 1903, as quoted ibid., p. 349.

20 Tirpitz, notes on the visit to Hubertusstock on 12 October 1903, as quoted ibid., p. 350.

21 Tirpitz, addendum to his notes for Hubertusstock, 18 October 1903, as cited ibid., pp. 351f.

22 Tirpitz, notes on the visit to Hubertusstock on 12 October 1903, cited ibid., p. 350.

23 Kaiser Wilhelm II to Reich Navy Office, 10 October 1903, as cited in Grießmer, *Linienschiffe*, pp. 18f.

24 Tirpitz, notes for the audience with the Kaiser on 14 November 1903, as quoted in Berghahn, *Tirpitz-Plan*, p. 351.

25 Kaiser Wilhelm II to Tirpitz, 14 November 1903, quoted ibid., pp. 353f.

26 Prince Heinrich of Prussia to Tirpitz, 25 November 1903, as cited ibid., p. 354.

27 Berghahn, *Tirpitz-Plan*, p. 354.

28 Tirpitz, addendum to his notes for Hubertusstock, 18 October 1903, cited ibid., p. 353.

29 Ibid., pp. 351f.

30 Zedlitz-Trützschler, diary for 1 October 1904, *Zwölf Jahre*, pp. 81f.

31 Tirpitz, notes on the events and negotiations of September 1904, as cited in Berghahn, *Tirpitz-Plan*, p. 375.

32 Berghahn, *Tirpitz-Plan*, pp. 349f.

33 Grießmer, *Linienschiffe*, p. 19.

34 Ibid., p. 24.

35 Zedlitz-Trützschler, diary for 1 October 1904, *Zwölf Jahre*, pp. 81ff.

36 Berghahn, *Tirpitz-Plan*, pp. 359ff.

37 Kaiser Wilhelm II, marginal comment of 12 August 1912 on Tirpitz to Kaiser Wilhelm II, 5 August 1912, as cited ibid., p. 364, note 40.

38 Kaiser Wilhelm II, memorandum entitled 'Einiges über Panzerkreuzer' of November 1903, ibid., p. 361. See the extensive summary of the published article in Axel Grießmer, *Große Kreuzer der Kaiserlichen Marine 1906–1918. Konstruktionen und Entwürfe im Zeichen des Tirpitz-Planes*, Bonn 1996, pp. 8f.

39 Berghahn, *Tirpitz-Plan*, pp. 361f.; Kaiser Wilhelm II to Tsar Nicholas II, 9 January 1904; Goetz, *Briefe Wilhelms II. an den Zaren*, No. XXXI, pp. 106ff. and 335f.

40 Kaiser Wilhelm II, pencilled note to Senden-Bibran, November 1903, Archiv des vormals regierenden preußischen Königshauses, Burg Hohenzollern, Hechingen.

41 Kaiser Wilhelm II, pencilled note to Senden-Bibran, November 1903, ibid.

42 Kaiser Wilhelm II to Senden-Bibran, no date [December 1903], BA-MA Freiburg-im-Breisgau, Senden-Bibran Papers, N160/1, fol. 74.

43 Kaiser Wilhelm II to Senden-Bibran, no date [December 1903], ibid., fol. 65f.

44 Kaiser Wilhelm II to Senden-Bibran, no date [December 1903], ibid., fol. 75.

45 Kaiser Wilhelm II to Tsar Nicholas II., 9 January 1904, Goetz, *Briefe Wilhelms II. an den Zaren*, No. XXXI, pp. 106–8 and 335f.

46 Tirpitz, memorandum of 29 January 1904, 'Was ist ein Großer Kreuzer', as quoted in Berghahn, *Tirpitz-Plan*, pp. 362–4; Grießmer, *Große Kreuzer*, p. 9.

47 Prince Heinrich of Prussia, diary for 31 January 1904, MSM Hamburg.

48 Grießmer, *Große Kreuzer*, p. 18.

49 Kaiser Wilhelm II, marginal notes on Tirpitz's memorandum of 29 January 1904, as cited in Berghahn, *Tirpitz-Plan*, pp. 364f.

50 See Grießmer, *Große Kreuzer*, p. 10.

51 Kaiser Wilhelm II to Tirpitz, 23 February 1904, Kaiser Wilhelm II, manuscript entitled 'L.: Zur Diskussion über Panzerkreuzer', Berghahn, *Tirpitz-Plan*, p. 367. Analysed in Grießmer, *Große Kreuzer*, pp. 8f.

52 H [i.e. Albert Hopman], 'Zu dem Aufsatz: "Einiges über Panzerkreuzer"', *Marine Rundschau*, 15 (1904), pp. 220–2.

53 Tirpitz to Kaiser Wilhelm II, 25 February 1904; Tirpitz, memorandum on the audience of 27 February 1904, as cited in Berghahn, *Tirpitz-Plan*, pp. 367f.

54 Kaiser Wilhelm II, 'Erwiderungswort' of 17 March 1904, ibid., p. 368.

55 Fischel to Senden-Bibran, 24 March 1904, ibid., p. 368.

56 Senden, minute deposited in the files on the Kaiser's orders on 7 April 1904, ibid.

57 Tirpitz to Prince Heinrich of Prussia, 6 May 1904, as quoted ibid., pp. 368f.

58 Prince Heinrich of Prussia to Tirpitz, 15 May 1904, quoted ibid., pp. 369f.

59 Kaiser Wilhelm II to Tirpitz, 28 April 1905, BA-MA Freiburg-im-Breisgau, RM3/v. 5, printed in part in Grießmer, *Große Kreuzer*, pp. 23f. See also Berghahn, *Tirpitz-Plan*, p. 452.

60 Kaiser Wilhelm II, marginal notes on the report of the naval attaché in Rome of 1 May 1905, BA-MA Freiburg, RM3/v. 5.

61 Kaiser Wilhelm II, comparative shipping tables, sent by Senden to Tirpitz on 4 May 1905, ibid.

62 Müller, diary for 2 and 4 May 1905, BA-MA Freiburg-im-Breisgau, Müller Papers. See also the conflict of the Kaiser and Senden with Tirpitz over the boat construction plans of the British Admiral Lord Victor Montagu, which Wilhelm and Senden wanted to try out in Kiel but which Tirpitz refused to countenance. Montagu to Senden, 5 May and 27 June 1905, Senden to Tirpitz, 22 May 1905, Tirpitz to Senden, 23 May 1905 BA-MA Freiburg-im-Breisgau, RM2/123.

63 Tirpitz to Kaiser Wilhelm II, 6 May 1905, BA-MA Freiburg-im-Breisgau, RM3/v. 5; Berghahn, *Tirpitz-Plan*, p. 452.

64 Kaiser Wilhelm II to Tirpitz, 7 May 1905, BA-MA Freiburg-im-Breisgau, RM3/v. 5; Berghahn, *Tirpitz-Plan*, p. 452; Grießmer, *Linienschiffe*, pp. 28f.

65 Müller, diary for 2 and 4 May 1905, BA-MA Freiburg-im-Breisgau, Müller Papers.

66 Müller to Tirpitz, 7 May 1905, BA-MA Freiburg-im-Breisgau, RM3/v. 5.

67 Naval Cabinet, 'Submission to the Kaiser' of 10 May 1905, Berghahn, *Tirpitz-Plan*, pp. 452f.

68 Müller to Tirpitz, 12 May 1905, passing on a marginal note of the Kaiser's and Tirpitz's comment thereon, BA-MA Freiburg-im-Breisgau, RM3/v. 5.

69 Müller to Kaiser Wilhelm II, 10 May 1905, as quoted in Berghahn, *Tirpitz-Plan*, p. 453; Müller, diary for 10 and 12 May 1905, BA-MA Freiburg-im-Breisgau, Müller Papers.

70 Tirpitz, minute of 13 May 1905, BA-MA Freiburg-im-Breisgau, RM3/v. 5. See Berghahn, *Tirpitz-Plan*, p. 453.

71 Trotha, notes on Eickstedt's oral assessment of the Kaiser's project for a fast capital ship, 9 May 1905, ibid., p. 452.

72 Müller to Tirpitz, 11 July 1905; Tirpitz to Müller, 19 July 1905, ibid., p. 454.

73 Tirpitz to Trotha, 19 July 1905, as cited ibid., p. 456.

74 Trotha to Tirpitz, 3 August 1905, quoted ibid.

75 Müller, diary for 14 March, 10 and 21 April and 24 July 1906, BA-MA Freiburg-im-Breisgau, Müller Papers.

76 Hopman, diary for 26 November 1906, BA-MA Freiburg-im-Breisgau, Hopman Papers, N 326/6, printed in Epkenhans, *Leben eines 'Wilhelminers'*, p. 140.

77 Müller, diary for 13 March 1907, BA-MA Freiburg-im-Breisgau, Müller Papers.

78 Ibid. See Harald Fock, 'Des Kaisers Preisausschreiben', *Marine Rundschau*, 1977, pp. 112–17, 183–7, 299–303 and 384–9.

79 Vittorio Cuniberti, 'An Ideal Warship for the British Navy', *All The World's Fighting Ships*, 1903. See Marder, *Anatomy of British Sea Power*, p. 527; Berghahn, *Tirpitz-Plan*, p. 434.

80 Kaiser Wilhelm II, marginal notes on Coerper's reports of 7 January and 20 February 1905, as cited ibid., p. 465.

81 Grießmer, *Linienschiffe*, pp. 26f.

82 Kaiser Wilhelm II, marginal note on Coerper's report of 27 May 1905, as quoted in Berghahn, *Tirpitz-Plan*, p. 465. See Grießmer, *Linienschiffe*, p. 28.

83 Hintze, report of 2 June 1905 with the Kaiser's marginal notes, Berghahn, *Tirpitz-Plan*, p. 465.

84 Müller, diary for 6 July 1905, BA-MA Freiburg-im-Breisgau, Müller Papers.

85 Kaiser Wilhelm II to Tirpitz, 20 and 24 July 1905, BA-MA Freiburg-im-Breisgau, RM3/v 5 and RM2/1601. See Berghahn, *Tirpitz-Plan*. p. 454.

86 Tirpitz to Kaiser Wilhelm II, 30 July 1905, as quoted ibid., pp. 454f.

87 Tirpitz to Scheer, 3 September 1905, ibid., p. 466; Grießmer, *Linienschiffe*, p. 30.

88 Senden to Tirpitz, 3 September 1905, Berghahn, *Tirpitz-Plan*, p. 467.

89 Tirpitz to Scheer, 6 September 1905, as cited ibid., p. 468.

90 Ibid.

91 See Capelle to Tirpitz, 8 September 1905, quoted in Berghahn, *Tirpitz-Plan*, pp. 469f.

92 Ibid., p. 470.

93 Ibid., pp. 472–5 and 479.

94 See Deist, *Flottenpolitik und Flottenpropaganda*. pp. 171–94.

95 Kaiser Wilhelm II to Menges, 6 May 1905, as cited in Berghahn, *Tirpitz-Plan*, p. 487.

96 Müller, diary for 22 May 1905, BA-MA Freiburg-im-Breisgau, Müller Papers.

97 Berghahn, *Tirpitz-Plan*, pp. 488f.

98 Müller, diary for 22 and 27 May 1905, BA-MA Freiburg-im-Breisgau, Müller Papers.

99 Kaiser Wilhelm II to King Wilhelm II von Württemberg, 15 June 1905, as quoted in Berghahn, *Tirpitz-Plan*, p. 489, note 61.

100 Tirpitz, dictation of 7 November 1905, Tirpitz, *Aufbau der deutschen Weltmacht*, p. 21. See Berghahn, *Tirpitz-Plan*, p. 22.

101 Hohenthal, report of 15 November 1905, as cited ibid., p. 492.

102 Berghahn, *Tirpitz-Plan*, p. 492.

103 Müller, diary for 6 November 1905, BA-MA Freiburg-im-Breisgau, Müller Papers.

104 Tirpitz, *Aufbau der deutschen Weltmacht*, p. 21. See Berghahn, *Tirpitz-Plan*, pp. 492f.

105 Tirpitz to Bülow, 8 November 1905, BA-MA Freiburg-im-Breisgau, Tirpitz Papers, N 253/6, cited in Berghahn, *Tirpitz-Plan*, pp. 494f.

106 Tirpitz to Loebell, 16 November 1905, BA-MA Freiburg-im-Breisgau, Tirpitz Papers, N 253/6, cited in Berghahn, *Tirpitz-Plan*, pp. 495–9.

107 Müller, diary for 10 February 1906, BA-MA Freiburg-im-Breisgau, Müller Papers.

108 Kaiser Wilhelm II, marginal note on the article 'The Recent Developments at the Admiralty', *The Tribune*, 12 February 1906, BA-MA Freiburg-im-Breisgau, Tirpitz Papers, N 253/6.

109 Tirpitz, minute of 11 November 1905, *Aufbau der deutschen Weltmacht*, p. 23.

110 Tirpitz, notes for the audience with the Kaiser on 3 February 1906, ibid., p. 24.

111 Senden-Bibran, memorandum of 6 February 1906, printed ibid., p. 25.

112 Tirpitz, memorandum on the events of February 1906, ibid., pp. 25–8.

113 Müller to Tirpitz, 15 February 1906, printed ibid., pp. 28f.

114 Müller, diary for 5, 6 and 9–16 March 1906, BA-MA Freiburg-im-Breisgau, Müller Papers.

115 Kaiser Wilhelm II, marginal note on an article in the *Neue Politische Korrespondenz* of 16 March 1906, printed in Tirpitz, *Aufbau der deutschen Weltmacht*, pp. 30f.

116 Tirpitz, dictation of 9 April 1906, ibid., p. 34.

117 Tirpitz to Kaiser Wilhelm II, 4 April 1906, ibid., pp. 31f.

118 Kaiser Wilhelm II to Tirpitz, 5 April 1906, ibid., pp. 32f.

119 Tirpitz, dictation of 9 April 1906, ibid., pp. 33f.

120 Trotha, minute of 3 May 1906, printed ibid., pp. 34f.

121 Ibid.

122 Ibid.

123 Prince Heinrich of Prussia, diary for 19 May and 26 September 1906, MSM Hamburg.

124 Tirpitz to Prince Heinrich of Prussia, 25 December 1905, as cited in Berghahn, *Tirpitz-Plan*, p. 506.

125 Kaiser Wilhelm II to Tirpitz, 20 May 1906, as quoted ibid., p. 512, note 27. See Trotha, notes on the events of May 1906, Tirpitz, *Aufbau der deutschen Weltmacht*, pp. 35f.

126 Hunold von Ahlefeld to Tirpitz, 2 July 1906, as quoted in Berghahn, *Tirpitz-Plan*, p. 512.

127 Müller, diary for 10 February 1906, BA-MA Freiburg-im-Breisgau, Müller Papers.

128 Müller to Tirpitz, 11 July 1906, quoted in Berghahn, *Tirpitz-Plan*, p. 513.

129 Berghahn, *Tirpitz-Plan*, pp. 505 and 508.

130 Zedlitz-Trützschler, diary for 19 April 1907, *Zwölf Jahre*, pp. 158f.

131 Kaiser Wilhelm II, marginal comments on Stumm's report of 27 April 1907, *Große Politik*, XXI/2, No. 7217.

132 Hardinge to Knollys, 23 and 31 October 1906, RA VIC/W 50/28 and 34.

133 Hardinge to Knollys, 25 June 1907, RA VIC/W 52/3.

134 Hardinge to Lascelles, 16 January 1907, RA VIC/W 51/13.

135 Grey to Knollys, 12 November 1906, RA VIC/W 50/45.

136 Kaiser Wilhelm II, marginal comments on two reports by Metternich of 31 January 1907, *Große Politik*, XXI/2, Nos. 7205 and 7206.

137 Kaiser Wilhelm II, marginal note on Metternich's report of 30 January 1907, ibid., No. 7204.

138 Kaiser Wilhelm II, marginal notes on Stumm's report of 20 April 1907, ibid., XXIII/1, No. 7927.

139 Kaiser Wilhelm II, marginal comments on Stumm's report of 10 May 1906, ibid., No. 7809.

140 Kaiser Wilhelm II, marginal notes on Stumm's report of 4 May 1907, ibid., No. 7931. Cf. the Kaiser's comments on Monts's report of 18 April 1907, ibid., XXI/2, No. 7215.

141 Kaiser Wilhelm II, marginal notes on Stumm's report of 20 April 1907, ibid., XXIII/1, No. 7927.

142 Müller, diary for 27 October 1906, BA-MA Freiburg-im-Breisgau, Müller Papers; Kaiser Wilhelm II, marginal notes on Stumm's reports of 20 April and 4 May 1907, *Große Politik*, XXIII/1, Nos. 7927 and 7931. See also his comments on Monts's report of 18 April 1907, ibid., XXI/2, No. 7215.

143 Kaiser Wilhelm II, marginal notes on Stumm's report of 4 May 1907, ibid., XXIII/1, No. 7931. Cf. his comments on Monts's report of 18 April 1907, ibid., XXI/2, No. 7215.

144 Kaiser Wilhelm II, marginal comments on both of Metternich's reports of 31 January 1907, ibid., Nos. 7205 and 7206.

145 Kaiser Wilhelm II, marginal comment on Stumm's report of 27 April 1907, ibid., No. 7217.

146 Tschirschky to Tirpitz, 7 September 1906; Sternburg to Auswärtiges Amt, 9 October 1906, ibid., XXIII/1, Nos. 7817–18.

147 Pourtalès to Kaiser Wilhelm II, 13 October 1906, with the Kaiser's comment of 15 October 1906, ibid., No. 7820; Pourtalès to Sternburg, 16 October 1906, ibid., No. 7821.

148 Coerper, reports of 23 and 31 May 1906, Berghahn, *Tirpitz-Plan*, p. 511; Grießmer, *Linienschiffe*, p. 49.

149 Kaiser Wilhelm II, marginal note on Coerper's report of 31 May 1906, as cited in Berghahn, *Tirpitz-Plan*, p. 512.

150 Berghahn, *Tirpitz-Plan*, pp. 522–4.

151 Müller, diary for 30 October 1906, 4 and 27 January 1907, BA-MA Freiburg-im-Breisgau, Müller Papers.

152 Kaiser Wilhelm II to Tirpitz, 14 June 1907, Berghahn, *Tirpitz-Plan*, pp. 565f.; Müller, diary for 15 June 1907, BA-MA Freiburg-im-Breisgau, Müller Papers.

153 See Berghahn, *Tirpitz-Plan*, pp. 525–31.

154 Tirpitz to Prince Heinrich of Prussia, 28 January 1907, printed in Tirpitz, *Aufbau der deutschen Weltmacht*, pp. 36f. See Berghahn, *Tirpitz-Plan*, pp. 538 and 556f.

155 Tirpitz to Trotha, 3 February 1907, Staatsarchiv Bückeburg, Trotha Papers, A 362.

156 Tirpitz, notes for the audience with the Kaiser on 9 March 1907, as cited in Berghahn, *Tirpitz-Plan*, p. 561. See Müller, diary for 9 March 1907, BA-MA Freiburg-im-Breisgau, Müller Papers.

157 Berghahn, *Tirpitz-Plan*, p. 566.

158 See ibid., pp. 561–5; Grießmer, *Linienschiffe*, p. 61.

159 Tirpitz, notes for the audience with the Kaiser on 27 May 1907; Kaiser Wilhelm II to Tirpitz, 14 June 1907, Berghahn, *Tirpitz-Plan*, pp. 565f.

160 Tirpitz to Bülow, 14 August 1907, cited ibid., pp. 579f.

161 Tirpitz to Kaiser Wilhelm II., 7 September 1907, cited ibid., p. 580.

162 Müller, diary for 26–30 September 1907, BA-MA Freiburg-im-Breisgau, Müller Papers.

163 Kaiser Wilhelm II., marginal note on an article in the *Berliner Lokalanzeiger* on 17 April 1907, quoted in Berghahn, *Tirpitz-Plan*, p. 583.

164 Tirpitz, notes for the audience with the Kaiser, September 1907, cited ibid., pp. 583f.

165 Tirpitz, notes for the audience with the Kaiser on 29 September 1907, as cited ibid., p. 588.

166 Berghahn, *Tirpitz-Plan*, p. 589.

19 THE ZENITH OF PERSONAL MONARCHY. THE KAISER AND THE
GOVERNMENT ON THE EVE OF THE GREAT CRISIS

1 Holstein to David, 13 May 1906, *Holstein Papers*, IV, No. 980.
2 Zedlitz-Trützschler, diary for 13 March 1906, *Zwölf Jahre*, p. 145.
3 Zedlitz-Trützschler to his father, 15 September 1907, ibid., pp. 167–70.
4 Zedlitz-Trützschler, diary for 26 November 1907, ibid., p. 177.
5 Zedlitz-Trützschler, diary for 18 December 1907, ibid., p. 183.
6 Hinzpeter to Kaiser Wilhelm II, 1 September 1906, GStA Berlin, BPHA Rep. 53J Lit. H Nr 1.
7 Spitzemberg, diary for 22 July 1906, Vierhaus, *Tagebuch*, pp. 462f.
8 Spitzemberg, diary for 18 September 1906, ibid., p. 464.
9 Ibid.
10 Spitzemberg, diary for 17 October 1906, ibid., p. 466.
11 Spitzemberg, diary for 16 January and 13 March 1907, ibid., pp. 469f.
12 Zedlitz-Trützschler, diary for February 1906, *Zwölf Jahre*, pp. 133f.
13 Holstein to David, 29 August 1906, *Holstein Papers*, IV, No. 990.
14 See Spitzemberg, diary for 22 April 1906, Vierhaus, *Tagebuch*, pp. 459f.
15 Bülow to Kaiser Wilhelm II, 20 May 1906, GStA Berlin, BPHA Rep. 53J Lit B Nr 16a.
16 Bülow to Kaiser Wilhelm II, 31 May 1906, ibid.
17 See Spitzemberg, diary for 16 January and 11 October 1906, Vierhaus, *Tagebuch*, pp. 455 and 465.
18 Zedlitz-Trützschler, diary for 13 March 1906, *Zwölf Jahre*, p. 145.
19 Zedlitz-Trützschler to his father, 15 September 1907, ibid., pp. 167–70.
20 Holstein to David, 13 May 1906, *Holstein Papers*, IV, No. 980.
21 Szögyény to Goluchowski, 19 August 1906, HHStA Vienna, Hofnachrichten: Preußen; Harden to Holstein, 3 September 1906, *Holstein Papers*, IV, No. 993. On the Podbielski crisis see Clark, *Kaiser Wilhelm II*, pp. 102f.
22 Monts to Holstein, 11 September 1906, *Holstein Papers*, IV, No. 994.
23 Karl F. Nowak and Friedrich Thimme, eds., *Erinnerungen und Gedanken des Botschafters Anton Graf Monts*, Berlin 1932 (cited below as Monts, *Erinnerungen und Gedanken*), p. 158. See below, pp. 545–51.
24 Spitzemberg, diary for 8 October 1906, Vierhaus, *Tagebuch*, p. 465.
25 Berckheim to Marschall, 8 November 1906, Fuchs, *Großherzog von Baden*, IV, No. 2583, note 4.
26 For the Köller-Krise see Röhl, *The Kaiser's Personal Monarchy*, pp. 721–31.
27 Rogge, *Friedrich von Holstein, Lebensbekenntnis*, p. 268.
28 Fürst Chlodwig zu Hohenlohe-Schillingsfürst, *Denkwürdigkeiten. Im Auftrag des Prinzen Alexander zu Hohenlohe-Schillingsfürst herausgegeben von Friedrich Curtius*, 2 vols., Stuttgart 1906–7; Kaiser Wilhelm II to Bülow, 7 October 1906, as quoted in Gutsche, *Wilhelm II.*, p. 124.
29 Kaiser Wilhelm II to Fürst Philipp-Ernst zu Hohenlohe-Schillingsfürst, October 1906, as cited in Bülow, *Denkwürdigkeiten*, II, p. 251.
30 Berckheim to Marschall, 15 October 1906, Fuchs, *Großherzog von Baden*, IV, No. 2570. See Spitzemberg, diary for 14 October 1906; Vierhaus, *Tagebuch*, p. 465.
31 David to Holstein, 25 November 1906, *Holstein Papers*, IV, No. 1007.
32 Cited in Holstein to David, 19 November 1906, ibid., No. 1005.
33 Bülow, *Denkwürdigkeiten*, II, p. 252.
34 Prince Alexander von Hohenlohe-Schillingsfürst to Fürst Hermann zu Hohenlohe-Langenburg, 13 October 1906, Hohenlohe-Zentralarchiv Schloß Neuenstein, Hermann Hohenlohe-Langenburg Papers, Bü. 298.

35 Prince Alexander von Hohenlohe-Schillingsfürst to Fürst Hermann zu Hohenlohe-Langenburg, 16 October 1906, ibid.

36 Fürst Hermann zu Hohenlohe-Langenburg to Kaiser Wilhelm II, 17 October 1906, GStA Berlin, BPHA Rep. 53J Lit. H Nr 6.

37 Kaiser Wilhelm II to Fürst Hermann zu Hohenlohe-Langenburg, 20 October 1906, ibid. See below, pp. 514f.

38 See Loth, *Katholiken im Kaiserreich*, pp. 110ff.

39 See Spitzemberg, diary for 25 March 1906, Vierhaus, *Tagebuch*, p. 457; Loth, *Katholiken im Kaiserreich*, pp. 11f. See Herbert Gottwald, 'Evangelischer Bund zur Wahrung der deutsch-protestantischen Interessen', in Dieter Fricke and Werner Fritsch, eds., *Lexikon zur Parteiengeschichte. Die bürgerlichen und kleinbürgerlichen Parteien und Verbände in Deutschland (1789–1945)*, 4 vols., Leipzig 1984, II, pp. 580ff.; Armin Müller-Dreyer, *Konfession in Politik, Gesellschaft und Kultur des Kaiserreichs. Der Evangelische Bund 1886–1914*, Gütersloh 1998.

40 See Lerman, *The Chancellor as Courtier*, p. 153; Terence F. Cole, 'Kaiser versus Chancellor: The Crisis of Bülow's Chancellorship 1905–6', in Richard J. Evans, ed., *Society and Politics in Wilhelmine Germany*, London 1978, p. 49.

41 Kaiser Wilhelm II to Bülow, 2 July 1906, PA AA R 3628; Müller, diary for 2 July 1906, BA-MA Freiburg-im-Breisgau, Müller Papers.

42 Bülow to Kaiser Wilhelm II, 17 July 1906, BPHA Rep. 53J Lit. B Nr 16a.

43 Bülow, *Denkwürdigkeiten*, II, p. 258.

44 Ibid.

45 Loth, *Katholiken im Kaiserreich*, p. 118.

46 Thus the Centre party leader Carl Bachem on 20 December 1906, as cited ibid., p. 119, note 90.

47 See Spitzemberg, diary for 26 May 1906, Vierhaus, *Tagebuch*, pp. 460f.

48 Bülow, *Denkwürdigkeiten*, II, pp. 269f.

49 Ibid., p. 270. See Theodor Eschenburg, *Das Kaiserreich am Scheideweg. Bassermann, Bülow und der Block. Nach unveröffentlichten Papieren aus dem Nachlass Ernst Bassermanns*, Berlin 1929, p. 41.

50 Peter-Christian Witt, *Die Finanzpolitik des Deutschen Reiches von 1903 bis 1913. Eine Studie zur Innenpolitik des Wilhelminischen Deutschlands*, Lübeck and Hamburg 1970, p. 155.

51 GStA Berlin, Rep. 90a B III 2b Nr 6, Bd. 153; Bethmann Hollweg to Bülow, 11 December 1906, BA Koblenz, Bülow Papers, No. 64. Cf. Berckheim to Marschall, 12 December 1906, Fuchs, *Großherzog von Baden*, IV, No. 2591.

52 See above, pp. 501–3.

53 Kaiser Wilhelm II to Fürstenberg, 12 December 1906, FFA Donaueschingen.

54 Hopman, diary for 13 December 1906, BA-MA Freiburg-im-Breisgau, Hopman Papers, N 326/6.

55 Berckheim to Marschall, 14 December 1906, Fuchs, *Großherzog von Baden*, IV, No. 2593.

56 Princess Marie Radziwill, *Briefe vom deutschen Kaiserhof 1889–1915*, Berlin 1936, p. 290.

57 Spitzemberg, diary for 16 December 1906 and 27 January 1907, Vierhaus, *Tagebuch*, pp. 469f.

58 See Mommsen, *War der Kaiser an allem schuld?*, p. 125.

59 Bülow, speech of 13 December 1906, in Huber, *Dokumente zur deutschen Verfassungsgeschichte*, II, No. 292.

60 Bülow to Liebert, 31 December 1906, in Ernst von Liebert, *Aus einem bewegten Leben*, Munich 1925, pp. 180f. See Bodman to Marschall, 3 January 1907, Fuchs, *Großherzog von Baden*, IV, No. 2603.

61 See Dieter Fricke, 'Der deutsche Imperialismus und die Reichstagswahlen von 1907', *Zeitschrift für Geschichtswissenschaft* 9, 1961, 554 ff.

62 Spitzemberg, diary for 8 and 14 December 1906, Vierhaus, *Tagebuch*, p. 468.

63 Holzing-Berstett to his mother, 23 December 1906, GLA Karlsruhe, Holzing-Berstett Papers, Zug. 1989, Nr 116/11.

64 Ibid.

65 Bernhardi to Holzing-Berstett, 18 December 1906, GLA Karlsruhe, Holzing-Berstett Papers, Zug. 1989, Nr 116/65.

66 Charlotte Hereditary Princess of Saxe-Meiningen to Schweninger, 24 December 1906, BA Berlin, Schweninger Papers, Nr 131.

67 Berckheim to Marschall, 28 January 1907, Fuchs, *Großherzog von Baden*, IV, No. 2611.

68 For the election results in Bavaria and Baden see Bodman to Marschall, 6 February 1907, Dusch to Grand Duke Friedrich I of Baden, 10 February 1907, Fuchs, *Großherzog von Baden*, IV, Nos. 2617 and 2621.

69 Spitzemberg, diary for 27 January 1907, Vierhaus, *Tagebuch*, p. 228.

70 Otto Hötzsch, ed., *Fürst Bülows Reden nebst urkundlichen Beiträgen zu seiner Politik, Bd. 3, 1907–1909*, Berlin 1909, p. 241. See Fesser, *Reichskanzler Fürst von Bülow*, p. 99.

71 Kaiser Wilhelm II to Grand Duke Friedrich I von Baden, 30 January 1907, Fuchs, *Großherzog von Baden*, IV, No. 2614. For Wilhelm II's delight at the outcome of the elections see also Müller, diary for 27 January and 6 February 1907, BA-MA Freiburg-im-Breisgau, Müller Papers.

72 Charlotte Hereditary Princess of Saxe-Meiningen to Schweninger, 6 February 1907, BA Berlin, Schweninger Papers, Nr 131.

73 See Holstein to Bülow, 8 February 1907, *Holstein Papers*, IV, No. 1009.

74 Kaiser Wilhelm II to Fürstenberg, 8 February 1907, FFA Donaueschingen; Chelius to Fürstenberg, 3 March 1907, ibid.; Holzing-Berstett to his wife, no date [August 1907], GLA Karlsruhe, Holzing-Berstett Papers, Nr 116/1.

75 Holstein, diary for 17 February 1907, *Holstein Papers*, IV, No. 1010.

76 Charlotte Hereditary Princess of Saxe-Meiningen to Schweninger, 6 and 16 February 1907, BA Berlin, Schweninger Papers, Nr 131.

77 See Fesser, *Reichskanzler Fürst von Bülow*, pp. 128ff.; Gerd Fesser, 'Zur Genesis des Reichsvereinsgesetzes. Staatsorgane, bürgerliche Parteien und Vereinsgesetzgebung im Deutschen Reich 1906 bis 1908', in Boris A. Aisin and Willibald Gutsche, eds., *Forschungsergebnisse zur Geschichte des deutschen Imperialismus vor 1917*, Berlin 1980, pp. 107ff.

78 Hötzsch, *Fürst Bülows Reden*, III, p. 133.

79 Berckheim to Marschall, 26 June 1907, Fuchs, *Großherzog von Baden*, IV, No. 2640.

80 GStA Berlin, Rep. 90a B III 2b, No. 6, Bd. 154, Bl. 288 R. See Fesser, *Reichskanzler Fürst von Bülow*, p. 100.

81 Berckheim to Marschall, 25 and 26 June 1907, Fuchs, *Großherzog von Baden*, IV, Nos. 2639–40.

82 Bülow to Valentini, 8 August 1907, GStA Berlin, Geheimes Zivilkabinett, 2.2.1 No. 667, Bl. 44R–45.

83 Ernst Johann, ed., *Reden des Kaisers. Ansprachen, Predigten and Trinksprüche Wilhelms II.*, Munich 1977, p. 122; Obst, *Die politischen Reden*, pp. 285–7.

84 Bülow to Kaiser Wilhelm II, 9 September 1907, GStA Berlin, BPHA Rep. 53J Lit. B Nr 16a. See also Bülow, minutes of the meeting of the Prussian Ministry of State on 5 October 1907, cited in Fesser, *Reichskanzler Fürst von Bülow*, p. 102.

85 See ibid., pp. 128ff.; also Fesser, 'Zur Genesis des Reichsvereingesetzes', pp. 107ff.

86 Prince Hohenlohe to Aehrenthal, 6 November 1907, HHStA Vienna, PA III Preußen, Karton 165, Bl. 18f.

87 Szögyény to Aehrenthal, 22 January 1908, ibid., Bl. 57.

88 Szögyény to Aehrenthal, 10 December 1907, ibid., Bl. 135f.

89 Spitzemberg diary for 12 April 1907, Vierhaus, *Tagebuch*, p. 472.

90 Spitzemberg, diary for 9 June 1907, ibid., p. 473.

91 Harden to Holstein, 18 September 1907, *Holstein Papers*, IV, No. 1049.

92 Holstein to Stülpnagel, 31 August 1907, Rogge, *Friedrich von Holstein, Lebensbekenntnis*, p. 287.

93 Ibid., p. 278.

94 Ibid., p. 279.

95 Spitzemberg, diary for 21 April 1907, Vierhaus, *Tagebuch*, p. 472.

96 Zedlitz-Trützschler to his father, 15 September 1907, *Zwölf Jahre*, pp. 167ff.

97 August Eulenburg to Fürstenberg, 16 September 1907, FFA Donaueschingen.

98 Zedlitz-Trützschler to his father, 15 September 1907, *Zwölf Jahre*, pp. 167ff.

99 Bülow to Kaiser Wilhelm II, 9 September 1907, BPHA Rep. 53J Lit. B Nr 16a.

100 Ibid.

101 Kaiser Wilhelm II to Hermann Fürst zu Hohenlohe-Langenburg, 28 September 1907, Hohenlohe-Zentralarchiv Schloß Neuenstein, Hermann Hohenlohe-Langenburg Papers, Bü. 268.

102 Hermann Fürst zu Hohenlohe-Langenburg to Kaiser Wilhelm II, 1 October 1907, ibid.

103 Hermann Fürst zu Hohenlohe-Langenburg to his son Ernst, 2 October 1907, ibid., 'Briefe von Papa von 1902–1907'; Ernst Hereditary Prince zu Hohenlohe-Langenburg to his father, 3 October 1907, ibid., Hermann Hohenlohe-Langenburg Papers, Bü. 268.

104 Hermann Fürst zu Hohenlohe-Langenburg to Kaiser Wilhelm II, 3 October 1907, ibid.

105 Ernst Hereditary Prince zu Hohenlohe-Langenburg to his father, 3 October 1907, ibid.

106 Bülow to Hermann Fürst zu Hohenlohe-Langenburg, 4 October 1907, ibid.

107 Hermann Fürst zu Hohenlohe-Langenburg to Bülow, 4 October 1907, ibid.

108 Hermann Fürst zu Hohenlohe-Langenburg to Kaiser Wilhelm II, 5 October 1907, ibid.

109 Hermann Fürst zu Hohenlohe-Langenburg to Bülow, 5 October 1907, ibid.

110 Kaiser Wilhelm II to Hermann Fürst zu Hohenlohe-Langenburg, 6 October 1907, ibid.

111 Kaiser Wilhelm II to Hermann Fürst zu Hohenlohe-Langenburg, 18 October 1907, ibid., Bü. 269.

112 See Spitzemberg, diary for 9 October 1907, Vierhaus, *Tagebuch*, p. 475.

113 Bülow to Holstein, 22 and 29 September 1907, *Holstein Papers*, IV, Nos. 1050 and 1052.

114 Holstein to Bülow, 26 September and 4 October 1907, ibid., Nos. 1051 and 1054.

115 Zedlitz-Trützschler, diary for 26 November 1907, *Zwölf Jahre*, p. 173.

116 Spitzemberg, diary for 15 June 1908, Vierhaus, *Tagebuch*, p. 483.

117 Zedlitz-Trützschler, diary for 18 December 1907, *Zwölf Jahre*, p. 181.

118 Szögyény to Aehrenthal, 22 January 1908, HHStA Vienna, PA III Preußen, Karton 165, Bl. 57.

119 Rogge, *Friedrich von Holstein, Lebensbekenntnis*, p. 303. See Spitzemberg, diary for 14 January 1908, Vierhaus, *Tagebuch*, p. 480.

120 Bülow, *Denkwürdigkeiten*, II, p. 324.

121 Hopman, diary for 30 March 1908, BA-MA Freiburg-im-Breisgau, Hopman Papers, N 326/6.

122 Spitzemberg, diary for 31 March 1908, Vierhaus, *Tagebuch*, p. 482. See Fiebig-von Hase, 'Die Rolle Kaiser Wilhelms II. in den deutsch-amerikanischen Beziehungen', p. 232.

123 Holstein to Bülow, 21 May 1908, *Holstein Papers*, IV, No. 1089. Holstein, memorandum of 15 June 1908, ibid., No. 1097. See also *Große Politik*, XXV, Nos. 8746–7.

124 Jagemann to Brauer, 10 March 1902, Fuchs, *Großherzog von Baden*, IV, No. 2270.

125 See below, pp. 844ff.

126 Tschirschky to Bülow, 7 July 1906; Bülow to Tschirschky, 16 July 1906, cited in Marschall, *Reisen und Regieren*, pp. 54f. See Klaus Meyer, *Theodor Schiemann als politischer Publizist*, Frankfurt a.M. and Hamburg 1956.

127 See Rüdiger vom Bruch, 'Adolf von Harnack und Wilhelm II.', in Otto Gerhard Oexle and Kurt Nowak, eds., *Adolf von Harnack. Theologe, Historiker, Wissenschaftspolitiker*, Göttingen 2001; Christian Nottmeier, *Adolf von Harnack und die deutsche Politik 1890–1930*, Tübingen 2004.

128 See Geoffrey G. Field, *Evangelist of Race. The Germanic Vision of Houston Stewart Chamberlain*, New York 1981.

129 Bülow, *Denkwürdigkeiten*, I, pp. 144 and 249.

130 Ibid., I, pp. 430 and 526f.

131 Ibid., III, p. 313.

132 Ibid., I, pp. 526f.

133 Waldersee, diary for 19 January 1903, GStA Berlin, Waldersee Papers; Meisner, III, pp. 201f.

134 See Ernst von Dryander, *Erinnerungen aus meinem Leben*, Bielefeld and Leipzig 1922, pp. 227–30.

135 See Christian Wiese, *Wissenschaft des Judentums and protestantische Theologie im wilhelminischen Deutschland. Ein Schrei ins Leere?*, Tübingen 1999, pp. 190–8.

136 Kaiser Wilhelm II to Admiral von Hollmann, 15 February 1903, with corrections and addenda in Bülow's hand, GStA Berlin, BPHA Rep. 53, Nr 235.

137 See Thomas Hartmut Benner, *Die Strahlen der Krone. Die religiöse Dimension des Kaisertums unter Wilhelm II. vor dem Hintergrund der Orientreise 1898*, Marburg 2001, pp. 123–8. See also Klaus Erich Pollmann, 'Wilhelm II. und der Protestantismus', in Stefan Samerski, ed., *Wilhelm II. und die Religion. Facetten einer Persönlichkeit und ihres Umfelds*, Berlin 2001, pp. 91–103.

138 Waldersee, diary for 21 February 1903, GStA Berlin, Waldersee Papers; Meisner, III, pp. 207f.

139 Adolf von Harnack, 'Der Brief Sr. Majestät des Kaisers an den Admiral Hollmann', *Preußische Jahrbücher* 111, 1903, 584–9.

140 Kaiser Wilhelm II to Harnack, 2 March 1903, Staatsbibliothek Berlin, Harnack Papers.

141 Harnack to Kaiser Wilhelm II, 2 March 1903, ibid.

142 See Nottmeier, *Adolf von Harnack*, pp. 251f.

143 Ibid., pp. 233f.

144 Chamberlain to Kaiser Wilhelm II, 26 December 1909, ibid., pp. 234f.

145 See the correspondence between Wilhelm II and Chamberlain in Houston Stewart Chamberlain, *Briefe 1882–1924 und Briefwechsel mit Kaiser Wilhelm II.*, 2 vols., Munich 1928, II, pp. 131ff.

146 See Eulenburg to Kaiser Wilhelm II, 13 February 1905, *Eulenburgs Korrespondenz*, III, No. 1504; Kaiser Wilhelm II to Chamberlain, 9 May 1905, Chamberlain, *Briefe*, II, p. 216; Chamberlain to Kaiser Wilhelm II, 5 July 1906, ibid., p. 220.

147 Chamberlain to Kaiser Wilhelm II, 20 February 1902, ibid., pp. 148–65.

148 For the development of the Kaiser's anti-Semitic prejudices over the years, see Röhl, *Kaiser and his Court*, pp. 190–212, and Chapter 46 below.

20 'KINGS ARE ONLY HUMAN, AFTER ALL.' SCANDALS AT THE HOHENZOLLERN COURT

1 Holzing to his wife, 14 May 1907, GLA Karlsruhe, Holzing-Berstett Papers, Nr 116/19.

2 Holzing to his wife, no date [August 1907], ibid.

3 Hopman, diary for 20 January 1908, BA-MA Freiburg-im-Breisgau, Hopman Papers; Zedlitz-Trützschler, diary for 25 January 1908, *Zwölf Jahre*, pp. 189f.

4 Kaiser Wilhelm II to Grand Duke Friedrich I of Baden, 3 March 1906, Fuchs, *Großherzog von Baden*, IV, No. 2549. See Martin Kohlrausch, *Der Monarch im Skandal. Die Logik der Massenmedien und die Transformation der wilhelminischen Monarchie*, Berlin 2005; Isabel V. Hull, *The Entourage of Kaiser Wilhelm II 1888–1918*, Cambridge 1982.

5 Zedlitz-Trützschler, diary for 17 April 1906 and 24 February 1907, *Zwölf Jahre*, pp. 148–50.

6 Walter Goetz, 'Kaiser Wilhelm II.', unpublished book manuscript, p. 457, BA Koblenz, Goetz Papers, N 1215/351.

7 Kaiser Wilhelm II, speech held in Bremen on 22 March 1905, cited above, pp. 336f. See Penzler, *Reden Kaiser Wilhelms II. in den Jahren 1901–Ende 1905*, pp. 240–44; Obst, *Die politischen Reden*, pp. 263–6; Obst, 'Einer nur ist Herr im Reiche', pp. 277ff.

8 Hopman, diary for 25 November 1906, Epkenhans, *Leben eines 'Wilhelminers'*, p. 140.

9 Kaiser Wilhelm II, speech of 13 November 1910 in Beuron, FFA Donaueschingen, Irma Fürstenberg Papers.

10 Gräfin Alice zu Lynar, née Gräfin von Wedel, 'Meine Hofdamenjahre in Potsdam und Berlin 1908–1911', unpublished manuscript, in the author's private archive.

11 Kaiser Wilhelm II to Hausminister von Wedell, May 1902, cited in Röhl, *Kaiser and his Court*, p. 98. See above, pp. 151–4.

12 Kaiser Wilhelm II, marginal comment of 27 December 1907 on the petition of Prince Friedrich Wilhelm of Prussia of 26 December 1907, Archiv des vormals regierenden preußischen Königshauses, Burg Hohenzollern, Hechingen.

13 Kaiser Wilhelm II to Prince Friedrich Wilhelm of Prussia, 25 December 1909, ibid.

14 Kaiser Wilhelm II to Fürstenberg, 23 December 1908, FFA Donaueschingen.

15 Kaiser Wilhelm II, remark of 20 March 1908, cited in Zedlitz-Trützschler, *Zwölf Jahre*, p. 191. See below, pp. 1200–4.

16 See Röhl, *Young Wilhelm*, pp. 485ff. and 502ff.; see also Röhl, *The Kaiser's Personal Monarchy*, pp. 197ff.

17 W. E. Elisabeth geschiedene Gräfin von Wedel-Bérard, *Meine Beziehungen zu S.M. Kaiser Wilhelm II. Aufklärung über den Königsmord in Italien. Die Dreyfus-Affaire im Lichte der Wahrheit!*, Zürich 1900. Her second book *Aus den Katakomben!!!* was published in Florence in January 1901. On the smuggling of banned books into Germany see Dönhoff, report from Dresden of 18 January 1904; circular instruction of the Prussian Minister of the Interior, Hammerstein, to all Regierungspräsidenten, 26 March 1904, PA AA R 3475.

18 See Chapter 19 of Röhl, *Young Wilhelm*.

19 Wedel-Bérard to Radolin, 25 June 1902, PA AA R 3474.

20 Wedel-Bérard to the Commandant of Berlin, 10 February 1903, ibid.

21 Wedel-Bérard to Radolin, 13 September and 30 December 1902, 22 January, 21 March and 29 April, 15, 17 and 31 July, 6 November 1903, ibid.

22 Mühlberg to Bülow, 31 July 1903; Mühlberg to Miessner, 4 and 14 August 1903, PA AA R 3475.

23 Consul Marschall von Bieberstein to Auswärtiges Amt, 6 November 1903, ibid.

24 Marschall von Bieberstein to Auswärtiges Amt, 29 January 1904, ibid.

25 Marschall von Bieberstein to Auswärtiges Amt, 4 February, 9 and 28 April 1904; Auswärtiges Amt to Lucanus, 8 February and 28 May 1904; Auswärtiges Amt to Marschall von Bieberstein, 27 April 1904; Lucanus to Bülow, 2 and 27 June 1904, ibid.

26 Marschall von Bieberstein to Bülow, 15 and 26 July 1904; Bülow to Lucanus, 31 July 1904; Lucanus to Bülow, 13 August 1904, ibid.

27 Marschall von Bieberstein to Bülow, 1 December 1904 and 15 June 1905; Director of the asylum to Marschall von Bieberstein, 22 June 1905, PA AA R 3476.

28 Mühlberg to Marschall von Bieberstein, no date, ibid.

29 Marschall von Bieberstein to Bülow, 30 September 1905, ibid.

30 Hereditary Princess Charlotte of Saxe-Meiningen to Empress Frederick, 28 January 1899, AdHH Schloß Fasanerie; Empress Frederick to Crown Princess Sophie of Greece, May 1899, Lee, *The Empress Frederick Writes to Sophie*, p. 302.

31 Müller, diary for 27 and 28 April and 2 and 3 May 1905, BA-MA Freiburg-im-Breisgau, Müller Papers; Kaiser Wilhelm II to Max Egon Fürst zu Fürstenberg, 3 May 1905, FFA Donaueschingen; Chelius to Fürstenberg, 6 August 1905, FFA Donaueschingen; Valentini, memorandum of April 1909, BA Koblenz, Valentini Papers, Kl. Erw. Nr 341–1, printed in abbreviated form in Valentini, *Kaiser und Kabinettschef*, pp. 109ff.

32 Admiral Lord Montagu's letters to Kaiser Wilhelm II are in BA-MA Freiburg-im-Breisgau, RM2/123. Cf. Victor A. Montagu, *Reminiscences*, London 1910.

33 Kaiser Wilhelm II to Victor Montagu, 7 October 1905, in the author's private archive.

34 Kaiser Wilhelm II to Mary Montagu, 17 October 1905, ibid. See Victor Montagu to Kaiser Wilhelm II, 27 October 1905, BA-MA Freiburg-im-Breisgau, RM2/123.

35 See Chapter 22, below.

36 Harden to Rathenau, 26 August 1912, Hellige and Schulin, *Briefwechsel Rathenau-Harden*, No. 352. See below, pp. 1206ff.

37 Rodd to Grey, 16 July 1906, TNA, FO 800/78, fols. 20–2. I am grateful to Dr Patrick Salmon for sharing this fascinating document with me.

38 Zedlitz-Trützschler, diary for 30 December 1908, *Zwölf Jahre*, pp. 202ff.

39 Martin Kohlrausch, *Der Monarch im Skandal. Die Logik der Massenmedien und die Transformation der wilhelminischen Monarchie*, Berlin 2005, p. 233 et passim.

40 See in particular Peter Winzen, *Freundesliebe am Hof Kaiser Wilhelms II.*, Norderstedt 2010; Winzen, *Das Ende der Kaiserherrlichkeit*; Winzen, *Im Schatten Wilhelms II.*; and Winzen, *Reichskanzler Bernhard von Bülow*.

41 Varnbüler to Soden, 7 December 1902, cited in Winzen, 'Krupp', pp. 435f.

42 Kaiser Wilhelm II, speech in Essen on 26 November 1902, printed in Obst, *Die politischen Reden*, pp. 250–2; see Obst, *'Einer nur ist Herr im Reiche'*, pp. 264–71. For the political furore caused by the speech see above, pp. 139ff.

43 Varnbüler to Soden, 7 December 1902, cited in Winzen, 'Krupp', p. 439.

44 *Vorwärts*, 28 November 1902, cited in Winzen, 'Krupp', pp. 440f.

45 See the evidence assembled in Winzen, 'Krupp', pp. 441f. with notes 77 to 79.

46 Harold James, *Krupp: A History of the Legendary German Firm*, Princeton and Oxford 2012, pp. 116–22.

47 Hans von Tresckow, *Von Fürsten und anderen Sterblichen. Erinnerungen eines Kriminal-kommissars*, Berlin 1922, pp. 127–30; Winzen, 'Krupp', pp. 420f.

48 See Dieter Richter, 'Friedrich Alfred Krupp auf Capri. Ein Skandal und seine Geschichte', in Michael Epkenhans and Ralf Stremmel, eds., *Friedrich Alfred Krupp. Ein Unternehmer im Kaiserreich*, Munich 2010, pp. 157–77.

49 Willi A. Boelcke, ed., *Krupp und die Hohenzollern in Dokumenten. Krupp-Korrespondenz mit Kaisern, Kabinettschefs und Ministern 1850–1918*, Frankfurt a.M. 1970, p. 158.

50 Hollmann to Krupp, 3 October 1902, as cited in Winzen, 'Krupp', p. 423.

51 See the account of these dramatic events in Winzen, 'Krupp', pp. 424–6. Both Kuno Moltke and Philipp Eulenburg's brother Fredi attempted to have their wives certified as insane when their marriages failed.

52 Krupp to Kaiser Wilhelm II, 13 October 1902, printed in Boelcke, *Krupp und die Hohenzollern*, pp. 160f. See Winzen, 'Krupp', p. 426 with notes 35 and 37.

53 Winzen, 'Krupp', p. 437.

54 See McLean, 'Kaiser Wilhelm and his Hessian Cousins', pp. 41ff.

55 Prince Heinrich of Prussia to Kaiser Wilhelm II., 8 November 1901, PA AA R 3062.
56 Kaiser Wilhelm II to Grand Duke Ernst Ludwig of Hessen, 11 November 1901, ibid. Quoted in part in Lothar Machtan, 'Wilhelm II. als oberster Sittenrichter: Das Privatleben der Fürsten und die Imagepolitik des letzten deutschen Kaisers', *Zeitschrift für Geschichtswissenschaft*, 1/2006, 7–9.
57 Kaiser Wilhelm II, marginal notes of 21 November 1901 on Johann Hohenlohe's telegram from Darmstadt of 18 November 1901, PA AA R 3062.
58 Zedlitz-Trützschler, *Zwölf Jahre*, p. 23.
59 See above, p. 525.
60 Zedlitz-Trützschler, *Zwölf Jahre*, p. 23.
61 Zedlitz-Trützschler, ibid., pp. 21–34.
62 Brandenstein to Hülsen-Haeseler, 7 April 1907, Archiv des vormals regierenden preußischen Königshauses, Burg Hohenzollern, Hechingen, Kaiser Wilhelm II Papers.
63 Ibid.
64 Zedlitz-Trützschler, diary for 14 June 1907, *Zwölf Jahre*, pp. 163f.
65 Hülsen-Haeseler, Instruction for Schenck with personal comments by Kaiser Wilhelm II of 15 May 1907, Archiv des vormals regierenden preußischen Königshauses, Burg Hohenzollern, Hechingen, Kaiser Wilhelm II Papers.
66 Zedlitz-Trützschler, diary for 14 June 1907, *Zwölf Jahre*, pp. 163–5.
67 Th. Ziehen, medical assessment of 24 October 1907, Archiv des vormals regierenden preußischen Königshauses, Burg Hohenzollern, Hechingen, Kaiser Wilhelm II Papers.
68 Prince Joachim Albrecht of Prussia to Kaiser Wilhelm II, 28 February 1908 with the Kaiser's marginal notes, ibid.
69 Szögyény to Aehrenthal, 14 April 1908, HHStA Vienna, Hofnachrichten: Preußen.
70 Zedlitz-Trützschler, diary for 20 March 1908, *Zwölf Jahre*, pp. 190f.
71 Harden to Holstein, 28 February 1907, *Holstein Papers*, IV, No. 1012.
72 See Zedlitz-Trützschler, diary for 19 and 20 March 1907, *Zwölf Jahre*, pp. 153ff.
73 Zedlitz-Trützschler, diary for 20 March 1907, ibid., p. 157.
74 Harden, 'Roulette', *Die Zukunft* 59, 27 April 1907, 117–30.
75 Zedlitz-Trützschler, diary for 7 and 16 June 1907, *Zwölf Jahre*, pp. 162f. and 167.
76 See Röhl, *The Kaiser's Personal Monarchy*, pp. 664–76.
77 See Karsten Hecht, 'Die Harden-Prozesse. Strafverfahren, Öffentlichkeit und Politik im Kaiserreich', unpublished Dr.jr. dissertation, University of Munich 1997, p. 9.
78 Ibid., pp. 118–20.
79 See below, pp. 566.
80 Einem, speech in the Reichstag of 29 November 1907, *Stenographische Berichte über die Verhandlungen des Reichstages*, XII/1, 1907/08; vol. 229, pp. 1913ff.
81 Kaiser Wilhelm II, marginal notes on Metternich's two dispatches of 1 November 1907, PA AA R 3709. See below, pp. 587f.

21   PRINCE EULENBURG'S DOWNFALL. THE CAMPAIGN AGAINST THE LIEBENBERG 'CAMARILLA'

1 See Martin Kohlrausch, *Der Monarch im Skandal. Die Logik der Massenmedien und die Transformation der wilhelminischen Monarchie*, Berlin 2005, p. 233 et passim.
2 Bülow's diabolical involvement in the destruction of the Liebenberg Round Table has been masterfully analysed by Peter Winzen in his recent books *Im Schatten Wilhelms II.* and *Das Ende der Kaiserherrlichkeit*.
3 Zedlitz-Trützschler, diary for 17 April 1906, *Zwölf Jahre*, pp. 148f.; Fesser, *Reichskanzler Fürst von Bülow*, p. 116.

4　Rogge, *Friedrich von Holstein, Lebensbekenntnis*, p. 268. See above, pp. 501–3.

5　Schiemann, diary for 7 April 1906, cited in *Eulenburgs Korrespondenz*, III, p. 2122. See Eulenburg to Kaiser Wilhelm II, 7 April 1906, ibid., No. 1511. See in particular Kohlrausch, *Der Monarch im Skandal*, pp. 186–242; Claudia Bruns, 'Skandale im Beraterkreis um Kaiser Wilhelm II. Die homoerotische "Verbündelung" der "Liebenberger Tafelrunde" als Politikum', in Susanne Zur Nieden, ed., *Homosexualität und Staatsräson: Männlichkeit, Homophobie und Politik in Deutschland 1900–1945*, Frankfurt a.M. and New York 2005, pp. 52–80; Hull, *The Entourage of Kaiser Wilhelm II*, pp. 45–145.

6　*Deutsche Gedenkhalle: Bilder aus der vaterländischen Geschichte. Schriftleitung: Julius von Pflugk-Harttung; Leitung des illustrativen Teils Hugo von Tschudi; veranstaltet von Max Herzig*, Berlin and Leipzig 1906. This luxury book was priced at 5,000 marks and went through numerous editions up to 1939. See *Eulenburgs Korrespondenz*, III, pp. 2101f. Also see Pflugk-Harttung to Kaiser Wilhelm II, 18 and 19 January 1907, Hohenlohe-Zentralarchiv, Schloß Neuenstein, Hermann Hohenlohe-Langenburg Papers, Bü. 318.

7　Harden, *Zukunft* No. 55 of 28 April 1906. Harden had made similar assertions in articles on 17 November and 8 December 1906.

8　Holstein to Radolin, 23 April 1906, *Holstein Papers*, IV, No. 966. See also Holstein to Stülpnagel, 7 June 1906, Rogge, *Friedrich von Holstein, Lebensbekenntnis*, p. 256.

9　Holstein to Radolin, 7 March 1906, *Holstein Papers*, IV, No. 940.

10　Holstein to Schiemann, 9 April 1906, cited in *Eulenburgs Korrespondenz*, III, p. 2122.

11　Schiemann to Holstein, 25 April 1906, Holstein to Schiemann, 28 April 1906, *Holstein Papers*, IV, Nos. 968 and 972.

12　Holstein to Eulenburg, 1 May 1906, ibid., No. 973.

13　Holstein to Varnbüler, 4 May 1906, Mühlberg to Eulenburg, 4 May 1906, Tschirschky to Varnbüler, 5 May 1906, Varnbüler, memorandum of May 1906, Varnbüler to Eulenburg, 11 and 14 May 1906, Eulenburg to Varnbüler, 12 and 13 May 1906, Varnbüler to Tschirschky, 14 May 1906, Tschirschky to Eulenburg, 17 May 1906, *Eulenburgs Korrespondenz*, III, Nos. 1512–21.

14　See ibid., p. 2130. See also below, pp. 551ff.

15　Eulenburg to Varnbüler, 13 May 1906, *Eulenburgs Korrespondenz*, III, No. 1518.

16　See Spitzemberg, diary for 22 April and 11 October 1906, Vierhaus, *Tagebuch*, pp. 459f. and 465.

17　Bülow, *Denkwürdigkeiten*, II, p. 262.

18　Ibid., p. 261.

19　Rogge, *Friedrich von Holstein, Lebensbekenntnis*, p. 265.

20　See 'The Broken Spell' in Röhl, *The Kaiser's Personal Monarchy*, pp. 1045–56.

21　Zedlitz-Trützschler, diary for 7 June 1907, *Zwölf Jahre*, pp. 159f.

22　Zedlitz-Trützschler, diary for 26 November 1907, ibid., pp. 175f.

23　Winzen, *Das Ende der Kaiserherrlichkeit*; Winzen, *Im Schatten Wilhelms II.*; Winzen, *Freundesliebe am Hof Kaiser Wilhelms II.*; Winzen, *Reichskanzler Bernhard von Bülow*.

24　Schiemann, diary for 7–9 April 1906, GStA Berlin, Schiemann Papers.

25　Spitzemberg, diary for 12 November 1906, Vierhaus, *Tagebuch*, p. 467.

26　Spitzemberg, diary for 9 and 11 November 1906, ibid., pp. 466f.

27　See Eulenburg to Kaiser Wilhelm II, September 1906, *Eulenburgs Korrespondenz*, III, No. 1523. Cf. August Eulenburg to Philipp Eulenburg, 31 August 1906, ibid., p. 2134, note 1.

28　August Eulenburg to Philipp Eulenburg, 21 October 1906, ibid., No. 1524.

29　Radziwill, *Briefe vom deutschen Kaiserhof*, pp. 258ff.; Eulenburg to his son Friedrich-Wend, 11 November 1906, *Eulenburgs Korrepondenz*, III, No. 1525; Zedlitz-Trützschler, diary for 26 November 1907, *Zwölf Jahre*, pp. 173f.

30 Holstein to Ida von Stülpnagel, cited in Rogge, *Friedrich von Holstein, Lebensbekenntnis*, p. 296.

31 Harden, *Zukunft* of 9 November 1907, p. 423. See Helmuth Rogge, *Holstein und Harden. Politisch-publizistisches Zusammenspiel zweier Außenseiter des Wilhelminischen Reiches*, Munich 1959, pp. 212f.

32 Radziwill, *Briefe vom deutschen Kaiserhof*, pp. 258ff.

33 Eulenburg to his son Friedrich-Wend, 11 November 1906, *Eulenburgs Korrepondenz*, III, No. 1525.

34 Radziwill, *Briefe vom deutschen Kaiserhof*, pp. 258ff.

35 See Spitzemberg, diary for 9 November 1906, Vierhaus, *Tagebuch*, pp. 466f.; Rogge, *Holstein und Harden*, p. 101; Fesser, *Reichskanzler Bernhard Fürst von Bülow*, p. 95.

36 Berckheim to Marschall, 8 November 1906, Fuchs, *Großherzog von Baden*, IV, No. 2583. See Bodman to Marschall, 15 November 1906, ibid., No. 2584.

37 Spitzemberg, diary for 15 November 1906, Vierhaus, *Tagebuch*, p. 467.

38 Bülow, speech in the Reichstag of 14 November 1906, *Stenographische Berichte über die Verhandlungen des Reichstages*, p. 3650.

39 Ibid.

40 Bülow, *Denkwürdigkeiten*, II, p. 266.

41 Holstein, diary for 11 November 1906, *Holstein Papers*, IV, No. 1004.

42 Bodman to Marschall, 15 November 1906, Fuchs, *Großherzog von Baden*, IV, No. 2584.

43 Harden, 'Praeludium', *Zukunft* of 17 November 1906.

44 Harden, 'Dies irae', *Zukunft* of 24 November 1906.

45 Hecht, 'Harden-Prozesse', pp. 34–41.

46 Eulenburg to Kaiser Wilhelm II, 11 December 1906, *Eulenburgs Korrespondenz*, III, No. 1526 with notes 3 and 4.

47 Charlotte Hereditary Princess of Saxe-Meiningen to Schweninger, 12 November, 13 and 24 December 1906, BA Berlin, Schweninger Papers, Nr 131. See Harden to Holstein, 3 October 1907, *Holstein Papers*, IV, No. 1053.

48 Charlotte Hereditary Princess of Saxe-Meiningen to Schweninger, 28 November 1906, BA Berlin, Schweninger Papers, Nr 131.

49 Charlotte Hereditary Princess of Saxe-Meiningen to Schweninger, 10 and 18 November 1907, ibid., quoted in Machtan, 'Wilhelm II. als oberster Sittenrichter', pp. 14f.

50 Harden, 'Symphonie', *Zukunft* of 2 February 1907; 'Wilhelm der Friedliche', *Zukunft* of 6 April 1907.

51 See Bülow, *Denkwürdigkeiten*, II, pp. 309f. and *Eulenburgs Korrespondenz*, III, pp. 2143f., note 4.

52 Harden, 'Monte Carlino', *Zukunft* of 13 April 1907.

53 Harden, 'Roulette', *Zukunft* of 27 April 1907, 118.

54 Tschirschky to Monts, 25 May 1907, Monts, *Erinnerungen und Gedanken*, pp. 451 and 580. See Rogge, *Holstein und Harden*, p. 157.

55 Bülow, speech in the Reichstag of 28 November 1907, *Stenographische Berichte über die Verhandlungen des Reichstages, XII. Legislatur-Periode, 1. Session, 60. Sitzung*, pp. 1880f.

56 Wolfgang Pfeiffer-Belli, ed., *Harry Graf Kessler, Tagebücher 1918–1937*, Frankfurt a.M. 1961, p. 505.

57 Harden to Holstein, 10 May 1907, *Holstein Papers*, IV, No. 1031.

58 Harden to Holstein, 17 July 1907, ibid., No. 1045.

59 See Rogge, *Holstein und Harden*, p. 157.

60 Berckheim to Marschall, 26 May 1907, Fuchs, *Großherzog von Baden*, IV, No. 2637. See Hecht, 'Harden-Prozesse', pp. 43–8; Crown Prince Wilhelm, *Erinnerungen des Kronprinzen Wilhelm*, Stuttgart and Berlin 1922, p. 13; Hans von Tresckow, *Von Fürsten und*

anderen Sterblichen. Erinnerungen eines Kriminalkommissars, Berlin 1922, p. 172; Paul Herre, *Kronprinz Wilhelm. Seine Rolle in der deutschen Politik*, Munich 1954, p. 26.

61 Harden to Holstein, 28 February 1907, *Holstein Papers*, IV, No. 1012.

62 Crown Prince Wilhelm, *Erinnerungen*, p. 106. See Machtan, 'Wilhelm II. als oberster Sittenrichter', p. 12.

63 Berckheim to Marschall, 26 May 1907, Fuchs, *Großherzog von Baden*, IV, No. 2637. Also Tresckow, *Von Fürsten und anderen Sterblichen*, pp. 164ff.

64 Müller, diary for 4 May 1907, BA-MA Freiburg-im-Breisgau, Müller Papers.

65 Harden to Holstein, 12 May 1907, *Holstein Papers*, IV, No. 1032.

66 Harden to Holstein, 15 June 1907, ibid., No. 1042.

67 See Spitzemberg, diary for 26 and 31 May 1907, Vierhaus, *Tagebuch*, p. 472.

68 Harden, 'Schlußvortrag', *Zukunft* of 9 November 1907; 'Der Prozeß', *Zukunft* of 23 November 1907.

69 Müller, diary for 13–16, 22, 24 and 26 May 1907, BA-MA Freiburg-im-Breisgau, Müller Papers.

70 Bernhard Hereditary Prince of Saxe-Meiningen to his father, Duke Georg II, undated fragment [May 1907], ThStaMgn, Hausarchiv 341.

71 Spitzemberg, diary for 26 and 31 May and 9 and 22 June 1907, Vierhaus, *Tagebuch*, pp. 472f.

72 Kessel to Eulenburg, 4 May 1907, *Eulenburgs Korrespondenz*, III, No. 1527.

73 Eulenburg to Kaiser Wilhelm II, 5 May 1907, ibid., No. 1528.

74 Ibid., p. 2146, note 5.

75 August Eulenburg to Philipp Eulenburg, 12 May 1907, ibid., No. 1530.

76 Harden to Holstein, 24 and 26 May 1907, *Holstein Papers*, IV, Nos. 1037–8.

77 Müller, diary for 30 May 1907, BA-MA Freiburg-im-Breisgau, Müller Papers.

78 Berckheim to Marschall, 26 May 1907, Fuchs, *Großherzog von Baden*, IV, No. 2637.

79 Bülow, *Denkwürdigkeiten*, II, pp. 293 and 312. Cf. Rogge, *Holstein und Harden*, pp. 163f. See Eulenburg's comment on Hahnke's letter of 26 May 1908, *Eulenburgs Korrespondenz*, III, No. 1544.

80 Harden to Holstein, 1 June 1907, *Holstein Papers*, IV, No. 1039.

81 Harden to Holstein, 31 December 1907 and 30 March 1908, ibid., Nos. 1071 and 1081.

82 Such, at any rate, was Varnbüler's assumption. See the diary of his sister Hildegard von Spitzemberg for 22 June and 7 November 1907, Vierhaus, *Tagebuch*, pp. 473 and 477.

83 Spitzemberg, diary for 7 and 16 November 1907, ibid., p. 477. On the behaviour of Hahnke and Hülsen-Haeseler in the Eulenburg affair, see Radziwill, *Briefe vom deutschen Kaiserhof*, pp. 309f.

84 Emil Graf Görtz to Kaiser Wilhelm II, 13 May 1907, GStA Berlin, BPHA Rep. 53J Lit. G Nr 5.

85 Harden to Holstein, 26 May 1907, *Holstein Papers*, IV, No. 1038. See above, pp. 560f.

86 Bülow, *Denkwürdigkeiten*, II, pp. 293 and 312. Cf. Rogge, *Holstein und Harden*, pp. 163f. On Fürstenberg's own homoerotic orientation see the character sketch '"Ein halber Ausländer" – Max Egon II. Fürst zu Fürstenberg (1863–1941)', in Winzen, *Freundesliebe am Hof Kaiser Wilhelms II.*, pp. 79–89. See also below, p. 1204.

87 Bülow, *Denkwürdigkeiten*, II, p. 311.

88 Eulenburg to Bülow, 12 May 1907, *Eulenburgs Korrespondenz*, III, No. 1529.

89 Bülow to Eulenburg, 17 May 1907, ibid., No. 1531.

90 Eulenburg to Bülow, 5 June 1907, ibid., No. 1536.

91 Bülow to Eulenburg, 31 May 1907, ibid., No. 1534.

92 Bülow to Loebell, 27 December 1908, quoted in Hellige and Schulin, *Briefwechsel Rathenau-Harden*, p. 522. See also Rogge, *Holstein und Harden*, p. 257.

93 Varnbüler, unpublished memoirs, as cited in *Eulenburgs Korrespondenz*, III, p. 2150, note 2.

94 Harden to Holstein, 3 June 1907, *Holstein Papers*, IV, No. 1040.

95 Harden to Holstein, 15 June 1907, ibid., No. 1042.

96 Harden to Holstein, 20 June 1907, ibid., No. 1043; Harden to Rathenau, 16 and 20 June 1907, Hellige and Schulin, *Briefwechsel Rathenau-Harden*, Nos. 200 and 202.

97 Harden to Isenbiel, 7 July 1908, cited in *Eulenburgs Korrespondenz*, III, p. 2184, note 2.

98 Varnbüler, unpublished memoirs, as cited ibid., p. 2150, note 2.

99 Moltke to Varnbüler, 31 March 1891, ibid., I, p. 39; Varnbüler to Moltke, 15 April, 7 May and 4 June 1898, ibid., III, No. 1366 and No. 1373 with note 2.

100 Spitzemberg, diary for 30 June 1908, Vierhaus, *Tagebuch*, pp. 483f.

101 Varnbüler to Moltke, 24 October 1912, *Eulenburgs Korrespondenz*, III, No. 1556. See Spitzemberg, diary for 6 December 1913, Vierhaus, *Tagebuch*, p. 564.

102 Eulenburg to Bülow, 4 June 1907, *Eulenburgs Korrespondenz*, III, No. 1535.

103 Eulenburg to Bülow, 5 June 1907, ibid., No. 1536.

104 See Hecht, 'Harden-Prozesse', pp. 86–91.

105 Ibid., pp. 69–85.

106 Harden to Holstein, 15 June 1907, *Holstein Papers*, IV, No. 1042; Harden to Rathenau, 6 June 1907, Hellige and Schulin, *Briefwechsel Rathenau-Harden*, No. 196; Harden, 'Nur ein paar Worte', *Zukunft* of 15 June 1907; Hecht, 'Harden-Prozesse', pp. 81–5.

107 Harden to Holstein, 13 October 1907, *Holstein Papers*, IV, No. 1055.

108 Hecht, 'Harden-Prozesse', pp. 55f.

109 Ibid., pp. 56–68.

110 Bülow to Kaiser Wilhelm II, 24 December 1907, cited in *Eulenburgs Korrespondenz*, III, p. 2160, note 2.

111 As cited in Hecht, 'Harden-Prozesse', p. 129. See Machtan, 'Wilhelm II. als oberster Sittenrichter', pp. 14f.

112 Bernstein, cited in *Zukunft* of 12 October 1907.

113 Cited in Hecht, 'Harden-Prozesse', pp. 107–9.

114 Hecht, 'Harden-Prozesse', pp. 114–17.

115 Ibid.

116 Ibid.

117 As cited ibid., p. 149.

118 Ibid., pp. 123f.

119 See the evidence in ibid., pp. 141–8.

120 As cited ibid., pp. 149f. and 155.

121 Ibid., pp. 160–74.

122 See Spitzemberg, diary for 29 October 1907, Vierhaus, *Tagebuch*, p. 476.

123 Hopman, diary for 27 October 1907, Epkenhans, *Leben eines 'Wilhelminers'*, p. 145.

124 Zedlitz-Trützschler, diary for 26 November 1907, *Zwölf Jahre*, pp. 170–3. See also the view of Knesebeck cited in Spitzemberg, diary for 30 October 1907, Vierhaus, *Tagebuch*, p. 476.

125 Loebell to Bülow, 23 October 1907, cited in *Eulenburgs Korrespondenz*, III, p. 2165, note 2; Lerman, *Chancellor as Courtier*, pp. 199f.

126 Bülow to Kaiser Wilhelm II, 26 October 1907, printed in *Holstein Papers*, IV, No. 1057.

127 Hecht, 'Harden-Prozesse', p. 99.

128 Loebell to Bülow, 26 October 1907, cited in *Eulenburgs Korrespondenz*, III, p. 2160, note 2.

129 Zedlitz-Trützschler, diary for 26 November 1907, *Zwölf Jahre*, pp. 171f.; Spitzemberg, diary for 7 November 1907, Vierhaus, *Tagebuch*, p. 477.

130 See below, pp. 585–8.

131 Hötzsch, *Fürst Bülows Reden*, III, pp. 69f.

132 *Stenographische Berichte über die Verhandlungen des Reichstages, XII. Legislaturperiode, 28–30 November 1907*, pp. 1875–974.

133 Zedlitz-Trützschler, diary for 18 December 1907, *Zwölf Jahre*, pp. 181f.

134 Podbielski to Loebell, 12 December 1907, cited in Rogge, *Holstein und Harden*, pp. 253f.

135 Harden to Holstein, 25 November and 12 December 1907, *Holstein Papers*, IV, Nos. 1062 and 1065.

136 Hecht, 'Harden-Prozesse', pp. 178–80.

137 Adolf Brand, *Fürst Bülow and die Abschaffung des § 175. Flugschrift der Gemeinschaft der Eigenen – philosophische Gesellschaft für Sittenverbesserung und Lebenskunst*, 10 September 1907. See Hecht, 'Harden-Prozesse', pp. 251f. Also see Harden to Holstein, 11 September 1907, *Holstein Papers*, IV, No. 1048; Holstein to Harden, 12 September 1907, Rogge, *Holstein und Harden*, pp. 205–10; Tresckow, *Von Fürsten and anderen Sterblichen*, p. 193. Most especially, see Winzen, *Ende der Kaiserherrlichkeit*, passim.

138 Harden to Holstein, 21 April 1907, *Holstein Papers*, IV, No. 1019; Berckheim to Marschall, 26 May 1907, Fuchs, *Großherzog von Baden*, IV, No. 2637. See above, p. 557.

139 Winzen, *Bernhard Fürst von Bülow*, p. 11; Lerman, *Chancellor as Courtier*, p. 199.

140 Bülow to Loebell, 27 September 1907, as cited in Winzen, *Bernhard Fürst von Bülow*, p. 11; Lerman, *Chancellor as Courtier*, p. 199.

141 Winzen, *Bernhard Fürst von Bülow*, pp. 11–13 and 46.

142 Bülow's statement under oath of 6 November 1907, as quoted in Hecht, 'Harden-Prozesse', p. 257.

143 Winzen, *Bernhard Fürst von Bülow*, pp. 12f.

144 Lerman, *Chancellor as Courtier*, pp. 198f.; *Eulenburgs Korrespondenz*, III, p. 1944, note 1.

145 Ibid., I, p. 12 and p. 109, note 6.

146 See Harden to Holstein, 9 July 1908, *Holstein Papers*, IV, No. 1105.

147 Brand, *Fürst Bülow and die Abschaffung des § 175*, as quoted in Hecht, 'Harden-Prozesse', p. 251. See Harden to Holstein, 17 January and 21 April 1907, *Holstein Papers*, IV, Nos. 1008 and 1019; Rogge, *Holstein und Harden*, pp. 157f., *Eulenburgs Korrespondenz*, III, pp. 2143f., note 4; Eulenburg to Isenbiel, 11 May 1908, ibid., No. 1543. See also Bülow, *Denkwürdigkeiten*, II, pp. 309f.

148 Eulenburg to Bülow, 28 February 1893; Bülow to Eulenburg, 13 March 1893 and 16 November 1894, *Eulenburgs Korrespondenz*, II, Nos. 776, 785 and 1050. See above all Winzen, *Bernhard Fürst von Bülow*, pp. 63–5; and the same author's recent studies, listed in note 23 above.

149 Bülow's testimony of 6 November 1907, as quoted in Hecht, 'Harden-Prozesse', p. 259.

150 Eulenburg's testimony of 6 November 1907, as quoted ibid., p. 261.

151 Hecht, 'Harden-Prozesse', pp. 180ff.

152 Bülow to Kaiser Wilhelm II, 24 December 1907, BA Berlin, R 43/798 b; Charlotte Hereditary Princess of Saxe-Meiningen to Schweninger, 23 and 25 December 1907, BA Berlin, Schweninger Papers, Nr 131; Bernhard Hereditary Prince of Saxe-Meiningen to his father, Duke Georg II, 10 January 1908, ThStaMgn, Hausarchiv 341. See Machtan, 'Wilhelm II. als oberster Sittenrichter', pp. 15f.

153 Kaiser Wilhelm II to Chamberlain, 23 December 1907, Chamberlain, *Briefe*, II, pp. 226f.

154 Bernstein, testimony of 21 April 1908, as quoted in Hecht, 'Harden-Prozesse', p. 301.

155 Hecht, 'Harden-Prozesse', pp. 320–36.

156 Spitzemberg, diary for 5 January 1908, Vierhaus, *Tagebuch*, p. 479.

157 Zedlitz-Trützschler, diary for 8 January 1908, *Zwölf Jahre*, pp. 183f.

158 Rogge, *Friedrich von Holstein, Lebensbekenntnis*, p. 301.

159 Ibid.

160 Zedlitz-Trützschler, diary for 8 January 1908, *Zwölf Jahre*, pp. 183f.

161 See Harden's letters to Holstein of March and April 1908, *Holstein Papers*, Nos. 1078ff.

162 Hecht, 'Harden-Prozesse', pp. 340f.

163 Harden to Bernstein, 19 January 1908, cited in Bernd Uwe Weller, *Maximilian Harden und die Zukunft*, Bremen 1970, p. 341; see also Hecht, 'Harden-Prozesse', p. 341.

164 'Harden und Fürst Eulenburg', *Neue Freie Volkszeitung*, 25 March 1908, as quoted ibid., p. 343.

165 See the details in *Eulenburgs Korrespondenz*, III, pp. 2168f.; Hecht, 'Harden-Prozesse', p. 352.

166 Spitzemberg, diary for 17 May 1908, Vierhaus, *Tagebuch*, p. 483.

167 Varnbüler to Laemmel, 22 April 1908, *Eulenburgs Korrespondenz*, III, No. 1539. Similar: Monts to Bülow, 23 July 1908, quoted ibid., pp. 2184f., note 2.

168 Eulenburg to his son Friedrich-Wend, 5 and 6 May 1908, ibid., No. 1541.

169 Machtan, 'Wilhelm II. als oberster Sittenrichter', p. 16.

170 Beseler to Kaiser Wilhelm II, 1 May 1908, cited in *Eulenburgs Korrespondenz*, III, p. 2176, note 3. See Eulenburg's written refutation of 23 April 1908 of the assertions made by Riedel and Ernst, ibid., No. 1540.

171 Beseler to Kaiser Wilhelm II, 9 May 1908, cited ibid., p. 2177, note 2. Also see Augusta Eulenburg to her son Sigwart, 8 May 1908, ibid., No. 1542.

172 See Johannes Haller, *Aus dem Leben des Fürsten Philipp zu Eulenburg-Hertefeld*, Berlin 1924, pp. 400ff.; Rogge, *Holstein und Harden*, pp. 283f.; Weller, *Harden*, p. 195; Hellige and Schulin, *Briefwechsel Rathenau-Harden*, pp. 551–6; Hecht, 'Harden-Prozesse', p. 386.

173 Kaiser Wilhelm II to Fürstenberg, 11 May 1908, FFA Donaueschingen.

174 Spitzemberg, diary for 30 June 1908, Vierhaus, *Tagebuch*, pp. 483f. See also ibid., p. 515.

175 Beseler to Kaiser Wilhelm II, 2 June 1908, cited in *Eulenburgs Korrespondenz*, III, p. 2183, note 4. See Radziwill, *Briefe vom deutschen Kaiserhof*, pp. 31f.; Rogge, *Holstein und Harden*, pp. 301f.; Hecht, 'Harden-Prozesse', pp. 270f.

176 Eulenburg to Ernst, 22 December 1907, cited in Hecht, 'Harden-Prozesse', pp. 387f.; statement of the prosecution against Eulenburg, 5 June 1908, ibid., p. 388.

177 Beseler to Kaiser Wilhelm II, 5 June 1908, cited in *Eulenburgs Korrespondenz*, III, pp. 2184f., note 2.

178 Radziwill, *Briefe vom deutschen Kaiserhof*, p. 308.

179 Beseler to Kaiser Wilhelm II, 8 July 1908, cited in *Eulenburgs Korrespondenz*, III, pp. 2184f., note 2.

180 Beseler to Kaiser Wilhelm II, 17, 18 and 20 July 1908, cited ibid., pp. 2184f., note 2.

181 Wahnschaffe to Bülow, 17 July 1908, cited ibid., pp. 2184f., note 2.

182 Kaiser Wilhelm II to Bülow, 18 July 1908, printed in Rogge, *Holstein und Harden*, p. 314.

183 Beseler to Kaiser Wilhelm II, 26 September 1908, cited in *Eulenburgs Korrespondenz*, III, pp. 2184f., note 2.

184 Spitzemberg, diary for 9 June 1909, Vierhaus, *Tagebuch*, p. 506.

185 Ibid.

186 Beseler to Kaiser Wilhelm II, 4, 13 and 29 June 1908, cited in *Eulenburgs Korrespondenz*, III, pp. 2184f., note 2. See Hecht, 'Harden-Prozesse', pp. 389f.

22 THE KAISER'S VISIT TO WINDSOR AND HIGHCLIFFE,
NOVEMBER TO DECEMBER 1907

1 Campbell-Bannerman to Knollys, 28 December 1906, RA VIC/R 27/130. For the 'atmosphere of distrust' which characterised the Kaiser's visit see Reinermann, *Der Kaiser in England*, pp. 290–324.

2 Kaiser Wilhelm II to Princess Louise Duchess of Argyll, 27 December 1906, RA VIC/Add Mss/A 17/1040.

3 Grand Duchess Augusta of Mecklenburg-Strelitz to Mary Princess of Wales, 26 February 1906; Mary Princess of Wales to Grand Duchess Augusta of Mecklenburg-Strelitz, 27 March 1906, RA GV/CC 32/21 and 24/47.

4 See for example the correspondence between Cope, Probyn and August Eulenburg, September 1905 to March 1906, RA PP EVII/C 15608; Kaiser Wilhelm II to King Edward VII, 25 and 26 December 1906; King Edward VII to Kaiser Wilhelm II, 26 December 1906, RA VIC/W 50/125–30; King Edward VII to Kaiser Wilhelm II, 14 June 1907, PA AA R 3705; Spender to Knollys, 17 October 1907, Knollys Papers RA VIC/Add C 07/2/Q; Paget to King Edward VII, 14 September 1907, RA VIC/W 52/4; Hardinge to King Edward VII, 20 September 1907, RA VIC/W 52/29.

5 Hardinge to Knollys, 7 August 1907, Knollys Papers, RA VIC/Add C 07/2/Q. See also Hardinge to King Edward VII, 22 October 1906, RA VIC/W 50/26; Hardinge to Bryce, 7 September 1907, Bodleian Library, Oxford University, James Bryce Mss., USA 27.

6 Kaiser Wilhelm II, marginal comments on Hans-Adolf von Bülow to Reich Chancellor, 26 August 1907, PA AA R 3707.

7 Hardinge to Grey, 7 April 1907, Gooch and Temperley, *British Documents*, VI, No. 44.

8 Hardinge to King Edward VII, 30 April 1907, RA VIC/W 51/74.

9 Hardinge to Knollys, 3 June 1907, RA VIC/W 51/107. The King's letter of invitation of 14 June 1907 is to be found in PA AA R 3705.

10 Metternich to Mühlberg, 16 June 1907, Mühlberg to Jenisch, 16 June 1907, ibid. See also Metternich's report of 11 July 1907, PA AA R 3706.

11 Jenisch to Mühlberg, 17 June 1907, PA AA R 3705. See *Große Politik*, XXI/2, p. 514, note.

12 Metternich to Mühlberg, Mühlberg to Jenisch, 18 June 1907, PA AA R 3705.

13 Jenisch to Mühlberg, 19 June 1907, ibid.

14 Kaiser Wilhelm II to King Edward VII, RA VIC/W 65/87. The German draft and a copy of the English letter are in PA AA R 3705. King Edward VII to Kaiser Wilhelm II, 25 June 1907, ibid.; Kaiser Wilhelm II to King Edward VII, 2 July 1907; Jenisch to Bülow, 2 July 1907, PA AA R 3706, copy in GStA Berlin, BPHA Rep. 53J Lit. G Nr 11. See also King Edward VII to Kaiser Wilhelm II, 16 July 1907, PA AA R 3706.

15 Hopman, diary for 27 June and 25 July 1907, BA-MA Freiburg-im-Breisgau, Hopman Papers N 326/6. Cf. Epkenhans, *Leben eines 'Wilhelminers'*, p. 143.

16 Kaiser Wilhelm II, marginal comments on Miquel's report of 9 October 1907, *Große Politik*, XXV/1, No. 8538.

17 See above, pp. 568f.

18 Kaiser Wilhelm II to King Edward VII, 31 October 1907, RA VIC/W 52/47.

19 King Edward VII to Kaiser Wilhelm II, 31 October 1907, RA VIC/W 52/48.

20 King Edward VII to Knollys, 31 October 1907, RA VIC/W 52/46.

21 Grey to Knollys, 1 November 1907, RA VIC/W 52/53.

22 Hardinge to Knollys, 1 November 1907, RA VIC/W 52/52.

23 Metternich to Bülow, 1 November 1907, PA AA R 3709.

24 Ibid.

25 Kaiser Wilhelm II, marginal notes on Metternich's two reports of 1 November 1907, PA AA R 3709. See the sarcastic account of the incident in Bülow, *Denkwürdigkeiten*, II, pp. 305f.

26 August Eulenburg to Auswärtiges Amt, 5 November 1907, PA AA R 3709.

27 Schoen, *Erlebtes*, p. 56.

28 Müller, diary for 13 November 1907, BA-MA Freiburg-im-Breisgau, Müller Papers.

29 Kaiser Wilhelm II to Bülow, 13 November 1907, PA AA R 3709.

30 Bülow to Kaiser Wilhelm II, 13 November 1907, ibid.

31 Kaiser Wilhelm II to Bülow, 14 November 1907, PA AA R 3710.

32 Mary Princess of Wales to Grand Duchess Augusta of Mecklenburg-Strelitz, 15 November 1907, RA GV/CC 24/93.

33 Hardinge to Bryce, 2 December 1907, Bodleian Library, Oxford University, Bryce Mss, USA 27/184.

34 Foreign Office memorandum of 9 November 1907 in RA VIC/W 52/55; undated memoranda of the Auswärtiges Amt in PA AA R 3706 and R 3628.

35 For Wilhelm's earlier role in the Baghdad railway project see above, pp. 88–95.

36 Grey to King Edward VII, 13 November 1907, RA VIC/W 52/58.

37 Kaiser Wilhelm II to Bülow, 14 November 1907, PA AA R 3710.

38 Schoen, *Erlebtes*, pp. 57f.

39 Grey, Hardinge and Haldane, memorandum of 14 November 1907, Gooch and Temperley, *British Documents*, VI, No. 62.

40 Haldane, dictation of 15 November 1907, RA VIC/W 52/61, printed ibid., No. 63.

41 Hardinge to Knollys, RA VIC/W 52/62.

42 Grey to Knollys, 16 November 1907, RA VIC/W 52/65, printed in Gooch and Temperley, *British Documents*, VI, No. 66.

43 Grey to Bertie, 16 November 1907, ibid., No. 65.

44 See Isvolsky to Benckendorff, 6 December 1907, printed ibid., p. 101.

45 Schoen, *Erlebtes*, p. 58. See Canis, *Abgrund*, pp. 263ff.

46 See below, Chapter 25.

47 Metternich to Bülow, 7 November 1907, PA AA R 3709.

48 Stumm, report from London of 25 November 1907, PA AA R 3711.

49 Stuart Wortley to his wife, 1 December 1907, printed in Peter Winzen, *Das Kaiserreich am Abgrund. Die Daily-Telegraph-Affäre and das Hale-Interview von 1908. Darstellung and Dokumentation*, Stuttgart 2002, pp. 94–6.

50 Stuart Wortley to his wife, 2 December 1907, printed ibid., pp. 97f.

51 Stuart Wortley to his wife, 7 December 1907, printed ibid., pp. 98f.

52 Stuart Wortley to his wife, 1 December 1907, printed ibid., pp. 94–6.

53 See Reinermann, *Der Kaiser in England*, pp. 321f.

54 The original wording here was: 'England and Germany are the only two great Protestant Powers in Europe and have, therefore, every reason . . .'

55 Kaiser Wilhelm II, interview in the *Manchester Daily Dispatch*, 4 December 1907, as cited in the articles 'The German Emperor and German Policy' in *The Times* of 4 and 6 December 1907.

56 'The German Emperor and German Policy', *The Times*, 5 and 6 December 1907. For this incident see Geppert, *Pressekriege*, pp. 264f.

57 Hardinge to Knollys, 4 December 1907, RA VIC/W 52/70.

58 Hardinge to Knollys, 4 December 1907, Grey to Lascelles, 4 December 1907, RA VIC/W 52/71 and 72.

59 Hardinge to Knollys, 6 December 1907, RA VIC/W 52/75.

60 See below, pp. 667ff.

61 Sternburg to Bülow, 21 December 1907, with marginal notes by Kaiser Wilhelm II, PA AA R 3711.

62 Emil Reich, *Germany's Swelled Head*, Walsall Press, 1907.

63 Wallace to Knollys, 1 October 1907, RA VIC/W 52/32.

64 Wallace to Knollys, 11 October 1907, RA VIC/W 52/40.

23   THE HOT SUMMER OF 1908. ON THE VERGE OF WAR WITH BRITAIN

1 Salis to Grey, 19 November and 4 December 1907; Dumas to Salis, 2 December 1907, Gooch and Temperley, *British Documents*, VI, Nos. 41 and 42.

2 Hardinge to Knollys, 6 December 1907, RA VIC/W 52/75.

3 Ibid.

4 In March 1908 the Austrian ambassador reported from London that a significant group of MPs and Lords believed that Germany was planning to land 200,000 men in England. Canis, *Abgrund*, p. 265, note 24. In a popular book entitled *Kaiser Wilhelm II. und König Eduard VII.* published in Dresden the previous year, Rudolf Martin had proposed an invasion of England by airborne troops. Ibid., p. 261, note 6.

5 Charles à Court Repington, 'German Naval Policy', *The Times*, 10 September 1907.

6 Esher, letter of 22 January 1908, published in *The Times* on 6 February 1908.

7 Fisher to King Edward VII, 14 March 1908, RA VIC/W 59/14.

8 Dumas to Lascelles, 3 February 1908; Lascelles to Grey, 4 February 1908, with minutes by Crowe, Hardinge and Grey of 10 February 1908, Gooch and Temperley, *British Documents*, VI, No. 80. See Dumas's lengthy report of 12 February 1908 on the Imperial Navy with critical comments by Crowe, Hardinge and Grey, ibid., No. 81. The pamphlet, referred to by Crowe, written by Oberleutnant Franz Freiherr von Edelsheim of the General Staff, on Germany's naval operations had been published in Berlin in 1901. See Fiebig-von Hase, *Lateinamerika*, I, pp. 480, 484 and 495. See also the report of the British military attaché Colonel Frederick Trench of 27 April 1908 stressing the danger of a surprise attack by the German Fleet, Gooch and Temperley, *British Documents*, VI, No. 94. The reports of the naval attachés in Berlin are now available in Matthew S. Seligmann, ed., *Naval Intelligence from Germany. The Reports of the British Naval Attachés in Berlin, 1906–1914*, Aldershot 2007. See also Matthew S. Seligmann, *Spies in Uniform. British Military and Naval Intelligence on the Eve of the First World War*, Oxford 2006; and Matthew S. Seligmann's recent work *The Royal Navy and the German Threat 1901–1914: Admiralty Plans to Protect British Trade in a War against Germany*, Oxford 2012.

9 Hardinge to Knollys, 22 January 1908, RA VIC/W 52/93.

10 Kaiser Wilhelm II to Bülow, 30 December 1907, *Große Politik*, XXV/1, No. 8557.

11 Sir C. Macdonald to Grey, 27 November 1908, RA Knollys Papers.

12 See Fiebig-von Hase, 'Die Rolle Wilhelms II. in den deutsch-amerikanischen Beziehungen', p. 251; Macdonald to Grey, 27 November 1908, RA Knollys Papers.

13 Kaiser Wilhelm II, marginal note on Bülow to Speck von Sternburg, 17 October 1907, *Große Politik*, XXV/1, No. 8551.

14 Kaiser Wilhelm II to Bülow, 30 December 1907, ibid., No. 8557.

15 Kaiser Wilhelm II, marginal notes on the report of Count Rex from China of 7 December 1907, ibid., No. 8556.

16 Kaiser Wilhelm II to Bülow, 30 December 1907, ibid., No. 8557.

17 Bülow, *Denkwürdigkeiten*, II, p. 324. For the Tweedmouth letter affair see also Cecil, *Wilhelm II: Emperor and Exile*, pp.129ff.; Lee, *King Edward VII*, II, pp. 604ff. For the reaction in the British press see Reinermann, *Der Kaiser in England*, pp. 325–32.

18 Müller, diary for 16 February 1908, BA-MA Freiburg-im-Breisgau, Müller Papers.

19 Kaiser Wilhelm II to Lord Tweedmouth, 16 February 1908, first mentioned in public in *The Times* on 6 March 1908. For the text of the letter see Tirpitz, *Aufbau der deutschen Weltmacht*, pp. 58–63; *Große Politik*, XXIV, No. 8181. The Admiralty's papers on the Tweedmouth letter are in the Bodleian Library, Oxford University.

20 Kaiser Wilhelm II to King Edward VII, 14 February 1908, Tweedmouth to Knollys, 19 February 1908, Cambridge University Library, Esher Papers, ESHR 10/53; Tweedmouth to Knollys, 18 February 1908, RA VIC/W 59/8.

21 King Edward VII to Kaiser Wilhelm II, 22 February 1908, *Große Politik*, XXIV, No. 8183.

22 Müller, diary for 24 and 25 February 1908, BA-MA Freiburg-im-Breisgau, Müller Papers.

23 Metternich's report is cited in Bülow, *Denkwürdigkeiten*, II, p. 325. On the reaction of the British Foreign Office see Repington to Esher, 5 and 14 March 1908, Cambridge University Library, Esher Papers, ESHR 10/53.

24 Bülow, *Denkwürdigkeiten*, II, pp. 324f.

25 Tirpitz, *Aufbau der deutschen Weltmacht*, pp. 57f.; Müller diary for 16, 24 and 25 February and also 23 and 24 March 1908, BA-MA Freiburg-im-Breisgau, Müller Papers; Kaiser Wilhelm II to Tirpitz, 31 March 1908, Tirpitz to Kaiser Wilhelm II, 1 April 1908, BA-MA Freiburg-im-Breisgau, Tirpitz Papers, N 253/8. On 1 April 1908 Admiral von Müller noted: 'H.M. received glowing telegram of thanks from Tirpitz, who has been called to the House of Lords.'

26 Radziwill to Robilant, 14 March 1908, printed in Cyril Spencer Fox, ed., *This Was Germany. An Observer at the Court of Berlin. Letters of Princess Marie Radziwill to General di Robilant 1908–1915*, London 1937 (cited below as *Letters of Princess Marie Radziwill*), pp. 23f.

27 Bülow to Kaiser Wilhelm II, 6 March 1908, *Große Politik*, XXIV, No. 8187.

28 Esher, diary for 14 March 1908, Cambridge University Library, Esher Papers, ESHR 2/11.

29 Metternich to Bülow, 6 March 1908; Bülow to Kaiser Wilhelm II, 6 March 1908 with the Kaiser's marginal note, *Große Politik*, XXIV, No. 8187.

30 Ibid.

31 Metternich to Bülow, 9 March 1908; Schoen to Metternich, 14 March 1908, *Große Politik*, XXIV, Nos. 8194 and 8196.

32 Metternich to Bülow, 6 March 1908; Bülow to Kaiser Wilhelm II, 6 March 1908 with the Kaiser's marginal note, ibid., No. 8187.

33 See Hopman, diary for 8–10 March 1908, BA-MA Freiburg-im-Breisgau, Hopman Papers, N 326/6.

34 Harden to Holstein, 8 March 1908, *Holstein Papers*, IV, No. 1076.

35 Radziwill to Robilant, 10 March 1908, printed in *Letters of Princess Marie Radziwill*, pp. 22f.

36 Bülow, *Denkwürdigkeiten*, II, p. 324.

37 Ibid., p. 325.

38 Radziwill to Robilant, 14 March 1908, printed in *Letters of Princess Marie Radziwill*, p. 23.

39 Metternich to Bülow, 6 March 1908, Bülow to Kaiser Wilhelm II, 6 March 1908 with the Kaiser's marginal note, *Große Politik*, XXIV, No. 8187; Kaiser Wilhelm II, marginal note on Metternich to Bülow, 8 March 1908, ibid., No. 8193.

40 Kaiser Wilhelm II, marginal comments on Metternich to Bülow, 8 March 1908, ibid.

41 Kaiser Wilhelm II, marginal comments on Pourtalès's reports of 9 and 12 June, *Große Politik*, XXV/2, Nos. 8803 and 8807.

42 Hardinge to Bryce, 4 December 1908, cited below, pp. 642f.

43 See the reports of Pourtalès, the ambassador in St Petersburg, of 5, 9 and 12 June 1908 with the marginal comments of Kaiser Wilhelm II, *Große Politik*, XXV/2, Nos. 8802, 8803 and 8807.

44 Kaiser Wilhelm II, speech of 29 May 1908, cited ibid., p. 456. Cf. Zedlitz-Trützschler, *Zwölf Jahre*, pp. 193f. and Obst, *'Einer nur ist Herr im Reiche'*, pp. 292ff.

45 Kaiser Wilhelm II, marginal comments on Pourtalès's report of 12 June 1908 and Metternich's report of 15 June 1908, *Große Politik*, XXV/2, Nos. 8808 and 8812. See also Kaiser Wilhelm II to Bülow, 19 July 1908, ibid., p. 457, note.

46 Kaiser Wilhelm II, marginal notes of 24 August 1908 on an article in the *Dortmunder Zeitung* of 20 August 1908, PA AA R 3712.

47 Bülow, *Denkwürdigkeiten*, II, p. 325. See above, pp. 615f.

48 Bülow to Kaiser Wilhelm II, 17 June 1908, *Große Politik*, XXV/2, No. 8815. See Bülow's comments of 25 June 1908, cited in Gutsche, *Wilhelm II*, p. 126. Also Canis, *Abgrund*, pp. 269f.

49 Kaiser Wilhelm II, marginal comment on Bülow's submission of 17 June 1908, *Große Politik*, XXV/2, No. 8815.

50 Kaiser Wilhelm II, marginal notes on Metternich to Bülow, 20 and 25 June 1908, ibid., Nos. 8817 and 8821.

51 See below, p. 621.

52 Treutler, telegram to Auswärtiges Amt, 21 June 1908, PA AA R 3691. Cf. the fullsome account of the Kaiser's visit to Hamburg filed by the Prussian minister to the Hanseatic cities Count von Götzen on 24 June 1908, which was circulated to the embassies in London, Paris and Petersburg on Wilhelm's orders. PA AA R 3751.

53 Kaiser Wilhelm II, speech of 23 June 1908 in Brunsbüttel, as cited in *Große Politik*, XXV/2, p. 488. See Müller, diary for 23 June 1908, BA-MA Freiburg-im-Breisgau, Müller Papers.

54 Müller, diary for 6 July 1908, ibid.

55 Ernst Erbprinz zu Hohenlohe-Langenburg to his father, 2 July 1908, Hohenlohe-Zentralarchiv, Schloß Neuenstein, Hermann Hohenlohe-Langenburg Papers, Bü. 73.

56 Müller, diary for 29 June 1908, BA-MA Freiburg-im-Breisgau, Müller Papers. See Ralph R. Menning and Carol Bresnahan Menning, '"Baseless Allegations": Wilhelm II and the Hale Interview of 1908', *Central European History*, 16, 1983, 372.

57 Hopman, diary for 30 June 1908, Epkenhans, *Leben eines 'Wilhelminers'*, p. 148.

58 Hopman, diary for 13 July 1908, ibid., p. 148.

59 Müller, diary for 7 and 9 July 1908, BA-MA Freiburg-im-Breisgau, Müller Papers.

60 Kaiser Wilhelm II, marginal note on Metternich's report of 9 July 1908, PA AA R 3751.

61 Kaiser Wilhelm II to Bülow, 6 July 1908, *Große Politik*, XXIV, No. 8214 and XXV/2, No. 8755. See XXV/2, p. 375, where the editors dispute the 'full authenticity' of the Kaiser's account. For the Sanjak railway crisis of early 1908, see F. R. Bridge, *Great Britain and Austria-Hungary 1906–1914: A Diplomatic History*, London 1972, pp. 77–93.

62 Kaiser Wilhelm II, marginal notes on Metternich's report of 10 July 1908, *Große Politik*., XXIV, No. 8215.

63 Kaiser Wilhelm II, marginal comments on Metternich's report of 16 July 1908, ibid., No. 8217. See below, pp. 631f.

64 Jacobi to Kaiser Wilhelm II, 4 and 5 July 1908, with the Kaiser's marginal comments, *Große Politik*, XXV/2, Nos. 8826 and 8850. See also Pourtalès's report of 9 July 1908, ibid., No. 8851.

65 Kaiser Wilhelm II to Bülow, 15 July 1908, PA AA R 2099. See *Große Politik*, XXV/2, p. 490, note.

66 Kaiser Wilhelm II, marginal note on Pourtalès's report of 6 July 1908, cited ibid.

67 See above, pp. 608–11.

68 Kaiser Wilhelm II, marginal notes on a report from Count Rex of 1 June 1908, *Große Politik*, XXV/1, No. 8563.

69 Kaiser Wilhelm II, marginal note on an article in the French newspaper *Matin* of 21 July 1908, cited in Winzen, *Kaiserreich am Abgrund*, p. 176; Bülow to Bethmann Hollweg, 25 June 1910, cited ibid., p. 69. For the Hale interview see Cecil, *Wilhelm II: Emperor and Exile*, pp. 141f.

70 Hale, memorandum of his interview with the Kaiser on 19 July 1908, printed in Winzen, *Kaiserreich am Abgrund*, pp. 344–8. See ibid., pp. 72f.

71 Hale to Reick, 19 July 1908, cited ibid., p. 70

72 Editor of the *New York Times* to Northcliffe, early August 1908, printed ibid., pp. 343f.

73 Hale, memorandum of his interview with the Kaiser on 19 July 1908, printed in Winzen, *Kaiserreich am Abgrund*, pp. 344–8.

74 Ibid.

75 Menning and Menning, 'Baseless Allegations', p. 375.

76 Roosevelt to Root, 8 August 1908, printed in Roosevelt, *The Letters*, VI, p. 1164; Fiebig-von Hase, 'Rolle Kaiser Wilhelms II. in den deutsch-amerikanischen Beziehungen', p. 253f.

77 Roosevelt to Reid, 6 January 1909, Roosevelt, *The Letters*, VI, p. 1467.

78 Roosevelt to Lee, 17 October 1908, ibid., pp. 1292–4. The letter was not sent. See Menning and Menning, 'Baseless Allegations', pp. 376f.

79 Root to Carnegie, 3 April 1909, as cited in Philip C. Jessup, *Elihu Root*, 2 vols., New York 1938, II, p. 310.

80 See above, p. 623.

81 Northcliffe to Tyrrell, 21 August 1908, Menning and Menning, 'Baseless Allegations', pp. 377ff. See Metternich to Bülow, 16 November 1908, printed in Winzen, *Kaiserreich am Abgrund*, No. 72.

82 See Menning and Menning, 'Baseless Allegations', pp. 389f.; Winzen, *Kaiserreich am Abgrund*, p. 75.

83 Hardinge to Knollys, 12 November 1908, RA Knollys Papers.

84 King Edward VII, marginal note, as cited in Menning and Menning, 'Baseless Allegations', p. 379.

85 King Edward VII to Knollys, 25 November 1908, as cited in Lee, *King Edward VII*, II, p. 622.

86 Hardinge to Knollys, 18 November 1908 with a comment by King Edward VII, RA Knollys Papers.

87 Bertie to Grey, 30 November and 4 December 1908, as cited in Menning and Menning, 'Baseless Allegations', p. 388.

88 Grey to Bertie, 1 December 1908, Gooch and Temperley, *British Documents*, VI, No. 142.

89 Hardinge to Knollys, 12 November 1908, RA Knollys Papers. See Bryce to Bertie, 9 November 1908, National Archives, Kew, F.O. 800/82, Grey Papers.

90 Cambon to Pichon, 25 November 1908, *Documents diplomatiques français*, 2nd series, XI, No. 566.

91 Eisendecher to Bülow, 29 November 1908, Winzen, *Kaiserreich am Abgrund*, No. 91. See ibid., pp. 87f.

92 Kaiser Wilhelm II, marginal notes on Metternich to Bülow, 15 and 30 June 1908, *Große Politik*, XXV/2, No. 8811 and XXIV, No. 8212. See ibid., XXV/2, p. 486, note.

93 Kaiser Wilhelm II, marginal note on the article 'King and Russia' in *The Westminster Gazette* of 20 May 1908, PA AA R 3712.

94 Kaiser Wilhelm II, marginal note on Metternich to Bülow, 27 May 1908, ibid. Cf. *Große Politik*, XXIV, p. 87, note.

95 Schoen to Kaiser Wilhelm II, 4 July 1908, Treutler to Schoen, 8 July 1908, ibid., XXV/2, Nos. 8824–5.

96 Bülow to Kaiser Wilhelm II, 5 July 1908, PA AA R 3712.

97 Kaiser Wilhelm II to Bülow, 9 July 1908, ibid.

98 Bülow to Kaiser Wilhelm II, [July 1908], *Große Politik*, XXIV, No. 8216.

99 King Edward VII to Kaiser Wilhelm II, 13 July 1908, GStA Berlin, BPHA Rep. 53J Lit. G Nr 11; PA AA R 3712.

100 King Edward VII to Kaiser Wilhelm II, 20 July and 3 August 1908; Kaiser Wilhelm II to King Edward VII, 29 July 1908, PA AA R 3712.

101 Bülow, *Denkwürdigkeiten*, II, p. 322.

102 Kaiser Wilhelm II, marginal comments on Metternich's report of 16 July 1908, *Große Politik*, XXIV, No. 8217.

103 Kaiser Wilhelm II, marginal comments of 3 August 1908 on Metternich's report of 1 August 1908, PA AA R 5780. Cf. *Große Politik*, XXIV, No. 8219. See Bülow's instruction to Metternich of 5 August 1908, ibid., No. 8220. The semi-official publication *Nauticus*.

Jahrbuch für Deutschlands Seeinteressen had been in the forefront of the campaign for German naval expansion since 1899.

104 Bülow, marginal comments on Metternich's report of 1 August 1908, PA AA R 5780. See Holstein's memorandum of 15 August 1908, *Holstein Papers*, IV, No. 1116.

105 Ponsonby to George Prince of Wales, August 1908, RA GV/AA 53/21.

106 Hardinge to George Prince of Wales, August 1908, RA GV/AA 53/22.

107 See Hammann, *Bilder aus der letzten Kaiserzeit*, pp. 141–4; Tirpitz, *Aufbau der deutschen Weltmacht*, pp. 69–72; *Große Politik*, XXIV, Nos. 8225–6; Bülow, *Denkwürdigkeiten*, II, pp. 321ff.

108 Kaiser Wilhelm II to Bülow, 12 and 13 August 1908, printed in Hammann, *Bilder aus der letzten Kaiserzeit*, pp. 141–4; *Große Politik*, XXIV, Nos. 8225–6; Tirpitz, *Aufbau der deutschen Weltmacht*, pp. 69–72. See also Bülow, *Denkwürdigkeiten*, II, pp. 321ff.

109 Ibid., pp. 321–4.

110 Zedlitz-Trützschler, diary for 18 March 1909, *Zwölf Jahre*, pp. 225f.

111 Jenisch to Auswärtiges Amt, 12 August 1908, *Große Politik*, XXIV, No. 8227. See Holstein's memorandum of 15 August 1908, *Holstein Papers*, IV, No. 1116.

112 Ponsonby to George Prince of Wales, August 1908, RA GV/AA 53/21.

113 Hardinge to George Prince of Wales, 17 August 1908, RA GV/AA 53/22.

114 See Chapter 24.

115 Hardinge, memorandum of 16 August 1908, Gooch and Temperley, *British Documents*, VI, No. 117; copy in Bodleian Library, Oxford University, James Bryce Mss, Folder USA 28, fol. 134–7.

116 See above, pp. 620–2.

117 See the marginal note 'aha! then why not an entente with us?', written by Kaiser Wilhelm II on Metternich's report of 10 July 1908, *Große Politik*, XXIV, No. 8215.

118 Kaiser Wilhelm II, marginal notes on Metternich's report of 1 August 1908, PA AA R 5780. Printed in *Große Politik*, XXIV, No. 8219.

119 Kaiser Wilhelm II, marginal notes on Metternich's report of 11 August 1908, ibid., No. 8228. For Metternich's reporting on naval matters see Tirpitz, *Aufbau der deutschen Weltmacht*, pp. 72–94; Bülow, *Denkwürdigkeiten*, II, p. 321.

120 Kaiser Wilhelm II, marginal comments on Brockdorff-Rantzau's report of 19 August 1908, *Große Politik*, XXIV, No. 8230. See also Brockdorff-Rantzau to Flotow, 27 August 1908, cited ibid., p. 135, note.

121 See above, pp. 628–30.

122 Hardinge to Bryce, 4 December 1908, Bodleian Library, Oxford University, James Bryce Mss, Folder USA 28.

24 'OUR KAISER AND HIS PEOPLE!' THE CRISIS OF WILHELM'S
PERSONAL MONARCHY

1 Bülow to Einem, 1 July 1906, cited in Bülow, *Denkwürdigkeiten*, II, pp. 226ff.

2 Metternich, report of 11 July 1906 with marginal notes by Kaiser Wilhelm II, PA AA R 3628.

3 Bülow to Kaiser Wilhelm II, 17 July 1906, GStA Berlin, BPHA Rep. 53J Lit B Nr 16a.

4 Ibid.

5 Kaiser Wilhelm II to Grand Duke Friedrich I of Baden, 1 February 1906, Fuchs, *Großherzog von Baden*, IV, No. 2544.

6 Kaiser Wilhelm II to Grand Duke Friedrich I of Baden, 30 January 1907, ibid., No. 2614.

7 Kaiser Wilhelm II to Fürstenberg, 9 and 18 May 1906, FFA Donaueschingen; Chelius to Fürstenberg, 21 May 1906, ibid.

8 Wedel, report of 30 May 1906, PA AA R 3648.

9　See above, pp. 646ff.

10　Kaiser Wilhelm II to Fürstenberg, 12 December 1906, FFA Donaueschingen.

11　See below, p. 650.

12　Kaiser Wilhelm II to Bülow, 5 June 1906, Bülow to Tschirschky, 5 June 1906, PA AA R 3648.

13　Minutes of the meeting of the Prussian Ministry of State on 31 August 1906, GStA Berlin, I. HA, Rep. 90a, B III 2 b, No. 6, Bd. 153, Bl. 16ff.

14　Ibid.

15　Holstein to Bülow, 26 September 1907, *Holstein Papers*, IV, No. 1051. See below, p. 661.

16　Spitzemberg, diary for 9 November 1906, Vierhaus, *Tagebuch*, p. 466.

17　Spitzemberg, diary for 24 November 1907, ibid., p. 478.

18　Spitzemberg, diary for 12 April 1907, ibid., p. 472.

19　Spitzemberg, diary for 24 July 1908, ibid., p. 485.

20　Monts to Holstein, 11 September 1906, *Holstein Papers*, IV, No. 994. See Thomas Kühne, 'Demokratisierung und Parlamentarisierung: Neue Forschungen zur politischen Entwicklungsfähigkeit Deutschlands vor dem Ersten Weltkrieg', *Geschichte und Gesellschaft*, 31, 2005, 293–316.

21　Zedlitz-Trützschler, diary for February 1906, *Zwölf Jahre*, p. 137.

22　Hinzpeter to Kaiser Wilhelm II, 31 March 1907, PA AA R 3901.

23　Hinzpeter to Kaiser Wilhelm II, 20 January 1907, ibid. The Badenese envoy in Munich expressed himself in a similarly pessimistic vein. Bodman to Marschall, 22 January 1907, Fuchs, *Großherzog von Baden*, IV, No. 2609.

24　Hinzpeter to Kaiser Wilhelm II, 1 September 1906, GStA Berlin, BPHA Rep. 53J Lit. H Nr 1.

25　See below, pp. 656f.

26　Bülow to Kaiser Wilhelm II, 17 July 1906, GStA Berlin, BPHA Rep. 53J Lit. B Nr 16a.

27　Szögyény to Goluchowski, 19 August 1906, HHStA Vienna, Hofnachrichten: Preußen.

28　Bülow to Kaiser Wilhelm II, 17 July 1906, GStA Berlin, BPHA Rep. 53J Lit. B Nr 16a.

29　Minutes of the meetings of the Prussian Ministry of State on 17 and 25 July 1906, *Die Protokolle des Preussischen Staatsministeriums*, IX, p. 178.

30　See the leading article 'Der Kaiser und die Majestätsbeleidigung' in the *Vossische Zeitung*, 28 January 1907.

31　Minutes of the meeting of the Prussian Ministry of State on 23 March 1907, GStA Berlin, Rep. 90a, B III 2b No. 6, Bd. 154, Bl. 174ff. See *Die Protokolle des Preussischen Staatsministeriums*, IX, p. 192.

32　Minutes of the meetings of the Prussian Ministry of State on 17 and 25 July 1906, ibid., p. 178.

33　Jost Rebentisch, *Die vielen Gesichter des Kaisers. Wilhelm II. in der deutschen und britischen Karikatur (1888–1918)*, Berlin 2000, pp. 58f. and 309.

34　Zedlitz-Trützschler, diary for 19 March 1907, *Zwölf Jahre*, pp. 153f. See also Dominik Petzold, '"Monarchische Reklamefilms"? Wilhelm II. im neuen Medium der Kinematographie', in Nils Freytag and Dominik Petzold, eds., *Das 'lange' 19. Jahrhundert: Alte Fragen und neue Antworten*, Munich 2007, pp. 201–20.

35　Moltke, diary for 9 February 1905, Moltke, *Erinnerungen, Briefe, Dokumente*, p. 316.

36　Zedlitz-Trützschler, diary for 20 March 1907, *Zwölf Jahre*, p. 157.

37　Kaiser Wilhelm II to Wedel, 2, 11, 20, 21 and 25 April 1907; Tschirschky to Kaiser Wilhelm II, 10 April 1907; Wedel to Auswärtiges Amt, 29 April 1907, PA AA R 3476.

38　Kaiser Wilhelm II, marginal comments on Tschirschky's submission of 20 August 1906, *Große Politik*, XXIII/1, No. 7813.

39 Tschirschky to Bülow, 12 December 1906, Bülow to Tschirschky, 14 December 1906, cited ibid., pp. 81f., note.
40 Kaiser Wilhelm II to Bülow, March 1906, GStA Berlin, BPHA Rep. 53 Nr 328.
41 Zedlitz-Trützschler, diary for 13 March 1906, *Zwölf Jahre*, p. 144.
42 August Eulenburg to Valentini, 30 August 1908, GStA Berlin, I. HA, Rep. 89, Nr 3086.
43 Johann, *Reden des Kaisers*, p. 115. See also Joachim Haferkorn, *Bülows Kampf um das Reichskanzleramt im Jahre 1906*, Würzburg and Aumühle 1939, pp. 106ff.; Obst, *Die politischen Reden*, pp. 280–2; Obst, '*Einer nur ist Herr im Reiche*', pp. 286ff.
44 See Hellige and Schulin, *Briefwechsel Rathenau-Harden*, No. 173, note 3.
45 Harden to Holstein, 27 October 1906, *Holstein Papers*, IV, No. 1001.
46 See above, pp. 551ff.
47 Spitzemberg, diary for 15 November 1906, Vierhaus, *Tagebuch*, p. 467.
48 Weber to Naumann, 14 December 1906, in M. Rainer Lepsius and Wolfgang J. Mommsen, eds., *Max-Weber-Gesamtausgabe*, II/5: *Briefe 1906–1908*, Tübingen 1990, p. 202.
49 See above, pp. 656f.
50 Anon., *Unser Kaiser und sein Volk! Deutsche Sorgen. Von einem Schwarzseher*, Freiburg-im-Breisgau and Leipzig 1906.
51 Spitzemberg, diary for 26 November 1906, Vierhaus, *Tagebuch* pp. 467f.
52 Holstein to Harden, 19 and 22 November 1906, printed in Rogge, *Holstein und Harden*, pp. 104f.
53 *Unser Kaiser und sein Volk!*, p. 16.
54 Ibid., p. 21.
55 Ibid., p. 22.
56 Ibid., pp. 23f.
57 Ibid., pp. 9f. and 19ff.
58 Ibid., pp. 25–8.
59 Ibid., pp. 39ff.
60 Ibid., pp. 10f.
61 See above, p. 301.
62 *Unser Kaiser und sein Volk!*, pp. 33f.
63 Ibid., pp. 30f.
64 Ibid., p. 47.

25 NEMESIS. WILHELM II AND THE *DAILY TELEGRAPH* AFFAIR

1 Kaiser Wilhelm II to Miss Mary Montagu, 27 August 1908, copy in the author's private archive. See also Flotow to Aehrenthal, 1 September 1908, HHStA Vienna, Hofnachrichten: Preußen.
2 Spitzemberg, diary for 2 September 1908, Vierhaus, *Tagebuch*, p. 487.
3 Bülow, *Denkwürdigkeiten*, II, pp. 338ff.; Theodor Eschenburg, 'Die Daily-Telegraph-Affäre. Nach unveröffentlichten Dokumenten', *Preußische Jahrbücher* 214 (1928), 206–9; Wilhelm Schüssler, *Die Daily-Telegraph-Affäre. Fürst Bülow, Kaiser Wilhelm und die Krise des Zweiten Reiches 1908*, Göttingen 1952, pp. 24–7; Friedrich Freiherr Hiller von Gaertringen, *Fürst Bülows Denkwürdigkeiten. Untersuchungen zu ihrer Entstehungsgeschichte und ihrer Kritik*, Tübingen 1956, pp. 134–9. Cf. Johannes Haller, *Die Aera Bülow. Eine historisch-politische Studie*, Stuttgart, Berlin 1922, pp. 140f.
4 Winzen, *Kaiserreich am Abgrund*.
5 See Edward Frederick Lawson Burnham, *Peterborough Court. The Story of The Daily Telegraph*, London 1955, p. 151; Esher to Knollys, 6 November 1908, Brett and Esher,

Journals and Letters of Reginald Viscount Esher, II, p. 356; Winzen, *Kaiserreich am Abgrund*, p. 112, note 8.

6 Varnbüler to Weizsäcker, 19 November 1908, printed ibid., No. 82. For the *Daily Telegraph* affair see also Kohlrausch, *Der Monarch im Skandal*, pp. 243–62; Clark, *Kaiser Wilhelm II*, pp. 172ff.; Mommsen, *War der Kaiser an allem schuld?*, pp. 142ff.; Volker Ullrich, *Als der Thron ins Wanken kam. Das Ende des Hohenzollernreiches 1890–1918*, Bremen 1993, pp. 39–63; Cecil, *Wilhelm II: Emperor and Exile*, pp. 123ff.

7 Canis, *Abgrund*, p. 674.

8 Kaiser Wilhelm II to King Edward VII, 1 February 1906, RA VIC/X 37/62. See the draft submitted to the Kaiser by Bülow, GStA Berlin, BPHA Rep. 53J Lit. G. Nr 11.

9 See above, Chapter 1.

10 Kaiser Wilhelm II to Miss Mary Montagu, 17 October 1905, copy in the author's private archive.

11 See above, pp. 594–8.

12 J. L. Bashford, 'Kaiser Wilhelm II', *The Strand Magazine*, January 1908, cited in Winzen, *Kaiserreich am Abgrund*, p. 110, note 4. See Geppert, *Pressekriege*, pp. 264f.

13 Hardinge to Knollys, 28 October 1908, Knollys Papers, RA VIC/Add C 07/2/Q. Similar: Hardinge to Bryce, 4 December 1908, Bodleian Library, Oxford University, James Bryce Mss, Folder USA 28, fol. 173.

14 See Bülow to Hammann, 12 September 1908, in Hammann, *Bilder aus der letzten Kaiserzeit*, p. 50.

15 Spring Rice to Knollys, 4 November 1908, Knollys Papers, RA VIC/Add C 07/2/Q. Cf. *Große Politik*, XXIV, p. 167, note; Fesser, *Reichskanzler Bernhard Fürst von Bülow*, p. 106.

16 Stuart Wortley to the editor of the *Daily Telegraph*, 7 July 1930, Winzen, *Kaiserreich am Abgrund*, No. 129. See Burnham, *Peterborough Court*, p. 150.

17 Of fundamental importance: Winzen, *Kaiserreich am Abgrund*, pp. 19–67. See Thomas G. Otte, '"An Altogether Unfortunate Affair": Great Britain and the *Daily Telegraph* Affair', *Diplomacy & Statecraft* 5, No. 2 (July 1994), 296–333; Geppert, *Pressekriege*, pp. 265ff. See also Cecil, *Wilhelm II: Emperor and Exile*, pp. 123–45; Clark, *Kaiser Wilhelm II*, pp. 172–7.

18 August Eulenburg to Stuart Wortley, 14 June 1908, quoted in Winzen, *Kaiserreich am Abgrund*, p. 100. See Robert Franklin, *The Fringes of History. The Life and Times of Edward Stuart Wortley*, Christchurch 2003, p. 92.

19 Stuart Wortley to the editor of the *Daily Telegraph*, 7 July 1930, Winzen, *Kaiserreich am Abgrund*, No. 129.

20 Kaiser Wilhelm II, marginal comment on Stumm's report from London of 8 September 1908, *Große Politik*, XXIV, No. 8245. Bülow gave his approval to the Kaiser's remarks on 16 September 1908. Winzen, *Kaiserreich am Abgrund*, pp. 99f.

21 Stuart Wortley to Kaiser Wilhelm II, 23 September 1908, printed ibid., No. 5.

22 Kaiser Wilhelm II to Stuart Wortley, 30 September 1908, printed ibid., p. 103.

23 See Chapter 23.

24 Kaiser Wilhelm II, marginal comment of 12 October 1908 on Marschall's telegram from Constantinople of 11 October 1908, *Große Politik*, XXVI/1, No. 9026.

25 See below, pp. 795ff.

26 See below, p. 795.

27 Jenisch to Bülow, 30 September 1908, *Große Politik*, XXIV, No. 8249; Winzen, *Kaiserreich am Abgrund*, No. 7.

28 Jenisch to Bülow, 30 September 1908, printed ibid., No. 6.

29 Winzen, *Kaiserreich am Abgrund*, pp. 19–23.

30 Bülow to Auswärtiges Amt, 2 October 1908, *Große Politik*, XXIV, No. 8250; Winzen, *Kaiserreich am Abgrund*, No. 7.

31 Spitzemberg, diary for 29 November 1908, Vierhaus, *Tagebuch*, p. 494; Winzen, *Kaiserreich am Abgrund*, p. 104, note 3.

32 Stemrich to Bülow, 5 and 7 October 1908, *Große Politik*, XXIV, No. 8251; Winzen, *Kaiserreich am Abgrund*, No. 8 with note 2.

33 See the evidence in ibid., No. 9 and No. 10 with notes.

34 On the return journey from Rominten see the revealing account in Zedlitz-Trützschler, *Zwölf Jahre*, pp. 204f.

35 Schoen, *Erlebtes*, pp. 95f. See Winzen, *Kaiserreich am Abgrund*, pp. 107–9.

36 Ibid., pp. 108f. with notes 2–5 and p. 125, note 3.

37 Jenisch to Kaiser Wilhelm II, 15 October 1908, printed ibid., No. 11; Jenisch to Bülow, 15 October 1908, ibid., No. 12.

38 Kaiser Wilhelm II to Stuart Wortley, 15 October 1908; Stuart Wortley to Kaiser Wilhelm II, 22 October 1908, ibid., Nos. 13 and 14; *Große Politik*, XXIV, No. 8253. Also Harry Lawson to Stuart Wortley, 28 October 1908, quoted ibid., p. 114, note 2.

39 Bülow, marginal note of 26 October 1908 on Stuart Wortley to Kaiser Wilhelm II, 22 October 1908, ibid., p. 114.

40 See the extended entry in Spitzemberg, diary for 26 September 1909, Vierhaus, *Tagebuch*, p. 512. Also Winzen, *Kaiserreich am Abgrund*, p. 129, note 2.

41 'The German Emperor and England. Personal Interview. Frank Statement of World Policy. Proofs of Friendship', *The Daily Telegraph*, 28 October 1908, printed in facsimile in Bülow, *Denkwürdigkeiten*, II, p. 352. A German translation appeared in the evening edition of *Der Tag* on 28 October 1908, see Winzen, *Kaiserreich am Abgrund*, No. 16.

42 Quoted in Burnham, *Peterborough Court*, pp. 151f.

43 King Edward VII, marginal notes on Lord Burnham to Knollys, 3 November 1908, and Lascelles to Knollys, 31 October 1908, RA VIC/Add CO7/2/Q.

44 See Harden to Holstein, 15 November 1908, Holstein Papers, IV, No. 1151.

45 Whitelaw Reid to Knollys, 22 December 1908, RA VIC/Add C 07/2/Q.

46 See the profound analysis of the agitated mood in Germany in Kohlrausch, *Der Monarch im Skandal*, especially pp. 243–301.

47 See Hammann, *Um den Kaiser*, p. 66; and Winzen, *Kaiserreich am Abgrund*, No. 15 with notes.

48 Spitzemberg, diary for 30 October 1908, Vierhaus, *Tagebuch*, pp. 488f.

49 Spitzemberg, diary for 1 November 1908, ibid., pp. 489f. See Radziwill, *Briefe vom deutschen Kaiserhof*, pp. 314f.

50 Maximilian Harden, 'Gegen den Kaiser', *Zukunft*, 7, 11 and 21 November 1908.

51 Harden to Holstein, 15 November 1908, *Holstein Papers*, IV, No. 1151; Harden, 'Gegen den Kaiser', *Zukunft* of 7 November 1908, cited in Winzen, *Kaiserreich am Abgrund*, p. 179, note 2.

52 Charlotte Hereditary Princess of Saxe-Meiningen to Schweninger, 18 November 1908, BA Berlin, Schweninger Papers, Nr 131.

53 Charlotte Hereditary Princess of Saxe-Meiningen to Schweninger, 5 December 1908, ibid. See Bülow's memorandum of 12 November 1908 on the mood in the Bundesrat committee for foreign affairs, printed in Winzen, *Kaiserreich am Abgrund*, No. 66.

54 Holstein to Bülow, 18 December 1908, *Holstein Papers*, IV, No. 1170.

55 As cited in Adolf Stein to Colmar von der Goltz, 7 December 1908, BA-MA Freiburg-im-Breisgau, von der Goltz Papers, N 737/22. See also Bülow, *Denkwürdigkeiten*, II, p. 363.

56 Valentini, manuscript 'Aufzeichnungen', Valentini Papers, BA Koblenz Kl. Erw. Nr 341–1. Cf. Valentini, *Kaiser und Kabinettschef*, pp. 98f.

57 Salis to Grey, 30 October 1908, Gooch and Temperley, *British Documents*, VI, pp. 201f.

58 See Zedlitz-Trützschler to his father, 30 November 1908, *Zwölf Jahre*, p. 196.

59 Bülow to Kaiser Wilhelm II, 30 October 1908, *Große Politik*, XXIV, No. 8257.

60 Kaiser Wilhelm II, marginal note on Bülow's submission of 30 October 1908, ibid., p. 181.

61 Jenisch to Bülow, 4 November 1908, printed in Winzen, *Kaiserreich am Abgrund*, No. 44. See ibid., pp. 38f. and p. 148, note 3.

62 See the detailed account in ibid., pp. 39–41.

63 Müller, diary for 31 October 1908, BA-MA Freiburg-im-Breisgau, Müller Papers.

64 Quoted in Berckheim to Marschall, 2 November 1908, Winzen, *Kaiserreich am Abgrund*, No. 33; see ibid., p. 39.

65 Hugo Graf von Lerchenfeld-Köfering, *Erinnerungen und Denkwürdigkeiten, 1843–1925*, Berlin 1934, p. 379.

66 Berckheim to Marschall, 2 November 1908, Winzen, *Kaiserreich am Abgrund*, No. 33.

67 Winzen, *Bernhard Fürst von Bülow*, pp. 134ff.

68 Jenisch to Bülow, 4 November 1908, Winzen, *Kaiserreich am Abgrund*, No. 44.

69 See the evidence cited ibid., pp. 172f., note 1.

70 Jenisch to Bülow, 4 November 1908, ibid., No. 44.

71 Hülsen-Haeseler to Müller, 8 November 1908, BA-MA Freiburg-im-Breisgau, Müller Papers, diary for the year 1908, fols. 399–402. Cf. Görlitz, *Der Kaiser*, pp. 70f.; Zedlitz-Trützschler to his father, 30 November 1908, *Zwölf Jahre*, p. 196.

72 Georg Freiherr von Hertling, speech in the Reichstag on 10 November 1908, as cited in Winzen, *Kaiserreich am Abgrund*, No. 56.

73 Ernst Bassermann, speech in the Reichstag on 10 November 1908, ibid., No. 52.

74 Otto Wiemer, speech in the Reichstag on 10 November 1908, ibid., No. 53.

75 Georg Freiherr von Hertling, speech in the Reichstag on 10 November 1908, ibid., No. 56.

76 Declaration of the Centre party in the Reichstag, 10 November 1908, ibid., pp. 208f., note 4.

77 Paul Singer, speech in the Reichstag on 10 November 1908, ibid., No. 54.

78 Wolfgang Heine, speech in the Reichstag on 11 November 1908, ibid., p. 51.

79 Ibid., pp. 51f.

80 Bülow, speech in the Reichstag on 10 November 1908, ibid., No. 55.

81 Conrad Haussmann, speech in the Reichstag on 11 November 1908, ibid., No. 58.

82 Wolfgang Heine, speech in the Reichstag on 11 November 1908, quoted ibid., p. 53. See Valentini, *Kaiser und Kabinettschef*, p. 100.

83 See Winzen, *Kaiserreich am Abgrund*, pp. 53f.

84 Gustav Roesicke, memorandum of 13 November 1908, printed ibid., No. 60.

85 Elard von Oldenburg-Januschau, speech in the Reichstag on 11 November 1908, ibid., pp. 217f., note 10.

86 Reinhold von Sydow, 'Fürst Bülow und die Reichsfinanzreform 1908/09. Glossen zum Bülow-Buch', in Friedrich Thimme, ed., *Front wider Bülow. Staatsmänner, Diplomaten und Forscher zu seinen Denkwürdigkeiten*, Munich 1931, p. 120.

87 Karl von Einem, *Erinnerungen eines Soldaten 1853–1933*, Leipzig 1933, pp. 120f.

88 Müller, diary for 30 October 1908, BA-MA Freiburg-im-Breisgau, Müller Papers.

89 Bülow, *Denkwürdigkeiten*, II, p. 363; cf. Einem, *Erinnerungen*, p. 121. See Winzen, *Kaiserreich am Abgrund*, p. 213, note 3.

90 Minutes of the meeting of the Prussian Ministry of State on 11 November 1908, printed ibid., No. 61.

91 Bülow to Kaiser Wilhelm II, 11 November 1908; Jenisch to Bülow, 12 November 1908, cited ibid., pp. 226f., note 1.

92 Harden to Rathenau, 9 November 1908, Hellige and Schulin, *Briefwechsel Rathenau-Harden*, No. 244.

93 Winzen, *Kaiserreich am Abgrund*, p. 210, note 2; Zedlitz-Trützschler, diary for 30 December 1908 and 2 January 1909, *Zwölf Jahre*, pp. 202–7.

94 Ottokar Czernin, *Im Weltkriege*, Berlin and Vienna 1919, p. 73.

95 Zedlitz-Trützschler to his father, 30 November 1908, *Zwölf Jahre*, pp. 196–8.

96 Müller, diary for 10 November 1908, BA-MA Freiburg-im-Breisgau, Müller Papers.

97 Kaiser Wilhelm II, speech of 10 November 1908, Johann, *Reden des Kaisers*, pp. 122f.

98 Zedlitz-Trützschler to his father, 30 November 1908, *Zwölf Jahre*, pp. 196–8.

99 Müller, diary for 11 November 1908, BA-MA Freiburg-im-Breisgau, Müller Papers. Cf. Görlitz, *Der Kaiser*, p. 71.

100 Valentini, *Kaiser und Kabinettschef*, p. 101.

101 Valentini, diary for 14 November 1908, BA Koblenz, Valentini Papers, Kl. Erw. Nr 341–1, cf. Valentini, *Kaiser und Kabinettschef*, pp. 102f.

102 Spitzemberg, diary for 30 November 1908, Vierhaus, *Tagebuch*, p. 495.

103 Zedlitz-Trützschler to his father, 30 November 1908, *Zwölf Jahre*, pp. 196–8.

104 Valentini, *Kaiser und Kabinettschef*, p. 101.

105 Valentini, memorandum of 20 November 1908 on his conversation with the Kaiser in Donaueschingen on 13 November 1908, copy, GStA Berlin, I. HA, Rep. 89, Nr 3068, fols. 189f.

106 Valentini, diary for 13 November 1908, BA Koblenz, Valentini Papers, Kl. Erw. Nr 341–1, printed in Valentini, *Kaiser und Kabinettschef*, p. 102.

107 Valentini, memorandum 'Das Drama von Donaueschingen', BA Koblenz, Valentini Papers, Kl. Erw. Nr 341–1. Cf. Valentini, *Kaiser und Kabinettschef*, p. 103. See also the retrospective account of Count Zedlitz in Zedlitz-Trützschler, diary for 8 February 1909, *Zwölf Jahre*, pp. 216ff. According to some accounts General Count Hülsen-Haeseler was wearing a tutu for his performance.

108 Zedlitz-Trützschler, diary for 26 November 1908, ibid., pp. 194f.

109 Valentini, diary for 15 November 1908, BA Koblenz, Valentini Papers, Kl. Erw. Nr 341–1, cf. Valentini, *Kaiser und Kabinettschef*, pp. 103f.

110 Holstein to Bülow, 16 and 17 November 1908, *Holstein Papers*, IV, Nos. 1154–5.

111 Hammann, *Um den Kaiser*, p. 73.

112 Hammann, memorandum of December 1908, printed in Winzen, *Kaiserreich am Abgrund*, No. 105.

113 The statement is printed ibid., No. 75. See Kaiser Wilhelm II, *Ereignisse und Gestalten*, p. 99.

114 Bülow to Holstein, 17 November 1908, *Holstein Papers*, IV, No. 1156. See Holstein's reply of the same day, ibid., No. 1157.

115 Hertling to his son Karl, 21 November 1908, printed in Karl Graf von Hertling, 'Bülow, Hertling, Zentrum', in Friedrich Thimme, *Front wider Bülow, Staatsmänner, Diplomaten und Forscher zu seinen Denkwürdigkeiten*, Munich 1931, pp. 143f. See also Lerchenfeld's report of 19 November 1908, printed in Winzen, *Kaiserreich am Abgrund*, No. 81.

116 Charlotte Hereditary Princess of Saxe-Meiningen to Schweninger, 18 November 1908, BA Berlin, Schweninger Papers, Nr 131.

117 Valentini, diary for 17 November 1908, BA Koblenz, Valentini Papers, Kl. Erw. Nr 341–1, printed in Valentini, *Kaiser und Kabinettschef*, p. 104. See also Zedlitz-Trützschler to his father, 30 November 1908, *Zwölf Jahre*, p. 196–8.

118 Einem, as cited from the original manuscript of his *Erinnerungen* in Winzen, *Kaiserreich am Abgrund*, p. 252, note 8.

119 Bülow to Holstein, 7 December 1908, *Holstein Papers*, IV, No. 1163.

120 Kaiser Wilhelm II to Felix von Müller, 22 February 1909; Müller to Kaiser Wilhelm II, 28 February 1909, printed in Winzen, *Kaiserreich am Abgrund*, Nos. 106 and 108.

121 Schiemann, diary for 12, 15 and 16 March 1909, printed ibid., Nos. 111 and 113. Cf. Valentini, *Kaiser und Kabinettschef*, pp. 106–8. Also Kaiser Wilhelm II, marginal

comment on Bethmann Hollweg's telegram of 28 September 1909, *Große Politik*, XXIV, No. 8272; Bethmann Hollweg to Auswärtiges Amt, 29 September 1909; Stemrich to Kiderlen-Wächter, 6 October 1909, Winzen, *Kaiserreich am Abgrund*, No. 120 with note 2 and pp. 331f., note 3.

122 Bülow to Jenisch, 12 November 1908, printed ibid., No. 67.

123 Prince Heinrich of Prussia, diary for 16–18 November 1908, MSM Hamburg.

124 Harden to Rathenau, 20 November 1908, Hellige and Schulin, *Briefwechsel Rathenau-Harden*, No. 246.

125 Kaiser Wilhelm II to Max Egon and Irma zu Fürstenberg, 22 November 1908, FFA Donaueschingen.

126 Bülow, marginal comment of 17 November 1908 on Metternich's telegram from London of 16 November 1908; Bülow to Metternich, 18 November 1908, printed in Winzen, *Kaiserreich am Abgrund*, Nos. 72 and 79. For the crisis occasioned by the Hale interview see ibid., pp. 68–88.

127 Bülow to Kaiser Wilhelm II, 21 November 1908 with the Kaiser's marginal comment of the same day, printed ibid., No. 84.

128 See above, pp. 622–8.

129 On 23 November 1908 the *Berliner Tageblatt* reprinted the reports that had appeared in the *New York World* on 21 November and the London *Observer* on 22 November 1908. See Winzen, *Kaiserreich am Abgrund*, p. 82 and No. 262, notes 3 and 4.

130 Kaiser Wilhelm II. to Bülow, 23 November 1908, cited ibid., p. 262, note 2.

131 Seele to Bülow, 23 November 1908, cited ibid., p. 262, note 1.

132 Zedlitz-Trützschler, diary for 26 November 1908, *Zwölf Jahre*, pp. 194f.

133 Bülow, minute of 23 November 1908, as cited in Winzen, *Kaiserreich am Abgrund*, p. 262, note 1.

134 Spitzemberg, diary for 30 November 1908, Vierhaus, *Tagebuch*, p. 495. See Valentini, *Kaiser und Kabinettschef*, p. 105.

135 *Erinnerungen des Kronprinzen Wilhelm*, pp. 92–4.

136 Kaiser Wilhelm II to Fürstenberg, 25 November 1908, FFA Donaueschingen.

137 Zedlitz-Trützschler to his father, 30 November 1908, *Zwölf Jahre*, pp. 196–8. See below, Chapter 27.

138 Zedlitz-Trützschler, diary for 22 December 1908, ibid., pp. 198–201.

139 Zedlitz-Trützschler, diary for 2 January 1909, ibid., p. 206.

140 Zedlitz-Trützschler, diary for 30 December 1908, ibid., pp. 202ff.

26   UPHEAVAL IN THE BALKANS. KAISER WILHELM AND THE BOSNIAN ANNEXATION CRISIS OF 1908 TO 1909

1 Bülow, *Denkwürdigkeiten*, II, p. 337.

2 See Röhl, *The Kaiser's Personal Monarchy*, pp. 944–54.

3 Kaiser Wilhelm II, marginal note on Marschall's report of 5 November 1901, as quoted in *Holstein Papers*, IV, p. 418. The report is printed without the Kaiser's comment in *Große Politik*, XVIII/1, No. 5460.

4 See Röhl, *The Kaiser's Personal Monarchy*, pp. 987f.

5 Holstein to Bülow, January 1906, *Holstein Papers*, IV, No. 919.

6 Kaiser Wilhelm II, marginal comments of 13 November 1905 on Bülow's submission of 13 November 1905, *Große Politik*, XXII, No. 7566.

7 Kaiser Wilhelm II, marginal note on Metternich to Bülow, 19 October 1908, ibid., XXVI/1, No. 9056.

8 Mudra to von der Goltz, 19 April 1907, BA-MA Freiburg-im-Breisgau, von der Goltz Papers, N 737/14.

9 Bülow to Auswärtiges Amt, 25 July 1908, cited in *Holstein Papers*, IV, No. 1112, note 6. For the effects of the Young Turk revolt on Anglo-German relations, see Schöllgen, *Imperialismus und Gleichgewicht*, pp. 239–45.

10 Kaiser Wilhelm II, marginal comments on Kiderlen-Wächter's report from Therapia and Pourtalès's report of 27 July 1908, *Große Politik*, XXV/2, Nos. 8881 and 8884; Bülow to Holstein, 28 July 1908, *Holstein Papers*, IV, No. 1112. See also Metternich's report of 14 August 1908 with marginal notes by Kaiser Wilhelm II, *Große Politik*, XXV/2, No. 8906.

11 Kaiser Wilhelm II, marginal comments on Kiderlen-Wächter's report and Pourtalès's report of 27 July 1908, *Große Politik*, XXV/2, Nos. 8881 and 8884.

12 Kaiser Wilhelm II, marginal comments of late August 1908 on Metternich's report of 14 August 1908, ibid., No. 8906.

13 Ibid.

14 See Marschall's report of 4 September 1908, *Große Politik*, XXV/2, No. 8911. On the Young Turk revolution see Feroz Ahmad, *The Young Turks. The Committee of Union and Progress in Turkish Politics 1908–1920*, Oxford 1969; Ernest E. Ramsaur, *The Young Turks. Prelude to the Revolution of 1908*, Princeton, NJ 1957; Schöllgen, *Imperialismus und Gleichgewicht*, pp. 239ff.

15 Kaiser Wilhelm II, marginal comment on Bülow to Jenisch, 7 October 1908, *Große Politik*, XXVI/1, No. 8992. See also his note on Marschall's telegram of 9 October 1908, ibid., No. 9002.

16 Kaiser Wilhelm II, marginal comments on Tschirschky's report from Vienna of 25 October 1908, ibid., XXVI/2, No. 9213.

17 See Röhl, *The Kaiser's Personal Monarchy*, pp. 121 and 987.

18 Kaiser Wilhelm II, marginal comments on Brockdorff-Rantzau's report from Vienna of 24 September 1908, *Große Politik*, XXVI/1, No. 8952.

19 See Heinz Alfred Gemeinhardt, *Deutsche und österreichische Pressepolitik während der Bosnischen Krise 1908/09*, Husum 1980, pp. 84ff. See also F. R. Bridge, *Great Britain and Austria-Hungary 1906–1914. A Diplomatic History*, London 1972, pp. 111–38; Clark, *Kaiser Wilhelm II*, pp. 186ff.; Schöllgen, *Imperialismus und Gleichgewicht*, pp. 253–74; Mommsen, *Großmachtstellung und Weltpolitik*, pp. 201ff.; Cecil, *Wilhelm II: Emperor and Exile*, pp. 175ff.

20 Bülow to Aehrenthal, 21 July 1908, cited in *Große Politik*, XXVI/1, p. 34, note. For Bülow's 'policy of strength' in the crisis see Canis, *Abgrund*, pp. 265ff.

21 Schoen to Bülow, 5 September 1908, *Große Politik*, XXVI/1, No. 8927.

22 Aehrenthal to Bülow, 26 September 1908, ibid., No. 8934.

23 Hötzsch, *Fürst Bülows Reden*, III, p. 187; Bülow to Auswärtiges Amt, 7 October 1908, *Große Politik*, XXVI/1, No. 9011. See Fesser, *Reichskanzler Bernhard Fürst von Bülow*, p. 120.

24 Bülow to Aehrenthal, 30 October 1908, *Große Politik*, XXVI/1, No. 9079.

25 Bülow to Schlözer, 25 June 1908, ibid., XXV/2, No. 8820.

26 Pourtalès to Bülow, 13 November 1908, ibid., XXVI/1, No. 9112.

27 George W. F. Hallgarten, *Imperialismus vor 1914. Die soziologischen Grundlagen der Außenpolitik europäischer Großmächte vor dem Ersten Weltkrieg*, 2 vols., Munich 1963, II, p. 109.

28 See Ralf Forsbach, *Alfred von Kiderlen-Wächter (1852–1912). Ein Diplomatenleben im Kaiserreich*, 2 vols., Göttingen 1997, I, pp. 161ff.

29 Walter Markov, *Grundzüge der Balkandiplomatie. Ein Beitrag zur Geschichte der Abhängigkeitsverhältnisse*, ed. Fritz Klein and Irene Markov, Leipzig 1999, p. 113.

30 Emperor Franz Joseph to Kaiser Wilhelm II, 29 September 1908; Bülow to Kaiser Wilhelm II, 5 October 1908; Tschirschky to Auswärtiges Amt, 28 September 1908; Aehrenthal to Bülow, 26 September 1908, *Große Politik*, XXVI/1, Nos. 8978, 8939, 8934 and 8936.

31 Kaiser Wilhelm II, marginal note on Tschirschky's telegram of 28 September 1908, ibid., No. 8936. See above, p. 700.

32 Kaiser Wilhelm II, marginal comment on Bülow's submission of 5 October 1908, published in facsimile in Bülow, *Denkwürdigkeiten*, II, pp. 336f. Cf. *Große Politik*, XXVI/1, No. 8939 and the Kaiser's marginal note 'Annexion!?' on Schoen to Bülow, 5 September 1908, ibid., No. 8927.

33 Kaiser Wilhelm II, marginal note on Bülow to Jenisch, 7 October 1908, ibid., No. 8992. See above, pp. 697f. Schöllgen, *Imperialismus und Gleichgewicht*, p. 253.

34 Kaiser Wilhelm II to Emperor Franz Joseph, 14 October 1908, *Große Politik*, XXVI/1, No. 9006. Kaiser Wilhelm II, speech from the throne to the Prussian Landtag on 20 October 1908, cited in *Holstein Papers*, IV, No. 1145, note 8.

35 Kaiser Wilhelm II, marginal note on Marschall's telegram of 9 October 1908, *Große Politik*, XXVI/1, No. 9002.

36 Kaiser Wilhelm II, marginal note on Marschall's telegram of 11 October 1908, ibid., No. 9026.

37 Holstein to Bülow, 8, 10 and 11 October 1908, *Holstein Papers*, IV, Nos. 1138, 1139 and 1141.

38 Bülow, *Denkwürdigkeiten*, II, pp. 341f.

39 See Pourtalès to Bülow, 1 November 1908, *Große Politik*, XXVI/1, No. 9085, note.

40 Kaiser Wilhelm II, marginal note on Miquel's report from St Petersburg of 12 October 1908, ibid., No. 9041. On the conflict over the Sanjak railway see F. R. Bridge, 'The Sanjak of Novibazar Railway Project', in T. G. Otte and Keith Neilson, eds., *Railways and International Politics. Paths of Empire, 1848–1945*, London 2006, pp. 59–93.

41 Kaiser Wilhelm II, marginal note on Metternich's report from London of 14 October 1908, *Große Politik*, XXVI/1, No. 9040. See the Kaiser's comments on Schoen's memorandum of 20 October 1908, ibid., XXVI/2, No. 9202, together with his marginalia on Pourtalès's report from St Petersburg of 1 November 1908, ibid., XXVI/1, No. 9085.

42 Kaiser Wilhelm II, marginal note on Tschirschky's telegram from Vienna of 17 October 1908, ibid., XXVI/2, No. 9279.

43 Kaiser Wilhelm II, marginal note on Romberg's report from Sofia of 15 October 1908, ibid., No. 9276.

44 Kaiser Wilhelm II, marginal note on Tschirschky's telegram from Vienna of 17 October 1908, ibid., No. 9279.

45 Radolin to Auswärtiges Amt, 17 October 1908, ibid., XXVI/1, No. 9050.

46 Kaiser Wilhelm II, marginal comment on Radolin to Auswärtiges Amt, 17 October 1908, ibid.

47 Szögyény, report of 21 October 1908, in *Österreich-Ungarns Außenpolitik von der Bosnischen Krise 1908 bis zum Kriegsausbruch 1914. Diplomatische Aktenstücke des österreichisch-ungarischen Ministeriums des Äußern*, 9 vols., Vienna and Leipzig 1930, I, No. 362. See Röhl, *The Kaiser's Personal Monarchy*, pp. 764f.

48 Kaiser Wilhelm II, marginal comment on Marschall's report from Therapia of 26 October 1908, *Große Politik*, XXVI/1, No. 9104.

49 See Schoen to Kaiser Wilhelm II, 16 October 1908, ibid., No. 9046.

50 Kaiser Wilhelm II, marginalia on Metternich's telegram from London of 15 October 1908, ibid., No. 9045.

51 Kaiser Wilhelm II, marginal note on Lancken's telegram from Paris of 15 October 1908, ibid., No. 9044.

52 Kaiser Wilhelm II, marginal note on Radolin's telegram from Paris of 17 October 1908, ibid., No. 9050.

53 Kaiser Wilhelm II, marginal note on Radolin's telegram from Paris of 20 October 1908, ibid., No. 9058. See above, pp. 455ff.

54 Bülow to Kaiser Wilhelm II, 22 October 1908 with the Kaiser's marginalia, ibid., No. 9061.

55 Bülow to Kaiser Wilhelm II, 25 October 1908, GStA Berlin, BPHA Rep. 53J Lit. B Nr 16a.

56 See above, pp. 692–5 and below, pp. 730ff.

57 For Fürstenberg's influence on the Kaiser, see Peter Winzen, 'Ein halber Ausländer' – Max Egon II. Fürst zu Fürstenberg (1863–1941), in Winzen, *Freundesliebe am Hof Kaiser Wilhelms II.*, Norderstedt 2010, pp. 79–89.

58 Kaiser Wilhelm II to Archduke Franz Ferdinand, 25 October 1908, MOL Budapest, 183 db.

59 Isvolsky to Nelidow, 5 November 1908, in Benno von Siebert, ed., *Diplomatische Aktenstücke zur Geschichte der Ententepolitik der Vorkriegsjahre*, 2 vols., Berlin 1921, I, pp. 71f.

60 Bülow to Kaiser Wilhelm II, 1 November 1908, *Große Politik*, XXVI/1, No. 9179. Jenisch to Bülow, 4 November 1908, as cited in Peter Winzen, 'Der Krieg in Bülows Kalkül: Katastrophe der Diplomatie oder Chance zur Machtexpansion?', in Jost Dülffer and Karl Holl, eds., *Bereit zum Krieg. Kriegsmentalität im wilhelminischen Deutschland 1890–1914*, Göttingen 1986, p. 171.

61 Kaiser Wilhelm II to Bülow, 5 November 1908, *Große Politik*, XXVI/1, No. 9086.

62 Kaiser Wilhelm II to Bülow, 6 November 1908, ibid., No. 9087.

63 See above, pp. 685ff.

64 Kaiser Wilhelm II to Fürstenberg, 1 December 1908, FFA Donaueschingen.

65 Szögyény to Aehrenthal, 9 December 1908, HHStA, Vienna, PA III Preußen, Karton 167, Bl. 231–3.

66 Kaiser Wilhelm II to Archduke Franz Ferdinand, 16 December 1908, MOL Budapest No. 183 db. Printed with several errors in Robert A. Kann, 'Kaiser Wilhelm II. und Thronfolger Franz Ferdinand in ihrer Korrespondenz', in Kann, *Erzherzog Franz Ferdinand Studien*, Vienna 1976, pp. 54f. Cited below, p. 735.

67 Kaiser Wilhelm II, marginal comments on Pourtalès's report of 9 December 1908, *Große Politik*, XXVI/1, No. 9146.

68 Kaiser Wilhelm II, marginal note on Pourtalès's report of 3 June 1908, cited in Canis, *Abgrund*, p. 269.

69 Posadowsky-Wehner, report of 10 December 1908, ibid., No. 9149.

70 Kaiser Wilhelm II, marginal comment on Posadowsky-Wehner's report of 10 December 1908, ibid. Canis, *Abgrund*, p. 304.

71 Pourtalès to Bülow, 11 December 1908, *Große Politik*, XXVI/1, No. 9152.

72 Kaiser Wilhelm II, marginal comments on Pourtalès's report of 11 December 1908, ibid.

73 Pourtalès, telegram of 12 December 1908, *Große Politik*, XXVI/1, No. 9180.

74 Kaiser Wilhelm II to Bülow, 13 December 1908, ibid., No. 9181.

75 Bülow to Kaiser Wilhelm II, 14 December 1908, ibid., No. 9182.

76 Kaiser Wilhelm II, marginal comments of 14 December 1908 on Bülow's submission of the same day, ibid.

77 Schoen, memorandum of 15 December 1908, *Große Politik*, XXVI/1, No. 9184; Bülow to Kaiser Wilhelm II, 29 January 1909, ibid., No. 9197. See Forsbach, *Kiderlen-Wächter*, I, pp. 273ff.

78 Kaiser Wilhelm II to Archduke Franz Ferdinand, 31 December 1908, MOL Budapest Nr 183 db. Printed – again with some errors – in Kann, 'Wilhelm II. und Thronfolger Franz Ferdinand in ihrer Korrespondenz', pp. 56f.

79 For this incident see below, pp. 736ff.

80 Bülow to Kaiser Wilhelm II, 11 January 1919, GStA Berlin, BPHA Lit. B Nr 16a vol. IV. Printed in part in Fesser, *Traum vom Platz an der Sonne*, p. 135.

81 Kaiser Wilhelm II to Archduke Franz Ferdinand, 14 January 1909, MOL Budapest, Nr. 183db. See Zedlitz-Trützschler, diary for 13 January 1909, *Zwölf Jahre*, pp. 207ff.

82 Kaiser Wilhelm II to Archduke Franz Ferdinand, 14 January 1909, MOL Budapest, Nr 183db.

83 Tsar Nicholas II to Kaiser Wilhelm II, 25 December 1908, *Große Politik*, XXVI/2, No. 9187; Bernd Schwertfeger, *Die Diplomatischen Akten des Auswärtigen Amtes 1871–1914. Ein Wegweiser durch das große Aktenwerk der Deutschen Regierung*, part 5, Berlin 1926, pp. 244f.

84 Kaiser Wilhelm II to Tsar Nicholas II, 8 January 1909. The original letter is in the Moscow State Archive and is printed correctly in Goetz, *Briefe Wilhelms II. an den Zaren*, No. LX, pp. 395–9. Cf. the draft prepared by the Auswärtiges Amt on 5 January 1909, printed in *Große Politik*, XXVI/2, No. 9188, with the note on pp. 388f.

85 Kaiser Wilhelm II to Tsar Nicholas II, 8 January 1909, Goetz, *Briefe Wilhelms II. an den Zaren*, pp. 395–8. See the Tsar's reply of 12 January 1909 in *Große Politik*, XXVI/2, No. 9194.

86 See Oskar Regele, *Feldmarschall Conrad. Auftrag und Erfüllung 1906–1918*, Vienna and Munich 1955, p. 57.

87 Moltke, marginal note on Conrad von Hötzendorf's letter of 1 January 1909, as quoted in Schäfer, 'Moltke und der Kriegsausbruch', BA-MA Freiburg-im-Breisgau, KGFA W10/50439.

88 Moltke to Conrad, 21 January 1909, printed in Franz Freiherr Conrad von Hötzendorf, *Aus meiner Dienstzeit*, 5 vols., Vienna 1921–5, I, p. 379. See Erwin Hölzle, ed., *Quellen zur Entstehung des Ersten Weltkrieges. Internationale Dokumente 1901–1914*, Darmstadt 1995, No. 22.

89 Kaiser Wilhelm II, marginal comment on Pourtalès's report of 25 January 1909, *Große Politik*, XXVI/2, No. 9195.

90 Kaiser Wilhelm II, marginal notes on Bülow's submission of 29 January 1909, ibid., No. 9197.

91 Archduke Franz Ferdinand to Kaiser Wilhelm II, draft, no date [February 1909], MOL Budapest, 183db. Cited in part in Kann, 'Wilhelm II. und Franz Ferdinand in ihrer Korrespondenz', pp. 61–4.

92 Kaiser Wilhelm II to Archduke Franz Ferdinand, 12 February 1909, MOL Budapest, 183db XI,7. Printed in part – with some errors – in Kann, 'Wilhelm II. und Franz Ferdinand in ihrer Korrespondenz', pp. 58–61. Cf. Kaiser Wilhelm II to Emperor Franz Joseph, 12 February 1909, *Große Politik*, XXVI/2, No. 9374.

93 Kaiser Wilhelm II, marginal note of early March 1909 on Hintze's report of 24 February 1909, ibid., No. 9342.

94 Kaiser Wilhelm II, marginal note of 20 February 1909 on Bülow's letter of 19 February 1909, ibid., No. 9379.

95 Kaiser Wilhelm II, marginal comments on Bülow to Kaiser Wilhelm II, 20 and 21 February 1909 and Tschirschky to Bülow, 20 February 1909, ibid., Nos. 9381, 9382 and 9384.

96 Kaiser Wilhelm II, marginal note on Pourtalès's report of 20 February 1909, ibid., No. 9387.

97 Tschirschky to Bülow, 20 February 1909 with approving marginal note by Kaiser Wilhelm II, ibid., No. 9382.

98 Bülow to Kaiser Wilhelm II, 22 February 1909, ibid., No. 9388.

99 Kaiser Wilhelm II, marginal note on Bülow's letter of 22 February 1909, ibid., No. 9388.

100 Kaiser Wilhelm II, marginal notes on Marschall's telegram of 24 February 1909, ibid., No. 9389.

101 Ibid. See also the Kaiser's marginal notes of 4 March 1909 on Bülow's submission of 2 March 1909, *Große Politik*, XXVI/2, No. 9411.

102 Kaiser Wilhelm II, marginal comment on Tschirschky's report of 24 February 1909, ibid., No. 9391.

103 Ibid., p. 624, note. A similar comment is made by Schwertfeger, *Diplomatische Akten*, p. 59. See Forsbach, *Kiderlen-Wächter*, I, p. 287.

104 Hausen, memorandum of 3 March 1909 on his conversation with Kaiser Wilhelm II on 1 March 1909, Sächsisches Hauptstaatsarchiv Dresden, Hausen Papers, Nr 36. I am most grateful to Dr Annika Mombauer for sharing this document with me. See Artur Brabant, *Generaloberst Max Freiherr von Hausen – Ein deutscher Soldat*, Dresden 1926, pp. 241f.

105 Holstein, memorandum of 8 March 1909, *Holstein Papers*, IV, No. 1184.

106 Kaiser Wilhelm II, marginal note on Ratibor's report of 3 March 1909, *Große Politik*, XXVI/2, No. 9415.

107 Kaiser Wilhelm II, marginal note on Pourtalès's report of 12 March 1909, ibid., No. 9436.

108 Hintze to Kaiser Wilhelm II, 13 March 1909, ibid., No. 9428.

109 Kaiser Wilhelm II, marginal note on Hintze's report of 13 March 1909, ibid.

110 Kaiser Wilhelm II, marginal note on Hintze's telegram of 14 March 1909, *Große Politik*, XXVI/2, No. 9439. See also the Kaiser's marginalia on Hintze's report of 1 April 1909, ibid., No. 9504.

111 Gemeinhardt, *Deutsche und österreichische Pressepolitik während der Bosnischen Krise 1908/09*, p. 352.

112 Kaiser Wilhelm II, marginal notes on Ratibor's telegram from Belgrade and on Pourtalès's telegram from St Petersburg of 15 March 1909, *Große Politik*, XXVI/2, Nos. 9431 and 9433.

113 Kaiser Wilhelm II, marginal notes on Pourtalès's telegram from St Petersburg of 19 March 1909, ibid., No. 9518.

114 Pourtalès to Auswärtiges Amt, 17 March 1909, ibid., No. 9451.

115 Kaiser Wilhelm II, marginal note on Pourtalès's report of 17 March 1909, ibid.

116 Bülow to Pourtalès, 21 March 1909, *Große Politik*, XXVI/2, No. 9460.

117 Pourtalès to Auswärtiges Amt, 22 March 1909, ibid., No. 9464.

118 Kaiser Wilhelm II, marginal note on Pourtalès's report of 22 March 1909, ibid.

119 Tsar Nicholas II to Kaiser Wilhelm II, 22 March 1909, *Große Politik*, XXVI/2, No. 9465; Schwertfeger, *Diplomatische Akten*, pp. 254f.

120 Bülow to Tschirschky, 24 March 1909, *Große Politik*, XXVI/2, No. 9468.

121 Hardinge to King Edward VII, 17, 26 and 31 March 1909, RA VIC/W 55/12, 14–15.

122 Kaiser Wilhelm II, marginal notes on Tschirschky's telegram from Vienna of 19 March 1909, *Große Politik*, XXVI/2, No. 9519; Kaiser Wilhelm II, marginal note on Radolin's report of 25 March 1909, ibid., No. 9476.

123 Kaiser Wilhelm II, marginal note on Metternich's telegram of 25 March 1909, ibid., No. 9474.

124 Kaiser Wilhelm II, marginal note on Metternich's report of 26 March 1909, ibid., No. 9482.

125 Kaiser Wilhelm II, marginal note on Pourtalès's telegram of 26 March 1909, ibid., No. 9481.

126 Kaiser Wilhelm II, marginal notes on Tschirschky's telegrams of 21 and 24 March 1909, ibid., Nos. 9521–2.

127 Kaiser Wilhelm II, marginal note on Tschirschky's report of 26 March 1909, ibid., No. 9478.

128 Kaiser Wilhelm II to Irma Fürstenberg, 4 April 1909, FFA Donaueschingen. See below, p. 741.

129 Kaiser Wilhelm II to Archduke Franz Ferdinand, 9 April 1909, MOL Budapest, 183db, XI/8. Cf. Kann, 'Wilhelm II. und Franz Ferdinand in ihrer Korrespondenz', p. 65.

130 Friedrich Freiherr von der Goltz and Wolfgang Förster, eds., *Generalfeldmarschall Colmar Freiherr von der Goltz. Denkwürdigkeiten*, Berlin 1929, p. 333.

131 Moltke to Conrad, 14 September 1909, printed in Conrad, *Aus meiner Dienstzeit*, I, p. 165. See Mombauer, *Moltke*, pp. 114–19.

132 Moltke to his niece Maria, 11 April 1909, printed in Andreas Bracher and Thomas Meyer, eds., *Helmuth von Moltke 1848–1916. Dokumente zu seinem Leben und Wirken*, Basel 2005, No. 301.

133 Zedlitz-Trützschler, diary for 26 March 1909, *Zwölf Jahre*, p. 226.

134 Zedlitz-Trützschler, diary for 9 April 1909, *Zwölf Jahre*, pp. 226f.

135 Jagow to Bülow, 10 June 1909, *Große Politik*, XXVI/2, No. 9550.

136 Pourtalès to Bülow, 6 May 1909, ibid., No. 9532.

137 Kaiser Wilhelm II to Tsar Nicholas II, 3 April 1909, Goetz, *Briefe Wilhelms II. an den Zaren*, p. 399.

138 Kaiser Wilhelm II to Tsar Nicholas II, 8 May 1909, ibid., pp. 400–2.

139 Hintze to Kaiser Wilhelm II, 29 May 1909, with the Kaiser's marginalia, *Große Politik*, XXVI/2, No. 9545.

140 Bülow to Tirpitz, 26 November 1924, BA Koblenz, Bülow Papers, Nr 126, Bl. 36.

141 See Dietrich Geyer, *Der russische Imperialismus. Studien über den Zusammenhang von innerer und auswärtiger Politik 1860–1914*, Göttingen 1977, p. 206.

142 Sir Edward Grey (Viscount Grey of Fallodon), *Twenty-five Years*, 2 vols., London 1925, I, pp. 172ff. (translated into German as *Fünfundzwanzig Jahre Politik 1892–1916. Memoiren*, 2 vols., Munich 1926).

143 As cited in Massie, *Dreadnought*, p. 608.

144 Geyer, *Der russische Imperialismus*, p. 195.

27   THE 'PANTOMIME': FROM BÜLOW TO BETHMANN HOLLWEG

1 Bülow to Bethmann Hollweg, 28 September 1909, copy, BA Koblenz, Valentini Paperts, Nr 13/1, printed in *Große Politik*, XXIV, No. 8271. See Bülow to Loebell, 29 September 1909, Loebell to Valentini, 3 October 1909, BA Koblenz, Valentini Papers, Nr 13/1.

2 Zedlitz-Trützschler to his father, 30 November 1908, *Zwölf Jahre*, p. 197; cf. Spitzemberg, diary for 30 November 1908, Vierhaus, *Tagebuch*, p. 495.

3 Szögyény to Aehrenthal, 9 December 1908, HHStA, Vienna, PA III Preußen, Karton 167, Bl. 231–3.

4 For the group of 'Kaisertreuen' see Bülow, *Denkwürdigkeiten*, II, pp. 477ff. See also Hull, *The Entourage of Kaiser Wilhelm II*, pp. 146ff.

5 Zimmermann to Bülow, 6 December 1908, BA Koblenz, Bülow Papers, Nr 33. See Fesser, *Reichskanzler Bernhard Fürst von Bülow*, p. 124; Adolf Stein to Colmar von der Goltz, 7 December 1908, BA-MA Freiburg-im-Breisgau, von der Goltz Papers, N 737 Mappe 22.

6 Ernst Rudolf Huber, *Deutsche Verfassungsgeschichte seit 1789, IV: Struktur und Krisen des Kaiserreichs*, Stuttgart, Berlin, Cologne and Mainz 1982, pp. 312ff.

7 Kaiser Wilhelm II to Archduke Franz Ferdinand, 16 December 1908, MOL Budapest Nr 183 db. Printed with several errors in Kann, 'Wilhelm II. und Franz Ferdinand in ihrer Korrespondenz', pp. 54f. See below, p. 735.

8 Mary Montagu to Kaiser Wilhelm II, 17 November 1908, GStA Berlin, BPHA Rep. 53 Nr 190; Kaiser Wilhelm II to Mary Montagu, 21 November 1908, copy in the author's private archive.

9 Zedlitz-Trützschler, diary for 22 December 1908, *Zwölf Jahre*, pp. 198–201. See below, p. 736.

10 See Zedlitz-Trützschler, diary for 26 November 1908, *Zwölf Jahre*, pp. 194f.

11 For Wilhelm II's relationship with the Fürstenbergs see the penetrating essay '"Ein halber Ausländer" – Max Egon II. Fürst zu Fürstenberg (1863–1941)', in Peter Winzen, *Freundesliebe am Hof Kaiser Wilhelms II.*, Norderstedt 2010, pp. 79–89.

12 Fürstenberg to Kaiser Wilhelm II, 21 November 1908, GStA Berlin, BPHA Rep. 53J Lit F Nr 3. I was unable to find the Kaiser's account of his audience with Bülow in the Fürstlich Fürstenbergsches Archiv Donaueschingen.

13 Fürstenberg to Kaiser Wilhelm II, 29 November 1908, FFA Donaueschingen.

14 Rathenau to Harden, 4 December 1908, Hellige and Schulin, *Briefwechsel Rathenau-Harden*, No. 249. See Zedlitz-Trützschler, diary for 29 November 1908, *Zwölf Jahre*, pp. 195f.

15 Bülow, *Denkwürdigkeiten*, II, p. 440.

16 Kaiser Wilhelm II to Fürstenberg, 23 December 1908, FFA Donaueschingen.

17 Kaiser Wilhelm II to Fürstenberg, 1 December 1908, ibid. Cf. Zedlitz-Trützschler, diary for 2 January 1909, *Zwölf Jahre*, pp. 206f.

18 See Holstein's letter to Bülow of 8 December 1908, *Holstein Papers*, IV, No. 1165.

19 Kaiser Wilhelm II to Fürstenberg, 23 December 1908, FFA Donaueschingen.

20 Fürstenberg to Kaiser Wilhelm II, 24 December 1908, GStA Berlin, BPHA Rep. 53J Lit. F Nr 3.

21 Kaiser Wilhelm II to Archduke Franz Ferdinand, 16 December 1908, MOL Budapest Nr 183 db. Printed with several errors in Kann, 'Wilhelm II. und Franz Ferdinand in ihrer Korrespondenz', pp. 54f.

22 Zedlitz-Trützschler to his father, 30 November 1908, *Zwölf Jahre*, pp. 196–8.

23 Reischach to Holzing-Berstett, 8 December 1908, GLA Karlsruhe, Holzing-Berstett Papers, Zug. 1989 Nr 116/65.

24 See above, pp. 714f.

25 Extracts from Schlieffen's article are printed in Ernst Jäckh, ed., *Kiderlen-Wächter – der Staatsmann und Mensch. Briefwechsel und Nachlaß*, 2 vols., Berlin and Leipzig 1924, II, pp. 20f., note 1.

26 Holstein to Bülow, 6 January 1909, *Holstein Papers*, IV, No. 1176.

27 Bülow to Holstein, 13 January 1909, ibid., No. 1178.

28 Bülow to Holstein, 10 January 1909, ibid., No. 1177.

29 Bülow to Kaiser Wilhelm II, 11 January 1919, GStA Berlin, BPHA Lit. B Nr 16a vol. IV.

30 Fürstenberg to Kaiser Wilhelm II, 9 January 1909, GStA Berlin, BPHA Rep. 53J Lit. F Nr 3.

31 Kaiser Wilhelm II to Fürstenberg, 11 January 1909, FFA Donaueschingen. Cited in Röhl, *Kaiser and his Court*, p. 206.

32 Zedlitz-Trützschler, diary for 13 January 1909, *Zwölf Jahre*, pp. 207ff.

33 Hardinge, memorandum of 11 February 1909, Bodleian Library, Oxford University, James Bryce Mss, Folder USA 28. For the Kaiser's growing anti-Semitism see Cecil, *Wilhelm II: Emperor and Exile*, pp. 332–47; Röhl, *Kaiser and his Court*, pp. 190–212.

34 Müller, diary for 2 February 1909, BA-MA Freiburg-im-Breisgau, Müller Papers.

35 See the view of Crown Prince Wilhelm, expressed on 21 November 1908, that Bülow had behaved 'like a traitor' towards his father, Thimme, *Front wider Bülow*, p. 123. See Valentini, *Kaiser und Kabinettschef*, p. 106.

36 Zedlitz-Trützschler, diary for 14 January 1909, *Zwölf Jahre*, p. 210.

37 Zedlitz-Trützschler, diary for 20 January 1909, ibid., pp. 212f.

38 Bülow to Kaiser Wilhelm II, 13 February 1909 with the Kaiser's marginal comments of the same day, GStA Berlin, BPHA Rep. 53J Lit. B Nr 16a. See Winzen, *Kaiserreich am Abgrund*, p. 307, note 2.

39 Valentini, *Kaiser und Kabinettschef*, p. 106. See Fesser, *Reichskanzler Bernhard Fürst von Bülow*, p. 124. Also Spitzemberg, diary for 15 February 1909, Vierhaus, *Tagebuch*, p. 499.

40 Kaiser Wilhelm II to Grand Duchess Luise of Baden, 5 February 1909, GStA Berlin, BPHA Rep. 53 Nr 81.
41 Valentini, memorandum of 24 February 1909, GStA Berlin, Valentini Papers, Nr 27.
42 Kaiser Wilhelm II to Müller, 22 February 1909, GStA Berlin, BPHA Rep, 53 Nr 243, printed in Winzen, *Kaiserreich am Abgrund*, No. 106. See Müller's memorandum of 26 February and his reply to the Kaiser of 28 February 1909, ibid., Nos. 107–8.
43 See Bülow, *Denkwürdigkeiten*, II, pp. 440ff.; Müller, diary for 12 March 1909, BA-MA Freiburg-im-Breisgau, Müller Papers.
44 Valentini, *Kaiser und Kabinettschef*, pp. 106ff.; Bernhard Schwertfeger, 'Fürst Bülow und Rudolf von Valentini', in Thimme, *Front wider Bülow*, pp. 314ff. Cf. Witt, *Die Finanzpolitik des Deutschen Reiches von 1903–1913*, p. 270, note 435; Huber, *Deutsche Verfassungsgeschichte*, IV, p. 314, note 48.
45 Zedlitz-Trützschler, diary for 12 March 1909, *Zwölf Jahre*, pp. 223f. Cf. Müller, diary for 12 March 1909, BA-MA Freiburg-im-Breisgau, Müller Papers.
46 Kaiser Wilhelm II to Irma Fürstenberg, 4 April 1909, FFA Donaueschingen.
47 Valentini, memorandum of April 1909, BA Koblenz, Valentini Papers, Kl. Erw. Nr 341–1, printed in somewhat abbreviated form in Valentini, *Kaiser und Kabinettschef*, pp. 109ff.
48 Szögyény to Aehrenthal, 14 April 1909, HHStA, Vienna, PA III Preußen, Karton 168, after fol. 45.
49 Valentini, memorandum of April 1909, BA Koblenz, Valentini Papers, Kl. Erw. Nr 341–1, printed in slightly shortened form in Valentini, *Kaiser und Kabinettschef*, pp. 109ff.
50 Bülow, *Denkwürdigkeiten*, II, p. 469.
51 Hiller von Gaertringen, *Bülows Denkwürdigkeiten*, p. 309.
52 Kaiserin Auguste Viktoria to Hermann Fürst zu Hohenlohe-Langenburg, 7 June 1909, Hohenlohe-Zentralarchiv, Schloß Neuenstein, Hermann Hohenlohe-Langenburg Papers, Bü. 110; Kessel to Kaiser Wilhelm II, 2 May 1909, GStA Berlin, BPHA Rep. 53J Lit. K Nr 4. See Valentini's memorandum of April 1909, BA Koblenz, Valentini Papers, Kl. Erw. Nr 341/1; Valentini, *Kaiser und Kabinettschef*, pp. 109ff.
53 Bülow to Kaiser Wilhelm II, 11 April 1909, *Große Politik*, XXVI/2, No. 9507.
54 Kessel to Kaiser Wilhelm II, 2 May 1909, GStA Berlin, BPHA Rep. 53J Lit. K Nr 4.
55 Valentini, *Kaiser und Kabinettschef*, pp. 109ff. See Kaiser Wilhelm II to Tsar Nicholas II, 8 May 1909, printed in Goetz, *Briefe Wilhelms II. an den Zaren*, No. LXII, pp. 400ff. On the genesis of this letter see *Große Politik*, XXVI/2, p. 786.
56 Lyncker to Goltz, 20 April 1909; Goltz to Kaiser Wilhelm II, 20 April 1909, BA-MA Freiburg-im-Breisgau, von der Goltz Papers, N 737 Zug. 228/95. Also Schoen to Goltz, 8 June 1909, ibid., Mappe 25.
57 Kaiser Wilhelm II, marginal note on Schoen's telegram of 17 April 1909, *Große Politik*, XXVII/1, No. 9582.
58 Kaiser Wilhelm II to Bülow, 18 April 1909, ibid., No. 9585.
59 Kaiser Wilhelm II, marginal note on Bülow's telegram of 17 April 1909, ibid., No. 9582.
60 Kaiser Wilhelm II to Bülow, 21 April 1909, ibid., No. 9589.
61 Sydow, 'Fürst Bülow und die Reichsfinanzreform 1908/09', in Thimme, *Front wider Bülow*, p. 116. On the background see Witt, *Die Finanzpolitik des Deutschen Reiches von 1903–1913*, pp. 199–316.
62 See Holstein to Bülow, 20 January 1909, *Holstein Papers*, IV, No. 1179.
63 Bülow, statement in the Prussian House of Deputies on 10 January 1908, in Huber, *Dokumente zur deutschen Verfassungsgeschichte*, III, No. 11.
64 Rudolf Martin, *Deutsche Machthaber*, Berlin and Leipzig 1910, pp. 342f.; Hiller von Gaertringen, *Bülows Denkwürdigkeiten*, p. 240.
65 Valentini to Loebell, 6 May 1909, BA Koblenz, Loebell Papers, Nr 14.

66 Bülow, *Denkwürdigkeiten*, II, pp. 457ff.

67 Kaiser Wilhelm II, marginal note on Hintze's telegram of 30 May 1909, PA AA R 3630.

68 Bülow to Kaiser Wilhelm II, 10 June 1909 with the Kaiser's approving marginal notes of the same day, PA AA R 15058.

69 Valentini to Loebell, 28 May 1909, BA Koblenz, Loebell Papers, Nr 14.

70 See Hötzsch, *Fürst Bülows Reden*, III, p. 223.

71 Hiller von Gaertringen, *Bülows Denkwürdigkeiten*, p. 219, note 34. See Huber, *Deutsche Verfassungsgeschichte*, IV, p. 317.

72 Valentini, *Kaiser und Kabinettschef*, pp. 120f.

73 Müller, diary for 26 June 1909, BA-MA Freiburg-im-Breisgau, Müller Papers.

74 Fesser, *Reichskanzler Bernhard Fürst von Bülow*, p. 128.

75 Kaiser Wilhelm II to Archduke Franz Ferdinand, 9 July 1909, MOL Budapest, 183 db, XI/9. Printed in Kann, 'Wilhelm II. und Franz Ferdinand in ihrer Korrespondenz', pp. 67f.

76 Valentini, *Kaiser und Kabinettschef*, p. 121.

77 Müller, diary for 6 July 1909, BA-MA Freiburg-im-Breisgau, Müller Papers.

78 Harden to Rathenau, 9 November 1908; Rathenau to Harden, 9 November 1908; Hellige and Schulin, *Briefwechsel Rathenau-Harden*, Nos. 244 and 245.

79 Kaiser Wilhelm II to Fürstenberg, 23 December 1908, FFA Donaueschingen.

80 Müller, diary for 26 February 1909, BA-MA Freiburg-im-Breisgau, Müller Papers.

81 See above, pp. 740ff.

82 Valentini, *Kaiser und Kabinettschef*, p. 121.

83 Valentini, memorandum entitled 'Bülows Sturz, Bethmanns Ernennung, Juni/Juli 1909', BA Koblenz, Valentini Papers, Kl. Erw. Nr 341–1, fol. 149, printed with some modifications in Valentini, *Kaiser und Kabinettschef*, p. 121.

84 Kaiserin Auguste Viktoria, view expressed to Dr Alfred Haehner on 26 October 1920, Haehner Papers, Stadtarchiv Köln, Tagebuch Nr 8, later addenda, p. 158.

85 Szögyény to Aehrenthal, 6 July 1909, HHStA Vienna, PA III Preußen, Karton 167, Bl. 181.

86 See Krethlow, *Generalfeldmarschall Colmar Freiherr von der Goltz*, pp. 264–6.

87 Valentini, *Kaiser und Kabinettschef*, p. 122.

28 WILHELM AND THE DIRECTION OF FOREIGN POLICY UNDER BETHMANN HOLLWEG

1 Heine, Kanzlererziehung, *Simplicissimus*, 30 August 1909.

2 Kaiser Wilhelm II to Archduke Franz Ferdinand, 14 December 1909, MOL Budapest, 183 db, XI, 12.

3 Bülow, *Denkwürdigkeiten*, II, p. 510; Canis, *Abgrund*, p. 342 with note 10.

4 Szögyény to Berchtold, 12 August 1913, *Österreich-Ungarns Außenpolitik*, VII, pp. 116–18.

5 Kaiser Wilhelm II to Archduke Franz Ferdinand, 13 August 1909, MOL Budapest 183 db, XI/10. Printed in Kann, 'Wilhelm II. und Franz Ferdinand in ihrer Korrespondenz', pp. 68f.

6 Kaiser Wilhelm II to Archduke Franz Ferdinand, 30 January 1910, MOL Budapest 183 db, XI/13, fols. 128–30, printed in part in 'Kann, Wilhelm II. und Franz Ferdinand in ihrer Korrespondenz', pp. 71f. See below, pp. 760f. See also Kaiser Wilhelm II to Fürstenberg, 18 February 1910, FFA Donaueschingen.

7 Battenberg, 'Notes of a Statement Made by the German Emperor . . . on May 20th 1911', 23 May 1911, RA GV/O 2580/1. See below, pp. 792f.

8 See Jürgen Angelow, *Kalkül und Prestige. Der Zweibund am Vorabend des Ersten Weltkrieges*, Cologne, Weimar and Vienna 2000, in particular pp. 151–284.

9 Kaiser Wilhelm II, marginal note on Jagow's report of 19 November 1909, *Große Politik*, XXVII/1, No. 9889.

10 Kaiser Wilhelm II, marginal notes on Tschirschky's report of 13 November 1909, ibid., No. 9781.

11 Bethmann Hollweg to Aehrenthal, 15 November 1909, HHStA Vienna, Geh. XXXVIII.

12 Kaiser Wilhelm II to Archduke Franz Ferdinand, 25 November 1909, MOL Budapest, 183 db, XI/11, printed in part in Kann, 'Wilhelm II. und Franz Ferdinand in ihrer Korrespondenz', pp. 69f.

13 Bethmann Hollweg to Kaiser Wilhelm II, 15 September 1910, Große Politik, XXVII/2, No. 9943.

14 Kaiser Wilhelm II, marginal comments on Bethmann Hollweg's telegram of 15 September 1910, ibid., No. 9943. Cf. ibid., XXVII/1, p. 270.

15 Kaiser Wilhelm II, marginal comments on Bethmann Hollweg's telegram of 17 September 1910, ibid., No. 9795.

16 See Schöllgen, Imperialismus und Gleichgewicht, passim.

17 Kaiser Wilhelm II, marginal notes on Brockdorff-Rantzau's telegram from Vienna of 17 August 1909, Große Politik, XXVII/1, No. 9666.

18 Kaiser Wilhelm II, marginal notes on Marschall's telegram of 6 November 1909, ibid., XXVII/2, No. 9974.

19 Kaiser Wilhelm II, marginal notes on Marschall's report of 22 November 1909, ibid., No. 9978. See also the Kaiser's marginalia on Pourtalès's report of 25 November 1909, ibid., XXVII/1, No. 9890.

20 Jenisch to Bethmann Hollweg, 23 November 1909, Bethmann Hollweg to Kaiser Wilhelm II, 24 November 1909, ibid., XXVII/2, Nos. 9979–80.

21 Kaiser Wilhelm II, marginal comments on Schoen's report of 26 January 1910 and Tschirschky's telegram of 3 February 1910, ibid., XXVII/1, Nos. 9686 and 9694.

22 Kaiser Wilhelm II, marginal comments on Tschirschky's telegram of 4 June 1910, ibid., No. 9707.

23 Kaiser Wilhelm II, marginal note on Wangenheim's telegram of 9 June 1910, ibid., No. 9708.

24 Kaiser Wilhelm II, marginal comments on Pourtalès's report of 16 June 1910, ibid., No. 9713. For Wilhelm's position on the Crete question see also his marginalia on Kühlmann's report of 17 June 1910, ibid., No. 9714.

25 Kaiser Wilhelm II, marginal notes on Marschall's telegrams of 17 and 20 October 1910, ibid., XXVII/2, Nos. 10051–2.

26 Kaiser Wilhelm II, marginalia of 22 October 1910 on Bethmann Hollweg's submission of 21 October 1910, ibid., No. 10053.

27 Kaiser Wilhelm II to Archduke Franz Ferdinand, 13 August 1909, MOL Budapest 183 db, XI/10. Printed in Kann, 'Wilhelm II. und Franz Ferdinand in ihrer Korrespondenz', pp. 68f.

28 Kaiser Wilhelm II to Grand Duchess Luise von Baden, 1 February 1910, GStA Berlin, BPHA Rep. 53 Nr 82.

29 Kaiser Wilhelm II to Archduke Franz Ferdinand, 30 January and 9 February 1910, MOL Budapest 183 db, XI/13 and 14, fols. 128–32, printed in part in Kann, 'Wilhelm II. und Franz Ferdinand in ihrer Korrespondenz', pp. 71ff.

30 Kaiser Wilhelm II to Fürstenberg, 17 March 1910, FFA Donaueschingen.

31 Kaiser Wilhelm II, marginal note on Marschall's telegram of 6 June 1910, Große Politik, XXVII/1, No. 9815.

32 Kaiser Wilhelm II, marginal notes on Brockdorff-Rantzau's telegram from Vienna of 11 September 1909, ibid., No. 9731.

33 Kaiser Wilhelm II to Fürstenberg, 17 March 1910, FFA Donaueschingen. See also Katrin Boeckh, Von den Balkankriegen zum Ersten Weltkrieg: Kleinstaatenpolitik und ethnische Selbstbestimmung auf dem Balkan, Munich 1996, p. 65.

34 Spitzemberg, diary entry for 12 and 16 January 1910, Vierhaus, *Tagebuch*, p. 517.
35 Findley to Hardinge, 22 June 1910, National Archives, Kew, Hardinge Papers, F.O. 800/192, fols. 272f. See also Kaiser Wilhelm II to Bethmann Hollweg, 21 May 1910, PA AA R 5791.
36 See the sixteen marginal comments Kaiser Wilhelm II penned on Bethmann Hollweg's report of 15 September 1909, *Große Politik*, CCVI/2, No. 9568. See also his comments on Pourtalès's report of 25 November 1909, ibid., XXVVV/1, No. 9890 and on Schoen's report of 7 May 1910, ibid., XXVII/2, No. 10113.
37 Kaiser Wilhelm II to Archduke Franz Ferdinand, 13 August 1909, MOL Budapest 183 db, XI/10. Printed in Kann, 'Wilhelm II. und Franz Ferdinand in ihrer Korrespondenz', pp. 68f.
38 Kaiser Wilhelm II, marginal note on Isvolsky's letter to Osten-Sacken of 4 November 1909, *Große Politik*, XXVII/1, No. 9888 annex.
39 Kaiser Wilhelm II, marginal notes on Pourtalès's report of 18 September 1909, ibid., XXVI/2, No. 9569.
40 See ibid., XXVII/1, pp. 421f., note.
41 For the agreement of Racconigi see Afflerbach, *Dreibund*, pp. 661−6. The text is printed in *Große Politik*, XXVII/1, pp. 415f.
42 Kaiser Wilhelm II, marginal note on Mirbach's report of 4 November 1909, ibid., No. 9887.
43 Kaiser Wilhelm II, marginal notes on Tschirschky's report of 30 October 1909, ibid., No. 9885.
44 Ibid.
45 Kaiser Wilhelm II, marginal notes on Jagow's report of 19 November 1909, ibid., No. 9889.
46 Kaiser Wilhelm II, marginal notes on Bethmann Hollweg's submission of 9 November 1909, ibid., No. 9888.
47 Kaiser Wilhelm II, marginal notes on Tschirschky's report of 30 October 1909, ibid., No. 9885.
48 Kaiser Wilhelm II, marginal notes on Bethmann Hollweg's submission of 9 November 1909, ibid., No. 9888. See also the Kaiser's marginalia on Wangenheim's report of 11 December 1909, ibid., No. 9739.
49 Tschirschky, report of 12 September 1909, PA AA R 3649.
50 Holzing-Berstett to his wife, 19 and 27 November 1909, GLA Karlsruhe, Holzing-Berstett Papers, Zug. 1989 Nr 116/32.
51 See above, Chapter 26, pp. 717f.
52 Kaiser Wilhelm II to Archduke Franz Ferdinand, 14 December 1909, MOL Budapest 183 db, XI/12. Partly printed in Kann, 'Wilhelm II. und Franz Ferdinand in ihrer Korrespondenz', pp. 70f.
53 Rhemen zu Barensfeld to Rumerskirch, 21 January 1910, MOL Budapest 183 db.
54 Kaiser Wilhelm II, marginal comments on Tschirschky's reports of 24 January and 1 February 1910, *Große Politik*, XXVII/2, Nos. 9900 and 9904. Wilhelm II expressed himself in similar vein to the Austro-Hungarian military attaché, see Bienerth to Conrad von Hötzendorf, 10 February 1910, Kriegsarchiv Vienna, Conrad-Archiv, B2/16, fols. 69f. On the activities of Wesselitzky in London see Geppert, *Pressekriege*, pp. 207−9.
55 Kaiser Wilhelm II, marginal comment on Tschirschky's report of 17 February 1910, *Große Politik*, XXVII/2, No. 9910.
56 Kaiser Wilhelm II to Archduke Franz Ferdinand, 30 January 1910, MOL Budapest 183 db, XI/13, fols. 128−30; printed in part in Kann, 'Wilhelm II. und Franz Ferdinand in ihrer Korrespondenz', pp. 71f.
57 Ibid.

58 Kaiser Wilhelm II to Archduke Franz Ferdinand, 9 February 1910, MOL Budapest 183 db, XI/14, fols. 132ff.; printed in part in Kann, 'Wilhelm II. und Franz Ferdinand in ihrer Korrespondenz', pp. 72f.

59 Kaiser Wilhelm II to Fürstenberg, 18 February 1910, FFA Donaueschingen.

60 Fürstenberg to Kaiser Wilhelm II, 20 February 1910, GStA Berlin, BPHA Rep. 53J Lit. F Nr 3; Kaiser Wilhelm II to Fürstenberg, 22 February 1910, FFA Donaueschingen.

61 See above, pp. 759f.

62 Kaiser Wilhelm II to Moltke, 10 January 1910, GStA Berlin, BPHA Rep. 53J Lit. M Nr 11.

63 Kaiser Wilhelm II to Tsar Nicholas II, 11 January 1910, Goetz, *Briefe Wilhelms II. an den Zaren*, pp. 404f. See also the numerous marginalia the Kaiser wrote on Pourtalès's report of 12 January 1910, *Große Politik*, XXXII, No. 11675.

64 Hintze to Kaiser Wilhelm II, 19 August 1910, ibid., XXVII/2, No. 9956.

65 Kaiser Wilhelm II to Bethmann Hollweg, 26 August 1910, ibid., No. 9955.

66 Kaiser Wilhelm II, marginal comments on Pourtalès's report of 12 August 1910, ibid., No. 9951.

67 Kaiser Wilhelm II, marginal comment on Pourtalès's report of 23 August 1910, ibid., No. 9574.

68 Kaiser Wilhelm II, marginal comments on Pourtalès's report of 22 August 1910, ibid., No. 9953.

69 Kaiser Wilhelm II, marginal comments on Pourtalès's reports of 12 and 26 August 1910, ibid., Nos. 9951 and 9954.

70 Plessen to Bethmann Hollweg, 17 September 1910, ibid., No. 9957; Bethmann Hollweg to Plessen, 23 September 1910, cited in Hürter, *Hintze*, p. 46.

71 Kaiser Wilhelm II, marginal comment on Hintze's report of 19 August 1910, Kaiser Wilhelm II to Bethmann Hollweg, 26 August 1910, *Große Politik*, XXVII/2, Nos. 9955 and 9956.

72 Bethmann Hollweg to Kaiser Wilhelm II, 15 September 1910, ibid., No. 9943. See above, pp. 752f.

73 Kaiser Wilhelm II, marginalia on Bethmann Hollweg's telegram of 15 September 1910, *Große Politik*, XXVII/2, No. 9943. See also ibid., XXVII/1, p. 270.

74 See Canis, *Abgrund*, pp. 372–402.

75 Tsar Nicholas II to Kaiser Wilhelm II, 29 August and 26 September 1910; Kaiser Wilhelm II to Tsar Nicholas II, 29 August 1910, PA AA R 3632; Kaiser Wilhelm II to Tsar Nicholas II, 1 November 1910, GStA Berlin, BPHA Rep. 53 Lit. T No. 1.

76 Kaiser Wilhelm II, marginal notes on the report from Freiherr von Jenisch of 13 October 1910 from Darmstadt, *Große Politik*, XXVII/2, No. 10148.

77 Ibid.

78 Kaiser Wilhelm II, marginalia on Bethmann Hollweg's submission of 1 November 1910, *Große Politik*, XXVII/2, No. 10152.

79 The official programme for the Tsar's visit is to be found in PA AA R 3633.

80 Kiderlen to Jenisch, 10 November 1910, *Große Politik*, XXVII/2, p. 838, note. Nicholas also expressed his delight: see Hintze to Müller, 24 March 1911, Hürter, *Hintze*, No. 59.

81 Jenisch to Bethmann Hollweg, 11 November 1910, PA AA R 3633.

82 Jenisch to Bethmann Hollweg, 19 November 1910, cited in Hürter, *Hintze*, p. 46.

83 Kaiser Wilhelm II to Bethmann Hollweg, 20 November 1910, ibid.

84 Bethmann Hollweg to Kaiser Wilhelm II, 21 November 1910; Müller to Kaiser Wilhelm II, 22 November 1910, ibid., pp. 46f.

85 Kaiser Wilhelm II to Tsar Nicholas II, no date [late November 1910] and 24 December 1910, Goetz, *Briefe Wilhelms II. an den Zaren*, pp. 405–7.

86 Tsar Nicholas II to Kaiser Wilhelm II, 2 December 1910, as quoted in Hürter, *Hintze*, p. 47.

87 Hürter, *Hintze*, pp. 49f.

88 Bethmann Hollweg to Kaiser Wilhelm II, 6 November 1910, Kaiser Wilhelm II to Emperor Franz Joseph; Emperor Franz Joseph to Kaiser Wilhelm II, 9 November 1910, *Große Politik*, XXVII/2, No. 10153 with annex.

89 Bienerth to Conrad, no date [January 1911], Kriegsarchiv Vienna, Generalstab, Militärattaché Berlin, Nr 11.

90 Bethmann Hollweg to Aehrenthal, 14 November 1910, *Große Politik*, XXVII/2, No. 10160.

91 Bethmann Hollweg to Aehrenthal, 23 December 1910, HHStA Vienna, Geh. XXXVIII.

92 Kaiser Wilhelm II, marginal note on a report in the *Lokal-Anzeiger* of 10 December 1910, cited in *Große Politik*, XXVII/2, p. 866, note.

93 Bethmann Hollweg to Kaiser Wilhelm II, 11 December 1910, ibid., No. 10169.

94 Kaiser Wilhelm II, marginal notes on Bethmann Hollweg's submission of 11 December 1910, ibid.

95 *Große Politik*, XXVII/2, p. 868, note.

29 THE KING IS DEAD, OR NEW HOPES OF AN AGREEMENT WITH ENGLAND

1 Metternich's report of 25 October 1909 with marginal notes by Kaiser Wilhelm II, *Große Politik*, XXVII/1, No. 9570. At this time the Kaiser expressed his enthusiasm for the writings of a certain Dr von Peetz on the subject of England and the continent. Kaiser Wilhelm II to Archduke Franz Ferdinand, 13 August 1909, MOL Budapest 183 db, XI/10. Printed in Kann, 'Wilhelm II. und Franz Ferdinand in ihrer Korrespondenz', pp. 68f.

2 See Epkenhans, *Die wilhelminische Flottenrüstung*, pp. 31ff. See Tirpitz to Bülow, 4 January 1909, *Große Politik*, XXVIII, No. 10247; Kaiser Wilhelm II to Bülow, 3 April 1909, ibid., No. 10294.

3 Bethmann Hollweg to Aehrenthal, 15 November 1909, HHStA Vienna, Geh. XXXVIII.

4 Kaiser Wilhelm II to Bethmann Hollweg, 22 August 1909; Bethmann Hollweg to Kaiser Wilhelm II, 25 August 1909, *Große Politik*, XXVIII, Nos. 10332–3. See also Schöllgen, *Imperialismus und Gleichgewicht*, pp. 287–91.

5 Kaiser Wilhelm II to Bethmann Hollweg, 30 September 1909, *Große Politik*, XXX, No. 10342.

6 Tyrrell to Knollys, 1 September 1909, RA Knollys Papers, VIC/Add C 07/2/Q.

7 Hardinge to Knollys, 26 August 1909, ibid.

8 Hardinge to Knollys, 7 September 1909, ibid.

9 Hardinge to Knollys, 26 August and 7 September 1909, ibid.

10 Hardinge to Knollys, 10 November 1909, ibid.

11 Hardinge to Knollys, 27 January 1910, RA VIC/W 55/89.

12 Knollys to Hardinge, 13 November 1909, cited in McLean, *Royalty and Diplomacy*, p. 208.

13 Knollys to Esher, 17 September 1910, Cambridge University Libary, Esher Papers ESHR 4/3.

14 Metternich's report of 25 October 1909 with marginal notes by Kaiser Wilhelm II, *Große Politik*, XXVII/1, No. 9570.

15 Metternich, report of 10 February 1910 with Kaiser Wilhelm II's marginal comments, *Große Politik*, XXVIII, No. 10371.

16 Kaiser Wilhelm II to Mary Montagu, December 1909, in the author's private archive.

17 Kaiser Wilhelm II to Mary Montagu, 8 January 1910, ibid.

18 Kaiser Wilhelm II, marginal comments of 24 December 1909 on Bethmann Hollweg's submission of 23 December 1909, *Große Politik*, XXXII, No. 11668.

19 Kaiser Wilhelm II, marginal notes on Mumm's telegram of 2 January 1910, *Große Politik*, XXXII, No. 11671. See also Wilhelm II's marginalia on Pourtalès's report of 12 January 1910, ibid., No. 11675.

20 Kaiser Wilhelm II, marginal comments on Montgelas's report of 31 January 1910, *Große Politik*, XXXII, No. 11690.

21 Kaiser Wilhelm II to Archduke Franz Ferdinand, 30 January 1910, MOL Budapest 183 db, XI/13, fols. 128–30; printed in part in Kann, 'Wilhelm II. und Franz Ferdinand in ihrer Korrespondenz', pp. 71f.

22 Kaiser Wilhelm II to Archduke Franz Ferdinand, 9 February 1910, MOL Budapest 183 db, XI/14, fols. 132ff.; printed in part in Kann, 'Wilhelm II. und Franz Ferdinand in ihrer Korrespondenz', pp. 72f.

23 The text of the agreement is printed in *Große Politik*, XXXII, No. 11707, annex.

24 Kaiser Wilhelm II, marginal notes on Metternich's report of 24 June 1910, *Große Politik*, XXXII, No. 11704.

25 Zedlitz-Trützschler, diary for 22 February 1910, *Zwölf Jahre*, pp. 235f.

26 Kaiser Wilhelm II to King Edward VII, 31 January 1910, RA VIC/X 37/65.

27 Hill, memorandum of 4 February 1910, Rochester University Library, Hill Papers. I am most grateful to Dr Ragnhild Fiebig-von Hase for showing me this important document.

28 For President Roosevelt's visit to Germany see *Große Politik*, XXVIII, pp. 322ff.

29 Roosevelt to Trevelyan, 1 October 1911, in Roosevelt, *The Letters*, VII, pp. 394–9, and Roosevelt to David Gray, 5 October 1911, ibid., pp. 409–11. See Fiebig-von Hase, 'The Uses of "Friendship"', pp. 150f. and 154.

30 The photographs are reproduced in Stefan Loran, *The Life and Times of Theodore Roosevelt*, Garden City, NY 1959.

31 Holzing-Berstett to his wife, 21 May 1910, GLA Karlsruhe, Holzing-Berstett Papers, Nr 116/21. Cf. Cecil, *Wilhelm II: Emperor and Exile*, p. 154. On Edward VII's death and its possible effect on Anglo-German relations see Reinermann, *Der Kaiser in England*, pp. 365–83.

32 Metternich to Bethmann Hollweg, 25 May 1910, PA AA R 3714.

33 Kaiser Wilhelm II to King George V, 7 and 23 May and 29 October 1910, RA GV/AA 55/101, 55/224 and 43/138.

34 Kaiser Wilhelm II to Bethmann Hollweg, 7 May 1910, *Große Politik*, XXVIII, pp. 321f.

35 Bethmann Hollweg to Metternich, 17 May 1910, ibid., No. 10387. Also in ibid., XXVII/2, No. 10120.

36 Kaiser Wilhelm II to Bethmann Hollweg, 19 May 1910, ibid., XXVIII, p. 324.

37 Kaiser Wilhelm II to Bethmann Hollweg, 20 May 1910, ibid., No. 10389. On the Kaiser's talks with Pichon see Hellige and Schulin, *Briefwechsel Rathenau-Harden*, Nos. 292–5.

38 Kaiser Wilhelm II to Bethmann Hollweg, 21 May 1910, *Große Politik*, XXVIII, No. 10388.

39 Metternich to Bethmann Hollweg, 24 May 1910, ibid., No. 10391.

40 Kaiser Wilhelm II to Bethmann Hollweg, 23 May 1910, ibid., No. 10390.

41 Ibid.

42 Kaiser Wilhelm II, marginal note on Bethmann Hollweg's telegram of 21 May 1910, ibid., XXVII/2, No. 10125.

43 Metternich to Bethmann Hollweg, 25 May 1910, PA AA R 3714.

44 Kaiser Wilhelm II to King George V, 8 July 1910, RA Geo V 0.69.

45 King George V to Kaiser Wilhelm II, July 1910, RA GV/O 69/1a.

46 Kaiser Wilhelm II, marginal comments on Pourtalès's report of 12 August 1910, *Große Politik*, XXVII/2, No. 9951.

47 Kaiser Wilhelm II, marginal comment of August 1910 on the British government's memorandum of 26 July 1910, ibid., XXVIII, No. 10401.

48 Kaiser Wilhelm II to Bethmann Hollweg, 30 September 1910, ibid., No. 10412.

49 Bethmann Hollweg to Kaiser Wilhelm II, 1 October 1910 with the Kaiser's marginal notes, ibid., No. 10413.

50 Kaiser Wilhelm II, marginal comments on Bethmann Hollweg's submission of 28 September 1910, ibid., XXXII, No. 11728; Canis, *Abgrund*, pp. 364ff.

51 King George V to Kaiser Wilhelm II, 9 and 21 February 1911, GStA Berlin, BPH Rep. 53 Nr 258–9; King George V to Kaiser Wilhelm II, 12 February 1911 with Bethmann Hollweg's comment of 13 February 1911, PA AA R 3714.

52 Kaiser Wilhelm II to King George V, 15 February 1911, RA GV/AA 43/152. On the reaction of the British press to the Kaiser's visit see Reinermann, *Der Kaiser in England*, pp. 384–401.

53 Memorandum of the British government of March 1911, RA VIC/Add C 07/2.

54 Tirpitz, *Aufbau der deutschen Weltmacht*, pp. 189f.

55 Kaiser Wilhelm II, marginalia on Widenmann's report of 14 March 1911, *Große Politik*, XXVIII, No. 10434.

56 Widenmann to Tirpitz, 14 March 1911, ibid., No. 10434.

57 Kaiser Wilhelm II to Tirpitz, 14 May 1911, ibid., No. 10444.

58 Bethmann Hollweg to Kaiser Wilhelm II, 15 May 1911, ibid., No. 10445.

59 Kaiser Wilhelm II to Bethmann Hollweg, 18 May 1911, PA AA R 3715.

60 Bethmann Hollweg, record of his conversation with the Kaiser of 23 May 1911, *Große Politik*, XXIX, No. 10562; see also ibid., XXVIII, pp. 415f., note.

61 Kaiser Wilhelm II, marginal comments on the newspaper article 'Der Besuch des deutschen Kaiserpaares in England', in the *Wiener Politische Correspondenz*, 22 May 1911, PA AA R 3715.

62 Seebohm's dispatch of 25 April 1911, Tirpitz, *Aufbau der deutschen Weltmacht*, p. 192.

63 Bethmann Hollweg, record of his conversation with the Kaiser of 23 May 1911, *Große Politik*, XXIX, No. 10562; see also ibid., XXVIII, pp. 415f., note.

64 Battenberg, 'Notes of a Statement Made by the German Emperor to Prince Louis of Battenburg on board his yacht on May 20th 1911', 23 May 1911, RA Geo V 0.2580/1.

65 Asquith to Knollys, 24 May 1911, RA GV/O 2580/2.

66 Tyrrell, 2 July 1911, cited in Zara S. Steiner, *Britain and the Origins of the First World War*, London 1977, p. 75.

30 AGADIR: THE LEAP OF THE *PANTHER*

1 See above, p. 445.

2 See for example Harden's article 'Diptychon' in the *Zukunft* of 17 July 1909; Harden to Rathenau, 24 July 1909, Hellige and Schulin, *Briefwechsel Rathenau-Harden*, p. 589.

3 Kaiser Wilhelm II, marginal comment on Wangenheim's telegram from Tangier of 3 October 1908, *Große Politik*, XXIV, No. 8371.

4 Kaiser Wilhelm II, marginalia on Bülow to Jenisch of 7 November 1908, ibid., No. 8400. See also Jenisch to Auswärtiges Amt, 7 November 1908, cited ibid., pp. 366f., note. On the Casablanca incident see Winzen, *Kaiserreich am Abgrund*, pp. 41f. and 153–5.

5 Bülow, comment on Jenisch's telegram of 8 November 1908, cited in *Große Politik*, XXIV, p. 368, note.

6 Kaiser Wilhelm II, marginal note on Bülow to Auswärtiges Amt, 29 August 1908, *Große Politik*, XXIV, No. 8417.

7 See Bülow to Hammann, 12 September 1908, printed in Hammann, *Bilder aus der letzten Kaiserzeit*, pp. 50f.

8 Kaiser Wilhelm II to Auswärtiges Amt, 24 September 1908, cited in *Große Politik*, XXIV, p. 430, note. See also Jenisch to Stemrich, 24 September 1908, quoted ibid.

9 Kaiser Wilhelm II, marginal notes of 26 September 1908 on Stemrich's submission of 25 September 1908, ibid., No. 8448.

10 Kaiser Wilhelm II to Bethmann Hollweg, 25 November 1909, ibid., XXIX, No. 10484.

11 Bethmann Hollweg to Kaiser Wilhelm II, 25 November 1909, ibid., No. 10485.

12 Kaiser Wilhelm II, marginalia on Bethmann Hollweg's telegram of 25 November 1909; Bethmann Hollweg to Kaiser Wilhelm II, 26 November 1909, ibid., Nos. 10485–6.

13 Kaiser Wilhelm II to Bethmann Hollweg, 22 April 1911, ibid., No. 10538. Cf. Müller, diary for 12 September 1911, BA-MA Freiburg-im-Breisgau, Müller Papers.

14 Jenisch to Kiderlen, 30 April 1911, *Große Politik*, XXIX, No. 10548.

15 Harden to Rathenau, 15 August 1911, Hellige and Schulin, *Briefwechsel Rathenau-Harden*, No. 317.

16 Kiderlen, minute of 6 June 1911, Jäckh, *Kiderlen-Wächter*, II, p. 122.

17 Mommsen, *War der Kaiser an allem schuld?*, p. 174, declares the 'leap of the Panther' to have been 'almost exclusively the work of Kiderlen-Wächter'.

18 As quoted in Emily Oncken, *Panthersprung nach Agadir. Die deutsche Politik während der Zweiten Marokkokrise 1911*, Düsseldorf 1981, pp. 112f.

19 Kiderlen, memorandum of 3 May 1911, *Große Politik*, XXIX, No. 10549.

20 On the collaboration of Kiderlen-Wächter with the Pan-German League at the time of Agadir see Thomas Meyer, *'Endlich eine Tat, eine befreiende Tat …' Alfred von Kiderlen-Wächters 'Panthersprung nach Agadir' unter dem Druck der öffentlichen Meinung*, Husum 1996, p. 147; Forsbach, *Kiderlen-Wächter*, II, pp. 423ff.; Michael Peters, *Der Alldeutsche Verband am Vorabend des Ersten Weltkrieges (1908–1914). Ein Beitrag zur Geschichte des völkischen Nationalismus im spätwilhelminischen Deutschland*, Frankfurt a.M. 1992, pp. 111ff.; Klaus Wernecke, *Der Wille zur Weltgeltung. Außenpolitik und Öffentlichkeit am Vorabend des Ersten Weltkrieges*, Düsseldorf 1970, pp. 29ff.

21 See Fischer, *Krieg der Illusionen*, p. 121.

22 Oncken, *Panthersprung nach Agadir*, p. 187; Meyer, *'Endlich eine Tat, eine befreiende Tat …'*; Forsbach, *Kiderlen-Wächter*; Geoffrey Barraclough, *From Agadir to Armageddon. Anatomy of a Crisis*, London 1982; Jean-Claude Allain, *Agadir 1911. Une crise impérialiste en Europe pour la conquête du Maroc*, Paris 1976; Jost Dülffer, Martin Kröger and Rolf-Harald Wippich, eds., *Vermiedene Kriege. Deeskalation von Konflikten der Großmächte zwischen Krimkrieg und Erstem Weltkrieg (1856–1914)*, Munich 1997, pp. 615ff.; Wolfgang J. Mommsen, *Bürgerstolz und Weltmachtstreben. Deutschland unter Wilhelm II. 1890 bis 1918*, Berlin 1995, p. 463; Afflerbach, *Dreibund*, pp. 675–86.

23 The French text is printed in *Große Politik*, XXIX, No. 10578; cf. Schwertfeger, *Diplomatische Akten*, V, p. 3071.

24 See Forsbach, *Kiderlen-Wächter*, II, pp. 563ff.

25 As quoted in Hans Fenske, ed., *Unter Wilhelm II. 1890–1918*, Darmstadt 1982, pp. 303f.

26 Karl-Dietrich Erdmann, ed., *Kurt Riezler, Tagebücher, Aufsätze, Dokumente*, Göttingen 1972 (cited below as Riezler, *Tagebücher*), No. 510.

27 Kiderlen, memorandum of 3 May 1911, *Große Politik*, XXIX, No. 10549. See above, p. 798.

28 Jäckh, *Kiderlen-Wächter*, II, p. 122.

29 Kaiser Wilhelm II, marginal comment on Bethmann Hollweg's telegram of 10 July 1911, *Große Politik*, XXIX, No. 10600.

30 Bethmann Hollweg, memorandum of 23 May 1911, ibid., No. 10562.

31 General Sir John French, Conversations with the German Emperor, 2 and 3 August 1911, PRO FO 800/107. My thanks to Dr Ragnhild Fiebig-von Hase for bringing my attention to this document.

32 Müller, diary for 26 December 1911, BA-MA Freiburg-im-Breisgau, Müller Papers.

33 Kaiser Wilhelm II, marginalia on Bethmann Hollweg's submissions of 10 and 11 July 1911, *Große Politik*, XXIX, Nos. 10565 and 10600. See below, p. 802.

34 Müller, diary for 24–8 June 1911, BA-MA Freiburg-im-Breisgau, Müller Papers.

35 As quoted in Forsbach, *Kiderlen-Wächter*, II, p. 454, note 255.

36 Kaiser Wilhelm II, marginal comment on Bethmann Hollweg's telegram of 10 July 1911, *Große Politik*, XXIX, No. 10600. See below, p. 802.

37 Müller, diary for 12 September 1911, BA-MA Freiburg-im-Breisgau, Müller Papers.

38 Kiderlen to Auswärtiges Amt, 26 June 1911, *Große Politik*, XXIX, No. 10576.

39 Müller, diary for 12 September 1911, BA-MA Freiburg-im-Breisgau, Müller Papers. See Müller's diary for 26 and 28 June 1911, ibid.

40 Müller, diary for 12 September 1911, ibid.

41 Müller, diary for 6 July 1911, ibid. For the remainder of the northern cruise see Müller, diary for 5 to 29 July 1911, ibid.

42 Zimmermann, memorandum of 12 June 1911, *Große Politik*, XXIX, No. 10572, note; Cambon to Gouppi, 22 June 1911, *Documents diplomatiques français*, 2nd series, XIII, No. 364.

43 Bethmann Hollweg to Kaiser Wilhelm II, 10 July 1911, *Große Politik*, XXIX, No. 10600.

44 Kaiser Wilhelm II, marginal comment on Bethmann Hollweg's telegram of 10 July 1911, ibid.

45 Treutler to Auswärtiges Amt, 11 July 1911, *Große Politik*, XXIX, No. 10601. Treutler transmitted the complete text of the Kaiser's marginalia to the Auswärtiges Amt on the following day, ibid., note.

46 Bethmann Hollweg to Kaiser Wilhelm II, 15 July 1911, ibid., No. 10607.

47 Kaiser Wilhelm II, marginal note on Bethmann Hollweg's telegram of 15 July 1911, ibid.

48 Ibid.

49 Treutler to Auswärtiges Amt, 17 July 1911, Kiderlen to Bethmann Hollweg, 17 July 1911, *Große Politik*, XXIX, Nos. 10609–10.

50 Text in Jäckh, *Kiderlen-Wächter*, II, pp. 128–30 and 132–4.

51 Kiderlen's letter of resignation, 17 July 1911, ibid., pp. 128ff.

52 Kiderlen's second letter of resignation, 19 July 1911, ibid., pp. 133f.

53 Bethmann Hollweg to Kaiser Wilhelm II, 20 July 1911; Bethmann Hollweg to Auswärtiges Amt, 21 July 1911, *Große Politik*, XXIX, Nos. 10613–4.

54 Forsbach, *Kiderlen-Wächter*, II, p. 477.

55 Metternich to Bethmann Hollweg, 22 July 1911, *Große Politik*, XXIX, No. 10621, note. On the background to the speech see Bentley B. Gilbert, 'Pacifist to Interventionist. David Lloyd George in 1911 and 1914: Was Belgium an Issue?', *Historical Journal*, 28, 1985, 871ff. For a recent, very critical account see Clark, *Sleepwalkers*, pp. 209ff.

56 As cited in Massie, *Dreadnought*, p. 732.

57 See F. R. Bridge and Roger Bullen, *The Great Powers and the European States System*, London 2005, pp. 303ff.

58 Lloyd George to Knollys, 29 July 1911, Stamfordham to Knollys, 29 July 1911, RA Knollys Papers.

59 Müller, diary for 26 July and 12 September 1911, BA-MA Freiburg-im-Breisgau, Müller Papers.

60 Müller, diary for 28 July 1911, ibid.

61 Hammann, memorandum of 30 July 1911, as quoted in Riezler, *Tagebücher*, pp. 178f., note.

62 Riezler, diary for 30 July 1911, ibid., No. 512. See Mommsen, *Bürgerstolz und Weltmacht-streben*, p. 465.

63 Müller, diary for 29–30 July 1911, BA-MA Freiburg-im-Breisgau, Müller Papers. See Forsbach, *Kiderlen-Wächter*, II, pp. 497f.

64 Riezler, *Tagebücher*, No. 512.

65 Forsbach, *Kiderlen-Wächter*, II, pp. 498f.

66 Spitzemberg, diary for 2 August 1911, Vierhaus, *Tagebuch*, p. 531.

67 Riezler, *Tagebücher*, No. 511.

68 See Schoen to Auswärtiges Amt, 27 July 1911, *Große Politik*, XXIX, No. 10678, note; Afflerbach, *Dreibund*, p. 683.

69 Reinermann, *Der Kaiser in England*, p. 404.

70 Jenisch to Auswärtiges Amt, 9 August 1911, *Große Politik*, XXIX, No. 10699, note. See Spitzemberg, diary for 7 August 1911, Vierhaus, *Tagebuch*, pp. 531f.

71 Jenisch to Auswärtiges Amt, 9 August 1911, *Große Politik*, XXIX, No. 10699, note.

72 Ibid.

73 Bienerth to Conrad von Hötzendorf, 10 October 1911, Kriegsarchiv Vienna, Generalstab, Militär-attaché Berlin, Nr 11.

74 Spitzemberg, diary for 8 August 1911, Vierhaus, *Tagebuch*, p. 532.

75 Forsbach, *Kiderlen-Wächter*, II, pp. 499–501.

76 Jenisch to Auswärtiges Amt, 9 August 1911, *Große Politik*, XXIX, No. 10698.

77 Eyck, *Das Persönliche Regiment Wilhelms II.*, p. 589.

78 Kaiser Wilhelm II, marginal note on Kiderlen's telegram of 8 August 1911, *Große Politik*, XXIX, No. 10698.

79 Kaiser Wilhelm II to Kiderlen, 9 August 1911, ibid., No. 10696.

80 Jenisch to Auswärtiges Amt, 9 August 1911, ibid., No. 10698.

81 Kiderlen, memorandum of 18 August 1911, Jäckh, *Kiderlen-Wächter*, II, pp. 138f.

82 Hartmut Pogge von Strandmann, ed., *Walther Rathenau Tagebuch 1907–1922*, Düsseldorf 1967 (cited below as Rathenau, *Tagebuch*), p. 152.

83 Moltke, *Erinnerungen, Briefe, Dokumente*, p. 362. See Mombauer, *Moltke*, p. 124.

84 Bienerth to Conrad von Hötzendorf, 10 October 1911; Bienerth to Schemua, 8 January 1912, Kriegsarchiv Vienna, Generalstab, Militär-attaché Berlin, Nr 11 and 12.

85 Müller, diary for 1 August 1911, BA-MA Freiburg-im-Breisgau, Müller Papers.

86 Kaiser Wilhelm II, marginal note on Kiderlen's telegram of 26 July 1911, *Große Politik*, XXIX, No. 10628.

87 Kaiser Wilhelm II, marginal note on Metternich's report of 3 August 1911, ibid., No. 10637.

88 Kaiser Wilhelm II to Kiderlen, 9 August 1911, ibid., No. 10696, see above, p. 809.

89 Kaiser Wilhelm II, marginal note on Kiderlen to Jenisch, 17 August 1911, *Große Politik*, XXIX, No. 10712.

90 Kaiser Wilhelm II to Bethmann Hollweg, 28 August 1911, ibid., No. 10724.

91 Bienerth to Conrad von Hötzendorf, 31 August 1911, Kriegsarchiv Vienna, Generalstab Militär-attaché Berlin, Nr 11.

92 Kiderlen to Jenisch, 29 September 1911, *Große Politik*, XXIX, No. 10750.

93 Kaiser Wilhelm II, marginal notes on Kiderlen's telegram of 29 September 1911, ibid.

94 Conrad von Hötzendorf, record of his conversation with Kageneck on 9 September 1911, Kriegsarchiv Vienna, Conrad-Archiv, B.2 Nr 16 fol. 348. See Günter Kronenbitter, *'Krieg im Frieden'. Die Führung der k. u. k. Armee und die Großmachtpolitik Österreich-Ungarns 1906–1914*, Munich 2003, p. 360.

95 Bienerth to Conrad von Hötzendorf, 12 October 1911, Kriegsarchiv Vienna, Conrad-Archiv B. 2 Nr 16/210, Geh. No. 54/1911; copy in Generalstab Militär-attaché Berlin, 11.

96 Kaiser Wilhelm II, marginal note on Bethmann Hollweg's telegram of 2 November 1911, *Große Politik*, XXIX, No. 10771.

97 Text ibid., No. 10772.

98 *Stenographische Berichte über die Verhandlungen des Reichstages*, 12. Legislaturperiode, 2. Session, Bd. 268, Berlin 1911, p. 7735.

99 Kaiser Wilhelm II, memorandum of 11 January 1912, *Große Politik*, XXXI, No. 11345.

31 'THE ENEMY IDENTIFIED.' THE ACCELERATION OF THE NAVAL RACE
AND THE GROWING MENACE OF WAR

1 Bienerth to Schemua, 15 January 1912, Kriegsarchiv Vienna, Generalstab, Militär-attaché Berlin, Nr 12.

2 Kaiser Wilhelm II to Bethmann Hollweg, 26 September 1911, BA-MA Freiburg-im-Breisgau, RM3/v 9. Cited more fully below, pp. 820–3.

3 Jenisch to Kiderlen, 28 September 1911, *Große Politik*, XXXI, No. 11308; Lerchenfeld to Podewils, 9 November 1911, cited in Epkenhans, *Die wilhelminische Flottenrüstung*, p. 106; Kaiser Wilhelm II, marginal note on the article 'British Royal Visit to Germany' in *The Standard*, 23 September 1911, PA AA R 3715.

4 Kaiser Wilhelm II, marginal comment on Kiderlen's submission of 24 September 1911, *Große Politik*, XXX/1, No. 10830. See also the Kaiser's marginalia on Metternich's report of 22 October 1911, ibid., No. 10905. Further his marginal notes on Marschall's report of 4 December 1911, ibid., No. 10987.

5 See above all Epkenhans, *Die wilhelminische Flottenrüstung*, pp. 93–112. See also Geppert, *Pressekriege*, pp. 289ff.; Mommsen, *Großmachtstellung und Weltpolitik*, pp. 228ff.

6 Tirpitz to Capelle, 12 August 1911, Tirpitz, *Aufbau der deutschen Weltmacht*, pp. 203–6.

7 Kaiser Wilhelm II, marginal note on Metternich's report of 30 August 1911, *Große Politik*, XXXI, No. 11307.

8 Kaiser Wilhelm II, marginal note on an article in *The Times* of 18 August 1911 and also on an article in the *Frankfurter Zeitung* of 20 August 1911, cited ibid., pp. 3f., note.

9 Kaiser Wilhelm II, speech of 27 August 1911, Johannes Penzler, ed., *Die Reden Kaiser Wilhelms II. in den Jahren 1906–1912*, Leipzig 1913, pp. 264–7. See also Obst, *Die politischen Reden*, pp. 343f.; Obst, *'Einer nur ist Herr im Reiche'*, pp. 318-20. Wilhelm's aunt Luise of Baden congratulated him on his 'marvellous' speech: Grand Duchess Luise of Baden to Kaiser Wilhelm II, 28 and 29 August 1911, GStA Berlin, BPHA Rep. 51 W Nr 2a.

10 Kaiser Wilhelm II, marginal note on Bülow's report of 28 August 1911, PA AA R 3691.

11 See above, pp. 618f.

12 Tirpitz, *Aufbau der deutschen Weltmacht*, p. 225.

13 Hopman, diary for 16 November 1911, Epkenhans, *Leben eines 'Wilhelminers'*, pp. 172f.

14 Tirpitz to Bethmann Hollweg, 30 August 1911; notes on a conversation of 31 August 1911, Tirpitz, *Aufbau der deutschen Weltmacht*, pp. 207–9.

15 Tirpitz, notes on a conversation of 1 September 1911, ibid., p. 209.

16 Müller, diary for 13 September 1911, BA-MA Freiburg-im-Breisgau, Müller Papers. See below, p. 819.

17 Müller, diary for 12 September 1911, ibid.

18 Typically August von Heeringen to Tirpitz, 6 December 1911, BA-MA Freiburg-im-Breisgau, RM3/v 9.

19 Müller, diary for 12 September 1911, BA-MA Freiburg-im-Breisgau, Müller Papers. See Hopman, diary for 10 September 1911, Epkenhans, *Leben eines 'Wilhelminers'*, p. 157.

20 Müller, diary for 12 September 1911, BA-MA Freiburg-im-Breisgau, Müller Papers.

21 Ibid.

22 Ibid. See below, p. 825.

23 Müller, diary for 12 September 1911, BA-MA Freiburg-im-Breisgau, Müller Papers. Hürter, *Hintze*, pp. 49f.

24 See Epkenhans, *Die wilhelminische Flottenrüstung*, p. 97.

25 Müller, diary for 13 September 1911, BA-MA Freiburg-im-Breisgau, Müller Papers. See Tirpitz, *Aufbau der deutschen Weltmacht*, pp. 212f.

26 See Capelle to Tirpitz, 11 September 1911, Tirpitz to Capelle, 13 September 1911, ibid., pp. 209–12.

27 Heeringen to Bethmann Hollweg, 7 October 1911, ibid., p. 221; Dähnhardt's memorandum of 16 October 1911, cited in Epkenhans, *Leben eines 'Wilhelminers'*, p. 163, note 43. See Epkenhans, *Die wilhelminische Flottenrüstung*, pp. 98–101. See also Lambi, *Navy and German Power Politics*, pp. 370f.

28 Müller, diary for 25–6 September 1911, BA-MA Freiburg-im-Breisgau, Müller Papers.

29 Müller, 'Leitsätze aus dem Imm. Vortrag des Staatssekretärs d. R.M.A. betr. weitere Flottenvermehrung', 26 September 1911, BA-MA Freiburg-im-Breisgau, RM3/v 9.

30 Müller, draft of an autograph letter from Kaiser Wilhelm II to Bethmann Hollweg, 26 September 1911, ibid. See Jenisch to Bethmann Hollweg, 28 September 1911, *Große Politik*, XXXI, No. 11308.

31 Kaiser Wilhelm II to Bethmann Hollweg, 26 September 1911, BA-MA Freiburg-im-Breisgau, RM3/v 9.

32 Müller, diary for 3 and 4 October 1911, BA-MA Freiburg-im-Breisgau, Müller Papers.

33 Hopman, diary for 2 October 1911, Epkenhans, *Leben eines 'Wilhelminers'*, pp. 158f.

34 Hopman, diary for 5 October 1911, ibid., pp. 160f.

35 See Lambi, *Navy and German Power Politics*, p. 364.

36 Tirpitz, 'Denkschrift über äußerste Zurückhaltung der Immediatbefehlshaber in der Frage der weiteren Entwickelung der Marine', September 1911, cited in Epkenhans, *Leben eines 'Wilhelminers'*, p. 159, note 23.

37 Müller, diary for 27 September 1911, BA-MA Freiburg-im-Breisgau, Müller Papers.

38 Bethmann Hollweg to Heeringen, 4 October 1911, BA-MA Freiburg-im-Breisgau, RM3/v 9; Bethmann Hollweg to Tirpitz, 4 October 1911, Tirpitz, *Aufbau der deutschen Weltmacht*, pp. 218–20.

39 Tirpitz to Bethmann Hollweg, 7 October 1911, Heeringen to Bethmann Hollweg, 7 October 1911, BA-MA Freiburg-im-Breisgau, RM3/v 9, printed in part in Tirpitz, *Aufbau der deutschen Weltmacht*, pp. 220–4.

40 Tirpitz to Kaiser Wilhelm II, 7 October 1911, BA-MA Freiburg-im-Breisgau, RM3/v 9.

41 Holtzendorff to Bethmann Hollweg, 25 October 1911, ibid.

42 Jenisch to Bethmann Hollweg, 28 September 1911, *Große Politik*, XXXI, No. 11308.

43 Kaiser Wilhelm II, marginal notes on Metternich's report of 9 October 1911 and on an article in the *Kreuzzeitung* of 11 October 1911, ibid., No. 11310.

44 Müller, diary for 13 October 1911, BA-MA Freiburg-im-Breisgau, Müller Papers; Görlitz, *Der Kaiser*, pp. 94f.

45 Müller, diary for 14 October 1911, BA-MA Freiburg-im-Breisgau, Müller Papers.

46 Ibid. Cf. Tirpitz, *Aufbau der deutschen Weltmacht*, p. 226.

47 Müller, diary for 14 October 1911, BA-MA Freiburg-im-Breisgau, Müller Papers.

48 Müller, diary for 15 October 1911, ibid.

49 Müller, diary for 14 October 1911, ibid.

50 Müller, diary for 15 and 17 October 1911, ibid.

51 Hopman, diary for 15 October 1911, Epkenhans, *Leben eines 'Wilhelminers'*, p. 162.

52 Müller to Tirpitz, 15 October 1911, Tirpitz, *Aufbau der deutschen Weltmacht*, p. 226.

53 Hopman, diary for 16 October 1911, Epkenhans, *Leben eines 'Wilhelminers'*, pp. 162f.

54 Müller, diary for 28 October 1911, BA-MA Freiburg-im-Breisgau, Müller Papers; Müller, 'Notiz zum Immediatvortrag mit Randbemerkung Tirpitz', ibid., RM3/v 9; Epkenhans, *Leben eines 'Wilhelminers'*, p. 166, note 59. See Tirpitz to August von Heeringen, 15 December 1911, BA-MA Freiburg-im-Breisgau, Admiralstab.

55 Müller, diary for 3 November 1911, BA-MA Freiburg-im-Breisgau, Müller Papers.

56 Müller, diary for 4 November 1911, ibid.

57 Hopman, diary for 4 November 1911, Epkenhans, *Leben eines 'Wilhelminers'*, p. 168.

58 Hopman, diary for 10 November 1911, ibid., p. 170.

59 See *Stenographische Berichte über die Verhandlungen des Reichstages*, 9 and 10 November 1911, 12. Legislaturperiode, II Session, Bd. 268, pp. 7723–30.

60 Tirpitz, *Aufbau der deutschen Weltmacht*, pp. 229 and 256f.

61 See Hopman's biting comments in Epkenhans, *Leben eines 'Wilhelminers'*, pp. 170f.

62 Varnbüler to Weizsäcker, 3 December 1911, cited in Epkenhans, *Die wilhelminische Flottenrüstung*, p. 107, note 94. Also Lerchenfeld to Podewils, 9 November 1911, cited ibid., p. 106.

63 Kaiser Wilhelm II to Bethmann Hollweg, 11 November 1911, *Große Politik*, XXXI, No. 11319.

64 Tirpitz, *Aufbau der deutschen Weltmacht*, p. 229.

65 Kaiser Wilhelm II to Tirpitz, 11 November 1911, Tirpitz, *Aufbau der deutschen Weltmacht*, pp. 228f.

66 Tirpitz, memorandum of 14 November 1911, ibid., pp. 256f.

67 Müller, diary for 14 November 1911, BA-MA Freiburg-im-Breisgau, Müller Papers.

68 Tirpitz, *Aufbau der deutschen Weltmacht*, p. 257; Müller to Tirpitz, 15 November 1911, BA-MA Freiburg-im-Breisgau, RM2/1764; Hopman, diary for 15 November 1911, Epkenhans, *Leben eines 'Wilhelminers'*, p. 172.

69 Müller to Valentini, 16 November 1911, ibid., p. 172, note 88.

70 Müller, diary for 14 and 15 November 1911, BA-MA Freiburg-im-Breisgau, Müller Papers.

71 Müller, diary for 28 November 1911, ibid.; Görlitz, *Der Kaiser*, p. 100. See below, pp. 835ff.

72 Bethmann Hollweg to Kaiser Wilhelm II, 28 November 1911, Epkenhans, *Leben eines 'Wilhelminers'*, p. 176, note 100; Tirpitz, *Aufbau der deutschen Weltmacht*, p. 261.

73 Bethmann Hollweg to Josias von Heeringen, 4 December 1911, BA-MA Freiburg-im-Breisgau, RM3/v 9; cf. Tirpitz, *Aufbau der deutschen Weltmacht*, p. 265; Hopman, diary for 29 and 30 November, 1–4 December 1911, Epkenhans, *Leben eines 'Wilhelminers'*, pp. 176–8. Also Epkenhans, *Die wilhelminische Flottenrüstung*, pp. 103f. See below, pp. 860–2.

74 Müller, diary for 29 November 1911, BA-MA Freiburg-im-Breisgau, Müller Papers. Cf. Görlitz, *Der Kaiser*, p. 101.

75 Müller, diary for 9 December 1911, BA-MA Freiburg-im-Breisgau, Müller Papers. See Lerchenfeld to Podewils, 11 December 1911, cited in Lambi, *Navy and German Power Politics*, pp. 369f.

76 Kaiser Wilhelm II to Müller, 9 December 1911, BA-MA Freiburg-im-Breisgau, RM3/v 9, printed in Tirpitz, *Aufbau der deutschen Weltmacht*, pp. 263–5.

77 Müller, diary for 9 December 1911, BA-MA Freiburg-im-Breisgau, Müller Papers.

78 Müller, diary for 23 and 24 December 1911, ibid.

79 Müller, diary for 26 December 1911, ibid.

80 Müller, diary for 6 and 9 January 1912, ibid.

81 Müller, diary for 9 January 1912, ibid.

82 Müller, diary for 10 January 1912, ibid.

83 Müller, diary for 15 January 1912, ibid.

84 See Tirpitz, *Aufbau der deutschen Weltmacht*, pp. 268–79.

85 Churchill to Grey, 31 January 1912, cited in R. S. Churchill, *Winston S. Churchill, II, Companion Part 3, 1911–14*, London 1969, p. 1504. See also Nicholas A. Lambert, *Sir John Fisher's Naval Revolution*, Columbia, SC 2002, pp. 249–52.

86 Grey to McKenna, 15 September 1911, Grey to Nicolson, 17 September 1911, Gooch and Temperley, *British Documents*, VII, Nos. 646–7.

87 Arthur J. Marder, ed., *Fear God and Dread Nought. The Correspondence of Admiral of the Fleet Lord Fisher of Kilverstone*, 3 vols., London 1952–9, II, p. 419.

88 Varnbüler to Weizsäcker, 3 December 1911, cited in Epkenhans, *Die wilhelminische Flottenrüstung*, p. 108.

32 'ALREADY LEADER OF THE UNITED STATES OF EUROPE?'
WILHELM AND THE DEBACLE OF THE HALDANE MISSION

1 On the Haldane Mission see Canis, *Abgrund*, pp. 459–79; Forsbach, *Kiderlen-Wächter*, II, pp. 579ff.; Mommsen, *Großmachtstellung und Weltpolitik*, pp. 228ff.; Cecil, *Wilhelm II: Emperor and Exile*, pp. 170ff.; Fischer, *Krieg der Illusionen*, pp. 182ff.; Stephen E. Koss, *Lord Haldane. Scapegoat for Liberalism*, New York and London 1969, pp. 65ff.; Massie, *Dreadnought*, pp. 790–817.

2 Widenmann, reports of 14, 28 and 30 October 1911, with the Kaiser's marginalia, printed in Tirpitz, *Aufbau der deutschen Weltmacht*, pp. 229–35.

3 Kaiser Wilhelm II, marginal note on Bethmann Hollweg's submission of 24 November 1911, *Große Politik*, XXXI, No. 11322. See the Kaiser's marginal notes on the article 'Die Voraussetzungen der britischen Politik' by Carl Peters in *Der Tag* of 7 January 1912, BA-MA Freiburg-im-Breisgau, Tirpitz Papers, N 253/26a.

4 Müller, diary for 28 November 1911, BA-MA Freiburg-im-Breisgau, Müller Papers; Görlitz, *Der Kaiser*, p. 100.

5 Metternich, reports of 1 and 24 November 1911 with the Kaiser's marginalia, *Große Politik*, XXXI, No. 11316 and XXIX, No. 10660. See ibid., No. 10653, and Tirpitz, *Aufbau der deutschen Weltmacht*, pp. 235–42.

6 Kaiser Wilhelm II to Bethmann Hollweg, *Große Politik*, XXXI, No. 11323.

7 Kaiser Wilhelm II, marginal comments on Metternich's report of 28 November 1911, ibid., No. 10662.

8 Hopman, diary for 28 and 30 October and 28 November 1911, Epkenhans, *Leben eines 'Wilhelminers'*, pp. 166f. and 175.

9 Kaiser Wilhelm II to Archduke Franz Ferdinand, 6 December 1911, MOL Budapest, 183 db, XI, 17. Cf. Kann, 'Wilhelm II. und Franz Ferdinand in ihrer Korrespondenz', p. 74.

10 Kaiser Wilhelm II, marginal notes on Marschall's report of 4 December 1911, *Große Politik*, XXX/1, No. 10985. See also Kaiser Wilhelm II, marginalia of 12 December 1911 on Bethmann Hollweg's submission of 11 December 1911, ibid., No. 10993.

11 Kaiser Wilhelm II, marginal comments on Metternich's report of 20 December 1911, ibid., No. 11344.

12 Kaiser Wilhelm II, marginal comments on the article 'German Expansion' in the *Spectator* of 9 December 1911, BA-MA Freiburg-im-Breisgau, Tirpitz Papers N 253/26a. For the colonial aspects of the Haldane mission see Michael Fröhlich, *Von Konfrontation zur Koexistenz: die deutsch-englischen Kolonialbeziehungen in Afrika zwischen 1884 und 1914*, Bochum 1990, pp. 294f.

13 Kaiser Wilhelm II, marginal notes on Kühlmann's report of 8 January 1912, *Große Politik*, XXXI, No. 11345.

14 Kaiser Wilhelm II, comments on Kühlmann's report of 11 January 1912, ibid., No. 11346, copy in BA-MA Freiburg-im-Breisgau, Tirpitz Papers, N 253/26a.

15 Müller, diary for 10 and 11 January 1912, BA-MA Freiburg-im-Breisgau, Müller Papers.

16 Müller, diary for 7 February 1912, ibid.; cf. Görlitz, *Der Kaiser*, p. 112.

17 Lamar Cecil, *Albert Ballin. Business and Politics in Imperial Germany, 1888–1918*, Princeton NJ 1967, p. 182; Jonathan Steinberg, 'Diplomatie als Wille und Vorstellung: Die Berliner Mission Lord Haldanes im February 1912', in Herbert Schottelius and Wilhelm Deist, *Marine und Marinepolitik im kaiserlichen Deutschland 1871–1914*, Düsseldorf 1972, pp. 263–82.

18 Kaiser Wilhelm II, marginal notes on Metternich's telegram of 12 February 1912, *Große Politik*, XXXI, No. 11366. See also Wilhelm's marginalia on Tirpitz's letter to him of 9 October 1917, ibid., No. 11426.

19 Görlitz, *Der Kaiser*, p. 102.

20 Kaiser Wilhelm II, marginal comment on the article 'The Foundations of British Policy, VI. Towards an Anglo-German Détente' in the *Westminster Gazette* of 20 December 1911, forwarded by Müller to Bethmann Hollweg on 8 January 1912, Niedersächsisches Staatsarchiv Bückeburg, Trotha Papers, Depos. 18 A 226. See Eyck, *Das Persönliche Regiment Wilhelms II.*, p. 593.

21 Churchill to Cassel, 8 January 1912, Cassel to Ballin, 9 January 1912, Steinberg, 'Diplomatie als Wille und Vorstellung', p. 274.

22 Churchill to Cassel, 26 January 1912, Cassel, 'Aufzeichnungen', 27 to 30 January 1912, *Große Politik*, XXXI, No. 11347 annex II. The British memorandum is printed ibid., No. 11347. See Steinberg, 'Diplomatie als Wille und Vorstellung', pp. 274f.

23 Müller, diary for 29 January 1912, BA-MA Freiburg-im-Breisgau, Müller Papers.

24 Ibid.

25 Müller, diary for 31 January 1912, BA-MA Freiburg-im-Breisgau, Müller Papers. Cf. Görlitz, *Der Kaiser*, pp. 110f.

26 Müller, diary for 3 February 1912, ibid. Cf. Görlitz, *Der Kaiser*, p. 111.

27 Kaiser Wilhelm II, marginal notes on Tirpitz's letter to him of 9 October 1917, *Große Politik*, XXXI, No. 11426.

28 Kaiser Wilhelm II to Auswärtiges Amt, 4 February 1912, Tirpitz, *Aufbau der deutschen Weltmacht*, pp. 280f. See *Große Politik*, XXXI, No. 11347 annex II.

29 Müller, diary for 4 February 1912, BA-MA Freiburg-im-Breisgau, Müller Papers.

30 Ibid.

31 Tirpitz to Müller, 25 February 1912, BA-MA Freiburg-im-Breisgau, Tirpitz Papers, N 253/26a; quoted in part in Steinberg, 'Diplomatie als Wille und Vorstellung', p. 276.

32 Kaiser Wilhelm II to Tirpitz, 5 February 1912, Tirpitz, *Aufbau der deutschen Weltmacht*, p. 281.

33 Kaiser Wilhelm II, notes for Tirpitz of 6 February 1912, ibid., p. 283f.

34 Kaiser Wilhelm II, comments on Kühlmann's report of 11 January 1912, *Große Politik*, XXXI, No. 11346, copy in BA-MA Freiburg-im-Breisgau, Tirpitz Papers, N 253/26a. See above, pp. 842–4.

35 Müller, diary for 7 February 1912, BA-MA Freiburg-im-Breisgau, Müller Papers. Cf. Görlitz, *Der Kaiser*, p. 112. See above, p. 844.

36 Tirpitz, record of the conversation with Haldane on 9 February 1912, BA-MA Freiburg-im-Breisgau, Tirpitz Papers N 253/179. Cf. Tirpitz, *Aufbau der deutschen Weltmacht*, pp. 286–9.

37 Nicolson, memorandum for King George V of 15 September 1911, RA GV/M 160A.

38 Nicolson to Bertie, 8 February 1912, Cedric James Lowe and Michael Lawrence Dockrill, eds., *The Mirage of Power: British Foreign Policy, 1902–22*, 3 vols., London 1972, III, p. 451. See also the minutes by Nicolson and Crowe of 12 February 1912, Gooch and Temperley, *British Documents*, VI, pp. 506f.

39 See Steinberg, 'Diplomatie als Wille und Vorstellung', pp. 276f.

40 'Diary of Lord Haldane's Visit to Berlin', 8 February 1912, RA GV/M 450/11, printed in Gooch and Temperley, *British Documents*, VI/2, No. 506.

41 Cassel to Kaiser Wilhelm II, delivered by Ballin on 7 February 1912, Tirpitz, *Aufbau der deutschen Weltmacht*, pp. 281f.

42 'Diary of Lord Haldane's Visit to Berlin', 8 February 1912, RA GV/M 450/11, printed in Gooch and Temperley, *British Documents*, VI/2, No. 506.

43 Bethmann Hollweg, memorandum of 12 February 1912 on the negotiations with Lord Haldane, *Große Politik*, XXXI, No. 11362. See Fischer, *Krieg der Illusionen*, pp. 182ff.

44 'Diary of Lord Haldane's Visit to Berlin', 8 February 1912, RA GV/M 450/11, printed in Gooch and Temperley, *British Documents*, VI/2, No. 506; Bethmann Hollweg, memorandum of 12 February 1912, *Große Politik*, XXXI, No. 11362–3; Bethmann Hollweg to Metternich, 12 February 1912, ibid., No. 11364.

45 Tirpitz, notes of 9 February 1912, BA-MA Freiburg-im-Breisgau, Tirpitz Papers, N 253/26a; printed in Tirpitz, *Aufbau der deutschen Weltmacht*, p. 284.

46 Tirpitz to Müller, 8 February 1912, ibid., p. 282. See also Tirpitz to Kaiser Wilhelm II, 9 October 1917, *Große Politik*, XXXI, No. 11426. Also the article 'Lord Haldane and Germany' in the *Manchester Guardian*, 1 September 1917.

47 Kaiser Wilhelm II, marginal notes on Ballin's letter of 8 February 1912, *Große Politik*, XXXI, No. 11358.

48 Kaiser Wilhelm II to Müller, 9 February 1912, cited according to the copy in Admiral von Müller's hand in Tirpitz Papers, BA-MA Freiburg-im-Breisgau, N 253/26a, printed in Tirpitz, *Aufbau der deutschen Weltmacht*, pp. 285f.

49 Müller, diary for 8–9 February 1912, BA-MA Freiburg-im-Breisgau, Müller Papers; 'Diary of Lord Haldane's Visit to Berlin', 9 February 1912, RA GV/M 450/11.

50 Müller, diary for 8–9 February 1912, BA-MA Freiburg-im-Breisgau, Müller Papers.

51 Kaiser Wilhelm II to Bethmann Hollweg, 9 February 1912, *Große Politik*, XXXI, No. 11359.

52 Kaiser Wilhelm II to Ballin, 9 February 1912, cited in Bernhard Huldermann, *Albert Ballin*, Oldenburg, 1922, pp. 256f.

53 'Diary of Lord Haldane's Visit to Berlin', 9 February 1912, RA GV/M 450/11, printed in Gooch and Temperley, *British Documents*, VI/2, No. 506.

54 Müller, diary for 10 February 1912, BA-MA Freiburg-im-Breisgau, Müller Papers; Görlitz, *Der Kaiser*, pp. 113f.

55 Rathenau, diary for 13 February 1912, as quoted in Rathenau, *Tagebuch*, pp. 156f. Cf. Haldane to his mother, 11 February 1912, as quoted in Dudley Sommer, *Haldane of Cloane. His Life and Times, 1856–1928*, London 1960, p. 263.

56 Tirpitz, notes on his audience with the Kaiser on 24 February 1912, BA-MA Freiburg-im-Breisgau, Tirpitz Papers N 253/26a. Cf. Tirpitz, *Aufbau der deutschen Weltmacht*, pp. 295f.

57 Müller, note of 24 February 1912, BA-MA Freiburg-im-Breisgau, Tirpitz Papers N 253/26a; Müller, diary for 24 February 1912, BA-MA Freiburg-im-Breisgau, Müller Papers; Görlitz, *Der Kaiser*, p. 114.

58 Tirpitz, notes on his conversation with Kiderlen on 22 February 1912; Müller to Kaiser Wilhelm II, 23 February 1912, BA-MA Freiburg-im-Breisgau, Tirpitz Papers N 253/26a. See Tirpitz, *Aufbau der deutschen Weltmacht*, pp. 290–2.

59 Müller, diary for 22 February 1912, BA-MA Freiburg-im-Breisgau, Müller Papers; Görlitz, *Der Kaiser*, p. 114.

60 Kaiser Wilhelm II, marginal note on Bethmann Hollweg's submission of 19 February 1912, Tirpitz, *Aufbau der deutschen Weltmacht*, p. 294.

61 Kaiser Wilhelm II to Kiderlen-Wächter, 24 February 1912, copy in BA-MA Freiburg-im-Breisgau, Tirpitz Papers N 253/26a, printed in Tirpitz, *Aufbau der deutschen Weltmacht*, pp. 292f.

62 Kiderlen-Wächter to Kaiser Wilhelm II, 24 February 1912, copy in BA-MA Freiburg-im-Breisgau, RM3/v 9, also in Tirpitz Papers N 253/26a.

63 Metternich, report of 22 February 1912, Tirpitz, *Aufbau der deutschen Weltmacht*, pp. 296–8.

64 Müller to Kaiser Wilhelm II, 25 February 1912, copy in BA-MA Freiburg-im-Breisgau, Tirpitz Papers, N 253/26a.

65 Müller, diary for 25 February 1912, BA-MA Freiburg-im-Breisgau, Müller Papers; cf. Görlitz, *Der Kaiser*, p. 114.

66 Tirpitz to Müller, 26 February 1912, BA-MA Freiburg-im-Breisgau, RM3/v 9; copy ibid., Tirpitz Papers, N 253/26a, printed in Tirpitz, *Aufbau der deutschen Weltmacht*, pp. 298–300.

67 Müller to Tirpitz, 26 February 1912, BA-MA Freiburg-im-Breisgau, Tirpitz Papers N 253/26b; Müller, diary for 26 February 1912, BA-MA Freiburg-im-Breisgau, Müller Papers.

68 Kaiser Wilhelm II to Bethmann Hollweg, 26 February 1912, copy in BA-MA Freiburg-im-Breisgau, RM3/v 9, also in Tirpitz Papers N 253/26a, printed in Tirpitz, *Aufbau der deutschen Weltmacht*, pp. 301f.

69 Kaiser Wilhelm II, marginalia on Metternich's report of 24 February 1912, copy in BA-MA Freiburg-im-Breisgau, RM3/v 9, printed in Tirpitz, *Aufbau der deutschen Weltmacht*, pp. 302f.; *Große Politik*, XXXI, No. 11374.

70 Kaiser Wilhelm II to Bethmann Hollweg, 27 February 1912, copy in BA-MA Freiburg-im-Breisgau, RM3/v 9, also ibid., Tirpitz Papers N 253/26b, printed in Tirpitz, *Aufbau der deutschen Weltmacht*, pp. 306–8.

71 Valentini, diary for 28 February 1912, BA Koblenz, Thimme Papers, Nr 26. See also: Müller, diary for 5 March 1912, BA-MA Freiburg-im-Breisgau, Müller Papers; Görlitz, *Der Kaiser*, p. 116.

72 Müller, diary for 27–8 February 1912, BA-MA Freiburg-im-Breisgau, Müller Papers; cf. Görlitz, *Der Kaiser*, p. 115.

73 Korvettenkapitän Karl von Müller to Widenmann, 4 March 1912 with marginal notes by Tirpitz, BA-MA Freiburg-im-Breisgau, Tirpitz Papers N 253/26b; cf. Tirpitz, *Aufbau der deutschen Weltmacht*, pp. 314f.

74 Bethmann Hollweg to Kaiser Wilhelm II, 28 February 1912, BA-MA Freiburg-im-Breisgau, Tirpitz Papers N 253/26b, printed in Tirpitz, *Aufbau der deutschen Weltmacht*, pp. 306–8. See Bethmann Hollweg to Metternich, 4 March 1912, *Große Politik*, XXXI, No. 11381.

75 Bethmann Hollweg to Kaiser Wilhelm II, 4 March 1912, with the Kaiser's marginal notes, copy in BA-MA Freiburg-im-Breisgau, Tirpitz Papers N 253/26b; cf. *Große Politik*, XXXI, No. 11382.

76 Kaiser Wilhelm II to Bethmann Hollweg, 4 March 1912, *Große Politik*, XXXI, p. 153, note.

77 Kaiser Wilhelm II to Bethmann Hollweg, 4 March 1912, ibid., No. 11383.

78 Kaiser Wilhelm II to Bethmann Hollweg, 5 March 1912, ibid., No. 11386. Cf. Tirpitz, *Aufbau der deutschen Weltmacht*, p. 317.

79 Kaiser Wilhelm II to Metternich, 5 March 1912, copy in BA-MA Freiburg-im-Breisgau, Tirpitz Papers N 253/26b, printed in Tirpitz, *Aufbau der deutschen Weltmacht*, p. 317.

80 Metternich, report of 1 March 1912, copy in BA-MA Freiburg-im-Breisgau, Tirpitz Papers N 253/26b, printed in Tirpitz, *Aufbau der deutschen Weltmacht*, pp. 308–10; *Große Politik*, XXXI, No. 11380.

81 Kaiser Wilhelm II, marginal comments on Metternich's report of 1 March 1912, copy in BA-MA Freiburg-im-Breisgau, Tirpitz Papers N 253/26b, printed in Tirpitz, *Aufbau der deutschen Weltmacht*, pp. 308–10; *Große Politik*, XXXI, No. 11380.

82 Kaiser Wilhelm II to Bethmann Hollweg, 5 March 1912, copy in BA-MA Freiburg-im-Breisgau, Tirpitz Papers N 253/26b, printed in *Große Politik*, XXXI, No. 11385.

83 Kaiser Wilhelm II to Metternich, 5 March 1912, copy in BA-MA Freiburg-im-Breisgau, Tirpitz Papers N 253/26b, printed in *Große Politik*, XXXI, No. 11387.

84 Müller, diary for 5 March 1912, BA-MA Freiburg-im-Breisgau, Müller Papers; cf. Görlitz, *Der Kaiser*, p. 116.

85 Rathenau, diary for 16 February 1912, Rathenau, *Tagebuch*, p. 158.

86 Bethmann Hollweg to Kaiser Wilhelm II, 6 March 1912, printed in Tirpitz, *Aufbau der deutschen Weltmacht*, pp. 318–20.

87 Müller, diary for 7 March 1912, BA-MA Freiburg-im-Breisgau, Müller Papers; cf. Görlitz, *Der Kaiser*, p. 116.

88 Kaiser Wilhelm II, marginal notes on Metternich's report of 7 March 1912, *Große Politik*, XXXI, No. 11392; cf. Tirpitz, *Aufbau der deutschen Weltmacht*, p. 321.

89 Müller, diary for 9 March 1912, BA-MA Freiburg-im-Breisgau, Müller Papers; cf. Görlitz, *Der Kaiser*, p. 117.

90 Tirpitz to Müller, 10 March 1912, Tirpitz, *Aufbau der deutschen Weltmacht*, pp. 322–4.

91 Tirpitz, record of his conversation with Kaiser Wilhelm II on 11 March 1912, BA-MA Freiburg-im-Breisgau, Tirpitz Papers N 253/26b, printed in Tirpitz, *Aufbau der deutschen Weltmacht*, pp. 324f.

92 Kaiser Wilhelm II, marginal notes on Bethmann Hollweg's submission of 12 March 1912, as cited in *Große Politik*, XXXI, No. 11393; cf. the version printed in Tirpitz, *Aufbau der deutschen Weltmacht*, pp. 325f. See also the Kaiser's marginal notes on Bethmann Hollweg's submission of 14 March 1912, ibid., pp. 326f., and Kaiser Wilhelm II to Valentini, 14 March 1912, BA Koblenz, Valentini Papers, Kl. Erw. Nr 341-2.

93 Müller, diary for 17 March 1912, BA-MA Freiburg-im-Breisgau, Müller Papers; cf. Görlitz, *Der Kaiser*, p. 117.

94 Haldane, minute of 12 March 1912, 'Very Secret', RA GV/M 450/14.

95 Tyrrell to Knollys, 13 March 1912, RA GV/M 450/10.

96 Metternich to Auswärtiges Amt, 14 March 1912, *Große Politik*, XXXI, No. 11399.

97 Grey to Goschen, 15 March 1912, RA VIC/Add C 07/2/Q, printed in Gooch and Temperley, *British Documents*, VI/2, No. 539.

98 Grey to Goschen, 16 March 1912, RA VIC/Add C 07/2/Q, printed in Gooch and Temperley, *British Documents*, VI/2, No. 544.

99 Müller, diary for 17 March 1912, BA-MA Freiburg-im-Breisgau, Müller Papers; cf. Görlitz, *Der Kaiser*, pp. 117f.

100 Müller to Tirpitz, 18 March 1912, BA-MA Freiburg-im-Breisgau, Tirpitz Papers N 253/26b; Tirpitz, *Aufbau der deutschen Weltmacht*, p. 328.

101 Kaiser Wilhelm II, marginal notes on Metternich's report of 17 March 1912, *Große Politik*, XXXI, No. 11403-4.

102 Bethmann Hollweg to Kaiser Wilhelm II, 17 March 1912, ibid., No. 11405.

103 Kaiser Wilhelm II, marginal comment of 18 March 1912 on Bethmann Hollweg's submission of 17 March 1912, ibid. Cf. the Kaiser's marginal notes on Metternich's telegram of 19 March 1912, ibid., No. 11410. Also Müller, diary for 18 March 1912, BA-MA Freiburg-im-Breisgau, Müller Papers; cf. Görlitz, *Der Kaiser*, p. 118.

104 Müller, diary for 18 March 1912, BA-MA Freiburg-im-Breisgau, Müller Papers; cf. Görlitz, *Der Kaiser*, p. 118. Tirpitz, memorandum on his audience with the Kaiser on 18 March 1912, Tirpitz, *Aufbau der deutschen Weltmacht*, pp. 329–31. See the instruction the Kaiser drafted on 18 March for Metternich but did not send off, *Große Politik*, XXXI, pp. 187f.

105 Tirpitz, *Aufbau der deutschen Weltmacht*, pp. 328f. See Müller, diary for 19 March 1912, BA-MA Freiburg-im-Breisgau, Müller Papers; cf. Görlitz, *Der Kaiser*, p. 119.

106 Kaiser Wilhelm II to King George V, 18 March 1912, printed in Tirpitz, *Aufbau der deutschen Weltmacht*, pp. 331f.

107 Fürstenberg, diary entry for 1 April 1912, quoted in Winzen, *Freundesliebe am Hof Kaiser Wilhelms II.*, p. 85.

108 Kaiser Wilhelm II, marginal comment of 31 March 1912 on Bethmann Hollweg's submission of 28 March 1912, *Große Politik*, XXXI, No. 11422, annex.

109 Ibid.

110 Valentini to his wife, 23 and 29 March 1912, BA Koblenz, Valentini Papers, Kl. Erw. 341-3.

111 Kaiser Wilhelm II to Mary Montagu, 7 May 1912, copy in the author's private archive.

112 Valentini to Bethmann Hollweg, 2 May 1912, GStA Berlin, Valentini Papers, Nr 2.

113 Ibid.

114 Müller to Tirpitz, 23 April 1912, BA-MA Freiburg-im-Breisgau, Tirpitz Papers N 253/26b.

115 Kaiser Wilhelm II to Auswärtiges Amt, 24 April 1912, PA AA R 3477.

116 Colonel Pomiankowski, report of 4 May 1912, Kriegsarchiv Vienna, 14/476ff.

117 Kaiser Wilhelm II, marginal notes of 12 December 1911 on Bethmann Hollweg's submission of 11 December 1911, *Große Politik*, XXX/1, No. 10993; cf. ibid., No. 10985.

118 Pomiankowski, report of 4 May 1912, Kriegsarchiv Vienna, 14/476ff.

119 Pomiankowski, report of 9 June 1912, ibid., 14/498ff.

120 Marschall's death gave rise to much comment. Cf. Grand Duchess Luise of Baden to Kaiser Wilhelm II, 24 September 1912, GStA Berlin, BPHA Rep. 51 W Nr 2a; Hereditary Princess Charlotte of Saxe-Meiningen to Schweninger, 1 October 1912, BA Berlin, Schweninger Papers, 90 Sch 4, Nr 132/142ff.; Harden to Rathenau, 24 September 1912, Hellige and Schulin, *Briefwechsel Rathenau-Harden*, No. 355.

121 Bethmann Hollweg to Kaiser Wilhelm II, 25 September 1912, GStA Berlin, BPHA Rep. 53J Lit. B Nr 7.

122 Winzen, *Im Schatten Wilhelms II.*, pp. 474ff.

123 Ibid.

124 Kaiser Wilhelm II to Bethmann Hollweg, 30 September 1912, ibid.

125 Kaiser Wilhelm II, marginal notes of 4 October 1912 on Bethmann Hollweg's submission of 3 October 1912, ibid., printed in part in John C. G. Röhl, *Zwei deutsche Fürsten zur Kriegsschuldfrage. Lichnowsky und Eulenburg und der Ausbruch des Ersten Weltkriegs. Eine Dokumentation*, Düsseldorf 1971, p. 16. Cf. Hans-Günter Zmarzlik, *Bethmann Hollweg als Reichskanzler 1909–1914. Studien zu Möglichkeiten und Grenzen seiner innerpolitischen Machtstellung*, Düsseldorf 1957, p. 28.

126 Lichnowsky to Kaiser Wilhelm II, 11 October 1912, Bethmann Hollweg, 11 October 1912, GStA Berlin, Rep. 53 E III Nr 8. See Zmarzlik, *Bethmann Hollweg*, p. 38, note 1.

127 Kaiser Wilhelm II, marginal notes on an article in the *Daily Express* of 27 May 1912 and on the article 'Das deutsch-englische Problem' in the *Frankfurter Zeitung* of 26 May 1912, *Große Politik*, XXXI, No. 11424 with note.

128 Kaiser Wilhelm II, marginal notes of 4 October 1912 on Bethmann Hollweg's submission of 3 October 1912, GStA Berlin, BPHA Rep. 53J Lit. B Nr 7, printed in part in Röhl, *Zwei deutsche Fürsten zur Kriegsschuldfrage*, p. 16. Cf. Zmarzlik, *Bethmann Hollweg*, p. 28.

129 Reischach to Fürstenberg, 2 January 1913, FFA Donaueschingen.

33   NOVEMBER 1912: THE STRATEGIC SWITCH FROM WEST TO EAST

1 See Forsbach, *Kiderlen-Wächter*, II, pp. 541ff.; Fischer, *Krieg der Illusionen*, pp. 137ff.

2 See above, pp. 798f.

3 Heinrich Claß, 'West-Marokko deutsch!', *Flugschriften des Alldeutschen Verbandes*, No. 29, Munich 1911. The passage omitted in the printed text is quoted in Willibald Gutsche, ed., *Herrschaftsmethoden des deutschen Imperialismus 1897/98 bis 1917*, Berlin 1977, p. 144.

4 Daniel Frymann [i. e. Heinrich Claß], *Wenn ich der Kaiser wär'. Politische Wahrheiten und Notwendigkeiten*, Leipzig 1912, cf. Roger Chickering, 'Die Alldeutschen erwarten den Krieg', in Dülffer and Holl, *Bereit zum Krieg*, p. 25. See also Peters, *Der Alldeutsche Verband am Vorabend des Ersten Weltkrieges.*

5 Friedrich von Bernhardi, *Deutschland und der nächste Krieg*, Berlin 1912.

6 See Bienerth to Schemua, 15 January 1912, cited above, p. 814.

7 Holger Afflerbach, *Falkenhayn. Politisches Denken und Handeln im Kaiserreich*, Munich 1994, p. 76.

8 Ibid., pp. 78f.

9 Spitzemberg, diary for 2 August 1911, Vierhaus, *Tagebuch*, p. 531.

10 Hopman, diary for 23 August 1911, Epkenhans, *Leben eines 'Wilhelminers'*, pp. 156f.

11 Crown Prince Wilhelm to Kaiser Wilhelm II, 5 November 1911, GStA Berlin, 2.2.1 Nr 670/1.

12 Crown Prince Wilhelm to Kaiser Wilhelm II, 31 December 1911, GStA Berlin, BPHA Rep. 54 Nr 18.

13 Bienerth to Conrad von Hötzendorf, 11 November 1911, Kriegsarchiv Vienna, Generalstab Militär-attaché Berlin, Nr 11. See also Conrad's memorandum on his audience with Emperor Franz Joseph on 15 November 1911, during which the monarch expressed his dismay at the German Crown Prince's behaviour towards parliament. Ibid., Conrad-Archiv B 2 Nr 16 fol. 362f.

14 Müller to Bethmann Hollweg, 25 December 1912, PA AA R 3744; Gutsche, *Wilhelm II.*, p. 148.

15 General Sir John French, 'Conversations with the German Emperor', 2 and 3 August 1911, National Archives Kew, FO 800/107. I thank Dr Ragnhild Fiebig-von Hase for drawing my attention to this source.

16 Knollys to Esher, 24 and 27 August 1911, Cambridge University Library, Esher Papers ESHR 10/52.

17 Müller, diary for 14 October 1911, BA-MA Freiburg-im-Breisgau, Müller Papers, cited above, p. 829.

18 Kaiser Wilhelm II, marginal notes on an article by Zorn in the *Kölnische Zeitung*, 30 December 1911, Niedersächsisches Staatsarchiv Bückeburg, Trotha Papers, E Nr 2.

19 Reinhold Koser, *Geschichte Friedrichs des Großen*, 4 vols., Berlin 1912–14.

20 Kaiser Wilhelm II, speech of 24 January 1912, BA-MA Freiburg-im-Breisgau, Tirpitz Papers, N 253/26. I thank Professor Michael Epkenhans for showing me this document.

21 Kaiser Wilhelm II, marginal note on an article in the *Leipziger Tageblatt* of 27 January 1912, PA AA R 3477, cited in Gutsche, *Wilhelm II.*, p. 142. See also Mackensen's speech of 27 January 1912, BA-MA Freiburg-im-Breisgau, Mackensen Papers, N 39/441.

22 Colonel Sir A. Davidson, record of a conversation with the King of Greece, 1 June 1912, RA GV/M 450/16.

23 Kaiser Wilhelm II to Moltke, 23 May 1912, GStA Berlin, BPHA Rep 53J, Lit. T Nr 1.

24 Critique of His Majesty the Kaiser at the end of the manoeuvres of 1912, BA-MA Freiburg-im-Breisgau, Moltke Papers, N78/23.

25 Colonel Sir A. Davidson, record of a conversation with the King of Greece, 1 June 1912, RA GV/M 450/16.

26 Kaiser Wilhelm II, marginal note on Bethmann Hollweg's submission of 29 June 1912, PA AA R 3634.

27 Kaiser Wilhelm II, marginal comments on Pourtalès's telegram of 29 June 1912, PA AA R 3634.

28 Kaiser Wilhelm II to Emperor Franz Joseph, 6 July 1912, *Große Politik*, XXXI, No. 11541. See the response of Kiderlen in Jäckh, *Kiderlen-Wächter*, II, p. 152.

29 See Von der Goltz to Lyncker, 14 September 1912, BA-MA Freiburg-im-Breisgau, von der Goltz Papers, N 737 Zug. 228/95.

30 Kaiser Wilhelm II, marginal comments on Zimmermann's telegram of 4 August 1912, *Große Politik*, XXXIII, No. 12079.

31 *Große Politik*, XXXIII, pp. 42f., note.

32 Jenisch to Bethmann Hollweg, 1 and 2 October 1912, PA AA R 3477.

33 Kaiser Wilhelm II, marginal note on Bethmann Hollweg's telegram of 1 October 1912, *Große Politik*, XXXIII, No. 12192.

34 Holzing-Berstett to his wife, 1 October 1912, GLA Karlsruhe, Holzing-Berstett Papers, 69 Zug. 1989 Nr 116/19.

35 Jenisch to Bethmann Hollweg, 1 October 1912, PA AA R 3477.

36 Bethmann Hollweg to Jenisch, 1 October 1912, PA AA R 3477.

37 Jenisch to Bethmann Hollweg, 2 October 1912, PA AA R 3477.

38 Kaiser Wilhelm II, marginal note on Bethmann Hollweg's telegram of 1 October 1912, *Große Politik*, XXXIII, No. 12192.

39 Kaiser Wilhelm II, marginal notes of 3 October 1912 on Stolberg's telegrams from Vienna of 20 and 26 September 1912, *Große Politik*, XXXIII, Nos. 12154 and 12168.

40 Kaiser Wilhelm II, marginal comments of 3 October 1912 on Stolberg's telegram from Vienna of 26 September 1912, *Große Politik*, XXXIII, No. 12168.

41 Kaiser Wilhelm II, marginal notes to Waldthausen's telegram from Bucharest, 3 October 1912, *Große Politik*, XXXIII, No. 12215.

42 Kaiser Wilhelm II, marginal notes on Kiderlen-Wächter's telegram of 4 October 1912, *Große Politik*, XXXIII, No. 12216.

43 Kaiser Wilhelm II, marginal note on Kanitz's telegram from Belgrade of 1 October 1912, *Große Politik*, XXXIII, No. 12186.

44 Kaiser Wilhelm II to Kiderlen-Wächter, 4 October 1912, cited from the manuscript original in GStA Berlin, BPHA Rep. 53J Lit. K Nr 5, printed in Jäckh, *Kiderlen-Wächter*, II, pp. 189f., and also *Große Politik*, XXXIII, No. 12225.

45 Kaiser Wilhelm II, marginal comments on telegrams from Tschirschky of 6 October and Wangenheim of 8 October 1912, *Große Politik*, XXXIII, Nos. 12235 and 12242.

46 Kaiser Wilhelm II, marginal comments on Bethmann Hollweg's telegram of 24 October 1912, *Große Politik*, XXXIII, No. 12294.

47 Kaiser Wilhelm II, marginal comments on telegrams from Tschirschky of 6 October and Wangenheim of 8 October 1912, *Große Politik*, XXXIII, Nos. 12235 and 12242.

48 Kaiser Wilhelm II, marginal note on Below-Saleske's telegram from Sofia of 1 October 1912, *Große Politik*, XXXIII, No. 12185.

49 Kaiser Wilhelm II, marginal note on Bethmann Hollweg's telegram of 1 October 1912, *Große Politik*, XXXIII, No. 12192.

50 Kaiser Wilhelm II, marginal notes on Kiderlen-Wächter's memorandum of 16 October 1912, *Große Politik*, XXXIII, No. 12277.

51 Kaiser Wilhelm II, marginal note on Griesinger's telegram of 25 October 1912, *Große Politik*, XXXIII, No. 12297.

52 Kaiser Wilhelm II, marginal note of 26 October 1912 on Griesinger's telegram of 25 October 1912, PA AA R 14238, omitted in *Große Politik*, XXXIII, No. 12297.

53 Bienerth to Schemua, 2 November 1912, Kriegsarchiv Vienna, Generalstab, Militärattaché Berlin, 237/12.

54 Wangenheim reported from Constantinople on 21 November 1912 that the news that the Kaiser had congratulated his sister the Crown Princess of Greece on the capture of Saloniki with the words 'Hurra, hurra, hurra, hurra' had caused consternation in Turkey. Wilhelm denied using these words but not the congratulatory telegram itself. Kaiser Wilhelm II, marginal note on Wangenheim's dispatch of 21 November 1912, PA AA Türkei 203. On the rumpus in Germany see the article 'Wieder einmal ein Kaiser-Telegramm' in the

Kieler Zeitung, 17 November 1912, and the item 'Der Kaiser und die Griechen' in the *Braunschweigische Landeszeitung*, 17 November 1912, ibid.; also Charlotte Hereditary Princess of Saxe-Meiningen to Schweninger, BA Berlin, Schweninger Papers, Nr 132.

55 Kaiser Wilhelm II, marginal comments of 3 November 1912 on Kiderlen-Wächter's submission of the same day, *Große Politik*, XXXIII, No. 12320.

56 Hopman, diary for 4 November 1912, Epkenhans, *Leben eines 'Wilhelminers'*, p. 254.

57 Kaiser Wilhelm II, marginal instruction of 4 November 1912, *Große Politik*, XXXIII, No. 12319.

58 Kaiser Wilhelm II, marginal comment on a telegram of the Wolff news agency of 4 November 1912, *Große Politik*, XXXIII, No. 12321, Kaiser Wilhelm II, marginal comment on Wangenheim's dispatch of 7 November 1912, ibid., No. 12342.

59 Kaiser Wilhelm II, marginal comment on Wangenheim's dispatch of 7 November 1912, ibid., No. 12342.

60 Kaiser Wilhelm II to Bethmann Hollweg, 6 November 1912, *Große Politik*, XXXIII, p. 323, note. Cf. Bethmann Hollweg's record of a conversation of 7 November 1912, ibid.

61 Kaiser Wilhelm II, marginal comments of 15 November 1912 on Wangenheim's letter of 7 November and his telegram of 14 November 1912; Kaiser Wilhelm II to Kiderlen-Wächter, 15 November 1912, *Große Politik*, XXXIII, No. 12364 and Nos. 12378–9.

62 Kaiser Wilhelm II, marginal notes of early December 1912 on Trummler's report of 25 November 1912, BA-MA Freiburg-im-Breisgau, RM2/1775 and on the article 'Balkanflotte und Meerengendurchfahrt' in the *Neue Preußische Kreuzzeitung*, 29 November 1912, ibid., RM2/198.

63 Kaiser Wilhelm II to Auswärtiges Amt, 1 December 1912, *Große Politik*, XXXIII, No. 12468.

64 *Große Politik*, XXXIII, p. 441, note. See Jenisch to Auswärtiges Amt, 2 December 1912 with note, *Große Politik*, XXXIII, No. 12469.

65 Moltke had also advised restraint on Austria-Hungary. See Bienerth to Schemua, 13 October 1912, Kriegsarchiv Vienna, Generalstab, Militärattaché Berlin, 222/12.

66 Kaiser Wilhelm II to Kiderlen-Wächter, 7 November 1912, *Große Politik*, XXXIII, No. 12339.

67 Holzing-Berstett to his wife, 1 October 1912, GLA Karlsruhe, Holzing-Berstett Papers, 69 Zug. 1989 Nr 116/19.

68 Kaiser Wilhelm II to Kiderlen-Wächter, 9 November 1912, *Große Politik*, XXXIII, No. 12348.

69 Kaiser Wilhelm II, marginal notes on Kiderlen-Wächter's telegram of 4 October 1912, *Große Politik*, XXXIII, No. 12216.

70 Jenisch to Auswärtiges Amt, 5 October 1912, *Große Politik*, XXXIII, Nos. 12223–4.

71 Kaiser Wilhelm II, marginal comments of 11 October 1912 on Kiderlen-Wächter's memorandum of 9 October 1912, *Große Politik*, XXXIII, No. 12256.

72 Kaiser Wilhelm II, marginal comments on Pourtalès's telegram from St Petersburg of 12 October 1912, *Große Politik*, XXXIII, No. 12264.

73 Kaiser Wilhelm II, marginal comments of 11 October 1912 on Kiderlen-Wächter's memorandum of 9 October 1912, *Große Politik*, XXXIII, No. 12256. See above, p. 890. See also Kiderlen-Wächter to Jenisch, 12 October 1912, Jäckh, *Kiderlen-Wächter*, II, pp. 190f.; *Große Politik*, XXXIII, No. 12263. Further: Kaiser Wilhelm II to Kiderlen-Wächter, 14 September 1912, *Große Politik*, XXXII, No. 12026; Kaiser Wilhelm II to Kiderlen-Wächter, 8 December 1912, *Große Politik*, XXXIX, No. 15613, cited below, p. 904f.

74 Hans Herzfeld, *Die deutsche Rüstungspolitik vor dem Weltkrieg*, Bonn 1923, pp. 47ff.; Bethmann Hollweg, memorandum of 17 March 1913, *Große Politik*, XXXIX, No. 15634.

75 Kaiser Wilhelm II to Kiderlen-Wächter, 9 November 1912, *Große Politik*, XXXIII, No. 12348.

76 Bethmann Hollweg to Kiderlen-Wächter, 9 November 1912, *Große Politik*, XXXIII, p. 302, note.

77 Kaiser Wilhelm II, memorandum of [11] November 1912, *Große Politik*, XXXIII, No. 12349.

78 August Eulenburg to Kiderlen-Wächter, 11 November 1912, PA AA R 3477.

79 Tschirschky to Kiderlen-Wächter, 17 November 1912; Kiderlen-Wächter to Tschirschky, 19 November 1912, *Große Politik*, XXXIII, No. 12397. See Hull, *The Entourage of Kaiser Wilhelm II*, p. 156.

80 Kaiser Wilhelm II, marginal note on Kiderlen-Wächter's submission of 19 November 1912, *Große Politik*, XXXIII, No. 12395. See also his marginal comments on Lichnowsky's telegram of 19 November 1912, ibid., No. 12399.

81 Kaiser Wilhelm II, marginal comments of 20 November 1912 on Tschirschky's report from Vienna of 18 November 1912, *Große Politik*, XXXIII, No. 12402.

82 Tschirschky, coded telegram of 21 November 1912 from Budapest, *Große Politik*, XXXIII, No. 12404.

83 Bienerth to Schemua, 4 December 1912, Kriegsarchiv Vienna, Generalstab, Militärattaché Berlin 12, 254/12. Cited in Kronenbitter, '*Krieg im Frieden*', p. 397.

84 Kaiser Wilhelm II, marginal notes on Tschirschky's telegram of 21 November 1912; Kaiser Wilhelm II to Kiderlen Wächter, 21 November 1912, *Große Politik*, XXXIII, Nos. 12404–5.

85 Kaiser Wilhelm II to Kiderlen-Wächter, 21 November 1912, cited from the manuscript original in GStA Berlin, BPHA Rep. 53J Lit. K Nr 5; *Große Politik*, XXXIII, No. 12405.

86 See the interpretation offered by the editors of the *Große Politik*, XXXIII, pp. 373f., and also XXXIX, pp. 325f., notes.

87 Mandelssohn to Bienerth, 19 November 1912; Bienerth to Schemua, 4 December 1912, Kriegsarchiv Vienna, Generalstab, Militärattaché Berlin 12, 254/12.

88 Austro-Hungarian General Staff to Bienerth, Bienerth to General Staff, 20 November 1912 Kriegsarchiv Vienna, Generalstab, Militärattaché Berlin 12, 244/12. See Kronenbitter, '*Krieg im Frieden*', pp. 396ff.

89 See Moltke to Auswärtiges Amt, 21 November 1912, *Große Politik*, XXXIII, No. 12412.

90 Bienerth to Schemua, 19 November 1912, Kriegsarchiv Vienna, Generalstab, Militärattaché Berlin 12, 243/12.

91 Schemua, 'Bericht über meinen Aufenthalt in Berlin am 22. d. M.', printed in E. C. Helmreich, 'An Unpublished Report on Austro-German Military Conversations of November, 1912', *Journal of Modern History* 5, June 1933, pp. 205–7. Also published in Stephan Verosta, *Theorie und Realität von Bündnissen. Heinrich Lammasch, Karl Renner und der Zweibund (1897–1914)*, Vienna 1971, pp. 627–31.

92 Archduke Franz Ferdinand, reports of 22 November 1912, *Österreich-Ungarns Außenpolitik*, IV, Nos. 4571 and 4559. See Szögyény's dispatches of 24 and 25 November 1912, ibid., Nos. 4594 and 4606.

93 Bienerth to Schemua, 4 December 1912, Kriegsarchiv Vienna, Generalstab, Militärattaché Berlin, 254/12.

94 Kaiser Wilhelm II, marginal comments of 22 November 1912 on the two reports from Pourtalès of 20 November 1912, *Große Politik*, XXXIII, Nos. 12415 and 12417. Cf. Müller, diary for 22 and 23 November 1912, BA-MA Freiburg-im-Breisgau, Müller Papers. See also Bernd F. Schulte, *Vor dem Kriegsausbruch 1914. Deutschland, die Türkei und der Balkan*, Düsseldorf 1980, pp. 82f.

95 Kronenbitter, *Krieg im Frieden*, p. 402. See note 132, ibid., p. 397.

96 Wenninger to Kress von Kressenstein, 25 November 1912, Bayer. HStA Munich, Abt. IV (Kriegsarchiv), MKr. 41, printed in part in John C. G. Röhl, 'An der Schwelle zum Weltkrieg. Eine Dokumentation über den "Kriegsrat" vom 8. Dezember 1912',

Militärgeschichtliche Mitteilungen 21, 1977, p. 129. See also Moltke to Josias von Heeringen, 25 November 1912, *Kriegsrüstung und Kriegswirtschaft, bearbeitet im Reichsarchiv, Anlagen zum ersten Band*, Berlin No. 48, 1930. But cf. August von Heeringen to Tirpitz, 30 November 1912, BA-MA Freiburg-im-Breisgau, RM3/4370.

97 Charlotte Hereditary Princess of Saxe-Meiningen to Schweninger, 23 November 1912, BA Berlin, Schweninger Papers, Nr 132.

98 Josias von Heeringen to Moltke, 29 November 1912, *Kriegsrüstung und Kriegswirtschaft*, No. 49.

99 Moltke to Heeringen, 2 December 1912, *Kriegsrüstung und Kriegswirtschaft*, No. 50.

100 Dorothy von Moltke to her parents, 22 October 1912, cited from the translation in Dorothy von Moltke, *Ein Leben in Deutschland. Briefe aus Kreisau und Berlin 1907–1934*, Munich 1999, pp. 35f.

34   DETERRENCE: THE UNRESOLVED PROBLEM OF BRITAIN'S NEUTRALITY

1 See above, p. 894.

2 Lichnowsky to Kaiser Wilhelm II, 23 November 1912, GStA Berlin, BPHA Rep. 53J Lit. L Nr 5, cited in Röhl, *Zwei deutsche Fürsten zur Kriegsschuldfrage*, p. 17. English translation in John C. G. Röhl, *1914: Delusion or Design? The Testimony of Two German Diplomats*, London, 1973. Karl von Eisendecher also sent the Kaiser a letter urging him to seek better relations with England, BA-MA Freiburg-im-Breisgau, RM2/1765.

3 August von Heeringen to Kiderlen-Wächter, 25 November 1912, ibid., RM3/4370.

4 Heeringen, notes for his audience with the Kaiser, December 1912, ibid., RM5/898.

5 Holtzendorff to Tirpitz, 26 November 1912, ibid., RM5/1926.

6 Tirpitz to Heeringen, 30 November 1912, ibid., RM2/1775.

7 Müller, diary for 25 and 26 November 1912, ibid., Müller Papers.

8 Kiderlen-Wächter, statement of 26 November 1912 in the foreign affairs committee of the Bundesrat, *Große Politik*, XXXIII, No. 12474; Bethmann Hollweg, speech of 2 December 1912 in the Reichstag, *Stenographische Berichte über die Verhandlungen des Reichstages, 13. Legislaturperiode*, Bd. 286, Sp. 2472ff.

9 Bienerth to Schemua, 4 December 1912, Kriegsarchiv Vienna, Generalstab, Militärattaché Berlin, 254/12.

10 Kaiser Wilhelm II to Bethmann Hollweg, 29 November 1912, GStA Berlin, Rep. 53J Lit. T. Nr 1.

11 Kaiser Wilhelm II to Auswärtiges Amt, 1 December 1912, cited above, p. 888. See Kaiser Wilhelm II to Archduke Franz Ferdinand, 2 December 1912, MOL Budapest, Franz Ferdinand Papers, 183 db, XI/18. See also Kaiser Wilhelm II to Chamberlain, 2 December 1912, Chamberlain, *Briefe 1882–1924*, II, pp. 239f.

12 Müller, diary for 3 December 1912, BA-MA Freiburg-im-Breisgau, Müller Papers.

13 Kaiser Wilhelm II to Luise, Grand Duchess of Baden, 26 November and 1 December 1912, GStA Berlin, BPHA Rep. 53J Lit. T Nr 1.

14 Prince Heinrich of Prussia, diary for 30 November to 9 December 1912, printed in Röhl, 'An der Schwelle zum Weltkrieg', pp. 98f.

15 Battenberg to King George V, 5 December 1912, RA GV/M 520 A/1.

16 Prince Heinrich of Prussia, diary for 30 November to 9 December 1912, printed in Röhl, 'An der Schwelle zum Weltkrieg', No. 2; Prince Heinrich of Prussia to Kaiser Wilhelm II, 14 December 1912, ibid., No. 18.

17 King George V to Grey, 8 December 1912, printed in Sir Harold Nicolson, *King George the Fifth. His Life and Reign*, London 1952, p. 206.

18 Grey to King George V, 9 December 1912, ibid., pp. 206f.; Cambon to Jonnart, 23 January 1913, RA GV/M 520 A/8.

19 Benckendorff to Sazonov, 22 January 1913, printed in Benno von Siebert, ed., *Graf Benckendorffs diplomatischer Schriftwechsel*, 3 vols., Berlin 1928, III, No. 833.

20 Cambon to Jonnart, 23 January 1913, RA GV/M 520 A/8. See also Mensdorff to Berchtold, 22 December 1912, *Österreich-Ungarns Außenpolitik*, V, No. 5028.

21 See below, pp. 1058–62.

22 Prince Heinrich of Prussia to King George V, 14 December 1912, Nicolson, *George the Fifth*, pp. 207f.

23 Ibid. The King's reply of 22 December is in Prince Heinrich's Papers, MSM Hamburg, Mappe 20b.

24 Prince Heinrich of Prussia to Kaiser Wilhelm II, 11 December 1912, BA-MA Freiburg-im-Breisgau, RM2/1765, printed in Tirpitz, *Aufbau der deutschen Weltmacht*, pp. 363f. On the Kaiser's orders copies were sent to Bethmann Hollweg, Kiderlen-Wächter and Tirpitz.

25 Lichnowsky, report of 3 December 1912, *Große Politik*, XXXIX, No. 15612; Tirpitz, *Aufbau der deutschen Weltmacht*, pp. 361f. On the orders of the Kaiser Lichnowsky's dispatch was circulated to the General Staff, the Admiralty Staff and the Reich Navy Office.

26 Kaiser Wilhelm II, marginal comments of 8 December 1912 on Lichnowsky's report of 3 December 1912, *Große Politik*, XXXIX, No. 15612; Tirpitz, *Aufbau der deutschen Weltmacht*, pp. 361f.

27 Kaiser Wilhelm II to Kiderlen-Wächter, 8 December 1912, *Große Politik*, XXXIX, No. 15613.

28 Kaiser Wilhelm II to Archduke Franz Ferdinand, 9 December 1912, cited from the original in MOL Budapest, Franz Ferdinand Papers, 183 db, XI/19. Cf. Kann, 'Wilhelm II. und Franz Ferdinand in ihrer Korrespondenz', pp. 74f.; Röhl, 'An der Schwelle zum Weltkrieg', No. 8.

29 Claparède, report of 10 December 1912, as cited in Terence F. Cole, 'German Decision-Making on the Eve of the First World War: The Records of the Swiss Embassy in Berlin', in Röhl, *Der Ort Kaiser Wilhelms II.*, pp. 62f.

30 Kaiser Wilhelm II, marginal notes on Prince Heinrich's letter of 11 December 1912, BA-MA Freiburg-im-Breisgau, RM2/1765. See above, pp. 902f.

31 Kaiser Wilhelm II to Prince Heinrich of Prussia, 12 December 1912, Röhl, 'An der Schwelle zum Weltkrieg', No. 12. The Kaiser expressed himself in very similar terms in a letter to Karl von Eisendecher, 12 December 1912, ibid., No. 13.

32 Lerchenfeld to Hertling, 14 December 1912, printed in Ernst Deuerlein, ed., *Briefwechsel Hertling-Lerchenfeld 1912–1917*, Boppard am Rhein 1973, pp. 189ff. Published in part in Karl Alexander von Müller, 'Neue Urkunden', *Süddeutsche Monatshefte*, July 1921, 293ff.

33 Kaiser Wilhelm II to Ballin, 15 December 1912, as cited in Huldermann, *Ballin*, pp. 273f.

34 Lerchenfeld to Hertling, 14 December 1912, quoted above, p. 907.

35 Bethmann Hollweg to Kiderlen-Wächter, 17 December 1912, *Große Politik*, XXXIX, No. 15559; Bethmann Hollweg to Eisendecher, 20 December 1912, Röhl, 'An der Schwelle zum Weltkrieg', No. 36. See below, pp. 912f.

36 Müller, diary for 8 December 1912, as cited in Röhl, 'An der Schwelle zum Weltkrieg', No. 4. See Leuckart von Weißdorf to Hausen, 12 December 1912, ibid., No. 14, printed in full in Helmut Otto and Karl Schmiedel, eds., *Der erste Weltkrieg. Dokumente*, Berlin 1977, No. 6.

37 William Michaelis, Lebenserinnerungen, BA-MA Freiburg-im-Breisgau, Michaelis Papers, N 164/4. I thank Professor Michael Epkenhans for showing me this important document.

38 Hopman, diary for 9 December 1912, Epkenhans, *Leben eines 'Wilhelminers'*, pp. 268–70.

39 Görlitz, *Der Kaiser*; John C. G. Röhl, 'Admiral von Müller and the Approach of War, 1911–1914', *The Historical Journal* XII, 4 (1969), 651–73. On the controversy surrounding the famous 'war council' see Clark, *Kaiser Wilhelm II*, pp. 195ff.; Wolfgang J. Mommsen, 'Der Topos vom unvermeidlichen Krieg: Außenpolitik und öffentliche Meinung im Deutschen Reich im letzten Jahrzehnt vor 1914', in Wolfgang J. Mommsen, *Der autoritäre Nationalstaat. Verfassung, Gesellschaft und Kultur im deutschen Kaiserreich*, Frankfurt a.M. 1990, pp. 392ff.

40 Wenninger to Kreß von Kressenstein, 15 December 1912, as cited in Röhl, 'An der Schwelle zum Weltkrieg', No. 22.

41 Bethmann Hollweg, memorandum of 20 December 1912, cited ibid., No. 34. Cf. *Große Politik*, XXXIII, No. 12496.

42 Fischer, *Krieg der Illusionen*, pp. 231ff. et passim.

43 Kaiser Wilhelm II, marginal notes on Lichnowsky's report of 20 December 1912, *Große Politik*, XXXIV/1, No. 12561.

44 Bethmann Hollweg to Kaiser Wilhelm II, 18 December 1912, with the remark 'aha!' by the Kaiser in the margin, ibid., XXXIX, No. 15560.

45 Bethmann Hollweg to Eisendecher, 20 December 1912, printed in Röhl, 'An der Schwelle zum Weltkrieg', No. 36. See Kiderlen-Wächter to Eisendecher, 19 December 1912, ibid., No. 35.

46 Eisendecher to Kaiser Wilhelm II, 23 December 1912, printed ibid., No. 39.

47 Bethmann Hollweg, memorandum of 14 December 1912, *Große Politik*, XXXIX, No. 15623.

48 Bethmann Hollweg to Kaiser Wilhelm II, 18 December 1912, ibid., No. 15560. See Lichnowsky's report of 9 December 1912 on the probable response of England in the event of a continental war, ibid., XXXIII, No. 12489.

49 Müller, diary for 8 December 1912, printed in Röhl, 'An der Schwelle zum Weltkrieg', No. 4.

50 Kaiser Wilhelm II, marginal notes on Bethmann Hollweg's submission of 18 December 1912, *Große Politik*, XXXIX, No. 15560.

51 Müller to Tirpitz, 4 January 1913, cited in Röhl, 'An der Schwelle zum Weltkrieg', p. 94; cf. Tirpitz, *Aufbau der deutschen Weltmacht*, p. 370.

52 Müller, diary for 4 January 1913, cited in Röhl, 'An der Schwelle zum Weltkrieg', 94.

53 Müller, diary for 5 January 1913, ibid.

54 Ibid.

55 Bethmann Hollweg, memorandum of 17 March 1913, *Große Politik*, XXXIX, No. 15634.

56 Müller, diary for 6 January 1911, cited in Röhl, 'An der Schwelle zum Weltkrieg', 94; Müller to Tirpitz, 6 January 1913, Tirpitz, *Aufbau der deutschen Weltmacht*, pp. 370f.

57 Bethmann Hollweg to Kaiser Wilhelm II, 18 December 1912, *Große Politik*, XXXIX, No. 15560, cited above, pp. 913f.

58 Bethmann Hollweg to Kaiser Wilhelm II, 18 December 1912, ibid.

59 Urbanski, 'Analyse der deutschen Wehrvorlage', 14 April 1913, Kriegsarchiv Vienna, 1913 47 4/27.

60 Mudra, notes on a conversation of 10 December 1912 between Bethmann Hollweg and Colmar von der Goltz, as cited in Schulte, *Vor dem Kriegsausbruch 1914*, p. 156.

35 'BERLIN HAS WARNED US OFF AGAIN.' THE 'POSTPONED RACIAL WAR AGAINST SLAVDOM'

1 Buchanan to Stamfordham, 20 February 1913, RA GV/M 421/15.

2 See the agitated marginal notes the Kaiser wrote on the Wolff agency telegram of 28 December 1912 and on Lichnowsky's reports of 9 and 10 January 1913, *Große Politik*, XXXIV/1, Nos. 12581, 12650 and 12658.

3 Szögyény to Berchtold, 17 December 1912, as cited in Röhl, 'An der Schwelle zum Weltkrieg', No. 29. But cf. the critical marginal comments of the Kaiser of 28 December on what he termed the 'megalomania' of the Turks, *Große Politik*, XXXIV/1, No. 12581.

4 Szögyény to Berchtold, 17 December 1912, cited in Röhl, 'An der Schwelle zum Weltkrieg', No. 29.

5 Ibid.

6 Kaiser Wilhelm II, marginal comment in the Wolff agency telegram of 4 January 1913, *Große Politik*, XXXIV/1, No. 12609. See also the Kaiser's marginal notes on Lucius's report from St Petersburg of 8 January 1913, ibid., No. 12649.

7 Berchtold to Archduke Franz Ferdinand, 13 January 1913, Franz Ferdinand Papers, MOL Budapest, 231 db Bl. 3 D 5.

8 Kronenbitter, *Krieg im Frieden*, pp. 406 and 409.

9 Conrad to Berchtold, 27 January 1913, Kriegsarchiv Vienna, Conrad-Archiv, B 3 Nr 17.

10 Colloredo-Mannsfeld to Austro-Hungarian War Ministry, naval section, 26 January 1913, Kriegsarchiv Vienna, Conrad-Archiv, B 2 Nr 17/48. See Kronenbitter, *Krieg im Frieden*, p. 410, note 194.

11 Wenninger, report of 28 January 1913, Bayer. HStA Munich, Militärbevollmächtigter Bd. I.

12 Berchtold to Conrad, 8 February 1913, Kriegsarchiv Vienna, Conrad-Archiv, B 3 17 Nr 51.

13 Bethmann Hollweg to Berchtold, 10 February 1913, MOL Budapest, Franz Ferdinand Papers, 231 db Bl 9 D 6, printed in *Große Politik*, XXXIV/1, No. 12818. See Hugo Hantsch, *Leopold Graf Berchtold. Grandseigneur und Staatsmann*, 2 vols., Graz, Vienna and Cologne 1963, I, p. 388. Also Canis, *Abgrund*, pp. 511f.

14 Berchtold to Archduke Franz Ferdinand, 11 February 1913, MOL Budapest, Franz Ferdinand Papers, 231 db Bl 9 D 6. See Hantsch, *Berchtold*, I, p. 388.

15 Moltke to Conrad, 10 February 1913, printed in Conrad, *Aus meiner Dienstzeit*, III, pp. 144–7. See also *Große Politik*, XXXIV/1, No. 12824 annex. See Norman Stone, 'Moltke-Conrad: Relations between the Austro-Hungarian and German General Staffs, 1909–14', *The Historical Journal* 9, 1966, 204–11.

16 Conrad to Moltke, 15 February 1913, printed in full in Conrad, *Aus meiner Dienstzeit*, III, pp. 147–51.

17 Bienerth to Conrad von Hötzendorf, 26 February 1913, printed ibid., III, pp. 151–3.

18 Kageneck to Moltke, 1 March 1913, cited in Kronenbitter, *Krieg im Frieden*, p. 412, note 208.

19 Szögyény, report of 30 January 1913, *Österreich-Ungarns Außenpolitik*, V, No. 5604.

20 Bienerth, report on a conversation with the Chief of the German General Staff, 26 February 1913, Conrad-Archiv, B 3 17 Nr 75.

21 Cited in Theodor Reismann-Grone, *Der Erdenkrieg und die Alldeutschen*, Mühlheim, Ruhr 1919, pp. 66f. See Thomas Lindemann, *Die Macht der Perzeptionen und Perzeptionen von Mächten*, Berlin 2000, p. 215.

22 Bienerth, report on a conversation with the Chief of the German General Staff, 26 February 1913, Conrad-Archiv, B 3 17 Nr 75.

23 Kaiser Wilhelm II to Archduke Franz Ferdinand, 24 February 1913, cited from the original in MOL Budapest, Franz Ferdinand Papers, 183 db, XI, 20. Cf. *Große Politik*, XXXIV/1, Nos. 12891–2. See Kann, 'Wilhelm II. und Franz Ferdinand in ihrer Korrespondenz', pp. 76–80.

24 Berchtold to Archduke Franz Ferdinand, 19 February 1913 with the draft of a personal letter to be sent to Tsar Nicholas II, MOL Budapest, Franz Ferdinand Papers 231 db D 7.

25 Kaiser Wilhelm II to Archduke Franz Ferdinand, 28 February 1913, MOL Budapest, Franz Ferdinand Papers, 183 db, XI/21. But cf. the Kaiser's marginal notes on Tschirschky's report of 27 February 1913, *Große Politik*, XXXIV/1, No. 12914.

26 Kaiser Wilhelm II, marginal comments on Jagow's telegram of 6 April 1913, ibid., XXXIV/2, No. 13093. For the Scutari crisis see Boeckh, *Von den Balkankriegen zum Ersten Weltkrieg*, pp. 46ff.; Hantsch, *Berchtold*, I, pp. 381ff.

27 Kaiser Wilhelm II, marginal notes on Jagow's telegram of 7 April 1913, *Große Politik*, XXXIV/2, No. 13097.

28 Conrad to Berchtold, 22 March 1913, Kriegsarchiv Vienna, Conrad-Archiv Nr 108.

29 Conrad to Potiorek, 7 April 1913, ibid.

30 Conrad to Potiorek, 15 April 1913, Conrad to Berchtold, 15 April 1913, ibid.

31 Kaiser Wilhelm II, marginal comments on Flotow's telegram of 23 March 1913, *Große Politik*, XXXIV/2, No. 13011.

32 Kaiser Wilhelm II, marginal notes on Lichnowsky's telegram of 26 March 1913, ibid., No. 13021.

33 Kaiser Wilhelm II, marginal comments on Pourtalès's telegram of 26 March 1913, ibid., No. 13024.

34 Tschirschky, report of 4 April 1913 with the marginal comment 'Ja' by the Kaiser, ibid., No. 13087. See Gutsche, *Wilhelm II.*, p. 149.

35 Kaiser Wilhelm II, marginal notes on Kageneck's report of 5 April 1913, *Große Politik*, XXXIV/2, No. 13095.

36 Kaiser Wilhelm II, marginal comments on Jagow's submission of 1 April 1913, ibid., No. 13060.

37 Kaiser Wilhelm II, marginal comments on Lichnowsky's telegram of 2 April 1913, ibid., No. 13070.

38 Kaiser Wilhelm II, marginal note on Jagow's telegram 6 April 1913, ibid., No. 13093.

39 August Eulenburg to Jagow, 17 April 1913, PA AA R 3477.

40 Kaiser Wilhelm II, marginal notes on Lichnowsky's telegram of 23 April 1913, *Große Politik*, XXXIV/2, No. 13191.

41 Kaiser Wilhelm II, marginal notes on Jagow's telegram of 24 April 1913, ibid., No. 13195.

42 Kaiser Wilhelm II, marginal notes on Pourtalès's telegram of 24 April 1913, ibid., No. 13198.

43 Treutler to Auswärtiges Amt, 23 April 1913, ibid., No. 13190. See also Kaiser Wilhelm II, marginal notes on Lichnowsky's telegram of 27 April 1913, ibid., No. 13216.

44 Wenninger, report of 28 April 1913, Bayer. HStA Munich, Militärbevollmächtigter, Bd. I.

45 Tschirschky to Jagow with the Kaiser's marginal note, 28 April 1913, *Große Politik*, XXXIV/2, No. 13230.

46 Kaiser Wilhelm II, marginal notes on Tschirschky's telegram of 28 April 1913, ibid., No. 13231.

47 Jagow to Tschirschky, 28 April 1913, as cited in Fischer, *Krieg der Illusionen*, p. 298.

48 Kaiser Wilhelm II, marginal note on Tschirschky's telegram of 29 April 1913, *Große Politik*, XXXIV/2, No. 13238.

49 Kaiser Wilhelm II, marginal comments on Tschirschky's telegram of 30 April 1913, ibid., No. 13243.

50 Kaiser Wilhelm II, marginal comments on Tschirschky's telegram of 1 May 1913, ibid., No. 13252.

51 Wenninger, report of 2 May 1913, Bayer. HStA Munich, Militärbevollmächtigter, Bd. I.

52 Wenninger, report of 5 May 1913, ibid.

53 Wenninger, report of 6 May 1913, ibid.

54 Berchtold, diary for 5 May 1913, Hantsch, *Berchtold*, I, p. 420.

55 Bienerth to Conrad, 20 May 1913, Conrad, *Aus meiner Dienstzeit*, III, p. 328.

56 Bienerth to Conrad, 21 June 1913, ibid., pp. 368f.

57 Kaiser Wilhelm II, marginal comment on Pourtalès's report of 6 May 1913, *Große Politik*, XXXIV/2, No. 13282. See also the Kaiser's comments on Pourtalès's report of 17 May 1913, ibid., XXXIX, No. 15645.

58 Kaiser Wilhelm II, marginal notes on Lucius's reports of 24 and 26 May 1913, PA AA R 3634.

59 Stamfordham, 'Notes on a Conversation with the German Emperor', 25 May 1913, RA GV/M 450/18.

60 Pohl to Tirpitz, 9 June 1913, Tirpitz to Pohl, 14 June 1913, BA-MA Freiburg-im-Breisgau, RM5/v 1608.

61 Kaiser Wilhelm II, marginal comments on Lichnowsky's report of 13 January 1913 and on the Wolff agency telegram of 14 January 1913, *Große Politik*, XXXIV/1, Nos. 12677–8. See also the Kaiser's remarks on the Wolff telegram of 15 January 1913, ibid., No. 12687. In the same vein: Kaiser Wilhelm II to Auswärtiges Amt, 11 January 1913, ibid., No. 12662; and the Kaiser's marginal note on Lichnowsky's dispatch of 9 January 1913 and on Zimmermann to Lichnowsky, 10 January 1913, ibid., Nos. 12650–1.

62 Kaiser Wilhelm II, marginal comment on Below-Saleske's telegram from Sofia of 28 March 1913, ibid., XXXIV/2, No. 13044. See also Kaiser Wilhelm II, marginal comment on Schoen's report from Paris of 13 March 1913, ibid., No. 12970.

63 Kaiser Wilhelm II, marginal note on Lichnowsky's telegram of 9 June 1913, *Große Politik*, XXXV, No. 13378.

64 Kaiser Wilhelm II, marginal comments on Lichnowsky's telegram of 31 January 1913, ibid., XXXIV/1, No. 12773.

65 Kaiser Wilhelm II, marginal comment on Lichnowsky's telegram of 1 February 1913, Kaiser Wilhelm II, marginal comments on Lichnowsky's telegram of 11 February 1913, ibid., Nos. 12775 and 12825.

66 Kaiser Wilhelm II, marginal comments on Wangenheim's report of 28 January 1913, ibid., No. 12754.

67 Kaiser Wilhelm II, marginal notes on Pourtalès's report of 14 July 1913, ibid., XXXV, No. 13595.

68 Kaiser Wilhelm II, marginal comments on Lichnowsky's report of 13 August 1913, ibid., XXXVI/1, No. 13778. The Kaiser's comments were telegraphed to the Auswärtiges Amt on 16 August, ibid., No. 13781.

69 Kaiser Wilhelm II, marginal note on Pourtalès's telegram of 5 March 1913, ibid., XXXIV/2, No. 12934.

70 Kaiser Wilhelm II, marginal comments on Tschirschky's report of 5 March 1913, ibid., No. 12937. See Jagow to Berchtold, 23 March 1913, and Tschirschky to Jagow, 20 March 1913, ibid., Nos. 13069 and 13000.

71 See Fischer, *Krieg der Illusionen*, pp. 300ff.

72 Kaiser Wilhelm II, marginal comment on Below-Saleske's telegram from Sofia of 28 March 1913, *Große Politik*, XXXIV/2, No. 13044.

73 Kaiser Wilhelm II, marginal comments on Jagow's report of 26 April 1913, ibid., XXXVIII, No. 15439.

74 Kaiser Wilhelm II, marginal note on Schulenburg's report of 30 April 1913, as cited in Fischer, *Krieg der Illusionen*, p. 429.

75 Stamfordham, 'Notes on a Conversation with the German Emperor', 25 May 1913, RA GV/M 450/18.

76 Jagow to Wangenheim, 28 July 1913, as cited in Gutsche, *Wilhelm II.*, p. 150.

77 See Fischer, *Krieg der Illusionen*, pp. 300f.

78 Kaiser Wilhelm II, marginal comments on Flotow's telegram from Rome of 2 April 1913, *Große Politik*, XXXIV/2, No. 13069.

79 Rheinbaben to Hopman, 18 April 1913, BA-MA Freiburg-im-Breisgau, Tirpitz Papers, N 253/424.

80 Kaiser Wilhelm II to Archduke Franz Ferdinand, 27 May 1913, MOL Budapest, Franz Ferdinand Papers, 183 db fols. 193–5, printed in Kann, 'Wilhelm II. und Franz Ferdinand in ihrer Korrespondenz', pp. 81–3.

81 Stamfordham to Nicolson, 7 and 10 January 1914, RA GV/M 450/19–20.

82 Kaiser Wilhelm II, marginal comments on Tschirschky's report of 14 June 1913, *Große Politik*, XXXV, No. 13395.

83 Archduke Franz Ferdinand to Berchtold, 24 July 1913, as cited in Kann, 'Wilhelm II. und Franz Ferdinand in ihrer Korrespondenz', p. 83, note 79.

84 Berchtold to Archduke Franz Ferdinand, 6 June 1913, MOL Budapest, Franz Ferdinand Papers, 231 db D 9.

85 Berchtold, diary for late June 1913, Hantsch, *Berchtold*, II, p. 441.

86 Berchtold, diary for 5 July 1913, ibid., p. 447.

87 See Fischer, *Krieg der Illusionen*, p. 310.

88 Kaiser Wilhelm II, marginal comment on Pourtalès's report of 6 June 1913, *Große Politik*, XXXV, No. 13373. For the Second Balkan war see Boeckh, *Von den Balkankriegen zum Ersten Weltkrieg*, pp. 55ff.; Schulte, *Vor dem Kriegsausbruch 1914*.

89 Kaiser Wilhelm II, marginal note on Lichnowsky's report of 9 June 1913, *Große Politik*, XXXV, No. 13378.

90 Kaiser Wilhelm II, marginal comment on Lichnowsky's telegram of 15 June 1913, ibid.

91 Colloredo-Mannsfeld, report of 7 September 1913, *Österreich-Ungarns Außenpolitik*, VI, No. 7672.

92 Conrad, record of a conversation with Kaiser Wilhelm II on 8 September 1913, Conrad, *Aus meiner Dienstzeit*, III, pp. 431f.

93 See Fischer, *Krieg der Illusionen*, p. 308.

94 Berchtold to Archduke Franz Ferdinand, 28 July 1913, MOL Budapest, Franz Ferdinand Papers, 231 db D 10.

95 Conrad to Berchtold, 30 July 1913, printed in Conrad, *Aus meiner Dienstzeit*, III, pp. 409–11.

96 Kaiser Wilhelm II to Auswärtiges Amt, 16 August 1913, *Große Politik*, XXXVI/1, No. 13781.

97 Circular instruction of 17 August 1913; Tschirschky, report of 22 August 1913, cited ibid., p. 30, note.

98 Wenninger, report of 12 August 1913, Bayer, HStA Munich, Militärbevollmächtigter, Bd. I. See also Moltke to Conrad, 27 August 1913, Conrad, *Aus meiner Dienstzeit*, III, pp. 429f.

99 Bienerth to Conrad, 27 June 1913, ibid., pp. 423f.

100 Moltke to Conrad, 29 June 1913, ibid., pp. 424–6.

101 Archduke Franz Ferdinand to Kaiser Wilhelm II, 7 September 1913, quoted in Treutler to Auswärtiges Amt, 7 September 1913, *Große Politik*, XXXIX, No. 15709.

102 Kaiser Wilhelm II to Archduke Franz Ferdinand, 8 September 1913, ibid., No. 15710.

103 Ibid., pp. 325f.

104 Conrad, record of a conversation with Kaiser Wilhelm II on 8 September 1913, Conrad, *Aus meiner Dienstzeit*, III, pp. 431f. Conrad to Emperor Franz Joseph, 20 September 1913, ibid., annex 4, pp. 720–3.

105 Wedel to Auswärtiges Amt, 29 September 1913, *Große Politik*, XXXVI/1, No. 13865.

106 Conrad, record of conversations with Moltke on 7 and 8 September 1913, Conrad, *Aus meiner Dienstzeit*, III, pp. 432f.

107 Ibid., pp. 460ff. and 724ff.

108 Kageneck, report of 9 October 1913, *Große Politik*, XXXVI/1, No. 14159.

109 Conrad, *Aus meiner Dienstzeit*, III, p. 463.

110 Stolberg, telegram of 15 October 1913, *Große Politik*, XXXVI/1, No. 14160.

111 Zimmermann to Wedel, 16 October 1913, Zimmermann to Tschirschky, 16 October 1913, Zimmermann to Lichnowsky, 16 October 1913, ibid., Nos. 14161–2 and 14164.

112 Stolberg, telegram of 17 October 1913, ibid., No. 14170.

113 Hindenburg to Bethmann Hollweg, 14 October 1913, Zimmermann to Lichnowsky, 17 October 1913, Kühlmann to Auswärtiges Amt, 18 October 1913, ibid., Nos. 14165–6 and 14169.

114 Wedel to Auswärtiges Amt, 17 October 1913, ibid., No. 14172.

115 Kaiser Wilhelm II, marginal note on Stolberg's telegram of 18 October 1913, ibid., No. 14170.

116 Conrad, record of a conversation with Kaiser Wilhelm II on 18 October 1913, Conrad, *Aus meiner Dienstzeit*, III, pp. 469f.

117 Kaiser Wilhelm II to Archduke Franz Ferdinand, 8 September and 26 October 1913, *Große Politik*, XXXIX, Nos. 15710–11; Kaiser Wilhelm II to Emperor Franz Joseph, 26 October 1913, Emperor Franz Joseph to Kaiser Wilhelm II, 27 October 1913, PA AA R 3650. See also Kaiser Wilhelm II to Archduke Franz Ferdinand, 2 November 1913, MOL Budapest, Franz Ferdinand Papers, 183 db.

118 Berchtold, memorandum of 28 October 1913 on his conversation with Kaiser Wilhelm II on 26 October 1913, *Österreich-Ungarns Außenpolitik*, VII, No. 8934.

119 Tschirschky to Bethmann Hollweg, 28 October 1913, as cited in Fischer, *Krieg der Illusionen*, p. 317.

36 KAISER AND REICH. WILHELM'S PERSONAL MONARCHY ON THE EVE OF WAR

1 See Bernd Sösemann, 'Hollow-Sounding Jubilees: Forms and Effects of Public Self-Display in Wilhelmine Germany', in Annika Mombauer and Wilhelm Deist, eds., *The Kaiser. New Research on Wilhelm II's Role in Imperial Germany*, Cambridge 2003, pp. 37–62. See also Sabine Behrenbeck and Alexander Nützenadel, eds., *Inszenierungen des Nationalstaats*, Cologne 2000; Friedrich Zipfel, 'Kritik der Öffentlichkeit an der Person und an der Monarchie Wilhelms II. bis zum Ausbruch des Weltkrieges', unpublished Dr Phil dissertation, University of Berlin 1952.

2 See Astrid M. Eckert, *Kampf um die Akten. Die Westalliierten und die Rückgabe von deutschem Archivgut nach dem Zweiten Weltkrieg*, Stuttgart 2004; Bernd Faulenbach, *Ideologie des deutschen Weges. Die deutsche Geschichte in der Historiographie zwischen Kaiserreich und Nationalsozialismus*, Munich 1980.

3 Fritz Hartung, 'Verantwortliche Regierungen, Kabinette und Nebenregierungen im konstitutionellen Preußen 1848–1918', *Forschungen zur Brandenburgischen und Preußischen Geschichte* 44, 1932, pp. 1–45 and 302–73; Fritz Hartung, 'Das persönliche Regiment Kaiser Wilhelms II.', *Sitzungsberichte der Deutschen Akademie zu Berlin*, Berlin 1952, 1–20.

4 Zmarzlik, *Bethmann Hollweg*, pp. 28f. et passim. Cf. Klaus Hildebrand, *Bethmann Hollweg. Der Kanzler ohne Eigenschaften? Urteile der Geschichtsschreibung. Eine kritische Bibliographie*, Düsseldorf 1970; Konrad H. Jarausch, *The Enigmatic Chancellor. Bethmann Hollweg and the Hubris of Imperial Germany*, London 1973.

5 Bienerth, dispatch of 21 February 1913, Kriegsarchiv Vienna, 1913 47/4–5 R; cf. Bienerth to Conrad von Hötzendorf, 26 February 1913, printed in Conrad, *Aus meiner Dienstzeit*, III, pp. 151–3.

6 Bethmann Hollweg to Valentini, 26 August 1911, GStA Berlin, Valentini Papers, Nr 2.

7 On the building of the Olympic stadium in Berlin see Christiane Eisenberg. *'English Sports' und Deutsche Bürger. Eine Gesellschaftsgeschichte 1800–1939*, Paderborn, Munich, Vienna and Zürich 1999, pp. 278–83.

8 Prince Heinrich of Prussia, diary for 12–18 June 1913, MSM Hamburg, Prince Heinrich Papers.

9 Duke Georg II of Saxe-Meiningen to his wife, 7 June 1913, ThStaMgn, HA 334.

10 Kaiser Wilhelm II to the First Regiment of Foot Guards, 13 June 1913, Archiv des vormals regierenden preußischen Königshauses, Burg Hohenzollern, Hechingen.

11 Duke Georg II of Saxe-Meiningen to his wife, 12 June 1913, ThStaMgn, HA 334.

12 Adolf von Achenbach et al., *Unser Kaiser. Fünfundzwanzig Jahre der Regierung Kaiser Wilhelms II. 1888–1913*, Berlin, Leipzig, Vienna and Stuttgart 1913. See also Hans Schöningen, *Kaiser Wilhelm II. und seine Zeit in Wort und Bild*, Hamburg 1913.

13 Philipp Zorn et al., *Deutschland unter Kaiser Wilhelm II.*, 3 vols., Berlin 1914. For critical comments on Bülow's account see Schoen to Bülow, 1 December 1913 with marginal remarks by Kaiser Wilhelm II of 24 December 1913, GStA Berlin, BPHA Rep. 53 E 1.

14 Berger to Rheinbaben, [November 1912], cited in Rheinbaben to Valentini, 30 November 1913, GStA Berlin, Valentini Papers, Nr 23.

15 Canis, *Abgrund*, p. 529.

16 Bethmann Hollweg to Eisendecher, 25 June 1913, cited ibid.

17 Kaiser Wilhelm II, speech in Königsberg on 25 August 1910, Schultheß, *Europäischer Geschichtskalender*, 26. Jahrgang (1910), pp. 391f. See the text of the speech, heavily redacted for publication, in Obst, *Die politischen Reden*, pp. 314–16. For the critical reception of this and other speeches see Sösemann, 'Hollow-Sounding Jubilees', p. 47.

18 Kaiser Wilhelm II, speech of 6 March 1913 in Bremen, Wolff's Telegraphisches Bureau, 6 March 1913.

19 Mackensen, speech of 27 January 1913, BA-MA Freiburg-im-Breisgau, Mackensen Papers, N 39/441.

20 Mackensen, speech of 10 March 1913, ibid. See also Mackensen's speech of 24 October 1912, ibid.

21 Mackensen, speech of 27 January 1914, ibid.

22 Chamberlain to Kaiser Wilhelm II, 21 January 1914, Richard-Wagner-Gedenkstätte, Bayreuth, Chamberlain Papers, printed in Chamberlain, *Briefe*, II, p. 243.

23 Westarp, speech of 26 April 1914, BA Berlin, Westarp Papers, Nr 25.

24 *Neue Preußische Kreuz-Zeitung*, 15 June 1913, cited in Sösemann, 'Hollow-Sounding Jubilees', p. 53.

25 Kaiser Wilhelm II to Crown Prince Wilhelm, 22 November 1913, printed in Hartmut Pogge von Strandmann, 'Staatsstreichpläne, Alldeutsche und Bethmann Hollweg', in Hartmut Pogge von Strandmann and Imanuel Geiss, *Die Erforderlichkeit des Unmöglichen. Deutschland am Vorabend des ersten Weltkrieges*, Frankfurt a.M. 1965, pp. 37–9.

26 Cambon to Pichon, 22 November 1913, as cited in Lindemann, *Perzeptionen*, p. 177.

27 Cited in King Friedrich August of Saxony to Kaiser Wilhelm II, 12 March 1912, Zmarzlik, *Bethmann Hollweg*, p. 70.

28 Kaiser Wilhelm II, marginal note on Bethmann Hollweg's submission of 31 May 1913, quoted ibid., p. 74, note 1.

29 Kaiser Wilhelm II, marginal note on Bülow's report of 20 May 1913, PA AA 3744, cited in part in Gutsche, *Wilhelm II.*, p. 149. See also Bethmann Hollweg to Ballin, 26 May 1913, Ballin to Bethmann Hollweg, 29 May 1913, PA AA R 3477.

30 Treutler to Auswärtiges Amt, 27 April 1913, ibid.

31 Thomas Mann, *Betrachtungen eines Unpolitischen*, Berlin 1918.

32 Tirpitz, memoir of a conversation with Kaiser Wilhelm II on 11 March 1912, in Tirpitz, *Aufbau der deutschen Weltmacht*, p. 324.

33 Bethmann Hollweg to Kaiser Wilhelm II, 20 March 1913 with the Kaiser's marginal comments; Kaiser Wilhelm II to Bethmann Hollweg, 23 March 1913, as cited in Zmarzlik, *Bethmann Hollweg*, pp. 27f.

34 Kaiser Wilhelm II to Crown Prince Wilhelm, 22 November 1913, printed in full in Pogge von Strandmann, 'Staatsstreichpläne, Alldeutsche und Bethmann Hollweg', pp. 37–9. See also Zmarzlik, *Bethmann Hollweg*, p. 30.

35 Bethmann Hollweg to Kaiser Wilhelm II, 14 January 1913, cited ibid., p. 25.

36 Bethmann Hollweg to Kaiser Wilhelm II, 26 January 1914, cited ibid., pp. 40 and 138.

37 Müller, diary for 12 September 1911, BA-MA Freiburg-im-Breisgau, Müller Papers.

38 Bethmann Hollweg to Eisendecher, 2 June 1913, as cited in Lindemann, *Perzeptionen*, pp. 164f.

39 See below, p. 978.

40 Wahnschaffe to Valentini, 9 April 1914, GStA Berlin, Valentini Papers, Nr 21. Cited in part in Zmarzlik, *Bethmann Hollweg*, p. 129, note 2.

41 Adolf Wermuth, *Ein Beamtenleben. Erinnerungen*, Berlin 1922, p. 287.

42 Valentini to Bethmann Hollweg, 2 May 1912, draft, GStA Berlin, Valentini Papers, Nr 2.

43 Hopman to Trotha, 21 February 1914, Staatsarchiv Bückeburg, Trotha Papers, A 135.

44 Kaiser Wilhelm II, marginal note on Bethmann Hollweg's submission of 9 August 1911, as cited in Zmarzlik, *Bethmann Hollweg*, p. 135.

45 Cf. ibid., pp. 12f.

46 See Eberhard von Vietsch, *Theobald von Bethmann Hollweg. Staatsmann zwischen Macht und Ethos*, Boppard am Rhein 1969, p. 165.

47 Plettenberg to his wife, 6 March 1913, Plettenberg Papers, in private hands, Essen.

48 Müller to Trotha, 31 August 1912, Staatsarchiv Bückeburg, Trotha Papers, A 227.

49 Pogge von Strandmann, 'Staatsstreichpläne, Alldeutsche und Bethmann Hollweg', pp. 14f. Cf. Valentini, diary for 19 and 22 November 1913, typescript copies in BA Koblenz, Thimme Papers, Nr 26.

50 Gebsattel, 'Gedanken über einen notwendigen Fortschritt in der inneren Entwicklung Deutschlands', September 1913, as cited in Pogge von Strandmann, 'Staatsstreichpläne, Alldeutsche und Bethmann Hollweg', pp. 16–18.

51 Bethmann Hollweg to Crown Prince Wilhelm, 15 November 1913, printed ibid., pp. 32–6.

52 Kaiser Wilhelm II to Crown Prince Wilhelm, 22 November 1913, printed ibid., pp. 37–9.

53 Crown Prince Wilhelm to Kaiser Wilhelm II, no date [late November 1913], GStA Berlin, 2.2.1 Nr 670/1.

54 Ibid.

55 Szögyény, dispatch of 16 December 1913, HHStA Vienna, Hofnachrichten F2.

56 Valentini, diary for 8 January 1914, BA Koblenz, Thimme Papers, Nr 26.

57 Paul Liman, *Der Kronprinz. Gedanken über Deutschlands Zukunft*, Minden 1914.

58 Ibid.

59 Wahnschaffe to Valentini, 26 May 1914 with a marginal comment by Valentini of 27 May 1914, GStA Berlin, 2.2.1 Nr 670/1.

60 Müller to Trotha, 28 December 1913, Staatsarchiv Bückeburg, Trotha Papers, A 227.

61 See the nineteen-page assessment by Kaiser Wilhelm II of the manoeuvres of 1912, BA-MA Freiburg-im-Breisgau, Moltke Papers, N 78/23; cf. Bienerth to Schemua, 4 June 1912, Kriegsarchiv Vienna, Generalstab, Militärattaché Berlin, Nr 12/12.

62 Vice Admiral Heeringen to Bethmann Hollweg, 10 June 1912, BA-MA Freiburg-im-Breisgau, RM5; Kaiser Wilhelm II, marginal comments on Kühlmann's reports from London of 16 and 18 September 1912, *Große Politik*, XXXI, Nos. 11595–6; see also his notes on von der Lancken's report of 22 September 1912 from Paris, ibid., No. 11599.

63 Bienerth to Schemua, 4 June 1912, Kriegsarchiv Vienna, Generalstab, Militärattaché Berlin, Nr 12/12.

64 See Zmarzlik, *Bethmann Hollweg*, pp. 31–3.

65 For the Zabern affair and its significance see Zmarzlik, *Bethmann Hollweg*, pp. 85–144; Fischer, *Krieg der Illusionen*, pp. 407–12; Hans-Ulrich Wehler, 'Der Fall Zabern', in Hans-Ulrich Wehler, *Krisenherde des Kaiserreichs 1871–1918. Studien zur deutschen Sozial- und Verfassungsgeschichte*, Göttingen 1979, pp. 70–89; David Schoenbaum, *Zabern 1913, Consensus Politics in Imperial Germany*, London 1982; Kirsten Zirkel, 'Vom Militaristen zum Pazifisten. Politisches Leben und Wirken des Generals Berthold von Deimling vor dem Hintergrund der Entwicklung Deutschlands vom Kaiserreich zum Dritten Reich', unpublished Dr Phil. dissertation, University of Düsseldorf 2006, pp. 123ff.; Gerd Fesser, '. . .ein Glück, wenn jetzt Blut fließt. . .' Die Zabernaffäre 1913/14, *Geschichte, Erziehung, Politik* 8, 1997, 351–9; Richard W. Mackey, *The Zabern Affair, 1913–1914*, Lanham 1991.

66 As cited in Zirkel, 'Deimling', p. 125.

67 Wedel to Bethmann Hollweg, 23 November 1913, ibid., p. 128.

68 Wedel to Bethmann Hollweg, 27 November 1913, ibid.

69 See Wedel to Bethmann Hollweg, 17 November 1913, cited in part in *Große Politik*, XXXIX, p. 229, note.

70 Treutler to Bethmann Hollweg, 4 December 1913, quoted in Zirkel, 'Deimling', p. 134, note 104.

71 Kaiser Wilhelm II, marginal note on an article in the *Leipziger Tageblatt* of 2 December 1913, cited in *Große Politik*, XXXIX, p. 230, note.

72 Kaiser Wilhelm II, marginal note on Schoen's report from Paris of 26 November 1913, ibid., No. 15658. See also below, p. 982.

73 Crown Prince Wilhelm to Kaiser Wilhelm II, no date [late November 1913], GStA Berlin, 2.2.1 Nr 670/1.

74 Crown Prince Wilhelm to Kaiser Wilhelm II, 21 February 1914, ibid.

75 Crown Prince Wilhelm to Deimling and Reuter, late November 1913, as cited in Zirkel, 'Deimling', p. 143. See Valentini to Bethmann Hollweg, 29 December 1913, ibid., note 142.

76 Wedel to Bethmann Hollweg, 23 November 1913, cited in Zmarzlik, *Bethmann Hollweg*, p. 115, note 2.

77 Wedel to Kaiser Wilhelm II, 30 November 1913; Kaiser Wilhelm II to Wedel, 30 November 1913, ibid., pp. 115 and 131.

78 Kaiser Wilhelm II to Wedel, 29 November 1913, Kaiser Wilhelm II to Deimling, 29 November 1913, ibid., pp. 114f.; Zirkel, 'Deimling', p. 132.

79 Wedel to Kaiser Wilhelm II, 1 December 1913, cited ibid., p. 133, note 101.

80 Bethmann Hollweg to Treutler, 29 November 1913, cited ibid., p. 133, note 102.

81 Bethmann Hollweg to Kaiser Wilhelm II, 3 December 1913, Kaiser Wilhelm II to Bethmann Hollweg, 4 December 1913, as cited in Zmarzlik, *Bethmann Hollweg*, p. 120; see also Zirkel, 'Deimling', p. 135.

82 Treutler to Bethmann Hollweg, 30 November 1913, Zmarzlik, *Bethmann Hollweg*, p. 115, note 5; Valentini, diary for 30 November 1913, typescript copy in BA Koblenz, Thimme Papers, Nr 26; cf. Valentini to Fürstenberg, 14 December 1913, FFA Donaueschingen.

83 Kaiser Wilhelm II, marginal note on Kühne's report of 2 December 1913, cited in Zmarzlik, *Bethmann Hollweg*, p. 119, note 4.

84 See ibid., pp. 116f.

85 *Stenographische Berichte über die Verhandlungen des Reichstags*, XIII. Legislaturperiode, 1. Session, 1913/14, Band 291, pp. 6155ff. and 6197.

86 Fischer, *Krieg der Illusionen*, p. 409. See Zirkel, 'Deimling', p. 137 and Afflerbach, *Falkenhayn*, p. 119.

87 Wahnschaffe, memorandum of 5 December 1913 of conversations with Spahn and Payer, Zmarzlik, *Bethmann Hollweg*, p. 119.

88 Hopman, diary for 8 December 1913, Epkenhans, *Leben eines 'Wilhelminers'*, p. 345.

89 Zmarzlik, *Bethmann Hollweg*, p. 119.

90 Bethmann Hollweg to Kaiser Wilhelm II, 4 December 1913, ibid., p. 121; Valentini, diary for 4 and 6 December 1913, typescript copies in BA Koblenz, Thimme Papers, Nr 26.

91 As cited in Zirkel, 'Deimling', p. 136.

92 Ibid., pp. 136f.

93 Wahnschaffe, minute of 5 December 1913, cited in Zmarzlik, *Bethmann Hollweg*, p. 120.

94 Bethmann Hollweg to Kaiser Wilhelm II, 3 December 1913, cited in Zmarzlik, *Bethmann Hollweg*, p. 120. See also Zirkel, *Deimling*, p. 135. See above, p. 976.

95 Crown Prince Wilhelm to Kaiser Wilhelm II, April 1914, GStA Berlin, 2.2.1 Nr 670/1.

96 Valentini to Bethmann Hollweg, 26 March 1914, GStA Berlin, Valentini Papers, Nr 2.

97 Wahnschaffe to Valentini, 9 April 1914, ibid., Nr 21.

37 'WITH HEAD HELD HIGH AND HAND ON SWORD-HILT!'
PREPARATIONS FOR WAR 1913 TO 1914

1 Pellé to Millerand, 26 May 1912, *Documents diplomatiques français*, 3rd series, III, No. 45.

2 Buchanan to Stamfordham, 7 April 1913, RA GV/P 284A/8.

3 Maurice Paléologue, 'La Russie des Tsars', *Revue des Deux Mondes*, 1921, I, p. 229. See also the view expressed by the French President Raymond Poincaré to E. Judet on 14 March 1914, referred to in *Große Politik*, XXXIX, p. 231, note.

4 See the photographs of the gigantic Fridtjov statue by Eduard Unger and the statue of King Bele designed by the Kaiser's boyhood friend Emil Count Görtz in Marschall, *Reisen und Regieren*, pp. 80ff.

5 Kaiser Wilhelm II, speech in Balestrand on 31 July 1913, the text of which was sent by Treutler to the Auswärtiges Amt on 26 July 1913 for publication, PA AA R 3754. See Kaiser Wilhelm II to Mary Montagu, 22 July 1913, copy in the author's private archive.

6 Gutsche, *Wilhelm II.*, p. 151. But cf. Clark, *Kaiser Wilhelm II*, pp. 189–202; Clark, *Sleepwalkers*, passim. See the important analyses by Stig Förster, 'Im Reich des Absurden: Die Ursachen des Ersten Weltkrieges', in Bernd Wegner, ed., *Wie Kriege entstehen. Zum historischen Hintergrund von Staatenkonflikten*, Paderborn, Munich, Vienna and Zürich 2000, pp. 211–52; Annika Mombauer, *The Origins of the First World War. Controversies and Consensus*, London 2002; Samuel R. Williamson Jr and Ernest R. May, 'An Identity of Opinion: Historians and July 1914', *The Journal of Modern History*, June 2007, 335–87; Holger Afflerbach and David Stevenson, eds. *An Improbable War? The Outbreak of World War I and European Political Culture before 1914*, Oxford and New York 2007.

7 Kaiser Wilhelm II, marginal notes on Jagow's telegrams of 15 and 16 April 1913, *Große Politik*, XXXIX, No. 15687–8.

8 Kaiser Wilhelm II, marginal note on Schoen's dispatch from Paris of 26 November 1913, ibid., No. 15658. Cited above, p. 974.

9 This was the assertion made by the Kaiser to the German Social Democrat Anton Fendrich at Charleville in 1915, Anton Fendrich, *Hundert Jahre Tränen, 1848–1948*, Karlsruhe 1953, pp. 127f.

10 See above, pp. 622–8.

11 See above, pp. 309–11.

12 Baron [Eugène] Beyens, *Deux années à Berlin, 1912–1914*, 2 vols., Paris 1931, II, p. 39f. See the textual analysis of this document in Jean Stengers, 'Guillaume II et le Roi Albert à Potsdam en novembre 1913', *Bulletin de la Classe des Lettres et des Sciences Morales et Politique*, 6th series, 4, 1993, . 227–53.

13 Ibid., pp. 234f.

14 Melotte to the Belgian War Minister, 25 November 1913, cited ibid., pp. 235f.

15 Kaiser Wilhelm II, marginal note on Schoen's report of 26 November 1913, *Große Politik*, XXXIX, No. 15658; Stengers, 'Guillaume II et le Roi Albert', 236-41.

16 Kaiser Wilhelm II, marginal comment on Pourtalès's report of 13 December 1913, *Große Politik*, XXXVIII, No. 15483.

17 Kaiser Wilhelm II, marginal note on Schoen's report of 11 February 1914, ibid., XXXVI/2, No. 14413.

18 Stengers, 'Guillaume II et le Roi Albert', 232-4.

19 Jules Cambon to Pichon, 22 and 24 November 1913, *Documents diplomatiques français*, 3rd series, VIII, pp. 653f. and 660.

20 Maurice Paléologue, *Au Quai d'Orsay à la veille de la tourmente, Journal 1913-1914*, Paris 1947, p. 239. On the reaction in Paris to Cambon's revelations see Stengers, 'Guillaume II et le Roi Albert', 248f.

21 Isvolsky to Sazonov, 4 December 1913, printed in Friedrich Stieve, *Der diplomatische Schriftwechsel Iswolskys, 1911-1914*, 3 vols., Berlin 1924, III, pp. 368f.

22 Paul Cambon, *Correspondance, 1870-1924*, Paris 1946, III, p. 55.

23 Stengers, 'Guillaume II et le Roi Albert', 250f.

24 'Rapport présenté à la Conférence des Préliminaires de paix par la Commission des responsabilités des auteurs de la guerre et sanctions', printed in *La Paix de Versailles. La Documentation Internationale*, 13 vols., Paris 1929-32, p. 461. See Fritz Dickmann, 'Die Kriegsschuldfrage auf der Friedenskonferenz von Paris 1919', *Historische Zeitschrift* 197/1, August 1963.

25 *Deutschland schuldig? Deutsches Weißbuch über die Verantwortlichkeit der Urheber des Krieges*, Berlin 1919, pp. 75f.

26 Kaiser Wilhelm II, marginal notes on Pourtalès's reports of 23 and 25 January 1913, *Große Politik*, XXXVIII, No. 15284 and XXXIV/1, No. 12729.

27 Kaiser Wilhelm II, marginal comment of 23 November 1913 on Jagow's submission of the same day, ibid., XXXVIII, No. 15452.

28 Kaiser Wilhelm II, marginal comment on Wangenheim's report of 3 December 1913, ibid., No. 15461.

29 Kaiser Wilhelm II, marginal comments on Wangenheim's telegram of 19 December 1913, ibid., No. 15492.

30 Kaiser Wilhelm II to Tsar Nicholas II, 26 February 1914, Goetz, *Briefe Wilhelms II. an den Zaren*, p. 416.

31 Kaiser Wilhelm II, marginal comments on Tschirschky's report of 11 February 1914, *Große Politik*, XXXVIII, No. 15434.

32 Goschen to Nicolson, 21 March 1914, National Archives, Kew, Nicolson Papers, F.O. 800/373.

33 Kaiser Wilhelm II, marginal comments on Pourtalès's report of 25 February 1914, *Große Politik*, XXXIX, No. 15841.

34 Crown Prince Wilhelm to Kaiser Wilhelm II, 21 February 1914 with a marginal remark by the Kaiser, GStA Berlin, 2.2.1 Nr 670/1.

35 See below, p. 1101.

36 Bienerth, report on the forthcoming session of the Reichstag, late December 1913, with comments by the Austro-Hungarian General Staff, Kriegsarchiv Vienna, Generalstab, Militärattaché Berlin 1913 47/4-44.

37 See Wernecke, *Wille zur Weltgeltung*, passim.

38 Wenninger to Kress von Kressenstein, 6 March 1914, Bayer. HStA Munich, MKr 41.

39 Kaiser Wilhelm II, marginal comments on Pourtalès's report of 11 March 1914, *Große Politik*, XXXIX, No. 15844.

40 See below, pp. 1009ff.

41 See below, pp. 997–1002.

42 Lichnowsky to Jagow, 16 May 1914 with the Kaiser's comment of 25 May 1914, Jagow to Kaiser Wilhelm II, 22 May 1914 with the Kaiser's comment of 24 May 1914, PA AA R 3716.

43 Prince Heinrich of Prussia to Kaiser Wilhelm II, 15 April 1913, ibid.

44 Prince Heinrich of Prussia, diary for 4 March to 8 May 1914, MSM Hamburg, Prince Heinrich Papers; Szögyény to Berchtold 10 February 1914, HHStA Vienna, Hofnachrichten F 2.

45 Kaiser Wilhelm II, marginal comments on Schoen's report of 12 March 1913, *Große Politik*, XXXIX, No. 15614.

46 Kaiser Wilhelm II, marginal comments on Kühlmann's report of 10 October 1913, ibid., No. 15577.

47 Kaiser Wilhelm II, marginal note on Kühlmann's telegram of 20 October 1913, ibid., No. 15578.

48 Kaiser Wilhelm II, marginal notes on Kühlmann's report of 11 December 1913, ibid., No. 15586.

49 Bethmann Hollweg to Kaiser Wilhelm II, 8 February 1914, ibid., No. 15590.

50 Kaiser Wilhelm II to Bethmann Hollweg, 9 February 1914, ibid., No. 15591.

51 Hopman to Trotha, 21 February 1914, Staatsarchiv Bückeburg, Trotha Papers, A 135.

52 Hopman to Trotha, 29 December 1913, ibid.

53 Hopman to Trotha, 21 February 1914, ibid.

54 Pohl, notes for his forthcoming audience with the Kaiser of 25 May 1914 with minute, BA-MA Freiburg-im-Breisgau, RM5/v 900, fol. 222.

55 Schulz, memorandum on the speech held by Tirpitz on 9 October 1913, BA-MA Freiburg-im-Breisgau, Tirpitz Papers, N 253/423. I thank Professor Michael Epkenhans warmly for drawing my attention to this key document.

56 State Secretary of the Reich Office of the Interior to Tirpitz, 18 and 23 March 1914, Tirpitz to Ingenohl, 25 March 1914, BA-MA Freiburg-im-Breisgau, RM5/v 1828; Commander of the High Seas Fleet to the Naval Commissar for the Kaiser Wilhelm Canal, 19 March 1914, ibid.

57 Delbrück to Tirpitz, 14 May 1914, ibid.

58 Reich Navy Office to Admiralty Staff, 16 April 1914, BA-MA Freiburg-im-Breisgau, RM5/v 1881; Tirpitz to Pohl, 16 May 1914, ibid.

59 Tirpitz to Müller, 23 April 1913, BA-MA Freiburg-im-Breisgau, RM5/v 1828.

60 Pohl to Müller, 2 May 1913, Müller to Pohl, 28 May 1913, BA-MA Freiburg-im-Breisgau, RM2/v 1816.

61 Marschall to Müller, 24 May 1913, BA-MA Freiburg-im-Breisgau, RM5/v 1828.

62 See Röhl, *The Kaiser's Personal Monarchy*, p. 929.

63 Pohl, memorandum 'Zum Immediatvortrag' of 17 October 1913 with subsequent minute of 20 October 1913, BA-MA Freiburg-im-Breisgau, RM5/v 899 fols. 411–15.

64 Pohl, memorandum 'Zum Immediatvortrag' of 24 April 1913 with subsequent minute of 29 April 1913, ibid., fols. 303–12. See also Pohl, 'Denkschrift zu den Allerhöchsten Befehlen an Seiner Majestät Schiffe im Auslande für den Kriegsfall', ibid., fols. 318–45.

65 Pohl, memorandum 'Zum Immediat-Vortrag' of 12 March 1914, approved by the Kaiser on 17 March 1914, BA-MA Freiburg-im-Breisgau, RM5/v 900, fols. 176–8.

66 Wedel to Jagow, 19 July 1914, Imanuel Geiss, ed., *Julikrise und Kriegsausbruch*, 2 vols., Hanover 1963–4, I, No. 147. See below, p. 1039.

67 See Matthew S. Seligmann, *The Royal Navy and the German Threat, 1901-1914: Admiralty Plans to Protect British Trade in a War Against Germany*, Oxford 2012.

68   Matthew S. Seligmann, 'New Weapons for New Targets: Sir John Fisher, the Threat from Germany, and the Building of H.M.S. *Dreadnought* and H.M.S. *Invincible*, 1902-1907', *International History Review* XXX/2 (June 2008), 303–31.

69   Pohl, memorandum 'Zum Immediatvortrag' of 5 May 1914 with subsequent minute of 26 May 1914, BA-MA Freiburg-im-Breisgau, RM5/v 900, fols. 199–204.

70   Pohl, memorandum 'Zum Immediatvortrag' of 15 May 1914 with subsequent minute of 9 June 1914, ibid., fols. 244–67.

71   Pohl, memorandum 'Zum Immediatvortrag' of 25 May 1914 with subsequent minute of 10 June 1914, ibid., fols. 231–40.

72   Tirpitz to Pohl, 18 June 1914, BA-MA Freiburg-im-Breisgau, RM5/v 1828.

73   Pohl to Tirpitz, 21 June 1914, ibid.

74   Müller, diary for 8 December 1912, cited above, pp. 909f.

75   'Direktiven für unser Verhalten gegenüber Holland und Belgien in einem Kriege Deutschlands mit England und Frankreich', 24 August 1912, BA-MA Freiburg-im-Breisgau, RM5/v 1608.

76   Straub to Conrad, 14 June 1913, Kriegsarchiv Vienna, Nr 243.

77   Bienerth, dispatch of 24 September 1913, Kriegsarchiv Vienna, 1913 47/4 35. See also Szeptycki, dispatch of 30 July 1913, Conrad, *Aus meiner Dienstzeit*, III, pp. 427–9. See Afflerbach, *Dreibund*, pp. 769ff.

78   Pohl, memorandum 'Zum Immediatvortrag' of 10 June 1913, BA-MA Freiburg-im-Breisgau RM5/v 899.

79   Pohl, minute of 30 July 1913 on the memorandum 'Zum Immediatvortrag' of 26 June 1913, ibid., fol. 380–8.

80   Pohl, memorandum 'Zum Immediatvortrag' of 26 May 1914 with subsequent minutes, BA-MA Freiburg-im-Breisgau, RM5/v 900, fol. 182–92.

81   Tschirschky, report of 25 March 1914, PA AA R 3650. See Tisza's memorandum of 15 March 1914 with Berchtold's numerous marginal comments, *Österreich-Ungarns Außenpolitik*, No. 9482.

82   Berchtold to Archduke Franz Ferdinand, 27 March 1914, MOL Budapest, Franz Ferdinand Papers, 231 db fols. 209–13.

83   Kaiser Wilhelm II to Fürstenberg, 26 March 1914, FFA Donaueschingen. Cf. Kaiser Wilhelm II to Grand Duchess Luise of Baden, 28 March 1914, GStA Berlin, BPHA Rep. 53, Nr 88; Kaiser Wilhelm II to Archduke Franz Ferdinand, 28 March 1914, MOL Budapest, Franz Ferdinand Papers, 183 db.

84   Valentini to Bethmann Hollweg, 26 March 1914, GStA Berlin, Valentini Papers, Nr 2.

85   Pacelli to Gaspari, 30 June 1917, in Hubert Wolf et al., eds., Kritische Online-Edition der Nuntiaturberichte Eugenio Pacellis (1917–29), Dokument Nr 366.

86   Valentini, diary for 27 March 1914, typescript copy in BA Koblenz, Thimme Papers, Nr 26.

87   Müller to Trotha, 7 April 1914, Staatsarchiv Bückeburg, Trotha Papers, A 226.

88   Kaiser Wilhelm II, marginal comments on Griesinger's report from Belgrade of 11 March 1914, *Große Politik*, XXXVIII, No. 15539.

89   Kaiser Wilhelm II, marginal notes on Flotow's report of 12 May 1914, ibid., No. 15551.

90   Bethmann Hollweg to Kaiser Wilhelm II, 5 and 6 April 1914, Kaiser Wilhelm II to Bethmann Hollweg, 5 April 1914, ibid., XXXVI/2, Nos. 14333 and 14335 with notes. See Kaiser Wilhelm II to Archduke Franz Ferdinand, 6 April 1914, MOL Budapest, Franz Ferdinand Papers, 183 db, fols. 215f.

91   On the attitude of Austria-Hungary to Wied see Kronenbitter, *'Krieg im Frieden'*, pp. 430ff.

92   Kaiser Wilhelm II, marginal comments on Flotow's telegram of 25 May 1914, *Große Politik*, XXXVI/2, No. 14452.

93   Kaiser Wilhelm II, marginal notes on Winckel's telegram of 29 May 1914, ibid., No. 14462.

94 Kaiser Wilhelm II, marginal note on Flotow's report of 30 May 1914, ibid., No. 14469.

95 Kaiser Wilhelm II, marginal comment on Flotow's report of 23 May 1914, ibid., No. 14451.

96 Kaiser Wilhelm II, marginal notes on Flotow's telegram of 30 May 1914, ibid., No. 14463.

97 Kaiser Wilhelm II, marginal notes on Flotow's second telegram of 30 May 1914, ibid., No. 14464.

98 Goschen to King George V, 6 June 1914, RA GV/P 586/3.

99 Kaiser Wilhelm II, marginal comments on Flotow's report from Rome of 17 June 1914, PA AA R 4284. Cf. *Große Politik*, XXXVI/2, No. 14498, where the Kaiser's final comment has been omitted. See also the Kaiser's concluding remark on Winckel's telegram from Valona of 22 June 1914, ibid., No. 14506.

100 Kaiser Wilhelm II, marginal notes of 1 July 1914 on Griesinger's report from Belgrade of 30 June 1914, ibid., No. 14522.

38 SUMMER 1914: THE DECISION FOR WAR

1 Kaiser Wilhelm II to Wilhelm Dörpfeld, 11 April 1914, MSM Hamburg, Karpf Papers.

2 Kaiser Wilhelm II to Grand Duchess Luise of Baden, 24 April 1914, GStA Berlin, BPHA Rep. 53, Nr 89. In similar vein: Kaiser Wilhelm II to Fürstenberg, 28 April 1914, FFA Donaueschingen.

3 Kaiser Wilhelm II to Grand Duchess Luise von Baden, 24 April 1914, GStA Berlin, BPHA Rep. 53, Nr 89.

4 Kaiser Wilhelm II to Mary Montagu, 3 May 1914, copy in the author's private archive.

5 Beyens to Davignon, 25 July 1914, Imanuel Geiss, ed., *Julikrise und Kriegsausbruch 1914*, 2 vols., Hanover 1963–4, I, No. 396.

6 Fleuriau to Bienvenu-Martin, 27 July 1914, ibid., II, No. 537.

7 See above, p. 750. Szögyény to Berchtold, 12 August 1913, *Österreich-Ungarns Außenpolitik*, VII, pp. 116ff.

8 Joseph Redlich, diary for 13 June 1915, Annika Mombauer, *The Origins of the First World War. Diplomatic and Military Documents*, Manchester 2013, No. 320; for Hoyos see below, p. 1023.

9 Conrad, *Aus meiner Dienstzeit*, III, p. 597.

10 Waldersee to Kageneck, 31 May 1914, cited in Kronenbitter, 'Macht der Illusionen', pp. 525f.; Mombauer, *Diplomatic and Military Documents*, No. 89.

11 Lerchenfeld, report of 6 June 1914, *Bayerische Dokumente zum Kriegsausbruch und zum Versailler Schuldspruch*, Munich 1925, No. 1.

12 See in particular Förster, 'Im Reich des Absurden'; Afflerbach, *Falkenhayn*; Mombauer, *Moltke*; Kronenbitter, '*Krieg im Frieden*'; Afflerbach and Stevenson, *An Improbable War?*; Günther Kronenbitter, 'Die Macht der Illusionen. Julikrise und Kriegsausbruch 1914 aus der Sicht des deutschen Militärattachés in Wien', *Militärgeschichtliche Zeitschrift* (formerly *Militärgeschichtliche Mitteilungen*) 57, 1998, 519–51.

13 Wenninger to Kress von Kressenstein, 29 July 1914, Geiss, *Julikrise und Kriegsausbruch*, II, No. 704. See below, pp. 1085ff. Cf. Leuckart von Weißdorff to Carlowitz, 29 July 1914, Geiss, *Julikrise und Kriegsausbruch*, II, No. 705.

14 Lerchenfeld to Hertling, 31 July 1914, ibid., No. 918.

15 Waldersee, 'Denkschrift über Deutschlands militärische Lage May 1914', 18 May 1914, BA-MA Freiburg-im-Breisgau, KGFA W-10/50279, Nr 94. See the translation of this document in Mombauer, *Diplomatic and Military Documents*, No. 85. See also Mombauer, *Moltke*, pp. 177f.

16 As cited in Egmont Zechlin, 'Motive und Taktik der Reichsleitung 1914', *Der Monat* 209, February 1966, 92.

17 See Ragnhild Fiebig-von Hase, 'Amerikanische Friedensbemühungen in Europa, 1905–1914', in Norbert Finzsch and Hermann Wellenreuther, eds., *Liberalitas*, Stuttgart 1992, pp. 312ff. See also Colonel Edward House to Kaiser Wilhelm II, 8 July 1914, in Arthur Stanley Link, ed., *The Papers of Woodrow Wilson*, 69 vols., Princeton, NJ, 1966–94, XXX, pp. 266f.

18 House to Wilson, 3 June 1914, ibid., pp. 139f.

19 Edward House, diary for 1 June 1914, printed in Charles Seymour, ed., *The Intimate Papers of Colonel House*, 2 vols., London 1926 (cited below as House, *Intimate Papers*), I, pp. 259–64.

20 Ibid., pp. 266ff.

21 Kaiser Wilhelm II, marginal comment on Wangenheim's report from Therapia of 8 June 1914, *Große Politik*, XXXVI/2, No. 14603.

22 Conrad, *Aus meiner Dienstzeit*, IV, pp. 38f. But cf. ibid., pp. 36f.

23 Kaiser Wilhelm II, marginal notes on an article in the *Berliner Lokal-Anzeiger* of 14 June 1914, Karl Kautsky, *Die deutschen Dokumente zum Kriegsausbruch. Im Auftrag des Auswärtigen Amtes*, ed. Max Montgelas und Walter Schücking, 4 vols., Charlottenburg 1919, No. 2.

24 Bethmann Hollweg to Lichnowsky, 16 June 1914, Kautsky, *Deutsche Dokumente*, No. 3. See Gutsche, *Wilhelm II.*, p. 153.

25 Wenninger to Kress von Kressenstein, 16 June 1914, Bayer. HStA Munich, Abt. IV, Mkr. 41.

26 See Bernd Sösemann, 'Die Bereitschaft zum Krieg. Sarajewo 1914', in Alexander Demandt, ed., *Das Attentat in der Geschichte*, Cologne, Weimar and Vienna 1996, pp. 295–320.

27 Max Warburg, *Aus meinen Aufzeichnungen*, Glückstadt 1952.

28 Müller, diary for 18–27 June 1914, BA-MA Freiburg-im-Breisgau, Müller Papers.

29 Goschen to King George V, 6 June 1914, RA GV/P 586/3.

30 House to Wilson, 3 June and 3 July 1914, *Papers of Woodrow Wilson*, XXX, pp. 139f. and 247f. See also House, diary for 17 July 1914, House, *Intimate Papers*, I, pp. 266ff.

31 Müller, memorandum of 27 November 1918, p. 1; cf. Walter Görlitz, ed., *Regierte der Kaiser? Kriegstagebücher, Aufzeichnungen und Briefe des Chefs des Marine-Kabinetts Admiral Georg Alexander von Müller 1914–1918*, Göttingen, Berlin and Frankfurt a.M. 1959, pp. 29f.

32 Kaiser Wilhelm II, marginal note on an article in the *Daily News* of 26 June 1914, cited in *Große Politik*, XXXIX, p. 106.

33 See *Der Krieg zur See 1914–1918*, 22 vols. in 7 parts, Berlin 1920–41, supplementary volumes Frankfurt a.M. 1964–6, Section 1: *Der Krieg in der Nordsee*, I, p. 2.

34 Wedel to Jagow, 25 June 1914, *Große Politik*, XXXIX, No. 15602.

35 Müller, diary for 28 June 1914, BA-MA Freiburg-im-Breisgau, Müller Papers; Prince Heinrich of Prussia, diary for 28 June 1914, MSM Hamburg.

36 Diary of an unknown court official, 30 June–2 July 1914, Archiv des vormals regierenden preußischen Königshauses, Burg Hohenzollern, Hechingen. Unfortunately the entries for 3 and 4 July 1914 are missing in this otherwise informative document. See Lüder Meyer-Arndt, *Die Julikrise 1914. Wie Deutschland in den ersten Weltkrieg stolperte*, Cologne and Vienna 2006, p. 19. See also Müller, diary for 1 July 1914, BA-MA Freiburg-im-Breisgau, Müller Papers, together with Müller's later account, written on 27 November 1918, entitled 'A Contribution to the History of the Outbreak of the World War (based on the diaries)', ibid., printed in Görlitz, *Regierte der Kaiser?*, pp. 29–41.

37 Waldersee to Zimmermann, 4 July 1914, PA AA R 996.

38 See the *Norddeutsche Allgemeine Zeitung*, Nos. 152 and 153, 2 and 3 July 1914. Reischach to Seckendorff, 2 July 1914, Prince Heinrich Papers, Schleswig-Holsteinisches Landesarchiv Schleswig, Abt. 395, Nr 42/I.

39 Eiswaldt to Auswärtiges Amt, 1 July 1914, Kautsky, *Deutsche Dokumente*, No. 6a.

40 Berchtold, memorandum of 3 July 1914, Geiss, *Julikrise und Kriegsausbruch 1914*, I, No. 14; Rumbold to Grey, 3 July 1914, Gooch and Temperley, *British Documents*, XI, No. 26; Mombauer, *Diplomatic and Military Documents*, No. 115.

41 Kaiser Wilhelm II, instruction to Tschirschky, cited in Bethmann Hollweg to Tschirschky, 2 July 1914, Kautsky, *Deutsche Dokumente*, No. 6b. See Tschirschky's report of 2 July 1914 on his audience with Emperor Franz Joseph, ibid., No. 9.

42 Müller, diary for 3 July 1914, BA-MA Freiburg-im-Breisgau, Müller Papers.

43 Crown Prince Wilhelm to Kaiser Wilhelm II, no date, received by the Kaiser on 5 July 1914, GStA Berlin, I. HA, Rep. 89, Nr 670/1.

44 Crown Prince Wilhelm to Bethmann Hollweg, 9 July 1914, GStA Berlin, BPHA Rep. 54 Nr 10/2.

45 Salza Lichtenau to Vitzthum, 2 July 1914, Geiss, *Julikrise und Kriegsausbruch*, I, No. 11. The Saxon military attaché Leuckart von Weißdorff reported in similar vein after a conversation with Waldersee. Leuckart to Carlowitz, 3 July 1914, ibid., No. 15.

46 Salza Lichtenau to Vitzthum, 2 July 1914, ibid., No. 11.

47 Hoyos, memorandum of his conversation with Naumann, 1 July 1914, ibid., No. 6.

48 Waldersee to Zimmermann, 4 July 1914, PA AA R 996.

49 Friedrich Thimme, 'Fürst Lichnowskys "Memoirenwerk"', *Archiv für Politik und Geschichte*, 10, 1928, 42f. Cf. Röhl, *Zwei deutsche Fürsten zur Kriegsschuldfrage*, pp. 20f. and 39–64.

50 Thimme, 'Lichnowskys "Memoirenwerk"', 31.

51 Pohl to Tirpitz, 3 July 1914, BA-MA Freiburg-im-Breisgau, RM5/v 1926.

52 Capelle to State Secretary of the Reich Office of the Interior, 9 July 1914, ibid.

53 Reich Navy Office to Commander of the High Seas Fleet, 22 and 23 July 1914, Naval Commissar for the Kaiser Wilhelm Canal to Reich Navy Office, 25 July 1914, ibid. See Hopman to Tirpitz, 24 July 1914, Volker R. Berghahn and Wilhelm Deist, 'Kaiserliche Marine und Kriegsausbruch 1914. Neue Dokumente zur Julikrise', *Militärgeschichtliche Mitteilungen* 1, 1970, No. 13.

54 See above, p. 1018.

55 See above, p. 1017.

56 Salza Lichtenau to Vitzthum, 2 July 1914, Geiss, *Julikrise und Kriegsausbruch*, I, No. 12. See above, pp. 1016f.

57 Tschirschky to Bethmann Hollweg, 2 July 1914, with approving marginal notes by Kaiser Wilhelm II, Geiss, *Julikrise und Kriegsausbruch*, I, No. 10.

58 Kaiser Wilhelm II, marginal note of 20 July 1914 on Pourtalès's report of 13 July 1914, Kautsky, *Deutsche Dokumente*, No. 53.

59 Tisza to Emperor Franz Joseph, 1 July 1914, Geiss, *Julikrise und Kriegsausbruch*, I, No. 8.

60 Kaiser Wilhelm II, marginal notes of 1 July 1914 on Griesinger's report from Belgrade of 27 June 1914, *Große Politik*, XXXVI/2, No. 14521.

61 Hoyos, memorandum of his conversation with Naumann, 1 July 1914, Geiss, *Julikrise und Kriegsausbruch*, I, No. 6.

62 See Conrad, *Aus meiner Dienstzeit*, IV, pp. 33f. Also Tisza to Emperor Franz Joseph, 1 July 1914, Geiss, *Julikrise und Kriegsausbruch*, I, No. 8.

63 Emperor Franz Joseph to Kaiser Wilhelm II, 2 July 1914, ibid., No. 9.

64 Kaiser Wilhelm II, marginal comment on Waldthausen's report from Bucharest of 16 June 1914, *Große Politik*, XXXVIII, No. 15532.

65 Waldersee to Zimmermann, 4 July 1914, PA AA R 996.

66 Kaiser Wilhelm II, marginal notes on Tschirschky's report of 30 July 1914, Kautsky, *Deutsche Dokumente*, No. 7; Mombauer, *Diplomatic and Military Documents*, No. 108.

See further Wilhelm II's underlinings and marginal comments on the report from Belgrade of 30 June 1914, ibid., No. 10.

67 See Berchtold's memorandum of 3 July 1914, Geiss, *Julikrise und Kriegsausbruch*, I, No. 14.

68 Forgáchs, memorandum of 4 July 1914, ibid., No. 19.

69 *Norddeutsche Allgemeine Zeitung*, No. 156, 7 July 1914.

70 Emperor Franz Joseph to Kaiser Wilhelm II, 2 July 1914, Kautsky, *Deutsche Dokumente*, No. 13.

71 Szögyény to Berchtold, 5 July 1914, Geiss, *Julikrise und Kriegsausbruch*, I, No. 21. See also Bethmann Hollweg to Tschirschky, 6 July 1914, Kautsky, *Deutsche Dokumente*, No. 15; and Berchtold to Tisza, 6 July 1914, Geiss, *Julikrise und Kriegsausbruch*, I, No. 28.

72 Kageneck to Moltke, 7 July 1914, ibid., No. 44. On Kageneck's role see Kronenbitter, 'Die Macht der Illusionen'.

73 Szögyény to Berchtold, 5 July 1914, Geiss, *Julikrise und Kriegsausbruch*, I, No. 21. Also Szögyény to Berchtold, 21 July 1914, ibid., No. 179.

74 Theobald von Bethmann Hollweg, *Betrachtungen zum Weltkrieg*, 2 vols., Berlin 1919, I, pp. 134ff. Cf. the diary of Adjutant-General Hans von Plessen for 5 July 1914, Holger Afflerbach, ed., *Der Kaiser als Oberster Kriegsherr im Ersten Weltkrieg. Quellen aus der militärischen Umgebung des Kaisers 1914–1918*, Munich 2005, No. P 4, cited below, p. 1025. Afflerbach describes the gathering in the Neues Palais as an almost formal meeting. Afflerbach, *Falkenhayn*, p. 149.

75 Bethmann Hollweg, *Betrachtungen zum Weltkrieg*, I, pp. 134ff.

76 Written submission by Falkenhayn to the parliamentary committee of enquiry, 1919, Geiss, *Julikrise und Kriegsausbruch*, I, No. 23b.

77 Plessen, diary entry for 5 July 1914, Afflerbach, *Kriegsherr*, No. P 4.

78 See above, pp. 1019f.

79 Zenker, statement of 8 November 1919, Kautsky, *Deutsche Dokumente*, p. xvi.

80 Hopman, diary entry for 7 July 1914, Epkenhans, *Leben eines 'Wilhelminers'*, pp. 384f. See Hopman to Tirpitz, 6 July 1914, printed in Berghahn and Deist, 'Kaiserliche Marine und Kriegsausbruch 1914', No. 1. Cf. Falkenhayn to Moltke, 5 July 1914, Geiss, *Julikrise und Kriegsausbruch*, I, No. 23 a). For Falkenhayn's evidently mistaken view of the Reich Chancellor's aims see Afflerbach, *Falkenhayn*, pp. 149–51.

81 Bertrab's statement of 20 October 1919, Kautsky, *Deutsche Dokumente*, pp. xivf.

82 Waldersee's statement of 25 October 1919, ibid., p. xv.

83 Hilmar Freiherr von dem Bussche-Haddenhausen, memorandum of 30 August 1917, ibid., annex VIII, p. 171.

84 See above, pp. 1024f. and Waldersee's statement of 25 October 1919, ibid., p. xv.

85 Hopman, diary for 6 July 1914, Epkenhans, *Leben eines 'Wilhelminers'*, pp. 382–4.

86 Hopman to Tirpitz, 9 and 13 July 1914, Berghahn and Deist, 'Kaiserliche Marine und Kriegsausbruch 1914', Nos. 4 and 6. Of some significance is Hopman's remark that the question of whether the *Panther* should set sail or not was being keenly followed by the Auswärtiges Amt, since in answering it the Kaiser would have to commit himself one way or the other on whether he was expecting a war. Ibid., No. 4.

87 Hopman to Tirpitz, 7 and 9 July 1914, ibid., Nos. 3 and 4. See also Behncke's statement to the parliamentary committee of enquiry in 1919, cited in Geiss, *Julikrise und Kriegsausbruch*, I, p. 229.

88 Falkenhayn to Moltke, 5 July 1914, ibid., No. 23; Bertrab to Moltke, 6 July 1914, ibid., No. 33; Alfred von Wegerer, *Der Ausbruch des Weltkrieges 1914*, 2 vols., Berlin 1939, I, p. 135. See the correspondence between Hopman and Tirpitz in Berghahn and Deist, 'Kaiserliche Marine und Kriegsausbruch 1914', pp. 37–58.

89 Waldersee's statement to the committee of enquiry, cited in Geiss, *Julikrise und Kriegs-ausbruch*, I, p. 97.

90 See in particular Mombauer, *Moltke*, pp. 191ff.

91 Imanuel Geiss, ed., *Juli 1914. Die europäische Krise und der Ausbruch des Ersten Weltkrieges*, Munich 1965, p. 69.

92 Falkenhayn to Moltke, 5 July 1914, Geiss, *Julikrise und Kriegsausbruch*, I, No. 23a.

93 Capelle's statement of 8 October 1919, ibid., No. 32a.

94 Schoen, report of 18 July 1914, ibid., No. 138.

95 Fischer, *Krieg der Illusionen*, p. 692. Cf. the account compiled by Admiral von Müller in the aftermath of Germany's defeat on 27 November 1918, pp. 3f; in Görlitz, *Regierte der Kaiser?*, p. 31.

96 Szögyény to Berchtold, 6 July 1914, Geiss, *Julikrise und Kriegsausbruch*, I, No. 27. See Bethmann Hollweg to Tschirschky, 6 July 1914, ibid., No. 34. Also Bethmann Hollweg, *Betrachtungen zum Weltkrieg*, I, p. 136; Conrad, *Aus meiner Dienstzeit*, IV, pp. 53ff.

97 Berchtold to Tisza, 8 July 1914, cited in Gutsche, *Wilhelm II.*, p. 160. On Tschirschky's role in the July Crisis see Hatzfeldt, *Heinrich von Tschirschky*, pp. 37–43.

98 Szögyény to Berchtold, 12 July 1914, Geiss, *Julikrise und Kriegsausbruch*, I, No. 75.

99 Graf Alexander Hoyos, 'Meine Mission nach Berlin', printed in Fritz Fellner, 'Die "Mission Hoyos"', in Wilhelm Alff, ed., *Deutschlands Sonderung von Europa 1862–1945*, Frankfurt a.M., Bern and New York 1984, pp. 309–16. See Clark, *Sleepwalkers*, pp. 412ff. See also the informative report of the Bavarian chargé d'affaires in Berlin, Schoen, of 18 July 1914, Geiss, *Julikrise und Kriegsausbruch*, I, No. 138.

100 Hopman to Tirpitz, 9 July 1914, Berghahn and Deist, 'Kaiserliche Marine und Kriegs-ausbruch 1914', No. 4. See also Hopman, diary for 8 July 1914, *Epkenhans, Leben eines 'Wilhelminers'*, p. 386.

39 THE KAISER'S LAST NORWEGIAN CRUISE

1 Müller, diary for 6 July 1914, BA-MA Freiburg-im-Breisgau, Müller Papers; *Nord-deutsche Allgemeine Zeitung*, No. 157, 8 July 1914.

2 Fischer, *Krieg der Illusionen*, p. 692; Willi A. Boelcke, ed., *Krupp und die Hohenzollern in Dokumenten*, Frankfurt a.M. 1970, p. 222; Gutsche, *Wilhelm II.*, p. 160; Lindemann, *Perzeptionen*, pp. 177f. See Dietrich von Bethmann Hollweg's recollections of the Kaiser's (and the Chancellor's) determination this time to let it come to war in Redlich's diary for 13 June 1915, Mombauer, *Diplomatic and Military Documents*, No. 320.

3 Kaiser Wilhelm II to Prince Heinrich of Prussia, 6 July 1914, Prince Heinrich Papers, Schleswig-Holsteinisches Landesarchiv Schleswig, Abt. 395, Nr 13.

4 Lyncker to his wife, 21 and 22 July 1914, Afflerbach, *Kriegsherr*, No. L 2–3. On the Kaiser's last Scandinavian cruise see also Cecil, *Wilhelm II: Emperor and Exile*, pp. 201ff.; Marschall, *Reisen und Regieren*, pp. 168–80.

5 See ibid., p. 171.

6 On 19 July 1914 Wedel reported that the intention was to remain at Balholm until about 30 July, then to call in at Bergen for a day to take on coal before returning to Swinemünde. Wedel to Jagow, 19 July 1914, Kautsky, *Deutsche Dokumente*, No. 79. See also Behncke to Jagow, 21 July 1914, ibid., No. 96.

7 The secret telegrams from Tschirschky and Stolberg of 7, 8, 10, 13 and 17 July from Vienna, Griesinger's dispatches of 6 and 8 July from Belgrade, the 'top-secret' telegram sent by Quadt on 9 July 1914 from Athens and also Waldburg's reports of 10 and 11 July 1914 from Bucharest were all forwarded to the Kaiser – if in some cases in shortened form – in this first phase of the crisis. See ibid., Nos. 18, 19, 19a, 24, 27, 28, 29, 32, 40, 41

and 65. Lichnowsky's reports from London of 17 and 20 July 1914 were also sent on to the Kaiser. Ibid., Nos. 76 and 92. Once the crisis reached its climax around 23 July all the relevant dispatches were forwarded by the Wilhelmstrasse to Wilhelm in Balholm. See Müller's account of 27 November 1918, p. 5, in Görlitz, *Regierte der Kaiser?*, p. 32.

8 Manfried Rauchensteiner, *Der Tod des Doppeladlers. Österreich-Ungarn und der Erste Weltkrieg*, Graz, Vienna and Cologne 1993, p. 75. The Prussian War Minister, von Falkenhayn, was aware that Austria-Hungary intended in advance to declare any Serbian response 'as unsatisfactory ... It is intent on the big showdown.' As cited in Hans von Zwehl, *Falkenhayn*, Berlin 1926, p. 56. See also Redlich's diary for 23-4 July 1914, Mombauer, *Diplomatic and Military Documents*, No. 205.

9 See Lindemann, *Perzeptionen*, pp. 142f.

10 Kaiser Wilhelm II, marginal notes on Tschirschky's report from Vienna of 10 July 1914, Kautsky, *Deutsche Dokumente*, No. 29.

11 Kaiser Wilhelm II, marginal notes on Tschirschky's report of 14 July 1914, Geiss, *Julikrise und Kriegsausbruch*, I, No. 91.

12 Kaiser Wilhelm II to Emperor Franz Joseph, sent on 14 July 1914, Kautsky, *Deutsche Dokumente*, Nos. 25 and 26.

13 Kaiser Wilhelm II, marginal notes on Wangenheim's telegram from Constantinople of 21 July 1914, ibid., No. 99.

14 Kaiser Wilhelm II, marginal notes on Tschirschky's report from Vienna of 14 July 1914, Geiss, *Julikrise und Kriegsausbruch*, I, Nos. 91 and 92.

15 Kaiser Wilhelm II, marginal notes on Tschirschky's report of 10 July 1914, ibid., No. 66. See Rauchensteiner, *Tod des Doppeladlers*, p. 75.

16 Herman Frobenius, *Des deutschen Reiches Schicksalsstunde*, Berlin 1914 (also published as *Germany's Hour of Destiny*, New York, 1914). The telegram was printed in *Vorwärts* on 16 July 1914, see Epkenhans, *Leben eines 'Wilhelminers'*, p. 390, note 154. For the incident see Herre, *Kronprinz Wilhelm*, pp. 39f. and 51.

17 Jagow to Bethmann Hollweg, 19 July 1914, as cited in Lindemann, *Perzeptionen*, p. 146. See Hopman, diary for 16 July 1914, Epkenhans, *Leben eines 'Wilhelminers'*, pp. 389f.

18 Bethmann Hollweg to Crown Prince Wilhelm, draft of 17 July 1914, sent on 19 July 1914, GStA Berlin, BPHA Rep. 54 Nr 10/3. Cited in part in John C. G. Röhl, 'Vorsätzlicher Krieg? Die Ziele der deutschen Politik im Juli 1914', in Wolfgang Michalka, *Der Erste Weltkrieg. Wirkung, Wahrnehmung, Analyse*, Munich and Zürich 1994, pp. 203f.

19 Bethmann Hollweg to Kaiser Wilhelm II, 20 July 1914, Kautsky, *Deutsche Dokumente*, No. 84.

20 Kaiser Wilhelm II to Crown Prince Wilhelm, 21 July 1914, ibid., No. 105.

21 Crown Prince Wilhelm to Kaiser Wilhelm II, Crown Prince Wilhelm to Bethmann Hollweg, 23 July 1914, ibid., Nos. 132 and 133.

22 Riezler, *Tagebücher*, p. 190.

23 Wangenheim to Auswärtiges Amt, 19 July 1914, with marginal notes by Kaiser Wilhelm II, Kautsky, *Deutsche Dokumente*, No. 81.

24 Wangenheim to Auswärtiges Amt, 21 July 1914, with marginal notes by Kaiser Wilhelm II, ibid., No. 99.

25 Kaiser Wilhelm II, marginal note of 26 July 1914 on the report from Sofia of 25 July 1914, ibid., No. 162.

26 Jagow to Kaiser Wilhelm II, 23 July 1914, with marginal notes by the Kaiser, *Große Politik*, XXXVI/2, No. 14647. See King Constantine of Greece to Kaiser Wilhelm II, 27 July 1914, Kautsky, *Deutsche Dokumente*, No. 243.

27 Wangenheim, report from Constantinople of 22 July 1914, with marginal notes by the Kaiser, ibid., No. 117. See *Große Politik*, XXXVI/2, No. 14648. See also Wedel to Jagow,

Jagow to Wangenheim, Wangenheim to Jagow, 24 July 1914, Kautsky, *Deutsche Dokumente*, Nos. 141, 144 and 147.

28 Kaiser Wilhelm II, marginal comment of 24 July 1914 on Wangenheim's telegram from Therapia of 23 July 1914, ibid., No. 149.

29 See ibid., p. 162.

30 See Wangenheim to Jagow, 28 July 1914, Bethmann Hollweg to Wangenheim, 28 July 1914, Geiss, *Julikrise und Kriegsausbruch*, II, Nos. 574 and 586. See below, pp. 1099–104.

31 See Bunsen to Grey, 30 July 1914, Geiss, *Julikrise und Kriegsausbruch*, II, No. 845 with the minute by Arthur Nicolson and the editor's note.

32 See Müller, diary for 6 July 1914, BA-MA Freiburg-im-Breisgau, Müller Papers; see also above, p. 1029.

33 Müller, diary for 19 July 1914, ibid.

34 See above, pp. 1032f.

35 See Berghahn and Deist, 'Kaiserliche Marine und Kriegsausbruch 1914', Nos. 6 and 11.

36 Kaiser Wilhelm II, marginal notes of 27 or 28 July 1914 on Pourtalès's report of 24 July 1914, Kautsky, *Deutsche Dokumente*, No. 203.

37 Kaiser Wilhelm II, marginal notes on Pourtalès's report from St Petersburg of 13 July 1914, ibid., No. 53.

38 Kaiser Wilhelm II, marginal notes of 23 July 1914 on Pourtalès's report of 21 July 1914, ibid., No. 120.

39 Kaiser Wilhelm II, marginal notes on Jagow's telegram of 23 July 1914 forwarding Lichnowsky's dispatch of 22 July 1914, ibid., No. 121.

40 Ibid., p. 143 and No. 140.

41 Tschirschky to Jagow, 24 July 1914, received on the *Hohenzollern* on 25 July 1914 at 8.15 hours. Ibid., No. 151.

42 Müller, diary for 25 July 1914, BA-MA Freiburg-im-Breisgau, Müller Papers.

43 Müller, account of 27 November 1918, printed in Görlitz, *Regierte der Kaiser?*, p. 33.

44 Ibid.

45 Kaiser Wilhelm II, marginal notes on the report of the Norddeich telegraphic agency of 24 July 1914, GStA Berlin, Eberhardt Papers, Rep. 92 Nr 18.

46 Kaiser Wilhelm II, marginal note on Reichenau's report of 26 July 1914, Geiss, *Julikrise und Kriegsausbruch*, II, No. 441a; Behncke's memorandum of his conversation with Jagow on 20 July 1914, Berghahn and Deist, 'Kaiserliche Marine und Kriegsausbruch 1914', No. 10.

47 Griesinger to Jagow, 24 July 1914, received on the *Hohenzollern* on 25 July 1914 at 15.45 hours, Kautsky, *Deutsche Dokumente*, No. 158.

48 Kaiser Wilhelm II, marginal notes of 25 July 1914 (afternoon) on Griesinger's report from Belgrade of 24 July 1914, ibid., No. 159.

49 Müller, diary for 25 July 1914, BA-MA Freiburg-im-Breisgau, Müller Papers. Cf. Müller's account of 27 November 1918, printed in Görlitz, *Regierte der Kaiser?*, p. 34.

50 Wedel to Jagow, 25 July 1914, Kautsky, *Deutsche Dokumente*, No. 173.

51 Wedel to Jagow, 19 July 1914, Geiss, *Julikrise und Kriegsausbruch*, I, No. 147.

52 Jagow to Wedel, 20 July 1914, Kautsky, *Deutsche Dokumente*, No. 90. See Cecil, *Albert Ballin*, p. 189.

53 See Behncke to Jagow, 22 July 1914, Kautsky, *Deutsche Dokumente*, No. 111. The Admiralty Staff's assessment was telegraphed to the Kaiser in Balholm on 3 July 1914.

54 Jagow to Bethmann Hollweg, 22 July 1914, ibid., No. 115. Behncke's statement to the parliamentary committee of enquiry 1919, Geiss, *Julikrise und Kriegsausbruch*, I, p. 229.

55 Müller, diary for 23 July 1914, BA-MA Freiburg-im-Breisgau, Müller Papers.

56 Behncke's memorandum on his conversation with Jagow and Stumm on 20 July 1914, Berghahn and Deist, 'Kaiserliche Marine und Kriegsausbruch 1914', No. 10; Hopman to

Tirpitz, 21 July 1914, ibid., No. 11; Hopman, diary for 21 July 1914, Epkenhans, *Leben eines 'Wilhelminers'*, pp. 391f.

57 Müller, diary for 19 July 1914, BA-MA Freiburg-im-Breisgau, Müller Papers. See Admiral von Müller's telegram to the Admiralty Staff of 19 July 1914, Kautsky, *Deutsche Dokumente*, No. 82. Also Hopman to Tirpitz, 20 July 1914, Berghahn and Deist, 'Kaiserliche Marine und Kriegsausbruch 1914', No. 9; Hopman, diary for 20 July 1914, Epkenhans, *Leben eines 'Wilhelminers'*, p. 391.

58 See Behncke's memorandum on his conversation with Jagow and Stumm on 20 July 1914, Berghahn and Deist, 'Kaiserliche Marine und Kriegsausbruch 1914', No. 10, and Hopman to Tirpitz, 21 July 1914, ibid., No. 11.

59 Bethmann Hollweg to Jagow, 21 July 1914, Kautsky, *Deutsche Dokumente*, No. 101. See the response of the Admiralty Staff and the Auswärtiges Amts, ibid., Nos. 111 and 115. Also Bethmann Hollweg to Jagow, 22 July 1914, Geiss, *Julikrise und Kriegsausbruch*, I, No. 205; Behncke's memorandum on his conversation with Jagow and Stumm on 20 July 1914, Berghahn and Deist, 'Kaiserliche Marine und Kriegsausbruch 1914', No. 10.

60 Kaiser Wilhelm II to Admiralty Staff, 23 July 1914, ibid., p. 57, note 114; *Der Krieg zur See, Nordsee*, I, p. 9.

61 Bethmann Hollweg to Wedel, 23 July 1914, Geiss, *Julikrise und Kriegsausbruch*, I, No. 235.

62 Hopman to Tirpitz, 22 July 1914, Berghahn and Deist, 'Kaiserliche Marine und Kriegsausbruch 1914', No. 12. Cf. Hopman, diary for 22 July 1914, Epkenhans, *Leben eines 'Wilhelminers'*, pp. 392f.

63 Behncke to Kaiser Wilhelm II, 23 July 1914, Berghahn und Deist, 'Kaiserliche Marine und Kriegsausbruch 1914', p. 57, note 117. See Hopman to Tirpitz, 24 July 1914, ibid., No. 13.

64 Ibid. Also Hopman, diary for 24 and 25 July 1914, Epkenhans, *Leben eines 'Wilhelminers'*, pp. 394–6.

65 Müller, diary for 24 July 1914, BA-MA Freiburg-im-Breisgau, Müller Papers. See Admiralty Staff to Jagow, 24 July 1914, Kautsky, *Deutsche Dokumente*, No. 175.

66 Zimmermann, memorandum of 25 July 1914, ibid., No. 174; Hopman, diary for 25 July 1914, Epkenhans, *Leben eines 'Wilhelminers'*, p. 396.

67 Müller, diary for 25 July 1914, BA-MA Freiburg-im-Breisgau, Müller Papers. Cf. Hopman, diary for 25 July 1914, Epkenhans, *Leben eines 'Wilhelminers'*, p. 396 with note 81.

68 Müller, diary for 25 July 1914, BA-MA Freiburg-im-Breisgau, Müller Papers. See Hopman, diary for 25 July 1914, Epkenhans, *Leben eines 'Wilhelminers'*, p. 396.

69 Professor Rheindorf's record of a conversation with Kurt Riezler on 20 May 1931, printed in Bernd F. Schulte, *Die Verfälschung der Riezler Tagebücher*, Frankfurt a.M., Bern, New York 1985, p. 175.

70 Müller, diary for 26 July 1914, BA-MA Freiburg-im-Breisgau, Müller Papers. Cf. Müller's account of 27 November 1918, printed in Görlitz, *Regierte der Kaiser?*, p. 35.

71 Bethmann Hollweg to Kaiser Wilhelm II, 25 July 1914, Geiss, *Julikrise und Kriegsausbruch*, I, No. 352.

72 Kaiser Wilhelm II, marginal notes of 26 July 1914 on Bethmann Hollweg's dispatch of 25 July 1914, Kautsky, *Deutsche Dokumente*, No. 182.

73 Müller, diary for 26 July 1914, BA-MA Freiburg-im-Breisgau, Müller Papers. Cf. Müller's account of 27 November 1918, printed in Görlitz, *Regierte der Kaiser?*, p. 35. Kaiser Wilhelm's telegram in reply is printed in Kautsky, *Deutsche Dokumente*, No. 231.

74 Erich von Müller to Reich Navy Office, 26 July 1914, ibid., No. 207.

75 Bethmann Hollweg to Kaiser Wilhelm II with the latter's marginal notes, 26 July 1914, ibid., No. 221.

76 Jagow to Wedel, 18 July 1914, ibid., No. 67. See Behncke's memorandum of his conversation with Jagow on 20 July 1914, Berghahn and Deist, 'Kaiserliche Marine und

Kriegsausbruch 1914', No. 10. Also Hopman, diary for 21 July 1914, Epkenhans, *Leben eines 'Wilhelminers'*, pp. 391f.

77 Lyncker to his wife, 21 July 1914, Afflerbach, *Kriegsherr*, No. L 2.

78 Lyncker to his wife, 22 July 1914, ibid., No. L 3.

79 Ibid.

80 Ibid.

81 Müller, diary for 23 July 1914, BA-MA Freiburg-im-Breisgau, Müller Papers.

82 Lyncker to his wife, 23 July 1914, Afflerbach, *Kriegsherr*, No. L 4.

83 Kaiser Wilhelm II to Admiralty Staff, 23 July 1914, Berghahn and Deist, 'Kaiserliche Marine und Kriegsausbruch 1914', p. 57, note 114; *Der Krieg zur See, Nordsee*, I, p. 9.

84 Müller, diary for 25 July 1914, BA-MA Freiburg-im-Breisgau, Müller Papers. Cf. Müller's account of 27 November 1918, printed in Görlitz, *Regierte der Kaiser?*, p. 34.

85 Müller's account of 27 November 1918, printed in Görlitz, *Regierte der Kaiser?*, p. 34.

86 Müller, diary for 25 July 1914, BA-MA Freiburg-im-Breisgau, Müller Papers; Müller's account of 27 November 1918, printed in Görlitz, *Regierte der Kaiser?*, p. 34.

87 Kaiser Wilhelm II, marginal notes on Tschirschky's report from Vienna of 24 July 1914, Kautsky, *Deutsche Dokumente*, No. 155. The dispatch was received on the *Hohenzollern* at noon on 26 July.

88 Kaiser Wilhelm II, marginal notes of 26 July 1914 on Lichnowsky's report from London of 24 July 1914, ibid., No. 157.

89 Wedel to Jagow, 26 July 1914, ibid., p. 171.

90 Kaiser Wilhelm II, marginal notes on Schoen's report from Paris of 24 July 1914, ibid., No. 154. The telegram was received by the Kaiser late in the evening of 25 July.

91 Kaiser Wilhelm II, marginal notes on Pourtalès's report from St Petersburg of 24 July 1914, ibid., No. 148.

92 Kaiser Wilhelm II, marginal notes on Pourtalès's report of 25 July 1914, Geiss, *Julikrise und Kriegsausbruch*, I, No. 283.

40 CONFUSION IN POTSDAM: THE FEAR OF BRITAIN'S INVOLVEMENT

1 Lyncker to his wife, 25–7 July 1914, BA-MA Freiburg-im-Breisgau, Lyncker Papers, MSg1/3251, Afflerbach, *Kriegsherr*, No. L 6. See Mombauer, *Diplomatic and Military Documents*, No. 231.

2 August Eulenburg to Kaiser Wilhelm II, 28 July 1914, GStA Berlin, I. HA, Rep. 89, Nr 3087.

3 Bethmann Hollweg to Kaiser Wilhelm II, 25 July 1914, received on the *Hohenzollern* on 26 July, 23.50 hours, Kautsky, *Deutsche Dokumente*, No. 191.

4 Chelius to Kaiser Wilhelm II, 25 July 1914, received on 27 July, 04.00 hours, ibid., No. 194.

5 Chelius to Kaiser Wilhelm II, 26 July 1914, ibid., No. 291.

6 Bethmann Hollweg to Kaiser Wilhelm II with the latter's marginal comments, 26 July 1914, received 27 July, 04.00 hours, ibid., No. 197.

7 Bethmann Hollweg to Kaiser Wilhelm II, 26 July 1914, cited in Gutsche, *Wilhelm II.*, p. 164.

8 Müller, diary for 27 July 1914, BA-MA Freiburg-im-Breisgau, Müller Papers. Cf. Müller, memorandum of 27 November 1918, printed in Görlitz, *Regierte der Kaiser?*, p. 35.

9 Ibid.

10 Hopman, diary for 27 July 1914, Epkenhans, *Leben eines 'Wilhelminers'*, pp. 399–401.

11 See *Der Krieg zur See, Nordsee*, I, p. 17.

12 Bethmann Hollweg to Kaiser Wilhelm II, 27 July 1914, Kautsky, *Deutsche Dokumente*, No. 245.

13 Moltke to his wife, 27 July 1914, Moltke, *Erinnerungen, Briefe, Dokumente*, p. 381.

14 Plessen, diary for 27 July 1914, Mombauer, *Diplomatic and Military Documents*, No. 266.

15 Bethmann Hollweg discussed these reports and telegrams from Pourtalès, Tschirschky and Flotow with the Kaiser at their meeting in Potsdam on 27 July. See Kautsky, *Deutsche Dokumente*, Nos. 204, 205, 213, 216, 217 and 220.

16 Schoen to Jagow, telegrams of 26 July 1914, ibid., Nos. 235 and 240.

17 Pourtalès to Jagow, telegrams of 26 and 27 July 1914, ibid., Nos. 216, 230, 238 and 242.

18 Bethmann Hollweg, marginal comment of 27 July 1914 on Pourtalès's telegram of 26 July 1914, ibid., No. 229. Wilhelm von Stumm's draft for a dispatch from the Kaiser to the Tsar is printed ibid., No. 233.

19 See Tschirschky's telegram to Jagow, 21 July 1914, shown to the Kaiser in Balholm on 22 July, ibid., No. 104.

20 Kaiser Wilhelm II, marginal notes of 26 July 1914 on Flotow's report from Rome of 24 July 1914, ibid., No. 168; Mombauer, *Diplomatic and Military Documents*, No. 197.

21 Flotow to Bethmann Hollweg, 25 July 1914, with a minute by the Chancellor of 27 July 1914, ibid., No. 244.

22 Jagow to Tschirschky, 27 July 1914, ibid., No. 267.

23 Müller, diary for 27 July 1914, BA-MA Freiburg-im-Breisgau, Müller Papers. Cf. Müller, memorandum of 27 November 1918, printed in Görlitz, *Regierte der Kaiser?*, pp. 35f. On the Chancellor's assessment of the situation on this day see his telegram to Kaiser Wilhelm II of 27 July 1914, Geiss, *Julikrise und Kriegsausbruch*, II, No. 489.

24 Weizsäcker to his father, 28 July 1914, as cited in Epkenhans, *Leben eines 'Wilhelminers'*, p. 401, note 207.

25 Falkenhayn, diary for 27 July 1914, Afflerbach, *Falkenhayn*, p. 154.

26 Kaiser Wilhelm II, marginal notes on Flotow's telegram of 27 July 1914, Kautsky, *Deutsche Dokumente*, No. 249.

27 Ibid.

28 Kaiser Wilhelm II, marginal note on Schoen's telegram of 27 July 1914, Kautsky, *Deutsche Dokumente*, No. 252.

29 Tschirschky to Jagow, 27 July 1914, ibid., No. 257.

30 Bethmann Hollweg to Brockdorff-Rantzau, draft telegram of 27 July 1914 with a marginal note by the Chancellor, sent on 29 July 1914, ibid., No. 371.

31 Naval attaché Erich von Müller to Reich Navy Office, 26 July 1914, ibid., No. 207.

32 Weizsäcker to his father, 28 July 1914, as cited in Epkenhans, *Leben eines 'Wilhelminers'*, p. 401, note 207. Müller, diary for 27 July 1914, BA-MA Freiburg-im-Breisgau, Müller Papers. Cf. Müller, memorandum of 27 November 1918, printed in Görlitz, *Regierte der Kaiser?*, pp. 35f. Also Riezler, *Tagebücher*, p. 191; Tirpitz, *Erinnerungen*, pp. 218–24; Alfred von Tirpitz, *Deutsche Ohnmachtspolitik im Weltkriege*, Hamburg and Berlin 1926, p. 7.

33 Lichnowsky to Jagow, 26 July 1914, with deletions and marginal comments by Bethmann Hollweg of 27 July 1914, Kautsky, *Deutsche Dokumente*, No. 236. Also Lichnowsky to Jagow, 27 July 1914, ibid., Nos. 265, 266 and 301. See Schoen to Jagow, 26 July 1914, ibid., No. 235.

34 Lichnowsky to Jagow, 26 July 1914, with deletions and marginal comments by Bethmann Hollweg of 27 July 1914, ibid., No. 236.

35 Bethmann Hollweg, minute on Lichnowsky's dispatch of 26 July 1914, ibid., No. 236.

36 Bethmann Hollweg, minute of 28 July 1914 on Pourtalès's report of 27 July 1914, ibid., No. 282.

37 Lichnowsky to Jagow, 27 July 1914, ibid., No. 258. See Friedrich Kießling, *Gegen den großen Krieg? Entspannung in den internationalen Beziehungen 1911–1914*, Munich 2002, pp. 281ff.

38 See Kautsky, *Deutsche Dokumente*, No. 283.

39 Müller, diary for 28 July 1914, BA-MA Freiburg-im-Breisgau, Müller Papers. Cf. Müller, memorandum of 27 November 1918, printed in Görlitz, *Regierte der Kaiser?*, p. 36. See the dispatches from Bucharest, Constantinople and Cetinje of 26 and 27 July 1914, which were laid before the Kaiser on the morning of 28 July 1914.

40 Bethmann Hollweg to Tschirschky, 27 July 1914, Kautsky, *Deutsche Dokumente*, No. 277.

41 Szögyény to Berchtold, 27 July 1914, Geiss, *Julikrise und Kriegsausbruch*, II, No. 479.

42 Bethmann Hollweg to Kaiser Wilhelm II, 27 July 1914, Kautsky, *Deutsche Dokumente*, No. 283.

43 Jagow to Kaiser Wilhelm II, 27 July 1914, ibid., No. 270.

44 Kaiser Wilhelm II, marginal comment of 28 July 1914 on the Serbian response of 25 July 1914 to the Austrian ultimatum, ibid., No. 271.

45 Plessen, diary for 28 July 1914, Mombauer, *Diplomatic and Military Documents*, No. 276.

46 Kaiser Wilhelm II to Jagow, 28 July 1914, ibid., No. 293. Mombauer, *Diplomatic and Military Documents*, No. 277.

47 Hopman, diary for 28 July 1914, Epkenhans, *Leben eines 'Wilhelminers'*, pp. 401–3. See Valentini to his wife, 30 July 1914, BA Koblenz, Valentini Papers, Kl. Erw. Nr 341–4.

48 Kaiser Wilhelm II, marginal comment on Bethmann Hollweg's submission of 29 July 1914, GStA Berlin, BPHA Rep 53J, Lit. B Nr 7.

49 Tschirschky to Jagow, two telegrams of 28 July 1914, submitted to the Kaiser on that same day, Kautsky, *Deutsche Dokumente*, Nos. 311 and 313.

50 Bethmann Hollweg to Tschirschky, 28 July 1914, ibid., No. 323.

51 Bethmann Hollweg to Kaiser Wilhelm II, 28 July 1914, ibid., No. 308. See the Kaiser's marginal comments on the dispatch from General von Chelius of 29 July 1914, ibid., No. 344.

52 Tirpitz, *Ohnmachtspolitik*, pp. 2ff.

53 Kaiser Wilhelm II, marginal notes on the telegram from General von Chelius of 29 July 1914, Kautsky, *Deutsche Dokumente*, No. 343; marginal comments of 30 July 1914 on Lichnowsky's telegram of 29 July 1914, ibid., No. 368; marginal comments of 30 July 1914 on Schoen's telegram of 29 July 1914, ibid., No. 367.

54 Kaiser Wilhelm II, marginal comments on the telegram from Chelius of 28 July 1914, ibid., No. 337.

55 Falkenhayn, diary for 28 July 1914, Afflerbach, *Falkenhayn*, p. 154.

56 Falkenhayn, diary for 29 July 1914, ibid., p. 156. Cf. Zwehl, *Falkenhayn*, p. 56.

57 See above, pp. 899–904.

58 Prince Heinrich of Prussia, diary for 22–5 July 1914, MSM Hamburg, Prince Heinrich Papers.

59 Ibid., 26 July 1914.

60 King George V to Prince Heinrich of Prussia, 25 July 1914, MSM Hamburg, Prince Heinrich Papers, Mappe 9.

61 Prince Heinrich of Prussia to King George V, 26 July 1914, RA PS/GV/Q 1167/16.

62 See below, pp. 1079–83. See Headlam Morley to Sir William Tyrrell, 3 February 1921, Tyrrell to Stamfordham, 4 February 1921, Stamfordham to Tyrrell, 7 February 1921, RA PS/GV/Q 1167/12–14.

63 Kaiser Wilhelm II to Reich Navy Office and Admiralty Staff, 31 July 1914, Kautsky, *Deutsche Dokumente*, No. 474. See below, pp. 1077f.

64 Prince Heinrich of Prussia, diary for 26 July 1914 with a later addendum, MSM Hamburg, Prince Heinrich Papers.

65 King George V, diary for 26 July 1914, RA.

66 King George V, minute dated 26 July 1914, supposedly written 'directly after the interview', RA GV/Q 1167/15. See RA GV/Q 1167/11814; Nicolson, *George the Fifth*, pp. 245f.

67 Nicolson to Grey, 26 July 1914, *British Documents*, Gooch and Temperley, XI, No. 144.

68 Lichnowsky to Jagow, 26 July 1914, Kautsky, *Deutsche Dokumente*, No. 201.

69 Naval attaché Erich von Müller to Reich Navy Office, 26 July 1914, ibid., No. 207. The telegram arrived in Berlin at 16.00 hours. Hopman, diary for 26 July 1914, Epkenhans, *Leben eines 'Wilhelminers'*, pp. 397–9. For German assessments of British public opinion in the July crisis see Schramm, *Das Deutschlandbild in der britischen Presse*, pp. 277ff.

70 Prince Heinrich of Prussia, diary for 26 July 1914, MSM Hamburg, Prince Heinrich Papers.

71 Rainer von Hessen, ed., *Wolfgang Prinz von Hessen: Aufzeichnungen*, Kronberg 1986, p. 39.

72 See below, pp. 1077f.

73 See above, p. 1060.

74 Prince Heinrich of Prussia to Kaiser Wilhelm II, 28 July 1914, certified copy in the Trotha Papers, Staatsarchiv Bückeburg. A further certified copy is to be found in GStA Berlin, BPHA, Rep. 52 V1 Nr 13a. See Mombauer, *Diplomatic and Military Documents*, No. 281.

75 Prince Heinrich of Prussia, reader's letter to *Süddeutsche Zeitung*, 21 December 1921; Kurt Jagow, 'Buckingham Palace 26. Juli 1914, King George V. und Prinz Heinrich', *Berliner Monatshefte* XVI, July/August 1938. See Nicolson, *George the Fifth*, pp. 245f.

76 Wenninger to Kress von Kressenstein, 30 July 1914, printed in Bernd F. Schulte, 'Neue Dokumente zu Kriegsausbruch und Kriegsverlauf 1914', *Militärgeschichtliche Mitteilungen* 25, 1979, 138.

77 Prince Heinrich of Prussia, diary for 29 July 1914, MSM Hamburg, Prince Heinrich Papers.

78 See Kurt Jagow, 'Der Potsdamer Kronrat. Geschichte und Legende nach zum Teil unbekannten Quellen', *Süddeutsche Monatshefte* 25/11 (1928).

79 See Afflerbach, *Falkenhayn*, p. 154.

80 Falkenhayn, diary for 29 July 1914, ibid., pp. 155f. Cf. Zwehl, *Falkenhayn*, p. 56.

81 See Geiss, *Julikrise und Kriegsausbruch*, II, p. 237.

82 Müller, diary for 29 July 1914, BA-MA Freiburg-im-Breisgau, Müller Papers. Cf. Müller, memorandum of 27 November 1918, printed in Görlitz, *Regierte der Kaiser?*, pp. 36f.

83 Tirpitz, *Ohnmachtspolitik*, pp. 2–4. See Hopman, diary for 29 July 1914, Epkenhans, *Leben eines 'Wilhelminers'*, pp. 403f.

84 Wenninger to Kress von Kressenstein, 29 July 1914, Geiss, *Julikrise und Kriegsausbruch*, II, No. 704. See also Leuckart von Weißdorff to Carlowitz, 29 July 1914, ibid., No. 705.

85 Wenninger to Kress von Kressenstein, 30 July 1914, Schulte, 'Neue Dokumente zu Kriegsausbruch', p. 138.

86 Leuckart von Weißdorff to Carlowitz, 29 July 1914, Geiss, *Julikrise und Kriegsausbruch*, II, No. 705.

87 Varnbüler to Weizsäcker, 29 July 1914, ibid., No. 706.

88 Falkenhayn, diary for 29 July 1914, Afflerbach, *Falkenhayn*, p. 157.

89 See Kautsky, *Deutsche Dokumente*, No. 233. See above, p. 1049.

90 Bethmann Hollweg to Kaiser Wilhelm II, 28 July 1914, Kautsky, *Deutsche Dokumente*, No. 308.

91 Kaiser Wilhelm II to Tsar Nicholas II, 28 July 1914, Kautsky, *Deutsche Dokumente*, No. 335. The Kautsky edition records the amendments made by the Kaiser to the draft submitted by the Auswärtiges Amt. See Mombauer, *Diplomatic and Military Documents*, No. 285. For the reception of the telegram in St Petersburg see the daily record of the Russian Foreign Ministry for 29 July 1914, ibid., No. 305.

92 Tsar Nicholas II to Kaiser Wilhelm II, 29 July 1914, Kautsky, *Deutsche Dokumente*, No. 332; Mombauer, *Diplomatic and Military Documents*, No. 286.

93 Kaiser Wilhelm II, marginal comment on Bethmann Hollweg's submission of 29 July 1914, GStA Berlin, BPHA Rep. 53J, Lit. B Nr 7. See also Tirpitz, *Ohnmachtspolitik*, pp. 2f.

94 Kaiser Wilhelm II, marginal note of 30 July 1914 on Pourtalès's report of 26 July 1914, Kautsky, *Deutsche Dokumente*, No. 288.

95 Kaiser Wilhelm II, marginal notes on the telegram from the Tsar, 29 July 1914, ibid., No. 332. See also the Kaiser's comment on the telegram from General von Chelius of 28 July 1914, ibid., No. 337.

96 Bethmann Hollweg to Kaiser Wilhelm II, 29 July 1914, GStA Berlin, BPHA Rep. 53J Lit. B Nr 7.

97 Kaiser Wilhelm II to Tsar Nicholas II, 29 July 1914, Kautsky, *Deutsche Dokumente*, No. 359.

98 Tsar Nicholas II to Kaiser Wilhelm II, 29 July 1914, ibid., No. 366; Mombauer, *Diplomatic and Military Documents*, No. 289. Italics here and in the following quotation denote Wilhelm's underlinings.

99 Tsar Nicholas II to Kaiser Wilhelm II, 30 July 1914, Kaustky, *Deutsche Dokumente*, No. 390.

100 Kaiser Wilhelm II, marginal notes on the Tsar's telegram of 30 July 1914, ibid.

101 See Gerhard Ritter, *Staatskunst und Kriegshandwerk. Das Problem des 'Militarismus' in Deutschland*, 4 vols., Munich 1954–68, II, p. 384, note 34.

102 Geiss, *Julikrise und Kriegsausbruch*, II, p. 286, note 3.

103 Kaiser Wilhelm II, marginal notes on Bethmann Hollweg's submission of 29 July 1914, Kautsky, *Deutsche Dokumente*, No. 399.

104 Kaiser Wilhelm II to Tsar Nicholas II, 30 July 1914, ibid., No. 420.

105 Bethmann Hollweg to Kaiser Wilhelm II, 30 July 1914, ibid., No. 408.

106 Bethmann Hollweg to Kaiser Wilhelm II, 30 July 1914, with an approving comment by the Kaiser, ibid., No. 407.

107 Tirpitz, *Ohnmachtspolitik*, pp. 2ff.

108 Bethmann Hollweg to Goschen (by word of mouth), 29 July 1914, Kautsky, *Deutsche Dokumente*, No. 373.

109 Goschen to Grey, 29 July 1914, with the damning minute by Eyre Crowe: 'It is clear that Germany is practically determined to go to war, and that the one restraining influence so far has been the fear of England joining in the defence of France and Belgium.' Gooch and Temperley, *British Documents*, XI, No. 293. See also Geiss, *Julikrise und Kriegsausbruch*, II, No. 745; Mombauer, *Diplomatic and Military Documents*, No. 301.

110 Müller, diary for 30 July 1914, BA-MA Freiburg-im-Breisgau, Müller Papers.

111 Prince Heinrich of Prussia to King George V, 30 July 1914, Kautsky, *Deutsche Dokumente*, No. 417. The original is to be found in RA PS/GV/Q 1549/5. See Prince Heinrich of Prussia, diary for 30 July 1914, MSM Hamburg, Prince Heinrich Papers.

112 See Hopman, diary for 29 July 1914, Epkenhans, *Leben eines 'Wilhelminers'*, pp. 403f.

113 Müller, diary for 30 July 1914, BA-MA Freiburg-im-Breisgau, Müller Papers. Cf. Müller, memorandum of 27 November 1918, printed in Görlitz, *Regierte der Kaiser?*, p. 37. See also Wenninger to Kress von Kressenstein, 30 July 1914, Schulte, 'Neue Dokumente zu Kriegsausbruch', p. 139.

114 Pohl, 'Denkschrift über den O-Plan gegen Frankreich und Russland bei einem Krieg Dreibund gegen Zweibund', 24 July 1914, with marginal notes by Pohl of 30 July 1914, BA-MA Freiburg-im-Breisgau, RM5/v 900; Pohl, 'Operationsbefehl für den Ostseekriegsschauplatz', 30 July 1914, ibid., RM5/v 1676.

115 Pohl to the Commander of the High Seas Fleet, Admiral von Ingenohl, 30 July 1914, ibid. See the slightly different operation plan for warfare in the North Sea which Pohl submitted to the Kaiser during his audience, cited in Epkenhans, *Leben eines 'Wilhelminers'*, pp. 406f., note 243.

116 Pohl, 'Grundzüge für das Verhalten gegen den englischen Truppentransport', 30 July 1914, BA-MA Freiburg-im-Breisgau, RM5/v 1676.

117 Pohl, 'Befehle für unser Verhalten gegenüber den Neutralen', 30 July 1914, ibid.

118 Boedicker to Delbrück, 31 July 1914, BA-MA Freiburg-im-Breisgau, RM5/v 1926.

119 Hopman, diary for 30 July 1914, Epkenhans, *Leben eines 'Wilhelminers'*, pp. 405–7.

120 Kaiser Wilhelm II, marginal comment on Bethmann Hollweg's submission of 30 July 1914, Kautsky, *Deutsche Dokumente*, No. 407.

121 Kaiser Wilhelm II, marginal comments of 30 July 1914 on the article 'Efforts towards Peace' in the *Morning Post*, ibid., No. 402. Cf. the comments made by the Kaiser on two articles in the *Daily Chronicle* of 29 July 1914, ibid., No. 382.

122 Kaiser Wilhelm II, marginal notes of 30 July 1914 on Lichnowsky's report of 29 July 1914, ibid., No. 368. See Mombauer, *Diplomatic and Military Documents*, No. 296.

123 Kaiser Wilhelm II, marginal comment of 30 July 1914 on a dispatch from St Petersburg of 30 July 1914, Kautsky, *Deutsche Dokumente*, No. 401; Mombauer, *Diplomatic and Military Documents*, No. 322.

124 Kaiser Wilhelm II, marginal comment on Wangenheim's report of 29 July 1914, cited in Gutsche, *Wilhelm II.*, p. 167.

125 Kaiser Wilhelm II to Emperor Franz Joseph, 30 June 1914, Kautsky, *Deutsche Dokumente*, No. 437.

126 Bethmann Hollweg to Tschirschky, 30 July 1914, ibid., No. 441. See Bethmann Hollweg's minute on his telegram to the Kaiser, 30 July 1914, ibid., No. 440, note 1.

127 Prince Heinrich of Prussia, diary for 30 July 1914, MSM Hamburg, Prince Heinrich Papers.

128 Valentini to his wife, 31 July 1914, BA Koblenz, Valentini Papers, Kl. Erw. Nr 341–4. Cf. Valentini to Major von Harbou, 28 January 1919, printed in Valentini, *Kaiser und Kabinettschef*, pp. 125–8 and Valentini, diary for 30 July 1914, typescript copy, BA Koblenz, Thimme Papers, Nr 26.

129 King George V to Prince Heinrich of Prussia, 30 July 1914, with marginal comments by Kaiser Wilhelm II, Kautsky, *Deutsche Dokumente*, No. 452. The original is in Prince Heinrich's papers in the Schleswig-Holseinisches Landesarchiv in Schleswig, Abt. 355 Nr 148. A copy is to be found in RA PS/GV/Q 1549/. See also Mombauer, *Diplomatic and Military Documents*, No. 310.

130 See Geiss, *Julikrise und Kriegsausbruch*, II, p. 382. See the optimistic assessment of Prince Heinrich in Hopman, diary for 31 July 1914, Epkenhans, *Leben eines 'Wilhelminers'*, p. 407. See below, p. 1081.

131 Kaiser Wilhelm II, marginal comment of 31 July 1914 on Bethmann Hollweg's submission of 30 July 1914, Kautsky, *Deutsche Dokumente*, No. 466.

132 Kaiser Wilhelm II, marginal notes of 31 July 1914 on the telegram from Chelius of 30 July 1914, ibid., No. 445.

133 Valentini to his wife, 31 July 1914, BA Koblenz, Valentini Papers, Kl. Erw. Nr 341–4.

134 Kaiser Wilhelm II to Reich Navy Office and Admiralty Staff, 31 July 1914, Kautsky, *Deutsche Dokumente*, No. 474. A certified copy can be found in StA Bückeburg, Trotha Papers, Nr A257. A further copy is kept in GStA Berlin, BPHA Rep. 53 E I Weltkrieg 1. For the reaction of Tirpitz and Bethmann Hollweg to this document see Tirpitz, *Ohnmachtspolitik*, pp. 10f. See also Görlitz, *Regierte der Kaiser?*, pp. 37f.

135 Pourtalès's report was dated 27 July; it reached Berlin on the 29th and was laid before the Kaiser on 30 July 1914. Kautsky, *Deutsche Dokumente*, No. 339 and No. 474, note 12.

136 Müller, diary for 31 July 1914, BA-MA Freiburg-im-Breisgau, Müller Papers. Cf. Müller, memorandum of 27 November 1918, printed in Görlitz, *Regierte der Kaiser?*, pp. 37f.

137 Tirpitz, *Ohnmachtspolitik*, pp. 10f.

138 Kaiser Wilhelm II to President Woodrow Wilson, 14 August 1914, in *Papers of Woodrow Wilson*, XXX, pp. 382f. See James Watson Gerard, *My Four Years in Germany*, London

1917, pp. 199–202 and pp. 433–8. Cf. the version of this telegram printed in the *Daily Telegraph* on 6 August 1917.

139 Montgomery to Stamfordham, 11 August 1917, RA PS/GV/Q 1167/4; Stamfordham to Montgomery, 13 August 1917, RA PS/GV/Q 1167/6.

140 Kaiser Wilhelm II to King George V, 31 July 1914, RA GV/Q 1549/8.

141 Kaiser Wilhelm II to Reich Navy Office and Admiralty Staff, 31 July 1914, ibid., No. 474. See above, pp. 1077–9.

142 Kaiser Wilhelm II, marginal notes on Tschirschky's report of 30 July 1914, Kautsky, *Deutsche Dokumente*, No. 433.

143 Prince Heinrich of Prussia, diary for 30 July 1914, MSM Hamburg, Prince Heinrich Papers.

144 But see Bethmann Hollweg to Tschirschky, 30 July 1914, Kageneck to Waldersee, 30 July 1914, Mombauer, *Diplomatic and Military Documents*, Nos. 316 and 317.

41 INTO THE ABYSS: THE OUTBREAK OF WAR

1 Wenninger to Kress von Kressenstein, 30 July 1914, Schulte, 'Neue Dokumente zu Kriegsausbruch', pp. 138f.

2 Szögyény to Berchtold, 2 August 1914, Geiss, *Julikrise und Kriegsausbruch*, II, No. 1063. See below, p. 1096.

3 Kaiser Wilhelm II, marginal note of 3 August 1914 to the telegram from King Constantine of Greece of 2 August 1914, Kautsky, *Deutsche Dokumente*, No. 702. See below, p. 1102.

4 Szögyény to Berchtold, 2 August 1914, Geiss, *Julikrise und Kriegsausbruch*, II, No. 1063. See below, p. 1096.

5 General Karl Freiherr von Plettenberg, 'Erinnerungen', in private hands, Essen.

6 See Afflerbach, *Falkenhayn*, pp. 157f.

7 Falkenhayn, diary for 30 July 1914, ibid., pp. 158f. See also Wenninger to Kress von Kressenstein, 30 July 1914, Schulte, 'Neue Dokumente zu Kriegsausbruch', pp. 138f.

8 Hans von Haeften, 'Meine Erlebnisse aus den Mobilmachungstagen 1914', BA-MA Freiburg-im-Breisgau, Haeften Papers, N 35/1.

9 Pourtalès to Auswärtiges Amt, 31 July 1914, Kautsky, *Deutsche Dokumente*, No. 473. See Paléologue to Viviani, 30 July 1914, Geiss, *Julikrise und Kriegsausbruch*, II, No. 836.

10 Wenninger, diary for 31 July 1914, printed in Schulte, 'Neue Dokumente zu Kriegsausbruch', pp. 139f. See also Afflerbach, *Falkenhayn*, p. 161.

11 Lerchenfeld to Hertling, 31 July 1914, Geiss, *Julikrise und Kriegsausbruch*, II, No. 918.

12 Müller, diary for 31 July 1914, BA-MA Freiburg-im-Breisgau, Müller Papers. Cf. Görlitz, *Regierte der Kaiser?*, pp. 37f.

13 Wenninger, diary for 31 July 1914, printed in Schulte, 'Neue Dokumente zu Kriegsausbruch', pp. 139f.

14 Prince Heinrich of Prussia, diary for 31 July 1914, MSM Hamburg, Prince Heinrich Papers.

15 Lerchenfeld to Hertling, 31 July 1914, Geiss, *Julikrise und Kriegsausbruch*, II, No. 918.

16 Szögyény to Berchtold, 31 July 1914, ibid., II, No. 868. See also Lyncker's diary for 31 July 1914, below, p. 1088.

17 Falkenhayn, diary for 31 July 1914, Afflerbach, *Falkenhayn*, pp. 159f. Cf. Wenninger, diary for 31 July 1914, printed in Schulte, 'Neue Dokumente zu Kriegsausbruch', pp. 139f.

18 Bethmann Hollweg to Tschirschky, 31 July 1914, Kautsky, *Deutsche Dokumente*, No. 479.

19 Kaiser Wilhelm II to Tsar Nicholas II, 31 July 1914, ibid., No. 480.

20 Lyncker, diary for 31 July 1914, Afflerbach, *Kriegsherr*, No. L 7.

21 Falkenhayn, diary for 31 July 1914, BA-MA Freiburg-im-Breisgau, W10/50635. See Afflerbach, *Falkenhayn*, pp. 160f.

22 Kaiser Wilhelm II, speech from the Schloß, special edition of the *Berliner Lokal-Anzeiger* of 31 July 1914, as cited in Geiss, *Julikrise und Kriegsausbruch*, II, p. 560. See Obst, *Die politischen Reden*, p. 362.

23 Falkenhayn, diary for 31 July 1914, BA-MA Freiburg-im-Breisgau, W-10/50635.

24 Müller, diary for 1 August 1914, BA-MA Freiburg-im-Breisgau, Müller Papers. Cf. Görlitz, *Regierte der Kaiser?*, pp. 38f., where this key passage has been changed to read: 'In both speeches the correct and entirely justified claim is made that we are the attacked.'

25 For the importance of representing Russia as the aggressor in order to win over the German people for the war, see Sven Oliver Müller, *Nationalismus in Deutschland und Großbritannien im Ersten Weltkrieg*, Göttingen 2002, pp. 117ff.; Wolfgang Kruse, *Krieg und nationale Integration. Eine Neuinterpretation des sozialdemokratischen Burgfriedensschlusses 1914/15*, Essen 1993; Susanne Miller, *Burgfrieden und Klassenkampf. Die deutsche Sozialdemokratie im Ersten Weltkrieg*, Düsseldorf 1974.

26 Tsar Nicholas II to Kaiser Wilhelm II, 31 July 1914, Kautsky, *Deutsche Dokumente*, No. 487.

27 Lyncker, diary for 31 July 1914, Afflerbach, *Kriegsherr*, No. L 7.

28 Bethmann Hollweg to Tschirschky, 31 July 1914, Kautsky, *Deutsche Dokumente*, No. 479.

29 Kaiser Wilhelm II to Emperor Franz Joseph, 31 July 1914, ibid., No. 503. See also Kaiser Wilhelm's marginal note of 5 August 1914 on Wangenheim's telegram of 4 August 1914, ibid., No. 856. Also Wenninger, diary for 31 July 1914, Schulte, 'Neue Dokumente zu Kriegsausbruch', pp. 139f.

30 Szögyény to Berchtold, 31 July 1914, Geiss, *Julikrise und Kriegsausbruch*, II, No. 868. See also Wilhelm II's remarks of 1 August to the Austrian diplomat Friedrich von Larisch, reported in Szögyény to Berchtold, 1 August 1914, ibid., No. 976.

31 Szögyény to Berchtold, 31 July 1914, ibid., No. 868.

32 Emperor Franz Joseph to Kaiser Wilhelm II, 1 August 1914, Kautsky, *Deutsche Dokumente*, No. 601. For the chaotic circumstances of the Austrian mobilisation in the summer of 1914 see in particular Norman Stone, 'Die Mobilmachung der österreichisch-ungarischen Armee 1914', *Militärgeschichtliche Mitteilungen* 2, 1974, pp. 67–95.

33 Tsar Nicholas II to Kaiser Wilhelm II, 1 August 1914, ibid., No. 546.

34 Falkenhayn, diary for 31 July 1914, BA-MA Freiburg-im-Breisgau, W 10/50635. Cf. Afflerbach, *Falkenhayn*, p. 162.

35 Haeften, 'Meine Erlebnisse aus den Mobilmachungstagen 1914', BA-MA Freiburg-im-Breisgau, Haeften Papers, N 35/1, pp. 29f.

36 Falkenhayn, diary for 1 August 1914, BA-MA Freiburg-im-Breisgau, W 10/50635. Cf. Afflerbach, *Falkenhayn*, p. 162. See Zwehl, *Falkenhayn*, pp. 58f.

37 Ibid.

38 Wenninger, diary for 2 August 1914, Schulte, 'Neue Dokumente zu Kriegsausbruch', p. 142.

39 Lichnowsky to Auswärtiges Amt, 1 August 1914, Kautsky, *Deutsche Dokumente*, No. 562. See Lichnowsky's second telegram, ibid., No. 570.

40 Haeften, 'Meine Erlebnisse aus den Mobilmachungstagen 1914', BA-MA Freiburg-im-Breisgau, Haeften Papers, N 35/1, p. 31.

41 Lyncker, diary for 1 August 1914, Afflerbach, *Kriegsherr*, No. L 8.

42 Müller, diary for 1 August 1914, BA-MA Freiburg-im-Breisgau, Müller Papers; Görlitz, *Regierte der Kaiser?*, pp. 38f.

43 Moltke, *Erinnerungen, Briefe, Dokumente*, pp. 19ff. See Mombauer, *Moltke*, pp. 216ff.

44 Max v. Mutius, 'Lebenserinnerungen', vol. II, p. 205, unpublished manuscript, BA-MA, N 195/2, as cited in Afflerbach, *Kriegsherr*, pp. 132f., note 36.

45 Ibid.

46 Moltke, *Erinnerungen, Briefe, Dokumente*, pp. 19ff. See also Haeften, 'Meine Erlebnisse aus den Mobilmachungstagen 1914', BA-MA Freiburg-im-Breisgau, Haeften Papers, N 35/1, pp. 32ff. The three Cabinet chiefs also recorded this conflict. See Müller, diary for 1 August 1914, BA-MA Freiburg-im-Breisgau, Müller Papers. Cf. Görlitz, *Regierte der Kaiser?*, pp. 38f.; Valentini, *Kaiser und Kabinettschef*, pp. 127f.; Lyncker, diary for 1 August 1914, Afflerbach, *Kriegsherr*, No. L 8.

47 Haeften, 'Meine Erlebnisse aus den Mobilmachungstagen 1914', BA-MA Freiburg-im-Breisgau, Haeften Papers, N 35/1, pp. 34f.

48 Falkenhayn, diary for 1 August 1914, BA-MA Freiburg-im-Breisgau, W 10/50635.

49 Ibid.; cf. Afflerbach, *Falkenhayn*, pp. 165–8.

50 Müller, diary for 1 August 1914, BA-MA Freiburg-im-Breisgau, Müller Papers. Cf. Görlitz, *Regierte der Kaiser?*, pp. 38f.; Falkenhayn, diary for 1 August 1914, cited in Afflerbach, *Falkenhayn*, p. 164; Zwehl, *Falkenhayn*, pp. 58f.

51 Falkenhayn, diary for 1 August 1914, BA-MA Freiburg-im-Breisgau, W 10/50635. Cf. Afflerbach, *Falkenhayn*, p. 164.

52 Bethmann Hollweg to Lichnowsky, 1 August 1914, Kautsky, *Deutsche Dokumente*, No. 578. See Jagow to Lichnowsky and to Schoen, 1 August 1914, ibid., Nos. 579 and 587.

53 Kaiser Wilhelm II to King George V, 1 August 1914, RA GV/Q 1549/12.

54 Haeften, 'Meine Erlebnisse aus den Mobilmachungstagen 1914', BA-MA Freiburg-im-Breisgau, Haeften Papers, N 35/1, pp. 34f.

55 Moltke, *Erinnerungen, Briefe, Dokumente*, p. 22.

56 Lichnowsky to Auswärtiges Amt, 1 August 1914, Kautsky, *Deutsche Dokumente*, No. 570.

57 Müller, diary for 1 August 1914, BA-MA Freiburg-im-Breisgau, Müller Papers. Cf. Görlitz, *Regierte der Kaiser?*, pp. 38f.

58 Kaiser Wilhelm II to Tsar Nicholas II, 1 August 1914, Kautsky, *Deutsche Dokumente*, No. 600.

59 Geiss, *Julikrise und Kriegsausbruch*, II, p. 570.

60 Emperor Franz Joseph to Kaiser Wilhelm II, 1 August 1914, Kautsky, *Deutsche Dokumente*, No. 601.

61 Szögyény to Berchtold, 2 August 1914, Geiss, *Julikrise und Kriegsausbruch*, II, No. 1063.

62 Sir Edward Grey, draft of a telegram from King George V to Kaiser Wilhelm II, 1 August 1914, RA GV/Q 1549/7. See Kautsky, *Deutsche Dokumente*, No. 612. Also Lichnowsky to Auswärtiges Amt, 1 August 1914, ibid., No. 603.

63 Moltke, *Erinnerungen, Briefe, Dokumente*, pp. 22f.

64 Haeften, 'Meine Erlebnisse aus den Mobilmachungstagen 1914', BA-MA Freiburg-im-Breisgau, Haeften Papers, N 35/1, pp. 36ff.

65 Lichnowsky to Jagow, 1 August 1914, Kautsky, *Deutsche Dokumente*, No. 596.

66 Tirpitz, *Ohnmachtspolitik*, pp. 20f.

67 Falkenhayn, diary for 1 August 1914, BA-MA Freiburg-im-Breisgau, W 10/50635, Afflerbach, *Falkenhayn*, p. 162, note 67.

68 Gutsche, *Herrschaftsmethoden*, No. 89. Also Willibald Gutsche, *Sarajevo 1914*, Berlin 1984, p. 141.

69 Bethmann Hollweg to Jagow, 15 August 1919, printed in Wolfgang Schumann and Ludwig Nestler, eds., *Weltherrschaft im Visier*, Berlin 1975, No. 19. See Gutsche, *Sarajevo*, p. 140.

70 Bethmann Hollweg to Kaiser Wilhelm II, 2 August 1914, Kautsky, *Deutsche Dokumente*, No. 629.

71 Jagow to Flotow, 2 August 1914, Bethmann Hollweg to Lichnowsky, 2 August 1914, Bethmann Hollweg to Flotow, 2 August 1914, Jagow to Lichnowsky, 3 August 1914, ibid., Nos. 690, 693, 694 and 710. See also Nos. 717, 719 and 782. Further: Krafft von Dellmensingen, war diary, 3 August 1914, BA-MA Freiburg-im-Breisgau, KGFA, W10/50642.

72 Tirpitz, *Ohnmachtspolitik*, pp. 21f.

73 Kaiser Wilhelm II, marginal notes of 2 August 1914 to Lichnowsky's telegram of 1 August 1914, Kautsky, *Deutsche Dokumente*, No. 596.

74 Goschen to Nicolson, 1 August 1914, Geiss, *Julikrise und Kriegsausbruch*, II, No. 1059.

75 Kaiser Wilhelm II, marginal note of 2 or 3 August 1914 on the article 'Was wird England tun?' in *Berliner Tageblatt*, 2 August 1914, Kautsky, *Deutsche Dokumente*, No. 661. See Kaiser Wilhelm II, marginal note of 3 August 1914 on Lichnowsky's telegram of 3 August 1914, ibid., No. 764.

76 In March 1906 Wilhelm II had written, 'Italy will only stay with us so long as we are on friendly terms with England.' Cited in Afflerbach, *Dreibund*, p. 568. See the reflections of Rudini on this point of 3 April 1906, ibid., p. 407.

77 Kaiser Wilhelm II, marginal note on Lichnowsky's telegram of 1 August 1914, Kautsky, *Deutsche Dokumente*, No. 570.

78 See above, pp. 1033–5.

79 See Kaiser Wilhelm II, marginal note on Tschirschky's report of 28 July 1914 with the minute by Bethmann Hollweg, Kautsky, *Deutsche Dokumente*, No. 328.

80 See above, pp. 1049f.

81 Szögyény to Berchtold, 31 July 1914, Geiss, *Julikrise und Kriegsausbruch*, II, No. 868.

82 Szögyény to Berchtold, 2 August 1914, ibid., II, No. 1063.

83 Reichenau to Bethmann Hollweg, 26 July 1914 with marginal notes by Kaiser Wilhelm II of 31 July 1914, ibid., No. 441a.

84 Jagow to Flotow, 31 July 1914, ibid., No. 904.

85 Kleist to Kaiser Wilhelm II, 3 August 1914, Kautsky, *Deutsche Dokumente*, No. 771. For the toning-down of the Kaiser's letter by Flotow see the report of the Austro-Hungarian ambassador Kajetan von Mérey of 4 August 1914, Afflerbach, *Dreibund*, pp. 845f.

86 See above, pp. 1049f.

87 See also Kaiser Wilhelm II's marginal note of 5 August 1914 on the stance Italy was taking: 'Blödsinn!! But with England they are in agreement.' Kautsky, *Deutsche Dokumente*, No. 840.

88 Flotow to Auswärtiges Amt, 2 August 1914, ibid., No. 675.

89 Kaiser Wilhelm II, marginal notes of 2 August 1914 on Flotow's telegram of 1 August 1914, ibid., No. 614. Cf. Kaiser Wilhelm II, marginal notes on Tschirschky's telegram of 3 August 1914, ibid., No. 700.

90 Kaiser Wilhelm II, marginal note on Bollati's telegram to Jagow of 3 August 1914, ibid., No. 756; Kaiser Wilhelm II, marginal notes on King Victor Emmanuel's telegram of 3 August 1914, ibid., No. 755.

91 Kleist to Kaiser Wilhelm II, 3 August 1914, ibid., No. 771.

92 Kaiser Wilhelm II to Emperor Franz Joseph, 2 August 1914, with the Kaiser's addendum of 3 August 1914, ibid., No. 766. See Müller, diary for 3 August 1914, BA-MA Freiburg-im-Breisgau, Müller Papers.

93 Kaiser Wilhelm II, marginal notes on Kleist's telegram of 4 August 1914, Kautsky, *Deutsche Dokumente*, No. 850.

94 Kaiser Wilhelm II to King Constantine of Greece, draft, approved by the Kaiser on 31 July 1914, ibid., No. 466.

95 Kaiser Wilhelm II, marginal notes of 3 August 1914 on the telegram from King Constantine of Greece of 2 August 1914, ibid., No. 702.

96 Kaiser Wilhelm II to King Carol of Romania, 31 July 1914, ibid., No. 472.

97 Kaiser Wilhelm II, marginal note of 2 August 1914 on Tschirschky's report of 1 August 1914, ibid., No. 597.

98 Kaiser Wilhelm II, marginal notes of 3 August 1914 on Waldthausen's telegram of 3 August 1914, ibid., No. 699.

99 Kaiser Wilhelm II, marginal notes of 3 August 1914 on Wangenheim's telegram of 3 August 1914, ibid., No. 795.

100 Kaiser Wilhelm II, marginal note of 4 August 1914 on Waldthausen's telegram of 4 August 1914, ibid., No. 811. See also ibid., Nos. 794, 795, 854 and 868.

101 For Turkey's decision to enter the war on the side of the Central Powers see Feroz A. K. Yasamee, 'Ottoman Empire', in Keith Wilson, ed., *Decisions for War 1914*, London 1995, pp. 229–68.

102 Lerchenfeld to Hertling, 4 August 1914, Kautsky, *Deutsche Dokumente*, annex IV, No. 33.

103 Kaiser Wilhelm II, marginal notes of 2 August 1914 on Below's telegram from Brussels of 1 August, ibid., No. 584.

104 Kaiser Wilhelm II, marginal note of 3 August 1914 on the protest note of Luxembourg's Prime Minister Eyschen, 3 August 1914, ibid., No. 730.

105 Below to Auswärtiges Amt, 3 August 1914, ibid., No. 735. The ultimatum, which had been drafted on 29 July, is printed ibid., No. 376.

106 King Albert of the Belgians to Kaiser Wilhelm II, 1 August 1914, ibid., No. 765.

107 Ibid., note 2.

108 Kaiser Wilhelm II to King Albert of the Belgians, 3 August 1914, ibid., No. 783. See ibid., No. 778.

109 King Albert of the Belgians to Kaiser Wilhelm II, 4 August 1914, ibid., No. 837.

110 See above, p. 1098.

111 Kaiser Wilhelm II to Bethmann Hollweg, 3 August 1914, Kautsky, *Deutsche Dokumente*, No. 780. See ibid., Nos. 667 and 810.

112 Goschen to Jagow, 4 August 1914, received by the Kaiser at 7.45 p.m., ibid., No. 839. See Thomas G. Otte, 'A "German Paperchase": The "Scrap of Paper" Controversy and the Problem of Myth and Memory in International History', *Diplomacy and Statecraft*, 18: 2007, pp. 53–87.

113 Kaiser Wilhelm II, marginal note of 4 August 1914 on Goschen to Jagow, 2 August 1914, Kautsky, *Deutsche Dokumente*, No. 720.

114 Kaiser Wilhelm II, speech from the throne of 4 August 1914, included in Müller, diary for 4 August 1914, pp. 263f., BA-MA Freiburg-im-Breisgau, Müller Papers. See Obst, *Die politischen Reden*, pp. 364–6.

115 Müller, diary for 4 August 1914, BA-MA Freiburg-im-Breisgau, Müller Papers.

116 See F. R. Bridge, 'The British Declaration of War on Austria-Hungary in 1914', *Slavonic and East European Review* 47, 1969.

117 Walter Page to President Wilson, 9 August 1914, *Papers of Woodrow Wilson*, XXX, pp. 366–71.

42 THE SUPREME WAR LORD IN THE FIRST WORLD WAR

1 See the recent study by Lothar Machtan, *Die Abdankung. Wie Deutschlands gekrönte Häupter aus der Geschichte fielen*, Berlin 2008.

2 Holger Afflerbach, ed., *Kaiser Wilhelm II. als Oberster Kriegsherr im Ersten Weltkrieg. Quellen aus der militärischen Umgebung des Kaisers 1914–1918*, Munich 2005.

3 Kuno Graf von Westarp, *Konservative Politik im letzten Jahrzehnt des Kaiserreiches*, 2 vols., Berlin 1935, I, p. 408.

4 Schoen to Hertling, 26 July 1914, Deuerlein, *Briefwechsel Hertling-Lerchenfeld*, I, No. 106.

5 See above, p. 1089.

6 Wolfdieter Bihl, ed., *Deutsche Quellen zur Geschichte des Ersten Weltkrieges*, Darmstadt 1991, p. 49.

7 Hammann, *Um den Kaiser*, p. 144, note 1.

8 Mathilde Gräfin von Keller, *Vierzig Jahre im Dienst der Kaiserin. Ein Kulturbild aus den Jahren 1881–1921*, Leipzig 1935, p. 301.

9 See above, pp. 1106f.

10 GStA Berlin, I. HA, Rep. 89, Nr 213, Bl. 218.

11 See Thomas Raithel, *Das 'Wunder' der inneren Einheit. Studien zur deutschen und französischen Öffentlichkeit bei Beginn des Ersten Weltkriegs*, Bonn 1996; Jeffrey Verhey, *Der 'Geist von 1914' und die Erfindung der Volksgemeinschaft*, Hamburg 2000.

12 Mommsen, *War der Kaiser am allem schuld?*, pp. 222f.; Wilhelm Deist, 'Kaiser Wilhelm II. als Oberster Kriegsherr', in Röhl, *Der Ort Kaiser Wilhelms II.*, p. 40; Wilfried Rogasch, '"Mit Anstand untergehen . . ." Kaiser Wilhelm II. als "Oberster Kriegsherr"', in Hans Wilderotter and Klaus-D. Pohl, eds., *Der letzte Kaiser. Wilhelm II. im Exil*, Gütersloh 1991, p. 101.

13 Evelyn Fürstin Blücher von Wahlstatt, *Tagebuch 1914–1919*, Munich 1924, pp. 11f. See also Röhl, *Kaiser and his Court*, p. 9.

14 See Röhl, 'Vorsätzlicher Krieg?', pp. 193ff.

15 Wahnschaffe to Valentini, 29 June 1915, GStA Berlin, Valentini Papers, Nr 21.

16 Schultheß, *Deutscher Geschichtskalender* 30 (1914), part 2, p. 132; Obst, *Die politischen Reden*, p. 366.

17 Viktoria Luise, Duchess of Brunswick-Lüneburg, *Ein Leben als Tochter des Kaisers*, Göttingen and Hanover 1965, p. 135.

18 Bülow, *Denkwürdigkeiten*, III, p. 146.

19 Groener, *Lebenserinnerungen*, p. 144.

20 Kaiserin Auguste Viktoria to Kaiser Wilhelm II, 12 August 1914, typescript copy dated 17 August 1942, Kaiser Wilhelm II Papers, Burg Hohenzollern.

21 Haeften, 'Meine Erlebnisse aus den Mobilmachungstagen 1914', BA-MA Freiburg-im-Breisgau, N 35/1; Bethmann Hollweg to Delbrück, 9 September 1914, Egmont Zechlin, 'Friedensbestrebungen und Revolutionierungsversuche im Ersten Weltkrieg', *Aus Politik und Zeitgeschichte*, Nos. 20, 24 and 25 (1961) and 20 and 22 (1963), 42.

22 Müller, diary for 6 August 1914, Görlitz, *Regierte der Kaiser?*, p. 44. See Mombauer, *Moltke*, pp. 225f.

23 For the organisation of the German High Command see below, pp. 1122–7.

24 Plessen's oral statement to the Reichsarchiv, 10 April 1923, BA-MA Freiburg-im-Breisgau, W-10/50897, cf. *Der Weltkrieg 1914–1918. Die militärischen Operationen zu Lande*, edited by the Reichsarchiv, 14 vols., Berlin 1925–44, XIII–XIV: Koblenz 1956, I, p. 440.

25 Lyncker to his wife, 24 August 1914, Afflerbach, *Kriegsherr*, No. L 18.

26 Müller, diary for 21 August 1914, Görlitz, *Regierte der Kaiser?*, p. 50.

27 Josef Stürgkh, *Im Deutschen Großen Hauptquartier*, Leipzig 1921, p. 30.

28 Plessen, diary for 24 August 1914, Afflerbach, *Kriegsherr*, No. P 14.

29 Groener, *Lebenserinnerungen*, p. 165. See Mombauer, *Moltke*, pp. 247ff.

30 Dommes, memorandum of 2 October 1922, BA-MA Freiburg-im-Breisgau, Dommes Papers, N 512.

31 See the recent studies by Wolfram Pyta, *Hindenburg. Herrschaft zwischen Hohenzollern und Hitler*, Berlin 2007, pp. 91ff. et passim; and Anna von der Goltz, *Hindenburg. Power, Myth, and the Rise of the Nazis*, Oxford 2009.

32 Cited in Fritz Klein, *Deutschland im Ersten Weltkrieg*, 3 vols., Berlin 1968–9, I, p. 317.

33 Moltke, *Erinnerungen, Briefe, Dokumente*, p. 24. But see Plessen, diary for 11 September 1914, Afflerbach, *Kriegsherr*, No. P 32.

34 Plessen, diary for 12 September 1914, ibid., No. P 33; cf. Moltke, *Erinnerungen, Briefe, Dokumente*, p. 25.

35 Plessen to Holzing-Berstett, 10 November 1914, GLA Karlsruhe, Holzing-Berstett Papers, Zug. 1989 Nr 116/65. See the evidence in Mombauer, *Moltke*, pp. 265f.

36 Plessen, diary for 12 September 1914, Afflerbach, *Kriegsherr*, No. P 33.

37 Plessen, diary for 14 September 1914, ibid., No. P 35.

38 Cf. Stürgkh, *Hauptquartier*, pp. 78f. et passim.

39 Afflerbach, *Falkenhayn*, p. 188.

40 Mombauer, *Moltke*, pp. 269ff.

41 Kurt Riezler, diary for 2 January 1915, Riezler, *Tagebücher*, No. 588.

42 Afflerbach, *Kriegsherr*, p. 26. See above, p. 976.

43 Holger Afflerbach, 'Wilhelm II as Supreme Warlord in the First World War', in Annika Mombauer and Wilhelm Deist, eds., *The Kaiser. New Research on Wilhelm II's Role in Imperial Germany*, Cambridge 2003, p. 201; Erich von Falkenhayn, *Die Oberste Heeresleitung 1914–1916 in ihren wichtigsten Entschließungen*, Berlin 1920, p. 3.

44 See above, pp. 300f.

45 Kaiser Wilhelm II to Moltke, 15 August 1914, BA-MA Freiburg-im-Breisgau, RH 18/1881.

46 Wild von Hohenborn to his wife, 7 June 1915, Helmut Reichold, ed., *Adolf Wild von Hohenborn. Briefe und Tagebuchaufzeichnungen des preußischen Generals als Kriegsminister und Truppenführer im Ersten Weltkrieg*, Boppard am Rhein 1986, No. 38 (cited below as Wild, *Briefe*).

47 Wenninger, diary for 31 August 1914, Schulte, 'Neue Dokumente zu Kriegsausbruch', No. 38.

48 Klepsch-Kloth to Bolfras, 7 September 1916, Peter Broucek, 'Der k. u. k. Delegierte im Deutschen Großen Hauptquartier Generalmajor Alois Klepsch-Kloth von Roden und seine Berichterstattung 1915/16', *Militärgeschichtliche Mitteilungen* 1, 1974, p. 126, note 76.

49 Hopman, diary for 2 October 1914, Epkenhans, *Leben eines 'Wilhelminers'*, p. 450. For the influence of Wilhelm II on the operational plans of the navy see below, pp. 1149–55.

50 Müller, diary for 6 November 1914, Görlitz, *Regierte der Kaiser?*, p. 68.

51 Wild von Hohenborn, memorandum of 25 June 1916, Wild, *Briefe*, No. 107.

52 Plessen, diary for 23 November 1914, Afflerbach, *Kriegsherr*, No. P 108.

53 Ibid. See also ibid., No. P 90 (7 November 1914): 'H.M. is furious over the paucity of the information he receives on how our operations are going.'

54 See e. g. Hopman, diary for 17 November 1914, 23 November 1914, 26 March 1915, Epkenhans, *Leben eines 'Wilhelminers'*, pp. 503, 506 and 585; Müller, diary for 28 July 1918, Görlitz, *Regierte der Kaiser?*, pp. 397f. On the banality of the Kaiser's everyday life at General Headquarters see below, pp. 1127ff.

55 Lyncker to his wife, 4 June and 22 August 1917, Afflerbach, *Kriegsherr*, Nos. L 621 and L 660.

56 Thaer to his wife, 15 June 1916, Albrecht von Thaer, *Generalstabsdienst an der Front und in der OHL*, ed. Siegfried Kaehler, Göttingen 1958, p. 69.

57 Fritz von Lossberg, *Meine Tätigkeit im Weltkriege 1914–1918*, Berlin 1939, pp. 164f.

58 Plettenberg to his wife, 4 October 1914, Plettenberg Papers, in private hands, Essen; Redern, diary for 29 October 1914, BA-MA Freiburg-im-Breisgau, KGFA, W 10/50676. See also Wild von Hohenborn, memorandum of 14 August 1916, Wild, *Briefe*, No. 134. For another example of the Kaiser's loss of authority in the army see Erich von Manstein, *Aus einem Soldatenleben 1887–1939*, Bonn 1958, pp. 53f., note.

59 Groener, *Lebenserinnerungen*, p. 267. See also the highly critical comments of von der Schulenburg, memorandum of 5 January 1919, BA-MA Freiburg-im-Breisgau, KGFA, W-10/50742.

60 *Der Weltkrieg*, V, p. 8.

61 Theodor Wolff, diary for 23 March 1915, Wolff, *Tagebücher*, I, No. 119, recording a conversation with Count Bogdan von Hutten-Czapski.

62 Afflerbach, *Falkenhayn*, pp. 211–17 et passim.

63 Ibid.

64 Ibid., p. 230; Ekkehard P. Guth, 'Der Gegensatz zwischen dem Oberbefehlshaber Ost und dem Chef des Generalstabes des Feldheeres 1914/15. Die Rolle des Major v. Haeften im Spannungsfeld zwischen Hindenburg, Ludendorff und Falkenhayn', *Militärgeschichtliche Mitteilungen* 35, 1984, p. 104.

65 Hopman, diary for 30 June 1917 (based on Jagow's account), Epkenhans, *Leben eines 'Wilhelminers'*, p. 995.

66 Afflerbach, *Falkenhayn*, pp. 235–42.

67 Pyta, *Hindenburg*, pp. 91ff. et passim; Anna von der Goltz, *Hindenburg*. Also Jesko von Hoegen, *Der Held von Tannenberg: Genese und Funktion des Hindenburg-Mythos*, Cologne 2007.

68 Müller, diary for 3 July 1916, Görlitz, *Regierte der Kaiser?*, p. 200. Cf. Karl-Heinz Janßen, ed., *Die graue Exzellenz. Zwischen Staatsraison und Vasallentreue. Aus den Papieren des kaiserlichen Gesandten Karl Georg von Treutler*, Frankfurt a.M. 1971, p. 215 (Wilhelm II: 'He was not going to allow himself to be deposed . . . and did not want to abdicate in favour of the people's tribune Hindenburg.')

69 Bethmann Hollweg to Wahnschaffe, 7 January 1915, Zechlin, 'Friedensbestrebungen', No. 26.

70 Lyncker to his wife, 11 December 1915, Afflerbach, *Kriegsherr*, No. L 320.

71 Guth, 'Gegensatz', p. 101.

72 Niemann, record of a conversation with the Kaiser in Doorn on 25 February 1934, certified as correct by Wilhelm II, BA-MA Freiburg-im-Breisgau, W-10/50705, as cited in Afflerbach, *Falkenhayn*, p. 365.

73 For Falkenhayn and the Battle of Verdun see Afflerbach, *Falkenhayn*, pp. 360–464; see also Holger Afflerbach, 'Planning Total War? Falkenhayn and the Battle of Verdun 1916', in Roger Chickering and Stig Förster, eds., *Great War, Total War. Combat and Mobilization on the Western Front, 1914–1918*, Cambridge 2000; Hermann Wendt, *Verdun 1916. Die Angriffe Falkenhayns im Maasgebiet mit Richtung auf Verdun als strategisches Problem*, Berlin 1931.

74 Afflerbach, *Falkenhayn*, pp. 424–36; Bethmann Hollweg, *Betrachtungen zum Weltkrieg*, II, p. 45; Karl-Heinz Janßen, 'Der Wechsel in der Obersten Heeresleitung 1916', *Vierteljahres-hefte für Zeitgeschichte* 7, 1959; Ritter, *Staatskunst und Kriegshandwerk*, III, pp. 226–42. For the Kaiser's attitude see Plessen, diary for 3–5 July 1916, Afflerbach, *Kriegsherr*, Nos. P 505 and P 506.

75 Afflerbach, *Falkenhayn*, pp. 431–3.

76 Bethmann Hollweg to Grünau, 23 June 1916, as cited in Ritter, *Staatskunst und Kriegs-handwerk*, III, p. 227 with note 24.

77 Groener, *Lebenserinnerungen*, p. 320; for a full account of Falkenhayn's dismissal see Afflerbach, *Falkenhayn*, pp. 437–50.

78 Max Bauer, *Der große Krieg in Feld und Heimat. Erinnerungen und Betrachtungen*, Tübingen 1921, p. 104.

79 Müller, diary for 27 August 1916, Görlitz, *Regierte der Kaiser?*, p. 216. See also Valentini, diary for 27 August 1916, BA Koblenz, typescript copy, Thimme Papers, Nr 26 ('H.M. plagued by severe depression and dangerous ideas'); Valentini to his wife, 30 August 1916, BA Koblenz, Kl. Erw. 341–6 ('severe collapse of the All-Highest nerves').

80 Plessen, diary for 28 August 1916, Afflerbach, *Kriegsherr*, No. P 538; Valentini, *Kaiser und Kabinettschef*, p. 139.

81 Lyncker to his wife, 29 August 1916, Afflerbach, *Kriegsherr*, No. L 460; Plessen, diary for 28 August 1916, ibid., No. P 538; Müller, diary for 28 August 1916, Görlitz, *Regierte der Kaiser?*, p. 216.

82 Ritter, *Staatskunst und Kriegshandwerk*, III, p. 235.

83 Wild von Hohenborn, memorandum of 7 March 1916, Wild, *Briefe*, No. 76.

84 See Matthew Stibbe, 'Kaiser Wilhelm II: The Hohenzollerns at War', in Matthew Hughes and Matthew Seligmann, eds., *Leadership in Conflict 1914–1918*, Barnsley 2000.

85 For the organisation of the German High Command see Walther Hubatsch, 'Großes Hauptquartier 1914–1918, Zur Geschichte einer deutschen Führungseinrichtung'. *Ostdeutsche Wissenschaft* 5, 1958.

86 Mombauer, *Moltke*, pp. 235–7.

87 Afflerbach, *Falkenhayn*, p. 245. See Mewes to his wife, 24 August 1914, Mewes Papers, in private hands, Munich, and Wenninger, diary for 21 August 1914, Schulte, 'Neue Dokumente zu Kriegsausbruch', No. 26.

88 Wild von Hohenborn, memorandum of 20 January [1916], Wild, *Briefe*, No. 67.

89 Janßen, *Exzellenz*, p. 162.

90 Riezler, diary for 2 January 1915, Riezler, *Tagebücher*, No. 588 et passim.

91 Hammann, *Bilder aus der letzten Kaiserzeit*, p. 129.

92 Ritter, *Staatskunst und Kriegshandwerk*, IV, p. 332.

93 See in particular Valentini's memorandum of 11 January 1917, Valentini, *Kaiser und Kabinettschef*, pp. 147f.; cf. also Müller to Trotha, 23 May 1916, StA Bückeburg, Trotha Papers, A 226; Hull, *The Entourage of Kaiser Wilhelm II*, pp. 270f.

94 Müller to Plessen, 2 September 1916, Görlitz, *Regierte der Kaiser?*, p. 219; cf. Müller, diary for 8 January 1917, ibid., p. 247.

95 Lyncker to his wife, 28 June 1917, Afflerbach, *Kriegsherr*, No. L 642.

96 Müller, diary for 27 June 1917, Görlitz, *Regierte der Kaiser?*, p. 297; on the Kaiser's refusal to accept the advice of his entourage to go to Berlin see Valentini to his wife, 12 September 1915 and 17 May 1916, BA Koblenz, Kl. Erw. 341–5/6.

97 Müller, diary for 27 June–4 July 1917, Görlitz, *Regierte der Kaiser?*, pp. 297–300; Plessen to Countess Brockdorff, 4 July 1917, Afflerbach, *Kriegsherr*, No. P 645; Valentini, *Kaiser und Kabinettschef*, p. 157.

98 Müller, diary for 5 August 1916, Görlitz, *Regierte der Kaiser?*, p. 208.

99 Mewes to his wife, 6 August 1916, Mewes Papers, in private hands, Munich.

100 Mommsen, *War der Kaiser an allem schuld?*, p. 226.

101 Prussian Ministry of State, submission to the monarch of 14 November 1914, GStA Berlin, Rep. 90, Nr 1952.

102 Müller, diary for 31 May 1915, Görlitz, *Regierte der Kaiser?*, p. 105. Similarly critical of the Kaiser's chairmanship is the diary for 26 August 1915, ibid., p. 125.

103 Lyncker to his wife, 3 March 1916, Afflerbach, *Kriegsherr*, No. L 344.

104 Müller, diary for 4 March 1916, Görlitz, *Regierte der Kaiser?*, p. 163. See also Grünau to Bethmann Hollweg, 19 August 1916, André Scherer and Jacques Grunewald, eds., *L'Allemagne et les problèmes de la paix pendant la première guerre mondiale. Documents extraits des archives de l'Office allemand des Affaires étrangères*, 4 vols., Paris 1962–76, I, No. 306 with note, p. 435.

105 Audiences of 3 and 4 March 1915, Ritter, *Staatskunst und Kriegshandwerk*, III, pp. 205f. See ibid., pp. 210–14, for a further example.

106 See e. g. Wild von Hohenborn, memorandum of 10 March 1916, Wild, *Briefe*, No. 79.

107 Müller to Niedner, 27 February 1927 and Niedner to Müller, 1 March 1927; Müller, diary for 18 April 1915, Görlitz, *Regierte der Kaiser?*, pp. 97–9; Tirpitz to his wife, 23–9 March 1915, Tirpitz, *Erinnerungen*, pp. 457–63; cf. Robert Merton, *Erinnernswertes aus meinem Leben das über das Persönliche hinausgeht*, Frankfurt a.M. 1955, p. 47.

108 Hull, *The Entourage of Kaiser Wilhelm II*, p. 269; Bruno Thoß, 'Nationale Rechte, militärische Führung und Diktaturfrage in Deutschland 1913–1923', *Militärgeschichtliche Mitteilungen* 42, 1987.

109 Plessen to Holzing-Berstett, 23 November 1914, GLA Karlsruhe, Holzing-Berstett Papers, Zug. 1989 Nr 116/65.

110 Valentini to his wife, 19 August 1914, BA Koblenz, Valentini Papers, Kl. Erw. 341–4.

111 Ilsemann, diary for 12 September 1918, Harald von Koenigswald, ed., *Der Kaiser in Holland. Aufzeichnungen des letzten Flügeladjutanten Kaiser Wilhelms II.*, 2 vols., Munich 1968, I, p. 15. The Kaiser's daily life during the war is well documented in the Papers of his three Cabinet chiefs: Admiral von Müller's diary (Görlitz, *Regierte der Kaiser?*); the letters of Moriz von Lyncker (Afflerbach, *Kriegsherr*); and Valentini's records (BA Koblenz, Kl. Erw. 341–4–6). The Papers of Fritz Mewes, Wilhelm's Flügeladjutant from 1916, have also been drawn upon in this chapter.

112 Lerchenfeld to Hertling, 30 April/1/2 May 1915, *Briefwechsel Hertling-Lerchenfeld*, I, No. 171.

113 Müller, diary for 22 November 1915, Görlitz, *Regierte der Kaiser?*, p. 140.

114 Müller, diary for 11 December 1914, ibid., p. 74; Friedrich von Berg, *Friedrich von Berg als Chef des Geheimen Zivilkabinetts 1918. Erinnerungen aus seinem Nachlaß*, ed. Heinrich Potthoff, Düsseldorf 1971, p. 166; cf. Müller, diary for 6 September 1918, Görlitz, *Regierte der Kaiser?*, p. 410; Ilsemann, diary for 23 May 1922, Koenigswald, *Kaiser in Holland*, I, pp. 216f.

115 Lyncker to his wife, 29 November 1916 and 29 September 1916, Afflerbach, *Kriegsherr*, Nos. L 525 and L 489. See Hull, *The Entourage of Kaiser Wilhelm II*, p. 266 for further examples.

116 Pacelli to Gaspari, 30 June 1917, in Hubert Wolf et al., eds., 'Kritische Online-Edition der Nuntiaturberichte Eugenio Pacellis (1917–1929)', Dokument Nr 366.

117 Valentini to his wife, 27 August 1914, BA Koblenz, Kl. Erw. 341–4.

118 Mewes to his wife, 17 and 24 August 1914, Mewes Papers, in private hands, Munich; Valentini to his wife, 31 August and 29 October 1914, BA Koblenz, Kl. Erw. 341–4; Reischach to Holzing-Berstett, 7 September 1915, GLA Karlsruhe, Holzing-Berstett Papers, Zug. 1989, No. 116/65; Crown Prince Wilhelm as cited in Müller, diary for 16 October 1916, Görlitz, *Regierte der Kaiser?*, p. 231.

119 Mewes to his wife, 24 August 1914, Mewes Papers, in private hands, Munich.

120 Kessel, diary for 4 December 1914, GStA Berlin, BPHA Rep.53a, Nr 29, quoted in Cecil, *Wilhelm II: Emperor and Exile*, p. 217; Lerchenfeld to Hertling, 30 June 1915, *Briefwechsel Hertling-Lerchenfeld*, I, No. 194. Matthew Stibbe, *German Anglophobia and the Great War, 1914–1918*, Cambridge 2001. Cf. Prince Heinrich of Prussia to his brother-in-law, Grand Duke Ernst Ludwig of Hessen-Darmstadt, 3 October 1914, Großherzoglich Hessisches Familienarchiv Darmstadt.

121 Pohl, diary for 4 September 1914, Hugo von Pohl, *Aus Aufzeichnungen und Briefen während der Kriegszeit*, Berlin 1920, p. 48; Wenninger, diary for 6 September 1914, cited in Bernd F. Schulte, *Europäische Krise und Erster Weltkrieg. Beiträge zur Militärpolitik des Kaiserreichs 1871–1914*, Frankfurt a.M and Bern 1983, p. 259; Kaiser Wilhelm II, marginal note on a report of 9 August 1914, PA-AA, R 20880, fols. 8f., cited in John Horne and Alan Kramer, *German Atrocities 1914. A History of Denial*, New Haven and London 2001, pp. 18f.; Karl Alexander von Müller, *Mars und Venus. Erinnerungen: 1914–1919*, Stuttgart 1954, II, p. 102.

122 Cited in Ritter, *Staatskunst und Kriegshandwerk*, III, p. 24.

123 Müller, diary for 4 September 1914, BA-MA Freiburg-im-Breisgau, Müller Papers, N 159/4, fol. 292. This passage was omitted in Görlitz, *Regierte der Kaiser?*, p. 54f. It is worth noting, however, that even the normally level-headed Valentini believed that such a measure would be unavoidable in view of the unimaginable number of prisoners of war (Valentini to his wife, 4 September 1914, BA Koblenz, Kl. Erw. 341–4). Valentini frequently expressed concern over how the masses of prisoners (280,000 by mid September 1914) were to be fed (Valentini to his wife, 31 August and 12 September 1914, ibid.).

124 Lyncker to his wife, 29 November 1916, Afflerbach, *Kriegsherr*, No. L 525.

125 Müller to Trotha, 7 April 1914, Staatsarchiv Bückeburg, Trotha Papers, A 226.

126 Müller, diary for 16 February 1917, BA-MA Freiburg-im-Breisgau, Müller Papers, N 159/5 fol. 325.

127 'Acta betreffend Operation Kaiser Wilhelms II. am 15 February 1917', GStA Berlin, BPHA Rep. 53 R I Nr 2.

128 Széchényi to Kálnoky, 9 January 1889, cited on pp. 25f. of Röhl, *The Kaiser's Personal Monarchy.*

129 Karl Freiherr von Plettenberg to his wife, 8 November 1914, Plettenberg Papers, in private hands, Essen. See Theodor Wolff, diary for 5 December 1914, Wolff, *Tagebuch*, I, No. 61.

130 Walter Mühlhausen and Gerhard Papke, eds., *Kommunalpolitik im Ersten Weltkrieg. Die Tagebücher Erich Koch-Wesers 1914 bis 1918*, Munich 1999, p. 180.

131 Charlotte Hereditary Princess of Saxe-Meiningen to Schweninger, 18 July 1912, BA Berlin, Schweninger Papers, Nr 132. Flotow, report of 27 August 1912, HHStA Vienna, Hofnachrichten F2. See Röhl, *The Kaiser's Personal Monarchy*, pp. 1056–67.

132 Stürgkh, *Hauptquartier*, p. 76.

133 Thaer, diary for 16 March 1915, Thaer, *Generalstabsdienst*, p. 29.

134 Hutten-Czapski, *Sechzig Jahre*, II, p. 181; cf. Heinrich Prinz von Schönburg-Waldenburg, *Erinnerungen aus kaiserlicher Zeit*, Leipzig 1929, pp. 234f. See Alfred Niemann, *Kaiser und Revolution. Die entscheidenden Ereignisse im Großen Hauptquartier*, Berlin 1922, p. 43.

135 Lyncker to his wife, 17 November 1914, Afflerbach, *Kriegsherr*, No. L 98; see Hull, *The Entourage of Kaiser Wilhelm II*, p. 267. Also Plessen, diary for 9 July 1915, Afflerbach, *Kriegsherr*, No. P 347.

136 Valentini to his wife, 30 December 1916, BA Koblenz, Kl. Erw. 341–6.

137 Wild von Hohenborn to his wife, 15 November 1914, Wild, *Briefe*, No. 19; cf. Groener, *Lebenserinnerungen*, p. 187.

138 Grünau to Bethmann Hollweg, 18 July 1916, cited in Afflerbach, *Falkenhayn*, p. 437; Wild von Hohenborn, diary for 28 August 1916, Wild, *Briefe*, No. 142. For Plessen's role see Afflerbach, *Kriegsherr*, pp. 608–11 and 615–18.

139 Lyncker to his wife, 28 May 1917, ibid., No. L 614.

140 Müller, diary for 26 June 1917, Görlitz, *Regierte der Kaiser?*, p. 296. For a similar incident see Müller's diary for 11 November 1917, ibid., p. 332.

141 Valentini to his wife, 9 August 1916, BA Koblenz, Kl. Erw. 341–6.

142 Valentini to his wife, 28 December 1914, BA Koblenz, Kl. Erw. 341–4. On the growing influence of the Kaiserin during the war see Andreas Dorpalen, 'Empress Auguste Victoria and the Fall of the German Monarchy', *American Historical Review* 58/3, 1952, and Afflerbach, *Kriegsherr*, pp. 46–50.

143 Kaiser Wilhelm II to Prince Joachim of Prussia and Princess Marie Auguste of Anhalt, 6 March 1916, GStA Berlin, BPHA Rep. 53 J Lit. P Nr 8, fols. 8–9.

144 For this famous episode see Müller, diary for 30 June 1916, Görlitz, *Regierte der Kaiser?*, pp. 197f.

145 Lyncker to his wife, 19 May 1917, Afflerbach, *Kriegsherr*, No. L 605.

146 Friedrich Payer, *Von Bethmann Hollweg bis Ebert. Erinnerungen und Bilder*, Frankfurt a.M. 1923, pp. 174f. Payer here describes the so-called 'Crown Councils' at which no one spoke but Wilhelm II.

147 Elisabeth Fehrenbach, *Wandlungen des deutschen Kaisergedankens 1871–1918*, Munich and Vienna 1969, pp. 216–18; Kohlrausch, *Monarch im Skandal*, pp. 305–11; Bernd Sösemann, 'Der Verfall des Kaisergedankens im Ersten Weltkrieg', in John C. G. Röhl, *Der Ort Kaiser Wilhelms II. in der deutschen Geschichte*, Munich 1991.

148 Plessen, diary for 5 July 1916, Afflerbach, *Kriegsherr*, No. P 506; Wild von Hohenborn to his wife, 5 July 1916, Wild, *Briefe*, No. 117.

149 Eugen Zimmermann to Valentini, 12 August 1915, GStA Berlin, I. HA, Rep. 89, Nr 3087. Kaiser Wilhelm II decided against such a publication at this time. Civil Cabinet to August Scherl Verlag, 20 August 1915, ibid.

150 Bogdan Krieger, *Der Kaiser im Felde*, Berlin 1916; see Krieger to Holzing-Berstett, 5 April 1916, GLA Karlsruhe, Holzing-Berstett Papers, Nr 116/41.

151 Mewes to his wife, 16 and 30 September 1916, Mewes Papers, in private hands, Munich.

152 Groener, *Lebenserinnerungen*, p. 325; Crown Prince Rupprecht of Bavaria, diary for 21 September 1916, Eugen von Frauenholz, ed., *Rupprecht, Kronprinz von Bayern, Mein Kriegstagebuch*, 3 vols., Munich 1929, II, p. 29; *Das Werk des Untersuchungsausschusses der Deutschen Verfassungsgebenden Nationalversammlung und des Deutschen Reichstages 1919–1926. Verhandlungen / Gutachten / Urkunden. Vierte Reihe: Die Ursachen des Deutschen Zusammenbruchs im Jahre 1918*. 12 vols., Berlin 1925–9, VII/1, p. 349.

153 Wahnschaffe to Valentini, 3 August 1916, GStA Berlin, VI. HA, Valentini Papers, Nr 21.

154 Karl Hampe, diary for 27 September 1916, Karl Hampe, *Kriegstagebuch 1914–1918*, ed. Folker Reichert and Eike Wolgast, Munich 2004, p. 443.

155 Minutes of the meeting of the military and civilian departments in the Prussian War Ministry, 25 May 1917, Wilhelm Deist, ed., *Militär und Innenpolitik im Weltkrieg 1914–1918*, 2 vols., Düsseldorf 1970, II, No. 326a. For the monarchist propaganda campaign see Kohlrausch, *Monarch im Skandal*, pp. 309f.; Klaus-D. Pohl, 'Der Kaiser im Zeitalter seiner technischen Reproduzierbarkeit. Wilhelm II. in Fotografie und Film', in Hans Wilderotter and Klaus-D. Pohl, eds., *Der letzte Kaiser. Wilhelm II. im Exil*, Gütersloh and Munich 1991, p. 16.

156 Lersner to Auswärtiges Amt, 29 April 1917, as cited in Martin Kitchen, *The Silent Dictatorship. The Politics of the German High Command under Hindenburg and Luden-dorff, 1916–1918*, London 1976, p. 63, note 2.

43   THE KAISER'S WAR AIMS

1 Edward House, notes of 27 January 1916, House, *Intimate Papers*, II, p. 139.

2 Müller, diary for 14 August 1916, Görlitz, *Regierte der Kaiser?*, p. 211; cf. Grünau to Auswärtiges Amt, 15 August 1916, Scherer and Grunewald, *L'Allemagne*, I, No. 305. See also Andersen, Report on visit to Berlin and Charleville, 16–20 March 1915, RA/PS/GV/01177/22.

3 Valentini to his wife, 27 June 1915, BA Koblenz, Kl. Erw. 341–5; Hopman, diary for 11 January 1916, Epkenhans, *Leben eines 'Wilhelminers'*, pp. 765f.

4 Wahnschaffe to Valentini, 29 June 1915, GStA Berlin, Valentini Papers, Nr 21.

5 Bethmann Hollweg to Valentini, 9 December 1915, GStA Berlin, Valentini Papers, Nr 2. See Grünau to Bethmann Hollweg, 9 May 1916, cited in Gutsche, *Wilhelm II.*, p. 175. See also Eugen Zimmermann to Valentini, 12 August 1915, GStA Berlin, 2.2.1 Nr 3087; Bethmann Hollweg to Grünau, 3 July 1917, Gutsche, *Wilhelm II.*, p. 182.

6 Kaiser Wilhelm II, 'Aufruf an das deutsche Volk', 31 July 1915, BA-MA Freiburg-im-Breisgau, N 247/25. See Wolff, diary for 1 and 3 August 1915, Sösemann, *Theodor Wolff, Tagebücher*, II, Nos. 193 and 194.

7 Kaiser Wilhelm II, marginal note on Czernin's memorandum, no date [April 1917], Scherer and Grunewald, *L'Allemagne*, II, No. 68, annex, p. 108, note 23; Kaiser Wilhelm II, marginal note on Wedel to Auswärtiges Amt, 16 July 1917, ibid., No. 168, p. 268, notes 7 and 9.

8 See Röhl, *1914: Delusion or Design?*

9 August Eulenburg to Lichnowsky, 6 August 1915, Stàtni archiv Opava, Lichnowsky Papers.

10 Hugo Freiherr von Reischach to Max Freiherr von Holzing-Berstett, 7 September 1915 and 4 May 1916, GLA Karlsruhe, Holzing-Berstett Papers, Zug. 1989 Nos. 116/65 and 116/41.

11 Bethmann Hollweg to Delbrück, 9 September 1914, printed in Fritz Fischer, *Griff nach der Weltmacht. Die Kriegszielpolitik des kaiserlichen Deutschland 1914/1918*, Düsseldorf 1961, pp. 110–13 (translated into English as *Germany's Aims in the First World War*, London 1967, pp. 103–6). The complete text of the so-called September Programme was first published in Werner Basler, *Deutschlands Annexionspolitik in Polen und im Baltikum 1914–1918*, Berlin 1962, pp. 381ff.

12 Andersen, Report on visit to Berlin and Charleville, 16–20 March 1915, RA/PS/GV/ 01177/22. See Fischer, *Griff nach der Weltmacht*, pp. 223ff.

13 Burián, diary for 29 November 1915, HHStA Vienna (translated from the Hungarian).

14 Kaiser Wilhelm II, marginal note on an article by Andrássy, 12 January 1918, Werner Hahlweg, ed., *Der Friede von Brest-Litowsk. Ein unveröffentlichter Band aus dem Werk des Untersuchungsausschusses der Deutschen Verfassungsgebenden Nationalversammlung und des Deutschen Reichstages*, Düsseldorf 1971, No. 184.

15 Bethmann Hollweg to Delbrück, 9 September 1914, printed in Fischer, *Griff nach der Weltmacht*, pp. 110–13.

16 Bülow, Merkbuch F, cited in Fesser, *Bülow*, pp. 142f.

17 August Eulenburg to Valentini, 24 July 1915, GStA Berlin, Valentini Papers, Nr 23. Hugo Freiherr von Reischach to Max Freiherr von Holzing-Berstett, 7 September 1915, GLA Karlsruhe, Holzing-Berstett Papers, Zug. 1989 Nr 116/65, cited above, p. 1137.

18 Loebell to Valentini, 18 December 1914; Loebell, 'Gedanken über den Friedensschluß', GStA Berlin, Valentini Papers, Nr 13 Bd. 1.

19 Ludendorff to Moltke, 1 April 1915, Moltke Papers, in private hands, Basel.

20 Ludendorff to Moltke, 27 April 1915, Moltke Papers, in private hands, Basel.

21 Ballin to Wolff, 13 July 1915, Sösemann, *Theodor Wolff, Tagebücher*, II, p. 890

22 Karl-Dietrich Erdmann, ed., *Kurt Riezler. Tagebücher, Aufsätze, Dokumente*, Göttingen 1972, p. 201.

23 Bethmann Hollweg to Delbrück, 9 September 1914, printed in Basler, *Deutschlands Annexionspolitik in Polen und im Baltikum 1914–1918*, pp. 381ff. See Fischer, *Griff nach der Weltmacht*, pp. 119–22.

24 Riezler, diary entry for 9 October 1914, *Tagebücher*, p. 215.

25 Riezler, diary entry for 22 August 1914, ibid., p. 201.

26 Müller, diary entry for 18 February 1915, Görlitz, *Regierte der Kaiser?*, p. 91.

27 Müller, diary entry for 20 October 1915, ibid., p. 137.

28 Lerchenfeld to Hertling, 2 November 1915, *Briefwechsel Hertling-Lerchenfeld*, I, No. 225.

29 Grünau to Auswärtiges Amt, 2 January 1917, Scherer and Grunewald, *L'Allemagne*, I, No. 455. See also p. 655, note 1.

30 Kaiser Wilhelm II, marginal note of 2 March 1918, cited in Fischer, *Griff nach der Weltmacht*, p. 585.

31 Kaiser Wilhelm II, marginal comments 'agreed' and 'very good' on Holtzendorff's memorandum of 29 October 1915, cited in Fischer, *Griff nach der Weltmacht*, p. 332.

32 Müller, diary for 17 September 1917, Görlitz, *Regierte der Kaiser?*, pp. 320f. For the Vatican's appeal for peace and Kühlmann's peace feelers in England see Ritter, *Staatskunst und Kriegshandwerk*, IV, pp. 26–89; Wolfgang Steglich, *Die Friedenspolitik der Mittelmächte 1917/18*, Wiesbaden 1964; Wolfgang Steglich, *Der Friedensappell Papst Benedikts XV. vom 1 August 1917 und die Mittelmächte. Diplomatische Aktenstücke des Deutschen*

Auswärtigen Amtes, des Bayerischen Staatsministeriums des Äußeren und des Britischen Auswärtigen Amtes aus den Jahren 1915–1922, Wiesbaden 1970; Wolfgang Steglich, *Die Friedensversuche der kriegführenden Mächte im Sommer und Herbst 1917. Quellenkritische Untersuchungen, Akten und Vernehmungsprotokolle*, Wiesbaden 1984; Wolfgang Steglich, *Verhandlungen des 2. Unterausschusses des Parlamentarischen Untersuchungsausschusses über die päpstliche Friedensaktion von 1917*, Wiesbaden 1974.

33 As cited in Steglich, *Friedenspolitik*, p. 561; Kühlmann, *Erinnerungen*, pp. 469ff.; Georg Michaelis, *Für Volk und Staat. Eine Lebensgeschichte*, Berlin 1922, pp. 344f.

34 Kaiser Wilhelm II to Michaelis, no date [10/11 September 1917], in William Michaelis, *Geschichte in Wissenschaft und Unterricht* 12, 1961, 433f.

35 See Röhl, *The Kaiser's Personal Monarchy*, pp. 493ff.

36 Bogdan Graf Hutten-Czapski to Kaiser Wilhelm II, 5 November 1916, Kaiser Wilhelm II to Hutten-Czapski, 8 November 1916, BA Berlin, Hutten-Czapski Papers, Nr 303. See Hutten-Czapski, *Sechzig Jahre Politik*, II, pp. 307f. Fischer, *Griff nach der Weltmacht*, p. 159.

37 Hutten-Czapski to Kaiser Wilhelm II., 8 August 1914, BA Berlin, Hutten-Czapski Papers.

38 Müller, diary entry for 12 October 1915, Görlitz, *Regierte der Kaiser?*, p. 136.

39 Hutten-Czapski, record of a conversation with Kaiser Wilhelm II, 13 June 1916, BA Berlin, Hutten-Czapski Papers.

40 Hutten-Czapski to Kaiser Wilhelm II, 5 November 1916, Kaiser Wilhelm II to Hutten-Czapski, 8 November 1916, BA Berlin, Hutten-Czapski Papers, Nr 303; Hutten-Czapski, *Sechzig Jahre Politik*, II, pp. 307–8.

41 Kaiser Wilhelm II, marginal note on Jagow's memorandum of 14 November 1915, cited in Fischer, *Griff nach der Weltmacht*, p. 258.

42 Hohenlohe to Burián, 9 February 1916, cited in Gutsche, *Wilhelm II.*, p. 178.

43 Kaiser Wilhelm II, marginal note on an article in *Die Post* of 17 February 1916, GStA Berlin, BPHA Rep. 53 Nr 276, cited in Gutsche, *Wilhelm II.*, p. 179.

44 Wedel to Zimmermann, 29 November 1916, cited in Gutsche, *Wilhelm II.*, p. 181.

45 Fischer, *Griff nach der Weltmacht*, pp. 569 and 685f.; Thaer, diary for 8 January 1918, Thaer, *Generalstabsdienst*, p. 156; Ritter, *Staatskunst und Kriegshandwerk*, IV, pp. 194f.

46 Niall Ferguson, *The Pity of War*, London 1998 (translated into German as *Der falsche Krieg. Der Erste Weltkrieg und das zwanzigste Jahrhundert*, Stuttgart 1999).

47 See Matthew Stibbe, *German Anglophobia and the Great War, 1914–1918*, Cambridge 2001.

48 Crown Prince Wilhelm to Kaiser Wilhelm II, 6 February 1916, GStA Berlin, 2.2.1 Nr 670/1.

49 Crown Prince Wilhelm to Kaiser Wilhelm II., 6 October 1914, ibid. See Bethmann Hollweg to Loebell, no date [October 1914], not sent, GStA Berlin, Valentini Papers, Nr 13 Bd. 1.

50 Crown Prince Wilhelm to Ernst Ludwig Grand Duke of Hessen-Darmstadt, 6 February 1915, Großherzoglich Hessisches Familienarchiv Darmstadt.

51 Crown Prince Wilhelm to Kaiser Wilhelm II, 26 January 1916, GStA Berlin, BPHA Rep. 54 Nr 18/6; Tirpitz to Kaiser Wilhelm II, 27 April 1916, BA-MA Freiburg-im-Breisgau, Tirpitz Papers, N 253/8.

52 Anonymous memorandum sent by Crown Prince to Kaiser Wilhelm II and passed on by him to the heads of the Civil and Military Cabinets on 21 October 1914, GStA Berlin, 2.2.1 Nr 670/1.

53 Prince Heinrich of Prussia to Ernst Ludwig Grand Duke of Hessen-Darmstadt, 3 October 1914, HStA Darmstadt, D 24 36/4.

54 Wolff, diary for 16 and 23 October 1914, Sösemann, *Theodor Wolff Tagebücher*, I, Nos. 37 and 41.

55 Valentini, diary entries for 1 February, 1 and 26 April and 5 September 1916, typescript copy, BA Koblenz, Thimme Papers Nr 26.

56 House, 27 January 1916, House, *Intimate Papers*, II, pp. 138f.

57 Kaiser Wilhelm II, marginal notes of 14 May 1917, cited in Fischer, *Griff nach der Weltmacht*, p. 456.

58 Kaiser Wilhelm II, marginal comment on Pourtalès to Jagow, 30 July 1914, Imanuel Geiss, ed., *July 1914. The Outbreak of the First World War: Selected Documents*, London 1967.

59 Jagow to Wangenheim, 15 August 1914, cited in Gutsche, *Wilhelm II.*, p. 173.

60 Lyncker to his wife, 19 August 1914, BA-MA Freiburg-im-Breisgau, Lyncker Papers, MSg 1/3251; Afflerbach, *Kriegsherr*, No. L 12.

61 Kaiser Wilhelm II to Michaelis, no date [September 1917], William Michaelis, *Geschichte in Wissenschaft und Unterricht* 12, 1961. pp. 433f.

62 Philipp Scheidemann, *Memoirs of a Social Democrat*, 2 vols., London 1928, II, pp. 381 and 427.

63 Kaiser Wilhelm II, 26 March 1918, quoted in Müller, *Regierte der Kaiser?*, p. 366.

64 Kaiser Wilhelm II to Houston Stewart Chamberlain, 15 January 1917, Chamberlain Papers, Richard-Wagner-Gedenkstätte, Bayreuth. An abbreviated version is printed in Chamberlain, *Briefe*, II, pp. 250f. See also Kaiser Wilhelm II to Chamberlain, 25 November 1914, ibid., pp. 244f.

65 Kaiser Wilhelm II, marginal note on an article in the *Frankfurter Zeitung*, 17 June 1918, PA-AA, R 3843. See Gutsche, *Wilhelm II.*, p. 185.

66 Tirpitz, undated memorandum, Tirpitz, *Ohnmachtspolitik*, p. 34.

67 Minute of 22 July 1915, ibid., p. 257.

68 Clark, *Kaiser Wilhelm II*, p. 227; Matthew Stibbe, 'Germany's "Last Card": Wilhelm II and the Decision in Favour of Unrestricted Submarine Warfare in January 1917', in Annika Mombauer and Wilhelm Deist, eds., *The Kaiser. New Research on Wilhelm II's Role in Imperial Germany*, Cambridge 2003, p. 220. For concrete examples of the Kaiser's direct involvement in naval operations see Hopman's diary in Epkenhans, *Leben eines 'Wilhelminers'*, p. 593, note 554 (10 November 1914), pp. 674 and 896 (12 August 1915 and 5 October 1916), p. 964, note 64 (14 March 1917).

69 Tirpitz, *Ohnmachtspolitik*, p. 126.

70 General von Einem refers to the fleet as Wilhelm's 'toy for Kiel Week' in his diary for 27 March 1915, BA-MA Freiburg-im-Breisgau, N 324/12, as cited in Epkenhans, *Leben eines 'Wilhelminers'*, p. 587, note 177. Admiral Hopman also writes in his diary for 13 January 1916 of 'Williams toy', ibid., p. 768.

71 Carl Axel Gemzell, *Organization, Conflict, and Innovation. A Study of German Naval Strategic Planning, 1880–1940*, Stockholm 1973, pp. 176–9; Tirpitz, *Erinnerungen*, pp. 298f.

72 Hopman, diary for 27 March 1915, in Epkenhans, *Leben eines 'Wilhelminers'*, p. 586.

73 Paul G. Halpern, *A Naval History of World War I*, Annapolis 1994, p. 287.

74 Müller, diary for 4 February 1915, Görlitz, *Regierte der Kaiser?*, pp. 87f.; cf. Janßen, *Exzellenz*, pp. 191f.; Tirpitz, *Ohnmachtspolitik*, pp. 303ff.

75 Karl Helfferich, *Der Weltkrieg*, 3 vols., Karlsruhe 1925, II, p. 303. See also Pohl to his wife, 9 January 1915, Pohl, *Aus Aufzeichnungen und Briefen*, pp. 100f.

76 Gerard, *My Four Years in Germany*, pp. 251–3.

77 Gerhard Granier, ed., *Die deutsche Seekriegsleitung im Ersten Weltkrieg. Dokumentation*, 4 vols., Koblenz 1999–2004, III, pp. 90–3 and Nos. 323–69; Joachim Schröder, *Die U-Boote des Kaisers. Die Geschichte des deutschen U-Boot-Krieges gegen Großbritannien im Ersten Weltkrieg*, Lauf a. d. Pregnitz 2001, pp. 126–70.

78 Afflerbach, *Falkenhayn*, p. 377; Jarausch, *Enigmatic Chancellor*, pp. 275f.; Müller, diary for 27 May–7 June 1915, Görlitz, *Regierte der Kaiser?*, pp. 104–7.

79 Kaiser Wilhelm II, marginal comment on Tirpitz's letter of resignation, Tirpitz, *Ohnmachtspolitik*, p. 350.

80 Tirpitz, *Erinnerungen*, p. 359.

81 Kaiser Wilhelm II, marginal comment on Tirpitz's submission of 7 September 1915, ibid., p. 428.

82 Granier, *Seekriegsleitung*, III, pp. 92f. with Nos. 357–69; Schröder, *U-Boote des Kaisers*, pp. 171–83.

83 Estimates varied from two to eight months for Britain to capitulate. See Tirpitz, *Ohnmachtspolitik*, pp. 450 and 466.

84 Afflerbach, *Falkenhayn*, pp. 378ff.

85 Müller, diary for 15 January 1916, Görlitz, *Regierte der Kaiser?*, p. 147.

86 Bethmann Hollweg to Jagow, 5 March 1916, Tirpitz, *Ohnmachtspolitik*, p. 499.

87 For Wilhelm II's hesitation see Müller, diary for 18 August and 25 August 1916, Görlitz, *Regierte der Kaiser?*, pp. 156 and 159; Treutler to Bethmann Hollweg, 17 January 1916, Janßen, *Exzellenz*, pp. 195f.

88 Bethmann Hollweg, memorandum of 29 February 1916, Bethmann Hollweg, *Betrachtungen zum Weltkrieg*, II, pp. 260ff.

89 For the following see Jarausch, *Enigmatic Chancellor*, pp. 285f.

90 Müller to Tirpitz, 5 March 1916, Tirpitz, *Ohnmachtspolitik*, p. 491; Müller, diary for 13 March 1916, Görlitz, *Regierte der Kaiser?*, p. 166; Lyncker to his wife, 14 March 1916, Afflerbach, *Kriegsherr*, No. L 355.

91 Afflerbach, *Falkenhayn*, pp. 390ff.

92 Janßen, *Exzellenz*, p. 206.

93 Müller, diary for 9 March 1916, Görlitz, *Regierte der Kaiser?*, p. 164.

94 Schröder, *U-Boote des Kaisers*, pp. 211–19.

95 The text of the note is printed in *Deutscher Geschichtskalender 1916*, I, 2, pp. 854–60.

96 Ritter, *Staatskunst und Kriegshandwerk*, III, pp. 209f.

97 Afflerbach, *Falkenhayn*, p. 399.

98 Bethmann Hollweg to Auswärtiges Amt, 30 April 1916, as cited ibid., pp. 399f., note 1081.

99 Holtzendorff, memorandum, in Arno Spindler, *Der Handelskrieg mit U-Booten*, 5 vols., I–IV: Berlin 1932–41, V: Frankfurt a.M. 1966, pp. 143f.; Müller, diary for 30 April 1916, Görlitz, *Regierte der Kaiser?*, pp. 172f.

100 Stibbe, 'Germany's "Last Card"', pp. 229 and 233.

101 Lyncker to his wife, 26 January 1917, Afflerbach, *Kriegsherr*, No. L 550.

102 Riezler, diary for 31 January 1917, Riezler, *Tagebücher*, No. 685.

103 Halpern, *Naval History*, pp. 310–29.

104 Kaiser Wilhelm II, speech in Wilhelmshaven, 5 June 1916, BA-MA Freiburg-im-Breisgau, RM 2/1970, fols. 38–42. The Kaiser's more exuberant phrases were toned down for publication. See Obst, *Die politischen Reden*, pp. 381–3; Obst, '*Einer nur ist Herr im Reiche*', pp. 359–80.

105 David Stevenson, *1914–1918. Der Erste Weltkrieg*, Düsseldorf 2006, p. 309.

106 Kitchen, *Silent Dictatorship*, pp. 111–17.

107 See the minutes of the meeting of the Prussian Ministry of State, 14 December 1916, GStA Berlin, I. HA, Rep. 90a, B III 2 b Nr 6, Bd. 165, fols. 388–96.

108 Kaiser Wilhelm II to Bethmann Hollweg, 31 October 1916, Scherer and Grunewald, *L'Allemagne*, I, No. 356.

109 Arthur N. Davis, *The Kaiser I Knew*, London 1918, p. 152. See also Stibbe, 'Germany's "Last Card"', p. 231.

110 *Schulthess' europäischer Geschichtskalender 1916*, I, p. 371; *Schulthess' Deutscher Geschichtskalender 1916*, 2, pp. 1086ff.

111 Müller, diary for 8 January 1917, Görlitz, *Regierte der Kaiser?*, p. 247.

112 Müller, diary for 8–9 January 1915, ibid., pp. 247–9; Ritter, *Staatskunst und Kriegshandwerk*, III, pp. 368–85.

113 Müller, diary for 9 January 1917, Görlitz, *Regierte der Kaiser?*, pp. 248f.; see Valentini, *Kaiser und Kabinettschef*, pp. 145f.; Karl E. Birnbaum, *Peace Moves and U-Boat-Warfare*, Stockholm 1958, pp. 315–27.

114 As cited in Fischer, *Griff nach der Weltmacht*, p. 398, note 101.

115 Czernin, *Im Weltkriege*, pp. 196f.

116 Plessen to Gräfin Brockdorff, 21 July 1918, Afflerbach, *Kriegsherr*, No. P 694.

117 Grünau to Bethmann Hollweg, 27 March 1917, Deist, *Militär und Innenpolitik*, II, No. 267.

118 Kaiser Wilhelm II to Bethmann Hollweg, Bethmann Hollweg to Kaiser Wilhelm II, 11 April 1917, Herbert Michaelis and Ernst Schraepel, eds., *Ursachen und Folgen. Vom deutschen Zusammenbruch 1918 und 1945 bis zur staatlichen Neuordnung Deutschlands in der Gegenwart. Eine Urkunden- und Dokumentensammlung zur Zeitgeschichte*, 26 vols., Berlin 1958–80, II, No. 271 A,d) and No. 271 A,e).

119 Kaiser Wilhelm II, war aims programme of 19 April 1917, Fischer, *Griff nach der Weltmacht*, pp. 448f.

120 Ibid., pp. 449–53.

121 Kaiser Wilhelm II, war aims programme of 13 May 1917, Fischer, *Griff nach der Weltmacht*, pp. 457f.; Gutsche, *Wilhelm II.*, p. 183.

122 Kaiser Wilhelm II to Bethmann Hollweg, telegram, 11 April 1917; Bethmann Hollweg, acknowledgement, 12 April 1917, Werner Hahlweg, ed., *Lenins Rückkehr nach Rußland 1917. Die deutschen Akten*, Leiden 1957, Nos. 54 and 58.

123 Berchtold, record of 28 October 1913 of his conversation with Kaiser Wilhelm II on 26 October 1913, *Österreich-Ungarns Außenpolitik*, VII, No. 8934, See above, pp. 950–3.

124 Quoted in Klaus Wiegrefe, Florian Altenhöner, Georg Bönisch, Heiko Buschke, Wladimir Pyliow and Anika Zeller, 'Revolutionär Seiner Majestät. Die gekaufte Revolution. Wie Kaiser Wilhelm II. Lenins Octoberrevolution finanzierte', *Der Spiegel*, No. 50, 10 December 2007, p. 40.

125 Kaiser Wilhelm II, marginal notes on Czernin's exposé, no date, annex to Grünau to Bethmann Hollweg, 14 April 1917, Scherer and Grunwald, *L'Allemagne*, II, No. 68.

126 Kaiser Wilhelm II to Michaelis, 3 September 1917, cited in Fischer, *Griff nach der Weltmacht*, p. 604.

127 Kaiser Wilhelm II, marginal note of January 1918, cited in Machtan, *Abdankung*, p. 89.

128 Kaiser Wilhelm II, quoted by Westarp in the Reichstag on 19 March 1918, Fischer, *Griff nach der Weltmacht*, p. 665.

129 Kaiser Wilhelm II, marginal note of 10 January 1918, cited in Fischer, *Griff nach der Weltmacht*, p. 822.

130 Cited in Machtan, *Abdankung*, p. 137.

131 Kaiser Wilhelm II, marginal note of 10 March 1918, cited in Machtan, *Abdankung*, p. 90f. See below, p. 1161f.

132 Kaiser Wilhelm II, marginal note of April 1918, cited in Machtan, *Abdankung*, pp. 107 and 137.

133 Kaiser Wilhelm II, marginal note on Lucius's report of 1 May 1918, cited in Winfried Baumgart, *Deutsche Ostpolitik 1918. Von Brest-Litowsk bis zum Ende des Ersten Weltkrieges*, Vienna and Munich 1966, p. 102, note 40.

134 For the negotiations at Brest-Litovsk see Fischer, *Griff nach der Weltmacht*, pp. 627–74; Kitchen, *Silent Dictatorship*, pp. 157–87; Steglich, *Friedenspolitik*, pp. 313–412.

135 Müller, diary for 13 January 1918, Görlitz, *Regierte der Kaiser?*, p. 343. See Kaiser Wilhelm II, marginal note on an article in the *Berliner Börsenzeitung* of 9 January 1918 entitled 'Herr von Kühlmann', cited in Hahlweg, *Frieden von Brest-Litowsk*, No. 171.

136 Kaiser Wilhelm II, marginal notes on articles in *Vorwärts*, 4 and 6 January 1918, in Hahlweg, *Friede von Brest-Litowsk*, Nos. 146 and 160.

137 Kaiser Wilhelm II, marginal note on an article in the *Norddeutsche Allgemeine Zeitung*, 5 March 1918, cited ibid., No. 405.

138 Kaiser Wilhelm II, marginal notes on the minutes of the meeting of the 'committee for political and territorial questions' at Brest-Litovsk, 12 January 1918, ibid., No. 137.

139 Kaiser Wilhelm II, marginal notes on the same committee's meetings of 10, 13 and 18 January 1918, ibid., Nos. 176, 195 and 219.

140 Kühlmann, *Erinnerungen*, p. 526; cf. Max Hoffmann, *Der Krieg der versäumten Gelegenheiten*, Munich 1923, pp. 203f.

141 Kühlmann, *Erinnerungen*, pp. 526f.

142 Valentini, *Kaiser und Kabinettschef*, p. 190.

143 Müller, diary for 8 January 1918, Görlitz, *Regierte der Kaiser?*, p. 342.

144 Hindenburg to Kaiser Wilhelm II, 7 January 1918, Hertling to Hindenburg, 12 January 1918, Hindenburg to Hertling, 14 January 1918, Kaiser Wilhelm II to Hindenburg, no date, all in Erich Ludendorff, ed., *Urkunden der Obersten Heeresleitung über ihre Tätigkeit 1916/18*, Berlin 1920, pp. 452–68. See Kühlmann, *Erinnerungen*, pp. 535–42; Karl Graf von Hertling, *Ein Jahr in der Reichskanzlei*, Freiburg-im-Breisgau 1919, p. 59; Ritter, *Staatskunst und Kriegshandwerk*, IV, pp. 125f. with notes 37 and 38.

145 Kaiser Wilhelm II, marginal notes on the minutes of the meeting of the 'committee for political and territorial questions' at Brest-Litovsk, 11 January 1918, in Hahlweg, *Friede von Brest-Litowsk*, No. 180. Similar marginal remarks by the Kaiser can be found on Wedel's report of 19 January 1918 and on an article in the *Norddeutsche Allgemeine Zeitung* of 20 January 1918 entitled 'Die Hemmungen in Brest-Litowsk', ibid., Nos. 227 and 232.

146 Minutes of the Crown Councils of 13 February 1918 and 12 March 1918, cited in Baumgart, *Deutsche Ostpolitik*, p. 25 and Fischer, *Griff nach der Weltmacht*, p. 682.

147 Kaiser Wilhelm II, marginal note on Mirbach's report of 13 May 1918, cited in Baumgart, *Deutsche Ostpolitik*, p. 212, note 14.

148 Ibid., p. 273, note 59.

149 Kaiser Wilhelm II, marginal notes on an article in the *Norddeutsche Allgemeine Zeitung* of 7 February 1918 entitled 'Die neue Verhandlungsphase in Brest', Hahlweg, *Frieden von Brest-Litowsk*, No. 286.

150 Bussche to Grünau, 29 June 1918, cited in Baumgart, *Deutsche Ostpolitik*, p. 85.

151 Ibid., pp. 187f.

152 Kaiser Wilhelm II, marginal note on an article in the *Münchener Allgemeine Zeitung* of 10 March 1918, entitled 'Die Unzufriedenen', Hahlweg, *Frieden von Brest-Litowsk*, No. 413; Baumgart, *Deutsche Ostpolitik*, p. 68, note 30.

153 Kaiser Wilhelm II, marginal note on an article in the *Berliner Tageblatt*, 31 December 1918, cited in Hahlweg, *Frieden von Brest-Litowsk*, No. 129.

154 Crown Council of 18 December 1917, Fischer, *Griff nach der Weltmacht*, pp. 629f.

155 Finnish Foreign Ministry to Prince Friedrich Karl of Hesse, October 1918, cited in Rainer von Hessen, ed., *Wolfgang Prinz von Hessen: Aufzeichnungen*, Kronberg im Taunus 1986, p. 106. See Fischer, *Griff nach der Weltmacht*, pp. 674ff. and 809ff.

156 Kaiser Wilhelm II, marginal note, summer 1918, cited in Fischer, *Griff nach der Weltmacht*, p. 562.

44 DOWNFALL. THE COLLAPSE OF THE HOHENZOLLERN MONARCHY

1 Gunther Mai, '"Verteidigungskrieg" und "Volksgemeinschaft". Staatliche Selbstbehauptung, nationale Solidarität und soziale Befreiung in Deutschland in der Zeit des Ersten Weltkrieges (1900–1925)', in Michalka, *Der Erste Weltkrieg*, pp. 586f.; Verhey, *Der Geist von 1914*, pp. 266f.

2 Jarausch, *Enigmatic Chancellor*, pp. 308ff.

3 Bethmann Hollweg, *Betrachtungen zum Weltkrieg*, II, pp. 179f.; cf. Jarausch, *Enigmatic Chancellor*, pp. 317–20.

4 Jarausch, *Enigmatic Chancellor*, pp. 327ff.

5 Ludwig Bergsträsser, *Die preußische Wahlrechtsfrage und die Entstehung der Osterbotschaft 1917*, Tübingen 1929, p. 140, note.

6 Valentini, diary for 5 April 1917, typescript copy, BA Koblenz, Thimme Papers, Nr 26.

7 The text is printed in *Schulthess' europäischer Geschichtskalender 1917*, I, pp. 398f.

8 See Lyncker to Bethmann Hollweg, 8 May 1917, Westarp, *Konservative Politik*, II, p. 243; Bethmann Hollweg, *Betrachtungen zum Weltkrieg*, II, pp. 191ff.; Riezler, diary for 13 May 1917, Riezler, *Tagebücher*, No. 723; Philipp Scheidemann, *Der Zusammenbruch*, Berlin 1921, pp. 168ff.; Valentini, *Kaiser und Kabinettschef*, pp. 152f.

9 Kaiser Wilhelm II to Bethmann Hollweg, 12 May 1917, GStA Berlin, BPHA Rep. 53 J Lit. B Nr 7, fols. 7–11, printed in Deist, *Militär und Innenpolitik*, II, No. 296.

10 See Ritter, *Staatskunst und Kriegshandwerk*, III, pp. 251ff.; Helfferich, *Weltkrieg*, II, pp. 264–6; Valentini, diary for 1917, typescript copy, BA Koblenz, Thimme Papers, Nr 26; Jarausch, *Enigmatic Chancellor*, pp. 264ff.

11 Riezler, diary for 22 November 1916, Riezler, *Tagebücher*, No. 685.

12 Mewes to his wife, 9 December 1916, Mewes Papers, in private hands, Munich. Valentini also remarked on the Kaiser's relief at handing over responsibility to Hindenburg and Ludendorff (Valentini to his wife, 30 August 1916, BA Koblenz, Kl. Erw. 341–6).

13 Bethmann Hollweg, *Betrachtungen zum Weltkrieg*, II, p. 191.

14 Erich Ludendorff, *Meine Kriegserinnerungen 1914–1918*, Berlin 1919, p. 356; see also Ludendorff to Drews, 8 December 1917, Erich Ludendorff, ed., *Urkunden der Obersten Heeresleitung über ihre Tätigkeit 1916/18*, Berlin 1920, pp. 291ff.

15 On 20 April 1917 the SPD called for peace negotiations to begin.

16 See above, pp. 1156ff.; Fischer, *Griff nach der Weltmacht*, pp. 453–9; Müller, diary for 24 April 1917, Görlitz, *Regierte der Kaiser?*, p. 279. See also Bethmann's minute quoted in Westarp, *Konservative Politik*, II, p. 85; Valentini, diary for 23 April 1917, typescript copy, BA Koblenz, Thimme Papers, Nr 26.

17 Ritter, *Staatskunst und Kriegshandwerk*, III, pp. 482–551.

18 Plessen, diary for 24 June 1917, Afflerbach, *Kriegsherr*, No. P 643. See Valentini, *Kaiser und Kabinettschef*, pp. 153ff.; Valentini, diary for 24 June 1917, typescript copy, BA Koblenz, Thimme Papers, Nr 26.

19 Erich Matthias, ed., *Der Interfraktionelle Ausschuß 1917/18*, 2 vols., Düsseldorf 1959, p. xxv; Scheidemann, *Zusammenbruch*, pp. 160ff.

20 Minutes of the meeting of the main committee on 6 July 1917, *Der Hauptausschuß des Deutschen Reichstages 1915–1918*, 4 vols., Düsseldorf 1981–3, III, No. 166. See Jarausch, *Enigmatic Chancellor*, pp. 370f.

21 Plessen, diary for 7 July 1917, Afflerbach, *Kriegsherr*, Nr P 647; see Müller, diary for 8 July 1917, Görlitz, *Regierte der Kaiser?*, pp. 300f.

22 Valentini, *Kaiser und Kabinettschef*, p. 158; see Riezler, *Tagebücher*, pp. 444f., note 3; Mertz von Quirnheim, memorandum of 9 July 1917, Deist, *Militär und Innenpolitik*, II, No. 314.

23 Müller, diary for 10 July 1917, Görlitz, *Regierte der Kaiser?*, p. 302.

24 Valentini, *Kaiser und Kabinettschef*, pp. 158f.

25 Ibid., p. 159.

26 Ibid.

27 Plessen, diary for 9 July 1917, Afflerbach, *Kriegsherr*, No. P 649.

28 Müller, diary for 9 July 1917, Görlitz, *Regierte der Kaiser?*, p. 301.

29 Ibid.

30 Wolff, diary for 10 July 1917, Wolff, *Tagebücher*, I, No. 571.

31 Minutes of the Crown Council of 9 July 1917, Leo Stern, ed., *Die Auswirkungen der großen sozialistischen Oktoberrevolution auf Deutschland*, 4 vols., Berlin 1959, II, No. 143.

32 Valentini, *Kaiser und Kabinettschef*, p. 160.

33 Ibid., pp. 161f. See Bethmann Hollweg, memoranda of 11 July and 14 July 1917, *Ursachen und Folgen*, I, Nos. 227 and 231.

34 Bethmann Hollweg, *Betrachtungen zum Weltkrieg*, II, p. 222; Helfferich, *Weltkrieg*, III, p. 121; Valentini, *Kaiser und Kabinettschef*, pp. 162f.

35 *Schulthess' europäischer Geschichtskalender 1917*, I, pp. 687f.

36 Hohenlohe to Czernin, 10/11 July 1917, HHStA Vienna, PA III, 173, as cited in Jarausch, *Enigmatic Chancellor*, p. 375.

37 Wolff, diary for 12 July 1917, Wolff, *Tagebücher*, I, No. 573.

38 See the Crown Prince's own account of these developments in Herre, *Kronprinz*, pp. 87ff.

39 The minutes are printed in Ludendorff, *Urkunden*, pp. 408–11. See also Bauer, *Der große Krieg*, pp. 141f.; Eduard David, diary for 12 July 1917, in Eduard David, *Das Kriegstagebuch des Reichstagsabgeordneten Eduard David 1914 bis 1918*, Düsseldorf 1966, pp. 243f.; Payer, *Bethmann Hollweg*, pp. 31ff.

40 Valentini, *Kaiser und Kabinettschef*, p. 165.

41 Müller, diary for 12 July 1917, Görlitz, *Regierte der Kaiser?*, p. 303; Valentini, *Kaiser und Kabinettschef*, p. 164.

42 See Kühlmann, *Erinnerungen*, p. 537.

43 Hammann, *Bilder aus der letzten Kaiserzeit*, p. 77.

44 Bethmann Hollweg, memorandum of 14 July 1917, *Ursachen und Folgen*, I, No. 231.

45 Valentini, *Kaiser und Kabinettschef*, p. 168.

46 Müller, diary for 14 July 1917, Görlitz, *Regierte der Kaiser?*, p. 304.

47 Plessen, diary for 13 July 1917, Afflerbach, *Kriegsherr*, No. P 653. See also Berg, *Erinnerungen*, pp. 120f.; Magnus von Braun, *Von Ostpreußen bis Texas: Erlebnisse und Zeitgeschichtliche Betrachtungen eines Ostpreußen*, Stollhamm 1955, pp. 113–16; Bülow, *Denkwürdigkeiten*, III, pp. 267f.; Helfferich, *Weltkrieg*, III, pp. 131f.; Kühlmann, *Erinnerungen*, pp. 501f.; Valentini, *Kaiser und Kabinettschef*, pp. 166ff.

48 Valentini, diary for 13 July 1917, typescript copy, BA Koblenz, Thimme Papers, Nr 26.

49 Cf. Afflerbach, *Kriegsherr*, p. 32.

50 See the trenchant study by Lothar Machtan, *Die Abdankung. Wie Deutschlands gekrönte Häupter aus der Geschichte fielen*, Berlin 2008, pp. 113 et passim.

51 Haußmann, diary for 14 October 1917, Conrad Haußmann, *Schlaglichter. Reichstagsbriefe und Aufzeichnungen*, ed. Ulrich Zeller, Frankfurt a.M. 1924, p. 131.

52 Minutes of the joint session of the SPD leadership and the SPD Reichstag members, 23 September 1917, Erich Matthias and Eberhard Pikart, eds., *Die Reichstagsfraktion der deutschen Sozialdemokratie 1898 bis 1918*, 2 vols., Düsseldorf 1966, II, No. 492b; Michaelis, *Für Volk und Staat*, p. 328; Matthias, *Der Interfraktionelle Ausschuß*, I, No. 29; Wolff, diary for 23 August 1917, Wolff, *Tagebücher*, I, No. 595. For the Chancellorship of Michaelis see Bert Becker, *Georg Michaelis. Preußischer Beamter – Reichskanzler – Christlicher Reformer. 1857–1936. Eine Biographie*, Paderborn, Munich, Vienna and Zürich 2007, pp. 354–525.

53 Matthias, *Der Interfraktionelle Ausschuß*, I, No. 49.

54 Matthias Erzberger, *Erlebnisse im Weltkrieg*, Stuttgart and Berlin 1920, p. 53.

55 For the devastating impression left by the Kaiser's meeting with the parliamentarians see Braun, *Ostpreußen*, pp. 119f.; David, diary for 20 July 1917, David, *Kriegstagebuch*, p. 249; Erzberger, *Erlebnisse*, pp. 53f.; Helfferich, *Weltkrieg*, III, p. 161; Payer, *Bethmann Hollweg*, pp. 42f.; Plessen, diary for 20 July 1917, Afflerbach, *Kriegsherr*, No. P 659; Philipp Scheidemann, *Memoirs of a Social Democrat*, 2 vols., London 1928, II, pp. 378–82; Eugen Schiffer, *Ein Leben für den Liberalismus*, Berlin 1951, pp. 57ff.; Molkenbuhr, diary for 21 July 1917, Matthias and Pikart, *Reichstagsfraktion*, II, p. 315, note 2; Westarp, *Konservative Politik*, II, pp. 473f.. See also Cecil, *Wilhelm II: Emperor and Exile*, p. 255.

56 Erzberger, *Erlebnisse*, p. 54.

57 Scheidemann, *Memoirs*, pp. 378–82; Machtan, *Abdankung*, pp. 117–19.

58 Matthias, *Der Interfraktionelle Ausschuß*, I, No. 50; cf. Michaelis, *Für Volk und Staat*, pp. 360f.; *Hauptausschuß*, III, No. 172.

59 Meeting of the joint parliamentary committee of 8 October 1917, *Hauptausschuß*, III, No. 187; *Stenographische Berichte über die Verhandlungen des Reichstages*, 13. Legislaturperiode, 2. Session, Bd. 310, pp. 3714ff.

60 Matthias, *Der Interfraktionelle Ausschuß*, I, No. 48.

61 Müller, diary for 9 October 1917, Görlitz, *Regierte der Kaiser?*, p. 324; cf. Kühlmann, *Erinnerungen*, pp. 501f.

62 Müller, diary for 21 October 1917, Görlitz, *Regierte der Kaiser?*, p. 326.

63 Matthias, *Der Interfraktionelle Ausschuß*, I, Nos. 55 and 57; Udo Bermbach, *Vorformen parlamentarischer Kabinettsbildung in Deutschland. Der interfraktionelle Ausschuß 1917/18 und die Parlamentarisierung der Reichsregierung*, Cologne 1967, pp. 172ff.

64 Valentini, *Kaiser und Kabinettschef*, p. 175; cf. Matthias, *Der Interfraktionelle Ausschuß*, I, Nos. 57d and 58; Michaelis, *Für Volk und Staat*, p. 368.

65 Valentini, *Kaiser und Kabinettschef*, p. 177; Matthias, *Der Interfraktionelle Ausschuß*, I, No. 63.

66 Valentini, *Kaiser und Kabinettschef*, p. 177.

67 Karl Graf von Hertling, *Ein Jahr in der Reichskanzlei*, Freiburg-im-Breisgau, 1919, p. 14; Michaelis, *Für Volk und Staat*, p. 383; Valentini, *Kaiser und Kabinettschef*, pp. 178f.

68 Valentini, *Kaiser und Kabinettschef*, p. 179.

69 Bermbach, *Vorformen parlamentarischer Kabinettsbildung*, pp. 187–200.

70 Machtan, *Abdankung*, p. 124.

71 Valentini, *Kaiser und Kabinettschef*, p. 181.

72 Scheidemann, *Memoirs of a Social Democrat*, II, p. 427. See Schiffer, *Liberalismus*, p. 61.

73 Kühlmann, *Erinnerungen*, pp. 512f.; Müller, diary for 8 November 1917, Görlitz, *Regierte der Kaiser?*, p. 331.

74 Ibid.; cf. Plessen, diary for 10 November 1917, Afflerbach, *Kriegsherr*, No. P 680. See Mewes to his wife, 3 and 4 November 1917, Mewes Papers, in private hands, Munich.

75 Müller, diary for 16 November 1917, Görlitz, *Regierte der Kaiser?*, p. 333.

76 Hindenburg to Kaiser Wilhelm II, 16 January 1918, Deist, *Militär und Innenpolitik*, II, No. 420; Hertling, *Ein Jahr in der Reichskanzlei*, pp. 55f.; Valentini, *Kaiser und Kabinettschef*, pp. 190f.; Valentini, diary for 13 and 15 January 1918, typescript copy, BA Koblenz, Thimme Papers, Nr 26.

77 Valentini, *Kaiser und Kabinettschef*, pp. 190f.; on the Kaiserin's role see above, p. 1168.

78 Valentini, *Kaiser und Kabinettschef*, p. 210.

79 Müller, diary for 17 January 1918, Görlitz, *Regierte der Kaiser?*, p. 345.

80 Dieter Storz, '"Aber was hätte anders geschehen sollen?" Die deutschen Offensiven an der Westfront 1918', in Jörg Duppler and Gerhard P. Groß, eds., *Kriegsende 1918. Ereignis, Wirkung, Nachwirkung*, Munich 1999; also *Der Weltkrieg*, XIV, pp. 100–259.

81 Müller, diary for 23 and 26 March 1918, Görlitz, *Regierte der Kaiser?*, pp. 365f. See above, p. 1149.

82 Mewes to his wife, 17 April 1918, Mewes Papers, in private hands, Munich; Niemann, *Kaiser und Revolution*, pp. 40f.

83 Crown Prince Rupprecht of Bavaria, diary for 19 February and 29 March 1918, Frauenholz, *Kriegstagebuch*, II, pp. 330f. and 364; Horst Mühleisen, *Kurt Freiherr von Lersner. Diplomat im Umbruch der Zeiten 1918–1920. Eine Biographie*, Göttingen 1988, pp. 27f.

84 Kühlmann, *Erinnerungen*, pp. 572f.

85 Kühlmann, speech in the Reichstag, 24 June 1918, *Schulthess' europäischer Geschichtskalender 1918*, I, pp. 202–10.

86 Berg, *Erinnerungen*, p. 150.

87 On Hintze's appointment see Hürter, *Hintze*, pp. 75–8.

88 Berg, *Erinnerungen*, p. 152; Lyncker to his wife, 15–20 July 1918, Afflerbach, *Kriegsherr*, No. L 760–5; Müller, diary for 16 and 20 July 1918, Görlitz, *Regierte der Kaiser?*, pp. 394f.

89 *Der Weltkrieg*, XIV, pp. 446–87.

90 For the dramatic collapse of morale in the German army in the summer and autumn of 1918 see especially Wilhelm Deist, 'Verdeckter Militärstreik im Kriegsjahr 1918?', in Wolfram Wette, ed., *Der Krieg des kleinen Mannes. Eine Militärgeschichte von unten*, Munich and Zürich 1992; Klaus Latzel, 'Die mißlungene Flucht vor dem Tod. Töten und Sterben vor und nach 1918', in Duppler and Groß, *Kriegsende 1918*; Volker Ullrich, 'Zur inneren Revolutionierung der wilhelminischen Gesellschaft des Jahres 1918', ibid.; Benjamin Ziemann, 'Enttäuschte Erwartung und kollektive Erschöpfung. Die deutschen Soldaten an der Westfront 1918 auf dem Weg zur Revolution', ibid.

91 Niemann, *Kaiser und Revolution*, p. 45; Müller, diary for 11 August 1918, Görlitz, *Regierte der Kaiser?*, pp. 401f.

92 See the details in Machtan, *Abdankung*, pp. 141f.

93 See Bauer, *Der große Krieg*, p. 210; Hintze to Auswärtiges Amt, 3 January 1919, Hürter, *Hintze*, No. 254; Ludendorff, *Kriegserinnerungen*, p. 553; Ludendorff, *Urkunden*, pp. 499–502; Golo Mann and Andreas Burckhardt, eds., *Max von Baden, Erinnerungen und Dokumente*, Stuttgart 1968, p. 287 (cited below as Max von Baden, *Erinnerungen*).

94 See Hürter, *Hintze*, p. 486, note 2.

95 Minutes of the conference in General Headquarters, 14 August 1918, Ludendorff, *Urkunden*, pp. 499–502.

96 Machtan, *Abdankung*, pp. 146 and 152.

97 Müller, diary for 2 September 1918, Görlitz, *Regierte der Kaiser?*, p. 406; see also Ilsemann, diary for 12 September 1918, Koenigswald, *Kaiser in Holland*, I, pp. 15–17.

98 Müller, diary for 17 August 1918, Görlitz, *Regierte der Kaiser?*, p. 402.

99 Max von Baden to Kaiser Wilhelm II, 15 August 1918, Max von Baden, *Erinnerungen*, pp. 290f.

100 Niemann, *Kaiser und Revolution*, pp. 78–80.

101 William Manchester, *Krupp. Chronik einer Familie*, Munich 1978, p. 300; Niemann, *Kaiser und Revolution*, p. 81; Berg, *Erinnerungen*, p. 169; Ilsemann, diary for 12 September 1918, Koenigswald, *Kaiser in Holland*, I, pp. 15–17; Müller, diary for 10 September 1918, Görlitz, *Regierte der Kaiser?*, p. 411.

102 See Obst, *Die politischen Reden*, pp. 405–12.

103 Müller, diary for 13, 16 and 22 September 1918, Görlitz, *Regierte der Kaiser?*, pp. 413–17; Ilsemann, diary for 23 May 1922, Koenigswald, *Kaiser in Holland*, I, pp. 216f.

104 Cited in Machtan, *Abdankung*, p. 153.

105 The Austro-Hungarian note of 14 September 1918 is printed in *Schulthess' europäischer Geschichtskalender 1918*, II, pp. 54–7.

106 Hintze to Auswärtiges Amt, 3 January 1919, Hürter, *Hintze*, No. 254; cf. ibid., pp. 103f.; Klaus Schwabe, *Deutsche Revolution und Wilson-Frieden. Die amerikanische und deutsche Friedensstrategie zwischen Ideologie und Machtpolitik 1918/19*, Düsseldorf 1971, pp. 95–105.

107 Memorandum by Stumm, Rosenberg and Bergen, 28 September 1918, in Scherer and Grunewald, *L'Allemagne*, IV, No. 280.

108 Thaer, diary for 30 September 1918, Thaer, *Generalstabsdienst*, p. 235.

109 Müller, diary for 29 September 1918, Görlitz, *Regierte der Kaiser?*, pp. 420ff.

110 For the negotiations in Spa on 29 September 1918 see the works listed in Matthias, *Der Interfraktionelle Ausschuß*, II, p. 739, note 3.

111 The text of the decree of 30 September 1918 is printed in *Schulthess' europäischer Geschichtskalender 1918*, I, p. 314. For details see Heinrich Potthoff, 'Der Parlamentarisierungserlaß vom 30. September 1918', *Vierteljahrshefte für Zeitgeschichte* 20, 1972.

112 See Machtan, *Abdankung*, p. 152.

113 Clemens von Delbrück, *Die wirtschaftliche Mobilmachung in Deutschland*, ed. Joachim von Delbrück, Munich 1924, pp. 265f.

114 See Lerchenfeld to Dandl, 1 October 1918, in Erich Matthias and Rudolf Morsey, eds., *Die Regierung des Prinzen Max von Baden*, Düsseldorf 1962, No. 5, especially p. 28.

115 Niemann, *Kaiser und Revolution*, p. 93.

116 Cf. Bermbach, *Vorformen parlamentarischer Kabinettsbildung*, pp. 269–72.

117 For the background to Hertling's dismissal see ibid., pp. 219–70. See also the report by Bussche and Haeften of 2 October 1918 to the party leaders, Ludendorff, *Urkunden*, pp. 535–40.

118 See Max von Baden, *Erinnerungen*, p. 334; Machtan, *Abdankung*, p. 166.

119 For the formation of the government of Max von Baden see the forthcoming biography by Lothar Machtan, *Des Kaisers letzter Kanzler. Prinz Max von Baden. Biographie eines Unglücks*, Frankfurt a.M. 2013, especially Chapter 8. See also Bermbach, *Vorformen parlamentarischer Kabinettsbildung*, pp. 285–306; Matthias and Morsey, *Regierung Max*, pp. 3–64; Max von Baden, *Erinnerungen*, pp. 308–61; Manfred Rauh, *Die Parlamentarisierung des Deutschen Reiche*s, Düsseldorf 1977, pp. 434–44.

120 Previously Wilhelm II had refused to countenance the appointment of a younger 'colleague' as Reich Chancellor. See Valentini, *Kaiser und Kabinettschef*, pp. 177f.; Machtan, *Abdankung*, pp.169ff.; Machtan, *Max von Baden*, Chapter 8.

121 See Huber, *Deutsche Verfassungsgeschichte*, V, pp. 535–669; Ulrich Kluge, *Die deutsche Revolution 1918/1919*, Frankfurt a.M. 1985, pp. 39–53; Eberhard Kolb, ed., *Vom Kaiserreich zur Weimarer Republik*, Cologne 1972; Ullrich, *Als der Thron ins Wanken kam*, pp. 179–221.

122 See Nipperdey, *Deutsche Geschichte*, II, pp. 867–71.

123 The German–American exchange of notes of October/November 1918 is published in *Schulthess' europäischer Geschichtskalender 1918*, II, pp. 608–18.

124 Quoted in Michael Balfour, *The Kaiser and his Times*, London 1964, p. 396. For Prince Max's role in the abdication crisis see Machtan, *Max von Baden*, Chapter 9.

125 Riezler, diary for 13 April 1917, Riezler, *Tagebücher*, No. 715.

126 See Ritter, *Staatskunst und Kriegshandwerk*, IV, pp. 414–50.

127 Quoted in Balfour, *Kaiser and his Times*, p. 397.

128 Kaiser Wilhelm II to Prinz Max von Baden, telegram, 16 October 1918, Matthias and Morsey, *Regierung Max*, p. 218, note 3.

129 Minutes of the meeting of the 'war cabinet', 17 October 1918, Matthias and Morsey, *Regierung Max*, No. 63.

130 Max von Baden, *Erinnerungen*, pp. 428–45.

131 See Adolf Stutzenberger, *Die Abdankung Kaiser Wilhelms II. Die Entstehung und Entwicklung der Kaiserfrage und die Haltung der Presse*, Berlin 1937; Kohlrausch, *Monarch im Skandal*, pp. 311–21; Wolff, diary for 15, 16, 21 and 31 October and 1–9 November 1918, Wolff, *Tagebücher*, Nos. 787f., 792f. 794–802.

132 Woodrow Wilson, *Papers*, I, p. 538.

133 Army order of 24 October 1918, *Amtliche Urkunden zur Vorgeschichte des Waffenstillstands*, Berlin 1924, No. 76 b; see Haeften's account in Matthias and Morsey, *Regierung Max*, No. 86.

134 Prinz Max von Baden to Kaiser Wilhelm II, 25 October 1918, Matthias and Morsey, *Regierung Max*, No. 94; cf. Max von Baden, *Erinnerungen*, p. 475.

135 Niemann, *Kaiser und Revolution*, p. 116; Ilsemann, diary for 26 October 1918, Koenigswald, *Kaiser in Holland*, I, pp. 28–30.

136 See the typescript notes in BA Koblenz, Solf Papers, Nr 11; Plessen, diary for 26 October 1918, Afflerbach, *Kriegsherr*, No. P 704.

137 See Max von Baden, *Erinnerungen*, pp. 482ff.

138 Ilsemann, diary for 24 October 1918, Koenigswald, *Kaiser in Holland*, I, p. 25.

139 Ilsemann, diary for 25 October 1918, ibid., pp. 25–7. See also Machtan, *Abdankung*, p. 187.

140 Kaiser Wilhelm II, speech to the new secretaries of state, 21 October 1918, *Ursachen und Folgen*, II, No. 390; decree of 28 October 1918, *Schulthess' europäischer Geschichtskalender 1918*, I, pp. 398f.

141 Kohlrausch, *Monarch im Skandal*, pp. 309f.

142 See the evidence in Cecil, *Wilhelm II: Emperor and Exile*, pp. 286f.

143 Payer, *Bethmann Hollweg*, p. 148; Max von Baden, *Erinnerungen*, pp. 498–501; Solf to Hammann, 23 January 1919, Hammann, *Bilder aus der letzten Kaiserzeit*, pp. 135–8; Viktoria Luise, Duchess of Brunswick-Lüneburg, *Ein Leben*, p. 201.

144 See Machtan, *Abdankung*, p. 208.

145 Johannes Vogel, memorandum of a conversation with Kaiser Wilhelm II in Spa on 3 November 1918, BA-MA Freiburg-im-Breisgau, Mackensen Papers, N 39/39.

146 Drews, report of his reception by Kaiser Wilhelm II in Spa on 1 November 1918, Matthias and Morsey, *Regierung Max*, No. 115; Vogel, memorandum of a conversation with Kaiser Wilhelm II in Spa on 3 November 1918, BA-MA Freiburg-im-Breisgau, Mackensen Papers, N 39/39; Ilsemann, diary for 1 November 1918, Koenigswald, *Kaiser in Holland*, I, pp. 30–2; Crown Prince Rupprecht of Bavaria, diary for 4 November 1918, Frauenholz, *Kriegstagebuch*, II, p. 473; Schiffer, *Leben für den Liberalismus*, pp. 135 and 137.

147 Ilsemann, diary for 19 November 1918, Koenigswald, *Kaiser in Holland*, I, pp. 55–60 et passim.

148 Ilsemann, diary for 6 and 8 November 1918, ibid., I, pp. 34f.

149 Groener, *Lebenserinnerungen*, p. 438; see also Thaer, diary for 9 November 1918, Thaer, *Generalstabsdienst*, pp. 257–9.

150 Groener, *Lebenserinnerungen*, p. 438; cf. Alfred Niemann, *Revolution von oben – Umsturz von unten. Entwicklung und Verlauf der Staatsumwälzung in Deutschland 1914–1918*, Berlin 1928, pp. 350f.

151 Max von Baden, *Erinnerungen*, pp. 595ff.; see Ilsemann, diary for 9 November 1918, Koenigswald, *Kaiser in Holland*, I, pp. 36ff.; Plessen, diary for 9 November 1918, Afflerbach, *Kriegsherr*, No. P 708.

152 Max von Baden, *Erinnerungen*, p. 597; cf. the accounts of Heilbronn and Simon in Matthias and Morsey, *Regierung Max*, Nos. 146 and 148.

153 Max von Baden, *Erinnerungen*, p. 598.

154 Max von Baden, declaration of 9 November 1918, *Schulthess' europäischer Geschichtskalender 1918*, I, p. 451.

155 See Ilsemann, diary for 9 November 1918, Koenigswald, *Kaiser in Holland*, I, p. 43; Niemann, *Kaiser und Revolution*, pp. 136–47; Niemann, *Revolution von oben*, pp. 325–473; Plessen, diary for 9 November 1918, Afflerbach, *Kriegsherr*, No. P 708; Kuno Graf von Westarp, *Das Ende der Monarchie am 9. November 1918*, Stollhamm 1952.

156 Stewart Roddie, memorandum of 29 June 1921, RA GV/M 1515/36.

45   THE UNICORN IN WINTER. A NEW LIFE IN EXILE

1 Jan Bank, 'Der Weg des Kaisers ins Exil', in Hans Wilderotter and Klaus-D. Pohl, eds., *Der letzte Kaiser. Wilhelm II. im Exil*, Gütersloh and Munich 1991, pp. 105f. See Clark, *Kaiser Wilhelm II*, pp, 245ff.; Cecil, *Wilhelm II: Emperor and Exile*, pp. 296ff.; Kohlrausch, *Monarch im Skandal*, pp. 386ff.

2 Kaiser Wilhelm II, abdication, 28 November 1918, GStA Berlin, BPHA Rep. 53 Nr 203.

3 Sally Marks, '"My Name is Ozymandias": The Kaiser in Exile', *Central European History*, XVI/2, June 1983, 129 and 132; Hans Wilderotter, 'Haus Doorn. Die verkleinerte Kopie eines Hofstaats', in Wilderotter and Pohl, *Der letzte Kaiser*, p. 116.

4 Requisitions of 13 and 30 November 1918, printed in Kurt Heinig, *Hohenzollern. Wilhelm II. und sein Haus. Der Kampf um den Kronbesitz*, Berlin 1921, pp. 73–6; Graf August zu Eulenburg to Prussian Ministry of Finance, 6 January, 7 June, 1 September and 15 October 1919, cited in Wilderotter, 'Haus Doorn', pp. 113f. and 120. For the total amount transmitted see ibid., note 8 and Heinig, *Hohenzollern*, p. 141. Cf. Marks, 'Kaiser in Exile', 131f.; Koenigswald, *Kaiser in Holland*, I, p. 90; Prince Eitel Friedrich of Prussia to Kaiser Wilhelm II, 29 November 1919, Archiv des vormals regierenden preußischen Königshauses, Burg Hohenzollern, Hechingen.

5 August Eulenburg, correspondence with Prussian Ministry of Finance, 17 May to 2 June 1921, cited in Wilderotter, 'Haus Doorn', p. 115 with note 11.

6 Ibid., p. 119 with note 32.

7 See the lists printed ibid., p. 121, note 33. Also Gutsche, *Wilhelm II.*, pp. 200f.

8 Speeches by Müller and Scheidemann at the SPD conference in September 1919, cited in Otmar Jung, *Volksgesetzgebung. Die 'Weimarer Erfahrungen' aus dem Fall der Vermögensauseinandersetzungen zwischen Freistaaten und ehemaligen Fürsten*, Hamburg 1990, pp. 465f. See also the angry reaction of Maximilian Harden in the *Zukunft* of 27 November 1920, pp. 252f.

9 Ilsemann, diary for 20 June 1926; Koenigswald, *Kaiser in Holland*, II, p. 40.

10 'Gesetz über die Vermögensauseinandersetzung zwischen dem Preußischen Staate und den Mitgliedern des vormals regierenden Preußischen Königshauses', 29 October 1926, Gutsche, *Wilhelm II.*, p. 202.

11 The tax statement of 26 October 1942 is to be found in GStA Berlin, BPHA Rep. 53 Nr 390–5. Gutsche, *Wilhelm II.*, p. 225; Wilderotter, 'Haus Doorn', p. 115.

12 Kaiser Wilhelm II to Margarethe Landgravine of Hesse, 19 April 1929, AdHH Schloss Fasanerie.

13 Wilderotter, 'Haus Doorn', p. 113.

14 Kaiser Wilhelm II, 4 May 1920, as cited in Gutsche, *Wilhelm II.*, p. 202.

15 Further details in Wilderotter, 'Haus Doorn', pp. 116ff.

16 Haehner, diary, Stadtarchiv Cologne, passim. But see Koenigswald, *Kaiser in Holland*, I, pp. 193f.

17 Kaiser Wilhelm II to Irma Fürstenberg, 16 May 1922, FFA Donaueschingen; Haehner, diary for April 1922, Stadtarchiv Cologne.

18 Haehner, diary for 30 December 1920, ibid.

19 RA GV/Q 1114/81-7 and Q 1560/1-52. For the agitation of the winter of 1918 to 'Hang the Kaiser' see Reinermann, *Kaiser in England*, pp. 471ff.; Thomas Wittek, *Auf ewig Feind? Das Deutschlandbild in den britischen Massenmedien nach dem Ersten Weltkrieg*, Munich 2005, pp. 215ff.

20 Marks, 'Kaiser in Exile', 132f. For the problem of extradition in general see Walter Schwengler, *Völkerrecht, Versailler Vertrag und Auslieferungsfrage: die Strafverfolgung wegen Kriegsverbrechen als Problem des Friedensschlusses 1919/20*, Stuttgart 1982.

21 Rosen, *Aus einem diplomatischen Wanderleben*, III/IV, pp. 249f.

22 Marks, 'Kaiser in Exile', 133.

23 See below, p. 1201.

24 Ilsemann, diary for 11 December 1918, Koenigswald, *Kaiser in Holland*, I, pp. 72ff.

25 Ibid., pp. 71-81, 86 and 92f.; Haehner, diary for 5 April 1921, Stadtarchiv Cologne.

26 Koenigswald, *Kaiser in Holland*, I, p. 86; Marks, 'Kaiser in Exile', 135f.

27 Koenigswald, *Kaiser in Holland*, I, pp. 88f.

28 Haehner, diary for November 1920, Stadtarchiv Cologne.

29 Marks, 'Kaiser in Exile', 136.

30 *La Paix de Versailles. La Documentation Internationale*, 13 vols., Paris 1929-32, III; Marks, 'Kaiser in Exile', 137.

31 Ibid., pp. 137ff. See George Sylvester Viereck, *The Kaiser on Trial*, New York 1937, passim.

32 Rosen to Kaiser Wilhelm II, 4 May 1919, Archiv des vormals regierenden preußischen Königshauses, Burg Hohenzollern, Hechingen; Koenigswald, *Kaiser in Holland*, I, pp. 105f.

33 Ibid., I, pp. 107f.; Marks, 'Kaiser in Exile', 140.

34 Hankey, minute of 5 July 1919, RA GV/Q 1560/9; Stamfordham to Davies, 7 and 11 July 1919, RA GV/Q 1560/10 and 17.

35 Plessen to Gräfin Brockdorff, 2 June 1919, printed in Afflerbach, *Kriegsherr*, No. P 711; Müller to Kaiser Wilhelm II, 10 June 1919, GStA Berlin, BPHA Rep. 53 E I Weltkrieg Nr 6; cf. Jörg-Uwe Fischer, *Admiral des Kaisers. Georg Alexander von Müller als Chef des Marinekabinetts Wilhelms II.*, Frankfurt a.M. 1992, pp. 283ff. See also Marks, 'Kaiser in Exile', 141-4. See below, p. 1197.

36 Kaiser Wilhelm II, marginal notes on a letter from General von Schubert, 12 May 1919, Kaiser Wilhelm II to Cardinal Felix von Hartmann, 28 May 1919, printed in Koenigswald, *Kaiser in Holland*, I, p. 319.

37 Esher to Stamfordham, 8 July 1919, RA GV/Q 1560/12.

38 See above, chapters 38-41.

39 Haehner, diary for 29-30 November, 1, 13-14 December 1919, Stadtarchiv Cologne; Ilsemann, diary for 1 December 1919, Koenigswald, *Kaiser in Holland*, I, p. 127; Graham to Curzon, 17 December 1919, RA PS/PSO/GV/C/Q 1560/22.

40 Graham to Curzon, 17 December 1919, RA PS/PSO/GV/C/Q 1560/22.

41 Haehner, diary for 28 November 1919, Stadtarchiv Cologne.

42 Haehner, diary for 15 December 1919, ibid.

43 Haehner, diary for 13 January 1920, ibid.

44 Alan Kramer, *Dynamic of Destruction. Culture and Mass Killing in the First World War*, Oxford 2007.

45 Clemenceau to the government of the Netherlands, 16 January 1920, RA PS/PSO/GV/Q 1560/28.

46 Marks, 'Kaiser in Exile', 148.
47 Haehner, diary for 22 January 1920, Stadtarchiv Cologne.
48 Kaiser Wilhelm II to Margarethe Landgravine of Hesse, 2 February 1920, AdHH Schloss Fasanerie.
49 Haehner, diary for 26 January, 13 and 28 February 1920, Stadtarchiv Cologne. See below, p. 1228.
50 Gooch and Temperley, *British Documents*, IX, pp. 624 and 628ff.; Marks, 'Kaiser in Exile', 152f.
51 'Réponse à La Hollande', 14 February 1920, RA GV/Q 1560/41.
52 Marks, 'Kaiser in Exile', 150–3; Hardinge to Graham, January 1920, Gooch and Temperley, *British Documents*, IX, p. 624; Stamfordham to King George V, 4 February 1920, RA PS/PSO/GV/C/Q 1560/37.
53 Memorandum of 17 February 1920, RA GV/K 1415/15.
54 Crown Prince Wilhelm to the kings of England, Belgium and Italy, the Emperor of Japan and the presidents of France and the USA, 9 February 1920, Kaiser Wilhelm II to Crown Prince, 10 February 1920, GStA Berlin, BPHA Rep. 54 E 1 Auswärtiges. Haehner, diary for 10–11 February 1920, Stadtarchiv Cologne. See below, pp. 1241f.
55 Note of 13 February 1920, cited in Marks, 'Kaiser in Exile', 158ff.; Graham to Stamfordham, 18 February 1920, RA PS/PSO/GV/C/P 512/5.
56 Kaiser Wilhelm II, declaration of 10 March 1920, BA-MA Freiburg-im-Breisgau, Dommes Papers, N 512/21; Haehner, diary for 9 March 1920, Stadtarchiv Cologne; Koenigswald, *Kaiser in Holland*, I, pp. 147f.; Marks, 'Kaiser in Exile', pp. 162f.; Gooch and Temperley, *British Documents*, IX, pp. 706–10.
57 Queen Wilhelmina, decree of 16 March 1920, Gooch and Temperley, *British Documents*, VII, p. 552.
58 Haehner, diary for 7 March 1921, Stadtarchiv Cologne.
59 Haehner, diary for 13–17 March (Amerongen) and 5 May (Wieringen) 1920, ibid.
60 See Annika Saerbeck, 'Kaiser ohne Amt und Zukunft. Zum politischen, weltanschaulichen und monarchischen Selbstverständnis Wilhelms II. in den ersten Jahren seines holländischen Exils', unpublished MA dissertation, University of Bremen 2007.
61 See Lothar Machtan, *Der Kaisersohn bei Hitler*, Hamburg 2006, pp. 73–83; Dorpalen, 'Empress Auguste Victoria'; Edgar Vincent Viscount D'Abernon, *Ein Botschafter der Zeitenwende, Memoiren*, 3 vols., Leipzig 1930, III, p. 98.
62 Haehner, diary for 19 November 1919, Stadtarchiv Cologne.
63 Haehner, diary for 4 December 1919, ibid.
64 Ibid.
65 John C. G. Röhl, Martin Warren and David Hunt, eds., *Purple Secret. Genes, 'Madness' and the Royal Houses of Europe*, London 1998, p. 154.
66 Haehner, diary for 5 and 6 November 1922, Stadtarchiv Cologne.
67 See Röhl, *The Kaiser's Personal Monarchy*, pp. 643f.
68 Haehner, later addenda, October 1920, diary No. 8, p. 152, Stadtarchiv Cologne.
69 Haehner, diary for 28 January and 23 February 1924, ibid.
70 Haehner, diary for 17 May 1921, ibid.
71 Haehner, diary for 19 November 1919, ibid.; Ilsemann, diary for 4 December 1919, Koenigswald, *Kaiser in Holland*, I, p. 128.
72 Kaiser Wilhelm II, declaration of 23 November 1918, BA-MA Freiburg-im-Breisgau, Dommes Papers, N 512/21.
73 Haehner, later addenda, July 1920, diary Nr 8, pp. 147f., Stadtarchiv Cologne.
74 Haehner, later addenda, July 1920, ibid.
75 Haehner, diary for 11 December 1919 and 5 November 1922, ibid.

76 For the marital crisis of Prince August Wilhelm and his wife see the detailed account in Machtan, *Kaisersohn*, pp. 105–20.

77 Haehner, diary for 9 and 20 December 1919 and 1 January 1920, Stadtarchiv Cologne, cited in Machtan, *Kaisersohn*, pp. 112f.; Ilsemann, diary for 6 November 1919, Koenigswald, *Kaiser in Holland*, I, pp. 121 and 245.

78 Haehner, diary for 6 December 1920, Stadtarchiv Cologne.

79 Ilsemann, diary for 10 October 1924, Koenigswald, *Kaiser in Holland*, II, p. 17.

80 Haehner, diary for 28–9 November and 6–8 December 1919, Stadtarchiv Cologne.

81 Haehner, diary for 29 November and 5 December 1920, ibid.

82 Haehner, diary for 6–8 December 1919, 22 December 1920 and 25 January 1921, ibid.

83 Ilsemann, diary for 28 August 1921, Koenigswald, *Kaiser in Holland*, I, p. 185.

84 Ilsemann, diary for 2 July 1922, ibid., I, p. 228. See below, pp. 1210f.

85 See Röhl, *The Kaiser's Personal Monarchy*, p. 1067.

86 Haehner, diary for 20 December 1919, Stadtarchiv Cologne.

87 Haehner, diary for 9 December 1919 and 22 January 1920, ibid.

88 Haehner, later addenda, June 1920, diary Nr 8, pp. 141–6, ibid.

89 Kaiser Wilhelm II, marginal note on a newspaper article, January 1920, Archiv des vormals regierenden preußischen Königshauses, Burg Hohenzollern, Hechingen.

90 A detailed account of Prince Joachim's disturbed condition and suicide was sent by his brother Eitel Friedrich to their father in Doorn. Prince Eitel Friedrich to Kaiser Wilhelm II, 18 July 1920, Archiv des vormals regierenden preußischen Königshauses, Burg Hohenzollern, Hechingen.

91 Haehner, later addenda, June 1920, diary Nr 8, pp. 141–6, Stadtarchiv Cologne; Kaiser Wilhelm II to Plessen, 29 July 1920, BA-MA Freiburg-im-Breisgau, Plessen Papers, MSg 1/3117; Kaiser Wilhelm II to Mackensen, 12 August 1920, BA-MA Freiburg-im-Breisgau, Mackensen Papers, N 39/39.

92 Haehner, diary for 25 November 1920, 22 December 1920 and 12 April 1921, Stadtarchiv Cologne.

93 Kaiser Wilhelm II to Margarethe Landgravine of Hesse, 21 and 30 October 1921, AdHH Schloss Fasanerie.

94 Haehner, diary for 24 November 1919, Stadtarchiv Cologne. Fürstenberg visited the Kaiser in Doorn in February 1923, ibid., 21 February 1923.

95 Haehner, diary for 20 December 1920, Stadtarchiv Cologne.

96 Ilsemann, diary for 30 August 1921, Koenigswald, *Kaiser in Holland*, I, p. 187.

97 Haehner, diary for 21, 28–9 August and 4 September 1921, Stadtarchiv Cologne. Also Ilsemann, diary for 28 August 1921, Koenigswald, *Kaiser in Holland*, I, p. 186.

98 Haehner, diary for 6 April 1923, Stadtarchiv Cologne.

99 Haehner, diary for 4 November 1919, ibid.

100 Haehner, diary for 11 and 14 April 1921, ibid.

101 Haehner, diary for 17 and 20 April 1921, ibid.

102 Kaiser Wilhelm II to Irma Fürstenberg, 19 April 1921, FFA Donaueschingen.

103 Haehner, diary for 25 April 1921, Stadtarchiv Cologne.

104 Haehner, diary for 13 April 1921, ibid.

105 Haehner, diary for 17 November 1920, ibid.

106 Haehner, diary for 21 April 1921, ibid.

107 Haehner, diary for 29 October 1924, ibid.

108 Haehner, diary for 11, 16 and 17 May and 8 August 1921, ibid.; Crown Prince Wilhelm to Mackensen, 24 May 1921, BA-MA Freiburg-im-Breisgau, Mackensen Papers, N 39/42.

109 Haehner, diary for 10 July and 15 September 1921, Stadtarchiv Cologne. For Frau Dr Hammar from Finland see the diary for 14 October 1923, ibid.

110 Haehner, diary for 21 and 28–9 August 1921, Stadtarchiv Cologne. Also Ilsemann, diary for 28 August 1921, Koenigswald, *Kaiser in Holland*, I, p. 186.

111 Ilsemann, diary for 1 September 1921, ibid., I, pp. 187f.

112 Ilsemann, diary for 23 September 1921, ibid., I, pp. 190f.

113 Haehner, diary for 30 September 1921, Stadtarchiv Cologne.

114 Ilsemann, diary for 16 October 1921, Koenigswald, *Kaiser in Holland*, I, pp. 191f.

115 Kaiser Wilhelm II to Margarethe Landgravine of Hesse, 15 and 16 October 1921, AdHH Schloss Fasanerie. See Lady Susan Townley, *Indiscretions*, New York 1922.

116 Haehner, diary for January 1922, Stadtarchiv Cologne.

117 Ilsemann, diary for 16 October and 28 December 1921, Koenigswald, *Kaiser in Holland*, I, pp. 191f. and 195.

118 Kaiser Wilhelm II to Margarethe Landgravine of Hesse, 15 and 16 October 1921, AdHH Schloss Fasanerie.

119 Haehner, diary for 5 November 1922, Stadtarchiv Cologne.

120 Haehner, diary for 27 January 1922, ibid.

121 Haehner, diary for February–March 1922, ibid.

122 Ilsemann, diary for 22 March 1922, Koenigswald, *Kaiser in Holland*, I, p. 203.

123 Haehner, diary for May 1922, Stadtarchiv Cologne.

124 Friedhild den Toom and Sven Michael Klein, *Hermine – die zweite Gemahlin von Wilhelm II.*, Greiz 2007, pp. 44ff.

125 Kaiser Wilhelm II to Fürstenberg, 8 and 14 October 1922, FFA Donaueschingen.

126 Haehner, diary for October 1922, Stadtarchiv Cologne.

127 Haehner, diary for 16 October 1922, ibid.

128 Kaiser Wilhelm II to Irma Fürstenberg, 14 September 1922, FFA Donaueschingen; Haehner, diary for 3, 5, 18 and 27 October 1922, Stadtarchiv Cologne. See also 4 August 1923, ibid.; Ilsemann, diary for 13 and 18 June and 10 July 1922, Koenigswald, *Kaiser in Holland*, I, pp. 220ff. and 231.

129 Haehner, diary for June 1922, Stadtarchiv Cologne.

130 Ibid.; Machtan, *Kaisersohn*, p. 121.

131 Haehner, diary for June 1922, Stadtarchiv Cologne.

132 Haehner, diary for 5 and 6 November 1922, ibid.

133 Toom and Klein, *Hermine*, pp. 52–7.

134 Haehner, diary for 25 October 1923, Stadtarchiv Cologne.

135 The marriage treaty of 5 November 1922 is to be found in GStA Berlin, BPH Rep. 53 Nr 399. See Toom and Klein, *Hermine*, pp. 44ff.

136 Kaiser Wilhelm II to Margarethe Landgravine of Hesse, 25 November 1922, AdHH Schloss Fasanerie.

137 Haehner, diary for 22, 29 and 30 December 1922, Stadtarchiv Cologne.

138 Haehner, diary for 2 January 1923, ibid.

139 Haehner, diary for 23 January and 2 and 4 August 1923, ibid.

140 Haehner, diary for 2 and 4 August 1923, ibid.

141 Haehner, diary for 6 August 1923, ibid.

142 Haehner, diary for 25 October 1923, ibid.

143 Haehner, diary for 12 August 1923, ibid. See also the entry for 4 September 1923, ibid.

144 Haehner, diary for 11 May and 8 August 1921, ibid.

145 Cf. Friedrich Wilhelm, Prinz von Preußen, *Das Haus Hohenzollern 1918–1945*, Munich and Vienna 1985 (reissued as '*Gott helfe unserem Vaterland'. Das Haus Hohenzollern 1918–1945*, Munich 2003).

46 'BLOOD MUST FLOW, MUCH BLOOD!' THE KAISER
AND THE 'SWINISH' WEIMAR REPUBLIC

1 Kaiser Wilhelm II, 22 August 1934, cited according to the original text of Sigurd von Ilsemann's diary in Röhl, *The Kaiser and his Court*, p. 15.

2 Wolfgang Krauel, diary for 24 October 1919, *Mitteilungen der Friedrich List-Gesellschaft*, Fasc. 6, Nr 13, October 1968, pp. 311–21. See also Ilsemann, diary for 2 June 1919, Koenigswald, *Kaiser in Holland*, I, pp. 103f.

3 Wilhelm II, *Vergleichende Geschichtstabellen von 1878 bis zum Kriegsausbruch 1914*, Leipzig 1921.

4 Haehner, diary for 10 May 1921, Stadtarchiv Cologne.

5 Wilhelm II, *Ereignisse und Gestalten in den Jahren 1878–1918*, Berlin and Leipzig 1922; Dommes to Zimmermann, 8 March 1922, Zimmermann to Dommes, 18 April 1922, BA-MA Freiburg-im-Breisgau, Dommes Papers, N 512/17; Zimmermann to August Eulenburg, 24 April 1922, Zimmermann to Kaiser Wilhelm II, 23 November 1922, Archiv des vormals regierenden preußischen Königshauses, Burg Hohenzollern, Hechingen.

6 Kurt Koehler to Dommes, 11 June 1922, ibid. By early 1923 more than 260,000 copies had been sold. Kaiser Wilhelm II to Margarethe Landgravine of Hesse, 15 February 1923, AdHH Schloss Fasanerie.

7 Valentini to Thimme, 30 January 1923, BA Koblenz, Thimme Papers, Nr 26.

8 Wahnschaffe to Valentini, 5 July 1922, GStA Berlin, Valentini Papers, Nr 21; Valentini to Hermann Fürst zu Hatzfeldt-Trachenberg, BA Koblenz, Kl. Erw. 670/5.

9 Heilbronn to Solf, 7 November 1922, BA Koblenz, Solf Papers, Nr 111.

10 Müller to Valentini, 10 November 1922, GStA Berlin, Valentini Papers, Nr 15. See also Ilsemann, diary for 16 September and 19 October 1922, Koenigswald, *Kaiser in Holland*, I, pp. 241 and 246.

11 Tirpitz, *Erinnerungen*. Wilhelm II's letters to Tsar Nicholas II were published in 1920 in the USA, the UK, France and Germany. See the appalled reaction of Professor Johannes Haller (Tübingen) to Eulenburg, 30 August 1919 and 11 January 1920, printed in *Eulenburgs Korrespondenz*, III, Nos. 1585 and 1593.

12 Emil Ludwig, *Wilhelm der Zweite*, Berlin 1925. Dommes to Fürstenberg, 3 and 27 October 1925, FFA Donaueschingen.

13 Kaiser Wilhelm II to Viereck, 24 February, 12 and 25 March and 13 September 1928, 7 January 1929, Houghton Library Harvard, Nos. 69, 72, 79 and 83; Kaiser Wilhelm II to Bigelow, 9 March 1927 and 10 March 1929, New York Public Library, Bigelow Papers, IV.

14 Wilhelm II, *Aus meinem Leben 1859–1888*, Berlin and Leipzig 1927.

15 Wilhelm II, 'Zur Geschichte der Doorner Arbeitsgemeinschaft', 18 January 1927, as cited in Gutsche, *Ein Kaiser im Exil*, p. 73; Wilhelm II, *Erinnerungen an Korfu*, Berlin and Leipzig 1924; Wilhelm II, *Studien zur Gorgo*, Berlin 1936. For the 'Doorner Arbeitsgemeinschaft' see Christoph Johannes Franzen, 'Eine Symbiose zwischen Wissenschaft und Politik. Leo Frobenius und Wilhelm II.', in Karl-Heinz Kohl and Editha Platte, eds., *Gestalter und Gestalten. 100 Jahre Ethnologie in Frankfurt am Main*, Frankfurt a.M. 2006, pp. 21–45. See especially Christoph Johannes Franzen, Karl-Heinz Kohl and Marie-Luise Recker, eds., *Der Kaiser und sein Forscher. Der Briefwechsel zwischen Wilhelm II. und Leo Frobenius (1924–1938)*, Stuttgart 2012.

16 The extensive correspondence between Wilhelm II and George Sylvester Viereck is to be found in the Houghton Library Harvard. The Kaiser's letters to his American friend Poultney Bigelow are in the New York Public Library. Barnes visited the Kaiser in Doorn in 1927.

17 Kaiser Wilhelm II to Viereck, 9 March 1927, Houghton Library Harvard, Viereck Papers, No. 53.

18 Kaiser Wilhelm II to Viereck, 6 November 1928, ibid. No. 82; Kaiser Wilhelm II to Prince Louis Ferdinand of Prussia, 3 March 1929, New York Public Library, Bigelow Papers.

19 Kaiser Wilhelm II to Bigelow, 24 October 1930, ibid., III.

20 George Sylvester Viereck, *The Kaiser on Trial*, New York 1937; Kaiserin Hermine to Margarethe Landgravine of Hesse, 28 December 1937, AdHH Schloss Fasanerie.

21 Kaiser Wilhelm II to Fürstenberg, 3 July 1927, FFA Donaueschingen; Kaiser Wilhelm II to Nowak, 3 May 1928, GStA Berlin, BPHA Rep. 53 Nr 237. See also Cecil, *Wilhelm II: Emperor and Exile*, pp. 308f.

22 See above, pp. 15f. Kaiser Wilhelm's correspondence with General Waters on the English edition of his mother's letters is to be found in RA GV/O 2578/3–6. For Nowak – who suffered a 'nervous collapse' as a result – and his involvement see Kaiser Wilhelm II to Margarethe Landgravine of Hesse, 16 March 1929, AdHH Schloss Fasanerie. See also Sir Horace Rumbold to King George V, 18 October 1929, RA GV/P 586/130.

23 Nowak, memoranda on his visits to Doorn, 1927–30, BA Berlin, Nowak Papers, Nr 48; Nowak to Dommes, 23 April 1931, Dommes to Nowak, 30 April 1931, BA Berlin, Nowak Papers, Nr 49; Kaiser Wilhelm II to Fürstenberg, 15 May 1931, FFA Donaueschingen.

24 Kaiser Wilhelm II to Nowak, 22 June, 9 and 16 July 1931; Nowak to Kaiser Wilhelm II, 1, 2, 14, 20 and 29 July 1931, GStA Berlin, Nowak Papers, Nr 20.

25 I am grateful to Dr Johannes Seidl, archivist of the University of Vienna, for researching Karl Friedrich Nowak's family background.

26 Kaiser Wilhelm II to Fürstenberg, 15 May 1931, FFA Donaueschingen. Both volumes of Hohenlohe's memoirs were translated into English.

27 See Kaiser Wilhelm II, marginal notes and comments of July 1929 on the third volume of Bismarck's *Gedanken und Erinnerungen*, GStA Berlin, BPHA Rep. 53 Nr 170.

28 Both Lydia Franke and Erich Eyck were forced to emigrate in 1933. See Lydia Franke, *Die Randbemerkungen Wilhelms II. in den Akten der auswärtigen Politik als historische und psychologische Quelle*, Berlin 1933; Erich Eyck, *Die Monarchie Wilhelms II. nach seinen Briefen, seinen Randbemerkungen und Zeugnissen seiner Freunde*, Berlin 1924; Eyck, *Das Persönliche Regiment Wilhelms II.*

29 See Ernst Graf von Reventlow, *Glanz und Tragödie Wilhelms II.*, Stuttgart 1938; Ernst Graf von Reventlow, *Von Potsdam nach Doorn*, Berlin 1940.

30 Jacques Daniel Chamier, *Fabulous Monster*, London 1934. (Translated into German as *Ein Fabeltier unserer Zeit. Glanz und Tragödie Wilhelms II.*, Vienna 1937; reprinted as J. Daniel Chamier, *Als Deutschland mächtig schien. Die Ära Wilhelms II.*, Berlin 1954. Printed again as *Wilhelm II. Der Deutsche Kaiser. Eine Biographie von Daniel Chamier. Mit einem Geleitwort Seiner Kaiserlichen Hoheit Louis Ferdinand Prinz von Preussen*, Munich and Berlin 1989.)

31 Kaiser Wilhelm II, marginal comments on Chamier's *Fabeltier*, November 1934, GStA Berlin, Rep. 92 Beseler Papers, Nr 20.

32 Haehner, diary for 17 April 1923, Stadtarchiv Cologne.

33 Haehner, diary for 23 June 1921, ibid.

34 Haehner, diary for 24 August 1923, ibid.

35 Haehner, diary for 7 June 1921, ibid.

36 Haehner, diary for 14 June 1921, ibid.

37 Haehner, diary for 11 August 1921, ibid.

38 Ilsemann, diary for 12 May 1928, Koenigswald, *Kaiser in Holland*, II, p. 96.

39 Kaiser Wilhelm II to Willy Pastor, 1919, as cited in Willibald Gutsche, *Ein Kaiser im Exil. Der letzte deutsche Kaiser Wilhelm II. in Holland. Eine kritische Biographie*, Marburg 1991, p. 24. See also Haehner, diary for 5–6 December 1919, Stadtarchiv Cologne; Ilsemann, diary for 6 November 1919, Koenigswald, *Kaiser in Holland*, I, p. 121.

40 Krauel, diary for 24 October 1919, *Mitteilungen der List-Gesellschaft*, Fasc. 6, No. 13, October 1968, pp. 311–21.

41 Friedrich Karl Landgrave of Hesse, notebook for early February 1920, cited in Rainer von Hessen, *Wolfgang Prinz von Hessen: Aufzeichnungen*, p. 125; Machtan, *Kaisersohn*, p. 103. See also Ilsemann, diary for 7 February 1920, Koenigswald, *Kaiser in Holland*, I, pp. 144f.

42 Kaiser Wilhelm II to Mackensen, 12 August 1920, BA-MA Freiburg-im-Breisgau, Mackensen Papers, N 39/39.

43 Haehner, diary for 6 March 1921, Stadtarchiv Cologne.

44 Haehner, diary for 17 April 1923, ibid.

45 Haehner, diary for 10 January 1920, ibid.

46 Haehner, diary for 8 November 1919, ibid.

47 Haehner, diary for 26 January 1920, ibid.

48 Haehner, diary for 13 November 1919, ibid.; Krauel, diary for 24 October 1919, *Mitteilungen der List-Gesellschaft*, Fasc. 6, No. 13, October 1968, pp. 311–21.

49 Haehner, diary for 10 May 1921, Stadtarchiv Cologne.

50 Kaiser Wilhelm II to Fürstenberg, 4 May 1919, FFA Donaueschingen; Prince Heinrich of Prussia to Kaiser Wilhelm II, 5 April 1927, GStA Berlin, BPHA Rep. 52 V1 Nr 13; Kaiser Wilhelm II to Margarethe Landgravine of Hesse, 18 November 1929, AdHH Schloss Fasanerie.

51 Haehner, diary for 15 December 1919, Stadtarchiv Cologne.

52 Haehner, diary for 12 December 1920, ibid.

53 Haehner, diary for 30 August 1921, ibid.

54 Haehner, diary for 27 August 1921, ibid.

55 Haehner, diary for 30 August and 3–4 September 1921, ibid.

56 Kessler, diary for 3 April 1923, Pfeiffer-Belli, *Harry Graf Kessler, Tagebücher 1918–1937*, p. 383. 'His fate was merited', commented the Kaiser on 12 July 1930 in a letter to General Waters, RA GV/O 2578/19.

57 Kaiser Wilhelm II, marginal note on a submission of the Rathenaubund of 19 November 1928, cited in Gutsche, *Kaiser im Exil*, p. 78.

58 Haehner, diary for 30 November and 24 December 1920, Stadtarchiv Cologne.

59 Kaiser Wilhelm II, 'Notizen', no date; Kaiser Wilhelm II to Kan, 12 February 1920, Archiv des vormals regierenden preußischen Königshauses, Burg Hohenzollern, Hechingen.

60 Kaiser Wilhelm II to Bigelow, 2 March 1928, copy in ibid.

61 Haehner, diary for 2 November 1922, Stadtarchiv Cologne.

62 Ilsemann, diary for 15 March 1920, Koenigswald, *Kaiser in Holland*, I, p. 149.

63 Haehner, diary for 13 March 1920, Stadtarchiv Cologne.

64 Ilsemann, diary for 22 March 1920, Koenigswald, *Kaiser in Holland*, I, p. 149.

65 Haehner, diary for 8 and 11 November 1923, Stadtarchiv Cologne.

66 Ilsemann, diary for 12 November 1923, Koenigswald, *Kaiser in Holland*, I, pp. 300ff.

67 Kaiser Wilhelm II to Mackensen, 19 December 1923, BA-MA Freiburg-im-Breisgau, Mackensen Papers, N 39/39.

68 Haehner, diary for 19 April 1921, Stadtarchiv Cologne.

69 Kaiser Wilhelm II, sermon, spring 1925, cited in Gutsche, *Kaiser im Exil*, pp. 66f.

70 Kaiser Wilhelm II to Tirpitz, 1 January 1925, BA-MA Freiburg-im-Breisgau, Tirpitz Papers, N 253/452.

71 Kaiser Wilhelm II, marginal note on a letter from Fritz von Unruh of 8 September 1928; Kaiser Wilhelm II to Unruh, 13 September 1928, as cited in Gutsche, *Kaiser im Exil*, p. 116.

72 Kaiser Wilhelm II, to Grumme-Douglas, 8 August 1931, Archiv des vormals regierenden preußischen Königshauses, Burg Hohenzollern, Hechingen.

73 Haehner, diary for 10 May 1921, Stadtarchiv Cologne.

74 Haehner, diary for 23 March 1921, ibid.

75 Haehner, diary for 12 December 1920, ibid.

76 Haehner, diary for 26 September 1922, ibid.

77 Ilsemann, diary for 27 April 1926, Koenigswald, *Kaiser in Holland*, II, p. 36.

78 Haehner, diary for 21 September 1922, Stadtarchiv Cologne.

79 Ilsemann, diary for 2 February 1927, Koenigswald, *Kaiser in Holland*, II, p. 49.

80 Ilsemann, diary for 21 January 1927, ibid., p. 46.

81 Krauel, diary for 24 October 1919, *Mitteilungen der List-Gesellschaft*, Fasc 6, No. 13, October 1968, pp. 311–21.

82 Kaiser Wilhelm II, sermon of 6 June 1926, cited in Gutsche, *Kaiser im Exil*, p. 76.

83 Ilsemann, diary for 9 June 1919, Koenigswald, *Kaiser in Holland*, I, p. 106.

84 Kaiser Wilhelm II to Ludendorff, 1919, photocopy in the author's private archive.

85 Kaiser Wilhelm II, marginal comment on Ludendorff's letter of 9 August 1927, BA-MA Freiburg-im-Breisgau, Mackensen Papers, N 39/39.

86 Kaiser Wilhelm II to Mackensen, 12 August 1920, ibid.

87 Mackensen, memorandum of 21 August 1920, John C. G. Röhl, *Kaiser, Hof und Staat. Wilhelm II. und die deutsche Politik*, Munich 1987, p. 218.

88 Krauel, diary for 24 October 1919, *Mitteilungen der List-Gesellschaft*, Fasc. 6, No. 13, October 1968, pp. 311–21.

89 Haehner, diary for 6 and 7 May 1921, Stadtarchiv Cologne.

90 Kaiser Wilhelm II to Plessen, 31 July 1921, BA-MA Freiburg-im-Breisgau, Plessen Papers, MSg 1/3117.

91 Haehner, diary for 4 May 1923, Stadtarchiv Cologne.

92 Krauel, diary for 24 October 1919, *Mitteilungen der List-Gesellschaft*, Fasc. 6, No. 13, October 1968, pp. 311–21.

93 Ilsemann, diary for 12 November 1923, Koenigswald, *Kaiser in Holland*, I, p. 303.

94 Ilsemann, diary for 9 February 1927, ibid., II, p. 48.

95 Haehner, diary for 10 July 1921, Stadtarchiv Cologne.

96 Kaiser Wilhelm II to Fürstenberg, 27 January 1920, FFA Donaueschingen.

97 Kaiser Wilhelm II to Curt von Morgen, 6 February 1920, BA-MA Freiburg-im-Breisgau, Morgen Papers, N 227/39.

98 Kaiser Wilhelm II to Max Buchner, 6 February 1920, BA Koblenz, Buchner Papers, N 88/121. A similar view was expressed in the Kaiser's letter to Dörpfeld of 14 February 1920, BA Koblenz, Kl. Erw. Nr 578/1.

99 Haehner, diary for 13 February 1920, Stadtarchiv Cologne.

100 Haehner, diary for 28 February 1920, ibid.

101 Haehner, diary for 3–9 October 1923, ibid.

102 Ilsemann, diary for 7 October 1923, Koenigswald, *Kaiser in Holland*, I, p. 287.

103 Kaiser Wilhelm II to Dörpfeld, December 1923, GStA Berlin, BPHA Rep. 53 Nr 118.

104 Frobenius to Wilhelm von Dommes, 20 June 1925, in Franzen et al., *Der Kaiser und sein Forscher*, No. 12.

105 See in particular Kaiser Wilhelm II, draft for an 'interview', December 1926, ibid., No. 22a.

106 Kaiser Wilhelm II, manuscript 'Was soll Locarno?', 22 November 1925, FFA Donaueschingen. See also Kaiser Wilhelm II to Reischach, 25 November 1925, BA-MA Freiburg-im-Breisgau, Mackensen Papers, N 39/256; Kaiser Wilhelm II to Viereck, 12 October and 21 November 1926, Houghton Library Harvard, Viereck Papers, Nos. 43 and 47.

107 Kaiser Wilhelm II, manuscript of 28 April 1931, as cited in Gutsche, *Kaiser im Exil*, p. 72.

108 Krauel, diary for 24 October 1919, *Mitteilungen der List-Gesellschaft*, Fasc. 6, No. 13, October 1968, pp. 311–21.

109 See Armin Phal-Traughber, *Der antisemitisch-antifreimaurerische Verschwörungsmythos in der Weimarer Republik und im NS-Staat*, Vienna 1993.

110 Haehner, diary for 12 February 1920, Stadtarchiv Cologne.

111 Haehner, diary for 10 January 1920, ibid.

112 Wolfgang Krauel, 'Ein Besuch beim deutschen Kaiserpaar in Amerongen am 24. Oktober 1919', in *Mitteilungen der Friedrich List-Gesellschaft*, Fasc. 6, No. 13, 1968, pp. 311–21.

113 Haehner, diary for 16 February 1920, Stadtarchiv Cologne.

114 Kaiser Wilhelm II to Cramon, 4 January 1927, BA-MA Freiburg-im-Breisgau, Cramon Papers, N 266/34. See Kaiser Wilhelm II, marginal notes on a letter from Plessen of 6 January 1927, ibid., Dommes Papers, N 512/18. See also Cramon to Kaiser Wilhelm II, 10 February 1927, BA-MA Freiburg-im-Breisgau, Cramon Papers, N 266/33. But cf. the book published in 1929 by Max Buchner, the leader of the Catholic group within the DNVP, entitled *Kaiser Wilhelm II., seine Weltanschauung und seine Stellung zu den deutschen Katholiken*, Leipzig, 1929. Kaiser Wilhelm's comments of 11 February 1929 on the book and the letter of thanks written to Buchner by Kaiserin Hermine on 11 December 1928 are to be found in BA Koblenz, Buchner Papers, N 88/121 and 112. Wilhelm's letter to Buchner is reproduced as facsimile in Hans Rall, 'Zur persönlichen Religiosität Kaiser Wilhelms II', *Zeitschrift für Kirchengeschichte*, 1984/2, 382–94.

115 Kaiser Wilhelm II to Edmund Stinnes, 30 August 1931, BA Koblenz, Kl. Erw. 625/1; Kaiser Wilhelm II to von der Heydt, Stadtarchiv Wuppertal, von der Heydt Papers.

116 Haehner, diary for 4 June 1921, Stadtarchiv Cologne. See also the entry for 1 March 1923, ibid.

117 Kaiser Wilhelm II to Fürstenberg, 31 January 1923, FFA Donaueschingen.

118 Haehner, diary for 24 October 1924, Stadtarchiv Cologne.

119 Kaiser Wilhelm II to Bigelow, 4 September 1928, New York Public Library, Bigelow Papers, IV.

120 Kaiser Wilhelm II to Mackensen, 2 December 1919, cited in Röhl, *Kaiser and his Court*, p. 210.

121 Gottfried zur Beek [in reality Ludwig Müller von Hausen] ed., *Die Geheimnisse der Weisen von Zion. Auf Vorposten*, Charlottenburg 1919. On the genesis of this poisonous diatribe see Norman Cohn, *Warrant for Genocide. The Myth of the Jewish World Conspiracy and the Protocols of the Elders of Zion*, London 1967.

122 Artur Dinter, *Die Sünde wider das Blut. Ein Zeitroman*, Leipzig 1917.

123 Friedrich Wichtl, *Weltfreimauerei, Weltrevolution, Weltrepublik. Eine Untersuchung über Ursprung und Endziele des Weltkrieges*, Munich 1921.

124 Friedrich Andersen, *Der Deutsche Heiland*, Munich 1921.

125 Houston Stewart Chamberlain, *Mensch und Gott. Betrachtungen über Religion und Christentum*, Munich 1921.

126 Haehner, diary for 11 November 1919, Stadtarchiv Cologne.

127 Haehner, diary for 3 December 1919, ibid., cited in part in Machtan, *Kaisersohn*, p. 144. For the influence of Artur Dinter's hugely popular novel *Die Sünde wider das Blut* (1917) see Manfred Bosch, '"Rasse und Religion sind eins!" Artur Dinters "Die Sünde wider das Blut" oder: Autopsie eines furchtbaren Bestsellers', *Die Ortenau*, 1991, pp. 596–621; George M. Kren and Rodler F. Morris, 'Race and Spirituality. Artur Dinter's Theosophical Antisemitism', *Holocaust and Genocide Studies* 6, No. 3, 1993, 233–52.

128 Haehner, diary for 2 December 1920, Stadtarchiv Cologne.

129 Haehner, diary for 8 March 1921, ibid., cited in part in Machtan, *Kaisersohn*, p. 144. The Kaiser was already expressing such views in autumn 1919. Krauel, diary for 24 October 1919, *Mitteilungen der List-Gesellschaft*, Fasc. 6, No. 13, October 1968, pp. 311–21.

130 Haehner, diary for 10 January 1924, ibid., cited in Machtan, *Kaisersohn*, p. 144.

131 Friedrich Schmitt-Ott, *Erlebtes und Erstrebtes, 1860–1950*, Wiesbaden 1952, p. 195.

132 Haehner, diary for 15 August 1921, Stadtarchiv Cologne.

133 Haehner, diary for 10 March 1923, ibid.

134 Kaiser Wilhelm II to Ludendorff, 26 August 1927, BA-MA Freiburg-im-Breisgau, Mackensen Papers, N 39/39.

135 Chamberlain, *Mensch und Gott*.

136 Friedrich Andersen, *Der Deutsche Heiland*, Munich 1921; Haehner, diary for 7 October 1922, Stadtarchiv Cologne.

137 Ibid.

138 Haehner, diary for 3 September 1921, ibid., cited in part in Machtan, *Kaisersohn*, p. 144; Kaiser Wilhelm II to Chamberlain, 21 September 1921 and 1 March 1922, Chamberlain, *Briefe*, II, pp. 260 and 262f.

139 Kaiser Wilhelm II to Chamberlain, 12 March 1923, ibid., II, pp. 265–73.

140 Kaiser Wilhelm II to court preacher Vogel, 10 March 1923, BA-MA Freiburg-im-Breisgau, Mackensen Papers, N 39/39.

141 Kaiser Wilhelm II to Chamberlain, 3 June 1923, Chamberlain, *Briefe*, II, pp. 273ff. See also Kaiser Wilhelm II to Frobenius, 20–3 May 1929 and 25 June 1929, in Franzen et al., *Der Kaiser und sein Forscher*, Nos. 66 and 67.

142 Haehner, diary for 30 October 1924, Stadtarchiv Cologne.

143 Kaiser Wilhelm II to Eva Chamberlain-Wagner, 14 April 1927, Richard-Wagner-Gedenkstätte, Bayreuth, Eva Chamberlain Papers. See Gutsche, *Kaiser im Exil*, p. 77.

144 Hans Blüher, *Die Aristie des Jesus von Nazareth*, 1921.

145 Kaiser Wilhelm II to Blüher, 29 August 1929, GStA Berlin, BPHA Rep. 53 Nr 352.

146 Kaiser Wilhelm II, manuscript 'Vatikan und Völkerbund', June 1926, FFA Donaueschingen; cited in part in Gutsche, *Kaiser im Exil*, p. 78.

147 Kaiser Wilhelm II to Viereck, 18 February 1926, Houghton Library Harvard, Viereck Papers, No. 36.

148 Kaiser Wilhelm II to Viereck, 21 April 1926, ibid. No. 41.

149 Kaiser Wilhelm II, manuscript 'The Jew Today', Archiv des vormals regierenden preußischen Königshauses, Burg Hohenzollern, Hechingen.

150 Kaiser Wilhelm II to Bigelow, 14 April 1927, New York Public Library, Bigelow Papers, IV, cited in Röhl, *Kaiser and his Court*, p. 210.

151 Kaiser Wilhelm II to Bigelow, 1 August 1928, New York Public Library, Bigelow Papers, IV.

152 Kaiser Wilhelm II to Bigelow, 18 October 1927, ibid., cited in Röhl, *Kaiser and his Court*, p. 210.

153 Kaiser Wilhelm II to Bigelow, 28 June 1929, New York Public Library, Bigelow Papers, IV.

154 Kaiser Wilhelm II to Bigelow, 15 August 1927, cited in Röhl, *Kaiser and his Court*, p. 210.

155 See the photograph of Princess Irène of Prussia and her sister Tsarina Alexandra with their families, taken at Wolfsgarten on 1 November 1910, in Michael, Prince of Greece, *Nicholas and Alexandra: The Family Albums*, London 1992, pp. 96f. Here Irène is seen wearing a pendant in the shape of a swastika.

156 Prince Heinrich of Prussia to Sontag, 8 December 1920, BA Koblenz, Sontag Papers, Nr 16. I am grateful to Dr Björn Hofmeister for drawing my attention to this document.

157 Haehner, diary for November 1920, Stadtarchiv Cologne.

158 See for example Brigitte Hamann, *Hitlers Wien. Lehrjahre eines Diktators*, Munich 1996; Wolfgang Meyer zu Uptrup, *Kampf gegen die 'jüdische Weltverschwörung'*, Berlin 2003.

47 MONARCH BY THE GRACE OF HITLER? WILHELM II AND THE THIRD REICH

1 Haehner, diary for April 1922, Stadtarchiv Cologne.
2 Haehner, later addenda, June 1920, diary Nr 8, pp. 138–40, ibid.
3 See Groener, *Lebenserinnerungen*, p. 451; Machtan, *Kaisersohn*, p. 83.
4 Ibid., pp. 83ff. See Haehner, later addenda, September 1920, diary Nr 8, p. 149, Stadtarchiv Cologne.
5 Haehner, diary for 25 October 1923, ibid.
6 See above, p. 1199.
7 Kaiser Wilhelm to Crown Prince Wilhelm, 10 February 1920, GStA Berlin, BPHA Rep. 54 E 1 Auswärtiges.
8 Haehner, diary for 16 February 1920, Stadtarchiv Cologne.
9 Crown Prince Wilhelm to Kaiser Wilhelm II, 31 May 1922 with the Kaiser's marginal notes of 3 June 1922, Archiv des vormals regierenden preußischen Königshauses, Burg Hohenzollern, Hechingen.
10 Viscount D'Abernon, diary for 2 August 1924, cited in Machtan, *Kaisersohn*, p. 154; Ilsemann, diary for 22 August 1924, Koenigswald, *Kaiser in Holland*, II, pp. 13f.
11 Kaiserin Hermine to Margarethe Landgravine of Hesse, 19 and 25 November 1923, AdHH Schloss Fasanerie.
12 Haehner, diary for 21 October 1923, Stadtarchiv Cologne.
13 Haehner, diary for 10 November 1923, ibid.
14 Kaiserin Hermine to Margarethe Landgravine of Hesse, 25 November and 26 December 1923, AdHH Schloss Fasanerie.
15 Berg to Kaiser Wilhelm II, 29 March, 20 May and 1 June 1926, Archiv des vormals regierenden preußischen Königshauses, Burg Hohenzollern, Hechingen.
16 Nationalverband Deutscher Offiziere to Mackensen, 18 January 1927, Cramon to Mackensen, 23 January 1927, Mackensen to Kaiser Wilhelm II, 8 February 1927, BA-MA Freiburg-im-Breisgau, Mackensen Papers, N 39/261; Kaiser Wilhelm II to Margarethe Landgravine of Hesse, 12 February 1927, AdHH Schloss Fasanerie; Kaiserin Hermine to Mackensen, 8 March 1927, BA-MA Freiburg-im-Breisgau, Mackensen Papers, N 39/41. See August von Mackensen, 'Kaiser Wilhelm II. und die alte Wehrmacht', *Der Aufrechte. Ein Kämpfer für christlich-deutsche Erneuerung*, 5 March 1927.
17 Kaiser Wilhelm II, 'Anweisung an die Deutschen als Richtlinien für ihr Denken und Wirken', 10 July 1927, BA Koblenz, Kl. Erw. Nr 578/2, copy in BA-MA Freiburg-im-Breisgau, Mackensen Papers, N 39/256. See also Kaiser Wilhelm II, 'Richtlinien für Monarchisten', 14 January 1928, Archiv des vormals regierenden preußischen Königshauses, Burg Hohenzollern, Hechingen; BA-MA Freiburg-im-Breisgau, Dommes Papers, N 512/18; Mackensen Papers, N 39/262.
18 Kaiser Wilhelm II, undated directives of 1927, in Friedrich Wilhelm, Prinz von Preußen, *Haus Hohenzollern*, pp. 83f. Cf. Gutsche, *Kaiser im Exil*, pp. 104f. See also Kaiser Wilhelm II, 'Anweisung für die vaterländische Arbeit'; 'Ziel der vaterländischen Arbeit', July 1928, Archiv des vormals regierenden preußischen Königshauses, Burg Hohenzollern, Hechingen, copy in BA-MA Freiburg-im-Breisgau, Mackensen Papers, N 39/256.
19 Gerhard Granier, *Magnus von Levetzow. Seeoffizier, Monarchist und Wegbereiter Hitlers. Lebensweg und ausgewählte Dokumente*, Boppard am Rhein 1982, pp. 252ff.
20 Kaiser Wilhelm II to Bigelow, 31 January 1929, New York Public Library, Bigelow Papers, IV.
21 Gutsche, *Kaiser im Exil*, p. 113.
22 Machtan, *Kaisersohn*, pp. 132 and 136.

23 Ibid., p. 157.
24 Valentini to Bethmann Hollweg, 24 November 1920, GStA Berlin, Valentini Papers, Nr 2/112–4. For the relationship between the Hohenzollerns and National Socialism see also Stephan Malinowski, *Vom König zum Führer. Sozialer Niedergang und politische Radikalisierung im deutschen Adel zwischen Kaiserreich und NS-Staat*, Berlin 2003, pp. 505ff.
25 Prince Heinrich of Prussia to Kaiser Wilhelm II, 12 March 1924, GStA Berlin, BPHA Rep. 52 V1 Nr 13.
26 Kaiser Wilhelm II to Grumme-Douglas, 20 June 1929, Archiv des vormals regierenden preußischen Königshauses, Burg Hohenzollern, Hechingen.
27 Machtan, *Kaisersohn*, pp. 159f. See Friedrich Christian, Prinz zu Schaumburg-Lippe, *Zwischen Krone und Kerker*, Wiesbaden 1952; Anon., [Friedrich Wilhelm Prinz zur Lippe] *Politische Beichte eines Deutschen Prinzen*, Leipzig 1925.
28 Machtan, *Kaisersohn*, pp. 164ff.
29 Ibid., pp. 171 and 173.
30 Ilsemann, diary for 10 May 1930, Koenigswald, *Kaiser in Holland*, II, p. 142; Machtan, *Kaisersohn*, pp. 180 and 184.
31 Ibid., pp. 167f. Cf. Gutsche, *Kaiser im Exil*, p. 108.
32 Ilsemann, diary for 1 February 1930, Koenigswald, *Kaiser in Holland*, II, p. 133.
33 Granier, *Levetzow*, pp. 154 and 291.
34 Ilsemann, diary for 17–20 January 1931, Koenigswald, *Kaiser in Holland*, II, pp. 153–6.
35 Granier, *Levetzow*, pp. 167 and 300ff.; Gutsche, *Kaiser im Exil*, p. 131; Machtan, *Kaisersohn*, pp. 223–7.
36 Ilsemann, diary for 23 March 1931, Koenigswald, *Kaiser in Holland*, II, p. 165.
37 Hanfstaengl, cited in Machtan, *Kaisersohn*, p. 225.
38 Ilsemann, diary for 25 December 1931, Koenigswald, *Kaiser in Holland*, II, pp. 175f.
39 Levetzow, memorandum of 30 November 1931, Granier, *Levetzow*, pp. 167 and 312ff.
40 Ilsemann, diary for 13 February 1932, Koenigswald, *Kaiser in Holland*, II, pp. 183f.
41 Otto Dietrich, *12 Jahre bei Hitler*, Munich 1955, p. 245; Machtan, *Kaisersohn*, p. 233.
42 Ilsemann, diary for 20–1 May 1932, Koenigswald, *Kaiser in Holland*, II, pp. 192–5.
43 Kaiserin Hermine to Margarethe Landgravine of Hesse, 20 April 1932, AdHH Schloss Fasanerie; Machtan, *Kaisersohn*, p. 230 with note 171, also pp. 240ff.
44 Ilsemann, diary for 12 January 1932, cited in Granier, *Levetzow*, p. 173 and Machtan, *Kaisersohn*, p. 230. See the detailed account in Pyta, *Hindenburg*, pp. 674ff.
45 Ilsemann, diary for 20 July 1932, Koenigswald, *Kaiser in Holland*, II, pp. 199f.
46 Klaus W. Jonas, *Der Kronprinz Wilhelm*, Frankfurt a.M. 1962, p. 230; Gutsche, *Kaiser im Exil*, p. 140.
47 Crown Prince Wilhelm, cited in Machtan, *Kaisersohn*, p. 244.
48 Crown Prince Wilhelm to Hitler, 25 September 1932, Hitler to Crown Prince Wilhelm, 28 September 1932, printed in Friedrich Wilhelm, Prinz von Preußen, *Haus Hohenzollern*, pp. 103ff. See also Machtan, *Kaisersohn*, pp. 243ff.
49 Ibid., pp. 229, 246 and 259.
50 Kaiser Wilhelm II to Prince August Wilhelm of Prussia, 11 February 1932, cited ibid., p. 257.
51 For these negotiations see the authoritative account in Pyta, *Hindenburg*, pp. 714ff.
52 Kaiser Wilhelm II to Crown Prince Wilhelm, 17 September 1932, GStA Berlin, BPHA Rep. 53 Nr 176, printed in Willibald Gutsche and Joachim Petzold, 'Das Verhältnis der Hohenzollern zum Faschismus', *Zeitschrift für Geschichtswissenschaft* 34/7, 1986, No. 2.
53 Ilsemann, diary for 3 October 1932, Koenigswald, *Kaiser in Holland*, II, p. 204.
54 Crown Prince Wilhelm to Kaiser Wilhelm II, 1 October 1932, Crown Prince Wilhelm to Hitler, 25 September 1932, Hitler to Crown Prince Wilhelm, 28 September 1932, GStA

Berlin, BPHA Rep. 54 Nr 37, printed in Friedrich Wilhelm Prinz von Preußen, *Haus Hohenzollern*, pp. 102–8.

55 Ilsemann, diary for 4 October 1932, Koenigswald, *Kaiser in Holland*, II, pp. 205f.

56 Kaiser Wilhelm II to Margarethe Landgravine of Hesse, 10 November and 31 December 1932, AdHH Schloss Fasanerie.

57 Machtan, *Kaisersohn*, pp. 271–9.

58 Kaiser Wilhelm II to Margarethe Landgravine of Hesse, 24 January 1933, AdHH Schloss Fasanerie.

59 Kaiser Wilhelm II, marginal note on Dommes's report of 25 January 1933, cited in Gutsche, *Kaiser im Exil*, p. 159.

60 Ilsemann, diary for 1 February 1933, Koenigswald, *Kaiser in Holland*, II, pp. 212f.

61 Kaiserin Hermine to Buchner, 6 February 1933, BA Koblenz, Buchner Papers, Nr 114.

62 For the so-called 'Tag von Potsdam' see Pyta, *Hindenburg*, pp. 820ff.

63 Ilsemann, diary for 21 March 1933, Koenigswald, *Kaiser in Holland*, II, p. 215.

64 Ilsemann, diary for 3 April 1933, ibid., p. 217.

65 Ilsemann, diary for 25 March 1933, ibid., p. 216.

66 Dommes, memorandum of 15 May 1933 on Hitler's attitude to the monarchy, printed in Gutsche and Petzold, 'Verhältnis der Hohenzollern zum Faschismus', Nr 5.

67 Ilsemann, diary for 2 June 1933, Koenigswald, *Kaiser in Holland*, II, pp. 222f.

68 Cramon to Hindenburg, October 1933, BA-MA Freiburg-im-Breisgau, Cramon Papers, N 266/46; Hindenburg to Cramon, 23 October 1933, ibid., N 266/25. See Pyta, *Hindenburg*, pp. 841f.

69 Kaiser Wilhelm II to Mackensen, 5 December 1933, BA-MA Freiburg-im-Breisgau, Mackensen Papers, N 39/39.

70 See Pyta, *Hindenburg*, pp. 840f.

71 Dommes, memorandum of 26 September 1933, GStA Berlin, BPHA Rep. 53 Nr 167/1.

72 Dommes, memorandum on his reception by Hitler on 24 October 1933, ibid. Nr 167/3, printed in Gutsche and Petzold, 'Verhältnis der Hohenzollern zum Faschismus', Nr 7.

73 For Göring's decree see Malinowski, *Vom König zum Führer*, pp. 508ff. and 550f. See also Pyta, *Hindenburg*, pp. 842f.

74 Ilsemann, diary for 1 February 1934, Koenigswald, *Kaiser in Holland*, II, pp. 250f. See Dommes to Hitler, 2 February 1934, GStA Berlin, BPHA Rep. 53 Nr 167/4.

75 Kaiser Wilhelm II to Margarethe Landgravine of Hesse, 2 April 1934, AdHH Schloss Fasanerie.

76 Kaiser Wilhelm II, telegram of 22 November 1933, cited in Friedrich Wilhelm Prinz von Preußen, *Haus Hohenzollern*, p. 139. Also Gutsche, *Kaiser im Exil*, pp. 177f. and 254; Machtan, *Kaisersohn*, p. 324.

77 Dommes, memorandum on his meeting with Hitler on 27 April 1934, GStA Berlin, BPHA Rep. 53 Nr 167/6, printed in Friedrich Wilhelm, Prinz von Preußen, *Haus Hohenzollern*, pp. 136–9.

78 Kaiser Wilhelm II to Bigelow, 15 May 1933, New York Public Library, Bigelow Papers, III.

79 Kaiser Wilhelm II to Hamilton, 20 March 1933, cited in Gutsche, *Kaiser im Exil*, p. 161.

80 Kaiserin Hermine to Cramon, 19 May 1933, BA-MA Freiburg-im-Breisgau, Cramon Papers, N 266/21.

81 Kaiser Wilhelm II to Margarethe Landgravine of Hesse, 7 July 1933, AdHH Schloss Fasanerie.

82 Kaiser Wilhelm II to Margarethe Landgravine of Hesse, 13 October 1933, ibid.

83 See the Kaiser's reaction in Ilsemann, diary for 2 July 1934, Koenigswald, *Kaiser in Holland*, II, pp. 264ff.

84 Machtan, *Kaisersohn*, pp. 342–4.

85 Ilsemann, diary for 17 May 1935, Koenigswald, *Kaiser in Holland*, II, p. 280.

86 Kaiser Wilhelm II to Margarethe Landgravine of Hesse, 12 August 1934, AdHH Schloss Fasanerie.

87 Kaiserin Hermine to Beckmann, 30 May 1934, extract cited in the J. A. Stargardt catalogue No. 685 (2006), p. 424.

88 Kaiserin Hermine to Margarethe Landgravine of Hesse, 11 March 1935, AdHH Schloss Fasanerie.

89 Kaiserin Hermine to Mackensen, 3 December 1935, BA-MA Freiburg-im-Breisgau, Mackensen Papers, N 39/41.

90 Kaiserin Hermine to Lindenberg, 28 December 1935, GStA Berlin, BPHA Rep. 53 Nr 187.

91 Kaiser Wilhelm II to Waters, 11 March 1936, RA Geo V O 2578/69.

92 Kaiser Wilhelm II to Waters, 15 March 1936, RA Geo V O 2578/70.

93 Kaiserin Hermine to Margarethe Landgravine of Hesse, 1 January 1937, AdHH Schloss Fasanerie.

94 Kaiser Wilhelm II to Bigelow, 8 August 1936, New York Public Library, Bigelow Papers, II.

95 Kaiser Wilhelm II to Margarethe Landgravine of Hesse, 8 November 1936, AdHH Schloss Fasanerie.

96 Kaiserin Hermine to Mackensen, 4 December 1936, BA-MA Freiburg-im-Breisgau, Mackensen Papers, N 39/41.

97 Kaiser Wilhelm II to Margarethe Landgravine of Hesse, 26 January 1937, AdHH Schloss Fasanerie.

98 Kaiserin Hermine to Friedrich Karl Landgrave of Hesse, 29 April 1938, ibid.

99 Kaiserin Hermine to Beckmann, 2 February 1938, extract cited in the J. A. Stargardt catalogue No. 685 (2006), p. 425.

100 Kaiser Wilhelm II to Margarethe Landgravine of Hesse, 16 June 1938, AdHH Schloss Fasanerie.

101 Kaiser Wilhelm II to Queen Mary, 1 October 1938, RA Geo V CC 46/270.

102 Kaiser Wilhelm II to Margarethe Landgravine of Hesse, 9 October 1938, AdHH Schloss Fasanerie.

103 Kaiser Wilhelm II to Margarethe Landgravine of Hesse, 7 November 1938, ibid.

104 Kaiser Wilhelm II to Waters, 12 December 1938, RA Geo V O 2578/96.

105 Kaiser Wilhelm II to Margarethe Landgravine of Hesse, 2 and 10 April 1939, AdHH Schloss Fasanerie.

106 Kaiserin Hermine to Margarethe Landgravine of Hesse, 19 April 1939, ibid.

107 Kaiserin Hermine to Margarethe Landgravine of Hesse, 9 May 1939, ibid.

108 Kaiser Wilhelm II to Queen Mary, 30 August 1939, RA GV/CC 45/1199.

109 Kaiserin Hermine to Buchner, 5 October 1939, BA Koblenz, Buchner Papers, N 88/115.

110 Kaiserin Hermine to Fürstenberg, 9 October 1939, FFA Donaueschingen.

111 Kaiser Wilhelm II to Margarethe Landgravine of Hesse, 18 October 1939, AdHH Schloss Fasanerie.

112 Kaiserin Hermine to Margarethe Landgravine of Hesse, 22 December 1939, ibid.

113 Kaiserin Hermine to Prince Franz Joseph of Prussia, 8 December 1939, cited in Gutsche, *Kaiser im Exil*, p. 197.

114 Kaiserin Hermine to Beckmann, 29 December 1939, extract cited in the J. A. Stargardt catalogue No. 685 (2006), p. 425.

115 Kaiser Wilhelm II to Margarethe Landgravine of Hesse, 17 April 1940, AdHH Schloss Fasanerie.

116 Kaiserin Hermine to Catalina von Pannwitz, 20 May 1940, cited in Gutsche, *Kaiser im Exil*, p. 201.

117 Kaiserin Hermine to Viktoria Luise, Duchess of Brunswick-Lüneburg, 15 July 1940, Archiv des vormals regierenden preußischen Königshauses, Burg Hohenzollern, Hechingen, cited in Gutsche, *Kaiser im Exil*, p. 206.

118 Ibid., pp. 200f.

119 Kaiser Wilhelm II to Bigelow, 14 September 1940 and 13 January 1941, New York Public Library, Bigelow Papers, I.

120 Kaiserin Hermine to Margarethe Landgravine of Hesse, 20 May 1940, AdHH Schloss Fasanerie.

121 Kaiserin Hermine to Margarethe Landgravine of Hesse, 1 June 1940, ibid.; Kaiserin Hermine to Princess of Solms-Braunfels, 6 June 1940, BA-MA Freiburg-im-Breisgau, Mackensen Papers, N 39/41.

122 Kaiser Wilhelm II to Margarethe Landgravine of Hesse, 30 May 1940, AdHH Schloss Fasanerie.

123 Kaiser Wilhelm II to Niemann, 31 May 1940, cited in Gutsche, *Kaiser im Exil*, p. 204.

124 Kaiser Wilhelm II to Hitler, 19 June 1940, BA-MA Freiburg-im-Breisgau, Cramon Papers, N 266/47, also cited in Gutsche, *Kaiser im Exil*, p. 204. Hitler's letter of thanks of 25 June 1940 is printed ibid. See also Mackensen to Kaiser Wilhelm II, 18 January 1941, BA-MA Freiburg-im-Breisgau, Mackensen Papers, N 39/39.

125 Kaiser Wilhelm II to Jagow, 5 July 1940, cited in Gutsche, *Kaiser im Exil*, p. 205.

126 Kaiser Wilhelm II to Bigelow, 14 September 1940, New York Public Library, Bigelow Papers, I, cited in part in Röhl, *Kaiser and his Court*, p. 211.

127 Kaiser Wilhelm II to Bigelow, 21 November 1940, New York Public Library, Bigelow Papers, I.

128 Kaiser Wilhelm II to Margarethe Landgravine of Hesse, 3 November 1940, AdHH Schloss Fasanerie.

129 Kaiserin Hermine to Max Trippenbach, 6 November 1940, GStA Berlin, BPHA Rep. 53 Nr 421.

130 Kaiser Wilhelm II to Margarethe Landgravine of Hesse, 3 November 1940, AdHH Schloss Fasanerie.

131 Kaiserin Hermine to Margarethe Landgravine of Hesse, 25 July 1940; Kaiser Wilhelm II to Margarethe Landgravine of Hesse, 1 February 1941, ibid.

132 See above, pp. 1231–9.

133 Kaiser Wilhelm II to Bigelow, 4 July 1933, New York Public Library, Bigelow Papers, III.

134 Ilsemann, diary for 24 November 1938, Koenigswald, *Kaiser in Holland*, II, pp. 314f. See Friedrich Wilhelm Prinz von Preußen, *Haus Hohenzollern*, p. 185.

135 Kaiser Wilhelm II to Queen Mary, 13 November 1938, RA GV/CC 46/272. See Clark, *Kaiser Wilhelm II*, p. 250.

136 Kaiser Wilhelm II to Alwina Gräfin von der Goltz, 28 July and 7 August 1940, printed in Willibald Gutsche, 'Illusionen des Exkaisers. Dokumente aus dem letzten Lebensjahr Kaiser Wilhelms II. 1940/41', *Zeitschrift für Geschichtswissenschaft* 39, 1991, 1028–32.

137 Kaiser Wilhelm II to Niemann, 24 December 1940, printed ibid., 1032–4.

138 Kaiser Wilhelm II to Margarethe Landgravine of Hesse, 3 November 1940, cited in Röhl, *Kaiser and his Court*, p. 211.

139 Kaiser Wilhelm II to Margarethe Landgravine of Hesse, 20 April 1941, AdHH Schloss Fasanerie.

140 Kaiser Wilhelm II to Friedrich Fürst von Hohenzollern-Sigmaringen, 15 January 1941, Kaiser Wilhelm II to Prinz Heinrich XXXIII Reuß, 15 March 1941, Kaiser Wilhelm II to Crown Prince Wilhelm, 26 May 1941, Archiv des vormals regierenden preußischen Königshauses, Burg Hohenzollern, Hechingen.

141 Dr Schulze, 'Bericht vom 18. September über das Befinden Kaiser Wilhelms II.', ibid.

142 Dr Sotier, 'Bericht vom 4. Februar 1937 über das Befinden Kaiser Wilhelms II.', ibid.
143 Dr Classmann to Dr Schulze, 18 March 1938, ibid.
144 Classmann and Schulze, report of 27 March 1938, ibid.
145 Dommes to Mackensen, 28 December 1940, BA-MA Freiburg-im-Breisgau, Mackensen Papers, N 39/66.
146 Dr von Ortenberg, 'Ärztlicher Bericht über die letzten Tage Seiner Majestät des Kaisers und Königs vom 1. bis 4. Juni 1941', BA-MA Freiburg-im-Breisgau, Dommes Papers, N 512/24.
147 Dommes, 'Zum Heimgang Seiner Majestät des Kaisers und Königs Wilhelm II., Juni 1941', ibid.

Archival sources

1. Richard-Wagner-Gedenkstätte, Bayreuth:
   Papers of Eva Chamberlain
   Papers of Houston Stewart Chamberlain
2. Bundesarchiv (BA) Berlin:
   Files of the Reichskanzlei (R 43) (the Reich Chancellor's office)
   Papers of Bogdan Graf von Hutten-Czapski
   Papers of Karl Friedrich Nowak
   Papers of Ernst Schweninger
   Papers of Kuno Graf von Westarp
3. Geheimes Staatsarchiv (GStA) Preußischer Kulturbesitz Berlin:
   Brandenburg-Preußisches Hausarchiv (BPHA)
   Files of the Geheimes Zivilkabinett (the Kaiser's Secret Civil Cabinet)
   Files of the Prussian Ministry of the Interior
   Minutes of the Prussian Ministry of State
   Papers of Dora von Beseler
   Papers of Magnus von Eberhardt
   Papers of Karl Friedrich Nowak
   Papers of Theodor Schiemann
   Papers of Rudolf von Valentini
   Papers of Alfred Graf von Waldersee
4. Politisches Archiv des Auswärtigen Amtes (PA AA) Berlin:
   Asservat Nr 4
   Files of the Political Division
5. Staatsbibliothek zu Berlin, Preußischer Kulturbesitz, Handschriftenabteilung:
   Papers of Adolf von Harnack
6. Niedersächsisches Staatsarchiv Bückeburg:
   Papers of Adolf von Trotha
7. Magyar Orszagos Levéltar (MOL) Budapest:
   Papers of Archduke Franz Ferdinand
8. Cambridge University Library:
   Papers of Viscount Reginald Esher
9. Cumbria Record Office Carlisle:
   Papers of Lord Lonsdale

10. Stadtarchiv Cologne:
    Papers of Alfred Haehner
11. Großherzoglich Hessisches Familienarchiv Darmstadt:
    Papers of Grand Duke Ernst Ludwig of Hesse and the Rhine
12. Hessisches Staatsarchiv (HStA) Darmstadt:
    Papers of Grand Duke Ernst Ludwig of Hesse and the Rhine
13. Fürstlich Fürstenbergisches Archiv (FFA) Donaueschingen:
    Papers of Irma Fürstin zu Fürstenberg
    Papers of Max Egon II Fürst zu Fürstenberg
14. Sächsisches Hauptstaatsarchiv Dresden:
    Papers of Max von Hausen
15. Archiv der Hessischen Hausstiftung (AdHH) Schloss Fasanerie:
    Papers of the Empress Frederick
    Papers of Margarethe Landgravine of Hesse
    Papers of Victoria Princess zu Schaumburg-Lippe
16. Bundesarchiv-Militärarchiv (BA-MA) Freiburg-im-Breisgau:
    Files of the Admiralty Staff (RM5)
    Files of the Kaiser's Naval Cabinet (RM2)
    Files of the Kriegsgeschichtliches Forschungsamt
    Files of the Reich Navy Office (RM3)
    Papers of August von Cramon
    Papers of Wilhelm Dommes
    Papers of Colmar Freiherr von der Goltz
    Papers of Wilhelm Groener
    Papers of Hans von Haeften
    Papers of Albert Hopman
    Papers of Moriz Freiherr von Lyncker
    Papers of August von Mackensen
    Papers of William Michaelis
    Papers of Helmuth von Moltke
    Papers of Curt von Morgen
    Papers of Georg Alexander von Müller
    Papers of Max von Mutius
    Papers of Hans von Plessen
    Papers of Gustav Freiherr von Senden-Bibran
    Papers of Alfred von Tirpitz
17. Marine- und Schiffahrtsmuseum (MSM) Hamburg:
    Papers of Johannes von Karpf
    Papers of Prince Heinrich of Prussia
18. Houghton Library Harvard:
    Papers of George Sylvester Viereck
19. Archiv des vormals regierenden preußischen Königshauses, Burg Hohenzollern, Hechingen:
    Papers of Kaiser Wilhelm II
20. Generallandesarchiv (GLA) Karlsruhe:
    Papers of Max Freiherr von Holzing-Berstett
21. The National Archives, Kew:
    Papers of Sir Edward Grey
    Papers of Sir Charles Hardinge
    Papers of Henry Marquess of Lansdowne
    Papers of Sir Arthur Nicolson

22. Bundesarchiv (BA), Koblenz:
    Papers of Max Buchner
    Papers of Bernhard Fürst von Bülow
    Papers of Walter Goetz
    Papers of Friedrich Wilhelm von Loebell
    Papers of Wilhelm Solf
    Papers of Franz Sontag
    Papers of Friedrich Thimme
    Papers of Rudolf von Valentini
23. Thüringisches Staatsarchiv Meiningen (ThStaMgn):
    House Archive of the ducal family of Saxe-Meiningen
24. Bayerisches Hauptstaatsarchiv (HStA) Munich:
    Reports of the Bavarian military plenipotentiary in Berlin
25. Hohenlohe-Zentralarchiv, Schloß Neuenstein:
    Papers of Ernst Prince zu Hohenlohe-Langenburg
    Papers of Hermann Fürst zu Hohenlohe-Langenburg
26. New York Public Library:
    Papers of Poultney Bigelow
27. Stàtni archiv Opava:
    Papers of Prince Karl Max von Lichnowsky
28. Bodleian Library, Oxford University:
    Papers of James Bryce
    Admiralty's papers on the Tweedmouth letter
29. Rochester University Library:
    Papers of David Jayne Hill
30. Schleswig-Holsteinisches Landesarchiv Schleswig:
    Papers of Prince Heinrich of Prussia
31. Centre for German–Jewish Studies, University of Sussex:
    Papers of Siegfried Sommer
32. Rijksarchief Utrecht:
    Papers of Kaiser Wilhelm II
33. Haus-, Hof- und Staatsarchiv (HHStA) Vienna:
    Ambassadors' reports from Berlin
    Hofnachrichten: Preußen
    Kabinettsarchiv Geheimakten
34. Kriegsarchiv Vienna:
    Papers of Franz Freiherr Conrad von Hötzendorf
35. National Archives Washington DC:
    Records of the Department of State
    Dispatches from US Ministers to Denmark
36. Royal Archives (RA) Windsor:
    Papers of King Edward VII
    Papers of King George V
    Papers of Sir Francis Knollys
    Papers of Prince Christian of Schleswig-Holstein
    Papers of Queen Victoria
37. Stadtarchiv Wuppertal:
    Papers of Eduard Freiherr von der Heydt

38. Privately held papers:
   Papers of Paul Hoffmann, Freiburg
   Papers of Friedrich Mewes, Munich
   Papers of Karl Freiherr von Plettenberg, Essen
   The author's private archive

Bibliography

D'Abernon, Edgar Vincent Viscount, *Ein Botschafter der Zeitenwende, Memoiren*, 3 vols., Leipzig 1930

Achenbach, Adolf von et al., *Unser Kaiser. Fünfundzwanzig Jahre der Regierung Kaiser Wilhelms II. 1888–1913*, Berlin, Leipzig, Vienna and Stuttgart 1913

Afflerbach, Holger, *Der Dreibund. Europäische Großmacht- und Allianzpolitik vor dem Ersten Weltkrieg*, Vienna, Cologne and Weimar 2002

    Falkenhayn. Politisches Denken und Handeln im Kaiserreich, Munich 1994

    'Planning Total War? Falkenhayn and the Battle of Verdun 1916', in Roger Chickering and Stig Förster, eds., *Great War, Total War. Combat and Mobilization on the Western Front, 1914–1918*, Cambridge 2000

    'Wilhelm II as Supreme Warlord in the First World War', in Annika Mombauer and Wilhelm Deist, eds., *The Kaiser. New Research on Wilhelm II's Role in Imperial Germany*, Cambridge 2003

    ed., *Kaiser Wilhelm II. als Oberster Kriegsherr im Ersten Weltkrieg. Quellen aus der militärischen Umgebung des Kaisers 1914–1918*, Munich 2005

Afflerbach, Holger and Stevenson, David, eds., *An Improbable War? The Outbreak of World War I and European Political Culture Before 1914*, Oxford and New York 2007

Ahmad, Feroz, *The Young Turks. The Committee of Union and Progress in Turkish Politics 1908–1920*, Oxford 1969

Allain, Jean-Claude, *Agadir 1911. Une crise impérialiste en Europe pour la conquête du Maroc*, Paris 1976

Alter, Peter, 'Herausforderer der Weltmacht. Das Deutsche Reich im britischen Urteil', in Klaus Hildebrand, ed., *Das Deutsche Reich im Urteil der großen Mächte und europäischen Nachbarn (1871–1945)*, Munich 1995

Amtliche Urkunden zur Vorgeschichte des Waffenstillstandes 1918. Auf Grund der Akten der Reichskanzlei, des Auswärtigen Amtes und des Reichsarchivs hrsg. vom Auswärtigen Amt und vom Reichsministerium des Innern, Berlin 1924

Andersen, Friedrich, *Der Deutsche Heiland*, Munich 1921

Anderson, Pauline R., *The Background of Anti-English Feeling in Germany 1890–1902*, Washington 1939

Angelow, Jürgen, *Kalkül und Prestige. Der Zweibund am Vorabend des Ersten Weltkrieges*, Cologne, Weimar and Vienna 2000

Anon., *Unser Kaiser und sein Volk! Deutsche Sorgen. Von einem Schwarzseher*, Freiburg-im-Breisgau and Leipzig 1906

[Friedrich Wilhelm Prinz zur Lippe], *Politische Beichte eines Deutschen Prinzen*, Leipzig 1925

Balfour, Michael, *The Kaiser and his Times*, London 1964

Bank, Jan, 'Der Weg des Kaisers ins Exil', in Hans Wilderotter and Klaus-D. Pohl, eds., *Der letzte Kaiser, Wilhelm II. im Exil*, Gütersloh and Munich 1991

Barraclough, Geoffrey, *From Agadir to Armageddon. Anatomy of a Crisis*, London 1982

Basler, Werner, *Deutschlands Annexionspolitik in Polen und im Baltikum 1914–1918*, Berlin 1962

Bauer, Max, *Der große Krieg in Feld und Heimat. Erinnerungen und Betrachtungen*, Tübingen 1921

Baumgart, Winfried, *Deutsche Ostpolitik 1918. Von Brest-Litowsk bis zum Ende des Ersten Weltkrieges*, Vienna and Munich 1966

Baumont, Maurice, *L'Affaire Eulenburg*, Geneva 1973

Bayerische Dokumente zum Kriegsausbruch und zum Versailler Schuldspruch, Munich 1925

Beale, Howard K., 'Theodore Roosevelt, Wilhelm II. und die deutsch-amerikanischen Beziehungen', *Die Welt als Geschichte* 15, 1955

Bebel, August, *Ausgewählte Reden und Schriften*, 10 vols., Munich 1978–80

Becker, Bert, *Georg Michaelis. Preußischer Beamter – Reichskanzler – Christlicher Reformer. 1857–1936. Eine Biographie*, Paderborn, Munich, Vienna and Zürich 2007

Beek, Gottfried zur [in reality Ludwig Müller von Hausen] ed., *Die Geheimnisse der Weisen von Zion. Auf Vorposten*, Charlottenburg 1919

Behrenbeck, Sabine and Nützenadel, Alexander, eds., *Inszenierungen des Nationalstaats*, Cologne 2000

Benner, Thomas Hartmut, *Die Strahlen der Krone. Die religiöse Dimension des Kaisertums unter Wilhelm II. vor dem Hintergrund der Orientreise 1898*, Marburg 2001

Berg, Friedrich von, *Friedrich von Berg als Chef des Geheimen Zivilkabinetts 1918. Erinnerungen aus seinem Nachlaß*, ed. Heinrich Potthoff, Düsseldorf 1971

Berghahn, Volker R., *Der Tirpitz-Plan. Genesis und Verfall einer innenpolitischen Krisenstrategie unter Wilhelm II.*, Düsseldorf 1971

'Zu den Zielen des deutschen Flottenbaus unter Wilhelm II.', *Historische Zeitschrift* 210/1, 1970

Berghahn, Volker R. and Deist, Wilhelm, 'Kaiserliche Marine und Kriegsausbruch 1914. Neue Dokumente zur Julikrise', *Militärgeschichtliche Mitteilungen* 1, 1970

Bergsträsser, Ludwig, *Die preußische Wahlrechtsfrage und die Entstehung der Osterbotschaft 1917*, Tübingen 1929

Bermbach, Udo, *Vorformen parlamentarischer Kabinettsbildung in Deutschland. Der interfraktionelle Ausschuß 1917/18 und die Parlamentarisierung der Reichsregierung*, Cologne 1967

Bernhardi, Friedrich von, *Deutschland und der nächste Krieg*, Berlin 1912

Bescheiden betreffende de buitenlandse politiek van Nederland, 1848–1919, third series, The Hague 1958

Bethmann Hollweg, Theobald von, *Betrachtungen zum Weltkrieg*, 2 vols., Berlin 1919

Beyens, [Eugène] Baron, *Deux années à Berlin, 1912–1914*, 2 vols., Paris 1931

Bihl, Wolfdieter, ed., *Deutsche Quellen zur Geschichte des Ersten Weltkrieges*, Darmstadt 1991

Birnbaum, Karl E., *Peace Moves and U-Boat-Warfare*, Stockholm 1958

Bismarck, Otto von, *Gedanken und Erinnerungen*, 3 vols., Berlin and Stuttgart 1898–1929

Blaschke, Olaf, *Katholizismus und Antisemitismus im Deutschen Kaiserreich*, Göttingen 1997

Blücher von Wahlstatt, Evelyn Fürstin, *Tagebuch 1914–1919*, Munich 1924

Blüher, Hans, *Die Aristie des Jesus von Nazareth*, 1921

Boeckh, Katrin, *Von den Balkankriegen zum Ersten Weltkrieg: Kleinstaatenpolitik und ethnische Selbstbestimmung auf dem Balkan*, Munich 1996

Boelcke, Willi A., ed., *Krupp und die Hohenzollern in Dokumenten, Krupp-Korrespondenz mit Kaisern, Kabinettschefs und Ministern 1850–1918*, Frankfurt a.M. 1970

Bosch, Manfred, '"Rasse und Religion sind eins!" Artur Dinters "Die Sünde wider das Blut" oder: Autopsie eines furchtbaren Bestsellers', *Die Ortenau* 1991

Brabant, Artur, *Generaloberst Max Freiherr von Hausen – Ein deutscher Soldat*, Dresden 1926

Bracher, Andreas and Meyer, Thomas, eds., *Helmuth von Moltke 1848–1916. Dokumente zu seinem Leben und Wirken*, Basel 2005

Brand, Adolf, *Fürst Bülow und die Abschaffung des § 175. Flugschrift der Gemeinschaft der Eigenen – philosophische Gesellschaft für Sittenverbesserung und Lebenskunst*, 10 September 1907

Braun, Magnus von, *Von Ostpreußen bis Texas: Erlebnisse und Zeitgeschichtliche Betrachtungen eines Ostpreußen*, Stollhamm 1955

Brechtken, Magnus, *Scharnierzeit 1895–1907. Persönlichkeitsnetze und internationale Politik in den deutsch-britisch-amerikanischen Beziehungen vor dem Ersten Weltkrieg*, Mainz 2006

Brett, Maurice V. and Esher, O., eds., *The Journals and Letters of Reginald Viscount Esher*, 4 vols., London 1934–8

Bridge, F. R., 'The British Declaration of War on Austria-Hungary in 1914', *Slavonic and East European Review* 47, 1969

　Great Britain and Austria-Hungary 1906–1914: A Diplomatic History, London 1972

　'The Sanjak of Novibazar Railway Project', in T. G. Otte and Keith Neilson, eds., *Railways and International Politics. Paths of Empire, 1848–1945*, London 2006

Bridge, F. R. and Bullen, Roger, *The Great Powers and the European States System*, London 2005

Broucek, Peter, 'Der k. u. k. Delegierte im Deutschen Großen Hauptquartier Generalmajor Alois Klepsch-Kloth von Roden und seine Berichterstattung 1915/16', *Militärgeschichtliche Mitteilungen* 1, 1974

Bruch, Rüdiger vom, 'Adolf von Harnack und Wilhelm II.', in Otto Gerhard Oexle and Kurt Nowak, eds., *Adolf von Harnack. Theologe, Historiker, Wissenschaftspolitiker*, Göttingen 2001

Brunn, Gerhard, *Deutschland und Brasilien (1889–1914)*, Cologne and Vienna 1971

Bruns, Claudia, 'Skandale im Beraterkreis um Kaiser Wilhelm II. Die homoerotische "Verbündelung" der "Liebenberger Tafelrunde" als Politikum', in Susanne Zur Nieden, ed., *Homosexualität und Staatsräson: Männlichkeit, Homophobie und Politik in Deutschland 1900–1945*, Frankfurt a.M. and New York 2005

Buchner, Max, *Kaiser Wilhelm II., seine Weltanschauung und seine Stellung zu den deutschen Katholiken*, Leipzig 1929

Bucholz, Arden, *Moltke, Schlieffen and Prussian War Planning*, Providence and Oxford 1991

Buckle, George Earle, ed., *The Letters of Queen Victoria*, third series, 3 vols., London 1930

Bülow, Bernhard Fürst von, *Denkwürdigkeiten*, 4 vols., Berlin 1930–1

Burnham, Edward Frederick Lawson, *Peterborough Court. The Story of The Daily Telegraph*, London 1955

Cambon, Paul, *Correspondance, 1870–1924*, Paris 1946

Canis, Konrad, *Von Bismarck zur Weltpolitik. Deutsche Außenpolitik 1890 bis 1902*, Berlin 1997

　Der Weg in den Abgrund. Deutsche Außenpolitik 1902–1914, Paderborn, Munich, Vienna and Zürich 2011

Cecil, Lamar, *Albert Ballin. Business and Politics in Imperial Germany, 1888–1918*, Princeton, NJ 1967

　'Coal for the Fleet That Had to Die', *American Historical Review* 69/4, 1964

Wilhelm II: Emperor and Exile, 1900–1941, Chapel Hill, London 1996

Wilhelm II: Prince and Emperor, 1859–1900, Chapel Hill, London 1989

Chamberlain, Houston Stewart, *Briefe 1882–1924 und Briefwechsel mit Kaiser Wilhelm II.*, 2 vols., Munich 1928

Mensch und Gott. Betrachtungen über Religion und Christentum, Munich 1921

Chamier, Jacques Daniel, *Fabulous Monster*, London 1934 (translated into German as *Ein Fabeltier unserer Zeit. Glanz und Tragödie Wilhelms II.*, Vienna 1937; reprinted as J. Daniel Chamier, *Als Deutschland mächtig schien. Die Ära Wilhelms II.*, Berlin 1954. Printed again as *Wilhelm II. Der Deutsche Kaiser. Eine Biographie von Daniel Chamier. Mit einem Geleitwort Seiner Kaiserlichen Hoheit Louis Ferdinand Prinz von Preußen*, Munich and Berlin 1989)

Chickering, Roger, 'Die Alldeutschen erwarten den Krieg', in Jost Dülffer and Karl Holl, eds., *Bereit zum Krieg. Kriegsmentalität im wilhelminischen Deutschland, 1890–1914*, Göttingen 1986

Churchill, R. S., *Winston S. Churchill, II, Companion Part 3, 1911–14*, London 1969

Clark, Christopher, *Kaiser Wilhelm II*, London 2000

The Sleepwalkers. How Europe Went to War in 1914, London 2012

Claß, Heinrich, 'West-Marokko deutsch!', *Flugschriften des Alldeutschen Verbandes*, No. 29, Munich 1911

Cohn, Norman, *Warrant for Genocide. The Myth of the Jewish World Conspiracy and the Protocols of the Elders of Zion*, London 1967

Cole, Terence F., 'German Decision-Making on the Eve of the First World War: The Records of the Swiss Embassy in Berlin', in John C. G. Röhl, ed., *Der Ort Kaiser Wilhelms II. in der deutschen Geschichte*, Munich 1991

'Kaiser Versus Chancellor: The Crisis of Bülow's Chancellorship 1905–6', in Richard J. Evans, ed., *Society and Politics in Wilhelmine Germany*, London 1978

Conrad von Hötzendorf, Franz Freiherr, *Aus meiner Dienstzeit*, 5 vols., Vienna 1921–5

Cowles, Virginia, *Wilhelm der Kaiser*, Frankfurt a.M., Berlin 1967

Craig, Gordon A., *Germany 1866–1945*, Oxford 1978

Czernin, Ottokar, *Im Weltkriege*, Berlin and Vienna 1919

Dabringhaus, Sabine, 'An Army on Vacation? The German War in China, 1900–1901', in Manfred F. Boemeke, Roger Chickering and Stig Förster, eds., *Anticipating Total War: The German and American Experiences, 1871–1914*, Cambridge 1999

David, Eduard, *Das Kriegstagebuch des Reichstagsabgeordneten Eduard David 1914 bis 1918*, Düsseldorf 1966

Davis, Arthur N., *The Kaiser I Knew*, London 1918

Dehio, Ludwig, *Gleichgewicht oder Hegemonie. Betrachtungen über ein Grundproblem der neuen Staatengeschichte*, Darmstadt 1996

Deist, Wilhelm, *Flottenpolitik und Flottenpropaganda. Das Nachrichtenbureau des Reichsmarineamtes 1897–1914*, Stuttgart 1976

'Kaiser Wilhelm II. als Oberster Kriegsherr', in John C. G. Röhl, ed., *Der Ort Kaiser Wilhelms II. in der deutschen Geschichte*, Munich 1991

'Verdeckter Militärstreik im Kriegsjahr 1918?', in Wolfram Wette, ed., *Der Krieg des kleinen Mannes. Eine Militärgeschichte von unten*, Munich and Zürich 1992

ed., *Militär und Innenpolitik im Weltkrieg 1914–1918*, 2 vols., Düsseldorf 1970

DeJonge, J. A., *Wilhelm II*, Amsterdam 1986

Delbrück, Clemens von, *Die wirtschaftliche Mobilmachung in Deutschland*, ed. Joachim von Delbrück, Munich 1924

Delbrück, Hans, 'Deutschland, Transvaal und der Besuch des Kaisers in England. Die neue Flottenforderung', *Preußische Jahrbücher* 98, 1899

Deuerlein, Ernst, ed., *Briefwechsel Hertling-Lerchenfeld 1912–1917*, 2 vols., Boppard am Rhein 1973

Deutsche Gedenkhalle: Bilder aus der vaterländischen Geschichte, Berlin and Leipzig 1906

Deutschland schuldig? Deutsches Weißbuch über die Verantwortlichkeit der Urheber des Krieges, Berlin 1919

Devleeshouwer, Robert, *Les Belges et le Danger de Guerre, 1910–1914*, Louvain, Paris 1958

Dickmann, Fritz, 'Die Kriegsschuldfrage auf der Friedenskonferenz von Paris 1919', *Historische Zeitschrift* 197, 1963

Dietrich, Otto, *12 Jahre bei Hitler*, Munich 1955

Dinter, Artur, *Die Sünde wider das Blut. Ein Zeitroman*, Leipzig 1917

Documents diplomatiques français 1871–1914, ed. Ministère Étrangère, 41 vols., Paris 1929–36

Domann, Peter, *Sozialdemokratie und Kaisertum unter Wilhelm II.*, Wiesbaden 1974

Dorpalen, Andreas, 'Empress Auguste Victoria and the Fall of the German Monarchy', *American Historical Review* 58/3, 1952

Dryander, Ernst von, *Erinnerungen aus meinem Leben*, Bielefeld and Leipzig 1922

Dülffer, Jost, *Regeln gegen den Krieg? Die Haager Friedenskonferenzen 1899 und 1907 in der internationalen Politik*, Frankfurt a.M., Berlin 1981

    Kröger, Martin and Wippich, Rolf-Harald, eds., *Vermiedene Kriege. Deeskalation von Konflikten der Großmächte zwischen Krimkrieg und Erstem Weltkrieg 1865–1914*, Munich 1997

Eckardstein, Hermann Freiherr von, *Lebenserinnerungen und Politische Denkwürdigkeiten*, 2 vols., Leipzig 1919–20

Eckert, Astrid M., *Kampf um die Akten. Die Westalliierten und die Rückgabe von deutschem Archivgut nach dem Zweiten Weltkrieg*, Stuttgart 2004

Ehlert, Hans, Epkenhans, Michael, and Groß, Gerhard P., eds., *Der Schlieffenplan. Analysen und Dokumente*, Paderborn, Munich, Vienna and Zürich 2006

Einem, Karl von, *Erinnerungen eines Soldaten 1853–1933*, Leipzig 1933

Eisenberg, Christiane, *'English Sports' und Deutsche Bürger. Eine Gesellschaftsgeschichte 1800–1939*, Paderborn, Munich, Vienna and Zürich 1999

Elst, Baron Van der, 'La Préméditation de l'Allemagne', *Revue de Paris*, 1 August 1923

Epkenhans, Michael, *Die wilhelminische Flottenrüstung 1908–1914. Weltmachtstreben, industrieller Fortschritt, soziale Integration*, Munich 1991

    ed., *Albert Hopman. Das ereignisreiche Leben eines 'Wilhelminers'. Tagebücher, Briefe, Aufzeichnungen 1901 bis 1920*, Munich 2004

Erdmann, Karl-Dietrich, ed., *Kurt Riezler. Tagebücher, Aufsätze, Dokumente*, Göttingen 1972

Ernst Ludwig, Grand Duke of Hesse and the Rhine, *Erinnertes*, Damstadt 1983

Erzberger, Matthias, *Erlebnisse im Weltkrieg*, Stuttgart and Berlin 1920

Eschenburg, Theodor, 'Die Daily-Telegraph-Affäre. Nach unveröffentlichten Dokumenten', *Preußische Jahrbücher* 214, 1928

    Das Kaiserreich am Scheideweg. Bassermann, Bülow und der Block. Nach unveröffentlichten Papieren aus dem Nachlass Ernst Bassermanns, Berlin 1929

Esherik, Joseph W., *The Origins of the Boxer Uprising*, Berkeley 1987

Eyck, Erich, *Die Monarchie Wilhelms II. nach seinen Briefen, seinen Randbemerkungen und Zeugnissen seiner Freunde*, Berlin 1924

    Das Persönliche Regiment Wilhelms II. Politische Geschichte des Deutschen Kaiserreiches von 1890 bis 1914, Zürich 1948

Falkenhayn, Erich von, *Die Oberste Heeresleitung 1914–1916 in ihren wichtigsten Entschließungen*, Berlin 1920

Fasseur, Cees, *Wilhelmina. De jonge Koningin*, Amsterdam 1998

Faulenbach, Bernd, *Ideologie des deutschen Weges. Die deutsche Geschichte in der Historiographie zwischen Kaiserreich und Nationalsozialismus*, Munich 1980

Fehrenbach, Elisabeth, *Wandlungen des deutschen Kaisergedankens 1871–1918*, Munich and Vienna 1969

Fellner, Fritz, 'Die "Mission Hoyos"', in Wilhelm Alff, ed., *Deutschlands Sonderung von Europa 1862–1945*, Frankfurt a.M., Bern and New York 1984

'Die Verstimmung zwischen Wilhelm II. und Eduard VII. im Sommer 1905', *Mitteilungen des österreichischen Staatsarchivs* XI, 1958

Vom Dreibund zum Völkerbund. Studien zur Geschichte der internationalen Beziehungen, 1882–1919, Vienna and Munich 1994

Fendrich, Anton, *Hundert Jahre Tränen, 1848–1948*, Karlsruhe 1953

Fenske, Hans, ed., *Unter Wilhelm II. 1890–1918*, Darmstadt 1982

Ferguson, Niall, *The Pity of War*, London 1998 (translated into German as *Der falsche Krieg. Der Erste Weltkrieg und das zwanzigste Jahrhundert*, Stuttgart 1999)

Fesser, Gerd, 'Gelbe Gefahr', in Kurt Pätzold and Manfred Weißbecker, eds., *Schlagwörter und Schlachtrufe*, Leipzig 2002, I

'"... ein Glück, wenn jetzt Blut fließt ..." Die Zabernaffäre 1913/14', *Geschichte, Erziehung, Politik* 8, 1997

Reichskanzler Bernhard Fürst von Bülow, Berlin 1991

Der Traum von Platz an der Sonne. Deutsche 'Weltpolitik' 1897–1914, Bremen 1996

'Zur Genesis des Reichsvereinsgesetzes. Staatsorgane, bürgerliche Parteien und Vereinsgesetzgebung im Deutschen Reich 1906 bis 1908', in Boris A. Aisin and Willibald Gutsche, eds., *Forschungsergebnisse zur Geschichte des deutschen Imperialismus vor 1917*, Berlin 1980

Fiebig-von Hase, Ragnhild, 'Amerikanische Friedensbemühungen in Europa, 1905–1914', in Norbert Finzsch and Hermann Wellenreuther, eds., *Liberalitas*, Stuttgart 1992

Lateinamerika als Konfliktherd der deutsch-amerikanischen Beziehungen 1890–1903, 2 vols., Göttingen 1986

'Die Rolle Kaiser Wilhelms II. in den deutsch-amerikanischen Beziehungen 1890–1914', in John C. G. Röhl, ed., *Der Ort Kaiser Wilhelms II. in der deutschen Geschichte*, Munich 1991

'The Uses of "Friendship". The "Personal Regime" of Wilhelm II and Theodore Roosevelt, 1901–1909', in Annika Mombauer and Wilhelm Deist, eds., *The Kaiser. New Research on Wilhelm II's Role in Imperial Germany*, Cambridge 2003

Field, Geoffrey G., *Evangelist of Race. The Germanic Vision of Houston Stewart Chamberlain*, New York 1981

Fischer, Fritz, *Griff nach der Weltmacht. Die Kriegszielpolitik des kaiserlichen Deutschland 1914/18*, Düsseldorf 1961

Krieg der Illusionen. Die deutsche Politik von 1911 bis 1914, Düsseldorf 1969

Fischer, Jörg-Uwe, *Admiral des Kaisers. Georg Alexander von Müller als Chef des Marinekabinetts Wilhelms II.*, Frankfurt a.M. 1992

Fock, Harald, 'Des Kaisers Preisausschreiben', *Marine Rundschau*, 1977, 112–17, 183–7, 299–303, 384–9

Forsbach, Ralf, *Alfred von Kiderlen-Wächter (1852–1912). Ein Diplomatenleben im Kaiserreich*, 2 vols., Göttingen 1997

Förster, Stig, 'Im Reich des Absurden: Die Ursachen des Ersten Weltkrieges', in Bernd Wegner, ed., *Wie Kriege entstehen. Zum historischen Hintergrund von Staatenkonflikten*, Paderborn, Munich, Vienna and Zürich 2000

Forstmeier, Friedrich, 'Deutsche Invasionspläne gegen die USA um 1900', *Marine Rundschau* 68, 1971

Fox, Cyril Spencer, ed., *This Was Germany. An Observer at the Court of Berlin. Letters of Princess Marie Radziwill to General di Robilant 1908–1915*, London 1937

Franke, Lydia, *Die Randbemerkungen Wilhelms II. in den Akten der auswärtigen Politik als historische und psychologische Quelle*, Berlin 1933

Franklin, Robert, *The Fringes of History. The Life and Times of Edward Stuart Wortley*, Christchurch 2003

Franzen, Christoph Johannes, 'Eine Symbiose zwischen Wissenschaft und Politik. Leo Frobenius und Wilhelm II.', in Karl-Heinz Kohl and Editha Platte, eds., *Gestalter und Gestalten. 100 Jahre Ethnologie in Frankfurt am Main*, Frankfurt a.M. 2006, pp. 21–45

    Kohl, Karl-Heinz and Recker, Marie-Luise, eds., *Der Kaiser und sein Forscher. Der Briefwechsel zwischen Wilhelm II. und Leo Frobenius (1924–1938)*, Stuttgart 2012

Frauenholz, Eugen von, ed., *Rupprecht, Kronprinz von Bayern, Mein Kriegstagebuch*, 3 vols., Munich 1929

Frey, Marc, *Der Erste Weltkrieg und die Niederlande. Ein neutrales Land im politischen und wirtschaftlichen Kalkül der Kriegsgegner*, Berlin 1998

Freytag-Loringhoven, Gustav Freiherr von, *Menschen und Dinge, wie ich sie in meinem Leben sah*, Berlin 1923

Fricke, Dieter, 'Der deutsche Imperialismus und die Reichstagswahlen von 1907', *Zeitschrift für Geschichtswissenschaft* 9, 1961

Fricke, Dieter, and Fritsch, Werner, eds., *Lexikon zur Parteiengeschichte. Die bürgerlichen und kleinbürgerlichen Parteien und Verbände in Deutschland (1789–1945)*, 4 vols., Leipzig 1984

Friedrich Christian, Prinz zu Schaumburg-Lippe, *Zwischen Krone und Kerker*, Wiesbaden 1952

Friedrich Wilhelm, Prinz von Preußen, *Das Haus Hohenzollern 1918–1945*, Munich and Vienna 1985 (reissued as '*Gott helfe unserem Vaterland*'. *Das Haus Hohenzollern 1918–1945*, Munich 2003)

Frobenius, Herman, *Des deutschen Reiches Schicksalsstunde*, Berlin 1914 (also published as *Germany's Hour of Destiny*, New York, 1914)

Fröhlich, Michael, *Von Konfrontation zur Koexistenz: die deutsch-englischen Kolonialbeziehungen in Afrika zwischen 1884 und 1914*, Bochum 1990

Frymann, Daniel [i.e. Heinrich Claß], *Wenn ich der Kaiser wär'. Politische Wahrheiten und Notwendigkeiten*, Leipzig 1912

Fuchs, Walther Peter, ed., *Großherzog Friedrich I. von Baden und die Reichspolitik 1871–1907*, 4 vols., Stuttgart 1968–80

Garvin, James L., *The Life of Joseph Chamberlain*, 3 vols., London 1934

Geiss, Imanuel, ed., *Juli 1914. Die europäische Krise und der Ausbruch des Ersten Weltkrieges*, Munich 1965

    ed., *Julikrise und Kriegsausbruch 1914*, 2 vols., Hanover 1963–4

    ed., *July 1914. The Outbreak of the First World War: Selected Documents*, London 1967

Gemeinhardt, Heinz Alfred, *Deutsche und österreichische Pressepolitik während der Bosnischen Krise 1908/09*, Husum 1980

Gemzell, Carl Axel, *Organization, Conflict, and Innovation. A Study of German Naval Strategic Planning, 1880–1940*, Stockholm 1973

Geppert, Dominik, *Pressekriege. Öffentlichkeit und Diplomatie in den deutsch-britischen Beziehungen (1896–1912)*, Munich 2007

Gerard, James Watson, *My Four Years in Germany*, London 1917

Geyer, Dietrich, *Der russische Imperialismus. Studien über den Zusammenhang von innerer und auswärtiger Politik 1860–1914*, Göttingen 1977

Gilbert, Bentley B., 'Pacifist to Interventionist. David Lloyd George in 1911 and 1914: Was Belgium an Issue?', *Historical Journal* 28, 1985

Goetz, Walter, ed., *Briefe Wilhelms II. an den Zaren 1894–1914*, Berlin 1920

Goltz, Anna von der, *Hindenburg. Power, Myth, and the Rise of the Nazis*, Oxford 2009

Goltz, Friedrich Freiherr von der and Förster, Wolfgang, eds., *Generalfeldmarschall Colmar Freiherr von der Goltz. Denkwürdigkeiten*, Berlin 1929

Gooch, George P. and Temperley, Harold, eds., *British Documents on the Origin of the War, 1898–1914*, 11 vols., London 1926–38

Gottwald, Herbert, 'Evangelischer Bund zur Wahrung der deutsch-protestantischen Interessen', in Dieter Fricke, Werner Fritsch et al., eds., *Lexikon zur Parteiengeschichte. Die bürgerlichen und kleinbürgerlichen Parteien und Verbände in Deutschland (1789–1945)*, 4 vols., Leipzig 1984

Görlitz, Walter, ed., *Der Kaiser ... Aufzeichnungen des Chefs des Marinekabinetts Admiral Georg Alexander von Müller über die Ära Wilhelms II.*, Göttingen 1965

ed., *Regierte der Kaiser? Kriegstagebücher, Aufzeichnungen und Briefe des Chefs des Marine-Kabinetts Admiral Georg Alexander von Müller 1914–1918*, Göttingen, Berlin and Frankfurt a.M. 1959

Granier, Gerhard, *Magnus von Levetzow. Seeoffizier, Monarchist und Wegbereiter Hitlers. Lebensweg und ausgewählte Dokumente*, Boppard am Rhein 1982

ed., *Die deutsche Seekriegsleitung im Ersten Weltkrieg. Dokumentation*, 4 vols., Koblenz 1999–2004

Grenville, J. A. S., *Lord Salisbury and Foreign Policy. The Close of the Nineteenth Century*, London 1964

Grey, Sir Edward (Viscount Grey of Fallodon), *Twenty-five Years*, 2 vols., London 1925 (translated into German as *Fünfundzwanzig Jahre Politik 1892–1916. Memoiren*, 2 vols., Munich 1926)

Grießmer, Axel, *Große Kreuzer der Kaiserlichen Marine 1906–1918. Konstruktionen und Entwürfe im Zeichen des Tirpitz-Planes*, Bonn 1996

Linienschiffe der Kaiserlichen Marine 1906–1918. Konstruktionen zwischen Rüstungskonkurrenz und Flottengesetz, Bonn 1999

Grimm, T., 'Die Boxerbewegung in China, 1898–1901', *Historische Zeitschrift* 224, 1977

Groener, Wilhelm, *Lebenserinnerungen. Jugend, Generalstab, Weltkrieg*, ed. Friedrich Freiherr von Gaertringen, Göttingen 1957

Groh, Dieter, *Negative Integration und revolutionärer Attentismus: die deutsche Sozialdemokratie am Vorabend des Ersten Weltkrieges*, Frankfurt a.M. 1973

Groh, Dieter, and Brandt, Peter, *'Vaterlandslose Gesellen'. Sozialdemokratie und Nation 1860–1990*, Munich 1992

Gust, Wolfgang, *Das Imperium der Sultane. Eine Geschichte des Osmanischen Reiches*, Munich 1995

Guth, Ekkehard P., 'Der Gegensatz zwischen dem Oberbefehlshaber Ost und dem Chef des Generalstabes des Feldheeres 1914/15. Die Rolle des Major v. Haeften im Spannungsfeld zwischen Hindenburg, Ludendorff und Falkenhayn', *Militärgeschichtliche Mitteilungen* 35, 1984

Gutsche, Willibald, 'Illusionen des Exkaisers. Dokumente aus dem letzten Lebensjahr Kaiser Wilhelms II. 1940/41', *Zeitschrift für Geschichtswissenschaft* 39, 1991

Ein Kaiser im Exil. Der letzte deutsche Kaiser Wilhelm II. in Holland. Eine kritische Biographie, Marburg 1991

Sarajevo 1914, Berlin 1984

Wilhelm II. Der letzte Kaiser des Deutschen Reiches. Eine Biographie. Berlin 1991

ed., *Herrschaftsmethoden des deutschen Imperialismus 1897/98 bis 1917*, Berlin 1977

Gutsche, Willibald, and Petzold, Joachim, eds., 'Das Verhältnis der Hohenzollern zum Faschismus', *Zeitschrift für Geschichtswissenschaft* 34/7, 1986, No. 2

Haferkorn, Joachim, *Bülows Kampf um das Reichskanzleramt im Jahre 1906*, Würzburg and Aumühle 1939

Hahlweg, Werner, ed., *Der Friede von Brest-Litowsk. Ein unveröffentlichter Band aus dem Werk des Untersuchungsausschusses der Deutschen Verfassungsgebenden Nationalversammlung und des Deutschen Reichstages*, Düsseldorf 1971

    ed., *Lenins Rückkehr nach Rußland 1917. Die deutschen Akten*, Leiden 1957

Hale, Oron James, *Publicity and Diplomacy with Special Reference to England and Germany 1890–1914*, New York 1940

Haller, Johannes, *Die Aera Bülow. Eine historisch-politische Studie*, Stuttgart and Berlin 1922

    Aus dem Leben des Fürsten Philipp zu Eulenburg-Hertefeld, Berlin 1924

Hallgarten, George W. F., *Imperialismus vor 1914. Die soziologischen Grundlagen der Außenpolitik europäischer Großmächte vor dem Ersten Weltkrieg*, 2 vols., Munich 1963

Halpern, Paul G., *A Naval History of World War I*, Annapolis 1994

Hamann, Brigitte, *Hitlers Wien. Lehrjahre eines Diktators*, Munich 1996

Hammann, Otto, *Bilder aus der letzten Kaiserzeit*, Berlin 1922

    Um den Kaiser, Berlin 1919

    Zur Vorgeschichte des Weltkrieges. Erinnerungen aus den Jahren 1897–1906, Berlin 1918

Hampe, Karl, *Kriegstagebuch 1914–1918*, ed. Folker Reichert and Eike Wolgast, Munich 2004

Hantsch, Hugo, *Leopold Graf Berchtold. Grandseigneur und Staatsmann*, 2 vols., Graz, Vienna and Cologne 1963

Harnack, Adolf von, 'Der Brief Sr. Majestät des Kaisers an den Admiral Hollmann', *Preußische Jahrbücher* 111, 1903, 584–9

Hartung, Fritz, 'Das persönliche Regiment Kaiser Wilhelms II.', *Sitzungsberichte der Deutschen Akademie zu Berlin*, Berlin 1952

    'Verantwortliche Regierungen, Kabinette und Nebenregierungen im konstitutionellen Preußen 1848–1918', *Forschungen zur Brandenburgischen und Preußischen Geschichte*, 44, 1932, 1–45 and 302–73

Haslip, Joan, *Der Sultan. Das Leben Abd al-Hamids II.*, Munich 1968

Hatzfeldt, Friedrich Graf von, *Heinrich von Tschirschky im Spiegel der Archive und der Geschichtsliteratur*, Cologne 1996

Der Hauptausschuß des Deutschen Reichstages 1915–1918, 4 vols., Düsseldorf 1981–3

Haußmann, Conrad, *Schlaglichter. Reichstagsbriefe und Aufzeichnungen*, ed. Ulrich Zeller, Frankfurt a.M. 1924

Hecht, Karsten, 'Die Harden-Prozesse. Strafverfahren, Öffentlichkeit und Politik im Kaiserreich', unpublished Dr.jur. dissertation, University of Munich, 1997

Heilbron, Fritz, 'Deutsche Intriguen gegen England während des Burenkriegs', *Deutsche Revue*, September 1908

Heinig, Kurt, *Hohenzollern. Wilhelm II. und sein Haus. Der Kampf um den Kronbesitz*, Berlin 1921

Helfferich, Karl, *Georg von Siemens. Ein Lebensbild aus Deutschlands großer Zeit*, 3 vols., Berlin 1923

    Der Weltkrieg, 3 vols., Karlsruhe 1925

Hell, Jürgen, *Der Griff nach Südbrasilien: Die Politik des Deutschen Reiches zur Verwandlung der drei brasilianischen Südstaaten in ein überseeisches Neudeutschland (1890–1914)*, unpublished D.Phil. thesis, Rostock 1966

Hellige, Hans Dieter and Schulin, Ernst, eds., *Walther Rathenau Gesamtausgabe*, VI: *Briefwechsel Walther Rathenau – Maximilian Harden*, Munich and Heidelberg 1983

Helmreich, E. C., 'An Unpublished Report on Austro-German Military Conversations of November, 1912', *Journal of Modern History* 5, June 1933, 205–7

Hering, Rainer, *Konstruierte Nation. Der Alldeutsche Verband 1890 bis 1939*, Hamburg 2003

Herre, Franz, *Kaiserin Friedrich. Victoria, Eine Engländerin in Deutschland*, Stuttgart 2006

Herre, Paul, *Kronprinz Wilhelm. Seine Rolle in der deutschen Politik*, Munich 1954

Hertling, Karl Graf von, 'Bülow, Hertling, Zentrum', in Friedrich Thimme, ed., *Front wider Bülow. Staatsmänner, Diplomaten und Forscher zu seinen Denkwürdigkeiten*, Munich 1931
Ein Jahr in der Reichskanzlei, Freiburg-im-Breisgau 1919

Herwig, Holger H., 'Admirals versus Generals. The War Aims of the Imperial German Navy, 1914–1918', *Central European History* 5, 1972

Herwig, Holger H. and Trask, David F., 'Naval Operations Plans Between Germany and the United States of America, 1898–1913, A Study of Strategic Planning in an Age of Imperialism', *Militärgeschichtliche Mitteilungen* 2, 1970, 5–32

Herzfeld, Hans, *Die deutsche Rüstungspolitik vor dem Weltkrieg*, Bonn 1923

Hessen, Rainer von, ed., *Wolfgang Prinz von Hessen: Aufzeichnungen*, Kronberg im Taunus 1986

Hessen, Wolfgang Prinz von, 'Zum Geleit', in E. C. Conte Corti, *Wenn ... Sendung und Schicksal einer Kaiserin*, Graz, Vienna and Cologne 1954

Hildebrand, Klaus, *Bethmann Hollweg. Der Kanzler ohne Eigenschaften? Urteile der Geschichtsschreibung. Eine kritische Bibliographie*, Düsseldorf 1970
Das vergangene Reich. Deutsche Außenpolitik von Bismarck bis Hitler, 1871–1945, Stuttgart 1995

Hiller von Gaertringen, Friedrich Freiherr, *Fürst Bülows Denkwürdigkeiten. Untersuchungen zu ihrer Entstehungsgeschichte und ihrer Kritik*, Tübingen 1956

Hillgruber, Andreas, 'Zwischen Hegemonie und Weltpolitik. Das Problem der Kontinuität von Bismarck bis Bethmann Hollweg', in Michael Stürmer, ed., *Das kaiserliche Deutschland. Politik und Gesellschaft 1870–1918*, Kronberg, 1977

Hobson, Rolf, *Maritimer Imperialismus. Seemachtideologie, seestrategisches Denken und der Tirpitzplan 1875 bis 1914*, Munich 2004

Hoegen, Jesko von, *Der Held von Tannenberg: Genese und Funktion des Hindenburg-Mythos*, Cologne 2007

Hoffmann, Dieter, *Der Sprung ins Dunkle. Oder wie der 1. Weltkrieg entfesselt wurde*, Leipzig 2010

Hoffmann, Max, *Der Krieg der versäumten Gelegenheiten*, Munich 1923

Hohenlohe-Schillingsfürst, Fürst Chlodwig zu, *Denkwürdigkeiten. Im Auftrag des Prinzen Alexander zu Hohenlohe-Schillingsfürst herausgegeben von Friedrich Curtius*, 2 vols., Stuttgart 1906–7

Hölzle, Erwin, ed., *Quellen zur Entstehung des Ersten Weltkrieges. Internationale Dokumente 1901–1914*, Darmstadt 1995

Horne, John and Kramer, Alan, eds., *German Atrocities 1914. A History of Denial*, New Haven and London 2001

Hötzsch, Otto, ed., *Fürst Bülows Reden nebst urkundlichen Beiträgen zu seiner Politik, Bd. 3, 1907–1909*, Berlin 1909

Hubatsch, Walther, 'Großes Hauptquartier 1914–1918. Zur Geschichte einer deutschen Führungseinrichtung', *Ostdeutsche Wissenschaft* 5, 1958

Huber, Ernst Rudolf, ed., *Deutsche Verfassungsgeschichte seit 1789, IV: Struktur und Krisen des Kaiserreichs*, Stuttgart, Berlin, Cologne and Mainz, 1982
ed., *Dokumente zur deutschen Verfassungsgeschichte*, 3 vols., Stuttgart 1963–78

Huldermann, Bernhard, *Albert Ballin*, Oldenburg 1922

Hull, Isabel V., *Absolute Destruction. Military Culture and the Practices of War in Imperial Germany*, Ithaca and London 2005
'Bernhard von Bülow (1849–1929)', in Wilhelm von Sternburg, ed., *Die deutschen Kanzler von Bismarck bis Schmidt*, Königstein 1985, pp. 69–85

The Entourage of Kaiser Wilhelm II 1888–1918, Cambridge 1982

'Prussian Dynastic Ritual and the End of Monarchy', in Carole Fink, Isabel V. Hull and MacGregor Knox, eds., *German Nationalism and the European Response, 1890–1945*, Norman, OK and London 1985

Hürter, Johannes, ed., *Paul von Hintze. Marineoffizier, Diplomat, Staatssekretär. Dokumente einer Karriere zwischen Militär und Politik, 1903–1918*, Munich 1998

Hutten-Czapski, Bogdan Graf von, *Sechzig Jahre Politik und Gesellschaft*, 2 vols., Berlin 1936

Jäckh, Ernst, ed., *Kiderlen-Wächter – der Staatsmann und Mensch. Briefwechsel und Nachlaß*, 2 vols., Berlin and Leipzig 1924

Jagemann, Eugen von, *75 Jahre des Erlebens und Erfahrens, 1849–1924*, Heidelberg 1925

Die Deutsche Reichsverfassung, Heidelberg 1904

Jagow, Kurt, 'Buckingham Palast 26. Juli 1914. König Georg V. und Prinz Heinrich', *Berliner Monatshefte* XVI, July/August 1938

'Der Potsdamer Kronrat. Geschichte und Legende nach zum Teil unbekannten Quellen', *Süddeutsche Monatshefte* 25/11, 1928

James, Harold, *Krupp: A History of the Legendary German Firm*, Princeton and Oxford 2012

Janßen, Karl-Heinz, 'Der Wechsel in der Obersten Heeresleitung 1916', *Vierteljahreshefte für Zeitgeschichte* 7, 1959

ed., *Die graue Exzellenz. Zwischen Staatsraison und Vasallentreue. Aus den Papieren des kaiserlichen Gesandten Karl Georg von Treutler*, Frankfurt a.M. 1971

Jarausch, Konrad H., *The Enigmatic Chancellor. Bethmann Hollweg and the Hubris of Imperial Germany*, London 1973

Jerussalimski, A. S., *Die Außenpolitik und die Diplomatie des deutschen Imperialismus Ende des 19. Jahrhunderts*, Berlin 1954

Jessup, Philip C., *Elihu Root*, 2 vols., New York 1938

Johann, Ernst, ed., *Reden des Kaisers. Ansprachen, Predigten and Trinksprüche Wilhelms II.*, Munich 1977

Jonas, Klaus W., *Der Kronprinz Wilhelm*, Frankfurt a.M. 1962

Jonas, Manfred, *The United States and Germany, a Diplomatic History*, Ithaca 1984

Jung, Otmar, *Volksgesetzgebung. Die 'Weimarer Erfahrungen' aus dem Fall der Vermögensauseinandersetzungen zwischen Freistaaten und ehemaligen Fürsten*, Hamburg 1990

Kann, Robert A., 'Kaiser Wilhelm II. und Thronfolger Franz Ferdinand in ihrer Korrespondenz', in Robert A. Kann, *Erzherzog Franz Ferdinand Studien*, Vienna 1976, pp. 46–85

Kantorowicz, Hermann, *Der Geist der englischen Politik und das Gespenst der Einkreisung Deutschlands*, Berlin 1929

Kautsky, Karl, *Die deutschen Dokumente zum Kriegsausbruch. Im Auftrag des Auswärtigen Amtes* ed. Max Montgelas and Walter Schücking, 4 vols., Charlottenburg 1919

Keller, Mathilde Gräfin von, *Vierzig Jahre im Dienst der Kaiserin. Ein Kulturbild aus den Jahren 1881–1921*, Leipzig 1935

Kelly, Patrick J., *Tirpitz and the Imperial German Navy*, Bloomington 2011

Kennedy, Paul, *The Rise of the Anglo-German Antagonism, 1860–1914*, London and Boston 1980

ed., *The War Plans of the Great Powers, 1880–1914*, Boston 1985

Kießling, Friedrich, *Gegen den großen Krieg? Entspannung in den internationalen Beziehungen 1911–1914*, Munich 2002

Kitchen, Martin, *The Silent Dictatorship. The Politics of the German High Command under Hindenburg and Ludendorff, 1916–1918*, London 1976

Klein, Fritz, *Deutschland von 1897/98 bis 1917*, Berlin 1986

Deutschland im Ersten Weltkrieg, 3 vols., Berlin 1968–9

Klein, Thoralf, 'Der Boxeraufstand als interkultureller Konflikt: zur Relevanz eines Deutungsmusters', in Susanne Kuß and Bernd Martin, eds., *Das Deutsche Reich und der Boxeraufstand*, Munich 2002, pp. 35–58

Kluge, Ulrich, *Die deutsche Revolution 1918/1919*, Frankfurt a.M. 1985

Koenigswald, Harald von, ed., *Der Kaiser in Holland. Aufzeichnungen des letzten Flügeladjutanten Kaiser Wilhelms II.*, 2 vols., Munich 1968

Kohlrausch, Martin, *Der Monarch im Skandal. Die Logik der Massenmedien und die Transformation der wilhelminischen Monarchie*, Berlin 2005

Kolb, Eberhard, ed., *Vom Kaiserreich zur Weimarer Republik*, Cologne 1972

König, Wolfgang, *Wilhelm II. und die Moderne. Der Kaiser und die technisch-industrielle Welt*, Paderborn, Munich, Vienna and Zürich 2007

Koser, Reinhold, *Geschichte Friedrichs des Großen*, 4 vols., Berlin 1912–14

Koss, Stephen E., *Lord Haldane. Scapegoat for Liberalism*, New York and London 1969

Kramer, Alan, *Dynamic of Destruction. Culture and Mass Killing in the First World War*, Oxford 2007

Krauel, Wolfgang, 'Ein Besuch beim deutschen Kaiserpaar in Amerongen am 24. Oktober 1919', in *Mitteilungen der Friedrich List-Gesellschaft*, Fasc. 6, No. 13, 1968, pp. 311–21

Kreiner, Josef, ed., *Der Russisch-Japanische Krieg (1904/05)* Göttingen 2005

Kren, George M. and Morris, Rodler F., 'Race and Spirituality. Artur Dinter's Theosophical Antisemitism', in *Holocaust and Genocide Studies* 6, No. 3. 1993, 233–52.

Krethlow, Carl Alexander, *Generalfeldmarschall Colmar Freiherr von der Goltz Pascha. Eine Biographie*, Paderborn, Munich, Vienna and Zürich 2012

Der Krieg zur See 1914–1918, 22 vols. in 7 parts, Berlin 1920–41, supplementary volumes Frankfurt a.M. 1964–6

Krieger, Bogdan, *Der Kaiser im Felde*, Berlin 1916

Kriegsrüstung und Kriegswirtschaft, bearbeitet im Reichsarchiv, Anlagen zum ersten Band, Berlin 1930

Kronenbitter, Günther, *'Krieg im Frieden'. Die Führung der k. u. k. Armee und die Großmachtpolitik Österreich-Ungarns 1906–1914*, Munich 2003

  'Die Macht der Illusionen. Julikrise und Kriegsausbruch 1914 aus der Sicht des deutschen Militärattachés in Wien', *Militärgeschichtliche Zeitschrift* (formerly *Militärgeschichtliche Mitteilungen)* 57, 1998

Kruse, Wolfgang, *Krieg und nationale Integration. Eine Neuinterpretation des sozialdemokratischen Burgfriedensschlusses 1914/15*, Essen 1993

Kuczynski, Jürgen, *Amerikanische Krisen und Monopolbildung in deutschen diplomatischen Berichten*, Berlin 1968

Kühlmann, Richard von, *Erinnerungen*, Heidelberg 1948

Kühne, Thomas, 'Demokratisierung und Parlamentarisierung: Neue Forschungen zur politischen Entwicklungsfähigkeit Deutschlands vor dem Ersten Weltkrieg', *Geschichte und Gesellschaft* 31, 2005, 293–316.

Kuß, Susanne, 'Deutsche Soldaten während des Boxeraufstandes in China: Elemente und Ursprünge des Vernichtungskrieges', in Susanne Kuß and Bernd Martin, eds., *Das Deutsche Reich und der Boxeraufstand*, Munich 2002, pp. 165–81

Kuß, Susanne and Martin, Bernd, eds., *Das Deutsche Reich und der Boxeraufstand*, Munich 2002

Lambert, Nicholas A., *Sir John Fisher's Naval Revolution*, Columbia, SC 2002

Lambi, Ivo Nikolai, *The Navy and German Power Politics 1862–1914*, Boston, London and Sydney 1984

Lambsdorff, Gustav Graf von, *Die Militärbevollmächtigten Kaiser Wilhelms II. am Zarenhofe 1904–1914*, Berlin 1937

Lammerting, Kristin, *Meteor. Die kaiserlichen Segelyachten*, Cologne 1999

Latzel, Klaus, 'Die mißlungene Flucht vor dem Tod. Töten und Sterben vor und nach 1918', in Jörg Duppler and Gerhard P. Groß, eds., *Kriegsende 1918. Ereignis, Wirkung, Nachwirkung*, Munich 1999

Lee, A. G., ed., *The Empress Frederick Writes to Sophie*, London 1955

Lee, Sir Sidney, *King Edward VII. A Biography*, 2 vols., London 1925

Lepsius, J., Mendelssohn-Bartholdy, A. and Thimme, F., eds., *Die Große Politik der europäischen Kabinette, 1871–1914*, 40 vols., Berlin, 1922–7

Lepsius, M. Rainer and Mommsen, Wolfgang J., eds., *Max-Weber-Gesamtausgabe*, II/5: *Briefe 1906–1908*, Tübingen 1990

Lerchenfeld-Köfering, Hugo Graf von, *Erinnerungen und Denkwürdigkeiten, 1843–1925*, Berlin 1934

Lerman, Katharine Anne, 'Bismarck's Heir: Chancellor Bernhard von Bülow and the National Idea 1890–1918', in John Breuilly, ed., *The State of Germany. The National Idea in the Making, Unmaking and Remaking of a Modern Nation-State*, London 1993

   The Chancellor as Courtier. Bernhard von Bülow and the Governance of Germany, 1900–1909, Cambridge 1990

   'The Decisive Relationship. Kaiser Wilhelm II and Chancellor Bernhard von Bülow 1900–1905', in John C. G. Röhl and Nicolaus Sombart, eds., *Kaiser Wilhelm II. New Interpretations*, Cambridge 1982

   'The Kaiser's Elite? Wilhelm II and the Berlin Adminstration, 1890–1914', in Annika Mombauer and Wilhelm Deist, eds., *The Kaiser. New Research on Wilhelm II's Role in Imperial Germany*, Cambridge 2003

Lichtervelde, Comte Louis de, *Léopold of the Belgians*, New York and London 1929

Liebert, Ernst von, *Aus einem bewegten Leben*, Munich 1925

Liman, Paul, *Der Kronprinz. Gedanken über Deutschlands Zukunft*, Minden 1914

Lindemann, Thomas, *Die Macht der Perzeptionen und Perzeptionen von Mächten*, Berlin 2000

Link, Arthur Stanley, ed., *The Papers of Woodrow Wilson*, 69 vols., Princeton, NJ, 1966–94

Loran, Stefan, *The Life and Times of Theodore Roosevelt*, Garden City, NY 1959

Lossberg, Fritz von, *Meine Tätigkeit im Weltkriege 1914–1918*, Berlin 1939

Loth, Wilfried, *Katholiken im Kaiserreich. Der politische Katholizismus in der Krise des wilhelminischen Deutschlands*, Düsseldorf 1984

Lowe, Cedric James and Dockrill, Michael Lawrence, eds., *The Mirage of Power: British Foreign Policy, 1902–22*, 3 vols., London 1972

Lübben, Jost, *Die Nordwestdeutsche Zeitung 1895 bis 1933/45. Ein Beitrag zur Entwicklung und politischen Ausrichtung der Generalanzeigerpresse in Deutschland*, Bremerhaven 1999

Ludendorff, Erich, *Meine Kriegserinnerungen 1914–1918*, Berlin 1919

   ed., *Urkunden der Obersten Heeresleitung über ihre Tätigkeit 1916/18*, Berlin 1920

Ludwig, Emil, *Wilhelm der Zweite*, Berlin 1925

Macalpine, Ida, Hunter, Richard, and Rimington, Claude, 'Porphyria in the Royal Houses of Stuart, Hanover and Prussia: A Follow-up Study of George III's Illness', *British Medical Journal*, 1968

Machtan, Lothar, *Die Abdankung. Wie Deutschlands gekrönte Häupter aus der Geschichte fielen*, Berlin 2008

   Des Kaisers letzter Kanzler. Prinz Max von Baden. Biographie eines Unglücks, Frankfurt a.M. 2013

   Der Kaisersohn bei Hitler, Hamburg 2006

   'Wilhelm II. als oberster Sittenrichter: Das Privatleben der Fürsten und die Imagepolitik des letzten deutschen Kaisers', *Zeitschrift für Geschichtswissenschaft* 1/2006

Mackensen, August von, 'Kaiser Wilhelm II. und die alte Wehrmacht', in *Der Aufrechte. Ein Kämpfer für christlich-deutsche Erneuerung*, 5 March 1927

Mackey, Richard W., *The Zabern Affair, 1913–1914*, Lanham 1991

McLean, Roderick R., 'Dreams of a German Europe: Kaiser Wilhelm II and the Treaty of Björkö of 1905', in Annika Mombauer and Wilhelm Deist, eds., *The Kaiser. New Research on Wilhelm II's Role in Imperial Germany*, Cambridge 2003

'Kaiser Wilhelm II and the British Royal Family: Anglo-German Dynastic Relations in Political Context, 1890–1914', *History* 86/284, October 2001

'Kaiser Wilhelm II and His Hessian Cousins: Intra-state Relations in the German Empire and International Dynastic Politics, 1890–1918', *German History* 19/1, 2001

Royalty and Diplomacy in Europe, 1890–1914, Cambridge 2001

Mai, Gunther, '"Verteidigungskrieg" und "Volksgemeinschaft". Staatliche Selbstbehauptung, nationale Solidarität und soziale Befreiung in Deutschland in der Zeit des Ersten Weltkrieges (1900–1925)', in Wolfgang Michalka, ed., *Der Erste Weltkrieg. Wirkung, Wahrnehmung, Analyse*, Munich 1994

Malinowski, Stephan, *Vom König zum Führer. Sozialer Niedergang und politische Radikalisierung im deutschen Adel zwischen Kaiserreich und NS-Staat*, Berlin 2003

Manchester, William, *Krupp. Chronik einer Familie*, Munich 1978

Mann, Golo and Burckhardt, Andreas, eds., *Max von Baden, Erinnerungen und Dokumente*, Stuttgart 1968

Mann, Thomas, *Betrachtungen eines Unpolitischen*, Berlin 1918

Manstein, Erich von, *Aus einem Soldatenleben 1887–1939*, Bonn 1958

Manzenreiter, Johann, *Die Bagdadbahn als Beispiel für die Entstehung des Finanzimperialismus in Europa (1872–1903)*, Bochum 1982

Marder, Arthur J., *British Naval Policy 1880–1905. The Anatomy of British Sea Power*, London 1941

From the Dreadnought to Scapa Flow, 5 vols., London 1961–71

ed., *Fear God and Dread Nought. The Correspondence of Admiral of the Fleet Lord Fisher of Kilverstone*, 3 vols., London 1952–9

Markov, Walter, *Grundzüge der Balkandiplomatie. Ein Beitrag zur Geschichte der Abhängigkeitsverhältnisse*, ed. Fritz Klein and Irene Markov, Leipzig 1999

Marks, Sally, '"My Name is Ozymandias": The Kaiser in Exile', *Central European History* 16/2, June 1983

Marschall, Birgit, *Reisen und Regieren. Die Nordlandfahrten Kaiser Wilhelms II.*, Heidelberg 1991

Martin, Bernd, 'Die Ermordung des deutschen Gesandten Clemens von Ketteler am 20. Juni 1900 in Peking und die Eskalation des "Boxerkrieges"', in Susanne Kuß and Bernd Martin, eds., *Das Deutsche Reich und der Boxeraufstand*, Munich 2002

Martin, Rudolf, *Deutsche Machthaber*, Berlin, Leipzig 1910

Kaiser Wilhelm II. und König Eduard VII., Dresden 1907

Massie, Robert K., *Dreadnought. Britain, Germany and the Coming of the Great War*, New York 1991

Matthias, Erich, ed., *Der Interfraktionelle Ausschuß 1917/18*, 2 vols., Düsseldorf 1959

Matthias, Erich and Morsey, Rudolf, eds., *Die Regierung des Prinzen Max von Baden*, Düsseldorf 1962

Matthias, Erich and Pikart, Eberhard, eds., *Die Reichstagsfraktion der deutschen Sozialdemokratie 1898 bis 1918*, Düsseldorf 1966

Max, Prinz von Baden, *Erinnerungen und Dokumente*, Berlin and Leipzig 1927

Mayer, Martin, *Geheime Diplomatie und öffentliche Meinung. Die Parlamente in Frankreich, Deutschland und Großbritannien und die erste Marokkokrise 1904–1906*, Düsseldorf 2002

Mehnert, Ute, 'German Weltpolitik and the American Two-Front Dilemma: The "Japanese Peril" in German–American Relations, 1904–1917', *The Journal of American History* 82, 1996, 1452–77

Meisner, Heinrich Otto, ed., *Denkwürdigkeiten des General-Feldmarschalls Alfred Graf von Waldersee*, 3 vols., Stuttgart and Berlin 1922–3

Menning, Ralph R. and Menning, Carol Bresnahan, '"Baseless Allegations": Wilhelm II and the Hale Interview of 1908', *Central European History* 16, 1983

Merton, Robert, *Erinnernswertes aus meinem Leben das über das Persönliche hinausgeht*, Frankfurt a.M. 1955

Meyer, Klaus, *Theodor Schiemann als politischer Publizist*, Frankfurt a.M. and Hamburg 1956

Meyer, Thomas, *'Endlich eine Tat, eine befreiende Tat . . .' Alfred von Kiderlen-Wächters 'Panthersprung nach Agadir' unter dem Druck der öffentlichen Meinung*, Husum 1996

Meyer-Arndt, Lüder, *Die Julikrise 1914. Wie Deutschland in den ersten Weltkrieg stolperte*, Cologne and Vienna 2006

Meyer zu Uptrup, Wolfgang, *Kampf gegen die 'jüdische Weltverschwörung'*, Berlin 2003

Michael, Prince of Greece, *Nicholas and Alexandra: The Family Albums*, London 1992

Michaelis, Georg, *Für Volk und Staat. Eine Lebensgeschichte*, Berlin 1922

Michaelis, Herbert and Schraepel, Ernst, eds., *Ursachen und Folgen. Vom deutschen Zusammenbruch 1918 und 1945 bis zur staatlichen Neuordnung Deutschlands in der Gegenwart. Eine Urkunden- und Dokumentensammlung zur Zeitgeschichte*, 26 vols., Berlin 1958–80

Michaelis, William, 'Der Reichskanzler Michaelis und die päpstliche Friedensaktion von 1917', *Geschichte in Wissenschaft und Unterricht* 12, 1961

Miller, Susanne, *Burgfrieden und Klassenkampf. Die deutsche Sozialdemokratie im Ersten Weltkrieg*, Düsseldorf 1974

Mitchell, Nancy, *The Danger of Dreams: German and American Imperialism in Latin America*, Chapel Hill 1997

Moltke, Dorothy von, *Ein Leben in Deutschland. Briefe aus Kreisau und Berlin 1907–1934*, Munich 1999

Moltke, Eliza von, ed., *Generaloberst Helmuth von Moltke, Erinnerungen, Briefe, Dokumente 1877–1916*, Stuttgart 1922

Mombauer, Annika, *Helmuth von Moltke and the Origins of the First World War*, Cambridge 2001

    The Origins of the First World War. Controversies and Consensus, London 2002

    'Wilhelm, Waldersee, and the Boxer Rebellion', in Annika Mombauer and Wilhelm Deist, eds., *The Kaiser. New Research on Wilhelm II's Role in Imperial Germany*, Cambridge 2003, pp. 91–118

    ed., *The Origins of the First World War. Diplomatic and Military Documents*, Manchester 2013

Mombauer, Annika and Deist, Wilhelm, eds., *The Kaiser. New Research on Wilhelm II's Role in Imperial Germany*, Cambridge 2003

Mommsen, Wolfgang J., *Bürgerstolz und Weltmachtstreben. Deutschland unter Wilhelm II. 1890 bis 1918*, Berlin 1995

    'Zur Entwicklung des Englandbildes der Deutschen seit dem Ende des 18. Jahrhunderts', in Lothar Kettenacker, Manfred Schlenke and Hellmut Seier, eds., *Studien zur Geschichte Englands und der deutsch-britischen Beziehungen. Festschrift für Paul Kluke*, Munich 1981, pp. 375–97

    Großmachtstellung und Weltpolitik. Die Außenpolitik des Deutschen Reiches 1870–1914, Berlin 1993

    'Der Topos vom unvermeidlichen Krieg: Außenpolitik und öffentliche Meinung im Deutschen Reich im letzten Jahrzehnt vor 1914', in Wolfgang J. Mommsen, *Der autoritäre Nationalstaat. Verfassung, Gesellschaft und Kultur im deutschen Kaiserreich*, Frankfurt a.M. 1990

War der Kaiser an allem schuld? Wilhelm II. und die preußisch-deutschen Machteliten, Munich 2002

Monger, George, *The End of Isolation: British Foreign Policy 1900–1907*, London 1963

Montagu, Victor A., *Reminiscences*, London 1910

Moritz, Albrecht, *Das Problem des Präventivkrieges in der deutschen Politik während der ersten Marokkokrise*, Bern and Frankfurt a.M. 1974

Mossolov, Aleksandr A., *At the Court of the Last Tsar*, London 1935

Mühleisen, Horst, *Kurt Freiherr von Lersner. Diplomat im Umbruch der Zeiten 1918–1920. Eine Biographie*, Göttingen 1988

Mühlhausen, Walter and Papke, Gerhard, eds., *Kommunalpolitik im Ersten Weltkrieg. Die Tagebücher Erich Koch-Wesers 1914 bis 1918*, Munich 1999

Müller, Karl Alexander von, *Mars und Venus. Erinnerungen: 1914–1919*. Stuttgart 1954

'Neue Urkunden', *Süddeutsche Monatshefte*, July 1921

ed., *Chlodwig zu Hohenlohe-Schillingsfürst, Denkwürdigkeiten der Reichskanzlerzeit*, Stuttgart, Berlin 1931

Müller, Sven Oliver, *Nationalismus in Deutschland und Großbritannien im Ersten Weltkrieg*, Göttingen 2002

Müller-Dreyer, Armin, *Konfession in Politik, Gesellschaft und Kultur des Kaiserreichs. Der Evangelische Bund 1886–1914*, Gütersloh 1998

Nicolson, Harold, *King George the Fifth. His Life and Reign*, London 1952

Niemann, Alfred, *Kaiser und Revolution. Die entscheidenden Ereignisse im Großen Hauptquartier*, Berlin 1922

Revolution von oben – Umsturz von unten. Entwicklung und Verlauf der Staatsumwälzung in Deutschland 1914–1918, Berlin 1928

Nipperdey, Thomas, *Deutsche Geschichte 1866–1918*, 2 vols., Munich 1990

Nottmeier, Christian, *Adolf von Harnack und die deutsche Politik 1890–1930*, Tübingen 2004

Nowak, Karl F. and Thimme, Friedrich, eds., *Erinnerungen und Gedanken des Botschafters Anton Graf Monts*, Berlin 1932

Obst, Michael A., '"Die fürchterliche Stimme". Kaiser Wilhelm II. als politischer Redner', unpublished D.Phil Dissertation, University of Düsseldorf 2007

'Einer nur ist Herr im Reiche.' Kaiser Wilhelm II. als politischer Redner, Paderborn, Munich, Vienna and Zürich 2010

ed., *Die politischen Reden Kaiser Wilhelms II. Eine Auswahl*, Paderborn, Munich, Vienna and Zürich 2011

O'Connor, Richard, *The Spirit Soldiers: A Historical Narrative of the Boxer Rebellion*, New York 1973

Olusoga, David and Erichsen, Casper W., *The Kaiser's Holocaust. Germany's Forgotten Genocide*, London 2010

Oncken, Emily, *Panthersprung nach Agadir. Die deutsche Politik während der Zweiten Marokkokrise 1911*, Düsseldorf 1981

Österreich-Ungarns Außenpolitik von der Bosnischen Krise 1908 bis zum Kriegsausbruch 1914. Diplomatische Aktenstücke des österreichisch-ungarischen Ministeriums des Äußeren, 9 vols., Vienna and Leipzig 1930

Otte, Thomas G., 'An Altogether Unfortunate Affair': Great Britain and the Daily Telegraph Affair, *Diplomacy & Statecraft* 5, 1994, 296–333

'A "German Paperchase": The "Scrap of Paper" Controversy and the Problem of Myth and Memory in International History', *Diplomacy and Statecraft* 18, 2007, 53–87

Otto, Helmut and Schmiedel, Karl, eds., *Der erste Weltkrieg. Dokumente*, Berlin 1977

Overlack, Peter, 'German War Plans in the Pacific, 1900–1914', *The Historian* 69, 1998, 579–93

La Paix de Versailles. La Documentation Internationale, 13 vols., Paris 1929–32

Pakula, Hannah, *An Uncommon Woman. The Empress Frederick, Daughter of Queen Victoria, Wife of the Crown Prince of Prussia, Mother of Kaiser Wilhelm*, New York 1995

Paléologue, Maurice, *Un Grand Tournant de la Politique Mondiale 1904–1906*, Paris 1934
   Guillaume II et Nicolas II, Paris 1935
   'La Russie des Tsars', *Revue des Deux Mondes*, 1921, I
   Au Quai d'Orsay à la veille de la tourmente, Journal 1913–1914, Paris 1947

Payer, Friedrich, *Von Bethmann Hollweg bis Ebert. Erinnerungen und Bilder*, Frankfurt a.M. 1923

Penzler, Johannes, ed., *Fürst Bülows Reden nebst urkundlichen Beiträgen zu seiner Politik*, 3 vols., (III ed. Otto Hötzsch) Berlin 1907–9,
   ed., *Die Reden Kaiser Wilhelms II. 1896–1900*, Leipzig 1904
   ed., *Die Reden Kaiser Wilhelms II. 1901–Ende 1905*, Leipzig 1906
   ed., *Die Reden Kaiser Wilhelms II. in den Jahren 1906–1912*, Leipzig 1913

Peters, Michael, *Der Alldeutsche Verband am Vorabend des Ersten Weltkrieges (1908–1914). Ein Beitrag zur Geschichte des völkischen Nationalismus im spätwilhelminischen Deutschland*, Frankfurt a.M. 1992

Petropoulos, Jonathan, *Royals and the Reich. The Princes von Hessen in Nazi Germany*, Oxford 2006

Petzold, Dominik, *Der Kaiser und das Kino. Herrschaftsinszenierung, Populärkultur und Filmpropaganda im wilhelminischen Zeitalter*, Paderborn, Munich, Vienna and Zürich 2012
   '"Monarchische Reklamefilms"? Wilhelm II. im neuen Medium der Kinematographie', in Nils Freytag and Dominik Petzold, eds., *Das 'lange' 19. Jahrhundert: Alte Fragen und neue Antworten*, Munich 2007, pp. 201–20

Pfeiffer-Belli, Wolfgang, ed., *Harry Graf Kessler, Tagebücher 1918–1937*, Frankfurt a.M. 1961

Phal-Traughber, Armin, *Der antisemitisch-antifreimaurerische Verschwörungsmythos in der Weimarer Republik und im NS-Staat*, Vienna 1993

Pogge von Strandmann, Hartmut, 'Der Kaiser und die Industriellen. Vom Primat der Rüstung', in John C. G. Röhl, ed., *Der Ort Kaiser Wilhelms II. in der deutschen Geschichte*, Munich 1991, pp. 111–29
   'Rathenau, Wilhelm II and the Perception of *Wilhelminismus*', in Annika Mombauer and Wilhelm Deist, eds., *The Kaiser. New Research on Wilhelm II's Role in Imperial Germany*, Cambridge 2003, pp. 259–80
   'Staatsstreichpläne, Alldeutsche und Bethmann Hollweg', in Hartmut Pogge von Strandmann and Imanuel Geiss, *Die Erforderlichkeit des Unmöglichen. Deutschland am Vorabend des ersten Weltkrieges*, Frankfurt a.M. 1965
   ed., *Walther Rathenau Tagebuch 1907–1922*, Düsseldorf 1967

Pohl, Hugo von, *Aus Aufzeichnungen und Briefen während der Kriegszeit*, Berlin 1920

Pohl, Klaus-D., 'Der Kaiser im Zeitalter seiner technischen Reproduzierbarkeit. Wilhelm II. in Fotografie und Film', in Hans Wilderotter and Klaus-D. Pohl, eds., *Der letzte Kaiser. Wilhelm II. im Exil*, Gütersloh and Munich 1991

Pollmann, Klaus Erich, 'Wilhelm II. und der Protestantismus', in Stefan Samerski, ed., *Wilhelm II. und die Religion. Facetten einer Persönlichkeit und ihres Umfelds*, Berlin 2001

Pommerin, Reiner, *Der Kaiser und Amerika. Die USA in der Politik der Reichsleitung 1890–1917*, Cologne and Vienna 1986

Ponsonby, Sir Frederick, *Letters of the Empress Frederick*, London 1929 (translated into German as *Briefe der Kaiserin Friedrich*, Berlin 1929)
   Recollections of Three Reigns, London 1951

Potthoff, Heinrich, 'Der Parlamentarisierungserlaß vom 30. September 1918', *Vierteljahrshefte für Zeitgeschichte* 20, 1972

Preston, Diana, *China's War on Foreigners*, London 2002

Die Protokolle des Preussischen Staatsministeriums 1817–1934/38, Acta Borussica, Neue Folge, ed. Reinhold Zilch for the Berlin-Brandenburgische Akademie der Wissenschaften, 1. series, IX, Hildesheim, Zürich and New York 2001

Puhle, Hans-Jürgen, *Agrarische Interessenpolitik und preußischer Konservatismus im wilhelminischen Reich (1893–1914). Ein Beitrag zur Analyse des Nationalismus in Deutschland am Beispiel des Bundes der Landwirte und der Deutsch-Konservativen Partei*, Bonn and Bad Godesberg 1975

Purcell, Victor, *The Boxer Uprising. A Background Study*, Cambridge 1963

Pyta, Wolfram, *Hindenburg. Herrschaft zwischen Hohenzollern und Hitler*, Berlin 2007

Radziwill, Princess Marie, *Briefe vom deutschen Kaiserhof 1889–1915*, Berlin 1936

Raithel, Thomas, *Das 'Wunder' der inneren Einheit. Studien zur deutschen und französischen Öffentlichkeit bei Beginn des Ersten Weltkriegs*, Bonn 1996

Rall, Hans, 'Zur persönlichen Religiosität Kaiser Wilhelms II.', *Zeitschrift für Kirchengeschichte*, 1984/2, 382–94

Ramsaur, Ernest E., *The Young Turks. Prelude to the Revolution of 1908*, Princeton, NJ 1957

Rassow, Peter and Born, Karl Erich, eds., *Akten zur Staatlichen Sozialpolitik in Deutschland 1890–1914*, Wiesbaden 1959

Rathenau, Walther, *Hauptwerke und Gespräche, Walther-Rathenau-Gesamtausgabe*, ed. Ernst Schulin, Munich 1977, II

Rauchensteiner, Manfried, *Der Tod des Doppeladlers. Österreich-Ungarn und der Erste Weltkrieg*, Graz, Vienna and Cologne 1993

Rauh, Manfred, *Die Parlamentarisierung des Deutschen Reiches*, Düsseldorf 1977

Raulff, Heiner, *Zwischen Machtpolitik und Imperialismus. Die deutsche Frankreichpolitik 1904/06*, Düsseldorf 1976

Rebentisch, Jost, *Die vielen Gesichter des Kaisers. Wilhelm II. in der deutschen und britischen Karikatur (1888–1918)*, Berlin 2000

Regele, Oskar, *Feldmarschall Conrad. Auftrag und Erfüllung 1906–1918*, Vienna and Munich 1955

Reich, Eric, *Germany's Swelled Head*, London, 1907

Reichold, Helmut, ed., *Adolf Wild von Hohenborn. Briefe und Tagebuchaufzeichnungen des preußischen Generals als Kriegsminister und Truppenführer im Ersten Weltkrieg*, Boppard am Rhein 1986

Reid, Michaela, *Ask Sir James. Sir James Reid, Personal Physician to Queen Victoria and Physician-in-Ordinary to Three Monarchs*, London 1987

Reimann, Josef, *Fürst Bülows Denkwürdigkeiten und die deutsche Marokkopolitik (1897–1909)*, Würzburg 1935

Reinermann, Lothar, *Der Kaiser in England. Wilhelm II. und sein Bild in der britischen Öffentlichkeit*, Paderborn, Munich, Vienna and Zürich 2001

Reismann-Grone, Theodor, *Der Erdenkrieg und die Alldeutschen*, Mühlheim, Ruhr 1919

Reventlow, Ernst Graf von, *Glanz und Tragödie Wilhelms II.*, Stuttgart 1938

Von Potsdam nach Doorn, Berlin 1940

Rich, Norman, *Friedrich von Holstein. Politics and Diplomacy in the Era of Bismarck and Wilhelm II*, 2 vols., Cambridge 1965

Rich, Norman and Fisher, M. H., eds., *The Holstein Papers. The Memoirs, Diaries and Correspondence of Friedrich von Holstein 1837–1909*, 4 vols., Cambridge 1956–63

Richter, Dieter, 'Friedrich Alfred Krupp auf Capri. Ein Skandal und seine Geschichte', in Michael Epkenhans and Ralf Stremmel, eds., *Friedrich Alfred Krupp. Ein Unternehmer im Kaiserreich*, Munich 2010

Ritter, Gerhard, *Der Schlieffenplan. Kritik eines Mythos*, Munich 1956

   Staatskunst und Kriegshandwerk. Das Problem des 'Militarismus' in Deutschland, 4 vols., Munich 1954–68

Rogasch, Wilfried, '"Mit Anstand untergehen …" Kaiser Wilhelm II. als "Oberster Kriegsherr"', in Hans Wilderotter and Klaus-D. Pohl, eds., *Der letzte Kaiser. Wilhelm II. im Exil*, Gütersloh 1991

Rogge, Helmuth, *Holstein und Harden. Politisch-publizistisches Zusammenspiel zweier Außenseiter des Wilhelminischen Reiches*, Munich 1959

   ed., *Friedrich von Holstein, Lebensbekenntnis in Briefen an eine Frau*, Berlin 1932

Röhl, John C. G., *1914: Delusion or Design? The Testimony of Two German Diplomats*, London, 1973

   'Admiral von Müller and the Approach of War, 1911–1914', *The Historical Journal* XII, 4, 1969

   'The Emperor's New Clothes', in John C. G. Röhl and Nicolaus Sombart, eds., *Kaiser Wilhelm II. New Interpretations*, Cambridge 1982

   The Kaiser and his Court. Wilhelm II and the Government of Germany, Cambridge 1994

   Kaiser, Hof und Staat. Wilhelm II. und die deutsche Politik, Munich 1987

   'Kaiser Wilhelm II. und der deutsche Antisemitismus', in John C. G. Röhl, *Kaiser, Hof und Staat. Wilhelm II. und die deutsche Politik*, Munich 2002, pp. 203–22

   'An der Schwelle zum Weltkrieg. Eine Dokumentation über den "Kriegsrat" vom 8. Dezember 1912', *Militärgeschichtliche Mitteilungen* 21, 1977

   'Vorsätzlicher Krieg? Die Ziele der deutschen Politik im Juli 1914', in Wolfgang Michalka, ed., *Der Erste Weltkrieg. Wirkung, Wahrnehmung, Analyse*, Munich and Zürich 1994

   Wilhelm II., Der Aufbau der persönlichen Monarchie 1888–1900, Munich 2001

   Wilhelm II., Die Jugend des Kaisers 1859–1888, Munich 1993

   Wilhelm II. The Kaiser's Personal Monarchy 1888–1900, Cambridge 2004

   Wilhelm II. Der Weg in den Abgrund 1900–1941, Munich 2008

   Young Wilhelm. The Kaiser's Early Life 1859–1888, Cambridge 1998

   Zwei deutsche Fürsten zur Kriegsschuldfrage. Lichnowsky und Eulenburg und der Ausbruch des Ersten Weltkriegs. Eine Dokumentation, Düsseldorf 1971

   ed., *Der Ort Kaiser Wilhelms II. in der deutschen Geschichte*, Munich 1991

   ed., *Philipp Eulenburgs politische Korrespondenz*, 3 vols., Boppard am Rhein 1976–83

Röhl, John C. G. and Sombart, Nicolaus, eds., *Kaiser Wilhelm II. New Interpretations*, Cambridge 1982

   Warren, Martin and Hunt, David, eds., *Purple Secret. Genes, 'Madness' and the Royal Houses of Europe*, London 1998

Rohrbach, Paul, *Die Bagdadbahn*, Berlin 1911

Roosevelt, Theodore, *The Letters*, ed. Elting E. Morison, John M. Blum and John J. Buckley, 8 vols., Cambridge, MA 1951–4

Rosen, Friedrich, *Aus einem diplomatischen Wanderleben*, Berlin 1931–59

Rosenbach, Harald, *Das Deutsche Reich, Großbritannien und der Transvaal (1896–1902)*, Göttingen 1993

Rüger, Jan, *The Great Naval Game: Britain and Germany in the Age of Empire*, Cambridge 2007

Saerbeck, Annika, 'Kaiser ohne Amt und Zukunft. Zum politischen, weltanschaulichen und monarchischen Selbstverständnis Wilhelms II. in den ersten Jahren seines holländischen Exils', unpublished MA dissertation, University of Bremen 2007

Samerski, Stefan, ed., *Wilhelm II. und die Religion. Facetten einer Persönlichkeit und ihres Umfelds*, Berlin 2001

Sarkin, Jeremy, *Germany's Genocide of the Herero: Kaiser Wilhelm II, his General, his Settlers, his Soldiers*, Cape Town 2011

Savinsky, Alexander, 'Guillaume II et la Russie. Ses dépêches à Nicolas II 1903–1905', *Revue des deux Mondes* 12, 1922, 765–802

Scheidemann, Philipp, *Memoirs of a Social Democrat*, 2 vols., London 1928
  Der Zusammenbruch, Berlin 1921
Schenk, Willy, *Die deutsch-englische Rivalität vor dem ersten Weltkrieg in der Sicht deutscher Historiker*, Aarau 1967
Scherer, André and Grunewald, Jacques, eds., *L'Allemagne et les problèmes de la paix pendant la première guerre mondiale. Documents extraits des archives de l'Office allemand des Affaires étrangères*, 4 vols., Paris 1962–76
Schiffer, Eugen, *Ein Leben für den Liberalismus*, Berlin 1951
Schimmelpenninck van der Oye, David, *Towards the Rising Sun. Russian Ideologies of Empire and the Path to War with Japan*, DeKalb, IL 2006
Schloßmacher, Norbert, 'Der Antiultramontanismus im Wilhelminischen Deutschland. Ein Versuch', in Wilfried Loth, ed., *Deutscher Katholizismus im Umbruch zur Moderne*, Stuttgart 1991, pp. 164–98
Schmidt, Erwin and Kasdorff, Hans, eds., *Hundert Jahre Erziehung der Jugend auf Schloß Plön 1868–1968*, Plön 1968
Schmitt-Ott, Friedrich, *Erlebtes und Erstrebtes, 1860–1950*, Wiesbaden 1952
Schoen, Wilhelm Freiherr von, *Erlebtes. Beiträge zur politischen Geschichte der neuesten Zeit*, Stuttgart and Berlin 1921
Schoenbaum, David, *Zabern 1913. Consensus Politics in Imperial Germany*, London 1982
Schöllgen, Gregor, *Imperialismus und Gleichgewicht. Deutschland, England und die orientalische Frage 1871–1914*, Munich 2000
Schönburg-Waldenburg, Heinrich Prinz von, *Erinnerung aus kaiserlicher Zeit*, Leipzig 1929
Schöningen, Hans, *Kaiser Wilhelm II. und seine Zeit in Wort und Bild*, Hamburg 1913
Schottelius, Herbert and Deist, Wilhelm, eds., *Marine und Marinepolitik im kaiserlichen Deutschland 1871–1914*, Düsseldorf 1972
Schramm, Martin, *Das Deutschlandbild in der britischen Presse 1912–1919*, Berlin 2007
Schröder, Hans-Jürgen, *Deutschland und Amerika in der Epoche des Ersten Weltkrieges 1900–1924*, Stuttgart 1993
Schröder, Joachim, *Die U-Boote des Kaisers. Die Geschichte des deutschen U-Boot-Krieges gegen Großbritannien im Ersten Weltkrieg*, Lauf a.d. Pregnitz 2001
Schulte, Bernd F., *Die deutsche Armee 1900–1918. Zwischen Beharren und Verändern*, Düsseldorf 1977
  Europäische Krise und Erster Weltkrieg. Beiträge zur Militärpolitik des Kaiserreichs 1871–1914, Frankfurt a.M. and Bern 1983
  Vor dem Kriegsausbruch 1914. Deutschland, die Türkei und der Balkan, Düsseldorf 1980
  'Neue Dokumente zu Kriegsausbruch und Kriegsverlauf 1914', *Militärgeschichtliche Mitteilungen* 25, 1979
  Die Verfälschung der Riezler Tagebücher, Frankfurt a.M., Bern and New York 1985
Schultheß, *Deutscher Geschichtskalender*
  Europäischer Geschichtskalender
Schumann, Wolfgang and Nestler, Ludwig, eds., *Weltherrschaft im Visier*, Berlin 1975
Schüssler, Wilhelm, *Die Daily-Telegraph-Affäre. Fürst Bülow, Kaiser Wilhelm und die Krise des Zweiten Reiches 1908*, Göttingen 1952
Schwabe, Klaus, *Deutsche Revolution und Wilson-Frieden. Die amerikanische und deutsche Friedensstrategie zwischen Ideologie und Machtpolitik 1918/19*, Düsseldorf 1971
Schwengler, Walter, *Völkerrecht, Versailler Vertrag und Auslieferungsfrage: die Strafverfolgung wegen Kriegsverbrechen als Problem des Friedensschlusses 1919/20*, Stuttgart 1982
Schwertfeger, Bernhard, *Die Diplomatischen Akten des Auswärtigen Amtes 1871–1914. Ein Wegweiser durch das große Aktenwerk der Deutschen Regierung*, 8 vols., Berlin 1923–7

'Fürst Bülow und Rudolf von Valentini', in Friedrich Thimme, ed., *Front wider Bülow. Staatsmänner, Diplomaten und Forscher zu seinen Denkwürdigkeiten*, Munich 1931

ed., *Kaiser und Kabinettschef. Nach eigenen Aufzeichnungen und dem Briefwechsel des Wirklichen Geheimen Rats Rudolf von Valentini*, Oldenburg i.O. 1931

Seeger, Charles Louis, ed., *The Memoirs of Alexander Iswolsky*, London 1920

Seligmann, Matthew S., 'Military Diplomacy in a Military Monarchy? Wilhelm II's Relations with the British Service Attachés in Berlin, 1903–1914', in Annika Mombauer and Wilhelm Deist, eds., *The Kaiser. New Research on Wilhelm II's Role in Imperial Germany*, Cambridge 2003

'New Weapons for New Targets: Sir John Fisher, the Threat from Germany, and the Building of H.M.S. Dreadnought and H.M.S. Invincible, 1902–1907', *International History Review* XXX/2, June 2008, 303–31

The Royal Navy and the German Threat 1901–1914: Admiralty Plans to Protect British Trade in a War Against Germany, Oxford 2012

Spies in Uniform. British Military and Naval Intelligence on the Eve of the First World War, Oxford 2006

ed., *Naval Intelligence from Germany. The Reports of the British Naval Attachés in Berlin, 1906–1914*, Aldershot 2007

Seymour, Charles, ed., *The Intimate Papers of Colonel House*, 2 vols., London 1926

Siebert, Benno von, ed., *Diplomatische Aktenstücke zur Geschichte der Ententepolitik der Vorkriegsjahre*, 2 vols., Berlin 1921

Graf Benckendorffs diplomatischer Schriftwechsel, 3 vols., Berlin 1928

Smith, Iain R., *The Origins of the South African War, 1899–1902*, London and New York 1996

Sommer, Dudley, *Haldane of Cloane. His Life and Times, 1856–1928*, London 1960

Sösemann, Bernd, 'Die Bereitschaft zum Krieg. Sarajewo 1914', in Alexander Demandt, ed., *Das Attentat in der Geschichte*, Cologne, Weimar and Vienna 1996

'Hollow-Sounding Jubilees: Forms and Effects of Public Self-Display in Wilhelmine Germany', in Annika Mombauer and Wilhelm Deist, eds., *The Kaiser. New Research on Wilhelm II's Role in Imperial Germany*, Cambridge 2004, pp. 37–62

'Die sog. Hunnenrede Wilhelms II. Textkritische und interpretatorische Bemerkungen zur Ansprache des Kaisers vom 27. Juli 1900 in Bremerhaven', *Historische Zeitschrift* 222, 1976, 342–58

'Der Verfall des Kaisergedankens im Ersten Weltkrieg', in John C. G. Röhl, ed., *Der Ort Kaiser Wilhelms II. in der deutschen Geschichte*, Munich 1991

ed., *Theodor Wolff, Tagebücher 1914–1919. Der Erste Weltkrieg und die Entstehung der Weimarer Republik in Tagebüchern, Leitartikeln und Briefen des Chefredakteurs des 'Berliner Tageblatt' und Mitbegründers der 'Deutschen Demokratischen Partei'*, 2 vols., Boppard am Rhein 1984

Spindler, Arno, *Der Handelskrieg mit U-Booten [Der Krieg zur See, Abteilung III]*, 5 vols., I–IV: Berlin 1932–41; V: Frankfurt a.M. 1966

Steglich, Wolfgang, *Bündnissicherung oder Verständigungsfrieden. Untersuchungen zu dem Friedensangebot der Mittelmächte vom 12. Dezember 1916*, Göttingen 1958

Der Friedensappell Papst Benedikts XV. vom 1. August 1917 und die Mittelmächte. Diplomatische Aktenstücke des Deutschen Auswärtigen Amtes, des Bayerischen Staatsministeriums des Äußeren und des Britischen Auswärtigen Amtes aus den Jahren 1915–1922, Wiesbaden 1970

Die Friedenspolitik der Mittelmächte 1917/18, Wiesbaden 1964

Die Friedensversuche der kriegführenden Mächte im Sommer und Herbst 1917. Quellenkritische Untersuchungen, Akten und Vernehmungsprotokolle, Wiesbanden 1984

Verhandlungen des 2. Unterausschusses des Parlamentarischen Untersuchungsausschusses über die päpstliche Friedensaktion von 1917, Wiesbaden 1974

Stein, Adolf, *Bülow und der Kaiser*, Berlin 1931

Stein, Hermann von, *Erlebnisse und Betrachtungen aus der Zeit des Weltkrieges*, Leipzig 1919

Steinberg, Jonathan, 'Diplomatie als Wille und Vorstellung: Die Berliner Mission Lord Haldanes im Februar 1912', in Herbert Schottelius and Wilhelm Deist, eds., *Marine und Marinepolitik im kaiserlichen Deutschland 1871–1914*, Düsseldorf 1972

'Germany and the Russo-Japanese War', *American Historical Review*, 75/2, 1970

Steiner, Zara S., *Britain and the Origins of the First World War*, London 1977

Stengers, Jean, 'Guillaume II et le Roi Albert à Potsdam en novembre 1913', *Bulletin de la Classe des Lettres et des Sciences Morales et Politique*, 6th series, 4, 1993

Stenographische Berichte über die Verhandlungen des Reichstages, Berlin 1871–1918

Stern, Leo, ed., *Die Auswirkungen der großen sozialistischen Oktoberrevolution auf Deutschland*, 4 vols., Berlin 1959

Stevenson, David, *1914–1918. Der Erste Weltkrieg*, Düsseldorf 2006

Stibbe, Matthew, *German Anglophobia and the Great War, 1914–1918*, Cambridge 2001

'Germany's "Last Card": Wilhelm II and the Decision in Favour of Unrestricted Submarine Warfare in January 1917', in Annika Mombauer and Wilhelm Deist, eds., *The Kaiser. New Research on Wilhelm II's Role in Imperial Germany*, Cambridge 2003

'Kaiser Wilhelm II: The Hohenzollerns at War', in Matthew Hughes and Matthew Seligmann, eds., *Leadership in Conflict 1914–1918* Barnsley 2000

Stieve, Friedrich, *Der diplomatische Schriftwechsel Iswolskys, 1911–1914*, 3 vols., Berlin 1924

Stingl, Werner, *Der Ferne Osten in der deutschen Politik vor dem Ersten Weltkrieg (1902–1914)*, Frankfurt a.M. 1978

Stone, Norman, 'Die Mobilmachung der österreichisch-ungarischen Armee 1914', *Militärgeschichtliche Mitteilungen* 2, 1974, 67–95

'Moltke-Conrad: Relations between the Austro-Hungarian and German General Staffs, 1909–14', *The Historical Journal* 9, 1966, 204–11

Storz, Dieter, '"Aber was hätte anders geschehen sollen?" Die deutschen Offensiven an der Westfront 1918', in Jörg Duppler and Gerhard P. Groß, eds., *Kriegsende 1918. Ereignis, Wirkung, Nachwirkung*, Munich 1999

Strouse, Jean, *Morgan. American Financier*, New York 1999

Stubmann, Peter Franz, *Albert Ballin. Leben und Werk eines deutschen Reeders*, Berlin 1927

Stürgkh, Josef, *Im Deutschen Großen Hauptquartier*, Leipzig 1921

Stutzenberger, Adolf, *Die Abdankung Kaiser Wilhelms II. Die Entstehung und Entwicklung der Kaiserfrage und die Haltung der Presse*, Berlin 1937

Sydow, Reinhold von, 'Fürst Bülow und die Reichsfinanzreform 1908/09. Glossen zum Bülow-Buch', in Friedrich Thimme, ed., *Front wider Bülow. Staatsmänner, Diplomaten und Forscher zu seinen Denkwürdigkeiten*, Munich 1931

Thaer, Albrecht von, *Generalstabsdienst an der Front und in der OHL*, ed. Siegfried Kaehler, Göttingen 1958

Thimme, Friedrich, 'Fürst Lichnowskys "Memoirenwerk"', *Archiv für Politik und Geschichte* 10, 1928

ed., *Front wider Bülow. Staatsmänner, Diplomaten und Forscher zu seinen Denkwürdigkeiten*, Munich 1931

Thoß, Bruno, 'Nationale Rechte, militärische Führung und Diktaturfrage in Deutschland 1913–1923', *Militärgeschichtliche Mitteilungen* 42, 1987

Tirpitz, Alfred von, *Der Aufbau der deutschen Weltmacht*, Stuttgart and Berlin 1924

Deutsche Ohnmachtspolitik im Weltkriege, Hamburg and Berlin 1926

Erinnerungen, Leipzig 1919

Toom, Friedhild den and Klein, Sven Michael, *Hermine – die zweite Gemahlin von Wilhelm II.*, Greiz 2007

Townley, Lady Susan, *Indiscretions*, New York 1922

Tresckow, Hans von, *Von Fürsten und anderen Sterblichen. Erinnerungen eines Kriminalkommissars*, Berlin 1922

Ullrich, Volker, *Als der Thron ins Wanken kam. Das Ende des Hohenzollernreiches 1890–1918*, Bremen 1993

 'Zur inneren Revolutionierung der wilhelminischen Gesellschaft des Jahres 1918', in Jörg Duppler and Gerhard P. Groß, eds., *Kriegsende 1918. Ereignis, Wirkung, Nachwirkung*, Munich 1999

 Die nervöse Großmacht. Aufstieg und Untergang des deutschen Kaiserreichs 1871–1918, Frankfurt a.M. 1997

Vagts, Alfred, *Deutschland und die Vereinigten Staaten in der Weltpolitik*, 2 vols., New York 1935

Vale, Vivian, *The American Peril. Challenge to Britain on the North Atlantic 1901–1904*, Manchester 1984

Verhey, Jeffrey, *Der 'Geist von 1914' und die Erfindung der Volksgemeinschaft*, Hamburg 2000

Verosta, Stephan, *Theorie und Realität von Bündnissen. Heinrich Lammasch, Karl Renner und der Zweibund (1897–1914)*, Vienna 1971

Vickers, Hugo, *Gladys Duchess of Marlborough*, New York 1979

Viereck, George Sylvester, *The Kaiser on Trial*, New York 1937

Vierhaus, Rudolf, ed., *Das Tagebuch der Baronin Spitzemberg. Aufzeichnungen aus der Hofgesellschaft des Hohenzollernreiches*, Göttingen 1960

Vietsch, Eberhard von, *Theobald von Bethmann Hollweg. Staatsmann zwischen Macht und Ethos*, Boppard am Rhein 1969

Viktoria Luise, Duchess of Brunswick-Lüneburg, *Bilder der Kaiserzeit*, Göttingen 1970

 Ein Leben als Tochter des Kaisers, Göttingen and Hanover 1965

Vogel, Barbara, *Deutsche Rußlandpolitik. Das Scheitern der deutschen Weltpolitik unter Bülow 1900–1906*, Düsseldorf 1973

Walker, Alexander, *Audrey. Her Real Story*, London 1994

Warburg, Max, *Aus meinen Aufzeichnungen*, Glückstadt 1952

Wedel-Bérard, W. E. Elisabeth geschiedene Gräfin von, *Aus den Katakomben!!!*, Florence 1901

 Meine Beziehungen zu S.M. Kaiser Wilhelm II. Aufklärung über den Königsmord in Italien. Die Dreyfus-Affaire im Lichte der Wahrheit!, Zürich 1900.

Wedel Jarlsberg, Fredrik, *1905: Kongevalget*, Oslo 1946

Wegerer, Alfred von, *Der Ausbruch des Weltkrieges 1914*, 2 vols., Berlin 1939

Wehler, Hans-Ulrich, *Deutsche Gesellschaftsgeschichte*, 5 vols., Munich 1987–2008

 Krisenherde des Kaiserreichs 1871–1918. Studien zur deutschen Sozial- und Verfassungsgeschichte, Göttingen 1979

Weick, Curd-Torsten, *Die schwierige Balance: Kontinuitäten und Brüche deutscher Türkeipolitik*, Münster 2002

Weller, Bernd Uwe, *Maximilian Harden und die Zukunft*, Bremen 1970

Der Weltkrieg 1914–1918. Die militärischen Operationen zu Lande, edited by the Reichsarchiv, 14 vols., I–XII: Berlin 1925–44; XIII–XIV: Koblenz 1956

Wendt, Hermann, *Verdun 1916. Die Angriffe Falkenhayns im Maasgebiet mit Richtung auf Verdun als strategisches Problem*, Berlin 1931

Das Werk des Untersuchungsausschusses der Deutschen Verfassunggebenden Nationalversammlung und des Deutschen Reichstages 1919–1926. Verhandlungen / Gutachten / Urkunden. Vierte Reihe: Die Ursachen des Deutschen Zusammenbruchs im Jahre 1918, 12 vols., Berlin 1925–9

Wermuth, Adolf, *Ein Beamtenleben. Erinnerungen*, Berlin 1922

Wernecke, Klaus, *Der Wille zur Weltgeltung. Außenpolitik und Öffentlichkeit im Kaiserreich am Vorabend des Ersten Weltkrieges*, Düsseldorf 1970

Westarp, Kuno Graf von, *Das Ende der Monarchie am 9. November 1918*, Stollhamm 1952
Konservative Politik im letzten Jahrzehnt des Kaiserreiches, 2 vols., Berlin 1935

White, J. A., *The Diplomacy of the Russo-Japanese War*, Princeton 1964

Wichtl, Friedrich, *Weltfreimauerei, Weltrevolution, Weltrepublik. Eine Untersuchung über Ursprung und Endziele des Weltkrieges*, Munich 1921

Wiegrefe, Klaus, Altenhöner, Florian, Bönisch, Georg, Buschke, Heiko Pyliow, Wladimir and Zeller, Anika, 'Revolutionär Seiner Majestät. Die gekaufte Revolution. Wie Kaiser Wilhelm II. Lenins Octoberrevolution finanzierte', *Der Spiegel* 50, 10 December 2007

Wielandt, Ute and Kaschner, Michael, 'Die Reichstagsdebatten über den deutschen Kriegseinsatz in China: August Bebel und die "Hunnenbriefe"', in Susanne Kuß and Bernd Martin, eds., *Das Deutsche Reich und der Boxeraufstand*, Munich 2002, pp. 183–201

Wiese, Christian, *Wissenschaft des Judentums und protestantische Theologie im wilhelminischen Deutschland. Ein Schrei ins Leere?*, Tübingen 1999

Wild von Hohenborn, Adolf, *Briefe und Tagebuchaufzeichnungen des preußischen Generals als Kriegsminister und Truppenführer im Ersten Weltkrieg*, ed. Helmut Reichold, Boppard am Rhein 1986

Wilderotter, Hans, 'Haus Doorn. Die verkleinerte Kopie eines Hofstaats', in Hans Wilderotter and Klaus-D. Pohl, eds., *Der letzte Kaiser. Wilhelm II. im Exil*, Gütersloh 1991

Wilderotter, Hans and Pohl, Klaus-D., eds., *Der letzte Kaiser. Wilhelm II. im Exil*, Gütersloh 1991

Wilhelm II., *Ereignisse und Gestalten in den Jahren 1878–1918*, Berlin and Leipzig 1922
Erinnerungen an Korfu, Berlin and Leipzig 1924
Aus meinem Leben 1859–1888, Berlin and Leipzig 1927
Studien zur Gorgo, Berlin 1936
Vergleichende Geschichtstabellen von 1878 bis zum Kriegsausbruch, Leipzig 1921

Wilhelm, Crown Prince, *Erinnerungen des Kronprinzen Wilhelm*, Stuttgart and Berlin 1922

Williamson, Samuel R. Jr and May, Ernest R., 'An Identity of Opinion: Historians and July 1914', *The Journal of Modern History*, June 2007, 335–87

Wilson, Keith, ed., *Decisions for War 1914*, London 1995

Winzen, Peter, *Bernhard Fürst von Bülow. Weltmachtstratege ohne Fortune – Wegbereiter der großen Katastrophe*, Göttingen, Zürich 2003
Bülows Weltmachtkonzept. Untersuchungen zur Frühphase seiner Außenpolitik 1897–1901, Boppard am Rhein 1977
Das Ende der Kaiserherrlichkeit. Die Skandalprozesse um die homosexuellen Berater Wilhelms II. 1907–1909, Cologne and Weimar 2010
Die Englandpolitik Friedrich von Holsteins 1895–1901, Cologne 1975
'Der erste politische Homosexualitätsskandal im Kaiserreich: Friedrich Alfred Krupp (1854–1902)', *Archiv der Kulturgeschichte* 93. Band, Heft 2, 2011, 415–50
Freundesliebe am Hof Kaiser Wilhelms II., Norderstedt 2010
'"Ein halber Ausländer" – Max Egon II. Fürst zu Fürstenberg (1863–1941)', in Peter Winzen, *Freundesliebe am Hof Kaiser Wilhelms II.*, Norderstedt 2010
Das Kaiserreich am Abgrund. Die Daily-Telegraph-Affäre und das Hale-Interview von 1908. Darstellung und Dokumentation, Stuttgart 2002
'Der Krieg in Bülows Kalkül: Katastrophe der Diplomatie oder Chance zur Machtexpansion?', in Jost Dülffer and Karl Holl, eds., *Bereit zum Krieg. Kriegsmentalität im wilhelminischen Deutschland 1890–1914*, Göttingen 1986
Reichskanzler Bernhard von Bülow. Mit Weltmachtphantasien in den Ersten Weltkrieg, Regensburg 2013

Im Schatten Wilhelms II. Bülows und Eulenburgs Poker um die Macht im Kaiserreich, Cologne 2011

Wipperfürth, Christian, *Von der Souveränität zur Angst. Britische Außenpolitik und Sozialökonomie im Zeitalter des Imperialismus*, Stuttgart 2004

Witt, Peter-Christian, *Die Finanzpolitik des Deutschen Reiches von 1903 bis 1913. Eine Studie zur Innenpolitik des Wilhelminischen Deutschlands*, Lübeck and Hamburg 1970

Wittek, Thomas, *Auf ewig Feind? Das Deutschlandbild in den britischen Massenmedien nach dem Ersten Weltkrieg*, Munich 2005

Wittenauer, Volker, *Im Dienste der Macht. Kultur und Sprache am Hof der Hohenzollern. Vom Großen Kurfürst bis zu Wilhelm II.*, Paderborn 2007

Wittgenstein, Ludwig, *Vermischte Bemerkungen. Eine Auswahl aus dem Nachlass* (1895), 1946

Wolf, Hubert et al., eds., 'Kritische Online-Edition der Nuntiaturberichte Eugenio Pacellis (1917–1929)'

Wolff, David, ed., *The Russo-Japanese War in Global Perspective: World War Zero*, Leiden 2007

Yasamee, Feroz, 'Colmar Freiherr von der Goltz and the Boer War', in Keith Wilson, ed., *The International Impact of the Boer War*, New York 2001

'Ottoman Empire', in Keith Wilson, ed., *Decisions for War 1914*, London 1995, pp. 229–68.

Zechlin, Egmont, 'Friedensbestrebungen und Revolutionierungsversuche im Ersten Weltkrieg', *Aus Politik und Zeitgeschichte*, Nos. 20, 24 and 25 (1961) and 20 and 22 (1963)

'Motive und Taktik der Reichsleitung 1914', *Der Monat* 209, February 1966

Zedlitz-Trützschler, Robert Graf von, *Zwölf Jahre am deutschen Kaiserhof*, Stuttgart, Berlin and Leipzig 1925

Ziemann, Benjamin, 'Enttäuschte Erwartung und kollektive Erschöpfung. Die deutschen Soldaten an der Westfront 1918 auf dem Weg zur Revolution', in Jörg Duppler and Gerhard P. Groß, eds., *Kriegsende 1918. Ereignis, Wirkung, Nachwirkung*, Munich 1999

Zipfel, Friedrich, 'Kritik der Öffentlichkeit an der Person und an der Monarchie Wilhelms II. bis zum Ausbruch des Weltkrieges', unpublished Dr Phil dissertation, University of Berlin 1952

Zirkel, Kirsten, 'Vom Militaristen zum Pazifisten. Politisches Leben und Wirken des Generals Berthold von Deimling vor dem Hintergrund der Entwicklung Deutschlands vom Kaiserreich zum Dritten Reich', unpublished Dr Phil dissertation, University of Düsseldorf 2006

Zmarzlik, Hans-Günter, *Bethmann Hollweg als Reichskanzler 1909–1914. Studien zu Möglichkeiten und Grenzen seiner innerpolitischen Machtstellung*, Düsseldorf 1957

Zorn, Philipp et al., *Deutschland unter Kaiser Wilhelm II.*, 3 vols., Berlin 1914

Zwehl, Hans von, *Falkenhayn*, Berlin 1926

Index

plans against Denmark, 304–5; and Büchsel's war plans, 314, 322; reputation, 314; silence in Wilhelm's presence, 314–15; dines with Wilhelm, 318; cooperation with Büchsel, 319; and preventive war against France, 323–4; dismissed, 660; and Boer War plans, 682; fear of encirclement of Germany, 714, 737; Wilhelm reads article to commanding generals, 715, 736

Schlieffen, Count Hermann, 326, 518

Schmidt, Caesar (publisher), 526

Schmitt-Ott, Friedrich, 1220, 1235

Schmitz, Bruno, 525

Schoen, Hans von, 1109

Schoen, Wilhelm, Freiherr von: appointed envoy in Copenhagen, 105; on Germany's Russian policy, 164; on alliances with smaller European countries, 231; discusses naval/military policy with Wilhelm, 297; in war games, 299; and Wilhelm's role in Moroccan crisis (1905), 329; accompanies Wilhelm on visit to Tangier, 340, 344; on Wilhelm's imperious behaviour, 345; and German desire to annex Denmark, 387–8; and Isvolsky in Copenhagen, 389; on Danish neutrality, 390; succeeds Alvensleben as ambassador in St Petersburg, 425; on Russian defection to French, 429; succeeds Tschirschky as Foreign Secretary, 514, 516; Varnbüler proposed as replacement in St Petersburg, 551; on success of Wilhelm's official visit to Britain (1907), 588; in discussion on Baghdad railway with British ministers, 591–3; and Wilhelm's policy on China, 608; not shown Wilhelm's letter to Tweedmouth, 611; learns of Wilhelm's letter to Tweedmouth, 615; cancels Wilhelm's order refusing British officers to attend German manoeuvres, 629; and Wilhelm's *Daily Telegraph* interview, 663, 671–2, 674, 677; and Austrian annexation of Bosnia-Herzegovina, 701; and Wilhelm's proposals for Russian alliance, 713; disparages Bülow, 746; Roosevelt meets, 778; and Wilhelm's dismissal of French peace proposals, 1045

Scholl, Friedrich von, 14, 300, 341, 802

Schöllgen, Gregor, 88

Schönstedt, Karl Heinrich, 102, 119

Schorlemer, Clemens, Baron von, 978, 1168

Schuckmann, Bruno von, 33

Schulenburg, General Friedrich, Count von der, 286, 1186

Schulz (valet), 693

Schwarze (industrialist), 144

Schweinitz, Hans Lothar von, 713

Schweninger, Ernst, 147, 158, 532, 556, 1131

Schwerin, Count (former Court Chamberlain), 1246, 1249

Schwerin-Löwitz, Hans, Count, 957

Schwertfeger, Rudolf, 326

Scutari, 918, 920, 925, 928–9, 932, 935

Seckendorff, Albert von, 224

Seckendorff, Götz, Count von, 16, 202, 247, 331, 400–1

Second World War (1939–45): outbreak, 1259

Sedan, Battle of (1870), 960

Seeband, William, 572–3

Ségur, Pierre de, 215

Selborne, William Waldegrave Palmer, 2nd Earl of, 168

Seligmann, Matthew, 999

Sell, Ulrich, Baron von, 1008, 1220

Senden-Bibran, Admiral Gustav Freiherr von: intrigues with Paulis, 176–7, 181, 228–9, 237, 239, 241, 318, 322; encourages battlefleet-building programme, 467, 486; differences with Tirpitz, 468–9, 472, 479, 489; offers resignation, 469; Wilhelm praises, 482; and Navy League, 484; drafts letter declining Tirpitz's resignation, 487

Serbia: regicide, 701, 722; nationalist movement, 701; partitioning, 701; prospective war with Austria (1908), 705–6, 708, 715, 719, 723, 726; Russia declines to support, 710; seeks compensation for annexation of Bosnia-Herzegovina, 715, 719; Wilhelm's hostility to, 722, 894, 906, 1037, 1066; and prospective Greek war with Turkey, 754; British influence in, 755; Austria denies access to Adriatic, 889, 891, 923; in Balkan wars, 882–3, 885–6, 888; Russian support for against Austria, 889, 909, 1036, 1047, 1103; danger of war with Austria (1912), 889; Austrian militancy towards, 891, 898–9, 908, 911, 916, 922, 945, 948, 951; Austria delays attack on, 916, 918; Wilhelm expects to give way, 919; Berchtold's conciliatory policy on, 920; conflict with Bulgaria, 922, 943; attack on Scutari, 925–6; Wilhelm expects Italy to join Austria against, 927; possible intervention in Scutari crisis, 930; Wilhelm casts as aggressor, 930; Wilhelm promotes rapprochement with Austria, 938, 947; Austrian ultimatum to (18